THE NEW AMERICAN
Webster
HANDY COLLEGE
DICTIONARY

**INCLUDES ABBREVIATIONS, GEOGRAPHICAL
NAMES, FOREIGN WORDS AND PHRASES,
FORMS OF ADDRESS**

ALBERT and LOY MOREHEAD
Editors

Expanded Edition prepared by
Philip D. Morehead and
Andrew T. Morehead

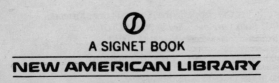

A SIGNET BOOK

NEW AMERICAN LIBRARY

SIGNET, SIGNET CLASSIC, MENTOR, ONYX, PLUME, MERIDIAN
and NAL BOOKS *are published by NAL PENGUIN INC.,*
1633 Broadway, New York, New York 10019

100   101   102   103   104   105   106   107

CONTENTS

Prepared and Edited by

The National Lexicographic Board

ALBERT H. MOREHEAD, *Chairman and General Editor*
WALDEMAR VON ZEDTWITZ, *President*
LOY C. MOREHEAD, *Vice President & Secretary;* LOYD F. GEHRES,
SALVATORE RAMONDINO, *Vice Presidents;* DONALD D. WOLF, WILLIAM C.
CAMPBELL, GEORGE H. COPELAND, JACK LUZZATTO.

Staff for the New American Handy College Dictionary

ALBERT *and* LOY MOREHEAD, *Editors*
GEOFFREY MOTT-SMITH, *Managing Editor.* WILLIAM T. ATWOOD, WILLIAM C.
CAMPBELL, JACK LUZZATTO, RICHARD HOWARD, *Associate Editors.* JANE
MCDOWELL, *Drawings.* (Incorporating in part *The New American Webster
Dictionary,* LOYD F. GEHRES, *Editor-in-Chief.*)

Consultants

HOW TO USE THIS DICTIONARY

This dictionary supplies the spelling, syllabication, pronunciation, and meaning of the most useful words of the English language as it is spoken in the United States. Abbreviations, foreign words and phrases, and the names and descriptions of places may be found in the pages following the main vocabulary.

Words are not listed separately when they are identical in spelling and pronunciation and differ only in etymology.

SPELLING

Where a word may correctly be spelled in more than one way, we have generally preferred the simplest way. Space does not permit us to include every spelling for which there is authority. The user of this dictionary may rely upon finding a correct way to spell his word, but it will not necessarily be *the only* correct way.

SYLLABICATION

Each word in its first spelling is divided into syllables, either by stress marks or by dots. The syllable preceding the mark (′) is primarily stressed; a syllable preceding the mark (″) receives secondary stress. The dots should not be confused with hyphens. When a word is to be hyphenated in spelling, it is marked with a bold, long hyphen (-).

It is not conventionally proper to divide a word, at the end of a line, at any place except where a stress mark, dot or hyphen appears. Even where the dictionary shows a division into syllables, it is not good style to leave a single letter of a word on one line; for example, words like *abound, alike, glossy,* should not be divided between lines.

GUIDE TO PRONUNCIATION

a	as in fat	û	as in pull	ngg	as in finger
ā	as in fate	ə	as in comma,	nk	as in ink (pro-
ä	as in far		label,		nounced
â	as in fall		pupil,		ingk)
á	as in ask		censor,	p	as in pen
ā	as in dare		focus	r	as in rat
e	as in met	b	as in but	s	as in sit, this
ē	as in mete	ch	as in chair	sh	as in she
ê	as in her	d	as in day	t	as in to
è	as in maybe	f	as in fill	th	as in thin
i	as in pin	g	as in go	th	as in then
ī	as in pine	h	as in hat	v	as in van
o	as in not	hw	as in when	w	as in win
ō	as in note	j	as in joke	y	as in yet
oo	as in spoon	k	as in keep	z	as in zone, quiz
ô	as in or	kt	as in act	zh	as in azure
oi	as in oil	l	as in late	ö	as in Ger. *schön*
ow	as in owl	m	as in man	ü	as in Fr. *tu*
u	as in tub	n	as in nod	ṅ	as in Fr. *bon*
ū	as in mute	ng	as in sing	kh	as in blockhouse

6

The criterion for pronunciation is the best usage in regions where there is no marked peculiarity of speech and in normal conversation rather than in formal speech.

Where the respelling of a word for pronunciation would be in all respects the same as the original spelling, the word is not respelled.

Most of the diacritical marks are self-explanatory, but some suggest comment:

ə (the upside-down e, called the schwa) marks the **a** in comma **e** in label **i** in pupil **o** in censor **u** in focus	Any unaccented vowel tends to become an ''uh'' sound. The use of the ə does not mean you must not pronunce the actual vowel; with meticulous speakers the original vowel sound remains recognizable. Say *char-i-ty* if you wish, but with equal confidence—and much more company—you may say *char-ə-ty.* The schwa is also used to indicate certain ''lost'' vowel sounds, as in the word *garden,* where the *n* is merely a nasal utterance following the gard-.
à as in ask	However you pronounce *ask, laugh, aunt*—with the *a* as in *cat,* or as in *father,* or somewhere in between—that is how you should render this à.
ô as in corn; horn, torn	Traditionally, dictionaries say that the sound of *o* in *corn, horn, morn* is different from the sound of *o* in *worn, torn, sworn;* that *horse* and *hoarse, border* and *boarder, born* and *borne,* are not pronounced the same. We do not make this distinction. In the few regions where it is made, the *r* is not pronounced.
ė to represent the *y* in story	The terminal *y* is rendered as short *i* in other dictionaries. Along with the writers of popular songs, we hear it, from coast to coast, as an unstressed long *e.*
nk as in ink	This is actually pronounced *ngk;* but since it is never pronounced any other way, it seems unnecessary to respell a word each time *nk* occurs.

Compound words are not respelled for pronunciation if each element is pronounced elsewhere in the dictionary. A derivative form is respelled for pronunciation only to the extent necessary: *odd'i·ty* (-ə-tė).

INFLECTIONAL FORMS

In the formation of plurals, inflection of verbs, and comparison of adjectives and adverbs, only irregular forms are specified in the dictionary. In the absence of specific exception, it should be assumed that the following rules apply.

PLURAL FORMS OF NOUNS

1. Usually, form the plural by adding -*s* to the singular noun. The -*s* is pronounced *z,* unless *s* is easier.

2. Usually add -*es* to a singular noun ending in a sibilant sound. The -*es* then forms a new syllable, pronounced -*iz.* Thus: *dresses* (dres'iz), *matches* (mach'iz).

If the singular noun ends in a sibilant but has a silent terminal *e*, add only -*s*, but the new syllable still occurs: *base, bases* (bā′siz).

3. When a noun ends in *y* preceded by a consonant, the plural form is -*ies: dairy, dairies* (dār′ĕz). But when the terminal *y* is preceded by a vowel, add merely -*s: day, days*.

4. The plural form of a noun ending in a consonant and *o* is -*oes: hero, heroes* (hir′ōz). But when a vowel precedes the terminal *o* add merely -*s: radio, radios* (rā′dĕ-ōz″).

POSSESSIVE FORMS

1. To form the possessive, add *'s* to a singular noun or to a plural noun not ending in *s*: a *man's* voice, the *horse's* mouth, the *fish's* tail, *men's* lives. The pronunciation follows the rules for regular plurals: *fish's* is the same as *fishes* (fish′iz).

2. To form the possessive of a plural noun ending in *s*, add the apostrophe (') alone: the *workers'* wages.

3. The foregoing rules apply also to proper names: *John's* book, John *Harris's* house, the *Smiths'* party. It is incorrect to write *the Harris' ages* instead of *Harrises'*.

4. The possessive forms of pronouns are usually irregular and are given in the dictionary.

INFLECTION OF REGULAR VERBS

1. The present indicative tense uses the infinitive in all cases except third person singular, which is regularly formed the same as the plurals of nouns (see preceding paragraphs). Thus: *to like, I like, you like, we like, they like,* but *he, she,* or *it likes*.

2. The past tense (preterit) is formed by adding -*d* or -*ed* to the infinitive, according as the latter does or does not end with *e*. The -*ed* forms a new syllable after *d* or *t*, and is pronounced -*id*: to want, *wanted* (wont′id); to end, *ended* (en′did). In other cases the -*d* or -*ed* does not form a new syllable and is pronounced *d* or *t*, whichever is easier: to play, *played* (plăd); to match, *matched* (macht). A terminal *y* preceded by a consonant changes to -*ied*: to bury, *bur'ied*.

3. The past participle is the same as the preterit.

4. The present participle is formed by adding -*ing* to the infinitive, from which the terminal *e* (if any) is dropped. Thus: to jump, *jump'ing*; to hate, *hat'ing*; to grapple *grap'pling*; to bury, *bur'y-ing*.

5. A consonant preceded by a short vowel is doubled: to can, *canned* (kand), *can'ning*. (These forms are regularly given in the dictionary.)

6. Many of the fundamental verbs are irregular, as *be, have, go, run, make,* etc. All forms of the auxiliary verbs *be* and *have* are given in the text under the infinitives. The forms of the other irregular verbs are given after the infinitive, in square brackets [   ], in the order: preterit, past participle, present participle. When the preterit and past participle are the same form, it is not repeated. When only one syllable is shown, it replaces the last syllable only of the word previously spelled out: *fit* [fit′ted, -ting].

7. Regular and irregular verbs alike form their other tenses as follows. *Present perfect:* add the past participle to the present indicative of *have*. (Thus: to go, I have gone.) *Past perfect, or pluperfect*: add the past participle to the preterit of *have*. (Thus: to go, I had gone.) *Present progressive:* add the present participle to the present indicative of *be*. (Thus: to go, I am going.) *Past progressive;* add the present participle to the preterit of *be*. (Thus: to go, I was going.) *Passive voice*: add the past participle to the appropriate tense of *be*. (Thus: to call, I am called, I was called, I have been called, I had been called, etc.) *Future tense*: add the infinitive to the appropriate tense of *will* or *shall*. (Thus: to call, I will call, I shall call, I shall be called, etc.) *Subjunctive mood*: add the infinitive to *would* or *should* (active voice) or the past participle to the subjunctive form of *be* (passive voice). (Thus: to call, if I should call, if I should be called.) *Imperative mood*: use the infinitive. (Thus: to go, Go!)

COMPARISON OF ADJECTIVES AND ADVERBS

1. The main vocabulary lists only the positive forms of adjectives and adverbs. The regular formation of the comparative is to add *-r* or *-er* to the positive; of the superlative, to add *-st* or *-est* (according as the positive does or does not end in *e*). A consonant preceded by a short vowel is doubled: *mad, mad′der, mad′dest*. For words ending in *y*, the forms are *-ier, -iest*. Often the regular formation makes for awkward pronunciation; in such a case, for the comparative, precede the positive by *more*; for the superlative, precede it by *most*. In general, this alternative is followed for words of three of more syllables.

2. For adjectives and adverbs compared irregularly, the text appends the comparative and superlative in square brackets [ ]: good [bet′ter, best].

THE FORMATION OF ADDITIONAL WORDS

1. This dictionary lists hundreds of prefixes, suffixes, and other word elements from which additional words can be formed and the meanings of other words can be inferred.

2. The adjectival forms ending in *-ful, -some, -like*, and *-less* are generally omitted from the dictionary.

3. Adverbs are regularly formed from adjectives by the addition of *-ly*: bright, *bright′ly*. When the adjective ends in *-y*, this letter regularly changes to *i*, making the terminal *-ily*: heavy, *heav′i·ly*. When the adjective ends in *-le* preceded by a consonant, the adverb is formed by changing the final *e* to *y*: idle, *i′dly*. Virtually all regular adverbial forms are omitted from the dictionary.

4. Nouns of agency are regularly formed by adding *-er* to a verb: *to pound, pound′er*, one who or that which pounds. The rules follow those for forming the comparatives of adjectives: *to bury, bur′i·er; to pine, pin′er; to dig, dig′ger*. Most of the regular forms are omitted from the dictionary. Such nouns when formed by adding *-or, -ist, -eer*, etc. are given in the dictionary.

AMERICAN, BRITISH AND CANADIAN SPELLINGS

The preferred spellings in this dictionary follow American usage. In the following cases British (and, when indicated, Canadian) usage differs:

1. Many nouns such as *honor, armor* (U.S.) are spelled *honour, armour* (Brit. & Can.). Similar variation between *o* and *ou* occurs in a few other words, as *molt* (U.S.), *moult* (Brit. & Can.); *smolder* (U.S.), *smoulder* (Brit. & Can.)

2. Most verbs ending in *-ize* (U.S. & Can.) are spelled *-ise* (Brit.): *realize* (U.S. & Can.), *realise* (Brit.).

3. Many words ending in *-er* (U.S.) are spelled *-re* (Brit. & Can.): *center, fiber* (U.S.), *centre, fibre* (Brit. & Can.).

4. In forms of verbs ending in *l* preceded by a short vowel, the *l* is not usually doubled (U.S.) and is usually doubled (Brit. & Can.): *traveled, traveling, traveler* (U.S.), *travelled, travelling, traveller* (Brit. & Can.).

A

A, a (ā) first letter of the English alphabet.
—*adj., indef. art.* one; any.

a- *pref.* **1,** not. **2,** in, on. **3,** an intensive, as in *arouse.*

AA (ā'ā') *n.* antiaircraft fire.

aard'vark" (ärd'värk") *n.* an African ant-eating mammal; groundhog.

ab- *pref.* away from; off.

a"ba·cá' (ä"bä-kä') *n.* a Philippine palm; its fiber, used in making hemp.

a·back' (ə-bak') *adv.* toward the rear.
—**taken aback,** disconcerted.

ab'a·cus (ab'ə-kəs) *n.* a calculating device consisting of beads strung on rods in a frame.

a·baft' (ə-baft') *adv. & prep.* (*Naut.*) toward the stern; behind.

ab"a·lo'ne (ab"-ə-lō'nė) *n.* a large snail abundant on the Pacific coast.

a·ban'don (ə-ban'dən) *v.t.* give up; leave; forsake; cast away. —*n.* freedom from restraint. —**a·ban'doned,** *adj.* reckless; dissolute. —**a·ban'don·ment,** *n.*

a·base' (ə-bās') *v.t.* reduce in rank or estimation. —**a·base'ment,** *n.*

a·bash' (ə-bash') *v.t.* make ashamed or dispirited; embarrass.

a·bate' (ə-bāt') *v.t.* beat down; reduce; moderate. —*v.i.* diminish; lessen. —**a·bate'ment,** *n.*

ab"at·toir' (ab"ə-twär') *n.* slaughterhouse.

ab·bé' (a-bā') *n.* a French ecclesiastic.

ab'bess (ab'es) *n.* the head of a convent.

ab'bey (ab'ė) *n.* a monastery or convent.

ab'bot (ab'ət) *n.* the head of a monastery.
—**ab'ba·cy** (ab'ə-sė) *n.*

ab·bre'vi·ate" (ə-brē'vė-āt') *v.t.* shorten by omission of some parts.

ab·bre'vi·a'tion (-ā'shən) *n.* **1,** abridgment. **2,** a shortened form, esp. of a word.

ABC's (ā"bē"sēz') *n.pl.* **1,** the alphabet. **2,** (*often sing.*) the basic facts or principles of a subject.

ab'di·cate" (ab'də-kāt') *v.i. & t.* renounce or relinquish an office, power, or right. —**ab'di·ca'tion,** *n.* —**ab'di·ca"tor,** *n.*

ab'do·men (ab'də-mən) *n.* the lower part of the human body, between thorax and pelvis. —**ab·dom'i·nal** (ab-dom'i-nəl) *adj.*

ab·duct' (ab-dukt') *v.t.* carry away by force; kidnap. —**ab·duc'tion,** *n.* —**ab·duc'tor,** *n.*

a·beam' (ə-bēm') *adv.* at right angles to the keel of a ship; in a sideward direction.

a·bed' (ə-bed') *adv.* in bed.

a·bele' (ə-bēl') *n.* the white poplar tree.

Ab'er·deen" An'gus (ab'ər-dēn" ang'gəs) one of a breed of hornless beef cattle.

ab·er'rant (ab-er'ənt) *adj.* straying from the right course; wandering. —**ab·er'rance, ab·er'ran·cy,** *n.*

ab"er·ra'tion (ab"ə-rā'shən) *n.* **1,** departure from a normal course. **2,** deviation from truth or moral rectitude. **3,** apparent displacement of a heavenly body, due to its motion relative to the earth. **4,** any disturbance of light rays that prevents accurate focusing.

a·bet' (ə-bet') *v.t.* [**a·bet'ted, -ting**] encourage; aid by approval, esp. in bad conduct. —**a·bet'ment,** *n.* —**a·bet'ter, a·bet'tor,** *n.*

a·bey'ance (ə-bā'əns) *n.* temporary suspension or inactivity.

ab·hor' (ab-hôr') *v.t.* [**-horred', -hor'ring**] regard with extreme repugnance; detest.

ab·hor'rence (ab-hor'əns) *n.* strong hatred; detestation. —**ab·hor'rent,** *adj.* detestable; disgusting.

a·bide' (ə-bīd') *v.i.* [*pret. & p.p.* **a·bode'**] **1,** remain; continue. **2,** dwell. **3,** (with *by*) stand firm. —*v.i. & t.* [**a·bid'ed**] put up with; tolerate.

ab'i·gail" (ab'ə-gāl") *n.* a lady's maid.

a·bil'i·ty (ə-bil'ə-tė) *n.* **1,** state of being able; possession of qualities necessary. **2,** competence; skill; a particular talent.

-a·bil'i·ty *suf.* marking noun forms of adjectives ending in *-able.*

ab'ject (ab'jekt) *adj.* **1,** low in condition or estimation; hopeless. **2,** servile; despicable. —**ab·ject'ness,** *n.*

ab·jure' (ab-jûr') *v.t.* renounce solemnly or on oath; repudiate; forswear. —**ab"ju·ra'tion** (ab"jə-rā'shən) *n.*

ab'la·tive (ab'lə-tiv) *n. & adj.* a grammatical case denoting agency, place, etc., in certain inflected languages, as Latin.

a·blaze' (ə-blāz') *adv. & adj.* **1,** on fire. **2,** brilliantly lighted up. **3,** very excited; angry.

a'ble (ā'bəl) *adj.* [**a'bler, a'blest**] **1,** having the means or power to be or act. **2,** having marked intellectual qualifications; talented. —**a'ble-bod"ied,** *adj.* of strong body; physically competent. —**able-bodied seaman,** a fully qualified merchant seaman.

-a·ble (ə-bəl) *suf.* denoting ability, liability, tendency.

a·bloom' (ə-bloom') *adv. & adj.* in blossom.

ab·lu'tion (ab-loo'shən) *n.* washing; cleansing, esp. ceremonial.

---

ab'ne·gate" (ab'nə-gāt") *v.t.* renounce or deny oneself (own rights or powers). —**ab"ne·ga'tion,** *n.*

ab·nor'mal (ab-nôr'məl) *adj.* not ordinary; unusual; deviating from a type or standard. —**ab"nor·mal'i·ty** (ab"nôr-mal'ə-tė) *n.* the state or an instance of being abnormal.

a·board' (ə-bôrd') *adv. & prep.* on board (a ship, train, or other conveyance).

a·bode' (ə-bōd') *n.* **1,** dwelling place. **2,** sojourn; continuance. —*v.* pret. & p.p. of *abide.*

a·bol'ish (ə-bol'ish) *v.t.* put an end to; annul; destroy. —**a·bol'ish·ment,** *n.*

ab"o·li'tion (ab'ə-lish'ən) *n.* **1,** destruction; annulment. **2,** the extinction of Negro slavery. —**ab"o·li'tion·ism,** *n.* advocation of abolition, esp. of Negro slavery. —**ab"o·li'tion·ist,** *n.*

A-'bomb" (ā'bom") *n.* atom bomb.

a·bom'i·na·ble (ə-bom'i-nə-bəl) *adj.* detestable; abhorrent. —**Abominable Snowman,** snowman (def. 2).

a·bom'i·nate" (ə-bom'ə-nāt") *v.t.* hate extremely; abhor; detest.

a·bom"i·na'tion (-nā'shən) *n.* **1,** intense aversion. **2,** a detestable quality, act, or condition.

ab"o·rig'i·nal (ab'ə-rij'i-nəl) *adj.* **1,** pert. to earliest times or conditions; primitive. **2,** indigenous.

ab"o·rig'i·nes (-nėz) *n.pl.* [*sing.* **-ne** (-nė)] earliest inhabitants.

a·bort' (ə-bôrt') *v.i.* **1,** miscarry in giving birth. **2,** remain rudimentary; fail to develop. —*v.t.* cause to miscarry or to fail. —**a·bor'tive,** *adj.*

a·bor'tion (ə-bôr'shən) *n.* **1,** untimely birth; miscarriage. **2,** expulsion or removal of the human fetus. **3,** any fruit or product in a state of arrested development. —**a·bor'tion·ist,** *n.* one who induces abortions, usu. illegal.

a·bound' (ə-bownd') *v.i.* be plentiful or prevalent; be filled (with).

a·bout' (ə-bowt') *adv.* **1,** in every direction; all around. **2,** near in time or place; approximately. **3,** on the point of; in readiness. **4,** at work; astir. —*prep.* **1,** in regard to. **2,** near to. **3,** on the outside of; surrounding. —**a·bout-"face',** *n.* reversal of attitude or position.

a·bove' (ə-buv') *adv. & prep.* **1,** in a higher place than; superior to. **2,** greater in quantity or degree (than). —*adj.* forementioned.

a·bove'board" *adj. & adv.* without deceit.

ab"ra·ca·dab'ra (ab"rə-kə-dab'rə) *n.* **1,** a cabalistic word-charm. **2,** mumbo-jumbo.

a·brade' (ə-brād') *v.i. & t.* wear away by friction.

a·bra'sion (ə-brā'shən) *n.* **1,** act or result of abrading. **2,** a scraped spot.

a·bra'sive (-siv) *n.* any material for abrading, grinding, or polishing. —*adj.* tending to wear down; rough.

a·breast' (ə-brest') *adj. & adv.* side by side; to the same degree.

a·bridge' (ə-brij') *v.t.* **1,** shorten, as by omission or condensation. **2,** cut off; curtail. —**a·bridg'ment,** *n.*

a·broad' (ə-brâd') *adv.* **1,** in a foreign country; absent. **2,** in circulation; astir.

ab'ro·gate" (ab'rə-gāt") *v.t.* repeal or annul by authoritative act. —**ab"ro·ga'tion,** *n.*

ab·rupt' (ə-brupt') *adj.* **1,** changing or terminating suddenly; discontinuous. **2,** precipitous. —**ab·rupt'ness,** *n.*

ab'scess (ab'ses) *n.* localized collection of pus in the body tissues. —*v.i.* form an abscess.

ab·scis'sa (ab-sis'ə) *n.* (*Geom.*) the distance of a point from a vertical line of reference.

ab·scond' (ab-skond') *v.i.* hide or depart suddenly, esp. to avoid legal process.

ab'sence (ab'səns) *n.* **1,** state or period of being away. **2,** lack.

ab'sent (ab'sənt) *adj.* not present; not in a certain place; away. —*v.t.* (ab-sent') keep (oneself) away; withdraw.

ab"sen·tee' (ab"sən-tē') *n.* one who is absent, as from his job. —*adj.* not present or in residence. —**ab"sen·tee'ism,** *n.*

ab'sent-mind"ed *adj.* preoccupied; forgetful. —**ab'sent-mind"ed-ness,** *n.*

ab'sinthe (ab'sinth) *n.* a liqueur made from wormwood and brandy.

ab'so·lute" (ab'sə-loot') *adj.* **1,** unqualified; unlimited. **2,** perfect; complete. **3,** positive; fixed; entirely determined; irrevocable. —*n.* something absolute. —**ab'so·lute"ness,** *n.* —**absolute pitch,** the ability to identify or reproduce any given pitch. —**absolute zero,** the temperature at which (in theory) all molecular motion ceases, about -459.6°F, -273.2°C. —**the Absolute,** God.

ab"so·lu'tion (ab"sə-loo'shən) *n.* **1,** act of absolving. **2,** forgiveness of sins; remission of punishment for sins.

ab'so·lut"ism (ab'sə-loo"tiz-əm) *n.* **1,** advocacy of autocratic government. **2,** any doctrine held without reservations. —**ab"so·lut'ist,** *adj. & n.*

ab·solve' (ab-solv') *v.t.* **1,** pardon; free from penalty. **2,** release from an obligation.

ab·sorb' (ab-sôrb') *v.t.* **1,** suck up a liquid; take in; assimilate. **2,** swallow, engulf, or engross completely. **—ab·sorbed′**, *adj.* preoccupied.

ab·sorb′ent (-ənt) *adj.* readily sucking up. **—ab·sorb′en·cy,** *n.*

ab·sorb′ing *adj.* very interesting.

ab·sorp′tion (ab-sôrp′shən) *n.* **1,** act of absorbing; assimilation. **2,** preoccupation. **—ab·sorp′tive,** *adj.*

ab·stain′ (ab-stān′) *v.i.* refrain (usually, from pleasurable action).

ab·ste′mi·ous (ab-stē′mė-əs) *adj.* moderate, temperate, esp. as to food and drink. **—ab·ste′mi·ous·ness,** *n.*

ab·sten′tion (ab-sten′shən) *n.* act of abstaining. **—ab·sten′tious,** *adj.*

ab′sti·nence (ab′sti-nəns) *n.* self-restraint in satisfaction of appetite. **—ab′sti·nent,** *adj.*

ab·stract′ (ab-strakt′) *v.t.* **1,** consider in general terms. **2,** take away; steal. **3,** (ab′strakt) reduce to a summary; epitomize. **—n.** (ab′strakt) **1,** a summary or inventory. **2,** the essential aspects of a subject. **—adj.** (ab′strakt) conceived in general or theoretical terms. **—ab·stract′ed,** *adj.* inattentive; preoccupied.

ab·strac′tion (ab-strak′shən) *n.* **1,** act of abstracting. **2,** state of being preoccupied or inattentive. **3,** an abstract idea, concept, etc.

ab·struse′ (ab-stroos′) *adj.* **1,** difficult to comprehend. **2,** profound. **—ab·struse′ness,** *n.*

ab·surd′ (ab-sêrd′) *adj.* contrary to common sense or sound judgment; logically impossible; ridiculous. **—n.** man's existence as meaningless and without purpose.

ab·surd′i·ty (-ə-tė) *n.* quality of being absurd; something that is absurd.

a·bun′dance (ə-bun′dəns) *n.* copious supply or quantity; plenteousness. **—a·bun′dant,** *adj.*

a·buse′ (ə-būz′) *v.t.* **1,** put to a wrong or bad use; misapply. **2,** do wrong to; injure; violate; defile. **3,** attack with contumelious language; revile. **—n.** (-būs′) improper use; injury; insult. **—a·bu′sive** (-bū′siv) *adj.*

a·but′ (ə-but′) *v.t.* [**a·but′ted, -ting**] rest against; be contiguous to. **—a·but′tal** (-əl), *n.*

a·but′ment (-mənt) *n.* **1,** a junction. **2,** a supporting base.

a·bys′mal (ə-biz′məl) *adj.* like an abyss; immeasurably deep or low.

a·byss′ (ə-bis′) *n.* bottomless pit; gulf; any deep, immeasurable space. Also, **a·bysm′** (a-biz′am). **—a·bys′sal** (-əl) *adj.*

a·ca′cia (ə-kā′shə) *n.* **1,** (*cap.*) a genus of shrubby plants. **2,** gum arabic. **3,** the locust tree.

ac′a·deme″ (ak′ə-dēm″) *n.* academic environment.

ac″a·dem′ic (ak″ə-dem′ik) *adj.* **1,** conforming to set rules or traditions; conventional. **2,** pert. to a college or other institution of higher learning. **3,** theoretical. **—ac″a·dem′i·cal·ly,** *adv.* **—ac″a·dem′i·cism** (-ə-siz-əm) *n.*

a·cad″e·mi′cian (ə-kad″ə-mish′ən) *n.* a member of a society for the promotion of an art or science.

a·cad′e·my (ə-kad′ə-mė) *n.* **1,** a school for instruction in a particular art or science. **2,** a private college-preparatory school. **3,** an association of adepts for the promotion of an art or science.

a·can′thus (ə-kan′thəs) *n.* **1,** a spiny shrub of Europe and Africa. **2,** a conventionalized representation of its leaf, used as an ornament in architecture.

a cap·pel′la (ä-kə-pel′ə) (*Ital., Music*) without accompaniment.

ac′a·rid (ak′ə-rid) *n.* a mite or tick.

ac·cede′ (ak-sēd′) *v.i.* (with *to*) **1,** give assent; yield. **2,** come into possession of; attain.

ac·cel″er·an′do (ak-sel″ə-rän′dō) *adj. & adv.* (*Music*) gradually increasing in speed. **—n.** a speeding up.

ac·cel′er·ate″ (ak-sel′ə-rāt″) *v.i.* increase in speed. **—v.t.** cause to move or develop faster.

ac·cel″er·a′tion (ak-sel″ə-rā′shən) *n.* **1,** act of accelerating. **2,** increase in speed; the rate of such increase.

ac·cel″er·a′tor (ak-sel′ə-rā″tər) *n.* **1,** a pedal for opening and closing the throttle of an automobile. **2,** a substance for hastening a chemical reaction.

ac′cent (ak′sent) *n.* **1,** special emphasis; stress placed on a particular syllable in uttering a word. **2,** manner of utterance; peculiarity of pronunciation, as *a foreign accent.* **3,** a mark attached to a letter, syllable, or musical note, to show pronunciation, stress, octave, etc. **—v.t.** (also ak-sent′) **1,** utter with emphasis. **2,** mark to show stress, etc.

ac·cen′tu·ate″ (ak-sen′choo-āt″) *v.t.* stress; emphasize. **—ac·cen″tu·a′tion,** *n.*

ac·cept′ (ak-sept′) *v.t. & i.* **1,** receive with approval; take in a formal way. **2,** agree to; give credence to. **—ac·cept′a·ble,** *adj.* worthy of approval.

ac·cept′ance (ak-sep′təns) *n.* **1,** act of accepting; approval. **2,** (*Com.*) a bill one has agreed to pay later.

ac″cep·ta′tion (ak″sep-tā′shən) *n.* meaning; sense.

ac′cess (ak′ses) *n.* **1,** means of approach

or admission. **2**, condition of being approachable. **—ac·ces'si·ble**, *adj.*

ac·ces'sion (ak-sesh'ən) *n*. **1**, attainment of a right or office. **2**, something added; increment. **3**, agreement; consent.

ac·ces'so·ry (ak-ses'ə-rè) *n*. **1**, an added and subordinate part. **2**, (*Law*) one who aids or abets a felony without being present at its commission. *—adj.* **1**, belonging to. **2**, contributory.

ac·ciac"ca·tu'ra (ät-chäk"kə-too'rə) *n*. (*Music*) a grace note half a step below its principal.

ac'ci·dent (ak'si-dənt) *n*. **1**, an unfortunate occurrence; mishap; catastrophe. **2**, any chance or fortuitous event.

ac"ci·den'tal (-den'təl) *adj*. **1**, happening by chance. **2**, subsidiary.

ac·cip'i·ter (ak-sip'ə-tər) *n*. a long-tailed hawk.

ac·claim' (ə-klām') *v.t.* **1**, applaud. **2**, proclaim with general approval.

ac"cla·ma'tion (ak"lə-mā'shən) *n*. a demonstration of joy or approval; election by such a demonstration. **—ac·clam'a·to·ry** (ə-klam'ə-tôr-è) *adj.*

ac·cli'mate (ə-klī'mət) *v.t. & i.* accustom or become accustomed to a new climate or environment. Also, **ac·cli'ma·tize'** (-mə-tīz"). **—ac"cli·ma'tion, ac·cli"ma·ti·za'tion**, *n.*

ac·cliv'i·ty (ə-kliv'ə-tè) *n*. an upward slope.

ac'co·lade" (ak'ə-lād") *n*. a ceremony conferring honor, as knighthood.

ac·com'mo·date" (ə-kom'ə-dāt") *v.t.* **1**, make suitable; adapt. **2**, do a kindness to; serve; furnish. *—v.i.* come into adjustment or conformance. **—ac·com'mo·dat"ing**, *adj.* obliging; considerate.

ac·com"mo·da'tion (ə-kom"ə-dā'shən) *n*. **1**, adaptation. **2**, readiness to serve. **3**, anything that supplies a want. **4**, (*pl.*) lodgings.

ac·com'pa·ni·ment (ə-kum'pə-nè-mənt) *n*. **1**, something subordinate added to a principal thing. **2**, (*Music*) harmony supplied to support solo voices.

ac·com'pa·ny (ə-kum'pə-nè) *v.t.* **1**, go with; be associated with. **2**, (*Music*) provide accompaniment for (a voice, etc.). **—ac·com'pa·nist**, *n.*

ac·com'plice (ə-kom'plis) *n*. an associate in a crime.

ac·com'plish (ə-kom'plish) *v.t.* **1**, bring to pass; do; complete. **2**, achieve; gain. **—ac·com'plished**, *adj.* talented; skillful. **—ac·com'plish·ment**, *n*. performance; attainment.

ac·cord' (ə-kôrd') *v.i.* be in harmony;

agree. *—v.t.* **1**, bring into agreement; adjust. **2**, render; concede. *—n.* agreement. **—ac·cord'ance**, *n.* **—ac·cord'ant**, *adj.*

ac·cord'ing (ə-kôr'ding) *adv.* **1**, (with *to* or *as*) in conformance with; in proportion to. **2**, (with *to*) as said by. **—ac·cord'ing·ly**, *adv.* so; hence; consequently.

ac·cor'di·on (ə-kôr'dè-ən) *n*. a handheld keyboard wind instrument with metal reeds, operated by a bellows. *—adj.* pleated like the bellows of an accordion. **—ac·cor'di·on·ist**, *n.*

ac·cost' (ə-kâst') *v.t.* approach and speak to; address.

ac·count' (ə-kownt') *n*. **1**, a record of pecuniary transactions. **2**, enumeration. **3**, explanatory statement; recital of facts. **4**, advantage. *—v.i.* **1**, keep records, esp. of money. **2**, give explanation. *—v.t.* impute. **—on account**, in part payment. **—on account of**, because of.

ac·count'a·ble (-ə-bəl) *adj*. **1**, able to be explained. **2**, liable. **3**, responsible. **—ac·count"a·bil'i·ty**, *n.*

ac·count'ant (-ənt) *n*. one who practices accounting. **—ac·count'an·cy**, *n.*

ac·count'ing *n*. **1**, the keeping and auditing of financial records. **2**, a statement of transactions; account.

ac·cout'er (ə-koo'tər) *v.t.* equip, esp. for military service; attire. **—ac·cou'ter·ments** (-mənts) *n.pl.* personal clothing; equipment.

ac·cred'it (ə-kred'it) *v.t.* **1**, accept as true; believe. **2**, ascribe or attribute to. **3**, confer authority upon; certify.

ac·crete' (ə-krēt') *v.i.* grow together; adhere. *—v.t.* add to.

ac·cre'tion (ə-krē'shən) *n*. act or result of accreting; increase; an added part.

ac·cru'al (ə-kroo'əl) *n*. that which accrues; in accounting, an amount entered on the books but payable or receivable in the future.

ac·crue' (ə-kroo') *v.i.* happen in due course; result from natural growth.

ac·cu'mu·late" (ə-kū'myə-lāt") *v.t.* collect or bring together; amass. *—v.i.* increase in size, quantity, or number. **—ac·cu"mu·la'tion**, *n.* **—ac·cu'mu·la"tive**, *adj.*

ac'cu·ra·cy (ak'yû-rə-sè) *n*. correctness; precision.

ac'cu·rate (ak'yû-rət) *adj*. correct; true; in exact conformity with a standard. **—ac'cu·rate·ness**, *n.*

ac·curs'ed (ə-kêr'sid) *adj*. doomed to misfortune; detestable. Also, **ac·curst'**. **—ac·curs'ed·ness**, *n.*

ac"cu·sa'tion (ak"yû-zā'shən) *n*. **1**, act of accusing. **2**, a charge of wrongdoing. Also, **ac·cu'sal** (ə-kū'zəl).

ac·cu'sa·tive (ə-kū'zə-tiv) *n. & adj.* a grammatical case denoting the direct object of a verb.

ac·cuse' (ə-kūz') *v.t.* charge with guilt or blame.

ac·cus'tom (ə-kus'təm) *v.t.* familiarize by custom or use. **—ac·cus'tomed,** *adj.* **1,** customary; usual. **2,** wonted.

ace (ās) *n.* **1,** a playing card or face of a die marked with a single pip. **2,** a point won without contest, as in tennis. **3,** an expert; adept. **4,** a very small quantity or degree. **5,** a fighter pilot who has downed five or more enemy planes. *—v.t.* win a point from (an opponent) without contest. *—adj.* of highest rank or proficiency; excellent. **—ace in the hole, 1,** a card dealt face down. **2,** (*Colloq.*) a concealed advantage.

ac'er·bate" (as'ər-bāt") *v.t.* embitter; exasperate.

a·cerb'i·ty (ə-sėr'bə-tė) *n.* **1,** sourness of taste. **2,** harshness of temper or expression.

ac'er·ose" (as'ə-rōs") *adj.* shaped like a needle.

ac·et"a·min'o·phen(a-set"ə-min'ə-fən)*n.* a drug used to relieve pain and reduce fever.

ac"et·an'i·lide (as"i-tan'ə-lid) *n.* a compound used to reduce fever or relieve pain.

ac'e·tate" (as'ə-tāt") *n.* (*Chem.*) a salt of acetic acid. **—cellulose acetate,** a thermoplastic compound.

a·ce'tic (ə-sē'tik) *adj.* pert. to vinegar.

a·ce'ti·fy (a-sē'tə-fī) *v.t.* convert to acid or vinegar.

ac'e·tone" (as'ə-tōn") *n.* a distillate of acetates, used as a solvent.

a·cet'y·lene (ə-set'ə-lin) *n.* a gas used as an illuminant and to produce a very hot flame.

ache (āk) *n.* continued pain. *—v.i.* **1,** suffer enduring pain. **2,** (*Colloq.*) yearn. **—ach'y** (-ē) *adj.*

a·chieve' (ə-chēv') *v.t. & i.* execute successfully; accomplish.

a·chieve'ment (-mənt) *n.* act or result of achieving; consummation; a notable deed.

A·chil'les heel (ə-kil'ēz) a vulnerable spot.

ach"ro·mat'ic (ak"rə-mat'ik) *adj.* free from coloration, as *achromatic lens,* one that transmits light without decomposing it. **—ach"ro·mat'i·cal·ly,** *adv.*

Ach"ro·my'cin (ak"rə-mī'sin) *n.* (*T.N.*) an antibiotic drug.

ac'id (as'id) *n.* **1,** any substance with a sour taste. **2,** (*Chem.*) a compound in which hydrogen can be replaced by a metal. **3,** (*Slang*) LSD, a drug producing hallucinations. *—adj.* **—a·cid'i·ty,** *n.* **—ac'id·i·fy,** *v.t.* acetify. **—acid test,** a definitive test of quality, value, etc.

ac"i·doph'i·lus milk (as"i-dof'ə-ləs) a fermented milk used medicinally.

ac"i·do'sis (as"i-dō'sis) *n.* excess acidity of the blood.

a·cid'u·lous (a-sid'yə-ləs) *adj.* somewhat acid; slightly sour.

-a·cious (ā-shəs) *suf.* forming adjectives from nouns ending in *-acity.*

-a·ci·ty (as-ə-tè) *suf.* the quality of being, or a tendency to be.

ack (ak) *n.* (*Brit.*) the letter A. **—ack'ack",** *n.* antiaircraft fire.

ac·knowl'edge (ak-nol'ij) *v.t.* **1,** admit the existence or truth of. **2,** give evidence of recognizing or realizing; certify the receipt of. **—ac·knowl'edg·ment,** *n.*

ac'me (ak'mē) *n.* the top or highest point.

ac'ne (ak'nē) *n.* a disease characterized by pimply skin eruption.

ac'o·lyte" (ak'ə-līt") *n.* **1,** a novice, esp. in a religious order. **2,** an attendant; assistant.

ac'o·nite" (ak'ə-nīt") *n.* **1,** a plant, monkshood or wolfbane. **2,** a medicinal tincture of this plant.

a'corn (ā'kôrn) *n.* the nut of the oak tree.

a·cous'tic (ə-koos'tik) *adj.* pert. to sound, hearing, or acoustics. **—a·cous'ti·cal·ly,** *adv.*

a·cous'tics (-tiks) *n.* **1,** (*sing.*) the science of sound. **2,** (*pl.*) the sound-reflecting properties (of a structure, etc.).

ac·quaint' (ə-kwānt') *v.t.* make familiar with; inform.

ac·quaint'ance (-əns) *n.* **1,** personal knowledge. **2,** a person known only slightly. **—ac·quaint'ance·ship,** *n.*

ac"qui·esce' (ak"wē-es') *v.i.* (with *in*) consent; agree. **—ac·qui·es'cence,** *n.* **—ac·qui·es'cent,** *adj.* yielding; submissive.

ac·quire' (ə-kwīr') *v.t.* obtain; gain. **—ac·quire'ment,** *n.*

ac"qui·si'tion (ak"wə-zish'ən) *n.* **1,** the act of acquiring. **2,** something acquired.

ac·quis'i·tive (ə-kwiz'ə-tiv) *adj.* tending to acquire; avaricious; grasping. **—ac·quis'i·tive·ness,** *n.*

ac·quit' (ə-kwit') *v.t.* [**ac·quit'ted, -ting**] **1,** pronounce not guilty; release, as from an obligation. **2,** discharge or pay, as a debt. **—acquit oneself,** behave.

ac·quit'tal (-əl) *n.* act or result of acquitting; exoneration.

a'cre (ā'kər) *n.* a measure of area, 43,560 sq. ft. **—a'cre·age,** *n.*

ac'rid (ak'rid) *adj.* sharp or biting to the tongue; pungent; severe. **—a·crid'i·ty, ac'rid·ness,** *n.*

ac'ri·mo"ny (ak'rə-mō"nē) *n.* bitterness of temper or expression. **—ac"ri·mo'ni·ous,** *adj.*

ac'ro·bat (ak'rə-bat) *n.* a gymnastic performer. —**ac'ro·bat'ic,** *adj.* —**ac''ro·bat'- i·cal·ly,** *adv.*

ac''ro·bat'ics (-iks) *n.sing. & pl.* the feats of an acrobat; agility.

ac'ro·nym'' (ak'rə-nim'') *n.* a word made from the initial letters of a term or phrase, as *WAC* (Women's Army Corps.)

ac''ro·pho'bi·a (ak''rə-fō'bē-ə) *n.* fear of high places.

a·crop'o·lis (ə-krop'ə-lis) *n.* 1, a settlement located on an eminence. 2, (*cap.*) the citadel of Athens.

a·cross' (ə-krâs') *prep.* from side to side of; transverse to; on the other side of. —*adv.* from side to side; crosswise. —**across-the-board,** *adj.* all-inclusive. —**come across,** 1, encounter by chance. 2, (*Colloq.*) pay up; tell the truth.

a·cros'tic (ə-krâs'tik) *n. & adj.* a composition in which the initial letters of lines form a word or phrase.

a·cryl'ic (ə-kril'ik) *adj.* pert. to an acid used in certain plastics, as lucite and plexiglass, and in paints.

act (akt) *v.i.* 1, do something; exert energy or force in any way. 2, exert influence; operate. 3, perform on the stage. 4, (with *up*) be unruly; behave eccentrically. —*v.t.* (often with *out*) do; perform; transact; represent by action. —*n.* 1, anything done; an exertion of energy or force; deed. 2, a law, ordinance, decree, or judgment, etc. 3, individual performance in a varied program. 4, a main division of a play. —**act of God,** an unforeseeable or unpreventable natural event.

ACTH *n.* a pituitary derivative used in combating rheumatic fever, arthritis, etc.

act'ing *adj.* 1, functioning. 2, serving temporarily.

ac·tin'ic (ak-tin'ik) *adj.* pert. to chemical reactions caused by radiant energy, as in a photographic emulsion by sunlight. —**ac· tin'i·cal·ly,** *adv.*

ac'tin·ide (ak'tin-īd) *adj.* any of a series of radioactive elements similar to actinium.

ac·tin'i·um (ak-tin'ē-əm) *n.* a radioactive chemical element resembling the rare earths, no. 89, symbol Ac.

ac'tion (ak'shən) *n.* 1, something done; an exertion of energy or force; act. 2, state of being active; continued influence; behavior; conduct. 3, a sequence of events; the main story of a play or narrative; a battle. 4, an operating mechanism, as of a watch. 5, a legal proceeding. 6, (*Slang*) the profits or spoils of some activity. —**ac'tion·a·ble,** *adj.* giving ground for a lawsuit.

ac'ti·vate'' (ak'tə-vāt'') *v.t.* make active; hasten action; put into operation. —**acti-**

vated **charcoal,** a highly absorbent form of carbon. —**ac''ti·va'tion,** *n.* —**ac'ti·va''tor,** *n.*

ac'tive (ak'tiv) *adj.* 1, engaged in action; busy; brisk; agile. 2, having the power to function, operate, or influence. 3, (*Gram.*) denoting the verb-form of action performed by the subject. —**ac'tive·ness,** *n.*

ac'tiv·ism (ak'tiv-iz-əm) *n.* a doctrine advocating the use of force. —**ac'ti·vist,** *n.*

ac·tiv'i·ty (ak-tiv'ə-tē) *n.* 1, state of being active. 2, a function; event.

ac'tor (ak'tər) *n.* one who acts, esp. a stage-player. —**ac'tress,** *n.fem.*

ac'tu·al (ak'choo-əl) *adj.* 1, of real existence. 2, now existing; present. —**ac''tu·al- ize'',** *v.t.*

ac''tu·al'i·ty (ak''choo-al'ə-tē) *n.* 1, real existence. 2, something real. 3, (*pl.*) actual circumstances; realities.

ac'tu·ar·y (ak'choo-er-ē) *n.* one who calculates insurance risks. —**ac''tu·ar'i·al,** *adj.*

ac'tu·ate'' (ak'choo-āt'') *v.t.* put or incite into action. —**ac''tu·a'tion,** *n.*

a·cu'men (ə-kū'mən) *n.* mental acuteness; keenness of perception or insight.

ac'u·punc''ture (ak'yû-punk''chər) *n.* an ancient method of therapy and pain relief by puncturing the body with needles.

a·cute' (ə-kūt') *adj.* 1, sharp-pointed; intense; shrill. 2, keen in perception or penetration; susceptible of slight impressions; discriminating. —**acute accent,** the mark (´), as in the French é. —**acute angle** (*Geom.*) one of less than 90°. —**a·cute'ness,** **a·cu'i·ty** (ə-kū'ə-tē) *n.*

-a·cy (ə-sē) *suf.* forming nouns denoting quality or state.

ad *n.* (*Colloq.*) advertisement. —**ad'man,** *n.* one who writes ads.

ad- *pref.* denoting addition, direction, or tendency.

ad'age (ad'ij) *n.* a pithy saying; proverb; old saying.

a·da'gio (ə-dä'zhō) *adj. & adv.* (*Music*) slow. —*n.* a movement in slow time. —**adagio dance,** a dance, usually for two, characterized by much posturing.

ad'a·mant (ad'ə-mənt) *adj.* hard; hard-hearted; unyielding. —*n.* any extremely hard mineral, as diamond. —**ad''a·man'tine** (ad''ə-man'tīn) *adj.*

Ad'am's apple the prominent formation of thyroid cartilage at the front of a man's throat.

a·dapt' (ə-dapt') *v.t.* make suitable; alter to fit. —**a·dapt'a·ble,** *adj.* easy to adapt; readily able to conform. —**ad''ap·ta'tion** (ad''əp-tā'shən) *n.*

add (ad) *v.t.* 1, increase by attaching more;

annex. **2,** unite in one sum or aggregate. —*v.i.* **1,** supply as an addition. **2,** perform arithmetical addition. —**ad′di·tive** (-ə-tiv) *n. & adj.*

ad′dend (ad′end) *n.* a number to be added.

ad·den′dum (ə-den′dəm) *n. [pl.* **-da** (-də)] something that is added, as the appendix of a book.

ad′der (ad′ər) *n.* any of several common vipers.

ad′dict (ad′ikt) *n.* one who has a confirmed habit, as the overuse of drugs. —*v.t.* (ə-dikt′) (fol. by *to*) cause addiction in; devote or give oneself (to). —**ad·dict′ed,** *adj.* —**ad·dic′tion,** *n.*

ad·di′tion (ə-dish′ən) *n.* **1,** the act or process of adding or uniting. **2,** the arithmetical operation of finding a sum, expressed by the symbol + . **3,** anything added. —**ad·di′tion·al,** *adj.* added; extra.

ad′dle (ad′əl) *v.t. & i.* make or become muddled or confused.

ad·dress′ (ə-dres′) *v.t.* **1,** speak or write to. **2,** direct attention to. **3,** direct for transmission. **4,** pay court to as a lover. —*n.* **1,** a formal utterance in speech or writing directed to a body of persons. **2,** the place where a person lives or may be reached. **3,** personal bearing; manner of speech. —**ad·dress′ee** (-ē) *n.*

ad·duce′ (ə-dūs′) *v.t.* bring forward as a reason or explanation; cite as evidence.

-ade (ād) *suf.* denoting **1,** action or result of action. **2,** a drink.

ad′e·noid (ad′ə-noid″) *n.* (usually *pl.*) a swollen lymphatic tissue in the pharynx that often impedes breathing. —**ad″e·noid′al,** *adj.*

ad′ept (ad′ept) *n.* one who has attained proficiency. —*adj.* (ə-dept′) skillful; expert. —**a·dept′ness,** *n.*

ad′e·quate (ad′i-kwət) *adj.* equal to requirement or occasion; sufficient; suitable. —**ad′e·qua·cy** (-kwə-sē) *n.*

ad·here′ (ad-hir′) *v.i.* **1,** stick fast; become joined. **2,** hold closely, as to an idea or course; be devoted. —**ad·her′ence,** *n.*

ad·her′ent (-ənt) *n.* one who follows a leader or supports a cause.

ad·he′sion (ad-hē′zhən) *n.* adherence between unlike particles.

ad·he′sive (ad-hē′siv) *adj.* sticky; tenacious; adhering. —*n.* that which sticks. —**ad·he′sive·ness,** *n.*

ad hoc (ad′hok′) (*Lat.*) relating exclusively to the subject in question.

a·dieu′ (ə-dū′) (*Fr.*) *interj. & n. [pl.* **-dieus′;** **-dieux′** (-dūz′)] farewell; good-bye.

a·dios′ (ä-dyōs′) *interj.* (*Sp.*) good-bye.

ad′i·pose″ (ad′i-pōs″) *adj.* fatty. —*n.* body fat, esp. on the kidneys. —**ad″i·pos′i·ty** (-pos′ə-tē) *n.*

ad′it *n.* an entrance or passageway.

ad·ja′cent (ə-jā′sənt) *adj.* lying near, close, or contiguous; adjoining. —**ad·ja′cen·cy** (-sən-sē) *n.*

ad′jec·tive (aj′ek-tiv) *n.* (*Gram.*) a word used to qualify, limit, or define a noun, as: *a large* book.

ad·join′ (ə-join′) *v.t. & i.* be adjacent; be in contact; abut.

ad·journ′ (ə-jêrn′) *v.t. & i.* **1,** suspend a sitting till another day, as of a legislature or court. **2,** defer; postpone. —**ad·journ′ment,** *n.*

ad·judge′ (ə-juj′) *v.t.* **1,** decide by judicial opinion; pronounce, decree, or award formally. **2,** judge; deem.

ad·ju′di·cate″ (ə-joo′di-kāt″) *v.t. & i.* adjudge; determine judicially. —**ad·ju″di·ca′tion,** *n.* —**ad·ju′di·ca″tor,** *n.*

ad′junct (a′junkt) *n.* something added to another. —*adj.* additional, esp. in a subordinate sense.

ad·jure′ (ə-jûr′) *v.t.* command, charge, or bind earnestly and solemnly. —**ad″ju·ra′tion** (aj″ə-rā′shən) *n.*

ad·just′ (ə-just′) *v.t.* **1,** make to fit or conform; adapt. **2,** put in order; regulate. **3,** bring to a satisfactory result; settle. —**ad·just′ment,** *n.*

ad′ju·tant (aj″ə-tənt) *n.* **1,** a military executive officer or aide. **2,** an assistant. **3,** an East Indian stork.

ad-lib′ *v.t. & i.* [**-libbed′, -lib′bing**] (*Colloq.*) improvise (lines or action not in the script, etc.). —*n.* something improvised.

ad·min′is·ter (ad-min′əs-tər) *v.t.* **1,** manage as an agent; conduct; superintend. **2,** make application of; supply; dispense. —*v.i.* (with *to*) bring aid. Also, **ad·min′is·trate″** (-trāt″).

ad·min″is·tra′tion (-strā′shən) *n.* **1,** conduct. **2,** any body of persons entrusted with ultimate executive powers. —**ad·min′is·tra″tive,** *adj.*

ad·min′is·tra″tor (ad-min′i-strā″tər) *n.* one who administers; executor. —**ad·min′is·tra″trix** (-triks) *n.fem.*

ad′mi·ra·ble (ad′mə-rə-bəl) *adj.* worthy of admiration; excellent. —**ad′mi·ra·ble·ness,** *n.*

ad′mi·ral (ad′mə-rəl) *n.* **1,** a naval officer of highest rank. **2,** the commander of a fleet.

ad′mi·ral·ty (ad′mə-rəl-tē) *n.* **1,** the office of admiral. **2,** the administration of a navy. **3,** maritime law.

ad″mi·ra′tion (ad″mə-rā′shən) *n.* act of admiring; approval.

ad·mire′ (ad-mīr′) *v.t.* regard with approbation, esteem, or affection. —*v.i.* (*Dial.*) wish (to). —**ad·mir′er,** *n.* one who admires; (*Colloq.*) a suitor.

ad·mis′si·ble (ad-mis′ə-bəl) *adj.* that may be conceded or allowed. —**ad·mis″si·bil′i·ty,** *n.*

ad·mis′sion (ad-mish′ən) *n.* **1,** the act of entering or admitting, or being allowed to enter. **2,** entrance fee. **3,** an acknowledgment or confession that something is true.

ad·mit′ *v.t. & i.* [-**mit′ted,** -**ting**] **1,** allow to enter; give means or right of entry. **2,** concede as valid; acknowledge to be true. —**ad·mit′tance** (-əns) *n.* permission or right to enter; admission.

ad·mix′ture (ad-miks′chər) *n.* **1,** the act of mixing or mingling, esp. of different substances. **2,** something added; ingredient. —**ad′mix,** *v. & n.*

ad·mon′ish *v.t.* **1,** reprove mildly. **2,** warn against something; exhort; guide. —**ad·mon′ish·ment,** *n.*

ad″mo·ni′tion (ad″mə-nish′ən) *n.* reproof; advice; warning. —**ad·mon′i·to·ry** (ad-mon′ə-tôr-ē) *adj.*

ad nau′se·am (ad-nâ′zē-əm) (*Lat.*) to the extent of causing disgust or boredom.

a·do′ (ə-doo′) *n.* action; bustle; trouble.

a·do′be (ə-dō′bē) *n.* a sun-dried block of mud used in building.

ad″o·les′cence (ad″ə-les′əns) *n.* the age of human life between puberty and adulthood, from about 14 to 25 (men) or 12 to 21 (women).

ad″o·les′cent (-ənt) *adj.* of or characteristic of adolescence. —*n.* an adolescent boy or girl.

a·dopt′ (ə-dopt′) **1,** take or receive as one's own. **2,** (of a council or legislature) vote to accept. —**a·dop′tion,** *n.* —**a·dop′tive,** *adj.*

a·dor′a·ble (ə-dôr′ə-bəl) *adj.* worthy of the utmost love or admiration. —**a·dor′a·ble·ness,** *n.*

ad″o·ra′tion (ad″ə-rā′shən) *n.* act of adoring or worshiping.

a·dore′ (ə-dôr′) *v.t.* **1,** regard with utmost love, esteem, or respect. **2,** worship as divine.

a·dorn′ (ə-dôrn′) *v.t.* decorate; dress with ornaments; embellish. —**a·dorn′ment,** *n.*

ad·re′nal (ə-drē′nəl) *adj.* near or on the kidneys; of the adrenal glands.

ad·ren′a·lin (ə-dren′ə-lin) *n.* a drug used to stimulate heart action.

a·drift′ (ə-drift′) *adv. & adj.* floating at random; not moored; swayed by any chance impulse.

a·droit′ (ə-droit′) *adj.* dextrous; skillful; ingenious. —**a·droit′ness,** *n.*

ad·sorp′tion (ad-sôrp′shən) *n.* condensation of a gas on the surface of a solid. —**ad·sorb′,** *v.t.* —**ad·sor′bate** (-bāt) *n.*

ad′u·late″ (ad′ū-lāt″) *v.t.* show feigned devotion to; flatter servilely. —**ad″u·la′tion,** *n.* —**ad′u·la·to·ry** (-lə-tôr-ē) *adj.*

ad′ult *n.* a person or animal grown to full size and strength. —*adj.* (ə-dult′) full-grown; mature; legally of age. —**a·dult′hood,** *n.*

a·dul′ter·ant (ə-dul′tər-ənt) *n.* a baser ingredient. —*adj.* serving to adulterate.

a·dul′ter·ate″ (ə-dul′tə-rāt″) *v.t.* debase by addition or substitution of interior ingredients; make impure. —**a·dul″ter·a′tion,** *n.*

a·dul′ter·er (ə-dul′tər-ər) *n.* one who commits adultery. —**a·dul′ter·ess** (-əs) *n.fem.*

a·dul′ter·y (ə-dul′tə-rē) *n.* illicit relations between a married person and another than his lawful spouse. —**a·dul′ter·ous,** *adj.*

ad·um′brate (ad-um′brāt) *v.t.* give a faint shadow or outline of; foreshadow. —**ad″um·bra′tion,** *n.*

ad·vance′ (ad-vâns′) *v.t.* **1,** bring forward; raise; enhance; promote. **2,** supply beforehand; furnish on credit. —*v.i.* **1,** move forward. **2,** make progress; improve; increase in quantity or price. —*n.* **1,** forward movement; a step forward; an improvement. **2,** money or goods supplied beforehand or on credit. **3,** the foremost part, as of an army. —**ad·vance′ment,** *n.* —**advance man,** someone sent ahead to make arrangements, etc. (as for a tour).

ad·van′tage (ad-vân′tij) *n.* **1,** any favorable circumstance. **2,** benefit; gain; profit. **3,** superiority. —**ad″van·ta′geous** (ad″vən-tā′jəs) *adj.*

ad′vent *n.* **1,** arrival. **2,** (*cap.*) the coming of Christ into the world.

ad″ven·ti′tious (ad″vən-tish′əs) *adj.* not intrinsic to the subject; accidentally or casually acquired; foreign.

ad·ven′ture (ad-ven′chər) *n.* **1,** a remarkable occurrence; a noteworthy event; a hazardous enterprise. **2,** activity of a hazardous or exciting nature. —*v.t. & i.* embark upon; take the risk of; dare. —**ad·ven′tur·er,** *n.* a bold person; explorer; soldier of fortune. —**ad·ven′tur·ess,** *n.fem.* (*Derogatory*) a female adventurer; a social climber. —**ad·ven′tur·ous,** *adj.* **1,** risky. **2,** daring.

ad′verb (ad′vêrb) *n.* (*Gram.*) a word used to qualify, clarify, limit or extend a verb or adjective, or another adverb. —**ad·ver′bi·al,** *adj.*

ad′ver·sar·y (ad′vər-ser-ē) *n.* an opponent in a contest; enemy.

ad·verse' (ad-vers') *adj.* **1,** contrary in purpose or effect; opposite. **2,** harmful to one's interests; unfortunate.

ad·ver'si·ty (ad-ver'sə-tē) *n.* ill fortune; an unfortunate happening.

ad·vert' (ad-vert') *v.i.* (with *to*) refer; turn attention.

ad·ver·tise'' (ad'vər-tīz'') *v.t. & i.* **1,** make public announcement of; give information concerning. **2,** praise or otherwise promote, as in selling wares.

ad''ver·tise'ment (-mənt; also, ad-ver'-tiz-mənt) *n.* a notice (esp. paid) in a publication, etc.

ad'ver·tis''ing (ad'vər-tīz''ing) *n.* the art and practice of promoting enterprises, esp. by paid public notices.

ad·vice' (ad-vīs') *n.* **1,** counsel as to a course of action; suggestion. **2,** information; communication of news.

ad·vis'a·ble (ad-vī'zə-bəl) *adj.* wise to do. —**ad·vis''a·bil'i·ty,** *n.*

ad·vise' (ad-vīz') *v.t.* **1,** give counsel to; offer an opinion to. **2,** urge as wise or prudent; recommend. **3,** give information to. —*v.i.* take or offer advice. —**ad·vised',** *adj.* considered, as in ill-advised. —**ad·vi'-sed·ly,** *adv.* with good reason; deliberately. —**ad·vise'ment,** *n.* consideration.

ad·vi'so·ry (ad-vī'zə-rē) *adj.* giving advice; consultative.

ad'vo·ca·cy (ad'və-kə-sè) *n.* act of advocating; espousal; support.

ad'vo·cate'' (ad'və-kāt'') *v.t.* plead in favor of; defend in argument; support. —*n.* (-kət) one who pleads or espouses a cause.

adz *n.* a cutting tool, comprising a blade fixed at right angles to a handle, used for rough trimming.

ae- see *e-* or *ai-.*

ae'gis (ē'jis) *n.* egis.

Ae·o'li·an harp (ē-ō'lē-ən) a boxlike stringed instrument sounded by the wind.

a'er·ate'' (ā'ər-āt'') *v.t.* **1,** expose freely to air. **2,** charge with air, carbon dioxide, or other gas. —**a''er·a'tion,** *n.* —**a'er·a''tor,** *n.*

aer'i·al (er'ē-əl) *adj.* **1,** of, produced by, or inhabiting air. **2,** high in the air. **3,** light in weight or substance; visionary. **4,** graceful; ethereal. —*n.* a radio antenna. —**aer'i·al·ist,** *n.* a trapeze acrobat.

aer'ie (âr'ē; ir'ē) *n.* **1,** an eagle's nest. **2,** a dwelling on a height.

aer'o- (âr-ə) *pref.* pert. to **1,** air; **2,** gas; **3,** aircraft or aviation.

aer''o·bat'ics (-bat'iks) *n.sing.* or *pl.* the performance of aerial stunts with an airplane or glider; those stunts.

aer'obe (âr'ōb) *n.* a bacterium requiring

oxygen for life. —**aer·o'bic,** *adj.* —**aer·o'-bic·al·ly,** *adv.*

aer''o·do·net'ics (-dō-net'iks) *n.* the science of gliding. —**aer''o·do·net'ic,** *adj.*

aer'o·drome'' *n.* airdrome.

aer''o·dy·nam'ics *n.sing.* a branch of mechanics treating of air and other gases in motion.

aer'o·naut'' (âr'ə-nât'') *n.* one who flies in the air; a balloonist.

aer''o·nau'tics (-nâ'tiks) *n.* **1,** flight in aircraft. **2,** the art or science of flying. —**aer''o·nau'tic,** *adj.* —**aer''o·nau'ti·cal·ly,** *adv.*

aer'o·sol (-sol) *n.* **1,** a gas bearing another substance. **2,** a container that discharges such a gas.

aer'o·space'' *n.* the area including the earth's atmosphere and space beyond. —*adj.* pert. to aerospace, or vehicles or travel therein.

aer'o·stat *n.* lighter-than-air aircraft.

aer'o·train *n.* a propeller-driven vehicle supported by a cushion of air over a single rail.

a·far' (ə-fär') *adv.* from a distance; far away.

af'fa·ble (af'ə-bəl) *adj.* easy to approach (esp. of one in high station); courteous; gracious. —**af''fa·bil'i·ty,** *n.*

af·fair' (ə-fär') *n.* **1,** a matter, action, business, or concern requiring attention and effort. **2,** a particular event or performance. **3,** an involvement of love. **4,** (*pl.*) pecuniary interests or relations.

af·fect' (ə-fekt') *v.t.* **1,** produce an effect or change on; influence. **2,** impress deeply. **3,** make a show of; feign; imitate; adopt; assume the character of. —*n.* (af'ekt) feeling; emotion.

af''fec·ta'tion (af''ek-tā'shən) *n.* artificiality of manner; pretension to qualities not actually possessed.

af·fect'ed *adj.* **1,** influenced; impaired. **2,** artificial in manner or conduct. **3,** moved by emotion.

af·fect'ing *adj.* pitiful.

af·fec'tion (ə-fek'shən) *n.* **1,** good will; love. **2,** the result, act, or state of being influenced. —**af·fec'tion·ate** (-ət) *adj.* loving; warm-hearted.

af'fer·ent (af'ər-ənt) *adj.* leading inward to a central organ or nerve.

af·fi'ance (ə-fī'əns) *v.t.* bind in promise of marriage; betroth.

af''fi·da'vit (af''i-dā'vit) *n.* (*Law*) a written and sworn declaration of alleged facts.

af·fil'i·ate'' (ə-fil'ē-āt'') *v.i. & t.* bring into association; unite in action and interest; join with. —*n.* (-ē-ət) an associate; a branch organization. —**af·fil′i·a′tion,** *n.*

af·fin′i·ty (ə-fin′ə-tē) *n.* **1,** a natural liking for, or attraction to, a person or thing. **2,** inherent likeness or agreement between things.

af·firm′ (ə-fêrm′) *v.t.* **1,** assert positively; declare to be a fact. **2,** confirm; ratify. —*v.i.* (*Law*) declare solemnly, in lieu of swearing upon oath. —**af′fir·ma′tion** (af′-ər-mā′shən) *n.*

af·firm′a·tive (ə-fêr′mə-tiv) *adj.* positive in form, not negative. —*n.* **1,** a word or phrase expressing assent, agreement, or affirmation. **2,** the side favoring a proposition. —**affirmative action,** a positive effort made by employers to hire members of minority groups.

af·fix′ (ə-fix′) *v.t.* **1,** add or append. **2,** fasten or attach. —*n.* (af′iks) that which is added or attached.

af·fla′tus (ə-flā′təs) *n.* mental force or inspiration; evinced by religious, poetical, or oratorical expression.

af·flict′ (ə-flikt′) *v.t.* distress with mental or bodily pain; torment.

af·flic′tion (ə-flik′shən) *n.* **1,** distress; pain. **2,** a cause of distress; an ill or disease. —**af·flic′tive,** *adj.*

af′flu·ence (af′loo-əns) *n.* **1,** an abundant supply, as of material wealth. **2,** a flowing toward, as of a tributary watercourse.

af′flu·ent (af′loo-ənt) *adj.* **1,** flowing freely. **2,** rich; wealthy.

af·ford′ (ə-fôrd′) *v.t.* **1,** be able; have the means. **2,** yield; produce; furnish.

af·for′est (ə-for′əst) *v.* to plant with trees.

af·fray′ (ə-frā′) *n.* a noisy quarrel; brawl; disturbance.

af·front′ (ə-frunt′) *n.* a personally offensive act or word; an open manifestation of disrespect or contumely. —*v.t.* insult openly; make ashamed or confused.

Af′ghan (af′gan) *n.* **1,** a native of Afghanistan. **2,** a breed of hound. **3,** (*l.c.*) a kind of woolen blanket or shawl.

a·fi″cio·na′do (ə-fē″shə-nä′dō) *n.* enthusiast; devotee.

a·field′ (ə-fēld′) *adv.* abroad; off the beaten track; away from home.

a·fire′ (ə-fīr′) *adv. & adj.* burning.

a·flame′ (ə-flām′) *adv. & adj.* on fire.

a·float′ (ə-flōt′) *adv. & adj.* **1,** borne on the water. **2,** moving about; in circulation.

a·flut′ter (ə-flut′ər) *adj.* **1,** fluttering. **2,** mildly excited; agitated.

a·foot′ (ə-fût′) *adv. & adj.* **1,** walking. **2,** in progress.

a·fore′said (ə-fôr′sed) *adj.* which was

mentioned previously. Also, **a·fore′men″-tioned.**

a·fore′thought″ (ə-fôr′thât″) *adj.* premeditated.

a·foul′ (ə-fowl′) *adv. & adj.* in a state of collision or entanglement.

a·fraid′ (ə-frād′) *adj.* impressed with fear or apprehension.

A-′frame″ (ā′-) *n.* a building having triangular front and rear walls and a long peaked roof descending nearly to the ground.

Af′ri·can (af′ri-kən) *adj.* pert. to Africa, its inhabitants, or their languages. —*n.* a native of Africa; a Negro.

Af″ri·kaans′ (af″ri-kans′) *n.* one of the two official languages of the Union of So. Africa.

Af″ri·kan′der (af″ri-kan′dər) *n.* Boer. Also, **Af″ri·ka′ner** (-kä′nər).

Af′ro (af′rō) *n.* (*Colloq.*) **1,** a short, round, bushy hairstyle. **2,** African style of dress; esp., dashiki. —*adj.* (*Colloq.*) Afro-American.

Af″ro-A·mer′i·can (af″rō-) *adj. & n.* pert. to American Negroes. Also, *colloq.*, **Af′ro.**

aft *adv.* (*Naut.*) in, near, or toward the stern of a ship.

af′ter (âf′tər) *prep.* **1,** later in time; subsequent to. **2,** behind in place; in the rear of; below in rank. **3,** in pursuit of; with desire for. **4,** according to; in proportion to; in imitation of. —*adv. & adj.* **1,** later in time. **2,** behind or below in place. **3,** (*Naut.*) aft.

af′ter·birth″ *n.* the placenta.

af′ter·burn″er *n.* a device for burning fuel in the hot exhaust gases of a turbojet engine to provide extra thrust.

af′ter·math″ *n.* what comes after; the consequences.

af′ter·noon′ *n. & adj.* the part of the day from noon to night.

af′ter·thought″ *n.* a belated idea or act.

af′ter·ward (-wərd) *adv.* later in time; subsequently. Also, **af′ter·wards.**

a·gain′ (ə-gen′) *adv.* **1,** once more; another time; anew. **2,** in addition; moreover. **3,** back; in the opposite direction.

a·gainst′ (ə-genst′) *prep.* **1,** in an opposite direction to. **2,** in contact with; toward; upon. **3,** adverse or hostile to. **4,** in provision for; in exchange for.

a·gape′ (ə-gāp′; ə-gap′) *adv. & adj.* with the mouth wide open.

a′ga·pe″ (ä′gä-pā″) *n.* Christian brotherly love.

a′gar (ä′gär) *n.* a gelatinous culture medium made from certain seaweeds.

ag′ate (ag′ət) *n.* **1,** a variety of quartz. **2,** a child's marble made of agate or of glass in imitation of agate. **3,** (*Printing*), 5½-point type.

a·ga've (ə-gā'vē) *n.* a genus of plants found chiefly in Mexico; the century plant.

age (āj) *n.* **1,** the length of time during which a being or thing has existed. **2,** the lifetime of an individual; duration of existence. **3,** a particular period of history; the people and events of an era. **4,** (*Colloq.*) a long time. —*v.i.* grow old. —*v.t.* **1,** bring to maturity. **2,** make old. —**age'less,** *adj.* unchanging. —**of age,** having reached legal majority.

-age (ij) *suf.* forming nouns denoting condition, effect, result, etc.

a'ged (ā'jəd) *adj.* **1,** old; having lived a long time. **2,** (ājd) having the age of, as *aged twenty years.*

age'less (-ləs) *adj.* never growing old; unchanging.

a'gen·cy (ā'jən-sē) *n.* **1,** a means of producing effects or exerting power; an instrument. **2,** the office and duties of an agent. **3,** a commercial or government office furnishing a particular public service.

a·gen'da (ə-jen'də) *n.pl.* [*sing.* **-dum**] **1,** items of business to be brought before a council, etc. **2,** (*construed as sing.*) a list of such items.

a'gent (ā'jənt) *n.* **1,** a person acting on behalf of another. **2,** a representative, as of a commercial firm or government bureau; an official. **3,** an active cause, as (*Chem.*) a substance that produces a reaction.

ag·glom'er·ate" (ə-glom'ə-rāt") *v.i. & t.* collect in a mass. —*adj.* (-ət) piled together; in a dense cluster. —*n.* a cluster, as of rock fragments. —**ag·glom"er·a'tion,** *n.*

ag·glu'ti·nate" (ə-gloo'tə-nāt") *v.i. & t.* unite or cause to adhere, as with glue. —*adj.* adhering by or as by glue. —**ag·glu"ti·na'tion,** *n.*

ag·glu'ti·nin (ə-gloo'tin-ən) *n.* any organic substance which causes red blood cells or bacteria to agglutinate.

ag'gran·dize" (ag'rən-dīz") *v.t.* **1,** make greater in power, wealth, or rank; widen in scope; extend. **2,** magnify; exaggerate. —**ag·gran'dize·ment** (ə-grán'diz-mənt) *n.*

ag'gra·vate" (ag'rə-vāt") *v.t.* **1,** intensify; make more serious or troublesome. **2,** (*Colloq.*) irritate; provoke. —**ag"gra·va'tion,** *n.*

ag'gre·gate" (ag'ri-gāt") *v.t.* **1,** collect into a sum, mass, or body. **2,** amount to (a number). —*v.i.* come together. —*n.* (ag'rə-gət) **1,** gross amount. **2,** (*Geol.*) rock formed of a mixture of different minerals. —*adj.* (-gət) total; combined. —**ag"gre·ga'tion,** *n.*

ag·gress' (ə-gres') *v.i.* begin a quarrel.

ag·gres'sion (ə-gresh'ən) *n.* **1** an act of hostility; an assault or encroachment. **2,** offensive action in general.

ag·gres'sive (ə-gres'iv) *adj.* **1,** tending to attack or be hostile. **2,** vigorous. —**ag·gres'sive·ness,** *n.*

ag·gres'sor (ə-gres'ər) *n.* one who begins a quarrel or starts a war without adequate provocation.

ag·grieved' (ə-grēvd') *p. adj.* offended; having cause to feel vexed. —**ag·grieve',** *v.t.*

a·ghast' (ə-gàst') *adj.* struck with amazement; filled with sudden fright and horror.

ag'ile (aj'əl) *adj.* able to move quickly; active; nimble.

a·gil'i·ty (ə-jil'ə-tē) *n.* ability to move quickly; nimbleness.

ag'i·tate" (aj'ə-tāt") *v.t.* **1,** force into violent motion; shake briskly; perturb. **2,** call attention to by speech or writing. —*v.i.* engage in discussion or debate. —**ag"i·ta'tion,** *n.* —**ag'i·ta"tor,** *n.*

a·glow' (ə-glō') *adj.* glowing.

ag'nate (ag'nāt) *adj.* related on the father's side. —*n.* a kinsman on the father's side.

ag·nos'tic (ag-nos'tik) *n.* one who holds that ultimate causes (as God) are unknowable. —*adj.* holding this view. —**ag·nos'-ti·cal·ly,** *adv.* —**ag·nos'ti·cism** (ag-nos'ti-siz-əm) *n.*

a·go' (ə-gō') *adv. & adj.* in past time.

a·gog' (ə-gog') *adj. & adv.* in a state of excitement, curiosity, or eager desire.

-a·gon (ə-gon) *suf.* denoting a plane geometrical figure, as *pentagon.*

a·gon'ic (ə-gon'ik) *adj.* not forming an angle.

ag'o·nize" (ag'ə-nīz") *v.i.* suffer violent anguish. —*v.t.* distress with extreme pain.

ag'o·ny (ag'ə-nē) *n.* **1,** extreme and prolonged mental or bodily pain. **2,** the death struggle.

ag"o·ra·pho'bi·a (ag"ə-rə-fō'bē-ə) *n.* morbid fear of open spaces.

a·gou'ti (ə-goo'tē) *n.* a rabbitlike rodent of Central and So. Amer.

a·grar'i·an (ə-grâr'ē-ən) *adj.* **1,** pert. to land or property rights in land. **2,** agricultural; rural. —*n.* one who favors an equal division of landed property.

a·gree' (ə-grē') *v.i.* **1,** give assent; consent. **2,** be of one opinion or mind; arrive at a settlement. **3,** be consistent; harmonize. **4,** be similar; correspond; coincide. —*v.t.* concede.

a·gree'a·ble (-ə-bəl) *adj.* **1,** pleasing to the mind or senses. **2,** conformable; willing to consent. —**a·gree"a·bil'i·ty,** *n.*

a·gree'ment (-mənt) *n.* **1,** concord; harmony. **2,** a contract; bargain.

ag'ri·cul'ture (ag'ri-kul"chər) *n.* the cultivation of the ground to raise food; husbandry; farming. —**ag"ri·cul'tur·al,** *adj.* —**ag"ri·cul'tur·ist,** *n.*

ag·ro- (ag-rō) *pref.* soil; field.

a·gron'o·my (ə-gron'ə-mē) *n.* the science of crop production and soil management.

a·ground' (ə-grownd') *adj. & adv.* on the ground; stranded.

a'gue (ā'gū) *n.* a malarial fever marked by intermittent paroxysms of chills and sweating.

ah (ä) *interj.* of understanding, agreement, or almost any emotion.

a·ha' (ä-hä') *interj.* of surprise, triumph, or contempt.

a·head' (ə-hed') *adv.* **1,** in or to the front; in advance. **2,** forward; onward.

a·hem' (ə-hem') *interj.* to attract attention, as by an affected cough.

a·hoy' (ə-hoi') *interj.* used to attract attention of persons at a distance.

aid (ād) *v.t.* **1,** give support or relief to; help. **2,** promote the accomplishment of; facilitate. —*n.* **1,** assistance; support. **2,** he who or that which gives help.

aide (ād) *n.* an assistant; esp. (*Mil.*) a secretarial assistant to an officer. Also, **aide-'de-camp'** (-də-kamp').

ai'grette (ā'gret) *n.* a plume of feathers worn on the head.

ai'ki·do' (ī'kē-dō') *n.* a Japanese art of self-defense.

ail (āl) *v.t.* affect with pain. —*v.i.* feel pain; be unwell.

ai'ler·on (ā'lə-ron) *n.* a hinged flap in the wing of an airplane, controlling its horizontal position.

ail'ment (-mənt) *n.* illness; malady.

aim (ām) *v.t.* point at something; fix in a certain direction, as *aim a gun.* —*v.i.* (with an infinitive) strive toward; intend. —*n.* **1,** the direction in which something is aimed. **2,** the act of aiming. **3,** the thing aimed at; target; intention; purpose. —**aim'less,** *adj.* without purpose or direction.

ain't (ānt) vulgar form of am not, is not, are not, has not, have not.

Ai'nu (ī'noo) *n.* one of an aboriginal race of Japan; their language.

air (âr) *n.* **1,** the earth's atmosphere; the particular mixture of nitrogen, oxygen, etc., of which it is composed. **2,** a light breeze. **3,** space; scope. **4,** utterance abroad; publication. **5,** outward appearance; personal mien or bearing. **6,** (*pl.*) affected manners. **7,** a tune; a principal melody. —*v.t.* **1,** expose to the air; let air into; ventilate. **2,** bring to public notice; proclaim. **3,** (*Slang*) broadcast; put on the air. —*adj.* **1,** operated by compressed air, as *air brake.* **2,** for or by aircraft, as *air base, air raid.* —**air brush,** an atomizer for applying liquid paint. —**air cavalry,** an army unit transported by air for the purpose of reconnaissance or for ground action elsewhere. —**air curtain, air door,** a stream of compressed air, usu. heated or cooled, directed across an opening and replacing a door. —**air cushion, 1,** an inflated cushion. **2,** [also, **air bag**] a device for cushioning shock or equalizing pressure. —**air force,** the branch of the military forces controlling aircraft. —**air lift,** use of aircraft as the sole means of transportation to a place. —**air lock,** an airtight compartment used as a passageway into a compressed-air chamber. —**air pocket,** a downward current of air. —**air waves,** the media. —**get the air,** (*Slang*) be dismissed. —**in the air, 1,** rumored. **2,** uncertain.

air'borne" (-bôrn") *adj.* supported by the air; in flight.

air'bus" *n.* a very large, luxurious airliner.

air'coach" *n.* a low-priced air passenger transport service.

air-"con·di'tion·ing *n.* a system of indoor ventilation and temperature control. Also, **air cooling.** —**air-"con·di'tion,** *v.t.*

air'craft" (âr'kraft") *n.* any type of machine that flies in the air, whether lighter or heavier than air.

air'drome" (-drōm") *n.* airport. Also, **aer'o·drome".**

air'drop" *v.t.* deliver (personnel or supplies) by dropping from an aircraft with the aid of a parachute. —*n.* such delivery.

Aire'dale" (âr'dāl") *n.* a breed of large terriers.

air'field" (âr'fēld") *n.* a place leveled and surfaced on which aircraft alight; an airport.

air'foil" (âr'foil") *n.* any surface on an aircraft used for steering, lifting, etc., by the flow of air upon it.

air'line" *n.* a company furnishing air transport on fixed schedules.

air'lin"er *n.* a passenger airplane.

air'man (-mən) *n.* [*pl.* -**men**] aviator.

air'plane" (âr'plān") *n.* an engine-driven aircraft heavier than air.

air'port" (âr'pôrt") *n.* an airfield having some attendant facilities for handling aircraft and their passengers, and freight.

air'ship" (âr'ship") *n.* an engine-driven aircraft lighter than air.

air'tight" *adj.* **1,** sealed against air. **2,** (of an argument, etc.) flawless.

air'wor"thy (âr'wêr"thē) *adj.* of aircraft, safe to fly.

air·y (ār′ė) *adj.* **1,** like air; unsubstantial. **2,** open to a free current of air; well-ventilated. **3,** flimsy; unreal; visionary. **4,** light in manner or movement; sprightly. **5,** affectedly lofty; pretentious. —**air′i·ness,** *n.*

aisle (īl) *n.* a passageway giving access, as to the seats in a church or theater.

a·jar′ (ə-jär′) *adv. & adj.* partly open (said of a door).

a·kim′bo (ə-kim′bō) *adv. & adj.* in a sharp bend (said of the arms when the hands are placed on the hips and the elbows are extended sideward).

a·kin′ (ə-kin′) *adj.* **1,** related by blood. **2,** similar in nature.

-al (əl) *suf.* pertaining to.

à la (ä′lä) (*Fr.*) in the fashion of; according to. —**à la carte** (kärt) from the bill of fare; not on the dinner. —**à la king,** cooked in a cream sauce. —**à la mode,** served with ice cream.

al′a·bas″ter (al′ə-bas″tər) *n.* a marblelike mineral, often white, used for ornamental purposes. —*adj.* like alabaster; white.

a·lac′ri·ty (ə-lak′rə-tė) *n.* cheerful willingness; eager promptitude.

a′lar (ā′lər) *adj.* having wings; pert. to wings.

a·larm′ (ə-lärm′) *n.* **1,** a warning of approaching danger; an urgent summons; a signal for attention. **2,** any mechanical device for giving such a signal. **3,** sudden fear; apprehension of danger. —*v.t.* **1,** fill with anxiety or apprehension; frighten. **2,** give notice of danger to; rouse.

a·larm′ist (-ist) *n.* one disposed to expect or prophesy calamity.

a·las′ (ə-làs′) *interj.* of sorrow or pity.

a′late (ā′lāt) *adj.* having wings or membranes like wings.

alb *n.* a white robe worn by a priest.

al′ba·core″ (al′bə-kôr″) *n.* a food fish of the mackerel family.

al′ba·tross″ (al′bə-trâs″) *n.* a web-footed seabird of the petrel family.

al·be′it (âl-bē′it) *conj.* although; notwithstanding that.

al·bi′no (al-bī′nō) *n.* [*pl.* **-nos**] a person or animal having a whitish coloring. —**al′bi·nism** (al′bə-niz-əm) *n.*

al′bum (al′bəm) *n.* a book of blank leaves for the insertion of photographs, stamps, phonograph records, or the like.

al·bu′men (al-bū′mən) *n.* the white of an egg.

al·bu′min (al-bū′min) *n.* a protein occurring in the body.

al′che·my (al′kə-mė) *n.* the doctrines and processes of early and medieval chemists. —**al′che·mist,** *n.*

al′co·hol″ (al′kə-hâl″) *n.* **1,** a liquid, ethyl hydrate derived by fermentation or distillation from organic substances. **2,** any intoxicating liquor containing alcohol.

al″co·hol′ic (-hol′ik) *adj.* of or containing alcohol. —*n.* one suffering from alcoholism. —**al″co·hol′i·cal·ly,** *adv.*

al′co·hol·ism (-iz-əm) *n.* addiction to excessive drinking of alcoholic liquors; dipsomania.

al′cove (al′kōv) *n.* a covered recess, bay, or niche.

al′der (âl′dər) *n.* any of numerous shrubs and trees abundant in temperate climates.

al′der·man (âl′dər-mən) *n.* [*pl.* **-men**] a municipal official; in the U.S. he usually represents a ward in a legislative body.

Al′der·ney (âl′dər-nė) *n.* one of a breed of dairy cattle.

ale (āl) *n.* a beverage made from malt, similar to beer but containing more alcohol.

a′le·a·tor″y (ā′lė-ə-tôr″ė) *adj.* pert. to or governed by chance. Also, **a″le·a·tor′ic.**

a·lem′bic (ə-lem′bik) *n.* a beaker.

a·lert′ (ə-lėrt′) *adj.* **1,** vigilantly attentive; watchful. **2,** brisk, nimble. —*v.t.* warn of or activate for impending danger. —*n.* **1,** a warning signal. **2,** a state of vigilant readiness. —**a·lert′ness,** *n.*

ale′wife (āl′wīf) *n.* a No. Amer. fish similar to the shad.

a·lex′i·a (ə-lek′sė-ə) *n.* loss of the faculty of understanding written language.

al·fal′fa (al-fal′fə) *n.* a forage plant extensively cultivated in the U.S.; lucerne.

al′ga (al′gə) *n.* [*pl.* **al′gae** (-jė)] any of a numerous class of plants that grow in sea and fresh water.

al′ge·bra (al′jə-brə) *n.* **1,** a branch of mathematics concerned with generalizing the arithmetic operations and analyzing equations. **2,** any system of compact notation for dealing with generalizations. —**al″ge·bra′ic**(-brā′ik)*adj.* —**al″ge·bra′i·cal·ly,**adv.

-al·gi·a (al′jə) *suf.* pain.

al′go·rism (al′gə-riz-əm) *n.* **1,** the system of Arabic numbers. **2,** calculation; arithmetic.

al′go·rithm (al′gə-rith-əm) *n.* a method of computation.

a′li·as (ā′lė-əs) *n.* an assumed name. —*adv.* also known as.

al′i·bi″ (al′ə-bī″) *n.* (*Law*) a plea of having been elsewhere at the time an offense is alleged to have been committed; (*Colloq.*) any excuse.

al′i·dade″ (al′ə-dād″) *n.* a straight edge attached to a telescope or a graduated circle, for sighting or measured angles.

al′ien (āl′yən) *adj.* **1,** not residing in the

country of one's citizenship. **2,** different in nature; foreign; adverse or hostile. —*n.* one who is estranged or excluded; a foreigner.

al·ien·a·ble (āl′yə-nə-bəl) *adj.* capable of being sold or transferred.

al·ien·ate″ (āl′yə-nāt″) *v.t.* **1,** repel or turn away in feeling; estrange. **2,** (*Law*) transfer title or property to another.

al″ien·a′tion (āl″yə-nā′shən) *n.* **1,** the act of alienating or being alienated. **2,** derangement; insanity.

al′ien·ist (āl′yən-ist) *n.* a psychiatrist, esp. one who pronounces upon legal insanity.

a·light′ (ə-līt′) *v.i.* **1,** dismount. **2,** disembark after a flight. —*adv. & adj.* glowing with light or fire.

a·lign′ (ə-līn′) *v.t. & i.* form into a line; straighten. Also, **a·line′**. —**a·lign′ment,** *n.*

a·like′ (ə-līk′) *adv.* in the same manner, form, or degree; in common; equally. —*adj.* having resemblance; similar; having no marked difference.

al′i·ment (al′ə-mənt) *n.* anything that nourishes or sustains; food; support. —**al″i·men′ta·ry** (al″ə-men′tə-rē) **canal,** the entire food passage.

al″i·men·ta′tion (al″i-men-tā′shən) *n.* **1,** act of nourishing or being nourished. **2,** maintenance; sustenance.

al′i·mo″ny (al′ə-mō″nē) *n.* an allowance directed to be paid by a person to a former spouse after divorce.

al′i·quant (al′i-kwənt) *adj.* (*Math.*) contained in another number but not dividing it evenly.

al′i·quot (al′i-kwot) *adj.* (*Math.*) of a divisor, not leaving a remainder.

a·live′ (ə-līv′) *adj.* **1,** living; existent. **2,** active; animated. **3,** open to impressions; susceptible. **4,** filled with living things.

al′ka·li″ (al′kə-lī″) *n.* (*Chem.*) any of numerous substances that have the power of neutralizing acids and forming salts; a base. —**al″ka·line** (-līn) *adj.* —**al″ka·lin′i·ty** (-lin′ə-tē) *n.*

al′ka·loid (al′kə-loid) *n.* any of certain compounds of nitrogen.

al′kyd (al′kīd) *n.* a resin made from fatty acids and glycerol.

all (âl) *adj. & pron.* the whole quantity or number of (as to substance, extent, degree, duration, etc.). —*adj.* every; any. —*adv.* wholly; entirely. —*n.* a totality of things or qualities. —**all in,** (*Colloq.*) worn out; exhausted.

Al′lah (ä′lä) *n.* (*Moslem*) God.

all-″A·mer′i·can *adj.* **1,** the best or one of the best in the U.S. **2,** composed wholly of Americans. **3,** typically American. —*n.* an all-American player.

all-″a·round′ *adj.* versatile; complete. Also, **all-″round′**.

al·lay′ (ə-lā′) *v.t.* **1,** make quiet or calm; pacify. **2,** make less violent; mitigate.

al″le·ga′tion (al″ə-gā′shən) *n.* **1,** act of alleging. **2,** an assertion or plea.

al·lege′ (ə-lej′) *v.t.* **1,** declare positively. **2,** assert without proof. —**al·leg′ed·ly** (-əd-lē) *adv.* according to allegation.

al·le′giance (ə-lē′jəns) *n.* **1,** the obligation of a person to his state or government. **2,** fidelity to a person or principle; devotion.

al′le·go″ry (al′ə-gôr″ē) *n.* the discussion or representation of a subject, not directly stated, through another analogous to it. —**al″le·gor′i·cal** (al″ə-gor′i-kəl) *adj.*

al″le·gret′to (al″ə-gret′ō) (*Music*) *adv. & adj.* quicker than andante, but not so quick as allegro. —*n.* an allegretto movement or work.

al·le′gro (ə-lā′grō) (*Music*) *adj.* brisk; lively. —*n.* an allegro movement or work.

al″le·lu′ia (al″ə-loo′yə) *n. & interj.* praise ye the Lord.

al′ler·gen (al′ər-jən) *n.* a substance that causes an allergenic reaction.

al·ler′gic (ə-lêr′jik) *adj.* having an allergy (to something); (*Colloq.*) averse.

al′ler·gy (al′ər-jē) *n.* abnormal sensitiveness to certain foods or substances. —**al′ler·gist,** *n.*

al·le′vi·ate″ (ə-lē′vē-āt″) *v.t.* remove in part; lessen; mitigate. —**al·le″vi·a′tion,** *n.*

al′ley (al′ē) *n.* **1,** [also, **al′ley·way″**] a narrow passageway; a back street. A long, narrow rink for sports, as bowling. **3,** a large playing-marble.

all-′fired″ (âl′fīrd″) *adv.* (*Colloq.*) greatly; very.

al·li′ance (ə-lī′əns) *n.* **1,** state of being allied or joined together, as in marriage or political confederation. **2,** the aggregate of persons or parties allied. **3,** the instrument of an alliance, as a treaty. **4,** kinship; similarity.

al·lied′ (ə-līd′) *adj.* **1,** joined together by compact or treaty. **2,** similar or related.

al′li·ga″tor (al′ə-gā″tər) *n.* a large lizardlike reptile, akin to the crocodile. —**alligator pear,** avocado.

al·lit″er·a′tion (ə-lit″ə-rā′shən) *n.* repetition of the same initial letter or sound in two or more nearby words, as *foolish fancy*. —**al·lit′er·ate,** *v.i.*

al′lo·cate″ (al′ə-kāt″) *v.t.* set apart for a particular purpose; allot; assign. —**al″lo·ca′tion,** *n.*

al″lo·cu′tion (al″ə-kū′shən) *n.* a formal address.

al·lop′a·thy (ə-lop′ə-thē) *n.* treatment of

disease by the agents that produce effects different from the symptoms of the disease. —**al′lo·path″**, *n.* —**al″lo·path′ic**, *adj.* —**al″lo·path′i·cal·ly**, *adv.*

al·lot′ (ə-lot′) *v.t.* [**al·lot′ted, al·lot′ting**] **1,** distribute as by lot; parcel out; apportion. **2,** set apart; appoint; assign for a particular purpose.

al·lot′ment (-mənt) *n.* **1,** act of allotting; distribution. **2,** a portion or share; an assigned quantity.

al′lo·trope″ (al′ə-trōp″) *n.* any of several different physical forms in which a chemical element may occur, as coal or diamond, both carbon. —**al″lo·trop′ic**, *adj.* —**al″lo·trop′i·cal·ly**,*adv.*—**al·lot′ro·py** (ə-lot′rə-pē), **al·lot′ro·pism** (-piz-əm) *n.*

all-″out′ *adj.* with full vigor.

al·low′ (ə-low′) *v.t.* **1,** permit; grant; yield; assign. **2,** admit; concede. **3,** make provision (for); take into account. **4,** (*Dial.*) aver; believe.

al·low′ance (ə-low′əns) *n.* **1,** a share or allotment, esp. of money granted to defray expenses. **2,** an addition or deduction, as the allowable difference from prescribed dimensions in machining. **3,** admission or acceptance; sanction.

al′loy (al′oi) *n.* **1,** a mixture of two or more metals, intimately fused. **2,** an admixture; a deleterious component; taint. —*v.t.* (ə-loi′) **1,** mix. **2,** debase by admixture.

all right 1, in good condition; correct; correctly; unharmed. **2,** expression of assent or agreement; very well; yes.

all′spice″ (âl′spīs″) *n.* the berry of a W. I. tree; pimento.

all-′star″ *adj.* **1,** comprising outstanding examples of a certain field. **2,** pert. to a member of such a group. —*n.* a member of an all-star group.

al·lude′ (ə-lood′) *v.i.* (with *to*) refer casually or indirectly.

al·lure′ (ə-lûr′) *v.t.* attract by some proposed pleasure or advantage; entice. —*n.* charm. —**al·lure′ment**, *n.* —**al·lur′ing**, *adj.* tempting; charming.

al·lu′sion (ə-loo′shən) *n.* a casual reference; a slight or incidental mention. —**al·lu′sive** (-siv) *adj.*

al·lu′vi·um (ə-loo′vē-əm) *n.* [*pl.* **-a** (-ə)] a deposit of sand formed by flowing water. —**al·lu′vi·al**, *adj.*

al·ly′ (ə-lī′) *v.t. & i.* join together; combine with; associate. —*n.* one joined with another in a common enterprise; a confederate.

al′ma ma′ter (äl′mə-mä′tər) one's school or college.

al′ma·nac″ (âl′mə-nak″) *n.* a yearly calendar showing the times of certain events, as the rising and setting of the sun and moon, the changes of the moon, the tides, dates of holidays, etc.

al·might′y (âl-mī′tē) *adj.* **1,** supremely powerful; of boundless sufficiency. **2,** (*Colloq.*) extreme. —*n.* (*cap.*) God.

al′mond (ä′mənd) *n.* **1,** a tree found in subtropical climates. **2,** the edible kernel of its fruit. **3,** the color of the kernel, light brown. **4,** anything shaped like an almond kernel.

al′mon·er (al′mən-ər) *n.* a giver of alms. —**al′mon·ry** (-rē) *n.*

al′most (âl′mōst) *adv.* nearly all; for the most part; very nearly; all but.

alms (ämz) *n.pl.* what is given to the poor or needy; anything bestowed in charity. —**alms′house″**, *n.* poorhouse.

al′oe (al′ō) *n.* **1,** an African plant used in making drugs and fiber. **2,** the American century plant. **3,** (*pl.*) a bitter purgative drug made from the juice of the aloe.

a·loft′ (ə-lâft′) *adv. & adj.* in the air; above the ground; (*Naut.*) in the upper rigging.

a·lo′ha (ə-lō′ə) (*Hawaiian*) *interj.* of well-wishing, used as both a greeting and a farewell.

a·lone′ (ə-lōn′) *adj.* apart from or to the exclusion of other persons or things; solitary; single. —*adv.* solely; only.

a·long′ (ə-lâng′) *prep.* in a longitudinal direction through, over, or by the side of. —*adv.* **1,** lengthwise. **2,** onward. **3,** in company; together.

a·long′side *adv. & prep.* along or by the side of; beside.

a·loof′ (ə-loof′) *adv.* at a distance, but within view; withdrawn. —*adj.* reserved; indifferent. —**a·loof′ness**, *n.*

a·loud′ (ə-lowd′) *adv.* audibly; with the natural tone of the voice as distinguished from whispering.

alp *n.* a high mountain.

al·pac′a (al-pak′ə) *n.* **1,** a domesticated sheeplike ruminant of South America. **2,** its hair; a fabric made from the hair. **3,** any glossy fabric made in imitation of alpaca.

al′pen·stock″ (al′pən-) *n.* a long, strong staff with a sharp iron point.

al′pha (al′fə) *n.* the first letter of the Greek alphabet (A, α), corresponding to English a. —**alpha particle**, a positively-charged particle. —**alpha ray**, a stream of alpha particles.

al′pha·bet″ (al′fə-bet″) *n.* the letters of a language in their customary order. —**al″pha·bet′i·cal** (-i-kəl) *adj.* in that order.

—**al′pha·bet·ize″** (-bə-tīz″) *v.t.* put into alphabetical order.

al″pha·nu·mer′ic (al″fə-noo-mer′ik) *adj.* consisting of or utilizing letters and numerals.

al′pine (al′pīn) *adj.* **1,** mountainous; high; elevated. **2,** (*cap.*) pert. to the Alps.

al·read′y (âl-red′ē) *adv.* previously to the present or a specified time.

al·right′ *adj. & adv.* (*Colloq.*) all right.

al′so (âl′sō) *adv.* in addition; too; likewise; further.

al′so-ran″ *n.* **1,** in a horse race, a horse not finishing 1st, 2nd, or 3rd. **2,** an unsuccessful contestant. **3,** a person of small importance; a failure.

al′tar (âl′tər) *n.* a structure, as a block of stone or a table, at which religious rites are performed.

al′tar·piece″ *n.* a reredos.

al′ter (âl′tər) *v.t.* make some change in; cause to vary; modify. —*v.i.* become different; change. —**al″ter·a′tion,** *n.*

al″ter·ca′tion (âl″tər-kā′shən) *n.* an angry or noisy dispute; wrangle. —**al′ter·cate″,** *v.i.*

al″ter e′go (âl″tər-ē′gō) (*Lat.*) one's other self; an inseparable companion.

al′ter·nate (âl′tər-nāt″) *v.i.* **1,** follow one another in time or place reciprocally. **2,** move or change in turn from one place or condition to another. —*v.t.* do or perform in turns, or in succession. —*adj.* (-nət) **1,** following by turns, recurrently or in succession. **2,** every other one of a series. —*n.* (-nət) a person authorized to take the place of another in his absence. —**al′ter·na′tion,** *n.*

alternating current electric current that reverses its direction of flow, usually 120 times per second.

al·ter′na·tive (âl-tėr′nə-tiv) *n.* one of a set of mutually exclusive choices or possibilities. —*adj.* **1,** affording a choice. **2,** mutually exclusive.

al′ter·na″tor (âl′tər-nā″tər) *n.* an electric generator for producing alternating current.

al·though′ (âl-thō′) *conj.* in spite of the fact that; even admitting that.

al·tim′e·ter (al-tim′ə-tər) *n.* an instrument for measuring altitudes.

al′ti·tude″ (al-ti-tood″) *n.* the distance upward, esp. from sea level to a point in the atmosphere; height.

al′to (al′tō) (*Music*) *adj.* higher than tenor. —*n.* [*pl.* **-tos**] **1,** a high male or low female voice. **2,** a part in the range of such a voice. **3,** any of several instruments.

al″to·geth′er (âl″tə-geth′ər) *adv.* wholly; entirely. —**in the altogether,** (*Colloq.*) nude.

al′tru·ism (al′troo-iz-əm) *n.* regard for the welfare of others; benevolent practices.

—**al′tru·ist,** *n.* —**al″tru·is′tic,** *adj.* —**al″tru·is′ti·cal·ly,** *adv.*

al′um (al′əm) *n.* any of numerous bitter, astringent compounds used in drugs and dyes.

a·lu′mi·num (ə-loo′mə-nəm) *n.* a metallic chemical element, much used in alloys because of its light weight, no. 13, symbol Al. Also (*Brit.*) **al″u·min′i·um** (al″ū-min′-ē-əm).

a·lum′nus (ə-lum′nəs) *n.* [*pl.* **-ni** (-nī)] a graduate or former student of a school or college. —**a·lum′na** [*pl.* **-nae** (-nē)] *n. fem.*

al′ways (âl′wėz) *adv.* **1,** throughout all time; uninterruptedly. **2,** at every recurring time.

am *v.* 1st person sing. of *be.*

a·main′ (ə-mān′) *adv.* **1,** with force, strength, or violence. **2,** full speed; hastily. **3,** exceedingly.

a·mal′gam (ə-mal′gəm) *n.* **1,** an alloy of mercury with another metal. **2,** any mixture or compound.

a·mal′ga·mate″ (ə-mal′gə-māt″) *v.t. & i.* **1,** mix or come together; blend; unite. **2,** combine with a metal. —**a·mal″ga·ma′tion,** *n.*

a·man″u·en′sis (ə-man″ū-en′sis) *n.* [*pl.* **-ses** (sēz)] a person who writes what another dictates; a secretary.

am′a·ranth (am′ə-ranth) *n.* any of various flowering plants.

am″a·ryl′lis (am″ə-ril′is) *n.* **1,** a bulbous plant, the belladonna lily. **2,** (*cap.*) a shepherdess.

a·mass′ (ə-mas′) *v.t.* collect in a mass or heap; bring together in great amount.

am′a·teur″ (am′ə-chûr″) *n.* **1,** one who pursues an activity for pleasure instead of for material gain. **2,** one who is unskillful; a dilettante. —*adj.* not professional. —**am″a·teur′ish,** *adj.* unskillful. —**am′a·teur·ism,** *n.*

am′a·tive (am′ə-tiv) *adj.* loving.

am′a·to″ry (am′ə-tôr″ē) *adj.* pert. to lovemaking.

a·maze′ (ə-māz′) *v.t.* cause to feel great astonishment, surprise, or wonder. —**a·maze′ment,** *n.*

am′a·zon″ (am′ə-zon″) *n.* a large and strong, or quarrelsome, woman.

am·bas′sa·dor (am-bas′ə-dər) *n.* a diplomatic agent of highest rank. —**am·bas′sa·dor′i·al** (-dôr′ē-əl) *adj.* —**am·bas′sa·dress,** *n. fem.*

am′ber (am′bər) *n.* **1,** a mineralized resin on which rubbing produces a negative electric charge. **2,** the pale yellow color of amber. —*adj.* like amber; yellow.

---

fat, fāte, fär, fâre, fâll, àsk; met, hē, hėr, maybè; pin, pīne; not, nōte, ôr, tool

am·ber·gris (am'bər-grēs") *n.* a morbid secretion of the sperm whale, prized for making perfume.

am·bi- *pref.* meaning both, or on both sides. Also, **am·phi-**.

am"bi·dex'trous (am"bi-deks'trəs) *adj.* apt with both hands. **—am"bi·dex·ter'i·ty,** *n.*

am'bi·ent (am'bē-ənt) *adj.* surrounding; circling about. **—am'bi·ence, am'bi·ance,** *n.* surroundings; environment.

am·bi·gu'i·ty (am-bi-gū'ə-tē) *n.* state of being ambiguous; double meaning.

am·big'u·ous (am-big'ū-əs) *adj.* of doubtful purport; open to various interpretations; having a double meaning.

am'bit *n.* boundary; compass.

am·bi'tion (am-bish'ən) *n.* eager desire for distinction, power, or fame.

am·bi'tious (am-bish'əs) *adj.* having much ambition; eager for success.

am·biv'a·lence (am-biv'ə-ləns) *n.* mixed or conflicting feelings. **—am·biv'a·lent,** *adj.*

am'ble (am'bəl) *v.i.* move easily and gently, like a walking horse.

am·bro'sia (am-brō'zhə) *n.* **1,** in Greek legend, the food of the gods. **2,** a fruit dessert topped with coconut. **—am·bro'sial** (-zhəl) *adj.*

am'bu·lance (am'bū-ləns) *n.* a vehicle for carrying the sick or wounded. **—ambulance chaser,** a lawyer who unethically solicits as clients the victims of an accident.

am'bu·late" (am'bū-lāt") *v.i.* move about from place to place. **—am"bu·la'tion,** *n.* **—am'bu·lant, am'bu·la·to"ry** (-tôr"ē) *adj.*

am"bus·cade' (am"bəs-kād') *n. & v.* ambush.

am'bush (am'bûsh) *v.t.* attack unexpectedly from a hidden position. **—n. 1,** the act of lying concealed for a surprise attack. **2,** a place of concealment.

a·me'ba (ə-mē'bə) *n.* a one-celled animal that continually changes shape to engulf and absorb its food. Also, **a·moe'ba.**

a·mel'io·rate" (ə-mēl'yə-rāt") *v.t. & i.* make or become better, more satisfactory, or more tolerable. **—a·mel'io·ra'tion,** *n.* **—a·mel'io·ra·tive,** *adj.*

a·men' (ā'men') *interj. & adv.* be it so (an expression of invocation or endorsement at the end of a prayer). **—n.** an expression of fervent assent.

a·me'na·ble (ə-mē'nə-bəl) *adj.* **1,** disposed to yield; submissive. **2,** liable, as to control or claim. **—a·me"na·bil'i·ty, a·me'na·ble·ness,** *n.*

a·mend' (ə-mend') *v.t.* **1,** make better; correct; improve. **2,** alter. **—v.i.** become better; reform. **—n.** (*pl.*) compensation for loss or injury; recompense. **—a·mend'a·to·ry** (-ə-tôr·ē) *adj.*

a·mend'ment (-mənt) *n.* **1,** correction; improvement. **2,** a change, as in a law; (*cap.*) a change in the Constitution of the U. S.

a·men'i·ty (ə-men'ə-tē) *n.* **1,** the quality of being pleasant or agreeable. **2,** (*pl.*) pleasant aspects; conveniences; social courtesies.

a·merce' (ə-mērs') *v.t.* punish by a fine or by any arbitrary penalty.

A·mer'i·can (ə-mer'i-kən) *adj. & n.* pert. to any country of the Western Hemisphere, esp. the U. S., its people, customs, etc. **—American cheese,** a mild cheddar cheese. **—American plan,** a system whereby a hotel's charge includes room and meals.

A·mer"i·ca'na (ə-mer"i-ka'nə) *n.pl.* materials (documents, antiques, etc.) bearing on Amer. history.

am"er·i'ci·um (am"ə-ris(h)'ē-əm) *n.* a radioactive chemical element, no. 95, symbol Am, produced artificially from plutonium.

Am'er·ind (am'ər-ind) *n.* an Amer. Indian or Eskimo.

am'e·thyst (am'ə-thist) *n.* **1,** a bluish variety of quartz used in making ornaments. **2,** a violet sapphire. **3,** a light purple or violet color.

a'mi·a·ble (ā'mē-ə-bəl) *adj.* **1,** pleasing; lovable. **2,** friendly; kindly. **—a"mi·a·bil'i·ty, a'mi·a·ble·ness,** *n.*

am'i·ca·ble (am'i-kə-bəl) *adj.* exhibiting friendliness; peaceable; harmonious. **—am"·i·ca·bil'i·ty,** *n.*

am'ice (am'is) *n.* **1,** a priestly vestment worn at Mass. **2,** a furred hood or cape.

a·mid' (ə-mid') *prep.* in the midst of or surrounded by. Also, **a·midst'.**

a·mid'ships" (ə-mid'ships") *adv.* midway of the length of a ship.

a·mi'no acid (ə-mē'nō) any of a large group of organic compounds which are basic constituents of proteins.

Am'ish (äm'ish) *adj.* of a certain sect of Mennonites.

a·miss' (ə-mis') *adv.* in a faulty manner; out of proper course of order. **—adj.** improper; faulty.

am'i·ty (am'ə-tē) *n.* friendship; pleasant relations, esp. between nations.

am·me"ter (am'mē"tər) *n.* an instrument for measuring amperes.

am'mo (am'ō) *n.* (*Slang*) ammunition.

am·mo'ni·a (ə-mōn'yə) *n.* **1,** a gaseous compound of nitrogen and hydrogen. **2,** a solution of this gas in water. **—am·mo'ni·ate"** (-āt") *v.t.*

am"mu·ni'tion (am"ū-nish'ən) *n.* **1,** materials used in discharging firearms, etc., as bullets, explosives, etc. **2,** means for retaliation or defense, as evidence, etc.

am·ne'sia (am-nē'zhə) *n.* loss of memory. **—am·ne'sic** (-zik) *adj.*

am'nes·ty (am'nəs-tē) *n.* a general pardon for a whole class of offenses against a government.

a·moe'ba (ə-mē'bə) *n.* ameba.

a·mok' (ə-mok') *adv.* amuck.

a·mong' (ə-mung') *prep.* **1,** in the midst of; in association with; in the class or group of. **2,** with or by the whole of. **3,** to each of. Also, **a·mongst'** (ə-mungst').

a·mon"til·la'do (ə-mon"tə-lä'dō) *n.* a dry sherry.

a·mor'al (a-môr'əl) *adj.* **1,** neither moral nor immoral; nonmoral. **2,** having no sense of moral responsibility. **—a"mo·ral'i·ty,** *n.*

am'o·rous (am'ə-rəs) *adj.* **1,** inclined to love; loving. **2,** indicating or conveying love. **—am'o·rous·ness,** *n.*

a·mor'phous (ə-môr'fəs) *adj.* **1,** having no determinate form; of irregular shape. **2,** of no particular kind; heterogeneous. **—a·mor'phous·ness, a·mor'phism** (-fiz-əm) *n.*

am'or·tize" (am'ər-tīz") *v.t.* extinguish (a debt) by means of a sinking fund. **—am'or·ti·za'tion,** *n.*

a·mount' (ə-mownt') *n.* **1,** the sum of two or more quantities. **2,** a sum quantity, value, or import, viewed as a whole. **—v.i.** (with *to*) add up; reach in quantity or degree.

a·mour' (ä-mûr') *n.* a love affair.

am'per·age (am'pir-ij) *n.* the measure of a current in amperes.

am'pere (am'pir) *n.* a unit of electromotive force, one volt·acting against the resistance of one ohm.

am'per·sand" (am'pər-sand") *n.* the character &: and.

am·phet'a·mine (am-fet'ə-mēn) *n.* a drug used to relieve nasal congestion and as a stimulant.

am·phib'i·an (am-fib'ē-ən) *n.* an amphibious animal, plant, or airplane.

am·phib'i·ous (am-fib'ē-əs) *adj.* capable of living or operating both on land and in water.

am'phi·the"a·ter (am'fə-thē"ə-tər) *n.* a circular or oval arena, usu. for sports, surrounded by tiers of seats on a sloping gallery.

am'pho·ra (am'fə-rə) *n.* [*pl.* **-rae** (-re)] a two-handled vessel.

am"pi·cil'lin (am"pə-sil'ən) *n.* an antibiotic drug.

am'ple (am'pəl) *adj.* **1,** large in extent or amount; copious. **2,** plentifully sufficient. **—am'ple·ness,** *n.*

am'pli·fi"er (am'plə-fī"ər) *n.* a device for increasing the amplitude of electrical impulses.

am'pli·fy" (am'plə-fī") *v.t.* make larger in extent or importance; enlarge. **—am"·pli·fi·ca'tion,** *n.*

am'pli·tude" (am'pli-tood") *n.* **1,** extension in space; largeness. **2,** (of a wave) the distance or magnitude of a crest or trough from the mean value. **—amplitude modulation,** a system of radio transmission.

am·poule' (am-pool') *n.* a sealed glass bulb holding one or more doses of a hypodermic injection. Also, **am'pule** (-pūl).

am'pu·tate" (am'pū-tāt") *v.t.* cut off (a limb). **—am"pu·ta'tion,** *n.* **—am"pu·tee',** *n.*

Am'trak *n.* a nationwide system of passenger railroad service in the U.S.

a·muck' (ə-muk') *adv.* in a frenzied manner. **—run amuck,** indiscriminately attack everyone encountered.

am'u·let (am'ū-let) *n.* an object superstitiously worn to bring good luck, avert illness, etc.

a·muse' (ə-mūz') *v.t.* excite pleasure or mirth in; entertain; divert.

a·muse'ment (-mənt) *n.* **1,** pleasurable interest; mirth. **2,** that which amuses; a pastime. **—amusement park,** a commercial park for entertainment, usu. having rides and booths.

an *adj.* a: the indefinite article, used before a word beginning with a vowel sound.

a·nab'a·sis (ə-nab'ə-sis) *n.* [*pl.* **-ses** (-sēz)] a long march by a military force.

a·nach'ro·nism (ə-nak'rə-niz-əm) *n.* an error in respect to dates or the order of historical events. **—a·nach"ro·nis'tic** (-nis'-tik) *adj.* **—a·nach"ro·nis'ti·cal·ly,** *adv.*

an"a·con'da (an"ə-kon'də) *n.* any large snake; boa constrictor.

an'a·gram" (an'ə-gram") *n.* a word or phrase formed from another by transposition of the letters.

a'nal (ā'nəl) *adj.* pert. to the anus.

an"al·ge'sia (an"əl-jē'zhə) *n.* inability of a part to feel pain.

an"al·ge'sic (an"əl-jē'zik) *n.* a remedy to relieve pain. **—adj.** relieving pain.

an'a·log" (an'ə-lâg") *adj.* employing measurement along scales rather than by numerical counting. **—analog computer,** a computer that expresses interrelationships between variables.

a·nal'o·gous (ə-nal'ə-gəs) *adj.* corresponding; similar.

an'a·logue (an'ə-log) *n.* something analogous to another.

a·nal'o·gy (ə-nal'ə-jē) *n.* similarity or

agreement between one thing and another; resemblance; comparison.

a·nal′y·sand, (ə-nal′ə-sand) *n.* a client of an analyst.

a·nal′y·sis (ə-nal′ə-sis) *n.* [*pl.* **-ses** (-sēz)] **1,** the separation of a complex material or conception into its elements. **2,** determination of causes from results; induction. **3,** an abstract; summary.

an′a·lyst (an′ə-list) *n.* **1,** one who analyzes. **2,** a psychoanalyst.

an·a·lyt′i·cal (an-ə-lit′i-kəl) *adj.* being or pert. to analysis. Also, **an·a·lyt′ic.**

an′a·lyze″ (an′ə-līz″) *v.t.* **1,** separate into its elements; determine the constituents of. **2,** examine critically.

an′a·pest″ (an′ə-pest″) *n.* a foot in poetry, two unstressed syllables followed by a stressed one. —**an″a·pes′tic,** *adj.*

an′arch·ism (an′ər-kiz-əm) *n.* the political doctrine that all governments should be abolished.

an′arch·ist (an′ər-kist) *n.* **1,** a social rebel; insurrectionist. **2,** a believer in anarchism. —**an″ar·chis′tic,** *adj.*

an′ar·chy (an′ər-kè) *n.* **1,** general disorder from lack of government. **2,** anarchism. —**an·ar′chic** (an-ärk′ik), **an·ar′chi·cal,** *adj.*

a·nath′e·ma (ə-nath′ə-mə) *n.* **1,** a denunciation, accompanied by excommunicaton, by an ecclesiastical authority. **2,** any solemn execration or curse. **3,** something accursed. —**a·nath′e·ma·tize″,** *v.t.* curse.

a·nat′o·my (ə-nat′ə-mè) *n.* **1,** the structure of an animal or plant body. **2,** the science of structure; the art of dissecting bodies to determine their structure. —**an″·a·tom′i·cal,** *adj.* —**a·nat′o·mize,** *v.t.* dissect.

-ance (əns) *suf.* same as **-ence.**

an′ces·tor (an′ses-tər) *n.* a foregoing person or organism (usually deceased) from whom one is descended; forebear; progenitor. —**an′ces·tress,** *n. fem.*

an·ces′tral (an-ses′trəl) *adj.* pert. to ancestry or an ancestor.

an′ces·try (an′ses-trè) *n.* a series of ancestors; line of descent.

an′chor (ang′kər) *n.* **1,** a device for securing a vessel to the ground under water by means of a cable. **2,** any device that holds in place, gives security or stability. —*v.t.* fix firmly in place. —*v.i.* drop anchor.

an′chor·age (-ij) *n.* a place suitable for anchoring.

an′cho·rite″ (ang′kə-rīt″) *n.* a recluse; hermit. Also, **an′cho·ret″** (-ret″).

an′chor·man″ *n. masc.* [*pl.* **-men**]—**anchorwoman,** *n. fem.* **1,** the principal

newscaster of a news broadcast. **2,** the moderator of a panel, discussion group, etc. **3,** (*Sports*) the last contestant in a relay race.

an′cho·vy (an′chō-vè) *n.* a small fish similar to the herring.

an·cien′ ré·gime′ (äë-syañ′rä-zhēm′) (*Fr.*) **1,** in France, the political and social system before the Revolution of 1789. **2,** any old or former system.

an′cient (ān′shənt) *adj.* **1,** having existed in the remote past. **2,** very old. —**Ancient of Days,** God.

an′cil·lar″y (an′sə-ler′ē) *adj.* **1,** serving in a subordinate or auxiliary capacity. **2,** (*Colloq.*) related. —*n.* (*pl.*) (*Mil.*) auxiliary forces, as of supply, transport, etc.

-an·cy (ən-sè) *suf.* same as **-ence, -ency.**

and *conj.* in addition; also; too.

an·dan′te (an-dan′tè) (*Music*) *adj.* & *adv.* moderately slow. —*n.* an andante movement or work. —**an·dan·ti′no,** *adj.*, *adv.* & *n.* somewhat faster than andante.

and′i″ron (and′ī″ərn) *n.* one of a pair of iron stands used to support wood burned in an open hearth.

an′dro- (an′drō) *pref.* man; male.

an′dro·gen (an′drə-jən) *n.* a substance, such as male sex hormones, that enhances masculinity.

an·drog′y·nous (an-droj′ə-nəs) *adj.* hermaphroditic.

an′droid *n.* an automaton in human form.

an·dros′ter·one″ (an-dros′tə-rōn″) *n.* a male sex hormone.

an′ec·dote″ (an′ek-dōt″) *n.* a short narrative of an occurrence. —**an″ec·do′tal,** *adj.*

a·ne′mi·a (ə-nē′mè-ə) *n.* quantitative deficiency of blood. —**a·ne′mic,** *adj.* —**a·ne′mi·cal·ly,** *adv.*

an″e·mom′e·ter (an″ə-mom′ə-tər) *n.* a device for measuring the velocity of the wind.

a·nem′o·ne (ə-nem′ə-nè) *n.* **1,** a wild flower. **2,** a small sea animal.

a·nent′ (ə-nent′) *prep.* (*Archaic*) in regard to; concerning.

an′er·oid″ (an′ər-oid″) *adj.* using no fluid.

an″es·the′sia (an″əs-thē′zhə) *n.* (*Med.*) loss of feeling, esp. as induced by certain drugs.

an″es·the″si·ol′o·gist (an″əs-thē″zè-ol′ə-jist) *n.* a physician specializing in the administering of anesthetics; anesthetist. —**an″es·the″si·ol′o·gy,** *n.*

an″es·thet′ic (-thet′ik) *n.* a drug that induces anesthesia.

an·es′the·tist (ə-nes′thə-tist) *n.* one who administers an anesthetic.

an·es′the·tize″ (ə-nes′thə-tīz″) *v.t.* administer an anesthetic to.

---

an'eu·rysm (an'yə-riz-əm) *n.* a permanent dilation of a blood vessel.

a·new' (ə-nū') *adv.* once more; again; in a new form.

an'gel (ān'jəl) *n.* **1,** an attendant of God, esp. a messenger. **2,** a kindly woman. **3,** (*Colloq.*) a financial backer. —**an·gel'ic** (an-jel'ik) *adj.* —**an·gel'i·cal·ly,** *adv.* —**an·gel food cake,** a light white cake made with flour, sugar, and egg whites.

an'gel·fish" *n.* **1,** a shark of the N. Atlantic. **2,** any of several beautifully colored tropical fish.

an·gel'i·ca (an-jel'i-kə) *n.* **1,** a plant of the carrot family. **2,** a wine or liqueur flavored with angelica.

an'ger (ang'gər) *n.* a strong emotion of displeasure and resentment; wrath. —*v.t.* excite to anger.

an·gi'na pec'to·ris (an-jī'nə pek'tə-ris) a spasm in the chest, symptom of a heart disease.

an'gle (ang'gəl) *n.* **1,** an enclosure or space formed by two intersecting lines or planes. **2,** (*Geom.*) that proportion of a circular arc intercepted by such lines. **3,** an angular projection; a corner. **4,** a point of view; an aspect or phase. —*v.t. & i.* form into an angle. —*v.i.* **1,** fish with hook and line. **2,** try to obtain by artful means. —**an'gler,** *n.* a fisherman. —**an'gling,** *n.* the art of fishing. —**angle iron,** a metal support, usu. in the form of a right angle.

an'gle·worm" *n.* an earthworm.

An'gli·can (ang'gli-kən) *adj.* pert. to the Church of England.

An'gli·cism (ang'glə-siz-əm) *n.* something peculiarly English.

an'gli·cize" (ang'gli-sīz") *v.t.* adapt to English form or custom.

An'glo- (ang'glō) *pref.* pert. to England or the English.

An'glo-Sax'on (-sak'sən) *adj. & n.* pert. to the early Germanic inhabitants of England, their language, or their descendants.

An·go'ra (ang-gôr'ə) *n.* **1,** a long-haired domestic cat. **2,** a breed of long-haired goat. **3,** a fabric (usually called mohair) woven from the hair of a goat.

an"gos·tu'ra (ang"gəs-tyûr'ə) *n.* the bitter bark of a tropical Amer. shrub, used medicinally. —**Angostura Bitters,** (*T.N.*) a bitter aromatic tonic (not containing angostura bark).

an'gry (ang'grē) *adj.* **1,** feeling anger; expressive of anger; tempestuous. **2,** sore; inflamed.

ang'strom (ang'strəm) *n.* a unit in measuring wave length.

an'guish (ang'gwish) *n.* acute bodily or mental distress; extreme pain. —*v.t. & i.* afflict with pain; suffer anguish.

an'gu·lar (ang'gū-lər) *adj.* **1,** having or forming angles, corners, or projections. **2,** bony; gaunt. **3,** stiff in manner. —**an·gu·lar'i·ty** (-lar'ə-tė) *n.*

an·hy'drous (an-hī'drəs) *adj.* (*Chem.*) having lost all water. —**an·hy'dride** (-drid), *n.*

an'il *n.* a W. I. shrub that yields indigo.

an'i·line (an'ə-lin) *n.* a liquid used in making dyes, perfumes, etc.

an"i·mad·ver'sion (an"ə-mad-vėr'zhən) *n.* **1,** a slurring remark; blame. **2,** unfavorable bias. —**an"i·mad·vert',** *v.i.*

an'i·mal (an'ə-məl) *n.* **1,** any living thing not a plant. **2,** any animal other than man. **3,** a brutish person. —*adj.* **1,** belonging to the realm or nature of animals. **2,** pert. to the bodily appetites or functions of man. —**an'i·mal·ism,** *n.* —**an"i·mal'i·ty** (-mal'ə-tė) *n.*

an"i·mal'cule (an"i-mal'kūl") *n.* a minute animal.

an'i·mate" (an'ə-māt") *v.t.* **1,** give life to. **2,** infuse with vigor or liveliness. **3,** incite to action. **4,** produce in the manner of an animated cartoon. —*adj.* (-mət) having life; lively. —**an'i·mat"ed,** *adj.* full of spirit; vigorous. —**an"i·ma'tion,** *n.* —**animated cartoon,** a series of cartoons photographed in sequence to give the illusion of motion.

an'i·mism (an'i-miz-əm) *n.* belief in the existence of the soul; general belief in spiritual beings. —**an'i·mist,** *n.*

an"i·mos'i·ty (an"ə-mos'ə-tė) *n.* active enmity; hatred; ill-will.

an'i·mus (an'ə-məs) *n.* **1,** animosity. **2,** a grudge.

an·i"on (an'ī"ən) *n.* a negatively charged ion.

an'ise (an'is) *n.* a Mediterranean plant whose seed (*aniseed*) is used in making drugs, perfumes, and liqueurs.

an"i·sette' (an"i-set') *n.* an anise-flavored liqueur.

ankh (angk) *n.* in Egyptian art, the symbol of eternal life, a cross with a loop at the top (☥).

an'kle (ang'kəl) *n.* the joint connecting the foot with the leg.

ank'let (ang'klet) *n.* **1,** a low sock that reaches just above the ankle. **2,** a bracelet or other ornament worn on the lower leg.

an'nals (an'əlz) *n. pl.* **1,** a history of events recorded year by year. **2,** historical records generally. —**an'nal·ist,** *n.*

an·neal' (ə-nēl') *v.t.* treat (glass, metals, etc.) by heating and gradually cooling, which toughens the substance and removes brittleness.

an·nex' (ə-neks') *v.t.* **1,** attach at the end; affix. **2,** unite or join, esp. a smaller thing to a larger. —*n.* (an'eks) something annexed, as a subsidiary building; a supplement. —**an"nex·a'tion,** *n.*

An'nie Oak'ley (an'ē-ōk'lē) (*Slang*) a free ticket or pass, as to the theater.

an·ni'hi·late" (ə-nī'ə-lāt") *v.t.* destroy utterly; reduce to nothing. —**an·ni"hi·la'tion,** *n.*

an"ni·ver'sa·ry (an"ə-vėr'sə-rē) *n.* **1,** the annually recurring date of a past event. **2,** the celebration of such a date. —*adj.* recurring each year.

an'no Do·mi·ni (an'ō-dom'ə-nī) (*Lat.*) in the year of our Lord.

an'no·tate" (an'ō-tāt") *v.t. & i.* furnish with explanatory or critical notes; comment upon in notes. —**an"no·ta'tion,** *n.*

an·nounce' (ə-nowns') *v.t.* make known formally; give notice of; publish; proclaim. —**an·nounce'ment** (-mənt) *n.* **1,** act of announcing. **2,** what is announced; a formal notice.

an·noun'cer (ə-nown'sər) *n.* one who announces, esp. commercials, news, etc. on radio, television, etc.

an·noy' (ə-noi') *v.t. & i.* be troublesome or vexatious to; irk and harass. —**an·noy'ance,** *n.*

an'nu·al (an'ū-əl) *adj.* **1,** occurring or returning once a year. **2,** lasting or continuing one year. —*n.* **1,** a plant or animal whose natural term of life is one year or season. **2,** a book published once a year, or covering the events of a year.

an·nu'i·ty (ə-nū'ə-tē) *n.* a periodical payment of money, usually a fixed amount in each year. —**an·nu'i·tant** (-tənt) *n.* one receiving an annuity.

an·nul' (ə-nul') *v.t.* [-nulled', -nul'ling] make null or void; abolish. —**an·nul'ment,** *n.*

an'nu·lar (an'ū-lər) *adj.* having the form of a ring.

an·nun"ci·a'tion (ə-nun"sē-ā'shən) *n.* (usually *cap.*) **1,** the announcement by Gabriel to Mary that she would bear Jesus. **2,** a feast day commemorating this, March 25. —**an·nun'ci·ate,** *v.t.* announce.

an'ode (an'ōd) *n.* the positive pole of a battery; an electrode that emits positive ions.

an'od·ize (-īz) *v.t.* to coat (a metal) with a protective film by electrolysis.

an'o·dyne" (an'ə-dīn") *n. & adj.* **1,** a drug that relieves pain. **2,** anything that relieves mental pain or distress.

a·noint' (ə-noint') *v.t.* pour oil upon, as

in a religious ceremony. —**a·noint'ment,** *n.*

a·nom'a·ly (ə-nom'ə-lē) *n.* deviation from the common rule; something abnormal or irregular. —**a·nom'a·lous,** *adj.*

a·non' (ə-non') *adv.* (*Archaic*) in a short time; soon.

an"o·nym'i·ty (an"ə-nim'ə-tē) *n.* state of being anonymous.

a·non'y·mous (ə-non'ə-məs) *adj.* lacking the name of the author, composer, contributor, etc.; from an unacknowledged source.

a·noph'e·les" (ə-nof'ə-lēz") *n.* [*pl.* -les"] the mosquito that carries malaria.

an'o·rak (an'ə-rok) *n.* a windproof jacket with an attached hood.

an"o·rex'i·a (an"ə-rek'sē-ə) *n.* loss of appetite.

an·oth'er (ə-nuth'ər) *adj.* **1,** one more; an additional. **2,** a different; of distinct kind. —*pron.* one additional, or a different, person or thing.

an'swer (an'sər) *n.* **1,** a reply or response. **2,** the solution of a problem. —*v.t. & i.* **1,** make a reply or response (to). **2,** serve or suit. **3,** atone (for).

an'swer·a·ble *adj.* **1,** capable of being answered. **2,** (with *for*) liable.

ant *n.* a small insect that lives in communities.

-ant (ənt) *suf.* **1,** denoting a doer. **2,** forming participial adjectives: equivalent to **-ing.**

ant·ac'id (ant-as'id) *n. & adj.* a drug or reagent for neutralizing acids.

an·tag'o·nism (an-tag'ə-niz-əm) *n.* mutual resistance or opposition of two forces in action.

an·tag'o·nist (an-tag'ə-nist) *n.* an active opponent. —**an·tag"o·nis'tic,** *adj.* opposed; unfriendly; hostile. —**an·tag"o·nist'ti·cal·ly,** *adv.*

an·tag'o·nize" (an-tag'ə-nīz") *v.t.* incur the ill will of; make hostile.

ant·arc'tic (ant-tärk'tik) *adj.* near or at the South Pole. —*n.* (*cap.*) the South Polar regions.

an'te (an'tē) *n.* a compulsory bet made by a card player before seeing his cards. —*v.i. & t.* [-ted (-tēd), -te·ing] make such a bet.

an·te- (an-tē) *pref.* meaning before.

ant'eat"er *n.* a toothless mammal of tropical Amer. that feeds on ants or termites.

an"te·ce'dent (an"tə-sē'dənt) *adj.* existing or going before, in time or place. —*n.* **1,** (*Gram.*) the noun or phrase for which a pronoun stands. **2,** (*Math., Logic*) the first of two correlative parts, as the first term of a ratio. **3,** (*pl.*) one's origin, previous associations, or avowed principles. —**an"te·ce'dence,** *n.*

an'te·cham"ber *n.* a room leading into another; waiting room.

an'te·date" *v.t.* **1,** precede in time. **2,** date before the true time. **3,** ascribe to an earlier time.

an'te·lope" (an'tə-lōp") *n.* a horned ruminant related to cattle.

an'te me·ri'di·em (an'tē-mə-rid'é-əm) (*Lat.*) before noon.

an·ten'na (an-ten'ə) *n.* **1,** a conducting wire from which radio waves are sent or received. **2,** [*pl.* **-nae** (-ē)] one of the appendages occurring in pairs on the head of an insect, also called *feelers*.

an·te'ri·or (an-tir'é-ər) *adj.* **1,** situated at the front; placed before. **2,** (of a human or animal body) toward the front; toward the head.

an'te·room" *n.* a smaller room giving access to a larger; waiting room; reception room.

an'them (an'thəm) *n.* **1,** a sacred hymn. **2,** a song of devotion or patriotism.

an'ther (an'thər) *n.* (*Bot.*) the part of a stamen bearing pollen.

an·thol'o·gist (an-thol'ə-jist) *n.* the compiler of an anthology.

an·thol'o·gy (an-thol'ə-jē) *n.* a collection in one volume of writings of various authors.

an'thra·cite (an'thrə-sīt) *n.* hard coal. —*adj.* coal-black.

an'thrax (an'thraks) *n.* a malignant bacterial disease of cattle and man.

an'thro·po- (an'thrə-pō) *pref.* pert. to a human being; man.

an'thro·poid" (an'thrə-poid") *adj.* resembling man.

an"thro·pol'o·gy (an"thrə-pol'ə-jē) *n.* **1,** the general science of man. **2,** the science of man's origin, early development, and culture. —**an"thro·pol'o·gist,** *n.*

an·ti- (an-tē) *pref.* against; opposed to.

an"ti·bi·ot'ic (an'ti-bī-ot'ik) *n.* a substance derived from certain organisms that tends to destroy harmful organisms.

an'ti·bod"y (an'ti-bod"ē) *n.* an immunizing agent within the human body that counteracts malignant bacteria.

an'tic (an'tik) *n.* (chiefly *pl.*) escapade; (*pl.*) ludicrous behavior; capers.

An'ti·christ" (an'tē-krīst") *n.* the personification of the force of evil.

an·tic'i·pate" (an-tis'ə-pāt") *v.t.* **1,** expect; foresee. **2,** realize beforehand. **3,** be ahead of time or of another; forestall. —**an·tic'i·pa'tion,** *n.* —**an·tic'i·pa·to"ry** (-ə-pə-tôr"ē) *adj.*

an"ti·cli'max (an"ti-klī'maks) *n.* an abrupt descent in style or subject from lofty ideas

or expression; ludicrous contrast with what has preceded. —**an"ti·cli·mac'tic** (-klī-mak'tik) *adj.*

an'ti·dote" (an'ti-dōt") *n.* **1,** a drug that counteracts the effect of a poison. **2,** any remedy against disease or injurious influence.

an'ti·freeze" *n.* a substance that reduces the freezing point of water.

an'ti·gen (an'ti-jən) *n.* any substance or organism, such as bacteria, that stimulates the production of an antibody.

an'ti·he"ro *n.* a protagonist lacking the qualities usu. associated with a hero.

an"ti·his'ta·mine" (an"tē-his'tə-mēn") *n.* a medicine used in treatment of allergic reactions.

an"ti·log'a·rithm *n.* the number of which a given number is the logarithm.

an"ti·ma·cas'sar (an"tē-mə-kas'ər) *n.* an ornamental protective covering for the arm or back of a chair, sofa, etc.

an'ti·mat"ter *n.* a hypothetical form of matter with properties the reverse of those of ordinary matter.

an'ti·mo"ny (an'tə-mō"nē) *n.* a metallic chemical element, no. 51, symbol Sb.

an'ti·nov"el *n.* a literary work similar in length to a novel, but lacking the usual character and plot development.

an'ti·par"ti·cle *n.* a particle of antimatter.

an"ti·pas'to (än'tē-päs'tō) *n.* (*It.*) an appetizer; hors d'oeuvres.

an"ti·pa'thy (an-tip'ə-thē) *n.* dislike. —**an"ti·pa·thet'ic** (an"tē-pə-thet'ik) *adj.* —**an"ti·pa·thet'i·cal·ly,** *adv.*

an'ti·phon (an'ti-fon) *n.* **1,** a psalm, hymn, or prayer sung responsively. **2,** a prelude or conclusion to some part of a service.

an·tiph'o·ny (an-tif'ə-nē) *n.* **1,** alternate singing by two parts of a choir. **2,** a composition arranged to be so chanted. —**an·tiph'o·nal,** *adj.*

an·tip'o·des (an-tip'ə-dēz) *n.pl.* places diametrically opposite each other on the earth. —**an·tip'o·dal,** *adj.*

an'ti·pope" *n.* a usurper of the papal office.

an'ti·quar"y (an'ti-kwär"ē) *n.* a collector of or expert on antiques or matters ancient. —**an"ti·quar'i·an** (-kwär'é-ən) *n. & adj.*

an'ti·quat·ed (an'ti-kwā-tid) *adj.* grown old; obsolete.

an·tique' (an-tēk') *adj.* belonging to former times; old-fashioned. —*n.* a relic of antiquity. —*v.t.* so treat (a piece of furniture, etc.) so as to make it appear to be an antique.

an·tiq'ui·ty (an-tik'wə-tē) *n.* **1,** ancient

times; former ages. **2,** the quality of being ancient.

an″ti-Sem′i·tism (-sem′i-tiz-əm) *n.* prejudice against the Jewish people. —**an″ti-Sem′ite** (-sem′īt), *n.* —**an″ti-Se·mit′ic** (-sə-mit′ik) *adj.*

an″ti·sep′tic (an″ti-sep′tik) *adj.* & *n.* destructive of microörganisms that cause disease. —**an″ti·sep′ti·cal·ly,** *adv.* —**an″ti·sep′sis,** *n.*

an″ti·so′cial *adj.* not inclined to seek or enjoy the company of others.

an·tith′e·sis (an-tith′ə-sis) *n.* [*pl.* **-ses** (-sēz)] **1,** direct opposition; marked contrast. **2,** what is directly opposite. —**an″ti·thet′i·cal** (an″ti-thet′i-kəl) *adj.*

an″ti·tox′in (an″ti-tok′sin) *n.* a substance that counteracts a toxin or poison.

an″ti·trust′ *adj.* opposed to combinations or trusts that result in monopoly.

an″ti·ven′in *n.* an antidote to poison injected by a snake bite or scorpion sting.

ant′ler (ant′lər) *n.* one of the branching horns of an animal of the deer family.

an′to·nym (an′tə-nim) *n.* a word meaning exactly the opposite of a given word.

an′trum (an′trəm) *n.* a cavity; hole.

a′nus (ā′nəs) *n.* the posterior opening of the alimentary canal.

an′vil (an′vəl) *n.* **1,** a heavy iron block on which metalwork is laid for beating. **2,** a bone of the ear.

anx·i′e·ty (ang-zī′ə-tē) *n.* **1,** uneasiness of mind from care or apprehension. **2,** concern or solicitude.

anx′ious (ank′shəs) *adj.* **1,** full of anxiety; worried. **2,** earnestly desirous. —**anx′ious·ness,** *n.*

an′y (en′ē) *adj.* & *pron.* one, or some, indiscriminately from a larger number. —*adv.* to whatever extent; in whatever degree; at all.

an′y·bod″y *pron.* any person.

an′y·how′ *adv.* **1,** in any way. **2,** in any case.

an′y·one′ *pron.* any person.

an′y·thing″ *pron.* any thing, fact, or deed.

an′y·way′ *adv.* **1,** in any way. **2,** in any case; nevertheless.

an′y·where′ *adv.* in or to any place.

ao′ dai (ä-ō′dī) *n.* traditional Vietnamese woman's dress.

a·or′ta (ā-ôr′tə) *n.* the chief artery of the human body, issuing from the heart.

a′ou·dad (ä′oo-däd) *n.* a wild sheep of N. Afr.

a·pace′ (ə-pās′) *adv.* speedily.

a·pache′ *n.* **1,** (ə-päsh′) (*Fr.*) a Parisian rowdy or gangster. **2,** (ə-pach′ē) (*cap.*) a

certain American Indian tribe or member of it.

a·part′ (ə-pärt′) *adv.* **1,** with parts separated; in pieces. **2,** at one side; separately from; aside from.

A·part′heid″ (ə-pärt′hāt″) *n.* segregation of races in South Africa.

a·part′ment (ə-pärt′mənt) *n.* **1,** a set of rooms designed for tenancy as a unit. **2,** a single room.

ap″a·thet′ic (ap″ə-thet′ik) *adj.* lacking feeling; expressing or being apathy. —**ap″a·thet′i·cal·ly,** *adv.*

ap′a·thy (ap′ə-thē) *n.* lack of feeling; absence of emotion; indifference.

ape (āp) *n.* **1,** any of several anthropoid animals, the gorilla, chimpanzee, orangutan, or gibbon. **2,** an imitator; a mimic. —*v.t.* imitate. —**go ape,** (*Slang*) get excited.

a·pe·ri·tif′ (ə-per-i-tēf′) *n.* (*Fr.*) an alcoholic drink taken before a meal.

ap′er·ture (ap′ər-chûr) *n.* an opening; hole; gap.

a′pex (ā′peks) *n.* the highest point of anything; top; peak; climax.

a·pha′sia (ə-fā′zhə) *n.* loss of the faculty of understanding written or spoken language. —**a·pha′sic,** *adj.*

a′phid (ā′fid) *n.* a plant louse.

aph′o·rism (af′ə-riz-əm) *n.* a concise statement of a principle. —**aph′o·rist,** *n.* —**aph′o·ris′tic,** *adj.* —**aph′o·rize,** *v.t.*

aph″ro·dis′i·ac (af″rə-diz′ē-ak) *adj.* & *n.* stimulating sexual desire.

a′pi·ar″y (ā′pē-âr″ē) *n.* a place where bees are kept.

ap′i·cal (ap′ə-kəl) *adj.* being or pert. to an apex.

a·piece′ (ə-pēs′) *adv.* for each.

ap′ish (ā′pish) *adj.* apelike.

a·plomb′ (ə-plom′) *n.* self-confidence; assurance of manner.

ap′o- (ap′ə) *pref.* from; away from.

a·poc′a·lypse (ə-pok′ə-lips) *n.* **1,** a revelation. **2,** (*cap.*) the book Revelation in the New Testament of the Bible. —**a·poc″a·lyp′tic** (-lip′tik) *adj.* —**a·poc″a·lyp′ti·cal·ly,** *adv.*

A·poc′ry·pha (ə-pok′rə-fə) *n. pl.* certain books of the Old Testament whose canonicity is disputed.

a·poc′ry·phal (ə-pok′rə-fəl) *adj.* **1,** of doubtful authorship or authenticity. **2,** spurious.

ap′o·gee (ap′ə-jē) *n.* the point of greatest distance from the earth, in an orbit.

a·pol″o·get′ic (ə-pol″ə-jet′ik) *adj.* expressing regret; constituting an apology. —**a·pol″o·get′i·cal·ly,** *adv.*

a·pol'o·gist (ə-pol'ə-jist) *n.* one who seeks to justify a cause.

a·pol'o·gize" (ə-pol'ə-jīz") *v.i.* offer an excuse; express regret.

a·pol'o·gy (ə-pol'ə-jē) *n.* 1, an expression of regret for a slight or injury. 2, something said or written in defense or vindication.

ap'o·plex"y (ap'ə-plek"sē) *n.* sudden loss of consciousness or mobility from rupture of a blood vessel in the brain. —**ap"o·plec'tic**, *adj.* —**ap"o·plec'ti·cal·ly**, *adv.*

a·pos'ta·sy (ə-pos'tə-sē) *n.* total desertion of one's professed principles, faith, or party. —**a·pos'tate"** (-tāt") *n.* & *adj.* —**a·pos'ta·tize**, *v.i.*

a pos·te'ri·o"ri (ā'pos-tir'ē-ôr"ē) (*Lat.*) from later; after observing what has occurred.

a·pos'tle (ə-pos'əl) *n.* 1, (*cap.*) one of the twelve disciples chosen by Christ to preach the gospel. 2, a pioneer of any great moral reform. —**ap"os·tol'ic** (ap"ə-stol'ik) *adj.* —**ap"os·tol'i·cal·ly**, *adv.*

a·pos'tro·phe (ə-pos'trə-fē) *n.* 1, a mark of punctuation (') indicating the omission of one or more letters. 2, a direct address to a person or persons, interpolated in a speech or writing. —**a·pos'tro·phize"** (-fīz") *v.t.*

a·poth'e·car"y (ə-poth'ə-ker"ē) *n.* one who deals in drugs; pharmacist.

ap'o·thegm (ap'ə-them) *n.* a short, pithy, instructive saying; a maxim.

a·poth"e·o'sis (ə-poth"ē-ō'sis) *n.* [*pl.* **-ses** (-sēz)] glorified personification of a principle or idea. —**ap"o·the'o·size"** (ap"ə-thē'ə-sīz") *v.t.* deify; exalt.

ap·pall' (ə-pâl') *v.t.* fill with fear or horror. Also, **ap·pal'**.

ap"pa·ra'tus (ap"ə-rā'təs) *n.* all the equipment used for some purpose.

ap·par'el (ə-par'əl) *n.* 1, clothing, esp. outer garments. 2, outward aspect; guise. —*v.t.* clothe.

ap·par'ent (ə-par'ənt) *adj.* 1, in plain view; capable of being clearly perceived; obvious. 2, seeming in appearance, not necessarily real.

ap"pa·ri'tion (ap"ə-rish'ən) *n.* a ghostly appearance; specter; phantom.

ap·peal' (ə-pēl') *v.i.* 1, call for aid, sympathy, or mercy; make an earnest entreaty. 2, resort. 3, be attractive; excite interest. —*v.i.* & *t.* (*Law*) apply for review to a higher court. —*n.* 1, a call or entreaty for aid, etc. 2, attractiveness. 3, (*Law*) application for review. —**ap·peal'ing**, *adj.* arousing admiration or sympathy.

ap·pear' (ə-pir') *v.i.* 1, become visible. 2, seem to be. 3, be known; be obvious. 4,

come into public view; be published. 5, (*Law*) come formally before a tribunal.

ap·pear'ance (-əns) *n.* 1, act of appearing. 2, outward look; aspect; semblance. 3, a coming to a place; presence. 4, (*pl.*) indications; circumstances.

ap·pease' (ə-pēz') *v.t.* 1, allay (anger or strife); placate, esp. by concession 2, satisfy (an appetite or demand). —**ap·pease'ment**, *n.* act of appeasing; partial submission to a threatening nation.

ap·pel'lant (ə-pel'ənt) *n.* one who appeals. —*adj.* appellate.

ap·pel'late (-ət) *adj.* (*Law*) 1, concerned with an appeal. 2, having the duty to hear appeals.

ap"pel·la'tion (ap"ə-lā'shən) *n.* 1, the word by which a thing or person is called; name; title. 2, the act of naming.

ap·pend' (ə-pend') *v.t.* add; attach; subjoin. —**ap·pend'age** (-ij) *n.* an added and subordinate part.

ap"pen·dec'to·my (ap"ən-dek'tə-mē) *n.* removal of the vermiform appendix.

ap·pen"di·ci'tis (a-pen"də-sī'tis) *n.* (*Pathol.*) inflammation of the vermiform appendix.

ap·pen'dix (ə-pen'diks) *n.* [*pl.* **-dix·es**, **-di·ces"** (-də-sēz")] a section added but not essential to a document or book. —**vermiform appendix**, a sac attached to the human intestine.

ap"per·tain' (ap"ər-tān') *v.i.* belong as a part or member; belong by association or normal relation.

ap'pe·tite" (ap'ə-tīt") *n.* 1, craving for food. 2, any strong desire. 3, inclination to satisfy a want.

ap'pe·tiz"er (ap'ə-tīz"ər) *n.* a snack to whet the appetite.

ap'pe·tiz"ing *adj.* appealing to the appetite or taste.

ap·plaud' (ə-plâd') *v.t.* & *i.* 1, show approval of; commend; praise. 2, acclaim by clapping the hands.

ap·plause' (ə-plâz') *n.* 1, act of applauding. 2, a loud expression of approval, as by handclapping.

ap'ple (ap'əl) *n.* an edible fruit, or the tree on which it grows. —**apple butter**, a thick spiced applesauce used as jam. —**the Big Apple**, (*Colloq.*) New York City.

ap'ple·jack" *n.* a strong alcoholic liquor or brandy made from cider.

ap'ple·sauce" *n.* 1, a sauce of boiled apples. 2, (*Slang*) nonsense.

ap·pli'ance (ə-plī'əns) *n.* 1, a tool or utensil for a particular use. 2, act of applying or putting to use.

ap'pli·ca·ble (ap'li-kə-bəl) *adj.* capable

of being applied; suitable; relevant. —**ap'''pli·ca·bil'i·ty**, *n*.

ap'pli·cant (ap'li-kənt) *n*. one who applies, as for a job.

ap''pli·ca'tion (ap''li-kā'shən) *n*. **1**, the act of applying. **2**, something applied, as a salve. **3**, relevance; bearing. **4**, a request or petition. **5**, close attention; diligence.

ap'pli·ca'tor (ap'li-kā'tər) *n*. a utensil for applying something.

ap''pli·que' (ap''li-kā') *adj*. added by sewing, pasting, cementing, etc. —*n*. ornamentation so added.

ap·ply' (ə-plī') *v.t*. **1**, bring into physical contact; lay on. **2**, put to use; bring into operation. **3**, devote to a particular purpose. **4**, give earnestly. —*v.i*. **1**, be applicable or pertinent. **2**, request or appeal. —**ap·plied'**, *adj*. put to practical use.

ap·pog'gia·tu'ra (ə-poj'ə-tûr'ə) *n*. (*Music*) a grace note preceding its principal and taking a portion of its time.

ap·point' (ə-point') *v.t*. **1**, nominate or assign; designate. **2**, fix by decree; prescribe. **3**, provide with necessary equipment; rig. —**ap·poin'tive**, *adj*. done or filled by appointment.

ap·point'ment (ə-point'mənt) *n*. **1**, the act of appointing. **2**, an office held by a person appointed. **3**, an agreement to meet at a stipulated time. **4**, (*pl*.) furnishings; equipment.

ap·por'tion (ə-pôr'shən) *v.t*. divide and allot proportionally. —**ap·por'tion·ment**, *n*.

ap·pose' (ə-pōz') *v.t*. put near together. —**ap''po·si'tion** (ap''ə-zish'ən) *n*.

ap'po·site (ap'ə-zit) *adj*. applicable; suitable; well-adapted.

ap·prais'al (ə-prā'zəl) *n*. act or result of appraising; estimate.

ap·praise' (ə-prāz') *v.t*. estimate the quality or value of, esp. in money. —**ap·prais'er**, *n*. one who estimates the value of property.

ap·pre'ci·a·ble (ə-prē'shē-ə-bəl) *adj*. capable of being estimated; large or intense enough to be perceived.

ap·pre'ci·ate (ə-prē'shē-āt') *v.t*. **1**, recognize the worth of; esteem duly. **2**, be fully conscious of. **3**, raise in value. —*v.i*. rise in value. —**ap·pre''ci·a'tion**, *n*. —**ap·pre'ci·a·tive** (-ə-tiv) *adj*. duly grateful.

ap''pre·hend' (ap''rē-hend') *v.t*. **1**, seize physically; take into custody; arrest. **2**, grasp mentally; understand. **3**, have fear of; anticipate. —**ap''pre·hen'si·ble** (-hen'sə-bal) *adj*.

ap''pre·hen'sion (ap''rē-hen'shən) *n*. **1**, act of apprehending. **2**, result of apprehending; arrest; understanding.

ap''pre·hen'sive (-siv) *adj*. uneasy or fearful about future events. —**ap''pre·hen'sive·ness**, *n*.

ap·pren'tice (ə-pren'tis) *n*. one who works under tutelage to learn a trade. —**ap·pren'tice·ship**, *n*.

ap·prise' (ə-prīz') *v.t*. give notice; inform.

ap·proach' (ə-prōch') *v.t. & i*. **1**, draw near to; advance toward. **2**, be similar to in quality or degree. **3**, make advances or proposals to. —*n*. **1**, the act of approaching. **2**, method or means of access; avenue. **3**, nearness; proximity.

ap''pro·ba'tion (ap''rə-bā'shən) *n*. approval; commendation.

ap·pro'pri·ate'' (ə-prō'prē-āt') *v.t*. **1**, allot (money) for a specific use. **2**, take possession of. —*adj*. (-ət) suitable; applicable. —**ap·pro'pri·ate·ness**, *n*.

ap·pro'pri·a'tion (-ā'shən) *n*. **1**, money set aside for a specific purpose. **2**, act of appropriating.

ap·prov'al (ə-proov'əl) *n*. act or effect of approving; commendation; approbation. —**on approval**, without obligation to buy.

ap·prove' (ə-proov') *v.t*. **1**, pronounce good; admit the propriety or excellence of. **2**, sanction officially; ratify. —*v.i*. judge favorably; be pleased.

ap·prox'i·mate (ə-prok'sə-mət) *adj*. **1**, nearly correct or precise. **2**, close together; very similar in form or degree. —*v.i*. (-māt') be nearly like. —**ap·prox'i·mate·ly**, *adv*. nearly; about. —**ap·prox''i·ma'tion**, *n*.

ap·pur'te·nance (ə-pêr'tə-nəns) *n*. **1**, (*Law*) a right or privilege belonging to a property. **2**, an accessory part; appendage. **3**, (*pl*.) furnishings; apparatus. —**ap·pur'te·nant**, *adj*.

a'pri·cot'' (ā'prə-kot') *n*. **1**, the fruit of a tree resembling the plum and peach. **2**, the apricot tree. **3**, a light orange color.

A'pril (ā'prəl) *n*. the fourth month of the year.

a pri·o'ri (ā'prē-ôr'ē) (*Lat*.) from before; before knowing what will occur.

a'pron (ā'prən) *n*. **1**, an outer garment worn to protect the clothing. **2**, any protective shield or flange.

ap''ro·pos' (ap''rə-pō') *adv*. **1**, to the purpose; opportunely. **2**, (with *of*) in reference to. —*adj*. appropriate.

apse (aps) *n*. an alcove or recess, usually semicircular and vaulted.

apt *adj*. **1**, suited to its purpose. **2**, quick in learning. **3**, having a tendency; inclined. —**apt'ness**, *n*.

ap'ti·tude (ap'ti-tood) *n*. fitness; innate ability.

aq'ua (ak'wə) *pref*. water.

---

aq′ua·cade″ (-kād″) *n.* a spectacular musical entertainment, with feats performed in the water.

aq′ua·cul″ture *n.* the cultivation of fish or produce in water.

Aq′ua-Lung″ (ak′wə-lung″) *n.* (*T.N.*) an underwater breathing apparatus using compressed-air cylinders.

aq′ua·ma·rine′ (ak′wə-mə-rēn′) *n.* **1,** a bluish-green color. **2,** semiprecious stone.

aq′ua·naut″ (-nât″) *n.* a diver who spends extended periods of time under water.

aq′ua·plane″ (ak′wə-plān″) *n.* a board towed behind a motorboat for carrying a surf-rider. —*v.i.* **1,** ride on such a board. **2,** hydroplane.

a·quar′i·um (ə-kwâr′ē-əm) *n.* a tank or building in which are kept living aquatic animals and plants.

A·quar′i·us (ə-kwâr′ē-əs) *n.* a constellation, the Water Bearer (see *zodiac*).

a·quat′ic (ə-kwat′ik) *adj.* **1,** pert. to water. **2,** living or done in water. —**a·quat′i·cal·ly,** *adv.*

aq′ua·tint″ (ak′wə-tint″) *n.* **1,** a method of engraving. **2,** a print so made.

aq′ua·vit″ (ä′kwə-vēt″) *n.* a strong alcoholic liquor; schnapps.

aq′ue·duct″ (ak′wi-dukt″) *n.* an artificial channel or conduit for conducting water from one place to another.

a′que·ous (ā′kwē-əs) *adj.* like water; containing or formed by water.

aq′ui·line (ak′wə-lin) *adj.* **1,** pert. to the eagle. **2,** (of a nose) like an eagle's beak.

ar″a·besque′ (ar″ə-besk′) *n.* **1,** style of fanciful decoration. **2,** a posture in ballet.

Ar′a·bic (ar′ə-bik) *adj.* pert. to Arabia, or its language, or to *Arabic numerals:* 0, 1, 2, 3, etc.

ar′a·ble (ar′ə-bəl) *adj.* fit for plowing and tillage. —**ar″a·bil′i·ty,** *n.*

Ar·a·ma′ic (ar-ə-mā′ik) *n. & adj.* a Semitic language, used by Jesus.

ar′bi·ter (är′bi-tər) *n.* **1,** one who has power to judge and decide. **2,** arbitrator; umpire.

ar′bi·trage (är′bi-trij) *n.* simultaneous purchase and sale of commodities in different markets to profit from unequal prices.

ar′bi·trar″y (är′bə-trār″ē) *adj.* **1,** not regulated by fixed rule or law. **2,** despotic. **3,** capricious; unreasonable. —**ar′bi·trar″i·ness,** *n.*

ar′bi·trate″ (är′bi-trāt″) *v.t.* **1,** act as a formal umpire between contestants. **2,** submit to arbitration. —**ar″bi·tra′tion,** *n.* settlement of a dispute by lay judges, out of court. —**ar′bi·tra′tor,** *n.*

ar′bor (är′bər) *n.* **1,** a bower formed by foliage trained over a lattice. **2,** a shaft or supporting bar in a machine. Also, **ar′bour.** —**ar·bo′re·al** (-bôr′ē-əl) *adj.* pert. to or living in trees.

ar″bo·re′tum (är″bə-rē′təm) *n.* a park in which trees or shrubs are cultivated, usu. for scientific purposes.

ar″bor·vi′tae (-vī′tē) *n.* an evergreen tree; the red cedar.

ar·bu′tus (är-bū′təs) *n.* **1,** any of several evergreen shrubs with scarlet berries. **2,** a creeping vine with fragrant white and pink flowers.

arc (ärk) *n.* **1,** a segment of a circle. **2,** any bow-shaped curve. **3,** a spark or luminescence caused by a flow of current across a gap between two electrical terminals. —*v.i.* form an arc; travel in a curved path.

ar·cade′ (är-kād′) *n.* **1,** a roofed passageway; a covered avenue lined with shops. **2,** an amusement center.

ar·cane′ (är-kān′) *adj.* secret.

arch (ärch) *n.* **1,** a building structure in the shape of a curve concave from below, supported at its extremities. **2,** anything that resembles an arch. —*v.t.* **1,** span with an arch. **2,** curve like an arch. —*adj.* **1,** chief; preëminent. **2,** sly; roguish.

arch- (ärch; ärk) *pref.* first; chief.

-arch (ärk) *suf.* ruler.

ar″chae·ol′o·gy (är″kē-ol′ə-jē) *n.* the study of past cultures through their surviving relics. —**ar″chae·o·log′i·cal,** *adj.* —**ar″chae·ol′o·gist,** *n.*

ar·cha′ic (är-kā′ik) *adj.* **1,** of an earlier period; antiquated. **2,** (*Lexic.*) not in current usage, but familiar in surviving earlier literature. —**ar′cha·ism** (-iz-əm) *n.*

arch′an″gel (ärk′-) *n.* a chief angel.

arch′bish″op (ärch′-) *n.* a bishop of highest rank.

arch″di′o·cese (ärch″-) *n.* the diocese or see of an archbishop. —**arch″di·oc′e·san,** *adj.*

arch′duke″ (ärch′-) *n.* title of former Austrian royal princes.

arch′er (är′chər) *n.* **1,** one who uses a bow and arrow. **2,** (*cap.*) the constellation of Sagittarius. —**arch′er·y** (-ē) *n.*

ar′che·type″ (är′ki-tīp″) *n.* an original model; prototype.

arch′fiend′ (ärch″-) *n.* **1,** a vicious person. **2,** (often *cap.*) the devil; Satan.

ar″chi·pel′a·go″ (är″kə-pel′ə-gō″) *n.* a group of many islands.

ar′chi·tect″ (är′kə-tekt″) *n.* **1,** one who designs buildings. **2,** the planner or maker of anything.

ar″chi·tec·ton′ics (är″ki-tek-ton′iks) *n.* **1,** the science of construction or structure. **2,**

the science of systematizing knowledge. —ar″chi·tec·ton′ic, *adj.*

ar″chi·tec′ture (-tek′chər) *n.* **1,** the designing of buildings. **2,** style of building. —**ar″chi·tec′tur·al,** *adj.*

ar′chi·trave″ (är′ki-trāv″) *n.* **1,** the lowest layer of a structure supported by columns, resting immediately on the head of the column. **2,** a molding.

ar′chives (är′kīvz) *n.pl.* **1,** documents preserved for their political or historical value. **2,** the place where such documents are kept. —**ar′chi·vist** (-kə-vist) *n.*

arch′way (ärch′wā) *n.* an entrance or passage under an arch.

-ar·chy (är-kė) *suf.* government; rule.

arc-′jet″ *adj.* pert. to an engine in which gases are heated by an electric arc.

arc′light″ *n.* a lamp producing light by means of an electric arc.

arc′tic (ärk′tik) *adj.* near or at the North Pole. —*n.* (*cap.*) the North Polar regions.

ar′dent (är′dənt) *adj.* **1,** fervent in feeling; intense; passionate. **2,** burning; fiery; glowing. —**ar′den·cy,** *n.*

ar′dor (är′dər) *n.* **1,** intensity of feeling; zeal; passion. **2,** fiery heat. Also, **ar′dour.**

ar′du·ous (är′dū-əs) *adj.* requiring prolonged effort; wearisome. —**ar′du·ous·ness,** *n.*

are (är) *v.* 1st person pl. of *be.*

are (âr; är) *n.* a unit of surface measure, 100 sq. meters.

ar′e·a (âr′ė-ə) *n.* **1,** amount of surface; extent in general; scope. **2,** a region or tract. —**area code,** any of a series of 3-digit call numbers used to designate various telephone calling areas in the U.S. and Canada.

a·re′na (ə-rē′nə) *n.* the enclosure in which an athletic contest is held.

aren't (ärnt) *contraction* are not.

ar′gent (är′jənt) *adj.* like silver, esp. in color.

ar′gon (är′gon) *n.* a colorless, odorless, inert gaseous element present in air, no. 18, symbol A.

ar′go·sy (är′gə-sė) *n.* a merchant vessel or fleet carrying a rich cargo.

ar′got (är′gō) *n.* the slang or cant of a particular class, as of thieves.

ar′gue (är′gū) *v.i.* engage in intellectual dispute. —*v.t.* **1,** state reasons for and against; discuss. **2,** maintain; seek to prove.

ar′gu·ment (är′gū-mənt) *n.* **1,** discussion of a controversial nature; debate. **2,** a statement or chain of reasoning tending to induce belief. **3,** an abstract or summary of a writing or speech. —**ar″gu·men·ta′tion,** *n.*

ar·gu·men′ta·tive (är-gyə-men′tə-tiv) *adj.* disposed to argue; contentious.

Ar′gy·rol″ (är′ji-rōl″) *n.* (*T.N.*) an antiseptic containing silver.

a′ri·a (ä′rė-ə) *n.* **1,** a vocal solo, with or without accompaniment. **2,** any tune.

ar′id *adj.* **1,** lacking moisture; parched with heat. **2,** uninteresting. —**a·rid′i·ty** (ə-rid′ə-tè) *n.*

Ar′i·es (âr′ėz) *n.* a northern constellation, the Ram (see *zodiac*).

a·rise′ (ə-rīz′) *v.i.* [**a·rose′,** **a·ris′en** (-riz′ən)] **1,** come into being or action. **2,** get up; move upward.

ar″is·toc′ra·cy (ar″is-tok′rə-sè) *n.* **1,** government by a privileged upper class. **2,** any class having special privileges or considered superior.

a·ris′to·crat (ə-ris′tə-krat) *n.* a member of the aristocracy, or one who behaves like a nobleman. —**a·ris″to·crat′ic,** *adj.* —**a·ris″to·crat′i·cal·ly,** *adv.*

a·rith′me·tic (ə-rith′mə-tik) *n.* the art of computation, the most elementary branch of mathematics. —**a·rith″me·ti′cian** (-tish′ən) *n.* —**arithmetic progression,** a sequence of numbers, each different from the number preceding it by the same amount, as 1, 3, 5, 7, etc.

ar″ith·met′i·cal (ar″ith-met′i-kəl) *adj.* of or by arthmetic. Also, **ar″ith·met′ic.**

ark (ärk) *n.* **1,** the vessel built by Noah to save those chosen from the Flood; a large boat or building. **2,** the chest containing the Covenant (between God and the Jews).

arm (ärm) *n.* **1,** the upper limb of the human body, extending from shoulder to hand. **2,** anything like an arm in form or position. **3,** range of authority; power. **4,** a branch, esp. of military forces. **5,** (usually *pl.*) a weapon. —*v.t. & i.* equip with arms; provide what is necessary for security or defense.

ar·ma′da (är-mä′də) *n.* a fleet of warships.

ar″ma·dil′lo (är″mə-dil′ō) *n.* [*pl.* **-los**] a So. and Central Amer. mammal having hard scales.

Ar″ma·ged′don (är″mə-ged′ən) *n.* **1,** the place of the final battle between good and evil. **2,** any battle or struggle of a decisive nature.

ar′ma·ment (är′mə-mənt) *n.* **1,** the totality of weapons with which a military unit is armed. **2,** the act of arming.

ar′ma·ture (är′mə-chûr) *n.* **1,** defensive armor; protective covering. **2,** a supporting or connecting member.

arm′chair″ *n.* a chair with side arms.

arm′ful″ *n.* **1,** as much as the arms can hold. **2,** (*Colloq.*) a stout or shapely girl.

ar′mi·stice (är′mi-stis) *n.* a temporary suspension of hostilities; truce. —**Armistice Day,** Veterans Day.

arm′let (-lət) *n.* **1,** an ornamental band or bracelet worn around the upper arm. **2,** a small inlet of the sea.

ar·moire′ (är-mwär′) *n.* a large cupboard or wardrobe.

ar′mor (är′mər) *n.* **1,** any covering worn for protection against offensive weapons. **2,** anything that protects.

ar·mor′i·al (är-môr′ē-əl) *adj.* pert. to heraldic bearings.

ar′mor·y (är′mə-rē) *n.* a place for storing or manufacturing weapons.

arm′pit″ *n.* the hollow under the arm at the shoulder.

arm-′twist″ing *n.* (*Colloq.*) persuasion.

ar′my (är′mē) *n.* **1,** a large body of men trained for war on land, excluding naval and (usually) air forces. **2,** any large body of persons.

ar′ni·ca (är′ni-kə) *n.* a medicinal tincture used on wounds and bruises.

a·ro′ma (ə-rō′mə) *n.* an agreeable odor; fragrance. —**ar″o·mat′ic** (ar″ə-mat′ik) *adj.* —**ar″o·mat′i·cal·ly,** *adv.*

a·round′ (ə-rownd′) *prep. & adv.* **1,** on all sides; encircling. **2,** from place to place; here and there. **3,** (*Colloq.*) near at hand; approximately. **4,** rotating.

a·rouse′ (ə-rowz′) *v.t.* excite into action; awaken; put in motion.

ar·peg′gi·o (är-pej′yō) *n.* (*Music*) the sounding of the notes of a chord in succession instead of simultaneously.

ar′rack (ar′ək) *n.* an Oriental liquor made from rice, molasses, or other materials.

ar·raign′ (ə-rān′) *v.t.* **1,** (*Law*) call into court to answer a charge. **2,** accuse. —**ar·raign′ment,** *n.*

ar·range′ (ə-rānj′) *v.t.* **1,** put in proper order. **2,** come to an agreement; settle. **3,** make preparation; plan. **4,** (*Music*) adapt for performance by particular voices or instruments. —**ar·range′ment,** *n.*

ar′rant (ar′ənt) *adj.* **1,** manifest; notorious. **2,** downright; thorough.

ar·ray′ (ə-rā′) *n.* **1,** regular order or arrangement; an orderly assemblage. **2,** a display. **3,** raiment or apparel. —*v.t.* **1,** place in order or in a display. **2,** dress; bedeck.

ar·rears′ (ə-rirz′) *n.pl.* that which is overdue, as an unpaid debt.

ar·rest′ (ə-rest′) *v.t.* **1,** take (a person) into custody; seize; capture. **2,** stop forcibly; check or hinder. **3,** catch the attention of. —*n.* **1,** detention under legal warrant. **2,** capture; restraint; stoppage. —**ar·rest′ing,** *adj.* striking.

ar·riv′al (ə-rī′vəl) *n.* **1,** the act, fact, or

time of arriving at a place. **2,** a person or thing that arrives.

ar·rive′ (ə-rīv′) *v.i.* **1,** reach a certain point. **2,** come; occur. **3,** attain a position of eminence or success.

ar′ro·gant (ar′ə-gənt) *adj.* aggressively haughty. —**ar′ro·gance,** *n.*

ar′ro·gate″ (ar′ə-gāt″) *v.t.* assume, demand, or appropriate unduly or presumptuously. —**ar″ro·ga′tion,** *n.*

ar′row (ar′ō) *n.* **1,** a rodlike missile weapon made to be shot from a bow. **2,** an angular sign, like the head of an arrow, used to point direction.

ar′row·head″ (-hed″) *n.* **1,** a hard, pointed tip for an arrow. **2,** a wedge-shaped mark.

ar′row·root″ *n.* **1,** a tropical Amer. plant; the starch obtained from it. **2,** any similar starch used in food products.

ar·roy′o (ə-roi′ō) *n.* a small gulch or ravine.

ar′se·nal (är′sə-nəl) *n.* a manufactory or storehouse for military arms and supplies.

ar′se·nic (är′sə-nik) *n.* **1,** a volatile chemical element, no. 33, symbol As. **2,** a poison derived therefrom. —**ar·sen′i·cal** (-sen′i-kəl) *adj.*

ar′son (är′sən) *n.* the malicious burning of a building.

art (ärt) *n.* **1,** any system of rules and traditional methods for the practice of a craft, trade, or profession; the application of knowledge and skill. **2,** works designed to give intellectual pleasure, as music, sculpture, and esp. pictorial representation. **3,** skillful workmanship. **4,** cunning; guile. —**Art Dec′o** (dek′ō) a style of decorative art popular in the 1920's and 1930's. —**Art Nou·veau′** (noo-vō′) a style of decorative and architectural art of the late 19th century.

ar·te″ri·o·scle·ro′sis (är-tir″ē-ō-skle-rō′sis) *n.* a thickening of the blood vessels.

ar′ter·y (är′tə-rē) *n.* **1,** any of the large vessels that convey blood from the heart to another part of the body. **2,** a main channel of conveyance or transportation. —**ar·te′ri·al** (-tir′ē-əl) *adj.*

ar·te′sian well (är-tē′zhən) a deep well in which water rises by subsurface pressure.

art′ful (ärt′fəl) *adj.* **1,** crafty; wily. **2,** skillful. —**art′ful·ness,** *n.*

ar·thri′tis (är-thrī′tis) *n.* inflammation of a joint. —**ar·thrit′ic** (-thrit′ik) *adj.*

ar′ti·choke″ (är′ti-chōk″) *n.* a thistlelike plant with an edible head.

ar′ti·cle (är′tə-kəl) . **1,** a separate item; a separate portion of anything. **2,** a literary composition on a specific topic. **3,** (*Gram.*)

a word used before a noun, marking its application. **—definite article,** the. **—indefinite article,** a or an.

ar·tic'u·late" (är-tik'ū-lāt") v.t. & i. **1,** say or speak distinctly, with clear separation of syllables. **2,** unite by joints. —adj. (-lət) **1,** able to speak; expressive. **2,** having joints; segmented. **3,** clear; distinct. **—ar·tic"u·la'tion,** n.

ar'ti·fact" (är'ti-fakt") n. a man-made object, esp. from prehistoric times.

ar'ti·fice (är'tə-fis) n. **1,** a crafty device. **2,** trickery. **—ar·tif'i·cer** (är-tif'ə-sər) n.

ar"ti·fi'cial (är"tə-fish'əl) adj. **1,** man-made; contrived by human skill. **2,** assumed; pretended; fictitious. **3,** full of affectation. **—ar"ti·fi"ci·al'i·ty** (är"ti-fish"ē-al'ə-tē) n. **—artificial horizon,** an aircraft position relative to the surface of the earth. **—artificial respiration,** expansion and contraction of the lungs by hand or machine, to restore or maintain breathing. **—artificial satellite,** any object or device propelled by rockets beyond the atmosphere and caused to revolve in an orbit.

ar·til'ler·y (är-til'ə-rē) n. **1,** all heavy, mounted firearms; cannons. **2,** troops servicing such firearms.

ar'ti·san (är'tə-zən) n. one skilled in an industrial craft.

art'ist (är'tist) **1,** one who pursues a pictorial art, esp. a painter. **2,** [also, **ar·tiste'** (-tēst')] a performer in an art of entertainment. **3,** a person of special skill. **—artis'tic,** adj. **—ar·tis'ti·cal·ly,** adv. **—art'ist·ry** (-rē) n.

art'less (ärt'ləs) adj. simple and natural; free from guile; sincere. **—art'less·ness,** n.

art'y (är'tē) adj. (Colloq.) affectedly or superficially interested in the fine arts. Also, **art'sy** (ärt'sē).

-ar·y (er-ē) suf. forming adjectives: pertaining to.

Ar'yan (är'yən) adj. & n. **1,** European or Asiatic (in race). **2,** (incorrectly) gentile; Nordic. Also, **Ar'i·an** (ar'ē-ən).

as (az) adv. in that degree; to that extent; so far. —conj. **1,** to the same degree or extent; in similar manner. **2,** at the same time. **3,** because. **4,** for example. —pron. that or who.

as"a·fet'i·da (as"ə-fet'i-də) n. a herb or a pungent drug made from it.

as·bes'tos (az-bes'təs) n. a mineral used for fireproofing.

as·cend' (ə-send') v.i. go upward; rise. —v.t. climb; mount.

as·cend'ant (ə-sen'dənt) adj. **1,** rising. **2,** dominant. —n. (with the) superiority. **—as·cend'an·cy,** n.

as·cen'sion (ə-sen'shən) n. a rising, esp. (cap.) of Christ into heaven.

as·cent' (ə-sent') n. **1,** act of ascending; a climbing or moving upward; rise. **2,** an upward slope.

as"cer·tain' (as"ər-tān') v.t. find out by examination; determine. **—as"cer·tain'·ment,** n.

as·cet'ic (ə-set'ik) adj. extreme in self-restraint or self-denial. —n. a recluse or hermit. **—as·cet'i·cal·ly,** adv. **—as·cet'i·cism** (-i-siz-əm) n.

a·scor'bic acid (ə-skôr'bik) vitamin C, used to combat scurvy.

as'cot (as'kət) n. a broad necktie folded like a scarf.

as·cribe' (ə-skrīb') v.t. attribute to a cause or source; impute. **—as·crip'tion** (ə-skrip'-shən) n.

a·sep'tic (ə-sep'tik) adj. free of germs that cause disease or decay. **—a·sep'ti·cal·ly,** adv.

a·sex'u·al (ā-sek'shoo-əl) adj. not having or involving sex.

ash n. **1,** the incombustible residue that remains after burning. **2,** (pl.) human remains. **3,** a hardwood tree. **—ash tray,** a dish for tobacco ashes. **—Ash Wednesday,** the Wednesday on which Lent begins.

ash'en (ash'ən) adj. **1,** pale; gray. **2,** pert. to the ash tree.

ash'lar (ash'lər) n. a block of building stone; such stones collectively. Also, **ash'-ler.**

a·shore' (ə-shôr') adv. to or on land, not water.

ash'y (ash'ē) adj. pale as ashes. **—ash'i·ness,** n.

A"si·at'ic (ā"zhē-at'ik) adj. pert. to Asia or its inhabitants. —n. a native of Asia. Also, **A'sian** (ā'zhən). **—Asiatic flu** or **Asian flu,** a mild form of influenza, usually lasting 5 days.

a·side' (ə-sīd') adv. **1,** on or to one side; apart or separately. **2,** out of consideration or regard. —n. (Stage) a private remark to the audience.

as'i·nine' (as'ə-nīn') adj. obtrusively silly; stupid. **—as"i·nin'i·ty** (-nin'ə-tē) n.

ask (ásk) v.t. & i. **1,** put a question (to); interrogate. **2,** seek to obtain; request. **3,** inquire (about). **4,** invite.

a·skance' (ə-skans') adv. distrustfully; from the side, as a glance.

a·skew' (ə-skū') adv. in an oblique position; out of line; awry.

a·slant' (ə-slánt') adj. & adv. slanting; oblique.

---

a·sleep' (ə-slēp') *adv.* & *adj.* **1,** sleeping; numb. **2,** inactive.

asp *n.* a poisonous snake.

as·par'a·gus (ə-spar'ə-gəs) *n.* a plant having edible shoots.

as'pect (as'pekt) *n.* **1,** one of the ways in which a thing may be viewed or contemplated. **2,** outward appearance; facial expression. **3,** view.

as'pen (as'pən) *adj.* tremulous; quivering. —*n.* a poplar tree.

as·per'i·ty (as-per'ə-tē) *n.* harshness of temper; severity.

as·perse' (ə-spèrs') *v.t.* make false or foul charges against; slander. —**as·per'sion** (-zhən) *n.*

as'phalt (as'fält) *n.* a bituminous substance used for paving, etc. —**asphalt jungle,** a large city, esp. its high crime areas.

as'pho·del (as'fə-del) *n.* a plant of the lily family.

as·phyx'i·a (as-fik'sē-ə) *n.* extreme lack of oxygen; suffocation.

as·phyx'i·ate' (as-fiks'ē-āt″) *v.t.* & *i.* kill or die by deprivation of oxygen; suffocate. —**as·phyx″i·a'tion,** *n.*

as'pic (as'pik) *n.* a clear jelly made of meat or vegetables.

as'pi·rate″ (as'pə-rāt″) *v.t.* pronounce with an audible emission of breath. —*n.* & *adj.* (-rət) the sound represented by h.

as″pi·ra'tion (as″pə-rā'shən) *n.* **1,** desire; ambition. **2,** breathing.

as·pire' (ə-spīr') *v.i.* be ardently desirous, esp. for something spiritual. —**as·pir'-ant,** *n.*

as'pi·rin (as'pə-rin) *n.* a drug used to relieve pain and reduce fever.

ass (as) *n.* **1,** a horselike beast of burden; the donkey. **2,** a stupid person; a fool.

as·sail' (ə-sāl') *v.t.* attack; belabor with entreaties or abuse. —**as·sail'ant,** *n.* attacker.

as·sas'sin (ə-sas'in) *n.* one who kills another by secret assault.

as·sas'si·nate″ (ə-sas'ə-nāt″) *v.t.* kill violently and treacherously. —**as·sas″si·na'tion,** *n.*

as·sault' (ə-sält') *v.t.* attack by physical means; assail with argument, abuse. —*n.* an attack. —**assault and battery,** (*Law*) assault with offensive or violent touching of another.

as·say' (ə-sā') *v.t.* test; analyze, esp. metallic ore.

as·se·gai″ (as'ə-gī″) *n.* **1,** a So. Afr. hardwood tree, similar to the dogwood. **2,** a slender spear or javelin. —*v.t.* strike or kill with an assegai. Also, **as'sa·gai″.**

as·sem'blage (ə-sem'blij) *n.* persons or things assembled.

as·sem'ble (ə-sem'bəl) *v.t.* **1,** bring together in one place. **2,** fit together. —*v.i.* come together; congregate.

as·sem'bler (-blər) *n.* a computer program which translates instructions into machine language.

as·sem'bly (ə-sem'blē) *n.* **1,** act of bringing or coming together. **2,** a group; congregation. **3,** a legislative body.

as·sent' (ə-sent') *v.i.* express agreement or approval; concur. —*n.* (as'ent) agreement; acquiescence.

as·sert' (ə-sèrt') *v.t.* **1,** state as true; declare; aver. **2,** claim and defend.

as·ser'tion (ə-sèr'shən) *n.* **1,** act of asserting. **2,** statement; claim; affirmation.

as·ser'tive (-tiv) *adj.* positive; overbearing. —**as·ser'tive·ness,** *n.*

as·sess' (ə-ses') *v.t.* **1,** estimate the value of (property) as a basis for taxation. **2,** impose a tax, charge, or fine. —**as·sess'-ment,** *n.* —**as·ses'sor,** *n.*

as'set (as'et) *n.* **1,** anything advantageous. **2,** (usually *pl.*) items of property available; total resources.

as·sev'er·ate″ (ə-sev'ə-rāt″) *v.t.* aver solemnly and positively. —**as·sev″er·a'tion,** *n.*

as″si·du'i·ty (as″i-dū'ə-tē) *n.* quality of being assiduous; diligence.

as·sid'u·ous (ə-sij'oo-əs) *adj.* diligent; attentive; unremitting. —**as·sid'u·ous·ness,** *n.*

as·sign' (ə-sīn') *v.t.* **1,** set apart; allot; transfer. **2,** appoint, as to office or duties. **3,** specify; designate; ascribe; refer. —*n.* (*Law*) [also, **as″sign·ee'** (as″ə-nē')] one to whom property is transferred.

as″sig·na'tion (as″ig-nā'shən) *n.* an appointment for an illicit love meeting.

as·sign'ment (-mənt) *n.* **1,** act of assigning. **2,** something assigned to be done; task; mission. **3,** a document attesting to a transfer of interest.

as·sim'i·late″ (ə-sim'ə-lāt″) *v.t.* **1,** take in and incorporate; absorb and digest. **2,** make similar; bring into conformity; adapt. —*v.i.* assimilate something. —**as·sim″i·la'tion,** *n.*

as·sist' (ə-sist') *v.t.* give help; aid. —*v.i.* be present; attend.

as·sist'ance (-əns) *n.* act of assisting; help; aid.

as·sist'ant (-ənt) *n.* a helper.

as·size' (ə-sīz') *n.* **1,** a session of a legislature. **2,** (*pl.*) a term of sittings of an English court.

as·so'ci·ate″ (ə-sō'shē-āt″) *v.t.* **1,** link together in some conceptual relationship. **2,** join in partnership; combine in a union. —*v.i.* consort together; unite. —*n.* (-ət) **1,** a partner, confederate, or companion. **2**, anything that usually accompanies another. —*adj.* (-ət) **1**, allied; concomitant. **2**, having subordinate membership.

as·so″ci·a′tion (ə-sō″sē-ā′shən) *n.* **1**, act of associating. **2**, state of being associated; partnership; combination. **3**, a society, league, etc.

as′so·nance (as′ə-nəns) *n.* resemblance in spoken sound, without strict rhyme. —**as′so·nant**, *adj.*

as·sort′ (ə-sôrt′) *v.t.* separate and distribute according to kind; classify; arrange.

as·sort′ment (-mənt) *n.* **1**, act of assorting. **2**, a diversified group or collection.

as·suage′ (ə-swāj′) *v.t.* lessen; mitigate; pacify. —**as·suage′ment**, *n.* —**as·sua′sive** (ə-swā′siv) *adj.*

as·sume′ (ə-soom′) *v.t.* **1**, take for granted without proof. **2**, take upon oneself; undertake. **3**, take the appearance of; pretend to possess. **4**, take for oneself; appropriate.

as·sump′tion (ə-sum′shən) *n.* **1**, act of assuming. **2**, a supposition or hypothesis. **3**, (*cap.*) bodily acceptance into heaven, esp. of the Virgin Mary.

as·sur′ance (ə-shûr′əns) *n.* **1**, an earnest statement intended to give confidence. **2**, freedom from doubt. **3**, boldness; impudence. **4**, a promise or pledge; surety. **5**, insurance.

as·sure′ (ə-shûr′) *v.t.* **1**, make sure or certain; make secure or stable. **2**, make confident; convince.

as′symp·tote″ (as′im-tōt″) *n.* a straight line considered as tangent to a curve but that does not meet the curve at any distance less than infinity. —**as″ymp·tot′ic** (-tot′ik) *adj.*

as′ta·tine″ (as′tə-tēn″) *n.* an unstable radioactive chemical element, one of the halogens, no. 85, symbol At, a product of radioactive decay.

as′ter (as′tər) *n.* any of many species of common flowers having colored petals around a yellow disk.

as′ter·isk (as′tər-isk) *n.* a symbol (*) used in printing.

a·stern′ (ə-stêrn′) *adv.* & *adj.* (*Naut.*) to the rear; behind.

as′ter·oid″ (as′tər-oid″) *n.* any of the many small planets located chiefly between Mars and Jupiter.

as·the′ni·a (as-thē′né-ə) *n.* loss of strength; bodily weakness.

asth′ma (az′mə) *n.* a disorder of respiration, marked by labored breathing. —**asth·mat′ic** (-mat′ik) *adj.* —**asth·mat′i·cal·ly**, *adv.*

a·stig′ma·tism (ə-stig′mə-tiz-əm) *n.* defect of the eye producing imperfect focus. —**as″tig·mat′ic** (as″tig-mat′ik) *adj.*

a·stir′ (ə-stêr′) *adv.* & *adj.* on the move; active; out of bed.

as·ton′ish (ə-ston′ish) *v.t.* strike with wonder; surprise; amaze. —**as·ton′ish·ment**, *n.*

as·tound′ (ə-stownd′) *v.t.* strike with amazement; astonish greatly.

as′tra·khan (as′trə-kən) *n.* **1**, the fur of the Karakul lamb. **2**, a fabric resembling it.

as′tral (as′trəl) *adj.* **1**, pert. to the stars; stellar. **2**, star-shaped.

a·stray′ (ə-strā′) *adv.* & *adj.* away from the proper path; wandering.

a·stride′ (ə-strīd′) *prep.* with one leg on each side of. Also, **a·strad′dle** (ə-strad′əl) *adj.*

as·tringe′ (ə-strinj′) *v.t.* contract; draw together. —**as·trin′gen·cy**, *n.*

as·trin′gent (ə-strin′jənt) *n.* a substance used to contract the bodily tissues and so diminish discharge, as of blood. —*adj.* **1**, tending to constrict. **2**, severe; austere.

as·tro- (as-trə) *pref.* star.

as′tro·labe″ (as′trə-lāb″) *n.* an astronomical instrument.

as·trol′o·gy (ə-strol′ə-jē) *n.* the study of the supposed influence of the stars and planets on human affairs. —**as·trol′o·ger** (-jər) *n.*

as′tro·naut (as′trə-nât) *n.* the pilot of or a traveler in a space ship. —**as″tro·nau′tics**, *n.sing.* the science of space travel.

as″tro·nom′i·cal (as″trə-nom′i-kəl) *adj.* **1**, pert. to astronomy. **2**, huge.

as·tron′o·my (ə-stron′ə-mé) *n.* the general science of all celestial bodies. —**as·tron′o·mer**, *n.*

as″tro·phys′ics *n.* the branch of astronomy dealing with the physical properties of heavenly bodies; astronomical physics. —**as″tro·phys′i·cal**, *adj.*

as·tute′ (ə-stoot′) *adj.* keen in discernment; sagacious; cunning. —**as·tute′ness**, *n.*

a·sun′der (ə-sun′dər) *adv.* & *adj.* into separate parts; in a position apart.

a·sy′lum (ə-sī′ləm) *n.* **1**, an institution for the care of the insane or afflicted. **2**, any place of refuge.

at *prep.* used in many idiomatic phrases to imply local or relative position, direction of motion or activity, time, order, condition, circumstance, etc.

at′a·brine (at′ə-brin) *n.* (*T.N.*) a drug used against malaria.

at′a·vism (at′ə-viz-əm) *n.* reversion to distant hereditary traits or characteristics. —**at″a·vis′tic** (-vis′tik) *adj.* —**at″a·vis′ti·cal·ly**, *adv.*

ate (āt) *v.* pret. of *eat*.

at″el·ier′ (at″əl-yā′) *n.* a studio; workshop.

a′the·ism (ā′thē-iz-əm) *n.* the doctrine that there is no God. —**a′the·ist**, *n.* —**a″the·is′·tic** (-is′tik) *adj.* —**a″the·is′ti·cal·ly**, *adv.*

ath″e·nae′um (ath″ə-nē′əm) *n.* an institution of learning; a library.

a·the′ni·um (a-thē′nē-əm) *n.* einsteinium.

ath′lete (ath′lēt) *n.* one who engages in exercises of physical agility and strength. —**athlete's foot,** a fungous skin disease.

ath·let′ic (ath-let′ik) *adj.* **1,** like an athlete; strong. **2,** pert. to athletics. —**ath·let′i·cal·ly,** *adv.*

ath·let′ics (-iks) *n.pl.* sports requiring physical prowess.

a·thwart′ (ə-thwôrt′) *adv. & prep.* **1,** from side to side; crosswise. **2,** perversely.

-a′tion (ā′shən) *suf.* forming nouns denoting the act, process, result, effect, or cause (of the root word).

at′las (at′ləs) *n.* a bound collection of maps.

at′mos·phere″ (at′məs-fir″) *n.* **1,** the entire gaseous envelope of the earth; the air. **2,** a unit of pressure, about 15 pounds per square inch. **3,** environment; predominant aspect or mood. —**at″mos·pher′ic** (-fer′ik) *adj.* —**at″mos·pher′i·cal·ly,** *adv.* —**at″mos·pher′ics,** *n.pl.* static.

at′oll (at′ol; ə-tol′) *n.* an island enclosing a lagoon.

at′om (at′əm) *n.* **1,** the smallest particle having the properties of a specific chemical element. **2,** anything extremely small. —**a·tom′ic** (ə-tom′ik) *adj.* —**a·tom′i·cal·ly,** *adv.* —**atomic clock,** an extremely accurate clock regulated by discharge of atoms. —**atomic number,** the number of protons in the nucleus of a certain atom. —**atomic pile,** an installation consisting of a mass of radioactive matter and apparatus permitting controlled nuclear fission. —**atomic weight,** the average weight of the atoms of a given element.

atom bomb a bomb caused to explode by fission of the nuclei of its atoms. Also, **atomic bomb.**

at′om·ize″ (at′ə-mīz″) *v.t.* reduce to bits, esp. to spray. —**at′om·iz″er,** *n.* a device for reducing liquid to a fine spray.

a·ton′al (a-tō′nəl) *adj.* (*Music*) having no key. —**a″to·nal′i·ty** (a″tō-nal′ə-tē) *n.*

a·tone′ (ə-tōn′) *v.i.* make amends for sin or error. —**a·tone′ment,** *n.*

a·top′ (ə-top′) *adv. & prep.* on top of.

a′tri·um (ā′trē-əm) *n.* [*pl.* **-a** (-ə)] the main room of an ancient Roman house.

a·tro′cious (ə-trō′shəs) *adj.* extremely wicked, criminal, or cruel; heinous. —**a·tro′·cious·ness,** *n.*

a·troc′i·ty (ə-tros′ə-tē) *n.* an atrocious act; wickedness.

at′ro·phy (at′rə-fē) *n.* a wasting away or arrested development, from defective nutrition or lack of use. —*v.i.* waste away.

at′ro·pine (at′rə-pin) *n.* a medicinal drug derived from belladonna.

at·tach′ (ə-tach′) *v.t.* **1,** fasten; affix. **2,** appoint; assign. **3,** (*Law*) seize by legal authority. **4,** bind by ties of affection or interest.

at″ta·ché′ (at″ə-shā′) *n.* a minor diplomatic officer.

at·tach′ment (ə-tach′mənt) *n.* **1,** act of attaching; state of being attached. **2,** something added, as a part to a machine.

at·tack′ (ə-tak′) *v.t.* **1,** fall upon with force or violence; assault; assail. **2,** begin to work upon; begin to affect. —*n.* **1,** a violent onset or assault. **2,** the offensive in a military conflict. **3,** a seizure or illness.

at·tain′ (ə-tān′) *v.t.* reach or achieve; accomplish.

at·tain′der (-dər) *n.* nullification of civil rights of one convicted of a high crime.

at·tain′ment (-mənt) *n.* **1,** act of attaining. **2,** an acquired personal ability, honor, etc.

at·taint′ (ə-tānt′) *v.t.* disgrace; taint.

at′tar (at′ər) *n.* an essential oil of roses.

at·tempt′ (ə-tempt′) *v.t.* make an effort to do; endeavor; undertake. —*n.* **1,** an effort to do something. **2,** attack; assault.

at·tend′ (ə-tend′) *v.t. & i.* **1,** be present at. **2,** go with; accompany. **3,** take care of; minister to; serve. **4,** listen to; heed. —**at·tend′ance,** *n.*

at·tend′ant (-ənt) *n.* one who attends another. —*adj.* attending.

at·ten′tion (ə-ten′shən) *n.* **1,** direction of the mind to an object of sense or thought. **2,** observant care; notice. **3,** an act of care, civility, or courtesy. **4,** (*Mil.*) a certain prescribed erect posture.

at·ten′tive (-tiv) *adj.* **1,** observant; intent. **2,** polite; (*Colloq.*) wooing. —**at·ten′tive·ness,** *n.*

at·ten′u·ate″ (ə-ten′ū-āt″) *v.t. & i.* **1,** make or become thin. **2,** weaken in force; lessen in quantity, value, or degree. —**at·ten″u·a′tion,** *n.*

at·test′ (ə-test′) *v.t.* **1,** bear witness to; declare to be true or genuine. **2,** give proof or evidence of. —**at″tes·ta′tion** (at″es-tā′shən) *n.*

at′tic (at′ik) *n.* a room directly under the roof; a garret.

at·tire′ (ə-tīr′) *v.t.* dress; clothe; adorn. —*n.* clothing; apparel.

at′ti·tude″ (at′ə-tood″) *n.* **1,** a position or manner indicative of feeling, opinion, or intention toward a person or thing. **2**, a bodily posture; position.

at·ti·tu'di·nize" (at-i-too'di-nīz") *v.i.* assume an attitude, esp. affectedly.

at·tor'ney (ə-tēr'nē) *n.* **1**, [also, **attorney-at-law**] a lawyer. **2**, one empowered to transact business for another; an agent. —**attorney general**, the chief law officer and legal head of a state or nation.

at·tract' (ə-trakt') *v.t.* **1**, draw toward (itself) by inherent physical force; cause to cohere with. **2**, invite; allure.

at·trac'tion (ə-trak'shən) *n.* **1**, act of attracting; power to attract. **2**, (*Theater*) an act, motion picture, etc.

at·trac'tive (-tiv) *adj.* appealing; likable; good-looking. —**at·trac'tive·ness,** *n.*

at·trib'ute (ə-trib'yût) *v.t.* consider as belonging, as a possession, quality, or cause; ascribe; impute. —*n.* (at'ri-būt") characteristic; anything attributed, as a property, quality, or cause. —**at"tri·bu'tion** (at"rə-bū'shən) *n.*

at·tri'tion (ə-trish'ən) *n.* **1**, the act of wearing away, or of being worn down, by friction; abrasion. **2**, loss of personnel due to causes other than dismissal, as death or retirement.

at·tune' (ə-toon') *v.t.* make harmonious.

au'burn (â'bẽrn) *n.* a reddish-brown color.

auc'tion (âk'shən) *n.* a public sale in which goods are sold to the highest bidder. —*v.t.* sell by auction. —**auc"tion·eer'** (-ir') *n.*

au·da'cious (â-dā'shəs) *adj.* **1**, bold; daring; intrepid. **2**, unrestrained; impudent.

au·dac'i·ty (â-das'ə-tē) *n.* boldness; impudence.

au'di·ble (â'də-bəl) *adj.* loud enough to be heard. —**au"di·bil'i·ty,** *n.*

au'di·ence (â'dē-əns) *n.* **1**, an assembly of hearers or spectators; the persons reached by a publication, radio, etc. **2**, a formal interview; a hearing. **3**, liberty or opportunity of being heard.

au'di·o" (â'dē-ō") *adj.* pert. to audible sound waves. —*n.* the audio or radio portion of a broadcast.

au·di·o- (â-dē-ō) *pref.* hearing.

au'di·on" (â'dē-on") *n.* a vacuum tube used in radio.

au'di·o·phile" *n.* one interested in sound and sound reproduction.

au'dit (â'dit) *n.* an official examination and verification of accounts or dealings. —*v.t.* & *i.* examine and certify accounts.

au·di'tion (â-dish'ən) *n.* **1**, the sense or act of hearing. **2**, a hearing or performance for test purposes, as by a musician. —*v.i.* & *t.* perform, or cause to perform, as a test.

au'di·tor (â'di-tər) *n.* **1**, a hearer; listener. **2**, one who audits accounts.

au"di·to'ri·um (â"də-tôr'ē-əm) *n.* a large room, space, or building for containing an audience or spectators.

au'di·to"ry (â'də-tôr'ē) *adj.* pert. to the sense or organs of hearing. Also, **au'di·tive.**

au'ger (â'gər) *n.* a tool for boring holes.

aught (ât) *n.* **1**, anything whatever. **2**, naught. —*adv.* in any respect; at all.

aug·ment' (âg-ment') *v.t.* cause to increase; add to. —*v.i.* increase. —**aug"men·ta'tion,** *n.*

au'gur (â'gər) *v.t.* & *i.* **1**, predict from omens; foretell. **2**, be a sign of; presage. —*n.* a prophet.

au'gu·ry (â'gyû-rē) *n.* **1**, prophecy divination. **2**, an omen.

au·gust' (â-gust') *adj.* highly dignified; imposing; eminent.

Au'gust (â'gəst) *n.* the eighth month of the year.

auk (âk) *n.* a diving bird found in northern regions.

aunt (ánt) *n.* **1**, the sister of one's father or mother. **2**, the wife of one's uncle.

au pair (ō-per') *pert.* to a person (usu. foreign) who does domestic duties in exchange for room and board.

au'ra (â'rə) *n.* **1**, a supposed force or imponderable matter emanating from a body and surrounding it like an atmosphere. **2**, a distinctive character or quality.

au'ral (â'rəl) *adj.* pert. to the ear or to hearing.

au're·ole" (ôr'ē-ōl") *n.* a halo or nimbus.

au"re·o·my'cin (ôr"ē-ō-mī'sin) *n.* an antibiotic used in treatment of certain virus diseases.

au'ri·cle (â'rə-kəl) *n.* **1**, the outer ear. **2**, one of the chambers of the heart. —**au·ric'u·lar** (â-rik'yə-lər) *adj.*

au·rif'er·ous (â-rif'ər-əs) *adj.* containing gold.

au·ro'ra (â-rôr'ə) *n.* **1**, morning twilight; the dawn of anything. **2**, an atmospheric phenomenon causing night lights in polar regions, **aurora bo"re·al'is** (bôr"ē-al'is) in the north, **aurora aus·tra'lis** (â-strā'lis) in the south. —**au·ro'ral,** *adj.*

aus'pice (â'spis) *n.* **1**, (*pl.*) favoring influence; protection or patronage. **2**, a favorable circumstance.

aus·pi'cious (â-spish'əs) *adj.* well-omened; betokening success. —**aus·pi'cious·ness,** *n.*

aus·tere' (â-stir') *adj.* **1**, severely simple; unadorned. **2**, serious; morally strict. **3**, harsh; stern; rigorous.

aus·ter'i·ty (âs-ter'ə-tē) *n.* **1,** state of being austere; harshness. **2,** simplicity in living.

aus'tral (â'strəl) *adj.* southern; lying in the southern hemisphere.

au'tar·chy (â'tär-kè) *n.* **1,** absolute power; autocracy. **2,** self-government. **3,** economic self-sufficiency (of a country). —**au·tar'·chic** (â-tär'kik) *adj.*

au·then'tic (â-then'tik) *adj.* **1,** actually of the ascribed authorship or origin; genuine. **2,** duly authorized. —**au·then'ti·cal·ly,** *adv.* —**au·then·tic'i·ty** (-tis'ə-tē) *n.*

au·then'ti·cate" (â-then'ti-kāt") *v.t.* make valid; attest to the genuineness of. —**au·then"ti·ca'tion,** *n.*

au'thor (â'thər) *n.* **1,** the originator or creator of anything. **2,** one who writes literary works. —*v.t.* (*Colloq.*) write. —**au'·thor·ess,** *n.fem.* —**au'thor·ship,** *n.*

au·thor'i·tar'i·an (ə-thor"ə-târ'ē-ən) *adj.* favoring rule by absolute authority. —*n.* an advocate of such rule.

au·thor'i·ta'tive (-tā"tiv) *adj.* based on authority; authentic.

au·thor'i·ty (ə-thor'ə-tē) *n.* **1,** the right to govern, control, or command. **2,** a person or group having such right. **3,** power or influence derived from reputation. **4,** an expert on a subject; an accepted source of information or counsel.

au"thor·i·za'tion (â"thə-ri-zā'shən) *n.* act or result of authorizing; authority to act.

au'thor·ize" (â'thə-riz") *v.t.* give authority, warrant, or legal power to; empower (a person).

au'tism (â'tiz-əm) *n.* excessive involvement in oneself; daydreaming. —**au·tis'tic,** *adj.*

au'to (â'tō) *n.* automobile.

au·to- (â-tō) *pref.* meaning self.

au"to·bi·og'ra·phy (â"tə-bī-og'rə-fè) *n.* a biography of a person written by himself. —**au"to·bi'o·graph'i·cal,** *adj.*

au'to·clave" (â'tə-klāv") *n.* a pressure cooker.

au·toc'ra·cy (â-tok'rə-sè) *n.* government by an absolute monarch.

au'to·crat" (â'tə-krat") *n.* one who rules by inherent right, subject to no restrictions. —**au"to·crat'ic,** *adj.* —**au"to·crat'i·cal·ly,** *adv.*

au"to·da·fe' (â"tō-də-fā') *n.* a public declaration of judgment, under the Inquisition.

au"to·gi'ro (â"tō-jī'rō) *n.* a propeller-driven aircraft supported in flight by a freely-rotating windmill-like rotor.

au'to·graph" (â'tə-gråf") *n.* **1,** one's own signature. **2,** one's own handwriting. **3,** an original handwritten manuscript.

au'to·mat" (â'tə-mat") *n.* a restaurant where food is vended by automatic coin-machines.

au"to·mat'ic (â"tə-mat'ik) *adj.* **1,** having the power of self-motion. **2,** operated by self-acting machinery. **3,** following inevitably as a consequence. **4,** done without volition; reflex; habitual. —*n.* an automatic pistol. —**au"to·mat'i·cal·ly,** *adv.*

au"to·ma'tion (â"tə-mā'shən) *n.* the handling and fabrication of materials by automatic machinery, esp. when no part of the process is done by hand. —**au'to·mate",** *v.t. & i.*

au·tom'a·ton" (â-tom'ə-ton") *n.* [*pl.* -ta (-tä)] **1,** a machine actuated to operate for some time without external guidance; a mechanical figure actuated by concealed machinery. **2,** a person who acts in a monotonous routine manner. —**au·tom'a·tism,** *n.*

au'to·mo·bile" (â'tə-mə-bēl") *n.* a vehicle propelled by a self-contained engine and designed to travel on ordinary roads. —*adj.* (-mō'bəl) self-propelled. —**au"to·mo·bil'ist,** *n.*

au"to·mo'tive (â"tə-mō'tiv) *adj.* **1,** pert. to self-propelled vehicles, esp. automobiles. **2,** self-propelling.

au·ton'o·my (â-ton'ə-mé) *n.* self-government; independence. —**au·ton'o·mous,** *adj.*

au"to·pi'lot *n.* an automatic guidance system for ships and aircraft; automatic pilot.

au'top"sy (â'top"sè) *n.* dissection and inspection of a dead body to discover the cause of death.

au"to·sug·ges'tion *n.* an effort to produce physical effects on oneself by thinking they will occur.

au'tumn (â'təm) *n.* the third season of the year, between summer and winter; also called *fall.* —**au·tum'nal** (â-tum'nəl) *adj.*

aux·il'ia·ry (âg-zil'yə-rè) *adj.* **1,** giving help or support. **2,** subordinate; additional.

a·vail' (ə-vāl') *v.i. & t.* have force or efficacy; serve. —*n.* efficacy; advantage. —**avail oneself of,** make use of.

a·vail'a·ble (-ə-bəl) *adj.* obtainable; at one's disposal. —**a·vail"a·bil'i·ty,** *n.*

av'a·lanche" (av'ə-lanch") *n.* the sudden fall of a mass of ice and debris down the side of a mountain.

a·vant'-garde' (a-vâê'gärd') *n. & adj.* (*Fr.*) vanguard.

av'a·rice (av'ə-ris) *n.* inordinate desire for wealth; greed; covetousness. —**av"a·ri'cious** (-rish'əs) *adj.*

a·vast' (ə-vast') *interj.* (*Naut.*) stop! hold!

av'a·tar" (av'ə-tär") *n.* (*Hindu*) incarnation of a deity.

A've Ma·ri'a (ä'vä-mä-rē'ə) a prayer, the

Hail Mary, from Luke 1:28,42 and other sources.

a·venge' (ə-venj') v.t. exact satisfaction or vengeance for or on behalf of.

av'e·nue" (av'ə-nū") n. 1, a wide street. 2, any roadway of approach, passageway, or means of access.

a·ver' (ə-vēr') v.t. [**a·verred', a·ver'ring**] declare in a positive manner; affirm with confidence.

av'er·age (av'ər-ij) n. 1, the mean value of a series of quantities, determined by dividing their sum by their number. 2, any mean, typical, or normal number, quantity, degree, quality, etc. —adj. intermediate, typical, or normal. —v.i. 1, determine an average of. 2, result in an average of.

a·verse' (ə-vērs') adj. 1, disposed against; reluctant. 2, turned away from in position.

a·ver'sion (ə-vēr'zhən) n. 1, dislike. 2, that which is disliked.

a·vert' (ə-vērt') v.t. 1, ward off; prevent. 2, turn away.

a'vi·ar"y (ā'vē-er'ē) n. an enclosure in which birds are kept.

a"vi·a'tion (ā"vē-ā'shən) n. the art or science of flying in the air, esp. in heavier-than-air aircraft.

a'vi·a"tor (ā'vē-ā"tər) n. a member of an aircraft's operating crew, esp. a pilot. —a'vi·ate, v.i. —a'vi·a'trix, n.fem.

av'id adj. eager. —a·vid'i·ty (ə-vid'ə-tē) n. eagerness.

a"vi·on'ics (ā"vē-on'iks) n. the use of electronic devices in aviation. —a"vi·on'ic, adj.

av"o·ca'do (av"ə-kä'dō) n. [pl. -dos] n. a tropical American fruit: the alligator pear.

av"o·ca'tion (av"ə-kā'shən) n. an occupation pursued for pleasure or diversion; a hobby.

a·void' (ə-void') v.t. keep away from; shun; refrain from. —a·void'ance, n.

av"oir·du·pois' (av"ər-də-poiz') n. the system of weights in which the ounce, pound, and ton are used.

a·vouch' (ə-vowch') v.t. 1, vouch for; guarantee. 2, acknowledge frankly.

a·vow' (ə-vow') n. declare openly; admit or confess frankly; acknowledge. —a·vow'al (ə-vow'əl) n.

a·vun'cu·lar (ə-vung'kū-lər) adj. like or pert. to an uncle.

a·wait' (ə-wāt') v.t. 1, wait for; look for and expect. 2, lie in store for.

a·wake' (ə-wāk') v.i. & t. [-woke', -waked', -wak'ing] 1, wake up. 2, call into being or action; bestir. —adj. 1, not sleeping. 2, alert; vigilant.

a·wak'en (ə-wā'kən) v.i. & t. awake.

—a·wak'en·ing, n. a sudden awareness or excitement.

a·ward' (ə-wôrd') v.t. bestow as a prize or reward, or as something due. —n. 1, anything awarded. 2, a decision of a judge or arbiter.

a·ware' (ə-wār') adj. conscious (of); informed; cognizant.

a·wash' (ə-wosh') adv. & adj. (Naut.) just at water level.

a·way' (ə-wā') adv. 1, from this place; off; apart; aside. 2, out of one's presence, possession, or attention. —adj. 1, absent. 2, distant.

awe (â) n. fear mingled with admiration or reverence. —v.t. inspire with awe.

a·weigh' (ə-wā') adj. of an anchor, raised so that a ship may sail.

awe'some (-səm) adj. inspiring awe. —awe'some·ness, n.

awe'struck" adj. feeling awe.

aw'ful (â'fəl) adj. 1, inspiring reverential fear. 2, (Colloq.) extremely bad or unpleasant. —adv. [also, aw'ful·ly] (Colloq.) very. —aw'ful·ness, n.

a·while' (ə-hwīl') adv. for a short time.

awk'ward (âk'wərd) adj. 1, lacking dexterity or skill; clumsy. 2, ungraceful; uncouth. 3, ill-adapted for use. 4, difficult to handle or deal with; requiring caution. 5, embarrassing. —awk'ward·ness, n.

awl (âl) n. a tool for punching small holes in leather, wood, etc.

awn'ing (â'ning) n. a cloth or metal covering, usu. movable, placed above a door or window; a sunshade.

a·woke' (ə-wōk') v. pret. of awake.

a·wry' (ə-rī') adv. & adj. away from a true direction or position; askew; perverse.

ax (aks) n. 1, a cutting tool or weapon, comprising a heavy-bladed head fixed to a handle. 2, (Slang) a musical instrument. —v.t. 1, trim with an ax. 2, (Slang) discharge from employment; injure. Also, **axe.** —get the ax, (Slang) be discharged.

ax'i·om (ak'sē-əm) n. 1, a proposition deemed to be self-evident and assumed without proof. 2, a universal proposition, amply proved, easily verifiable, or generally accepted. —ax'i·o·mat'ic (-mat'ik) adj. —ax"i·o·mat'i·cal·ly, adv.

ax'is (ak'sis) n. [pl. -es (-sēz)] 1, the line about which a rotating body turns. 2, the line with respect to which a body or structure is symmetrical. 3, a principal supporting member. 4, (cap.) the military alliance of Germany and Italy in World War II. —ax'i·al (ak'sē-əl) adj.

ax'le (ak'səl) n. the pin or shaft on which

tub, cūte, pŭll; labəl; oil, owl, go, chip, she, thin, then, sing, ink; see p. 6

a wheel turns, or which turns with it on a bearing.

ax'o·lotl" (ak'sə-lot"əl) *n.* a salamander of the U.S. and Mexico.

ax'on (aks'on) *n.* the branch of a neuron that carries impulses away from the cell body.

a"yah·tol'lah (äyə-tōlə) *n.* a Moslem religious leader of the Shiite sect.

aye (ī) *adv. & n.* **1,** yes. **2,** always. Also, **ay.**

Ayr'shire (ãr'shər) *n.* one of a breed of dairy cattle.

a·zal'ea (ə-zāl'yə) *n.* a plant bearing brightly-colored flowers.

az'i·muth (az'ə-məth) *n.* **1,** an angle measured clockwise from north to south. **2,** (*Astron.*) this angle measured on a horizon circle.

Az'tec (az'tek) *adj.* pert. to an aboriginal American Indian group.

az'ure (azh'ər) *adj. & n.* sky blue.

B

B, b (bē) second letter of the English alphabet.

baa (bä) *v.i.* **[baaed, baa'ing]** *& n.* bleat.

bab'bitt (bab'it) *n.* **1,** [also, **Babbitt metal**] an alloy of tin, lead, copper and antimony. **2,** (*l.c.*) a smug, conformist, middle-class Amer. businessman.

bab'ble (bab'əl) *v.i.* **1,** talk idly; chatter. **2,** utter words imperfectly; prattle —*v.t.* utter incoherently—*n.* chatter; prattle.

babe (bāb) *n.* **1,** baby. **2,** (*Slang*) girl.

ba'bel (bā'bəl) *n.* confused and overpowering sound; discord.

ba'bies'-breath" (bā'bēz-) *n.* a plant with small white or pink flowers.

ba·boon' *n.* any of several large monkeys.

ba·bush'ka (bə-boosh'kə) *n.* a woman's scarf worn over the head and tied under the chin.

ba'by (bā'bē) *n.* **1,** a very young child; infant. **2,** a childish person. **3,** the youngest child. **4,** (*Slang*) pet (term of endearment). —*adj.* **1,** suited for a baby; infantile. **2,** small. —*v.t.* pamper. —**ba'by·hood,** *n.*

ba'by·sit' *v.i.* act as a temporary nurse for a child. —**ba'by·sit"ter,** *n.*

bac"ca·lau're·ate (bak"ə-lôr'ē-ət) *adj.* pert. to or designating an address given before a graduating class.

bac"ca·rat' (bäk"ä-rä') *n.* a gambling game played with cards.

bac'cha·nal" (bäk'ə-nal") *n.* **1,** a drunken orgy. **2,** a reveler; carouser. —**bac"cha·na'li·an** (-nä'lē-ən) *adj. & n.*

Bac'chic (bak'ik) *adj.* **1,** pert. to Bacchus or bacchanalian rites. **2,** (*l.c.*) jovially or riotously intoxicated.

bach'e·lor (bach'ə-lər) *n.* **1,** an unmarried man. **2,** recipient of a college degree. —**bach'e·lor·hood",** *n.*

bach"e·lor·ette' (bach"ə-lər-et') *n.* a young unmarried woman.

ba·cil'lus (bə-sil'əs) *n.* [*pl.* **-li** (-lī)] a rod-shaped bacterium.

back (bak) *n.* **1,** the spinal, posterior, or dorsal side or surface of an animal. **2,** the rear or hind part of anything. **3,** support or stiffening in general. **4,** a player and his position in certain athletic games, as football. —*v.t.* **1,** furnish with a back; support or favor. **2,** cause to move backward. —*v.i.* (often with *up*) go backward. —*adv.* **1,** toward the rear. **2,** toward the past. —**back'er,** *n.* a financial sponsor, as of a person or enterprise. —**back and fill,** shilly-shally. —**back talk,** an insolent or argumentative reply.

back'beat" *n.* the characteristic driving beat of rock music.

back'bite" (bak'bīt") *v.t. & i.* speak evil of (an absent person).

back'board" *n.* a board or rigid sheet used as backing or reinforcement; esp. the board placed behind the basket on a basketball court.

back'bone" (bak'bōn") *n.* **1,** the human spine or vertebral column; any similar supporting or stiffening member. **2,** firmness; resolution.

back'date" *v.t.* antedate.

back'fire" *n.* **1,** a premature explosion in a gasoline engine. **2,** a fire set to check a forest fire. **3,** a result opposite to what was intended. —*v.i.* produce a backfire.

back'gam"mon (bak'gam"ən) *n.* a game played by moving pieces (*stones*) on a board in accordance with casts of dice.

back'ground" *n.* **1,** the more distant objects and planes of sight in a view or picture. **2,** antecedent events and circumstances, in relation to a person or later event.

back'hand" *n.* writing that slopes to the left. —*adj.* performed with the hand turned back outward, as a backhand stroke in tennis.

back'hand"ed *adj.* **1,** backhand. **2,** oblique in meaning; ironic.

back'lash" *n.* **1,** jarring recoil of badly fitted or worn parts, as in a machine. **2,** a snarl of a fishing line in the reel. **3,** a strong reaction, esp. to social change.

back'log" (bak'lôg") n. something in reserve; unfilled orders on hand.

back'or'der v.t. hold an order for (merchandise temporarily out of stock) to be filled at some later date.

back'slide" (bak'slīd") v.i. relapse into evil ways; retrogress.

back'stairs" adj. indirect; underhand; secret.

back'stop" n. 1, a screen. 2, in baseball, the catcher.

back'track" v.i. 1, return over the same course; retreat. 2, withdraw from an agreement, project, etc.

back'up" n. a substitute or alternative.

back'ward (bak'wərd) adv. [also, back'-wards] 1, toward the back or rear. 2, with back foremost; reverse. 3, in reverse order. 4, toward or in past time. —adj. 1, late in time; slow; unprogressive. 2, reluctant; shy.

back'wash" n. 1, water or air thrown back by an oar, propeller, etc. 2, aftermath.

back'wa"ter n. 1, a pool of water, often stagnant, held back by a dam, etc. 2, a situation or place considered stagnant or backward. —adj. (Colloq.) rustic; lacking culture.

back'woods" (bak'wûdz") adj. primitive; uncultivated.

ba'con (bā'kən) n. meat from the back and sides of the hog, salted and dried.

bac·te'ri·a (bak-tir'ē-ə) n.pl. [sing. -um] vegetable microorganisms that cause fermentation, decay, disease, etc. —bac·te'ri·al, adj.

bac·te'ri·cide (bak-tir'ə-sīd) n. an agent that destroys bacteria. —bac·te"ri·ci'dal, adj.

bac·te"ri·ol'o·gy (bak-tir"ē-ol'ə-jē) n. the science dealing with bacteria. —bac·te"ri·o·log'i·cal (-ə-loj'i-kəl) adj. —bac·te"ri·ol'o·gist, n.

bad adj. [worse, worst] 1, wicked; vicious. 2, not good; defective; not valid. 3, hurtful; noxious. 4, unfavorable; unfortunate. 5, sick. —n. any thing or condition that is bad. —bad'ness, n. —bad blood, a feeling of enmity. —bad egg, (Slang) a scoundrel.

bade (bad) v. pret. of bid.

badge (baj) n. a token, mark, or device worn to show allegiance, honors, etc.

badg'er (baj'ər) n. a carnivorous mammal prized for its fur. —v.t. pester; harass.

bad'i·nage' (bad"ə-näzh') n. playful banter; raillery.

bad'lands" n.pl. a barren region with eroded rock formations.

bad'ly (-lē) adv. 1, with bad effect. 2, (Colloq.) very much.

bad'min·ton (bad'min-tən) n. an outdoor game similar to tennis played with rackets (battledores) and shuttlecocks.

bad'mouth" v.t. (Slang) speak ill of.

baf'fle (baf'əl) v.t. disconcert by interposing obstacles; frustrate; confuse. —n. 1, an obstacle. 2, a device or structure for deflecting light, sound, etc. —baf'fle·ment, n.

bag n. 1, a portable receptacle made of a flexible material, capable of being closed at the mouth. 2, a suitcase. 3, anything formed like or serving the purpose of a bag. 4, the contents of a bag; an amount taken or collected. 5, (Slang) an old woman. 6, (Slang) function or purpose in life. —v.t. [bagged, bag'ging] capture. —v.i. 1, swell out; bulge. 2, hang loosely.

bag'a·telle' (bag"ə-tel') n. 1, anything trifling. 2, a game played by striking balls with a cue.

ba'gel (bā'gəl) n. a ring-shaped roll.

bag'gage (bag'ij) n. 1, containers, as trunks, suitcases, etc., used by a traveler. 2, a saucy young woman.

bag'gy (bag'ē) adj. bulging; hanging loosely. —bag'gi·ness, n.

bag'pipe" (bag'pīp") n. a Scottish musical instrument with several reed pipes, one melodic and the rest drones, actuated by a wind bag.

ba·guette' (ba-get') n. 1, a gem cut oblong. 2, a narrow oblong shape.

bah (bä) interj. of disgust or contempt.

bail' (bāl) n. (Law) security given to obtain the temporary release of a prisoner. —v.t. grant or obtain release of a prisoner in bail. —bails'man, n. one who gives bail. —bail out, 1, remove (water) from a boat with a bucket or pump. 2, jump from an airplane with a parachute. 3, assist, esp. financially.

bai'ley (bā'lē) n. [pl. -leys] the outermost fortification of a castle. —Old Bailey, the English criminal court.

bail'iff (bā'lif) n. a deputy officer of a court of law.

bail'i·wick (bāl'ə-wik) n. an area of jurisdiction, activity, or influence.

bait (bāt) n. 1, a lure placed on a fishhook or in a trap. 2, any device of allurement. —v.t. 1, place bait on or in. 2, torment; tease. —bait-and-switch, adj. pert. to an unethical sales method involving advertisement of an item, often nonexistent, at a very low price to lure customers, with the intent to induce them subsequently to purchase a different, higher-priced item.

baize (bāz) *n*. a feltlike woolen fabric.

bake (bāk) *v.t. & i*. **1,** cook by dry heat. **2,** harden by heat. —*v.i.* become baked. —**baked Alaska,** a dessert of cake and ice cream, topped with meringue, and quickly browned in an oven. —**baking powder,** a preparation of baking soda and an acid, used for leavening. —**baking soda,** sodium bicarbonate.

Ba′ke·lite″ (bā′kə-līt″) *n*. (*T.N.*) a thermosetting plastic made of phenol and formaldehyde.

bak′er (bā′kər) *n*. one whose business is baking bread. —**baker's dozen,** thirteen.

bak′er·y (bā′kə-rē) *n*. a baker's shop or plant.

bak′la·va (bak′lə-və) *n*. a layered pastry filled with nuts and honey.

bal″a·lai′ka (bal′ə-lī′kə) *n*. a Russian musical instrument of the guitar type.

bal′ance (bal′əns) *n*. **1,** an instrument for weighing. **2,** equal distribution of weight; a state of equilibrium; harmonious arrangement of parts. **3,** mental stability; good judgment. **4,** equality between two sides of an account. **5,** an excess or remainder. —*v.t.* **1,** bring into balance or equilibrium. **2,** arrange in harmonious form. **3,** weigh; estimate; compare. **4,** equalize two sides of an account. —*v.i.* come into equilibrium; be harmonious. —**balance of payments,** the difference in value between a country's exports and imports. —**balance of power,** an equilibrium of power (between states).

bal·bo′a (bal-bō′ə) *n*. the monetary unit of Panama.

bal·brig′gan (bal-brig′ən) *n*. unbleached cotton, used chiefly for underwear.

bal′co·ny (bal′kə-nē) *n*. **1,** a platform projecting from a wall, having an outer railing or parapet. **2,** an elevated tier of seats in a theater.

bald (bâld) *adj*. **1,** destitute of hair or other natural covering. **2,** bare; unadorned. **3,** undisguised. —**bald′ing,** *adj*. becoming bald. —**bald′ness,** *n*.

bal′da·chin (bal′də-kin) *n*. **1,** a canopy over an altar, throne, etc. **2,** a heavy, ornate silk fabric.

bal′der·dash″ (bâl′dər-dash″) *n*. a nonsensical jumble of words.

bald-′faced″ (-fāst″) *adj*. bare-faced.

bal′dric (bal′drik) *n*. an ornamented belt, worn diagonally over one shoulder.

bale (bāl) *n*. **1,** a large bundle of merchandise, closely compressed and bound. **2,** sorrow; woe. —*v.t.* pack into bales.

ba·leen′ (bə-lēn′) *n*. a flexible, bony substance from a whale; whalebone.

bale′ful (bāl′fəl) *adj*. menacing; malign. —**bale′ful·ness,** *n*.

balk (bâk) *n*. **1,** an obstacle; a check or defeat. **2,** a blunder or failure. **3,** (*Baseball*) a penalizable feint by the pitcher. **4,** a heavy wooden timber. —*v.t.* hinder; thwart. —*v.i.* stop at an obstacle; refuse to act or continue. —**balk′y,** *adj*.

ball (bâl) *n*. **1,** any round or roundish body; sphere; globe. **2,** any of various games played with balls, as *football, baseball*. **3,** (*Baseball*) a pitch not struck at by the batter and ruled to be too high, low, or wide. **4,** a solid projectile fired from a gun. **5,** a social assembly for dancing. **6,** (*Slang*) a highball. —*v.t.* (with *up*) (*Slang*) disarrange; confuse. —**on the ball,** (*Slang*) alert.

bal′lad (bal′əd) *n*. a simple narrative poem; a sentimental song.

bal·lade′ (bä-läd′) *n*. **1,** a poem of three stanzas and an envoy. **2,** (*Music*) a composition in a romantic mood.

bal′last (bal′əst) *n*. **1,** heavy material carried to increase stability or decrease buoyancy. **2,** crushed stone, etc., forming the bed of a railroad.

bal″le·ri′na (bal′ə-rē′nə) *n*. a female ballet dancer.

bal′let (bal′ā) *n*. **1,** a theatrical pantomime of dancing and music. **2,** a stylized form of solo and group dancing. **3,** a troupe of professional dancers.

bal·let′o·mane (ba-let′ō-mān) *n*. an enthusiastic spectator of ballet dancing.

bal·lis′tics (bə-lis′tiks) *n*. the science of the motion of projectiles.

bal·loon′ (bə-loon′) *n*. **1,** an airship that derives its lift from a large bag inflated with a gas lighter than air. **2,** an inflated rubber bag, used as a child's toy. **3,** (in cartoons) a loop enclosing words represented as issuing from the mouth of a speaker. —*v.i.* swell out. —**bal·loon′ist,** *n*.

bal′lot (bal′ət) *n*. **1,** a ticket or other device for marking an individual vote. **2,** the casting of ballots; the whole number of votes recorded. —*v.i.* **1,** vote by ballot. **2,** draw lots.

ball′point″ pen a fountain pen with a minute ball bearing for a point.

ball′room″ *n*. a room for dancing.

bal′ly·hoo″ (bal′ė-hoo″) *n*. (*Slang*) crude or blatant advertising. —*v.t.* promote by ballyhoo.

balm (bäm) *n*. **1,** any of various aromatic resinous substances. **2,** anything that soothes or mitigates pain.

balm′y *adj*. **1,** mild. **2,** fragrant. **3,** (*Slang*) mildly insane. —**balm′i·ness,** *n*.

ba·lo′ney (bə-lō′nē) *n*. **1**, (*Colloq*.) bologna. **2**, (*Slang*) nonsense; humbug.

bal′sa (bâl′sə) *n*. a tree having exceedingly light wood.

bal′sam (bâl′səm) *n*. **1**, balm. **2**, transparent turpentine. **3**, any plant or tree yielding balsam.

bal′us·ter (bal′ə-stər) *n*. an ornamental upright post giving support to a rail.

bal″us·trade′ (bal″ə-strād′) *n*. a row of balusters topped by a rail.

bam·boo′ *n*. **1**, a woody tropical grass. **2**, its hollow stem. —**bamboo curtain**, an ideological and political barrier in the Far East.

bam·boo′zle (bam-boo′zəl) *v.t.* deceive by trickery; mystify.

ban *v.t.* [**banned, ban′ning**] forbid; prohibit. —*n*. **1**, prohibition. **2**, denunciation.

ba′nal (bā′nəl; bə.nal′) *adj*. commonplace; trite. —**ba·nal′i·ty** (bə-nal′ə-tē) *n*.

ba·nan′a (bə-nan′ə) *n*. a tropical fruit. —**bananas**, *adj*. (*Slang*) crazy. —**banana seat**, a long, slim bicycle saddle with an upward-curving back.

band *n*. **1**, a flat strip of flexible material, used to bind, confine, trim, or ornament. **2**, a stripe; a zone marked off from adjacent areas. **3**, a company of persons traveling or acting together. **4**, a group of musicians playing together, esp. a group not including stringed instruments. —*v.t. & i.* unite.

band′age (ban′dij) *n*. cloth used to bind up a wound.

ban·dan′na (ban-dan′ə) *n*. a large colored handkerchief.

band′box″ (band′boks″) *n*. a hat box; a small compartment or room.

ban·deau′ (ban-dō′) *n*. a band worn on the head.

ban′de·role″ (ban′də-rōl″) *n*. a ribbon, streamer, or small flag.

ban′di·coot″ (ban′di-koot″) *n*. **1**, a large E. Indian rat. **2**, a small marsupial of Australia.

ban″do·leer′ (ban″də-lir′) *n*. a cartridge belt worn over the shoulders. Also, **ban″·do·lier′**.

ban′dit *n*. a robber, esp. one of a band of marauders. —**ban′dit·ry**, *n*.

band′stand″ *n*. a platform on which a musical band plays.

band′wag″on *n*. **1**, a vehicle carrying a musical band in a parade. **2**, (*Slang*) the successful side, as in an election.

ban′dy (ban′dē) *v.t.* strike, throw, or pass back and forth; give and take. —*adj*. crooked. —**ban′dy-leg″ged**, *adj*. having bowlegs.

bane (bān) *n*. **1**, a deadly poison. **2**, anything that destroys or spoils. —**bane′ful**, *adj*. very inimical.

bang *n*. **1**, a loud, explosive noise, of a gun, etc. **2**, (*Colloq*.) energy; spirit. **3**, (*Slang*) thrill. **4**, (usu. *pl*.) a fringe of short, evenly-cut hairs over the forehead. —*v.t.* **1**, knock about; drub; slam. **2**, (with *up*) (*Slang*) smash; damage. —*v.i.* **1**, strike violently. **2**, make a sudden, loud noise. —*adv*. suddenly; loudly.

ban′gle (bang′gəl) *n*. an ornamental bracelet without a clasp.

bang-′up″ *adj*. (*Slang*) first-rate.

ban′ish *v.t.* put in exile; drive away; dismiss. —**ban′ish·ment**, *n*.

ban′is·ter (ban′is-tər) *n*. a baluster or balustrade.

ban′jo (ban′jō) *n*. [*pl*. **-jos**] a musical stringed instrument with a circular head. —**ban′jo·ist**, *n*.

bank *n*. **1**, a long pile or ridge, as of earth. **2**, a slope; the border of a watercourse. **3**, an elevated plateau in the sea or a river; a shoal. **4**, lateral inclination. **5**, a tier, as of keys on an organ. **6**, an institution for receiving and lending money; the quarters of such an institution. **7**, a store, fund, reserve, or depository. —*v.t.* **1**, provide with or form into a bank. **2**, give a lateral inclination to. **3**, cover up (a fire). **4**, deposit in a bank. —*v.i.* **1**, act as a banker. **2**, depend or rely (on).

bank′er (-ər) *n*. one who conducts or works in a bank. —**bank′ing**, *n*.

bank′note″ *n*. a piece of paper money.

bank′roll″ *n*. money supply; funds. —*v.t.* (*Slang*) supply the capital for (a venture).

bank′rupt *n*. (*Law*) one who is adjudged insolvent. —*adj*. unable to pay debts; bereft. —*v.t.* make bankrupt. —**bank′rupt·cy** (-sē) *n*.

ban′ner (ban′ər) *n*. **1**, a flag, pennant, or other device emblematic of a country, faith, etc. **2**, anything displayed as a profession of principles. **3**, a headline extending across the full width of a newspaper. —*adj*. foremost; leading.

banns (banz) *n. pl.* notice of an intended marriage.

ban′quet (bang′kwit) *n*. a rich entertainment of food and drink.

ban·quette′ (bang-ket′) *n*. **1**, a ledge along the inside of a parapet. **2**, a bench; shelf.

ban′shee″ (ban′shē″) *n*. a wailing spirit that heralds death.

ban′tam (ban′təm) *n*. **1**, a small-sized variety of chicken. **2**, any small animal. —*adj*. very small.

ban′tam·weight″ *n*. a boxer of 112 to 118 pounds.

---

ban'ter (ban'tər) *n.* playful talk; good-humored raillery. —*v.t. & i.* make fun of; chaff.

Ban'tu (ban'too) *n. & adj.* pert. to a large family of Negro tribes of Africa.

ban'yan (ban'yən) *n.* an E. Ind. fig tree.

ban'zai" (bän'zī") *interj.* (Jap.) may he (it) live 10,000 years!

bap'tism (bap'tiz-əm) *n.* a sacrament of the Christian church, signalized by sprinkling with or immersion in water. —**baptis'mal** (-tiz'məl) *adj.*

Bap'tist *n.* a member of a certain Christian denomination.

bap'tis·ter·y (bäp'tis-tré) *n.* a place, font or tank used in baptism.

bap'tize" (-tīz") *v.t.* **1,** administer baptism to. **2,** christen; name. **3,** cleanse spiritually.

bar (bär) *n.* **1,** a rod used as an obstruction or guard. **2,** anything that obstructs. **3,** a band or stripe; anything of oblong shape. **4,** a room where liquors are sold: *barroom.* **5,** lawyers as a whole; the legal profession. **6,** any tribunal. **7,** (*Music*) a vertical line marking the division between measures; a measure. —*v.t.* **[barred, bar'ring] 1,** shut out; exclude. **2,** block; close. —*prep.* except.

barb (bärb) *n.* **1,** a pointed part projecting backward, as on a fishhook. **2,** a beardlike growth or member. —**barbed,** *adj.* **1,** having a hooked point. **2,** spiteful.

bar·bar'i·an (bär-bâr'é-ən) *n.* a man in a primitive, savage, or uncivilized state. —*adj.* uncivilized.

bar·bar'ic (bär-bar'ik) *adj.* **1,** of or like barbarians. **2,** magnificent but crude. —**bar·bar'i·cal·ly,** *adv.*

bar'ba·rism (bär'bə-riz-əm) *n.* **1,** lack of civilization. **2,** something barbarous. **3,** a word, phrase, form, etc., alien to accepted usage.

bar·bar'i·ty (bär-bâr'ə-té) *n.* **1,** brutality; cruelty. **2,** crudeness.

bar'bar·ous (bär'bə-rəs) *adj.* **1,** uncultured; crude. **2,** brutal; cruel. —**bar'barous·ness,** *n.*

bar'be·cue" (bär'bə-kū") *n.* **1,** a social gathering where animal carcasses are roasted whole; any cookout. **2,** a large grille or frame for roasting. —*v.t.* **1,** broil or roast (a carcass) whole. **2,** cook (meat or fish) in a highly seasoned sauce.

bar'bell" *n.* a bar with adjustable weights used in weightlifting.

bar'ber (bär'bər) *n.* one whose occupation is to shave the beard, cut and dress the hair. —*v.t.* trim or dress the facial hair of.

bar'ber"ry (bär'be"ré) *n.* a shrub whose roots yield a bitter tonic.

bar·bette' (bär-bet') *n.* (*Mil.*) a gun platform or housing.

bar'bi·can (bär'bi-kən) *n.* an outpost, usu. a tower, defending the approach to a castle, bridge, etc.

bar'bi·tal" (bär'bə-tâl") *n.* a sleep-producing drug.

bar·bit'u·rate" (bär-bit'yû-rät") *n.* one of various sedative drugs.

bar'ca·role" (bär'kə-rōl") *n.* a boating song.

bard (bärd) *n.* poet; minstrel.

bare (bâr) *adj.* **1,** without clothing or covering; naked; nude. **2,** without usual furniture or equipment. **3,** bald; unadorned. **4,** open to view; not concealed. **5,** scarcely or just sufficient. —*v.t.* lay open to view; denude; strip. —**bare'ness,** *n.*

bare'back" *adv. & adj.* without a saddle.

bare'faced" (-fāst") *adj.* **1,** boldly open; undisguised. **2,** shameless.

bare'foot" *adj.* with bare feet.

bare'ly (-lé) *adv.* **1,** only; just. **2,** openly; nakedly.

barf (bärf) *v.i.* (*Slang*) vomit.

bar'fly" *n.* (*Colloq.*) one who frequents barrooms.

bar'gain (bär'gən) *n.* **1,** an agreement as to sale or exchange of goods. **2,** an advantageous purchase. —*v.i.* discuss terms of sale; haggle.

barge (bärj) *n.* **1,** an unpowered boat for transporting goods. **2,** any capacious, slow-moving, or ceremonial vessel. —*v.i.* **1,** move in a slow, heavy manner. **2,** (with *in*) (*Colloq.*) intrude. **3,** (with *into*) (*Colloq.*) collide with.

bar'i·tone" (bar'ə-tōn") *n. & adj.* **1,** a male voice intermediate between bass and tenor. **2,** a musical instrument having analogous range.

bar'i·um (bâr'é-əm) *n.* a chemical element, no 56, symbol Ba.

bark (bärk) *n.* **1,** the abrupt cry of a dog. **2,** any similar cry or sound by an animal or person. **3,** the outer covering of the stems of woody plants. **4,** a small three-masted ship. —*v.i.* **1,** utter a harsh sound like the bark of a dog. **2,** speak gruffly; make a clamor. —*v.t.* remove bark from; rub off the skin of.

bark'er (bär'kər) *n.* (*Colloq.*) a person who urges passers-by to enter a theater, etc.

bar'ley (bär'lé) *n.* a cereal plant widely cultivated for food and the making of liquors.

bar mitz'vah (bär-mitz'və) *n.* **1,** a Jewish boy who has attained his 13th birthday. **2,** the ceremony recognizing that attainment.

barn (bärn) *n.* an outbuilding of a farm,

used for storing grain and housing cattle and horses.

bar'na·cle (bär'nə-kəl) *n.* a small marine crustacean that attaches itself tenaciously to rocks and ships.

barn'storm" (bärn'stôrm") *v.i.* (*Colloq.*) tour rural areas, lecturing or performing publicly.

bar·o- (bär-ə) *pref.* pressure; weight.

ba·rom'e·ter (bə-rom'ə-tər) *n.* an instrument for measuring atmospheric pressure.

bar'on (bar'ən) *n.* **1,** a nobleman of the lowest rank of peerage. **2,** a powerful person in industry, business, or finance. **—bar'on·ess,** *n. fem.* **—ba·ro'ni·al** (bə-rō'nē-əl), *adj.*

bar'on·age (-ij) *n.* **1,** the whole body of barons. **2,** a baron's rank.

bar'on·et" (bar'ə-net") *n.* a hereditary noble below a baron and above a knight. **—bar'·on·et·cy** (-sē) *n.* his rank.

bar'o·ny (bar'ə-nē) *n.* the estate or rank of a baron.

ba·roque' (bə-rōk') *adj.* **1,** in or pert. to a style of art and ornamentation characterized by grotesque or exaggerated forms. **2,** fantastic; grotesque. **—n.** baroque art or style.

bar'rack (bar'ək) *n.* (usually *pl.*) a large building for lodging soldiers.

bar"ra·cu'da (bar"ə-koo'də) *n.* a large, fierce tropical game fish.

bar·rage' (bə-räzh') *n.* **1,** (*Mil.*) a barrier of sustained artillery fire. **2,** a sustained flow.

bar'ra·try (bar'ə-trē) *n.* **1,** (*Law*) the defrauding of the owners of a ship by its master or crew. **2,** purchase or sale of offices of church or state. **3,** persistent instigation of litigation.

bar'rel (bar'əl) *n.* **1,** a cylindrical vessel of wooden staves bound together with hoops. **2,** any similar container or part, as the tube of a gun. **—barrel organ,** a hand organ.

bar'ren (bar'ən) *adj.* **1,** incapable of producing offspring; sterile. **2,** unproductive; unprofitable. **3,** destitute of interest or attraction. **—bar'ren·ness,** *n.*

bar·rette' (bə-ret') *n.* a clasp for a woman's hair.

bar"ri·cade' (bar"ə-kād') *n.* **1,** a hastily-made fortification against the advance of any enemy. **2,** any temporary barrier. **—v.t.** block.

bar'ri·er (bar'ē-ər) *n.* **1,** any fence or structure erected to bar passage. **2,** any natural obstacle to passage or communication. **3,** anything that hinders or prevents progress, access, etc. **4,** a limit or boundary. **—barrier reef,** a coral reef parallel to the shore, separated from it by a lagoon.

bar'ris·ter (bar'is-tər) *n.* (*Brit.*) a lawyer who tries cases in court.

bar'row (bar'ō) *n.* **1,** a frame with handles, for carrying a load; a wheelbarrow. **2,** a heap, esp. a burial mound.

bar·tend"er *n.* one who mixes and serves drinks at a bar.

bar'ter (bär'tər) *v.i. & t.* exchange goods without the use of money. **—n.** this method of exchange.

bas'al (bā'səl) *adj.* basic. **—basal metabolism,** rate of expenditure of energy by the body at rest.

ba·salt' (bə-sâlt') *n.* a dark, dense, igneous rock.

base (bās) *n.* **1,** the bottom of anything, considered as its support. **2,** a fundamental principle; foundation. **3,** the starting point of action or reckoning; the first ingredient of a concoction. **4,** a principal seat of direction or supply; a depot. **5,** in baseball, one of the four corners of playing diamond. **—v.t.** **1,** place on a foundation; found. **2,** establish as a fact or conclusion. **—adj.** **1,** morally low; mean in spirit. **2,** low in rank; inferior in value. **—base'ness,** *n.*

base'ball" *n.* an athletic game in which a ball is batted to advance runners around a circuit of bases; the ball used in this game.

base'board" *n.* boarding that lines the interior wall of a room, next to the floor.

base'born" *adj.* **1,** of low or mean parentage. **2,** born out of wedlock; illegitimate.

base'ment (bās'mənt) *n.* a story of a building below the entrance level, usually underground.

ba·sen'ji (bə-sen'jē) *n.* a So. African breed of hound.

bash *v.t.* strike with crushing force. **—n.** **1,** a smashing blow. **2,** (*Slang*) a good time; a wild party.

bash'ful (bash'fəl) *adj.* timorous in approach to other persons; diffident; shy. **—bash'ful·ness,** *n.*

bas'ic (bā'sik) *adj.* **1,** pert. to a base or standard. **2,** fundamental. **—n.** (*all caps*) a computer language **—bas'i·cal·ly,** *adv.*

bas'il (baz'əl) *n.* an herb used as flavoring.

ba·sil'i·ca (bə-sil'i-kə) *n.* a church or other building with a broad nave flanked by rows of columns.

bas'i·lisk (bas'ə-lisk) *n.* **1,** a fabulous creature supposed to kill by its breath or look. **2,** a tropical lizard.

ba'sin (bā'sən) *n.* **1,** a shallow, circular vessel for holding liquids. **2,** a lowland.

ba'sis (bā'sis) *n.* [*pl.* **-ses** (-sēz)] **1,** a

fundamental principle; foundation; groundwork. **2**, principal ingredient.

bask (bàsk) *v.i.* thrive as the object of benign influence, as warmth, etc.

bas′ket (bas′kit) *n.* **1**, a container woven of pliable reeds, etc. **2**, the contents or capacity of a basket. **3**, (*Basketball*) a wire hoop supporting an open net, fixed to a backboard; the score for throwing the ball through the hoop. —**basket case**, (*Slang*) one who has had all four limbs amputated; hence, a totally ineffectual person. —**basket weave**, a criss-cross weave.

bas′ket·ball″ *n.* an indoor athletic game in which the object is to throw an inflated leather ball through a hoop or basket; the ball used in this game.

Basque (bàsk) *n.* **1**, a people of No. Spain, or their language. **2**, (*l.c.*) a tight blouse.

bas-re·lief″ (bä′rə-lēf″) *n.* sculpture with the figures projecting only slightly from the surface; low relief.

bass (bās) *adj.* (*Music*) low in pitch or range. —*n.* **1**, [also, **bas′so**] a man who sings bass. **2**, a bass instrument, esp. the bass viol. —**bass′ist**, *n.* one who plays the bass viol.

bass (bas) *n.* **1**, a perchlike food fish. **2**, a tree, the basswood or linden.

bas′set (bas′it) *n.* a hound dog with short legs and long body.

bas′set horn (bas′ət) a tenor clarinet.

bas″si·net′ (bas″i-net′) *n.* a hooded basket used as a baby's cradle.

bas′so (bas′ō) *n.* bass.

bas·soon′ (ba-soon′) *n.* a musical instrument the baritone of the double-reed wind family.

bast *n.* the fibrous inner bark of certain trees, used for making matting.

bas′tard (bas′tərd) *n.* an illegitimate child. —*adj.* **1**, of illegitimate birth. **2**, spurious; impure.

bas′tard·ize (-īz″) *v.t.* **1**, make a bastard of. **2**, adulterate; debase.

bas′tar·dy (-dè) *n.* **1**, act of begetting a bastard. **2**, illegitimacy.

baste (bāst) *v.t.* **1**, sew with temporary stitches. **2**, moisten (meat) while cooking. **3**, beat with a stick.

bas·tille′ (bas-tēl′) *n.* a prison, esp. one conducted oppressively.

bas″ti·na′do (bas″ti-nā′dō) *n.* punishment by beating the feet with a stick; the stick used.

bas′tion (bas′chən) *n.* **1**, a walled fortification projecting from a main rampart. **2**, a fortified sector.

bat *n.* **1**, a heavy club or cudgel. **2**, the club used to strike the ball in certain games.

3, a nocturnal flying mammal. **4**, (*Slang*) a spree. —*v.t.* [**bat′ted, -ting**] strike with a bat; have a turn at batting.

batch (bach) *n.* **1**, a quantity prepared for, or produced by, one operation. **2**, a quantity or group from a larger aggregation.

bate (bāt) *v.t.* lessen or restrain.

bath (bàth) *n.* **1**, a washing of the body in water. **2**, equipment for a bath: the fluid or a bathtub.

bathe (bāth) *v.t. & i.* **1**, take or administer a bath. **2**, immerse or be immersed in a liquid.

bath′house″ *n.* a seaside building where bathers disrobe.

bath mitz′vah (bäth-mits′və) *n.* **1**, a Jewish girl who has attained her 13th birthday. **2**, the ceremony recognizing that attainment.

ba·thom′e·ter (bə-thom′i-tər) *n.* an instrument for measuring ocean depths.

ba′thos (bā′thos) *n.* **1**, a ludicrous descent from the elevated to the commonplace. **2**, mawkish pathos.

bath′robe″ *n.* a loose robe worn instead of clothing; dressing gown.

bath′room″ *n.* a room containing bathing and other toilet facilities.

bath′tub″ *n.* a tub in which a person lies to bathe.

bath′y·sphere″ (bath′is-fir″) *n.* an apparatus lowered into deep waters for observation from a spherical compartment. —**bath′y·scaphe″** (-skäf″) a bathysphere with a wedge-shaped underportion to permit greater descent.

ba·tik′ (bə-tēk′) *n.* a method of printing colors on cloth, by covering with wax portions to be unprinted.

ba·tiste′ (bə-tēst′) *n.* a plain, thin cotton fabric.

ba·ton′ *n.* **1**, a staff or club carried as a symbol of authority. **2**, a wand used in conducting an orchestra.

bat·tal′ion (bə-tal′yən) *n.* (*Mil.*) a body of troops, of variable number but usually less than a regiment.

bat′ten (bat′ən) *v.i.* feed gluttonously; grow fat; thrive. —*v.t.* **1**, fatten. **2**, furnish with battens. **3**, (*Naut.*) cover with tarpaulins secured by battens. —*n.* a light strip of wood; slat.

bat′ter (bat′ər) *v.t. & i.* beat persistently; pound violently. —*n.* **1**, a mixture of flour, eggs, etc. for making bread or pastry; any mixture of similar consistency. **2**, one who wields a bat, as in baseball.

bat′ter·y (bat′ə-rè) *n.* **1**, a device for producing an electric current or storing electricity. **2**, a unit of artillery; a group of guns. **3**, a set of similar machines or de-

---

fat, fāte, fär, fāre, fåll, àsk; met, hē, hėr, maybè; pin, pīne; not, nōte, ôr, tool vices. **4.** (*Baseball*) the pitcher and catcher together. **5,** (*Law*) the unlawful beating of another.

bat′ting (bat′ing) *n.* cotton or wool in matted sheets for quilts or bedcovers.

bat′tle (bat′əl) *n.* a fight, hostile encounter, or engagement between opposing forces. —*v.t. & i.* engage in battle; struggle; content. —**battle fatigue,** a neurosis affecting soldiers in active warfare. —**battle royal,** a fight in which each of several contestants opposes each other.

bat′tle-ax″ *n.* **1,** an ax used as a weapon. **2,** (*Slang*) a shrewish old woman.

bat′tle-dore″ (-dôr″) *n.* the racket used in badminton.

bat′tle-field″ *n.* the field or place where a battle is fought. Also, **bat′tle-ground″.**

bat′tle-ment (-mənt) *n.* a parapet on a fort, castle, etc. having openings for shooting through.

bat′tle-ship″ (bat′əl-ship″) *n.* the most heavily armed type of warship.

bat′ty (bat′ē) *adj.* (*Slang*) foolish or crazy. Also, **bats.**

bau′ble (bâ′bəl) *n.* a trinket of little value.

baud (bâd) *n.* a unit of data transmission, usu. one dot or one bit per second.

baux′ite (bâk′sīt) *n.* the ore from which aluminum is derived.

bawd′y (bâ′dē) *adj.* lewd; indecent. —**bawd′i-ness,** *n.*

bawl (bâl) *v.i. & t.* shout clamorously; cry vehemently; wail. —**bawl out,** (*Colloq.*) scold.

bay (bā) *n.* **1,** a recess in a shore; an inlet; a large cove or small gulf. **2,** a turret projecting outward from a wall; a niche or alcove. **3,** a compartment of space. **4,** any of several trees, as laurel. **5,** the deep-toned bark of a hunting dog. **6,** a horse of reddish-brown color. —*v.i.* bark with a deep, prolonged sound. —**at bay,** trapped, as by hunting dogs. —**bay rum,** a fragrant skin and hair lotion. —**bay window, 1,** a group of windows projecting from a room in a floor-level recess. **2,** (*Slang*) a fat belly.

bay′ber·ry (ba′ber-ē) *n.* **1,** a shrub or tree of the myrtle family; its berry. **2,** a W. Indian tree; its oil, used in *bay rum.*

bay′o·net (bā′ə-net) *n.* a steel weapon for stabbing or slashing, attached to the barrel of a rifle. —*v.t.* stab with a bayonet.

bay′ou (bi′oo) *n.* a cove of a lake; a sluggish watercourse.

ba·zaar′ (bə-zär′) *n.* **1,** a market place. **2,** a sale of miscellaneous goods for charitable purposes.

ba·zoo′ka (bə-zoo′kə) *n.* (*Mil.*) a tubular rocket launcher portable by one or two persons.

BB (bē′bē) *n.* a pellet of lead shot used in a type of air rifle (*BB gun*).

be (bē) *v.i.* [*present indicative:* **I am; you are** (*Archaic,* **thou art**); **he is; we, you, they are;** *pret.* **I, he was; we, you, they were;** *p.p.* **been** (bin); **be′ing**] **1,** (as substantive) exist; live; have reality; occur; take place; remain in a condition. **2,** (as copulative) a link between a subject and a predicate, as *I am* here; an element in participial and infinitive phrases, as it is *being* done; we wish to *be* informed. **3,** (as auxiliary) used with a participle to form a progressive, as he *is* reading; we *have been* waiting; used to indicate passive voice, as it *was* repaired.

be- (bē) *pref.* **1,** affect with, as *becloud.* **2,** take off or away, as *behead.*

beach (bēch) *n.* the part of a shore washed by the tide or waves. —*v.t.* run or haul (a boat) upon a beach. —**beach buggy,** a motor vehicle with oversize tires for use on sand beaches. —**beach wagon,** a station wagon.

beach′comb″er (-kō″mər) *n.* an outcast living on a tropical beach.

beach′head″ *n.* a military position on an enemy shore.

bea′con (bē′kən) *n.* **1,** a lighthouse, signal buoy, or other fixed marker that guides ships or aircraft. **2,** anything that warns or guides.

bead (bēd) *n.* **1,** a small ball pierced with a hole for stringing with others. **2,** (*pl.*) a necklace or rosary. **3,** a drop of liquid; a bubble, as in froth. **4,** any small globular body or mass; —*v.t.* ornament with beads. —**bead′y,** *adj.* like or containing beads.

bea′dle (bē′dəl) *n.* a minor official having disciplinary duties.

bea′gle (bē′gəl) *n.* a small, long-eared hunting dog.

beak (bēk) *n.* **1,** the horny bill of a bird. **2,** the snout, jaws, or similar part of any animal.

beak′er (bē′kər) *n.* a glass vessel.

beam (bēm) *n.* **1,** a horizontal supporting member. **2,** a lever or piston. **3,** the greatest width of a ship. **4,** a bundle of parallel rays of light; a focused train of electronic waves. —*v.t. & i.* **1,** emit rays; form like a beam of light. **2,** smile radiantly.

bean (bēn) *n.* **1,** the edible seed of a leguminous plant. **2,** any oval or roundish seed, berry, nut, or lump. **3,** a plant producing seed in the shape of beans. **4.** (*Slang*) head; (*pl.*) money; spirit. —*v.t.* (*Slang*) strike on the head.

bean′er·y (bēn′ə-rē) *n.* a cheap restaurant.

bean′ie (bē′nē) *n.* a child's skullcap.

bean'o (bē'nō) *n.* a form of bingo.

bear (bâr) *v.t.* [**bore, borne**] 1, hold up; support; carry; convey. 2, put up with; accept; endure; sustain. 3, bring forward; render. 4, possess; show; exercise. 5, give birth to. 6, produce by natural growth. —*v.i.* 1, remain firm; be patient. 2, (with *on*) press; have effect or reference. 3, move or tend in a specific direction; be situated. 4, produce offspring, fruit, etc. —*n.* 1, a large omnivorous mammal, covered with heavy fur. 2, a person likened to a bear, as gruff, clumsy, predatory, etc. 3, a trader in financial stocks who sells short in the belief prices will go down. —**Great Bear, Little Bear,** two constellations.

beard (bird) *n.* 1, the growth of hair on the face of a man, esp. the chin. 2, a tuft of hair, bristle, etc.

bear'ing (bâr'ing) *n.* 1, the manner in which a person bears or comports himself; carriage; behavior. 2, the act or capability of producing offspring, fruit, etc. 3, a supporting member of a structure or machine; a fixed part supporting a moving part. 4, the relation of parts; mode of connection; implication. 5, the compass direction of one object from another. 6, (*pl.*) position; orientation.

bear'ish *adj.* 1, surly. 2, pessimistic. —**bear'ish·ness,** *n.*

beast (bēst) *n.* 1, any four-footed animal. 2, a brutal, coarse, or otherwise beastlike human. —**beast'ly** (-lē) *adj.* very unpleasant.

beat (bēt) *v.t.* [**beat, beat'en, beat'ing**] 1, strike repeatedly. 2, move repeatedly; flutter; (*Music*) mark time by strokes. 3, dash with force. 4, overcome; vanquish; surpass; baffle. 5, (*Slang*) swindle. 6, (with *up*) give a beating to. —*v.i.* 1, strike repeated blows; strike (against). 2, throb; pulsate. —*n.* 1, a stroke, blow, or throb. 2, a series of regular strokes, as the ticking of a watch. 3, accent or stress. 4, an assigned or habitual course of travel. 5, (*Slang*) publication of a news story in advance of rival newspapers. —*adj.* 1, exhausted. 2, of or pert. to the beat generation. —**beat generation,** a youth culture of the 1940's to the 1960's characterized by rock music and the use of drugs.

be·at'i·fy" (bē-at'ə-fī") *v.t.* 1, make supremely happy. 2, (*Rom. Cath. Ch.*) declare to be blessed and therefore worthy of certain honors. —**be"a·tif'ic** (bē"ə-tif'ik) *adj.* —**be·at"i·fi·ca'tion,** *n.*

be·at'i·tude" (bē-at'ə-tūd") *n.* 1, blessedness; bliss. 2, (*cap.*) any of Jesus's statements on blessedness in the Sermon on the Mount.

beat'nik (bēt'nik) *n.* a member of the beat generation.

beat-'up" *adj.* (*Slang*) dilapidated; broken down.

beau (bō) *n.* 1, a male lover; swain. 2, a man fussy of his dress; a fop.

Beau'fort scale (bō'fərt) a scale of wind velocities, ranging from 0 (calm) to 12 (hurricane).

beau'te·ous (bū'tē-əs) *adj.* beautiful. —**beau'te·ous·ness,** *n.*

beau·ti'cian (bū-tish'ən) *n.* one who owns or works in a beauty parlor.

beau'ti·ful (bū'ti-fəl) *adj.* having beauty; lovely.

beau'ti·fy" (bū'ti-fī") *v.t. & i.* make or become beautiful. —**beau"ti·fi·ca'tion,** *n.*

beau'ty (bū'tē) *n.* 1, the quality of an object of sense or thought that arouses admiration, approval, or pleasure. 2, a particular trait, grace, or charm that pleases. 3, an object possessing beauty, esp. a woman. —**beauty parlor** *or* **salon,** an establishment where hairdressing, manicuring, etc., are performed.

beaux-arts' (bō-zärts'; *Fr.* -zär') *n.pl.* (*Fr.*) the fine arts.

bea'ver (bē'vər) *n.* 1, an amphibious rodent prized for its fur. 2, a hat made of beaver fur; a man's high silk hat. 3, a heavy woolen cloth.

bea'ver·board" *n.* a light sheathing material of wood fiber.

be'bop (bē'bop) *n.* (*Slang*) bop.

be·calm' (bē-käm') *v.t.* make calm or still. —**be·calmed',** *adj.* (*Naut.*) motionless, by lack of wind.

be·cause' (bē-kâz') *conj.* for the reason that; since. —*adv.* (with *of*) by reason; on account.

bêche-'de-mer' (besh'də-mer') *n.* (*Fr.*) trepang.

beck (bek) *n.* a beckoning gesture.

beck'on (bek'ən) *v.i. & t.* 1, signal to approach by a gesture of the hand or head. 2, lure; entice.

be·cloud' (bē-klowd') *v.t.* obscure; make unclear.

be·come' (bē-kum') *v.i.* [**-came', -com'ing**] change (into a state or condition); come into being as. —*v.t.* befit in appearance; grace. —**be·com'ing,** *adj.* attractive; appropriate.

bed *n.* 1, an article of furniture, on which one sleeps. 2, any place of rest or repose. 3, any bottom layer or foundation; the ground in which plants are grown; the bottom of a body of water; the lowest layer of a road. —*v.t.* [**bed'ded, bed'ding**] 1, shelter. 2, seat firmly in a substance. —*v.i.* go to bed.

---

bed′bug″ *n.* a small blood-sucking insect that infests beds.

bed′cham″ber *n.* a room for sleeping.

bed′clothes″ *n. pl.* the sheets, covers, etc. placed on a bed.

bed′ding *n.* bedclothes.

be·deck′ (bė-dek′) *v.t.* decorate; hang ornaments on.

be·dev′il (bė-dev′əl) *v.t.* torment maliciously; confuse. —**be·dev′il·ment,** *n.*

be·diz′en (bė-dī′zən) *v.t.* dress gaudily. —**be·diz′en·ment,** *n.*

bed′lam (bed′ləm) *n.* **1,** wild uproar and confusion. **2,** a lunatic asylum. —**bed′lam·ite,** *n.*

Bed′ou·in (bed′û-win) *n.* **1,** one of the Arabs of the Asian and Afr. desert. **2,** any nomad or wanderer.

bed′pan″ *n.* **1,** a warming pan. **2,** a toilet pan for use of one confined to bed.

be·drag′gled (bė-drag′əld) *adj.* untidy or soiled, as clothes; unkempt.

bed′rid″den (bed′rid″ən) *adj.* not strong or well enough to rise from bed.

bed′rock″ *n.* **1,** the solid rock beneath the surface soil. **2,** the lowest stratum. **3,** any firm foundation.

bed′room″ *n.* a room designed to be slept in.

bed′spread″ *n.* an outer cover for a bed, usually decorative.

bed′stead″ *n.* the framework of a bed.

bee (bē) *n.* **1,** any of a family of insects that live in colonies and gather honey. **2,** a social gathering.

beech (bēch) *n.* a smooth-barked tree found in temperate regions. —**beech′en,** *adj.* —**beech′nut″,** *n.* the nut of the beech tree.

beef (bēf) *n.* **1,** the meat of a bovine animal. **2,** [*pl.* **beeves**] a steer, bull, or cow. **3,** (*Colloq.*) muscle; flesh. **4,** (*Colloq.*) a complaint. —*v.i.* (*Colloq.*) complain. —**beef′burg″er,** *n.* an all-beef hamburger. —**beef′eat″er,** *n.* (*Slang*) an English soldier. —**beef′steak″,** *n.* a slice from the best cuts of beef. —**beef′y** (-ē) *adj.* brawny.

bee′line″ (bē′līn″) *n.* a direct line.

been (bin) *v.* p.p. of *be.*

beep (bēp) *n.* a short, usu. high-pitched, sound. —*v.i.* make this sound.

beer (bir) *n.* **1,** an alcoholic beverage made from grain. **2,** any fermented nonalcoholic beverage.

bees′wax″ (bēz′waks″) *n.* wax secreted by bees to make honeycomb.

beet (bēt) *n.* a plant with a dark red fleshy root, used as food or to produce sugar.

bee′tle (bē′təl) *n.* **1,** any of an order of insects. **2,** a heavy mallet or pestle. **3,** (*Slang*) a slow racehorse. —*v.t.* beat; ram.

—*v.i.* **1,** jut out. **2,** move swiftly; scamper.

bee′tle-browed″ (-browd″) *adj.* **1,** having projecting eyebrows. **2,** scowling; sullen or menacing.

beeves (bēvz) *n.* pl. of *beef.*

be·fall′ (bė-fâl′) *v.i.* happen; occur. —*v.t.* happen to.

be·fit′ (bė-fit′) *v.t.* [**-fit′ted, -ting**] be suitable for; be appropriate to.

be·fogged′ (bė-fogd′) *adj.* in a fog; bewildered or muddled.

be·fore′ (bė-fôr′) *prep.* **1,** earlier than; previous to. **2,** in the future. **3,** ahead of in position; in front of. **4,** in precedence of; in preference to. **5,** in the presence of. —*conj.* **1,** previous to the time when. **2,** rather than. —*adv.* **1,** ahead; in advance. **2,** previously; sooner. —**be·fore′hand″,** *adv.* in advance of a usual or appointed time.

be·foul′ (bė-fowl′) *v.t.* make foul.

be·friend′ (bė-frend′) *v.t.* act as a friend to; aid; favor.

be·fud′dle (bė-fud′əl) *v.t.* stupefy with liquor; muddle; confuse.

beg *v.t. & i.* [**begged, beg′ging**] **1,** ask as alms; live by asking alms. **2,** ask as a favor.

be·get′ (bė-get′) *v.t.* [**-got′, get′ting**] **1,** procreate; generate (of the male parent). **2,** produce as an effect. —**be·got′ten,** *adj.* sired; fathered.

beg′gar (beg′ər) *n.* **1,** one who begs. **2,** one who is very poor. **3,** fellow; rogue. —*v.t.* **1,** make a beggar of; impoverish. **2,** exhaust the resources of. —**beg′gar·ly,** *adj.* —**beg′gar·y,** *n.*

be·gin′ (bė-gin′) *v.t. & i.* [**-gan′, -gin′ning**] **1,** take the first step in an action; commence; start. **2,** come into existence; arise. —**be·gin′ner,** *n.* one just beginning to learn or do something; a novice.

be·gin′ning *n.* **1,** a start or starting point; an early stage. **2,** origin; source.

be·gone′ (bė-gân′) *interj. & v.* go away!

be·go′ni·a (bi-gō′nė-ə) *n.* a tropical plant having showy flowers.

be·grime′ (bė-grīm′) *v.t.* soil.

be·grudge′ (bė-gruj′) *v.t.* **1,** be disinclined to give or allow. **2,** be envious of another's possession of.

be·guile′ (bė-gīl′) *v.t.* **1,** delude with guile; deceive. **2,** amuse; divert; pass (time). —**be·guile′ment,** *n.*

be·guine′ (bə-gēn′) *n.* a So. Amer. dance; its music.

be·half′ (bė-hâf′) *n.* interest; favor.

be·have′ (bė-hāv′) *v.i.* **1,** conduct oneself or itself; act or operate. **2,** comport oneself properly.

be·hav′ior (bė-hāv′yər) *n.* manner of behaving; deportment; habits or tendencies.

be·head′ (bė-hed′) v.t. cut off the head of.

be′he·moth (bē′ə-məth; bə-hē′-) n. a huge, powerful person or animal.

be·hest′ (bė-hest′) n. a command.

be·hind′ (bė-hīnd′) prep. 1, at the back of; in the rear of; on the farther side of; beyond. 2, less advanced than; inferior to. 3, later than. —adv. 1, toward the back or rear. 2, in arrears; slow. —n. (Colloq.) posterior; buttocks.

be·hind′hand″ adv. late; in arrears.

be·hold′ (bė-hōld′) v.t. [-held′, -hold′ing] observe with care; look at; see. —interj. look!

be·hold′en (bė-hōl′dən) adj. held by an obligation; grateful.

be·hoof′ (bė-hoof′) n. advantage.

be·hoove′ (bė-hoov′) v.t. (with expletive it) be fitting or necessary.

beige (bāzh) n. a light tan color.

be′ing (bē′ing) n. 1, existence; life. 2, a creature; a human.

be·jew′el (bė-joo′əl) v.t. adorn with jewels; spangle.

be·la′bor (bė-lā′bər) v.t. 1, beat soundly; thump. 2, assail persistently, as with criticism.

be·lat′ed (bė-lā′tid) adj. coming late or too late.

be·lay′ (bė-lā′) v.t. fasten (a rope) by winding it around a pin or cleat. —interj. stop! desist!

bel can′to (bel kän′tō) (Ital.) a style of operatic singing emphasizing beautiful tone and line.

belch v.i. 1, eject wind noisily from the stomach through the mouth; eructate. 2, issue in spurts. —v.t. eject violently; emit spasmodically. —n. an eructation; a burst, as of smoke, etc.

bel′dam (bel′dəm) n. an old woman; a hag.

be·lea′guer (bė-lē′gər) v.t. surround, as in laying siege to.

bel′fry (bel′frė) n. 1, a tower for a bell. 2, the part of a steeple or other structure in which a bell is hung.

be·lie′ (bė-lī′) v.t. 1, give a false representation of. 2, show to be false; contradict.

be·lief′ (bė-lēf′) n. 1, the act of believing; faith. 2, an accepted opinion.

be·lieve′ (bė-lēv′) v.t. 1, accept as true. 2, give credence to.

be·lit′tle (bė-lit′əl) v.t. make lower in importance; disparage.

bell (bel) n. 1, a hollow metal device giving forth a resonant or tinkling sound when struck. 2, a cup-shaped object suggesting a bell. 3, a nautical unit of time. 4, a flared part, as the mouth of a horn, etc. 5, (pl.) bell-bottom trousers. —v.i. swell out. —v.t. attach a bell to. —**bell jar,** a bell-shaped glass cover. —**bell metal,** a hard alloy of copper and tin.

bel′la·don″na (bel″ə-don′ə) n. a medicinal herb.

bell-′bot″tom adj. of trousers, having legs with flared bottoms. —**bell-′bot″toms,** n.pl.

bell′boy″ (bel′boi″) n. an attendant in a hotel. Also **bell′man″,** (Colloq.) **bell′hop″.**

belle (bel) n. a beautiful woman, a favorite of admirers.

bel′li·cose″ (bel′ə-kōs″) adj. warlike; pugnacious. —**bel·li·cos′i·ty** (-kos′ə-tė) n.

bel·lig′er·ent (bə-lij′ər-ənt) adj. 1, pert. to war. 2, given to waging war; bellicose. 3, at war. —n. a country at war. —**bellig′er·ence,** n.

bel′low (bel′ō) v.i. & t. make a loud, hollow noise; roar. —n. a loud outcry.

bel′lows (bel′ōz) n. 1, an instrument for producing a current of air, a kind of box with collapsible sides. 2, something resembling a bellows.

bell′weth″er (-weth″ər) n. a sheep (usually wearing a bell) that leads the flock.

bel′ly (bel′ė) n. 1, the part of a vertebrate animal between its breast and groin; the abdomen; the stomach. 2, the inside of anything. —v.i. & t. bulge. —**belly flop,** a dive resulting in a landing flat on the belly. —**belly laugh,** a deep, raucous laugh; guffaw.

bel′ly·ache″ n. colic. —v.i. (Slang) complain; gripe.

bel′ly·but″ton n. (Colloq.) navel.

bel′ly·dance″ n. a woman's dance characterized by gyrating motions of the abdominal area.

be·long′ (bi-lâng′) v.i. 1, (with to) be a property or concern (of). 2, have place (in).

be·long′ing (bi-lâng′ing) n. 1, the state of being a member, part, adjunct, etc. 2, a possession.

be·lov′ed (bė-luv′id) adj. greatly loved. —n. one greatly loved.

be·low′ (bė-lō′) adv. 1, in a lower place; beneath. 2, at a later point in a writing. —prep. 1, lower than, in position or direction; under; beneath. 2, inferior to.

belt n. 1, a flexible band worn around the waist. 2, a similar endless loop. 3, a stripe; a zone. —v.t. 1, gird. 2, beat, as with a belt. —**black, brown,** etc., **belt,** levels of proficiency in judo.

be·lu′ga (bə-loo′gə) n. 1, a white sturgeon of the Black Sea; its roe, made into caviar. **2,** the white whale.

bel″ve·dere′ (bel″və-dir′) *n.* an upper story of a building that has a fine view.

be·mused′ (bé-mūzd′) *adj.* **1,** confused. **2,** lost in thought.

Ben′a·dryl (ben′ə-dril) *n.* (*T.N.*) a drug for the relief of hay fever.

bench *n.* **1,** a long seat. **2,** the office of judge; the judiciary. **3,** a stout table; workbench. **4,** a shelf. **—bench mark,** a point of reference for making measurements.

bend *v.t.* [*pret. & p.p.* **bent**] **1,** put a curve or crook in. **2,** turn in a different direction. **3,** force into submission. —*v.i.* become curved or crooked. —*n.* **1,** a curve or crook. **2,** a knot. **3,** (*pl.*) a disease caused by rapid emergence from compression. **—bend′er,** *n.* (*Slang*) a drinking spree.

be·neath′ (bé-nēth′) *adv.* in a lower place, condition, rank, etc; underneath. —*prep.* below.

ben′e·dict (ben′ə-dikt) *n.* a bridegroom.

Ben″e·dic′tine (ben″ə-dik′tēn) *n.* **1,** a monk of the order of St. Benedict. **2,** a liqueur. —*adj.* pert. to St. Benedict or the Benedictines.

ben″e·dic′tion (ben″ə-dik′shən) *n.* **1,** the act of pronouncing a blessing. **2,** a blessing.

ben″e·fac′tion (ben″ə-fak′shən) *n.* **1,** the doing of good. **2,** a benefit conferred, esp. a charitable donation. **—ben′e·fac″tor,** *n.*

ben′e·fice (ben′ə-fis) *n.* an ecclesiastical position providing a living.

be·nef′i·cent (bə-nef′i-sənt) *adj.* conferring benefit; charitable. **—be·nef′i·cence,** *n.*

ben″e·fi′cial (ben″ə-fish′əl) *adj.* **1,** helpful; profitable. **2,** pert. to a benefit.

ben″e·fi′ci·ar·y (ben″ə-fish′é-er-é) *n.* a recipient of benefits.

ben′e·fit (ben′ə-fit) *n.* **1,** advantage; profit. **2,** an act of kindness. **3,** an activity, as a theatrical performance, to raise money for a charitable purpose. —*v.i.* [**-fit′ted, -ting**] derive a benefit (from). —*v.t.* be beneficial to.

be·nev′o·lent (bə-nev′ə-lənt) *adj.* manifesting a desire to do good; kind. **—be·nev′o·lence,** *n.*

be·night′ed (bé-nī′tid) *adj.* in a state of mental darkness; in deep ignorance.

be·nign′ (bé-nīn′) *adj.* **1,** of a kind disposition; gracious. **2,** favorable; propitious. **—be·nig′ni·ty** (bé-nig′nə-té) *n.*

be·nig′nant (bé-nig′nənt) *adj.* kindly; benign. **—be·nig′nan·cy,** *n.*

ben′i·son (ben′i-sən) *n.* a blessing.

ben′ny (ben′é) *n.* (*Slang*) **1,** an overcoat. **2,** a Benzedrine tablet.

bent *adj.* **1,** curved or crooked. **2,** determined; resolved. —*n.* tendency; inclination. —*v.* pret. & p.p. of *bend.*

Ben′ze·drine″ (ben′zə-drēn″) *n.* (*T.N.*) a type of amphetamine.

ben′zene (ben′zēn) *n.* a volatile liquid derived from coal, used as a solvent and fuel.

ben′zine (ben′zēn) *n.* a volatile liquid obtained from petroleum, used in cleaning, etc.

ben′zo·ate (ben′zō-ət) *n.* a salt obtained from benzoin, used as a food preservative.

ben′zo·caine″ (ben′zə-kān) *n.* a local anesthetic.

ben′zo·in (ben′zō-in) *n.* a fragrant resin used in perfumes and drugs. **—ben·zo′ic** (-ik) *adj.*

ben′zol (ben′zâl) *n.* a form of benzene used as a motor fuel, etc.

be·queath′ (bé-kwēth′) *v.t.* dispose of (property) by will. **—be·queath′al** (-əl) *n.*

be·quest′ (bé-kwest′) *n.* a legacy.

be·rate′ (bé-rāt′) *v.t.* scold.

Ber′ber (bėr′bėr) *n. & adj.* pert. to a No. Afr. people inhabiting Barbary and the Sahara, or their language.

ber·ceuse′ (ber-söz′) *n.* a lullaby.

be·reave′ (bé-rēv′) *v.t.* [*pret. & p.p.* often **be·reft′**] take away from, esp. by death. **—be·reave″ment,** *n.*

be·reft′ (bé-reft′) *adj.* deprived; destitute.

be·ret′ (bə-rā′) *n.* a round, soft, visorless cap.

ber′i·ber′i (ber′é-) *n.* a vitamin-deficiency disease.

ber·ke′li·um (bėr-kē′lé-əm) *n.* an unstable, radioactive, metallic element, no. 97, symbol Bk, produced artificially from americium.

ber·lin′ (bər-lin′) *n.* **1,** a large, four-wheeled, closed carriage. **2,** [also, **ber·line′**] a type of limousine.

Bermuda onion a large, mild variety of Spanish onion.

Bermuda shorts short pants reaching almost to the knees.

ber′ry (ber′é) *n.* **1,** any small pulpy fruit. **2,** a dry kernel, as of coffee. —*v.i.* **1,** produce berries. **2,** gather berries.

ber′serk′ (bėr′sėrk) *adj.* in a frenzy; amuck.

berth (bėrth) *n.* **1,** a sleeping compartment; bunk. **2,** a storage space; a dock. **3,** a job. **4,** a position, as in a competition. —*v.i. & t.* enter or place in a berth.

ber′tha (bėr′thə) *n.* a short cape or collar worn by women.

ber′yl (ber′əl) *n.* **1,** a mineral occurring in many colors, prized as a gem. **2,** a blue-green color.

be·ryl′li·um (bə-ril′ē-əm) *n.* a metallic chemical element, no. 4, symbol Be.

be·seech′ (bē-sēch′) *v.t.* ask urgently; entreat; implore; solicit.

be·seem′ (bē-sēm′) *v.t.* be fit for or worthy of.

be·set′ (bē-set′) *v.t.* [**be·set′, -set′ting**] attack from all sides; assail; harass.

be·shrew′ (bē-shroo′) *v.t.* put a curse on.

be·side′ (bē-sīd′) *prep.* **1,** at the side of; near. **2,** in addition to. **3,** apart from; not connected with. —*adv.* besides.

be·sides′ (bē-sīdz′) *adv.* **1,** moreover; further. **2,** in addition. **3,** otherwise; else. —*prep.* beside.

be·siege′ (bē-sēj′) *v.t.* **1,** lay siege to. **2,** harass, as with demands, etc.

be·smirch′ (bē-smėrch′) *v.t.* soil; sully the honor of.

be′som (bē′zəm) *n.* a broom of twigs.

be·sot′ted (bē-sot′id) *adj.* **1,** stupefied, as with drink. **2,** addicted to drink. —**be·sot′,** *v.t.*

be·speak′ (bē-spēk′) *v.t.* [**be·spoke′, be·spo′ken**] **1,** show; indicate. **2,** order in advance.

best *adj.* **1,** superlative of *good.* **2,** largest. —*adv.* **1,** superlative of *well.* **2,** with most advantage or success. **3,** most fully. —*n.* the utmost; the highest quality. —*v.t.* defeat; surpass. —**best man,** chief attendant of the bridegroom at a wedding.

bes′tial (bes′chəl) *adj.* **1,** like a beast; brutal. **2,** pert. to beasts. —**bes·tial′i·ty** (-chal′ə-tē) *n.*

be·stir′ (bes-stër′) *v.t. & i.* [**-stirred′, -stir′ring**] agitate; rouse.

be·stow′ (bē-stō′) *v.t.* **1,** give; confer as a gift. **2,** deposit; consign. —**be·stow′al,** *n.*

be·stride′ (bē-strīd′) *v.t.* [**be·strode′, be·strid′den**] **1,** sit astride of; straddle. **2,** step over or across.

bet *v.t. & i.* [**bet, bet′ting**] pledge as forfeit upon some contingency; wager. —*n.* **1,** a wager. **2,** the stake.

be′ta (bā′tə) *n.* the second letter of the Greek alphabet (B, β). —**beta particle,** an electron emitted by a radioactive substance. —**beta ray,** a stream of beta particles.

be·take′ (bē-tāk′) *v.t.* [**-took′, -tak′ing**] take (oneself) to a place; go.

be′ta·tron″ (bā′tə-tron″) *n.* a device for accelerating electrons to high velocity.

bête noire (bet-nwär′) (*Fr.*) an aversion; object of dislike.

be·think′ (bē-think′) *v.t.* [*pret. & p.p.* **-thought′**] remind (oneself); recall.

be·tide′ (bē-tīd′) *v.i. & t.* come to pass; happen (to).

be·times′ (bē-tīmz′) *adv.* (*Archaic*) early; soon.

be·to′ken (bē-tō′kən) *v.t.* be a token or visible sign of; indicate.

be·tray′ (bē-trā′) *v.t.* **1,** deliver treacherously to an enemy. **2,** be unfaithful in (a trust). **3,** reveal unconsciously. —**be·tray′-al,** *n.*

be·troth′ (bē-trâth′) *v.t.* engage to take or give in marriage. —**be·troth′al,** *n.*

bet′ter (bet′ər) *adj.* **1,** comparative of *good.* **2,** larger. **3,** improved in health. —*adv.* comparative of *well.* —*v.t.* **1,** improve. **2,** surpass. —*n.* **1,** something or someone superior. **2,** [also, **bet′tor**] one who bets. —**bet′ter·ment,** *n.* act or effect of bettering; improvement. —**better than,** (*Colloq.*) more than.

be·tween′ (bē-twēn′) *prep.* **1,** in the space that separates (two things). **2,** intermediate in time, quantity, or degree. **3,** in joint interest or action of. **4,** involving; concerning. —*adv.* intermediate in space, time, etc.

be·twixt′ (bē-twikst′) *prep.* between.

bev′a·tron″ (bev′ə-tron″) *n.* a device for accelerating electrons, protons, etc.

bev′el (bev′əl) *n.* **1,** an angle other than a right angle between two lines or surfaces. **2,** an instrument for measuring or cutting a bevel. —*v.t. & i.* cut or slant obliquely. —*adj.* oblique.

bev′er·age (bev′ər-ij) *n.* any liquid fit for drinking.

bev′y (bev′ē) *n.* a flock of birds or girls.

be·wail′ (bē-wāl′) *v.t. & i.* mourn aloud (for).

be·ware′ (bē-wâr′) *v.i. & t.* be wary (of), cautious, or vigilant.

be·wil′der (bē-wil′dər) *v.t.* lead into perplexity; confuse. —**be·wil′der·ment,** *n.*

be·witch′ (bē-wich′) *v.t.* **1,** please extremely; charm; fascinate. **2,** cast a spell upon. —**be·witch′ing,** *adj.*

be·yond′ (bē-yond′) *prep. & adv.* **1,** on the other side of; farther on than. **2,** more than; superior to. **3,** outside the reach or limits of.

bez′el (bez′əl) *n.* a beveled face or part.

bhang (bang) *n.* **1,** an E. Indian hemp plant. **2,** a narcotic obtained from it.

bi- (bī) *pref.* two; twice; once in every two.

bi·al′y (bē-al′ē) *n.* a flat, onion-flavored breakfast roll.

bi′as (bī′əs) *n.* **1,** an oblique line or direction. **2,** prejudice. —*v.t.* prejudice; warp. —*adj. & adv.* oblique; unbalanced.

bi·ath'lon (bī-ath'lon) *n.* an athletic competition combining cross-country skiing and marksmanship.

bib *n.* a cloth worn over the breast to protect the clothing.

bib'e·lot (bib'ə-lō) *n.* any small article prized for beauty or rarity.

Bi'ble (bī'bəl) *n.* **1,** the collection of sacred writings of the Christian religion, comprising the Old and New Testaments. **2,** (*l.c.*) any book regarded as authoritative. —**Bib'li·cal** (bib'li-kəl) *adj.*

bib·li·o- (bib'lē-ō) *pref.* **1,** book. **2,** Bible.

bib"li·og'ra·phy (bib"lē-og'rə-fē) *n.* **1,** classification of books. **2,** a list of books. —**bib"li·o·graph'i·cal,** *adj.*

bib'li·o·phile" (bib'lē-ō-fīl") *n.* a lover of books.

bib'u·lous (bib'yə-ləs) *adj.* addicted to drinking liquor. —**bib'u·lous·ness,** *n.*

bi·cam'er·al (bī-kam'ər-əl) *adj.* (of a legislature) comprising two houses.

bi·car'bon·ate of soda (bī-kär'bə-nət) a white, crystalline, alkaline substance, commonly called *baking soda.*

bi"cen·ten'ni·al *adj.* the 200th anniversary.

bi'ceps (bī'seps) *n.* a muscle having a double origin at one end, esp. that on the upper arm.

bi·chlor'ide (bī-klôr'īd) *n.* a compound in which each molecule contains two atoms of chlorine.

bick'er (bik'ər) *v.i.* & *n.* engage in a petulant quarrel; wrangle.

bi'con·cave" *adj.* concave on both sides.

bi'con·vex" *adj.* convex on both sides.

bi'cron (bī'kron) *n.* one billionth of a meter.

bi·cus'pid (bī-kus'pid) *adj.* having two cusps or points. —*n.* a double-pointed tooth.

bi'cy·cle (bī'sik-əl) *n.* a vehicle having two wheels in line.

bid *v.t.* **1,** [**bade, bid'den, -ding**] command; invite. **2,** [*pret.* & *p.p.* **bid**] offer a price or. —*v.i.* make an offer. —*n.* **1,** an amount or thing offered. **2,** an effort. **3,** an invitation. —**bid'der,** *n.* —**bid fair,** appear likely.

bid'dy (bid'ē) *n.* **1,** a chicken, esp. a hen. **2,** a cackling woman.

bide (bīd) *v.t.* & *i.* pause; await.

bi·det' (bi-det'; bē-dā') *n.* **1,** a small horse. **2,** a low basin used for bathing the genital area.

bi·en'ni·al (bī-en'ē-əl) *adj.* happening every two years.

bier (bir) *n.* a framework on which a coffin is laid before burial.

biff (bif) *v.t.* (*Colloq.*) strike sharply. —*n.* a blow.

bi·fo'cal (bī-fō'kəl) *adj.* having two lenses. —*n.* (*pl.*) eyeglasses having lenses for near and far vision.

bi'fur·cate" (bī'fər-kāt") *v.* divide into two branches. —*adj.* two-branched.

big *adj.* [**big'ger, -gest**] **1,** large in size, extent, degree, etc. **2,** important. **3,** generous, tolerant. —**big brother,** (*Slang*) government, esp. oppressive government. —**big shot,** bigwig. —**big top,** the circus.

big'a·my (big'ə-mē) *n.* the crime of having two wives or husbands at the same time. —**big'a·mist,** *n.* —**big'a·mous,** *adj.*

big'·foot" *n.* sasquatch.

big'horn" *n.* a wild sheep of the Rocky Mountains.

bight (bīt) *n.* **1,** a bend, as of a coastline; a bay. **2,** a loop in rope.

big'ot (big'ət) *n.* a person intolerant of creeds, opinions, etc. other than his own. —**big'ot·ry** (-rē) *n.*

big'wig" *n.* (*Colloq.*) a high-ranking person.

bike (bīk) *n.* (*Colloq.*) bicycle.

bi·ki'ni (bi-kē'nē) *n.* a woman's scanty two-piece bathing suit.

bi·lat'er·al (bī-lat'ər-əl) *adj.* having two sides.

bil'ber"ry (bil'ber"ē) *n.* a flowering shrub; its berry.

bile (bīl) *n.* **1,** a secretion of the liver. **2,** ill nature; peevishness.

bilge (bilj) *n.* **1,** the bulging or broadest part, as of a ship or barrel. **2,** (*Slang*) buncombe; obscenity. —**bilge water,** evil-smelling water that collects in the hold of a ship.

bi·lin'gual (bī-ling'gwəl) *adj.* **1,** able to speak two languages. **2,** expressed in two languages. —**bi·lin'gual·ism,** *n.* —**bi·lin'guist,** *n.*

bil'ious (bil'yəs) *adj.* having an excess of bile. —**bil'ious·ness,** *n.*

-bil'i·ty (bil'ə-tē) *suf.* forming nouns of adjectives ending in *-able* and *-ible.*

bilk *v.t.* defraud; swindle.

bill (bil) *n.* **1,** an account of money owed. **2,** a written order to pay money. **3,** a piece of paper money. **4,** a proposed law. **5,** a list or public notice: *handbill.* **6,** the horny beak of a bird. —*v.t.* **1,** enter on a bill; send a bill to. **2,** engage or schedule on a theatrical program. —**bill and coo,** make love sentimentally. —**bill of fare,** a list of dishes available in a restaurant. —**bill of lading,** a list of goods received for transportation. —**Bill of Rights,** constitutional law guaranteeing civil liberties. **—bill of sale,** a document transferring possession.

bill'board" *n.* a large board for posting of advertisements.

bil'let (bil'it) *n.* **1,** a sleeping space or lodging, esp. for a soldier or sailor. **2,** assignment; job. **3,** a ticket; a written note [also, bi-lā']. **4,** a stick of wood, esp. for fuel. *—v.t.* assign to a lodging or place.

bil'let-doux" (bě'yä-doo') *n.* (*Fr.*) a love letter.

bill'fold" *n.* a wallet.

bil'liards (bil'yərdz) *n.* a game played with balls driven by cues on a rectangular table. **—bil'liard,** *n.* a scoring shot in this game; carom.

bill'ing *n.* **1,** act of sending or listing on a bill. **2,** advertisement of a performer's name on a program.

bil'lings·gate" (bil'ingz-gāt") *n.* coarse and abusive language.

bil'lion (bil'yən) *n.* **1,** (*U.S.*) a thousand millions: also (*Brit.*) **mil'liard. 2,** (*Brit.*) a million millions.

bil'low (bil'ō) *n.* a large sea wave; any similar surging mass. *—v.i.* surge like a sea wave. **—bil'low·y,** *adj.*

bil'ly (bil'ē) *n.* a small bludgeon, esp. a policeman's club.

bil'ly-goat" *n.* a male goat.

bi·met'al·lism (bī-met'ə-liz-əm) *n.* use of both gold and silver as a monetary standard.

bin *n.* a storage compartment.

bi'na·ry (bī'nə-rē) *adj.* **1,** having two parts or components. **2,** based on the radix 2.

bin·au'ral (bi-nôr'əl) *adj.* pert. to, involving, or designed for the use of both ears.

bind (bīnd) *v.t.* [*pret.* & *p.p.* **bound**] **1,** make fast with a band; fasten; cause to cohere. **2,** form a border on. **3,** obligate; compel. *—v.i.* **1,** stick fast; cohere. **2,** be obligatory.

bind'er (bīn'dər) *n.* **1,** one who binds. **2,** a device for binding; a cover in which loose pages are held. **3,** an adhesive; cement. **—bind'er·y,** *n.* a place where books are bound.

bind'ing (bīn'ding) *n.* that which binds: the cover of a bound book, a reinforcing strip, etc.

bindle stiff (*Slang*) a hobo.

binge (binj) *n.* (*Slang*) spree.

bin'go (bing'gō) *n.* a game based on lotto. *—interj.* a cry of triumph.

bin'na·cle (bin'ə-kəl) *n.* the stand that holds a ship's compass.

bi·noc'u·lar (bə-nok'yə-lər) *adj.* having or requiring two eyes. *—n.* (*pl.*) a telescope or microscope with two eyepieces.

bi·no'mi·al (bī-nō'mē-əl) *adj.* having two parts. *—n.* an algebraic expression, as *a + b.*

bi'o (bī'ō) *n.* (*Colloq.*) a biography.

bi·o- (bī-ō, bī-ə) *pref.* **1,** life; living things. **2,** biological.

bi"o·chem'is·try *n.* the chemistry of life and living things.

bi'o·clean" *adj.* free or almost free from harmful organisms.

bi"o·de·grad'a·ble (-dē-grād'ə-bəl) *adj.* able to be decomposed by bacterial action.

bi·og'ra·phy (bī-og'rə-fē) *n.* **1,** a history of the life of a person. **2,** such histories collectively. **—bi"o·graph'i·cal,** *adj.*

bi·ol'o·gy (bī-ol'ə-jē) *n.* the general science of the structure and processes of living organisms. **—bi"o·log'i·cal,** *adj.* **—bi·ol'o·gist,** *n.*

bi'ome (bī'ōm) *n.* any community of plants and animals.

bi"o·med'i·cine *n.* a branch of medicine concerned with human survival under stress.

bi·on'ic (bī-on'ik) *adj.* relating biological functions and engineering.

bi"o·phys'ics *n.* the physics of life and living things.

bi'op·sy (bī'op-sē) *n.* the removal of tissue or fluids from the body for examination.

bi'o·rhythm (bī'ō-rith-əm) *n.* an innately controlled biological or physical process. **—bi"o·rhyth'mic,** *adj.*

bi·ot'ic (bī-ot'ik) *adj.* pert. to life.

bi'o·tin (bī'ə-tin) *n.* vitamin H, found in liver, egg yolk, etc.

bi'o·tron" (bī'ə-tron") *n.* a chamber for study of the effects of environment on living organisms.

bi'o·type" (bī'ə-tīp") *n.* a group of organisms having the same hereditary constitution. **—bi"o·typ'ic** (-tip'ik) *adj.*

bi·par'ti·san (bī-pär'ti-zən) *adj.* representing or involving two parties.

bi·par'tite (bī-pär'tīt) *adj.* having or divided into two corresponding parts.

bi'ped (bī'ped) *n.* a two-footed animal.

bi'plane" (bī'plān") *n.* an airplane with two wings in tier.

birch (bērch) *n.* a tree having smooth bark, often white; its wood.

Birch'er (bēr'chər) *n.* (*Slang*) a member of the John Birch Society, a reactionary political organization.

bird (bērd) *n.* **1,** any feather-covered vertebrate animal whose forelimbs form wings. **2,** (*Brit. slang*) an attractive young girl. **—bird's-'eye",** *adj.* general; cursory, as a view. **—bird of paradise,** a bird with brilliant plumage, found in New Guinea.

bird'ie (bēr'dė) n. (Golf) a score on a hole of one under par.

bi'reme (bī'rēm) n. an ancient galley having two banks of oars on each side.

bi·ret'ta (bə-ret'ə) n. a stiff cap worn by Roman Catholic priests.

birth (bērth) n. 1, act of being born. 2, the bringing forth of offspring. 3, lineage; descent. 4, the origin or inception of anything.

birth'day" n. the day of one's birth, or any anniversary of it.

birth'mark" n. a congenital blemish on the body.

birth'place" n. the place where one was born.

birth'right" n. inheritance.

birth'stone" n. a gem associated with a certain month or period.

bis'cuit (bis'kit) n. 1, (U.S.) a small, soft cake made from leavened dough. 2, (Brit.) a flat, hard cake made from unleavened dough; a cracker. 3, anything in the shape of a biscuit. 4, plastic material in process of shaping, molding, or baking.

bi·sect' (bī-sekt') v.t. 1, cut into two parts. 2, divide into two equal parts. —**bi·sec'tion,** n.

bi·sex'u·al (bī-sek'shoo-əl) adj. 1, combining both sexes; hermaphroditic. 2, applying to both sexes. —n. a person both homo- and heterosexual. —**bi''sex·u·al'i·ty,** n.

bish'op (bish'əp) n. 1, a high officer of a church. 2, a chess piece. —**bish'op·ric** (-rik) n. the diocese or office of a bishop; see.

bis'muth (biz'məth) n. a metallic element, no. 83, symbol Bi.

bi'son (bī'sən) n. a large animal of the ox family; the buffalo.

bisque (bisk) n. 1, a thickened soup. 2, unglazed porcelain. 3, a handicap allowed a weaker player.

bis·sex'tile (bī-seks'til) adj. pert. to the extra day of leap year. —n. a leap year.

bis'tro (bis'trō) n. a small café.

bit n. 1, a small piece or quantity of anything. 2, any small coin; a money value of 12½ cents. 3, the mouthpiece of a horse's bridle. 4, the essential part of a cutting tool. 5, (Colloq.) a routine or pattern of behavior; specialty. 6, a unit of memory capacity, as in a computer. 7, a unit of information, the result of a choice between two alternatives: in a binary computer, between 0 and 1. —v. pret. of bite.

bitch (bich) n. 1, a female of the dog family. 2, (Slang) a malicious woman. 3, (Slang) a complaint. —v.i. (Slang) complain. —v.t. (with up) (Slang) bungle; spoil.

bite (bīt) v.t. [bit (bit), bit'ten (bit'ən), bit'ing] 1, grip or pierce with the teeth. 2, sting. 3, take firm hold of. 4, eat into; corrode. —v.i. 1, take a bait; accept something deceptive. 2, take hold; act with effect. —n. 1, the act of biting. 2, a piece bitten off. 3, a small quantity of food.

bit'stock" n. a handle for a bit or drill; brace.

bit'ten (bit'ən) v. p.p. of bite.

bit'ter (bit'ər) adj. 1, having a harsh taste. 2, hard to bear; disagreeable. 3, cruel; sarcastic. —n. (pl.) a liquor having a bitter taste. —**bit'ter·ness,** n.

bit'tern (bit'ərn) n. a No. Amer. heron.

bi·tu'men (bi-tū'mən) n. any of a class of natural substances such as petroleum and asphalt. —**bi·tu'mi·nous,** adj.

bi'valve" (bī'valv") n. a mollusk having two shells, as the oyster. —adj. two-shelled.

biv'ou·ac" (biv'oo-ak") n. an unsheltered encampment or camp. —v.i. [biv'ou·acked", -ack"ing] encamp without shelter.

bi·zarre' (bi-zär') adj. odd; whimsical; grotesque. —**bi·zarre'ness,** n.

blab v.t. [blabbed, blab'bing] utter thoughtlessly; disclose. —v.i. talk indiscreetly.

blab'ber (blab'ər) v.i. 1, mumble. 2, blab; talk idly.

black (blak) n. 1, the color of coal; strictly, the absence of all color or of all illumination. 2, a Negro. —adj. 1, entirely or relatively dark. 2, dismal; wicked; evil; calamitous. 3, Negro. —v.t. put blacking on. —**black box,** a device whose function is known, but whose components and method of operation are concealed. —**Black Death,** bubonic plague. —**black eye, 1,** a bruise near the eye. 2, (Colloq.) disgrace. —**black fly,** a very small fly or gnat with a venomous bite. —**black gold,** (Colloq.) oil. —**black hole,** (Astron.) a theoretical celestial body considered to be a collapsed star. —**black humor** or **comedy,** humor characterized by a cynical, ironic, often grotesque view of the human condition. —**black light,** invisible ultraviolet or infrared light. —**black lung,** a disease caused by breathing coal dust. —**black magic,** magic used malevolently. —**Black Maria** (mə-rī'ə) (Slang) a police patrol wagon used to transport prisoners. —**black market,** the selling of goods in violation of legal restrictions. —**black mar"ket·eer',** one who sells goods on the black market. —**Black Muslim** (mus'ləm) a member of a Negro religious organization following the tenets of Islam. —**Black Nationalism,** a Negro movement advocating political separation of Negroes and whites by formation of a Negro nation either within the boundaries of the U.S. or

abroad. **—black out,** lose consciousness.
—Black Power, a movement among American blacks to achieve political and economic power without integration. **—black sheep,** a disgraceful member of a family or group. **—Black Shirt,** a member of the Fascist party of Italy. **—Black Studies,** the study of Negro history and culture. **—black tie,** semiformal evening wear for men. **—black widow,** a kind of poisonous spider.

black'a·moor (blak'ə-mûr) *n.* a Negro.

black-"and-blue' *adj.* discolored by bruising.

black'ball" *v.t.* reject; ostracize.

black'ber"ry *n.* a thorny vine, or its fruit.

black'bird" *n.* any of various birds having dark plumage.

black'board" *n.* a slate bulletin board. **—blackboard jungle,** (*Slang*) an urban school whose students are unusually disorderly or destructive.

black'en (-ən) *v.t. & i.* make or become black.

black'guard (blag'ərd) *n.* a scoundrel. **—black'guard·ly,** *adj.*

black'head" *n.* **1,** a secretion of fatty matter in a skin follicle. **2,** a disease of poultry.

black'ing *n.* shoe polish.

black'jack" (blak'jak") *n.* **1,** a club with a heavy head and a short elastic shaft. **2,** card game: *twenty-one.* —*v.t.* **1,** hit with a blackjack. **2,** coerce.

black'leg" *n.* **1,** a disease of cattle. **2,** a strikebreaker; scab. **3,** a swindler; a crooked gambler.

black'list" *n.* a list of persons in disfavor. —*v.t.* **1,** vote against (a candidate for club membership). **2,** put on a blacklist.

black'mail" *n.* extortion of a bribe for silence. —*v.t.* threaten exposure unless paid.

black'out" *n.* **1,** the extinguishing of lights as a protection against enemy airplanes. **2,** unconsciousness; a faint. **3,** loss of memory.

black'smith" (blak'smith") *n.* a worker in iron, esp. a horseshoer.

black'thorn" *n.* a prickly shrub.

black'top" *n.* a bituminous substance for paving roads, etc. —*v.t.* pave with blacktop.

blad'der (blad'ər) *n.* **1,** a body sac in which urine is retained. **2,** any elastic sac or bag.

blade (blād) *n.* **1,** the sharpened part of a cutting or piercing weapon or tool; the weapon or tool itself, esp. a sword. **2,** the leaf of a plant; the broad part of a leaf. **3,** any broad thin part, as of an oar. **4,** a gay or rakish fellow.

blah (blä) *adj.* **1,** listless; debilitated. **2,** dull; uninteresting. **—the blahs,** (*Slang*) boredom; listlessness.

blain (blān) *n.* an inflammatory swelling; a blister.

blame (blām) *v.t.* charge with an error or fault. —*n.* imputation of error or fault; censure. **—blame'wor"thy,** *adj.* culpable.

blanch (blanch) *v.t.* make white or pale. —*v.i.* become pale.

bland *adj.* **1,** suave. **2,** affable; kindly. **3,** mild; balmy. **4,** oily; nonirritating or nonstimulating (of foods or medicines). **—bland'ness,** *n.*

blan'dish *v.t.* coax or cajole with flattery or caresses. **—blan'dish·ment,** *n.*

blank *adj.* **1,** empty; bare; void of something usual or necessary to completeness. **2,** not written or printed on. **3,** showing no emotion; unresponsive. **4,** complete; unmitigated. **5,** white or pale. —*n.* **1,** a space from which something is absent or omitted; a vacancy. **2,** a printed form or space not filled out by writing. **3,** a rough-fashioned wood or metal part to be finished by tooling. —*v.t.* **1,** (with *out*) make blank. **2,** (*Colloq.*) keep an opponent in a game from scoring. **—blank'ness,** *n.* **—blank check,** (*Colloq.*) unlimited authority. **—blank verse,** unrhymed but metrical verse.

blan'ket (blang'kit) *n.* **1,** a large piece of heavy cloth, used as a bedcovering. **2,** any extensive or close covering, as of snow. —*adj.* widespread; comprehensive. —*v.t.* cover with or as with a blanket.

blare (blâr) *v.i.* give out a brazen sound; bellow. —*v.t.* sound loudly; proclaim. —*n.* **1,** a trumpet's sound. **2,** blatancy in sound, color, etc.

blar'ney (blär'nē) *n.* wheedling talk; cajolery. —*v.t. & i.* flatter; cajole.

bla·sé' (blä-zā) *adj.* satiated with pleasure; bored.

blas·pheme' (blas-fēm') *v.i.* speak irreverently of God or sacred things. —*v.t.* **1,** speak impiously of (God, etc.). **2,** speak evil of; revile. **—blas'phe·mous,** *adj.* **—blas'phe·my** (-fə-mē) *n.*

blast (blást) *n.* **1,** a forcible stream or sudden gust of air. **2,** the blowing of a horn, whistle, etc.; the sound of a wind instrument. **3,** an explosion; a charge of explosives. **4,** a blight. —*v.t.* **1,** shatter with explosives. **2,** ruin; destroy; cause to shrivel. **—blast furnace,** a smelting furnace in which fuel is burned under a forced draft of air. **—blast off,** take off (said esp. of rockets).

blat (blat) *v.i.* bleat —*v.t.* (*Colloq.*) blurt; blab.

bla'tant (blā'tənt) *adj.* **1,** offensively

loud-voiced; noisy. **2,** obtrusive. **—bla'-tan·cy** (-tən-sē) *n.*

blath'er (blath′ər) *v.* talk or say foolishly. **—n.** foolish talk.

blath'er·skite (″ -skīt″) *n.* a voluble, foolish talker.

blaze (blāz) *n.* **1,** flame or fire. **2,** any dazzling display, brilliant sunlight; a bright flame; a hot glow. **3,** a sudden outburst of fire, passion, etc. **4,** a white spot on the face of a horse, cow, etc. **5,** a mark made on a tree to indicate a path or boundary. **6,** (*pl.*) (*Slang*) hell. **—v.i.** burst into flame; burn brightly; shine. **—v.t.** **1,** exhibit vividly; proclaim. **2,** mark with a blaze.

blaz'er (blā′zər) *n.* **1,** coat for sports wear, usu. brightly colored or navy blue. **2,** a pan for use over a flame. **3,** (*Colloq.*) anything intensely hot or bright.

bla'zon (blā′zən) *v.t.* **1,** depict or describe in heraldic terms. **2,** adorn. **3,** display; proclaim. **—n.** **1,** a coat of arms. **2,** pompous display. **—bla'zon·ry,** *n.*

bleach (blēch) *v.t. & i.* make or become white, pale, or colorless. **—n.** a bleaching agent.

bleach'ers (blē′chərz) *n. pl.* unsheltered seats on a playing field.

bleak (blēk) *adj.* **1,** desolate and windswept. **2,** cold; piercing. **3,** cheerless; dreary. **—bleak'ness,** *n.*

blear (blir) *v.t.* dim (the eyes) with tears, etc. **—adj.** (of the eyes) sore or dimmed. **—blear'y,** *adj.*

bleat (blēt) *n.* the cry of a sheep, goat, or calf. **—v.i.** utter such a cry.

bled *v.* pret. & p.p. of *bleed.*

bleed (blēd) *v.i.* [**bled**] **1,** emit blood. **2,** exude fluid. **3,** flow out; run together. **4,** feel pity, sorrow, or anguish. **—v.t.** **1,** cause to lose blood, sap, etc.; make flow; drain out. **2,** (*Colloq.*) extort money from, as by overcharge or blackmail. **3,** (*Printing*) allow (a picture) to run off the page; trim (a page) so as to cut into the printing. **—bleed'er,** *n.* a hemophiliac.

bleep (blēp) *n.* a short, high-pitched sound; beep. **—v.t.**

blem'ish *v.t.* deface; mar; damage. **—n.** defect; flaw; stain.

blench *v.i.* draw back; flinch; quail.

blend *v.t.* **1,** mix inseparably. **2,** mix so as to obtain a desired combination of qualities. **—v.i.** **1,** combine into a harmonious whole. **2,** pass imperceptibly into one another. **—n.** **1,** the act of blending. **2,** something formed by blending; a smooth mixture; a harmonious whole.

bless (bles) *v.t.* **1,** consecrate by a religious rite. **2,** invoke God's favor upon. **3,** make happy, fortunate, or prosperous. **4,** praise; extol. **—bless'ed** (-ed), **blessed,** or **blest,** *adj.* **—bless'ed event,** the birth of a child.

bless'ing *n.* **1,** a short prayer for divine approval. **2,** a fortunate occurrence. **3,** benediction; approval.

blew (bloo) *v.* pret. of *blow.*

blight (blīt) *n.* **1,** any widespread disease of plants. **2,** any similar malignant and destructive influence. **—v.t.** **1,** cause to wither or decay. **2,** ruin; frustrate.

blimp *n.* an airship with a nonrigid gas bag.

blind (blīnd) *adj.* **1,** lacking or having lost the sense of sight. **2,** lacking in discernment; unable to understand or judge. **3,** irrational; undiscriminating; heedless. **4,** out of sight; hidden; unlighted. **5,** having no opening or outlet. **6,** done without seeing. **—v.t.** **1,** deprive of sight. **2,** make obscure; conceal. **3,** impair the perception or judgment of. **—n.** **1,** something that obstructs vision or excludes light. **2,** something that masks a purpose or action. **3,** a rude shelter for hunters. **—blind'ness,** *n.* **—blind alley,** a street blocked at one end; an impasse. **—blind date,** an engagement with a stranger. **—blindman's buff,** a game of tag in which the person searching is blindfolded. **—blind spot, 1,** an area of poor visibility, reception, etc. **2,** a part of the retina not sensitive to light. **3,** an area of impaired judgment.

blind'fold *n.* a bandage over the eyes. **—v.t.** put a blindfold on.

blink *v.i.* **1,** wink rapidly and repeatedly. **2,** shine unsteadily; glimmer. **—v.t.** **1,** catch sight of. **2,** regard with indifference; ignore. **—n.** **1,** a wink or gleam. **2,** a glance or glimpse.

blink'er *n.* **1,** an intermittent signal lights; flasher. **2,** (*pl.*) [also, **blind'ers**] shades for horses' eyes.

blintz (blints) *n.* a thin rolled pancake with a filling.

blip *n.* an image on a radar screen.

bliss (blis) *n.* **1,** supreme happiness; spiritual joy. **2,** gladness. **—bliss'ful,** *adj.*

blis'ter (blis′tər) *n.* **1,** a vesicle on the skin. **2,** any similar swelling, as in a coat of paint; an air bubble in a metal casting. **—v.t.** **1,** raise a blister on. **2,** vituperate; mortify. **—v.i.** become blistered.

blithe (blīth) *adj.* merry; joyous; glad; light-hearted. **—blithe'ness,** *n.* **—blithe'-some** (-səm) *adj.* merry; gay.

blith'er·ing (blith′ə-ring) *adj.* talking foolishly.

blitz (blits) *n.* **1,** a violent and highly mobile attack by combined military forces of different types. **2,** any sudden or over-whelming onslaught. —*v.t.* attack with a blitz.

blitz′krieg″ (blits′krēg″) *n.* (*Ger.*) lightning warfare; blitz.

bliz′zard (bliz′ərd) *n.* **1,** a heavy fall of snow. **2,** a violent windstorm with sleet or dry snow.

bloat (blōt) *v.t.* **1,** cause to swell or distend. **2,** make vain or conceited. **3,** cure (fish) by smoking. —*v.i.* puff up; dilate. —*n.* a dietary ailment of cattle, sheep, and horses.

bloat′er (-ər) *n.* a fish cured by salting and smoking, like herring.

blob *n.* a small globe of liquid; a drop, bubble, or lump.

bloc (blok) *n.* a group of persons acting together for a particular interest.

block (blok) *n.* **1,** a solid mass of stone, wood, metal, etc. **2,** a solid mass used as a table for heavy work; a form on which something is molded or shaped. **3,** a base on which an engraving is mounted for printing. **4,** a platform, as that mounted by an auctioneer. **5,** a case containing one or more pulleys, for rigging rope tackles. **6,** an obstruction; the condition of being obstructed. **7,** the area of a town bounded by two intersecting pairs of two adjacent streets. **8,** a portion or section treated as a unit. **9,** a section of a railway, divided for signaling purposes. —*v.i.* **1,** mount on or fit with a block. **2,** (usually with *out*) plan or sketch roughly. **3,** obstruct; check. —**block′age** (-ij) *n.* an obstruction.

block·ade′ (blok-ād′) *n.* **1,** the barring of entrance to and exit from a place, esp. a port or coast. **2,** any obstruction of passage or progress. —*v.t.* shut up or obstruct by a blockade.

block′bust″er *n.* **1,** a large explosive aerial bomb. **2,** something large or effective. **3,** a real estate operator.

block′head″ (blok′hed″) *n.* a stupid person.

block′house″ *n.* a house of heavy timber used as a fort.

bloke (blōk) *n.* (*Brit. slang*) a fellow.

blond *adj.* [*fem.* **blonde** (blond)] light-colored, esp. as to hair and skin. —*n.* a person with light hair and fair skin. —**blond′ness,** *n.*

blood (blud) *n.* **1,** the fluid that circulates in the arteries and veins of animals. **2,** any vital fluid; the sap or juice of plants. **3,** descent; lineage; racial heritage. **4,** a person of high spirit; a rake. —**bad blood,** enmity. —**blood bank,** a supply of whole blood or plasma. —**blood count,** a count of red and white blood cells per unit of

volume. —**blood group,** all persons having the same blood type. —**blood relation,** a person related by birth. —**blood type,** the class of blood determined by agglutination. —**blood vessel,** any vein or artery. —**in cold blood,** deliberately.

blood′hound″ *n.* a keen-scented tracking dog.

blood′less *adj.* **1,** done without bloodshed. **2,** pale. **3,** lacking courage.

blood′let″ting (-let″ing) *n.* **1,** removal of blood from the body, as by opening a vein. **2,** bloodshed.

blood′mo·bile″ (blud′mə-bēl″) *n.* a vehicle equipped as a mobile blood donation center.

blood′shed″ *n.* slaughter.

blood′shot″ *adj.* (of eyes) streaked with red.

blood′stone″ *n.* a variety of chalcedony, green with spots of red.

blood′suck″er *n.* **1,** a leech. **2,** an extortioner.

blood′thirst″y *adj.* eager to kill. —**blood′-thirst″i·ness,** *n.*

blood′y (blud′ē) *adj.* **1,** covered with blood; gory. **2,** marked by great bloodshed. **3,** (*Brit.*) a vulgar expletive. —**blood′i·ness,** *n.* —**Bloody Mary,** a beverage made from vodka and tomato juice.

bloom *n.* **1,** the flower of a plant. **2,** the state of blossoming; a flourishing condition. **3,** a rosy glow or other evidence of youth or good health. **4,** a powdery deposit or coating, as on plums, cabbage leaves, etc. **5,** a rough-rolled ingot of steel. —*v.i.* **1,** produce blossoms. **2,** flourish; be in good health. **3,** glow with color. —**bloom′er,** *n.* a blunder.

bloom′ers (bloo′mərz) *n. pl.* loose trousers gathered at the knees, for women.

bloom′ing *adj.* (*Slang*) confounded: an expletive of little or no meaning.

bloop′er (bloo′pər) *n.* a blunder, esp. one on radio or television.

blos′som (blos′əm) *n.* **1,** the flower of a plant. **2,** the state of bearing flowers. —*v.i.* **1,** produce blossoms. **2,** become mature; develop.

blot *n.* **1,** a spot or stain, as of ink on paper. **2,** an erasure or obliteration. **3,** a blemish, as upon character or reputation. **4,** in backgammon, a piece exposed to being hit. —*v.t.* [**blot′ted, -ting**] **1,** stain; spatter. **2,** efface; obliterate. **3,** dry with a blotter. —*v.i.* form a stain; become stained.

blotch (bloch) *n.* a large irregular spot or blot. —*v.t.* blot; blur.

blot′ter (blot′ər) *n.* **1,** a piece of absorbent paper used to remove excess ink. **2,** a

journal book, esp. as used in a police station.

blot′to (blot′ō) *adj.* (*Slang*) drunk.

blouse (blows) *n.* **1,** a loose garment worn
on the upper body, esp. by women and
children. **2,** an outer garment reaching to
the knees, often belted, worn by both sexes
in Russia and elsewhere.

blow (blō) *v.i.* [**blew, blown** (blōn), **blow′
ing**] **1,** produce a current of air. **2,** be
carried about by or as by wind. **3,** make a
whistling sound; give out sound. **4,** breathe
hard; pant. **5,** (with *up* or *out*) explode. **6,**
(with *over*) subside. **7,** (*Colloq.*) boast. **8,**
produce flowers; blossom. —*v.t.* **1,** drive
by a current of air. **2,** force air into or
through, in order to clear, cause to sound,
inflate, etc. **3,** scatter or shatter, as by
exploding. **4,** (with *up*) inflate; enlarge. **5,**
(*Slang*) squander. —*n.* **1,** a blast of air; a
gale of wind. **2,** a stroke with the hand; a
thump. **3,** a sudden shock or calamity.

blow′gun″ *n.* a weapon from which missiles are expelled by one's blowing.

blow′hard″ *n.* (*Colloq.*) a braggart.

blow′out″ *n.* **1,** a sudden escape of air or
liquid, as from a ruptured tire, steam pipe,
etc. **2,** (*Colloq.*) a spree.

blow′pipe″ *n.* a pipe through which air is
forced.

blow′torch″ *n.* a portable gas heating
appliance, used for welding, soldering, etc.

blow′up″ *n.* **1,** an explosion; outburst. **2,**
a photographic enlargement.

blowz′y (blow′zē) *adj.* **1,** disheveled; untidy. **2,** fat and ruddy; red-faced.

blub′ber (blub′ər) *n.* the fat of whales.
—*v.i.* weep with a contorted face. —*v.t.*
say tearfully.

blu′cher (bloo′kər) *n.* **1,** a shoe in which
tongue and upper are cut from one piece. **2,**
a short boot.

bludg′eon (bluj′ən) *n.* a heavy-headed
club. —*v.t.* **1,** hit with a bludgeon. **2,** bully;
coerce.

blue (bloo) *n.* **1,** the color of the clear sky;
a hue between green and violet in the spectrum. **2,** (*Poetic*) the sky; the sea. —*adj.* **1,**
of blue color; azure. **2,** (of the skin) livid,
as from cold or fear. **3,** depressed; despond-
ent. **4,** dismal; unpromising. **5,** strict in
morals; puritanical. **6,** risqué; profane. —*v.t.*
make blue; dye blue. —**blue baby,** a baby
born with an oxygen deficiency. —**blue
cheese,** a strong cheese streaked with blue,
as Roquefort. —**blue law,** a law forbidding
or regulating certain activities on Sunday.
—**blue ribbon,** first prize.

blue′bell″ (bloo′bel″) *n.* any of various
plants having blue bell-shaped flowers.

blue′ber″ry *n.* the small, bluish, edible
fruit of various shrubs.

blue′bird″ *n.* a blue songbird of eastern
U.S.

blue′blood″ *n.* (*Colloq.*) an aristocrat.

blue′bon″net *n.* the state flower of Texas.

blue′book″ *n.* **1,** a directory of socially
prominent persons. **2,** an examination book.

blue′bot″tle (bloo′bot″əl) *n.* **1,** a large fly
of blue-green color. **2,** any of several plants
with blue flowers; the cornflower.

blue′chip″ *adj.* considered among the most
successful or profitable in its field.

blue′col″lar *adj.* pert. to those workers
whose employment entails the wearing of
work clothes or protective gear.

blue′fish″ *n.* any of various edible fishes.

blue′grass″ *n.* **1,** a variety of grass. **2,** a
kind of country music.

blue′jack″et *n.* a sailor.

blue′jeans″ *n.* jeans.

blue-′pen′cil *v.t.* edit; cancel.

blue′print″ (bloo′print″) *n.* **1,** a photographic process that produces a print with
white lines on a blue field. **2,** such a print.
3, any detailed plan. —*v.t.* make a blue-
print of.

blue-″rib′bon, *adj.* **1,** prize-winning. **2,**
of a jury, composed of prominent citizens.

blues (blooz) *n.* **1,** a style of mournful
jazz music. **2,** a feeling of despondency.

blue′stock″ing *n.* a person who affects
learning or intellectual tastes.

bluff (bluf) *v.t. & i.* mislead by a pretense
of strength, influence, etc. —*n.* **1,** the act
of bluffing. **2,** a broad, steep, face of a hill
or headland. —*adj.* **1,** somewhat abrupt in
manner; rough and hearty; frank. **2,** having
a broad front or face.

blu′ing (bloo′ing) *n.* a bluish dye used to
whiten clothes after washing.

blun′der (blun′dər) *n.* a gross or stupid
mistake. —*v.i.* **1,** make such a mistake. **2,**
move blindly or clumsily. —*v.t.* confuse;
bungle.

blun′der·buss″ (-bus″) *n.* a musket with
flaring mouth.

blunt *adj.* **1,** having a rounded or thick
point or edge; not sharp. **2,** rough in manner or speech; abrupt; plain-spoken. —*v.t.*
make blunt; impair the force or keenness
of. —**blunt′ness,** *n.*

blur (blēr) *v.t.* [**blurred, blur′ring**] **1,**
make indistinct; obscure without effacing.
2, sully; stain. **3,** dim the perception or
susceptibility of. —*v.i.* become indistinct.
—*n.* **1,** a blot, smudge, or smear. **2,** a
confused appearance. —**blur′ry,** *adj.*
—**blur′ri·ness,** *n.*

blurb (blêrb) *n.* a laudatory advertisement, esp. of a book.

blurt (blêrt) *v.t.* utter suddenly; divulge inadvertently.

blush *v.i.* **1,** become red in the face from shame or embarrassment. **2,** be ashamed. **3,** become red or rosy. —*n.* **1,** a reddening of the face. **2,** a pink tinge. —**blush'er** *n.* a cosmetic applied to the face.

blus'ter (blus'tər) *v.i.* **1,** be loud and boastful; swagger; utter empty menaces. **2,** roar. —*n.* boastful utterance.

bo'a (bō'ə) *n.* **1,** any of various large snakes that kill by constricting, as *boa constrictor*. **2,** a long neckpiece worn by women.

boar (bôr) *n.* **1,** the wild hog. **2,** an uncastrated domesticated hog.

board (bôrd) *n.* **1,** a long, thin cut of timber. **2,** a flat slab of wood used for some specific purpose, as for ironing, posting notices, playing games. **3,** a table, esp. for food. **4,** provision for daily meals. **5,** a group of officials acting together. **6,** border; edge. —*v.t.* **1,** cover with boards. **2,** furnish with daily meals. **3,** go on or into (a ship, train, vehicle). —*v.i.* be supplied with daily meals. —**board'ing house,** a lodging house where meals are served.

boast (bōst) *v.i.* **1,** speak vaingloriously or exaggeratedly of one's own worth, property, deeds, etc. **2,** speak with laudable pride. —*v.t.* **1,** speak of with vanity or exultation. **2,** take pride in possessing. —*n.* **1,** something boasted of. **2,** bragging speech. —**boast'ful,** *adj.*

boat (bōt) *n.* **1,** a vessel for transport on water, esp. a small one moved by oars. **2,** an open dish, as for gravy. —*v.i.* & *t.* go or transport by boat. —**boat'ing,** *n.* the sport of going in boats. —**boat'er,** *n.* one who boats.

boat'swain (bō'sən; bōt'swān") *n.* a superior seaman in charge of anchors, cables, etc.

bob *n.* **1,** a jerk; jerking motion. **2,** any small dangling object: a weight on a plumb line; a float on a fishing line. **3,** a style of short haircut. **4,** a kind of sled. **5,** (*Brit.*) a shilling. —*v.i.* **[bobbed, bob'bing]** move jerkily; go up and down quickly. —*v.t.* **1,** cut short. **2,** hit lightly.

bob'bin (bob'in) *n.* a reel or spool for holding thread, yarn, or wire.

bob'ble (bob'əl) *v.t.* fumble. —*v.i.* bob; move jerkily. —*n.* fumble.

bob'by (bob'ē) *n.* a policeman.

bobby pin a clip for the hair.

bobby socks ankle-length socks. Also, **bobby sox.** —**bobby sox'er** (sok'sər) a teen-age girl.

bob'cat" *n.* an Amer. wildcat.

bob'o·link" (bob'ə-link") *n.* an American songbird.

bob'sled" *n.* a long sled with two sets of runners turning independently.

bob'white" (bob'hwīt") *n.* an American quail or partridge.

bock (bok) *n.* a dark beer, usually the first brew of the spring season.

bode (bōd) *v.t.* & *i.* be an omen (of); portend; betoken.

bod'ice (bod'is) *n.* **1,** a laced outer garment covering the upper body, worn by women. **2,** a close-fitting waist or body of a gown.

bod'i·ly (bod'ə-lē) *adj.* pert. to the body; corporeal.

bod'kin *n.* **1,** a blunt needle for drawing tape through a hem or loop. **2,** an awl for making holes in cloth, etc. **3,** (*Obs.*) a dagger.

bod'y (bod'ē) *n.* **1,** the physical structure of an animal. **2,** the main portion of this structure, excluding the head, appendages, etc. **3,** the main part of anything; a vehicle exclusive of wheels, etc.; a speech or treatise exclusive of introduction, appendix, etc. **4,** anything existing in three-dimensional space; a solid; anything having inertia or mass. **5,** weight, density, consistency, or other attribute of a solid. **6,** a group of persons or things collectively. —**body politic,** a people, their government, and form of government collectively. —**body language,** physical gestures and signals, often unconscious. —**body stocking,** a close-fitting one-piece garment.

bod'y·guard" *n.* a private guard; an escort.

Boer (bôr) *n.* a So. Afr. native of Dutch descent.

bog *n.* an area of wet and spongy ground; marsh. —*v.t.* & *i.* **[bogged, bog'ging]** sink in a bog; flounder among obstacles.

bo'gey (bō'gē) *n.* (*Golf*) a score of par on a hole (*Brit.*) or one over par (*U.S.*).

bog'gle (bog'əl) *v.i.* **1,** draw back in fright or alarm; shy; shrink. **2,** be clumsy or bungling. —*v.t.* **1,** amaze; astound.

bo'gie (bō'gē) *n.* bogy.

bo'gus (bō'gəs) *adj.* counterfeit; spurious; sham.

bo'gy (bō'gē) *n.* a troublesome imp; hobgoblin; anything that annoys. Also, **bo'gie.**

Bo·he'mi·an (bō-hē'mē-ən) *adj.* pert. to Bohemia or Bohemians, or the Czech language. —*n.* (*l.c.*) one who lives a gay, unconventional life.

boil *v.i.* **1,** change from liquid to gas under the influence of heat. **2,** be agitated, as by bubbles of gas rising to the surface of a heated liquid; be excited, esp. by anger. —*v.t.* **1,** cause to boil. **2,** cook by boiling. **3,** (with *down*) abridge; condense. —*n.* **1,** the act or condition of boiling. **2,** an inflammatory and suppurating sore on the skin. —**boil′er,** *n.* a vessel in which a liquid is boiled, esp. a tank in which water is converted to steam to operate an engine or furnish heat. —**boil′ing point,** the point at which a liquid will boil; of water, 212° F., 100° C.

boil′er·mak″er *n.* (*Slang*) a mixture of whiskey and beer.

bois′ter·ous (boi′stər-əs) *adj.* **1,** noisy and violent; clamorous. **2,** coarse and unrestrained. —**bois′ter·ous·ness,** *n.*

bo′la (bō′la) *n.* a So. Amer. missile weapon, comprising two heavy balls connected by a cord.

bold (bōld) *adj.* **1,** daring; brave; courageous. **2,** overstepping usual bounds; forward; impudent. **3,** requiring or exhibiting courage. **4,** standing out to view; conspicuous. **5,** steep; abrupt. —**bold′ness,** *n.*

bold′face″ *n.* a type face with thick lines. —*adj.* **1,** being, or set in, boldface. **2,** [also, **bold′faced″**] bold; impudent.

bole (bōl) *n.* the trunk of a tree.

bo·le′ro (bō-lâr′ō) *n.* [*pl.* -**ros**] **1,** a lively Spanish dance in triple time. **2,** a short close-fitting jacket reaching only to the waist.

bo·li·var′ (bō-lè-vär′) *n.* the monetary unit of Venezuela.

boll (bōl) *n.* a pod or seed vessel of cotton, flax, and other plants. —**boll weevil,** a beetle infesting cotton bolls.

bol′lix (bol′iks) *v.t.* (*Colloq.*) **1,** frustrate; defeat. **2,** baffle. **3,** (often with *up*) mix up; botch.

bo′lo (bō′lō) *n.* a heavy single-edged knife. —**bolo tie,** a string tie with a clasp.

bo·lo′gna (bə-lōn′yə) *n.* a variety of sausage named for Bologna, Italy.

Bol′she·vik (bol′shə-vik) *n.* [*pl.* -**vi″ki** (-vē″kè)] a member of the controlling Communist party in Russia. —**Bol′she·vism,** *n.* the doctrines of this party. —**Bol′she·vist,** *n.*

bol′ster (bōl′stər) *n.* **1,** a long cylindrical pillow. **2,** anything resembling a bolster, used to pad or prop. —*v.t.* prop up; support.

bolt (bōlt) *n.* **1,** a metal pin, usually threaded at one end to receive a nut. **2,** the movable pin or bar of a lock that engages the fixed socket or frame. **3,** an arrow used in a crossbow. **4,** a bundle or roll, as of cloth or wallpaper. **5,** a stream of lightning; thunderbolt. **6,** a sudden spring; the act of running away; desertion of a political party or

candidate. —*v.t. & i.* **1,** fasten with a bolt. **2,** run away from; desert. **3,** swallow (food) hastily. —*adv.* abruptly; stiffly.

bo′lus (bō′ləs) *n.* a large pill or lump of medicine.

bomb (bom) *n.* **1,** an explosive missile, not fired from a gun. **2,** a mass of lava ejected from a volcano. **3,** (*Slang*) an unsuccessful play, etc.; (*Brit. slang*) a smashing success. **4,** (*Slang*) something inferior. —*v.t. & i.* hurl bombs at or on.

bom·bard′ (bom-bärd′) *v.t.* **1,** attack with bombs. **2,** attack with artillery. **3,** assail violently. **4,** attack (a molecule, etc.) with a stream of particles. —*n.* the earliest type of cannon. —**bom″bar·dier′** (bom″bər-dir′) *n.*

bom′bast *n.* high-sounding, extravagant, or stilted words. —**bom·bas′tic,** *adj.* —**bom·bas′ti·cal·ly,** *adv.*

bombe (bâmb) *n.* a layered ice cream dessert.

bomb′er (bom′ər) *n.* an airplane used to drop bombs.

bomb′shell″ *n.* **1,** a bomb. **2,** a sudden and devastating event.

bomb′sight″ *n.* a device for aiming bombs dropped by aircraft.

bo′na-fide″ (bō′nə-fīd″) (*Lat.*) **1,** in good faith; without fraud. **2,** made in good faith; genuine.

bo·nan′za (bō-nan′zə) *n.* **1,** a rich mass of ore. **2,** any lucky find or profitable enterprise.

bon′bon″ *n.* a piece of candy.

bond *n.* **1,** anything that binds, fastens, or confines. **2,** something that unites people; a cause of union. **3,** something that constrains action; an obligation or duty. **4,** a written promise or obligation to pay money, perform a duty, etc.; an insurance agreement. **5,** an interest-bearing certificate of indebtedness of a corporation or government. **6,** a substance for compacting particles into a solid mass. **7,** a close-compacted variety of paper. —*v.t.* **1,** put under bond. **2,** place a bonded debt upon. **3,** form into a compact mass. —*v.i.* hold together; adhere solidly.

bond′age (bon′dij) *n.* **1,** involuntary servitude; slavery. **2,** the state of being under obligation, restraint, or captivity.

bond′man (-mən) *n.* [*pl.* -**men**] a male slave. —**bond′wom″an, bond′maid″,** *n. fem.*

bonds′man (bondz′mən) *n.* [*pl.* -**men**] a surety.

bone (bōn) *n.* **1,** any of the pieces of which the skeleton of a vertebrate is composed. **2,** the hard tissue of which the skeleton is made. **3,** any of various similar hard substances, as ivory. **4,** something made of bone or the like; a domino; a die; a strip of whalebone or metal for stiffening a corset. —*v.t.* **1,** remove the bones from. **2,** put bone or bones into. —*v.i.* (with *up*) (*Slang*) study hard; cram.

bone'black" *n.* a substance made of burnt bones used for coloring and as a filter for coloring matter.

bone-'dry" *adj.* completely dry.

bone'head" *n.* a stupid person.

bon'er (bō'nər) *n.* (*Colloq.*) a foolish mistake; a blunder.

bon'fire" (bon'fīr") *n.* a fire built in the open.

bong *n.* the sound of a bell; any similar sound. —*v.* ring or cause to ring like a bell.

bon'go (bong'gō) *n.* **1,** large African antelope. **2,** a small tuned drum played with the fingers.

bon'i·face" (bon'i-fās") *n.* the keeper of an inn.

bo·ni'to (bə-nē'tō) *n.* an Atlantic food fish like the mackerel.

bon'kers (bong'kərz) *adj.* (*Slang*) crazy.

bon'net (bon'it) *n.* **1,** a covering for the head worn by women and children, usually tied with ribbons under the chin. **2,** protective cover; the hood of an automobile.

bon'ny (bon'ē) *adj.* pretty.

bo'nus (bō'nəs) *n.* a sum of money given over and above what is required to be paid.

bon'y (bō'nē) *adj.* **1,** of, like, or full of bones. **2,** thin. —**bon'i·ness,** *n.*

boo *interj.* expressing contempt or disapproval, or used to frighten. —*v.t.* show contempt for; disapprove. —*v.i.* utter a boo.

boob *n.* (*Slang*) a fool. —**boob tube,** (*Slang*) television.

boo'by (boo'bē) *n.* **1,** [also, **boob**] a stupid person. **2,** the contestant who finishes lowest or last in a game. **3,** any of various gannets. —**booby hatch,** (*Colloq.*) a mental institution. —**booby prize,** an award for the worst performance in a competition. —**booby trap,** a stratagem to deceive the unwary; a hidden explosive or mine.

boo'dle (boo'dəl) *n.* money fraudulently obtained in public service. —*v.t.* obtain money by corruption.

boo'gie·woo'gie (bû'gē-wû'gē) *n.* a form of jazz music.

book (bûk) *n.* **1,** a written or printed composition of considerable length. **2,** a number of sheets of paper bound together. **3,** a similar bundle of tickets, stamps, tobacco leaves, etc. **4,** (*cap.*) the Bible. **5,** a written record; the script of a play; the libretto of an opera. —*v.t. & i.* **1,** enter in a book; record. **2,** engage place for; engage the

services of; schedule. **3,** charge (with a criminal offense).

book'case" *n.* a set of shelves for books.

book'ie (-ē) *n.* (*Slang*) bookmaker.

book'ish (bûk'ish) *adj.* **1,** given to reading. **2,** formal or stilted.

book'keep"ing (bûk'kē"ping) *n.* the theory and practice of keeping records of money transactions.

book'let (-lət) *n.* a book having few pages and often no cover.

book'mak"er *n.* one who accepts bets, esp. on horse races.

book'mo·bile" *n.* a mobile lending library or bookstore.

book'plate" *n.* a label pasted in a book, bearing the owner's name.

book'worm" *n.* **1,** an insect larva that feeds on bookbindings. **2,** a person devoted to books and reading.

Bool'e·an algebra (bool'ē-ən) a system of algebra that proceeds deductively from a set of unproved axioms concerning the use of certain undefined symbols.

boom *n.* **1,** a prolonged hollow sound. **2,** a rapid heightening or increase of interest, activity, popularity, prices, etc. **3,** a spar used to extend the foot of certain kinds of sails. **4,** the movable arm of a derrick. **5,** a barrier set up in water, of logs, chains, etc. —*v.t.* **1,** say or give forth with a prolonged resonant sound. **2,** promote vigorously. —*v.i.* **1,** make a booming sound; swell in magnitude; flourish.

boom'er·ang" (boo'mə-rang") *n.* **1,** a missile weapon of the Australian aborigines, which returns to the thrower if it misses the target. **2,** a scheme or enterprise that recoils with injurious effect.

boon *n.* **1,** a benefit enjoyed; something to be thankful for. **2,** a favor asked. —*adj.* convivial.

boon'docks" (boon'doks") *n.* **1,** the jungle. **2,** (*Slang*) rural regions; the sticks.

boon'dog"gle (boon'dog"əl) *v.i.* (*Slang*) do useless, unproductive work. —*n.* useless, unproductive work.

boor (bûr) *n.* **1,** one who is rude, unmannerly, or clownish. **2,** a rustic. —**boor'ish,** *adj.*

boost *v.t.* **1,** shove upward; lift from below; raise. **2,** aid by speaking well of; promote. —*n.* **1,** an upward shove. **2,** an act of assistance or promotion.

boost'er (-ər) *n.* **1,** a device to increase applied power. **2,** a zealous supporter.

boot *n.* **1,** a foot covering that reaches high above the ankle, usually to the knee. **2,** (*Brit.*) a shoe that covers the ankle. **3,** any of several kinds of protective covering;

a footband for a horse; an apron for the driver's seat of a vehicle. **4,** (*Brit.*) the trunk (of an automobile). **5,** a blow with the foot; a kick. **6,** (*Slang*) dismissal. —*v.t.* **1,** kick. **2,** (*Slang*) dismiss. **3,** (*Colloq.*) bungle. **4,** put boots on. —**boot′er·y,** *n.* —**boot camp,** a military basic training camp. —**to boot,** in addition.

boot′black″ *n.* one who shines shoes.

boot′ee (boo′tē) *n.* **1,** a baby's knitted foot-covering. **2,** a woman's soft overshoe.

booth *n.* **1,** a temporary structure as for the display of wares, for voting, etc. **2,** a small room or compartment, as for projecting motion pictures.

boot′jack″ *n.* a device for pulling off boots.

boot′leg″ *n.* liquor transported or sold illegally. —*v.t. & i.* [**-legged″, -leg′ging**] deal in (liquor or other commodity) unlawfully. —*adj.* made, transported or sold illegally. —**boot′leg″ger,** *n.*

boot′less (boot′ləs) *adj.* of no advantage; useless; futile.

boot′lick″ *v.t.* (*Slang*) toady to; fawn upon.

boo′ty (boo′tē) *n.* **1,** spoil taken from an enemy in war; anything seized by violence. **2,** any prize or gain.

booze (booz) (*Colloq.*) *n.* intoxicating liquor. —*v.i.* drink immoderately. —**booz′y,** *adj.*

bop *n.* a type of jazz music.

bo·rac′ic acid (bə-ras′ik) boric acid.

bo′rax (bôr′aks) *n.* **1,** a white crystalline mineral used as a flux and cleansing agent. **2,** (*Slang*) inferior merchandise.

bor·del′lo (bôr-del′ō) *n.* a brothel. Also, **bor′del** (bôr′dəl).

bor′der (bôr′dər) *n.* **1,** a side or edge; limit or boundary. **2,** a line separating two countries, etc.; the area near such a line; frontier. **3,** something marking a boundary; an ornamental strip; a frame of lines. —*v.t.* **1,** enclose or adorn with a border. **2,** be a boundary to. **3,** lie at the boundary of; adjoin. —*v.i.* touch upon; abut; approach closely.

bore (bôr) *v.t.* **1,** pierce or gouge out with an auger or drill. **2,** penetrate forcibly. **3,** weary or annoy by tedious iteration, dullness, etc. —*v.i.* **1,** make a hole with a rotary cutting instrument. **2,** advance by persistent thrusting. —*n.* **1,** a hole made by or as if by boring. **2,** the internal diameter of a circular hole or a hollow cylinder; the caliber of a gun. **3,** a tiresome or annoying person. **4,** a cause of ennui. **5,** a periodic and forceful flow of tidal water through a narrow channel. —**bore′some,** *adj.*

bo′re·al (bôr′ē-əl) *adj.* **1,** pert. to the north wind. **2,** northern.

bore′dom (-dəm) *n.* state of being bored; ennui.

bor′ic (bôr′ik) *adj.* containing boron. —**boric acid,** a substance obtained from borax, used in solution as a mild antiseptic and eye wash.

born (bôrn) *adj.* **1,** brought forth by birth. **2,** congenital.

borne (bôrn) *v.* p.p. of *bear.* —*adj.* **1,** carried. **2,** endured.

bo′ron (bôr′on) *n.* a chemical element, no. 5, symbol B.

bor′ough (bēr′ō) *n.* **1,** an incorporated municipality smaller than a city. **2,** one of the administrative divisions of a city, as in New York.

bor′row (bor′ō) *v.t.* **1,** obtain temporary possession or use of; take (a thing) on pledge to return it or an equivalent. **2,** take and adopt (words, ideas) from a foreign source. **3,** transfer (units) in arithmetical subtraction. —*v.i.* receive a loan.

borsch (bôrsh) *n.* a beet soup. Also, **borsht** (bôrsht).

bor′zoi (bôr′zoi) *n.* a Russian wolfhound.

bosh *n.* utter nonsense; nothing.

bosk′y (bos′kē) *adj.* overgrown with bushes; shady.

bo′s′n (bō′sən) *n.* boatswain.

bos′om (bûz′əm) *n.* **1,** the human breast. **2,** the enclosure formed by the breast and arms; embrace. **3,** the breast as the supposed seat of tender emotions. **4,** the part of a garment that covers the breast. —*adj.* intimate; familiar. —*v.t.* **1,** embrace; cherish. **2,** conceal.

boss (bâs) *n.* **1,** an overseer of workmen; superintendent; manager. **2,** one who controls a political party. **3,** a rounded protuberance, knob, stud, or enlarged part. —*v.t.* be the boss of; manage; direct. —*v.i.* **1,** be boss. **2,** be domineering. —*adj.* chief; master. —**boss′ism,** *n.* —**boss′y,** *adj.*

bos″sa no′va (bâs″ə-nō′və) *n.* a Brazilian dance.

Boston terrier (bâs′tən) a small short-haired dog, a cross between the bulldog and the bull terrier. Also, **Boston bull.**

bot′a·ny (bot′ə-nē) *n.* **1,** the general science of plant life. **2,** the plants of a region. —**bo·tan′i·cal** (bə-tan′i-kəl) *adj.* —**bot′a·nist** (bot′ə-nist) *n.*

botch (boch) *v.t.* spoil by unskillful work; bungle. —*n.* a poorly-done piece of work. —**botch′y,** *adj.*

both (bōth) *adj. & pron.* the one and the other (of two); the pair or couple together. —*adv. & conj.* including the two; equally; alike.

both′er (both′ər) *v.t. & i.* give trouble to;

annoy; pester; bewilder. —*n*. **1,** someone or something that bothers. **2,** the state of being annoyed or worried. —*interj.* [also (*Colloq.*) **both″er·a′tion**] expressing mild vexation or perplexity. —**both′er·some** (-səm) *adj.* causing trouble; perplexing.

bot′tle (bot′əl) *n.* **1,** a vessel for holding liquids, usually of glass. **2,** the contents or capacity of a bottle. **3,** intoxicating liquor. —*v.t.* **1,** put in a bottle. **2,** (often with *up*) shut in; restrain forcibly. —**bot′tle·neck′**, *n.* a point at which progress is retarded by congestion.

bot′tom (bot′əm) *n.* **1,** the lowest or deepest part of anything; the base, foundation, or root; the under side. **2,** the ground under any body of water. **3,** the hull of a ship; the part of the hull below the wales; a ship generally. **4,** the buttocks. **5,** the fundamental aspect; basic principles. **6,** the lowland along a watercourse. —*adj.* **1,** [also, **bot′tom·most″**] lowest; undermost. **2,** fundamental. —*v.t.* **1,** furnish with a bottom. **2,** use as a base. **3,** get to the bottom of; fathom. —*v.i.* **1,** be based; rest. **2,** run aground. **3,** (with *out*) reach the lowest point. —**bottom line,** (*Colloq.*) the final result, esp. the ultimate cost, of a project, etc.

bot′u·lism (boch′ə-liz-əm) *n.* poisoning due to a toxin produced by certain bacteria in preserved foods.

bou·clé′ (boo-klā′) *adj.* woven with looped yarn to produce a knitted effect.

bou′doir (boo′dwär) *n.* a woman's bedroom or private sitting room.

bouf·fant′ (boo-fän′) *adj.* puffed out; flared.

bou″gain·vil′lae·a (boo″gən-vil′ē-ə) *n.* a tropical woody vine with red or purple flowers.

bough (bow) *n.* a branch of a tree.

bought (bât) *v.* pret. & p.p. of *buy.*

bouil″la·baisse′ (boo″yə-bäs′) *n.* a highly seasoned fish stew.

bouil′lon (bûl′yon) *n.* a clear soup, the liquid from boiling meat, etc.

boul′der (bōl′dər) *n.* a large detached rock.

boul′e·vard″ (bûl′ə-värd″) *n.* a broad street, esp. one shaded by trees or used as a promenade.

bounce (bowns) *v.i.* **1,** spring back like an elastic ball; recoil. **2,** move with a spring or leap. —*v.t.* **1,** cause to spring or rebound. **2,** (*Slang*) eject or dismiss summarily. —*n.* **1,** a rebound; a sudden leap. **2,** elasticity or resilience. **3,** (*Slang*) expulsion or dismissal. **4,** bluster; impudence. —**boun′cer**, *n.* (*Slang*) one employed to eject disorderly patrons. —**boun′cing**, *adj.* vigorous; big.

bound (bownd) *v.i.* **1,** jump; move by leaps. **2,** bounce back; rebound. —*v.t.* **1,** cause to bounce or leap. **2,** be the boundary of; limit. **3,** name the boundaries of. —*n.* **1,** a jump, leap, or rebound. **2,** a limiting line or boundary. **3,** something that binds or restrains. **4,** (*pl.*) territory near a boundary, or enclosed by it. —*adj.* **1,** made fast by a band or bond; tied; fettered. **2,** under obligation or compulsion. **3,** destined; determined; resolved. **4,** traveling (to); destined (for).

bound′a·ry (bown′də-rē) *n.* a bounding line; something that marks a limit.

bound′er (bown′dər) *n.* (*Colloq.*) a vulgar, ill-bred person; an upstart.

boun′te·ous (bown′tē-əs) *adj.* bountiful. —**boun′te·ous·ness**, *n.*

boun′ti·ful (bown′ti-fəl) *adj.* **1,** generous in giving. **2,** plentiful; abundant. —**boun′ti·ful·ness**, *n.*

boun′ty (bown′tē) *n.* **1,** liberality in giving; generosity. **2,** a favor given benevolently. **3,** a premium offered by a government to encourage a certain activity, as the destruction of pests.

bou·quet′ (bō-kā′; boo-) *n.* **1,** a bunch of flowers. **2,** the characteristic aroma of a wine.

Bour′bon (bûr′bən) *n.* **1,** name of a French royal family. **2,** (bẽr′bən) a whiskey made from corn.

bour·geois′ (bûr-zhwä′) *n.* a person of the middle class; a tradesman, or one owning property. —*adj.* middle-class. —**bour″geoi·sie′** (-zē) *n.*

bourne (bûrn) *n.* **1,** boundary; limit. **2,** goal; destination. Also, **bourn.**

bout (bowt) *n.* **1,** a contest between two persons, esp. of physical strength or endurance. **2,** a period of struggle, as against illness. **3,** a turn or round, as of work.

bou·tique′ (boo-tēk′) *n.* a small store, esp. one specializing in fashionable clothing or accessories.

bou″ton·nière′ (boo″tən-yär′) *n.* a flower in the buttonhole.

bo′vine (bō′vīn) *adj.* **1,** of the family that includes the ox; oxlike. **2,** stolid; dull. —*n.* a bovine animal.

bow *v.i.* **1,** bend; curve; stoop. **2,** tend; turn; yield; submit. **3,** bend the body or head in salutation, worship, etc. **4,** make a debut. **5,** (with *out*) resign; retire. —*v.t.* **1,** cause to bend, stoop, or turn. **2,** force to submit; subdue. —*n.* **1,** a bend of the body or head in salutation, etc. **2,** the forward end of a ship.

---

fat, fāte, fär, fāre, fâll, ȧsk; met, hē, hẽr, maybè; pin, pīne; not, nōte, ôr, tool

bow (bō) *n.* **1,** a weapon for shooting arrows, comprising a long elastic stick bent in a curve by a string attached to both ends. **2,** a device in similar form, for playing a musical stringed instrument. **3,** a knot in cord or ribbon having one or more prominent loops. **4,** a bend or curve. **5,** something curved; a rainbow; an ear-piece to hold eyeglasses in place. —*adj.* bent like a bow; curved. —*v.t. & i.* **1,** bend; curve. **2,** use a bow (in playing an instrument).

bowd′ler·ize″ (bowd′lər-īz″) *v.t.* expurgate or paraphrase prudishly.

bow′el (bow′əl) *n.* **1,** the intestine of an animal; (*pl.*) the entire alimentary canal below the stomach. **2,** (*pl.*) the inner parts of anything.

bow′er (bow′ər) *n.* **1,** a shelter made with boughs or vines. **2,** (*Poetic*) a rustic cottage; a boudoir. **3,** a playing-card jack.

bow′ie knife (bō′ē) a daggerlike hunting knife.

bowl (bōl) *n.* **1,** a deep dish or basin; a large drinking-cup. **2,** something bowl-shaped; a rounded hollow in the ground; the container of a spoon or tobacco-pipe. **3,** a stadium for athletic contests, etc. **4,** a ball used in bowls or bowling. —*v.i.* **1,** play at bowls or bowling. **2,** move with rapid easy motion. —*v.t.* **1,** roll or trundle. **2,** (with *over* or *down*) knock down; upset; disconcert. —**bowl′ing,** *n.* a game of knocking down pins with a ball.

bowl′der (bōl′dər) *n.* boulder.

bow′leg″ (bō′leg″) *n.* **1,** an outward curvature of the leg. **2,** a leg so curved. —**bow′leg″ged,** *adj.*

bowl′er (bō′lər) *n.* (*Brit.*) a derby hat.

bowls (bōlz) *n.sing.* an outdoor game of rolling balls toward a goal.

bow′man (bō′mən) *n.* [*pl.* **-men**] a soldier armed with a bow and arrows.

bow′sprit″ (bow′-) *n.* a large, forward spar.

box (boks) *n.* **1,** a container, case, or receptacle, esp. one that is rectangular. **2,** a compartment or cell of a larger enclosure; a space in a theater barred off by curtains or rails. **3,** a small shelter; a countryhouse for temporary use; a booth for sentries, railroad workers, etc. **4,** a housing or casing; a protective part. **5,** a socket, pit, or hollow part. **6,** an area marked out by a border, esp. rectangular; a bordered section of printed matter on a newspaper; a place where the batter stands in baseball. **7,** a blow with the hand. **8,** an evergreen shrub; its wood. —*v.t.* **1,** put in a box. **2,** enclose; confine; house. **3,** strike with the hand, esp. the ear. **4,** engage in a fist-fight or boxing match. —*v.i.* **1,** fight with the fists. **2,** fight cautiously; spar. —**box office, 1,** a ticket booth in a theater. **2,** (*Slang*) receipts from sale of tickets.

box′er (bok′sər) *n.* **1,** one who fights with his fists; a pugilist. **2,** a large smooth-coated dog.

box′ing (bok′sing) *n.* fighting with the fists; pugilism. —**Boxing Day,** the first weekday after Christmas, a holiday in some countries.

boy (boi) *n.* **1,** a male child, esp. before the beginning of youth. **2,** any male person, regarded familiarly or as immature. **3,** a male servant. —**boy′hood″,** *n.* —**boy′ish,** *adj.* like a boy, in manner or appearance.

boy′cott (boi′kot) *v.t.* combine with others to abstain from buying, using, patronizing, etc. (a business, product, etc.), as a means of coercing or intimidating. —*n.* **1,** the act of boycotting. **2,** an instance of boycotting.

boy′sen·ber″ry (boi′zən-ber″ē) *n.* a large fruit like a blackberry.

bra (brä) *n.* brassiere. —**bra′less,** *adj.*

brace (brās) *n.* **1,** something that holds parts together or in place. **2,** something that makes strong, rigid, firm, or steady. **3,** a piece of timber strengthening a framework; a wire band to straighten the teeth; a truss or support for weak body joints; a bitstock for holding bits or drills. **4,** (*pl.*) trouser suspenders. **5,** a symbol [{}] for joining printed lines or musical staves; bracket. **6,** a pair or couple. —*v.t.* **1,** join, fix, or strengthen with a brace. **2,** make steady, firm, or tight; increase the tension of. **3,** stimulate; fortify in resolution. —*v.i.* (with *up*) fortify one's resolution or vigor.

brace′let (brās′lət) *n.* **1,** an ornamental band worn on the arm. **2,** any similar circlet or shackle; a handcuff.

bra·ce′ro (brə-se′rō) *n.* a Mexican laborer admitted to the U.S. for seasonal work.

bra′chi·al (brā′kē-əl) *adj.* **1,** pert. to the arm, foreleg, wing, or other forelimb of a vertebrate. **2,** like an arm.

brack′en (brak′ən) *n.* **1,** a large fern. **2,** a tract overgrown with ferns.

brack′et (brak′it) *n.* **1,** a supporting piece for a shelf; a small shelf on such a piece. **2,** one of a pair of marks ([ ]) used like a parenthesis; a mark ({) grouping several items. **3,** a group of persons of similar condition, esp. taxpayers. —*v.t.* **1,** support by a bracket. **2,** enclose in brackets. **3,** group persons in or as in a bracket. **4,** (of gunfire) straddle.

brack′ish (brak′ish) *adj.* (of water) salty; stale. —**brack′ish·ness,** *n.*

brad *n.* a small, slender nail.

brae (brā) *n.* (*Scot.*) a slope; hillside.

brag v.i. [bragged, brag'ging] boast; swagger. —n. a boast.

brag'ga·do'ci·o" (brag"ə-dō'shē-ō") n. [pl. -os" (-ōz")] 1, vain boasting. 2, a braggart.

brag'gart (brag'ərt) n. a boastful person.

brah'ma (brä'mə) n. a large Asiatic domestic fowl, widely bred in the U.S.

Brah'man (brä'mən) n. [pl. -mans] 1, a member of the priestly and highest caste of Hindus. 2, (Colloq.) a member of an old and prominent family in Boston. Also, **Brah'min. —Brah'man·ism,** n.

braid (brād) v.t. 1, interlace three strands, as of hair; plait. 2, weave, as a rug, by braiding. —n. 1, ornamental tape. 2, a length of braided hair.

Braille (brāl) n. a system of raised printing, read by touch, for the blind.

brain (brān) n. 1, a mass of nerve matter in the skull; the organ of thought, consciousness, and body control. 2, (often pl.) intelligence. —v.t. kill by beating out the brain. **—brain drain,** (Colloq.) the loss of scientists, philosophers, etc., from one country to another. **—brain wave,** (Colloq.) a sudden inspiration.

brain'child" n. a product of the creative imagination.

brain'sick" adj. crazy. **—brain'sick"ness,** n.

brain'storm" n. a sudden aberration or inspiration.

brain trust a group of expert advisers. **—brain'trust"er,** n.

brain'wash"ing n. intense and prolonged indoctrination to change one's beliefs. **—brain'wash",** v.t.

brain'y (brā'nē) adj. intelligent. **—brain'i·ness,** n.

braise (brāz) v.t. of meat, brown and stew slowly.

brake (brāk) n. 1, a device for slowing or stopping a vehicle or machine. 2, fig., a retarding influence. 3, a thicket. —v.t. apply a brake.

brake'man (-mən) n. [pl. -men] an assistant to a railroad conductor.

bram'ble (bram'bəl) n. a thorny shrub. **—bram'bly,** adj.

bran n. the outer coat of wheat or other grains, used as a breakfast cereal and flour.

branch (branch) n. 1, a limb; a bough. 2, an offshoot or subdivision. 3, a stream or small river. 4, a subordinate office. —v.i. put forth branches; diverge. **—branch water,** (Colloq.) tap water.

brand n. 1, a piece of burning wood; an ember. 2, an identifying mark made with a hot iron; the iron implement so used. 3, any identifying mark. 4, an article identified by a brand. 5, quality as indicated by a brand. 6, a mark of infamy; stigma. —v.t. mark with, or as with, a brand; stigmatize. **—brand-'new",** adj. unused.

bran'dish v.t. flourish; wave.

bran'dy (bran'dē) n. an alcoholic liquor distilled from wine, cider, etc. —v.t. flavor with or steep in brandy. **—bran'died** (-dēd) adj.

brash adj. 1, reckless; impetuous. 2, impudent. **—brash'ness,** n.

brass (bras) n. 1, an alloy of copper and zinc. 2, a brass wind instrument; such instruments collectively. 3, (Colloq.) assurance; impudence. 4, (Slang) persons in authority, esp. (Mil.) brass hats. **—brass tacks,** (Colloq.) precise facts or details.

bras'sard (bras'ärd) n. 1, a mourning band on the sleeve. 2, a badge or identifying mark worn on the arm.

bras"se·rie' (bras"ə-rē') n. a restaurant serving beer and food; a tavern.

brass'ie (-ē) n. a brass-soled golf club (No. 2 wood).

bras·siere' (brə-zir') n. a woman's undergarment, a band having cups to support the breasts.

brass'y (-ē) adj. 1, having a metallic sound. 2, (Colloq.) impudent. **—brass'i·ness,** n.

brat n. an unruly or spoiled child.

bra·va'do (brə-vä'dō) n. 1, swaggering defiance; boastful truculence. 2, a bully.

brave (brāv) adj. 1, courageous. 2, splendid; handsome. —n. an American Indian warrior. —v.t. face with courage; defy. **—brave'ness,** n. **—brav'er·y,** n. courage.

bra'vo (brä'vō) interj. Well done! —n. a thug; assassin.

bra·vu'ra (brə-vyûr'ə) n. 1, (Music) a passage requiring great skill or spirit of the performer. 2, daring; bravery.

brawl (brál) n. 1, a noisy quarrel. 2, a wild, noisy party. —v.i. 1, quarrel noisily. 2, carouse.

brawn (brán) n. 1, powerful muscles; muscular strength. 2, flesh of the boar. **—brawn'y,** adj.

bray (brā) n. the harsh cry of an ass, or a sound resembling it. —v.i. make such a sound. —v.t. pound; crush to powder.

braze (brāz) v.t. 1, join with a solder containing brass. 2, make of or cover with brass.

bra'zen (brā'zən) adj. 1, made of brass. 2, giving forth the sound of vibrating brass. 3, impudent; shameless. —v.t. (with out) face with impudence. **—bra'zen·ness,** n.

bra'zier (brā'zhər) n. 1, a worker in brass. 2, a vessel in which coal or charcoal is burned.

bra·zil' (brə-zil') *n.* a red dye from various tropical trees. —**Brazil nut, a** So. Amer. tree; its nut.

breach (brēch) *n.* **1,** a break or separation; a violation, as of a law; a quarrel. **2,** a gap broken in a wall or the like. **3,** an interruption. —*v.t.* make a break in.

bread (bred) *n.* **1,** a food made of flour or meal and generally leavening, baked in loaves. **2,** food in general. —*v.t.* cover with bread crumbs. —**break bread,** dine.

bread'fruit" *n.* a pulpy fruit of a tree found in the So. Seas, baked for food.

bread'stuff" *n.* grain, flour, or meal used to make bread.

breadth (bredth) *n.* **1,** the measure of an object from side to side; width. **2,** liberality; freedom from narrowness. **3,** wide extent; broadness.

bread'win"ner (bred'win"ər) *n.* the principal working member and supporter of a family.

break (brāk) *v.t.* [**broke, bro'ken, break'ing**] **1,** shatter violently; rupture; crack. **2,** interrupt; destroy the continuity of. **3,** destroy the integrity of; change into smaller units, as *break* a dollar bill. **4,** tame; train. **5,** violate, as a law. **6,** be first to tell, as news. **7,** demote, as an officer. **8,** weaken; soften, as a fall. **9,** exceed or surpass, as a record. **10,** (with *into*) (*Law*) enter by force with criminal intent. **11,** render bankrupt or penniless. **12,** (with *down*) separate into component parts; analyze. **13,** (with *off*) discontinue. —*v.i.* **1,** be shattered, ruptured, or cracked. **2,** change gait (of a horse), tone (of a voice), etc. **3,** discharge, as a sore. **4,** begin suddenly, as day. **5,** (with *in*) force one's way. **6,** (with *down*) succumb to illness or emotion. **7,** (with *up*) disband; separate. —*n.* **1,** a breach; a fracture. **2,** an interruption; a gap; a suspension. **3,** a sudden change. **4,** an instrumental solo in a jazz performance. —**break'age,** *n.*

break'down" *n.* **1,** a collapse, as from illness. **2,** an analysis.

break'er *n.* a breaking wave.

break'fast (brek'fəst) *n.* the first meal of the day.

break'front" *n.* a large, high cabinet with recessed center or sides.

break'neck" (brāk'nek") *adj.* dangerously fast.

break'through" *n.* **1,** a penetration, as by military forces. **2,** an important development or discovery.

break-up' *n.* disintegration; ruin.

break'wa"ter (brāk'wâ"tər) *n.* a sea wall to protect a harbor, swimming area, etc.

bream (brēm) *n.* [*pl.* **bream**] any of several American food fishes.

breast (brest) *n.* **1,** the front of the upper body, enclosing the lungs; the chest. **2,** a mammary gland or the flesh covering it. **3,** the chest regarded as the seat of human emotion. —*v.t.* **1,** push against with the breast. **2,** face courageously.

breast'pin" *n.* a brooch.

breast'work" *n.* a protective wall, as of earth.

breath (breth) *n.* **1,** the air inhaled or exhaled in a respiration. **2,** a respiration. **3,** a light breeze. **4,** ability to breathe. **5,** a faint scent. **6,** a trifle; a trivial speech. —**breath'y,** *adj.*

breathe (brēth) *v.i.* **1,** draw air into and expel it from the lungs; live. **2,** pause; rest. —*v.t.* **1,** inhale and exhale. **2,** speak softly; whisper. **3,** allow to rest. —**breath'er** (brē'thər) *n.* a short rest.

breath'less (breth'ləs) *adj.* **1,** panting. **2,** in suspense; thrilled; astounded. —**breath'less·ness,** *n.*

breath'tak"ing (breth'tā"king) *adj.* rendering one breathless, as from astonishment, fright, etc.

breech (brēch) *n.* the rear part of anything, esp. a gun; the buttocks.

breech'cloth" *n.* a garment wrapped around the buttocks.

breech'es (brich'iz) *n.* **1,** short pants, reaching from waist to knee. **2,** (*Colloq.*) trousers.

breeches buoy (brich'iz) a lifesaving apparatus for transporting a person to safety, as from a sinking ship.

breed (brēd) *v.t.* [*pret.* & *p.p.* **bred**] **1,** beget; produce offspring. **2,** cause to produce offspring; mate. **3,** bring up; rear. —*v.i.* beget; produce; be produced. —*n.* a distinctive race or kind. —**breeder reactor,** a nuclear reactor in which fissionable material is produced.

breed'ing *n.* **1,** genetic strain or background. **2,** gentility.

breeze (brēz) *n.* a light wind. —*v.i.* **1,** blow lightly. **2,** (*Colloq.*) travel fast without great effort.

breeze'way" *n.* a covered passageway, usu. connecting two buildings.

breez'y (brē'zè) *adj.* **1,** mildly windy. **2,** fresh; airy; (*Colloq.*) pert. —**breez'i·ness,** *n.*

breth'ren (breth'rin) *n.pl.* **1,** brothers. **2,** associates.

breve (brēv) *n.* **1,** (*Music*) a double whole note (see *note*). **2,** (*Print.*) a diacritical mark (˘).

bre·vet' (brə-vet') *n.* formerly, a temporary commission of high military rank. —*v.t.* [**bre·vet'ted, -vet'ting**] promote by brevet.

bre'vi·ar·y (brē'vē-er-ē) n. a book of daily prayers.

brev'i·ty (brev'ə-tē) n. shortness; terseness.

brew (broo) v.t. **1,** produce by fermenting grains, as ale. **2,** steep, as tea. —n. the beverage so produced.

brew'er (-ər) n. a maker of beer. —**brew'er·y** (brŭr'ē) n. a place where beer or ale is brewed. —**brew'mas"ter,** n. chief brewer.

bri'ar (brī'ər) n. brier.

bri·ard' (brē-ärd') n. a breed of French working dog.

bribe (brīb) n. a gift or promise given unethically in return for a favor. —v.t. make or offer a bribe. —**brib'er·y** (brī'bə-rē) n.

bric-'a·brac" (brik'ə-brak") n. unusual small objects of art; knick-knacks.

brick (brik) n. **1,** a rectangular block of molded and baked, or dried, clay. **2,** any solid resembling a brick. **3,** (Colloq.) a good fellow. —adj. made of brick. —v.t. (often with up) build with bricks. —**brick'lay"er,** n. one who builds with brick.

brick'bat" n. **1,** a brick or piece of a brick. **2,** an insulting remark. —v.t. [-**bat'-ted, -bat'ting**] throw a brickbat at.

brid"al (brī'dəl) adj. pert. to a bride, her wedding, attendants, etc.

bride (brīd) n. a woman at, or immediately before or after, her wedding.

bride'groom" n. a man at, or immediately before or after, his wedding.

brides'maid" (brīdz'-) n. a bride's attendant, usu. unmarried.

bridge (brij) n. **1,** a pathway spanning a stream, valley, or road; anything that spans a gap. **2,** the bony structure of the nose. **3,** a raised platform on a ship. **4,** a device for raising the strings of a stringed instrument from the sounding board. **5,** a device for measuring electrical resistance. **6,** a card game. **7,** a device for holding false teeth in place. —v.t. build a bridge across; cross; span. —**bridge'head",** n. a position held on the enemy's shore of a river.

bri'dle (brī'dəl) n. **1,** the head part of a harness for a horse, etc. **2,** a restraint. —v.t. restrain; check. —v.i. toss the head, in contempt, deprecation, etc. —**bridle path,** a road reserved for horseback riders.

Brie (brē) n. a soft white cheese.

brief (brēf) adj. short; terse; succinct. —n. a concise summary. —v.t. **1,** condense. **2,** give brief instructions to. —**brief'ness,** n.

brief'case" n. a leather bag for carrying documents; portfolio.

bri'er (brī'ər) n. **1,** a thorny shrub. **2,** a root used for making pipes for smoking.

brig n. **1,** a square-rigged sailing ship. **2,** a ship's jail.

bri·gade' (bri-gād') n. **1,** a military unit, two or more regiments. **2,** an organized body of persons.

brig"a·dier' (brig"ə-dir') n. [in the U.S. Army, **brigadier general**] an officer ranking next above colonel.

brig'and (brig'ənd) n. a robber; highwayman.

brig'an·tine (brig'an-tēn; -tīn) n. a type of two-masted sailing vessel.

bright (brīt) adj. **1,** having the quality of reflecting light; shining; glowing; clear. **2,** sunny; fair. **3,** clever; mentally alert. **4,** vivacious; happy. —**bright'en** (-ən) v.t. & i. make or become bright. —**bright'ness,** n.

bril'liance (bril'yəns) n. **1,** sparkling appearance; luster; magnificence. **2,** outstanding mental superiority; vivacity.

bril'liant (bril'yənt) adj. **1,** lustrous; glittering; sparkling. **2,** marked by high intelligence, ability, or achievement. —n. a many-faceted gem.

bril'lian·tine" (bril'yən-tēn") n. **1,** an oily preparation for the hair. **2,** a glossy dress fabric.

brim n. the edge; a projecting rim. —**brim'ful",** adj. as full as can be.

brim'stone" (brim'stōn") n. sulphur. —adj. greenish yellow.

brin'dled (brin'dəld) adj. gray or brownish streaked with darker colors.

brine (brīn) n. **1,** a strong solution of salt in water. **2,** the sea. —**brin'y,** adj.

bring v.t. [pret. & p.p. **brought** (brât)] **1,** carry or conduct to where the speaker is (so distinguished from take); fetch. **2,** produce; yield. **3,** (often with around) induce; persuade. **4,** command as a price. **5,** (with up) rear, as a child.

brink n. an edge, as of a cliff or the like; verge.

brink'man·ship" n. the policy or practice of pursuing a dangerous course of action almost to the limit.

bri·oche' (brē-osh') n. [pl. -**oches'** (-osh')] a sweet roll or bun.

bri·quette' (bri-ket') n. a compacted block of loose material, esp. of coal dust used for fuel.

brisk adj. **1,** lively; quick; swift; vivacious. **2,** sharp; stimulating. —**brisk'ness,** n.

bris'ket n. a cut of meat from the breast.

bris'ling (bris'ling) n. a small herring; a size or grade of sardine.

bris'tle (bris'əl) n. a stiff hair. —v.i. stand erect, as fur on a frightened cat; evince resentment. —**bris'tly,** adj.

bris'tling (bris'ling) *adj.* **1**, stubbly; prickly. **2**, resentful.

Bristol board a fine pasteboard used in drawing and printing.

britch'es (brich'əz) *n.* breeches.

Brit'ish *adj.* pert. to Great Britain, its people, customs, etc. —**Brit'ish·er**, *n.*

British thermal unit a unit of heat, the quantity required to raise 1 lb. of water 1° F. Also, **BTU.**

Brit'on (brit'ən) *n.* a native of Great Britain.

brit'tle (brit'əl) *adj.* **1**, fragile; easily snapped apart; crisp. **2**, highstrung; lacking strength. —*n.* a hard, brittle candy. —**brit'tle·ness**, *n.*

broach (brōch) *n.* **1**, a tool for piercing. **2**, a brooch. —*v.t.* **1**, pierce; open. **2**, introduce, as a subject.

broad (brâd) *adj.* **1**, wide. **2**, of great extent; widespread. **3**, liberal; inclusive. **4**, indelicate; plainspoken. **5**, pronounced openly and sustained, as the *broad a* in *father.* —*n.* (*Vulgar*) a woman. —**broad'en**, *v.t. & i.* —**broad jump**, an athletic contest.

broad'cast" (brâd'kåst") *adj.* widely published, disseminated, or scattered. —*n.* a widely disseminated radio program. —*v.t. & i.* [*pret. & p.p.* **-cast"** or **-cast"ed**] publish or spread widely.

broad'cloth" (brâd'klâth") *n.* **1**, a fine, smooth-finish woolen cloth. **2**, a cotton material with a silky luster.

broad'loom" *n.* carpeting fabric woven on a wide loom.

broad'mind"ed *adj.* free from prejudice or bigotry; liberal.

broad'side" (brâd'sīd") *n.* **1**, the side of a ship above the water line. **2**, a simultaneous discharge of all guns on one side of a warship; fig., any concerted attack. **3**, a large printed sheet.

broad'sword" *n.* a sword with a broad blade.

bro·cade' (brō-kād') *n.* a rich silken fabric with a raised pattern.

broc'co·li (brok'ə-lė) *n.* a vegetable with edible stalks and flower heads.

bro·chette' (brō-shet') *n.* a small spit or skewer.

bro·chure' (brō-shûr') *n.* a pamphlet.

bro'gan (brō'gən) *n.* a heavy leather boot.

brogue (brōg) *n.* **1**, a dialectal pronunciation of English, esp. that of the Irish. **2**, a low shoe.

broil *v.t. & i.* **1**, cook by direct exposure to an open fire, as on a grill. **2**, subject to great heat. **3**, fret; stew. —*n.* a portion of meat, esp. mixed meats, cooked by broiling.

broil'er (-ər) *n.* **1**, a pan, oven, or stove holding a grill for broiling. **2**, a young fowl to be broiled.

broke (brōk) *v.* pret. of *break.* —*adj.* (*Slang*) without money; penniless.

bro'ken (brō'kən) *adj.* **1**, rough or hilly, as terrain. **2**, shattered; cracked; not in repair. **3**, imperfectly spoken, as a language. **4**, infirm; in poor health. **5**, violated, as a vow. **6**, tamed to obedience; crushed in spirit. —*v.* p.p. of *break.* —**broken home**, a family of which the parents have separated or divorced.

bro"ken-down' *adj.* in bad repair; not operating; decrepit.

bro'ken-heart'ed (brō'kən-här'tid) *adj.* disappointed to the point of despair.

bro'ker (brō'kər) *n.* an agent who buys or sells insurance or property, esp. stocks and bonds on commission.

bro'ker·age (-ij) *n.* **1**, a broker's business or office. **2**, a commission paid to a broker.

bro'mide (brō'mīd) *n.* **1**, a compound of bromine, used as a sedative. **2**, (*Colloq.*) a trite remark. —**bro·mid'ic** (brō-mid'ik) *adj.*

bro'mine (brō'mēn) *n.* a reddish-brown chemical element, no. 35, symbol Br.

bron'chi (brong'kī) *n. pl.* [*sing.* **-chus** (-kəs)] the two main branches of the windpipe. —**bron'chi·al** (brong'kė-əl) *adj.*

bron·chi'tis (brong-kī'təs) *n.* inflammation in the bronchial tubes.

bron'cho·scope" (brong'kə-skōp") *n.* a tubular instrument that can penetrate to the bronchi or lungs, for inspection or treatment.

bron'co (brong'kō) *n.* in the western U.S., a small wild or unbroken horse. Also, **bron'cho.**

bron"to·sau'rus (bron"tə-sôr'əs) *n.* a prehistoric gigantic reptile of the dinosaur group.

bronze (bronz) *n.* **1**, an alloy of copper and tin. **2**, the color brown with tinges of red and yellow. —*v.t. & i.* make or become this color, esp. (of persons) by suntanning. —*adj.* of this color. —**Bronze Age**, a period when bronze implements were first used, about 3,500 B.C.

brooch (brōch) *n.* an ornamental pin.

brood *n.* the young hatched in one nest or of one mother. —*v.t. & i.* **1**, sit (on eggs). **2**, ponder moodily. —**brood'er**, *n.* **1**, a heated device for raising baby chicks. **2**, a moody person. —**brood'y**, *adj.* preoccupied.

brook (brûk) *n.* a small stream. —*v.t.* bear; put up with.

broom *n.* **1**, a brush for sweeping. **2**, a

shrub of the pea family. —**broom'stick**", *n.* the handle of a broom.

broth (brâth) *n.* a thin soup.

broth'el (broth'əl) *n.* a house where lovemaking (often illicit) is afforded.

broth'er (bruth'ər) *n.* **1,** a male relative having the same parents as another. **2,** a fellow man. **3,** a member of a religious order, club, society, etc. **4,** a fellow black.

broth'er·hood" (bruth'ər-hûd") *n.* **1,** fellowship. **2,** a fraternity of men; its members collectively.

broth'er-in-law" *n.* [*pl.* **broth'ers-**] **1,** the brother of one's spouse. **2,** the husband of one's sister.

broth'er·ly (-lè) *adj.* sympathetic; kind; befitting a brother. —**broth'er·li·ness,** *n.*

brough'am (broo'əm) *n.* **1,** a carriage with a straight front. **2,** a similar body for a chauffeur-driven automobile.

brought (brât) *v.* pret. & p.p. of *bring.*

brou'ha·ha (broo'hä-hä) *n.* hubbub; uproar; hullabaloo.

brow *n.* **1,** the forehead. **2,** the edge of the top of a cliff or hill.

brow'beat" (brow'bēt") *v.t.* bully; intimidate.

brown *n.* a shade between orange and black. —*adj.* of this color. —*v.t. & i.* make or become brown. —**brown betty,** a baked fruit pudding. —**brown shirt,** a Nazi. —**brown study,** a reverie.

brown'ie (brow'nè) *n.* **1,** a good-natured elf supposed to do chores at night. **2,** a kind of cookie. **3,** (*cap.*) a junior Girl Scout.

brown'out" *n.* a partial blackout, to save electricity or to protect against air raids.

brown'stone" *n.* a reddish-brown sandstone; a house built with it.

browse (browz) *n.* twigs, tender shoots, etc., as food for animals. —*v.i.* **1,** feed on or crop twigs, leaves, etc. **2,** read idly here and there, as in a book or library.

bru'in (broo'in) *n.* a bear, from a name given a bear in fairy tales.

bruise (brooz) *n.* an injury caused by a blow that discolors but does not break the skin. —*v.t.* inflict such an injury upon. —**bruis'er,** *n.* a fight; a powerful-looking man.

bruit (broot) *v.t.* make known publicly, as by rumor.

brum'ma·gem (brum'ə-jəm) *adj.* cheap; spurious.

brunch *n.* (*Colloq.*) breakfast eaten at or near lunch time.

bru·nette' (broo-net') *adj.* (*fem.*) having dark eyes and hair. —*n.* a brunette person. Also, **bru·net'.**

brunt *n.* the main force of an attack or shock; the principal burden.

brush *n.* **1,** a thicket; scrub. **2,** lopped-off branches of trees. **3,** an implement with hair bristles, wire, etc., attached to a handle or back, for painting, scrubbing, etc. **4,** a bushy tail. **5,** a light touch; a graze. **6,** a minor conflict; a skirmish. —*v.t.* **1,** sweep, rub, clean, etc. with a brush. **2,** remove with or as with a brush. **3,** touch lightly in passing. **4,** (with *off*) dismiss brusquely. —*v.i.* **1,** (with *by*) sweep past. **2,** (with *up*) practice; refresh one's memory. —**brush'off**", *n.* a brusque refusal or dismissal.

brusque (brusk) *adj.* abrupt; curt. —**brusque"ness,** *n.*

Brus'sels sprout (brus'əlz) a vegetable whose edible buds resemble miniature cabbage heads.

brut (broot; *Fr.* brü) *adj.* of wine, very dry.

bru'tal (broo'təl) *adj.* cruel. —**bru·tal'i·ty** (-tal'ə-té) *n.*

bru'tal·ize" (broo'tə-līz") *v.t. & i.* **1,** make or become brutal. **2,** to treat brutally. —**bru"tal·i·za'tion,** *n.*

brute (broot) *n.* **1,** a beast. **2,** a savage, cruel person. —*adj.* like a beast; not sensitive or reasoning.

brut'ish (broo'tish) *adj.* like an animal; stupid; savage. —**brut'ish·ness,** *n.*

bry'o·ny (brī'ə-nè) *n.* a vine of the gourd family.

bub'ble (bub'əl) *n.* **1,** a thin film of liquid holding gas or air. **2,** a small bead of gas or air in a liquid. **3,** an unsound project or idea. —*v.i.* give forth bubbles; boil; effervesce; be aerated, esp. with a gurgling sound, as a brook. —**bubble gum,** chewing gum that stretches to a strong film.

bub'ble·top" *adj.* of a car, having a transparent plastic covering (usu. bulletproof).

bu'bo (bū'bō) *n.* an inflammatory swelling of a lymph gland, esp. in the groin. —**bu·bon'ic** (-bon'ik), *adj.* —**bubonic plague,** a deadly, epidemic disease, marked by inflammation of the lymphatic glands.

buc"ca·neer' (buk"ə-nir') *n.* a pirate.

buck (buk) *n.* **1,** the male of various animals. **2,** a fop. **3,** (*Slang*) a dollar. **4,** a sawhorse. —*v.i.* **1,** make a sudden, twisting leap, said of a horse. **2,** (*Colloq.*) demur; suddenly object. —*v.t.* **1,** throw off by bucking. **2,** (*Colloq.*) go against. **3,** in Amer. football, charge into (the opponents' line). —**pass the buck,** (*Slang*) shift the responsibility to another.

buck'a·roo" (buk'ə-roo") *n.* a cowboy.

buck'board" (buk'bôrd") *n.* a light horse-drawn wagon.

buck'et (buk'it) n. **1,** a vessel for carrying water or other fluids, usually in the shape of an inverted truncated cone; a pail. **2,** a scoop, as on a dredge. —**bucket seat,** a seat with a rounded back, for one person. —**bucket shop,** a fraudulent stockbroker's office. —**kick the bucket** (Slang) die.

buck'eye'' (buk'ī'') n. **1,** a tree or its inedible nutlike seed. **2,** (cap.) a native of Ohio.

buck fever a beginner's fear.

buck'le (buk'əl) n. **1,** a clasp for joining loose ends, as of a belt or strap. **2,** a bend or kink in metal. —v.t. **1,** fasten with a buckle. **2,** crumple; bend. —v.i. **1,** (often with down) apply oneself with vigor. **2,** crumple; warp.

buck'ler (buk'lər) n. a round shield carried on the arm.

buck'ram (buk'rəm) n. a coarse, stiffened fabric, used in bookbinding, millinery, etc.

buck'saw'' (buk'sâ'') n. a saw blade set in a large quadrangular frame.

buck'shot'' n. a large size of shot used in hunting.

buck'skin'' (buk'skin'') n. **1,** leather made of deer or sheep skin. **2,** (pl.) garments made of buckskin.

buck'thorn'' (buk'thôrn'') n. any of various shrubs and trees with prickly branches.

buck'tooth'' (buk'tooth'') n. a tooth that sticks out. —**buck'toothed''**, adj.

buck'wheat'' (buk'hwēt'') n. a cereal plant whose seeds are ground into flour; this flour.

bu·col'ic (bū-kol'ik) adj. pastoral; rustic. —n. a poem dealing with simple country life. —**bu·col'i·cal·ly,** adv.

bud n. **1,** an undeveloped swelling on a plant that may open into a leaf or flower. **2,** a person or thing in an early stage of development. **3,** a debutante. —v.i. [**bud'ded, -ding**] sprout.

Bud'dha (bŭd'ə) n. **1,** the title of saint, in Buddhism. **2,** a conventionalized statue of Gautama Buddha, founder of Buddhism.

Bud'dhism (bŭd'iz-əm) n. an Asiatic religion that teaches self-denial. —**Bud'dhist** (-ist) n. & adj.

bud'dy (bud'ē) n. (Colloq.) a friend; pal.

budge (buj) v.t. & i. move; stir.

budg'er·i·gar'' (buj'ə-rē-gar'') n. a parakeet. Also, **budg'ie** (ē).

budg'et (buj'it) n. an estimate of future financial income and outgo. —v.t. plan (expenditures) by making a budget. —**budg'et·ar·y** (-er-ē) adj.

buff (buf) n. **1,** a dull-yellow leather; a military coat made of it. **2,** a dull-yellowish color. —v.t. polish by vigorous rubbing with a soft substance.

buf'fa·lo'' (buf'ə-lō'') n. a kind of wild ox, esp. the Amer. bison. —v.t. (Slang) **1,** baffle; hoodwink. **2,** overawe; intimidate.

buff'er (buf'ər) n. **1,** a polisher. **2,** anything that serves to deaden the shock of striking forces. —**buffer state,** a small neutral nation situated between larger, potentially hostile nations. —**buffer zone,** a demilitarized area between hostile forces.

buf'fet (buf'it) n. a slap; any blow. —v.t. **1,** beat. **2,** contend against.

buf·fet' (bə-fā') n. **1,** a sideboard; a public refreshment counter. **2,** food set out for guests to help themselves. —adj. served informally.

buf'fo (bûf'ō) n. [pl. **-fi** (-fē)] a male singer of comic operatic roles.

buf·foon' (bə-foon') n. a clownish jester. —**buf·foon'er·y** (-ə-rē) n. the pranks or behavior of a buffoon.

bug n. **1,** one of an order of insects that suck vital fluids. **2,** (Colloq.) any crawling insect. **3,** (Slang) a disease germ. **4,** (Slang) a fanatic; a zealot. **5,** (Slang) a small microphone for secretly recording conversations. **6,** (Slang) defect. —v.t. **1,** (Slang) install a microphone in (a room, etc.) for secretly recording conversations. **2,** (Colloq.) bother; annoy.

bug'a·boo'' (bug'ə-boo'') n. a fancied object of terror. Also, **bug'bear''.**

bug'eye'' n. **1,** a staring or protruding eye. **2,** a small sailboat. —**bug'eyed''**, adj.

bug'gy (bug'ē) n. a single-seated, horse-drawn vehicle for two persons, open but with a folding top.

bug'house'' n. (Slang) an insane asylum.

bu'gle (bū'gəl) n. a trumpetlike brass wind instrument. —v.i. **1,** blow a bugle. **2,** of the elk, utter a cry. —**bu'gler,** n.

build (bild) v.t. [pret. & p.p. **built** (bilt)] **1,** construct; fashion; erect. **2,** found. **3,** increase and strengthen. **4,** (with in) install. —v.i. construct something, esp. a house. —n. bodily figure or shape; form; make or brand of manufacture. —**build'ing,** n. any architectural structure, as a house.

bulb n. **1,** the rounded underground stem of certain plants, as the lily, onion, etc. **2,** anything shaped like a bulb, as the lamp of an electric light. —**bulb'ous,** adj.

bulge (bulj) n. an outward swelling; a rounded protuberance. —v.t. & i. swell outward.

bulk n. **1,** extent or volume, as of massed substance. **2,** an aggregate; a large quantity. **3,** the major part. **4,** massed food fiber that promotes intestinal activity. —v.i. loom large. —**bulk'y,** adj.

bulk'head'' (bulk'hed'') n. a wall or compartment protruding from a main body, as to protect it.

bull (bûl) *n*. **1,** the male of any animal of the ox family, and of various other large animals. **2,** one who tries to raise the price of stocks. **3,** a papal edict. **4,** a ludicrous blunder in language. **5,** (*Slang*) pompous talk; buncombe.

bull'dog" (bûl'dâg") *n*. a powerful, short-haired dog. —*adj*. tenacious; stubborn. —*v.t. & i*. in western U. S., throw (a calf steer) by twisting its neck. —**bulldog edition,** the earliest edition of a morning newspaper.

bull'doze" (bûl'dōz") *v.t.* coerce; bully; frighten. —**bull'doz"er,** *n.* a tractor-driven pushing blade for clearing land, building roads, etc.

bul'let (bûl'ət) *n.* a small missile to be fired from a firearm.

bul'le·tin (bûl'ə-tən) *n.* **1,** a short, official news report. **2,** a periodical journal, as of an organization.

bull'fight" *n.* a combat between a man and a bull, held in an arena for spectators' amusement.

bull'finch" (bûl'finch") *n.* any of various finches.

bull'frog" (bûl'frog") *n.* an Amer. frog with a bellowing croak.

bull'head"ed (bûl'hed"id) *adj.* obstinate. —**bull'head"ed·ness,** *n.*

bull'horn" *n.* a loudspeaker.

bul'lion (bûl'yən) *n.* uncoined gold or silver.

bull market a rising trend in stock prices.

bull'ock (bûl'ək) *n.* an ox; steer.

bull'pen" *n.* a place where relief pitchers warm up.

bull's-'eye" (bûlz'ī") *n.* **1,** a thick disk of glass in a deck, roof, etc. **2,** a convex lens for concentrating rays of light. **3,** the center of a target; a shot that reaches it.

bul'ly (bûl'ē) *n.* a tormentor of those smaller or weaker. —*v.t.* hector with threats and bluster. —*adj. & interj.* (*Colloq.*) fine; first-rate.

bul'rush" (bûl'rush") *n.* **1,** any of various rushes or reedy plants. **2,** (*Bib.*) the papyrus plant.

bul'wark (bûl'wərk) *n.* **1,** a wall for defense; rampart. **2,** any means of protection.

bum (*Slang*) *v.i.* [**bummed, bum'ming**] loaf; beg. —*v.t.* get by sponging or begging. —*n.* a worthless fellow; a beggar. —*adj.* worthless.

bum'ble·bee" (bum'bəl-bē") *n.* a large, hairy, humming bee.

bum'bling *adj.* clumsy; ineffectual.

bum'mer (bum'ər) *n.* (*Slang*) something bad or unpleasant; a bad drug trip.

bump *n.* **1,** a thump; collision. **2,** a swelling caused by a blow; any rounded elevation or protuberance. —*v.t.* strike together or against. —*v.i.* **1,** collide heavily. **2,** jolt along. —**bump'y,** *adj.* —**bump off** (*Slang*) kill; murder.

bump'er (bum'pər) *n.* **1,** a device, as a protective bar or pad, to deaden the shock of a collision. **2,** a glass filled to the top. —*adj.* (*Colloq.*) very large.

bump'kin *n.* an awkward fellow.

bump'tious (bump'shəs) *adj.* (*Colloq.*) ebullient; brash.

bun *n.* **1,** a sweetened biscuit. **2,** a wad of coiled hair as part of a hairdress.

bu'na (boo'nə) *n.* a synthetic rubber.

bunch *n.* a cluster of things of the same kind growing, grouped, or fastened together. —*v.t. & i.* make into or form a bunch.

bun'co (bung'ko) *n.* (*Colloq.*) a swindle; confidence game.

bun'combe (bung'kəm) *n.* (*Colloq.*) humbug; nonsense. Also, **bunk'um.**

bun'dle (bun'dəl) *n.* **1,** articles packed together; a pack; a package. **2,** (*Colloq.*) a large quantity. —*v.t.* **1,** tie in a package. **2,** (with *off*) dispose of hurriedly. —*v.i.* **1,** (often with *off*) depart hurriedly. **2,** lie in the same bed without undressing.

bung *n.* a stopper for the hole in a cask; the hole itself: *bunghole.*

bun'ga·low" (bung'gə-lō") *n.* a one-story house. —**bun'ga·loid",** *adj.*

bun'gle (bung'gəl) *v.t. & i.* perform clumsily. —**bung'ler,** *n.*

bun'ion (bun'yən) *n.* a chronic enlargement of the first joint of the big toe.

bunk *n.* **1,** a frame built against a wall for use as a bed. **2,** buncombe. —*v.i.* (with *together*) share the same bed.

bunk'er (bung'kər) *n.* **1,** a bin for storage, esp. a ship's coal bin. **2,** in golf, a sand pit.

bun'ny (bun'ē) *n.* a rabbit.

Bun'sen burner (bun'sən) a burner producing a single jet of hot flame produced by mixture of gas with air.

bunt *v.t. & i.* **1,** butt. **2,** in baseball, tap (the ball) without swinging the bat. —*n.* a hit so made.

bun'ting *n.* **1,** a light fabric, esp. used for flags, streamers, etc. **2,** a small songbird. **3,** an infant's outer garment.

buoy (boi) *n.* **1,** an anchored float to guide navigation. **2,** a life-saving device. —*v.t.* (often with *up*) keep from sinking; hence, sustain morally; encourage.

---

buoy'an·cy (boi'ən-sè) n. **1,** ability to float. **2,** lightheartedness. —**buoy'ant,** adj.

bur (bėr) n. any rough, prickly seed covering. Also, **burr.**

bur'ble (bėr'bəl) n. **1,** a bubbling noise. **2,** excited or confused speech. —v.i. **1,** bubble; gush. **2,** make a burbling noise.

bur'den (bėr'dən) n. **1,** something carried; a load. **2,** something borne with difficulty, as care, grief, etc. **3,** an encumbrance. **4,** a main theme; a refrain. —v.t. **1,** load. **2,** encumber; tax. Also, **bur'then** (bėr'thən). —**bur'den·some,** adj.

bur'dock (bėr'dok) n. a common burbearing weed.

bu'reau (byûr'ō) n. **1,** a chest of drawers; a dresser. **2,** an executive branch or office of a government or business.

bu·reauc'ra·cy (byû-rok'rə-sè) n. control or great influence in government by minor officials.

bu'reau·crat'' (byûr'ə-krat'') n. a jobholder in a bureaucracy. —**bu''reau·crat'ic,** adj. —**bu''reau·crat'i·cal·ly,** adv.

bu·rette' (byû-ret') n. a graduated measuring tube with a stopcock. Also, **bu·ret'.**

burg (bėrg) n. (Colloq.) a town.

bur'geon (bėr'jən) v.i. sprout buds.

-burg'er (bėr'gər) suf. patty of ground meat, usu. served on a round bun.

bur'gess (bėr'jis) n. **1,** a municipal official or councilman. **2,** a full voting citizen.

burgh (bėrg) n. town; borough. —**burgh'-er,** n.

bur'glar (bėr'glər) n. one who breaks into a house with intent to rob. —**bur'glar·ize''** (-īz'') [also, colloq., **bur'gle** (-gəl)] v.t. break into and rob. —**bur'gla·ry,** n.

bur'go·mas''ter (bėr'gə-mås''tər) n. a mayor, in Ger. and Dutch towns.

Bur'gun·dy (bėr'gən-dè) n. any of various wines from the Burgundy region of France.

bur'i·al (ber'è-əl) n. interment; the act of burying or state of being buried.

bu'rin (byûr'in) n. an engraving tool for cutting furrows in metal.

bur'lap (bėr'lap) n. a coarse fabric of hemp or jute, used for bags, etc.

bur·lesque' (bėr-lesk') n. **1,** an imitation of a literary or dramatic work for comic effect; a parody. **2,** a theatrical entertainment characterized by coarse comedy. —v.t. caricature; parody.

bur'ly (bėr'lè) adj. stout; brawny. —**bur'li·ness,** n.

burn (bėrn) v.t. [**burned** or **burnt, burn'-ing**] **1,** destroy by fire. **2,** scorch; injure by heat or radiation. **3,** produce by fire. **4,** consume as fuel. **5,** inflame. —v.i. **1,** be on fire. **2,** become charred or scorched. **3,** suffer from too much heat or radiation. **4,** become inflamed, as with emotion. **5,** (Slang) be electrocuted. —n. **1,** an injury caused by fire, heat, or radiation. **2,** the firing of an engine.

bur'nish (bėr'nish) v.t. make bright by polishing, esp. metal.

bur·noose' (bėr-noos') n. a hooded cloak worn by Arabs.

burp (bėrp) (Colloq.) n. a belch. —v.i. belch. —v.t. hold (a baby) so it will belch gas from the stomach. —**burp gun,** an automatic pistol.

burr (bėr) n. **1,** a roughness left by a tool in cutting metal, wood, etc. **2,** a bur. **3,** a guttural pronunciation of the letter r. **4,** a dentist's drill. —v.t. **1,** make rough or jagged. **2,** pronounce with a burr.

bur'ro (bėr'ō) n. [pl. **-ros**] a small donkey.

bur'row (bėr'ō) n. a hole dug in the ground by an animal. —v.i. dig into the ground.

bur'sa (bėr'sə) n. a sac between body joints.

bur'sar (bėr'sər) n. a treasurer.

bur'sa·ry (bėr'sə-rè) n. **1,** a treasury. **2,** a scholarship.

bur·si'tis (bėr-sī'tis) n. inflammation of the bursa.

burst (bėrst) v.i. [**burst, burst'ing**] **1,** break from internal pressure; explode. **2,** break or give way. **3,** (with a prep.) display (sudden emotion). **4,** appear or go suddenly. —v.t. rupture. —n. **1,** an outburst. **2,** an explosion. **3,** a rush; a spurt.

bur'y (ber'è) v.t. **1,** put underground; inter; entomb. **2,** cover or conceal from sight or attention. **3,** wholly engage (oneself), as in thought.

bus n. **1,** a large public motor vehicle; omnibus. **2,** (Slang) any automobile. —v.t. (Colloq.) transport by bus.

bus'boy'' n. a waiter's assistant in a restaurant.

bush (bûsh) n. **1,** a low, woody shrub. **2,** uncleared land; scrub. **3,** brush. —adj. (Slang) amateur; inferior. —**bushed,** adj. (Colloq.) fatigued; worn out. —**bush league,** a minor league. —**bush leaguer,** (Colloq.) an incompetent amateur.

bush'el (bûsh'əl) n. a unit of dry measure; four pecks.

bu'shi·do'' (boo'shè-dō'') n. the chivalric code of the Jap. gentry and officer class.

bush'ing (bûsh'ing) n. **1,** a metal lining in which an axle or shaft turns. **2,** an insulating lining for a hole.

bush'man (bûsh'mən) n. [pl. **-men**] a

member of a savage aboriginal tribe in Australia or (often *cap.*) Africa.

bush'mas"ter (bûsh'mǎs"tər) *n.* a poisonous snake of tropical Amer.

bush'whack"er (bûsh'hwak"ər) *n.* (*Colloq.*) a backwoodsman; a hillbilly. —**bush'-whack"**, *v.t.* ambush.

bush'y (-ē) *adj.* formed like a bush; dense in growth, as a beard. —**bush'i·ness**, *n.*

busi'ness (biz'nəs) *n.* **1,** occupation; calling. **2,** a commercial enterprise; a company. **3,** commercial pursuits in general; capital engaged in trade or industry. **4,** industrial activity; the condition of businessmen collectively. **5,** duty; aim. **6,** affair; a matter of interest or concern. **7,** in the theater, action illustrative of the script.

busi'ness·like" *adj.* methodical; efficient; attentive to the business at hand.

busi'ness·man" *n.* [*pl.* **-men"**] a man engaged in business.

bus'kin *n.* a short soft boot.

bus'man (-mən) *n.* a driver or conductor of a bus. —**busman's holiday,** a holiday spent in activity similar to one's regular work.

buss (bus) *v.t.* kiss.

bust *n.* **1,** a sculptured likeness of the head and shoulders of a person. **2,** the human chest or bosom. **3,** (*Colloq.*) a failure; in cards, a worthless hand. **4,** (*Colloq.*) a spree. —*v.i.* (*Colloq.*) burst; fail. —*v.t.* (*Slang*) arrest. —**bust'ed,** *adj.* (*Colloq.*) out of money.

bus'tard (bus'tərd) *n.* a large cranelike bird.

bus'ter (bus'tər) *n.* (*Colloq.*) a boy or man (a patronizing term).

Buster Brown a boy's costume comprising a short jacket and knee-length pants.

bus'tle (bus'əl) *v.i.* be fussily busy. —*n.* **1,** stir; ado. **2,** a pad under the back of a woman's skirt.

bus'y (biz'ē) *adj.* **1,** actively occupied. **2,** crowded with activity, as a *busy day.* —*v.t.* keep occupied. —**bus'y·ness,** *n.*

bus'y·bod"y (biz'ē-bod"ē) *n.* a prying or meddling person.

but *adv.* only. —*prep.* except; besides. —*conj.* **1,** unless. **2,** nevertheless; though. **3,** on the contrary. **4,** whether.

bu'tane (bū'tān) *n.* a flammable petroleum derivative, used as a fuel, etc.

butch (bûch) *adj.* (*Slang*) very masculine in appearance or behavior.

butch'er (bûch'ər) *n.* **1,** one who slaughters animals for food and dresses meat for market; a seller of meat. **2,** one who kills brutally. —*v.t.* **1,** kill and dress for food. **2,**

murder wantonly. **3,** botch, spoil. —**butch'-er·y,** *n.* slaughter.

but'ler (but'lər) *n.* a manservant, usually the head servant of a large household.

butt (but) *n.* **1,** a wine cask. **2,** the thicker end of anything, as of a tool, log, etc. **3,** a target; the object of criticism, a joke, etc. **4,** a push with the head. —*v.i.* **1,** strike something with the head. **2,** collide. **3,** abut. —*v.t.* strike with the head.

butte (būt) *n.* a steep-sided hill.

but'ter (but'ər) *n.* **1,** a fatty substance made by churning cream. **2,** any butterlike substance. —*v.t.* **1,** spread with butter. **2,** (*Colloq.*) (with *up to*) flatter; ingratiate oneself with. —**but'ter·y,** *adj.*

but'ter·cup" (but'ər-kup") *n.* a meadow plant with yellow flowers.

but'ter·fat" *n.* the fat in milk.

but'ter·fin"gers *n.* (*Colloq.*) a fumbler; a person who drops things.

but'ter·fly" (but'ər-flī") *n.* **1,** an insect with broad, brilliantly colored wings. **2,** (*Colloq.*) a gay, fickle woman.

but'ter·milk" (but'ər-milk") *n.* the mildly acid liquid left after butter is churned.

but'ter·nut" (but'ər-nut") *n.* the Amer. white walnut; the tree; its oily fruit.

but'ter·scotch" (but'ər-skoch") *n.* a hard candy made of brown sugar, corn syrup, and water.

but'tocks (but'əks) *n. pl.* the fleshy part of the hips; the rump.

but'ton (but'ən) *n.* **1,** a knob or disk used on clothes as an ornament or a fastener. **2,** any buttonlike object or device. —*v.t. & i.* fasten with buttons.

but'ton-down" *adj.* **1,** of a shirt, having collars held down by buttons. **2,** (*Slang*) lacking originality.

but'ton·hole" (but'ən-hōl") *n.* the loop or slit for a button. —*v.t.* **1,** make such a slit in. **2,** (*Colloq.*) detain in conversation.

but'tress (but'ris) *n.* **1,** masonry built against a wall or building for strength and support. **2,** any prop. —*v.t.* prop; brace.

bux'om (buk'səm) *adj.* plump; healthy. —**bux'om·ness,** *n.*

buy (bī) *v.t.* [**bought** (bât), **buy'ing**] **1,** obtain in exchange for money; purchase. **2,** obtain by any sacrifice. **3,** bribe. **4,** (*Slang*) accept; believe. —*n.* (*Colloq.*) something purchased. —**buy'er,** *n.* a purchaser; a departmental manager in a store. —**buyer's market,** a business condition in which supply exceeds demand.

buzz (buz) *n.* **1,** a humming sound, as of bees. **2,** a confused murmur. **3,** (*Slang*) a telephone call. —*v.t.* **1,** (*Slang*) swoop down upon in an airplane, as a prank. **2,** enlighten privately. **3,** (with *off*) leave. —*v.i.* **1,** make a humming sound. **2,** (*Colloq.*) be very active. **3,** (*Colloq.*) telephone to. —**buzz bomb,** a bomb self-propelled by a rocket or jet engine.

buz'zard (buz'ərd) *n.* **1,** a hawklike bird. **2,** an Amer. vulture.

buzz'saw" *n.* a circular saw.

bwa'na (bwä'nə) *n.* master.

by (bī) *prep.* **1,** beside; near. **2,** along; over. **3,** past and beyond. **4,** through the action or agency of. **5,** in or to the amount of. **6,** before; no later than. —*adv.* **1,** near; beside. **2,** aside. **3,** past.

by- (bī) *pref.* **1,** secondary. **2,** out of the way. **3,** near.

by-'and-by' (bī'ən-bī') *adv.* in the near future. —*n.* the future.

bye (bī) *n.* **1,** in a tournament, an idle round in which a competitor nevertheless advances. **2,** goodbye.

by'gone" (bī'gon") *adj.* of times past; former. —*adv.* past. —*n.* (*pl.*) deeds done in the past.

by'law" (bī'lâ") *n.* a regulation or rule adopted by a corporation or organization.

by-'line" (bī'līn") *n.* the line naming the author of a story or article.

by-'pass" (bī'pas") *n.* an alternative route, as a road or pipe. —*v.t.* avoid and progress beyond.

by'path" *n.* **1,** a side or private road. **2,** an indirect route or course; a detour.

by-'play" *n.* a diversion; secondary action.

by-'prod"uct (bī'prod"əkt) *n.* a secondary product, produced incidentally to the manufacture of something else.

by'stand"er (bī'stan"dər) *n.* a spectator.

byte (bīt) *n.* a group of binary digits or bits processed by a computer as a unit.

by'way" (bī'wā") *n.* a side road.

by'word" (bī'wērd") *n.* **1,** a proverb; a motto or slogan. **2,** a pet expression.

By·zan'tine (bi-zan'tin; biz'ən-tēn", -tīn") *adj.* **1,** pert. to Byzantium. **2,** ornate; elaborate.

C

C, c (sē) the third letter of the English alphabet. **2,** the Roman numeral for 100.

cab (kab) *n.* **1,** a horse-drawn or motor vehicle for public hire. **2,** the driver's compartment of a truck or locomotive.

ca·bal' (kə-bal') *n.* **1,** a secret scheme or intrigue. **2,** a group of secret plotters.

cab'a·la (kab'ə-lə) *n.* any occult science. —**cab"a·lis'tic,** *adj.*

ca·ba'ña (kə-bä'nyə) *n.* **1,** a small cabin. **2,** a private bathhouse.

cab"a·ret' (kab"ə-rā') *n.* a restaurant that provides entertainment.

cab'bage (kab'ij) *n.* a vegetable plant having edible leaves formed into a thick compact head.

cab'by (kab'ē) *n.* (*Colloq.*) taxicab driver. Also, **cab'bie.**

cab'in (kab'in) *n.* **1,** cottage; hut. **2,** a room in a ship or airplane.

cab'i·net (kab'i-nət) *n.* **1,** a piece of furniture used as a cupboard. **2,** a small meeting room. **3,** an advisory council. —*adj.* **1,** pert. to a council. **2,** of a certain small size.

ca'ble (kā'bəl) *n.* **1,** a thick, strong rope or chain. **2,** a number of wires for conducting electricity, bound together in a cylindrical sheath. **3,** [also, **ca'ble·gram"**] a telegram sent by submarine cable. **4,** (*Naut.*) a unit of length. —*v.t. & i.* furnish with cables; communicate by cable.

cab'o·chon" (kab'ə-shon") *n.* a gem polished but not cut in facets.

ca·boo'dle (kə-boo'dəl) *n.* (*Colloq.*) the whole crowd or collection.

ca·boose' (kə-boos') *n.* a car on a freight train fitted for use of the crew.

cab"ri·o·let' (kab"rē-ə-lā') *n.* **1,** a light, two-wheeled carriage. **2,** an automobile with a folding top.

ca·ca'o (kə-kä'ō) *n.* a tropical evergreen tree whose seeds are the source of cocoa and chocolate.

cac"cia·to're (kach"ə-tôr'ē) *adj.* simmered with herbs and seasonings.

cache (kash) *n.* **1,** a place of storage or concealment, esp. underground. **2,** a store of provisions, treasure, etc. so concealed. —*v.t.* hide.

ca·chet' (ka-shā') *n.* **1,** a seal, as on a letter. **2,** a mark of authentication or distinction; a special postmark.

cack'le (kak'əl) *n.* **1,** the shrill repeated cry of a goose or hen. **2,** silly chatter; noisy laughter. —*v.i.* chatter; laugh noisily.

ca·coph'o·ny (kə-kof'ə-nē) *n.* a combination of discordant sounds; dissonance. —**ca·coph'o·nous,** *adj.*

cac'tus (kak'təs) *n.* [*pl.* **-ti** (-tī)] a leafless spiny desert plant.

cad (kad) *n.* an ill-bred or contemptible person. —**cad'dish,** *adj.*

ca·dav'er (kə-dav'ər) *n.* a dead body; corpse. —**ca·dav'or·eus,** *adj.*

cad'die (kad'ē) *n.* a boy engaged to carry the clubs of a golf player. —*v.i.* act as a caddie. Also, **cad'dy.**

cad'dy (kad'ē) *n.* **1,** a small can or chest for holding tea, etc. **2,** caddie.

ca′dence (kā′dəns) *n.* **1,** rhythmic flow. **2,** a fall in pitch or tempo. **3,** (*Music*) a sequence of chords expressing conclusion, finality, or repose. **4,** the beat or rate of a rhythm.

ca·den′za (kə-den′zə) *n.* a passage in showy style for a soloist in a concerto.

ca·det′ (kə-det′) *n.* **1,** a young man in training for army service. **2,** a younger son.

cadge (kaj) *v.t.* peddle or beg.

cad′mi·um (kad′mē-əm) *n.* a metallic chemical element, no. 48, symbol Cd.

ca′dre (kä′dər) *n.* a permanently organized group of persons forming the framework of a larger unit.

ca·du′ce·us (kə-doo′sē-əs) *n.* [*pl.* **-i″** (-ī″)] a winged staff: symbol of the medical profession.

cae′cum (sē′kəm) *n.* the inner end of the large intestine to which the vermiform appendix is attached.

Cae·sar′e·an (si-zār′ē-ən) *adj.* pert. to Caesarean operation or section, delivery of a baby by cutting into the womb.

cae·su′ra (sē-zhûr′ə) *n.* a natural break or pause, due to sense, in a line of poetry.

ca·fé′ (ka-fā′) *n.* a restaurant or barroom.

caf′fe·te′ri·a (kaf″ə-tir′ē-ə) *n.* a self-service restaurant.

caf′feine (kaf′ēn) *n.* a bitter alkaloid having a stimulating effect.

caf′tan (kaf′tən) *n.* a long garment with long sleeves worn in the Near East.

cage (kāj) *n.* an enclosure made of wires or bars. —*v.t.* put in a cage. **—cage′ling,** *n.* a caged animal; a prisoner. **—cag′er,** *n.* (*Colloq.*) a basketball player.

cag′y (kā′jē) *adj.* (*Colloq.*) wary; shrewd. Also, **cag′ey.**

ca·hoots″ (kə-hoots′) *n.pl.* (*Colloq.*) secret partnership.

cai′man (kā′mən) *n.* [*pl.* **-mans**] a So. Amer. alligator. Also, **cay′man.**

cairn (kârn) *n.* **1,** a heap of stones, erected as a monument. **2,** a small dog of a terrier breed.

cais′son (kā′sən) *n.* **1,** a large boxlike structure with an open bottom, used in submarine excavation. **2,** a floating structure used as a dock, etc. **3,** a wagon for ammunition. **—caisson disease,** the bends.

cai′tiff (kā′tif) *n.* (*Archaic*) a wicked or mean person.

ca·jole′ (kə-jōl′) *v.t. & i.* persuade by flattery; wheedle. **—ca·jol′er·y,** *n.*

cake (kāk) *n.* **1,** a sweet food baked from dough. **2,** any loaflike mass, as of soap. —*v.* form or become formed into a compact mass; cohere.

cake′walk″ *n.* a dance.

cal′a·bash″ (kal′ə-bash″) *n.* any of various gourds or gourd trees.

cal′a·boose″ (kal′ə-boos″) *n.* (*Slang*) a jail.

cal′a·mine″ (kal′ə-mīn″) *n.* a white mineral, an ore of zinc, used medicinally.

ca·lam′i·ty (kə-lam′ə-tē) *n.* a great misfortune or cause of distress; disaster. **—ca·lam′i·tous,** *adj.*

cal·car′e·ous (kal-kār′ē-əs) *adj.* containing calcium carbonate; chalky.

cal′ci·fy″ (kal′sə-fī″) *v.t. & i.* harden or become hard by deposit of calcium. **—cal″ci·fi·ca′tion,** *n.*

cal′ci·mine″ (kal′sə-mīn″) *n.* a thin water-soluble paint, usually white. —*v.t.* whitewash. Also, **kal′so·mine″.**

cal′cine (kal′sīn) *v.t.* heat in order to fuse, crumble, oxidize, etc. **—cal″ci·na′-tion,** *n.*

cal′cite (kal′sīt) *n.* calcium carbonate.

cal′ci·um (kal′sē-əm) *n.* a chemical element, no. 20, symbol Ca, found in bone, chalk, lime, etc.

cal′cu·late″ (kal′kū-lāt″) *v.t.* **1,** ascertain by mathematics; compute. **2,** plan. **3,** (*Colloq.*) intend; guess. —*v.i.* reckon. **—cal′cu·la·ble,** *adj.* **—cal′cu·lat″ing,** *adj.* shrewd; scheming. **—cal″cu·la′tion,** *n.* **—cal′cu·la″tor,** *n.*

cal′cu·lus (kal′kyə-ləs) *n.* **1,** (*Math.*) any system of computation or analysis by a specialized algebraic notation. **2,** a small stone, as a gallstone.

cal′dron (kâl′drən) *n.* a large kettle. Also, **caul′dron.**

cal″e·fac′tion (kal″ə-fak′shən) *n.* heating. **—cal″e·fac′to·ry** (-tə-rē) *adj.*

cal′en·dar (kal′ən-dər) *n.* **1,** any system of division of time. **2,** a table of days, weeks, and months. **3,** a list, register, or catalog; a list of cases to be tried in a court. —*v.t.* enter in a calendar; register.

cal′en·der (kal′ən-dər) *n.* a machine for pressing, drying or glazing paper, cloth, etc. —*v.t.* treat in a calender.

cal′ends (kal′əndz) *n.pl.* in ancient Rome, the first day of the month.

ca·len′du·la (kə-len′jə-lə) *n.* any of various flowering plants including the marigold.

calf (kåf) *n.* [*pl.* **calves** (kåvz)] **1,** the young of certain animals, as cow, elephant, seal, whale. **2,** calfskin leather. **3,** the thick fleshy part of the human leg, below the knee.

cal′i·ber (kal′ə-bər) *n.* **1,** diameter, esp. of the hollow inside of a cylinder. **2,** capacity of mind; degree of importance. Also, **cal′i·bre.**

cal′i·brate″ (kal′ə-brāt″) *v.t.* mark (a measuring instrument) with graduations; verify or rectify. —**cal′i·bra′tion**, *n*.

cal′i·co (kal′ə-kō″) *n*. a printed cotton cloth.

cal′i·for′ni·um (kal″ə-fôr′né-əm) *n*. an unstable, radioactive chemical element, no. 98, symbol Cf, produced artificially from curium.

cal′i·per (kal′ə-pər) *n*. (usually *pl*.) a measuring instrument for determining diameters. —*v.t.* & *i*. measure with calipers.

ca′liph (kā′lif) *n*. title of a sovereign in Mohammedan countries. —**cal′iph·ate** (-āt), *n*.

cal″is·then′ics (kal″əs-then′iks) *n.pl*. light gymnastics.

calk (kâk) *v.t.* make (a boat, boiler, tank, etc.) watertight. —*n*. **1**, [also, **caulk′ing**] a material used to calk. **2**, a metal spike or spur on the bottom of a shoe. Also, **caulk**.

call (kâl) *v.t.* **1**, utter loudly; announce; proclaim. **2**, attract or demand the attention of; summon. **3**, give a name to; designate; characterize. **4**, telephone to. —*v.i.* **1**, shout. **2**, make a short visit. —*n*. **1**, a cry or shout. **2**, the characteristic cry of an animal or bird; the note of a bugle or horn. **3**, a notice, summons, or invitation. **4**, a short visit. —**call girl**, a prostitute.

cal′la (kal′ə) *n*. [also, **calla lily**] a plant with a large white flower and bright yellow spadix.

call′back″ *n*. a recall, as of a product for repair of defects, a candidate for another hearing, etc.

cal·lig′ra·phy (kə-lig′rə-fé) *n*. fancy handwriting.

call′ing *n*. **1**, profession or vocation. **2**, act of summoning, etc. —**calling card**, a card bearing one's name.

cal·li′o·pe (kə-lī′ə-pé) *n*. a musical instrument employing steam whistles.

cal·los′i·ty (kə-los′ə-té) *n*. **1**, a hardened part; a callus. **2**, a callous condition.

cal′lous (kal′əs) *adj*. **1**, hard; hardened. **2**, unfeeling; unkind. —*n*. callus. —**cal′-lous·ness**, *n*.

cal′low (kal′ō) *adj*. very immature. —**cal′-low·ness**, *n*.

cal′lus (kal′əs) *n*. a hardened or thickened part of the skin.

calm (käm) *adj*. **1**, quiet; still. **2**, serene; tranquil. —*n*. the state of being calm. —*v.t.* & *i*. (often with *down*) quiet. —**calm′ness**, *n*.

cal′o·mel″ (kal′ə-mel″) *n*. a medicine, mercurous chloride, used as a purgative.

cal′o·rie (kal′ə-ré) *n*. a measure of heat, and of the energy-producing property of

food. —**ca·lor′ic** (kə-lôr′ik) *adj*. —**cal″o·rif′ic** (kal″ə-rif′ik) *adj*. producing heat.

cal′u·met″ (kal′ū-met″) *n*. an Indian ceremonial tobacco pipe.

ca·lum′ni·ate″ (kə-lum′né-āt″) *v.t.* slander. —**ca·lum″ni·a′tion**, *n*.

cal′um·ny (kal′əm-né) *n*. a false accusation of crime or misconduct; slander. —**ca·lum′ni·ous**, *adj*.

cal′va·ry (kal′və-ré) *n*. **1**, a picture or sculpture of the scene of the Crucifixion. **2**, (*cap*.) the place where Christ was crucified.

calve (kâv) *v.i.* bear a calf.

calves (kâvz) *n*. pl. of *calf*.

Cal′vin·ism (kal′vin-iz-əm) *n*. the theological doctrines of John Calvin; Presbyterianism. —**Cal′vin·ist**, *n*. —**Cal″vin·is′-tic**, *adj*.

cal·vi′ti·es″ (kal-vish′é-éz″) *n*. baldness.

ca·lyp′so (kə-lip′sō) *n*. a style of song of the Brit. W. Indies.

ca′lyx (kā′liks) *n*. the outermost envelope of a flower; the sepals.

cam (kam) *n*. an eccentric wheel or part for converting rotary motion into linear or irregular motion.

ca″ma·ra′de·rie (kä″mə-rä′də-ré) *n*. comradeship.

cam′ber (kam′bər) *n*. a slight curve or arch.

cam′bi·um (kam′bé-əm) *n*. a layer of tissue between bark and wood.

cam′bric (kām′brik) *n*. a closely-woven fabric of cotton or linen. —**cambric tea**, hot water, cream, and sugar.

came (kām) *v*. pret. of *come*.

cam′el (kam′əl) *n*. **1**, a large, ruminant quadruped with two humps, used in Asia and Afr. as a beast of burden; Bactrian camel. **2**, dromedary. —**cam″el·eer′** (kam″ə-lir′) *n*. a camel driver.

ca·mel′lia (kə-mēl′yə) *n*. an evergreen plant bearing red or white flowers.

ca·mel′o·pard″ (kə-mel′ə-pärd″) *n*. the giraffe.

Cam′em·bert″ (kam′əm-bär″) *n*. a soft-ripening cheese.

cam′e·o″ (kam′é-ō″) *n*. **1**, a stone or shell decorated with raised carving. **2**, a brief story or play. **3**, a small role performed by a well-known personality.

cam′er·a (kam′ər-ə) *n*. **1**, a photographic apparatus for recording an image on a sensitized surface. **2**, the private chamber of a judge. —**cam′er·a·man″**, *n*. —**in camera**, in private.

camera lu′ci·da (loo′si-də) an optical instrument for projecting an image to be traced or copied on paper.

camera ob·scu´ra (ob-skyûr´ə) a dark-ened room or box in which a real image of an external object is projected and viewed.

cam´i·on (kam´é-ən) *n*. **1,** a cart for heavy loads. **2,** a military truck.

cam´i·sole (kam´ə-sōl˝) *n*. **1,** a woman's blouse. **2,** a straight jacket.

cam´o·mile (kam´ə-mīl˝) *n*. a herb used to make a medicinal tea.

cam´ou·flage (kam´ə-fläzh˝) *n*. **1,** (*Mil.*) disguise of objects that cannot be wholly concealed. **2,** any disguise; false pretense. —*v.t.* disguise. —**cam˝ou·fleur´** (-flêr´) *n*.

camp (kamp) *n*. **1,** a place for the erection of temporary shelters. **2,** a group of tempo-rary lodgings, as for lumbermen. **3,** a cabin in the wilderness. **4,** fig., a group or sect. **5,** something interesting or entertaining be-cause of its banality or archaism. —*v.i.* **1,** live in a camp. **2,** (with *on*) follow per-sistently; haunt. —**camp´er,** *n*. motor home; caravan. —**camp chair,** a folding chair. —**camp follower, 1,** a prostitute. **2,** an observer who is not a member, as of a movement.

cam·paign´ (kam-pān´) *n*. **1,** military op-erations during one season or in a definite enterprise. **2,** a series of activities directed to a single purpose, as for election to public office.

cam˝pa·ni´le (kam˝pə-nē´lè) *n*. a bell tower.

cam·pan´u·la (kam-pan´yə-lə) *n*. the bellflower.

cam´phor (kam´fər) *n*. **1,** a vegetable or synthetic gum used in medicine, plastics, etc. **2,** an oriental tree. —**cam´phor·ate˝** (-āt˝) *v.i.* —**cam´phor·at˝ed** (-ā˝tid) *adj*.

cam´pus (kam´pəs) *n*. the grounds of a college or university.

can (kan) *aux. v.* [*pret.* **could**] **1,** have the ability or power to; be able to. **2,** (*Colloq.*) may; have permission to. —*n*. **1,** a metal container or receptacle. **2,** (*Slang*) jail. —*v.t.* [**canned** (kand), **can´ning**] **1,** seal in a con-tainer. **2,** (*Colloq.*) dismiss from employment. **3,** record, as on film or tape. **4,** (*Slang*) cease.

Ca·na´di·an bacon (kə-nādé-ən) bacon from the pork loin.

ca·nail´le (ka-nä´yə) *n*. (*Fr.*) riffraff.

ca·nal´ (kə-nal´) *n*. **1,** an artificial water-way for navigation or irrigation. **2,** any channel, duct, or passage conveying or containing a fluid.

can´a·pé (kan´ə-pé) *n*. a small piece of bread or toast bearing a morsel of appetiz-ing food.

ca·nard´ (kə-närd´) *n*. a false story; a hoax.

ca·nar´y (kə-nār´è) *n*. **1,** a songbird, widely

domesticated as a household pet. **2,** a light yellow color.

ca·nas´ta (kə-näs´tə) *n*. a card game based on rummy.

can´can (kan´kan) *n*. a posturing dance with high kicking.

can´cel (kan´səl) *v.t.* **1,** draw lines across (something written) so as to deface. **2,** make void; annul. **3,** compensate for; offset; neu-tralize. —**can˝cel·la´tion,** *n*.

can´cer (kan´sər) *n*. a malignant tumor; any evil that grows and spreads. —**can´-cer·ous,** *adj*.

Can´cer (kan´sər) *n*. a northern constella-tion, the Crab (see *zodiac*).

can˝de·la´brum (kan˝də-lä´brəm) *n*. [*pl.* **-bra** (-brə), **-brums**] an ornamental branched candlestick.

can·des´cent (kan-des´ənt) *adj*. glowing. —**can·des´cence,** *n*.

can´did (kan´did) *adj*. outspoken; frank. —**can´did·ness,** *n*.

can´di·date (kan´də-dāt˝) *n*. one who seeks an office or honor. —**can´di·da·cy** (-də-sè) *n*.

can´dle (kan´dəl) *n*. a rod of wax, tallow, or paraffin with an embedded wick, burned to give sustained light. —*v.t.* examine (esp. eggs) by holding between the eye and a light. —**candle power,** a measure of illu-mination.

Can´dle·mas (-məs) *n*. a Christian reli-gious festival, Feb. 2, commemorating the purification of the Virgin Mary.

can´dle·pin˝ (kan´dəl-pin˝) *n*. a nearly cylindrical bowling pin, tapering in at top and bottom. —**can´dle·pins˝,** *n.sing*. a bowling game using candlepins and a small round ball.

can´dle·stick˝ *n*. a holder for a candle.

can´dle·wick˝ *n*. **1,** the wick of a candle. **2,** a tufted cotton bedspread.

can´dor (kan´dər) *n*. frankness; sincerity. Also, **can´dour.**

can´dy (kan´dé) *n*. any of a variety of confections containing sugar. —*v.t.* **1,** cook with much sugar or syrup. **2,** make agreea-ble. —**candy strip´er** (strī´pər) (*Slang*) a teenage volunteer nurses' aid.

cane (kān) *n*. **1,** a walking stick. **2,** the woody stem of certain plants, as sugar cane, bamboo. **3,** pliable woody fibers. —*v.t.* **1,** flog with a cane. **2,** make or weave with cane. —**cane´brake˝,** *n*. a thicket of canes.

ca·nine´ (kā´nīn) *adj*. pert. to dogs. —*n*. **1,** any dog or member of the dog family. **2,** a long, pointed tooth.

can´is·ter (kan´is-tər) *n*. a small can or box; a caddy.

can´ker (kang´kər) *n*. an ulcerous sore,

esp. in the mouth. —*v.t. & i.* infect or become infected with canker; fig., poison or corrupt slowly. —**can′ker·ous**, *adj.*

can′na (kan′ə) *n.* a tropical flowering plant.

can′na·bis (kan′ə-bis) *n.* hemp.

can′nel coal (kan′əl) a variety of coal that ignites readily and burns brightly.

can′ner (kan′ər) *n.* one who cans food for preservation. —**can′ner·y**, *n.* a place where foods are canned.

can′ni·bal (kan′ə-bəl) *n.* **1**, a person who eats human flesh. **2**, any animal that eats the flesh of its own kind. —**can′ni·bal·ism**, *n.* —**can″ni·bal·is′tic**, *adj.* —**can″ni·bal·is′·ti·cal·ly**, *adv.*

can′ni·bal·ize″ *v.t.* **1**, eat the flesh of. **2**, remove parts of (a machine, etc.) to use in another place.

can′non (kan′ən) *n.* **1**, a large, mounted gun for hurling projectiles. **2**, (*Brit.*) a carom in billiards. —*v.i.* discharge cannons. —**can″non·eer′** (-ə-nir′) *n.* —**can′non·ry** (-rē) *n.*

can′non·ade″ (kan″ə-nād′) *n.* concentrated cannon fire. —*v.t. & i.* bombard.

can′not (kan′ot) *v.* can not.

can′ny (kan′ē) *adj.* wary; prudent; sagacious. —**can′ni·ness**, *n.*

ca·noe′ (kə-noo′) *n.* a light, round-bottomed boat pointed at both ends, propelled by paddling. —*v.i.* go in a canoe. —**ca·noe′ist**, *n.*

can′on (kan′ən) *n.* **1**, any rule, law, or body of law, esp. ecclesiastical. **2**, genuine books, esp. of the Bible. **3**, a church officer. —**ca·non′i·cal** (kə-non′i-kəl) *adj.* —**can″on·ic′i·ty** (-nis′ə-tē) *n.* —**can′on·ize″** (-īz″) *v.t.* designate as a saint.

ca′ñon (kan′yən) *n.* canyon.

can′on·ess (kan′ən-əs) *n.* a woman who lives in a convent, but has not taken a nun's vows.

can′o·py (kan′ə-pē) *n.* a suspended covering over a bed, entrance, etc.

cant (kant) *n.* **1**, insincere speech or writing, esp. conventional pretense to high ideals or aims. **2**, the special vocabulary or speech of a profession or class, as the whine of beggars; argot. **3**, a tilt, slant, or obliquity. **4**, a salient angle. —*v.i.* **1**, utter cant. **2**, tilt; list. —*v.t.* **1**, make oblique; bevel. **2**, tip; upset.

can′t (kånt) *contraction* cannot.

can·ta′bi·le (kan-tä′bə-lē) *n., adj. & adv.* (*Music*) (in) a flowing or songlike manner.

can′ta·loupe″ (kan′tə-lōp″) *n.* a variety of muskmelon.

can·tan′ker·ous (kan-tang′kər-əs) *adj.* perverse in disposition; cross; ill-natured. —**can·tan′ker·ous·ness**, *n.*

can·ta′ta (kən-tä′tə) *n.* a choral composition, sacred or secular.

can·teen′ (kan-tēn′) *n.* **1**, a shop, bar, or recreation hall in a military camp, barracks, etc. **2**, a portable container for water.

can′ter (kan′tər) *n.* a gait of a horse; an easy gallop. —*v.i.* ride at a canter.

can′thus (kan′thəs) *n.* the corner of the eye.

can″ti·lev″er (kan′tə-lev″ər; -lē″vər) *adj.* supported at one end.

can′tle (kan′təl) *n.* the upward curve at the rear of a saddle.

can′to (kan′tō) *n.* a main division of a long poem.

can′ton (kan′tən) *n.* a subdivision of a country; a small district.

can·ton′ment (kan-ton′mənt) *n.* a military camp, esp. a large one.

can′tor (kan′tər) *n.* the singing leader in a cathedral or synagogue.

ca·nuck′ (kə-núk′) *n. & adj.* (*Slang*) French-Canadian.

can′vas (kan′vəs) *n.* **1**, a heavy cloth of hemp or flax. **2**, something made of canvas, esp. a sail, a tent, or an oil painting.

can′vas·back″ *n.* a No. Amer. wild duck.

can′vass (kan′vəs) *v.t.* **1**, traverse (a district) for purposes of questioning or solicitation. **2**, examine; discuss. —*v.i.* solicit votes, opinions, etc. —*n.* **1**, a campaign of soliciting votes, opinions, etc. **2**, examination; investigation; discussion.

can′yon (kan′yən) *n.* a narrow valley with steep sides; a ravine. Also, **ca′ñon.**

cap (kap) *n.* **1**, a covering for the head. **2**, something resembling a cap, esp. a covering for an opening. **3**, the head or top; the acme. **4**, a noise-making or explosive device. —*v.t.* [**capped, cap′ping**] **1**, cover with a cap. **2**, complete; bring to a climax; surpass.

ca′pa·ble (kā′pə-bəl) *adj.* **1**, (with *of*) having the ability, capacity, inclination, etc. **2**, competent; efficient. —**ca″pa·bil′i·ty**, *n.*

ca·pa′cious (kə-pā′shəs) *adj.* capable of holding much; roomy. —**ca·pa′cious·ness**, *n.*

ca·pac′i·tance (kə-pas′ə-təns) *n.* the ability of a condenser to store an electrical charge.

ca·pac′i·tate″ (kə-pas′ə-tāt″) *v.t.* make capable; give legal powers to. —**ca·pac′i·ta″·tion**, *n.*

ca·pac′i·tor (kə-pas′ə-tər) *n.* an electrical condenser.

ca·pac′i·ty (kə-pas′ə-tē) *n.* **1**, the power of receiving or containing. **2**, cubic contents; volume. **3**, ability; power to act. **4**, function; role.

cap-"a·pie' (kap"ə-pē') *adv.* from head to foot.

ca·par'i·son (kə-par'i-sən) *n.* 1, an ornamental covering for a horse. 2, equipment; clothing. —*v.t.* equip; bedeck.

cape (kāp) *n.* 1, a loose outer garment, covering the shoulders. 2, a piece of land jutting from the coast into a sea or lake. 3, a small one-story house.

ca'per (kā'pər) *v.i.* leap or skip about; frolic. —*n.* 1, a leap or skip. 2, a prank. 3, a plant whose bud is used for seasoning; the pickled bud.

cap'il·lar"y (kap'ə-ler"ē) *adj.* 1, pert. to a tube of small bore. 2, pert. to the surface tension of a liquid. 3, resembling hair. —*n.* a minute tube or vessel. —**cap"il·lar'i·ty,** *n.*

cap'i·tal (kap'ə-təl) *n.* 1, the city that is the official seat of the government of a country or of a subdivision. 2, a capital letter. 3, the head of a pillar. 4, wealth used in trade; the net worth of a business. 5, the owners of capital wealth, collectively. —*adj.* 1, principal; most important. 2, excellent. 3, pert. to the seat of government. 4, (of letters) of the large size used at the beginnings of sentences. 5, (of a crime) punishable by death. —**capital goods,** facilities or goods used to produce other goods. —**capital punishment,** the death penalty. —**capital ship,** a warship of largest size.

cap'i·tal·ism (-iz-əm) *n.* the economic system in which the ownership and exploitation of wealth are left largely in private hands.

cap'i·tal·ist *n.* 1, one with wealth invested for profit. 2, one who favors capitalism. —**cap"i·tal·is'tic,** *adj.* —**cap"i·tal·is'ti·cal·ly,** *adv.*

cap'i·tal·ize" (-īz") *v.t.* 1, provide capital for; use as capital. 2, use to advantage. 3, begin with a capital letter. —**cap"i·tal·i·za'tion,** *n.*

cap"i·ta'tion (kap"ə-tā'shən) *n.* 1, a census. 2, a poll tax.

cap'i·tol (kap'ə-təl) *n.* the chief office building of a government; statehouse.

ca·pit'u·late" (kə-pich'ə-lāt") *v.i.* surrender on stipulated terms. —**ca·pit"u·la'tion,** *n.*

ca'pon (kā'pon) *n.* a castrated rooster.

cap'o·ral (kap'ə-rəl) *n.* a kind of tobacco.

cap"puc·ci'no (ka"pə-chē'nō) *n.* espresso coffee topped with whipped cream.

ca·price' (kə-prēs') *n.* 1, a sudden change of mind or humor; a whim. 2, fickleness. —**ca·pri'cious** (-prē'shəs) *adj.*

ca·pric'ci·o (ka-prēt'chō) *n.* 1, (*Music*) a free, whimsical composition. 2, a caprice.

Cap'ri·corn" (kap'ri-kôrn") *n.* a constellation, the Goat (see *zodiac*).

cap'ri·ole (kap'rē-ōl) *n.* a leap or caper.

cap·size' (kap-sīz') *v.i.* & *t.* overturn; upset (esp. of a boat).

cap'stan (kap'stən) *n.* a type of windlass, a drum rotating on an upright axle, manually operated.

cap'sule (kap'səl) *n.* 1, a gelatin case enclosing a dose of medicine. 2, a small casing or envelope. 3, the crew compartment of a spacecraft.

cap'tain (kap'tən) *n.* 1, one in authority; chief; leader. 2, (*Mil.*) a rank between lieutenant and major. 3, (*Naval*) a rank between commander and commodore or admiral. 4, the master of any ship. —*v.t.* command.

cap'tion (kap'shən) *n.* a headline or title. —*v.t.* supply a caption for.

cap'tious (kap'shəs) *adj.* faultfinding; hypercritical. —**cap'tious·ness,** *n.*

cap'ti·vate" (kap'ti-vāt") *v.t.* enthrall by charm; fascinate. —**cap"ti·va'tion,** *n.*

cap'tive (kap'tiv) *n.* a prisoner. —*adj.* captured; held prisoner. —**cap·tiv'i·ty** (kap-tiv'ə-tē) *n.*

cap'tor (kap'tər) *n.* one who captures.

cap'ture (kap'chər) *v.t.* take prisoner; seize; win. —*n.* 1, act of capturing. 2, who or what is captured.

cap·u'chin (kap'yû-shin) *n.* 1, a long-tailed South American monkey. 2, a hooded cloak. 3, (*cap.*) an order of Franciscan monks.

cap"y·ba'ra (kap"i-bä'rə) *n.* a So. Amer. rodent. Also, **cap"i·ba'ra.**

car (kär) *n.* 1, automobile. 2, any of a variety of vehicles. 3, an elevator. 4, a compartment for passengers or freight. —**car hop,** a serving person in a drive-in restaurant. —**car jockey,** (*Slang*) a garage attendant.

ca"ra·ba'o (kär"ə-bä'ō) *n.* a large animal of the ox family; a water buffalo.

car"a·bin·eer" (kar"ə-bə-nir") *n.* a rifleman.

car'a·cole" (kar'ə-kōl") *n.* a half turn. —*v.i.* turn; go zigzag.

car'a·cul (kar'ə-kəl) *n.* the curly fleece of the newborn Astrakhan sheep.

ca·rafe' (kə-raf') *n.* a glass water bottle; decanter.

car'a·mel (kar'ə-məl) *n.* 1, burnt sugar, as used for flavoring. 2, a kind of candy. —**car'a·mel·ize",** *v.t.* & *i.*

car'a·pace" (kar'ə-pās") *n.* the hard covering or shell of an animal.

car'at (kar'ət) *n.* 1, a unit of weight for

precious stones. **2**, a measure of purity of gold. Also, **kar'at.**

car'a·van" (kar'ə-van") *n.* **1**, a group of travelers banded together for safety, esp. in desert regions of Asia and Africa. **2**, a large covered wagon; van. **3**, (*Brit.*) a house trailer.

car"a·van'sa·ry (kar"ə-van'sə-rē) *n.* an inn for caravan travelers.

car'a·vel" (kar'ə-vel") *n.* a small Portuguese sailing vessel.

car'a·way" (kar'ə-wā") *n.* a pungent seed used as a flavoring.

car'bide (kär'bīd) *n.* a chemical compound, esp. **calcium carbide,** used to make acetylene gas.

car'bine (kär'bīn) *n.* a short-barreled rifle. **—car"bi·neer',** *n.*

car·bo- (kär-bō) *pref.* carbon.

car"bo·hy'drate (kär"bō-hī'drāt) *n.* a class of compounds of carbon, hydrogen, and oxygen, important in foods, as sugar and starch.

car"bo·lat"ed (kär'bə-lā"tid) *adj.* treated with carbolic acid.

car·bol'ic (kär-bol'ik) *adj.* pert. to **carbolic acid,** or phenol, a disinfectant.

car'bon (kär'bən) *n.* **1**, a chemical element, no. 6., symbol C, that occurs pure as diamond and graphite, impurely as coal, and in compounds to form organic substances. **2**, a rod of carbon used as an electrode. **3**, [**carbon paper**] a piece of paper backed with black preparation, for making duplicate copies; a copy so made. **—car·bon'ic** (-bon'ik) *adj.* **—car'bon·ize,** *v.t.* **—carbon black,** lamp black. **—carbon dioxide,** [also, **carbonic acid gas**] a heavy, colorless gas; dry ice. **—carbon 14,** a radioactive isotope of carbon used in dating archaeological and geological samples. **—carbon monoxide,** a colorless, odorless, poisonous gas. **—carbon tetrachloride** (tet"rə-klôr'īd) a non-inflammable liquid used in fire extinguishers and as a solvent in cleaning fluids

car'bon·ate" (kär'bə-nāt") *v.t.* charge (water) with carbon dioxide. **—carbonated water,** soda water.

car'bon-date" *v.t.* determine the age of (an object) by measuring its content of carbon 14.

Car"bo·run'dum (kär"bə-run'dəm) *n.* (*T.N.*) an abrasive made of silicon and carbon.

car'boy (kär'boi) *n.* a large glass bottle protected with wickerwork or wood, for holding acids, etc.

car'bun·cle (kär'bung-kəl) *n.* **1**, a garnet

or its color. **2**, a circumscribed inflammation exuding pus.

car'bu·re'tor (kär'bə-rā"tər) *n.* a device for vaporizing a fuel to produce a combustible gas. **—car'bu·ret"** (-rāt") *v.t.* **—car"·bu·re'tion,** *n.*

car'cass (kär'kəs) *n.* the dead body of an animal.

car·cin'o·gen (kär-sin'ə-jən) *n.* a substance that causes cancer. **—car"cin·o·gen"ic,** *adj.*

car"ci·no'ma (kär"sə-nō'mə) *n.* (*Med.*) a malignant growth in body tissues; cancer.

card (kärd) *n.* **1**, a piece of thick paper or thin pasteboard, usually rectangular and printed, as *calling card, membership card, greeting card.* **2**, one of a set of such pieces printed for playing games: *playing card;* (*pl.*) any game played with such cards. **3**, a program of events; a bill of fare. **4**, (*Colloq.*) an amusing person. **5**, a brush or other implement for combing fibers. **—v.t. 1**, comb (fibers). **2**, list; schedule.

car'da·mom (kär'də-məm) *n.* the aromatic seed of an E. Indian herb, used as a spice. Also, **car'da·mon** (-mən).

card'board" *n.* thin stiff pasteboard.

car'di·ac" (kär'dē-ak") *adj.* **1**, pert. to the heart. **2**, pert. to the upper part of the stomach.

car'di·gan (kär'də-gən) *n.* a close-fitting wool jacket or sweater, opening in the front.

car'di·nal (kär'də-nəl) *adj.* **1**, of first importance; chief; fundamental. **2**, deep red. **—n. 1**, a member of the Sacred College of the Rom. Cath. Church. **2**, a No. Amer. finch. **3**, a deep red color. **—cardinal numbers,** one, two, etc., as distinguished from first, second, etc. **—cardinal points,** the compass directions.

car'di·nal·ate" (kär'də-nə-lāt") *n.* **1**, the rank of cardinal. **2**, the body of cardinals.

car·di·o- (kär-dē-ō) *pref.* heart.

car'di·o·gram" *n.* a record made by a cardiograph.

car'di·o·graph" *n.* an instrument for recording heart action. **—car"di·o·graph'ic,** *adj.*

card'sharp" *n.* a professional swindler at card games. Also, **card'sharp"er.**

care (kār) *n.* **1**, attention; heed; solicitude; anxiety. **2**, a cause of worry, etc. **3**, protection; charge. **—v.i. 1**, be concerned, etc. **2**, provide (for). **3**, have an inclination (to) or affection (for).

ca·reen' (kə-rēn') *v.i.* **1**, sway or lean to one side, as a ship. **2**, (*Colloq.*) run or move at full speed; career.

ca·reer' (kə-rir') *n.* **1**, a general course of action, esp. progress in a lifework. **2**, a

calling pursued as a lifework. **3,** speed.
—*v.i.* run or move at full speed.

care'free" *adj.* free of anxiety or worry.

care'ful (kār'fəl) *adj.* employing care; cautious. **—care'ful·ness,** *n.*

care'less (kār'ləs) *adj.* **1,** inattentive; negligent; reckless. **2,** unworried. **—care'less·ness,** *n.*

ca·ress' (kə-res') *v.t.* touch with the hand to express affection. —*n.* an act of affection.

car'et (kar'ət) *n.* the mark (∧) used to show where to insert additional matter in a written or printed line.

care'tak"er *n.* a watchman or janitor.

care'worn" *n.* showing fatigue, etc., from worry.

car'fare" *n.* the charge for a ride on a streetcar, bus, etc.

car'go (kär'gō) *n.* the goods or merchandise carried by a ship.

car'i·bou" (kar'ə-boo") *n.* a No. Amer. reindeer.

car'i·ca·ture (kar'i-kə-chûr) *n.* a picture or verbal description that ludicrously exaggerates the characteristics of the thing depicted. —*v.t.* make a caricature of. **—car'i·ca·tur"ist,** *n.*

car'ies (kār'ēz) *n.* decay, esp. of teeth. **—car'i·ous** (-ē-əs) *adj.*

car'il·lon" (kar'ə-lon") *n.* a set of bells tuned to play melodies. **—car"il·lon·neur'** (-lə-nēr') *n.*

Car"i·o·ca (kar'ē-ō'kə) *n.* **1,** a native of Rio de Janeiro. **2,** (*l.c.*) a dance set to So. Amer. music; its music.

cark'ing (kär'king) *adj.* worrisome; anxious.

car'load" *n.* capacity or contents of a railroad freight car.

car·min'a·tive (kär-min'ə-tiv) *adj.* tending to reduce flatulence.

car'mine (kär'min) *n. & adj.* a purplish-red color.

car'nage (kär'nij) *n.* the slaughter of many; a massacre.

car'nal (kär'nəl) *adj.* pert. to the body; not spiritual. **—car·nal'i·ty** (-nal'ə-tē) *n.*

car·na'tion (kär-nā'shən) *n.* **1,** a fragrant flower. **2,** a shade of pink.

car·nau'ba (kär-now'bə) *n.* the wax palm of Brazil; its wax.

car·nel'ian (kär-nēl'yən) *n.* a reddish, semi-precious stone.

car'ni·val (kär'nə-vəl) *n.* **1,** riotous revelry. **2,** the feasting season immediately preceding Lent. **3,** an amusement park set up temporarily.

car'ni·vore" (kär'nə-vôr") *n.* any animal

living chiefly on flesh. **—car·niv'o·rous** (-niv'ə-rəs) *adj.*

car'ob (kar'əb) *n.* a Mediterranean tree; its seed pod, used as fodder and as a flavoring.

car'ol (kar'əl) *n.* a song of joy, esp. one sung at Christmas. —*v.i. & t.* sing joyously; celebrate in song.

car'om (kar'əm) *n.* **1,** (*Billiards*) a shot in which the cue ball is made to strike two other balls. **2,** any glancing blow or rebound. —*v.i.* rebound.

car'o·tene" (kar'ə-tēn") *n.* a hydrocarbon found in carrots and other plants, a source of vitamin A. Also, **car'o·tin** (-tin).

ca·rot'id (kə-rot'id) *n.* an artery leading to the head.

ca·rouse' (kə-rowz') *v.i.* drink freely; revel noisily. **—ca·rous'al,** *n.*

carp (kärp) *v.i.* find fault. —*n.* any of several fresh-water food fishes.

car'pal (kär'pəl) *adj.* pert. to the wrist.

car'pel (kär'pəl) *n.* (*Bot.*) a seed vessel in the pistil.

car'pen·ter (kär'pən-tər) *n.* a builder or repairer of wooden structures. **—car'pen·try,** *n.*

car'pet (kär'pit) *n.* a heavy cloth floor covering. —*v.t.* cover with, or as with carpet. **—car'pet·ing,** *n.* such fabric.

car'pet·bag"ger (-bag"ər) *n.* one who carries all his possessions in one bag, esp. a Northerner in the South after the Civil War.

car pool an arrangement by which persons take turns driving each other (to work, shopping, etc.). **—car'pool",** *v.i.*

car'port" *n.* a roofed but otherwise open shelter for an automobile.

car'ra·geen" (kar'ə-gēn") *n.* an edible seaweed; Irish moss. **—car"ra·gee'nin** (-gē'nin) *n.* food additive made from carrageen.

car'rel (kar'əl) *n.* a cubicle in a library for study or reading.

car'riage (kar'ij) *n.* **1,** a wheeled vehicle for the conveyance of persons. **2,** any part of a machine or apparatus that carries another part. **3,** manner of carrying one's person; posture. **4,** the act of carrying, conveying, or transporting. **—carriage trade,** wealthy customers.

car'ri·er (kar'ē-ər) *n.* **1,** a company, as a railroad, engaged in public transportation. **2,** a naval vessel designed to carry airplanes. **3,** underwriter; insurer. **4,** one who delivers newspapers. **—carrier pigeon,** a pigeon trained to fly home, used to carry messages.

car'ri·on (kar'ē-ən) *n.* dead and putrefying flesh.

car'rot (kar'ət) *n.* a plant having an edible orange-yellow root.

---

fat, fāte, fär, fåre, fåll, åsk; met, hē, hēr, maybē; pin, pīne; not, nōte, ôr, tool

car″rou·sel′ (kar″ə-sel′) *n.* a merry-go-round.

car′ry (kar′ė) *v.t.* **1,** transport from place to place; convey. **2,** bear the weight of; support. **3,** adopt (a bill or motion); obtain election from (an electorate). **4,** be possessed of. **5,** transfer. **6,** keep (goods) in stock; have available for sale. —*v.i.* **1,** reach a distance, as a voice or missile. **2,** be adopted, as by a vote. **3,** (with *on*) display emotion. **4,** (with *on*) continue. —*n.* **1,** distance traversed. **2,** a portage. —**carrying charge,** interest.

cart (kärt) *n.* a two-wheeled vehicle. —*v.t.* transport in a cart.

cart′age (kär′tij) *n.* **1,** conveyance in a cart. **2,** a fee therefore.

carte blanche (kärt′blänsh′) (*Fr.*) unlimited authority.

car·tel′ (kär-tel′) *n.* a syndicate formed to seek a business monopoly.

cart′er (-ər) *n.* a truckman.

car′ti·lage (kär′tə-lij) *n.* a firm, elastic substance in the body; gristle. —**car″ti·lag′i·nous** (-laj′i-nəs) *adj.*

car·tog′ra·phy (kär-tog′rə-fė) *n.* the art and science of making maps. —**car·tog′ra·pher,** *n.* —**car″to·graph′ic,** *adj.* —**car″to·graph′i·cal·ly,** *adv.*

car′ton (kär′tən) *n.* a cardboard box, usually large.

car·toon′ (kär-toon′) *n.* **1,** a preparatory drawing (for a painting, sculpture, etc.). **2,** a drawing, often in caricature, made as a commentary on current events, or to illustrate a joke or narrative. —**car·toon′ist,** *n.*

car′tridge (kär′trij) *n.* **1,** a cylindrical metal or cardboard case holding a charge of powder and shot. **2,** any similar sealed container.

cart′wheel″ *n.* **1,** a lateral handspring. **2,** (*Slang*) a large coin.

carve (kärv) *v.t. & i.* cut with an edged tool, esp. with skill.

car″y·at′id (kar″ė-at′id) *n.* a sculptured figure of a woman used as a supporting column.

car′wash″ *n.* an automatic machine for washing automobiles.

ca·sa′ba (kə-sä′bə) *n.* a variety of muskmelon. Also, **cas·sa′ba.**

cas·cade′ (kas-kād′) *n.* **1,** a waterfall; a series of waterfalls. **2,** something likened to waterfalls.

cas·ca′ra (kas-kar′ə) *n.* **1,** a kind of buckthorn. **2,** a laxative made from its bark.

case (kās) *n.* **1,** that which happens; actual circumstances. **2,** a particular instance among like instances. **3,** a question, problem, or state of things requiring discussion or deci-

sion; a cause of legal action. **4,** a statement of facts and reasons relevant to a decision. **5,** an instance of disease; a patient. **6,** (*Gram.*) one of the categories in the inflection of nouns, as *nominative case.* **7,** an outer covering or sheath; a box or receptacle. —*v.t.* **1,** put in a case; enclose. **2,** (*Slang*) survey, as for criminal intent. —**lower case,** small (letters). —**upper case,** capital (letters).

case′hard″en *v.t.* harden the surface of (metal), as by heat.

ca′se·in (kā′sė-in) *n.* a protein precipitated from milk.

case′ment (kās′mənt) *n.* a hinged frame for a glass window.

ca·serne′ (kə-zern′) *n.* a small barracks.

cash (kash) *n.* **1,** currency; specie. **2,** immediate payment. —*v.t.* exchange (a check, etc.) for cash. —**cash in** (*Colloq.*) **1,** terminate a speculation, usually with profit. **2,** die. —**cash register,** a machine that holds and records money received.

cash′ew (kash′oo) *n.* a tropical American tree or its fruit, a small edible nut.

cash·ier′ (ka-shir′) *n.* an employee or officer who receives money, makes change, etc.; a treasurer. —*v.t.* dismiss in disgrace. —**cashier's check,** a check drawn by a bank for payment from its own treasury.

cash′mere (kash′mir) *n.* **1,** a fabric made from the hair of Kashmir goats. **2,** a twilled wool fabric.

cas′ing (kā′sing) *n.* a protective case or covering; a frame.

ca·si′no (kə-sē′nō) *n.* [*pl.* **-nos**] **1,** a building or room for indoor games. **2,** [also, **cas·si′no**] a card game.

cask (kåsk) *n.* **1,** a barrel for holding liquids. **2,** its capacity.

cas′ket (kås′kit) *n.* **1,** a small box, esp. for jewels. **2,** a coffin.

cas·sa′va (kə-sä′və) *n.* a tropical plant cultivated for its starchy roots.

cas′se·role″ (kas′ə-rōl″) *n.* a baking dish with a cover; food cooked and served in such a dish.

cas·sette′ (kə-set′) *n.* **1,** a lightproof case for holding photographic or X-ray film. **2,** a compact container of recording tape.

cas′sia (kash′ə) *n.* **1,** a Chinese tree, or cinnamon obtained from it. **2,** a tropical tree or its pulpy pods, which yield senna.

cas′sock (kas′ək) *n.* a long, close-fitting clerical coat.

cas′so·war″y (kas′ə-wär″ė) *n.* a large, flightless bird of Australia.

cast (kåst) *v.t.* [*pret. & p.p.* **cast**] **1,** throw; hurl; fling. **2,** throw off; shed. **3,** plan; contrive; arrange; compute. **4,** select actors for (a play); assign (an actor) to a rôle. **5,** pour (molten metal, plaster, etc.) into a mold; make by this process. —*v.i.* **1,** throw. **2,** calculate; conjecture. —*n.* **1,** a throw. **2,** what is cast; something molded [also, **cast'-ing**]. **3,** the list of actors in a play. **4,** tendency; expression; tinge. **5,** a computation.

cas″ta·net′ (kas″tə-net′) *n.* a shell of hard wood, used in pairs as clappers to provide a rhythmic beat.

cast′a·way″ (kast′ə-wā″) *n.* a person marooned, as by shipwreck.

caste (kåst) *n.* **1,** one of the hereditary social classes among the Hindus. **2,** any group united by its social position.

cas·tel·lat′ed (kas′tə-lā″tid) *adj.* built like a castle; having turrets and battlements. —**cas″tel·la′tion,** *n.*

cast′er (kås′tər) *n.* **1,** one who or that which casts. **2,** a small wheel attached to the leg of a piece of furniture. **3,** a small cruet or shaker.

cas′ti·gate″ (kas′tə-gāt″) *v.t.* **1,** criticize severely. **2,** punish; correct. —**cas″ti·ga′-tion,** *n.*

cas′tile (kas′tēl) *n.* soap made with olive oil and soda.

cast-'i″ron (kåst′ī″ərn) *adj.* **1,** made of cast iron, an alloy of iron, carbon, etc. **2,** inflexible. **3,** hardy.

cas′tle (kås′əl) *n.* **1,** a fortified residence of feudal times. **2,** a fortress. **3,** an imposing building. **4,** a chess piece, the rook. —*v.t. & i.* in chess, exchange the places of the king and rook. —**cas″tling,** *n.* a move in chess. —**castle in the air,** a daydream.

cas′tor oil (kas′tər) thick oil obtained from a bean (*castor bean*), used as a cathartic or lubricant.

cas′trate (kas′trāt) *v.t.* emasculate. —**cas·tra′tion,** *n.*

cas′u·al (kazh′ū-əl) *adj.* **1,** happening by chance; offhand. **2,** careless; negligent. **3,** occasional; irregular. —*n.* **1,** a worker employed only irregularly. **2,** a casualty. —**cas′u·al·ness,** *n.*

cas′u·al·ty (kazh′ū-əl-tē) *n.* **1,** an accident involving bodily injury or death. **2,** a person injured accidentally. **3,** (*Mil.*) a soldier lost through enemy action.

cas′u·ist·ry (kazh′oo-is-trē) *n.* specious reasoning. —**cas′u·ist,** *n.*

ca′sus bel′li (ka′səs-bel′ī) (*Lat.*) a cause or justification for war.

cat (kat) *n.* **1,** a domesticated animal of the feline family. **2,** any feline animal, as lion, tiger, etc. **3,** (*Colloq.*) a spiteful woman. **4,** a whip formed of several thongs: *cat-o′-nine-tails.* **5,** a caterpillar tractor. —**cat nap,** a short sleep.

ca·tab′o·lism (kə-tab′ə-liz-əm) *n.* destructive metabolism. —**cat″a·bol′ic** (kat″ə-bol′ik) *adj.*

cat′a·clysm (kat′ə-kliz-əm) *n.* a violent, usually destructive, upheaval. —**cat″a·clys′mic,** *adj.* —**cat″a·clys′mi·cal·ly,** *adv.*

cat′a·comb″ (kat′ə-kōm″) *n.* (usually *pl.*) an underground burial vault.

cat′a·falque″ (kat′ə-falk″) *n.* a dais for display of a coffin at a ceremonious public funeral.

cat′a·lep″sy (kat′ə-lep″sè) *n.* a morbid condition of muscular rigidity, loss of sensation, etc. —**cat″a·lep′tic,** *adj.*

cat′a·log″ (kat′ə-lâg″) *n.* a list of separate items; a register; a series of explanatory notes. —*v.t.* **1,** list. **2,** describe in explanatory notes. Also, **cat′a·logue″.**

ca·tal′pa (kə-tal′pə) *n.* a flowering tree of Asia and America.

ca·tal′y·sis (kə-tal′y-sis) *n.* acceleration of a chemical reaction by a substance which itself remains unaffected. —**cat′a·lyst** (kat′ə-list) *n.* the substance used in catalysis. —**cat′a·lyt′ic,** *adj.* —**catalytic converter,** an antipollution device. —**cat′a·lyze″,** *v.t. & i.*

cat″a·ma·ran′ (kat″ə-mə-ran′) *n.* **1,** a raft. **2,** a boat with connected parallel hulls. **3,** a scold.

cat′a·mount″ (kat′ə-mownt″) *n.* a wild animal of the feline family; the cougar; the lynx.

cat′a·pult″ (kat′ə-pult″) *n.* a contrivance for hurling; a launching device for airplanes. —*v.t.* hurl by recoil. —*v.i.* leap suddenly.

cat′a·ract″ (kat′ə-rakt″) *n.* **1,** a large or spectacular waterfall; any furious downpour of water. **2,** a disease of the eye, characterized by opacity of the lens.

ca·tarrh′ (kə-tär′) *n.* inflammation of the mucous membrane, esp. in the nose and throat. —**ca·tarrh′al,** *adj.*

ca·tas′tro·phe (kə-tas′trə-fè) *n.* a sudden or extreme disaster. —**cat″a·stroph′ic** (kat″ə-strof″ik) *adj.* —**cat″a·stroph′i·cal·ly,** *adv.*

cat″a·to′ni·a (kat″ə-tō′nè-ə) *n.* a muscular rigidity and insensitivity, symptom of certain mental disorders. —**cat″a·ton′ic** (kat″ə-ton′ik) *adj.*

cat′boat″ (kat′bōt″) *n.* a small sailboat.

cat′call″ *n.* a cry expressing disapproval, as in a theater.

catch (kach) *v.t.* **[caught], 1,** capture after pursuing; seize. **2,** overtake; intercept; reach. **3,** halt; check. **4,** entrap; deceive. **5,** get; receive; incur. **6,** understand; perceive. **7,** (*Colloq.*) see or hear (a performer or act). —*v.i.* take hold; become entangled. —*n.* **1,** the act of catching. **2,** a device for stopping or checking motion. **3,** what is caught. **4,** (*Colloq.*) something desirable to catch, as a matrimonial prospect. **5,** a trick; ruse; hindrance. **—catch′ing,** *adj.* infectious.

catch′pen′ny *adj.* designed to be sold readily, though of little worth.

catch′up (kech′əp) *n.* ketchup.

catch′word″ *n.* **1,** a slogan. **2,** a word at the top of a dictionary page, to show the first or last main entry on it. **3,** a word at the bottom of a page to show the first word of the next page.

catch′y (kach′ē) *adj.* quick to win attention and favor.

cat″e·che′sis (kat″ə-kē′sis) *n.* [*pl.* **-ses** (-sēz)] oral religious instruction. **—cat″e·chet′ic** (-ket′ik) *adj.*

cat′e·chism (kat′ə-kiz-əm) *n.* a series of questions and the answers to them. **—cat′·e·chize″** (-kīz″) *v.t.*

cat″e·chu′men (kat″ə-kū′mən) *n.* a student.

cat″e·gor′i·cal (kat″ə-gôr′i-kəl) *adj.* **1,** stated unconditionally; explicit. **2,** pert. to a category.

cat′e·go″ry (kat′ə-gôr′ē) *n.* a comprehensive division or class. **—cat′e·go·rize″,** *v.t.*

cat′e·nar·y (kat′ə-ner-ē) *n.* the curve assumed by a suspended cord.

ca′ter (kā′tər) *v.i.* make provision, as of food, service, etc. **—ca′ter·er,** *n.* a purveyor of food.

cat′er-cor″nered (kat′ər-kôr″nərd) *adj.* diagonal.

cat′er·pil″lar (kat′ə-pil″ər) *n.* the wormlike larva of a moth or butterfly. **—adj.** (*T.N.*) moving on treads, as some tractors.

cat′er·waul″ (kat′ər-wâl″) *v.i.* howl or screech like a cat. **—n.** such a sound.

cat′fish″ (kat′fish″) *n.* any of many smooth-skinned, blunt-headed fishes.

ca·thar′sis (kə-thär′sis) *n.* **1,** (*Med.*) purgation. **2,** any cleansing or release, as of pent-up emotions. **—ca·thar′tic** (-tik) *adj. & n.*

ca·the′dral (kə-thē′drəl) *n.* **1,** the principal church in a diocese. **2,** any imposing church edifice.

cath′e·ter (kath′ə-tər) *n.* a tube used to drain the bladder. **—cath′e·ter·ize″,** *v.t.*

cath′ode (kath′ōd) *n.* the negative pole of an electric current; a negative electrode. **—cathode ray,** electrons issued from the cathode.

cath′o·lic (kath′ə-lik) *adj.* **1,** universal in extent, character, or application. **2,** (*cap.*) pert. to the Roman Catholic Church, or to any of certain other Christian churches. **—n.** (*cap.*) a member of a Catholic church.

—Ca·thol′i·cism (kə-thol′ə-siz-əm) *n.*

—cath″o·lic′i·ty (-lis′ə-tē) *n.* universality.

cat′i·on (kat′ē-ən) *n.* a positively charged ion, molecule, or radical.

cat′kin (kat′kin) *n.* a scaly or downy spike of flowers.

cat′nip (kat′nip) *n.* a plant of the mint family, relished by cats.

cat′s-′eye″ *n.* a chatoyant gem.

cat′s-′paw″ (kats′pâ″) *n.* a dupe.

cat′sup (kat′sup) *n.* ketchup.

cat′tail″ (kat′tāl″) *n.* a marsh plant with velvety spikes of brown flowers.

cat′tle (kat′əl) *n.* **1,** bovine animals. **2,** livestock generally.

cat′ty (kat′ē) *adj.* malicious. Also, **cat′tish.** **—cat′ti·ness,** *n.*

cat′ty-cor″nered (kat′ē-kôr″nərd) *adj.* catercornered.

cat′walk″ (kat′wâk″) *n.* a narrow suspended path, as on a ship.

Cau·ca′sian (kâ-kā′zhən) *adj. & n.* ''white'' in race.

Cau′ca·soid (kâ′kə-zoid) *adj.* of the ''white'' race; Caucasian.

cau′cus (kâ′kəs) *n.* a meeting of the leaders of a political party. **—v.i.** meet to discuss party policy.

cau′dal (kâ′dəl) *adj.* **1,** like a tail. **2,** at or near the tail.

caught (kât) *v.* pret. & p.p. of *catch.*

caul (kâl) *n.* a sac sometimes covering the head of a child at birth, once thought to augur good luck.

caul′dron (kâl′drən) *n.* caldron.

cau′li·flow″er (kâ′lə-flow″ər) *n.* **1,** a plant whose flower forms a compact head. **2,** the edible flower. **—cauliflower ear,** an ear mutilated, as in boxing.

caulk (kâk) *v.t.* calk.

cau·sal′i·ty (kâ-zal′ə-tē) *n.* the relation of cause and effect.

cau·sa′tion (kâ-zā′shən) *n.* **1,** act of causing. **2,** a cause. **3,** causality.

cause (kâz) *n.* **1,** that which produces an effect or a result. **2,** the reason or motive for an action. **3,** a subject of discussion or debate; a case for judicial decision. **4,** a doctrine, view, or side of a question. **—v.t.** make occur or be; bring about. **—caus′al,** *adj.*

cause cé·lè′bre (se-leb′rə) any famous legal case.

cau″se·rie′ (kō″zə-rē′) *n.* **1,** informal talk; a chat. **2,** a brief essay.

cause′way″ *n.* a raised road; a paved highway.

caus′tic (kâs′tik) *adj.* **1,** capable of burning, corroding, or destroying animal tissue.

---

tub, cūte, pûll; labəl; oil, owl, go, chip, she, thin, *th*en, sing, ink; *see p. 6*

2, severely critical or sarcastic. —*n.* a caustic substance. —**caus′ti·cal·ly,** *adv.*

cau′ter·ize″ (kâ′tər-īz″) *v.t.* burn with a hot iron or a caustic, as morbid flesh. —**cau″ter·i·za′tion,** *n.* —**cau′ter·y,** *n.*

cau′tion (kâ′shən) *n.* **1,** prudence in regard to danger; wariness. **2,** a warning of danger. —*v.t.* warn; admonish. —**cau′tion·ar·y** (-ner-ē) *adj.*

cau′tious (-shəs) *adj.* wary. —**cau′tious·ness,** *n.*

cav′al·cade″ (kav′əl-kād″) *n.* a procession of persons on horseback or in carriages.

cav″a·lier′ (kav″ə-lir′) *n.* **1,** a horseman; knight. **2,** a courtly or gallant person; a man who escorts a woman. —*adj.* haughty; disdainful; discourteously offhand.

cav′al·ry (kav′əl-rē) *n.* military troops that serve on horseback. —**mechanized cavalry,** troops serving in motor vehicles.

cav″a·ti′na (kav″ə-tē′nə) *n.* a simple song.

cave (kāv) *n.* a hollow place in a hillside, esp. a natural underground cavity of large size. —*v.i.* (with *in*) collapse.

ca′ve·at″ (ka′vē-at″) *n.* **1,** a warning. **2,** (*Law*) notice to suspend action until further hearing. —**caveat emp′tor** (emp′tôr) (*Lat.*) let the buyer beware.

cav′ern (kav′ərn) *n.* a cave.

cav′ern·ous (-əs) *adj.* **1,** containing caves. **2,** hollow; gaping.

cav′i·ar″ (kav′ē-är″) *n.* roe of fish, esp. sturgeon, prepared as a relish.

cav′il (kav′əl) *v.i.* find fault without good reason; carp. —*n.* a captious objection.

cav′i·ty (kav′ə-tē) *n.* any hollow place or space; esp., a hole in a tooth.

ca·vort′ (kə-vôrt′) *v.i.* prance about; caper.

caw (kâ) *n.* the call of a crow, or any similar sound.

cay (kā; kē) *n.* a small island.

cay·enne′ (kī-en′) *n.* a red pepper.

cay·use′ (kī-ūs′) *n.* an Indian pony.

cease (sēs) *v.i.* **1,** stop doing an action; desist; come to rest. **2,** come to an end. —*v.t.* discontinue. —**cease′less,** *adj.* without stopping.

cease-′fire″ *n.* a suspension of military action.

ce′dar (sē′dər) *n.* any of several coniferous trees.

cede (sēd) *v.t.* yield and surrender to another; grant.

ce·dil′la (si-dil′ə) *n.* a sign (ç) indicating a c that is pronounced as s.

ceil′ing (sē′ling) *n.* **1,** the interior overhead surface, as of a room. **2,** the maximum altitude an aircraft can reach, or from which it has clear visibility of the earth. —**ceiling price,** a maximum established by law.

Cel′a·nese″ (sel′ə-nēz″) *n.* (*T.N.*) a rayon fabric or yarn.

cel′e·brate″ (sel′ə-brāt″) *v.t.* **1,** commemorate (a day or event) with festivities, ceremonies, etc. **2,** perform (rites). **3,** make known with honor or praise; extol. —*v.i.* make merry. —**cel′e·brant,** *n.* —**cel″e·brat″ed,** *adj.* famous. —**cel″e·bra′tion,** *n.*

ce·leb′ri·ty (sə-leb′rə-tē) *n.* a famous person.

ce·ler′i·ty (sə-ler′ə-tē) *n.* rapidity of motion; swiftness.

cel′er·y (sel′ə-rē) *n.* a plant whose stalks are used as a food.

ce·les′ta (sə-les′tə) *n.* a keyboard glockenspiel. Also, **ce·leste′** (sə-lest′).

ce·les′tial (sə-les′chəl) *adj.* **1,** pert. to the sky. **2,** heavenly; divine.

cel′i·ba·cy (sel′ə-bə-sē) *n.* the state of being unmarried. —**cel′i·bate,** *adj. & n.*

cell (sel) *n.* **1,** one of many like rooms, as in a prison. **2,** any small room. **3,** a group forming a unit in an organization, political party, etc. **4,** the structural unit of organic life. **5,** a device for producing an electric current chemically.

cel′lar (sel′ər) *n.* a room or rooms under a building, partly or wholly underground. —**cel′lar·age** (-ij) *n.* cellar space; storage space in a cellar; a charge for such space.

cel″lar·et′ (sel″ə-ret′) *n.* a cabinet for wine bottles.

cel′lo (chel′ō) *n.* [*pl.* -**los**] violoncello. —**cel′list,** *n.*

cel′lo·phane″ (sel′ə-fān″) *n.* a transparent plastic sheeting.

cel′lu·lar (sel′ū-lər) *adj.* pert. to, or consisting of, cells.

cel′lu·loid″ (sel′yə-loid″) *n.* a nitrocellulose plastic compound.

cel′lu·lose″ (sel′yə-lōs″) *n.* the chief constituent of the cell walls of all plants, used in making plastic fibers, feed, fertilizers, etc.

Cel′si·us (sel′sē-əs) *adj.* centigrade.

Celt′ic (sel′tik) *adj.* pert. to the Celts, a people including the Irish, Welsh, Gaels, and Bretons. —*n.* a Celtic language. Also, **Kelt′ic.**

cem′ba·lo (chem′bə-lō) *n.* **1,** a dulcimer. **2,** a harpsichord.

ce·ment′ (si-ment′) *n.* **1,** any of various adhesive plastic substances. **2,** pulverized limestone and clay, used in making concrete; Portland cement. —*v.t. & i.* join; bind.

cem'e·ter"y (sem'ə-ter"ē) *n.* a burial ground.

ce'no·bite" (se'nə-bīt") *n.* a member of a religious community. **—ce"no·bit'ic** (-bit'ik) *adj.* **—ce'no·bit"ism** (-bit"iz-əm) *n.*

cen'o·taph" (sen'ə-taf") *n.* an empty tomb as a memorial to someone buried elsewhere.

Cen"o·zo'ic (sen"ə-zō'ik) *adj.* pert. to a geological era, the age of man.

cen'ser (sen'sər) *n.* a vessel or pan in which incense is burned.

cen'sor (sen'sər) *n.* **1,** one empowered to judge the fitness of manuscripts, communications, etc. for publication. **2,** one who censures; a faultfinder. **—v.t.** judge critically; examine for fitness; delete as unsuitable. **—cen'sor·ship,** *n.*

cen·sor'i·ous (sen-sôr'ē-əs) *adj.* faultfinding; carping. **—cen·sor'i·ous·ness,** *n.*

cen'sure (sen'shər) *v.t.* reprove. **—n.** reproof.

cen'sus (sen'səs) *n.* registration and enumeration of the population.

cent (sent) *n.* In U. S. coinage, a copper coin worth .01 dollar.

cen'taur (sen'tôr) *n.* a mythological animal half horse and half man.

cen"te·nar'i·an (sen"tə-nār'ē-ən) *n.* a person aged 100 or more years.

cen"te·nar'y (sen"tə-ner'ē) *adj.* pert. to or consisting of 100. **—n.** a 100-year period. **—cen"te·nar'i·an,** *n.*

cen·ten'ni·al (sen-ten'ē-əl) *n. & adj.* the 100th anniversary.

cen'ter (sen'tər) *n.* **1,** the point equidistant from all extremities; the mid-point. **2,** the area near the middle. **3,** a pivot or axis. **4,** a principal object. **5,** position of a player in various games. **6,** a political party of moderate views. **—v.i. & t.** be or place at the center. Also, **cen'tre. —cen'trist,** *n.* a political moderate.

cen'ter·board" *n.* a board lowered through the keel of a sailboat, to provide stability.

cen'ter·fold" *n.* the central facing pages of a magazine, usu. with an additional foldout page or pages, showing a photograph, map, etc.

cen'ti- (sen'tə) *pref.* **1,** 100. **2,** 1/100th. **—cen'ti·gram,** *n.* 1/100th gram. **—cen'ti·me"ter,** *n.* 1/100th meter.

cen'ti·are" (sen'tē-âr") *n.* a square meter.

cen'ti·grade" (sen'tə-grād") *adj.* pert. to the thermometer on which boiling and freezing points of water are 100° and 0° respectively. Also, **Cel'si·us.**

cen'ti·pede" (sen'tə-pēd") *n.* any of various insects having many legs.

cen'tral (sen'trəl) *adj.* in the center; conveniently located. **—n.** a telephone operator. **—cen·tral'i·ty,** *n.*

cen'tral·ize" (sen'trə-līz") *v.t. & i.* **1,** put or come together at or near the center. **2,** bring or come under one control. **—cen"tral·i·za'tion,** *n.*

cen·trif'u·gal (sen-trif'yə-gəl) *adj.* radiating or flying off or out, from a center.

cen'tri·fuge" (sen'tri-fūj") *n.* a machine that whirls a mixture to separate its ingredients.

cen·trip'e·tal (sen-trip'ə-təl) *adj.* progressing or stressed toward, or held to, the center.

cen·tu'ri·on (sen-tyûr'ē-ən) *n.* **1,** in ancient Rome, a military officer of medium rank, commanding 100 men. **2,** a person of one hundred years of age or more.

cen'tu·ry (sen'chə-rē) *n.* **1,** a period of 100 years. **2,** 100 of anything.

ce·phal'ic (sə-fal'ik) *adj.* pert. to the head or skull.

ce·ram'ics (sə-ram'iks) *n. pl.* **1,** clay or porcelain objects. **2,** the art or manufacture of such objects. **—ce·ram'ic,** *adj.*

ce're·al (sir'ē-əl) *adj.* pert. to edible grain or seeds. **—n.** a food prepared from corn, wheat, etc.

cer"e·bel'lum (ser"ə-bel'əm) *n.* the rear lobe of the brain.

cer'e·bral (ser'ə-brəl) *adj.* pert. to the cerebrum or brain. **—cerebral palsy,** a crippling disease, characterized by paralysis or spasms, due to brain injury.

cer'e·brate" (ser'ə-brāt") *v.i.* think.

cer'e·brum (ser'ə-brəm) *n.* the front portion of the brain.

cere'ment (sir'mənt) *n.* **1,** the cloth in which a body is wrapped for embalming. **2,** (*pl.*) grave clothes.

cer"e·mo'ni·al (ser"ə-mō'nē-əl) *adj.* pert. to or being a ceremony or rite; formal. **—n.** rite.

cer"e·mo'ni·ous (ser"ə-mō'nē-əs) *adj.* **1,** elaborately polite. **2,** ceremonial. **—cer"e·mo'ni·ous·ness,** *n.*

cer'e·mo"ny (ser'ə-mō"nē) *n.* **1,** a formal occasion; rite. **2,** usages of politeness.

ce·rise' (sə-rēs') *adj.* cherry red.

ce'ri·um (sir'ē-əm) *n.* a metallic chemical element of the rare-earth group, no. 58, symbol Ce.

cer'tain (sêr'tən) *adj.* **1,** sure to occur; inevitable. **2,** established as true or sure. **3,** free from doubt; confident. **4,** definite; specified. **5,** unspecified in amount, degree or identity; some. **—cer'tain·ty,** *n.*

cer'tain·ly (-lē) *adv.* with certainty; without doubt. **—interj.** of course!

---

cer·tif'i·cate (sẽr-tif'i-kət) *n.* **1,** a document of attestation. **2,** a written testimonial as to status, qualifications, etc. **3,** a banknote, bond, or similar financial document. —*v.t.* (-kāt') certify by such a document. —**cer''ti·fi·ca'tion,** *n.*

cer'ti·fy'' (sẽr'tə-fī'') *v.t.* attest to the truth or validity of. —**cer'ti·fied check,** a check guaranteed by a bank.

cer'ti·tude'' (sẽr'tə-tūd'') *n.* certainty; complete freedom from doubt.

ce·ru'le·an (sə-roo'lē-ən) *adj.* sky blue; light blue.

ce·ru'men (sə-roo'mən) *n.* earwax.

cer'vix (sẽr'viks) *n.* **1,** the neck. **2,** a constricted necklike part. —**cer'vi·cal,** *adj.*

ce'si·um (sē'zē-əm) *n.* a rare, monovalent metallic element, no. 55, symbol Cs.

ces·sa'tion (se-sā'shən) *n.* ceasing or discontinuance of action or motion.

ces'sion (sesh'ən) *n.* the act of ceding; transfer of rights or property; surrender.

cess'pool'' (ses'pool'') *n.* a pit for the reception of sewage.

ce·ta'cean (sə-tā'shən) *adj.* pert. to whales.

cha-'cha' (chä'chä') *n.* a Latin Amer. ballroom dance; its music.

chafe (chāf) *v.t.* **1,** abrade or roughen by friction. **2,** vex; annoy. —**chaf'ing dish,** a warming dish with its own heater.

chaff (chaf) *n.* **1,** the residue left from threshing grain. **2,** finely-chopped straw for cattle food. **3,** gentle banter; raillery. —*v.t. & i.* tease; banter.

chaf'fer (chaf'ər) *v.i.* bargain; haggle. —*n.* haggling.

chaf'finch (chaf'inch) *n.* a common European finch.

cha·grin' (shə-grin') *n.* mental disquiet or grief; self-dissatisfaction. —*v.t.* render crestfallen.

chain (chān) *n.* **1,** a connected series of links of metal or other material. **2,** something that binds, restrains, or fetters. **3,** (*pl.*) bondage. **4,** a series of connected phenomena, events, objects, etc. **5,** a measuring instrument, 66 feet long (*surveyor's chain*) or 100 feet long (*engineer's chain*). —*v.t.* fasten with a chain; unite; restrain. —**chain gang,** a group of prisoners chained together. —**chain letter,** a letter sent from person to person according to a certain plan. —**chain reaction,** a series in which each effect causes the next one. —**chain store,** one of a group of retail stores owned and managed by the same company.

chain-'smoke'' *v.* to smoke (cigarettes, etc.) continuously.

chair (chãr) *n.* **1,** a seat with a back, for one person. **2,** a chairperson; the office of chairperson. **3,** a position of authority; a professorship, as, the *chair* of physics. —*v.t.* act as chairperson of.

chair'man (-mən) *n.* [*pl.* **-men** (-mən)] a presiding officer. —**chair'man·ship,** *n.* —**chair'per''son,** *n.* —**chair'wom''an,** *n. fem.*

chaise (shāz) *n.* **1,** an open horsedrawn vehicle; shay. **2,** [also, **chaise longue** (lâng)] an armchair whose seat extends to form a couch.

chal·ced'o·ny (kal-sed'ə-nē) *n.* a variety of quartz; a semiprecious stone.

chal·co- (chal-kō) *pref.* copper.

cha·let' (shä-lā') *n.* a style of country house, with a wide heavy roof.

chal'ice (chal'is) *n.* a cup-shaped vessel from which the wine is administered at communion.

chalk (châk) *n.* **1,** a soft whitish variety of limestone. **2,** a crayon or cube of such substance. —*v.t.* **1,** treat with chalk. **2,** (with *up*) write; score; earn. —**chalk'-board'',** *n.* blackboard. —**chalk'y,** *adj.* like chalk; very pale.

chal'lah (khä'lə) *n.* a loaf of white leavened egg bread used by Jews.

chal'lenge (chal'inj) *n.* **1,** a call to battle or debate. **2,** a demand for explanation or identification. **3,** an objection. —*v.t.* **1,** invite to battle or debate. **2,** demand explanation of, etc. **3,** take exception to; object to.

chal'lis (shal'ē) *n.* a light cotton, wool, or rayon fabric, usu. printed.

cham'ber (chām'bər) *n.* **1,** a room, esp. an inner or secluded room; a bedroom. **2,** a legislative body or its meeting place. **3,** any enclosed space, hollow, or cavity. **4,** (*pl.*) a private office or apartment, esp. of a judge or lawyer. **5,** [also, **chamber pot**] a pot used as a urinal.

cham'ber·lain (chām'bər-lin) *n.* **1,** one responsible for the management of rooms. **2,** a supervisory official; treasurer.

cham'ber·maid'' *n.* a girl servant who takes care of bedrooms.

cham'bray (sham'brā) *n.* a kind of gingham.

cha·me'le·on (kə-mē'lē-ən) *n.* **1,** a lizardlike reptile that can adapt its coloration to that of its surroundings. **2,** a fickle person.

cham'fer (cham'fər) *n.* a bevel on the edge of a board or other solid, usually of 45°. —*v.t.* bevel.

cham'ois (sham'ē) *n.* **1,** a Europ. antelope. **2,** its skin, or similar soft leather.

champ *v.t. & i.* bite into small pieces; munch; chew. —*n.* champion.

cham·pagne' (sham-pān') *n.* a sparkling white wine.

cham'pi·on (chăm'pē-ən) *n.* **1**, the winner of a contest. **2**, one who defends a person or a cause. —*adj.* first among all competitors; preeminent. —*v.t.* defend; support. —**cham'pi·on·ship**, *n.* **1**, supremacy. **2**, support or defense.

chance (chăns) *n.* **1**, accident; fortuity. **2**, hazard; risk. **3**, a favorable contingency; an opportunity. **4**, an unexpected event. **5**, (often *pl.*) probability; likelihood. —*v.i. & t.* **1**, occur by accident. **2**, hazard. —*adj.* due to chance. —**chan'cy**, *adj.* (*Colloq.*)

chan'cel (chăn'səl) *n.* an enclosed space about the altar of a church.

chan'cel·ler·y (chăn'sə-lə-rē) *n.* chancery.

chan'cel·lor (chăn'sə-lər) *n.* **1**, the judge in a court of equity or chancery. **2**, a high or the highest officer of certain universities, courts, etc.

chance-'med"ley *n.* **1**, killing by accident or self-defense. **2**, haphazardness.

chan'cer·y (chăn'sə-rē) *n.* **1**, a court of equity. **2**, an office of public records. **3**, [also, **chan'cel·ler·y**] the court or office of a chancellor. —**in chancery**, in a helpless or embarrassing position.

chan'cre (shang'kər) *n.* a sore, esp. the initial lesion of syphilis.

chan'croid (shang'kroid) *n.* a venereal sore.

chan"de·lier' (shan"də-lir') *n.* a branched cluster of lights hung from a ceiling.

chan'dler (chăn'dlər) *n.* **1**, a dealer in specific supplies, provisions, etc. **2**, a maker of candles. —**chan'dler·y**, *n.*

change (chānj) *v.t.* **1**, make different; alter. **2**, replace by another; substitute. **3**, give and take reciprocally; exchange. —*v.i.* become different; pass from one condition or state to another. —*n.* **1**, alteration; modification; transformation. **2**, substitution; exchange. **3**, variety; novelty. **4**, money of small denomination; coins. —**change'ling**, *n.* a child secretly substituted for another. —**change of life**, menopause.

change'a·ble (chān'jə-bəl) *adj.* variable; fickle; inconstant.

chan'nel (chan'əl) *n.* **1**, the bed of a waterway; a navigable waterway. **2**, a means of access; a route. **3**, a furrow or groove. **4**, a frequency band, as in radio. **5**, (*pl.*) the prescribed routing of an application or order. —*v.t.* **1**, direct into a particular course. **2**, cut or form a channel in.

chan'son (shän'sən) *n.* (*Fr.*) a song.

chant (chănt) *n.* **1**, a song in which an indefinite number of syllables are intoned on each note, as in canticle-singing. **2**, any monotonous song or singing. —*v.t. & i.* sing; intone in a monotonous manner.

chan·teuse' (shan-töz') *n.* a woman singer, esp. of popular music.

chant'ey (chan'tē) *n.* a tune sung, esp. by sailors, to set the rhythm of united physical labor.

chan'ti·cleer" (chan'tə-klir") *n.* a cock; a male fowl.

chan'try (chăn'trē) *n.* a chapel attached to a church, used for minor services.

Chan·u·kah (khän'ə-kə) *n.* Hanukkah.

cha'os (kā'os) *n.* the absence of form or order; utter confusion. —**cha·ot'ic** (-ot'ik) *adj.* —**cha·ot'i·cal·ly**, *adv.*

chap *v.t. & i.* [**chapped, chap'ping**] (of the skin) split in clefts; crack and roughen. —*n.* fellow; a familiar term for a man or boy.

chap"ar·ral' (chap"ə-ral') *n.* a dense thicket.

cha·peau' (sha-pō') *n.* (*Fr.*) [*pl.* **-peaux'** (-pō')] a hat.

chap'el (chap'əl) *n.* **1**, a small church; a subordinate place of worship in a church. **2**, a room for religious services in a school; the services held there.

chap'er·on" (shap'ə-rōn") *n.* an older person, usu. a married woman, accompanying younger unmarried women. —*v.t. & i.* attend as a chaperon.

chap'fal"len (chap'fâl"ən) *adj.* dejected.

chap'lain (chap'lin) *n.* a clergyman serving a special group, as a legislature, army, navy, etc.

chap'let (chap'lit) *n.* **1**, a wreath, as of flowers, worn on the head. **2**, a string of beads.

chaps *n. pl.* seatless riding breeches worn by American cowboys.

chap'ter (chap'tər) *n.* **1**, a main division of a book or treatise. **2**, a council; assemblage. **3**, a branch of an association, fraternity, etc.

char (chär) *v.t.* [**charred, char'ring**] burn to charcoal; scorch. —*v.i.* **1**, become charcoal. **2**, do menial household tasks. —**char'wom"an**, *n.* a domestic servant hired by the day.

char'a·banc' (shär'ə-bank") *n.* a bus, esp. one for sightseeing or excursions.

char'ac·ter (kar'ik-tər) *n.* **1**, the aggregate of properties and qualities that distinguishes one person or thing from another. **2**, a trait. **3**, good qualities. **4**, a person, esp. (*Colloq.*) an odd one; an actor or rôle in a play. **5**, a mark made in writing, printing, etc.

char"ac·ter·is'tic (-is'tik) *n.* a distinguishing quality or trait. —*adj.* typical. —**char"ac·ter·is'ti·cal·ly**, *adv.*

char'ac·ter·ize" (-īz") *v.t.* describe in terms of characteristics. **—char"ac·ter·i·za'tion,** *n.*

cha·rade' (shə-rād') *n.* (often *pl.*) a game of pantomime acting to convey words and their syllables.

char'broil" (chär'-) *v.t.* (*Colloq.*) to broil over charcoal embers.

char'coal" (chär'kōl") *n.* the residue of wood or other organic material reduced to carbon by imperfect combustion.

chard (chärd) *n.* a spinachlike vegetable: *Swiss chard.*

charge (chärj) *v.t.* **1,** put a load on or in; fill or occupy with something to be carried or retained. **2,** command; enjoin. **3,** accuse; blame. **4,** ask as a price; hold liable for payment. **5,** defer payment for. **6,** attack by rushing violently against. *—v.i.* make an onset. *—n.* **1,** a load; a burden; a filling. **2,** a command or instruction. **3,** a duty, responsibility, or encumbrance. **4,** an accusation. **5,** a price, cost, or fee. **6,** a violent onslaught. **—charge account,** an established line of credit with a retail store, bank, etc. **—charge card,** credit card.

char·gé' d'af·faires' (shär-zhä'dä-fär') [*pl.* **char·gés'** (shär-zhä'-)] a diplomatic officer who is temporarily in charge of an embassy or legation.

charg'er (chär'jər) *n.* **1,** a warhorse. **2,** a large platter or tray.

char'i·ot (char'ē-ət) *n.* **1,** an ancient two-wheeled horse-drawn vehicle. **2,** a carriage. **—char"i·ot·eer'** (-tir') *n.* the driver of a chariot.

cha·ris'ma (kə-riz'mə) *n.* a power for eliciting enthusiastic popular support attributed to a person or a position. **—char"is·mat'ic** (kăr"is-mat'ik) *adj.*

char'i·ty (char'ə-tē) *n.* **1,** the quality of sympathetic understanding; philanthropy; tolerance. **2,** alms. **3,** an organization devoted to the relief of the unfortunate. **—char'i·ta·ble,** *adj.*

char'la·tan (shär'lə-tən) *n.* a pretender; quack; mountebank.

char'ley horse (chär'lē) (*Colloq.*) a cramp in a muscle of arm or leg.

Charles'ton (chärlz'tən) *n.* a dance popular in the 1920's.

char'lotte (shär'lət) *n.* a molded dessert. **—charlotte russe** (roos), Bavarian cream in a mold with ladyfingers.

charm (chärm) *n.* **1,** personal attractiveness; irresistible power to please or attract. **2,** a symbol of occult power, as an amulet. *—v.t. & i.* fascinate; enchant; captivate. **—charm'ing,** *adj.* highly attractive.

char'nel (chär'nəl) *n.* a place where dead bodies are deposited.

chart (chärt) *n.* **1,** a map; a drawn or written guide. **2,** a systematic record of development or change. *—v.t.* make a map of; record.

char'ter (chär'tər) *n.* **1,** a written instrument giving a right or privilege. **2,** a fundamental statement of purpose and scope; a constitution. *—v.t.* **1,** authorize; empower. **2,** lease or hire.

char·treuse' (shär-trûz') *n.* **1,** a liqueur. **2,** a greenish yellow color.

char'y (chär'ē) *adj.* very cautious; suspicious. **—char'i·ness,** *n.*

chase (chās) *v.t.* **1,** [also, **give chase (to)**] follow after in order to overtake, capture, or kill; pursue; hunt. **2,** drive away. **3,** decorate (metal) by tooling. *—v.i.* move briskly. *—n.* **1,** the act of chasing. **2,** what is chased; quarry. **3,** the sport of hunting. **4,** a frame in which type is locked for printing.

chas'er (chā'sər) *n.* **1,** a milder drink taken after liquor. **2,** (*Colloq.*) a roué.

chasm (kaz'əm) *n.* **1,** a deep gulf or fissure. **2,** a wide divergency.

chas'sis (shas'ē) *n.* [*pl.* **-sis**] **1,** a supporting framework. **2,** the frame, wheels, and engine of an automobile, without the body; a radio receiving apparatus without a cabinet.

chaste (chāst) *adj.* **1,** abstaining from carnal love. **2,** pure; not ornate or fanciful in design.

chas'ten (chā'sən) *v.t.* **1,** punish; reprimand. **2,** make chaste..

chas·tise' (chas-tīz') *v.t.* punish, esp. corporally. **—chas·tise'ment,** *n.*

chas'ti·ty (chas'tə-tē) *n.* quality or state of being chaste.

chas'u·ble (chaz'yə-bəl) *n.* an ecclesiastical outer vestment.

chat *v.i.* [**chat'ted, -ting**] converse desultorily; make talk. **—chat'ty,** *adj.*

cha·teau' (sha-tō') *n.* [*pl.* **-teaux'** (-tōz')] a French castle; an elaborate country house.

cha·toy'ant (shə-toi'ənt) *adj.* changeable in color or luster.

chat'tel (chat'əl) *n.* a movable piece of personal property.

chat'ter (chat'ər) *v.i.* **1,** make rapid clacking sounds having little or no meaning. **2,** talk rapidly but aimlessly. **3,** vibrate noisily. *—n.* **1,** chattering sounds as made by monkeys, birds, etc. **2,** idle or senseless talk; gossip. **—chat'ter·box",** *n.* (*Slang*) one who talks incessantly.

chauf'feur (shō'fər) *n.* one hired to drive an automobile.

chau·tau'qua (shə-tâ'kwə) *n.* a community assembly for educational or recreational purposes.

chau′vin·ism (shō′və-niz-əm) *n.* **1**, excessive and blindly prejudiced patriotism. **2**, excessive devotion to a cause. **3**, [also, **male chauvinism**] belief that the male should or does have predominance over the female. —**chau′vin·ist,** *n.* —**chau″vin·is′-tic,** *adj.* —**chau″vin·is·ti·cal·ly,** *adv.*

cheap (chēp) *adj.* **1**, available at a low price. **2**, of little value. **3**, miserly; mean; petty. **4**, unfair, dishonorable. —**cheap′en,** *v.t. & i.* lessen in price, value, or reputation. —**cheap′ness,** *n.* —**cheap shot,** (*Slang*) an unfair comment.

cheap′skate″ *n.* a stingy person.

cheat (chēt) *v.t.* **1**, mislead; defraud; swindle. **2**, escape from; elude. —*v.i.* **1**, practice deception or trickery. **2**, be unfaithful. —*n.* **1**, a swindler, esp. a card sharper. **2**, an impostor. **3**, an act of fraud.

check (chek) *n.* **1**, an obstruction, hindrance, or stop; a device for stopping. **2**, a stoppage or rebuff. **3**, a test of operation; verification of accounts; investigation or examination (often **check-up**). **4**, a mark (√) indicating disposition or approval. **5**, a written order to a bank to pay money. **6**, a piece of paper used as a receipt, token, etc. **7**, one of a pattern of squares alternating in color. **8**, in chess, jeopardy of the king. **9**, a counter; a poker chip. —*v.t.* **1**, impede; stop. **2**, test; verify; investigate. **3**, make a check mark (√) upon. **4**, put or accept in temporary custody. **5**, send (baggage) under privilege of a passenger ticket. **6**, in chess, threaten to capture (the king). —*v.i.* **1**, make a test or investigation. **2**, prove to be right or accurate. **3**, pause; stop. **4**, in poker, stay in without betting. —*interj.* (*Colloq.*) correct! All right! —**check in,** register (at a hotel, etc.). —**check out, 1**, itemize. **2**, depart. **3**, (*Slang*) die. —**in check,** in chess, of the king, in jeopardy.

check′er (chek′ər) *n.* **1**, one who checks; a record-keeper. **2**, one of the pieces for checkers. —**check′ered** (-ərd) *adj.* marked with a pattern of squares of alternating color.

check′ers (chek′ərz) *n.sing.* a game for two played on a checkered board (*checkerboard*).

check′mate″ *n.* **1**, (*Chess*) a position in which one's king is attacked and cannot escape capture. **2**, defeat; frustration. —*v.t.* put in checkmate; overthrow.

check′off″ (chek′âf″) *n.* the withholding of union dues from a payroll on behalf of the union.

Ched′dar (ched′ər) *n.* a smooth variety of English or American cheese.

cheek (chēk) *n.* **1**, the side of the face below the eye-line. **2**, impudence; overweening self-assurance. —**cheek′y,** *adj.* impudent.

cheep (chēp) *n.* the high cry of a young bird; chirp. —*v.t. & i.* chirp.

cheer (chir) *n.* **1**, state of mind. **2**, gaiety; animation. **3**, a shout of joy; applause. —*v.t. & i.* **1**, encourage. **2**, applaud with shouts. —**cheers,** *interj.* a toast.

cheer′ful (-fəl) *adj.* full of cheer; blithe. —**cheer′ful·ness,** *n.*

cheer′i·o″ (chir′ē-ō″) *n. & interj.* hello or goodbye.

cheer′y (-ē) *adj.* in good spirits; gay. —**cheer′i·ness,** *n.*

cheese (chēz) *n.* a food made of aged milk solids.

cheese′burg″er (chēz′bėr″gər) *n.* a hamburger grilled with cheese.

cheese′cake″ *n.* **1**, a kind of pie. **2**, (*Slang*) suggestive pictures of women.

cheese′cloth″ *n.* a coarse cotton cloth of open texture.

chees′y (chē′zē) *adj.* (*Colloq.*) unsubstantial; shoddy.

chee′tah (chē′tə) *n.* a leopardlike animal of Asia and Africa.

chef (shef) *n.* a head cook.

chef-d'oeu′vre (she-dövr′) *n.* (*Fr.*) a masterpiece.

chem′i·cal (kem′i-kəl) *adj.* pert. to chemistry. —*n.* a substance produced by or used in a chemical process. —**chemical warfare,** use of chemical or bacterial agents against an enemy.

che·min–′de·fer′ (shə-man′də-fer′) *n.* a gambling game, a variety of baccarat.

che·mise′ (shə-mēz′) *n.* a loose-fitting undergarment.

chem′is·try (kem′is-trē) *n.* the general science of the composition, properties, and phenomena of elementary substances. —**chem′ist,** *n.*

chem·o- (kēm-ō; kem-ō) *pref.* chemical; chemically.

chem′ur·gy (kem′ər-jē) *n.* a branch of applied chemistry dealing with industrial uses of agricultural products.

che·nille′ (shə-nēl′) *n.* **1**, a fluffy yarn of cotton, silk, etc. **2**, a fabric woven with such yarn.

cheque (chek) *n.* (*Brit.*) check.

cher′ish *v.t.* hold dear; treat with affection; nurse.

che·root′ (shə-root′) *n.* a cigar with square, open ends.

cher′ry (cher′ē) *n.* **1**, a tree bearing small, red, pitted fruit; its wood; its fruit. **2**, a bright red color.

---

cherry'stone" n. 1, the pit of a cherry. 2, a small quahog clam.

cher'ub (cher'əb) n. 1, [pl. **cher'u·bim**] an angel represented as a child with wings. 2, a child with a round, plump face; a beautiful or innocent person. —**che·ru'bic** (che-roo'bik) adj. —**che·ru'bi·cal·ly**, adv.

cher'vil n. a plant used for seasoning.

chess (ches) n. a game for two played on a board of 64 checkered squares (chessboard).

chest n. 1, a box, esp. a strong one for holding valuables. 2, the human body between the neck and belly; the thorax. 3, [also, **chest of drawers**] a bureau for clothes, etc. 4, a public fund, as for charity.

ches'ter·field" (ches'tər-fēld") n. 1, a single-breasted overcoat. 2, a kind of sofa.

chest'nut (ches'nut) n. 1, a tree of the beech family; its wood; its edible nut. 2, a reddish brown color. 3, (Slang) a hackneyed joke; anything repeated to the point of staleness. —adj. reddish brown.

chest'y (ches'tē) adj. (Slang) conceited.

che·val' glass (shə-val') a long mirror pivoted in a frame.

chev"a·lier' (shev"ə-lir') n. 1, knight; a gallant man. 2, a rank of membership in an honorable order.

chev'i·ot (shev'ē-ət) n. a worsted fabric of twill weave.

chev'ron (shev'rən) n. a striped badge denoting military rank.

chew (choo) v.t. 1, bite and grind with the teeth. 2, meditate on; discuss. —n. a portion chewed, as of tobacco. —**chew'y**, adj. —**chew the rag**, (Slang) converse at length.

chi (kī) n. the twenty-second letter of the Greek alphabet (X, x).

chi·a"ro·scu'ro (kē-är"ə-skûr'ō) n. 1, the distribution of light and shade in a picture. 2, a drawing in black and white.

chic (shēk) adj. stylish; fashionable.

chi·can'er·y (shi-kā'nə-rē) n. adroit but dishonest maneuvering or scheming.

chi·ca'no (chē-kä'nō) n. an American of Mexican descent.

chi'chi" (shē'shē") adj. 1, ornamental; showy. 2, affected; pretentious. 3, chic. —n. something chichi.

chick (chik) n. 1, a young chicken or other bird. 2, (Slang) a young girl.

chick'a·dee" (chik'ə-dē") n. a small No. Amer. bird of the titmouse family.

chick'en (chik'ən) n. 1, a young domestic fowl. 2, (Slang) a girl; a young woman. 3, (Slang) coward. —adj. (Slang) cowardly; timid. —**chicken feed**, a small sum of money. —**chick"en·heart'ed**, adj. timid. —**chicken pox**, a mild, contagious,

eruptive disease. —**chicken wire**, a lightweight wire fencing.

chick'pea" n. a plant of the pea family; its hard, edible seed.

chic'le (chik'əl) n. a gum from certain trees, the basis of chewing gum.

chic'o·ry (chik'ə-rē) n. 1, a plant whose root is used as a substitute or adulterant for coffee. 2, a salad herb.

chide (chīd) v.t. & i. reprove mildly.

chief (chēf) n. 1, the head man; commander; leader. 2, the most important part or aspect. —adj. highest in rank or importance. —**Chief Executive**, the President.

chief'tain (-tən) n. the leader of a tribe, clan, or band.

chif·fon' (shi-fon') n. a thin, gauzelike fabric.

chif"fo·nier' (shif"ə-nir') n. a chest of drawers; a bureau.

chig'ger (chig'ər) n. 1, the larva of certain mites whose bite causes severe itching. 2, a flea; the chigoe.

chi'gnon (shēn'yon) n. a coil of hair, worn at the back of the neck by women.

chi·hua'hua (chē-wä'wä) n. a breed of tiny dog.

chil'blain" (chil'blān") n. a sore, esp. on the foot, resulting from exposure to cold.

child (chīld) n. [pl. **chil'dren** (chil'drən)] a young human offspring; an infant, boy or girl. —**with child**, pregnant. —**child'like"**, adj. —**child's play**, a very easy task.

child'birth" n. the giving birth to a child; parturition.

child'hood" n. the state or time of being a child.

child'ish adj. 1, immature. 2, silly. —**child'ish·ness**, n.

chil'dren (chil'drən) n. 1, pl. of child. 2, all the members of any group having a common experience, nationality, origin, etc.

chil'i (chil'ē) n. a hot seasoning made of dried pods of red pepper. —**chili con car'ne** (kon-kär'nē) a Mexican dish of meat and chili, usu. with beans.

chill (chil) n. 1, an acute sensation of cold, often with shivering. 2, a degree of cold. —v.t. 1, make cold. 2, dispirit; discourage. —v.i. be fearful. —**chill'er**, n. a frightening novel, story, etc. —**chill'y**, adj. —**chill factor**, windchill.

chime (chīm) n. 1, a bell or tube producing a bell-like tone; a set of such bells. 2, harmonious sound or relation; concord. —v.i. 1, produce harmonious sounds. 2, harmonize; agree. 3, (with in) add one's word; agree. —v.t. give forth (a sound).

chi·me'ra (ki-mir'ə) n. 1, a mythical monster, part lion, goat, and serpent. 2, a fantastic or vain hope. —**chi·mer'i·cal** (ki-mer'i-kəl) *adj.*

chim'ney (chim'nè) *n.* **1,** a tube, duct, or flue to carry off smoke. **2,** a volcanic vent. —**chimney pot,** a tubular cover put on top of a chimney to increase the draft.

chim"pan·zee' (chim"pan-zē') *n.* a large anthropoid ape of W. Africa. Also, *colloq.,* **chimp.**

chin *n.* the point of a jaw.—*v.i.* [**chinned, chin'ning**] (*Slang*) chat; talk. —**chin one-self,** pull one's body upward toward an elevated horizontal bar, for exercise.

chi'na (chī'nə) *n.* porcelain ware; dishes; crockery.

Chi'na·town' *n.* the Chinese quarter of a city.

chinch *n.* **1,** a bedbug. **2,** an insect that attacks grain plants.

chin·chil'la (chin-chil'ə) *n.* a small, fur-bearing rodent of South America; its fur.

chine (chīn) *n.* **1,** the backbone of an animal. **2,** a cut of meat across the back-bone. **3,** a ridge.

Chi·nese' (chī-nēz') *adj.* pert. to China. —*n.* **1,** the language of China. **2,** one descended from the people of China.

chink *n.* a small rift, fissure, or cleft. —*v.i.* **1,** crack. **2,** make a sharp metallic sound. —*v.t.* **1,** split. **2,** fill up cracks; calk.

chi'no (chē'nō) *n.* **1,** a cotton fabric. **2,** an article of clothing made from this fabric.

Chi·nook' (chi-nûk') *n.* **1,** an Amer. Indian tribe. **2,** (*l.c.*) a warm, dry wind of the Rocky Mountains.

chintz (chints) *n.* a printed cotton fabric, usually glazed. —**chint'zy,** *adj.* (*Colloq.*) cheap.

chip *n.* **1,** a small fragment, as of wood or stone. **2,** a small disk used as a counter or token; poker chip. —*v.t.* [**chipped, chip'-ping**] cut or knock off fragments from. —*v.i.* **1,** break off in small pieces. **2,** (often with *in*) contribute a chip or money. —**a chip on one's shoulder,** a belligerent attitude. —**in the chips,** well off; wealthy.

chip'board' *n.* a coarse paperboard.

chip'munk *n.* a small squirrellike rodent.

chip'per (chip'ər) *v.i.* chirp; twitter. —*adj.* (*Colloq.*) lively; gay.

chi·ro- (kī-rō) *pref.* hand.

chi·rog'ra·phy (kī-rog'rə-fè) *n.* hand-writing.

chi'ro·man"cy (kī'rə-man"sè) *n.* palm-istry.

chi·rop'o·dy (kī-rop'ə-dè) *n.* the treat-ment of foot ailments. —**chi·rop'o·dist,** *n.*

chi"ro·prac'tic (kī"rō-prak'tik) *n.* the treatment of ailments by manipulating the bones. —**chi'ro·prac"tor,** *n.*

chirp (chērp) *n.* a short, shrill sound made by birds or insects. —*v.i.* utter with a chirp.

chir'rup (chir'əp) *n. & v.* chirp.

chis'el (chiz'əl) *n.* a bladed tool for cut-ting wood or metal. —*v.t. & i.* **1,** cut or trim with a chisel. **2,** (*Slang*) seek an undue advantage; cheat. —**chis'el·er,** *n.*

chit *n.* **1,** a pert young person (esp. a girl) or animal. **2,** a memorandum of indebtedness for a minor purchase.

chit'chat' *n.* idle talk.

chit'ter·ling (chit'ər-ling) *n.* (usu.*pl.*) part of the small intestine, esp. of swine, cooked as food.

chiv'al·ry (shiv'əl-rè) *n.* **1,** the institution of medieval knighthood. **2,** gallantry; honor. —**chiv'al·ric, chiv'al·rous,** *adj.*

chive (chīv) *n.* (usually *pl.*) an onionlike herb used for seasoning.

chlo'ral (klôr'əl) *n.* a hypnotic prepara-tion from chlorine. —**chloral hydrate,** a solution of this substance.

chlor'dane (klôr'dān) *n.* an insecticide.

chlo'ride (klôr'īd) *n.* a compound of chlo-rine and one other element.

chlor'i·nate" (klôr'ə-nāt") *v.t.* combine or treat with chlorine. —**chlor"in·a'tion,** *n.*

chlo'rine (klôr'ēn) *n.* a gaseous chemical element, no. 17, symbol Cl.

chlo'ro·form" (klôr'ə-fôrm") *n.* a vola-tile, colorless liquid used as an anesthetic.

chlo'ro·phyll (klôr'ə-fil) *n.* the green coloring principle in plants.

chock (chok) *n.* a block of wood or stone used as a stop to prevent rolling. —**chock"-full',** *adj.* full.

chock'a·block" (chok'ə-blok") *adj.* snugly fitted; crowded.

choc'o·late (chok'ə-lit) *n.* **1,** a food or flavoring made from the cacao bean. **2,** a beverage or candy flavored with it. **3,** a dark brown color.

choice (chois) *n.* **1,** the act of choosing. **2,** opportunity or right to choose; option. **3,** what is chosen; preference; alternative. **4,** the best part. —*adj.* superior; select; excel-lent. —**choice'ness,** *n.*

choir (kwīr) *n.* **1,** a chorus in a church; a group of angels singing. **2,** the choir's section in a church.

choke (chōk) *v.t.* **1,** stop the breath of by stopping the windpipe; strangle. **2,** stop by filling; obstruct; stifle. —*v.i.* **1,** suffer con-striction of the windpipe. **2,** be crammed full or overcrowded. **3,** (with *up*) be over-come by emotion or fear. —*n.* **1,** a con-striction of blockage in a passage. **2,** an instrument for shutting off air from the carburetor of a gas engine. **3,** the central, inedible part of an artichoke. **—chok′er,** *n.* a high or tight collar or necklace.

chol′er (kol′ər) *n.* anger; ill-temper; irascibility. **—chol′er·ic,** *adj.*

chol′er·a (kol′ər-ə) *n.* **1,** an infectious disease, often fatal; the plague. **2,** a less serious disorder of the digestive organs.

cho·les′ter·ol (kə-les′tə-rol) *n.* a fatty alcohol found in bile, gallstones, etc., a possible cause of atherosclerosis.

chomp *v.* champ.

choose (chooz) *v.t.* [**chose** (chōz), **cho′sen**] select from two or more; give preference to; decide upon. **—***v.i.* make a choice. **—choos′y,** *adj.* (*Colloq.*) hard to please.

chop *v.t.* [**chopped, chop′ping**] **1,** cut with a quick blow; hew. **2,** cut into pieces; mince. **—***v.i.* **1,** make heavy strokes, as with an ax. **2,** turn or shift suddenly. **—***n.* **1,** a cutting stroke; a hard blow. **2,** a slice of meat cut from the loin, containing the rib. **3,** a brisk, irregular motion of waves. **4,** (usu. *pl.*) the jaw. **—chop′per,** *n.* (*Colloq.*) a helicopter. **—chop suey** (soo′ē) a stew served in Chinese restaurants.

chop′py (-ē) *adj.* rough; jerky.

chop′stick″ *n.* **1,** a pencil-sized stick, two of which are used together by many Asian peoples as an eating utensil. **2,** (*pl.*) a short waltz for piano, played with two outstretched forefingers.

cho′ral (kôr′əl) *adj.* pert. to a chorus or choir.

cho·rale′ (kə-rál′) *n.* **1,** a simple sacred tune. **2,** a chorus (sense 3).

chord (kôrd) *n.* **1,** a cord; a string of a musical instrument; an anatomical cord. **2,** a group of three or more tones sounding simultaneously. **3,** a straight line intersecting a curve at two points. **4,** a connecting member, as of a bridge truss.

chore (chôr) *n.* a minor job; (*pl.*) routine household duties.

cho·re′a (kô-rē′ə) *n.* a spasmodic nervous disease; St. Vitus.' dance.

cho″re·og′ra·phy (kôr″ē-og′rə-fē) *n.* the art of dancing; composition of exhibition dances. **—chor′e·o·graph″,** *v.t. & i.* **—cho″re·og′ra·pher,** *n.* a designer of dances.

cho′rine (kôr′ēn) *n.* (*Slang*) a chorus girl.

chor′is·ter (kôr′is-tər) *n.* a member of a chorus.

chor′tle (chôr′təl) *n.* a gleeful chuckle. **—***v.* chuckle and snort.

cho′rus (kôr′əs) *n.* **1,** a group of persons singing together. **2,** any group acting together in support of a soloist or principal. **3,** a composition for a chorus; a refrain; the

principal melody of a popular song. **4,** a group of dancers or singers, or an interlocutor, who explain the action of a drama. **—***v.t.* utter in concert.

chose (chōz) *v.* pret. of *choose.*

cho′sen (chō′zən) *v.* p.p. of *choose.*

chow *n.* **1,** [also, **chow-′chow′**] a Chinese breed of dog. **2,** (*Slang*) food; meals.

chow′chow″, *n.* **1,** a mixed, highly-seasoned dish; a pickle preserve. **2,** (-chow′) chow. **—chow mein** (mān) a Chinese dish of meat, vegetables, and fried noodles.

chow′der (-dər) *n.* a thick soup, usually of sea food, as clams.

chrism (kriz′əm) *n.* consecrated oil.

Christ (krīst) *n.* the Messiah; Jesus, as fulfilling his prophesied coming.

chris′ten (kris′ən) *v.t.* **1,** baptize and receive into the Christian church. **2,** give a name to.

Chris′ten·dom (kris′ən-dəm) *n.* the Christian world; all Christians.

Chris′tian (kris′chən) *n.* one who professes the religious principles of Jesus Christ. **—***adj.* pert. to these religious principles or any church based on them. **—Chris″ti·an′i·ty,** *n.* **—Christian name,** given name; first name. **—Christian Science,** the religious system of the Church of Christ, Scientist, that emphasizes the treatment of disease by mental and spiritual means.

Christ′mas (kris′məs) *n.* the festival celebrating the birth of Christ; Dec. 25.

chro·mat′ic (krō-mat′ik) *adj.* **1,** pert. to color. **2,** (*Music*) involving tones foreign to the diatonic scale. **—chro·mat′i·cal·ly,** *adv.*

chrome (krōm) *n.* chromium, esp. in alloy or as a source of pigments. **—chro′mic,** *adj.*

chro′mi·um (krō′mē-əm) *n.* a metallic chemical element, no. 24, symbol Cr.

chro′mo (krō′mō) *n.* a lithograph in colors, esp. a copy of a painting.

chro·mo- (krō-mə) *pref.* **1,** color. **2,** chromium.

chro′mo·some″ (krō′mə-sōm″) *n.* a thread-like body in a germ cell, a carrier of hereditary characters.

chron- *pref.* of time. Also, **chron·o-.**

chron′ic (kron′ik) *adj.* of long standing; inveterate; continual. **—chron′i·cal·ly,** *adv.*

chron′i·cle (kron′i-kəl) *n.* an account of events in order of time; a history. **—***v.t.* record or narrate in order of time. **—chron′i·cler,** *n.*

chron′o·graph″ (kron′ə-graf″) *n.* a stopwatch.

chron″o·log′i·cal (kron″ə-loj′i-kəl) *adj.* arranged in order of time.

chro·nol′o·gy (krə-nol′ə-jē) *n.* **1,** the sci-

---

ence of determining the dates or historical order of past events. **2,** a statement of the order in time of particular events.

chro·nom'e·ter (krə-nom'ə-tər) *n.* a clock of great accuracy. **—chro·nom'e·try,** *n.*

chrys'a·lis (kris'ə-lis) *n.* the pupa of certain insects, as the moth.

chrys·an'the·mum (kri-san'thə-məm) *n.* a large flower.

chrys'o·lite" (kris'ə-līt") *n.* a semiprecious stone, green or yellow.

chub *n.* any of several freshwater or marine fishes.

chub'by (chub'ē) *adj.* plump.

chuck (chuk) *n.* **1,** a device to grip work in a turning machine. **2,** a cut of beef. **—v.t. 1,** pat, usually on the chin. **2,** toss (often with *out*). **—chuck it,** (*Slang*) desist; quit. **—chuck wagon,** a wagon equipped with cooking facilities.

chuck'le (chuk'əl) *v.i.* laugh in a suppressed manner. **—n.** a subdued laugh.

chuck-'luck" (chuk'luk") *n.* a game of betting on casts of three dice.

chug *n.* a short explosive sound. **—v.i.** [**chugged, chug'ging**] make such sounds.

chug'a·lug" (chug'ə-lug") *v.t. & i.* drink the contents of a container without stopping.

chuk'ka (chuk'ə) *n.* an ankle-high boot.

chuk'ker (chuk'ər) *n.* one of the periods of play in polo.

chum *n.* an intimate; a close companion. **—chum'my,** *adj.*

chump *n.* **1,** (*Colloq.*) a blockhead. **2,** a block of wood.

chunk *n.* **1,** an irregular solid piece, as of coal; a lump. **2,** a considerable amount. **—chunk'y,** *adj.* stocky; thickset.

church (chērch) *n.* **1,** an edifice for religious worship; the chief services held there. **2,** a body or organization of Christian believers; a denomination. **—church'ly,** *adj.* devout.

church'key" *n.* a can opener.

church'man (-mən) *n.* **1,** a clergyman. **2,** an active member of a church. **—church'-wo"man,** *n.fem.*

churl (chērl) *n.* a surly or coarse person. **—churl'ish,** *adj.* rude; surly.

churn (chērn) *n.* **1,** a device for agitating milk, to separate the butter fats from it. **2,** a similar agitating device. **—v.t.** agitate (milk) to make butter. **—v.i. 1,** operate a churn. **2,** be nervously excited or agitated.

chute (shoot) *n.* **1,** an inclined trough, channel, or duct, esp. for the conveyance of fluid solids, as sand, by gravity. **2,** any channel providing a steep descent. **—'chute,** *n.* a parachute.

chut'ney (chut'nē) *n.* an E. Indian condiment of mangoes, herbs and spices.

chutz'pa (khûts'pə) *n.* (*Colloq.*) effrontery; gall.

chyle (kīl) *n.* a fluid produced as part of digestion.

ciao (chow) *interj.* (*Ital.*) (*Colloq.*) hello; goodbye.

ci·ca'da (si-kā'də) *n.* an insect that makes a shrill sound by vibrating certain membranes, as esp. the locust.

cic'a·trix (sik'ə-triks) *n.* [*pl.* **-tri'ces** (-trī'sēz)] the new tissue that forms a scar. Also, **cic'a·trice** (-tris).

cic'e·ly (sis'ə-lē) *n.* a plant of the parsley family.

cic"e·ro'ne (sis"ə-rō'nē) *n.* a guide.

-cide (sīd) *suf.* denoting a killer (of), or the act of killing. **— -cid'al,** *suf.* forming adjectives.

ci'der (sī'dər) *n.* expressed apple juice, fresh or slightly fermented.

ci·gar' (si-gär') *n.* a cylindrical roll of tobacco leaves, for smoking.

cig"a·rette' (sig"ə-ret') *n.* shredded or granular tobacco contained within a paper tube, for smoking. Also, **cig"a·ret'.**

cig"a·ril'lo (sig"ə-ril'ō) *n.* a small, thin cigar.

cil'i·a (sil'ē-ə) *n.pl.* [*sing.* **-um** (-əm)] the eyelashes; similar short hairs or hairlike processes. **—cil'i·ar·y** (-er-ē) *adj.*

cinch (sinch) *n.* **1,** a saddle-girth. **2,** (*Colloq.*) anything easy or sure of accomplishment. **—v.t. 1,** tighten, as a surrounding band. **2,** assure.

cin·cho'na (sin-kō'nə) *n.* a tropical tree; its bark, yielding quinine.

cinc'ture (sink'chər) *n.* a girdle; a belt. **—v.t.** engirdle; encircle.

cin'der (sin'dər) *n.* a sandlike globular particle of burned matter; (*pl.*) ashes. **—cinder block,** a concrete building block containing coal cinders.

cin'e·ma (sin'ə-mə) *n.* a motion picture; a motion picture theater. **—cin"e·mat'ic,** *adj.*

Cin'e·ma·scope" (sin'ə-mə-skōp") *n.* (*T.N.*) a wide-screen motion-picture system utilizing a special wide-angle lens.

cin'e·ma·theque" (-tek") *n.* a motion-picture theater, esp. one showing experimental films.

cin"e·ma·tog'ra·phy (-tog'rə-fē) *n.* the art or science of motion-picture photography. **—cin"e·ma"to·graph'ic,** *adj.* **—cin"e·ma·tog'ra·pher,** *n.*

Cin"e·ra'ma (sin"ə-rä'mə) *n.* (*T.N.*) a motion-picture system featuring a wide field of view, formed by projecting on a curved screen three films taken simultaneously from different angles.

cin″e·rar′i·um (sin″ə-rär′ē-əm) *n.* [*pl.* **-a** (-ə)] a place of deposit for the ashes of cremated dead.

cin′na·bar″ (sin′ə-bär″) *n.* a red mercuric sulfide: an ore of mercury.

cin′na·mon (sin′ə-mən) *n.* the dried bark of a certain tree used as a spice. —*adj.* light brown.

ci′pher (sī′fər) *n.* **1,** the digit zero (0). **2,** any Arabic numeral. **3,** a secret code; the message written in it; the key to it. —*v.t.* calculate numerically.

cir′ca (sër′kə) *prep.* (*Lat.*) about.

cir′cle (sër′kəl) *n.* **1,** a closed curve, the locus of all points equidistant from a fixed point, or center, within. **2,** a ring. **3,** a cycle; a series culminating in a return to the starting point. —*v.t.* travel around the outside of. —*v.i.* move in a circle.

cir′clet (sër′klit) *n.* a ring.

cir′cuit (sër′kit) *n.* **1,** a closed path providing continuous passage of fluids or electricity. **2,** a route regularly followed; an itinerary. —**cir′cuit·ry,** *n.* —**circuit breaker,** a thermal electric switch.

cir·cu′i·tous (sër-kū′i-təs) *adj.* not direct; roundabout. —**cir·cu′i·tous·ness,** *n.*

cir′cu·lar (sër′kyə-lər) *adj.* **1,** in the shape of a circle. **2,** roundabout; wandering. —*n.* a letter or brochure for general circulation.

cir′cu·late (sër′kū-lāt″) *v.i.* move through a circuit; (of persons) move about among other people. —*v.t.* disseminate; spread. —**cir′cu·la·to″ry,** *adj.*

cir″cu·la′tion (sër″kū-lā′shən) *n.* **1,** the act of diffusion or dissemination. **2,** continuous passage through a closed system, as the blood.

cir·cum- (sër-kəm) *pref.* going around.

cir″cum·ci′sion (sër″kəm-sizh′ən) *n.* removal of the foreskin of males, esp. as a religious rite. —**cir′cum·cise″** (-sīz″) *v.t.*

cir·cum′fer·ence (sər-kum′fər-əns) *n.* the distance around a circle, sphere, or other closed curved figure or object.

cir′cum·flex″ (sër′kəm-fleks″) *n.* a diacritical mark (^), as ê.

cir″cum·lo·cu′tion (sër″kəm-lō-kū′shən) *n.* studied indirectness of speech; evasion of a point.

cir″cum·scribe′ (sër″kəm-skrīb′) *v.t.* limit; bound; restrain within fixed bounds. —**cir″cum·scrip′tion** (-skrip′shən) *n.*

cir′cum·spect″ (sër′kəm-spekt″) *adj.* careful of one's behavior; discreet. —**cir″cum·spec′tion,** *n.*

cir′cum·stance″ (sër′kəm-stans″) *n.* **1,** a concomitant condition or situation; one of

the factors influencing a decision. **2,** (*pl.*) existing conditions; economic status. **3,** (*Archaic*) ceremonious display.

cir″cum·stan′tial (-stan′shəl) *adj.* **1,** pert. to circumstances. **2,** based on incidental details; presumptive. —**cir″cum·stan″ti·al′i·ty,** *n.*

cir″cum·stan′ti·ate (sër″kəm-stan′shē-āt″) *v.t.* support with evidence; prove to be true; document. —**cir″cum·stan·ti·a′tion,** *n.*

cir″cum·vent′ (sër″kəm-vent′) *v.t.* evade (an impediment) by going around it; outwit. —**cir″cum·ven′tion,** *n.*

cir′cus (sër′kəs) *n.* **1,** a traveling show, including acrobats, clowns, wild animal displays, etc.; the company of performers in such show. **2,** any entertaining display likened to a circus; a good time. **3,** a circular area, as an arena or (*Brit.*) an open space where several streets converge.

cir·rho′sis (si-rō′sis) *n.* a disease, esp. of the liver, characterized by hardening of tissues.

cir′ro- (sir′ō) *pref.* cirrus.

cir′rus (sir′əs) *n.* [*pl.* **-ri** (-rī)] a cloud formation notably long, stratified, and of filamentous structure.

cis- (sis) *pref.* on this side of, as *cisalpine,* on this (the Roman) side of the Alps.

cis′tern (sis′tərn) *n.* an underground tank to hold a supply of fresh water.

cit′a·del (sit′ə-dəl) *n.* a fortress, usually at the edge of a town.

ci·ta′tion (sī-tā′shən) *n.* **1,** act or result of citing; a citing; quotation. **2,** a commendatory mention. **3,** an official summons.

cite (sīt) *v.t.* **1,** mention in specific connection; quote; refer to in support. **2,** summon officially, as to a court.

cith′a·ra (sith′ə-rə) *n.* an ancient musical instrument like a lyre.

cith′ern (sith′ərn) *n.* an ancient musical instrument like a guitar. Also, **cither, cittern** (sit′ərn).

cit′i·fied″ (sit′i-fīd″) *adj.* having the habits of a city dweller. —**cit′i·fy″,** *v.t.*

cit′i·zen (sit′ə-zən) *n.* **1,** an enfranchised member of a state or nation. **2,** civilian. —**cit′i·zen·ry** (-rē) *n.* citizens collectively. —**cit′i·zen·ship,** *n.* —**citizen's band,** one of several radio bands for private communications.

cit′ric acid (sit′rik) an acid found in lemons and similar fruit.

cit′ron (sit′rən) *n.* a fruit resembling the lemon; a candied preserve made of its rind.

cit″ron·el′la (sit″rə-nel′ə) *n.* an oil used in perfumes and soaps, and to repel insects.

cit′rus (sit′rəs) *n.* a species of tree, including the lime, lemon, etc. —*adj.* [also, **cit′rous**] containing citric acid.

cit′y (sit′é) *n.* a large or important town. —**city hall**, the building in which the chief officials of a city government have their offices; (*fig.*) city government.

cit′y-state′ *n.* a city having independent sovereignty.

civ′et (siv′it) *n.* **1**, a glandular secretion of the civet cat, used in perfumery. **2**, the civet cat, a feline of Asia and Africa.

civ′ic (siv′ik) *adj.* pert. to the affairs of a city or community, or to citizenship.

civ′ics (siv′iks) *n.sing.* the study of the processes of government and duties of citizenship.

civ′il (siv′əl) *adj.* **1**, pert. to the state, its laws, administration, etc. **2**, pert. to a private citizen; not military, ecclesiastic, etc. **3**, courteous; polite. **4**, within a nation, as a *civil war.* —**civil defense**, defense of civilians against air raids, etc. —**civil disobedience**, noncooperation with government officers, as a method of protest. —**civil engineering**, the engineering of public-works construction, as bridges. —**civil law**, laws relating to private matters, rather than criminal, ecclesiastical, or military. —**civil liberty**, freedom of individual action and opinion. —**civil rights**, personal rights, as freedom of speech and freedom of assembly. —**civil service**, nonelected, permanent government employees collectively.

ci·vil′ian (si-vil′yən) *n.* one engaged in civil, not military, pursuits. —*adj.* not military.

ci·vil′i·ty (si-vil′ə-té) *n.* politeness.

civ″i·li·za′tion (siv″i-lə-zā′shən) *n.* **1**, civilized peoples, states and facilities collectively. **2**, act of civilizing.

civ′i·lize″ (siv′ə-līz″) *v.t.* educate in the usages of organized society.

civ′vies (siv′éz) *n.pl.* (*Colloq.*) civilian clothes (as opposed to military uniform). Also, **civ′ies.**

clab′ber (klab′ər) *n.* soured, coagulated milk, not fully separated into curds and whey. —*v.i.* coagulate.

clack (klak) *n.* a quick, sharp, repeated sound. —*v.t. & i.* **1**, make a sharp, repeated sound; let the tongue vibrate. **2**, prattle.

clad (klad) *v.* clothed; dressed.

claim (klām) *v.t.* **1**, assert a right to; demand. **2**, (*Colloq.*) assert as fact; contend. —*n.* a demand for something due; the thing demanded. —**claim′ant**, *n.* —**claim′ing race**, a horse race among horses offered for sale at the same price.

clair·voy′ance (klâr-voi′əns) *n.* extrasensory sight or perception. —**clair·voy′ant**, *n. & adj.*

clam (klam) *n.* **1**, any of several varieties of bivalve mollusks. **2**, an uncommunicative person. —*v.i.* **1**, gather clams. **2**, (with *up*) (*Colloq.*) stop talking.

clam′bake″ *n.* **1**, a picnic at which clams are baked. **2**, any social gathering.

clam′ber (klam′bər) *v.i.* ascend by climbing, often with difficulty.

clam′my (klam′é) *adj.* cold and damp. —**clam′mi·ness**, *n.*

clam′or (klam′ər) *n.* noise; noisy ado; a vociferous demand or complaint. —*v.i.* make an outcry; demand loudly. Also, **clam′our.** —**clam′or·ous**, *adj.*

clamp (klamp) *n.* a device for holding objects, or fastening them together temporarily. —*v.t.* fasten with or as with a clamp. —*v.i.* (with *down*) become strict.

clam′shell″ *n.* **1**, the shell of a clam. **2**, a dredging bucket having two hinged jaws.

clan (klan) *n.* **1**, a family or tribe, esp. Scottish. **2**, any social set; clique. —**clan′nish**, *adj.* —**clans′man** (klanz′mən) *n.* a kinsman. —**clans′wo″man**, *n.fem.*

clan·des′tine (klan-des′tin) *adj.* secret; covert; furtive.

clang (klang) *n.* the sound of a gong or hammer; the ring of metal when struck. —*v.i. & t.* make such a sound.

clan′gor (klang′ər) *n.* **1**, a clanging sound. **2**, clamor.

clank (klank) *n.* a sharp, metallic sound. —*v.t.* strike (an object) to produce such a sound. —*v.i.* give out such a sound.

clap (klap) *v.t.* [**clapped, clap′ping**] **1**, strike together (as the hands) producing a sharp sound. **2**, place or dispose of hastily. —*v.i.* strike with the hands together, for applause, attention, etc. —*n.* **1**, the sound of clapping hands; applause. **2**, a blow with the flat of the hand. **3**, (*Vulgar*) gonorrhea.

clap′board (klab′ərd) *n.* a wood siding for houses, in which the boards overlap.

clap′per (klap′ər) *n.* the tongue of a bell.

clap′trap″ (klap′trap″) *n.* insincere and diversionary talk; nonsense.

claque (klak) *n.* a group of persons hired to applaud a performer.

clar′et (klar′ət) *n.* a red wine from Bordeaux; its color.

clar′i·fy″ (klar′ə-fī″) *v.t. & i.* **1**, make clear to the sight or understanding. **2**, free from turbidity; become clear. —**clar″i·fi·ca′tion**, *n.*

clar″i·net′ (klar″ə-net′) *n.* a single-reed woodwind instrument.

---

tub, cūte, púll; labəl; oil, owl, go, chip, she, thin, *th*en, sing, ink; *see p.* 6

clar′i·on (klar′ē-ən) *adj.* obtrusively clear and high-pitched, as a trumpet's sound.

clar′i·ty (klar′ə-tè) *n.* clearness.

clash (klash) *v.i.* collide so as to make a loud, harsh noise; meet in conflict. —*v.t.* strike together violently and noisily. —*n.* a collision of physical objects, opinions, etc.; conflict.

clasp (klásp) *n.* **1,** a small latch for holding two things together. **2,** a joining of the hands; an embrace. —*v.t.* fasten together; embrace; grasp.

class (klås) *n.* **1,** order or rank, esp. of persons; caste. **2,** a category. **3,** a group of persons with a common interest, esp. such a group in student session. **4,** (*Colloq.*) smartness; beauty; modishness. —*v.t.* arrange according to class; classify. —**class action,** pert. to a legal suit brought on behalf of a group of people with a common complaint.

clas′sic (klas′ik) *n.* **1,** a creation of enduring value or esteem, as a musical or literary composition. **2,** a standard; a perfect specimen. **3,** (*pl.*) the literature of Greece and Rome. —*adj.* characterized by enduring value. —**clas′si·cal,** *adj.*

clas′si·cism (klas′i-siz-əm) *n.* **1,** purity and simplicity of style. **2,** advocacy of such a style. —**clas′si·cist,** *n.*

clas″si·fi·ca′tion (klas″i-fi-kā′shən) *n.* **1,** act of classifying. **2,** a class or category.

clas′si·fied″ (klas′i-fīd″) *adj.* **1,** arranged by topic, group, etc. **2,** (*Mil.*) secret, confidential, or restricted. —**classified ad,** a want ad, etc., arranged with others of the same nature.

clas′si·fy″ (klas′ə-fī″) *v.t.* **1,** sort into groups having common characteristics. **2,** assign a place in a group. **3,** (*Mil.*) place (a document) in a category of secrecy.

class′y (klas′ē) *adj.* (*Slang*) highgrade; modish.

clat′ter (klat′ər) *n.* a rattling or clashing sound, as of dishes roughly handled. —*v.i.* make such a sound.

clause (klåz) *n.* **1,** a sentence element containing at least a subject and verb. **2,** a stipulation, modification, or condition of a document; a paragraph. —**claus′al,** *adj.*

claus″tro·pho′bi·a (klås″trə-fō′bē-ə) *n.* a morbid fear of being shut in or confined.

clav′i·chord″ (klav′ə-kôrd″) *n.* an ancient musical instrument, precursor of the piano.

clav′i·cle (klav′ə-kəl) *n.* the collarbone.

clav′i·er (klav′ē-ər; klə-vir′) *n.* (*Music*) a keyboard instrument; a keyboard.

claw (klâ) *n.* **1,** a hook or talon on a limb, esp. the foot, of a living creature. **2,** a tool or device for grasping. —*v.t. & i.* scratch; tear or rend.

clay (klā) *n.* **1,** plastic earth in the form of thick mud, used in making brick, for modeling, etc. **2,** the human body. **3,** one easily influenced.

clean (klēn) *adj.* **1,** free from dirt or irrelevant substances; pure; unadulterated. **2,** free from error or sin. **3,** fastidious. —*v.t.* remove foreign or superfluous material from; wash. —**clean′ness,** *n.* —**clean up,** (*Colloq.*) make much money. —**come clean,** (*Colloq.*) confess.

clean-′cut″ *adj.* **2,** shapely and clean-looking. **2,** sharply outlined; definite.

clean′er *n.* **1,** one who cleans. **2,** a washing agent.

clean′ly (klen′lē) *adj.* clean. —**clean′li·ness,** *n.*

cleanse (klenz) *v.t.* **1,** clean; dryclean. **2,** absolve or free from guilt; purify. —**cleans′er** (klen′zər) *n.*

clear (klir) *adj.* **1,** easily understood or perceived; not turbid or cloudy; unobstructed; transparent. **2,** untroubled, innocent. —*v.t.* **1,** remove burdens or obstructions from; clarify; free from debt, encumbrance or accusation. **2,** make a net profit of. **3,** jump over. **4,** (with *up*) explain lucidly; solve. **5,** (often with *away* or *off*) remove; sweep away. —*v.i.* **1,** (often with *up*) become bright or unclouded. **2,** (of a check) be paid. **3,** (often with *out*) depart hastily; go. —**clear′ness,** *n.*

clear′ance (-əns) *n.* **1,** act of clearing. **2,** the space between two objects; room to pass. **3,** approval as free from objection; permission to proceed.

clear′cut″ *adj.* distinct; obvious.

clear′ing (klir′ing) *n.* a tract of land cleared of trees. —**clearing house,** a coöperative institution through which banks settle their mutual accounts.

cleat (klēt) *n.* a crosspiece serving to join and strengthen a number of longitudinal strips; a similar crosspiece attached to increase traction.

cleav′age (klē′vij) *n.* **1,** act or result of cleaving, splitting, or division. **2,** the depression between a woman's breasts.

cleave (klēv) *v.i.* **1,** adhere; stick; cling. **2,** come apart; divide; split. —*v.t.* split; rend asunder; force apart.

cleav′er (klē′vər) *n.* a heavy knife for chopping through bone.

clef (klef) *n.* (*Music*) a character placed at the beginning of a staff to indicate the location of the governing tonality.

cleft (kleft) *n.* a crack; crevice; split. —*v. p.p.* of *cleave.*

clem′a·tis (klem′ə-tis) *n.* a climbing vine bearing small white flowers.

clem'en·cy (klem'ən-sē) n. mildness; leniency; mercy.

clem'ent (klem'ənt) adj. **1,** merciful; lenient. **2,** mild; agreeable.

clench (klench) v.t. close tightly, as the fist or teeth.

clere'sto"ry (klir'stôr"ē) n. the upper part of a building, esp. a church, rising above the roofs and lighted with windows.

cler'gy (klēr'jē) n. priests, ministers, or ecclesiastical officials collectively. **—cler'-gy·man** (-mən) n. any member of the clergy.

cler'ic (kler'ik) n. a clergyman.

cler'i·cal (kler'ə-kəl) adj. **1,** pert. to the clergy or to affairs of the church. **2,** pert. to written records, copies, or to office work.

clerk (klērk) n. **1,** a salesperson in a shop. **2,** an assistant in an office. **3,** an official of a branch of government who keeps records. **4,** (Archaic) a lay officer of the church; any literate person. **—v.i.** serve as a clerk. **—clerk'ly,** adj. **—clerk'ship,** n.

clev'er (klev'ər) adj. **1,** shrewd; quick to learn; skillful; quick-witted. **2,** ingenious. **—clev'er·ness,** n.

clev'is (klev'is) n. a U-shaped device for attaching a wagon, etc., to a drawbar for pulling.

clew (kloo) n. clue.

cli·ché' (klē-shā') n. (Fr.) an outworn expression; a stale or trite remark; literally, a stereotype.

click (klik) n. a small, sharp snap. **—v.i. 1,** make such a sound. **2,** (Colloq.) be successful.

cli'ent (klī'ənt) n. a customer, esp. the recipient of professional, esp. legal, services.

cli"en·tele' (klē"ən-tel'; klī'-) n. a body of clients of a lawyer, doctor, etc.; the customers of a business establishment.

cliff (klif) n. an abrupt wall of rock; precipice.

cliff'hang"er n. **1,** an event whose outcome is uncertain until the very end. **2,** an adventure serial.

cli·mac'ter·ic (klī-mak'tər-ik) n. a critical period, esp. the menopause. **—adj.** pert. to a critical time.

cli·mac'tic (klī-mak'tik) adj. pert. to a climax. **—cli·mac'ti·cal·ly,** adv.

cli'mate (klī'mit) n. the customary pattern of the weather for any specific locality. **—cli·mat'ic,** adj. **—cli·mat'i·cal·ly,** adv.

cli'max (klī'maks) n. **1,** the culmination of one or more events. **2,** the highest point of action, stress, motion, etc. **3,** the most effective point of a narrative, drama, or argument. **4,** orgasm. **—v.t.** bring to the highest or most effective point.

climb (klīm) v.t. & i. **1,** ascend with effort; toil upward. **2,** rise slowly. **3,** (with down) descend. **—n.** an ascent.

clime (klīm) n. (Poetic) a place or region of the earth.

clinch (klinch) v.t. **1,** secure tightly; fasten by bending the point (of a nail, etc.) sideways after driving it through; clench. **2,** make certain of; consolidate. **—v.i.** (Colloq.) embrace; in boxing, grasp the opponent with the arms. **—n.** the result of clinching. **—clinch'er,** n. that which clinches, esp. a decisive argument.

cling (kling) v.i. [**clung, cling'ing**] adhere; be fastened to; hold tenaciously to. **—cling'y,** adj.

cling'stone" n. a peach whose stone clings to the flesh of the fruit.

clin'ic (klin'ik) n. **1,** a place for medical examination and treatment, often free, for experimental or instructive purposes. **2,** a class or meeting dealing with problems of a specific field of study. **—clin'i·cal,** adj. **1,** pert. to or used in medical practice. **2,** analytical. **—clini'cian** (kli-ni'shən) n.

clink (klink) n. **1,** a high-pitched, fine sound, as of struck glass. **2,** (Slang) a jail.

clink'er (kling'kər) n. **1,** a vitreous residue of various fuels; a piece of slag. **2,** (Colloq.) error; boner.

clip (klip) n. **1,** a mechanical clasping device, as a paper clip, cartridge clip. **2,** a fast gait. **3,** punch; blow **—v.t.** [**clipped** (klipt), **clip'ping**] **1,** fasten together by a spring-actuated device. **2,** cut, as with shears; truncate. **3,** cuff with a glancing blow. **4,** (Slang) cheat. **—clip joint,** (Slang) an establishment that overcharges its customers.

clip'per (klip'ər) n. **1,** any of various tools that cut by shearing. **2,** something that travels swiftly, esp. a square-rigged, speedy sailing ship, or an airliner.

clip'ping n. a piece clipped or cut out.

clique (klēk; klik) n. a small exclusive social coterie. **—cli'quish** (-kish) adj.

clit'o·ris (klit'ə-ris) n. a small protuberance on the external genital parts of a female.

clo·a'ca (klō-ā'kə) n. [pl. **-cae** (-sē)] **1,** a sewer. **2,** a privy. **3,** a cavity in certain animals. **—clo·a'cal,** adj.

cloak (klōk) n. **1,** a loose-fitting, sleeveless outer garment. **2,** a disguise; pretext; cover. **—v.t.** cover; conceal. **—cloak'-room",** n. a room where coats, hats, etc., are left temporarily. **—cloak and dagger,** pert. to espionage or secrecy.

clob'ber (klob'ər) v.t. (Slang) **1,** pummel; punish. **2,** frustrate; spoil. **3,** defeat soundly.

cloche (klâsh) n. **1,** a bell-shaped woman's hat. **2,** a bell-shaped or deep concave glass cover.

clock (klok) *n.* **1,** a stationary timepiece. **2,** a vertical ornament on the ankle of a sock. —*v.t.* (*Colloq.*) measure the speed of; time.

clock′wise″ (klok′wīz″) *adj.* in the direction of travel of a clock's hands: from left to right around a circle.

clock′work″ *n.* the mechanism of a clock, or one similarly exact and inexorable.

clod (klod) *n.* **1,** a compacted chunk of earth. **2,** a stupid, stolid person. —**clod′-dish,** *adj.*

clod′hop″per *n.* **1,** a rustic; boor. **2,** (*pl.*) heavy work shoes.

clog (klog) *n.* **1,** a block or encumbrance; any impediment or hindrance. **2,** a type of thick-soled, often wooden, shoe. **3,** a dance in which heavy shoes tap the rhythm: *clog dance.* —*v.t.* **[clogged, clog′ging]** encumber; hinder; impede. —*v.i.* **1,** become clogged. **2,** dance a clog dance.

cloi″son·né′ (kloi″zə-nā′) *n.* decorative work of enamel sections in a pattern of metal strips.

clois′ter (klois′tər) *n.* **1,** an arched walk surrounding a courtyard; an arcade or colonnade. **2,** a place of religious retirement. —**clois′tered** (-tərd) *adj.* **1,** secluded. **2,** having a cloister. —**clois′tral** (-trəl) *adj.*

clone (klōn) *v.t.* grow (an organism) from a single cell by asexual reproduction. —*n.* an organism so produced.

clop (klop) *n. & v.* make the sound of a hoof or wooden shoe against pavement.

close (klōz) *v.t.* **1,** stop up; shut. **2,** join; fill, as a gap. **3,** finish; conclude. —*v.i.* **1,** unite; come together. **2,** (with *in*) approach; draw near. **3,** come to an end; terminate. **4,** consummate a sale or agreement. **5,** fight in bodily contact; grapple. —*n.* **1,** conclusion; termination. **2,** (klōs) an enclosed yard; court. —*adj.* (klōs) **1,** near to; in contact with. **2,** restricted in space; wanting fresh air; stuffy. **3,** compact; dense. **4,** secretive; reticent. **5,** (*Colloq.*) penurious; miserly. —*adv.* (klōs) **1,** near. **2,** in a closed manner. —**close′ness** (klōs′-) *n.* —**close call** (klōs) (*Colloq.*) a narrow escape. —**closed car,** an automobile having windows and a hard top. —**closed circuit,** television transmission by wire to a limited number of receivers. —**closed shop,** a shop employing union members only.

close-′fist″ed (klōs′-) *adj.* stingy.

close-′knit″ (klōs′-) *adj.* firmly bound together.

close′out (klōz′owt) *n.* a sale to liquidate stock.

clos′et (kloz′it) *n.* a small room for retirement or storage. —**clos′et·ed,** *adj.* shut up in a private room.

close-′up″ (klōs′-) *n.* a near view; a picture taken at close range.

clo′sure (klō′zhər) *n.* **1,** act of closing; state of being closed. **2,** that which closes, as a bottle cap.

clot (klot) *n.* soft or fluid matter, as blood or cream, coagulated into a mass. —*v.t. & i.* **[clot′ted, -ting]** form a clot. —**clot′ty,** *adj.*

cloth (klâth) *n.* **1,** fabric woven from filaments of wool, cotton, etc. **2,** (*pl.* klâthz) a specific piece of such material for a designated purpose. **3,** the professional dress of a clergyman. —*adj.* made of cloth.

clothe (klōth) *v.t.* **[clothed** or **clad, cloth′-ing]** attire; cover with, or as with, clothing.

clothes (klōz) *n.pl.* **1,** wearing apparel. **2,** cloth coverings, esp. for beds. —**clothes′-horse″,** *n.* (*Slang*) a person on whom clothes are unusually becoming. —**clothes′pin″,** *n.* a small clip for fastening clothes on a line. —**clothes′press″,** *n.* a chest or closet for storing clothes. —**clothes′tree″,** *n.* an upright pole with arms for hanging hats and coats.

cloth′ier (klōth′yər) *n.* a manufacturer or retailer of clothes.

cloth′ing (klō′thing) *n.* wearing apparel; cloth coverings in general.

clo′ture (klō′chər) *n.* a stopping of a debate by parliamentary rule.

cloud (klowd) *n.* **1,** white or gray masses of suspended water or ice particles at varying heights above the earth. **2,** anything resembling a cloud, as dust. **3,** anything that darkens, threatens, or obscures. —*v.t.* **1,** obscure; darken. **2,** place under suspicion; sully. —*v.i.* grow cloudy; become obscured. —**cloud′y,** *adj.* —**cloud chamber,** a vapor chamber for studying the movements of particles. —**cloud nine,** (*Colloq.*) a feeling of well-being.

cloud′ber″ry *n.* a variety of raspberry.

cloud′burst″ *n.* a heavy rainfall.

clout (klowt) *v.t.* strike with the hand; cuff. —*n.* **1,** a blow. **2,** in baseball, a hard hit. **3,** (*Colloq.*) influence.

clove (klōv) *n.* **1,** one of the small bulbs from the mother-bulb, as a clove of garlic. **2,** a spice, the dried flower buds of the clove tree.

clo′ven (klō′vən) *adj.* parted; divided; split.

clo′ver (klō′vər) *n.* a common garden plant, useful as forage.

clo′ver·leaf″ *n.* an arrangement of road intersections to avoid direct crossings.

---

fat, fāte, fär, fâre, fâll, åsk; met, hē, hêr, maybè; pin, pīne; not, nōte, ôr, tool

clown (klown) *n.* **1,** a comedian, esp. in a circus; a buffoon. **2,** (*Archaic*) a rustic; an uncouth person. —*v.i. & t.*act the buffoon; parody. —**clown'er·y,** *n.* —**clown'ish,** *adj.* rude or comical.

cloy (kloi) *v.t. & i.* surfeit; seem excessive (to).

club (klub) *n.* **1,** a stick to be used as a weapon; a cudgel; a bat or stick as used in various games. **2,** any playing card designated by the trefoil (♣). **3,** a group of persons joined by a common interest; its quarters. —*v.t.* [**clubbed, club'bing**] **1,** strike or beat with a club. **2,** use as a weapon. **3,** pool; unite. —*v.i.* (with *together*) unite; act jointly. —**club car,** a railroad car equipped with a lounge, buffet, and other conveniences for passengers. —**club chair,** an easy chair. —**club sandwich,** a large multilayer sandwich with chicken, bacon, tomatoes, lettuce, and mayonnaise. —**club steak,** any of various cuts of beefsteak.

club'foot' *n.* a deformed foot.

cluck (kluk) *n.* **1,** the sound made by suddenly separating the tongue from the hard palate. **2,** the sound of a hen calling her chicks. —*v.i.* utter such sounds.

clue (kloo) *n.* a hint, indication or tangible guide to the solution of a mystery or problem. Also, **clew.**

clump (klump) *n.* **1,** a shapeless mass of solid material. **2,** a cluster of trees or shrubs. —*v.i.* walk heavily and clumsily. —**clump'y,** *adj.*

clum'sy (klum'zè) *adj.* awkward; blundering; ill-adapted. —**clum'si·ness,** *n.*

clung (klung) *v.* pret. & p.p. of *cling.*

clunk (klunk) *n.* a dull, heavy, metallic sound. —*v.i.* make such a sound. —**clunk'er,** *n.* (*Slang*) something inferior; a lemon.

clus'ter (klus'tər) *n.* a closely grouped number of things, as fruits or persons; a bunch. —*v.i. & t.* bunch together. —**cluster college,** a small specialized residential college within a university.

clutch (kluch) *v.t.* **1,** grasp with the hands. **2,** (with *at*) try to grasp. —*v.i.* try to seize something. —*n.* **1,** (often *pl.*) a strong grip; powerful control. **2,** a device to engage a driven member with the driving force. **3,** a brood of eggs or chickens. **4,** (*pl.*) (*Slang*) a critical situation.

clut'ter (klut'ər) *n.* a disorderly state or litter. —*v.t.* (often with *up*) strew in confusion.

Clydes'dale'' (klīdz'dāl'') *n.* **1,** a breed of heavy draft horses. **2,** a breed of small Skye terriers.

clys'ter (klīs'tər) *n.* an enema.

co- (kō) *pref.* as one of two or more; jointly.

coach (kōch) *n.* **1,** carriage; passenger vehicle. **2,** a tutor or instructor. —*v.t.* instruct; train. —**coach'man** (-mən) *n.*

co·ad'ju·tor (kō-aj'ə-tər) *n.* an assistant, as of a bishop or prelate.

co·ag'u·late'' (kō-ag'yə-lāt'') *v.i.* become clotted or congealed. —*v.t.* curdle; congeal. —**co·ag'u·lant,** *n.* —**co·ag''u·la'tion,** *n.*

coal (kōl) *n.* **1,** a blackish carbonaceous mineral used as fuel. **2,** a lump of coal; (*pl.*) any burning lumps. —**coal oil,** kerosene.

co''a·lesce'' (kō''ə-les') *v.i.* grow together; unite. —**co''a·les'cence,** *n.*

co''a·li'tion (kō''ə-lish'ən) *n.* **1,** a temporary alliance. **2,** fusion into one mass.

coarse (kôrs) *adj.* **1,** of rough finish or texture. **2,** crude; unrefined. —**coars'en** (kôr'sən) *v.t.* make coarse. —**coarse'ness,** *n.*

coast (kōst) *n.* the shore line; land by the sea. —*v.i.* proceed without power, by gravity or inertia. —**coast'al,** *adj.* —**Coast Guard,** a U. S. armed service.

coast'er (-ər) *n.* **1,** a vehicle that will coast, as a sled. **2,** a small table mat. **3,** a serving tray on wheels. **4,** a roller coaster. —**coaster brake,** a bicycle brake operated by the pedals.

coat (kōt) *n.* **1,** an outer garment with sleeves. **2,** anything that covers the entire surface, as paint, an animal's fur, etc. —*v.t.* cover with a bonded or close-fitting layer of anything. —**coat'ing,** *n.* a layer of some substance, as paint. —**coat of arms,** a shield distinctively emblazoned.

co·au'thor *n.* one of two or more persons who write or compose something together. —*v.t.* write or compose together.

coax (kōks) *v.t. & i.* beg by fondling or flattery; wheedle; cajole.

co·ax'i·al (kō-ak'sē-əl) *adj.* having a common axis; but (of a cable) capable of transmitting different and distinguishable impulses.

cob (kob) *n.* **1,** the spike upon which grains of corn grow: *corncob*. **1,** a small, strong horse. **3,** the male swan.

co'balt (kō'bâlt) *n.* a hard metallic element, no. 27, symbol Co. —*adj.* deep blue.

cob'ble (kob'əl) *v.t. & i.* make or repair shoes; mend or patch, esp. clumsily.

cob'bler (kob'lər) *n.* **1,** a shoemaker. **2,** a dessert or drink made with fruit.

cob'ble·stone'' *n.* a paving stone with convex upper surface.

CO'BOL (kō'bâl) *n.* a standardized language for programming a computer (*common business oriented language*).

co'bra (kō'brə) *n.* a poisonous snake of Asia and India.

cob'web" (kob'web") *n.* **1,** the net spun by the spider. **2,** any similar flimsy structure.

co'ca (kō'kə) *n.* the dried leaf of a So. Amer. shrub, used medicinally as a tonic, or mild stimulant.

co·caine' (kō'kān') *n.* an alkaloid of coca, used as an anesthetic and narcotic.

coc'cyx (kok'siks) *n.* [*pl.* **coc·cy'ges** (-sī'jēz)] a small bone at the base of the spinal column. —**coc·cyg'e·al** (-sij'ē-əl) *adj.*

coch"i·neal' (koch"ə-nēl') *n.* a scarlet dye made from dried Central Amer. insects.

coch'le·a (kok'lē-ə) *n.* [*pl.* **-ae"** (-ē")] a spiral canal in the internal ear. —**coch'·le·ar** (-ər) *adj.*

cock (kok) *n.* **1,** the male of various birds, esp. of domestic fowl; a rooster. **2,** a leader. **3,** a conical pile of hay. **4,** an upward tilt, as of a head, hat, etc. **5,** a faucet or valve. —*v.t.* **1,** turn up on one side. **2,** draw back the hammer of (a gun). —**cocked hat,** a hat with a wide brim turned up in flaps. —**knock into a cocked hat,** destroy; discredit.

cock·ade' (-ād') *n.* a rosette worn on the hat as a badge.

cock'a·ma"mie (kok'ə-mā"mē) *adj.* (*Slang*) absurd; ridiculous.

cock-'and-bull' (kok'ən-bûl') *adj.* of a story, absurd, but told as true.

cock"a·too' (-ə-too') *n.* a crested Australian parrot.

cock'a·trice (kok'ə-tris) *n.* a fabulous deadly serpent.

cock'crow" *n.* dawn.

cock'er (-ər) *n.* a small long-haired hunting dog: *cocker spaniel.*

cock'er·el (-ər-əl) *n.* a young cock.

cock'eyed' (-īd") *adj.* **1,** cross-eyed. **2,** (*Slang*) twisted; absurd. **3,** (*Slang*) drunk.

cock'horse' *n.* a child's rocking horse.

cock'le (kok'əl) *n.* **1,** a weed. **2,** an edible mollusk with two fluted shells. **3,** a shallow boat. —**cockles of the heart,** inmost depths of feeling.

cock'ney (kok'nē) *n.* a native of the East End of London; the dialect of this region.

cock'pit" *n.* **1,** the space for pilots in an airplane or motor boat. **2,** a recess in the after deck of a yacht, etc. **3,** a place for cockfighting.

cock'roach" *n.* an insect infesting houses.

cocks'comb" (koks'kōm") *n.* a crimson-flowered plant: the *celosia.*

cock'sure' *adj.* overconfident.

cock'tail" *n.* a mixed drink, or dish of fruit, shellfish, etc. served before a meal.

—**cocktail sauce,** a mixture of ketchup, horseradish, and spices.

cock'y (kok'ē) *adj.* conceited. —**cock'i·ness,** *n.*

co'co (kō'kō) *n.* the coconut palm.

co'coa (kō'kō) *n.* **1,** a powder made from cacao seed; a hot drink made from this powder and milk. **2,** a brown color. —**cocoa butter,** a waxy substance made from cacao seeds.

co'co·nut" (kō'kə-nut") *n.* the large, hard fruit of a tropical tree (*coconut palm*).

co·coon' (kə-koon') *n.* a silky case in which certain larvae develop.

co·cotte' (kō-kot') *n.* a harlot.

cod (kod) *n.* a No. Atlantic food fish. Also, **cod'fish".**

co'da (kō'də) *n.* a concluding section of a musical composition.

cod'dle (kod'əl) *v.t.* **1,** humor; pamper. **2,** cook in hot but not boiling water.

code (kōd) *n.* **1,** a systematized collection of laws. **2,** any set of rules. **3,** a system of signals for telegraphic or secret communication. —*v.t.* **1,** codify. **2,** encode.

co'deine (kō'dēn) *n.* a narcotic derivative of opium.

co'dex (kō'deks) *n.* [*pl.* **-di·ces"** (-də-sēz")] a manuscript, esp. of a classic book.

codg'er (koj'ər) *n.* (*Colloq.*) an old person.

cod'i·cil (kod'ə-səl) *n.* a supplement to a will.

cod'i·fy" (kod'i-fī") *v.t.* arrange systematically; reduce to a code. —**cod"i·fi·ca'tion,** *n.*

cod'piece" *n.* a flap hanging over the opening in the front of men's breeches.

co·ed" (kō'ed") *n.* (*Colloq.*) a female student in a coeducational college.

co"ed·u·ca'tion *n.* education of students of both sexes together. —**co"ed·u·ca'tion·al,** *adj.*

co"ef·fi'cient (kō"ə-fish'ənt) *n.* a multiplier.

co·e'qual *adj. & n.* equal in extent, rank, power, etc. —**co"e·qual'i·ty,** *n.*

co·erce' (kō-ērs') *v.t.* compel by force. —**co·er'cion** (-shən) *n.*

co·e'val (kō-ē'vəl) *adj.* of the same age; contemporary.

co"ex·ist' *v.i.* exist together or at the same time. —**co"ex·ist'ence,** *n.* —**co"ex·ist'ent,** *adj.*

co"ex·tend' *v.i.* extend equally in space or time. —**co"ex·ten'sive,** *adj.*

cof'fee (kâf'ē) *n.* **1,** a drink made from the seeds of a tropical shrub; the shrub or seeds (coffee beans). **2,** a brown color. —**coffee house, 1,** a public room where coffee and other refreshments are served. **2**, a café; nightclub. —**coffee shop,** a restaurant serving simple meals. —**coffee table,** a low, usu. long, table set before a sofa.

cof'fer (kâf'ər) *n.* a chest, esp. one for valuables.

cof'fer·dam'' *n.* a watertight enclosure built in water, pumped dry to allow construction work.

cof'fin (kâf'in) *n.* a box in which a corpse is buried.

cog (kog) *n.* a tooth on a gear wheel (*cogwheel*). —**cog railway,** a railway used on steep slopes that employs a cog wheel for traction.

co'gent (kō'jənt) *adj.* convincing; forcible. —**co'gen·cy,** *n.*

cog'i·tate'' (koj'ə-tāt'') *v.i. & t.* ponder; plan. —**cog''i·ta'tion,** *n.*

co'gnac (kōn'yak) *n.* a Fr. brandy.

cog'nate (kog'nāt) *adj.* related. —*n.* something related. —**cog·na'tion,** *n.*

cog·ni'tion (kog-nish'ən) *n.* the process of acquiring a conscious awareness; perception; cognizance.

cog'ni·zance (kog'ni-zəns) *n.* **1,** awareness; notice. **2,** range of observation. —**cog'ni·zant,** *adj.*

cog·no'men (kog-nō'mən) *n.* **1,** a surname. **2,** among Romans, the third or family name. **3,** a nickname.

co·hab'it (kō-hab'it) *v.i.* live together, esp. as husband and wife. —**co·hab''i·ta'tion,** *n.*

co·here' (kō-hir') *v.i.* **1,** stick together. **2,** be logically consistent or connected. —**co·her'ence,** *n.* —**co·her'ent,** *adj.*

co·he'sion (kō-hē'zhən) *n.* a sticking together of like particles. —**co·he'sive** (-siv) *adj.*

co'hort (kō'hôrt) *n.* **1,** a band, esp. of warriors. **2,** (*Colloq.*) comrade.

coif (koif) *n.* **1,** a close-fitting peasant cap. **2,** a nun's hood-shaped cap. —*v.t.* provide with a headdress.

coif·feur' (kwä-fêr') *n.* a hairdresser.

coif·fure' (kwä-fyûr') *n.* a manner of arranging the hair; a headdress.

coil (koil) *v.t. & i.* twist into spiral shape. —*n.* a length of coiled rope, wire, pipe, etc.

coin (koin) *n.* a piece of metal authorized for use as money. —*v.t.* **1,** make (metal) into money. **2,** make (money) by minting metal. **3,** invent, as a word. **4,** (*Colloq.*) gain (money) rapidly. —**coin'er,** *n.* a counterfeiter.

coin'age (koin'ij) *n.* **1,** the act or process of coining; money coined. **2,** currency. **3,** a thing invented.

co''in·cide' (kō''in-sīd') *v.i.* **1,** occupy the same space or time. **2,** correspond exactly. **3,** concur; agree.

co·in'ci·dence (kō-in'si-dəns) *n.* **1,** exact correspondence in space or time. **2,** a notable occurrence of events apparently accidental. —**co·in''ci·dent, co·in''ci·den'tal,** *adj.*

co'i·tus (kō'i-təs) *n.* sexual intercourse. Also, **co·i'tion** (kō-ish'ən).

coke (kōk) *n.* **1,** a fuel, the solid residue of coal baked but not burned. **2,** (*Slang*) cocaine. **3,** (*T.N.*) a soft drink: *Coca-Cola*.

co'la (kō'lə) *n.* **1,** kola. **2,** a carbonated soft drink flavored with an extract of the kola nut.

col'an·der (kol'ən-dər) *n.* a strainer used in cooking.

cold (kōld) *adj.* **1,** below the temperature comfortable to the body; chilling. **2,** lacking bodily heat. **3,** not heated. **4,** unresponsive; indifferent; lacking in enthusiasm. —*n.* **1,** a condition of low temperature. **2,** a sensation produced by lack of heat. **3,** an ailment affecting the mucous membranes of the nose and throat. —**cold'ness,** *n.* —**catch cold,** become sick with a cold. —**cold cream,** a cosmetic. —**cold duck,** a mixture of sparkling Burgundy and champagne. —**cold feet,** (*Colloq.*) lack or loss of courage. —**cold shoulder,** a rebuff; deliberate disregard. —**cold sore,** a blister in the mouth. —**cold storage,** long-term storage. —**cold turkey,** (*Slang*) complete withdrawal from drugs as a cure for addiction. —**cold war,** a period of bitterly unfriendly diplomatic relations.

cold'blood''ed (-blud''id) *adj.* **1,** deliberate; unsympathetic; cruel. **2,** pert. to fishes and reptiles. —**cold'blood''ed·ness,** *n.*

cole (kōl) *n.* a plant of the cabbage family; rape.

cole'slaw'' (kōl'slâ'') *n.* finely sliced cabbage.

col'ic (kol'ik) *n.* severe griping abdominal pains. —**col'ick·y,** *adj.*

col''i·se'um (kol''ə-sē'əm) *n.* a large public amphitheater.

co·li'tis (kō-lī'tis) *n.* inflammation of the colon.

col·lab'o·rate'' (kə-lab'ə-rāt'') *v.i.* **1,** work with another, esp. in writing. **2,** in wartime, work with the enemy. —**col·lab''o·ra'tion,** *n.* —**col·lab''o·ra'tion·ist,** *n.* one who works with the enemy. —**col·lab'o·ra'tor,** *n.* a joint author.

col·lage' (kə-läzh') *n.* (*Art*) a composition made of fragments of different materials stuck together.

col·lapse' (kə-laps') *v.i. & t.* **1,** break, fall in, or give way. **2,** fail. **3,** break down physically. **4,** fold up intentionally, as an umbrella. —*n.* a sudden failure or falling in. —**col·laps'i·ble,** *adj.*

col'lar (kol'ər) *n.* a band or harness worn around the neck. —*v.t.* **1,** put a collar on. **2,** grasp by the collar. **3,** (*Slang*) seize; apprehend.

col'lar·bone" *n.* a bone connecting the breastbone with the shoulder blade; the clavicle.

col'lard (kol'ərd) *n.* a kind of kale.

col·late' (kə-lāt') *v.t.* **1,** compare in detail. **2,** put (pages, etc.) in proper order.

col·lat'er·al (kə-lat'ər-əl) *adj.* **1,** attendant on, but subordinate to, the main issue. **2,** side by side; parallel. **3,** descended from the same ancestor, but in a different line. —*n.* something given as additional security for a loan.

col·la'tion (ko-lā'shən) *n.* **1,** act of collating. **2,** a light meal.

col'league (kol'ēg) *n.* a professional associate.

col·lect' (kə-lekt') *v.t.* **1,** gather together. **2,** receive payment of. **3,** get (contributions, etc.) from others. **4,** acquire as a hobby. **5,** regain command of (oneself). —*v.i.* assemble; accumulate. —*n.* (kol'ekt) a short prayer. —**col·lec'tion,** *n.* —**col·lec'tor,** *n.*

col·lec'tive (kə-lek'tiv) *adj.* **1,** combined. **2,** belonging to, or exercised by, an aggregate of persons. **3,** treating a number of objects as one unit, as a *collective noun.* —*n.* a collective enterprise. —**col·lec'tiv·ism,** *n.* the socialistic principle of state ownership. —**col·lec'tiv·ize,** *v.i. & t.* —**collective bargaining,** the process of fixing wages, hours, and other conditions for work for all employees by negotiation between their chosen representatives and the employer.

col·leen' (ko-lēn') *n.* (*Irish*) girl.

col'lege (kol'ij) *n.* **1,** an institution of higher learning. **2,** one of the separate schools of a university. **3,** a body of men having certain powers and rights.

col·le'gi·an (kə-lē'jē-ən) *n.* a college student.

col·le'gi·ate (kə-lē'jē-ət) *adj.* **1,** pert. to a college or college customs. **2,** pert. to a church allied with others.

col·lide' (kə-līd') *v.i.* come into violent contact; conflict.

col'lie (kol'ē) *n.* a Scot. sheep dog.

col'lier (kol'yər) *n.* **1,** a coal miner. **2,** a vessel for shipping coal. —**col'lier·y,** *n.* a coal mine.

col·lin'e·ar (kə-lin'ē-ər) *adj.* lying in the same straight line.

col'lins (kol'inz) *n.* a tall cocktail of liquor, lemon juice, sugar, and carbonated water.

col·li'sion (kə-lizh'ən) *n.* act or result of colliding; clash.

col'lo·cate" (kol'ə-kāt") *v.t.* place side by side; arrange in order. —**col"lo·ca'tion,** *n.*

col·lo'di·on (kə-lō'dē-ən) *n.* a cellulose solution used as a protective coating.

col'loid (kol'oid) *n.* (*Chem.*) a substance that, when dispersed in another medium, forms particles larger than molecules but smaller than particles of suspension.

col·lo'qui·al (kə-lō'kwē-əl) *adj.* belonging to ordinary, everyday speech. —**col·lo'qui·al·ism,** *n.*

col·lo'qui·um (kə-lō'kwē-əm) *n.* a conference; discussion.

col'lo·quy (kol'ə-kwē) *n.* **1,** a conversation. **2,** a discussion; conference.

col·lude' (kə-lood') *v.i.* conspire together. —**col·lu'sion** (-loo'zhən) *n.* —**col·lu'sive** (-siv) *adj.*

col·lyr'i·um (kə-lir'ē-əm) *n.* [*pl.* **-a** (-ə)] an eyewash.

co·logne' (kə-lōn') *n.* a fragrant toilet water.

co'lon (kō'lən) *n.* **1,** the large intestine. **2,** a mark (:) of punctuation, introducing an example or conclusion.

colo'nel (kēr'nəl) *n.* a military officer ranking between lieutenant colonel and brigadier general. —**colo'nel·cy** (-sē) *n.*

co·lo'ni·al (kə-lō'nē-əl) *adj.* being or pert. to a colony. —*n.* a native of a colony. —**co·lo'ni·al·ism,** *n.*

col'on·nade" (kol'ə-nād") *n.* a series of columns.

col'o·ny (kol'ə-nē) *n.* **1,** a body of people who settle in a new country but remain subject to the mother country; the place of settlement. **2,** people of one nationality or occupation living close together. —**col'o·nist,** *n.* —**col'o·nize"** (-nīz") *v.t. & i.*

col'o·phon" (kol'ə-fon") *n.* a publisher's emblem.

col'or (kul'ər) *n.* **1,** any of the hues of the rainbow; also, any tint or shade made by mixing these hues. **2,** complexion. **3,** a pigment. **4,** outward appearance; general characteristics. **5,** (*pl.*) a flag. **6,** (*pl.*) a symbolic colored ribbon or ornament; the clothes of a jockey. **7,** (*Colloq.*) commentary in a sports broadcast. —*v.t.* **1,** dye. **2,** misrepresent. —*v.i.* blush. Also, **col'our.** —**col"or·a'tion,** *n.* —**col'or·ant,** *n.* —**color line,** systematic segregation by races.

col"o·ra·tu'ra (kul"ə-rə-tyûr'ə) *n.* **1,** florid passages in vocal music. **2,** a singer of coloratura, esp. a soprano of high range.

col'or·blind" *adj.* unable to distinguish different colors normally.

col'or·cast" *n.* a television broadcast in color. —*v.i. & t.* to broadcast in color.

col'or-code" *v.t.* color (a wire, etc.) for purposes of identification.

col'ored (-ərd) *adj.* **1,** having color. **2,** belonging to a nonwhite race, esp. the Negro race. **3,** biased; deceptive.

col'or·fast" *adj.* having color that will not fade, wash out, etc.

col'or·ful (-fəl) *adj.* **1,** full of color. **2,** picturesque; dramatic.

col'or·ing *n.* **1,** complexion; hue. **2,** dye.

col'or·less *adj.* **1,** without color. **2,** lacking interest.

co·los'sal (kə-los'əl) *adj.* huge; gigantic.

co·los'sus (kə-los'əs) *n.* a gigantic statue; any great thing or person.

co·los'to·my (kə-los'tə-mē) *n.* a surgical operation to form an artificial opening to the colon.

co·los'trum (kə-los'trəm) *n.* milk secreted for several days before and after childbirth.

col'por"teur (kol'pôr"tər) *n.* a peddler of books, esp. religious books.

colt (kōlt) *n.* **1,** a young male horse. **2,** (*cap.*) (*T.N.*) a type of revolver. —**colt'ish,** *adj.*

col'um·bine" (kol'əm-bīn") *n.* a plant having spurred flowers.

co·lum'bi·um (kə-lum'bē-əm) *n.* niobium.

col'umn (kol'əm) *n.* **1,** an upright pillar supporting some part of a building. **2,** anything resembling a pillar in use, position, or appearance. **3,** a vertical row of figures or type. **4,** a regular department in a newspaper. **5,** a formation or line of soldiers or ships. —**co·lum'nar** (kə-lum'nər) *adj.*

col'um·nist (kol'əm-ist) *n.* the writer of a regular newspaper feature.

com- (kom) *pref.* with; jointly; entirely.

co'ma (kō'mə) *n.* **1,** a state of prolonged stupor, caused by injury, disease, or poison. **2,** the head of a comet.

com'a·tose" (kom'ə-tōs") *adj.* **1,** in a coma. **2,** lethargic.

comb (kōm) *n.* **1,** a toothed instrument for arranging the hair, currying horses, carding wool or fibers, etc. **2,** a rooster's crest. **3,** reticulated cells, as a honeycomb. —*v.t.* **1,** dress (hair); card (wool, etc.). **2,** search thoroughly.

com'bat (kom'bat) *n.* a fight; a battle. —*v.t. & i* (kəm-bat') fight against; oppose. —**com'bat·ant** (-bə-tənt) *n. & adj.* —**com·bat'ive,** *adj.*

com"bi·na'tion (kom"bə-nā'shən) *n.* **1,** a coming together so as to form a group, sum, product, etc.; the group, etc. so formed. **2,** a one-piece undergarment. **3,** the series of numbers which when dialed will open a keyless lock.

com·bine' (kəm-bīn') *v.t. & i.* join; unite. —*n.* (kom'bīn") **1,** a harvesting machine. **2,** (*Colloq.*) a union of important persons, parties, or corporations. —**com·bin"a·to'-ri·al** (kəm-bī"nə-tôr'ē-əl) *adj.*

com'bo (kom'bō) *n.* (*Slang*) combination; esp. a small jazz or dance band.

com·bus'tion (kəm-bus'chən) *n.* the act or process of burning. —**com·bus'ti·ble,** *adj. & n.*

come (kum) *v.i.* [**came** (kām), **come, com'-ing**] **1,** move toward; approach. **2,** arrive, in space, time, or sequence. **3,** appear as the result of something; be derived from. **4,** become. **5,** happen; occur. **6,** extend to a given point. **7,** be attained or acquired. —**come across, 1,** meet. **2,** deliver. —**come around, 1,** recover. **2,** submit. —**come off,** succeed; occur. —**come over,** happen to. —**come through, 1,** survive. **2,** produce as expected. —**come to,** regain consciousness.

come'back" *n.* (*Colloq.*) **1,** a recovery of lost position. **2,** a retort.

co·me'di·an (kə-mē'dē-ən) *n.* an actor or writer of comedy. —**co·me"di·enne'** (-en') *n.fem.*

com'e·do" (kom'ə-dō") *n.* a blackhead.

come'down" *n.* a humiliating experience.

com'e·dy (kom'ə-dē) *n.* **1,** a light, amusing drama ending happily. **2,** the comic element in anything. **3,** any comic incident.

come'ly (kum'lē) *adj.* good-looking. —**come'li·ness,** *n.*

come-'on" *n.* (*Slang*) a lure; gimmick.

com'er (kum'ər) *n.* (*Colloq.*) one likely to be successful.

co·mes'ti·ble (kə-mes'tə-bəl) *n. & adj.* edible.

com'et (kom'it) *n.* a moving celestial body with a luminous tail.

come·up'pance (-up'əns) *n.* (*Slang*) a humiliating or humbling experience.

com'fit (kum'fit) *n.* a bonbon.

com'fort (kum'fərt) *v.t.* console. —*n.* **1,** solace; consolation. **2,** one who brings solace. **3,** the feeling of consolation. **4,** a state or feeling of well-being and content. **5,** (*pl.*) things that contribute to such a state. **6,** a bed covering. —**comfort station,** rest room.

com'fort·a·ble (kum'fərt-ə-bəl) *adj.* **1,** affording ease. **2,** free from pain or distress. **3,** (*Colloq.*) sufficient.

com'fort·er *n.* **1,** a bedcovering. **2,** a scarf. **3,** one who comforts. **4,** (*cap.*) the Holy Spirit.

com'fy (kum'fē) *adj.* (*Colloq.*) comfortable.

com'ic (kom'ik) *adj.* **1,** pert. to comedy. **2,** comical; funny. —*n.* **1,** a comedian. **2,** (*pl.*) comic pictures, esp. in a newspaper; funny papers. **3,** [also, **comic book**] a magazine presenting stories in cartoon style. —**com'i·cal,** *adj.* droll; funny; exciting mirth. —**comic strip,** a series of drawings in cartoon style, developing a narrative.

com'i·ty (kom'ə-tē) *n.* courtesy, esp. between nations.

com'ma (kom'ə) *n.* **1,** a punctuation mark (,) indicating a brief or minor pause. **2,** a caesura.

com·mand' (kə-mànd') *v.t. & i.* **1,** order or require with authority. **2,** exercise supreme power (over). **3,** overlook, as from a height. —*n.* **1,** an order. **2,** authority to order. **3,** power to control; mastery; complete knowledge or skill. **4,** a naval or military force under the control of a certain officer. —**command performance,** a theatrical performance before a king, etc.

com"man·dant' (kom"ən-dänt') *n.* the officer in command of a military installation, fortress, etc.

com"man·deer' (kom"ən-dir') *v.t.* **1,** seize for military purposes. **2,** seize arbitrarily.

com·mand'er (kə-man'dər) *n.* **1,** a leader; chief officer. **2,** in the U.S. Navy, the rank next below captain.

com·mand'ing (kə-man'ding) *adj.* **1,** in command. **2,** imperative; imperious. **3,** affording a panoramic view. **4,** impressive.

com·mand'ment (kə-mand'mənt) *n.* **1,** a command; a charge. **2,** one of the Ten Commandments.

com·man'do (kə-màn'dō) *n.* [*pl.* **-dos**] a member of a body of picked troops for raiding enemy territory.

com·mem'o·rate" (kə-mem'ə-rāt') *v.t.* **1,** honor the memory of in a formal manner. **2,** serve as a memento of. —**com·mem"o·ra'tion,** *n.* —**com·mem'o·ra"tive,** *adj.*

com·mence' (kə-mens') *v.t. & i.* begin.

com·mence'ment (-mənt) *n.* **1,** a beginning; **2,** the graduation exercises of a school or college.

com·mend' (kə-mend') *v.t.* **1,** praise. **2,** recommend. **3,** entrust or give in charge. —**com·mend'a·ble,** *adj.* —**com·mend'a·to·ry,** *adj.*

com"men·da'tion (kom"ən-dā'shən) *n.* a citation of praise.

com·men'su·ra·ble (kə-men'shə-rə-bəl) *adj.* comparable in measure; proportionate.

com·men'su·rate (kə-men'shə-rət) *adj.* **1,** of equal size. **2,** corresponding in amount, degree, or size; comparable. **3,** adequate.

com'ment (kom'ent) *n.* **1,** a remark or observation, esp. a note explaining or criticizing a book. **2,** talk; gossip. —*v.i.* make remarks.

com"men·tar"y (kom'ən-tär"ē) *n.* an explanatory discourse.

com"men·ta"tor (kom'ən-tā"tər) *n.* one who reports and comments on current events.

com'merce (kom'ērs) *n.* **1,** trade on a large scale, esp. between countries; business. **2,** any intercourse.

com·mer'cial (kə-mēr'shəl) *adj.* **1,** pert. to, or engaged in, or accruing from, trade. **2,** suitable or designed for sale. —*n.* the advertising material on a radio or television program. —**com·mer'cial·ism** (-iz-əm) *n.* principles and practices of commerce; mercenary spirit. —**com·mer'cial·ize"** (-īz") *v.t.* exploit; turn to account. —**commercial traveler,** a traveling salesman.

com·min'gle (kə-ming'gəl) *v.t. & i.* mingle together; blend.

com"mi·nute' (kom"i-nūt') *v.t.* pulverize. —**com"mi·nu'tion,** *n.*

com·mis'er·ate" (kə-miz'ə-rāt') *v.t.* pity; condole with. —**com·mis"er·a'tion,** *n.*

com"mis·sar' (kom"ə-sär') *n.* the head of a government department in the U.S.S.R. —**com"mis·sar'i·at** (-sär'ē-ət) *n.* a department of a military or (in the U.S.S.R.) government organization.

com'mis·sar"y (kom'ə-sär"ē) *n.* **1,** a store supplying food and supplies, as in a camp. **2,** a deputy.

com·mis'sion (kə-mish'ən) *n.* **1,** the act of doing or perpetrating. **2,** a warrant to inquire and report. **3,** a body of persons entrusted with special duties. **4,** a matter entrusted to another; assignment. **5,** authority to act as agent; also, the fee paid. **6,** a document conferring naval or military rank. **7,** an order to make or perform a work of art; the fee accompanying such an order. —*v.t.* **1,** delegate; appoint. **2,** confer rank or authority on. **3,** equip (a ship) for active service. **4,** order (as a work of art) to be made or performed.

com·mis'sion·er *n.* **1,** the head of a commission or of one of certain governmental departments. **2,** an agent.

com·mit' (kə-mit') *v.t.* [**com·mit'ted, -ting**] **1,** entrust to another's care. **2,** consign to custody. **3,** perpetrate (a sin, crime, etc.). **4,** refer to a committee, as a bill. **5,** involve in risk. **6,** bind (oneself); pledge. **7,** authorize the confinement of (a person) in a mental institution.

com·mit'ment (-mənt) *n.* **1,** act of committing. **2,** a pledge; something undertaken. Also, **com·mit'tal** (-əl) *n.*

com·mit'tee (kə-mit'ė) *n.* a body of persons appointed for specific duties. **—com·mit'tee·man** (-mən) *n.* **—com·mit'tee·wom"an**, *n.fem.*

com·mode' (kə-mōd') *n.* a small bedside cupboard.

com·mo'di·ous (kə-mō'dė-əs) *adj.* roomy and spacious. **—com·mo'dious·ness**, *n.*

com·mod'i·ty (kə-mod'ə-tė) *n.* 1, an article of commerce. 2, a useful thing.

com'mo·dore" (kom'ə-dôr") *n.* the senior or commanding officer of more than one ship or yacht; in the U. S. Navy, a rank next above captain.

com'mon (kom'ən) *adj.* 1, shared by, or equally true of, two or more; joint; united. 2, public; general. 3, familiar; usual. 4, not notable; ordinary. 5, vulgar; coarse. —*n.* 1, a tract of public land; a park. 2, (*pl.*) a college dining hall; its food. 3, (*pl.*) (*cap.*) the elective house of Parliament. **—common carrier**, a company that transports for hire. **—common law**, the system of law based on custom and court decisions, not statutes. **—Common Market**, a European customs union established in 1958. **—common noun**, a noun designating any of a class. **—common sense**, good judgment in simple matters. **—common stock**, shares of ownership of a company, having voting rights but no fixed dividend.

com'mon·al·ty (kom'ən-əl-tė) *n.* 1, the common people. 2, the members of a corporation.

com'mon·er (kom'ən-ər) *n.* a person without noble rank.

com'mon·place" (kom'ən-plās") *adj.* 1, ordinary; not unusual or original. 2, hackneyed; trite.

com'mon·wealth" (kom'ən-welth") *n.* a state or union of states.

com·mo'tion (kə-mō'shən) *n.* 1, violent agitation. 2, disorder; public unrest.

com'mu·nal (kom'yoo-nəl) *adj.* pert. to, or owned by, a community; public.

com·mune' (kə-mūn') *v.i.* 1, interchange thoughts and feelings; converse. 2, take Communion. —*n.* (kom'ūn) a community.

com·mu'ni·cant (-kənt) *n.* one who communicates; one who takes communion.

com·mu'ni·cate" (kə-mū'ni-kāt") *v.t.* convey, impart. —*v.i.* 1, converse; get in touch by letter, etc. 2, be connected, as rooms. **—com·mu'ni·ca·ble**, *adj.*

com·mu"ni·ca'tion (-kā'shən) *n.* 1, act of communicating. 2, a message. 3, a means or way of communicating; passage.

com·mu'ni·ca·tive (-kə-tiv) *adj.* informative; talkative.

com·mun'ion (kə-mūn'yən) *n.* 1, a sharing; fellowship. 2, (*cap.*) celebration of the Lord's Supper.

com·mu"ni·qué' (kə-mū"nə-kā') *n.* an official communication or bulletin.

com'mu·nism (kom'yə-niz-əm) *n.* a social theory that the common people should own all property and means of production. **—com'mu·nize"** (-nīz") *v.t.*

com'mu·nist (kom'yə-nist) *adj.* pert. to a political party or government advocating communism, esp. (*cap.*) in the U.S.S.R. —*n.* an advocate of such theory, or member of such government or such party.

com·mu'ni·ty (kə-mū'nə-tė) *n.* 1, all persons living in a particular locality. 2, a group having interests or religion in common. 3, joint sharing.

com'mu·tate" (kom'yû-tāt") *v.t.* change the direction of (an electric current). **—com'mu·ta"tor**, *n.*

com·mute' (kə-mūt') *v.t.* substitute another thing for, esp. to reduce the severity of a penalty, obligation, etc. —*v.i.* travel daily between a city and suburb. **—com"mu·ta'tion**, *n.* **—com·mut'er**, *n.*

comp (komp) *n.* (*Slang*) a complimentary ticket, as for a concert.

com·pact' (kəm-pakt') *adj.* 1, closely packed together; solid; dense. 2, concise. —*v.t.* 1, pack together closely; condense. 2, form; compound. —*n.* (kom'pakt) 1, a small case containing powder and rouge. 2, an agreement; treaty. 3, a small car. **—compact'or**, *n.*

com·pan'ion (kəm-pan'yən) *n.* 1, an associate; comrade. 2, a paid attendant. 3, a mate; one of a pair of matched objects. **—com·pan'ion·a·ble**, *adj.* agreeable; friendly. **—com·pan'ion·ate** (-ət) *adj.* of or like a companion.

com·pan'ion·ship *n.* friendship.

com·pan'ion·way" *n.* a stair from deck to cabins on a ship.

com'pa·ny (kum'pə-nė) *n.* 1, a group of persons assembled, working, or associating together. 2, someone to talk or commune with. 3, guests. 4, a business firm. 5, a military unit; a ship's crew. **—part company**, separate.

com'pa·ra·ble (kom'pə-rə-bəl) *adj.* capable of being, or worthy to be, compared.

com·par'a·tive (kəm-par'ə-tiv) *adj.* 1, relative; based on comparison. 2, (*Gram.*) expressing a higher degree, as when modified by *more.* —*n.* (*Gram.*) a comparative form.

com·pare' (kəm-pār') *v.t.* 1, represent as similar. 2, note the resemblance and differences of. 3, (*Gram.*) give the degrees of comparison of. —*v.i.* admit of comparison. —*n.* comparison.

com·par'i·son (kəm-par'i-sən) *n.* 1, act of comparing. 2, an illustration; simile. 3, a comparable state or condition. **4,** (*Gram.*) the inflection of an adjective or adverb to show difference in degree.

com·part'ment (kəm-pärt'mənt) *n.* a chamber, cell, or space partitioned off. —*v.t.* divide into compartments. —**com·part'-ment'al·ize** (-men'təl-īz) *v.t.*

com'pass (kum'pəs) *n.* **1,** extent within limits; boundary; range. **2,** an instrument showing the magnetic North. **3,** (often *pl.*) an instrument with two legs pivoted at one end, for describing circles, etc. —*v.t.* **1,** encompass; encircle. **2,** accomplish.

com·pas'sion (kəm-pash'ən) *n.* sympathy, esp. pity. —**com·pas'sion·ate,** *adj.* sympathetic; merciful.

com·pat'i·ble (kəm-pat'ə-bəl) *adj.* **1,** consistent. **2,** congenial; harmonious. —**compat''i·bil'i·ty,** *n.*

com·pa'tri·ot (kəm-pā'trē-ət) *n.* **1,** a fellow countryman. **2,** (*Colloq.*) colleague. —*adj.* of the same country.

com'peer (kom'pir) *n.* an associate, equal, or fellow.

com·pel' (kəm-pel') *v.t.* **[-pelled', -pel'-ling]** coerce; oblige.

com·pen'di·um (kəm-pen'dē-əm) *n.* a summary. —**com·pen'di·ous,** *adj.* concise.

com'pen·sate'' (kom'pən-sāt'') *v.t. & i.* **1,** make up (for); offset. **2,** pay (for); recompense. —**com·pen'sa·to·ry,** *adj.*

com''pen·sa'tion (kom''pən-sā'shən) *n.* **1,** act or result of compensating; offset; pay. **2,** regular payments, in lieu of wages, to a worker injured on the job: *workmen's compensation.*

com·pete' (kəm-pēt') *v.i.* contend with another; vie.

com'pe·tence (kom'pə-təns) *n.* **1,** fitness; adequacy. **2,** sufficient means for living comfortably.

com'pe·tent (-tənt) *adj.* **1,** capable; adequate. **2,** authorized.

com''pe·ti'tion (kom''pə-tish'ən) *n.* **1,** rivalry; the struggle for trade, preëminence, etc. **2,** a match between contestants. —**competi'tive** (kəm-pet'ə-tiv) *adj.*

com·pet'i·tor (kəm-pet'i-tər) *n.* **1,** one who competes. **2,** opponent; rival.

com·pile' (kəm-pīl') *v.t.* collect from various sources, esp. literary material for a book. —**com''pi·la'tion** (kom''pə-lā'shən) *n.*

com·pla'cen·cy (kəm-plā'sən-sè) *n.* self-satisfaction. Also, **com·pla'cence.** —**compla'cent,** *adj.*

com·plain' (kəm-plān') *v.i.* **1,** express pain, resentment, etc.; find fault. **2,** make a formal charge. —**com·plain'ant,** *n.* plaintiff.

com·plaint' (kəm-plānt') *n.* **1,** an expression of discontent, pain, etc. **2,** a bodily ailment. **3,** (*Law*) a statement of the cause of action in a civil suit.

com·plai'sant (kəm-plā'zənt) *adj.* agreeable; compliant. —**com·plai'sance,** *n.*

com'ple·ment (kom'plə-mənt) *n.* **1,** that which fills up or completes. **2,** one of two parts needed to form a whole. —*v.t.* (-ment') fill out; complete. —**com''ple·men'ta·ry,** *adj.* —**complementary colors,** pairs of colors that produce gray when mixed.

com·plete' (kəm-plēt') *adj.* **1,** having all its parts; whole. **2,** absolute; thorough. **3,** concluded. —*v.t.* **1,** supply what is lacking to. **2,** finish. —**com·ple'tion** (-plē'shən) *n.*

com·plex' (kəm-pleks') *adj.* **1,** composed of many parts. **2,** involved; complicated; perplexing. —*n.* (kom'pleks) **1,** a complex condition or situation. **2,** an intricate assemblage of related buildings. **3,** (*Psych.*) a group of emotional experiences, often having an unsuspected effect. **4,** (*Colloq.*) an obsession. —**complex number,** a number expressed as the sum of a real number and an imaginary number.

com·plex'ion (kəm-plek'shən) *n.* **1,** the hue or texture of the skin, esp. of the face. **2,** general appearance; aspect.

com·plex'i·ty (kom-plek'sə-tè) *n.* intricacy.

com·pli'ant (kəm-plī'ənt) *adj.* complying; yielding to the wishes of others. —**compli'ance,** *n.*

com'pli·cate'' (kom'plə-kāt'') *v.t.* **1,** render intricate or involved. **2,** aggravate. —**com''pli·ca'tion,** *n.*

com'pli·cat''ed *adj.* complex; (*Colloq.*) confusing.

com·plic'i·ty (kəm-plis'ə-tè) *n.* the state of being an accomplice.

com'pli·ment (kom'plə-mənt) *n.* **1,** an expression of praise or admiration. **2,** (*pl.*) formal greetings. —*v.t.* (-ment'') **1,** utter a compliment to. **2,** present with a gift or other favor. **3,** congratulate.

com''pli·men'ta·ry (kom''plə-men'tə-rè) *adj.* **1,** conveying or given as a compliment. **2,** given free.

com'plin (kom'plin) *n.* the last of the seven canonical hours; the service for it. Also, **com'pline.**

com·plot' (kəm-plot') *v.* plot together; conspire. —*n.* (kom'plot') a conspiracy.

com·ply' (kəm-plī') *v.i.* acquiesce in another's wish, command, etc.

com·po'nent (kəm-pō'nənt) *adj.* forming a part of. —*n.* a constituent part.

com·port' (kəm-pôrt') *v.t.* behave (oneself). —*v.i.* (with *with*) accord; fit, suit. —**com·port'ment,** *n.* behavior.

com·pose' (kəm-pōz') *v.t.* **1,** form by putting parts together. **2,** be the parts of. **3,** construct in some creative way, esp. original music. **4,** calm; quiet. **5,** settle (differences); adjust. **6,** set (type). —*v.i.* write music. —**com·posed'**, *adj.* calm; serene. —**com·pos'er,** *n.* one who composes music.

com·pos'ite (kəm-pos'it) *adj. & n.* **1,** made up of distinct parts. **2,** (*Bot.*) having small flowers arranged compactly.

com''po·si'tion (kom''pə-zish'ən) *n.* act or result of composing; a piece of music, essay, etc.; a compound; structure.

com·pos'i·tor (kəm-poz'ə-tər) *n.* one who sets type.

com'post (kom'pōst) *n.* a mixture of decaying leaves, etc., used as fertilizer.

com·po'sure (kəm-pō'zhər) *n.* serenity; calmness.

com'pote (kom'pōt) *n.* **1,** stewed fruit. **2,** a small dish.

com·pound' (kəm-pownd') *v.t.* **1,** combine (two or more ingredients). **2,** form by mixing or joining. **3,** fail to prosecute (a criminal) for a consideration. —*adj.* (kom'pownd) composed of two or more elements. —*n.* (kom'pound) **1,** something compound. **2,** an enclosure for houses; a reserved area, or area of confinement (as for prisoners, foreigners, etc.). —**compound fracture,** an open wound as well as a broken bone. —**compound interest,** interest paid on accrued interest, as well as on the capital.

com''pre·hend' (kom''prē-hend') *v.t.* **1,** include within a certain extent of time or space. **2,** understand.

com''pre·hen'si·ble (kom''prē-hen'sə-bəl) *adj.* understandable; intelligible. —**com''-pre·hen'si·bil'i·ty,** *n.*

com''pre·hen'sion (kom''prē-hen'shən) *n.* **1,** act or result of comprehending; power to comprehend. **2,** inclusion; perception.

com''pre·hen'sive (kom''prē-hen'siv) *adj.* of large scope; inclusive. —**com''pre·hen'-sive·ness,** *n.*

com·press' (kəm-pres') *v.t.* reduce the bulk of by applied pressure; pack tightly together; condense. —*n.* (kom'pres) a soft pad used to apply moisture, pressure, etc. —**com·pres'sion** (-presh'ən) *n.* —**com·pres'sor** (-pres'ər) *n.* a device for compressing, esp. gas or air.

com·prise' (kəm-prīz') *v.t.* **1,** include. **2,** consist of.

com'pro·mise'' (kom'prə-mīz'') *n.* **1,** the settlement of differences by mutual concessions. **2,** a middle course; something intermediate. —*v.t.* **1,** adjust by compromise. **2,** expose to suspicion or scandal. —*v.i.* make a compromise.

comp·trol'ler (kən-trōl'ər) *n.* a chief ac-

counting officer. Also, **con·trol'ler.** —**comp·trol'ler·ship,** *n.*

com·pul'sion (kəm-pul'shən) *n.* **1,** the act of compelling; coercion. **2,** impulse.

com·pul'sive (-siv) *adj.* (*Psych.*) pert. to or compelled by a force of which the subject is not conscious.

com·pul'so·ry (-sə-rē) *adj.* **1,** compelling. **2,** obligatory.

com·punc'tion (kəm-punk'shən) *n.* a slight regret or prick of conscience.

com·pute' (kəm-pūt') *v.t. & i.* calculate; reckon. —**com''pu·ta'tion,** *n.*

com·put'er (kəm-pū'tər) *n.* **1,** that which computes. **2,** a computing machine, esp. an automatic electronic machine.

com·put'er·ize'' *v.t. & i.* use or provide with computers. —**com·put'er·i·za'tion,** *n.*

com'rade (kom'rəd) *n.* **1,** a close friend. **2,** a fellow member. **3,** a title of address in some Communist countries. —**com'rade·ship,** *n.*

con (kon) *v.t.* [**conned, con'ning**] **1,** pore over; learn. **2,** (*Slang*) swindle. **3,** direct the course of (a ship). —*n.* (*Slang*) a convict. —*adv.* against. —**con game,** (*Slang*) a confidence game. —**con man,** (*Slang*) a confidence man. —**conning tower,** the pilot house of a warship.

con- *pref.* a form of **com-.**

con·cat'e·nate'' (kon-kat'ə-nāt') *v.t.* link together. —**con·cat''e·na'tion,** *n.*

con·cave' (kon-kāv') *adj.* with an outline or surface curved like the inside of a ball; curved inward. —**con·cav'i·ty** (kən-kav'ə-tē) *n.*

con·ceal' (kən-sēl') *v.t.* keep secret or hidden; secrete; hide. —**con·ceal'ment,** *n.*

con·cede' (kən-sēd') *v.t.* **1,** grant, as a right or privilege. **2,** admit as true. **3,** give up as lost (as an election). —*v.i.* yield; admit defeat.

con·ceit' (kən-sēt') *n.* **1,** an exaggerated opinion of one's own ability, etc. **2,** a quaint or humorous fancy. —**con·ceit'ed,** *adj.* vain.

con·ceive' (kən-sēv') *v.t. & i.* **1,** form in the mind; believe; have a feeling. **3,** become pregnant (with young). —**con·ceiv'-a·ble,** *adj.* believable.

con'cen·trate'' (kon'sən-trāt'') *v.t.* **1,** bring together at one point; focus. **2,** increase the strength of by removing foreign elements. —*v.i.* **1,** meet at a common center. **2,** employ all one's power or attention.

con''cen·tra'tion (kon''sən-trā'shən) *n.* **1,** act or result of concentrating; assembly; intensification. **2,** close attention or application, as in study. —**concentration camp,** a camp in which prisoners or refugees are confined.

con·cen'tric (kən-sen'trik) *adj.* having a common center. **—con·cen'tri·cal·ly,** *adv.*

con'cept (kon'sept) *n.* a mentally conceived image; an idea or thought. **—con·cep'tu·al,** *adj.* **—con·cep'tu·al·ize,** *v.t.*

con·cep'tion (kən-sep'shən) *n.* 1, act or effect of conceiving; an idea; notion. 2, fertilization; pregnancy. 3, beginning.

con·cern' (kən-sērn') *v.t.* 1, relate to. 2, (with *in* or *with*) interest or occupy. 3, disturb; trouble. *—n.* 1, a matter of interest. 2, solicitude; anxiety. 3, a business firm. **—con·cern'ing,** *prep.* relating to; about.

con·cert (kon'sērt) *n.* 1, agreement in a plan or design. 2, a musical performance. 3, musical harmony; unison. *—v.t.* contrive or plan by agreement. **—con·cert'ed,** *adj.* in unison; harmonious. **—con'cert·ize** (-īz) *v.i.* give a concert or concerts. **—in concert,** in unison; together.

con''cer·ti'na (kon''sər-tē'nə) *n.* a small accordion, hexagonal in shape.

con'cert·mas''ter *n.* the leader of an orchestra (after the conductor), usu. the leader of the first violins. **—con'cert·mis''tress,** *n. fem.*

con·cer'to (kən-cher'tō) *n.* [*pl.* **-tos** (-tōz)] a musical composition, usually for a solo instrument with accompaniment.

con·ces'sion (kən-sesh'ən) *n.* 1, the act or effect of conceding; the thing or point conceded. 2, a grant or lease by an authority to a business. **—con·ces''sion·aire'** (-ə-nâr') *n.* the recipient of such a grant or lease.

conch (konk; konch) *n.* a sea mollusk; its large, spiral shell.

con·cierge' (kôṅ-syerzh') *n.* (*Fr.*) a doorkeeper or janitor.

con·cil'i·ate'' (kən-sil'ē-āt'') *v.t.* overcome the hostility of; pacify. **—con·cil''i·a'tion,** *n.* **—con·cil'i·a·to·ry** (-ə-tôr-ē) *adj.*

con·cise' (kən-sīs') *adj.* brief and compact; terse. **—con·cise'ness,** *n.*

con·ci'sion (kən-sizh'ən) *n.* 1, conciseness. 2, a cutting off; schism.

con'clave (kon'klāv) *n.* 1, a private assembly. 2, the meeting of the cardinals for election of a Pope.

con·clude' (kən-klood') *v.t.* 1, bring to an end; finish; decide finally; determine. 2, deduce; infer. *—v.i.* 1, come to an end. 2, decide.

con·clu'sion (kən-kloo'zhən) *n.* 1, the end. 2, the final part or stage. 3, a result; outcome. 4, a proposition inferred logically from premises. **—con·clu'sive** (-siv) *adj.* decisive.

con·coct' (kən-kokt') *v.t.* 1, combine and

prepare, as in cooking. 2, devise; contrive, as a plot. **—con·coc'tion,** *n.*

con·com'i·tant (kon-kom'ə-tənt) *adj.* attending; going together. *—n.* an accompanying thing or circumstance. **—con·com'i·tance, con·com'i·tan·cy,** *n.*

con'cord (kon'kôrd) *n.* 1, harmony; unanimity. 2, peace. 3, an agreement; a treaty.

con·cord'ance (kon-kôr'dəns) *n.* 1, agreement. 2, an index of words, as of those in the Bible. **—con·cord'ant,** *adj.*

con·cor'dat (kon-kôr'dat) *n.* a treaty.

con'course (kon'kôrs) *n.* 1, a throng; crowd. 2, an open place, as a public square. 3, a wide street or arcade.

con'crete (kon'krēt) *adj.* 1, existing in material form; real, not abstract. 2, specific, not general. 3, consisting of concrete. *—n.* a building material made of sand, cement, etc. *—v.i.* harden. **—con·crete'ness,** *n.* **—con·cre'tion,** *n.*

con'cu·bine'' (kon'kū-bīn'') *n.* a woman cohabiting with a man but not married to him. **—con·cu'bi·nage** (-bə-nij) *n.*

con·cu'pis·cence (kon-kū'pə-səns) *n.* sensual appetite or desire. **—con·cu'pis·cent,** *adj.*

con·cur' (kən-kēr') *v.i.* [**-curred', -curring**] 1, happen together; coincide; exist side by side. 2, agree in opinion. 3, (with *in*) act jointly. **—con·cur'rence,** *n.* **—con·cur'rent,** *adj.*

con·cus'sion (kən-kush'ən) *n.* the shock occasioned by a collision or blow.

con·demn' (kən-dem') *v.t.* 1, express disapprobation of; censure. 2, find guilty; sentence to punishment. 3, pronounce unfit for use. 4, claim for public use. **—con''dem·na'tion,** *n.*

con·dense' (kən-dens') *v.t. & i.* 1, make more compact. 2, express in fewer words. 3, compress; reduce (gas, vapor) to a liquid or solid. **—con'dens·ate** (kon'dən-sāt'') *n.* **—con''den·sa'tion,** *n.* **—condensed milk,** evaporated milk with sugar added.

con·dens'er (-sər) *n.* a device for liquefying vapors, concentrating light rays or electric current, etc.

con''de·scend' (kon''di-send') *v.i.* 1, deal as an equal with one of inferior rank. 2, waive ceremony or dignity; deign (to do something). 3, deal patronizingly, as though conscious of superior rank. **—con''de·scen'sion,** *n.*

con''de·scend'ing *adj.* 1, complaisant; not haughty. 2, patronizing.

con·dign' (kən-dīn') *adj.* fitting; deserved.

con'di·ment (kon'də-mənt) *n.* something to give relish to food, as pepper.

con·di'tion (kən-dish'ən) *n.* 1, a mode or

state of being of a person or thing. **2,** social rank. **3,** state of health. **4,** a stipulation or provision; a prerequisite. —*v.t.* **1,** limit by, or subject to, a condition. **2,** put into a certain condition. **3,** modify the behavior, attitude, etc., of (a person or animal). —**con·di′tion·al,** *adj.* provisional.

con·dole′ (kən-dōl′) *v.i.* express sympathy for grief or misfortune. —**con·do′lence,** *n.*

con′dom (kon′dəm) *n.* a contraceptive or prophylactic device worn by the male.

con″do·min′i·um (kon″də-min′ē-əm) *n.* **1,** joint sovereignty over a territory by two or more nations. **2,** a cooperative apartment building or development jointly owned by its tenants who also own their own dwellings.

con·done′ (kən-dōn′) *v.t.* forgive, overlook, extenuate, or justify (another's offense, shortcomings, etc.). —**con·done′ment, con″do·na′tion** (kon″də-nā′shən) *n.*

con′dor (kon′dər) *n.* a large So. Amer. vulture.

con·duce′ (kən-doos′) *v.i.* (with *to*) contribute to a result. —**con·du′cive** (-siv) *adj.*

con·duct′ (kən-dukt′) *v.t.* **1,** act as leader of; guide; escort. **2,** manage; carry on. **3,** behave (oneself). **4,** transmit; convey. —*v.i.* act as a conductor. —*n.* (kon′dukt) **1,** management. **2,** deportment. **3,** escort. —**con·duc′tion,** *n.* —**con·duc′tive,** *adj.*

con·duct′ance (kən-duk′təns) *n.* the ability of a substance to conduct electricity.

con″duc·tiv′i·ty (kon″duk-tiv′ə-tē) *n.* power of transmitting heat, electricity, etc.

con·duc′tor (kən-duk′tər) *n.* **1,** one who leads, guides, or manages; esp. the director of an orchestra or chorus. **2,** the person in charge of a train, trolley car, etc. **3,** a substance that transmits heat, electricity, etc. —**con·duc′tress,** *n.fem.*

con′duit (kon′dit) *n.* a channel or tube that conducts fluids, electric wires, etc.

cone (kōn) *n.* **1,** a solid generated by a line passing through a fixed point and a given plane curve. **2,** anything resembling this figure.

Con″e·sto′ga wagon (kon″ə-stō′gə) a heavy, covered wagon.

con·fab′u·late″ (kən-fab′yə-lāt″) *v.i.* converse. —**con′fab,** *n. & v.i.* (*Colloq.*).

con·fect′ (kən-fekt′) *v.t.* **1,** make from ingredients; construct. **2,** make into a confection.

con·fec′tion (kən-fek′shən) *n.* **1,** a sweet preparation, esp. candy. **2,** a frilly dress. —**con·fec′tion·a·ry,** *adj.* —**con·fec′tion·er,** *n.* one who sells candy. —**con·fec′tion·er·y** (-ner-ē) *n.* his shop.

con·fed′er·a·cy (kən-fed′ə-rə-sē) *n.* **1,** a league; alliance. **2,** (*cap.,* with *the*) the eleven southern states that seceded from the U. S. in 1860-61.

con·fed′er·ate (kən-fed′ər-ət) *adj.* **1,** united in a league; party to a confederation. **2,** (*cap.*) pert. to the Confederacy. —*n.* **1,** a member of a confederation. **2,** an accomplice. —*v.t. & i.* (-rāt″) unite in a league. —**con·fed′er·a′tion,** *n.* a league.

con·fer′ (kən-fër′) *v.t.* [**-ferred′, -fer′ring**] (with *on*) bestow. —*v.i.* consult together. —**con′fer·ee′** (kon″fə-rē′) *n.*

con′fer·ence (kon′fər-əns) *n.* **1,** a meeting for consultation or discussion. **2,** a league, as of churches, athletic teams, etc.

con·fess′ (kən-fes′) *v.t.* **1,** admit (having done something discreditable); acknowledge (guilt or belief). **2,** (of a priest) hear the confession of. —*v.i.* admit a crime, fault, etc. —**con·fes′sed·ly** (-id-lē) *adj.* by confession.

con·fes′sion (kən-fesh′ən) *n.* the act or a statement of confessing. —**con·fes′sion·al** (-əl) *n.* a booth where a priest hears confessions.

con·fes′sor (kən-fes′ər) *n.* a priest who hears confessions.

con·fet′ti (kən-fet′ē) *n.* bits of colored paper thrown about in merrymaking.

con″fi·dant′ (kon″fi-dänt′) *n.* one trusted with secrets. —**con″fi·dante′,** *n.fem.*

con·fide′ (kən-fīd′) *v.t.* **1,** entrust. **2,** reveal privately. —*v.i.* (with *in*) **1,** have trust. **2,** entrust a secret.

con′fi·dence (kon′fi-dəns) *n.* **1,** firm trust; reliance. **2,** self-assurance; boldness. **3,** an assured state of mind. **4,** a state of trust and intimacy. **5,** a secret confided. —**confidence game,** a scheme to obtain money fraudulently. —**confidence man,** a swindler.

con′fi·dent (kon′fi-dənt) *adj.* **1,** firmly trustful; sure. **2,** bold; self-assured. **3,** optimistic.

con″fi·den′tial (kon″fi-den′shəl) *adj.* **1,** secret; private. **2,** entrusted with private affairs. **3,** intimate. —**con″fi·den″ti·al′i·ty,** *n.*

con·fig″u·ra′tion (kən-fig″yə-rā′shən) *n.* **1,** form. **2,** placement.

con·fine′ (kən-fīn′) *v.t.* **1,** restrict within bounds; imprison. **2,** keep indoors, as by sickness, esp. by childbirth. —*n.* (kon′fīn) (usu. *pl.*) a boundary or border. —**confine′ment,** *n.*

con·firm′ (kən-fërm′) *v.t.* **1,** establish more firmly; strengthen. **2,** put past doubt; verify. **3,** make valid. **4,** admit to church membership. —**con″fir·ma′tion,** *n.* —**confirm′a·to″ry,** *adj.*

con·firmed′ (kən-fërmd′) *adj.* **1,** settled. **2,** inveterate; chronic.

con·fis·cate (kon'fis-kāt") *v.t.* **1,** appropriate, by way of penalty, to public use. **2,** take away by, or as if by, authority. —**con"fis·ca'tion,** *n.*

con"fla·gra'tion (kon"flə-grā'shən) *n.* a large-scale fire.

con·flict' (kən-flikt') *v.i.* clash; be contrary. —*n.* (kon'flikt) **1,** a combat. **2,** discord; antagonism. —**conflict of interest,** a situation in which the demands of one job adversely or illegally affect the demands of another.

con'flu·ence (kon'flŭ-əns) *n.* **1,** a flowing together as of streams; their place of meeting. **2,** the coming together of people; a crowd. Also, **con'flux** (-fluks). —**con'flu·ent,** *adj.*

con·form' (kən-fôrm') *v.t.* bring into harmony; adapt. —*v.i.* be in accord; comply.

con"for·ma'tion (kon"fôr-mā'shən) *n.* **1,** structure. **2,** adaptation.

con·form'ist *n.* one who conforms, esp. to the usages of the Church of England.

con·form'i·ty (-ə-tē) *n.* accordance; agreement.

con·found' (kon-fownd') *v.t.* **1,** throw into confusion; perplex; astound. **2,** mistake for another. —**con·found'ed,** *adj.* (*Colloq.*) damnable.

con'frere (kon'frār) *n.* a colleague.

con·front' (kən-frunt') *v.t.* **1,** stand facing; meet. **2,** meet in hostility. **3,** bring face to face (with). —**con"fron·ta'tion** (kon"frən-tā'shən) *n.*

con·fuse' (kən-fūz') *v.t.* **1,** throw into disorder. **2,** perplex; disconcert. **3,** mistake for another. —**con·fu'sion,** *n.*

con·fute' (kən-fūt') *v.t.* prove false; disprove. —**con"fu·ta'tion,** *n.*

con'ga (kong'gə) *n.* **1,** a Cuban dance. **2,** a tall bass drum beaten with the hands.

con·geal' (kən-jēl') *v.t.* & *i.* **1,** freeze; stiffen; harden, esp. as an effect of cold. **2,** coagulate; clot. —**con"ge·la'tion** (kon"jə-lā'shən) *n.*

con·gen'ial (kən-jēn'yəl) *adj.* **1,** kindred; like; sympathetic. **2,** agreeable; pleasing. —**con·ge"ni·al'i·ty,** *n.*

con·gen'i·tal (kən-jen'ə-təl) *adj.* existing at birth.

con'ger (kong'gər) *n.* a large marine eel.

con·ge·ries" (kon'jə-rēz") *n.sing.* & *pl.* collection into one heap; an aggregation.

con·gest' (kən-jest') *v.t.* **1,** overcrowd. **2,** overfill with blood. —**con·ges'tion,** *n.*

con·glom'er·ate (kən-glom'ər-ət) *adj.* collected or clustered together. —*n.* **1,** a mass of varied and incongruous materials. **2,** a rock made of pieces of gravel. **3,** a company that operates businesses in a wide variety of unrelated fields. —*v.t.* & *i.* (-rāt") collect into a mass. —**con·glom"er·a'tion,** *n.*

con·grat'u·late" (kən-grach'ə-lāt") *v.t.* express (to a person) pleasure at his or her happiness or triumph; felicitate. —**con·grat"u·la'tion,** *n.*

con'gre·gate" (kon'gri-gāt") *v.t.* & *i.* gather together; assemble.

con"gre·ga'tion (kon"gri-gā'shən) *n.* **1,** act of congregating. **2,** a gathering, esp. of persons for religious worship.

con"gre·ga'tion·al *adj.* **1,** pert. to a congregation. **2,** (*cap.*) pert. to a certain Protestant denomination. —**Con"gre·ga'tion·al·ism,** *n.* —**Con"gre·ga'tion·al·ist,** *adj.* & *n.*

con'gress (kon'gris) *n.* **1,** a formal meeting of delegates for discussion; a conference. **2,** (*cap.*) the legislative body of the U.S. **3,** intercourse. —**con·gres'sion·al** (kən-gresh'ən-əl) *adj.* —**con'gress·man,** *n.* (often *cap.*) a member of the U.S. Congress. —**con'gress·wom"an,** *n.fem.*

con'gru·ent (kong'groo-ənt) *adj.* **1,** agreeing; harmonious. **2,** (*Geom.*) superposable. —**con'gru·ence,** *n.*

con·gru'i·ty (kong-groo'ə-tē) *n.* congruousness.

con'gru·ous (kong'groo-əs) *adj.* well adapted; appropriate; consistent. —**con'gru·ous·ness,** *n.*

con'ic (kon'ik) *adj.* [also, **con'i·cal**] having the shape of or like a cone. —*n.* [also, **conic section**] (*Geom.*) an ellipse, parabola, or hyperbola.

co'ni·fer (kon'i-fər) *n.* a cone-bearing plant. —**co·nif'er·ous** (kō-nif'ər-əs) *adj.*

con·jec'ture (kən-jek'chər) *n.* an opinion not founded on sufficient evidence; a guess; a surmise. —*v.t.* & *i.* guess. —**con·jec'tur·al,** *adj.*

con·join' (kən-join') *v.t.* & *i.* join; associate. —**con·joint',** *adj.*

con'ju·gal (kon'jə-gəl) *adj.* pert. to marriage; connubial. —**con"ju·gal'i·ty,** *n.*

con'ju·gate" (kon'jə-gāt") *v.t.* give in order the forms of (a verb). —*adj.* formed in a pair; coupled. —**con'ju·ga"tive,** *adj.*

con"ju·ga'tion (-gā'shən) *n.* **1,** inflection of verbs. **2,** conjunction.

con·junct' (kən-junkt') *adj.* joined together; united. —**con·junc'tive,** *adj.*

con·junc'tion (kən-junk'shən) *n.* **1,** act of joining. **2,** union; connection. **3,** a word that joins sentences, clauses, phrases, or words, as *and*.

con·junc"ti·vi'tis (kən-junk"tə-vī'tis) *n.* inflammation of the mucous membrane of the eyelids.

---

con·junc′ture (kən-junk′chər) *n.* **1,** a combination of circumstances. **2,** a crisis.

con′jure (kon′jər) *v.t. & i.* **1,** call up or bring about by, or as if by, magic; practice magic. **2,** straighten (hair). **3,** (kon-jûr′) entreat solemnly. —**con″ju·ra′tion,** *n.*

con′jur·er (kon′jər-ər) *n.* a magician. Also, **con′jur·or.**

conk (konk) (*Slang*) *v.t.* thump. —*v.i.* (with *out*) fail; stop running.

con·nect′ (kə-nekt′) *v.t. & i.* **1,** associate mentally. **2,** join; associate closely. **3,** (with *with*) establish communication or juncture. **4,** (*Slang*) attain one's goal or object. —**con·nec′tive,** *adj. & n.*

con·nec′tion (kə-nek′shən) *n.* **1,** the state of being connected; union; a connecting part. **2,** family relationship; a distant relative. **3,** (*pl.*) influential friends. **4,** continuity of words or ideas. **5,** a bond; tie. **6,** (often *pl.*) a meeting of trains, etc., for transfer of passengers. **7,** (*Slang*) a source of smuggled goods, esp. narcotics.

con·nip′tion (kə-nip′shən) *n.* (*Colloq.*) hysterical excitement.

con·nive′ (kə-nīv′) *v.i.* secretly abet or permit a wrong. —**con·niv′ance,** *n.*

con″nois·seur′ (kon″ə-sēr′) *n.* a discriminating critic.

con·note′ (kə-nōt′) *v.t.* imply; suggest; denote secondarily. —**con″no·ta′tion,** *n.*

con·nu′bi·al (kə-noo′bē-əl) *adj.* pert. to marriage; conjugal.

con′quer (kong′kər) *v.t.* **1,** subdue by force. **2,** overcome; surmount. **3,** resist, as temptation, a bad habit, etc. —**con′quer·or,** *n.*

con′quest (kon′kwest) *n.* **1,** subjugation by force; victory. **2,** that which is subdued or won.

con·quis′ta·dor″ (kon-kwis′tə-dôr″) *n.* a Spanish conqueror of the New World.

Con′rail″ (kon′rāl″) *n.* a government railway network in the U.S.

con″san·guin′i·ty (kon″sang-gwin′ə-tē) *n.* relationship by blood. —**con″san·guin′e·ous** (-ē-əs) *adj.*

con′science (kon′shəns) *n.* one's moral sense of right and wrong.

con″sci·en′tious (kon″shē-en′shəs) *adj.* **1,** scrupulous. **2,** careful; meticulous. —**conscientious objector,** one who refuses to fight for his country, for moral or religious scruple.

con′scion·a·ble (kon′shən-ə-bəl) *adj.* conforming to one's conscience; just.

con′scious (kon′shəs) *adj.* **1,** aware of one's existence, feelings, and thoughts. **2,** in a waking, not comatose, state. **3,** aware. **4,** intentional. —**con′scious·ness,** *n.*

con′script (kon′skript) *n.* one pressed into military or naval service. —*v.t.* (kən-skript′) draft. —**con·scrip′tion,** *n.*

con′se·crate″ (kon′si-krāt″) *v.t.* dedicate to a sacred purpose or service. —**con″se·cra′tion,** *n.*

con·sec′u·tive (kən-sek′ū-tiv) *adj.* succeeding one another in regular order.

con·sen′sus (kən-sen′səs) *n.* **1,** agreement in opinion, feeling, etc. **2,** general agreement, as of opinion.

con·sent′ (kən-sent′) *v.i.* agree; yield; accede. —*n.* voluntary compliance; permission. —**con·sen′tient** (-shənt) *adj.* agreeing; unanimous.

con′se·quence (kon′sə-kwens) *n.* **1,** that which follows as the result of some preceding act, cause, etc. **2,** significance. **3,** distinction; importance in rank, etc.

con′se·quent (kon′sə-kwent) *adj.* **1,** resulting. **2,** following logically. —**con′se·quent·ly,** *adv.* in consequence of; therefore.

con″se·quen′tial (kon″si-kwen′shəl) *adj.* **1,** important. **2,** consequent.

con″ser·va′tion (kon″sər-vā′shən) *n.* preservation, esp. of natural resources. —**con″ser·va′tion·ist,** *n.*

con·serv′a·tive (kən-sēr′və-tiv) *adj.* **1,** opposed to change. **2,** moderate; not extreme. **3,** protecting from loss, waste, or injury. **4,** preservative. —*n.* a conservative person. —**con·serv′a·tism,** *n.*

con·serv′a·to″ry (-tôr′ē) *n.* **1,** a greenhouse. **2,** a school, esp. of music.

con·serve′ (kən-sērv′) *v.t.* preserve from loss, waste, etc. —*n.* (kon′sērv) a fruit preserve. —**con″ser·va′tor** (kon′sər-vā″tər) *n.*

con·sid′er (kən-sid′ər) *v.t.* **1,** ponder; study. **2,** make allowance for. **3,** hold in esteem. **4,** believe; judge. —*v.i.* reflect; meditate.

con·sid′er·a·ble *adj.* **1,** notable; important. **2,** not small. —*n.* (*Colloq.*) a large amount or degree.

con·sid′er·ate (-ət) *adj.* thoughtful of others.

con·sid″er·a′tion *n.* **1,** careful reflection. **2,** thoughtfulness of others. **3,** something to be reckoned with. **4,** motive; reason. **5,** a fee; compensation. **6,** importance.

con·sid′ered (-ərd) *adj.* **1,** taken into account. **2,** deliberate; intentional.

con·sid′er·ing *prep.* taking into account; in view of.

con·sign′ (kən-sīn′) *v.t.* **1,** hand over; commit formally. **2,** assign. **3,** send or address (goods) to, for sale or custody. —**con·sign′or,** *n.* **con″sign·ee′** (kon″sī-nē′) *n.*

con·sign′ment (-mənt) *n.* **1,** act of consigning; something consigned; a shipment. **2,** the condition that goods received will not be paid for unless they are sold.

con·sist′ (kən-sist′) *v.i.* (with *of*) be composed; (with *in*) exist.

con·sist′en·cy (-ən-sė) *n.* **1,** solidity; degree of density, esp. of liquids. **2,** harmony; correspondence. **3,** state of being consistent.

con·sist′ent (-ənt) *adj.* **1,** congruous; in accord. **2,** conforming regularly to the same pattern, habits, principles, etc.

con·sis′to·ry (kən-sis′tə-rė) *n.* an ecclesiastical council or meeting; its meeting place.

con″so·la′tion (kon″sə-lā′shən) *n.* act or effect of consoling; solace.

con·sole′ (kən-sōl′) *v.t.* comfort in time of sorrow; solace.

con′sole (kon′sōl) **1,** the cabinet containing the keyboard, etc. of an organ. **2,** a floor cabinet, as for a radio. **3,** a supporting bracket.

con·sol′i·date″ (kən-sol′ə-dāt″) *v.t.* **1,** make solid or firm; strengthen. **2,** unite firmly in one body; combine; merge. —**con·sol″i·da′tion,** *n.*

con″som·mé′ (kon″sə-mā′) *n.* a strong, clear meat soup.

con′so·nant (kon′sə-nənt) *adj.* **1,** agreeing in sound. **2,** consistent. **3,** relating to consonants. —*n.* an alphabetical element other than a vowel. —**con′so·nance,** *n.*

con′sort (kon′sôrt) *n.* **1,** a husband or wife. **2,** the spouse of a more important person. **3,** a vessel sailing with another. —*v.i.* (kən-sôrt′) (with *with*) associate; agree.

con·sor′ti·um (kən-sôr′tē-əm) *n.* **1,** international business agreement; cartel. **2,** society; association. **3,** a meeting; colloquium.

con·spec′tus (kən-spek′təs) *n.* an outline or summary of a subject.

con·spic′u·ous (kən-spik′ū-əs) *adj.* **1,** easily seen. **2,** attracting attention; notable; important. —**con·spic′u·ous·ness,** *n.*

con·spir′a·cy (kən-spir′ə-sė) *n.* a combination of persons for an evil purpose; a plot. —**con·spir′a·tor,** *n.* one who joins in a conspiracy.

con·spire′ (kən-spīr′) *v.i.* **1,** combine for an unlawful purpose; plot secretly. **2,** concur to one end.

con′sta·ble (kon′stə-bəl) *n.* an officer of the peace; a policeman.

·con·stab′u·lar·y (kən-stab′yə-ler-ė) *n.* a body of constables; police. —*adj.* [also, **con·stab′u·lar** (-lər)] pert. to police work.

con′stan·cy (kon′stən-sė) *n.* state of being constant; fidelity; stability.

con′stant (kon′stənt) *adj.* **1,** regularly recurring. **2,** ceaseless. **3,** steadfast; resolute. **4,** unvarying. —*n.* **1,** something constant or unchanging. **2,** (*Math.*) a quantity which does not change value.

con″stel·la′tion (kon″stə-lā′shən) *n.* a group of fixed stars.

con″ster·na′tion (kon″stər-nā′shən) *n.* terrified amazement; dismay.

con′sti·pate″ (kon′sti-pāt″) *v.t.* **1,** cause constipation in. **2,** clog; impede movement in.

con″sti·pa′tion (kon″sti-pā′shən) *n.* difficulty in moving the bowels.

con·stit′u·en·cy (kən-stich′oo-ən-sė) *n.* a body of voters, customers, etc.

con·stit′u·ent (kən-stich′oo-ənt) *n.* **1,** a necessary part. **2,** a voter or resident in a legislative district. —*adj.* being one necessary part.

con′sti·tute″ (kon′sti-tūt″) *v.t.* **1,** make up; form as a necessary part. **2,** establish by lawful authority. **3,** appoint.

con″sti·tu′tion (kon″sti-too′shən) *n.* **1,** natural composition, qualities, structure, etc. **2,** a code of principles or laws forming the basis of a government or organization; the document of such a code.

con″sti·tu′tion·al (-əl) *adj.* **1,** inherent; basic; essential. **2,** beneficial to health. **3,** pert. to or in accordance with a written constitution. —*n.* an exercise, as a walk. —**con″sti·tu″tion·al′i·ty** (-al′ə-tė) *n.*

con·strain′ (kən-strān′) *v.t.* **1,** compel; oblige. **2,** bind; confine. **3,** repress; restrain. —**con·straint′,** *n.*

con·strict′ (kən-strikt′) *v.t.* cause to shrink; cramp; crush. —**con·stric′tion,** *n.* —**con·strict′ive,** *adj.* —**con·stric′tor,** *n.*

con·struct′ (kən-strukt′) *v.t.* **1,** build; make. **2,** frame in the mind. —*n.* (kon′strukt) something constructed. —**con·struc′tor,** *n.*

con·struc′tion (kən-struk′shən) *n.* **1,** the act or method of building or constructing; a structure; an interpretation. **2,** (*Gram.*) arrangement and connection of words in a sentence. **3,** act of construing. —**con·struc′tion·ist,** *n.* one who interprets (something written).

con·struc′tive (-tiv) *adj.* **1,** building; beneficial to progress. **2,** inferential.

con·strue′ (kən-stroo′) *v.t.* **1,** analyze grammatically. **2,** translate. **3,** interpret.

con″sub·stan″ti·a′tion (kon″səb-stan″-shē-ā′shən) *n.* the doctrine that the blood and body of Christ coexist in and with the bread and wine of the Eucharist.

con′sul (kon′səl) *n.* **1,** a diplomatic officer or agent of a government in a foreign country. **2,** (*Hist.*) a chief magistrate. —**con′su·lar,** *adj.* —**con′su·late** (-sə-lət) *n.*

con·sult′ (kən-sult′) *v.t.* **1,** ask the advice of; refer to. **2,** consider; have regard for. —*v.i.* confer. —**con·sult′ant,** *n.*

con″sul·ta′tion (kon″səl-tā′shən) *n.* act of consulting; conference. —**con·sul′ta·tive** (kən-sul′tə-tiv) *adj.* advisory.

con·sume′ (kən-soom′) *v.t.* **1,** devour; eat; destroy. **2,** use up; spend, as time. —**con·sum′er,** *n.* the ultimate user of a commodity. —**con·sum′er·ism,** *n.* a movement to protect the rights of the consumer.

con′sum·mate″ (kon′sə-māt″) *v.t.* bring to completion or perfection. —*adj.* (kən-sum′it) complete; perfect. —**con″sum·ma′tion,** *n.*

con·sump′tion (kən-sump′shən) *n.* **1,** the act or effect of consuming; the amount consumed. **2,** tuberculosis of the lungs.

con·sump′tive (-tiv) *adj.* wasteful. —*n. & adj.* (one) affected with tuberculosis.

con′tact (kon′takt) *n.* **1,** a meeting or touching of two things or (*Colloq.*) persons. **2,** a business or social acquaintance or introduction. —*v.t. & i.* (*Colloq.*) get in touch (with). —**contact lens,** a thin plastic shell fitted to the front of the eyeball under the eyelids to correct vision. —**contact man,** a go-between.

con·ta′gion (kən-tā′jən) *n.* **1,** the communication of a disease by contact; the disease; plague. **2,** rapid spread of disease, feelings, etc.

con·ta′gious (kən-tā′jəs) *adj.* **1,** communicable; spreading. **2,** (*Colloq.*) hard to resist. —**con·ta′gious·ness,** *n.*

con·tain′ (kən-tān′) *v.t.* **1,** keep within bounds; restrain; enclose. **2,** comprise; have a capacity of; hold. —**con·tain′er,** *n.* a vessel, can, box, bottle, etc.

con·tain″er·i·za′tion (kən-tān″ər-i-zā′-shən) *n.* the use in shipping of large containers that are transported as units in specially equipped transports.

con·tam′i·nate″ (kən-tam′i-nāt″) *v.t.* make impure by mixture; taint; pollute. —**con·tam′i·nant,** *n.* —**con·tam″i·na′tion,** *n.*

con·temn′ (kən-tem′) *v.t.* scorn.

con·tem·plate″ (kon′təm-plāt″) *v.t.* **1,** view or reflect upon attentively. **2,** intend; expect. —*v.i.* meditate. —**con″tem·pla′tion,** *n.* —**con′tem·pla″tive,** *adj.*

con·tem″po·ra′ne·ous (kən-tem″pə-rā′-nē-əs) *adj.* contemporary.

con·tem′po·rar″y (kən-tem′pə-rer″ē) *adj.* **1,** living or occurring at the same time. **2,** of the same age. —*n.* a person contemporary with another.

con·tempt′ (kən-tempt′) *n.* **1,** the act of despising. **2,** a feeling of disdain. **3,** (*Law*) defiance of a court, etc.

con·tempt′i·ble (kən-temp′tə-bəl) *adj.*

meriting scorn; despicable. —**con·tempt″i·bil′i·ty,** *n.*

con·temp′tu·ous (kən-temp′choo-əs) *adj.* expressing disdain; scornful. —**con·temp′-tu·ous·ness,** *n.*

con·tend′ (kən-tend′) *v.i.* **1,** compete; struggle in opposition. **2,** assert in argument.

con′tent (kon′tent) *n.* **1,** (*pl.*) all that is contained in a receptacle. **2,** (*pl.*) subject matter, as of a book. **3,** the gist or substance, as of a sermon, etc. **4,** capacity.

con·tent′ (kən-tent′) *adj.* satisfied; easy in mind. —*v.t.* satisfy. —**con·tent′ed,** *adj.* satisfied; placidly happy. —**con·tent′ment,** *n.*

con·ten′tion (kən-ten′shən) *n.* **1,** act of contending; a struggle, debate, etc. **2,** rivalry; strife.

con·ten′tious (kən-ten′shəs) *adj.* argumentative. —**con·ten′tious·ness,** *n.*

con′test (kon′test) *n.* **1,** a struggle; fight; controversy. **2,** a competitive game. —*v.t.* (kən-test′) **1,** compete or vie for. **2,** challenge; dispute. —**con·test′ant,** *n.* one who competes.

con′text (kon′tekst) *n.* related or adjoining passages of a book, etc. —**con·tex′tu·al,** *adj.*

con·tig′u·ous (kən-tig′ū-əs) *adj.* touching at the border; adjoining. —**con″ti·gu′i·ty,** *n.*

con′ti·nence (kon′tə-nəns) *n.* **1,** self-restraint, esp. of sexual appetite. **2,** the ability to retain voluntarily a bodily discharge, as urine.

con′ti·nent (kon′ti-nənt) *n.* **1,** one of the six principal land masses of the globe. **2,** (*cap.,* with *the*) the mainland of Europe. —*adj.* exercising continence; chaste. —**con″ti·nen′tal,** *adj.* pert. to a continent, esp. (*cap.*) the mainland of Europe.

con·tin′gen·cy (kən-tin′jən-sē) *n.* **1,** a circumstance; what may happen. **2,** dependence.

con·tin′gent (kən-tin′jənt) *adj.* **1,** depending on something not certain; conditional. **2,** accidental. —*n.* **1,** a quota; a delegation. **2,** a fighting unit; detachment.

con·tin′u·al (kən-tin′ū-əl) *adj.* constant; often repeated.

con·tin′u·ance (-əns) *n.* **1,** a keeping on; duration. **2,** uninterrupted succession. **3,** (*Law*) postponement.

con·tin″u·a′tion (-ā′shən) *n.* **1,** act of continuing; state of being continued. **2,** an extension or prolongation.

con·tin′ue (kən-tin′ū) *v.t.* **1,** prolong; extend. **2,** keep on with; not cease from. **3,** resume the course of. **4,** retain, as in office.

—*v.i.* **1,** persist; keep on. **2,** resume after interruption. **3,** abide or stay. **4,** last; endure.

con″ti·nu′i·ty (kon″ti-nū′ə-tè) *n.* **1,** unbroken connection or sequence. **2,** a script for a motion picture, radio show, etc.

con·tin′u·ous (kən-tin′ū-əs) *adj.* without cessation or interruption.

con·tin′u·um (kən-tin′ū-əm) *n.* [*pl.* **-a** (-ə)] **1,** a continuous whole. **2,** continuity. —**space-time continuum,** four-dimensional space, of which the dimensions are length, breadth, thickness, and time.

con·tort′ (kən-tôrt′) *v.t. & i.* twist out of shape.

con·tor′tion (kən-tôr′shən) *n.* a twisting out of shape. —**con·tor′tion·ist,** *n.* a performer who contorts his body.

con′tour (kon′tûr) *n. & adj.* the outline, as of a figure, coast, etc. —*v.t.* form the outline of; mark with contour lines. —**contour farming,** prevention of erosion by tilling land according to its shape. —**contour line,** a line connecting all points of equal elevation.

con·tra- (kon-tra) *pref.* against; opposite.

con′tra·band″ (kon′trə-band″) *adj.* prohibited by law from being imported or exported. —*n.* **1,** smuggling. **2,** smuggled goods.

con′tra·bass″ (-bās″) *adj.* denoting a musical instrument of deepest pitch or range in its family. —*n.* double bass.

con′tra·bas·soon′ *n.* an instrument similar to the bassoon but pitched an octave lower.

con″tra·cep′tion (kon″trə-sep′shən) *n.* birth control. —**con″tra·cep′tive,** *n. & adj.*

con′tract (kon′trakt) *n.* **1,** a legal or business agreement. **2,** in certain games, the highest bid. **3,** (*Slang*) an agreement for murder. —*v.t.* (kən-trakt′) **1,** make smaller; condense; abridge. **2,** acquire (a habit, disease, etc.); incur; enter into. —*v.i.* **1,** enter into an agreement. **2,** shrink.

con·trac′tile (kən-trak′til) *adj.* having the function or power of contracting, as a muscle.

con·trac′tion (-shən) *n.* **1,** a shrinking; shrinkage. **2,** a shortened form of a word or phrase.

con·trac′tor (-tər) *n.* one who agrees to undertake a project, esp. in construction.

con·trac′tu·al (kən-trak′choo-əl) *adj.* pert. to a contract.

con″tra·dict′ (kon″trə-dikt′) *v.t.* **1,** assert the contrary of. **2,** deny the words of. **3,** be contrary to. —**con″tra·dic′tion,** *n.* —**con″tra·dic′to·ry,** *adj.*

con″tra·dis·tinc′tion *n.* direct contrast.

con″tra·in′di·cate *v.t.* discourage the use of (a treatment, etc.).

con·tral′to (kən-tral′tō) *n.* [*pl.* **-tos**] the lowest female voice.

con·trap′tion (kən-trap′shən) *n.* (*Colloq.*) a contrivance or gadget.

con″tra·pun′tal (kon″trə-punt′əl) *adj.* pert. to counterpoint.

con″tra·ri′e·ty (kon″trə-rī′ə-tè) *n.* **1,** contrariness. **2,** adversity.

con″tra·ri·wise″ (kon′trer-è-wīz″) *adv.* **1,** in the opposite way or sense. **2,** perversely.

con′tra·ry (kon′trer-è) *adj.* **1,** diametrically opposed; opposite. **2,** conflicting. **3,** perverse. —*n.* the opposite in sense or meaning. —**con′tra·ri·ness,** *n.*

con·trast′ (kən-trást′) *v.t. & i.* compare by showing differences. —*n.* (kon′trast) **1,** the act of contrasting. **2,** a striking difference. **3,** the ratio between light and dark in a scene.

con″tra·vene′ (kon″trə-vēn′) *v.t.* **1,** conflict with. **2,** violate. —**con″tra·ven′tion,** *n.*

con′tre·temps″ (kôñ′trə-täñ″) *n.* [*pl.* **con′tre·temps″**] an embarrassing occurrence.

con·trib′ute (kən-trib′yət) *v.t.* **1,** give with others, as to a charity. **2,** write for a magazine, etc. —*v.i.* have a share; be of use. —**con″tri·bu′tion** (-bū′shən) *n.* —**con·trib′u·tive,** *adj.* —**con·trib′u·tor,** *n.* —**con·trib′u·to·ry,** *adj.* helping toward a result.

con·trite′ (kən-trīt′) *adj.* humbly penitent. —**con·tri′tion** (-trish′ən) *n.*

con·triv′ance (kən-trī′vəns) *n.* **1,** a mechanical device. **2,** a means of doing.

con·trive′ (kən-trīv′) *v.t.* devise or bring about by clever planning. —*v.i.* **1,** scheme. **2,** (with *to*) manage to.

con·trol′ (kən-trōl′) *v.t.* [**-trolled′, -trol′ling**] **1,** exercise power over; restrain; govern; dominate. **2,** regulate. **3,** verify by comparison. —*n.* **1,** restraint. **2,** authority to govern, regulate, or manage. **3,** (often *pl.*) the apparatus for operating a machine. —**con·trol′ler,** *n.* comptroller.

con″tro·ver′sial (kon″trə-vér′shəl) *adj.* being or causing a controversy.

con′tro·ver″sy (kon′trə-vér″sè) *n.* contention; an argument or debate.

con′tro·vert″ (kon″trə-vért″) *v.t.* **1,** argue against; dispute or deny. **2,** discuss; debate. —**con″tro·vert′i·ble,** *adj.*

con′tu·ma·cy (kon′tyū-mə-sè) *n.* contempt of authority. —**con″tu·ma′cious** (-mā′shəs) *adj.*

con′tu·me·ly (kon′tyū-mə-lè) *n.* contemptuous abuse. —**con″tu·me′li·ous** (-mē′lé-əs) *adj.*

---

fat, fāte, fär, fâre, fâll, àsk; met, hē, hèr, maybè; pin, pīne; not, nōte, ôr, tool

con·tuse' (kən-tooz') v.t. bruise. **—con·tu'sion** (-zhən) n. a bruise.

co·nun'drum (kə-nun'drəm) n. a riddle; a hard question.

con''ur·ba'tion (kon''ər-bā'shən) n. a continuous network of cities and towns.

con''va·lesce' (kon''və-les') v.i. recover gradually after sickness. **—con''va·les'·cence,** n. **—con''va·les'cent,** adj. & n.

con·vec'tion (kən-vek'shən) n. 1, transfer of heat, electricity, etc., in a fluid. 2, (*Meteor.*) upward or downward movement of part of the atmosphere. **—con·vec'tive,** adj. **—con·vect',** v.

con·vene' (kən-vēn') v.t. & i. assemble for some public purpose.

con·ven'ience (kən-vēn'yəns) n. 1, suitability; accessibility; opportuneness. 2, (often pl.) that which adds to comfort. **—con·ven'ient,** adj. **—convenience food,** packaged food designed for easy preparation.

con'vent (kon'vənt) n. a home of nuns; nunnery.

con·ven'tion (kən-ven'shən) n. 1, an assembly; a formal meeting. 2, an agreement, esp. international. 3, a fixed custom or usage. **—con·ven'tion·eer',** n.

con·ven'tion·al (-əl) adj. 1, conforming to custom; conservative. 2, arbitrarily established. **—con·ven'tion·al'i·ty,** n.

con·verge' (kən-vērj') v.i. 1, incline toward each other, as lines; tend to meet. 2, intersect. **—con·ver'gence,** n. **—con·ver'·gent,** adj.

con·ver'sant (kən-vēr'sənt) adj. acquainted; well-informed.

con''ver·sa'tion (kon''vər-sā'shən) n. informal, familiar talk. **—con''ver·sa'tion·al,** adj. **—con''ver·sa'tion·al·ist,** n.

con·verse' (kən-vērs') v.i. talk informally. —n. (kon'vērs) informal talk; conversation.

con'verse (kon'vērs) adj. transposed; reversed. —n. the reverse; opposite.

con·ver'sion (kən-vēr'shən) n. act or effect of converting; change.

con·vert' (kən-vērt') v.t. 1, change into another form; exchange. 2, persuade to change in policy, religion, etc. 3, (*Law*) appropriate illegally. —n. (kon'vērt) a converted person, esp. as to religion. **—con·vert'er, con·vert'or,** n.

con·vert'i·ble adj. 1, capable of being converted. 2, of an automobile, having a folding top. —n. 1, a convertible automobile. 2, a sofa which changes into a bed. **—con·vert''i·bil'i·ty,** n.

con·vex' (kon-veks') adj. curved like the outside surface of a sphere. **—con·vex'i·ty,** n.

con·vey' (kən-vā') v.t. 1, carry from one place to another; transport. 2, transmit. 3, communicate; impart. 3, (*Law*) transfer title of.

con·vey'ance n. 1, act or result of conveying. 2, a vehicle. 3, (*Law*) a transfer of title; the document effecting such transfer.

con·vey'or n. a contrivance for conveying, as a moving belt.

con·vict' (kən-vikt') v.t. prove or find guilty. —n. (kon'vikt) a convicted prisoner.

con·vic'tion (kən-vik'shən) n. 1, act or effect of convicting or convincing. 2, a firm belief.

con·vince' (kən-vins') v.t. 1, cause (a person) to believe. 2, (*Colloq.*) persuade. **—con·vinc'ing,** adj. assuring by proof; persuasive.

con·viv'i·al (kən-viv'ē-əl) adj. 1, fond of feasting; gay; jovial. 2, festive. **—con·viv''i·al'i·ty,** n.

con''vo·ca'tion (kon''vō-kā'shən) n. 1, act or result of convoking. 2, an assembly.

con·voke' (kən-vōk') v.t. summon to assemble.

con'vo·lute'' (kon'və-loot'') adj. rolled up; coiled. —v.t. form into a coil, spiral, or whorl. **—con''vo·lut'ed,** adj. complicated. **—con''vo·lu'tion,** n.

con'voy' (kən-voi') v.t. escort for protection. —n. (kon'voi) a protecting force or ship; a fleet or group under escort.

con·vulse' (kən-vuls') v.t. 1, contract spasmodically. 2, disturb violently. 3, cause to laugh uncontrollably. **—con·vul'sion,** n. **—con·vul'sive** (-siv) adj.

co'ny (kō'nē) n. rabbit fur dyed to imitate sealskin.

coo (koo) v.i. murmur like a pigeon or dove; talk fondly.

cook (kûk) v.t. 1, prepare (food) by heating; apply heat to. 2, (with *up*) concoct. 3, (*Colloq.*) ruin. 4, (*Slang*) falsify. —v.i. 1, undergo cooking. 2, work as a cook. —n. one who cooks food. **—cook'er·y** (-ə-rē) n.

cook'book'' n. a book of recipes for cooking. Also, **cookery book.**

cook'ie (kûk'ē) n. a small, flat cake. Also, **cook'y.**

cook'out'' n. an outing at which food is cooked and served.

cook'top'' n. a cooking surface.

cool (kool) adj. 1, neither warm nor very cold. 2, calm; not excited. 3, lacking cordiality. 4, (of colors) green, blue, or violet. 5, (*Colloq.*) not overstated. 6, (*Slang*) excellent. 7, (*Slang*) all right. —v.t. & i. 1, make or become cool or cooler. 2, (with *off*) become less angry, excited, etc. 3,

(with *it*) (*Slang*) relax. —**cool'ant** (-ənt) *n.*
—**cool'ness**, *n.*

cool'er *n.* **1**, a cold room or space. **2**, a cold drink. **3**, (*Slang*) jail.

coo'lie (koo'lē) *n.* an unskilled laborer.

coon (koon) *n.* raccoon. —**coon's age**, (*Slang*) a long time.

coop (koop) *n.* **1**, a small crate or pen, as for poultry. **2**, any small place. **3**, (*Slang*) jail. —*v.t.* **1**, (with *up*) confine. **2**, (*Slang*) sleep during working hours; said of policemen.

co-·'op (kō'op) *n.* a cooperative.

coop'er (koo'pər) *n.* one who makes barrels and casks. —**coop'er·age** (-ij) *n.*

co·op'er·ate" (kō-op'ə-rāt") *v.i.* work together toward a common goal. —**co·op"er·a'tion**, *n.*

co·op'er·a·tive (-tiv) *adj.* **1**, willing to cooperate. **2**, owned by those it serves, as a store by its customers. —*n.* [also, **co-·'op**] a cooperative store, business, etc.

co-opt' (kō-opt') *v.t.* elect or appoint as a member; absorb.

co·or'di·nate" (kō-ôr'də-nāt") *v.t.* bring into harmony or proper relation. —*adj.* (-nət) of the same rank or degree. —*n.* (-nət) (*Math.*) one of a set of numbers that determine the location of a point, line, etc., in a space. —**co·or'di·na"tor**, *n.*

co·or"di·na'tion (-nā'shən) *n.* **1**, act of coordinating. **2**, harmonious combination. **3**, ability to combine muscular functions effectively.

coot (koot) *n.* **1**, a swimming and diving bird. **2**, (*Colloq.*) a fool.

coot'ie (koo'tē) *n.* (*Slang*) a louse.

cop (kop) *n.* (*Slang*) a policeman. —*v.t.* [**copped, cop'ping**] **1**, steal. **2**, catch. —**cop a plea**, (*Slang*) turn state's evidence. —**cop out**, (*Slang*) give up; back out.

co'pal (kō'pəl) *n.* a resin used in varnishes.

co·part'ner *n.* a partner or associate. —**co·part'ner·ship"**, *n.*

cope (kōp) *n.* a mantle worn by priests. —*v.i.* contend or struggle successfully.

cope'stone" *n.* **1**, a stone used in a coping. **2**, the top or crowning piece of a structure.

cop'ing (kō'ping) *n.* the uppermost stones or bricks in a wall.

coping saw a narrow-bladed saw for cutting curves.

co'pi·ous (kō'pē-əs) *adj.* abundant; plentiful. —**co'pi·ous·ness**, *n.*

cop-'out" (kop'out") *n.* (*Slang*) the act or an instance of copping out; an excuse.

cop'per (kop'ər) *n.* **1**, a tough, ductile metallic element, no. 29, symbol Cu. **2**, its

color, reddish brown. **3**, a penny **4**, (*Slang*) a policeman. —**cop'per·y**, *adj.*

cop'per·head" *n.* a venomous Amer. snake.

cop'pice (kop'is) *n.* a thicket of small trees; a copse.

cop'ra (kop'rə) *n.* the dried meat of the coconut, yielding oil.

copse (kops) *n.* a thicket.

cop'u·la (kop'yə-lə) *n.* **1**, a link or coupling. **2**, (*Gram.*) the verb *to be*.

cop'u·late" (-lāt") *v.i.* unite. —**cop"u·la'tion**, *n.* —**cop'u·la"tive** (-lā"tiv) *adj.*

cop'y (kop'ē) *n.* **1**, an imitation; a reproduction. **2**, one of a number of duplicates, as a book, magazine, etc. **3**, matter to be set in type. —*v.t.* **1**, make a copy of. **2**, imitate. —**cop'y·ist**, *n.*

cop'y·cat" *n.* (*Colloq.*) one who copies another's behavior, writings, etc.

cop'y·hold"er *n.* an assistant to a proofreader.

cop'y·read"er *n.* one who edits copy.

cop'y·right" *n.* the sole right to reproduce a literary or artistic work. —*v.t.* secure such right on.

co·quette' (kō-ket') *n.* a flirt.

cor'al (kôr'əl) *n.* **1**, a hard, horny skeleton of tiny marine animals; a hard, compact mass formed of these skeletons. **2**, a yellowish-red color. —**coral snake**, a venomous snake of the so. U.S.

cor'bel (kôr'bəl) *n.* a bracket. —*v.t.* support or furnish with corbels.

cord (kôrd) *n.* **1**, string or small rope. **2**, any ropelike structure; a tendon. **3**, a cubic measure, 8 x 4 x 4 ft., used esp. for firewood. **4**, rib or ridge in a textile. —**cord'age**, *n.* cords, ropes, etc.

cor'dial (kôr'jəl) *adj.* friendly; hearty. —*n.* **1**, a sweet, aromatic liquor; liqueur. **2**, a stimulating beverage or medicine. —**cor·dial'i·ty** (-jal'ə-tē) *n.*

cor·dil'le·ra (kôr-dil'ə-rə) *n.* an extensive chain of mountains.

cord'ite (kôr'dīt) *n.* a smokeless explosive powder.

cor'do·ba (kôr'də-bə) *n.* the monetary unit of Nicaragua.

cor'don (kôr'dən) *n.* **1**, a series or line, as of forts. **2**, an ornamental braid.

cor'do·van (kôr'də-vən) *n.* a goatskin or horsehide leather; its color, a dark grayish-brown.

cor'du·roy" (kôr'də-roi") *n.* a heavy, ribbed fabric; (*pl.*) trousers of this fabric.

core (kôr) *n.* **1**, the innermost or essential part; pith. **2**, the center of an apple, pear, etc.

co"re·op'sis (kôr'ē-op'sis) *n.* a plant with a bright-yellow flower.

co-"re·spond'ent (kō"rə-spon'dənt) *n.* a joint defendant in a divorce suit.

Cor'fam (kôr'fam) *n.* (*T.N.*) a synthetic leather substitute, used in making shoes, etc.

co"ri·an'der (kôr'ē-an'dər) *n.* an herb; its seeds, used in cookery.

cork (kôrk) *n.* 1, the light, elastic outer bark of a species of oak. 2, a piece of cork used as a stopper for a bottle. —*v.t.* seal; stop up.

cork'age (-ij) *n.* a restaurant's charge for serving a patron's liquor.

cork'er (-ər) *n.* (*Slang*) a good fellow, thing, joke, etc.

cork'ing *adj.* (*Slang*) very good.

cork'screw" *n.* a metal spiral used for drawing out cork stoppers. —*adj.* twisted; tortuous. —*v.i.* follow a tortuous course.

corm (kôrm) *n.* a fleshy underground stem resembling a bulb.

cor'mo·rant (kôr'mə-rənt) *n.* a large fish-eating sea bird. —*adj.* greedy.

corn (kôrn) *n.* 1, a single seed of a cereal plant. 2, grain: in the U. S., maize; in England, wheat; in Scotland, oats. 3, a callus, esp. on a toe. 4, (*Slang*) triteness; mawkishness. —*v.t.* preserve (beef) in brine. —**corn pone** (pōn) a hard cake made of corn meal. —**corn sugar,** dextrose. —**corn syrup,** syrup made from cornstarch.

corn'ball" *adj.* (*Slang*) corny.

corn'cob" *n.* the hard core of an ear of corn.

cor'ne·a (kôr'nē-ə) *n.* the firm transparent covering of the eye.

cor'ne·ous (kôr'nē-əs) *adj.* horny.

cor'ner (kôr'nər) *n.* 1, the intersection of, or the space between, two converging lines or surfaces; a point where streets meet; an angle. 2, a nook. 3, a region; a remote place. 4, an awkward position. 5, a monopoly. —*v.t.* 1, force into a difficult position. 2, monopolize —**cut corners, 1,** take a short cut. 2, economize.

cor'ner·stone" *n.* a stone, often inscribed, at a corner of a building; hence, a basis.

cor·net' (kôr-net') *n.* a brass musical instrument similar to the trumpet.

corn'flow"er *n.* any of several blue or white flowers.

cor'nice (kôr'nis) *n.* 1, an ornamental molding at the top edge of a wall. 2, an ornamented piece of wood or metal used to conceal drapery hardware.

corn'starch" *n.* starch obtained from corn, used in puddings, etc.

cor"nu·co'pi·a (kôr"nū-kō'pē-ə) *n.* a horn overflowing with fruit, symbolizing abundance.

corn'y (kôr'nē) *adj.* (*Slang*) trite.

co·rol'la (kə-rol'ə) *n.* the petals of a flower collectively.

cor'ol·lar"y (kor'ə-ler'ē) *n.* 1, (*Math.*) a proposition proved incidentally in proving another. 2, a natural sequence or concomitant result.

co·ro'na (kə-rō'nə) *n.* 1, the luminous circle on the rim of the sun; a similar luminous effect. 2, a halo; crown. 3, a kind of long cigar. —**co·ro'nal,** *adj.*

cor'o·nach (kôr'ə-nəkh) *n.* a dirge.

cor'o·nar"y (kor'ə-ner'ē) *adj.* 1, like a crown. 2, pert. to arteries around the heart.

cor"o·na'tion (kor'ə-nā'shən) *n.* the crowning of a king or queen.

cor'o·ner (kor'ə-nər) *n.* the presiding officer at an inquest into a cause of death.

cor'o·net (kor'ə-net) *n.* 1, a crown indicating noble rank. 2, an ornamental headdress.

cor'po·ral (kôr'pə-rəl) *n.* the lowest noncommissioned army officer. —*adj.* pert. to the body. —**corporal punishment,** punishment inflicted on the body, as flogging.

cor'po·rate (kôr'pə-rət) *adj.* 1, being or pert. to a corporation. 2, pert. to a body.

cor"po·ra'tion (kôr'pə-rā'shən) *n.* 1, a company or association chartered to act as an individual. 2, a governing body. 3, (*Slang*) a fat belly.

cor·po're·al (kôr-pôr'ē-əl) *adj.* bodily; material; not spiritual. —**cor·po"re·al'i·ty,** *n.*

corps (kôr) *n.* [*pl.* **corps** (kôrz)] 1, persons associated in some way, considered as a group. 2, (*Mil.*) a unit of two or more divisions; the officers of any unit; a special detail. —**corps'man** (kôrz'mən) *n.*

corpse (kôrps) *n.* a dead body.

cor'pu·lence (kôr'pyə-ləns) *n.* fatness; obesity. —**cor'pu·lent,** *adj.*

cor'pus (kôr'pəs) *n.* 1, the body of a human or animal. 2, a body of writings, as laws.

cor'pus·cle (kôr'pəs-əl) *n.* 1, a minute body or cell in the blood. 2, a minute particle.

cor·ral' (kə-ral') *n.* an enclosure for horses or cattle. —*v.t.* [**-ralled', -ral'ling**] 1, pen up. 2, seize; collect.

cor·rect' (kə-rekt') *v.t.* 1, note or mark errors in; edit. 2, rectify. 3, discipline. —*adj.* 1, true; accurate. 2, conforming to good taste, etc. —**cor·rec'tive,** *adj.* & *n.* —**cor·rect'ness,** *n.*

cor·rec'tion (kə-rek'shən) *n.* 1, act of correcting. 2, an emendation; rectification; adjustment; rebuke; discipline.

cor·rec'tion·al (-əl) *adj.* **1,** tending to or intended for correction or reformation. **2,** pert. to a penal institution. **3,** corrective.

cor're·late" (kor'ə-lāt") *v.t.* show or find to be related or connected. **—cor"re·la'·tion,** *n.*

cor·rel'a·tive (kə-rel'ə-tiv) *adj.* **1,** having a mutual relation. **2,** (*Gram.*) complementary, as *neither* and *nor*.

cor"re·spond' (kor"ə-spond') *v.i.* **1,** be similar or analogous. **2,** conform; match; fit. **3,** communicate by letter. **—cor"re·spond'ence,** *n.* **—correspondence school,** a school that instructs its students by mail.

cor"re·spond'ent (-ənt) *n.* **1,** a writer of letters. **2,** a reporter or agent in a distant place.

cor'ri·dor (kor'i-dər) *n.* **1,** a narrow passageway. **2,** a narrow tract giving access from a country to an outlying territory, city, etc., or the sea.

cor"ri·gen'dum (kôr"ə-jen'dəm) *n.* [*pl.* **-da** (-də)] something to be corrected, esp. in print.

cor'ri·gi·ble (kôr'ə-jə-bəl) *adj.* capable of being corrected or reformed. **—cor"ri·gi·bil'i·ty,** *n.*

cor·rob'o·rate" (kə-rob'ə-rāt") *v.t.* confirm (another's report). **—cor·rob"o·ra'tion,** *n.* **—cor·rob'o·ra·tive,** *adj.*

cor·rode' (kə-rōd') *v.t. & i.* wear or eat away gradually, esp. by chemical action.

cor·ro'sion (kə-rō'zhən) *n.* act or effect of corroding; a gradual eating or wearing away. **—cor·ro'sive** (-siv) *adj. & n.*

cor'ru·gate" (kor'ə-gāt") *v.t. & i.* make wrinkles or folds (in). **—cor"ru·ga'tion,** *n.* **—corrugated paper,** wrapping paper formed in ridges, for strength, then pasted between two flat sheets to form a board.

cor·rupt' (kə-rupt') *adj.* **1,** dishonest; open to bribery. **2,** debased; evil. **3,** tainted. **—v.t. 1,** influence for evil; bribe; pervert. **2,** make impure; taint; injure. **—cor·rupt'·i·ble,** *adj.* **—cor·rupt'ness,** *n.*

cor·rup'tion (kə-rup'shən) *n.* act or effect of corrupting; dishonesty; perversion.

cor·sage' (kôr-säzh') *n.* a small bouquet of flowers to be worn.

cor'sair (kôr'sâr) *n.* a pirate.

cor"se·let' *n.* **1,** (kor"se-let') a woman's undergarment. **2,** (kors'let) armor for the upper body.

cor'set (kôr'sit) *n.* a stiffened girdle worn to shape the figure.

cor·tege' (kôr-tezh') *n.* **1,** a procession. **2,** a retinue.

cor'tex (kôr'teks) [*pl.* **-ti·ces"** (-ti-sēz")] *n.* **1,** bark, as of a tree. **2,** the layer of gray matter covering the brain. **—cor'ti·cal,** *adj.* **—cor'ti·cate** (-ti-kət) *adj.*

cor'ti·sone (kôr'ti-sōn) *n.* a hormone used in treating various diseases.

co·run'dum (kə-run'dəm) *n.* a very hard mineral used as an abrasive and, in some forms, a gem (ruby, sapphire, etc.).

cor'us·cate" (kôr'ə-skāt") *v.i.* emit vivid flashes of light; sparkle; gleam. **—cor"us·ca'tion,** *n.*

cor·vette' (kôr-vet') *n.* a small warship used as an escort.

cor'vine (kôr'vin) *adj.* pert. to the crow.

cor"y·phée' (kôr"ə-fā') *n.* a ballet dancer.

cos (kos) *n.* a kind of lettuce.

co·sig'na·to·ry *adj.* uniting with others in signing an agreement. **—n.** [also, **co·sign'er**] a cosignatory person or power.

cos·met'ic (koz-met'ik) *n.* a preparation for beautifying the skin. **—adj.** serving to beautify.

cos'mic (kos'mik) *adj.* **1,** pert. to the universe; vast. **2,** orderly. **—cos'mi·cal·ly,** *adv.* **—cosmic rays,** certain rays or streams of particles, present in space, of which the exact nature is not known.

cos·mo- (koz-mə) *pref.* of the cosmos.

cos'mo·drome" *n.* a Russian aerospace center.

cos·mog'o·ny (koz-mog'ə-nē) *n.* a theory or story of the origin of the universe.

cos·mol'o·gy (koz-mol'ə-jē) *n.* the branch of philosophy concerned with the origin and attributes of the universe, such as space, time, and causality. **—cos"mo·log'i·cal,** *adj.* **—cos·mol'o·gist,** *n.*

cos'mo·naut" (kos'mə-nât") *n.* a Russian astronaut.

cos·mop'o·lis (kos-mop'ə-lis) *n.* **1,** a city inhabited by persons of many nationalities. **2,** a city of international importance.

cos"mo·pol'i·tan (koz"mə-pol'ə-tən) *adj.* **1,** familiar with all the world; at home anywhere. **2,** peopled from all the world, as a city. **—n.** [also, **cos·mop'o·lite**] a cosmopolitan person.

cos'mos (koz'məs) *n.* **1,** the universe as an ordered whole. **2,** a tall annual plant with daisylike flowers.

Cos'sack (kos'ak) *n.* one of a Russian tribe famous as cavalrymen.

cost (kâst) *n.* **1,** the price paid, or to be paid, for a thing or service; expense; outlay. **2,** loss of any kind; suffering. **—v.t.** [*pret. & p.p.* **cost**] **1,** have as a price. **2,** cause the loss of. **—v.i.** cause expenditure or loss.

cos'tard (kos'tərd) *n.* a large apple of England.

---

cos′tive (kos′tiv) *adj.* **1,** tending to cause constipation. **2,** constipated.

cost′ly (-lē) *adj.* expensive. **—cost′li·ness,** *n.*

cost-′plus″ *n.* a fixed surcharge.

cos′tume (kos′tūm) *n.* **1,** dress in general; a particular style of dress. **2,** fancy dress; dress for stage wear. *—v.t.* furnish with a costume. **—cos′tum·er,** *n.* **—costume jewelry,** jewelry not containing precious stones.

co′sy (kō′zē) *adj.* cozy. **—co′si·ness,** *n.*

cot (kot) *n.* a small, light bed.

cote (kōt) *n.* a pen or coop.

co′te·rie (kō′tə-rē) *n.* a social group; set; clique.

co·til′lion (kō-til′yən) *n.* **1,** a fancy square dance. **2,** a ball.

cot′tage (kot′ij) *n.* a small house. **—cot′-tag·er,** *n.* **—cottage cheese,** a soft cheese made from sour milk curds.

cot′ter (kot′ər) *n.* **1,** a Scottish peasant. **2,** a split pin or bolt: *cotter pin.*

cot′ton (kot′ən) *n.* a soft white fibrous mass from a plant (cotton plant); thread spun, cloth woven, etc. from cotton. *—v.i.* (with *to* or *up to*) (*Colloq.*) become friendly or attached (to). **—cot′ton·y,** *adj.*

cot′ton·mouth″ *n.* a venomous snake of so. U.S.: *water moccasin.*

cot′ton·seed″ *n.* & *adj.* the seeds of cotton, which yield an oil.

cot′ton·tail″ *n.* a white-tailed rabbit.

cot′ton·wood″ (kot′ən-wŭd″) *n.* an Amer. tree of the poplar family; the abele.

cot″y·le′don (kot″ə-lē′dən) *n.* (*Bot.*) the primary leaf of a plant.

couch (kowch) *n.* a lounge; a small bed. *—v.t.* **1,** express (meaning) in words. **2,** set; lay.

cou·chette′ (koo-shet′) *n.* **1,** a sleeping compartment on a train. **2,** a berth.

cou′gar (koo′gər) *n.* a large tawny Amer. wildcat; the puma.

cough (kâf) *v.i.* **1,** expel air from the lungs with effort and noise. **2,** (with *up*) expel by coughing, as phlegm; (*Slang*) surrender; pay out. *—n.* an act of coughing; a disease that causes coughing. **—cough drop,** a medicinal lozenge for soothing the throat.

could (kŭd) *v.* pret. of *can.*

cou′lee (koo′lē) *n.* a deep ravine.

cou·lomb′ (koo-lōm′) *n.* a unit of electric current.

coun′cil (kown′səl) *n.* a deliberative assembly. **—coun′cil·man** (-mən) *n.*′**—coun′-cil·or,** *n.* **—coun′cil·wom″an,** *n.fem.*

coun′sel (kown′səl) *n.* **1,** an interchange of opinions; consultation. **2,** advice. **3,** a

lawyer; legal representative(s). *—v.t.* & *i.* advise; recommend. **—coun′se·lor,** *n.*

count (kownt) *v.t.* **1,** enumerate one by one; reckon. **2,** consider; deem. *—v.i.* **1,** name numbers in order. **2,** be of value. **3,** (with *on*) depend; rely. **4,** (with *in*) include. *—n.* **1,** the act of reckoning. **2,** the result obtained. **3,** (*Law*) a charge in an indictment. **4,** a rank and title of nobility. **—count′down″,** *n.* a process of counting the seconds remaining before an event, esp. the launching of a spacecraft, is to occur.

coun′te·nance (kown′tə-nəns) *n.* **1,** the face. **2,** expression of the face. **3,** favor; approval. *—v.t.* aid; encourage; show approval of.

count′er (kown′tər) *n.* **1,** a device for keeping count; a token. **2,** a bench or case over which goods are sold. **3,** the opposite or contrary. *—adj.* contrary; opposite. *—adv.* contrary. *—v.t.* & *i.* **1,** oppose; contradict. **2,** retaliate; strike back.

coun′ter- *pref.* denoting: **1,** opposition. **2,** oppositeness. **3,** a complement.

coun″ter·act′ *v.t.* offset; neutralize. **—coun″ter·ac′tion,** *n.* **—coun″ter·act′ive,** *adj.*

coun′ter·at·tack″ *n.* an attack made to offset an enemy attack. *—v.i.* deliver a retaliatory attack (against).

coun″ter·bal″ance *n.* a weight or influence offsetting another. *—v.t.* offset with a counterbalance.

coun″ter·clock′wise *adj.* & *adv.* in reverse of clockwise.

coun′ter·cul″ture *n.* a subculture whose values and habits differ from those of society.

coun″ter·es′pi·o·nage *n.* the detection or frustration of enemy espionage.

coun′ter·feit″ (kown′tər-fit) *adj.* forged; spurious. *—n.* an imitation, esp. of a coin or banknote. *—v.t.* & *i.* imitate (money, etc.) fraudulently. **—coun′ter·feit·er,** *n.*

coun′ter·foil″ *n.* a part of a document, as the stub of a check, retained by the issuer.

coun″ter·in·tel″li·gence *n.* measures taken to combat an enemy's information gathering systems.

coun′ter·mand″ (kown′tər-mànd′) *v.t.* revoke; overrule.

coun′ter·of·fen″sive *n.* counterattack.

coun′ter·pane″ *n.* a bedspread.

coun′ter·part″ *n.* **1,** a duplicate; facsimile. **2,** complement.

coun′ter·point″ (kown′tər-point″) *n.* (*Music*) the combining of different melodies.

coun′ter·poise″ *n.* a balancing weight; equilibrium.

coun″ter·pro·duc′tive *adj.* tending to

produce results opposite those desired; self-defeating.

coun"ter·rev"o·lu'tion *n.* a revolution seeking to restore a former state of things. —**coun"ter·rev"o·lu'tion·ar·y,** *adj. & n.*

coun'ter·sign" *v.t.* add an authenticating signature to. —*n.* a password.

coun'ter·sink" *v.t.* **1,** enlarge (a hole) to receive the head of a screw or nail. **2,** sink (the head of a screw) flush with the surface. —*n.* a reamer for chamfering a hole.

coun'ter·spy" *n.* a spy who spies on other spies.

coun'ter·ten"or. *n.* **1,** a man's falsetto voice; a male alto. **2,** a high tenor.

coun'ter·vail' (-vāl') *v.t.* counteract; offset.

coun'ter·weight" *n.* a weight used to balance another.

count'ess (kown'tis) *n.fem.* the wife of a count or earl.

count'less (-ləs) *adj.* so numerous as to be uncountable.

coun'tri·fied" (kun'trə-fīd") *adj.* (*Colloq.*) rustic in dress, manners, etc.

coun'try (kun'trē) *n.* **1,** land in general; a region; a particular kind of region. **2,** a nation, its territory or people. **3,** any rural region. —*adj.* pert. to, or characteristic of, rural regions. —**country and western,** a kind of music. —**country club,** a club with a golf course. —**the old country,** the foreign land from which a person or his ancestors emigrated, esp. Europe.

coun'try·man (-mən) *n.* [*pl.* **-men**] **1,** a native of one's own country. **2,** a rustic.

coun'try·side" *n.* the surrounding (rural) scene.

coun'ty (kown'tē) *n.* **1,** a political division of a state; its inhabitants. **2,** the domain of a count.

coup (koo) *n.* a sudden strategic move; a blow; stroke. —**coup' de grâce'** (koo"də-gräs') (*Fr.*) a merciful finishing blow. —**coup" d'é·tat'** (koo"dā-tä') (*Fr.*) a political stroke; a revolution —**coup d'oeil** (koo-döē') (*Fr.*) a glance.

cou·pé' (koo-pā') *n.* **1,** a two-doored closed automobile. **2,** a closed carriage for two.

cou'ple (kup'əl) *n.* **1,** two of a kind. **2,** a man and woman associated together. —*v.t.* connect; link; pair. —**coup'ler,** *n.*

coup'let (kup'lət) *n.* two successive rhyming lines.

coup'ling (kup'ling) *n.* a device for connecting things, as railroad cars, etc.

cou'pon (koo'pon) *n.* a slip to be detached from a bond, advertisement, etc. and exchanged for something.

cour'age (kėr'ij) *n.* lack of fear; bravery; valor.

cou·ra'geous (kə-rā'jəs) *adj.* intrepid; brave.

cour'i·er (kėr'ē-ər) *n.* **1,** a messenger. **2,** a paid escort of travelers.

course (kôrs) *n.* **1,** a moving forward; passage. **2,** the line of motion. **3,** the path or ground covered; a place for playing golf; a race track. **4,** progressive phases, as in a disease. **5,** a series, as of lectures, studies, etc. **6,** method of procedure. **7,** a succession of acts, practices, etc. **8,** any part of a meal served at one time. —*v.t.* run, hunt, or chase after. —*v.i.* move swiftly. —**of course,** obviously; certainly; yes, indeed.

cours'er (kôr'sər) *n.* **1,** a ploverlike bird. **2,** (*Poetic*) a swift horse.

court (kôrt) *n.* **1,** a space enclosed by buildings: *courtyard.* **2,** a level area for certain games, as tennis. **3,** a sovereign's household; a general reception by him. **4,** a sovereign's authority. **5,** a hall of justice; a session there; the judge or judges presiding. —*v.t.* **1,** seek the favor of. **2,** woo. **3,** aspire to; invite. —*v.i.* woo. —**court'ly,** *adj.* elegant; refined; polite.

cour'te·ous (kėr'tē-əs) *adj.* showing courtesy; polite.

cour'te·san (kôr'tə-zən) *n.* a harlot.

cour'te·sy (kėr'tə-sē) *n.* **1,** kind and thoughtful behavior toward another; politeness; gracious attention. **2,** a favor or indulgence.

court'house" *n.* a building for law courts and governmental offices.

cour'ti·er (kôr'tē-ər) *n.* a person in attendance at a royal court.

court-"mar'tial *n.* [*pl.* **courts-"mar'tial**] a military or naval court. —*v.t.* try by court-martial.

court'ship" *n.* a wooing, esp. of a woman.

court'yard" *n.* an enclosed yard in or near a building.

cous'in (kuz'ən) *n.* **1,** a child of one's uncle, aunt, or cousin. **2,** (*Slang*) a dupe. —*v.t.* (*Slang*) dupe. —**cous'in·ly,** *adj.*

cous"in-ger'man (-jėr'mən) *n.* [*pl.* **cous"ins-ger'man**] first cousin.

cou·ture' (koo-tyûr') *n.* dress design.

cou·tu·rier' (koo-tûr-yā') *n.* a male dressmaker and designer. —**cou·tu·rière'** (-yär') *n.fem.*

cove (kōv) *n.* **1,** a sheltered inlet. **2,** (*Brit. Slang*) fellow; man.

cov'en (kuv'ən) *n.* band of witches, esp. thirteen.

cov'e·nant (kuv'ə-nənt) *n.* a solemn agreement. —*v.t. & i.* promise.

cov'er (kuv'ər) *v.t.* **1,** put something over or upon; lie upon; close the opening of; shield; protect; coat; clothe. **2,** extend over the entire surface of; hide; screen. **3,** travel or pass over. **4,** include; comprise. **5,** aim at directly, as with a gun. **6,** insure for some specified risk. **7,** (*Colloq.*) report the news of (an event, place, etc.) —*v.i.* **1,** be spread or lie over an entire thing or surface. **2,** replace a hat. —*n.* **1,** something laid or lying over a thing to close, conceal, or protect it. **2,** a screen; disguise. **3,** shelter. **4,** table fittings for one person. —**cover charge,** a restaurant's extra charge for a floor show. —**cover girl,** a young woman whose picture is used to decorate the cover of a magazine. —**cover story, 1,** a story which is advertized on the cover of a magazine. **2,** a story used to conceal the truth, provide an alibi, etc.

cov′er·age (-ij) *n.* **1,** protection by insurance or funds in reserve. **2,** the reporting of news; the extent or quality of the reports.

cov′er·alls (-âlz) *n.pl.* protective work garments.

cov′er·let *n.* a bedspread.

cov′ert (kuv′ərt) *adj.* **1,** secret; hidden. **2,** sheltered. —*n.* a thicket; hiding place, esp. for game.

cov′er·up″ *n.* action taken to conceal information, as of an embarrassing or illegal event.

cov′et (kuv′it) *v.t.* long for; desire enviously. —**cov′et·ous,** *adj.*

cov′ey (kuv′ė) *n.* a small flock of birds, esp. quail.

cow (kow) *n.* the female of various large animals, esp. of domestic cattle. —*v.t.* intimidate.

cow′ard (kow′ərd) *n.* one who shrinks from pain or danger. —**cow′ard·ice** (-is) *n.* —**cow′ard·ly,** *adj.*

cow′bird″ *n.* a small No. Amer. blackbird.

cow′boy″ *n.* a worker on a cattle ranch. Also, **cow′hand, cow′punch″er.** —**cow′-girl″,** *n.fem.*

cow′catch″er *n.* the guarding front frame of a locomotive.

cow′er (kow′ər) *v.i.* bend down or crouch in fear, shame, etc.

cow′hide″ *n.* leather from the skin of cattle.

cowl (kowl) *n.* **1,** a monk's hooded garment; its hood. **2,** the front of an automobile's body.

cow′lick *n.* an unruly tuft of hair.

cowl′ing *n.* a metal cover or housing.

cow′man (kow′mən) *n.* [*pl.* **-men**] an owner of cattle; rancher.

cow′poke″ (kow′pōk″) *n.* cowboy.

cow′pox″ (kow′poks″) *n.* an eruptive disease of cows, caused by a virus used in smallpox vaccination.

cow′rie (kow′rė) *n.* a small marine shell, used for costume jewelry and by various peoples for money.

cow′slip (kow′slip) *n.* the marsh marigold.

cox′comb″ (koks′kōm″) *n.* **1,** a jester's cap. **2,** a vain, conceited fellow.

cox′swain (kok′sən) *n.* a helmsman of a rowed boat.

coy (koi) *adj.* exhibiting pretended shyness. —**coy′ness,** *n.*

coy·o′te (kī-ō′tė) *n.* a small tawny wolf of western No. Amer.

coy′pu (koi′poo) *n.* a So. Amer. rodent.

coz′en (kuz′ən) *v.t.* cheat; defraud. —**coz′en·age,** *n.*

co′zy (kō′zė) *adj.* warm and snug. —*n.* a padded cover, as for a teapot. —**co′zi·ness,** *n.*

crab (krab) *n.* **1,** an edible crustacean. **2,** (*Colloq.*) a cross, surly person. **3,** a tree, the crab apple; its fruit. **4,** (*cap.*) a northern constellation; a sign of the Zodiac: Cancer. —*v.i.* [**crabbed, crab′bing**] **1,** fish for crabs. **2,** (*Colloq.*) find fault. —**crab grass,** a common lawn weed.

crab′ap″ple *n.* a variety of small, sour apple.

crab′bed (krab′id) *adj.* **1,** peevish; cross. **2,** cramped; illegible.

crab′by (-ė) *adj.* grouchy; surly.

crack (krak) *v.i. & t.* **1,** snap with a sudden sharp sound. **2,** split without separating. **3,** of a voice, break. **4,** (*Colloq.*) lose effectiveness or courage. **5,** (*Colloq.*) tell (a joke). **6,** distill (petroleum) under pressure. **7,** (with *down*) enforce regulations strictly; punish severely. —*n.* **1,** a sharp snapping sound or report. **2,** a narrow fissure; slight break. **3,** a resounding blow. **4,** (*Slang*) an attempt. **5,** (*Slang*) a gibe. —*adj.* (*Colloq.*) expert; excellent.

cracked (krakt) *adj.* **1,** broken. **2,** (*Colloq.*) crazy.

crack′er *n.* **1,** a thin, crisp biscuit. **2,** a poor white farmer of Ga. and Fla. —**crack′ers,** *adj.* (*Slang*) crazy.

crack′er·jack″ *adj.* [also, **crack′ing**] (*Colloq.*) excellent; first-class. —*n.* a popcorn confection.

crack′le (krak′əl) *v.i.* emit repeated, sharp, snapping noises. —*n.* pottery with fine cracks in the glaze. —**crack′ly,** *adj.*

crack′ling *n.* the crisp browned skin of roast pork.

crack′pot″ *n.* (*Slang*) an eccentric person. —*adj.* eccentric; crazy.

cracks′man (-mən) *n.* [*pl.* **-men**] a burglar.

crack-'up *n.* **1,** a crash. **2,** collapse; defeat. **3,** (*Colloq.*) a physical or mental breakdown.

-cra·cy (krə-sē) *suf.* denoting government or governing body.

cra'dle (krā'dəl) *n.* a baby's crib, usually on rockers; hence, birthplace; origin; infancy. —*v.t.* place in, or hold as in, a cradle. —**cat's cradle,** a game played by forming designs with an endless loop of string; a design so formed.

craft (krȧft) *n.* **1,** [*pl.* **craft**] a vessel; boat; ship, etc. **2,** a trade requiring manual skill; a guild. **3,** skill; dexterity. **4,** cunning; guile.

crafts'man (-mən) *n.* [*pl.* **-men**] an artisan. —**crafts'man·ship,** *n.*

craft'y (-ē) *adj.* guileful. —**craft'i·ness,** *n.*

crag (krag) *n.* a steep, rugged rock. —**crag'gy,** *adj.*

cram (kram) *v.t.* [**crammed, cram'ming**] **1,** fill overfull; pack or stuff in. **2,** eat greedily. —*v.i.* **1,** stuff oneself. **2,** study intensely for an examination.

cramp (kramp) *n.* **1,** a sudden, painful contraction of a muscle. **2,** (*pl.*) griping pain in the abdomen. —*v.t.* hinder from free action; hamper; confine narrowly. —**cramped,** *adj.* too small or close.

cran'ber"ry (kran'ber"ē) *n.* the tart red berry of a bog plant; the plant.

crane (krān) *n.* **1,** a large, long-legged wading bird. **2,** a machine for lifting and moving heavy weights; derrick. —*v.i. & t.* stretch out (the neck).

cra'ni·um (krā'nē-əm) *n.* the part of the skull containing the brain. —**cra'ni·al,** *adj.*

crank (krangk) *n.* **1,** a device, as a bent axle, for imparting or converting rotary motion. **2,** an eccentric person. —*v.i. & t.* operate by a crank.

crank'case" *n.* the housing for the crankshaft and its neighboring parts.

crank'shaft" *n.* the cranking shaft of an (esp. automobile) engine.

crank'y (krang'kē) *adj.* irritable; hard to please. —**crank'i·ness,** *n.*

cran'ny (kran'ē) *n.* crevice; crack.

crape (krāp) *n.* crepe.

craps (kraps) *n.sing.* a gambling dice game. —**crap'shoot"er,** *n.* —**crap out,** lose. —**shoot craps,** play the game of craps.

crap'u·lent (krap'yə-lənt) *adj.* sick from excessive eating or drinking.

crash (krash) *n.* **1,** a loud harsh sound of things breaking. **2,** a collision. **3,** financial failure or ruin. **4,** a coarse, rough fabric of linen or cotton. —*v.t. & i.* **1,** smash; shatter. **2,** (*Slang*) intrude. **3,** (*Slang*) recover

from a drug-induced experience. **4,** (*Slang*) spend the night; sleep.

crash-'dive" *v.i.* of a submarine, dive suddenly, to escape detection or attack.

crass (kras) *adj.* gross; obtuse. —**crass'ness,** *n.*

-crat (krat) *suf.* denoting a ruler; a member of a ruling body; or an advocate of a form of government.

crate (krāt) *n.* a box made of wooden slats. —*v.t.* put into a crate or protecting frame.

cra'ter (krā'tər) *n.* **1,** the mouth of a volcano. **2,** the pit made by an exploding bomb or shell.

cra·vat' (krə-vat') *n.* a necktie.

crave (krāv) *v.t.* **1,** long for. **2,** beg for.

cra'ven (krā'vən) *n.* a cowardly, abject person. —*adj.* cowardly.

crav'ing (krā'ving) *n.* extreme desire.

craw (krȧ) *n.* the crop of a bird. —**stick in one's craw,** rankle.

craw'fish" (krȧ'fish") *n.* a crustacean resembling a lobster. Also, **cray'fish** (krā'-). —*v.i.* (*Colloq.*) retreat from a position or opinion.

crawl (krȧl) *v.i.* **1,** move on hands and knees or by drawing the body along the ground. **2,** advance slowly or feebly. **3,** be or feel overrun by creeping things. **4,** humiliate oneself to regain favor. —*n.* **1,** a creeping progress. **2,** a fast swimming stroke. —**crawl'y,** *adj.*

cray'on (krā'ən) *n.* a stick of chalk, wax, etc. for drawing or writing. —*v.t.* draw with crayons.

craze (krāz) *v.t. & i.* make or become insane. —*n.* **1,** a fad. **2,** a crack in the glaze of pottery.

cra'zy (krā'zē) *adj.* insane; wildly excited. —**cra'zi·ness,** *n.* —**crazy bone,** funnybone. —**crazy quilt,** a patchwork quilt.

creak (krēk) *v.i.* make a squeaking noise. —**creak'y,** *adj.*

cream (krēm) *n.* **1,** the rich, oily part of milk. **2,** something smooth like cream, as a sauce, paste, etc. **3,** the choice part of anything. **4,** a yellowish-white color. —*v.t.* **1,** beat to a smooth consistency. **2,** (*Slang*) whip soundly; thrash. —**cream'y,** *adj.* —**cold cream,** a cosmetic ointment. —**cream of tartar,** potassium bitartrate, an ingredient in baking powder.

cream'er *n.* a cream pitcher.

cream'er·y (-ə-rē) *n.* a factory where butter and cheese are made.

crease (krēs) *n.* a long thin mark made by folding; a wrinkle. —*v.t. & i.* make or become wrinkled.

cre·ate' (krē-āt') *v.t.* **1,** bring into being;

cause to exist. **2,** invest with rank. **3,** give rise to; originate.

cre·a'tion (krē-ā'shən) *n.* **1,** act or result of creating; invention; an original product. **2,** the world or universe. **3,** a woman's dress, hat, etc., of new and original design.

cre·a'tive (-tiv) *adj.* inventive; originating. **—cre·a'tive·ness,** *n.*

cre·a'tor (-tər) *n.* **1,** one who creates. **2,** (*cap.*) God.

crea'ture (krē'chər) *n.* **1,** a living animal or human. **2,** one created or controlled by another.

crèche (kresh) *n.* a tableau of the crib of Jesus in the stable of Bethlehem.

cre'dence (krē'dəns) *n.* belief.

cre·den'tials (kri-den'shəls) *n. pl.* attesting documents.

cre·den'za (kri-den'zə) *n.* a small sideboard, buffet, or table.

cred'i·ble (kred'ə-bəl) *adj.* worthy of belief; believable. **—cred"i·bil'i·ty,** *n.* **—credibility gap,** lack of confidence or trust between two entities (as between a government and its public).

cred'it (kred'it) *n.* **1,** faith; belief. **2,** credibility. **3,** an acknowledgment of worth or accomplishment. **4,** good reputation, esp. in financial affairs; borrowing power. **5,** a sum in a person's favor in an account. **—v.t. 1,** believe; have faith in. **2,** acknowledge the worth of; record a payment received, etc. **—credit card,** a card used to purchase goods, etc., on credit.

cred'it·a·ble *adj.* deserving of esteem or praise.

cred'i·tor (kred'i-tər) *n.* one to whom money is owed.

cre'do (krē'dō) *n.* [*pl.* **-dos** (-dōz)] a statement of beliefs; a creed.

cre·du'li·ty (kre-dū'lə-tē) *n.* willingness to believe; gullibility.

cred'u·lous (krej'ə-ləs) *adj.* too willing to believe; gullible.

creed (krēd) *n.* **1,** a brief statement of belief, esp. religious. **2,** a sect; denomination; belief.

creek (krēk) *n.* a small river.

creel (krēl) *n.* **1,** a wickerwork basket for carrying fish. **2,** a framework for holding bobbins or spools in a spinning mill.

creep (krēp) *v.i.* [*pret. & p.p.* **crept** (krept)] **1,** move with the body close to the ground. **2,** move slowly, feebly, or stealthily. **3,** crawl. **4,** grow along the ground. **—n. 1,** a creeping movement. **2,** (*Slang*) a disgusting person. **3,** (*pl.*) a sensation of horror.

creep'er *n.* **1,** a vine. **2,** (*pl.*) a garment worn by infants.

creeps *n.pl.* a sensation of horror.

creep'y *adj.* creeping; causing horror. **—creep'i·ness,** *n.*

cre'mate (krē'māt) *v.t.* reduce to ashes, as a corpse. **—cre·ma'tion,** *n.*

cre'ma·to·ry (krē'mə-tôr-ē) *n.* a furnace for cremation. Also, **cre"ma·to'ri·um** (-tôr'-ē-əm).

crème de ca·ca'o (krem'də-kə-kä'ō) *n.* (*Fr.*) a liqueur flavored with chocolate.

crème de menthe (krem'də-mänt') (*Fr.*) a mint-flavored liqueur.

cren'el (kren'əl) *n.* an opening in a battlement; embrasure. **—cren'el·ate** (-āt") *adj.* **—cren"el·a'tion,** *n.*

Cre'ole (krē'ōl) *n.* **1,** an American of Fr. or Sp. ancestry. **2,** (*Colloq.*) erroneously, a person part Negro. **—adj.** in the style (as of cooking), dialect, etc. of Creoles.

cre'o·sote" (krē'ə-sōt") *n.* an oily liquid from wood tar, an antiseptic and preservative.

crepe (krāp) *n.* a crinkled fabric, usually of silk, often worn in black as a sign of mourning. Also, **crape. —crepe de chine** (-də-shēn) a very thin silk crepe. **—crêpes Suzette** (krāp'soo-zet') *Fr.* pancakes cooked in burning liqueurs.

crep'i·tate" (krep'ə-tāt") *v.i.* crackle. **—crep'i·tant,** *adj.* **—crep"i·ta'tion,** *n.*

crept (krept) *v.* pret. & p.p. of *creep.*

cre·pus'cu·lar (kri-pus'kyə-lər) *adj.* pert. to twilight; dim.

cre·scen'do (krə-shen'dō) (*Music*) *adj. & adv.* gradually increasing in force or loudness. **—n.** a gradual increase in force or loudness.

cres'cent (kres'ənt) *adj.* **1,** growing; increasing. **2,** shaped like the new moon. **—n.** something in this shape.

cress (kres) *n.* a plant of the mustard family with crisp, pungent leaves.

crest (krest) *n.* **1,** a comb or tuft on a bird's head. **2,** the top of a helmet; the figure above an escutcheon. **3,** the top; peak, as of a hill, wave, etc. **—v.i.** form a crest; rise to a maximum.

crest'fall"en *adj.* dejected; abashed.

cre'tin (krē'tin) *n.* a person with a congenital thyroid deficiency, usu. resulting in idiocy. **—cre'tin·ism,** *n.*

cre·tonne' (kri-ton') *n.* an unglazed printed cotton fabric.

cre·vasse' (krə-vas') *n.* a crack, as in a glacier or levee.

crev'ice (krev'is) *n.* a crack; fissure.

crew (kroo) *n.* a working force of men, esp. of a ship or train. **—v.** pret. of *crow.*

crew'el (kroo'əl) *n.* a worsted embroidery yarn.

crib (krib) *n.* **1,** a high-sided bed for a

child. **2,** a slatted bin for storage of grain. **3,** (*Colloq.*) trot. —*v.t.* [**cribbed, crib'bing**] **1,** confine. **2,** (*Colloq.*) plagiarize; prepare (a language lesson) from a translation. —**crib'ber,** *n.* —**crib death,** a sudden fatal affliction of unknown cause that strikes babies.

crib'bage (krib'ij) *n.* a card game.

crick (krik) *n.* **1,** a painful spasm, esp. of the neck or back. **2,** (*Dial.*) creek.

crick'et (krik'it) *n.* **1,** a jumping insect. **2,** a Brit. ball game similar to baseball. **3,** (*Colloq.*) fair play.

cri'er (krī'ər) *n.* one who cries, as a hawker or public announcer.

crime (krīm) *n.* **1,** an offense punishable by law. **2,** (*Colloq.*) a foolish or reprehensible act.

crim'i·nal (krim'i-nəl) *adj.* pert. to or constituting crime. —*n.* a person guilty of a crime. —**crim″i·nal'i·ty,** *n.*

crim'i·nol'o·gy (krim″i-nol'ə-jē) *n.* the study of crime or crime-detection. —**crim″i·nol'o·gist,** *n.*

crimp (krimp) *v.t.* pinch into folds or flutings; give a wavy appearance to. —*n.* a fluting; a wave, as in hair. —**put a crimp in,** (*Slang*) hinder; obstruct.

crim'son (krim'zən) *n. & adj.* a deep-red color.

cringe (krinj) *v.i.* wince; shrink, esp. with fear or servility.

crin'kle (kring'kəl) *v.t. & i.* make wrinkles or ripples (in); twist. —**crink'ly,** *adj.*

crin'o·line (krin'ə-lin) *n.* **1,** a stiff cotton fabric. **2,** a hoop skirt.

crip'ple (krip'əl) *n.* a physically disabled person. —*v.t.* lame; disable.

cri'sis (krī'sis) *n.* [*pl.* **-ses** (-sēz)] a decisive point or condition; a turning point; a climax.

crisp (krisp) *adj.* **1,** brittle; crumbly; short, as pastry; not limp. **2,** fresh. **3,** pithy; terse. **4,** crinkled; tightly curled. —*v.t.* curl; crimp. —*v.i.* become crisp. —**crisp'ness,** *n.*

criss'cross″ *adj.* formed in or marked by crossing lines. —*adv.* crosswise. —*n.* crisscross mark or pattern. —*v.i. & t.* form or mark (with) a crisscross.

cri·te'ri·on (krī-tir'ē-ən) *n.* [*pl.* **-a** (-ə)] a standard for comparison or judgment.

crit'ic (krit'ik) *n.* **1,** one who appraises the merit of others' works, esp. artistic or literary. **2,** one who censures.

crit'i·cal (krit'i-kəl) *adj.* **1,** censorious. **2,** pert. to criticism. **3,** pert. to a crisis.

crit'i·cism (krit'i-siz-əm) *n.* the act or judgment of a critic.

crit'i·cize″ (krit'i-sīz″) *v.t. & i.* judge as a critic, esp. adversely.

cri·tique' (kri-tēk') *n.* a critical review.

crit'ter (krit'ər) *n.* (*Dial.*) creature.

croak (krōk) *n.* a hoarse, guttural sound, as of a frog. —*v.i.* **1,** utter a croak. **2,** (*Slang*) die. —*v.t.* (*Slang*) kill.

croak'er (krō'kər) *n.* **1,** a frog or croaking fish. **2,** (*Slang*) a doctor.

cro·chet' (krō-shā') *n.* a kind of knitting done with one hooked needle. —*v.t. & i.* make such work.

crock (krok) *n.* an earthenware vessel or jar. —**crocked** (krokt) *adj.* (*Slang*) drunk.

crock'er·y (-ə-rē) *n.* earthenware dishes.

Crock-'Pot″ *n.* (*T.N.*) an electric earthenware pot for slow cooking with low heat.

croc'o·dile″ (krok'ə-dīl″) *n.* a large hornyskinned aquatic reptile. —**crocodile tears,** insincere grief.

cro'cus (krō-kəs) *n.* a dwarf bulb flowering in earliest spring.

crois·sant' (krwä-sän') *n.* a light crescentshaped roll.

crom'lech (krom'lek) *n.* a prehistoric stone monument.

crone (krōn) *n.* an old woman.

cro'ny (krō'nē) *n.* a chum.

crook (krûk) *n.* **1,** a bend; curve; hook. **2,** a bent or curved staff, part, tool, etc. **3,** a dishonest person. —*v.t. & i.* bend; curve.

crook'ed (krûk'id) *adj.* **1,** not straight; winding. **2,** dishonest. —**crook'ed·ness,** *n.*

croon (kroon) *v.t. & i.* sing softly and plaintively.

crop (krop) *n.* **1,** plants grown and harvested; the useful yield of a particular plant, field, or season. **2,** a riding whip. **3,** a pouch in a bird's gullet. **4,** hair cut close to the head. —*v.t.* [**cropped, crop'ping**] **1,** cut or bite off the tips of. **2,** cut short, as a tail, hair, etc. —*v.i.* (with *up*) appear unexpectedly.

crop'per (krop'ər) *n.* a fall from horseback; hence, a failure. —**come a cropper,** fail.

cro·quet' (krō-kā') *n.* a lawn game of driving balls through wickets.

cro·quette' (krō-ket') *n.* a fried portion of finely minced meat, rice, etc.

cro'sier (krō'zhər) *n.* crozier.

cross (krâs) *n.* **1,** two intersecting stakes, bars, or lines; (*cap.*) the cross on which Christ died; a replica of this as a religious symbol. **2,** hence, a burden; misfortune. **3,** an intermixture of breeds. —*adj.* **1,** transverse; intersecting. **2,** contrary; opposed. **3,** peevish; fretful. **4,** hybrid. —*v.t.* **1,** draw (a line) or place (a thing) across another. **2,** (with *out*) cancel. **3,** go across. **4,** make the sign of the cross on or over. **5,** meet and pass. **6,** thwart; oppose. **7,** mix the breed of. —*v.i.* **1,** intersect. **2,** pass from one side to the other. **3,** meet and pass. **4,** interbreed. —**cross fire,** shooting from different positions so the lines cross. —**cross purposes,** conflicting purposes or tactics. —**cross section,** a cut through a solid; hence, a view of all parts or aspects.

cross- *pref.* **1,** across; transverse. **2,** opposing; antagonistic; counter.

cross′bar″ *n.* a transverse bar.

cross′bones″ *n.* crossed bones, a symbol of piracy.

cross′bow″ (-bō″) *n.* a bow mounted on a catapulting device.

cross′breed″ *v.t.* [*pret. & p.p.* **-bred″**] mix (breeds).

cross′cut″ *adj.* **1,** cut across the grain. **2,** adapted for cutting across.

cross-″ex·am′ine *v.t.* question a hostile witness or person. Also, **cross-″ques′tion.**

cross′eyed″ (-īd″) *adj.* having one or both eyes directed abnormally.

cross′hatch″ *v.t.* mark with crossed sets of parallel lines, as to shade a drawing. —*n.* an area so marked.

cross′ing *n.* **1,** an intersection of roads. **2,** a place suitable for crossing a road, river, etc. **3,** act of opposing.

cross′patch″ *n.* (*Colloq.*) a cross person.

cross-′pol″li·na′tion *n.* the transfer of pollen from one flower to another. —**cross-′pol′li·nate″,** *v.t.*

cross-ref′er·ence *n.* a note directing attention to another part of the same document. —**cross-″re′fer′,** *v.i.*

cross′roads″ *n.* **1,** an intersection of roads. **2,** a critical point in time.

cross′town″ *adj.* across the width of a town.

cross′wise″ *adv.* across. Also, **cross′-ways″.**

cross′word″ puzzle a game of fitting defined words to squares in a diagram.

crotch (kroch) *n.* the angle where two branches, legs, etc. divide.

crotch′et (kroch′it) *n.* **1,** an odd notion; a whim. **2,** (*Music*) a quarter note (see *note*).

crotch′et·y (kroch′it-ē) *adj.* given to odd or eccentric fancies; cranky.

cro′ton (krō′tən) *n.* any of various tropical herbs and shrubs yielding *croton oil*, a powerful purgative.

crouch (krowch) *v.i.* stoop low.

croup (kroop) *n.* a disease of young children marked by difficult breathing and hoarse coughing. —**croup′y,** *adj.*

crou′pi·er (kroo′pē-ər) *n.* (*Fr.*) an employee of a gambling casino.

crou′ton (kroo′ton) *n.* a small piece of toast put in soup, etc.

crow (krō) *v.i.* **1,** [*pret.* also **crew**] utter the cry of a rooster. **2,** brag; gloat. —*n.* **1,** a rooster's cry. **2,** a large, glossy black bird; raven.

crow′bar″ (krō′bär″) *n.* a heavy iron bar used for prying.

crowd (krowd) *n.* **1,** a multitude; throng. **2,** the populace. **3,** (*Colloq.*) a clique; coterie. —*v.t.* **1,** squeeze; cram. **2,** fill to excess. —*v.i.* come in numbers; swarm.

crow′foot″ *n.* [*pl.* **-foots″**] a plant with leaves divided like a bird's foot.

crown (krown) *n.*.**1,** a monarch's jeweled headdress; hence, the sovereign; royal authority. **2,** a wreath for the head. **3,** the highest part of anything. **4,** the exposed part of a tooth. **5,** an English silver coin, 5 shillings. —*v.t.* **1,** put a crown on. **2,** confer honor or sovereignty upon. **3,** put the finishing touch to. **4,** (*Colloq.*) hit on the head. —**crown prince,** the heir apparent to a throne. —**crown saw,** a rotary saw formed of a hollow cylinder with teeth in its edge.

crow's-′foot″ *n.* [*pl.* **-feet**] a wrinkle shaped like a bird's foot.

crow's-′nest″ *n.* a lookout's perch.

cro′zier (krō′zhər) *n.* the pastoral staff of a bishop or abbot. Also, **cro′sier.**

cru′cial (kroo′shəl) *adj.* decisive; critical.

cru′ci·ble (kroo′sə-bəl) *n.* a caldron for melting ores, metals, etc.

cru′ci·fer (kroo′sə-fər) *n.* a cross-bearer in a religious procession.

cru′ci·fix″ (kroo′si-fiks″) *n.* a representation of Christ on the cross.

cru″ci·fix′ion (kroo″sə-fik′shən) *n.* **1,** the act of crucifying. **2,** (*cap.*) the death of Christ on the cross.

cru′ci·form″ (kroo′sə-fôrm″) *adj.* cross-shaped.

cru′ci·fy″ (kroo′si-fī″) *v.t.* **1,** put to death by attaching to a cross. **2,** berate; scourge.

crude (krood) *adj.* **1,** in a raw or unprepared state. **2,** unrefined; unpolished. —**crude′-ness, cru′di·ty,** *n.* —**crude oil,** unrefined petroleum.

cru′el (kroo′əl) *adj.* deliberately causing suffering to others; pitiless. —**cru′el·ty** (-tē) *n.*

cru′et (kroo′it) *n.* a glass vial, as for oil or vinegar.

cruise (krooz) *v.i.* **1,** drive or sail about with no definite destination. **2,** patrol a beat in a police car. **3,** operate a conveyance at the speed of maximum efficiency. **4,** (*Slang*) search for a sexual partner. —*n.* an ocean trip for pleasure.

cruis′er (kroo′zər) *n.* **1,** a warship somewhat smaller than a battleship. **2,** a small yacht. **3,** a police car.

crul′ler (krul′ər) *n.* a ring or twist of deep-fried cake; a doughnut.

crumb (krum) *n.* **1,** a small fragment, esp. of bread. **2,** (*Slang*) an insignificant person. —**crumb′y,** *adj.*

crum′ble (krum′bəl) *v.t. & i.* break into small bits; disintegrate. —**crum′bly** (-blē) *adj.*

crum′my (krum′ē) *adj.* (*Slang*) of poor quality; inferior; shabby.

crum′pet (krum′pət) *n.* an unsweetened muffin, usually toasted before served.

crum′ple (krum′pəl) *v.t. & i.* rumple; wrinkle.

crunch (krunch) *v.t. & i.* chew, grind, or trample noisily.

crup′per (krup′ər) *n.* a strap holding a riding saddle steady.

cru·sade′ (kroo-sād′) *n.* a zealous campaign to defend a cause. —*v.i.* participate in a crusade. —**cru·sad′er,** *n.* one engaged in a crusade, esp. (*cap.*) in the "holy wars" of the Middle Ages.

cruse (krooz) *n.* an earthen bottle or jar.

crush (krush) *v.t.* **1,** squeeze out of shape; mash; rumple. **2,** grind into bits. **3,** conquer. —*v.i.* be pressed out of shape. —*n.* **1,** sudden, violent pressure. **2,** a crowd. **3,** (*Slang*) an infatuation; the object of it.

crust (krust) *n.* **1,** a hard outer layer or coating; the outside of bread, a pie, etc. **2,** an end (heel) of a loaf of bread. **3,** either of the two casings of a pie. **4,** (*Slang*) nerve. —**crust′y,** *adj.* surly; curt.

crus·ta′cean (krus-tā′shən) *n.* a hard-shelled, usually aquatic, animal, as a crab, lobster, etc.

crutch (kruch) *n.* **1,** a support to fit under the arm, used by the lame. **2,** any means of support. **3,** a person, thing, fact, etc., that gives solace.

crux (kruks) *n.* a critical and puzzling point or phase.

cru·zei′ro (kroo-zā′rō) *n.* the monetary unit of Brazil.

cry (krī) *v.i.* **1,** call loudly. **2,** weep. **3,** utter a characteristic sound, as an animal. —*v.t.* **1,** proclaim. **2,** offer (wares) by shouting. —*n.* **1,** any vehement outcry. **2,** a shout to attract attention. **3,** a fit of weeping. —**a far cry,** something almost entirely different.

cry′ba″by *n.* (*Colloq.*) a chronic complainer.

cry·o- (krī-ō) *pref.* cold; icy.

cry″o·gen′ics (krī″ə-jen′iks) *n.* (*Physics*) the study of very low temperatures.

cry·on′ics (krī-on′iks) *n.sing.* the practice of freezing a dead diseased human being for possible future thawing and cure.

crypt (kript) *n.* **1,** an underground vault. **2,** a secret code or cipher.

cryp′tic (krip′tik) *adj.* hidden; secret; occult. —**cryp′ti·cal·ly,** *adv.*

cryp′to·graph (krip′tə-graf) *n.* **1,** a device for putting text into cipher. **2,** [also, **cryp′to·gram**] a message in secret code or cipher. —**cryp·tog′ra·pher** (-tog′rə-fər) *n.* —**cryp·tog′ra·phy,** *n.*

crys′tal (kris′təl) *n.* **1,** transparent quartz. **2,** a glass of unusual brilliance. **3,** the transparent disk over a watch face. **4,** a characteristically faceted body or particle. **5,** an electrical device for determining frequency. —*adj.,* clear. —**crys′tal·line** (-lin) *adj.*

crys′tal-clear′ *adj.* (*Colloq.*) obvious; evident.

crys′tal·lize″ (-līz″) *v.i. & t.* take, or cause to take, definite form or shape, esp. in crystals. —**crys″tal·li·za′tion,** *n.*

cub (kub) *n.* **1,** the young of the fox, bear, wolf, lion, and tiger. **2,** a child. **3,** a junior Boy Scout. **4,** a tyro. —*adj.* untrained.

cub′by·hole″ (kub′ē-) *n.* a small compartment or room. Also, **cub′by.**

cube (kūb) *n.* **1,** a solid with six square faces, at right angles. **2,** the square of a number again multiplied by the number. —*v.t.* **1,** raise to the third power. **2,** cut into cubes. —**cu′bic,** *adj.*

cu′beb (kū′beb) *n.* the dried fruit of an E. Indian shrub, used medicinally.

cu′bi·cle (kū′bə-kəl) *n.* a small room or compartment.

Cub′ism (kū′biz-əm) *n.* a form of modern art characterized by the use of geometrical forms. —**cub′ist,** *n. & adj.*

cu′bit (kū′bit) *n.* an ancient measure of length, about 18 inches.

cuck′old (kuk′əld) *n.* the husband of an unfaithful wife. —*v.t.* seduce the wife of.

cuck′oo (koo′koo) *n.* a Europ. bird uttering a sound like "cuckoo." —*adj.* (*Colloq.*) crazy. —**cuckoo clock,** a clock from which a puppet cuckoo pops out to call the hour.

cu′cum·ber (kū′kum-bər) *n.* a trailing plant; its long, green, edible fruit.

cud (kud) *n.* **1,** swallowed food brought up for rechewing by a ruminant. **2,** (*Slang*) a wad for chewing. —**chew the cud,** ruminate.

cud′dle (kud′əl) *v.t.* hug; embrace; fondle. —*v.i.* lie close and snug. —**cud′dle·some** (-səm) *adj.* affectionate. —**cud′dly,** *adj.*

cudg′el (kuj′əl) *n.* a short thick club. —*v.t.* beat with a club.

cue (kū) *n.* **1,** a guiding suggestion; hint. **2,** in a play, the spoken words that signal the next speech or action. **3,** a tapering rod, used to strike a billiard ball. **4,** a pigtail. **5,** a queue; line. —*v.t.* remind or signal to (an actor). —**cue ball,** in billiards, the ball first struck by the cue.

cuff (kuf) *n.* **1,** an ornamental band or fold, as on a sleeve. **2,** a slap. —*v.t.* slap. —**cuff link,** a device for fastening a shirt cuff. —**on the cuff,** (*Slang*) on credit.

cui·rass′ (kwi-ras′) *n.* a piece of body armor; a breastplate.

Cui″se·naire′ rod (kwē″zə-nâr′) any of a set of colored rods of varied lengths used for teaching arithmetic.

cui·sine′ (kwi-zēn′) *n.* kitchen; mode of cooking.

cul-′de-sac″ (kul′də-sak″) *n.* **1,** a blind alley. **2,** any duct or cavity with only one opening.

-cule (kūl) *suf.* small; diminutive.

cu′li·nar″y (kū′lə-ner″ē) *adj.* pert. to cooking or to the kitchen.

cull (kul) *v.t.* select and gather. —*n.* a rejected item.

cul′mi·nate″ (kul′mə-nāt″) *v.i.* reach the highest point. —**cul″mi·na′tion,** *n.*

cu·lottes′ (kū-lots′) *n.pl.* full trousers worn by women, having the appearance of an undivided skirt.

cul′pa·ble (kul′pə-bəl) *adj.* deserving censure; blameworthy. —**cul″pa·bil′i·ty,** *n.*

cul′prit (kul′prit) *n.* an offender; the guilty one.

cult (kult) *n.* the persons and rites associated with an object of worship or veneration.

cul′ti·vate″ (kul′tə-vāt″) *v.t.* **1,** prepare or condition (land) for crops. **2,** promote the growth of; foster; develop; refine. **3,** seek the society of. —**cul′ti·vat″ed,** *adj.* —**cul″·ti·va′tion,** *n.* —**cul′ti·va″tor,** *n.* a plowing machine.

cul′ture (kul′chər) *n.* **1,** a state of civilization; customs; esp., a high level of development. **2,** the growing of bacteria for scientific use; the product of such culture. **3,** tillage. **4,** improvement; refinement. —**cul′tur·al,** *adj.* —**cul′tured,** *adj.* —**culture shock,** the sense of disorientation caused by one of a certain cultural level encountering a society of a level markedly higher or lower.

cul′vert (kul′vərt) *n.* a conduit under a road, railroad, etc.

cum′ber (kum′bər) *v.t.* overload; hamper; impede. —**cum′ber·some, cum′brous,** *adj.* unwieldy; burdensome.

cum′in (kum′ən) *n.* a plant with aromatic seeds, used medicinally and for flavoring.

cum lau′de (kûm-low′dē) (*Lat.*) with praise.

cum′mer·bund″ (kum′ər-bund″) *n.* a sash.

cu′mu·la″tive (kū′myə-lā″tiv) *adj.* increasing by accumulation.

cu′mu·lus (kū′myə-ləs) *n.* [*pl.* **-li** (-lī)] a cloud in the form of heaped-up white masses.

cu·ne′i·form″ (kū-nē′ə-fôrm″) *adj.* wedge-shaped, as the characters in ancient Persian, etc. inscriptions.

cun′ning (kun′ing) *adj.* ingenious; sly; (*Colloq.*) cute. —*n.* **1,** skill; expertise. **2,** craftiness; guile.

cup (kup) *n.* a bowl-shaped vessel, usually with a handle, to drink from; its contents or capacity; anything of similar concavity. —**cup′ful** (-fûl) *n.* —**cupped,** *adj.* held to form a hollow, as the hands. —**in one's cups,** tipsy; drunk.

cup′board (kub′ərd) *n.* a cabinet or closet fitted with shelves.

cup′cake″ *n.* a small cake.

cu·pid′i·ty (kū-pid′ə-tē) *n.* immoderate greed; avarice.

cu′po·la (kū′pə-lə) *n.* **1,** a dome rising above a roof. **2,** a furnace for melting iron.

cur (kėr) *n.* **1,** a snappish dog. **2,** a surly, ill-bred fellow.

cu″ra·çao′ (kyûr″ə-sow′) *n.* a liqueur flavored with orange peel.

cu·ra′re (kyû-rä′rē) *n.* a poisonous substance obtained from a So. Amer. plant.

cu′rate (kyûr′it) *n.* an assistant to a rector or vicar. —**cu′ra·cy** (-ə-sē) *n.*

cur′a·tive (kyûr′ə-tiv) *adj.* curing. —*n.* a remedy.

cu·ra′tor (kyû-rā′tər) *n.* the custodian of a museum, art gallery, etc. —**cu·ra′tor·ship,** *n.*

curb (kėrb) *v.t.* **1,** hold in check; control. **2,** pull to the curb of the street. —*n.* **1,** a check; restraint. **2,** [also, **curb′stone″**] the raised edge of a street. **3,** a minor securities market.

curd (kėrd) *n.* coagulated milk solids.

cur′dle (kėr′dəl) *v.t. & i.* congeal, as into curd.

cure (kyûr) *n.* **1,** restoration to health. **2,** a method of treatment. **3,** a remedy. —*v.t.* **1,** heal; make well. **2,** remedy (an evil). **3,** preserve by drying or salting. —**cure-′all″,** *n.* a panacea.

cu·ré′ (kyû-rā′) *n.* (*Fr.*) a parish priest.

cu·ret′tage (kyə-red′ij) *n.* the scraping of a bodily cavity.

cu·rette′ (kyə-ret′) *n.* a scoop-shaped surgical instrument.

cur′few (kėr′fū) *n.* a time or signal (as a bell) after which all, or certain, persons must be indoors.

cu′ri·a (kyûr′ē-ə) *n.* [*pl.* **-ae″** (-ē″)] **1,** the administrative bodies through which the Pope governs the Roman Catholic Church

(Curia Romana). **2,** the senate house of ancient Rome. **3,** the senate of other Italian cities.

cu'rie (kyûr'ê) *n.* a unit of radioactivity.

cu'ri·o (kyûr'ê-ō) *n.* an object of art, esp. if rare or unusual.

cu″ri·os'i·ty (kyûr″ê-os'ə-tê) *n.* **1,** state of being curious. **2,** a rare or unusual thing.

cu'ri·ous (kyûr'ê-əs) *adj.* **1,** eager to learn; inquisitive; prying. **2,** (*Colloq.*) strange; odd; rare.

cu'ri·um (kyûr'ê-əm) *n.* an unstable, radioactive, metallic element, no. 96, symbol Cm.

curl (kērl) *n.* **1,** a ringlet of hair. **2,** something spiral-shaped. —*v.t. & i.* **1,** form into, or take the form of, a curl; coil. **2,** play at curling. —**curl'y,** *adj.* —**curling iron,** a heated rod for curling hair.

cur'lew (kēr'loo) *n.* a wading bird with a long, slender bill.

curl'i·cue″ (kēr'li-kū″) *n.* a fancy twist or curl. Also, **curl'y·cue″.**

curl'ing (kēr'ling) *n.* a Scot. game, similar to bowls, played on ice.

cur·mudg'eon (kər-muj'ən) *n.* a churlish person.

cur'rant (kēr'ənt) *n.* **1,** a shrub bearing red acid berries; the berry. **2,** a small seedless raisin.

cur'ren·cy (kēr'ən-sê) *n.* **1,** the state of being current; circulation. **2,** money in actual use.

cur'rent (kēr'ənt) *adj.* **1,** widely circulated; prevalent. **2,** belonging to the immediate present. —*n.* **1,** a moving stream of water, air, electricity, etc. **2,** general course, as of events, opinions, etc.

cur·ric'u·lum (kə-rik'yə-ləm) *n.* **1,** a regular course of study. **2,** an accepted schedule; routine. —**cur·ric'u·lar,** *adj.*

cur'ry (kēr'ê) *v.t.* **1,** rub down (a horse) with a comb. **2,** dress (leather). —*n.* a spice, sauce flavored with it, or food served with such a sauce, from India. —**cur'ry-comb″,** *n.* —**curry favor,** seek favor by flattery or cajolery.

curse (kērs) *n.* **1,** the invoking of evil on a person; the evil inflicted. **2,** an invocation of evil; oath; profanity. **3,** an affliction; bane. —*v.t.* **1,** call down evil upon; swear at profanely. **2,** blaspheme. **3,** harm; afflict. —*v.i.* swear profanely. —**curs'ed** (-sid) *adj.*

cur'sive (kēr'siv) *adj.* in script.

cur'so·ry (kēr'sə-rê) *adj.* hasty and superficial, as an examination, a glance, etc.

curt (kērt) *adj.* short; abrupt. —**curt'ness,** *n.*

cur·tail' (kər-tāl') *v.t.* cut short; diminish

in force, extent, quantity, or duration. —**cur·tail'ment,** *n.*

cur'tain (kēr'tən) *n.* **1,** fabric hung to adorn or conceal, as at windows, before a stage, etc. **2,** a wall connecting two towers, etc. **3,** (*pl.*) (*Slang*) the end; ruin or death. —*v.t.* conceal. —**curtain call,** a reappearance of an actor, to receive applause. —**curtain raiser,** an act before the main show.

curt'sy (kērt'sê) *n.* a woman's deep bow with genuflection. Also, **curt'sey.**

cur·va'ceous (kēr-vā'shəs) *adj.* (*Colloq.*) of a woman, having a well-rounded figure.

cur'va·ture (kēr'və-chūr) *n.* a curving or degree of curve.

curve (kērv) *n.* a continuous bent line without angles. —*v.t. & i.* bend from a straight line.

cur'vet (kēr'vit) *n.* a leap of a horse with all four legs in the air. —*v.t. & i.* (cause to) so leap.

cush'ion (kûsh'ən) *n.* **1,** a pillow or soft pad. **2,** something elastic to absorb shock. **3,** the padded rim of a billiard table. **4,** something to ease a hardship or absorb a blow. —*v.t.* **1,** hold or place in a soft base. **2,** absorb the impact or shock of.

cush'y (kûsh'ê) *adj.* (*Slang*) easy; soft; pleasant.

cusp (kusp) *n.* a point, as on the crown of a tooth or a crescent. —**cusp'ate** (-āt) *adj.*

cus'pid (kus'pid) *n.* a pointed tooth; canine.

cus'pi·dor″ (kus'pə-dôr″) *n.* a spittoon.

cuss (kus) (*Colloq.*) *v.i. & t.* swear (at); curse. —*n.* a fellow. —**cuss'ed** (-id) *adj.* (*Colloq.*) obstinate; perverse.

cus'tard (kus'tərd) *n.* a cooked dessert of eggs and milk.

cus·to'di·an (kus-tō'dê-ən) *n.* a caretaker; guardian; janitor.

cus'to·dy (kus'tə-dê) *n.* **1,** guardianship; care, esp. in trust. **2,** imprisonment; arrest. —**cus·to'di·al** (kəs-tō'dê-əl) *adj.*

cus'tom (kus'təm) *n.* **1,** usual practice or habit; convention. **2,** patronage. **3,** (*pl.*) duties levied on imported goods. —*adj.* made or making to order. —**cus'tom-built″,** *adj.* built to an individual's specifications. —**cus'tom·ize,** *v.t.* —**custom house,** a government office for collecting customs duties. —**cus'tom-made″,** *adj.* make to order for an individual customer. —**customs union,** an international agreement on tariff policies.

cus'tom·ar″y (kus'tə-mer″ê) *adj.* **1,** usual. **2,** established by custom.

cus'tom·er (kus'tə-mər) *n.* one who buys goods from another; a patron.

cus'tom·ize" (-īz") *v.t.* (*Colloq.*) make or alter to a customer's order.

cut (kut) *v.t.* [**cut, cut'ting**] **1,** penetrate or sever with a sharp edge; gash; reap; trim. **2,** intersect; divide into parts. **3,** cause pain to; injure; insult. **4,** hit; strike (at). **5,** shape, as a garment. **6,** abridge; reduce. **7,** absent oneself from. **8,** refuse to recognize; snub. —*v.i.* **1,** make a slit or gash. **2,** admit of being cut. **3,** go by a shorter route. **4,** (often with *out*) (*Slang*) leave. —*n.* **1,** the act or result of cutting. **2,** an engraved block for printing a picture; a picture so printed. **3,** style; manner. **4,** a glancing blow at a ball that causes it to spin. —**a cut above,** better than. —**cut'-and-dried",** *adj.* by rote; invariable. —**cut in, 1,** move in sharply or suddenly. **2,** interrupt. **3,** add (an ingredient to a mixture). —**cut out** (with *for* or *to be*), apt; suited. —**cut up,** act foolish or frivolous.

cu·ta'ne·ous (kū-tā'nē-əs) *adj.* pert. to the skin.

cut'a·way" *n.* a long tailcoat.

cut'back" *n.* **1,** a return to earlier events in a novel, movie, etc. **2,** a reduction; retrenchment.

cute (kūt) *adj.* **1,** winning; attractive. **2,** coy. —**cute'ness,** *n.* —**cute'sy** (-sē) *adj.* (*Colloq.*) very cute.

cu'ti·cle (kū'tə-kəl) *n.* **1,** the outer layer of skin. **2,** the skin at the base of a fingernail.

cut'lass (kut'ləs) *n.* a short sword with a wide curved blade.

cut'ler (kut'lər) *n.* one who makes, repairs, or sells cutlery.

cut'ler·y (kut'lə-rē) *n.* edged or cutting tools collectively.

cut'let (kut'lit) *n.* **1,** a thin slice of meat. **2,** a croquette.

cut'off" *n.* **1,** a shorter way. **2,** a valve. **3,** (*Music*) a signal (as by a conductor) to stop playing or singing. **4,** (*pl.*) short pants formed by cutting off the legs of long pants.

cut'purse" *n.* a pickpocket.

cut-'rate" *adj.* **1,** selling merchandise at a discount. **2,** cheap.

cut'ter *n.* **1,** one who or that which cuts. **2,** a swift ship; launch. **3,** a sleigh.

cut'throat" *n.* a thug. —*adj.* relentless.

cut'ting (kut'ing) *n.* something cut off, as a shoot of a plant or a newspaper clipping. —*adj.* **1,** piercing; penetrating. **2,** sarcastic.

cut'tle·fish" (kut'əl-fish") *n.* a marine mollusk.

cut'up" *n.* a prankster; a boisterous fellow.

cut'worm" *n.* a caterpillar that cuts plants off near the ground.

-cy (sē) *suf.* of nouns [*pl.* **-cies**] denoting: **1,** qualities or abstract entities; **2,** arts or professions; **3,** offices.

cy'an (sī'an) *n.* greenish-blue. —**cy·an'ic** (-ik) *adj.*

cy'a·nide" (sī'ə-nīd") *n.* potassium cyanide, a deadly poison.

cy·an'o·gen (sī-an'ə-jən) *n.* a colorless, poisonous gas.

cy"ber·na'tion (sī"bər-nā'shən) *n.* the automatic control of a process by use of computers.

cy"ber·net'ics (sī"ber-net'iks) *n.sing.* the comparative study of calculating machines and the human nervous system.

cy'borg (sī'bôrg) *n.* a human being, modified by the provision of artificial organs.

cy'cla·mate" (sī'klə-māt") *n.* a sweetening agent.

cyc'la·men (sik'lə-mən) *n.* a plant of the primrose family.

cy'cle (sī'kəl) *n.* **1,** a period of years in which certain phenomena recur; any long period; an age. **2,** a series or round. **3,** one double alternation of alternating current. **4,** a bicycle, tricycle, etc. —*v.i.* **1,** return to the beginning or original condition; move in cycles. **2,** ride on a bicycle. —**cy'clic,** *adj.* —**cy'cli·cal·ly,** *adv.*

cy'clist (sī'klist) *n.* a bicycle rider.

cy'cloid (sī'kloid) *adj.* resembling or arranged in a circle. —*n.* a curve generated by a point on a circle that rolls on a straight line.

cy'clone (sī'klōn) *n.* a storm caused by rotating winds; hurricane. —**cy·clon'ic** (sī-klon'ik) *adj.*

cy"clo·pe'dic (sī"klə-pē'dik) *adj.* pert. to a cyclopedia (encyclopedia); hence, of great range. —**cy"clo·pe'di·cal·ly,** *adv.*

cy"clo·ra'ma (sī"klə-ra'mə) *n.* a pictorial representation of a scene in natural perspective in a cylindrical room.

cy'clo·tron" (sī'klə-tron") *n.* an apparatus for bombarding the nuclei of atoms with other atomic particles.

cyg'net (sig'nit) *n.* a young swan.

cyl'in·der (sil'in-dər) *n.* **1,** a solid generated by the revolution of a rectangle on one of its sides. **2,** any body or space having this shape; the piston chamber of an engine, etc. —**cy·lin'dri·cal** (sə-lin'dri-kəl) *adj.*

cym'bal (sim'bəl) *n.* (*Music*) one of a pair of metal concave plates that ring when struck together. —**cym'bal·ist,** *n.*

cyn'ic (sin'ik) *n.* a sneering faultfinder. —**cyn'i·cism** (-siz-əm) *n.*

---

tub, cūte, pûll; labəl; oil, owl, go, chip, she, thin, *th*en, sing, ink; *see p. 6*

cyn'i·cal (sin'i-kəl) *adj.* incredulous of man's goodness; sarcastic.

cy'no·sure" (sī'nə-shûr") *n.* a center of attention.

cy'press (sī'prəs) *n.* a cone-bearing evergreen tree.

cyst (sist) *n.* (*Pathol.*) a diseased sac in the body. —**cys'tic,** *adj.* —**cystic fibrosis,** a hereditary disease of infants and young children.

cys·ti'tis (sis-tī'tis) *n.* inflammation of the urinary bladder.

cy·tol'o·gy (sī-tol'ə-jē) *n.* the science treating of cells.

cy'to·plasm (sī'tə-plaz-əm) *n.* the protoplasm of a cell, exclusive of the nucleus. —**cy"to·plas'mic,** *adj.*

czar (zär) *n.* **1,** the title of the former emperors of Russia. **2,** a despot. **3,** a person of great wealth or power. Also, **tsar.** —**cza·ri'na** (zä-rē'nə) *n.fem.*

czar'das (chär'däsh) *n.* a Hungarian dance.

Czech (chek) *n. & adj.* of the Slavic people of Bohemia in Czechoslovakia, their language, etc.

D

D, d (dē) **1,** the fourth letter of the English alphabet. **2,** (*cap.*) Roman numeral for 500.

dab *v.t. & i.* [**dabbed, dab'bing**] touch lightly; pat; moisten in spots. —*n.* **1,** a gentle blow. **2,** a small amount; bit. **3,** a flat fish.

dab'ble (dab'əl) *v.i.* **1,** splash or play in water. **2,** do anything in a superficial manner. —**dab'bler** (-lər) *n.*

dab'chick" *n.* a small grebe.

da ca'po (dä-kä'pō) (*Ital.;music*) from the beginning.

dace (dās) *n.* a small river fish.

da'cha (dä'chə) *n.* a Russian villa.

dachs'hund" (däks'hûnd") *n.* a small dog with a small body and very short legs.

Da'cron (dā'krən) *n.* a yarn or fabric made of a certain plastic.

dac'tyl (dak'təl) *n.* a metrical foot: one syllable stressed then two unstressed, as ten'der·ly. —**dac·tyl'ic,** *adj.*

dac"ty·lol'o·gy (dak"tə-lol'ə-jē) *n.* conversing by means of the fingers; language of the deaf and dumb.

dad *n.* (*Colloq.*) father. Also, **dad'dy** (-ē).

da'da (dä'dä) *n.* a style in art producing meaningless or apparently irrational expressions. —**da'da·ism,** *n.*

dad'dy-long'legs" *n.* [*pl.* **-legs"**] an insect, the harvestman.

da'do (dā'dō) *n.* **1,** the part of a pedestal between the base and the cornice. **2,** a decorative covering for the lower part of a wall.

dae'dal (dē'dəl) *adj.* (*Poetic*) intricate.

daf'fo·dil (dăf'ə-dil) *n.* an early spring flower, yellow in color, of the narcissus family.

daf'fy (dăf'ē) *adj.* (*Colloq.*) crazy; silly. —**daf'fi·ness,** *n.*

daft (dăft) *adj.* foolish; silly; insane.

dag'ger (dag'ər) *n.* **1,** a pointed short straight weapon for stabbing. **2,** a reference mark (†) in printing.

da·guerre'o·type" (də-ger'ə-tīp") *n.* **1,** an early process in photography. **2,** a picture produced by such process.

dahl'ia (dăl'yə) *n.* a plant bearing large, brilliantly colored flowers.

dai'ly (dā'lē) *adj. & adv.* happening every day; diurnal. —*n.* a newspaper published every day. —**daily double,** a bet on two horses, one each in the first two races of a day's card, both of which must win to win the bet. —**daily dozen,** (*Colloq.*) a series of setting-up exercises.

dain'ty (dān'tē) *adj.* of delicate beauty or exquisite taste; neat; fastidious. —*n.* a delicacy; tidbit. —**dain'ti·ness,** *n.*

dai'qui·ri (dī'kə-rē) *n.* a cocktail of rum, lemon or lime juice, and sugar.

dair'y (dâr'ē) *n.* **1,** a milk farm. **2,** a building where milk is made into butter and cheese. **3,** a company or shop that makes or sells dairy products. —**dair'y·ing,** *n.* the business of running a dairy. —**dair'y·maid** (-mād) *n.* —**dair'y·man** (-mən) *n.*

da'is (dā'is) *n.* a raised platform.

dai'sy (dā'zē) *n.* **1,** a common spring wildflower. **2,** (*Slang*) something considered highly.

Da·lai' La'ma (dä-lī'lä'mə) title of the former sovereign and religious leader of Tibet.

dale (dāl) *n.* a small valley; a space between two hills.

dal'ly (dal'ē) *v.i.* **1,** play without seriousness; trifle, esp. with another's affections. **2,** idle; delay. —**dal'li·ance** (dal'yəns) *n.*

Dal·ma'tian (dal-mā'shən) *n.* a breed of dog having a white coat with dark spots.

dal·mat'ic (dal-mat'ik) *n.* a loose-fitting ecclesiastical vestment.

dal'ton (dâl'tən) *n.* a unit of atomic mass.

dal'ton·ism (dâl'tə-niz-əm) *n.* colorblindness, esp. as to red and green.

dam *n.* **1,** a wall to confine a flow of water, as a river, and raise its level; a floodgate. **2,** any barrier or obstruction that stops a flow. **3,** the female parent of a

quadruped. —*v.t.* **[dammed, dam'ming] 1,** build a dam across (a stream, etc.). **2,** confine; shut up.

dam'age (dam'ij) *n.* **1,** hurt; harm; injury; loss. **2,** (*pl.*) (*Law*) money awarded for a loss sustained. —*v.t.* hurt; injure.

dam'a·scene'' (dam'ə-sēn'') *v.t.* decorate (metal) with a damask-like pattern. —*n.* damask.

dam'ask (dam'əsk) *n. & adj.* **1,** linen or silk woven into patterns, esp. for table linen. **2,** a rose color.

dame (dām) *n.* **1,** (*Slang*) a woman. **2,** (*cap.*) a British title of honor given to women, equivalent to Sir.

damn (dam) *v.t. & i.* **1,** condemn to hell. **2,** curse; swear. **3,** pronounce bad; censure. —*n.* an oath. —**damned,** *adj.* consigned to perdition; detestable.

dam'na·ble (dam'nə-bəl) *adj.* worthy of condemnation.

dam·na'tion (dam-nā'shən) *n.* **1,** condemnation. **2,** eternal punishment.

damp *adj.* moderately wet; moist. —*n.* **1,** a condition of extreme humidity; moisture. **2,** a poisonous vapor in coal mines. —*v.t.* **1,** moisten; wet. **2,** dispirit; deaden. **3,** extinguish; smother. —**damp'en** (-ən) *v.t. & i.* make or become damp. —**damp'ness,** *n.*

damp-'dry'' *v.t.* dry partially.

damp'en (-ən) *v.t. & i.* **1,** make or become damp. **2,** deaden. **3,** depress.

damp'er (dam'pər) *n.* **1,** something that checks or discourages. **2,** a metal plate in a flue to regulate draft. **3,** (*Music*) a device in a piano to check vibration of the strings.

dam'sel (dam'zəl) *n.* a maiden; girl. —**damsel fly,** a slender-bodied, brilliantly colored insect.

dam'son (dam'zən) *n.* a black plum.

dance (dåns) *v.i.* **1,** move the body and feet rhythmically to music. **2,** move quiveringly from emotion. **3,** bound up and down. —*v.t.* cause to move up and down. —*n.* **1,** a succession of ordered steps and movements to music; any similar ordered succession of movements. **2,** a tune to which people dance. **3,** a party for dancing; ball. —**danc'er,** *n.*

dan'de·li''on (dan'də-lī''ən) *n.* a common herb with a large, bright yellow flower.

dan'der (dan'dər) *n.* **1,** scurf from an animal's coat. **2,** (*Colloq.*) temper; anger.

dan'dle (dan'dəl) *v.t.* move (an infant) up and down in the arms or on the knee; fondle.

dan'druff (dan'drəf) *n.* a crust that forms on the scalp and comes off in small scales or dust.

dan'dy (dan'dē) *n.* **1,** a dude; fop. **2,** (*Slang*) something especially acceptable or excellent. —*adj.* very good; quite suitable. —**dan'di·fy,** *v.t.* make a dandy of. —**dan'dy·ism,** *n.* —**dandy fever,** dengue.

dan'ger (dān'jər) *n.* exposure to injury, loss, pain, or other evil.

dan'ger·ous (-əs) *adj.* **1,** not safe; hazardous. **2,** causing danger.

dan'gle (dang'gəl) *v.* hang or cause to hang loosely.

Dan'ish pastry (dā'nish) a kind of sweet roll. Also, **Dan'ish.**

dank *adj.* unpleasantly damp; humid; moist. —**dank'ness,** *n.*

dan·seuse' (dä-sûz') *n.* a female professional dancer.

daph'ne (daf'nē) *n.* a shrub bearing fragrant flowers.

dap'per (dap'ər) *adj.* **1,** carefully dressed and groomed (of a man); neat; trim. **2,** little and active.

dap'ple (dap'əl) *v.t.* mark with different-colored spots.

dare (dār) *v.t.* **1,** challenge; defy. **2,** face boldly. —*v.i.* [*pret.* **dared** or **durst** (dêrst)] have courage; venture. —*n.* a challenge. —**dar'ing,** *n.* boldness; recklessness; intrepidity.

dare'dev''il (dār'dev''əl) *n.* a reckless person. —*adj.* rash; venturesome; reckless. —**dare''dev''il·try,** *n.*

dark (därk) *adj.* **1,** without illumination; unlighted. **2,** not light in color, as skin or a shade. **3,** shaded; obscure; concealed. **4,** gloomy; dreary; morose; glowering. **5,** wicked; sinister. —*n.* **1,** absence of light; nightfall. **2,** secrecy. **3,** ignorance. **4,** a color or shade not light. —**dark horse,** a long shot. —**dark'ness,** *n.* —**in the dark,** uninformed.

dark'en (där'kən) *v.t. & i.* **1,** make or become dark or darker. **2,** make or become sad, angry, etc.

dar'kle (där'kəl) *v.i.* **1,** loom in the dark. **2,** grow dark or gloomy. —**dark'ling,** *adj. & adv.* in the dark; obscure.

dark'room'' *n.* a darkened room, used for handling and developing photographic film.

dark'some (-səm) *adj.* (*Poetic*) dark; gloomy.

dark'y (där'kē) *n.* (*Offensive*) a Negro.

dar'ling (där'ling) *n. & adj.* favorite; dear; beloved.

darn (därn) *v.t.* **1,** mend by interweaving stitches of yarn or thread. **2,** (*Colloq.*) damn (*a mild form*). —*adj.* [also, **darned**] damned. —*n.* **1,** a torn spot so mended. **2,** a mild oath.

dar'nel (där'nəl) *n.* a common field weed.

darning needle 1, a large needle for darning clothes. **2,** a dragonfly.

dart (därt) *n.* **1,** a pointed missile, usually thrown by the hand as a weapon or in a game. **2,** (*pl.*) a game of target shooting with darts. **3,** a sudden, swift progressive movement; a dash. **4,** a short seam. —*v.t. & i.* **1,** throw or thrust suddenly. **2,** suddenly spring or start forward.

dart'er (där'tər) *n.* a perchlike fresh-water fish.

dar'tle (där'təl) *v.* dart repeatedly.

Dar'von (där'von) *n.* (*T.N.*) a pain-killing drug.

dash *v.t.* **1,** strike or thrust suddenly and violently, so as to shatter. **2,** sprinkle; spatter. **3,** (with *off*) sketch or write, in a hasty manner. **4,** cast down; frustrate. —*v.i.* rush violently, esp. for a brief distance. —*n.* **1,** a sudden and violent blow or thrust. **2,** a splashing of a liquid; a small amount of a fluid added to a concoction, as for flavoring. **3,** a vigorous, energetic manner; striking appearance or behavior. **4,** a horizontal stroke (—) used in punctuation to signify a sudden change of thought. **5,** a long signal in telegraphic code, transcribed as —. **6,** a swift rush, esp. a short race. —**cut a dash,** show off.

dash'board″ (dash'bôrd″) *n.* a panel facing the driver of a vehicle.

dash'er (dash'ər) *n.* **1,** that which dashes. **2,** a plunging arm in a machine.

da·shi'ki (da-shē'kē) *n.* a brightly colored African robe or tunic.

dash'ing *adj.* high-spirited; gay; romantic.

dash'pot″ *n.* a device for dampening or cushioning movement, as in a meter.

das'tard (das'tərd) *n.* a coward. —**das'tard·ly,** *adj.* cowardly; mean; reprehensible.

da'ta (dā'tə) *n.pl.* [*sing.* **da'tum**] facts or truths given or admitted and used as a basis for conclusions. —**data bank,** the place in a computer where information is stored. —**data processing,** the preparation of information for, or the processing of information by, a computer. —**data processor,** a computer.

da″ta·ma'tion (da″tə-mā'shən) *n.* automatic data processing.

date (dāt) *n.* **1,** the time or period of an event, usually stated by year and often month and day. **2,** a time of execution, as marked on a document, etc. **3,** (*Colloq.*) an appointment; engagement. **4,** a tree, the date palm, or its edible fruit. —*v.t.* **1,** mark with a time. **2,** note or set the time of. **3,** (*Colloq.*) make an appointment with, in courtship. —*v.i.* exist from a point in time. —**dating**

bar, an establishment catering to singles. —**to date,** until the present time.

dat'ed (dāt'id) *adj.* **1,** marked with a date; classified by date. **2,** old-fashioned.

date line 1, a line in a publication giving the date of an issue or of the report. **2,** [also, **international date line**] an imaginary line near 180° longitude, west of which it is one day later than to the east. Also, **date'line**″.

da'tive (dā'tiv) *n. & adj.* a grammatical case signifying the indirect object.

da·tu'ra (də-tyū'rə) *n.* a poisonous plant with a disagreeable odor and narcotic properties.

daub (dâb) *v.t. & i.* **1,** smear or cover roughly. **2,** spread or pat (a substance) on something. **3,** paint badly or coarsely. —*n.* **1,** a spot of paint, etc.; a smear. **2,** an inartistic painting. —**daub'er,** *n.* an inept painter.

daugh'ter (dâ'tər) *n.* **1,** a girl or woman considered with reference to her parents. **2,** a female descendant of any degree. —**daugh'ter-in-law**″, *n.* a son's wife. —**daugh'ter·ly,** *adj.* like or befitting a daughter.

daunt (dânt) *v.t.* intimidate; discourage. —**daunt'less,** *adj.* fearless; intrepid.

dau'phin (dâ'fin) *n.* title of the heir apparent to the crown of France (1349-1830).

dav'en·port″ (dav'ən-pôrt″) *n.* a sofa, often one convertible to a bed.

dav'it (dav'it) *n.* an apparatus for suspending, lowering, or hoisting a boat or anchor.

daw'dle (dâ'dəl) *v.i. & t.* (*Colloq.*) idle; loiter; trifle; waste time.

dawn (dân) *n.* **1,** the break of day. **2,** the beginning of anything. —*v.i.* **1,** begin to grow light. **2,** begin to open or expand. **3,** begin to be evident.

day (dā) *n.* **1,** the period between the rising and setting of the sun. **2,** the time of one revolution of the earth on its axis, 24 hours. **3,** (often *pl.*) an epoch; era. **4,** a definite period of glory, influence, activity, etc. —**call it a day,** cease effort or work. —**day bed,** a couch that may be used as a bed. —**day-'care**″ **center,** a supervised place where children can be left, usu. while parents work. —**day nursery,** a day-care center for pre-school children.

day'book″ *n.* a journal; a diary.

day'break″ *n.* dawn; sunrise.

day'dream″ *n.* a train of fanciful thoughts while awake.

day letter a telegram sent by day but at a reduced rate for deferred delivery.

day'light″ *n.* direct, not reflected, light from the sun. —**daylight saving time,** a reckoning of time, used in summer, that sets timepieces ahead by one hour in order to afford an extra period of daylight.

day'time″ *n*. the hours between sunrise and sunset.

daze (dāz) *n*. a sensation of confusion or bewilderment. —*v.t.* stun; bewilder; astound.

dazzle (daz′əl) *v.t.* overpower with an excess of light, brilliance, or magnificence.

de- (dè) *pref.* **1**, down, as in *degrade*. **2**, off; away; not; as in *detach, deformed*. **3**, same as *dis-*.

dea′con (dē′kən) *n*. a cleric or layman who assists a minister. —**dea′con·ess**, *n.fem.* —**dea′con·ry**, *n.*

de·ac′ti·vate″ *v.t.* **1**, render inactive or safe. **2**, demobilize. —**de·ac″ti·va′tion**, *n.*

dead (ded) *adj*. **1**, not living; not existing; deceased. **2**, void; useless; forgotten. **3**, complete, as *a dead stop*; exact. **4**, lacking feeling; lacking the power to rebound; dull. **5**, lacking interest, appeal, or flavor. —*adv.* completely; exactly. —*n*. **1**, that or those which no longer exist. **2**, an extreme or culminating point. —**dead end**, a point at which a street or other passageway stops abruptly; (*fig.*) a procedure, etc., without likelihood of a successful outcome. —**dead heat**, a race in which two or more contestants finish exactly even. —**dead letter**, a letter that is unclaimed or cannot be delivered. —**dead reckoning**, the calculation of a ship's place at sea from the log and compass. —**dead weight**, **1**, a heavy, oppressive burden. **2**, the weight of a container or structure apart from its contents or load.

dead′beat″ *n.* (*Slang*) one who avoids paying.

dead′en (ded′ən) *v.t.* **1**, deprive of sensation; make less acute; dull; weaken; retard; lessen. **2**, make soundproof.

dead′eye″ *n.* **1**, a device used by seamen to extend the shrouds and stays. **2**, (*Slang*) an expert rifleman.

dead′head″ *n.* (*Colloq.*) one who obtains any privilege without paying for it.

dead′line″ *n.* a time on or before which a task must be completed.

dead′lock″ *n.* an impasse.

dead′ly (ded′lè) *adj*. **1**, able to kill; lethal. **2**, relentless; malignant. **3**, suggestive of death or deadness. **4**, (*Colloq.*) exceedingly dull. —**dead′li·ness**, *n.* —**deadly sins**, the seven sins regarded in Christian religion as the source of all others: pride, covetousness, lust, anger, gluttony, envy, sloth.

dead′pan″ (*Slang*) *adj*. lacking expression of any feeling, as the face. —*n.* a face that has no expression.

dead′wood″ *n.* **1**, dead trees or branches. **2**, something discarded or useless.

deaf (def) *adj*. **1**, unable to hear. **2**, refusing to listen; unpersuaded. —**deaf′ness**, *n.*

deaf′en (-ən) *v.t.* **1**, make deaf. **2**, seem too loud to (someone). —**deaf′en·ing**, *adj.* unpleasantly loud.

deaf-′mute″ *n.* one who is both deaf and dumb.

deal (dēl) *v.t.* [*pret. & p.p.* **dealt** (delt)] **1**, apportion; distribute. **2**, deliver, as a blow. —*v.i.* **1**, (with *out*) dispose (of); be concerned; negotiate. **2**, (with *in*) trade; do business. **3**, distribute playing cards in a game. —*n.* **1**, a transaction; a business arrangement; an agreement. **2**, a portion; a large quantity. **3**, the distribution of cards, the cards as distributed, and the play of them. —**a good** (or **great**) **deal**, a large amount or degree; much.

deal′er (dē′lər) *n.* **1**, a merchant; one who buys and resells the product of another. **2**, one who deals (cards). —**deal′er·ship″**, *n.* the right to sell a manufacturer's product in a specific territory.

deal′ing (dē′ling) *n.* **1**, behavior; conduct. **2**, (usually *pl.*) business transactions.

dean (dēn) *n.* **1**, an ecclesiastical title, the head of a cathedral. **2**, the faculty head of a university or college. **3**, the senior member of any group. —**dean′er·y** (-ə-rè) *n.* the residence of a dean.

dear (dir) *adj*. **1**, beloved. **2**, valuable. **3**, costly. **4**, a perfunctory salutation in letters, as *Dear Sirs*. —*n.* a term of endearment; darling. —**dear′ness**, *n.*

dearth (dērth) *n.* scarcity; lack.

death (deth) *n.* **1**, the act of dying; cessation, esp. of life. **2**, (*cap.*) the personification of the inevitability of death. **3**, lack of existence; the state of being dead. **4**, a plague; a fatal disease. —**death′bed″** *n.* the bed in which a person dies. —**death′less**, *adj*. immortal; of enduring value. —**death′ly**, *adv*. suggestive of death. —**death house**, a section of a prison reserved for persons condemned to death. —**death row**, a cell block for prisoners condemned to death.

death′trap″ *n.* a structure or situation dangerous to life.

death′watch″ *n.* **1**, a vigil kept over a dying person. **2**, a guard set over a person condemned to death. **3**, a ticking beetle.

deb *n.* (*Colloq.*) debutante.

de·ba′cle (dā-bä′kəl) *n.* **1**, an utter failure; a sudden inglorious end. **2**, a stampede; panic. **3**, a sudden breaking of a jam of ice, logs, etc., in a river.

de·bar′ (di-bär′) *v.t.* [**de·barred′**, **-bar′-ring**] shut out; exclude; preclude. —**de·bar′-ment**, *n.*

de·bark′ (di-bärk′) *v.i. & t.* leave a ship

to go ashore; disembark; land from a vessel. —**de"bar·ka'tion,** *n.*

de·base' (di-bās') *v.t.* degrade; adulterate. —**de·base'ment,** *n.*

de·bat'a·ble (di-bāt'ə-bəl) *adj.* subject to question or doubt; moot.

de·bate' (di-bāt') *v.i. & t.* **1,** discuss; engage in an argument for and against; dispute; contend. **2,** reflect; consider. —*n.* **1,** a controversy; a contest by argument. **2,** a quarrel.

de·bauch' (di-bâch') *v.t.* corrupt; ruin. —*v.i.* engage in wild and dissipated living. —*n.* an intemperate party; carousal. —**deb'·au·chee'** (deb"ô-chē') *n.*

de·bauch'er·y (-ə-rė) *n.* immoral and excessive indulgence.

de·ben'ture (di-ben'chər) *n.* **1,** a writ acknowledging a debt. **2,** an unsecured interest-bearing bond.

de·bil'i·tate" (di-bil'ə-tāt") *v.t.* weaken; enfeeble. —**de·bil"i·ta'tion,** *n.*

de·bil'i·ty (di-bil'ə-tė) *n.* feebleness.

deb'it *n.* **1,** a recorded item of money owed; a charge. **2,** an entry on the left-hand side of the ledger, which carries all items charged to an account. —*v.t.* charge with or as a debt.

deb"o·nair' (deb"ə-nār') *adj.* gay; lighthearted; affable; courteous.

de·bouch' (di-boosh') *v.i.* come out; emerge, as from a narrow passage into the open. —**de·bouch'ment,** *n.*

de"brief' (dē"brēf') *v.t.* interrogate about a mission just completed.

de·bris' (de-brē') *n.* fragments of a former whole; rubbish; ruins.

debt (det) *n.* **1,** that which is owed. **2,** an obligation to make payment in money or kind. —**debt'or,** *n.* one who owes something.

de·bug' *v.t.* remove the errors from, as a computer program.

de·bunk' (dė-bunk') *v.t.* (*Colloq.*) strip of sham; show the truth of.

de·but' (di-bū') *n.* a first public appearance. —*v.i.* make a debut.

deb'u·tante" (deb'yû-tänt") *n.* a young woman during her first season in society.

dec·a- (dek'ə) *pref.* ten; tenfold.

dec'ade (dek'ād) *n.* **1,** a period of ten consecutive years. **2,** a set of ten.

dec'a·dence (dek'ə-dəns) *n.* a process or state of decay or deterioration. —**dec'a·dent,** *adj.*

dec'a·gram *n.* a metric unit of weight, 10 grams.

de·caf'fein·ate" (dē-kaf'ə-nāt") *v.t.* remove the caffeine from.

dec"a·he'dron (dek"ə-hē'drən) *n.* a solid figure having 10 faces.

de·cal"co·ma'ni·a (di-kal"kə-mā'-nē-ə) *n.* a picture or design that can be transferred to wood, glass, china, or other smooth surfaces. Also (*Colloq.*) **de·cal'.**

Dec'a·logue" (dek'ə-lâg") *n.* the Ten Commandments.

de·camp' (di-kamp') *v.i.* **1,** march off; break camp. **2,** depart unceremoniously; run away.

de·cant' (di-kant') *v.t.* **1,** pour gently, as liquor from its sediment. **2,** transfer (a liquor) from one container to a smaller one. —**de·cant'er,** *n.* a fancy bottle from which liquor is served.

de·cap'i·tate" (di-kap'i-tāt") *v.t.* cut off the head of; behead. —**de·cap"i·ta'tion,** *n.*

de·cath'lon (di-kath'lon) *n.* an athletic contest consisting of ten separate track or field events.

de·cay' (di-kā') *v.i. & t.* become dead matter; rot; decompose; deteriorate. —*n.* **1,** loss of soundness, health, substance, etc.; deterioration. **2,** dead or decomposed matter.

de·cease' (di-sēs') *n.* death; demise. —*v.i.* die.

de·ce'dent (di-sē'dent) *n.* (*Law*) one who is dead.

de·ceit' (di-sēt') *n.* **1,** the act of deceiving; fraud; cheating; artifice. **2,** something that tricks or deceives. —**de·ceit'ful,** *adj.* tending to deceive.

de·ceive' (di-sēv') *v.t.* give a false impression to; mislead; delude; cheat; trick. —*v.t.* be untruthful; lie; misrepresent.

de·cel'er·ate" (dė-sel'ə-rāt") *v.t. & i.* lessen the speed of; slow down. —**de·cel"er·a'tion,** *n.*

De·cem'ber (di-sem'bər) *n.* the twelfth month of the year.

de'cen·cy (dē'sən-sė) *n.* state or quality of being decent.

de·cen'ni·al (di-sen'ė-əl) *adj.* occurring once in 10 years; marking the end of a ten-year period. —*n.* observance of a tenth anniversary.

de'cent (dē'sənt) *adj.* **1,** respectable; ethical; moral. **2,** in good taste; becoming suitable; proper. **3,** virtuous; modest. **4,** fair; good enough.

de·cen'tral·ize" *v.t. & i.* separate and distribute (offices, duties, etc.) of a government or agency.

de·cep'tion (di-sep'shən) *n.* **1,** the act of misleading. **2,** a misrepresentation; artifice; fraud. —**de·cep'tive,** *adj.* intended to or tending to deceive.

dec'i- (des'ə) *pref.* one-tenth; divided by ten.

dec'i·bel" (des'ə-bel) *n.* a unit for measuring the loudness of sounds. *Abbr.*, dB.

de·cide' (di-sīd') *v.i.* **1,** make up one's mind; settle or determine a question; render a decision. **2,** choose; exercise an option; —*v.t.* **1,** determine; settle. **2,** arbitrate. —**de·cid'ed,** *adj.* **1,** unmistakable. **2,** determined.

de·cid'u·ous (di-sij'oo-əs) *adj.* **1,** shedding the leaves annually, as trees. **2,** falling off, as leaves; transitory.

dec'i·mal (des'ə-məl) *adj.* pert. to 10 or tenths. —*n.* a fraction with a power of ten for its denominator. —**decimal point,** a dot to show that the number following is a decimal.

dec'i·mate" (des'ə-māt) *v.t.* destroy a great number of, literally one tenth. —**dec"i·ma'-tion,** *n.*

de·ci'pher (di-sī'fər) *v.t.* **1,** translate from cipher to clear language; decode. **2,** find the meaning of. —**de·ci'pher·ment,** *n.*

de·ci'sion (di-sizh'ən) *n.* **1,** the act of making up one's mind. **2,** determination; resolution. **3,** a judgment, as of a court of law.

de·ci'sive (di-sī'siv) *adj.* final; conclusive; resolute. —**de·ci'sive·ness,** *n.*

deck (dek) *n.* **1,** the floor of a ship. **2,** a package, as of playing cards. **3,** a tape deck. —*v.t.* **1,** (often with *out*) adorn **2,** knock down. —**on deck,** (*Colloq.*) at hand.

deck'le (dek'əl) *n.* **1,** a device used in paper-making. **2,** the ragged edge characteristic of handmade paper. —**deck'le-edged",** *adj.*

de·claim' (di-klām') *v.i. & t.* **1,** speak or write in an oratorical or pompous style. **2,** make a formal speech.

dec"la·ma'tion (dek"lə-mā'shən) *n.* act or result of declaiming. —**de·clam'a·to·ry** (di-klam'ə-tôr-ē) *adj.*

dec"la·ra'tion (dek"lə-rā'shən) *n.* **1,** act of declaring. **2,** statement; assertion. **3,** (*Cards*) the high bid.

de·clar'a·tive (di-klar'ə-tiv) *adj.* positive; constituting a statement. Also, **de·clar'a·to·ry** (-tôr-ē).

de·clare' (di-klâr') *v.t. & i.* **1,** assert explicitly; state; say. **2,** announce; proclaim formally. **3,** bid.

dé·clas·sé' (dā-klä-sā') (*Fr.*) *adj.* having lost social standing.

de·clas'si·fy" *v.t.* remove (a document) from a classification of secrecy limiting its distribution.

de·clen'sion (di-klen'shən) *n.* **1,** descent.

2, deterioration. **3,** (*Gram.*) inflection of nouns, etc.

de·cline' (di-klīn') *v.i.* **1,** bend or slant down; droop. **2,** approach termination; deteriorate. **3,** refuse. **4,** (*Gram.*) inflect, as a noun or adjective. —*v.t.* **1,** depress; bend down. **2,** refuse; reject. —*n.* **1,** a falling off; decay. **2,** a gradual diminishing. —**dec"li·na'tion** (dek"li-nā'shən) *n.*

de·cliv'i·ty (di-kliv'ə-tē) *n.* a downward slope.

de·coct' (di-kokt') *v.t.* extract by boiling. —**de·coc'tion,** *n.*

de·code' (dē-kōd') *v.t.* translate a message from code.

dé"col·le·tage' (dā"kol-ə-täzh') *n.* (*Fr.*) a low-necked gown, or the wearing of it.

dé"col·le·té' (dā"kol-tā') *adj.* low-necked, as an evening gown.

de"com·pose' (dē"kəm-pōz') *v.t. & i.* **1,** resolve into its original parts. **2,** decay. —**de"com·po·si'tion,** *n.*

de"con·ges'tant (dē"kən-jes'tənt) *n.* a medication which relieves nasal or sinal congestion.

de"con·trol' *v.t.* make free of restrictions; deregulate.

dé·cor' (dā-kôr') *n.* (*Fr.*) a plan or theme of decorative arrangement, esp. of a room.

dec'o·rate" (dek'ə-rāt) *v.t.* **1,** embellish; ornament. **2,** reward or distinguish, as with a medal. **3,** paint; refinish. **4,** design and outfit (a room, show window, etc.). —**dec'o·ra"tor,** *n.*

dec"o·ra'tion (dek"ə-rā'shən) *n.* **1,** act of decorating. **2,** an ornament, medal ribbon, etc. —**dec'o·ra·tive** (-rə-tiv) *adj.* adding beauty; ornamental.

dec'o·rous (dek'ə-rəs) *adj.* well-behaved; proper; seemly.

de·co'rum (di-kôr'əm) *n.* propriety.

dé"cou·page' (dā"koo-päzh') *n.* the act or result of decorating with paper cutouts.

de·coy' (di-koi') *n.* **1,** a live or imitation bird used as a lure to attract wild fowl. **2,** a stratagem. **3,** one who allures, as into a trap. —*v.t. & i.* lure; entice.

de·crease' (di-krēs') *v.i. & t.* become or make less; diminish; reduce. —*n.* (dē'krēs) a reduction; diminution; falling off.

de·cree' (di-krē') *n.* an edict; a law; a judgment, esp. of a court of equity. —*v.t. & i.* order; promulgate.

dec're·ment (dek'rə-mənt) *n.* **1,** the act of becoming less; decrease. **2,** (*Math.*) negative increment.

de·crep'it (di-krep'it) *adj.* weakened, esp. by age; infirm. —**de·crep'i·tude"** (-tood") *n.*

de·crep'i·tate" (di·krep'ə-tāt") *v.i. & t.*

crackle, esp. in roasting. **—de·cres″i·ta′-tion,** *n.*

de·cre·scen′do *adv. & adj.* gradually decreasing in loudness. **—n.** a gradual decrease in loudness.

de·crim′i·nal·ize″ (de-krim′i-nǝl-īz″) *v.t.* remove criminal penalties for use, possession, etc., of.

de·cry′ (di-krī′) *v.t.* blame; deplore; disparage; censure.

dec′u·ple (dek′yû-pǝl) *adj.* tenfold. **—n.** a number repeated 10 times.

de·cus′sate (de-kus′āt) *v.t. & i.* intersect, like an X. **—adj.** intersecting. **—de″cus-sa′tion,** *n.*

ded′i·cate″ (ded′i-kāt″) *v.t.* **1,** set aside or mark for a specific purpose, esp. testimonial; consecrate; devote. **2,** inscribe or address (a book, etc.) to someone. **—ded″-i·ca′tion,** *n.* **—ded′i·ca·to·ry** (ded′i-kǝ-tôr-ē) *adj.*

de·duce′ (di-doos′) *v.t.* derive or conclude by reasoning. **—de·duc′i·ble,** *adj.*

de·duct′ (di-dukt′) *v.t.* take away; subtract. **—de·duct′i·ble,** *adj.* capable of being subtracted.

de·duc′tion (di-duk′shǝn) *n.* **1,** act or result of deducting or deducing. **2,** reasoning from the general to the particular. **—de·duc′tive,** *adj.*

deed (dēd) *n.* **1,** a thing done; an act. **2,** an exploit. **3,** a legal document for conveying real estate. **—v.t.** transfer by deed.

dee′jay″ (dē′jā″) *n.* (*Slang*) a disk jockey.

deem (dēm) *v.t.* hold as an opinion; think; judge.

deep (dēp) *adj.* **1,** extending far downward, backward, or within. **2,** studiously engaged; absorbed. **3,** implicated; involved. **4,** profound; abstruse. **5,** wise; penetrating. **6,** low in pitch. **7,** dark and rich in color; intense. **8,** heartfelt. **—n. 1,** the sea. **2,** the culminating point. **—deep′en,** *v.t. & i.* increase in depth. **—deep′ness,** *n.* **—go off the deep end,** (*Colloq.*) be rash, extreme, or intemperate in behavior or expression.

Deep′freeze″ *n.* (*T.N.*) a cabinet in which food can be frozen and stored.

deep-fry′ *v.t.* fry in boiling oil or fat.

deep′seat″ed *adj.* firmly imbedded.

deep-set′ *adj.* placed far downward or inward, as *deep-set eyes.*

deer (dir) *n.* [*pl.* **deer**] a ruminant mammal, the male of which bears deciduous horns or antlers.

de·es′ca·late (de-es′kǝ-lāt) *v.t. & i.* to reduce the scope or intensity of. **—de·es″-ca·la′tion,** *n.*

de·face′ (di-fās′) *v.t.* mar the face or surface of; disfigure. **—de·face′ment,** *n.*

de fac′to (dē-fak′tō) (*Lat.*) in fact; actual.

de·fal′cate (di-fal′kāt) *v.i.* misappropriate money, etc.; embezzle. **—de″fal·ca′tion** (dē″-fal-kā′shǝn) *n.* act of defalcating; the amount so taken.

de·fame′ (di-fām′) *v.t.* dishonor by injurious reports; slander. **—def″a·ma′tion** (def″ǝ-mā′shǝn) *n.* **—de·fam′a·to·ry** (di-fam′ǝ-tôr-ē) *adj.*

de·fault′ (di-fâlt′) *v.i. & t.* **1,** fail in fulfilling an obligation or duty, esp. legal or financial. **2,** (*Sports*) lose (a match) by failure to appear. **—n.** a deficiency; failure of duty.

de·feat′ (di-fēt′) *v.t.* **1,** conquer or overcome, in a battle or contest. **2,** thwart; baffle. **—n.** a setback; the act of defeating or being defeated; a loss. **—de·feat′ism,** *n.* the will to surrender without fighting. **—de·feat′ist,** *n.*

def′e·cate″ (def′ǝ-kāt″) *v.t.* clear of impurities. **—v.i.** have a bowel movement. **—def″e·ca′tion,** *n.*

de′fect (dē′fekt) *n.* **1,** a fault; an imperfection. **2,** a deficiency. **—v.i.** (di-fekt′) desert. **—de·fec′tion** (-fek′shǝn) *n.*

de·fec′tive (di-fek′tiv) *adj.* **1,** imperfect. **2,** subnormal (in intelligence). **—n.** a subnormal person. **—de·fec′tive·ness,** *n.*

de·fend′ (di-fend′) *v.t. & i.* **1,** guard against danger; shield. **2,** vindicate; uphold. **3,** contest (in court).

de·fend′ant (di-fen′dǝnt) *n.* (*Law*) one who is sued.

de·fend′er (di-fen′dǝr) *n.* **1,** one who guards. **2,** one who resists attack.

de·fense′ (di-fens′) *n.* **1,** resistance against assault. **2,** a fortification; a safeguard. **3,** a speech in vindication. **4,** (*Law*) the argument and evidence of the defendant; the defendant and his counsel. Also, **defence.** **—de·fense′less,** *adj.* helpless; vulnerable. **—de·fen′si·ble,** *adj.* capable of being defended.

de·fen′sive (di-fen′siv) *adj.* **1,** pert. to defense or to that which defends. **2,** [also, **on the defensive**] defending; fearing or expecting attack. **—n. 1,** resistance to attack. **2,** a defending party or side. **—de·fen′-sive·ness,** *n.*

de·fer′ (di-fēr′) *v.i. & t.* [**-ferred′, -fer′-ring**] **1,** yield to another's opinion. **2,** delay; postpone. **—de·fer′ment,** *n.* postponement.

def′er·ence (def′ǝ-rǝns) *n.* submission to the judgment of another; respect. **—def″er·en′tial** (-ren′shǝl) *adj.* respectful.

de·fi′ance (di-fī′ǝns) *n.* **1,** a challenge to fight. **2,** contempt of authority or an opposing force. **—de·fi′ant,** *adj.* full of antagonism; challenging.

de·fi'cient (di-fish'ənt) *adj.* inadequate; imperfect. —**de·fi'cien·cy**, *n.*

def'i·cit (def'ə-sit) *n.* a shortage, esp, in money; the excess of liabilities over assets. —**deficit spending**, the spending of money raised by borrowing rather than through taxation or earned revenue.

de·file' (di-fīl') *v.t.* soil; befoul; desecrate; sully. —*v.t.* march off in a line. —*n.* a narrow mountain passage. —**de·file'- ment**, *n.* corruption; desecration.

de·fine' (di-fīn') *v.t.* **1,** set the limits of; prescribe. **2,** state the meaning of; describe; explain.

def'i·nite (def'ə-nit) *adj.* **1,** having fixed or clear limits; exact; certain. **2,** positive; unequivocal. —**definite article,** (*Gram.*) in English, *the.* —**def'i·nite·ness,** *n.*

def''i·ni'tion (def''ə-nish'ən) *n.* act or effect of defining; a statement of the meaning of a word.

de·fin'i·tive (di-fin'ə-tiv) *adj.* conclusive; fixed; final. —**de·fin'i·tive·ness,** *n.*

de·flate' (di-flāt') *v.t.* **1,** remove the air or gas from; reduce in size or importance. **2,** lower, as prices.

de·fla'tion (di-flā'shən) *n.* **1,** act of deflating. **2,** a decrease in volume and circulation of money.

de·flect' (di-flekt') *v.i. & t.* turn aside; bend away. —**de·flec'tion,** *n.* —**de·flec'- tive,** *adj.*

def''lo·ra'tion (def''lə-rā'shən) *n.* act or result of deflowering.

de·flow'er (di-flow'ər) *v.t.* **1,** strip of flowers. **2,** despoil of beauty. **3,** ravish.

de·fog' *v.t.* remove the fog or mist from.

de·fo'li·ate'' (di-fō'lē-āt'') *v.t. & i.* strip (a tree) of leaves. —**de·fo'li·ant** (-ənt) *n. & adj.* —**de·fo''li·a'tion,** *n.*

de·for'est *v.t.* clear of forests; remove trees from. —**de·for''est·a'tion,** *n.*

de·form' (di-fôrm') *v.t.* **1,** mar the natural shape of; disfigure. **2,** render ugly; spoil. —**de''for·ma'tion** (dē''fôr-mā'shən) *n.* —**de·formed',** *adj.* misshapen.

de·form'i·ty (di-fôr'mə-tē) *n.* physical malformation; defect in shape or structure.

de·fraud' (di-frâd') *v.t.* deprive of, by misrepresenting; cheat; dupe.

de·fray' (di-frā') *v.t.* pay for. —**de·fray'al,** *n.*

de·frost' (dē-frâst') *v.t.* **2,** thaw out (frozen foods). —**de·frost'er,** *n.* a device for melting frost on a wildshield.

deft *adj.* dextrous; skillful. —**deft'ness,** *n.*

de·funct' (di-funkt') *adj.* dead.

de·fuse' *v.t.* **1,** remove the fuse from;

disarm. **2,** render (a situation) less volatile by removal of dangerous elements.

de·fy' (di-fī') *v.t.* **1,** challenge; dare. **2,** brave; show contempt for.

de·gauss' (dē-gâs') *v.t.* to make nonmagnetic.

de·gen'er·a·cy (di-jen'ə-rə-sē) *n.* state of being degenerate; corruptness.

de·gen'er·ate'' (di-jen'ə-rāt'') *v.i.* pass from a better to an inferior state; deteriorate. —*adj.* (-ət) degraded; worthless. —*n.* (-ət) one of low morals. —**de·gen''er·a'tion,** *n.*

de·grade' (di-grād') *v.t.* **1,** reduce in rank or degree. **2,** demean; debase. **3,** decompose chemically. —**de·grad'a·ble,** *adj.* —**deg''ra·da'tion** (deg''rə-dā'shən) *n.*

de·gree' (di-grē') *n.* **1,** a step in a series. **2,** a stage of progress. **3,** grade; rank; station. **4,** (*Gram.*) a stage in the comparison of an adjective or adverb. **5,** a title indicating academic rank or achievement. **6,** a unit of temperature. **7,** intensive quantity; extent; measure. **8,** (*Geom.,* etc.) the 360th part of the circumference of a circle. **9,** the symbol (°) following a number. **10,** (*Law*) a distinction in culpability.

de·his'cence (di-his'əns) *n.* (*Bot.*) the opening of the capsules of plants to discharge seeds or pollen. —**de·his'cent,** *adj.*

de·hu'man·ize'' (dē-hū'mə-nīz'') *v.t.* make inhuman or impersonal.

de·hy'drate (dē-hī'drāt) *v.t. & i.* deprive of, or lose, water. —**de''hy·dra'tion,** *n.*

de''ice' (dē''īs') *v.t.* remove ice from. —**de''ic·ers,** *n.pl.* attachments on airplane wings, that vibrate to shake off ice.

de'i·fy'' (dē'ə-fī'') *v.t.* make a god of; worship; exalt. —**de''i·fi·ca'tion** (-fi-kā'shən) *n.*

deign (dān) *v.i.* condescend; stoop (to an act). —*v.t.* grant.

de'ism (dē'iz-əm) *n.* belief in God. —**de'- ist,** *n.*

de'i·ty (dē'ə-tē) *n.* **1,** divine nature. **2,** a god or goddess.

de·ject' (di-jekt') *v.t.* cast down; dishearten. —**de·ject'ed,** *adj.* sad; depressed. —**de·jec'tion,** *n.* sadness; gloom; discouragement.

dek·a- (dek-ə) *pref.* deca-.

de·late' (di-lāt') *v.t.* spread abroad; make public. —**de·la'tion,** *n.*

de·lay' (di-lā') *v.i. & t.* **1,** procrastinate; wait; put off; defer; postpone. **2,** retard; detain. —*n.* a putting off; a postponement; a stay.

de'le (dē'lē) *v.t.* take out; delete.

de·lec'ta·ble (di-lek'tə-bəl) *adj.* delightful; very pleasing. —**de·lec''ta·bil'i·ty,** **de''lec·ta'tion** (dē''lek-tā'shən) *n.*

del′e·gate (del′i-gət) *n.* one who acts for or represents another or a group; an emissary. —*v.t.* (-gāt″) **1**, entrust; empower. **2**, send as a representative with power to transact business; depute.

del″e·ga′tion (del″i-gā′shən) *n.* **1**, act of delegating; what is delegated. **2**, a group of delegates.

de·lete′ (di-lēt′) *v.t.* take out; expunge; erase. —**de·le′tion**, *n.*

del″e·te′ri·ous (del″ə-tir′ē-əs) *adj.* injurious. —**del″e·te′ri·ous·ness**, *n.*

delft *n.* **1**, [also, **delf, delft′ware**] a kind of pottery decorated in colors. **2**, a shade of blue.

del′i (del′ē) *n.* (*Colloq.*) delicatessen.

de·lib′er·ate (di-lib′ər-āt″) *v.i. & t.* reflect carefully; consider. —*adj.* (-ət) **1**, careful; unhurried. **2**, intentional.

de·lib″er·a′tion (di-lib″ə-rā′shən) *n.* **1**, act of deliberating; careful thought. **2**, (*pl.*) conference or discussion among a deliberative body.

de·lib′er·a″tive (di-lib′ə-rā″tiv) *adj.* reflecting and weighing carefully. —**deliberative body**, a legislature, committee, etc.

del′i·ca·cy (del′i-kə-sē) *n.* the state or act of being delicate; a delicate thing, esp. a choice food.

del′i·cate (del′i-kət) *adj.* **1**, minutely perfect; exquisite. **2**, requiring tact or skill. **3**, fragile; of a weak constitution. **4**, considerate; tactful; sensitive. **5**, choice, as food.

del″i·ca·tes′sen (del″ə-kə-tes′ən) *n.pl.* prepared foods, as salads, cooked meats. —*n.sing.* a store where these are sold.

de·li′cious (di-lish′əs) *adj.* highly pleasing to the taste or smell; delightful. —**de·li′cious·ness**, *n.*

de·light′ (di-līt′) *n.* a high degree of pleasure or satisfaction, or that which affords it. —*v.t. & i.* thrill with pleasure. —**de·light′-ful**, *adj.* very enjoyable; very attractive.

de·light′ed *adj.* greatly pleased. —*interj.* (I accept) with pleasure!

de·lim′it (dē-lim′it) *v.t.* place limits on; mark the limits of.

de·lin′e·ate (di-lin′ē-āt″) *v.t.* mark the outline of; describe; depict; sketch. —**de·lin″e·a′tion**, *n.*

de·lin′quent (di-ling′kwənt) *n.* one who fails to perform a duty or to fill an obligation; an offender; a culprit. —*adj.* **1**, neglectful of a duty or obligation. **2**, guilty of a crime or misdeed. —**de·lin′quency**, *n.*

del′i·quesce′ (del″ə-kwes′) *v.i.* melt; become liquid from absorbing moisture. —**del″i·ques′cence**, —**del″i·ques′cent**, *adj.*

de·lir′i·um (di-lir′ē-əm) *n.* **1**, a temporary disordered mental state, marked by delusions. **2**, violent excitement; mad rapture. —**de·lir′i·ous**, *adj.* —**delirium tre′-mens** (trē′mənz) delirium induced by excessive drinking of alcoholic liquor.

de·liv′er (di-liv′ər) *v.t.* **1**, set free; liberate; release. **2**, give or hand over; transport to a consignee. **3**, surrender; yield. **4**, give birth to. **5**, cast, as a blow; throw, as a ball. **6**, utter; enunciate.

de·liv′er·ance (-əns) *n.* **1**, delivery, esp. from restraint; rescue. **2**, an expressed thought; a pronouncement.

de·liv′er·y (-ē) *n.* **1**, act of delivering; transport of goods, letters, etc. **2**, a handing over. **3**, release; rescue. **4**, the giving of birth. **5**, manner of delivering. **6**, something delivered.

dell (del) *n.* a small shady valley; a glen.

del·phin′i·um (del-fin′ē-əm) *n.* a handsome garden plant; the larkspur.

del′ta (del′tə) *n.* **1**, the fourth letter of the Greek alphabet (Δ, δ). **2**, a triangular deposit at the mouth of a river split into branches. —**delta wing**, a triangular, sweptback airplane wing.

del′toid *adj.* triangular. —*n.* the shoulder muscle.

de·lude′ (di-lood′) *v.t.* convince that something false is true; deceive; cheat.

del′uge (del′ūj) *n.* a heavy downpour of rain; a flood. —*v.t.* **1**, overflow. **2**, overwhelm.

de·lu′sion (di-loo′zhən) *n.* **1**, a false belief. **2**, a persistent and false mental conception of facts as they relate to oneself.

de·lu′sive (di-loo′siv) *adj.* **1**, being a delusion. **2**, deluding.

de·lu′so·ry (di-loo′sə-rē) *adj.* tending to delude; delusive.

de luxe (di luks′) (*Fr.*) of highest quality; luxurious.

delve (delv) *v.i.* **1**, dig. **2**, carry on laborious and continued research.

dem′a·gogue″ (dem′ə-gog″) *n.* **1**, an unprincipled popular orator or leader. **2**, a rabble rouser. —**dem″a·gog″uer·y** (-ə-rē) *n.* —**dem″a·gog′ic** (-goj′ik) *adj.* —**dem″a·gog′i·cal·y**, *adv.*

de·mand′ (di-mánd′) *v.t.* **1**, claim by right. **2**, ask insistently. **3**, require; need; call for. —*n.* **1**, an authoritative claim. **2**, an urgent request. **3**, that which is demanded. **4**, the state of being sought after. **5**, (*Econ.*) the desire to purchase goods coupled with the power to do so. —**de·mand′ing**, *adj.* **1**, arduous, difficult. **2**, hard to please.

de″mar·ca′tion (dē″mär-kā′shən) *n.* a marking of bounds. —**de·mar′cate** (dē-mär′kāt) *v.*

dé·marche' (dā-märsh') n. (Fr.) a way of procedure; a move or step, esp. one involving a change of policy.

de·mean' (di-mēn') v.t. **1**, debase; lower. **2**, (Archaic) comport or behave oneself.

de·mean'or (di-mēn'ər) n. behavior; bearing. Also, **de·mean'our**.

de·ment'ed (di-men'ted) adj. insane.

de·men'tia (di-men'shə) n. impairment of the mental powers; insanity. —**dementia prae'cox** (prē'koks) a mental disorder occurring usu. at puberty.

de·mer'it (dē-mer'it) n. **1**, a fault. **2**, a mark given for bad conduct or deficiency.

dem·i- (dem-ē; -i) pref. **1**, half. **2**, inferior.

dem'i·god" n. **1**, an inferior or minor deity. **2**, a being half god and half human.

dem'i·john" (dem'i-jon") n. a large jug, usually incased in wicker.

de·mil'i·ta·rize" (dē-mil'i-tə-rīz") v.t. **1**, remove troops, fortifications, etc. from. **2**, transfer from military to civil control. —**de·mil"i·ta·ri·za'tion**, n.

dem'i·monde" (dem'i-mond") n. women of poor reputation; the world in which they move. —**dem'i·mon·daine"** (-dān") n. a member of the demimonde.

de·mise' (di-mīz') n. **1**, death. **2**, transfer of an estate by death. —v.t. & i. transfer, as an estate.

de·mit' (di-mit') v.t. [**-mit'ted, -ting**] resign.

dem'i·tasse" (dem'i-tàs") n. a small cup of, or for, black coffee.

dem'o (dem'ō) n. (Slang) a demonstrator, used for selling.

de·mo'bi·lize" (dē-mō'bə-līz") v.t. disband, as troops. —**de·mo"bi·li·za'tion** (-li-zā'shən) n.

de·moc'ra·cy (di-mok'rə-sē) n. **1**, government by the people. **2**, political and social equality in general; belief in this. —**de·moc'ra·tize"** (-rə-tīz") v.t.

dem'o·crat" (dem'ə-krat") n. **1**, a believer in democracy. **2**, one who treats all others as his equals. **3**, (cap.) a member of the Democratic political party in the U.S. —**dem"o·crat'ic**, adj. —**dem"o·crat'i·cal·ly**, adv.

de·mod'ed (dē-mō'did) adj. out of fashion. Also, **dé"mo·dé'** (dā"mō-dā').

de·mod'u·late" (dē-moj'ə-lāt") v.t. detect (radio waves). —**de·mod"u·la'tion,** n.

de·mog'ra·phy (di-mog'rə-fē) n. the science of vital statistics relating to deaths, births, etc. —**de·mog'ra·pher,** n. —**dem"o·graph'ic** (dem'ə-graf'ik) adj.

de·mol'ish (de-mol'ish) v.t. throw or pull down; destroy. —**dem"o·li'tion** (dem"ə-

lish'ən) n. —**demolition derby,** an automobile contest in which contestants try to demolish their opponents' cars.

demon (dē'mən) n. **1**, an evil spirit; a devil. **2**, a wicked or cruel person. **3**, (Colloq.) an energetic person. —**de·mo'ni·ac** (di-mō'nē-ak), **de"mo·ni'a·cal** (dē"mō-nī'ə-kəl) adj. —**de·mon'ic** (di-mon'ik) adj.

de·mon'e·tize" (dē-mon'ə-tīz") v.t. withdraw from use as money. —**de·mon"e·ti·za'tion** (-ti-zā'shən) n.

de"mon·ol'o·gy (dē"mən-ol'ə-jē) n. **1**, the study of demons or the belief in them. **2**, the doctrines of demon worshipers. —**de"mon·ol'o·gist,** n.

de·mon'stra·ble (di-mon'strə-bəl) adj. capable of proof by demonstration. —**de·mon"stra·bil'i·ty,** n.

dem'on·strate" (dem'ən-strāt") v.t. & i. **1**, describe or explain by use of examples. **2**, establish the truth of by reasoning; prove. **3**, exhibit and put to test publicly. **4**, point out; make evident. **5**, make a show of force; assemble to show approval or protest.

dem"on·stra'tion (-strā'shən) n. **1**, act of demonstrating; exhibition; display. **2**, manifestation of feelings; a show of force, protest, etc.

de·mon'stra·tive (di-mon'strə-tiv) adj. **1**, strongly exhibiting one's feelings. **2**, conclusive, as proof. **3**, (Gram.) pointing out an object, as this, that. —**de·mon'stra·tive·ness,** n.

dem'on·stra"tor (dem'ən-strā"tər) n. one who or that which demonstrates, esp. an automobile so used.

de·mor'al·ize" (di-môr'ə-līz") v.t. **1**, corrupt. **2**, deprive of spirit or energy; dishearten. **3**, throw into confusion or disorder. —**de·mor"al·i·za'tion** (-li-zā'shən) n.

de·mote' (di-mōt') v.t. reduce in rank or class. —**de·mo'tion,** n.

de·mot'ic (dē-mot'ik) adj. of the common people; popular.

de·mul'cent (de-mul'sənt) adj. softening; mollifying; soothing.

de·mur' (di-mēr') v.i. [**-murred', -mur'ring**] take exception; object. —n. objection. —**de·mur'ral,** n.

de·mure' (di-myûr') adj. **1**, affectedly modest; prim. **2**, sedate. —**demure'ness,** n.

de·mur'rage (di-mēr'ij) n. detention of a vessel or freight car beyond the time stipulated; the charge for such delay.

de·mur'rer (di-mēr'ər) n. (Law) a plea that the case be dismissed though the facts alleged are conceded.

den n. **1**, a cave for a wild beast. **2**, a

de·na'ture (dē-nā'chər) *v.t.* change the nature of, esp. of alcohol to render it unfit to drink.

den'drite (den'drīt) *n.* **1,** the branching outer part of a neuron. **2,** a veining in certain impure minerals.

den·dro- (den-drō) *pref.* tree.

-den'dron (den'drən) *suf.* tree.

den'e·gate'' (den'i-gāt'') *v.t.* deny. —**den'-e·ga'tion,** *n.*

den'gue (deng'gā) *n.* a tropical disease: *dandy-fever.*

de·ni'al (di-nī'əl) *n.* **1,** the act of contradiction; negation. **2,** refusal to grant a request. **3,** a refusal to accept or acknowledge. **4,** restraint of personal desires; poverty.

de·nier' (də-nir') *n.* the measure of weight or fineness of a yarn.

den'i·grate'' (den'i-grāt'') *v.t.* blacken in reputation; defame. —**den''e·gra'tion,** *n.*

den'im (den'əm) *n.* a coarse twilled cotton cloth.

den'i·zen (den'ə-zən) *n.* a dweller; an inhabitant.

de·nom'i·nate'' (di-nom'ə-nāt'') *v.t.* give a specific name to; designate.

de·nom'i·na'tion (di-nom''i-nā'shən) *n.* **1,** act of naming; a name. **2,** a religious sect. **3,** a unit in a series, as of quantity, value, etc.

de·nom'i·na''tor (di-nom'i-nā''tər) *n.* (*Math.*) the part of a fraction that represents the divisor: in ½, 2 is the denominator.

de·note' (di-nōt') *v.t.* **1,** point out and identify; designate. **2,** be a sign or symptom of; indicate. —**de''no·ta'tion** (dē''nō-tā'shən) *n.* —**de·no'ta·tive** (dē-nō'tə-tiv) *adj.*

dé''noue·ment' (dā''noo-män') *n.* the solution of a plot, as in a play.

de·nounce' (di-nowns') *v.t.* **1,** blame or brand publicly; stigmatize. **2,** inform against; condemn. **3,** announce the intention of abrogating a treaty. —**de·nounce'ment,** *n.*

dense (dens) *adj.* **1,** having great closeness of parts; thick; compact. **2,** stupid. —**dense'ness, den'si·ty** (-sə-tē) *n.*

dent *n.* a small hollow or depression made by a blow. —*v.t. & i.* make a dent (in).

den'tal (den'təl) *adj.* pert. to the teeth.

den'ti·frice (den'tə-fris) *n.* a preparation for cleaning the teeth.

den'tin *n.* the hard tissue of a tooth, under the enamel. Also, **den'tine.**

den'tist *n.* a doctor for the teeth. —**den'-tist·ry** (-rē) *n.* the science of treating the teeth; dental surgery.

den·ti'tion (den-tish'ən) *n.* **1,** the kind,

number, and arrangement of the teeth in a man or animal. **2,** teething.

den'ture (den'chər) *n.* a set of false teeth.

de·nu'cle·ar·ize'' (dē-noo'klē-ə-rīz'') *v.t.* remove nuclear weapons or technology from.

de·nude' (di-nūd') *v.t.* strip or divest of all covering.

de·nun''ci·a'tion (di-nun''sē-ā'shən) *n.* act or result of denouncing. —**de·nun'ci·ate,** *v.t.* —**de·nun'ci·a·to·ry** (-ə-tôr-ē) *adj.*

de·ny' (di-nī') *v.t.* **1,** refuse to admit the truth of; contradict. **2,** refuse to give or grant. **3,** refuse to accept or admit. **4,** renounce; disown —**deny oneself,** do without.

de·o'dar'' (dē'ə-där') *n.* an E. Indian evergreen tree.

de·o'dor·ant (dē-ōd'ə-rənt) *n.* a preparation that destroys unpleasant odor. —*adj.* deodorizing.

de·o'dor·ize'' (dē-ō'də-rīz'') *v.t.* remove odor from. —**de·o''dor·i·za'tion,** *n.*

de·part' (di-pärt') *v.i.* **1,** go or move away; leave (often with *from*). **2,** deviate; abandon. **3,** die. —**de·par'ture** (di-pär'chər) *n.* —**the departed,** the deceased.

de·part'ment (di-pärt'ment) *n.* a separate part or division of a complex system; a branch of a business, government, etc. —**de·part''men'tal** (di-pärt''men'təl) *adj.* pert. to a department; organized into departments. —**de·part''men'tal·ize,** *v.t.* —**department store,** a retail store dealing in many different kinds of merchandise.

de·pend' (di-pend') *v.i.* **1,** be contingent upon something; hang. **2,** (with *on* or *upon*) repose confidence; rely. **3,** (with *on*) rely upon for maintenance. —**de·pend'-a·ble,** *adj.* reliable; trustworthy. —**de·pen'dence,** *n.*

de·pen'den·cy (di-pen'dən-sē) *n.* **1,** dependence. **2,** an appurtenance. **3,** a territory that is dependent upon, but not a part of, a nation.

de·pen'dent (di-pen'dənt) *adj.* **1,** depending (on) or subject (to). **2,** conditional. **3,** hanging down. —*n.* [also, **de·pen'dant**] one who is supported by another.

de·per'son·al·ize'' *v.t.* render impersonal; remove the personality of.

de·pict' (di-pikt') *v.t.* portray by a picture or words. —**de·pic'tion,** *n.*

dep'i·late'' (dep'ə-lāt'') *v.t.* remove the hair from —**dep''i·la'tion,** *n.*

de·pil'a·to·ry (di-pil'ə-tôr-ē) *n.* a preparation for removing unwanted hair. —*adj.* capable of removing hair.

de·plane' *v.i.* disembark from an airplane.

de·plete' (di-plēt') *v.t.* exhaust by drawing away, as resources, strength, vital powers. —**de·ple'tion**, *n.*

de·plore' (di-plôr') *v.t.* regret; lament. —**de·plor'a·ble**, *adj.* lamentable; calamitous.

de·ploy' (di-ploi') *v.t. & i.* (*Mil.*) spread out on a more extended front. —**de·ploy'ment**, *n.*

de·pone' (di-pōn') *v.i.* (*Law*) give testimony under oath; depose. —**de·po'nent** (-ənt) *n.*

de·pop'u·late" (dē-pop'yə-lāt") *v.t.* deprive of inhabitants, as by killing or expelling them. —**de·pop"u·la'tion**, *n.*

de·port' (di-pôrt') *v.t.* **1,** transport forcibly; exile. **2,** behave (oneself). —**de"por·ta'tion** (dē"pôr-tā'shən) *n.* —**de"por·tee'**, *n.*

de·port'ment (-mənt) *n.* behavior, conduct.

de·pose' (di-pōz') *v.t. & i.* **1,** remove from a high office. **2,** testify. —**de·pos'al** (-əl) *n.*

de·pos'it (di-poz'it) *v.t.* **1,** lay down; put; precipitate. **2,** place in safekeeping, esp. money in a bank. —*n.* **1,** anything entrusted, as money in a bank. **2,** a pledge; a part payment. **3,** that which is laid, thrown down, or settled, as sand from a body of water. **4,** a natural accumulation of a mineral in the earth.

dep"o·si'tion (dep"ə-zish'ən) *n.* **1,** act or effect of deposing. **2,** sworn testimony. —**de·pos'i·to·ry** (di-poz'ə-tôr-ē) *n.* a place where something is deposited; a bank.

de'pot (dē'pō) *n.* **1,** a warehouse; a railroad station. **2,** (*Mil.*) a redistribution point for supplies.

de·prave' (di-prāv') *v.t.* pervert; corrupt. —**de·prav'i·ty** (di-prav'ə-tè) *n.*

dep're·cate" (dep'rə-kāt") *v.t.* plead against; express disapproval of. —**dep"re·ca'tion**, *n.* —**dep're·ca·to·ry** (-kə-tôr-ē) *adj.*

de·pre'ci·ate" (di-prē'shè-āt") *v.i. & t.* **1,** become worth less; lessen the value of. **2,** belittle. —**de·pre"ci·a'tion**, *n.* a decrease in value; the amount of the decrease.

dep're·date" (dep'rə-dāt") *v.t. & i.* lay waste; plunder. —**dep"re·da'tion**, *n.*

de·press' (di-pres') *v.t.* **1,** press or move downward. **2,** weaken. **3,** sadden. —**de·pres'sive** (-iv) *adj.* —**de·pres'sor**, *n.*

de·pres'sant (di-pres'ənt) *n. & adj.* a sedative.

de·pressed' (di-prest') *adj.* **1,** dejected. **2,** in a state of economic depression. **3,** lowered in position, amount, intensity, etc. **4,** indented; concave.

de·pres'sion (di-presh'ən) *n.* **1,** act of depressing, or state of being depressed. **2,**

a hollow. **3,** an unwarranted and prolonged condition of emotional dejection. **4,** a period of decline in business activity.

dep"ri·va'tion (dep"ri-vā'shən) *n.* **1,** act of depriving; loss. **2,** poverty; want.

de·prive' (di-prīv') *v.t.* **1,** divest; strip. **2,** withhold; prevent from possessing.

de·pro'gram *v.t.* rid or attempt to rid (a person) of beliefs acquired from a previous indoctrination.

depth *n.* **1,** deepness; distance measured downward, inward, or backward. **2,** intensity. **3,** profundity. **4,** (*pl.*) utmost depression of spirits. —**depth charge,** a mine set to explode at a certain depth.

dep"u·ta'tion (dep"yû-tā'shən) *n.* **1,** appointment to act for another. **2,** a group of duties.

de·pute' (di-pūt') *v.t.* **1,** appoint as an agent. **2,** assign to an agent.

dep'u·tize" (dep'yû-tīz") *v.t.* appoint as agent.

dep'u·ty (dep'yə-tè) *n.* a representative assistant, or agent esp. of a public officer; one deputed.

de·rail' (dē-rāl') *v.i. & t.* run (a train) off the track. —**de·rail'ment**, *n.*

de·rail'leur (də-rā'lər) *n.* a multiple-speed gear mechanism for a bicycle.

de·range' (di-rānj') *v.t.* **1,** disarrange. **2,** disorder the mind of. —**de·range'ment**, *n.*

der'by (dĕr'bè) *n.* **1,** a man's hat with a stiff rounded crown and narrow brim. **2,** (*cap.*) any of several horse races.

de·reg'u·late" *v.t.* free from regulation (esp. governmental); decontrol.

der'e·lict (der'ə-likt) *adj.* **1,** abandoned. **2,** unfaithful. —*n.* **1,** anything abandoned, esp. a ship. **2,** an outcast. **3,** one guilty of neglect. —**der"e·lic'tion**, *n.*

de·ride' (di-rīd') *v.t.* laugh at contemptuously; mock. —**de·ri'sive** (-rī'siv) *adj.*

de·ri'sion (di-rizh'ən) *n.* **1,** act of deriding; ridicule. **2,** an object of ridicule or mockery.

der"i·va'tion (der"i-vā'shən) *n.* **1,** act of deriving. **2,** source.

de·riv'a·tive (di-riv'ə-tiv) *n. & adj.* what is derived.

de·rive' (di-rīv') *v.t. & i.* **1,** draw or receive from a source or origin. **2,** deduce; infer. **3,** trace the development of (a word).

derm-, -derm (dĕrm) *pref. & suf.* skin.

der"ma·tol'o·gy (dĕr"mə-tol'ə-jè) *n.* the science of the skin and its diseases. —**der"ma·tol'o·gist**, *n.* a practitioner in this science.

der'ma (dĕr'mə) *n.* the true skin, below the epidermis. Also, **der'mis.**

der″ma·ti′tis (dẽr″mǝ-tī′tis) *n.* inflammation of the skin.

der·nier′ cri (der-nyä′krē′) (*Fr.*) the last word; the latest thing.

der′o·gate″ (der′ǝ-gāt″) *v.t. & i.* detract from; disparage; depreciate. —**der″o·ga′tion,** *n.* —**de·rog′a·to·ry** (di-rog′ǝ-tôr-ė), **de·rog′a·tive,** *adj.*

der′rick (der′ik) *n.* **1,** an apparatus for hoisting; a crane. **2,** the framework over an oil well.

der′ring-do′ (der′ing-doo′) *n.* daring deeds; heroism.

der′rin·ger (der′in-jǝr) *n.* an antique short-barreled pistol.

der′vish (dẽr′vish) *n.* a member of a Mohammedan religious cult.

de·sal′i·nate″ (dė-sal′ǝ-nāt″) *v.t.* remove the salt from. Also, **de·sal′i·nize″** (-nīz″), **de·salt′.**

des′cant (des′kant) *n.* **1,** a melody. **2,** a variation; varied discourse. —*v.t.* (deskant′) **1,** sing. **2,** enlarge upon a topic.

de·scend′ (di-send′) *v.i.* **1,** move downward. **2,** slope downward. **3,** proceed from an original; be derived. **4,** lower oneself morally or socially. **5,** (with *upon*) come suddenly, violently, or in a hostile manner. —*v.t.* go down upon or along. —**de·scend′ent,** *adj.*

de·scend′ant (di-sen′dǝnt) *n.* one descended from an ancestor.

de·scent′ (di-sent′) *n.* **1,** act or process of descending. **2,** a downward passage or slope. **3,** ancestral lineage.

de·scribe′ (di-skrīb′) *v.t.* **1,** portray in words. **2,** trace out; outline.

de·scrip′tion (di-skrip′shǝn) *n.* **1,** the act of representing a thing by words or pictures or signs; such a representation. **2,** a category. —**de·scrip′tive,** *adj.* serving to describe.

de·scry′ (di-skrī′) *v.t.* catch sight of; detect.

des′e·crate″ (des′ǝ-krāt″) *v.t.* treat with sacrilege; profane. —**des″e·cra′tion,** *n.*

de·seg′re·gate″ *v.t. & i.* rid of segregation. —**de·seg″re·ga′tion,** *n.*

de″se·lect′ *v.t.* discharge (a trainee) from a training program.

de·sen′si·tize″ *v.t.* make insensitive or less sensitive.

des′ert (dez′ǝrt) *n.* **1,** a dry sandy wasteland. **2,** a wilderness.

de·sert′ (di-zẽrt′) *v.t. & i.* **1,** abandon; forsake. **2,** leave (the army, etc.) without leave and not intending to return. —*n.* (often *pl.*) something deserved. —**de·sert′er,** *n.* one who deserts, esp. from military service. —**de·ser′tion** (di-zẽr′shǝn) *n.*

de·serve′ (di-zẽrv′) *v.t. & i.* be entitled to receive, as reward or punishment; be worthy of. —**de·serv′ing,** *adj.* meritorious; worthy.

des′ic·cate″ (des′ǝ-kāt″) *v.i. & t.* **1,** dry up; wither. **2,** preserve (food) by drying. —**des′ic·cant** (-kǝnt) *n.* —**des″ic·ca′tion,** *n.*

de·sid″er·a′tum (di-sid″ǝ-rā′tǝm) *n.* [*pl.* **-ta** (-tǝ)] something desired or needed.

de·sign′ (di-zīn′) *v.t.* **1,** draw a plan or outline of; sketch. **2,** plan a detailed pattern. **3,** plan; contrive. **4,** intend; purpose. —*v.i.* do original artwork; make an original plan. —*n.* **1,** a preliminary drawing; a plan. **2,** the arrangement of details in a piece of art. **3,** a scheme, esp. a hostile scheme. —**de·sign′er,** *n.*

des′ig·nate″ (dez′ig-nāt″) *v.t.* **1,** mark; point out; specify. **2,** name. **3,** appoint. —**des″ig·na′tion,** *n.*

de·sign′ing *adj.* craftily planning; artful. —*n.* the art of design.

de·sire′ (di-zīr′) *v.t.* **1,** wish or long for; crave. **2,** ask for; solicit. —*n.* **1,** a wish; craving; longing. **2,** sensual feeling. **3,** a request; **4,** an object wished for. —**de·sir′a·ble,** *adj.* worth desiring. —**de·sir′ous,** *adj.* feeling desire.

de·sist′ (di-zist′) *v.i.* stop; forbear.

desk *n.* **1,** a table for writing, reading, or study. **2,** an official position or assignment, esp. in journalism. **3,** a small department, as of a foreign office. **4,** a hotel counter. —**desk′work″,** *n.* clerical work.

des′o·late (des′ǝ-lǝt) *adj.* **1,** solitary; lonely; miserable. **2,** uninhabited; abandoned. **3,** barren; ravaged. —*v.t.* (-lāt″) make desolate. —**des″o·la′tion,** *n.*

de·spair′ (di-spâr′) *v.i.* give up all hope. —*n.* utter lack of hope.

des′patch′ (di-spach′) *v.t. & n.* dispatch.

des″per·a′do (des″pǝ-rä′dō) *n.* a reckless outlaw.

des′per·ate (des′pǝr-ǝt) *adj.* **1,** driven by despair; frantic; reckless. **2,** beyond hope. **3,** extremely dangerous. —**des″per·a′tion,** *n.*

des′pi·ca·ble (des′pi-kǝ-bǝl) *adj.* to be despised; contemptible.

de·spise′ (di-spīz′) *v.t.* look down upon; scorn.

de·spite′ (di-spīt′) *prep.* notwithstanding; in spite of.

de·spoil′ (di-spoil′) *v.t.* pillage; plunder. —**de·spoil′ment,** *n.* —**de·spo″li·a′tion** (di-spō″lė-ā′shǝn) *n.*

de·spond′ent (di-spon′dǝnt) *adj.* depressed; melancholy. —**de·spond′en·cy,** *n.*

des′pot (des′pǝt) *n.* an absolute ruler; a tyrant. —**des·pot′ic** (-pot′ik) *adj.* —**pot′i·cal·ly,** *adv.* —**des′pot·ism,** *n.*

des·sert' (di-zĕrt') *n.* a sweet served as the last course of a meal.

des"ti·na'tion (des"ti-nā'shən) *n.* **1,** the predetermined end of a journey. **2,** the purpose for which anything is intended.

des'tine (des'tin) *v.t.* **1,** set apart; appoint for a special purpose. **2,** predetermine unalterably, as by divine decree.

des'ti·ny (des'tə-nē) *n.* **1,** fate; fortune. **2,** the inevitable.

des'ti·tute" (des'tə-toot") *adj.* **1,** (with *of*) wholly lacking (something needed). **2,** indigent; extremely poor. —**des"ti·tu'tion,** *n.*

de·stroy' (di-stroi') *v.t.* **1,** totally demolish; ruin; spoil. **2,** annihilate; slay. —**de·stroy'er,** *n.* **1,** one who destroys. **2,** a type of naval vessel.

des·truct' (des-trukt') *v.i.* be destroyed by a built-in device. Also, **self-"des'truct'.**

des·truc'tion (des-struk'shən) *n.* **1,** the act of destroying; a scene of ruin. **2,** a force that destroys. —**de·struc'ti·ble,** *adj.*

des·truc'tive (-iv) *adj.* **1,** destroying. **2,** causing damage; hurtful.

des'ue·tude" (des'wə-tūd") *n.* disuse.

des'ul·to·ry (des'əl-tôr-ē) *adj.* aimless; disconnected; unmethodical.

de·tach' (di-tach') *v.t.* **1,** unfasten; disunite; separate. **2,** (*Mil.*) dispatch on a distinct mission.

de·tached' (-tacht') *adj.* **1,** separate; independent. **2,** impartial in judgment. **3,** preoccupied; aloof.

de·tach'ment (di-tach'mənt) *n.* **1,** (*Mil.*) troops or ships detached for a special task. **2,** aloofness.

de·tail' (di-tāl') *v.t.* **1,** express by particulars; enumerate. **2,** (*Mil.*) appoint to a special duty. —*n.* **1,** an individual part; a particular. **2,** (*Mil.*) selection of an individual or a body of troops for a special service; those selected. —**de·tailed',** *adj.* complete in all particulars.

de·tain' (di-tān') *v.t.* **1,** hold back; prevent from proceeding; delay. **2,** (*Law*) hold in custody. —**de·ten'tion,** *n.*

de·tect' (di-tekt') *v.t.* find out; discover (what is hidden or obscure). —**de·tec'tion,** *n.* —**de·tec'tor,** *n.*

de·tec'tive (di-tek'tiv) *n.* a person whose occupation is investigating crimes.

de·tent' (di-tent') *n.* a mechanical part that stops or checks motion, as a lock, catch, or pawl.

dé·tente' (dā-tänt') *n.* a relaxation, esp. of political relations between countries.

de·ter' (di-tĕr') *v.t.* [**-terred', -ter'ring**] discourage and stop, esp. by inciting fear or doubt. —**de·ter'ment,** *n.*

de·ter'gent (di-tĕr'jənt) *n.* a cleansing substance. —*adj.* cleansing.

de·te'ri·o·rate" (di-tir'ē-ə-rāt") *v.i. & t.* grow worse; reduce in worth; impair. —**de·te"ri·o·ra'tion,** *n.*

de·ter'mi·nate (di-tĕr'mi-nət) *adj.* definite; fixed.

de·ter"mi·na'tion (di-tĕr"mi-nā'shən) *n.* **1,** act of determining. **2,** a definite decision. **3,** firmness. **4,** exact measurement.

de·ter'mine (di-tĕr'min) *v.t.* **1,** resolve; decide. **2,** find out; ascertain. **3,** bring to a conclusion; end. **4,** give direction to. **5,** restrict. **6,** decree; ordain. —*v.i.* come to a decision. —**de·ter'mi·na·tive** (-nə-tiv) *adj.* —**de·ter'mined,** *adj.* resolute; firm.

de·ter'rent (di-tĕr'ənt) *adj.* deterring. —*n.* that which deters.

de·test' (di-test') *v.t.* dislike intensely; abhor. —**de·test'a·ble,** *adj.* hateful. —**de"tes·ta'tion** (dē"tes-tā'shən) *n.*

de·throne' (dē-thrōn') *v.t.* remove from a reigning or controlling position; depose. —**de·throne'ment,** *n.*

det'o·nate" (det'ə-nāt") *v.i. & t.* explode or cause to explode; explode loudly. —**det"o·na'tion,** *n.* —**det'o·na"tor,** *n.* a substance that causes explosion, as of a bomb.

de'tour (dē'tûr) *n.* a roundabout way used when the main road is temporarily closed. —*v.i. & t.* go around.

de·tox'i·fy" (dē-tok'sə-fī") *v.t.* to remove poison or the effects of poison from. —**de·tox"i·fi·ca'tion,** *n.*

de·tract' (di-trakt') *v.t. & i.* (with *from*) disparage; reduce; take away a part, esp. from reputation. —**de·trac'tion,** *n.* —**de·trac'tive,** *adj.* —**de·trac'tor,** *n.*

de·train' (dē-trān') *v.i. & t.* get off a railroad train. —**de·train'ment,** *n.*

det'ri·ment (det'rə-mənt) *n.* an injury or loss, or that which causes it. —**det"ri·men'tal** (-men'təl) *adj.*

de·tri'tus (di-trī'təs) *n.* (*Geol.*) loose particles eroded from solid rock by water or ice.

deuce (doos) *n.* **1,** (*Cards or Dice*) two. **2,** (*Tennis*) a tied score in a game. —**the deuce!** an exclamation of annoyance. —**deuc'ed** (doo'sid) *adj.* (*Colloq.*) confounded; annoying.

de'us ex ma'chi·na (dē'əs-eks-mäk'i-nə) (*Lat.*) a god from a machine; (*fig.*) a person, event, or object unexpectedly introduced into a story to resolve the plot.

deu·te'ri·um (doo-tir'ē-əm) *n.* a heavy isotope of hydrogen.

deu'ter·on (doo'tə-ron) *n.* the deuterium atom. Also, **deu'ton** (doo'ton).

de·val′u·ate″ (dē-val′ū-āt″) *v.t.* lower the value of, esp. of currency. Also, **de·val′ue.** —**de·val″u·a′tion,** *n.*

dev′as·tate″ (dev′ə-stāt″) *v.t.* **1,** lay waste; pillage. **2,** (*Colloq.*) disappoint greatly.

de·vel′op (di-vel′əp) *v.i. & t.* **1,** advance or expand to a more complex or complete form; train; improve. **2,** unfold gradually; disclose; become apparent. **3,** process a photographic film, causing the image to become visible. **4,** elaborate; explain in full detail.

de·vel′op·ment (-mənt) *n.* **1,** act of developing or being developed. **2,** what is developed; a new or newly discovered event or fact. **3,** a group of buildings or land planned for buildings built or to be built by the same contractor. **4,** (*Music*) a section of a work in which themes previously announced are elaborated.

de′vi·ate″ (dē′vē-āt″) *v.i. & t.* turn aside from a course; digress from a line of reasoning. —*n.* a deviant; sexual pervert.

de·vice′ (di-vīs′) *n.* **1,** a contrivance; a gadget. **2,** a scheme; trick. **3,** a heraldic design, as on a coat of arms. **4,** (*pl.*) will; inclination; pleasure.

dev′il (dev′əl) *n.* **1,** (*cap.*) the supreme evil spirit; Satan. **2,** any evil spirit; a demon. **3,** a cruel, fiendish person. **4,** a reckless person, as a *daredevil.* **5,** an expletive: *the devil!* **6,** a printer's errand boy. —*v.t.* **1,** (*Colloq.*) bother; torment. **2,** in cooking, season highly. —**dev′il·ish,** *adj.* **1,** fiendish. **2,** roguish. —**dev′il·ment, dev′il·try** (-trē) *n.* mischief; roguishness. —**devil's advocate,** one who takes a position for the sake of argument, without necessarily accepting it. —**devil's food,** a rich chocolate cake.

dev′il·fish″ *n.* a large marine animal, esp. an octopus.

dev′il·ish *adj.* **1,** like a devil. **2,** (*Colloq.*) excessive. —*adv.* (*Colloq.*) extremely.

devil-may-care *adj.* reckless; casual.

de′vi·ous (dē′vē-əs) *adj.* out of the direct or common way; circuitous. —**de′vi·ous·ness,** *n.*

de·vise′ (di-vīz′) *v.t. & i.* **1,** think out; concoct; scheme. **2,** transmit (property) by will; bequeath. —*n.* a will; the act of transmitting by will. —**di·vis′er, di·vi′sor,** *n.* —**de·vi·see″** (-zē″) *n.*

de·vi·tal·ize″ (dē-vī′tə-līz″) *v.t.* deprive of vitality; weaken in force or effect. —**de·vi″tal·i·za′tion,** *n.*

de·void′ (di-void′) *adj.* (with *of*) empty; destitute or lacking.

de·volve′ (di-volv′) *v.t. & i.* transmit or delegate to another; (with *upon*) pass to. —**dev″o·lu′tion** (dev″ə-loo′shən) *n.*

de·vote′ (di-vōt′) *v.t.* **1,** give or apply, as time to a hobby. **2,** consecrate or dedicate. —**de·vot′ed,** *adj.* ardently attached; dedicated.

dev′o·tee′ (dev″ə-tē′) *n.* one ardently devoted, as to religion; a zealot.

de·vo′tion (di-vō′shən) *n.* **1,** act of devoting; dedication; consecration. **2,** piety; godliness. **3,** affection; love; zeal. **4,** (*pl.*) prayers; religious worship.

de·vour′ (di-vowr′) *v.t.* **1,** swallow up; eat ravenously. **2,** consume; destroy. **3,** absorb; take in, as a book.

de·vout′ (di-vowt′) *adj.* devoted to religion or religious worship. —**de·vout′ness,** *n.*

dew (dū) *n.* small drops of moisture condensed from the atmosphere at night. —**dew′y,** *adj.* —**dew point,** the temperature at which dew forms.

dew′ber″ry (dū′ber′ē) *n.* a trailing plant or its fruit, similar to a blackberry.

dew′claw″ *n.* a useless inner claw in the foot of some dogs.

dew-′drop″ *n.* a globule of dew.

dew′lap″ (doo′lap″) *n.* the pendulous skin under the throat of some animals.

dew′y (dū′ē) *adj.* **1,** moist with or like dew. **2,** fresh; young. —**dew′i·ness,** *n.*

Dex′e·drine″ (dek′sə-drēn″) *n.* (*T.N.*) an amphetamine used as a stimulant.

dex·ter′i·ty (deks-ter′ə-tē) *n.* manual or mental adroitness; skill. —**dex′ter·ous** (deks′tər-əs) *adj.*

dex′trin (dek′strin) *n.* a gummy product of starch, used as mucilage, etc.

dex′tro- (dek′strō) *pref.* right; turning to the right.

dex′trose (deks′trōs) *n.* a form of sugar, obtained commercially from starch.

dex′trous (deks′trəs) *adj.* dexterous.

dhole (dōl) *n.* a wild Asiatic dog.

dhow (dow) *n.* a light Arab sailing vessel.

di- (dī; di) *pref.* two; twofold; double.

di′a·be′tes (dī″ə-bē′tis) *n.* a disease commonly due to the inability of the body to use sugar. —**di″a·bet′ic** (-bet′ik) *adj. & n.*

di″a·bol′ic (dī″ə-bol′ik) *adj.* devilish; infernal. Also, **di″a·bol′i·cal.**

di·ac′o·nal (dī-ak′ə-nəl) *adj.* of or pert. to a deacon.

di″a·crit′i·cal (dī″ə-krit′ə-kəl) *adj.* serving to distinguish. —**diacritical mark,** also, **di″a·crit′ic,** a mark that indicates the exact pronunciation of a letter; accent mark.

di′a·dem″ (dī′ə-dem″) *n.* **1,** a crown. **2,** a jeweled headband.

di″ag·nose″ (dī″əg-nōs″) *v.t.* ascertain; analyze; determine the nature of, esp. of a disease.

di''ag·no'sis (dī''əg-nō'sis) *n.* [*pl.* **-ses** (-sēz)] analysis of present condition, esp. of a disease. —**di''ag·nos'tic** (-nos'tik) *adj.* —**di''·ag·nos'ti·cal·ly,** *adv.*

di''ag·nos·ti'cian (dī''əg-nos-tish'ən) *n.* a doctor skilled in making diagnoses.

di·ag'o·nal (dī-ag'ə-nəl) *adj.* **1,** extending, as a line, from one angle to another not adjacent, within a polygon. **2,** oblique; slanting; marked by oblique lines. —*n.* a diagonal line or direction.

di'a·gram (dī'ə-gram) *n.* a chart or plan, esp. a drawing made for demonstrating or graphic analysis. —*v.t.* chart; plan in detail. —**di'a·gram·mat'ic** (-grə-mat'ik) *adj.* —**di'a·gram·mat'i·cal·ly,** *adv.*

di'al (dī'əl) *n.* **1,** the face on which time is indicated, as on a clock or *sundial.* **2,** any face on which a pointer indicates something, as pressure. **3,** the round index disk on a telephone, used to signal for connections. —*v.t.* measure or signal for, with a dial. —**dial tone,** a buzzing signal indicating that a telephone's dial may be used.

di'a·lect (dī'ə-lekt) *n.* **1,** the special idiom of a locality or class. **2,** jargon. —**di'a·lec'tal,** *adj.*

di''a·lec'tic (dī''ə-lek'tik) *adj.* **1,** relating to the art of reasoning or discussion. **2,** pert. to dialect. —*n.* **1,** the art of debating, or of logical discussion. **2,** (*pl.*) logic. —**di''·a·lec'ti·cal·ly,** *adv.* —**di''a·lec·ti'cian,** *n.*

di'a·logue (dī'ə-lâg) *n.* **1,** conversation between two or more persons. **2,** speeches spoken in a play. Also, **di'a·log.**

di·al'y·sis (dī-al'ə-sis) *n.* [*pl.* **-ses** (-sēz)] the separation of substances by passing them through a membrane. —**di''a·lyt'ic** (dī''ə-lit'ik) *adj.*

di·am'e·ter (dī-am'ə-tər) *n.* a line dividing a circle into halves; its length.

di''a·met'ri·cal (dī''ə-met'ri-kəl) *adj.* **1,** pert. to a diameter. **2,** absolute; complete. Also, **di''a·met'ric.**

dia'mond (dī'mənd) *n.* **1,** a form of pure carbon, extremely hard and brilliant; a precious stone. **2,** a quadrilateral, esp. a rhombus, viewed with an angle uppermost (◇). **3,** a playing card so marked. **4,** a baseball field, esp. the infield.

dia'mond·back *n.* **1,** a kind of rattlesnake. **2,** a kind of terrapin.

di''a·net'ics (dī''ə-net'iks) *n. sing.* a proposed therapy for mental disorders, esp. neuroses.

di''a·pa'son (dī''ə-pā'zən) *n.* **1,** the entire range of a voice or an instrument. **2,** correct tune or pitch.

di'a·per (dī'ə-pər) *n.* **1,** an infant's breech cloth. **2,** a white unbleached linen or cotton fabric with a woven pattern.

di·aph'a·nous (dī-af'ə-nəs) *adj.* transparent or translucent.

di'a·phragm (dī'ə-fram) *n.* **1,** the muscular partition that separates the thorax from the abdomen; the midriff. **2,** any thin piece of metal that serves as a partition, as the vibrating disk of a telephone. **3,** a contraceptive device; pessary. —**di'a·phrag·mat'ic** (-frag-mat'ik) *adj.* —**di'a·phrag·mat'i·cal·ly,** *adv.*

di''ar·rhe'a (dī''ə-rē'ə) *n.* abnormally frequent evacuation of the bowels. —**di''ar·rhet'ic** (-ret'ik) *adj.*

di'a·ry (dī'ə-rē) *n.* a daily record; journal. —**di'a·rist,** *n.*

di·as'po·ra (dī-as'pə-rə) *n.* **1,** (often *cap.*) the Jews living among the Gentiles after the Babylonian captivity. **2,** the dispersion of a religious or political sect after conquest of its homeland.

di·as'to·le (dī-as'tə-lē) *n.* the rhythmical dilation of the heart.

di'a·ther''my (dī'ə-thĕr''mē) *n.* (*Pathol.*) treatment with radiant heat. —**di'a·ther''·mic,** *adj.*

di'a·tom (dī'ə-təm) *n.* any of a large family of microscopic, one-celled sea and freshwater plants.

di''a·ton'ic (dī''ə-ton'ik) *adj.* (*Music*) pert. to a normal scale—major or minor—of eight tones to the octave. —**di''a·ton'i·cal·ly,** *adv.*

di'a·tribe'' (dī'ə-trīb) *n.* a bitter and abusive denunciation.

di·az'e·pam (dī-az'ə-pam) *n.* a tranquilizer and muscle-relaxing drug.

dib'ble (dib'əl) *n.* a gardening tool for making holes in the ground.

dice (dīs) *n.* (*pl.* of **die**) small cubes, esp. those having each face stamped with a different number of spots, used in games and in gambling. —*v.t.* cut into small cubes, as food. —*v.i.* play at dice.

di'cey (dī'sē) *adj.* (*Slang*) dangerous; risky.

di·chot'o·my (dī-kot'ə-mē) *n.* a subdivision into two parts.

dick (dik) *n.* (*Slang*) a detective.

dic'kens (dik'ənz) *interj.* devil; deuce.

dick'er (dik'ər) *v.i.* bargain; barter; haggle. —*n.* a haggling deal.

dick'ey (dik'ē) *n.* **1,** a child's bib. **2,** a separate or false shirt front. **3,** a woman's garment covering only the chest and worn under a suit coat or a bodice. **4,** a seat at the back of a vehicle. **5,** a small bird.

Dick test a test to determine susceptibility to scarlet fever.

Dic'ta·phone'' (dik'tə-fōn) *n.* a recording machine used for dictating: a trade name.

dic'tate (dik'tāt) *v.t. & i.* **1,** express orally for another to write down. **2,** prescribe with authority; command. —n. **1,** an order; a command. **2,** a guiding principle; a maxim. —**dic·ta'tion,** n.

dic'ta·tor (dik'tā-tər) n. **1,** a person exercising unlimited powers of government; an absolute ruler. **2,** one who dictates. —**dic"ta·to'ri·al** (dik"tə-tôr'ē-əl) adj. —**dic'ta·tor·ship,** n.

dic'tion (dik'shən) n. **1,** manner of expression or choice of words in speaking or writing. **2,** enunciation.

dic'tion·ar·y (dik'shə-ner-ē) n. a book defining and listing in alphabetical order the principal words of a language, or a particular class of words.

Dic'to·graph" (dik'tə-graf") n. (T.N.) a recording instrument used chiefly for obtaining evidence.

dic'tum (dik'təm) n. [pl. **-ta** (-tə)] a positive or authoritative statement.

did v. pret. of do.

di·dac'tic (dī-dak'tik) adj. instructive; expository. —**di·dac'ti·cal·ly,** adv.

did'dle (did'əl) v.i. & t. (Colloq.) **1,** waste time; dawdle. **2,** swindle.

di'do (dī'dō) n. (Colloq.) a prank; a caper.

di·dym'i·um (dī-dim'ē-əm) n. a mixture of neodymium and praesodymium, once thought to be a single element.

die (dī) v.i. [**died, dy'ing**] **1,** cease to live; expire. **2,** come to an end. **3,** (with away or out) fade away. **4,** (with for) (Colloq.) desire keenly. —n. **1,** an engraved stamp used for impressing a design. **2,** any of various mechanical devices, as a tool for cutting the threads of screws. **3,** sing. of dice.

die'hard" n. & adj. one who resists to the end; conservative.

diel'drin (dēl'drən) n. an insecticide.

di"e·lec'tric (dī"ə-lek'trik) n. a nonconducting substance. —adj. nonconducting.

di·er'e·sis (dī-er'ə-sis) n. [pl. **-ses** (-sēz)] **1,** the separate pronunciation of two adjacent vowels. **2,** a mark (¨) indicating such pronunciation.

die'sel (dē'zel) n. an internal-combustion engine employing the heat of compression to ignite fuel oil.

di'et (dī'ət) n. **1,** food and drink regularly consumed. **2,** a prescribed course of food. **3,** regimen. **4,** a formal public assembly. —v.i. eat according to a diet. —**di'e·tar·y** (-ter-ē) adj.

di"e·tet'ics (dī"ə-tet'iks) n. the science of regulating the diet.

di"e·ti'tian (dī"ə-tish'ən) n. one trained to plan meals.

dif'fer (dif'ər) v.i. **1,** be unlike or distinct (with from). **2,** (with with) disagree, in opinion.

dif'fer·ence (dif'ər-əns) n. **1,** a dissimilarity; a distinction. **2,** a controversy; a dispute. **3,** discrimination. **4,** (Math.) the remainder after a number has been subtracted.

dif'fer·ent (dif'ər-ənt) adj. unlike; not the same.

dif"fer·en'tial (dif"ə-ren'shəl) n. **1,** (Math.) an infinitesimal difference between two values of a variable quantity. **2,** in automobiles, a gear arrangement that allows the outer driving wheel to turn faster on a curve. —adj. making, showing, or having a difference.

dif"fer·en'ti·ate" (dif"ə-ren'shē-āt") v.t. & i. make, constitute, or observe a difference (between). —**dif"fer·en'ti·a'tion,** n.

dif'fi·cult" (dif'ə-kult") adj. **1,** presenting an obstacle or perplexing problem; not easy; hard to do or understand; arduous. **2,** hard to please or persuade; not compliant; troublesome.

dif'fi·cul·ty (dif'ə-kul-tē) n. **1,** that which is hard to understand or to overcome. **2,** a troublesome or embarrassing situation; (pl.) want of money. **3,** an objection; reluctance.

dif'fi·dence (dif'ə-dəns) n. want of self-confidence; shyness. —**dif'fi·dent,** adj.

dif·frac'tion (di-frak'shən) n. **1,** in optics, the modification of light or deflection of its rays. **2,** a modification of sound waves passing by a large building, etc. —**dif·fract',** v. —**dif·frac'tive,** adj.

dif·fuse' (di-fūz') v.t. & i. pour out and spread; send out in all directions; scatter. —adj. (di-fūs') **1,** widely spread. **2,** verbose. —**dif·fu'sion** (-zhən) n. —**dif·fu'sive** (-siv) adj.

dig v.t. & i. (**dug, dig'ging**) **1,** turn up, or scoop out, as earth, with a trowel or spade; excavate. **2,** work hard; find out by effort or research. **3,** (with in) make a hole or trench for military protection. **4,** (with up) unearth; bring to light. **5,** (Slang) enjoy; appreciate. —n. **1,** a thrust; a poke. **2,** (Colloq.) a sarcastic remark. —**dig'ger,** n.

di·gest' (di-jest') v.t. **1,** convert food in the body for assimilation. **2,** assimilate mentally; think over. —n. (dī'jest) a condensed collection or summary. —**di·gest'i·ble,** adj.

di·ges'tion (di-jes'chən) n. act or process of assimilating food. —**di·ges'tive,** adj.

dig'ger (dig'ər) n. **1,** that which digs. **2,** the stinger of an insect.

dig'gings (dig'ingz) n. **1,** an excavation or mine. **2,** (Colloq.) living quarters.

dig'it (dij'it) n. **1,** a finger or toe; **2,** any number under ten. —**dig'i·tal** (-i-təl) adj. —**digital computer,** a computer operating directly with digits.

dig"i·tal'is (dij"ə-tal'is) n. **1,** a genus of

plants, esp. the foxglove. **2,** a drug obtained from its leaves used as a heart stimulant.

dig′ni·fy″ (dig′nə-fī″) v.t. **1,** confer honor upon; ennoble. **2,** give an undeservedly important name to. **—dig′ni·fied,** adj. marked by dignity; noble; stately.

dig′ni·tar·y (dig′ni-ter-ē) n. one who holds an exalted rank or office.

dig′ni·ty (dig′nə-tē) n. **1,** worthiness; high rank. **2,** self-respecting or noble mien or deportment; importance. **3,** a high office or title.

di′graph (dī′graf) n. two letters representing a single sound, as th in the.

di·gress′ (di-gres′) v.i. turn away from the main subject; deviate; wander. **—di·gres′sion** (-gresh′ən) n. **—di·gres′sive,** adj.

di·he′dral (dī-hē′drəl) adj. **1,** having two plane faces, as a crystal. **2,** forming an angle, as between the walls of a room.

dike (dīk) n. **1,** an embankment built to prevent flooding by a river or the ocean. **2,** a channel for water.

Di·lan′tin (dī-lan′tin) n. (T.N.) a drug used in treating epilepsy.

di·lap′i·date″ (di-lap′ə-dāt″) v.t. & i. ruin, or fall into partial or total ruin. **—di·lap′i·dat″ed,** adj. **—di·lap″i·da′tion,** n.

di·late′ (dī-lāt′) v.t. & i. **1,** expand; make larger; distend. **2,** expatiate (upon). **—di·la′tion, dil″a·ta′tion** (dil″ə-tā′shən), n. **—di·la′tor,** n.

dil′a·to·ry (dil′ə-tôr-ē) adj. given to delay; procrastinating.

dil′do (dil′dō) n. (Vulgar) an artificial substitute for an erect penis.

di·lem′ma (di-lem′ə) n. a choice between alternatives equally undesirable.

dil″et·tante′ (dil″ə-tänt′) n. one who pursues art or literature for amusement; a dabbler.

dil′i·gence (dil′ə-jəns) n. **1,** constant and persistent attention to one's work; industry. **2,** a public stagecoach. **—dil′i·gent,** adj.

dill (dil) n. an aromatic herb.

dil′ly (dil′ē) n. (Colloq.) something unusually good or striking.

dil′ly·dal″ly (dil′ē-dal″ē) v.i. (Colloq.) loiter; waste time; vacillate.

dil′u·ent (dil′ū-ənt) n. a fluid used to dilute another.

di·lute′ (di-loot′) v.t. weaken by an admixture of water or other liquid; reduce in strength. **—di·lu′tion,** n.

di·lu′vi·al (di-loo′vē-əl) adj. **1,** pert. to a flood or deluge. **2,** pert. to any debris deposited by a flood.

dim adj. [dim′mer, -mest] **1,** not bright

or clear; not well lighted. **2,** obscure; vague; not understood. **3,** not comprehending clearly. —v.i. & t. [dimmed, dim′ming] make dim or dimmer. **—dim′ness,** n.

dime (dīm) n. a U. S. silver coin worth ten cents. **—dime novel,** a paperbound novel of adventure or romance. **—dime store,** a five-and-ten-cent store.

di·men′sion (di-men′shən) n. measure in one direction; length, breadth, or thickness. **—di·men′sion·al,** adj.

di·min′ish v.t. & i. make less or smaller by any means; lessen. **—dim″i·nu′tion** (dim″i-nū′shən) n.

di·min″u·en′do (di-min″yû-en′dō) n. (Music) a gradual lessening of the volume of sound.

di·min′u·tive (di-min′ū-tiv) adj. very small; tiny. —n. **1,** a small thing or person. **2,** a word form denoting smallness, affection, etc.

dim′i·ty (dim′ə-tē) n. a thin cotton fabric with woven corded stripes.

dim′mer (dim′ər) n. **1,** a device that reduces the intensity of a light. **2,** (pl.) dim lights. —adj. more dim.

dim-′out″ n. a partial reduction in lighting in a city, to conserve electricity or escape attacking aircraft.

dim′ple (dim′pəl) n. **1,** a natural hollow in some soft part of the body, as in the cheek. **2,** a dent. —v.i. show a dimple, as by smiling.

dim′wit″ n. (Slang) a dull-witted or stupid person.

din n. a continued clattering or ringing noise; a clamor.

di·nar′ (dē-när′) n. the monetary unit of Yugoslavia, Iraq, Algeria, and other countries.

dine (dīn) v.i. eat the chief meal of the day. —v.t. give a dinner to or for.

din′er (dī′nər) n. **1,** one taking dinner. **2,** a railroad car, or similar structure, where meals are served.

di·nette′ (dī-net′) n. a small room or alcove in which to eat.

ding n. [also, **ding-′dong″**] the sound of a bell.

ding′a-ling′ (ding′ə-ling′) n. (Slang) a stupid person.

ding′bat″ n. an eccentric or silly person.

din′ghy (ding′ē) n. a small boat, usually for rowing.

din′gle (ding′gəl) n. a secluded valley.

din′go (ding′gō) n. a wild dog of Australia.

ding′us (ding′əs) n. (Slang) a gadget.

din′gy (din′jē) adj. dirty; not fresh; tarnished. **—din′gi·ness,** n.

dink'y (dink'ē) *adj.* small; tiny. —*n.* [also **dink'ey**] a little locomotive.

din'ner (din'ər) *n.* **1,** the principal meal. **2,** an entertainment; banquet. —**dinner jacket,** a man's semiformal jacket; tuxedo.

di'no·saur'' (dī'nə-sôr'') *n.* an extinct gigantic reptile. —**di''no·sau'ri·an** (-ē-ən) *adj.*

dint *n.* **1,** a dent. **2,** a power; force.

di'o·cese'' (dī'ə-sēs'') *n.* the district under the care of a bishop. —**di·oc'e·san** (dī-os'i-sən) *adj.*

di'ode (dī'ōd) *n.* in electronics, a vacuum tube or semiconductor device used as a rectifier.

di''o·ram'a (dī''ə-ram'ə) *n.* a continuous painting exhibited in a dark room with spectacular lighting effects. —**di''o·ram'ic,** *adj.*

di·ox'ide (dī-ok'sīd) *n.* (*Chem.*) an oxide having two oxygen atoms per molecule.

dip *v.t.* [**dipped, dip'ping**] **1,** immerse temporarily in a liquid. **2,** lower and raise, as a bird's wings. **3,** scoop up. —*v.i.* **1,** plunge into temporarily. **2,** (with *into*) investigate; be interested. **3,** incline downward. **4,** sink. —*n.* **1,** the act or result of dipping; a short swim. **2,** a sloping downward. **3,** a hollow; depression. **4,** a liquid to dip something in, as for tinting or disinfection. **5,** a pickpocket. **6,** (*Slang*) an ineffectual person.

diph·the'ri·a (dif-thir'ē-ə) *n.* an infectious disease in which a membrane forms over the air passage.

diph'thong (dif'thâng) *n.* two adjacent vowels pronounced in one syllable.

di·plo'ma (di-plō'mə) *n.* a certificate given by a school or college showing graduation. —**dip'lo·mate''** (dip'lə-māt'') *n.* —**diploma mill,** (*Slang*) an educational institution granting diplomas fraudulently or without proper standards.

di·plo'ma·cy (di-plō'mə-sē) *n.* **1,** the art of negotiation between nations. **2,** tact.

dip'lo·mat'' (dip'lə-mat'') *n.* **1,** an official representative of a country. **2,** one skilled in diplomacy. Also, **di·plo'ma·tist** (di-plō'-mə-tist).

dip''lo·mat'ic (-ik) *adj.* **1,** pert. to the work of a diplomat. **2,** tactful. —**dip''lo·mat'i·cal·ly,** *adv.*

di'pole'' (dī'pōl'') *n.* a pair of equal and opposite electric charges or magnetic poles. —**di·po'lar** (dī-pō'lər) *adj.*

dip'per (dip'ər) *n.* **1,** a utensil for ladling or scooping out something. **2,** (*cap.*) either of two constellations: *Big Dipper; Little Dipper.*

dip'py (dip'ē) *adj.* (*Slang*) **1,** crazy or eccentric. **2,** foolish.

dip''so·ma'ni·a (dip''sə-mā'nē-ə) *n.* an irresistible craving for intoxicants. —**dip''-so·ma'ni·ac,** *n.*

dip'stick'' *n.* a measuring stick used for checking fluid levels.

dip'tych (dip'tik) *n.* **1,** an ancient two-leaved writing tablet. **2,** a pair of pictures or carvings hinged together.

dire (dīr) *adj.* dreadful; fearful; disastrous. —**dire'ful,** *adj.* —**dire'ness,** *n.*

di·rect' (di-rekt') *v.t.* **1,** aim or point toward an object. **2,** point out a course to. **3,** regulate; guide or lead. **4,** order; command. **5,** address (a letter); address (words) to a person. **6,** conduct an orchestra or choir. **7,** control the interpretation and dramatic performance of (a play, opera, etc.). —*adj.* **1,** straightforward; open; sincere. **2,** personal; firsthand. —**di·rect'ness,** *n.* —**direct current,** electric current that flows always in the same direction.

di·rec'tion (di-rek'shən) *n.* **1,** relative position, as along a line or to a place. **2,** act of directing; administration; management. **3,** the act of aiming or pointing out a course. **4,** an order; a regulation; instruction. —**di·rec'tion·al,** *adj.*

di·rec'tive (di-rek'tiv) *n.* an instruction; a statement of policy.

di·rect'ly (-lē) *adv.* **1,** in a direct line, course, or manner. **2,** immediately. **3,** expressly; clearly; precisely.

di·rec'tor (di-rek'tər) *n.* one who directs, esp. a company or theatrical production. —**di·rec'to·rate** (-ət) *n.* a body of directors. —**di·rec''tor'i·al** (-tôr'ē-əl) *adj.* —**di·rec'tor·ship,** *n.* —**di·rec'tress** (-trəs) *n.fem.*

di·rec'to·ry (di-rek'tə-rē) *n.* **1,** a book listing names and addresses. **2,** (*cap.*) a French government, 1795-99, during the French Revolution.

dirge (dērj) *n.* music or poetry expressing grief; a funeral hymn.

dir'i·gi·ble (dir'i-jə-bəl) *n.* a large cigar-shaped rigid airship, capable of being steered. —*adj.* capable of being directed or steered.

dirk (dērk) *n.* a dagger.

dirn'dl (dērn'dəl) *n.* a colorful peasant dress.

dirt (dērt) *n.* **1,** any filthy substance, as dust, mud, etc. **2,** earth or soil. **3,** anything mean or worthless; gossip. —*adj.* granular; unpaved, as a road. —**do one dirt,** (*Colloq.*) treat one abusively. —**eat dirt,** be humiliated.

dirt-'cheap' *adj. & adv.* very cheap or cheaply.

dirt'y (dēr'tē) *adj.* **1,** soiling. **2,** unclean; sullied. **3,** base; low; contemptible. **4,** rainy (of the weather). **5,** obscene; pornographic. —*v.t.* sully. —**dirt'i·ness,** *n.*

dis- *pref.* **1**, separate; not joined. **2**, not; negation in an active sense (thus: something *unproved* may never have been tried, something *disproved* has been tried and found false). [In addition to words defined in the text, the following words may be defined by assuming active lack or negation of the root word, which see in each case.]

dis″ac·cord′	dis·fa′vor
dis″af·firm′	dis·har′mo·ny
dis″al·low′	dis·hon′est
dis″ap·pro·ba′ tion	dis·in″cli·na′tion
	dis″in·fec′tion
dis″ar·range′	dis″in·gen′u·ous
dis″as·sem′ble	dis·join′
dis″as·so′ci·ate′	dis·junc′tion
dis″be·lief′	dis·loy′al
dis″be·lieve′	dis″o·blige′
dis·bur′den	dis·pir′it
dis″con·nect′	dis″pro·por′tion
dis″con·tin′u·ance	dis·rel′ish
dis·coun′te·nance	dis″re·mem′ber
dis″em·bark′	dis′re·spect′
dis″em·bar′rass	dis·robe′
dis″em·bod′y	dis·rup′ture
dis″em·ploy′	dis·ser′vice
dis″en·chant′	dis·sim′i·lar
dis″en·cum′ber	dis″si·mil′i·tude
dis″en·gage′	dis·sym′me·try
dis″en·tan′gle	dis·trust′
dis″en·twine′	dis·un′ion
dis″es·tab′lish	dis″u·nite′
dis″es·teem′	dis·use′

dis·a′ble (dis-ā′bəl) *v.t.* deprive of physical, mental, or legal power; incapacitate. —**dis″a·bil′i·ty,** *n.*

dis″a·buse′ (dis″ə-būz′) *v.t.* set right; undeceive.

dis″ad·van′tage (dis″əd-văn′tij) *n.* **1**, that which prevents success or makes it difficult. **2**, a loss to profit, reputation, etc.; a drawback. —**dis″ad·van′taged,** *adj.* deprived of the basic requirements for normal development; underprivileged. —**dis·ad″van·ta′geous,** *adj.*

dis″af·fect′ *v.t.* make unfriendly or discontented. —**dis″af·fec′tion,** *n.* ill will.

dis″a·gree′ *v.i.* **1**, (with *with*) differ. **2**, quarrel. **3**, be incompatible or unsuitable. —**dis″a·gree′a·ble,** *adj.* bad-tempered; distasteful.

dis″a·gree′ment *n.* **1**, act of disagreeing. **2**, a quarrel; controversy. **3**, discrepancy; difference.

dis″ap·pear′ *v.i.* pass out of sight or existence; vanish. —**dis″ap·pear′ance,** *n.*

dis″ap·point′ (dis″ə-point′) *v.t. & i.* fail

to fulfill the expectations of (someone). —**dis″ap·point′ment,** *n.*

dis″ap·prove′ *v.t. & i.* **1**, condemn. **2**, decline to sanction. —*v.i.* feel or express disfavor (with *of*). —**dis″ap·prov′al,** *n.*

dis·arm′ (dis-ärm′) *v.t.* **1**, deprive of weapons. **2**, deprive of resentment; make friendly. —*v.i.* reduce or curtail military power. —**dis·ar′ma·ment,** *n.* —**dis·arm′ing,** *adj.* inducing friendliness.

dis″ar·ray′ (dis″ə-rā′) *v.t.* **1.** divest; disrobe. **2**, throw into disorder; rout. —*n.* **1**, confusion. **2**, disorderly dress.

dis·as′ter (di-zas′tər) *n.* a great misfortune; a catastrophe. —**dis·as′trous,** *adj.*

dis″a·vow′ *v.t.* disown; deny; repudiate. —**dis″a·vow′al,** *n.*

dis·band′ *v.i. & t.* dissolve, as a band or group; dismiss, as troops from an army. —**dis·band′ment,** *n.*

dis·bar′ (dis-bär′) *v.t.* [**-barred′, -bar′-ring**] withdraw the right (of a lawyer) to practice law. —**dis·bar′ment,** *n.*

dis·burse′ (dis-bėrs′) *v.t.* pay out; expend. —**dis·burse′ment,** *n.*

disc (disk) *n.* disk.

dis·card′ (dis-kärd′) *v.t.* cast off; reject; throw away as useless. —*n.* (dis′kärd″) **1**, something cast off. **2**, a place of disposal.

dis·cern′ (di-zėrn′) *v.t. & i.* distinguish by the eye or the intellect; perceive; discriminate. —**dis·cern′i·ble,** *adj.* —**dis·cern′ing,** *adj.* discriminating; keen. —**dis·cern′ment,** *n.*

dis·charge′ (dis-chärj′) *n.* **1**, the act of unloading. **2**, the act of firing a missile or a weapon. **3**, removal by taking away, settlement, or payment. **4**, a flowing out; emission. **5**, freeing, as of a prisoner; release, as of a soldier (also, a certificate of such release); dismissal, as of an employee. **6**, that which is emitted. **7**, performance; execution. —*v.t.* **1**, unload. **2**, emit (as water). **3**, set free; dismiss; absolve. **4**, fulfill (a duty); execute. **5**, fire, as a gun.

dis·ci′ple (di-sī′pəl) *n.* one who adheres to the doctrines of another; a follower, esp. (often *cap.*) an Apostle.

dis″ci·pli·nar′i·an (dis″ə-pli-nâr′ē-ən) *n.* an exacting master.

dis′ci·pli·nar″y (dis′ə-pli-ner″ē) *adj.* pert. to or promoting discipline.

dis′ci·pline (dis′ə-plin) *n.* **1**, mental and moral training. **2**, obedience to rules. **3**, correction; chastisement. **4**, a set of regulations; regimen. **5**, a course of study; a science or art. —*v.t.* **1**, train. **2**, chastise.

dis·claim′ (dis-klām′) *v.t.* renounce; deny; disown. —**dis·claim′er,** *n.* a statement of disavowal.

---

tub, cūte, pûll; labəl; oil, owl, go, chip, she, thin, *th*en, sing, ink; *see p. 6*

dis·close' (dis-klōz') *v.t.* bring to light; uncover; make known. **—dis·clo'sure** (-klō'-shər) *n.*

dis'co (dis'kō) *n. & adj.* (*Colloq.*) (pert. to) a discotheque or its music.

dis·col'or (dis-kul'ər) *v.t. & i.* 1, alter the natural hue of. 2, stain. **—dis·col"or·a'tion**, *n.*

dis"com·bob'u·late (dis"kəm-bob'ū-lāt) *v.t.* confuse; disconcert.

dis·com'fit (dis-kum'fit) *v.t.* embarrass; frustrate. **—dis·com'fi·ture** (-fi-chər) *n.*

dis·com'fort *n.* uneasiness; pain.

dis"com·mode' (dis"kə-mōd') *v.t.* put to inconvenience; trouble.

dis"com·pose' (dis"kum-pōz') *v.t.* unsettle; agitate; disturb. **—dis"com·po'sure** (-pō'zhər) *n.* embarrassment.

dis"con·cert' (dis"kən-sērt') *v.t.* 1, perturb; confuse. 2, throw into disorder.

dis·con'so·late (dis-kon'sə-lət) *adj.* without consolation; sorrowful.

dis·con·tent' *n.* want of satisfaction; uneasiness of mind. *—v.t.* make unhappy. **—dis"con·tent'ed**, *adj.* not contented; restive; unhappy. **—dis"con·tent'ment**, *n.*

dis"con·tin'u·ance *n.* lack of continued connection.

dis"con·tin'ue *v.t.* cease; break off; interrupt. *—v.i.* come to a stop or end. **—dis"con·tin"u·a'tion**, *n.* **dis"con·tin'u·ous**, *adj.*

dis·con"ti·nu'i·ty *n.* a gap; lack of cohesion.

dis'cord (dis'kôrd) *n.* 1, want of agreement; contention; strife. 2, (*Music*) want of harmony; a dissonance. 3, any confused noise. **—dis·cord'ance, dis·cord'an·cy**, *n.* **—dis·cord'ant**, *adj.*

dis'co·theque" (dis'kə-tek") *n.* a nightclub where dance music is provided, usu. by recorded music.

dis'count (dis'kownt) *v.t.* 1, deduct from the settlement of, as of a bill or charge account. 2, disregard; make allowance for exaggeration. 3, lessen effectiveness of by anticipating the outcome. 4, (*Com.*) buy or sell for less than face value, as a promissory note before maturity. *—n.* a deduction. **—discount rate**, rate of interest charged by the Federal Reserve Bank on borrowed money.

dis·cour'age (dis-kēr'ij) *v.t.* 1, cause to lose spirit or hope. 2, obstruct by opposition. 3, dissuade (with *from*). **—dis·cour'age·ment**, *n.*

dis'course (dis'kôrs) *n.* 1, expression of ideas by words; a conversation. 2, a formal discussion or written treatment of a subject. *—v.i.* (dis-kôrs') converse; talk.

dis·cour'te·ous *adj.* uncivil; rude.

dis·cour'te·sy *n.* 1, incivility; ill manners; rudeness. 2, an impolite act.

dis·cov'er (dis-kuv'ər) *v.t.* gain first sight or knowledge of something hitherto unknown. **—dis·cov'er·er**, *n.*

dis·cov'er·y (-ē) *n.* 1, act of discovering. 2, something discovered.

dis·cred'it *v.t.* 1, not to believe. 2, injure the reputation of; destroy confidence in. *—n.* 1, a loss of reputation or honor. 2, doubt; disbelief. **—dis·cred'it·a·ble**, *adj.* blameworthy.

dis·creet' (dis-krēt') *adj.* careful of appearances; tactful. **—dis·creet'ness**, *n.*

dis·crep'an·cy (dis-krep'ən-sē) *n.* an unexplained difference; inconsistency. **—dis·crep'ant**, *adj.*

dis·crete' (dis-krēt') *adj.* 1, separate. 2, discontinuous. **—dis·crete'ness**, *n.*

dis·cre'tion (dis-kresh'ən) *n.* 1, act or state of being discreet. 2, judgment; power to decide. **—dis·cre'tion·a·ry** (-er-ē) *adj.*

dis·crim'i·nate" (dis-krim'ə-nāt") *v.i. & t.* 1, judge (respective merits). 2, treat differently on the basis of race, class, sex, etc. **—dis·crim'i·nat"ing**, *adj.* showing good taste. **—dis·crim"i·na'tion**, *n.* **—dis·crim'·in·a·to"ry**, *adj.*

dis·cur'sive (dis-kēr'siv) *adj.* rambling from topic to topic; digressive. **—dis·cur'sive·ness**, *n.*

dis'cus (dis'kəs) *n.* a heavy disk used in weight-throwing contests.

dis·cuss' (dis-kus') *v.t.* 1, talk about; debate. 2, speak or write about; explain. **—dis·cus'sant**, *n.* **—dis·cus'sion** (dis-kush'ən) *n.*

dis·dain' (dis-dān') *v.t. & i.* 1, look down upon; scorn; despise. 2, not deign or stoop. *—n.* scorn. **—dis·dain'ful**, *adj.*

dis·ease' (di-zēz') *n.* a condition of ill health; malady. *—v.t.* infect with disease.

dis"em·bow'el (dis"em-bow'əl) *v.t.* 1, eviscerate. 2, stab in the abdomen, as in harakiri. **—dis"em·bow'el·ment**, *n.*

dis"en·fran'chise *v.t.* disfranchise. **—dis"en·fran'chise·ment**, *n.*

dis·fig'ure (dis-fig'yər) *v.t.* mar; deface. **—dis·fig'ure·ment**, *n.*

dis·fran'chise *v.t.* 1, deprive of rights of citizenship, esp. the right to vote. 2, deprive of a franchise. **—dis·fran'chise·ment**, *n.*

dis·gorge' (dis-gôrj') *v.t. & i.* throw out or emit, esp. violently; vomit. **—dis·gorge'·ment**, *n.*

dis·grace' (dis-grās') *n.* acute shame; ignominy; loss of reputation. *—v.t.* shame; discredit. **—dis·grace'ful**, *adj.* shameful.

dis·grun'tled (dis-grun'təld) *adj.* not contented; cross. **—dis·grun'tle,** v.t. **—disgrun'tle·ment,** n.

dis·guise' (dis-gīz') v.t. conceal the identity or real nature of; give a misleading appearance to. —n. a covering that masks or misleads.

dis·gust' n. extreme repugnance; loathing. —v.t. cause to feel loathing; offend.

dish n. **1,** a receptacle or vessel, esp. for food. **2,** a particular prepared food. **3,** (Slang) something very welcome, as a very attractive woman. **4,** fact or degree of concavity. —v.t. **1,** (often with out or up) serve, as food. **2,** make concave.

dis"ha·bille' (dis"ə-bēl') n. **1,** the state of being carelessly dressed; undress. **2,** a loose morning dress.

dish'cloth" n. a cloth with which dishes are washed.

dis·heart'en (dis-här'tən) v.t. cause to lose spirit or courage.

di·shev'el (di-shev'əl) v.t. muss, esp. the clothing or hair; tousle. **—di·shev'el·ment,** n.

dis·hon'or (dis-on'ər) v.t. **1,** bring shame upon. **2,** fail to meet (an obligation). —n. disgrace. **—dis·hon'or·a·ble,** adj.

dish'pan" n. a pan in which dishes are washed.

dish'rag" n. dishcloth.

dish'wash"er n. a machine for washing (and, usu., drying) dishes.

dish'wa"ter n. water in which dishes will be or have been washed.

dis"il·lu'sion v.t. deprive of illusions; disenchant. —n. freedom from illusions. **—dis"il·lu'sion·ment,** n.

dis"in·fect' v.t. remove infection or a source of infection from. **—dis"in·fect'ant,** n. a preparation for disinfecting.

dis"in·her'it v.t. cut off (an heir) from an inheritance. **—dis"in·her'i·tance,** n.

dis·in'te·grate" v.i. & t. separate into parts; go to pieces. **—dis·in"te·gra'tion,** n.

dis"in·ter' v.t. [-terred', -ter'ring] dig up something buried; unearth. **—dis"in·ter'ment,** n.

dis·in'ter·est·ed (dis-in'tə-res-tid) adj. unbiased; unselfish. **—dis·in'ter·est,** n.

dis·joint'ed adj. not coherent; not properly connected.

dis·junct' (dis-junkt') adj. disconnected; distinct.

disk n. **1,** any flat circular plate or surface. **2,** (Colloq.) a phonograph record. Also, **disc.** **—disk brake,** a friction brake employing two disks. **—disk jockey,** a radio announcer who plays phonograph records.

dis·like' n. fixed aversion or distaste. —v.t. feel aversion toward. **—dis·lik'a·ble,** adj.

dis"lo·cate' v.t. **1,** displace; put out of joint or position. **2,** interrupt the continuity or order of. **—dis"lo·ca'tion,** n.

dis·lodge' v.t. remove or drive from a habitation or a position occupied. **—dislodg'ment,** n.

dis'mal (diz'məl) adj. gloomy; dreary; cheerless; doleful. **—dis'mal·ness,** n.

dis·man'tle (dis-man'təl) v.t. **1,** strip of equipment or defenses. **2,** take to pieces. **—dis·man'tle·ment,** n.

dis·may' (dis-mā') v.t. utterly dishearten. —n. complete loss of courage; fright.

dis·mem'ber (dis-mem'bər) v.t. **1,** tear limb from limb. **2,** separate into parts. **—dis·mem'ber·ment,** n.

dis·miss' (dis-mis') v.t. **1,** send away; order or give permission to depart. **2,** discard; discharge from employment. **3,** put out of mind, as a subject. **4,** (Law) of a court, etc., refuse to continue to hear (an action, etc.). **—dis·miss'al,** n.

dis·mount' v.i. get off, as from a horse or bicycle. —v.t. **1,** unhorse. **2,** remove from a frame or setting, as a jewel. **3,** take apart, as a machine.

dis"o·be'di·ence n. refusal to obey. **—dis"o·be'di·ent,** adj.

dis"o·bey' v.t. & i. neglect or refuse to obey.

dis·or'der n. **1,** lack of order; confusion. **2,** tumult; disturbance of the peace. **3,** disturbance of the body or mind; a diseased state. —v.t. **1,** put in improper arrangement. **2,** unsettle the normal conditions of body or mind.

dis·or'dered adj. **1,** confused. **2,** mentally ill.

dis·or'der·ly adj. **1,** untidy. **2,** unruly; immoral. **—dis·or'der·li·ness,** n. **—disorderly house,** a house of prostitution.

dis·or'gan·ize" v.t. destroy the system or arrangement of. **—dis·or"gan·i·za'tion,** n. a breaking down or absence of system.

dis·or'i·ent v.t. confuse; cause to lose one's bearings. Also, **dis·or'i·en·tate".**

dis·own' v.t. refuse to admit ownership or responsibility.

dis·par'age (dis-par'ij) v.t. speak slightingly of; discredit. **—dis·par'age·ment,** n.

dis'pa·rate (dis'pə-rət) adj. essentially different; unequal. **—dis·par'i·ty** (dis-par'ə-tē) n.

dis·pas'sion n. freedom from passion or emotion; impartiality. **—dis·pas'sion·ate,** adj.

dis·patch' (dis-pach') v.t. **1,** send off or away. **2,** transact speedily; kill. —n. **1,** a sending off or away. **2,** dismissal. **3,** speed; haste. **4,** a written message. Also, **despatch.**

dis·pel' (dis-pel') *v.t.* [-**pelled'**, -**pel'ling**] drive off or away.

dis·pen'sa·ry (dis-pen'sə-rē) *n.* **1**, a place where medicines are given out. **2**, a public medical clinic.

dis"pen·sa'tion (dis"pən-sā'shən) *n.* **1**, act of dispensing. **2**, that which is dispensed by God to man. **3**, a relaxation of a law, esp. ecclesiastical.

dis·pen'sa·to·ry (dis-pen'sə-tôr-ē) *adj.* pert. to the dispensing of medicines. —*n.* **1**, a pharmacist's manual. **2**, a dispensary.

dis·pense' (dis-pens') *v.t.* **1**, deal out; distribute. **2**, administer, as laws. **3**, excuse; exempt. —*v.i.* **1**, (with *with*) permit the omission of; do without. **2**, compound (drugs, prescriptions). —**dis·pen'sa·ble,** *adj.*

dis·perse' (dis-pērs') *v.t.* **1**, scatter; diffuse. **2**, dissipate; cause to vanish. —*v.i.* separate. —**dis·per'sal** (-səl), **dis·per'sion** (-zhən) *n.*

dis·place' *v.t.* **1**, put out of the usual or proper place; remove from office. **2**, replace. —**displaced person,** one driven from his home by war.

dis·place'ment *n.* **1**, act of displacing. **2**, the weight or volume of water displaced by a submerged body. **3**, the volume swept out by a piston.

dis·play' (dis-plā') *v.t. & i.* show; exhibit; make manifest. —*n.* an exhibition. —*adj.* **1**, of type, large and designed to attract notice. **2**, used to display merchandise.

dis·please' *v.t. & i.* offend; be disagreeable (to). —**dis·pleas'ure,** *n.* vexation.

dis·port' (dis-pôrt') *v.i.* make merry; play.

dis·pose' (dis-pōz') *v.t.* **1**, place in a particular order; arrange. **2**, regulate; adjust. **3**, incline the mind or heart of. —*v.i.* **1**, (with *of*) part with. **2**, control. —**dis·pos'a·ble,** *adj.* —**dis·pos'al,** *n.*

dis"po·si'tion (dis"pə-zish'ən) *n.* **1**, an arrangement of parts. **2**, definite settlement; ultimate destination. **3**, innate temper; natural tendency of the mind.

dis·pos·sess' (dis"pə-zes') *v.t.* deprive of actual occupancy; dislodge. —**dis"pos·ses'-sion,** *n.*

dis·proof' *n.* proof to the contrary; refutation.

dis·prove' *v.t.* prove to be false or erroneous.

dis"pu·ta'tion (dis"pū-tā'shən) *n.* a controversy; debate. —**dis"pu·ta'tious,** *adj.*

dis·pute' (dis-pūt') *v.i.* argue; debate; wrangle. —*v.t.* argue about or against. —*n.* a controversy; a quarrel. —**dis·put'a·ble,** *adj.* —**dis·put'ant,** *n.*

dis·qual'i·fy' *v.t.* make unfit or ineligible. —**dis·qual"i·fi·ca'tion,** *n.*

dis·qui'et (dis-kwī'ət) *v.t.* deprive of peace; make uneasy or restless. —*n.* an uneasy feeling or state; unrest. —**dis·qui'e·tude** (-ə-tood) *n.*

dis"qui·si'tion (dis"kwi-zish'ən) *n.* a dissertation; treatise.

dis"re·gard' *v.t.* ignore. —*n.* failure to observe; neglect. —**dis"re·gard'ful,** *adj.*

dis"re·pair' *n.* the state of being in bad condition.

dis"re·pute' *n.* loss or want of good reputation. —**dis·rep'u·ta·ble** *adj.* of low character.

dis·rupt' *v.t. & i.* break asunder; separate forcibly. —**dis·rup'tion,** *n.* —**dis·rup'tive,** *adj.*

dis·sat'is·fy' *v.t.* fail to satisfy or please; render discontented. —**dis·sat"is·fac'tion,** *n.*

dis·sect' (di-sekt') *v.t.* **1**, cut in pieces; separate the parts of. **2**, examine point by point; analyze. —**dis·sec'tion,** *n.*

dis·sem'ble (di-sem'bəl) *v.t. & i.* **1**, give a false impression about; conceal one's real motives. **2**, pretend to disregard or ignore. —**dis·sem'blance** (-bləns) *n.*

dis·sem'i·nate" (di-sem'ə-nāt") *v.t.* scatter abroad; sow. —**dis·sem"i·na'tion,** *n.*

dis·sen'sion (di-sen'shən) *n.* violent disagreement; strife; discord.

dis·sent' (di-sent') *v.i.* feel or express a negative opinion. —*n.* difference of opinion. —**dis·sent'er,** *n.* one who disagrees, esp. with the doctrines of the Church of England.

dis·sen'tient (di-sen'shənt) *adj.* dissenting. —*n.* one who dissents. —**dis·sen'tious** (-shəs) *adj.*

dis"ser·ta'tion (dis"ər-tā'shən) *n.* a formal discourse or essay.

dis·sev'er (di-sev'ər) *v.t.* separate; divide. —**dis·sev'er·ance,** *n.*

dis'si·dence (dis'ə-dəns) *n.* difference in opinion; disagreement. —**dis'si·dent,** *adj. & n.*

dis·sim'u·late" (di-sim'yə-lāt") *v.t. & i.* disguise; make pretense; feign. —**dis·sim"u·la'tion,** *n.*

dis'si·pate" (dis'i-pāt") *v.t.* **1**, scatter; dispel. **2**, expend wastefully. —*v.i.* **1**, come to an end or vanish. **2**, act dissolutely. —**dis'si·pa'tion,** *n.*

dis'si·pat"ed (-id) *adj.* **1**, dissolute. **2**, dispersed.

dis·so'ci·ate" (di-sō'shē-āt") *v.t.* sever the connection of; separate. —**dis·so"ci·a'tion,** *n.*

dis'so·lute (dis'ə-loot) *adj.* loose in behavior and morals; wanton. —**dis'so·lute-ness,** *n.*

dis″so·lu′tion (dis″ə-loo′shən) *n.* act of dissolving or being dissolved.

dis·solve′ (di-zolv′) *v.t.* **1,** liquefy by means of heat or absorption. **2,** disunite; separate into parts; break up. **3,** solve; explain, as a mystery. —*v.i.* **1,** become fluid. **2,** come to an end; crumble or waste away. **3,** disappear gradually; fade from sight. —**dis·sol′u·ble** (di-sol′yû-bəl) *adj.*

dis′so·nance (dis′ə-nəns) *n.* **1,** an inharmonious combination of sounds. **2,** disagreement; discord. —**dis′so·nant,** *adj.*

dis·suade′ (di-swād′) *v.t.* change from a purpose by advice, persuasion, or argument. —**dis·sua′sion** (-zhən) *n.*

dis′taff (dis′tàf) *n.* **1,** a cleft stick for holding wool, flax, etc. in spinning. **2,** woman, her activities or work. —**distaff side,** the female line of descent in a family.

dis′tance (dis′təns) *n.* **1,** measure of interval in space or time. **2,** remoteness. —*v.t.* get far ahead of; surpass; outstrip.

dis′tant (dis′tənt) *adj.* **1,** situated at a different point in space or time. **2,** remote; far off. **3,** haughty; cool; reserved.

dis·taste′ (dis-tāst′) *n.* aversion; dislike. —**dis·taste′ful,** *adj.* displeasing; offensive.

dis·tem′per (dis-tem′pər) *n.* **1,** a serious disease of animals, esp. dogs. **2,** bad humor. **3,** mural paint or painting using eggs as sizing.

dis·tend′ *v.t.* dilate; expand. —*v.i.* swell. —**dis·ten′si·ble** (-ten′sə-bəl) *adj.* —**disten′tion,** *n.*

dis′tich (dis′tik) *n.* (*Poetry*) a couplet.

dis·till′ (dis-til′) *v.i.* fall in drops. —*v.t.* **1,** let fall in drops. **2,** purify. **3,** extract by process of distillation. —**dis′til·late,** *n.*

dis″til·la′tion (dis″tə-lā′shən) *n.* **1,** the vaporization and subsequent condensation of a liquid. **2,** a distilled liquid.

dis·till′er·y (dis-til′ə-rè) *n.* a place where alcoholic liquors other than ale or beer are made.

dis·tinct′ (dis-tinkt′) *adj.* **1,** separate; different. **2,** well-defined; not blurred; very plain; unmistakable; clear. —**dis·tinct′-ness,** *n.*

dis·tinc′tion (dis-tink′shən) *n.* **1,** act of distinguishing. **2,** a distinguishing quality or characteristic; difference in general. **3,** an honor; eminence; superiority.

dis·tinc′tive (dis-tink′tiv) *adj.* **1,** different; marking a difference. **2,** characteristic. —**dis·tinc′tive·ness,** *n.*

dis·tin′guish (dis-ting′gwish) *v.t.* **1,** mark, recognize, or see as distinct or different. **2,** separate by classification. **3,** discern critically; judge. **4,** treat with honor. —*v.i.* make a distinction (between). —**dis·tin′-**

guish·a·ble, *adj.* capable of being perceived and recognized. —**dis·tin′guished,** *adj.* eminent; celebrated.

dis·tort′ (dis-tôrt′) *v.t.* twist out of shape; pervert; misrepresent. —**dis·tor′tion,** *n.*

dis·tract′ (dis-trakt′) *v.t.* **1,** divert the attention of. **2,** confuse; bewilder. **3,** derange.

dis·tract′ed (-id) *adj.* **1,** diverted. **2,** bewildered.

dis·trac′tion (dis-trak′shən) *n.* **1,** act of distracting or being distracted. **2,** what distracts; a diversion. **3,** frenzy; (*Colloq.*) madness.

dis·traint′ (dis-trānt′) *n.* (*Law*) a seizing of property, as for debt. —**dis·train′,** *v.t.*

dis·trait′ (dis-trāt′) *adj.* abstracted; absentminded; inattentive.

dis·traught′ (dis-trât′) *adj.* bewildered; perplexed; deranged.

dis·tress′ (dis-tres′) *n.* **1,** pain or suffering of body or mind. **2,** calamity; adversity. **3,** the state of needing help; danger. —*v.t.* make miserable. —**dis·tress′ful,** *adj.* distressing.

dis·trib′ute (dis-trib′ūt) *v.t.* **1,** parcel out; apportion. **2,** classify. **3,** spread out. —**dis″tri·bu′tion** (dis″tri-bū′shən) *n.*

dis·trib′u·tor (dis-trib′yə-tər) *n.* **1,** one who distributes; esp., a wholesale dealer. **2,** a device for distributing, esp. electricity to the spark plugs of an engine.

dis′trict (dis′trikt) *n.* a section of a city or state; a region in general. —**district attorney,** the public prosecutor for a city or county.

dis·turb′ (dis-tērb′) *v.t.* **1,** agitate; disquiet; molest. **2,** interfere with; interrupt. —**dis·turbed′,** *adj.* mentally unsound; emotionally ill.

dis·turb′ance (-əns) *n.* **1,** something that disturbs; a feeling of disquiet; a disease. **2,** an illegally noisy commotion.

ditch (dich) *n.* a trench or channel dug in the earth. —*v.t.* **1,** drain by or surround with a ditch. **2,** throw or run into a ditch. **3,** (*Slang*) cast off; escape from.

dith′er (dith′ər) *n.* **1,** a nervous, excited state. **2,** commotion.

dith′y·ramb″ (dith′ə-ram″) *n.* a poem or discourse in impassioned mood.

dit′to (dit′ō) *n.* [*pl.* **-tos**] **1,** the same thing; expressed by two small marks (″). **2,** (*cap., T.N.*) a spirit duplicating process. —*v.t.* **1,** copy; repeat; echo. **2,** copy by the Ditto process.

dit′ty (dit′è) *n.* a little song.

di″u·ret′ic (dī″yû-ret′ik) *adj.* promoting urination. —**di″u·re′sis** (-rē′sis) *n.*

di·ur′nal (dī-ēr′nəl) *adj.* pert. to day; daily.

di·va (dē′vä) *n.* a prima donna.

div′a·gate″ (div′ə-gāt″) *v.i.* stray; digress. —**div″a·ga′tion,** *n.* digression.

di·van′ *n.* **1,** a kind of sofa. **2,** a certain area of theater seating. **3,** a council of state in Turkey.

dive (dīv) *v.i.* **1,** plunge head first downward or forward, esp. into water. **2,** submerge. **3,** engage deeply in anything. —*n.* **1,** a headfirst plunge, esp. into water. **2,** (*Slang*) a seamy place. **3,** (*Slang*) intentional loss of an athletic contest. —**dive bomber,** a bombing plane that aims its bombs by diving toward its target. —**div′er,** *n.*

di·verge′ (di-vērj′) *v.i.* **1,** branch off in different directions. **2,** take different courses or ways (of thought; of life). **3,** differ from a typical form. —**di·ver′gence, di·ver′gen·cy,** *n.* —**di·ver′gent,** *adj.*

di·verse′ (di-vērs′) *adj.* essentially different; varied. Also, **di′vers** (dī′vərz). —**di·verse′ness,** *n.*

di·ver″si·fy′ (di-vēr′si-fī″) *v.t.* give variety to. —**di·ver″si·fi·ca′tion** (-fi-kā′shən) *n.*

di·ver′sion (di-vēr′zhən) *n.* **1,** act of diverting. **2,** a turning aside; a detour. **3,** recreation; amusement; a pastime.

di·ver′si·ty (di-vēr′sə-tē) *n.* **1,** essential difference. **2,** variety.

di·vert′ (di-vērt′) *v.t.* **1,** turn aside or away from a course or an aim. **2,** amuse; entertain.

di·vest′ *v.t.* **1,** strip of clothes, arms, or equipment; despoil. **2,** deprive of rights, privileges, or authority. —**dives′ti·ture** (-ti-chər), **di·vest′ment,** *n.*

di·vide′ (di-vīd′) *v.t.* **1,** separate into parts or pieces; disjoin; sever the union of. **3,** make or keep distinct. **4,** distribute; share. **5,** (*Math.*) perform the process of division. —*v.i.* go apart. —*n.* a watershed. —**di·vid′ers,** *n.* compasses.

div′i·dend″ (div′ə-dend″) *n.* **1,** a sum to be divided and distributed, as to shareholders; the share of each. **2,** (*Math.*) a number or quantity to be divided by another.

div″i·na′tion (div″ə-nā′shən) *n.* the foretelling of the future or discovering of that which is hidden.

di·vine′ (di-vīn′) *adj.* **1,** of the nature of, proceeding from, or pert. to God; sacred. **2,** heavenly; excellent. —*n.* a clergyman. —*v.t.* learn by divination. —*v.i.* surmise. —**divine right,** the·doctrine that kings derive the right to rule directly from God.

di·vin′er (di-vīn′ər) *n.* **1,** one who divines. **2,** a rod supposed to locate subterranean water: *divining rod.*

di·vin′i·ty (di-vin′ə-tē) *n.* **1,** the character of being godly or divine. **2,** (*cap.*) God. **3,** a confection.

di·vis′i·ble (di-viz′ə-bəl) *adj.* capable of being divided, esp. (*Math.*) without a remainder. —**di·vis″i·bil′i·ty,** *n.*

di·vi′sion (di-vizh′ən) *n.* **1,** separation. **2,** a partition. **3,** a definite part; a self-sufficient unit of an army. **4,** disunion; discord. **5,** (*Math.*) the process of finding how many times a number (divisor) or quantity is contained in another (dividend).

di·vi′sion·al (-əl) *adj.* pert. to a division. —*n.* (*pl.*) examinations of candidates for academic degrees.

di·vi′sive (di-vī′siv) *adj.* tending to create dissension.

di·vi′sor (di-vī′zər) *n.* a number by which another is divided.

di·vorce′ (di-vôrs′) *n.* **1,** a legal dissolution of the marriage bond. **2,** complete separation. —*v.t.* obtain a divorce (from). —**di·vor″cée′** (-sā′) *n.* a divorced woman. —**di·vorce′ment,** *n.*

div′ot (div′ət) *n.* a piece of turf cut out by a golfer's club.

di·vulge′ (di-vulj′) *v.t.* tell or make known; reveal. —**di·vul′gence,** *n.*

div′vy (div′ē) *v.t.* (*Slang*) divide into portions.

Dix′ie (dik′sē) *n.* the southern states of the U.S. —**Dix′ie·crat″** (-krat″) *n.* a Democrat who places sectional before party interests.

Dix′ie·land″ *n.* **1,** Dixie. **2,** a style of jazz.

diz′zy (diz′ē) *adj.* **1,** having a whirling sensation in the head; giddy. **2,** causing dizziness. **3,** (*Slang*) silly; foolish. —**diz′zi·ness,** *n.*

DNA (dē′en′ā′) deoxyribonucleic acid, an essential constituent of chromosomes.

do (doo) *v.i.* [**did, done** (dun), **do′ing**] **1,** perform; carry out. **2,** perform the action or work required by the nature of the case, as *do one's hair.* **3,** cause; render. **4,** complete; finish. **5,** put forth; exert. **6,** (*Slang*) cheat; swindle. —*v.i.* **1,** work. **2,** act or behave. **3,** fare; prosper. **4,** serve the purpose. —*aux. v.* forming an emphatic pres. or past indicative with an infinitive, as *I did go.* —**do′a·ble,** *adj.* —**do away with,** destroy. —**do for,** destroy; kill —*n.* (*Colloq.*) **1,** bustle; ado. **2,** a party. —**do in, 1,** kill. **2,** swindle. —**do up, 1,** wrap. **2,** dress. —**make do,** use what is available.

do (dō) *n.* (*Music*) the first tone of a scale.

dob′bin (dob′in) *n.* a common name for a work horse.

Do′ber·man pin′scher (dō′bər-mən pin′shər) a breed of slender, smooth-coated dog.

doc (dok) *n.* (*Colloq.*) doctor.

do′cent (dō′sənt) *adj.* teaching. —*n.* instructor; lecturer.

doc′ile (dos′əl) *adj.* amenable; easily managed. —**do·cil′i·ty** (do-sil′ə-tē) *n.*

dock (dok) *n.* **1,** an enclosed water space in which a ship floats while being loaded or unloaded; a slip or pier; a wharf. **2,** the place where a prisoner stands in court. **3,** a coarse herb or weed. **4,** the stump of an animal's tail. —*v.t.* **1,** cut off; clip, as a dog's tail. **2,** deduct from, as wages. **3,** bring or draw (a vessel) into a dock. —*v.i.* **1,** arrive at a wharf or dock. **2,** join in space (as two spacecraft).

dock′age (-ij) *n.* **1,** act of docking. **2,** provision for docking a vessel; fee for use of a dock.

dock′et (dok′it) *n.* **1,** (*Law*) a list of cases for trial; any such agenda. **2,** (*Law*) a register of judgments. **3,** a package label. —*v.t.* **1,** summarize. **2,** enter in a court register. **3,** label; tag.

dock′yard *n.* a place where ships are built or repaired.

doc′tor (dok′tər) *n.* **1,** a physician. **2,** a person holding the highest degree a university can confer in his or her special field. —*v.t.* (*Colloq.*) **1,** treat medicinally. **2,** repair; patch up. **3,** adulterate; tamper with. —**doc′tor·ate** (-ət) *n.*

doc″tri·naire′ (dok″trə-nār′) *n.* one who acts by doctrine or theory without sufficient regard for practical considerations. —*adj.* obstinately impractical; theoretical.

doc′trine (dok′trin) *n.* a principle or body of principles; a tenet; a dogma. —**doc′-tri·nal,** *adj.*

doc′u·ment (dok′yə-mənt) *n.* a written or printed paper containing a record or statement. —*v.t.* (-mənt″) cite or provide documents for authority. —**doc″u·men′tal,** *adj.* —**doc″u·men·ta′tion,** *n.*

doc″u·men′ta·ry (dok″yə-men′tə-rē) *adj.* **1,** of or pert. to documents. **2,** factual and educational, as a film. —*n.* an educational motion picture consisting of factual sequences.

dod′der (dod′ər) *v.i.* tremble; shake; totter.

do·dec·a- (do-dek-ə) *pref.* twelve.

dodge (doj) *v.i. & t.* suddenly jump or step aside; evade. —*n.* an act of evasion; a trick, stratagem, or clever device.

do′do (dō′dō) *n.* **1,** an extinct flightless bird. **2,** (*Slang*) a stodgy, unimaginative person.

doe (dō) *n.* the female of the deer, most antelopes, the hare, and rabbit.

do′er (doo′ər) *n.* **1,** one who does (something). **2,** one who accomplishes a great deal.

does (duz) *v.* 3rd pers. sing., pres. ind., of *do.*

doe′skin″ *n.* **1,** a fine leather. **2,** a finely twilled woolen cloth.

doff (dof) *v.t.* take off (any article of dress).

dog (dâg; dog) *n.* **1,** a domesticated quadruped descended from different wild species of the genus *Canis,* as the wolf, fox, or jackal. **2,** a mechanical device for holding. **3,** a mean, worthless fellow. —*v.t.* [**dogged, dog′ging**] hound; keep at the heels of; worry. —**dog days,** the hottest period of summer. —**dog it,** give up, through fear. —**dog tag,** a dog's license plate; (*Slang*) a soldier's identification disk. —**go to the dogs,** (*Colloq.*) go to ruin. —**put on the dog,** (*Colloq.*) behave or dress pretentiously.

dog′bane″ *n.* an herb with an intensely bitter root.

dog′cart″ *n.* **1,** a light horse-drawn vehicle. **2,** a cart drawn by dogs.

doge (dōj) *n.* title of the former rulers of Venice and Genoa.

dog′ear″ *n.* **1,** a dog's ear. **2,** a frayed corner. —*v.t.* turn down the corner of a page. —*v.i.* fray.

dog′fight″ *n.* combat between war planes at close quarters.

dog′fish″ *n.* any of a variety of small sharks.

dog′ged (dog′id) *adj.* obstinate; persistent. —**dog′ged·ness,** *n.*

dog′ger·el (dâg′ər-əl) *n.* light, inept verse.

dog′gy (dâg′ē) *n.* (*Colloq.*) a dog. —*adj.* **1,** like a dog. **2,** pretentious. —**doggy bag,** a bag to bring restaurant leftovers home.

dog′house″ *n.* a hut for a dog. —**in the doghouse,** (*Slang*) in disfavor.

do′gie (dō′gē) *n.* a stray calf.

dog′ma (dâg′mə) *n.* a rigidly held principle or doctrine, esp. in a religion; precept. —**dog′ma·tism,** *n.*

dog·mat′ic (dâg-mat′ik) *adj.* **1,** pert. to a dogma. **2,** positive; adhering rigidly to a tenet. —**dog·mat′i·cal·ly,** *adv.*

dog-′tired′ *adj.* extremely tired.

dog′tooth″ *n.* [*pl.* **-teeth″**] **1,** eyetooth. **2,** an ornamental molding. —**dogtooth violet,** an early spring wild flower.

dog′trot″ *n.* a slow running gait.

dog′wood″ *n.* a shrub or tree bearing clusters of flowers.

do-″it-your·self′ *adj.* designed to be used or done by anyone. —**do-″it-your·self′er,** *n.*

doi′ly (doi′lē) *n.* a small ornamental mat for use on a table.

Dol′by (dōl′bē) *n.* (*T.N.*) a device for reducing noise on recordings. —**Dol′by·ize″** (-īz″) *v.t.*

dol'ce (dōl'che) (*Music*) *adj. & adv.* sweet and soft.

dol'drums (dōl'drəmz) *n.pl.* **1**, low spirits; the dumps. **2**, zones of calm in the ocean near the Equator.

dole (dōl) *n.* **1**, alms. **2**, (*Brit.*) money granted to the unemployed. —*v.t.* hand out sparingly.

dole'ful (dōl'fəl) *adj.* showing sorrow; sad. —**dole'ful·ness**, *n.*

doll (dol) *n.* **1**, a toy baby for children; a puppet. **2**, (*Slang*) a girl. —*v.i. & t.* (with *up*) put on one's best clothes.

dol'lar (dol'ər) *n.* **1**, the basis of decimal coinage. **2**, a coin or treasury certificate of one dollar value, in the U.S. worth 100 cents. —**dollar diplomacy**, use (by the U. S.) of money to implement foreign policy.

dol'lop (dol'əp) *n.* (*Colloq.*) a lump; mass.

dol'ly (dol'ē) *n.* **1**, diminutive of *doll.* **2**, any of several mechanical devices, esp. a low platform on rollers for moving heavy loads.

dol'men (dol'mən) *n.* (*Archaeol.*) one of a number of ancient structures, believed to be tombs, formed by a horizontal slab of rock set atop two or more upright stones.

dol'o·mite (dōl'ə-mīt″) *n.* a rock composed largely of calcium magnesium carbonate.

do'lor (dō'lər) *n.* sorrow.

do'lor·ous (dol'ər-əs) *adj.* sad; mournful. —**dol'or·ous·ness**, *n.*

dol'phin (dol'fin) *n.* a sea mammal of the whale family.

dolt (dōlt) *n.* a dull, stupid person.

-dom (dəm) *suf.* the estate, condition or rank of, as *kingdom.*

do·main' (dō-mān') *n.* **1**, territory owned or governed. **2**, sphere of action or knowledge.

dome (dōm) *n.* **1**, a hemispherical roof; a large cupola. **2**, (*Slang*) head.

do·mes'tic (də-mes'tik) *adj.* **1**, relating to the household. **2**, pert. to one's own country; not foreign. **3**, tame, as an animal. —*n.* a household servant. —**do·mes'ti·cal·ly**, *adv.*

do·mes'ti·cate″ (də-mes'ti-kāt″) *v.t.* convert to home life; tame. —**do·mes″ti·ca'tion**, *n.*

do″mes·tic'i·ty (dō″mes-tis'ə-tē) *n.* the state of liking home life.

dom'i·cile (dom'ə-səl) *n.* a place of residence.

dom'i·nant (dom'ə-nənt) *adj.* **1**, exercising rule or authority. **2**, most conspicuous; overshadowing. —**dom'i·nance**, *n.*

dom'i·nate″ (dom'ə-nāt″) *v.t. & i.* govern; control; hold control; be most conspicuous. —**dom″i·na'tion**, *n.*

dom″i·neer' (dom'ə-nir') *v.i. & t.* rule in an overbearing or arrogant manner; swagger; tyrannize. —**dom″i·neer'ing**, *adj.* overbearing.

Do·min'i·can (də-min'ə-kən) *n. & adj.* one of a Rom. Cath. religious order founded by St. Dominic in the early 13th century.

dom'i·nie (dom'ə-nē) *n.* a clergyman; priest.

do·min'ion (də-min'yən) *n.* **1**, supreme authority; control. **2**, a territory under a sovereign, now esp. one having strong powers of self-government. —**Dominion Day**, a legal holiday in Canada, July 1.

dom'i·no″ (dom'ə-nō″) *n.* **1**, a small tile of wood or bone, marked with dots; (*pl.*) a game played with such tiles. **2**, a masquerade costume, esp. a cloak; a half-mask. —**domino theory**, the theory that if one country is taken over by a Communist regime, the neighboring countries will soon be overrun in turn.

don *v.t.* [**donned, don'ning**] put on. —*n.* **1**, (*cap.*) a Spanish nobleman; his title: Sir, Mr. **2**, a fellow or tutor in an English university. —**do'ña** (dō'nyä) *n.fem.*

do'nate (dō'nāt) *v.t. & i.* bestow as a gift; contribute. —**do·na'tion**, *n.*

done (dun) *v.* p.p. of *do.* —*adj.* **1**, executed; completed. **2**, worn out; used up. **3**, (of meat) thoroughly cooked. **4**, proper.

don'jon (dun'jən) *n.* the inner tower, keep, or stronghold of a castle; dungeon.

don'key (dong'kē) *n.* **1**, the ass. **2**, a stupid or obstinate person.

don'ny·brook″ (don'ē-brúk″) *n.* free-for-all; public altercation.

do'nor (dō'nər) *n.* one who gives.

do'nut (dō'nut) *n.* doughnut.

doo'dad *n.* (*Colloq.*) **1**, a trinket; gewgaw. **2**, a title for something whose name is unknown or forgotten.

doo'dle (doo'dəl) *v.i.* **1**, (*Slang*) draw or scribble aimlessly. **2**, play a bagpipe.

doo'dle·bug″ (doo'dəl-bug″) *n.* **1**, an insect larva. **2**, a contrivance for locating water, minerals, etc., under the earth. **3**, (*Colloq.*) a Geiger counter.

doo'dle·sack″ *n.* bagpipe.

doo'hick″ey (doo'hik″ē) *n.* gadget; doodad.

doom *n.* **1**, destiny, esp. when unhappy or destructive; fate. **2**, a judgment; a sentence. **3**, the last judgment: *doomsday.* —*v.t.* condemn to ruin.

door (dôr) *n.* **1**, a barrier that swings on hinges or slides for opening or closing a passageway. **2**, any means of access, entrance, or exit.

door'keep"er *n.* one who guards an entrance.

door'man (-mən) *n.* [*pl.* **-men**] an attendant at the door of a hotel, club, etc.

door'step" *n.* threshold.

door'way" *n.* the opening in which a door is mounted.

dope (dōp) *n.* **1,** varnish, rubber cement, etc., used in waterproofing, etc. **2,** (*Colloq.*) a narcotic drug; such drugs collectively. **3,** information; a private hint. **4,** (*Slang*) a stupid person. —*v.t.* **1,** (*Colloq.*) drug. **2,** (*Slang*) (with *out*) solve, as a mystery. —**dop'ey,** *adj.*

Dopp'ler effect (däp'lər) an apparent change in the frequency of sound, light, or radio waves reaching an observer when the wave source and the observer are in motion relative to one another.

dor'mant (dôr'mənt) *adj.* in a state of rest or inactivity. —**dor'man·cy,** *n.*

dor'mer (dôr'mər) *n.* a window in a projection under a gable.

dor'mi·to·ry (dôr'mə-tôr-ė) *n.* a building or large room in which many persons sleep. Also, *colloq.*, **dorm.**

dor'mouse" (dôr'mows") *n.* [*pl.* **-mice"** (-mīs")] a squirrel-like hibernating rodent.

dor'sal (dôr'səl) *adj.* pert. to, on, or situated near, the back.

do'ry (dôr'ė) *n.* **1,** a small, flat-bottomed boat. **2,** an edible sea fish.

dose (dōs) *n.* **1,** a prescribed quantity of medicine to be taken at one time. **2,** anything disagreeable to take. **3,** (*Slang*) an attack of venereal disease. —*v.t.* give a dose to. —**dos'age,** *n.*

do·sim'e·ter (dō-sim'ə-tər) *n.* a device for measuring doses, as of X-rays.

dos'si·er" (dos'ė-ā") *n.* a complete file of information on a person or affair.

dot *n.* **1,** a minute, round spot; a speck. **2,** a dowry. —*v.t.* & *i.* [**dot'ted, -ting**] mark with a dot or dots. —**on the dot,** exactly on time.

dot'age (dō'tij) *n.* **1,** senility. **2,** excessive fondness.

do'tard (dō'tərd) *n.* an old, foolish man.

dote (dōt) *v.i.* **1,** be weak-minded from age. **2,** (with *on*) lavish extravagant fondness.

dot'ty (dot'ė) *adj.* (*Colloq.*) crazy.

dou'ble (dub'əl) *adj.* **1,** being a pair; duplicated. **2,** twofold; twice as much, as large, as thick, etc. **3,** folded once. —*n.* **1,** a twofold quantity or size. **2,** a duplicate; a counterpart. **3,** a fold. **4,** an understudy. **5,** esp. in bridge, an increase in scoring values. **6,** in baseball, a two-base hit. **7,** (*pl.*) esp. in tennis, play with two on a side.

—*v.t.* **1,** make double. **2,** contain twice as much or as many. **3,** fold once, as a blanket. **4,** repeat; duplicate. —*v.i.* **1,** increase or grow to twofold. **2,** turn in the opposite direction. —**doub'ly,** *adv.* —**double boiler,** a vessel for slow cooking over hot water or steam. —**double date,** (*Colloq.*) two unmarried couples joining in some social occasion. —**double dealing,** treachery. —**double jeopardy,** subjection to trial and possible punishment twice for the same offense. —**double meaning,** intentional ambiguity. —**double standard,** a dual moral code, as one stricter for women than for men. —**double take,** (*Slang*) sudden, delayed understanding. —**on the double,** at double rate; quickly.

double bass (*Music*) the largest and deepest-toned viol; bass viol.

dou'ble-bar'reled *adj.* **1,** having two barrels, as a gun. **2,** doubly effective.

dou'ble-breast'ed *adj.* (of a garment) made alike on both sides of the breast.

dou"ble-cross' *v.t.* (*Slang*) betray the confidence of. —*n.* betrayal.

dou'ble-deck'er *n.* **1,** a ship, bus, bunk, etc. having two decks or tiers. **2,** (*Colloq.*) a two-layered sandwich.

double-"en·ten'dre (doo"blonñ-tänd'rə) *n.* (*Fr.*) an expression having two meanings, one usu. risqué.

dou'ble·head'er (dub'əl-hed'ər) *n.* **1,** two separate games played consecutively by the same teams on the same day. **2,** a train drawn by two engines.

dou'ble-joint'ed *adj.* having unusually flexible joints, esp of the fingers.

dou'ble-knit" *n.* a kind of knitted fabric.

dou"ble-park" *v.t.* & *i.* park (an automobile) in the street, parallel with an automobile parked at the curb.

dou'ble-speak" *n.* inflated, often deliberately obscure language.

dou'blet (dub'lət) *n.* **1,** a pair of like things. **2,** one of such a pair. **3,** a close-fitting jacket formerly worn by men.

dou'ble-talk" *n.* rapid talk mingling real words with nonsense; gibberish.

dou·bloon' (dub-loon') *n.* a former Spanish gold coin, worth about five dollars.

doubt (dowt) *n.* **1,** an unsettled state of opinion; indecision. **2,** a matter of uncertainty. **3,** an objection. —*v.i.* feel doubt. —*v.t.* question the accuracy or honesty of. —**doubting Thomas,** a person disposed to doubt or question. —**doubt'less,** *adj.* & *adv.* certainly.

doubt'ful (-fəl) *adj.* **1,** feeling doubt; hesitant. **2,** unlikely.

douche (doosh) *n.* a liquid spray of water

to clean or heal some organ of the body, or the instrument or syringe used. —*v.i. & t.* so spray.

dough (dō) *n.* **1,** the paste for bread or pastry ready to be baked. **2,** (*Slang*) money.

dough'boy" a U.S. soldier, esp in World War I.

úough'nut" *n.* a ring-shaped cake fried in deep fat.

dough'ty (dow'tė) *adj.* fearless; strong. —**dough'ti·ness,** *n.*

dour (dûr) *adj.* hard; inflexible; sour in mien. —**dour'ness,** *n.*

douse (dows) *v.t.* **1,** immerse in or splash with water. **2,** extinguish. —*v.i.* search for water or minerals with a divining rod.

dove (duv) *n.* **1,** a pigeon or related bird. **2,** an emblem of innocence and affection. **3,** an advocate of peace.

dove'cot" (-kot") *n.* a doves' house. Also, **dove'cote"** (-kōt").

dove'tail" (duv'tāl") *v.i. & t.* fit or adjust exactly, esp. for space saving; work together harmoniously. —*n.* a mortise and tenon in somewhat the shape of a dove's tail.

dow'a·ger (dow'ə-jər) *n.* **1,** a widow endowed with property from her husband. **2,** (*Colloq.*) a dignified-looking elderly woman.

dow'dy (dow'dė) *adj.* slovenly; ill-dressed. —**dow'di·ness,** *n.*

dow'el (dow'əl) *n.* a pin or tenon used for fastening together two pieces of wood, stone, etc.

dow'er (dow'ər) *n.* **1,** the property that a woman brings to her husband at marriage; dowry. **2,** real estate granted by law, to a widow for her lifetime. **3,** one's portion of natural gifts. —*v.t.* supply with a dowry.

dow'itch·er (dow'ich-ər) *n.* a species of snipe.

down *adv.* **1,** [also, **down'ward** (-wərd)] in a descending direction; from higher to lower; from earlier to later times; from a greater to a less or lower rate. **2,** on the ground; at the bottom or lowest point; into disrepute. **3,** in writing; on paper. firmly; closely. —*adj.* **1,** downward. **2,** behind, in a score. **3,** dejected; ill-disposed. —*prep.* in a descending direction upon or along. —*n.* **1,** downward movement. **2,** a unit of play or progress in football. **3,** the soft feathers, as on a young bird; under-plumage. **4,** any soft hairy growth. **5,** a hill; a dune. —*v.i. & t.* go or cause to go down. —**down payment,** an initial payment on an installment purchase. —**down-to-earth,** *adj.* sensible; practical. —**down under,** in Australia or New Zealand.

down'cast" *adj.* dejected.

down'er (-ər) *n.* (*Slang*) **1,** a barbiturate depressant drug. **2,** a depressing event, report, etc.

down'fall" *n.* defeat; ruin.

down'grade" *n.* **1,** a downward slope or course. **2,** deterioration. —*v.t.* assign (a position or person) to lower status and salary.

down"heart'ed *adj.* discouraged.

down'hill" *adj. & adv.* in a descending direction down a slope.

down-'home' *adj.* informal; simple.

down'pour" *n.* heavy rainfall.

down'right" *adj.* **1,** direct; plain; blunt. **2,** complete; utter; absolute. —*adv.* thoroughly; completely. —**down'right"ness,** *n.*

down'shift" *v.i. & t.* shift into a lower gear.

down'stairs" *adv. & adj.* toward or on a lower floor.

down'town" *adv. & adj.* at, to, or of the business section of a city.

down'trod"den (-dən) *adv.* oppressed.

down'ward (-wərd) *adj.* [also, **down'-wards**] **1,** from a higher to a lower place, state, degree, etc. **2,** away from a source. —*adj.* descending.

down'y (dow'nė) *adj.* **1,** covered with down. **2,** like down; soft and fluffy. —**down'i·ness,** *n.*

dow'ry (dow'rė) *n.* the estate that a bride brings to her husband.

dowse (dows) *v.* douse.

dox·ol'o·gy (doks-ol'ə-jė) *n.* a hymn or psalm of praise of God.

doy'en (dwä'yen) *n.* a dean; senior member. —**doy·enne'** (dwä-yen') *n.fem.*

doze (dōz) *n.* a light sleep. —*v.i.* (often with *off*) nap.

doz'en (duz'ən) *n.* twelve units.

drab *adj.* [**drab'ber, -best**] **1,** of a yellowish-gray tint. **2,** monotonous; dull. —*n.* **1,** a dull gray or brown color. **2,** cloth of this color. —**drab'ness,** *n.*

drach'ma (dräkh'mə) *n.* the monetary unit of Greece.

dra·co'ni·an (dra-kō'nė-ən) *adj.* (of laws) rigorous; harshly oppressive.

draft (dråft) *n.* **1,** the act of drawing, dragging, or hauling. **2,** a drink. **3,** a heavy demand. **4,** conscription. **5,** the depth a loaded ship sinks in water. **6,** a written order for payment, as a check. **7,** a current of air; a device to produce or control the air flow. **8,** a first sketch; an outline. —*adj.* used for or capable of hauling. —*v.t.* make a draft of, upon, or from. Also, **draught.** —**draft'ee,** *n.* a conscript. —**on draft,** (of beer) drawn from a keg, not bottled.

drafts'man (dråfts'mən) *n.* [*pl.* **-men**] one who draws plans, sketches, or designs.

draft'y (dráf'tè) *adj.* causing or exposed to currents of air. —**draft'i·ness,** *n.*

drag *v.t. & i.* [**dragged, drag'ging**] 1, pull; haul. 2, (often with *along*) draw, move, or proceed slowly, heavily, or tiresomely. 3, draw a grapnel through a body of water in search of something; dredge. 4, harrow. 5, (with *out*) prolong tediously. 6, (*Slang*) race, esp. in automobiles. —*n.* 1, something designed to be dragged or hauled; a brake; an impediment; hindrance. 2, the act of dragging. 3, (*Slang*) influence. 4, (*Slang*) a street; district. 5, a puff, as on a cigarette. 6, (*Slang*) something boring or tiresome. 7, (*Slang*) a woman's dress worn by a man. —**in drag,** (*Slang*) of a man, dressed in women's clothing. —**drag strip,** a paved lane for automobile racing.

drag'gle (drag'əl) *v.t.* soil by dragging through the mud. —*v.i.* trail on the ground.

drag'net" *n.* 1, a net for fishing. 2, (*Colloq.*) a canvass, esp. by the police.

drag'o·man (drag'ō-mən) *n.* a professional interpreter or guide.

drag'on (drag'ən) *n.* a fabulous fire-breathing serpentine animal of great size and fierceness.

drag'on·fly" (drag'ən-flī") *n.* a large insect with two pairs of wings: the *devil's darning needle.*

dra·goon' (drə-goon') *n.* an armed cavalry soldier. —*v.t.* persecute or oppress by armed force.

drain (drān) *v.t. & i.* 1, draw off or flow off gradually. 2, empty or exhaust gradually. —*n.* 1, the act of draining. 2, a passage or pipe used for draining.

drain'age (drā'nij) *n.* 1, a gradual flowing off; that which flows off. 2, a system of sewers for draining. 3, area drained.

drake (drāk) *n.* the male duck.

dram *n.* 1, a unit of weight, one-sixteenth ounce in avoirdupois weight. 2, one-eighth of a fluid ounce. 3, a small drink, esp. of spirits.

dra'ma (drä'mə) *n.* 1, a literary composition written for the stage; a play. 2, that branch of literature dealing with the writing and production of plays; all plays, classic and modern. 3, a human course of events.

Dram'a·mine (dram'ə-mēn) *n.* (*T.N.*) a drug used to prevent motion sickness.

dra·mat'ic (drə-mat'ik) *adj.* 1, pert. to drama. 2, intensely interesting; eventful. —**dra·mat'i·cal·ly,** *adv.*

dra·mat'ics (drə-mat'iks) *n.pl.* stage plays. —*n.sing.* 1, the art or study of acting in, writing, and producing plays. 2, histrionics.

dram'a·tist (dram'ə-tist) *n.* a playwright.

dram'a·tize" (-tīz") *v.t.* 1, put in the form of a play. 2, express dramatically. —**dram"a·ti·za'tion** (-ti-zā'shən) *n.*

dram'a·tur"gy (dràm'ə-tēr"jè) *n.* the art or science of dramatic composition and representation. —**dram"a·tur'gi·cal,** *adj.*

drank *v.* p.t. of *drink.*

drape (drāp) *v.t.* 1, cover with or adorn with cloth or hangings. 2, arrange or adjust in folds. —*n.* a heavy curtain . —**drap'er,** *n.* a dealer in cloths.

dra'per·y (drā'pə-rè) *n.* textile fabrics used for draping; (*pl.*) curtains.

dras'tic (dras'tik) *adj.* having extreme and immediate effect; radical; harsh. —**dras'ti·cal·ly,** *adv.*

draught (dráft) 1, draft. 2, (*pl.*) checkers.

draw (drâ) *v.t.* [**drew** (droo), **drawn, drawing**] 1, pull; drag. 2, take out, as money from a bank. 3, derive; obtain from some source. 4, induce; attract, as a crowd. 5, deduce; infer. 6, inhale; suck in. 7, drain. 8, tie (a game). 9, (with *out*) extract the essence of; encourage to talk. 10, (often with *out*) stretch; lengthen; prolong. 11, obtain as due, as salary. 12, sketch in lines of words; make a picture or draft of. 13, disembowel; eviscerate (as poultry). 14, of a vessel, have a draft of. 15, play (a match) to a tie score. —*v.i.* 1, move (toward or away). 2, attract attendance. 3, sketch. 4, make a draft or a demand (upon). 5, be susceptible to a draft, as a pipe. 6, take a weapon out of its holster. 7, tie (a score). 8, draw lots. —*n.* 1, the act of drawing; that which is drawn. 2, a tie score. 3, movable part of a drawbridge. —**draw a bead on,** aim at. —**draw a line,** fix a limit or barrier. —**draw back,** retreat; cower.

draw'back" *n.* a disadvantage; a hindrance.

draw'bridge" *n.* a bridge that can be raised or turned to permit vessels to pass through.

draw'er (drôr) *n.* 1, a sliding box-shaped compartment in a piece of furniture. 2, (drâ'ər) one who draws, esp. a check or draft. 3, (*pl.*) (drôrz) an undergarment worn on the lower part of the body.

draw'ing (drâ'ing) *n.* 1, the art of sketching, esp. pictures; a picture or illustration; a plan. 2, the selection of the winners in a lottery. —**drawing card,** (*Colloq.*) a show or performer that attracts a large audience.

draw'ing·room" *n.* 1, a room used for the reception of company. 2, a private compartment in a railroad car.

drawl (drâl) *v.t. & i.* speak in a slow, dragged-out tone. —*n.* this manner of speech.

drawn (drân) *v.* p.p. of *draw.* —*adj.* 1, disemboweled, as a fowl prepared for

tub, cūte, púll; labəl; oil, owl, go, chip, she, thin, *th*en, sing, ink; *see p. 6* cooking. 2, strained from weariness or grief. 3, of a battle or contest, indecisive; tied.

dray (drā) n. a low horse-drawn cart for heavy loads. —**dray′age**, n. use of or charge for a dray. —**dray′horse″**, n. —**dray′man** (-mən) n.

dread (dred) v.t. & i. fear greatly; be in great fear. —n. 1, great fear. 2, awe. —adj. fearsome.

dread′ful (-fəl) adj. 1, causing great fear or awe. 2, frightful; shocking; horrible. —**dread′ful·ness**, n.

dread′nought″ (dred′nât″) n. a powerful battleship.

dream (drēm) n. 1, images or ideas occurring in the mind during sleep. 2, a vision of the fancy. 3, (Colloq.) something delightful. —v.i. & t. 1, imagine during sleep. 2, think idly; indulge in reverie. 3, plan vaguely; be unduly hopeful (of). 4, (with up) invent; devise. —**dream′er**, n. a visionary.

dream′land″ n. sleep; the realm of fancy.

dream′y (drē′mē) adj. 1, vague; fanciful. 2, peaceful. 3, delightful. —**dream′i·ness**, n.

drear′y (drir′ē) adj. dismal; gloomy; tedious. Also, **drear.** —**drear′i·ness**, n.

dreck (drek) n. (Slang) shoddy merchandise; trash; junk.

dredge (drej) n. a scooping machine or instrument for clearing a channel, as in a river. —v.t. & i. 1, clear out by use of a dredge. 2, sprinkle flour upon, as in roasting meat.

dregs (dregz) n.pl. worthless residue, as the sediment of liquors.

drench v.t. wet thoroughly.

dress (dres) v.t. 1, put clothes on; attire. 2, bandage, as a wound. 3, prepare; make ready. 4, put in orderly arrangement, as the hair; adorn. —v.i. 1, clothe oneself. 2, come into proper alignment. —n. 1, clothing; attire. 2, a woman's frock. 3, outward aspect; guise. 4, formal, as dress suit. —**dress circle**, a section of a theater. —**dress down**, censure; discipline. —**dress rehearsal**, a final rehearsal of a play, concert, etc. —**dress up**, put on one's best clothes.

dres·sage′ (dre-säzh′) n. the training of a horse in precision movements; the execution of such movements.

dress′er (-ər) n. 1, one who dresses another, esp. in the theater; one who adjusts, trims, etc. 2, a bedroom chest of drawers with a mirror; a bureau.

dress′ing (-ing) n. 1, the act of one who dresses. 2, bandages applied to a wound. 3, sauce or stuffing for food. 4, a sizing, as starch, for fabrics. —**dressing gown**, a bathrobe; lounging robe.

dress′ing-down″ n. (Colloq.) a severe reprimand; a thrashing.

dress′mak″er n. a seamstress.

dress′y (-ē) adj. (of clothes) stylish or formal. —**dress′i·ness**, n.

drew (droo) v. pret. of **draw**.

drib′ble (drib′əl) v.i. 1, fall in drops. 2, slaver. —v.t. 1, let fall in drops. 2, in some games, kick or bounce the ball forward. —n. a dripping of water.

drib′let (drib′lit) n. a tiny amount.

dri′er (drī′ər) n. 1, a substance that accelerates drying. 2, an apparatus for removing moisture. 3, an ingredient added to promote quick drying.

drift n. 1, the direction in which something is driven; the thing driven; the impelling force. 2, a heap of any matter driven together, as by wind. 3, a current, as of water; general current or intention; trend. —v.i. float or be carried at random by the force of wind or tide; hence, fig., be carried involuntarily into a course of action. —**drift′er**, n. a vagrant; hobo; one constantly on the move.

drift′wood″ n. wood and debris cast ashore by drift or tide.

drill (dril) n. 1, a tool for boring holes. 2, military training, esp. in parade exercises. 3, teaching by repeated exercises; a test; quiz. 4, an agricultural machine for planting seeds. 5, a heavy cotton fabric. —v.t. & i. 1, pierce with a drill. 2, exercise; train; quiz. 3, sow in rows, as wheat. —**drill′mas″ter**, n. a teacher, esp. of soldiers. —**drill press**, a machine for drilling.

drink v.t. [**drank, drunk, drink′ing**] 1, swallow (a liquid) 2, take in (a liquid) in any way; imbibe; absorb. 3, (often with in) take in through the senses. —v.i. 1, swallow water or other fluid; habitually imbibe alcoholic liquors. 2, (with to) salute in drinking. —n. 1, any liquid taken into the stomach. 2, alcoholic liquor. 3, a potion; a draught. 4, (with the) the ocean, sea, etc. —**drink′er**, n. one who habitually drinks liquor.

drip v.i. & t. [**dripped, drip′ping**] fall or let fall in drops. —n. 1, a falling in drops. 2, a receptacle for catching the overflow. 3, (Slang) an unattractive or boring person. —**drip′pings**, n.pl. fat that falls from meat in cooking.

drip-′dry′ v.i. & t. dry rapidly when hung up. —adj. designed for drip-drying.

drive (drīv) v.t. [**drove** (drōv), **driv′en** (driv′ən), **driv′ing**] 1, force to move, esp. forward; impel; hammer in. 2, set or direct in motion, as an automobile; carry forward. 3, chase (game); hunt. 4, incite to a course of action or a state of mind; urge; press.

—*v.i.* **1,** be impelled. **2,** move forcibly. **3,** be conveyed, as in an automobile. **4,** aim; tend. **5,** in golf, hit the ball off the tee. **6,** work energetically. —*n.* **1,** a trip in an automobile. **2,** a private road; driveway. **3,** the urging together of animals, as for roundup. **4,** a campaign to collect something, as money, members, sales. **5,** extreme haste or strong action. **6,** the power to drive; energy; ambition. —**drive at,** (*Colloq.*) mean to say.

drive-'in' *n.* a restaurant or theater serving people who remain in automobiles.

driv'el (driv'əl) *v.i.* **1,** drool; slaver. **2,** talk foolishly. —*n.* act or result of driveling.

driv'er (drī'vər) *n.* **1,** one who, or that which drives; a chauffeur. **2,** a form of golf club (No. 1 wood).

drive'way' *n.* a private lane.

driz'zle (driz'əl) *v.i.* rain in small drops. —*n.* a light rain.

drogue (drōg) *n.* a device used to slow down a boat, airplane, etc., or, attached to a harpoon line, to tire a whale.

droll (drōl) *adj.* facetious; comical; amusing. —**droll'er·y,** *n.*

drom'e·dar·y (drom'ə-der-ė) *n.* the Arabian one-humped camel.

drone (drōn) *v.i. & t.* utter a dull, unvaried sound, as a bee; hence, speak in a monotonous tone. —*n.* **1,** a monotonous, continued sound. **2,** the male honeybee. **3,** an idler. **4,** a robot airplane operated by remote control.

drool *v.i.* drivel; slaver, esp. with greed or anticipated pleasure.

droop *v.i.* **1,** sink or hang down, as from weakness or exhaustion. **2,** languish; decline. —*v.t.* let sink or hang down. —*n.* **1,** the act of drooping; a drooping state. **2,** (*Slang*) a killjoy. —**droop'y,** *adj.*

drop *n.* **1,** a small free-falling globule of liquid, as of rain; anything that resembles it; (*pl.*) a liquid medicine. **2,** a small quantity. **3,** a sudden fall or descent; the distance covered by such. **4,** a hanging; a curtain. **5,** a chute; a trapdoor. —*v.i. & t.* [**dropped, drop'ping**] **1,** fall or let fall in globules. **2,** drip. **3,** fall; descend. **4,** sink or let sink to a lower position, level, state, or condition. **5,** fall dead. **6,** let go; dismiss. **7,** utter or write in an offhand manner. **8,** (with *off*) diminish. **9,** (of cattle, etc.) give birth (to) —**drop'pings,** *n.pl.* animal dung. —**drop kick,** (*Football*) a kick given to a dropped ball on the rebound. —**drop out,** cease participation. —**drop shipment,** shipment by a manufacturer direct to his dealer's customer.

drop-"forge' *v.t.* forge (metal) by dropping a heavy weight (*drop hammer*) on it.

drop'out' *n.* one who has dropped out, esp. of school or society.

drop'per (drop'ər) *n.* a tube for dispensing liquid in drops.

drop'sy (drop'sė) *n.* an abnormal accumulation of serous fluid in the body. —**drop'si·cal** (-si-kəl) *adj.*

drosh'ky (drosh'kė) *n.* a Russian horse-drawn passenger vehicle, used as a cab.

dross (drâs) *n.* **1,** the waste matter thrown off from molten metal. **2,** any refuse.

drought (drowt) *n.* long-continued dry weather. Also, **drouth** (drowth).

drove (drōv) *v.* pret. of *drive.* —*n.* a number of cattle, sheep, etc. driven in a herd. —**drov'er,** *n.* a driver of or dealer in such animals.

drown *v.t. & i.* **1,** suffocate or be suffocated by immersion in water or other liquid. **2,** flood; submerge; overwhelm. **3,** (with *out*) prevent from being heard, by creating a louder or more pervasive noise.

drowse (drowz) *v.i.* be half asleep; be heavy or dull. —*n.* a half-sleep.

drow'sy (drow'zė) *adj.* sleepy. —**drow'si·ness,** *n.*

drub *v.t.* [**drubbed, drub'bing**] beat; cudgel. —**drub'bing,** *n.* a bad beating or defeat.

drudge (druj) *v.i.* labor at hard, uninteresting tasks. —*n.* an overworked person; a spiritless toiler. —**drudg'er·y** (-ə-rė) *n.*

drug *n.* **1,** any substance used in the composition or preparation of medicines. **2,** a narcotic. **3,** a commodity unsalable because of overproduction. —*v.t.* [**drugged, drug'ging**] **1,** mix or dose with drugs. **2,** surfeit.

drug'gist (-ist) *n.* a pharmacist.

drug'store" *n.* a store that deals in drugs and, usually, other merchandise.

dru'id (droo'id) *n.* a priest of the ancient Celts.

drum *n.* **1,** a musical instrument consisting of a hollow frame covered on the top by a tightly stretched membrane which is beaten with sticks in playing. **2,** anything drum-shaped. **3,** a fish. **4,** a membrane in the ear: *eardrum.* —*v.i.* [**drummed, drum'ming**] **1,** play a drum. **2,** tap on something with the fingers. **3,** sound like a drum; resound. —*v.t.* **1,** (*Mil.*) expel formally. **2,** impress, as an idea into someone. **3,** (with *up*) attract or solicit, as trade. —**drum major** or **majorette** (*fem.*), the leader of a marching corps of drummers or a band.

drum'lin *n.* (*Geol.*) a long narrow mound, formed by a glacier.

drum'mer (-ər) *n.* **1,** a traveling salesman. **2,** one who plays a drum.

drum'stick" *n.* **1,** a stick with which a drum is beaten. **2,** the leg of a fowl.

drunk *v.* p.p. of *drink* —*adj.* [also, **drunk'en** (-ən)] intoxicated by liquor. —*n.* **1,** a spree. **2,** an inebriated person. —**drunk'-en·ness,** *n.*

drunk'ard (-ərd) *n.* a person given to excessive drinking of liquor.

drupe (droop) *n.* a stone fruit, as the plum, cherry, or peach. —**drupe'let,** *n.* a small drupe, as a section of a berry, containing a hard seed.

dry (drī) *adj.* **1,** without moisture; not wet. **2,** not giving milk, as a *dry cow;* empty, as a *dry well.* **3,** thirsty. **4,** barren; uninteresting. **5,** grave in manner but humorous or sarcastic. **6,** free from sweetness, as certain wines. **7,** (*Colloq.*) of or pert. to prohibition of alcoholic beverages. —*v.t. & i.* free from or lose moisture. —*n.* (*Colloq.*) prohibitionist. —**dry'ness,** *n.* —**dry cell,** a sealed storage battery. —**dry dock,** a structure for holding a ship out of water, for repairs, etc. —**dry goods,** textile fabrics, etc. —**dry ice,** frozen carbon dioxide. —**dry measure,** a system of units of volume or capacity used in measuring dry commodities, as grain. —**dry point,** a process of engraving on copper with a sharp-pointed tool; an engraving so made. —**dry rot,** a fungous disease of timber or other plants; fig., a concealed inward decay, as of public morals. —**dry run,** a rehearsal; demonstration. —**dry up, 1,** become arid or barren. **2,** (*Colloq.*) stop talking. —**dry wall,** a prefabricated plaster wall panel.

dry'ad (drī'ad) *n.* a wood nymph.

dry-'clean" *v.t.* wash (clothes, etc.) in benzene, gasoline, etc.

dry'er (drī'ər) *n.* drier.

du'al (doo'əl) *adj.* relating to or consisting of two parts; twofold.

du·al'i·ty (doo-al'ə-tè) *n.* the state of being twofold.

dub *v.t.* [**dubbed, dub'bing**] **1,** confer a new dignity or name upon. **2,** rub or dress so as to make smooth. **3,** record from or on a previous sound track.

dub'bin (dub'in) *n.* a mixture of oil and tallow for dressing leather.

du·bi'e·ty (doo-bī'ə-tè) *n.* doubtfulness.

du'bi·ous (doo'bè-əs) *adj.* **1,** of questionable value. **2,** doubtful; hesitating. —**du'-bi·ous·ness,** *n.*

du'cal (doo'kəl) *adj.* of or pert. to a duke.

duc'at (duk'ət) *n.* **1,** a former Europ. gold coin. **2,** (*pl.*) (*Slang*) money.

du'ce (doo'chä) *n.* (*Ital.*) **1,** leader. **2,** (*cap.*) Benito Mussolini, head of the Fascist Italian state from 1922-1943.

duch'ess (duch'əs) *n.* the wife of a duke.

duch'y (duch'è) *n.* the territory of a duke or duchess; a dukedom.

duck (duk) *n.* **1,** any of many species of broad-, flat-billed water birds. **2,** (*Colloq.*) a likable person. **3,** a strong cotton or linen fabric; (*pl.*) clothes made of it. **4,** a diving inclination of the head. **5,** a brief dip or plunge in water. —*v.t. & i.* **1,** plunge testify into water. **2,** bob or bow the head suddenly. **3,** dodge by bending down or aside suddenly. **4,** evade.

duck'bill" *n.* the platypus.

duck'ling *n.* a young duck.

duck'pin" *n.* a small bowling pin; (*pl.*) a bowling game.

duck'y (duk'è) (*Colloq.*) *adj.* excellent. —*n.* (as a term of address) darling; dear.

duct (dukt) *n.* **1,** any tube or canal by which a fluid is conducted or conveyed. **2,** a pipe for electric cables or wires. —**duct-less gland,** any of certain glands, as the thyroid, giving off their secretions directly into the blood stream.

duc'tile (duk'təl) *adj.* **1,** capable of being drawn out into wire or threads. **2,** complying; easily led. —**duc·til'i·ty** (-til'ə-tè) *n.*

dud *n.* **1,** (*pl.*) (*Colloq.*) old clothes. **2,** a bomb, shell or firecracker that fails to explode. **3,** a failure.

dude (dood) *n.* **1,** an overdressed man; a fop. **2,** a city person; a tenderfoot. —**dud'-ish,** *adj.* —**dude ranch,** a resort modeled on a cattle ranch.

dudg'eon (duj'ən) *n.* resentment; sullen anger.

due (doo) *adj.* **1,** owed; payable. **2,** suitable. **3,** expected or looked for. **4,** attributable. —*n.* **1,** that which is owed or required; a debt; an obligation. **2,** (*pl.*) a toll; a fee. —**due'bill",** *n.* a written acknowledgment of a debt, made payable in goods or services. —**due to,** because of.

du'el (doo'əl) *n.* **1,** a premeditated combat between two persons with deadly weapons. **2,** any two-sided contest. —**du'el·ist,** *n.*

du·en'na (dū-en'ə) *n.* a chaperon.

du·et' (doo-et') *n.* (*Music*) a composition for two performers; the performance or performers.

duf'fel (duf'əl) *n.* **1,** a coarse woolen thick-napped cloth. **2,** a sportsman's or camper's outfit. —**duffel bag,** a large cloth carrying bag.

duf'fer (duf'ər) *n.* **1,** a peddler. **2,** (*Slang*) a stupid or inefficient person; a poor player at a game.

dug *v.* pret. & p.p. of *dig.* —*n.* **1**, an udder or breast. **2**, a teat or nipple.

du′gong (doo′gong) *n.* a large sea mammal.

dug′out″ *n.* **1**, a boat hollowed out from a log. **2**, a shelter in the ground, esp. in trench warfare.

dui′ker (dī′kər) *n.* a small Afr. antelope.

duke (dook) *n.* **1**, a hereditary title of nobility equivalent to or next below a prince. **2**, the ruler of a duchy. —**duke′dom** (-dəm) *n.*

dul′cet (dul′sit) *adj.* sweet; harmonious; agreeable.

dul′ci·mer (dul′sə-mər) *n.* a precursor of the pianoforte.

dull (dul) **1**, not understanding readily; stupid. **2**, tedious; boring; uninteresting. **3**, not quick or keen in perception. **4**, dismal; cheerless. **5**, not bright or clear; dim. **6**, not sharp; blunt. —*v.t.* & *i.* make or become dull. —**dull′ness**, *n.*

dull′ard (-ərd) *n.* a stupid person; a blockhead.

dulse (duls) *n.* an edible seaweed.

du′ly (doo′lē) *adv.* in a due manner; properly.

Du′ma (doo′mä) *n.* the former Russian lower house of parliament.

dumb (dum) *adj.* **1**, not having the power of speech. **2**, mute; silent. **3**, (*Colloq.*) stupid. —**dumb′ness**, *n.* —**dumb show**, pantomime.

dumb′bell″ *n.* **1**, a weight for gymnastic exercise. **2**, (*Slang*) a dolt.

dumb′wait″er *n.* an elevator to convey food or small articles.

dum′dum *n.* a soft-nosed bullet designed to spread on impact.

dum·found′ (dum-fownd′) *v.t.* strike dumb; confound.

dum′my (dum′ē) *n.* **1**, one who is dumb; a mute. **2**, a figurehead, model, effigy, etc. **3**, the high bidder's partner or his cards, exposed on the table, in bridge and other card games. **4**, (*Colloq.*) a stupid person; a dolt. —*adj.* sham; set up for appearances only.

dump *v.t.* **1**, throw down or let slide down (a mass or body of something); unload. **2**, sell (quantities of stocks, merchandise, etc.) regardless of price. —*n.* **1**, a place for dumping loads, esp. rubbish. **2**, (*Mil.*) a temporary storage place for supplies. **3**, (*pl.*) a state of depression; the doldrums.

dump′ish *adj.* morose; depressed in spirits. —**dump′ish·ness**, *n.*

dump′ling *n.* a lump of dough boiled in soup, stew, etc.

dump′ster (dump′stər) *n.* a large container used for disposal of trash, etc.

dump′y (-ē) *adj.* short and thick; squat. —**dump′i·ness**, *n.*

dun *v.t.* & *i.* [**dunned, dun′ning**] urge to pay a debt. —*n.* a demand for payment. —*adj.* of a dull grayish-brown color.

dunce (duns) *n.* a dull-witted stupid person; an ignoramus. —**dunce cap**, a cone of paper worn as a cap to mark a stupid student.

dun′der·head″ (dun′dər-) *n.* a dunce.

dune (doon) *n.* a hill of sand heaped up by the wind. —**dune buggy**, a vehicle with large balloon tires for traveling on sand, etc.

dung *n.* animal excrement; manure.

dun″ga·ree′ (dung″gə-rē′) *n.* **1**, a coarse cotton material generally blue. **2**, (*pl.*) work clothes made from this material.

dun′geon (dun′jən) *n.* **1**, a deep, dark place of confinement. **2**, the tower of a medieval castle.

dung′hill″ *n.* **1**, a heap of manure. **2**, anything mean, vile, or low.

dunk *v.t.* dip, esp. bread into coffee before eating it.

Dunk′ard (-ərd) *n.* one of a certain religious sect. Also, **Dunk′er.**

dun′nage (dun′ij) *n.* **1**, loose wood used to pack a ship's cargo. **2**, baggage.

du′o (doo′ō) *n.* a couple; pair.

du·o- *pref.* two.

du″o·dec′i·mal (doo″ə-des′ə-məl) *adj.* reckoning by twelves and the powers of twelve.

du″o·de′num (doo″ə-dē′nəm) *n.* the first portion of the small intestine, immediately connected with the stomach. —**du″o·de′-nal**, *adj.*

dupe (doop) *v.t.* deceive; trick; mislead. —*n.* a person easily deceived. —**dup′er·y**, *n.*

du′ple (doo′pəl) *adj.* double; twofold.

du′plex (doo′pleks) *adj.* **1**, double; twofold. —*n.* **1**, an apartment of two floors. **2**, a two-family house.

du′pli·cate (doo′plə-kit) *adj.* **1**, double; twofold. **2**, exactly like something done before. —*n.* an exact copy; a facsimile. —*v.t.* (-kāt″) make a copy or copies of. —**du″pli·ca′tion**, *n.* —**du′pli·ca″tor**, *n.*

du·plic′i·ty (doo-plis′ə-tē) *n.* bad faith; dissimulation; hypocrisy; double dealing.

du′ra·ble (dyûr′ə-bəl) *adj.* lasting; long-wearing; not perishable or changeable. —**du″ra·bil′i·ty**, *n.*

durable press treated to hold its shape after repeated washing.

du·ral′u·min (dyû-ral′yə-min) *n.* (*T.N.*) a strong and light alloy of aluminum.

dur′ance (dyûr′əns) *n.* imprisonment; involuntary confinement of any kind.

du·ra′tion (dyû-rā′shən) *n.* the length of time during which anything continues or lasts.

dur′bar (dēr′bär) *n.* in India, a prince's audience room, or an official audience or reception.

du·ress′ (dyû-res′) *n.* **1,** restraint of personal liberty; imprisonment. **2,** coercion.

dur′ing (dûr′ing) *prep.* in the time or course of; throughout the continuance of.

dur′mast (dēr′mast) *n.* a heavy, elastic variety of oak.

du′rum (dûr′əm) *n.* a hard wheat used in making macaroni.

dusk *n.* **1,** the state between light and darkness, esp. at twilight. **2,** partial darkness; shadow. **3,** swarthiness.

dusk′y (dus′kè) *adj.* dark, as at dusk. —**dusk′i·ness,** *n.*

dust *n.* **1,** fine, dry particles of earth or other matter. **2,** a dead body; remains. **3,** the ground; a low condition. **4,** a small quantity of any powdered substance sprinkled over something. —*v.t.* **1,** free from dust or sweep away dust from. **2,** sprinkle with a powder. —**dust bowl,** an area where the dry topsoil is blown about by the wind. —**dust cover,** a cover to keep out dust, as the jacket of a book.

dust′er (dus′tər) *n.* **1,** a cloth or implement for removing dust. **2,** a light overcoat. **3,** peignoir.

dust′y (dus′tè) *adj.* being covered with or charged with dust. —**dust′i·ness,** *n.*

Dutch (duch) *adj.* pert. to the Netherlands, its people or language. —**Dutch door,** a door with upper and lower sections that can be opened separately. —**Dutch oven,** a kettle for baking. —**Dutch treat,** a party in which each pays his share. —**Dutch uncle,** a severe but well-wishing critic. —**Dutch wife,** a bolster used as a sleeping companion. —**go Dutch,** each pay his own way. —**in Dutch,** in trouble.

du′te·ous (doo′tè-əs) *adj.* performing the duties required; obedient. —**du′te·ous·ness,** *n.*

du′ti·a·ble (doo′tè-ə-bəl) *adj.* subject to customs duty.

du′ti·ful (doo′ti-fəl) *adj.* **1,** duteous. **2,** loyal; diligent. —**du′ti·ful·ness,** *n.*

du′ty (doo′tè) *n.* **1,** good behavior owed to one's parents or superiors. **2,** service requisite to one's position. **3,** any moral obligation. **4,** a tax; excise or customs dues. —**du′ty-free″,** *adj.* not dutiable.

du′ve·tyn″ (doo′və-tēn″) *n.* a soft woolen cloth with a long nap.

dwarf (dwôrf) *n.* **1,** a person, animal or plant much below ordinary size. —*adj.* below average size. —*v.t.* **1,** hinder from growing; stunt. **2,** cause to seem small by comparison. —*v.i.* become less. —**dwarf′-ish,** *adj.*

dwell (dwel) *v.i.* [*pret. & p.p.* **dwelt** or **dwelled**] **1,** stay; remain. **2,** abide as a permanent resident; reside. **3,** (usually with *on*) dilate upon, as a topic. —**dwell′er,** *n.* a resident. —**dwell′ing,** *n.* a house for human occupation.

dwin′dle (dwin′dəl) *v.i.* diminish; become less; shrink; waste away.

dy′ad (dī′ad) *n.* **1,** two units treated as one. **2,** an element with a valence of two, as oxygen in H_2O. **3,** (*Biol.*) a secondary unit of organization; one of a pair of chromosomes.

dye (dī) *n.* **1,** a liquid or other matter used to change the color of something else. **2,** a particular color; tint. —*v.t.* [**dyed, dye′-ing**] change the color of, with a dye. —**dy′er,** *n.* —**dye′stuff″** *n.* a substance used for making dye. —**dyed′-in-the-wool″,** *adj.* confirmed in character; thoroughgoing.

dy·na- (dī-nə) *pref.* power.

dy·nam′ic (dī-nam′ik) *adj.* **1,** full of force and energy; active; potent. **2,** pert. to dynamics. —**dy·nam′i·cal·ly,** *adv.*

dy·nam′ics (dī-nam′iks) *n.* **1,** a branch of mechanics treating of motion. **2,** (construed as *pl.*) the principles of active operation in any field.

dy′na·mite″ (dī′nə-mīt″) *n.* **1,** an explosive, nitroglycerin mixed with sand. **2,** a precarious situation or plan. **3,** (*Colloq.*) something exciting. —*v.t.* blow up with dynamite.

dy′na·mo″ (dī′nə-mō″) *n.* [*pl.* **-mos″**] a machine that converts mechanical energy into electrical energy.

dy″na·mom′e·ter (dī″nə-mom′i-tər) *n.* an instrument for measuring force or power.

dy′nas·ty (dī′nəs-tè) *n.* **1,** a succession of rulers or monarchs of the same line or family. **2,** the period during which a dynasty rules. —**dy′nast,** *n.* a ruler. —**dy·nas′tic,** *adj.*

dyne (dīn) *n.* (*Physics*) the unit of force in the centimeter-gram-second system.

Dy′nel (dī′nel) *n.* (*T.N.*) a synthetic, flame-resistant fiber; the yarn or fabric made from it.

dys- (dis) *pref.* with difficulty; difficulty.

dys′en·ter″y (dis′ən-ter″è) *n.* a disease of the large intestine characterized by diarrhetic

---

discharge of blood and mucus from the bowels.

dys·func′tion (dis-funk′shən) *n.* (*Med.*) impaired functioning, as of a bodily organ.

dys·lex′i·a (dis-leks′ē-ə) *n.* an impairment of the ability to read. —**dys·lex′ic**, *adj.*

dys·pep′sia (dis-pep′shə) *n.* impaired power of digestion.

dys·pep′tic (dis-pep′tik) *adj.* & *n.* (a person) afflicted with dyspepsia, hence gloomy or irritable. —**dys·pep′ti·cal·ly**, *adv.*

dys·pro′si·um (dis-prō′sē-əm) *n.* a metallic element, no. 66, symbol Dy, one of the rare earths.

dys·tro·phy (dis′trə-fè) *n.* faulty nutrition.

E

E, e (ē) the fifth letter of the English alphabet.

each (ēch) *adj.* every (unit) (of a group or series considered one by one) —*pron.* every one individually. —*adv.* apiece.

ea′ger (ē′gər) *adj.* having keen desire or longing; being impatient, intent or earnest. —**ea′ger·ness**, *n.*

ea′gle (ē′gəl) *n.* **1,** a large bird of prey. **2,** a conventional representation of an eagle. **3,** a U. S. ten-dollar gold piece. **4,** in golf, two below par on a hole. —**ea′glet**, *n.* a young eagle.

ear (ir) *n.* **1,** the organ of hearing in mammals; the external part alone. **2,** the sense of hearing; ability to discriminate among sounds. **3,** attention; heed. **4,** something likened to an ear. **5,** the part of a cereal plant that contains the grains.

ear′drop″ *n.* **1,** an earring with a pendant. **2,** (usu. *pl.*) medication for the ear.

ear′drum″ *n.* the tympanum.

earl (ērl) *n.* a British nobleman ranking above a viscount and below a marquis. —**earl′dom**, *n.*

ear′ly (ēr′lē) *adv.* & *adj.* **1,** occurring near the beginning. **2,** of ancient date. **3,** before an appointed time. **4,** in the near future. —**ear′li·ness**, *n.* —**early bird**, early riser; first arrival.

ear′mark″ *n.* a mark of identification. —*v.t.* **1,** mark for identification. **2,** set aside for a specific purpose.

ear′muff″ *n.* one of a pair of coverings for warming the ears.

earn (ērn) *v.t.* **1,** gain in return for labor or service, or as profit. **2,** deserve; merit. —**earn′ings**, *n.pl.* wages; profits.

ear′nest (ēr′nəst) *adj.* **1,** serious in purpose or effort; sincere. **2,** diligent; zealous.

3, important; grave. **4,** showing sincerity. —*n.* a pledge. —**ear′nest·ness**, *n.* —**earnest money,** money given to bind a contract.

ear′phone″ *n.* a small speaker worn on the ear, for radio, telephone, etc.

ear′plug″ *n.* a stopper placed in the ear to reduce noise.

ear′ring″ *n.* an ornament worn on the ear.

ear′shot″ *n.* range of hearing.

ear′split″ting *adj.* extremely loud.

earth (ērth) *n.* **1,** the globe or planet we inhabit. **2,** the solid matter of the globe. **3,** the loose material of the globe's surface; sand, soil, etc. **4,** the inhabitants of the globe; the world. —**earth science,** a science, such as geography, geology, etc., that deals with the earth.

earth′bound″ *adj.* bound by earthly or mundane ties or interests.

earth′en (ēr′thən) *adj.* made of earth, clay, etc. —**earth′en·ware″**, *n.* vessels of baked clay.

earth′ling *n.* **1,** an inhabitant of the earth; a mortal. **2,** a worldly person.

earth′ly (-lē) *adj.* **1,** worldly; material. **2,** (*Colloq.*) possible; conceivable. —**earth′-li·ness**, *n.*

earth′nut″ *n.* an edible nut or plant part that grows underground; a tuber.

earth′quake″ *n.* a trembling or shaking of the earth's surface.

earth′shak″ing *adj.* (*Colloq.*) of great importance.

earth′work″ *n.* a structure of earth, as a rampart.

earth′worm″ *n.* any of various burrowing worms.

earth′y (ēr′thē) *adj.* **1,** of or like earth. **2,** worldly or coarse. —**earth′i·ness**, *n.*

ear′wax″ *n.* a yellowish secretion of glands of the external ear.

ear′wig″ *n.* a small harmless insect.

ease (ēz) *n.* **1,** physical comfort. **2,** mental tranquillity. **3,** freedom from difficulty; facility. **4,** unaffectedness. —*v.t.* **1,** put in a state of ease; rid of pain, anxiety, etc. **2,** lessen; mitigate. **3,** make less difficult. —*v.i.* (often with *off* or *up*) become less painful, severe, difficult, etc. —**at ease, 1,** in a state of ease. **2,** (*Mil.*) not at attention.

ea′sel (ē′zəl) *n.* a stand for supporting a picture, blackboard, etc.

ease′ment (ēz′mənt) *n.* **1,** the act of easing. **2,** (*Law*) a right to use land owned by another person.

east (ēst) *n.* **1,** one of the four cardinal points of the compass, 90 degrees clockwise from north. **2,** (usu. *cap.*) a region lying in this direction, as the Orient. —*adj.* in, toward or from the east.

East'er (ēs'tər) *n.* the festival commemorating the resurrection of Jesus Christ, observed on the first Sunday after the first full moon that occurs on or after March 21.

east'er·ly (-lē) *adj. & adv.* toward or from the east.

east'ern (-tərn) *adj.* in or pert. to the east. —**east'ern·er,** *n.*

east'ward (-wərd) *adj. & adv.* toward the east.

eas'y (ē'zē) *adj.* **1,** not difficult. **2,** comfortable; tranquil. **3,** not oppressive. —*adv.* (*Colloq.*) easily. —**eas'i·ness,** *n.* —**easy chair,** a comfortable chair. —**go** or **be easy on,** treat with restraint. —**on easy street,** in comfortable circumstances.

eas'y·go"ing *adj.* calm and unhurried in manner or pace.

eat (ēt) *v.t.* **1,** take into the mouth and swallow for nourishment (esp. of nonliquid food). **2,** consume by corrosion, rust, etc. —*v.i.* dine; consume food. —*n.* (*pl.*) (*Colloq.*) food. —**eat'a·bles,** *n.pl.* articles of food. —**eat crow,** accept defeat or humiliation. —**eat dirt** or **humble pie,** apologize humbly. —**eat one's words,** retract what one has said.

eat'er·y (ēt'ə-rē) *n.* (*Colloq.*) a lunchroom.

eau de co·logne' (ō"də-kə-lōn') *n.* cologne.

eaves (ēvz) *n.pl.* the edge of a roof overhanging the walls.

eaves'drop" *v.i.* listen secretly.

ebb (eb) *v.i.* flow back, as tidal water; recede; fall away. —*n.* **1,** a receding or ebbing. **2,** a decline.

eb'on·ite (eb'ə-nīt) *n.* hard rubber, esp. when black; vulcanite. —**eb'on·ize,** *v.t.*

eb'on·y (eb'ən-ē) *n.* a hard, durable wood from various trees. —*adj.* **1,** of ebony. **2,** black.

e·bul'li·ent (i-bul'yənt) *adj.* greatly excited or demonstrative; boiling. —**e·bul'li·ence,** *n.*

eb"ul·li'tion (eb"ə-lish'ən) *n.* **1,** a boiling up or overflow of liquid. **2,** an outburst of feeling, passion, etc.

ec·cen'tric (ek-sen'trik) *adj.* **1,** off center; not having the same center. **2,** elliptical, not circular. **3,** deviating from usual or recognized form; queer. —*n.* **1,** a queer or erratic person. **2,** a contrivance for transforming rotary to linear motion. —**ec·cen'tri·cal·ly,** *adv.* —**ec"cen·tric'i·ty** (ek"sən-tris'ə-tē) *n.*

ec·cle"si·as'tic (e-klē"zē-as'tik) *n.* a clergyman. —**ec·cle"si·as'ti·cal,** *adj.* pert. to the church or clergy.

ech'e·lon" (esh'ə-lon") *n.* **1,** a level of command. **2,** a steplike deployment of military or naval units.

ech'o (ek'ō) *n.* **1,** repetition of a sound by reflection of the sound waves. **2,** sympathetic response; one who so responds. —*v.i.* produce an echo. —*v.t.* repeat or imitate. —**ech·o'ic,** *adj.*

ech"o·lo·ca'tion *n.* the location of objects by use of radio waves, as in radar and sonar. Also, **ech"o·la'tion** (-lā'shən)

é·clair' (ā-klār') *n.* a frosted, filled cake.

é·clat' (ā-kla') *n.* brilliant effect; splendor.

ec·lec'tic (ek-lek'tik) *adj.* **1,** selective; not following any one school of thought. **2,** consisting of selections from various sources. —**ec·lec'ti·cal·ly,** *adv.* —**ec·lec'ti·cism,** *n.*

e·clipse' (i-klips') *n.* **1,** obscuration of the light of the sun by intervention of the moon (*solar eclipse*), or of the moon by intervention of the earth (*lunar eclipse*). **2,** any obscuration or diminution of light, brilliance, glory, etc. —*v.t.* **1,** cast a shadow upon. **2,** surpass.

e·clip'tic (i-klip'tik) *n. & adj.* the great circle which is the apparent annual path of the sun.

ec'logue (ek'log) *n.* a short pastoral poem.

ec'o·cide" (ek'ə-sīd") *n.* deliberate destruction of the natural environment.

e·col'o·gy (i-kol'ə-jē) *n.* **1,** (*Biol.*) the study of the relations between organisms and their environment. **2,** (*Sociol.*) the study of the causes and effects of the spatial distribution of population. —**e"co·log'i·cal** (ē"kə-loj'ə-kəl; ek"ə-) *adj.* —**e·col'o·gist,** *n.*

e"co·nom'ic (ē"kə-nom'ik; ek"ə-) *adj.* **1,** utilitarian. **2,** pert. to economics. —**e"co·nom'i·cal,** *adj.* thrifty.

e"co·nom'ics (ē"kə-nom'iks; ek"ə-) *n.* the science of the production and distribution of goods and services.

e·con'o·mist (i-kon'ə-mist) *n.* a scientist in the field of economics.

e·con'o·mize" (i-kon'ə-mīz") *v.i.* manage frugally.

e·con'o·my (i-kon'ə-mē) *n.* **1,** avoidance of or freedom from waste in expenditure or management; thrift. **2,** a system of management of resources, esp. pecuniary.

ec'o·sphere" (ek'ə-sfir") *n.* the part of the universe habitable by living organisms.

ec'o·sys"tem (ek'ə-sis"təm) *n.* an ecological community.

ec'ru (ek'roo) *adj. & n.* light tan.

ec'sta·sy (ek'stə-sē) *n.* overpowering emotion or exaltation; rapture. —**ec·stat'ic** (ek-stat'ik), *adj.* —**ec·stat'i·cal·ly,** *adv.*

ec·to- (ek'tō) *pref.* external; outer.

-ec'to·my (-ek'tə-mē) *suf.* surgical excision.

ec′to·plasm (ek′tə-plaz-əm) *n.* a visible exudation, in spiritualism.

é·cu′ (ā-kū′) *n.* [*pl.* **é·cus″** (ā-kū′)] (*Fr.*) **1**, a triangular shield of the middle ages. **2**, a 14th-century French coin.

ec″u·men′i·cal (ek″yū-men′i-kəl) *adj.* **1**, general; universal. **2**, belonging to the whole Christian church.

ec′ze·ma (eg′zə-mə) *n.* an inflammation of the skin, often attended by exudation of lymph.

-ed *suf.* **1**, possessed of: forming adjectives from nouns, as *moneyed*. **2**, forming past tenses of verbs.

E′dam (ēdəm) *n.* a yellow cheese.

ed′dy (ed′ē) *n.* a rotary motion in a stream of liquid or gas; a small whirl or vortex. —*v.i.* whirl; spin.

e′del·weiss′ (ā′dəl-vīs″) *n.* a flowering herb of alpine regions.

e·de′ma (ē-dē′mə) *n.* a disease in which body liquids collect in the tissues, causing swelling; dropsy. —**e·dem′ic** (ē-dem′ik) *adj.*

E′den (ē′dən) *n.* **1**, the garden that was the first home of Adam and Eve. **2**, any delightful region or residence; a paradise.

edge (ej) *n.* **1**, the extreme border or margin of anything; verge; brink; rim. **2**, the line of junction of two faces of a solid object; the sharpened side of a blade. **3**, sharpness; keenness; acuteness. **4**, (*Colloq.*) advantage. —*v.t.* **1**, put an edge or border on. **2**, sharpen. **3**, (often with *out*) defeat by a slight margin. —*v.i.* move sidewise; advance gradually. —**edg′ing**, *n.* a border. —**edg′y** (ej′ē) *adj.* irritable; nervous. —**on edge**, edgy; impatient.

edge′wise″ *adv.* **1**, in the direction of the edge. **2**, barely. Also, **edge′ways″**.

ed′i·ble (ed′ə-bəl) *adj.* fit to be eaten as food. —*n.* something eatable. —**ed″i·bil′i·ty**, *n.*

e′dict (ē′dikt) *n.* a decree or proclamation issued by an authority.

ed′i·fice (ed′ə-fis) *n.* a building, esp. one that is large and imposing.

ed′i·fy″ (ed′i-fī″) *v.t.* build up faith, belief, or knowledge in (a person); persuade; instruct. —**ed″i·fi·ca′tion** (-fi-kā′shən) *n.*

ed′it *v.t.* **1**, prepare (a manuscript) for publication by revising, correcting, etc. **2**, supervise (a publication) by collecting and preparing materials.

e·di′tion (i-dish′ən) *n.* the whole number of copies of a work printed at one time.

ed′i·tor (ed′i-tər) *n.* **1**, one who edits; one who corrects, compiles, etc. **2**, one who selects the contents of a publication.

ed″i·to′ri·al (ed″i-tôr′ē-əl) *n.* an article presenting the opinion of an editor. —*adj.*

pert. to editing or an editor. —**ed″i·to′ri·al·ize″** (-īz″) *v.i.* express an opinion, esp, in reporting news.

ed′u·cate″ (ed′yə-kāt″) *v.t.* **1**, impart knowledge and training to; develop mentally and morally by instruction. **2**, send to school; provide schooling for. —**ed′u·ca·ble**, *adj.*

ed″u·ca′tion (ed″yə-kā′shən) *n.* **1**, act or process of educating; instruction. **2**, the science of teaching; pedagogy. —**ed″u·ca′tion·al**, *adj.*

ed′u·ca″tor (ed′yə-kā″tər) *n.* a teacher.

e·duce′ (ē-dūs′) *v.t.* draw out; elicit; develop. —**e·duc′tion** (-duk′shən) *n.*

-ee *suf.* **1**, the object or recipient of, as *draftee*, one who is drafted. **2**, a person in a specified condition. **3**, a person that performs a specified action.

eel (ēl) *n.* an elongated fish without ventral fins, resembling a snake.

e′en (ēn) (*Poetic*) *n.* evening. —*adv.* even.

e′er (âr) *adv.* (*Poetic*) ever.

-eer (ir) *suf.* one whose profession, occupation, activity or residence is. Also, **-ier.**

ee′rie (ir′ē) *adj.* inspiring fear; strange; weird. —**ee′ri·ness**, *n.*

ef·face′ (e-fās′) *v.t.* **1**, rub out; erase; obliterate. **2**, make inconspicuous. —**ef·face′ment**, *n.*

ef·fect′ (e-fekt′) *n.* **1**, what is produced by a cause; something that follows as a consequence; a result. **2**, power to produce results; force; validity. **3**, the state of being operative, in force, or active. **4**, (*pl.*) property, esp. personal. —*v.t.* produce as a result; be the cause or agent of; make happen; achieve. —**take effect**, begin to operate.

ef·fec′tive (e-fek′tiv) *adj.* **1**, productive; efficient. **2**, having a desired effect; successful. —**ef·fec′tive·ness**, *n.*

ef·fec′tu·al (e-fek′choo-əl) *adj.* producing a desired effect. —**ef·fec″tu·al′i·ty**, *n.*

ef·fec′tu·ate″ (e-fek′choo-āt″) *v.t.* make happen; cause. —**ef·fec″tu·a′tion**, *n.*

ef·fen′di (e-fen′dē) *n.* a Turkish title of respect.

ef·fem′i·nate (e-fem′ə-nət) *adj.* having the qualities of the female sex; womanish (applied to men). —**ef·fem′i·na·cy** (-nə-sē) *n.*

ef′fer·ent (ef′ə-rənt) *adj.* carrying away or outward, as nerve impulses.

ef″fer·vesce′ (ef″ər-ves′) *v.i.* **1**, bubble and hiss, like a boiling liquid. **2**, exhibit excitement or liveliness. —**ef″fer·ves′cence**, *n.* —**ef″fer·ves′cent**, *adj.*

ef·fete′ (ə-fēt′) *adj.* worn out by age; staled by usage; exhausted.

ef″fi·ca′cious (ef″i-kā′shəs) *adj.* having power adequate to an intended purpose;

effective; effectual. —**ef'fi·ca·cy** (-kə-sé) *n.*

ef·fi'cient (i-fish'ənt) *adj.* **1,** adequate in performance or operation; capable; competent. **2,** (of a machine) giving a relatively high output of work. **3,** acting as a cause; producing an effect; causative. —**ef·fi'cien·cy,** *n.*

ef'fi·gy (ef'ə-jé) *n.* a life-sized sculptured likeness or dummy of a person.

ef"flo·resce' (ef"lō-res') *v.i.* **1,** burst into bloom; blossom. **2,** (Chem.) decompose into powdery substance. —**ef"flo·res'cence,** *n.* —**ef"flo·res'cent,** *adj.*

ef'flu·ence (ef'loo-əns) *n.* **1,** act of flowing out. **2,** an emanation. Also, **ef'flux** (ef'luks). —**ef'flu·ent** (-ənt) *adj. & n.*

ef·flu'vi·um (i-floo'vé-əm) *n.* [pl. **-a** (-ə)] an unpleasant vapor or emanation from something.

ef'fort (ef'ərt) *n.* **1,** voluntary exertion to perform an action. **2,** a strenuous attempt. **3,** a work; an achievement.

ef·fron'ter·y (i-frun'tə-ré) *n.* barefaced impropriety; shamelessness; impudence.

ef·ful'gent (i-ful'jənt) *adj.* radiantly bright. —**ef·fulge',** *v.t. & i.* —**ef·ful'gence,** *n.*

ef·fuse' (e-fūz') *v.t.* pour out; shed. —*v.i.* seep out; exude. —*adj.* (e-fūs') loosely spread out. —**ef·fu'sion** (i-fū'zhən) *n.* —**ef·fu'sive** (-siv) *adj.* gushing.

eft *n.* **1,** a newt. **2,** a small lizard.

e·gad' (i-gad') *interj.* a mild oath.

e·gal'i·tar'i·an (i-gal'ə-târ'é-ən) *adj.* advocating equal rights for all. —*n.* one who advocates this. —**e·gal'i·tar'i·an·ism,** *n.*

egg (eg) *n.* **1,** the reproductive cell and its envelopes, as formed in a female animal. **2,** this cell and its nourishment enclosed in a hard rounded shell, such as produced by birds. **3,** anything resembling a hen's egg. —*v.t.* (usu. with *on*) incite; urge.

egg'head" *n.* (usu. contemptuous) intellectual; highbrow.

egg'nog" (eg'nog") *n.* a drink made of beaten eggs, sugar, and milk, often with an alcoholic beverage.

egg'plant" *n.* a plant having edible egg-shaped fruit, sometimes yellow.

e'gis (ē'jis) *n.* protection; sponsorship. Also, **ae'gis.**

eg'lan·tine" (eg'lən-tīn") *n.* any of several brier plants.

e'go (ē'gō) *n.* [pl. **-gos**] the ''I''; that which feels, acts, and thinks; the self.

e"go·cen'tric (ē"gō-sen'trik) *adj.* self-centered; selfish; individualistic. —*n.* also an egocentric person.

e'go·ism (ē'gō-iz-əm) *n.* **1,** the doctrine that self-interest is the basis of all behavior. **2,** conceit. —**e'go·ist,** *n.*

e"go·ma·ni'a (ē"gō-mā'né-ə) *n.* abnormally developed egotism. —**e"go·ma'ni·ac,** *adj. & n.*

e'go·tism (ē'gə-tiz-əm) *n.* the habit of talking too much about oneself; conceit. —**e'go·tist,** *n.* —**e"go·tis'tic** (-tis'tik) *adj.* —**e"go·tis'ti·cal·ly,** *adv.*

e·gre'gious (i-grē'jəs) *adj.* **1,** (Archaic) remarkable; striking. **2,** extraordinarily flagrant. —**e·gre'gious·ness,** *n.*

e'gress (ē'gras) *n.* **1,** the act of going out; departure. **2,** a way for going out; an exit. —**e·gres'sion** (i-gresh'ən) *n.*

e'gret (ē'grət) *n.* **1,** any of various herons. **2,** a plume from an egret.

E·gyp'tian (i-jip'shən) *adj.* pert. to Egypt, its people, customs, etc. —*n.* a native of Egypt.

eh (ā) *interj.* what?

ei'der (ī'dər) *n.* a large sea duck, whose breast feathers are prized for stuffing pillows, etc. —**eider down, 1,** the down of the duck. **2,** a quilt made of it. **3,** a soft napped fabric of cotton or wool.

ei·det'ic (ī-det'ik) *adj.* based on intuition.

ei·do'lon (ī-dō'lən) *n.* [pl. **-la** (-lə)] **1,** an image or likeness. **2,** a specter or apparition.

eight (āt) *n. & adj.* the cardinal number between seven and nine, expressed by 8. —**eighth** (ātth) *adj. & n.*

eight ball in pool, a ball numbered 8 and colored black. —**behind the eight ball,** (Slang) in a predicament; helpless.

eigh"teen' (ā"tēn') *n. & adj.* eight plus ten, 18. —**eigh"teenth'** (-tēnth') *adj. & n.*

eight'y (ā'tē) *n. & adj.* eight times ten, 80. —**eight'i·eth** (-əth) *adj. & n.*

ein'stein"i·um (īn'stīn"é-əm) *n.* an unstable, radioactive chemical element, no. 99, symbol E, produced artificially.

ei'ther (ē'thər; ī'-) *adj.* **1,** one or the other of two. **2,** each of two. —*pron.* one or the other. —*adv.* also; further, esp. in emphatic denial. —*conj.* precedes the first of two coordinate alternatives, the second being preceded by *or*.

e·jac'u·late" (i-jak'yə-lāt") *v.t.* **1,** utter suddenly and briefly; exclaim. **2,** emit forcibly; discharge. —**e·jac'u·la'tion,** *n.*

e·ject' (i-jekt') *v.t.* throw out; drive away; expel; evict. —**e·jec'tion,** *n.* —**e·jec'tor,** *n.*

eke (ēk) *v.t.* (with *out*) **1,** obtain with difficulty. **2,** supplement. —*adv.* (Archaic) also.

e·kis'tics (é-kis'tiks) *n.* the science of urban planning and development.

e·lab'o·rate (i-lab'ə-rət) *adj.* **1,** worked out with great care or exactness. **2,** intricate; involved. —*v.t.* & *i.* (-rāt") work out with precision, in full detail; add details. —**e·lab'o·rate·ness,** *n.* —**e·lab"o·ra'tion,** *n.*

e·lan' (ē-lan') *n.* ardor; impetuous enthusiasm; dash.

e'land (ē'lənd) *n.* a large Afr. antelope.

e·lapse' (i-laps') *v.i.* (of time) pass away.

e·las'tic (i-las'tik) *adj.* **1,** tending to revert to an original shape after distortion (of a solid); tending to expand (as a gas). **2,** highly flexible. **3,** recovering original form or condition readily; buoyant. —*n.* an elastic cord or band. —**e·las'ti·cal·ly,** *adv.* —**e"las·tic'i·ty** (ē"las-tis'ə-tē) *n.*

e·las'to·mer (ē-las'tə-mər) *n.* an elastic substance.

e·late' (i-lāt') *v.t.* make proud or exultant; gratify. —**e·la'tion,** *n.* great joy.

el'bow (el'bō) *n.* **1,** the joint connecting the long bones of the arm. **2,** an angle or bend. —*v.t.* & *i.* push with the elbows; jostle. —**elbow grease,** (*Colloq.*) energetic labor with the hands. —**el'bow·room",** *n.* enough space for comfort.

eld'er (el'dər) *adj.* older; senior. —*n.* **1,** a senior in age. **2,** a leader or legislator in a tribe, community, or church. **3,** a shrub or small tree, bearing a reddish fruit.

el'der·ber'ry *n.* the small dark berry of the elder plant, used in wine, medicine, etc.

eld'er·ly (-lē) *adj.* rather old. —**eld'er·li·ness,** *n.*

eld'est (el'dəst) *adj.* oldest.

El"do·ra'do (el"də-rä'dō) *n.* a fabulously rich region; a golden opportunity.

e·lect' (i-lekt') *v.t.* **1,** select for office by vote. **2,** choose; prefer; determine in favor of. —*adj.* **1,** voted into office but not yet inducted. **2,** chosen. **3,** superior; select; choice. —*n.* a person or persons chosen or worthy to be chosen.

e·lec'tion (i-lek'shən) *n.* act of electing; balloting. —**e·lec"tion·eer'** (-ir') *v.i.* solicit votes.

e·lec'tive (i-lek'tiv) *adj.* **1,** chosen by election. **2,** having the duty or power to elect. **3,** optional. —*n.* an optional academic course.

e·lec'tor (i-lek'tər) *n.* **1,** one qualified to vote. **2,** in the U.S., a member of the electoral college. —**e·lec'to·rate** (-tər-ət) *n.* body of voters. —**e·lec'tress,** *n.fem.*

e·lec'tor·al (i-lek'tər-əl) *adj.* pert. to election or electors. —**electoral college,** the body of persons chosen by popular vote to elect the president and vice-president of the U.S.

e·lec'tric (i-lek'trik) *adj.* **1,** of or pert. to electricity. **2,** operated by the power of electricity. **3,** startling; exciting. Also, **e·lec'tri·cal** (-tri-kəl). —**electrical storm,** a lightning storm. —**electric chair,** a chairlike device used for electrocution. —**electric eye,** a photoelectric cell.

e·lec"tri'cian (i-lek"trish'ən) *n.* a craftsman skilled in making, repairing or operating electric equipment.

e·lec"tric'i·ty (i-lek"tris'ə-tē) *n.* **1,** a force, manifest in magnetism, lightning, etc., utilized by man for power, light, etc. **2,** a flow of electric current.

e·lec'tri·fy" (i-lek'tri-fī") *v.t.* **1,** charge with electricity. **2,** equip for operation by electricity. **3,** startle greatly; thrill. —**e·lec"·tri·fi·ca'tion** (-fi-kā'shən) *n.*

e·lec'tro- (i-lek-trō) *pref.* pert. to or employing electricity.

e·lec"tro·cute" (i-lek"trə-kūt") *v.t.* kill by electric shock. —**e·lec"tro·cu'tion,** *n.* —**e·lec"tro·cu'tion·ist,** *n.*

e·lec'trode (i-lek'trōd) *n.* a conductor of electricity, esp. the terminal of such a conductor.

e·lec"tro·lier' (i-lek"trō-lir') *n.* a support for electric lights, esp. one like a chandelier.

e·lec"trol'o·gist (i-lek-trol'ə-jist) *n.* one who removes warts, hair, etc., using electricity.

e·lec"trol'y·sis (i-lek"trol'ə-sis) *n.* the decomposition of a chemical compound by an electric current. —**e·lec"tro·lyt'ic** (-lit'ik) *adj.*

e·lec'tro·lyte" (i-lek'trə-līt") *n.* a liquid or solid that conducts electricity by flow of ions.

e·lec"tro·mag'net *n.* an iron core, magnetized by an electric current passing through a wire coiled around it. —**e·lec"tro·mag·net'ic,** *adj.* —**e·lec"tro·mag·net'i·cal·ly,** *adv.* —**e·lec"tro·mag'net·ism,** *n.*

e·lec"tro·mo'tive (i-lek"trə-mō'tiv) *adj.* pert. to, or producing, electric current.

e·lec'tron (i-lek'tron) *n.* one of the fundamental particles of matter, believed to be the unit of negative electricity. —**e·lec"·tron'ic,** *adj.* —**e·lec"tron'i·cal·ly,** *adv.* —**electron gun,** a cathode-ray tube. —**electronic music,** music produced by a synthesizer, or by altering natural sounds electronically (*musique concrète*).

e·lec"tron'ics *n.* the science dealing with the action of electrons.

e·lec"tro·plate" (i-lek"trə-plāt") *v.t.* coat with metal by electrolysis.

e·lec"tro·shock' *n.* a treatment for certain mental disorders using electric current.

Also, **electroshock therapy, shock treatment.**

e·lec″tro·stat′ic (-stat′ik) *adj.* producing or containing static electricity. —**e·lec″tro·stat′ics,** *n.sing.* the study of static electricity.

e·lec′tro·type″ (i-lek′trə-tīp″) *n.* a printing plate made by an electrolytic process; the print made from such a plate. —*v.t.* make an electrotype of.

el″ee·mos′y·nar·y (el″ə-mos′ə-ner-ė) *adj.* charitable.

el′e·gant (el′i-gənt) *adj.* having or exhibiting good taste; luxurious. —**el′e·gance,** *n.*

el·e′gi·ac (e-lē′jė-ak) *adj.* expressing sorrow.

el′e·gy (el′ə-jė) *n.* a mournful poem or song, esp. in lament for the dead. —**el′e·gist,** *n.* —**el′e·gize″** (-jīz″) *v.t.* & *i.*

el′e·ment (el′i-mənt) *n.* **1,** that of which anything is in part composed; component; constituent. **2,** (*Chem.*) one of the substances of which all matter is composed, believed to be formed by particles or forces common to all. **3,** (*pl.*) rudimentary principles of an art or science. **4,** that in which something exists; proper or natural environment. **5,** (*pl.*) atmospheric forces. **6,** (*pl.*) the bread and wine used in the Eucharist. —**el″e·men′tal,** *adj.* basic; primal.

el″e·men′ta·ry (-ə-rė) *adj.* simple; pert. to elements or first principles. —**elementary school,** kindergarten or first grade through seventh or eighth grades.

el′e·phant (el′ə-fənt) *n.* a large mammal of Afr. and India having a long prehensile proboscis or trunk and long ivory tusks. —**el″e·phan′tine** (-fan′tin) *adj.* huge. —**white elephant,** a burdensome or embarrassing possession.

el″e·phan·ti′a·sis (el″ə-fən-tī′ə-sis) *n.* a disease causing enlargement of bodily parts.

el′e·vate″ (el′i-vāt″) *v.t.* **1,** move to a higher level or station; raise; lift up. **2,** cheer.

el″e·va′tion (el″i-vā′shən) *n.* **1,** act of elevating. **2,** a high place; eminence. **3,** a drawing or plan of a vertical surface of a structure. **4,** altitude above the ground.

el′e·va″tor (el′i-vā″tər) *n.* **1,** a platform or small room capable of being raised or lowered to carry passengers or freight. **2,** a building for storage of grain, etc. **3,** a type of rudder on an airplane. —**elevator shoe** or **heel,** a very high heel, used to make one appear taller.

e·lev′en (i-lev′ən) *n.* & *adj.* the cardinal number between ten and twelve, expressed by 11. —**e·lev′enth** (-ənth) *adj.* & *n.* —**eleventh hour,** the last moment.

elf *n.* [*pl.* **elves** (elvz)] an imaginary tiny being of mischievous character; sprite; fairy. —**elf′in,** *adj.*

el′hi″ (el′hī″) *adj.* for use in grades 1 thru 12.

e·lic′it (i-lis′it) *v.t.* draw out; bring forth; evoke. —**e·lic″i·ta′tion,** *n.*

CHEMICAL ELEMENTS

actinium	mercury
aluminum	molybdenum
americium	neodymium
antimony	neon
argon	neptunium
arsenic	nickel
astatine	nìobium
barium	nitrogen
berkelium	nobelium
beryllium	osmium
bismuth	oxygen
boron	palladium
bromine	phosphorus
cadmium	platinum
calcium	plutonium
californium	polonium
carbon	potassium
cerium	praseodymium
cesium	promethium
chlorine	protactinium
chromium	radium
cobalt	radon
copper	rhenium
curium	rhodium
dysprosium	rubidium
einsteinium	ruthenium
erbium	rutherfordium
europium	samarium
fermium	scandium
fluorine	selenium
francium	silicon
gadolinium	silver
gallium	sodium
germanium	strontium
gold	sulfur
hafnium	tantalum
hahnium	technetium
helium	tellurium
holmium	terbium
hydrogen	thallium
indium	thorium
iodine	thulium
iridium	tin
iron	titanium
krypton	tungsten
lanthanum	uranium
lawrencium	vanadium
lead	xenon
lithium	ytterbium
lutetium	yttrium
magnesium	zinc
manganese	zirconium
mendelevium	

---

e·lide′ (i-līd′) *v.t.* omit or slur over, as in speech.

el′i·gi′ble (el′i-jə-bəl) *adj.* **1,** fit to be chosen; worthy or deserving of choice. **2,** available and desirable as a husband. **3,** legally qualified. —**el′i·gi·bil′i·ty,** *n.*

e·lim′i·nate″ (i-lim′i-nāt″) *v.t.* **1,** get rid of; remove. **2,** omit; ignore. **3,** expel; secrete. —**e·lim″i·na′tion,** *n.*

e·li′sion (i-lizh′ən) *n.* act or result of eliding; omission.

e·lite′ (ā-lēt′) *n.* a superior or choice part, esp. of a human society. —*adj.* select; elite. —**e·lit′ist,** *adj.* —**e·lit′ism,** *n.*

e·lix′ir (i-lik′sər) *n.* **1,** a supposed substance sought by alchemists to transmute baser metals into gold and to prolong life. **2,** a palatable medicine; any invigorating drink.

elk *n.* **1,** a large deer. **2,** the wapiti.

ell (el) *n.* **1,** an addition to a building at right angles to the main part. **2,** a measure of length, 45 inches.

el·lipse′ (i-lips′) *n.* the curve traced by a moving point, the sum of whose distances from two fixed points (the *foci*) remains constant; a closed curve, somewhat oval-shaped. —**el·lip′ti·cal** (i-lip′ti-kəl) *adj.*

el·lip′sis (i-lip′sis) *n.* [*pl.* **-ses** (-sēz)] the omission of words from a sentence, sometimes indicated by (. . .).

el·lip′soid (el-lip′soid) *n.* (*Geom.*) a solid figure, all plane sections of which are ellipses or circles. —**el·lip′soi·dal** (-əl) *adj.*

elm *n.* a tree with wide-spreading branches; its wood.

el″o·cu′tion (el″ə-kū′shən) *n.* the study and practice of effective public speaking. —**el″o·cu′tion·ar·y,** *adj.* —**el″o·cu′tion·ist,** *n.*

e·lon′gate (i-lâng′gāt) *v.t.* make longer; extend. —*v.i.* become long or longer. —**e″lon·ga′tion** (ē″long-gā′shən) *n.*

e·lope′ (i-lōp′) *v.i.* **1,** run away with a lover. **2,** break loose from ties; escape. —**e·lope′ment,** *n.*

el′o·quent (el′ə-kwənt) *adj.* **1,** having the power to speak vividly and appropriately. **2,** stirring; persuasive. —**el′o·quence,** *n.*

else (els) *adv.* otherwise; differently; instead. —*adj.* besides; in addition.

else′where″ (els′hwâr″) *adv.* in or to another place.

e·lu′ci·date″ (i-loo′si-dāt″) *v.t.* make clear; explain. —**e·lu″ci·da′tion,** *n.*

e·lude′ (i-lood′) *v.t.* avoid or escape by stratagem or deceit; evade.

e·lu′sion (i-loo′zhən) *n.* act of eluding; evasion.

e·lu′sive (i-loo′siv) *adj.* hard to grasp or catch; slippery. —**e·lu′sive·ness,** *n.*

e·lu′so·ry (i-loo′sə-rè) *adj.* tending to slip away; evasive.

elves (elvz) *n.* pl. of *elf.*

E·ly′si·um (i-liz′é-əm) *n.* **1,** in Gk. myth., the abode of the blessed after death. **2,** any place of exquisite happiness. —**E·ly′sian** (i-li′zhən) *adj.*

em *n.* a square space, in printing type: usually the pica, 12 points.

em- (em *or* im) *pref.* same as *en-*.

e·ma′ci·ate″ (i-mā′shè-āt″) *v.t.* make lean by gradual wasting away of flesh. —**e·ma″ci·a′tion,** *n.*

em′a·nate″ (em′ə-nāt″) *v.i.* flow out or issue; proceed from a source.

em″a·na′tion (em″ə-nā′shən) *n.* **1,** act or result of emanating. **2,** (*Chem.*) a gas given off by a radioactive substance.

e·man′ci·pate″ (i-man′si-pāt″) *v.t.* set free from a restraint; liberate. —**e·man″ci·pa′tion,** *n.* —**e·man′ci·pa″tor,** *n.*

e·mas′cu·late″ (i-mas′kyə-lāt″) *v.t.* **1,** castrate. **2,** deprive of manhood, strength, or vigor. —**e·mas″cu·la′tion,** *n.*

em·balm′ (em-bäm′) *v.t.* treat (a dead body) with balm, drugs, etc., to preserve it. —**em·balm′ment,** *n.*

em·bank′ *v.t.* enclose or confine with a ridge, as of earth. —**em·bank′ment,** *n.* a protecting bank or wall.

em·bar′go (em-bär′gō) *n.* a restraint, hindrance or prohibition, esp. of commerce or shipping by government order.

em·bark′ (em-bärk′) *v.i.* **1,** go aboard a ship. **2,** set out; make a start. —*v.t.* put or receive aboard a ship. —**em″bar·ka′tion,** *n.*

em·bar′rass (em-bar′əs) *v.t.* **1,** make self-conscious or ashamed; disconcert. **2,** perplex; hamper; impede. **3,** involve in financial difficulties. —**em·bar′rass·ment,** *n.*

em′bas·sy (em′bə-sè) *n.* **1,** an ambassador and his staff. **2,** the headquarters of this body.

em·bat′tled (em-bat′əld) *adj.* prepared for or involved in battle.

em·bed′ *v.t.* [**-bed′ded, -ding**] place in a bed; fix firmly in a surrounding substance.

em·bel′lish (em-bel′ish) *v.t.* **1,** beautify with ornamentation; adorn. **2,** add fictitious detail to (a tale). —**em·bel′lish·ment,** *n.*

em′ber (em′bər) *n.* a smoldering coal; (*pl.*) dying remains. —**Ember Days,** an annual period of three days of fasting and prayer, observed in certain Catholic and Protestant Churches.

em·bez′zle (em-bez′əl) *v.t.* take (property

in trust) for one's own use. —**em·bez'zle·ment**, *n.*

em·bit'ter (em-bit'ər) *v.t.* make resentful. —**em·bit'ter·ment**, *n.*

em·bla'zon (em-blā'zən) *v.t.* **1**, depict on a heraldic shield. **2**, decorate; illuminate. **3**, celebrate; proclaim. —**em·bla'zon·ment**, *n.* —**em·bla'zon·ry** (-rē) *n.* heraldic decoration.

em'blem (em'bləm) *n.* an object or a design symbolizing an idea, quality, or the like; a flag; a badge. —**em"blem·at'ic** (-mat'ik) *adj.* —**em"blem·at'i·cal·ly**, *adv.*

em·bod'y (em-bod'ē) *v.t.* **1**, invest with a body; make concrete; express in concrete form. **2**, collect into a body; organize. **3**, comprise; include. —**em·bod'i·ment**, *n.*

em·bold'en (em-bōl'dən) *v.t.* make bold; encourage.

em'bo·lism (em'bə-liz-əm) *n.* obstruction by a blood clot.

em·bon·point' (än-bôṅ-pwaṅ') *n.* (*Fr.*) plumpness; stoutness.

em·boss' (em-bâs') *v.t.* represent in raised designs or relief. —**em·boss'ment**, *n.*

em"bou·chure' (äm"bû-shûr') *n.* **1**, the mouth of a river or valley. **2**, the mouthpiece of a musical instrument; also, the adjustment of the lips in playing a wind instrument.

em·brace' (em-brās') *v.t.* **1**, clasp in the arms; hug. **2**, enclose; contain; include. **3**, take or receive willingly; adopt. —*n.* a hug; grasp.

em·bra'sure (em-brā'zhər) *n.* a flared opening for a window or door, having a larger aperture on one side of the wall than on the other.

em'bro·cate" (em'brō-kāt") *v.t.* moisten and rub (a bruised or injured part) with a liniment. —**em"bro·ca'tion**, *n.*

em·broi'der (em-broi'dər) *v.t.* **1**, decorate with ornamental needlework. **2**, embellish; elaborate. —**em·broi'der·y**, *n.*

em·broil' *v.t.* involve in contention or strife. —**em·broil'ment**, *n.*

em'bry·o" (em'brē-ō") *n.* **1**, an organism in its earliest stages of development after fertilization of the germ cell. **2**, the rudimentary or formative stage of anything. —*adj.* undeveloped. —**em"bry·on'ic** (-on'-ik) *adj.* undeveloped; rudimentary. —**em"-bry·on'i·cal·ly**, *adv.*

em"bry·ol'o·gy (em"brē-ol'ə-jē) *n.* the science of the origin and development of the embryo. —**em"bry·ol'o·gist** (-jist) *n.*

em·cee' (em'sē) *n.* master of ceremonies (from initials, M. C.). —*v.i. & t.* (*Colloq.*) act as master of ceremonies (for).

e·mend' (ē-mend') *v.t.* remove faults or errors from; revise; correct. Also, **e'men·date** (ē'men-dāt). —**e"men·da'tion**, *n.*

em'er·ald (em'ər-əld) *n. & adj.* **1**, a variety of beryl, prized as a gem. **2**, of its color, green. —**Emerald Isle**, Ireland.

e·merge' (i-mērj') *v.i.* rise out, as from water; come forth from something that conceals; become apparent. —**e·mer'gence** (-jəns) *n.* —**e·mer'gent**, *adj.*

e·mer'gen·cy (i-mēr'jən-sē) *n.* a sudden and urgent occasion for action; pressing necessity.

e·mer'i·tus (i-mer'i-təs) *adj.* retired from active duty but retaining honorary title.

e·mer'sion (i-mēr'shən) *n.* the act of emerging.

em'er·y (em'ə-rē) *n.* a mixture of pulverized minerals used as an abrasive.

e·met'ic (i-met'ik) *n.* a medicine to induce vomiting.

em'i·grant (em'i-grənt) *n.* one who emigrates. Also, **é·mi·gré'** (ā-mē-grā'). —*adj.* emigrating.

em'i·grate" (em'i-grāt") *v.i.* leave a country or region to settle elsewhere. —**em"i·gra'tion**, *n.*

em'i·nence (em'i-nəns) *n.* **1**, high repute. **2**, a hill. **3**, (*cap.*) title of honor of a cardinal.

em'i·nent (em'i-nənt) *adj.* **1**, high in rank, office, worth, etc. **2**, conspicuous; noteworthy. —**eminent domain**, the right of a government to buy property for public use.

e·mir' *n.* a Mohammedan prince.

em'is·sar·y (em'i-ser-ē) *n.* a person sent out on a mission; an agent.

e·mis'sion (i-mish'ən) *n.* **1**, the act of emitting or issuing. **2**, something issued; emanation.

e·mit' (i-mit') *v.t.* [-**mit'ted**, -**ting**] **1**, send forth; give out; utter. **2**, issue.

e·mol'lient (i-mol'yənt) *n.* a substance that softens or soothes.

e·mol'u·ment (i-mol'ū-mənt) *n.* salary or fees for services; gain.

e·mote' (ē-mōt') *v.i.* (*Colloq.*) to express emotion. —**e·mot'ive**, *adj.*

e·mo'tion (i-mō'shən) *n.* **1**, a state of mind in which feeling, sentiment, or attitude is predominant (over cognition and volition). **2**, a specific feeling, as love, joy, etc.

e·mo'tion·al (-əl) *adj.* **1**, pert. to or affecting the emotions. **2**, easily stirred. —**e·mo'tion·al·ism**, *n.*

em·pa·na'da (em-pə-nä'də) *n.* (*Span.*) a stuffed pastry turnover.

em'pa·thize" (-thīz") *v.i.* (with *with*) show empathy for.

em'pa·thy (em'pə-thē) *n.* **1**, sympathetic understanding of another person. **2**, projec-

tion of one's emotions on an object.
—em·path'ic (em-path'ik), em·pa·thet'ic (-thet'ik) adj.

em"pen·nage' (än"pə-näzh') n. the rear part of an airplane or airship.

em'per·or (em'pər-ər) n. the ruler of an empire.

em'pha·sis (em'fə-sis) n. [pl. -ses" (-sēz")] stress laid upon anything; vigor or force in expression. —emphat'ic (em-fat'ik) adj. —em·phat'i·cal·ly, adv.

em'pha·size" (em'fə-sīz") v.t. place emphasis on; stress.

em"phy·se'ma (em"fi-sē'mə) n. abnormal distention produced by gas or air in any part of the body, esp. the lungs.

em·pire (em'pīr) n. 1, a group of countries or peoples with a single government or emperor. 2, supreme power. 3, area of influence; domain.

em·pir'ic (em-pir'ik) n. 1, one who follows an empirical method. 2, a quack or charlatan. —em·pir'i·cism (-i-siz-əm) n.

em·pir'i·cal (em-pir'ə-kəl) adj. 1, derived from experience. 2, derived from observation without reliance on theory.

em·place'ment (im-plās'mənt) n. 1, a gun or battery. 2, a putting into place.

em·ploy' (em-ploi') v.t. 1, use. 2, give occupation to. —em·ploy·ee' (-ē") n. —em·ploy'er, n. —em·ploy'ment, n.

em·po'ri·um (em-pôr'ē-əm) n. [pl. -a (-ə)] a shop that sells a variety of articles; department store.

em·pow'er (em-pow'ər) v.t. authorize; commission; license. —em·pow'er·ment, n.

em'press (em'prəs) n. the wife of an emperor, or a woman ruler of an empire.

emp'ty (emp'tē) adj. 1, containing nothing. 2, lacking in effect, value, etc.; meaningless. 3, (Colloq.) hungry. —v.t. remove the contents of. —v.i. unload; discharge; become empty. —n. (Colloq.) an empty container or vehicle. —emp'ti·ness, n.

em"py·re'an (em"pə-rē'ən) n. the highest heaven, once supposed to be pure fire. —adj. celestial. —em"py·re'al, adj.

e'mu (ē'mū) n. a large flightless Australian bird.

em'u·late" (em'yə-lāt") v.t. strive to equal or excel; vie with. —em"u·la'tion, n. —em'u·lous, adj.

e·mul'si·fy" (i-mul'si-fī") v.t. make into an emulsion. —e·mul"si·fi·ca'tion, n.

e·mul'sion (i-mul'shən) n. a mixture of liquids, minute globules of one being suspended in a second that does not dissolve the first.

en n. (Print.) one-half em.

en- (en or in) pref. 1, in; into. 2, used to indicate a transitive verb.

-en (ən) suf. forming: 1, verbs from nouns and adjectives, as lengthen. 2, diminutive nouns, as maiden. 3, adjectives meaning made of, as golden.

en·a'ble (en-ā'bəl) v.t. make able; furnish with power, ability, or means; facilitate.

en·act' (en-akt') v.t. 1, make into a law; decree; accomplish. 2, act the part of (in a play). —en·act'ment, n.

e·nam'el (i-nam'əl) n. 1, a glassy substance applied to pottery, metalware, etc. 2, a paint that dries in a hard, glossy surface. 3, the outermost and hardest part of a tooth. —v.t. apply enamel to; coat. —e·nam'el·ware", n.

en·am'or (in-am'ər) v.t. inflame with love; charm; captivate. Also, en·am'our.

en·camp' (en-kamp') v.i. form or lodge in a camp.

en·camp'ment (-mənt) n. 1, the act of camping. 2, a camp.

en·cap'su·late" (in-kap'sə-lāt") v.t. encase in a capsule. —en·cap"su·la'tion, n.

en·case' (en-kās') v.t. enclose in or as in a case. —en·case'ment, n.

-ence (əns) suf. forming nouns denoting act, state or quality. Also, -en·cy (ən-sē)

en·ceinte' (än-sänt') adj. pregnant. —n. 1, fortifications of a castle or town. 2, the close of a cathedral.

en·ceph"a·li'tis (en-sef"ə-lī'tis) n. inflammation of the brain.

en·chant' (en-chánt') v.t. 1, put a magical spell upon. 2, delight to a high degree; charm; fascinate. —en·chant'ment, n. —en·chant'ress (-rəs) n.fem.

en·chase' (en-chās') v.t. 1, incrust with gems, etc.; inlay; ornament. 2, chase, as metalwork; engrave; emboss.

en"chi·la'da (en"chi-lä'dä) n. a Mexican dish with chili.

en·ci'pher (in-sī'fər) v.t. convert (a message) into cipher; encode.

en·cir'cle (en-sēr'kəl) v.t. 1, form a circle around; enclose. 2, move around; make a circle of. —en·cir'cle·ment, n.

en'clave' (en'klāv) n. a country wholly surrounded by a foreign country.

en·close' (en-klōz') v.t. 1, surround; shut in; confine. 2, insert in the same envelope. Also, in·close'.

en·clo'sure (en-klō'zhər) n. 1, act of enclosing. 2, something enclosed. 3, that which encloses, as a fence. Also, in·clo'sure.

en·code' (in-cōd') v.t. convert a message, etc.) into code or some other language of communication.

en·co'mi·um (en-kō'mē-əm) n. extravagant praise. **—en·co'mi·ast"**, *n*. **—en·co"-mi·as'tic**, *adj*.

en·com'pass (en-kum'pəs) *v.t.* **1,** surround; encircle. **2,** contain. **—en·com'-pass·ment**, *n*.

en'core (än'kôr) *n.* a repeated performance, or additional act. **—***v.t.* call for an encore of or by.

en·coun'ter (en-kown'tər) *v.t. & i.* **1,** meet, esp. by chance. **2,** meet in strife or contention. **—***n.* a meeting or conflict. **—encounter group,** a group of persons meeting for various kinds of social interaction, usu. for purposes of therapy or self-analysis.

en·cour'age (en-kėr'ij) *v.t.* **1,** inspire with courage or confidence; lead on; incite. **2,** support. **—en·cour'ag·ing**, *adj.* promoting optimism. **—en·cour'age·ment**, *n*.

en·croach' (en-krōch') *v.i.* enter upon the domain of another; trespass; make inroads. **—en·croach'ment**, *n*.

en·cum'ber (en-kum'bər) *v.t.* hinder, as with a load; burden with obligations or difficulties. **—en·cum'ber·ment**, *n*.

en·cum'brance (en-kum'brəns) *n.* **1,** a burden or hindrance. **2,** a legal obligation. **3,** a dependent, esp. a child.

en·cyc'li·cal (en-sik'li-kəl) *n.* a general letter from the Pope.

en·cy"clo·pe'di·a (en-sī"klə-pē'dē-ə) *n.* a work treating of various branches of knowledge, or various topics. **—en·cy"-clo·pe'dic**, *adj.* wide in scope; comprehensive. **—en·cy"clo·pe'di·cal·ly**, *adv.* **—en·cy"clo·pe'dist**, *n.* a writer of encyclopedias.

end *n.* **1,** one of the terminal points or parts of something that is longer than it is wide. **2,** an outermost boundary. **3,** the terminal moment in time; finish; cessation; the concluding part. **4,** death; extinction. **5,** purpose; aim. **6,** outcome; result. **7,** the position of a player in football and other games. **—***v.i.* **1,** come to an end; cease; finish. **2,** result. **—end run,** an evasion.

en·dan'ger (en-dān'jər) *v.t.* put into danger; expose to loss or injury. **—en·dan'-ger·ment**, *n*.

en·dear' (en-dir') *v.t.* make dear or beloved. **—en·dear'ment**, *n*.

en·deav'or (en-dev'ər) *v.i.* exert oneself to do something; strive. **—***n.* effort. Also, **en·deav'our**.

en·dem'ic (en-dem'ik) *adj.* peculiar to a locality or a people (esp. of disease). **—en·dem'i·cal·ly**, *adv*.

end'ing *n.* **1,** act of coming or bringing to a close; termination. **2,** the final stage or part.

en'dive (en'dīv) *n.* a plant whose leaves are used in salad.

end'less (-ləs) *adj.* **1,** extending without end in space or time; infinite. **2,** having the ends joined to form a ring. **—end'less·ness**, *n*.

end'most (end'mōst") *adj.* at the very end; most remote.

en·do- (en-dō) *pref.* within.

en'do·crine" (-krin") *adj.* secreting internally. **—endocrine glands,** various glands that directly affect certain organs of the body.

en·dorse' (en-dôrs') *v.t.* **1,** approve; ratify; sustain. **2,** write one's name or initials upon, as a mark of approval, payment received, obligation, etc. Also, **in·dorse'**. **—en·dorse'ment**, *n*.

en·dow' *v.t.* **1,** provide with a permanent source of income. **2,** bestow upon; give; furnish or equip. **—en·dow'ment**, *n*.

en'drin *n.* an insecticide.

en·due' (en-dū') *v.t.* endow with some quality, ability, etc.

en·dure' (en-dyûr') *v.t.* **1,** undergo; sustain. **2,** sustain without impairment or yielding. **3,** bear with patience; put up with. **—***v.i.* continue to exist. **—en·dur'ance**, *n*.

en·du'ro (en-dyû'rō) *n.* a long race, esp. for automobiles or motorcycles; a test of endurance.

end'ways" (-wāz") *adv.* **1,** with the end upward or forward. **2,** toward the ends; lengthwise. **3,** on end; end to end. Also, **end'wise"** (-wīz")

en'e·ma (en'ə-mə) *n.* an injection of a liquid into the rectum.

en'e·my (en'ə-mē) *n.* **1,** one who opposes or seeks to inflict injury on another. **2,** an opposing military force; a hostile foreign country, or a national of such a country. **3,** anything injurious or antagonistic.

en"er·get'ic (en"ər-jet'ik) *adj.* manifesting energy; vigorous in action; powerful in force or effect. **—en"er·get'i·cal·ly**, *adv*.

en'er·gy (en'ər-jē) *n.* **1,** vigor in the exertion of power; strength in action; forcefulness of expression. **2,** action; activity; operation. **3,** (*Physics*) capacity to produce motion or heat. **—en'er·gize"** (-jīz") *v.t.*

en'er·vate" (en'ər-vāt") *v.t.* deprive of nerve or strength; weaken. **—en"er·va'tion**, *n*.

en"fi·lade' (en"fə-lād') *n.* a position allowing fire down the length of a line of enemy troops, trenches, etc. **—***v.t.* attack in this manner.

en·force' (en-fôrs') *v.t.* **1,** put or keep in force; compel obedience to. **2,** impose by force. **—en·force'a·ble**, *adj.* **—en·force'-ment**, *n*.

en·fran'chise (en-fran'chīz) *v.t.* **1,** grant

a franchise to. **2,** give the right to vote. **—en·fran′chise·ment,** *n.*

en·gage′ (en-gāj′) *v.t.* **1,** obtain the services or use of; employ; hire. **2,** betroth. **3,** bind by pledge or promise. **4,** gain the attention of; attract. **5,** meet in conflict with. **6,** interlock. **—en·gag′ing,** *adj.* attractive; pleasing.

en′′ga·gé′ (än′′gä-zhä′) *adj.* (*Fr.*) committed to a cause.

en·gage′ment (-mənt) *n.* **1,** act or effect of engaging; state of being engaged. **2,** betrothal.

en·gen′der (en-jen′dər) *v.t.* give rise to; bring forth; cause; excite.

en′gine (en′jən) *n.* **1,** any machine that converts energy into work. **2,** any mechanical contrivance. **3,** a railroad locomotive.

en′′gi·neer′ (en′′jə-nir′) *n.* **1,** one who operates an engine. **2,** one versed in the principles and practice of any department of engineering. —*v.t.* **1,** plan or direct, as an engineer. **2,** contrive.

en′′gi·neer′ing *n.* **1,** the work or profession of an engineer. **2,** the science of making practical application of knowledge in any field. **3,** skillful management or contrivance.

en·gird′ (en-gērd′) *v.t.* surround; encircle; encompass. Also, **en·gir′dle.**

Eng′lish (ing′glish) *adj.* pert. to England, its people, customs, etc. —*n.* the English language. **—Basic English,** a select vocabulary of English words (orig. 750) intended as a teaching aid and an international language. **—English horn,** the alto instrument of the oboe family.

en·grave′ (en-grāv′) *v.t.* **1,** cut in; produce by incision of a surface, as wood, metal, stone; carve in sunken patterns. **2,** produce by etching with acid, as in photoengraving. **3,** impress deeply.

en·grav′ing *n.* **1,** the art of making designs by cutting or etching plates. **2,** an engraved plate. **3,** a print or impression from such a plate.

en·gross′ (en-grōs′) *v.t.* **1,** occupy wholly (as the attention of a person). **2,** write out in a document, in a special style of handwriting. **3,** monopolize the supply of. **—engross′ment,** *n.*

en·gulf′ *v.t.* swallow; submerge.

en·hance′ (en-hàns′) *v.t.* raise to a higher degree; intensify; make more important or effective. **—en·hance′ment,** *n.*

en′′har·mon′ic (en′′-) *adj.* (*Music*) having the same pitch but written differently, as C sharp and D flat.

e·nig′ma (i-nig′mə) *n.* a riddle; anything puzzling. **—en′′ig·mat′ic** (en′′ig-mat′ik; ē′′nig-) *adj.* **—en′′ig·mat′i·cal·ly,** *adv.*

en·join′ *v.t.* **1,** command (a person) to do something; prescribe (a course of conduct). **2,** (*Law*) prohibit or restrain by injunction.

en·joy′ (en-joi′) *v.t.* **1,** feel joy in doing or perceiving; find pleasure in. **2,** have possession or use of. **—en·joy′ment,** *n.*

en·kin′dle (en-kin′dəl) *v.t.* **1,** excite; inflame. **2,** set on fire.

en·lace′ (en-lās′) *v.t.* **1,** encircle. **2,** entangle; intertwine. **—en·lace′ment,** *n.*

en·large′ (en-lärj′) *v.t.* **1,** make larger; extend; augment. **2,** increase in capacity or scope; expand. —*v.i.* **1,** become larger; expand. **2,** be diffuse in speaking or writing; expatiate. **—en·large′ment,** *n.* act or result of enlarging; esp., a photograph extended in size.

en·light′en (en-līt′ən) *v.t.* give intellectual or spiritual light to; impart knowledge to; instruct. **—en·light′en·ment,** *n.*

en·list′ *v.t. & i.* **1,** enter, as a name on a list; enroll. **2,** engage in a service or cause, as a military service. **—en·list′ment,** *n.* **—enlisted man,** a male member of the U.S. armed forces who is not a commissioned officer, warrant officer, or cadet.

en·liv′en (en-lī1′vən) *v.t.* give life or activity to; animate; make vigorous or gay. **—en·liv′en·ment,** *n.*

en·mesh′ *v.t.* enclose in meshes; entangle.

en′mi·ty (en′mə-tè) *n.* hostility; hatred; ill will; antagonism.

en·no′ble (e-nō′bəl) *v.t.* elevate in rank, dignity, or worth. **—en·no′ble·ment,** *n.*

en′nui (än′′wē) *n.* weariness or discontent arising from satiety or lack of interest; boredom.

e·nor′mi·ty (i-nôr′mə-tè) *n.* **1,** something outrageously offensive or heinous. **2,** atrociousness.

e·nor′mous (i-nôr′məs) *adj.* **1,** greatly exceeding the usual size; huge; immense. **2,** extremely wicked; atrocious. **—e·nor′-mous·ness,** *n.*

e·nough′ (i-nuf′) *adj.* answering the purpose; adequate; sufficient; satisfactory. —*adv.* **1,** in sufficient quantity or degree. **2,** to a notable extent; fully.

en·plane′ (en-plān′) *v.i.* board an airplane.

en·rage′ (en-rāj′) *v.t.* excite rage in; provoke anger or fury in.

en·rap′ture (en-rap′chər) *v.t.* put in rapture; delight extremely.

en·rich′ (en-rich′) *v.t.* **1,** make rich; supply with abundant property. **2,** supply with anything (as knowledge) in abundance. **3,** make better in quality. **4,** fertilize, as soil. **—en·rich′ment,** *n.*

en·roll' (en-rōl') *v.i.* & *t.* enlist. **—en·roll'ment, en·rol'ment,** *n.*

en route (än-root') (*Fr.*) on the way.

en·sconce' (en-skons') *v.t.* **1,** settle firmly or snugly. **2,** cover; hide.

en·sem'ble (än-säm'bəl) *n.* **1,** the whole; all parts taken together. **2,** the costume of a person, esp. when all parts are in harmony.

en·shrine' (en-shrīn') *v.t.* **1,** enclose in or as in a shrine. **2,** preserve with care; cherish. **—en·shrine'ment,** *n.*

en·shroud' (en-shrowd') *v.t.* wrap in or as in a shroud; conceal.

en'sign (en'sīn) *n.* **1,** the identifying flag of a company of soldiers, army, nation, vessel, etc. **2,** a badge of rank or office; an emblem or token. **3,** (-sin) the lowest commissioned rank in the U.S. Navy. **—en'sign·ship,** *n.*

en'si·lage (en'sə-lij) *n.* fodder preserved in a silo or pit.

en·sile' (en-sīl') *v.t.* preserve in a silo; prepare as ensilage.

en·slave' (en-slāv') *v.t.* make a slave of; put in bondage. **—en·slave'ment,** *n.*

en·snare' (en-snār') *v.t.* trap. **—en·snare'-ment,** *n.*

en·sue' (en-soo') *v.i.* **1,** follow in order; come after. **2,** follow as a consequence.

en·sure' (en-shûr') *v.t.* **1,** make sure or certain to occur, come, or be. **2,** make safe or secure. **3,** insure.

-ent (ənt) *suf.* forming adjectives or nouns denoting doing or doer.

en·tail' (en-tāl') *v.t.* **1,** bring about; cause to ensue; involve as a consequence. **2,** impose as a burden. **3,** limit the inheritance of (property) to a specified line of heirs. **—en·tail'ment,** *n.*

en·tan'gle (en-tang'gəl) *v.t.* **1,** involve in difficulties; perplex. **2,** make complicated. **—en·tan'gle·ment,** *n.*

en·tente' (än-tänt') *n.* an understanding, esp. among nations friendly to one another. Also, **en·tente' cor·diale'** (kôr-dyal').

en'ter (en'tər) *v.t.* **1,** come into; go into; penetrate. **2,** put in; insert. **3,** become a member of; join; admit to membership. **4,** take the first step in; begin upon; become involved in. **5,** make a record of; register. **—***v.i.* **1,** come or go in. **2,** make a beginning. **3,** take an interest or part in an enterprise.

en·ter'ic (en-ter'ik) *adj.* intestinal. **—***n.* typhoid fever.

en·ter·i'tis (en''tə-rī'tis) *n.* inflammation of the intestines.

en'ter·prise (en''tər-prīz'') *n.* **1,** something undertaken; a project, mission, business, etc., esp. one requiring boldness and perse-

verance. **2,** boldness in undertakings. **—en'ter·pris''ing,** *adj.* ready and energetic in carrying out projects.

en''ter·tain' (en''tər-tān') *v.t.* **1,** afford amusement or diversion. **2,** accommodate as a guest. **3,** admit into the mind; give heed to; harbor; take under consideration. **—***v.i.* exercise hospitality; receive guests.

en''ter·tain'ment (-mənt) *n.* **1,** act or result of entertaining; state of being entertained. **2,** a show, party, etc.

en·thrall' (en-thrål') *v.t.* **1,** captivate; charm. **2,** put or hold in bondage. **—en·thrall'ment,** *n.*

en·throne' (en-thrōn') *v.t.* place on a throne; invest with authority. **—en·throne'ment,** *n.*

en·thuse' (en-thooz'; -thūz') *v.* (*Colloq.*) **—***v.t.* make enthusiastic. **—***v.i.* become enthusiastic; show enthusiasm.

en·thu'si·asm (en-thoo'zė-az-əm) *n.* **1,** absorbing possession of the mind by an interest, study, or pursuit; ardent interest. **2,** (*Archaic*) extravagant religious fervor. **—en·thu'si·ast,** *n.* **—en·thu''si·as'tic,** *adj.* **—en·thu''si·as'ti·cal·ly,** *adv.*

en·tice' (en-tīs') *v.t.* draw on by exciting hope or desire; allure; attract. **—en·tice'-ment,** *n.*

en·tire' (en-tīr') *adj.* whole; complete; not broken or diminished; intact. **—en·tire'-ness,** *n.*

en·tire'ty (-tė) *n.* **1,** the whole of something. **2,** completeness.

en·ti'tle (en-tī'təl) *v.t.* **1,** give a right to; furnish with grounds for a claim. **2,** give a title or name to.

en'ti·ty (en'tə-tė) *n.* **1,** something that has real existence; a thing. **2,** existence; being.

en·tomb' (en-toom') *v.t.* place in a tomb; bury. **—en·tomb'ment,** *n.*

en·to·mo- (en-tə-mə) *pref.* meaning ''insect.''

en''to·mol'o·gy (en''tə-mol'ə-jė) *n.* the study of insects. **—en''to·mo·log'i·cal,** *adj.* **—en''to·mol'o·gist,** *n.*

en''tou·rage' (än''tû-räzh') *n.* the attendants or followers of a person.

en·tr'acte' (än-trakt') *n.* **1,** an interval between acts of a play or opera. **2,** a musical piece, dance, etc., performed during this interval.

en'trails (en'trəlz) *n.pl.* **1,** the intestines or bowels. **2,** the internal parts or contents of anything.

en·train' (en-trān') *v.i.* board a train. **—***v.t.* put on a train.

en'trance (en'trəns) *n.* **1,** the act of entering. **2,** a means or place of access; an opening or passage for entering.

---

en·trance' (en-tràns') *v.t.* **1,** fill with delight or wonder; enrapture. **2,** put in a trance.

en'trant (en'trənt) *n.* one who enters, as into a club, college, competition, etc.

en·trap' *v.t.* [**-trapped', -trap'ping**] catch in a trap; snare. —**en·trap'ment,** *n.*

en·treat' (en-trēt') *v.t.* ask earnestly; implore; beseech.

en·treat'y (en-trē'tè) *n.* **1,** act of entreating. **2,** a prayer; petition.

en'tre·cote" (än"trə-kōt") *n.* a rib or sirloin steak.

en'tree (än'trā) *n.* **1,** (U. S.) the main dish of a dinner, other than a roast. **2,** a dish served between chief courses of a dinner. **3,** the right or privilege of entering.

en·trench' *v.t.* **1,** fortify by digging trenches around, or putting in a trench. **2,** establish in a position of security. —*v.i.* encroach; trespass. —**en·trench'ment,** *n.*

en'tre·pot" (än"trə-pō") *n.* **1,** a port or town to which goods are sent for distribution. **2,** a warehouse.

en"tre·pre·neur' (än"trə-prə-nër') *n.* **1,** an employer of workmen. **2,** one who undertakes an enterprise.

en'tre·sol" (än"trə-sōl") *n.* mezzanine.

en·tro·py (en'trə-pè) *n.* (*Physics*) **1,** a measure of the unavailable energy in a thermodynamic system. **2,** the ultimate result of the degradation of matter and energy in the universe.

en·trust' *v.t.* **1,** (with *to*) transfer or commit, with confidence. **2,** (with *with*) charge with a trust or responsibility.

en'try (en'trè) *n.* **1,** the act of entering; entrance. **2,** an opening or passage for entering; a vestibule. **3,** an item entered in a register, account book, etc.

en·twine' (en-twīn') *v.t. & i.* curl about or together. —**en·twine'ment,** *n.*

e·nu'mer·ate" (i-nū'mə-rāt") *v.t.* **1,** name one by one; mention separately. **2,** count; ascertain the number of. —**e·nu"mer·a'tion,** *n.*

e·nun'ci·ate" (i-nun'sè-āt") *v.t. & i.* utter or pronounce, as words or syllables, esp. with reference to manner. —*v.t.* proclaim; announce distinctly. —**e·nun"ci·a'tion,** *n.*

en·vel'op (en-vel'əp) *v.t.* surround entirely; form a covering about; wrap up. —**en·vel'op·ment,** *n.*

en've·lope (en'və-lōp) *n.* **1,** any covering or wrapping. **2,** a cover for a letter.

en·ven'om (en-ven'əm) *v.t.* **1,** make poisonous. **2,** imbue with malice.

en'vi·a·ble (en'vè-ə-bəl) *adj.* of an excellence to invite envy. —**en'vi·a·ble·ness,** *n.*

en'vi·ous (en'vè-əs) *adj.* feeling or showing envy. —**en'vi·ous·ness,** *n.*

en·vi'ron·ment (en-vī'rən-mənt) *n.* the aggregate of surrounding things or conditions; the totality of external influences on an organism. —**en·vi"ron·men'tal,** *adj.* —**en·vi"ron·men'tal·ist,** *n.* one dedicated to the preservation of the natural environment.

en·vi'rons (en-vī'rənz) *n.pl.* the region surrounding a place; outskirts or suburbs.

en·vis'age (en-viz'əj) *v.t.* **1,** visualize. **2,** confront.

en·vi'sion (en-vizh'ən) *v.t.* contemplate in imagination, esp. future events.

en'voy (en'voi) *n.* **1,** an agent sent on a mission, esp. diplomatic. **2,** a postscript to a composition.

en'vy (en'vè) *n.* a feeling of mortification or discontent excited by seeing the superiority or prosperity of another person; desire for the possessions or advantages of another; ill will combined with jealousy. —*v.t.* regard with envy.

en'zyme (en'zīm) *n.* a substance that acts as a catalyst in metabolism.

e·o- (è-ō) *pref.* early; primeval.

e"o·lith'ic (ē"ə-lith'ik) *adj.* pert. to the earliest period of the Stone Age.

e'on (ē'ən) *n.* **1,** an indefinitely long period of time. **2,** the longest division of geologic time.

ep'au·let" (ep'ə-let") *n.* an ornamental badge on the shoulder.

é·pée' (ā-pā') *n.* a thin, pointed sword used in fencing.

e·pergne' (i-pêrn') *n.* an ornamental table centerpiece.

e·phed'rine (i-fed'rin) *n.* a drug used to relieve nasal congestion.

e·phem'er·al (i-fem'ər-əl) *adj.* lasting only one day or a very short time; transitory.

epi- *pref.* to; against.

ep'ic (ep'ik) *adj.* **1,** pert. to a poem or poetry narrating in lofty style the achievements and adventures of a hero. **2,** of heroic character or style; imposing. —*n.* an epic poem or story. —**ep'i·cal·ly,** *adv.*

ep'i·cene" (ep'i-sēn") *adj.* both masculine and feminine.

ep'i·cen"ter (ep'ə-sen"tər) *n.* **1,** the parts of the earth immediately above the focus of an earthquake. **2,** focus; center.

ep'i·cure" (ep'ə-kyūr") *n.* **1,** one of refined taste in eating and drinking. **2,** one given to sensual pleasure. —**ep"i·cu·re'an** (-kyû-rē'ən) *adj. & n.*

ep"i·dem'ic (ep"ə-dem'ik) *adj.* (of a disease) appearing in a large number of cases at the same time in a locality. —*n.* a temporary prevalence of a disease in a community. —**ep''i·dem'i·cal·ly,** *adv.*

ep''i·der'mis (ep''ə-dêr'mis) *n.* the outermost skin, membrane, integument, or layer of an organic body.

ep''i·glot'tis (ep''i-glot'is) *n.* the flap of cartilage that covers the glottis during swallowing.

ep'i·gram (ep'ə-gram'') *n.* a terse, witty saying, usually satirical. —**ep''i·gram·mat'-ic** (-grə-mat'ik) *adj.* —**ep''i·gram·mat'i·cal·ly,** *adv.*

ep'i·graph'' (ep'ə-graf'') *n.* **1,** an inscription. **2,** a quotation or motto at the beginning of a book or chapter. —**ep''i·graph'ic,** *adj.*

e·pig'ra·phy (i-pig'rə-fè) *n.* **1,** the science of deciphering and explaining inscriptions. **2,** inscriptions collectively.

ep'i·lep''sy (ep'ə-lep''sè) *n.* a nervous disease characterized by muscular spasm and loss of consciousness.

ep''i·lep'tic (ep''ə-lep'tik) *adj.* pert. to epilepsy. —*n.* a person afflicted with epilepsy.

ep''i·logue'' (ep'ə-lâg'') *n.* the concluding part of a discourse; a section added at the end.

ep''i·neph'rine (ep''i-nef'rin) *n.* a drug used to stimulate the heart, etc.

E·piph'a·ny (i-pif'ə-nè) *n.* a Christian festival, Jan. 6.

e·pis'co·pa·cy (i-pis'kə-pə-sè) *n.* **1,** a form of church government in which the chief ministers are bishops. **2,** the office of a bishop. —**e·pis'co·pate** (-pət) *n.*

e·pis'co·pal (i-pis'kə-pəl) *adj.* **1,** pert. to a bishop. **2,** (*cap.*) designating a Protestant sect governed by bishops. —**E·pis''co·pa'lian** (-pāl'yən) *n.* a member of this sect.

ep'i·sode'' (ep'ə-sōd'') *n.* **1,** an incident in a series of events or a narrative; one happening. **2,** (*Music*) a digressive passage, as in a fugue. —**ep''i·sod'ic** (-sod'ik) *adj.* —**ep''i·sod·i·cal·ly,** *adv.*

e·pis''te·mol'o·gy (i-pis''tə-mol'ə-jè) *n.* the study of the nature, basis, limits, and validity of human knowledge.

e·pis'tle (i-pis'əl) *n.* a written communication; a letter, esp. a formal discourse, as (*cap.*) any of the apostolic letters in the New Testament. —**e·pis'to·lar·y** (-tə-ler-è) *adj.*

ep'i·taph'' (ep'ə-tàf'') *n.* **1,** a memorial inscription on a monument. **2,** any similar commemorative writing.

ep''i·tha·la'mi·um (ep''i-thə-lā'mè-əm) *n.* a song or poem in honor of a newly married person or pair.

ep'i·thet'' (ep'ə-thet'') *n.* a name or phrase used to characterize a person or thing. —**ep''i·thet'ic, ep''i·thet'i·cal,** *adj.*

e·pit'o·me (i-pit'ə-mè) *n.* a brief summary of a subject or writing; an abridgment or abstract. —**e·pit'o·mize''** (-mīz'') *v.t.*

ep'och (ep'ək) *n.* **1,** a period of time marked by distinctive events; a division of a geologic period. **2,** a point of time distinguished by some remarkable event. —**ep'och·al** (-əl) *adj.*

e·pox'y resin (è-pàks'è) *n.* a thermosetting resin used as an adhesive or a protective coating. Also, **epoxy.**

ep'si·lon'' (ep'sə-lon'') *n.* the fifth letter of the Greek alphabet (E, ε).

Ep'som salts (ep'səm) hydrated magnesium sulfate, used as a cathartic.

eq'ua·ble (ek'wə-bəl) *adj.* uniform in action, intensity, or state; even; steady; tranquil. —**eq''ua·bil'i·ty,** *n.*

e'qual (è'kwəl) *adj.* **1,** having one measure; the same in magnitude, quantity, degree, worth, etc. **2,** evenly balanced; level; uniform in operation. —*v.t.* be or become equal to; make or do something equal to. —**e·qual'i·ty** (i-kwol'ə-tè) *n.* —**equal time,** the requirement of a radio or television station to provide equal air time to all political candidates if time is provided to any.

e'qual·ize'' (è'kwə-līz'') *v.t.* make equal or uniform. —**e''qual·i·za'tion,** *n.*

e'qual·iz''er (è'kwə-līz''ər) *n.* **1,** a device for maintaining equal or uniform stress, potential, etc., among different parts of an apparatus. **2,** (*Slang*) a pistol.

e''qua·nim'i·ty (ē''kwə-nim'ə-tè) *n.* evenness of mind or temper; calmness under stress.

e·quate' (i-kwāt') *v.t.* state the equality of; put in an equation.

e·qua'tion (i-kwā'shən) *n.* (*Math.*) a statement of relation between two quantities, indicated by an *equals sign* (=) or other symbol.

e·qua'tor (i-kwā'tər) *n.* a circle dividing the surface of a sphere into two equal parts. —**e''qua·tor'i·al** (ē''kwə-tôr'è-əl) *adj.*

eq'uer·ry (ek'wə-rè) *n.* **1,** an attendant in a royal household. **2,** an officer in charge of horses.

e·ques'tri·an (i-kwes'trè-ən) *adj.* **1,** pert. to horsemen or horsemanship. **2,** mounted on horseback. —*n.* one who rides a horse. —**e·ques''tri·enne'** (-en') *n.fem.*

e·qui- (ē-kwə; ek-wē) *pref.* equal.

e''qui·dis'tant (ē''kwə-dis'tənt) *adj.* equally distant.

e''qui·lat'er·al (ē''kwə-lat'ər-əl) *adj.* having all sides of equal length.

e''qui·li'brate (ē''kwə-lī'brāt) *v.t. & i.* be or put in equal balance. —**e''qui·li·bra'tion,** *n.*

e″qui·lib′ri·um (ē″kwə-lib′rē-əm) n. 1, a state of rest or balance through equality of counteracting forces. 2, mental stability.

e′quine (ē′kwīn) adj. pert. to or like a horse. —n. a horse.

e′qui·nox″ (ē′kwi-noks″) n. either of the two annual occasions, about Mar. 21 and Sept. 22, when night and day are of equal length. —e″qui·noc′tial (-nok′shəl) adj.

e·quip′ (i-kwip′) v.t. [-quipped′, -quip′-ping] fit out with what is needed to execute an undertaking; rig for service.

eq′ui·page (ek′wə-pij) n. a carriage.

e·quip′ment (i-kwip′mənt) n. 1, act of equipping; state of being equipped. 2, that which equips; supplies; gear.

e′qui·poise″ (ē′kwə-poiz″) n. 1, equal distribution of weight. 2, a counterbalance.

eq′ui·ta·ble (ek′wi-tə-bəl) adj. fair. —eq′ui·ta·ble·ness, n.

eq″ui·ta′tion (ek″wə-tā′shən) n. horsemanship.

eq′ui·ty (ek′wi-tè) n. 1, impartial justice; fairness. 2, (Law) the application of common principles of fair dealing, to supplement statute law. 3, a net financial interest in a property.

e·quiv′a·lent (i-kwiv′ə-lənt) adj. 1, the same in magnitude, meaning, effect, etc. 2, corresponding in position or function. —n. substantially the same thing. —e·quiv′a·lence, n.

e·quiv′o·cal (i-kwiv′ə-kəl) adj. 1, of uncertain meaning; ambiguous. 2, of doubtful origin; dubious.

e·quiv′o·cate″ (i-kwiv′ə-kāt″) v.i. use ambiguous expressions; be evasive. —e·quiv′o·ca′tion, n.

-er (-ər) suf. 1, added to verbs to denote a person or implement performing the act; added to nouns to denote a performer, follower, or resident of. 2, forming the comparative degree of adjectives and adverbs.

e′ra (ir′ə) n. 1, a period of time of distinctive historical character. 2, (Geol.) a major period of geological time.

e·rad′i·cate″ (i-rad′i-kāt″) v.t. pull up by the roots; destroy utterly. —e·rad″i·ca′tion, n. —e·rad′i·ca″tor, n.

e·rase′ (i-rās′) v.t. rub or scratch out; clear (of writing, transcribed sound, etc.). —e·ras′er, n. a utensil, device or substance (as rubber) for erasing.

e·ras′ure (i-rā′shər) n. 1, act of erasing. 2, a place where something has been erased.

er′bi·um (ēr′bē-əm) n. a chemical element of the rare-earth group, no. 68, symbol Er.

ere (âr) prep. before (in time). —conj. before; sooner or rather than. —ere″long′, adv. before long.

e·rect′ (i-rekt′) v.t. 1, build; construct. 2, set up; establish; found. 3, raise to an upright position. —adj. upright. —e·rec′tile, adj. capable of being erected. —e·rec′tion, n.

er′e·mite″ (er′ə-mīt″) n. a hermit, esp. religious.

erg (ērg) n. a unit of work. Also, er′gon (ēr′gon).

er′go (ēr′gō) conj. (Lat.) therefore.

er·gos′ter·ol″ (ər-gos′tə-rōl″) n. a food supplement taken for its Vitamin D content.

er′got (ēr′gət) n. a fungus, in rye and other cereals, yielding a medicine used to check hemorrhage. —er′go·tism, n. a disease caused by ergot, marked by spasm and gangrene.

er′mine (ēr′min) n. 1, a white-furred weasel; its fur. 2, the office or dignity of a judge.

e·rode′ (i-rōd′) v.t. & i. wear away slowly. —e·ro′sive, adj.

e·rog′e·nous (i-roj′ə-nəs) adj. producing sexual desire.

e·ro′sion (i-rō′zhən) n. a washing or wearing away of the earth's surface.

e·rot′ic (i-rot′ik) adj. pert. to sexual love. —e·rot′i·cal·ly, adv. —e·rot′i·cism, n.

e·rot′i·ca (i-rot′i-kə) n.pl. erotic literature or art; pornography.

err (ēr; er) v.i. 1, go astray; be mistaken; blunder. 2, sin.

er′rand (er′ənd) n. 1, a special business entrusted to a messenger; a commission. 2, a short trip to execute a commission.

er′rant (er′ənt) adj. 1, wandering; roving. 2, deviating; erring.

er·rat′ic (i-rat′ik) adj. 1, wandering; off course. 2, tending to err. 3, eccentric. —er·rat′i·cal·ly, adv.

er·ra′tum (i-rä′təm) n. [pl. -ta (-tə)] an error in a book; misprint.

er·ro′ne·ous (i-rō′nē-əs) adj. incorrect. —er·ro′ne·ous·ness, n.

er′ror (er′ər) n. 1, a deviation from truth; a mistake; an inaccuracy. 2, moral wrongdoing; an offense. 3, difference from a true value or standard.

er′satz (er′zäts) adj. & n. (Ger.) substitute.

Erse (ērs) n. Gaelic.

erst′while″ (ērst′hwīl″) adj. former.

e·ruct′ (i-rukt′) v.t. & i. emit or issue violently, esp. wind from the stomach; belch. —e·ruc′tate (-tāt) v.t. & i. —e·ruc″ta′tion, n.

er″u·di′tion (er″û-dish′ən) n. knowledge gained by study; learning. —er′u·dite″ (-dīt″) adj.

e·rupt' (i-rupt') *v.i. & t.* burst forth suddenly and violently, like a volcano. —**e·rup'tive,** *adj.*

e·rup'tion (i-rup'shən) *n.* **1,** a bursting forth. **2,** a rash.

er''y·sip'e·las (er''ə-sip'ə-ləs) *n.* an acute, infectious skin disease.

er''y·the'ma (er''i-thē'mə) *n.* [*pl.* **-ma·ta** (-mə-tə)] redness of the skin due to local congestion or the blood.

es·ca·late' (es'kə-lāt') *v.t. & i.* increase the scope or intensity of.

es·ca·la''tor (es'kə-lā''tər) *n.* a moving stairway for transporting passengers from one level to another. —**escalator clause,** a provision in labor contracts permitting periodic adjustment of wage scales.

es·cal'lop (es-kol'əp) *v.t.* **1,** bake (food) in a sauce, with crumbs on top. **2,** scallop. —*n.* scallop.

es'ca·pade'' (es'kə-pād'') *n.* a wild prank; a foolish adventure.

es·cape' (es-kāp') *v.i.* **1,** get away or flee, as from capture or confinement; evade or avoid threatened harm. **2,** leak out, as a liquid. —*v.t.* slip away from; elude. —*n.* act of escaping. —**escape clause,** a provision in a contract that permits a party to it to evade provisions of the contract under certain circumstances. —**escape velocity,** the velocity required for a spacecraft to escape the pull of gravity.

es·cape'ment (es-kāp'mənt) *n.* a contrivance for alternately releasing and stopping a moving part, as in a clock.

es·cap'ism (es-kāp'iz-əm) *n.* diversion of thought from unpleasant reality. —**es·cap'·ist,** *n.*

es'ca·role'' (es'kə-rōl'') *n.* a broad-leaved variety of endive.

es·carp'ment (es-kärp'mənt) *n.* a precipitous slope; a cliff.

es''cha·tol'o·gy (es''kə-tol'ə-jé) *n.* the branch of theology that treats of last or final things, as death. —**es''cha·to·log'i·cal** (-tə-loj'i-kəl) *adj.*

es·chew' (es-choo') *v.t.* shun.

es·cort' (es-kôrt') *v.t.* accompany on a trip as a companion or protector; convoy. —*n.* (es'kôrt) one who escorts; a body of attendants.

es''cri·toire' (es''kri-twär') *n.* a writing desk or secretary.

es'crow (es'krō) *n.* a conditional contract of which the consideration is deposited in trust.

es·cu'do (es-koo'dō) *n.* [*pl.* **-dos**] a coin or monetary unit of various Spanish- and Portuguese-speaking countries.

es'cu·lent (es'kū-lənt) *adj.* fit to be used for food; edible.

es·cutch'eon (es-kuch'ən) *n.* the shield on which armorial bearings are emblazoned.

-ese (ēs *or* ēz) *suf.* denoting the language or inhabitants of a place or a situation; the jargon of an industry, etc.

Es'ki·mo'' (es'ki-mō'') *n.* [*pl.* **-mos''**] **1,** one of the race idigenous to arctic North America. **2,** a malemute or husky.

e·soph'a·gus (ė-sof'ə-gəs) *n.* [*pl.* **-gi** (-jī)] the food canal of an animal, from mouth to stomach; the gullet.

es''o·ter'ic (es''ə-tər'ik) *adj.* understood by, or intended for, only a select few; secret; mysterious. —**es''o·ter'i·cal·ly,** *adv.*

es·pa·drille'' (es'pə-dril'') *n.* a flat sandal.

es·pal'ier (es-pal'yər) *n.* **1,** a trellis for the branches of a fruit tree or bush. **2,** a tree or plant so grown.

es·pe'cial (es-pesh'əl) *adj.* **1,** special; distinguished from others of the same kind. **2,** exceptional.

Es''pe·ran'to (es''pə-rän'tō) *n.* a proposed universal language.

es'pi·o·nage (es'pė-ə-nij) *n.* the practice of spying.

es''pla·nade' (es''plə-nād') *n.* a public ground for walking or riding; a level, open area.

es·pouse' (es-powz') *v.t.* **1,** take as a spouse; wed. **2,** adopt or advocate, as a cause. —**es·pous'al,** *n.*

es·pres'so (es-pres'sō) *n.* (*Ital.*) coffee brewed with forced steam.

es·prit' (es-prē') *n.* liveliness; spirit; wit. —**esprit de corps** (də-kôr) morale.

es·py' (es-pī') *v.t.* catch sight of.

-esque (esk) *suf.* like; having the style or manner of, as *picturesque, arabesque.*

es·quire' (es-kwīr') *n.* **1,** a title of politeness, added after a man's last name in addressing him by letter; usually *Esq.* **2,** (*Hist.*) an attendant on a knight.

-ess (əs *or* is) *suf.* forming feminine nouns, as *seeress.*

es'say (es'ā) *n.* **1,** a literary composition on a particular subject. **2,** an effort or attempt. —*v.t.* (e-sā') endeavor; try. —**es'·say''ist,** *n.*

es'sence (es'əns) *n.* **1,** the distinctive characteristic of something. **2,** the inward nature or true substance of something. **3,** a liquid containing a substance in concentrated form, as a perfume.

es·sen'tial (ə-sen'shəl) *adj.* **1,** absolutely necessary; indispensable. **2,** relating to inmost nature; basic; fundamental. **3,** pert. to or yielding a liquid essence. —*n.* a basic part or aspect; an element. —**essential oil,**

a volatile oil in a plant giving it its characteristic odor or flavor.

es·tab'lish v.t. **1**, set up on a firm basis; found; fix. **2**, install, as in a position. **3**, show to be valid; prove.

es·tab'lish·ment (-mənt) n. **1**, act of establishing; state of being established. **2**, something established as a household, business, institution. **3**, (cap.) (Colloq.) the social institution and officials of a country or society.

es·tate' (es-tāt') n. **1**, a piece of landed property. **2**, a person's entire property and possessions. **3**, a person's worldly condition or circumstances; status; rank. **4**, a political or social class.

es·teem' (es-tēm') v.t. **1**, set a high value on; regard favorably. **2**, estimate; rate. —n. **1**, favorable opinion; respect. **2**, judgment of worth.

es'ter (es'tər) n. a chemical compound, analogous to a salt and often fragrant.

es'thete (es'thēt) n. one who cultivates appreciation of the beautiful.

es·thet'ic (es-thet'ik) adj. pert. to beauty. —n. a philosophy of beauty and good taste. Also, **aes·thet'ic.** —**es·thet'i·cal·ly,** adv.

es·thet'ics (-iks) n. the philosophy of beauty and good taste.

es'ti·ma·ble (es'ti-mə-bəl) adj. **1**, worthy of esteem. **2**, capable of being estimated or valued.

es'ti·mate'' (es'tə-māt'') v.t. form an opinion of, as to size, value, etc. —n. (es'tə-mət) an opinion, judgment, or approximate calculation; a tentative price or charge. —**es''ti·ma'tion** (-mā'shən) n. **1**, the act of estimating; opinion. **2**, esteem.

es'ti·val (es'tə-vəl) adj. pert. to summer.

es'ti·vate'' (es'tə-vāt'') v.i. pass the summer; esp. (Zool.) be dormant, as some mollusks. Also, **aes'ti·vate.** —**es''ti·va'tion,** n.

es·top' v.t. [-topped', -top'ping] prevent, bar, or stop. —**es·top'pel** (-əl) n.

es·trange' (es-trānj') v.t. cause to be hostile; alienate the affections of. —**estrange'ment,** n.

es'tri·ol'' (es'trē-ol'') n. a female sex hormone.

es'tro·gen (es'trə-jən) n. a substance that stimulates production of certain sex hormones.

es'trus (es'trəs) n. **1**, a passionate impulse or desire. **2**, (Zool.) heat; rut. Also, **oes'trus.**

es'tu·ar·y (es'choo-er-ē) n. the mouth of a river, subject to tides.

-et suf. diminutive, as owlet.

e'ta (ā'tə) the seventh letter of the Greek alphabet (H, η).

é''ta·gère' (ā''tä-zher') n. a many-shelved cabinet; whatnot.

et cet'er·a (et-set'ər-ə) (Lat.) and others; and so on: usually, **etc.,** abbr.

etch (ech) v.t. **1**, cut (the surface of a metal plate, etc.) with acid, in order to form a design. **2**, engrave with a stylus. —**etch'ing,** n. a printed impression from an etched plate.

e·ter'nal (i-tẽr'nəl) adj. **1**, existing throughout all time; without beginning or end. **2**, incessant. **3**, (cap.) God.

e·ter'ni·ty (i-tẽr'nə-tē) n. **1**, time without beginning or end; infinite duration. **2**, a seemingly endless period of time.

-eth suf. **1**, forming ordinal numbers, as twentieth. **2**, (Archaic) forming the third person singular of verbs, as he readeth, now he reads.

eth'ane (eth'ān) n. a colorless, combustible gas.

eth'a·nol (eth'ə-nâl) n. ethyl alcohol.

e'ther (ē'thər) n. **1**, a compound of sulfuric acid and alcohol, used as a solvent and anesthetic. **2**, the sky.

e·the're·al (i-thir'ē-əl) adj. **1**, airy; light; intangible. **2**, heavenly.

eth'ic (eth'ik) adj. ethical. —n. ethics.

eth'i·cal (eth'i-kəl) adj. in accordance with accepted principles of conduct.

eth'ics (eth'iks) n.pl. **1**, the principles of honor and morality. **2**, accepted rules of conduct. **3**, the moral principles of an individual.

E''thi·o'pi·an (ē''thē-ō'pē-ən) adj. pert. to Ethiopia. —n. **1**, a native of Ethiopia. **2**, (incorrectly) a Negro.

eth'nic (eth'nik) adj. **1**, pert. to a people distinguished by race, language, culture, etc. **2**, heathen; pagan. —**eth'ni·cal,** adj. —**eth·nic'i·ty** (-nis'ə-tē) n.

eth·no- (eth-nə-) pref. race; people; nation.

eth·nol'o·gy (eth-nol'ə-jē) n. the science of the origin, history, customs, etc., of peoples. —**eth''no·log'i·cal,** adj. —**eth·nol'ogist,** n.

e'thos (ē'thos) n. **1**, the character, ideals, etc., of a community or people. **2**, the quality of a work of art that produces a high moral impression, noble and universal.

eth'yl (eth'əl) n. (Chem.) a radical of alcohol. —**ethyl fluid,** tetraethyl lead, added to gasoline to reduce engine knock.

e''ti·ol'o·gy (ē''tē-ol'ə-jē) n. the study of causes. —**e''ti·o·log'i·cal,** adj. —**e''ti·ol'ogist,** n.

et'i·quette'' (et'i-ket'') n. the conventional requirements of polite behavior; proprieties of conduct; good manners.

tub, cūte, ṗull; labəl; oil, owl, go, chip, she, thin, then, sing, ink; see p. 6

-ette (et) *suf.* **1**, little, small, as *kitchenette*. **2**, feminine, as *suffragette*. **3**, imitation, as *leatherette*.

é·tude' (ā-tūd') *n.* a musical composition intended as an exercise in technique, but often of esthetic value; a study.

e·tui' (ā-twē') *n.* a small box, as for notions.

et"y·mol'o·gy (et"i-mol'ə-jē) *n.* **1**, the study of the structure and history of words. **2**, the derivation or history of a given word. —**et"y·mo·log'i·cal,** *adj.* —**et"y·mol'o·gist,** *n.*

eu"ca·lyp'tus (ū"kə-lip'təs) *n.* a tree of the myrtle family; its wood or aromatic oil.

Eu'cha·rist (ū'kə-rist) *n.* the sacrament of the Lord's Supper; Holy Communion.

eu'chre (ū'kər) *n.* a card game. —*v.t.* swindle; outsmart.

Eu'clid (ū'klid) *n.* **1**, the system of geometry of Euclid (c. 300 B.C.). **2**, geometry. —**Eu·clid'i·an** (ū-klid'ē-ən) *adj.*

eu·gen'ics (ū-jen'iks) *n.* the science of improving the human race through the regulation of parenthood. —**eu·gen'ic,** *adj.* —**eu·gen'i·cal·ly,** *adv.*

eu'lo·gy (ū'lə-jē) *n.* high praise; a speech or writing that lauds a person, esp. one deceased, or a thing. —**eu"lo·gis'tic** (-jis'tik) *adj.* —**eu"lo·gis'ti·cal·ly,** *adv.* —**eu'lo·gize"** (-jīz") *v.t.* deliver a eulogy about.

eu'nuch (ū'nək) *n.* a castrated man.

eu·pep'sia (ū-pep'shə) *n.* good digestion. —**eu·pep'tic** (-tik) *adj.*

eu'phe·mism (ū'fə-miz-əm) *n.* **1**, the use of a mild word in place of a plainer but possibly offensive one. **2**, a word or expression thus substituted. —**eu"phe·mis'tic** (-mis'tik) *adj.* —**eu"phe·mis'ti·cal·ly,** *adv.*

eu·phen'ics (ū-fen'iks) *n.* the science of improving the human species by modifying biological development.

eu·pho'ni·ous (ū-fō'nē-əs) *adj.* pleasing in sound. —**eu·pho'ni·ous·ness,** *n.*

eu·pho'ni·um (ū-fō'nē-əm) *n.* a tenor tuba.

eu'pho·ny (ū'fə-nē) *n.* harmonious arrangement of sounds, esp. of words. —**eu·phon'ic,** *adj.* —**eu·phon'i·cal·ly,** *adv.*

eu·pho'ri·a (ū-fôr'ē-ə) *n.* a feeling or state of well-being.

eu'phu·ism (ū'fū-iz-əm) *n.* an excessively ornate style in writing. —**eu"phu·is'tic,** *adj.* —**eu"phu·is'ti·cal·ly,** *adv.*

Eur·a'sian (yû-rā'zhən) *n.* a person of mixed Europ. and Asiatic blood. —*adj.* **1**, pert. to Europe and Asia as a single continental mass. **2**, of mixed European and Asiatic parentage.

eu·re'ka (yû-rē'kə) *interj.* I have found it!

Eu'ro·dol"lar (yû'rō-dol"ər) *n.* (*usu.pl.*) U.S. dollars circulating among European banks.

Eu"ro·pe'an (yûr"ə-pē'ən) *adj.* pert. to Europe. —*n.* a native of Europe. —**European plan,** in hotel-keeping, rental of room only, with meals not included.

eu·ro'pi·um (yû-rō'pē-əm) *n.* a rare-earth chemical element, no. 63, symbol Eu.

eu·ryth'mics (ū-riᵗʰ'miks) *n.* **1**, the science of harmonious bodily movements. **2**, a system of musical education through bodily movements.

eu·ryth'my (ū-riᵗʰ'mē) *n.* harmony of movement or proportion. —**eu·ryth'mic,** *adj.*

Eu·sta'chi·an tube (ū-stā'kē-ən) the canal between the eardrum and pharynx.

eu"tha·na'sia (ū"thə-nā'zhə) *n.* **1**, painless death. **2**, mercy-killing.

eu·then'ics (ū-then'iks) *n.* **1**, the science of adjusting living conditions to improve the human race. **2**, the science of improving growth conditions of plants and animals.

eu'tro·phy (ū'trə-fē) *n.* healthy nutrition. —**eu·troph'ic** (ū-trof'ik) *adj.*

e·vac'u·ate" (i-vak'ū-āt") *v.t.* **1**, make empty; free from something contained. **2**, vacate; withdraw from. **3**, excrete. —*v.i.* go elsewhere, esp. to avoid danger. —**e·vac"u·a'tion,** *n.*

e·vac'u·ee" (-ē") *n.* a person removed from a place of danger.

e·vade' (i-vād') *v.t.* **1**, escape from; avoid capture by; elude. **2**, circumvent by trickery. **3**, baffle.

e·val'u·ate" (i-val'ū-āt") *v.t.* **1**, ascertain the value or amount of. **2**, express numerically. —**e·val"u·a'tion,** *n.*

ev"a·nesce' (ev"ə-nes') *v.i.* fade away; disappear gradually; vanish. —**ev"a·nes'cence,** *n.* —**ev"a·nes'cent,** *adj.*

e·van'gel (i-van'jəl) *n.* the Christian gospel.

e"van·gel'i·cal (ē"van-jel'ə-kəl) *adj.* **1**, pert. to the Gospels or to evangelism. **2**, (of churches) adhering strictly to Protestant theology, esp. in interpretation of the Gospels.

e·van'ge·list (i-van'je-list) *n.* **1**, one of the apostles Matthew, Mark, Luke, John. **2**, a preacher of the gospel, esp. a revivalist. —**e·van'ge·lism,** *n.*

e·van'ge·lize" (-līz") *v.t. & i.* preach the gospel (to); convert to Christianity.

e·vap'o·rate" (i-vap'ə-rāt") *v.i.* **1**, pass off as vapor. **2**, disappear; be dissipated. —**e·vap"o·ra'tion,** *n.* —**evaporated milk,** milk concentrated by removal of some water by evaporation.

e·va'sion (i-vā'zhən) *n.* **1**, the act of evading. **2**, a trick or subterfuge; an equivocation.

e·va′sive (i-vā′siv) *adj.* **1,** using artifice to escape or avoid. **2,** escaping observation or understanding; elusive. —**e·va′sive·ness,** *n.*

eve (ēv) *n.* **1,** the night or the day before (a date, festival, etc.). **2,** the time just preceding an event. **3,** evening.

e′ven (ē′vən) *adj.* **1,** level; plane; smooth. **2,** uniform in action or character; unvarying. **3,** equal; on the same line or level. **4,** divisible by 2. **5,** whole; having no fractional part. **6,** not easily excited; placid. —*adv.* **1,** uniformly; equally; wholly; evenly. **2,** just; exactly; moreover; likewise; fully (used to emphasize or strengthen an assertion). —*v.t.* make even. —**e′ven·ness,** *n.* —**break even,** have neither a net profit nor a net loss. —**get even (with),** obtain revenge (upon).

e″ven-hand′ed (-han′did) *adj.* impartial; equitable; fair. —**e″ven-hand′ed·ness,** *n.*

eve′ning (ēv′ning) *n.* **1,** the latter part of the day; the time from sunset to darkness, or from first darkness to bedtime. **2,** the latter part or decline of any term of existence. —**evening star,** a bright planet, esp. Venus.

e′ven·song″ *n.* **1,** a song or hymn sung at evening. **2,** vespers.

e·vent′ (i-vent′) *n.* **1,** something that happens; an occurrence. **2,** an incident of special interest. **3,** an outcome, issue, or consequence. **4,** one item of a series.

e·vent′ful (-fəl) *adj.* **1,** full of striking events, as a period of time. **2,** having important results or outcome. —**e·vent′ful·ness,** *n.*

e′ven·tide″ (ē′vən-tīd″) *n.* evening.

e·ven′tu·al (i-ven′choo-əl) *adj.* **1,** happening or to happen finally; ultimate. **2,** contingent.

e·ven″tu·al′i·ty (i-ven″choo-al′ə-tē) *n.* an event that may come to pass.

e·ven′tu·ate″ (i-ven′choo-āt″) *v.i.* happen as an outcome; result. —**e·ven″tu·a′tion,** *n.*

ev′er (ev′ər) *adv.* **1,** at all times; always; continually. **2,** at any time. **3,** in any degree; at all.

ev′er·glade″ *n.* a tract of low, swampy ground.

ev′er·green″ *n.* a plant or tree that has green leaves throughout the entire year. —*adj.* always fresh.

ev″er·last′ing *adj.* **1,** perpetual; eternal. **2,** wearisome. —*n.* **1,** (*cap.*) God. **2,** a plant that does not wilt or fade when dried.

ev″er·more″ *adv.* forever after.

e·vert′ (i-vērt′) *v.t.* turn outward or inside out. —**e·ver′sion,** *n.*

ev′er·y (ev′rē) *adj.* **1,** each without exception; all (of an aggregate taken one by one). **2,** the greatest possible, in extent or degree.

ev′er·y·bod″y *n.* every person.

ev′er·y·day″ *adj.* commonplace; usual.

ev′er·y·one″ *n.* every person.

ev′er·y·thing″ *n.* all things.

ev′er·y·where″ *adv.* **1,** in all places. **2,** wherever.

e·vict′ (i-vikt′) *v.t.* expel, esp. by judicial order; dispossess. —**e·vic′tion,** *n.*

ev′i·dence (ev′i-dəns) *n.* **1,** the means of proving or disproving an alleged fact; testimony, exhibits, etc., offered as proof; an indication of proof. **2,** the state of being clear or certain. —*v.t.* show clearly; prove. —**ev″i·den′tial** (-den′shəl) *adj.* —**in evidence,** plainly visible; conspicuous.

ev′i·dent (ev′i-dənt) *adj.* plainly seen or perceived; manifest; obvious. —**ev′i·dent·ly,** *adv.* apparently.

e′vil (ē′vəl) *adj.* **1,** immoral; wicked. **2,** harmful; disastrous. **3,** bad; ill-reputed. —*n.* **1,** violation of moral principles; improper conduct. **2,** injury; misfortune. **3,** a cause of injury or mischief. **4,** a malady. —**e″vil·do′er,** *n.* one who sins. —**e′vil·ness,** *n.* —**evil eye,** a faculty of inflicting injury or bringing bad luck by a look; such a look. —**Evil One,** Satan.

e·vince′ (i-vins′) *v.t.* show clearly; exhibit; manifest; —**e·vince′ment,** *n.*

e·vis′cer·ate″ (i-vis′ə-rāt″) *v.t.* **1,** remove the viscera from; disembowel. **2,** deprive of essential parts. —**e·vis″cer·a′tion,** *n.*

e·voke′ (i-vōk′) *v.t.* bring into the mind; cause to appear; call forth. —**ev′o·ca·ble** (ev′ə-kə-bəl) *adj.* —**ev″o·ca′tion,** *n.* —**e·voc′a·tive** (i-vok′ə-tiv) *adj.*

ev″o·lu′tion (ev″ə-loo′shən) *n.* **1,** the act of evolving; formation, growth, or development. **2,** (*Biol.*) the continuous modification of organic species; the steps in adaptation to environment. **3,** something evolved. —**ev″o·lu′tion·a·ry,** *adj.*

e·volve′ (i-volv′) *v.t.* **1,** form gradually, as though by unfolding; develop. **2,** emit. —*v.i.* come into being, or change, gradually.

ewe (ū) *n.* a female sheep.

ew′er (ū′ər) *n.* a water pitcher with a wide mouth.

ex (eks) *prep.* **1,** without; not including. **2,** from. —*n.* **1,** the letter X. **2,** a former husband, boyfriend, etc.

ex- *pref.* **1,** out: out of. **2,** (hyphenated) formerly, as *ex-president.*

ex·ac′er·bate″ (eg-zas′ər-bāt″) *v.t.* embitter; make more bitter, angry or violent; irritate; aggravate. —**ex·ac″er·ba′tion,** *n.*

ex·act′ (eg-zakt′) *v.t.* compel to be paid or yielded; require. —*adj.* **1,** strictly accurate or correct. **2,** admitting of no deviation;

strict. —**ex·act′ing,** *adj.* holding to strict standards. —**ex·act′ness,** *n.*

ex·act′a (eg-zak′tə) *n.* perfecta.

ex·ac′tion (eg-zak′shən) *n.* something exacted; extortion.

ex·ac′ti·tude (eg-zak′ti-tood) *n.* preciseness; strictness.

ex·ag′ger·ate″ (eg-zaj′ə-rāt″) *v.t.* **1,** represent as large, important, etc., beyond the truth; magnify falsely. **2,** enlarge or increase abnormally. —*v.i.* overstate. —**ex·ag′ger·at″ed,** *adj.* unduly enlarged. —**ex·ag′ger·a′tion,** *n.*

ex·alt′ (eg-zâlt′) *v.t.* **1,** elevate in rank, honor, power, etc. **2,** praise; extol. **3,** inspire; elate. —**ex″al·ta′tion,** *n.*

ex·am′ (ig-zam′) *n.* (*Colloq.*) a test, in school, usu. requiring a written answer; any examination.

ex·am″i·na′tion (eg-zam″i-nā′shən) *n.* **1,** act or process of examining or being examined. **2,** a series of questions asked as a test.

ex·am′ine (eg-zam′in) *v.t.* **1,** look at carefully; inspect; scrutinize. **2,** inquire into; investigate. **3,** test; interrogate.

ex·am′ple (eg-zam′pəl) *n.* **1,** one of a number of things that shows the character of all; a sample. **2,** a specimen or instance serving to illustrate or explain. **3,** a model.

ex·as′per·ate″ (eg-zas′pə-rāt″) *v.t.* irritate extremely; annoy; make angry. —**ex·as″·per·a′tion,** *n.*

ex′ca·vate″ (eks′kə-vāt″) *v.t.* **1,** make a cavity or hollow in; dig into. **2,** form by scooping out material. **3,** unearth. —**ex″·ca·va′tion,** *n.* —**ex′ca·va″tor,** *n.*

ex·ceed′ (ek-sēd′) *v.t.* **1,** go beyond in quantity, degree, etc. **2,** be superior to; surpass. —*v.i.* be greater than others; excel. —**ex·ceed′ing·ly,** *adv.* extremely; (*Colloq.*) very.

ex·cel′ (ek-sel′) *v.t. & i.* [**-celled′, -cel′ling**] be superior (to); surpass; outdo.

ex′cel·lence (ek′sə-ləns) *n.* great merit or efficiency.

ex′cel·len·cy (ek′sə-lən-sē) *n.* (usually *cap.*) a title of address to certain high officials.

ex′cel·lent (ek′sə-lənt) *adj.* remarkably good; of superior merit.

ex·cel′si·or (ek-sel′sē-ər) *n.* wood shavings, used for packing.

ex·cept′ (ik-sept′) *prep.* leaving out; excluding; but for. —*conj.* **1,** with this exception; otherwise than. **2,** (*Archaic*) unless. —*v.t.* leave out; exclude. —*v.i.* make objection.

ex·cep′tion (ik-sep′shən) *n.* **1,** exclusion. **2,** something excepted; an instance not conforming to a general rule. **3,** an objection. **4,** slight anger or resentment. —**ex·cep′tion·a·ble,** *adj.* subject to objection. —**ex·cep′tion·al,** *adj.* unusual. —**take exception, 1,** make an objection. **2,** offense.

ex′cerpt (ek′sērpt) *n.* an extract from something written or printed. —*v.t.* (ek-sērpt′) cite or cull (such an extract).

ex·cess′ (ek-ses′; ek′ses) *n.* **1,** the state of being more or too much. **2,** a surplus or remainder. **3,** immoderate indulgence of the appetites. —*adj.* more than enough; extra.

ex·ces′sive (-siv) *adj.* **1,** superfluous. **2,** unduly great; extreme. —**ex·ces′sive·ness,** *n.*

ex·change′ (eks-chānj′) *v.t.* give in return for something else; give and receive reciprocally. —*v.i.* **1,** trade. **2,** be taken or received in exchanging. —*n.* **1,** the act of exchanging; mutual substitution. **2,** something given or received in exchanging; checks, drafts, etc. **3,** the rate at which one currency may be converted to another. **4,** a percentage or fee charged for exchanging. **5,** a place of exchange, as of stocks, drafts, etc.; a central telephone switchboard.

ex·cheq′uer (eks-chek′ər) *n.* **1,** a treasury, esp. a government treasury. **2,** (*Colloq.*) funds.

ex′cise (ek′sīz″) *n.* a tax imposed on commodities, occupations, etc., within a country. —*v.t.* **1,** impose an excise tax upon. **2,** cut off or out; delete. —**ex·ci′sion** (ek-sizh′ən) *n.*

ex·cite′ (ek-sīt′) *v.t.* **1,** arouse the emotions of; stimulate. **2,** stir; agitate. **3,** produce a magnetic field in. —**ex·cit′a·ble,** *adj.* easy to excite. —**ex″ci·ta′tion** (ek″sī-tā′shən) *n.*

ex·cit′ed *adj.* **1,** emotionally aroused. **2,** enthusiastic.

ex·cite′ment (ek-sīt′mənt) *n.* **1,** the state of being excited. **2,** commotion; ado.

ex·cit′ing *adj.* **1,** tending to stir up. **2,** causing enthusiasm; appealing.

ex·claim′ (eks-klām′) *v.i.* cry out in astonishment, alarm, etc.; speak with vehemence. —*v.t.* say loudly and vehemently.

ex″cla·ma′tion (eks″klə-mā′shən) *n.* the act of exclaiming; what is exclaimed. —**exclamation point,** the symbol (!) used in punctuation for vehement expression.

ex·clam′a·to·ry (es-klam′ə-tôr-ē) *adj.* **1,** spoken vehemently. **2,** marked with an exclamation point.

ex′clave″ (ek′sklāv″) *n.* a portion of a country physically separated from the main part.

ex·clude′ (ek-sklood′) *v.t.* **1,** shut out; omit. **2,** thrust out; eject; expel.

ex·clu′sion (ek-skloo′zhən) *n.* act of excluding; state of being excluded.

ex·clu′sive (ek-skloo′siv) *adj.* **1,** shutting out all others or all else from admission or consideration. **2,** incompatible with something else. **3,** (often with *of*) with the exception of. **4,** select; snobbish. **5,** (*Colloq.*) fashionable; stylish. **—ex·clu′sive·ness,** *n.*

ex·cog′i·tate″ (eks-koj′ə-tāt″) *v.t.* think out; contrive; devise. **—ex·cog″i·ta′tion,** *n.*

ex″com·mu′ni·cate″ (eks″kə-mū′ni-kāt″) *v.t.* cut off from communion or membership, esp. in respect to a church by ecclesiastical sentence. **—ex″com·mu″ni·ca′tion,** *n.*

ex·co′ri·ate″ (ek-skôr′ē-āt″) *v.t.* **1,** denounce or censure violently. **2,** remove the skin or outer covering from. **—ex·co′ri·a′tion,** *n.*

ex′cre·ment (eks′krə-mənt) *n.* waste matter eliminated from the living body, esp. the feces.

ex·cres′cence (ek-skres′əns) *n.* **1,** an abnormal outgrowth on a body, as a wart. **2,** a normal outgrowth, as hair. **—ex·cres′cent,** *adj.* superfluous.

ex·crete′ (ek-skrēt′) *v.t.* discharge from an organic body, as waste matter. **—ex·cre′ta** (-tə) *n.pl.* excreted matter. **—ex·cre′tion,** *n.* act of excreting; something excreted.

ex·cru′ci·at″ing (ek-skroo′shē-ā″ting) *adj.* extremely painful.

ex′cul·pate″ (eks′kul-pāt″) *v.t.* clear from a charge of fault or guilt; exonerate. **—ex″cul·pa′tion,** *n.* **—ex·cul′pa·to·ry** (eks-kulp′ə-tôr-ē) *adj.*

ex·cur′sion (ek-skēr′zhən) *n.* **1,** a journey, usually for a specific purpose, and return to the starting point; a jaunt. **2,** a train or boat ride at a reduced fare. **3,** a digression or deviation. **—ex·cur′sion·ist,** *n.* **—ex·cur′sive,** *adj.*

ex·cuse′ (ek-skūz′) *v.t.* **1,** pardon; forgive; overlook. **2,** apologize for; justify. **3,** release from an obligation or duty. **4,** refrain from exacting; remit. *—n.* (ek-skūs′) **1,** a plea offered or reason given for excusing. **2,** a pretext or subterfuge. **—ex·cus′a·ble** (ek-skūz′ə-bəl) *adj.*

ex′e·cra·ble (ek′si-krə-bəl) *adj.* detestable. **—ex′e·cra·ble·ness,** *n.*

ex′e·crate″ (ek′sə-krāt″) *v.t.* **1,** detest utterly; abhor. **2,** denounce as abominable; curse.

ex″e·cra′tion *n.* **1,** the act of execrating. **2,** curse; denunciation.

ex′e·cute″ (ek′sə-kūt″) *v.t.* **1,** do; perform; carry out. **2,** enact. **3,** put to death according to law. **—ex·ec′u·tant** (eg-zek′yū-tənt) *n.*

ex″e·cu′tion (ek″sə-kū′shən) *n.* **1,** act of executing. **2,** style or effectiveness of performance. **3,** capital punishment. **—ex″e·cu′tion·er,** *n.* the officer who inflicts capital punishment.

ex·ec′u·tive (eg-zek′yə-tiv) *adj.* **1,** concerned with doing, performing, or carrying into effect. **2,** pert. to management or administration. *—n.* a person or body having executive duties or abilities. **—Chief Executive,** the president of the U.S.

ex·ec′u·tor (eg-zek′yə-tər) *n.* one designated to perform specified duties, esp. the provisions of a will. **—ex·ec′u·trix** (-triks) *n. fem.*

ex″e·ge′sis (ek″sə-jē′sis) *n.* interpretation, esp. of the Scriptures. **—ex′e·gete″** (-jēt″) *n.* an expert at exegesis. **—ex″e·get′ic** (-jet′ik) *adj.*

ex·em′plar (eg-zem′plər) *n.* an example, esp. an ideal one; a model.

ex·em′pla·ry (eg-zem′plə-rē) *adj.* **1,** worthy of imitation. **2,** serving as a model or example.

ex·em′pli·fy″ (eg-zem′pli-fī″) *v.t.* **1,** explain or illustrate by an example. **2,** be an example of. **—ex·em″pli·fi·ca′tion** (-fi-kā′shən) *n.*

ex·empt′ (eg-zempt′) *v.t.* free from an obligation; except. *—adj.* excepted or released. **—ex·emp′tion,** *n.*

ex′er·cise″ (ek′sər-sīz″) *n.* **1,** exertion of mind or body for development or training. **2,** active performance or use. **3,** a composition, drill, device, etc., designed for practice. **4,** (usually *pl.*) ceremonies; rites. *—v.t.* **1,** employ actively; perform; use. **2,** give practice or training to. **3,** make uneasy; disturb. *—v.i.* take bodily exercise.

ex·ert′ (eg-zērt′) *v.t.* **1,** put to use, as strength, ability, power, etc. **2,** bestir (oneself) vigorously.

ex·er′tion (eg-sēr′shən) *n.* **1,** act of exerting. **2,** a great effort.

ex″ha·la′tion (eks″ə-lā′shən) *n.* **1,** act of exhaling. **2,** what is exhaled.

ex·hale′ (eks-hāl′) *v.i.* breathe out. *—v.t.* give off as a vapor.

ex·haust′ (eg-zâst′) *v.t.* **1,** draw out the entire contents of; make empty or useless. **2,** tire out; fatigue. *—n.* the exhalation of waste gases, as from an engine. **—ex·haust′i·ble,** *adj.*

ex·haus′tion (eg-zâs′chən) *n.* **1,** act of exhausting; state of being exhausted. **2,** complete expenditure; utter fatigue. **—ex·haus′tive,** *adj.* thorough.

ex·hib′it (eg-zib′it) *v.t.* **1,** offer to view; place on show. **2,** manifest as a quality of character. *—v.i.* hold an exhibition. *—n.* **1,**

exhibition. **2,** something exhibited; a concrete thing offered in evidence.

ex·hi·bi'tion (ek"sə-bish'ən) n. **1,** the act of exhibiting. **2,** a public display, as of works of art, goods, etc.

ex·hi·bi'tion·ist n. one who feels a compulsive urge to be noticed. —**ex"hi·bi'-tion·ism,** n.

ex·hib'i·tor (eg-zib'i-tər) n. one who displays, esp. the operator of a theater.

ex·hil'a·rate" (eg-zil'ə-rāt") v.t. make cheerful or joyous. —**ex·hil"a·ra'tion,** n.

ex·hort' (eg-zôrt') v.t. urge to a course of action; incite; admonish. —**ex"hor·ta'tion** (ek'sər-tā'shən) n.

ex·hume' (eks-hūm') v.t. dig up (something buried, esp. a body). —**ex"hu·ma'-tion** (ek"sū-mā'shən) n.

ex'i·gen·cy (ek'si-jən-sē) n. **1,** a state of affairs requiring prompt action; an emergency. **2,** pressing necessity. —**ex'i·gent,** adj.

ex·ig'u·ous (eg-zig'ū-əs) adj. scanty; sparse. —**ex·ig'u·ous·ness,** n.

ex'ile (eg'zīl) n. **1,** expulsion from one's country; banishment. **2,** prolonged absence from home or country. **3,** one exiled. —v.t. banish.

ex·ist' (eg-zist') v.i. have actual being; be; live.

ex·ist'ence (-əns) n. **1,** state of existing; life. **2,** reality. —**ex·ist'ent,** n.

ex"is·ten'tial (eg"zis-ten'shəl) adj. **1,** pert. to existence. **2,** expressing the fact of existence.

ex"is·ten'tial·ism (ek"sis-ten'shəl-iz-əm) n. a humanistic philosophy stating that each man is responsible for forming his self and must with his free will oppose his uncertain, purposeless, and seemingly hostile environment.

ex'it (ek'sit) n. **1,** a way of departure; a passage out. **2,** a departure. —v.i. go out or away.

ex" li'bris (eks" lē'bris) (Lat.) from the books (of).

ex·o- (ek-sō; ek-sə) pref. outside of.

ex"o·bi·ol'o·gy (ek"sō-bī-ol'ə-jē) n. the biology of outer space.

ex'o·crine (ek'sə-krin) adj. secreting externally.

ex'odus (ek'sə-dəs) n. a mass departure.

ex" of·fi'ci·o" (eks"ə-fish'ē-ō") (Lat.) by right of office.

ex·on'er·ate" (eg-zon'ə-rāt") v.t. relieve of blame or accusation; exculpate; clear. —**ex·on'er·a'tion,** n.

ex·or'bi·tant (eg-zôr'bə-tənt) adj. going beyond usual or proper bounds; excessive; inordinate. —**ex·or'bi·tance,** n.

ex'or·cise" (ek'sôr-sīz") v.t. **1,** expel (evil spirits) by magical or religious rites. **2,** rid of evil spirits, etc., by rites. —**ex'or·cism** (-siz-əm) n.

ex·or'di·um (eg-sôr'dē-əm) n. a beginning; esp., a preface or introduction. —**ex·or'di·al** (-əl) adj.

ex'o·sphere" (ek'sō-sfir") n. the outermost region of the atmosphere.

ex"o·ter'ic (ek"sə-ter'ik) adj. readily understood; commonplace.

ex·ot'ic (eg-zot'ik) adj. **1,** of foreign origin or character; strange. **2,** (Colloq.) striking in appearance. **3,** (Colloq.) pert. to strip tease. —n. **1,** anything exotic. **2,** (Colloq.) a strip-tease dancer. —**ex·ot'i-cal·ly,** adv.

ex·pand' (ek-spand') v.t. & i. **1,** increase in extent, bulk, amount, etc. **2,** spread or stretch out; unfold.

ex·panse' (ek-spans') n. an uninterrupted stretch or area.

ex·pan'sion (ek-span'shən) n. **1,** act of expanding; state of being expanded. **2,** an enlargement, increase, etc.

ex·pan'sion·ist n. an advocate of expansion, as of currency or territory. —**ex·pan'sion·ism** (-iz-əm) n.

ex·pan'sive (ek-span'siv) adj. **1,** wide; extensive; comprehensive. **2,** gregarious; sociable; friendly. —**ex·pan'sive·ness,** n.

ex·pa'ti·ate" (ek-spā'shē-āt") v.i. talk with copiously, as in writing. —**ex·pa"ti·a'tion,** n.

ex·pa'tri·ate (eks-pā'trē-ət) n. one living, as though permanently, away from his country. —v.t. (-āt") banish. —**ex·pa"tri·a'-tion,** n.

ex·pect' (ek-spekt') v.t. **1,** look forward to; anticipate; await as likely to happen or appear. **2,** (Colloq.) suppose; conclude.

ex·pec'tan·cy (ek-spek'tən-sē) n. **1,** act of expecting; expectation. **2,** that which is expected. **3,** contingency.

ex·pec'tant (-tənt) adj. expecting; eagerly awaiting.

ex"pec·ta'tion (ek"spek-tā'shən) n. **1,** act of expecting; expectancy. **2,** something expected or awaited, as a legacy. **3,** (pl.) prospects of future good fortune.

ex·pec'to·rant (ek-spek'tə-rənt) adj. promoting expectoration. —n. an expectorant medicine.

ex·pec'to·rate" (ek-spek'tə-rāt") v.i. & t. spit out from the mouth. —**ex·pec"to·ra'-tion,** n.

ex·pe'di·ent (ek-spē'dē-ənt) adj. **1,** serving to promote a desired object; advisable. **2,** conducive to present advantage or self-interest. —n. **1,** a means to an end. **2,** a makeshift. —**ex·pe'di·en·cy, ex·pe'di-ence,** n.

ex'pe·dite" (eks'pə-dīt") *v.t.* **1,** quicken the progress of. **2,** dispatch. —**ex'pe·dit"er,** *n.* one who directs the course of a project through a series of government or business departments.

ex"pe·di'tion (eks"pə-dish'ən) *n.* **1,** an excursion made by a company of persons for a specific purpose. **2,** the state of being expedited; promptness or speed. —**ex"-pe·di'tion·ar·y** (-er-ē) *adj.* making a journey.

ex"pe·di'tious (eks"pə-dish'əs) *adj.* quick. —**ex"pe·di'tious·ness,** *n.*

ex·pel' (ek-spel') *v.t.* [-**pelled', -pel'ling**] drive out or away; eject; emit. —**ex·pel'lant,** *adj. & n.*

ex·pend' (ek-spend') *v.t.* **1,** use up. **2,** pay out; spend. —**ex·pend'a·ble,** *adj.* dispensable; not too valuable to spare.

ex·pend'i·ture (ek-spen'di-chər) *n.* **1,** consumption; disbursement. **2,** something expended; outlay.

ex·pense' (ek-spens') *n.* **1,** cost; charge; an expenditure. **2,** (*pl.*) charges, incurred for another, to be reimbursed. **3,** damage or loss.

ex·pen'sive (ek-spen'siv) *adj.* high in price or cost. —**ex·pen'sive·ness,** *n.*

ex·pe'ri·ence (ek-spir'ē-əns) *n.* **1,** the process or fact of learning by personally observing, encountering, testing, or undergoing something. **2,** knowledge or skill gained by this process. **3,** a particular instance of observing, encountering, etc.; an event in which one is involved. —*v.t.* meet, undergo, or feel. —**ex·pe'ri·enced,** *adj.* adept or knowing through experience; expert.

ex·per'i·ment (ek-sper'ə-mənt) *n.* **1,** a trial or test. **2,** the process of learning by observation. —*v.i.* make a trial or test. —**ex·per"i·men·ta'tion,** *n.*

ex·per'i·men·tal (-men'təl) *adj.* **1,** done as a trial. **2,** based on observation, not theory.

ex'pert (eks'pért) *adj.* having great knowledge or skill; learned; dexterous. —*n.* one especially skilled or learned; an authority. —**ex·pert'ness,** *n.*

ex"per·tise' (eks"pér-tēz') *n.* specialized skill; know-how.

ex'pi·a·ble (eks'pē-ə-bəl) *adj.* capable of being atoned for; pardonable.

ex'pi·ate (eks'pē-āt') *v.t.* atone for; make amends for. —**ex"pi·a'tion,** *n.*

ex"pi·ra'tion (ek"spə-rā'shən) *n.* **1,** [also, **ex·pi'ry** (ek-spī'rē)] the end; termination. **2,** a breathing out.

ex·pir'a·to·ry (ek-spī'rə-tôr-ē) *adj.* pert. to emission of air from the lungs.

ex·pire' (ek-spīr') *v.i.* **1,** come to an end; die; close. **2,** breathe out; exhale. —*v.t.* breathe out; emit.

ex·plain' (ek-splān') *v.t.* **1,** make plain or clear to the mind. **2,** describe; interpret; analyze. **3,** show the cause or reason of; account for. **4,** (with *away*) nullify or remove the apparent import of. —*v.i.* give an explanation.

ex"pla·na'tion (ek"splə-nā'shən) *n.* **1,** the act of explaining; the facts or assertions that explain something. **2,** a clarification; solution; apology; excuse.

ex·plan'a·to·ry (ek-splan'ə-tôr-ē) *adj.* serving to explain.

ex'ple·tive (eks'plə-tiv) *adj.* added merely to fill out or to give emphasis (of a word or phrase). —*n.* an interjection; an oath or imprecation.

ex'pli·ca·ble (eks'pli-kə-bəl) *adj.* capable of being explained.

ex'pli·cate" (eks'pli-kāt') *v.t.* **1,** develop (an idea, etc.). **2,** analyze; explain. —**ex'-pli·ca'tion,** *n.*

ex·plic'it (ek-splis'it) *adj.* **1,** (of words, ideas) fully or clearly expressed, not merely implied; definite. **2,** (of persons) outspoken. —**ex·plic'it·ness,** *n.*

ex·plode' (ek-splōd') *v.i.* **1,** burst suddenly; fly to pieces with noise and violence. **2,** break into action, speech, etc., suddenly and vehemently. —*v.t.* **1,** cause to explode. **2,** disprove; discredit. **3,** bring into discredit; expose. —**ex·plod'ed,** *adj.* showing the component parts of (a mechanism) separated but with indication of their relationship.

ex'ploit (eks'ploit) *n.* a notable achievement; conspicuous act or deed. —*v.t.* (ek-sploit') **1,** make complete use of. **2,** turn to one's own advantage; utilize selfishly. —**ex"ploi·ta'tion,** *n.*

ex"plo·ra'tion (ek"splôr-ā'shən) *n.* **1,** the act of exploring. **2,** adventurous penetration of unknown territory. —**ex·plor'a·to·ry** (ek-splôr'ə-tôr-ē) *adj.*

ex·plore' (ek-splôr') *v.t.* **1,** travel over or through (a region) for purpose of observation and discovery. **2,** inquire into; examine; investigate. —*v.i.* engage in exploring.

ex·plor'er (ek-splôr'ər) *n.* one who explores unknown territories.

ex·plo'sion (eks-plō'zhən) *n.* the act of exploding; the loud noise attending such act.

ex·plo'sive (eks-plō'siv) *adj.* tending to explode. —*n.* that which explodes or causes explosion, as dynamite.

ex'po (ek'spō) *n.* (*Colloq.*) an exposition.

ex·po'nent (ek-spō'nənt) *n.* **1,** one who expounds or explains. **2,** representative, advocate, or symbol of something. **3,** (*Math.*) a superscript written after a quantity to indicate the power to which it is to be raised, as the ^{2} in 3^2 (= 3 x 3). —**ex″po·nen′tial** (-nen′shəl) *adj.*

ex·port′ (ek-spôrt′) *v.t.* send (a commodity) to another place or country for sale. —*n.* (eks′pôrt) **1,** something exported. **2,** the act or business of exporting. —*adj.* pert. to or suitable for exporting. —**ex″por·ta′tion,** *n.* —**ex·port′er,** *n.* one whose business is exporting merchandise.

ex·pose′ (ek-spōz′) *v.t.* **1,** lay open to view; uncover; reveal. **2,** show the secret intentions or motives of. **3,** leave unprotected. **4,** (*Photog.*) admit light to (a film or plate). —**ex·pos′al,** *n.* —**ex·pos′i·tor** (ek-spos′ə-tər) *n.* one who or that which explains or expounds.

ex″po·sé′ (ek″spō-zā′) *n.* an exposure, esp. of something discreditable.

ex″po·si′tion (ek″spə-zish′ən) *n.* **1,** an exhibit or show, as of products of art or manufacture. **2,** the act of exposing or explaining. **3,** a detailed explanation.

ex·pos′i·to·ry (ek-spoz′ə-tôr-ē) *adj.* serving to explain.

ex·pos′tu·late″ (ek-spos′chə-lāt″) *v.i.* reason earnestly; remonstrate. —**ex·pos″tu·la′tion,** *n.*

ex·po′sure (ek-spō′zhər) *n.* **1,** the act of exposing; the state of being exposed. **2,** in photography, the admission of light to a sensitized plate or film; the duration of such action. **3,** the compass direction faced; aspect.

ex·pound′ (ek-spownd′) *v.t.* set forth the principles of; explain.

ex·press′ (ek-spres′) *v.t.* **1,** put (thoughts, ideas) into tangible or communicable form, as words, pictures, etc. **2,** manifest; reveal; make explicit. **3,** press or squeeze out. **4,** send as express. —*adj.* **1,** made known clearly or explicitly; directly stated or represented; precise. **2,** special; specially direct and fast. —*adv.* specially; by express. —*n.* **1,** a specially direct and fast train or other carrier. **2,** a system of rapid transportation of packages and money; goods transported by this system. —**ex·press′i·ble,** *adj.* —**ex·press′ive·ness,** *adj.*

ex·pres′sion (ek-spresh′ən) *n.* **1,** the act of expressing. **2,** the word or phrase, picture, etc., that makes something known. **3,** the style in which something is expressed. **4,** outward manifestation; appearance of face; intonation of voice.

ex·pres′sion·ism (eks-presh′ən-iz-əm) *n.* (*Art*) **1,** the effort to convey the artist's inner feelings rather than to represent external reality. **2,** free expression of one's individuality in writing, painting, etc.

ex·press′way″ (ek-spres′wā″) *n.* a high-

speed, usually divided, limited-access highway.

ex·pres′sive (ek-spres′iv) *adj.* **1,** pert. to expression. **2,** revealing; readily understood. —**ex·pres′sive·ness,** *n.*

ex·pro′pri·ate″ (eks-prō′prē-āt″) *v.t.* **1,** take for public use by right of eminent domain. **2,** dispossess. —**ex·pro″pri·a′tion,** *n.* —**ex·pro′pri·a″tor,** *n.*

ex·pul′sion (ek-spul′shən) *n.* the act of expelling or being expelled.

ex·punge′ (ek-spunj′) *v.t.* blot or wipe out; erase; destroy. —**ex·punc′tion** (ek-spunk′shən) *n.*

ex′pur·gate″ (eks′pər-gāt″) *v.t.* purge or cleanse, esp. by deletion. —**ex″pur·ga′tion,** *n.* —**ex′pur·ga″tor,** *n.*

ex′qui·site (eks′kwi-zit) *adj.* **1,** exceedingly beautiful, fine, dainty, elegant, etc. **2,** giving pleasure or pain in the highest degree; intense; keen. **3,** very accurate; delicate in action or function. —**ex′qui·site·ness,** *n.*

ex′tant (ek′stənt) *adj.* in existence.

ex·tem″po·ra′ne·ous (ek-stem″pə-rā′nē-əs) *adj.* made, spoken, or performed without previous preparation; improvised at the moment. —**ex·tem″po·ra′ne·ous·ness,** *n.*

ex·tem′po·re (ek-stem′pə-rē) *adj. & adv.* impromptu.

ex·tem′po·rize″ (ek-stem′pə-rīz″) *v.t. & i.* speak extemporaneously; improvise.

ex·tend′ (ek-stend′) *v.t.* **1,** stretch out in space; carry forward; enlarge. **2,** continue in time; prolong; postpone. **3,** put forth; offer; bestow; impart. —*v.i.* **1,** be stretched or laid out. **2,** (with *to*) reach; include or cover. **3,** increase in length, duration, scope, etc. —**ex·tend′ed,** *adj.* stretched out; prolonged; extensive.

ex·ten′si·ble (ek-sten′sə-bəl) *adj.* capable of being extended.

ex·ten′sion (ek-sten′shən) *n.* **1,** the act of extending; state of being extended. **2,** an addition or prolongation. **3,** scope; range; extent.

ex·ten′sive (ek-sten′siv) *adj.* great in scope; thorough. —**ex·ten′sive·ness,** *n.*

ex·tent′ (ek-stent′) *n.* the space or degree to which something extends; length; bulk; size; limit.

ex·ten′u·ate″ (ek-sten′ū-āt″) *v.t.* make smaller in degree or appearance; make (a fault, crime, etc.) less blamable. —**ex·ten′u·at″ed,** *adj.* shrunken; thin. —**ex·ten″u·a′tion,** *n.*

ex·te′ri·or (ek-stir′ē-ər) *adj.* being outside; pert. to the outer surface, side, or part; outward; outlying. —*n.* the outer surface or part.

ex·ter'mi·nate" (ek-stēr'mi-nāt") *v.t.* destroy utterly; extirpate. **—ex·ter"mi·na'tion,** *n.*

ex'tern" (eks'tērn") *n.* a person connected with an institution but not residing there.

ex·ter'nal (ek-stēr'nəl) *adj.* **1,** exterior. **2,** located outside and apart; separate. **3,** pert. to the outside of the body. **4,** outside the mind; having material existence. **5,** pert. to outward manifestation. **—n.** (*pl.*) outward appearances, manners, etc. **—ex·ter'nal·ism,** *n.* **—ex"ter·nal'i·ty,** *n.* **—ex·ter'nal·ize,** *v.t. & i.*

ex·tinct' (ik-stinkt') *adj.* **1,** extinguished, as a fire. **2,** having ceased; out of existence; no longer living. **—ex·tinc'tion,** *n.*

ex·tin'guish (ek-sting'gwish) *v.t.* **1,** put out, as a fire; quench. **2,** put an end to; destroy; suppress. **—ex·tin'guish·er,** *n.* a device for putting out a fire. **—ex·tin'guish·ment,** *n.*

ex'tir·pate" (ek'stər-pāt") *v.t.* pull up by the roots; eradicate; destroy totally. **—ex"tir·pa'tion,** *n.*

ex·tol' (ek-stōl') *v.t.* [**-tolled', -tol'ling**] speak in laudatory terms of; praise highly.

ex·tort' (ek-stôrt') *v.t.* obtain by force or compulsion; wrest from another by intimidation.

ex·tor'tion (ek-stôr'shən) *n.* exaction of payment by threat; blackmail. **—ex·tor'tion·ate** (-ət) *adj.* exorbitant in price; demanding too much.

ex'tra (eks'strə) *adj.* more than what is usual, due, or expected; additional; supplementary. **—adv.** beyond the ordinary standard, amount or degree; unusually. **—n. 1,** something additional or superior. **2,** a special edition of a newspaper. **3,** an added worker, as an actor hired by the day.

ex·tra- *pref.* outside; beyond.

ex·tract' (ek-strakt') *v.t.* **1,** remove forcibly from a fixed position; pull out. **2,** separate, as a constituent part from the whole. **3,** derive from a particular source; deduce; select. **—n.** (ek'strakt) **1,** something extracted. **2,** a substance or preparation obtained by distillation or other chemical means. **3,** a passage from a book, etc.; excerpt; quotation. **—ex·trac'tor,** *n.*

ex·trac'tion (-shən) *n.* **1,** act of extracting. **2,** an extract or essence. **3,** descent; lineage; birth.

ex"tra·cur·ric'u·lar (ek"strə-kə-rik'yə-lər) *adj.* pert. to school activities outside the regular courses of study.

ex'tra·dite" (ek'strə-dīt") *v.t.* **1,** deliver up (a prisoner or fugitive) to another nation or jurisdiction. **2,** secure custody of a person by extradition. **—ex"tra·di'tion** (-dish'-ən) *n.*

ex·tra'dos (ek-strā'dōs) *n.* the upper or convex surface of an arch or vault.

ex"tra·mu'ral (ek"strə-myûr'əl) *adj.* outside the walls, as of a college; not confined to one's own base or group.

ex·tra'ne·ous (ek-strā'nē-əs) *adj.* not belonging or proper to a thing; not intrinsic or essential; foreign. **—ex·tra'ne·ous·ness,** *n.*

ex·tra·or'di·nar"y (ek-strôrdə-ner'ē) *adj.* **1,** not of the usual or regular kind. **2,** exceeding the common degree; remarkable; wonderful.

ex·trap'o·late" (ek-strap'ə-lāt") *v.t.* project on the basis of known data; surmise. **—ex·trap"o·la'tion,** *n.*

ex"tra·sen'so·ry *adj.* beyond the perception of the recognized senses.

ex"tra·ter·res'tri·al *adj.* beyond the limits of the earth.

ex"tra·ter"ri·to'ri·al *adj.* not subject to the jurisdiction of local authorities.

ex·trav'a·gant (ek-strav'ə-gənt) *adj.* **1,** wasteful of money; inclined to spend unnecessarily. **2,** high in price. **3,** profuse; irregular; fantastic. **—ex·trav'a·gance,** *n.*

ex·trav"a·gan'za (ek-strav"ə-gan'zə) *n.* a dramatic or musical show of elaborate or fantastic nature.

ex·treme' (ek-strēm') *adj.* **1,** utmost in degree, as largest, smallest, etc.; greatest in degree. **2,** farthest from the center. **3,** last; final. **4,** very immoderate in action, opinion, etc. **—n. 1,** the utmost or greatest degree. **2,** something immoderate or fantastic. **3,** the first or last. **—ex·treme'ly,** *adv.* exceedingly; very. **—ex·treme'ness,** *n.*

ex·trem'ist (ek-strē'mist) *n.* one who goes to extremes in opinions or actions. **—extrem'ism** (-iz-əm) *n.*

ex·trem'i·ty (ek-strem'ə-tē) *n.* **1,** the outer or terminal point; the limit or boundary. **2,** an end part; a hand, foot, etc. **3,** the utmost degree. **4,** (often *pl.*) a condition of great peril, distress, or want. **5,** (*pl.*) the last moments before death.

ex'tri·cate" (ek'strə-kāt") *v.t.* disentangle; set free; liberate. **—ex'tri·ca·ble,** *adj.* **—ex"tri·ca'tion,** *n.*

ex·trin'sic (ek-strin'sik) *adj.* **1,** being outside and separate; coming from without. **2,** not inherent or essential; extraneous. **—ex·trin'si·cal·ly,** *adv.*

ex'tro·vert" (ek'strə-vērt") *n. & adj.* (*Psychol.*) a person concerned chiefly with what is outside his own mind. **—ex"tro·ver'sion** (-vēr'zhən) *n.*

ex·trude' (ek-strood') *v.t.* **1,** thrust out; expel. **2,** form (a plastic product) by ejection through a shaped opening. **—v.i.** project outward; protrude. **—ex·tru'sion** (-zhən) *n.* **—ex·tru'sive,** *adj.*

ex·u'ber·ant (eg-zoo'bər-ənt) *adj.* **1,** effusive in feeling or expression; lavish. **2,** copious to excess; overflowing. —**ex·u'ber·ance,** *n.*

ex·ude' (eg-zood') *v.i.* ooze out, like sweat through the pores. —*v.t.* emit or discharge slowly. —**ex'u·date** (eks'ū-dāt") *n.* something exuded. —**ex"u·da'tion** (eks'ū-dā'-shən) *n.*

ex·ult' (eg-zult') *v.i.* show or feel self-congratulatory joy; rejoice in triumph. —**ex·ult'ant,** *adj.* rejoicing. —**ex"ul·ta'tion** (eks"əl-tā'shən) *n.*

ex'urb (eks'ẽrb) *n.* region beyond the city and suburbs, usually inhabited by the wealthy. —**ex·ur'ban·ite** (ek-sẽr'bən-īt) *n.* one who lives in the exurbs.

ex·ur'bi·a (ek-sẽr'bē-ə) *n.* the exurbs collectively.

ex·u'vi·ate' (eg-zoo'vē-āt") *v.t.* shed or cast off, as skin or shell; molt. —**ex·u"vi·a'tion,** *n.*

eye (ī) *n.* **1,** the organ of vision in man and the higher animals. **2,** vision; the field of sight; observation; watchful attention. **3,** mental view; opinion; estimation. **4,** something resembling an eye; a colored spot; a bud or shoot. **5,** a hole in an instrument or tool; a loop of rope or wire; a hook or catch. **6,** the center of a hurricane. —*v.t.* ogle; observe; watch. —**eye bank,** a storage facility for eye parts, esp. corneas, for transplant. —**eye opener, 1,** a surprising occurrence. **2,** a drink of liquor early in the day. —**eye shadow,** makeup used to color the eyelids.

eye'ball" *n.* the ball-like mass of the eye. —*v.t.* (*Slang*) stare at; ogle.

eye'brow" *n.* the ridge above the eye.

eye'ful (ī'fûl) *n.* **1,** (*Colloq.*) a full or satisfying look at something. **2,** (*Slang*) a beautiful girl.

eye'glass" *n.* **1,** (*pl.*) one of a pair of lenses worn before the eye to correct faulty vision. **2,** the eyepiece of an optical instrument.

eye'lash" *n.* one of the hairs growing at the edge of the eyelid.

eye'let (ī'lət) *n.* a small round hole, as in paper, leather, fabric, etc., bound around the rim.

eye'lid" *n.* the skin that moves over the eyeball.

eye'li"ner (ī'-lī"-nər) *n.* makeup used to outline the eye.

eye opener 1, a surprising occurrence. **2,** a drink of liquor early in the day.

eye'piece" *n.* the lens of an optical instrument to which the eye is applied.

eye'shade" *n.* a visor.

eye'sight" *n.* the faculty of seeing; vision.

eye'sore" *n.* an object of offensive appearance.

eye'spot" *n.* a visual organ of lower animals; any eyelike spot of color.

eye'strain" *n.* fatigue of the eye muscles caused by excessive or incorrect use of the eyes.

eye'tooth" *n.* either of the two canine teeth of the upper jaw. —**cut one's eye-teeth,** gain understanding through age and experience.

eye'wash" *n.* **1,** a lotion for the eyes. **2,** (*Slang*) specious talk; a lying excuse.

eye'wit"ness *n.* one who testifies concerning an occurrence which he has seen.

ey'rie (âr'ē; ī'rē) *n.* aerie.

F

F, f (ef) the sixth letter in the English alphabet.

fa (fä) *n.* (*Music*) the fourth tone of the diatonic scale.

Fa'bi·an (fā'bē-ən) *adj.* conservative; cautious in making change. —*n.* a member of the Fabian Society, a nineteenth-century socialist organization in Great Britian.

fa'ble (fā'bəl) *n.* **1,** a fictitious tale conveying a moral. **2,** a myth; legend. **3,** a lie. —**fa'bled,** *adj.* legendary; fictitious. —**fab'u·list** (fab'yə-list) *n.*

fab'ric (fab'rik) *n.* **1,** frame; structure; composition. **2,** a woven or knitted material; cloth.

fab'ri·cate" (fab'rə-kāt") *v.t.* **1,** build or manufacture. **2,** construct by assembling parts. **3,** concoct falsely. —**fab'ri·ca"tion,** *n.*

fab'u·lous (fab'yə-ləs) *adj.* **1,** mythical; not actual. **2,** incredible; hence, immense or great. —**fab'u·lous·ness,** *n.*

fa·cade' (fə-säd') *n.* **1,** the chief exterior face of a building. **2,** the superficial aspect of something.

face (fās) *n.* **1,** the front of the head; countenance. **2,** expression; a look. **3,** outward aspect. **4,** prestige; reputation. **5,** effrontery. **6,** the principal surface of anything. —*v.t.* **1,** have the face or front toward. **2,** meet boldly. **3,** cover the surface of, with anything. —*v.i.* front in any given direction. —**face card,** king, queen, or jack, in playing cards, —**face down,** abash; stare down. —**face up to,** confront boldly. —**face value, 1,** par or promised value. **2,** degree of validity claimed.

face-'lift"ing *n.* removal of wrinkles by plastic surgery. —**face-'lift",** *n.* such an operation.

face-'off" *n.* a method for putting the playing piece in play, as in hockey or la-crosse.

face-'sav"ing *adj.* serving to save one's prestige or pride.

fac'et (fas'it) *n.* **1,** one of the small surfaces of a cut gem. **2,** aspect, phase.

fa·ce'tious (fə-sē'shəs) *adj.* humorous; joking. **—fa·ce'tious·ness,** *n.*

fa'cial (fā'shəl) *adj.* of the face. *—n.* a facial massage.

-fa'cient (fā-shənt) *suf.* **1,** making; tending to make. **2,** that which makes.

fac'ile (fas'il) *adj.* **1,** ready; quick; skill-ful. **2,** affable. **3,** glib; flippant. **4,** easy to use.

fa·cil'i·tate" (fə-sil'ə-tāt") *v.t.* make easi-er. **—fa·cil"i·ta'tion,** *n.*

fa·cil'i·ty (fə-sil'ə-tē) *n.* **1,** ease. **2,** talent; dexterity. **3,** (*pl.*) conveniences. **4,** a build-ing, etc., designed to serve a particular purpose.

fac'ing (fās'ing) *n.* **1,** an outer covering, as of different stone on a wall. **2,** a material on the edge of a garment.

fac·sim'i·le (fak-sim'ə-lè) *n.* an exact copy.

fact (fakt) *n.* **1,** something known to have occurred or to be true. **2,** the quality of being actual. **3,** the statement of something done or known to be true. **—in fact,** truly; actually.

fac'tion (fak'shən) *n.* **1,** a group or clique in a party, state, etc., seeking to promote partisan interests. **2,** strife, discord. **—fac'tion·al,** *adj.* **—fac'tion·al·ism,** *n.*

fac'tious (fak'shəs) *adj.* opposing; con-tentious. **—fac'tious·ness,** *n.*

fac·ti'tious (fak-tish'əs) *adj.* artificial; sham; made-up. **—fac·ti'tious·ness,** *n.*

fac'tor (fak'tər) *n.* **1,** an agent, distribu-tor, or private banker. **2,** any contributing cause or element. **3,** (*Math.*) one of the numbers which when multiplied together produce a given result. *—v.t.* **1,** handle as agent; lend money on accounts receivable. **2,** (*Math.*) produce from given factors; separate into factors. **—fac'tor·age** (-ij) *n.* business or commission of a factor.

fac·to'ri·al (fak-tôr'ē-əl) *adj.* **1,** pert. to a factor. **2,** (*Math.*) the product of consecu-tive integers from an integer to 1, written (!), as $3! (= 3 \times 2 \times 1)$.

fac'to·ry (fak'tə-rē) *n.* **1,** a building for manufacturing. **2,** a place where goods, etc., are produced, esp. in quantity.

fac·to'tum (fak-tō'təm) *n.* a person hired to do all kinds of work.

fac'tu·al (fak'choo-əl) *adj.* **1,** pert. to facts. **2,** true; real; actual.

fac'u·la (fak'yə-lə) *n.* [*pl.* **-lae"** (-lē")] a spot or streak on the sun.

fac'ul·ta"tive (fak'əl-tā"tiv) *adj.* **1,** con-ferring or comprising a power. **2,** optional.

fac'ul·ty (fak'əl-tē) *n.* **1,** a physical or mental power. **2,** a special aptitude; ability; knack. **3,** the teaching body collectively of a school.

fad *n.* a passing style or interest. **—fad'-dish,** *adj.* **—fad'dist,** *n.* one who follows fads.

fade (fād) *v.i.* **1,** lose color, freshness, or vigor. **2,** grow dim; die gradually. *—v.t.* **1,** cause to fade. **2,** (*Slang*) accept a bet, in craps. **—fade'less,** *adj.* permanent; eternal.

fag *v.t. & i.* **[fagged, fag'ging]** weary; exhaust. *—n.* (*Slang*) a cigarette.

fag'ot (fag'ət) *n.* a bundle of sticks used for fuel. Also, **fag'got.**

fag'ot·ing *n.* a kind of ornamentation in embroidery. Also, **fag'got·ing.**

Fahr'en·heit" (far'ən-hīt") *n.* a thermo-metric scale on which $+32°$ is the freezing and $+212°$ the boiling point of water.

fa·ience' (fī-äns') *n.* a kind of glazed pot-tery with highly colored decoration.

fail (fāl) *v.i.* **1,** fall short; be deficient. **2,** become weaker. **3,** prove to be lacking in what is expected or desired. **4,** go bank-rupt. *—v.t.* **1,** not fulfill the expectations of; disappoint. **2,** assign a grade insufficient for passing.

fail'ing *n.* a fault. *—prep.* in the absence of; in default of.

faille (fāl; fīl) *n.* a ribbed silk or rayon fabric.

fail-'safe" *adj.* **1,** automatically compen-sating for a mistake or failure. **2,** irreversibly reacting (as to launch a counterattack) on the occurrence of certain predetermined con-ditions.

fail'ure (fāl'yər) *n.* **1,** the act of failing; a falling short; nonperformance; deterioration; bankruptcy. **2,** an unsuccessful person or thing.

fain (fān) *adv.* (*Archaic*) willingly; gladly.

faint (fānt) *adj.* **1,** not easily seen or heard; weak in tone, color, sound, etc.; indistinct; pale. **2,** feeble; weak; about to swoon. *—n.* a swoon. *—v.i.* swoon. **—faint"heart'-ed,** *adj.* diffident; timid. **—faint'ness,** *n.*

fair (fār) *adj.* **1,** good to look upon; beau-tiful. **2,** blond; light-colored. **3,** spotless; pure. **4,** legal; within bounds, as a hit ball in baseball. **5,** just; unbiased. **6,** passably good. **7,** clear; unclouded; bright; not stormy. **8,** womanly; feminine. *—adv.* **1,** according to rule. **2,** favorably; passably well. **3,** squarely. *—n.* **1,** a competitive exhibition of farm products, handwork, etc. **2,** a sale or bazaar, as for charity. **3**, a regular meeting, at a stated time and place, of buyers and sellers. —**fair′ness**, *n.* —**fair and square**, honest(ly). —**fair copy**, a final, corrected copy of a document. —**the fair sex**, women. —**fair shake**, a fair chance.

fair′haired″ (-hârd) *adj.* **1**, having blond hair. **2**, unduly favored.

fair′ly (-lẽ) *adv.* **1**, impartially; reasonably. **2**, tolerably; to a moderate degree. **3**, actually; positively.

fair′spo″ken *adj.* polite in speech.

fair-′trade″ agreement an agreement under which a retailer must not undersell minimum price levels set by a manufacturer.

fair′way″ (fâr′wā″) *n.* **1**, in golf, the mowed strip between tee and putting green. **2**, the navigable part of a river or harbor.

fair-′weath″er *adj.* (*Colloq.*) not dependable in time of trouble.

fair′y (fâr′ẽ) *n.* a tiny spirit capable of assuming various forms and of interfering in human affairs. —**fair′y·land″**, *n.* the land where fairies live; any enchanting place. —**fairy tale**, **1**, a story about fairies, for children. **2**, a preposterous tale; a lie.

faith (fāth) *n.* **1**, belief without proof; confidence; reliance. **2**, belief in God. **3**, loyalty; fidelity to an agreement or promise. **4**, a religious creed.

faith′ful (-fǝl) *adj.* **1**, loyal. **2**, conscientious. **3**, exact; true. —**faith′ful·ness**, *n.*

faith-′heal″ing *n.* the curing of ills by prayer and religious faith alone.

faith′less (-lǝs) *adj.* false to a promise or obligation. —**faith′less·ness**, *n.*

fake (fāk) *v.t. & i.* (*Colloq.*) **1**, imitate fraudulently; pretend; feign. **2**, improvise. —*adj.* not genuine. —*n.* **1**, a counterfeit; a fraudulent imitation. **2**, a false pretender; an impostor. —**fake book**, a book of popular songs, giving only melody and chord symbols.

fak′er *n.* **1**, one who fakes. **2**, a swindler.

fa·kir′ (fǝ-kir′) *n.* a religious mendicant, esp. Moslem or Hindu.

fal′chion (fal′chǝn) *n.* a broad-bladed sword with a curved edge.

fal′con (fâl′kǝn) *n.* a small, swift hawk, esp. one trained to hunt.

fal′con·ry (-rẽ) *n.* the sport of hunting with falcons.

fall (fâl) *v.i.* [**fell, fall′en, fall′ing**] **1**, drop or sink from a higher to a lower level; descend rapidly; decline. **2**, (sometimes with *down*) tumble to the ground, esp. after stumbling. **3**, die. **4**, come by chance. **5**, occur. **6**, pass from one condition to another. **7**, (with *away*) decline; (with *for*) be deceived by; (with *in*) take one's place in line; hence,

agree; (with *out*) quarrel; (with *through*) not come to exist; miscarry. —*n.* **1**, the act or result of falling. **2**, (often *cap.*) the season from Sept. 22 to Dec. 21; autumn. —**fall guy**, (*Slang*) victim; scapegoat; dupe. —**falling sickness**, epilepsy. —**falling star**, meteorite. —**fall off**, **1**, decrease; diminish. **2**, separate; withdraw.

fal′la·cy (fal′ǝ-sẽ) *n.* **1**, an error or flaw, esp. in reasoning. **2**, a false idea. —**falla′cious** (fǝ-lā′shǝs) *adj.*

fal′li·ble (fal′ǝ-bǝl) *adj.* apt to be mistaken; capable of committing error. —**fal″li·bil′i·ty**, *n.*

Fal·lo′pi·an tubes (fǝ-lō′pē-ǝn) *n.* the two tubes that conduct the egg from the ovaries to the uterus.

fall′out *n.* **1**, the falling of radioactive debris after a nuclear explosion. **2**, the debris itself. **3**, the reaction to or result of a statement or action.

fal′low (fal′ō) *adj.* **1**, plowed but not sowed. **2**, not in use; idle. **3**, a pale, yellowish color.

false (fâls) *adj.* **1**, not according to fact; untrue; erroneous; wrong. **2**, not truthful. **3**, treacherous; deceitful; disloyal. **4**, sham; artificial. —**false′ness**, *n.* —**false alarm**, **1**, an emergency alarm improperly or mistakenly sounded. **2**, any alarm or warning that turns out to be groundless.

false′hood″ (-hûd″) *n.* a lie.

fal·set′to (fâl-set′ō) *n.* [*pl.* **-tos**] a voice, esp. a man's voice, that is artificially high.

fal′sies (fâl′sēz) *n.pl.* forms worn by women to fill out their bosoms.

fal′si·fy″ (fâl′si-fī″) *v.t.* **1**, misrepresent; deceive. **2**, alter fraudulently. —**fal″si·fi·ca′tion** (-fi-kā′shǝn) *n.*

fal′si·ty (fâl′sǝ-tẽ) *n.* **1**, the quality of being false. **2**, a lie.

falt′boat″ (fâlt′-) *n.* a small collapsible boat. Also, **fold′boat″**.

fal′ter (fâl′tǝr) *v.i.* **1**, be unsteady; stumble. **2**, be hesitant in speech; stammer. **3**, waver, in action or purpose.

fame (fām) *n.* renown; widespread reputation; rumor. —**famed**, *adj.*

fa·mil′iar (fǝ-mil′yǝr) *adj.* **1**, closely intimate. **2**, well versed or acquainted. **3**, well known and remembered; common. **4**, overfree; presuming. —*n.* **1**, an intimate associate. **2**, a spirit or demon supposed to attend on a person, esp. a witch or wizard. —**fa·mil′ial** (fǝ-mil′yǝl) *adj.* —**fa·mil″i·ar′i·ty** (fǝ-mil″yǝr′ǝ-tẽ) *n.* —**fa·mil′iar·ize″** (-īz″) *v.t.* make well acquainted or well known.

fam′i·ly (fam′ǝ-lẽ) *n.* **1**, a household. **2**, kindred, esp. one's own spouse, parents, and children. **3**, descendants of a common ancestor; a tribe. **4**, lineage. **5**, a group of things with some common feature. —**family tree**, a genealogical chart. —**in a family way**, (*Slang*) pregnant.

fam'ine (fam'in) *n.* extreme scarcity of food; starvation.

fam'ish *v.t. & i.* starve; suffer extreme hunger. —**fam'ish·ment**, *n.*

fa'mous (fā'məs) *adj.* **1**, widely known; renowned; noted or notorious. **2**, (*Colloq.*) excellent. —**fa'mous·ly**, *adv.*

fam'u·lus (fam'yū-ləs) *n.* [*pl.* **-li″** (-lī″)] a servant or assistant.

fan *n.* **1**, a device for stirring the air, either mechanical or manual. **2**, (*Colloq.*) a devotee of a sport, hobby, etc. —*v.t. & i.* [**fanned, fan'ning**] **1**, drive air upon; wave a fan. **2**, rouse; excite. **3**, spread out like a fan. **4**, in baseball, strike out.

fa·nat'ic (fə-nat'ik) *n.* a zealot, esp. in religion. —*adj.* extreme; excessive. —**fanat'i·cal,** *adj.* —**fa·nat'i·cism,** *n.*

fan'ci·er (fan'sē-ər) *n.* one with a special interest, as in dogs or plants. —*adj.* comp. of *fancy.*

fan'ci·ful (fan'si-fəl) *adj.* **1**, whimsical; unreal. **2**, curiously designed.

fan'cy (fan'sē) *n.* **1**, the capacity for imaginative vision; an idea or notion of something unreal or fantastic but pleasing; a delusion. **2**, a whim. **3**, fondness; liking. —*adj.* **1**, chiefly imagined or imaginative; whimsical. **2**, not plain. **3**, of best quality; superfine. **4**, extravagant. **5**, done with skill. —*v.t.* **1**, imagine. **2**, suppose; assume. **3**, like; wish for; prefer. —**fan'cied,** *adj.* imaginary. —**fan'ci·ness,** *n.*

fan'cy-free″ *adj.* carefree; not in love.

fan·dan'go (fan-dang'gō) *n.* [*pl.* **-gos**] a lively Spanish dance; the music for it.

fan'dom (fan'dəm) *n.* (*Colloq.*) fans collectively (as of a sport).

fan'fare″ (fan'fār″) *n.* a flourish of trumpets; ceremony; ostentation.

fang *n.* a sharp tooth, esp. of an animal or poisonous snake.

fan'jet″ *n.* a jet engine with a special air intake for increased thrust.

fan'light″ *n.* a fan-shaped window above a door.

fan'ny (fan'ē) *n.* (*Slang*) buttocks.

fan'tail″ *n.* **1**, a fan-shaped end, part, or structure. **2**, a bird, fish, or plant having a fanlike tail or part. —*adj.* having such a part.

fan'tan″ *n.* **1**, a card game. **2**, a Chinese gambling game.

fan·ta'si·a (fan-tä'zhə) *n.* an unconventional musical piece.

fan·tas'tic (fan-tas'tik) *adj.* **1**, imagined or unreal and hardly possible. **2**, grotesque. —**fan·tas'ti·cal·ly,** *adv.*

fan'ta·sy (fan'tə-sē) *n.* **1**, unrestrained imagination. **2**, an illusory mental image; a visionary idea. Also, **phan'ta·sy.** —**fan'ta·size,** *v.i.*

far (fär) *adj.* [**far'ther** (-*th*ər), **-thest**] **1**, remote in time or space. **2**, more distant of the two. —*adv.* **1**, widely. **2**, by a great deal. **3**, to a definite distance, point, or degree. —**a far cry**, **1**, a great distance or length of time. **2**, disparate; incommensurate. —**as far as**, to the distance, extent, or degree that.

far'ad (far'əd) *n.* a unit of electrical capacitance.

farce (färs) *n.* **1**, a comedy of exaggerated humor. **2**, a mockery; a fiasco. —**far'ci·cal** (fär'si-kəl) *adj.*

fare (fār) *v.i.* **1**, proceed; go; travel. **2**, turn out; result. **3**, have good or bad health, fortune, or treatment. **4**, eat and drink. —*n.* **1**, the amount charged for passage; any charge or rate. **2**, a paying passenger. **3**, food served.

Far East a part of Asia including Japan, China, Vietnam, Korea, etc.

fare″well' (fār″wel') *interj.* goodbye. —*n.* a leave-taking.

far″fetched' (fär″fecht') *adj.* too complex or unnatural to be readily grasped or believed.

far″flung' (fär″flung') *adj.* **1**, widely dispersed. **2**, extensive.

fa·ri'na (fə-rē'nə) *n.* meal or flour made from cereal grains. —**fa″ri·na'ceous** (fa″rə-nā'shəs) *adj.*

farm (färm) *n.* a tract of land on which crops, animals, etc., are raised. —*v.t. & i.* **1**, use (land) as a farm. **2**, develop by cultivation. **3**, (with *out*) lease; assign.

farm'er (fär'mər) *n.* **1**, one who farms professionally. **2**, a rustic.

farm'ing *n.* agriculture.

farm'stead″ *n.* a farm and its buildings.

farm'yard″ *n.* the ground around buildings on a farm.

far'o (fār'ō) *n.* a card game.

far-'out' (*Slang*) *adj.* **1**, extreme. **2**, excellent; first-rate. —*interj.* excellent!

far·ra'go (fə-rä'gō) *n.* a confused mixture.

far'ri·er (far'ē-ər) *n.* one who shoes horses.

far'row (far'ō) *n.* a litter of pigs. —*v.t. & i.* give birth to (pigs).

far'sight″ed (fär'sī″tid) *adj.* **1**, able to perceive distant sights. **2**, having foresight. —**far″sight'ed·ness,** *n.*

far'ther (fär'*th*ər) *adj. & adv.* more remote or extended, with reference to distance: comp. of *far*.

far′ther·most″ *adj.* most remote.

far′thing (fär′thing) *n.* a former Brit. coin worth ¼ penny.

far′thin·gale″ (fär′thing-gāl″) *n.* a kind of hoop skirt.

fas′ces (fas′ēz) *n. pl.* [*sing.* **-cis**] a bundle of rods bound as a staff for an ax blade.

fas′ci·cle (fas′i-kəl) *n.* **1,** a bundle; cluster. **2,** a number of sheets bound together; a part of a printed work.

fas′ci·nate″ (fas′ə-nāt″) *v.t.* attract irresistibly; bewitch; enchant. —**fas″ci·na′tion,** *n.* —**fas′ci·na·tor,** *n.* a woman's lace scarf.

fas′cism (fash′iz-əm) *n.* a strongly nationalistic regime characterized by regimentation, rigid censorship, and suppression of opposition.

fas′cist (fash′ist) *n.* a supporter of fascism or a believer in its policies. —*adj.* reactionary; intolerant. —**fas·cis′tic** (fə-shis′tik) *adj.* —**fas·cis′ti·cal·ly,** *adv.*

fash′ion (fash′ən) *n.* **1,** prevailing mode, esp. of dress; present custom. **2,** people of polite society collectively. **3,** external shape; form. **4,** manner or way (of doing something). —*v.t.* make; fabricate; give a particular shape or form to. —**fashion plate,** a stylishly dressed person.

fash′ion·a·ble (-ə-bəl) *adj.* **1,** stylish. **2,** favored by polite society. —**fash′ion·a·ble·ness,** *n.*

fast (fåst) *adj.* **1,** moving at a rapid pace; swift; quick. **2,** without delay. **3,** conducive to rapidity, as a *fast track.* **4,** of a clock, showing too advanced time; of time (*Colloq.*) daylight saving. **5,** loose in morals; dissipated. **6,** firmly fixed; tight; steadfast. **7,** not subject to fading; lasting. —*adv.* **1,** rapidly. **2,** firmly; soundly. —*n.* voluntary abstinence from food. —*v.i.* abstain from eating. —**fast time,** daylight saving time.

fast′back″ *n.* a sloping automobile roof; a car with such a roof.

fas′ten (fås′ən) *v.t. & i.* **1,** attach firmly; fix firmly in position; make secure. **2,** direct (the eyes, etc.) steadily. —**fas′ten·ing,** *n.* a clasp, lock, hook, etc.

fast-′food″ *adj.* providing rapid preparation and service of food.

fas·tid′i·ous (fas-tid′ē-əs) *adj.* hard to please; overnice. —**fas·tid′i·ous·ness,** *n.*

fast′ness (fåst′nəs) *n.* **1,** state of being fast; speed. **2,** an impregnable place.

fast-′talk″ *v.t.* (*Slang*) persuade with glib or deceptive talk.

fat *adj.* [**fat′ter, -test**] **1,** bulging with much, or too much, flesh; corpulent; plump.

2, consisting of fat; greasy. **3,** rich in some desirable element. **4,** fertile; fruitful; profitable. —*n.* **1,** the oily solid substance in animal tissue, yellowish white in color; suet. **2,** the best part of anything. —**fat′ness,** *n.* —**chew the fat,** (*Slang*) chat; converse. —**fat cat,** (*Slang*) a wealthy person, esp. a contributor to a political campaign. —**a fat chance,** little or no chance. —**fat city,** (*Slang*) a state of material well-being. —**fat farm,** (*Slang*) a health spa.

fa′tal (fā′təl) *adj.* **1,** causing death or ruin. **2,** fateful. —**fa′tal·ness,** *n.*

fa′tal·ism (fā′tə-liz-əm) *n.* the belief that all events are predetermined and hence inevitable. —**fa′tal·ist,** *n.* —**fa″tal·is′tic,** *adj.*

fa·tal′i·ty (fā-tal′ə-tē) *n.* a fatal disaster; a death in a disaster.

Fa′ta Mor·ga′na (fā′tə-môr-gä′nə) a mirage seen on the coasts of Italy and Sicily.

fat′back″ *n.* salt pork.

fate (fāt) *n.* **1,** a power that supposedly predetermines what is to happen. **2,** destiny; lot. **3,** ultimate outcome.

fat′ed (fā′tid) *adj.* **1,** predetermined by fate. **2,** doomed.

fate′ful (-fəl) *adj.* **1,** momentous. **2,** controlled by destiny. **3,** prophetic. **4,** disastrous. —**fate′ful·ness,** *n.*

fat′head″ *n.* (*Colloq.*) a stupid person; dolt.

fa′ther (fä′thər) *n.* **1,** a male parent. **2,** (*cap.*) God. **3,** any ancestor. **4,** one who originates, makes possible, or inspires something. **5,** the title given to certain priests. **6,** one of the leading citizens. —**fa′ther·hood″,** *n.* —**fa′ther-in-law″** *n.* the father of one's husband or wife.

fa′ther·land″ *n.* one's native country.

fa′ther·ly (-lē) *adj.* paternal; like a father. —**fa′ther·li·ness,** *n.*

fath′om (fath′əm) *n.* a nautical measure of length, 6 feet. —*v.t.* **1,** measure in fathoms; reach the bottom of. **2,** understand thoroughly. —**fath′om·less** (-ləs) *adj.* too deep to fathom.

fa·tigue′ (fə-tēg′) *n.* **1,** weariness from physical or mental exertion. **2,** *pl.* work clothes. —*v.t.* weary with labor. —**fat′i·ga·ble,** *adj.*

fat′ted (fat′id) *adj.* fattened.

fat′ten (fat′ən) *v.t.* **1,** feed so as to make fat. **2,** enrich; increase. —*v.i.* become fatter.

fat′ty (fat′ē) *adj.* of or like fat. —**fatty acid,** any of a class of acids present in animal and vegetable fats.

fa·tu′i·ty (fə-too′ə-tē) *n.* **1,** fatuousness. **2,** a foolish act or idea.

fat′u·ous (fach′oo-əs) *adj.* complacently silly; inane. —**fat′u·ous·ness,** *n.*

fau′cet (fâ′sit) *n.* a device for controlling the flow of a liquid from a pipe or container; a tap.

fault (fâlt) *n.* **1,** whatever is not perfect or not satisfactory; a defect; flaw; imperfection; failing; error; mistake. **2,** a cause for blame. **3,** a break in continuity, esp. in rock formation. **4,** in tennis, etc., an improper service. —*v.t.* blame —**fault′find″-ing,** *adj.* given to carping. —**fault′less,** *adj.* perfect; irreproachable. —**fault′y,** *adj.* having some defects; erroneous; erratic.

faun (fân) *n.* a Roman rural deity, part goat and part man.

fau′na (fâ′nə) *n.* the animals of a region or period.

faux pas (fō-pä′) (*Fr.*) a false step; social error; mistake.

fa′vor (fā′vər) *n.* **1,** a spirit of approval, good will, or liking; partiality. **2,** an act of kindness, not of self-seeking. **3,** a small gift, esp. to a guest at a party; a token. **4,** in business idiom, a letter. —*v.t.* **1,** prefer. **2,** advocate; support. **3,** (*Colloq.*) resemble in facial aspect. Also, **fa′vour.**

fa′vor·a·ble (-ə-bəl) *adj.* **1,** inclined to approve; affirmative. **2,** advantageous. —**fa′vor·a·ble·ness,** *n.*

fa′vored (-vērd) *adj.* **1,** blessed. **2,** appealing. **3,** given special consideration.

fa′vor·ite (fā′vər-it) *adj.* preferred. —*n.* **1,** a person or thing preferred or popular. **2,** a contestant deemed most likely to win. —**fa′vor·it·ism,** *n.* partiality. —**favorite son,** at a U.S. presidential convention, a person favored as a nominee by the delegates from his state.

fawn (fân) *v.i.* show affection, as a dog, by hand-licking, etc.; hence, cringe and flatter. —*n.* **1,** a young deer. **2,** a very light tan color.

fax (faks) *n.* transmission of images by radio or wire; facsimile.

fay (fā) *n.* an elf; fairy. —*adj.* **1,** elfin. **2,** (*Slang*) effeminate; homosexual.

faze (fāz) *v.t.* (*Colloq.*) ruffle; daunt.

fe′al·ty (fē′əl-tē) *n.* fidelity, esp. to a lord.

fear (fir) *n.* **1,** anticipation of misfortune or pain; the state of being afraid. **2,** something dreaded. **3,** anxiety. **4,** reverent awe, as of God. —*v.t. & i.* feel fear (of).

fear′ful (-fəl) *adj.* **1,** timid; apprehensive. **2,** fearsome. —**fear′ful·ness,** *n.*

fear′less (-ləs) *adj.* feeling no fear. —**fear′-less·ness,** *n.*

fear′some (-səm) *adj.* causing fear; terrible. —**fear′some·ness,** *n.*

fea′si·ble (fē′zə-bəl) *adj.* **1,** possible of realization. **2,** suitable. —**fea″si·bil′i·ty,** *n.*

feast (fēst) *n.* **1,** a sumptuous meal. **2,**

festival, esp. religious. —*v.t.* **1,** entertain with a feast. **2,** gratify; delight. —*v.i.* **1,** have a feast. **2,** dwell with delight.

feat (fēt) *n.* an act of remarkable skill or valor.

feath′er (fe*th*′ər) *n.* **1,** one of the light outgrowths from a bird's skin. **2,** (*pl.*) plumage; hence, attire. **3,** something light. —*v.i. & t.* **1,** grow, or provide with, feathers. **2,** turn (an oar, a propeller shaft, etc.) almost to a horizontal position. —**feath′er·y,** *adj.*

feath′er·bed″ *n.* **1,** a mattress or thick quilt stuffed with feathers. **2,** (*Slang*) an easy task. —*v.i.* be paid for work not actually done.

feath′er·edge″ *n.* a very thin edge; the thinner edge, as of a board. —**feath′er·edged″,** *adj.*

feath′er·weight″ *n.* a boxer of 118 to 126 pounds.

fea′ture (fē′chər) *n.* **1,** any part of the face; (*pl.*) facial appearance. **2,** a distinctive or prominent characteristic. **3,** an item of unusual interest or attraction; an article in a magazine, newspaper, etc. **4,** a motion picture of full length; the main motion picture shown in a theater. —*v.t.* give prominence to.

feb′ri·fuge″ (feb′ri-fūj″) *n.* a medicine to combat fever. —**feb″ri·fu′gal** (-fū′gəl) *adj.* acting against fever.

fe′brile (fē′brəl) *adj.* feverish.

Feb′ru·ar·y (feb′roo-er-ē) *n.* the second month of the year.

fe′cal (fē′kəl) *adj.* pert. to feces.

fe′ces (fē′sēz) *n.pl.* excrement.

feck′less (fek′ləs) *adj.* feeble; ineffective.

fec′u·lent (fek′yə-lənt) *adj.* muddy; foul. —**fec′u·lence,** *n.*

fe′cund (fē′kund) *adj.* prolific; fertile. —**fe·cun·date″** (-dāt″) *v.* —**fe·cund′i·ty** (fi-kun′də-tē) *n.*

fed *v.* pret. & p.p. of *feed.* —*n.* (*cap.*) (*Slang*) a federal investigative agent.

fed′er·al (fed′ər-əl) *adj.* pert. to a nation formed by the union of several sovereign states.

fed′er·al·ism (fed′ər-ə-liz-əm) *n.* the doctrine or practice of federal government; advocacy of a strong federal government. —**fed′er·al·ist,** *n.* —**fed′er·al·ize,** *v.t. & i.*

fed′er·ate″ (fed′ə-rāt″) *v.t. & i.* join (states, clubs, etc.) in a union.

fed″er·a″tion (fed″ə-rā′shən) *n.* **1,** act of uniting or being united. **2,** league; confederacy. —**fed′er·a″tive** *adj.*

fe·do′ra (fə-dôr′ə) *n.* a man's soft felt hat.

fee (fē) *n.* **1,** a charge for services, privileges, etc. **2,** a tip. **3,** land held under a feudal overlord. —v.t. give a fee to. —**fee simple,** absolute ownership.

fee'ble (fē'bəl) adj. **1,** lacking energy or power; very weak; infirm. **2,** showing weakness; halfhearted; ineffective. —**fee'bleness,** n.

feed (fēd) v.t. & i. [pret. & p.p. **fed**] **1,** give food to. **2,** supply what is needed for the growth, operation, or maintenance of. **3,** satisfy; gratify. —v.i. take food; eat. —n. **1,** food, esp. for cattle, etc.; fodder. **2,** (Colloq.) a meal. **3,** a feeding mechanism. —**feed'bag",** n. a bag from which a horse feeds. —**fed up,** (Colloq.) disgusted by too much of something.

feed'back" n. a return of part of the output of a system to the input.

feed'lot" n. a place where animals are fed, esp. to fatten for slaughter.

feel (fēl) v.t. [pret. & p.p. **felt**] **1,** perceive by the sense of touch; examine by touching. **2,** have a sensation of; be conscious of being, as warm, happy, etc. **3,** know intuitively; infer. **4,** suffer the consequences of. **5,** [often with out] explore by touch; find (one's way) cautiously by any means. —v.i. **1,** have a sensation of any kind; perceive oneself to be (in a certain condition, as ill). **2,** touch something to feel it; grope. **3,** be capable of, or experience, emotion. **4,** seem to the touch. —n. **1,** tactile quality of an object, material, etc. **2,** feeling. **3,** act of feeling. **4,** (Colloq.) aptitude; understanding.

feel'er (fē'lər) n. **1,** palpus. **2,** something said or done to find out the views of others.

feel'ing (fē'ling) n. **1,** the sense of touch. **2,** sensation of any kind. **3,** emotion; the capacity to feel emotion. **4,** an unreasoned conviction. —**feel'ing·ly,** adv. **1,** emotionally. **2,** sympathetically.

feet (fēt) n. pl. of foot.

feign (fān) v.i. & t. pretend.

feint (fānt) n. an apparent aiming at one point when another is the real object of attack. —v.i. make a feint.

feis'ty (fī'stē) adj. **1,** quarrelsome. **2,** frisky.

feld'spar" (feld'spär") n. a mineral found in many common rocks, used in making porcelain.

fe·lic'i·tate" (fi-lis'ə-tāt") v.t. express happy sympathy with; congratulate. —**fe·lic"i·ta'tion,** n.

fe·lic'i·tous (fi-lis'ə-təs) adj. well chosen; apt. —**fe·lic'i·tous·ness,** n.

fe·lic'i·ty (fi-lis'ə-tē) n. **1,** happiness; a source of happiness. **2,** aptness; grace.

fe'line (fē'līn) n. an animal of the cat family. —adj. of the cat family; catlike; sly. —**fe·lin'i·ty** (fē-lin'ə-tē) n.

fell (fel) v.t. strike down by a blow or cut. —adj. ruthless; terrible. —v.i. pret. of fall. —n. pelt.

fel'lah (fel'ə) n. [pl. -**lahs**] a peasant or agricultural laborer.

fel'loe (fel'ō) n. the rim of a wheel when extended by spokes from a hub. Also, **fel'ly** (-ē).

fel'low (fel'ō) n. **1,** a comrade. **2,** one of a pair; a mate; an equal. **3,** (Colloq.) a person, esp. male. **4,** a member of a learned society. **5,** a graduate student on a fellowship. —adj. in the same class, occupation, or condition. —**fellow traveler,** one who supports an organization, esp. the Communist party, but is not a member. —**hail fellow,** a boisterously friendly acquaintance.

fel'low·ship (fel'ə-ship) n. **1,** a body of fellows or associates. **2,** companionship; community of interests. **3,** a grant of money for further study.

fel'on (fel'ən) n. **1,** a person convicted of a felony; a criminal. **2,** an acute inflammation near the fingernail or toenail.

fel'o·ny (fel'ə-nē) n. a major crime. —**fe·lo'ni·ous** (fə-lō'nē-əs) adj.

felt n. a pressed fabric made of wool, hair, or fur. —v. pret. & p.p. of feel.

fe'male (fē'māl) adj. **1,** of the sex bearing young or yielding offspring. **2,** feminine. **3,** (Mech.) concave for the reception of a fitting part. —n. a female person, animal, or thing.

fem'i·nine (fem'ə-nin) adj. **1,** relating to, or like, woman. **2,** (Gram.) of the gender to which words applying to women belong.

fem"i·nin'i·ty (-ə-tē) n. **1,** womanliness. **2,** females collectively.

fem'i·nism (fem'ə-niz-əm) n. advocacy of increased political activity or rights for women. —**fem'i·nist,** n.

fe'mur (fē'mər) n. the thigh bone. —**fem'o·ral** (fem'ə-rəl) adj.

fen n. low, marshy ground.

fence (fens) n. **1,** an enclosing barrier. **2,** (Slang) a receiver of stolen goods. —v.t. (usually with in) surround with a fence. —v.i. **1,** use a sword or foil for sport or in self-defense. **2,** parry; evade. —**fenc'er,** n. one skilled in swordplay.

fenc'ing n. **1,** swordplay, esp. for sport. **2,** fences collectively.

fend v.t. ward off. —v.i. make shift: fend for oneself.

fend'er (fen'dər) n. a protective guard, as on an automobile or before a fireplace.

fe·nes'tra (fi-nes'trə) n. a windowlike opening.

fen"es·tra'tion (fen"ə-strā'shən) n. windows, their number and location.

fen'nel (fen'əl) *n.* an aromatic herb, used in cookery.

fe'ral (fir'əl) *adj.* wild; untamed; hence, savage.

fer-de-lance' (fer-də-läns') *n.* a venomous snake.

fer'ment (fēr'ment) *n.* **1,** a substance that causes fermentation. **2,** commotion. —*v.t. & i.* (fər-ment') **1,** cause or undergo fermentation (in). **2,** excite; arouse; seethe.

fer″men·ta'tion (fēr″mən-tā'shən) *n.* **1,** the chemical change produced in a substance by the action of organisms, as when milk sours. **2,** unrest; agitation.

fer'mi·um (fēr'mē-əm) *n.* an unstable, radioactive metallic element, no. 100, symbol Fm, produced artificially.

fern (fērn) *n.* any of a large group of flowerless plants that propagate from spores. —**fern'er·y,** *n.*

fe·ro'cious (fə-rō'shəs) *adj.* very fierce; savage.

fe·roc'i·ty (fə-ros'ə-tē) *n.* cruel fierceness.

-fer·ous (fə-rəs) *suf.* containing; yielding; producing.

fer'ret (fer'it) *n.* a slim, lithe animal used to hunt rabbits and rats. —*v.t.* drive out of a hiding place; search out, as a criminal or a secret.

fer'ri-, fer'ro- (fer'ə) *pref.* iron.

Fer'ris wheel (fer'is) an amusement-park attraction, a large upright rotating wheel with seats for passengers.

fer″ro·con'crete *n.* reinforced concrete.

fer″ro·mag·net'ic *adj.* behaving like iron in a magnetic field.

fer'rous (fer'əs) *adj.* containing or derived from iron.

fer'rule (fer'ool) *n.* a metal ring or cap for strengthening a tool handle, end of a cane, etc. Also, **fer'ule.**

fer'ry (fer'ē) *n.* **1,** provision for conveying passengers or goods across water. **2,** the boat or raft so used: *ferryboat.* —*v.t.* transport on a ferry.

fer'tile (fēr'təl) *adj.* **1,** producing crops, offspring, etc., abundantly; fruitful; prolific. **2,** capable of reproducing or developing. —**fer·til'i·ty** (fər-til'ə-tē) *n.*

fer'ti·lize″ (fēr'tə-līz″) *v.t.* make productive, as by impregnating (an egg, etc.) or enriching (the soil). —**fer″ti·li·za'tion** (-li-zā'shən) *n.* —**fer'ti·liz″er,** a substance that enriches the soil, as manure.

fer'ule (fer'əl) *n.* **1,** a ruler for punishing children. **2,** (-ool) ferrule.

fer'vent (fēr'vənt) *adj.* **1,** earnest; ardent. **2,** hot; glowing. —**fer'ven·cy,** *n.*

fer'vid (fēr'vid) *adj.* glowing with enthusiasm; vehement. —**fer'vid·ness,** *n.*

fer'vor (fēr'vər) *n.* **1,** ardent feeling; zeal. **2,** intense heat. Also, **fer'vour.**

fes'cue (fes'kū) *n.* a grass much used for pasture or lawns.

fes'tal (fes'təl) *adj.* pert. to a feast: gala.

fes'ter (fes'tər) *v.i.* **1,** become filled with pus; suppurate. **2,** rankle.

fes'ti·val (fes'ti-vəl) *n.* **1,** a feast or celebration, religious or anniversary. **2,** a gathering for entertainment or rejoicing. —*adj.* festive; joyous.

fes'tive (fes'tiv) *adj.* pert. to a feast or festival; joyous; gay. —**fes'tive·ness,** *n.*

fes·tiv'i·ty (fes-tiv'ə-tē) *n.* **1,** gaiety; rejoicing. **2,** (*pl.*) festive observances or activities.

fes·toon' *n.* a rope of flowers, ribbons, etc., hung in a loop. —*v.t.* hang with festoons; decorate.

fe'tal (fē'təl) *adj.* pert. to a fetus.

fetch (fech) *v.t. & i.* **1,** go after and bring back. **2,** sell for. —**fetch'ing,** *adj.* (*Colloq.*) alluring; attractive.

fete (fāt) *n.* a festival. —*v.t.* entertain in honor of.

fet'id *adj.* having an offensive stench. —**fet'id·ness,** *n.*

fet'ish *n.* **1,** an object supposed to embody a spirit; totem. **2,** an object of abnormal love or passion. —**fet'ish·ism,** *n.* —**fet'ish·ist,** *n.*

fet'lock (fet'lok) *n.* a projection above and behind a horse's hoof; a tuft of hair at this point.

fet'ter (fet'ər) *n.* **1,** a shackle. **2,** a check; restraint. —*v.t.* confine in fetters; restrain.

fet'ter·bush″ (fet'ər-bûsh″) *n.* an evergreen shrub.

fet'tle (fet'əl) *n.* state of health or spirits; condition.

fet″tu·ci'ni (fet″ə-chē'nē) *n. pl.* (*Ital.*) noodles.

fe'tus (fē'təs) *n.* the unborn young of an animal.

feud (fūd) *n.* a long-standing strife between clans or families; a quarrel. —*v.i.* quarrel. —**feud'ist,** *n.*

feu'dal (fū'dəl) *adj.* **1,** pert. to the system under which a vassal held land in fief from a lord to whom he owed allegiance and certain services. **2,** pert. to the period of the feudal system, the Middle Ages. —**feu'dal·ism,** *n.* practice or advocacy of the feudal system or a similar modern system.

fe'ver (fē'vər) *n.* **1,** a body temperature higher than normal; in humans, more than 98.6°F.(37°C.). **2,** a disease marked by weakness and high temperature. **3,** intense agitation.

fe'ver·few" (fē'vər-fū") *n.* a perennial garden herb.

fe'ver·ish (fē'vər-ish) *adj.* **1,** having a fever. **2,** impatient; excited. —**fe'ver·ish·ness,** *n.*

few (fū) *adj.* not many. —*n.* **1,** a small group. **2,** (with *the*) the minority. —**quite a few,** (*Colloq.*) many.

fez *n.* a tasseled red cap formerly worn by Turks.

fi'an·cé' (fē"än-sā') *n.* a man engaged to be married. —**fi"an·cée',** *n.fem.*

fi·as'co (fé-as'kō) *n.* [*pl.* **-cos**] an ignominious failure.

fi'at (fī'ət) *n.* a decree or sanction. —**fiat money,** paper currency made legal tender by fiat, not convertible into coin.

fib *n.* a trivial lie. —*v.i.* [**fibbed, fib'bing**] tell a fib.

fi'ber (fī'bər) *n.* **1,** one of the fine threadlike parts forming plant and animal tissue. **2,** a substance made of these parts, esp. when capable of being spun or woven. **3,** quality; character. Also, **fi'bre.** —**fi'brous,** *adj.* —**fiber optics,** transparent fibers of glass or plastic used to transmit light.

fi'ber·board" *n.* a building material of compressed wood fiber.

fi'ber·fill" *n.* a man-made material used as stuffing for quilts, etc.

fi'ber·glass" *n.* glass drawn into a strong, pliable filament, used as a cord in automobile tires, in masses for insulation, or spun and woven into fabrics.

fi'ber·scope" *n.* a flexible instrument for viewing inaccessible areas.

fi·bro'sis (fi-brō'sis) *n.* excess production of fibrous tissue in an organ, etc.

fib'u·la (fib'ū-lə) *n.* the thinner of the two bones of the lower leg.

-fic (fik) *suf.* causing; producing.

-fi·ca'tion (fi-kā'shən) *suf.* a making or being made.

fiche (fēsh) *n.* microfiche.

fich'u (fish'oo) *n.* a triangular scarf of lace, muslin, etc.

fick'le (fik'əl) *adj.* inconstant; changeable. —**fick'le·ness,** *n.*

fic'tion (fik'shən) *n.* **1,** literature in which the plot and the characters are imaginary. **2,** a statement contrary to fact. —**fic'tion·al,** *adj.* —**fic'tion·al·ize",** *v.t.*

fic·ti'tious (fik-tish'əs) *adj.* **1,** imaginary. **2,** feigned. **3,** false. —**fic·ti'tious·ness,** *n.*

fic'tive (fik'tiv) *adj.* fictitious; imaginary; feigned.

fid'dle (fid'əl) *n.* a violin. —*v.i.* **1,** (*Colloq.*) play on the violin. **2,** move the hands and fingers idly; trifle. —**fid'dler,** *n.*

—**fiddler crab,** a small crab, one of whose claws is disproportionately large.

fid'dle-fad"dle (-fad"əl) *n.* (*Colloq.*) nonsense; trivialities.

fid'dle·sticks" (fid'əl-stiks") *interj.* nonsense!

fid'dling (fid'ling) *adj.* (*Colloq.*) trivial; ineffectual.

fi·del'i·ty (fi-del'ə-tē) *n.* **1,** faithfulness; loyalty. **2,** accuracy; exactness.

fidg'et (fij'it) *v.i.* **1,** make restless or uneasy movements; squirm. —*n.* (*pl.*) a restless mood. —**fidg'et·y,** *adj.*

fi·du'ci·ar·y (fi-doo'shē-er-ē) *adj.* pert. to a trustee. —*n.* a trustee.

fie (fī) *interj.* for shame!

fief (fēf) *n.* an estate held under feudal law.

field (fēld) *n.* **1,** a tract of cleared land for cultivation, pasture, etc.; an area considered in relation to a specific use, as sports, hunting. **2,** a wide expanse; an unimpeded course. **3,** a sphere of activity; a class of enterprise, interest, study, etc.; a business. **4,** a battlefield; a battle; warfare. **5,** a background, as of a photograph; a visible area; scope. **6,** a group considered as one for betting purposes; several unfavored horses in a race; several improbable numbers at dice; etc. —*v.t.* **1,** put a team into competition. **2,** catch and return (a ball). —**field day, 1,** an outing, esp. one devoted to athletic games. **2,** (*Colloq.*) an opportunity for unrestrained fun, etc. —**field glass, binoculars. —field goal, 1,** in football, a kick that sends the ball over the cross bar and between the goalposts. **2,** in basketball, a ball thrown through the basket. —**field hockey,** hockey played on a field with a ball. —**field house,** a building near an athletic field, housing dressing rooms, etc., and often a stadium. —**field marshal,** a high- or the highest-ranking military officer. —**field of honor,** the scene of a duel or battle. —**field rank** (*Mil.*) the rank of major to colonel (*field officer*).

field'er (-ər) *n.* (*Baseball*) **1,** a player whose side is not at bat. **2,** an outfielder.

field'piece" *n.* a cannon.

fiend (fēnd) *n.* **1,** a devil; a demon; a diabolically cruel person. **2,** (*Colloq.*) an addict of some practice, sport, etc. —**fiend'-ish,** *adj.* cruel.

fierce (firs) *adj.* **1,** eager to kill or injure; savage; ferocious. **2,** violent; raging; intense. —**fierce'ness,** *n.*

fi'er·y (fīr'ē) *adj.* **1,** glowing, etc., like fire; burning; hot. **2,** passionate; spirited. —**fi'er·i·ness,** *n.*

fi·es'ta (fē-es'tə) *n.* (*Span.*) a holiday or festival. esp. religious.

fife (fīf) *n.* a shrill musical instrument like a flute.

fif′teen′ (fif′tēn′) *n. & adj.* the cardinal number between fourteen and sixteen, expressed by 15. —**fif′teenth′** (-tēnth′) *n. & adj.*

fifth *n. & adj.* the ordinal of five, also written 5th. —*n.* **1,** one of 5 equal parts. **2,** a measure of liquor, one-fifth gallon. —**fifth column,** a body of citizens who serve enemy interests. —**fifth wheel,** (*Colloq.*) something superfluous. —**take the Fifth,** (*Colloq.*) refuse to testify or to answer a question, by invoking the Fifth Amendment to the U.S. Constitution, under which one cannot be required to testify against himself.

fif′ty (fif′tē) *n. & adj.* the cardinal number between forty-nine and fifty-one, expressed by 50. —**fif′ti·eth,** *n. & adj.* —**fifty-fifty,** *adv. & adj.* (*Colloq.*) in two equal shares.

fig *n.* a tropical tree; its pulpy, pear-shaped fruit.

fight (fīt) *v.i.* [*pret. & p.p.* **fought** (fât)] **1,** engage in combat. **2,** strive; contend. —*v.t.* **1,** war against. **2,** contend with. —*n.* **1,** a battle or contest. **2,** willingness to fight.

fight′er (-ər) *n.* **1,** one who fights. **2,** a warplane designed to fight enemy planes.

fig′ment (fig′mənt) *n.* something feigned or imagined; a pure invention.

fig″ur·a′tion (fig″yû-rā′shən) *n.* act or result of shaping, embellishing, or expressing by a figure.

fig′ur·a·tive (fig′yər-ə-tiv) *adj.* **1,** symbolical; not literal. **2,** full of figures of speech; flowery. —**fig′ur·a·tive·ness,** *n.*

fig′ure (fig′yər) *n.* **1,** form; shape; outline. **2,** a likeness of a form, as in art. **3,** the bodily form. **4,** an outline traced by a skater; a movement of a dance; the pattern of a fabric; a design, esp. an ornate one. **5,** a rhetorical symbol: *figure of speech.* **6,** a personage. **7,** a numerical symbol; (*pl.*) mathematics; computation. **8,** price. —*v.t.* **1,** (often with *out*) calculate; indicate by numbers. **2,** form; shape; portray, esp. in sculpture; see in imagination. **3,** ornament with a design. —*v.i.* **1,** take prominent part. **2,** (*Colloq.*) calculate; deduce. **3,** (with *on*) (*Colloq.*) count on; expect; anticipate.

fig′ure·head″ (fig′yər-hed″) *n.* **1,** an ornamental figure on a ship's bow. **2,** a person of nominal but no real authority.

fig′ur·ine″ (fig′yû-rēn′) *n.* a small work of sculpture; a statuette.

fil′a·ment (fil′ə-mənt) *n.* **1,** a fine thread-like fiber, as of a cobweb, wire, etc. **2,** the slender stalk bearing an anther in a flower.

fi′lar (fī′lər) *adj.* threadlike.

fil′bert (fil′bərt) *n.* the edible nut of the hazel; a hazelnut.

filch *v.t.* steal; pilfer.

file (fīl) *n.* **1,** a folder, case, or device for keeping papers in order; the papers so kept. **2,** a row of persons, esp. soldiers, one behind the other. **3,** a metal tool with a ridged surface for smoothing or cutting metal, wood, etc. —*v.t.* **1,** put (papers) in a file; record officially. **2,** smooth or cut with a file. —*v.i.* march in file. —**on file,** in a file and available for reference.

fi·let′ (fi-lā′) *n. & v.* fillet. —**filet mignon′** (min-yon′) a tenderloin of beefsteak.

fil′i·al (fil′ē-əl) *adj.* pert. to or appropriate to a son or daughter.

fil′i·bus″ter (fil′ə-bus″tər) *n.* **1,** the tactics, esp. in the U.S. Senate, of prolonged speaking to prevent or delay legislation. **2,** a freebooter. —*v.i.* **1,** speak in a filibuster. **2,** act like or be a freebooter.

fil′i·gree″ (fil′ə-grē″) *n. & adj.* ornamental openwork of fine wire. —*v.t.* make into or adorn with filigree.

fil′ing (fī′ling) *n.* (usually *pl.*) a scrap filed off a larger piece. —**filing cabinet,** a set of drawers for holding filed papers.

fill (fil) *v.t.* **1,** occupy the entire capacity of. **2,** make full; be perceptible throughout; pervade. **3,** occupy (a position); perform the duties of. **4,** secure an occupant or incumbent for (a job, etc.) **5,** put an appropriate substance into (a cavity, hole, crack, etc.); stop up. **6,** feed to satiation. **7,** carry out (an order). —*v.i.* take in a filling quantity. —*n.* **1,** enough to satisfy. **2,** a filling. —**fill′er,** *n.* material used for filling, esp. the inside tobacco of a cigar, a base paint to fill cracks, etc. —**fill′ing,** *n.* that which is used to fill, esp. to fill a cavity in a tooth, or the crust of a pie. —**filling station,** a service station. —**fill out, 1,** complete (a document) by writing in the blank spaces. **2,** become rounded, inflated, or filled.

fil′let (fil′et) **1,** a narrow band for the hair. **2,** a thin, narrow strip, as a molding. **3,** [also, **fi·let′** (fi-lā′)] a boneless piece of meat or fish. —*v.t.* [**fil·let′ed** (fi-lād′)] to remove bones, etc., from (a piece of meat or fish).

fil′lip (fil′əp) *n.* **1,** a snap of the fingers. **2,** a stimulus; incentive.

fil′ly (fil′ē) *n.* a young mare.

film *n.* **1,** a very thin layer, as of oil, coating the surface of something. **2,** a cellulose sheet, coated for photography; the developed negative of a picture. **3,** a mist; haze. **4,** a thin membrane. **5,** a motion picture. —*v.t.* photograph. —**film′dom** (-dəm) *n.* the motion picture industry. —**film′y,** *adj.*

film′strip″ *n.* a strip of film intended for still projection.

fil′ter (fil′tər) *n.* **1,** any porous material for trapping solids from a fluid or the air. **2,** any similar device, as for separating light rays. —*v.t. & i.* pass through a filter.

filth *n.* **1,** foul matter; a dirty condition. **2,** corruption; obscene matter. —**filth′i·ness,** *n.* —**filth′y,** *adj.*

fil′trate (fil′trāt) *v.t. & i.* filter. —*n.* filtered liquid. —**fil·tra′tion,** *n.*

fin *n.* **1,** a membranous winglike projection from the body of a fish; anything resembling it. **2,** (*Slang*) five dollars. —**finned, fin′ny,** *adj.*

fi·na′gle (fi-nā′gəl) *v.t. & i.* obtain or contrive unscrupulously.

fi′nal (fī′nəl) *adj.* **1,** last; ultimate. **2,** decisive. —*n.* (*pl.*) **1,** a deciding contest. **2,** the last college examinations. —**fi′nal·ist,** *n.* one competing in the deciding match. —**fi·nal′i·ty** (fī-nal′ə-tē) *n.* —**fi′nal·ize,** *v.t.* (*Colloq.*) make final or definite.

fi·na′le (fi-nä′lē) *n.* a closing scene, esp. of a musical performance.

fi·nance′ (fi-nans′; fī′nans) *n.* **1,** management of monetary affairs, esp. in banking and government. **2,** bankers, capitalists, and investors collectively. **3,** (*pl.*) monetary resources or revenue. —*v.t.* supply with money. —**fi·nan′cial** (-shəl) *adj.* —**finance company,** a company that lends money.

fin″an·cier′ (fin″ən-sir′) *n.* a capitalist or banker.

fin′back″ *n.* any of a genus of whales having large dorsal fins.

finch *n.* any of various small songbirds, as the sparrow.

find (fīnd) *v.t.* [*pret. & p.p.* **found**] **1,** locate by searching; come across by chance; discover. **2,** arrive at (a result, etc.); conclude; (*Law*) declare. —*n.* a valuable discovery. —**find′er,** *n.* one who or that which finds, esp. a device for locating a view for photographing.

find′ing *n.* **1,** a decision or verdict. **2,** (*pl.*) small accessories or materials.

fine (fīn) *adj.* **1,** pure, as unalloyed gold; superior in quality, texture, etc. **2,** delicate, not coarse; of small diameter; ground into very small particles; very thin or keen, as a blade. **3,** discriminating. **4,** elegant; handsome. —*n.* **1,** a money penalty for a breach of law. **2,** (fē′ne) (*Music*) the end (of a piece or repeated section). —*v.t.* punish by a fine. —**fine′ness,** *n.* the degree of purity, thinness, etc. —**fine arts,** painting, engraving, architecture, and sculpture. —**in fine,** in short; finally.

fin′er·y (fī′nə-rē) *n.* showy clothes and jewelry.

fine-′spun″ *adj.* **1,** drawn out in a fine thread. **2,** highly or artificially subtle.

fi·nesse′ (fi-nes′) *n.* **1,** delicate skill. **2,** cunning; artful management. **3,** in card games, a play to trap an opponent's card. —*v.t. & i.* **1,** use or achieve by artifice. **2,** attempt a finesse (of) at cards.

fin′ger (fing′gər) *n.* **1,** one of the five terminal members of the hand, esp. one other than the thumb. **2,** anything like or operating like a finger. —*v.t.* **1,** touch; handle. **2,** (*Slang*) inform against. **3,** perform with the fingers. —**fin′ger·ing,** *n.* (*Music*) the action or use of the fingers in playing. —**fin′ger·board″** *n.* the neck of a violin, guitar, etc. —**finger bowl,** a small dish of water for rinsing the fingers after a meal. —**finger wave,** a wave in the hair, done without a heated iron.

fin′ger·ling (fing′gər-ling) *n.* a finger-length fish.

fin′ger·nail″ *n.* the horny cap at the end of the finger.

fin′ger·print″ *n.* an impression of the lines on the tips of the fingers, used for identification.

fin′i·al (fin′ē-əl) *n.* the ornamental tip of a spire, cap on a shaft, etc.

fin′i·cal (fin′i-kəl) *adj.* unduly particular or fussy. Also, **fin′ick·ing, fin′ick·y.**

fi′nis (fin′is) *n.* the end.

fin′ish *v.t.* **1,** bring to an end; terminate. **2,** use up. **3,** complete; perfect. **4,** paint; polish. —*n.* **1,** the end. **2,** the final work done upon an object. **3,** the way in which something is finished, as furniture. **4,** social polish; poise. —**finishing school,** a private secondary school for girls.

fin′ished *adj.* **1,** completed; perfected; polished. **2,** highly accomplished.

fi′nite (fī′nīt) *adj.* having limits; restricted. —**fi′nite·ness,** *n.*

fink (*Slang*) *n.* **1,** a strikebreaker. **2,** an informer. —*v.i.* **1,** (with *out*) quit; give up; let down. **2,** (with *on*) inform against.

fin′nan had′die (fin′ən-had′ē) *n.* smoked haddock.

Finn′ish bath (fin′ish) a sauna followed by a plunge in cold water.

fiord (fyôrd) *n.* a narrow arm of the sea between high cliffs. Also, **fjord.**

fir (fẽr) *n.* an evergreen, cone-bearing tree or its wood.

fire (fīr) *n.* **1,** the heat and light caused by burning. **2,** a burning of fuel; a conflagration, as of a building, forest, etc. **3,** a discharge of firearms. **4,** ardor; zeal; brilliancy. —*v.t.* **1,** set ablaze. **2,** subject to great heat. **3,** animate; inspire. **4,** discharge, as a gun. **5,** (*Colloq.*) dismiss from a job. —**fire engine,** a motor vehicle equipped to combat fires. —**fire escape,** an outdoor stairway or other structure designed to be used for escape from a burning building. —**fire′storm**, **1**, a conflagration caused by bombing. **2**, a barrage of mail, etc. —**fire′tower**, a lookout tower used esp. to watch for forest fires. —**fir′ing line**, **1**, the line from which weapons fire is directed against an enemy. **2**, a vulnerable front line position.

fire′arm″ n. a weapon that propels a missile by an explosive.

fire′ball″ n. **1**, an early type of bomb. **2**, something like a ball of fire, as a luminous meteor. **3**, the cloud of hot, luminous gases produced by a nuclear explosion. **4**, (Colloq.) an extremely energetic person.

fire′bomb″ n. an incendiary bomb. —v.t. to attack with a firebomb.

fire′box″ n. the fuel chamber of a furnace or locomotive.

fire′brand″ n. **1**, a piece of burning wood. **2**, one who stirs up strife.

fire′break″ n. a strip of land cleared to check the spread of a forest fire.

fire′brick″ n. a brick capable of resisting high temperatures.

fire′bug″ n. (Colloq.) one who intentionally starts destructive fires.

fire′crack″er n. a small explosive-filled tube, set off to make a noise.

fire′damp″ n. a combustible gas occurring in coal mines.

fire′dog″ n. an andiron.

fire′fight″ n. an exchange of gunfire by opposing military forces.

fire′fight″er n. a fireman.

fire′fly″ n. a small beetle that emits light.

fire′man (-mən) n. [pl. -men] **1**, one employed to prevent or extinguish fires. **2**, one who tends a fire, as in a boiler; a stoker.

fire′place″ n. a recess lined with bricks or stones in which a fire is built for cooking or warmth.

fire′plug″ n. a street hydrant.

fire′proof″ adj. made of fire-resisting material.

fire′side″ n. the hearth; home.

fire′trap″ n. a building likely to be dangerous in case of fire.

fire′wa″ter n. (Colloq.) strong liquor.

fire′works″ n.pl. explosives set off to produce noise or display.

fir′kin (fẽr′kin) n. a small cask.

firm (fẽrm) adj. **1**, not easy to shake, move, press in, puncture, etc.; steady; rigid; compact; solid; tough. **2**, stanch; loyal. **3**, positive; unalterable. —n. a business partnership; a company. —**firm′ness**, n.

fir′ma·ment (fẽr′mə-mənt) n. the visible sky; the heavens.

fir′man (fẽr′mən) n. an edict issued by an Oriental sovereign.

first (fẽrst) adj. **1**, foremost in time, place, importance, etc. **2**, the ordinal of one. —adv. before all others in place, time, rank, etc. —n. a person or thing that is first. —**first aid**, emergency treatment of the injured. —**First Lady**, the wife of the U.S. president or of a state governor. —**first lieutenant**, an army officer ranking below a captain and above a second lieutenant. —**first off**, (Slang) in the first place. —**first person**, (Gram.) the relation between a verb and its subject, so called when the subject is the speaker. —**first water**, the highest degree of fineness.

first′class″ adj. of best quality.

first′hand″ adj. direct, not by hearsay.

first-′rate″ adj. of best quality; excellent. —adv. (Colloq.) very well.

firth (fẽrth) n. an arm of the sea.

fis′cal (fis′kəl) adj. pert. to financial matters, esp. governmental.

fish n. [pl. **fishes** or **fish**] **1**, a completely aquatic vertebrate, usually with scales and fins. **2**, (Slang) a dupe. —v.i. & t. **1**, try to catch fish. **2**, search for anything hidden. **3**, seek to get indirectly; draw out. —**fish and chips**, deep-fried fish with French fried potatoes. —**fish story**, (Colloq.) an exaggerated or unbelievable narrative; tall tale.

fish′er·man (-ər-mən) n. [pl. **men**] a person or vessel engaged in fishing.

fish′er·y (-ə-rē) n. **1**, the business of fishing. **2**, a fishing ground.

fish′eye″ lens a wide-angle lens giving 180° view.

fish′hook″ n. a hook used in catching fish.

fish′wife″ n. a scurrilous woman.

fish′y (-ē) adj. **1**, like fish in appearance, smell, etc. **2**, improbable; questionable. **3**, expressionless. —**fish′i·ness**, n.

fis′sile (fis′il; -əl) adj. fissionable.

fis′sion (fish′ən) n. a splitting into parts. —**fis′sion·a·ble**, adj. (of a chemical element) composed of atoms that will split.

fis′sure (fish′ər) n. a crack or cleft.

fist n. the hand clenched. —**fist′fight″**, n. a fight with the fists. —**fist′ful**, n.

fist′ic (-ik) adj. pert. to boxing.

fist′i·cuffs″ (-i-kufs″) n.pl. a fistfight.

fis′tu·la (fis′chŭ-lə) n. an ulcerous passage from an abscess or an internal organ to the surface. —**fis′tu·lar**, adj.

fit adj. [**fit′ter**, -**test**] **1**, proper; suitable. **2**, ready; prepared; in top condition. —v.t. [**fit′ted**, -**ting**] **1**, adapt. **2**, (often with out) equip; supply. —*v.i.* **1,** be meet or proper. **2,** be of the right shape, size, etc. —*n.* **1,** something that is suitable. **2,** a convulsion; a sudden attack, as of epilepsy. **3,** an outburst, as of emotion, energy, etc. —**fit′ness,** *n.*

fit′ful (fit′fəl) *adj.* capricious; intermittent. —**fit′ful·ness,** *n.*

fit′ter (-ər) *n.* one who fits clothes on others.

fit′ting (-ing) *adj.* suitable; proper. —*n.* **1,** act of fitting. **2,** (*pl.*) furnishings.

five (fīv) *n. & adj.* the cardinal number between four and six, expressed by 5. —**five-and-ten,** *n.* (*Colloq.*) a department store specializing in low-priced items. —**five-o′clock shadow,** (*Slang*) a light beard.

fix (fiks) *v.t.* **1,** fasten firmly. **2,** settle definitely; establish (a time or place). **3,** make fast or permanent, as dye. **4,** arrange; repair. **5,** prepare. **6,** (*Slang*) bribe. **7,** (*Colloq.*) castrate or spay (an animal). —*n.* (*Colloq.*) a predicament. —**fix′ings,** *n.pl.* (*Colloq.*) trimmings.

fix·a′tion (fik-sā′shən) *n.* **1,** the state of being fixed. **2,** an obsession. **3,** a premature cessation of emotional development.

fix′a·tive (fik′sə-tiv) *adj.* serving to fix; making stable or permanent. —*n.* a preservative substance, as varnish to a drawing, etc.

fix′ture (fiks′chər) *n.* **1,** an article of furniture attached to the room. **2,** a person or thing that cannot be removed.

fizz (fiz) *v.i.* **1,** make a hissing sound; effervesce. **2,** a mixed drink. —*n.* such a sound.

fiz′zle (fiz′əl) **1,** make a hissing sound. **2,** (*Colloq.*) peter out; fail.—*n.* act or effect of fizzling.

fjord (fyôrd) *n.* fiord.

flab *n.* (*Colloq.*) excess body fat.

flab′ber·gast″ (flab′ər-gast″) *v.t.* (*Colloq.*) confound; astonish.

flab′by (flab′ē) *adj.* **1,** lacking firmness; jellylike. **2,** feeble. —**flab′bi·ness,** *n.*

flac′cid (flak′sid) *adj.* soft; flabby. —**flac·cid′i·ty** (-sid′ə-tē), **flac′cid·ness,** *n.*

fla·con′ (flä-kän′) *n.* a small flask.

flag *n.* **1,** a piece of cloth bearing a design for display as a signal, standard, etc. **2,** an iris. **3,** a flagstone. —*v.t.* **[flagged, flag′ging] 1,** signal to with or as with a flag. **2,** pave with flagstones. —*v.i.* droop; grow languid. —**flag officer,** a naval officer of rank of commodore or higher.

flag′el·late″ (flaj′ə-lāt″) *v.t.* whip. —**flag′el·lant,** (-lənt) *n.* —**flag″el·la′tion,** *n.*

flag″eo·let′ (flaj″ə-let′) *n.* a woodwind instrument.

fla·gi′tious (flə-jish′əs) *adj.* grossly wicked. —**fla·gi′tious·ness,** *n.*

flag′on (flag′ən) *n.* a covered pitcher for liquors.

flag′pole″ *n.* a pole on which a flag is hung.

fla′grant (flā′grənt) *adj.* overtly outrageous. —**fla′gran·cy,** *n.*

flag′ship″ *n.* the ship of the officer commanding a fleet.

flag′staff″ *n.* a staff by which a flag is hung or supported.

flag′stone″ *n.* a flat paving stone.

flail (flāl) *n.* a hand tool for threshing grain. —*v.t. & i.* **1,** use a flail (on). **2,** whip; beat.

flair (flâr) *n.* **1,** discriminating taste. **2,** a liking; bent.

flak *n.* **1,** antiaircraft fire. **2,** (*Slang*) criticism; complaints.

flake (flāk) *n.* a small flat, scalelike particle. —*v.t. & i.* break or separate into flakes.

flak′y (flā′kē) *adj.* **1,** like or consisting of flakes. **2,** of pastry, very short; crumbly. **3,** (*Slang*) odd or unusual in style or behavior. —**flak′i·ness,** *n.*

flam *v.t.* **[flammed, flam′ming]** delude; cheat. —*n.* **1,** a trick; deception. **2,** a short roll on the drum.

flam·bé′ (fläm-bā′) *adj.* (*Fr.*) flaming.

flam′beau (flam′bō) *n.* **1,** a flaming torch. **2,** a large candlestick.

flam·boy′ant (flam-boi′ənt) *adj.* showy; ornate; gorgeous; florid. —**flam·boy′ance,** *n.*

flame (flām) *n.* **1,** burning gas or vapor; the luminous, quivering tongue it makes; (*pl.*) a state of combustion. **2,** burning zeal; ardor. **3,** (*Slang*) a sweetheart. —*v.i.* **1,** burn; shine. **2,** break out like flame, in anger or passion. —**flame thrower,** a weapon that throws a spray of burning oil.

fla·men′co (flə-meng′kō) *n.* an Andalusian gypsy dance.

flame′out″ *n.* the stalling of a jet engine.

flam′ing *adj.* **1,** fiery. **2,** passionate; violent. **3,** flagrant.

fla·min′go (flə-ming′gō) *n.* [*pl.* **-gos**] a long-legged tropical bird with scarlet plumage.

flam′ma·ble (flam′ə-bəl) *adj.* inflammable.

flange (flanj) *n.* a projecting rim.

flank *n.* **1,** an animal's side between ribs and hip. **2,** the side of anything. **3,** (*Mil.*) the extreme right or left of an army or fleet. —*v.t.* **1,** stand at the flank. **2,** go around, or turn, the flank of.

flan'nel (flan'əl) *n.* **1,** a soft woolen fabric. **2,** (*pl.*) men's trousers made of flannel. **3,** (*pl.*) woolen undergarments. —**flannel cake,** a pancake.

flan"nel·et' (flan"ə-let') *n.* a cotton fabric, used for wearing apparel. Also, **flan"-nel·ette'.**

flap *n.* **1,** anything broad, flat, and unusually flexible, hanging loose. **2,** the motion or noise of a swinging flap or wing. **3,** a slap. **4,** an argument; controversy. —*v.t.* [**flapped, flap'ping**] swing as a flap; beat (wings, etc.) up and down. —*v.i.* swing to and fro; flap wings.

flap'jack" *n.* a large pancake.

flap'pa·ble (flap'ə-bəl) *adj.* (*Colloq.*) easily disturbed or upset; excitable.

flap'per (-ər) *n.* **1,** a flap. **2,** a young duck or bird. **3,** (*Colloq.*) a brash teen-age girl. **4,** a young woman of the 1920's.

flare (flâr) *n.* **1,** a flaring, wavering light. **2,** a blazing light used as a signal. **3,** an outburst, as of temper. **4,** a spreading outward, as of a skirt. —*v.i.* **1,** be or form a flare. **2,** (often with *out* or *up*) burst into sudden flame, activity, or emotion. **3,** spread outward, as a skirt, etc. —**flare-'up",** *n.* a burst of anger or flame.

flash *n.* **1,** a sudden transitory burst of light or flame; an instantaneous outburst or sensation, as of wit, understanding, etc. **2,** a glimpse. **3,** an instant; a moment. **4,** (*Colloq.*) ostentation. **5,** a brief bulletin. —*v.i.* blaze momentarily; be temporarily visible, brilliant, notable, etc. —*v.t.* send forth suddenly, esp. a signal or bulletin. —**flash card,** a card used for drill in language, etc. —**flash gun,** a device that ignites a flash bulb. —**a flash in the pan,** a person, idea, etc., which is successful at first but which does not last. —**flash point,** the lowest temperature at which a vapor will ignite or explode.

flash'back" *n.* a scene or event from the past, in a novel or motion picture.

flash'bar" *n.* (*T.N.*) (*Photog.*) a row of flashbulbs in a single housing, ignited successively.

flash'bulb" *n.* (*Photog.*) a glass bulb containing magnesium foil and oxygen, giving a brief, brilliant flash of light when ignited.

flash'cube" *n.* (*Photog.*) a plastic cube containing four small flashbulbs arranged to fire in sequence.

flash'ing *n.* pieces of metal for waterproofing roofing joints.

flash'light" *n.* **1,** a small portable electric torch. **2,** a brilliant instantaneous light for taking pictures; a picture so taken.

flash'y (-ē) *adj.* showy; gaudy; momentarily brilliant. —**flash'i·ness,** *n.*

flask (flåsk) *n.* a narrow-necked glass or metal container.

flat *adj.* [**flat'ter, -test**] **1,** horizontally level and relatively smooth. **2,** spread out, lying, or fallen on a level surface; lying down; collapsed; (of feet) having fallen arches. **3,** without qualification; positive; exact. **4,** defeated; (*Slang*) penniless. **5,** dull; stale; insipid. **6,** (*Music*) below the true pitch. —*adv.* in a flat manner. —*n.* **1,** a plain; a shoal. **2,** the flat part of anything. **3,** (*Slang*) a deflated tire. **4,** (*Music*) a note, marked (♭), lowered a half tone in pitch. **5,** an apartment. —*v.t. & i.* [**flat'ted, -ting**] lower (the pitch). —**flat'ness,** *n.*

flat'boat" *n.* a large flat-bottomed boat for transporting goods.

flat'car" *n.* a roofless, sideless freight car.

flat'fish" *n.* a broad, flat fish with both eyes on the upper side.

flat'foot" [*pl.* -**feet"**] **1,** a deformity of the foot due to fallen arches. **2,** (*Slang*) a policeman. —**flat'foot'ed,** *adj.*

flat'i"ron *n.* an iron for pressing clothes.

flat-'out' *adv.* at maximum speed.

flat'ten (-ən) *v.t.* **1,** make flat. **2,** knock down. —*v.i.* become flat or level.

flat'ter (flat'ər) *v.t.* **1,** seek to gratify by undue praise. **2,** portray too favorably. —**flat'ter·y,** *n.* adulation.

flat-'top" *n.* an aircraft carrier.

flat'u·lent (flach'ə-lənt) *adj.* **1,** producing or having gas in the stomach. **2,** pretentious. —**flat'u·lence,** *n.*

flat'ware" (flat'wâr") *n.* **1,** table dishes that are flat, as plates. **2,** table utensils, usu. silver.

flaunt (flânt) *v.t. & i.* parade impudently; make a gaudy display (of).

flau'tist (flä'tist) *n.* a flutist.

fla'vor (flā'vər) *n.* **1,** that quality which affects the taste; usually the quality of appealing to the taste. **2,** a substance that imparts a distinctive taste. **3,** an interesting or distinctive quality in anything. —*v.t.* give flavor to. Also, **fla'vour.** —**fla'vor·ing,** *n.* a substance that flavors.

flaw (flâ) *n.* a defect; imperfection. —**flaw'-less,** *adj.* without a flaw; perfect.

flax (flaks) *n.* a blue-flowered plant grown for its fiber, used for making linen, and its seeds, for linseed oil. —**flax'seed",** *n.*

flax'en (flak'sən) *adj.* **1,** made of flax. **2,** of a light yellow color, as hair.

flay (flā) *v.t.* **1,** strip the skin from. **2,** censure severely.

flea (flē) *n.* a small, leaping, blood-sucking insect. —**flea'bite",** *n.* an inconsequential

injury. —**flea′bit″ten,** *adj.* (*Colloq.*) shabby; seedy. —**a flea in one's ear,** a warning hint; rebuke. —**flea market,** a market for secondhand goods, usu. held outdoors.

flea′bag″ *n.* **1,** an old, rundown hotel. **2,** a slatternly woman.

fleche (flesh) *n.* **1,** a slender spire. **2,** any of the points of a backgammon board.

fleck (flek) *n.* a speck or small spot. —*v.t.* mark with spots.

fled *v.* pret. & p.p. of *flee.*

fledg′ling (flej′ling) *n.* **1,** a young bird just able to fly. **2,** a young, inexperienced person.

flee (flē) *v.i. & t.* [*pret. & p.p.* **fled**] take flight (from); escape.

fleece (flēs) *n.* the woolly coat of a sheep. —*v.t.* swindle. —**fleec′y,** *adj.* soft and woolly; resembling fleece; as clouds.

fleet (flēt) *adj.* able to run fast; rapid; swift. —*n.* an organized group of ships or vehicles. —**fleet′ing,** *adj.* swiftly passing; transitory. —**fleet′ness,** *n.* —**Fleet Admiral,** highest rank in the U.S. Navy.

flesh *n.* **1,** the mass of muscular tissue, containing some fat, that constitutes the soft substance of the animal body. **2,** a similar substance, as of fruit. **3,** meat. **4,** kindred. **5,** bodily appetites or sensibilities. —*adj.* of the color of the skin. —**flesh′ly,** *adj.* corporeal; worldly or sensual. —**flesh′y,** *adj.* plump. —**in the flesh,** in person.

flesh′pot″ *n.* **1,** night club. **2,** (*pl.*) high living; luxury.

fletch′er (flech′ər) *n.* a maker of arrows.

fleur-″de-lis′ (flẽr″də-lē′) *n.* **1,** (*Hist.*) the royal emblem of France. **2,** the iris.

flew (floo) *v.* pret. of *fly.*

flex (fleks) *v.t.* **1,** bend, as a part of the body. **2,** contract (a muscle). —**flex′ion** (flek′shən) *n.*

flex′i·ble (flek′sə-bəl) *adj.* **1,** easily bent. **2,** adaptable. —**flex″i·bil′i·ty,** *n.*

flex′time″ *n.* a system which allows workers to choose their own schedule. Also, **flex′i·time″.**

flib′ber·ti·gib″bet (flib′ər-tē-jib″it) *n.* **1,** a frivolous or flighty person. **2,** an imp or friend.

flick (flik) *n.* a light, sharp blow, as with the finger or a whip. —*v.t.* so strike.

flick′er (flik′ər) *v.i.* **1,** vibrate; quiver. **2,** burn fitfully. —*n.* **1,** a wavering light. **2,** a briefly felt hope, feeling, etc. **3,** a large woodpecker. **4,** (*often pl.*) (*Slang*) a motion picture.

fli′er (flī′ər) *n.* **1,** one who or that which flies; an aviator. **2,** a handbill. **3,** a risk; a speculative or incidental financial venture. Also, **fly′er.**

flight (flīt) *n.* **1,** the act, mode, or power of flying. **2,** swift motion caused by any propelling force. **3,** the distance or course a bird, missile, aircraft, etc., flies. **4,** a number of creatures or things flying together. **5,** (*fig.*) an imaginative or extravagant excursion or soaring. **6,** hasty departure. **7,** the stairs from one landing or story to the next. —**flight′less,** *adj.* incapable of flying.

flight′y (flī′tē) *adj.* given to whims, disordered fancies, etc.; capricious. —**flight′i·ness,** *n.*

flim′flam″ *n. & v.t.* humbug.

flim′sy (flim′zē) *adj.* **1,** loosely constructed or woven; unsubstantial. **2,** weak; ineffectual. —**flim′si·ness,** *n.*

flinch *v.i.* shrink from anything painful or unpleasant.

fling *v.t. & i.* [*pret. & p.p.* **flung**] throw with violence; cast; hurl. —*n.* **1,** the act of flinging. **2,** a brief time of unrestrained pleasure. **3,** a lively dance. **4,** (*Colloq.*) a try.

flint *n.* a very hard, dark gray quartz that will strike sparks from steel. —**flint′y,** *adj.* obdurate. —**flint glass,** a heavy, brilliant glass containing lead. —**flint′lock″,** *n.* an old type of musket.

flip *n.* **1,** a flick; snap. **2,** a sweet drink, usually containing wine or liquor. —*v.t.* [**flipped, flip′ping**] toss lightly. —*adj.* [**flip′per, -pest**] (*Colloq.*) pert. —**flip side,** (*Colloq.*) the other side (of a record).

flip′pant (flip′ənt) *adj.* disrespectful; treating serious things lightly. —**flip′pan·cy,** *n.*

flip′per (flip′ər) *n.* **1,** a limb used for swimming, as of a seal. **2,** device in a pinball machine used to project the ball.

flirt (flẽrt) *v.i.* **1,** play at being in love, not seriously. **2,** trifle (with an idea). —*n.* a coquette.

flir·ta′tion (flẽr-tā′shən) *n.* a transient, not serious, love affair.

flir·ta′tious (flẽr-tā′shəs) *adj.* given to flirting. —**flir·ta′tious·ness,** *n.*

flit *v.i.* [**flit′ted, -ting**] move lightly and swiftly.

flit′ter (-ər) *v.i.* flutter.

fliv′ver (fliv′ər) *n.* (*Slang*) a small, cheap automobile.

float (flōt) *v.i.* **1,** be buoyed up by water or air. **2,** drift idly and gently. —*v.t.* **1,** cause to rest on, or rise to, the surface of a liquid. **2,** start; launch, as a company, rumor, etc. —*n.* **1,** something that floats, as an anchored raft, a buoy, etc. **2,** a decorated vehicle in a parade.

float′er *n.* **1,** (*Colloq.*) one who moves from place to place, esp. a laborer. **2,** an insurance policy that covers unspecified items.

float'ing *adj.* **1,** not attached. **2,** not fixed or settled.

floc'cu·lent (flok'yə-lənt) *adj.* like tufts of wool; fleecy; flaky. —**floc'cu·lence,** *n.*

flock (flok) *n.* **1,** a number of animals or birds of one kind keeping together; a congregation, esp. of a church. **2,** a tuft of wool, cotton, etc. **3,** powdered fibers of wool, cotton, etc. —*v.i.* congregate; go in crowds.

floe (flō) *n.* a mass of floating ice.

flog *v.t.* [**flogged, flog'ging**] thrash.

flood (flud) *n.* **1,** a great volume of water overflowing land; a deluge. **2,** a great outpouring, as of work, light, etc.; a superfluity, **3,** inflow of the tide. —*v.t. & i.* **1,** overflow. **2,** issue or rise in great quantity. —**flood tide,** a rising tide.

flood'gate" *n.* a gate regulating the flow of water in a channel; *fig.*, something that restrains an outburst.

flood'light" *n.* a bright light illuminating a large area.

floor (flôr) *n.* **1,** the bottom surface of a room, cave, the ocean, etc. **2,** a story of a building. **3,** the right to address a meeting. —*v.t.* **1,** furnish with a floor. **2,** (*Colloq.*) knock down; confound. —**floor'ing,** *n.* material of which a floor is made. —**floor show,** a show in a cabaret. —**floor'walk"er,** *n.* a supervisor of sales in a store.

floo'zy (floo'zē) *n.* (*Slang*) **1,** a prostitute. **2,** a loose woman. Also, **floo'zie, floo'sy.**

flop *v.i.* [**flopped, flop'ping**] **1,** thrash about; flap. **2,** fall down clumsily. **3,** (*Slang*) fail. —*n.* (*Slang*) a failure. —**flop'py,** *adj.* lacking rigidity. —**floppy disc,** a small, flexible plastic disc used for storing data in a computer.

flop'house" (flop'hows") *n.* (*Slang*) a very cheap hotel.

flo'ra (flôr'ə) *n.* plant life peculiar to a region or area.

flo'ral (flôr'əl) *adj.* of or pert. to flowers.

flor'id (flôr'id) *adj.* **1,** ruddy, as the complexion. **2,** highly ornate.

flor'in (flôr'in) *n.* **1,** the gulden. **2,** an Eng. two-shilling coin.

flo'rist (flôr'ist) *n.* one who raises or sells flowers as a business.

floss (flâs) *n.* **1,** the silky substance in certain plant pods. **2,** silk filaments used in embroidery, etc.

floss'y *adj.* **1,** like floss. **2,** (*Slang*) fancy.

flo'tage (flō'tij) *n.* **1,** buoyancy. **2,** things afloat; flotsam. **3,** a fee for transporting railroad cars on floats.

flo·ta'tion (flō-tā'shən) *n.* **1,** act or state

of floating. **2,** arrangement to receive a loan.

flo·til'la (flō-til'ə) *n.* a small fleet; a fleet of small vessels.

flot'sam (flot'səm) *n.* wreckage of a ship or its cargo, found floating.

flounce (flowns) *n.* **1,** a deep ruffle sewed at its upper edge, on a skirt. **2,** a petulant jerk of one's body. —*v.i.* move with a flounce.

floun'der (flown'dər) *v.i.* struggle awkwardly or helplessly. —*n.* a flatfish.

flour (flowr) *n.* the finely ground meal of grain, esp of wheat; hence, any fine, soft powder. —*v.t.* sprinkle with flour. —**flour'y,** *adj.*

flour'ish (flēr'ish) *v.i.* thrive; prosper; be active. —*v.t.* **1,** wave about; hence, flaunt. **2,** embellish with a flourish. —*n.* anything done by way of display, as a fanciful pen stroke, a fanfare, etc.

flout (flowt) *v.t. & i.* scoff (at).

flow (flō) *v.i.* **1,** both progress and move internally, as the stream of a liquid; circulate. **2,** issue from a source. **3,** proceed smoothly or evenly. **4,** rise, as the tide. —*n.* **1,** the act of flowing; the amount that flows. **2,** issuance; rise.

flow'er (flow'ər) *n.* **1,** the seed-producing part of a plant, esp. when colorful and fragrant; a blossom. **2,** a plant grown for its flowers. **3,** the state of efflorescence. **4,** the best part or finest example. **5,** youthful vigor. —*v.i.* blossom. —**flower child,** (*Slang*) a hippie.

flow'er·pot" *n.* a pot to hold earth in which a flower grows.

flow'er·y (-ē) *adj.* **1,** of flowers. **2,** florid; full of ornate phrases. —**flow'er·i·ness,** *n.*

flown (flōn) *v.* p.p. of *fly.*

flu (floo) *n.* influenza.

flub *n. & v.i.* blunder; blooper.

fluc'tu·ate" (fluk'chû-āt") *v.i.* change continually; vary irregularly; rise and fall, like waves. —**fluc"tu·a'tion,** *n.*

flue (floo) *n.* a passageway for smoke, etc., as in a chimney.

flu'ent (floo'ənt) *adj.* facile in speech; voluble; smoothly flowing. —**flu'en·cy,** *n.*

fluff (fluf) *n.* **1,** a light puff of dust or nap; a downy mass, as hair. **2,** (*Slang*) a mistake. —*v.t.* puff up in a light mass. —**fluff'y,** *adj.* soft and light.

flu'gel·horn" (floo'gəl-hôrn") *n.* a type of bugle.

flu'id (floo'id) *adj.* **1,** capable of flowing; esp. liquid or gaseous. **2,** not rigid or fixed. —*n.* a liquid or a gas. —**flu·id'i·ty** (-ə-tē) *n.* —**fluid dram,** a measure of capacity, ⅛ of a fluid ounce. —**fluid drive,** a transmission using a hydraulic pump. —**fluid ounce,** a measure of capacity, one sixteenth of a pint.

fluke (flook) *n.* **1,** that part of an anchor which catches and holds. **2,** the head of an arrow or harpoon; a lobe of a whale's tail. **3,** (*Slang*) an accidental stroke; a lucky chance. —**fluk′y,** *adj.* (*Colloq.*) unpredictable.

flume (floom) *n.* a natural or artificial channel for conveying water.

flum′mer·y (flum′ə-rė) *n.* **1,** agreeable nonsense. **2,** a porridge.

flum′mox (flum′əks) *v.t.* (*Slang*) confuse.

flung *v.* pret. & p.p. of *fling.*

flunk *v.t. & i.* (*Colloq.*) fail to award, or get, a passing grade. —**flunk out,** be dismissed, as from a school, for failure.

flunk′y (flung′kė) *n.* **1,** a liveried man-servant. **2,** a toady. Also, **flunk′ey.**

flu″o·res′cence (floo″ə-res′əns) *n.* the property of becoming self-luminous, or emitting radiation, when exposed to the direct action of light-rays; also, the emitted radiation. —**flu″o·resce′,** *v.i.* —**flu″o·res′cent,** *adj.* —**fluorescent light,** a mercury vapor lamp.

flu·o′ri·date″ (floor′ə-dāt″) *v.t. & i.* add a fluoride (to a water supply) in order to prevent tooth decay.

flu′o·ride″ (floo′ə-rīd″) *n.* a chemical compound of fluorine with another element.

flu′o·rine″ (floo′ə-rēn″) *n.* a corrosive, pungent, gaseous element, no. 9, symbol F. —**fluor′i·nate″** (flôr′ə-nāt″) *v.t.*

fluor′o·scope″ (flûr′ə-skōp″) *n.* a device for exposing objects to radiation, as x-ray, and viewing them on a screen.

flur′ry (flêr′ė) *n.* **1,** a sudden gust of wind. **2,** temporary ado or commotion. —*v.t.* fluster.

flush *v.i.* **1,** blush; glow. **2,** be startled from cover. —*v.t.* **1,** suffuse with color. **2,** elate; thrill. **3,** wash out with a copious flow of water. **4,** startle (a bird) from cover. —*n.* **1,** a blush; any warm coloring. **2,** a rush of water, as for cleansing. **3,** a rush of emotion; thrill. **4,** glow; vigor. **5,** a hand of cards all of the same suit. —*adj.* **1,** full; well filled. **2,** (*Colloq.*) prosperous; well supplied with money. **3,** in the same plane or line; level or even.

flus′ter (flus′tər) *v.t.* embarrass and confuse. —*n.* nervous confusion.

flute (floot) *n.* **1,** a tubular woodwind musical instrument. **2,** a groove or furrow, as in a pillar, or in a ruffle. —**flut′ed,** *adj.* grooved. —**flut′ist,** *n.*

flut′ter (flut′ər) *v.i. & t.* **1,** flap the wings rapidly, as a bird; hover. **2,** move or beat irregularly, as the heart. **3,** be agitated. **4,**

wave, as a flag. —*n.* **1,** quick irregular motion; rapid vibration. **2,** agitation; stir. —**flut′ter·y,** *adj.* habitually fluttering.

flu′vi·al (floo′vē-əl) *adj.* pert. to rivers.

flux (fluks) *n.* **1,** a flowing, as of a liquid. **2,** continual change. **3,** a substance used to promote fusing of metals, prevent oxidation, etc. —**flux′ion** (fluk′shən) *n.*

fly (flī) *v.i.* [**flew** (floo), **flown** (flōn), **fly′ing**] **1,** move more or less horizontally through the air, not touching ground; be airborne. **2,** pass swiftly. **3,** flee. **4,** wave in the air, as a flag. **5,** go by airplane. **6,** [*pret.* **flied** (flīd)] hit a baseball that is caught in the air. —*v.t.* **1,** cause to be airborne. **2,** operate, or travel over in, aircraft. **3,** flee from. —*n.* **1,** any of several two-winged insects, esp. the housefly. **2,** a fishhook disguised as a fly. **3,** a strip of cloth on a garment to hide a fastening. **4,** an extra roof for a tent. **5,** a baseball batted high in the air. —**flying boat,** a seaplane. —**flying buttress,** a supporting arch extending in the air from a wall to a pier. —**flying fish,** a fish with winglike fins, capable of brief flights out of the water. —**flying saucer,** a saucer-shaped illuminated object often reportedly seen in the skies. —**flying squirrel,** a squirrel having webs of skin, capable of long gliding leaps.

fly′blown″ *adj.* maggoty.

fly-′by-night″ *adj.* unreliable. —*n.* an unreliable person.

fly′catch″er *n.* a small insectivorous bird.

fly′leaf″ *n.* a blank leaf at the beginning or end of a book.

fly′pa″per *n.* sticky paper for catching flies.

fly′speck″ *n.* a fly's egg; a tiny spot.

fly′swat″ter (-swot″tər) *n.* a mat with a handle, for killing flies.

fly′way″ *n.* a migration route of birds.

fly′weight″ *n.* a boxer weighing 112 lbs. or less.

fly′wheel″ *n.* a heavy wheel that tends to stabilize the speed of a machine.

F number in photography, the effective aperture of a lens divided by its focal length.

foal (fōl) *n.* a young horse, ass, etc. —*v.i. & t.* bring forth (a foal).

foam (fōm) *n. & v.i.* froth. —**foam′y,** *adj.* —**foam rubber,** latex in spongelike form.

fob *n.* **1,** a short watch chain. **2,** a small pocket for a watch. —*v.t.* **1,** (with *off*) palm off. **2,** cheat; trick.

fo′c′s′le (fōk′səl) *n.* forecastle.

fo′cus (fō′kəs) *n.* [*pl.* **-cus·es** or **-ci** (-sī)] **1,** the point at which rays as of light, heat, etc., meet after reflection or refraction. **2,**

focal length. 3, an adjustment of eyes, camera, etc., for clear vision. 4, a center, as of interest, activity, etc. —v.t. 1, adjust the focus of. 2, bring into focus —fo'cal, adj. —focal length, the distance from a lens to the plane of its focus. —focal point, 1, the point of focus of a lens. 2, the center of attention.

fod'der (fod'ər) n. dried food, as hay, straw, etc., for livestock.

foe (fō) n. an enemy; an opponent. —foe'man (-mən) n. [pl. -men] an enemy in war.

fog n. 1, a heavy mist at or near the earth's surface. 2, mental confusion. —v.t. & i. [fogged, fog'ging] make or become obscure or cloudy. —fog'gy, adj. thick with mist; obscure.

fog'bound" adj. unable to navigate because of heavy fog.

fog'horn" n. a horn for warning of an approach through fog.

fo'gy (fō'gē) n. one who is averse to change or to new ideas.

foi'ble (foi'bəl) n. a whimsy; a weakness.

foil n. 1, a very thin sheet of metal. 2, anything that sets off something by contrast. 3, a blunted fencing sword. —v.t. baffle; frustrate.

foist v.t. palm off as genuine.

fold (fōld) v.t. 1, bend double, as cloth, paper, etc.; restore to original shape by folding once or more. 2, clasp together, as arms; bring toward the body; embrace. 3, wrap (something) by folding paper over it. —v.i. 1, double together. 2, (Slang) close down, as a play. —n. 1, a pleat. 2, a pen for sheep. 3, a flock of sheep; hence, any group under a leader, esp. a church congregation. —folding money, (Colloq.) paper money.

-fold suf. 1, multiplied by. 2, divided by.

fold'er (fōl'dər) n. 1, printed matter, as a map, circular, etc., folded into a booklet. 2, a stiff folded holder for loose papers.

fo'li·age (fō'lē-ij) n. the leaves of plants.

fo'li·ate" v.t. & i. (fō'lē-āt") 1, put forth or shape like leaves. 2, number the leaves of (a book). —adj. (-ət) 1, having leaves. 2, leaflike. —fo"li·a'tion, n.

fo'lic acid (fō'lik) Vitamin M (a B vitamin), found in liver and leaves.

fo'li·o" (fō'lē-ō") n. 1, a sheet of paper folded once. 2, a book of sheets folded once; a book of largest size. 3, a page number.

folk (fōk) n. 1, people in general. 2, (pl.) one's relatives; people of a certain class. —adj. originating or widely used among the common people, as folk song, folk music, folk dance.

folk'lore" n. the old traditions, beliefs, and superstitions of a people.

folk-'rock" n. & adj. (Music) pert. to music combining a rock beat with folk-song lyrics.

folk'sy (-sē) adj. sociable; friendly and unpretentious.

folk'ways" n.pl. traditional customs.

fol'li·cle (fol'ə-kəl) n. 1, a minute cavity or gland. 2, a dry one-celled seed vessel. —fol·lic'u·lar (fə-lik'yə-lər) adj.

fol'low (fol'ō) v.t. 1, come after in place or order of time; succeed. 2, pursue. 3, understand. 4, emulate; accept as a guide or leader. 5, result from. —v.i. 1, go or come after another. 2, arise as a natural consequence or inference; result. —fol'low·er, n. an adherent; disciple. —follow through, continue or complete an action started. —follow up, continue to pursue or take advantage of (an opportunity, etc.).

fol'low·ing n. a body of supporters or patrons. —adj. coming next in order or time.

fol'low-through" n. 1, completion of a stroke, as in golf or tennis. 2, exploitation of an advantage.

fol'low-up" n. an act, letter, circular, call, etc., to sustain the effectiveness of a previous one.

fol'ly (fol'ē) n. 1, lack of good sense; foolishness. 2, a foolish act or undertaking. 3, (pl.) a revue.

fo·ment' (fō-ment') v.t. stir up; incite. —fo"men·ta'tion, n.

fond adj. 1, loving. 2, foolishly tender or trusting; doting. 3, inclined toward. —fond'ness, n.

fon'dant (fon'dənt) n. a creamy sugar paste used in making candy.

fon'dle (fon'dəl) v.t. caress.

fon'due (fon'doo) n. a baked pudding made of grated cheese or chocolate, butter, and eggs.

font n. 1, a receptacle for baptismal water. 2, a full assortment of one size and style of printing type.

food n. 1, an edible substance, usually solid, for the nourishment of the body. 2, anything that sustains or nourishes.

food'stuff" n. a grocery item.

fool n. 1, a silly or stupid person. 2, a court jester. —v.t. dupe; mislead. —v.i. 1, play the fool. 2, spend time idly. 3, (with with) play or tamper (with). —fool'er·y, n. —fool's gold, a mineral which resembles gold.

fool'har'dy adj. foolishly rash. —fool'-har'di·ness, n.

fool'ish *adj.* silly; unwise. —**fool'ish·ness**, *n.*

fool'proof *adj.* surely effective, even if mismanaged.

fools'cap" (foolz'kap") *n.* a size of paper, about 13 x 17 inches.

foot (fût) *n.* [*pl.* **feet** (fēt)] **1,** the terminal part of the leg of a man or animal. **2,** anything that resembles a foot in shape, function, or position; the bottom or lowest point. **3,** a measure of length, 12 inches. **4,** tread; step. **5,** infantry. **6,** a group of syllables forming a metrical unit in a verse. —*v.t.* **1,** add up as numbers in a column. **2,** (*Colloq.*) pay, as a bill.

foot'age (-ij) *n.* length in feet.

foot'ball" *n.* a field game played with an inflated leather ball; the ball used.

foot-'can'dle *n.* a unit of illumination.

foot'fall" *n.* the sound of a footstep.

foot'hill" *n.* one of the lower hills at the base of a mountain range.

foot'hold" *n.* a secure position.

foot'ing *n.* **1,** a foothold. **2,** an assured position. **3,** a foundation. **4,** basis; relative standing.

foot'less (-ləs) *adj.* **1,** having no feet. **2,** without foundation or basis. **3,** (*Colloq.*) awkward; inept.

foot'lights" *n.pl.* **1,** the row of lights at floor level in front of a stage. **2,** the theater; stage; theatrical life.

foot'loose" *adj.* not tied down; free to travel.

foot'man (-mən) *n.* [*pl.* **-men**] a manservant for carriage, door, and table.

foot'note" *n.* an explanatory note at the foot of a page.

foot'pad" *n.* a highwayman.

foot-'pound" *n.* the energy required to raise one pound one foot.

foot'print" *n.* the mark made by a foot.

foot'sore" *adj.* **1,** having sore feet. **2,** tired of travel.

foot'step" *n.* **1,** a tread of a foot or the sound it makes. **2,** (*pl.*) the example set by a predecessor.

foot'stool" *n.* a low stool on which to rest one's feet while sitting.

foot'work" *n.* **1,** agility on foot. **2,** laborious walking.

foo'zle (foo'zəl) *v.t. & i.* bungle. —*n.* blunder. —**foo'zler** (-zlər) *n.*

fop *n.* a man too concerned with dressing stylishly. —**fop'per·y** (-ə-rē) *n.* —**fop'pish,** *adj.*

for (fôr) *prep.* **1,** in order to obtain. **2,** to be used by, or given to; adapted to; appropriate to. **3,** in favor of. **4,** in place of;

instead of; in consideration of. **5,** in honor of. **6,** because of; for want of. **7,** over the space of; during. **8,** toward. **9,** with regard to. —*conj.* because. —**for"as·much' as,** in view of the fact that; since.

for'age (fôr'ij) *n.* **1,** food for livestock, esp. pasturage. **2,** a search for food. —*v.i. & t.* raid for food.

fo·ra'men (fə-rā'mən) *n.* a hole or passage, esp. in a bone.

for'ay (fôr'ā) *n.* a raid for plunder. —*v.i.* make a raid; forage.

for·bear' (fôr-bâr') *v.t.* [**-bore'**, **-borne'**, **-bearing**] refrain or abstain from. —*v.i.* hold back; be patient or lenient. —**for·bear'-ance,** *n.*

for·bid' (fôr-bid') *v.t.* [**-bade'**, **-bid'den**, **-ding**] **1,** order (something) not to be done; refuse to permit; prohibit. **2,** order (someone) not to do something. —**for·bid'ding,** *adj.* repelling approach; disagreeable.

force (fôrs) *n.* **1,** the capacity for exerting strength; power; might. **2,** the power to coerce, persuade, convince, etc. **3,** meaning; import. **4,** military strength. **5,** a body of men prepared for action. **6,** (*pl.*) an army; physical resources. **7,** (*Physics*) the cause of motion, or a change in the motion, of a body. —*v.t.* **1,** compel by physical, mental, or moral means. **2,** extort by violence. **3,** effect by effort. **4,** compel the acceptance of. **5,** hasten the growth of. —**force'ful,** *adj.* powerful; effective.

forced *adj.* **1,** compulsory. **2,** strained; unnatural. **3,** caused by an emergency.

force'meat" *n.* meat chipped fine and seasoned, used as stuffing.

for'ceps (fôr'səps) *n.* an instrument for grasping or extracting; pincers.

for·ci·ble (fôr'sə-bəl) *adj.* **1,** effective; convincing. **2,** resulting from the use of brute force.

ford (fôrd) *n.* a shallow place where a river can be crossed by wading. —*v.t.* pass across by a ford.

fore (fôr) *n.* the front. —*adv.* in or toward the bow of a ship. —*adj.* at or near the front; ahead, in time, rank, etc. —*interj.* in golf, a warning to look out.

fore- (fôr) *pref.* **1,** front. **2,** previous; ahead of time. **3,** ahead in rank; superior.

fore-'and-aft' *adj.* (*Naut.*) lying or running in the general direction of the length of a vessel.

fore'arm" *n.* the arm between elbow and wrist.

fore'bear" *n.* an ancestor.

fore·bode' *v.t. & i.* **1,** presage. **2,** have a premonition of. —**fore·bod'ing,** *n.* a feeling that evil is impending.

fore′cast *n.* a prediction. —*v.t.* (fôr-kåst′) **1**, foresee. **2**, predict.

fore′cas·tle (fōk′səl) *n.* **1**, the forward part of the upper deck of a vessel. **2**, in merchant ships, the seaman's quarters. Also, **fo′c's'le.**

fore·close′ (fôr-klōz′) *v.t. & i.* (*Law*) take away the right to redeem (a mortgage). —**fore·clo′sure** (-klō′zhər) *n.*

fore′fa″ther *n.* an ancestor.

fore′fin″ger *n.* the finger next to the thumb.

fore′front″ *n.* the foremost place or part.

fore′go′ing *adj.* that precedes, as a previous part of something written.

fore′gone″ *adj.* **1**, past. **2**, settled in advance.

fore′ground″ *n.* the part of a picture, etc., represented as being nearest the observer.

fore′hand″ *adj.* **1**, made on the right side of the body (of a righthanded player), as a tennis stroke. **2**, done beforehand. —**fore′-hand″ed,** *adj.* **1**, ahead of time. **2**, prudent; thrifty.

fore′head (fôr′id) *n.* the front of the head or face above the eyes and below the hairline.

for′eign (for′in) *adj.* **1**, situated outside one's own land. **2**, relating to, or dealing with, other countries. **3**, alien; not native. **4**, not pertinent. —**for′eign·er,** *n.* a resident or native of another country.

fore″know′ *v.t.* [*pret. & p.p.* **-knew′**] know beforehand. —**fore·knowl′edge,** *n.*

fore′leg″ *n.* one of the front legs of an animal having four or more legs.

fore′lock″ *n.* a lock of hair at the forehead.

fore′man (-mən) *n.* [*pl.* **-men**] **1**, a superintendent of workers. **2**, the spokesman of a jury. —**fore′wom″an, fore′la″dy,** *n.fem.*

fore′mast″ *n.* the mast nearest the bow of a ship.

fore′most″ *adj. & adv.* first; chief.

fore′name″ *n.* first name. —**fore′named″,** *adj.* mentioned previously.

fore′noon″ *n.* morning.

fo·ren′sic (fə-ren′sik) *adj.* pert. to courts of law or to debate. —**for·en′si·cal·ly,** *adv.*

fore″or·di·na′tion (fôr″ôr-di-nā′shən) *n.* predestination.

fore′play″ *n.* sexual stimulation preceding intercourse.

fore′quar″ter *n.* one of the front quarters in cutting a carcass for meat.

fore′run″ner *n.* a predecessor; a precursor.

fore·see′ *v.t.* [**-saw′**, **-seen′**] predict; anticipate.

fore·shad′ow *v.t.* give notice or indication in advance.

fore″short′en *v.t.* **1**, gradually shorten the lines of (an object in a drawing) to give it the correct perspective. **2**, curtail.

fore′sight″ *n.* **1**, the power of foreseeing. **2**, prudent care for the future.

fore′skin″ *n.* the loose skin at the tip of the penis.

for′est (for′ist) *n.* a large area covered with a dense growth of trees. —**for′est·er,** *n.* one who works in a forest.

fore·stall′ *v.t.* thwart by action in advance.

for″est·a′tion (for″əs-tā′shən) *n.* the planting of forests.

for′est·ry (-rē) *n.* the science of caring for forests.

fore′taste″ *n.* anticipation. —*v.t.* (fôr-tāst′) have previous experience of.

fore·tell′ *v.t. & i.* [*pret. & p.p.* **-told′**] prophesy.

fore′thought″ *n.* anticipatory care.

fore·to·ken *v.t.* foreshadow. —*n.* (fôr-tō″kən) an omen.

for·ev′er (fôr-ev′ər) *adv.* **1**, eternally. **2**, continually.

fore″warn′ *v.t.* warn of a coming event.

fore″word′ *n.* a preface in a book.

for′feit (fôr′fit) *n.* **1**, a deposit, hostage, or agreed penalty surrendered through neglect, default, a crime, error, etc. **2**, a fine; penalty. —*v.i. & t.* surrender (a forfeit). —**for′fei·ture** (-fi-chər) *n.*

for″fend′ (fôr″fend′) *v.t.* (*Archaic*) forbid; avert.

for·gath′er (fôr-gath′ər) *v.i.* assemble; associate.

forge (fôrj) *v.t.* **1**, hammer into shape while malleable through heat. **2**, shape out in any way; fashion. **3**, imitate fraudulently (a signature). —*v.i.* move ahead slowly but surely. —*n.* a smithy. —**forg′ing,** *n.* a piece of forged metal.

for′ger·y (fôr′jə-rē) *n.* fraudulent imitation of a signature, document, etc.; the false signature or document.

for·get′ (fər-get′) *v.t.* [**for·got′**, **-got′ten** or **-got′**, **-get′ting**] **1**, be unable or fail to remember. **2**, omit or neglect (to act), unintentionally or willfully. **3**, (with *oneself*) act or speak improperly. —**for·get′ful,** *adj.* apt to forget; thoughtless. —**for·get′-ful·ness,** *n.*

for·get′-me-not″ *n.* a tiny blue flower.

for·give′ (fər-giv′) *v.t.* [**for·gave′**, **-giv′en**, **-giv′ing**] **1**, grant pardon for (something) or to (someone). **2**, remit (a debt). **3**, cease to resent. —**for·give′ness,** *n.* willingness to forgive. —**for·giv′ing,** *adj.* ready to forgive.

for·go' (fôr-gō') *v.t.* [**for·went'**, **-gone'**, **-go'ing**] give up; let pass.

fo'rint (fô'rint) *n.* the monetary unit of Hungary.

fork (fôrk) *n.* **1,** a pronged tool for digging, lifting, etc., or for handling food at table. **2,** a division or branch, as of a road, stream, etc.; the place of such division. —*v.t.* **1,** use a fork on. **2,** (with *over*) (*Colloq.*) surrender. —*v.i.* separate into branches. —**fork lift,** a vehicle with a pronged lifting platform.

for·lorn' (fôr-lôrn') *adj.* **1,** abandoned; forsaken. **2,** wretched. **3,** hopeless. —**for·lorn'ness,** *n.* —**forlorn hope, 1,** a desperate or hopeless enterprise. **2,** a group of soldiers picked for an expectedly perilous task.

form (fôrm) *n.* **1,** external shape; structure; style. **2,** the human body. **3,** something that determines shape; a mold or pattern. **4,** a particular kind or condition. **5,** type in a frame ready for printing. **6,** a prescribed practice, as for conduct, ritual, etc.; a ceremony. **7,** manner of doing something. **8,** physical fitness. **9,** a document with blanks to be filled in. **10,** (*Gram.*) a change in a word, as by spelling, inflection, etc. —*v.t.* **1,** make; shape. **2,** train; mold, as character. **3,** be an element of; constitute. **4,** organize. **5,** develop. —*v.i.* take a definite shape or arrangement; develop. —**form letter, 1,** a letter duplicated for sending to a number of people. **2,** a standardized letter.

-form (fôrm) *suf.* in the form of; shaped.

for'mal (fôr'məl) *adj.* **1,** adhering to established form or mode; conventional; ceremonious; precise. **2,** not familiar or friendly in manner; stiff. **3,** perfunctory. —*n.* (*Colloq.*) **1,** a formal occasion. **2,** an evening dress. —**for'mal·ize,** *v.t.*

for·mal'de·hyde'' (fôr-mal'də-hīd'') *n.* a gas, used in solution, as a preservative and disinfectant.

for'mal·ism (-liz-əm) *n.* strict adherence to prescribed or customary forms. —**for'-mal·ist,** *n. & adj.* —**for''mal·is'tic,** *adj.*

for·mal'i·ty (fôr-mal'ə-tė) *n.* **1,** rigid conformity to conventions. **2,** ceremony; a rule of procedure; a perfunctory act.

for'mat (fôr'mat) *n.* the general style, appearance, or organization (of a book, program, etc.).

for·ma'tion (fôr-mā'shən) *n.* **1,** the process of shaping. **2,** that which is shaped. **3,** formal structure or arrangement, esp. of troops.

for'ma·tive (fôr'mə-tiv) *adj.* **1,** forming; shaping. **2,** pert. to development.

for'mer (fôr'mər) *adj.* **1,** preceding in time. **2,** the earlier or first mentioned of two. —**for'mer·ly,** *adv.* in time past.

For·mi'ca (fôr-mī'kə) *n.* (*T.N.*) any of various laminated plastic products used in construction and in making furniture.

for'mi·da·ble (fôr'mi-də-bəl) *adj.* **1,** exciting fear. **2,** hard to accomplish; alarmingly difficult. —**for''mi·da·bil'i·ty, for'mi·da·ble·ness,** *n.*

for'mu·la (fôr'mū-lə) *n.* **1,** a fixed rule or form for saying or doing something. **2,** expression by symbols of the constituents of a chemical compound, or of a mathematical rule or principle. **3,** a recipe. —**for'-mu·la·rize'',** *v.t.* —**for'mu·lism,** *n.*

for'mu·late'' (fôr'mū-lāt'') *v.t.* express as a formula; put into definite words. —**for''-mu·la'tion,** *n.*

for'ni·cate'' (fôr'ni-kāt'') *v.i.* consummate a love affair when not married. —**for''ni·ca'tion,** *n.*

for·sake' (fôr-sāk') *v.t.* [**for·sook'** (-sûk'), **-sak'en** (-sā'kən), **-sak'ing**] renounce; abandon.

for·sooth' (fôr-sooth') *adv.* (*Archaic*) in truth; indeed.

for·swear' (fôr-swâr') *v.t.* [**for·swore'**, **-sworn'**, **swear'ing**] deny or renounce upon oath; abjure. —*v.i.* commit perjury. —**for·sworn',** *adj.* perjured.

for·syth'i·a (fôr-sith'ė-ə) *n.* a shrub bearing yellow flowers.

fort (fôrt) *n.* a strongly fortified place.

forte (fôrt) *n.* a strong point; one's special talent. —*adj. & adv.* (fôr'tė) (*Music*) loud; loudly.

for''te·pi·a'no (fôr''te-pė-ä'nō) *n.* (*Archaic*) a piano.

forth (fôrth) *adv.* **1,** onward or forward in time or place. **2,** into view; from under cover. **3,** away. —**and so forth,** et cetera.

forth'com''ing *adj.* **1,** approaching in time. **2,** available when needed.

forth'right'' *adj.* outspoken; direct. —*adv.* **1,** directly. **2,** immediately. —**forth'right''-ness,** *n.*

forth''with' *adv.* at once.

for'ti·eth (fôr'tė-əth) *adj. & n.* **1,** the ordinal of forty, also written 40th. **2,** one of 40 equal parts.

for''ti·fi·ca'tion (fôr''ti-fi-kā'shən) *n.* **1,** the act of strengthening. **2,** a fortified position.

for'ti·fy'' (fôr'ti-fī'') *v.t.* **1,** provide with military defenses. **2,** strengthen, against wear, etc. **3,** strengthen mentally, morally, or physically.

for·tis'si·mo'' (fôr-tis'i-mō'') *adj. & adv.* (*Music*) very loud.

for'ti·tude'' (fôr'tə-tūd'') *n.* the power to endure pain, hardship, etc.

fort'night'' (fôrt'nīt'') *n.* two weeks. **—fort'night''ly,** *adj. & adv.* (occurring) once each fortnight.

FOR'TRAN (fôr'tran) *n.* a computer language.

for'tress (fôr'tres) *n.* **1,** a fortified place; a group of forts. **2,** any stronghold.

for·tu'i·tous (fôr-tū'ə-təs) *adj.* coming by chance; accidental. **—for·tu'i·tous·ness,** **for·tu'i·ty,** *n.*

for'tu·nate (fôr'chə-nət) *adj.* **1,** having good fortune; lucky. **2,** resulting favorably.

for'tune (fôr'chən) *n.* **1,** success or failure as controlled or influenced by chance. **2,** wealth, esp. great wealth; good luck. **3,** chance; luck; destiny. **—fortune hunter,** one who seeks to marry for wealth.

for'ty (fôr'tē) *n. & adj.* the cardinal number between thirty-nine and forty-one, expressed by 40. **—forty winks,** (*Colloq.*) a short nap.

for'ty-five' *n.* (*Colloq.*) **1,** a .45 caliber revolver or pistol. **2,** 45 r.p.m. disk.

for''ty·nin'er (fôr'tē-nī'nər) *n.* one who participated in the California gold rush of 1849.

fo'rum (fôr'əm) *n.* a public meeting; any medium for public discussion; a tribunal.

for'ward (fôr'wərd) *adj.* **1,** near or toward the front. **2,** well-advanced. **3,** eager; ready. **4,** presumptuous; bold. **—adv.** **1,** onward; ahead; toward the front. **2,** forth; into view. **—v.t.** **1,** further; encourage. **2,** send (freight, etc.). **3,** send (a letter, etc.) on to a new and different address. **—n.** in sports, a player stationed near the opponent's goal; in football, a lineman. **—for'ward·ness,** *n.*

fos'sil (fos'əl) *n.* **1,** remains or traces of a prehistoric plant or animal found in earth, rocks, etc. **2,** an outdated person or thing. **—fos'sil·ize''** (-īz'') *v.t. & i.*

fos'ter (fâs'tér) *v.t.* **1,** nourish; bring up. **2,** cherish. **3,** promote the growth or development of. **—adj.** equivalent to parent or child though not so related by blood. **—fos'ter·ling,** *n.* foster child. **—foster home,** a home provided by foster parents. **—foster mother,** a woman who takes the place of a mother in caring for a child.

fought (fât) *v.* pret. & p.p. of *fight*.

foul (fowl) *adj.* **1,** disgusting to the senses by reason of decay, turpitude, filthiness, etc.; noisome; hateful. **2,** clogged, as a chimney; choked; entangled, as a rope. **3,** against the rules; out of legal bounds; unfair. **4,** base; vicious; scurrilous. **—n.** **1,** a violation of the rules. **2,** a collision. **—v.t.** **1,** defile. **2,** clog; entangle. **3,** collide with.

—v.i. **1,** become foul; commit a foul. **2,** (with *up*) (*Slang*) blunder. **—foul'ness,** *n.* **—fall foul of,** have trouble with; clash with.

fou·lard' (foo-lärd') *n.* a soft silk with a satin finish.

foul-'mouthed'' (-mowt͟hd'') *adj.* given to filthy or abusive speech.

found (fownd) *v.t.* **1,** lay the basis or foundation of, as a building. **2,** establish, as a business or a dynasty. **3,** (with *on*) base. **4,** cast (metal) in a mold. **5,** pret. & p.p. of *find*. **—n.** food and lodging.

foun·da'tion (fown-dā'shən) *n.* **1,** the base on which a building rests; hence, basis; underlying principle. **2,** an endowment, as for research, a charity, etc.

foun'der (fown'dər) *v.i.* **1,** fill and sink, as a ship. **2,** go lame, as a horse. **3,** fail utterly. **—n.** **1,** originator; charter member. **2,** one who casts metal.

found'ling (fownd'ling) *n.* a deserted infant of unknown parentage.

found'ry (fown'drē) *n.* a place where metal is cast.

fount (fownt) *n.* a fountain; a source.

foun'tain (fown'tən) *n.* **1,** a natural spring; a source of water. **2,** an artificial jet of water; a basin to receive it. **—fountain pen,** a pen containing a reservoir for ink.

foun'tain·head'' *n.* **1,** the head or source of a stream. **2,** a primary source, as of learning.

four (fôr) *n. & adj.* the cardinal number between three and five, expressed by 4. **—on all fours,** on four feet; on hands and knees (or feet).

four'flush''er (fôr'flush''ər) *n.* (*Slang*) a pretender.

four-'in-hand'' *n.* **1,** a long necktie tied in a slip knot. **2,** a team of four horses driven by one person.

four-'o'clock'' (fôr'ə-klok'') *n.* a plant whose flowers open in the afternoon and close the next morning.

four'some *n.* four persons; a quartet.

four'square'' *adj.* steady; frank.

four'teen' (fôr'tēn') *n. & adj.* the cardinal number between thirteen and fifteen, expressed by 14. **—four'teenth',** *n. & adj.*

fourth (fôrth) *adj. & n.* the ordinal of four; 4th. **—one of four equal parts. —fourth dimension,** time or duration, considered as a dimension in the space-time theory of relativity. **—fourth estate,** the press; journalists collectively. **—the Fourth,** July 4, Independence Day.

fowl *n.* **1,** a domestic hen or cock; its flesh as food. **2,** birds in general, esp. those used for food. **—fowl'er,** *n.* one who hunts wild birds. **—fowl'ing,** n. the hunting of birds. **—fowling piece,** a shotgun.

fox (foks) n. a wild animal of the wolf family, noted for its cunning. **2,** a crafty person. —v.t. (Slang) outwit. **—foxed,** adj. discolored, stained, or spotted. **—fox terrier,** a small, usu. smooth-coated, terrier. **—fox trot,** a type of ballroom dance.

fox'glove″ (foks'gluv″) n. a flowering plant, the source of digitalis.

fox'hole″ (foks'hōl″) n. a hastily dug pit for shelter from enemy fire.

fox'hound″ n. a breed of large, swift hounds trained for hunting.

fox'y (fok'sē) adj. **1,** clever; sly. **2,** foxed. **—fox'i·ness,** n.

foy'er (foi'ər) n. a lobby or entranceway, as of a hotel, theater, apartment, etc.

fra'cas (frā'kəs) n. a noisy fight.

frac'tion (frak'shən) n. **1,** a part of a unit, or of a whole. **2,** a scrap; a fragment. **—frac'tion·al,** adj.

frac'tion·ate″ (-āt″) v.t. (Chem.) separate by distillation, crystallization, etc. **—frac″-tion·a'tion,** n.

frac'tious (frak'shəs) adj. **1,** cross; peevish. **2,** unruly. **—frac'tious·ness,** n.

frac'ture (frak'chər) n. a breaking, esp. of a bone. —v.t. & i. break.

frag'ile (fraj'əl) adj. easily broken; delicate; brittle. **—fra·gil'i·ty** (frə-jil'ə-tē) n.

frag'ment (frag'mənt) n. **1,** a part broken off. **2,** an unfinished part, as of a poem. **—frag'men·ta″ry,** adj. incomplete. **—frag″-men·ta'tion,** n.

fra'grant (frā'grənt) adj. **1,** sweet-scented; pleasant. **2,** (Colloq.) having an unpleasant odor. **—fra'grance,** n.

frail (frāl) adj. **1,** fragile. **2,** morally or physically weak. —n. (Slang) a woman. **—frail'ty** (-tē) n.

frame (frām) v.t. **1,** construct; fit together. **2,** compose or devise, as a law or a poem; utter or express. **3,** surround with a frame, as a picture. **4,** (Slang) incriminate (a person) on false evidence. —n. **1,** something made of parts fitted and joined. **2,** any kind of structure for enclosing, supporting, or holding something. **3,** bodily structure. **4,** a state of mind; mood. **—frame house,** a house built of wood.

frame'up″ n. (Slang) something fraudulently prearranged.

frame'work″ n. the structure for supporting anything; an outline or basic plan.

franc (frank) n. the monetary unit of France, Belgium, and Switzerland.

fran'chise (fran'chīz) n. **1,** the right to vote. **2,** a special right granted, esp. by a government.

fran'ci·um (fran'sē-əm) n. an unstable radioactive chemical element, no. 87, symbol Fr.

franc'o·phone″ (frank'ə-fōn″) n. a person who speaks French, esp. as his principal language.

fran'gi·ble (fran'jə-bəl) adj. breakable. **—fran″gi·bil'i·ty,** n.

frank adj. unreserved in expressing one's sentiments; candid; undisguised. —n. **1,** the privilege of mailing letters free of postage. **2,** (Colloq.) frankfurter. —v.t. mark for free mailing. **—frank'ness,** n.

Frank'en·stein″ (frank'ən-stīn″) n. a fictional character who created a creature (Frankenstein's monster) that destroyed him.

frank'furt″er (-fēr″tər) n. a reddish sausage of beef and pork. Also, colloq., **frank.**

frank'in·cense″ (frank'in-sens″) n. a gum resin burned as incense.

fran'tic (fran'tik) adj. frenzied; wild with excitement, pain, or fear. **—fran'ti·cal·ly,** adv.

frappe (frap) n. a milk shake with ice cream.

frap·pé' (fra-pā') n. a mixed cold drink.

fra·ter'nal (frə-tēr'nəl) adj. **1,** brotherly. **2,** pert. to a fraternity.

fra·ter'ni·ty (frə-tēr'nə-tē) n. **1,** brotherliness. **2,** a society, or group, of men with common interests or tastes. **3,** a college society or club.

frat'er·nize″ (frat'ər-nīz″) v.t. associate in a friendly manner. **—frat″er·ni·za'tion,** n.

frat'ri·cide″ (frat'rə-sīd″) n. the killer or killing of a brother.

Frau (frow) n. (Ger.) a wife; Mrs. **—Fräu'-lein″** (froi'līn″) n. (Ger.) an unmarried woman; Miss.

fraud (frâd) n. **1,** deceit; a trick. **2,** (Law) dishonest practice; breach of confidence. **3,** (Colloq.) a cheat.

fraud'u·lent (frâ'dyə-lənt) adj. dishonest; based on or obtained by fraud. **—fraud'-u·lence,** n.

fraught (frât) adj. filled (with).

fray (frā) n. a battle; skirmish. —v.t. & i. ravel; wear thin, as cloth.

fraz'zle (fraz'əl) v.t. & i. (Colloq.) **1,** fray. **2,** exhaust; weary. —n. a ragged end; an exhausted state.

freak (frēk) n. **1,** an abnormal person, plant or thing. **2,** a whim; vagary. **—freak'-ish,** adj. **—freak out,** (Slang) **1,** lose control of oneself under the influence of drugs; have a "bad trip." **2,** experience similar reaction without drugs.

freck'le (frek'əl) *n.* a light-brown spot on the skin, caused by sunlight. —*v.t. & i.* cause or acquire freckles. —**freck'ly** *adj.*

free (frē) *adj.* **1,** enjoying personal liberty; not enslaved. **2,** enjoying civil or political liberty; self-governing. **3,** existing under civil liberty, as a country. **4,** unrestricted in opinion, choice, or action; independent. **5,** exempt, as from tax or restriction. **6,** obtained without cost; given without charge. **7,** lavish; profuse. **8,** not bound or restricted by force. **9,** unrestrained; unceremonious; not bound by fixed rules. **10,** not literal or exact. **11,** open to all. —*adv.* without charge. —*v.t.* unfetter; release; exempt; rid (with *of*). —**free agent,** a person not bound by contract, etc., and hence free to act. —**free lance,** a self-employed writer who may sell to whom he pleases. —**free love,** sexual relations or cohabitation without marriage. —**free port,** an area allowing free passage of goods without import duties. —**free trade,** commercial trading between countries without government-imposed duties, etc. —**free university,** an informally organized forum offering classes in subject matter not usually available in regular university courses. —**free verse,** verse without rhyme or regular meter.

-free (frē) *suf.* free of; lacking.

free'bie (frē'bē) *n.* (*Slang*) something obtained or given free of cost.

free'boot''er (frē'boo''tər) *n.* a pirate.

freed'man (frēd'mən) *n.* [*pl.* **-men**] a man who has been freed from slavery. —**freed'wom''an,** *n.fem.*

free'dom (-dəm) *n.* the state of being free; personal liberty or national independence. —**freedom of the press,** the right to publish fact and opinion without censorship.

free-'for-all'' *n.* (*Colloq.*) a contest or fight open to all.

free'hand'' *adj.* roughly drawn by hand. —**free'hand''ed,** *adj.* generous.

free'hold'' *n.* land owned outright.

free'lance'' *adj.* pert. to or produced by a free lance. —*v.i.* operate as a free lance.

free-'load''er *n.* (*Slang*) **1,** a parasite; sponge. **2,** a crasher, as at a party. —**free'-load'',** *v.i.*

Free'ma''son *n.* a member of the Free and Accepted Masons, a secret order. —**free'ma''son·ry,** *n.* sympathetic fellowship.

free'si·a (frē'zhē-ə) *n.* a flowering plant.

free'stone'' (frē'stōn'') *adj.* of a fruit, one whose pulp does not cling to the stone.

free'think''er *n.* a person of independent religious opinions.

free'way'' *n.* a toll-free highway.

free'wheel''ing *adj.* (*Colloq.*) **1,** free of restraint. **2,** nonchalant; carefree.

free'will'' *adj.* voluntary.

freeze (frēz) *v.t.* [**froze** (frōz), **fro'zen, freez'ing**] **1,** cause to congeal; change from a liquid to a solid state by loss of heat. **2,** form ice on or in; injure or kill by cold. **3,** fix at the present place, condition, price, etc. —*v.i.* **1,** be turned into, or covered with, ice. **2,** be injured or killed by intense cold. **3,** suffer from, or as from, cold. —*n.* a freezing condition, as of weather. —**freeze out,** exclude.

freeze-'dry'' *v.t.* dehydrate by freezing and removing moisture by vacuum.

freez'er *n.* **1,** a machine for freezing ice cream, etc. **2,** a cold storage cabinet.

freight (frāt) *n.* **1,** transportation of goods by a common carrier. **2,** goods so transported; cargo; shipment. **3,** the charge for handling. **4,** a train carrying freight. —*v.t.* **1,** load with, or as with, cargo. **2,** ship (goods) by freight. —**freight'er,** *n.* a ship used to transport goods.

French *adj.* pert. to France, its people, etc. —*n.* the language of France. —**French'man,** *n.* —**French cuffs,** folding cuffs. —**French doors** or **window,** a pair of doors opening in the middle. —**French dressing,** a salad dressing of oil, vinegar, salt, and spices. —**French fried potatoes,** also, **French fries,** strips of potato fried in deep fat. —**French horn,** a brass wind instrument having a coiled tube ending in a flaring mouth. —**French leave,** abrupt departure. —**French pancake,** crêpe. —**French toast,** bread, dipped in egg and milk and sautéed.

French'i·fy'' (fren'chi-fī'') *v.t.* (*Colloq.*) make French in taste, manners, or characteristics.

fre·net'ic (frə-net'ik) *adj.* frenzied. —**fre·net'i·cal·ly,** *adv.*

fren'zy (fren'zē) *n.* **1,** violent mental agitation. **2,** delirious excitement. —**fren'zied,** *adj.*

fre'on (frē'on) *n.* (*T.N.*) a gas used as a refrigerant.

fre'quen·cy (frē'kwən-sē) *n.* **1,** repeated occurrence. **2,** the rate of recurrence of a given event in a given time. —**frequency modulation,** in radio, alteration of wave length frequency to avoid distortion.

fre'quent (frē'kwənt) *adj.* **1,** happening often; occurring at short intervals. **2,** habitual; regular. —*v.t.* (*also,* frē-kwent') go often or habitually to. —**fre''quen·ta'tion** (-tā'shən) *n.* —**fre'quen·ta·tive** (-tə-tiv) *adj.*

fres'co (fres'kō) *n.* a mural painting on damp plaster.

fresh *adj.* **1,** having its original qualities; not faded, worn, or stale. **2,** novel; new;

recent. **3,** cool; refreshing; of wind, brisk. **4,** of water, not salt; of food, not canned, preserved, or salted; recently grown, picked, slaughtered, etc. **5,** rested; not tired; invigorated; healthy. **6,** of a cow, recently having calved. **7,** inexperienced. **8,** (*Slang*) impudent. —**fresh′ness,** *n.*

fresh′en (-ən) *v.t.* make fresh.

fresh′et (fresh′it) *n.* a sudden seasonal rise in the level of a stream.

fresh′man (-mən) *n.* [*pl.* -**men**] a student in his first year in high school or college.

fresh′wa′ter *adj.* **1,** living in or accustomed to inland waters, not the sea. **2,** inexperienced, insignificant, or rustic.

fret *v.i.* [**fret′ted,** -**ting**] **1,** be continuously perturbed by worry, anxiety, annoyance, or resentment. **2,** become worn or corroded. —*v.t.* **1,** vex; irritate. **2,** chafe; rub. —*n.* **1,** irritation. **2,** a carved ornamental pattern: *fretwork.* **3,** a small ridge across the fingerboard of a stringed instrument. —**fret′ful,** *adj.* fretting; restless; peevish. —**fret saw,** a saw used for ornamental woodwork.

Freud′i·an (froi′dē-ən) *adj.* pert. to the theories of Sigmund Freud relating to neurotic and psychopathic conditions.

fri′a·ble (frī′ə-bəl) *adj.* easily crumbled. —**fri′a·bil′i·ty,** *n.*

fri′ar (frī′ər) *n.* a member of certain Rom. Cath. religious orders. —**fri′ar·y,** *n.* a monastery.

fric″as·see′ (frik″ə-sē′) *n.* a dish of meat or fowl cut in pieces and cooked in gravy. —*v.t.* so cook.

fric′tion (frik′shən) *n.* **1,** the rubbing of two surfaces together; opposition; conflict. **2,** the resistance to relative motion between two surfaces in contact. **3,** lack of harmony; conflict. —**fric′tion·al,** *adj.* —**friction tape,** a water-resistant insulating adhesive tape.

Fri′day (frī′dē) *n.* the sixth day of the week.

fried (frīd) *v.* pret. & p.p. of *fry.* —*adj.* **1,** boiled in fat. **2,** (*Slang*) drunk.

friend (frend) *n.* **1,** a person on intimate and affectionate terms with another. **2,** a supporter; well-wisher. **3,** (*cap.*) a member of the Religious Society of Friends; a Quaker. —**friend′ly,** *adj.* amicable; not hostile; favorable. —**friend′li·ness,** *n.* —**friend′ship,** *n.* the state of being friendly toward or intimate with another.

frieze (frēz) *n.* **1,** an ornamental or sculptured band around a wall. **2,** a heavy woolen cloth.

frig′ate (frig′it) *n.* **1,** (*Hist.*) a sailing warship, relatively equivalent to the cruiser. **2,** a modern light warship.

fright (frīt) *n.* **1,** sudden fear or terror. **2,** (*Colloq.*) a grotesque person or thing.

fright′en (-ən) *v.t.* terrify.

fright′ful (-fəl) *adj.* **1,** terrible. **2,** (*Colloq.*) unpleasant. —**fright′ful·ness,** *n.*

frig′id (frij′id) *adj.* **1,** icy; wintry. **2,** chilly in manner; formal. **3,** emotionally unresponsive. —**fri·gid′i·ty** (fri-jid′ə-tē) *n.*

frill (fril) *n.* **1,** a gathered or pleated ruffle; a trimming. **2,** (*Colloq.*) (*pl.*) affectations. **3,** a fancy detail or accessory. —**frill′y,** *adj.*

fringe (frinj) *n.* **1,** a raveled edge on a fabric; a fancy edging of tassels or twisted threads. **2,** border; outskirts. **3,** an extreme and unrepresentative part of a group, party, doctrine, etc. —*v.t.* furnish with a fringe; border. —**fringe benefit,** a benefit given in addition to salary or wages.

frip′per·y (frip′ə-rē) *n.* worthless finery; ostentation.

Fris′bee (friz′bē) *n.* (*T.N.*) a saucer-shaped object thrown from person to person.

fri·sé′ (fri-zā′) *n.* an upholstery fabric, made of uncut loops.

frisk *v.i.* leap about; gambol. —*v.t.* (*Slang*) search (a person) for concealed weapons. —**frisk′y,** *adj.* playful.

frit′ter (frit′ər) *v.t.* waste on trifles, as time, energy, etc. —*n.* a small fried battercake.

fri·vol′i·ty (fri-vol′ə-tē) *n.* **1,** a frivolous act. **2,** merrymaking.

friv′o·lous (friv′ə-ləs) *adj.* **1,** not seriously intended; lacking in dignity; slight; trivial. **2,** silly; giddy. —**friv′o·lous·ness,** *n.*

friz *v.* form into crisp curls or tufts, as hair. —*n.* something frizzed. —**friz′zy,** *adj.*

friz′zle (friz′əl) *v.t.* **1,** friz. **2,** cook with sizzling noise. —**friz′zly,** *adj.*

fro (frō) *adv.* back. —**to and fro,** back and forth.

frock (frok) *n.* **1,** a dress. **2,** a coarse outer garment worn by a monk, etc. —**frock coat,** a man's long-skirted coat.

frog (frâg) *n.* **1,** a small, tailless amphibian with great leaping and swimming ability. **2,** a lump of mucus in the throat. **3,** a fastening made of a button and a loop. **4,** a device that permits the intersection of two railway tracks. **5,** a flower holder.

frog′man *n.* a specially trained underwater swimmer.

frol′ic (frol′ik) *v.i.* [-**icked,** -**ick·ing**] play merrily. —*n.* merrymaking; fun. —**frol′ic·some,** *adj.*

from *prep.* away; out of (a certain starting point); denoting removal, separation, distinction, etc.

frond *n.* a leaf of a fern, etc.

---

fat, fāte, fär, fâre, fâll, àsk; met, hē, hēr, maybē; pin, pīne; not, nōte, ôr, tool

front (frunt) *n.* **1,** the foremost part or face of anything. **2,** manner of facing anything. **3,** position directly before a person or thing. **4,** land along the edge of a river, bay, etc. **5,** in war, the scene of actual fighting. **6,** bearing or demeanor. **7,** (*Colloq.*) an outward manifestation of wealth or importance. **8,** (*Colloq.*) a figurehead. **9,** (*Meteor.*) the surface of contact of two unlike air masses. **10,** a temporary coalition of political parties. —*adj.* pert. to, or situated at, the front. —*v.t.* confront; have the front toward; face. —*v.i.* **1,** face in a certain direction. **2,** (with *for*) (*Colloq.*) lend one's name or prestige (to). —**front foot,** a foot of frontage.

front'age (frun'tij) *n.* the distance a lot extends along a street, body of water, etc.

fron'tal (frun'təl) *adj.* **1,** at or of the front. **2,** pert. to the bone of the forehead.

fron·tier' (frun-tir') *n.* **1,** that part of a country that borders another country or an unsettled region. **2,** undeveloped spheres of knowledge, etc.

fron'tis·piece'' (frun'tis-pēs'') *n.* an illustration facing the title page of a book.

front-'run'ner *n.* (*Colloq.*) the leader in a competition, contest, etc.

frost (frâst) *n.* **1,** frozen dew or vapor. **2,** freezing weather. **3,** a frozen state of the ground. **4,** (*Slang*) a failure. **5,** (*Colloq.*) a coolness between persons. —*v.t.* **1,** cover with frost. **2,** injure by freezing. **3,** ice (a cake). —**frost'ed,** *adj.* iced.

frost'bite'' *n.* injury to body tissues, caused by exposure to intense cold.

frost'ing *n.* **1,** a sugar coating for cake. **2,** a finish on metal or glass.

frost'y *adj.* **1,** cold. **2,** gray, as hair.

froth (frâth) *n.* **1,** mass of fine bubbles on the surface of a liquid, at the mouth of a hard-ridden horse, etc.; foam. **2,** anything light and trivial. —*v.t. & i.* foam.

froth'y *adj.* **1,** foaming. **2,** light; insubstantial.

frou'frou'' (froo'froo'') *n.* a rustling, esp. of a woman's silk dress.

fro'ward (frō'wərd) *adj.* willful; perverse. —**fro'ward·ness,** *n.*

frown *n.* a wrinkling of the brows, as in anger, perplexity, etc. —*v.i.* **1,** so wrinkle the brow. **2,** (with *upon*) disapprove.

frowz'y (frow'zē) *adj.* slovenly; unkempt. —**frowz'i·ness,** *n.*

froze (frōz) *v.* pret. of *freeze*.

fro'zen (frō'zən) *v.* **1,** congealed by cold. **2,** frigid. **3,** lacking emotion. **4,** refrigerated. **5,** fixed; not liquid, as assets. —*v.* p.p. of *freeze*.

fruc'ti·fy'' (fruk'tə-fī'') *v.t.* make productive. —*v.i.* bear fruit. —**fruc''ti·fi·ca'tion** (-fi-kā'shən) *n.*

fruc'tose (fruk'tōs) *n.* an intensely sweet sugar that occurs in honey.

fru'gal (froo'gəl) *adj.* economical; not wasteful; not lavish; sparing. —**fru·gal'i·ty** (froo-gal'ə-tė), *n.*

fruit (froot) *n.* **1,** any natural, useful yield of a plant. **2,** the seed of a plant and its enveloping tissues. **3,** the sweet fruit of certain trees and vines, as peach, pear, grape, etc. **4,** a result; consequence. —**fruit'er·er,** *n.* a dealer in fruit. —**fruit'ful,** *adj.* productive; profitable. —**fruit'less,** *adj.* unprofitable; barren.

fruit'cake'' *n.* **1,** a rich cake. **2,** (*Slang*) an eccentric; a crazy person.

fru·i'tion (froo-ish'ən) *n.* **1,** state of bearing fruit. **2,** realization; attainment, as of one's hopes.

fruit'y (-ė) *adj.* **1,** having the taste or flavor of fruit. **2,** spicy, as a story.

frump *n.* a dowdy woman. —**frump'ish,** *adj.*

frus'trate (frus'trāt) *v.t.* prevent from fulfilling plans, hopes, etc.; balk; thwart; nullify.

frus·tra'tion (frus-trā'shon) *n.* **1,** act of frustrating; state of being frustrated. **2,** extreme disappointment.

frus'tum (frus'təm) *n.* the remainder of a truncated cone or pyramid.

fry (frī) *v.t. & i.* **1,** cook or be cooked in hot fat. **2,** (*Slang*) be electrocuted. **3,** be subjected to extreme heat. —*n.* **1,** a young fish. **2,** a swarm or brood of young; young children.

fuch'sia (fū'shə) *n.* a shrub or plant with drooping reddish tubular flowers; the color of the flower.

fud'dle (fud'əl) *v.* [**-dled, -dling**] —*v.t.* muddle or intoxicate. —*v.i.* tipple.

fud'dy-dud'dy (fud'ė-dud'ė) *n.* **1,** a fogy. **2,** stuffed shirt.

fudge (fuj) *n.* **1,** nonsense. **2,** a creamy beaten chocolate candy. —*v.i.* cheat; hedge.

fu'el (fū'əl) *n.* **1,** combustible material burned to supply heat or power. **2,** a means of increasing passion, etc. —*v.t. & i.* furnish with, or take on, fuel. —**fuel injection,** a method of spraying fuel into the cylinders of an internal combustion engine.

fu'gi·tive (fū'jə-tiv) *adj.* **1,** fleeing; having run away. **2,** evanescent; fleeting. **3,** of literature, of passing interest; transitory. —*n.* one who flees from pursuit, duty, etc.

fugue (fūg) *n.* a musical composition in which the theme is reintroduced by various parts.

Füh'rer (fyü'rər) n. (Ger.) leader; applied esp. to Adolf Hitler.

-ful (-fəl) suf. **1,** full of; filled. **2,** characterized by. **3,** tending to, as harmful.

ful'crum (ful'krəm) n. the support on which a lever rests or turns.

ful·fill' (ful-fil') v.t. **1,** carry into effect, as a promise. **2,** perform, as a duty. **3,** satisfy, as a desire. Also, **ful·fil'. —ful-fill'ment,** n.

ful'gent (ful'jənt) adj. shining brightly. —**ful'gent·ness,** n.

fu·lig'i·nous (fū-lij'ə-nəs) adj. sooty; smoky. —**fu·lig'i·nous·ness,** n.

full (ful) adj. **1,** filled to capacity; holding all that can be held. **2,** complete according to standard; whole. **3,** rounded out; plump; ample. **4,** engrossed. **5,** abundantly supplied. **6,** at the peak of, as quality, force, volume, etc. —adv. **1,** entirely. **2,** exactly. —n. utmost extent. —**full'ness,** n. —**full stop,** a period.

full'back" n. in football, a player stationed behind the line.

full'blast' adj. **1,** operating at capacity. **2,** thorough; unrestrained. —adv. at capacity; thoroughly.

full·blood'ed adj. **1,** of unmixed ancestry. **2,** virile.

full·blown' adj. fully developed.

full-'bod"ied adj. having utmost flavor or strength, as a beverage.

full'er (ful'ər) n. **1,** one who treats cloth to thicken it. **2,** a hammer with a cylindrical striking surface. —**fuller's earth,** a claylike substance used as a filter and blotting material.

full-'fledged" adj. **1,** fully matured or developed. **2,** of first rank.

ful'mar (ful'mər) n. an Arctic sea bird related to the petrel.

ful'mi·nate" (ful'mi-nāt") v.t. & i. **1,** explode; detonate. **2,** (with against) issue denunciations. —**ful"mi·na'tion,** n.

ful'some (ful'səm) adj. cloying; offensively excessive; insincere. —**ful'some·ness,** n.

fu'ma·role" (fū'mə-rōl") n. a hole from which volcanic gases issue.

fum'ble (fum'bəl) v.i. & t. **1,** grope about awkwardly; handle clumsily. **2,** in sports, fail to hold (the ball). —n. a slip; misplay.

fume (fūm) n. (usually pl.) smoke, gas, vapor, esp. if noxious. —v.i. **1,** emit fumes. **2,** be vexed; fret. —**fumed,** adj. colored by fumes, as woodwork.

fu'mi·gate" (fū'mi-gāt") v.t. treat with fumes to disinfect or to destroy pests. —**fu'mi·gant,** n. —**fu"mi·ga'tion,** n. —**fu'-mi·ga"tor,** n.

fun n. anything that induces enjoyment, esp. mirthful; amusement; sport; joking.

fu·nam'bu·list (fū-nam'byə-list) n. a tightrope walker.

func'tion (funk'shən) n. **1,** proper action by which any person, organ, office, structure, etc., fulfills its purpose or duty. **2,** a public ceremony or occasion. **3,** (Math.) a quantity that depends on other quantities for its value. —v.i. perform a function; operate, in the natural or intended manner. —**func'tion·al** (-əl) adj. **1,** pert. to a function. **2,** designed to perform some function; useful. —**functional disease,** a disease characterized by a morbid change in the function, but not in the tissues, of an organ. —**func'tion·al·ism,** n. the doctrine that functional utility should determine design (of furniture, etc.). —**func'tion·ar·y** (-er-ē) n. an official.

fund n. **1,** a stock or supply, esp. of money, set apart for a purpose. **2,** a store of anything, as knowledge. **3,** (pl.) available cash. —v.t. **1,** convert (a temporary debt) into a permanent debt bearing interest. **2,** provide funding for.

fun"da·men'tal (fun"də-men'-təl) adj. serving as, or being an essential part of, a foundation; basic; primary; elementary. —n. a basic principle. —**fun"da·men'tal·ist,** n. one who accepts the Bible as literally true. —**fun"da·men'tal·ism,** n.

fu·ne'bri·al (fū-nē'brē-əl) adj. funereal.

fu'ner·al (fū'nər-əl) n. the ceremony of burying a dead person.

fu·ne're·al (fū-nir'ē-əl) adj. **1,** dark; gloomy; sad. **2,** pert. to a funeral.

fun'gi·cide (fun'ji-sīd) n. an agent for destroying fungous growths, as athlete's foot.

fun'gus (fung'gəs) n. any of a group of non-green plants, including the molds, toadstools, rusts, etc. —**fun'gous,** adj.

fu·nic'u·lar (fū-nik'ū-lər) adj. pert. to, or worked by, a rope or cable. —n. a mountain cable railway.

funk n. (Colloq.) **1,** cowering fear. **2,** a state of depression.

funk'y (funk'ē) adj. earthy; having a feeling of the blues.

fun'nel (fun'əl) n. **1,** a cone-shaped device for guiding something into a small opening. **2,** a smokestack. **3,** a shaft for ventilation.

fun'ny (fun'ē) adj. **1,** amusing; comical. **2,** (Colloq.) strange; odd. **3,** (pl.) (Colloq.) the comic strips; funny papers. —**fun'ni·ness,** n. —**funny farm,** (Colloq.) an insane asylum.

fun'ny·bone" n. **1,** a nerve in the elbow. **2,** sense of humor.

fur (fẽr) *n.* the soft, fine hair of certain animals; their dressed skins, used for clothing. —**furred,** *adj.*

fur'be·low" (fẽr'bə-lō") *n.* **1,** a plaited dress trimming; a flounce. **2,** any bit of finery.

fur'bish (fẽr'bish) *v.t.* polish; burnish; renovate.

fu'ri·ous (fyu̇r'ē-əs) *adj.* **1,** raging; full of fury. **2,** violent, as a wind. **3,** energetic. —**fu'ri·ous·ness,** *n.*

furl (fẽrl) *v.t.* roll up and fasten (a flag or sail).

fur'long (fẽr'lâng) *n.* a measure of length, 220 yards.

fur'lough (fẽr'lō) *n.* leave of absence for a soldier.

fur'nace (fẽr'nis) *n.* a structure in which fuel is burned to make heat.

fur'nish (fẽr'nish) *v.t.* supply with what is needed, esp. furniture; provide. —**fur'-nish·ings,** *n.pl.* fittings of any kind.

fur'ni·ture (fẽr'nə-chər) *n.* **1,** movable articles, as chairs, desks, etc., for equipping a house, office, etc. **2,** any necessary apparatus.

fu'ror (fyu̇r'ôr) *n.* **1,** great excitement. **2,** a prevailing craze.

fur'ri·er (fẽr'ē-ər) *n.* a maker of or dealer in fur garments.

fur'ring (fẽr'ing) *n.* **1,** fur for a garment. **2,** in building, thin boards providing a basis for laths, plaster, etc.

fur'row (fẽr'ō) *n.* **1,** a trench in the earth, esp. that made by a plow. **2,** a wrinkle. —*v.t.* make furrows in.

fur'ry (fẽr'ē) *adj.* **1,** covered with fur. **2,** made of or like fur. —**fur'ri·ness,** *n.*

fur'ther (fẽr'thər) *adj.* [*superl.* **fur'thest**] **1,** more remote or extended, in figurative senses; comp. of *far.* **2,** additional. —*adv.* **1,** to a greater distance or extent. **2,** also. —*v.t.* promote or advance, as a cause. —**fur'ther·ance,** *n.* advancement.

fur'ther·more" *adv.* besides; also.

fur'tive (fẽr'tiv) *adj.* sly; stealthy; done by stealth. —**fur'tive·ness,** *n.*

fu'run·cle (fyu̇r'ung-kəl) *n.* a boil.

fu'ry (fyu̇r'ē) *n.* **1,** violent passion; great anger. **2,** fierceness; violence.

furze (fẽrz) *n.* a shrub common waste lands in Europe; gorse.

fuse (fūz) *n.* **1,** a casing filled with combustible material for exploding a shell, blast, etc. **2,** a protective strip of fusible metal inserted in an electric circuit. —*v.t. & i.* **1,** melt with extreme heat. **2,** blend, as if melted together; weld. —**fus'i·ble,** *adj.* —**fus"i·bil'i·ty,** *n.*

fu'se·lage (fū'zə-lij) *n.* the body of an airplane.

fu·see' (fū-zē') *n.* **1,** a friction match that will burn in the wind. **2,** a warning flare.

fu'sel oil (fū'zəl) a poisonous liquid, a by-product of distilleries, used in solvents.

fu'si·form" (fū'zə-form") *adj.* spindle-shaped.

fu'sil·lade' (fū"ze-lād') *n.* simultaneous fire from many firearms.

fu'sion (fū'zhən) *n.* **1,** union by fusing. **2,** union of two or more political parties. **3,** in nuclear physics, union of parts of two atoms.

fuss (fus) *n.* **1,** much ado over trifles; bustle; confusion. **2,** (*Colloq.*) a petty quarrel. —*v.t.* worry, or be busy, over trifles. —*v.t.* confuse. —**fuss'y,** *adj.* unduly particular.

fuss'bud'get *n.* one who fusses about insignificant things.

fus'tian (fus'chən) *n.* **1,** a coarse cotton fabric. **2,** high-flown speech; bombast.

fus'ty (fus'tē) *adj.* **1,** musty; stuffy. **2,** old-fashioned. —**fus'ti·ness,** *n.*

fu'tile (fū'təl) *adj.* **1,** ineffectual. **2,** idle; trifling. —**fu·til'i·ty** (-til'ə-tē) *n.*

fu'ture (fū'chər) *adj.* **1,** yet to come or happen. **2,** relating to later time. —*n.* **1,** times to come. **2,** prospects. —**fu'tur·ism,** *n.* —**future shock,** inability to deal with the rapidity of social and technological change.

fu"tur·is'tic (fū"chər-is'tik) *adj.* anticipating the supposed art forms of the future. —**fu"tur·is'ti·cal·ly,** *adv.*

fu·tu'ri·ty (fū-tyu̇r'ə-tē) *n.* **1,** the future; the state of being yet to come. **2,** a horserace in which the entries are named long in advance.

fuzz (fuz) *n.* **1,** fine, fluffy particles of wool, cotton, etc.; down. **2,** (*Slang*) policeman; the police. —**fuzz'y,** *adj.* —**fuzz'-i·ness,** *n.* —**fuzz box,** an electronic device which gives a fuzzy quality to sound which is fed through it.

-fy (-fī) *suf.* forming verbs meaning: **1,** make, as *simplify,* make simple. **2,** become, as *solidify,* become solid.

G

G, g (jē) the seventh letter of the English alphabet.

g (gē) *n.* **1,** gravity; acceleration of gravity. **2,** a unit of force equal to the force of gravity. **3,** (*Slang*) a grand; one thousand dollars.

gab *v.i.* [**gabbed, gab'bing**] (*Colloq.*) talk

idly; chatter. —*n.* idle talk. —**gab'by**, *adj.* very talkative.

gab'ar·dine" (gab'ər-dēn") *n.* cloth of wool or cotton, similar to serge.

gab'ble (gab'əl) *v.i.* **1,** cackle, as geese. **2,** talk volubly; jabber. —*n.* act or result of gabbling.

gab'fest" *n.* (*Colloq.*) an informal get-together for conversation.

ga'ble (gā'bəl) *n.* the triangular expanse of wall between opposite edges of a sloping roof. —**ga'bled,** *adj.*

gad *n.* a pointed rod; a goad. —*v.i.* [**gad'-ded, -ding**] ramble about idly. —*interj.* a euphemism for God. —**gad'der, gad'a-bout",** *n.* one who travels about aimlessly.

gad'fly" (gad'flī") *n.* a stinging insect annoying to cattle.

gadg'et (gaj'it) *n.* any small device, esp. mechanical. —**gadg"e·teer'** (-ə-tir') *n.* one who makes or collects many gadgets.

gad"o·lin'i·um (gad"ə-lin'ē-əm) *n.* a metallic element of the rare-earth group, no. 64, symbol Gd.

Gael'ic (gā'lik) *adj.* pert. to the Celtic peoples, esp. Irish. —*n.* a language spoken by these peoples.

gaff (gaf) *n.* **1,** a stick with an iron hook, for landing fish. **2,** a spar to extend a sail. **3,** (*Slang*) persistent teasing; expense.

gaffe (gaf) *n.* a social blunder.

gaf'fer (-ər) *n.* **1,** an old man. **2,** a gang boss, esp. in a carnival.

gag *n.* **1,** a thing thrust into the mouth to prevent outcry; hence, restraint of free speech. **2,** (*Colloq.*) a joke. —*v.t.* [**gagged, gag'ging**] put a gag on; silence. —*v.i.* retch.

ga'ga (gä'gä) *adj.* (*Slang*) senseless.

gage (gāj) *n.* **1,** gauge. **2,** anything, as a glove, symbolizing a challenge.

gag'gle (gag'əl) *v.i.* [**-gled, -gling**] cackle. —*n.* a flock of geese.

gai'e·ty (gā'ə-tē) *n.* gayness; merrymaking; brightness.

gai'ly (gā'lē) *adv.* **1,** merrily. **2,** showily.

gain (gān) *v.t.* **1,** obtain (something valued or desired). **2,** acquire by accretion, as added weight. **3,** earn by effort. **4,** reach; arrive at. —*v.i.* **1,** benefit. **2,** make progress. **3,** put on weight. —*n.* **1,** profit. **2,** an increase. —**gain'ful,** *adj.* advantageous.

gain'er (gā'nər) *n.* a dive in which the diver faces forward and makes a backward somersault.

gain'say" (gān'sā") *v.t.* [**-said', -say'ing**] contradict; dispute.

gait (gāt) *n.* manner of running or walking. —**gait'ed,** *adj.* (of a horse) trained to various gaits.

gai'ter (gā'tər) *n.* a cloth or leather covering for the leg or ankle; a spat.

gal *n.* (*Colloq.*) a woman or girl.

ga'la (gā'lə) *n.* a festival. —*adj.* festive.

gal'an·tine (gal'ən-tēn) *n.* a dish of chicken, veal, etc., served cold.

gal'ax·y (gal'ək-sē) *n.* **1,** a luminous band of stars. **2,** (*cap.*) the Milky Way. **3,** an assemblage of splendid persons or things. —**ga·lac'tic** (gə-lak'tik) *adj.*

gale (gāl) *n.* **1,** a stiff wind. **2,** an outburst, as of laughter. **3,** a shrub.

ga·le'na (gə-lē'nə) *n.* a mineral, an important ore of lead and silver.

gal"i·ma'ti·as (gal"ə-mā'shē-əs) *n.* incoherent or nonsensical talk.

gall (gâl) *n.* **1,** a bitter secretion of the liver; bile. **2,** rancor. **3,** (*Slang*) impudence. **4,** a sore made by chafing. **5,** a lump made by insects on trees, esp. oaks. —*v.t. & i.* **1,** make sore by rubbing. **2,** vex; annoy. —**gall bladder,** a sac in which the bile is stored.

gal'lant (gal'ənt) *adj.* **1,** brave; chivalrous. **2,** honorable; noble. **3,** (gə-länt') courtly; attentive to women. —*n.* (gə-länt') **1,** a dashing man of fashion. **2,** a ladies' man. —**gal'lant·ry** (-trē) *n.*

gal'le·on (gal'ē-ən) *n.* a former Span. sailing vessel.

gal'ler·y (gal'ə-rē) *n.* **1,** a long narrow passage often open at one side; a veranda. **2,** a room or building for the exhibition of works of art. **3,** a balcony, as in a theater.

gal'ley (gal'ē) *n.* **1,** an ancient seagoing vessel propelled by oars and sails. **2,** a rowboat larger than a gig. **3,** the kitchen of a ship. **4,** an oblong, shallow tray to hold set-up type; a proof printed from this type.

gal'liard (gal'yərd) *n.* a lively dance.

Gal'lic (gal'ik) *adj.* pert. to the Gauls; French.

Gal'li·cism (gal'ə-siz-əm) *n.* **1,** a French idiom. **2,** a French word or phrase used in another language.

gal'li·um (gal'ē-əm) *n.* a rare metallic element, no. 31, symbol Ga.

gal'li·vant (gal'i-vant) *v.i.* seek pleasure frivolously; gad about.

gal'lon (gal'ən) *n.* a measure of capacity; four quarts.

gal'lop (gal'əp) *n.* a rapid, springing gait, esp. of a horse. —*v.t.* cause to gallop. —*v.i.* **1,** run or ride at a gallop. **2,** progress rapidly.

gal'lows (gal'ōz) *n.* a structure (*tree*) with two upright posts and a crossbar at the top, for hanging criminals.

gall'stone" (gâl'stōn") *n.* a stony mass formed in the gall bladder.

gal′lus·es (gal′ə-siz) *n.pl.* suspenders.

ga·loot′ (gə-loot′) *n.* (*Slang*) a clumsy or foolish fellow; yokel.

gal′op (gal′əp) *n.* 1, a lively dance. 2, the music for it.

ga·lore′ (gə-lôr′) *adj. & adv.* in plenty; in abundance.

ga·losh′ (gə-losh′) *n.* (usu. *pl.*) a high overshoe.

gal·van′ic (gal-van′ik) *adj.* 1, pert. to a current of electricity. 2, stimulating; electric; spasmodic. —**gal·van′i·cal·ly,** *adv.*

gal′va·nism (gal′və-niz-əm) *n.* production of electricity by chemical action.

gal′va·nize″ (gal′və-nīz″) *v.t.* 1, shock or stimulate, as by electricity. 2, plate or coat with metal by means of electricity. —**galvanized iron,** iron sheeting plated with zinc.

gal″va·nom′e·ter (gal″və-nom′ə-tər) *n.* an instrument for detecting and measuring the strength and direction of an electric current.

gam *n.* 1, a school of whales. 2, (*Slang*) the human leg.

gam′bit *n.* 1, in chess, an opening that loses a pawn or other piece but gains positional advantage. 2, any apparent sacrifice in expectation of later gain.

gam′ble (gam′bəl) *v.i.* 1, risk money on a game of chance. 2, hazard something of value on an uncertain event. —*v.t.* risk; (with *away*) lose by gambling. —*n.* a risk. —**gam′bler,** *n.* —**gam′bling,** *n.*

gam·boge′ (gam-bōj′) *n.* a resin used as a yellow pigment or medicine.

gam′bol (gam′bəl) *v.i.* leap or skip about in frolic. —*n.* frolic.

gam′brel (gam′brəl) *n.* a joint in the hind leg of a horse. —**gambrel roof,** a roof in two sections of different slope, the outer being steeper.

game (gām) *n.* 1, play; amusement. 2, a contest played according to rules; a division of a contest; a winning score. 3, a plan, scheme, or enterprise. 4, wild animals, birds, or fish hunted for food or sport. —*adj.* (*Slang*) 1, plucky. 2, willing. 3, lame. —*v.t. & i.* play games; gamble. —**game′ness,** *n.* —**game′ster** (-stər) *n.* a gambler. —**game theory,** the application of mathematical laws of probability to finding the best strategy for winning at games, war, politics, etc.

game′cock″ *n.* a cock bred to fight in exhibitions.

game′keep″er *n.* a private game warden.

games′man·ship (gāmz′mən-ship) *n.* the art of winning games, esp. by deception or trickery.

gam′ete (gam′ēt) *n.* (*Biol.*) a cell that unites with another for reproduction.

gam′in *n.* a neglected child; street urchin. —**gam′ine** (ga′mēn) *n.fem.*

gam′ing (gā′ming) *n.* the playing of a game for money.

gam′ma (gam′ə) *n.* the third letter of the Greek alphabet (Γ, γ). —**gamma glob′u·lin** (glob′yə-lin) a drug formerly used against infantile paralysis, often called **G.G.** —**gamma rays,** rays similar to x-rays, emitted by radioactive elements.

gam′mon (gam′ən) *n.* 1, a smoked ham. 2, trickery. 3, nonsense. 4, in backgammon, a won game of double value. —*v.t.* deceive.

gam′ut (gam′ət) *n.* 1, the whole range of accepted musical tones. 2, range; scope.

gam′y (gā′mē) *adj.* [-**i·er**, -**i·est**] 1, having the flavor of game. 2, spirited; plucky. 3, racy; off-color.

gan′der (gan′dər) *n.* 1, the male goose. 2, (*Slang*) a careful look.

gang *n.* a company of persons acting or going about together. —*v.i.* (with *up*) join forces against.

gang′land″ *adj.* pert. to the criminal underworld, esp. organized crime.

gan′gling (gang′gling) *adj.* awkwardly tall and thin. Also, **gan′gly** (-glē). —**gan′gle** (-gəl) *v.i.*

gan′gli·on (gang′glē-ən) *n.* 1, a knot on a nerve from which nerve fibers radiate. 2, a mass of gray matter in the central nervous system.

gang′plank″ *n.* a movable ramp to a ship.

gan′grene (gang′grēn) *n.* the rotting away of body tissue, due to stoppage of nourishment. —**gan′gre·nous,** *adj.*

gang′ster (gang′stər) *n.* a member of a lawless gang; a racketeer.

gang′way″ (gang′wā″) *n.* a passageway into or out of an enclosed space. —*interj.* stand aside! make way!

gan′net (gan′ət) *n.* a large sea bird.

gant′let (gànt′lət) *n.* 1, a form of punishment or hazing in which the victim runs between two lanes of men who strike him as he passes. 2, a series of unpleasant things or events. 3, gauntlet.

gan′try (gan′trē) *n.* a supporting structure, as a framework or bridge.

gaol (jāl) *n. & v.t.* (*Brit.*) jail.

gap *n.* 1, an opening; a vacant space. 2, a notch in a mountain ridge. 3, a break in continuity.

gape (gāp) *v.i.* 1, open the mouth wide; yawn. 2, be wide open. 3, look amazed. —*n.* breach; gap.

gar (gär) *n.* a fish with a long, sharp snout.

ga·rage' (gə-räzh') *n.* a building where motor vehicles are stored or repaired. —*v.t.* put, keep, or service in a garage. —**garage sale,** a personal sale of used merchandise, clothing, etc.

Gar'and rifle (gar'ənd) a kind of automatic repeating rifle.

garb (gärb) *n.* clothes, esp of a distinctive calling or period; attire. —*v.t.* clothe.

gar'bage (gär'bij) *n.* **1,** waste matter from a kitchen; refuse. **2,** a worthless assortment; nonsense.

gar·ban'zo (gär-ban'zō) *n.* the chickpea.

gar'ble (gär'bəl) *v.t.* twist, in order to misrepresent; distort; misquote.

gar'den (gär'dən) *n.* **1,** a plot of ground where flowers, fruits, or vegetables are grown. **2,** a delightful spot. —*v.i.* lay out or work in a garden. —**gar'den·er,** *n.* one who tends a garden, esp. one employed to do so. —**garden variety,** common; regular.

gar·de'nia (gär-dē'nyə) *n.* the white or yellow flower of a tropical shrub.

Gar·gan'tu·an (gär-gan'tū-ən) *adj.* enormous; gigantic.

gar'gle (gär'gəl) *v.i.* rinse the throat with medicinal liquid. —*n.* such a liquid.

gar'goyle (gär'goil) *n.* (*Archit.*) a grotesque stone image.

gar'ish (gar'ish) *adj.* showy; overdecorated. —**gar'ish·ness,** *n.*

gar'land (gär'lənd) *n.* **1,** a wreath of flowers or leaves. **2,** a literary anthology. —*v.t.* deck with garlands.

gar'lic (gär'lik) *n.* a bulb with a strong onionlike flavor. —**gar'lick·y,** *adj.*

gar'ment (gär'mənt) *n.* any article of clothing.

gar'ner (gär'nər) *v.t.* reap, gather, and store, as in a granary; collect.

gar'net (gär'nit) *n.* a clear deep-red stone, used as a gem.

gar'nish (gär'nish) *n.* a decoration, esp. for food. —*v.t.* **1,** adorn. **2,** garnishee. —**gar'nish·ment,** *n.*

gar"nish·ee' (gär"ni-shē') *v.t.* **[-eed'** (-ēd'), **-ee'ing]** (*Law*) attach a defendant's property which is in the possession of a third party, esp. wages. —*n.* a defendant whose property is attached.

gar'ni·ture (gär'ni-chər) *n.* decoration; trimming.

gar'ret (gar'ət) *n.* an attic.

gar'ri·son (gar'ə-sən) *n.* troops stationed in a fort or fortified town. —*v.t.* provide with or occupy as a garrison.

gar·rote' (gə-rōt') *v.t.* kill by strangulation.

gar·ru'li·ty (gə-roo'lə-tē) *n.* quality of being garrulous.

gar'ru·lous (gar'yə-ləs) *adj.* given to talking too much. —**gar'ru·lous·ness,** *n.*

gar'ter (gär'tər) *n.* a band or other device to keep up a stocking. —**garter snake,** a common and harmless striped snake.

gas *n.* **1,** any elastic, airlike fluid capable of indefinite expansion. **2,** such fluids used as anesthetic, fuel, etc. **3,** noxious fumes. **4,** (*Colloq.*) gasoline. —*v.i.* **[gassed, gas'sing]** (*Slang*) converse idly but at length. —*v.t.* poison with gas. —**gas'i·fy** (-i-fī) *v.t.* convert into gas. —**gas chamber,** a room in which a person is executed with gas. —**gas mask,** a mask worn for protection against poison gas. —**natural gas,** a mixture of gaseous hydrocarbons found in deposits in the earth often associated with petroleum, used as a fuel.

gas"con·ade' (gas"kə-nād') *n.* boastful talk.

gas'e·ous (-ē-əs) *adj.* of or like gas.

gash *n.* a deep slash or cut. —*v.t.* cut deeply.

gas'ket (gas'kit) *n.* a strip of material used to seal a joint; a washer.

gas'o·line (gas'ə-lēn") *n.* an inflammable liquid distilled from petroleum, used esp. as a motor fuel. Also, **gas'o·lene".**

gasp (gàsp) *n.* a convulsive catching of the breath. —*v.i.* labor for breath painfully. —*v.t.* utter with quick, short breaths. —**last gasp,** dying breath; final effort.

gas'sy (gas'ē) *adj.* **1,** full of or like gas. **2,** (*Colloq.*) talkative; boastful.

gas'tric (gas'trik) *adj.* pert. to the stomach. —**gas·tri'tis** (-trī'tis) *n.* inflammation of the stomach.

gas·tro- (gas-trō) *pref.* of or pert. to the stomach.

gas·tron'o·my (gas-tron'ə-mē) *n.* the art of preparing good food. —**gas'tro·nome** (-trə-nōm)*n.* —**gas"tro·nom'ic**(-trə-nom'ik) *adj.* —**gas"tro·nom'i·cal·ly,** *adv.*

gat *n.* (*Slang*) a pistol.

gate (gāt) *n.* **1,** an opening, esp. in a fence, hedge, or wall, for entrance and exit; a movable barrier at such an opening. **2,** an electronic device used in computers which emits a signal when certain input conditions are met. **3,** (*Slang*) the money received from sale of admission tickets. **4,** (*Slang*) dismissal.

gate'crash"er *n.* one who gains admission to a party, etc., without an invitation, or without paying.

gate'way" *n.* a means of access.

gath'er (gath'ər) *v.t.* **1,** bring together; assemble. **2,** cull; pick. **3,** acquire; gain;

amass. **4,** recover; marshal. **5,** infer. **6,** draw (cloth) into folds; pleat. —v.i. **1,** congregate. **2,** increase. **3,** come to a head, as a boil. —n. a fold or pleat in cloth. —**gath′-er·ing,** n. an assemblage.

Gat′ling gun an early type of machine gun having a cluster of barrels.

gauche (gōsh) adj. socially awkward. —**gau′che·rie** (gō′shə-rè) n.

Gau′cho (gow′chō) n. a cowboy of South America.

gaud′y (gâ′dè) adj. **1,** gay; bright. **2,** showy without taste. —**gaud′i·ness,** n.

gauge (gāj) n. **1,** a standard of measurement. **2,** a graduated instrument for measuring. **3,** an instrument for measuring flow. —v.t. **1,** measure. **2,** estimate. Also, **gage.**

gaunt (gânt) adj. thin; haggard. —**gaunt′-ness,** n.

gaunt′let (gânt′lət) n. **1,** a glove with a long, wide cuff. **2,** a challenge. **3,** a course beset by punishing or afflicting agencies. Also, **gant′let.**

gauss (gows) n. (Physics) a unit of magnetic induction.

gauze (gâz) n. a very thin, porous fabric of silk, cotton, wire, etc.

gave (gāv) v. pret. of give.

gav′el (gav′əl) n. a small mallet, used by a chairman or auctioneer.

ga·votte′ (gə-vot′) n. a dance similar to the minuet, but livelier.

gawk (gâk) n. an awkward fellow. —v.i. stare stupidly. —**gawk′y,** adj. clownish; clumsy.

gay (gā) adj. **1,** high-spirited; merry. **2,** bright; colorful; showy. **3,** dissipated; loose. **4,** homosexual. —n. a homosexual. —**gay′-e·ty** (-ə-tè) n. —**gay′ness,** n.

gaze (gāz) n. a fixed, intent look. —v.i. look at intently.

ga·ze′bo (gə-zē′bō) n. [pl. -bos or -boes] a summerhouse or garden pavilion.

ga·zelle′ (gə-zel′) n. a small, graceful antelope.

ga·zette′ (gə-zet′) n. **1,** a newspaper. **2,** an official government journal. —v.t. publish in such a journal.

gaz″et·teer′ (gaz″ə-tir′) n. a dictionary of geographical names.

gear (gir) n. **1,** equipment; apparatus; tools. **2,** a harness, as for horses, and its appurtenances. **3,** a wheel or part that engages another part of a machine, as by meshing teeth; a working unit of a machine, as steering gear. **4,** the adjustment of parts of a machine, with respect to speed or efficiency, as in high gear, in gear. —v.t. **1,** equip; harness. **2,** adjust the operation or speed of, with gears. —**gear′shift″,** n. a

mechanism for power transmission, as in an automobile.

geck′o (gek′ō) n. a small nocturnal lizard.

gee (jē) v.t., v.i. & interj. turn or move to the right. —v.i. (Colloq.) suit; fit. —interj. an expletive of mild feeling.

geek (gēk) n. (Slang) a gullible or feeble-minded person.

geese (gēs) n. pl. of goose.

gee′zer (gē′zər) n. (Slang) a queer fellow.

ge·fil′te fish (gə-fil′tə) chopped fish mixed with egg and seasonings, and cooked in broth.

Ge·hen′na (gi-hen′ə) n. a fiery place; hell.

Gei′ger counter (gī′gər) a device for detecting radioactivity.

gei′sha (gā′shə) n. a Japanese girl skilled in the art of entertaining people, esp. men.

gel (jel) n. (Chem.) a jellylike or solid material formed by the coagulation of a colloidal solution. —v.i. [gelled, gell′ing] form or become a gel.

gel′a·tin (jel′ə-tin) n. a granular transparent substance that congeals when cold; jelly. —**ge·lat′i·nous** (jə-lat′i-nəs) adj.

geld v.t. castrate. —**geld′ing,** n. a castrated animal, esp. a horse.

gel′id (jel′id) adj. very cold; icy. —**ge·lid′i·ty, gel′id·ness,** n.

gem (jem) n. **1,** a precious stone. **2,** an object of great beauty or worth.

gem′i·nate (jem′ə-nət) adj. in pairs, coupled. —v.t. & i. (-nāt″) double. —**gem″-i·na′tion,** n.

Gem′i·ni″ (jem′ə-nī″) n. a constellation, the Twins (see zodiac).

gems′bok (gemz′bok) n. a large straight-horned antelope of So. Afr.

ge·mut′lich (gə-müt′lish) adj. (Ger.) intimate; cheerful; warmhearted. —**ge·mut′-lich·keit″** (-kīt″) n.

gen′darme (zhän′därm) n. (Fr.) a policeman.

gen′der (jen′dər) n. in grammar, the classification as masculine, feminine, or neuter.

gene (jēn) n. (Biol.) an element in the germ cell, concerned with the transmission of hereditary characteristics.

ge″ne·al′o·gy (jē″nè-al′ə-jè) n. record of descent from an ancestor; pedigree. —**ge″ne·a·log′i·cal,** adj. —**ge″ne·al′o·gist,** n. one whose vocation is tracing pedigrees.

gen′er·a (jen′ə-rə) n. pl. of genus.

gen′er·al (jen′ər-əl) adj. **1,** pert. or applicable to all or most of an entire class or category; universal; not limited in scope. **2,** widespread. **3,** not specific or detailed; vague; indefinite. **4,** usual; ordinary. **5,** chief;

highest-ranking. —*n.* **1,** the highest-ranking army officer. **2,** any officer ranking above a colonel. **3,** the masses; the populace. —**gen′er·al·ship,** *n.* —**General Assembly,** an organ of the United Nations composed of all member nations, each of which has one vote. —**general delivery,** a department of a post office that holds mail until picked up; mail sent to that department. —**general practitioner,** a medical doctor not limiting his practice to a specialty. Also, **GP.**

gen″er·al·is′si·mo″ (jen″ər-ə-lis′i-mō″) *n.* a supreme military commander.

gen′er·al′i·ty (jen″ər-al′ə-tē) *n.* **1,** the majority. **2,** a statement that is essentially true but not specific.

gen′er·al·ize″ (jen′ər-ə-līz″) *v.i.* draw conclusions from varied evidence. —*v.t.* consider as or arrange by classes. —**gen″er·al·i·za′tion,** *n.*

gen′er·ate″ (jen′ə-rāt″) *v.t.* **1,** bring into life. **2,** produce; form. —**gen′er·a″tive,** *adj.*

gen″er·a′tion (jen″ə-rā′shən) *n.* **1,** production by natural or artificial means. **2,** the average difference in age between parent and child, usually counted as 30 years; each ancestor in a line of descent. **3,** all persons living at the same time. **4,** (*pl.*) descendants. —**generation gap,** (*Colloq.*) the difference in attitudes, mores, etc., between persons of different generations, esp. between parents and their children.

gen′er·a″tor (jen′ə-rā″tər) *n.* an apparatus for producing gas, steam, or electricity.

ge·ner′ic (ji-ner′ik) *adj.* **1,** pert. to a genus or class. **2,** general, not specific. —**ge·ner′i·cal·ly,** *adv.*

gen″er·os′i·ty (jen″ə-ros′ə-tē) *n.* quality of being generous; liberality.

gen′er·ous (jen′ər-əs) *adj.* **1,** free in giving; liberal. **2,** abundant. **3,** not mean or prejudiced.

gen′e·sis (jen′ə-sis) *n.* [*pl.* **-ses″** (-sēz″)] **1,** the origin of anything. **2,** (*cap.*) the first book of the Old Testament.

ge·net′ics (ji-net′iks) *n. pl.* the study of the evolution of species and of heredity. —**ge·net′ic,** *adj.* —**ge·net′i·cal·ly,** *adv.*

Ge·ne′va convention (jə-nē′və) an international agreement dealing with the treatment of sick, wounded, and prisoners, in time of war.

gen′ial (jēn′yəl) *adj.* **1,** friendly and kindly in manner; cordial; jovial. **2,** favorable to growth or comfort. —**ge″ni·al′i·ty** (jē″nē-al′ə-tē) *n.*

ge′nie (jē′nē) *n.* a mythical spirit having power to perform miraculous deeds.

gen′i·tal (jen′ə-təl) *adj.* pert. to reproduction of animals. —*n.* (*pl.*) [also, **gen″i·ta′li·a** (jen″ə-tā′lē-ə)] the organs of reproduction.

gen′i·tive (jen′ə-tiv) *n.* the grammatical case expressing possession or source; the possessive.

gen′ius (jēn′yəs) *n.* **1,** the guiding spirit of a person or place. **2,** natural fitness; aptitude; talent; bent. **3,** exceptional mental and creative power. **4,** a person with such power.

gen′o·cide″ (jen′ə-sīd″) *n.* deliberate extermination of an entire people.

gen′re (zhän′rə) *n.* **1,** variety, type. **2,** in painting, portrayal of scenes from everyday life.

gent (jent) *n.* (*Colloq.*) gentleman.

gen·teel′ (jen-tēl′) *adj.* affectedly refined. —**gen·teel′ness,** *n.*

gen′tian (jen′shən) *n.* an herb bearing a blue flower.

gen′tile (jen′tīl) *n.* **1,** (*Bible*) a person not a Jew. **2,** in respect to any religious group, an outsider.

gen·til′i·ty (jen-til′ə-tē) *n.* **1,** the state of being well-born or well-bred; all persons of good or noble birth. **2,** gentleness; softness.

gen′tle (jen′təl) *adj.* **1,** mild in manner or disposition; tender; peaceful; tame. **2,** not rough or harsh; kind. **3,** of good birth; belonging to the gentry. —*v.t.* (*Colloq.*) soften; subdue. —**gen′tle·ness,** *n.* —**gentle sex,** women.

gen′tle·folk″ *n.pl.* persons of good breeding.

gen′tle·man (jen′təl-mən) *n.* [*pl.* **-men** (-mən)] **1,** a man of good birth. **2,** an honorable man of fine feelings. **3,** (*pl.*) men; sirs. —**gen′tle·man·ly,** *adj.* refined; well-behaved. —**gen′tle·wom″an,** *n.fem.* —**gentlemen's agreement,** an agreement or promise binding as a matter of honor, but not of law.

gen′try (jen′trē) *n.* **1,** people of good breeding and, usually, wealth. **2,** people of a particular class or group.

gen′u·flect″ (jen′ū-flekt″) *v.i.* bend the knee, esp. in worship. —**gen″u·flec′tion, gen″u·flex′ion,** *n.*

gen′u·ine (jen′yū-in) *adj.* **1,** not counterfeit; authentic. **2,** real; sincere. —**gen′u·ine·ness,** *n.*

ge′nus (jē′nəs) *n.* [*pl.* **gen′er·a** (jen′ə-rə)] (*Biol.*) a group of animals or plants having close relationship.

-gen·y (jə-nē) *suf.* denoting origin.

ge·o- (jē-ə; -ō) *pref.* signifying earth.

ge′ode (jē′ōd) *n.* (*Geol.*) a hollow stone formed in concentric layers, often lined with crystals.

ge″o·des′ic (jē″ə-dē′sik) *adj.* pert. to the geometry of curved surfaces. —*n.* a line which is the shortest distance between its tèrminal points. —**geodesic dome,** a domed structure formed of interlocking polygons.

ge·od'e·sy (jē-od'ə-sē) *n.* the science of measuring the shape and area of the earth. —**ge"o·det'ic** (jē"ə-det'ik) *adj.*

ge·og'ra·phy (jē-og'rə-fē) *n.* the science that deals with the earth, its plants and animals, climate, population, industries, etc. —**ge·og'ra·pher,** *n.* —**ge"o·graph'i·cal,** *adj.*

ge·ol'o·gy (jē-ol'ə-jē) *n.* the science that deals with the history of the earth and its changes, esp. as recorded in its rocks. —**ge"o·log'i·cal,** *adj.* —**ge·ol'o·gist,** *n.*

ge·om'e·try (jē-om'ə-trē) *n.* that branch of mathematics dealing with the relations and measurements of lines, angles, surfaces, and solids. —**ge"o·met'ric** (jē"ə-met'rik), **ge"o·met'ri·cal,** *adj.* —**ge·om"e·tri'cian** (-trish'ən) *n.* —**geometric progression** or **series,** a series of numbers or terms, each of which is a constant multiple of the one preceding it, as 1, 2, 4, 8, etc.

ge"o·phys'ics (jē"ō-fiz'iks) *n.* the study of the structure of the earth and the physical forces that affect it.

ge"o·pol'i·tics (jē"ō-pol'ə-tiks) *n.* the study or application of political science in the light of geographical influences and objectives.

Geor'gian (jôr'jən) *adj.* pert. to the period (1714–1830) of the reigns of George I to George IV of England.

ge·ra'ni·um (jə-rā'nē-əm) *n.* **1,** a wild flower with pinkish-blue blossoms. **2,** a cultivated plant with large heads of white, pink, or red flowers.

ger'bil (jēr'bəl) *n.* a small burrowing rodent of Asia and Africa.

ger"i·at'rics (jer"ē-at'riks) *n.* the study and treatment of diseases attendant on old age.

germ (jērm) *n.* **1,** a microbe. **2,** the earliest stage of an organism. **3,** source; origin. —**germ cell,** a cell having the function of reproduction.

Ger'man (jēr'mən) *adj.* pert. to Germany, its people, or language. —*n.* a native, or the language, of Germany. —**Ger·man'ic** (-man'ik) *adj.* —**German measles,** a contagious disease resembling measles; rubella. —**German silver,** an alloy of copper, zinc, and nickel.

ger·mane' (jer-mān') *adj.* closely allied; relevant.

ger·ma'ni·um (jər-mā'nē-əm) *n.* a rare metallic element, no. 32, symbol Ge.

ger'mi·cide" (jēr'mi-sīd") *n.* a substance to destroy germs. —**ger'mi·cid'al,** *adj.*

ger'mi·nal (jēr'mə-nəl) *adj.* sprouting; budding.

ger'mi·nate" (jēr'mə-nāt") *v.i.* begin to grow; sprout. —**ger"mi·na'tion,** *n.*

ger"on·tol'o·gy (jer"ən-tol'ə-jē) *n.* the science that deals with the phenomena of old age.

ger'ry·man"der (ger'ē-man"dər; jer'-) *v.t.* change the boundaries of election districts to give one political party an unfair advantage.

ger'und (jer'ənd) *n.* a noun formed from a verb and ending in -*ing*.

ges'so (jes'ō) *n.* a preparation used as a base for painting.

gest (jest) *n.* **1,** a tale of adventure; a romance. **2,** deed; exploit. Also, **geste.**

ge·stalt' (gə-shtält') *n.* a structure (psychological, physical, or biological) having properties not derivable from the sum of its parts.

Ge·sta'po (gə-stä'pō) *n.* the state police of Nazi Germany.

ges'tate (jes'tāt) *v.t.* carry in the womb during pregnancy. —**ges·ta'tion,** *n.* pregnancy.

ges·tic'u·late" (jes-tik'yə-lāt") *v.i.* make gestures to convey meaning. —**ges·tic"u·la'tion,** *n.*

ges'ture (jes'chər) *n.* **1,** a movement of head or limbs to convey feeling or to emphasize or illustrate. **2,** something said or done for effect only. —*v.i.* make gestures.

Ge·sund'heit" (gə-zûnt'hīt") *interj.* (*Ger.*) your health!: said as a toast, or to a person who has sneezed.

get *v.t.* [**got, got** or **got'ten, get'ting**] **1,** acquire possession of, esp. by one's own efforts; obtain; receive. **2,** fetch. **3,** grasp; understand. **4,** cause to be or be done; cause to be; induce. **5,** produce; beget. —*v.i.* **1,** cause oneself to be or become; become. **2,** arrive. —*n.* offspring; a litter. —**get away (with),** *n.* escape (the consequences of). —**get back (at),** (*Slang*) obtain revenge (upon). —**get lost,** (*Slang*) go away! —**get off, 1,** depart. **2,** escape punishment. —**get on, 1,** progress; proceed; succeed. **2,** grow older. —**get through (to),** reach; establish communication with, esp. by telephone. —**get up, 1,** arise. **2,** assemble. —**get with (it),** (*Slang*) be or become up to date.

get'a·way" *n.* (*Slang*) escape.

get-'up *n.* (*Colloq.*) costume; manner of dress.

gew'gaw" (gū'gä") *n.* a piece of minor jewelry; bauble; plaything.

gey'ser (gī'zər) *n.* a hot spring that periodically spouts hot water and steam.

ghast'ly (gàst'lē) *adj.* **1,** very pale; haggard. **2,** morally shocking. —**ghast'li·ness,** *n.*

gher'kin (gĕr'kin) n. a small cucumber used for pickles.

ghet'to (get'ō) n. [pl. **-tos**] 1, the Jewish quarter in a city. 2, any ethnic quarter. 3, a slum.

ghost (gōst) n. 1, a disembodied human spirit, esp. such a spirit thought of as returning to haunt the living; a specter. 2, a mere shadow; a glimmering. —**ghost'ly,** adj. like a ghost. —**ghost writer,** an author for whose work another receives credit.

ghoul (gool) n. 1, an imaginary spirit who preys on the dead. 2, a grave robber. —**ghoul'ish,** adj.

G.I. abbr. Government Issue; (Slang) a soldier in the U.S. Army.

gi'ant (jī'ənt) n. 1, an imaginary being of superhuman size. 2, a person, animal, plant, or thing of great size. —adj. huge. —**gi'-ant·ess,** n.fem.

gib'ber (jib'ər) v.i. talk nonsense; babble.

gib'ber·ish (jib'ər-ish) n. inarticulate talk; nonsense.

gib'bet (jib'ət) n. a gallows. —v.t. 1, execute by hanging. 2, expose to ridicule, etc.

gib'bon (gib'ən) n. a small ape.

gib'bous (gib'əs) adj. convex, as the moon when more than half and less than full.

gibe (jīb) v.t. & i. mock; jeer; taunt. —n. a taunt.

gib'lets (jib'ləts) n.pl. the gizzard, liver, and heart of poultry.

gib'son (gib'sən) n. a cocktail of gin and vermouth with pearl onions.

gid'dy (gid'ē) adj. 1, dizzy. 2, causing dizziness. 3, frivolous. —**gid'di·ness,** n.

gift n. 1, something given; a donation; a present. 2, the right or power to give. 3, a natural talent. —**gift'ed,** adj. endowed with unusual talent.

gig n. 1, a light, two-wheeled carriage. 2, a ship's boat. 3, any fancy, unusual hairdo. 4, (Music) a playing engagement, as a concert.

gi·gan'tic (jī-gan'tik) adj. huge; enormous. —**gi·gan'ti·cal·ly,** adv.

gi·gan'tism (jī-gan'tiz-əm) n. abnormal increase in size of an organism or any of its parts.

gig'gle (gig'əl) n. a silly, half-suppressed laugh. —v.i. so laugh.

gig'o·lo (jig'ə-lō″) n. [pl. **-los**″] a man who, for pay, acts as an escort.

gig'ot (jig'ət) n. 1, a puffed sleeve. 2, a leg of mutton.

gigue (zhēg) n. (Fr.) a jig.

Gi'la monster (hē'lə) a large poisonous lizard of the American Southwest.

gild v.t. 1, overlay or coat with gold. 2, give a bright but misleading appearance to.

gild'ing n. 1, superficial or simulated gold. 2, material for gilding, as gold leaf.

gill (gil) n. 1, the breathing organ of fish. 2, (jil) a liquid measure, one-fourth of a pint.

gil'ly·flow″er (jil'ē-flow″ər) n. 1, a cultivated flower-bearing plant. 2, a kind of apple.

gilt n. 1, gilding, esp. with an imitation of gold. 2, a young sow. —adj. gilded; imitative of gold.

gilt-'edged″ adj. 1, having gilded edges. 2, of highest quality.

gim'bals (jim'bəlz) n.pl. rings used for suspending anything, as a mariner's compass, so that it will remain level at all times.

gim'crack″ (jim'krak″) n. an intricate but useless device or ornament; a gewgaw.

gim'let (gim'lit) n. 1, a hand tool for boring small holes. 2, a cocktail of vodka or gin and lime juice.

gim'mick (gim'ik) n. 1, any small, concealed device used for trickery, as by a magician. 2, any means of tricking the unwary, as a joker in a contract. 3, an inducement, as a premium, offered to make a sale.

gimp n. 1, a braid used for trimming. 2, one who limps; a cripple. —v.i. limp.

gin (jin) n. 1, an uncolored alcoholic liquor, distilled from grain. 2, a machine for separating the seeds from cotton. 3, a snare; trap. 4, [also, **gin rummy**] a card game for two. —v.t. put (cotton) through a gin.

gin'ger (jin'jər) n. 1, a tropical herb with a hot, spicy root, used in cooking and in medicine. 2, a tawny, yellowish color. 3, (Colloq.) vigor; vivacity.

gin'ger·bread″ (jin'jər-bred″) n. 1, a cake flavored with ginger. 2, excessively fancy decoration, in architecture.

gin'ger·ly (jin'jər-lē) adv. with extreme caution. —adj. slow and timid. —**gin'ger·li·ness,** n.

gin'ger·snap″ n. a thin brittle cookie flavored with ginger.

ging'ham (ging'əm) n. a cotton dress fabric woven in checks, plaids, or stripes.

gin·gi·vi'tis (jin-jə-vī'tis) n. inflammation of the gums.

gink'go (ging'kō) n. a tree with fan-shaped leaves, native to Japan and China.

gin'seng (jin'seng) n. a herb or shrub whose aromatic root is used in medicine.

gip'sy (jip'sē) n. gypsy.

gi·raffe' (jə-raf') n. an Afr. ruminant animal with extremely long neck and legs.

gird (gėrd) *v.t.* [*pret.* & *p.p.* **girt** or **gird'-ed**] **1,** confine with a belt; make fast by binding. **2,** encircle. **3,** prepare for action; equip.

gird'er (gėr'dər) *n.* a main supporting beam, esp. of steel.

gir'dle (gėr'dəl) *n.* **1,** a sash or belt for the waist. **2,** an elastic undergarment to support the abdomen and shape the body. **3,** a ring around a tree trunk. —*v.t.* bind; encircle.

girl (gėrl) *n.* **1,** a young woman or female child. **2,** a maidservant. **3,** (*Colloq.*) sweetheart. —**girl'hood"**, —**girl'ish**, *adj.* —**girl Friday,** a female assistant.

girl'friend" *n.* a female companion, sweetheart, or lover.

Girl Guide a member of the Girl Guides, an association of girls, similar to the Girl Scouts.

Girl Scout a member of the Girl Scouts, an association of girls 8 to about 18 years old.

girth (gėrth) *n.* **1,** a band around an animal's body to secure a saddle or load. **2,** the distance around anything cylindrical; circumference.

gis'mo (gis'mō) *n.* gizmo.

gist (jist) *n.* the essence or substance of a matter; pith.

give (giv) *v.t.* [**gave** (gāv), **giv'en**, **giv'-ing**] **1,** bestow; make a present of; donate. **2,** spend or pay, as money; exchange. **3,** supply; deliver; convey. **4,** (with *up*) yield; concede. **5,** utter; impart. —*v.i.* **1,** bestow alms. **2,** (usually with *in* or *up*) yield; surrender. **3,** afford an opening. —*n.* lack of resistance; elasticity. —**give off,** exude, emit, or produce. —**give way, 1,** fall back. **2,** surrender; give in.

give-'and-take' *n.* **1,** cooperative dealing by mutual concession and compromise. **2,** bantering conversation.

give'a·way" (giv'ə-wā") *n.* **1,** an unintentional betrayal; a revelation. **2,** something free; a premium; a bargain. —*adj.* being a giveaway.

giv'en (giv'ən) *adj.* **1,** addicted; inclined. **2,** granted; agreed. **3,** (of a name) first, not the surname.

giz'mo (giz'mō) *n.* gadget; contraption.

giz'zard (giz'ərd) *n.* the second stomach of a bird; a similar digestive organ in insects and earthworms.

gla'brous (glā'brəs) *adj.* (*Biol.*) devoid of hair or down; smooth.

gla·cé' (glä-sā') *adj.* **1,** glossy; smooth. **2,** covered with a hard, shiny sugar coating.

gla'cial (glā'shəl) *adj.* pert. to ice or glaciers.

gla'ci·ate (glā'shē-āt) *v.t.* **1,** cover with ice. **2,** (*Slang*) freeze (socially).

gla'cier (glā'shər) *n.* a slowly flowing mass or river of ice.

glad *adj.* [**glad'der, -dest**] **1,** joyful; bright; cheerful. **2,** joyous. —**glad'den** (-ən) *v.t.* & *i.* cause to be, or become, glad. —**glad'-ness,** *n.*

glade (glād) *n.* a clear space in a forest.

glad'i·a"tor (glad'ē-ā"tər) *n.* in ancient Rome, a man who fought in the arena with men or wild beasts.

glad"i·o'lus (glad"ē-ō'ləs) *n.* a bulbous plant with a tall spike of large flowers. Also, **glad"i·o'la** (-lə).

glad'some (glad'səm) *adj.* **1,** glad. **2,** causing gladness. —**glad'some·ness,** *n.*

glad'stone" bag a suitcase that opens into two equal compartments.

glair (glâr) *n.* the white of egg, used for sizing.

glam'our (glam'ər) *n.* alluring charm. Also, **glam'or.** —**glam'or·ize,** *v.t.* —**glam'or·ous,** *adj.*

glance (gläns) *n.* a brief, cursory look. —*v.i.* **1,** flash; gleam. **2,** take a hasty look. **3,** strike and be deflected.

gland *n.* an organ that secretes a substance to be used in the body. —**glan'du·lar** (glan'dyə-lər) *adj.*

glan'ders (glan'dərz) *n.* a contagious disease of horses.

glans (glanz) *n.* [*pl.* **glan'des** (glan'dēz)] the head of the penis or of the clitoris.

glare (glâr) *n.* **1,** a dazzling light. **2,** a fierce look. **3,** a slippery surface, as of ice. —*v.i.* **1,** shine dazzlingly. **2,** stare fiercely.

glar'ing *adj.* **1,** shining dazzlingly. **2,** obvious; notorious.

glas'phalt (glas'fâlt) *n.* a paving material composed of asphalt and glass.

glass (gläs) *n.* **1,** a hard, brittle substance, usually transparent, made of silicates fused at high heat. **2,** an article, as a mirror, tumbler, etc., made of this substance; a telescope or binocular: *spyglass.* **3,** a tumblerful; the amount of liquid in a tumbler. **4,** (*pl.*) spectacles. —**glass'ful",** *n.* —**glass wool,** massed glass fibers, used for insulation.

glass·ine' (gla-sēn') *n.* a thin transparent paper.

glass'y (gläs'ē) *adj.* **1,** like glass, esp. in smoothness. **2,** staring; expressionless. —**glass'i·ness,** *n.*

glau·co'ma (glâ-kō'mə) *n.* a disease of the eye, a hardening of the eyeball.

glaze (glāz) *v.t.* **1,** furnish with glass, as a window sash. **2,** overlay (pottery, cloth, paper) with a glossy, hard surface. —*v.i.*

become glassy. —*n.* a glassy appearance or sheen.

gla'zier (glā'zher) *n.* one who works with glass.

gleam (glēm) *n.* **1,** a brief flash of light. **2,** luster. —*v.i.* emit dim rays of light.

glean (glēn) *v.t. & i.* **1,** gather (grain) after the reapers; pick up leavings. **2,** gather (as information) by slow, careful selection.

glee (glē) *n.* **1,** mirth; delight. **2,** a musical piece for three or more voices. —**glee'ful,** *adj.* exultantly happy. —**glee club,** a choral group.

glen *n.* a narrow valley; dale.

glen·gar'ry (glen-gar'ē) *n.* a Scottish cap.

glib *adj.* [**glib'ber, -best**] fluent but insincere. —**glib'ness,** *n.*

glide (glīd) *v.i.* move smoothly and easily. —*n.* **1,** a smooth, easy motion. **2,** the downward flight, without engine power, of an airplane. **3,** a metal button used on furniture legs to reduce friction when moving.

glid'er (glī'dər) *n.* **1,** a motorless aircraft resembling an airplane. **2,** a suspended swing.

glim'mer (glim'ər) *n.* a faint and wavering light. —*v.i.* shine faintly. —**glim'mer·ing,** *n.* a faint trace, of light or anything.

glimpse (glimps) *n.* **1,** a momentary view. **2,** an inkling. —*v.t.* get a hasty view of.

glint *n.* a streaked reflection of light; a flash. —*v.i.* flash; sparkle.

glis·sade' (gli-säd') *n.* **1,** a sliding down a snow slope in a standing position. **2,** a glide in dancing.

glis·san'do (gli-sän'dō) *n.* (*Music*) the effect of sliding the finger across the keys or strings of an instrument.

glis'ten (glis'ən) *v.i.* shine with sparkling light; gleam.

glitch (glich) *n.* **1,** a sudden, brief surge of electrical power. **2,** a minor malfunction of an apparatus.

glit'ter (glit'ər) *v.i.* **1,** send off shoots of light, as a gem; sparkle. **2,** be brilliant or showy. —*n.* **1,** sparkling light. **2,** splendor; allure.

gloam'ing (glō'ming) *n.* twilight.

gloat (glōt) *v.i.* **1,** gaze or ponder with spite, lust, or greed. **2,** show joy at another's misfortune.

glob *n.* a globule.

glob'al (glō'bəl) *adj.* worldwide.

globe (glōb) *n.* **1,** a sphere; a ball-shaped body. **2,** the earth. **3,** a sphere bearing a map of the earth. **4,** something of nearspherical shape, as an incandescent lamp, bowl, etc.

globe'trot"ter *n.* one who travels all over the world.

glob'u·lar (glob'yə-lər) *adj.* spherical. —**glob'u·lar'i·ty** (-lar'ə-tē) *n.*

glob'ule (glob'ūl) *n.* a tiny, round particle.

glob'u·lin (glob'yû-lin) *n.* a protein soluble in pure water.

glock'en·spiel" (glok'ən-spēl") *n.* a musical instrument consisting of tuned bells or tubes played upon with hammers.

gloom *n.* **1,** dim shade; obscurity; cloudiness. **2,** melancholy; pessimism. —**gloom'y,** *adj.*

glop *n.* any thick semiliquid substance.

glo'ri·fy" (glôr'i-fī") *v.t.* **1,** worship. **2,** confer honor on. **3,** invest with beauty. —**glo"ri·fi·ca'tion,** *n.*

glo'ri·ous (glôr'ē-əs) *adj.* **1,** pert. to glory; blessed. **2,** illustrious; splendid. —**glo'ri·ous·ness,** *n.*

glo'ry (glôr'ē) *n.* **1,** exalted honor. **2,** splendor; radiance. **3,** celestial bliss. **4,** a source of pride. **5,** height of prosperity or renown. **6,** a halo. —*v.i.* exult; rejoice.

gloss (glâs) *n.* **1,** a smooth, mirrorlike finish; luster. **2,** a deceptive exterior. **3,** an explanation or annotation to clarify a word or phrase.

glos'sa·ry (glos'ə-rē) *n.* an explanatory list of terms used in a text.

gloss'y (-ē) *adj.* having a gloss or sheen; lustrous. —**gloss'i·ness,** *n.*

-glot *suf.* denoting mastery of (a specified number of) languages.

glot'tis (glot'is) *n.* the opening at the top of the windpipe and between the vocal cords. —**glot'tal** (-əl) *adj.*

glove (gluv) *n.* **1,** a covering for the hand, with compartments for the thumb and fingers. **2,** a padded covering for the hand, used in certain sports. —**glov'er,** *n.* a maker of gloves.

glow (glō) *v.i.* **1,** throw out heat and light without flame; display dull light. **2,** be flushed with heat or emotion; redden, as from exertion. **3,** shine brightly. —*n.* **1,** luminosity. **2,** brightness of color. **3,** ardor. **4,** bodily warmth.

glow'er (glow'ər) *v.i.* look menacing or angry; scowl; frown. —*n.* a frown; sullen stare.

glow'worm" (glō'wêrm") *n.* an insect or its larva that glows in the dark.

glox·in'i·a (glok-sin'ē-ə) *n.* a plant having large bell-shaped flowers.

gloze (glōz) *v.t.* (with *over*) gloss over; explain away.

glu'cose (gloo'kōs) *n.* a light-colored syrup obtained from starch, cane sugar, etc., by the action of acids.

glue (gloo) *n.* a sticky, soluble substance

that dries to a resinous hardness, used as an adhesive and sizing. —**glue′y**, *adj.*

glum *adj.* [**glum′mer, -mest**] disheartened; sullen. —**glum′ness**, *n.*

glut *v.t.* [**glut′ted, -ting**] fill to overflowing; satiate; overstock. —*n.* **1**, a surfeit. **2**, supply exceeding demand.

glu′ten (gloo′tən) *n.* a sticky substance, highly nutritious, found in flour.

glu′ti·nous (gloo′tə-nəs) *adj.* sticky.

glut′ton (glut′ən) *n.* an excessive eater; a greedy person. —**glut′ton·ous**, *adj.* —**glut′ton·y**, *n.* greed.

glyc′er·in (glis′ər-in) *n.* a colorless syrupy liquid used in cosmetics, explosives, etc.

gly′co·gen (glī′kə-jən) *n.* the sugar formed in the body from carbohydrates.

glyph (glif) *n.* **1**, (*Archit.*) a groove or channel, usu. vertical, as in a sculptured decoration. **2**, a symbol used for nonverbal communication.

glyp′tic (glip′tik) *adj.* pert. to carving and engraving.

G-′man″ (jē′man″) *n.* (*Slang*) an agent of the FBI.

gnarl (närl) *n.* a knot on a tree. —*v.t.* twist; knot. —**gnarled**, *adj.* full of knots; twisted.

gnash (nash) *v.t.* grate or grind (the teeth) together.

gnat (nat) *n.* any of several small biting insects.

gnaw (nâ) *v.t. & i.* **1**, bite or wear away with the front teeth. **2**, consume; torture, as if by continual biting. —**gnaw′ing**, *n.* a continuous feeling of discomfort, as from hunger or remorse.

gneiss (nīs) *n.* rock composed of layers of quartz, mica, etc.

gnome (nōm) *n.* **1**, a dwarf, esp. an imaginary one living in the earth and guarding its treasures. **2**, an aphorism. —**gnom′ic**, *adj.*

gno′mon (nō′mon) *n.* the arm on a sundial which by its shadow shows the time of day.

gnos′tic (nos′tik) *adj.* **1**, possessing mystic knowledge. **2**, (*cap.*) a believer in Gnosticism, a mystic, quasi-religious philosophy.

gnu (noo) *n.* an Afr. antelope resembling an ox.

go (gō) *v.i.* [**went, gone, go′ing**] **1**, move away (from where the speaker is); depart. **2**, be in motion; proceed; travel; be transported. **3**, succeed; fit; be suited. **4**, pass; elapse; cease to exist. **5**, extend; continue. **6**, operate; be in working order. **7**, be sold; be disposed of; be transferred. **8**, be a part of; belong. —*v.t. & i.* (*Colloq.*) say. —*n.*

(*Colloq.*) **1**, ambition; energy. **2**, a success. **3**, an agreement. **4**, an attempt; a try. **5**, a Jap. game of tactics. —**go back on**, (*Colloq.*) betray; fail to keep (one's word, etc.). —**go down**, (*Slang*) happen. —**go for**, (*Colloq.*) **1**, be attracted by; be infatuated with. **2**, attack. —**go in for**, **1**, participate in. **2**, enjoy. —**go it**, (*Colloq.*) endure. —**go one better**, (*Colloq.*) outdo; surpass. —**go over**, (*Colloq.*) succeed. —**go under**, (*Colloq*) fail; be ruined.

go′a (gō′ə) *n.* an antelope of Tibet.

goad (gōd) *n.* **1**, a sharp stick for driving cattle. **2**, any incentive. —*v.t.* spur on, with or as with a goad; urge.

go-′a·head″ *n.* approval to proceed.

goal (gōl) *n.* **1**, the point that limits a race. **2**, the place, in some games, that players must reach to score; the score for reaching such a place. **3**, any object of ambition or desire. —**goal′ie**, **goal′keep″er**, **goal′-tend″er**, *n.* in certain games, the player who guards the goal.

goat (gōt) *n.* **1**, an agile, horned ruminant animal about the size of a sheep, valued for its milk and hair. **2**, (*Colloq.*) the victim of a joke; an innocent sufferer. —**get one's goat**, (*Slang*) cause one to lose one's temper.

goat·ee′ (gō-tē′) *n.* a pointed beard.

goat′herd″ *n.* one who tends goats.

goat′skin″ *n.* leather made from the hide of a goat.

gob *n.* **1**, a mass or lump; a mouthful. **2**, (*Colloq.*) a sailor.

go′bang (gō′bang″) *n.* a Japanese game similar to go.

gob′bet (gob′it) *n.* a lump or fragment.

gob′ble (gob′əl) *v.t.* **1**, swallow hastily. **2**, (*Slang*) (often with *up*) seize greedily. —*v.i.* make a rattling noise in the throat, as a male turkey. —*n.* the cry of a male turkey. —**gob′bler**, *n.* a male turkey.

gob′ble·dy·gook″ (gob′əl-dē-gŭk″) *n.* **1**, obscure, inflated language; officialese. **2**, meaningless confusion of words; nonsense. **3**, specialized, technical language; jargon.

go-′be·tween″ *n.* an intermediary.

gob′let (gob′lit) *n.* a drinking glass with a stem and base.

gob′lin *n.* a surly, malicious sprite.

go′by (gō′bē) *n.* a small spiny-finned fish.

go′cart″ (gō′kärt″) *n.* **1**, a child's walker. **2**, a small baby carriage or stroller. **3**, a small-scale, often motorized, open racing car for children.

god *n.* **1**, (*cap.*) the Supreme Being, creator and master of all. **2**, any being considered as divine. **3**, an idol. **4**, a person or thing made the object of supreme devotion. —**god'dess** (-əs) *n.fem.*

god'child" *n.* a child one sponsors at baptism. —**god'daugh"ter, god'fa"ther, god'-moth"er, god'par"ent, god'son"**, *n.*

god'head" *n.* 1, divinity. 2, *(cap.)* God.

god'hood" *n.* divinity.

god'less (-ləs) *adj.* impious; wicked. —**god'less·ness**, *n.*

god'ly (-lė) *adj.* pious. —**god'li·ness**, *n.*

god'send" *n.* an unlooked-for acquisition or piece of good fortune.

God'speed" *interj.* God speed you: a wish for success or prosperity.

god'wit *n.* a water bird akin to the snipe.

go'fer (gō'fər) *n.* *(Slang)* an employee hired primarily to run errands. Also, **go'-pher.**

go·"get'ter *n.* *(Slang)* one who succeeds by vigorous pursuit of his object.

gog'gle (gog'əl) *v.i.* roll the eyes; blink. —**gog'gles**, *n.pl.* spectacles to protect against glare, dust, etc.

go·'go" (gō'gō") *adj. (Slang)* modern; fashionable. Also, **a go-go.**

go"ings-on' (gō"ingz-on') *n.* *(Colloq.)* events or actions; behavior.

goi'ter (goi'tər) *n.* morbid swelling of the thyroid gland.

gold (gōld) *n.* 1, a precious metallic element, no. 79, symbol Au, used in coinage and jewelry. 2, money; wealth. 3, a bright yellow color. —**gold brick, 1,** anything sold as valuable that proves to be worthless. 2, *(Slang)* in the U.S. Army, a soldier who cleverly evades onerous duty. —**gold digger,** *(Slang)* a woman whose interest in men is mainly mercenary. —**gold leaf,** gold beaten into thin leaves. —**gold mine,** *(Slang)* anything productive of great wealth. —**gold standard,** a standard of value for a monetary system based on gold.

gold-'brick" *(Colloq.) v.t.* swindle; cheat. —*v.i.* shirk a duty; loaf.

gold'en (gōl'dən) *adj.* 1, made of gold. 2, yellow. 3, most auspicious. 4, very precious; excellent. 5, most flourishing. 6, glamorous. 7, fiftieth: said of anniversaries. —**golden rule,** a rule of conduct: Do unto others as you would have them do unto you.

golden age an era of prosperity, progress, or development. —**golden ager,** *(Colloq.)* a senior citizen.

gold'en·rod" *n.* a wildflower with yellow flower-heads.

gold-'filled" *adj.* heavily goldplated.

gold'fish" *n.* a small yellow fish of the carp family.

gold'smith" *n.* a worker in gold.

golf *n.* a game played on an extensive course, in which the object is to drive a ball into a series of holes in the fewest number of strokes.

Gol·go·tha (gol'gə-thə) *n.* 1, Calvary. 2, any place of suffering and slaughter.

gol'ly (gol'ė) *interj.* an exclamation of delight or surprise.

-gon *suf.* denoting geometrical figures.

gon'ad *n.* in biology, a sex gland.

gon'do·la (gon'də-lə) *n.* 1, a narrow, one-oared boat used on the canals of Venice. 2, an open railroad freight car. 3, the control car of an airship. 4, a cable car. —**gon"do·lier'** (-lir') *n.* the oarsman of a gondola.

gone (gân) *v.* p.p. of **go.** —*adj.* 1, ruined; failing. 2, *(Colloq.)* (with *on*) in love; entranced. —**gon'er**, *n.* *(Slang)* a person or thing lost or past recovery.

gon'fa·lon (gon'fə-lən) *n.* a flag; standard.

gong (gâng) *n.* a metal disk giving a resonant tone when struck.

gon"or·rhe'a (gon"ə-rē'ə) *n.* a contagious disease of the genitals.

goo *n.* *(Slang)* a sticky substance. —**goo'ey** (-ė) *adj.*

goo'ber (goo'bər) *n.* the peanut.

good (gůd) *adj.* [**bet'ter, best**] 1, worthy of respect or commendation, by being beneficial, honest, noble, etc. 2, useful; suited to the purpose; skillful or competent. 3, virtuous; pure; well-behaved. 4, thorough; complete; considerable. 5, valid; genuine; worthy of being believed or trusted. 6, pleasant; agreeable. —*n.* 1, what is right, just, or desirable. 2, virtuous persons. 3, *(pl.)* merchandise, esp. textiles; possessions. 4, *(pl.)* *(Slang)* evidence of guilt. —*interj.* expressing agreement, approval, or congratulation. —**Good Book,** the Bible. —**good Samaritan,** one who helps another in distress. —**good will, 1,** kindly feeling; cheerful readiness. 2, the value to a business of its established position and patronage.

good'bye' (gůd'bī') *interj. & n.* 1, a word spoken when parting from another; farewell. 2, a parting, dismissal, or abandonment. Also, **good-'by'** [*pl.* **-bys'**], **good-"bye'**.

Good Friday the Friday before Easter.

good'ies (gůd'ėz) *n.pl.* candy.

good-"look'ing *adj.* handsome; comely.

good'ly (gůd'lė) *adj.* adequate in quality, amount, etc.

good-'na"tured *adj.* having a pleasant disposition; friendly and cheerful.

good'ness (gůd'nəs) *n.* 1, the state, quality or degree of being good. 2, heaven; providence. —*interj.* a mild exclamation.

good'y (gŭd'ė) *interj.* expressing delight. —*n.* (*Colloq.*) candy or delicacy. —**good'y-good'y,** *adj. & n.* priggish (person).

goof *n.* (*Slang*) a silly person. —*v.i.* make a mistake. —**goof'y,** *adj.* —**goof off,** (*Slang*) loaf.

goof'ball" *n.* (*Slang*) **1,** a sleeping pill. **2,** a crazy person.

gook (gŭk) *n.* sticky stuff.

goon *n.* **1,** (*Slang*) a hired thug. **2,** a stupid person.

goop *n.* **1,** (*Slang*) an uncouth person. **2,** a thick, viscid liquid; goo.

goose (goos) *n.* [*pl.* **geese** (gēs)] **1,** a large web-footed bird, esp. the female, similar to a duck; its flesh. **2,** a silly person. **3,** [*pl.* **goos'es**] a tailor's iron. —*v.t.* (*Slang*) jab (a person) in the backside. —**goose flesh,** a roughened condition of the skin caused by cold or fear. Also, **goose pimples.** —**goose step,** a stiff-kneed marching step, as used by German soldiers.

goose'ber"ry (goos'ber'ė) *n.* a tart, greenish-brown berry, used in preserves.

goose'neck" (goos'nek") *n.* anything curved like a goose's neck, esp. an iron or rubber coupling.

go'pher (gō'fər) *n.* **1,** a ground squirrel of the prairies. **2,** a burrowing rodent with large cheek pouches. **3,** (*Slang*) a gofer.

gore (gôr) *n.* **1,** a wedge-shaped piece of cloth used to vary width, as of a garment or sail. **2,** blood. —*v.t.* pierce, as with a horn.

gorge (gôrj) *n.* **1,** a narrow ravine. **2,** the gluttonous eating of a big meal; a feast. **3,** food consumed; what has been swallowed. —*v.t. & i.* eat greedily; stuff.

gor'geous (gôr'jəs) *adj.* showy; magnificent. —**gor'geous·ness,** *n.*

Gor"gon·zo'la (gôr"gən-zō'lə) *n.* a strong Italian cheese.

go·ril'la (gə-ril'ə) *n.* **1,** the largest known manlike ape. **2,** a powerful, brutal man.

gor'mand·ize" (gôr'mən-dīz") *v.i.* eat voraciously.

gorse (gôrs) *n.* a common Europ. weed; furze.

gor'y (gôr'ė) *adj.* **1,** like or covered with blood. **2,** involving bloodshed. —**gor'i·ness,** *n.*

gosh *interj.* a mild curse.

gos'hawk" (gos'hâk") *n.* a large hawk formerly used in falconry.

gos'ling (goz'ling) *n.* a young goose.

gos'pel (gos'pəl) *n.* **1,** the record of Christ's life and teachings. **2,** (*cap.*) any one of the first four books of the New Testament. **3,** any principle one believes in or preaches. **4,** absolute truth.

gos'sa·mer (gos'ə-mər) *n.* **1,** a cobweb.

2, any thin, filmy material. —*adj.* cobweblike; unsubstantial.

gos'sip (gos'ip) *n.* **1,** trifling talk, esp. about other persons. **2,** [also, **gos'sip·er**] an idle talker. —*v.i.* discuss other persons' affairs.

got *v.* pret. & p.p. of *get.*

Goth'ic (goth'ik) *adj.* designating a type of architecture with pointed arches and high, steep roofs. —*n.* a style of printing type without serifs.

got'ten (got'ən) *v.* p.p. of *get.*

gouache (gwäsh) *n.* a way of painting with water colors; a painting so made.

Gou'da (gow'də) *n.* a mild Dutch cheese.

gouge (gowj) *v.t.* **1,** scoop or tear out. **2,** (*Colloq.*) overcharge. **3,** (*Colloq.*) cheat. —*n.* a chisel.

gou'lash (goo'läsh) *n.* **1,** a highly seasoned stew. **2,** a jumble.

gourd (gôrd) *n.* **1,** the fleshy fruit of a vine related to the squash and cucumber. **2,** the dried shell of this fruit, used as a dipper or vessel.

gour·mand' (goor-mänd') *n.* **1,** a glutton. **2,** a lover of good food.

gour·met' (goor-mā') *n.* a lover of good eating; an epicure.

gout (gowt) *n.* a painful inflammation of the joints, esp. the big toe. —**gout'y,** *adj.* —**gout'i·ness,** *n.*

gov'ern (guv'ərn) *v.t. & i.* **1,** rule with authority. **2,** guide; control. **3,** determine.

gov'er·ness (guv'ər-nəs) *n.* a woman tutor for children.

gov'ern·ment (guv'ərn-mənt) *n.* **1,** regulation; management. **2,** a state's established form of political rule. **3,** the body of persons authorized to govern; the administration. —**gov"ern·men'tal** (-men'təl) *adj.*

gov'er·nor (guv'ər-nər) *n.* **1,** one who governs; esp. the head of a state of the U.S. **2,** a device for regulating the speed of an engine.

gown *n.* **1,** a woman's dress. **2,** a loose robe worn officially by judges, clergymen, etc.; fig., the academic world. —*v.t.* put a gown on; dress.

grab *v.t.* [**grabbed, grab'bing**] **1,** seize violently or suddenly; snatch. **2,** obtain by violent or illegal means. —*n.* seizure. —**grab'ber,** *n.*

grab'ble (grab'əl) *v.i.* **1,** grope about. **2,** sprawl; grovel.

grace (grās) *n.* **1,** ease and elegance of manner or movement; charm. **2,** (often *pl.*) liking; favor; good will. **3,** virtue; kindness; politeness. **4,** postponement, as of a penalty or obligation; clemency. **5,** a prayer for blessing at a meal. **6,** divine favor. —*v.t.* **1,**

adorn. 2, honor; favor. —**grace′ful**, *adj.* beautiful and elegant in form, manner, and esp. movement. —**grace note** (*Music*) a note not essential but ornamental.

gra′cious (grā′shəs) *adj.* 1, kindly; courteous. 2, charming; attractive. 3, generous; magnanimous. —*interj.* a mild expression of surprise. —**gra′cious·ness**, *n.*

grack′le (grak′əl) *n.* a blackbird.

grad *n.* (*Slang*) graduate.

gra′date (grā′dāt) *v.i.* pass gradually, as from one color to another. —*v.t.* 1, cause to gradate. 2, arrange by grades.

gra·da′tion (grā-dā′shən) *n.* 1, the act or process of classifying by grade, or becoming different in grade. 2, a grade differing only slightly from near grades.

grade (grād) *n.* 1, a step in any series, as of quality, etc.; degree. 2, relative position in any scale; rank; standing or a mark of standing. 3, one of the divisions of a school course; also, the pupils in any of these divisions. 4, the rate of ascent and descent of a highway or railroad; also, a slope. —*v.t.* 1, classify, as by relative quality; sort. 2, make (a slope) level. —**grade crossing**, two roads or tracks crossing at the same level. —**grade school**, a primary school, below high school.

gra′di·ent (grā′dē-ənt) *n.* the amount or angle of slope.

grad′u·al (gra′joo-əl) *adj.* changing by degrees; not sudden or abrupt.

grad′u·ate (gra′joo-ət) *n.* 1, one who has received an academic degree. 2, a measuring glass. —*adj.* 1, who has graduated. 2, pert. to academic graduates. —*v.t.* (-āt) 1, confer an academic degree upon. 2, mark with degrees; calibrate. —*v.i.* (-āt) 1, receive a degree or diploma. 2, pass gradually. —**grad″u·a′tion**, *n.*

graf·fi′to (grə-fē′tō) *n.* [*pl.* **-ti** (-tē)] an inscription or design written or scratched on a wall, stone, etc.

graft (gráft) *v.t.* 1, unite or mix living tissue or plant shoots, for joint growth or reproduction; crossbreed. 2, dishonestly accept (bribes, perquisites). —*n.* 1, the act of grafting; a part grafted. 2, dishonest use of office to get money or perquisites; anything so acquired.

gra′ham flour (grā′əm) wholewheat flour.

grail (grāl) *n.* a cup. —**Holy Grail**, in legend, the cup used by Jesus at the Last Supper.

grain (grān) *n.* 1, cereal grasses, or their seeds. 2, a tiny, hard particle. 3, the smallest unit of weight; an infinitesimal amount. 4, the direction in which fibers run; texture, as of wood, stone, etc. 5, the hair side of leather. —*v.t.* paint or emboss in the pattern of the grain of wood, leather, etc. —**grain′y**, *adj.* —**grain alcohol**, ethyl alcohol.

gram *n.* the unit of weight in the metric system, .0353 avoirdupois ounce.

-gram *suf.* denoting a writing, as *telegram*.

gram′mar (gram′ər) *n.* 1, the science of word-endings and inflectional forms. 2, mode of speaking and writing according to the principles of grammar. 3, a book on grammar. —**gram·mar′i·an** (grə-mâr′ē-ən) *n.* a student of grammar. —**grammar school** (*U.S.*) an elementary school, grades 1 to 8.

gram·mat′i·cal (grə-mat′i-kəl) *adj.* 1, pert. to grammar. 2, correct in grammar.

Gram′my (gram′ē) *n.* an award for excellence in phonograph recording.

gram′o·phone″ (gram′ə-fōn″) *n.* (*T.N.*) a phonograph.

gram′pus (gram′pəs) *n.* a large sea mammal related to the dolphin.

gran′a·ry (gran′ə-rē) *n.* a storage place for grain.

grand *adj.* 1, imposing in size or effect; majestic; splendid. 2, dignified; lofty; eminent. 3, belonging to high society; elegant. 4, main; comprehensive; all-embracing. 5, designating the second generation in ascent or descent, as *grandfather*, *grandson*. 6, (*Colloq.*) fine, very good. 7, (*Slang*) one thousand dollars. —**grand′ness**, *n.* —**grand duke**, 1, a royal prince, esp. in czarist Russia. 2, the ruler of a grand duchy, a principality ranking next below a kingdom. —**grand jury**, a jury that indicts. —**grand larceny**, the crime of stealing something of great value. —**grand opera**, a play in which all dialogue is sung. —**grand piano**, a piano with a horizontal, harp-shaped cabinet. —**grand tour**, a tour of Europe.

gran·dee′ (gran-dē′) *n.* a great nobleman; a man of comparable rank or pretensions.

gran′deur (gran′jûr) *n.* 1, grandness; illustriousness. 2, conspicuous splendor.

grandfather clock a large, pendulum clock. Also, **grandfather's clock.**

gran·dil′o·quent (gran-dil′ə-kwənt) *adj.* pompous, esp. in speech; bombastic. —**gran·dil′o·quence**, *n.*

gran′di·ose″ (gran′dē-ōs″) *adj.* 1, ostentatiously imposing. 2, bombastic; showy. —**gran″di·os′i·ty** (-os′ə-tē) *n.*

grand mal (grän′mäl′) *n.* (*Fr.*) epilepsy.

grand′stand″ *n.* the main structure for seating spectators at outdoor sporting events. —**grandstand play**, (*Slang*) a competitor's feat intended solely to impress an audience.

grange (grānj) *n.* 1, (*Archaic*) a farm. 2, (*cap.*) a national society of farmers; one of its branches.

gran'ite (gran'it) *n.* a hard, durable rock.

gra·niv'o·rous (gra-niv'ə-rəs) *adj.* feeding on grain.

gran'ny (gran'ē) *n.* **1,** grandmother; an old woman. **2,** an incorrectly tied square knot.

gra·no'la (grə-nō'lə) *n.* an oat cereal flavored with raisins, nuts, etc.

grant (gránt) *v.t.* **1,** convey by deed. **2,** give; bestow. **3,** concede to be true. —*n.* the act of granting; also, the thing (land, money, etc.) given. —**gran·tee'** (-tē') *n.* the recipient of a grant. —**grant'or,** *n.*

grants'man·ship (grantz'mən-ship'') *n.* the technique of applying for and obtaining financial grants. —**grants'man,** *n.*

gran'u·late'' (gran'yə-lāt'') *v.t.* **1,** grind or form into granules. **2,** roughen the surface of. —**gran''u·la'tion,** *n.*

gran'ule (gran'ūl) *n.* a fine grain or particle. —**gran'u·lar,** *adj.* composed of or formed in grains.

grape (grāp) *n.* **1,** a juicy berry growing in clusters on a vine. **2,** wine. **3,** grape-sized cannon shot: *grapeshot.*

grape'fruit'' *n.* a large citrus fruit.

grape'vine'' *n.* **1,** the vine that bears grapes. **2,** (*Colloq.*) word-of-mouth transmission of secret information.

graph (gráf) *n.* a diagram showing the successive values of a changing quantity. —*v.t.* mark such values on cross-ruled paper (*graph paper*).

-graph (gráf) *suf.* a writing or picturing, as in *telegraph, photograph.*

graph'ic (graf'ik) *adj.* **1,** pert. to the arts of drawing, printing, engraving, etc. **2,** vivid; lifelike. —**graph'i·cal·ly,** *adv.* —**graphic arts,** the pictorial arts: drawing, painting, engraving, etc.; sometimes also printing, process engraving, etc.

graph'ite (graf'it) *n.* a soft, greasy, natural carbon used in lead pencils and as a lubricant.

graph·ol'o·gy (gra-fol'ə-jē) *n.* the study of handwriting as an expression or indication of character. —**graph·ol'o·gist,** *n.*

-graphy (grə-fē) *suf.* writing or picturing, as in *photography, geography.*

grap'nel (grap'nəl) *n.* a hook with several prongs, for grappling.

grap'ple (grap'əl) *v.t.* **1,** lay fast hold of. **2,** (with *with*) deal with; try to overcome. —*v.i.* seize; come to close quarters with. —*n.* **1,** a grapnel. **2,** a clinch, as in wrestling. —**grap'pling iron,** grapnel.

grasp (grásp) *v.t.* **1,** seize and hold. **2,** understand. —*n.* **1,** a grip; clasp. **2,** possession. **3,** comprehension. —**grasp'ing,** *adj.* covetous; miserly.

grass (grás) *n.* **1,** green herbage sending up spikelike shoots or blades. **2,** any of a large family of plants with hollow stems and grainlike seed. **3,** a lawn; pasture. **4,** (*Slang*) marijuana.

grass'hop''per (grás'hop''ər) *n.* a large jumping insect destructive to crops.

grass'land (-lənd) *n.* permanent pasture.

grass'roots' *adj.* (*Colloq.*) emanating from the mass of people, as a cause, political movement, etc.

grass widow (*Colloq.*) a woman separated from her husband.

grass'y (-ē) *adj.* **1,** covered with grass. **2,** like grass.

grate (grāt) *v.t.* **1,** reduce to particles by rubbing on a rough surface. **2,** rub together with harsh sound. —*v.i.* **1,** make a rasping noise. **2,** cause irritation. —*n.* **1,** a frame of iron bars, as in a door or window. **2,** a box or frame of iron bars for holding burning fuel; a fireplace. —**grat'er,** *n.* a device for shredding or grating.

grate'ful (grāt'fəl) *adj.* **1,** thankful. **2,** soothing; pleasant.

grat'i·fy'' (grat'i-fī'') *v.t.* please; satisfy; indulge. —**grat''i·fi·ca'tion,** *n.*

grat'ing (grā'ting) *n.* a latticework of wood or metal.

gra'tis (grā'tis) *adv.* without charge.

grat'i·tude'' (grat'i-tood'') *n.* thankfulness.

gra·tu'i·tous (grə-tū'i-təs) *adj.* **1,** freely given. **2,** uncalled for. —**gra·tu'i·tous·ness,** *n.*

gra·tu'i·ty (grə-tū'i-tē) *n.* an extra payment, not owed; a tip.

grau'pel (grow'pəl) *n.* soft snow pellets.

gra·va'men (grə-vā'mən) *n.* (*Law*) the chief part of an accusation.

grave (grāv) *adj.* **1,** earnest; sedate; dignified. **2,** momentous; presenting a crisis. **3,** somber; not gay. **4,** (grä've) (*Music*) slow and solemn. —*n.* an excavation for the burial of a body; a tomb; hence, death. —*v.t.* engrave; impress (on the mind). —**grave'ness,** *n.* seriousness. —**grave accent,** the mark (ˋ) placed over a letter.

grav'el (grav'əl) *n.* fragments of rock larger than sand.

grav'en (grā'vən) *adj.* deeply carved or impressed; engraved.

grave'stone'' *n.* a marker placed where a person is buried; a tombstone.

grave'yard'' *n.* a cemetery. —**graveyard shift,** the last and latest work shift of the day, usu. beginning at midnight.

grav'i·tate'' (grav'ə-tāt'') *v.i.* **1,** yield to the force that draws bodies together. **2,** be attracted. —**grav''i·ta'tion,** *n.* —**grav''i·ta'tion·al,** *adj.* pert. to gravity or gravitation.

grav'i·ty (grav'ə-tē) *n*. **1**, the force that draws all objects toward the center of the earth. **2**, graveness.

gra·vure' (grə-vyûr') *n*. an intaglio printing process whereby liquid inks are deposited on paper from an engraved plate; such a plate; a print made by this process.

gra'vy (grā'vē) *n*. **1**, the juice that escapes from meat in cooking; also, a sauce made from this juice. **2**, (*Slang*) unearned profit. **3**, (*Slang*) graft. —**gravy boat**, a gravy dish. —**gravy train**, (*Slang*) a job yielding high income with little effort.

gray (grā) *n*. a shade between, or mixture of black and white. —*adj*. **1**, of this shade. **2**, cloudy; dismal. **3**, aged; (of hair) whitened by age. Also, **grey**. —**gray'ing**, *adj*. becoming gray. —**gray'ish**, *adj*. —**gray matter**, (*Colloq*.) brains; hence, intelligence. —**gray power**, political power of senior citizens collectively.

gray'beard" *n*. an old man.

gray'ling *n*. a freshwater fish similar to trout.

graze (grāz) *v.t.* **1**, put (cattle) to pasture. **2**, brush lightly in passing. **3**, inflict a surface wound. —*v.i.* **1**, feed on grass, etc., as cattle. **2**, (often with *against*) barely touch. —*n*. a grazing touch; abrasion.

grease (grēs) *n*. **1**, animal fat; any oily matter. **2**, an oily lubricant much more viscous than liquid oil. —*v.t.* (grēz) **1**, lubricate, esp. with grease. **2**, (*Slang*) flatter; bribe. —**grease paint**, theatrical make-up.

greas'y (grē'zē) *adj*. **1**, oily in feel or appearance. **2**, slippery. —**greas'i·ness**, *n*.

great (grāt) *adj*. **1**, conspicuously large or important; vast; numerous. **2**, extreme. **3**, long-continued. **4**, notable; renowned; magnificent. **5**, (*Colloq*.) most enjoyable. **6**, one step more remote in relationship, as *great-grandfather*, the father of a grandfather. —**great'ly**, *adv*. in or to a great degree. —**great'ness**, *n*. —**great-'aunt"**, *n*. the aunt of a parent; grandaunt. —**great circle**, any circle on a sphere having the same diameter as the sphere. —**Great Dane**, a breed of very large dog. —**great-un"cle**, *n*.

great'coat" *n*. (*Brit*.) overcoat.

grebe (grēb) *n*. any of several diving birds allied to the loons.

Gre'cian (grē'shən) *adj*. pert. to Greece, esp. to the ancient Greeks and their culture; Greek.

greed (grēd) *n*. undue desire; avarice. —**greed'y**, *adj*. —**greed'i·ness**, *n*.

Greek (grēk) *adj*. pert. to Greece, its people and language. —*n*. a native or the language of Greece.

green (grēn) *adj*. **1**, of the color of growing grass; a mixture of blue and yellow. **2**, unripe; immature; not dried, seasoned, etc. **3**, untrained; inexperienced. **4**, new; recent. **5**, pale; wan. —*n*. **1**, the color of growing grass. **2**, a common; a grassplot, esp. that around a hole on a golf course. **3**, (*pl.*) cut foliage, esp. evergreens, for decoration. **4**, (*pl.*) a cooked dish of leafy vegetables. **5**, (*Slang*) money, usu. paper money. —**green'ish**, *adj*. somewhat green. —**green'ness**, *n*. —**green light**, (*Colloq*.) permission to proceed. —**green manure**, a crop plowed under as fertilizer. —**green thumb**, the ability to make plants grow.

green'back" *n*. a piece of U. S. paper money.

green'er·y (grē'nə-rē) *n*. **1**, green vegetation or foliage. **2**, a place for raising plants.

green'eyed" (grēn'īd") *adj*. (*Colloq*.) jealous.

green'gage" (grēn'gāj") *n*. a fine-flavored plum.

green'horn" *n*. (*Colloq*.) an inexperienced person; ignoramus.

green'house" *n*. a glass house in which plants are grown.

green'room" *n*. a sitting room in a theater for the use of the performers when not on stage.

green'sward" (-swôrd") *n*. grassy land; a lawn.

greet (grēt) *v.t.* **1**, speak courteously to. **2**, welcome; receive.

greet'ing *n*. **1**, a spoken or written expression of salutation or good wishes. **2**, (*pl.*) a friendly message. —**greeting card**, a printed message of congratulation, good will, etc.

gre·gar'i·ous (gri-gâr'ē-əs) *adj*. tending to live, associate, or congregate with others of the same kind; fond of company; sociable. —**gre·gar'i·ous·ness**, *n*.

Gre·gor'i·an calendar (gri-gôr'ē-ən) the calendar now in use, introduced by Pope Gregory XIII in 1582.

Gregorian chant a song used in the ritual of the Roman Catholic Church.

grem'lin *n*. a mischievous imp.

gre·nade' (gri-nād') *n*. a small bomb, usu. thrown by hand.

gren"a·dier (gren'ə-dir') *n*. **1**, a soldier. **2**, a No. Atlantic fish.

gren"a·dine' (gren'ə-dēn') *n*. **1**, a flavoring syrup made from pomegranate juice. **2**, a dress fabric.

grew (groo) *v*. pret. of *grow*.

grey (grā) *adj*. & *n*. gray.

grey'hound" (grā'hownd") *n*. a breed of tall, very slender, fleet dog.

grid *n*. **1**, a grate or network of bars;

gridiron. **2**, a rigid lead plate for conducting current in a storage battery. **3**, a grating between the electrodes of a vacuum tube.

grid'dle (grid'əl) n. a flat metal plate, heated from beneath, for cooking. **—grid'dle·cake''**, n. a pancake.

grid'i''ron (grid'ī''ərn) n. **1**, a metal cooking utensil of separated bars on which food is broiled. **2**, a football field. **3**, the beams and tackle above a theater stage by which scenery is hung and moved.

grief (grēf) n. **1**, deep sorrow; also the cause of sorrow. **2**, disaster; failure.

griev'ance (grē'vəns) n. a real or fancied cause of complaint.

grieve (grēv) v.t. cause to suffer sorrow. —v.i. feel grief; mourn.

griev'ous (grē'vəs) adj. **1**, causing mental or physical pain, **2**, atrocious. **—griev'ous·ness**, n.

grif'fin (grif'in) n. a fabulous creature with an eagle's head and wings and a lion's body.

grift n. (Slang) gambling pursuits generally. **—grift'er**, n. a confidence man or dishonest professional gambler.

grill (gril) n. **1**, a gridiron. **2**, a hotel bar or restaurant. **3**, a dish of various broiled meats. —v.t. **1**, broil (food) on a grill. **2**, subject to persistent questioning.

grille (gril) n. a metal grating.

grim adj. [**grim'mer, -mest**] **1**, forbidding. **2**, uncompromising; unyielding. **3**, frightful; cruel. **—grim'ness**, n.

gri·mace' (gri-mās') n. a twisting of the face, expressive of pain, disgust, etc. —v.i. make a grimace.

gri·mal'kin n. **1**, a cat, esp. a female. **2**, a spiteful old woman.

grime (grīm) n. deeply ingrained dirt. **—grim'y**, adj. dirty.

grin n. a broad smile that shows the teeth. —v.i. [**grinned, grin'ning**] make a grin; smile broadly.

grind (grīnd) v.t. [**ground, grind'ing**] **1**, subject to friction between two abrasive surfaces, or against one surface, so as to reduce to particles, wear away, etc.; pulverize; grate; sharpen; smooth; machine; shape. **2**, operate (a grinding machine or wheel), as by pedaling or turning a handle. **3**, grit (the teeth); chew. **4**, oppress. —v.i. **1**, work at grinding. **2**, (Slang) work very hard. —n. **1**, a tedious routine. **2**, (Slang) a student who does nothing but study.

grind'er (grīn'dər) n. **1**, a device for grinding. **2**, (Slang) a large sandwich; a hero.

grind'stone'' n. a rotating abrasive wheel.

grin'go (gring'gō) n. in Latin Amer., an Anglo-Saxon person.

grip v.t. [**gripped, grip'ping**] **1**, grasp firmly. **2**, hold the interest of. —n. **1**, a firm grasp; the power of firmness of a grasp or hold. **2**, a ritual manner of clasping hands. **3**, a handle or hilt; a device for grasping or attaching. **4**, power; control. **5**, (Colloq.) a valise. **6**, (Slang) a stagehand.

gripe (grīp) v.t. squeeze painfully; distress, esp. cause colic in. —v.i. **1**, have pain in the bowels. **2**, (Slang) complain. —n. **1**, a pang of colic. **2**, (Colloq.) a complaint. **—grip'er**, n. a chronic grumbler.

grippe (grip) n. influenza.

gris'ly (griz'lē) adj. **1**, somewhat gray. **2**, gruesome; frightful. **—gris'li·ness**, n.

grist, n. grain to be ground.

gris'tle (gris'əl) n. cartilage. **—gris'tly** (-lē) adj. composed of, or like, cartilage; tough.

grit n. **1**, tiny, rough particles; sand. **2**, a rough sandstone. **3**, pluck. **4**, (pl. used as sing.) coarsely ground hominy. —v.t. & i. [**grit'ted, -ting**] grate; grind.

grit'ty (-ē) adj. **1**, sandy; dirty. **2**, plucky.

griz'zled (griz'əld) adj. mixed with gray, as hair.

griz'zly (griz'lē) adj. streaked with gray. **—grizzly bear**, a large savage bear of western No. America.

groan (grōn) n. a low, mournful sound uttered in pain or grief. —v.t. & i. utter such a sound.

groat (grōt) n. **1**, a former English silver coin worth fourpence. **2**, a very small sum. **3**, (pl.) crushed or coarsely ground grain.

gro'cer (grō'sər) n. a dealer in food supplies. **—gro'cer·ies** (-ēz) n.pl. food supplies. **—gro'cer·y**, n. a grocer's shop.

grog n. rum and water. **—grog'gy**, adj. confused and unsteady.

groin n. the depression between the abdomen and the thigh.

grom'met (grom'it) n. a ring or eyelet of metal.

groom n. **1**, a servant in charge of horses. **2**, a bridegroom. **3**, an attendant in a royal household. —v.t. **1**, tend (a horse). **2**, make neat and tidy. **3**, prepare (for a duty); coach; train. **—groom'ing**, n. personal appearance.

groove (groov) n. **1**, a channel cut by a tool; rut; furrow. **2**, an unprogressive routine; habit. **3**, (Slang) a pleasurable experience. —v.t. **1**, cut a groove in. **2**, (Slang) enjoy oneself. **—groov'y**, adj. (Slang) wonderful.

grope (grōp) v.i. feel about with the hands, as in the dark; seek aimlessly.

gros'grain" (grō'grān") *n.* a heavy corded silk fabric.

gross (grōs) *adj.* **1,** whole, without deductions; total. **2,** thick; fat; coarse; hence, vulgar, indelicate. **3,** dull; dense. **4,** flagrant. —*n.* twelve dozen; 144. —*v.t.* make a profit of, before deductions for expense or taxes. —**gross'ness,** *n.* vulgarity; indecency; obesity. —**gross national product,** the total value of the goods and services produced by a country during a specified period.

gro·tesque' (grō-tesk') *adj.* contorted; fantastic. —*n.* something grotesque. —**grotesque'ness,** *n.*

grot'to (grot'ō) *n.* a cavern, esp. an artificial one; a bower.

grouch (growch) *n.* (*Colloq.*) **1,** a fit of ill temper. **2,** a surly person. —*v.t.* complain. —**grouch'y,** *adj.*

ground (grownd) *n.* **1,** that part of the earth's surface that is not water; dry land; the composition of such surface; earth; soil. **2,** a specific region; area. **3,** a distance traversed. **4,** a foundation; subject matter; a basis; a reason. **5,** (*pl.*) a tract of land, esp. one attached to a dwelling. **6,** (*pl.*) waste matter in ground form, as *coffee grounds.* **7,** a conveyance of electrical current to the earth or a conductor of equivalent effect. —*adj.* **1,** prepared by grinding. **2,** at the level of the ground. —*v.t.* **1,** set on the ground. **2,** (*Aviation*) forbid to fly. **3,** connect electrical current with the earth, etc. **4,** run (a ship) aground. **5,** teach fundamentals to. **6,** pret. & p.p. of *grind.* —*v.i.* come to rest on the ground. —**cover ground,** make progress. —**give ground,** yield; retreat.

ground'er (grown'dər) *n.* (*Baseball*) a ball hit along the ground.

ground'hog" *n.* woodchuck. —**groundhog day,** Candlemas, Feb. 2.

ground'less (-ləs) *adj.* with no adequate reason.

ground'ling (grownd'ling) *n.* **1,** an animal or plant bound to or living close to the ground. **2,** a materialistic person.

ground'nut" *n.* (*Brit.*) the peanut.

ground'work" *n.* preparatory work; foundation; basis.

group (groop) *n.* a number of persons or things gathered or classified together, usually because of likeness or common purpose. —*v.t. & i.* combine in a unit.

group'er (groo'pər) *n.* an Atlantic food fish.

group'ie (groo'pē) *n.* (*Slang*) a person, esp. a young girl, who follows a celebrity, rock group, etc.

grouse (grows) *n.* **1,** [*pl.* **grouse**] any of several game birds. **2,** (*Slang*) a complaint. —*v.i.* (*Slang*) grumble.

grout (growt) *n.* a thin mortar mixed with gravel.

grove (grōv) *n.* a small wood; also, a group of cultivated fruit trees.

grov'el (gruv'əl) *v.i.* crawl or be prone upon the earth; hence, humble oneself.

grow (grō) *v.i.* [**grew** (groo), **grown** (grōn), **grow'ing**] **1,** increase in size, power, etc. **2,** arise naturally. **3,** become. —*v.t.* cause or permit to grow; plant and cultivate. —**grow up,** become adult; mature.

growl *n.* **1,** a deep snarling noise. **2,** a grumbling noise; complaint. —*v.t. & i.* make such a sound.

grown (grōn) *v.* p.p. of *grow.* —**grown'-up,** *n.* an adult.

growth (grōth) *n.* **1,** act, process, or result of growing. **2,** a mass of morbid tissue, as a tumor.

grub *v.t.* [**grubbed, grub'bing**] **1,** dig up by the roots. **2,** remove roots, etc., from (land). —*v.i.* dig in the ground; hence, toil. —*n.* **1,** the larva of an insect. **2,** (*Slang*) food. —**grub'by,** *adj.* dirty.

grub'stake" *n.* the necessities for subsistence, supplied as an investment.

grudge (gruj) *n.* a feeling of resentment; a cause of hostility.

gru'el (groo'əl) *n.* thin porridge.

gru'el·ing (groo'əl-ing) *adj.* arduous; exhausting.

grue'some (groo'səm) *adj.* horribly repulsive. —**grue'some·ness,** *n.*

gruff (gruf) *adj.* **1,** rough; hoarse. **2,** curt; surly. —**gruff'ness,** *n.*

grum'ble (grum'bəl) *n.* a growl; a discontented mutter. —*v.i.* complain in a mutter; growl.

grump'y (grum'pē) *adj.* surly; glum. —**grump'i·ness,** *n.*

grun'gy (grun'jē) *adj.* dirty; grubby. —**grun'gi·ness,** *n.*

grunt *n.* **1,** a deep guttural sound, as that made by a hog. **2,** (*Slang*) a foot soldier. —*v.t. & i.* utter a grunt.

gru·yère' (grə-yār') *n.* a stiff, pale-yellow cheese, often with small holes; Swiss cheese.

G-'string" *n.* **1,** on a musical instrument, a string tuned to G. **2,** a string used as a belt to hold up a breechcloth.

gua"ca·mo'le (gwä"kə-mō'lē) *n.* a seasoned mixture of avocado, tomato, and onions.

gua·na'co (gwä-nä'kō) *n.* a large So. Amer. quadruped.

gua'no (gwä'nō) *n.* [*pl.* **-nos**] a fertilizer made from the droppings of sea birds.

---

gua·ra'ni (gwä-rä'nė) *n.* the monetary unit of Paraguay.

guar"an·tee' (gar"ən-tē') *n.* **1,** a statement that a thing is as represented; warranty. **2,** (*Law*) a promise to be responsible for another's debt or failure; property pledged as security for this promise. —*v.t.* **1,** insure; promise. **2,** (*Law*) be responsible for. Also, **guar'an·ty'.** —**guar"an·tor"** (-tôr") *n.*

guard (gärd) *v.t.* protect; keep safe. —*v.i.* be cautious. —*n.* **1,** a means of defense. **2,** a watchful state. **3,** a person or group of persons who guard; a sentry. **4,** a device to prevent injury. —**guard'ed,** *adj.* wary; reticent. —**guard'house",** *n.* a military prison.

guard'i·an (gär'dė-ən) *n.* **1,** a warden. **2,** (*Law*) one entrusted with the person or property of another. —*adj.* guarding.

guards'man (gärdz'mən) *n.* [*pl.* **-men**] **1,** a guard. **2,** a member of the U.S. National Guard.

gua'va (gwä'və) *n.* the pulpy fruit of a tropical tree.

gu"ber·na·to'ri·al (goo"bər-nə-tôr'ė-əl) *adj.* pert. to a governor.

gudg'eon (guj'ən) *n.* **1,** a small fish used as bait. **2,** one easily duped or cheated. **3,** a pivot. —*v.t.* dupe; swindle.

guer'don (gēr'dən) *n.* a reward.

Guern'sey (gērn'zė) *n.* one of a breed of dairy cattle.

guer·ril'la (gə-ril'ə) *n.* a person engaged in irregular warfare. —**guerrilla theater,** drama of social issue usu. performed outside on the street.

guess (ges) *n.* an opinion reached at random or without reason; a conjecture. —*v.t.* **1,** form such an opinion; surmise. **2,** surmise correctly. —*v.i.* hazard an opinion. —**guess'work",** *n.* the act of guessing; procedure based on guessing.

guess'ti·mate (ges'tə-mət) *n.* (*Colloq.*) an estimate, esp. one based on intuition.

guest (gest) *n.* **1,** a person entertained at the home of another. **2,** a patron of a hotel, etc.

guf·faw' (gu-fâ') *n.* a boisterous laugh. —*v.i.* laugh coarsely.

guid'ance (gī'dəns) *n.* the act of guiding; direction; management.

guide (gīd) *v.t.* **1,** show the way to; escort. **2,** direct; manage. —*n.* **1,** a person or thing that directs. **2,** a controlling device, as on a machine. **3,** a guidebook. —**guided missile,** a rocket-driven explosive missile carrying radio apparatus by which its course may be corrected from the ground.

guide'book" *n.* a book of directions and information for travelers.

guide'line" *n.* a recommendation or principle for determining a course of action.

guide'post" *n.* a post bearing a sign to direct travelers.

gui'don (gī'dən) *n.* a flag or pennant; a soldier who carries it.

guild (gild) *n.* an association of persons in a common trade, or having a common interest.

guil'der (gil'dər) *n.* **1,** gulden. **2,** the Austrian florin.

guile (gīl) *n.* craft; cunning. —**guile'ful,** *adj.* —**guile'less,** *adj.* naïve.

guil'lo·tine" (gil'ə-tēn") *n.* a machine for decapitating a person.

guilt (gilt) *n.* **1,** the fact of having violated law or right. **2,** a sense of having committed a wrong. —**guilt'less,** *adj.* —**guilt'y,** *adj.*

guimpe (gamp) *n.* a woman's outer garment for the neck and shoulders.

guin'ea (gin'ė) *n.* a Brit. monetary unit, 21 shillings. —**guinea fowl,** an Afr. game bird, related to the pheasant. —**guinea hen,** a fowl domesticated for its meat and eggs. —**guinea pig,** a small, short-tailed rodent, much used in medical research; hence, a person used as a subject for experimentation.

guise (gīz) *n.* **1,** garb; dress; hence, semblance. **2,** cloak; cover.

gui·tar' (gi-tär') *n.* a six- or twelve-stringed musical instrument plucked with the fingers or a pick. —**gui·tar'ist,** *n.*

gulch *n.* a gorge; ravine.

gul'den (gûl'den) *n.* the monetary unit of the Netherlands, worth about 40 cents.

gulf *n.* **1,** an arm of the sea extending into the land. **2,** an abyss.

gull (gul) *n.* **1,** a web-footed sea bird. **2,** a dupe. —*v.t.* trick; cheat.

gul'let (gul'it) *n.* the throat.

gul'li·ble (gul'ə-bəl) *adj.* easily deceived. —**gul"li·bil'i·ty,** *n.*

gul'ly (gul'ė) *n.* a narrow ravine.

gulp *v.t.* swallow hastily. —*v.i.* gasp; choke. —*n.* the act of gulping; a quantity gulped.

gum *n.* **1,** the firm flesh in which the teeth are set. **2,** a sticky substance. **3,** a tree yielding a viscid resin. **4,** chewing gum. —*v.t.* [**gummed, gum'ming**] **1,** stick together with gum. **2,** (*Slang*) clog; impede. —*v.i.* become sticky. —**gum'my,** *adj.* —**gum'mi·ness,** *n.* —**gum up,** spoil. —**gum arabic,** a gum derived from the acacia, used in medicines, etc.

gum'bo (gum'bō) *n.* [*pl.* **-bos** (-bōz)] **1,** a soup or dish made with okra. **2,** (*Colloq.*) sticky mud.

---

tub, cūte, pûll; labəl; oil, owl, go, chip, she, thin, *th*en, sing, ink; *see p.* 6

gum'drop" *n.* a small candy made of gum arabic or gelatin.

gump'tion (gump'shən) *n.* (*Colloq.*) 1, initiative; self-reliance. 2, common sense.

gum'shoe" *n.* 1, (*Colloq.*) an overshoe. 2, (*Slang*) a detective.

gun *n.* 1, any of various portable firearms. 2, a cannon. 3, in airplanes, the throttle. —*v.t.* [**gunned, gun'ning**] 1, hurt with a gun. 2, (*with for*) pursue. 3, accelerate. —**at gunpoint,** with a gun pointing at one.

gun'boat" *n.* a small warship carrying mounted guns. —**gunboat diplomacy,** diplomatic relations based on actual or implied threat of military action.

gun'cot"ton *n.* cotton treated with nitric acid, used in explosives; cellulose nitrate.

gung ho (gung'hō') *adj.* (*Colloq.*) enthusiastic.

gun'man (-mən) *n.* [*pl.* **-men**] a hired ruffian. Also, **gun'fight"er.**

gun'ner (gun'ər) *n.* the operator of a gun or cannon.

gun'ner·y (-ē) *n.* 1, the making or operation of guns. 2, artillery.

gun'ny (gun'ē) *n.* a coarse fabric made of jute or hemp fiber.

gun'play" *n.* the firing of guns, esp. an exchange of shots.

gun'pow"der *n.* an explosive powder for use in guns, blasting, etc.

gun'run"ning *n.* the smuggling of firearms. —**gun'run"ner,** *n.*

gun'sling"er *n.* a gunman.

gun'smith" *n.* one who makes or repairs guns.

gun'wale (gun'əl) *n.* the upper edge of a ship's side.

gup'py (gup'ē) *n.* a very small fish.

gur'gle (gẽr'gəl) *v.i.* make a bubbling sound, as water flowing from a bottle. —*n.* this sound.

gu'ru (goo'roo) *n.* a personal teacher and intellectual (and usu. spiritual or mystical) guide.

gush *v.i.* 1, issue copiously and violently; flow out freely. 2, (*Colloq.*) display sentiment effusively. —*v.t.* emit copiously. —*n.* a spouting forth.

gush'er (gush'ər) *n.* 1, one given to sentimental display. 2, an oil well with a copious natural flow.

gush'y (gush'ē) *adj.* (*Colloq.*) overdemonstrative. —**gush'i·ness,** *n.*

gus'set (gus'ət) *n.* a triangular piece of cloth inserted in a garment.

gus'sy (gus'ē) *v.i. & t.* (with *up*) (*Colloq.*) dress up; make pretty.

gust *n.* 1, a sudden squall of wind. 2, an outburst. —*v.i.* blow (of wind).

gus'ta·to·ry (gus'tə-tôr-ē) *adj.* pert. to the sense of taste.

gus'to (gus'tō) *n.* zest; enjoyment.

gust'y (gus'tē) *adj.* coming in gusts or squalls; windy. —**gust'i·ness,** *n.*

gut *n.* 1, an intestine; (*pl.*) the bowels. 2, animal intestines used as a string: *catgut.* 3, a narrow defile; a channel. 4, (*pl.*) (*Slang*) stamina; courage. —*v.t.* [**gut'ted, gut'ting**] 1, disembowel. 2, plunder of contents; destroy the insides of. —*adj.* (*Slang*) 1, easy; simple. 2, basic; fundamental. 3, intuitive; nonintellectual. —**gut'sy,** *adj.* (*Slang*).

gut'ta-per'cha (gut'ə-pẽr'chə) *n.* the dried juice of certain trees, which forms a whitish puttylike material.

gut'ter (gut'ər) *n.* 1, a channel for carrying off water, as at the eaves of a roof or at a roadside. 2, a debased state of living or thinking.

gut'ter·snipe" (gut'ər-snīp") *n.* a person, esp. a child, of lowly origin; a gamin.

gut'tur·al (gut'ər-əl) *adj.* pert. to or formed in the throat; hoarse.

guy (gī) *n.* 1, a rope, chain, or wire used to steady something. 2, (*Slang*) a fellow. —*v.t.* (*Colloq.*) tease.

guz'zle (guz'əl) *v.t. & i.* drink too much or too rapidly.

gym·kha'na (jim-kä'nə) *n.* place where athletic events are held; the events themselves.

gym·na'si·um (jim-nā'zē-əm) *n.* 1, building or room for athletic exercises. Also, *colloq.,* **gym** (jim). 2, (often *cap.*) in some countries, a secondary school preparing students for university.

gym'nast (jim'nast) *n.* one skilled in acrobatic and similar physical exercises. —**gym·nas'tics,** *n.pl.* such exercises. —**gym·nas'tic,** *adj.* —**gym·nas'ti·cal·ly,** *adv.*

gy"ne·col'o·gy (gī"nə-kol'ə-jē) *n.* in medicine, the science of diseases of woman. —**gy"ne·col'o·gist,** *n.*

gy'no- (gī'nə) *pref.* female; woman.

gyp (jip) *n.* (*Slang*) a cheat; swindler. —*v.t.* [**gypped, gyp'ping**] cheat.

gyp'sum (jip'səm) *n.* a soft mineral, from which plaster of Paris is made.

gyp'sy (jip'sē) *n.* a member of a vagabond, dark-skinned race; the language of this race. Also, **gip'sy.**

gy'rate (jī'rāt) *v.i.* move spirally; rotate. —**gy·ra'tion,** *n.*

gy·rene' (jī-rēn') *n.* (*Slang*) a U. S. Marine.

gy'ro- (jī'rō) denoting a ring or circle.

gy'ro·com"pass (jī'rō-kum"pəs) *n.* a

motor-driven gyroscope placed with its axis parallel to that of the earth and thus indicating true north regardless of rotation of the earth and the movement of a ship.

gy′ro·scope″ (jī′rə-skōp′) *n.* an instrument employing a rotating wheel to stabilize ships, etc.

gyve (jīv) *n.* (usually *pl.*) a fetter for the leg; shackle. —*v.t.* fetter.

H

H, h (āch) the eighth letter of the English alphabet.

ha (hä) *interj.* expressing triumph or interrogation.

ha′ba·ne′ra (hä″bə-ne′rə) *n.* a Spanish dance.

ha′be·as·cor′pus (hā′bē-əs kôr′pəs) (*Law*) a writ demanding that a prisoner be given an immediate hearing or else be released.

hab′er·dash″er (hab′ər-dash″ər) *n.* a dealer in accessory articles of men's wear. —**hab′er·dash″er·y,** *n.* the shop of such a dealer.

ha·bil′i·ment (hə-bil′ə-mənt) *n.* (usu. *pl.*) clothing; garments.

hab′it *n.* **1,** a tendency or disposition to act in a certain way, acquired by repetition of such acts. **2,** a usual mode of action; a custom or usage. **3,** a characteristic trait. **4,** (often *pl.*) a costume appropriate to a vocation or occasion. **5,** addiction —*v.t.* clothe. —**hab′it·a·ble,** *adj.* capable of being lived in. —**hab′i·tant,** *n.*

hab′i·tat″ (hab′ə-tat″) *n.* the natural home of an animal or plant; the characteristics, as climate, etc., of such a region.

hab″i·ta′tion (hab″ə-tā′shən) *n.* **1,** a place of abode; a dwelling. **2,** the act of inhabiting.

ha·bit′u·al (ha-bich′oo-əl) *adj.* customary; by habit.

ha·bit′u·ate″ (ha-bich′oo-āt″) *v.t.* **1,** accustom. **2,** frequent. —**ha·bit′u·a′tion,** *n.*

hab′i·tude″ (hab′ə-tood″) *n.* habitual attitude; usual condition or character; custom.

ha·bit′u·é″ (hə-bich′oo-ā″) *n.* one who frequents a place.

ha·chure′ (ha-shûr′) *n.* shading of a drawing or map with lines; hatching.

ha″ci·en′da (hä″sē-en′də) (*Sp.*) *n.* a landed estate or the house on it.

hack (hak) *n.* **1,** a cut, gash, or notch. **2,** a tool for hacking, as an ax or hoe. **3,** a cough; an impediment in speech. **4,** a hackney; a taxicab. **5,** an overworked or jaded horse or person. **6,** a person hired to write according to demand. —*adj.* **1,** hired. **2,**

hackneyed; trite. —*v.t.* **1,** notch or chop irregularly; strike. **2,** (with *out*) produce without enjoyment. **3,** hackney. **4,** (*Slang*) do; perform. —*v.i.* **1,** make cuts or notches. **2,** cough repeatedly; stutter. **3,** drive a hackney or taxi-cab. **4,** write for hire. —**hack′ie, hack′man,** *n.* taxi driver.

hack′le (hak′əl) *n.* **1,** the neck feathers of a fowl. **2,** a comb for dressing hemp, etc. —*v.t.* **1,** comb. **2,** hack roughly.

hack′ney (hak′nē) *n.* a horse or carriage kept for hire. —*adj.* hired out. —*v.t.* make stale or trite by overuse. —**hack′neyed,** *adj.*

hack′saw″ (hak′sâ″) *n.* a saw for cutting metal.

had *v.* pret. & p.p. of *have.*

had′dock (had′ək) *n.* a No. Atlantic food fish similar to the cod.

Ha′des (hā′dēz) *n.* the abode of the dead; hell.

hadj (haj) *n.* the pilgrimage to Mecca. —**hadj′i** (haj′ē) *n.* a pilgrim.

haf′ni·um (haf′nē-əm) *n.* a metallic element, no. 72, symbol Hf.

haft (häft) *n.* the handle of a cutting or thrusting instrument.

hag *n.* **1,** a repulsive or malicious old woman. **2,** a witch or sorceress. **3,** a fish related to the lamprey.

hag′gard (hag′ərd) *adj.* wild-looking, as from terror, suffering, or fatigue. —**hag′-gard·ness,** *n.*

hag′gle (hag′əl) *v.i.* bargain in a petty manner; cavil. —*v.t.* cavil at. —*n.* dispute, esp. about price.

hag′i·o- (haj′ē-ō) *pref.* saint; sacred; holy.

ha′ha′ (hä″hä′) *n.* a laugh.

hai′ku (hī′koo) *n.* a Japanese lyric poem.

hail (hāl) *v.t.* **1,** salute; welcome; cheer. **2,** cry out to. **3,** pour down like hail. —*v.i.* pour down hail. —*n.* **1,** a cry or call to attract attention. **2,** a salutation or greeting. **3,** pellets of ice falling in showers: *hailstones.* —**Hail Mary!,** a prayer, the Ave Maria.

hail-′fel″low *n.* a pleasant or congenial companion.

hair (hâr) *n.* **1,** one or the aggregate of the numerous fine filaments growing from the skin of most animals. **2,** any fine filament. **3,** a very small distance or degree. —**hair trigger,** a trigger requiring very slight pressure to activate.

hair′cloth″ *n.* an upholstery or lining fabric made of horsehair.

hair′cut″ *n.* a cutting or clipping of the hair.

hair′do″ (-doo″) *n.* any particular style of arranging a woman's hair.

hair′dress″er *n.* one who cuts and arranges women's hair.

hair′line″ *n.* a very thin line.

hair′piece″ *n.* a patch of human or artificial hair; toupee.

hair′pin″ *n.* a bent piece of wire, used to hold the hair in place. —*adj.* bent in form of a U.

hair′rais″ing *adj.* frightening.

hair′split″ting *n.* & *adj.* the practice of making excessively fine distinctions.

hair′spray″ *n.* a substance sprayed on the hair to keep it in place.

hair′spring″ *n.* a fine spiral spring in a timepiece.

hair′y (-ė) *adj.* **1,** having much hair. **2,** (*Slang*) dangerous; difficult. —**hair′i·ness,** *n.*

hake (hāk) *n.* a sea fish.

hal′berd (hal′bərd) *n.* a medieval weapon, comprising a blade and spiked points on a long shaft.

hal′cy·on (hal′sė-ən) *n.* a marine bird, the kingfisher. —*adj.* calm; quiet; undisturbed.

hale (hāl) *v.t.* drag forcibly; haul; pull. —*adj.* in good health; robust.

half (hàf) *n.* [*pl.* **halves** (hàvz)] **1,** one of two equal parts into which something is divided. **2,** a tie score. **3,** 50 cents. —*adj.* **1,** being one half. **2,** partial; incomplete. —*adv.* **1,** to the extent or degree of a half. **2,** partly; somewhat. —**better half,** (*Slang*) wife. —**half brother** or **sister,** a brother or sister by one parent but not the other. —**half nelson** (nel′sən) a wrestling hold. —**half note,** (*Music*) a minim (see *note*). —**half pen·ny** (hā′pə-nė) *n.* a British bronze coin. Also, **half′pence″.** —**half step,** (*Music*) a semitone.

half-′and-half″ *n.* a mixture of equal portions, esp. milk and cream, or ale and beer.

half′back″ *n.* (*Football*) a player stationed behind the line.

half-′baked″ *adj.* not completely cooked; (*fig.*) uncompleted; immature.

half′breed″ *n.* an offspring of parents of different races.

half-′caste″ *n.* a person whose parents were of different castes.

half-″cocked″ *adj.* & *adv.* insufficiently prepared; superficial(ly).

half′heart″ed *adj.* showing little eagerness, enthusiasm, or generosity. —**half′-heart″ed·ness,** *n.*

half-′life″ *n.* the time required for half the atoms of a radioactive substance to undergo radioactive decay.

half-′mast″ *adv.* (of a flag) about half-

way down its pole, as a mark of mourning or distress. Also, **half-′staff″.**

half′tone″ *n.* **1,** a process of photoengraving using a fine wire screen. **2,** a plate or print so made.

half′track″ *n.* a motor truck having treads instead of rear wheels.

half′way″ *adv.* & *adj.* **1,** to or at half the distance or middle point. **2,** partial. —**half-way house,** a rehabilitation center.

half′wit″ *n.* a feeble-minded person. —**half′wit″ted,** *adj.*

hal′i·but (hal′ə-bət) *n.* any of several large flatfishes.

hal″i·to′sis (hal″ə-tō′sis) *n.* foul-odored breath.

hall (hâl) *n.* **1,** a building or a large room devoted to some public or common use. **2,** an antechamber or corridor giving entrance to other rooms. **3,** a main house.

hal′lah (häl′ə) *n.* challah.

hal″le·lu′jah (hal″ə-loo′yə) *interj.* Praise ye the Lord!

hall′mark″ (hâl′märk″) *n.* a mark, stamp, or attestation of quality.

hal·loo′ (ha-loo′) *interj.* to attract attention. —*v.i.* & *t.* shout; call.

hal′low (hal′ō) *v.t.* set apart as holy; regard as sacred; consecrate. —**hal′lowed** (hal′ōd, hal′ō-id) *adj.*

Hal″low·een′ (hal″ə-wēn) *n.* the evening of October 31, the eve of All Saints' Day.

hal·lu″ci·na′tion (hə-loo″sə-nā′shən) *n.* **1,** an apparent perception of something not actually perceptible. **2,** a false belief; illusion. —**hal·lu′ci·nate″,** *v.i.*

hal·lu′cin·o·gen (hə-loo″sə-nə-jən″) *n.* a drug that causes hallucinations. —**hal·lu″cin·o·gen′ic,** *adj.*

hall′way″ *n.* a vestibule; hall.

ha′lo (hā′lō) *n.* a circle of light around the head, as of a saint.

hal′o·gen (hal′ə-jən) *n.* any of the elements fluorine, chlorine, iodine, and bromine.

halt (hâlt) *v.i.* **1,** cease advancing; stop. **2,** waver; hesitate. —*v.t.* cause to halt. —*n.* a stop or pause. —*adj.* (*Archaic*) lame. —**halt′ing,** *adj.* hesitant.

hal′ter (hâl′tər) *n.* **1,** a rope or strap having a noose, for leading or confining an animal. **2,** a woman's waist held in place by bands tied around the back and neck.

hal′vah (häl′vä) *n.* a Turkish confection of sesame seeds and honey.

halve (hàv) *v.t.* **1,** divide into two equal parts. **2,** reduce to a half. **3,** make equal scores in (a contest).

hal′yard (hal′yərd) *n.* a rope for raising and lowering a yard, sail, flag, etc.

---

fat, fāte, fär, fâre, fâll, àsk; met, hē, hēr, maybė; pin, pīne; not, nōte, ôr, tool

ham *n.* **1,** the buttock of a hog; the meat from this quarter. **2,** the back of the knee; (*pl.*) the thighs. **3,** (*Slang*) an actor who overacts. **4,** (*Slang*) an amateur, esp. in radio. —*v.i.* [**hammed, ham′ming**] (*Slang*) overact.

ham′burg″er (ham′bẽr″gər) *n.* **1,** chopped beef: *hamburg steak.* **2,** a sandwich of such meat in a bun.

ham′let (ham′lit) *n.* a small village.

ham′mer (ham′ər) *n.* **1,** an instrument for driving nails, beating metal, etc., comprising a heavy solid head set on a handle. **2,** any of various instruments for pounding or striking. **3,** a metal ball with a flexible handle used in throwing contests. —*v.t. & i.* **1,** beat, drive, etc., with or as with a hammer. **2,** (with *out*) execute laboriously.

ham′mer·head″ (-hed″) *n.* a kind of shark.

ham′mer·lock″ *n.* a wrestling hold.

ham′mock (ham′ək) *n.* a heavy cloth or mesh suspended by cords, used as a bed.

ham′per (ham′pər) *v.t.* impede in motion or progress; hinder. —*n.* a large covered basket.

ham′ster (ham′stər) *n.* a small burrowing rodent.

ham′string *n.* a tendon at the back of the knee. —*v.t.* [*pret. & p.p.* **ham′strung″**] cripple; disable.

hand *n.* **1,** the end of the human arm, from wrist outward, comprising the palm and fingers; a corresponding part of certain animals. **2,** something resembling a hand, as a pointer on a clock. **3,** style of handwriting; a person's signature. **4,** a unit of linear measure, 4 inches. **5,** a manual laborer; an employee. **6,** help; aid; agency; participation. **7,** (often *pl.*) possession or control. **8,** the cards dealt to a player in a game; a player; the period from one deal to the next. —*adj.* **1,** of the hand; to be carried by or worn on the hand. **2,** operated or made by hand. —*v.t.* **1,** (often with *over*) deliver by hand. **2,** help; conduct. —**hand-in-glove,** very intimate; co-operating closely. —**hand organ,** a hurdy-gurdy. —**hand-to-mouth,** *adj.* barely supplying the minimum necessities of life; insecure. —**on hand,** available; present.

hand′bag″ *n.* a woman's purse.

hand′ball″ *n.* an athletic game.

hand′bill″ *n.* a printed notice.

hand′book″ *n.* **1,** a compact treatise; a guidebook. **2,** the business of a bookmaker.

hand′car″ *n.* a small hand-propelled railroad car.

hand′cuff″ *n.* (usually *pl.*) a shackle fitting on the wrist. —*v.t.* put handcuffs on.

-hand′ed (han′did) *suf.* supplied with or done by a specified number of hands.

hand′ful″ (-fùl″) *n.* **1,** what the hand can hold; a small quantity or number. **2,** (*Colloq.*) a difficult task.

hand′i·cap″ (han′di-kap″) *n.* **1,** an extra burden placed upon a superior competitor in a contest. **2,** any encumbrance or disadvantage. **3,** a contest in which some of the entrants are handicapped. —*v.t.* [**-capped″, -cap″ping**] **1,** place a handicap upon; rate. **2,** encumber; hinder. —**hand′i·cap″per,** *n.*

hand′i·craft″ (han′di-kráft″) *n.* **1,** skilled labor with the hands. **2,** a manual art. *Also,* **hand′craft″.**

hand′i·ly (han′də-lē) *adv.* **1,** skillfully. **2,** easily; conveniently.

hand′i·work″ (han′di-wẽrk″) *n.* **1,** work done or something made by hand. **2,** the result of an action.

hand′ker·chief (hang′ker-chif) *n.* a small cloth carried for wiping the face or nose, etc.

han′dle (han′dəl) *v.t.* **1,** touch, manipulate, manage, or control with the hands. **2,** deal with; treat of. **3,** make use of; deal in; buy and sell. —*n.* **1,** the part of an imple ment, instrument, tool, or weapon made to be gripped by the hand. **2,** a title, as Mr. **3,** (*Slang*) name or nickname. —**han′dler,** *n.*

han′dle·bar″ *n.* (usually *pl.*) one of the two bars with which a bicycle or motorcycle is steered.

hand′made″ *adj.* not made by machinery.

hand′maid″ *n.* a female servant.

hand-′me-down″ *n.* a garment or other thing previously used by someone else. —*adj.* second-hand.

hand′out″ *n.* (*Slang*) something given to a beggar.

hand′sel (han′səl) *n.* a gift; token.

hand′set″ *n.* a telephone receiver and transmitter mounted on one handle.

hand′some (hand′səm) *adj.* **1,** agreeable to the eye. **2,** large; generous. —**hand′-some·ness,** *n.*

hand′spring″ *n.* a somersault.

hand′writ′ing *n.* **1,** writing done by hand. **2,** a style of such writing.

hand′y (han′dė) *adj.* **1,** ready at hand; accessible. **2,** well-suited to use; easy to handle; convenient. **3,** skillful in using the hands; dexterous. —**hand′i·ness,** *n.*

han′dy·man″ *n.* [*pl.* **-men″**] a man employed to do odd jobs.

hang [*pret. & p.p.* **hung**] *v.t.* **1,** support from above and not from below; suspend. **2,** [*pret. & p.p.* **hanged**] suspend by the neck until dead. **3,** let dangle; let bend or droop downward. **4,** attach, as wallpaper.

5, cause (a jury) to fail to reach a verdict. —*v.i.* **1,** be suspended; dangle; swing freely. **2,** [*pret. & p.p.* **hanged**] be executed by hanging. **3,** be contingent or dependent. **4,** hold fast; cling. **5,** (with *around* or *out*) linger; loiter. **6,** impend. **7,** come to a standstill. —*n.* **1,** the way something hangs. **2,** (*Colloq.*) the precise meaning, function, operation, etc. **3,** a trifle (in expletives). —**hang fire, 1,** be slow to explode. **2,** be slow in acting. —**hang gliding,** the individual sport of soaring with the aid of a kitelike glider. —**hang out,** (*Slang*) frequent a place; reside.

hang′ar (hang′ər) *n.* a shed for housing aircraft.

hang′dog″ *adj.* **1,** mean-looking. **2,** dejected.

hang′er *n.* a device for hanging something, as clothes.

hang′er-on″ *n.* [*pl.* **hang′ers-on″**] a dependent; parasite.

hang′ing *n.* **1,** capital punishment on the gallows. **2,** a drapery, hung tapestry, etc.

hang′man (-mən) *n.* [*pl.* **-men**] an executioner.

hang′nail″ *n.* a tear in a fingernail or cuticle.

hang′out″ *n.* (*Slang*) a place one frequents.

hang′o″ver *n.* (*Colloq.*) a belated effect of a previous act or condition; esp., illness induced by excessive drinking of liquor.

hang′up *n.* (*Slang*) **1,** a problem. **2,** an obsession; phobia.

hank *n.* a skein, as of thread or yarn; a coil or knot.

han′ker (hang′kər) *v.i.* have an uneasy craving; yearn keenly. —**han′ker·ing,** *n.*

han′ky (hang′kè) *n.* (*Colloq.*) handkerchief.

han′ky-pan′ky (hang′kè-pang′kè) *n.* trickery; legerdemain.

han′som (han′səm) *n.* a two-passenger carriage with an elevated rear seat for the driver.

Ha′nuk·kah″ (hä′nú-kä″) *n.* the Jewish Feast of the Dedication.

hap″haz′ard (hap″haz′ərd) *adj.* occurring by chance; accidental; random. —*adv.* at random.

hap′less (hap′ləs) *adj.* unlucky; unfortunate. —**hap′less·ness,** *n.*

hap′pen (hap′ən) *v.i.* **1,** come to pass; take place; occur. **2,** occur by chance.

hap′pen·ing (hap′ən-ing) *n.* **1,** a theatrical event, usu. partially or wholly spontaneous, often involving audience participation. **2,** any spontaneous social occurrence.

hap′pen·stance″ (-stans″) *n.* a fortuitous happening.

hap′py (hap′ē) *adj.* **1,** glad; joyous; satisfied; pleased. **2,** giving pleasure; agreeable. **3,** lucky; fortunate. **4,** very fitting; apt; felicitous. —**hap′pi·ness,** *n.* —**hap′py-go-luck′y,** *adj.* unworried; irresponsible.

ha′ra-ki′ri (hä′rə-kir′ē) *n.* (*Jap.*) suicide by ripping open the abdomen with a knife.

ha·rangue′ (hə-rang′) *n.* a long vehement speech; a tirade. —*v.t. & i.* address in a harangue; declaim.

har′ass (har′əs) *v.t.* annoy by repeated attacks; disturb or torment persistently. —**har′ass·ment,** *n.*

har′bin·ger (här′bin-jər) *n.* a forerunner that gives notice of the coming of another.

har′bor (här′bər) *n.***1,** a bay, cove, etc., that affords shelter or anchorage for ships. **2,** a refuge. —*v.t.* **1,** give shelter to; protect; conceal. **2,** have in the mind, as suspicious feelings. Also, **har′bour.** —**har′bor·age,** *n.* shelter.

hard (härd) *adj.* **1,** solid in substance or texture; resistant to penetration or cutting; unyielding. **2,** enduring; resistant; tough. **3,** firmly formed; tight. **4,** difficult; not easy to do, understand, etc. **5,** requiring or displaying great energy or exertion. **6,** harsh; severe; violent. **7,** shrewd; unsentimental; unfriendly. **8,** intoxicating; strong. —*adv.* **1,** vigorously; earnestly; intently. **2,** roughly; harshly. **3,** fully; closely. —**hard′ness,** *n.* —**hard and fast,** inflexible. —**hard liquor,** spirituous liquor of high alcoholic content. —**hard money, 1,** coins. **2,** cash. —**hard of hearing,** somewhat deaf. —**hard up,** short of funds. —**hard water,** water that contains mineral salts resistant to dissolving soap.

hard′bit″ten *adj.* obstinate; tough.

hard″boiled′ (-boild′) *adj.* **1,** boiled until hard. **2,** (*Colloq.*) unpitying; disillusioned; sophisticated.

hard′en (här′dən) *v.t. & i.* make or become harder.

hard′fist″ed (-fis″tid) *adj.* stingy.

hard′hat″ *n.* **1,** a protective head covering. **2,** (*Colloq.*) a construction worker.

hard′head″ed *adj.* **1,** realistic; practical. **2,** obstinate.

har′di·hood″ (här′dē-hûd″) *n.* boldness; venturesome spirit.

hard′ly (-lē) *adv.* **1,** barely; not quite. **2,** not probable. **3,** harshly.

hard′nosed″ (-nōzd″) *adj.* (*Colloq.*) **1,** stubborn; persistent. **2,** determined.

hard′pan″ *n.* a layer of hard clay, etc., underlying soft soil.

hard′ship″ *n.* something that exacts endurance, as suffering, want, adversity.

hard'tack" *n.* hard, dry biscuits.

hard'top" *n.* an automobile with a fixed metal roof designed to resemble a convertible.

hard'ware" *n.* wares made of metal, as tools, cutlery, etc.

hard'wood" *n.* **1**, deciduous timber. **2**, any heavy, compact, closegrained wood, as oak, maple, etc.

har'dy (här'dè) *adj.* capable of resisting hardship; strong; enduring. —**har'di·ness,** *n.*

hare (hâr) *n.* a rodent similar to the rabbit.

hare'brained" (hâr'brând") *adj.* reckless; giddy. —**hare'brained"ness,** *n.*

hare'lip" (hâr'lip") *n.* a congenital deformation of the upper lip by a vertical cleft or fissure.

har'em (hâr'əm) *n.* **1**, the women in an Oriental residence; their quarters. **2**, (*Humorous*) a train of feminine admirers.

hark (härk) *v.i.* listen. —*interj.* Listen! Give attention! —**hark back,** retrace one's steps; revert.

hark'en (-ən) *v.i.* give heed.

har'le·quin (här'lə-kwin) *n.* a clown; a jester. —**har'le·qui·nade'** (-kwə-nād') *n.* a farce.

har'lot (här'lət) *n.* a prostitute.

harm (härm) *n.* physical or moral injury; damage; detriment; wrong; mischief. —*v.t.* injure; hurt; be detrimental to. —**harm'ful,** *adj.* injurious. —**harm'ful·ness,** *n.* —**harm'less,** *adj.* unable to harm. —**harm'less·ness,** *n.*

har·mon'ic (här-mon'ik) *adj.* **1**, pert. to harmony. **2**, in harmony; concordant. —**har·mon'i·cal·ly,** *adv.*

har·mon'i·ca (här-mon'ə-kə) *n.* a small musical instrument played by blowing; a mouth organ.

har·mon'ics (här-mon'iks) *n.* the science of musical sounds.

har·mo'ni·ous (här-mō'nè-əs) *adj.* **1**, pleasing to the ear or eye. **2**, agreeable; friendly. —**har·mo'ni·ous·ness,** *n.*

har·mo'ni·um (här-mō'nè-əm) *n.* a reed organ.

har'mo·nize" (här'mə-nīz) *v.t.* bring to accord or agreement. —*v.i.* sing in harmony. —**har"mo·ni·za'tion,** *n.*

har'mo·ny (här'mə-nè) *n.* **1**, (*Music*) the sound of two or more simultaneous tones; the structure and relationship of chords. **2**, a pleasing arrangement or combination of parts; congruity. **3**, agreement, as in sentiments or interests; accord; peace and friendship.

har'ness (här'nəs) *n.* **1**, the straps and other gear put on a horse or other draft animal; any similar arrangement of straps. **2**, (*Slang*) girdle. —*v.t.* **1**, put a harness on. **2**, link up for use; make useful application of. —**in harness,** employed; active; at work.

harp (härp) *n.* **1**, a musical instrument with strings played by plucking. **2**, (*Slang*) (sometimes offensive) an Irishman. —*v.i.* (*Colloq.*) (with *on*) speak or write of repetitiously. —**harp'ist,** *n.*

har·poon' (här-poon') *n.* a barbed spear attached to a rope, used in capturing large fish or whales. —*v.t.* strike with a harpoon.

harp'si·chord" (härp'si-kôrd") *n.* a keyboard musical instrument in which the strings are plucked by quills or quill-like plectrums.

har'py (här'pè) *n.* a repulsively greedy and unfeeling person, esp. a woman.

har'ri·dan (har'ə-dən) *n.* an odious old woman; a hag.

har'ri·er (har'è-ər) *n.* **1**, a breed of hunting dog. **2**, a cross-country runner. **3**, a hawk.

har'row (har'ō) *n.* an agricultural implement, as a heavy frame set with iron teeth, used to break up clods. —*v.t.* **1**, draw a harrow over. **2**, affect the feelings of; distress. —**har'row·ing,** *adj.* distressing.

har'ry (har'è) *v.t.* harass; ravage.

harsh (härsh) *adj.* **1**, rough to the senses; sharp, sour, discordant, irritating, etc. **2**, severe in character or effect; hard. —**harsh'ness,** *n.*

hart (härt) *n.* a male of the deer.

har'te·beest" (här'tə-bēst") *n.* a large So. Afr. antelope.

harts'horn" (härts'hôrn") *n.* **1**, the antler of the hart. **2**, a solution of ammonia in water or alcohol.

har'um-scar'um (hâr'əm-skâr'əm) *adj.* giddy; rash.

har'vest (här'vəst) *n.* **1**, the gathering of crops. **2**, the season for gathering crops; autumn. **3**, a crop gathered, as grain. **4**, a supply of anything gathered and stored; the product of any labor. —*v.t. & i.* gather or reap, as grain.

har'vest·er (här'vəs-tər) *n.* a machine that harvests grain.

has (haz) *v.* 3rd person singular of *have.*

has-'been" *n.* (*Colloq.*) a person formerly but no longer notable.

has'en·pfef"fer (hä'zən-pfef"ər) *n.* (*Ger.*) rabbit stew.

hash *n.* **1**, a dish of chopped meat and potatoes. **2**, any mixture, or muddle. **3**, (*Slang*) hashish. —*v.t.* **1**, make hash of. **2**, botch; bungle. —**hash mark, 1,** a military service stripe. **2**, a vertical stroke, as of a pencil. **3**, discuss.

hash'ish (hash'ēsh) *n.* a narcotic preparation made from Indian hemp.

hasp (hásp) *n.* a clasp for a door, etc.; a wire loop or hook.

has'sle (has'əl) *n.* (*Slang*) an argument; quarrel.

has'sock (has'ək) *n.* 1, a thick hard cushion used as a footstool. 2, a clump or tuft of coarse grass.

haste (hāst) *n.* 1, swiftness; promptness. 2, undue or rash quickness. —*v.i.* hasten.

has'ten (hā'sən) *v.i.* go, move, or act quickly; hurry. —*v.t.* cause to go fast or faster; accelerate.

hast'y (hās'tē) *adj.* 1, unduly hurried or accelerated. 2, thoughtless. —**hast'i·ness**, *n.* —**hasty pudding**, porridge.

hat *n.* a covering for the head, esp. one worn outdoors, having a crown and brim. —**pass the hat**, take a collection; ask for contributions.

hatch (hach) *v.t.* 1, bring forth young from (an egg). 2, contrive or produce (a plan, a result). 3, mark lines for shading (a drawing). —*v.i.* 1, emerge from a shell. 2, be contrived or produced. —*n.* 1, what is hatched; a brood. 2, a fine line, as in engraving. 3, an opening or door: *hatchway*. 4, a cover for such an opening. —**hatch'er·y** (-ə-rè) *n.* a place for hatching eggs. —**hatch'ing**, *n.* fine lines, usu. parallel, used in shading or modeling.

hatch'back'' *n.* an automobile with a sloped roof which opens in the rear.

hatch'et (hach'it) *n.* a short-handled ax for use by one hand. —**bury the hatchet**, make peace. —**hatchet job**, (*Colloq.*) a harsh verbal attack.

hatch'et·man'' *n.* [*pl.*-men''] a paid assassin; a gunman.

hatch'way'' *n.* 1, a rectangular opening in a ship's deck. 2, the opening of any trap door.

hate (hāt) *v.t.*1, regard with strong aversion or ill will; detest. 2, find unpalatable or unappealing. —*v.i.* feel hatred. —*n.* 1, passionate dislike or ill will. 2, something hated.

hate'ful (hāt'fəl) *adj.* 1, detestable; abhorrent. 2, malicious; malevolent. —**hate'ful·ness**, *n.*

hat'rack'' *n.* a rail or stand fitted with pegs to hold hats.

ha'tred (hā'trəd) *n.* passionate dislike; detestation.

hat'ter (hat'ər) *n.* one who makes or sells hats.

hau'berk (hâ'bərk) *n.* a coat of mail extending below the knees.

haugh'ty (hâ'tè) *adj.* disdainfully proud. —**haugh'ti·ness**, *n.*

haul (hâl) *v.t.* 1, pull or draw with force; move by pulling; drag. 2, (with *up*) call to account; arraign. —*v.i.* 1, pull; tug. 2, change direction; shift; veer. 3, (with *off*) withdraw; pull back the arm preparatory to a blow. —*n.* 1, a pulling with force. 2, the distance through which something is hauled. 3, a quantity gathered; (*Colloq.*) a valuable acquisition. —**haul'age**, *n.* the process of, or a fee for, hauling. —**haul'er**, *n.* one who hauls, esp. a truckman.

haunch (hânch) *n.* the fleshy part of the body above the thigh; hip.

haunt (hânt) *v.t.* 1, reappear to frequently after dying, as a ghost. 2, visit frequently. —*v.i.* reappear, as a specter. —*n.* 1, (often *pl.*) a place frequently visited. 2, (hant) (*Dial.*) a ghost, or his visiting ground.

haute' cou·ture' (ōt'koo-tür') (*Fr.*) high fashion.

hau·teur' (hō-tēr') *n.* haughtiness.

have (hav) *v.t.* [*present indicative:* **I have**; *you* **have** (*Archaic*, thou **hast**); *he* **has** (*Archaic*, **hath**); *we*, *you*, *they* **have**; *pret.* & *p.p.* **had**; **hav'ing**] 1, possess; own; hold. 2, acquire; obtain; receive. 3, contain; comprise; be in part. 4, hold in custody; control. 5, hold in the mind; entertain; maintain. 6, exhibit in action; exercise; show. 7, possess knowledge of; be affected with; experience. 8, procure to be done; permit; allow. 9, (with *on*) wear. 10, (*Slang*) outwit. —*aux. v.* used with a past participle to form a perfect tense, as I *have done* it, he *had gone*. —*n.* (*Colloq.*) a person or nation that has material wealth. —**have at**, attack. —**have it in for**, hold a grudge against.

ha'ven (hā'vən) *n.* a harbor; a place of shelter or asylum.

have-'not'' *n.* (*Colloq.*) a person or nation lacking in material wealth.

hav'er·sack'' (hav'ər-sak'') *n.* a bag for provisions; knapsack.

hav'oc (hav'ək) *n.* general destruction; devastation.

haw (hâ) *interj.* 1, a command to turn left. 2, an expression marking indecision in speech. 3, ha; a guffaw. —*v.i.* speak with hesitation.

hawk (hâk) *n.* 1, any of numerous birds of prey. 2, (*Colloq.*) an advocate of militaristic policies. 3, a hard cough; a noisy effort to clear the throat. —*v.t.* offer for sale; peddle. —*v.i.* 1, hunt with hawks. 2, try to cough. 3, peddle. —**hawk'er**, *n.* one who cries his wares; peddler.

hawk'eyed'' (hâk'īd'') *adj.* having keen vision.

haws (hâz) *n. pl.* a disease of the third eyelid of a horse.

haw′ser (hâ′zər) *n.* a rope or cable used on a ship for mooring, etc.

haw′thorn″ (hâ′thôrn″) *n.* a thorny shrub or small tree, much used in hedges.

hay (hā) *n.* grass cut and dried for use as fodder. —*v.i.* cut and dry grass for use as fodder. —**hay fever,** an allergic reaction to pollen with symptoms like those of a cold.

hay′cock″ *n.* a conical pile of hay in a field.

hay′mak″er *n.* (*Slang*) a decisive blow; knockout punch.

hay′seed″ *n.* (*Colloq.*) a rustic; a naïve person.

hay′stack″ *n.* a pile of hay.

hay′wire″ *adj.* (*Slang*) crazy; hopelessly confused.

haz′ard (haz′ərd) *n.* **1,** exposure to danger; risk; peril. **2,** a fortuitous event; chance; accident. **3,** something dangerous or obstructive; an obstacle. **4,** something risked. **5,** a dice game. —*v.t.* **1,** put up as a stake; expose to danger or loss. **2,** run the risk of incurring or bringing to pass. **3,** do or say tentatively. —**haz′ard·ous,** *adj.* dangerous.

haze (hāz) *n.* **1,** a thin mist or fog. **2,** obscurity; vagueness, as of thought. —*v.t.* play mischievous tricks on (a candidate for membership). —**haz′y,** *adj.* foggy; vague.

ha′zel (hā′zəl) *n.* **1,** any of several shrubs or small trees. **2,** a pale brown color. —**ha′zel·nut″,** *n.*

H-′bomb″ *n.* hydrogen bomb.

he (hē) *pron.* [*poss.* **his;** *obj.* **him**] **1,** the third person sing masc.; a male, other than the speaker and the person addressed. **2,** any male. —*adj.* (*Colloq.*) male.

head (hed) *n.* **1,** the uppermost part of the human body, above the neck; the skull with its contents and integuments; the corresponding part of any animal. **2,** the head regarded as the seat of intelligence; understanding; will; inclination. **3,** the position or person of a leader or chief. **4,** the highest or foremost part; the top or summit; the obverse of a coin. **5,** the source, as of a stream. **6,** culmination; crisis; force; pressure. **7,** something like a head in position, form, or function; a rounded protuberance; the compact inflorescence of a plant, as cabbage; the membrane of a drum. **8,** an individual, taken as one of a number. **9,** a subject or topic; a title or subtitle; heading; headline. **10,** (*Slang*) a dope addict; one who takes drugs, esp. LSD. —*adj.* **1,** being at the head; foremost; principal. **2,** coming from in front. —*v.t.* **1,** be the chief of. **2,** go to the front of; lead; precede. **3,** turn or direct in advancing. **4,** oppose; check; restrain. —*v.i.* **1,** go in a direction. **2,** origi-

nate. —**lose one's head,** become excited or panicky.

head′ache″ *n.* **1,** a pain in the head. **2,** (*Colloq.*) a troublesome person or circumstance.

head′cheese″ *n.* a loaf made of the head and feet of hogs.

-head′ed (hed′id) *suf.* **1,** having a specified kind of head or number of heads. **2,** having a specified mind or temperament, as *levelheaded.*

head′er (-ər) *n.* **1,** a brick or stone laid lengthwise across the thickness of a wall. **2,** (*Colloq.*) a plunge headfirst.

head′first′ *adv.* **1,** with the head foremost. **2,** rashly; impetuously.

head′gear″ *n.* a helmet; any covering for the head.

head′ing (hed′ing) *n.* **1,** a title or caption. **2,** something that forms a head or front. **3,** the compass point toward which a craft is directed.

head′land (hed′lənd) *n.* a point of land projecting into the sea; a cape.

head′light″ *n.* a lamp to illuminate the road ahead.

head′line″ *n.* a title in large type, as in a newspaper. —*v.t.* give prominent billing to; advertise. —**head′lin″er,** *n.* lead performer.

head′lock″ *n.* a wrestling hold.

head′long″ *adv.* & *adj.* **1,** hastily; rashly. **2,** with head foremost.

head′mas″ter *n.* the principal of a (usu. boys') school. —**head′mis″tress,** *n. fem.*

head-′on′ *adj.* & *adv.* with the head or front first.

head′phone″ *n.* a radio, telephone, or high-fidelity receiver held against the ear(s) by a clamp over the head. Also, **head′set″.**

head′quar″ters *n. pl.* or *sing.* **1,** a principal office or residence. **2,** a seat of command.

heads′man (hedz″mən) *n.* [*pl.*-**men**] an executioner.

head′stall″ *n.* that part of a bridle which encompasses the head.

head′stone″ *n.* a stone placed at the head of a grave.

head′strong″ *adj.* obstinate; willful.

head′wait″er *n.* maître d'hôtel.

head′wat″ers *n. pl.* the source and earliest tributaries of a river.

head′way″ *n.* **1,** motion or impetus forward. **2,** clear space in height, as under a bridge.

head′wind″ *n.* a wind blowing opposite to the direction of one's travel.

head′y (hed′ē) *adj.* exhilarating; intoxicating. —**head′i·ness,** *n.*

heal (hēl) v.t. **1,** make whole or sound; restore to health. **2,** cleanse; purify; remedy; repair. —v.i. grow whole or sound; get well. —**heal′er,** n. one who heals, not a physician.

health (helth) n. **1,** freedom from disease; good condition; normal and efficient functioning. **2,** bodily condition. **3,** a toast. —**health′ful,** adj. conducive to health. —**health′y,** adj. sound; in good condition.

heap (hēp) n. **1,** a collection of things laid together, esp. in a raised pile. **2,** (Colloq.) a large number or quantity. **3,** (Slang) an automobile. —v.t. **1,** put together; pile; amass. **2,** bestow bountifully. —**heap′ing,** adj. filled above the level of a retaining wall.

hear (hir) v.t. [**heard, hear′ing**] **1,** perceive by ear. **2,** listen to; give attention to. **3,** be informed of. —v.i. **1,** possess the sense of hearing. **2,** be told; learn by report. —**hear′er,** n. one of an audience. —**hear! hear!,** an exclamation expressing approval.

hear′ing n. **1,** ability to perceive by ear. **2,** an opportunity to be heard. **3,** an examination in a court of law. **4,** earshot. —**hearing aid,** a device to amplify sounds for the hard-of-hearing.

hear′say″ n. information communicated by another; gossip; rumor.

hearse (hērs) n. a vehicle for bearing a corpse to a burial ground.

heart (härt) n. **1,** the principal organ that causes blood to circulate in the body. **2,** this organ regarded as the seat of vitality intellect, emotion, etc. **3,** love; kindness; pity. **4,** courage; determination; enthusiasm. **5,** the inner, central, or essential part of anything. **6,** the symbol (♥); a playing card so marked. —**by heart,** by memory. —**take heart,** have courage. —**take to heart, 1,** think about earnestly. **2,** be queried about.

heart′ache″ n. mental anguish; sorrow or grief.

heart′break″ n. overwhelming sorrow or grief. —**heart′bro″ken,** adj.

heart′burn″ n. a burning sensation due to stomach acidity.

-heart′ed (här′tid) suf. having a specified kind of heart or sentiment.

heart′en (här′tən) v.t. incite with courage or good cheer; encourage.

heart′felt″ adj. felt deeply; sincere.

hearth (härth) n. **1,** a place where a fire is built; a section of floor in front of an open fire. **2,** the home or domestic circle; the fireside.

hearth′stone″ n. a stone or one of the stones forming a fireplace.

heart′land″ n. a region of special importance.

heart′less adj. unfeeling; cruel. —**heart′-less·ness,** n.

heart-′rend″ing adj. causing extreme grief or pity; harrowing.

heart′sick″ adj. unhappy; grieving. Also, **heart′sore″.** —**heart′sick″ness, heart′-sore″ness,** n.

heart′strings″ n.pl. the deepest feelings.

heart′throb″ n. a deep emotion or something that arouses it.

heart-′to-heart′ adj. confidential; unreservedly revealing, as a talk.

heart′y (här′tē) adj. **1,** friendly; cordial; affectionate. **2,** vigorous; enthusiastic; zealous. **3,** large; substantial. —n. a robust or brave person. —**heart′i·ness,** n.

heat (hēt) n. **1,** the condition, caused by friction, expenditure of energy, etc., that induces the sensation one feels when exposed to fire and causes substances to expand; the sensation, effect, etc., of being hot. **2,** high temperature; a hot condition, as of the atmosphere. **3,** passionate feeling; rage, vehemence, excitement, etc. **4,** the mating period of a female animal. **5,** one division of an athletic contest; one heating of metal in a furnace, etc. **6,** (Slang) the police or other authority. —v.t. **1,** make hot, hotter, or less cold. **2,** inflame with feeling. —v.i. **1,** become warmer. **2,** become excited. —**heat′ed,** adj. excited; angry.

heat′er n. **1,** a device for heating. **2,** (Slang) a handgun.

heath (hēth) n. **1,** a tract of uncultivated waste land. **2,** any of several evergreen shrubs.

hea′then (hē′thən) n. **1,** an irreligious person. **2,** a pagan.

heath′er (heth′ər) n. a variety of heath common in Scotland.

heave (hēv) v.t. **1,** lift with marked effort; raise with exertion. **2,** throw upward and outward; toss; hurl. **3,** utter laboriously or painfully. —v.i. **1,** be raised, thrown, or forced up; swell up; bulge out. **2,** rise and fall, as the ocean. **3,** breathe laboriously; pant. **4,** vomit. —n. **1,** the act of heaving; an upward thrust or movement. **2,** the surface displacement of a geological fault. **3,** (pl.) a respiratory disease of horses.

heav′en (hev′ən) n. **1,** the abode of God; the place or state of existence of the blessed, after death. **2,** (cap.) God; Providence. **3,** a state of bliss; supreme happiness or exaltation. **4,** (usually pl.) the visible sky; the firmament.

heav′en·ly (-lē) adj. **1,** blissful; sublime. **2,** pert. to heaven; in the heavens.

heav′en·ward (-wərd) *adv.* & *adj.* toward heaven; upward; aloft.

heav′y (hev′ē) *adj.* **1,** having much weight; hard to lift or move. **2,** of high specific gravity; dense. **3,** great volume, force, intensity, etc.; thick, coarse, broad, deep, loud, etc. **4,** serious; intense; somber; dull; ponderous; sluggish. **5,** hard to bear; hard to do. **6,** pregnant. —*n.* a villainous character in a play. —**heav′i·ness,** *n.* —**heavy hydrogen,** deuterium. —**heavy water,** water in which hydrogen atoms have been replaced by deuterium.

heav′y-du′ty *adj.* capable of withstanding great wear, strain, etc.

heav′y-hand″ed *adj.* **1,** oppressive. **2,** clumsy.

heav′y-heart″ed *adj.* sad; mournful; dejected.

heav′y-set″ *adj.* stout; stocky.

heav′y-weight″ *n.* a boxer or wrestler weighing more than 175 lbs.

heb·dom′a·dal (heb-dom′ə-dəl) *adj.* weekly.

he·bet′ic (hi-bet′ik) *adj.* pert. to or occurring during puberty; immature.

He·bra′ic (hė-brā′ik) *adj.* **1,** of or like the Hebrews; Jewish. **2,** in or pert. to Hebrew.

He′brew (hē′broo) *n.* **1,** a Semitic language; the official language of Israel. **2,** a Jew.

hec′a·tomb″ (hek′ə-tōm″) *n.* a great slaughter; a mass sacrifice.

heck′le (hek′əl) *v.t.* harass with questions, objections, jibes, etc.

hec′tare (hek′tār) *n.* a metric measure of land, 10,000 square meters or about 2½ acres.

hec′tic (hek′tik) *adj.* **1,** turbulent; excited; impassioned. **2,** feverish; consumptive.

hect·o- (hek-tə) *pref.* hundred.

hec′to·graph″ *n.* the process of copying writings by offset from a gelatin base.

hec′tor (hek′tər) *v.t.* bully; tease; harass. —*n.* a bully.

hedge (hej) *n.* a barrier or fence formed by bushes or small trees growing close together. —*v.t.* **1,** enclose by a hedge. **2,** surround; hem in; obstruct. **3,** protect (a bet) by betting on both sides. —*v.i.* **1,** avoid a decisive course; veer aside; hesitate. **2,** provide a means of retreat or escape; protect a risk by some offsetting transaction.

hedge′hog″ *n.* **1,** a small insectivorous mammal. **2,** the porcupine.

hedge′hop″ *v.i.* [**hopped″, -hop″ping**] fly an airplane dangerously near the ground.

he′don·ism (hē′də-niz-əm) *n.* the doctrine that pleasure or happiness is the highest good. —**he″don·ist,** *n.* —**he″don·is′tic,** *adj.* —**he″don·is′ti·cal·ly,** *adv.*

-he′dron (hē′drən) *suf.* denoting a solid figure with several faces.

heed (hēd) *v.t.* & *i.* give attention; observe; consider. —*n.* careful notice or consideration. —**heed′ful,** *adj.* —**heed′less,** *adj.* neglectful; unwary.

hee′haw″ (hē′hä″) *n.* the bray of an ass.

heel (hēl) *n.* **1,** the back part of the foot. **2,** the part of a stocking covering the heel; the rear support of a shoe. **3,** the rear, concluding, or final part of something. **4,** a tipping motion; a canted position. **5,** (*Slang*) a low character; a cad. —*v.t.* **1,** furnish with a heel. **2,** follow on the heels of; pursue. **3,** (*Colloq.*) arm; equip. **4,** cause to tilt. —*v.i.* **1,** tip to one side. **2,** run; dance.

heft *v.t.* heave; try the weight of by lifting. —*n.* weight.

heft′y (hef′tė) *adj.* **1,** heavy. **2,** muscular; strong. —**heft′i·ness,** *n.*

he·gem′o·ny (hi-jem′ə-nė) *n.* leadership or predominance, esp. by one member of a confederation of nations.

He·gi′ra (he-ji′rə) *n.* the flight of Mohammed from Mecca, A.D. 622.

heif′er (hef′ər) *n.* a female cow that has not produced a calf.

heigh (hā) *interj.* a cry for attention.

height (hīt) *n.* **1,** vertical distance above the ground or base; altitude; elevation. **2,** distance upward; stature. **3,** elevation of degree or condition; eminence. **4,** the state of being high; loftiness. **5,** the highest part; top; apex. **6,** the highest degree; the culminating point.

height′en (hī′tən) *v.t.* **1,** increase the height of. **2,** intensify. —*v.i.* **1,** become higher. **2,** become more intense.

hei′nous (hā′nəs) *adj.* wicked; reprehensible. —**hei′nous·ness,** *n.*

heir (âr) *n.* **1,** one who inherits property from another; one who will inherit. **2,** successor; beneficiary. —**heir′ess,** *n.fem.* —**heir apparent,** one who must inherit, if he survives. —**heir presumptive,** one who will inherit unless a more eligible candidate is born.

heir′loom″ (âr′loom″) *n.* a personal possession handed down from generation to generation in a family.

heist (hīst) (*Slang*) *n.* a burglary; the property stolen. —*v.t.* steal.

held *v.* pret. & p.p. of *hold.*

he″li·an′thus (hē″lė-an′thəs) *n.* a sunflower.

hel′i·cal (hel′i-kəl) *adj.* spiral.

hel′i·con (hel′i-kon) *n.* a bass tuba.

hel′i·cop″ter (hel′i-kop″tər) *n.* an aircraft

that is given vertical lift as well as propulsion by a horizontal propeller.

he·li·o- (hē-lē-ə) *pref.* sun.

he'li·o·graph" *n.* a device for signaling by reflecting the rays of the sun.

he'li·o·trope" (hē'lē-ə-trōp") *n.* **1,** a flower-bearing plant that turns toward the sun. **2,** a pale or pinkish purple color.

hel'i·pad *n.* a landing space for a helicopter.

hel'i·port" (hel'i-pôrt") *n.* an airport for helicopters.

he'li·um (hē'lē-əm) *n.* an inert gaseous chemical element, no. 2, symbol He.

he'lix (hē'liks) *n.* **1,** a spiral; a spiral part. **2,** a coil; the typical curve of a screw thread.

hell (hel) *n.* **1,** the abode or state of the wicked after death. **2,** any place or state of great suffering or misery. **3,** a place of low repute.

hell'bend"er (-ben"dər) *n.* **1,** a salamander. **2,** (*Slang*) a reckless debauch.

hell'bent" *adj.* (*Slang*) recklessly determined to have or do at all costs.

hell'cat" *n.* a violent woman.

Hel·len'ic (he-len'ik) *adj.* **1,** Greek. **2,** pert. to Amer. college fraternities and sororities.

hell'er (-ər) *n.* a wild or dissipated person.

hell'fire" *n.* **1,** the fire of hell. **2,** punishment; retribution.

hell'hound" *n.* a fiend.

hell'ion (hel'yən) *n.* a troublemaking, uncontrollable person.

hell'ish (-ish) *adj.* vile; unbearable. —**hell'ish·ness,** *n.*

hel·lo' (he-lō') *interj.* **1,** a greeting; a conventional salutation in telephoning. **2,** an exclamation of surprise.

helm *n.* **1,** the tiller or wheel controlling the rudder of a ship. **2,** the place or post of control.

hel'met (hel'mit) *n.* a protective covering for the head; any of various types of metal hats.

helms'man (helmz'mən) *n.* [*pl.* **-men**] a pilot.

hel'ot (hel'ət) *n.* a serf or slave.

help *v.t.* **1,** give aid to; assist in doing or attaining. **2,** bring relief to; succor; save. **3,** mitigate; relieve. **4,** repair; remedy. **5,** serve or distribute food (to). —*v.t.* give aid; be of service. —*n.* **1,** the act of helping; aid; relief; remedy. **2,** someone or something that helps; an assistant; servants, esp. domestic; a remedy. —**help'er,** *n.* an assistant. —**help'ful,** *adj.* useful. —**help'ing,** *n.* a portion of food served to a person at one time. —**help'less,** *adj.* entirely

ineffective or dependent; unable to move or perform.

help'mate" *n.* a spouse, esp. a wife. Also, **help'meet".**

hel'ter-skel'ter (hel'tər-skel'tər) *adj. & adv.* with confused haste or commotion; in a disorderly hurry. —*n.* confused action; bustle.

helve (helv) *n.* the handle of an ax.

hem *n.* **1,** a fold on the edge of a cloth, sewed down to prevent raveling. **2,** an edge, rim, or border. —*v.t.* [**hemmed, hem'ming**] **1,** form a hem on. **2,** (often with *in*) enclose; limit. —*v.i.* clear the throat. —*interj.* a clearing of the throat; a mild exclamation to attract attention. —**hem and haw,** hesitate in speaking.

he'man" (hē'man") *n.* (*Colloq.*) a muscular virile man.

he"ma·tol'o·gy (hē"mə-tol'ə-jē) *n.* a branch of biology dealing with the blood.

hem·i- (hem-ə) *pref.* half.

hem'i·sphere" (hem'ə-sfir") *n.* half of a sphere, esp. of the terrestrial globe or celestial sphere: the No. and So. hemispheres are regarded as divided by the equator, the W. and E. hemispheres by the Atlantic and Pacific Oceans. —**hem"i·spher'i·cal** (-sfer'ə-kəl) *adj.*

hem'lock (hem'lok) *n.* **1,** an herb from which is obtained a powerful sedative. **2,** an evergreen tree of the spruce family.

he·mo- (hē-mə) *pref.* blood.

he"mo·glo'bin (hē"mə-glō'bin) *n.* the coloring matter of the red blood corpuscles.

he"mo·phil'i·a (hē"mə-fil'ē-ə) *n.* an affliction in which the blood does not coagulate readily. —**he"mo·phil'i·ac,** *n.* one so afflicted.

hem'or·rhage (hem'ə-rij) *n.* a discharge of blood from a ruptured blood vessel.

hem'or·rhoid" (hem'ə-roid") *n.* a swelling of a vein in the rectum; a pile.

he'mo·stat" (hē'mə-stat") *n.* an instrument for checking hemorrhage.

hemp *n.* any of various fibrous shrubs, used for cordage, fabrics, and narcotic drugs. —**hemp'en,** *adj.*

hem'stitch" *n.* a hem joined where threads have been pulled to make a decorative pattern.

hen *n.* **1,** a female fowl, esp. a chicken. **2,** a censorious married woman.

hence (hens) *adv.* **1,** as a consequence; for this reason; therefore. **2,** from this time; in the future. **3,** from this place. **4,** from this source or origin.

hence"forth' *adv.* from this time onward.

hench'man (hench'mən) *n.* [*pl.* **-men**] an attendant or follower.

hen'na (hen'ə) *n.* an Asiatic shrub; a reddish-brown dye made from it. —*v.t.* dye (esp. hair) with henna.

hen'ner·y (-ə-rē) *n.* a hen house.

hen'peck" (hen'pek") *v.t.* domineer over (said of a wife who thus rules her husband).

hen'ry (hen'rē) *n.* a unit of inductance.

hep *adj.* (*Slang*) well-informed; being one of the elect. —**hep'cat"**, *n.* (*Slang*) one thoroughly conversant with jazz.

he·pat'ic (hi-pat'ik) *adj.* pert. to the liver.

hep"a·ti'tis (hep"ə-tī'tis) *n.* inflammation of the liver.

hep·ta- (hep-tə) *pref.* seven.

her (hėr) *pron.* obj. and poss. case of *she.*

her'ald (her'əld) *n.* **1,** an announcer; crier; publisher. **2,** one who proclaims in advance; forerunner; harbinger. **3,** a messenger. **4,** one who regulates the use of armorial bearings. —*v.t.* give tidings of; announce. —**he·ral'dic** (he-ral'dik) *adj.* —**her'ald·ry** (-rē) *n.* the art and science of armorial bearings.

herb (ėrb, hėrb) *n.* an annual plant whose stem does not become woody, often used for medicine, flavoring, etc. —**herb·ba'ceous** (hėr-bā'shəs) *adj.* —**herb'age**, *n.* herbs collectively or growing together. —**herb'al**, *adj.* —**herb'al·ist**, *n.* a collector or student of herbs.

her·bar'i·um (hėr-bār'ė-əm) *n.* **1,** a collection of dried plants, arranged systematically. **2,** a place where such a collection is kept.

her'bi·cide (her'bə-sīd) *n.* plant or weed killer.

her·biv'o·rous (hėr-biv'ə-rəs) *adj.* feeding on plants only. —**her'bi·vore"** (hėr'bi-vôr") *n.*

her·cu'le·an (hėr-kū'lė-ən) *adj.* having or requiring prodigious strength, endurance, etc.

herd (hėrd) *n.* **1,** a number of animals together. **2,** a mob; rabble. **3,** [also, **herd'er**] one who tends a herd. —*v.t.* drive together; tend or lead. —*v.i.* go together; unite.

herds'man (hėrds'mən) *n.* [*pl.* **-men**] one who tends a herd of animals.

here (hir) *adv.* **1,** in or toward this place. **2,** at this time or juncture. —*interj.* **1,** I am present. **2,** come here!

here'a·bout" *adv.* about or near this place. Also, **here'a·bouts"**

here·af'ter (-af'tėr) *adv.* **1,** in the future. **2,** beyond this place or juncture. —*n.* future time, esp. after death.

here'by" *adv.* by this means or agency; as a result of this.

he·red'i·tar·y (hi-red'ə-tār-ė) *adj.* **1,** passing naturally from parent to offspring; descending by inheritance. **2,** pert. to heredity.

he·red'i·ty (hə-red'ə-tē) *n.* the transmission of qualities or characteristics from parents to offspring.

here·in' *adv.* **1,** in this place. **2,** in view of this.

here·of' *adv.* of or concerning this.

her'e·sy (her'ə-sė) *n.* an unorthodox doctrine or opinion, esp. in religion.

her'e·tic (her'ə-tik) *n.* one who holds an unorthodox opinion. —*adj.* of such opinion. —**he·ret'i·cal** (hə-ret'i-kəl) *adj.*

here·to' *adv.* to this.

here"to·fore' *adv.* before this time.

here"up·on' *adv.* at or immediately following this time or event.

her'it·a·ble (her'ə-tə-bəl) *adj.* capable of being inherited. —**her"it·a·bil'i·ty,** *n.*

her'it·age (her'ə-tij) *n.* **1,** something inherited. **2,** a condition, lot, or portion acquired by being born.

her·maph'ro·dite" (hėr-maf'rə-dīt") *n.* an animal or plant having both male and female organs of generation. —**her·maph"ro·dit'ic** (-dit'ik) *adj.*

her·met'ic (hėr-met'ik) *adj.* made airtight by sealing, as a container. —**her·met'i·cal·ly,** *adv.*

her'mit (hėr'mit) *n.* one who lives alone and avoids the society of others; a recluse. —**her'mit·age,** *n.* the dwelling of a hermit.

her'ni·a (hėr'nė-ə) *n.* the protrusion of a bodily organ or tissue through its surrounding walls, esp. abdominal; a rupture. —**her'ni·ate** (-āt) *v.i.* rupture.

he'ro (hir'ō) *n.* **1,** a man admired for his courage, fortitude, prowess, nobility, etc. **2,** the principal male character in a play, story, or poem. **3,** a submarine sandwich.

he·ro'ic (hi-rō'ik) *adj.* **1,** pert. to or like a hero. **2,** having recourse to extreme measures; daring; drastic. **3,** larger than life-size (in art). —**he·ro'i·cal·ly,** *adv.*

he·ro'ics (hi-ro'iks) *n.* bombastic language; mawkish sentiment.

her'o·in (her'ō-in) *n.* a habit-forming drug, derivative of morphine.

her'o·ine (her'ō-in) *n.* a female hero.

her'o·ism (her'ō-iz-əm) *n.* heroic qualities or conduct.

her'on (her'ən) *n.* a wading bird with long legs, neck, and bill.

her"pe·tol'o·gy (hėr"pə-tol'ə-jė) *n.* the branch of zoölogy dealing with reptiles and amphibians. —**her"pe·tol'o·gist,** *n.*

her'pes (her'pēz) *n.* an inflammatory infection of the skin or mucous membrane. —**herpes zos'ter** (zos'tər) shingles.

her'ring (her'ing) *n.* any of numerous small food fishes.

her'ring·bone" (her'ing-bōn") *n.* & *adj.* a pattern of oblique parallel lines in tiers alternating in direction.

hertz (herts) *n.* [*pl.* **hertz**] a unit equaling one cycle (of a periodic process) per second.

hers (hērz) *pron.* poss. case of *she* used predicatively.

her·self' (hẽr-self') *pron.* emphatic and reflexive form of *her.*

hes'i·tan·cy (hez'i-tən-sė) *n.* hesitation.

hes'i·tant (hez'i-tənt) *adj.* hesitating or prone to hesitate; irresolute.

hes'i·tate" (hez'i-tāt") *v.i.* **1,** hold back in doubt or indecision. **2,** falter in speech; stammer. **3,** pause. —**hes"i·ta'tion,** *n.*

Hes'sian (hesh'ən) *n.* a native of Hesse (in Germany), esp. a soldier who fought against the U.S. in the Revolutionary War.

het·er·o- (het-ər-ə) *pref.* different; other.

het'er·o·dox" (het'ər-ə-doks") *adj.* not orthodox; heretical. —**het'er·o·dox"y,** *n.*

het"er·o·ge·ne·ous (het"ər-ə-jē'nė-əs) *adj.* **1,** different in kind; widely dissimilar. **2,** composed of parts of different kinds; not homogeneous. —**het"er·o·ge'ne·ous·ness,** *n.*

het"er·o·sex'u·al (het"ər-ə-sek'shoo-əl) *adj.* **1,** pert. to different sexes. **2,** manifesting sexual desire toward a member of the opposite sex. —*n.* a heterosexual person. —**het"er·o·sex"u·al'i·ty,** *n.*

heu·ris'tic (hyû-ris'tik) *adj.* serving to demonstrate or reveal the truth. —**heu·ris'tic·al·ly,** *adv.*

hew (hū) *v.t.* & *i.* [*p.p.* **hewed** or **hewn**] **1,** cut with an ax, sword, etc.; chop. **2,** carve.

hex (heks) *v.t.* practice witchcraft on. —*n.* a spell.

hex·a- (hek-sə) *pref.* six; sixfold.

hex"a·chlor'o·phene (heks"ə-klôr'ə-fēn) *n.* an antibacterial agent used esp. in soaps.

hex'a·gon" (heks'ə-gon") *n.* a plane figure having six sides. —**hex·ag'o·nal** (heks-ag'ə-nəl) *adj.*

hex'a·gram (heks'ə-gram) *n.* **1,** a six-pointed star; Mogen David. **2,** a six-sided figure.

hex"yl·res·or'cin·ol" (hek"sil-rə-zôr'sə-nōl") *n.* an antiseptic compound.

hey (hā) *interj.* to draw attention.

hey'day" (hā'dā") *n.* highest vigor; full strength; acme.

hi·a'tus (hī-ā'təs) *n.* a space where something is missing; a gap; break.

hi·ba'chi (hi-bä'chē) *n.* a small, charcoal-burning brazier.

hi·ber'nal (hī-bẽr'nəl) *adj.* pert. to winter.

hi·ber'nate" (hī'bər-nāt") *v.i.* pass the winter in seclusion and in a torpid condition, as do some animals. —**hi"ber·na'tion,** *n.*

Hi·ber'ni·an (hī-bẽr'nė-ən) *adj.* Irish. —*n.* a native of Ireland.

hi·bis'cus (hī-bis'kəs) *n.* a shrub having large, showy flowers.

hic'cup (hik'up) *n.* **1,** a spasmodic, involuntary, audible, cutting-off of indrawn breath. **2,** (*pl.*) such spasms. —*v.i.* have the hiccups. Also, **hic'cough** (hik'up).

hick (hik) (*Slang*) *n.* a person unfamiliar with city ways; a rustic. —*adj.* countrified.

hick'ey (hik'ė) *n.* **1,** an electronic fitting. **2,** (*Slang*) a mark on the skin caused by kissing.

hick'o·ry (hik'ə-rė) *n.* a No. Amer. tree or its tough, springy wood.

hi·dal'go (hi-dal'gō) *n.* a Spanish man of the lower nobility.

hide (hīd) *v.t.* [**hid** (hid), **hid'den** (hid'ən) or **hid, hid'ing** (hī'ding)] prevent from being discovered; secrete. —*v.i.* keep out of view. —*n.* **1,** the skin of an animal, raw or dressed. **2,** (*Slang*) the human skin.

hide-'a-bed" (hīd'ə-bed") *n.* (*T.N.*) a convertible sofa.

hide'a·way" *n.* a hiding place; retreat.

hide'bound" (hīd'bownd") *adj.* narrow and stubborn in opinion.

hid'e·ous (hid'ė-əs) *adj.* frightful in appearance or character. —**hid'e·ous·ness,** *n.*

hide-'out" *n.* a secret lodging; retreat.

hid'ing (hīd'ing) *n.* **1,** the state of being hidden. **2,** (*Colloq.*) a thrashing.

hie (hī) *v.i.* go in haste.

hi'er·arch" (hī'ə-rärk") *n.* one of authority in sacred matters. —**hi"er·ar'chal** (-əl) *adj.*

hi'er·ar"chy (hī'ə-rär"kė) *n.* **1,** a body of persons organized by rank, in church or government. **2,** a series of terms of different rank. —**hi"er·ar'chic, hi"er·ar'chi·cal,** *adj.*

hi"er·o·glyph'ic (hī"ər-ə-glif'ik) *adj.* **1,** pert. to a system of writing by conventionalized pictures, esp. ancient Egyptian. **2,** hard to decipher. —*n.* a hieroglyphic symbol.

hi"er·o·phant" (hī"ər-ə-fant") *n.* interpreter of sacred mysteries or esoteric principles.

hig'gle·dy-pig'gle·dy (hig'əl-dė-pig'əl-dė) *adj.* & *adv.* in disorder or confusion; topsy-turvy. —*n.* a jumble; confusion.

high (hī) *adj.* **1,** rising far above, or situated above, the ground or a base. **2,** elevated in rank, etc. **3,** expensive. **4,** intensified; large in measure or amount. **5,** (of meat) slightly tainted. **6,** in the upper range of sounds; shrill. **7,** (*Colloq.*) under the influence of alcohol or drugs; tipsy. —*adv.* at a high place or level; to a high degree. —*n.* **1,** something that is high or highest. **2,** the automobile gear giving greatest forward speed. **3,** an area of high atmospheric pressure. **4,** (*Slang*) the effects of a stimulant or psychedelic drug; a trip. —**high fidelity,** the reproduction or audio signals through their full frequency range with a minimum of distortion. —**high school,** the ninth or tenth to twelfth grades. —**high sea,** the open ocean. —**high time,** (*Colloq.*) almost too late.

high′ball″ *n.* **1,** a drink of whiskey diluted with water, seltzer, etc. **2,** a railroad signal used to show a clear track. —*v.i.* (*Colloq.*) go ahead rapidly.

high′bind″er (-bīn″dər) *n.* a paid criminal, esp. Chinese.

high′boy″ *n.* a tall chest of drawers.

high′brow″ *n.* (*Colloq.*) a person of intellectual tastes. —*adj.* intellectual; abstruse.

high′fa·lu′tin (hī″fə-loo′tən) *adj.* (*Colloq.*) pretentious.

high′flown″ *adj.* over-ambitious; (esp. of language) fancy.

high′fly″er *n.* one extravagant in aims or pretensions.

high-′hand′ed *adj.* overbearing; arbitrary. —**high-′hand′ed·ness,** *n.*

high-′hat″ *adj.* (*Slang*) snobbish. —*v.t.* treat condescendingly. —*n.* a percussion instrument formed of two cymbals.

high′land″ (-lənd) *n.* (often *pl.*) & *adj.* a mountainous region.

high′light″ *n.* **1,** the point of most intense light. **2,** a conspicuous part or event. —*v.t.* **1,** emphasize. **2,** in art, put highlight on.

high′ly (hī′lē) *adv.* **1,** in or to a great degree. **2,** favorably. **3,** in a high place or position.

high-″mind′ed *adj.* **1,** having exalted principles or motives. **2,** arrogantly proud. —**high-″min′ded·ness,** *n.*

high′ness (-nəs) *n.* **1,** the state of being high. **2,** (*cap.*) a title of address to royal persons.

high-′rise′ *adj.* & *n.* pert. to a building with many stories.

high′road″ *n.* **1,** a main road. **2,** any public route. **3,** an easy course.

high-′sound″ing *adj.* pretentious and imposing when read or spoken.

high′strung″ *adj.* nervous; tense.

high′tail″ *v.i.* (*Slang*) (with *it*) escape in a great hurry.

high-′ten″sion *adj.* in electricity, involving high potential, usu. 1000 volts or more.

high-′test″ *adj.* of gasoline, etc., having a relatively low boiling point and a high octane rating.

high′toned″ (-tōnd″) *adj.* **1,** high in pitch. **2,** (*Colloq.*) stylish.

high′way″ *n.* **1,** a main road. **2,** any public route, on land or water.

high′way·man (-mən) *n.* [*pl.* **-men**] a robber.

hi′jack″ (hī′jak″) *v.t.* (*Slang*) steal (contraband in transit).

hike (hīk) *v.i.* **1,** walk afield, for pleasure or training. **2,** (*Colloq.*) leave; walk away. **3,** raise with a jerk. —*n.* a walking trip; a march.

hi·lar′i·ous (hi-lār′ē-əs) *adj.* **1,** gay; exhilarated. **2,** causing great mirth. —**hi·lar′i·ty** (hi-lar′ə-tē) *n.*

hill (hil) *n.* **1,** a natural elevation of land. **2,** an artificial mound. —*v.t.* form into hills, as corn.

hill′bill″y *n.* a backwoods mountaineer. —*adj.* (esp. of music) in the style of mountain folksong.

hill′ock (hil′ək) *n.* a small hill.

hill′side″ *n.* the side of a hill; sloping ground.

hill′y (-ē) *adj.* **1,** abounding in hills. **2,** steep. —**hill′i·ness,** *n.*

hilt *n.* the handle of a weapon, esp. of a sword or dagger.

him *pron.* objective case of *he.*

him·self′ *pron.* emphatic form of *him*; reflexive form of *he.*

hind (hīnd) *adj.* [*superl.* **hind′most″** or **hind′er·most″** (hīn′dər-)] situated at the back; posterior. —*n.* a female deer.

hin′der (hin′dər) *v.t.* & *i.* prevent from acting or proceeding; impede.

hind′quar″ter *n.* **1,** the hind leg and loin of an animal, cut for meat. **2,** (*pl.*) the rump.

hin′drance (hin′drəns) *n.* **1,** act of hindering; a stopping or checking. **2,** an obstacle.

hind′sight″ *n.* judgment of what should have been done, after the result is known.

Hin′du (hin′doo) *n.* & *adj.* East Indian, in language and religion (Brahman). —**Hin′du·ism,** *n.*

hinge (hinj) *n.* **1,** a joint that permits movement, as for a door. **2,** a similar anatomical joint, as the knee. **3,** that on which something turns or depends; a controlling principle. —*v.i.* & *t.* **1,** turn or depend on. **2,** attach by a hinge.

hin′ny (hin′ē) *n.* **1,** a neigh. **2,** a mule.

hint *n.* a covert suggestion or implication; an indirect allusion. —*v.t.* & *i.* intimate; imply.

hin'ter·land" (hin'tər-land") n.**1**, territory lying back of a coastal region. **2**, a remote region.

hip n. **1**, the projecting, fleshy part of the body around the pelvis; the haunch. **2**, the hip joint. —adj. (Slang) informed. —interj. a sound used in cheering.

hip"hug"gers n. tight pants.

hipped (hipt) adj. (Slang) having an obsession.

hip"pie (hip'ē) n. a nonconformist person, usu. one who rejects conventional social behavior and dress, and often a user of drugs. Also, **hip'py.**

hip"po (hip'ō) n. (Colloq.) hippopotamus.

Hip"po·crat'ic oath (hip"ə-krat'ik) an oath embodying the obligations of a physician.

hip"po·drome" (hip'ə-drōm") n. an arena for spectacular exhibitions.

hip"po·pot'a·mus (hip"ə-pot'ə-məs) n. a large Afr. herbivorous pachydermatous mammal that frequents rivers and lakes.

hip'ster (hip'stər) n. (Slang) one who is up-to-date in attitudes and taste.

hir'cine (hẽr'sīn) adj. goatlike, esp. in odor.

hire (hīr) v.t. **1**, engage the services or use of, for pay; employ; rent. **2**, (sometimes with out) grant the services or use of, for pay. —v.i. (with out) lend one's services for pay. —n. **1**, wages; rental. **2**, the act of hiring or being hired. —**hire'ling**, n. one serving only for pay.

hir·sute' (hẽr-soot') adj. hairy. —**hir·sute'ness**, n.

his (hiz) pron. poss. form of he.

His·pan'ic (his-pan'ik) adj. Spanish.

hiss (his) v.t. & i. **1**, make a sound like that of the letter s prolonged. **2**, express disapproval by making this sound. —n. such a sound.

hist interj. **1**, listen! **2**, silence!

his'ta·mine" (his'tə-mēn") n. an organic ammonia compound released by the body tissues in certain reactions, as of the common cold.

his'to·gram" (his'tə-gram") n. a graph in the form of rectangles of equal width and varying lengths.

his·tol'o·gy (his-tol'ə-jē) n. the science that treats of organic tissues. —**his"to·log'i·cal**, adj.

his·to'ri·an (his-tôr'ē-ən) n. a writer of, or an authority on, history.

his·tor'ic (his-tôr'ik) adj. **1**, in or pert. to history. **2**, important in history. Also, **his·tor'i·cal.**

his"to·ric'i·ty (his"tə-ris'ə-tē) n. historical authenticity.

his"to·ri·og'ra·phy (hi-stôr"ē-og'rə-fē) n. the method of historical study. —**his"to·ri·og'ra·pher**, n.

his'to·ry (his'tə-rē) n. **1**, the branch of knowledge concerned with ascertaining and recording past events. **2**, an oral or written narrative of past events. **3**, a systematic description of natural phenomena.

his"tri·on'ic (his"trē-on'ik) adj. **1**, pert. to actors or acting. **2**, pretended; artificial; affected. —**his"tri·on'i·cal·ly**, adv.

his"tri·on'ics (-iks) n.pl. **1**, theatricals. **2**, artificial speech or manner.

hit v.t. & i. [**hit**, **hit'ting**] **1**, deal a blow to; strike; collide with. **2**, reach, as with a missile. **3**, move by a stroke. **4**, assail in speech. **5**, meet with; find; (with on) discover. **6**, agree with; suit. **7**, (Slang) kill. **8**, (Slang) burglarize. —n. **1**, a blow, impact, or collision. **2**, (Baseball) a safely batted ball. **3**, (Colloq.) a successful performance or enterprise. —**hit'ter**, n. —**hit'-and-run'**, adj. guilty of causing an automobile accident and not stopping to identify oneself. —**hit man**, a paid assassin.

hitch (hich) v.t. **1**, fasten as with a rope, esp. temporarily; tether. **2**, pull up; raise by jerks. —v.i. **1**, be fastened, entangled. **2**, move jerkily. **3**, (Colloq.) work smoothly together; agree. **4**, (Colloq.) hitchhike. —n. **1**, a joining or making fast. **2**, a device for attaching one thing to another, as a trailer to an automobile. **3**, a knot. **4**, a temporary stoppage or obstruction. **5**, a jerk; a limping gait. **6**, (Colloq.) a task; working period; prison sentence. —**hitch a ride**, hitchhike.

hitch'hike" (hich'hīk") v.i. (Colloq.) travel by begging rides in strangers' automobiles.

hith'er (hith'ər) adv. to this place. —adj. on the nearer side. —**hith"er·to'**, adv. up to this time.

hive (hīv) n. **1**, a swarm of bees; any shelter they inhabit. **2**, a roomful of busy people. —v.i. enter a hive.

hives (hīvz) n. an eruptive skin disease.

ho (hō) interj. to call attention, express surprise, amusement, etc.

hoa'gy (hō'gē) n. a submarine sandwich. Also, **hoa'gie.**

hoar (hôr) adj. **1**, white or gray, as frost. **2**, gray-haired with age. —**hoar'frost"**, n. frozen dew. —**hoar'y**, adj.

hoard (hôrd) n. a stock or store laid by for preservation or future use. —v.t. & i. **1**, amass; save. **2**, store up beyond one's own needs.

hoarse (hôrs) adj. **1**, deep and harsh to the ear; raucous. **2**, having a husky voice. —**hoars'en**, v.t. & i. render or become hoarse. —**hoarse'ness**, n.

hoax (hōks) *n.* a mischievous deception; a practical joke. —*v.t.* deceive.

hob *n.* **1,** a shelf or projection in a fireplace. **2,** a stick used as a target. **3,** (*Colloq.*) mischief.

hob'ble (hob'əl) *v.i.* limp; proceed haltingly. —*v.t.* **1,** fetter by tying the legs together. **2,** impede in any way. —*n.* **1,** a limping gait. **2,** a rope used to tie the legs of an animal. —**hob'bling,** *adj.* limping. —**hobble skirt,** a skirt with a band near the ankles.

hob"ble·de·hoy' (hob"əl-dē-hoi') *n.* a clumsy or awkward youth.

hob'by (hob'ē) *n.* **1,** an occupation pursued for recreation. **2,** a stick or rocking vehicle with a horse's head, for children: *hobbyhorse.*

hob'gob"lin *n.* **1,** a mischievous imp. **2,** something that arouses fear.

hob'nail" *n.* a large-headed nail protecting the sole of a heavy shoe.

hob'nob" *v.i.* [**-nobbed", -nob"bing**] associate constantly.

ho'bo (hō'bō) *n.* [*pl.* **-boes**] **1,** a tramp; vagrant. **2,** a migrant worker.

hock (hok) *n.* **1,** a protruding joint in the hind leg of a horse. **2,** a white Rhine wine. —*v.t.* **1,** hamstring. **2,** (*Colloq.*) pawn.

hock'ey (hok'ē) *n.* a game played with a puck and crooked sticks, either on the ground or on ice.

hock'shop" *n.* (*Colloq.*) pawnshop.

ho'cus (hō'kəs) *v.t.* deceive by trickery.

ho'cus-po'cus (hō'kəs-pō'kəs) *n.* **1,** a jocular incantation uttered by a conjurer. **2,** a conjurer's trick; deception. —*v.t.* & *i.* deceive.

hod *n.* **1,** a trough fixed on a long handle, for carrying bricks or mortar. **2,** a coal scuttle.

hodge'podge" (hoj'poj") *n.* an indiscriminate mixture; a jumble.

hoe (hō) *n.* a blade fixed on a long handle, for cultivating earth, cutting weeds, etc. —*v.t.* & *i.* use a hoe (on).

hoe'cake" *n.* a baked cornmeal cake.

hoe'down" (hō'-) *n.* a square dance.

hog *n.* **1,** a pig, sow, or boar; a swine. **2,** a domesticated swine fattened for market. **3,** (*Colloq.*) a greedy or filthy person. —*v.t.* [**hogged, hog'ging**] (*Slang*) take more than one's share of. —**hog'gish,** *adj.*

ho'gan (hō'gan) *n.* a Navajo Indian hut.

hog'back" *adj.* curved so as to be highest at the middle.

hogs'head" (hogz'hed") *n.* **1,** a large barrel or cask. **2,** a unit of capacity.

hog'tie" *v.t.* tie with all four feet together;

hence, impede the movements or actions of.

hog'wash" *n.* **1,** swill given to hogs. **2,** (*Colloq.*) trash; nonsense.

hog"wild" *adj.* (*Slang*) berserk.

hoi pol·loi' (hoi"pə-loi') (*Gk.*) the common people.

hoist *v.t.* raise or lift, esp. by machinery. —*n.* **1,** a contrivance for lifting, as an elevator. **2,** a lift or boost. ·

hoi'ty-toi'ty (hoi'tē-toi'tē) *adj.* **1,** giddy. **2,** haughty.

ho'kum (hō'kəm) *n.* (*Slang*) **1,** nonsense; buncombe. **2,** stereotyped humor.

hold (hōld) *v.t.* [*pret.* & *p.p.* **held**] **1,** keep fast, as in grasp of the hand; retain; cling to. **2,** keep back; withhold; restrain. **3,** have in possession; own; occupy. **4,** engage in; pursue; sustain. **5,** contain; have the capacity of. **6,** entertain in the mind; maintain. **7,** rule legally. **8,** (with *up*) rob. —*v.i.* **1,** maintain a grasp; adhere; cling. **2,** (often with *out*) maintain a position or condition. **3,** cease or pause; refrain. —*n.* **1,** the act of holding fast; grasp; grip. **2,** [also, **hold'er**] a part by which something is held, as a handle. **3,** something that fixes in place, supports, controls, or dominates. **4,** a place of security or confinement. **5,** the cargo space in a ship. **6,** (*Music*) a fermata. —**hold'ing,** *n.* property owned, esp. real estate or stocks. —**hold down, 1,** curb; check. **2,** (*Slang*) retain (a job, etc.). —**hold forth,** preach; harangue. —**hold over, 1,** postpone. **2,** keep in force or action. —**holding company, 1,** a company whose chief or sole business is to acquire the securities of other companies. **2,** an operating company that owns a controlling interest in the stock of another.

hold'o"ver *n.* a thing or condition retained from a previous time.

hold'up (hōld'up) *n.* (*Colloq.*) a robbery under threat of bodily injury.

hole (hōl) *n.* **1,** an opening; aperture; perforation. **2,** a hollow place; cavity; excavation. **3,** any place that is dark, secluded, or dingy; a hiding-place; a dungeon. **4,** (*Golf*) the course from one tee to the corresponding hole. **5,** (*Colloq.*) an embarrassing predicament. **6,** (*Colloq.*) a flaw. —*v.t.* put into a hole. —*v.i.* (with *up*) go into seclusion or hiding; hibernate. —**hole'y,** *adj.* perforated. —**hole up,** go into hiding.

hol'i·day" (hol'ə-dā") *n.* **1,** a commemorative day, fixed by law or custom, on which business is suspended. **2,** a vacation. —*adj.* festive; pert. to a holiday.

Hol'land·aise" sauce (hol'ən-dez") a sauce of egg yolks and butter seasoned with lemon or vinegar.

hol′ler (hol′ər) *v.t. & i. & n.* yell.

hol′low (hol′ō) *adj.* **1,** empty within; not solid. **2,** having a hole, cavity, or concavity; sunken, as cheeks. **3,** (of sound) low-pitched. **4,** of little worth; fruitless. **5,** insincere; false. **6,** hungry. —*n.* **1,** an empty space, hole, or cavity. **2,** a valley. —*v.t.* (with *out*) make hollow. —**hol′low·ness,** *n.*

hol′low·ware″ *n.* silver serving dishes.

hol′ly (hol′ē) *n.* a shrub with glossy leaves and red berries much used for Christmas decoration.

hol′ly·hock″ (hol′ē-hok″) *n.* a tall plant bearing large flowers.

hol′mi·um (hōl′mē-əm) *n.* a rare-earth metallic element, no. 7, symbol Ho.

hol·o- (hol-ə) *pref.* whole, entire.

hol′o·caust″ (hol′ə-kâst″) *n.* great destruction of life, esp. by fire.

hol′o·gram″ (hol′ə-gram″) *n.* an image produced on a sensitized surface by holography.

hol′o·graph″ (hol′ə-graf″) *n.* **1,** a document written in the hand of its author. **2,** a hologram. —*adj.* written in the hand of its author. —*v.* produce an image (of an object) using holography. —**holographic,** *adj.*

ho·log′ra·phy (hō-log′rə-fē) *n.* a kind of three-dimensional lensless photography using lasers. —**hol′o·graph″ic,** *adj.*

hol′ster (hōl′stər) *n.* a leather case for carrying a pistol.

ho′ly (hō′lē) *adj.* **1,** sacred; declared sacred by church authority. **2,** devoted to the service of God or the church; religious. **3,** pious; devout; saintly. —**hol′i·ness,** *n.* —**Holy Week,** the week preceding Easter.

hom′age (hom′ij) *n.* respect or reverence; tribute.

hom′burg (hom′bėrg) *n.* a style of man's felt hat.

home (hōm) *n.* **1,** the house, etc., where one resides; one's native land. **2,** the burrow or retreat of an animal. **3,** the region in which something is common or native. **4,** an institution for sheltering orphans, the aged, etc. **5,** in games, the goal or principal base. —*v.i.* (with *in*) aim or be directed (toward). —*adj.* **1,** domestic. **2,** to the point. —*adv.* **1,** at, to, or toward home. **2,** to the point; effectively; all the way. —**hom′ey,** *adj.* (*Colloq.*) —**hom′ing,** *adj.* trained to return home from great distances. —**home economics,** the art or study of household management. —**home stretch,** the final portion of a race, journey, effort, etc.

home′bod″y *n.* a person who would rather stay home than go out.

home′land″ *n.* one's native land.

home′made″ *adj.* made at home, not in a factory.

home′ma″ker *n.* one who manages a household; a housewife.

ho″me·o- (hō′mē-ə) *pref.* similar.

ho″me·op′a·thy (hō″mē-op′ə-thē) *n.* treatment of disease with drugs that produce symptoms similar to those of the disease. —**ho′me·o·path″,** *n.* —**ho″me·o·path′ic,** *adj.* —**ho″me·o·path′i·cal·ly,** *adv.*

hom′er (hō′mər) *n.* **1,** (*Baseball*) a home run. **2,** a homing pigeon.

home′sick″ *adj.* depressed by longing for home. —**home′sick″ness,** *n.*

home′spun″ *adj.* **1,** spun or woven at home, as cloth. **2,** plain; unpretentious.

home′stead″ *n.* land and dwelling occupied by their owner. —**home′stead″er,** *n.* one who establishes a homestead in unsettled territory.

home′work″ *n.* any work, esp. schoolwork, assigned to be done at home.

hom′i·cide″ (hom′ə-sīd″) *n.* the killing of one human being by another. —**hom′i·cid′al,** *adj.*

hom″i·let′ic (hom″ə-let′ik) *adj.* being or like a sermon. —**hom″i·let′i·cal·ly,** *adv.*

hom″i·let′ics (-iks) *n.* the composition or preaching of sermons.

hom′i·ly (hom′ə-lē) *n.* a moralizing discourse; a sermon.

hom′i·ny (hom′ə-nē) *n.* corn, ground or in hulled kernels, boiled in water or milk.

hom·o- (hom-ə) *pref.* the same.

ho″mo·ge′ne·ous (hō″mə-jē′nē-əs) *adj.* **1,** composed of parts of the same kind; not heterogeneous. **2,** alike in kind. —**ho″mo·ge·ne′i·ty** (-jə-nē′ə-tē) *n.*

ho·mog′e·nize″ (hə-moj′ə-nīz″) *v.t.* make homogeneous; mix thoroughly, as milk and cream. —**ho·mog″e·ni·za′tion,** *n.*

hom′o·graph″ (hom′ə-graf″) *n.* a word spelled the same as another but of different origin and meaning. —**hom″o·graph′ic,** *adj.*

ho·mol′o·gous (hə-mol′ə-gəs) *adj.* having the same relative position, proportion, value, or structure. —**ho·mol′o·gy** (-jē) *n.*

hom′o·nym″ (hom′ə-nim) *n.* a word like another in sound and (often) spelling, but different in meaning, as *bear* (carry) and *bear* (mammal).

hom′o·phile″ (hom′ə-fīl″) *adj.* pert. to homosexuality; being homosexual.

hom′o·phone″ (hom′ə-fōn″) *n.* a word pronounced like another but different in meaning and spelling, as *too* and *two.* —**hom″o·phon′ic** (-fon′ik) *adj.*

ho·moph′o·ny (hō-mof′ə-nē) *n.* **1,** sameness of sound. **2,** music having a principal melody or leading voice: *monody.*

ho″mo·sex′u·al (hō″mə-sek′shoo-əl) *adj.* feeling romantic love for persons of the same sex. —*n.* a homosexual person, esp. male. —**ho″mo·sex″u·al′i·ty,** *n.*

ho·mun′cu·lus (hō-mung′kyə-ləs) *n.* **1,** a dwarf. **2,** a manikin.

hon′cho (hon′chō) *n.* (*Slang*) boss; leader.

hone (hōn) *n.* a stone for sharpening razors, etc. —*v.t.* sharpen with a hone; whet. —*v.i.* (*Dial.*) yearn.

hon′est (on′ist) *adj.* **1,** having a sense of honor; upright and fair in dealing. **2,** sincere; truthful. **3,** genuine; unadulterated; virtuous. —**hon′es·ty,** *n.*

hon′ey (hun′ē) *n.* **1,** a sweet fluid produced by bees from the nectar of flowers. **2,** something sweet or delightful. **3,** a term of endearment. —**hon′eyed,** *adj.* sweet; fawning.

hon′ey·bee″ *n.* a bee that gathers honey.

hon′ey·comb″ *n.* **1,** a wax structure formed by bees for storing honey. **2,** any structure having many cells. —**hon′ey·combed″,** *adj.*

hon′ey·dew″ *n.* a sweet plant substance. —**honeydew melon,** a white-fleshed variety of muskmelon.

hon′ey·moon″ *n.* **1,** a trip taken alone by a newly married couple. **2,** a brief period of amity.

hon′ey·suck″le *n.* a sweet-scented shrub or vine.

honk *n.* **1,** the cry of a wild goose. **2,** a similar sound, esp. of a warning horn. —*v.i.* utter such a sound.

honk′y (honk′ē) *n.* (*Offensive*) a white man.

honk′y-tonk″ (-tonk″) *n.* (*Slang*) a cheap saloon or cabaret.

hon′or (on′ər) *n.* **1,** high esteem; deferential admiration. **2,** high reputation; credit for honesty, etc. **3,** fidelity to principles or obligations; fairness in dealing; conformance with high standards of behavior. **4,** high rank, achievement, or distinction. **5,** a title, decoration, diploma, etc. **6,** (preceded by *his* or *your*) a title of address to a mayor or judge. **7,** chastity in a woman. —*v.t.* **1,** hold in honor; respect. **2,** confer a mark of honor upon. **3,** treat with due respect; accept; credit; fulfill. Also, **hon′our.** —**do the honors,** act as host or hostess.

hon′or·a·ble (-ə-bəl) *adj.* **1,** worthy of respect. **2,** noble; upright. —**hon′or·a·ble·ness,** *n.*

hon″o·rar′i·um (on″ə-rār′ē-əm) *n.* [*pl.* **-a** (-ə)] a fee, as for professional services.

hon′or·ar·y (on′ər-er-ē) *adj.* **1,** conferring honor, without usual requirements, duties, etc. **2,** done or given in token of honor. **3,** dependent on honor for fulfillment.

hon″o·rif′ic (on″ə-rif′ik) *adj.* conferring or expressing honor. —*n.* a term of respectful address.

hooch *n.* (*Slang*) alcoholic liquor.

hood (hd) *n.* **1,** a covering for the head, often attached to a cloak, etc. **2,** any hood-shaped covering, as over an automobile engine. **3,** (*Slang*) a hoodlum.

-hood (hd) *suf.* the state or condition of being what is expressed by the foregoing word, as *likelihood,* the state of being likely.

hood′lum (hd′ləm) *n.* a rowdy; a ruffian.

hoo′doo (h′doo) *n.* **1,** voodoo. **2,** (*Colloq.*) bad luck; someone or something supposed to bring bad luck. —*v.t.* bring bad luck to.

hood′wink″ *v.t.* deceive; impose upon.

hoo′ey (h′ē) *n. & interj.* (*Slang*) nonsense.

hoof (hf) *n.* the horny casing that sheathes the foot of many quadrupeds; the entire foot. —*v.i.* (*Colloq.*) walk; dance. —**hoof′er,** *n.* (*Slang*) a professional dancer.

hook (hk) *n.* **1,** a curved or angular piece of metal or the like, used to catch, hold, or sustain something. **2,** anything so bent or curved, as a spit of land. **3,** a curved course, as of a ball hit or thrown; a swinging blow in boxing; (*Golf*) an oblique stroke, veering to the left. —*v.t.* **1,** use or make a hook. **2,** catch by artifice; trap. **3,** (*Slang*) pilfer. **4,** (with *up*) connect. —*v.i.* **1,** become attached. **2,** bend or curve. —**by hook or crook,** by any means. —**hook and eye,** a fastening device used on clothes.

hoo′kah (hk′ə) *n.* a pipe in which the smoke is cooled by being drawn through water. Also, **hoo′ka.**

hooked (hkt) *adj.* **1,** bent in a loop. **2,** having a hook or hooks. **3,** caught on or as on a hook. —**hook′ed·ness,** *n.*

hook′er (hk′ər) *n.* **1,** a boat. **2,** (*Slang*) a prostitute. **3,** (*Slang*) drink.

hook′up″ *n.* **1,** a diagram as of radio apparatus. **2,** a system of radio stations.

hook′worm″ *n.* a parasitic bloodsucking worm infesting the intestine.

hook′y (hk′ē) *adj.* **1,** full of hooks or barbs. **2,** hook-shaped. —**play hooky,** be absent from school unjustifiably.

hoo′li·gan (h′lə-gən) *n.* (*Slang*) a hoodlum.

hoop *n.* a circular band or ring, such as used on a barrel. —**hoop skirt,** a skirt stretched to bell-shape over a framework.

hoop′la (hp′lä) *n.* excitement; hullabaloo.

hoo·ray′ (hoo-rā′) *interj.* hurrah.

hoose′gow (hoos′gow) *n.* (*Slang*) a jail.

Hoo′sier (hoo′zhər) *n.* (*Slang*) a native of Indiana. —*adj.* of Indiana.

hoot *n.* **1,** the cry of an owl; any similar sound. **2,** a cry or noise of derision. —*v.i. & t.* utter this cry.

hootch (hooch) *n.* **1,** a thatched hut. **2,** (*Slang*) liquor.

hoot′e·nan″ny (hoo′tə-nan″ē) *n.* an assemblage of folk singers, usu. for public performance.

hop *v.i.* **1,** leap; move by short leaps. **2,** leap on one foot. **3,** (*Colloq.*) dance. **4,** (with *off*) begin a flight or journey. —*v.t.* [**hopped, hop′ping**] **1,** leap across. **2,** jump upon. —*n.* **1,** a short leap, esp. on one foot. **2,** a flight or journey. **3,** (*Colloq.*) a dance. **4,** (*Slang*) opium. **5,** a twining plant whose flowers (*hops*) are used in brewing.

hope (hōp) *v.t. & i.* expect or look forward to, with desire and confidence. —*n.* **1,** confidence in a future event; expectation of something desired. **2,** what is hoped for. **3,** something that arouses or justifies hope. —**hope′ful,** *adj.* —**hope′less,** *adj.* **1,** without hope. **2,** beyond repair, correction, or salvation.

hop′head″ *n.* (*Slang*) a user of drugs.

hopped′up″ (hopt′-) *adj.* (*Slang*) **1,** under the influence of drugs; doped. **2,** very excited; enthusiastic.

hop′per (hop′ər) *n.* **1,** one who or that which hops, as certain insects. **2,** a trough or chute in a storage tank through which grain, coal, etc., is discharged.

hop′sack″ing *n.* **1,** a material of hemp and jute. **2,** a rough-surfaced cotton or wool clothing fabric. Also, **hop′sack″.**

hop′scotch″ *n.* a children's game, played by hopping from square to square.

hor′a (hôr′ə) *n.* a round dance of Israel.

ho′ral (hôr′əl) *adj.* hourly; relating to hours.

horde (hôrd) *n.* **1,** a large troop or flock; a multitude. **2,** a tribe, esp. of Asiatic nomads.

hore′hound″ (hôr′hownd″) *n.* a perennial herb, used in making medicine and candy.

ho·ri′zon (hə-rī′zən) *n.* **1,** the apparent boundary between earth and sky. **2,** the limit of visual or intellectual perception.

hor·i·zon′tal (hor-i-zon′təl) *adj. & n.* parallel to the earth's surface; at right angles to a vertical line.

hor′mone (hôr′mōn) *n.* any of various substances normally secreted by glands.

horn (hôrn) *n.* **1,** a hard, spikelike growth on the head, as of cattle; the substance of which it is composed. **2,** something shaped like, or made of, or suggesting a horn, as a

cusp of the moon. **3,** any of a variety of musical wind instruments, usually made of brass; any of various noise-producing instruments. **4,** a megaphone. **5,** either of the alternatives of a dilemma. —*adj.* made of horn. —**horn′y,** *adj.* —**horn in,** intrude, as in a conversation.

horn′bill″ (hôrn′bil″) *n.* a large bird.

horn′book″ *n.* formerly, a writing tablet bound with animal horn used for school work.

hor′net (hôr′nit) *n.* a large insect of the wasp family.

horn′pipe″ (hôrn′pīp″) *n.* **1,** a old Welsh clarinet. **2,** a lively solo dance popular among sailors.

horn′swog″gle (hôrn′swog″əl) *v.t.* (*Slang*) swindle; hoax.

ho·rol′o·gy (hô-rol′ə-jē) *n.* the art of making timepieces. —**hor″o·log′ic** (hôr″ə-loj′ik) *adj.* —**ho·rol′o·gist,** *n.*

hor′o·scope″ (hor′ə-skōp″) *n.* a plan of the positions of the planets, used by astrologers. —**ho·ros′co·py** (hə-ros′kə-pē) *n.*

hor·ren′dous (hə-ren′dəs) *adj.* horrible; frightful.

hor′ri·ble (hor′ə-bəl) *adj.* exciting horror; dreadful; deplorable. —**hor′ri·ble·ness,** *n.*

hor′rid (hor′id) *adj.* unpleasant; disagreeable. —**hor′rid·ness,** *n.*

hor′ri·fy″ (hor′i-fī″) *v.t.* arouse horror. —**hor·rif′ic** (hə-rif′ik) *adj.*

hor′ror (hor′ər) *n.* **1,** a painful emotion of fear or abhorrence; an intense aversion. **2,** that which excites such a feeling.

hors d'oeuvres′ (ôr-dövr′) *n. pl.* (*Fr.*) assorted appetizers.

horse (hôrs) *n.* **1,** a large, solid-hoofed domesticated quadruped, a draft or riding animal. **2,** a male horse; a stallion. **3,** a troop of horses; cavalry. **4,** a supporting frame on legs. **5,** a gymnastic apparatus. —*v.t.* provide with a horse; put on horseback. —*v.i.* (*Slang*) be playful or boisterous. —**horse chestnut,** a flowering tree, as the Ohio buckeye; its seed. —**horse latitude,** a zone of relative calm, near 30° north or south latitude. —**horse opera,** a western. —**horse sense,** (*Colloq.*) good sense.

horse′back″ *n.* the part of a horse's back on which a rider sits.

horse′car″ *n.* a car drawn by a horse.

horse′feath″ers *interj.* (*Slang*) nonsense!

horse′fly″ *n.* gadfly.

horse′hair″ *n. & adj.* the mane and tail hair of a horse; a fabric woven from it.

horse′laugh″ *n.* a derisive laugh.

horse′less carriage an automobile.

horse′man (-mən) *n.* [*pl.* **-men**] the rider or trainer of a horse. —**horse′man·ship**, *n.* —**horse′wom″an**, *n.fem.*

horse′play″ *n.* boisterous behavior.

horse′pow″er *n.* a unit for measuring rate of work.

horse′rad″ish *n.* a cultivated plant; its root, ground and used as a condiment.

horse′shoe″ *n.* **1,** the U-shaped iron plate nailed to a horse's hoof; anything so shaped. **2,** (*pl.*) a game of quoits played with horseshoes.

horse′whip″ *n.* a whip for urging a horse. —*v.t.* [**-whipped″, -whip″ping**] beat with a whip.

hors′y (hôr′sè) *adj.* **1,** like a horse; gross. **2,** interested in horses or horse racing. —**hors′i·ness,** *n.*

hor′ta·to·ry (hôr′tə-tôr-è) *adj.* exhorting.

hor′ti·cul″ture (hôr′ti-kul″chər) *n.* the science and art of growing plants. —**hor″ti·cul′tur·al,** *adj.*

ho·san′na (hō-zan′ə) *interj. & n.* an exclamation in praise of God.

hose (hōz) *n.* **1,** a flexible tube for conveying water. **2,** [*pl.* **hose**] stockings or socks. —*v.t.* apply water through a hose.

ho′sier·y (hō′zhə-rè) *n.* stockings.

hos′pice (hos′pis) *n.* a shelter for travelers, or the destitute, maintained by a religious order.

hos′pi·ta·ble (hos′pi-tə-bəl) *adj.* **1,** happy to welcome and entertain guests. **2,** receptive, as to ideas. —**hos″pi·ta·ble·ness,** *n.*

hos′pi·tal (hos′pi-təl) *n.* an institution for the care and treatment of the sick and injured; any similar establishment, as for repairs.

hos″pi·tal′i·ty (hos″pə-tal′ə-tè) *n.* the reception of guests in a liberal and kindly way.

hos″pi·tal·i·za′tion (hos″pi-təl-i-zā′shən) *n.* insurance covering expenses incurred in a hospital. —**hos′pi·tal·ize″,** *v.t.* put or treat in a hospital.

host (hōst) *n.* **1,** one who entertains another, esp. in his own house. **2,** the proprietor of an inn or restaurant. **3,** a great number of persons or things. **4,** (*cap.*) the bread consecrated in the Eucharist. **5,** an animal or plant that provides nutrition to a parasite.

hos′tage (hos′tij) *n.* a person or thing held as a pledge or security for the performance of an action.

hos′tel (hos′təl) *n.* a lodging house or inn. Also, **hos′tel·ry** (-rè).

host′ess (hōs′tis) *n.* **1,** a female host. **2,** a woman who greets patrons in a restaurant, etc. **3,** a woman employed to entertain and assist patrons, as on an airplane, etc.

hos′tile (hos′təl) *adj.* **1,** opposed in feel-ing or action; antagonistic. **2,** relating to an enemy.

hos·til′i·ty (hos-til′i-tè) *n.* **1,** antagonism. **2,** (*pl.*) warfare.

hos′tler (hos′lər) *n.* a servant who tends horses at an inn.

hot *adj.* [**hot′ter, -test**] **1,** having or giving the sensation of heat; of high temperature. **2,** pungent to the taste; biting. **3,** ardent in feeling; vehement; passionate. **4,** fresh; keen; brisk. **5,** (*Slang*) exciting; (of music) heightened by rhapsodic improvisation. **6,** (*Slang*) wanted by the police. **7,** (*Slang*) in good form, as an athlete; on a lucky streak, as a gambler. **8,** (*Slang*) sexually excited or exciting. **9,** (*pl.*) (*Slang*) sexual desire.—**hot air,** (*Slang*) empty talk. —**hot dog,** (*Slang*) a frankfurter on a roll. —**hot line,** an emergency telephone line. —**hot plate,** a portable metal cooking or warming apparatus. —**hot rod,** (*Slang*) an automobile altered for greater speed.

hot′bed″ *n.* **1,** a glass-covered bed of soil. **2,** a place where growth is rapid.

hot′blood″ed *adj.* excitable; impetuous. —**hot′blood″ed·ness,** *n.*

hot′cake″ *n.* pancake.

hotch′potch″ *n.* hodgepodge.

ho·tel′ (hō-tel′) *n.* a public house that furnishes lodging, food, etc., to travelers or other guests.

hot′foot″ *adv.* hastily; speedily. —*v.i.* in haste.

hot′head″ed *adj.* of fiery temper; rash. —**hot′head″,** *n.* —**hot′head″ed·ness,** *n.*

hot′house″ *n.* a glass-covered area for raising plants.

hot′pants″ *n.pl.* pants with very short legs, usu. worn by women.

hot′shot″ *n.* (*Slang*) a particularly energetic and skillful person.

hot-′wire″ *adj.* operated by the expansion of a wire through which electricity is made to pass. —*v.t.* (*Slang*) to start an automobile by bypassing the ignition switch.

hound (hownd) *n.* **1,** any of various hunting dogs. **2,** any dog. **3,** (*Slang*) a mean, contemptible fellow. **4,** (*Slang*) an addict. —*v.t.* harass.

hour (owr) *n.* **1,** measure of time equal to 60 minutes or one twenty-fourth of a solar day. **2,** a time of day. **3,** an indefinite period of time; a particular or appointed time.

hour′glass″ *n.* a device for measuring time by the flow of sand.

hou′ri (hû′rè) *n.* a beautiful maiden in the Mohammedan paradise.

hour′ly (-lè) *adj. & adv.* occurring each hour; continual or often.

house (hows) n. [pl. **hous′es** (how′ziz)] **1,** a building for human use or occupation, esp. a dwelling. **2,** any place of abode. **3,** something that contains or houses; a cell or compartment. **4,** a household. **5,** a family including ancestors and descendants. **6,** a body of persons; a legislature; a commercial establishment; an audience in a theater. **7,** the management of a gaming house. —v.t. (howz) shelter.

house′boy″ n. a young male servant.

house′break″er n. a burglar.

house′brok″en adj. trained to live in a house, as an animal.

house′hold″ n. all the permanent residents of a dwelling house.

house′keep″ing n. the maintenance and management of a house, including the serving of meals. —**house′keep″er,** n.

house′maid″ n. a female domestic servant. —**housemaid's knee,** inflammation of the bursa of the kneecap.

house′warm″ing n. a party to celebrate occupancy of a new house.

house′wife″ n. a woman in charge of a household.

house′work″ n. cooking, cleaning, etc.

hous′ing (how′zing) n. **1,** houses collectively. **2,** the act of putting in a house; the business of providing houses. **3,** a cover, hood, or shield.

hove (hōv) v. pret. & p.p. of **heave**.

hov′el (huv′əl) n. a small, wretched house.

hov′er (huv′ər) v.i. **1,** remain over one place while fluttering in the air. **2,** linger about. **3,** continue in an undecided state.

hov′er·craft (huv′ər-kraft″) n. a motorized vehicle that travels over the surface of land or water supported on a cushion of air.

how adv. **1,** in what way or manner; by what means. **2,** to what extent; in what amount. **3,** in what state or condition. **4,** for what reason. —interj. a greeting.

how′dah (how′dä) n. a railed and canopied seat on the back of an elephant.

how·ev′er (how-ev′ər) conj. nevertheless; despite which. —adv. in whatever manner; to whatever extent or degree.

how′itz·er (how′it-sər) n. a rifled cannon for high-angle shots.

howl v.i. & t. **1,** utter a loud, prolonged, and mournful cry, as a wolf. **2,** cry out in pain, rage, etc. **3,** make a wailing sound, as the wind. **4,** laugh loudly. —n. such a cry. —howl′ing, adj. (Slang) great; wonderful.

howl′er (how′lər) n. **1,** one who or that which howls. **2,** a So. Amer. monkey. **3,** (Colloq.) an amusing blunder, joke, etc.

how″so·ev′er adv. **1,** in whatever manner. **2,** to whatever degree.

hoy′den (hoi′dən) n. a rowdy girl; a tomboy.

hua·ra′che (wə-rä′chē) n. a low-heeled sandal.

hub n. **1,** a block in the center of a wheel to which the spokes are joined. **2,** a center of intellectual, commercial, or other activity. —**the Hub,** Boston, Mass.

hub′bub (hub′ub) n. a noise as of many voices or sounds; uproar.

hub′cap″ n. a cover for the hub of a wheel.

huck′le·ber″ry (huk′əl-ber″ē) n. a low shrub or its dark-blue edible berry.

huck′ster (huk′stər) n. a street peddler, esp. of fruit and vegetables. —v.t. peddle.

hud′dle (hud′əl) v.t. draw closely together. —v.i. **1,** crowd together. **2,** (Colloq.) confer privately. —n. **1,** a confused mass; a crowd. **2,** (Colloq.) a secret conference.

hue (hū) n. **1,** a color; color in general. **2,** intensity of color. **3,** clamor, esp. in hue and cry.

huff (huf) n. a sudden swell of anger or resentment. —v.i. **1,** take offense. **2,** puff or blow; pant.

huff′ish adj. **1,** resentful; petulant. **2,** arrogant; swaggering. —**huff′ish·ness,** n.

huff′y adj. **1,** irascible; touchy. **2,** sulky. —**huff′i·ness,** n.

hug v.t. & i. [**hugged, hug′ging**] **1,** clasp tightly in the arms; embrace. **2,** cling to mentally. **3,** keep close to. —n. a close embrace.

huge (hūj) adj. very large. —**huge′ness,** n.

hug′ger-mug′ger (hug′ər-mug′ər) n. disorder; a muddle or jumble. —adj. **1,** confused. **2,** clandestine.

hu′la-hu′la (hoo′lə-hoo′lə) n. a Hawaiian dance. —**hula hoop,** a large hoop, usu. plastic, swung about the hips or waist.

hulk n. **1,** the hull of a ship, esp. one that is dismantled or wrecked. **2,** a bulky or unwieldy person or mass. —v.i. loom. —**hulk′ing,** adj.

hull (hul) n. **1,** the body of a ship, exclusive of masts and other superstructure. **2,** the fuselage of a seaplane. **3,** the shell, husk, etc., of a nut, fruit, or grain. —v.t. remove the hull of.

hul′la·ba·loo″ (hul′ə-bə-loo″) n. noisy confusion.

hum v.t. & i. [**hummed, hum′ming**] **1,** make a droning sound. **2,** vocalize with closed lips. **3,** make indistinct sounds; murmur. —n. a buzzing or droning sound. —interj. of hesitation, doubt, etc. —**hum′ming,** adj. **1,** buzzing, etc. **2,** intensely active.

hu′man (hū′mən) adj. pert. to man or

mankind; being a man; having the nature of man.

hu·mane' (hū-mān') *adj.* **1,** inclined to treat others, and animals, with kindness; benevolent; compassionate. **2,** (of a branch of knowledge) tending to refine. **—humane'ness,** *n.*

hu'man·ism (hū'mə-niz-əm) *n.* **1,** a system of thought predominantly centered on human interests. **2,** study of the humanities; literary culture. **—hu'man·ist,** *n.*

hu·man"i·tar'i·an (hū-man"ə-tār'ē-ən) *adj. & n.* concerned with the interests of all mankind; philanthropic.

hu·man'i·ty (hū-man'ə-tē) *n.* **1,** the human race; mankind. **2,** the quality of being human; human nature. **3,** humaneness. **4,** (usually *pl.*) any of the branches of learning embraced by philosophy, literature, languages, art, etc., excluding theology, natural and social sciences.

hu'man·ize" (hū'mə-nīz") *v.t.* make human or humane. **—hu"man·i·za'tion** (-i-zā'shən) *n.*

hu'man·kind" *n.* the human race; mankind.

hu'man·oid" (hū'mə-noid") *adj.* having human characteristics. **—n.** a humanoid being.

hum'ble (hum'bəl) *adj.* **1,** low in station; unimportant; lowly. **2,** meek or modest in manner. **—v.t.** abase; humiliate. **—hum'ble·ness,** *n.*

hum'bug *n.* **1,** a fraudulent trick; a hoax; sham. **2,** an impostor. **—v.t.** [-bugged, -bug·ging] delude.

hum"ding'er (hum"ding'ər) *n.* (*Slang*) a remarkable person or thing.

hum'drum" *adj.* monotonous.

hu'mer·us (hū'mər-əs) *n.* [*pl.* -i (-ī)] the bone of the upper arm.

hu'mid (hū'mid) *adj.* moist; damp.

hu·mid'i·fy" (hū-mid'ə-fī") *v.t.* make damper. **—hu·mid'i·fi·ca'tion,** *n.*

hu·mid'i·stat" (hū-mid'i-stat") *n.* a device for measuring humidity.

hu·mid'i·ty (hū-mid'ə-tē) *n.* dampness; moisture in the air.

hu'mi·dor" (hū'mə-dôr") *n.* a container fitted to keep its contents moist, as for tobacco.

hu·mil'i·ate" (hū-mil'ē-āt") *v.t.* subject to shame or disgrace; abase in estimation; mortify. **—hu·mil"i·a'tion,** *n.*

hu·mil'i·ty (hū-mil'ə-tē) *n.* modesty in self-estimation; humbleness.

hum'ming·bird" (hum'ing-bērd") *n.* a tiny bird whose wings hum from rapid vibration.

hum'mock (hum'ək) *n.* a knoll.

hu'mor (hū'mər) *n.* **1,** the quality of inciting laughter, or of perceiving what is comical; drollery; facetiousness. **2,** mental state; mood. **3,** caprice; whim. **4,** droll literature. **5,** (*Biol.*) any body fluid. **—v.t.** indulge; cater to the whims of. Also, **hu'mour. —hu'mor·ist,** *n.* a writer of humor. **—hu'mor·ous,** *adj.* funny; droll.

hu"mor·esque' (hū"mə-resk') *n.* a musical caprice.

hump *n.* a protuberance or swelling, esp. a natural or morbid curvature of the back. **—v.t. & i.** **1,** form or rise in a hump. **2,** (*Slang*) exert oneself.

hump'back" *n.* **1,** a hump on the back. **2,** one who has a humpback. **3,** a kind of whale.

humph (humf) *interj.* of contempt, doubt, dissatisfaction, etc.

hu'mus (hū'məs) *n.* decayed vegetable matter, important to the fertility of soil.

hunch *n.* **1,** hump. **2,** (*Colloq.*) a premonition or suspicion. **—v.t.** thrust out or up in a hump. **—v.i.** sidle or lunge forward. **—hunch'back",** *n.* humpback.

hun'dred (hun'drid) *n. & adj.* the cardinal number represented by 100, equal to ten times ten. **—hun'dredth,** *n. & adj.* the ordinal of this number, also written 100th.

hun'dred·fold" *adv. & adj.* a hundred times.

hun'dred·weight" *n.* 100 pounds in U.S., 112 pounds in England.

hung *v.* pret. & p.p. of *hang*.

hun'ger (hung'gər) *n.* **1,** craving for food. **2,** any strong desire. **—v.i.** feel hunger. **—hun'gry** (-grē) *adj.* **—hunger strike,** refusal to eat in an effort to force compliance with one's demands.

hung-up' *adj.* (*Slang*) **1,** disturbed; depressed. **2,** obsessed; addicted.

hunk *n.* (*Colloq.*) a large piece, lump, or chunk. **—hunk'y** [also, **hunk'y-do'ry** (-dôr'ē)] *adj.* (*Slang*) satisfactory; all right.

hun'ker (hung'kər) *v.i.* squat; crouch.

hunt *v.t. & i.* **1,** chase (animals) for the purpose of catching or killing. **2,** pursue; harry. **3,** look for; search. **—n.** **1,** the act or sport of chasing wild animals. **2,** a pack of hunting dogs; a group of hunters. **3,** any pursuit, search, or quest. **—hunt'er, hunts'man** (huntz'mən) *n.*

hur'dle (hēr'dəl) *n.* **1,** a barrier (as on a racetrack); a frame of crossed sticks, bars, etc., to be leaped over. **2,** an obstacle or difficulty. **—v.t.** **1,** leap over. **2,** circumvent or overcome by any means. **—hur'dler,** *n.*

hur'dy-gur'dy (hēr'dē-gēr'dē) *n.* a musical instrument played by turning a crank; a barrel organ.

hurl (hērl) *v.i. & t.* **1,** throw; fling. **2,** utter vehemently.

hurl'ing *n.* an Irish variant of hockey.

hur'ly-bur'ly (hēr'lè-bēr'lè) *n. & adj.* tumult; confusion.

hur·rah' (hə-rä') *interj.* of applause, approval, or elation.

hur'ri·cane" (hēr'ə-kān") *n.* a windstorm of intense severity; a tropical cyclone.

hur'ry (hēr'è) *v.i.* move or act with haste. —*v.t.* urge onward; impel to greater rapidity; hasten. —*n.* haste.

hurt (hērt) *v.t. & i.* **1,** cause bodily pain to. **2,** do harm or mischief to; injure; damage. **3,** grieve; distress. —*n.* **1,** an impairment; a wound, bruise, injury, etc. **2,** a cause of distress; an insult. —**hurt'ful,** *adj.* injurious.

hur'tle (hēr'təl) *v.i.* rush violently and noisily.

hus'band (huz'bənd) *n.* a married man, in relation to his wife. —*v.t.* manage prudently; economize. —**hus'band·man** (-mən) *n.* a farmer.

hus'band·ry (-rè) *n.* **1,** farming; agriculture. **2,** thrifty management; frugality.

hush *interj.* to command silence. —*v.i.* become quiet or silent. —*v.t.* **1,** silence. **2,** calm; soothe; allay. —*n.* silence or quiet, esp. after noise. —**hush money,** a bribe to buy silence.

hush'pup'py (hush'pup'è) *n.* **1,** a cornmeal fritter. **2,** (*cap., T.N.*) a lightweight rubber-soled shoe.

husk *n.* the outer covering of certain fruits and seeds, esp. corn. **2,** any similar dry covering. —*v.t.* remove the husk from.

hus'ky (hus'kè) *adj.* **1,** strong; burly. **2,** dry in the throat; hoarse. —*n.* a large Eskimo dog. —**hus'ki·ness,** *v.*

hus·sar' (hû-zär') *n.* a light-cavalryman.

hus'sy (huz'è) *n.* a willful girl; a mean or worthless woman.

hust'ings (hus'tingz) *n.sing.* a platform or place where political candidates speak.

hus'tle (hus'əl) *v.i. & t.* **1,** move or act energetically; make haste. **2,** move by pushing or crowding. **3,** spirit away. **4,** (*Slang*) swindle. **5,** (*Slang*) ply the trade of a prostitute.

hus'tler (hus'lər) *n.* **1,** an energetic worker. **2,** (*Slang*) a minor swindler. **3,** (*Slang*) a prostitute.

hut *n.* a small, rude dwelling; a cabin.

hutch (huch) *n.* **1,** a box or coop for confining a small animal. **2,** a hut; a fisherman's shanty.

hutz'pa (khúts'pə) *n.* chutzpah.

huz·za' (hə-zä') *interj.* hurrah.

hy'a·cinth (hī'ə-sinth) *n.* **1,** a bulbous plant having spikes of bell-shaped flowers. **2,** a semiprecious stone.

hy'brid (hī'brid) *n.* **1,** the offspring of animals or plants of different varieties, species, or genera; a crossbreed or mongrel. **2,** any product or mixture of two heterogeneous things. —*adj.* crossbred; diverse. —**hy'brid·ize",** *v.t.*

hy·dran'gea (hī-drān'jə) *n.* a shrub having showy clusters of flowers.

hy'drant (hī'drənt) *n.* a pipe for drawing water from a main pipe.

hy'drate (hī'drāt) *n.* any compound containing water in chemical combination. —**hy·dra'tion,** *n.*

hy·drau'lic (hī-drâ'lik) *adj.* operated by water or other liquid. —**hy·drau'li·cal·ly,** *adv.*

hy·drau'lics (-liks) *n.* the science and engineering application of the motion of liquids.

hy·dro- (hī-drō) *pref.* **1,** water. **2,** hydrogen.

hy"dro·car'bon *n.* an organic compound of hydrogen and carbon.

hy"dro·e·lec'tric *adj.* pert. to the generation of electricity by water power.

hy'dro·foil" (hī'drə-foil") *n.* a fin attached to a speedboat that lifts the hull above the water when a certain speed is reached.

hy'dro·gen (hī'drə-jən) *n.* a gas, the lightest of the chemical elements, no. 1, symbol H. —**hy·dro'gen·ate"** (hī-droj'ə-nāt") *v.t.* combine with hydrogen. —**hydrogen bomb,** an atomic bomb based on fusion of an isotope of hydrogen.

hy·drom'e·ter (hī-drom'i-tər) *n.* an instrument for measuring the specific gravity of liquids.

hy"dro·pho'bi·a (hī"drə-fō'bé-ə) *n.* **1,** rabies. **2,** morbid fear of water.

hy'dro·plane" *n.* **1,** a seaplane. **2,** a powerful motorboat designed to skim over the surface of the water. **3,** a horizontal rudder on a submersible boat. —*v.i.* skim the surface of water in, or as in, a hydroplane.

hy"dro·pon'ics (-pon'iks) *n.* the cultivation of plants in a nutrient solution instead of soil.

hy'drous (hī'drəs) *adj.* containing water.

hy·e'na (hī-è'nə) *n.* a carnivorous mammal of Afr. and Asia, whose cry resembles a laugh.

hy'giene (hī'jēn) *n.* the science that deals with the preservation of health.

hy"gi·en'ic (hī"jè-en'ik) *adj.* **1,** sanitary. **2,** pert. to hygiene. —**hy"gi·en'i·cal·ly,** *adv.*

hy·grom'e·ter (hī-grom'ə-tər) *n.* an instrument for measuring the humidity of the atmosphere.

hy'men (hī'mən) *n.* a membrane partly closing the vagina; maidenhead.

hy"me·ne'al (hī"mə-nē'əl) *adj.* pert. to marriage.

hymn (him) *n.* **1,** a song in worship of God. **2,** any song or ode of praise.

hym'nal (him'nəl) *n.* a book of hymns. —*adj.* pert. to hymns.

hymn'o·dy (him'nə-dē) *n.* the singing, composing, body, or study of hymns.

hype (hīp) *n.* (*Colloq.*) flattering publicity; puff.

hy·per- (hī-pər) *pref.* over; in excess; exaggerated.

hy·per'bo·la (hī-pėr'bə-lə) *n.* a curve, one of the conic sections.

hy·per'bo·le (hī-pėr'bə-lè) *n.* obvious exaggeration; an extravagant statement.

hy"per·bol'ic (hī"pər-bol'ik) *adj.* **1,** pert. to or being a hyperbola. **2,** of or being hyperbole.

hy"per·gol'ic (hī"pər-gol'ik) *adj.* self-igniting: said of fuels.

hy·per'tro·phy (hī-pėr'trə-fè) *n.* excessive development of an organ of the body.

hy'phen (hī'fən) *n.* the symbol (-) used to join the parts of compound words, indicate syllabication, etc. —**hy'phen·ate"** (-āt") *v.t.*

hyp·no'sis (hip-nō'sis) *n.* a condition similar to sleep, but usually induced artificially; a trance.

hyp·not'ic (hip-not'ik) *adj.* **1,** pert. to hypnosis; susceptible to hypnotism. **2,** inducing sleep. —**hyp·not'i·cal·ly,** *adv.*

hyp'no·tize" (hip'nə-tīz") *v.t.* put to sleep by persuasion or mental ascendancy. —**hyp'no·tism",** *n.* —**hyp'no·tist",** *n.*

hy'po (hī'pō) *n.* **1,** a photographic fixing agent. **2,** hypodermic.

hy·po- (hī-pō) *pref.* under.

hy"po·chon'dri·ac" (hī"pə-kon'drè-ak") *n. & adj.* one who is morbidly anxious about his health or suffers imagined ills. —**hy"po·chon'dri·a** (-ə) *n.*

hy·poc'ri·sy (hi-pok"rə-sè) *n.* false pretension to personal qualities or principles not actually possessed.

hyp'o·crite" (hip'ə-krit") *n.* one who pretends to beliefs, sentiments, etc., he does not actually feel. —**hyp"o·crit'i·cal,** *adj.*

hy"po·der'mic (hī"pə-dėr'mik) *adj.* under the skin. —*n.* **1,** a remedy applied under the skin. **2,** a syringe for hypodermic injection. —**hy"po·der'mi·cal·ly,** *adv.*

hy"po·gly·ce'mi·a (hī"pō-glī-sē'mè-ə) *n.* low level of sugar in the blood.

hy·pot'e·nuse" (hī-pot'ə-noos") *n.* the longest side of a right triangle.

hy·poth'e·cate" (hī-poth'thə-kāt") *v.t.* pledge to a creditor as security. —**hy·poth"e·ca'tion,** *n.*

hy·poth'e·sis (hī-poth'ə-sis) *n.* [*pl.* **-ses** (-sēz)] a tentative assertion about natural phenomena, assumed but not positively known; a postulate. —**hy·poth'e·size"** (-sīz") *v.t. & i.*

hy"po·thet'i·cal (hī"pə-thet'i-kəl) *adj.* **1,** taken as a hypothesis. **2,** conjectural; supposed.

hys'sop (his'əp) *n.* an aromatic flowering herb.

hys·ter·ec'to·my (his-tə-rek'tə-mè) *n.* surgical removal of the uterus.

hys·te'ri·a (his-tir'ē-ə) *n.* a disorder marked by violent emotional outbreaks.

hys·ter'ic (his-ter'ik) *n.* **1,** one subject to hysteria. **2,** (*pl.*) a fit of hysteria. —**hys·ter'i·cal,** *adj.*

I

I, i (ī) **1,** the ninth letter of the English alphabet. **2,** the personal pronoun, first person. **3,** (*cap.*) the Roman numeral one.

i·am'bic (ī-am'bik) *n.* an iamb or iambus, a foot in poetry constituting an unstressed then a stressed syllable, as *a·bout'*. —*adj.* (of verse) in iambics.

I·ber'i·an (ī-bir'ē-ən) *adj.* pert. to the region of Spain and Portugal.

i'bex (ī'beks) *n.* a Europ. wild goat with long, curved horns.

i'bis (ī'bis) *n.* a wading bird related to the heron and stork.

-i·ble (i-bəl) *suf.* same as **-able.**

-ic (ik) *suf.* forming adjectives: **1,** like. **2,** pert. to. **3,** composed of. Also, **-i·cal** (i-kəl).

ice (īs) *n.* **1,** the solid form of water, produced by freezing. **2,** any frozen liquid. **3,** a confection of frozen fruit juice. **4,** ice cream. **5,** icing. **6,** reserve; formality. **7,** (*Slang*) diamonds. **8,** (*Slang*) graft; bribes paid for freedom from arrest. —*v.t.* **1,** cool with ice. **2,** change into ice; freeze. **3,** cover with icing. —*v.i.* freeze. —*adj.* iced; icy. —**ice box,** a refrigerator. —**ice cream,** a frozen confection of cream, flavoring, and often eggs. —**ice milk,** frozen custard. —**ice water,** very cold water.

ice'berg" (īs'bėrg") *n.* **1,** a mass of ice floating at sea. **2,** (*Colloq.*) a cold, unemotional person.

ice'bound" *adj.* frozen in or obstructed by ice.

ice'man" *n.* [*pl.* **-men**] one who sells ice.

i'chor (ī'kôr) *n.* **1,** in Gk. mythology, the ethereal fluid flowing in the veins of the gods. **2,** an acrid watery discharge, as from an ulcer. —**i′chor·ous,** *adj.*

ich′thy·o- (ik′thē-ō) *pref.* fish.

ich″thy·ol′o·gy (ik″thē-ol′ə-jē) *n.* the study of fishes. —**ich′thy·o·log′i·cal,** *adj.* —**ich″-thy·ol′o·gist,** *n.*

i′ci·cle (ī′si-kəl) *n.* a spike of ice formed when dripping water freezes.

ic′ing (ī′sing) *n.* a preparation of sugar used for covering cakes, etc; frosting.

ick′y (ik′ē) *adj.* (*Colloq.*) **1,** sticky and unpleasant. **2,** disgusting.

i′con (ī′kon) *n.* a sacred image.

i·con′o·clast″ (ī-kon′ə-klåst″) *n.* one who challenges cherished beliefs. —**i·con′o-clasm,** *n.* —**i·con″o·clas′tic,** *adj.* —**i·con″o-clas′ti·cal·ly,** *adv.*

i·con′o·scope″ (ī-kon′ə-skōp″) *n.* the large cathode-ray tube of a TV camera.

-ics (iks) *suf.* forming nouns, denoting fields of knowledge or activity.

ic′tus (ik′təs) *n.* the moment of stress, as in a poetic line.

i′cy (ī′sē) *adj.* **1,** made of or abounding with ice. **2,** like ice; cold. —**i′ci·ly,** *adv.* —**i′ci·ness,** *n.*

id *n.* (*Psychoanal.*) a person's urge to pleasure and the exercise of the libido.

i·de′a (ī-dē′ə) *n.* **1,** something existing in the mind; conception; thought. **2,** an attitude of mind; opinion; belief; impression. **3,** a notion, vagary, or fantasy. **4,** a plan of action; purpose; intention.

i·de′al (ī-dē′əl) *n.* something imagined in a state of perfection; a goal; a model. —*adj.* **1,** perfect, highly desirable, worthy of emulation, etc. **2,** existing only in idea. **3,** not real; impractical; visionary.

i·de′al·ism (ī-dē′ə-liz-əm) *n.* **1,** a tendency to wish or believe things to be ideal, or better than they are. **2,** a constant effort to achieve perfection. —**i·de′al·ist,** *n.* —**i·de″al·is′tic,** *adj.* —**i·de″al·is′ti·cal·ly,** *adv.*

i·de′al·ize″ (ī-dē′ə-līz″) *v.t.* regard as ideal, usually in disregard of fact. —**i·de″al·i·za′tion,** *n.*

i·de′al·ly (ī-dē′ə-lē) *adv.* **1,** perfectly. **2,** if everything were as one wished.

i·den′ti·cal (ī-den′ti-kəl) *adj.* **1,** being the same. **2,** exactly or much alike.

i·den″ti·fi·ca′tion (ī-den″tə-fi-kā′shən) *n.* **1,** act of identifying. **2,** a mark or means of identifying.

i·den′ti·fy″ (ī-den′ti-fī″) *v.t.* **1,** recognize or establish as being a particular kind, individual, etc. **2,** show to be identical. **3,** associate (oneself) in feeling, interest, etc.

i·den′ti·ty (ī-den′tə-tē) *n.* **1,** what a thing or person is; a name, classification, etc. **2,**

recognizable individuality. **3,** sameness. **4,** exact or close likeness.

id′e·o·gram″ (id′ē-ə-gràm″) *n.* a written symbol that represents an idea directly. Also, **id′e·o·graph″** (-gráf″).

i″de·ol′o·gy (ī″dē-ol′ə-jē) *n.* **1,** the aggregate of ideas, beliefs, doctrines, etc., of a large group of persons; popularly, a system of government. **2,** the science of ideas. —**i″de·o·log′i·cal,** *adj.*

ides (īdz) *n.pl.* in ancient Rome, the 15th day of March, May, July, October; the 13th of other months.

id′i·o·cy (id′ē-ə-sē) *n.* the condition of an idiot.

id′i·om (id′ē-əm) *n.* **1,** a form of expression peculiar to a language. **2,** a dialect. **3,** the peculiar character of a language. **4,** a distinct style, as in music, art, etc.

id″i·o·mat′ic (id″ē-ə-mat′ik) *adj.* **1,** conforming to idiom. **2,** colloquial. —**id″i·o-mat′i·cal·ly,** *adv.*

id″i·o·syn′cra·sy (id″ē-ə-sin′krə-sē) *n.* a peculiarity, as of behavior.

id′i·ot (id′ē-ət) *n.* a person born mentally deficient, incapable of developing beyond a four-year mental level. —**id·i·ot′ic** (-ot′ik) *adj.* —**id·i·rot′i·cal·ly,** *adv.* —**idiot light,** a warning light on an automobile instrument panel.

i′dle (ī′dəl) *adj.* **1,** doing nothing; inactive; unemployed. **2,** not in use or operation. **3,** lazy; slothful. **4,** useless; ineffective; futile. **5,** trivial; pointless; groundless. —*v.i.* **1,** pass the time in idleness. **2,** move slowly; saunter; loiter. **3,** (of a machine) run while not connected to do work. —*v.t.* cause to be idle. —**i′dle·ness,** *n.*

i′dler (ī′dlər) *n.* **1,** a gear or device that idles. **2,** a loafer.

i′dol (ī′dəl) *n.* **1,** an image of a deity, used as an object of worship. **2,** a person or thing adored or revered. **3,** a phantom; a false idea. —**i′dol·ize″,** *v.t.*

i″dol′a·ter (ī″dol′ə-tər) *n.* an idol worshiper.

i·dol′a·try (ī-dol′ə-trē) *n.* the worship of idols. —**i·dol′a·trous,** *adj.*

i′dyl (ī′dəl) *n.* **1,** a descriptive or narrative poem, esp. pastoral. **2,** a simple, appealing episode or scene. —**i·dyl′lic** (-dil′ik) *adj.* simple.

-ier (ir) *suf.* same as **-er** or **-eer.**

if *conj.* **1,** in case that; supposing that; on condition that. **2,** whether. **3,** even though. —*n.* a condition; a supposition. —**if′fy,** *adj.* (*Colloq.*) uncertain; contingent.

ig′loo *n.* a domed Eskimo hut, made of blocks of snow and ice. Also, **ig′lu.**

ig′ne·ous (ig′nē-əs) *adj.* **1,** produced by

intense heat, as rock of volcanic origin. **2,** pert. to fire.

ig·nis fat·u·us (ig'nəs-fach'oo-əs) [*pl.* **ig'nes fat·u·i** (ig'nēz-fach'oo-ī)] **1,** a flickering light sometimes seen at night over a marsh. **2,** something misleading; a delusion.

ig·nite' (ig-nīt') *v.t.* & *i.* set on fire; begin to burn; kindle.

ig·ni'tion (ig-nish'ən) *n.* **1,** act of igniting; state of being ignited. **2,** a means, device, or process for igniting, esp. the electrical system of an internal combustion engine.

ig·no'ble (ig-nō'bəl) *adj.* **1,** low in character; base; dishonorable. **2,** low in birth or station. —**ig·no'ble·ness, ig''no·bil'i·ty,** *n.*

ig''no·min'i·ous (ig''nə-min'ē-əs) *adj.* causing or deserving humiliation, disgrace, or public contempt.

ig'no·min·y (ig'nə-min-ē) *n.* public disgrace.

ig''no·ra'mus (ig''nə-rā'məs) *n.* an ignorant person.

ig'no·rant (ig'nə-rənt) *adj.* **1,** having little or no knowledge; unlearned. **2,** unaware; uninformed. —**ig'no·rance,** *n.*

ig·nore' (ig-nôr') *v.t.* pass by without notice; pay no heed to.

i·gua'na (i-gwä'nə) *n.* a large lizard of tropical America.

il- *pref.* same as **in-,** but used before an *l.*

il''e·i'tis (il''ē-ī'tis) *n.* inflammation of the ileum.

il'e·um (il'ē-əm) *n.* the part of the small intestine between the jejunum and the large intestine.

il'i·ac'' (il'ē-ak'') *adj.* pert. to the ilium, the large anterior bone of the pelvis.

ilk *n.* sort, kind, family, class, etc.

ill (il) *adj.* **1,** impaired in health; unwell; sick. **2,** wicked; bad. **3,** causing evil; deleterious; malevolent. **4,** unfriendly; cross; crabbed. **5,** unfavorable; adverse. **6,** unskillful; bungling. —*adv.* **1,** wickedly. **2,** unfortunately; unfavorably; in a hostile manner. **3,** with difficulty or hardship; faultily. —*n.* **1,** a bodily ailment; disease. **2,** injury; harm; misfortune; trouble. —**ill'ness,** *n.* —**ill will,** hostility.

ill-''ad·vised'' (-əd-vīzd') *adj.* showing poor judgment; unwise.

ill-'bred'' *adj.* uncouth; impolite.

il·le'gal (i-lē'gəl) *adj.* contrary to law. —**il''le·gal'i·ty** (il''i-gal'ə-tē) *n.*

il·leg'i·ble (i-lej'ə-bəl) *adj.* impossible or hard to read. —**il·leg''i·bil'i·ty,** *n.*

il''le·git'i·mate (il''i-jit'ə-mət) *adj.* **1,** unlawful; invalid. **2,** born out of wedlock. —**il''le·git'i·ma·cy,** *n.*

ill-''fat'ed (-fā'təd) *adj.* **1,** doomed. **2,** unlucky.

ill-''fa''vored *adj.* ugly; unpleasant.

ill-''got'ten *adj.* obtained by illegal or dishonest means.

il·lic'it (i-lis'it) *adj.* **1,** unlawful; unlicensed. **2,** clandestine. —**il·lic'it·ness,** *n.*

il·lim'it·a·ble (i-lim'i-tə-bəl) *adj.* infinite; too great to measure.

il·lin'i·um (i-lin'ē-əm) *n.* promethium.

il·lit'er·ate (i-lit'ər-ət) *adj.* unable to read and write. —*n.* an illiterate person. —**il·lit'er·a·cy,** *n.*

il·log'i·cal (i-loj'i-kəl) *adj.* contravening or disregarding the rules of logic. —**il·log''i·cal'i·ty** (-kal'ə-tē) *n.*

ill-'starred'' *adj.* unfortunate.

il·lu'mi·nate'' (i-loo'mə-nāt'') *v.t.* **1,** furnish with a light; light up; enlighten. **2,** make clear; explain; elucidate. **3,** decorate in color by hand. —**il·lu''mi·na'tion,** *n.* —**il·lu'mi·na''tor,** *n.* Also, **il·lu'mine** (-min).

ill-''use' (-ūz') *v.t.* mistreat; abuse. —*n.* (-ūs') cruel or unjust treatment. Also, **ill-''us'age.**

il·lu'sion (i-loo'zhən) *n.* something that deceives the eye or mind; a mistaken perception or belief. —**il·lu'sive** (-siv), **il·lu'so·ry** (-sə-rē) *adj.*

il'lus·trate'' (il'ə-strāt'') *v.t.* **1,** furnish with pictures, diagrams, etc., to adorn or elucidate. **2,** make clear or intelligible, as with examples. —**il·lus'tra·tive** (i-lus'trə-tiv), *adj.*

il''lus·tra'tion (il''ə-strā'shən) *n.* **1,** something that illustrates, as a picture. **2,** act of illustrating.

il·lus'tra''tor (il'ə-strā''tər) *n.* an artist who makes illustrations for books or periodicals.

il·lus'tri·ous (i-lus'trē-əs) *adj.* very distinguished; conspicuous; eminent. —**il·lus'tri·ous·ness,** *n.*

im- *pref.* same as **in-,** but used before *b, m,* or *p.* [In addition to words defined in the text, the following words formed by prefixing **im-** (= not) have merely the negative sense of the positive term. For pronunciation of such words, listed below or defined in the text, refer to the vocabulary for the pronunciation of the positive term.]

im·bal'ance	im·pen'i·tent
im·meas'ur·a·ble	im''per·cep'ti·ble
im·mis'ci·ble	im·per'ish·a·ble
im·mit'i·ga·ble	im·per'ma·nent
im·mov'a·ble	im·per'me·a·ble
im·mu'ta·ble	im·per'son·al
im·pal'pa·ble	im''per·turb'a·ble
im·par'i·ty	im·plau'si·ble
im·pas'sa·ble	im·pol'i·tic
im·pas'si·ble	im·prac'ti·ca·ble
im·pen'e·tra·ble	im·prac'ti·cal

im″pre·cise′ **im·pro′bi·ty**
im·prob′a·ble **im·prov′i·dent**

im·age (im′ij) *n.* **1,** a representation of the form and features of a person or thing, in a picture, statue, etc. **2,** a reflection in a mirror. **3,** a mental picture; a written description; a figure of speech. **4,** any counterpart or copy; a likeness or similitude. **5,** symbol. —*v.t.* **1,** picture in the mind; imagine. **2,** make an image of.

im·age·ry (-rè) *n.* **1,** imaginative thought or expression. **2,** images collectively.

i·mag′i·nar·y (i-maj′ə-ner-è) *adj.* existing only in the imagination òr fancy; not real. —**imaginary number** or **part,** (*Math.*) the part of a complex number containing the imaginary unit (as ''3i'' in 5 + 3i). —**imaginary unit,** the positive square root of minus 1, symbol i.

i·mag″i·na′tion (i-maj″ə-nā′shən) *n.* **1,** the act or faculty of forming mental images of objects. **2,** the faculty of forming ideas and ideals. **3,** fancy, ideal, concept, etc.

im·ag′i·na·tive (i-maj′ə-nā-tiv) *adj.* having lively imagination.

im·ag′ine (i-maj′in) *v.t.* **1,** form a mental image of. **2,** think; believe; suppose; conjecture; guess, etc. —*v.i.* **1,** exercise the imagination. **2,** think; fancy. —**im·ag′i·na·ble,** *adj.*

i·ma′go (i-mā′gō) *n.* **1,** an insect in the adult stage. **2,** (*Psychol.*) an idealized concept of a parent, formed in childhood and retained in the adult unconscious mind.

i·mam′ (i-mäm′) *n.* a Moslem priest.

im·be·cile (im′bə-sil) *n.* a person of defective mentality, but above the level of an idiot. —**im″be·cil′ic,** *adj.* —**im″be·cil′i·ty,** *n.*

im·bed′ *v.t.* [**-bed′ded, -ding**] bury; set (in something).

im·bibe′ (im-bīb′) *v.t.* **1,** drink. **2,** absorb; take in.

im·bri·cate (im′brə-kət) *adj.* **1,** overlapping like tiles, as fish scales, etc. **2,** decorated with designs like overlapping tiles. Also, **im′bri·cat″ed** —*v.* (im-brì-kāt″) overlap like tiles. —**im″bri·ca′tion,** *n.*

im·bro′glio (im-brōl′yō) *n.* an intricate, confused, or perplexing state of affairs.

im·brue′ (im-broo′) *v.t.* wet; drench; stain.

im·bue′ (im-bū′) *v.t.* saturate; dye; impregnate, as with sentiments, opinions, etc. —**im·bue′ment,** *n.*

im′i·tate″ (im′ə-tāt″) *v.t.* **1,** copy in manner or action; follow as a model; mimic; simulate. **2,** make a copy of. —**im′i·ta·ble,** *adj.* —**im′i·ta″tive,** *adj.* —**im′i·ta″tor,** *n.*

im″i·ta′tion (im″ə-tā′shən) *n.* the act or a product of imitating; a copy, likeness, or counterfeit. —*adj.* made to imitate a genuine, and usually superior, article.

im·mac′u·late (i-mak′yə-lit) *adj.* **1,** perfectly clean; spotless. **2,** free from moral blemish; pure. —**im·mac′u·la·cy** (-lə-sè), —**im·mac′u·late·ness,** *n.*

im′ma·nent (im′ə-nənt) *adj.* remaining within; intrinsic. —**im′ma·nence,** *n.*

im″ma·te′ri·al (im″ə-tir′è-əl) *adj.* of little or no significance; irrelevant. —**im″ma·te′ri·al·ness,** *n.*

im″ma·ture′ (im″ə-tyûr′) *adj.* not ripe or fully developed; youthful. —**im″ma·tur′i·ty,** *n.*

im·me′di·a·cy (i-mē′dè-ə-sè) *n.* urgency, due to lack of intervening time.

im·me′di·ate (i-mē′dè-ət) *adj.* **1,** without any time intervening; instant. **2,** of the present moment. **3,** not separated; next; nearest. **4,** direct. —**im·me′di·ate·ness,** *n.*

im″me·mo′ri·al (im″ə-môr′è-əl) *adj.* of a time beyond memory, record, or knowledge.

im·mense′ (i-mens′) *adj.* **1,** very large; huge; vast. **2,** boundless. **3,** (*Slang*) excellent. —**im·men′si·ty** (i-men′sə-tè), a, **mense′ness,** *n.*

im·merse′ (i-mêrs′) *v.t.* **1,** plunge into, esp. deeply. **2,** involve or interest deeply. —**im·mer′sion** (-shən) *n.*

im′mi·grant (im′i-grənt) *n.* one who immigrates.

im′mi·grate″ (im′ə-grāt″) *v.i.* come to settle in a new habitat or country. —**im″mi·gra′tion,** *n.*

im′mi·nent (im′ə-nənt) *adj.* **1,** likely to occur soon; impending. **2,** jutting out; overhanging. —**im′mi·nence,** *n.*

im·mo′bile (i-mō′bil) *adj.* not movable or moving. —**im″mo·bil′i·ty,** *n.*

im·mo′bi·lize″ (i-mō′bə-līz″) *v.t.* render incapable of moving. —**im″mo″bi·li·za′tion,** *n.*

im·mod′er·ate (i-mod′ər-ət) *adj.* not confined to just or reasonable limits; intemperate. —**im·mod′er·a′tion,** *n.*

im·mod′est (i-mod′ist) *adj.* **1,** not proper; indecent. **2,** boastful. —**im·mod′es·ty,** *n.*

im′mo·late″ (im′ə-lāt″) *v.t.* kill as a sacrificial victim. —**im″mo·la′tion,** *n.*

im·mor′al (i-môr′əl) *adj.* not conforming to moral law. —**im″mo·ral′i·ty** (im″ə-ral′ə-tè) *n.* wickedness; vice.

im·mor′tal (i-môr′təl) *adj.* not subject to death, cessation, or oblivion. —*n.* one who is immortal. —**im″mor·tal′i·ty** (im″ôr-tal′ə-tè) *n.*

im·mor′tal·ize″ (-īz″) *v.t.* make immortal or forever famous. —**im·mor″tal·i·za′tion,** *n.*

im·mor·telle′ (im″ôr-tel′) *n.* a plant or flower that retains form and color when it dies.

im·mune′ (i-mūn′) *adj.* not liable; exempt, as from a disease. **—im·mu′ni·ty** (i-mū′-nə-tē) *n.*

im′mu·nize″ (im″yə-nīz″) *v.t.* protect, as from disease by inoculation. **—im″mu·ni·za′tion,** *n.*

im·mure′ (i-myûr′) *v.t.* surround with walls; confine. **—im·mure′ment,** *n.*

imp *n.* a small prankish sprite or child. **—imp′ish,** *adj.* mischievous.

im′pact (im′pakt) *n.* **1,** the striking of one body against another; collision. **2,** the force of a collision. **—***v.t.* (im-pakt′) press closely; pack in. **—im·pact′ed,** *adj.* tightly packed; wedged in. **—im·pac′tion,** *n.*

im·pair′ (im-pār′) *v.t. & i.* make or become worse; damage; weaken. **—im·pair′ment,** *n.*

im·pa′la (im-pä′lə) *n.* a large Afr. antelope.

im·pale′ (im-pāl′) *v.t.* **1,** thrust a sharpened stake through; transfix. **2,** fence in. **—im·pale′ment,** *n.*

im·pan′el (im-pan′əl) *v.t.* enroll or summon (a jury). **—im·pan′el·ment,** *n.*

im·part′ (im-pärt′) *v.t.* **1,** make known; tell. **2,** give; bestow; share. **—im″par·ta′tion,** *n.*

im·par′tial (im-pär′shəl) *adj.* not biased; equitable; just. **—im·par″ti·al′i·ty** (-shē·al′-ə-tē) *n.*

im·passe′ (im-pas′) *n.* a condition in which progress or escape is blocked; a deadlock.

im·pas′sion (im-pash′ən) *v.t.* move or affect with passion. **—im·pas′sioned,** *adj.* filled with emotion; ardent.

im·pas′sive (im-pas′iv) *adj.* **1,** free of emotion; unmoved; apathetic. **2,** serene; calm. **—im·pas′sive·ness, im″pas·siv′i·ty** (im″pə-siv′ə-tē) *n.*

im·pas′to (im-päs′tō) *n.* a thick covering of paint.

im·pa′tient (im-pā′shənt) *adj.* not tranquil; restive; eager. **—im·pa′tience,** *n.*

im·peach′ (im-pēch′) *v.t.* **1,** accuse (a public official) of misconduct. **2,** discredit; disparage. **—im·peach′ment,** *n.*

im·pec′ca·ble (im-pek′ə-bəl) *adj.* without fault or blemish; irreproachable. **—im·pec″ca·bil′i·ty,** *n.*

im″pe·cu′ni·ous (im″pə-kū′nē-əs) *adj.* without money; poor. **—im″pe·cu′ni·ous·ness,** *n.*

im·pe′dance (im-pē′dəns) *n.* (*Electricity*) the apparent resistance to the flow of an alternating current that corresponds to the actual resistance to the flow of a direct current.

im·pede′ (im-pēd′) *v.t.* check or retard the progress of; hinder; obstruct.

im·ped′i·ment (im-ped′ə-mənt) *n.* **1,** a load; hindrance. **2,** a physical defect that impairs speech. **3,** a bar to marriage. **—im·ped″i·men′ta** (-tə) *n.pl.* baggage.

im·pel′ *v.t.* [**-pelled′, pel′ling**] **1,** incite or constrain to an action; urge. **2,** drive onward.

im·pend′ *v.t.* be on the point of occurring; be imminent.

im·per′a·tive (im-per′ə-tiv) *adj.* **1,** expressing command; peremptory. **2,** not to be evaded; obligatory. **3,** (*Gram.*) of verbs, the mood expressing command. **—im·per′a·tive·ness,** *n.*

im·per′fect (im-pėr′fikt) *adj.* **1,** faulty; defective; incomplete. **2,** (*Gram.*) of verbs, expressing past but not completed action; past progressive, as, *he was singing.* **—im″per·fec′tion,** *n.*

im·per′fo·rate (im-pėr′fə-rit) *adj.* not pierced. **—***n.* a postage stamp not perforated for separation.

im·pe′ri·al (im-pir′ē-əl) *adj.* **1,** pert. to an empire or emperor. **2,** august; commanding. **3,** grand; superior in size or quality. **—***n.* **1,** a short narrow beard under the lower lip. **2,** a former Russian gold coin. **—imperial gallon,** a Brit. liquid measure, 1⅕ U.S. gallons.

im·pe′ri·al·ism (-iz-əm) *n.* the policy of expanding national territory. **—im·pe′ri·al·ist,** *n.* **—im·pe″ri·al·is′tic,** *adj.* **—im·pe″ri·al·is′ti·cal·ly,** *adv.*

im·per′il (im-per′əl) *v.t.* put in peril; endanger. **—im·per′il·ment,** *n.*

im·pe′ri·ous (im-pir′ē-əs) *adj.* **1,** domineering. **2,** imperative; urgent. **—im·pe′ri·ous·ness,** *n.*

im·per′son·ate″ (im-pėr′sə-nāt″) *v.t.* pretend to be; assume the character of; play the rôle of. **—im·per″son·a′tion,** *n.* **—im·per′son·a·tor,** *n.*

im·per′ti·nent (im-pėr′tə-nənt) *adj.* **1,** unmannerly in conduct; forward; insolent. **2,** not pertinent; irrelevant. **—im·per′ti·nence,** *n.*

im·per′vi·ous (im-pėr′vē-əs) *adj.* **1,** not permeable. **2,** resistant to persuasion. **—im·per′vi·ous·ness,** *n.*

im″pe·ti′go (im″pə-tī′gō) *n.* a contagious skin disease, esp. of children.

im·pet′u·ous (im-pech′oo-əs) *adj.* sudden and vehement in action. **—im·pet″u·os′i·ty** (-os′ə-tē), **im·pet′u·ous·ness,** *n.*

im′pe·tus (im′pə-təs) *n.* **1,** energy of motion; the power with which a moving body tends to maintain its velocity. **2,** impulse; incentive.

im·pi'e·ty (im-pī'ə-tė) *n.* lack of reverence; wickedness.

im·pinge' (im-pinj') *v.i.* (with *on, against,* etc.) **1,** collide. **2,** encroach. —**im·pinge'·ment,** *n.*

im'pi·ous (im'pē-əs) *adj.* lacking reverence for God; profane. —**im'pi·ous·ness,** *n.*

im·pla'ca·ble (im-plā'kə-bəl) *adj.* not to be placated or appeased; inexorable. —**im·pla'ca·ble·ness, im·pla''ca·bil'i·ty,** *n.*

im·plant' (im-plànt') *v.t.* **1,** plant in the mind; inculcate; instill. **2,** set in a place; imbed. —*n.* (im'plànt'') (*Med.*) something introduced into living tissue. —**im''plan·ta'tion.** *n.*

im'ple·ment (im'plə-mənt) *n.* **1,** an instrument, tool, or utensil. **2,** a means of doing or enacting; an agent. —*v.t.* (-ment'') **1,** enact; execute. **2,** provide with implements or means. —**im''ple·men·ta'tion,** *n.*

im'pli·cate'' (im'pli-kāt'') *v.t.* show to be involved or concerned with; entangle.

im''pli·ca'tion (im''pli-kā'shən) *n.* **1,** something implied; the act of implying. **2,** the condition of being implicated or involved.

im·plic'it (im-plis'it) *adj.* **1,** to be assumed, though not directly expressed; implied. **2,** unquestioning, as of faith. —**im·plic'it·ness,** *n.*

im·plode' (im-plōd') *v.t. & i.* burst inward.

im·plore' (im-plôr') *v.t.* **1,** beseech; entreat. **2,** request urgently.

im·plo'sion (im-plō'zhən) *n.* a bursting inward. —**im·plo'sive,** *adj.*

im·ply' (im-plī') *v.t.* **1,** suggest or indicate without expressing directly. **2,** necessarily involve; entail.

im''po·lite' (im''pə-līt') *adj.* discourteous. —**im''po·lite'ness,** *n.*

im·pon'der·a·ble (im-pon'dər-ə-bəl) *adj.* not to be weighed or evaluated; too vague to meditate upon. —**im·pon''der·a·bil'i·ty,** *n.*

im·port' (im-pôrt') *v.t.* **1,** bring in, as wares from a foreign country. **2,** denote; signify. **3,** have a bearing on. —*v.i.* be of importance. —*n.* (im'pôrt) **1,** something imported from abroad; the act or business of importing. **2,** meaning; implication. **3,** importance; consequence. —**im''por·ta'tion** (im''pôr-tā'shən) *n.*

im·por'tance (im-pôr'təns) *n.* state of being important.

im·por'tant (im-pôr'tənt) *adj.* **1,** of great weight in meaning, significance, or consequence. **2,** urgent. **3,** eminent; prominent; influential. **4,** pompous.

im''por·tune' (im''pôr-tūn') *v.t. & i.* **1,** beset with entreaties. **2,** ask for persistently; beg. —**im·por'tu·nate,** *adj.* —**im''por·tu'ni·ty,** *n.*

im·pose' (im-pōz') *v.t.* **1,** lay as a burden; levy, inflict, or enforce. **2,** palm off. **3,** obtrude (oneself) upon others. **4,** lay on; put; lay out (printing type) in proper order. —**im·pos'ing,** *adj.* stately; impressive.

im''po·si'tion (im''pə-zish'ən) *n.* **1,** act or manner of imposing. **2,** a burden placed on another's good will.

im·pos'si·ble (im-pos'ə-bəl) *adj.* **1,** non-existent or false; sure not to happen. **2,** that cannot be done; utterly impracticable. **3,** (*Colloq.*) very unattractive. —**im·pos''si·bil'i·ty,** *n.*

im'post (im'pōst) *n.* a tax or tribute, esp. a customs duty.

im·pos'tor (im-pos'tər) *n.* one who deceitfully assumes a false name or character.

im·pos'ture (im-pos'chər) *n.* false assumption of another's name, etc.; any sham or hoax.

im'po·tent (im'pə-tənt) *adj.* lacking strength, power, or virility. —**im'po·tence, im'po·ten·cy,** *n.*

im·pound' (im-pownd') *v.t.* **1,** shut in a pen; restrain within bounds. **2,** seize and keep in custody. —**im·pound'age, im·pound'ment,** *n.*

im·pov'er·ish (im-pov'ər-ish) *v.t.* **1,** make indigent. **2,** cause to deteriorate. —**im·pov'er·ish·ment,** *n.*

im'pre·cate'' (im'prə-kāt'') *v.t.* invoke a curse or evil upon. —**im''pre·ca'tion,** *n.*

im·preg'na·ble (im-preg'nə-bəl) *adj.* **1,** not to be taken or overcome by force; invincible. **2,** capable of being impregnated. —**im·preg''na·bil'i·ty,** *n.*

im·preg'nate (im-preg'nāt) *v.t.* **1,** make pregnant; fertilize. **2,** permeate or saturate. —*adj.* impregnated. —**im''preg·na'tion,** *n.*

im''pre·sa'ri·o'' (im''prə-sär'ė-ō'') *n.* a theatrical producer or manager, esp. of an opera company; any promoter.

im·press' (im-pres') *v.t.* **1,** affect deeply as to mind or feelings. **2,** fix firmly in the mind. **3,** press; stamp; imprint. **4,** seize for public use; force into service. —*n.* (im'press) **1,** a product of stamping or printing. **2,** distinctive appearance or character. —**im·press'i·ble,** *adj.*

im·pres'sion (im-presh'ən) *n.* **1,** effect produced, as by perception or sensation; an idea, image, etc., esp. if vague. **2,** the act of impressing; a mark, mold, copy, etc., made by pressing, stamping, or printing. **3,** an edition. —**im·pres'sion·a·ble,** *adj.* easily impressed; susceptible.

im·pres'sion·ism (-iz-əm) *n.* a style of nonobjective expression in art and music. —**im·pres'sion·ist,** *adj. & n.*

im·pres'sive (-siv) *adj.* tending to excite admiration. —**im·pres'sive·ness,** *n.*

im·press'ment (-mənt) *n.* a forcing into service.

im″pri·ma'tur (im″pri-mā'tər) *n.* an official license to publish.

im·print' *v.t.* produce or fix by, or as by, pressure; print; stamp. —*n.* (im'print) **1,** a distinctive mark; a maker's or seller's name, esp. a publisher's. **2,** effect produced; impression.

im·pris'on (im-priz'ən) *v.t.* put in prison; confine. —**im·pris'on·ment,** *n.*

im·promp'tu (im-promp'too) *adj.* **1,** done without previous preparation. **2,** hastily prepared; improvised. —*n.* an impromptu performance or composition. —*adv.* extemporaneously.

im·prop'er (im-prop'ər) *adj.* not proper; not moral; incorrect; indecorous. —**im·prop'er·ness,** *n.* —**improper fraction,** a fraction of which the numerator is equal to or greater than the denominator.

im″pro·pri'e·ty (im″prə-prī'ə-tfi) *n.* improper action; an error; a breach of propriety.

im·prove' (im-proov') *v.t.* **1,** make better. **2,** make (land) more valuable, esp. by erecting buildings. —*v.i.* become better; increase in value or utility.

im·prove'ment (-mənt) *n.* **1,** act or result of improving. **2,** construction, or a structure, that improves real property.

im'pro·vise″ (im'prə-vīz″) *v.t.* make or do hastily or without previous preparation; extemporize, esp. in music. —**im″pro·vi·sa'tion,** *n.*

im·pru'dent (im-proo'dənt) *adj.* indiscreet; rash. —**im·pru'dence,** *n.*

im'pu·dent (im'pyə-dənt) *adj.* offensively forward in behavior; insolent; saucy. —**im'pu·dence,** *n.*

im·pugn' (im-pūn') *v.t.* challenge as false. —**im·pugn'ment,** *n.*

im'pulse (im'puls) *n.* **1,** force acting suddenly; a thrust or push. **2,** a stimulation of the mind to action; a sudden inclination. **3,** the intensity or momentum of a force; induced motion; impetus. —**im·pul'sion,** *n.* —**im·pul'sive,** *adj.* impetuous.

im·pu'ni·ty (im-pū'nə-tfi) *n.* exemption from punishment.

im·pure' (im-pyūr') *adj.* **1,** not simple or homogeneous; mixed with extraneous matter; tainted. **2,** obscene. —**im·pure'ness,** *n.*

im·pur'i·ty (im-pyūr'ə-tfi) *n.* **1,** something not pure; a flaw. **2,** impureness. **3,** that

which makes impure, as a foreign ingredient, etc.

im·pute' (im-pūt') *v.t.* charge, ascribe, or attribute, esp. something discreditable. —**im″pu·ta'tion,** *n.*

in *prep.* denoting presence, existence, situation, inclusion, action, etc., within limits, as of place, time, condition, circumstances, etc. —*adv.* **1,** at, to, or toward (a place, condition, relation, etc.). **2,** inward; on the inside; at home; in occupancy. **3,** having the turn to play in a game. **4,** accepted; elected. —*adj.* (*Colloq.*) in vogue.

in- *pref.* **1,** in, as in *income.* **2,** used to form or intensify verbs, as *intrust;* often replaced by **en-. 3,** not: used to impart a negative sense, as in *inactive.* (See also **un-.**) [In addition to words defined in the text, the following words formed by prefixing **in-** (= not) have merely the negative sense of the positive term. For pronunciation of such words, refer to the vocabulary for the pronunciation of the positive term.]

in″a·bil'i·ty	in″cor·rupt'i·ble
in″ac·ces'si·ble	in·cur'a·ble
in·ac'cu·rate	in·cu'ri·ous
in·ac'tive	in″de·ci'pher·a·ble
in·ad'e·quate	in·dec'o·rous
in″ad·mis'si·ble	in″de·fen'si·ble
in″ad·vis'a·ble	in″de·fin'a·ble
in·al'ien·a·ble	in″de·scrib'a·ble
in·ap'pli·ca·ble	in″de·struct'i·ble
in″ap·pre'ci·a·ble	in·di'rect'
in″ap·pro'pri·ate	in″dis·cern'i·ble
in·apt'	in″dis·pen'sa·ble
in″ar·tis'tic	in″dis·put'a·ble
in·au'di·ble	in″dis·sol'u·ble
in″aus·pi'cious	in″dis·tinct'
in·cal'cu·la·ble	in″di·vis'i·ble
in·ca'pa·ble	in·ed'i·ble
in·cer'ti·tude	in″ef·fec'tive
in″ci·vil'i·ty	in″ef·fec'tu·al
in·cog'ni·zant	in·ef'fi·ca·cy
in″com·bus'ti·ble	in″ef·fi'cient
in″com·men'su·rate	in·e'las'tic
in″com·mu'ni·ca·ble	in·el'e·gant
in″com·plete'	in·el'i·gi·ble
in″com·pre·hen'si·ble	in·el'o·quent
in″com·press'ible	in″e·qual'i·ty
in″con·ceiv'a·ble	in″e·rad'i·ca·ble
in″con·clu'sive	in″es·cap'a·ble
in″con·sid'er·ate	in·ex'act'
in″con·sist'ent	in″ex·cus'a·ble
in″con·sol'a·ble	in″ex·haust'i·ble
in″con·test'a·ble	in″ex·pe'di·ent
in″con·tro·vert'i·ble	in″ex·pen'sive
in″cor·po're·al	in·ex'pert'
in″cor·rect'	in·ex'pi·a·ble
	in″ex·plic'a·ble
	in″ex·press'i·ble
	in″ex·tin'guish·a·ble

in·ex'tri·ca·ble
in''fe·li'ci·tous
in·fer'tile
in·fre'quent
in''har·mo'ni·ous
in·hos'pi·ta·ble
in''hu·mane'
in·im'i·ta·ble
in''ju·di'cious
in·jus'tice
in·nu'mer·a·ble
in''ob·ser'vant
in·op'er·a·ble
in·op''por·tune'
in·or'gan·ic
in·sa'ti·a·ble

in·sen'sate
in·sen'si·tive
in''sep'a·ra·ble
in''so·bri'e·ty
in·sol'u·ble
in''sub·stan'tial
in''suf'fer·a·ble
in''suf·fi'cient
in''sup·port'a·ble
in''sur·mount'a-
ble
in·trac'ta·ble
in''var'i·a·ble
in·ver'te·brate
in·vis'i·ble
in·vul'ner·a·ble

in''ad·vert'ent (in''əd-vėr'tənt) *adj.* **1,** unintentional; accidental. **2,** not attentive; negligent. —**in''ad·vert'ence,** *n.*

in·am''o·ra'ta (in-am''ə-rä'tə) *n.* a woman with whom one is in love.

in·ane' (in-ān') *adj.* void of sense or intelligence; silly. —**in·an'i·ty** (in-an'ə-te) *n.*

in·an'i·mate (in-an'i·mət) *adj.* not alive; quiescent.

in''a·ni'tion (in''ə-ni'shən) *n.* **1,** exhaustion from lack of nourishment; starvation. **2,** inanity.

in''ar·tic'u·late (in''är-tik'yə-lət) *adj.* **1,** not articulate. **2,** lacking facility in speech or expression. —**in''ar·tic'u·late·ness,** *n.*

in''as·much' as (in''əz-much') *adj.* **1,** in view of the fact; considering that. **2,** in so far as; to the degree of.

in''at·ten'tion (in''ə-ten'shən) *n.* failure to be attentive or thoughtful. —**in''at·ten'tive** (-tiv) *adj.*

in·au'gu·ral (in-â'gyū-rəl) *adj.* inaugurating; pert. to an inauguration.

in·au'gu·rate'' (in-â'gyə-rāt'') *v.t.* **1,** make a formal beginning of; initiate. **2,** install in office. —**in·aug''u·ra'tion,** *n.*

in''board'' (in'bôrd'') *adj.* & *adv.* **1,** inside a ship's hull. **2,** toward the inside.

in'born'' (in'bôrn'') *adj.* implanted by nature; innate.

in'bred'' *adj.* **1,** produced by inbreeding. **2,** innate.

in'breed''ing (in'brē''ding) *n.* the mating of closely-related individuals. —**in'breed'',** *v.i.*

In'ca (ing'kə) *n.* **1,** a member of an American Indian people of ancient Peru. **2,** a king of this people.

in''can·des'cent (in''kən-des'ənt) *adj.* **1,** rendered luminous by heat. **2,** white-hot; glowing; brilliant. —**in''can·des'cence,** *n.*

in''can·ta'tion (in''kan-tā'shən) *n.* the uttering of magical words.

in''ca·pac'i·tate'' (in''kə-pas'ə-tāt'') *v.t.*

render unfit; disqualify. —**in''ca·pac''i·ta'-tion,** *n.*

in''ca·pac'i·ty (-ə-te) *n.* inability to perform; incompetence.

in·car'cer·ate'' (in-kär'sə-rāt'') *v.t.* put or hold in prison. —**in·car''cer·a'tion,** *n.*

in·car'na·dine'' (in-kär'nə-dīn'') *adj.* flesh-colored.

in·car'nate (in-kär'nət) *adj.* embodied in flesh. —*v.t.* (-nāt) **1,** embody in flesh. **2,** typify. —**in''car·na'tion,** *n.* existence in bodily form.

in·cau'tious (in-kâ'shəs) *adj.* not cautious; done or uttered with insufficient thought or discretion. —**in·cau'tious·ness,** *n.*

in·cen'di·ar·y (in-sen'de·er-e) *adj.* **1,** pert. to arson. **2,** used in starting a fire. **3,** tending to excite violence; inflammatory. —*n.* **1,** one who or that which starts destructive fires. **2,** an agitator. —**in·cen'di·ar·ism** (-ə-riz-əm) *n.*

in'cense (in'sens) *n.* **1,** an aromatic material or the perfume it produces when burned. **2,** any agreeable odor.

in·cense' (in-sens') *v.t.* excite to anger or resentment; enrage. —**in·cense'ment,** *n.*

in·cen'tive (in-sen'tiv) *n.* something that incites to action; motive; spur. —*adj.* stimulating.

in·cep'tion (in-sep'shən) *n.* a beginning; initiation. —**in·cep'tive,** *adj.*

in·ces'sant (in-ses'ənt) *adj.* unceasing; continuing without interruption. —**in·ces'san·cy,** *n.*

in'cest (in'sest) *n.* illicit intercourse between closely related persons. —**in·ces'tu·ous** (in-ses'choo-əs) *adj.*

inch *n.* a unit of length, one twelfth of a foot. —*v.t.* & *i.* move by small degrees.

in·cho'ate (in-kō'it) *adj.* just begun; rudimentary. —**in·cho'ate·ness,** *n.*

inch'worm'' *n.* a measuring worm.

in'ci·dence (in'si-dəns) *n.* **1,** frequency or range of occurrence; extent of effects. **2,** manner or direction of a fall; course. **3,** partial coincidence.

in'ci·dent (in'si-dənt) *n.* **1,** an occurrence or event; a casual happening. **2,** an episode. **3,** a result or casual feature of something else. —*adj.* **1,** dependent; pertaining. **2,** falling or striking on something. **3,** likely to happen.

in''ci·den'tal (in''si-den'təl) *adj.* **1,** pert. to or constituting an incident. **2,** casual; minor.

in·cin'er·ate'' (in-sin'ə-rāt'') *v.t.* burn to ashes. —**in·cin''er·a'tor,** *n.* a furnace for burning waste.

in·cip'i·ent (in-sip'e-ənt) *adj.* beginning

to exist or appear. **—in·cip'i·ence, in·cip'i·en·cy,** *n.*

in·cise' (in-sīz') *v.t.* cut into; engrave.

in·ci'sion (in-sizh'ən) *n.* **1,** act of cutting into. **2,** a cut or gash.

in·ci'sive (in-sī'siv) *adj.* **1,** sharply expressive; penetrating; trenchant. **2,** adapted for cutting. **—in·ci'sive·ness,** *n.*

in·ci'sor (in-sī'zər) *n.* a tooth adapted for cutting.

in·cite' (in-sīt') *v.t.* **1,** move (a person) to action; urge or stimulate. **2,** stir up (an action); instigate. **—in·cite'ment,** *n.*

in·clem'ent (in-klem'ənt) *adj.* (of weather) harsh; tempestuous. **—in·clem'en·cy,** *n.*

in"cli·na'tion (in"klə-nā'shən) *n.* **1,** a preference or liking; disposition; bent. **2,** the act of inclining; the state of being inclined. **3,** a slanted position; the angle of a slant.

in·cline' (in-klīn') *v.t.* **1,** have a tendency or preference. **2,** be slanted or oblique. **3,** approximate. *—v.t.* **1,** give a tendency to. **2,** bend; bow; slant. *—n.* (in'klīn) a slope.

in·close' (in-klōz') *v.t.* enclose.

in·clude' (in-klood') *v.t.* **1,** contain as a part; take in; embrace or cover. **2,** be composed of; comprise. **—in·clu'sion** (-zhən) *n.*

in·clu'sive (in-kloo'siv) *adj.* **1,** including the stated limits. **2,** wide in extent; comprehensive. **—in·clu'sive·ness,** *n.* **—inclu·sive of,** including.

in·cog'ni·to" (in-kog'ni-tō") *adj. & adv.* with real name or identity concealed.

in"co·her'ent (in"kō-hir'ənt) *adj.* **1,** without apparent unity or connection; incongruous. **2,** not logical or coordinated in expression; confused; chaotic. **3,** lacking physical cohesion. **—in"co·her'ence,** *n.*

in'come (in'kum) *n.* **1,** money received as wages, interest, etc. **2,** profit. **—income tax,** tax levied on annual income.

in"com"ing *adj.* **1,** entering; approaching. **2,** coming in as occupant or successor. **3,** accruing.

in"com·mode' (in"kə-mōd') *v.t.* subject to inconvenience. **—in"com·mo'di·ous,** *adj.*

in"com·mu"ni·ca·do (in"kə-mū"ni-kä'dō) *adj.* shut off from any communication with others.

in·com'pa·ra·ble (in-kom'pə-rə-bəl) *adj.* **1,** without a rival; unequaled; matchless. **2,** not comparable. **—in·com"pa·ra·bil'i·ty,** *n.*

in·com·pat'i·ble (in"kəm-pat'ə-bəl) *adj.* not compatible; esp. of persons, unable to live together in harmony. **—in"com·pat·i·bil'i·ty,** *n.*

in·com'pe·tent (in-kom'pə-tənt) *adj.* not fit or capable. *—n.* one inadequate to a task, esp. mentally. **—in·com'pe·tence,** *n.*

in·con'gru·ous (in-kong'groo-əs) *adj.* **1,** out of place; unsuitable; inappropriate; inconsistent. **2,** comprised of inharmonious parts; disjointed. **—in"con·gru'i·ty** (in"kən-groo'ə-tē), **in·con'gru·ous·ness,** *n.*

in·con'se·quent (in-kon'sə-kwənt) *adj.* **1,** not consequent. **2,** fallacious. **3,** incongruous; irrelevant. **—in·con'se·quence,** *n.*

in"con·se·quen'tial (in"kon-sə-kwen'shəl) *adj.* **1,** of no importance or effect; trivial. **2,** not consequent.

in"con·sid'er·a·ble (in"kən-sid'ər-ə-bəl) *adj.* too few or small to matter; unimportant. **—in"con·sid'er·a·ble·ness,** *n.*·

in"con·spic'u·ous (in"kən-spik'yoo-əs) *adj.* too small or retiring to notice; not readily perceived. **—in"con·spic'u·ous·ness,** *n.*

in·con'stant (in-kon'stənt) *adj.* not loyal; not faithful. **—in·con'stan·cy,** *n.*

in·con'ti·nent (in-kon'tə-nənt) *adj.* not holding or held in; unrestrained; intemperate. **—in·con'ti·nence,** *n.*

in"con·ven'ience (in"kən-vēn'yəns) *n.* discomfort; trouble. *—v.t.* put to trouble. **—in"con·ven'ient,** *adj.* causing difficulty.

in·cor'po·rate" (in-kôr'pə-rāt') *v.t.* **1,** organize into a corporation; unite in a society, etc. **2,** combine; introduce as an integral part. *—v.i.* unite in a corporation, society, etc., or a body, mass, etc. *—adj.* (-rit) not corporeal; not having a material body. **—in·cor'po·ra'tion,** *n.*

in·cor'ri·gi·ble (in-kor'i-jə-bəl) *adj.* resistant to correction or reform; beyond reform. **—in·cor"ri·gi·bil'i·ty,** *n.*

in·cras'sate" (in-kras'āt") *v.t. & i.* thicken in consistency, as a liquid. *—adj.* thickened; swollen from fatness.

in·crease' (in-krēs') *v.t.* make greater; extend in bulk, size, number, degree, etc.; enlarge; augment; enhance. *—v.i.* become greater. **2,** multiply. *—n.* (in'krēs) **1,** the act of increasing. **2,** the amount, result, or product of increase. **—on the increase,** increasing.

in·cred'i·ble (in-kred'ə-bəl) *adj.* **1,** not believable. **2,** (*Colloq.*) extraordinary. **—in·cred"i·bil'i·ty,** *n.*

in"cre·du'li·ty (in"krə-dū'lə-tē) *n.* disbelief; skepticism. **—in·cred'u·lous** (in-krej'-ə-ləs) *adj.*

in'cre·ment (in'krə-mənt) *n.* something added; augmentation; growth.

in·crim'i·nate" (in-krim'ə-nāt") *v.t.* show to be involved in a crime; charge; accuse. **—in·crim"i·na'tion,** *n.*

in·crust' (in-krust') *v.t.* form into a crust;

cover or line with a hard coating. —in″crus·ta′tion, n.

in·cu·bate″ (in′kyə-bāt″) v.t. 1, hatch (eggs). 2, maintain at a temperature favorable to growth. 3, produce as though by hatching. —v.i. sit on eggs; brood. —in″cu·ba′tion, n. —in′cu·ba″tor, n. a heated apparatus for hatching eggs, nurturing babies, etc.

in·cu·bus (in′kyə-bəs) n. 1, a male demon imagined to disturb sleep; hence, a nightmare. 2, a burden.

in·cul′cate (in-kul′kāt) v.t. impress on the mind, as by admonition. —in″cul·ca′tion, n.

in·cul′pa·ble (in-kul′pə-bəl) adj. innocent; blameless.

in·cul′pate (in-kul′pāt) v.t. accuse of wrongdoing. —in″cul·pa′tion, n.

in·cum′bent (in-kum′bənt) adj. 1, resting on one as a duty or obligation. 2, leaning on something. —n. an office-holder. —in·cum′ben·cy, n.

in″cu·nab′u·la (in″kū-nab′yə-lə) n.pl. [sing. -lum (-ləm)] 1, the place or period of beginning and earliest development, as of a race, art, etc. 2, books printed before 1500 A.D. —in″cu·nab′u·lar, adj.

in·cur′ (in-kėr′) v.t. [in·curred′, -cur′ring] 1, encounter as an experience. 2, bring on oneself. —in·cur′rence, n.

in·cur′sion (in-kėr′zhən) n. a sudden running in; an inroad or invasion. —in·cur′sive (-siv) adj.

in·debt′ed (in-det′id) adj. owing; under obligation. —in·debt′ed·ness, n. fact of owing; amount owed.

in·de′cent (in-dē′sənt) adj. 1, not fit to be done, seen, or heard in polite company; indelicate. 2, immodest. —in·de′cen·cy, n.

in″de·ci′sion (in″di-sizh′ən) n. vacillation; irresolution.

in″de·ci′sive (-sī′siv) adj. 1, inconclusive. 2, unable to decide. —in″de·ci′sive·ness, n.

in·deed′ (in-dēd′) adv. in fact; in reality; in truth. —interj. expressing doubt, surprise or agreement.

in″de·fat′i·ga·ble (in″di-fat′ə-gə-bəl) adj. not easily fatigued; not yielding to fatigue. —in″de·fat″i·ga·bil′i·ty, n.

in·def′i·nite (in-def′ə-nit) adj. 1, having no fixed or specified limit; infinite. 2, vague. 3, indeterminate. —indefinite article, a or an. —in·def′i·nite·ness, n.

in·del′i·ble (in-del′ə-bəl) adj. not capable of being deleted or obliterated. —in·del″i·bil′i·ty, n.

in·del′i·cate (in-del′i-kət) adj. coarse; gross; immodest; unrefined. —in·del′i·ca·cy (-kə-sē) n.

in·dem′ni·fy″ (in-dem′nə-fī″) v.t. compensate for or guarantee against damage, loss, or expenses incurred. —in·dem′ni·fi·ca′tion, n.

in·dem′ni·ty (in-dem′nə-tē) n. 1, what is paid as compensation or reimbursement. 2, security given against damage or loss. 3, exemption from liability.

in·dent′ make a dent, notch, or recess in; begin (a line of writing) to the right of the left margin. —in″den·ta′tion (in″den-tā′shən) n.

in·den′ture (in-den′chər) n. 1, a contract binding a person to service, esp. an apprentice. 2, a sealed deed, contract, etc. —v.t. so bind.

in″de·pen′dence (in″di-pen′dəns) n. condition of being independent; freedom from control or influence. —Independence Day, July 4, on which the United States declared themselves sovereign.

in″de·pen′dent (in″di-pen′dənt) adj. 1, not contingent on something else for existence, operation, etc. 2, not influenced by others in opinion, conduct, etc. 3, not affiliated; sovereign in authority. 4, having ample income without working. —n. someone or something independent.

in-″depth′ adj. thorough; profound.

in″de·ter′min·a·ble (in″di-tėr′mə-nə-bəl) adj. incapable of being determined, limited, established, etc.

in″de·ter′mi·nate (in″di-tėr′mə-nət) adj. 1, not fixed or established; not precise or clear. 2, not determinable. —in″de·ter′mi·nate·ness, n.

in′dex (in′deks) n. [pl. in′dex·es, in′di·ces″ (in′də-sēz″)] 1, an alphabetized list of items and their locations. 2, a pointer; the symbol (☞). 3, a quality, trait, etc. 4, the forefinger. 5, (Math.) an operative symbol, as an exponent. 6, (cap.) a list of books forbidden to the Roman Catholic laity. —v.t. 1, furnish with or enter in an index. 2, point out. —index number, a percent of something expressed as a number without a percent sign.

India ink a black drawing ink.

In′di·an (in′dē-ən) adj. & n. 1, pert. to the aboriginal inhabitants of North and South America. 2, pert. to the inhabitants of India or the East Indies. —Indian club, a wooden club swung for exercise. —Indian corn, maize. —Indian file, single file. —Indian giver, a person who takes back a gift he made. —Indian summer, warm days late in the Fall.

India paper a very thin but tough paper, used chiefly for large reference works.

India rubber natural rubber; caoutchouc.

in′di·cate″ (in′di-kāt″) v.t. 1, point out;

direct attention to. **2,** imply. **—in″di·ca′·tion,** *n.*

in·dic′a·tive (in-dik′ə-tiv) *adj.* **1,** pointing out; betokening. **2,** (*Gram.*) expressing a statement or question.

in′di·ca″tor (in′di-kā″tər) *n.* an instrument or part that indicates.

in·di′ci·a (in-dish′ē-ə) *n.pl.* [*sing.* **-di′ci·um** (-dish′ē-əm)] **1,** discriminating marks. **2,** printed marks to show payment of postage, as by postage meters.

in·dict′ (in-dīt′) *v.t.* charge with an offense, esp. a criminal one. **—in·dict′ment,** *n.*

in·dif′fer·ent (in-dif′ər-ənt) *adj.* **1,** feeling no interest or anxiety; apathetic. **2,** unbiased; impartial. **3,** not making a difference. **4,** mediocre; moderate in amount or degree. **—in·dif′fer·ence,** *n.*

in·dig′e·nous (in-dij′ə-nəs) *adj.* originating in a particular region; native. **—in·dig′e·nous·ness,** *n.*

in′di·gent (in′di-jənt) *adj.* destitute; poor; needy. **—in′di·gence,** *n.*

in″di·gest′i·ble (in″di-jes′tə-bəl) *adj.* hard to digest or assimilate. **—in″di·gest″i·bil′i·ty,** *n.*

in″di·ges′tion (in″di-jes′chən) *n.* pain caused by inability to digest food properly.

in·dig′nant (in-dig′nənt) *adj.* feeling or showing anger, esp. righteous anger; resentful.

in″dig·na′tion (in″dig-nā′shən) *n.* righteous anger over injustice, etc.

in·dig′ni·ty (in-dig′nə-tē) *n.* an injury or affront to one's dignity; a slight; humiliation.

in′di·go″ (in′di-gō″) *n.* **1,** a dark blue dye. **2,** a violet-blue color.

in·dis·creet′ (in-dis-krēt′) *adj.* not prudent. **—in·dis·creet′ness,** *n.*

in·dis·cre′tion (-kresh′ən) *n.* act of being indiscreet; error of judgment.

in″dis·crim′i·nate (in″dis-krim′ə-nit) *adj.* not carefully selected; heterogeneous. **—in″dis·crim′i·na′tion,** *n.* **—in″dis·crim′i·nate·ness,** *n.*

in″dis·posed′ (in″dis-pōzd′) *adj.* **1,** somewhat sick or ill. **2,** not inclined; unwilling. **—in″dis·po·si′tion** (-pə-zish′ən) *n.*

in·dite′ (in-dīt′) *v.t.* put into verbal form; write or compose. **—in·dite′ment,** *n.*

in′di·um (in′dē-əm) *n.* a rare, silver-white metallic element, no. 49, symbol In.

in″di·vid′u·al (in″di-vij′oo-əl) *adj.* **1,** relating to one person or thing. **2,** not divisible without loss of identity. **3,** single; particular. **4,** having peculiar characteristics. **—n.** a single person, animal, or thing.

in·di·vid′u·al·ism (-iz-əm) *n.* independence in personal behavior. **—in·di·vid′u·al·ist,** *n.* **—in·di·vid″u·al·is′tic,** *adj.*

in·di·vid″u·al′i·ty (-al′ə-tē) *n.* the state of being distinct and unlike others; peculiar character.

in″di·vid′u·al·ize (in″di-vij′oo-ə-līz″) *v.t.* **1,** differentiate; distinguish. **2,** mention or consider separately. **—in″di·vid″u·al·i·za′tion,** *n.*

in″di·vid′u·ate″ (-āt″) *v.t.* individualize.

in·doc′tri·nate″ (in-dok′tri-nāt″) *v.t.* imbue with a particular belief or principle. **—in·doc″tri·na′tion,** *n.*

In′do-Eu″ro·pe′an (in′dō-) *adj.* pert. to a family of languages spoken chiefly in Europe.

in′do·lent (in′də-lənt) *adj.* **1,** lazy; sluggish. **2,** giving little pain. **—in′do·lence,** *n.*

in·dom′i·ta·ble (in-dom′i-tə-bəl) *adj.* that cannot be subdued or repressed. **—in·dom″·i·ta·bil′i·ty,** *n.*

in′door″ (in′dôr″) *adj.* in a building; not in open air. **—in′doors′,** *adv.*

in·dorse′ (in-dôrs′) *v.t.* endorse.

in·du′bi·ta·ble (in-doo′bi-tə-bəl) *adj.* not to be doubted; sure. **—in·du′bi·ta·ble·ness,** *n.*

in·duce′ (in-dūs′) *v.t.* **1,** lead by persuasion or influence; prevail upon; incite. **2,** produce or cause. **3,** produce by induction. **4,** infer.

in·duce′ment (-mənt) *n.* **1,** act or result of inducing. **2,** incentive.

in·duct′ (in-dukt′) *v.t.* **1,** install in office; initiate. **2,** enroll in military service.

in·duc′tance (in-duk′təns) *n.* the creation of an electromotive force by means of a varying current in an electric circuit.

in·duc′tion (in-duk′shən) *n.* **1,** installation of a person into office. **2,** the excitation of an electromagnetic field by a neighboring body, without direct contact. **3,** the process of drawing a general conclusion from particular facts. **4,** the act of inducing. **—in·duc′tive,** *adj.*

in·due′ (in-dū′) *v.t.* endow; supply.

in·dulge′ (in-dulj′) *v.t.* yield to or comply with (an inclination or person); humor. **—v.i.** yield to one's own inclination. **—in·dul′gent,** *adj.*

in·dul′gence (in-dul′jəns) *n.* **1,** gratification of desire. **2,** an extension of time. **3,** (*Rom. Cath.*) remission of punishment; relaxation of law.

in′du·rate (in′dyə-rət) *adj.* hardened.

in·dus′tri·al (in-dus′trē-əl) *adj.* pert. to large-scale manufacturing. **—in·dus′tri·al·ism,** *n.* **—in·dus′tri·al·ist,** *n.* **—industrial arts,** manual skills, and other skills related to industrial tools and techniques, taught as a course in school. **—industrial park,** a plot of land reserved for business and industrial buildings.

in·dus'tri·al·ize" (in-dus'trē-əl-īz") *v.t.* establish industries in (a country, city, etc.); organize the manufacturing activities of. —**in·dus"tri·al·i·za'tion,** *n.*

in·dus'tri·ous (in-dus'trē-əs) *adj.* hardworking; diligent; assiduous. —**in·dus'·tri·ous·ness,** *n.*

in'dus·try (in'dəs-trē) *n.* **1,** a manufacturing trade. **2,** manufacturing and business generally. **3,** diligence; application to tasks.

in·e'bri·ate" (in-ē'brē-āt") *v.t.* make drunk; intoxicate. —**in·e'bri·a'tion,** *n.*

in"e·bri'e·ty (in"i-brī'ə-tē) *n.* drunkenness.

in·ef'fa·ble (in-ef'ə-bəl) *adj.* inexpressible; too sacred to speak of. —**in·ef'fa·bil'i·ty,** *n.*

in"e·luc'ta·ble (in"i-luk'tə-bəl) *adj.* not to be eluded or overcome.

in·ept' *adj.* **1,** not apt, fit, or suited. **2,** inefficient. —**in·ept'ness, in·ep'ti·tude** (in-ep'tə·tood) *n.*

in·eq'ui·ta·ble (in-ek'wi-tə-bəl) *adj.* unfair; unjust.

in·eq'ui·ty (in-ek'wə-tē) *n.* injustice; something that is unfair.

in·ert' (in-ẽrt') *adj.* **1,** having no inherent power to move or act. **2,** lacking active properties. **3,** sluggish. —**in·ert'ness,** *n.*

in·er'tia (in-ẽr'shə) *n.* **1,** the property of matter whereby a body remains at rest or in uniform rectilinear motion unless acted upon by an external force. **2,** inertness; inactivity.

in·es'ti·ma·ble (in-es'tə-mə-bəl) *adj.* not to be estimated; beyond measure. —**in·es"ti·ma·bil'i·ty,** *n.*

in·ev'i·ta·ble (in-ev'i-tə-bəl) *adj.* **1,** unavoidable. **2,** sure to come or happen. —**in·ev"i·ta·bil'i·ty,** *n.*

in·ex'o·ra·ble (in-ek'sə-rə-bəl) *adj.* not to be persuaded or moved; unrelenting. —**in·ex'o·ra·ble·ness,** *n.*

in"ex·pe'ri·ence (in"ik-spir'ē-əns) *n.* lack of the knowledge or skill usually gained from experience. —**in"ex·pe'ri·enced,** *adj.*

in·fal'li·ble (in-fal'ə-bəl) *adj.* **1,** free from fallacy; not liable to error. **2,** unfailingly certain; trustworthy. —**in·fal"li·bil'i·ty,** *n.*

in·fa'mous (in'fə-məs) *adj.* notoriously evil; shamefully bad; wicked. —**in'fa·my** (in'fə-mē) *n.*

in'fan·cy (in'fən-sē) *n.* **1,** condition or period of being an infant. **2,** the earliest and formative period of a movement, nation, art, etc.

in'fant (in'fənt) *n.* **1,** a baby or young child. **2,** (*Law*) anyone under legal age. —*adj.* **1,** being an infant, legally a minor. **2,** incipient.

in·fan'ta (in-fan'tə) *n.* a daughter of the king of Spain or Portugal. —**in·fan'te** (-tā) *n.* a son of the king of Spain or Portugal, but not heir to the throne.

in·fan'ti·cide (in-fan'ti-sīd) *n.* the killer or killing of an infant.

in'fan·tile (in'fən-tīl") *adj.* being or like a baby. —**infantile paralysis,** poliomyelitis.

in'fan·try (in'fən-trē) *n.* soldiers that serve on foot; a branch of military forces. —**in'fan·try·man,** *n.*

in·fat'u·ate" (in-fach'oo-āt") *v.t.* inspire with foolish passion, esp. of love. —**in·fat"u·a'tion,** *n.*

in·fect' (in-fekt') *v.t.* **1,** impregnate with germs; affect with disease. **2,** imbue; taint. —**in·fec'tion,** *n.*

in·fec'tious (-shəs) *adj.* **1,** communicable by transmission of germs. **2,** spreading rapidly; hard to resist. —**in·fec'tious·ness,** *n.*

in·fer' (in-fẽr') *v.t. & i.* [**in·ferred', in·fer'ring**] conclude by reasoning; opine; derive from evidence.

in'fer·ence (in'fə-rəns) *n.* **1,** act of inferring. **2,** a conclusion or presumption. —**in"fer·en'tial** (-ren'shəl) *adj.*

in·fe'ri·or (in-fir'ē-ər) *adj.* **1,** lower in rank, grade, etc. **2,** markedly poor in quality. **3,** lower in place or position. —*n.* someone or something inferior. —**in·fe"ri·or'i·ty** (-or'ə-tē) *n.*

in·fer'nal (in-fẽr'nəl) *adj.* **1,** pert. to mythical lower regions. **2,** hellish; diabolical. **3,** (*Colloq.*) annoying; troublesome.

in·fer'no (in-fẽr'nō) *n.* [*pl.* **-nos**] hell; the nether regions.

in·fest' *v.t.* **1,** invade and swarm over, like vermin. **2,** pervade noxiously. —**in"fes·ta'tion,** *n.*

in'fi·del (in'fə-dəl) *adj.* **1,** having no religious faith. **2,** not of a particular religion. —*n.* an unbeliever.

in"fi·del'i·ty (in"fə-del'ə-tē) *n.* **1,** unfaithfulness; disloyalty. **2,** lack of faith.

in'field" (in'fēld") *n.* the baseball diamond; the four players (*infielders*) stationed there.

in'fight"ing (in'fīt"ing) *n.* rivalry within an organization or group.

in·fil'trate (in-fil'trāt) *v.t.* filter into or through; permeate. —**in"fil·tra'tion** (in"fəl-trā'shən) *n.*

in'fi·nite (in'fə-nit) *adj.* **1,** great beyond measurement or counting; without limit; interminable. **2,** absolute. —*n.* **1,** something limitless; boundless space. **2,** (*cap.*) God. —**in'fi·nite·ness,** *n.*

in"fin·i·tes'i·mal (in"fin-i-tes'ə-məl) *adj.* immeasurably small.

in·fin'i·tive (in-fin'ə-tiv) *n.* the form of a

verb merely expressing its sense: used after *to*, as *to go*.

in·fin'i·ty (in-fin'ə-tē) *n.* **1,** boundless extension; unlimited quantity or number. **2,** the condition of being infinite. **3,** (*Math.*) increase to immeasurable magnitude; the symbol (∞) denoting this.

in·firm' (in-fērm') *adj.* not in good health; weak; faltering.

in·fir'ma·ry (in-fēr'mə-rē) *n.* a place for the care of the sick or injured.

in·fir'mi·ty (in-fēr'mə-tē) *n.* illness; weakness.

in·flame' (in-flām') *v.t.* **1,** excite highly; make more violent; aggravate. **2,** affect with bodily inflammation. **3,** set on fire.

in·flam'ma·ble (in-flam'ə-bəl) *adj.* capable of burning; combustible. **—in·flam″ma·bil'i·ty,** *n.*

in″flam·ma'tion (in″flə-mā'shən) *n.* a morbid condition of the body characterized by heat, swelling, redness, etc.

in·flam'ma·to·ry (in-flam'ə-tôr-ē) *adj.* serving to inflame.

in·flate' (in-flāt') *v.t. & i.* **1,** fill with air or other gas; distend; swell. **2,** elate. **3,** (of currency, prices, etc.) raise or expand.

in·fla'tion *n.* a condition in which the money in circulation is excessive for the commodities on sale or being sold. **—in·fla'tion·ar·y,** *adj.*

in·flect' (in-flekt') *v.t.* **1,** turn from a direct course; bend. **2,** modulate (the voice); vary (a word) by inflection.

in·flec'tion (in-flek'shən) *n.* **1,** change of pitch or tone in speaking; modulation. **2,** variation of a word to show plurality, person, part of speech, etc. **3,** a bend or angle; a change of curvature. **—in·flec'tion·al** (-əl), **in·flec'tive,** *adj.*

in·flex'i·ble (in-flek'sə-bəl) *adj.* **1,** not to be bent; rigid. **2,** stubborn. **—in·flex″i·bil'i·ty,** *n.*

in·flict' (in-flikt') *v.t.* impose (something undesired); cause to be suffered or borne. **—in·flic'tion,** *n.*

in″flo·res'cence (in″flō-res'əns) *n.* **1,** the flowering part of a plant; flowers collectively; a flower. **2,** the fact or stage of blossoming. **—in″flo·res'cent,** *adj.*

in'flu·ence (in'floo-əns) *n.* **1,** power to control or affect others by authority, persuasion, example, etc. **2,** a person or thing that exerts such power. **—***v.t.* exercise influence on.

in″flu·en'tial (-en'shəl) *adj.* **1,** able to exert much influence. **2,** influencing.

in″flu·en'za (in″floo-en'zə) *n.* a highly contagious disease characterized by nasal catarrh, bronchial inflammation, and prostration.

in'flux'' (in'fluks″) *n.* **1,** a flowing in. **2,** the place where something flows in. **3,** invasion.

in'fo (in'fō) *n.* (*Slang*) information.

in·form' (in-fôrm') *v.t.* **1,** communicate facts to; make known to; tell. **2,** instruct. **—***v.i.* give information, esp. about a criminal.

in·for'mal (in-fôr'məl) *adj.* unconventional; familiar in manner; irregular. **—***n.* a party at which formal dress is not required. **—in″for·mal'i·ty** (in″fôr-mal'ə-tē) *n.*

in·form'ant (in-fôr'mənt) *n.* one who communicates facts.

in″for·ma'tion (in″fər-mā'shən) *n.* **1,** act or result of informing; news. **2,** an official criminal charge.

in·form'a·tive (in-fôr'mə-tiv) *adj.* imparting news or knowledge.

in·form'er (in-fôr'mər) *n.* **1,** one who exposes a wrongdoer to official punishment. **2,** informant.

in·fra- (in-frə) *pref.* below; beneath.

in·frac'tion (in-frak'shən) *n.* breach; violation.

in″fra·red' *n. & adj.* radiation outside the visible spectrum, at the red (lower-frequency) end.

in·fringe' (in-frinj') *v.t.* violate; transgress. **—***v.i.* encroach; trespass. **—in·fringe'ment,** *n.*

in·fu'ri·ate'' (in-fyûr'ē-āt″) *v.t.* make furious; enrage.

in·fuse' (in-fūz') *v.t.* **1,** cause to penetrate. **2,** permeate like a liquid; imbue. **3,** soak. **—in·fu'sion,** *n.*

in·gen'ious (in-jēn'yəs) *adj.* showing cleverness in contrivance or construction. **—in·gen'ious·ness,** *n.*

in″gé·nue' (an″zhə-nū') *n.* an ingenuous young woman, in a play.

in″ge·nu'i·ty (in″jə-nū'ə-tē) *n.* cleverness; inventiveness.

in·gen'u·ous (in-jen'ū-əs) *adj.* free from guile; candid; naïve. **—in·gen'u·ous·ness,** *n.*

in·gest' (in-jest') *v.t.* take into the body for digestion, as food. **—in·ges'tion,** *n.* **—in·ges'tive,** *adj.*

in'gle·nook'' (ing'gəl-nûk″) *n.* a corner near the fireplace of a dwelling.

in·glo'ri·ous (in-glôr'ē-əs) *adj.* dishonorable; shameful. **—in·glo'ri·ous·ness,** *n.*

in'got (ing'gət) *n.* a mass of metal roughly shaped by casting or rolling.

in·grain' (in-grān') *v.t.* fix firmly, as in the mind.

in'grate (in'grāt) *n.* one who is ungrateful.

in·gra′ti·ate″ (in-grā′shē-āt″) *v.t.* establish (oneself) in the favor of another. **—in·gra″ti·a′tion,** *n.*

in·grat′i·tude (in-grat′i-tood) *n.* ungratefulness.

in·gre′di·ent (in-grē′dē-ənt) *n.* an essential part of a compound or mixture; constituent; element.

in′gress (in′gres) *n.* entrance.

in′grown″ (in′grōn″) *adj.* grown into the flesh, as an *ingrown toenail.*

in·gur′gi·tate″ (in-gėr′jə-tāt″) *v.t.* swallow; gulp. **—in·gur″gi·ta′tion,** *n.*

in·hab′it *v.t.* live or dwell in.

in·hab′it·ant (-tənt) *n.* a resident.

in·hal′ant (in-hā′lənt) *n.* medicinal vapor; an apparatus for dispensing it.

in·hale′ (in-hāl′) *v.t.* draw in by or as by breathing. *—v.i.* breathe in. **—in″ha·la′tion** (in″hə-lā′shən) *n.* **—in″ha·la″tor,** *n.* an apparatus for facilitating normal respiration or the inhalation of medical preparations.

in·here′ (in-hir′) *v.i.* be a basic and inseparable element; be innate or intrinsic. **—in·her′ence,** *n.*

in·her′ent (in-hir′ənt) *adj.* belonging intrinsically; innate. **—in·her′ence, in·her′en·cy,** *n.*

in·her′it *v.t. & i.* **1,** receive (property, etc.) as an heir; acquire by gift or succession. **2,** receive (qualities, etc.) from progenitors; possess intrinsically. **—in·her′it·ance,** *n.* **—in·her′i·tor,** *n.* **—in·her′i·trix,** *n. fem.*

in·hib′it *v.t.* **1,** check or repress as an impulse. **2,** forbid; prohibit. **—in·hib′i·tive,** *adj.*

in″hi·bi′tion (in″ə-bish′ən) *n.* the checking, restraining, or blocking of a mental process, physiological reaction, etc.

in·hu′man (in-hū′mən) *adj.* **1,** cruel; bestial. **2,** supernatural. **—in″hu·man′i·ty,** *n.*

in·hume′ (in-hūm′) *v.t.* inter. **—in″hu·ma′tion,** *n.*

in·im′i·cal (in-im′i-kəl) *adj.* **1,** harmful. **2,** like an enemy; hostile.

in·iq′ui·tous (i-nik′wə-təs) *adj.* **1,** lacking equity; grossly unjust. **2,** wicked; sinful. **—in·iq′ui·ty** (-tė) *n.*

in·i′tial (i-nish′əl) *adj.* **1,** placed at the beginning. **2,** pert. to the beginning or first stage. *—n.* the first letter of a word. *—v.t.* mark with the initials of one's name.

in·i′ti·ate″ (i-nish′ē-āt″) *v.t.* **1,** set going; begin; originate. **2,** give instruction to. **3,** induct to membership in a club, etc. **—in·i″ti·a′tion,** *n.*

in·i′ti·a·tive (i-nish′ē-ə-tiv) *n.* **1,** readiness and ability to initiate, take the lead, contrive, etc. **2,** the first step; leading movement.

in·ject′ (in-jekt′) *v.t.* **1,** put in by driving force, as liquid into a cavity. **2,** insert; interject.

in·jec′tion (in-jek′shən) *n.* **1,** act or result of injecting; an enema, hypodermic, etc. **2,** a substance or thing injected. **3,** the process of boosting a spacecraft into orbit.

in·junc′tion (in-junk′shən) *n.* **1,** a command; order; admonition. **2,** the act of enjoining. **—in·junc′tive,** *adj.*

in′jure (in′jər) *v.t.* do harm to; hurt; damage; impair.

in·ju′ri·ous (in-jûr′ē-əs) *adj.* damaging; hurtful. **—in·ju′ri·ous·ness,** *n.*

in′ju·ry (in′jə-rė) *n.* act or result of injuring; hurt; damage.

ink *n.* **1,** a fluid used for writing or printing. **2,** an inky secretion ejected by certain animals for protection. *—v.t.* write or draw with ink; cover with ink.

ink′ling *n.* a vague idea or notion; a hint or intimation.

ink′well″ *n.* a cup for holding ink.

ink′y (-ė) *adj.* like ink; black.

in′laid″ (in′lād″) *adj.* **1,** set in a surface, as decorative material. **2,** formed or ornamented by this method.

in′land (in′lənd) *adj.* **1,** away from the coast or border. **2,** domestic to a country. *—adv.* toward the interior.

in-′law″ *n.* (*Colloq.*) a relative by marriage.

in·lay′ (in-lā′) *v.t.* [**in·laid′, in·lay′ing**] **1,** decorate with pieces set on the surface. **2,** apply to a surface, in a decorative pattern. **3,** graft (a shoot) upon a plant. *—n.* (in′lā″) **1,** something inlaid or for inlaying. **2,** a filling for a tooth.

in′let *n.* an arm of a sea or lake extending into the land.

in′mate (in′māt″) *n.* an inhabitant or lodger; one confined in an institution.

in me·mo′ri·am″ (in″mə-môr′ē-äm″) (*Lat.*) in memory (of).

in′most″ (in′mōst″) *adj.* farthest within; deepest.

inn (in) *n.* **1,** a hotel, esp. a small one. **2,** a tavern. **—inn′keep″er,** *n.*

in′nards (in′ərdz) *n.pl.* the viscera.

in·nate′ (i-nāt′) *adj.* existing in one from birth; inborn. **—in·nate′ness,** *n.*

in′ner (in′ər) *adj.* [*superl.* **in′ner·most″**] **1,** situated in or farther within. **2,** mental or spiritual; not outward. **3,** private; concealed. **—inner city,** the central part of a city, esp. that part occupied by slums. **—inner sanctum,** a private retreat.

in′ner·vate″ (in′ər-vāt″) *v.t.* stimulate

through the nerves; supply with nervous energy. —**in″ner·va′tion**, *n.*

in′ning (in′ing) *n.* **1,** (*Baseball*) a period in which each side has a turn at bat. **2,** (often *pl.*) a time of power.

in′no·cent (in′ə-sənt) *adj.* **1,** not guilty; upright; harmless. **2,** naïve; artless. **3,** devoid. —**in′no·cence**, *n.*

in·noc′u·ous (i-nok′ū-əs) *adj.* harmless. —**in·noc′u·ous·ness**, *n.*

in·nom′i·nate (i-nom′ə-nət) *adj.* anonymous; unnamed. —**innominate bone**, hipbone.

in′no·vate″ (in′ə-vāt″) *v.i. & t.* introduce something new. —**in″no·va′tion,** *n.* —**in′no·va″tor,** *n.*

in″nu·en′do (in″ū-en′dō) *n.* an insinuation; unfriendly hint.

in·oc′u·late″ (i-nok′yə-lāt″) *v.t.* **1,** inject an immunizing agent into. **2,** imbue. —**in·oc″u·la′tion,** *n.*

in″of·fen′sive (in″ə-fen′siv) *adj.* harmless; not annoying. —**in″of·fen′sive·ness,** *n.*

in·op′er·a·tive (in-op′ə-rə-tiv) *adj.* **1,** not operative or operating; destitute of activity or effect. **2,** (*Colloq.*) without meaning or effect.

in·or′di·nate (in-ôr′də-nət) *adj.* beyond proper limits; excessive.

in′pa″tient (in′pā″shənt) *n.* a hospital patient who is lodged there.

in′put (in′pût) *n.* **1,** the energy or power put in, as to operate a machine. **2,** the amount or share of a contribution.

in′quest (in′kwest) *n.* a legal inquiry, esp. as to the cause of death, before a jury.

in·qui′e·tude″ (in-kwī′ə-tūd″) *n.* unrest; uneasiness.

in·quire′ (in-kwīr′) *v.t. & i.* ask (about); seek knowledge (of). Also, **en·quire′.**

in·quir′y (in-kwīr′ē; in′kwə-rē) *n.* **1,** search for information or knowledge; interrogation; investigation. **2,** a question. Also, **en·quir′y.**

in″qui·si′tion (in″kwə-zish′ən) *n.* **1,** examination; a formal inquiry. **2,** (*cap.*) (*Hist.*) a court for the suppression of heresy.

in·quis′i·tive (in-kwiz′ə-tiv) *adj.* unduly curious; prying. —**in·quis′i·tive·ness,** *n.*

in·quis′i·tor (in-kwiz′i-tər) *n.* one who conducts an inquisition.

in′road″ (in′rōd″) *n.* a forcible or insidious encroachment; a raid.

in·sane′ (in-sān′) *adj.* crazy; not legally responsible for one's actions. —**in·san′i·ty** (in-san′ə-tē) *n.*

in·sa′ti·ate (in-sā′shē-it) *adj.* **1,** insatiable. **2,** not satisfied.

in·scribe′ (in-skrīb′) *v.t.* **1,** write or en-

grave; mark with letters or signs. **2,** write or draw inside of.

in·scrip′tion (in-skrip′shən) *n.* something inscribed, as on a monument or coin. —**in·scrip′tive,** *adj.*

in·scru′ta·ble (in-skroo′tə-bəl) *adj.* not to be read by scrutiny or investigation; unfathomable; incomprehensible. —**in·scru″ta·bil′i·ty,** *n.*

in′seam″ *n.* the seam from the crotch to the bottom of the trouser leg.

in′sect (in′sekt) *n.* **1,** any member of a class of tiny winged invertebrates. **2,** a contemptible person.

in·sec′ti·cide″ (in-sek′ti-sīd″) *n.* a substance to kill insects.

in″sec·tiv′o·rous (in″sek-tiv′ə-rəs) *adj.* feeding on insects.

in″se·cure′ (in″si-kyûr′) *adj.* **1,** feeling unsafe. **2,** not tightly fastened; not safe. —**in″se·cu′ri·ty,** *n.*

in·sem′i·nate″ (in-sem′ə-nāt″) *v.t.* sow seeds in; impregnate. —**in·sem″i·na′tion,** *n.*

in·sen′si·ble (in-sen′sə-bəl) *adj.* **1,** deprived of sensation; unconscious; unfeeling. **2,** imperceptible. —**in·sen′si·bil′i·ty,** *n.*

in·sert′ (in-sẽrt′) *v.t.* put in; place inside of or among. —*n.* (in′sẽrt) something inserted.

in·ser′tion (in-ser′shən) *n.* **1,** the act of inserting. **2,** an insert. **3,** the process of putting a spacecraft into orbit.

in′set″ *n.* something set in; an insert, esp. in a book, illustration, etc. —*v.t.* insert.

in·side′ (in-sīd′) *prep. & adv.* in or into; within a body or limit (of space or time). —*n.* **1,** the inner part; interior region; inner surface. **2,** the contents; (*pl.*) the alimentary tract; mental feelings. —*adj.* **1,** interior; internal. **2,** indoor. **3,** specially privileged. —**in·sid′er,** *n.* (*Colloq.*) one who has special access to secrets or privileges.

in·sid′i·ous (in-sid′ē-əs) *adj.* **1,** operating stealthily with evil effect. **2,** deceitful; treacherous. —**in·sid′i·ous·ness,** *n.*

in′sight″ (in′sīt″) *n.* **1,** penetrating discernment; intuition. **2,** a sudden awareness.

in·sig′ni·a (in-sig′nē-ə) *n. sing. & pl.* [*sing.* also **in·sig′ne** (-nē)] a badge of office or honor; an emblem.

in″sig·nif′i·cant (in″sig-nif′ə-kənt) *adj.* without importance; trivial. —**in″sig·nif′i·cance,** *n.*

in″sin·cere′ (in″sin-sir′) *adj.* not sincere; hypocritical. —**in″sin·cer′i·ty** (-ser′ə-tē) *n.*

in·sin′u·ate″ (in-sin′yû-āt″) *v.t.* **1,** hint or suggest indirectly; imply slyly. **2,** introduce by devious means or by slow degrees. —**in·sin″u·a′tion,** *n.*

in·sip′id *adj.* **1,** lacking flavor or savor. **2,** uninteresting; dull. —**in″si·pid′i·ty** (in″-si-pid′ə-tē) *n.*

in·sist′ *v.i.* **1,** (with *on*) enforce by command; assert or argue emphatically. **2,** persevere in action. —**in·sist′ence,** *n.* —**in·sist′ent,** *adj.*

in″so·la′tion (in″sō-lā′shən) *n.* radiant energy from the sun.

in′sole (in′sōl″) *n.* the inner sole of a shoe.

in′so·lent (in′sə-lənt) *adj.* contemptuously rude, disrespectful, or insulting. —**in′so·lence,** *n.*

in·sol′vent (in-sol′vənt) *adj.* having greater liabilities than assets; bankrupt. —**in·sol′ven·cy,** *n.*

in·som′ni·a (in-som′nē-ə) *n.* inability to sleep, esp. when chronic. —**in·som′ni·ac″** (-ak″) *n.*

in′so·much′ *adv.* inasmuch (as).

in·sou′ci·ant (in-soo′sē-ənt) *adj.* carefree; unconcerned. —**in·sou′ci·ance,** *n.*

in·spect′ (in-spekt′) *v.t.* look at closely; examine critically. —**in·spec′tion,** *n.* —**in·spec′tor,** *n.* one who inspects; a title of various executive or supervisory officers.

in″spi·ra′tion (in″spə-rā′shən) *n.* **1,** any influence, esp. supernatural or intuitive, that inspires thought or action; thought so suggested. **2,** the act of inspiring; the state of being inspired. —**in″spi·ra′tion·al,** *adj.*

in·spire′ (in-spīr′) *v.t.* **1,** stimulate to activity; animate; instigate; impel. **2,** breathe in; inhale. —**in·spir′a·to·ry** (-ə-tôr-ē) *adj.*

in·spir′it *v.t.* animate.

in·spis′sate (in-spis′āt) *v.t.* thicken (a liquid) by evaporation. —**in″spis·sa′tion,** *n.*

in″sta·bil′i·ty (in″stə-bil′ə-tē) *n.* unsteadiness; lack of firmness; changeability.

in·stall′ (in-stâl′) *v.t.* **1,** place in position for service or use. **2,** induct into office; seat.

in″stal·la′tion (in″stə-lā′shən) *n.* **1,** act or result of installing. **2,** something installed, as a fixed machine. **3,** a tract of land and the buildings thereon devoted to military use.

in·stall′ment (in-stâl′mənt) *n.* one part of anything divided for periodical receipt or issuance, as a debt, a serial story, etc. Also, **in·stal′ment.** —**installment plan,** a method of payment by installments.

in′stance (in′stəns) *n.* **1,** an event that is one of many; a case; an example. **2,** instigation; suggestion.

in′stant (in′stənt) *n.* **1,** a small or infinitesimal interval of time; a moment. **2,** the present time or moment. —*adj.* **1,** immediate. **2,** of present time, esp. of the present

month. —**in″stan·ta′ne·ous** (-tā′nē-əs) *adj.* done in an instant.

in·stan′ter (in-stan′tər) *adv.* without delay; immediately.

in·stead′ (in-sted′) *adv.* in place (of another).

in′step″ *n.* the arched upper surface of the human foot.

in′sti·gate″ (in′sti-gāt″) *v.t.* goad on, urge, or stimulate (a person); foment (an action). —**in″sti·ga′tion,** *n.* —**in′sti·ga″tor,** *n.*

in·still′ (in-stil′) *v.t.* **1,** infuse slowly into the mind or feelings. **2,** pour in by drops. —**in″stil·la′tion** (in″stə-lā′shən) *n.*

in′stinct (in′stinkt) *n.* **1,** an inborn tendency to act or respond in a particular way. **2,** aptitude. —**in·stinc′tive,** *adj.*

in′sti·tute″ (in′sti-toot″) *v.t.* set up; establish; appoint. —*n.* a corporate group, school, etc., devoted to scientific work, etc.

in″sti·tu′tion (in″sti-too′shən) *n.* **1,** an organization for the promotion of a particular object; the building it occupies. **2,** an established custom. **3,** act or result of instituting. —**in″sti·tu′tion·al,** *adj.*

in″sti·tu′tion·al·ize″ (-ə-līz″) *v.t.* **1,** establish as an institution. **2,** to place (a person) in an institution.

in·struct′ (in-strukt′) *v.t.* **1,** give directions to; order; command. **2,** train. **3,** apprise.

in·struc′tion (in-struk′shən) *n.* **1,** act or result of instructing; teaching. **2,** an order; direction.

in·struc′tive (-tiv) *adj.* serving to teach or inform. —**in·struc′tive·ness,** *n.*

in·struc′tor (-tər) *n.* a teacher; in colleges, one below professorial rank.

in′stru·ment (in′strə-mənt) *n.* **1,** any mechanical device or contrivance; a tool, implement, or apparatus. **2,** a contrivance for producing musical sounds. **3,** a formal legal document. **4,** an agent, agency, or means. —**in″stru·men′tal,** *adj.* —**in″stru·men′tal·ist,** *n.* one who performs on a musical instrument. —**in″stru·men·tal′i·ty,** *n.* agency. —**in″stru·men·ta′tion,** *n.* orchestration.

in″sub·or′di·nate (in″sə-bôr′də-nət) *adj.* disobedient; defiant. —**in″sub·or″di·na′tion,** *n.*

in′su·lar (in′sū-lər) *adj.* **1,** pert. to an island; detached; hemmed in. **2,** provincial; narrow-minded. —**in″su·lar′i·ty** (-lar′ə-tē) *n.*

in′su·late″ (in′sə-lāt″) *v.t.* **1,** shield with material that isolates from heat, sound, electricity, etc. **2,** isolate. —**in″su·la′tion,** *n.* —**in′su·la″tor,** *n.* that which insulates, esp. a nonconductor of electricity.

in′su·lin (in′sə-lin) *n.* a preparation from

the pancreas of animals, used in treating diabetes.

in·sult' *v.t.* cause to take offense; affront. —*n.* (in'sult) an affront to self-respect.

in·su'per·a·ble (in-soo'pər-ə-bəl) *adj.* incapable of being surmounted or overcome. —**in·su"per·a·bil'i·ty**, *n.*

in·sur'a·ble (in-shûr'ə-bəl) *adj.* acceptable to an underwriter. —**in·sur"a·bil'i·ty**, *n.*

in·sur'ance (in-shûr'əns) *n.* **1**, a contract whereby one party agrees to compensate another for loss through fire, death, etc. **2**, the business of insuring or underwriting. **3**, indemnity. **4**, assurance.

in·sure' (in-shûr') *v.t.* **1**, issue or obtain insurance on. **2**, assure.

in·sur'gent (in-sẽr'jənt) *adj.* revolting against established government; engaged in insurrection. —*n.* one who revolts. —**in·sur'gence**, *n.*

in"sur·rec'tion (in"sə-rek'shən) *n.* armed resistance to authority; a limited rebellion. —**in"sur·rec'tion·ar·y**, *adj.* —**in"sur·rec'tion·ist**, *n.*

in·tact' (in-takt') *adj.* remaining uninjured, unimpaired, whole, or complete. —**in·tact'ness**, *n.*

in·tagl'io (in-tăl'yō) *n.* **1**, incised engraving. **2**, the process of printing from engraved plates.

in'take" *n.* a taking or drawing in; consumption.

in·tan'gi·ble (in-tan'jə-bəl) *adj.* not able to be touched or grasped; vague. —**in·tan"gi·bil'i·ty**, *n.*

in'te·ger (in'tə-jər) *n.* a whole number, not fractional.

in'te·gral (in'tə-grəl) *adj.* **1**, being an essential part of a whole; component; intrinsic. **2**, being an integer; involving integers. **3**, entire.

in'te·grate" (in'tə-grāt") *v.t.* form into a whole; bring together. —**in'te·gra·ble** (-grə-bəl) *adj.* —**integrated circuit**, a complete circuit, comprising transistors, resistors, and other components, inseparably associated in a single miniature unit.

in·te·gra'tion (-grā'shən) *n.* act or effect of integrating; mixing of white persons and Negroes, as in schools.

in·teg'ri·ty (in-teg'rə-tè) *n.* **1**, fidelity to moral principles; honesty. **2**, soundness; completeness.

in·teg'u·ment (in-teg'yə-mənt) *n.* a natural covering, as skin, shell, rind, etc.

in'tel·lect" (in'tə-lekt") *n.* **1**, the mind in its aspect of knowing and understanding (but not of feeling or willing). **2**, mental capacity.

in"tel·lec'tu·al (in"tə-lek'choo-əl) *adj.*

pert. to, perceived by, or appealing to the intellect. —*n.* an intelligent and informed person.

in·tel'li·gence (in-tel'i-jəns) *n.* **1**, the power of knowing and understanding; mental capacity. **2**, news; information, esp. secret information. **3**, a staff of persons engaged in obtaining information. —**intelligence quotient**, a number representing a score made in an intelligence test; I.Q.

in·tel'li·gent (in-tel'i-jənt) *adj.* **1**, quick to understand. **2**, marked by or indicating intelligence.

in·tel"li·gent'si·a (in-tel"i-jen'sè-ə) *n.pl.* the highly educated classes; the intellectuals.

in·tel'li·gi·ble (in-tel'ə-jə-bəl) *adj.* capable of being understood; comprehensible. —**in·tel"li·gi·bil'i·ty**, *n.*

in·tem'per·ate (in-tem'pər-ət) *adj.* excessive; unrestrained; severe. —**in·tem'per·ance**, **in·tem'per·ate·ness**, *n.*

in·tend' *v.t.* have in mind as a purpose; plan to do, use, give, etc. —**in·tend'ed**, *n.* (*Colloq.*) fiancé(e).

in·tend'ant (in-ten'dənt) *n.* a manager or superintendent.

in·tense' (in-tens') *adj.* **1**, existing in high degree; strong; acute. **2**, vehement; earnest; ardent. —**in·tense'ness**, *n.*

in·ten'si·fy" (in-ten'si-fī") *v.t. & i.* make or become intense or more intense. —**in·ten"si·fi·ca'tion**, *n.*

in·ten'si·ty (-sə-tè) *n.* condition or degree of intenseness.

in·ten'sive (-siv) *adj.* extreme; very acute. —*n.* (*Gram.*) something that emphasizes, as *self* in *himself*. —**in·ten'sive·ness**, *n.*

in·tent' *n.* intention; aim; plan. —*adj.* **1**, firmly fixed or directed upon an object. **2**, earnest; sedulous.

in·ten'tion (-shən) *n.* **1**, the act of intending; something intended; purpose; aim. **2**, (*pl.*) (*Colloq.*) design with respect to proposing marriage. —**in·ten'tion·al**, *adj.* done purposely.

in·ter' (in-tẽr') *v.t.* [**in·terred'**, **in·ter'ring**] place in a grave or tomb; bury. —**in·ter'ment**, *n.*

in·ter- (in-tər) *pref.* between; among; together; mutually or reciprocally. [In addition to words defined in the text, the following words have the same sense as their root words, extended by the prefix to indicate interaction.]

in"ter·breed'	in"ter·de·nom'i-
in"ter·col·le'gi·	na'tion·al
ate	in"ter·de·pend'ent
in"ter·co·lo'ni·al	in'ter·faith"
in"ter·com·mu'ni·	in'ter·mix"
cate"	in"ter·o"ce·an'ic

in″ter·plan′e·tar·y
in″ter·play′
in″ter·plead′
in″ter·ra′cial
in″ter·scho·las′tic
in″ter·stel′lar
in″ter·trib′al
in″ter·twine′
in″ter·twist′
in″ter·weave′

in″ter·act′ *v.i.* act on each other or one another. —in″ter·ac′tion, *n.*

in·ter′ca·lar·y (in-tər′kə-ler-ė) *adj.* 1, inserted in the calendar as an extra day, month, or year. 2, interpolated.

in·ter′ca·late″ (in-tər′kə-lāt″) *v.t.* insert between others; interpolate. —in·ter″ca·la′tion, *n.*

in″ter·cede′ (in″tər-sēd′) *v.i.* mediate between two contending parties.

in″ter·cept′ (in″tər-sept′) *v.t.* 1, interpose between. 2, seize in passage; cut off. —*n.* (in′tər-sept″) 1, a crossing. 2, a message picked up off a radio, etc. 3, an interception. —in″ter·cep′tion, *n.* —in″ter·cep′tor, *n.* a fighter airplane.

in″ter·ces′sion (in″tər-sesh′ən) *n.* 1, act of interceding. 2, a prayer for mercy. —in″ter·ces′sor (-ses″ər) *n.*

in″ter·change′ *v.t.* 1, put each (of two things) in the place of the other. 2, transpose; exchange. 3, alternate; vary. —*v.i.* change reciprocally. —*n.* 1, mutual exchange; alternate succession. 2, an intersection of two or more routes in a highway system. —in″ter·change′a·ble (-ə-bəl) *adj.*

in′ter·com″ (in′tər-kom″) *n.* a device for talking between rooms or offices of the same house or suite.

in′ter·course″ (in′tər-kôrs″) *n.* 1, communication between persons; exchange of ideas; conversation. 2, sexual relations; coitus.

in′ter·dict″ (in′tər-dikt″) *v.t.* forbid peremptorily; restrain by injunction; debar. —*n.* 1, a prohibitory order or decree. 2, (*Rom. Cath.*) denial of certain sacraments. —in″ter·dic′tion, *n.*

in′ter·est (in′tər-ist) *n.* 1, a feeling of concern, curiosity, etc.; the object that arouses such feeling. 2, connection, esp. through investment, with a business. 3, benefit; advantage; profit. 4, (*pl.*) a group of persons or companies allied in business. 5, selfish consideration. 6, payment for the use of money; the rate or amount. —*v.t.* engage or excite the attention or curiosity of. —in′ter·est·ing, *adj.* attracting attention.

in′ter·face″ *v.i.* provide a link between two entities, regions, components, etc. —*n.* that which provides such a link.

in″ter·fere′ (in″tər-fir′) *v.i.* 1, thrust oneself into the affairs of others; meddle. 2, collide; be obstructive.

in″ter·fer′ence (in″tər-fir′əns) *n.* 1, act of interfering. 2, the interaction of waves of any kind, esp. the confusion of radio waves by extraneous waves.

in′ter·im (in′tər-im) *n.* an intervening time; the meantime. —*adj.* provisional; temporary.

in·te′ri·or (in-tir′ė-ər) *adj.* 1, being inside something; internal. 2, inland; domestic; indoor; mental. —*n.* the internal part; the inside, as of a room, country, etc.

in″ter·ject′ (in″tər-jekt′) *v.t.* thrust between other things; insert; interpolate.

in″ter·jec′tion (-jek′shən) *n.* 1, the act of interjecting. 2, an exclamatory utterance.

in″ter·lace′ (in″tər-lās′) *v.t.* weave together; intersperse.

in″ter·lard′ (in″tər-lärd′) *v.t.* mix or insert among other things; diversify.

in″ter·leave′ (-lēv′) *v.t.* 1, insert between leaves. 2, provide (a book) with interleaved blank pages or illustrations.

in″ter·line′ *v.t.* 1, insert between lines of writing. 2, furnish (a garment) with an extra lining. —in″ter·lin′e·ar (-lin′ė-ər) *adj.* between lines. —in″ter·lin′ing, *n.* an extra, inside lining.

in″ter·lock′ *v.t. & i.* 1, fasten or become fastened together. 2, be connected so as to operate simultaneously or in desired sequence. —*n.* (in′tər-lok″) 1, an interconnection. 2, a mechanical interdependence whereby the operation of one part activates or prevents the operation of another part.

in″ter·lo·cu′tion (in″tər-lō-kū′shən) *n.* conversation; dialogue.

in″ter·loc′u·tor (in″tər-lok′yû-tər) *n.* one with whom one is conversing.

in″ter·loc′u·to·ry (in″tər-lok′yû-tôr-ė) 1, of speech or conversation. 2, interpolated. 3, (of a legal ruling) not final.

in″ter·lope′ (in″tər-lōp′) *v.i.* intrude, as in a business, without right.

in′ter·lude″ (in′tər-lood″) *n.* 1, an intervening time, period, or stage; an episode of such time. 2, a short performance between acts.

in″ter·mar′ry *v.i.* marry within the limits of a family or group. —in″ter·mar′riage, *n.*

in″ter·me′di·a *adj.* relating to the combined use of several media.

in″ter·me′di·ar·y (in″tər-mē′dė-er-ė) *adj.* 1, intermediate. 2, serving as an intermediary. —*n.* a mediator; messenger; go-between.

in″ter·me′di·ate (in″tər-mē′dė-ət) *adj.* situated between two extremes; coming between, in position or degree; intervening. —*v.i.* (-āt″) mediate. —intermediate school, junior high school.

in″ter·mez′zo (in″tər-met′sō) *n.* [*pl.* -zos

or **-zi** (-sē)] a musical composition played between the acts of a play, etc.; an independent piece in similar style.

in·ter′mi·na·ble (in-tēr′mə-nə-bəl) *adj.* never ending; long drawnout.

in″ter·min′gle (in″tər-ming′gəl) *v.t.* mix together; combine.

in″ter·mis′sion (in″tər-mish′ən) *n.* a period of temporary cessation; a pause or recess.

in″ter·mit′ (in″tər-mit′) *v.* [**-mit′ted, -mit′ting**] stop temporarily; suspend; delay.

in″ter·mit′tent (in″tər-mit′ənt) *adj.* ceasing and recurring at intervals. —**in″ter·mit′tence,** *n.*

in·tern′ (in-tērn′) *v.t.* confine within prescribed limits, esp. hold aliens, ships, etc., during a war. —*n.* interne. —**in″ter·nee′** (-nē′) *n.* one interned as a prisoner of war. —**in·tern′ment,** *n.* —**in·tern′ship,** *n.*

in·ter′nal (in-tēr′nəl) *adj.* **1,** situated within something; enclosed; inside. **2,** pert. to an inner part; domestic; subjective. **3,** (of a medicine, etc.) to be taken into the body. —**internal combustion,** power generated by an explosion inside a chamber, as in the cylinder of a gasoline engine. —**internal medicine,** a branch of medicine dealing with the diagnosis and nonsurgical treatment of the internal organs.

in″ter·na′tion·al *adj.* **1,** pert. to the relations between nations. **2,** involving more than one nation. —*n.* (*cap.*) any of several international federations of socialist or communistic groups.

in·terne″ (in′tērn″) *n.* a doctor residing in a hospital for training.

in″ter·ne′cine (in″tər-nē′sin) *adj.* accompanied by mutual slaughter; extremely destructive.

in·tern′ist (in-tērn′ist) *n.* a physician, internal medicine specialist.

in·ter′po·late″ (in-tēr′pə-lāt″) *v.t.* insert between other things; introduce (something new or extraneous). —**in·ter″po·la′tion,** *n.*

in″ter·pose′ (in″tər-pōz′) *v.t.* place between or among; interrupt with. —*v.i.* come between things or persons, as an obstacle or mediator. —**in″ter·po·si′tion** (-pə-zish′ən) *n.*

in·ter′pret (in-tēr′prit) *v.t.* **1,** show the meaning of; explain; elucidate; translate. **2,** construe in a particular way, as a part in a play. —**in·ter″pre·ta′tion,** *n.* —**in·ter′pre·ta″tive, in·ter′pre·tive,** *adj.*

in″ter·reg′num (in″tər-reg′nəm) *n.* an interval between one reign and the next; a breach of continuity.

in·ter′ro·bang″ (in-ter′ə-bang″) *n.* a punctuation mark (‽) expressing both inquiry and exclamation.

in·ter′ro·gate″ (in-ter′ə-gāt″) *v.t. & i.* ask a question or questions (of). —**in·ter′ro·ga″tor,** *n.*

in·ter″ro·ga′tion (-gā′shən) *n.* **1,** a question or questioning. **2,** the symbol (?).

in″ter·rog′a·tive (in″tə-rog′ə-tiv) *adj.* asking a question. Also, **in″ter·rog′a·to·ry** (-tôr-ē).

in″ter·rupt′ (in″tə-rupt′) *v.t.* **1,** make a gap in; bring to a pause or stop. **2,** intrude upon the action or speech of. —**in″ter·rup′tion,** *n.*

in″ter·sect′ (in″tər-sekt′) *v.t. & i.* cut or divide; cross (one another).

in″ter·sec′tion (-sek′shən) *n.* **1,** the act of intersecting. **2,** a point where lines or roads meet.

in″ter·sperse″ (in″tər-spērs′) *v.t.* **1,** scatter among other things. **2,** diversify by placing various things here and there.

in″ter·state″ *adj.* between different states; in the U.S., concerning two or more states and so within Federal jurisdiction. —*n.* a highway in the Interstate Highway System.

in·ter′stice (in-tēr′stis) *n.* [*pl.* **in·ter′sti·ces** (-siz)] an intervening space; a small narrow opening.

in″ter·ur′ban *adj.* between cities. —*n.* a trolley car running between cities.

in′ter·val (in′tər-vəl) *n.* **1,** the time between two events. **2,** an intermission. **3,** the distance between two objects; a difference in degree, etc. **4,** an empty space; a gap.

in″ter·vene′ (in″tər-vēn′) *v.i.* **1,** happen between things, persons, or events. **2,** intercede; interfere. —**in″ter·ven′tion** (-ven′-shən) *n.*

in″ter·view″ (in″tər-vū″) *n.* **1,** a meeting of persons face to face. **2,** a questioning; examination. —*v.t.* meet to question.

in·tes′tate (in-tes′tāt) *adj.* **1,** having made no will. **2,** not bequeathed. —*n.* one who dies without having made a will. —**in·tes′ta·cy,** *n.*

in·tes′tine (in-tes′tin) *n.* the lower part of the alimentary tract; the bowel. —**in·tes′tin·al,** *adj.*

in′ti·ma·cy (in′ti-mə-sē) *n.* **1,** condition of being intimate. **2,** an act evidencing close familiarity with a person.

in′ti·mate″ (in′ti-mət) *adj.* **1,** close in personal relations; familiar; closely allied. **2,** personal; private. **3,** pert. to the inmost part or essential nature. —*n.* a close friend. —*v.t.* (-māt″) suggest; hint; imply. —**in″ti·ma′tion,** *n.* suggestion; a hint.

in·tim′i·date″ (in-tim′ə-dāt″) *v.t.* make timid or fearful; overawe. —**in·tim″i·da′-tion,** *n.*

in'to (in'too) *prep.* **1,** to and in, implying motion. **2,** (*Math.*) as a division of. **3,** (*Slang*) involved or interested in.

in·tol'er·a·ble (in-tol'ər-ə-bəl) *adj.* unbearable. **—in'tol'er·a·bil'i·ty, in'tol'er·a·ble·ness,** *n.*

in·tol'er·ant (in-tol'ər-ənt) *adj.* **1,** angered by contrary opinions or beliefs. **2,** unable to accept or bear. **—in·tol'er·ance,** *n.*

in"to·na'tion (in"tə-nā'shən) *n.* **1,** a particular modulation of the voice. **2,** the act of intoning. **3,** the relation of the pitch of a certain tone of a musical instrument or the voice to an accepted standard. **4,** the use of musical tones in speaking or chanting.

in·tone' (in-tōn') *v.t. & i.* **1,** utter in a singing voice; chant. **2,** utter in a particular tone, esp. a monotone.

in·tox'i·cant (in-tok'si-kənt) *n.* an intoxicating drink or drug.

in·tox'i·cate" (in-tok'si-kāt") *v.t.* **1,** make drunk with liquor. **2,** excite to elation, enthusiasm, etc. **3,** poison. **—***v.i.* cause intoxication. **—in·tox"i·ca'tion,** *n.*

in·tra- (in-trə) *pref.* within.

in·tra'dos (in-trā'dōs) *n.* the interior curve or surface of an arch or vault.

in"tra·mu'ral (in"trə-myūr'əl) *adj.* confined to, or within the walls or limits of, a school, city, etc.

in·tran'si·gent (in-tran'sə-jənt) *adj.* refusing to agree or compromise. **—***n.* one who is uncompromising. **—in·tran'si·gence,** *n.*

in·tran'si·tive (in-tran'sə-tiv) *adj.* (*Gram.*) of a verb, not acting directly on an object, as *I laugh, I go.*

in"tra·u'ter·ine (-ū'tər-in) *adj.* placed or found within the uterus. **—intrauterine device,** a contraceptive device placed within the uterus. Also, **IUD.**

in"tra·ve'nous (in"trə-vē'nəs) *adj.* within or into a vein.

in·trench' *v.t.* entrench, establish in a trench or similarly secure position. **—in·trench'ment,** *n.*

in·trep'id *adj.* undaunted; fearless. **—in"-tre·pid'i·ty** (in"trə-pid'ə-tē) *n.*

in'tri·cate (in'tri-kət) *adj.* perplexingly tangled; complex. **—in'tri·ca·cy** (-kə-sē) *n.*

in·trigue' (in-trēg') *v.t.* excite to interest or curiosity. **—***v.i.* engage in underhand plotting. **—***n.* a clandestine plot or love affair; plotting. **—in·tri'gant** (-trē'gənt) *n.*

in·trin'sic (in-trin'zik) *adj.* being an innate or essential part; inherent. **—in·trin'si·cal·ly,** *adv.*

in·tro- (in-trō; in-trə) *pref.* within; into; inward.

in"tro·duce' (in"trə-dūs') *v.t.* **1,** bring into notice, use, or practice. **2,** begin; provide

with a preface. **3,** present (a person) to another or to society. **4,** lead (a person) to a particular experience. **5,** put in; insert.

in"tro·duc'tion (in"trə-duk'shən) *n.* **1,** act or result of introducing. **2,** that which introduces, as a preface. **—in"tro·duc'to·ry** (-tə-rē) *adj.*

in·tro'it (in-trō'it) *n.* an antiphon sung at the beginning of mass or communion.

in"tro·spec'tion (in"trə-spek'shən) *n.* observation of one's own mental state.

in"tro·spec'tive (-tiv) *adj.* observing or tending to think about one's thoughts, feelings, etc.

in'tro·vert" (in'trə-vērt") *n.* a person chiefly concerned with his own thoughts. **—***v.t.* turn inward. **—in"tro·ver'sion** (-vēr'zhən) *n.*

in·trude' (in-trood') *v.t.* thrust in forcibly. **—***v.i.* thrust oneself in, esp. without warrant or welcome.

in·tru'sion (in-troo'zhən) *n.* **1,** act or result of intruding. **2,** an unwelcome visit or entrance.

in·tru'sive (in-troo'siv) *adj.* intruding; being an intrusion. **—in·tru'sive·ness,** *n.*

in·trust' *v.t.* entrust.

in"tu·i'tion (in"too-ish'ən) *n.* comprehension without effort of reasoning; instinctive knowledge. **—in·tu'it** (in-too'it) *v.i. & t.* **—in·tu'i·tive** (in-too'ə-tiv) *adj.*

in"un·date" (in'un-dāte") *v.t.* flood; deluge. **—in"un·da'tion,** *n.*

in·ure' (in-yûr') *v.t.* deaden the sensibility of; accustom; habituate. **—***v.i.* (*Law*) pass (to); serve. **—in·ure'ment,** *n.*

in·va·lid (in'və-lid) *n.* a sick or disabled person. **—***adj.* infirm; sickly.

in"val'id *adj.* not valid; without force.

in·val'i·date" (in-val'i-dāt") *v.t.* remove validity from; annul. **—in·val"i·da'tion,** *n.*

in·val'u·a·ble (in-val'ū-ə-bəl) *adj.* of immeasurably great value. **—in·val'u·a·ble·ness,** *n.*

in·var' (in-vär') *n.* a nickel-steel alloy.

in·va'sion (in-vā'zhən) *n.* act or result of invading. **—in·va'sive** (-siv) *adj.*

in·vec'tive (in-vek'tiv) *n.* vehement denunciation or vituperation. **—***adj.* censorious; abusive.

in·veigh' (in-vā') *v.i.* make a verbal attack.

in·vei'gle (in-vā'gəl) *v.t.* lead astray artfully; entice. **—in·vei'gle·ment,** *n.*

in·vent' *v.t.* **1,** be the first to devise; originate. **2,** fabricate, as a story. **—***v.i.* create something new. **—in·ven'tor,** *n.*

in·ven'tion (in-ven'shən) *n.* **1,** act of inventing. **2,** something invented; an original creation. **3,** a lie. **4,** imagination; skill or ingenuity in original contrivance.

in·ven'tive (in-ven'tive) *adj.* apt at inventing; creative. **—in·ven'tive·ness,***n.*

in'ven·to·ry (in'vən-tôr-ē) *n.* **1,** a descriptive list of articles; a catalog of contents, stock, etc. **2,** the value of a stock of goods. *—v.t.* list; catalog.

in"ver·ness' (in"vər-ness') *n.* a long, sleeveless cape.

in·verse' (in-vērs') *adj.* **1,** opposite or contrary in meaning, sense, application, etc. **2,** reversed in position or direction; inverted. *—n.* that which is inverse.

in·ver'sion (in-vēr'zhən) *n.* **1,** reversal; transposition. **2,** alteration of the natural order of words.

in·vert' (in-vērt') *v.t.* reverse in position or condition; turn over; transpose; reverse in meaning, application, tendency, etc. *—n.* (in'vert) the opposite or contrary thing.

in·vest' *v.t.* **1,** put (money) to profitable use. **2,** install; endow. **3,** dress. **4,** hem in; besiege. *—v.i.* invest money.

in·ves'ti·gate" (in-ves'ti-gāt") *v.t. & i.* examine in detail; inquire into. **—in·ves"ti·ga'tion,** *n.* **—in·ves'ti·ga"tor,** *n.*

in·ves'ti·ture (in-ves'ti-chər) *n.* **1,** act or effect of installing in office. **2,** a robe or token of office.

in·vest'ment (-mənt) *n.* act or result of investing; money invested.

in·vet'er·ate (in-vet'ər-ət) *adj.* firmly established or addicted by habit, custom, or usage. **—in·vet'er·a·cy,** *n.*

in·vid'i·ous (in-vid'ē-əs) *adj.* **1,** prompted by envy or ill will. **2,** unfair; odious. **—in·vid'i·ous·ness,** *n.*

in·vig'or·ate" (in-vig'ə-rāt") *v.t.* strengthen; animate. **—in·vig"or·a'tion,** *n.*

in·vin'ci·ble (in-vin'sə-bəl) *adj.* unconquerable. **—in·vin"ci·bil'i·ty, in·vin'ci·ble·ness,** *n.*

in·vi'o·la·ble (in-vī'ə-lə-bəl) *adj.* not to be violated; invulnerable. **—in·vi"o·la·bil'i·ty,** *n.*

in·vi'o·late (in-vī'ə-lət) *adj.* **1,** not desecrated, infringed, or impaired. **2,** not to be violated.

in"vi·ta'tion (in"vi-tā'shən) *n.* **1,** act of inviting. **2,** a request to be present; an allurement. **—in"vi·ta'tion·al** (-əl) *adj.* open by invitation only.

in·vite' (in-vīt') *v.t.* **1,** ask (a person) to come; request the presence of. **2,** solicit, allure, tempt, etc. **3,** lay oneself open to. *—n.* (in'vīt) (*Slang*) an invitation. **—in·vit'ing,** *adj.* alluring; tempting.

in"vo·ca'tion (in"vō-kā'shən) *n.* **1,** act of invoking. **2,** a prayer.

in'voice (in'vois) *n.* a list of items shipped; a bill for them. *—v.t.* list and bill for.

in·voke' (in-vōk') *v.t.* **1,** call on for aid or protection, esp. as addressing a deity. **2,** call for; utilize, as a law. **—in·voc'a·to·ry** (in-vok'ə-tôrē) *adj.*

in·vol'un·tar"y (in-vol'ən-ter"ē) *adj.* **1,** not willed or intentional. **2,** done unwillingly. **—in·vol'un·tar"i·ness,** *n.*

in'vo·lute" (in'və-loot") *adj.* rolled inward; involved; intricate. **—in"vo·lu'tion,** *n.* something involute.

in·volve' (in-volv') *v.t.* **1,** contain or include; entail; imply. **2,** affect or be affected by. **3,** combine inextricably; implicate. **4,** make intricate or complex. **—in·volve'ment,** *n.*

in'ward (in'wərd) *adv.* [also, **in'wards**] toward the inside or center; in the mind or soul. *—adj.* **1,** being within; directed toward the inside or center. **2,** pert. to inner parts; in the mind. **—in'ward·ness,** *n.*

in'ward·ly (-lē) *adv.* **1,** toward the inside or center. **2,** privately; secretly. **3,** in a low tone; not aloud.

i'o·dine" (ī'ə-dīn") *n.* **1,** a nonmetallic chemical element, used medicinally, no. 53, symbol I. **2,** an antiseptic solution: *tincture of iodine.* **—i'o·dize",** *v.t.* treat with iodine.

i'on (ī'ən) *n.* an atom or molecule bearing an electric charge.

i·o'ni·um (ī-ō'nē-əm) *n.* a radioactive chemical element, no. 90, symbol Io.

i'on·ize" (ī'ə-nīz") *v.t.* form ions in; change to ions. **—i"on·i·za'tion,** *n.*

i·on'o·sphere" (ī-on'ə-sfir") *n.* the outer regions of the earth's atmosphere, from about 60 miles outward.

i·o'ta (ī-ō'tə) *n.* **1,** the ninth letter of the Greek alphabet (I, ι). **2,** a small quantity.

I O U *n.* a written acknowledgment of a debt (= I owe you).

ip·e·cac" (ip'ə-kak") *n.* a So. Amer. shrub; an emetic drug made from it.

I.Q. (ī'kū') *n.* intelligence quotient.

ir- *pref.* not (the equivalent of **in-**, used before an initial r.) [In addition to words defined in the text, the following words formed by prefixing ir- (= not) have merely the negative sense of the positive term.]

ir·ra'tion·al	ir"re·me'di·a·ble
ir"re·claim'a·ble	ir"re·mov'a·ble
ir·rec'on·cil"a·ble	ir·rep'a·ra·ble
ir"re·cov'er·a·ble	ir"re·place'a·ble
ir·re·deem'a·ble	ir"re·press'i·ble
ir"e·duc'i·ble	ir"re·proach'
ir·ref'u·ta·ble	a·ble
ir·rel'e·vant	ir"re·sist'i·ble

ir·res'o·lute″   ir″rev'er·ent
ir″re·spon'sive   ir″re·vers'i·ble
ir″re·triev'a·ble   ir″rev'o·ca·ble

i·ras'ci·ble (i-ras'ə-bəl) *adj.* easily provoked to anger; hot-tempered. —**i·ras″ci·bil'i·ty**, *n.*

i'rate (ī'rāt) *adj.* angry; incensed.

ire (īr) *n.* anger; resentment. —*v.t.* irritate; enrage.

i·ren'ic (ī-ren'ik) *adj.* tending to promote peace. —**i·ren'i·cal·ly**, *adv.*

ir″i·des'cent (ir″ə-des'ənt) *adj.* glittering with changeable colors, like a rainbow. —**ir″i·des'cence**, *n.*

i·rid'i·um (i-rid'ē-əm) *n.* a metallic chemical element, similar to platinum, no. 77, symbol Ir.

i'ris (ī'ris) *n.* **1,** the colored diaphragm of the eye surrounding the pupil. **2,** any of various flowering plants. **3,** the rainbow, or a similar iridescence.

I'rish (ī'rish) *adj.* pert. to Ireland, its people, customs, etc. —*n.* the Gaelic language; Erse. —**I'rish·man**, *n.*

irk (ērk) *v.t.* annoy; bore. —**irk'some**, *adj.* boring; annoying. —**irk'some·ness**, *n.*

i'ron (ī'ərn) *n.* **1,** a metallic chemical element, no. 26, symbol Fe; this metal, widely fabricated. **2,** a tool; implement, utensil, weapon, etc.; a thing of this metal; a harpoon; (*Slang*) a gun; (*pl.*) shackles; an implement for pressing clothes; a type of golf club. **3,** something hard, rigid, unyielding, etc. **4,** a tonic containing iron. —*adj.* **1,** made of iron. **2,** like iron; hard; enduring, steadfast, etc. —*v.t. & i.* press (clothes, etc.). —**Iron Age,** a period when iron implements were first used, about 1000 B.C. —**Iron Curtain,** a barrier to travel and communication into and out of a country, by government restrictions and censorship. —**iron horse,** (*Colloq.*) **1,** a railroad locomotive. **2,** a bicycle or tricycle. —**iron lung,** a chamber in which a paralyzed person is placed to enable him to breathe.

i'ron·clad″ *adj.* **1,** armored, as a warship. **2,** unassailable; unbreakable, as an agreement.

i·ron'ic (ī-ron'ik) *adj.* **1,** being irony; sarcastic. **2,** frustrating. Also, **i·ron'i·cal.**

i'ron·stone″ *n.* a kind of pottery.

i'ro·ny (ī'rə-nē) *n.* **1,** a figure of speech: emphasis by stating the opposite; covert sarcasm. **2,** the frustration of hopes.

ir·ra'di·ate″ (i-rā'dē-āt″) *v.t.* **1,** throw rays of light upon. **2,** make clear. —*v.i.* emit rays or radiant energy. —**ir·ra'di·a'tion**, *n.*

ir″re·gard'less (ir″i-gärd'ləs) *adj.* (*Erroneous*) regardless.

ir·reg'u·lar (i-reg'yə-lər) *adj.* **1,** not reg-

ular. **2,** against the rules. **3,** (*Mil.*) not belonging to the established armed forces. —**ir″reg″u·lar'i·ty** (-lar'ə-tē) *n.*

ir″re·li'gious (ir″i-lij'əs) *adj.* **1,** not devout. **2,** profane. —**ir″re·li'gious·ness**, *n.*

ir″re·spec'tive (ir″i-spek'tiv) *adj.* regardless of; independent of.

ir″re·spon'si·ble (ir″i-spon'sə-bəl) *adj.* **1,** having no sense of responsibility; not trustworthy. **2,** not accountable, as for one's own actions. —**ir″re·spon″si·bil'i·ty**, *n.*

ir'ri·gate″ (ir'ə-gāt″) *v.t.* **1,** supply (land) with water through artificial channels. **2,** wash with a flow of liquid, as a wound. —**ir″ri·ga'tion**, *n.*

ir'ri·ta·ble (ir'ə-tə-bəl) *adj.* irascible. —**ir″ri·ta·bil'i·ty**, *n.*

ir'ri·tant (ir'ə-tənt) *n. & adj.* something that irritates.

ir'ri·tate″ (ir'ə-tāt″) *v.t.* **1,** excite to resentment or anger; vex; annoy. **2,** make sore or painful; chafe. —**ir″ri·ta'tion**, *n.*

ir·rup'tion (i-rup'shən) *n.* a bursting in; a sudden invasion. —**ir·rupt'**, *v.i.* —**ir·rup'tive**, *adj.*

is (iz) *v.* 3rd. pers. sing. pres. indicative of *be.*

-ise (īz) *suf.* same as **-ize.**

-ish *suf.* having some characteristics of.

i'sin·glass″ (ī'zing-glás″) *n.* **1,** a form of translucent gelatin. **2,** mica.

Is'lam (is'ləm) *n.* the Mohammedan religion; its followers and realm.

is'land (ī'lənd) *n.* **1,** a body of land entirely surrounded by water. **2,** something isolated or surrounded. —**is'land·er**, *n.* —**island universe,** a galaxy.

isle (īl) *n.* a small island. Also, **is'let** (ī'lət).

ism (iz'əm) *n.* a distinctive doctrine, theory, or practice.

-ism (iz-əm) *suf.* of nouns, implying practice, system, doctrine, theory, or principle.

i'so- (ī'sō) *pref.* **1,** equal. **2,** (*Chem.*) isomeric.

i'so·bar″ (ī'sə-bär″) *n.* a line connecting, on a map, all places where the barometric pressure is the same.

i'so·late″ (ī'sə-lāt″) *v.t.* **1,** place apart; make separate. **2,** single out; rid of extraneous matter.

i″so·la'tion (ī″sə-lā'shən) *n.* **1,** the act of isolating; the state of being isolated. **2,** a national policy of nonparticipation in international affairs. —**i″so·la'tion·ism**, *n.* pursuit or support of this policy. —**i″so·la'tion·ist**, *n.*

i'so·mer (ī'sə-mər) *n.* a chemical compound of the same composition (as another) but in different arrangement. —**i″so·mer'ic** (-mer'ik) *adj.*

i″so·met′ric (ī″sə-met′rik) *adj.* **1**, of equal measure; regularly spaced. **2**, of muscular contraction, taking place against resistance, but without lengthening or shortening of the muscle fibers.

i·sos′ce·les″ (ī-sos′ə-lēz″) *adj.* (of a triangle) having two equal sides.

i′so·therm″ (ī′sə-thěrm″) *n.* a line connecting all places that have the same mean temperature. —**i″so·ther′mal,** *adj.*

i″so·ton′ic (ī″sō-tän′ik) *adj.* of muscle contraction, taking place without resistance but with lengthening or shortening of the muscle fibers.

i′so·tope″ (ī′sə-tōp″) *n.* a chemical element, nearly identical (with another or others) but differing in atomic weight.

Is·ra·el′i (iz-rā′ə-lē) *adj. & n.* pert. to the modern country of Israel. —**Is′ra·el·ite″** (iz′rĕ-əl-īt″) *n.*

is′sue (ish′oo) *n.* **1,** the act of sending out; publication; emission. **2,** what is sent out, esp. a quantity issued at one time. **3,** an outflow; product, result, outcome, etc.; offspring or progeny. **4,** a point in question or dispute; a principal question. —*v.t.* **1,** send out; publish; promulgate; distribute. **2,** emit; discharge. —*v.i.* **1,** go or come out; flow out; emerge. **2,** arise as a result or yield. —**is′su·ance,** *n.*

-ist *suf.* of nouns denoting a supporter or adherent (of a doctrine, etc.), as *capitalist*; a practitioner or expert, as *strategist*; a performer on a named instrument, as *violinist*.

isth′mus (is′məs) *n.* a narrow strip of land connecting two larger bodies.

it *pron.* [*poss.* **its**] **1,** a personal pron., third person sing., neuter gender. **2,** a pron. of indefinite sense, as in *What is it?* **3,** a particle used for grammatical completeness in certain idiomatic constructions, as *It is ten o'clock. Let us call it a day.* —*n.* (*Colloq.*) **1,** a person who is the center of attention, or (esp. in children's games) solely given an onerous duty. **2,** (*Slang*) attractiveness to the opposite sex. —**it's** (its) *contraction* it is.

I·tal′ian (i-tal′yən) *adj. & n.* pert. to Italy or its inhabitants or language.

i·tal′ic (i-tal′ik) *n. & adj.* a style of type with sloped letters, thus: *italic.* —**i·tal′i·cize″** (-i-sīz″) *v.t.*

itch (ich) *v.i.* **1,** feel or produce an inclination to scratch an affected part. **2,** desire eagerly. —*n.* **1,** tingling sensation in the skin. **2,** an itching skin disease; scabies. **3,** a persistent desire. —**itch′y,** *adj.*

-ite (-īt) *suf.* **1,** denoting a supporter, follower, associate, or inhabitant. **2,** denoting

certain kinds of minerals, chemical compounds, etc.

i′tem (ī′təm) *n.* **1,** one article of a collection, list, etc. **2,** a separate article, particular, or piece, as in a newspaper.

i′tem·ize″ (ī′tə-mīz″) *v.t.* make a particularized list of. —**i″tem·i·za′tion** (-mi-zā′-shən) *n.*

it′er·ate″ (it′ə-rāt″) *v.t.* utter or say again or repeatedly. —**it″er·a′tion,** *n.* —**it′er·a·tive,** *adj.*

i·tin′er·ant (ī-tin′ə-rənt) *adj.* traveling from place to place. —*n.* a traveler. —**i·tin′er·an·cy,** *n.*

i·tin′er·ar·y (ī-tin′ə-rer-ē) *n.* a plan of travel, esp. a proposed route.

-i·tis (ī′təs) *suf.* (*Pathol.*) forming nouns, denoting an inflammation.

it·self′ *pron.* reflexive or emphatic form of *it.*

i′vo·ry (ī′və-rē) *n.* **1,** the bony substance of a tusk, esp. of an elephant. **2,** (*Slang*) a tooth; (*pl.*) piano keys; (*pl.*) dice. **3,** the color of ivory, creamy white. —**ivory tower,** a dream world.

i′vy (ī′vē) *n.* any of several climbing or trailing plants. —**Ivy League,** an association of colleges in the NE U.S.

-ize (īz) *suf.* forming verbs denoting application of the action denoted by the root, as *emphasize,* make emphatic.

iz′zard (iz′ərd) *n.* (*Colloq.*) z.

J

J, j (jā) the tenth letter of the English alphabet.

jab *v.t. & i.* [**jabbed, jab′bing**] strike suddenly and sharply; prod; poke. —*n.* a sharp thrust.

jab′ber (jab′ər) *v.i. & t.* talk rapidly in an incoherent way; chatter. —*n.* gibberish.

jab′ber·wock″y (jab′ər-wok″ē) *n.* gibberish; nonsensical speech.

ja·bot′ (zha-bō′) *n.* a frill or ruffle in a bosom of a shirt.

jac′a·mar (jak′ə-mär) *n.* a long-billed Amer. bird.

jac″a·ran′da (jak″ə-ran′də) *n.* a tall tropical tree valued for its wood.

jack (jak) *n.* **1,** a mechanical contrivance for lifting. **2,** an oscillating lever or fixed piece for transmitting motion. **3,** one of the face cards in a pack of playing cards; knave. **4,** a small flag. **5,** jackass; jackrabbit; jackdaw; any of several fishes, as the pike. **6,** a fellow. **7,** (*Slang*) money. —*v.t.* (usually with *up*) hoist; raise.

jack′al (jak′əl) *n.* a wild dog of Asia and Africa.

jack′a·napes″ (jak′ə-nāps″) *n.* an impertinent or obstreperous fellow.

jack′ass″ (-as″) *n.* **1,** a male donkey. **2,** a stupid or foolish person.

jack′boot″ *n.* a long boot reaching over the knee.

jack′daw″ (-dâ″) *n.* **1,** a Europ. crow. **2,** an Amer. grackle.

jack′et (jak′it) *n.* **1,** a tailless coat. **2,** any outer covering, as a protective wrapper on a book.

jack′ham″mer *n.* a pneumatic hand drill.

jack-′in-the-box″ *n.* a toy consisting of a box from which a compressed figure springs upward when the lid is released.

jack′knife″ (jak′nīf″) *n.* a large folding pocket knife.

jack-′of-all-trades′ *n.* a handyman.

jack-′o′lan″tern (jak′ə-lan″tərn) *n.* a carved hollowed pumpkin used for decorative illumination at Halloween.

jack pine a tree found in northern U. S. and Canada.

jack′pot″ *n.* an unusually large prize, esp. the largest prize.

jack′rab″bit *n.* a large hare.

jack′screw″ *n.* a jack for raising weights.

jack′straw″ *n.* **1,** an effigy made of straw. **2,** a man without substance or means; a dependent. **3,** (*pl.*) a child's game using straws or strips.

Jac″o·be′an (jak″ə-bē′ən) *adj.* pert. to or contemporary with James I of England.

Jac′o·bite (jak′ə-bīt) *n.* supporter of James II of England or the Stuart dynasty.

jade (jād) *n.* **1,** a green mineral prized for jewelry. **2,** a shade of green. **3,** a dissolute woman. **4,** an inferior or worn-out horse. —*v.t. & i.* make or become exhausted by overwork.

jae′ger (yā′gər) *n.* **1,** a predatory bird, the skua. **2,** a hunter. **3,** (*pl.*) (jā′gərz) long underwear.

jag *n.* **1,** a sharp notch or tooth. **2,** (*Slang*) a drinking spree.

jag′ged (jag′id) *adj.* having sharp projections; irregular.

jag′uar (jag′wär) *n.* a large, ferocious cat of Central and So. Amer.

ja″gua·ron′di (ja″gwə-ron′dē) *n.* a small tropical Amer. wildcat. Also, **ja″gua·run′-di** (-run′dē).

jai a·lai′ (hī′ä-lī′) a game resembling squash but played with basketlike rackets.

jail (jāl) *n.* a place of detention for convicted criminals or persons awaiting trial. —*v.t.* put in a jail. —**jail′er,** *n.* an officer of a jail.

jail′bird″ *n.* an ex-convict.

ja·lop′y (jə-lop′ē) *n.* (*Colloq.*) a decrepit automobile.

jal′ou·sie (jal′oo-zē; -ə-sē) *n.* a blind or shutter made of slats set at an angle to admit air but exclude sun and rain.

jam *v.t.* **[jammed, jam′ming] 1,** thrust or squeeze in so as to stick fast; crowd so as to hinder motion or extrication. **2,** interfere with (a radio broadcast) by another on the same frequency. —*v.i.* **1,** become wedged in place. **2,** (*Slang*) improvise together informally. **3,** (*Slang*) enliven. —*n.* **1,** an obstruction. **2,** a fruit preserve. **3,** (*Slang*) a predicament. —**jam session,** an impromptu jazz session.

jamb (jam) *n.* a vertical side member in the frame of a door or window.

jam″bo·ree′ (jam″bə-rē′) *n.* (*Slang*) a festive gathering.

jam-′packed″ *adj.* (*Colloq.*) full to capacity.

Jane Doe (*Law*) a female defendant or prisoner whose name is not known.

jan′gle (jang′gəl) *v.i. & t.* make a harsh or metallic sound. —*n.* **1,** a discordant sound. **2,** a quarrel or wrangle.

jan′i·tor (jan′ə-tər) *n.* the caretaker of a building; custodian. —**jan′i·tress,** *n.*

Jan′u·ar″y (jan′yû-er″ē) *n.* the first month of the year.

ja·pan′ (jə-pan′) *n.* a varnish that gives a hard, glossy finish.

Jap″a·nese′ (jap″ə-nēz′) *adj.* pert. to Japan. —*n.* **1,** the language of Japan. **2,** (-nēs′) one descended from the people of Japan.

jape (jāp) *n.* a joke or gibe.

ja·pon′i·ca (jə-pon′ə-kə) *n.* a shrub with scarlet flowers and yellow fruit; the Japanese quince.

jar (jär) *v.t. & i.* **[jarred, jar′ring] 1,** jolt suddenly; rattle; make a harsh sound. **2,** affect unpleasantly; annoy or disconcert. **3,** clash; be inharmonious. —*n.* **1,** a harsh impact; a shock. **2,** a clash; conflict; discord. **3,** a wide-mouthed vessel.

jar″di·nière′ (jär″də-nir′) *n.* an ornamental flowerpot.

jar′gon (jär′gən) *n.* **1,** confused or meaningless talk. **2,** language peculiar to a group or profession; cant.

jas′mine (jas′min) *n.* any of several shrubs bearing fragrant yellow or red flowers.

jas′per (jas′pər) *n.* a variety of quartz used for making ornaments.

ja′to (jā′tō) *n.* jet-assisted rake-off.

jaun′dice (jân′dis) *n.* **1,** a disease that causes a yellowish tinge in the skin. **2,** a state of feeling that colors judgment, as jealousy, envy, etc. —*v.t.* affect with prejudice or envy. —**jaun'diced** (-dist) *adj.* adversely biased.

jaunt (jânt) *n.* a short trip, made for pleasure.

jaun'ty (jân'tè) *adj.* **1,** sprightly. **2,** smart in appearance. —**jaun'ti·ness,** *n.*

jave'lin (jav'lin) *n.* a spear made to be thrown by hand.

jaw (jâ) *n.* **1,** either of the two bony structures that form the mouth. **2,** anything likened to a jaw, for holding or seizing. —*v.i.* (*Slang*) talk; chatter; scold.

jaw'bone" *n.* **1,** a bone of the jaw. **2,** (*Slang*) credit. —*v.i.* chatter; scold.

jaw'break"er (jâ'brā"kər) *n.* (*Colloq.*) **1,** any word hard to pronounce. **2,** a hard candy.

jay (jā) *n.* any of several common birds, as *blue jay.*

Jay'cee" (jā'sē") *n.* a member of a Junior Chamber of Commerce.

jay'walk" (jā'wâk") *v.i.* (*Colloq.*) cross a street against a traffic light, or between regular crossings.

jazz (jaz) *n.* **1,** dance music in a certain syncopated style. **2,** (*Slang*) foolishness; nonsense. —*v.t.* (*Slang*) (usu. with *up*) enliven. —*v.i.* (*Slang*) lie.

jazz'y (jaz'ē) *adj.* (*Slang*) [**-i·er, -i·est**] **1,** containing or in the style of jazz. **2,** wildly exciting or energetic.

jeal'ous (jel'əs) *adj.* **1,** feeling or actuated by envy or resentment, as of a more successful rival. **2,** proceeding from distrust. **3,** intolerant of rivalry. —**jeal'ous·y,** *n.*

jean (jēn) *n.* **1,** a twilled cotton fabric. **2,** (*pl.*) trousers or overalls of jean.

jeep (jēp) *n.* a small all-purpose military automobile.

jeer (jir) *v.i. & t.* scoff at; deride; mock. —*n.* gibe; taunt.

Je·ho'vah (jē-hō'və) *n.* the name of God in the Old Testament.

je'hu (jē'hū) *n.* a reckless driver of a cart or car.

je·june' (ji-joon') *adj.* deficient in sense, substance, or taste.

jell (jel) *v.i.* **1,** coagulate; become jelly. **2,** achieve a planned stage or form.

jel'ly (jel'ē) *n.* **1,** a semisolid food made by congealing fruit syrup or meat juice. **2,** any preparation of a soft, gelatinous consistency. —**jel'lied,** *adj.*

jel'ly·bean" *n.* a small oval candy with a soft chewy center.

jel'ly·fish" (jel'ē-fish") *n.* a marine invertebrate with a soft umbrella-shaped body, often with long tentacles.

jen'net (jen'ət) *n.* **1,** a small Span. horse. **2,** (also, **gen'et**) a female donkey.

jen'ny (jen'ē) *n.* **1,** a type of spinning machine. **2,** the female of some species, as the ass. **3,** an airplane used for training fliers.

jeop'ard·y (jep'ər-dē) *n.* risk; danger. —**jeop'ard·ize",** *v.t.* imperil.

jer·bo'a (jēr-bō'ə) *n.* a small rodent of No. Afr. and Asia; jumping mouse.

jer"e·mi'ad (jer'ə-mī'ad) *n.* lamentation; a complaining tirade.

jerk (jērk) *v.i. & t.* **1,** pull suddenly; tug or twist. **2,** cure (meat) in the sun. —*n.* **1,** a sudden start or thrust. **2,** (*Slang*) an inexpert or unsophisticated person.

jer'kin (jēr'kin) *n.* a sleeveless jacket.

jerk'wa"ter (jērk'wâ"tər) *adj.* (*Colloq.*) located away from a main line; provincial.

jerk'y (jēr'kē) *adj.* tending to jerk; spasmodic. —**jerk'i·ness,** *n.*

jer'ry (jer'ē) *n.* (*Brit.*) a nickname for a German or the Germans.

jer'ry·built" (jer'ē-bilt") *adj.* constructed hastily and with flimsy materials. —**jer'ry·build"** (-bild") *v.t.*

jer'sey (jēr'zē) *n.* **1,** a close-knitted fabric. **2,** a knitted shirt or jacket. **3,** (*cap.*) a breed of dairy cattle.

jest *v.i.* speak facetiously, playfully, or derisively. —*n.* a joke. —**jest'er,** *n.* a person retained to amuse a king; fool.

Jes'u·it (jezh'ū-it) *n.* a member of the Society of Jesus, a Roman Catholic religious order.

jet *n.* **1,** a gush of fluid from a spout. **2,** a spout. **3,** a black coal used in making ornaments. **4,** glossy black. **5,** an aircraft propelled by a jet engine. —*v.i. & t.* [**jet'ted, -ting**] spurt; emit. —*adj.* black. —**jet engine,** an engine producing motion by jet propulsion. —**jet lag,** disorientation resulting from a rapid change of time zone without adequate time for adjustment of the body's biological clock. —**jet propulsion,** propelling force exerted (on aircraft or rockets) by exhaust of gases from burning. —**jet set,** (*Colloq.*) wealthy, usu. young, persons who travel long distances for parties and other social events. —**jet stream,** a high-speed air current.

jet'li"ner (jet'lī"nər) *n.* a jet-propelled passenger airplane.

jet'port" *n.* an airport suitable for jet airplanes.

jet'sam (jet'səm) *n.* goods thrown overboard to lighten a ship.

jet'ti·son (jet'ə-sən) *v.t.* throw goods overboard, to lighten a ship.

jet'ty (jet'ē) *n.* **1,** a pier built in water to

Jew 292 jog

deflect currents or shelter an anchorage. **2,** a landing wharf.

Jew (joo) *n.* a descendant of the Hebrew people or follower of their religion; an Israelite. —**Jew′ish,** *adj.*

jew′el (joo′əl) *n.* **1,** a gem; a precious stone, cut and polished, for adornment or for uses requiring great durability, as in the bearings of a watch. **2,** anything valuable. —**jew′el·er,** *n.* a seller of jewelry.

jew′el·ry (-rė) *n.* gems and precious metals made into ornaments.

Jew′ry (joo′rė) *n.* **1,** Jews collectively. **2,** a ghetto.

jews′-harp″ (jooz′härp″) *n.* a metal reed in a round frame that is plucked and caused to sound different tones by movements of the mouth.

jez′e·bel (jez′ə-bel) *n.* an unscrupulous or vicious woman.

jib *n.* **1,** a triangular sail set foreward of a mast. **2,** a projecting arm, as in a gibbet or derrick.

jibe (jīb) *v.i.* **1,** shift abruptly from one side to the other, as the boom of a sail. **2,** (*Colloq.*) agree with; be in harmony with. —*n.* gibe.

jif′fy (jif′ė) *n.* (*Colloq.*) a moment.

jig *n.* **1,** a tool for holding or guiding, as on a drill or lathe. **2,** a lively dance in triple time. —*v.i. & t.* **[jigged, jig′ging]** dance or play a jig; jump about.

jig′ger (jig′ər) *n.* **1,** a mast or sail near the stern, as on a yawl. **2,** a mechanical device that operates with a jerky motion, as a tripper. **3,** a 1½-oz. measure.

jig′gle (jig′əl) *v.i. & t.* move to and fro in quick, jerky motion. —*n.* act of jiggling; a jiggling motion.

jig′saw″ *n.* a saw designed to cut designs in wood. —**jigsaw puzzle,** a picture cut into many pieces to be fitted together.

ji·had′ (ji-had′) *n.* **1,** a Mohammedan religious war against unbelievers. **2,** any war or crusade in support of doctrine.

jilt *v.t.* dismiss (a sweetheart).

Jim Crow segregation of Blacks.

jim-′dan′dy *adj.* (*Colloq.*) excellent; first-rate.

jim′my (jim′ė) *n.* **1,** a small prying tool used by burglars. **2,** (*pl.*) small chocolate sprinkles used on ice cream. —*v.t.* pry open.

jim′son weed (jim′sən) a noxious weed with white flowers; datura.

jin′gle (jing′gəl) *v.i. & t.* make tinkling sounds. —*n.* **1,** a metallic clinking sound. **2,** verse constructed more for sound than sense. **3,** verse set to music and used to advertise a product, service, etc.

jin′go (jing′gō) *n.* one who favors lavish armament or a bellicose foreign policy. —**jin′go·ism,** *n.*

jinks *n. pl.* (*Colloq.*) pranks; lively merrymaking; usually *high jinks.*

jinn (jin) *n.pl.* [*sing.* **jin·ni′** (jin-ė′)] in Mohammedan mythology, a class of spirits lower than angels.

jin·rik′i·sha (jin-rik′shä) *n.* a two-wheeled vehicle pulled by a man.

jinx (jinks) *n.* (*Colloq.*) a supposed influence for bad luck.

jit′ney (jit′nė) *n.* **1,** (*Colloq.*) a public cab. **2,** (*Slang*) a U. S. nickel.

jit′ter (jit′ər) *v.i.* show nervousness or apprehension. —*n.* nervousness. —**jit′-ter·y,** *adj.* very nervous.

jit′ter·bug″ *v.i.* **[-bugged″, -bug′ging]** dance to swing music with violent convulsive movements. —*n.* one who so dances.

jive (jīv) *n.* **1,** swing music. **2,** a patois of certain U.S. Blacks, used by jazz musicians. **3,** talk meant to deceive or confuse. —*v.t.* confuse, as by loud noise or rapid talk.

job *n.* **1,** one's profession, trade, or employment. **2,** a specific task or stint of work. **3,** (*Colloq.*) matter; state of affairs. —*v.i.* **[jobbed, job′bing]** do work by the piece. —*v.t.* **1,** portion out work. **2,** buy or sell in large or small quantities, for resale to retailers. —**job′ber·y,** *n.* corruption in a position of trust.

job′ber *n.* **1,** a wholesaler. **2,** one who does piecework.

jock (jok) *n.* (*Slang*) a male athlete.

jock′ey (jok′ė) *v.t. & i.* **1,** bring about by skillful maneuvering. **2,** obtain advantage by trickery. —*n.* a professional rider of race horses. —**car jockey,** (*Slang*) a garage attendant. —**disk jockey,** a radio announcer on a program of recorded music.

jock′strap″ (jok′strap″) *n.* a supporter worn by male athletes.

jo·cose′ (jō-kōs′) *adj.* facetious; humorous. —**jo·cos′i·ty** (-kos′ə-tė) *n.*

joc′u·lar (jok′yə-lər) *adj.* playful; joking. —**joc″u·lar′i·ty** (-lar′ə-tė) *n.*

joc′und (jok′ənd) *adj.* cheerful; merry. —**jo·cun′di·ty** (jō-kun′də-tė) *n.*

jodh′purs (jod′pərz) *n.pl.* riding breeches, close-fitting below the knee.

Joe (jō) *n.* (*Colloq.*) a fellow.

jo′ey (jō′ė) *n.* **1,** (*Colloq.*) a fellow. **2,** the young of any animal, esp. a young child or kangaroo.

jog *v.t.* **[jogged, jog′ging] 1,** push slightly; nudge. **2,** align the edges of (sheets of paper). —*v.i.* **1,** move with a jolting motion. **2,** (with *on* or *along*) proceed steadily or uneventfully. **3,** trot; amble. —*n.* **1,** a

fat, fāte, fär, fāre, fäll, åsk; met, hē, hėr, maybė; pin, pīne; not, nōte, ôr, tool poke; nudge. **2,** a projection; an irregularity of surface. **3,** a notch.

jog′gle (jog′əl) *v.i.* & *t.* move joltingly; jiggle.

John (jon) *n.* **1,** (*Slang*) a prostitute's client. **2,** (*l.c.*) (*Colloq.*) a toilet.

John Bull 1, an Englishman. **2,** the English people.

John Doe (*Law*) a male defendant or prisoner whose name is not known.

join *v.t.* & *i.* **1,** put together; combine. **2,** unite with; become a member of. **3,** connect. —*n.* a joint.

join′er (-ər) *n.* **1,** one who joins. **2,** woodworker; carpenter. **3,** (*Colloq.*) one who joins many organizations. —**join′er·y,** *n.* woodworking; carpentry.

joint *n.* **1,** a place where two things come together and are united; a seam; a hinge. **2,** a large cut of meat. **3,** (*Slang*) a disreputable place. **4,** (*Slang*) a marijuana cigarette. —*adj.* **1,** joined in relation or interest, as *joint* owners. **2,** shared by different individuals. —*v.t.* combine; unite closely; articulate.

join′ture (join′chər) *n.* (*Law*) an estate settled before marriage.

joist *n.* one of the horizontal timbers to which are fastened the boards of a floor or laths of a ceiling.

joke (jōk) *n.* something said or done to excite laughter; a jest. —*v.i.* say or do something playful; jest.

jok′er (jō′kər) *n.* **1,** one who jokes. **2,** an extra card in a pack of playing cards. **3,** a clause in a document that weakens its intended effect.

jol′li·fy″ (jol′ə-fī″) *v.* make or be jolly. —**jol″li·fi·ca′tion** (-fi-kā′shən) *n.*

jol′ly (jol′ē) *adj.* gaily cheerful; full of merriment. —*n.* (*pl.*) (*Slang*) excitement; pleasure. —**jol′li·ty** (-ə-tē) *n.* —**Jolly Rog′er** (rä′jər) a pirate flag.

jolt (jōlt) *v.t.* & *i.* shake with sudden jerks; move with a jerking motion. —*n.* a sudden jerk.

Jo′nah (jō′nə) *n.* one reputed to bring bad luck.

jon′gleur (jong′glər) *n.* a medieval wandering minstrel.

jon′quil (jong′kwil) *n.* a plant with pale yellow flowers.

jo′rum (jôr′əm) *n.* a large bowl for mixing liquors.

josh *v.t.* & *i.* (*Slang*) tease or chaff good-naturedly.

joss (jos) *n.* a Chinese god or idol.

jos′tle (jos′əl) *v.t.* push against; bump so as to render unsteady. —*v.i.* shove and be shoved about, as in a crowd.

jot *n.* a very small quantity. —*v.t.* [**jot′ted, -ting**] (usually with *down*) make a written memorandum of.

joule (jowl) *n.* a unit of work, equal to 10,000,000 ergs.

jounce (jowns) *v.i.* & *t.* shake up and down violently; bounce.

jour′nal (jēr′nəl) *n.* **1,** a record of daily transactions or events. **2,** a book for keeping such records. **3,** a newspaper or magazine.

jour′nal·ese′ (jēr″nə-lēz′) *n.* the style of writing characteristic of newspapers.

jour′nal·ism (jēr″nə-liz-əm) *n.* newspaper or magazine writing. —**jour′nal·ist,** *n.* —**jour″nal·is′tic,** *adj.* —**jour″nal·is·ti·cal·ly,** *adv.*

jour′ney (jēr′nē) *n.* a trip from one place to another. —*v.i.* travel.

jour′ney·man (-mən) *n.* [*pl.* **-men**] a trained worker at a skilled trade.

joust (jowst) *n.* a combat between armored knights with lances.

Jove (jōv) *n.* Jupiter, supreme god of the Romans. —**Jo′vi·an,** *adj.*

jo′vi·al (jō′vē-əl) *adj.* cheerful; gay; jolly. —**jo″vi·al′i·ty** (-al′ə-tē) *n.*

jowl *n.* **1,** the cheek. **2,** a fold of flesh hanging from the jaw.

joy (joi) *n.* an emotion of sudden pleasure; exultant satisfaction; keen delight. —**joy′ful, joy′ous,** *adj.* —**joy ride,** (*Colloq.*) **1,** a ride for pleasure in an automobile, esp. when the car is used surreptitiously or driven recklessly. **2,** a trip (usu. on drugs). —**joy stick,** the lever that controls the directions of an airplane's flight; any similar control.

ju′bi·lant (joo′bə-lənt) *adj.* triumphantly glad; exultant.

ju″bi·la′tion (joo″bə-lā′shən) *n.* rejoicing; glee.

ju′bi·lee″ (joo′bə-lē″) *n.* **1,** a special occasion or manifestation of joyousness. **2,** fiftieth anniversary.

Ju′da·ism (joo′də-iz-əm) *n.* the religion of Jews, or adherence to it. —**Ju·da′ic** (joo-dā′ik) *adj.*

judge (juj) *v.t.* **1,** hear and determine authoritatively, as a controversy. **2,** hold as an opinion; deem; consider. —*v.i.* **1,** pass judgment on a cause. **2,** make a critical determination; estimate the value or magnitude of anything. —*n.* **1,** a public officer empowered to administer justice; a magistrate. **2,** an arbiter; one qualified to judge.

judg′ment (juj′mənt) *n.* **1,** the act of judging. **2,** the ability to make accurate determinations; discernment. **3,** a decision, award, or sentence, as of a court of law.

ju′di·ca″tive (joo′di-kā″tiv) *adj.* having ability to judge; judging.

---

tub, cūte, půll; labəl; oil, owl, go, chip, she, thin, *th*en, sing, ink; *see p. 6*

ju'di·ca"tor (joo'di-kā"tər) *n.* one who acts as a judge; an arbiter.

ju'di·ca·to"ry (joo'di-kə-tôr'ē) *adj.* pert. to judgment or the courts. —*n.* **1,** a court of justice. **2,** administration of justice.

ju'di·ca·ture (joo'də-kə-chər) *n.* **1,** the administration of justice. **2,** the whole body of judges and courts. **3,** the jurisdiction of a court.

ju·di'cial (joo-dish'əl) *adj.* pert. to a judge, to a court of law, or to the administration of justice.

ju·di'ci·ar·y (joo-dish'ē-er-ē) *n.* **1,** the judicial branch of the government. **2,** judges collectively. —*adj.* pert. to court judges.

ju·di'cious (joo-dish'əs) *adj.* having or exercising sound judgment; prudent. —**ju·di'cious·ness,** *n.*

ju'do (joo'dō) *n.* a system of exercise and personal defense.

jug *n.* **1,** a vessel for holding liquids; pitcher. **2,** (*Slang*) a jail.

ju'gal (joo'gəl) *adj.* pert. to the cheekbone.

jug'ger·naut" (jug'ər-nât") *n.* an irresistible force.

jug'gle (jug'əl) *v.i.* **1,** perform feats of dexterity or legerdemain. **2,** practice artifice or imposture. —*v.t.* manipulate by trickery.

jug'gler (jug'lər) *n.* a performer of tricks of dexterity, as tossing and keeping balls in the air. —**jug'gler·y,** *n.*

jug'u·lar (jug'yə-lər) *adj.* pert. to the neck, or to one of the large veins in the neck.

juice (joos) *n.* **1,** the watery part of vegetables, esp. of fruits. **2,** the fluid part of an animal body or substance. **3,** (*Slang*) motor fuel. **4,** (*Slang*) electric current.

juic'y (joo'sē) *adj.* **1,** full of juice. **2,** interesting; pithy. —**juic'i·ness,** *n.*

ju·jit'su (joo-jit'soo) *n.* a Japanese method of wrestling.

ju'jube (joo'joob) *n.* **1,** the fruit of several tropical Asian and Amer. trees. **2,** a jellybean.

juke box (jook) (*Slang*) a coin-activated phonograph.

ju'lep (joo'lip) *n.* a sweet drink. —**mint julep,** iced bourbon whiskey flavored with mint leaves.

ju'li·enne (joo'lē-en) *adj.* of vegetables, cut into thin strips. —*n.* a clear soup containing such vegetables.

Ju·ly' (jû-lī') *n.* the seventh month of the year.

jum'ble (jum'bəl) *v.t.* mix in a confused mass; put together without order. —*v.i.* become mixed. —*n.* **1,** a confused mass or

collection. **2,** a state of disorder. **3,** a thin, crisp, ginger-flavored cake.

jum'bo (jum'bō) *n.* [*pl.* **-bos**] a very large individual of its kind. —*adj.* very large.

jump *v.i.* **1,** spring from the ground or from any support; leap. **2,** move with a leap; jolt; throb. **3,** rise abruptly in amount, intensity, etc. —*v.t.* **1,** spring or leap over. **2,** cause to leap or jolt. **3,** give no heed to; disregard. —*n.* **1,** the act of jumping; a leap. **2,** a sudden rise; a jolt. **3,** an omission; an abrupt transition. **4,** (*Colloq.*) a position of advantage; a head start. —**jump suit,** a one-piece suit worn by paratroopers; an article of clothing of a similar design for men or women.

jump'er (-ər) *n.* **1,** one who jumps. **2,** any mechanical device that operates with a jumping motion. **3,** a loose outer garment; (*pl.*) overalls.

jump'y (-ē) *adj.* nervous. —**jump'i·ness,** *n.*

jun'co (jung'kō) *n.* a snowbird.

junc'tion (junk'shən) *n.* **1,** act of joining or uniting; coalition. **2,** place of meeting or joining.

junc'ture (junk'chər) *n.* **1,** a point of time. **2,** a seam.

June (joon) *n.* the sixth month of the year.

jun'gle (jung'gəl) *n.* **1,** a dense growth of rank and tangled vegetation; a wilderness. **2,** (*Slang*) a camping-ground of tramps. —**asphalt jungle,** the city, esp. the inner city. —**jungle gym,** a playground structure for climbing.

jun'ior (joon'yər) *n.* **1,** one younger than another. **2,** one of less experience or inferior standing in his profession than another. **3,** a student in the next-to-last year of the high school or college course. —*adj.* **1,** younger. **2,** pert. to juniors. —**junior college,** a school teaching two years of a college course. —**junior high,** a school teaching grades 7, 8, and 9.

ju'ni·per (joo'nə-pər) *n.* a coniferous evergreen shrub, used in making gin and certain medicines.

junk *n.* **1,** worn-out or discarded material; trash. **2,** a Chinese sailing vessel. **3,** (*Slang*) narcotic drugs. —*v.t.* (*Colloq.*) throw away; discard. —**junk food,** food with low nutritional value. —**junk mail,** third-class mail.

Jun'ker (yûng'kər) *n.* a member of the German aristocratic class.

jun'ket (jung'kit) *n.* **1,** a custard, milk sweetened and flavored, curdled with rennet. **2,** a picnic; an excursion. **3,** an excursion paid for at the taxpayers' expense. —*v.i. & t.* feast; regale; go on a pleasure trip.

jun'kie (jung'kē) *n.* (*Slang*) a drug addict, esp. one addicted to heroin.

jun'ta (jun'tə, hün-) *n.* **1,** a consultative or legislative assembly, esp. Spanish. **2,** a revolutionary caretaker government (usu. military).

jun'to (jun'tō) *n.* [*pl.* **-tos**] a secret political combine.

Ju'pi·ter (joo'pi-tər) *n.* **1,** the chief god in Roman mythology. **2,** the largest planet in the solar system.

ju·rid'i·cal (jû-rid'ə-kəl) *adj.* relating to administrative law.

ju''ris·dic'tion (jûr''is-dik'shən) *n.* **1,** the right of making and enforcing laws. **2,** the domain over which a given authority extends.

ju''ris·pru'dence (jûr''is-proo'dəns) *n.* **1,** the science of law. **2,** the body of laws existing in a given state or nation.

ju'rist (jûr'ist) *n.* one who professes the science of law. —**ju·ris'tic,** *adj.*

ju'ror (jûr'ər) *n.* a member of a jury. *Also,* **ju'ry·man.**

ju'ry (jûr'ē) *n.* a group of persons appointed to hear evidence and decide facts. —*adj.* (*Naut.*) rigged in an emergency; makeshift.

just *adj.* **1,** right in law or ethics: **2,** fair-minded; good in intention; impartial. **3,** based on right; legitimate. **4,** in correct accordance with a standard. —*adv.* **1,** precisely. **2,** very nearly. **3,** barely; by a narrow margin. **4,** (*Colloq.*) wholly; positively. —**just'ness,** *n.* fairness.

jus'tice (jus'tis) *n.* **1,** conformity to moral principles or law; just conduct. **2,** merited reward or punishment. **3,** the administration of law; authority; jurisdiction. **4,** a judicial officer; a judge. —**justice of the peace,** a minor local judge.

jus'ti·fy'' (jus'tə-fī'') *v.t. & i.* **1,** prove or show to be just or conformable to justice, reason, law, etc. **2,** declare innocent or blameless. **3,** make precise; adjust; (*Printing*) make successive lines of type of equal length. —**jus''ti·fi'a·ble,** *adj.* defensible. —**jus''ti·fi·ca'tion,** *n.*

jut *v.i.* [**jut'ted, -ting**] (usually with *out*) extend beyond the main body or line. —*n.* a projection.

jute (joot) *n.* **1,** a plant that grows in warm, moist climate; its fiber. **2,** a coarse fabric made from jute.

ju've·nile (joo'və-nəl) *adj.* **1,** young; youthful. **2,** pert. to or suited for young persons. —*n.* a young person. —**ju''ve·nil'i·ty,** *n.*

ju''ve·nil'i·a (joo''və-nil'ē-ə) *n.pl.* works produced in youth.

jux''ta·pose' (juks''tə-pōz') *v.t.* place side by side or close together. —**jux''ta·po·si'tion** (-pə-zish'ən) *n.*

K

K, k (kā) the eleventh letter of the English alphabet.

kad'dish (kad'ish) *n.* [*pl.* **kad'di·shim** (-im)] **1,** the doxology of the Jewish ritual. **2,** the prayer for the dead.

Kai'ser (kī'zər) *n.* (*Ger.*) Emperor; esp. Wilhelm II, German emperor during World War I.

ka''ka·po' (kä''kä-pō') *n.* [*pl.* **-pos**] a large nocturnal parrot of New Zealand.

kale (kāl) *n.* **1,** a variety of cabbage with curled or wrinkled leaves. **2,** (*Slang*) money.

ka·lei'do·scope'' (kə-lī'də-skōp'') *n.* an optical instrument for creating, by reflection, colorful symmetrical patterns. —**ka·lei''do·scop'ic** (-skop'ik) *adj.* —**ka·lei''do·scop'i·cal·ly,** *adv.*

kal'so·mine'' (kal'sə-mīn'') *v.t. & n.* calcimine; whitewash.

ka''mi·ka'ze (kä''mi-kä'zē) *adj. & n. pl.* (*Jap.*) (aircraft pilots) sworn to make suicidal attacks.

Ka·nak'a (kə-nak'ə) *n.* a Hawaiian.

kan''ga·roo' (kang''gə-roo') *n.* a marsupial of Australia having powerful hind legs developed for leaping. —**kangaroo court,** an unofficial group that acts as a court of law.

ka·o'lin (kā'ə-lin) *n.* a white clay used in making porcelain.

ka'on (kā'än) *n.* an unstable meson.

ka'pok (kā'pok) *n.* a tropical tree whose seeds yield a silky wool used for stuffing cushions, etc.

kap'pa (kap'ə) *n.* the tenth letter of the Greek alphabet (K, κ).

ka·put' (kä-pût') *adj.* (*Colloq.*) ruined; done for.

kar'a·kul (kar'ə-kəl) *n.* an Asiatic breed of sheep; its fur.

ka·ra'te (kə-rä'tē) *n.* a Japanese system of self-defense.

kar'ma (kär'mə) *n.* **1,** in Hinduism and Buddhism, the ethical consequences of the totality of one's actions that determine the destiny of one's subsequent existence or existences until one has achieved spiritual liberation. **2,** fate; destiny. —**kar'mic** (kär'mik) *adj.*

ka'ty·did (kā'tē-did) *n.* a large Amer. grasshopper.

ka'va (kä'vä) *n.* a Polynesian shrub of the pepper family; a beverage made from it.

kay'ak (kī'ak) *n.* a light Eskimo boat made of sealskins.

kay'o (kā'ō) *v.t.* (*Slang*) knock out, in pugilism.

ka·zoo' (kə-zoo') *n.* a musical instrument or toy consisting of a tube containing a membrane that vibrates sympathetically when the player hums into the tube.

kedge (kej) *v.t. & i.* pull or warp (a ship) by the rope of an anchor. —*n.* a small anchor.

keel (kēl) *n.* **1,** a central longitudinal member from which a frame is built upwards, as on a ship. **2,** any central main stem, as on a leaf. —**keel over,** turn upside-down.

keel'haul" (kēl'hâl") *v.t.* (*Naut.*) **1,** haul (a person) under the keel of a ship for punishment. **2,** reprimand severely.

keen (kēn) *adj.* **1,** having a sharp edge or point. **2,** acutely harsh or painful; biting. **3,** having sharp perception of senses or mind. **4,** intense in feeling; ardent. —*n.* lamentation for the dead. —*v.i.* wail; lament (esp. for the dead). —**keen'ness,** *n.*

keep (kēp) *v.t.* [*pret. & p.p.* **kept**] **1,** maintain possession or custody of; retain. **2,** continue or maintain in action or conduct. **3,** carry out; perform; observe; fulfill. **4,** preserve; protect; care for; support. **5,** hold; detain; restrain. —*v.i.* **1,** continue (action, state, etc.). **2,** endure; last. —*n.* **1,** board and lodging; subsistence; maintenance. **2,** the stronghold of a castle. —**keep'er,** *n.* a guardian, guard, or warden. —**keep'ing,** *n.* congruity; appropriateness. —**for keeps,** permanently.

keep'sake" (kēp'sāk") *n.* a souvenir or memento.

kees'hond" (kās'händ") *n.* [*pl.* **kees'hon"-den** (-hän"dən)] a Dutch breed of companion dog.

keg *n.* a small barrel.

keg'ler (keg'lər) *n.* bowler. —**keg'ling,** *n.*

kelp *n.* a large brown seaweed.

Kel'vin *adj.* pert. to the thermometer similar to the Celsius scale but with its 0° fixed at absolute zero (-273.13° C. or -459.6° F.).

ken *n.* range of sight or knowledge.

ken'nel (ken'əl) *n.* a house for a dog or (also *pl.*) dogs. —*v.t. & i.* lodge in a kennel.

ke'no (kē'nō) *n.* a lottery game, precursor of bingo.

kep'i (kep'ē) *n.* a French military cap.

kept *v.* pret. & p.p. of *keep.*

ker'a·tin (ker'ə-tin) *n.* a protein which forms the basis of hair, horn, etc. —**ke-rat'i·nous** (kə-rat'i-nəs) *adj.*

kerb (kērb) *n.* (*Brit.*) street curb.

ker'chief (kēr'chif) *n.* **1,** a cloth worn as a headdress, esp. by women. **2,** handkerchief.

kerf (kērf) *n.* a cut, as made by a saw.

ker'nel (kēr'nəl) *n.* **1,** the substance, often edible, inside a nut or fruit stone. **2,** a grain or seed, as of corn. **3,** gist; nucleus.

ker'o·sene" (ker'ə-sēn") *n.* an oil, distilled from coal or petroleum, used for heat and illumination.

ker'sey (kēr'zē) *n.* a coarse woolen cloth, usu. ribbed.

ketch (kech) *n.* a small sailing vessel.

ketch'up (kech'əp) *n.* catchup.

ket'tle (ket'əl) *n.* a covered vessel for the heating of liquids or for cooking.

ket'tle·drum" *n.* **1,** a musical instrument consisting of a drumhead on a metal hemisphere, capable of being tuned. **2,** (*pl.*) tympani.

kew'pie (kū'pē) *n.* a caricatural picture or doll of a cherub.

key (kē) *n.* **1,** an instrument for opening and closing a lock, valve, circuit, etc. **2,** a control lever operated by the fingers, as on a telegraph, typewriter, piano, horn. **3,** something explanatory; a translation of cipher, symbols, problems, perplexities, etc. **4,** (*Music*) the tonic note or name of a scale; a key signature; the tonality implied by a sequence of chords. **5,** pitch; degree of intensity; tone or mood. **6,** a reef or low island near the coast; cay. —*adj.* principal; fundamental. —*v.t.* provide with a key or reference system. —**keyed up,** tense.

key'board" *n.* the row of keys for controlling a piano, typewriter, etc.

key'hole" *n.* the opening through which a key is inserted in a lock.

key'note" *n.* main theme or principle.

key'punch" *n.* a machine, operated from a keyboard, that punches holes or notches in cards for use in data-processing machines.

key'set" *n.* keyboard.

key'stone" *n.* the central stone bearing the pressure of other stones in an arch; hence, any essential member.

khak'i (kak'ē) *n.* an olive-drab or yellowish-brown color or cloth.

khan (kán) *n.* **1,** an Asiatic title of respect. **2,** a caravansary.

khe·dive' (kə-dēv') *n.* formerly, title of the Turkish viceroy of Egypt.

kib'ble (kib'əl) *v.t.* grind coarsely. —*n.* coarsely ground grain, etc.

kib·butz' (ki-bûts') *n.* [*pl.* **kib"·but·zim'** (ki"bût-sēm')] in Israel, a communally owned, operated, and organized collective farm or settlement.

kib'itz·er (kib'it-sər) *n.* an onlooker who

gives unwanted advice, esp. at a card game.
—**kib′itz**, *v.i.* & *t.*

ki′bosh (kī′bosh) *n.* (*Slang*) **1**, nonsense.
2, a ruinous curse or spell.

kick (kik) *v.t.* **1**, strike with the foot. **2**,
strike in recoiling. —*v.i.* **1**, thrust the foot
forward or outward. **2**, recoil, as a firearm.
3, (*Slang*) complain; resist. **4**, (with *in*)
(*Slang*) contribute. —*n.* **1**, a blow with the
foot. **2**, a recoil. **3**, (*Slang*) a complaint or
objection. **4**, (*Colloq.*) vigor; excitement or
thrill; the stimulating quality of liquor.

kick′back″ *n.* **1**, a violent reaction. **2**, the
return of a portion of a worker's pay to an
employer. **3**, (*Slang*) an amount returned,
as graft money.

kick′off″ *n.* **1**, in football, a place kick
made to commence play. **2**, an event that
begins something, as a fund drive.

kick′shaw″ (kik′shä″) *n.* **1**, something
fantastic and trifling. **2**, an unsubstantial
dish or food.

kick′stand″ *n.* the built-in stand for a
bicycle, motorcycle, etc.

kid *n.* **1**, a young goat. **2**, leather made
from the skin of a young goat. **3**, (*Colloq.*)
a child; youngster. —*v.t.* & *i.* [**kid′ded,
-ding**] (*Slang*) tease.

kid′nap *v.t.* abduct, or carry off forcibly
(a human being).

kid′ney (kid′nė) *n.* either of two bean-
shaped organs that excrete urine. —*adj.*
kidney-shaped.

kid′vid″ *n.* (*Slang*) a television show for
children.

kiel′ba·sa (kil′bä-sə) *n.* an uncooked
smoked Polish sausage.

kill (kil) *v.t.* **1**, put to death; slay. **2**, destroy; extinguish; nullify; cancel; veto; neu-
tralize. —*n.* **1**, the act of killing. **2**, the
culmination of a hunt or quest; an animal
killed. **3**, a creek or river.

kill′ing (kil′ing) *n.* **1**, the act of killing. **2**,
(*Colloq.*) a highly successful stroke of busi-
ness. —*adj.* **1**, deadly; exhausting. **2**,
(*Colloq.*) funny.

kill′joy″ *n.* one who spoils the enjoyment
of others.

kiln (kil) *n.* an oven for drying or baking,
as bricks. —*v.t.* bake.

kil·o- (kil-ə) *pref.* thousand;1,000 times.

kil′o·cy″cle (kil′ə-sī″kəl) *n.* 1,000 cycles
per second.

kil′o·gram″ (kil′ə-gram″) *n.* 1,000 grams,
equal to 2.2 pounds.

kil′o·me″ter (kil′ə-mē″tər) *n.* 1,000 meters, about .62 mile.

kil′o·watt″ (kil′ə-wot″) *n.* 1,000 watts.
—**kilowatt hour,** consumption of 1,000
watts throughout one hour.

kilt *n.* a short plaid skirt, esp. as worn by
Scotsmen.

kil′ter (kil′tər) *n.* (*Colloq.*) good working
condition.

ki·mo′no (kə-mō′nō) *n.* [*pl.* **-nos**] **1**, a
gownlike Japanese outer garment. **2**, a dressing gown; bathrobe.

kin *n.* **1**, one's relatives collectively. **2**,
relationship of those having common de-
scent. —*adj.* **1**, related by blood; of the
same family or clan. **2**, of the same kind or
nature. —**kin′ship,** *n.*

-kin *suf.* of diminutive nouns, as *lambkin.*

kind (kīnd) *n.* **1**, natural constitution or
character. **2**, a class of persons or things of
the same character; a category. **3**, an individual representative (of a class). —*adj.* of
a sympathetic nature; benevolent. —**kind
of,** (*Colloq.*) somewhat.

kin′der·gar″ten (kin′dər-gär″tən) *n.* a
school or class for children of pre-school
age. —**kin′der·gart″ner** (-gärt″nər) *n.*

kin′dle (kin′dəl) *v.t.* **1**, set on fire. **2**,
inspire; stir up. —*v.i.* **1**, catch fire. **2**, become animated.

kin′dling *n.* small pieces of material for
starting fires.

kind′ly (kīn′dlė) *adj.* agreeable; considerate. —*adv.* **1**, in a kind way. **2**, if
you please. —**kind′li·ness,** *n.*

kind′ness (-nəs) *n.* sympathetic nature;
benevolence.

kin′dred (kin′drəd) *n.* **1**, consanguinity.
2, kin; family or tribe. **3**, affinity. —*adj.* **1**,
related by birth or descent. **2**, akin; allied.
3, congenial.

kine (kīn) *n.pl.* (*Archaic*) cows.

kin″e·mat′ics (kin″ə-mat′iks) *n.sing.* a
branch of dynamics dealing with motion
considered apart from mass and force. Also,
cin″e·mat′ics (sin″-).

kin′e·scope″ (kin′ə-skōp″) *n.* (*T.N.*) **1**,
the tube and screen used in a television
receiver. **2**, a film record of a television
broadcast.

kin″es·the′sia (kin″əs-thē′zhə) *n.* the sensation of bodily tension or movement perceived through nerve ends in the muscles,
tendons, and joints.

ki·net′ic (ki-net′ik) *adj.* caused by or pert.
to motion. —**ki·net′i·cal·ly,** *adv.*

kin′folk″ *n.pl.* relatives.

king *n.* **1**, a male sovereign; a monarch. **2**,
a person or thing of preëminent rank in a
class. **3**, a playing card bearing the picture
of a king; the chief piece in chess; in checkers, a piece that has been crowned.
—**king′ly,** *adj.* majestic. —**king′ship,** *n.*

king′dom (-dəm) *n.* **1**, the realm of a
king. **2**, any society or classification. **3**,

one of the classes (animal, vegetable, mineral) of matter.

king'fish"er (-ər) *n.* a kind of diving bird.

king'pin" *n.* **1,** one of the bolts on which the steering axle of a vehicle pivots. **2,** (*Slang*) chief; boss.

king-'size" *adj.* **1,** extra-large. **2,** pert. to a bed made of two twin-size beds joined together.

kink *n.* **1,** a knotlike curl, as in a wire. **2,** a muscular cramp. **3,** a mental twist; obstinate notion; crotchet. —*v.i.* & *t.* twist; curl. —**kink'y** (-ē) *adj.*

kin'ka·jou" (king'kə-joo") *n.* an animal with a long, prehensile tail.

kins'man (kinz'mən) *n.* [*pl.* **-men**] a male relative.

ki·osk' (kē-osk') *n.* a small building, as a newsstand or booth.

kip'per (kip'ər) *v.t.* prepare (fish) by salting and smoking. —*n.* a fish so prepared, esp. a herring.

kis'met (kiz'met) *n.* fate; destiny.

kiss (kis) *v.t.* & *i.* **1,** touch (esp. the lips of another) with the lips, as a caress or salutation. **2,** touch gently in any way. —*n.* **1,** the act of kissing. **2,** a gentle touch or contact. **3,** a kind of candy. —**kiss'er,** *n.* (*Slang*) the face, mouth, or lips.

kit *n.* **1,** an assemblage of tools, materials, supplies, etc. **2,** a case for containing such an outfit. **3,** a small three-stringed violin. —**kit and caboodle,** everything; the whole lot.

kitch'en (kich'ən) *n.* a room in which food is cooked. —**kitch"en·ette'** (-ə-net') *n.* a very small kitchen. —**kitchen police,** soldiers assigned to help in preparing and serving meals; assignment to this duty. Also, **K.P.**

kite (kīt) *n.* **1,** a light contrivance, held captive by a long cord, designed to be supported in air by the wind. **2,** a variety of hawk. **3,** a fictitious commercial bill or check. —*v.t.* (*Slang*) cash (a check) against funds not yet deposited.

kith *n.* one's friends collectively (now used only in *kith and kin*).

kitsch (kitsh) *n.* anything pretentious and in poor taste.

kit'ten (kit'ən) *n.* a young cat. —**kit'ten·ish,** *adj.* playful.

kit'ty (kit'ē) *n.* **1,** a pool formed by card players to defray expenses, etc. **2,** in a card game, the widow. **3,** pet name for a cat. **3,** a collection or fund.

ki'wi (kē'wē) *n.* **1,** a flightless bird of New Zealand. **2,** (*Colloq.*) a nonflying aviation officer.

Klans'man (klanz'mən) *n.* [*pl.* **-men**] a member of the Ku Klux Klan.

kleen'ex (klē'neks) *n.* (*T.N.*) a soft paper handkerchief.

klep"to·ma'ni·a (klep"tə-mā'nē-ə) *n.* morbid addiction to stealing without regard to personal needs. —**klep"to·ma'ni·ac,** *n.*

Klieg light (klēg) a very bright electric light for motion-picture photography, etc.

kludge (klooj) *n.* (*Slang*) **1,** computer garbage. **2,** mismatched parts forming an imperfect whole.

klutz (kluts) *n.* (*Slang*) an inept or clumsy person.

knack (nak) *n.* aptitude; talent.

knap'sack" (nap'sak") *n.* a bag strapped to the shoulders.

knave (nāv) *n.* **1,** rascal. **2,** in playing cards, a jack. —**knav'er·y** (nā'və-rē) *n.* dishonesty. —**knav'ish,** *adj.* dishonest.

knead (nēd) *v.t.* manipulate (dough, plastic material, the body in massaging, etc.) by squeezing, pressing, and thumping.

knee (nē) *n.* **1,** the joint between the two main parts of the leg. **2,** a hinge; a sharp bend or crook. —*v.t.* strike with the knee.

knee'cap" *n.* the bone at the front of the knee joint.

kneel (nēl) *v.i.* [*pret.* & *p.p.* **knelt**] rest on one or both bended knees.

knell (nel) *n.* the sound of a bell, esp. when rung at a death and funeral.

knick'ers (nik'ərz) *n. pl.* short breeches gathered at the knee. Also, **knick'er-bock"ers** (-bok"ərz).

knick'knack" (nik'nak") *n.* an unsubstantial article of food, furniture, or dress.

knife (nīf) *n.* [*pl.* **knives** (nīvz)] a cutting tool; a sharp-edged blade with attached handle. —*v.t.* cut or stab with or as with a knife. —**knife switch,** an electric switch having a pivoted blade that can be pressed between two metal clips to make contact and complete the circuit.

knight (nīt) *n.* **1,** medieval mounted soldier of noble birth. **2,** a title (marked in the Brit. Empire by the title Sir) conferred on men in recognition of merit. **3,** a chivalrous person. **4,** a chess piece. —**knight'hood,** *n.* —**knight'ly,** *adj.*

knight-"er'rant *n.* [*pl.* **knights-"er'rant**] a knight who wandered in quest of adventure. —**knight-"er'rant·ry,** *n.*

knish (kə-nish') *n.* fried or baked dough stuffed with a filling.

knit (nit) *v.t.* & *i.* [**knit'ted, -ting**] **1,** make (fabric) by interlooping a single strand of yarn on needles. **2,** join closely. **3,** contract (one's brows). **4,** grow together, as bones. —*n.* **1,** a style or stitch in knitting. **2,** knitted work.

knob (nob) *n.* **1,** a rounded projection. **2,** a hill. —**knob'by** (-ė) *adj.*

knock (nok) *v.t.* **1,** hit; strike; rap. **2,** (*Slang*) criticize harshly. —*v.i.* **1,** strike a blow. **2,** collide. **3,** make a noise, as repeated blows or collisions; (of a motor) detonate. —*n.* **1,** the act of knocking. **2,** the sound of a knock. **3,** (*Slang*) a deprecating criticism or comment. —**knock down, 1,** sell finally, at auction. **2,** strike (an opponent) so that he falls, in pugilism. —**knocked down,** disassembled (as machinery) for shipment, storage, or repair. —**knock off, 1,** stop working. **2,** complete successfully. **3,** (*Slang*) kill. —**knock out,** eliminate or defeat finally; in pugilism, knock down (an opponent) so that he cannot rise and continue.

knock'er (-ər) *n.* **1,** one who knocks. **2,** a device for rapping at a door: *doorknocker.*

knock'kneed" (-nēd") *adj.* having legs that bend inward.

knock'out" *n.* **1,** victory won by knocking out an opponent. **2,** (*Slang*) a very prepossessing or beautiful thing or person. —**knockout drops,** chloral hydrate, when criminally used to drug someone.

knock'wurst" (näk'wėrst") *n.* a kind of sausage.

knoll (nōl) *n.* a small rounded hill.

knot (not) *n.* **1,** an interlacement of loops in a cord, rope, or ribbon, drawn tight into a bunch, made for fastening or ornament. **2,** any bunch, cluster, lump, knob, or protuberance. **3,** a bond of association; a tie. **4,** a puzzle, problem, or perplexity. **5,** a unit of speed, one nautical mile per hour. **6,** the embedded end of a tree branch. —*v.t.* [**knot'ted, -ting**] **1,** fasten with a knot; form a knot in. **2,** form lumps. —*v.i.* become knotted, snarled, or lumpy. —**knot'hole,** *n.* a hole left by the removal of a knot from wood. —**knot'ty** (-ė) *adj.*

knout (nowt) *n.* a whip or scourge. —*v.t.* flog with a knout.

know (nō) *v.t.* [**knew** (noo), **known** (nōn), **know'ing**] **1,** perceive as fact or truth. **2,** have information of; be acquainted with. **3,** recognize or distinguish in comparison. —*v.i.* **1,** have knowledge or information. **2,** have insight or perception.

know-'how' *n.* (*Colloq.*) expertness.

know'ing *adj.* aware; shrewd.

knowl'edge (nol'ij) *n.* **1,** awareness of facts, truths, or principles; cognizance. **2,** erudition. **3,** what is known; a body of accumulated facts. —**knowl'edge·a·ble,** *adj.* wise.

known (nōn) *v.* p.p. of *know.*

knuck'le (nuk'əl) *n.* **1,** a joint of the finger. **2,** a cut of meat, esp. from the knee. **3,** a protuberance; a hinge. —*v.i.* **1,** (with *down*) apply oneself earnestly to a task. **2,** (with *under*) submit; yield.

knurl (nėrl) *n.* one of a series of ridges, as on a thumbscrew, to afford a grip. —*v.t.* roughen.

KO (kā'yō) *n.* (*Slang*) knockout. Also, **K.O., k.o.**

ko·a'la (kō-ä'lə) *n.* a small Australian marsupial resembling a bear.

ko'bold (kō'bōld) *n.* a gnome.

Ko'dak (kō'dak) *n.* (*T.N.*) a small portable camera, esp. one with a universal lens.

kohl'ra"bi (kōl'rä"bė) *n.* a plant cultivated for its edible stem.

ko'la (kō'lə) *n.* a tree of the chocolate family; its seed (*kola nut*), used in drinks.

ko·lin'sky (kə-lin'skė) *n.* a Siberian mink, and its golden-brown fur.

kol·khoz' (kəl-kōz') *n.* in the U.S.S.R., a collective farm.

kom'on·dor" (kom'ən-dôr") *n.* a shaggy white Hungarian working dog.

kook *n.* (*Slang*) an eccentric or crazy person.

ko'peck (kō'pek) *n.* a former Russian coin.

Ko·ran' (kō-rän') *n.* the sacred book of the Mohammedans.

ko'sher (kō'shər) *adj.* **1,** conformant to Jewish dietary law. **2,** (*Slang*) approved; genuine. **3,** (*Slang*) proper; conventional.

kow"tow' *v.i.* **1,** touch the forehead to the ground. **2,** fawn; cringe. —*n.* a low bow.

kraal (kräl) *n.* **1,** a South African village. **2,** a cattle pen.

kraft (kráft) *n.* a heavy brown wrapping paper.

K·'ra"tion *n.* a concentrated food product used as an emergency field ration by the U.S. Army.

krem'lin *n.* **1,** a Russian castle. **2,** (*cap.*) former headquarters of the Soviet government, in Moscow.

kro'na (krō'nə) *n.* a Swedish coin.

kro'ne (krō'nə) *n.* any of various coins, Danish, Norwegian, or Austrian.

kryp'ton (krip'ton) *n.* an inert gaseous chemical element, no. 36, symbol Kr.

ku'dos (kū'dos) *n.* glory; praise.

Ku Klux Klan (koo'kluks'klan') a secret terroristic society in the U.S., opposed to Negroes, Jews, and Roman Catholics.

ku·lak' (koo-läk') *n.* formerly, a freeholding peasant, in Russia.

ku'miss (koo'mis) *n.* a beverage made from fermented milk.

kum'quat (kum'kwot) *n.* a subtropical

shrub with a pulpy citrus fruit, used chiefly for preserves.

kung'fu' (kung'foo') n. a Chinese martial art.

Kuo'min'tang' (kwō'min'tang') n. a former political party of China.

ku'vasz (koo'väs) n. a large white Hungarian working dog.

kvetch (kvech) v.i. (Slang) gripe.

kwa'shi·or''kor (kwa'shē-ôr''kər) n. malnutrition in children caused by protein deficiency.

ky'an·iz·ing (kī'ən-īz-ing) n. a process for preserving wood. —**ky'an·ize**, v.t.

Kyr'i·e'' e·le'i·son'' (kir'ē-ā''ā-lā'ə-son') (Gk.) a chant of prayer: Lord, have mercy.

L

L, l (el) the twelfth letter of the English alphabet.

la (lä) n. (Music) the sixth note of the diatonic scale. —interj. of surprise.

la'bel (lā'bəl) n. **1,** a slip of paper bearing a name, price, destination, or other particulars, to be fixed on an article or parcel. **2,** a mark or title of identification. **3,** any small strip or flap of paper, ribbon, etc. —v.t. attach or assign a label to.

la'bi·al (lā'bē-əl) adj. **1,** pert. to the lips or a liplike part. **2,** pert. to sounds produced by the lips, as p.

la'bile (lā'bil) adj. apt to lapse or err; unstable. —**la·bil'i·ty** (lə-bil'ə-tē) n.

la'bor (lā'bər) n. **1,** bodily toil for the earning of a livelihood. **2,** the class of persons engaged in such toil. **3,** hard work. **4,** a task. **5,** the pangs of childbirth; travail. —v.i. **1,** work; toil. **2,** be burdened or oppressed. **3,** be in travail. —v.t. work at persistently. Also, **la'bour.** —**Labor Day,** the first Monday in September, a federal legal holiday in the U.S. and Canada.

lab'o·ra·to·ry (lab'rə-tôr-ē) n. a room or building equipped for scientific research.

la'bored (lā'bərd) adj. done laboriously.

la·bo'ri·ous (lə-bôr'ē-əs) adj. **1,** not easy. **2,** diligent; assiduous. —**la·bo'ri·ous·ness,** n.

la·bur'num (lə-bėr'nəm) n. a small leguminous tree.

lab'y·rinth (lab'ə-rinth) n. **1,** an intricate combination of passages difficult to find a way through or out of; a maze. **2,** any thing or condition confusingly intricate. **3,** the canals in the human inner ear. —**lab''y·rin'thine** (-rin'thin) adj.

lac (lak) n. **1,** a resinous substance used in

making varnishes. **2,** shellac. **3,** (Pharm.) milk.

lace (lās) n. **1,** an ornamental fabric or net of fine threads. **2,** a cord used for drawing together edges of cloth or leather. **3,** ornamental cord or braid. —v.t. **1,** bind with a lace. **2,** intertwine. **3,** add spirits to, as coffee. **4,** (Colloq.) beat; thrash.

lac'er·ate'' (las'ə-rāt'') v.t. **1,** tear roughly; mangle. **2,** afflict. —**lac''er·a'tion,** n.

lach'ry·mal (lak'rə-məl) adj. pert. to weeping or tears.

lach'ry·mose'' (-mōs'') adj. tending to shed or induce tears.

lac'ing (lā'sing) n. **1,** a cord fastening. **2,** a beating.

lack (lak) n. **1,** deficiency or absence of something needed, desired, or usual. **2,** what is lacking. —v.t. & i. be without; be deficient (in).

lack''a·dai'si·cal (lak''ə-dā'zi-kəl) adj. languid; listless.

lack'ey (lak'ē) n. **1,** a manservant; a liveried attendant. **2,** a servile follower.

lack'lus''ter adj. dull.

la·con'ic (lə-kon'ik) adj. expressing much in few words; pithy. —**la·con'i·cal·ly,** adv.

lac'quer (lak'ər) n. **1,** a varnish made with natural or synthetic resins. **2,** decorative work covered with lacquer and polished. —v.t. coat with lacquer.

la·crosse' (lə-krâs') n. an athletic field game played with a small ball and longhandled rackets (crosses).

lac·ta'tion (lak-tā'shən) n. **1,** the formation or secretion of milk. **2,** the period of suckling. —**lac'tate** (-tāt) v.i. secrete milk.

lac'te·al (lak'tē-əl) adj. pert. to milk; resembling milk.

lac'tic (lak'tik) adj. pert. to or derived from milk. —**lactic acid,** an acid found in sour milk, etc.

lac'tose'' (lak'tōs'') n. milk sugar.

la·cu'na (lə-kū'nə) n. a gap.

lac'y (lā'sē) adj. netlike. —**lac'i·ness,** n.

lad n. a boy or youth.

lad'der (lad'ər) n. **1,** an apparatus for ascending, comprising a series of horizontal bars fixed to one or two vertical posts. **2,** a blemish in a fabric, caused by the breaking of a warp thread. **3,** any means or way of ascent. —**fish ladder,** a series of pools so positioned as to allow fish to swim over a dam.

lad'die (lad'ē) n. lad.

lade (lād) v.t. [p.p. **lad'en**] **1,** load; burden. **2,** bail out with a ladle.

lad'ing (lā'ding) n. a cargo.

la'dle (lā'dəl) n. a spoon for dipping; a

dipper. —*v.t.* dip out or convey with a ladle.

la·drone′ (la-drōn′) *n.* a robber; highwayman; thief; bandit.

la′dy (lā′dē) *n.* **1,** a woman of good breeding or social position. **2,** (*cap.*) a title in Brit. peerage. **3,** a wife; the mistress of a household. —*adj.* female.

la′dy·bug″ *n.* a small flying beetle. Also, **la′dy·bird″.**

la′dy·fin″ger *n.* a sponge cake shaped like a finger.

la′dy-kill″er *n.* (*Slang*) a man fascinating to women.

la′dy·like″ *adj.* befitting a lady, as in behavior.

la′dy·love″ *n.* sweetheart.

la′dy·ship″ *n.* title or rank of a lord's wife.

la′e·trile″ (lā′ə-tril″) *n.* a drug purported to be effective against some forms of cancer.

lag *v.i.* [**lagged, lag′ging**] **1,** move slowly; fall behind in progress; hang back. **2,** in games, drive a ball toward a line. —*n.* **1,** a falling behind; the amount of retardation. **2,** a hoop around a cylinder.

la′ger (lä′gər) *n.* aged beer.

lag′gard (lag′ərd) *n.* one who lags. —*adj.* lagging.

la·gniappe′ (lan-yap′) *n.* a tip; largess.

la·goon′ (lə-goon′) *n.* a shallow lake or channel.

la′ic (lā′ik) *adj.* pert. to the laity; secular.

laid (lād) *v.* pret. & p.p. of *lay.*

lain (lān) *v.* p.p. of *lie.*

lair (lâr) *n.* the den of a wild animal; a resting place.

laird (lârd) *n.* (*Scot.*) lord.

lais′sez faire (le′sā-fâr′) (*Fr.*) let alone; noninterference.

la′i·ty (lā′ə-tē) *n.* laymen; all those outside the clergy or a particular profession.

lake (lāk) *n.* **1,** a large body of water surrounded by land. **2,** a metallic pigment.

lal′ly·gag″ (lä′lē-gag″) *v.i.* (*Dial.*) loiter; dawdle. Also, **lol′ly·gag″.**

lam *v.t.* [**lammed, lam′ming**] (*Slang*) thrash; beat. —*v.i.* (*Slang*) run away.

la′ma (lä′mə) *n.* a priest or monk of the religion of Tibet.

la′ma·ser″y (lä′mə-ser″ē) *n.* a monastery of lamas.

La·maze′ technique (lä-mäz′) a method for childbirth without drugs, with the mother's active participation.

lamb (lam) *n.* **1,** a young sheep; its meat. **2,** one who is gentle, meek, or gullible.

lam·baste′ (lam-bāst′) *v.t.* whack; pound.

lamb′da (lam′də) *n.* the eleventh letter of the Greek alphabet (Λ, λ).

lam′bent (lam′bənt) *adj.* **1,** moving lightly; licking. **2,** softly bright; gleaming. —**lam′ben·cy** (-sē) *n.*

lamb′kin *n.* a little lamb.

lame (lām) *adj.* **1,** physically disabled; limping. **2,** ineffectual; halting. —*v.t.* make lame. —**lame duck,** (*Colloq.*) an officeholder soon to be succeeded. —**lame′ness,** *n.*

la·mé′ (la-mā′) *n.* a fabric made of metallic threads interwoven with silk, wool, or cotton.

la·mel′la (lə-mel′ə) *n.* a thin plate or scale. —**lam′el·lar** (lam′ə-lər), **lam′el·late,** *adj.*

la·ment′ (lə-ment′) *v.i.* & *t.* express sorrow (for); mourn; bewail. —*n.* an expression of grief; an elegy. —**lam′en·ta·ble** (lam′ən-tə-bəl) *adj.* regrettable. —**lam″en·ta′tion,** *n.*

lam′i·na (lam′ə-nə) *n.* **1,** a thin layer or scale. **2,** layers.

lam′i·nate″ (lam′ə-nāt″) *v.t.* press (layers) together. —*adj.* in layers. —**lam″i·na′tion,** *n.*

lamp *n.* **1,** a vessel for burning an illuminant; any device, chemical or electrical, for providing light. **2,** (*pl.*) (*Slang*) the eyes.

lamp′black″ *n.* soot used as a black pigment.

lam·poon′ *n.* a satire aimed at a person. —*v.t.* assail in a lampoon.

lam′prey (lam′prē) *n.* a snakelike fish.

la·nai′ (lə-nī′) *n.* veranda; terrace.

lance (lâns) *n.* a weapon comprising a sharp-pointed head on a long shaft. —*v.t.* prick or cut open.

lanc′er (lan′sər) *n.* **1,** a mounted soldier with a lance. **2,** (*pl.*) a kind of square dance.

lan′cet (lan′sit) *n.* a surgical knife. —**lancet arch,** an arch acutely pointed at the head.

land *n.* **1,** the surface of the earth, esp. the dry parts. **2,** a particular tract; a region or country. **3,** a tract as property; real estate. —*v.t.* **1,** discharge (passengers or freight); transfer to land. **2,** catch or capture. —*v.i.* **1,** disembark. **2,** arrive at a place or condition.

lan′dau (lan′dow) *n.* a carriage or automobile with a folding top.

land′ed (lan′did) *adj.* **1,** consisting of land, as landed property. **2,** owning land.

land′fall″ *n.* the land first sighted from the sea.

land′fill″ *n.* earth, gravel, etc., used to build up ground level or to fill in a swamp, etc.

land′hold″er *n.* an owner of land. Also, **land′own″er.**

land′ing *n.* **1,** a place where persons or

goods are landed. **2,** a platform in a staircase. —**landing gear,** the wheels, pontoons, etc., on which an aircraft rests on land or water.

land′la″dy *n.* a woman landlord.

land′locked″ (-lokt″) *adj.* (of water) sheltered or enclosed by land.

land′lord″ *n.* **1,** an owner of rented land, buildings, etc. **2,** the proprietor of a hotel, etc.

land′lub″ber (-lub″ər) *n.* one unaccustomed to being on a ship at sea.

land′mark″ *n.* **1,** a conspicuous object serving to bound or identify a place. **2,** a memorable event.

land office a government office for registration of deeds. —**land-office business,** (*Colloq.*) a highly successful operation.

land-′poor″ *adj.* owning much land but lacking capital because the land is unproductive or encumbered.

land′scape″ *n.* a view or picture of rural scenery. —*v.t.* beautify (land).

land′slide″ *n.* **1,** the falling of a large mass of earth down a steep slope. **2,** an overwhelming victory.

lands′man 1, (lantz′mən) *n.* [*pl.* -**leit** (-līt)] a fellow Jew from one's own E. European district or town. **2,** (landz′mən) [*pl.* -**men**] a person who lives and works on land.

lane (lān) *n.* **1,** a narrow passage; a rural road or path. **2,** a fixed route, as across an ocean.

lan′guage (lang′gwij) *n.* **1,** the aggregate of words comprising a system of communication between persons in speech or writing. **2,** such a system peculiar to a country, race, etc. **3,** expression of thought in any way. **4,** linguistics. **5,** diction.

lan′guid (lang′gwid) *adj.* **1,** sluggish from weakness, fatigue, or lack of energy. **2,** spiritless; listless. —**lan′guid·ness,** *n.*

lan′guish (lang′gwish) *v.i.* be languidly; droop, as from grief or longing. —**lan′-guish·ment,** *n.*

lan′guor (lang′gər) *n.* lack of spirit or vigor; dreaminess. —**lan′guor·ous,** *adj.*

lank *adj.* meagerly thin; gaunt. —**lank′y,** *adj.* slim and tall.

lan′o·lin (lan′ə-lin) *n.* a fat from sheep's wool, used in cosmetics, etc.

lan′tern (lan′tərn) *n.* **1,** a portable lamp. **2,** the lamp chamber of a lighthouse. —**lan′tern-jawed″** (-jâd″) *adj.* thin-faced, with bulging jaws.

lan′tha·nide″ (lan′thə-nīd″) *n.* any of the rare-earth elements. Also, **lan′tha·non″** (-nän″).

lan′tha·num (lan′thə-nəm) *n.* a metallic element, usu. included with the rare-earth elements, no. 57, symbol La.

lan′yard (lan′yərd) *n.* a short length of cord used in rigging, etc.

lap *n.* **1,** the platform formed by the thighs when one sits. **2,** support or shelter, like the mother's lap to the child. **3,** the part of one body that lies on another; overlap. **4,** the distance or material required to go around something once. **5,** a rotating wheel for cutting or polishing gems. **6,** the act or sound of lapping liquid. —*v.t.* [**lapped, lap′ping**] **1,** fold; wrap. **2,** cover partly. **3,** get ahead of (a competitor) by one circuit of the racecourse. **4,** cut or polish with a lap wheel. **5,** lick up (a liquid) with the tongue. **6,** wash against; lick. —*v.i.* **1,** be folded. **2,** overlap. **3,** ripple, as waves. —**lap dog,** a small pet dog.

la·pel′ (lə-pel′) *n.* a fold in the front of a coat below the collar.

lap′i·dar·y (lap′ə-der-ė) *n.* **1,** a skilled worker on gems. **2,** an engraver of monuments.

lap′in *n.* a rabbit; rabbit fur.

lap′is laz′u·li″ (lap′is laz′yû-lī″) *n.* a semiprecious stone; its color, sky-blue.

Lapp (lap) *n.* one of a people of Mongolian descent, inhabiting Lapland. Also, **Lapp′-land″er** (-lan″dər).

lap′pet (lap′it) *n.* a loosely-hanging part, as a flap; the wattle of a fowl.

lapse (laps) *n.* **1,** the passing by or away, as of time; termination or cessation, as of a privilege. **2,** a careless mistake; failure; error. —*v.i.* **1,** pass by or away gradually; end. **2,** deteriorate. **3,** err.

lap′wing″ *n.* a ploverlike Europ. bird; the pewit.

lar′board (lär′bərd) *adj.* (*Naut.*) left; port: opposite of *starboard.*

lar′ce·ny (lär′sə-nė) *n.* the wrongful taking of another's goods; theft. —**lar′ce-nous,** *adj.*

larch (lärch) *n.* a coniferous tree; its wood.

lard (lärd) *n.* a grease for cooking, prepared from hogs' fat. —*v.t.* **1,** grease. **2,** garnish or ornament.

lard′er (lär′dər) *n.* a pantry; a stock of food.

lar′don (lär′dən) *n.* a strip of salt pork, bacon, or suet, used for larding meat. Also, **lar·doon′** (lär-doon′).

large (lärj) *adj.* great in size, amount, number, degree, range, scale, etc. —**at large, 1,** not caught or confined. **2,** at length; fully. **3,** (*Politics*) representing no specified district. —**large′ly,** *adv.* in great part. —**large′ness,** *n.*

large-ʹheartʺed *adj.* sympathetic; generous. **—large-ʹheartʺed·ness**, *n.*

large-ʹscaleʺ *adj.* **1**, extensive. **2**, drawn to a larger scale, as a map.

lar·gessʹ (lär-jesʹ) *n.* a liberal gift; generous bestowal of gifts.

larʹgo (lärʹgō) (*Music*) *adj.* slow. *—n.* a slow movement or work **—larʹghetʹto** (lärget′tō) *adv. & adj.* (*Music*) somewhat slow.

larʹi·at (larʹē-ət) *n.* **1**, a lasso. **2**, a rope used to picket a horse.

lark (lärk) *n.* **1**, any of numerous songbirds. **2**, a merry adventure; jovial frolic. *—v.i.* play pranks.

larkʹspurʺ (lärkʹspēr″) *n.* a flowering plant; delphinium.

larʹrup (larʹəp) *v.t.* (*Colloq.*) flog; beat.

larʹva (lärʹvə) *n.* [*pl.* **-vae** (-vē)] the young of any animal that undergoes metamorphosis. **—larʹval**, *adj.*

larʹyn·giʹtis (lar″in-jī′tis) *n.* inflammation of the larynx.

larʹynx (larʹinks) *n.* the part of the windpipe containing the vocal cords. **—la·ryn′ge·al** (lə-rin′jē-əl) *adj.*

la·saʹgna (lə-zä′nyə) *n.* broad flat noodles, usu. served with a sauce.

lasʹcar (lasʹkər) *n.* an E. Indian sailor.

las·civʹi·ous (lə-siv′ē-əs) *adj.* **1**, inciting to lust. **2**, wanton; lewd. **—las·civ′i·ous·ness**, *n.*

laʹser (lā′zər) *n.* a device producing an intense, highly directional beam of light through *L*ight *A*mplification by *S*timulated *E*mission of (electromagnetic) *R*adiation.

lash *n.* **1**, the flexible part of a whip. **2**, a blow with a whip; a sweeping movement. **3**, a stroke of sarcasm or censure. **4**, eyelash. *—v.t.* **1**, flog. **2**, beat or dash against. **3**, assail violently with words. **4**, fasten with cord. *—v.i.* (with *out*) burst into violent action or speech.

lashʹing *n.* **1**, act or result of lashing or beating. **2**, tonguelashing. **3**, a rope used for binding or fastening.

lass (las) *n.* girl. Also, **lasʹsie** (-ē).

lasʹsi·tude (lasʹi-tūd) *n.* weariness; languor.

lasʹso (lasʹō) *n.* a rope with a noose used to catch animals. *—v.t.* catch in the noose of a lasso.

last (låst) *v.i.* **1**, continue to exist or progress; endure. **2**, continue unexhausted. *—n.* **1**, that which is after all others. **2**, end; conclusion. **3**, a model of the human foot, on which shoes are formed. *—adj.* **1**, being all others in time, place, order, etc. **2**, being all that remains; final. **3**, most recent; latest. *—adv.* **1**, after all others. **2**, finally. **3**, on the most recent occasion. **—lastʹing**, *adj.* enduring; permanent. **—lastʹly**, *adv.*

in the last place; in conclusion. **—at last**, finally. **—last straw**, the final burden, indignity, etc., that goes beyond the limit of one's endurance. **—Last Supper**, the supper of Christ and his disciples on the night of Christ's betrayal.

Lasʹtex (las′teks) *n.* (*T.N.*) elastic yarn consisting of silk, cotton, etc., wound around a latex rubber core.

latch (lach) *n.* a device for holding shut a door or gate. *—v.t.* lock.

latchʹet (lach′ət) *n.* shoestring.

late (lāt) *adj.* **1**, coming after the usual or proper time. **2**, protracted in time. **3**, coming near the end. **4**, recent. **5**, recently changed, ended, or deceased. *—adv.* **1**, after the usual or proper time. **2**, not long since. **—latʹer**, *adv.* after some passage of time. **—lateʹly**, *adv.* recently. **—lateʹness**, *n.* **—of late**, recently.

la·teenʹ (la·tēn′) *adj.* denoting a type of triangular sail.

laʹtent (lā′tənt) *adj.* hidden; dormant; undeveloped. **—laʹten·cy**, *n.*

latʹer·al (lat′ər-əl) *adj.* pert. to the side.

laʹtex (lā′teks) *n.* a milky liquid occurring in many plants, as rubber.

lath (låth) *n.* a narrow strip of wood; such strips collectively. **—lathʹy**, *adj.* slender.

lathe (lāth) *n.* a machine that rotates wood or metal while it is shaped by a tool. *—v.t.* shape in a lathe.

lathʹer (lath′ər) *n.* **1**, froth produced by soap and water. **2**, froth produced by profuse sweating. **3**, a state of excitement, fear, etc.

Latʹin *n.* **1**, the language spoken by the ancient inhabitants of Rome. **2**, a member of any Latin race. *—adj.* **1**, pert. to the Latin language. **2**, pert. to any people speaking a language derived from Latin. **—Latin American**, pert. to the Spanish- and Portuguese-speaking American countries. **—Latin Quarter**, a community of artists or section where they live.

latʹi·tudeʺ (lat′i-tūd″) *n.* **1**, freedom from narrow restriction. **2**, the distance of a point on the earth's surface from the equator. **—latʺi·tu′di·nal**, *adj.*

la·trineʹ (lə-trēn′) *n.* a privy.

latʹter (lat′ər) *adj.* **1**, being the second of two mentioned. **2**, more recent. **—Latter-day Saints**, the Mormons. **—latʹter·ly**, *adv.* **1**, recently. **2**, toward the end.

latʹtice (lat′is) *n.* an open network of laths, rods, etc.

laud (låd) *v.t.* praise highly; extol. **—laud′a·ble**, *adj.* worthy of praise.

lauʹda·num (lå′də-nəm) *n.* a medicinal tincture of opium.

laud′a·to·ry (lâd′ə-tôr-ē) *adj.* praising.

lauds (lâdz) *n.sing.* the second canonical hour, usu. beginning at dawn.

laugh (láf) *v.i.* **1,** make a convulsive or chuckling noise excited by merriment or pleasure. **2,** (with *at*) be amused by; deride. —*n.* an expression of mirth or joy by an explosive noise. —**laugh′a·ble,** *adj.* funny. —**laughing gas,** nitrous oxide, used as an anesthetic.

laugh′ing·stock″ *n.* a person or thing ridiculed.

laugh′ter (-tər) *n.* the act or sound of laughing.

launch (lânch) *v.t.* **1,** set or slide (a boat) into the water. **2,** give initial impulse to; set going. **3,** send forth; hurl. —*v.i.* begin action or speech. —*n.* a large open boat.

laun′der (lân′dər) *v.t. & i.* **1,** wash and iron (clothes). **2,** conceal the source or disposition (of money) by passing it through foreign banks. —**laun′der·er,** *n.* —**laun′dress,** *n.fem.*

Laun′dro·mat″ (lân′drə-mat″) *n. (T.N.)* an establishment offering coin-operated washing machines and dryers for public use.

laun′dry (lân′drē) *n.* **1,** an establishment for laundering. **2,** what is laundered.

lau′re·ate (lâ′rē-ət) *adj.* crowned with laurel, as a mark of honor. —*n.* one honored, esp. a poet.

lau′rel (lor′əl) *n.* **1,** a small evergreen tree; the bay tree. **2,** any of several trees and shrubs having similar leaves. **3,** a wreath of laurel leaves, as an emblem of honor. **4,** (*pl.*) honor for achievement.

la′va (lä′və) *n.* molten rock thrown out by a volcano.

la·va′bo (lə-vā′bō) *n.* **1,** a ritual act of hand-washing. **2,** a basin holding water for ablutions.

lav″a·liere′ (läv″ə-lir′) *n.* an ornament pendant from a chain.

lav′a·to·ry (lav′ə-tôr-ē) *n.* **1,** a small room for personal washing. **2,** a wash basin.

lave (lāv) *v.i. & t.* wash; bathe. —**la·vage′** (lə-väzh′) *n.*

lav′en·der (lav′ən-dər) *n.* **1,** an aromatic shrub used in perfumery. **2,** a pale blue-purple color.

lav′ish *adj.* extravagant; generous; abundant; profuse. —*v.t.* expend or bestow in generous amount. —**lav′ish·ness,** *n.*

law (lâ) *n.* **1,** a rule of action prescribed by an authority. **2,** a collection or system of such rules. **3,** jurisprudence; the profession dealing with legal procedure; the bar. **4,** a proposition asserting a natural truth. **5,** litigation. **6,** (*Colloq.*) a law-enforcement of-

ficer. **7,** (often *cap.*) the first five books of the Old Testament. —**law·a·bid″ing,** *adj.* obedient to the law. —**law′giv″er,** *n.* a legislator.

law′ful (-fəl) *adj.* allowed or sanctioned by law. —**law′ful·ness,** *n.*

law′less (-ləs) *adj.* **1,** contrary to or defiant of law. **2,** not regulated by laws. —**law′less·ness,** *n.*

law′mak″er *n.* a legislator.

law′man (lâ′mən) *n.* an officer of the law.

lawn (lân) *n.* **1,** a tract of ground covered by mowed grass. **2,** a thin linen or cotton fabric.

law·ren′ci·um (lâ-ren′sē-əm) *n.* a radioactive chemical element, no. 103, symbol Lw, produced artificially.

law′suit″ *n.* an action to seek justice in a civil court.

law′yer (lâ′yər) *n.* a legal counselor.

lax (laks) *adj.* **1,** lacking in strictness; careless; remiss. **2,** not tense or firm; relaxed. **3,** vague. —**lax′i·ty** (-ə-tē), **lax′ness,** *n.*

lax′a·tive (lak′sə-tiv) *n. & adj.* a mild purgative.

lay (lā) *v.t.* [*pret. & p.p.* **laid** (lād)] **1,** cause to lie; put in a position, situation, or condition (with *up, down, by, away,* etc.); arrange. **2,** overthrow; allay. **3,** contrive. **4,** wager. **5,** bring forth (eggs). **6,** impute; ascribe. —*v.i.* bring forth eggs. —*v.* pret. of *lie.* —*n.* **1,** relative position or arrangement. **2,** a lyric poem or song. —*adj.* pert. to the laity. —**lay an egg,** (*Slang*) fail; flop. —**lay′a·way″ plan,** a method of purchasing whereby the item to be purchased is reserved by a down payment until complete payment is given. —**lay for,** (*Colloq.*) prepare to attack. —**lay hold of,** seize; catch. —**lay off,** **1,** measure off; mark the boundaries of. **2,** discharge an employee, usu. temporarily. **3,** (*Slang*) stop; cease. —**lay out,** **1,** plan in detail. **2,** display. **3,** spend.

lay′er (lā′ər) *n.* **1,** a thickness of some material lying on another. **2,** that which lays.

lay·ette′ (lā-et′) *n.* an outfit of clothing, bedding, etc., for a newborn baby.

lay′man (-mən) *n.* [*pl.* **-men**] any member of the laity.

lay′off″ (lā′âf″) *n.* temporary suspension of employment.

lay′out″ (lā′owt″) *n.* **1,** a sketch, play, or design. **2,** an arrangement, as of furniture; a set of materials or tools; equipment.

lay′o″ver *n.* stopover.

la′zar (las′ər) *n.* a leper, esp. one who is a beggar.

laze (lāz) *v.i.* & *t.* lounge.

la′zy (lā′zē) *adj.* **1,** disinclined to exertion; indolent. **2,** slow; sluggish; languid. —**la′zi·ness,** *n.* —**lazy Su′san** (soo′zən) a revolving tray for food.

la′zy·bones″ *n.* (*Colloq.*) a lazy person.

lea (lē) *n.* a meadow.

leach (lēch) *v.t.* & *i.* wash or drain by percolation of liquid.

lead (led) *n.* **1,** a heavy, soft metal, chemical element, no. 82, symbol Pb. **2,** something made of lead; a weight, bullet, etc. **3,** graphite: *black lead.* —*v.t.* **1,** treat, weight, etc., with lead. **2,** (*Printing*) space between lines.

lead (lēd) *v.t.* [*pret.* & *p.p.* **led**] **1,** go before as a guide; conduct; influence; induce. **2,** direct; control. **3,** go or be first in. **4,** play as the first card. —*v.i.* **1,** act as a guide. **2,** provide passage or access; be conducive. **3,** go first; be in advance; be in command. **4,** make the first play. —*n.* **1,** guidance; direction. **2,** the condition of being first; precedence. **3,** a clue. **4,** the opening words of a story. **5,** the principal rôle. **6,** a wire for conducting electric current.

lead′en (led′ən) *adj.* **1,** made of lead. **2,** sluggish; gloomy. **3,** of a dull gray color.

lead′er (lē′dər) *n.* **1,** one who or that which leads; a chief director, etc. **2,** (*Brit.*) an editorial. **3,** (*Brit.*) a concertmaster. —**lead′er·ship,** *n.*

lead′ing (lē′ding) *adj.* **1,** guiding. **2,** principal. —*n.* (led′ing) (*Printing*) space between lines of type. —**leading question** (lē′-) (*Law*) a question suggesting or inducing a desired reply.

leaf (lēf) *n.* [*pl.* **leaves** (lēvz)] **1,** a flat green blade growing from a stem of a plant. **2,** petal. **3,** a sheet of paper; a page. **4,** a sheet of wood, metal, etc. —**leaf′y,** *adj.*

leaf′age (lē′fij) *n.* foliage.

leaf′let (-lət) *n.* a pamphlet or circular.

league (lēg) *n.* **1,** a confederation of states, parties, etc.; alliance; association. **2,** a measure of distance, about 3 miles. —*v.t.* & *i.* combine.

leak (lēk) *n.* **1,** an unintended aperture allowing the escape of a fluid; any avenue of unintended entrance or escape, as of information. **2,** the act of leaking. —*v.t.&i.* **1,** enter, escape, or allow to escape through an unintended crack, etc. **2,** release information without authorization, usu. to the news media.

leak′age (lē′kij) *n.* act of leaking; the amount that leaks.

leak′y (lē′kē) *adj.* not perfectly sealed. —**leak′i·ness,** *n.*

lean (lēn) *v.i.* **1,** deviate from an upright position; tilt; bend. **2,** incline in feeling, opinion, etc. **3,** rest against or rely on something. —*v.t.* cause to rest against something. —*n.* **1,** a slant. **2,** meat without fat. —*adj.* **1,** not fat or plump; thin; spare. **2,** containing no fat. **3,** scanty; meager. —**lean′ness,** *n.*

lean′ing *n.* a tendency; desire.

lean-′to″ *n.* a rude shelter slanting from the ground to supporting posts.

leap (lēp) *v.i.* **1,** spring through the air; jump; bound. **2,** start eagerly. —*v.t.* jump over or across; vault. —*n.* **1,** a jump or bound. **2,** a sudden rise or start. —**leap year,** a year occurring once every four years containing an extra day (Feb. 29).

leap′frog″ *n.* a gymnastic game.

learn (lērn) *v.t.* & *i.* **1,** acquire knowledge or skill (in). **2,** become informed of or acquainted (with). **3,** memorize. —**learn′ed** (lēr′nəd) *adj.* erudite. —**learn′er,** *n.* a student. —**learn′ing,** *n.* systematic knowledge.

lease (lēs) *v.t.* grant or obtain the use of (land, buildings, etc.) at a fixed rental. —*n.* a written instrument granting such use.

lease′hold″ *n.* property held under lease.

leash (lēsh) *n.* a cord or thong, esp. for restraining an animal. —*v.t.* hold in check.

least (lēst) *adj.* [*superl.* of **less**] little beyond all others. —**least′ways,** **least′wise,** *adv.* (*Colloq.*) at least. —**at least,** in any case. —**in the least,** at all.

leath′er (leth′ər) *n.* animal skin prepared for use by tanning, etc. —*v.t.* make, cover, or furnish with leather. —**leath′ern,** *adj.* made of leather. —**leath′er·y,** *adj.* tough, like leather.

leath″er·ette′ (-et′) *n.* imitation leather. Also, **leath″er·et′.**

leath′er·neck″ *n.* (*Slang*) a U.S. marine.

leave (lēv) *v.t.* [*pret.* & *p.p.* **left**] **1,** go away from; quit. **2,** let remain. **3,** omit; postpone. **4,** (*with off*) stop doing; desist from. **5,** have remaining; bequeath. —*v.i.* go away; depart. —*n.* **1,** permission. **2,** a period of absence by permission. **3,** departure. **4,** (*pl.*) pl. of *leaf.* —**leaved** (lēvd) *adj.* having a leaf or leaves.

leav′en (lev′ən) *n.* **1,** a batch of fermenting dough. **2,** an influence that effects a gradual change. —*v.t.* add leavening to; change.

leav′en·ing *n.* that which causes a leaven; yeast.

leave-′tak″ing *n.* farewell.

leav′ings *n.pl.* residue.

lech′er (lech′ər) *n.* a lewd man. —**lech′er·ous,** *adj.* —**lech′er·y,** *n.*

lec′i·thin (les′ə-thin) *n.* a fatty substance found in various body fluids, in pus, and in egg yolks.

lec'tern (lek'tərn) *n.* a reading stand.

lec'tor (lek'tər) *n.* a reader.

lec'ture (lek'chər) *n.* **1,** a discourse to an audience; an address. **2,** a long, tedious reprimand. —*v.t.* address; rebuke. —**lec'-tur·er,** *n.* one who delivers addresses.

led *v.* pret. & p.p. of *lead.*

ledge (lej) *n.* a flat projecting part; a rim; a shelf.

ledg'er (lej'ər) *n.* a book for recording debits and credits. —**ledger** or **leger line,** (*Music*) a short line above or below the staff extending its compass.

lee (lē) *n.* shelter; the side of a ship away from the wind. —**lee'ward** (-wərd) *adj.*

leech (lēch) *n.* **1,** a blood-sucking worm. **2,** an instrument for drawing out blood. **3,** a parasitic person.

leek (lēk) *n.* a bulbous plant allied to the onion.

leer (lir) *v.i.* cast a suggestive or malicious look. —*n.* an oblique glance. —**leer'y,** *adj.* (*Colloq.*) wary.

lees (lēz) *n.pl.* dregs.

lee'way' *n.* room for movement, expansion, discretion, etc.

left *adj.* pert. to the side or direction that is westward as one faces north. —*n.* **1,** the left side. **2,** (often *cap.*) radical political parties. —*v.* pret. of *leave.* —**New Left,** a loosely organized political movement composed largely of young people seeking radical social and economic change.

left'hand"ed *adj.* [also, **left'hand'**] **1,** preferring the use of the left hand. **2,** toward the left. **3,** (*Colloq.*) insincere. —*adv.* for or with the left hand.

left'ist *n.* a radical.

left'o"ver *n.* a bit of food saved from a meal.

left'wing" *adj.* pert. to the parties or doctrines of the left.

left'y (-ē) *n.* (*Colloq.*) **1,** one who is lefthanded. **2,** a political radical.

leg *n.* **1,** one of the limbs that support and move the human or animal body; any vertical supporting member. **2,** the part of a garment covering the leg. **3,** a straight segment. **4,** one contest of a series. —**leg'gy** (-ē) *adj.* having long legs. —**leg it,** walk; run fast. —**pull one's leg,** (*Slang*) fool one. —**shake a leg,** (*Slang*) hurry up.

leg'a·cy (leg'ə-sē) *n.* property left by will; a bequest.

le'gal (lē'gəl) *adj.* **1,** permitted or established by law; lawful. **2,** pert. to the practice or administration of law. —**le·gal'i·ty** (li-gal'ə-tē) *n.* lawfulness. —**le'gal·ize** (-īz") *v.t.* make legal. —**legal tender,** currency that must be accepted by a creditor.

leg'ate (leg'ət) *n.* an envoy.

leg"a·tee' (-ə-tē') *n.* one who receives a legacy.

le·ga'tion (li-gā'shən) *n.* the staff and headquarters of a diplomatic officer.

le·ga'to (li-gä'tō) *adj.* (*Music*) without breaks between the successive tones.

leg'end (lej'ənd) *n.* **1,** a widely-accepted but unverified story. **2,** an inscription; a caption; a written key. —**leg'end·ar·y,** *adj.*

leg"er·de·main' (lej"ər-də-mān') *n.* sleight of hand; conjuring.

-legged (legd *or* leg'gid) *suf.* having a specified leg or number of legs.

leg'gings (leg'ingz) *n.pl.* outer coverings for the legs.

leg'horn" *n.* **1,** a small domestic fowl. **2,** a hat made of straw from Livorno (Leghorn), Italy.

leg'i·ble (lej'ə-bəl) *adj.* that may be read; written plainly. —**leg"i·bil'i·ty,** *n.*

le'gion (lē'jən) *n.* **1,** a large body of armed men. **2,** any multitude of persons or things. —**le'gion·ar·y,** *adj.*

le"gion·naire' (lē"jə-nâr') *n.* a member of a legion. —**legionnaire's disease,** an acute respiratory infection, often fatal, apparently caused by airborne organisms transmitted by air conditioning.

leg'is·late" (lej'is-lāt") *v.i.* prepare and enact laws. —*v.t.* effect by legislation. —**leg'is·la"tor,** *n.*

leg"is·la'tion (lej"is-lā'shən) *n.* the enactment of laws; the laws. —**leg'is·la"tive,** *adj.*

leg'is·la"ture (lej'is-lā"chər) *n.* a body that prepares and enacts laws.

le·git' (lə-jit') *adj.* (*Slang*) legitimate; honest or respectable, as an occupation.

le·git'i·ma·cy (lə-jit'i-mə-sē) *n.* state of being legitimate; lawfulness.

le·git'i·mate (lə-jit'i-mət) *adj.* **1,** conforming to law; proper. **2,** born of parents legally married. **3,** logically correct; valid. **4,** regular; genuine. —*v.t.* (-māt") make or declare to be legitimate. —**le·git'i·mize"** (-mīz"), **le·git'i·ma·tize"** (-mə-tīz") *v.t.* —**le·git"i·mi·za'tion,** *n.*

leg'man" *n.* **1,** an agent working outside the office. **2,** a reporter covering news at the scene.

leg'ume (leg'ūm) *n.* a plant having pods that divide into halves, as peas and beans; the pods. —**le·gu'mi·nous** (lə-gū'mi-nəs) *adj.*

leg'work" *n.* travel, esp. walking, as required by a job.

le'i (lā'ē) *n.* (*Hawaiian*) a wreath of flowers around the neck.

lei'sure (lē'zhər) *n.* **1,** freedom from necessary occupation; spare time. **2,** convenience. —*adj.* unoccupied; idle. —**lei′sure-ly** (-lē) *adj. & adv.* without haste.

leit′mo·tif″ (līt′mō-tēf″) *n.* **1,** (*Music*) a recurring theme. **2,** a dominant motive or emotion. Also, **leit′mo·tiv″** (-tēf).

lem′ming (lem′ing) *n.* a mouselike rodent of northern regions.

lem′on (lem′ən) *n.* **1,** a subtropical tree; its citrus fruit. **2,** a pale yellow color. **3,** (*Colloq.*) something inferior; a failure. —*adj.* light yellow.

lem″on·ade′ (-ād′) *n.* a beverage of sweetened lemon juice and water.

le′mur (lē′mər) *n.* a small arboreal mammal related to the monkey.

lend *v.t.* [*pret. & p.p.* **lent**] **1,** give temporary custody and use of. **2,** give use of (money), usually for a consideration. **3,** impart; furnish; accommodate (oneself) to. —*v.i.* make a loan (of or to).

length *n.* **1,** distance along a line; linear measure. **2,** the longest dimension of a body. **3,** duration in time. **4,** a piece, stretch, period, etc.

length′en (leng′thən) *v.t. & i.* make or become longer.

length′wise″ *adv.* in the direction of the longest axis. Also, **length′ways″.**

length′y (leng′thē) *adj.* very long. —**length′i·ness,** *n.*

le′ni·ent (lē′nē-ənt) *adj.* disposed to act without severity; merciful; gentle. —**le′-ni·en·cy** (-sē), **len′i·ty** (len′ə-tē) *n.*

len′i·tive (len′ə-tiv) *adj. & n.* **1,** soothing. **2,** mildly laxative.

lens (lenz) *n.* **1,** transparent glass, etc., having one or two curved surfaces, for altering the direction of light rays. **2,** a similar structure in the eye: *crystalline lens*.

Lent *n.* an annual period of fasting or penitence in Christian ritual. —*v.* (*l.c.*) *pret. & p.p.* of *lend.* —**Lent′en,** *adj.*

len′til *n.* a leguminous plant.

len′to (len′tō) *adj. & adv.* (*Music*) slow; slowly.

Le′o (lē′ō) *n.* a constellation, the Lion (see *zodiac*).

le′o·nine″ (lē′ə-nīn″) *adj.* like a lion; pert. to a lion.

leop′ard (lep′ərd) *n.* a large ferocious animal of the cat family.

le′o·tard″ (lē′ə-tärd″) *n.* a close-fitting sleeveless garment worn by acrobats and dancers; (also *pl.*) tights.

lep′er (lep′ər) *n.* one afflicted with leprosy.

lep′re·chaun″ (lep′ri-kân″) *n.* a helpful sprite, in Irish folklore.

lep′ro·sy (lep′rə-sē) *n.* a chronic bacillic disease of the skin and nerves. —**lep′rous** (-rəs) *adj.*

Les′bi·an (lez′bē-ən) *n.* **1,** a resident of the island of Lesbos. **2,** a homosexual female.

lese maj′es·ty (lēz) an offense against, or indignity to, a sovereign or state's sovereignty.

le′sion (lē′zhən) *n.* an injury or wound.

less (les) *adv.* to a smaller extent or degree. —*adj.* [**less′er, least**] not so much, or so large, or so important; smaller in extent. —*prep.* minus.

-less (-ləs; -les) *suf.* without; lacking.

les·see′ (le-sē′) *n.* one to whom a lease is granted.

less′en (-ən) *v.t. & i.* make or become less.

les′son (les′ən) *n.* **1,** anything learned by study or experience. **2,** a session of instruction. **3,** a reproof or punishment. **4,** a reading from the Bible or other sacred text.

les′sor (les′ôr) *n.* one who grants a lease.

lest *conj.* for fear that; to avoid.

let *v.t.* [**let, let′ting**] **1,** allow; permit. **2,** lease; rent out; assign. **3,** propose, cause, or do (as in *Let us go*). —*v.i.* be leased or rented. —*adj.* in tennis, having hit the net. —**let on, 1,** divulge. **2,** pretend.

-let *suf.* little.

let′down″ *n.* **1,** a decrease in force or tension. **2,** disappointment.

le′thal (lē′thəl) *adj.* causing death.

leth′ar·gy (leth′ər-jē) *n.* disinclination to move; sluggishness. —**le·thar′gic** (lə-thär′jik) *adj.* —**le·thar′gi·cal·ly,** *adv.*

let′ter (let′ər) *n.* **1,** a sign representing a voiced sound; one of the characters in writing or printing. **2,** a written communication. **3,** (*pl.*) literature. **4,** literal wording. —*v.t.* mark with letters. —**letter bomb,** a bomb wrapped up and delivered with the mail. —**letter carrier,** postman. —**letter of credit,** a draft on one bank by another, usually given to a traveler. —**letter of marque** (märk) (*Hist.*) a state's license to a shipowner to confiscate foreign shipping.

let′tered (-ərd) *adj.* **1,** in separate letters, not script. **2,** learned.

let′ter·head″ *n.* a printed heading on letter paper.

let′ter·ing *n.* the letters (usu. hand-drawn) in an inscription, etc.

let′ter-per′fect *adj.* exactly correct.

let′ter·press″ *n. & adj.* printing by direct impression of inked type on paper.

let′ter·set″ *n.* an offset printing method.

let′tuce (let′əs) *n.* a plant with large green leaves, used in salad.

let′up″ *n.* a pause for rest.

leu (le-û) *n.* the monetary unit of Romania.

leu′co·cyte″ (loo′kə-sīt″) *n.* a white blood corpuscle.

leu·ke′mi·a (loo-kē′mē-ə) *n.* excessive production of white blood corpuscles.

lev *n.* the monetary unit of Bulgaria.

lev′ee (lev′ē) *n.* **1,** an embankment confining a river; a dike. **2,** a social reception, esp. for a large group.

lev′el (lev′əl) *adj.* **1,** being in a horizontal plane. **2,** having a smooth, even surface. **3,** (of two or more things) rising to the same elevation; equal in degree, etc. **4,** uniform; unbroken; even. —*n.* **1,** an imaginary line or plane parallel to the surface of water at rest. **2,** any instrument for determining such a line or plane. **3,** degree of elevation. **4,** a level surface. —*v.t.* **1,** make level. **2,** raze. **3,** aim. —*v.i.* **1,** seek or achieve a level condition. **2,** take aim; direct a purpose. **3,** (*Colloq.*) be honest or candid. —**lev′el·ness,** *n.*

lev′el·head″ed *adj.* calm and sound in judgment.

lev′er (lev′ər; lē′vər) *n.* **1,** a bar resting on and tending to rotate about a fixed point, the fulcrum, when force is applied at one end. **2,** a means or device used to achieve a desired end; tool.

lev′er·age (-ij) *n.* **1,** the action of a lever; the mechanical advantage it provides. **2,** force; coercion.

le·vi′a·than (li-vī′ə-thən) *n.* something of huge size, esp. a sea animal or ship.

Le′vis (lē′vīz) *n.pl.* (*T.N.*) tight-fitting trousers of blue denim; blue jeans.

lev′i·tate″ (lev′ə-tāt″) *v.i. & t.* float or cause to float in air. —**lev″i·ta′tion,** *n.*

lev′i·ty (lev′ə-tē) *n.* **1,** lack of seriousness; frivolity. **2,** lightness in weight.

lev′y (lev′ē) *v.t.* **1,** assess or collect (taxes). **2,** raise or gather (troops). **3,** stir up; set in motion. —*n.* an assessing or assessment.

lewd (lood) *adj.* lascivious; indecent; obscene. —**lewd′ness,** *n.*

lew′is·ite″ (loo′ə-sīt″) *n.* a gas-producing agent used in chemical warfare.

lex′i·cal (lek′si-kəl) *adj.* pert. to diction, vocabulary, or a lexicon.

lex″i·cog′ra·phy (lek″si-kog′rə-fē) *n.* the writing of dictionaries. —**lex″i·cog′ra·pher** (-kog′rə-fər) *n.* —**lex″i·co·graph′ic** (-kō-graf′ik) *adj.*

lex′i·con (lek′si-kən) *n.* **1,** a dictionary. **2,** a special vocabulary.

Ley′den jar (lī′dən) an early form of electrical condenser or battery.

lha″sa ap′so (lä″sä-äp′sō) a Tibetan breed of terrier with a long, heavy coat.

li″a·bil′i·ty (lī″ə-bil′ə-tē) *n.* **1,** the state of being liable. **2,** a debt; a debit.

li′a·ble (lī′ə-bəl) *adj.* **1,** under legal obligation; responsible; answerable. **2,** affected by a present or future influence, esp. injurious. **3,** (*Colloq.*) apt; likely; probable.

li′ai″son (lē′ā″zon″) *n.* **1,** contact maintained between independent forces. **2,** (*Colloq.*) an illicit affair.

li·a′na (lē-ä′nə) *n.* a tropical climbing or twining plant.

li′ar (lī′ər) *n.* one who tells a lie.

lib *n.* (*Slang*) liberation. —**lib′ber,** *n.* (*Slang*) a member of the Women's Liberation movement.

li·ba′tion (lī-bā′shən) *n.* **1,** a ceremonial pouring out of wine. **2,** (*Colloq.*) a drink; tippling.

li′bel (lī′bəl) *n.* defamation of a person in writing or printing. —**li′bel·ous,** *adj.*

lib′er·al (lib′ər-əl) *adj.* **1,** favoring progress and reform in social institutions, and the fullest practicable liberty of individual action. **2,** (*cap.*) (*Brit.*) of a certain political party. **3,** tolerant. **4,** not strict. **5,** bountiful; generous. —**lib′er·al·ism,** *n.* —**lib′er·al·ness,** *n.* —**liberal arts,** studies (as language, history, philosophy) providing general knowledge, rather than professional or vocational training.

lib″er·al′i·ty (lib″ə-ral′ə-tē) *n.* tolerance; generosity.

lib′er·al·ize″ (-īz″) *v.t.* give broader range or greater tolerance to. —**lib″er·al·i·za′tion,** *n.*

lib′er·ate″ (lib′ə-rāt″) *v.t.* set free. —**lib″er·a′tion** (-ā′shon) *n.* —**lib″er·a′tion·ist,** *adj. & n.*

lib″er·tar′i·an (lib″ər-tãr′ē-ən) *n.* an advocate of the utmost personal freedom. —*adj.* pert. to or advocating such freedom. —**lib″er·tar′i·an·ism,** *n.*

lib′er·tine (lib′ər-tēn″) *n. & adj.* a dissolute or licentious man.

lib′er·ty (lib′ər-tē) *n.* **1,** freedom from bondage, captivity, restraint, etc. **2,** permission granted. **3,** a presumptuous act. —**at liberty,** not engaged; not employed.

li·bid′i·nous (li-bid′ə-nəs) *adj.* lewd; lustful.

li·bi′do (li-bē′dō) *n.* the will to live; all one's energies and desires.

Li′bra (lī′brə) *n.* a constellation, the Balance (see *zodiac*).

li′brar″y (lī′brer″ē) *n.* **1,** a collection of books, records, etc. **2,** a room or building where such a collection is available. —**li·brar′i·an,** *n.* a skilled worker in a library.

li·bret′to (li-bret′ō) *n.* the text or words

of a musical composition, esp. an opera. —li·bret'tist, *n.* the writer of a libretto.

lice (līs) *n.* pl. of *louse.*

li'cense (lī'səns) *n.* 1, permission to do something, esp. a formal authorization; an official permit. 2, intentional unconventionality, in art. 3, undue freedom of action or speech. —*v.t.* grant permission for; issue a license to; authorize. —li"cen·see' (-sē) *n.* one to whom a license is granted. —li'-cens·er, li'cen·sor, *n.*

li·cen'ti·ate" (lī-sen'shē-āt") *n.* one licensed to practice a profession.

li·cen'tious (li-sen'shəs) *adj.* lewd; dissolute; immoral. —li·cen'tious·ness, *n.*

li'chee" (lē'chē") *n.* litchi.

li'chen (lī'kən) *n.* any of a variety of mosslike fungoid plants.

lic'it (lis'it) *adj.* lawful.

lick (lik) *v.t.* 1, pass the tongue over. 2, stroke lightly. 3, (*Colloq.*) thrash; whip; defeat. —*n.* 1, a stroke with or as with the tongue. 2, (*Colloq.*) a hard blow; a vigorous effort. 3, a natural deposit of salt which animals lick. 4, (*Colloq.*) gait.

lick"e·ty-split' (lik"ə-tē-) *adv.* (*Colloq.*) extremely fast.

lic'o·rice (lik'ə-ris) *n.* a leguminous plant; its roots, used as flavoring.

lid *n.* 1, a movable cover. 2, eyelid. 3, (*Colloq.*) a hat.

li'dar (lī'där) *n.* a device similar to radar using laser pulses instead of radio waves.

lie (lī) *v.i.* [lay (lā), lain (lān), ly'ing] 1, rest in a recumbent or prostrate position; stretch out horizontally. 2, be at rest; be buried; remain inactive. 3, (with *down*) rest, press, weigh, or depend. 4, be in a specified place, direction, or position; be found or occur. 5, consist; comprise. 6, (with *in*) be confined in childbirth. 7, (with *to*) head into the wind so as to be as stationary as possible (of a ship). 3, [*pret. & p.p.* lied] speak falsely; have a deceitful appearance. —*n.* 1, relative position, direction, etc. 2, a falsehood; a false appearance. —give the lie to, accuse of lying. —lie in, be confined in childbirth.

lie'der·krantz" (lē'dər-krants") *n.* 1, a German choral society. 2, (*cap.*) a strong, mellow cheese.

lief (lēf) *adv.* willingly; gladly.

liege (lēj) *n.* in feudal custom, a lord or vassal. —*adj.* loyal.

lien (lēn) *n.* the right to hold another's property while pressing a claim against him.

lieu (loo) *n.* place; stead.

lieu·ten'ant (loo-ten'ənt; *Brit.* lef-) *n.* 1, an officer next below the rank of captain (Army) or lieutenant commander (Navy). 2,

assistant; deputy. —lieu·ten'an·cy (-ən-sē) *n.* —lieutenant colonel, commander, general, officers of the grade next lower than colonel, commander, general, respectively. —lieutenant governor, the office in a U. S. state corresponding to vice-president in the U.S. government.

life (līf) *n.* 1, the aggregate of the powers of metabolism, reproduction, mobility, etc. 2, animals and plants collectively. 3, duration of existence. 4, a condition or course of living; career; station. 5, a biography. 6, animation; vivacity; vigor. —life belt, life jacket, life net, life raft, articles designed to protect one from drowning. —life buoy, a buoyant ring used to keep one afloat in the water. —life insurance, insurance whose proceeds are payable when the insured person dies. —life preserver, a buoyant belt to be worn when in the water. —life span, the longest period of expectancy of life.

life'boat" *n.* a boat in which to escape from a sinking ship.

life'guard" *n.* one who patrols a beach to rescue bathers in peril.

life'less (-ləs) *adj.* 1, without life; dead. 2, without spirit; dull; listless. —life'-less·ness, *n.*

life'line" *n.* 1, a cable by which a person can be hauled out of the water. 2, a vital line of transportation or communication.

life'long" *adj.* enduring throughout (one's) life.

lif'er (lī'fər) *n.* (*Slang*) one sentenced to prison until his death.

life-'style" *n.* a person's particular way of living.

life'time" *n.* 1, the duration of one's life. 2, (*Colloq.*) a relatively long time. —*adj.* throughout one's life.

life'work" *n.* the calling or occupation one adopts permanently.

lift *v.t.* 1, move upward in space; raise; elevate. 2, exalt. 3, display; sing loudly with (the voice). 4, (*Colloq.*) steal. —*v.i.* 1, exert lifting force. 2, rise. —*n.* 1, the act of raising or rising; the distance, force applied, or weight lifted. 2, a helping upward or onward; a ride. 3, (*Brit.*) an elevator. 4, exaltation of feeling.

lift'off" *n.* of an air- or spacecraft, the act or time of leaving the ground.

lig'a·ment (lig'ə-mənt) *n.* a band of tissue connecting bodily parts.

lig'a·ture" (lig'ə-chūr") *n.* 1, the act of tying up or binding; the band, bandage, etc., used. 2, a stroke connecting letters, notes in music, etc.; the joint character, as fl, Æ. —li'gate" (lī'gāt) *v.t.* join with a ligature.

li'ger (lī'gər) *n.* the offspring of a male lion and a female tiger.

light (līt) *n.* **1,** that which makes things visible; illumination. **2,** the state of being visible. **3,** electromagnetic radiation, esp. that to which the eye is sensitive. **4,** a source of illumination, as a lamp; a luminous body. **5,** daytime. **6,** a window or window pane. **7,** a means of igniting, as a match. **8,** clarification. **9,** (*pl.*) point of view; principles of conduct. **10,** that which is light. **11,** (*pl.*) lungs of an animal. —*adj.* **1,** illuminated, not dark. **2,** pale or whitish in color. **3,** of little weight; not heavy; not heavy enough. **4,** of little density or specific gravity. **5,** moderate. **6,** not burdensome or oppressive; easy. **7,** not serious or profound. —*v.t.* [*pret. & p.p.* **light'ed** or **lit**] **1,** illuminate. **2,** ignite. **3,** (with *up*) make bright. —*v.i.* **1,** catch fire; (often with *up*) become bright. **2,** dismount; alight. **3,** come to rest; land. **4,** (with *on*) come or meet by chance. **5,** (*Colloq.*) (with *into*) attack. **6,** (with *out*) depart suddenly or quickly. **7,** (with *up*) ignite a cigarette. —**light'ness,** *n.* —**light meter,** a photometer. —**light opera,** operetta.

light'en (-ən) *v.t. & i.* make or become light or lighter.

light'er (-ər) *n.* **1,** a device for igniting. **2,** a barge or boat for freight.

light'face" *n.* (*Printing*) a type having thin light lines (opposed to **boldface**).

light-'fin"gered *adj.* addicted to stealing.

light-'foot"ed *adj.* nimble in footwork.

light'head"ed *adj.* **1,** dizzy. **2,** frivolous.

light'heart"ed *adj.* carefree.

light heavyweight a boxer weighing 160 to 175 pounds.

light'house" *n.* a tower displaying a warning or guiding light.

light'ing *n.* a method or effect of illumination.

light'ning (līt'ning) *n.* a sudden flash of light by the discharge of atmospheric electricity. —**lightning bug,** firefly. —**lightning rod,** a metal rod designed to ground the charge from a stroke of lightning.

light'some (-səm) *adj.* **1,** cheerful; sportive. **2,** buoyant. —**light'some·ness,** *n.*

light'weight" *n.* **1,** a boxer weighing 127 to 135 pounds. **2,** (*Colloq.*) one of small importance or intellect.

light year the distance a ray of light travels in a year, about 5,880 billion miles.

lig'ne·ous (lig'nē-əs) *adj.* of or like wood.

lig'ni·fy (lig'nə-fī) *v.t. & i.* make or become woody.

lig'nin *n.* a tissue found in wood.

lig'nite (lig'nīt) *n.* imperfectly formed coal, resembling wood.

like (līk) *v.t.* regard with favor; be pleased with; feel affection toward; enjoy. —*v,i.* feel inclined; wish; choose. —*adj.* **1,** having resemblance; similar; analogous; corresponding. **2,** characteristic of. —*n.* something equivalent or similar. —*adv.* (*Colloq.*) likely; probably. —*prep.* similar to; in the manner of. —*conj.* (*Colloq.*) as; as though. —**lik'a·ble,** *adj.*

-like *suf.* resembling.

like'li·hood" (-lē-hûd") *n.* probability; expectancy.

like'ly (-lē) *adj.* **1,** probably destined to happen or be. **2,** credible. **3,** suitable; preferred. —**like'li·ness,** *n.*

like-'mind"ed *adj.* in agreement.

lik'en (lī'kən) *v.t.* represent as similar; compare.

like'ness (-nəs) *n.* **1,** a picture, etc., esp. a faithful one. **2,** resemblance.

like'wise" *adv.* **1,** also; moreover. **2,** in like manner.

lik'ing (lī'king) *n.* a feeling of preference, favor, or enjoyment.

li'lac (lī'lək) *n.* **1,** a shrub having large clusters of fragrant flowers. **2,** a pale purple color.

Lil"li·pu'tian (lil"i-pū'shən) *adj. & n.* of minute size; tiny.

lilt *n.* gay, lively rhythm or tone.

lil'y (lil'ē) *n.* any of various bulbous plants with showy bell- or horn-shaped flowers. —*adj.* **1,** pert. to the lily. **2,** white; pale; fair. **3,** pure; unsullied. —**lily-of-the-valley,** *n.* a type of lily. —**lily pad,** the floating leaf of the water lily.

lil'y-liv"ered *adj.* cowardly.

Li'ma bean (lī'mə) a bean with a flat, oval seed.

limb (lim) *n.* **1,** a member of an animal body apart from the head and trunk; a leg, arm, wing, etc. **2,** a large branch of a tree. **3,** a projecting part; an outgrowth, offshoot, etc. —**out on a limb,** (*Colloq.*) in a precarious situation.

lim'ber (lim'bər) *adj.* easily bent; flexible; supple. —*v.t. & i.* make limber; flex; exercise. —*n.* a wheeled carriage of a field gun.

lim'bo (lim'bō) *n.* **1,** a region where certain souls of the dead reside. **2,** fig., a place of oblivion or discard. **3,** a W. Indian dance.

Lim'burg"er (lim'bėr"gər) *n.* a kind of strong, soft cheese.

lime (līm) *n.* **1,** a tropical tree allied to the lemon; its greenish-yellow citrus fruit. **2,** oxide of calcium, prepared from limestone (*quicklime* or *unslaked lime*) used in cement and mortar. **3,** a sticky substance: birdlime. —**lim′y,** adj.

lime·ade′ (līm-ād′) n. a drink made of lime juice, sweetening, and water.

lime′light″ n. a strong light thrown on a stage; hence, publicity.

lim′er·ick (lim′ər-ik) n. a five-line stanza used in humorous verse.

lime′stone″ (līm′stōn″) n. rock composed chiefly of calcium carbonate.

lim′ey (lī′mē) n. (Colloq.; often offensive) a British sailor or ship.

lim′it n. **1,** an extreme point or line; boundary; terminal. **2,** a bound of any kind. —v.t. restrict; confine. —**lim″i·ta′tion,** n.

lim′it·ed n. an express train. —**limited company,** a corporation.

limn (lim) v.t. draw; portray.

lim′ou·sine″ (lim′ə-zēn″) n. an enclosed automobile. Slang, **lim′o** (lim′ō).

limp v.i. **1,** walk with a jerky or lame step. **2,** proceed in a halting, faulty manner. —n. a lame walk or gait. —adj. lacking rigidity or stiffness; flexible; flaccid. —**limp′ness,** n.

lim′pet (lim′pət) n. a sea mollusk.

lim′pid adj. transparent; clear; lucid. —**lim·pid′i·ty, lim′pid·ness,** n.

lin′age (lī′nij) n. **1,** the number of lines (of something in print). **2,** the amount paid per line (of a story, etc.).

linch′pin″ n. a pin that holds a wheel on an axle.

lin′den (lin′dən) n. a tree with wide heart-shaped leaves.

line (līn) n. **1,** a straight mark of little breadth; a band, stripe, furrow, wrinkle, etc. **2,** a string, cord, or rope. **3,** a row or rank. **4,** a row of written or printed letters; a verse of poetry; a short written message. **5,** a connected series. **6,** a boundary or limit. **7,** a connecting wire, pipe, etc. **8,** a railroad, steamship, or other transport service. **9,** a direction; a bearing. **10,** business or occupation. **11,** (Slang) flirtatious banter. **12,** (pl.) plan of construction or action; words to be spoken in a play. —v.t. **1,** bring into line; put in a row; mark with lines; delineate. **2,** provide with a lining. —v.i. (often with up) form in a row; become aligned. —**line drive,** in baseball, a low, hard-hit ball.

lin′e·age (lin′ē-ij) n. line of descent; family.

lin′e·al (lin′ē-əl) adj. in direct line of descent.

lin′e·a·ment (lin′ē-ə-mənt) n. a feature, esp. facial.

lin′e·ar (lin′ē-ər) adj. **1,** involving mea-

surement in only one dimension. **2,** composed of or involving lines.

line′back″er n. (Football) a player stationed behind the linemen.

line′man (-mən) n. [pl. -men] **1,** one who works on, or with, a line of wire, etc., as of long distance telephone. Also, **lines′-man.** **2,** in football, a player in the forward line.

lin′en (lin′ən) n. & adj. **1,** thread, yarn, or cloth made from flax. **2,** (often pl.) articles usu. (or formerly) made of linen, esp. shirts, bedsheets, etc.

lin′er (lī′nər) n. **1,** a ship, airplane, etc., of a transport line. **2,** any instrument for drawing lines. **3,** a material for lining. **4,** in baseball, a ball batted almost parallel to the ground; a line drive.

lines′man (līnz′mən) n. [pl. -men] **1,** in sports, an official who watches boundaries or lines of a playing field. **2,** a lineman.

line′up″ n. an array or combination of persons or things.

ling n. a marine food fish.

-ling suf. **1,** denoting connection with, as hireling. **2,** diminutive, as duckling.

lin′ger (ling′gər) v.i. **1,** remain beyond a usual or appointed time. **2,** dawdle; delay.

lin″ge·rie′ (lan″zhə-rē′) n. women's underclothing.

lin′go (ling′gō) n. (Colloq.) argot.

lin′gua fran′ca (ling′gwə-frang′kə) **1,** a mixed language used in some Mediterranean ports. **2,** any international dialect.

lin′gual (ling′gwəl) adj. **1,** pert. to language. **2,** pert. to the tongue.

lin′guist (ling′gwist) n. one who knows languages; a polyglot.

lin·guis′tics (ling-gwis′tiks) n. the science of language. —**lin·guis′tic,** adj. —**lin·guis′ti·cal·ly,** adv.

lin′i·ment (lin′ə-mənt) n. a soothing liquid medicine for the skin.

lin′ing (lī′ning) n. an interior coating or layer.

link n. **1,** one of the pieces comprising a chain. **2,** something that connects. **3,** a loop. **4,** a surveyor's unit of measure, 7.92 inches. **5,** (pl.) a golf course. —**link′age,** n.

lin′net (lin′it) n. a small Europ. songbird.

li·no′le·um (li-nō′lē-əm) n. a floor covering of heavily coated fabric.

lin′o·type″ (lī′nə-tīp″) n. (T.N.) a typesetting machine which casts each line as a unit.

lin′sang″ n. a civet cat of Java.

lin′seed″ (lin′sēd″) n. seed of flax.

lin′sey-wool′sey (lin′zē-wûl′zē) n. a cloth of wool and linen or cotton.

lint *n*. small bits of fiber or thread.

lin·tel (lin'təl) *n*. a horizontal beam over a doorway, etc.

li·on (lī'ən) *n*. **1,** a large, ferocious cat of Afr. and Asia. **2,** a strong, courageous man. **3,** a sought-after person; a celebrity. **—li'on·ess,** *n.fem.* **—lion's share,** the largest part.

li·on·heart″ed *adj*. courageous.

li·on·ize″ (-īz″) *v.t*. treat as a celebrity.

lip *n*. **1,** either of the two fleshy parts forming the opening of the mouth. **2,** (*pl.*) speech; utterance. **3,** (*Slang*) impudent talk. **4,** a liplike organ or part; rim; edge. **—lip reading,** the reading of the movements of another's lips, as by a deaf person. **—lip service,** insincere praise or agreement.

li′pase (lī'pās) *n*. an enzyme that breaks down fats into acids and glycerin.

lip′stick″ *n*. a stick of cosmetic used to color the lips.

liq′ue·fy″ (lik'wi-fī″) *v.t*. & *i*. make or become liquid. **—liq″ue·fac′tion,** *n*.

li·ques′cent (li-kwes'ənt) *adj*. **1,** melting; becoming liquid. **2,** tending to melt or liquefy. **—li·ques′cence,** *n*.

li·queur′ (li-kẽr') *n*. a sweet, flavored alcoholic liquor.

liq′uid (lik'wid) *n*. any fluid substance neither solid nor gaseous. **—adj**. **1,** being or pert. to a liquid. **2,** like a liquid: clear, transparent, flowing, etc. **3,** in cash or readily convertible to cash. **—li·quid′i·ty** (-ə-tē) *n*.

liq′ui·date″ (lik'wi-dāt″) *v.t*. & *i*. **1,** pay or settle (debts, etc.); convert to cash. **2,** finally close (business affairs, etc.). **3,** (*Slang*) kill. **—liq″ui·da′tion,** *n*.

liq′uor (lik'ər) *n*. **1,** a distilled alcoholic beverage. **2,** any liquid.

li′ra (lē'rä) *n*. [*pl*. **li′re**] the monetary unit of Italy, worth about 1/2 U. S. cent.

lisle (līl) *adj*. knitted of fine, strong cotton or linen yarn.

lisp *n*. the pronouncing of *s* and *z* like *th*. **—v.t**. & *i*. so pronounce.

lis′some (lis'əm) *adj*. supple.

list *n*. **1,** a record of a number of items; an enumeration. **2,** a leaning to one side, as of a ship. **3,** selvage. **4,** a ridge or furrow. **5,** (*pl.*) an arena for jousts. **—v.t**. make a record of; enter or arrange in a list. **—v.i**. **1,** tilt; careen. **2,** (*Archaic*) like; wish. **3,** (*Archaic*) listen. **—list price,** retail sales price.

lis′ten (lis'ən) *v.i*. **1,** try to hear. **2,** give heed; be compliant.

list′er (lis'tər) *n*. a plow for cutting furrows.

list′less (list'ləs) *adj*. indifferent; languid. **—list′less·ness,** *n*.

lit *v*. pret. & p.p. of *light*. **—adj**. (*Slang*) drunk.

lit′a·ny (lit'ə-nė) *n*. a ceremonial prayer with responses.

li′tchi (lē'chē) *n*. a Chinese tree; its sweet nut. Also, **li′chee.**

li′ter (lē'tər) *n*. a liquid measure, about 1.0567 U.S. quarts. Also, **li′tre.**

lit′er·a·cy (lit'ə-rə-sė) *n*. ability to read and write.

lit′er·al (lit'ər-əl) *adj*. **1,** in accordance with the strict meanings of words; not figurative or metaphorical. **2,** (of persons) strict in interpretation; unimaginative; prosaic. **3,** true to fact. **4,** pert. to letters of the alphabet. **—lit′er·al·ism,** *n*.

lit′er·ar·y (lit'ə-rer-ė) *adj*. **1,** pert. to literature. **2,** engaged in writing; learned in literature.

lit′er·ate (lit'ər-ət) *adj*. able to read and write. **—n**. one who is literate.

lit″e·ra′ti (lit″ə-rä'tē) *n.pl*. **1,** learned persons. **2,** the literary class.

lit′er·a′tim (lit″ər-ā'tim) *adj*. (*Lat.*) letter for letter.

lit′er·a·ture (lit'ər-ə-chûr) *n*. **1,** artistic writings. **2,** the aggregate of all writings of a people, period, topic, etc. **3,** literary work. **4,** (*Colloq.*) printed matter, esp. advertising pamphlets.

lith- *pref*. stone.

-lith *suf*. stone.

lithe (līth) *adj*. easily bent; pliant; flexible; supple. Also, **lithe′some** (-səm). **—lithe′-ness,** *n*.

lith′i·at″ed (lith'ė-ā″tid) *adj*. treated with lithium, which imparts a citrous flavor. **—lith′i·a water** (lith'ė-ə) lithiated water.

lith′i·um (lith'ė-əm) *n*. a metallic chemical element, no. 3, symbol Li.

lith·o- (lith-ə) *pref*. stone.

lith′o·graph″ (lith'ə-gráf″) *n*. a print produced by lithography. **—lith″o·graph′ic,** *adj*. **—lith″o·graph′i·cal·ly,** *adv*.

li·thog′ra·phy (li-thog'rə-fė) *n*. printing, now usually by offset, from a stone or equivalent surface of which certain parts are chemically treated to reject ink. **—li·thog′ra·pher,** *n*.

lith′o·sphere″ (lith'ə-sfir″) *n*. the earth's crust.

lit′i·gant (lit'i-gənt) *n*. a disputant at law.

lit′i·gate″ (lit'i-gāt″) *v.i*. & *t*. contest in court. **—lit″i·ga′tion,** *n*.

li·ti′gious (li-tij'əs) *adj*. quick to litigate. **—li·ti′gious·ness,** *n*.

lit′mus (lit'məs) *n*. a substance that changes color in reaction to acid or alkaline presence. **—litmus paper,** a paper used to test for acids and bases.

---

fat, fāte, fär, fâre, fâll, ásk; met, hē, hêr, maybė; pin, pīne; not, nōte, ôr, tool

lit'ter (lit'ər) *n*. **1**, a number of young brought forth at one birth. **2**, a portable bed. **3**, loose straw, etc., for bedding. **4**, rubbish; disorder. —*v.t.* scatter (things) about.

lit'ter·bug" (lit'ər-bug") *n*. (*Slang*) one who litters, esp. in public places.

lit'tle (lit'əl) *adj.* [less or **less'er, least;** or **lit'tler, -tlest**] **1**, small in size, amount, number, degree, or duration; not large or much. **2**, unimportant; low in station. **3**, petty; mean. —*adv.* **1**, in small degree; not much. **2**, not at all. —**lit'tle·ness,** *n*.

lit'tle·neck" *n*. a small edible clam.

lit'to·ral (lit'ə-rəl) *adj. & n.* shore.

lit'ur·gy (lit'ər-jē) *n*. a ritual of public worship. —**li·tur'gi·cal** (li-tēr'ji-kəl) *adj.*

liv'a·ble (liv'ə-bəl) *adj.* habitable; endurable.

live (liv) *v.i.* **1**, have life, as an animal or plant. **2**, remain alive; survive. **3**, continue in existence, operation, etc. **4**, dwell; reside. **5**, have experience. —*v.t.* pass (a kind of life); experience. —*adj.* (līv) **1**, having life; alive; energetic. **2**, burning; carrying electric current; unexploded (of a shell). **3**, performed at the time; not prerecorded. —**live wire** (līv) **1**, a wire carrying electric current. **2**, (*Slang*) a go-getter.

-lived (-līvd) *suf.* aged; having a specified life or existence.

live'li·hood" (līv'lē-hûd") *n*. an occupation that furnishes means of support.

live'long" (liv'-) *adj.* entire.

live'ly (līv'lē) *adj.* **1**, full of life. **2**, vivid; bright. **3**, buoyant; elastic. —**live'li·ness,** *n*.

liv'en (lī'vən) *v.t. & i.* make or become lively.

liv'er (liv'ər) *n*. **1**, the vital organ that secretes bile, etc. **2**, an animal liver as meat.

liv'er·ied (liv'ər-ēd) *adj.* uniformed.

liv'er·ish (liv'ər-ish) *adj.* **1**, having a disorder of the liver. **2**, disagreeable in manner.

liv'er·wurst" (liv'ər-wērst") *n*. liver sausage.

liv'er·y (liv'ə-rē) *n*. **1**, a uniform, esp. one worn by a domestic servant. **2**, the keeping and settling of horses for hire. —**liv'er·y·man",** *n*.

live'stock" (līv'-) *n*. useful domestic animals, esp. cattle.

liv'id *adj.* **1**, dull bluish in color, as a bruise. **2**, furiously angry. **3**, pallid; ashen. —**liv'id·ness,** *n*.

liv'ing (liv'-) *n*. livelihood; (*Brit.*) a rector's post. —**living room,** a parlor.

liz'ard (liz'ərd) *n*. a small four-legged reptile with a long scaly body.

lla'ma (lä'mə) *n*. a large ruminant of So. Amer.; its fine, soft hair.

lla'no (lä'nō) *n*. [*pl*. **-nos**] a plain.

lo (lō) *interj.* look!; behold!

load (lōd) *n*. **1**, that which is carried in a conveyance; the amount that can be carried or contained at one time. **2**, a burden; demand of work. **3**, electrical power supplied or required by a machine, etc. **4**, (*Slang*) too much liquor imbibed. —*v.t.* **1**, put a load on or into; fill; charge. **2**, weigh down; burden; encumber; oppress. —*v.i.* take on a load. —**load'ed,** *adj.* (*Slang*) drunk.

load'stone" *n*. lodestone.

loaf (lōf) *n*. [*pl*. **loaves** (lōvz)] a formed mass of bread, cake, or other food. —*v.i. & t.* lounge; idle away time.

loaf'er (-ər) *n*. **1**, an idler. **2**, a lounging shoe or slipper.

loam (lōm) *n*. **1**, soil rich in organic matter. **2**, a mixture of sand, sawdust, etc., used to make molds.

loan (lōn) *n*. something lent; the act of lending. —*v.t. & i.* (*Colloq.*) lend. —**loan shark,** a usurer.

loath (lōth) *adj.* reluctant.

loathe (lōth) *v.t.* hate; detest. —**loath'ing,** *n*. aversion, disgust, or hatred. —**loath'·some,** *adj.* hateful.

lob *v.t. & i.* [**lobbed, lob'bing**] strike or toss a ball so that it moves slowly in a high arc. —*n*. such a toss.

lob'by (lob'ē) *n*. **1**, a vestibule or anteroom. **2**, persons who seek to influence legislators. —*v.i.* solicit the support of legislators. —**lob'by·ist,** *n*.

lobe (lōb) *n*. a globular or rounded part, esp. of the ear or lung. —**lo'bar** (-ər) *adj.*

lob'lol·ly (lob'lol-ē) *n*. a bay or pine tree.

lo'bo (lō'bō) *n*. a large gray wolf of eastern U.S.

lo·bot'o·my (lō-bot'ə-mē) *n*. surgical cutting of brain tissue.

lob'ster (lob'stər) *n*. an edible marine crustacean having two large claws. —**lobster shift,** the working hours from midnight to 8 a.m.

lob'ule (lob'ūl) *n*. a small lobe, esp. of the brain. —**lob'u·late** (-yə-lət) *adj.*

lo'cal (lō'kəl) *adj.* **1**, pert. to situation in space; occurring in or particular to a specified place. **2**, (of a train, bus, etc.) stopping at many or all stations.

lo·cale' (-kal') *n*. the scene of specified events.

lo·cal'i·ty (-kal'ə-tē) *n*. a place; community; section.

lo'cal·ize'' (-īz'') v.t. restrict to a particular place. **—lo''cal·i·za'tion,** n.

lo'cate (lō'kāt) v.t. **1,** discover or describe the place or locality of. **2,** establish in a particular place; settle. **—lo·ca'tion,** n. **—on location,** of a motion picture, advertisement, etc., photographed or recorded at the actual place depicted, not in a studio.

loc'a·tive (lok'ə-tiv) adj. & n. (Gram.) denoting a case that indicates place.

loch (lokh) n. (Scot.) a lake.

lock (lok) n. **1,** a device that fastens and prevents the opening, detachment, movement, etc., of a door, part, etc.; a catch or brake. **2,** a boxlike enclosure in a watercourse, with gates at each end, for moving boats from one level to another. **3,** any of various wrestling holds. **4,** a tress of hair; (pl.) hair of the head. —v.t. **1,** fasten, secure, or arrest. **2,** close (a lock). **3,** (with up or in) shut in; confine; isolate. **4,** (with out) exclude forcibly. **5,** fix or unite firmly. —v.i. become locked. **—lock'age** (-ij) n. a system of locks; the fee paid to use them. **—lock step,** a method of marching.

lock'er (-ər) n. a cabinet that can be locked.

lock'et (-it) n. a hinged case worn on a necklace.

lock'jaw'' n. tetanus.

lock'out n. the closing of a plant by an employer to force worker's compliance.

lock'smith'' n. a skilled worker on locks.

lock'up'' n. (Colloq.) a jail.

lo'co (lō'kō) adj. (Slang) crazy, as from eating locoweed, an intoxicating plant.

lo''co·mo'tion (lō''kə-mō'shən) n. the act or power of moving from place to place.

lo''co·mo'tive (-tiv) adj. pert. to or having the power of locomotion. —n. the self-propelled vehicle that pulls a railroad train.

lo''co·mo'tor (-tər) adj. pert. to locomotion. **—locomotor a·tax'i·a** (ə-tak'sē-ə) a form of paralysis.

lo'co·weed'' n. a plant of Central Amer. containing a poison that produces temporary mental imbalance.

lo'cus (lō'kəs) n. [pl. **lo'ci** (lō'sī)] a place; locality.

lo'cust (lō'kəst) n. **1,** a variety of voracious grasshoppers or cicadas. **2,** a thorny, white-flowered tree.

lo·cu'tion (lō-kū'shən) n. style of speech; a phrase or expression.

lode (lōd) n. a mineral deposit or vein, esp. of metal ore.

lo'den (lō'dən) n. a woolen overcoat or outer jacket. Also, **loden coat.**

lode'star'' (lōd'stär'') n. a star that serves to guide, esp. Polaris.

lode'stone'' n. a mineral having magnetic attraction for iron. Also, **load'stone.**

lodge (loj) n. **1,** a temporary habitation. **2,** a fraternal society; its place. —v.t. **1,** provide lodging for; shelter; harbor. **2,** put in a place; deposit. **3,** file; deposit. —v.i. **1,** live in hired quarters. **2,** come to rest in a place. **—lodg'er,** n. one living in hired quarters. **—lodg'ing,** n. (often pl.) quarters hired for residence.

loess (les) n. a yellowish loam.

loft (lâft) n. **1,** the space directly under the roof of a building. **2,** a large room used for light manufacturing. **3,** a lifting stroke or impetus. —v.t. & i. send upward; rise.

loft'y (lâf'tē) adj. high; elevated; exalted. **—loft'i·ness,** n.

log (lâg) n. **1,** a bulky piece of timber; a section of the trunk or a large branch of a tree. **2,** a device for measuring the speed and progress of a ship; a record of this: logbook. **3,** a record or register. **4,** a stolid or stupid person. **5,** logarithm. —v.t. [**logged, log'ging**] **1,** cut into logs. **2,** record. —v.i. cut down trees; gather timber. **—log'ger,** n. one who cuts trees for lumber.

lo'gan·ber''ry (lō'gən-ber''ē) n. a berry similar to a blackberry.

log'a·rithm (log'ə-rith-əm) n. the exponent that must be applied to a fixed number (base) to produce a given number. **—log''·a·rith'mic** (-mik) adj.

loge (lōzh) n. a box or area of special seats in a theater.

log'ger·head'' (lâg'ər-hed'') n. a stupid person. **—at loggerheads,** engaged in dispute.

log'gia (loj'ə) n. a gallery or partly open room.

log'ic (loj'ik) n. the science of correct reasoning. **—lo·gi'cian** (lō-jish'ən) n.

log'i·cal (loj'i-kəl) adj. reasonable; persuasive; to be expected.

lo·gis'tics (lō-jis'tiks) n. (Mil.) the science of transport and supply. **—lo·gis'tic,** adj. **—lo·gis'ti·cal·ly,** adv.

log'jam'' n. **1,** a crowded mass of logs in a river. **2,** an impasse in work, negotiations, etc.

log'o·type'' (log'ə-tīp'') n. (Printing) a single piece of type containing two or more letters, a trademark, company symbol, etc. Also, **lo'go** (lō'gō).

log'roll''ing n. **1,** the rolling of floating logs with the feet. **2,** (Colloq.) the trading of favors among politicians.

-logue (lâg) suf. speech or writing. Also, **-log.**

lo'gy (lō'gē) adj. sluggish; dull.

loid *v.t.* (*Slang*) open a spring-locked door with a plastic card.

loin *n.* the part of a body between the lower ribs and hipbone; meat from this part of an animal. —**loin'cloth"**, *n.* a cloth worn around the hips.

loi'ter (loi'tər) *v.i.* **1**, linger idly. **2**, waste time; delay; lag.

loll (lol) *v.i.* lean or lie in a languid, indolent manner.

lol'la·pa·loo'za (lol'ə-pə-loo'zə) *n.* (*Slang*) something admirable or remarkable.

lol'li·pop" (lol'ē-pop") *n.* a kind of hard candy on the end of a stick.

lol'ly·gag" (lol'ē-gag") *v.i.* lallygag.

Lon'don broil (lun'dən) beefsteak served broiled and sliced.

lone (lōn) *adj.* **1**, being alone; solitary; isolated. **2**, unmarried.

lone'ly (-lē) *adj.* **1**, remote from other habitations. **2**, [also, **lone'some**] dejected from being alone. —**lone'li·ness, lone'some·ness,** *n.*

lo'ner (lō'nər) *n.* (*Colloq.*) a person liking or living in solitude.

long (lâng) *adj.* **1**, having great extent in time or space. **2**, having a specified length or duration. **3**, far away; distant in time. **4**, tall; great in amount, number, or ratio. —*adv.* **1**, to a protracted extent, esp. in time. **2**, to a specified extent. —*n.* **1**, a long time. **2**, something long. —*v.i.* feel a strong desire; yearn; hanker. —**long distance,** telephone service between different cities. —**long face,** an expression of dejection or depression. —**long green,** (*Slang*) paper money. —**long shot,** an entry, venture, etc., not very likely to win or to succeed. —**long ton,** 2,240 pounds.

long'boat" *n.* the principal boat carried aboard a merchant vessel.

long'drawn" *adj.* prolonged.

lon·ge'vi·ty (lân-jev'ə-tē) *n.* duration of life; long life.

long'hair" *n. & adj.* (*Colloq.*) overly intellectual or refined.

long'hand" *n.* ordinary handwriting.

long'horn" *n.* a kind of cattle.

long'ing *n.* prolonged desire.

lon'gi·tude" (lon'jə-tūd") *n.* distance on the earth's surface east or west of a given meridian, esp. that of Greenwich. —**lon"gi·tu'di·nal,** *adj.*

long play (*T.N.*) a 12-inch 33 1/3 r.p.m. phonograph record. —**long'play"ing,** *adj.*

long-'range" *adj.* designed to travel long distances.

long'shore'man (-mən) *n.* [*pl.* **-men**] one who loads or unloads ships.

long'stand"ing *adj.* existing or continuing for a long time.

long'suf'fer·ing *adj.* bearing injuries or provocations with patience.

long'term" *adj.* having a relatively long duration.

long'time" *adj.* longstanding.

long'wind"ed *adj.* tediously long (of a speech, etc.). —**long'wind"ed·ness,** *n.*

loo *n.* a popular Eng. card game.

loo'ey (loo'ē) *n.* (*Slang*) lieutenant. Also, **loo'ie.**

look (lûk) *v.i.* **1**, use the eyes; exercise the power of vision. **2**, afford a view or outlook. **3**, keep watch; take heed. **4**, expect or hope (for). **5**, appear. —*v.t.* **1**, (usually with *up*) try to find. **2**, suggest by a look or appearance. —*n.* **1**, a visual examination or search. **2**, the act of looking. **3**, (often *pl.*) outward appearance or aspect. —**look'ing glass,** a mirror. —**look sharp,** be alert or careful.

look'er *n.* **1**, a watcher. **2**, a handsome person. —**look"er-on',** *n.* a spectator.

look'out" *n.* **1**, a watch kept; a watchman; his post. **2**, (*Colloq.*) an object of care or concern.

look-'see" *n.* (*Colloq.*) a look.

loom *n.* a machine for weaving cloth from yarn or thread. —*v.i.* **1**, come into view indistinctly. **2**, seem large or portentous.

loon *n.* **1**, a fish-eating diving bird. **2**, a stupid person.

loon'y *adj. & n.* (*Colloq.*) crazy. —**loony bin,** (*Slang*) an insane asylum.

loop *n.* **1**, a portion of rope, ribbon, etc., doubled back on itself to form an open eye. **2**, something of similar shape. —*v.t.* form a loop in; make into a loop; encircle with a loop. —*v.i.* move in a loop. —**looped** (loopt) *adj.* (*Colloq.*) drunk. —**loop'y,** *adj.* (*Slang*) eccentric or crazy.

loop'hole" *n.* any means of escape or evasion.

loose (loos) *adj.* **1**, free from fetters or restraint; joined slackly or not at all; not tight or close; not bundled. **2**, open or porous. **3**, slack; diffuse; not concise. **4**, wanton; dissolute. —*v.t.* **1**, make loose; set free; release; untie. **2**, relax. —**loose'ness,** *n.* —**at loose ends,** unoccupied; disorderly.

loose-'leaf" *adj.* having leaves or sheets which can be removed easily.

loos'en (loo'sən) *v.t. & i* make or become loose or looser.

loot *n.* booty seized in war; plunder; spoils; something stolen. —*v.t.* pillage; rob. —**loot'er,** *n.*

lop *v.t.* [**lopped, lop'ping**] **1**, cut off; trim

by cutting off superfluous parts. **2,** let droop. —*v.i.* droop.

lope (lōp) *v.i.* move with a long, easy stride; canter. —*n.* this gait.

lop'sid″ed (lop′sī″did) *adj.* heavier on, or leaning to, one side. —**lop'sid″ed·ness,** *n.*

lo·qua'cious (lō-kwā′shəs) *adj.* talkative. —**lo·quac'i·ty** (-kwas′ə-tē) *n.*

lo'ran (lôr′an) *n.* an electronic device by which a navigator can determine his position from radio signals.

lord (lôrd) *n.* **1,** a master; a nobleman: a title of rank. **2,** (*cap.*) God; Jesus Christ. —**lord'ling,** *n.* a minor nobleman. —**lord'ship,** *n.*

lord'ly (-lė) *adj.* **1,** imperious; insolent. **2,** befitting a lord; magnificent. —**lord'li·ness,** *n.*

lore (lôr) *n.* the store of knowledge about a particular subject.

lor'e·lei″ (lôr′ə-lī″) *n.* a siren (def. l).

lor·gnette' (lôr-nyet′) *n.* eyeglasses mounted on a handle.

lor'i·keet″ (lôr′ə-kēt″) *n.* a small parrot, a kind of lory.

lorn (lôrn) *adj.* forsaken; desolate (*obs.* except in compounds, as *lovelorn*).

lor'ry (lor′ė) *n.* a truck, esp. (*Brit.*) a motor truck.

lo'ry (lôr′ė) *n.* a small Pacific parrot.

lose (looz) *v.t.* [*pret. & p.p.* **lost**] **1,** miss and not know where to find. **2,** be deprived of; be parted from. **3,** cease to have. **4,** cause or suffer defeat in (a game). —*v.i.* suffer loss; be defeated. —**los'er,** *n.*

loss (lâs) *n.* **1,** failure to hold, keep, or preserve. **2,** that which is lost. **3,** wastage. **4,** defeat; ruin. —**at a loss,** bewildered; uncertain. —**loss leader,** an item sold at a loss to attract customers.

lost (lâst) *adj.* **1,** no longer possessed. **2,** wasted. **3,** unable to find one's way. —*v.* pret. & p.p. of *lose.*

lot *n.* **1,** a station or condition determined by chance or destiny. **2,** a means of deciding something by chance. **3,** a distinct portion or parcel, esp. of land. **4,** (*Colloq.*) a great many; a great deal.

lo'tion (lō′shən) *n.* a liquid medicine for the skin.

lot'ter·y (lot′ə-rė) *n.* a method of selling numbered tickets and awarding prizes to the holders of certain numbers drawn by lot.

lot'to (lot′ō) *n.* a kind of lottery game; bingo.

lo'tus (lō′təs) *n.* **1,** a plant of Greek legend, possibly a jujube shrub or nettle tree. **2,** any of a variety of water lilies. **3,** a genus of leguminous plants. **4,** a sitting position in yoga, legs crossed over one another.

loud (lowd) *adj.* **1,** strongly audible. **2,** vehement; noisy. **3,** stormy; turbulent. **4,** urgent; emphatic. **5,** excessively showy; overdone. **6,** vulgar in manners or taste. —**loud'ness,** *n.*

loud'mouthed″ (-mowth̸d″) *adj.* arrogantly talkative. —**loud'mouth″,** *n.*

loud'speak″er *n.* a device for amplifying sound to make it widely audible.

lounge (lownj) *v.i.* **1,** move or recline listlessly; loll. **2,** pass the time idly. —*n.* **1,** a public waiting room. **2,** a kind of long sofa. **3,** an indolent gait or stooping posture.

loupe (loop) *n.* a magnifying glass held in the eye, used by jewelers, etc.

louse (lows) *n.* [*pl.* **lice** (līs)] **1,** a small blood-sucking insect; any of various other parasitic insects. **2,** (*Slang*) a contemptible person. —*v.t.* (with *up*) (*Slang*) muddle or bungle; execute poorly.

lous'y (low′zė) *adj.* **1,** infested with lice. **2,** (*Slang*) mean or contemptible. **3,** (*Slang*) abundantly supplied. —**lous'i·ness,** *n.*

lout (lowt) *n.* an awkward, uncouth, or boorish fellow. —**lout'ish,** *adj.*

lou'ver (loo′vər) *n.* a slit, esp. one of a number serving as air vents.

love (luv) *n.* **1,** affection for another person, esp. of the opposite sex. **2,** an object of affection; a sweetheart. **3,** any strong liking or affection. **4,** (in games) a score of zero. —*v.t. & i.* have love, affection, or liking for. —**lov'a·ble,** *adj.* —**love seat,** a settee for two.

love'bird″ *n.* **1,** a kind of parrot or parakeet, remarkable for the affection it shows its mate. **2,** (usu. *pl.*) lovers.

love'lorn″ *adj.* forsaken by a loved one.

love'ly (-lė) *adj.* beautiful; delightful. —**love'li·ness,** *n.*

lov'er (luv′ər) *n.* **1,** one who loves, esp. a man who loves a woman. **2,** one with a special liking for something.

love'sick″ *adj.* disconsolate because of unrequited love.

lov'ing *adj.* very affectionate. —**loving cup,** a large cup from which many can drink; such a cup used as a trophy.

low (lō) *adj.* **1,** situated not far above the ground or base; not high; below a usual or standard level. **2,** deep. **3,** prostrate or dead. **4,** not high in scale, quality, or degree; moderate; simple. **5,** inferior. **6,** base; mean; coarse. **7,** not many in number. **8,** not loud; soft; feeble. **9,** dejected; depressed. —*adv.* **1,** in a low position, degree, etc. **2,** cheaply. **3,** in low tone or pitch; quietly. —*n.* **1,** that which is low. **2,** a low point; a time or feeling of depression. **3,** (*Meteorol.*) a low-pressure area. **4,** the lowest gear ratio for forward progress in an automobile transmission. **5,** the sound uttered by cattle. —*v.i. & t.* sound or utter as cattle do; moo.

low'boy" *n.* a chest of drawers on short legs.

low'brow" *n. & adj.* (*Slang*) one of low intellectual tastes.

low'down' (*Slang*) *adj.* contemptible. —*n.* inside information.

low'er (lō'ər) *v.t.* **1,** cause to descend; take down. **2,** reduce; degrade; humble; humiliate. —*v.i.* **1,** decrease. **2,** descend; sink. —**low"er·case'**, *adj.* in letters not capitals.

low'er (low'ər) *v.i.* **1,** scowl; frown. **2,** appear dark and threatening.

low'key" *adj.* low in intensity; restrained.

low'land (lō'lənd) *n.* territory low in elevation.

low'ly (lō'lē) *adj.* humble. —**low'li·ness,** *n.*

low-'mind"ed *adj.* having a vulgar mind. —**low'mind"ed·ness,** *n.*

low-'rise" *adj.* having one or two stories and not equipped with elevators.

low-'spir"it·ed (-id) *adj.* dejected; depressed. —**low"spir'it·ed·ness,** *n.*

lox (loks) *n.* smoked salmon.

loy'al (loi'əl) *adj.* **1,** faithful; constant in devotion or regard. **2,** manifesting fidelity. —**loy'al·ist,** *n.* one who remains loyal to a government during a rebellion.

loy'al·ty (-tē) *n.* state of being loyal; fidelity.

loz'enge (loz'ənj) *n.* **1** a sweet pill. **2,** a diamond-shaped figure.

lu'au (loo'ow) *n.* an Hawaiian feast.

lub'ber (lub'ər) *n.* a clumsy or stupid fellow; an unskillful sailor. —**lub'ber·ly,** *adj.*

lube (loob) (*Slang*) *n.* lubrication. —*v.t.* lubricate.

lu'bri·cant (loo'bri-kənt) *n.* a material for lubricating, as grease.

lu'bri·cate" (loo'bri-kāt") *v.t.* **1,** apply oil or grease to. **2,** make smooth. —**lu"bri·ca'tion,** *n.*

lu'bri·cous (loo'bri-kəs) *adj.* **1,** smooth; slippery. **2,** unstable; shifty. **3,** lewd. —**lu·bric'i·ty** (loo-bris'ə-tē) *n.*

lu'cent (loo'sənt) *adj.* shining. —**lu'cence,** *n.*

lu·cerne' (loo-sẽrn') *n.* alfalfa.

lu'cid (loo'sid) *adj.* **1,** clear; easily understood; distinct. **2,** sane; rational. **3,** shining. —**lu·cid'i·ty,** *n.*

lu'cite (loo'sīt) *n.* (*T.N.*) a plastic having unusual transparency and properties of light transmission.

luck (luk) *n.* **1,** a trend of chance events. **2,** good fortune.

luck'y (-ē) *adj.* **1,** bringing good fortune; favorable. **2,** fortunate. **3,** chance; fortuitous. —**luck'i·ness,** *n.*

lu'cra·tive (loo'krə-tiv) *adj.* yielding gain; profitable.

lu'cre (loo'kər) *n.* money; profit (usually contemptuous).

lu'cu·brate" (loo'kyû-brāt") *v.i.* work or study laboriously, esp. at night. —**lu"cu·bra'tion,** *n.*

lu'di·crous (loo'di-krəs) *adj.* absurd; ridiculous. —**lu'di·crous·ness,** *n.*

luff (luf) *v.i.* turn the bow of a ship toward the wind. —*n.* the foreward edge of a fore-and-aft sail.

lug *v.t. & i.* [**lugged, lug'ging**] carry or drag with effort. —*n.* **1,** a yank, tug, or haul. **2,** a projecting earlike part; a tab, flange, or cam. **3,** a sluggish fellow.

luge (loozh) *n.* **1,** a small sled. **2,** an Olympic sledding event.

lug'gage (lug'ij) *n.* trunks, valises, etc.; baggage.

lug'ger (lug'ər) *n.* a vessel rigged with lugsails. —**lug'sail",** *n.* a quadrilateral sail.

lu·gu'bri·ous (loo-gū'brē-əs) *adj.* mournful; doleful; dejected. —**lu·gu'bri·ous·ness,** *n.*

lug'worm" *n.* an annelid marine worm much used for bait.

luke'warm" (look'wôrm") *adj.* **1,** tepid; **2,** unenthusiastic. —**luke'warm"ness,** *n.*

lull (lul) *v.t.* soothe; assuage; calm. —*v.i.* become quiet; subside. —*n.* a period of temporary quiet or rest.

lull'a·by" (lul'ə-bī") *n.* a song to lull a child to sleep.

lu'lu" (loo'loo") *n.* (*Slang*) an exceptional person or incident.

lum·ba'go (lum-bā'gō) *n.* rheumatic pain in muscles of the back.

lum'bar (lum'bər) *adj.* pert. to the loins.

lum'ber (lum'bər) *n.* timber sawed or split for use. —*v.i.* walk clumsily.

lum'ber·jack" *n.* one who cuts lumber.

lum'ber·yard" *n.* a place where building materials, esp. lumber, are sold.

lu'men (loo'mən) *n.* [*pl.* **lu'mi·na** (-mi-nə)] a unit of light flow.

lu'mi·nar·y (loo'mə-ner-ē) *n.* **1,** a celestial body, as the sun; a light. **2,** one who enlightens mankind.

lu"mi·nes'cence (loo"mə-nes'əns) *n.* emission of light without heat. —**lu"mi·nesce',** *v.i.* —**lu"mi·nes'cent,** *adj.*

lu´mi·nous (loo´mə-nəs) *adj.* **1,** giving out light. **2,** bright; resplendent. **3,** clear; lucid. **4,** intellectually brilliant. —**lu·mi·nos´i·ty** (-nos´ə-tē) *n.*

lum´mox (lum´əks) *n.* (*Colloq.*) a clumsy or stupid person.

lump *n.* **1,** a mass of solid matter with no particular shape. **2,** a protuberance, knob, or swelling. **3,** a dull, stolid person. —*adj.* in the form of a lump. —*v.t.* work into a mass; deal with as a whole. —*v.i.* **1,** form a lump. **2,** move heavily. —**lump´y, lump´ish, adj.** —**lump it,** endure something disagreeable.

lu´na·cy (loo´nə-sē) *n.* insanity.

lu´nar (loo´nər) *adj.* pert. to the moon.

lu´na·tic (loo´nə-tik) *n.* a crazy person. —*adj.* crazy. —**lunatic fringe,** (*Colloq.*) those who espouse the most extreme causes, cults, and isms.

lunch *n.* **1,** a midday meal. **2,** any light meal. —*v.i.* eat a lunch.

lunch´eon (lun´chən) *n.* lunch.

lun″cheon·ette´ (-et´) *n.* a modest restaurant. Also, **lunch´room″.**

lune (loon) *n.* a figure bounded by two arcs of circles; a crescent. —**lu´nate** (-nāt) *adj.* —**lu·nette´** (-net´) *n.* something crescent-shaped.

lung *n.* one of the two large spongy organs of breathing in man and the higher vertebrates. —**iron lung,** a chamber to assist respiration by alternations of air pressure.

lunge (lunj) *n.* a sudden forward movement. —*v.i.* so move.

lunk´head″ *n.* (*Colloq.*) a blockhead.

lu´pine (loo´pin) *adj.* pert. to a wolf.

lu´pus (loo´pəs) *n.* a bacterial skin disease.

lurch (lėrch) *v.i.* sway suddenly to one side; list; stagger. —*n.* **1,** an act of lurching. **2,** an untenable situation; bad defeat in a game.

lure (lûr) *n.* something used to allure, entice, or trap; a bait or decoy. —*v.t.* entice.

lu´rid (lûr´id) *adj.* **1,** lighted up with a fiery glare. **2,** sensational; exaggerated. —**lur´id·ness, n.**

lurk (lėrk) *v.i.* **1,** lie in concealment; exist unperceived or unsuspected. **2,** skulk; slink.

lus´cious (lush´əs) *adj.* very pleasing to taste or smell; delightful. —**lus´cious·ness, n.**

lush *adj.* **1,** fresh and juicy. **2,** luxuriant. —*n.* (*Slang*) a drunkard. —**lush´ness, n.**

lust *n.* intense longing for possession or enjoyment; passionate or lewd desire. —*v.i.* feel lust. —**lust´ful, adj.**

lus´ter (lus´tər) *n.* **1,** the quality of shining with light emitted or reflected; radiance; glitter. **2,** a glossy finish. **3,** distinction; brilliancy. Also, **lus´tre.** —**lus´trous, adj.**

lust´y (lus´tē) *adj.* vigorous; robust; healthy; lively. —**lust´i·ness, n.**

lute (loot) *n.* a medieval musical instrument similar to a mandolin. —**lu´ta·nist** (loo´tə-nist) *n.*

lu·te´ti·um (loo-tē´shē-əm) *n.* a rare-earth metallic element, no. 71, symbol Lu.

Lu´ther·an (loo´thə-rən) *adj.* & *n.* pert. to the Protestant Church founded by Martin Luther.

lux (luks) *n.* ´[*pl.* **lu´ces** (loo´sēz)] the international unit of illumination.

lux·u´ri·ant (lug-zhûr´ē-ənt) *adj.* **1,** growing or producing in abundance; plentiful; profuse. **2,** florid; superabundant. —**lux·u´ri·ance, n.**

lux·u´ri·ate″ (lug-zhûr´ē-āt″) *v.i.* enjoy luxury or abundance. —**lux·u″ri·a´tion, n.**

lux·u´ri·ous (lug-zhûr´ē-əs) *adj.* characterized by luxury.

lux´u·ry (luk´shə-rē) *n.* **1,** abundant means of self-indulgence. **2,** something enjoyable but not necessary; a delicacy.

-ly (-lė) *suf.* **1,** in a specified manner; forming adverbs, as *blindly.* **2,** like: forming adjectives, as *saintly.*

ly´can·thrope″ (lī´kən-thrōp″) *n.* a werewolf; an insane person who imagines himself to be a wolf. —**ly·can´thro·py** (lī-kan´thrə-pē) *n.*

ly·ce´um (lī-sē´əm) *n.* **1,** a literary association. **2,** a lecture hall.

lye (lī) *n.* a caustic solution of any alkaline salt, used in making soap.

ly″ing-in´ *adj.* confinement in childbirth.

lymph (limf) *n.* a yellowish alkaline fluid in animal bodies. —**lym´phoid** (-foid) *adj.* —**lymph node,** lymph gland.

lym·phat´ic (lim-fat´ik) *adj.* **1,** pert. to lymph. **2,** sluggish.

lynch (linch) *v.t.* execute (a person) without authority or process of law.

lynx (links) *n.* a wildcat. —**lynx-´eyed″,** *adj.* having acute eyesight.

ly″on·naise´ (lē″ə-nez´) *adj.* esp. of potatoes, cooked with butter, parsley, and onions.

lyre (līr) *n.* a stringed musical instrument of ancient Greece.

lyre´bird″ *n.* an Australian bird.

lyr´ic (lir´ik) *adj.* **1,** pert. to singing; songlike. **2,** concerned with thoughts and feelings; romantic. **3,** (of a voice) delicate in quality and without great range. —*n.* **1,** a lyric poem or song. **2,** (*Colloq.*) the words of a song. —**lyr´i·cal, adj.** —**ly´ri·cist, n.**

—ly·sis (lə-sis) *suf.* disintegration; destruction.

M

M, m (em) the thirteenth letter of the English alphabet.

ma (mä) *n.* (*Colloq.*) mother.

ma'am (màm; məm) *n.* (*Colloq.*) a term of address to women; madam.

ma·ca'bre (mə-kä'brə) *adj.* gruesome, as suggestive of the dance of death (*danse macabre*).

mac·ad'am (mə-kad'əm) *n.* a road of crushed stone, usually with an asphalt surface. —*adj.* made of such materials. —**mac·ad'am·ize''** (-īz'') *v.t.*

ma·caque' (mə-käk') *n.* a short-tailed monkey of Asia.

mac''a·ro'ni (mak''ə-rō'nē) *n.* thin tubes of dried wheat paste, as food.

mac''a·roon' (mak''ə-roon') *n.* a small sweet cake.

ma·caw' (mə-kâ') *n.* a long-tailed parrot of tropical America.

mace (mās) *n.* **1,** a clublike weapon. **2,** a spice resembling nutmeg. **3,** (*Cap., T.N.*) a chemical compound combining the effects of tear gas and nerve gas, used to control riots, etc.

mac''er·ate'' (mas'ə-rāt'') *v.t.* **1,** separate or soften by digestion or soaking. **2,** make thin. —*v.i.* grow thin; waste away. —**mac''er·a'tion,** *n.*

Mach (mäk) *adv.* in relation to the speed of sound at a given altitude, as *Mach 2* = twice the speed of sound (2 being the Mach number).

ma·che'te (mə-shet'ē) *n.* a heavy knife.

Mach''i·a·vel'li·an (mak''ē-ə-vel'ē-ən) *adj.* pert. to Niccolo di Bernardo Machiavelli, Italian statesman, or to his political philosophy of ruthlessness and unscrupulousness.

mach'i·nate'' (mak'ə-nāt'') *v.t. & i.* plan or plot, esp. with evil intent. —**mach''i·na'tion,** *n.*

ma·chine' (mə-shēn') *n.* **1,** any device that transfers or converts energy from one form to another, esp. for manufacturing. **2,** an automobile. **3,** a sewing machine. **4,** persons acting together for a common purpose, as a *political machine.* —*v.t.* grind to a smooth finish with a machine. —**machine gun,** a mounted rifle that fires automatically and continuously. —**machine language,** a means of communicating directly with a computer, without the need for translation.

ma·chin'er·y (mə-shē'nə-rē) *n.* **1,** machines or parts of machines, collectively.

2, a system, not mechanical, designed to keep anything going.

ma·chin'ist (mə-shē'nist) *n.* a skilled operator of precision machinery; a toolmaker.

ma·chis'mo (mä-chēs'mō) *n.* masculinity; virility.

ma'cho (mä'chō) *adj.* exhibiting machismo.

mack'er·el (mak'ər-əl) *n.* a food fish of the No. Atlantic.

mack'i·naw'' (mak'ə-nâ'') *n.* a short, woolen outer coat.

mack'in·tosh'' (mak'in-tosh'') *n.* a raincoat of rubber-coated cloth.

ma''cra·me' (ma''krə-mā') *n.* lacework made of knotted heavy string or cord.

mac·ro- (mak-rə) *pref.* large; great.

ma''cro·bi·ot'ic (-bī-ot'ik) *adj.* pert. to the use of diet to prolong life.

mac'ro·cosm (mak'rə-koz-əm) *n.* the great world; the universe.

ma'cron (mā'kron) *n.* the diacritical mark indicating a long vowel, as on ā.

mac''ro·scop'ic (mak''rə-skop'ik) *adj.* visible to the naked eye. —**mac''ro·scop'i·cal·ly,** *adv.*

mad *adj.* [**mad'der, -dest**] **1,** mentally deranged; irresponsible; irrational. **2,** of a dog, rabid. **3,** disorderly; ill-advised. **4,** infatuated; in love. **5,** (*Colloq.*) angry. —**mad'ness,** *n.*

mad'am (mad'əm) *n.* **1,** a polite term of address to a woman. **2,** a woman who operates a brothel. Also (*Fr.*) **ma·dame'** (mà-däm') [*pl.* **mes·dames'** (mā-däm')].

mad'cap'' (mad'kap'') *adj.* wild; flighty. —*n.* an unrestrained, adventurous person.

mad'den (mad'ən) *v.t.* make mad. **2,** infuriate.

mad'der (mad'ər) *n.* a herb; a dye, usually red, made from its root.

mad'ding (mad'ing) *adj.* (*Rare*) distracted; raging.

made (mād) *v.* pret. & p.p. of *make.* —*adj.* (*Colloq.*) **1,** artificially produced. **2,** assured of success.

ma·dei'ra (mə-dir'ə) *n.* a fine sherry wine.

mad''e·moi·selle' (mad''mwə-zel') *n.* [*pl.* **mes''de·moi·selles'** (mād''-)] (*Fr.*) an unmarried woman; miss.

made-'to-or'der *adj.* made specially for a customer; opposed to *ready-made.*

made-'up' (mād'up') *adj.* **1,** invented; fictional. **2,** adorned with cosmetics, as a face. **3,** put together; assembled.

mad'house'' *n.* **1,** a lunatic asylum. **2,** a place in a state of confusion.

mad'man'' *n.* [*pl.* **-men''**] an insane person. —**mad'wom''an,** *n.fem.*

Ma·don'na (mə-don'ə) *n.* a picture or statue of the Virgin Mary.

mad'ras (mad'rəs) *n.* a cotton fabric, usually with a bright-colored design.

mad'ri·gal (mad'ri-gəl) *n.* **1,** a medieval poem or song. **2,** any part song, esp. one without accompaniment.

mae·ce'nas (mī-sē'nəs) *n.* any generous patron of the arts.

mael'strom (māl'strəm) *n.* a whirlpool; great and destructive agitation.

mae'nad (mē'nad) *n.* **1,** a priestess of Bacchus. **2,** a frenzied woman. **—mae·nad'ic,** *adj.*

maes'tro (mīs'trō) *n.* [*pl.* **-tros**] a master, esp. an eminent musical composer or conductor.

Mae West (mā'west') an inflatable life jacket.

Ma'fi·a" (mä'fē-ä") *n.* a Sicilian criminal organization, the Black Hand, active also in other countries. **—ma·fi·o'so** (mä-fē-ō'zō) *n.* a member of the Mafia.

mag"a·zine" (mag"ə-zēn') *n.* **1,** a periodical publication, issued oftener than weekly. **2,** a depository for ammunition. **3,** a storehouse. **4,** a supply chamber, as in a weapon.

mag'da·lene" (mag'də-len") *n.* a reformed prostitute.

ma·gen'ta (mə-jen'tə) *n. & adj.* a color or dye, reddish purple.

mag'got (mag'ət) *n.* the larva of an insect; a worm. **—mag'got·y,** *adj.*

Ma'gi (mā'jī) *n. pl.* **1,** priests, in ancient Persia. **2,** the "Three Wise Men," Matt. 2:1–12.

mag'ic (maj'ik) *n.* **1,** the pretended art of controlling the supernatural; sorcery. **2,** legerdemain. **3,** charm; enchantment. *—adj.* [also **mag'i·cal**] **1,** as by supernatural agency. **2,** delightful. **—mag'i·cal·ly,** *adv.* **—magic lantern,** a projector. **—magic square,** an arrangement of integers in a square such that the sum of the numbers in each row, column, or diagonal is the same.

ma·gi'cian (mə-jish'ən) *n.* a conjurer.

Mag'i·cube" (maj'i-) *n.* (*T.N.*) a flashcube not requiring external electrical ignition.

mag"is·te'ri·al (maj"is-tir'ē-əl) *adj.* **1,** pert. to a magistrate. **2,** authoritative; imperious.

mag'is·trate" (maj'is-trāt") *n.* a minor judge or judicial officer. **—mag'is·tra·cy** (-trə-sē) *n.*

mag'ma (mag'mə) *n.* [*pl.* **mag'ma·ta** (-mə-tə)] *n.* (*Geol.*) the mass of molten material below the earth's crust.

mag·nan'i·mous (mag-nan'ə-məs) *adj.*

generous; high-minded; noble. **—mag"na·nim'i·ty** (mag"nə-nim'ə-tē) *n.*

mag'nate (mag'nāt) *n.* a person of importance, esp. in industry.

mag·ne'sia (mag-nē'zhə) *n.* an oxide of magnesium, used medicinally.

mag·ne'si·um (mag-nē'zhē-əm) *n.* a metallic chemical element, no. 12, symbol Mg.

mag'net (mag'nit) *n.* **1,** a body that attracts iron or steel; a lodestone. **2,** anything that draws persons toward it; an attraction. **—mag·net'ic** (-net'ik) *adj.* **—mag·net'i·cal·ly,** *adv.* **—magnetic field,** a space in which a magnetic force is present, as around a magnet or a conductor carrying an electric current.

mag'net·ism (mag'nə-tiz-əm) *n.* **1,** the properties of attraction. **2,** charm. **3,** act or result of magnetizing.

mag'ne·tite" (mag'nə-tīt") *n.* an iron ore, often with magnetic properties; lodestone.

mag'net·ize" (mag'nə-tīz") *v.t.* **1,** make a magnet of. **2,** attract; influence.

mag·ne'to (mag-nē'tō) *n.* [*pl.* **-tos**] a generator of electricity by use of magnets.

mag'ne·tron" (mag'nə-tron") *n.* a vacuum tube for producing short radio waves.

mag·ni- *pref.* large; great.

mag·nif'i·cent (mag-nif'ə-sənt) *adj.* **1,** great in size or extent. **2,** splendid; brilliant. **3,** noble; sublime. **—mag·nif'i·cence,** *n.*

mag·nif'i·co" (mag-nif'i-kō") *n.* a person of high rank or importance.

mag'ni·fy" (mag'nə-fī") *v.t.* **1,** make greater. **2,** make to appear greater. **3,** glorify; extol. **—mag"ni·fi·ca'tion,** *n.* **—mag'ni·fi"er,** *n.*

mag·nil'o·quent (mag-nil'ə-kwənt) *adj.* affectedly lofty. **—mag·nil'o·quence,** *n.*

mag'ni·tude" (mag'nə-tūd") *n.* **1,** physical greatness; relative size. **2,** importance; moral greatness. **3,** the measure of brightness of a star.

mag·no'li·a (mag-nō'lē-ə) *n.* an evergreen tree with large, fragrant blossoms.

mag'num (mag'nəm) *n.* **1,** a two-quart wine bottle. **2,** [*pl.* **-na** (-nə)] a wrist bone.

mag'num o'pus (ō'pəs) (*Lat.*) major work; great work.

mag'pie" (mag'pī") *n.* **1,** a noisy bird. **2,** a chattering person.

Mag'yar (mä'gyər) *n.* a member of the predominant Hungarian race; the language of Hungary.

ma"ha·ra'jah (mä"hə-rä'jə) *n.* a ruling prince in India. Also, **ma"ha·ra'ja. —ma"·ha·ra'nee** (-nē) *n. fem.*

ma·hat'ma (mə-hät'mə) *n.* a sage or saint in Brahmanism.

mah-'jongg" (mä'jâng") *n.* a Chinese game, played with domino-like tiles.

mahl'stick" (mäl'stik") *n.* a stick held by a painter as support for his brush.

ma·hog'a·ny (mə-hog'ə-nē) *n.* a tropical Amer. tree or its hard, reddish-brown wood.

Ma·hom'et·an (mə-hom'ə-tən) *n. & adj.* Mohammedan.

ma·hout' (mə-howt') *n.* the keeper and driver of an elephant.

maid (mād) *n.* **1,** a girl; an unmarried woman. **2,** a virgin. **3,** a female servant. —**maid in waiting,** a woman, often of noble birth, attendant on a queen or princess. —**maid of honor,** the chief unmarried attendant on a bride.

maid'en (mā'dən) *n.* **1,** an unmarried girl or woman. **2,** a virgin. **3,** a new, untried animal or thing; a horse that has not won a race. —*adj.* unmarried; unused; first or earliest. —**maid'en·hood,** *n.* —**maid'en·ly,** *adj.* —**maiden name,** the surname of a woman before marriage.

maid'en·hair" (mā'dən-hâr") *n.* a delicate, feathery fern.

maid'en·head" *n.* the hymen.

mail (māl) *n.* **1,** letters or packages sent by post. **2,** the postal system. **3,** flexible armor of metal rings, interlinked. —*v.t.* send by mail. —**mailed,** *adj.* armored.

mail·lot' (mä-yō') *n.* **1,** tights. **2,** a woman's one-piece bathing suit.

mail'man" *n.* [*pl.* **-men"**] one employed to deliver mail; letter carrier.

mail-'or"der *adj.* pert. to the business of ordering and delivering goods by mail.

maim (mām) *v.t.* **1,** disable, by wounding or mutilation. **2,** impair.

main (mān) *adj.* **1,** chief; principal. **2,** sheer; utmost; as, by *main strength.* —*n.* **1,** a principal pipe or duct. **2,** the open ocean. **3,** strength; force. —**main'ly,** *adv.* chiefly. —**main drag,** (*Slang*) the principal street of a town. —**main line, 1,** a principal highway, railroad line, etc. **2,** (*Slang*) a principal vein.

main'frame" *n.* a computer.

main'land (-lənd) *n.* a principal mass of land; a continent.

main'line" *v.i.* (*Slang*) inject a narcotic drug into a principal vein.

main'mast" (-məst) *n.* the principal mast of a ship. —**main'sail"** (-səl) *n.* the principal sail of a ship.

main'spring" *n.* **1,** the principal spring in a watch. **2,** chief source or motive.

main'stay" *n.* a chief support.

main'stream" *n.* the predominant current or tendency of a movement, discipline, etc.

main·tain' (mān-tān') *v.t.* **1,** preserve;

keep in condition. **2,** support; provide for. **3,** defend in argument. **4,** assert to be true. —**main'te·nance** (mān'tə-nəns) *n.*

mai'tai" (mī'tī") *n.* a cocktail made with rum, curaçao, and fruit juices.

maî"tre d'hô·tel' (me"tr-dō-tel') *n.* **1,** a butler; headwaiter. **2,** the owner or manager of a hotel. Also, **maître d'** (-dē').

maize (māz) *n.* **1,** a cereal plant; Indian corn, in the U.S. called corn. **2,** a yellow color.

ma·jes'tic (mə-jes'tik) *adj.* possessing majesty; grand; sublime. —**ma·jes'ti·cal·ly,** *adv.*

maj'es·ty (maj'is-tē) *n.* **1,** stateliness; grandeur. **2,** sovereignty. **3,** a royal personage.

ma·jol'i·ca (mə-jol'ə-kə) *n.* decorative enameled Ital. pottery.

ma'jor (mā'jər) *adj.* **1,** greater in importance, quantity, or extent. **2,** senior. **3,** of legal age. **4,** (*Music*) pert. to a certain scale or larger interval. —*n.* **1,** an army officer ranking next above captain. **2,** a principal field of study. —*v.t.* (with *in*) adopt as a principal field of study. —**major general,** the fourth-highest-ranking army officer. —**major league,** one of the highest-ranking leagues of professional baseball teams.

ma"jor·do'mo (-dō'mō) *n.* [*pl.* **-mos**] the manager of a large household or estate.

ma"jor·ette' (-et') *n.fem.* the leader of a marching band or formation. Also, **drum majorette.**

ma·jor'i·ty (mə-jor'ə-tē) *n.* **1,** the greater part or number; the excess of the greater over the smaller. **2,** full legal age. **3,** the military rank of a major. —**silent majority,** the presumed majority of the population which does not express its opinion in political action.

make (māk) *v.t.* [*pret. & p.p.* **made** (mād)] **1,** bring into being. **2,** form; put in condition. **3,** compel. **4,** appoint. **5,** constitute; compose. **6,** judge; infer; estimate. **7,** arrive at; reach; achieve. **8,** earn; acquire. **9,** (with *out*) discern; understand; (*Colloq.*) assert. **10,** (with *up*) fabricate, as a story; adorn with cosmetics, as one's face; arrange, as type for printing. **11,** (with *up to*) ingratiate oneself with. **12,** (*Slang*) seduce. —*v.i.* **1,** cause to be as specified. **2,** be of effect; operate. **3,** go (toward or away from). **4,** (with *out*) fare. **5,** (with *up*) become reconciled; prepare one's face with cosmetics. —*n.* **1,** construction; nature; brand. **2,** the process of manufacture. —**make away with, 1,** steal. **2,** kill. **3,** eat all of. —**make one's way,** succeed. —**make out, 1,** write out (a form). **2,** see. **3,** get along; manage. **4,** (*Colloq.*) pet. —**make over, 1,** alter; remodel. **2,** transfer title to; hand over.

—**make up, 1,** become reconciled. **2,** invent. **3,** prepare; apply cosmetics (to).

make-'be·lieve" *adj.* pretended. —*n.* pretense, as children's play.

make-'read'y *n.* adjustment to produce even printing.

make'shift" *n. & adj.* a temporary expedient.

make-'up" *n.* **1,** composition: character or nature. **2,** the arrangement of type, etc. for printing. **3,** cosmetics; the use of cosmetics or costume.

mak'ings (mā'kingz) *n.pl.* ingredients necessary for making or producing something.

mal- *pref.* bad; imperfect.

mal'a·chite" (mal'ə-kīt") *n.* copper carbonate, an ore of copper, also used as a gem.

mal''ad·just'ed (mal''ə-jus'tid) *adj.* **1,** badly adjusted. **2,** (*Psych.*) not fully adapted to social living. —**mal''ad·just'ment,** *n.*

mal''a·droit' (mal''ə-droit') *adj.* inexpert; awkward.

mal'a·dy (mal'ə-dē) *n.* **1,** a disease. **2,** any disordered state or condition.

ma·laise' (ma-lez') *n.* (*Fr.*) an indefinite feeling of uneasiness or discomfort.

ma'la·mute" (mä'lə-mūt") *n.* a kind of Alaskan working dog having heavy fur.

mal'a·prop''ism (mal''ə-prop''iz-əm) *n.* a blunder in speech, through ignorance of a word or meaning.

mal''ap·ro·pos' (mal''ap-rə-pō') *adj. & adv.* inappropriate.

ma'lar (mā'lər) *n.* the cheek bone.

ma·lar'i·a (mə-lār'ē-ə) *n.* an intermittent or remittent fever. —**ma·lar'i·al, ma·lar'i·ous,** *adj.*

ma·lar'key (mə-lär'kē) *n.* (*Slang*) empty talk; buncombe.

Ma·lay' (mə-lā') *n.* one of the race of brown men inhabiting the Malay Peninsula. —**Ma·lay'an,** *adj.*

mal'con·tent'' (mal'kən-tent'') *adj.* discontented. —*n.* a discontented person.

male (māl) *adj.* **1,** pertaining to the sex that begets young. **2,** characteristic of this sex; masculine. **3,** (*Mech.*) shaped to be inserted into a socket. —*n.* **1,** a man. **2,** a male animal.

mal''e·dic'tion (mal''ə-dik'shən) *n.* **1,** evil speaking. **2,** a curse.

mal''e·fac'tor (mal''ə-fak''tər) *n.* **1,** a lawbreaker. **2,** one who does evil. —**mal''e·fac'tion,** *n.*

ma·lef'ic (mə-lef'ik) *adj.* harmful; doing mischief.

ma·lef'i·cent (mə-lef'ə-sənt) *adj.* having an evil effect or intent. —**ma·lef'i·cence,** *n.*

ma'le·mute'' (mä'lə-mūt") *n.* a malamute.

ma·lev'o·lent (mə-lev'ə-lənt) *adj.* wishing evil to others; hostile. —**ma·lev'o·lence,** *n.*

mal·fea'sance (mal-fē'zəns) *n.* performance of a wrongful act. —**mal·fea'sant,** *adj.*

mal''for·ma'tion *n.* a faulty construction, as of a part of the body. —**mal·formed',** *adj.*

mal·func'tion *v.i.* operate imperfectly; fail to operate. —*n.* an act or instance of malfunctioning.

mal'ic (mal'ik) *adj.* pert. to apples.

mal'ice (mal'is) *n.* **1,** a disposition to inflict injury; ill will. **2,** a hostile act.

ma·li'cious (mə-lish'əs) *adj.* bearing malice; intending harm.

ma·lign' (mə-līn') *v.t.* speak ill of; defame. —*adj.* pernicious; malicious.

ma·lig'nant (mə-lig'nənt) *adj.* **1,** threatening danger. **2,** deadly or growing worse, as a cancerous tumor. —**ma·lig'nan·cy, ma·lig'ni·ty,** *n.*

ma·lin'ger (mə-ling'gər) *v.i.* feign illness. —**ma·ling'er·er,** *n.*

mall (mâl) *n.* **1,** a maul. **2,** a shaded public walk.

mal'lard (mal'ərd) *n.* the common wild duck.

mal'le·a·ble (mal'ē-ə-bəl) *adj.* **1,** capable of being extended by beating or rolling. **2,** adaptable. —**mal''le·a·bil'i·ty,** *n.*

mal'let (mal'it) *n.* **1,** a small wooden hammer. **2,** a long-handled club, as used in croquet or polo.

mal'low (mal'ō) *n.* a shrub or tree bearing pink or white flowers.

malm'sey (mäm'zē) *n.* a strong, sweet wine.

mal''nu·tri'tion (mal''noo-trish'ən) *n.* imperfect, or lack of, nutrition.

mal·o'dor·ous (mal-ō'dər-əs) *adj.* having an offensive odor. —**mal·o'dor·ous·ness,** *n.*

mal·prac'tice (mal-prak'tis) *n.* improper conduct, esp. by a physician.

malt (mâlt) *n.* **1,** partially germinated grain, used in brewing. **2,** ale. —**malt'ed milk,** a preparation of dried milk and malted cereals; a drink of this mixed with milk and fruit flavoring.

Mal·tese' (mâl-tēz') *adj.* pert. to the island of Malta. —**Maltese cat,** a bluish-gray breed of cat. —**Maltese cross,** a cross of four equal arms, notched and wider at the end.

malt'ose (mâl'tōs) *n.* malt sugar, produced by conversion of starch.

mal·treat' (mal-trēt') *v.t.* treat badly; abuse. —**mal·treat'ment,** *n.*

ma′ma (mä′mə) *n.* mamma.

mam′ba (mäm′bə) *n.* a poisonous African snake.

mam′bo″ (mäm′bō″) *n.* a lively ballroom dance.

mam′ma (mä′mə *or* mä-mä′) *n.* **1,** [also, **ma′ma**] mother. **2,** (mam′ə) [*pl.* **-mae** (-mē)] a gland secreting milk.

mam′mal (mam′əl) *n.* an animal whose young feed upon milk from the breast. —**mam·ma′li·an** (ma-mā′lē-ən) *adj.*

mam′ma·ry (mam′ə-rē) *adj.* pert. to the mammae or breasts.

mam·mog′ra·phy (mam-og′rə-fē) *n.* X-ray photography of the breast (usu. used to detect cancer).

mam′mon (mam′ən) *n.* **1,** material wealth. **2,** (*cap.*) the apotheosis of riches and avarice.

mam′moth (mam′əth) *n.* an extinct species of very large elephant. —*adj.* gigantic; immense.

mam′my (mam′ē) *n.* **1,** mother. **2,** a colored female nurse.

man *n.* [*pl.* **men**] **1,** a mammal of the genus Homo. **2,** a person; a human being. **3,** the human race; mankind. **4,** an adult human male. **5,** (*Colloq.*) a husband. **6,** a strong, virile, brave, or accomplished man. **7,** a piece in a game, as chess. **8,** (with *the*) (*Slang*) the police; authority, esp. white authority. —*v.t* [**manned, man′ning**] supply with men, as for service or defense. —**man about town,** a sophisticated, worldly man. —**man Friday,** a loyal servant or person; a slavish follower.

-man (mən) *suf.* [*pl.* **-men**] in compounds, denoting a man (or, often, person) who does, acts, has, etc., as indicated by the root word.

man′a·cle (man′ə-kəl) *n.* (usually *pl.*) a shackle; handcuff. —*v.t.* fetter; restrain.

man′age (man′ij) *v.t.* **1,** control physically, as a horse. **2,** control by direction or persuasion. **3,** contrive; bring about. —*v.i.* direct or control affairs. —**man′age·a·ble,** *adj.*

man′age·ment (-mənt) *n.* **1,** act of managing. **2,** owners and executives as distinguished from labor.

man′ag·er (man′ij-ər) *n.* one who directs any operations. —**man″a·ger′i·al** (-ə-jir′ē-əl) *adj.*

ma·ña′na (mä-nyä′nə) *adv.* & *n.* tomorrow; (*fig.*) (at) an indefinite time in the future.

man-′at-arms″ *n.* [*pl.* **men-′**] a soldier or armed attendant of medieval times.

man″a·tee′ (man″ə-tē′) *n.* a seacow; a large sea mammal.

Man·chu′ (man-choo′) *n.* a member of a tribe from Manchuria, long the rulers of China; their language. —**Man·chu′ri·an** (-chŭ′rē-ən) *adj.*

man·da′mus (man-dā′məs) *n.* (*Law*) a writ directing an inferior court, person, etc., to perform a specific act.

man′da·rin (man′də-rin) *n.* **1,** a Chinese official. **2,** a Chinese dialect. **3,** an Asiatic citrus fruit. **4,** a loose, wide sleeve; a woman's coat with such sleeves.

man′date (man′dāt) *n.* **1,** a command. **2,** an order or injunction, as from a superior court to an inferior one. **3,** a commission, as to one nation to manage the affairs of another.

man′da·to·ry (man′də-tôr-ē) *adj.* compulsory; officially required.

man′di·ble (man′də-bəl) *n.* a bone of the lower jaw. —**man·dib′u·lar** (-dib′yə-lər) *adj.*

man′do·lin″ (man′də-lin″) *n.* a musical instrument of the lute class, having metal strings in pairs.

man′drake (man′drāk) *n.* a poisonous herb of Europe. Also, **man·drag′o·ra** (man-drag′ə-rə).

man′drel (man′drəl) *n.* **1,** a cylindrical bar used to support work being turned on a lathe. **2,** a core for shaping metal or glass.

man′drill (man′dril) *n.* a large, ferocious Afr. baboon.

mane (mān) *n.* the long hair on the neck of some animals, as the horse or the lion. —**maned** (mānd) *adj.*

ma·nege′ (ma-nezh′) *n.* the art of training and riding horses; a riding school.

ma·neu′ver (mə-noo′vər) *n.* **1,** a planned and regulated strategic movement, particularly of troops or warships. **2,** an adroit move. —*v.t.* & *i.* manipulate; move skillfully. Also, **ma·noeu′vre.**

man′ful (-fəl) *adj.* brave. —**man′ful·ness,** *n.*

man′ga·nese″ (mang′gə-nēs″) *n.* a metallic chemical element, no. 25, symbol Mn. —**man·gan′ic** (man-gan′ik) *adj.*

mange (mānj) *n.* a skin disease of animals which causes loss of hair and eruptions.

man′gel-wur′zel (mang′gəl-wĕr′zəl) *n.* a beetlike root used as fodder.

man′ger (mān′jər) *n.* a trough or box for feeding animals.

man′gle (mang′gəl) *v.t.* **1,** cut or slash; disfigure. **2,** mar. **3,** press in a mangle. —*n.* a machine for ironing cloth.

man′go (mang′gō) *n.* the luscious, slightly acid fruit of a tropical tree.

man′grove (man′grōv) *n.* a tropical tree, a source of tannic acid.

man′gy (mān′jē) *adj.* **1,** infected with mange. **2,** shabby; mean; petty. —**man′gi·ness,** *n.*

man′han″dle *v.t.* **1,** handle roughly. **2,** move by manpower.

Man·hat′tan (man-hat′ən) *n.* a cocktail of whiskey and sweet vermouth.

man′hole″ *n.* a hole for entering a sewer, steam boiler, etc.

man′hood″ (-hûd″) *n.* **1,** the state or condition of being a man. **2,** courage; virility.

man-′hour″ *n.* a unit of work, that done by one man in one hour.

man′hunt″ *n.* a hunt for a man, as a lawbreaker.

ma′ni·a (mā′nē-ə) *n.* **1,** a form of insanity, marked by great excitement. **2,** a great desire or enthusiasm.

-ma·ni·a (mā′nē-ə) *suf.* denoting love or enthusiasm for.

ma′ni·ac (mā′nē-ak) *n.* a madman. —**ma·ni′a·cal** (mə-nī′ə-kəl) *adj.*

man′ic (man′ik) *adj.* pert. to or affected with mania. —**manic depressive,** having a mental disorder marked by recurrent cycles of excitation and depression.

ma″ni·cot′ti (ma″nə-kot′ē) *n.* pasta filled with ricotta and ham.

man′i·cure″ (man′ə-kyūr″) *n.* care of the hands and fingernails. —*v.t.* trim; polish. —**man′i·cur″ist,** *n.*

man′i·fest″ (man′ə-fest″) *adj.* readily perceived; obvious. —*v.t.* demonstrate; give evidence of. —*n.* a list of a shipment. —**man″i·fes·ta′tion,** *n.* a demonstration; display.

man″i·fes′to (man″ə-fes′tō) *n.* a public declaration; a proclamation.

man′i·fold″ (man′ə-fōld″) *adj.* **1,** of many kinds; varied. **2,** having many parts, features, or activities. **3,** numerous. —*n.* **1,** a carbon or duplicated copy; facsimile. **2,** thin paper for making many carbon copies. **3,** a pipe with several connections.

man′i·kin (man′ə-kin) *n.* **1,** a little man. **2,** a mannequin.

ma·nil′a (mə-nil′ə) *n.* **1,** a Philippine fiber used for cordage, heavy wrapping paper, etc. **2,** a cigar.

man′i·oc″ (man′ē-ok″) *n.* cassava; the starch derived from its roots.

man′i·ple (man′ə-pəl) *n.* a short narrow band worn over the left arm as a eucharistic vestment.

ma·nip′u·late″ (mə-nip′yə-lāt″) *v.t.* **1,** handle with skill. **2,** influence; manage. **3,** adapt or change. —**ma·nip′u·la·ble,** *adj.* —**ma·nip″u·la′tion,** *n.*

man′i·tou (man′i-too) *n.* an Indian spirit or god of nature.

man′kind″ *n.* the human race.

man′ly (-lē) *adj.* having the ideal qualities of a man. —**man′li·ness,** *n.*

man′na (man′ə) *n.* spiritual food.

man′ne·quin (man′ə-kin) *n.* **1,** a person who models clothes for sale. **2,** a dummy used by artists and tailors.

man′ner (man′ər) *n.* **1,** a mode of action; method. **2,** customary way of doing; habit; style. **3,** personal bearing and behavior. **4,** kind; sort. **5,** (*pl.*) polite, courteous deportment. —**man′ner·ly,** *adj.* —**man′ner·less,** *adj.*

man′nered (man′ərd) *adj.* **1,** having manners of a specified sort. **2,** affected or artificial in style.

man′ner·ism (man′ə-riz-əm) *n.* a habitual peculiarity of deportment or speech; idiosyncrasy.

man′nish (-ish) *adj.* unbecomingly masculine. —**man′nish·ness,** *n.*

ma·noeu′vre (mə-noo′vər) *v.* maneuver.

man-″of-war′ *n.* [*pl.* **men-″**] a warship.

ma·nom′e·ter (mə-nom′ə-tər) *n.* an instrument for measuring the pressure of gases or liquids. —**man″o·met′ric** (man″ə-met′rik) *adj.*

man′or (man′ər) *n.* in England, a landed estate, vested with certain rights. —**ma·no′ri·al** (mə-nôr′ē-əl) *adj.*

man′pow″er *n.* **1,** human muscle power. **2,** men available for work, warfare, etc.

man·qué′ (män-kā′) *adj.* (*Fr.*) unsuccessful; unfulfilled.

man′sard (man′särd) *n.* a roof having two slopes, one steeper than the other.

manse (mans) *n.* a parsonage.

man′sion (man′shən) *n.* a large and stately residence.

man′slaugh″ter (man′slå″tər) *n.* (*Law*) the unlawful killing of another without malice aforethought.

man′ta (man′tə) *n.* **1,** a coarse cotton cloth; a shawl or blanket made of this. **2,** a large ray; devilfish.

man′tel (man′təl) *n.* the facing above and around a fireplace. —**man′tel·piece″,** *n.* the shelf of a mantel.

man′tel·et (mant′lit) *n.* **1,** a short cape. **2,** a shield or screen.

man·til′la (man-til′ə) *n.* **1,** a lace headcovering. **2,** a light cloak.

man′tis *n.* [*pl.* **-tes** (-tēz)] a carnivorous insect: *praying mantis.*

man·tis′sa (man-tis′ə) *n.* the decimal part of a logarithm.

man′tle (man′təl) *n.* **1,** a loose cloak. **2,**

any covering. **3,** an incandescent hood for a gas jet. —*v.t.* & *i.* cover or be covered.

man'tra (man'trə) *n.* a sacred word or formula used in meditation.

man'u·al (man'ū-əl) *adj.* pert. to or done by the hands. —*n.* **1,** a book of instructions. **2,** a routine. **3,** an organ keyboard played by the hands.

man"u·fac'ture (man"yə-fak'chər) *n.* the making of goods, by hand or machinery. —*v.i.* engage in such a business. —*v.t.* **1,** make (goods); fabricate. **2,** produce artificially; invent. —**man"u·fac'tur·er,** *n.*

man"u·mis'sion (man"yə-mish'ən) *n.* liberation from slavery. —**man"u·mit',** *v.t.* liberate.

ma·nure' (mə-nyûr') *n.* any substance, chiefly animal feces, used to fertilize land.

man'u·script (man'yə-skript") *n.* **1,** a book or document written by hand. **2,** an original copy, not set in type. —*adj.* handwritten.

Manx (manks) pert. to the Isle of Man. —**Manx cat,** a tailless cat.

man'y (men'ē) *n.* a large number. —*adj.* [**more, most**] numerous.

Mao jacket (mow) a jacket with a high, broad collar.

mao tai (mow'tī') *n.* a strong Chinese liquor.

map *n.* **1,** a drawing of all or a part of the earth's surface, or the heavens; a chart. **2,** (*Slang*) the face. —*v.t.* [**mapped, map'ping**] **1,** draw a map. **2,** (often with *out*) plan.

ma'ple (mā'pəl) *n.* a shade tree, valued for its hard wood and for the sugar-producing sap of some species.

Ma·quis' (ma-kē') *n.sing.* & *pl.* the French underground in World War II. —**ma·qui·sard'** (ma-kė-zär') *n.* a member of the Maquis.

mar (mär) *v.t.* [**marred, mar'ring**] **1,** disfigure; scratch. **2,** impair in quality.

mar'a·bou' (mar'ə-boo") *n.* **1,** a large stork. **2,** a marabou's plume or feathers, used for trimming.

ma·ra'ca (mə-rä'kə) *n.* a hollow gourd containing loose pebbles, used as a percussion instrument.

ma·ras'ca (mə-räs'kə) *n.* a small black variety of cherry.

mar'a·schi'no (mar"ə-skē'nō) *n.* a cordial distilled from the marasca. —**maraschino cherries,** cherries in a syrup flavored with maraschino.

mar'a·thon" (mar'ə-thon") *n.* **1,** a footrace of about 26 miles. **2,** any test of endurance.

ma·raud' (mə-râd') *v.i.* rove in search of plunder. —**ma·raud'er,** *n.*

mar'ble (mär'bəl) *n.* **1,** hard crystalline limestone, used in sculpture and architecture. **2,** a small ball of glass, agate, etc., used in a child's game. **3,** (*pl.*) the game played with such balls. —*adj.* made of, or like, marble. —**mar'ble·ize,** *v.t.* —**marble cake,** a cake streaked like marble from the mixture of light and dark (usu. chocolate) batters.

mar'bling (mär'bling) *n.* **1,** an imitation of, or appearance like, variegated marble. **2,** layers of fat and lean in meat. —**mar'bled,** *adj.*

mar'ca·site" (mär'kə-sīt") *n.* a yellowish crystalline mineral, used in ornaments.

mar·cel' (mär-sel') *n.* a method of putting waves in hair.

march (märch) *v.i.* **1,** proceed on foot. **2,** walk with regular, concerted steps, as soldiers. —*v.t.* cause to march. —*n.* **1,** the act of marching; progress from one place to another. **2,** the distance of a single marching. **3,** a musical composition, to whose rhythm persons march. **4,** border land; a frontier.

March *n.* the third month of the year.

mar'chion·ess" (mär'shə-nes") *n.* the wife or widow of a marquess. Also, **mar·che'sa** (mär-kā'zə).

march'pane" (märch'pān") *n.* marzipan.

march-'past" *n.* procession.

Mar'di gras' (mär'dē-grä') the celebration of Shrove Tuesday.

mare (mār) *n.* a female horse.

mare's-'nest" (märz'nest") *n.* a nonexistent discovery; a hoax.

mare's-'tail" *n.* **1,** any of various plants. **2,** (*pl.*) long, narrow cirrus clouds.

mar'ga·rine" (mär'gə-rin) *n.* oleomargarine.

mar'ga·ri'ta (mär'gə-rē'tə) *n.* a cocktail made of tequila, lemon juice, and orange liqueur.

mar'gin (mär'jin) *n.* **1,** a bordering space, as along a river, or on a letter or page. **2,** allowance for error or security, as in a business transaction. **3,** the difference between selling price and cost.

mar'gi·nal (-əl) *adj.* **1,** on the edge. **2,** making little or no provision for error.

mar'grave (mar'grāv) *n.* a title of certain German nobles. —**mar'gra·vine"** (-grə-vēn") *n.fem.*

mar'gue·rite' (mär"gə-rēt') *n.* a daisylike flower.

mar'i·gold" (mar'i-gōld") *n.* a flower, usually yellow or orange.

ma"ri·jua'na (mä"rə-hwä'nə) *n.* a hemplike plant whose leaves are smoked in cigarettes as a narcotic.

ma·rim'ba (mə-rim'bə) *n.* a musical instrument having strips of wood that produce bell-like tones when struck with hammers.

ma·ri'na (mə-rē'nə) *n.* a boat basin equipped to store and service small boats.

mar''i·nade' (mar''ə-nād') *n.* **1,** a sauce used in marinating. **2,** a pickle preserve.

mar''i·na'ra (mär''ə-när'ə) *adj.* made with tomatoes, onions, garlic, and seasonings.

mar'i·nate'' (mar'ə-nāt'') *v.t.* preserve by salting or pickling; steep in dressing. —**mar''i·na'tion,** *n.*

ma·rine' (mə-rēn') *adj.* pert. to the sea, or navigation; nautical. —*n.* **1,** shipping in general. **2,** a soldier serving on a ship; in U. S. (*cap.*) a member of the Marine Corps.

mar'i·ner (mar'ə-nər) *n.* a seaman.

mar''i·o·nette' (mar''ē-ə-net') *n.* a puppet moved by strings.

mar'i·tal (mar'i-təl) *adj.* pert. to marriage or the married condition.

mar'i·time'' (mar'i-tīm'') *adj.* pert. to or bordering on the sea.

mar'jo·ram (mär'jə-rəm) *n.* an aromatic herb used as a flavoring.

mark (märk) *n.* **1,** a visible impression, as a line, stain, etc. **2,** a distinguishing symbol or peculiarity. **3,** a significant indication. **4,** a symbol denoting ownership or origin, as a *trade mark.* **5,** a rating or grade, as in school. **6,** a target; a goal or aim. **7,** a Ger. monetary unit. **8,** a standard. —*v.t.* **1,** make a mark on. **2,** notice. —**mark time, 1,** (*Mil.*) move the feet as in marching but without advancing. **2,** suspend progress; pause and wait. —**marked** (märkt) *adj.* branded; conspicuous; doomed.

mark'down'' *n.* **1,** a marking for sale at a reduced price. **2,** the amount of such reduction.

mark'er (mär'kər) *n.* **1,** anything used as a mark; a counter, tombstone, etc. **2,** (*Slang*) a memorandum; an I O U.

mar'ket (mär'kit) *n.* **1,** an assemblage of people, or a place, for buying and selling; a store. **2,** trade; rate of sale; demand. —*v.t.* offer for sale; sell. —**mar'ket·a·ble,** *adj.* —**market place,** an open space in a town where markets are held.

marks'man (märks'mən) *n.* one skilled in shooting. —**marks'man·ship,** *n.*

mark'up'' *n.* the amount added to a cost price, for profit.

mar'lin (mär'lin) *n.* a large game fish.

mar'line·spike'' (mär'lin-spīk'') *n.* (*Naut.*) an iron spike used in twisting or splicing rope.

mar'ma·lade'' (mär'mə-lād'') *n.* a preserve containing pieces of fruit.

mar·mo're·al (mar-môr'ē-əl) *adj.* of marble.

mar'mo·set'' (mär'mə-zet'') *n.* a small Central Amer. monkey.

mar'mot (mär'mət) *n.* any of various rodents, as the woodchuck.

ma·roon' (mə-roon') *v.t.* abandon on a desolate island; isolate. —*adj. & n.* dark red.

mar·quee' (mär-kē') *n.* a projecting roof above a door or sidewalk.

mar'que·try (mär'kə-trē) *n.* inlaid work on furniture.

mar'quis (mär'kwis) *n.* a nobleman, ranking between a count or earl and a duke. Also (*Brit.*) **mar'quess, mar·che'se** (märkā'ze). —**mar·quise'** (mär-kēz') *n.fem.* wife of a marquis.

mar''qui·sette' (mär''kwi-zet') *n.* a light, gauzelike fabric.

mar'riage (mar'ij) *n.* **1,** the legal union of a man and a woman; a wedding. **2,** the state of being married or united. —**mar'riage·a·ble,** *adj.* eligible to be married.

mar·ron' (ma-rōñ') *n.* a chestnut, esp. candied. —**marrons gla·cées'** (gla-sā') candied chestnuts.

mar'row (mar'ō) *n.* **1,** a soft tissue in the interior of the bones. **2,** the essence; the real meaning. **3,** vitality.

mar'ry (mar'ē) *v.t.* **1,** unite in wedlock. **2,** take for husband or wife. —*v.i.* wed.

Mars (märz) *n.* **1,** the planet fourth from the sun and nearest the earth. **2,** the Roman god of war.

Mar''seil·laise' (mär''sā-yez') *n.* the French national song.

marsh (märsh) *n.* low, wet land; a swamp. —**marsh'y,** *adj.* —**marsh gas,** a toxic inflammable gas.

mar'shal (mär'shəl) *n.* **1,** a high military officer. **2,** a judicial, or police, officer. **3,** a person in charge of ceremonies, etc. —*v.t.* arrange in order; gather.

marsh'mal''low (märsh'mal''ō) *n.* a confection of gelatin and sugar.

mar·su'pi·al (mär-soo'pē-əl) *n.* a mammal having a *marsupium,* or external pouch, for its young, as the kangaroo.

mart (märt) *n.* a market.

mar'ten (mär'tən) *n.* an Amer. fur-bearing animal; its fur.

mar'tial (mär'shəl) *adj.* warlike; military; soldierly. —**martial law,** rule by military, not civil, authority.

Mar'tian (mär'shən) *adj.* pert. to the planet Mars. —*n.* a supposed inhabitant of this planet.

mar'tin (mär'tən) *n.* a swallowlike bird.

mar''ti·net' (mär''tə-net') *n.* a rigid disciplinarian.

mar'tin·gale'' (mär'tən-gāl'') *n.* **1,** in a

orse's harness, a strap between the girth
nd the bit. **2,** (*Naut.*) a short spar under
he bowsprit.

nar·ti'ni (mär-tē'nē) *n.* a cocktail of gin
and dry vermouth.

nar'tyr (mär'tər) *n.* one who suffers in
defense of a belief or cause. **—mar'tyr-
lom,** *n.* **—mar'tyr·ize"** (-īz") *v.t.*

mar'vel (mär'vəl) *n.* a wonderful or ex-
raordinary thing. **—***v.t. & i.* wonder at; be
moved by wonder. **—mar'vel·ous,** *adj.* ex-
raordinary.

Marx'ism (märk'siz-əm) *n.* the socialistic theory originated by the German econ-
omist, Karl Marx. **—Marx'i·an,** *adj.*
—Marx'ist, *n.*

Mary Jane (mār'ē-jān') (*Slang*) marijuana.

mar'zi·pan" (mär'zə-pan") *n.* an almond
confection. Also, **march'pane".**

mas·car'a (mas-kar'ə) *n.* a cosmetic used
on the eyelashes.

mas'cot (mas'kət) *n.* an animal or person
supposed to bring good luck.

mas'cu·line (mas'kyə-lin) *adj.* male;
manly; (of a woman) mannish. **—mas'cu-
lin'i·ty,** *n.*

ma'ser (mā'sər) *n.* a device that amplifies
or produces electromagnetic waves through
*M*icrowave *A*mplification by *S*timulated
*E*mission of *R*adiation.

mash *n.* a pulpy mixture, esp. of grain,
etc., for feed, distilling, etc. **—***v.t.* crush;
make into a mash.

mash'er (-ər) *n.* **1,** a machine or implement for crushing. **2,** (*Slang*) a man who
makes amorous advances to women with
whom he is not acquainted.

mash'ie (mash'ē) *n.* a golf club used in
making lofting shots, No. 5 iron.

mask (mäsk) *n.* **1,** a covering for the face,
worn for disguise, protection, etc. **2,** anything that conceals; a pretense. **3,** a masquerade. **4,** a likeness of a face, cast in
plaster. **—***v.t. & i.* disguise or conceal.

mas'o·chism (mas'ə-kiz-əm) *n.* pleasure
derived from self-suffering or humiliation.
—mas'o·chist, *n.* **—mas'o·chis'tic,** *adj.*

ma'son (mā'sən) *n.* **1,** one who builds with
brick, stone, etc. **2,** (*cap.*) a Freemason.
—Ma·son'ic (mə-son'ik) *adj.* **—Mason
jar,** a glass jar with an airtight closure.

Mason-Dixon line a surveyor's line, the
boundary between Pennsylvania and Maryland, once considered as separating slave
from free territory.

Ma'son·ite" (mā'sə-nīt") *n.* (T.N.) sheets
of pressed wood fiber, used for partitions
and as insulation.

ma'son·ry (mā'sən-rē) *n.* **1,** stonework.
2, (*cap.*) Freemasonry.

masque (mäsk) *n.* **1,** a dramatic entertainment. **2,** a masquerade.

mas"quer·ade' (mas"kə-rād') *n.* **1,** a gathering where masks are worn. **2,** a disguise;
concealment; false pretense. **—***v.i.* go about
under false pretenses.

mass (mas) *n.* **1,** a body of matter; a lump.
2, a quantity of matter in a body. **3,** an
assemblage of particles or things, as troops.
4, (*pl.*) the proletariat. **5,** the bulk; the
greater part. **6,** bulk; magnitude. **7,** (*cap.*) a
church service. **—***v.t.* collect into a mass.
—*v.i.* assemble. **—mass meeting,** a large
or general assembly. **—mass number,** the
sum of the numbers of protons and neutrons
in an atomic neucleus.

mas'sa·cre (mas'ə-kər) *n.* the indiscriminate wholesale killing of humans. **—***v.t.*
kill; defeat decisively.

mas·sage' (mə-säzh') *n.* treatment of the
muscles by rubbing, kneading, etc. **—***v.t.*
so treat.

mas·seur' (ma-sēr') *n.* one who massages
therapeutically. **—mas·seuse'** (ma-sûz')
n.fem.

mas'sif (mas'if) *n.* the dominant part of a
mountain range.

mas'sive (mas'iv) *adj.* **1,** bulky; heavy.
2, substantial; imposing. **—mas'sive·ness,**
n.

mass-"pro·duce' *v.t.* produce in large
quantities, esp. by automatic machines.
—mass-"pro·duc'tion, *n.*

mast (mäst) *n.* **1,** a vertical support for
yards, sails, etc., on a ship. **2,** any tall
pole. **3,** food for hogs, etc.

mas·tec'to·my (mas-tek'tə-mē) *n.* the removal of a breast.

mas'ter (mäs'tər) *n.* **1,** one who has chief
authority or control. **2,** one eminently skilled
in an occupation, art, or science. **—***adj.* **1,**
chief or principal; predominant. **2,** eminently
skilled. **—***v.t.* become master of; subdue.
—master hand, an expert. **—master key,**
a key opening many locks. **—master of
ceremonies,** a person who introduces the
speakers, performers, etc., as at a show.
Also, **M.C. —master sergeant,** a noncommissioned officer, ranking just below sergeant major (in the Air Force, just below
senior master sergeant).

mas'ter·ful (-fəl) *adj.* **1,** authoritative;
domineering. **2,** masterly. **—mas'ter·ful-
ness,** *n.*

mas'ter·ly (-lē) *adj.* skilled. **—mas'ter-
li·ness,** *n.*

mas'ter·mind" *n.* one who plans and directs an undertaking. **—***v.t.* plan and control (an undertaking).

mas′ter·piece″ *n*. a work of surpassing excellence. Also, **mas′ter·work″**.

mas′ter·y (más′tə-rè) *n*. power of control; command.

mast′head″ *n*. **1**, the top of a ship's mast. **2**, a statement of ownership, etc., in a newspaper.

mas′tic (mas′tik) *n*. **1**, a resin. **2**, a cement used in masonry or plastering.

mas′ti·cate (mas′tə-kāt″) *v.t. & i*. **1**, chew. **2**, crush or knead into pulp. —**mas″-ti·ca′tion**, *n*.

mas′tiff (más′tif) *n*. a large dog.

mas·ti′tis (mas-tī′tis) *n*. inflammation of the breast.

mas′to·don″ (mas′tə-don″) *n*. an extinct, elephantlike mammal.

mas′toid *n*. a bony prominence below and behind the ear. —*adj*. **1**, pert. to the mastoid. **2**, shaped like a nipple. —**mas″-toid·i′tis**, inflammation of the mastoid.

mas′tur·ba′tion (mas′tər-bā′shən) *n*. sexual self-gratification. —**mas′tur·bate″**, *v.i.*

mat *n*. **1**, a piece of fabric, woven of straw, etc., used on the floor, on a table, etc. **2**, a thick mass, as of weeds or hair. **3**, a lusterless surface. **4**, a matrix, in printing. **5**, a border placed around a picture, inside the frame (if any). —*v.t.* [**mat′ted, -ting**] **1**, cover with, or form into, a mat. **2**, finish with a dull surface. —*v.i.* become entangled. —*adj*. dull in surface.

mat′a·dor″ (mat′ə-dôr″) *n*. in a bullfight, the one who kills the bull.

match (mach) *n*. **1**, an equal; a peer. **2**, a pair; a mating. **3**, a contest, as in golf. **4**, a chemically-tipped piece of wood, etc., that ignites on friction. —*v.t.* mate; bring into agreement; equal. —*v.i.* contend; correspond; suit; harmonize. —**match′less**, *adj*. having no equal.

match′lock″ *n*. a musket in which the powder was ignited by a slow-burning cord.

match′mak″er *n*. one who arranges matrimonial matches, or athletic contests.

mate (māt) *n*. **1**, a husband or wife. **2**, one of a pair; a counterpart. **3**, an habitual associate. **4**, an officer on a merchant ship. **5**, checkmate. —*v.t.* join as a mate; marry; pair. —*v.i.* **1**, take a mate; marry. **2**, copulate.

ma·te′ri·al (mə-tir′ē-əl) *n*. **1**, a constituent principle or element; substance; raw matter to be developed. **2**, a textile fabric. —*adj*. **1**, physical; corporeal; not spiritual. **2**, important; essential.

ma·te′ri·al·ism (-iz-əm) *n*. devotion to material, rather than spiritual, needs or interests; self-interest. —**ma·te′ri·al·ist**, *n*.

—**ma·te″ri·al·is′tic**, *adj*. —**ma·te″ri·al·is′ti·cal·ly**, *adv*.

ma·te′ri·al·ize″ (-īz″) *v.t. & i*. give or assume, material form or perceptible existence (to) —**ma·te″ri·al·i·za′tion**, *n*.

ma·te′ri·al·ly (-ə-lē) *adv*. to an important extent.

ma·té·ri·el′ (mə-tir-ē-el′) *n*. equipment and supplies, esp. military.

ma·ter′nal (mə-tēr′nəl) *adj*. pert. to, befitting, or related to, a mother.

ma·ter′ni·ty (mə-tēr′nə-tē) *n*. state of being a mother.

math *n*. (*Colloq*.) mathematics.

math″e·mat′i·cal (math″ə-mat′i-kəl) *adj*. **1**, pert. to mathematics. **2**, exact; precise.

math″e·mat′ics (math″ə-mat′iks) *n. sing.* the science of numbers in all their relations and applications. —**math″e·ma·ti′cian** (-mə-tish′ən) *n*.

mat′in·al (mat′ə-nəl) *adj*. pert. to matins or morning.

mat′i·nee′ (mat″ə-nā′) *n*. a daytime dramatic performance.

mat′ins (mat′inz) *n.pl.* **1**, one of the seven canonical hours, beginning properly at midnight. **2**, a morning service.

ma′tri- *pref*. mother.

ma′tri·arch (mā′trē-ärk) *n*. a woman having chief authority in a household. —**ma″tri·ar′chal**, *adj*.

ma′tri·ar″chy (mā′trē-är″kē) *n*. a social system ruled by mothers or women.

mat′ri·cide″ (mat′ri-sīd″) *n*. the killer or killing of one's mother.

ma·tric′u·late″ (mə-trik′yə-lāt″) *v.t. & i*. enroll, or be enrolled, in a college. —**ma·tric′u·lant**, *n*. —**ma·tric″u·la′tion**, *n*.

mat′ri·mo″ny (mat′rə-mō″nē) *n*. the ceremony or sacrament of marriage. —**mat′ri·mo′ni·al**, *adj*.

ma′trix (mā′triks) *n*. [*pl.* **-tri·ces** (-tri-sēz)] **1**, that which forms or determines. **2**, a mold. **3**, (*Math*.) a rectangular array of quantities, such as a determinant.

ma′tron (mā′trən) *n*. **1**, a married woman. **2**, a woman in charge, as in an institution. —**ma′tron·ly**, *adj*. like a matron in manner or appearance; staid. —**matron of honor**, a married woman, attendant of the bride at a wedding.

matte (mat) *n*. **1**, an impure product of the smelting of certain ores. **2**, mat (def. 3).

mat′ted (mat′id) *adj*. covered with, or formed into, a mat or tangled mass.

mat′ter (mat′ər) *n*. **1**, the substance of which physical objects consist. **2**, any particular kind of substance, as *printed matter*. **3**, pus. **4**, the substance, as of a book. **5**, a thing of consequence; affair; business. —*v.i.*

1, be of consequence. **2,** form or excrete pus.

mat′ter-of-course′ *adj.* in the natural course of things.

mat′ter-of-fact′ *adj.* **1,** commonplace. **2,** unimaginative.

mat′ting (mat′ing) *n.* matted fabric; material for making mats.

mat′tock (mat′ək) *n.* a tool like a pickax, but with one end broad.

mat′tress (mat′ris) *n.* a cloth case filled with padding, used as or on a bed.

mat′u·rate″ (mach′ú-rāt″) *v.i.* suppurate. —**mat″u·ra′tion,** *n.* —**ma·tur′a·tive** (mə-tū′rə-tiv) *adj.*

ma·ture′ (mə-tyûr′) *adj.* complete in natural growth; ripe; fully developed. —*v.t. & i.* age; become mature. —**ma·tu′ri·ty,** *n.*

ma·tu′ti·nal (mə-tū′tə-nəl) *adj.* in the morning.

mat′zoth (mät′sōth) *n. pl.* [*sing.* **mat′zo** (-zə)] unleavened bread.

maud′lin (mâd′lin) *adj.* tearfully, or drunkenly, sentimental.

maul (mâl) *n.* a heavy hammer. —*v.t.* handle roughly.

maun′der (mân′dər) *v.i.* talk or move about in a rambling way.

mau″so·le′um (mâ″sə-lē′əm) *n.* a grand and stately tomb.

mauve (mōv) *n. & adj.* a color or dye, pale bluish purple.

ma′ven (mā′vən) *n.* an expert. Also, **ma′vin.**

mav′er·ick (mav′ər-ik) *n.* **1,** an unbranded cow or calf. **2,** a dissenter.

ma′vis (mā′vis) *n.* the Europ. song-thrush.

ma·vour′neen (mə-vûr′nēn) *n.* (*Irish*) my darling.

maw (mâ) *n.* the throat; gullet.

mawk′ish (mâ′kish) *adj.* nauseating; sickeningly sentimental. —**mawk′ish·ness,** *n.*

max′i- (mak′sē) *pref.* especially large, long, etc.

max′i·dress″ *n.* a woman's ankle-length dress. —**max′i·skirt″,** *n.* a woman's ankle-length skirt. Also, *colloq.,* **max′i.**

max·il′la (mak-sil′ə) *n.* [*pl.* **-lae** (-ē)] the upper jawbone. —**max′il·lar·y** (mak′sə-ler-ē) *adj.*

max′im (mak′sim) *n.* a pithy expression of a general truth, or a rule of conduct.

max′i·mum (mak′si-məm) *n.* [*pl.* **-ma** (-mə) or **-mums**] & *adj.* the greatest quantity or amount possible. —**max′i·mal** (-məl) *adj.* —**max′i·mize** (mīz) *v.t.* make as great as possible.

max′well (maks′wel) *n.* a unit of magnetic flux.

may (mā) *aux. v.* [*pret.* **might** (mīt)] expressing possibility, permission, wish, or contingency.

May *n.* the fifth month of the year.

Ma′ya (mä′yə) *n.* a member of a race formerly inhabiting Central America; their language. —**Ma′yan,** *adj. & n.*

may′be (mā′bē) *adv.* perhaps.

May Day 1, May 1, often celebrated with a spring festival, and also by organized labor and the Communist Party. **2,** a call of distress.

may′flow″er (mā′flow′ər) *n.* a spring-flowering plant, esp. the trailing arbutus.

may′fly *n.* an insect having a short adult life; an ephemerid.

may′hem (mā′hem) *n.* the infliction of serious bodily injury.

may″on·naise′ (mā″ə-nāz′) *n.* a thick salad dressing. Also, *colloq.,* **may′o** (mā′ō).

may′or (mā′ər) *n.* the principal officer of a municipality. —**may′or·al** (mā′ər-əl) *adj.* —**may′or·al·ty,** *n.* —**may′or·ess,** *n. fem.*

May′pole″ *n.* a pole around which persons dance on May Day, holding streamers attached to its top.

May wine a white wine flavored with woodruff and orange slices.

maze (māz) *n.* **1,** a labyrinth; a deception. **2,** bewilderment. —**maz′y,** *adj.*

ma′zel tov″ (mä′zəl-tov″) *interj.* (*Yiddish*) good luck; congratulations.

ma·zu′ma (mə-zoo′mə) *n.* (*Slang*) money.

ma·zur′ka (mə-zēr′kə) *n.* a lively Polish dance.

mbi′ra (em-bir′ə) *n.* an Afr. musical instrument.

McCoy, the (**real**) (mə-koi′) the real person or thing, not a substitute.

me (mē) *pron.* obj. of *I.*

mead (mēd) *n.* **1,** a fermented liquor of honey and yeast. **2,** (*Poetic*) meadow.

mead′ow (med′ō) *n.* a piece of land for raising hay or for pasture. —**meadow lark,** a yellow-breasted starling.

mea′ger (mē′gər) *adj.* lean; thin; without richness or fullness; scanty. —**mea′ger·ness,** *n.*

meal (mēl) *n.* **1,** a regular repast; sufficient food to satisfy the appetite. **2,** edible grain ground to a powder. **3,** any coarsely ground substance. —**meal ticket, 1,** a ticket for a meal at a restaurant. **2,** (*Slang*) a person or job depended upon for meals or financial support.

meal′y (mē′lē) *adj.* **1,** resembling, or covered with, meal. **2,** pale, as the complexion. —**meal′i·ness,** *n.*

meal′y·mouthed″ (mē′lė-mow*th*d″) *adj.* inclined to speak evasively; insincere.

mean (mēn) *v.t.* [*pret. & p.p.* **meant** (ment)] **1,** intend; purpose; have in mind for a particular use. **2,** signify; denote; express. —*v.i.* have intentions of some kind. —*adj.* **1,** inferior in quality; low in station; of small importance. **2,** miserly; stingy. **3,** (*Colloq.*) nasty; vicious; in poor health. **4,** (*Slang*) skillful. —*n.* **1,** something midway between two extremes. **2,** (*pl.*) what implements a plan; resources, esp. pecuniary. —**mean′y, mean′ie** (-ė) *n.* an unpleasant, often cruel, person. —**mean′ness,** *n.*

me·an′der (mė-an′dər) *v.i.* wander aimlessly; pursue a winding course.

mean′ing (mē′ning) *n.* that which is expressed; significance; import. —*adj.* significant. —**mean′ing·ful,** *adj.*

mean′time″ (mēn′tīm″) *n.* the intervening time. —*adv.* in the interval. Also, **mean′while″.**

mea′sles (mē′zəlz) *n.* an infectious, eruptive disease, chiefly in children.

mea′sly (mē′zlė) *adj.* **1,** infected with measles. **2,** (*Slang*) poor; inadequate. —**mea′sli·ness,** *n.*

meas′ure (mezh′ər) *n.* **1,** a unit or standard for determining extent, volume, quantity, etc., by comparison. **2,** any standard of comparison, estimation, or judgment. **3,** the instrument, act, or system of measurement. **4,** any definite quantity measured. **5,** a legislative bill. **6,** a rhythmical unit or movement, in poetry, music, or dance. —*v.t.* ascertain the extent of; estimate; appraise. —**meas′ure·less,** *adj.* unlimited. —**meas′ur·ing worm,** a type of caterpillar.

meas′ured *adj.* **1,** ascertained or regulated by measure. **2,** regular; deliberate.

meas′ure·ment (-mənt) *n.* **1,** act of measuring. **2,** the dimension, etc., ascertained.

meat (mēt) *n.* **1,** the flesh of animals, used for food. **2,** the edible part of anything; the material part; gist. —**meat′y,** *adj.* **1,** like meat. **2,** pithy.

Mec′ca (mek′ə) *n.* the holy city of Islam, goal of Moslem pilgrims; hence, a goal.

me·chan′ic (mə-kan′ik) *n.* **1,** [also, **mech′-ani′cian** (mek″ə-nish′ən)] a skilled worker with tools. **2,** a sharper at cards, dice, etc.

me·chan′i·cal (mə-kan′ə-kəl) *adj.* **1,** pert. to, operated by, or produced by, a mechanism or machine. **2,** artificial; not spontaneous; lacking in life or spirit. **3,** effected by physical forces; materialistic. —*n.* a layout for printing.

me·chan′ics (mə-kan′iks) *n.* **1,** the science of mechanical forces and motion. **2,** the science of machinery and mechanical appliances.

mech′an·ism (mek′ə-niz-əm) *n.* **1,** machinery. **2,** the agency by which an effect is produced or a purpose accomplished. **3,** mechanical execution. **4,** a belief that the processes of life are fully explainable by the laws of physics and chemistry. —**mech″a·nis′tic,** *adj.*

mech′a·nize″ (mek′ə-nīz″) *v.t.* **1,** make mechanical. **2,** (*Mil.*) equip with armored motor vehicles. —**mech″a·ni·za′tion,** *n.*

med′al (med′əl) *n.* a coinlike piece of metal inscribed to commemorate an event. —**med′al·ist,** *n.* one who has won a medal. —**Medal of Honor,** the highest U.S. military medal.

me·dal′lion (mə-dal′yən) *n.* a large carved medal.

med′dle (med′əl) *v.i.* interfere unjustifiedly. —**med′dler** (-lər) *n.* —**med′dle·some,** *adj.* disposed to meddle.

me′di·a (mē′dė-ə) *n.* **1,** *pl.* of **medium. 2,** [*pl.* **-ae** (-ė)] the middle wall of an artery.

me′di·al (mē′dė-əl) *adj.* intermediate; average; ordinary.

me′di·an (mē′dė-ən) *adj.* being the dividing line or plane between two parts; middle.

me′di·ate″ (mē′dė-āt″) *v.t. & i.* reconcile (opposing forces); settle (a dispute); effect an agreement between others. —**me″di·a′tion,** *n.* —**me′di·a′tor,** *n.*

med′ic (med′ik) *n.* (*Colloq.*) **1,** a doctor. **2,** a member of a medical corps.

Med′i·caid″ (med′i-kād″) *n.* a government program of medical aid for the financially underprivileged.

med′i·cal (med′i-kəl) *adj.* **1,** pert. to the science or practice of medicine. **2,** curative.

me·dic′a·ment (mə-dik′ə-mənt) *n.* any substance for healing wounds or curing disease.

Med′i·care″ (med′i-kâr″) *n.* a government program of medical aid for the aged.

med′i·cate″ (med′i-kāt″) *v.t.* treat with medicine.

med″i·ca′tion *n.* **1,** the use of medicine. **2,** a remedy.

med′i·cine (med′ə-sən) *n.* **1,** the science of treating disease or preserving health. **2,** a substance for treating disease; a remedy. —**me·dic′i·nal** (mə-dis′ə-nəl) *adj.* —**medicine ball,** a heavy ball, thrown for exercise. —**medicine man,** among primitive peoples, a healer by magic.

med′i·co″ (med′i-kō″) *n.* [*pl.* **-cos**] (*Slang*) a doctor.

---

fat, fāte, fär, fâre, fâll, åsk; met, hē, hėr, maybė; pin, pīne; not, nōte, ôr, tool

me″di·e′val (mē″dè-ē′vəl) *adj.* pert. to, or characteristic of, the Middle Ages. Also, **me″di·ae′val.**

me′di·o′cre (mē′dè-ō″kər) *adj.* of moderate quality; ordinary. —**me″di·oc′ri·ty** (-ok′rə-tè) *n.*

med′i·tate″ (med′i-tāt″) *v.t.* intend; plan. —*v.i.* brood. —**med″i·ta′tion,** *n.* —**med′i·ta′tive,** *adj.*

me′di·um (mē′dè-əm) *n.* **1,** something intermediate; a mean. **2,** an intervening substance, person, agency, or instrumentality, through which something exists or an effect is produced; in spiritualism, a person through whom the dead speak. **3,** [usually *pl.*, **me′di·a**] a publication, or other means of mass communication, used by an advertiser. —*adj.* intermediate. —**me″di·um·is′tic,** *adj.* pert. to or having the abilities of a medium (def. 2).

med′lar (med′lər) *n.* a small tree, or its apple-like fruit.

med′ley (med′lè) *n.* a mixture; a combination, as of songs.

me·dul′la (mi-dul′ə) *n.* (*Anatomy*) the marrow or center of an organ, etc. —**medulla ob″lon·ga′ta** (ob″long-gä′tə) the part of the brain adjoining the spinal cord.

meed (mēd) *n.* (*Archaic*) recompense; reward.

meek (mēk) *adj.* submissive; humble. —**meek′ness,** *n.*

meer′schaum (mir′shəm) *n.* a silicate used for the bowls of tobacco pipes.

meet (mēt) *v.t.* [*pret. & p.p.* **met**] **1,** come together, or into contact, with. **2,** encounter; welcome. **3,** conform to; answer; refute. —*v.i.* **1,** (often with *with*) come together; combine; agree. **2,** come into contact. —*n.* a meeting, as of huntsmen. —*adj.* suitable.

meet′ing *n.* **1,** a coming together; a junction. **2,** an encounter, sometimes hostile, as a duel. **3,** an assembly or gathering. —**meeting house,** a church.

meg·a- (meg-ə) *pref.* **1,** great. **2,** a million times.

meg′a·buck″ *n.* (*Slang*) one million dollars.

meg′a·cy″cle (meg′ə-sī″kəl) *n.* a million cycles: applied to wave lengths. Also, **meg′-a·hertz″.**

meg′a·death″ *n.* the death of one million persons.

meg′a·lith″ (meg′ə-lith″) *n.* a huge stone.

meg·al·o- (meg-ə-lə) *pref.* very large.

meg″a·lo·ma′ni·a *n.* a mania or delusion of greatness or wealth. —**meg″a·lo·ma′-ni·ac,** *n.*

meg″a·lop′o·lis (meg″ə-läp′ə-ləs) *n.* **1,** a

very large city. **2,** the heavily populated region around a large city; urban area.

meg′a·phone″ (meg′ə-fōn″) *n.* an instrument for magnifying sound.

me′grim (mē′grim) *n.* **1,** (*pl.*) lowness of spirit; "the blues." **2,** a headache.

mei·o′sis (mī-ō′sis) *n.* a process of cell division in which the number of chromosomes is halved.

mel′a·mine″ (mel′ə-mīn″) *n.* a type of thermoplastic.

mel″an·cho′li·a (mel″ən-kō′lè-ə) *n.* a mental disease marked by great depression of spirits. —**mel″an·cho′li·ac,** *n. & adj.*

mel′an·chol′y (mel′ən-kol′è) *n.* a gloomy state of mind; depression. —*adj.* sad. —**mel″an·chol′ic,** *adj.* —**mel″an·chol′i·cal·ly,** *adv.*

Mel″a·ne′sian (mel″ə-nē′zhən) *adj.* pert. to one of the principal regions of island groups in the So. Pacific.

mé·lange′ (mā-länzh′) *n.* a mixture; a medley.

mel′a·nin (mel′ə-nin) *n.* the dark pigment in the hair, skin, etc. —**me·lan′ic** (mə-lan′ik) *adj.*

mel′a·nism (mel′ə-niz-əm) *n.* abnormal development of dark pigmentation in the skin.

mel·a·no- (mel-ə-nō) *pref.* black.

mel″a·no′ma (mel″ə-nō′mə) *n.* a dark pigment skin tumor.

Mel′ba toast (mel′bə) bread sliced very thin and well browned.

meld *n.* a scoring combination of cards. —*v.t. & i.* **1,** announce or exhibit such cards. **2,** blend; merge.

me·lée′ (mā-lā′) *n.* a general hand-to-hand fight.

mel′io·rate″ (mēl′yə-rāt″) *v.t. & i.* make or become better. —**mel″io·ra′tion,** *n.*

mel·lif′lu·ous (mə-lif′loo-əs) *adj.* smoothly and sweetly flowing; flowing with honey. Also, **mel·lif′lu·ent,** —**mel·lif′lu·ence, mel·lif′lu·ous·ness,** *n.*

mel′low (mel′ō) *adj.* **1,** soft, esp. from ripeness. **2,** softened; matured; good-humored. —*v.t. & i.* make or become mellow. —**mel′low·ness,** *n.*

me·lo′de·on (mə-lō′dè-ən) *n.* a small organ.

me·lod′ic (mə-lod′ik) *adj.* tuneful; pert. to melody. —**me·lod′i·cal·ly,** *adv.*

me·lo′di·ous (mə-lō′dè-əs) *adj.* musical; tuneful. —**me·lo′di·ous·ness,** *n.*

mel′o·dra″ma (mel′ə-drä″mə) *n.* a play with a sensational plot and exaggerated sentiment.

mel″o·dra·mat′ic (-drə-mat′ik) *adj.* affecting undue sentiment. —**mel″o·dra·mat′-**

i·cal·ly, adv. **—mel″o·dra·mat′ics,** n.sing. & pl.

mel′o·dy (mel′ə-dē) n. a tune; the air of a musical composition; a succession of musical tones.

mel′on (mel′ən) n. a large fruit with a juicy flesh inside a rind.

melt v.t. & i. **1,** make or become liquid through heat. **2,** dissolve. **3,** dwindle; blend. **4,** be softened to tenderness, sympathy, etc. **—melting pot,** a country or city that assimilates and unites immigrants of various national origins.

mem′ber (mem′bər) n. **1,** a part of any aggregate or whole. **2,** a part of the body; a vital organ; a limb. **3,** each of the persons composing a society, party, or legislative body. **—mem′ber·ship″,** n. the state of being a member, as of a party; the total number of such members.

mem′brane (mem′brān) n. a sheet of thin tissue, lining an organ, connecting parts, etc. **—mem′bra·nous** (-brə-nəs) adj.

me·men′to (mə-men′tō) n. [pl. **-tos**] a reminder; a souvenir.

mem′o (mem′ō) n. [pl. **-os**] a memorandum.

mem′oir (mem′wär) n. **1,** a record of facts. **2,** (pl.) a narrative of facts and events, esp. of one's own life.

mem″o·ra·bil′i·a (mem″ər-ə-bil′ē-ə) n.pl. [sing. **mem″o·ra′bi·le** (-rab′ə-lē)] memorable events.

mem′o·ra·ble (mem′ə-rə-bəl) adj. worthy to be remembered.

mem″o·ran′dum (mem″ə-ran′dəm) n. [pl. **-dums** or **-da** (-də)] **1,** a record. **2,** a note to help the memory.

me·mo′ri·al (mə-môr′ē-əl) n. **1,** a commemorative monument, etc. **2,** a petition. **—**adj. commemorating. **—me·mo′ri·al·ize″** (-īz″) v.t. **—Memorial Day,** a federal legal holiday, the last Monday in May.

mem′o·rize″ (mem′ə-rīz″) v.t. commit to memory. **—mem″o·ri·za′tion,** n.

mem′o·ry (mem′ə-rē) n. **1,** the mental capacity of retaining and reviving impressions; remembrance; recollection. **2,** the state of being remembered. **3,** that which is remembered. **4,** the device or location, as in a computer, where data is stored.

men n. pl. of man.

men′ace (men′is) n. a threat or threatening. **—**v.t. threaten.

mé·nage′ (mā-näzh′) n. a household.

me·nag′er·ie (mə-naj′ə-rē) n. a collection or exhibition of wild animals.

mend v.t. repair; make whole; correct; improve. **—**v.i. improve in health; become whole. **—**n. **1,** a mended place. **2,** recovery from sickness.

men·da′cious (men-dā′shəs) adj. **1,** untrue. **2,** untruthful. **—men·dac′i·ty** (-das′-ə-tē) n.

men″de·le′vi·um (men″də-lē′vē-əm) n. a radioactive chemical element, no. 101, symbol Md.

men′di·cant (men′di-kənt) n. a beggar. **—**adj. begging. **—men′di·can·cy,** n.

men·ha′den (men-hā′dən) n. [pl. **men·ha′den**] a marine fish of the eastern U.S., used in making fertilizer.

men′hir n. an upright ornamental stone.

me′ni·al (mē′nē-əl) n. **1,** a domestic servant. **2,** a servile person. **—**adj. lowly; servile.

men″in·gi′tis (men″in-jī′tis) n. inflammation of the membranes of the brain and spinal cord.

Men′no·nite″ (men′ə-nīt″) n. a member of a certain fundamentalist Protestant sect.

men′o·pause″ (men′ə-pâz″) n. the final cessation of the menses; change of life.

me·no′rah (mə-nô′rə) n. the Judaic seven-branched candelabrum.

Mensch (mensh) n. (Colloq.) a human being, esp. one with compassion for one's fellow person.

men′ses (men′sēz) n.pl. the monthly discharge from the uterus.

men′stru·ate″ (men′stroo-āt″) v.i. discharge the menses. **—men′stru·al,** adj. **—men″stru·a′tion,** n.

men′sur·a·ble (men′shər-ə-bəl) adj. measurable. **—men″su·ra′tion,** n. the process of measuring.

men′sur·al (men′shər-əl) adj. pert. to measure.

-ment (mənt) suf. the act, fact, or result of doing (the root word).

men′tal (men′təl) adj. pert. to, or performed by, the mind or intellect. **—mental deficiency, mental retardation,** subnormal intellectual development, often caused by a defect in the central nervous system.

men′tal·ist (-ist) n. mind reader.

men·tal′i·ty (men-tal′ə-tē) n. **1,** mental capacity. **2,** the mind.

men′thol (men′thol) n. a crystalline substance derived from oil of peppermint, useful in treating nasal disorders. **—men′tho·lat″ed,** adj. treated with or containing menthol.

men′tion (men′shən) v.t. refer to briefly or incidentally. **—**n. a brief reference.

men′tor (men′tôr) n. a wise adviser; a trusted teacher and counselor.

men′u (men′ū) n. a bill of fare.

---

fat, fāte, fär, fâre, fâll, àsk; met, hē, hêr, maybē; pin, pīne; not, nōte, ôr, tool

me·ow' (mĕ-ow') *n.* the whining sound made by a cat. —*v.i.* so cry.

me·per'i·dine" (mə-per'ə-dēn") *n.* a synthetic, morphine-like narcotic drug.

me·phi'tis (mi-fī'tis) *n.* a noxious or poisonous exhalation; a stench. —**me·phit'ic** (-fit'ik) *adj.*

mer'can·tile (mēr'kən-til) *adj.* pert. to merchants or trading; commercial. —**mer'can·til·ism,** *n.*

Mer·ca'tor projection (mēr-kā'tər) a method of map-making in which the meridians and parallels of latitude are straight lines, intersecting at right angles.

mer'ce·nar"y (mēr'sə-ner"ē) *adj.* serving only for gain; avaricious. —*n.* a hired soldier; a hireling.

mer'cer (mēr'sər) *n.* a dealer in cloth. —**mer'cer·y,** *n.*

mer'cer·ize" (mēr'sə-rīz") *v.t.* treat cotton fabric with caustic alkali, to increase its luster and strength.

mer'chan·dise" (mēr'chən-dīs") *n.* commodities bought and sold. —*v.t. & i.* (-dīz") market.

mer'chant (mēr'chənt) *n.* one who buys and sells commodities. —**merchant marine,** ships used in commerce; their crews.

mer'chant·man (mēr'chənt-mən) *n.* [*pl.* -men] a trading vessel.

mer·ci' (mer-sē') *interj.* (*Fr.*) thank you.

mer'ci·ful (mēr'si-fəl) *adj.* compassionate; lenient.

mer'ci·less (-ləs) *adj.* pitiless. —**mer'ci·less·ness,** *n.*

mer·cu'ri·al (mər-kyûr'ē-əl) *adj.* **1,** [also, **mer·cur'ic**] pert. to mercury. **2,** sprightly; changeable.

mer·cu'ro·chrome" (mər-kyûr'ə-krōm") *n.* an antiseptic or germicide.

mer'cu·ry (mēr'kyə-rē) *n.* **1,** a fluid metallic element, no. 80, symbol Hg. **2,** (*cap.*) the planet nearest the sun. —**mer'cur·ous,** *adj.*

mer'cy (mēr'sē) *n.* **1,** compassionate leniency toward an enemy or wrongdoer. **2,** discretionary power to punish or spare. —**mercy killing,** the painless putting to death of persons suffering from incurable diseases; euthanasia. —**mercy seat,** the throne of God.

mere (mir) *adj.* simple; only. —*n.* a lake; pond. —**mere'ly** (-lē) *adv.* simply; solely.

mer"e·tri'cious (mer"ə-trish'əs) *adj.* deceitfully alluring; tawdry. —**mer"e·tri'cious·ness,** *n.*

mer·gan'ser (mər-gan'sər) *n.* a fish-eating duck.

merge (mērj) *v.i.* **1,** be absorbed; lose identity. **2,** unite. —*v.t.* cause to be absorbed or unite.

merg'er (mēr'jər) *n.* a uniting of two or more businesses.

me·rid'i·an (mə-rid'ē-ən) *n.* **1,** a great circle, of the earth or the heavens, passing through the poles; half of this circle. **2,** the zenith; midday. —**me·rid'i·o·nal,** *adj.*

me·ringue' (mə-rang') *n.* a white-of-egg and sugar coating for pastry.

me·ri'no (mə-rē'nō) *n.* [*pl.* -nos] a sheep prized for its fine wool.

mer'it *n.* **1,** a commendable quality; worthiness. **2,** (*pl.*) the qualities by which something is evaluated. —*v.t.* deserve.

mer"i·to'ri·ous (mer"i-tôr'ē-əs) *adj.* deserving of praise or reward.

merle (mērl) *n.* the Europ. blackbird.

mer'lin (mēr'lin) *n.* a small hawk.

mer'maid" (mēr'mād") *n.* an imaginary marine woman, with the tail of a fish. —**mer'man",** *n.masc.*

mer'ry (mer'ē) *adj.* **1,** festive. **2,** mirthful. —**mer'ri·ment,** *n.*

mer"ry-an'drew (mer"ē-an'droo) *n.* a clown; buffoon.

mer'ry-go-round" (mer'ē-gō-rownd") *n.* a revolving platform fitted with hobbyhorses, etc.

mer'ry·mak"er (-mā'kər) *n.* a reveler. —**mer'ry·mak"ing,** *n.*

mer·thi'o·late" (mər-thī'ə-lāt") *n.* (*T.N.*) a red liquid compound of mercury used as an antiseptic and germicide.

me'sa (mā'sə) *n.* a tableland.

més·al'li·ance (mā-zal'ē-əns) *n.* a marriage with a social inferior.

mes·cal' (mes-kal') *n.* **1,** a cactus. **2,** an intoxicating beverage.

mes'ca·line" (mes'kə-lēn") *n.* a crystalline, hallucinogenic compound. Also, **mez'ca·line".**

mesh *n.* an open space of a net; a network. —*v.t.* **1,** entangle; enmesh. **2,** engage, as gear teeth. —*v.i.* become engaged; work efficiently (with another).

mesh'work *n.* network.

mes'mer·ism (mes'mə-riz-əm) *n.* hypnotism. —**mes·mer'ic** (-mer'ik) *adj.* —**mes'mer·ist,** *n.* —**mes'mer·ize",** *v.t.*

mes·o- (mez-ə) *pref.* middle.

mes"o·lith'ic (me"zə-lith'ik) *adj.* pert. to an early period of the Stone Age.

me'son (mā'sän) *n.* an unstable nuclear particle of variable charge, first found in cosmic rays. Also, **mes'o·tron".**

me'so·sphere" *n.* an atmospheric layer above the ionosphere.

mes'o·tron" (mez'ə-tron") *n.* a meson.

Mes″o·zo′ic (mez″ə-zō′ik) *adj.* pert. to a geological era, the age of reptiles.

mes·quite′ (mes-kēt′) *n.* a shrub of the Southwest U. S., on which grazing cattle feed.

mess (mes) *n.* **1,** an untidy condition or mass. **2,** a confused situation. **3,** a group taking meals together; such a meal. —*v.t.* make untidy; muddle. —*v.i.* **1,** eat in company. **2,** act or work haphazardly.

mes′sage (mes′ij) *n.* a verbal or written communication.

mes′sen·ger (mes′ən-jər) *n.* one who bears a message or goes on an errand.

Mes·si′ah (mə-sī′ə) *n.* **1,** the prophesied deliverer of the Jews; a savior. **2,** to Christians, Jesus Christ. —**Mes″si·an′ic** (mes″ē-an′ik) *adj.*

mess′mate″ *n.* an associate in a ship's mess.

mess′y (-ė) *adj.* untidy. —**mess′i·ness,** *n.*

mes·ti′zo (mes-tē′zō) *n.* a person of mixed blood, as Spanish and Amer. Indian. —**mes·ti′za,** *n.fem.*

met *v.* pret. & p.p. of *meet.*

met·a- (met-ə) *pref.* along with; after; over; also denoting change or transformation.

me·tab′o·lism (mə-tab′ə-liz-əm) *n.* the chemical process of absorbing food. —**met″·a·bol′ic** (met″ə-bol′ik) *adj.* —**me·tab′o·lite** (-līt) *n.* a product of metabolism.

met″a·car′pus (met″ə-kär′pəs) *n.* [*pl.* **-pi** (pī)] the part of the hand between the wrist and the fingers.

met″a·gal′ax·y *n.* the entire material universe, including all seen and unseen galaxies. —**met″a·ga·lac′tic,** *adj.*

met′al (met′əl) *n.* an elementary substance possessing opacity, conductivity, plasticity, and a peculiar luster, as gold, silver, etc.; an alloy of such substances. —**me·tal′lic** (mə-tal′ik) *adj.* —**me·tal′li·cal·ly,** *adv.*

met′al·loid″ (met′ə-loid″) *n.* an element having some but not all of the properties of a metal.

met′al·lur″gy (met′ə-lẽr″jē) *n.* the science of separating metals from their ores, treating metals, and compounding alloys. —**met″·al·lur′gic,** *adj.* —**met′al·lur″gist,** *n.*

met″a·mor′pho·sis (met″ə-môr′fə-sis) *n.* a complete change of form, structure, or appearance. —**met″a·mor′phic,** *adj.* —**met″·a·mor′phose** (-fōz) *v.t. & i.*

met′a·phor (met′ə-fər) *n.* a figure of speech, based on some resemblance of a literal to an implied subject. —**met″a·phor′·i·cal** (-for′i-kəl) *adj.* —**met″a·phor′ic,** *adj.*

met″a·phys′ics (met″ə-fiz′iks) *n.* philosophy in general; particularly the science of essential principles, or the more abstruse or abstract principles. —**met″a·phys′i·cal,** *adj.* concerned with the abstract. —**met″a·phy·si′cian,** *n.*

met′a·plasm (met′ə-plaz-əm) *n.* the lifeless matter included with protoplasm in a cell.

me·tas′ta·sis (mə-tas′tə-sis) *n.* **1,** a change of substance. **2,** transference of a disease to another part of the body. **3,** a sudden rhetorical transition. —**met″a·stat′ic,** *adj.*

met″a·tar′sus (met″ə-tär′sus) *n.* [*pl.* **-si** (-sī)] the foot bone between the ankle and toes. —**met″a·tar′sal,** *adj.*

Met″a·zo′a (met″ə-zō′ə) *n.* all those animals which are above the Protozoa, and have two or more cells. —**Met″a·zo′an,** *adj. & n.*

mete (mēt) *v.t.* apportion by measure.

me·temp″sy·cho′sis (mə-temp″sə-kō′sis) *n.* [*pl.* **-ses** (-sēz)] the passing of the soul after death into another body; reincarnation.

me′te·or (mē′tė-ər) *n.* matter from space that becomes luminous upon entering the earth's atmosphere.

me″te·or′ic (-or′ik) *adj.* **1,** pert. to a meteor. **2,** transiently brilliant. —**me″te·or′·i·cal·ly,** *adv.*

me′te·or·ite″ (-īt″) *n.* a mass of stone or metal that reaches the earth from outer space.

me′te·or·oid″ (-oid″) *n.* a small meteor.

me″te·or·ol′o·gy (mē″tė-ə-rol′ə-jē) *n.* the scientific study of the atmosphere, the weather, etc. —**me″te·or·o·log′i·cal,** *adj.*

me′ter (mē′tər) *n.* **1,** the metric unit of length, 39.37 inches. **2,** poetic or musical rhythm or measure. **3,** an instrument that measures, as gas, water, etc. —*v.t.* measure or record by a meter. Also, **me′tre.**

me′ter·maid″ *n.* a policewoman assigned to check for parking violations.

meth′a·done″ (meth′ə-dōn″) *n.* a synthetic, morphine-like narcotic drug.

meth′ane (meth′ān) *n.* an inflammable natural gas.

meth′a·nol″ (meth′ə-nol″) *n.* wood alcohol.

meth′e·drine″ (meth′ə-drēn″) *n.* an amphetamine drug; speed.

meth′od (meth′əd) *n.* systematic procedure; a plan or system of conduct or action. —**me·thod′i·cal,** *adj.* following a method; orderly. —**meth′od·ize″,** *v.t.*

Meth′od·ist (meth′ə-dist) *n.* a member of the United Methodist Church, a principal Protestant sect. —**Meth′od·ism,** *n.*

meth″od·ol′o·gy (meth″ə-dol′ə-jē) *n.* **1,** a system of methods. **2,** the branch of logic dealing with the principles of reasoning in scientific inquiry.

meth'yl (meth'il) *n.* a derivative of methane. **—methyl alcohol**, wood alcohol.

me·tic'u·lous (mə-tik'yə-ləs) *adj.* finically careful. **—me·tic'u·lous·ness**, *n.*

mé·tier' (mā-tyā') *n.* **1**, profession; trade. **2**, appropriate field or surroundings.

mé·tis' (mā-tēs') *n.* **1**, a person of mixed blood; halfbreed. **2**, a crossbred animal. Also, **mé·tif'** (-tēf').

met'ra·zol (met'rə-zōl") *n.* (*T.N.*) a drug, a heart and lung stimulant.

met'ric (met'rik) *adj.* **1**, pert. to the meter (measure of length). **2**, pert. to measurement. **—metric system**, a decimal system of weights and measures.

met'ri·cal (met'ri-kəl) *adj.* composed in meter, as verse.

met'ri·cize' (met'ri-sīz") *v.t.* convert to the metric system. **—met"ri·ca'tion**, *n.*

met'ro (met'rō) *n.* **1**, the Paris subway; any subway. **2**, metropolitan region. *—adj.* metropolitan.

met'ro·nome" (met'rə-nōm") *n.* a mechanical contrivance for signaling intervals of time.

me·trop'o·lis (mə-trop'ə-lis) *n.* the chief city of a country or region.

met"ro·pol'i·tan (met"rə-pol'ə-tən) *adj.* characteristic of a metropolis. *—n.* **1**, an inhabitant of a metropolis. **2**, (*cap.*) a title in the Orthodox Church, equivalent to archbishop.

-me·try (mə-trē) *suf.* measurement.

met'tle (met'əl) *n.* natural temperament; courage. **—met'tle·some**, *adj.* spirited.

mew (mū) *n.* **1**, an enclosure. **2**, (*pl.*) a set of stables around a court. **3**, meow. *—v.i.* meow.

mewl (mūl) *v.i.* whine; whimper.

Mex'i·can (mek'si-kən) *adj. & n.* pert. to Mexico, its language or inhabitants.

mez'za·nine" (mez'ə-nēn") *n.* **1**, a low story between two principal stories. **2**, a theater balcony.

mezzo- (met'sō-) *pref.* intermediate.

mez'zo-so·pran'o *n.* a voice intermediate between soprano and contralto.

mez'zo·tint" *n.* an engraving made by roughening a copper or other metallic surface.

mho (mō) *n.* a unit of electrical conductivity.

mi (mē) *n.* (*Music*) the third tone in the diatonic scale.

mi·aou' (mė-ow') *n. & v.i.* meow.

mi·as'ma (mī-az'mə) *n.* noxious emanation.

mi'ca (mī'kə) *n.* a mineral, readily separable into thin sheets.

mice (mīs) *n.* pl. of *mouse*.

Mick'ey (mik'ē) *n.* (*Slang*) a drink containing knockout drops or a purgative. Also, **Mickey Finn**.

micro- (mī-krō) *pref.* **1**, very small. **2**, one-millionth part. Also, before vowels, **mi'cr-**.

mi'crobe (mī'krōb) *n.* a germ; a bacterium. **—mi·cro'bic**, *adj.*

mi"cro·bi·ol'o·gy *n.* the branch of biology dealing with microorganisms.

mi"cro·com·pu'ter *n.* a small computer, esp. for personal or small-business use.

mi'cro·cosm (mī'krə-koz-əm) *n.* **1**, a little world; a world in miniature. **2**, fig., man.

mi'cro·dot" *n.* printed matter reduced photographically to the size of a dot.

mi'cro·fiche" (-fēsh") *n.* a card or sheet of microfilm containing information considerably reduced in size.

mi'cro·film" (mī'krə-film") *n.* the film used in microphotography.

mi'cro·graph" *n.* **1**, a pantograph for drawing and engraving in microscopic size. **2**, a photograph or drawing of an object as seen through a microscope. **—mi·crog'raph·y** (mī-krog'rə-fē) *n.*

Mi'cro·groove" (mī'krə-groov") *n.* cap. *T.N.* **1**, an extremely narrow groove in a long-playing phonograph record. **2**, such a record.

mi·crom'e·ter (mī-krom'ə-tər) *n.* a precision instrument for measuring distances in thousandths of an inch or less.

mi'cron (mī'kron) *n.* [*pl.* **-cra** (-krə), **-crons**] one millionth of a meter.

Mi"cro·ne'sian (mī"krə-nē'zhən) *adj.* pert. to a certain group of very small islands in the So. Pacific.

mi"cro·or'gan·ism (mī"krō-ôr'gə-niz-əm) *n.* an organism of microscopic size; a microbe, germ, etc.

mi'cro·phone" (mī-krə-fōn") *n.* an instrument that transforms sound waves into variations in an electric current; used esp. in telephonic and radio transmission and in recording.

mi"cro·pho'to·graph" *n.* a minute film reproduction, esp. of printed or written matter, read by enlargement on a screen. **—mi"cro·pho·tog'ra·phy**, *n.*

mi'cro·scope" (mī'krə-skōp") *n.* an instrument that magnifies objects not visible to the naked eye.

mi"cro·scop'ic (-skop'ik) *adj.* **1**, pert. to a microscope. **2**, extremely small. **—mi"cro·scop'i·cal·ly**, *adv.*

---

tub, cūte, pûll; labəl; oil, owl, go, chip, she, thin, *th*en, sing, ink; *see p. 6*

mi·cro·sur″ger·y *n.* extremely delicate surgery performed under a microscope.

mi′cro·tome″ (mī′krə-tōm″) *n.* an instrument for cutting tissue, etc., into thin sections for examination under the microscope.

mi′cro·wave″ (mī′krə-wāv″) *n.* (*Radio*) a very small electromagnetic wave having a wavelength less than one meter. —**microwave oven,** a cooking machine using microwaves to heat food.

mid *adj.* middle. —*prep.* amid; among.

mid′air″ *adj.* occurring in the air.

mid′day″ (mid′dā″) *n.* the middle of the day; noon.

mid′dle (mid′əl) *adj.* **1,** equally distant from the extremes or limits. **2,** intermediate; intervening. —*n.* **1,** the center; a middle point or area. **2,** the waist; the stomach. —**Middle Ages,** the period between classical antiquity and the Renaissance, roughly A.D. 500 to 1400. —**middle class,** an intermediate social or economic class. —**middle ear,** (*Anat.*) the tympanum. —**Middle East, 1,** a region including Iran, Iraq, and Afghanistan, and sometimes Burma, Tibet, and India. **2,** (*Brit.*) the Near East (def. 1). Also, **Mid′east″. —middle-of-the-road,** *adj.* neutral; midway between extremes. —**middle school,** a division in some schools, often corresponding to junior high school. —**Middle West,** the north central states of the U.S.

mid′dle-aged′ (mid′əl-ājd′) *adj.* intermediate in range; from about 45 to 60 years old.

mid′dle·man″ (mid′əl-man″) *n.* [*pl.* -men] an intermediary; esp. in business, a wholesaler or retailer.

mid′dle·weight″ (mid′əl-wāt″) *n.* a boxer weighing 148 to 160 lbs.

mid′dling (mid′ling) *adj.* **1,** of medium quality or size. **2,** (*Colloq.*) in moderate health.

mid′dy (mid′ē) *n.* **1,** a loose blouse with a sailor collar: *middy blouse.* **2,** a midshipman.

midge (mij) *n.* a small fly.

midg′et (mij′it) *n.* a very small person or thing.

mid′i·dress″ (mid′ē-) *n.* a woman's dress of mid-calf length. —**mid′i·skirt″,** *n.* a woman's skirt of mid-calf length. Also, *colloq.,* **mid′i.**

mid′i″ron (mid′ī″ərn) *n.* a golf club used for long approach shots, No. 2 iron.

mid′land (mid′lənd) *adj.* in the interior of a country; inland.

mid′night″ (mid′nīt″) *n.* 12 o'clock at night. —*adj.* **1,** at midnight. **2,** intensely black or dark. —**midnight sun,** the sun visible at midnight during the summer in arctic or antarctic regions.

mid′riff (mid′rif) *n.* **1,** the diaphragm. **2,** a dress open at the midriff.

mid′ship″man (mid′ship″mən) *n.* [*pl.* -men] one in training to be a naval officer; his rank.

midst *n.* an interior or central position; middle.

mid′stream″ *n.* the middle of a stream, current of affairs, etc.

mid′sum″mer *n.* the middle of summer; the summer solstice. —**mid′win″ter,** *n.* the winter solstice.

mid′way″ (mid′wā″) *adj.* halfway. —*n.* a place for side shows at a fair.

Mid′west′ *n.* Middle West.

mid′wife″ (mid′wīf″) *n.* a woman who assists at childbirth. —**mid′wife″ry,** *n.*

mien (mēn) *n.* a person's bearing, manner, appearance.

miff (mif) *v.t.* (*Colloq.*) offend.

might (mīt) *n.* effective power; ability. —*aux. v.* pret. of *may.*

might′y (mī′tē) *adj.* powerful; momentous. —*adv.* (*Colloq.*) very. —**might′i·ness,** *n.*

mi″gnon·ette′ (min″yə-net′) *n.* a fragrant garden plant.

mi′graine (mī′grān) *n.* a severe headache, sometimes accompanied by nausea.

mi′grant (mī′grənt) *n.* one who or that which migrates. —*adj.* migrating.

mi′grate (mī′grāt) *v.i.* **1,** go from one country or place of residence to settle in another. **2,** move periodically from one region or latitude to another, esp. birds. —**mi·gra′tion,** *n.* —**mi′gra·to·ry,** *adj.*

mi·ka′do (mi-kä′dō) *n.* formerly, the emperor of Japan.

mike (mīk) (*Slang*) *n.* a microphone. —*v.t.* measure with a micrometer.

mil *n.* a unit of length, .001 of an inch.

milch *adj.* giving milk, as a cow.

mild (mīld) *adj.* even-tempered; gentle; temperate; moderate in intensity or degree; not severe, as weather; not sharp, as flavor. —**mild′ness,** *n.*

mil′dew (mil′doo) *n.* **1,** a fungus disease of plants. **2,** a white fungus coating on fabrics, leather, etc., from exposure to moisture. —*v.t. & i.* become covered with mildew.

mile (mīl) *n.* a Brit. and Amer. unit of distance, 5,280 ft. (*statute mile*) on land, 6,080 ft. (*nautical mile*) at sea.

mile′age (mī′lij) *n.* **1,** the miles traveled in a given time. **2,** a fixed charge per mile. **3,** a traveling allowance.

mile′post″ *n.* **1,** a post marking the distance in miles along a highway. **2**, (*fig.*) an important point of time, as in a lifetime.

mil′er (mīl′ər) *n.* a runner trained to race a mile.

mile′stone″ (mīl′stōn″) *n.* **1**, a stone distance-marker along a highway. **2**, an important event in life; a birthday.

mil′i·ar′i·a (mil″ē-âr′ē-ə) *n.* an inflammatory skin disease. —**mil′i·ar·y,** *adj.*

mi·lieu′ (mē-lyū′) *n.* surroundings; environment.

mil′i·tant (mil′i-tənt) *adj.* **1**, aggressive. **2**, engaged in warfare. —*n.* one engaged in warfare. —**mil′i·tan·cy,** *n.*

mil′i·ta·rism (mil′ə-tə-riz-əm) *n.* extreme emphasis on military power in state policy. —**mil′i·ta·rist,** *n.* —**mil″i·ta·ris′tic,** *adj.*

mil′i·ta·rize″ (mil′i·tə-rīz″) *v.t.* equip or prepare for war. —**mil″i·tar·i·za′tion,** *n.*

mil′i·tar″y (mil′ə-ter″ē) *adj.* **1**, pert. to the army, a soldier, or affairs of war; soldierly. **2**, pert. to any arm or instrument of warfare. —*n.* the army.

mil′i·tate″ (mil′ə-tāt″) *v.i.* have weight or force, against or for.

mi·li′tia (mi-lish′ə) *n.* a body of citizen soldiers, called out only in emergencies. —**mi·li′tia·man,** *n.*

milk *n.* **1**, a whitish liquid secreted by the mammary glands of female mammals for feeding their young. **2**, any liquid resembling this. —*v.t.* **1**, extract milk from a cow, etc. **2**, extract; draw out; exploit. —**milk fever,** a fever coincident with lactation. —**milk leg,** thrombosis and swelling of the large veins of the leg. —**milk of magnesia,** a mild laxative. —**milk shake,** an iced drink of milk, a flavoring syrup, and usu. ice cream, shaken together. —**milk tooth,** one of the temporary teeth of a young child or animal; baby tooth.

milk′maid″ *n.* a girl who milks cows.

milk′man″ *n.* [*pl.* **-men**] a man who delivers milk for a dairy.

milk′sop″ *n.* a soft, effeminate man.

milk′weed″ (milk′wēd″) *n.* a plant having milky juice.

milk′wort″ (milk′wērt″) *n.* a flowering herb or shrub.

milk′y (mil′kē) *adj.* **1**, like milk. **2**, white. —**milk′i·ness,** *n.* —**Milky Way,** a luminous band in the heavens, composed of innumerable stars.

mill (mil) *n.* **1**, a manufacturing establishment; factory. **2**, a building equipped to grind grain into flour. **3**, any of various machines for grinding, or otherwise working materials into proper form. **4**, one tenth of a cent in U. S. money. —*v.i.* move in a circle, as cattle. —*v.t.* **1**, grind, etc., in or

with a mill. **2**, groove the edge of (a coin, etc.).

mil·len′ni·um (mi-len′ē-əm) *n.* **1**, a thousand years; a thousandth anniversary. **2**, any period of universal happiness. —**mil·len′ni·al** (-əl) *adj.*

mill′er (mil′ər) *n.* **1**, one who operates a grain mill. **2**, a small moth.

mil′let (mil′it) *n.* a cereal grass, grown for grain or fodder.

mil·li- (mil-ə) *pref.* thousand; in the metric system, one-thousandth. —**mil′li·gram″,** 1/1000th gram. —**mil′li·me″ter,** *n.* 1/1000th meter.

mil′liard (mil′yərd) *n.* (*Brit.*) one thousand million; billion.

mil′li·ner (mil′ə-nər) *n.* one who makes or sells women's hats. —**mil′li·ner″y,** *n.* women's hats.

mill′ing *n.* **1**, act or process of grinding, etc. **2**, the grooves or ridges on the edge of a coin. **3**, a slow circulating movement in a crowd of persons, cattle, etc. **4**, (*Slang*) a thrashing.

mil′lion (mil′yən) *n.* one thousand times one thousand; 1,000,000.

mil″lion·aire′ (mil″yə-nâr′) *n.* a person worth a million dollars, pounds, etc.; a very rich person.

mil′lionth (mil′yənth) *adj. & n.* the ordinal of one million, also written 1,000,000th; one of one million equal parts.

mil′li·pede″ (mil′ə-pēd″) *n.* any of several insects with a many-segmented body.

mill′race″ (mil′rās″) *n.* the current of water that drives a mill, or the channel in which it flows.

mill′stone″ (mil′stōn″) *n.* **1**, one of two heavy circular stones between which grain is ground. **2**, a heavy burden.

mi′lo (mī′lō) *n.* a milletlike sorghum grown in the U.S. for forage.

milque′toast″ (milk′tōst″) *n.* (*Slang*) a timid person.

mil′reis″ (mil′rās″) *n.* the monetary unit of Brazil.

milt *n.* **1**, the reproductive organs of male fish. **2**, fish sperm. —*adj.* breeding. —*v.t.* fertilize (roe) with milt.

mime (mīm) *n.* **1**, a mummer. **2**, in ancient drama, a farce.

mim′e·o·graph″ (mim′ē-ə-gräf″) *n.* (*T.N.*) a device for duplicating letters, etc., by means of stencils. —*v.t.* copy by mimeograph. Also, *colloq.,* **mim′e·o** (-ō).

mim′ic (mim′ik) *v.t.* [**mim′icked, mim′ick·ing**] imitate, esp. derisively. —*n.* an imitator; one apt at mimicking. —*adj.* **1**, imitative. **2**, simulated, esp. on a smaller scale.

mim'ic·ry (-rē) *n.* act or result of mimicking.

mi·mo'sa (mi-mō'sə) *n.* a tropical tree or shrub having globular flowers. **—mim"o·sa'ceous** (mim"ə-sā'shəs) *adj.*

min"a·ret' (min"ə-ret') *n.* a slender minaret attached to a mosque.

min'a·to"ry (min'ə-tôr'ē) *adj.* menacing.

mince (mins) *v.t.* **1,** cut into small pieces. **2,** speak of euphemistically; minimize; moderate. *—v.i.* walk daintily; act or speak with affected delicacy. **—minc'ing,** *adj.* affectedly elegant.

mince'meat" (mins'mēt") *n.* **1,** a pie filling of minced suet, fruits, etc. **2,** anything chopped into small pieces.

mind (mīnd) *n.* **1,** that with which a living being feels, wills, and thinks; the ego. **2,** the intellect, as distinguished from feeling and volition; intellectual ability. **3,** reason; sanity. **4,** opinion; inclination; disposition. **5,** purpose; intention. **6,** memory. *—v.t.* & *i.* **1,** pay attention to; obey. **2,** take care of; attend to. **3,** care about; object to.

mind-'blow"ing *adj.* (*Colloq.*) shocking; surprising.

-mind'ed *suf.* **1,** inclined. **2,** having such a mind, as *high-minded, weak-minded.*

mind-'ex·pand"ing *adj.* (of drugs) causing an apparent increase in one's sensitivity and understanding.

mind'ful (-fəl) *adj.* aware. **—mind'ful·ness,** *n.*

mind'less *adj.* thoughtless; heedless.

mind-'read"ing *n.* the art of reading or discerning another's thoughts. **—mind'-read"er,** *n.*

mine (mīn) *pron.* poss. of *I;* belonging to me. *—n.* **1,** a deposit of mineral ores or coal, or the excavation made for removing them. **2,** an abounding source of anything. **3,** a charge of explosives submerged in the water or buried on land. **4,** an excavated passage for placing explosives under enemy fortifications. *—v.t.* & *i.* **1,** extract ores, etc. **2,** make subterranean passages. **3,** lay explosive mines. **—min'er,** *n.* **—min'ing,** *n.* **—mine field,** an area on land or water systematically covered with mines. **—mine layer,** a naval vessel specially equipped for placing mines. **—mine sweeper,** a naval vessel that clears away mines.

min'er·al (min'ər-əl) *n.* **1,** an inorganic substance occurring in nature, of a definite chemical composition and definite structure. **2,** anything inorganic. *—adj.* **1,** of or pert. to minerals. **2,** containing minerals. **—mineral oil, 1,** petroleum. **2,** a laxative. **—mineral water,** water naturally or artificially impregnated with metallic salts. **—mineral wool,** an insulating material made from slag.

min'er·al·ize" (-īz") *v.t.* **1,** change (metal) to ore. **2,** change (organic matter) to a mineral; petrify. **3,** impregnate with minerals. *—v.i.* collect mineral specimens. **—min"er·al·i·za'tion,** *n.*

min"er·al'o·gy (min"ər-al'ə-jē) *n.* the science of minerals. **—min"er·al'o·gist,** *n.*

min"e·stro'ne (min"ə-strō'nē) *n.* an Ital. soup containing vegetables, herbs, etc.

min'gle (ming'gəl) *v.t.* & *i.* **1,** mix; blend; unite. **2,** associate.

mi·ni- (min-ē) *pref.* especially small, short, etc.

min'i·a·ture (min'ē-ə-chər) *n.* **1,** anything represented on a greatly reduced scale. **2,** anything small, esp. a portrait. *—adj.* small. **—min'i·a·tur·ize",** *v.t.*

min'i·bike" *n.* a small motorcycle.

min'i·bus" *n.* a van or small bus.

min'i·cam" (-kam") *n.* a miniature camera, esp. for television.

min'i·com·pu'ter *n.* a small computer, esp. for small-business use.

min'i·dress" *n.* a very short dress for women. **—min'i-skirt",** *n.* a very short skirt for women. Also, *colloq.,* **min'i.**

min'im (min'əm) *n.* **1,** the smallest unit of liquid measure, about one drop. **2,** something very small. **3,** (*Music*) an eighth note.

min'i·mize" (min'ə-mīz") *v.t.* **1,** reduce to a minimum. **2,** belittle.

min'i·mum (min'ə-məm) *n.* the least possible, or lowest actual, degree, amount, etc. **—min'i·mal,** *adj.* **—minimal art,** a movement, esp. in painting and sculpture, rejecting complexity and tradition.

min'ion (min'yən) *n.* **1,** an obsequious favorite, as of a prince. **2,** a subordinate.

min'is·ter (min'is-tər) *n.* **1,** a clergyman; pastor. **2,** a diplomatic envoy. **3,** (esp. *Brit.*) a high state official, esp. head of a department. *—v.i.* (with *to*) attend; care for; contribute. **—min'is·trant** (-trənt) *n.* & *adj.*

min"is·te'ri·al (-tir'ē-əl) *adj.* pert. to a minister or ministry.

min"is·tra'tion (-trā'shən) *n.* the act of serving or helping; an act of service or aid. **—min'is·tra"tive,** *adj.*

min'is·try (min'is-trē) *n.* **1,** the office or function of a clergyman or minister of state. **2,** the clergy, or the ministers of state, collectively. **3,** (*Brit.*) an administrative department of the government.

mink *n.* a fur-bearing aquatic animal; its fur.

min'ne·sing"er (min'ə-sing"ər) *n.* German lyric poet and singer of the 12th and 13th centuries.

min'now (min'ō) *n.* a small freshwater fish.

mi·nor (mī'nər) *adj.* **1,** lesser in importance, size, or extent. **2,** under legal age. **3,** (*Music*) pert. to a certain scale or smaller interval. —*n.* **1,** one not of legal age. **2,** a secondary field of study. —**minor league,** any of the leagues of baseball teams other than the two major leagues.

mi·nor'i·ty (mi-nor'ə-tē) *n.* **1,** the lesser part or number; less than half. **2,** a less numerous party or group, as political or racial, among a more numerous. **3,** the state of being below legal age.

min'ster (min'stər) *n.* a church or cathedral.

min'strel (min'strəl) *n.* **1,** originally, an itinerant musician or singer, esp. of ballads. **2,** a blackfaced singer or comedian. —**min'strel·sy,** *n.*

mint *n.* **1,** any of several aromatic herbs. **2,** a mint-flavored confection. **3,** a place where money is coined under governmental authority. **4,** a vast amount. —*adj.* unused (of a postage stamp). —*v.t.* coin (money). —**mint julep,** a drink made of whiskey, sugar, ice, and fresh mint.

mint'age (-ij) *n.* the process, result, or cost of minting.

min'u·end" (min'ū-end") *n.* a number from which another number is to be subtracted.

min'u·et' (min"ū-et') *n.* a slow and stately ballroom dance.

mi'nus (mī'nəs) *prep.* **1,** less (by a certain amount). **2,** lacking. —*adj.* **1,** less than nothing; negative. **2,** (*Math.*) denoting subtraction, as the minus sign (−).

mi·nus'cule (mi-nus'kūl) *adj.* small, esp. of letters; not capital.

min'ute (min'it) *n.* **1,** the sixtieth part of an hour; 60 seconds. **2,** a short space of time. **3,** a moment; a point of time. **4,** a summary; a rough draft. **5,** (*pl.*) a record of the proceedings at a meeting. **6,** the sixtieth part of a degree. —*adj.* quickly prepared. —**minute steak,** a very thin cut of beefsteak that cooks very quickly.

mi·nute' (mī-nūt') *adj.* **1,** extremely small in size. **2,** very small in scope. —**mi·nute'ness,** *n.*

min'ute·man" (min'it-man") *n.* [*pl.* -**men**] **1,** an Amer. militiaman of Revolutionary times. **2,** (*pl.*, *cap.*) a reactionary political group.

mi·nu'ti·ae (mi-nū'shē-ē) *n.pl.* [*sing.* -**a** (-ə)] trivial details.

minx (minks) *n.* a pert girl.

mir (mēr) *n.* formerly, a community of Russian peasants, holding land in common.

mir'a·cle (mir'ə-kəl) *n.* **1,** an act or happening attributed to supernatural power. **2,** a wonderful thing.

mi·rac'u·lous (mi-rak'yə-ləs) *adj.* being, or like, a miracle; wonderful.

mi·rage' (mi-räzh') *n.* an optical illusion by which images of distant objects can be seen.

mire (mīr) *n.* **1,** wet, slimy ground; deep mud. **2,** filth. —*v.t.* **1,** sink or fix in mire. **2,** soil with filth. **3,** involve in difficulties. —*v.i.* sink in mire. —**mir'y,** *adj.* muddy; filthy.

mir'ror (mir'ər) *n.* **1,** a surface that reflects clear images; a looking glass. **2,** anything that gives a true picture or reflection. —*v.t.* reflect; imitate.

mirth (mērth) *n.* festive gaiety; amusement; laughter.

mirth'ful *adj.* **1,** full of mirth. **2,** causing mirth. —**mirth'less,** *adj.*

mis- *pref.* **1,** bad; wrong; erroneous. **2,** negative. **3,** hating.

mis"ad·ven'ture *n.* a mishap; ill fortune.

mis'an·thrope" (mis'ən-thrōp") *n.* a hater of mankind. Also, **mis·an'thro·pist** (mis-an'thrə-pist).

mis·an'thro·py (mis-an'thrə-pē) *n.* dislike of, or evil deeds toward, mankind. —**mis"an·throp'ic** (mis"ən-throp'ik) *adj.* —**mis"an·throp'i·cal·ly,** *adv.*

mis"ap·pre·hend' *v.t.* misunderstand. —**mis"ap·pre·hen'sion,** *n.*

mis"ap·pro'pri·ate' *v.t.* put to a wrong or dishonest use, as funds. —**mis"ap·pro'-pri·a'tion,** *n.*

mis"be·got'ten (mis"bē-got'ən) *adj.* illegitimate.

mis"be·have' *v.i.* behave badly. —**mis"-be·hav'ior,** *n.*

mis"be·lieve' *v.t.* doubt.

mis·cal'cu·late" *v.t. & i.* calculate incorrectly. —**mis"cal·cu·la'tion,** *n.*

mis·car'riage (mis-kar'ij) *n.* **1,** failure to arrive at a just result, as of justice. **2,** failure to arrive at destination, as a letter. **3,** untimely or premature delivery of young. —**mis·car'ry,** *v.i.*

mis"ce·ge·na'tion (mis"i-jə-nā'shən) *n.* interbreeding between races.

mis"cel·la'ne·ous (mis"ə-lā'nē-əs) *adj.* consisting of a mixture; diversified; varied.

mis"cel·la'ny (mis'ə-lā'nē) *n.* a collection of literary compositions on varied subjects. Also, **mis"cel·la'ne·a** (-ə) *n.pl.*

mis·chance' *n.* a mishap; ill luck.

mis'chief (mis'chif) *n.* **1,** an injury; a petty annoyance; trouble. **2,** a cause or source of trouble.

mis'chie·vous (mis'chə-vəs) *adj.* **1,** injurious; annoying. **2,** fond of mischief; teasing. —**mis'chie·vous·ness,** *n.*

mis·ci·ble (mis'ə-bəl) *adj.* capable of being mixed. —**mis"ci·bil'i·ty,** *n.*

mis"con·ceive' *v.t. & i.* misunderstand. —**mis"con·cep'tion,** *n.*

mis·con'duct (mis-kon'dukt) *n.* **1,** improper conduct. **2,** unlawful conduct, as by an official, lawyer, etc. —*v.t.* (mis"kən-dukt') mismanage.

mis"con·strue' *v.t.* misinterpret. —**mis"con·struc'tion,** *n.*

mis·count' *v.t.* count incorrectly. —*n.* (mis'kownt) a wrong count.

mis'cre·ant (mis'krē-ənt) *n.* a villain; a scoundrel. —*adj.* villainous. —**mis'cre·an·cy** (-ən-sē) *n.*

mis·cue' (mis'kū) *n.* **1,** a slip of the cue (at billiards). **2,** a failure to take a hint, or to answer one's cue (in the theater). —*v.i.* make a miscue.

mis·deed' *n.* a wicked action.

mis"de·mean'or (mis"də-mē'nər) *n.* **1,** (*Law*) an offense less serious than a felony. **2,** misbehavior.

mis"di·rect' *v.t.* **1,** give erroneous information or instruction to. **2,** address incorrectly (a letter, etc.). —**mis"di·rec'tion,** *n.*

mise en scène (mē"zän-sen') (*Fr.*) **1,** stage setting. **2,** staging; direction.

mi'ser (mī'zər) *n.* an avaricious, niggardly person; one who hoards money. —**mi'ser·ly,** *adj.* —**mi'ser·li·ness,** *n.*

mis'er·a·ble (miz'ər-ə-bəl) *adj.* **1,** wretched; unhappy; poor. **2,** manifesting, causing, or attended with, misery. **3,** mean; contemptible. **4,** (*Colloq.*) ailing.

mis'er·y (miz'ə-rē) *n.* **1,** physical or mental suffering; wretchedness; poverty. **2,** a cause of suffering. **3,** (*Colloq.*) a bodily ailment.

mis·fea'sance (mis-fē'zəns) *n.* the misuse of power; a wrongful exercise of lawful authority.

mis·fire' *v.i.* **1,** fail to explode or fire. **2,** go wrong; not produce the desired effect.

mis·fit' *n.* **1,** something that does not fit, as a garment of the wrong size; state of being unsuitable. **2,** a person poorly adapted to his job, society, etc.

mis·for'tune *n.* **1,** bad luck; adversity. **2,** a mishap; a calamity.

mis·giv'ing *n.* a feeling of doubt or apprehension.

mis·guide' *v.t.* advise badly; mislead.

mis·han'dle *v.t.* handle badly or roughly; maltreat.

mis'hap *n.* an unfortunate occurrence.

mish'mash" *n.* a jumble.

mis"in·form' *v.t.* give false information to. —**mis"in·for·ma'tion,** *n.*

mis"in·ter'pret *v.t.* understand, or explain, incorrectly.

mis·judge' *v.t. & i.* have an unjust or incorrect opinion (of). —**mis·judg'ment,** *n.*

mis·lay' *v.t.* [*pret. & p.p.* **mis·laid'**] **1,** lay away and forget. **2,** place incorrectly.

mis·lead' (mis-lēd') *v.t.* lead astray; lead into error; delude.

mis·man'age *v.t. & i.* manage badly. —**mis·man'age·ment,** *n.*

mis·match' *v.t.* match inaccurately or unsuitably. —*n.* a wrong or poor match, esp. a mésalliance.

mis·no'mer (mis-nō'mər) *n.* a misapplied term, name, or designation; a misnaming.

mi·sog'a·my (mi-sog'ə-mē) *n.* hatred of marriage. —**mi·sog'a·mist,** *n.*

mi·sog'y·ny (mi-soj'ə-nē) *n.* hatred of women. —**mi·sog'y·nist,** *n.*

mis·place' *v.t.* **1,** put in a wrong place. **2,** bestow unwisely, as confidence.

mis'print' *n.* a typographical error. —*v.* (mis-print') print incorrectly.

mis·pri'sion (mis-prizh'ən) *n.* **1,** concealment of the crime of another, esp. of treason. **2,** any serious offense, esp. in a position of trust.

mis"pro·nounce' *v.t. & i.* pronounce incorrectly. —**mis"pro·nun"ci·a'tion,** *n.*

mis·quote' *v.t. & i.* quote incorrectly. —**mis"quo·ta'tion,** *n.*

mis·read' (mis-rēd') *v.t.* misinterpret.

mis"rep·re·sent' *v.t.* represent falsely or imperfectly. —**mis"rep·re·sen·ta'tion,** *n.*

mis·rule' *v.t.* govern badly. —*n.* **1,** bad or unwise rule. **2,** disorder.

miss (mis) *v.t.* **1,** fail to reach or attain what is aimed at, expected, or desired. **2,** feel the want of, or absence of. **3,** avoid. **4,** overlook. —*v.i.* fail to attain; be unsuccessful. —*n.* **1,** a failure to accomplish, etc. **2,** a girl; an unmarried woman.

mis'sal (mis'əl) *n.* a prayer book.

mis·shap'en (mis-shā'pən) *adj.* deformed. —**mis·shap'en·ness,** *n.*

mis'sile (mis'əl) *n.* an object or weapon that can be hurled or shot.

miss'ing (mis'ing) *adj.* absent; lacking. —**missing link,** a hypothetical primate proposed as having linked ape and man, in evolution.

mis'sion (mish'ən) *n.* **1,** a sending; a charge to go and perform a specific service or duty. **2,** a delegation so sent. **3,** the service or duty for which one is sent. **4,** a self-imposed duty or function. **5,** an organized effort for the spread of religion in foreign lands.

mis'sion·ar"y (mish'ə-ner"ē) *n.* one sent to spread his religion or philosophy in a foreign land or to persons not of the same persuasion.

mis·si·sau·ga (mis″i-sâ′gə) *n.* a kind of snake.

mis′sive (mis′iv) *n.* a written message.

mis·speak′ *v.* [**mis·spoke′, mis·spo′ken**] speak or say incorrectly.

mis·spell′ *v.t.* spell incorrectly. —**mis·spelt′**, *adj.*

mis·spent′ *adj.* squandered. —**mis·spend′**, *v.t.*

mis·state′ *v.t.* state incorrectly or misleadingly. —**mis·state′ment**, *n.*

mis·step′ *n.* **1**, a stumble. **2**, a mistake in conduct.

mist *n.* **1**, a cloud of minute globules of water, near the ground; a fog. **2**, a precipitation much finer than rain. **3**, a haze; something that veils or obscures. —*v.t. & i.* make or become misty.

mis·take′ (mi-stāk′) *v.t.* [**mis·took′** (-tûk′), **mis·tak′en, -tak′ing**] choose erroneously; regard (something) as other than it is; misunderstand. —*v.i.* be in error. —*n.* an error in action, opinion, or judgment. —**mis·tak′en**, *adj.* **1**, erroneous. **2**, being in error.

mis′ter (mis′tər) *n.* a conventional title for a man, usually written Mr.

mis·time′ (mis-tīm′) *v.t.* say or do inopportunely.

mis′tle·toe″ (mis′əl-tō″) *n.* a parasitic plant, with white berries, used in Christmas decorations.

mis′tral (mis′trəl) *n.* a cold, dry northwest wind from the Mediterranean.

mis·treat′ *v.t.* treat badly; abuse. —**mis·treat′ment**, *n.*

mis′tress (mis′tris) *n.* **1**, a woman who has authority or control, as of a house or servants. **2**, the female owner, as of a dog. **3**, a woman serving as wife without being married.

mis·tri′al (mis-trī′əl) *n.* (*Law*) a trial not concluded because of error, or because of disagreement of the jury.

mis·trust′ *n.* lack of trust; suspicion. —*v.t. & i.* distrust. —**mis·trust′ful**, *adj.*

mist′y (mis′tė) *adj.* **1**, accompanied by, or resembling, mist. **2**, indistinct; obscure. **3**, (*Colloq.*) tearful. —**mist′i·ness**, *n.*

mis″un·der·stand′ *v.t. & i.* [*pret. & p.p.* **mis″un·der·stood′**] misinterpret; understand wrongly.

mis″un·der·stand′ing *n.* **1**, disagreement. **2**, a misconception.

mis″un·der·stood′ *adj.* **1**, incorrectly interpreted. **2**, unappreciated.

mis·us′age *n.* **1**, improper use, as of words. **2**, bad treatment.

mis·use′ (mis-ūz′) *v.t.* **1**, make a false or improper use of. **2**, maltreat. —*n.* (mis-ūs′) improper use; abuse.

mite (mīt) *n.* **1**, a very small sum of money, or contribution. **2**, a very small person or thing. **3**, an insect that infests plants and foods.

mi′ter (mī′tər) *n.* **1**, the official headdress of a bishop. **2**, a surface cut for a miter joint, a joining of two pieces beveled at equal angles. **3**, a jig or form for cutting such a surface. —*v.t.* cut so as to join in a miter joint. Also, **mi′tre.**

mit′i·gate (mit′ə-gāt″) *v.t. & i.* lessen or moderate in severity. —**mit″i·ga′tion**, *n.*

mi·to′sis (mī-tō′sis) *n.* a process of cell division in which the number of chromosomes is doubled.

mitt (mit) *n.* **1**, a long glove without fingers. **2**, (*Baseball*) a thickly padded glove. **3**, a mitten. **4**, (*Slang*) a hand.

mit′ten (mit′ən) *n.* a glove that encloses the four fingers together and the thumb separately.

mix (miks) *v.t.* **1**, unite or blend into one mass. **2**, mingle indiscriminately; crossbreed. **3**, (with *up*) confuse. —*v.i.* **1**, become mixed. **2**, associate. —*n.* a mixture.

mixed (mikst) *adj.* **1**, blended by mixing. **2**, indiscriminate; assorted. **3**, (*Colloq.*) mentally confused. —**mixed number**, a number consisting of an integer and a fraction.

mix′er (-ər) *n.* **1**, one who or that which mixes. **2**, a sociable person. **3**, a party.

mix′ture (miks′chər) *n.* the act, state, or result of mixing; a conglomeration; medley.

mix′up″ (miks′up″) *n.* a confused situation; a tangle.

miz′zen·mast″ (miz′ən-mást″) *n.* the after or third mast of a vessel. Also, **miz′zen.**

mne·mon′ic (ni-mon′ik) *adj.* pert. to or assisting the memory. —*n.* an aid in remembering —**mne·mon′i·cal·ly**, *adv.* —**mne·mon′ics**, *n.sing.* a technique for improving the memory.

mo′a (mō′ə) *n.* a large extinct bird of N. Z.

moan (mōn) *v.i.* **1**, utter a low inarticulate sound expressive of suffering. **2**, make a similar sound, as the wind. —*n.* such a sound.

moat (mōt) *n.* a deep, water-filled trench around a fortified place.

mob *n.* **1**, an incoherent, disorderly crowd of people. **2**, any assemblage of persons or things (used disparagingly). **3**, the common mass of people. —*v.t.* [**mobbed, mob′bing**] crowd around or attack.

mo′bile (mō′bəl) *adj.* **1**, easily moving or movable. **2**, changing easily; facile; responsive. —*n.* a sculpture whose parts may be moved by a breeze. **—mo·bil'i·ty** (mō-bil'-ə-tė) n. **—mobile home,** a house trailer.

mo'bi·lize" (mō'bə-līz") v.t. & i. organize or put in readiness for service. **—mo"bi·li·za'tion,** n.

mob·oc'ra·cy (mob-ok'rə-sė) n. rule by the mob.

mob'ster (mob'stər) n. (Slang) one of a criminal mob; gangster.

moc'ca·sin (mok'ə-sən) n. **1,** a shoe of soft leather. **2,** a venomous water snake.

mo'cha (mō'kə) n. **1,** a choice coffee. **2,** a flavor of chocolate and coffee. **3,** a fine glove leather.

mock (mok) v.t. **1,** ridicule; deride; mimic. **2,** defy; deceive. —v.i. scoff; jeer. —adj. being an imitation, as a mock battle. **—mock orange,** a shrub, the common syringa. **—mock turtle soup,** a soup made of veal or other meat and seasoned to imitate turtle soup.

mock'er·y (mok'ə-rė) n. **1,** ridicule; object of ridicule. **2,** an imitation; a travesty.

mock-'he·ro'ic adj. & n. (a work) burlesquing the heroic style.

mock'ing·bird" (mok'ing-bėrd") n. an imitative song bird of the So. U. S.

mock-'up" (mok'up") n. **1,** a model, built to scale, as of a machine. **2,** a layout of printed or other matter.

mod adj. (Colloq.) **1,** a style of dress fashionable in the 1960's. **2,** up-to-date.

mode (mōd) n. **1,** a manner of acting or doing; method. **2,** the manner of existence or action of anything. **3,** the customary usage; the prevailing fashion. **4,** (Music) a form of scale. **5,** (Gram.) mood. **—mod'al** (mō'dəl) adj.

mod'el (mod'əl) n. **1,** a standard for imitation or comparison. **2,** a copy, usually in miniature. **3,** an image for later reproduction. **4,** a subject for an artist. **5,** one employed to wear and display clothes, pose for pictures, etc. —adj. **1,** serving as a model. **2,** exemplary. —v.t. & i. **1,** form according to, or make, a model. **2,** act as a model.

mo'dem (mō'dem) n. a device for converting signals from one mode of transmission to another.

mod'er·ate (mod'ər-it) adj. **1,** restrained; temperate; kept or keeping within reasonable limits. **2,** medium; mediocre. —n. one who avoids extreme opinions or actions. —v.t. & i. (mod'ə-rāt") **1,** make or become less severe or intense. **2,** preside over a meeting. **—mod"er·a'tion,** n. temperance. **—mod'er·a"tor,** n. a presiding officer.

mod"e·ra'to (mōd"ə-rä'tō) adj. & adv. (Music) moderate in tempo.

mod'ern (mod'ərn) adj. pert. to or characteristic of present or recent times. —n. a person of the present era, or of modern tastes.

mod'ern·ism (-iz-əm) n. practice or advocacy of radically new customs, design, etc. **—mod'ern·ist,** n. & adj. **—mod"ern·is'tic,** adj.

mod'ern·ize" (-īz") v.t. & i. make or become modern; renovate. **—mod"ern·i·za'tion,** n.

mod'est (mod'ist) adj. **1,** manifesting humility, propriety, and restraint. **2,** moderate. **3,** decent; decorous. **—mod'es·ty,** n.

mod'i·cum (mod'ə-kəm) n. a small or moderate quantity.

mod'i·fy" (mod'ə-fī") v.t. **1,** change the properties, form, or function of. **2,** moderate. **3,** (Gram.) qualify or describe (another word). **—mod"i·fi·ca'tion,** n. **—mod'i·fi"er,** n.

mod'ish (mō'dish) adj. fashionable. **—mod'ish·ness,** n.

mo·diste' (mō-dēst') n. a maker or seller of women's hats, dresses, etc.

mod'u·lar (moj'oo-lər) adj. pert. to modulation; of a module.

mod'u·late" (moj'ə-lāt") v.t. **1,** make softer in tone; regulate. **2,** vary or inflect the sound or utterance of. **3,** (Radio) vary the frequency of the transmitted wave. **—mod"u·la'tion,** n. **—mod'u·la"tor,** n.

mod'ule (moj'ool) n. **1,** a unit of measure, esp. of building materials. **2,** a standardized unit. **3,** an independent unit of a space vehicle.

mo'dus op"e·ran'di (mō'dəs-op"ə-ran'dī) (Lat.) method of working.

mo'gul (mō'gəl) n. an important person; a member of the (orig. Mongolian) ruling class.

mo'hair" (mō'hâr") n. the fleece of an Angora goat; a fabric made of it.

Mo·ham'med·an (mō-ham'ə-dən) n. a follower of Mohammed or his religion. —adj. Moslem.

Mohs scale (mōz) a numerical scale for expressing the hardness of minerals.

moi'e·ty (moi'ə-tė) n. **1,** a half part. **2,** a share.

moil v.i. work hard. —n. drudgery. **—moil'er,** n.

moire (mwär) n. a watered silk or wool fabric.

moi·ré' (mwä-rā') adj. watered; wavelike.

moist adj. damp; slightly wet; tearful (of the eyes). **—moist'ness,** n.

mois'ten (mois'ən) v.t. & i. make or become damp.

mois'ture (mois'chər) *n.* diffused wetness. —**mois'tur·ize**, *v.t.* —**mois'tur·iz·er**, *n.*

mo'lar (mō'lər) *n.* a grinding tooth.

mo·las'ses (mō-las'iz) *n.* a dark syrup produced in making sugar.

mold (mōld) *n.* **1,** a shape or form, esp. for shaping molten or plastic material. **2,** something shaped in or on a mold, or the shape imparted to it. **3,** native character. **4,** a furry fungus growth, esp. on food or decaying matter. **5,** soft, rich earth. —*v.t.* shape, form, or fashion, esp. in or on a mold. —*v.t. & i.* make or become fungus mold. Also, **mould.** —**mold'y,** *adj.* covered with fungus mold.

mold'board'' (mōld'bôrd'') *n.* the curved surface of a plow blade.

mold'er (mōl'dər) *v.i. & t.* turn to mold or dust by natural decay. —*n.* one who molds.

mold'ing (mōl'ding) *n.* **1,** (*Archit.*) a decorative border. **2,** something molded.

mole (mōl) *n.* **1,** a small dark permanent blemish on the human skin. **2,** a small mammal, living chiefly underground. **3,** a massive stone breakwater.

mol'e·cule'' (mol'ə-kūl'') *n.* **1,** the smallest possible physical unit of an element or compound, composed of atoms. **2,** a very small particle. —**mo·lec'u·lar** (mə-lek'yə-lər) *adj.*

mole'hill'' *n.* **1,** a small mound of earth raised by burrowing moles. **2,** an unimportant obstacle.

mole'skin'' (mōl'skin'') *n.* **1,** a stout cotton fabric. **2,** the soft gray fur of the mole.

mo·lest' (mə-lest') *v.t.* trouble; interfere with injuriously. —**mo''les·ta'tion** (mō''les-tā'shən) *n.*

moll (mol) *n.* (*Slang*) the woman companion of a gangster.

mol'li·fy (mol'ə-fī'') *v.t.* **1,** soften. **2,** soothe; appease. —**mol''li·fi·ca'tion,** *n.* —**mol'li·fi''er,** *n.*

mol'lusk (mol'əsk) *n.* an invertebrate animal with a soft body and usually a hard shell, as a snail or oyster. Also, **mol'lusc.**

mol'ly·cod''dle (mol'ē-kod''əl) *n.* a pampered boy. —*v.t.* pamper.

Mol'o·tov'' cocktail (mol'ə-tof'') a bottle of gasoline ignited and hurled as an antitank weapon.

molt (mōlt) *v.t. & i.* shed feathers (as a bird) or skin (as a reptile). Also, **moult.**

mol'ten (mōl'tən) *adj.* melted.

mo·lyb'de·num (mə-lib'də-nəm) *n.* an element used in alloys, no. 32, symbol Mo. —**mo·lyb'dic,** *adj.*

mom *n.* (*Colloq.*) mamma; mother. Also, **mom'my** (-ē).

mom-'and-pop' (mom'ən-pop') *adj.*

(*Colloq.*) of a business, etc., operated by a family.

mo'ment (mō'mənt) *n.* **1,** an indefinitely small space of time; a minute. **2,** the present time; instant. **3,** importance; consequence.

mo'men·tar''y (mō'mən-ter'ē) *adj.* very brief. —**mo''men·tar'i·ly** (-tär'ə-lē) *adv.* for a moment; at any moment.

mo·men'tous (mō-men'təs) *adj.* of great consequence. —**mo·men'tous·ness,** *n.*

mo·men'tum (mō-men'təm) *n.* impetus; the quantity of motion of a body: the mass times the velocity.

mon'ad *n.* **1,** (*Biol.*) a single-celled organism. **2,** (*Chem.*) an element having a valence of one. **3,** a unit. —**mo·nad'ic,** *adj.*

mon'arch (mon'ərk) *n.* a hereditary sovereign; king; ruler. —**mo·nar'chal** (mə-när'kəl) *adj.*

mon'ar·chy (mon'ər-kē) *n.* a government headed by a monarch. —**mon'ar·chism** (-kiz-em) *n.* —**mon'ar·chist** (-kist) *n.* one who favors such form of government.

mon'as·ter·y (mon'ə-ster-ē) *n.* the premises occupied by monks.

mo·nas'tic (mə-nas'tik) *adj.* pert. to austere life in seclusion, as of monks. —**mo·nas'ti·cism,** *n.*

mon·aur'al (mon-ôr'əl) *adj.* **1,** pert. to or for use with one ear. **2,** monophonic.

Mon'day (mun'dē) *n.* the second day of the week.

Mo·nel' metal (mō-nel') (*T.N.*) a nonrusting alloy of nickel.

mon'e·tar·ism (mon'ə-tə-riz''əm) an economic theory dealing with the effects of money in circulation.

mon'e·tar·y (mon'ə-ter-ē) *adj.* of or pert. to money.

mon'e·tize'' (mon'ə-tīz'') *v.t.* legalize as, or coin into, money.

mon'ey (mun'ē) *n.* **1,** coin; stamped metal or banknotes authorized as a medium of exchange. **2,** available assets; wealth; credit. —**mon'eyed,** *adj.* wealthy. —**money of account,** a monetary unit used in computation but not issued as a coin or note. —**money order,** an order for payment of money, esp. one issued at a post office.

mon'ey·bags'' *n.sing.* (*Slang*) a rich man.

mon'ger (mung'gər) *n.* **1,** a dealer, as a *fishmonger.* **2,** one sordidly active, as a *scandalmonger.*

Mon·gol'i·an (mon-gō'lē-ən) *adj. & n.* **1,** pert. to Mongolia or to the yellow-skinned races of eastern Asia. **2,** [also, **Mon'gol·oid** (-gə-loid)] afflicted with Mongolism.

Mon'gol·ism (mong'gə-liz-əm) *n.* the abnormal condition of a mentally deficient child born with slanting eyes, large tongue, flattened skull, etc.; Down's syndrome.

mon'goose (mong'goos) *n.* [*pl.* **-goos·es**] a slender ferretlike animal of India.

mon'grel (mong'grəl) *n.* **1**, a dog of mixed breed. **2**, any plant, animal, or thing of mixed breed or elements. —*adj.* mixed; not pure.

mon'i·ker (mon'ə-kər) *n.* (*Slang*) a name or nickname.

mon'ism (mon'iz-əm) *n.* the metaphysical doctrine that mind and matter are not separate substances. —**mon'ist,** *n.*

mo·ni'tion (mō-nish'ən) *n.* a warning.

mon'i·tor (mon'i-tər) *n.* **1**, a pupil charged with overseeing other pupils. **2**, one who admonishes; a warning. —*v.t. & i.* listen to radio or television broadcasts for checking purposes. —**mon'i·tor·ship",** *n.*

mon'i·to"ry (mon'i-tôr'ē) *adj.* admonishing. —*n.* an admonishing letter.

monk (munk) *n.* a man withdrawn from the world under religious vows. —**monk'ish,** *adj.* —**monk's cloth,** a coarse fabric used for draperies.

mon'key (mung'kē) *n.* **1**, any mammal of the order *Primates* except man, the lemur, and the apes. **2**, a mischievous child or person. **3**, any of various machines. —*v.t.* (*Colloq.*) trifle; fool. —**monkey business,** (*Slang*) playful, mischievous, or deceitful behavior. —**monkey jacket,** a sailor's jacket. —**mon'key·shine",** *n.* (*Slang*) a mischievous prank. —**monkey suit,** (*Slang*) a tailcoat. —**monkey wrench,** an adjustable wrench.

monks'hood (munks'hûd) *n.* a plant having a hooded flower.

mon·o- (mon-ə) *pref.* single; alone.

mon'o·chord" *n.* an instrument with one string and a movable bridge.

mon'o·chrome" (mon'ə-krōm") *n.* a painting in different shades of a single color. —**mon'o·chro·mat'ic,** *adj.* pert. to one color or one wave length.

mon'o·cle (mon'ə-kəl) *n.* an eyeglass for one eye. —**mo·noc'u·lar,** (mə-nok'yə-lər) *adj.* having, pert. to, or intended for, one eye.

mon'o·dy (mon'ə-dē) *n.* **1**, a musical composition in which one voice-part predominates. **2**, a mourner's lament, in a poem or ode. —**mo·nod'ic** (mə-nod'ik) *adj.*

mo·nog'a·my (mə-nog'ə-mē) *n.* the practice of marrying only once, or being married to only one person at a time. —**mo·nog'a·mist,** *n.* —**mo·nog'a·mous,** *adj.*

mon'o·gram" (mon'ə-gram") *n.* a design

combining two or more letters, esp. initials.

mon'o·graph" (mon'ə-gràf") *n.* a treatise on a single subject. —**mon"o·graph'ic,** *adj.*

mon"o·ki'ni (-kē'nē) *n.* **1**, a topless bathing suit. **2**, very brief men's shorts.

mon'o·lith (mon'ə-lith) *n.* a single stone; a structure of a single stone, as an obelisk. **mon"o·lith'ic** (-ik) *adj.* **1**, formed from a single block of stone; massive; solid. **2**, formed from, or produced in or on, a single silicon chip.

mon'o·logue" (mon'ə-lâg") *n.* a discourse, poem, or dramatic part, by a single speaker. Also, **monolog.** —**mon'o·log"ist,** *n.*

mon"o·ma'ni·a *n.* an exaggerated interest in one thing; a specific delusion. —**mon"o·ma'ni·ac,** *n.*

mon"o·met'al·lism (mon"ə-met'ə-liz"əm) *n.* the use of one metal only as a monetary standard.

mo·no'mi·al (mo-nō'mē-əl) *adj. & n.* an algebraic expression) consisting of only one term.

mon"o·nu·cle·o'sis (mon"ō-noo-clē-ō'sis) *n.* an infectious disease characterized by an abnormal increase in the number of white blood cells with one nucleus in the bloodstream.

mon"o·pho'bi·a *n.* morbid dread of being alone.

mon"o·phon'ic (mon"ə-fän'ik) *adj.* **1**, consisting of a solo voice with accompaniment. **2**, having only one part. **3**, pert. to sound transmission on a single channel. —**mo·noph'o·ny** (mə-nof'ə-nē) *n.*

mon'o·plane" *n.* an airplane with one pair of wings.

mo·nop'o·list (mə-nop'ə-list) *n.* one who establishes or advocates a monopoly. —**mo·nop"o·lis'ti·cal·ly,** *adv.*

mo·nop'o·lize" (-līz") *v.t.* have exclusive control or possession of.

mo·nop'o·ly (mə-nop'ə-lē) *n.* **1**, exclusive control of a commodity. **2**, an exclusive privilege to carry on a traffic or service. **3**, the subject of, or a company having, a monopoly.

mon'o·rail" **1**, a single rail serving as the track for a train that either hangs from it or straddles it. **2**, a train that uses a monorail.

mo"no·so'dium glu'ta·mate (gloo'tə-mət) *n.* a flavor enhancer (MSG).

mon'o·syl'la·ble *n.* a word of one syllable. —**mon"o·syl·lab'ic,** *adj.*

mon'o·the"ism (mon'ə-thē'iz-əm) *n.* the doctrine or belief that there is but one God. —**mon'o·the"ist,** *n. & adj.* —**mon"o·the·is'tic,** *adj.*

mon·o·tone″ (mon′ə-tōn″) *n.* **1,** (*Music*) a single unvaried tone. **2,** speaking or singing without inflection or variation in pitch. **3,** sameness of style in writing.

mo·not′o·nous (mə-not′ə-nəs) *adj.* **1,** continued in the same tone. **2,** tiresome.

mo·not′o·ny (mə-not′ə-nė) *n.* boring lack of variety; sameness.

mon′o·type″ (mon′ə-tīp″) *n.* **1,** (*T.N.*) a machine for setting type, which sets each character separately; type set by such a machine. **2,** a print from a picture painted on a metal plate.

mon·sieur′ (mə-syû′) *n.* [*pl.* **messieurs′** (mā-syû′; mes′ərz)] (*Fr.*) **1,** mister. **2,** sir.

Mon·si′gnor (mon-sēn′yər) *n.* a title given to certain dignitaries of the Rom. Cath. Church.

mon·soon′ *n.* the seasonal wind, or the rainy season, of So. Asia.

mon′ster (mon′stər) *n.* **1,** a fabulous half-human animal. **2,** an abnormal or malformed animal or plant. **3,** a huge animal. **4,** a morally deformed person. —*adj.* huge.

mon′strance (mon′strəns) *n.* (*R.C.Ch.*) a receptacle in which the host is presented for adoration.

mon·stros′i·ty (mon-stros′ə-tė) *n.* state of being monstrous; anything monstrous.

mon′strous (mon′strəs) *adj.* **1,** abnormal. **2,** huge. **3,** frightful; shocking. —**mon′-strous·ness,** *n.*

mon·tage′ (mon-täzh′) *n.* the combination of elements of different pictures, esp. photographic.

Mon″tes·so′ri method (mon″tə-sôr′ė) a method of training young children emphasizing self-education through guidance rather than control.

Mon″te·zu′ma′s revenge (mon″tə-zoo′-məz) (*Slang*) diarrhea, esp. when contracted in Mexico.

month (munth) *n.* **1,** one-twelfth of a solar year, about 30 days; four weeks. **2,** any of the twelve parts of the calendar year, as January, etc.

month′ly (-lė) *adj.* once a month; every month; continuing for a month. —*n.* **1,** a periodical published once a month. **2,** (*pl.*, *slang*) menses.

mon′u·ment (mon′yə-mənt) *n.* **1,** a memorial structure or statue; a tomb or tombstone. **2,** any enduring memorial. —**mon″-u·men′tal,** *adj.* imposing; notable.

moo *n.* the sound a cow makes.

mooch (*Slang*) *v.i.* **1,** skulk; hang about. **2,** make love by petting. —*v.t.* get without payment; cadge.

mood *n.* **1,** state of mind or feeling; disposition. **2,** (*pl.*) fits of uncertainty or gloom-

iness. **3,** (*Gram.*) any of a series of verb inflections that denote whether a verb expresses fact, wish, question, etc.

mood′y (moo′dė) *adj.* gloomy; sullen; pensive. —**mood′i·ness,** *n.*

moon *n.* **1,** the heavenly body that revolves around the earth monthly and shines by the sun's reflected light. **2,** a lunar month. **3,** any planetary satellite. **4,** anything resembling an orb or a crescent. —*v.i.* behave listlessly or idly. —**moon′y,** *adj.* listless. —**moon blindness,** a disease of horses.

moon′beam″ *n.* a beam of light from the moon.

moon′calf″ *n.* an imbecile.

moon′flow″er *n.* a night-blooming plant.

moon′light″ *n. & adj.* the light of the moon. —*v.i.* (*Colloq.*) work at a second job, usu. at night. —**moon′lit″,** *adj.*

moon′shine″ *n.* **1,** moonlight. **2,** nonsensical talk. **3,** (*Colloq.*) illicitly distilled liquor. —*v.t. & i.* distill (liquor) illicitly. —**moon′shin″er,** *n.* (*Colloq.*) an illicit distiller.

moon′stone″ *n.* a variety of feldspar used as a gem.

moon-′struck″ *adj.* crazed or bemused.

moor (mûr) *n.* a tract of open waste land, often swampy; heath. —*v.t. & i.* secure (esp. a ship) in one place, by cables or anchors. —**moor′age,** *n.* a place for mooring.

Moor (mûr) *n.* any member of the dark-skinned No. African Moslem people who formerly occupied Spain.

moor′ing *n.* the cables for, or the place of, mooring.

Moor′ish (mûr′ish) *adj.* pert. to the Mohammedan Arabs of northwest Africa.

moose (moos) *n.sing. & pl.* a large antlered animal of the deer family.

moot *adj.* debatable.

mop *n.* **1,** a bunch of yarn, etc., on a handle, for washing floors. **2,** a thick mass (as of hair). —*v.t.* [**mopped, mop′ping**] clean with or as with a mop; wipe clean.

mop′board″ *n.* a baseboard.

mope (mōp) *v.i.* be listless, gloomy, or melancholy. —**mop′ish,** *adj.*

mo′ped″ (mō′ped″) *n.* a motorbike (def. 1).

mop′pet (mop′it) *n.* a doll; a little girl; a child.

mo·quette′ (mō-ket′) *n.* a thick velvety carpet.

mo·raine′ (mə-rān′) *n.* the accumulation of boulders, gravel, etc., deposited by a glacier.

mor′al (mor′əl) *adj.* **1,** pert. to the distinction between right and wrong, and the rules of right conduct. **2,** conforming to these rules. **3,** based on ethical, rather than legal rights. **4,** ethically or virtually, but not literally, true, as a *moral victory.* —*n.* **1,** the moral lesson in a fable, experience, etc. **2,** moral conduct or character.

mo·rale′ (mə-ral′) *n.* moral or mental condition as regards courage, confidence, etc.

mor′al·ism (-iz-əm) *n.* **1,** belief in the practice of morality apart from religion. **2,** a maxim. —**mor′al·ist,** *n.* a moral person; a student or teacher of morality.

mor·al′i·ty (mə-ral′ə-tē) *n.* quality of being moral; virtue. —**morality play,** a type of medieval drama in which the characters personified moral qualities.

mor′al·ize″ (-īz″) *v.i. & t.* reflect on or explain in a moral sense.

mor′al·ly (-lē) *adv.* **1,** virtuously. **2,** virtually.

mo·rass′ (mə-ras′) *n.* a marsh; bog.

mor″a·to′ri·um (môr″ə-tôr′ē-əm) *n.* an authorization, as to delay payment. —**mor′a·to·ry,** *adj.*

mo′ray (môr′ā) *n.* a savage eel.

mor′bid (môr′bid) *adj.* **1,** diseased. **2,** mentally unhealthy. —**mor·bid′i·ty, mor′bid·ness,** *n.*

mor·da′cious (môr-dā′shəs) *adj.* violent in action; biting; acrid. —**mor·dac′i·ty** (-das′ə-tē) *n.*

mor′dant (môr′dənt) *adj.* **1,** biting; sarcastic. **2,** having the property to fix colors. —**mor′dan·cy,** *n.*

mor′dent (môr′dənt) *n.* (*Music*) a melodic embellishment.

more (môr) *adj.* **1,** [*superl.* **most**] in greater measure or number. **2,** additional. —*n.* a greater or additional quantity or number. —*adv.* to a greater extent.

mo·reen′ (mə-rēn′) *n.* a heavy wool, or wool and cotton, fabric.

mo·rel′ (mə-rel′) *n.* an edible mushroom.

mo·rel′lo (mə-rel′ō) *n.* a dark-red variety of cherry.

more·o′ver *adv.* further; besides.

mo′res (môr′ēz) *n.pl.* customs of behavior.

Mo·resque′ (mô-resk′) *adj. & n.* (pert. to) a Moorish style of decoration.

mor″ga·nat′ic (môr″gə-nat′ik) *adj.* denoting a marriage between a man of high rank and a woman who does not share his rank. —**mor″ga·nat′i·cal·ly,** *adv.*

morgue (môrg) *n.* **1,** a place where the bodies of unknown dead persons are kept until identified. **2,** the reference files of a newspaper.

mor′i·bund″ (môr′ə-bund″) *adj.* in a dying state.

Mor′mon (môr′mən) *n.* a member of the Church of Jesus Christ of Latter-Day Saints.

morn (môrn) *n.* morning.

morn′ing (môr′ning) *n.* **1,** the period between midnight and noon, or dawn and noon. **2,** the early part of anything. Also, **morn.** —**morning sickness,** nausea in the morning, often accompanying early pregnancy. —**morning star,** the planet Venus.

morn′ing-glo″ry (môr′ning-glôr′ē) *n.* a climbing plant with cone-shaped flowers.

mo·roc′co (mə-rok′ō) *n.* a fine goatskin leather.

mo′ron (môr′on) *n.* **1,** a person whose mentality does not develop beyond the 12-year-old level. **2,** (*Colloq.*) a fool; stupid person. —**mo·ron′ic,** *adj.*

mo·rose′ (mə-rōs′) *adj.* sullenly ill-humored. —**mo·rose′ness,** *n.*

morph-, mor·pho- (môrf; môr-fə) *pref.* form; as a *suf.,* **-morph, -mor·phic, -mor·phous.**

mor′phine (môr′fēn) *n.* a habit-forming narcotic, used medicinally to dull pain.

mor·phol′o·gy (môr-fol′ə-jē) *n.* the science of form and structure, as of animals and plants. —**mor″pho·log′ic, mor″pho·log′i·cal,** *adj.* —**mor·phol′o·gist,** *n.*

mor′ris (môr′is) *n.* an old English pastoral dance. Also, **morris dance.**

Mor′ris chair a large armchair with an adjustable back and removable cushions.

mor′row (mor′ō) *n.* the next day after this.

Morse code (môrs) an alphabet of dots, dashes, and spaces, used in telegraphy and signaling.

INTERNATIONAL MORSE CODE

A	·—	N	—·	1	·————	;	—·—·—·
B	—···	O	———	2	··———	'	·————·
C	—·—·	P	·——·	3	···——	:	———···
D	—··	Q	——·—	4	····—		
E	·	R	·—·	5	·····	/	—··—·
F	··—·	S	···	6	—····	( )	—·——·—
G	——·	T	—	7	——···		
H	····	U	··—	8	———··	á	·——·—
I	··	V	···—	9	————·	ä	·—·—
J	·———	W	·——	0	—————	é	··—··
K	—·—	X	—··—	,	——··——	ñ	——·——
L	·—··	Y	—·——	.	·—·—·—	ö	———·
M	——	Z	——··	?	··——··	ü	··——

mor′sel (môr′səl) *n.* a small piece or quantity, esp. of food.

mor′tal (môr′təl) *adj.* **1,** subject to death; hence, human. **2,** deadly; fatal. **3,** implacable. **4,** grievous. —*n.* a human being.

mor·tal′i·ty (môr-tal′ə-tē) *n.* **1,** the condition of being mortal. **2,** deaths; death rate.

mor'tar (môr'tər) *n.* **1,** a bowl or device in which substances are pounded and ground. **2,** a cannon, firing at high angles; a similar device for hurling lifelines, etc. **3,** a mixture of cement used in building.

mor'tar·board" *n.* **1,** a board for holding mortar. **2,** an academic cap with a flat, square top.

mort'gage (môr'gij) *n.* (*Law*) a conditional conveyance of property as security for a loan. —*v.t.* put a mortgage on. —**mort"ga·gor'** (-jôr') *n.* one who so pledges property. —**mort"ga·gee'** (-jē') *n.* one who grants such a loan.

mor·ti'cian (môr-tish'ən) *n.* an undertaker.

mor'ti·fy" (môr'tə-fī") *v.t. & i.* **1,** humiliate. **2,** subject (the body) to ascetic discipline. **3,** affect with gangrene. —**mor"ti·fi·ca'tion,** *n.*

mor'tise (môr'tis) *n.* a cavity or recess to receive an inserted part, e.g., a tenon in joining wood. —*v.t.* make, or fasten by, a mortise.

mor'tu·ar"y (môr'choo-er"ē) *n.* a place for temporary reception of the dead. —*adj.* pert. to burial or death.

mo·sa'ic (mō-zā'ik) *n.* a picture or decoration composed of small pieces of material, separate photographs, etc. —*adj.* **1,** pert. to a mosaic. **2,** composed of diverse elements. **3,** (*cap.*) pert. to Moses or his writings.

Mo·selle' (mō-zel') *n.* a German white wine.

mo'sey (mō'zē) *v.i.* (*Slang*) stroll.

Mos'lem (mos'ləm) *adj. & n.* Muslim.

mosque (mosk) *n.* a Mohammedan place of worship.

mos·qui'to (mə-kē'tō) *n.* an insect that bites animals and draws blood. —**mosquito boat,** a fast motorboat equipped with torpedoes.

moss (mâs) *n.* a plant growing in tufts or mats, usually green, on moist ground, rocks, etc. —**moss'y,** *adj.*

moss'back" *n.* a person of antiquated or conservative opinions.

most (mōst) *adj.* greatest in quantity or number. —*n.* **1,** the greatest quantity or number. **2,** the majority. —*adv.* **1,** to the greatest extent. **2,** (*Colloq.*) almost.

-most *suf.* a superlative: foremost.

most'ly (-lē) *adv.* chiefly; mainly.

mot (mō) *n.* a witticism.

mote (mōt) *n.* a speck, as of dust.

mo·tel' (mō-tel') *n.* motor court.

mo·tet' (mō-tet') *n.* a contrapuntal vocal composition, usu. sacred.

moth (mâth) *n.* **1,** a nocturnal insect resembling the butterfly. **2,** a larva that destroys woolen fabrics. —**moth'y,** *adj.* —**moth ball,** a ball of naphthalene to repel clothes moths.

moth·eat"en *adj.* shabby.

moth'er (muth'ər) *n.* **1,** a female parent. **2,** an elderly woman. **3,** the superior of a convent, etc. **4,** one who exercises the authority or protective care of a mother; a matron. **5,** a slimy substance formed by bacteria in vinegar, etc., during fermentation. —*adj.* **1,** maternal. **2,** native; giving origin. —*v.t.* **1,** give origin to. **2,** protect tenderly or solicitously. —**moth'er·hood,** *n.* —**mother hubbard** (hub'ərd) a full loose gown for women. —**mother superior,** the woman superintendent of a convent. —**mother wit,** common sense.

moth'er-in-law" *n.* the mother of one's wife or husband.

moth'er·land" *n.* the land of one's birth or ancestry.

moth'er·ly (-lē) *adj. & adv.* like or befitting a mother. —**moth'er·li·ness,** *n.*

moth'er-of-pearl' *n.* the iridescent lining of an oyster shell, etc.

mo·tif' (mō-tēf') *n.* a dominant theme; a short musical phrase.

mo'tile (mō'təl) *adj.* (*Biol.*) capable of moving spontaneously. —**mo·til'i·ty,** *n.*

mo'tion (mō'shən) *n.* **1,** the process, power, or manner of moving. **2,** a movement; gesture. **3,** a proposal; suggestion; application. —*v.t. & i.* direct by a motion or gesture. —**motion picture,** consecutive pictures shown so as to give an illusion of motion. —**motion sickness,** nausea induced by motion, as in a car, airplane, etc.

mo'ti·vate" (mō'tə-vāt") *v.t.* provide with a motive; induce. —**mo"ti·va'tion,** *n.*

mo'tive (mō'tiv) *n.* **1,** a mental force that induces an act; a determining impulse. **2,** intention; purpose; design. —*adj.* **1,** causing, or pert. to, motion. **2,** constituting a motive.

mot'ley (mot'lē) *adj.* **1,** composed of discordant elements; heterogeneous. **2,** consisting of, or wearing, a combination of different colors.

mo'to·cross" (mō'tō-) *n.* a cross-country motorcycle race.

mo'tor (mō'tər) *n.* **1,** a source of mechanical power. **2,** a machine that transforms the energy of water, steam, electricity, etc., into mechanical energy; engine. **3,** an automobile: *motor car.* —*adj.* **1,** causing or imparting motion. **2,** pert. to an automobile. —*v.i.* ride in an automobile. —**motor court,** a group of cabins serving as an inn for motorists. —**motor home,** a large van outfitted for occupancy. —**motor scooter,**

a two-wheeled motorized vehicle less powerful than a motorcycle and having a seat that the driver does not straddle.

mo'tor·bike' *n.* **1,** a bicycle propelled by a detachable motor. **2,** (*Colloq.*) a motorcycle.

mo'tor·boat' *n.* a boat propelled by a gas or electric engine.

mo'tor·cade" (-kād") *n.* a procession of automobiles.

mo'tor·car" *n.* automobile.

mo'tor·cy"cle *n.* a two-wheeled automotive vehicle for one or two passengers.

mo'tor·drome" (-drōm") *n.* a track for motorcycle or automobile racing.

mo'tor·ist *n.* one who travels in an automobile.

mo'tor·ize" (-īz") *v.t.* **1,** furnish with a motor. **2,** equip with motor-driven vehicles. **—mo'tor·i·za'tion,** *n.*

mo'tor·man (mō'tər-mən) *n.* [*pl.* **-men**] the operator of a trolley car, etc.

mot'tle (mot'əl) *v.t.* mark with different colored spots. **—n.** a diversifying spot or blotch; variegated coloring. **—mot'tled,** *adj.*

mot'to (mot'ō) *n.* a phrase, or word, expressive of one's guiding principle.

moue (moo) *n.* (*Fr.*) a pout.

mou·lage' (moo-läzh') *n.* a plaster mold of a footprint, etc., to be used as evidence.

mould (mōld) *n.* mold.

moult (mōlt) *n.* molt.

mound (mownd) *n.* **1,** a natural or artificial elevation of earth. **2,** a raised mass of anything, as hay. **—v.t.** heap up.

mount (mownt) *v.t.* **1,** get up on; ascend. **2,** place at an elevation; set in proper position. **3,** equip with or place on a horse. **4,** preserve and stuff (as an animal skin). **—v.i. 1,** ascend. **2,** rise in amount. **—n. 1,** the act of mounting. **2,** a horse, etc., for riding. **3,** a support; setting. **4,** a mountain or hill.

moun'tain (mown'tən) *n.* **1,** a considerable and abrupt elevation of land. **2,** something resembling this in size. **3,** something relatively very large. **—mountain goat,** a long-haired antelope of the Rocky Mountains. **—mountain laurel,** an evergreen shrub with poisonous leaves. **—mountain lion,** a cougar.

moun"tain·eer' (-ir') *n.* **1,** one who lives in a mountainous region. **2,** a mountain climber.

moun'tain·ous *adj.* **1,** abounding in mountains. **2,** resembling a mountain; huge. **—moun'tain·ous·ness,** *n.*

moun'te·bank" (mown'tə-bank") *n.* a charlatan; an itinerant seller of quack medicines.

mount'ed (mown'tid) *adj.* **1,** riding, or serving while riding, as police on horseback. **2,** fixed on a support, etc.

moun'tie (mown'tē) *n.* (*Colloq.*) a mounted policeman, esp. (*cap.*) of Canada.

mount'ing *n.* a support; setting.

mourn (môrn) *v.i. & t.* **1,** feel or express sorrow, esp. for the dead. **2,** wear or display the customary tokens of sorrow. **3,** regret the loss of; deplore.

mourn'er *n.* one who mourns, esp. (at a funeral) a relative. **—mourners' bench,** at a revival meeting, a seat for penitent sinners.

mourn'ful (-fəl) *adj.* **1,** sorrowful. **2,** gloomy; dreary. **—mourn'ful·ness,** *n.*

mourn'ing *n.* the conventional tokens of sorrow, as black dress, etc.

mouse (mows) *n.* [*pl.* **mice** (mīs)] a small rodent. **—v.i. & t.** (mowz) hunt for mice; prowl about; search stealthily.

mous'er (mow'zər) *n.* an animal, esp. a cat, that catches mice.

mous·sa'ka (moo-sä'kə) *n.* a dish of ground meat and eggplant.

mousse (moos) *n.* a frozen dessert of whipped cream, etc.

mousse"line' (moos"lēn') *n.* (*Fr.*) **1,** muslin. **2,** a very light fabric. **3,** a very thin blown glass used for goblets.

mous·tache' (mus-tash') *n.* mustache.

mous'y (mow'sē) *adj.* resembling a mouse; drab; colorless; quiet. **—mous'i·ness,** *n.*

mouth (mowth) *n.* [*pl.* **mouths** (mow*th*z)] **1,** the opening, through or in which an animal takes food, masticates, and gives vocal utterance; the oral cavity. **2,** a similar opening, as of a cave, a vise, etc. **3,** the end of a river. **—v.t.** (mow*th*) **1,** utter pompously. **2,** put into, or rub with, the mouth. **3,** form (words) without uttering sound. **—v.i.** declaim pompously; make a grimace. **—mouth organ,** a harmonica.

mouth'ful *n.* **1,** enough to fill the mouth. **2,** (*Slang*) a sage remark.

mouth'piece" (mowth'pēs") *n.* **1,** a part of an instrument, etc., forming a mouth, or to which the mouth is applied. **2,** a person, newspaper, etc., acting as a spokesman for others. **3,** (*Slang*) a lawyer.

mouth'wash" *n.* an antiseptic mouth-cleaning fluid used as a gargle.

mouth'wat"er·ing (-wât"ər-ing) *adj.* (*Colloq.*) appetizing; savorous.

mouth'y (mow'thē) *adj.* loudmouthed. **—mouth'i·ness,** *n.*

mou'ton (moo'ton) *n.* sheep's wool used as fur in garments.

move (moov) *v.i. & t.* **1,** change from one place or residence to another; be or set in motion; advance. **2,** have a regular motion, esp. revolve. **3**, be sold (as stock); circulate (as in society); take action. **4**, make an application or proposal. **5**, arouse (the emotions of); touch the feelings of. —*n.* **1**, the act of moving; a change of residence; an action toward an end. **2**, in a game, the right or turn to play. —**mov'a·ble,** *adj.* & *n.* a piece of furniture not fixed in place; an article of personal property.

move'ment (moov'mənt) *n.* **1**, the act or manner of moving. **2**, a change of positions, as troops or ships. **3**, the progress of events; a tendency or trend. **4**, the suggestion of action, as in a painting. **5**, the works (of a watch, etc.). **6**, (*Music*) a principal division of a composition.

mov'er (moo'vər) *n.* **1**, a truckman who moves household things. **2**, (*Colloq.*) one who accomplishes things.

mov'ie (moo'vē) *n.* (*Colloq.*) a motion picture. —**mov'ie·go''er,** *n.*

mov'ing (moov'ing) *adj.* **1**, having or creating motion. **2**, actuating. **3**, exciting the emotions. —**moving picture,** motion picture. —**moving staircase** or **stairway,** an escalator.

mow (mō) *v.t.* & *i.* [*p.p.* **mowed** or **mown** (mōn)] **1**, cut down (grass, etc.) with a machine or scythe. **2**, cut down men in battle. —*n.* (mow) a place in a barn for storing hay.

mox'ie (mok'sē) *n.* (*Slang*) courage; pluck.

moz·ar'ab (mō-za'rəb) *n.* a Spanish Christian at the time of the Moslem domination of Spain. —**moz·ar'a·bic** (-ik) *adj.*

moz''za·rel'la (mot''sə-rel'ə) *n.* a soft white Ital. cheese.

Mr. (mis'tər) *abbr.* [*pl.* **Messrs.;** see *monsieur*] mister.

Mrs. (miz'iz) *abbr.* [*pl.* **Mmes.;** see *madame*] mistress: a title before the surname of a married woman.

Ms. (miz) *abbr.* [*pl.* **Mses.**] a title before the surname of a woman without regard to her marital status.

mu (mū) *n.* the 12th letter of the Greek alphabet (M, μ).

much *adj.* [**more, most**] in great quantity. —*n.* **1**, a great quantity. **2**, a great or important thing. —*adv.* **1**, to a great extent. **2**, approximately.

mu'ci·lage (mū'sə-lij) *n.* **1**, an adhesive gum or glue. **2**, a gummy secretion in plants. —**mu''ci·lag'i·nous** (-laj'ə-nəs) *adj.*

muck (muk) *n.* **1**, filth; dirt. **2**, manure. **3**, highly organic soil. **4**, useless rock. —**muck'y,** *adj.*

muck'rake'' (muk'rāk'') *v.i.* (*Colloq.*) expose political corruption.

mu'cous (mū'kəs) *adj.* pert. to, or secret-

ing, mucus. —**mucous membrane,** the membrane lining an internal organ.

mu'cus (mū'kəs) *n.* a viscid fluid secreted in the mucous membrane.

mud *n.* wet, soft earth; mire. —**mud dauber,** a wasp.

mud'cat'' (mud'kat'') *n.* a large catfish.

mud'dle (mud'əl) *v.t.* & *i.* **1**, mix up; confuse. **2**, confuse mentally; intoxicate. **3**, make muddy or turbid. —*n.* **1**, a mess. **2**, intellectual confusion.

mud'dle-head''ed *adj.* mentally confused or stupid; not thinking clearly.

mud'dler (mud'lər) *n.* **1**, a stick for mixing drinks. **2**, one who acts confusedly or haphazardly.

mud'dy (mud'ē) *adj.* **1**, covered or filled with mud. **2**, not clear; obscure. —*v.t.* make muddy. —**mud'di·ness,** *n.*

mud'guard'' *n.* a fender, as on an automobile.

mud hen a marsh bird, esp. a coot.

mud'sling''er *n.* one who makes unwarranted attacks on the character of an opponent, as in a political campaign. —**mud'-sling''ing,** *n.*

mud'suck''er (mud'suk''ər) *n.* a Calif. fish.

muen'ster (mön'stər) *n.* a soft, mild Alsatian cheese.

mu·ez'zin (mū-ez'in) *n.* the crier who calls Mohammedans to prayer.

muff (muf) *n.* a cylindrical cover for warming both hands. —*v.t.* & *i.* (*Colloq.*) perform clumsily; bungle.

muf'fin (muf'in) *n.* a small round bread.

muf'fle (muf'əl) *v.t.* **1**, wrap up, esp. in a cloak or scarf. **2**, deaden (sound) by wrapping. —*v.i.* (with *up*) wrap oneself well.

muf'fler (muf'lər) *n.* **1**, a scarf. **2**, a device for deadening sound, as on an engine.

muf'ti (-tē) *n.* **1**, civilian dress. **2**, a Mohammedan religious officer.

mug *n.* **1**, a cup with a handle. **2**, (*Slang*) the mouth; the face; a wry expression. —*v.t.* & *i.* [**mugged, mug'ging**] (*Slang*) **1**, photograph. **2**, throttle from behind. **3**, grimace. **4**, overact.

mug'ger (mug'ər) *n.* **1**, a crocodile. **2**, one who mugs.

mug'gy (mug'ē) *adj.* (of weather, etc.) humid and hot. —**mug'gi·ness,** *n.*

mug'wump'' *n.* an independent in politics.

muk'luk *n.* an Eskimo sealskin or reindeer-skin boot or slipper.

mu·lat'to (mū-lat'ō) *n.* the offspring of a white person and a Black. —*adj.* light-brown in color.

mul'ber'ry (mul'ber"ē) *n.* **1,** a tree or its berrylike, collective fruit. **2,** a dull reddish-purple color.

mulch *n.* a protective covering of straw, etc., around trees, etc.

mulct (mulkt) *v.t.* deprive of something by penalty or trickery. —*n.* a fine.

mule (mūl) *n.* **1,** the offspring of a mare and a male donkey. **2,** a stubborn person. **3,** a machine for spinning cotton. **4,** a slipper open at the heel. **5,** (*Slang*) a drug smuggler. —**mul'ish,** *adj.* stubborn.

mu"le·teer' (mū"lə-tir') *n.* a driver of mules: *mule skinner.*

mu'ley (mū'lē) *n.* a cow. —*adj.* (of cattle) hornless.

mull (mul) *v.i.* ponder. —*v.t.* **1,** make a failure of. **2,** heat, sweeten, and spice, as wine or ale. **3,** think over. —*n.* a kind of muslin.

mul'lein (mul'in) *n.* any of various flowering plants or weeds.

mul'let (mul'it) *n.* any of various marine or fresh-water fishes.

mul'li·gan (mul'ə-gən) *n.* (*Slang*) a meat and vegetable stew.

mul"li·ga·taw'ny (mul"ē-gə-tâ'nē) *n.* a soup flavored with curry.

mul'lion (mul'yən) *n.* a vertical division between lights of a window or panels of wainscoting. —*v.t.* divide by mullions.

mul·ti- *pref.* many.

mul"ti·far'i·ous (mul"ti-fār'ē-əs) *adj.* having many differing parts.

Mul'ti·graph" (mul'ti-gráf") *n.* (*T.N.*) a small printing press.

mul"ti·lat'er·al *adj.* **1,** having many sides. **2,** including more than two nations, as a pact.

mul"ti·me'di·a *adj.* involving several different media, as of communication, entertainment, etc.

mul"ti·mil'lion·aire' *n.* one who owns property worth several millions of dollars.

mul"ti·na'tion·al *adj.* including or involving several different countries.

mul"ti·par'tite (mul"tē-pär'tīt) *adj.* **1,** having many parts. **2,** of or between three or more nations.

mul'ti·ple (mul'ti-pəl) *adj.* manifold; having many parts, individuals, etc. —*n.* (*Math.*) the product of multiplying a number by a whole number. —**multiple sclerosis,** a hardening of the tissues in various parts of the body, affecting the nervous system and causing defects in speech and sight, and weakness.

mul'ti·ple-choice' *adj.* involving several choices, one of which must be chosen.

mul'ti·plex" (-pleks") *adj.* **1,** manifold.

2, repeated many times. **3,** pert. to a system of transmitting several signals simultaneously on the same circuit or channel. —*v.t. & i.* encode or send (messages, etc.) by a multiplex system.

mul"ti·pli·cand' (mul"tə-pli-kand') *n.* a number to be multiplied by another.

mul"ti·pli·ca'tion (mul"tə-pli-kā'shən) *n.* act or process of multiplying; often indicated by the multiplication sign (× or •).

mul"ti·plic'i·ty (mul"tə-plis'ə-tē) *n.* a great number.

mul'ti·ply" (mul'ti-plī") *v.t. & i.* **1,** increase the number or quantity. **2,** increase by propagation or procreation. **3,** (*Math.*) add as many units of one number as there are units in a second number. —**mul'ti·pli"er,** *n.*

mul'ti·tude" (mul'ti-tood") *n.* a great number; a crowd of persons. —**mul"ti·tu'di·nous,** *adj.*

mul"ti·ver'si·ty (-vėr'sə-tē) *n.* (*Colloq.*) a very large university.

mul"ti·vi'ta·min *n. & adj.* (a vitamin supplement) combining several different vitamins in one tablet, liquid, etc.

mum *adj.* [**mum'mer, -mest**] silent. —*n.* (*Colloq.*) **1,** a chrysanthemum. **2,** mother.

mum'ble (mum'bəl) *v.i. & t.* **1,** speak inarticulately or indistinctly. **2,** chew with the gums. —*n.* an inarticulate sound.

mum'ble·ty·peg" (mum'bəl-ti-peg") *n.* a game played with a knife.

mum'bo jum'bo (mum'bō-jum'bō) **1,** an object of superstitious awe; a fetish. **2,** senseless incantation.

mum'mer (mum'ər) *n.* one who wears a mask; a disguised reveler.

mum'mer·y (mum'ə-rē) *n.* **1,** a performance of mummers; burlesque. **2,** insincere ceremony.

mum'mi·fy" (mum'ə-fī") *v.t. & i.* make or become a mummy. —**mum"mi·fi·ca'tion,** *n.*

mum'my (mum'ē) *n.* **1,** a human body embalmed by the ancient Egyptians; any desiccated corpse. **2,** a withered living being. **3,** (*Colloq.*) mother.

mumps *n.* an inflammation and swelling of the parotid glands.

munch *v.t. & i.* chew continuously and noisily.

mun'dane (mun'dān) *adj.* pert. to the world or universe; worldly. —**mun·dane'ness,** *n.*

mu·nic'i·pal (mū-nis'i-pəl) *adj.* pert. to the government of a city.

mu·nic"i·pal'i·ty (mū-nis"i-pal'ə-tē) *n.* a city or town having corporate existence.

mu·nif'i·cent (mū-nif'i-sənt) *adj.* generous; spending liberally. **—mu·nif′i·cence,** *n.*

mu·ni′tion (mū-nish′ən) *n.* (usually *pl.*) materials for carrying on war, esp. ammunition.

mu′on (mū′on) *n.* a short-lived subatomic particle.

mu′ral (myŭr′əl) *adj.* pert. to, or placed on, a wall. *—n.* a painting or photograph directly on or covering a wall.

mur′der (mēr′dər) *n.* homicide with malice aforethought. *—v.t.* **1,** kill with premeditated malice. **2,** kill barbarously. **3,** mar by poor execution. **—mur′der·er,** *n.* **—mur′der·ess,** *n.fem.*

mur′der·ous *adj.* pert. to, or capable of, murder; deadly. **—mur′der·ous·ness,** *n.*

mu″ri·at′ic acid (myŭr″ē-at′ik) hydrochloric acid.

murk (mērk) *n.* haze; gloom.

murk′y (mēr′kē) *adj.* **1,** dark. **2,** obscured; hazy. **—murk′i·ness,** *n.*

mur′mur (mēr′mər) *n.* **1,** a low, indistinct sound; a subdued hum, as of voices, a brook, the wind, etc. **2,** a muttered complaint. **3,** an abnormal sound in the body, esp. the heart. *—v.t. & i.* utter (such a sound). **—mur′mur·ous,** *adj.*

Mur′phy's Law (mûr′fēz) (*Slang*) the observation that anything that can go wrong will go wrong.

mur′rain (mur′ən) *n.* a disease of cattle, esp. anthrax.

mus′ca·dine (mus′kə-din) *n.* **1,** a variety of grape grown in the U.S. **2,** a variety of pear.

mus′cat (mus′kət) *n.* a variety of grape. **—mus″ca·tel′** (-tel′) *n.* a sweet wine made from the muscat.

mus′cle (mus′əl) *n.* **1,** a fixed bunch of fibers in an animal body which produces movement by contracting and dilating. **2,** muscular strength; brawn. *—v.i.* (with *in*) (*Colloq.*) force one's way in. **—mus′cle-bound″,** *adj.* having inelastic muscles.

Mus′co·vite″ (mus′kə-vīt″) *adj. & n.* of or pert. to Muscovy (Russia), its people or language.

mus′cu·lar (mus′kyə-lər) *adj.* of or pert. to muscle; very strong. **—mus″cu·lar′i·ty,** *n.* **—muscular dystrophy,** a hereditary disease characterized by progressive weakening of the muscles.

mus′cu·la·ture (mus′kyə-lə-chər) *n.* the number, kind, and arrangement of muscles in a part of or in the whole body.

muse (mūz) *v.i. & t.* **1,** ponder; reflect. **2,** gaze meditatively. *—n.* **1,** a poet's inspiration or genius. **2,** (*cap.*) a goddess presiding over one of the arts. **—mus′ing,** *adj. & n.*

mu·sette′ (mū-zet′) *n.* **1,** an early French

bagpipe; a composition for this instrument. **2,** a kind of oboe. **—musette bag,** an army officer's bag for personal belongings.

mu·se′um (mū-zē′əm) *n.* a building for an exhibit of art, science, etc.

mush *n.* **1,** anything soft and pulpy. **2,** a food, made of meal and water. **3,** (*Colloq.*) maudlin sentiment. **4,** a journey over snow with a dog team. *—v.i.* drive a dog team.

mush′room″ *n.* any of various large fungi, esp. the edible varieties. *—v.i.* grow or spread rapidly.

mush′y (-ē) *adj.* **1,** pulpy. **2,** sentimental. **—mush′i·ness,** *n.*

mu′sic (mū′zik) *n.* **1,** the combining of sounds and tones as a form of artistic expression. **2,** a composition rendered by instruments or singing voices; a copy or copies of such a composition. **3,** any pleasing combination of sounds, as of the wind. **—music box,** a mechanical musical instrument.

mu′si·cal (-əl) *adj.* **1,** pert. to, producing, or skilled in, music. **2,** melodious; harmonious. *—n.* [also, **musical comedy**] a light drama composed chiefly of music. **—mu″si·cal′i·ty,** *n.*

mu″si·cale′ (mū″zi-kal′) *n.* a program of music.

mu·si′cian (mū-zish′ən) *n.* one who composes or performs music.

mu″si·col′o·gy (mū″zi-kol′ə-jē) *n.* the study of the history, forms, and methods of music. **—mu″si·col′o·gist,** *n.*

musk *n.* an odoriferous animal secretion used in perfumery. **—musk′y,** *adj.*

mus′keg *n.* a bog.

mus′kel·lunge″ (mus′kə-lunj″) *n.* a large, fresh-water game fish.

mus′ket (mus′kit) *n.* a hand gun for soldiers.

mus″ket·eer′ (mus″kə-tir′) *n.* a soldier, orig. one who carried a musket.

mus′ket·ry (-rē) *n.* **1,** troops armed with muskets. **2,** firing practice.

musk′mel″on (musk′mel″ən) *n.* a small sweet variety of melon.

musk ox a ruminant mammal intermediate between the sheep and the ox.

musk′rat″ *n.* a No. Amer. aquatic rodent; its fur.

Mus′lim (muz′ləm) *adj.* pert. to the Mohammedan religion or civilization. *—n.* a Mohammedan.

mus′lin (muz′lin) *n.* a cotton fabric, esp. used for sheets.

muss (mus) *n.* an untidy or confused state. *—v.t.* disarrange. **—muss′y,** *adj.*

mus′sel (mus′əl) *n.* any bivalve mollusk, esp. the fresh-water clam.

---

tub, cūte, pûll; labəl; oil, owl, go, chip, she, thin, *th*en, sing, ink; *see p. 6*

must *v.i.* be obliged or compelled to. —*n.* **1,** (*Colloq.*) a necessary thing. **2,** new wine. —*adj.* (*Colloq.*) required.

mus'tache (mus'tash) *n.* the hair on a man's upper lip. Also, **mous·tache'**, **mus·ta'chio** (mus-tä'shō) *n.*

mus'tang *n.* an Amer. wild horse.

mus'tard (mus'tərd) *n.* a plant; its seed made into a paste, used as a condiment or medicinally. —**mustard gas,** a chemical liquid used in warfare. —**mustard plaster,** a poultice containing mustard, used as a counterirritant, as for chest colds.

mus'te·line'' (mus'tə-līn'') *adj.* designating a large family of fur-bearing mammals.

mus'ter (mus'tər) *v.t.* **1,** assemble, esp. troops. **2,** (with *in*) enlist; (with *out*) discharge. **3,** (with *up*) gather; summon (up). —*v.i.* assemble. —*n.* assembly; enrollment list.

mus'ty (mus'tè) *adj.* **1,** having a stale odor or taste. **2,** antiquated. —**mus'ti·ness,** *n.*

mu'tate (mū'tāt) *v.t. & i.* change; alter. —**mu'ta·ble,** *adj.* —**mu'tant,** *adj. & n.*

mu·ta'tion *n.* (*Biol.*) a sudden change in characteristics.

mute (mūt) *adj.* **1,** silent; not speaking. **2,** incapable of speech. —*n.* **1,** one incapable of speech. **2,** a device to deaden the resonance of a musical instrument. —*v.t.* deaden the resonance of. —**mute'ness,** *n.*

mu'ti·late'' (mū'tə-lāt'') *v.t.* maim or disfigure, esp. by depriving of a limb. —**mu'ti·la'tion,** *n.*

mu'ti·neer'' (mū'tə-nir'') *n.* one who commits mutiny.

mu'ti·nous (-nəs) *adj.* **1,** being or pert. to mutiny. **2,** rebellious.

mu'ti·ny (mū'tə-nè) *n.* a revolt, esp. by soldiers or seamen, against lawful authority. —*v.i.* revolt.

mutt (mut) *n.* (*Slang*) **1,** a stupid person. **2,** a mongrel dog.

mut'ter (mut'ər) *v.t. & i.* utter indistinctly in a low tone; grumble.

mut'ton (mut'ən) *n.* the flesh of a grown sheep, used as food.

mut'ton·chops'' *n.pl.* side whiskers when the chin is clean-shaven.

mu'tu·al (mū'choo-əl) *adj.* **1,** preferred, exerted, or performed by, each of two with respect to the other; reciprocal. **2,** pert. alike to both or all sides; shared alike. **3,** denoting a company whose members share the expenses and the profits. —**mu'tu·al'i·ty,** *n.* reciprocity. —**mutual fund,** an investment company whose resources are pooled and invested.

muu'muu'' (moo'moo'') *n.* a loose Hawaiian dress.

Mu'zak (mū'zak) *n.* (*T.N.*) pre-recorded music transmitted to hotels, offices, etc.; hence, (*l.c.*) canned music.

mu·zhik' (moo-zhik') *n.* a Russian peasant.

muz'zle (muz'əl) *n.* **1,** the mouth of a gun barrel. **2,** the jaws and nose of an animal. **3,** a device to prevent an animal from biting. —*v.t.* **1,** equip with a muzzle to prevent biting. **2,** restrain from speech.

muz'zy (muz'é) *adj.* dazed.

my (mī) *pron.* poss. form of *I.* —*interj.* expressing surprise.

my''as·the'ni·a (mī''əs-thē'nè-ə) *n.* abnormal muscle weakness.

my·col'o·gy (mī-kol'ə-jè) *n.* **1,** the study of fungi. **2,** the fungi of a region. —**my''co·log'i·cal,** *adj.*

my''e·li'tis (mī''ə-lī'tis) *n.* inflammation of the spinal chord. —**my''e·lit'ic** (-lit'ik) *adj.*

My'lar (mī'lär) *n.* (*T.N.*) a polyester film.

my'na (mī'nə) *n.* an Asiatic bird, sometimes taught to talk. Also, **mi'na; my'nah.**

my·o- (mī-ō) *pref.* muscle.

my·o'pi·a (mī-ō'pè-ə) *n.* nearsightedness. —**my·op'ic** (-op'ik) *adj.* —**my·ope',** *n.*

my·o'sis (mī-ō'sis) *n.* abnormal contraction of the pupil of the eye. —**my·ot'ic** (-ot'ik) *adj.*

my''o·so'tis (mī''ə-sō'tis) *n.* the forget-me-not.

myr'i·ad (mir'è-əd) *n. & adj.* **1,** ten thousand. **2,** many.

myr'mi·don'' (mèr'mə-don'') *n.* a follower who obeys without question or scruple.

myrrh (mèr) *n.* an aromatic resin of certain plants, used for incense.

myr'tle (mèr'təl) *n.* any of various evergreen plants.

my·self' (mī-self') *pron.* [*pl.* **our·selves'**] **1,** an emphatic form of *I.* **2,** the reflexive form of *me.*

mys·te'ri·ous (mis-tir'è-əs) *adj.* pert. to a mystery; obscure; puzzling. —**mys·te'ri·ous·ness,** *n.*

mys'ter·y (mis'tə-rè) *n.* **1,** a fact or phenomenon whose meaning or cause is unknown; an enigma or puzzle. **2,** a story or novel about crime, esp. murder. **3,** a religious sacrament; (*pl.*) ancient religious rites. —**mystery play,** a medieval religious drama based on the Scriptures.

mys'tic (mis'tik) *adj.* **1,** known only to those of special comprehension or especially initiated; obscure. **2,** occult. **3,** pert. to mystery or mysticism. —*n.* one who believes in, or practices, mysticism. —**mys'ti·cal,** *adj.*

mys'ti·cism (mis'tə-siz-əm) *n.* a mode of

thought founded on spiritual illumination or intuition.

mys'ti·fy" (mis'tə-fī") *v.t.* perplex; bewilder. —**mys"ti·fi·ca'tion**, *n.*

mys·tique' (mis-tēk') *n.* semimystical beliefs and attitudes surrounding a person, institution, etc., and endowing him or it with a special aura and significance.

myth (mith) *n.* **1,** a legendary story; fable. **2,** a fictitious person, thing, or happening. —**myth'i·cal,** *adj.*

my·thol'o·gy (mi-thol'ə-jē) *n.* a body or system of myths concerning a particular person or race. —**myth"o·log'i·cal** (mith"ə-loj'i-kəl) *adj.*

N

N, n (en) the fourteenth letter of the English alphabet.

nab *v.t.* [**nabbed, nab'bing**] (*Colloq.*) **1,** seize suddenly. **2,** arrest.

na'bob (nā'bob) *n.* a very rich man, esp. one whose riches were acquired in the Far East.

na·celle' (nə-sel') *n.* a cabin or enclosed shelter on an aircraft.

na'cre (nā'kər) *n.* mother-of-pearl.

na'dir (nā'dər) *n.* **1,** that point of the heavens directly below the observer. **2,** the lowest point.

nag *v.t. & i.* [**nagged, nag'ging**] annoy by constant scolding or urging. —*n.* (*Colloq.*) a horse, esp. an inferior horse.

nai'ad (nī'ad) *n.* a water nymph of springs and streams.

nail (nāl) *n.* **1,** the horny covering at the end of a finger or toe. **2,** a slender pointed piece of metal, used to hold things together, esp. wood. —*v.t.* **1,** fasten with nails. **2,** (*Colloq.*) catch; secure. **3,** detect and expose.

nail'set" *n.* a metal punch for sinking the head of a nail.

nain'sook (nān'sûk) *n.* a fine, soft cotton fabric.

na·ive' (nä-ēv') *adj.* unsophisticated; artless. —**na·ive"té'** (-tā') *n.*

na'ked (nā'kid) *adj.* **1,** unclothed; nude. **2,** without the usual covering; bare; exposed. **3,** plain; undisguised. **4,** (*Law*) lacking in some essential detail required for confirmation, authentication, etc.

nam'by-pam'by (nam'bē-pam'bē) *adj.* insipid; inanely sentimental.

name (nām) *n.* **1,** a word by which a person, place, or thing is known. **2,** a descriptive word or title. **3,** reputation, good or bad. **4,** fame; great reputation. **5,** a family; clan. **6,** a famous person. —*v.t.* **1,** give a name to. **2,** mention; specify. **3,** appoint. **4,** identify.

name'less (-ləs) *adj.* **1,** obscure. **2,** anonymous. **3,** illegitimate. **4,** indescribable or unmentionable. —**name'less·ness,** *n.*

name'ly (-lē) *adv.* that is to say.

name'sake" *n.* one who is named for another.

nan·keen' (nan-kēn') *n.* **1,** a yellow cotton cloth. **2,** (*pl.*) trousers made of it. **3,** (*cap.*) a type of porcelain. Also, **nan·kin'.**

nan'ny (nan'ē) *n.* **1,** a child's word for nurse. **2,** a female goat.

na'no- (na'nō) *pref.* one billionth.

nap *n.* **1,** the soft, fuzzy surface of some fabrics. **2,** a short sleep. —*v.t.* [**napped, nap'ping**] **1,** take a short sleep. **2,** be off guard.

na'palm (nā'pâm) *n.* jellied gasoline, used in incendiary weapons.

nape (nāp) *n.* the back of the neck.

na'per·y (nā'pə-rē) *n.* table linens.

naph'tha (naf'thə) *n.* a volatile liquid distilled from petroleum, used for dry cleaning, etc.

naph'tha·lene" (naf'thə-lēn") *n.* a coal tar derivative, used for dyes or as a moth repellent.

nap'kin *n.* a small square of cloth or paper, esp. one used at table.

na·po'le·on (nə-pō'lē-ən) *n.* **1,** a former Fr. gold coin. **2,** a rich layered pastry. **3,** a high boot.

narc (närk) *n.* (*Slang*) a federal narcotics inspector.

nar·cis'sism (när-sis'iz-əm) *n.* an abnormal tendency to admire one's own perfections. Also, **nar'cism.**

nar·cis'sus (när-sis'əs) *n.* a spring-flowering, bulbous plant, as the daffodil and jonquil.

nar·co'sis (när-kō'sis) *n.* stupor induced by drugs. Also, **nar'co·tism** (när'kə-tiz-əm). —**nar'co·tize,** *v.t.* stupefy; affect with a narcosis.

nar·cot'ic (när-kot'ik) *n. & adj.* a drug that dulls the senses, relieves pain, and produces sleep.

nard (närd) *n.* an aromatic ointment made from an E. Indian herb; the herb.

nar'es (när'ēz) *n.pl.* [*sing.* **nar'is**] the nostrils. —**nar'i·al,** *adj.*

nar'ghi·le (nar'gi-le) *n.* an Oriental tobacco pipe; hookah.

nark (närk) *n.* (*Slang*) an informer.

nar'rate" (na'rāt") *v.t. & i.* give an account (of); relate. —**nar·ra'tion,** *n.* —**nar'·ra"tor,** *n.*

nar′ra·tive (nar′ə-tiv) *n.* a story. —*adj.* of or being a story.

nar′row (nar′ō) *adj.* **1,** of small width; not broad. **2,** limited in extent, resources, point of view, etc. **3,** with little margin; close. —*v.t. & i.* lessen; contract. —*n.* (*pl.*) the shallow part of a river; a strait. —**nar′row-gauge″,** *adj.* having (railroad) tracks less than the usual 56½ inches apart. —**nar′row-mind″ed,** *adj.* shallow; intolerant; bigoted. —**nar′row·ness,** *n.*

nar′thex (när′theks) *n.* vestibule.

nar′whal (när′wəl) *n.* an arctic sea mammal, related to the whale, with a long, straight tusk.

nar′y (năr′ė) *adj.* (*Dial.*) not a; no.

na′sal (nā′zəl) *adj.* pert. to the nose; pronounced through the nose. —**na′sal·ize″,** *v.t.* pronounce through the nose.

nas′cent (năs′ənt) *adj.* beginning to exist or to grow. —**nas′cen·cy,** *n.*

nas·tur′tium (na-stēr′shəm) *n.* a plant bearing fragrant flowers.

nas′ty (nas′tė) *adj.* **1,** physically filthy; offensive. **2,** indecent; objectionable. **3,** stormy, as weather. **4,** troublesome. **5,** vicious. —**nas·ti·ness,** *n.*

na′tal (nā′təl) *adj.* pert. to one's birth. —**na·tal′i·ty** (nə-tal′ə-tė) *n.* birthrate.

na′tant (nā′tənt) *adj.* swimming; floating.

na·ta′tion (na-tā′shən) *n.* the art or act of swimming. —**na″ta·to′ri·um,** (na″tə-tôr′ė-əm) *n.* a swimming pool. —**na′ta·to″ry,** *adj.*

na′tion (nā′shən) *n.* **1,** a race of people having a common descent, language, and culture. **2,** a body of people constituting a political unit under one government.

na′tion·al (nash′ən-əl) *adj.* common to the whole nation; public; governmental. —*n.* a citizen. —**national debt,** money owed by the federal government to private individuals or organizations. —**National Guard,** the militia of the U. S. states, each commanded by the governor except in wartime. —**National Socialism,** the German government under Hitler.

na′tion·al·ism (nash′ə-nə-liz-əm) *n.* advocacy of the utmost political advancement of one's nation or people. —**na′tion·al·ist,** *n.* —**na″tion·al·is′tic,** *adj.*

na″tion·al′i·ty (nash″ə-nal′ə-tė) *n.* **1,** membership in a particular nation. **2,** a race of people; a nation.

na′tion·al·ize″ (-īz″) *v.t.* place under government control or ownership. —**na″tion·al·i·za′tion,** *n.*

na′tive (nā′tiv) *adj.* **1,** pert. to one by birth or by the place of one's birth. **2,** not

of foreign origin or production. **3,** natural; innate. —*n.* **1,** one born in a certain place or country. **2,** one of the original inhabitants. —**na′tive-born″,** *adj.*

na·tiv′i·ty (nā-tiv′ə-tė) *n.* **1,** birth; also, time, place, and manner of birth. **2,** (*cap.*) the birth of Christ.

NATO (nā′tō) *n. & adj.* North Atlantic Treaty Organization, a group of nations cooperating to oppose the spread of communism.

nat′ty (nat′ė) *adj.* (*Colloq.*) smartly spruce; trim. —**nat′ti·ness,** *n.*

nat′u·ral (nach′ə-rəl) *adj.* **.1,** not artificial; formed by nature. **2,** pert. to, or in a state of, nature. **3,** proper; reasonable; not unusual. **4,** innate. **5,** easy; unaffected; kindly. **6,** (*Music*) neither sharp nor flat. **7,** (of children) illegitimate. —*n.* **1,** something that is natural. **2,** (*Colloq.*) a person or thing sure to succeed. **3,** an idiot. —**nat′u·ral·ness,** *n.* —**natural history,** the study of plant and animal life, behavior, etc. —**natural selection,** survival of the fittest.

nat′u·ral·ism (-iz-əm) *n.* **1,** close adherence to nature or reality in painting, poetry, etc. **2,** a view of the world which takes account only of natural elements and forces.

nat′u·ral·ist (-ist) *n.* a scholar of plant and animal life.

nat′u·ral·ize″ (-īz″) *v.t.* admit (an alien) to citizenship. —**nat′u·ral·i·za′tion,** *n.*

na′ture (nā′chər) *n.* **1,** the material universe; the forces at work in the universe, independently of man or his acts. **2,** the essential character of a person or thing. **3,** kind; sort.

naught (nât) *n.* **1,** nothing. **2,** a zero; a cipher (0).

naugh′ty (nâ′tė) *adj.* **1,** disobedient. **2,** improper. —**naugh′ti·ness,** *n.*

nau′sea (nâ′shə) *n.* **1,** an inclination to vomit. **2,** a feeling of disgust.

nau′se·ate″ (nâ′sė-āt″) *v.t.* sicken.

nau′seous (nâ′shəs) *adj.* causing nausea. —**nau′seous·ness,** *n.*

nautch (nâch) *n.* an Indian ballet.

nau′ti·cal (nâ′ti-kəl) *adj.* pert. to ships, seamen, or navigation.

nau′ti·lus (nâ′tə-ləs) *n.* a mollusk with a spiral chambered shell.

na′val (nā′vəl) *adj.* pert. to a navy.

nave (nāv) *n.* **1,** the main body of a church from chancel to entrance. **2,** the hub of a wheel.

na′vel (nā′vəl) *n.* the depression in the center of the abdomen. —**navel orange,** a type of small, seedless orange.

nav′i·ga·ble (nav′i-gə-bəl) *adj.* **1,** affording passage to ships. **2**, capable of being steered, as a dirigible.

nav′i·gate″ (nav′i-gāt″) *v.t. & i.* **1**, travel by water; sail over or on. **2**, sail or steer a ship. —**nav″i·ga′tion**, *n.* —**nav′i·ga″tor**, *n.* one who plots the course of ships or aircraft.

na′vy (nā′vė) *n.* **1**, all the war vessels of a nation. **2**, (usually *cap.*) a nation's naval organization. —**navy bean**, a variety of small, white bean. —**navy blue**, a deep, dark blue.

nay (nā) *n.* **1**, no; a refusal. **2**, a negative vote. —*adv.* not only so, but; indeed.

Naz″a·rene′ (naz″ə-rēn′) *n. & adj.* of or pert. to Nazareth. —**the Nazarene**, Jesus Christ.

Na′zi (not′sė) *n.* a member of the former National Socialist party, which controlled Germany 1933 to 1945. —**Na′zism** (not′-siz-əm) *n.* the principles of this party, quasi-fascistic and racist.

N-′bomb″ *n.* neutron bomb.

Ne·an′der·thal″ (nė-an′dər-täl″) *adj.* pert. to a species of man existing in the paleolithic period.

neap (nēp) *adj.* designating the lowest high tide in the lunar month.

near (nir) *adj.* **1**, not remote; close to; close. **2**, closely akin. **3**, intimate, as friends. **4**, on the left (opposed to *off*). **5**, (*Colloq.*) stingy. —*adv.* **1**, not far off. **2**, closely. **3**, nearly. —*prep.* close by or to. —*v.i. & t.* come close (to). —**near-″by′**, *adj., adv. & prep.* close at hand. —**near′ness**, *n.* —**near beer**, a malt liquor with a very low alcoholic content.

Near East 1, a region including southwestern Asia (Syria, Turkey, Jordan, etc.) and sometimes the Balkans and Egypt. **2**, (*Brit.*) the Balkans.

near′ly *adv.* **1**, closely. **2**, almost.

near′sight″ed *adj.* able to see clearly only at short distances; myopic. —**near′-sight″ed·ness**, *n.*

neat (nēt) *adj.* **1**, tidy; orderly. **2**, adroit; effective. **3**, pure; undiluted. —**neat′ness**, *n.*

neb′bish (neb′ish) *n.* a meek or uninteresting person.

neb′u·la (neb′yə-lə) *n.* [*pl.* **-lae** (-lė), **-las**] a luminous patch in the sky made by distant star clusters or masses of gas. —**neb′u·lar**, *adj.*

neb′u·lous (neb′yə-ləs) *adj.* **1**, cloudy; hazy. **2**, indistinct; vague; confused. —**neb″-u·los′i·ty, neb′u·lous·ness**, *n.*

nec′es·sar″y (nes′ə-ser″ė) *adj.* **1**, inevitably resulting from the nature of things. **2**, required; essential; indispensable. —*n.* an

essential thing. —**nec″es·sar′i·ly** (-ə-lė) *adv.* inevitably.

ne·ces′si·tate″ (nə-ses′ə-tāt″) *v.t.* render unavoidable; compel.

ne·ces′si·tous (nə-ses′ə-təs) *adj.* very poor; needy.

ne·ces′si·ty (nə-ses′ə-tė) *n.* **1**, the state or fact of being inevitable or necessary. **2**, something essential, esp. to existence. **3**, poverty; great need. **4**, compulsion.

neck (nek) *n.* **1**, the slender part of the body between the head and shoulders. **2**, in a garment, the part closest to the neck. **3**, something resembling a neck; an isthmus. —*v.i.* (*Slang*) kiss and pet.

neck′er·chief (nek′ər-chif) *n.* a scarf worn around the neck. Also, **neck′cloth″**.

neck′lace (nek′ləs) *n.* any flexible ornament worn around the neck.

neck′tie″ (nek′tī″) *n.* a decorative band worn around the neck. —**neck′tie party**, (*Slang*) a public hanging, esp. without trial.

neck′wear″ *n.* neckties, etc.

nec·ro- (nek-rō) *pref.* dead; death; corpse.

ne·crol′o·gy (nek-rol′ə-jė) *n.* **1**, an obituary. **2**, a list of persons who have died. —**ne·crol′o·gist**, *n.*

nec′ro·man″cy (nek′rə-man″sė) *n.* **1**, divination by conversing with the dead. **2**, magic in general.

ne·crop′o·lis (nek-rop′ə-lis) *n.* a cemetery, esp. of ancient times.

ne·cro′sis (ne-krō′sis) *n.* death of bodily tissue; gangrene. —**ne·crot′ic** (-krot′ik) *adj.*

nec′tar (nek′tər) *n.* **1**, in mythology, the wine of the gods. **2**, any delicious drink. **3**, a sweet secretion. —**nec′tar·ous**, *adj.*

nec″ta·rine′ (nek″tə-rēn′) *n.* a form of peach with a smooth skin.

née (nā) *adj.* born; whose maiden name was.

need (nēd) *n.* **1**, necessity or lack; urgent want. **2**, time of difficulty; emergency. **3**, poverty. —*v.t.* be in want of. —*v.i.* **1**, be obliged. **2**, be necessary. —**need′ful**, *adj.* necessary; requisite.

nee′dle (nē′dəl) *n.* **1**, a slender pointed instrument with a hole for thread, used in sewing. **2**, any of various similar instruments, as for knitting, in a phonograph, on a hypodermic syringe, etc. **3**, a leaf of a pine tree. **4**, the pointer on the dial of an instrument, esp. the magnetized pointer in a compass. **5**, something resembling a needle, as an obelisk. —*v.t.* (*Colloq.*) vex or goad by repeated gibes.

nee′dle·point″ *n.* **1**, lace made on a paper pattern. **2**, a kind of embroidery.

need′less (-ləs) *adj.* unnecessary. —**need′-less·ness**, *n.*

---

tub, cūte, pûll; labəl; oil, owl, go, chip, she, thin, *th*en, sing, ink; *see p. 6*

nee′dle·work″ *n.* sewing or embroidery.

need′y (nē′dē) *adj.* very poor. —**need′-i·ness**, *n.*

ne′er (nâr) *contraction* never.

ne′er-′do-well″ (nâr′doo-wel″) *n.* an idle, worthless person.

ne·far′i·ous (ni-fār′ē-əs) *adj.* unspeakably wicked. —**ne·far′i·ous·ness**, *n.*

ne·gate′ (ne-gāt′) *v.t.* deny; nullify. —**ne·ga′tion**, *n.*

neg′a·tive (neg′ə-tiv) *adj.* **1,** expressing denial or refusal; not affirmative; not positive. **2,** lacking positive or distinguishing qualities. **3,** (*Math.*) denoting subtraction; minus. **4,** having an excess of electrons. —*n.* **1,** a negative statement, reply, or word. **2,** in a debate, the side that denies or refutes. **3,** (*Photog.*) a plate or film from which a print is made; the image in reverse. —*v.t.* refuse assent. —**negative income tax,** a method of public relief; guaranteed annual income. —**neg′a·tiv·ism**, *n.* a tendency to view the world with a skeptical attitude.

neg·lect′ (ni-glekt′) *v.t.* **1,** disregard. **2,** be remiss about; leave uncared for. **3,** fail in duty or performance through carelessness. —*n.* **1,** lack of attention or care. **2,** negligence. —**neg·lect′ful**, *adj.* careless.

neg″li·gee′ (neg″lə-zhā′) *n.* a woman's loose, informal house gown.

neg′li·gent (neg′lə-jənt) *adj.* **1,** guilty of or characterized by neglect, esp. of duty. **2,** (*Law*) failing to exercise due care. —**neg′li·gence**, *n.*

neg′li·gi·ble (neg′li-jə-bəl) *adj.* of little importance. —**neg″li·gi·bil′i·ty**, *n.*

ne·go′ti·a·ble (ni-gō′shē-ə-bəl) *adj.* capable of being negotiated; transferable. —**ne·go″ti·a·bil′i·ty**, *n.*

ne·go′ti·ate″ (ni-gō′shē-āt″) *v.i.* discuss with others the terms of a diplomatic, political, or business matter. —*v.t.* **1,** bring about by mutual discussions. **2,** sell (notes, securities, etc.). **3,** (*Colloq.*) handle. —**ne·go′ti·ant**, *n.* —**ne·go″ti·a′tion**, *n.*

Ne·gri′to (ni-grē′tō) *n.* a member of one of the dwarfish Negroid peoples of Asia or Africa.

Ne′gro (nē′grō) *n.* a member of the darkest-skinned, or black, race. —*adj.* of, or pert. to, this race. —**Ne′gress**, *n.fem.* —**Ne′groid** (-groid) *adj.*

ne′gus (neg′əs) *n.* a beverage of hot water and wine, sweetened and spiced.

Neh′ru jacket (nā′roo) Mao jacket.

neigh (nā) *n.* the prolonged cry of a horse; a whinny. —*v.i.* whinny.

neigh′bor (nā′bər) *n.* **1,** one who lives near another. **2,** a person or thing next or near another. **3,** a fellow being. —*v.t.* ad-

join; be near to. Also, **neighbour.** —**neigh′-bor·ing,** *adj.* nearby.

neigh′bor·hood″ *n.* **1,** the vicinity; a district of a particular kind. **2,** the persons in a locality.

neigh′bor·ly (-lē) *adj.* appropriate to a neighbor; accommodating. —**neigh′bor·li·ness**, *n.*

nei′ther (nē′thər, nī′-) *adj.*, *adv.*, *conj.* & *pron.* not either.

nel′son (nel′sən) *n.* a hold in wrestling.

Nem′bu·tal″ (nem′byŭ-tâl″) *n.* a barbiturate used as a sedative and analgesic.

nem′e·sis (nem′ə-sis) *n.* [*pl.* **-ses″** (-sēz″)] an agent of vengeance.

ne·o- (nē-ō) *pref.* new; recent.

ne″o·clas′si·cism *n.* any revival of classic style in the arts. —**ne″o·clas′sic,** *adj.*

ne″o·dym′i·um (nē″ō-dim′ē-əm) *n.* a rare-earth metallic element, no. 60, symbol Nd.

ne″o·lith′ic (nē″ō-lith′ik) *adj.* pert. to the later stone age.

ne·ol′o·gism (nē-ol′ə-jiz-əm) *n.* a new word, usage, or expression. Also, **ne·ol′o·gy.**

ne′on (nē′on) *n.* an inert gaseous element, no. 10, symbol Ne, much used in electric signs.

neph′rite (nef′rīt) *n.* a variety of jade.

ne′o·phyte″ (nē′ə-fīt″) *n.* **1,** a beginner; a novice. **2,** a convert.

ne′o·plasm″ (nē′ə-plaz″-əm) *n.* any morbid growth, as a tumor. —**ne″o·plas′tic,** *adj.*

ne′o·plas″ty (nē′ə-plas″tē) *n.* restoration by plastic surgery.

ne′o·prene″ (nē′ə-prēn″) *n.* a kind of synthetic rubber.

ne″o·ter′ic (nē″ə-ter′ik) *adj.* recent; modern. —*n.* a modern writer, etc.

ne·pen′the (ni-pen′thē) *n.* anything that induces forgetfulness of pain or care.

neph′ew (nef′ū) *n.* a son of one's sister or brother.

ne·phri′tis (ne-frī′tis) *n.* inflammation of the kidneys.

nep′o·tism (nep′ə-tiz-əm) *n.* undue favoritism to relatives. —**ne·pot′ic** (nə-pot′ik) *adj.* —**ne·pot′i·cal·ly,** *adv.*

nep·tu′ni·um (nep-tū′nē-əm) *n.* an artificially produced radioactive element, no. 93, symbol Np.

ne′re·id (nir′ē-id) *n.* a sea nymph.

nerve (nērv) *n.* **1,** a bundle of fibers, one of many conveying impulses of motion and sensation from the brain to all parts of the body. **2,** force; energy. **3,** courage. **4,** (*pl.*) acute nervousness. **5,** (*Slang*) audacity. —*v.t.* give strength or courage to. —**nerve**

cell, 1, any cell of the nervous system. 2, a ganglion. —**nerve gas**, a chemical weapon which attacks the nervous system.

nerve'less (-ləs) adj. 1, lacking courage. 2, listless; weak. —**nerve'less·ness**, n.

nerv'ous (nėrv'əs) adj. 1, made up of, or affecting, the nerves. 2, high-strung; easily agitated. 3, timid; uneasy. —**nerv'ous·ness**, n. —**nervous breakdown**, a condition characterized by fatigue, lethargy, worry, and lack of energy. —**nervous system**, the bodily system that receives stimuli and transmits impulses.

ner'vure (ner'vyûr) n. a vein in a leaf or insect's wing.

nerv'y (nėr'vē) adj. brash; bold.

nes'cience (nesh'əns) n. ignorance. —**nes'cient**, adj.

ness (nes) n. a promontory or cape.

-ness (nəs) suf. quality or state of being (the root word); added to adjectives to form nouns. (A terminal -y regularly changes to -i before -ness.)

nest n. 1, a place used by or made by birds, insects, turtles, etc., for laying eggs and hatching young. 2, any snug retreat. 3, a graduated set of articles, as bowls, tables, etc., fitted one within the other. —v.i. sit on or build a nest. —**nest egg**, a fund of money saved for an emergency.

nes'tle (nes'əl) v.i. & t. 1, lie close and snug. 2, settle comfortably; snuggle.

nest'ling (nest'ling; nes'-) n. a young bird in the nest.

net n. 1, a contrivance made of coarse string tied in meshes, for catching fish, birds, etc. 2, a snare; a trap. 3, a fine fabric of open mesh for dresses, veils, etc. 4, anything woven or tied in meshes. 5, clear profit. —adj. 1, remaining as profit after all necessary deductions (taxes, expenses, etc.). 2, without discount. —v.t. [**net'ted, -ting**] 1, capture, as with a net. 2, spread a net over. 3, earn as clear profit.

neth'er (neth'ər) adj. under; lower. —**neth'er·most**, adj. lowest, deepest, etc. —**neth'er·ward** (-wərd) adv. toward the depths. —**nether world**, hell.

net'ting (net'ing) n. any meshed fabric of thread, rope, wire, etc.

net'tle (net'əl) n. a coarse herb with stinging hairs. —v.t. vex. —**net'tle·some** (-səm) adj.

net'work" n. 1, anything of intersecting lines resembling a net. 2, a chain of radio or television stations.

neu'ral (nyûr'əl) adj. pert. to the nerves or the nervous system.

neu·ral'gia (nyū-ral'jə) n. an acute intermittent pain along the course of a nerve. —**neu·ral'gic**, adj. —**neu·ral'gi·cal·ly**, adv.

neu"ras·the'ni·a (nyûr"əs-thē'nē-ə) n. nervous exhaustion. —**neu"ras·then'ic** (-then'ik) adj. & n.

neu·ri'tis (nyû-rī'tis) n. inflammation or continued pain in a nerve.

neu·ro- (nyû-rō) pref. nerve.

neu·rol'o·gy (nyû-rol'ə-jē) n. the branch of science dealing with the nervous system and its diseases. —**neu"ro·log'i·cal**, adj. —**neu·rol'o·gist**, n.

neu'ron (nyûr'on) n. a nerve cell. Also, **neu'rone** (-ōn).

neu"ro·pa·thol'o·gy n. (Med.) the study of the diseases of the nervous system. —**neu"ro·pa·thol'o·gist**, n.

neu·ro'sis (nyû-rō'sis) n. [pl. -ses (sēz)] a functional nervous disease or emotional disorder. —**neu·rot'ic** (-rot'ik) adj. & n. —**neu·rot'i·cal·ly**, adv.

neu'ter (noo'tər) adj. 1, (Gram.) neither masculine nor feminine. 2, (Zool.) sexless; (Bot.) asexual. —v.t. render neuter.

neu'ter·cane" (nyoo'tər-kān') n. a subtropical cyclone.

neu'tral (noo'trəl) adj. 1, taking neither side in a war, quarrel, or dispute. 2, with no decided qualities or characteristics; indifferent. 3, of a color, gray; subdued in tone. —n. a neutral power, one of its subjects or its vessels. —**neutral spirits**, ethyl alcohol of higher than 190 proof.

neu·tral'i·ty (noo-tral'ə-tē) n. state of being neutral.

neu'tral·ize" (noo'trə-līz") v.t. 1, render neutral or inactive. 2, counteract. —**neu"tral·i·za'tion**, n.

neu·tri'no (noo-trē'nō) n. a neutral particle.

neu'tron (noo'tron) n. a minute uncharged particle of matter. —**neutron bomb**, a high-energy bomb which kills living things but inflicts little physical damage on buildings, etc.

nev'er (nev'ər) adv. 1, not ever. 2, not at all. —**never-never land**, 1, wilderness. 2, an imaginary place. 3, an imagined existence.

nev"er·more' adj. never again.

nev'er-say-"die' adj. indomitable; unconquerable.

nev"er·the·less' (nev"ər-thə-les') adv. & conj. in spite of that; yet.

ne'vus (ne'vəs) n. [pl. -vi (-vī)] a mole or birthmark.

new (noo) adj. 1, recently made, discovered, invented, etc. 2, unfamiliar. 3, not the same as before; different. 4, not used before. 5, starting afresh; unaccustomed. 6, not previously well known. —adv. recently; freshly. —**new'ish**, adj. —**new'-**

ness, *n.* —**new math**, a system of teaching mathematics based on set theory. —**new moon**, the phase of the moon when it is in conjunction with the sun, its dark side turned toward the earth.

new′born″ *adj.* **1,** born recently. **2,** re-born.

new′com″er *n.* one recently arrived.

new′el (noo′əl) *n.* **1,** the center pillar of a flight of winding stairs. **2,** a post on a stairway.

new″fan′gled (-fang′gəld) *adj.* novel. —**new·fan′gled·ness,** *n.*

new-′fash″ioned *adj.* **1,** made in a new form or style. **2,** lately come into fashion.

New′found·land (noo′fənd-lənd) *n.* a very large, shaggy dog.

new′ly (noo′lē) *adv.* **1,** recently; lately. **2,** anew; afresh.

new′ly·wed″ *n.* a person recently married.

news (nooz) *n.sing.* **1,** tidings, esp. of recent public events. **2,** the reports published in a newspaper. **3,** (*Colloq.*) a matter not previously known. —**news′boy″,** *n.,* **news·girl″,** *n.fem.* a boy or girl who sells or delivers newspapers. —**news′cast″,** *n.* a radio broadcast of current news. —**news′-deal″er,** *n.* a person who sells newspapers. —**news′man″,** *n.,* **news′wom″an,** *n.fem.* a person who writes, edits, reports, etc., the news. —**news′pa″per,** *n.* a printed publication giving chiefly news. —**news′print″,** *n.* a cheap paper used in newspapers. —**news′reel″,** *n.* motion pictures of current events. —**news′stand″,** *n.* a stand where newspapers are sold.

news′let″ter *n.* a periodical news bulletin, usu. for a particular special interest group.

news′mon″ger *n.* a gossip.

new′speak″ *n.* the intentional use of ambiguous and misleading language.

news′wor″thy *adj.* worthy of being reported as news; of general interest.

news′y (noo′zfi) *adj.* full of news; informative. —**news′i·ness,** *n.*

newt (noot) *n.* a small, semiaquatic salamander.

New Testament the books of the Holy Bible relating to Jesus Christ or Christianity.

New Year a year just beginning. —**New Year's Day,** Jan. 1. —**New Year's Eve,** Dec. 31.

next (nekst) *adj. & adv.* **1,** nearest. **2,** immediately following in time, place, order, etc. —*prep.* nearest to.

nex′us (nek′səs) *n.* [*pl.* **nex′us**] **1,** a tie; link. **2,** a connected series.

ni′a·cin (nī′ə-sin) *n.* nicotinic acid.

nib *n.* **1,** the point of anything, esp. of a pen. **2,** a bird's beak.

nib′ble (nib′əl) *v.i. & t.* bite off small pieces (of). —*n.* a small bite.

nib′lick (nib′lik) *n.* a golf club for high lofting shots; no. 9 iron.

nibs (nibz) *n.* (*Colloq.*) an important person, as *his nibs* or *her nibs.*

nice (nīs) *adj.* **1,** requiring precision or tact. **2,** subtle, as a distinction. **3,** delicately sensitive; minutely accurate. **4,** fastidious; refined; discriminating. **5,** (*Colloq.*) pleasing or pleasant; attractive; kind. —**nice′-ness,** *n.*

nice-′nel′ly·ism (-nel′ē-iz-əm) *n.* a euphemism.

ni′ce·ty (nī′sə-tē) *n.* **1,** precision; accuracy. **2,** a minute distinction or detail. **3,** something choice. **4,** (usu. *pl.*) refinement.

niche (nich) *n.* **1,** a recess in a wall, as for a vase, statue, etc. **2,** a suitable place or position.

ni′chrome (nik′rōm) *n.* an alloy of nickel, chromium, and iron.

nick (nik) *n.* **1,** a notch. **2,** a slightly chipped place, as on a dish. **3,** the exact moment (of time). —*v.t.* make a notch in; chip.

nick′el (nik′əl) *n.* **1,** a hard silvery-white metallic element much used in alloys, no. 28, symbol Ni. **2,** a U. S. 5-cent coin. —**nickel** or **German silver,** an alloy of nickel, copper, and zinc, used for tableware, etc.

nick″el·o′de·on (nik′ə-lō′dē-ən) *n.* **1,** a movie theater with an admission price of five cents. **2,** a juke box.

nick′er (nik′ər) *v.i.* **1,** neigh. **2,** laugh; snicker. —*n.* a neigh; a vulgar laugh.

nick′name″ (nik′nām″) *n.* an additional or substitute name.

nic′o·tine″ (nik′ə-tēn″) *n.* a poisonous colorless, oily liquid extracted from tobacco. —**nic′o·tin″ic acid,** a B vitamin derived from nicotine; niacin.

ni′dus (nī′dəs) *n.* [*pl.* **-di** (-dī)] **1,** a nest, esp. for insects' eggs. **2,** a place where disease germs may develop.

niece (nēs) *n.* a daughter of one's brother or sister.

Niel′son rating (nēl′sən) a system of ranking (television programs) on the basis of the estimated number of viewers.

nif′ty (nif′tē) (*Slang*) *adj.* smart; stylish. —*n.* a smart remark.

nig′gard (nig′ərd) *n.* a stingy person; a miser. —*adj.* **1,** niggardly. **2,** scanty; inadequate.

nig'gard·ly (nig'ərd-lē) *adj.* stingy; miserly. —**nig'gard·li·ness,** *n.*

nig'gle (nig'əl) *v.t. & i.* **1,** trifle (with); perform too meticulously. **2,** cheat.

nigh (nī) *adj., adv. & prep.* near.

night (nīt) *n.* **1,** the time from sunset to sunrise. **2,** nightfall. **3,** darkness; also, a time of affliction or ignorance. —**night blindness,** poor vision at night; nyctalopia. —**night crawler,** a large earthworm. —**night letter,** a telegram transmitted at a reduced rate, during the night. —**night owl,** a person accustomed to late hours.

night'cap" (nīt'kap") *n.* **1,** a cap worn at night in bed. **2,** a drink taken just before retiring. **3,** the last event in an evening program.

night'clothes, *n.pl.* bedclothes.

night'club" *n.* a cabaret.

night'dress" *n.* a garment worn in bed.

night'fall" *n.* the coming of night.

night'gown" *n.* **1,** a dressing gown. **2,** a loose shift worn in bed.

night'hawk" *n.* **1,** any of various nocturnal hawks. **2,** (*Colloq.*) night owl.

night'ie (-ē) *n.* (*Colloq.*) a nightgown.

night'in·gale" (nīt'ən-gāl") *n.* a European thrush famous for its song.

night'ly (-lē) *adj.* **1,** happening at night. **2,** happening every night. **3,** pert. to night. —*adv.* every night.

night'mare" *n.* **1,** any oppressive terrifying dream. **2,** any threatening, haunting thought or experience. —**night'mar"ish,** *adj.*

night'rid"er *n.* a member of a lawless band that commits crimes of violence at night.

night'shade" *n.* any of several poisonous plants, as belladonna or henbane.

night'shirt" *n.* a loose knee-length garment formerly worn in bed by men.

night'spot" *n.* (*Colloq.*) a night club.

night'stick *n.* a billy.

night'time" *n.* night.

night'y (-ē) *n.* nightie.

ni'hil·ism (nī'ə-liz-əm) *n.* **1,** a doctrine that denies moral principles and social obligations. **2,** an extreme anarchistic movement. —**ni'hil·ist,** *n.* —**ni"hil·is'tic,** *adj.*

-nik *suf.* designating one who advocates or is associated with.

nil *n.* nothing.

nim'ble (nim'bəl) *adj.* **1,** lively; quick; agile. **2,** alert; acute. —**nim'ble·ness,** *n.*

nim'bus (nim'bəs) *n.* in art, a bright cloud or a halo around the head of a divine or saintly person.

nin'com·poop" (nin'kəm-poop") *n.* a simpleton.

nine (nīn) *n. & adj.* the cardinal number between eight and ten, expressed by 9. —**ninth,** *adj. & n.* —**nine days' wonder,** an event or person arousing short-lived excitement.

nine'pins" *n.sing.* a bowling game using nine pins.

nine'teen" (nīn'tēn") *n. & adj.* nine plus ten: 19. —**nine'teenth,** *adj. & n.* —**nineteenth hole,** (*Colloq.*) a clubhouse, bar, or other place where golfers gather after playing a round.

nine'ty (nīn'tē) *n. & adj.* ten times nine: 90. —**nine'ti·eth,** *adj. & n.*

nin'ny (nin'ē) *n.* a simpleton.

ni'non (nē'non) *n.* a sheer chiffon fabric.

ni·o'bi·um (nī-ō'bē-əm) *n.* a steel-gray metallic element, no. 41, symbol Nb.

nip *v.t.* [**nipped, nip'ping**] **1,** pinch; bite. **2,** pinch off. **3,** benumb; blast, as by cold. **4,** check in growth, as a plot. **5,** drink in sips. —*n.* **1,** a pinch; bite. **2,** chill or sting in the air. **3,** a small drink. —**nip and tuck,** (in a contest) almost exactly even; unpredictable in outcome. —**nip in the bud,** arrest at the start of development.

nip'per (nip'ər) *n.* **1,** the large claw of a crab or lobster. **2,** (*pl.*) pincers. **3,** (*Colloq.*) a small boy.

nip'ple (nip'əl) *n.* **1,** the milk duct of the female breast. **2,** the mouthpiece of a nursing bottle. **3,** a short piece of pipe threaded at both ends.

Nip"pon·ese' (nip"ə-nēz') *n. & adj.* Japanese.

nip'py (nip'ē) *adj.* sharp; biting.

nir·va'na (nir-vä'nə) *n.* a state of detachment and dispassion.

Ni'sei' (nē'sā') *n.* a native U. S. citizen of Japanese ancestry.

Nis'sen hut (nis'ən) a shelter in the form of a metal half-cylinder.

nit *n.* the egg or young of a parasitic insect, as the louse.

ni'ter (nī'tər) *n.* nitrate of potassium, a white salt used in gunpowder; saltpeter. Also, **ni'tre.**

ni'ton (nī'ton) *n.* radon.

nit'pick" *v.i.* concentrate on petty details.

ni'trate (nī'trāt) *n.* a chemical compound of nitric acid, used as a fertilizer.

nit'ric (nī'trik) *adj.* **1,** containing nitrogen. **2,** pert. to niter. —**nitric acid,** a corrosive compound of nitrogen, used in making dyes, explosives, plastics, etc.

ni'tri·fy (nī'tri-fī) *v.t.* **1,** combine with nitrogen. **2,** impregnate with nitrates, as soil. —**ni"tri·fi·ca'tion,** *n.*

ni"tro·cel'lu·lose (nī"trə-sel'yə-lōs) *n.* a plastic compound of nitrogen and cellulose.

ni·tro·gen (nī'trə-jən) n. a colorless, odorless gaseous element, no. 7, symbol N, forming four-fifths of the volume of the earth's atmosphere.

ni"tro·glyc'er·in (nī"trə-glis'ər-in) n. a highly explosive oil.

ni'trous (nī'trəs) adj. containing nitrogen.
—**nitrous oxide,** an anesthetic (laughing) gas.

nit"ty-grit'ty (nit"ē-grit'ē) n. (Slang) the essential facts, issues, elements, etc.

nit'wit n. (Slang) a stupid person.

nix (niks) n., adv. & interj. (Slang) nothing; no. —v.t. (Slang) veto. —n. a water sprite.

nix'ie (-ē) n. 1, a female nix. 2, an improperly addressed and undeliverable piece of mail.

no (nō) adv. a word of denial, refusal, or dissent; a negative. —adj. not any; not at all. —n. 1, a denial or refusal. 2, a negative vote.

nob n. (Slang) 1, a socially-prominent person. 2, the head.

No·bel' Prize (nō-bel') a prize in money (about $40,000) given for an achievement in science, literature, or the advancement of peace, endowed by Alfred Nobel, Swed. inventor.

no·bel'i·um (nō-bel'ē-əm) n. a radioactive chemical element, no. 102, symbol No, produced artificially.

no·bil'i·ty (nō-bil'ə-tē) n. state of being noble.

no'ble (nō'bəl) adj. 1, of high birth, rank, or title. 2, of lofty character. 3, stately; imposing. 4, admirably conceived or executed. 5, choice; excellent. —n. a peer: nobleman.

no·blesse' o·blige' (nâ-bles'â-blēzh') (Fr.) the supposed moral and social obligations of the nobility.

no'bod"y (nō'bod"ē) n. 1, no one. 2, a person of no social standing.

nock (nok) n. a notch in a bow or arrow.

noct- (nokt) pref. night.

noc·tur'nal (nok-tēr'nəl) adj. 1, pert. to, or occurring in, the night. 2, active at night, as certain animals.

noc'turne (nok'tərn) n. a meditative pensive musical piece.

nod n. an inclination of the head, as in a greeting; approval, command, etc. —v.t. & i. [nod'ded, -ding] 1, incline the head in assent, etc. 2, drowse; become inattentive.

nod'dy (nod'ē) n. 1, a simpleton; fool. 2, a shore bird.

node (nōd) n. 1, a knot; knob. 2, a hard swelling. 3, a point of intersection, as of two great circles. 4, a point in a vibrating body that remains relatively at rest.
—**nod'al** (nō'dəl) adj.

nod'ule (nod'ūl) n. a little knot or lump.
—**nod'u·lous,** adj.

no'dus (nō'dəs) n. 1, a knot. 2, a complication, as in a drama.

No·el' (nō-el') n. Christmas.

no-'fault" adj. of a type of insurance under which claims are paid without regard to fault.

no-'frills" adj. of a type of reduced-fare service, as on an airplane, offering few or no extra benefits.

nog'gin (nog'in) n. 1, a small mug. 2, a small amount of liquor; a gill. 3, (Colloq.) the head.

Noh (nō) n. a type of Japanese dance-drama. Also, **No.**

noil n. a short fiber, esp. of wool.

noise (noiz) n. 1, a sound of any kind, esp. when loud or disagreeable. 2, outcry; clamor. —v.t. spread the report of; make public. —**nois'y,** adj. full of, or making, loud sounds.

noi'some (noi'səm) adj. 1, ill-smelling; disgusting. 2, injurious.

no'mad (nō'mad) n. a member of a roving tribe; a wanderer. —**no·mad'ic,** adj. —**no·mad'i·cal·ly,** adv.

no man's land 1, territory between entrenched enemy forces. 2, wasteland.

nom de guerre (nōm"də-gār') (Fr.) a pseudonym assumed for a certain activity.

nom de plume (nom'də-ploom") (Fr.) a pen name.

no'men·cla"ture (nō'mən-klā"chər) n. a system of names.

nom'i·nal (nom'i-nəl) adj. 1, existing in name only; so-called. 2, so small as to be virtually nothing. 3, pert. to a name. —**nominal value,** the named or face value; par value.

nom'i·nate" (nom'ə-nāt") v.t. 1, propose for an elective office. 2, appoint to an office. —**nom"i·na'tion,** n.

nom'i·na·tive (nom'i-nā-tiv) adj. 1, requiring nomination. 2, (Gram.) designating the case of the subject of a verb. —n. this case.

nom'i·nee" (nom'i-nē") n. a person nominated for office.

non- pref. used freely before nouns, adjectives, and adverbs with the general meaning of not, being less emphatic than un- or in-.

non'age (non'ij) n. legal minority; immaturity.

non"a·ge·nar'i·an (non"ə-jə-nār'ē-ən) n. a person 90 years of age or older, but less than 100.

non″ag·gres′sion *n.* a refraining from aggression, esp. in international relations.

non′a·gon″ (non′ə-gon″) *n.* a polygon having nine sides and nine angles.

non″a·ligned′ (-ə-līnd′) *adj.* neutral, as of a nation.

non′bel·lig′er·ent *n. & adj.* (being) a nation that is not at war but is openly assisting a nation at war.

nonce (nons) *n.* the time being; this one time. —**nonce word,** a word coined and used on a single occasion.

non′cha·lance (non′shə-ləns) *n.* coolness; disinterested self-possession. —**non′cha·lant** (-lənt) *adj.*

non′com′ (non′kom″) *n.* (*Colloq.*) a noncommissioned officer.

non″com′bat·ant *n.* **1,** a person in the armed forces whose duties do not include fighting. **2,** a civilian in wartime.

non″com·mis′sioned *adj.* not having a commission, as an officer of the rank of corporal or sergeant.

non″com·mit′tal (-kə-mit′əl) *adj.* not committing oneself or itself to a positive view or course.

non″com·pli′ance *n.* failure or refusal to comply; disobedience.

non″con·duc′tor *n.* a substance that does not readily conduct electricity, heat, etc.

non″con·form′i·ty *n.* refusal or failure to conform, esp. to some established church. —**non″con·form′ist,** *n.*

non″co·op·er·a′tion *n.* **1,** failure to work together harmoniously. **2,** refusal to perform civic duties in protest against an unpopular administration.

non′dair′y *adj.* not containing any milk products.

non′de·script″ (non′də-skript″) *adj.* not easily classified; of no particular kind or sort.

none (nun) *pron.* **1,** no one. **2,** not any. —*adv.* in no degree. —*adj.* not any. —**none″the·less′,** *adv.* no less; nevertheless.

non″ef·fec′tive *n.* a soldier or sailor not fit for duty.

non·en′ti·ty (non-en′tə-tē) *n.* **1,** a person or thing of no importance. **2,** something not exciting.

nones (nōnz) *n.* **1,** in ancient Rome, the 7th of March, May, July, and October, and the 5th of other months. **2,** the fifth canonical hour, beginning about 3:00 p.m.; a service at this hour.

non″es·sen′tial *adj. & n.* (something) not essential or necessary.

none′such′ (nun′such″) *n.* a person or thing that has no equal.

none″the·less′ *adv.* nevertheless.

non″ex·ist′ence *n.* condition of not existing; something that does not exist. —**non″ex·ist′ent,** *adj.*

non·fea′sance (non-fē′zəns) *n.* (*Law*) omission to do something that should have been done.

non″fic′tion *n.* literature dealing with real persons and events, as history or biography.

non″hero′ *n.* a person or character lacking the usual attributes of a hero.

non″in·ter·ven′tion *n.* refusal to intervene, esp. in the affairs of other nations.

non″pa·reil′ (non″pə-rel′) *n. & adj.* **1,** (some one or thing) having no equal; peerless. **2,** a size of type. **3,** a kind of chocolate candy coated with small sugar pellets. —*n.* a brightly colored finch of the So. U.S.

non′per′son *n.* **1,** a person treated or ignored as though nonexistent. **2,** a person with no standing in society.

non·plus′ *v.t.* perplex; confound.

non″prof′it *adj.* not intended to earn a profit, as an incorporated charity.

non·res′i·dent *adj.* exercising rights or performing duties (as of franchise, membership, position, etc.) while residing relatively far away. —*n.* one who lives elsewhere.

non″sec·tar′i·an (non″sek-tār′ē-ən) *adj.* favoring no particular religious sect, as a school, association, etc.

non′sense *n.* senseless or absurd words, ideas, or conduct. —**non·sen′si·cal,** *adj.*

non se′qui·tur (non-sek′wi-tər) (*Lat.*) a conclusion which does not logically follow from its premises.

non′stop′ *adj. & adv.* without a single stop, as a journey.

non″sup·port′ *n.* (*Law*) failure to provide maintenance by one who is obligated to do so.

non″un′ion *adj.* **1,** not conforming to trade-union requirements. **2,** not having membership in, or a contract with, a trade-union.

non″vi′o·lence *n.* **1,** abstention on principle from all forms of violence. **2,** the doctrine of such abstention in the effort to achieve one's objectives.

noo′dle (noo′dəl) *n.* **1,** dough rolled into thin, flat, strips; a form of macaroni. **2,** (*Slang*) the head.

nook (nûk) *n.* a recess; an out-of-the-way corner or retreat.

noon (noon) *n.* **1,** twelve o'clock midday; 12 M. **2,** (*Colloq.*) a recess for lunch. —**noon′day″,** *adj.* at noon. —**noon′time″, noon′tide″,** *n.* noon.

---

noose (noos) *n.* **1,** a loop with a sliding knot, as in a lasso. **2,** (with *the*) death by hanging.

no′pal (nō′pəl) *n.* a cactus, the prickly pear.

nor (nôr) *conj.* and not; neither.

Nor′dic (nôr′dik) *adj.* pert. to or designating a Caucasian race characterized by blond hair, blue eyes, and tall stature, as the Scandinavians and Anglo-Saxons. —*n.* a person of Nordic ancestry.

norm (nôrm) *n.* **1,** a standard; pattern. **2,** a type.

nor′mal (nôr′məl) *adj.* **1,** conforming to a certain type or standard; regular; average. **2,** free from mental defect. —*n.* the standard; the average. —**nor′mal·cy, nor·mal′i·ty,** *n.* state of being normal; a normal condition. —**nor′mal·ize″,** *v.t. & i.* make or become normal; standardize. —**nor′ma·tive,** *adj.* —**normal school,** a college where teachers are trained.

Nor′man (nôr′mən) *n.* [*pl.* **-mans**] **1,** one of the French who conquered England in 1066. **2,** a native of Normandy. —*adj.* of the Normans or Normandy.

Norse (nôrs) *adj.* **1,** pert. to ancient Scandinavia. **2,** Norwegian.

north (nôrth) *n.* **1,** the point of the compass on the right hand of a person facing the setting sun; the direction toward that point. **2,** a region or country lying north of another; (*cap.,* with *the*) in the U.S., the region lying north of Maryland, the Ohio River, and Missouri. —*adj. & adv.* in, toward, or from the direction of north. —**north′er·ly** (nôr′thər-lē) *adj.* in or toward the north. —**north′ward,** *adv.*

north″east′ *n. & adj.* midway between north and east. —**north″east′er,** (nôr-ēs′tər) *n.* a gale from the northeast. —**north″east′ern,** *adj.*

north′er (nôr′thər) *n.* a strong, cold wind from the north.

north′ern (nôr′thərn) *adj.* pert. to, living in, coming from, or going toward the north. —**north′ern·er,** *n.* a resident or native of the north. —**northern lights,** the aurora borealis. —**north′ern·most″,** *adj.* furthest north.

north′land (-lənd) *n.* **1,** a northern region, or the northern part of any country. **2,** (*cap.*) the Scandinavian Peninsula.

North Pole 1, the north end of the earth's axis of rotation. **2,** the zenith of this point.

North Star Polaris, a bright star near the North Pole of the heavens.

north″west′ *n. & adj.* midway between north and west. —**north″west′er** (nôr-wes′tər) *n.* a gale from the northwest. —**north″west′ern,** *adj.*

Nor·we′gian (nôr-wē′jən) *adj. & n.* pert. to Norway, its language or inhabitants.

nor′west′er (nôr-wes′tər) *n.* a seaman's oilskin raincoat.

nose (nōz) *n.* **1,** that feature of the face above the mouth, containing the nostrils or respiratory passage; the organ of smell. **2,** sense of smell, as of a dog. **3,** something likened to a nose in shape; the forward or projecting part of anything. —*v.t. & i.* **1,** detect by smell. **2,** rub with the nose. **3,** push slowly forward, as a ship. **4,** (with *out*) (*Colloq.*) defeat by a narrow margin. **5,** pry curiously. —**nose′bleed″,** a bleeding from the nose. —**nose cone,** the part of a space vehicle that contains the instrumentation and that returns to earth at the end of a mission; the forward end of a rocket or missile. —**nose′dive″,** a headlong plunge of an airplane. —**nose′gay″,** *n.* a bouquet. —**nos′ey, nos′y,** *adj.* prying.

nosh *n. & v.i.* (*Slang*) snack.

no·′show″ *n.* (*Colloq.*) a person who does not show up, as for a reserved space.

nos·tal′gia (nos-tal′jə) *n.* homesickness; sentimental recollection of the past. —**nos·tal′gic** (-jik) *adj.* —**nos·tal′gi·cal·ly,** *adv.*

nos·tol′o·gy (nos-tol′ə-jē) *n.* the study of senility.

nos′tril (nos′trəl) *n.* an external opening of the nose.

nos′trum (nos′trəm) *n.* **1,** a medicine, esp. a quack remedy. **2,** any cure-all scheme or device.

not *adv.* a word expressing denial, refusal, or negation.

no′ta be′ne (nō′tə-bē′nē) (*Lat.*) note well; mark carefully. **N.B.**

no′ta·ble (nō′tə-bəl) *adj.* worthy of note; remarkable; eminent. —*n.* a prominent or important person. —**not″a·bil′i·ty,** *n.*

no′ta·rize″ (nō′tə-rīz″) *v.t.* attest to (a sworn statement).

no′ta·ry (nō′tə-rē) *n.* a person licensed to attest deeds, take affidavits, etc.: *notary public.* —**no·tar′i·al** (nō-tār′ē-əl) *adj.*

no·ta′tion (nō-tā′shən) *n.* **1,** the act of taking notes; a note. **2,** a system, or set of symbols, for representing numbers and quantities by symbols, in mathematics and music. —**no′tate** (-tāt) *v.t.*

notch (noch) *n.* **1,** a nick or slot in the edge of something. **2,** a narrow defile between mountains.

notch′back″ *n.* an automobile roof having a deck at the rear.

note (nōt) *n.* **1,** a mark or record to assist the memory. **2,** fame or distinction; importance or consequence. **3,** notice; heed. **4,** an annotation, as in a book. **5,** a memorandum. **6,** a short letter; also, a formal diplomatic communication. **7,** (*pl.*) a brief record of facts, impressions, a speech, etc. **8,** a written promise to pay. **9,** a sound; cry; a musical tone or a symbol of it in musical notation. —*v.t.* **1,** observe carefully. **2,** make a record of. **3,** make mention of. —**note′-book″,** *n.* a book of blank pages for making notes. —**note′wor′thy,** *adj.* notable.

1   2   3   4   5   6   7   8   9

NOTES: **1,** double whole note (breve). **2,** whole note (semibreve). **3,** half note (minim). **4,** quarter note (crochet). **5,** eighth note (quaver). **6,** sixteenth note (semiquaver). **7,** thirty-second note (demisemiquaver). **8,** sixty-fourth note (hemidemisemiquaver). **9,** a group of thirty-second notes.

not′ed *adj.* **1,** famous; well known. **2,** noticed.

noth′ing (nuth′ing) *n.* **1,** that which does not exist; absence of everything; not anything. **2,** a trifle. **3,** a zero. —*adv.* in no way. —**noth′ing·ness,** *n.* nonexistence.

no′tice (nō′tis) *n.* **1,** observation; attention; cognizance. **2,** any written statement giving an order, information, or warning. **3,** a brief review, as of a book, play, etc. **4,** public attention. —*v.t.* **1,** perceive; observe. **2,** remark upon; acknowledge. **3,** heed. —**no′tice·a·ble,** *adj.*

no′ti·fy′ (nō′ti-fī″) *v.t.* give attention to; inform. —**no″ti·fi·ca′tion,** *n.*

no′tion (nō′shən) *n.* **1,** a general idea; a somewhat vague belief. **2,** a view; opinion. **3,** a whim; a fancy. **4,** (*pl.*) various small wares. —**no′tion·al,** *adj.*

no″to·ri′e·ty (nō″tə-rī′ə-tē) *n.* state or fact of being notorious.

no·to′ri·ous (nō-tôr′ē-əs) *adj.* widely but not favorably known.

not″with·stand′ing *adv.* nevertheless. —*prep.* in spite of. —*conj.* although.

nou′gat (noo′gət) *n.* a glazed candy. —**nou′ga·tine,** *n.* a chocolate-covered nougat.

nought (nât) *adv., adj. & n.* naught.

noun (nown) *n.* (*Gram.*) a word denoting a person, place, thing, or concept.

nour′ish (nēr′ish) *v.t.* **1,** supply with substances that are assimilated and maintain life and growth; feed. **2,** foster; maintain.

nour′ish·ment (-mənt) *n.* **1,** feeding. **2,** food.

nou″veau riche′ (noo″vō-rēsh′) (*Fr.*) newly rich.

no′va (nō′və) *n.* a star that increases greatly in brightness and then gradually wanes.

nov′el (nov′əl) *adj.* previously unknown; unusual; new and striking. —*n.* a long narrative portraying fictitious characters and events in a realistic manner. —**nov″el·ette′,** *n.* a short novel. —**nov′el·ist,** *n.* a writer of novels. —**nov′el·ize″,** *v.t.*

no·vel′la (nō-vel′la) *n.* [*pl.* **-le** (-le)] a short story.

nov′el·ty (nov′əl-tē) *n.* **1,** the quality of being new and fresh. **2,** a new experience or thing. **3,** a new or unusual article of trade.

No·vem′ber (nō-vem′bər) *n.* the eleventh month of the year.

no·ve′na (no-vē′nə) *n.* a devotion consisting of nine days of prayer.

nov′ice (nov′is) *n.* **1,** a beginner. **2,** a monk or nun who has not yet taken vows.

no·vit′i·ate (nō-vish′ē-ət) *n.* a probationary period.

no″vo·caine″ (nō′və-kān″) *n.* (*T.N.*) a local anesthetic.

now *adv.* **1,** at the present time; at once. **2,** but lately. **3,** nowadays; under existing circumstances. —*conj.* since. —*n.* this very time. —**now′a·days″,** *adv.* at present; in this age.

no′way″ *adv.* in no way, manner, or degree. Also, **no′ways″.**

no′where″ (nō′hwâr″) *adv.* in, at, or to no place; not anywhere.

no′wise″ (nō′wīz″) *adv.* in no way.

nox′ious (nok′shəs) *adj.* injurious. —**nox′-ious·ness,** *n.*

noz′zle (noz′əl) *n.* a terminal spout, as on a hose or pipe.

nth (enth) *adj.* **1,** (*Math.*) being the last term, or any at random, of a series. **2,** superlative.

nu (noo) *n.* the thirteenth letter of the Greek alphabet (N, γ).

nu·ance′ (noo-äns′) *n.* a delicate degree or shade of difference.

nub *n.* **1,** a knob. **2,** (*Colloq.*) the gist of a story.

nub′bin (nub′in) *n.* **1,** a small piece. **2,** an underdeveloped corn ear.

nub′ble (nub′əl) *n.* **1,** a small piece or lump. **2,** a protuberance. —**nub′bly,** *adj.* lumpy.

nu′bi·a (noo′bē-ə) *n.* a wrap of soft fleecy material worn by women.

nu′bile (noo′bil) *adj.* marriageable. —**nu-bil′i·ty,** *n.*

nu′cle·ar (noo′klē-ər) *adj.* **1,** being or pert. to a nucleus. **2,** pert. to the study of atomic nuclei. —**nu′cle·ate** (-ət) *adj.* —**nuclear energy,** energy released by the fusion or fission of atomic nuclei. **—nuclear fission,** the breakdown of the atomic nucleus of an element into two or more nuclei of lower atomic number, part of the mass being converted into energy. **—nuclear fusion,** the fusion of atomic nuclei to transform elements, with release of large quantities of energy. **—nuclear physics,** the branch of physics that deals with the structure and transformations of nuclei.

nu·cle′ic acid (noo-klā′ik) any of several complex acids found in all living cells.

nu′cle·on (noo′klē-än) *n.* a proton or neutron, esp. in a nucleus.

nu″cle·on′ics (noo″klē-on′iks) *n.sing.* nuclear physics.

nu′cle·us (noo′klē-əs) *n.* [*pl.* **-i** (-ī)] **1,** a central mass about which other matter collects; a starting point for growth or development. **2,** (*Biol.*) the kernel of a cell. **3,** (*Physics*) the center of an atom.

nude (nood) *adj.* naked; bare. *—n.* in art, an undraped figure. **—nude′ness,** *n.* **—nud′ism,** *n.* the practice of going naked. **—nud′ist,** *n.*

nudge (nuj) *v.t.* prod gently, as a hint or signal. *—n.* a gentle prod.

nu′di·ty (noo′də-tē) *n.* nudeness.

nu′ga·to″ry (noo′gə-tôr″ē) *adj.* **1,** worthless. **2,** ineffectual.

nug′get (nug′ət) *n.* a lump, esp. of native gold.

nui′sance (noo′səns) *n.* an annoying or obnoxious person or thing.

null (nul) *adj.* **1,** of no effect. **2,** nonexistent. **—null and void,** utterly without validity.

nul′li·fy″ (nul′i-fī″) *v.t.* **1,** render invalid. **2,** make ineffective. **—nul″li·fi·ca′tion,** *n.*

nul′li·ty (nul′ə-tē) *n.* something invalid, null, without legal force, etc.

numb (num) *adj.* without sensation; powerless to feel or act. *—v.t.* make numb. **—numb′ness,** *n.*

num′ber (num′bər) *n.* **1,** the sum of an aggregation of persons or things. **2,** the symbol that stands for this sum. **3,** a particular numeral assigned to one of a series. **4,** (*Gram.*) inflection of nouns depending on quantity, as singular or plural. **5,** a large, but not precisely counted, aggregation. **6,** (*pl.*) a considerable aggregation; superiority. **7,** (*pl.*) a type of lottery. **8,** one issue of a periodical. **9,** a musical composition; a verse; a recitation; an act, as in vaudeville; (*Colloq.*) a routine; bit. *—v.t.* **1,** count. **2,** include in a class. **3,** assign a number to. **4,** limit in number. **—num″ber·less,** *adj.* too many to number; countless. **—numbers game** or **pool** or **racket,** an illegal lottery.

nu′mer·al (noo′mər-əl) *n. & adj.* a symbol or word denoting a number, as 9 or nine.

nu′mer·ate″ (noo′mə-rāt″) *v.t.* enumerate; count. **—nu′mer·a·ble,** *adj.* **—nu″mer·a′tion,** *n.*

nu′mer·a″tor (noo′mə-rā″tər) *n.* in a fraction, the number above the line showing how many parts of a unit are taken.

nu·mer′i·cal (noo-mer′i-kəl) *adj.* pert. to, or expressed in, numbers.

nu″mer·ol′o·gy (noo″mə-rol′ə-jē) *n.* the study of the occult meaning of numbers. **—nu″mer·ol′o·gist,** *n.*

nu′mer·ous (noo′mər-əs) *adj.* a great many. **—nu′mer·ous·ness,** *n.*

nu″mis·mat′ics (noo″miz-mat′iks) *n.* the science of coins and medals. **—nu″mis·mat′ic,** *adj.* **—nu·mis′ma·tist,** *n.*

num′skull″ (num′skul″) *n.* a dolt.

nun *n.* a woman living under religious vows in a convent. **—nun′ner·y** (-ə-rē) *n.* a convent.

nun·ci·o″ (nun′shē-ō″) *n.* a diplomatic agent of the Pope. **—nun′ci·a·ture** (-ə-chər) *n.* the office or term of a nuncio.

nup′tial (nup′shəl) *adj.* pert. to marriage or a wedding ceremony. *—n.* (*pl.*) a wedding.

nurse (nērs) *n.* **1,** a woman in charge of young children. **2,** one who cares for the sick. *—v.t.* **1,** take care of, as children or invalids. **2,** suckle; feed from the breast. **3,** foster; encourage. **—nurs′ing home,** a private home for elderly persons and invalids.

nurse′maid″ *n.* a maid who takes care of children. *—v.t.* act as nursemaid to.

nurs′er·y (nēr′sə-rē) *n.* **1,** a room set apart for children. **2,** day nursery. **3,** a place where young trees, shrubs, and plants are grown for sale. **—nurs′er·y·man** (-mən) *n.* one whose business is the growing of young trees, plants, etc. **—nursery rhyme,** a story for children written in rhymed verse.

nurs′ling (nērs′ling) *n.* **1,** an infant. **2,** any person or thing receiving tender care.

nur′ture (nēr′chər) *v.t.* **1,** give nourishment to; feed. **2,** rear; train.

nut *n.* **1,** the fruit of certain trees, consisting of a kernel in a hard shell; the kernel itself. **2,** a small perforated metal block internally threaded to fit a bolt. **3,** a difficult problem. **4,** (*Slang*) the head. **5,** (*Slang*) fixed expenses; overhead. **6,** (*Slang*) a crazy person.

nu·ta′tion (noo-tā′shən) *n.* **1,** a wedding. **2,** (*Pathol.*) an involuntary shaking of the head. **—nu′tant,** (noo′tənt) *adj.*

nut′crack″er (nut′krak″ər) *n.* **1,** an instrument for cracking nuts. **2,** a Europ. bird that feeds on nuts.

nut′hatch″ (nut′hach″) *n.* a small bird that creeps on tree trunks.

nut′meg *n.* the seed of an East Indian tree, used as a spice.

nu′tri·a (noo′trē-ə) *n.* the coypu or its fur, resembling beaver.

nu′tri·ent (noo′trē-ənt) *n.* & *adj.* (something) affording nutrition.

nu′tri·ment (noo′tri-mənt) *n.* nourishment.

nu·tri′tion (noo-trish′ən) *n.* **1,** the process by which food is converted into living tissue. **2,** the act of nourishing; food. —**nu·tri′tion·al,** *adj.* —**nu·tri′tion·ist,** *n.* —**nu·tri′tious,** *adj.* nourishing. —**nu′tri·tive** (-trə-tiv) *adj.*

nuts (nutz) (*Slang*) *interj.* of disgust or defiance. —*adj.* crazy.

nut′shell″ *n.* **1,** the shell of a nut. **2,** a pithy condensation; summary. —**in a nutshell,** in few words.

nut′ty (-ē) *adj.* **1,** like a nut, esp. in flavor. **2,** (*Slang*) crazy. —**nut′ti·ness,** *n.*

nuz′zle (nuz′əl) *v.t.* & *i.* **1,** dig, push, or rub with the nose. **2,** nestle; snuggle.

nyc″ta·lo′pi·a (nik″tə-lō′pē-ə) *n.* night blindness.

ny′lon (nī′lon) *n.* a synthetic thermoplastic product that can be spun into fibers of great toughness and elasticity, used in hosiery, clothing, bristles, cordage, etc.

nymph (nimf) *n.* **1,** (*Myth.*) a semidivine maiden inhabiting streams, forests, hills, etc. **2,** a beautiful young woman. **3,** the young of certain insects.

nym″pho·ma′ni·a (nim″fə-mā′nē-ə) *n.* uncontrollable amorous passion in women. —**nym″pho·ma′ni·ac,** *n.*

O

O, o (ō) **1,** the fifteenth letter of the English alphabet. **2,** (*cap.*) as a numeral, zero.

oaf (ōf) *n.* a simpleton; a lout. —**oaf′ish,** *adj.*

oak (ōk) *n.* a valuable hardwood tree, whose fruit is the acorn. —**oak′en,** *adj.* —**Oak Leaf Cluster,** an insignia, traditionally in the shape of oak leaves, signifying that a medal previously awarded has been earned again.

oa′kum (ō′kəm) *n.* loose rope fibers, used for calking ships.

oar (ôr) *n.* **1,** a shaft of wood, broad at one end, for rowing a boat. **2,** an oarsman. —**oar′lock″,** *n.* a U-shaped oar rest on the

side of a boat. —**oars′man** (ôrz′mən) *n.* a rower.

o·a′sis (o-ā′sis) *n.* [*pl.* **-ses** (-sēz)] a fertile spot in a desert; a watering place.

oat (ōt) *n.* a cereal plant or its seeds, used for food, esp. for horses. —**oat′en,** *adj.* —**feel one's oats,** feel lively. —**sow (one's) wild oats,** indulge in youthful excesses.

oath (ōth) *n.* **1,** a solemn statement, with God as witness. **2,** a curse.

oat′meal″ *n.* **1,** crushed and hulled oats. **2,** oat porridge.

ob- *pref.* **1,** toward; facing. **2,** against. **3,** upon or over.

ob″bli·ga′to (ob″lə-gä′tō) *n.* [*pl.* **-tos, -ti** (-tē)] (*Music*) an accompaniment of independent importance.

ob′du·rate (ob′dyə-rət) *adj.* resisting entreaty; hardhearted. —**ob′du·ra·cy,** *n.*

o′be·ah (ō′bē-ə) *n.* a religion of the W. Indies employing witchcraft; a fetish used in that religion.

o·be·di·ent (ō-bē′dē-ənt) *adj.* submissive to authority; willing to obey. —**o·be′di·ence,** *n.*

o·bei′sance (ō-bā′səns) *n.* **1,** a bow, as a mark of deference. **2,** deference. —**o·bei′sant,** *adj.*

ob′e·lisk (ob′ə-lisk) *n.* **1,** a four-sided shaft of stone tapering to a pyramidal apex. **2,** (*Printing*) the dagger (†).

o·bese′ (ō-bēs′) *adj.* very fat. —**o·bes′i·ty,** *n.*

o·bey′ (ō-bā′) *v.t.* comply with the command of. —*v.i.* do as bidden.

ob·fus′cate (ob-fus′kāt) *v.t.* darken; obscure; bewilder. —**ob″fus·ca′tion,** *n.*

o′bi (ō′bē) *n.* **1,** a broad sash worn by Japanese women. **2,** obeah.

O′bie (ō′bē) *n.* one of several awards given annually for excellence in off-Broadway theaters.

ob′i·ter dic′tum (ob′i-tər-dik′təm) (*Lat.*) a passing remark; an incidental opinion.

o·bit′u·ar″y (ō-bich′oo-er″ē) *n.* a notice, esp. in a newspaper, of a person's death, with a brief biography. Also, *colloq.,* **o′bit.** —*adj.* pert. to the death of a person or persons.

ob′ject (ob′jikt) *n.* **1,** a material thing. **2,** a person or thing to which action or feeling is directed. **3,** purpose; goal; aim. **4,** (*Gram.*) a word or clause toward which the action of the verb is directed. —**object lesson,** a practical illustration or example.

ob·ject′ (əb-jekt′) *v.i.* offer opposition; disapprove.

ob·jec′ti·fy (ob-jek′tə-fī) *v.t.* give form and shape to. —**ob·jec″ti·fi·ca′tion,** *n.*

ob·jec′tion (ob-jek′shən) *n.* **1,** an expression of opposition or disapproval. **2,** an adverse reason.

ob·jec'tion·a·ble (-ə-bəl) *adj.* undesirable; unpleasant.

ob·jec'tive (-tiv) *n.* **1,** a goal; aim. **2,** the lens nearest the object observed, as in a microscope. —*adj.* **1,** dealing with external facts and not with thoughts and feelings. **2,** free from personal prejudices; unbiased. —**objective case,** (*Gram.*) the case of the direct object of a verb. —**ob"jec·tiv'i·ty** (ob"jek-tiv'ə-tē) *n.*

ob·jet' d'art' (ob-zhe"där') [*pl.* **objets d'art** (ob-zhe"-)] (*Fr.*) a small work of art.

ob·jur·gate" (ob'jər-gāt") *v.t.* berate; rebuke. —**ob"jur·ga'tion,** *n.* —**ob·jur'ga·to·ry** (əb-jer'gə-tôr-ē) *adj.*

ob'late (ob'lāt) *adj.* flattened at the poles. —*n.* (*Rom. Cath.*) a secular person devoted to monastic work.

ob·la'tion (ob-lā'shən) *n.* a religious offering; sacrifice.

ob'li·gate" (ob'lə-gāt") *v.t.* bind by some legal or moral tie, sense of duty, etc.

ob"li·ga'tion (-gā'shən) *n.* **1,** the binding power of a promise, contract, sense of duty, etc. **2,** a debt. **3,** the state of being bound to do something.

ob·lig'a·to"ry (ob-lig'ə-tôr"ē) *adj.* compulsory; necessary.

o·blige' (ə-blīj') *v.t.* **1,** bind, constrain, or compel by any physical, moral, or legal force or influence. **2,** lay under obligation by some favor; render a favor to. —**o·blig'ing,** *adj.* accommodating; courteous.

ob·lique' (ə-blēk') *adj.* **1,** slanting. **2,** indirectly aimed or expressed. —**ob·liq'ui·ty** (ə-blik'wə-tē) *n.* —**oblique angle,** an angle other than a right or straight angle.

ob·lit'er·ate" (ə-blit'ə-rāt") *v.t.* blot out; efface entirely. —**ob·lit"er·a'tion,** *n.*

ob·liv'i·on (ə-bliv'ē-ən) *n.* **1,** the state of being forgotten. **2,** forgetfulness. —**ob·liv'i·ous,** *adj.* forgetful; unmindful.

ob'long (ob'lâng) *adj.* **1,** longer than broad and with sides parallel. **2,** elongated. —*n.* a rectangle.

ob'lo·quy (ob'lə-kwē) *n.* **1,** abusive language; slander. **2,** disgrace.

ob·nox'ious (əb-nok'shəs) *adj.* odious; objectionable. —**ob·nox'ious·ness,** *n.*

o'boe (ō'bō) *n.* a double-reed woodwind instrument with a penetrating tone. —**o'bo·ist,** *n.*

ob·scene' (əb-sēn') *adj.* offensive to modest sensibilities (said of words, pictures, etc.); indecent; lewd. —**ob·scen'i·ty** (-sen'ə-tē) *n.*

ob·scur'ant (əb-skyūr'ənt) *n.* one who strives to prevent inquiry, enlightenment,

or reform. —**ob·scur'ant·ism,** *n.* —**ob·scur'ant·ist,** *n.*

ob·scure' (əb-skyūr') *adj.* **1,** vague; not clearly expressed. **2,** murky; dim. **3,** remote; hidden. **4,** humble; lowly. —**ob·scure'ness,** *n.*

ob·scu'ri·ty (əb-skūr'ə-tē) *n.* **1,** state of being obscure. **2,** lack of fame or recognition.

ob'se·quies (ob'sə-kwēz) *n.pl.* funeral rites.

ob·se'qui·ous (əb-sē'kwē-əs) *adj.* fawning; servile; deferential. —**ob·se'qui·ous·ness,** *n.*

ob·serv'ance (əb-zēr'vəns) *n.* **1,** the act of complying with some law, custom, rule, etc. **2,** a customary rite or ceremony.

ob·serv'ant (əb-zēr'vənt) *adj.* **1,** taking keen notice. **2,** apt at noticing details; attentive; mindful.

ob"ser·va'tion (ob"zər-vā'shən) *n.* **1,** the act of seeing and noting; notice. **2,** the observing of scientific phenomena; the record so obtained. **3,** a remark or comment. **4,** the faculty of observing.

ob·serv'a·to"ry (ob-zēr'və-tôr"ē) *n.* **1,** a building equipped with instruments for studying natural phenomena. **2,** a high tower for affording an extensive view.

ob·serve' (əb-zērv') *v.t.* **1,** take note of; watch. **2,** remark; comment. **3,** comply with; obey. **4,** celebrate with due ceremony. —**ob·serv'er,** *n.* a spectator.

ob·sess' (əb-ses') *v.t.* dominate the mind.

ob·ses'sion (-sesh'ən) *n.* **1,** excessive preoccupation with an idea or delusion. **2,** the idea or delusion.

ob·sid'i·an (ob-sid'ē-ən) *n.* a dark volcanic rock resembling glass.

ob"so·les'cent (ob"sə-les'ənt) *adj.* becoming obsolete. —**ob"so·les'cence,** *n.*

ob'so·lete" (ob'sə-lēt") *adj.* gone out of use; out of date. —**ob'so·lete"ness,** *n.*

ob'sta·cle (ob'stə-kəl) *n.* an obstruction; hindrance.

ob·stet'rics (əb-stet'riks) *n.* the medical science of care during pregnancy and childbirth. —**ob·stet'ric, ob·stet'ri·cal,** *adj.* —**ob"ste·tri'cian** (ob"stə-trish'ən) *n.*

ob'sti·nate (ob'sti-nət) *adj.* stubbornly persistent. —**ob'sti·na·cy,** *n.*

ob·strep'er·ous (əb-strep'ər-əs) *adj.* noisy; unruly. —**ob·strep'er·ous·ness,** *n.*

ob·struct' (əb-strukt') *v.t.* **1,** block so as to prevent passing; interfere with. **2,** retard; delay. **3,** shut out from sight, as a view.

ob·struc'tion (-struk'shən) *n.* **1,** a barrier or hindrance. **2,** systematic and persistent efforts to delay legislation. —**ob·struc'tion·ist,** *n.* one who willfully impedes progress, esp. in a legislative body. —**ob-struc'tive**, adj.

ob·tain' (əb-tān') v.t. get possession of, esp. by some effort; acquire. —v.i. be established or in vogue.

ob·trude' (əb-trood') v.t. **1,** thrust forward unasked. **2,** push out; form by forcing through an opening of proper shape. —v.i. intrude. —**ob·tru'sion**, (-zhən) n. —**ob-tru'sive** (-siv) adj. given to intruding; showy, distracting, etc.

ob·tund' v.t. reduce the force or intensity of; dull; blunt; deaden.

ob·tuse' (əb-toos') adj. **1,** not sensitive; stupid. **2,** blunt in form. **3,** of angles, larger than a right angle. —**ob·tuse'ness**, n.

ob·verse' (ob-vêrs') adj. **1,** facing the observer; on the top or front side. **2,** (Bot.) narrower at the base than at the top. —n. (ob'vêrs) **1,** the side of a coin bearing the head or main design. **2,** a counterpart. —**ob·vert'** (əb-vêrt') v.t.

ob'vi·ate' (ob'vē-āt') v.t. meet and clear away, as difficulties; make unnecessary. —**ob''vi·a'tion** (-ā'shən) n.

ob'vi·ous (ob'vē-əs) adj. plainly seen or understood; evident. —**ob'vi·ous·ness**, n.

oc''a·ri'na (ok''ə-rē'nə) n. an egg-shaped musical wind instrument.

oc·ca'sion (ə-kā'zhən) n. **1,** a special event, ceremony, etc. **2,** reason; motive; need. **3,** opportunity; a favorable moment. **4,** a cause; that which brings about an unexpected result. **5,** a particular time; the time of a special happening.

oc·ca'sion·al (-əl) adj. **1,** occurring now and then. **2,** incidental.

oc'ci·dent (ok'si-dənt) n. the west; esp., Europe and the Western Hemisphere. —**oc''ci·den'tal**, adj.

oc'ci·put'' (ok'si-put'') n. the back part of the skull. —**oc·cip'i·tal** (ok-sip'ə-təl) adj.

oc·clude' (ə-klood') v.t. **1,** shut in or out; also, close, as pores. **2,** absorb. —**oc·clu'sion** (-zhən) n.

oc·cult' (o-kult') adj. **1,** beyond ordinary understanding. **2,** secret; known only to the initiated. **3,** dealing with the supernatural or magical: the occult sciences. —n. something occult or supernatural. —**oc·cult'ism**, n. —**oc·cult'ist**, adj.

oc''cul·ta'tion (ok''ul-tā'shən) n. the disappearance from view, esp. of a star or planet.

oc'cu·pan·cy (ok'yə-pən-sē) n. act of occupying; state of being an occupant.

oc'cu·pant (ok'yə-pənt) n. one who resides in a place; a tenant.

oc''cu·pa'tion (ok''yə-pā'shən) n. **1,** possession; occupancy. **2,** the stationing of a controlling forces in enemy territory. **3,** means of filling one's time; regular employment; a job. —**oc''cu·pa'tion·al**, adj. pert. to an occupation, esp. a trade. —**occupational therapy**, the treatment of mental and physical disorders by suitable work.

oc'cu·py'' (ok'yə-pī'') v.t. **1,** become established in, as a building, enemy territory, etc. **2,** hold, as an office. **3,** take up or fill, as space, time, attention, etc. **4,** engage the attention of; employ.

oc·cur' (ə-kêr') v.i. [oc·curred', -cur'ring] **1,** take place; happen. **2,** come to mind. **3,** be found; exist. —**oc·cur'rence**, n. a happening. —**oc·cur'rent**, adj.

o'cean (ō'shən) n. **1,** the body of salt water covering three-fourths of the earth's surface; any of the five great divisions of this body. **2,** a vast amount. —**o''ce·an'ic** (-shē-an'ik) adj.

o'cean·aut'' (-nât) n. aquanaut.

o''ce·an'ics (o''shē-an'iks) n.sing. the study of the ocean.

o''cean·og'ra·phy (ō''shən-äg'rə-fē) n. a branch of geography dealing with the ocean and its phenomena.

o·cel'lus (ō-sel'əs) n. **1,** an eyelike spot of color, as in a peacock's tail. **2,** one of the minute single eyes of insects and various other animals. —**o·cel'lar** (-ər), adj. —**o·cel'late** (-ət) adj.

o'ce·lot'' (ō'sə-lot'') n. an Amer. leopardlike cat.

o'cher (ō'kər) n. an earth containing iron, used as a yellow or orange pigment. Also, **o'chre**.

o'clock' (ə-klok') adv. on the clock; hours, etc., since noon or midnight.

oct- (okt) pref. eight.

oc'ta·gon'' (ok'tə-gon'') n. a polygon with eight sides and eight angles. —**oc·tag'o·nal** (ok-tag'ə-nəl) adj.

oc'tane (ok'tān) n. **1,** an isomeric hydrocarbon found in petroleum. **2,** the measure of the power-producing quality of gasoline. —**octane number** or **rating**, a number representing the antiknock property of gasoline.

oc'tant (ok'tant) n. **1,** the eighth part of a circle, 45°. **2,** a navigational instrument resembling a sextant.

oc'tave (ok'tiv) n. (Music) **1,** a note eight diatonic degrees above or below another note. **2,** an interval of eight degrees. **3,** the whole series of notes within this interval. **4,** (Poetry) a group of eight lines.

oc·ta'vo (ok-tā'vō) adj. of a book, having pages about 6 x 9 inches, or somewhat less; written 8vo.

oc·tet' (ok-tet') *n.* a group of, or a composition for, eight voices or instruments.

Oc·to'ber (ok-tō'bər) *n.* the tenth month of the year.

oc"to·ge·nar'i·an (ok"tə-jə-nār'é-ən) *n.* a person at least 80 but less than 90 years of age.

oc'to·pus (ok'tə-pəs) *n.* a sea mollusk having eight arms with sucking disks.

oc"to·roon' (ok"tə-roon') *n.* a person having one-eighth Negro blood.

oc'u·lar (ok'yə-lər) *adj.* **1,** pert. to the eye. **2,** perceived by the eye; visual. —*n.* the eyepiece of an optical instrument.

oc'u·list (ok'yə-list) *n.* a doctor who examines and treats the eye; ophthalmologist.

OD (ō'dē') *v.i.* (*Slang*) take an overdose of a drug, often with fatal results.

o'da·lisque (ō'də-lisk) *n.* a female slave in a harem. Also, **o'da·lisk.**

odd (od) *adj.* **1,** eccentric; queer; strange. **2,** casual; occasional; differing from the ordinary. **3,** not paired; lacking a mate. **4,** extra; left over after an even division; not exactly divisible by two. **5,** a small surplus; a little more. —*adv.* more or less. —**odd'-ness,** *n.*

odd'ball" *n.* an eccentric person.

odd'i·ty (-ə-tē) *n.* a strange person or thing.

odd'ment (od'mənt) *n.* an odd article; a remnant.

odds (odz) *n.pl.* **1,** excess in favor of one as compared with another; advantage; superiority. **2,** balance of probability. **3,** in sports, a handicap. **4,** variance; disagreement. —**odds-'on',** *adj.* likely to win. —**at odds,** in disagreement. —**odds and ends,** miscellaneous articles.

ode (ōd) *n.* a lyric poem of exalted and dignified style. —**od'ic,** *adj.*

o'di·ous (ō'dē-əs) *adj.* deserving of hate; repugnant. —**o'di·ous·ness,** *n.*

o'di·um (ō'dē-əm) *n.* **1,** hatred. **2,** disgrace. **3,** censure; reproach.

o·dom'e·ter (ō-dom'ə-tər) *n.* an instrument for measuring the distance traveled by a wheeled vehicle.

o"don·tol'o·gy (ō"don-tol'ə-jē) *n.* the science relating to the teeth.

o'dor (ō'dər) *n.* **1,** effect on the sense of smell, pleasant or unpleasant. **2,** fame. Also, **o'dour.** —**in bad odor,** in ill repute.

o"dor·if'er·ous (ō"də-rif'ər-əs) *adj.* giving forth an odor. —**o·dor·if'er·ous·ness,** *n.*

o'dor·ous (ō'dər-əs) *adj.* having an odor, esp. a fragrant one.

od'ys·sey (äd'ə-sē) *n.* a long wandering; an intellectual or spiritual quest.

Oed'i·pus complex (ed'ə-pəs) uncon-

scious attachment of a son to his mother. —**oed'i·pal** (-pəl) *adj.*

o'er (ôr) *adv. & prep.* (*Poetic*) over.

oer'sted (ēr'sted) *n.* a unit of magnetic intensity.

of (uv) *prep.* **1,** indicating separation, derivation, source, or origin: from. **2,** concerning; about. **3,** indicating composition or substance. **4,** indicating possession: belonging to. **5,** containing.

off (âf) *adv.* **1,** away; at, or to, a distance. **2,** not on, touching, or attached. **3,** so as to stop or end entirely. **4,** away from work. —*prep.* **1,** away from. **2,** deviating from standard. **3,** to seaward of. **4,** less than. **5,** temporarily relieved of. **6,** (*Slang*) refraining from. —*adj.* **1,** on the right side of a vehicle or animal (opposed to *near*) **2,** disengaged, as an *off* day. **3,** below normal. **4,** disconnected; discontinued. **5,** provided for. **6,** (*Colloq.*) in error. —**off and on,** intermittently. —**take off,** leave.

of'fal (âf'əl) *n.* refuse; garbage.

off'beat" *n.* (*Music*) an unaccented part of a measure. —*adj.* **1,** stressing the offbeat. **2,** unusual; eccentric.

off-"Broad'way (-brâd'wā) *adj.* pert. to professional theater in New York not in the traditional commercial theaters or district. —**off-"off-"Broad'way,** *adj.* pert. to the more experimental or avant-garde New York theater.

off-'chance" *n. & adj.* a remote possibility.

off-col'or *adj.* **1,** of poor color; inferior, as a gem. **2,** (*Colloq.*) improper.

of·fend' (ə-fend') *v.t.* cause resentment in; displease. —*v.i.* **1,** sin. **2,** cause indignation, dislike, or resentment.

of·fend'er *n.* **1,** one who offends; a culprit. **2,** an aggressor.

of·fense' (ə-fense') *n.* **1,** an attack; assault. **2,** a cause of displeasure; an affront. **3,** anger; annoyance. **4,** a sin. **5,** [also, **of'fense**] the attacking side. Also, **of·fence'.**

of·fen'sive (ə-fen'siv) *adj.* **1,** offending. **2,** attacking. —*n.* **1,** the state of being the attacker. **2,** an aggressive campaign; an attack. —**of·fen'sive·ness,** *n.*

of'fer (of'ər) *v.t. & i.* **1,** present or put forward for acceptance. **2,** put forward, as a suggestion; propose; suggest. **3,** volunteer (to do something). **4,** present as an act of devotion to God. **5,** present for sale. **6,** tender as a bid. —*n.* the act of offering; condition of being offered; a proposal; a bid. —**of'fer·ing,** *n.* something offered; a gift, esp. in an offertory.

of'fer·to"ry (of'ər-tôr'ē) *n.* the offering and collection of gifts at a religious service; the rites at that time.

off'hand" *adj. & adv.* **1,** impromptu. **2,** free and easy. —**off'hand"ed,** *adj.* casual.

of'fice (ôf'is) *n.* **1,** a position of trust, esp. in public service. **2,** the duties of such a position. **3,** official employment. **4,** a service or task. **5,** a prescribed form of worship. **6,** a room for transacting business. **7,** the quarters and staff of a governmental department. —**office boy, 1,** a young employee who does errands and menial tasks. **2,** a person treated like an office boy.

of'fi·cer (ôf'ə-sər) *n.* **1,** a holder of public or civil office. **2,** a person of (usually, commissioned) rank in the army, navy, etc. **3,** a policeman. **4,** an executive in a society, corporation, etc.

of·fi'cial (ə-fish'əl) *n.* a person holding office. —*adj.* **1,** pert. to an office or to the discharge of the duties of an office. **2,** properly authorized. **3,** formal. —**offi'cial·dom** (-dəm) *n.* the official class. —**offi'cial·ism,** *n.* red tape.

of·fi'ci·ate (-shē-āt") *v.i.* **1,** act in an official capacity, esp. on some special occasion. **2,** conduct a religious service. —**offi'ci·ant,** *n.* —**offi"ci·a'tion,** *n.*

of·fi'cious (ə-fish'əs) *adj.* acting unduly important; meddling; obtrusive. —**offi'cious·ness,** *n.*

off'ing *n.* a place or result to be reached in the future but at present remote. —**in the offing,** in the near future.

off'ish *adj.* (*Colloq.*) reserved or distant in manner. —**off'ish·ness,** *n.*

off-'key" *adj.* **1,** out of tune. **2,** unusual; abnormal.

off-'load" *v.t.* unload (from a truck, etc.).

off'print" *n.* a separate reprint of a magazine, etc., article. —*v.t.* make an offprint of.

off-'sea"son *adj. & n.* (pert. to) a less busy period of the year for a business, sport, etc.

off'set" *v.t.* [-set", -set"ting] **1,** place (one thing) over another; balance. **2,** (of printing) blot. —*n.* **1,** something that balances or compensates. **2,** the start. **3,** a type of lithography.

off'shoot" *n.* **1,** a branch from a main stem. **2,** a lateral branch, as of a family.

off'shore" *adv. & adj.* **1,** a short distance out to sea. **2,** away from the shore.

off'side" *adj.* (*Sports*) away from the proper side; ahead of the ball or puck.

off'spring" (âf'spring") *n.* a child or children; a descendant.

off-"the-rec'ord *adj.* unofficial; informal.

off'track" *adj.* handled away from the track, as of parimutuel betting.

off-'white" *adj.* of a grayish white.

oft (âft) *adv.* (*Poetic*) often.

of'ten (âf'ən) *adv.* many times; in many cases. Also, **oft, of'ten·times".**

o·gee' (ō-jē') *n.* an S-shaped curve.

o'give (ō'jiv) *n.* **1,** a pointed arch. **2,** a diagonal rib in a Gothic vault. —**o·giv'al** (ō-jī'vəl) *adj.*

o'gle (ō'gəl) *v.i. & t.* stare (at) covetously; leer.

OG'PU (og'poo) *n.* formerly, the security police of the U.S.S.R.

o'gre (ō'gər) *n.* **1,** in fairy tales, a man-eating giant. **2,** a terrifying person.

oh (ō) *interj.* expressing surprise, pain, etc.

ohm (ōm) *n.* the unit of electrical resistance. —**ohm'age,** *n.* —**ohm'ic,** *adj.* —**ohm'me"ter,** *n.* a device to measure resistance.

-oid *suf.* like; resembling.

oil *n.* **1,** any of various vegetable, animal, or mineral substances that tend to reduce the friction of surfaces rubbing against each other, are inflammable and are used for heat, lubrication, medicines, perfumes, etc. **2,** in art, a paint made of oil mixed with pigment; a picture painted in oils. —*v.t.* **1,** lubricate or treat with oil. **2,** (*Colloq.*) placate; flatter. —**oil'er,** *n.* a tankship for transporting oil. —**oil color,** a pigment ground in oil. —**strike oil,** (*Colloq.*) make a profitable discovery.

oil'cloth" *n.* cloth coated with a glossy, water-resistant substance.

oil'pa"per *n.* paper waterproofed by being steeped in oil.

oil'skin" *n.* **1,** a cloth made waterproof with oil. **2,** (*pl.*) garments made of this cloth.

oil'stone" *n.* a fine-grained variety of quartz, used for whetstones.

oil'y (oi'lē) *adj.* **1,** like oil. **2,** smooth in manner; unctuous; fawning. —**oil'i·ness,** *n.*

oink *n.* the cry of a pig. —*v.i.* make this sound.

oint'ment (oint'mənt) *n.* a salve for healing or beautifying the skin.

O.K. (ō-kā') (*Colloq.*) *adj. & adv.* satisfactory; all right. —*v.t.* approve. Also, **o·kay'.**

o·ka'pi (ō-kä'pē) *n.* an Afr. mammal related to the giraffe.

o'kie (ō'kē) *n.* (*Opprobious*) a migrant worker.

o'kra (ō'krə) *n.* a vegetable grown for its green mucilaginous pods.

-ol·a·try (ol-ə-trē) *suf.* worship of.

old (ōld) *adj.* **1,** advanced in years; having existed or lived long, or for most of its life span. **2,** of a (specified) age. **3,** of long standing. **4,** experienced. **5,** not new, fresh, or recent. **6,** not modern; antique. **7,** belonging to an earlier time, stage, etc. —**old′ness,** n. —**Old Glory,** the flag of the U.S.; the Stars and Stripes. —**old guard,** a conservative faction. —**old hand,** a person of much experience or skill. —**old hat,** old-fashioned; out of date. —**old lady,** (*Colloq.*) **1,** one's mother or wife. **2,** one in command. —**old maid, 1,** an elderly woman who has never married. **2,** (*Colloq.*) a prim, fastidious person. **3,** a children's card game. —**old man,** (*Colloq.*) **1,** one's father or husband. **2,** one in command. —**Old Testament,** all the books of the Holy Bible written before the Christian era. —**Old World,** Europe and Asia.

old′en (ōl′dən) *adj.* ancient.

old-fash′ioned *adj.* **1,** holding to old ideas or customs. **2,** out of style. —*n.* a cocktail of sweetened whiskey, soda, bitters, and fruit.

old′ie (ōld′ē) *n.* (*Colloq.*) something old.

old-′school *adj.* having customs, education, etc., of a bygone age.

old′ster (-stər) *n.* an elderly person.

old-′style *adj.* according to the Julian calendar, several days earlier than the modern calendar.

old-′time″ *adj.* of, or characteristic of, old times. —**old-′tim′er,** n. (*Colloq.*) one who has grown old in a place, profession, etc.

o·le′ (ō-lā′) *interj.* of approval or encouragement.

o″le·ag′i·nous (ō″lē-aj′ə-nəs) *adj.* oily; unctuous. —**o″le·ag′i·nous·ness,** n.

o″le·an′der (ō″lē-an′dər) *n.* a poisonous evergreen shrub with showy red or white blossoms.

o′le·in (ō′lē-in) *n.* an oily substance found in most animal and vegetable fats and oils.

o″le·o·mar′ga·rine (ō″lē-ō-mär′jə-rin) *n.* an animal and vegetable fat used like butter; margarine. Also, **o′le·o″.**

ol·fac′to·ry (ol-fak′tə-rē) *adj.* pert. to the sense of smell.

ol′i·gar″chy (ol′ə-gär″kē) *n.* government in which power is in the hands of a few. —**ol″i·gar′chic,** adj.

o′li·o″ (ō′lē-ō″) *n.* **1,** a stew. **2,** a medley; miscellany.

ol′ive (ol′iv) *n.* **1,** an evergreen tree of warm climates grown for its fruit, wood, or oil; its small, oval fruit, ripe or green. **2,** a yellowish-green color. —**olive branch,** a symbol of peace. —**olive drab, 1,** a dull greenish brown. **2,** a woolen cloth of this color, used for military uniforms. —**olive oil,** oil pressed from olives, used in food and medicines.

ol′la (ol′ə) *n.* a wide-mouthed jar.

O·lym′pi·ad (o-lim′pē-ad) *n.* **1,** in ancient Greece, the four-year period between Olympic games. **2,** a modern tournament of Olympic games.

O·lym′pic games (ō-lim′pik) **1,** athletic contests in ancient Greece. **2,** international athletic contests, held every four years in a different country.

om *n.* a word used as a mantra.

o′mah″ (ō′mä″) *n.* the sasquatch.

om′buds·man (äm′buds-mən) *n.* a government official who investigates complaints from the public.

o·me′ga (ō-mē′gə) *n.* the twenty-fourth and last letter of the Greek alphabet (Ω, ω).

om′e·let (om′lit) *n.* beaten eggs cooked as a pancake. Also, **om′e·lette.**

o′men (ō′mən) *n.* a sign or event prophetic of the future; an augury.

om′i·cron (om′i-kron″) *n.* the fifteenth letter of the Greek alphabet (O, o).

om′i·nous (om′i-nəs) *adj.* foretelling disaster; threatening. —**om′i·nous·ness,** n.

o·mis′sion (ō-mish′ən) *n.* **1,** neglect or failure to do something. **2,** the act of leaving out; the thing left out.

o·mit′ (ō-mit′) *v.t.* [**o·mit′ted, -ting**] **1,** leave out. **2,** leave undone; neglect.

om·ni- (om-nə) *pref.* all.

om′ni·bus″ (om′nə-bus″) *n.* **1,** a large passenger motor vehicle. **2,** a volume of related literary works. —*adj.* comprising or providing for many objects or items.

om″ni·far′i·ous (-fār′ē-əs) *adj.* of all varieties, forms, or kinds.

om·nif′er·ous (om-nif′ə-rəs) *adj.* producing all kinds.

om·nip′o·tent (om-nip′ə-tənt) *adj.* having infinite power. —**om·nip′o·tence,** n.

om″ni·pres′ent *adj.* present everywhere at the same time. —**om″ni·pres′ence,** n.

om·nis′cient (om-nish′ənt) *adj.* all-knowing. —**om·nis′cience,** n.

om″ni·um-ga′ther·um (om″nē-əm-ga′-thə-rəm) *n.* a hodge-podge.

om·niv′o·rous (om-niv′ə-rəs) *adj.* eating both animal and vegetable foods; devouring everything. —**om·niv′o·rous·ness,** n.

on *prep.* **1,** above and in contact with. **2,** dependent on; supported by. **3,** near or adjacent to. **4,** in regard to. **5,** at the time of. **6,** (*Colloq.*) at the expense of. —*adv.* **1,** in or into place or position. **2,** in progress. **3,** into action or use. **4,** forward. —**on to,** (*Slang*) aware of.

on′a·ger (on′ə-jər) *n.* **1,** a wild ass of

Central Asia. **2,** a medieval war-engine for throwing large boulders.

o'nan·ism (ō'nə-niz-əm) *n.* **1,** uncompleted sexual intercourse. **2,** masturbation. —**o'nan·ist,** *n.* —**o'nan·is'tic,** *adj.*

once (wuns) *adv.* **1,** at one time; formerly. **2,** one time only. **3,** even for one time; ever. —*conj.* whenever; as soon as. —*n.* one time. —**at once, 1,** simultaneously. **2,** immediately.

once-'o"ver *n.* (*Slang*) a single, comprehensive inspection.

one (wun) *n.* **1,** the lowest whole number, expressed by 1 (ordinal, *first*). **2,** a single person or thing; a unit. —*adj.* **1,** a single. **2,** any. **3,** some. **4,** the same. **5,** united. —*pron.* someone; anyone. —**all one,** all the same. —**one by one,** singly. —**one-night stand,** a theatrical performance scheduled for one night only.

one-'horse" *adj.* (*Colloq.*) small and unimportant.

one'ness (-nəs) *n.* **1,** unity. **2,** uniformity. **3,** constancy in feeling or purpose.

one-'li'ner (-lī'nər) *n.* (*Colloq.*) a short joke.

on'er·ous (on'ər-əs) *adj.* burdensome. —**on'er·ous·ness,** *n.*

one·self' *pron.* reflexive form of *one.* —**be oneself,** behave as usual.

one'sid"ed *adj.* **1,** unequal. **2,** unfair; partial. —**one'sid"ed·ness,** *n.*

one-'time" *adj.* former.

one-'to-one' *adj.* involving interaction between two persons.

one-'track" *adj.* **1,** having one track. **2,** (*Colloq.*) narrow; restricted.

one-'way" *adj.* permitting traffic in one direction only.

on'ion (un'yən) *n.* a plant with a pungent edible bulb.

on'ion·skin" (un'yən-skin") *n.* a very thin translucent paper.

on'look"er (-ər) *n.* spectator.

on'ly (ōn'lē) *adj.* **1,** single; sole. **2,** best. —*adv.* **1,** alone; solely. **2,** merely; no more than. —*conj.* but; excepting that.

on"o·mat"o·poe'ia (on"ə-mat"ə-pē'ə) *n.* imitation of natural sounds in word formation or rhetoric. —**on"o·mat"o·po·et'ic** (-pō-et'ik) *adj.*

on'rush" *n.* a rush forward.

on'set" *n.* **1,** an attack. **2,** a beginning; start.

on'side" *adj. & adv.* (*Sports*) at or toward the proper position.

on'slaught" (on'slât") *n.* a violent attack.

on'to (on'too) *prep.* to a place on; upon.

on·to- (on-tə) *pref.* existence; being.

on·tog'e·ny (on-toj'ə-nè) *n.* the entire development and history of an individual organism. —**on"to·ge·net'ic,** *adj.*

on·tol'o·gy (on-tol'ə-jē) *n.* the branch of metaphysics dealing with the nature of being. —**on"to·log'i·cal,** *adj.* —**on·tol'o·gist,** *n.*

o'nus (ō'nəs) *n.* a burden; a charge.

on'ward (on'wərd) *adv. & adj.* toward the front; forward. —**on'wards,** *adv.*

on'yx (on'iks) *n.* a quartz with parallel colored bands.

o·o- (ō-ə) *pref.* egg.

oo'dles (oo'dəlz) *n.pl.* (*Colloq.*) a large quantity.

oo'long (oo'lâng) *n.* a variety of tea.

oomph (oomf) *n.* (*Slang*) **1,** sex appeal. **2,** energy; pep.

ooze (ooz) *n.* soft mud or slime, esp. on the bed of the ocean. —*v.i.* seep or leak slowly. —**oo'zy,** *adj.*

o·pac'i·ty (ō-pas'ə-tē) *n.* state of being opaque.

o'pah (ō'pä) *n.* a brilliantly colored oceanic food fish.

o'pal (ō'pəl) *n.* an iridescent mineral valued as a gem. —**o'pal·ine** (-in) *adj.*

o·pal·esce' (ō-pə-les') *v.i.* give forth a play of colors like an opal. —**o"pal·es'cence,** *n.* —**o"pal·es'cent,** *adj.*

o·paque' (ō-pāk') *adj.* **1,** not letting light through. **2,** dull. **3,** obscure. **4,** stupid. —**o·paque'ness,** *n.*

o'pen (ō'pən) *adj.* **1,** permitting passage through; not shut or closed. **2,** without a cover; not protected. **3,** unfilled, as a position; unengaged, as time. **4,** free to use; public. **5,** unrestrained; unrestricted. **6,** undecided. **7,** without concealment; frank. **8,** spread out; unfolded. **9,** exposed. **10,** immune from attack. —*v.t.* **1,** unfasten; raise the covering of; move aside. **2,** remove obstructions from. **3,** unfold; spread out. **4,** reveal; disclose. **5,** make accessible, esp. for trade, settlement, etc. **6,** start; initiate. **7,** make an opening in. —*v.i.* **1,** afford a view, entrance, or egress, etc. **2,** unfold; come apart; become open. **3,** become more visible. **4,** commence. —*n.* **1,** the outdoors. **2,** public view. —**o'pen·er,** *n.* —**o'pen'ness,** *n.* —**open door,** in diplomacy; free and equal trade opportunities for all. —**open shop,** a shop open to non-union labor.

o"pen-air' *adj.* happening out of doors.

o'pen-and-shut' *adj.* perfectly obvious.

o"pen-end' *adj.* having no predetermined duration or amount. Also, **o"pen-end'ed.**

o'pen-hand"ed *adj.* generous.

o'pen-hearth" *adj.* pert. to a process of making steel.

o'pen·ing *n.* **1,** a beginning. **2,** an open

space; a gap, breach, clearing, etc. **3**, a business opportunity; vacancy. **4**, a formal beginning, as of a sale, a theatrical production, etc.

o′pen-mind″ed *adj.* unprejudiced. —**o′- pen·mind″ed·ness**, *n.*

o′pen-mouthed″ (-mow*th*d″) *adj.* gaping with astonishment.

o′pen-work″ *n.* ornamental work, such as lace, embroidery, etc., made with openings in the material.

op′er·a (op′ər-ə) *n.* **1**, a drama wholly sung. **2**, *pl.* of *opus.* —**op′er·at′ic**, *adj.* —**op′er·at′i·cal·ly**, *adv.* —**opera glass**, a small binocular. Also, **opera glasses.**

op′er·a·ble (op′ər-ə-bəl) *adj.* permitting surgical treatment.

op′er·ate″ (op′ə-rāt″) *v.i.* **1**, perform or be at work; act. **2**, be effective. **3**, perform a surgical operation. **4**, deal heavily in securities, etc. —*v.t.* direct the working of. —**op′er·ant** (-ənt) *adj. & n.*

op″er·a′tion (op″ər-ā′shən) *n.* **1**, act or method of working; action; agency. **2**, (*Mil.*) a strategic project, movement, or campaign. **3**, surgical treatment. **4**, a business transaction. —**op″er·a′tion·al**, *adj.*

op′er·a·tive (op′ə-rə-tiv) *adj.* **1**, acting; effective. **2**, practical. **3**, pert. to surgical operations. —*n.* **1**, a workman. **2**, a private detective.

op′er·a″tor (-tər) *n.* **1**, one who runs something. **2**, one who makes connections in a telephone exchange. **3**, a speculator. **4**, (*Math.*) a letter or other character signifying an operation to be performed.

op″er·et′ta (op″ə-ret′ə) *n.* a drama set to gay music.

oph′i·cleide″ (of′ə-klīd″) *n.* an early form of the tuba.

o·phid′i·an (ō-fid′ē-ən) *adj.* pert. to snakes.

oph·thal′mic (of-thal′mik) *adj.* pert. to the eye.

oph″thal·mol′o·gy (of″thəl-mol′ə-jē) *n.* the study of the eye and its diseases. —**oph″thal·mol′o·gist**, *n.*

oph·thal′mo·scope″ (of-thal′mə-skōp″) *n.* an instrument for examining the interior of the eye, esp. the retina. —**oph·thal″mo·scop′ic**, *adj.*

o′pi·ate (ō′pē-ət) *n. & adj.* **1**, a narcotic drug, esp. one containing opium. **2**, anything that dulls sensation.

o·pine′ (ō-pīn′) *v.i. & t.* give an opinion; think.

o·pin′ion (ə-pin′yən) *n.* **1**, a conclusion; view. **2**, a view held by many at once: public opinion. **3**, estimation; judgment.

o·pin′ion·at″ed (ə-pin′yə-nā″tid) *adj.* obstinate in one's opinion.

o′pi·um (ō′pē-əm) *n.* a narcotic drug derived from the poppy.

o·pos′sum (ō-pos′əm) *n.* a marsupial of the So. U.S.

op·po′nent (ə-pō′nənt) *n.* an antagonist; adversary.

op″por·tune′ (op″ər-tūn″) *adj.* timely; appropriate. —**op″por·tune′ness**, *n.*

op″por·tun′ism (op″ər-tū″niz-əm) *n.* quickness to grasp opportunities, often unscrupulously. —**op″por·tun′ist**, *n.*

op·por·tu′ni·ty (op″ər-tū″nə-tē) *n.* a favorable occasion or time.

op·pose′ (ə-pōz′) *v.t.* **1**, set against or opposite to (something else). **2**, be hostile to; object to; resist. **3**, contrast; offset. —**op·pos′a·ble**, *adj.*

op′po·site (op′ə-zit) *adj.* **1**, situated on the other side; facing. **2**, going the other way. **3**, radically different. —*n.* something opposite. —**opposite number**, a person having the same rank or duties as one, but in a different country, company, etc.

op″po·si′tion (op″ə-zish′ən) *n.* **1**, act of opposing; state of being opposite. **2**, resistance; antagonism. **3**, the political party opposed to the party in power.

op·press′ (ə-pres′) *v.t.* **1**, lie heavily on (the mind); weigh down. **2**, treat tyrannically. —**op·pres′sion** (-presh′ən) *n.* —**op·pres′sive** (-pres′iv) *adj.* —**op·pres′sor**, *n.* a tyrant.

op·pro′bri·ous (ə-prō′brē-əs) *adj.* abusive; insulting; vile. —**op·pro′bri·um**, *n.* infamy; reproach.

op·pugn′ (ə-pūn′) *v.t.* oppose, as by argument; attack or resist. —**op·pug′nant** (ə-pug′nənt) *adj.* —**op·pug′nan·cy** (-nən-sē) *n.*

opt *v.i.* make a choice.

op′tic (op′tik) *adj.* pert. to vision or to the eye. —*n.* (*Slang*) the eye. —**op′ti·cal**, *adj.* —**optical art**, a movement, esp. in painting and sculpture, specializing in geometric construction, optical illusion, and mechanical devices. Also, **op art.**

op·ti′cian (op-tish′ən) *n.* one who makes and sells eyeglasses, etc.

op′tics *n.* the science that deals with vision and light.

op′ti·mism (op′tə-miz-əm) *n.* **1**, the belief that good will prevail. **2**, cheerful hopefulness. —**op′ti·mist**, *n.* —**op″ti·mis′·tic**, *adj.* —**op″ti·mis′ti·cal·ly**, *adv.*

op′ti·mum (op′ti-məm) *n. & adj.* the best; the most favorable. —**op′ti·mal** (-məl) *adj.* —**op′ti·mize** (-mīz) *v.t.* make best use of.

op′tion (op′shən) *n.* **1**, the right or power

of choice. **2,** the thing that is or may be chosen. **3,** a purchased right to buy later. **—op'tion·al,** *adj.*

op·tom'e·try (op-tom'ə-trè) *n.* the measurement of vision and fitting of glasses. **—op·tom'e·trist,** *n.*

op'u·lent (op'yə-lənt) *adj.* wealthy; abundantly supplied. **—op'u·lence,** *n.*

o'pus (ō'pəs) *n.* [*pl.* **op'e·ra**] a work, esp. of music. **—o'pus·cule"** (-kūl") *n.* a minor work; a small book.

or (ôr) *conj.* a connective between words, clauses, terms, etc., indicating an alternative or explanation.

-or (ôr, ər) *suf.* denoting **1,** nouns of agency, as *operator.* **2,** adjectives of comparison, as *major.*

or'a·cle (or'ə-kəl) *n.* **1,** a deity that utters answers to questions; hence, an authoritative voice. **2,** the answers given. **—o·rac'u·lar** (â-rak'yə-lər) *adj.*

o'ral (ôr'əl) *adj.* **1,** spoken; not written. **2,** pert. to the mouth.

or'ange (or'inj) *n.* **1,** the round, juicy, deep yellow citrus fruit of a tropical evergreen tree; the tree. **2,** a reddish-yellow color. **—orange pe'koe** (pē'kō) a black tea from Ceylon or India. **—orange stick,** a rod of orangewood used in manicuring.

or"ange·ade' (-ād') *n.* a drink of orange juice mixed with water and sugar.

Or'ange·man (-mən) *n.* [*pl.* **-men**] an Irish Protestant.

or'ange·wood" *n.* the wood of the orange tree.

o·rang'u·tan' (ō-rang'ū-tan") *n.* an ape of Borneo and Sumatra.

o·rate' (ō-rāt') *v.i.* (*Humorous*) deliver an oration.

o·ra'tion (ō-rā'shən) *n.* a formal and dignified public speech.

or'a·tor (or'ə-tər) *n.* an eloquent public speaker.

or"a·to'ri·o (ôr"ə-tôr'è-ō) *n.* a composition for choral singing, usually on a sacred theme.

or'a·to·ry (or'ə-tôr-è) *n.* **1,** eloquent public speaking. **2,** a place for prayer. **—or"a·tor'i·cal,** *adj.*

orb (ôrb) *n.* **1,** a sphere; globe; esp., a heavenly body. **2,** (*Poetic*) the eye. **—or·bic'u·lar** (ôr-bik'yə-lər) *adj.*

or'bit (ôr'bit) *n.* **1,** a regular circuit or path, esp. of a planet around a star or a satellite around a planet. **2,** the eye socket. **—***v.i. & t.* travel or cause to travel in an orbit (around). **—or'bit·al,** *adj.*

or'chard (ôr'chərd) *n.* a grove of fruit trees.

or'ches·tra (ôr'kis-trə) *n.* **1,** a group of players on various musical instruments. **2,** the main floor of a theater. **—or·ches'tral,** *adj.*

or"ches·tra'tion (ôrk"əs-trā'shən) *n.* **1,** music arranged in separate parts for an orchestra. **2,** the planning of a stratagem. **—or'ches·trate",** *v.t. & i.*

or·ches'tri·on (ôr-kes'trè-ən) *n.* a mechanical musical instrument that imitates the sound of an orchestra.

or'chid (ôr'kid) *n.* **1,** any of a large order of tropical plants with brilliant flowers. **2,** a bluish purple. **—or"chi·da'ceous** (-dā'shəs) *adj.*

or·dain' (ôr-dān') *v.t.* **1,** decree; enact. **2,** appoint. **3,** confer holy orders upon.

or·deal' (ôr-dēl') *n.* a severe test; a trying experience.

or'der (ôr'dər) *n.* **1,** an authoritative direction; a command. **2,** a direction to buy, sell, or furnish something. **3,** a sequence; systematic arrangement. **4,** class; kind; rank. **5,** a classification of plants and animals. **6,** a prescribed mode of procedure. **7,** (*pl.*) religious ordination; clerical rank. **8,** a society of persons, esp. monastic. **9,** an honorary society or institution. **10,** conformity to law or authority. **—***v.t.* **1,** command; bid. **2,** direct; manage. **3,** give an order for. **—***v.i.* give a command. **—in order to,** for the purpose of. **—out of order, 1,** not in accordance with parliamentary rules. **2,** not in working condition.

or'der·ly (ôr'dər-lè) *adj.* **1,** arranged in order; neat; tidy. **2,** well managed. **3,** peaceable. **—***n.* **1,** an officer's aide. **2,** a male hospital attendant. **—or'der·li·ness,** *n.*

or'di·nal (ôr'də-nəl) *adj.* defining a thing's position in a series, as first, second, etc. **—***n.* an ordinal number.

or'di·nance (ôr'də-nəns) *n.* a law or decree; a regulation.

or'di·nar"y (ôr'də-ner"è) *adj.* **1,** usual; customary. **2,** mediocre. **—***n.* **1,** the usual condition, etc. **2,** a regular meal at a fixed price; an inn serving such a meal.

or"di·na'tion (ôr"də-nā'shən) *n.* act or effect of ordaining.

ord'nance (ôrd'nəns) *n.* **1,** heavy artillery. **2,** weapons of all kinds, ammunition, etc.

or'dure (ôr'dyûr) *n.* excrement; dung.

ore (ôr) *n.* a mineral or rock from which metal is extracted.

o·re'ga·no (ō-re'gə-nō) *n.* an aromatic herb.

or'gan (ôr'gən) *n.* **1,** a part of a plant or animal body which does some vital work. **2,** a medium of communication, esp. a sectarian or political newspaper. **3,** a large musical instrument played by releasing compressed air through pipes (*pipe organ*); an instrument providing similar sound electronically (*electronic organ*). **4,** any of various other wind instruments, as a barrel organ, mouth organ, etc. —**or'gan·ist,** *n.* —**organ grinder,** one who operates a hand organ in the streets and solicits money. —**organ loft,** the place where the pipes of an organ are placed.

or'gan·dy (ôr'gən-dè) *n.* a sheer, stiffened muslin.

or·gan'ic (ôr-gan'ik) *adj.* **1,** pert. to an organ of the body. **2,** pert. to or derived from plant and animal matter; containing carbon. **3,** systematized. **4,** structural. —**or·gan'i·cal·ly,** *adv.*

or'gan·ism (ôr'gə-niz-əm) *n.* any living thing; any whole with interdependent parts.

or"gan·i·za'tion (ôr"ga-nə-zā'shən) *n.* **1,** the process of organizing. **2,** that which is organized, as a business, a club, etc.

or'gan·ize (ôr'gə-nīz") *v.t.* **1,** unite the separate elements of into a smoothly working unit. **2,** set going; start. —*v.i.* combine. —**organized labor,** workers belonging to labor unions.

or·gan'za (ôr-gan'zə) *n.* a light, stiff fabric of silk, rayon, etc.

or'gasm (ôr'gaz-əm) *n.* a crisis or consummation in love-making. —**or·gas'tic,** *adj.*

or'gy (ôr'jè) *n.* **1,** a drunken carousal. **2,** excessive indulgence. —**or"gi·as'tic,** *adj.* —**or"gi·as'ti·cal·ly,** *adv.*

or'i·bi (ôr'i-bè) *n.* a small So. Amer. antelope.

o'ri·el (ō'rè-əl) *n.* a large bay window projecting from an upper story.

o'ri·ent (ôr'è-ənt) *n.* **1,** the east. **2,** (*cap.*) the Asiatic countries. —*v.t.* [also, **o'ri·en·tate"**] **1,** place so as to face the east. **2,** adjust with relation to circumstances, facts, etc. —**o"ri·en·ta'tion,** *n.*

o"ri·en'tal (ôr"è-en'təl) *adj.* **1,** eastern. **2,** (often *cap.*) of the Far East. —*n.* a native or inhabitant of the Orient.

or'i·fice (or'ə-fis) *n.* a mouthlike aperture.

o"ri·ga'mi (or"ə-gä'mè) *n.* the Japanese art of paper folding.

or'i·gin (or'ə-jin) *n.* **1,** a source; a beginning. **2,** (often *pl.*) ancestry.

o·rig'i·nal (ə-rij'i-nəl) *adj.* **1,** occurring first. **2,** not copied or imitated. **3,** novel; fresh. **4,** creative; inventive. —*n.* a model, pattern, or first and authentic example. —**o·rig"i·nal'i·ty** (-nal'ə-tè) *n.*

o·rig'i·nate" (ə-rij'i-nāt") *v.t. & i.* begin; initiate. —**o·rig"i·na'tion,** *n.* —**o·rig'i·na"tor,** *n.*

o'ri·ole" (ôr'è-ōl") *n.* an Amer. bird with black and orange plumage.

O·ri'on (ō-rī'ən) *n.* a constellation near the Equator.

or'i·son (or'i-zən) *n.* a prayer.

or'lon (ôr'lon) *n.* a synthetic fabric used for outer clothing.

or'mo·lu" (ôr'mə-loo") *n.* **1,** gold prepared for gilding. **2,** imitation gold.

or'na·ment (ôr'nə-mənt) *n.* **1,** anything that beautifies or adorns. **2,** a person who confers grace or honor to his position, society, etc. —*v.t.* adorn. —**or"na·men'tal** (-men'təl) *adj.* —**or"na·men·ta'tion,** *n.*

or·nate' (ôr-nāt') *adj.* elaborately adorned. —**or·nate'ness,** *n.*

or'ner·y (ôr'nə-rè) *adj.* (*Dial.*) of ugly disposition; hard to manage.

or"ni·thol'o·gy (ôr"ni-thol'ə-jè) *n.* the study of birds. —**or"ni·tho·log'i·cal** (-thə-loj'i-kəl) *adj.* —**or"ni·thol'o·gist,** *n.*

o·ro·tund' (ôr'ə-tund") *adj.* **1,** rich and full (of the voice). **2,** pompous (of rhetoric or delivery).

or'phan (ôr'fən) *n.* a child bereft by death of its parents. —*adj.* **1,** bereft of parents. **2,** unprotected. **3,** of or to orphans. —*v.t.* bereave of parents. —**or'phan·age** (-ij) *n.* a home for orphans. —**or'phan·hood",** *n.*

or'rer·y (ôr'ə-rè) *n.* a machine representing the motions and phases of the planets; a planetarium.

or'ris (or'is) *n.* a kind of iris; its root, used for perfume.

or'thi·con (ôr'thi-kon) *n.* a television camera.

or·tho- (ôr-thə) *pref.* straight; upright; correct.

or"tho·don'tia (ôr"thə-don'shə) *n.* the dental science of straightening the teeth. —**or"tho·don'tist,** *n.*

or"tho·don'tics (ôr"thə-dän'tiks) *n.sing.* a branch of dentistry dealing with irregularities of the teeth and the correction of them, esp. by mechanical means.

or'tho·dox" (ôr'thə-doks") *adj.* **1,** holding sound, generally accepted views, esp. on religion. **2,** approved; conventional. —**Orthodox Church,** a Christian church in eastern Europe. —**or'tho·dox"y** (-è) *n.*

or·thog'o·nal (ôr-thog'ə-nəl) *adj.* of right angles; rectangular.

or·thog'ra·phy (ôr-thog'rə-fè) *n.* correct spelling. —**or'tho·graph'ic,** *adj.*

or"tho·pe'dic (ôr"thə-pē'dik) *adj.* (*Med.*) pert. to or employed in the correction of deformities. —**or"tho·pe'di·cal·ly,** *adv.* —**or"tho·pe'dist,** *n.*

or"tho·pe'dics (-pē'diks) *n.* prevention

or correction of physical deformities, esp. in children.

or'to·lan (ôr'tə-lən) *n.* a Europ. bunting; the bobolink.

-or·y (ôr-ē; ə-rē) *suf.* **1,** pert. to; characterized by; effecting; expressing. **2,** a place for; an instrument for.

o'ryx (ō'riks) *n.* a large straight-horned Afr. antelope.

or'zo (ôr'zō) *n.* rice-shaped pasta.

Os'car (os'kər) *n.* (*Colloq.*) the statuette signifying an Academy Award, given anually for various achievements in motion pictures.

os'cil·late (os'ə-lāt') *v.i.* **1,** move to and fro, as a pendulum. **2,** vacillate; fluctuate. —**os"cil·la'tion,** *n.* —**os'cil·la'tor,** *n.*

os·cil'lo·scope" (ə-sil'ə-skōp") *n.* an instrument for tracing a graphic picture of an electric wave on a fluorescent screen.

os'cu·late" (os'kyə-lāt") *v.t. & i.* kiss. —**os'cu·lant** (-lənt) *adj.* —**os"cu·la'tion,** *n.*

-ose (ōs) *suf.* **1,** full of. **2,** like. **3,** used to name various carbohydrates.

o'sier (ō'zhər) *n.* a willow whose twigs are used for baskets, etc.

-o·sis (ō-sis) *suf.* [*pl.* **-o·ses** (-sēz)] abnormal condition of.

os'mi·um (oz'mē-əm) *n.* a hard, heavy metallic element, no. 76, symbol Os, similar to platinum.

os·mo'sis (oz-mō'sis) *n.* the tendency of liquids to pass through porous partitions and become diffused.

os'prey (os'prē) *n.* a large fish-eating bird.

os'se·ous (os'ē-əs) *adj.* made of or like bone.

os'si·fy" (os'i-fī") *v.t. & i.* change into bone. —**os'si·fi·ca'tion,** *n.*

os'su·ar·y (os'ū-er-ē) *n.* a vessel or place for the bones of the dead.

os·ten'si·ble (os-ten'sə-bəl) *adj.* appearing outwardly; professed.

os"ten·ta'tion (os"ten-tā'shən) *n.* a pretentious display. —**os"ten·ta'tious,** *adj.*

os·te·o- (os-tē-ō) *pref.* bone.

os"te·ol'o·gy (os"tē-ol'ə-jē) *n.* the science dealing with the bones.

os"te·op'a·thy (os"tē-op'ə-thē) *n.* a system of medicine which holds that disease is chiefly due to derangement of the bones. —**os"te·o·path'** (os"tē-ə-path") *n.*

os"ti·na'to (os"ti-nä'tō) *n.* (*Ital.*) a short melodic phrase repeated over and over at the same pitch.

os'tra·cize" (os'trə-sīz") *v.t.* banish from society, etc. —**os'tra·cism,** *n.*

os'trich *n.* a very large flightless bird of Africa, valued for its plumes.

o·tal'gi·a (ō-tal'jē-ə) *n.* earache.

oth'er (u*th*'ər) *adj.* **1,** different from the one just mentioned. **2,** the remaining one or ones. **3,** additional. **4,** different; not the same. —*adv.* otherwise. —*pron.* **1,** the second of two. **2,** a different person or thing.

oth'er·wise" *adv.* in a different way. —*conj.* else.

oth"er·world'ly *adj.* concerned with the world of supposed existence after death. —**oth"er·world'li·ness,** *n.*

o'tic (ō'tik) *adj.* of the ear.

o'ti·ose" (ō'shē-ōs") *adj.* **1,** inactive; idle. **2,** careless; ineffective; futile. —**o"ti·os'i·ty** (-os'ə-tē) *n.*

o·ti'tis (ō-tī'tis) *n.* inflammation of the ear.

o·tol'o·gy (ō-tol'ə-je) *n.* the science of the ear and its diseases. —**o·tol'o·gist,** *n.*

ot'ter (ot'ər) *n.* an aquatic animal; its dark-brown fur.

ot'to·man (ot'ə-mən) *n.* **1,** a cushioned footstool or bench. **2,** a corded fabric. **3,** (*cap.*) a Turk.

ou"bli·ette' (oo"blē-et') *n.* a dungeon or pit with an opening only at the top.

ouch (owch) *interj.* an exclamation of pain.

ought (ât) *aux. v.* be bound, or obliged, or sure (to): followed by an infinitive.

oui'ja (wē'jə) *n.* a board and pointer supposed mystically to spell out words.

ounce (owns) *n.* **1,** a measure of weight, one-twelfth of a pound troy, one-sixteenth of a pound avoirdupois. **2,** one-sixteenth of a pint: *fluid ounce.* **3,** the snow leopard of Asia.

our (owr) *pron. & adj.* poss. form of *we.* —**ours,** *pron.* form of *our* used predicatively. —**our·selves',** *pron.*

-ous (əs) *suf.* **1,** full of; having; like. **2,** (*Chem.*) in a compound, denoting a lower valence than that denoted by -ic.

oust (owst) *v.t.* drive out. —**oust'er,** *n.* ejection.

out (owt) *adv.* **1,** away from or not in a place, position, state, etc. **2,** into sight or existence; forth. **3,** to exhaustion, extinction, or conclusion. **4,** at variance; in error; minus. **5,** not in vogue. **6,** by reason of. **7,** (*Baseball*) temporarily retired from action. —*n.* (*Colloq.*) **1,** a means of escape or excuse. **2,** (*pl.*) bad terms. **3,** one who is out. —*v.i.* become known.

out- *pref.* beyond; outside; outer: used in many compounds.

out'age (-ij) *n.* a period of suspension of operation or service.

out-'and·out' *adj.* absolute; complete.

out-"bal'ance *v.t.* outweigh.

out·bid' *v.t.* bid more than.

out'board" *adj. & adv.* on or to the outside of a boat; away from the center.

out'bound" *adj.* going away.

out·brave' *v.t.* **1,** surpass in daring or courage. **2,** overcome; defy successfully.

out'break" *n.* **1,** a sudden eruption; an outburst. **2,** a riot or insurrection.

out'build"ing *n.* a small, detached building, subordinate to another.

out'burst" *n.* a sudden pouring forth; an outbreak of emotion.

out'cast" *n.* **1,** a person cast out, as from home. **2,** discarded matter.

out·class' *v.t.* be ahead of; surpass.

out'come" *n.* the result, consequence, or issue.

out'crop" *n.* rock projecting upward through the ground.

out'cry" *n.* a loud cry, as of distress; clamor. —*v.t.* cry louder than.

out·dat'ed *adj.* obsolete; out-of-date; antiquated. —**out·date'**, *v.t.*

out·dis'tance *v.t.* go farther than.

out·do' *v.t.* do better than; surpass; excel.

out'door" *adj.* in open air, not in a building. —**out·doors'**, *adv. & n.*

out'er (ow'tər) *adj.* **1,** exterior. **2,** farther out. —**out'er·most**", *adj.* farthest out. —**outer space**, **1,** space beyond the earth's atmosphere. **2,** interstellar space.

out·face' *v.t.* **1,** face or stare down. **2,** confront boldly; defy.

out'field" *n.* the part of a baseball field outside the diamond; the three players (*outfielders*) stationed there.

out'fit" *n.* **1,** equipment for a special purpose, trade, etc.; fittings. **2,** a special group of persons, as a company, a military unit. —*v.t.* **[-fit'ted, -ting]** equip.

out·flank' *v.t.* go beyond the extent of (an army's) flank.

out·fox' *v.t.* outwit.

out'go" *n.* **1,** expenditure. **2,** outflow.

out'go"ing *adj.* **1,** going out; vacating; retiring. **2,** extrovert.

out·grow' *v.t.* **1,** grow too large or able for. **2,** surpass in growing.

out'growth" *n.* a natural development or result; an offshoot.

out·guess' *v.t.* penetrate the designs of; outwit.

out'house" *n.* **1,** an outbuilding. **2,** a privy.

out'ing *n.* a pleasure trip.

out'land" *n.* outlying land. —*adj.* foreign. —**out'land"er**, *n.* a foreigner; stranger.

out·land'ish (owt-lan'dish) *adj.* unfamiliar; bizarre; odd.

out·last' *v.t.* last longer than; outlive.

out'law" *n.* a habitual criminal. —*v.t.* **1,** make illegal or legally unenforceable. **2,** deprive of the protection of the law. —**out'law"ry**, *n.*

out'lay" *n.* expenditure, as of money, effort, etc.

out'let" *n.* **1,** a means of exit or escape. **2,** a market for goods. **3,** a letting out; discharge.

out'line" *n.* **1,** the line tracing the exterior shape of an object. **2,** a drawing showing only this shape. **3,** a rough draft, as of a speech, plan, etc. **4,** a summary; (*pl.*) the gist. —*v.t.* make an outline of; describe briefly.

out·live' *v.t.* live longer than.

out'look" *n.* **1,** a view or scene from a place. **2,** the prospect for the future. **3,** mental attitude.

out'ly"ing (owt'lī"ing) *adj.* remote from the center; outside a boundary.

out"mod'ed (-mō'did) *adj.* out of fashion.

out'most" *adj.* outermost.

out·num'ber *v.t.* be more numerous than.

out-'of-date' *adj.* no longer in style; antiquated; obsolete.

out-"of-door' *adj.* outside; outdoor. —**out-"of-doors'**, *adv. & n.*

out-"of-the-way' *adj.* secluded.

out'pa"tient *n.* a person treated at, but not staying in, a hospital.

out'post" *n.* a station distant from an army; troops stationed there as a guard.

out'pour" *n.* a pouring out; effusion. Also, **out'pour"ing.**

out'put" *n.* **1,** production of goods, crops, work, etc. **2,** the amount produced; yield.

out'rage" *n.* **1,** a shameful wrong. **2,** cruel or wanton violence. —*v.t.* **1,** assault. **2,** transgress shamefully. **3,** offend grossly.

out·ra'geous (-rāj'əs) *adj.* flagrantly contrary to law, order, or decency. —**out·ra'geous·ness**, *n.*

out·rank' *v.t.* rank higher than.

ou·tré' (oo-trā') (*Fr.*) *adj.* **1,** extravagantly odd or exaggerated. **2,** improper.

out·reach' *v.t. & i.* **1,** extend beyond; surpass. **2,** outwit. —*n.* (out'rēch") the extent of effectiveness or influence.

out'rid"er *n.* a horseback rider attending a carriage.

out'rig"ger *n.* a projection from the side of a ship or boat, to give stability, support oars, etc.

out'right" *adv.* **1,** all at once; entirely. **2,** openly. —*adj.* **1,** complete; total. **2,** unqualified.

out·run' *v.t.* run faster than.

out·set *n.* the beginning.

out·shine' *v.t.* shine more brightly than; surpass in fame.

out"side' *n.* **1,** the region beyond an enclosure or boundary. **2,** the outer surface; external aspect. **3,** the utmost limit. —*adj.* **1,** external. **2,** coming from beyond a given place or group. **3,** apart from one's regular occupation. —*adv.* **1,** on or to the outer side. **2,** outdoors. —*prep.* **1,** outward from. **2,** beyond. **3,** (*Colloq.*) except for. —**out"·sid'er,** *n.* one not belonging to a particular set, etc.

out'size" *n.* a size not standard; esp., an unusually large size. —**out'sized",** *adj.*

out'skirts (owt'skẽrtz) *n.pl.* an outer part; a bordering district.

out'smart' *v.t.* (*Colloq.*) outwit.

out'spo"ken (owt'spō"kən) *adj.* frank; said without reserve.

out·stand'ing *adj.* **1,** prominent; notable. **2,** not paid or settled. **3,** standing apart; detached; opposing.

out'sta"tion *n.* an outpost.

out·stay' *v.t.* stay longer than.

out·strip' *v.t.* get ahead of; surpass; outdo.

out'take" *n.* material prepared (for a film, etc.) and subsequently eliminated.

out·talk' *v.t.* **1,** talk longer or more effectively than. **2,** overpower by talking.

out·vote' *v.t.* defeat in an election or a vote.

out'ward (-wərd) *adj.* **1,** going away. **2,** external; seen from the outside. **3,** visible. —*adv.* [also, **out'wards**] toward the outside; out.

out·wear' *v.t.* **1,** last longer than. **2,** wear out; exhaust.

out·weigh' *v.t.* exceed in weight, importance, or influence.

out·wit' *v.t.* get the better of by superior cleverness.

out'work" *n.* one of the minor defenses constructed in advance of the main fortification.

out·worn' *adj.* **1,** obsolete; outgrown. **2,** worn out, as clothes; exhausted.

ou'zel (oo'zəl) *n.* the Europ. blackbird.

ou'zo (oo'zō) *n.* an anise-flavored Gk. liqueur.

o'val (ō'vəl) *adj.* elliptical. —**Oval Office,** the office of the President of the U.S., where he conducts official business.

o'va·ry (ō'və-rē) *n.* the organ in a female in which the egg cells are formed. —**o·var'i·an** (ō-vâr'ē-ən) *adj.*

o·vate' (ō-vāt') *adj.* egg-shaped.

o·va'tion (ō-vā'shən) *n.* enthusiastic public acclaim.

ov'en (uv'ən) *n.* a chamber, as in a stove, for baking or drying.

[The following words may be defined by assuming the prefix *over-* to mean "excessive" in the case of nouns; "too much, too far, too long," etc., in the case of verbs; "too" or "excessively" in the case of adjectives and adverbs.]

o"ver·a·bun'dance, *n.*	o"ver·ex·er·cise", *v.i. & t.*	o"ver·scru'pu·lous, *adj.*
o"ver·ac'tive, *adj.*	o"ver·ex·ert', *v.i.*	o"ver·sell', *v.t. & i.*
o"ver·am·bi'tious, *adj.*	o"ver·ex·pan'sion, *n.*	o"ver·sen'si·tive, *adj.*
o"ver·anx'ious, *adj.*	o"ver·ex·pose', *v.t.*	o"ver·set', *v.i.*
o"ver·bold', *adj.*	o"ver·fa·mil'iar, *adj.*	o"ver·sim"pli·fi·ca'tion, *n.*
o"ver·bur'den, *v.t.*	o"ver·fa·tigue', *v.t.*	o"ver·sim'pli·fy", *v.t. & i.*
o"ver·bus'y, *adj.*	o"ver·feed', *v.t.*	o"ver·spread', *adj. & v.t.*
o"ver·buy', *v.i. & t.*	o"ver·fill', *v.t.*	o"ver·stay', *v.i.*
o"ver·cap'i·tal·ize", *v.t.*	o"ver·fond', *adj.*	o"ver·stim'u·late", *v.t.*
o"ver·care'ful, *adj.*	o"ver·has'ty, *adj.*	o"ver·stock', *v.t.*
o"ver·cau'tious, *adj.*	o"ver·heat', *v.t. & i.*	o'ver·stock", *n.*
o"ver·charge', *v.i. & t.*	o"ver·in·dulge', *v.i.*	o"ver·strict'", *adj.*
o"ver·con'fi·dent, *adj.*	o"ver·load', *v.t.*	o"ver·stu'di·ous, *adj.*
o"ver·con·serv'a·tive, *adj.*	o"ver·long', *adv. & adj.*	o"ver·sub·scribe', *v.t.*
o"ver·cook', *v.t.*	o"ver·mod'est, *adj.*	o"ver·sus·pi'cious, *adj.*
o"ver·crit'i·cal, *adj.*	o"ver·pay', *v.t. & i.*	o"ver·sweet', *adj.*
o"ver·crowd', *v.t.*	o"ver·pay'ment, *n.*	o"ver·talk'a·tive, *adj.*
o"ver·cu'ri·ous, *adj.*	o"ver·plump', *adj.*	o"ver·task', *v.t.*
o"ver·do', *v.i. & t.*	o"ver·pop'u·la'tion, *n.*	o"ver·tax', *v.t.*
o"ver·done', *adj.*	o"ver·praise', *v.t.*	o"ver·tire', *v.t. & i.*
o"ver·ea'ger, *adj.*	o"ver·pro·duce', *v.i. & t.*	o"ver·trained', *adj.*
o"ver·eat', *v.i.*	o"ver·pro·duc'tion, *n.*	o"ver·val'u·a'tion, *n.*
o"ver·e·mo'tion·al, *adj.*	o"ver·qual'i·fied, *adj.*	o"ver·val'ue, *v.t.*
o"ver·em'pha·size", *adj.*	o"ver·re·li'gious, *adj.*	o"ver·ve'he·ment, *adj.*
o"ver·en·thu'si·as'tic, *adj.*	o"ver·ripe', *adj.*	o"ver·write', *v.i. & t.*
o"ver·ex·cite', *v.t.*	o"ver·rule', *v.t.*	o"ver·zeal'ous, *adj.*

---

o'ver (ō'vər) *prep*. **1,** higher than; above; covering. **2,** above and across; to or on the other side of. **3,** more than. **4,** during. **5,** about; concerning. **6,** in preference to. —*adv*. **1,** on the top. **2,** across. **3,** yonder; on the other side. **4,** from one to another. **5,** so as to show the other side. **6,** above the rim or top. **7,** from beginning to end. **8,** in excess. **9,** once more. **10,** at one end. **11,** (*Colloq*.) successfully. —*adj*. **1,** higher up. **2,** in excess; surplus. **3,** finished; past. —**over and above,** in addition to; besides.

o·ver- *pref*. over; beyond; extra.

o″ver·act′ *v.i. & t.* be excessively dramatic; overplay.

o″ver·age′ *adj*. beyond the proper age; too old.

o′ver·age (-ij) *n*. excess of goods, money, etc.

o′ver·all *adj*. extending to both or all extremes; covering all parts. —*n.* (*pl.*) a one-piece outer garment worn to protect the clothes.

o″ver·awe′ *v.t.* restrain or subdue by awe, fear, or superior influence.

o″ver·bal′ance *v.t.* **1,** outweigh. **2,** tip over.

o″ver·bear′ing (-bâr′ing) *adj*. haughty; arrogant; dictatorial.

o″ver·bid′ *v.t.* bid higher than. —*v.i.* bid too much. —*n.* a higher bid.

o″ver·blown′ *adj*. **1,** past the time of blossoming. **2,** pretentious.

o′ver·board′ *adv*. **1,** off a ship into the water. **2,** (*Colloq.*) to a rash or extravagant extent.

o″ver·book′ *v.t.* accept more reservations for (an airplane, concert, etc.) than there are seats available.

o′ver·call″ *v.t. & n.* bid higher than (another bid), in a card game.

o″ver·cast′ *adj*. **1,** darkened, esp. by clouds. **2,** sewn by long stitches over an edge, as to prevent raveling.

o′ver·clothes″ *n.pl.* outer garments, as for outdoor wear.

o″ver·cloud′ *v.t. & i.* overspread with clouds; make or become gloomy.

o′ver·coat″ *n.* a long outer coat, esp. for cold weather.

o″ver·come′ *v.t.* **1,** defeat; conquer. **2,** successfully resist (an impulse, etc.). —*adj*. feeling great emotion.

o′ver·dose″ *n.* an excessive dose, as of medicine. —*v.t.* (ō″vər-dōs′) give too large a dose to.

o′ver·draft″ *n.* **1,** a draft exceeding one's credit balance, esp. at a bank. **2,** any excess draft or demand. **3,** an air draft above a fire, or passing downward.

o″ver·draw′ *v.t. & i.* **1,** draw out or back too much or too far. **2,** exaggerate in depicting.

o″ver·dress′ *v.i. & t.* dress too ostentatiously.

o″ver·drive′ *v.t.* drive or work too hard; push to excess. —*n.* (ō′vər-drīv″) a gear arrangement whereby a wheel or propeller rotates faster than the driving shaft.

o″ver·due′ *adj*. due at a previous time; past due.

o″ver·es′ti·mate″ (-māt″) *v.t. & i.* **1,** rate too highly. **2,** estimate to be more than the reality. —*n.* (-mət) an excessive estimate. —**o″ver·es″ti·ma′tion,** *n.*

o″ver·flow′ *v.t. & i.* **1,** flood. **2,** run over the edge or boundary (of). —*n.* (ō′vər-flō″) **1,** a flowing over; that which flows over. **2,** an outlet for excess fluid.

o″ver·grown′ *adj*. covered with a growth of vegetation, hair, etc.

o″ver·hand′ *adj. & adv.* with the hand above or raised.

o″ver·hang′ *v.t. & i.* **[-hung, -hang′ing] 1,** extend or project over. **2,** impend; threaten. —*n.* (ō′vər-hang″), a projecting part; the extent of this projection.

o′ver·haul″ *v.t.* **1,** examine or repair thoroughly. **2,** overtake. —*n.* inspection.

o′ver·head″ *adj*. **1,** above one's head; in the sky. **2,** applicable to all; average. —*n.* the fixed expenses of a business, as for rent, etc. —*adv.* (ō″vər-hed′) **1,** aloft; on high. **2,** so as to be completely submerged.

o″ver·hear′ *v.t. & i.* hear without the speaker's knowledge or intention.

o″ver·joy′ *v.t.* make exceedingly glad; overcome with joy. —**o″ver·joyed′,** *adj*.

o′ver·kill″ *n.* the nuclear capacity to destroy many times the total population of an enemy nation or of the world.

o″ver·land′ (-lənd″) *adj. & adv.* across dry land; by land.

o″ver·lap′ *v.t. & i.* cover partly and extend beyond. —*n.* (ō′vər-lap″) the part lapping over.

o′ver·lay″ *v.t.* **1,** place on something else. **2,** cover, esp. with a decorative layer. —*n.* (ō′vər-lā″) something laid on something else.

o″ver·leap′ *v.t.* **1,** leap over; pass beyond. **2,** omit; disregard.

o″ver·look′ *v.t.* **1,** fail to notice. **2,** ignore; condone. **3,** afford a view of, from a higher position. **4,** supervise.

o′ver·lord″ *n.* a master; a chief lord.

o′ver·ly (-lē) *adv*. excessively.

o″ver·match′ *v.t.* **1,** surpass. **2,** put in competition against another greatly superior.

o″ver·much′ *adj. & adv.* too much. —*n.* an excessive amount.

o′ver·night″ *adj.* **1,** done during the night. **2,** intended for one night's use. —*adv.* (ō″vər-nīt′) during the night. —*n.* **1,** the previous evening or night. **2,** (*Colloq.*) an overnight pass or trip.

o′ver·pass″ *n.* a bridge over a road. —*v.t.* (ō″vər-pàs′) *v.t.* go over or beyond; surmount.

o″ver·play′ *v.t. & i.* act or make a play with more force than is proper; exaggerate.

o″ver·pleased′ (-plēzd′) *adj.* too pleased (used chiefly in the negative, to express dissatisfaction).

o″ver·pow′er *v.t.* **1,** conquer or subdue by superior force. **2,** overwhelm, as with emotion. **3,** equip with too much power.

o″ver·rate′ *v.t.* value too highly; overestimate.

o″ver·reach′ *v.t. & i.* **1,** stretch beyond. **2,** reach too far; miss. **3,** outwit.

o″ver·ride′ *v.t.* **1,** prevail over; outweigh; overrule. **2,** trample down. **3,** extend over; overlap.

o″ver·run′ *v.t.* **1,** swarm over in great numbers. **2,** roam over; spread throughout. **3,** run beyond; exceed. **4,** take possession of (a country) by invasion. —*n.* (o′ver-run″) the act or result of exceeding (a budget, limit, etc.).

o′ver·seas′ (-sēz′) *adj.* **1,** situated beyond a sea; foreign. **2,** pert. to sea travel. —*adv.* (ō″vər-sēz′) beyond a sea; abroad.

o″ver·see′ *v.t.* **1,** supervise; direct. **2,** observe; watch. —**o′ver·se″er,** *n.*

o″ver·shad′ow *v.t.* **1,** darken, as by casting a shadow on. **2,** cause to seem less important.

o′ver·shoe″ *n.* a shoe worn over another; a waterproof shoe, as a rubber or galosh.

o″ver·shoot′ *v.t. & i.* shoot or go beyond (a proper mark or limit).

o′ver·shot″ *adj.* **1,** driven from above, as a water wheel. **2,** with the upper jaw overhanging the lower, as on a dog.

o′ver·sight″ *n.* **1,** an omission or error due to failure to notice. **2,** supervision; care.

o′ver·size″ *adj.* larger than is usual or proper. —*n.* an oversize article. Also, **o′ver·sized″.**

o′ver·skirt″ *n.* an outer skirt, esp. one worn over another.

o″ver·sleep′ *v.i.* sleep too late.

o″ver·state′ *v.t.* state too strongly; exaggerate. —**o″ver·state′ment,** *n.*

o″ver·step′ *v.t.* go beyond; transgress.

o″ver·strung′ *adj.* **1,** too tightly strung. **2,** highly nervous.

o″ver·stuffed″ (-stuft″) *adj.* (of furniture) covered with thick stuffing and upholstery.

o′vert (ō′vērt) *adj.* plain to the view; open.

o″ver·take′ *v.t.* catch up with, as in pursuing.

o′ver-the-count′er *adj.* **1,** sold direct to buyers, as in a retail store. **2,** aboveboard.

o″ver·throw′ *v.t.* **1,** defeat; force out of power; put an end to. **2,** knock down; upset. —*n.* defeat; demolition.

o′ver·time″ *n.* **1,** time spent working after regular hours; pay for such work. **2,** an extra period beyond the usual, as in sports. —*adj. & adv.* requiring extra time. —*v.t.* (ō″vər-tīm′) give too much time to, as in photographic processes.

o′ver·tone″ *n.* **1,** a higher, secondary tone of a basic musical tone. **2,** (*pl.*) additional meaning; connotation.

o″ver·top′ *v.t.* **1,** rise above. **2,** exceed. **3,** surpass; outdo.

o′ver·trick″ *n.* in bridge, a trick won in excess of the contract.

o″ver·trump′ *v.t.* play a higher trump than.

o″ver·ture″ (ō′vər-chûr″) *n.* **1,** an orchestral prelude to an opera, play, etc. **2,** a proposal; a suggestion that negotiations begin.

o″ver·turn′ *v.t. & i.* **1,** overthrow. **2,** upset; capsize.

o′ver·view″ *n.* a comprehensive survey or view.

o″ver·ween′ing (ō″vər-wē′ning) *adj.* arrogant; presumptuous.

o″ver·weigh′ *v.t.* **1,** exceed in weight. **2,** weigh down; oppress. —**o′ver·weight″** (-wāt″) *adj.*

o″ver·whelm′ *v.t.* **1,** cover, bury, load, or weigh upon overpoweringly; crush; oppress. **2,** overcome with emotion.

o″ver·work′ *v.i.* work too hard. —*v.t.* **1,** weary with too much work. **2,** excite excessively. **3,** elaborate too much. —*n.* (ō′vər-wêrk″) extra work.

o″ver·wrought′ *adj.* **1,** weary or nervous, esp. from overwork or excitement. **2,** too elaborate.

o′vi·duct″ (ō′vi-dukt″) *n.* the duct or passage through which the ovum or egg of an animal passes from the ovary.

o′vine (ō′vīn) *adj.* pert. to sheep.

o·vip′a·rous (ō-vip′ə-rəs) *adj.* producing eggs.

o′void (ō′void) *adj.* egg-shaped.

o′vu·late″ (o′vū-lāt″) *v.i.* produce or lay an egg or eggs. —**o″vu·la′tion,** *n.*

o′vule (ō′vūl) *n.* a rudimentary egg or seed.

o'vum (ō'vəm) *n.* [*pl.* **o'va** (-və)] the female reproductive cell.

owe (ō) *v.t.* **1,** be under obligation to pay, render, etc. **2,** be indebted to or for. —**ow'ing,** *adj.* owed; due. —**owing to,** because of.

owl *n.* **1,** a nocturnal bird of prey, with hooked beak and strong claws. **2,** a solemn person. **3,** a person of nocturnal habits. —**owl'et,** *n.* a young, or small, owl. —**owl'ish,** *adj.* affecting a solemn or wise manner.

own (ōn) *v.t.* **1,** possess by right. **2,** admit; concede. —*adj.* belonging to or concerning only oneself or itself. —**own'er,** *n.* —**own'-er·ship",** *n.*

ox (oks) *n.* [*pl.* **ox'en** (-ən)] the emasculated adult male of the domestic cattle family.

ox·al'ic acid (oks-al'ik) a poisonous acid used in bleaching, dyeing, etc.

ox'a·lis (ok'sə-lis) *n.* a plant with white or pink flowers.

ox'blood" **1,** the blood of an ox. **2,** a deep red color.

ox'bow" (oks'bō") *n.* **1,** in a yoke, the U-shaped piece that fits over the neck of the animal. **2,** a U-shaped bend in a river.

ox'eye" (oks'ī") *n.* **1,** a daisylike plant. **2,** a small U.S. shore bird, as the sandpiper.

ox'ford (oks'fərd) *n.* **1,** a low shoe. **2,** a cotton or rayon fabric used as shirting. —**oxford gray,** a dark gray.

ox'ide (ok'sīd) *n.* a compound of oxygen with another element.

ox'i·dize" (ok'sə-dīz") *v.t. & i.* combine with oxygen. —**ox'i·dant** (-dənt) *n.* —**ox"i·da'tion,** *n.*

ox"y·a·cet'y·lene (ok"sē-ə-set'ə-lēn) *adj.* pert. to a gas that burns with a very hot flame, used for welding and cutting metal.

ox'y·gen (ok'sə-jən) *n.* a gaseous element, no. 8, symbol O, colorless, odorless, and essential to all life. —**ox'y·gen·ate"** (-āt") *v.t.* —**oxygen mask,** a mask worn over the nose and kept supplied with oxygen. —**oxygen tent,** an enclosure supplied with oxygen in which a patient is kept for aid in breathing.

o'yez (ō'yes; -yez) *interj.* hear! attention!

oys'ter (ois'tər) *n.* an edible saltwater bivalve mollusk. —**oyster plant,** a vegetable, the salsify.

o'zone (ō'zōn) *n.* **1,** an ionized form of oxygen. **2,** (*Colloq.*) pure air.

P

P, p (pē) the sixteenth letter of the English alphabet.

pa (pä) *n.* (*Colloq.*) papa.

pab'u·lum (pab'yə-ləm) *n.* **1,** food. **2,** insipid ideas.

pa'ca (pä'kə) *n.* a large spotted rodent of So. Amer.

pace (pās) *n.* **1,** a single step or its distance. **2,** mode or rate of walking or progressing; gait; speed. **3,** a gait of horses. **4,** (*pl.*) gaits; accomplishments. —*v.t.* **1,** set the rate for. **2,** (usu. with *off*) measure by counting steps. **3,** walk back and forth across. —*v.i.* walk in even steps; go at a pace. —**pac'er,** *n.* a pacing horse.

pace'mak"er *n.* **1,** one who sets the pace, as in a race; a leader. **2,** a machine for regulating the heartbeat.

pace'set"ter *n.* pacemaker (def. 1)

pa·chi'si (pa-chē'zē) *n.* parcheesi.

pach'y·derm" (pak'i-dêrm") *n.* a thick-skinned quadruped, esp. an elephant or rhinoceros. —**pach"y·der'ma·tous,** *adj.*

pach"y·san'dra (pak"i-san'drə) *n.* an evergreen plant used as a ground cover.

pa·cif'ic (pə-sif'ik) *adj.* peaceable; conciliatory; calm. —*n.* (*cap.*) the Pacific Ocean. —**pa·cif'i·cal·ly,** *adv.*

pac'i·fi"er (pas'i-fī"ər) *n.* a simulated nipple for a baby.

pac'i·fism (-fiz-əm) *n.* opposition to war for any reason. —**pac'i·fist,** *n.*

pac'i·fy" (-fī") *v.t.* appease; calm. —**pac"i·fi·ca'tion,** *n.*

pack (pak) *n.* **1,** a bundle tied up; a packing; a package, esp. of cards or cigarettes. **2,** a group of persons or animals; a gang. —*v.t.* **1,** put in a bundle or a piece of baggage. **2,** compress; cram; fill (a space). **3,** carry, esp. on the back. **4,** (with *off*) send away. —*v.i.* stow personal things for traveling. —*adj.* that carries things. —**pack animal,** a beast of burden. —**pack rat, 1,** a desert rodent. **2,** a hoarder.

pack'age (-ij) *n.* **1,** a small wrapped bundle. **2,** (*Colloq.*) a comprehensive plan or proposition. —*v.t.* put into a package, esp. for marketing. —**pack'ag·ing,** *n.* —**package store,** a liquor store.

pack'er (-ər) *n.* one who packs; esp., a wholesale supplier of meat.

pack'et (-it) *n.* **1,** a small, compact bundle or portion. **2,** a small merchant ship.

pack'ing *n.* material for a protective wad.

pack'sack" *n.* a large knapsack.

pack'sad"dle *n.* a pair of sacks or bags joined with straps and hung over the back of a pack animal.

pack'thread" *n.* a heavy twine.

pact (pakt) *n.* an agreement.

pad *n.* **1,** a small wad of something soft; a cushion. **2,** the soft sole of an animal's paw. **3,** a leaf of a water lily. **4,** a writing tablet. **5,** (*Slang*) quarters where a person lives or sleeps. **6,** (*Slang*) graft. —*v.t.* [**pad′-ded, -ding**] **1,** fill out or cushion with pads. **2,** add needless or fraudulent items to. —*v.i.* walk or trot steadily. —**pad′ding,** *n.*

pad′dle (pad′əl) *n.* a short oar; a similar broad-bladed implement. —*v.i. & t.* **1,** propel (a canoe). **2,** dabble (as the feet) in shallow water. **3,** spank. —**paddle wheel,** a large wheel with boards around the rim for propelling a boat (*paddle boat*).

pad′dock (pad′ək) *n.* a small enclosed field near a stable.

pad′dy (pad′ē) *n.* **1,** rice in the husk, either in the field or gathered. **2,** a field where rice is grown.

pad′dy wagon (pad′ē) *n.* an enclosed police truck used to carry prisoners. Also, **Black Maria.**

pad′dy·whack″ *n.* (*Colloq.*) **1,** an Irishman. **2,** a disturbance.

pa′di·shah″ (pa′di-shä″) *n.* great king; emperor.

pad′lock″ (pad′lok″) *n.* a portable lock with a hinged arm. —*v.t.* fasten with a padlock; close officially.

pad′nag″ *n.* an easygoing saddle horse.

pa′dre (pä′drē) *n.* **1,** a priest. **2,** a chaplain.

pae′an (pē′ən) *n.* a song of joy.

pa′gan (pā′gən) *n.* an idolater. —*adj.* heathenish; irreligious. —**pa′gan·dom,** *n.* —**pa′gan·ism,** *n.* —**pa′gan·ize,** *v.t.*

page (pāj) *n.* **1,** one side of a printed leaf of a book, etc. **2,** a messenger boy, esp. one in an honorary position. —*v.t.* **1,** number the pages of. **2,** summon (a person) from a crowd by calling his name.

pag′eant (paj′ənt) *n.* a showy spectacle. —**pag′eant·ry** (-rē) *n.*

page′boy″ *n.* a hairstyle in which the hair is curled under at the shoulder.

pag′i·nate″ (paj′i-nāt″) *v.t.* number the pages of. —**pag′i·na′tion,** *n.*

pa·go′da (pə-gō′də) *n.* in the Far East, a many-storied tower.

paid (pād) *v.* pret. & p.p. of *pay.*

pail (pāl) *n.* an open vessel for carrying liquids; a bucket.

pain (pān) *n.* **1,** suffering of body or mind. **2,** (*pl.*) great care. —*v.t.* cause suffering to. —**pain′ful,** *adj.*

pain′kill″er *n.* an anesthetic.

pains′tak″ing (pānz′tāk″ing) *adj.* very careful.

paint (pānt) *n.* **1,** a pigmented oil or liquid that forms a coloring or protective coating when dry. **2,** rouge. **3,** a pinto horse. —*v.t. & i.* **1,** apply paint (to). **2,** portray, esp.

with oil paints on canvas; make paintings. —**paint′er,** *n.* one who paints (houses, etc., or paintings) professionally. —**paint′ing,** *n.* a painted picture.

pair (pâr) *n.* **1,** a matched set of two things. **2,** a married couple. **3,** two cards of the same rank. —*v.t. & i.* **1,** match (two things). **2,** (often with *off* or *up*) join or go off in couples.

pais′ley (pāz′lē) *n. & adj.* a thin, soft woolen fabric.

pa·jam′as (pə-jäm′əz) *n.pl.* loose coat and trousers for sleeping or lounging. Also, *Brit.,* **py·jam′as.**

pal *n.* (*Slang*) friend; chum.

pal′ace (pal′is) *n.* **1,** the residence of a sovereign. **2,** a magnificent building.

pal′a·din (pal′ə-din) *n.* a heroic champion.

pal″an·quin′ (pal″ən-kēn′) *n.* a litter borne by men.

pal′at·a·ble (pal′ə-tə-bəl) *adj.* tasty; acceptable. —**pal″at·a·bil′i·ty,** *n.*

pal′ate (pal′it) *n.* **1,** the roof of the mouth. **2,** the sense of taste; liking. —**pal′a·tal,** *adj.*

pa·la′tial (pə-lā′shəl) *adj.* grand, like (or as in) a palace.

pa·lat′i·nate″ (pə-lat′i-nāt″) *n.* a palatine's state or domain.

pal′a·tine″ (pal′ə-tīn″) *adj.* having royal privileges. —*n.* a palatine nobleman.

pa·lav′er (pə-lav′ər) *n.* idle talk; cajolery. —*v.i.* chat.

pale (pāl) *adj.* **1,** wan; lacking color; in a light shade. **2,** faint; lacking brilliance. —*n.* **1,** a pointed stake; picket. **2,** a strictly bounded area. —*v.t. & i.* make wan; dim. —**pale′ness,** *n.* —**beyond the pale,** out of bounds.

pale′face″ *n.* a white person (supposedly so called by Amer. Indians).

pa·le·o- (pā-lē-ə) *pref.* **1,** remote in the past. **2,** early; primitive.

pa″le·og′ra·phy (pā″lē-og′rə-fē) *n.* the study of ancient written documents and methods of writing; those methods collectively. —**pa″le·og′ra·pher,** *n.* —**pa″le·o·graph′ic,** *adj.*

pa″le·o·lith′ic (pā″lē-ə-lith′ik) *adj.* pert. to the Old Stone Age.

pa″le·on·tol′o·gy (pā″lē-ən-tol′ə-jē) *n.* the scientific study of life in past geologic periods. —**pa″le·on·to·log′i·cal,** *adj.* —**pa″le·on·tol′o·gist,** *n.*

Pa″le·o·zo′ic (pā″lē-ə-zō′ik) *adj.* pert. to a geological era, the age of invertebrates.

pal′ette (pal′it) *n.* the thin board on which an artist mixes his colors.

pal′frey (pâl′frē) *n.* a saddle horse.

pal'imp·sest" *n.* a parchment from which one writing has been erased to make way for another.

pal'in·drome" (pal'in-drōm") *n.* a word or sentence whose letters read the same backwards as forwards, as *level*.

pal'ing (pāl'ing) *n.* a row of pales; fencing.

pal'i·node" (pal'ə-nōd") *n.* a retraction. —*v.* recant. —**pal"in·o'di·al** (-dē-əl) *adj.*

pal'i·sade' (pal"ə-sād') *n.* **1,** a fence of pointed stakes. **2,** (*pl.*) a line of sheer cliffs.

pall (pâl) *n.* **1,** a cloth thrown over a coffin. **2,** the coffin. **3,** a gloomy, blanketing effect. —*v.i.* become boring. —*v.t.* satiate; depress.

pal·la'dium (pə-lā'dē-əm) *n.* **1,** a rare metallic element of the platinum group, no. 46, symbol Pd. **2,** any safeguard; esp. of liberty or rights. —**pal·la'dous** (-dəs) *adj.* containing palladium.

pall'bear"er *n.* a coffin-bearer at a funeral.

pal'let (pal'it) *n.* **1,** a board for drying ceramics, bricks, etc. **2,** a bed of straw or rags. **3,** palette.

pal'li·ate" (pal'ē-āt") *n.* **1,** make excuses for, as a crime. **2,** relieve without curing, as a disease. —**pal"li·a'tion,** *n.* —**pal'li·a"tive,** *n. & adj.*

pal'lid (pal'id) *adj.* pale; wan.

pall-"mall" (pel"mel') *n.* an old game in which a wooden ball was driven through a raised ring at the end of an alley; the alley.

pal'lor (pal'ər) *n.* paleness.

palm (päm) *n.* **1,** that surface of the hand toward which the fingers bend; a similar part, as of a glove. **2,** any of various tropical trees. **3,** a leaf of this tree as a symbol of victory. —*v.t.* **1,** conceal in the hand. **2,** (with *off*) get rid of unfairly. —**Palm Sunday,** the Sunday before Easter, commemorating Christ's entry into Jerusalem.

pal'mate (päl'māte) *adj.* **1,** like a hand with the fingers extended. **2,** web-footed. —**pal·ma'tion,** *n.*

palm'er (-ər) *n.* a pilgrim returning from the Holy Land.

pal·met'to (pal-met'ō) *n.* [*pl.* **-tos**] a palm tree with fan-shaped leaves.

palm'is·try (pä'mis-trē) *n.* fortune-telling from the markings of the palm. —**palm'ist,** *n.*

palm'y (pä'mē) *adj.* flourishing.

pal"o·mi'no (pal"ə-mē'nō) *n.* [*pl.* **-nos**] a gray or golden horse, usually with near-white mane and tail, bred in the southwest U.S.

pa·loo'ka (pə-loo'kə) *n.* (*Slang*) an inept or inexperienced person.

pal'pa·ble (pal'pə-bəl) *adj.* readily perceived; obvious. —**pal'pa·ble·ness,** *n.*

pal'pate (pal'pāt) *v.t.* examine by touch; manipulate. —**pal·pation,** *n.*

pal'pi·tate" (pal'pə-tāt") *v.i.* pulsate; throb. —**pal"pi·ta'tion,** *n.*

pal'pus (pal'pəs) *n.* [*pl.* **-pi** (-pī)] a sense organ of an insect, crustacean, etc.. Also, **palp.**

pal'sy (pâl'zē) *n.* paralysis; commonly, uncontrolled shaking. —*v.t.* paralyze. —**pal'sied,** *adj.*

pal'ter (pâl'tər) *v.i.* play false; trifle.

pal'try (pâl'trē) *adj.* worthless; trifling. —**pal'tri·ness,** *n.*

pal'u·dal (pal'yə-dəl) *adj.* marshy.

pam'pas (pam'pəz) *n.pl.* in So. Amer., vast treeless plains. —**pam·pe'an** (pam-pē'ən) *adj.*

pam'per (pam'pər) *v.t.* overindulge; humor.

pam·pe'ro (päm-per'ō) *n.* [*pl.* **-ros**] a cold, dry wind of Argentina and Brazil.

pam'phlet (pam'flit) *n.* a small printed tract; a booklet. —**pam"phlet·eer**' (-flə-tir") *n.* a writer of polemical essays.

pan *n.* **1,** a hollow vessel for cooking. **2,** any similar shallow vessel. **3,** a depression. —*v.t. & i.* [**panned, pan'ning**] **1,** cook or wash in a pan. **2,** (*Slang*) criticize harshly. **3,** yield gold. **4,** (with *out*) succeed. **5,** move (a camera) toward or away from its object, or so as to follow a moving object.

pan- *pref.* all; every; united.

pan"a·ce'a (pan"ə-sē'ə) *n.* a remedy for all ills.

pa·na'da (pə-nä'də) *n.* a bread pudding.

pan'a·ma" (pan'ə-mä") *n.* a hat woven of fine leaf shoots or straws.

Pan-"A·mer'i·can *adj.* embracing all the sovereign countries of the Western Hemisphere; lit., all-American.

pan"a·tel'a (pan"ə-tel'ə) *n.* a cigar that is relatively long and slender. Also, **pan"e·tel'a.**

pan'cake" (pan'kāk") *n.* **1,** a thin, fried battercake. **2,** in aviation, an abrupt, almost vertical landing. **3,** a flat facial paint.

pan"chro·mat'ic (pan"krō-mat'ik) *adj.* sensitive to light of all colors.

pan'cre·as (pan'krē-əs) *n.* a large gland secreting a digestive fluid (*pancreatin*); as meat, called *sweetbread*. —**pan"cre·at'ic,** *adj.*

pan'da (pan'də) *n.* **1,** a raccoonlike animal of India. **2,** [**giant panda**] a bearlike animal of Tibet.

pan·dem'ic (pan-dem'ik) *adj.* **1,** common

to or characteristic of a whole people. **2,** affecting a very high proportion of the population (of a country or an area), as a disease.

pan″de·mo′ni·um (pan″də-mō′nē-əm) *n.* a wild, lawless uproar.

pan′der (pan′dər) *n.* **1,** one who assists to gratify their baser passions. **2,** a pimp. —*v.i.* act as a pander.

pan′dit *n.* in India, a wise person; scholar.

pan-dow′dy (pan-dow′dė) *n.* a pudding of bread and apples baked together.

pane (pān) *n.* a sheet of glass in a door or window; a rectangular section, as in a ceiling.

pan″e·gyr′ic (pan″ə-jir′ik) *n.* an oration or writing of high praise.

pan′el (pan′əl) *n.* **1,** a flat section, raised or sunken, in a wall, door, etc. **2,** a strip inserted in a skirt. **3,** a list of eligible jurors; a group of speakers. —*v.t.* form with, divide into, or decorate with panels. **—pan′·eled,** *adj.* **—pan′el·ing,** *n.* **—panel truck,** a small, fully enclosed truck, usu. used for deliveries.

pan′el·ist (-ist) *n.* a member of a panel; one of several persons who discuss events, play games, etc., on a radio or television show.

pan″e·tel′a (pan″ə-tel′ə) *n.* panatela.

pang *n.* a sudden sharp pain or feeling of emotion.

pan·go′lin (pan-gō′lin) *n.* a scaly anteater of Afr. and Asia.

pan′han·dle *n.* **1,** the handle of a pan. **2,** (often *cap.*) a narrow strip of land extending from a territory. —*v.i. & t.* (*Slang*) beg. **—pan′han″dler** (-dlər) *n.* (*Slang*) a street beggar who is not an invalid.

Pan′hel·len′ic (pan″hə-len′ik) *adj.* **1,** embracing all the states of ancient Greece. **2,** representing all fraternities and sororities in a college.

pan′ic (pan′ik) *n.* **1,** a sudden, extreme fright. **2,** rapidly spreading alarm, esp. in financial circles. **3,** (*Colloq.*) something extremely funny. **4,** any of several species of grass. —*v.t. & i.* affect or be affected with panic. **—pan′ick·y** (-ik-ė) *adj.* **—pan′ic-strick″en, pan′ic-struck″,** *adj.*

pan′nier (pan′yər) *n.* a basket, usually of wicker, esp. one of a pair.

pan′o·ply (pan′ə-plė) *n.* **1,** a full set of armor. **2,** splendid array.

pan″o·ram′a (pan″ə-ràm′ə) *n.* an unbroken or widely extended view. **—pan″o·ram′ic,** *adj.* **—pan″o·ram′i·cal·ly,** *adv.*

pan″pipe″ *n.* a simple wind instrument

consisting of reeds or tubes of graduated length. Also, **Pan′s pipes.**

pan′sy (pan′zė) *n.* **1,** a plant of the violet family, with velvety, variously colored flowers. **2,** (*Slang*) a pantywaist.

pant *v.i.* **1,** breathe deeply and rapidly; throb. **2,** yearn.

pan″ta·lets′ (pan″tə-letz′) *n.pl.* a woman's long drawers.

pan″ta·loons′ (pan″tə-loonz′) *n.pl.* trousers.

pant′dress″ *n.* a dress with a divided skirt.

pan′the·ism (pan′thė-iz-əm) *n.* **1,** the doctrine that the existing universe is God. **2,** the worship of all gods. **—pan′the·ist,** *n.* **—pan″the·is′tic,** *adj.* **—pan″the·is′ti·cal·ly,** *adv.*

pan′the·on″ (pan′thė-on″) *n.* **1,** a dedicated building, as a temple or mausoleum. **2,** (*cap.*) a temple of ancient Rome, dedicated to all the gods.

pan′ther (pan′thər) *n.* **1,** a leopard. **2,** the American puma or cougar.

pan′ties (pan′tėz) *n.pl.* (*Colloq.*) a woman's short drawers.

pan′tile (pan′tīl) *n.* a roofing tile in the shape of a horizontal S.

pan′to·graph″ (pan′tə-gráf″) *n.* **1,** an instrument for copying a drawing to a given scale. **2,** the extensible wire contact on an electric locomotive. **—pan″to·graph′ic,** *adj.* **—pan″to·graph′i·cal·ly,** *adv.*

pan″to·mime″ (pan′tə-mīm″) *n.* acting, or a play, done solely by gestures and facial expressions. —*v.t. & i.* express by pantomime. **—pan″to·mim′ic** (-mim′ik) *adj.*

pan′try (pan′trė) *n.* a small room for storing food and dishes.

pants *n.pl.* (*Colloq.*) **1,** trousers. **2,** drawers.

pant′suit″ *n.* a women's ensemble of jacket and pants.

pan′ty-hose″ *n.* stockings and panties combined in one garment worn by women.

pan′ty-waist″ *n.* **1,** a child's undergarment. **2,** (*Slang*) a childish or timorous person; an effeminate man.

pan′zer (pan′zər) *adj.* (*Ger.*) armored, as a division of troops.

pap *n.* a soft food for babies or invalids.

pa′pa (pä′pə) *n.* father.

pa′pa·cy (pä′pə-sė) *n.* the office, term, jurisdiction, or institution of the Pope. **—pa′pal,** *adj.*

pa·pa·raz′zo (pä-pä-rät′sō) *n.* a photographer specializing in celebrities.

pa·paw′ (pâ-pâ′) *n.* a tree of the southern U.S. or its edible fruit.

---

tub, cūte, pûll; labəl; oil, owl, go, chip, she, thin, *th*en, sing, ink; *see p.* 6

pa·pa'ya (pə-pä'yə) *n.* a tropical tree or its sweet, juicy fruit.

pa'per (pā'pər) *n.* **1,** a thin, flexible material made in sheets of pressed wood pulp, rag fiber, etc. **2,** a newspaper. **3,** an essay; article. **4,** a document; (*pl.*) credentials. **5,** bank notes; bills of exchange. —*adj.* of or on paper. —*v.t.* **1,** cover with wallpaper. **2,** fill (a theater) with an unpaying audience. —**pa'per·y,** *adj.* —**paper clip,** a metal clip for holding sheets of paper together. —**paper nautilus,** a variety of thin-shelled sea mollusk. —**paper tiger,** an individual or organization outwardly powerful but in reality weak or ineffectual.

pap'er·back" *adj.* bound with paper, instead of cardboard, etc. —*n.* a paperback book.

pa'per·board" *n.* cardboard.

pa'per·hang"er *n.* one who hangs wallpaper as a trade.

pa'per·weight" *n.* a weight to hold down loose papers.

pa'per·work" *n.* the writing of records, reports, etc.

pa"pier-ma·ché' (pā"pər-mə-shā') *n.* a plastic material of ground or compressed paper.

pa·pil'la (pə-pil'ə) *n.* [*pl.* **-lae** (-ē)] a small nipplelike projection. —**pap'il·lar·y** (pap'ə-ler-ē) *adj.*

pa"pil'lon" (pa"pē-yōn') *n.* a breed of toy dog related to the spaniel.

pap'il·lote (pap'ə-lōt) *n.* **1,** a curl-paper used by women to hold their hair in place. **2,** a frilled ring of paper used to decorate a lamb chop.

pa'pist (pā'pist) *n.* one who favors Roman Catholicism or papal supremacy.

pa·poose' (pa-poos') *n.* a No. Amer. Indian baby.

pa'pri·ka (pä'pri-kä) *n.* a mild red pepper.

Pap test a test to detect cancer in smears of various bodily secretions, esp. from the cervix and the vagina. Also, **Pap smear.**

pap'u·la (pap'yə-lə) *n.* [*pl.* **-lae** (-lè)] a pimple. Also, **pap'ule.** —**pap'u·lar,** *adj.*

pa·py'rus (pə-pī'rəs) *n.* a paper made by the ancient Egyptians; a manuscript written on it.

par (pär) *n.* **1,** full or nominal value of money, stocks, etc. **2,** equal footing. **3,** an accepted standard; (*Golf*) a score for each hole based on length and two putts for the green.

pa'ra (pä'rä) *n.* the monetary unit of Turkey, worth about 10 U. S. cents.

pa·ra- (par-ə) *pref.* **1,** beside; beyond. **2,** (*Med.*) faulty; abnormal.

par'a·ble (par'ə-bəl) *n.* a fictitious story pointing a moral.

pa·rab'o·la (pə-rāb'ə-lə) *n.* a curve formed by the intersection of a cone by a plane parallel to its side. —**par"a·bol'ic** (par"ə-bol'ik) *adj.*

par'a·chute" (par'ə-shoot") *n.* an apparatus to retard the speed of a falling body. —*v.i.* descend by parachute. —**par'a·chut"ist,** *n.*

par'a·clete" (par'ə-klēt") *n.* the Holy Ghost or Holy Spirit.

pa·rade' (pə-rād') *n.* **1,** a formal procession; troops assembled for review. **2,** a display; a passing in review. —*v.t. & i.* pass in review.

par'a·digm (par'ə-dim) *n.* (*Gram.*) a list of the inflected forms of a word.

par'a·dise" (par'ə-dīs") *n.* **1,** heaven. **2,** a place of extreme beauty or of supreme happiness. **3,** (*cap.*) the garden of Eden. —**par"a·dis'i·ac** (-dis'ē-ak) *adj.*

par'a·dox" (par'ə-doks") *n.* **1,** a seemingly absurd but possibly true statement. **2,** something self-contradictory. —**par"a·dox'i·cal,** *adj.*

par'af·fin (par'ə-fin) *n.* **1,** an odorless, waxy substance used for candles, sealing, etc. **2,** (*Brit.*) kerosene. Also, **par'af·fine.**

par'a·foil" (par'ə-foil") *n.* a self-inflating parachute.

par'a·glid"er *n.* a parachute used for reentering spacecraft, etc.

par'a·gon" (par'ə-gon") *n.* a model of perfection.

par'a·graph" (par'ə-gráf") *n.* **1,** a separate section of a writing, usually having an indented first line, or marked by the sign (¶). **2,** a brief item, as in a newspaper.

par'a·keet" (par'ə-kēt") *n.* a small, long-tailed parrot.

par·al'de·hyde" (pə-ral'də-hīd") *n.* a liquid used as a sedative and hypnotic.

par'al·lax" (par'ə-laks") *n.* the apparent shifting of an object when the observer's position changes.

par'al·lel" (par'ə-lel") *adj.* **1,** of lines or planes, never intersecting; equidistant at all points. **2,** similar; analogous. —*n.* **1,** something parallel or similar to another. **2,** comparison. **3,** one of the imaginary lines indicating degrees of latitude. —*v.t.* **1,** compare. **2,** run parallel to. **3,** correspond to. —**par'al·lel"ism,** *n.* —**parallel circuit,** a circuit in which each device receives its current independently of others on the same circuit.

par"al·lel'e·pi"ped (-ə-pī'pid) *n.* a solid figure with six sides, all parallelograms.

par″al·lel′o·gram″ (-ə-gram″) *n.* a quadrilateral whose opposite sides are parallel.

pa·ral′y·sis (pə-ral′ə-sis) *n.* complete or partial loss of power to feel or move. **—par″a·lyt′ic** (par″ə-lit′ik) *adj. & n.*

par′a·lyze (par′ə-līz″) *v.t.* **1,** affect with paralysis. **2,** render helpless or ineffective.

par″a·me′ci·um (pa″rə-mē′shē-əm) *n.* [*pl.* **-ci·a** (-shē-ə)] a one-celled, slipper-shaped protozoan.

par″a·med′i·cal *adj. & n.* (pert. to) a person who assists a physician.

pa·ram′e·ter (pə-ram′ə-tər) *n.* (*Math.*) a variable quantity whose values depend on the special case.

par″a·mil′i·tar″y *adj.* being supplementary to regular military forces.

par′a·mount (par′ə-mownt″) *adj.* superior to all others.

par′a·mour (par′ə-mûr″) *n.* a lover, esp. an illicit one.

par′ang *n.* a large, heavy knife used by Malays.

par″a·noi′a (par″ə-noi′ə) *n.* insanity marked by delusions of grandeur or persecution. **—par″a·noid, par″a·noi′ac,** *n.*

par′a·pet (par′ə-pət) *n.* **1,** (*Mil.*) a rampart; breastwork. **2,** a low wall at the edge of a balcony, bridge, etc.

par″a·pher·nal′ia (par″ə-fər-nāl′yə) *n.pl.* **1,** personal belongings. **2,** equipment; trappings.

par′a·phrase″ (par′ə-frāz″) *n.* an expression of the same meaning in other words. **—v.t. & i.** restate.

par″a·ple′gi·a (par″ə-plē′jē-ə) *n.* paralysis from the waist down. **—par″a·pleg′ic** (-plēj′ik) *n. & adj.*

par″a·pro·fes′sion·al *adj. & n.* (pert. to) one who assists a professional.

par″a·psy·chol′o·gy *n.* the study of phenomena not explainable by accepted laws of nature.

par′a·sang (par′ə-sang″) *n.* an ancient Persian measure, about 3½ miles.

par′a·site″ (par′ə-sīt″) *n.* a person, animal, or plant that lives in or on or at the expense of another (called the *host*). **—par″a·sit′ic** (-sit′ik), **par″a·sit′i·cal,** *adj.*

par′a·sol″ (par′ə-sâl″) *n.* a light umbrella used as a dainty sunshade.

par″a·thy′roid *adj.* designating any of four small hormone-producing glands beside the thyroid gland. **—n.** an extract of these glands, or their secretions, used in treating tetany.

par′a·troop″er (par′ə-troo″pər) *n.* a soldier dropped by parachute in enemy territory. **—par′a·troops″,** *n.pl.*

par′a·vane″ (par′ə-vān″) *n.* a device to protect vessels against mines.

par′boil″ (pär′boil″) *v.t.* **1,** cook partially in boiling water. **2,** overheat.

par′cel (pär′səl) *n.* **1,** a package. **2,** a small piece, as of land. **3,** an integral part: *part and parcel.* **—v.t.** separate and dole out. **—parcel post,** postal transmission of packages.

parch (pärch) *v.t. & i.* **1,** dry out by heat. **2,** shrivel; dry up.

par·chee′si (pär-chē′zē) *n.* a game resembling backgammon, played with counters and dice. Also, **pa·chi′si, par·chi′si.**

parch′ment (-mənt) *n.* sheep- or goatskin prepared to take writing; paper resembling it; a document written on it.

pard (pärd) *n.* (*Slang*) partner.

par′don (pär′dən) *v.t.* excuse; forgive, as a person or offense; free (a person) from penalty. **—n.** a release from punishment. **—par′don·a·ble,** *adj.*

pare (pâr) *v.t.* **1,** cut or shave off the skin or edge of. **2,** reduce.

par″e·gor′ic (par″ə-gor′ik) *n.* a medicine for relieving pain or diarrhea. **—adj.** relieving pain.

par′ent (pâr′ənt) *n.* **1,** a father or mother; a progenitor. **2,** a cause; source. **—par′ent·age** (-tij) *n.* **—pa·ren′tal** (pə-ren′təl) *adj.* **—par′ent·hood″,** *n.*

pa·ren′the·sis (pə-ren′thə-sis) *n.* [*pl.* **-ses** (-sēz)] **1,** an inserted explanatory word, clause, etc. **2,** either of the curves ( ) enclosing insertions. **—par″en·thet′i·cal,** *adj.*

pa·re′sis (pə-rē′sis) *n.* partial paralysis. **—pa·ret′ic** (-ret′ik) *adj. & n.*

par ex″cel·lence′ (pär ek″sə-läns′) (*Fr.*) above all others.

par·fait′ (pär-fā′) *n.* **1,** a frozen dessert of whipped cream, egg, etc. **2,** ice cream in a glass with a flavored syrup and whipped cream.

pa·ri′ah (pə-rī′ə) *n.* an outcast.

pa·ri′e·tal (pə-rī′ə-təl) *adj.* **1,** pert. to a wall-like structure, esp. the sides of the skull. **2,** resident within, or having charge over, the walls or buildings of a college. **—n.** (*pl.*) the rules of conduct for a dormitory, etc.

par″i·mu′tu·el (par″ē-mū′choo-əl) *n.* (usually *pl.*) a method of dividing the money bet on horse races, etc., among winning bettors.

par′ing (pâr′ing) *n.* something pared off; slice; peel.

Paris green a poisonous green powder used as a pigment and as an insecticide.

par′ish *n.* **1,** the district under a clergyman's care. **2,** a county.

pa·rish′ion·er (pə-rish′ən-ər) *n.* a member of a church parish.

par′i·ty (par′ə-tē) *n.* equality; equality with or equivalence to a fixed value or standard.

park (pärk) *n.* **1,** ground set apart for public use, esp. for recreation or sports. **2,** the grounds adjoining a country house. —*v.t. & i.* leave (an automobile) temporarily on a street or in a lot. —**industrial park,** an area zoned for industrial and business use and characterized by coordinated plant design.

par′ka (pär′kə) *n.* a shirtlike coat made of fur or fleece-lined woolen, usually hooded.

Par′kin·son′s disease (pär′kin-sunz) a progressive nervous disorder.

park′way″ *n.* a wide, landscaped thoroughfare.

par′lance (pär′ləns) *n.* way of speaking; language.

par·lay′ (pär-lā′) *v.t.&i.* bet a previously won bet and its winnings. —*n.* (pär′lā) such a bet.

par′ley (pär′lē) *n.* a conference, esp. between hostile parties. —*v.i.* confer; hold a parley.

par′lia·ment (pär′lə-mənt) *n.* a legislative assembly, esp. (*cap.*) of Great Britain.

par″lia·men′ta·ry (-men′tə-rē) *adj.* pert. to the rules of procedure of legislative bodies. —**par″lia·men·tar′i·an** (-tär′ē-ən) *n.* one versed in such procedure.

par′lor (pär′lər) *n.* **1,** a reception or lounging room. **2,** a private meeting or dining room in a hotel, etc.; a shop. Also, **par′lour.** —**parlor car,** an extra-fare railroad car.

par′lor·maid″ *n.* housemaid.

par′lous (pär′ləs) *adj.* dangerous.

Par″me·san′ cheese (pär″mə-zän′) a dry Ital. cheese made from skim milk.

Par·nas′sus (pär-nas′əs) *n.* a center of, or inspiration for, poetic or artistic works.

pa·ro′chi·al (pə-rō′kē-əl) *adj.* **1,** pert. to a parish. **2,** local; provincial. —**parochial school,** one maintained by a church parish, esp. Rom. Cath.

par′o·dy (par′ə-dē) *n.* a humorous imitation of an author′s or artist′s style; a burlesque. —*v.t.* imitate (an author, etc.) in a derisive manner. —**par′o·dist,** *n.*

pa·role′ (pə-rōl′) *n.* **1,** a prisoner′s promise not to escape. **2,** a conditional release from prison. —*v.t.* release on parole.

pa·rot′id (pə-rot′id) *adj.* **1,** designating either of two salivary glands adjacent to the ears. **2,** near the ears.

par′ox·ysm (par′ək-siz-əm) *n.* a spasm; violent outburst.

par·quet′ (pär-kā′) *n.* **1,** [also, **par′quet-**

ry (-ket-rē)] inlaid flooring of different woods. **2,** the main floor of a theater.

par′ri·cide″ (par′ə-sīd″) *n.* the killer or killing of one′s parent.

par′rot (par′ət) *n.* **1,** a tropical bird of brilliant plumage, capable of imitating speech. **2,** one who echoes the words of another. —*v.t.* imitate.

par′ry (par′ē) *v.t.* turn aside; ward off. —*n.* a warding off.

parse (pärs) *v.t.* resolve (a sentence) into its grammatical parts.

par′sec″ (pär′sek″) *n.* a unit of distance, about 3.26 light years.

Par′see (pär′sē) *n.* a member of a Zoroastrian sect in India.

par′si·mo″ny (pär′sə-mō″nē) *n.* excessive frugality. —**par″si·mo′ni·ous,** *adj.* stingy.

pars′ley (pärs′lē) *n.* an herb with aromatic leaves used as a garnish and seasoning.

pars′nip (pärs′nip) *n.* a plant with a white, edible root.

par′son (pär′sən) *n.* a clergyman; preacher.

par′son·age (-ij) *n.* the residence of a clergyman, provided by the church.

part (pärt) *n.* **1,** a piece of a whole; a section; an essential element, as of a machine. **2,** a person′s share or duty. **3,** a role, as in a play. **4,** in music, the melody assigned to any voice or instrument. **5,** a side in a dispute. **6,** (*pl.*) abilities. **7,** a division in the hair. —*v.t.* **1,** divide into sections. **2,** separate; hold apart. —*v.i.* **1,** become separated or sundered. **2,** (with *with*) let go. —**part′i·ble,** *adj.* —**part′ing,** *n.* —**part and parcel,** an integral part. —**part of speech,** a classification of the form or function of a word, as noun, adjective, etc. —**part song,** a choral composition, usu. in four parts and unaccompanied.

par·take′ (pär-tāk′) *v.i.* [-**took′,** -**tak′en**] have or take a share.

par·terre′ (pär-tär′) *n.* **1,** the rear of a theater′s main floor. **2,** an ornamental pattern of flower beds.

par″the·no·gen′e·sis (pär″thə-nō-jen′ə-sis) *n.* reproduction from an unfertilized egg.

par′tial (pär′shəl) *adj.* **1,** affecting a part only; not total. **2,** (with *to*) having a liking for. **3,** biased. —*n.* an overtone. —**par″ti·al′i·ty** (-shē-al′ə-tē) *n.*

par·tic′i·pant (pär-tis′i-pənt) *n.* one who participates.

par·tic′i·pate″ (pär-tis′i-pāt″) *v.i.* have a share; take part in something. —**par·tic″i·pa′tion,** *n.*

par′ti·ci″ple (pär′tə-sip″əl) *n.* a part of a

verb showing characteristics of both verb and adjective. **—par″ti·cip′i·al,** (-ē-əl) *adj.*

par′ti·cle (pär′tə-kəl) *n.* **1,** a minute piece or amount. **2,** a part of speech, as an article *(the),* conjunction, etc.

par″ti·col″ored (pär-tē-kul″ərd) *adj.* variegated.

par·tic′u·lar (pər-tik′yə-lər) *adj.* **1,** belonging or relating to a single person, place, or thing; not general. **2,** apart from others; separate. **3,** unusual; notable. **4,** detailed; careful. **5,** nice; fastidious. **—n.** an item; detail. **—par·tic″u·lar′i·ty** (-lar′ə-tē) *n.* **—par·tic′u·lar·ize″,** *v.t.* specify in detail. **—par·tic′u·lar·ly,** *adv.* especially; specifically.

par·tic′u·late (pär-tik′yə-lət) *adj.* consisting of separate particles.

par′ti·san (pär′tə-zən) *n.* **1,** an adherent, often biased, of a party or cause. **2,** a guerrilla. **—adj.** **1,** pert. or belonging to a political party. **2,** biased. **—par′ti·san·ship,** *n.*

par·ti′tion (pär-tish′ən) *n.* **1,** division; separation. **2,** that which separates, esp. a dividing wall. **—v.t.** **1,** divide by a partition. **2,** divide into shares.

par′ti·tive (pär′ti-tiv) *adj.* **1,** serving to divide into parts. **2,** indicating a part, as *some.* **—n.** a partitive word.

part′ly (pärt′lē) *adv.* in part; in some degree; not wholly.

part′ner (pärt′nər) *n.* one who is associated with another, as in business, dancing, marriage, etc.

part′ner·ship″ *n.* **1,** the state of being partners. **2,** a business firm of partners, not incorporated.

par′tridge (pär′trij) *n.* a game bird; the quail; ruffed grouse.

part-′time″ *adj.* requiring less than the usual working time.

par″tu·ri′tion (pär″tyū-rish′ən) *n.* childbirth. **—par·tur′i·ent,** *adj.*

par′ty (pär′tē) *n.* **1,** a body of persons; a detachment of troops; an organization of persons acting together politically. **2,** a person concerned in some action, as a contract; *(Colloq.)* a person. **3,** a social gathering. **—party line, 1,** a telephone line shared by different houses. **2,** the dogma of a political party. **—party wall,** a wall common to two houses.

par′ve·nu″ (pär′və-nū″) *n.* an upstart; one newly rich.

par′vis (pär′vis) *n.* an outer court, front yard, porch, or portico of a church, palace, etc.; a room over such a porch.

pas (pä) *n. (Fr.)* a step in dancing; a dance.

pas′chal (pas′kəl) *adj.* pert. to Easter, or to the Passover.

pa·sha′ (pə-shä′) *n.* a Turkish title of authority. Also, **pa·cha′.** **—pa·sha′lik** (pə-shä′lik) *n.* territory governed by a pasha.

pas′quin (pas′kwin) *n.* a lampoon; satire. Also, **pas″quin·ade′** (-ād′).

pass (pás) *v.i.* **1,** move from one place or condition to another. **2,** vanish; (often with *away* or *on*) die. **3,** be enacted, as a law. **4,** undergo a test or pursue a course of study successfully. **5,** occur; happen. **6,** (with *on*) pronounce an opinion. **7,** go by unnoticed. **8,** be accepted at face value. **9,** take no action; decline to bid. **—v.t. 1,** go by or over. **2,** spend, as time. **3,** undergo successfully. **4,** gain the approval of; give legal effect to. **5,** utter; pronounce. **6,** hand over; transfer. **—n. 1,** an act of passing. **2,** a defile in the mountains. **3,** state of affairs, as a *sorry pass.* **4,** a free ticket; *(Mil.)* a written leave of absence. **5,** *(Slang)* a feinted blow. **6,** *(Slang)* an amorous advance. **—bring to pass,** cause to happen. **—come to pass,** happen. **—pass muster,** be found up to standard. **—pass out,** *(Colloq.)* faint. **—pass the buck,** shift responsibility.

pass′a·ble *adj.* **1,** navigable; traversable. **2,** only fairly good.

pas″sa·cag′li·a (päs″sə-kä′lyə) *n.* a musical composition on a ground bass.

pas′sage (pas′ij) *n.* **1,** a passing or moving. **2,** a means of passing; a channel, alley, etc. **3,** a voyage, usu. by sea; accommodations for it. **4,** an excerpt from a book, speech, etc. **5,** enactment, as of a law. **6,** an interchange, as of vows, blows, etc. **7,** lapse, as of time.

pas′sage·way″ *n.* passage (def. 2).

pass′book″ *n.* a bank book.

pas·sé′ (på-sā′) *adj.* outmoded.

pas′sel (pas′əl) *n. (Dial.)* a large number.

pas′sen·ger (pas′ən-jər) *n.* a traveler on some form of conveyance. **—passenger-mile,** *n.* one passenger transported one mile.

passe″ par·tout′ (passpär-too′) *(Fr.)* **1,** a means by which one can pass anywhere, as a master key. **2,** a picture mounting.

pass″er-by′ *n. [pl.* **pass″ers-by′]** one who happens to go by.

pas′ser·ine (pas′ər-in) *adj. & n.* pert. to or belonging to the order of perching birds, embracing more than half of all birds.

pass-′fail′ *adj.* of a grading system employing only two levels of achievement, pass or fail.

pas′sim (pas′im) *adv. (Lat.)* at different places; here and there.

pass′ing *n.* death. **—adj. 1,** now happening; current. **2,** cursory. **3,** fleeting. **—passing note,** *(Music)* a transitional, unaccented note, not a part of the harmony.

pas'sion (pash'ən) n. 1, intense emotion: anger; rage; ardent love; zeal; enthusiasm. 2, the object of admiration. 3, (cap.) the sufferings of Christ in his last days, in preparation for the Crucifixion. —**pas'sion-ate** (-ət) adj. —**Passion play, 1**, a dramatic representation of scenes from the Passion of Jesus. 2, similar dramatic treatment of the suffering and death of a famous religious or spiritual leader.

pas'sive (pas'iv) adj. 1, unresisting; not opposing. 2, not acting, but acted upon; (Gram.) naming that form of a transitive verb in which the subject is acted upon. —**pas'sive-ness**, n.

pas-siv'i-ty (pə-siv'ə-tè) n. unresisting acceptance.

pass'key" n. a master key.

Pass'o"ver n. the feast of unleavened bread (Ex. 12).

pass'port" n. 1, official permission to travel. 2, a means to an end. 3, a document of identification.

pass'word" n. a secret word to distinguish friend from foe or to prove authorization to enter.

past (pàst) adj. 1, gone by in time. 2, just gone by. 3, no longer in office. 4, (Gram.) indicating a time gone by. —n. 1, bygone time; events of that time. 2, a person's past history, esp. a discreditable one. —prep. beyond in time, position, or condition. —adv. by.

pas'ta (päs'tə) n. a dough of flour and water, shaped, and used dry.

paste (pàst) n. 1, an adhesive substance, usually one containing starch. 2, dough for pastry or macaroni, etc. 3, a material ground to a creamy consistency. 4, a compound used for making artificial gems. —v.t. 1, cause to adhere with paste. 2, (Slang) wallop.

paste'board" n. 1, a board made from paper pasted or pressed together. 2, (Slang) a ticket or playing card. —adj. flimsy; unsubstantial.

pas-tel' (pas-tel') n. a pale and light shade of color; a drawing with pastel crayons.

pas'tern (pas'tərn) n. the part of a horse's foot between the fetlock and the hoof.

pas'teur-ize" (pas'tə-rīz") v.t. partially sterilize a liquid, as milk, by heating it. —**pas"teur-i-za'tion**, n.

pas-tiche' (pas-tēsh') n. a medley, combining various works or styles; potpourri. Also, **pas-tic'cio** (-tē'chō).

pas-tille' (pas-tēl') n. 1, a cone of incense. 2, a medicated lozenge.

pas'time" (pàs'tīm") n. an agreeable occupation; amusement.

pas'tor (pàs'tər) n. a minister in charge of a parish; a clergyman. —**pas'tor-ate** (-ət) n.

pas'tor-al (-əl) adj. 1, pert. to the duties of a pastor. 2, pert. to shepherds or country life. —n. a work, esp. a poem, dealing with country life.

pas"to-rale' (pas"tə-räl') n. a musical composition suggestive of rustic life.

pas-tra'mi (pəs-trä'mè) n. smoked, highly seasoned beef.

pas'try (pàs'trè) n. food with a shortened crust, as pies, patties, etc.

pas'ture (pàs'chər) n. grassland for grazing cattle. —v.t. put to graze. —**pas'tur-age** (-ij) n.

past'y (pàs'tè) adj. 1, of or like paste. 2, pale. —n. 1, a meat pie. 2, a patch used by exotic dancers to cover the nipple. —**past'i-ness**, n.

pat v.t. [**pat'ted, -ting**] tap or stroke gently with the hand. —n. 1, a light blow. 2, a small molded mass. —adj. [**pat'ter, -test**] apt. —adv. exactly.

pat-'a-cake" (pat'ə-kāk") n. a children's game played to a nursery rhyme. Also, **pat'ty-cake"**.

patch (pach) n. 1, a piece of cloth, metal, etc., used to cover a hole or worn place. 2, a small piece, as a plot of ground. —v.t. 1, mend with a patch. 2, (with up) repair; reconcile. —**patch test**, a skin test for tuberculosis. —**patch'y**, adj.

patch'board" n. a board allowing interconnection of various devices in different combinations.

patch'cord" n. an electrical wire used for connections on a patchboard.

patch'work" n. something made up of fragments of different kinds, colors, or shapes.

pate (pàt) n. the top of the head.

pâ-té' (pä-tā') n. 1, an appetizer made of chopped liver. 2, a pasty (def. 1). —**pâté de foie gras** (-də-fwä-grä') a paste made of fat goose livers.

pa-tel'la (pə-tel'ə) n. the kneecap.

pat'en (pat'ən) n. the plate holding consecrated bread.

pat'ent (pat'ənt; pā'-) n. an official document (letters patent) granting a privilege, esp. a temporary monopoly to an inventor. —adj. 1, open for all to read; plain; obvious. 2, patented. —v.t. obtain a patent for. —**pat"ent-ee'** (pat"ən-tē') n. one to whom a patent is issued. —**patent leather**, a leather or coated fabric with a hard, glossy surface. —**patent medicine**, a packaged medicine with patented name.

pa-ter'nal (pə-tēr'nəl) adj. 1, fatherly. 2, inherited from, or related through, a father.

pa·ter′nal·ism (-iz-əm) *n.* excessive governmental regulation. —**pa·ter″nal·is′tic,** *adj.* —**pa·ter″nal·is′ti·cal·ly,** *adv.*

pa·ter′ni·ty (pə-tēr′nə-tē) *n.* male parentage; fatherhood.

pa′ter·nos″ter (pā′tər-nos″tər) *n.* a prayer, esp. the Lord's Prayer.

path (páth) *n.* **1,** a footway; any road. **2,** course; track. —**path′way″,** *n.*

pa·thet′ic (pə-thet′ik) *adj.* exciting pity. —**pa·thet′i·cal·ly,** *adv.* —**pathetic fallacy,** ascription of human attributes to inanimate objects.

path′find″er *n.* a pioneer.

-path·ic (path-ik) *suf.* disease.

path·o- (path-ə) *pref.* disease.

path′o·gen′ (path′ə-jən) *n.* a cause of disease. —**path″o·gen′ic** (path″ə-jen′ik) *adj.* causing disease.

pa·thol′o·gy (pə-thol′ə-jē) *n.* the science of the nature and origin of disease. —**path″o·log′i·cal,** *adj.* —**pa·thol′o·gist,** *n.*

pa′thos (pā′thos) *n.* a quality that evokes pity or sadness.

-path·y (pə-thē) *suf.* **1,** feeling. **2,** disease.

pa′tience (pā′shəns) *n.* **1,** endurance of pain or provocation without complaint. **2,** the power to wait calmly. **3,** perseverance. **4,** (*Cards*) solitaire.

pa′tient (pā′shənt) *adj.* having patience. —*n.* a person under medical care.

pat′i·na (pat′ə-nə) *n.* a film that forms on a surface, esp. of bronze; a mellowing due to age.

pa′ti·o″ (pá′tē-ō″) *n.* a courtyard.

pat′ois (pat′wä) *n.* a dialect.

patri- (pat-rē) *pref.* father.

pa′tri·arch″ (pā′trē-ärk″) *n.* **1,** a father or ruler of a tribe. **2,** a high church dignitary. **3,** a venerable old man. —**pa″tri·ar′chal,** *adj.* —**pa′tri·ar″chate** (-kit) *n.* —**pa″tri·ar″chy,** *n.* government by the father or fathers.

pa·tri′cian (pə-trish′ən) *n.* an aristocrat. —*adj.* of noble birth.

pat′ri·cide″ (pat′rə-sīd″) *n.* the killer or killing of one's father. —**pat″ri·cid′al** (-əl) *adj.*

pat′ri·mon″y (pat′rə-mō″nē) *n.* **1,** an inheritance from any ancestor. **2,** the endowment of a church. —**pat″ri·mo′ni·al,** *adj.*

pa′tri·ot (pā′trē-ət) *n.* one who loves and defends his country. —**pa″tri·ot′ic** (-ot′ik) *adj.* —**pa″tri·ot′i·cal·ly,** *adv.* —**pa′tri·ot·ism,** *n.*

pa·trol′ (pə-trōl) *v.t.* & *i.* [**patrolled′, -trol′ling**] traverse as a guard. —*n.* **1,** the act of patrolling; a person or troop that patrols. **2,** a unit of Boy Scouts, etc.

—**pa·trol′man,** *n.* a policeman. —**patrol wagon,** a police vehicle for transporting prisoners; Black Maria.

pa′tron (pā′trən) *n.* **1,** an influential supporter or donor. **2,** a guardian saint. **3,** a regular customer of a shop. —**pa′tron·ess,** *n.fem.*

pa′tron·age (-ij) *n.* **1,** support; favor. **2,** customers. **3,** the power to appoint jobholders.

pa′tron·ize″ (-īz″) *v.t.* **1,** give one's support or custom to. **2,** treat with condescension.

pat″ro·nym′ic (pat″rə-nim′ik) *n.* a family name. —*adj.* being or pert. to a family name.

pat′sy (pat′sē) *n.* (*Slang*) the unwitting victim of a scheme, plot, or practical joke; a dupe; gull.

pat′ten (pat′ən) *n.* a shoe with a wooden sole.

pat′ter (pat′ər) *v.i.* **1,** make quick, short taps; run with short steps. **2,** talk glibly. —*v.t.* repeat mechanically. —*n.* **1,** a succession of light taps. **2,** rapid, glib speech.

pat′tern (pat′ərn) *n.* **1,** an example; ideal. **2,** a model to be copied. **3,** a decorative design. —*v.t.* (with *after*) make conform (to some pattern).

pat′ty (pat′ē) *n.* **1,** a cup-shaped shell of pastry. **2,** a shaped mound of chopped meat.

pat′ty-cake″ (pat′ē-kāk″) *n.* pat-a-cake.

pau′ci·ty (pâ′sə-tē) *n.* smallness of quantity or number.

paunch (pânch) *n.* the belly.

pau′per (pâ′pər) *n.* a destitute person; a recipient of charity. —**pau′per·ism,** *n.* —**pau′per·ize″** (-īz″) *v.t.* impoverish.

pause (pâz) *n.* an interval of silence or inaction. —*v.i.* stop, hesitate, or linger for a time.

pav′an (pav′ən) *n.* a slow, stately dance. Also, **pav′ane.**

pave (pāv) *v.t.* **1,** cover with bricks, cement, etc. **2,** facilitate. —**pave′ment, pav′-ing,** *n.* a paved surface, as a sidewalk.

pa·vil′ion (pə-vil′yən) *n.* a light building or tent for recreation, etc.

paw (pâ) *n.* an animal's foot with nails or claws. —*v.t.* & *i.* **1,** strike or scrape with the foot. **2,** touch, stroke, or handle rudely.

pawl (pâl) *n.* a short pivoted bar acting as a brake in a machine.

pawn (pân) *n.* **1,** the chess piece of lease value; hence, a person used as a tool. **2,** a pledge; something pawned. —*v.t.* deposit as security for a loan. —**pawn′bro″ker,** *n.* a person licensed to lend money on pledged property. —**pawn′shop″,** *n.*

pay (pā) *v.t.* [**paid** (pād), **pay′ing**] **1,** compensate (a person) for services rendered or goods supplied. **2**, discharge, as a debt; hand over, as money. **3**, render, as a compliment. **4**, be profitable to. —*v.i.* **1**, discharge a debt. **2**, be advantageous. —*n.* **1**, wages; salary. **2**, employment for gain. —**pay'a·ble**, *adj. & n.* (amount) due. —**pay dirt**, **1**, earth containing a remunerative quantity of gold. **2**, (*Colloq.*) something profitable. —**pay out**, **1**, expend. **2**, let out. —**pay station**, or **telephone**, a public coin-operated telephone.

pay'day" *n.* the day on which employees receive their pay.

pay·ee' (pā-ē') *n.* one who receives payment.

pay'load" *n.* the weight a vehicle carries in freight or paying passengers.

pay'mas"ter *n.* the official who pays laborers, troops, etc.

pay'ment (-mənt) *n.* **1**, act of paying. **2**, that which is paid.

pay'off" *n.* (*Slang*) a final reckoning.

pay·o'la (pā-ō'lə) *n.* a bribe paid to receive a certain service.

pay'roll" *n.* a list of persons to be paid (wages), or the wages paid.

pea (pē) *n.* the round, edible green seed of a leguminous vine; the vine. —**pea jacket**, a heavy woolen coat worn by sailors.

peace (pēs) *n.* **1**, freedom from war or civil disorder. **2**, a contract to end war. **3**, harmony in human relations. **4**, tranquility; quietness. —**peace'a·ble**, *adj.* not quarrelsome; loving peace. —**Peace Corps**, a volunteer organization of the U.S. government that sends skilled persons abroad to help underdeveloped countries. —**peace officer**, a policeman, constable, sheriff, etc. —**peace pipe**, the calumet.

peace'ful (-fəl) *adj.* **1**, quiet; tranquil. **2**, peaceable. —**peace'ful·ness**, *n.*

peace'nik *n.* (*Colloq.*) an advocate of the cause of peace.

peace'time" *n.* a period of not being at war.

peach (pēch) *n.* **1**, a round juicy fruit with a fuzzy, red-tinged skin; the tree bearing it. **2**, a yellowish-red color. **3**, (*Slang*) a person highly approved of. —*v.i.* (*Slang*) inform.

peach'y (-ė) *adj.* **1**, peachlike. **2**, (*Slang*) excellent. —**peach'i·ness**, *n.*

pea'cock" (pē'kok") *n.* a male bird with long brilliant tail feathers. —**pea'fowl"**, *n.* a peacock or peahen. —**pea'hen"**, *n. fem.*

peak (pēk) *n.* **1**, the pointed end of anything. **2**, a steep mountain. **3**, a visor. **4**, the highest point. —*v.i.* look sickly; be-

come emaciated. —**peak'ed** (-id) *adj.* thin; sickly.

peal (pēl) *n.* the loud ringing of a bell, or of thunder, laughter, etc. —*v.t. & i.* ring.

pea'nut" (pē'nut") *n.* **1**, a plant of the pea family whose pods ripen under ground; its edible nutlike seed. **2**, a small person. —**peanut butter**, a paste made of ground peanuts.

pear (pār) *n.* the juicy fruit of a tree related to the apple; the tree.

pearl (pėrl) *n.* **1**, a hard lustrous body found in the shells of certain mollusks and valued as a gem. **2**, a pale, bluish-gray color. **3**, a size of type. —**pearl'y**, *adj.* like pearl; lustrous.

pear'main" (-mān") *n.* a variety of apple.

peas'ant (pez'ənt) *n.* a countryman; rustic. —**peas'ant·ry** (-rė) *n.*

peat (pēt) *n.* partly decomposed vegetable matter found in bogs, used, when dried, for fuel.

peb'ble (peb'əl) *n.* a small stone worn smooth by water. —*v.t.* grain, as leather. —**peb'bly**, *adj.*

pe·can' (pi-kán') *n.* a species of hickory tree or its thin-shelled nut.

pec"ca·dil'lo (pek"ə-dil'ō) *n.* a trifling offense.

pec'cant (pek'ənt) *adj.* sinning; guilty; causing offense. —**pec'can·cy** (-kən-sė) *n.*

pec'ca·ry (pek'ə-rė) *n.* a hoglike animal of tropical America.

peck (pek) *n.* **1**, a unit of capacity: in dry measure, 8 quarts or one-fourth of a bushel. **2**, a quick, sharp stroke, as with a bird's beak or a pointed tool. **3**, (*Colloq.*) a kiss. —*v.t. & i.* **1**, strike or pick up with, or as with, the beak. **2**, nag. **3**, eat in bits. **4**, (*Colloq.*) kiss. —**peck'ing order**, (*Colloq.*) a hierarchy.

pec'tin (pek'tin) *n.* a substance that causes jelling. —**pec'tic**, *adj.*

pec'to·ral (pek'tə-rəl) *adj.* pert. to the chest.

pec'u·late" (pek'yə-lāt") *v.t. & i.* embezzle. —**pec"u·la'tion**, *n.*

pe·cul'iar (pi-kūl'yər) *adj.* **1**, characteristic of or belonging exclusively to. **2**, special. **3**, odd; queer. —**pe·cu"li·ar'i·ty**, *n.*

pe·cu'ni·ar"y (pi-kū'nė-er"ė) *adj.* pert. to, or consisting of, money.

ped'a·gogue" (ped'ə-gog") *n.* a schoolteacher. Also, **ped'a·gog"**. —**ped'a·go"gy** (-gō"jė) *n.* —**ped"a·gog'i·cal** (-goj'i-kəl) *adj.*

ped'al (ped'əl) *adj.* pert. to the foot. —*n.* a lever worked by the foot, as of a bicycle, organ, etc. —*v.t. & i.* work the pedals (of).

ped'ant (ped'ənt) *n.* one who parades or overvalues his learning. —**pe·dan'tic** (pə-dan'tik) *adj.* —**pe·dan'ti·cal·ly,** *adv.* —**ped'-ant·ry** (-rē) *n.*

ped'dle (ped'əl) *v.i. & t.* sell from house to house. —**ped'dler,** *n.*

ped'er·as"ty (ped'ə-ras"tē) *n.* anal intercourse, esp. between man and boy.

ped'es·tal (ped'is-təl) *n.* a supporting base, as of a column.

pe·des'tri·an (pə-des'trē-ən) *n.* one who walks. —*adj.* **1,** walking. **2,** prosaic; unimaginative.

pe"di·at'rics (pē"dē-at'riks) *n.* (*Med.*) the medical care and treatment of children. —**pe"di·a·tri'cian** (pē"dyə-trish'ən) *n.*

ped'i·cab" (ped'i-kab") *n.* a foot-propelled vehicle for hire.

ped'i·cure" (ped'ə-kyûr") *n.* the care of the feet.

ped'i·gree" (ped'ə-grē") *n.* **1,** lineage; descent. **2,** a genealogical record. —**ped'i-greed",** *adj.* of known and pure breeding.

ped'i·ment (ped'ə-ment) *n.* a triangular gable over the front of a building.

ped'lar (ped'lər) *n.* peddler.

pe"do·don'tia (pē"dō-don'shə) *n.* dentistry as applied to children.

pe·dom'e·ter (pi-dom'ə-tər) *n.* a watch-shaped instrument for recording steps taken in walking.

peek (pēk) *v.i.* peep slyly. —*n.* a sly peep. —**peek'a·boo"** (-ə-boo") *n.* a child's peeking game.

peel (pēl) *v.t.* strip the rind, skin, or bark from. —*v.i.* become stripped. —*n.* [also, **peel'ing**] the rind.

peen (pēn) *n.* the shaped top of a hammer's head.

peep (pēp) *v.i.* **1,** begin to appear. **2,** peer slyly or furtively. **3,** chirp; cheep. —*n.* **1,** a sly or furtive look. **2,** a glimpse. **3,** the cry of a small bird. **4,** (*Slang*) a military automobile, larger than a jeep. —**peep'er,** *n.* a young frog. —**peep'hole",** *n.*

peer (pir) *n.* **1,** an equal; match. **2,** a nobleman. —*v.i.* look sharply or curiously. —**peer'age,** *n.* the nobility. —**peer'ess,** *n.fem.* —**peer'less,** *adj.* matchless.

peeve (pēv) (*Colloq.*) *v.t. & i.* make or become ill-tempered. —*n.* an annoyance.

pee'vish (pē'vish) *adj.* fretful; irritable. —**pee'vish·ness,** *n.*

pee'wee" (pē'wē") *n.* (*Dial.*) **1,** a small child, person, or animal; a runt. **2,** a small marble.

peg *n.* **1,** a tapering pin of wood or metal. **2,** (*Brit.*) a drink of liquor. —*v.t.* [**pegged, peg'ging**] **1,** fasten or mark with pegs. **2,** set at a certain price. —**peg leg,** a wooden leg. —**take down a peg,** humble.

peg'board" *n.* a perforated board used for hanging things with pegs.

peign·oir' (pān-wär') *n.* a woman's dressing gown; duster.

pe"jo·ra'tion (pej"ə-rā'shən) *n.* **1,** deterioration. **2,** a change for the worse in the meaning of a word.

pe·jo'ra·tive (pi-jôr'ə-tiv) *adj.* disparaging; depreciating. —*n.* a disparaging term.

Pe"king·ese" (pē"kə-nēz") *n.* a small Chinese dog.

pe'koe (pē'kō) *n.* a black India tea.

pel'age (pel'ij) *n.* the hair, fur, or other soft covering of a mammal.

pe·lag'ic (pə-laj'ik) *adj.* marine; oceanic.

pel"er·ine' (pel"ə-rēn') *n.* a woman's cape with pointed ends.

pelf *n.* booty; money.

pel'i·can (pel'ə-kən) *n.* a large water bird with a pouch under its bill.

pel·la'gra (pə-lā'grə) *n.* a disease, characterized by dermatitis, affecting the nervous system, caused by deficient diet.

pel'let (pel'ət) *n.* a little ball of dough, lead, etc.; a pill.

pell-'mell' (pel'mel') *adv.* in confusion; headlong.

pel·lu'cid (pə-loo'sid) *adj.* **1,** clear; limpid. **2,** easily understood; perfectly clear.

pe·lo'ta (pe-lō'tə) *n.* jai alai.

pel"o·ton' (pel"ə-ton') *n.* a type of ornamental glass.

pelt *n.* **1,** a hide, esp. with fur. **2,** a blow; a beating down, as of rain. —*v.t.* assail with missiles. —*v.i.* **1,** beat violently. **2,** move rapidly.

pel'vis *n.* [*pl.* **-ves** (-vēz)] the basin-shaped group of bones that support the spine. —**pel'vic** (-vik) *adj.*

pem'mi·can (pem'ə-kən) *n.* a dried meat paste, made into cakes.

pen *n.* **1,** a small enclosure for animals. **2,** an instrument for writing with ink. —*v.t.* [**penned, pen'ning**] **1,** shut in; enclose. **2,** write. —**pen name,** a pseudonym.

pe'nal (pē'nəl) *adj.* pert. to or inflicting punishment. —**pe'nal·ize** (-īz") *v.t.* inflict a penalty upon.

pen'al·ty (pen'əl-tē) *n.* a punitive forfeit; punishment.

pen'ance (pen'əns) *n.* self-inflicted punishment for sin.

pe·na'tes (pə-nä'tēz) *n.pl.* the household gods of the ancient Romans.

pence (pens) *n.pl.* (*Brit.*) pennies.

pen'chant (pen'chənt) *n.* a strong inclination or predilection.

pen'cil (pen'səl) *n.* **1,** a cylinder, as of wood, enclosing a soft, solid substance for writing, marking, etc. **2,** rays of light diverging from or converging to a given point. —*v.t.* write, draw, or mark with, or as with, a pencil.

pend *v.i.* hang, as if balanced; await settlement.

pend′ant (pen′dənt) *n.* a hanging ornament.

pend′ent (pen′dənt) *adj.* **1,** hanging. **2,** pending. —**pend′den·cy,** *n.*

pen′du·lous (pen′jə-ləs) *adj.* hanging loosely. —**pen′du·lous·ness,** *n.*

pen′du·lum (pen′jə-ləm) *n.* a weight suspended on a swinging arm.

pen′e·trate″ (pen′i-trāt″) *v.t.* **1,** pierce into or through. **2,** enter and become part of; permeate. **3,** see into; understand. —*v.i.* enter and make way. —**pen′e·tra·ble,** *adj.* —**pen′e·tra″tive,** *adj.* keen. —**pen″e·tra′tion,** *n.*

pen′guin (peng′gwin) *n.* a flightless aquatic bird.

pen″i·cil′lin (pen″ə-sil′ən) *n.* a powerful, bacteria-killing substance obtained from a green mold (*penicillium*).

pen·in′su·la (pə-nin′sə-lə) *n.* a body of land almost surrounded by water. —**pen·in′su·lar,** *adj.*

pe′nis (pē′nis) *n.* the male organ through which sperm and urine are discharged.

pen′i·tent (pen′ə-tənt) *adj.* repentant; contrite. —*n.* a penitent person. —**pen′i·tence,** *n.* —**pen″i·ten′tial** (-ten′shəl) *adj.*

pen″i·ten′tia·ry (pen″ə-ten′shə-rē) *n.* a prison for criminals.

pen′knife″ *n.* a pocket knife.

pen′light″ *n.* a small flashlight.

pen′man (-mən) *n.* [*pl.* **-men**] one skilled in handwriting. —**pen′man·ship,** *n.* handwriting.

pen′nant (pen′ənt) *n.* a long, narrow flag, often one awarded to a victor.

pen′nate (pen′āt) *adj.* winged.

pen′non (pen′ən) *n.* a small triangular flag.

pen′ny (pen′ē) *n.* **1,** a copper coin worth one U.S. cent. **2,** (*Brit.*) formerly, one-twelfth of a shilling, now one-hundredth of a pound. —**pen′ni·less,** *adj.* destitute. —**penny arcade,** an amusement center. —**penny-wise and pound-foolish,** niggardly in unimportant matters. —**pretty penny,** a fairly large sum of money.

pen′ny-pinch″er *n.* a niggardly person.

pen′ny·roy″al *n.* **1,** a plant of the mint family. **2,** any of various herbs.

pen′ny·weight″ *n.* a measure of weight, one-twentieth of a troy ounce.

pe·nol′o·gy (pē-nol′ə-jē) *n.* the science of prison management. —**pe″no·log′i·cal** (pē″nə-loj′i-kəl) *adj.* —**pe·nol′o·gist,** *n.*

pen′sion (pen′shən) *n.* **1,** a regular payment for past services. **2,** (pän-sē-ân″) (*Fr.*) a boarding house. —*v.t.* retire and pay a pension to. —**pen′sion·er,** *n.* one who is pensioned.

pen′sive (pen′siv) *adj.* reflective; thoughtful. —**pen′sive·ness,** *n.*

pen′stock″ *n.* a trough or pipe for conveying water, as to a water wheel.

pent *adj.* (often with *up*) confined; shut up.

pen·ta- (pen-tə) *pref.* five.

pen′ta·cle (pen′tə-kəl) *n.* **1,** a five-pointed star. **2,** hexagram.

pen′ta·gon (pen′tə-gon) *n.* a five-sided figure. —**pen·tag′o·nal** (-tag′ə-nəl) *adj.*

pen·tam′e·ter (pen-tam′ə-tər) *n.* & *adj.* (a line of verse) having five metrical feet.

Pen′ta·teuch″ (pen′tə-tūk″) *n.* the first five books of the Bible.

Pen′te·cost″ (pen′tə-kâst″) *n.* a Christian festival, Whitsunday.

pent′house″ (pent′hows″) *n.* an apartment or house on the roof of a building.

pe·nu′che (pə-noo′chē) *n.* a kind of fudge.

pe′nult (pē′nult) *n.* the next-to-last syllable.

pe·nul′ti·mate (pi-nul′ti-mət) *adj.* next to last.

pe·num′bra (pi-num′brə) *n.* **1,** partial shadow. **2,** a fringe. **3,** the gray border around a sunspot. —**pe·num′bral,** *adj.*

pe·nur′i·ous (pə-nyûr′ē-əs) *adj.* stingy; miserly. —**pe·nur′i·ous·ness,** *n.*

pen′u·ry (pen′yə-rē) *n.* extreme poverty.

pe′on (pē′on) *n.* in Lat. Amer., a day-laborer. —**pe′on·age,** *n.* virtual slavery; serfdom.

pe′o·ny (pē′ə-nē) *n.* a plant bearing large, globular flowers.

peo′ple (pē′pəl) *n.* **1,** a whole of a particular body or group of persons. **2,** (*n.pl.*) the populace; the masses. **3,** (*n. pl.*) (*Colloq.*) persons; relatives. —*v.t.* populate.

pep (*Slang*) *n.* energy; vigor. —*v.t.* [**pepped, pep′ping**] (with *up*) stimulate. —**pep′py,** *adj.* —**pep talk,** a brief speech designed to excite or encourage the listener.

pep′lum (pep′ləm) *n.* a short fitted overskirt.

pep′per (pep′ər) *n.* **1,** a pungent spice. **2,** a garden plant or its edible fruit. —*v.t.* **1,** season with pepper. **2,** sprinkle (on); pelt. —**pepper pot,** any of various highly seasoned stews.

pep′per-and-salt′ *adj.* mixed black and white.

---

fat, fāte, fär, fâre, fâll, ȧsk; met, hē, hér, maybē; pin, pīne; not, nōte, ôr, tool

pep'per·corn" n. **1,** the berry of the pepper plant. **2,** a small particle.

pep'per·mint" (pep'ər-mint") n. a pungent herb, its oil, or candy flavored with it.

pep'per·y (-ė) adj. **1,** hot; biting. **2,** hottempered. —**pep'per·i·ness,** n.

pep'sin n. a digestive substance in the gastric juice. —**pep'tic,** adj. pert. to digestion.

per (pėr) prep. **1,** by means of; through. **2,** for or to each.

per- (per) pref. **1,** through. **2,** thoroughly; utterly; very. **3,** (Chem.) the maximum or an unusual amount.

per"ad·ven'ture (pėr'-) adv. perhaps.

per·am'bu·late" (pər-am'byə-lāt") v.i. walk about. —**per·am"bu·la'tion,** n. —**per·am'bu·la·to·ry** (-lə-tôr'ė) adj.

per·am'bu·la"tor (-lā'tər) n. a baby carriage. Also, **pram.**

per an'num (an'əm) (Lat.) each year.

per·cale' (pər-kāl') n. a closely woven cotton fabric.

per cap'i·ta (kap'ə-tə) (Lat.) per person.

per·ceive' (pər-sēv') v.t. become aware of through the senses or the understanding. —**per·ceiv'a·ble,** adj.

per·cent' (pər-sent') n. parts per hundred, symbol (%).

per·cent'age (-ij) n. **1,** rate or proportion per hundred; proportion; commission. **2,** (Colloq.) profit; advantage.

per·cen'tile (pər-sen'tīl; -til) n. one of 100 equal consecutive groups arranged in order of magnitude, or the points dividing them. —adj. pert. to a percentile or to a division by percentiles.

per'cept (pėr'sept) n. a perception. —**per·cep'tu·al** (pər-sep'shoo-əl) adj.

per·cep'ti·ble (pər-sep'tə-bəl) adj. perceivable. —**per·cep"ti·bil'i·ty,** n.

per·cep'tion (pər-sep'shən) n. the act or faculty of perceiving; something perceived.

per·cep'tive (-tive) adj. quick to perceive. —**per·cep'tive·ness,** n.

perch (pėrch) n. **1,** any of various edible fishes. **2,** any of several units of measure, as a rod, a sq. rod, etc. **3,** a support, esp. a roost for birds. —v.t. place on a perch. —v.i. roost.

per·chance' (pər-chàns') adv. perhaps.

Per'che·ron" (pėr'chə-ron") n. one of a breed of draft horses.

per·cip'i·ent (pər-sip'ė-ənt) adj. perceiving. —**per·cip'i·ence,** n.

per'co·late" (pėr'kə-lāt") v.t. pass (a liquid) through a porous substance. —v.i. seep; filter. —**per"co·la'tion,** n. —**per'co·la"tor,** n. a pot for cooking coffee.

per·cus'sion (pər-kush'ən) n. the forcible striking of one body against another. —**per·cuss',** v.t. —**per·cus'sion·ist,** n. —**percussion cap,** a cap filled with powder on the end of a cartridge. —**percussion instrument,** a drum, cymbals, etc.

per di'em (pər-dē'əm) (Lat.) **1,** by the day. **2,** a fixed allowance for each day's expenses; daily expense account.

per·di'tion (pər-dish'ən) n. **1,** utter ruin. **2,** eternal damnation.

per·dur'a·ble (pər-) adj. everlasting; imperishable.

per"e·gri·na'tion (per'ə-grə-nā'shən) n. a wandering about from place to place.

per'e·grine (per'ə-grin) adj. foreign; migratory; wandering. —n. a swift, courageous kind of falcon. Also, **per'e·grin.**

per·emp'to·ry (pə-remp'tə-rė) adj. **1,** admitting no refusal. **2,** dogmatic; dictatorial.

per·en'ni·al (pə-ren'ė-əl) adj. **1,** lasting several years, as a plant. **2,** long-lasting; continuing. —n. a perennial plant.

per'fect (pėr'fikt) adj. **1,** complete in every detail. **2,** without defect; flawless. **3,** of the highest type. **4,** exact; precise. **5,** thoroughly learned or skilled. **6,** (Colloq.) utter; complete. **7,** (Gram.) denoting the tense of a verb that expresses completed action. —n. the perfect tense. —v.t. (pər-fekt') **1,** complete; finish. **2,** make perfect. —**per·fec'tion** (pər-fek'shən), n. —**per'fect·ness,** n. —**per·fec'tion·ist,** n. & adj. —**per·fec'tion·ism,** n.

per·fec'ta (pər-fek'tə) n. a wager requiring correct choice of first and second place in exact order to win; exacta.

per·fec'to (pėr-fek'tō) n. a shape of cigar.

per'fi·dy (pėr'fə-dė) n. breach of faith; treachery. —**per·fid'i·ous,** adj.

per'fo·rate" (pėr'fə-rāt") v.t. bore through; make a series of holes in. —adj. perforated.

per"fo·ra'tion (pėr'fə-rā'shən) n. **1,** act of perforating. **2,** a hole or row of holes, as in paper.

per·force' (pər-fôrs') adv. of necessity.

per·form' (pər-fôrm') v.t. **1,** carry out; do. **2,** discharge, as a duty, etc. **3,** act (a play or part); render (music). —v.i. **1,** work; operate. **2,** act, sing, or play in public. —**performing arts,** those arts, as drama, music, etc., which involve public performance.

per·form'ance (-əns) n. **1,** the act of performing; execution. **2,** a thing performed. **3,** a musical, dramatic, or other entertainment. **4,** efficiency.

per·fume' (pər-fūm') v.t. make fragrant. —n. **1,** a pleasant scent; aroma. **2,** a volatile sweet-smelling liquid.

per·fum′er·y (pər-fūm′ə-rē) *n.* **1,** perfumes in general. **2,** a place where perfumes are made or sold.

per·func′to·ry (pər-funk′tə-rē) *adj.* done merely from a sense of duty; casual; superficial.

per′go·la (pēr′gə-lə) *n.* a latticework over a walk; an arbor.

per·haps′ (pər-haps′) *adv.* maybe.

pe′ri (pir′ē) *n.* an elf; fairy.

per″i·cyn′thi·on (per″ə-sin′thē-on) *n.* the point nearest the moon in the lunar orbit of a satellite.

per′i·dot (per′ə-dot) *n.* green chrysolite, used as a gem.

per′i·gee (per′ə-jē) *n.* the point of the orbit of a satellite of the earth which is nearest the earth. —**per″i·ge′al, per″i·ge′an,** *adj.*

per″i·he′li·on (-hē′lē-ən) *n.* [*pl.* **-li·a** (-lē-ə)] the point of the orbit of a planet or comet which is nearest the sun.

per′il (per′əl) *n.* danger; risk. —*v.t.* imperil. —**per′il·ous,** *adj.*

per·im′e·ter (pə-rim′i-tər) *n.* the outer boundary; circumference.

pe′ri·od (pir′ē-əd) *n.* **1,** an era; epoch. **2,** a specified division of time; a recurring event or its duration. **3,** the sign (.) marking the end of a declarative sentence. **4,** termination.

pe″ri·od′ic (pir″ē-od′ik) *adj.* recurring at regular intervals. —**pe″ri·o·dic′i·ty** (-ə-dis′ə-tē) *n.* —**periodic table** or **chart,** a grouping of the atomic elements by atomic numbers or weights.

pe″ri·od′i·cal (pir″ē-od′ə-kəl) *adj.* **1,** periodic. **2,** published at regular intervals. —*n.* a periodical magazine.

per″i·pa·tet′ic (per″ə-pə-tet′ik) *adj.* walking about; itinerant.

pe·riph′er·y (pə-rif′ə-rē) *n.* the outer boundary line. —**pe·riph′er·al,** *adj.*

pe·rique′ (pə-rēk′) *n.* a strong-flavored tobacco from Louisiana.

per′i·scope″ (per′ə-skōp″) *n.* an instrument for seeing above or around an obstacle.

per′ish *v.i.* waste away; disappear; die. —**per′ish·a·ble,** *adj. & n.* mortal; easily spoiled, as goods.

per″i·stal′sis (per″ə-stal′sis) *n.* involuntary muscular movements of some organs, esp. the alimentary canal.

per′i·style″ *n.* a row of columns surrounding a building, an open court, etc.; the enclosed space.

per″i·to·ne′um (per″ə-tə-nē′əm) *n.* the membrane lining the abdominal cavity.

per″i·to·ni′tis (per″ə-tə-nī′tis) *n.* inflammation of the peritoneum.

per′i·wig (per′i-wig) *n.* peruke.

per′i·win″kle (per′ə-wing″kəl) *n.* a trailing evergreen plant with blue flowers; myrtle.

per′jure (pēr′jər) *v.t.* make (oneself) guilty of perjury. —**per′jured,** *adj.* constituting, or guilty of, perjury. —**per′jur·er,** *n.*

per′ju·ry (pēr′jə-rē) *n.* the willful giving of false testimony under oath.

perk (pērk) *v.t. & i.* (with *up*) lift (one's head, ears) eagerly; be cheered. —*n.* (*Slang*) perquisite. —**perk′y,** *adj.* jaunty; pert.

per′ma·frost″ (pēr′mə-) *n.* permanently or perennially frozen subsoil, usu. in arctic regions.

perm′al·loy″ (pērm′ə-loi″) *n.* (*T.N.*) an iron-nickel alloy easily magnetized and demagnetized.

per′ma·nent (pēr′mə-nənt) *adj.* lasting; fixed, not temporary. —**per′ma·nence,** *n.* —**permanent press,** a treatment for fabrics which permits them to hold their shape after washing. —**permanent wave** [also, *colloq.,* **permanent** or **perm**] a long-lasting artificial wave for the hair.

per′me·a·ble (pēr′mē-ə-bəl) *adj.* porous. —**per″me·a·bil′i·ty,** *n.*

per′me·ate″ (pēr′mē-āt″) *v.t. & i.* seep through the pores (of); penetrate; spread through. —**per″me·a′tion,** *n.*

per·mis′si·ble (pər-mis′ə-bəl) *adj.* allowable. —**per·mis″si·bil′i·ty,** *n.*

per·mis′sion (pər-mish′ən) *n.* act of permitting; consent; license.

per·mis′sive (pər-mis′iv) *adj.* **1,** permitted. **2,** permitting.

per′mit (pēr′mit) *n.* a written license to do something. —*v.t.* (pər-mit′) [**per′mit′ted, -ting**] **1,** allow. **2,** give formal consent to. —*v.i.* make possible.

per″mu·ta′tion (pēr″mū-tā′shən) *n.* any possible arrangement of any units in a group.

per·mute′ (pər-mūt′) *v.t.* **1,** alter. **2,** make permutations of.

per·ni′cious (pər-nish′əs) *adj.* highly destructive; ruinous. —**per·ni′cious·ness,** *n.*

per·nick′et·y (pər-nik′ə-tē) *adj.* (*Colloq.*) persnickety.

per″o·ra′tion (per″ə-rā′shən) *n.* an emphatic or summarizing conclusion of a speech. —**per′o·rate″** (-rāt″) *v.i.*

per·ox′ide (pə-rok′sīd) *n.* **1,** a chemical compound with a high oxygen content. **2,** hydrogen peroxide, an antiseptic liquid.

per″pen·dic′u·lar (pēr″pən-dik′yə-lər) *adj.* **1,** perfectly vertical. **2,** (*Geom.*) meeting a line or surface at right angles. —*n.* a vertical line. —**per″pen·dic″u·lar′i·ty,** *n.*

per′pe·trate″ (pēr′pə-trāt″) *v.t.* commit (a crime); be guilty of. —**per″pe·tra′tion,** *n.* —**per′pe·tra″tor,** *n.*

---

fat, fāte, fär, fâre, fâll, àsk; met, hē, hêr, maybè; pin, pīne; not, nōte, ôr, tool

per·pet′u·al (pər-pech′oo-əl) *adj.* **1,** everlasting. **2,** continuous.

per·pet′u·ate″ (-āt″) *v.t.* cause to continue indefinitely; preserve from oblivion. —**per·pet″u·a′tion,** *n.*

per″pe·tu′i·ty (pĕr″pə-tū′ə-tē) *n.* endless existence or duration.

per·plex′ (pər-pleks′) *v.t.* make confused or bewildered; puzzle. —**per·plex′i·ty,** *n.*

per′qui·site (pĕr′kwi-zit) *n.* extra payment received because of one's regular work, as a tip.

per′se·cute″ (pĕr′si-kūt″) *v.t.* *harass* persistently, esp. make suffer for divergent principles. —**per″se·cu′tion,** *n.* —**per′se·cu″tor,** *n.*

per″se·vere′ (pĕr″sə-vir′) *v.i.* persist in something undertaken. —**per″se·ver′ance,** *n.*

Per′sian (pĕr′zhən) *adj. & n.* pert. to ancient Persia, or Iran, its people or language. —**Persian blinds,** adjustable shutters for the outside of a window. Also, **per·siennes′** (per-zyen′). —**Persian lamb,** the fur of the older Karakul lamb.

per′si·flage″ (pĕr′si-fläzh″) *n.* flippant, bantering talk.

per·sim′mon (pər-sim′ən) *n.* a tree or its pulpy, acid fruit.

per·sist′ (pər-zist′) *v.i.* **1,** continue despite opposition. **2,** endure; recur. —**per·sis′tence, per·sist′en·cy,** *n.* —**per·sist′ent,** *adj.*

per·snick′e·ty (pər-snik′ə-tē) *adj.* (*Colloq.*) excessively meticulous. Also, **per·nick′e·ty.**

per′son (pĕr′sən) *n.* **1,** a human being. **2,** the human body. **3,** (*Gram.*) the distinction between the speaker (*first person*), person spoken to (*second person*), and person spoken of (*third person*).

-per·son (pĕr-sən) *suf.* designating an agent of unspecified sex.

per·so′na (pər-sō′nə) *n.* [*pl.* **-nae** (-nė)] (*Lat.*) **1,** person; personality. **2,** façade; mask. **3,** (*pl.*) the characters in a play.

per′son·a·ble (-ə-bəl) *adj.* attractive in manner and appearance.

per′son·age (-ij) *n.* **1,** an important person. **2,** a part or character in a play.

per′son·al (-əl) *adj.* **1,** one's own; private. **2,** done by oneself, not a representative or representation. **3,** (of a remark) invidious. **4,** (*Gram.*) denoting person. **5,** of property, movable.

per·son·al′i·ty (pĕr-sən-al′ə-tē) *n.* **1,** distinctive character; individuality. **2,** (*pl.*) gossip. **3,** (*Colloq.*) celebrity.

per′son·al·ize″ (-īz″) *v.t.* **1,** typify; make personal. **2,** mark or identify, as by initialing. —**per″son·al″i·za′tion,** *n.*

per′son·al·ty (-tē) *n.* (*Law*) personal property; movable possessions.

per·so′na non gra′ta (pər-sō′nə-nōn-grä′tə) (*Lat.*) an unacceptable or unwanted person.

per·son′i·fy″ (pər-son′ə-fī″) *v.t.* **1,** attribute human qualities to (an object, quality, etc.). **2,** exemplify; typify. —**per·son″i·fi·ca′tion,** *n.*

per″son·nel′ (pĕr″sə-nel′) *n.* employees (of a particular employer).

per·spec′tive (pər-spek′tiv) *n.* **1,** point of view. **2,** the proper relative position of objects or phenomena one perceives.

per″spi·ca′cious (pĕr″spə-kā′shəs) *adj.* mentally acute. —**per″spi·cac′i·ty** (-kas′ə-tē) *n.*

per·spic′u·ous (pər-spik′ū-əs) *adj.* easily understood; lucid. —**per″spi·cu′i·ty** (-spi-kū′ə-tē) *n.*

per·spire′ (pər-spīr′) *v.i. & t.* excrete waste fluids through the pores; sweat. —**per″spi·ra′tion,** *n.*

per·suade′ (pər-swād′) *v.t.* prevail upon by argument or entreaty; convince.

per·sua′sion (pər-swā′zhən) *n.* **1,** act or effect of persuading. **2,** a conviction; way of thinking. —**per·sua′si·ble,** *adj.* —**per·sua′sive** (-siv) *adj.* serving to persuade.

pert (pĕrt) *adj.* saucy; impudent. —**pert′·ness,** *n.*

per·tain′ (pər-tān′) *v.i.* (with *to*) **1,** belong as a part. **2,** have reference or relation; relate; bear upon; be connected with.

per″ti·na′cious (pĕr″ti-nā′shəs) *adj.* stubbornly holding to an opinion, purpose, etc. —**per″ti·nac′i·ty** (-nas′ə-tē) *n.*

per′ti·nent (pĕr′tə-nənt) *adj.* to the point; appropriate; relevant; pertaining. —**per′ti·nence,** *n.*

per·turb′ (pər-tĕrb′) *v.t.* agitate; disturb greatly. —**per″tur·ba′tion,** *n.*

per·tus′sis (pər-tus′əs) *n.* whooping cough.

pe·ruke′ (pə-rook′) *n.* a wig.

pe·ruse′ (pə-rooz′) *v.t.* read attentively. —**pe·rus′al,** *n.*

Pe·ru′vi·an (pə-roo′vė-ən) *adj.* of or pert. to Peru. —*n.* a native or citizen of Peru.

per·vade′ (pər-vād′) *v.t.* spread through every part of; permeate. —**per·va′sive,** *adj.*

per·verse′ (pər-vĕrs′) *adj.* self-willed; contrary. —**per·verse′ness,** —**per·ver′si·ty,** *n.*

per·vert′ (pər-vĕrt′) *v.t.* **1,** divert from its intended meaning, use, etc. **2,** lead astray; corrupt. —*n.* (pĕr′vĕrt) a perverted person. —**per·ver′sion** (-zhən) *n.*

Pe′sach (pe′säk) *n.* the Passover.

pe·se′ta (pə-sā′tə) *n.* the monetary unit of Spain.

pes'ky (pes'kė) *adj.* (*Colloq.*) troublesome. **—pes'ki·ness,** *n.*

pe'so (pā'sō) *n.* [*pl.* **-sos**] a coin of varying value used in Latin Amer.

pes'sa·ry (pes'ə-rė) *n.* **1,** any of various appliances placed in the vagina for support or medication. **2,** a diaphragm (def. 3).

pes'si·mism (pes'ə-miz-əm) *n.* a tendency to expect the worse. **—pes'si·mist,** *n.* **—pes'si·mis'tic,** *adj.* **—pes'si·mis'ti·cal·ly,** *adv.*

pest *n.* **1,** a pestilence. **2,** a person or thing that annoys; nuisance.

pes'ter (pes'tər) *v.t.* annoy; harass.

pest'house" *n.* a hospital ward isolated because of infectious disease.

pest'i·cide" (pest'ə-sīd") *n.* an agent (as a chemical) used to kill pests.

pes·tif'er·ous (pes-tif'ər-əs) *adj.* **1,** bearing infection; noxious. **2,** (*Colloq.*) annoying. **—pes·tif'er·ous·ness,** *n.*

pes'ti·lence (pes'tə-ləns) *n.* a devastating epidemic disease. **—pes"ti·len'tial** (-len'-shəl) *adj.*

pes'ti·lent (pes'tə-lənt) *adj.* **1,** poisonous. **2,** injurious to morals. **3,** troublesome.

pes'tle (pes'əl) *n.* a tool for pounding substances in a mortar.

pet *n.* **1,** an animal or bird that is cherished. **2,** a favorite. **3,** a sulking mood. *—adj.* **1,** loved and fondled. **2,** favorite. **3,** expressing fondness. *—v.t.* & *i.* [**pet'ted, -ting**] **1,** fondle; engage in amorous caresses. **2,** sulk.

pet'al (pet'əl) *n.* a leaf of a flower.

pe·tard' (pi-tärd') *n.* an ancient cannon or bomb attached to a gate or wall, to blow a hole in it.

pet'cock" *n.* a small faucet.

pe'ter (pē'tər) *v.i.* (*Colloq.*) (with *out*) become exhausted.

pe'ter·sham (pē'tər-shəm) *n.* a heavy overcoat; the woolen cloth of which it was made.

pet'i·ole" (pet'ė-ōl") *n.* a leafstalk.

pe·tite' (pə-tēt') *adj.* (*Fr.*) little. **—pe·tite'ness,** *n.*

pe'tit four' (pet'ė-fôr') [*pl.* **pe'tits fours'** (pet'ė-fôrz')] a small frosted cake covered completely with icing.

pe·ti'tion (pə-tish'ən) *n.* **1,** an earnest entreaty; prayer. **2,** a formal written request. *—v.t.* address a petition to. **—pe·ti'tion·er,** *n.*

pe'tit jury (pet'ė) a jury that decides the facts of a case in a court trial.

pet'nap"ping *n.* (*Colloq.*) stealing of a pet, esp. for ransom.

pet'rel (pet'rəl) *n.* a sea bird.

pet'ri·fy" (pet'rə-fī") *v.t.* & *i.* **1,** turn into stone. **2,** paralyze or stupefy, as with fear. **—pet"ri·fac'tion,** *n.*

pet·ro- (pet-rō) *pref.* **1,** stone. **2,** oil.

pet'ro·dol"lar *n.* a dollar earned, esp. by a foreign country, from the sale of crude oil.

pe·trog'ra·phy (pi-trog'rə-fė) *n.* the scientific study and classification of rocks. **—pet"ro·graph'ic** (pet"rə-graf'ik) *adj.*

pet'rol (pet'rəl) *n.* gasoline.

pet"ro·la'tum (pet"rə-lā'təm) *n.* an oil obtained from petroleum.

pe·tro'le·um (pə-trō'lė-əm) *n.* unrefined oil obtained from the earth.

pe·trol'o·gy (pi-trol'ə-jė) *n.* the study of rocks.

pet'ti·coat" (pet'ė-kōt") *n.* a woman's underskirt.

pet'ti·fog"ger (pet'ė-fog"ər) *n.* a scheming lawyer. **—pet'ti·fog",** *v.i.*

pet'tish (pet'ish) *adj.* peevish. **—pet'tish·ness,** *n.*

pet'ty (pet'ė) *adj.* on a small scale; trivial; mean. **—pet'ti·ness,** *n.* **—petty cash,** cash on hand for minor expenditures. **—petty officer,** a noncommissioned officer in the Navy.

pet'u·lant (pech'ə-lənt) *adj.* peevish; capricious. **—pet'u·lance,** *n.*

pe·tu'ni·a (pə-tū'nė-ə) *n.* a plant or its funnel-shaped flower.

pew (pū) *n.* a bench for worshipers in a church.

pe'wee (pē'wė) *n.* a small Amer. flycatcher; the phoebe.

pew'ter (pū'tər) *n.* an alloy of tin and lead, antimony, or bismuth.

pe·yo'te (pā-yō'tė) *n.* a stimulant drug derived from mescal.

pH a measure of the acidity or alkalinity of a solution.

pha·e'ton (fā'ə-tən) *n.* **1,** a light four-wheeled carriage. **2,** a convertible sedan.

-phage (fāj) *suf.* an eater of. **— -pha·gous** (fā-gəs) *suf.* forming adjectives.

phag'o·cyte" (fag'ə-sīt") *n.* a white corpuscle in the blood, capable of destroying bacteria.

pha·lan'ger (fə-lan'jər) *n.* a long-tailed arboreal marsupial of Australia.

pha'lanx (fā'lanks) *n.* **1,** a body of troops in close formation; a solid group. **2,** [*pl.* **pha·lan'ges** (fə-lan'jėz)] any of the bones of the fingers or toes.

phal'a·rope" (fal'ə-rōp") *n.* a small coastal wading bird.

phal'lus (fal'əs) *n.* a symbol or image of the male reproductive organ. **—phal'lic,** *adj.*

---

phan′tasm (fan′taz-əm) *n.* **1**, a specter. **2**, fantasy; an illusion.

phan·tas″ma·go′ri·a (fan-taz″mə-gôr′ē-ə) *n.* **1**, a succession of illusive images, as in a dream. **2**, a similar fantastic exhibition.

phan′ta·sy (fan′tə-sē) *n.* fantasy.

phan′tom (fan′təm) *n.* an apparition; specter; something unreal. —*adj.* illusive; ghostly.

Phar′aoh (fãr′ō) *n.* a title of ancient Egyptian kings.

phar′i·see″ (far′ə-sē″) *n.* one who follows the letter, not the spirit, of the (religious) law. —**phar″i·sa′ic** (-sā′ik) *adj.* —**phar″-i·sa′i·cal·ly,** *adv.*

phar″ma·ceu′tics (fär″mə-soo′tiks) *n.* pharmacy (def. 1). —**phar″ma·ceu′tic, phar″ma·ceu′ti·cal,** *adj.*

phar″ma·col′o·gy (-kol′ə-gē) *n.* the science of drugs. —**phar″ma·co·log′i·cal,** (-kə-loj′ə-kəl) *adj.* —**phar″ma·col′o·gist,** *n.*

phar″ma·co·poe′ia (-kō-pē′yə) *n.* an official list of drugs and medicines.

phar′ma·cy (fär′mə-sē) *n.* **1**, the art of compounding drugs according to prescription. **2**, a drugstore. —**phar′ma·cist** (-sist) *n.*

phar′ynx (far′inks) *n.* [*pl.* **pha·ryn′ges** (fə-rin′jēz), **phar′ynx·es**] the passage connecting the mouth with the esophagus. —**pha·ryn′ge·al** (fə-rin′jē-əl) *adj.* —**phar″-yn·gi′tis** (-jī′təs) *n.*

phase (fāz) *n.* the aspect in which a thing appears; a stage.

pheas′ant (fez′ənt) *n.* a long-tailed game bird.

phe″no·bar′bi·tal″ (fē″nō-bär′bi-tâl″) *n.* a drug used as a hypnotic.

phe′nol (fē′nol) *n.* carbolic acid.

phe·nom′e·non″ (fi-nom′ə-non″) *n.* [*pl.* **-na** (-nə)] **1**, any observable fact in nature. **2**, an odd or notable thing. —**phe·nom′e·nal,** *adj.*

phew (fū) *interj.* of disgust, weariness, relief, or surprise.

phi (fī) *n.* the twenty-first letter of the Greek alphabet (Φ, φ).

phi′al (fī′əl) *n.* vial.

phil- (fil) *pref.* loving; fond of.

phi·lan′der (fi-lan′dər) *v.i.* make trifling love to a woman; flirt.

phi·lan′thro·py (fi-lan′thrə-pē) *n.* **1**, love of mankind; altruism. **2**, a benevolent act, gift, etc. —**phil″an·throp′ic** (fil″ən-throp′ik) *adj.* —**phil″an·throp′i·cal·ly,** *adv.* —**phi·lan′thro·pist** (-thrə-pist) *n.*

phi·lat′e·ly (fi-lat′ə-lē) *n.* the collecting and study of stamps and related postal materials. —**phi·lat′e·list,** *n.*

-phile (fil) *suf.* one who loves.

phil″har·mon′ic (fil″här-mon′ik) *adj.* **1**, fond of or devoted to music. **2**, a type of orchestra.

phi·lip′pic (fi-lip′ik) *n.* an oration full of bitter invective.

Phil′ip·pine (fil′ə-pēn) *adj.* pert. to the Philippine Islands or Republic.

Phi·lis′tine (fi-lis′tin) *n.* an uncultured, materialistic person.

phil′o·den′dron (fil″ə-den′drən) *n.* a tropical Amer. climbing plant.

phi·lol′o·gy (fi-lol′ə-jē) *n.* the science of the origins, laws, etc., of languages. —**phil″o·log′i·cal,** *adj.* —**phi·lol′o·gist,** *n.*

phi·los′o·pher (fi-los′ə-fer) *n.* **1**, a student of philosophy. **2**, a philosophical person. —**philosopher's stone,** a magical substance believed by alchemists to have the power, among others, to change base metal into gold.

phil″o·soph′i·cal (fil″o-sof′ə-kəl) *adj.* **1**, pert. to philosophy. **2**, serene in adversity. Also, **phil″o·soph′ic.**

phi·los′o·phy (fi-los′ə-fē) *n.* **1**, the science dealing with the general causes and principles of things. **2**, personal attitude. —**phi·los′o·phize″** (-fiz″) *v.i.*

phil′ter (fil′tər) *n.* a love potion. Also, **phil′tre.**

phle·bi′tis (fli-bī′tis) *n.* inflammation of a vein.

phle·bot′o·my (fle-bot′ə-mē) *n.* bloodletting as a therapeutic measure; bleeding.

phlegm (flem) *n.* **1**, thick mucus secreted in throat and bronchi. **2**, sluggishness; apathy.

phleg·mat′ic (fleg-mat′ik) *adj.* **1**, apathetic; unexcitable. **2**, pert. to phlegm. —**phleg·mat′ic·al·ly,** *adv.*

phlo·gis′ton (flō-jis′tən) *n.* fire considered as an element present but latent in all combustible substances and released when burning occurs.

phlox (floks) *n.* a tall summer perennial bearing large flower heads.

-phobe (fōb) *suf.* one who fears or hates.

pho′bi·a (fō′bē-ə) *n.* an irrational fear or dread.

phoe′be (fē′bē) *n.* a bird, a small American fly-catcher; pewee; pewit.

phoe′nix (fē′niks) *n.* a fabled bird that burned itself and rose from its own ashes.

phon- (fōn) *pref.* sound; voice; speech.

phone (fōn) *n.* & *v.* (*Colloq.*) telephone.

-phone (fōn) *suf.* **1**, sound. **2**, speaking.

pho·net′ic (fō-net′ik) *adj.* pert. to speech sounds; in spelling, using always the same symbol for each sound. —**pho·net′i·cal·ly,** *adv.* —**pho·net′ics,** *n.sing.*

phon′ic (fon′ik) *adj.* pert. to sound, esp.

speech sounds. **—phon′ics,** *n.sing.* the use of phonetics in teaching reading.

pho′no·graph″ (fō′nə-gráf″) *n.* a machine for reproducing recorded sounds. **—pho′no·graph″ic,** *adj.*

pho′ny (fō′nē) (*Colloq.*) *adj.* fake; spurious. **—***n.* a fake or faker.

phooo′ey (foo′ē) *interj.* of disgust.

phos′gene (fos′jēn) *n.* a poisonous gas formerly used in chemical warfare.

phos′phate (fos′fāt) *n.* **1,** a compound of phosphorous used as a fertilizer. **2,** an effervescent drink.

phos′phor (fos′fər) *n.* a chemical that gives off visible light when struck by ultraviolet radiation.

phos″pho·res′cence (fos″fə-res′əns) *n.* the property of giving out luminous light without sensible heat. **—phos″pho·res′cent,** *adj.*

phos′pho·rus (fos′fə-rəs) *n.* a waxy, luminous nonmetallic element, no. 15, symbol P. **—phos′phor·ous,** *adj.*

phot (fot) *n.* a unit of illumination.

pho′to (fō′tō) *n.* photograph. **—photo finish,** a race so close that the winner must be determined from a photograph.

pho·to- (fō′tō) *pref.* **1,** light. **2,** photographic.

pho′to·cop″y *n.* a photographic reproduction of printing, drawing, etc. **—***v.t. & i.* make a photocopy (of). Also, **pho″to·dup′li·cate,** *n. & v.t.*

pho″to·e·lec′tric cell a device for controlling an electric circuit by light falling on it: *electric eye.* Also, **pho″to·cell″.**

pho″to·en·grav′ing *n.* a reproduction of pictures on letterpress printing plates by a photographic process. **—pho″to·en·grave′,** *v.t.*

pho″to·gen′ic (-jen′ik) *adj.* easy to photograph effectively.

pho′to·graph″ (fō′tə-gráf″) *n.* a picture made by exposing a chemically treated surface to light. **—***v.t.* make a photograph of. **—***v.i.* **1,** take photographs. **2,** be a (good, bad, etc.) subject for photography. **—pho″to·graph′ic,** *adj.* **—pho″to·graph′i·cal·ly,** *adv.*

pho·tog′ra·phy (fə-tog′rə-fē) *n.* the taking of photographs. **—pho·tog′ra·pher,** *n.*

pho·tom′e·ter (fō-tom′ə-tər) *n.* an instrument for measuring the intensity of light; light meter.

pho″to·mi′cro·graph″ (-mī′krə-gráf″) *n.* a photograph taken through a microscope. **—pho″to·mi·crog′ra·phy** (-mī-krog′rə-fē) *n.*

pho′ton (fō′ton) *n.* a particle of radiant energy moving with the velocity of light.

pho″to·off′set *n.* lithography from plates made photographically.

pho′to·play″ *n.* a motion picture.

pho′to·sphere″ *n.* the gaseous, luminous envelope of the sun.

pho′to·stat″ *n.* (*T.N.*) a facsimile or negative copy, photographed directly onto paper. Also, **stat. —pho″to·stat′ic,** *adj.*

pho″to·syn′the·sis *n.* the process by which plants make carbohydrates from light and air.

phrase (frāz) *n.* **1,** a group of words used as though one. **2,** a short, pithy expression. **3,** (*Music*) a group of notes played or sung connectedly in a particular way. **—***v.t.* express in words.

phra″se·ol′o·gy (frā″zē-ol′ə-jē) *n.* choice of words.

phre·net′ic (fri-net′ik) *adj.* **1,** insane; violent. **2,** fanatic; zealous. **—phre·net′i·cal·ly,** *adv.*

phren′ic (fren′ik) *adj.* **1,** pert. to the diaphragm. **2,** mental.

phre·nol′o·gy (fre-nol′ə-jē) *n.* character-reading from the form of the skull. **—phre·nol′o·gist,** *n.*

phthi′sis (thī′sis) *n.* **1,** tuberculosis of the lungs. **2,** bodily decay.

phy·col′o·gy (fī-kol′ə-jē) *n.* the branch of botany dealing with algae.

phy·lac′ter·y (fə-lak′tə-rē) *n.* **1,** a small leather box containing scriptures, worn by pious Jews. **2,** an amulet; talisman.

phy·lo- (fī-lō) *pref.* tribe or race.

phy·log′e·ny (fī-loj′ə-nē) *n.* racial history; the evolution of a type or species of animal or plant. Also, **phy″lo·gen′e·sis** (fī″lə-). **—phy″lo·gen′ic, phy″lo·ge·net′ic,** *adj.*

phy′lum (fī-ləm) *n.* [*pl.* **-la** (-lə)] a primary division of the animal or vegetable kingdom.

phys″i·at′rics (fiz″ē-at′riks) *n.* a system of medicine founded on the healing powers of nature.

phys′ic (fiz′ik) *n.* a medicine; specif., a cathartic.

phys′i·cal (fiz′i-kəl) *adj.* **1,** pert. to the body. **2,** pert. to nature or to the material. **3,** pert. to physics. **—** (*Colloq.*) a medical examination. **—physical education,** instruction in hygiene, exercises for the body, etc.

phy·si′cian (fə-zish′ən) *n.* a healer; esp. a doctor of medicine.

phys′ics (fiz′iks) *n.* the science dealing with the properties of matter and energy. **—phys′i·cist** (-i-sist) *n.*

phy·si·o- (fiz-ē-ō) *pref.* **1,** nature; natural. **2,** physical.

---

fat, fāte, fär, fâre, fåll, åsk; met, hē, hêr, maybė; pin, pīne; not, nōte, ôr, tool

phys″i·og′no·my (fiz″ē-og′nə-mē) *n.* the face; external aspect.

phy·si·og′ra·phy (fiz-ē-og′rə-fē) *n.* physical geography or geophysics.

phys″i·ol′o·gy (fiz″ē-ol′ə-jē) *n.* the science dealing with the processes of living. —**phys″i·o·log′i·cal,** *adj.* —**phys″i·ol′o·gist,** *n.*

phys″i·o·ther′a·py *n.* treatment of disease by the use of heat, massage, etc. —**phys″i·o·ther′a·pist,** *n.*

phy·sique′ (fi-zēk′) *n.* the structure and development of the body.

phy·to- (fī-tō) *pref.* plant; plant life; vegetable.

pi (pī) *n.* **1,** the sixteenth letter of the Greek alphabet (Π, π), also (π) denoting the ratio of the circumference of a circle to its diameter, about 3.1416. **2,** a jumbled mass of printing type. —*v.t.* [**pied, pie′ing**] jumble (type).

pi″a·nis′si·mo″ (pē″ə-nis′i-mō″) *adj. & adv.* very soft.

pi·an′ist (pē-an′ist; pē′ə-nist) *n.* one who plays on the piano.

pi·an′o (pē-an′ō) *n.* [*pl.* -**os**] a large stringed musical instrument with a keyboard. —*adj. & adv.* soft. —**pi·an′o·forte″** (-fôrt″) *n.* a piano. —**piano roll,** a roll of heavy paper on which is recorded mechanically, by means of holes, the notes of a work as performed by a pianist, to be reproduced on a player piano.

pi·as′ter (pē-as′tər) *n.* a coin, of varying value, of various countries, as Turkey and Egypt.

pi·az′za (pē-az′ə) *n.* **1,** a porch. **2,** (pē-át′sə) a public square or walk.

pi′broch (pē′brokh) *n.* a wild, irregular kind of bagpipe music.

pi′ca (pī′kə) *n.* (*Printing*) 12 points; a type of this pitch.

pic′a·dor″ (pik′ə-dôr″) *n.* a mounted bullfighter.

pic″a·resque′ (pik″ə-resk′) *adj.* (of fiction) episodic and dealing with rogues.

pic″a·yune′ (pik″ə-ūn′) *adj.* trifling; of little value.

pic′ca·lil″li (pik′ə-lil″ē) *n.* a pickle of chopped vegetables.

pic′co·lo″ (pik′ə-lō″) *n.* [*pl.* -**los″**] a small, high-pitched flute. —**pic′co·lo·ist,** *n.*

pick (pik) *n.* **1,** any of various pointed tools, large or small, as for loosening rock, chopping ice, etc.; a pickax. **2,** a handgathered crop. **3,** first choice; hence, the choicest. —*v.t.* **1,** prick, pierce, clean, open, etc., with a pointed tool. **2,** (often with *up*) acquire; gain; gather, as crops; take up; lift; pluck. **3,** (often with *out*) choose; select. **4,**

rob; open (a lock) without a key. **5,** pull apart; shred. **6,** provoke (a quarrel); (with *on*) nag unfairly; tease. —*v.i.* **1,** use a pointed instrument. **2,** nibble at food. **3,** select. **4,** (with *up*) improve; recover. —**pick′er,** *n.* one who chooses wisely. —**pick′y,** *adj.* choosy; finicky.

pick′a·back″ *adv.* (riding) on a person's back and shoulders.

pick′a·nin″ny (pik′ə-nin″ē) *n.* (*Offensive*) a Negro child.

pick′ax″ *n.* a heavy, wooden-handled digging tool.

pick′er·el (pik′ər-el) *n.* an edible fish of the pike family.

pick′et (pik′it) *n.* **1,** a pointed stake. **2,** a small body of troops sent out to scout, guard, etc. **3,** a person, as a striking workman, stationed outside a place to protest its operations. —*v.i. & t.* **1,** be or post a picket outside a place. **2,** tether.

pick′ings (-ingz) *n.pl.* (*Colloq.*) opportunity to glean or pilfer.

pick′le (pik′əl) *n.* **1,** a food preserved in brine or a vinegar solution. **2,** (*Colloq.*) a difficult or dangerous situation. —*v.t.* preserve as a pickle. —**pick′led,** *adj.* (*Slang*) drunk.

pick′-me-up″ *n.* a stimulating drink.

pick′pock″et *n.* one who steals from others' pockets.

pick-′up *n.* **1,** an acquaintance met without an introduction. **2,** power of acceleration. **3,** a small open-body motor truck. **4,** (*Slang*) improvement, as in business. **5,** a device that receives audio or video signals, as a microphone. **6,** reception of sounds or images for broadcasting. —*adj.* made of odds and ends.

pic′nic (pik′nik) *n.* a short trip for an outdoor meal. —*v.i.* [**pic′nicked, -nick′-ing**] go on a picnic. —**pic′nick·er,** *n.*

pi′cot (pē′kō) *n.* a small projecting loop on the edge of lace, fabric, etc.

pic′to·graph″ (pik′tə-graf″) *n.* a pictorial symbol used in writing. —**pic″to·graph′ic,** *adj.* —**pic·tog′ra·phy,** (-tog′rə-fē) *n.*

pic·tor′i·al (pik-tôr′ē-əl) *adj.* expressed in, consisting of, or illustrated by pictures.

pic′ture (pik′chər) *n.* **1,** a painting, photograph, etc., depicting a person, object, or scene; an image; likeness. **2,** a description in words. **3,** (often *pl.*) (*Colloq.*) a motion picture. —*v.t.* **1,** portray, depict. **2,** imagine. —**picture tube,** a kinescope. —**picture window,** a large window offering a panoramic view.

Pic′ture·phone″ *n.* (*T.N.*) a type of telephone providing both audio and visual communication.

---

tub, cūte, pûll; labəl; oil, owl, go, chip, she, thin, *th*en, sing, ink; *see p.* 6

pic·tur·esque' (pik-chər-esk') *adj.* colorful; vivid. —**pic·tur·esque'ness,** *n.*

pid'dle (pid'əl) (*Colloq.*) *v.i.* **1,** dawdle; putter. **2,** urinate. —*v.t.* waste (time). —**pid'dling,** *adj.* trifling; petty.

pidg'in (pij'ən) *n.* a dialect formed of limited vocabulary and simplified grammar; esp., *pidgin English,* used between oriental and English-speaking traders.

pie (pī) *n.* **1,** food baked in a pastry crust. **2,** pi (def. 2).

pie'bald (pī'bâld") *adj.* having patches of color. —*n.* a piebald animal, esp. a horse.

piece (pēs) *n.* **1,** a fragment; a part or portion; a tract. **2,** a separate article, as of furniture, etc. **3,** an amount of work to be done. **4,** a definite quantity, as of cloth. **5,** one of the figures used in a game, as chess. **6,** a short literary or musical composition. **7,** a coin. **8,** a rifle or cannon. —*v.t.* (often with *out*) extend or enlarge by adding material. —**piece goods,** dry goods. —**piece of eight,** an old Span. coin.

piece'meal *adv.* bit by bit; gradually.

piece'work" *n.* work paid for by the piece or job.

pied (pīd) *adj.* of several colors.

pied-'à-terre' (pyäd'a-târ') *n.* [*pl.* **-terres'** (-târ')] (*Fr.*) a place (as an apartment) where one can stay when necessary.

pied'mont (pēd'mont) *n.* located at the base of a mountain or mountain range.

pie-'eyed' (-īd") *adj.* drunk.

pie'plant" *n.* rhubarb.

pier (pir) *n.* **1,** a breakwater; a wharf projecting into the water. **2,** a support of a bridge span. **3,** solid masonry between windows, etc. —**pier glass,** a large high mirror.

pierce (pirs) *v.t.* **1,** make a hole in. **2,** stab; enter painfully. **3,** force a way into or through. **4,** wound or affect keenly. —**pierc'ing,** *adj.* (of sound) shrill.

pi'e·ty (pī'ə-tē) *n.* reverence for God; devoutness.

pi·e"zo·e·lec'tric (pē-ā"zō-ē-lek'trik) *adj.* having the capacity to transform vibrations into electric current.

pif'fle (pif'əl) *n.* (*Slang*) nonsense.

pig *n.* **1,** a hog, esp. a young one. **2,** a greedy or dirty person. **3,** a mass of cast molten metal. **4,** (*Vulgar*) a policeman.— **pig'let** (-lit) *n.* a small or young pig. —**pig iron,** crude iron cast into molds for further processing. —**pig Latin,** dog Latin.

pi'geon (pij'ən) *n.* **1,** a dove or related bird. **2,** (*Slang*) a dupe. —**clay pigeon,** a disk of baked clay used as a target in trap shooting.

pi'geon-heart"ed *adj.* easily frightened; meek.

pi'geon·hole" *n.* a small open compartment in a desk. —*v.t.* **1,** file in a pigeonhole; lay aside and ignore. **2,** classify.

pi'geon-toed" (-tōd") *adj.* having the toes turned in.

pig'gish (pig'ish) *adj.* like a pig; gluttonous or dirty. —**pig'gish·ness,** *n.*

pig'gy (-gē) *n.* a small pig. —**piggy bank,** a hollow statuette of a pig, used as a savings bank; any similar savings receptacle.

pig'gy·back" *adv.* **1,** pickaback. **2,** on a railroad flatcar. —*n.* a system of freight transport utilizing special railroad flatcars to carry truck trailers.

pig'head"ed *adj.* stubborn.

pig'ment (pig'mənt) *n.* **1,** coloring matter. **2,** the natural coloring matter in the tissues of an animal or plant. —**pig'men·tar·y,** *adj.* —**pig"men·ta'tion,** *n.*

pig'skin" *n.* **1,** leather from pigs' skin. **2,** (*Colloq.*) a football.

pig'sty" *n.* sty. Also **pig'pen".**

pig'tail" *n.* a long hanging braid of hair.

pike (pīk) *n.* **1,** a steel-pointed weapon; a lance. **2,** an edible fresh-water fish. **3,** a main road; turnpike.

pik'er (pī'kər) *n.* (*Slang*) one who bets or spends in a small way.

pike'staff" *n.* a staff with a metal point on the end.

pi·laf' (pi-läf') *n.* a dish of boiled rice and meat. Also, **pi·lau'** (-low').

pi·las'ter (pi-las'tər) *n.* a rectangular column built partly in a wall.

pil'chard (pil'chərd) *n.* **1,** a small marine fish, like a herring. **2,** a sardine.

pile (pīl) *n.* **1,** soft hair; nap on cloth. **2,** a large supporting timber, etc., set in the ground. **3,** a massive edifice. **4,** a heap or mass. **5,** a pyre. **6,** (*Colloq.*) a large quantity; a fortune. **7,** a series of metal plates for producing electric current. **8,** an atomic pile. **9,** (*pl.*) hemorrhoids. —*v.t.* **1,** heap up. **2,** load. —*v.i.* (with *up*) form a heap; accumulate. —**pile driver,** a machine which drives piles by dropping a heavy weight (*drop hammer*) upon them.

pile-'up" *n.* **1,** a collision involving several automobiles, people, etc. **2,** congestion, as in the air.

pil'fer (pil'fər) *v.t. & i.* steal surreptitiously in small amounts. —**pil'fer·er,** *n.*

pil'grim *n.* **1,** one who travels, esp. to a holy place as an act of devotion. **2,** (*cap.*) one of the earliest English settlers in Massachusetts. —**pil'grim·age,** *n.* a journey.

pill (pil) *n.* **1,** a small tablet of medicine.

2, (*Slang*) a ball, as in baseball. **3,** (*Slang*) a disagreeable person.

pil′lage (pil′ij) *v.t. & i.* plunder, esp. in war; sack. —*n.* plunder.

pil′lar (pil′ər) *n.* a supporting or ornamental column; any mainstay.

pill′box″ *n.* **1,** a small box for pills. **2,** (*Mil.*) a low, fortified machine-gun position.

pil′lion (pil′yən) *n.* an extra rear saddle or motorcycle seat.

pil′lo·ry (pil′ə-rē) *n.* a frame to hold an offender for exposure to public ridicule. —*v.t.* **1,** punish in the pillory. **2,** invoke scorn upon.

pil′low (pil′ō) *n.* a soft cushion to rest the head upon. —*v.t.* lay on a pillow. —**pil′lowcase″, pil′low·slip″,** *n.* a cover for a pillow.

pi′lot (pī′lət) *n.* **1,** one who steers or controls a ship or aircraft. **2,** a leader; guide. **3,** a prototype. —**pilot lamp,** an indicator lamp on a motor, etc. —*v.t.* direct the course of. —**pilot light,** a small flame from which to ignite a larger.

pils′ner (pilz′nər) *n.* **1,** a light Bohemian beer. **2,** a tall tapering glass.

pi·men′to (pi-men′tō) *n.* [*pl.* **-tos**] *n.* **1,** the berry of a W. Indies tree; allspice; also, the tree. **2,** pimiento.

pi·mien′to (pi-myen′tō) *n.* [*pl.* **-tos**] a sweet red pepper.

pimp *n.* an agent or exploiter of prostitutes. —*v.i.* pander.

pim′per·nel″ (pim′pər-nel″) *n.* a plant with flowers which close in bad weather.

pim′ple (pim′pəl) *n.* a small eruption on the skin. —**pim′ply,** *adj.*

pin *n.* **1,** a pointed piece, esp. of thin wire, to join or attach things; a peg or bolt; a fastening device employing a pin. **2,** a piece of jewelry attached by a pin; a brooch. **3,** any of various pieces cut from a cylinder, as used in machines, bowling, etc. —*v.t.* [**pinned, pin′ning**] **1,** hold fast, esp. with a pin. **2,** (*Colloq.*) give a fraternity pin to (a girl) as a token of intention to become engaged. —**pin money,** a small amount of money, usu. for personal expenses. —**pins and needles,** a tingling sensation. —**on pins and needles,** nervous or tense; insecure.

pi′ña co·la′da (pē′nyə-kə-lä′dä) a drink of rum, pineapple juice, and coconut.

pin′a·fore″ (pin′ə-fôr″) *n.* a child's apron or sleeveless dress.

pin′ball″ *n.* a bagatelle game in which the scores are electrically recorded.

pince-′nez″ (paṅs′nā′) *n.* (*Fr.*) eyeglasses held on the nose by a spring.

pin′cers (pin′sərz) *n.pl.* or *sing.* **1,** a gripping tool, two arms hinged off-center. **2,**

the gripping claws of lobsters, crabs, etc. **3,** (*Mil.*) simultaneous attacks from different directions. Also, **pinch′ers** (pin′chərz).

pinch *v.t. & i.* **1,** nip or squeeze between two surfaces. **2,** cramp; afflict, as with cold, poverty, etc.; be frugal. **3,** (*Slang*) capture; arrest. **4,** (*Slang*) steal. —*n.* **1,** a squeeze; nip. **2,** a tiny amount. **3,** painful stress. **4,** a critical juncture; emergency. **5,** (*Slang*) a raid; arrest.

pinch-′hit″ *v.i.* in baseball, go to bat for another; act as substitute, esp. in an emergency.

pin′cush″ion *n.* a small cushion in which to keep pins.

pine (pīn) *n.* a cone-bearing evergreen tree with needle-shaped leaves; its timber. —*v.i.* **1,** grieve; languish. **2,** long (for).

pin′e·al (pin′ē-əl) *adj.* shaped like a pine cone. —**pineal body** or **gland,** a small vestigial organ of unknown function attached to the brain.

pine′ap″ple (pīn′ap″əl) *n.* **1,** a tropical plant or its sweet, juicy cone-shaped fruit. **2,** a small bomb in this shape.

pin′feath″ers *n.* feather stems just emerging.

ping *n.* **1,** the whistling sound of a projectile. **2,** motor knock. —*v.i.* make a pinging sound.

ping-′pong″ *n.* (*T.N.*) table tennis.

pin′head″ *n.* (*Colloq.*) **1,** a person with a very small head. **2,** a dolt.

pin′hole″ *n.* a tiny hole or dent.

pin′ion (pin′yən) *n.* **1,** a small gear wheel. **2,** the end segment of a bird's wing; a feather; a wing. —*v.t.* restrain, as by cutting the wings or pinning the arms.

pink *n.* **1,** a garden plant or its spicy, fringed flower. **2,** a light-red color. **3,** a person mildly inclined to communism. **4,** the best degree. —*v.t.* **1,** pierce; prick. **2,** finish with a serrated edge.

pink′eye″ *n.* a contagious disease of the eye; conjunctivitis.

pink′ie (-ē) *n.* the little finger.

pink′ster (-stər) *n.* Whitsuntide. Also, **pinx′ter.** —**pinkster flower,** a variety of azalea.

pin′nace (pin′is) *n.* a light, two-masted vessel; a small boat.

pin′na·cle (pin′ə-kəl) *n.* **1,** a sharp point or peak; a spire. **2,** the highest point; acme.

pin′nate (pin′āt) *adj.* shaped like a feather.

pi′noch″le (pē′nuck″əl) *n.* a card game.

pin′ñon (pin′yən) *n.* a variety of pine tree; its fruit.

pin′point″ *n.* extreme exactitude; a pin's

point or similar fineness. —v.t. locate exactly, as for precision bombing.

pin′set″ter n. an automatic device in a bowling alley that sets up the pins and returns the ball. Also, **pin′spot″ter** (T.N.).

pin′stripe″ adj. (of a fabric) having thin lines of a different color. —n. **1,** a fabric so woven. **2,** any such line or stripe.

pint (pīnt) n. a measure of capacity, 16 liquid oz., one-half quart.

pin′tail″ n. a wild duck with a pointed tail.

pin′to (pin′tō) adj. mottled. —n. a piebald horse or pony.

pin-′up girl an attractive young woman or her picture.

pin′wheel″ n. **1,** a wheel that spins on a pin when blown upon. **2,** revolving fireworks.

pinx′ter (pink′stər) n. pinkster.

pin′y (pī′nė) adj. of the pine.

pi″o·neer′ (pī″ə-nir′) n. one who goes ahead; an early settler. —v.t. & i. do or be first.

pi′ous (pī′əs) adj. **1,** godly; devout. **2,** pretending piety. —**pi′ous·ness,** n.

pip n. **1,** a disease of fowls. **2,** a small seed, as of an apple; something like it, as a spot on dice, a suit symbol on playing cards, etc. **3,** a spot on a radar screen. **4,** (Slang) something remarkable.

pipe (pīp) n. **1,** a long tube for conveying a fluid. **2,** a tube and its attached bowl, for smoking. **3,** one of the tubes of an organ. **4,** (Archaic) a musical wind instrument. **5,** a shrill voice; a bird's note. **6,** a wine measure, usu. 126 gallons. —v.t. **1,** supply with, or convey by or as by, pipe. **2,** (Naut.) summon or salute with the sound of a whistle or pipe. **3,** utter in a shrill voice; whistle. —v.i. **1,** chirp; whistle. **2,** play on a pipe. —**pipe down,** (Slang) be quiet. —**pipe dream,** a vain hope. —**pipe up,** (Colloq.) speak up.

pipe′line″ n. **1,** a pipe for conveying oil or gas over long distances. **2,** a means of obtaining secret information.

pip′er n. a flutist or bagpiper. —**pay the piper, 1,** bear the costs (of something). **2,** suffer the consequences (of an action).

pipe′stem″ n. the stem of a pipe. —adj. (Colloq.) very thin, as a person's legs.

pi·pette′ (pī-pet′) n. a small tube. Also, **pi·pet′.**

pip′ing (pī′ping) n. a trim of covered cord. —**piping hot,** very hot.

pip′it n. a small bird resembling the lark that sings in flight.

pip′pin (pip′in) n. **1,** a variety of apple. **2,** (Slang) something lovely.

pip′squeak″ n. (Slang) an unimportant, usu. small person, esp. one who is obtrusive or presumptuous.

pi′quant (pē′kənt) adj. agreeably pungent; attractive though racy. —**pi′quan·cy,** n.

pique (pēk) v.t. **1,** wound the pride of; nettle. **2,** arouse the interest of. —n. wounded pride; umbrage.

pi·qué′ (pė-kā′) n. a ribbed fabric.

pi·quet′ (pi-ket′) n. a card game for two.

pi·ran′ha (pi-ron′yə) n. a small tropical fish, voracious and typically vicious.

pi′rate (pī′rət) n. **1,** a sea-robber; his ship. **2,** hijacker. **3,** one who steals a literary or artistic idea. —v.t. **1,** rob at sea. **2,** publish without legal right. —**pi′ra·cy** (pī′rə-sė) n. —**pi·rat′i·cal** (pī-rat′i-kəl) adj.

pi·rogue′ (pi-rōg′) n. a canoe hollowed out from the trunk of a tree.

pir″ou·ette′ (pir″ə-wet′) n. in ballet dancing, a spinning on the toes.

pis″ca·to′ri·al (pis″kə-tôr′ė-əl) adj. pert. to fishing or fishermen.

Pis′ces (pis′ēz) n. a constellation, the Fish (see zodiac).

pis·ci- (pis-i) pref. fish.

pish interj. nonsense!

pis′mire″ (pis′mīr″) n. an ant.

pis·ta′chi·o″ (pis-tä′shė-ō″) n.[pl. -os″ (-ōz″)] a tree bearing a greenish edible nut; the nut.

pis′til n. (Bot.) the seed-bearing organ of a flower.

pis′tol (pis′təl) n. a small firearm held and fired by one hand. —**pis′tol-whip″,** v.t. beat with a pistol.

pis·tole′ (pis-tōl′) n. a former gold coin of various countries, esp. Spain.

pis′ton (pis′tən) n. a cylinder moving within a fitting bore to impart motion.

pit n. **1,** a hole in the ground; an abyss; a mine, or shaft in a mine. **2,** a depression; a small scar. **3,** a small arena; (Brit.) the cheaper seats in a theater. **4,** an area for trading in a stock or grain exchange, etc. **5,** the stone of a fruit. **6,** (pl.) (Slang) the worst. —v.t. [**pit′ted, -ting**] **1,** make scars in. **2,** match (one person or force) against another. **3,** remove the pits from, as fruit. —**pit viper,** a snake having a deep pit in the skin between the eye and the nostril.

pit′a·pat″ (pit′ə-pat″) n. a succession of taps; a light quick step.

pitch (pich) v.t. **1,** hurl; toss; throw. **2,** set up, as a tent. **3,** (Music) start (a tune) by sounding the keynote. —v.i. **1,** toss something; specif., throw a ball to a batter. **2,** encamp. **3,** plunge headlong; slant; incline; slope. **4,** (with on or upon) decide. **5,** rise and fall, as a ship at sea. —n. **1,** a throw;

toss. **2,** a headlong fall. **3,** the fore-and-aft plunging of a ship. **4,** the extreme point or degree or height or depth. **5,** slope; a declivity. **6,** (*Music*) highness or lowness of tone. **7,** a thick black substance; tar. **—pitch dark,** complete dark. **—pitch in,** (*Colloq.*) set to work with energy. **—pitch into,** (*Colloq.*) attack. **—pitch pipe,** a harmonica-like device for giving the pitch (as to singers, etc.).

pitch-'black" *adj.* as black as pitch.

pitch'blende" (pich'blend") a lustrous black mineral, a source of radium and uranium.

pitch'er (-ər) *n.* **1,** a vessel with a handle for holding liquids. **2,** the player in baseball who pitches. **3,** a golf club for lofting shots, No. 7 iron.

pitch'fork" *n.* a tool for lifting hay.

pitch'man" *n.* [*pl.* **-men"**] a hawker.

pit'e·ous (pit'ē-əs) *adj.* sad; arousing pity. **—pit'e·ous·ness,** *n.*

pit'fall" *n.* a trap; a hidden danger.

pith *n.* **1,** the spongy tissue in the stems of certain plants. **2,** the essential part; gist. **3,** vigor. **—pith'y,** *adj.*

pit'i·a·ble (pit'ē-ə-bəl) *adj.* deserving pity. **—pit'i·a·ble·ness,** *n.*

pit'i·ful (-fəl) *adj.* **1,** deserving pity. **2,** paltry. **—pit'i·ful·ness,** *n.*

pit'i·less (-ləs) *adj.* unmerciful. **—pit'i·less·ness,** *n.*

pi'ton (pē'ton) *n.* in mountain climbing, a metal spike driven into rock or ice, used to secure a rope.

pit'tance (pit'əns) *n.* a very small and inadequate quantity, esp. of money.

pit'ter-pat"ter (pit'ər-pat"ər) *n.* pit-a-pat.

pi·tu'i·tar"y (pi-tū'ə-ter"ē) *adj.* pert. to a small endocrine gland.

pit'y (pit'ē) *n.* **1,** a feeling of compassion for another's grief or suffering. **2,** a cause of regret. **—v.t.** feel compassion for.

più (pyoo) *adv.* (*Ital.*) more.

piv'ot (piv'ət) *n.* a pin on which an object turns; hence, a cardinal or critical point. **—v.i.** turn; hinge. **—piv'ot·al,** *adj.*

pix'i·lat"ed (pik'sə-lā"tid) *adj.* (*Colloq.*) mentally eccentric.

pix'y (pik'sē) *n.* a mischievous elf. Also, **pix'ie.**

piz'za (pēt'tsə) *n.* an Italian baked dish resembling a pie, made of leavened bread dough rolled out into a thin sheet (usu. round) and topped with a tomato and cheese sauce and other seasonings. **—piz"ze·ri'a** (pēt'tsə-rē'ə) *n.* a restaurant specializing in pizza.

piz"zi·ca'to (pit"sə-kä'tō) *adj.* played by plucking the strings with the fingers.

plac'ard (plak'ərd) *n.* a notice posted in a public place; poster. **—v.t.** place a poster on.

pla'cate (plā'kāt) *v.t.* pacify; conciliate. **—pla'ca·to·ry,** (-kə-tôr-ē) *adj.*

place (plās) *n.* **1,** region; locality; spot; a particular spot or building. **2,** room to stand or sit in. **3,** the proper or allocated position for anything. **4,** a job; situation. **5,** social status; duty. **6,** second in a horse race. **—v.t.** **1,** put or set in a particular position; set in order; arrange. **2,** find a home or job for. **3,** put; repose. **4,** locate; identify, as by association. **—v.i.** finish second. **—place kick,** (*Football*) a kick of the ball held upright on the ground. **—place setting,** the necessary eating utensils for one person. **—take place,** occur.

pla·ce'bo (plə-sē'bō) *n.* **1,** (*Med.*) an inert medicine prescribed to humor or pacify a patient. **2,** (*Rom. Cath. Ch.*) the vespers for the dead. **3,** a control dose given to one of two groups in a medical experiment.

place'ment (-mənt) *n.* **1,** act or result of placing. **2,** employment. **3,** a place kick.

pla·cen'ta (plə-sen'tə) *n.* the organ in the womb to which the fetus is attached.

plac'er (plā'sər) *n.* in mining, a place where sand, gravel, etc., is washed for gold.

plac'id (plas'id) *adj.* serene; unruffled. **—pla·cid'i·ty,** *n.*

plack'et (plak'it) *n.* a slit in a skirt, coat tail, etc.

pla'gi·a·rism (plā'jə-riz-əm) *n.* the offering of another's artistic or literary work as one's own. **—pla'gi·a·rist,** *n.* **—pla'gi·a·rize",** *v.t. & i.*

plague (plāg) *n.* **1,** a pestilential epidemic disease. **2,** severe trouble; scourge. **3,** (*Colloq.*) a nuisance. **—v.t.** **1,** harass; annoy. **2,** afflict with the plague. **—pla'guy,** *adj.*

plaice (plās) *n.* a kind of flatfish or flounder.

plaid (plad) *n.* a wool fabric with a tartan or similar pattern; the pattern itself. **—adj.** having a crossbarred pattern.

plain (plān) *adj.* **1,** flat; level; unobstructed; open. **2,** easily understood. **3,** sheer; downright. **4,** without a figured pattern. **5,** not handsome or fancy; homely. **6,** simple; sincere; frank. **—n.** an extent of level country. **—plain'ness,** *n.*

plain'clothes"man (-mən) *n.* [*pl.* **-men**] a detective not in uniform.

plains'man (plānz'mən) *n.* [*pl.* **-men**] a dweller on an undeveloped plain.

plain'song" *n.* a liturgical chant.

plain-'spo″ken *adj.* frank. **—plain-″spo′ken·ness,** *n.*

plaint (plānt) *n.* **1,** a sad song; lamentation. **2,** a complaint.

plain'tiff (plān'tif) *n.* (*Law*) the person who brings suit.

plain'tive (plān'tiv) *adj.* mournful. **—plain'tive·ness,** *n.*

plait (plāt) *n.* **1,** a braid, as of hair. **2,** an overlapping fold; pleat. **—v.t.** braid (hair).

plan *n.* **1,** a diagram or drawing, esp. of an uncompleted structure. **2,** arrangement of parts in a certain design. **3,** a formulated scheme for getting something done. **—v.t.** [**planned, plan'ning**] **1,** make a design or diagram of. **2,** devise ways and means for. **—v.i.** decide on future acts. **—plan'ner,** *n.* **—planned parenthood,** the advance planning of family size by parents; (*cap.*) an organization dedicated to promoting this.

plane (plān) *adj.* level; flat.—*n.* **1,** a flat or level surface. **2,** a grade or level, as of thought, etc. **3,** an airplane. **4,** a tool for smoothing wood. **5,** a type of tree, as the sycamore.—*v.t.* smooth with a plane.—*v.i.* to glide, as in a hydroplane.

plan'et (plan'it) *n.* a celestial body revolving around the sun. **—plan'e·tar·y,** *adj.*

plan″e·tar'i·um (plan″i-târ′ē-əm) *n.* [*pl.* **-a** (-ə)] a device to represent the heavenly bodies and their movement; the auditorium or building housing it.

plan'e·tar'y (plan'ə-ter'ē) *adj.* **1,** pert. to a planet or the planets. **2,** pert. to system of gears, esp. an automobile transmission.

plan″e·tes'i·mal (plan″ə-tes′ə-məl) *n.* one of numerous small solid heavenly bodies which may have united to form the planets and moons of our solar system.

plan'et·oid *n.* a minor planet; asteroid.

plank *n.* **1,** a long, thick board. **2,** an item of a political party's platform.—*v.t.* **1,** cover with planks. **2,** (with *down*) pay; deliver. **3,** cook and serve on a board.

plank'ton (plank'tən) *n.* the microscopic animals and plants that drift freely in natural bodies of water and on which most marine life feeds.

plant (plănt) *n.* **1,** a living organism, lacking voluntary motion, usually rooted in and growing from the soil. **2,** a seedling or cutting; anything planted. **3,** a factory; a business building and its equipment.—*v.t.* **1,** put in the ground to grow. **2,** set firmly in position. **3,** implant or engender, as ideas, etc. **4,** (*Slang*) secrete (something) to trick or incriminate someone **—plant louse,** aphid.

plan'tain (plan'tin) *n.* **1,** a common weed with broad leaves. **2,** a tropical tree; its bananalike fruit.

plan·ta'tion (plan-tā'shən) *n.* a large estate on which cotton or sugar, etc., is cultivated.

plant'er *n.* **1,** a rich farmer; a plantation owner. **2,** a small plant-holder. **—planter's punch,** a sweetened drink of rum and lemon or lime juice.

plaque (plak) *n.* **1,** an ornamental or commemorative tablet. **2,** a patch of skin disease. **3,** mucus containing bacteria on a tooth.

plash *n.* **1,** a splash. **2,** a puddle. —*v.t. & i.* **1,** splash. **2,** bend down and interweave the branches of, as a hedge.

plas'ma (plaz'mə) *n.* **1,** the liquid part of blood, lymph, or milk. **2,** charged particles. **3,** a green quartz.

plas'ter (plås'tər) *n.* **1,** a wet paste of lime, sand, water, etc., that dries to a hard smooth finish. **2,** a remedy spread on cloth and applied to the body. —*v.t.* **1,** apply plaster to. **2,** spread on. **—plas'tered,** *adj.* (*Slang*) drunk. **—plas'ter·ing,** *n.* **—plaster of Paris,** a white paste used in molding.

plas'ter·board″ *n.* a layered building material for walls, etc.

plas'tic (plas'tik) *adj.* **1,** capable of being molded, esp. by pressure; pliant. **2,** (*Slang*) phony; not trustworthy. —*n.* a plastic substance, esp. one of a group of synthetic materials used as substitutes for wood, metal, etc. **—plas'ti·cal·ly,** *adv.* **—plastic arts,** the arts of modeling or molding plastic materials, as plaster, clay, etc. **—plastic surgery,** surgery to correct deformities or repair mutilations. **—plastic wood,** a plastic that dries to the consistency of wood.

plas·tic'i·ty (plas-tis′ə-tē) *n.* state of being plastic.

plate (plāt) *n.* **1,** a thin flat sheet of metal, glass, etc.; such a sheet used or prepared for any purpose, as printing, photography, etc. **2,** a shallow dish for food; its contents. **3,** gold and silver table dishes and utensils. **4,** a denture; a setting for false teeth. **5,** in an electron tube, the electrode to which the electrons flow. **6,** in baseball, home base. —*v.t.* apply a coating of metal to. **—plate glass,** a superior kind of thick glass, rolled and polished, used for mirrors, shop windows, etc.

pla·teau' (pla-tō') *n.* **1,** an extent of elevated land; a tableland. **2,** a period of area of little change.

plat'en (plat'ən) *n.* **1,** the plate that presses paper against printing type. **2,** the roller of a typewriter.

plat'form (plat'fôrm) *n.* **1,** a raised flooring. **2,** a statement of political policies.

plat'i·num (plat'ə-nəm) *n.* a precious silver-white metallic element, no. 78, symbol Pt. —**platinum blonde,** a woman with hair of extremely pale yellow.

plat′i·tude″ (plat′i-tood″) n. a trite, obvious remark. —**plat′i·tu′di·nous,** adj.

pla·ton′ic (plə-ton′ik) adj. solely spiritual; not sensual. —**pla·ton′i·cal·ly,** adv.

pla·toon′ (plə-toon′) n. a body of troops, comprising several squads.

plat′ter (plat′ər) n. **1,** a broad shallow dish for serving food. **2,** phonograph record.

plat′y·pus (plat′ə-pəs) n. a small, egg-laying, aquatic mammal with a bill like a duck's.

plau′dit (plâ′dit) n. (usually pl.) applause.

plau′si·ble (plâ′zə-bəl) adj. seemingly true or trustworthy. —**plau″si·bil′i·ty,** n.

play (plā) v.i. **1,** move lightly and quickly; flicker; dart. **2,** engage in a game; take recreation. **3,** act; behave. **4,** act on the stage; perform music. —v.t. **1,** engage in (a game); compete against; bet on. **2,** perform upon (a musical instrument). **3,** perform (a play, musical composition, trick, etc.); assume the role of. **4,** put in operation or motion. —n. **1,** brisk or free motion; freedom; scope. **2,** amusement; diversion; fun; jest. **3,** a dramatic work. **4,** in a game, one's turn to act; the move made or action taken. —**make a play for,** try to obtain; solicit; woo. —**play around,** (Colloq.) flirt; dally. —**play at,** do inexpertly or half-heartedly. —**play back,** replay, as a record. —**play down,** depreciate. —**play down to,** (Colloq.) treat in a condescending manner. —**playing card,** one of the pasteboard or plastic cards, 2¼ or 2½ by 3½ inches, used in many games. —**play on words,** a pun. —**play up,** emphasize.

play′act″ v.i. **1,** pretend; make believe. **2,** behave artificially.

play′bill″ n. a theater program.

play′boy″ n. (Slang) a rich, frivolous man.

play′er n. a performer in a game, play, etc. —**player piano,** a piano which automatically plays music recorded mechanically on piano rolls.

play′ful adj. frolicsome; jocular. —**play′-ful·ness,** n.

play′girl″ n. (Slang) a frivolous young woman.

play′go″er n. one who regularly attends plays.

play′ground″ n. a field for games, etc.

play′house″ n. **1,** theater. **2,** a small house for children's play.

play′let (plā′lit) n. a short dramatic play.

play′mate″ n. a companion at play. Also, **play′fel″low.**

play-′off″ n. a contest to decide a previous tie.

play′thing″ n. a toy.

play′wright″ n. a dramatist.

pla′za (plä′zə) n. an open square.

plea (plē) n. **1,** an entreaty. **2,** pretext; excuse. **3,** (Law) a defendant's answer to the charge against him. —**plea bargaining,** agreement in advance of trial between prosecution and defense for a certain plea and sentence.

plead (plēd) v.i. **1,** (with with) try to persuade; beg; implore. **2,** (Law) present a plea. —v.t. urge or allege as an excuse or defense. —**plead′ings,** n.pl. statements made in court.

pleas′ance (plez′əns) n. a secluded formal garden attached to a mansion.

pleas′ant (plez′ənt) adj. agreeable. —**pleas′ant·ness,** n.

pleas′ant·ry (plez′ən-trē) n. **1,** banter. **2,** a jest.

please (plēz) v.t. give satisfaction or delight to. —v.i. **1,** give satisfaction. **2,** choose; wish; think fit. —adv. if you so wish: a polite form in imperative construction, short for if [it] you please, as in please do this. —**pleas′ing,** adj. attractive; agreeable.

pleas′ure (plezh′ər) n. **1,** a feeling of enjoyment or delight. **2,** a cause or source of this feeling. **3,** desire; preference. —**pleas′-ur·a·ble,** adj.

pleat (plēt) n. a fold, as of cloth. —v.t. lay in folds.

plebe (plēb) n. at Annapolis or West Point, a fourth-classman (freshman).

ple·be′ian (pli-bē′ən) adj. pert. to the common people; vulgar. —n. one of the common people.

pleb′i·scite″ (pleb′ə-sīt″) n. a vote by the whole people.

plebs (plebz) n.sing. [pl. **ple′bes** (plē′bēz)] in ancient Rome, the populace.

plec′trum (plek′trəm) n. a small flat implement for plucking the strings of a musical instrument.

pledge (plej) n. **1,** a thing given as security. **2,** a promise. **3,** a candidate for admission to a fraternity or sorority who has not yet been initiated. —v.t. **1,** pawn. **2,** promise, esp. a donation.

ple′na·ry (plē′nə-rē) adj. **1,** full; unqualified. **2,** fully attended or constituted.

plen″i·po·ten′ti·ar″y (plen″i-pō-ten′shē-er″ē) n. an emissary, as an ambassador, with full powers. —adj. having full powers.

plen′i·tude″ (plen′i-tood″) n. abundance; fullness.

plen′te·ous (plen′tē-əs) adj. abundant. —**plen′te·ous·ness,** n.

plen'ti·ful (plen'ti-fəl) *adj.* **1,** ample. **2,** fruitful. **—plen'ti·ful·ness,** *n.*

plen'ty (plen'tė) *n.* an adequate supply; abundance.

ple'num (plē'nəm) *n.* **1,** fullness; the opposite of vacuum. **2,** a quantity of air, etc., under greater than atmospheric pressure. **3,** a full meeting or assembly.

pleth'o·ra (pleth'ə-rə) *n.* overfullness; superabundance.

pleu'ra (plûr'ə) *n.* the membrane lining of the chest. **—pleu'ral,** *adj.* **—pleu·ris'tic,** *adj.*

pleu'ri·sy (plûr'ə-sė) *n.* inflammation of the pleura.

plex'i·glass'' (plek'sə-glås'') *n.* (*T.N.*) a clear thermoplastic compound.

plex'us (plek'səs) *n.* a network, as of blood vessels and nerve fibers. **—plex'i·form,** *adj.*

pli'a·ble (plī'ə-bəl) *adj.* **1,** flexible. **2,** compliant. **—pli''a·bil'i·ty,** *n.*

pli'ant (plī'ənt) *adj.* supple; pliable. **—pli'an·cy,** *n.*

pli'ers (plī'ərz) *n.pl.* pincers with long, blunt jaws.

plight (plīt) *n.* **1,** condition; predicament. **2,** a pledge. **—v.t. 1,** pledge, as one's word, honor, etc. **2,** betroth.

Plim'soll mark (plim'səl) a line showing a ship's safe load capacity.

plinth *n.* the slab at the base of a column, pedestal, statue, etc.

pli'o·film'' (plī'ə-) *n.* a plastic that forms flexible, transparent sheets, used for raincoats, etc.

plod *v.i.* [**plod'ded, -ding**] **1,** trudge. **2,** toil; drudge. **—plod'der,** *n.*

plop *n.* the sound of something falling into water with little splashing. **—v.i. & t.** [**plopped, plop'ping**] fall, drop, or set with a plop.

plot *n.* **1,** a small piece of ground. **2,** a plan or map. **3,** an intrigue; conspiracy. **4,** the plan of a novel, play, etc. **—v.t.** [**plot'ted, -ting**] **1,** chart; map; plan. **2,** contrive. **—v.i.** conspire. **—plot'ter,** *n.*

plov'er (pluv'ər) *n.* a shore bird akin to the sandpiper.

plow *n.* an implement that furrows and turns over the soil; a similar instrument, as a snow plow. **—v.t. & i. 1,** till with a plow. **2,** move, cleave, or push through. Also, **plough. —plow'man** (-mən) *n.*

plow'share'' *n.* the cutting blade of a plow.

ploy (ploi) *n.* **1,** a game; an escapade or trick. **2,** a stratagem or remark that subtly puts an antagonist at a disadvantage in a game or in argument or conversation.

pluck (pluk) *v.t.* **1,** pull off or up; pick. **2,** strip (a fowl) of feathers. **3,** jerk; twitch. **4,** twang, as a banjo. **5,** (*Slang*) rob; fleece. **—n. 1,** a twitch; tug; twang. **2,** courage; spirit. **—pluck'y,** *adj.* spirited; courageous.

plug *n.* **1,** a stopper. **2,** a connection, as for a hose, an electrical wire, etc. **3,** a cake of tobacco. **4,** (*Colloq.*) a favorable remark. **5,** (*Slang*) something unfit or worthless, esp. a horse. **6,** an artificial lure in fishing. **—v.t.** [**plugged, plug'ging**] **1,** stop up with a plug. **2,** (*Colloq.*) shoot. **3,** (*Colloq.*) publicize. **—v.i.** work steadily. **—plug'ger,** *n.* a dogged worker. **—plug-ug'ly,** *n.* (*Slang*) a rowdy; tough; gangster's henchman.

plug·o'la (plug-ō'lə) *n.* (*Slang*) payola paid to receive a plug on radio or TV.

plum *n.* **1,** the juicy, smooth-skinned fruit of a tree similar to the peach; the tree. **2,** a raisin. **3,** a prize or reward; a good thing. **4,** a bluish-red color.

plum'age (ploo'mij) *n.* **1,** feathers. **2,** (*Humorous*) bright or fancy clothing.

plumb (plum) *n.* **1,** a ball of lead dropped on a line (*plumb line*) for testing perpendicularity, depth, etc. **2,** the vertical. **—v.t.** test by a plumb line. **—adj.** vertical. **—adv. 1,** vertically. **2,** exactly. **3,** (*Colloq.*) utterly.

plum·ba'go (plum-bā'gō) *n.* graphite, used in lead pencils, etc.

plumb'er (plum'ər) *n.* a worker on water pipes, bathroom fixtures, steam fitting, etc. **—plumber's helper,** a plunger.

plumb'ing *n.* **1,** the trade of a plumber. **2,** piping and attached fixtures.

plume (ploom) *n.* a feather or bunch of feathers. **—v.t.** preen or adorn (oneself).

plum'met (plum'it) *n.* a plumb. **—v.i.** plunge straight down.

plump *v.i. & t.* **1,** drop suddenly and heavily. **2,** support (as a candidate) vigorously. **—n.** a heavy fall. **—adj.** fat; well-rounded. **—adv.** heavily; flatly. **—plump'ness,** *n.*

plun'der (plun'dər) *v.t.* rob; take by force. **—n. 1,** robbery. **2,** booty.

plunge (plunj) *v.t.* **1,** thrust suddenly (into a liquid, flesh, etc.). **2,** cast or throw (into a state or condition, as war, debt, etc.). **—v.i. 1,** dive or leap. **2,** rush headlong. **3,** bet recklessly. **—n.** a sudden dive or leap.

plung'er *n.* **1,** a mechanical part that moves up and down, as a piston. **2,** an implement for unclogging a toilet. **3,** (*Slang*) a reckless gambler.

plunk *v.i.* make a quick, hollow, heavy, often metallic sound. **—v.t. 1,** twang. **2,** drop or slap down. **—n.** the sound of plunking.

plu″per′fect (ploo″pēr′fikt) *adj. & n.* (*Gram.*) past perfect, as *I had done it.*

plu′ral (plůr′əl) *adj.* designating more than one. —*n.* (*Gram.*) a plural form.

plu·ral′i·ty (plŭ-ral′ə-tė) *n.* the receipt of more votes than any other candidate; the amount of excess.

plus *adj.* **1,** indicating addition. **2,** additional. **3,** positive; greater than zero. —*prep.* with the addition of. —*n.* **1,** the plus sign (+). **2,** something additional. —**plus fours,** long baggy knickerbockers.

plush *n.* a fabric like velvet, but with a longer pile. —*adj.* (*Colloq.*) luxurious; showy.

plu·toc′ra·cy (ploo-tok′rə-sė) *n.* **1,** government by the rich. **2,** the influential rich.

plu′to·crat″ (ploo′tə-krat″) *n.* **1,** a very rich person. **2,** an adherent of plutocracy. —**plu″to·crat′ic,** *adj.* —**plu″to·crat′i·cal·ly,** *adv.*

plu·to′ni·um (ploo-tō′nė-əm) *n.* a radioactive chemical element, no. 94, symbol Pu.

plu′vi·ous (ploo′vė-əs) *adj.* pert. to rain; rainy. —**plu′vi·al,** *adj.*

ply (plī) *n.* a layer or strand. —*v.t.* **1,** wield diligently. **2,** work at steadily. **3,** address persistently, as with questions. **4,** offer (to someone) frequently and persistently, as drink. —*v.t.* travel a course regularly.

ply′wood″ *n.* several layers of wood laminated together.

pneu·mat′ic (nū-mat′ik) *adj.* **1,** pert. to air. **2,** inflated with air. **3,** worked by compressed air. —**pneu·mat′i·cal·ly,** *adv.*

pneu·mo- (noo-mō) *pref.* the lungs.

pneu·mo′ni·a (noo-mō′nyə) *n.* inflammation of the tissues of the lungs. —**pneu·mon′ic** (-mon′ik) *adj.*

poach (pōch) *v.t. & i.* **1,** cook (egg) by breaking it into boiling water. **2,** trespass, esp. to hunt or fish. —**poach′er,** *n.* a trespasser.

pock (pok) *n.* a pus-filled eruption, as in smallpox. —**pock′mark″,** *n.*

pock′et (pok′it) *n.* **1,** a pouch inserted in a garment; its contents, esp. money. **2,** a cavity or hollow. —*adj.* of small size. —*v.t.* **1,** put in a pocket. **2,** appropriate; accept. **3,** suppress. —**in one's pocket,** under one's domination or control. —**line one's pockets,** get much money. —**pocket battleship,** a heavily armed vessel, smaller than usual because of treaty limitations. —**pocket billiards,** a game of sinking balls in pockets on a billiard table. —**pocket park,** a small city park. —**pocket veto,** the holding of a bill by a chief executive until it expires by law, in effect, a veto.

pock′et·book″ *n.* a purse.

pock′et·knife″ *n.* a folding knife to be carried in the pocket.

po′co (pō′kō) *adv.* (*Ital.*) somewhat. —**poco a poco,** *adv.* little by little; gradually.

pod *n.* **1,** the seed case of certain plants, as the pea or bean. **2,** a podlike container, as a spacecraft compartment, an airline bus, etc.

po·di′a·try (pō-dī′ə-trė) *n.* (*Med.*) the treatment of disorders of the feet. —**po·di′a·trist,** *n.*

po′di·um (pō′dė-əm) *n.* [*pl.* **-a** (-ə)] a speaker's or conductor's platform; dais.

po′em (pō′im) *n.* a composition in verse; lofty or imaginative writing or artistic expression.

po′e·sy (pō′ə-sė) *n.* **1,** poetry. **2,** the art of writing poetry.

po′et (pō′it) *n.* **1,** one who writes poems or is capable of lofty artistic expression. —**po′et·ess,** *n.fem.* —**poet laureate,** the official poet of a state or nation.

po′et·as″ter (pō′it-as″tər) *n.* a writer of poor verse.

po·et′ic (pō-et′ik) *adj.* **1,** of or pert. to poetry. **2,** befitting poetry. Also, **po·et′i·cal.** —**poetic justice,** an ideal distribution of rewards and punishments. —**poetic license,** deviation from form to achieve a poetic effect.

po′et·ry (-rė) *n.* **1,** expression in poems. **2,** poems collectively. **3,** poetic qualities, spirit, or feeling. Also, **po′e·sy** (-zė).

po·go′ni·a (pə-gō′nė-ə) *n.* a type of orchid usu. having a single pale rose flower.

po′go stick (pō′gō) a pole with a spring, for leaping great distances.

po′grom (pō′grəm) *n.* an organized massacre, esp. of Jews.

poi *n.* a Hawaiian dish made from the root of the taro.

poign′ant (poin′yənt) *adj.* biting; painfully acute; affecting. —**poign′an·cy,** *n.*

poin·ci·a′na (poin-sė-a′nə) *n.* a tropical tree bearing showy orange or scarlet flowers.

poin·set′ti·a (poin-set′ė-ə) *n.* a plant with large scarlet leaves.

point *n.* **1,** a sharp or tapering end. **2,** a telling or essential feature. **3,** precise degree. **4,** aim; purpose. **5,** an exact spot or time . **6,** a unit of counting, measuring, or scoring. **7,** a unit of measurement for type; about 1/72 of an inch. **8,** one of the divisions of a compass. **9,** the period, esp. as a decimal mark. —*v.t.* **1,** aim. **2,** (with *out*) indicate the direction or position of. **3,** (with *up*) emphasize. —*v.i.* **1,** indicate direction with, or as with, the finger. **2,** tend; lead. **3,** face. —**pointy,** *adj.* pointed. —**point of**

no return, the place or moment in a journey or proceedings when one can no longer return or retreat. **—point of order,** a question as to whether proceedings are according to parliamentary law. **—point of view,** one's aspect of a subject or thing.

point-'blank" adj. direct; straightforward.

point'ed (-id) adj. sharp; pertinent; intended to affect a person. **—point'ed·ness,** n.

point'er (-ər) n. **1,** a hand on a clock, etc. **2,** a tapering rod for pointing. **3,** a hunting dog. **4,** a bit of advice; a tip.

poin'til·lism (pwan'tə-liz-əm) n. a method of Fr. impressionist painters in which color is applied in small dots on a white field.

point'less (-ləs) adj. meaningless; purposeless. **—point'less·ness,** n.

poise (poiz) n. **1,** equilibrium. **2,** carriage; bearing; self-possession. **—v.t. & i.** balance.

poi'son (poi'zən) n. **1,** a substance that causes injury or death upon ingestion, contact, or injection. **2,** any baneful influence or doctrine. **—v.t.** give poison to; corrupt or spoil with poison. **—poi'son·ous,** adj. **—poison ivy, oak, sumac,** plants that cause irritation of the skin.

poke (pōk) v.t. **1,** thrust away, down, or through. **2,** jab; prod, as with a stick. **—v.i.** **1,** search; pry; grope. **2,** make a thrust. **3,** dawdle. **—n. 1,** a thrust; nudge. **2,** a projecting brim on a bonnet. **3,** a bag; sack. **4,** a dawdler.

pok'er (pō'kər) n. **1,** a steel bar for stirring a fire. **2,** a card game. **—poker face,** (Colloq.) an expressionless face.

pok'y (pō'kè) adj. **1,** slow; boring. **2,** of a room, small and shabby. **—n.** (Colloq.) a jail. Also, **pok'ey. —pok'i·ness,** n.

po'lar (pō'lər) adj. pert. to, or at, the poles of a sphere, esp. of the earth. **—polar bear,** a large, creamy-white bear of the Arctic.

Po·la'ris (pō-lār'is) n. the North Star; the polestar.

po·lar'i·ty (pō-lār'ə-tè) n. the property whereby like magnetic poles attract and unlike poles repel each other.

po"lar·i·za'tion (pō"lər-ə-zā'shən) n. a state in which light rays exhibit different qualities in different directions. **—po'lar·ize"** (-īz") v.t.

po'lar·oid" n. (T.N.) **1,** an optical glass used to polarize light: to reduce glare, create the illusion of three-dimensional pictures, etc. **2,** a camera which takes pictures with a film that develops rapidly by itself.

pol'der (pōl'der) n. reclaimed marshland that has been brought under cultivation.

pole (pōl) n. **1,** either end óf the axis of a

sphere; specif. either end (North Pole or South Pole) of the earth's axis. **2,** either end of a magnet or terminal of an electric cell. **3,** a long, slender, tapering piece of wood. **4,** a measure of length, a rod, 5½ yds. **5,** (cap.) a native of Poland. **—v.t. 1,** propel by a pole. **2,** support by poles. **—pole vault,** an athletic contest of leaping, aided by a long pole.

pole'ax" n. **1,** a battle-ax with a hook or spike opposite the blade. **2,** an ax with a hammer face opposite the blade, for slaughtering cattle. **—v.t.** fell with or as with a poleax.

pole'cat" (pōl'kat") n. **1,** a small Europ. animal of the weasel family. **2,** in the U.S., a skunk.

po·lem'ic (pō-lem'ik) n. argument about doctrines. **—po·lem'i·cal,** adj. **—po·lem'ics,** n.sing. the art or practice of disputation.

pole'star" n. **1,** the North Star. **2,** a guide; lodestar.

po·lice' (pə-lēs') n.sing. & pl. **1,** the civil department that maintains order and enforces the law. **2,** (Mil.) the work of keeping a camp clean. **—v.t. 1,** guard and maintain order in. **2,** clean up, as a camp. **—police dog,** a German shepherd dog. **—police state,** a territory, country, etc., governed by a repressive government.

po·lice'man (-mən) n. [pl. **-men**] a member of a police force. **—po·lice'wom"an,** n.fem.

pol'i·cy (pol'ə-sè) n. **1,** a course of conduct based on principle or advisability. **2,** a contract of insurance. **3,** a form of lottery.

pol"i·o·my"e·li'tis (pol"è-ō-mī"ə-lī'tis) n. a spinal paralysis; infantile paralysis. Also, **pol'i·o.**

pol'ish v.t. **1,** make smooth and glossy, as by rubbing. **2,** give elegance or refinement to. **—n. 1,** a smooth, glossy finish. **2,** a mixture for polishing. **3,** refinement; elegance. **—polish off,** dispose of quickly.

Pol'ish (pō'lish) adj. & n. of or pert. to Poland, its people, language, etc.

Po·lit'bu"ro (pə-lit'byûr"ō) n. a policyforming committee in the Communist Party of the U.S.S.R.

po·lite' (pə-līt') adj. **1,** courteous; wellbred. **2,** refined. **—po·lite'ness,** n.

pol'i·tic (pol'ə-tik) adj. **1,** consisting of citizens. **2,** wise; expedient. **3,** shrewd; crafty.

po·lit'i·cal (pə-lit'i-kəl) adj. pert. to governmental affairs or to politics. **—political science,** the science of the principles and conduct of government.

pol"i·ti'cian (pol"ə-tish'ən) n. **1,** one skilled or active in politics. **2,** a statesman.

---

fat, fāte, fär, fåre, fåll, åsk; met, hē, hér, maybè; pin, pīne; not, nōte, ôr, tool

po·lit′i·cize″ (pǝ-lit′ǝ-sīz″) *v.i.* engage in political discussion or action. —*v.t.* make the subject of political discussion or dispute.

pol′i·tick″ (-tik″) *v.i.* engage in politics.

po·lit′i·co (pǝ-lit′i-kō) *n.* a politician.

pol′i·tics (pol′ǝ-tiks) *n.sing.* **1,** the science of government. **2,** the activities of a political party. **3,** (construed as *pl.*) political opinions.

pol′i·ty (pol′ǝ-tē) *n.* the system of a government.

pol′ka (pōl′kǝ) *n.* a lively dance; the music for it. —*v.i.* dance the polka. —**polka dots,** a pattern of round spots on a fabric.

poll (pōl) *n.* **1,** the voting at an election; the number of votes cast. **2,** (*pl.*) a place of voting. **3,** a survey of opinion. **4,** the head. —*v.t.* **1,** register the votes of; ask the opinions of. **2,** receive as votes. **3,** clip; shear; cut off. —**poll tax,** a tax on individuals who vote.

pol′lack (pol′ǝk) *n.* a marine food fish of the cod family.

pol′lard (pol′ǝrd) *n.* **1,** a tree cut back nearly to the trunk, to produce a dense head of branches. **2,** a stag, ox, etc., without horns.

pol′len (pol′ǝn) *n.* the fertilizing element of a plant, a fine yellow powder. —**pollen count,** a measure of the pollen in the air.

pol′li·nate″ (pol′ǝ-nāt″) *v.t.* fertilize (a flower). —**pol″li·na′tion,** *n.*

pol′li·wog″ (pol′ē-wog″) *n.* a tadpole.

poll′ster (pōl′stǝr) *n.* one who takes a poll, as of individual opinions.

pol·lute′ (pǝ-loot′) *v.t.* make impure; soil; defile. —**pol·lu′tion,** *n.*

Pol″ly·an′na (pol″ē-an′ǝ) *n.* an overoptimistic person.

po′lo (pō′lō) *n.* a game similar to hockey but played on horseback. —**polo shirt,** a short-sleeved knitted shirt.

pol″o·naise′ (pol″ǝ-nāz′) *n.* **1,** a stately Polish dance; the music for it. **2,** an outer dress for women.

po·lo′ni·um (pǝ-lō′nē-ǝm) *n.* a radioactive element, no. 84, symbol Po.

pol′ter·geist″ (pōl′tǝr-gīst″) *n.* a noisy and mischievous ghost.

pol·troon′ *n.* a coward. —**pol·troon′er·y,** *n.*

pol·y- (pol-ē) *pref.* many.

pol′y·an′dry (-an″drē) *n.* the state or practice of having more than one husband at the same time. —**pol″y·an′drous,** *adj.*

pol″y·chrome″ *adj.* having various colors. —*n.* a work of art done in several colors. Also, **pol″y·chro·mat′ic,** *adj.*

pol″y·clin′ic *adj.* treating various diseases.

—*n.* a hospital or clinic that treats various diseases.

pol″y·dac′tyl *adj.* having too many fingers or toes. —**pol″y·dac′tyl·ism,** *n.*

pol″y·es′ter (päl″ē-es′tǝr) *n.* **1,** an ester used in making fibers, resins, and plastics. **2,** a polyester fiber, often blended with other fibers (as cotton or wool). **3,** a polyester resin used for making packaging or backing films or for molding and laminating.

pol″y·eth′yl·ene *adj.* a type of plastic.

po·lyg′a·my (pǝ-lig′ǝ-mē) *n.* the state or practice of having more than one mate (husband or, esp., wife) at the same time. —**po·lyg′a·mist,** *n.* —**po·lyg′a·mous,** *adj.*

pol′y·glot″ *adj.* knowing or comprising several languages.

pol′y·gon″ *n.* a closed plane figure with many sides and angles.

pol′y·graph″ (päl′ē-graf″) *n.* a device that records tracings of several different signals at once (as of blood pressure, respiration, etc.).

po·lyg′y·ny (pǝ-lig′ǝ-nē) *n.* the state or practice of having more than one female mate or wife at the same time. —**po·lyg′y·nous** (-nǝs) *adj.*

pol″y·he′dron (-hē′drǝn) *n.* [*pl.* **-dra** (-drǝ)] a many-sided solid.

pol′y·math″ (-math″) *n.* a person having extensive knowledge.

pol′y·mer (-mǝr) *n.* a chemical compound with very complex and heavy molecules.

Pol″y·ne′sian (pol″i-nē′zhǝn) *adj. & n.* of or pert. to the peoples of the So. Pacific islands called Oceania.

pol″y·no′mi·al (-nō′mē-ǝl) *adj.* containing many names or terms. —*n.* an algebraic expression consisting of two or more terms. —**pol″y·no′mi·al·ism,** *n.*

pol′yp (pol′ip) *n.* **1,** an invertebrate marine animal. **2,** a small tumor.

po·lyph′o·ny (pǝ-lif′ǝ-nē) *n.* **1,** (*Music*) a combining of two or more individual but harmonizing melodies. **2,** a multiplicity of sounds (as in an echo). —**pol″y·phon′ic** (pol″ē-fän′ik) *adj.*

pol″y·sty′rene *n.* a clear, hard plastic.

pol′y·syl′la·ble *n.* a word having many (usually four or more) syllables. —**pol″y·syl·lab′ic** (-si-lab′ik) *adj.*

pol″y·tech′nic *adj.* teaching many sciences. —*n.* a technical school.

pol′y·the·ism″ *n.* belief in more than one god. —**pol′y·the″ist,** *n.* —**pol″y·the·is′tic,** —**pol″y·the·is′ti·cal,** *adj.*

pol′y·to′nal *adj.* (*Music*) having more than one tonal center or key. —**pol″y·to·nal′i·ty,** *n.*

pol″y·un·sat′u·rat·ed *adj.* of animal or

vegetable fats, having molecules with many double or triple bonds (associated with lower concentration of cholesterol in the blood). —**pol″y·un·sat′u·rate** (-rit) n.

pol′y·ur′e·thane″ (päl′ė-yůr′ə-thān″) n. any of various polymers used in making resins, flexible and rigid foams, and elastic, rubberlike substances.

pol″y·vi′nyl n. one of several thermoplastic vinyls.

pom′ace (pum′is) n. a crushed pulpy residue.

po·made′ (pō-mād′) n. a scented ointment.

pome (pōm) n. the typical fruit of the apple family. —**po·ma′ceous** (-mā′shəs) adj.

pome′gran″ate (pom′gran″it) n. a tropical tree; its pulpy fruit.

Pom″er·a′ni·an (pom″ə-rā′nė-ən) n. a small, long-haired dog.

pom′mel (pum′əl) n. a rounded knob on a saddle, etc. —v.t. pummel.

pomp n. splendor; showy display.

pom′pa·dour″ (pom′pə-dôr″) n. a hairdress, the hair straight back from the forehead.

pom′pa·no″ (pom′pə-nō″) n. a food fish of tropical seas.

pom-′pom″ n. 1, a many-barreled antiaircraft gun. 2, pompon. —**pom-pom girl,** a prostitute.

pom′pon n. 1, a fluffy ball of feathers, wool, etc. 2, a globelike flower, as a chrysanthemum.

pomp′ous (pom′pəs) adj. ostentatiously dignified or lofty. —**pom·pos′i·ty** (-pos′ə-tė), **pom′pous·ness,** n.

pon′cho (pon′chō) n. [pl. **-chos**] 1, a blanket used as a cloak, with a hole in it for the head. 2, a similar rainproof cloak.

pond n. a body of standing water usu. smaller than a lake.

pon′der (pon′dər) v.t. & i. reflect (upon or over); consider deeply.

pon′der·ous (pon′der-əs) adj. very heavy; hence, unwieldy; tedious. —**pon′der·ous·ness,** n.

pone (pōn) n. a cornmeal bread.

pon·gee′ (pon-jė′) n. a soft silk fabric.

pon′iard (pon′yərd) n. a dagger.

pon′tiff (pon′tif) n. a bishop; specif. the Pope. —**pon·tif′i·cal,** adj.

pon·tif′i·cate (pon-tif′i-kət) n. the office of a bishop. —v.i. (-kāt″) assume an air of infallibility; speak pompously. —**pon·tif′-i·ca′tion,** n.

pon·toon′ n. 1, a flat-bottomed boat. 2, a floating support for a temporary bridge; a buoy. 3, a float for a seaplane.

po′ny (pō′nė) n. 1, a horse of a small, stocky breed. 2, (Slang) a trot; crib. 3, a

small liqueur glass. —**pony express,** a system of mail delivery by relays of horses and riders.

po′ny·tail″ n. a woman's hairstyle.

pooch n. (Slang) dog.

poo′dle (poo′dəl) n. a breed of dog with wiry curled hair.

pooh (poo) interj. of contempt. —**pooh-″pooh′,** v.t. treat with contempt; make light of.

pool n. 1, a still, deep place in a river; a pond; puddle. 2, an open tank of water for swimming. 3, pocket billiards. 4, the totality of bets made on a contingency; pot. 5, a combination of business interests or investors. —v.t. put into a common fund.

poop n. 1, a raised deck in a ship's stern. 2, (Slang) information. —v.t. (of a wave or a gust of wind) strike. —**pooped,** adj. (Slang) fatigued.

poor (pûr) adj. 1, needy; not rich. 2, lacking desirable qualities; inferior. 3, spiritless. 4, unfortunate; to be pitied. 5, humble. —**poor boy,** (Colloq.) a submarine sandwich. —**poor farm,** a farm for paupers.

poor′house″ n. a home for paupers.

poor′ly (-lė) adv. & (Erroneous) adj. not well.

poor-′mouth″ (Slang) v.i. use one's alleged poverty as an excuse. —v.t. disparage.

pop n. 1, a short explosive sound. 2, a soft drink. 3, (Colloq.) papa. —v.i. [**popped, pop′ping**] 1, make such a sound; burst. 2, appear or disappear suddenly. —v.t. 1, cause to burst or explode. 2, put (in) quickly. —adj. popular. —**pop art,** a movement, esp. in painting and sculpture, dealing with objects from everyday life and borrowing the techniques of commercial art. —**pop the question,** (Colloq.) propose marriage.

pop′corn″ n. a maize whose kernels burst when heated.

Pope (pōp) n. the bishop of Rome, leader of the Rom. Cath. Church. —**pop′ish,** adj. (Offensive) pert. to this church.

pop′eyed″ (-īd″) adj. having bulging eyes.

pop′gun″ n. a toy gun.

pop′in·jay″ (pop′in-jā″) n. 1, a woodpecker. 2, a vain person.

pop′lar (pop′lər) n. a tree with light soft wood; the wood.

pop′lin n. a ribbed fabric.

pop′o″ver n. a light muffin.

pop′pet (pop′it) n. a valve that opens by lifting from its seat.

pop′py (pop′ė) n. a flowering plant with a milky narcotic juice.

pop′py·cock″ (pop′ė-kok″) n. (Colloq.) nonsense; vain talk.

---

fat, fāte, fär, fâre, fâll, àsk; met, hē, hėr, maybė; pin, pīne; not, nōte, ôr, tool

pop-'top' *adj.* of a can, having a removable tab for opening.

pop'u·lace (pop'yə-lis) *n.* the common people; the multitude.

pop'u·lar (pop'yə-lər) *adj.* **1,** pert. to, or intended for, the common people. **2,** generally liked. **—pop"u·lar'i·ty** (-lar'ə-tē) *n.* **—pop'u·lar·ize"** (-īz") *v.t.* **—popular front,** a temporary coalition of political parties.

pop'u·late" (pop'yə-lāt") *v.t.* supply with inhabitants.

pop"u·la'tion (pop"yə-lā'shən) *n.* **1,** total number of inhabitants of a place. **2,** the process of populating. **—population explosion,** an unusually large increase in annual population growth.

pop'u·lism (pop'yə-liz-əm) *n.* a political philosophy in support of the common people. **—pop'u·list,** *adj. & n.*

pop'u·lous (pop'yə-ləs) *adj.* thickly inhabited. **—pop'u·lous·ness,** *n.*

por'ce·lain (pôr'sə-lin) *n.* a fine, white, translucent china.

porch (pôrch) *n.* **1,** a covered approach to a doorway. **2,** a veranda.

por'cine (pôr'sīn) *adj.* pert. to swine.

por'cu·pine" (pôr'kyə-pīn") *n.* a small animal with sharp spines on its body and tail.

pore (pôr) *n.* a tiny opening, esp. in the skin. **—v.i.** (with *over*) meditate; ponder.

por'gy (pôr'jē) *n.* a small, edible sea fish.

pork (pôrk) *n.* the flesh of swine as food. **—pork'er,** *n.* a swine, esp. a young hog fattened for market. **—pork barrel,** a government grant used for political patronage. **—pork'y,** *adj.* porklike; fat.

pork'pie" *n.* a flat, low-crowned hat.

por'no (pôr'nō) (*Slang*) *adj.* pornographic. **—n.** pornography. Also, **porn.**

por·nog'ra·phy (pôr-nog'rə-fē) *n.* obscene art, writings, etc. **—por"no·graph'ic,** *adj.* **—por"no·graph'i·cal·ly,** *adv.*

por'ous (pôr'əs) *adj.* permeable by fluids. **—po·ros'i·ty** (pə-ros'ə-tē), **por'ous·ness,** *n.*

por'phy·ry (pôr'fə-rē) *n.* a hard, purplish-red rock embedded with crystals. **—por"phy·rit'ic,** *adj.*

por'poise (pôr'pəs) *n.* a whale-like sea mammal, about 6 ft. long.

por'ridge (pôr'ij) *n.* a thin boiled cereal.

por'rin·ger (pôr'in-jər) *n.* a dish for cereal.

port (pôrt) *n.* **1,** a coast city where ships load and unload; a harbor; a haven. **2,** a porthole; an outlet. **3,** the left side of a ship. **4,** a sweet, dark-red wine. **—v.t.** **1,** turn (the helm) to the left. **2,** (*Mil.*) hold (a rifle) diagonally across the body. **—port of**

call, an intermediate stop in an itinerary, shipping route, etc. **—port of entry,** a port where imports can enter.

port'a·ble (pôrt'ə-bəl) *adj.* capable of being carried; easily conveyed. Also, **port'a·tive,** *adj.* **—port"a·bil'i·ty,** *n.*

por'tage (pôr'tij) *n.* **1,** the act or place of carrying boats overland from one stream to another. **2,** a fee for conveyance.

por'tal (pôr'təl) *n.* a doorway. **—portal-to-portal,** *adj.* of salary, including time spent traveling to and from one's working place.

por"ta·men'to (pôr"tə-men'tō) *n.* (*Music*) a gliding from one tone to another.

port·cul'lis (pôrt-kul'is) *n.* a gate that slides up and down, esp. as used in medieval castles.

por·tend' (pôr-tend') *v.t.* give a warning of; presage.

por'tent (pôr'tent) *n.* a dire or evil omen.

por·ten'tous (pôr-ten'təs) *adj.* **1,** foreshadowing evil. **2,** solemn. **—por·ten'tous·ness,** *n.*

por'ter (pôr'tər) *n.* **1,** one who carries baggage; a sleeping-car attendant. **2,** a doorkeeper or janitor. **3,** a heavy, dark beer. **—por'ter·age,** *n.* transport or fees for it. **—por'tress,** *n.fem.*

por'ter·house" (pôr'tər-hows") *n.* a choice cut of beef; a T-bone steak.

port·fo'lio (pôrt-fō'lē-ō) *n.* **1,** a flat case for carrying documents; a brief case. **2,** the office of a cabinet minister. **3,** an itemized account of securities, etc., held by an investor.

port'hole" (pôrt'hōl") *n.* a round window in a ship's side; an aperture in a wall.

por'ti·co (pôr'ti-kō") *n.* a roof supported by columns, used as a porch or a detached shed.

por"tiere' (pôr"tyâr') *n.* a curtain hung in a doorway.

por'tion (pôr'shən) *n.* **1,** a part of a whole. **2,** a share. **3,** lot; destiny. **4,** a dowry. **—v.t.** **1,** allot in shares. **2,** dower.

port'ly (pôrt'lē) *adj.* **1,** fat; stout. **2,** stately; dignified. **—port'li·ness,** *n.*

port·man'teau (pôrt-man'tō) *n.* a traveling bag or suitcase. **—portmanteau word,** a word made by combining parts of other words, as brunch (*br*eakfast and l*unch*).

por'trait (pôr'trit) *n.* a picture of a person, esp. one done in oils. **—por'trai·ture** (-trə-chər), **por'trait·ist,** *n.*

por·tray' (pôr-trā') *v.t.* **1,** picture; describe vividly. **2,** enact. **—por·tray'al,** *n.*

Por'tu·guese (pôr'tyə-gēz) *adj. & n.* of or pert. to the people of Portugal, their language, etc. **—Portuguese man-of-war,**

a tropical, brilliantly colored marine invertebrate, with tentacles over 10 feet long.

por″tu·la′ca (pôr″chə-lä′kə) *n.* a low-growing annual plant.

pose (pōz) *v.t.* **1,** place (a model) suitably. **2,** propound, as a question. —*v.i.* **1,** act as a model. **2,** make a pretense. —*n.* **1,** attitude; position. **2,** an affectation.

pos′er (pō′zər) *n.* **1,** [also, **po·seur′** (-zēr′)] an affected person; pretender. **2,** a puzzling question.

posh *adj.* (*Colloq.*) luxurious; exclusive.

pos′it (poz′it) *v.t.* **1,** put in place or relation; dispose. **2,** present as a fact or datum; stipulate.

po·si′tion (pə-zish′ən) *n.* **1,** the place occupied by a person or thing; situation. **2,** bodily attitude or posture. **3,** point of view; opinion. **4,** rank; station, esp. high standing. **5,** a job; occupation. —*v.t.* put in proper position; locate. —**po·si′tion·al,** *adj.*

pos′i·tive (poz′ə-tiv) *adj.* **1,** stated explicitly; definite. **2,** confident; dogmatic. **3,** affirmative. **4,** real; actual; of numbers, greater than zero; plus. **5,** proving the presence of something in question. **6,** in photography, showing light and shade as in the original. **7,** noting the simple form of an adjective or adverb. **8,** of electricity, having a deficiency of electrons. —*n.* something positive. —**pos′i·tive·ness,** *n.*

pos′i·tron″ (poz′ə-tron″) *n.* a particle of positive electricity having the same mass as an electron.

pos′se (pos′ē) *n.* a body of men helping a law officer.

pos·sess′ (pə-zes′) *v.t.* **1,** have as one's property; own; have as a quality. **2,** obtain power over; dominate. —**pos·ses′sor,** *n.*

pos·sessed′ (pə-zest′) *adj.* **1,** in possession (of). **2,** afflicted by evil spirits.

pos·ses′sion (pə-zesh′ən) *n.* **1,** the state of having or controlling. **2,** something owned.

pos·ses′sive (-zes′iv) *adj.* **1,** pert. to ownership; jealous in ownership. **2,** (*Gram.*) denoting a possessor. —**pos·ses′sive·ness,** *n.*

pos′si·ble (pos′ə-bəl) *adj.* **1,** capable of existing, occurring, or being done. **2,** that may do; worth consideration. **3,** conceivable. —**pos″si·bil′i·ty,** *n.*

pos′si·bly (pos′ə-blē) *adv.* by any possibility; perhaps.

pos′sum (pos′əm) *n.* (*Colloq.*) an opossum. —**play possum,** feign death.

post (pōst) *n.* **1,** an upright timber or stake. **2,** a station; assignment; job. **3,** a military station or its garrison; a trading station. **4,** a system or means of conveying letters, packages, etc.; the mail. —*v.t.* **1,** fasten (a no-tice) in a public place. **2,** mail (a letter). **3,** station at a post, as a sentry. **4,** transfer to, or enter in, a ledger. **5,** (*Colloq.*) supply with information. —*v.i.* **1,** travel in haste. **2,** move up and down in the saddle, when riding. —**post chaise,** a horsedrawn coach. —**post exchange,** (also *cap.*) a store or canteen for soldiers at an army post. Abbrev. **PX.** —**post office, 1,** formerly, the government department for the transmission of mail; now, the Postal Service. **2,** a branch office of the Postal Service.

post- *pref.* after.

post′age (pōs′tij) *n.* the fee for conveying letters or packages; mailing charges. —**postage meter,** a machine which prints postage on mail and records accumulated postage expenditures. —**postage stamp,** an official stamp showing prepayment of postage.

post′al (pōs′təl) *adj.* pert. to the mail service. —**postal card,** postcard. —**postal note,** a check issued by the post office for transmission of money; a postal money order. —**Postal Service,** a U.S. government corporation that handles the mail.

post′card″ *n.* a card prepared for correspondence on one section or side, and address on the other.

post″date′ *v.t.* **1,** date (a contract, check, etc.) with a date later than the current one. **2,** be subsequent to in time.

post′er *n.* a posted notice; a placard.

poste′ res·tante′ (pōst″res-tänt′) (*Fr.*) a place where mail is held until called for.

pos·te′ri·or (pos-tir′ē-ər) *adj.* **1,** located in the back or rear. **2,** later. —*n.* the rump.

pos·ter′i·ty (pos-ter′ə-tē) *n.* **1,** descendants collectively. **2,** all future generations.

pos′tern (pos′tərn) *n.* a rear or secondary entrance.

post′fix″ *v.t.* add at the end; suffix.

post·grad′u·ate *adj.* pert. to study after graduation from a school or college. —*n.* a postgraduate student.

post′haste″ *adv.* by fastest means; speedily.

post′hu·mous (pos′tū-məs) *adj.* **1,** done by or awarded to a person now dead. **2,** born after the father's death.

pos·til′lion (pōs-til′yən) *n.* a rider on one of a team of two or four horses.

post′lude″ (pōst′lood″) *n.* (*Music*) an added or concluding piece.

post′man (-mən) *n.* [*pl.* **-men**] a mail carrier.

post′mark″ *n.* an official mark canceling a postage stamp and giving the date and place of mailing.

post′mas″ter *n.* a person in charge of

a post office. —**post′mis″tress**, *n.fem.*
—**Postmaster General**, the official in charge of the Postal Service.

post″me·rid′i·an (pōst″mə-rid′ē-ən) *adj.* occurring after noon.

Post me·rid′·i·em (-əm) (*Lat.*) after noon, usu. abbr. P.M.

post-″mor′tem (pōst″môr′təm) *adj.* after death. —*n.* 1, an autopsy. 2, (*Slang*) discussion of card play after a game.

post·na′sal *adj.* behind the nose.

post′paid″ *adj.* with postage prepaid.

post·par′tum (-pär′təm) *adj.* of or occurring after birth.

post·pone′ (pōst-pōn′) *v.t.* defer until later; delay. —**post·pone′ment**, *n.*

post′script (pōst′skript″) *n.* a paragraph added to a letter finished and signed; any added part.

pos′tu·lant (pos′chə-lənt) *n.* a candidate for membership, esp. in a religious order.

pos′tu·late″ (pos′chə-lāt″) *v.t. & i.* assert or assume as a basis for reasoning. —*n.* (-lət) 1, an assumption; hypothesis. 2, a prerequisite.

pos′ture (pos′chər) *n.* 1, bodily position; carriage. 2, attitude. —*v.i.* pose.

post″war″ *adj.* after the (most recent) war.

po′sy (pō′zē) *n.* a flower.

pot *n.* 1, a round deep vessel, as for cooking. 2, an aggregate of stakes to be won; a prize. 3, a wicker basket for catching fish, lobsters, etc. 4, (*Colloq.*) potbelly. 5, (*Slang*) marijuana. —*v.t.* [**pot′ted, -ting**] 1, preserve in pots; plant in a pot. 2, shoot (game) for food. —**go to pot** (*Colloq.*) go to pieces; be ruined. —**pot cheese**, cottage cheese. —**pot roast**, braised beef. —**pot shot**, a random shot, or one at close range.

po′ta·ble (pō′tə-bəl) *adj.* drinkable. —*n.* (*pl.*) beverages.

pot′ash″ *n.* a white chemical obtained by leaching wood ashes.

po·tas′si·um (pə-tas′ē-əm) *n.* a soft, silvery-white metallic element, no. 19, symbol K, used in drugs, fertilizers, etc. —**po·tas′sic**, *adj.*

po·ta′to (pə-tā′tō) *n.* a plant or its important edible tuber. —**potato chip**, a fried thin slice of potato. Also, **small potatoes**, (*Slang*) something or someone insignificant.

pot′bel″ly *n.* (*Colloq.*) a fat or protruding belly.

pot′boil″er *n.* a work of art or literature produced solely for making a living.

po·teen′ (pō-tēn′) *n.* in Ireland, illicitly distilled liquor. Also, **po·theen′** (-thēn′).

po′ten·cy (pō′ten-sē) *n.* state or quality of being potent; power; ability.

po′tent (pō′tənt) *adj.* 1, wielding power; strong; effective. 2, capable of procreation.

po′ten·tate″ (pō′tən-tāt″) *n.* a ruler; monarch.

po·ten′tial (pə-ten′shəl) *adj.* 1, possible. 2, latent. —*n.* something that has the possibility of becoming actual. —**po·ten′ti·al′·i·ty** (-shē-al′ə-tē) *n.*

pot′head″ *n.* (*Slang*) one who uses marijuana, esp. to excess.

poth′er (poth′ər) *n.* confusion; bustle. —*v.t.* bother; perplex. —*v.i.* make a commotion.

pot′herb″ *n.* a plant boiled for food or used for seasoning.

pot′hold″er *n.* a thick cloth used as protection for the hand when picking up a hot utensil.

pot′hole″ *n.* a round depression (in a rock, road, etc.) caused by erosion, traffic, etc.

pot′hook″ (pot′hůk″) *n.* 1, a hook used to lift or suspend pots. 2, any S-shaped figure, as in writing; (*Humorous*) any stenographic symbol.

po′tion (pō′shən) *n.* a drink, as of medicine or poison.

pot′latch (pot′lach) *n.* a ceremonious distribution of gifts.

pot′luck″ (pot′luk″) *n.* whatever food is on hand, without special buying.

pot′pie″ *n.* 1, a meat pie. 2, a stew of meat and dumplings.

pot·pour′ri (pot-pûr′ē; pō-poo-rē′) *n.* a mixture or medley of spices, foods, musical or literary compositions, etc.

pot′sherd″ (-shêrd″) *n.* a broken piece of earthenware.

pot′tage (pot′ij) *n.* a stew.

pot′ted (pot′id) *adj.* 1, put into, cooked, or preserved in a pot. 2, (*Slang*) tipsy; drunk.

pot′ter (pot′ər) *n.* one who makes pottery. —*v.i.* busy oneself over trifles; loiter; dawdle. —**potter′s field**, a place for the burial of paupers or criminals. —**potter′s wheel**, a rotating disk on which a potter shapes clay.

pot′ter·y (-ē) *n.* dishes, vases, etc., molded from clay and baked.

pot′ty (-ē) *n.* (*Colloq.*) toilet. —*adj.* (*Slang*) slightly crazy.

pouch (powch) *n.* 1, a small bag or sack. 2, a marsupium.

poult (pōlt) *n.* the young of the domestic fowl, pheasant, etc.

poul′tice (pōl′tis) *n.* a soft, warm mass applied to a sore spot.

poul′try (pōl′trē) *n.* domestic fowls collectively. —**poul′ter·er**, *n.* a dealer in poultry.

---

tub, cūte, půll; labəl; oil, owl, go, chip, she, thin, *th*en, sing, ink; *see p.* 6

pounce (powns) *v.i.* (often with *on* or *upon*) swoop and seize suddenly. —*n.* a sudden spring.

pound (pownd) *n.* **1,** a measure of weight, 16 avoirdupois or 12 troy ounces. **2,** the Brit. monetary unit; its symbol (£). **3,** an enclosure for stray animals. —*v.t.* **1,** beat; pummel. **2,** crush. —*v.i.* **1,** hammer away steadily. **2,** plod heavily. —**pound′age,** *n.* —**pound cake,** a rich, sweet cake.

pound′al (pown′dəl) *n.* the force which, acting for one second upon a mass of one pound, gives it a velocity of one foot per second.

pound-′fool″ish *adj.* spending large sums without due regard to value.

pour (pôr) *v.t.* **1,** cause to flow downward in a stream. **2,** send forth copiously. —*v.i.* **1,** flow. **2,** rain hard. **3,** issue in great numbers.

pout (powt) *v.i.* protrude the lips, as in sullenness. —*n.* a sulky mood.

pout′er pigeon a pigeon with a puffed-out crop.

pov′er·ty (pov′ər-tē) *n.* **1,** lack of money; need. **2,** lack; scarcity. —**pov′er·ty-strick′en,** *adj.* impoverished.

pow′der (pow′dər) *n.* **1,** a mixture of fine, dry particles, as pulverized talc used as a cosmetic; gunpowder; a dose of medicinal powder. **2,** (*Slang*) sudden departure. —*v.t.* **1,** sprinkle with or as with powder. **2,** reduce to powder. —**pow′der·y,** *adj.* —**powder blue,** a pale blue. —**powder keg,** a situation liable to explode, as in war. —**powder puff, 1,** a pad for applying powder. **2,** an effeminate man. —**powder room,** a lavatory for women. —**take a powder,** (*Slang*) depart quickly or suddenly.

pow′er (pow′ər) *n.* **1,** ability to do or act. **2,** physical or mental strength or energy; influence; control. **3,** an influential person; a nation considered as a military force. **4,** the magnifying capacity of a lens. **5,** any of the products obtained by multiplying a number by itself repeatedly; as, 2 x 2 = 4 (*2nd* power) x 2 = 8 (*3rd* power), etc. —**power of attorney,** legal authority to act for another. —**power politics,** diplomacy based on the threat of force.

pow·er- *pref.* impelled by an engine.

pow′er·boat″ *n.* motorboat.

pow′er·drive″ *n.* (*T.N.*) a type of automatic transmission.

pow′er·ful *adj.* strong; influential; mighty. —**pow′er·ful·ness,** *n.*

pow′er·house″ *n.* **1,** a plant for generating electricity. **2,** (*Colloq.*) something very strong.

pow′er·less *adj.* helpless; without authority. —**pow′er·less·ness,** *n.*

pow′wow″ *n.* **1,** among N. Amer. Indians, a ceremony or conference. **2,** (*Colloq.*) any conference. —*v.i.* confer.

pox (poks) *n.* a disease marked by eruptive pocks.

prac′ti·ca·ble (prak′ti-kə-bəl) *adj.* capable of being done or used. —**prac″ti·ca·bil′i·ty,** *n.*

prac′ti·cal (prak′ti-kəl) *adj.* **1,** usable; useful. **2,** taught by, or derived from experience; advisable. **3,** inclined to action rather than theory. **4,** pert. to actual practice or action; not theoretical. —**prac″ti·cal′i·ty,** *n.* —**practical joke,** one that causes discomfort or embarrassment to someone. —**practical nurse,** an experienced nurse who is not registered and not a graduate of a nursing school.

prac′ti·cal·ly (-ē) *adv.* **1,** in practice; actually. **2,** (*Colloq.*) nearly; in effect.

prac′tice (prak′tis) *n.* **1,** actual performance. **2,** frequent performance; custom; usage. **3,** the exercise of a profession, esp. medical. **4,** repeated exercise, to gain skill —*v.t.* **1,** carry out in action. **2,** do repeatedly, esp. to gain skill. **3,** follow as a profession. —*v.i.* **1,** perform certain acts often. **2,** engage in a profession. Also (*Brit.*) **prac′tise.** —**prac′ticed,** *adj.* skilled; proficient.

prac·ti′tion·er (prak-tish′ən-ər) *n.* **1,** one engaged in a profession. **2,** in Christian Science, an authorized healer.

prag·mat′ic (prag-mat′ik) *adj.* **1,** based on utility or effect; practical. **2,** matter-of-fact. **3,** dogmatic. —**prag·mat′i·cal·ly,** *adv.* —**prag′ma·tism,** *n.*

prai′rie (prâr′ē) *n.* a broad, level, treeless grassland. —**prairie chicken,** a kind of grouse. —**prairie dog,** a rodent of Amer. prairies. —**prairie schooner,** a covered wagon. —**prairie wolf,** a coyote.

praise (prāz) *v.t.* **1,** commend warmly. **2,** glorify the attributes of (God). —*n.* compliments; applause.

praise′wor″thy *adj.* commendable. —**praise′wor′thi·ness,** *n.*

pra′line (prä′lēn) *n.* a confection of browned sugar and nuts.

pram *n.* perambulator.

prance (prāns) *v.i.* **1,** step proudly (of a horse's gait). **2,** strut. —*n.* a prancing gait or stride.

pran′di·al (pran′dē-əl) *adj.* pert. to a meal, esp. dinner.

prank *n.* a playful or mischievous act. —**prank′ish,** *adj.* —**prankster,** *n.*

pra″se·o·dym′i·um (prä″zē-ō-dim′ē-əm) *n.* a rare-earth metallic element, no. 59, symbol Pr.

prate (prāt) *v.t. & i.* chatter; babble; talk too much.

prat'fall'' (prat'fâl'') *n.* a fall on the buttocks.

prat'tle (prat'əl) *v.i.* talk idly, like a child. —*n.* such talk.

prawn (prân) *n.* an edible shrimp-like crustacean.

prax'is (prak'sis) *n.* **1,** art learned by experience. **2,** established practices; customs. **3,** a manual or textbook of such practices.

pray (prā) *v.i.* ask God's grace. —*v.t.* **1,** beg; entreat. **2,** petition for. —*adv.* (*Archaic*) please.

prayer (prâr) *n.* **1,** a supplication to God; (*pl.*) a religious service. **2,** entreaty; petition. —**prayer book,** a book of forms for prayers. —**prayer shawl,** a tallith.

prayer'ful (-fəl) *adj.* **1,** devout. **2,** entreating. —**prayer'ful·ness,** *n.*

praying mantis an insect with long forelegs.

pre- (prē) *pref.* before, in time, place, rank, sequence, etc.

preach (prēch) *v.t. & i.* **1,** deliver (a sermon). **2,** advocate earnestly; exhort. **3,** give advice importunately. —**preach'ment,** *n.* —**preach'y,** *adj.* moralizing; didactic.

preach'er *n.* **1,** a clergyman. **2,** anyone who preaches.

preach'i·fy'' (-ə-fī'') *v.i.* (*Colloq.*) give prolonged, tiresome moral advice.

pre'am''ble (prē'am''bəl) *n.* introductory remarks; a preface.

pre·am'pli·fi''er *n.* an electronic device used to modify a signal for an amplifier. Also, *colloq.,* **pre'amp.**

pre''ar·range' *v.t.* arrange beforehand. —**pre''ar·range'ment,** *n.*

pre·car'i·ous (pri-kār'ē-əs) *adj.* uncertain; insecure. —**pre·car'i·ous·ness,** *n.*

pre·cau'tion (pri-kâ'shən) *n.* **1,** an act done in advance to assure safety or benefit. **2,** prudent foresight. —**pre·cau'tion·ar·y,** *adj.*

pre·cede' (prē-sēd') *v.t. & i.* go before in place, time, rank, or importance. —**pre·ced'ing,** *adj.*

prec'e·dence (pres'i-dəns) *n.* **1,** the act of going before. **2,** the right of taking a more honored position.

prec'e·dent (pres'i-dənt) *n.* an identical or analogous previous example. —*adj.* (prē-sē'dənt) preceding.

pre·cen'tor (prē-sen'tər) *n.* one who leads singing in church; a soloist. —**pre·cen'tor·ship'',** *n.*

pre'cept (prē'sept) *n.* a rule for moral conduct; maxim. —**pre·cep'tor,** *n.* a teacher. —**pre·cep'tress,** *n.fem.*

pre'cinct (prē'sinkt) *n.* **1,** district. **2,** (*pl.*) environs.

pre''ci·os'i·ty (presh''ē-os'ə-tē) *n.* overniceness; affectation.

pre'cious (presh'əs) *adj.* **1,** of great value. **2,** held in great esteem; dear. **3,** overrefined; affectedly clever or delicate. —*adv.* (*Colloq.*) very. —**pre'cious·ness,** *n.*

prec'i·pice (pres'ə-pis) *n.* a very steep or overhanging cliff. —**pre·cip'i·tous** (pri-sip'-i-təs) *adj.*

pre·cip'i·tant (pri-sip'ə-tənt) *adj.* rushing headlong; abrupt; hasty. —*n.* an agent that causes precipitation. —**pre·cip'i·tan·cy,** *n.*

pre·cip'i·tate'' (pri-sip'ə-tāt'') *v.t.* **1,** cast headlong. **2,** cause to happen suddenly or too soon. **3,** (*Chem.*) change from a state of solution to solid form. —*v.i.* (*Chem.*) separate from a solution, as a solid. —*adj.* (-tət) **1,** headlong. **2,** acting hastily and unwisely. **3,** extremely sudden or abrupt.

pre·cip''i·ta'tion (pri-sip''i-tā'shən) *n.* **1,** act of hurling down or falling headlong. **2,** impetuous action. **3,** (*Chem.*) the process or effect of precipitating. **4,** rain, sleet, or snow; the quantity that falls.

pre·cip'i·tous (pri-sip'ə-təs) *adj.* **1,** overhasty; rash. **2,** steep.

pré·cis' (prā-sē') *n.* a concise summary.

pre·cise' (pri-sīs') *adj.* **1,** exactly defined; definite; accurate. **2,** punctilious; formal. **3,** exact; identical. —**pre·cise'ness,** *n.*

pre·ci'sian (pri-sizh'ən) *n.* a stickler for the rules.

pre·cis'ion (pri-sizh'ən) *n.* preciseness; accuracy.

pre·clude' (pri-klood') *v.t.* impede; prevent. —**pre·clu'sion,** *n.* —**pre·clu'sive,** *adj.*

pre·co'cious (pri-kō'shəs) *adj.* prematurely developed, esp. mentally. —**pre·co'cious·ness, pre·coc'i·ty** (pri-kos'ə-tē) *n.*

pre''con·ceive' *v.t.* form an idea or opinion of in advance. —**pre''con·cep'tion,** *n.*

pre''con·di'tion (prē''-) *n.* a requirement for beginning something as negotiations.

pre·cur'sor (pri-kēr'sər) *n.* a predecessor; a premonitory forerunner. —**pre·cur'so·ry** (-sə-rē) *adj.*

pre·da'cious (pri-dā'shəs) *adj.* predatory. Also, **pre·da'ceous.** —**pre·dac'i·ty** (-das'ə-tē) *n.*

pred'a·to''ry (pred'ə-tôr'ē) *adj.* **1,** plundering. **2,** preying upon others.

pred''e·ces'sor (pred''i-ses'ər) *n.* one who preceded another in the same position, etc.

pre''des''ti·na'tion *n.* **1,** the belief that God has ordained all events to come. **2,** fate; destiny.

pre·des'tine *v.t.* decide the course or fate of beforehand.

pre''de·ter'mine *v.t.* **1,** decide or ascertain beforehand. **2,** predestine.

pre·dic'a·ment (pri-dik'ə-mənt) *n.* a trying or dangerous situation; a dilemma.

pred'i·cate (pred'ə-kət) *n.* **1,** (*Gram.*) the part of a sentence that tells something about the subject. **2,** what is predicated. —*v.t.* (-kāt') **1,** assert; declare. **2,** base.

pred'i·ca″tive (pred'i-kā″tiv) *adj.* of an adjective, being in the predicate and modifying the subject, as *clear* in *the sky is clear*.

pre·dict' (pri-dikt') *v.t. & i.* foretell; prophesy. —**pre·dic'tion,** *n.*

pre″di·lec'tion (prē″də-lek'shən) *n.* partiality; liking.

pre″dis·pose' (prē″dis-pōz') *v.t.* **1,** give a tendency or inclination to. **2,** dispose in advance. —**pre″dis·po·si'tion,** *n.* innate tendency.

pre·dom'i·nate″ (pri-dom'i-nāt″) *v.i. & t.* prevail (over); control; be the chief element. —**pre·dom'i·nance,** *n.* —**pre·dom'i·nant,** *adj.*

pree'mie (prē'mē) *n.* (*Colloq.*) a premature baby.

pre·em'i·nent (prē-em'i-nənt) *adj.* eminent above others. —**pre·em'i·nence,** *n.*

pre·empt' (prē-empt') *v.t. & i.* occupy; seize; buy before another can. —**pre·emp'tion,** *n.* —**pre·emp'tive,** *adj.* —**pre·emp'tor,** *n.*

preen (prēn) *v.t.* **1,** smooth (feathers) with the beak. **2,** trim or adorn (oneself).

pre·fab'ri·cate″ *v.t.* manufacture parts of, for later assembly, as houses. Also, *colloq.,* **pre'fab.** —**pre″fab'ri·ca'tion,** *n.*

pref'ace (pref'is) *n.* an introduction, as to a book or speech. —*v.t.* **1,** give a preface to. **2,** introduce; precede. —**pref'a·to·ry,** *adj.*

pre'fect (prē'fekt) *n.* **1,** a chief magistrate; an administrative head. **2,** a monitor in school. —**pre'fec·ture** (-fek-shər) *n.*

pre·fer' (pri-fėr') *v.t.* [**preferred', -fer'ring**] **1,** choose, rather than another; like more. **2,** advance; bring forward. —**pref'er·a·ble** (pref'ər-ə-bəl) *adj.* —**preferred stock,** stock that receives a dividend before common stock.

pref'er·ence (pref'ə-rəns) *n.* **1,** act of preferring; choice; favor. **2,** preferred or superior position.

pref″er·en'tial (pref″ər-en'shəl) *adj.* favored; based on preference.

pre·fer'ment (pri-fėr'mənt) *n.* promotion.

pre·fig'ure *v.t.* **1,** presage. **2,** imagine in advance. —**pre·fig″u·ra'tion,** *n.* —**pre·fig'u·ra·tive,** *adj.* —**pre·fig'ure·ment,** *n.*

pre'fix (prē'fiks) *v.t.* fix or place before. —*n.* in compound words, one or more letters or syllables that go before and qualify another word.

preg'na·ble (preg'nə-bəl) *adj.* capable of being taken by force.

preg'nant (preg'nənt) *adj.* **1,** carrying unborn young. **2,** fertile; inventive. **3,** full of significance. —**preg'nan·cy,** *n.*

pre·hen'sile (pri-hen'sil) *adj.* fitted for grasping or holding, as claws.

pre″his·tor'ic *adj.* preceding recorded history. —**pre″his·tor'i·cal·ly,** *adv.*

pre·judge' *v.t.* judge or condemn before proper inquiry.

prej'u·dice (prej'ə-dis) *n.* **1,** an opinion, often unfavorable, formed without adequate reasons; bias. **2,** disadvantageous effect. —*v.t.* **1,** cause prejudice in. **2,** damage. —**prej″u·di'cial** (-dish'əl) *adj.*

prel'ate (prəl'ət) *n.* a high ecclesiastical dignitary. —**prel'a·cy,** *n.*

pre·lim'in·ar″y (pri-lim'i-ner″ē) *adj.* leading up to something more important. —*n.* (usu. *pl.*) a preparatory act, feature, test, etc.

prel'ude (prel'ūd) *n.* **1,** something preliminary or introductory. **2,** (*Music*) an introductory movement. —*v.t.* introduce.

pre'ma·ture″ *adj.* happening before maturity or too soon; overhasty.

pre″med'i·cal *adj.* preparing for the study of medicine. Also, *colloq.,* **pre'med'.**

pre·med'i·tate″ *v.t. & i.* consider or plan beforehand. —**pre·med″i·ta'tion,** *n.*

pre'mi·er (prē'mē-ər) *adj.* chief; foremost. —*n.* the chief minister of state; prime minister.

pre·mière' (pri-myâr'; *Colloq.* pri-mir') *n.* a first performance; opening. —*v.t. & i.* (*Colloq.*) have or present a première (of).

prem'ise (prem'is) *n.* **1,** a previous statement from which something is inferred or concluded. **2,** (*pl.*) real estate; a building and grounds.

pre'mi·um (prē'mē-əm) *n.* **1,** a prize; reward; anything given as an inducement. **2,** an amount to be paid for insurance. **3,** an excess of value over cost.

pre·mo'lar (prē-mō'lər) *adj.* situated in front of the molar teeth. —*n.* a premolar tooth.

pre″mo·ni'tion (prē″mə-nish'ən) *n.* a foreboding, as of impending danger.

pre·mon'i·to·ry (pri-mon'ə-tôr-ē) *adj.* forewarning.

pre″na'tal *adj.* occurring or existing before birth.

pre·oc'cu·py″ (prē-ok'yə-pī″) *v.t.* take the attention of, to the exclusion of other matters; engross; absorb. —**pre·oc'cu·pied″,** *adj.* —**pre·oc″cu·pa'tion,** *n.*

pre″or·dain' *v.t.* decree beforehand. —**pre″or·di·na'tion,** *n.*

prep *adj.* (*Colloq.*) preparatory; as, a *prep school.* —*v.t.* (*Slang*) prepare, as for an operation.

prep″a·ra′tion (prep″ə-rā′shən) *n.* the act, means, or result of preparing.

pre·par′a·to·ry (pri-par′ə-tôr-ē) *adj.* serving to make ready. —**preparatory school,** a school preparing students to enter college. Also, **prep school.**

pre·pare′ (pri-pâr′) *v.t.* **1,** make ready for a particular purpose. **2,** instruct. **3,** provide; fit out. **4,** make; manufacture; compound. **5,** cook; concoct. —*v.i.* **1,** put things in readiness. **2,** make oneself ready.

pre·par′ed·ness *n.* the state of being prepared, esp for war.

pre·pay′ (pré-pā′) *v.t.* pay or pay for in advance. —**pre′paid″,** *adj.*

pre·pon′der·ate″ (pri-pon′də-rāt″) *v.i.* exceed in weight, influence, number, etc.; prevail. —**pre·pon′der·ance,** *n.* —**pre·pon′der·ant,** *adj.*

prep″o·si′tion (prep″ə-zish′ən) *n.* (*Gram.*) a part of speech serving to show the relation between a noun or pronoun and some other word. —**prep″o·si′tion·al,** *adj.*

pre″pos·sess′ (prē″pə-zes′) *v.t.* **1,** impress favorably at the outset; dominate, as a prejudice. —**pre″pos·sess′ing,** *adj.* arousing favorable bias.

pre·pos′ter·ous (pri-pos′tər-əs) *adj.* contrary to common sense; utterly absurd. —**pre·pos′ter·ous·ness,** *n.*

pre′puce (prē′pūs) *n.* the foreskin.

pre·req′ui·site *adj.* necessary as an antecedent condition. —*n.* something needed in advance or at the outset.

pre·rog′a·tive (pri-rog′ə-tiv) *n.* a right or privilege inherent in one's office or position.

pres′age (pres′ij) *n.* an omen; foreboding. —*v.t.* (pri-sāj′) give a warning of; foretell.

pres′by·ter (prez′bi-tər) *n.* **1,** a Presbyterian elder or minister. **2,** a title of some clergymen.

Pres″by·te′ri·an (prez″bi-tir′é-ən) *adj.* & *n.* pert. to a Prot. church governed by its ministers and elders.

pres′by·ter″y (-ter″é) *n.* **1,** a ruling council of a church; its jurisdiction. **2,** a priest's residence.

pre-school′ *adj.* of the time in a child's life before it enters school (usu. 6 years of age).

pre′sci·ence (presh′é-əns) *n.* foreknowledge; foresight. —**pre′sci·ent** (-ənt) *adj.*

pre·scribe′ (pré-skrīb′) *v.t.* **1,** lay down beforehand as a rule. **2,** advise the use of (a medicine). —*v.i.* **1,** lay down rules. **2,** advise remedies.

pre′script (prē′skript) *n.* a rule.

pre·scrip′tion (pri-skrip′shən) *n.* **1,** authoritative directions, esp. for a medicine. **2,** the medicine. —**pre·scrip′tive,** *adj.*

pres′ence (prez′əns) *n.* **1,** the fact of being present. **2,** immediate vicinity. **3,** a person's bearing, demeanor, etc. **4,** a spirit. —**presence of mind,** alertness in emergencies.

pres′ent (prez′ənt) *adj.* **1,** being at the place in question; here. **2,** being or occurring at this time; not past or future. —*n.* **1,** time now passing. **2,** the present tense. **3,** a gift.

pre·sent′ (pri-zent′) *v.t.* **1,** make a gift to; offer as a gift. **2,** introduce; exhibit; display. —**pre·sent′a·ble,** *adj.* in fit shape to be offered or seen.

pres″en·ta′tion (prez″ən-tā′shən) *n.* **1,** act of presenting. **2,** something presented; an exhibition, show, etc.

pre·sen′ti·ment (pri-zen′tə-mənt) *n.* a foreboding; premonition.

pres′ent·ly (-lé) *adv.* **1,** soon. **2,** at this time.

pre·sent′ment (-mənt) *n.* **1,** presentation. **2,** (*Law*) a statement or charge of an offense by a Grand Jury, based on its own knowledge.

pres″er·va′tion (prez″ər-vā′shən) *n.* act or effect of preserving.

pre·serv′a·tive (pri-zerv′ə-tiv) *adj.* & *n.* serving to keep alive or sound.

pre·serve′ (pri-zērv′) *v.t.* **1,** keep safe or free from harm. **2,** keep alive or permanent. **3,** retain (a quality, condition). **4,** keep (food) from decay by canning, etc. —*n.* **1,** (usu. *pl.*) fruit, jam, or jellies. **2,** ground set aside for the protection of game.

pre·side′ (pri-zīd′) *v.i.* act as chairperson of a meeting; act as head.

pres′i·den·cy (prez′i-dən-sé) *n.* **1,** office, function, etc., of a president. **2,** a territory governed by a president.

pres′i·dent (prez′i-dənt) *n.* **1,** (often *cap.*) the highest executive officer of a republic, company, club, college, etc. **2,** a chairperson. —**pres″i·den′tial** (-den′shəl) *adj.*

pre·sid′i·um (pri-sid′i-əm) *n.* **1,** an administrative or executive committee. **2,** (*cap.*) the permanent committee within the Supreme Soviet.

press (pres) *v.t.* **1,** bear down upon; weigh heavily upon. **2,** compress; squeeze out. **3,** clasp in the arms. **4,** smooth or flatten by pressure. **5,** thrust upon others; push; thrust aside. **6,** urge on; hurry. **7,** conscript; draft. —*v.i.* **1,** bear heavily. **2,** crowd. **3,** hurry.

—*n.* **1,** a crowding pressure. **2,** urgency. **3,** a chest, as for clothes. **4,** a machine that exerts pressure, as for printing. **5,** the practice and industry of printing or publishing. **6,** periodicals, newspapers, and their representatives, collectively. —**press'ing,** *adj.* urgent; persistent. —**press agent,** one employed to solicit favorable publicity.

—**press conference,** an interview given to the collected press at an appointed time.

press'man (-mən) *n.* [*pl.* -**men**] operator of a printing press.

press'mark" *n.* the catalogue number of a library book.

pres'sure (presh'ər) *n.* **1,** a bearing down; squeezing. **2,** the exertion of influence or authority. **3,** trouble; burden. **4,** demand, on one's time or energy. —**pressure cook-er,** an airtight vessel for cooking food under high steam pressure. —**pressure group,** a group using lobbying, propaganda, etc., to influence decisions, such as legislation.

—**pressure point,** a region of the body where it is possible to obstruct blood circulation and produce fainting or necrosis.

pres'sur·ize" (presh'ər-īz") *v.t.* supply with compressed air to increase the air pressure.

pres"ti·dig"i·ta'tion (pres"tə-dij"ə-tā'shən) *n.* sleight of hand. —**pres"ti·dig'i·ta"tor,** *n.*

pres·tige' (pres-tēzh') *n.* influence arising from reputation or esteem. —**pres·tig'ious** (-tij'əs) *adj.*

pres'to (pres'tō) *adv.* quickly.

pre·sume' (pri-zoom') *v.t.* **1,** take for granted; assume. **2,** take upon oneself; dare. —*v.i.* behave with undue familiarity. —**pre·sum'a·ble,** *adj.*

pre·sump'tion (pri-zump'shən) *n.* **1,** the act of presuming. **2,** something believed on inconclusive evidence. **3,** arrogance; boldness.

pre·sump'tive (pri-zump'tiv) *adj.* justifying or based on presumption.

pre·sump'tu·ous (pri-zump'tyū-əs) *adj.* arrogant; overbold. —**pre·sump'tu·ous-ness,** *n.*

pre"sup·pose' (prē"sə-pōz') *v.i.* **1,** assume in advance. **2,** imply as an antecedent fact. —**pre"sup·po·si'tion,** *n.*

pre·tend' (pri-tend') *v.t.* **1,** make believe; feign. **2,** profess falsely. —*v.i.* **1,** make pretense. **2,** assert a claim, as to a throne, etc. **3,** (with *to*) venture; aspire.

pre·tend'er (-ər) *n.* **1,** one who makes a false show, as of learning. **2,** a claimant, esp. to a throne.

pre·tense' (pri-tens'; prē'tens) *n.* **1,** a sham; false profession; pretext. **2,** a claim. Also, **pre·tence'.**

pre·ten'sion (pri-ten'shən) *n.* **1,** a claim; allegation. **2,** (often *pl.*) ostentation.

pre·ten'tious (pri-ten'shəs) *adj.* ostentatious; showy. —**pre·ten'tious·ness,** *n.*

pre·ter- (prē-tər) *pref.* beyond; more than.

pret'er·it (pret'ər-it) *adj.* (*Gram.*) expressing action or existence in the past. —*n.* the past tense.

pre"ter·nat'u·ral *adj.* extraordinary.

pre'text (prē'tekst) *n.* an ostensible reason; excuse.

pret'ti·fy" (prit'i-fī") *v.t.* make pretty, esp. by gaudy embellishment.

pret'ty (prit'ē) *adj.* pleasing, esp. to the eye; attractive. —*adv.* (*Colloq.*) fairly; tolerably. —**pret'ti·ness,** *n.*

pret'zel (pret'səl) *n.* a hard dry biscuit crusted with salt, in form of a stick or knot.

pre·vail' (pri-vāl') *v.i.* **1,** be victorious. **2,** (with *on* or *upon*) persuade. **3,** be prevalent.

prev'a·lent (prev'ə-lənt) *adj.* of wide use or occurrence; widespread. —**prev'a·lence,** *n.*

pre·var'i·cate" (pri-var'ə-kāt") *v.i.* be evasive; lie. —**pre·var"i·ca'tion,** *n.* —**pre·var'-i·ca"tor,** *n.*

pre·vent' (pri-vent') *v.t.* hinder or keep from doing or happening; impede.

pre·ven'ta·tive (pri-ven'tə-tive) *n.* that which prevents. —*adj.* preventing; precautionary. Also, **pre·ven'tive.**

pre·ven'tion (pri-ven'shən) *n.* act or effect of preventing.

pre'view" (prē'vū") *n.* **1,** an advance showing, as of a motion picture before general release. **2,** [also, **pre'vue"**] an excerpt from a motion picture shown to advertise it. —*v.t.* show or see in advance.

pre'vi·ous (prē'vē-əs) *adj.* earlier; prior; foregoing. —**pre'vi·ous·ness,** *n.*

pre·vi·sion (prē-vizh'ən) *n.* foreknowledge; premonition.

pre·war' *adj.* before the (most recent) war.

prex'y (prek'sē) *n.* (*Slang*) president.

prey (prā) *n.* **1,** an animal killed by another for food. **2,** any victim. **3,** predatory habits, as *a bird of prey.* —*v.i.* (with *on* or *upon*) **1,** seize and devour an animal. **2,** plunder.

price (prīs) *n.* **1,** a consideration, esp. money, demanded in exchange for something. **2,** cost or sacrifice. **3,** the offer of a reward. **4,** an acceptable bribe. —*v.t.* set or ask the price of. —**price'less,** *adj.* invaluable. —**price control,** legislative control of pricing. —**price support,** government intervention in the market to maintain a predetermined price level. —**price war,** a competition between businessmen through use of unusually low prices.

prick (prik) *n*. **1,** a tiny hole or wound made by a pointed instrument. **2,** a stinging sensation. —*v.t.* **1,** make a tiny hole in. **2,** cause sharp pain to. **3,** (with *up*) raise (ears) as does a dog or horse.

prick′le (prik′əl) *n*. a small thorn-like projection. —*v.i.* tingle; sting. —**prick′ly,** *adj*. —**prickly pear,** a variety of cactus; its fruit. —**prickly heat,** an inflammation of the sweat glands.

pride (prīd) *n*. **1,** a sense of one's own worth; self-respect. **2,** undue self-esteem; haughtiness. **3,** a feeling or object of delight. —*v.t.* be proud of (oneself). —**pride′-ful,** *adj*.

prie-″dieu (prē″dyö′) *n*. (*Fr.*) a kneeling desk for prayer.

priest (prēst) *n*. a person authorized to perform religious rites. —**priest′craft″,** *n*. —**priest′ess,** *n.fem.* —**priest′hood,** *n*. —**priest′ly,** *adj*.

prig *n*. **1,** one who makes a show of virtue. **2,** (*Slang*) a thief. —*v.t.* [**prigged, prig′ging**] (*Slang*) steal. —**prig′gish,** *adj*.

prim *adj*. [**prim′mer, -mest**] stiffly formal; demure. —**prim′ness,** *n*.

pri′ma·cy (prī′mə-sē) *n*. state of being first in rank, importance, etc.

pri′ma don′na (prē′mə-don′ə) the principal female singer in an opera.

pri′mal (prī′məl) *adj*. **1,** original; primeval. **2,** primary.

pri·ma′ri·ly (prī-mer′ə-lē) *adv*. **1,** principally. **2,** at first; originally.

pri′ma″ry (prī′mer″ē) *adj*. coming first; chief; principal; original; earliest; preliminary; elementary. —*n*. **1,** the first. **2,** an election to nominate candidates. —**primary colors,** in the spectrum, red, green, and blue; in pigments, red, yellow, and blue. —**primary school,** a school offering the first three grades of elementary school and sometimes kindergarten.

pri′mate (prī′mit) *n*. **1,** an archbishop. **2,** (-māt″) one of an order of animals that includes man, the apes, etc.

prime (prīm) *adj*. **1,** first in order of time, rank, degree. **2,** of highest quality. **3,** of a number, divisible only by itself and unity. —*n*. **1,** the first part; earliest stage. **2,** the part of highest quality. **3,** the period of greatest vigor. —*v.t.* prepare; make ready; supply with priming. —**prime meridian,** the meridian which passes through Greenwich, England, 0°. —**prime minister,** in some countries, the chief executive or cabinet officer. —**prime time,** in broadcasting, the evening hours during which the largest audience is tuned in.

prim′er *n*. **1,** (prī′mər) that which primes; an instrument or charge to promote ignition. **2,** (prim′ər) an elementary textbook, esp. a reader.

pri·me′val (prī-mē′vəl) *adj*. pert. to earliest times; primitive.

prim′ing (prī′ming) *n*. **1,** powder, fuel, etc. used to ignite a charge, as in a firearm. **2,** the adding of liquids to a pump, to start it. **3,** a first coat of paint.

prim′i·tive (prim′ə-tiv) *adj*. **1,** early in the history of the world or man; original. **2,** simple; crude. **3,** basic. —*n*. **1,** an untrained artist. **2,** a basic form of a word or equation.

pri″mo·gen′i·ture (prī″mə-jen′ə-chər) *n*. **1,** the fact of being the first born. **2,** the eldest son's right of inheritance or succession. —**pri″mo·gen′i·tor,** *n*.

pri·mor′di·al (prī-môr′dē-əl) *adj*. original; earliest.

primp *v.i. & t*. dress (oneself) with elaborate care; prink.

prim′rose″ (prim′rōz″) *n*. a spring-flowering plant; its yellow flower. —**primrose path,** devotion to pleasure.

prince (prins) *n*. **1,** a ruler of a principality or small state. **2,** a monarch. **3,** the title of a son of a sovereign. **4,** a title of high nobility. **5,** a preeminent person. —**prince′-dom,** *n*. —**prin′cess,** *n. fem.* —**prince consort,** the husband of a reigning female sovereign.

prince′ly *adj*. **1,** royal. **2,** lavish; magnificent. —**prince′li·ness,** *n*.

prin′ci·pal (prin′sə-pəl) *adj*. first in rank or importance; chief. —*n*. **1,** one who takes a leading part. **2,** the head of a school. **3,** capital bearing interest. **4,** the employer of an agent. **5,** the chief perpetrator of a crime. —**principal parts,** the principal inflected forms of a verb.

prin″ci·pal′i·ty (prin″sə-pal′ə-tē) *n*. the domain of a prince.

prin′ci·ple (prin′sə-pəl) *n*. **1,** a fundamental truth or doctrine on which others are based. **2,** (*pl.*) rules of conduct or ethical behavior. —**prin′ci·pled,** *adj*.

prink *v.t. & i*. dress up; adorn.

print *n*. **1,** a mark made by impression. **2,** a seal or die. **3,** anything printed; (of a book) publication. **4,** cloth stamped with a design. —*v.t.* **1,** impress; stamp. **2,** produce (reading matter from type, a photograph from a film, etc.). **3,** form (letters) in imitation of type. —**printed circuit,** a circuit made by depositing conducting material on a surface between two terminals.

print′er (-ər) *n*. **1,** one whose business or trade is printing. **2,** a device for copying (not applied to printing machinery). **3,** a high-speed typewriter. **—printer's devil,** an errand boy in a print shop.

print'ing n. **1,** the process of producing the printed portion of books, etc. **2,** the use of capital letters only, in handwriting. **3,** something printed.

print-'out″ n. the typed or printed output of a computer, etc.

pri'or (prī′ər) adj. preceding in time, order, or importance. —adv. (with to) previous. —n. a superior in a religious order or house (priory). **—pri'or·ess,** n.fem.

pri·or'i·ty (prī-or′ə-tè) n. **1,** the state of being prior. **2,** a right of precedence.

prise (prīz) v.t. pry (def. 1).

prism (priz′əm) n. **1,** a solid figure whose sides are parallelograms and whose ends are similar equal polygons and parallel. **2,** a transparent body that separates light into its component colors. **—pris·mat'ic,** adj.

pris'on (priz′ən) n. a jail; any place of confinement. **—pris'on·er,** one confined in or as in prison or forcibly restrained.

pris'sy (pris′è) adj. (Colloq.) prim. **—pris'·si·ness,** n.

pris'tine (pris′tēn) adj. original; primitive; unspoiled.

pri'va·cy (prī′və-sè) n. state of being private or alone.

pri'vate (prī′vit) adj. **1,** personal; not public. **2,** secret, confidential; being alone. **3,** retired; secluded. —n. a soldier of lowest rank. **—private detective,** a detective not working for an official police force. **—private eye,** a private detective.

pri″va·teer' (prī″və-tir′) n. a ship operating under a letter of marque; its commander.

pri·va'tion (prī-vā′shən) n. want; destitution.

priv'et (priv′it) n. an evergreen shrub, much used for hedges.

priv'i·lege (priv′ə-lij) n. a special advantage enjoyed by a person. —v.t. **1,** grant a privilege to. **2,** (with from) exempt. **3,** authorize.

priv'i·leged (-lijd) adj. **1,** favored. **2,** exempt. **3,** confidential.

priv'y (priv′è) adj. **1,** (with to) admitted to a secret. **2,** private. —n. a small building used as a toilet. **—privy council,** a small advisory body.

prize (prīz) n. **1,** a reward given as a symbol of superiority. **2,** anything highly valued. **3,** a ship seized from an enemy. —v.t. **1,** value highly. **2,** [also, **prise**] pry. —adj. **1,** worthy of or given as a prize. **2,** outstanding; superior. **—prize fight,** a professional boxing match. **—prize ring,** prize-fighting as a profession.

pro (prō) n. [pl. **pros**] **1,** a proponent. **2,** (Colloq.) a professional, esp. in sports. —adv. for the affirmative. —prep. for.

pro- pref. **1,** in favor of. **2,** on behalf of.

pro'a (prō′ə) n. a Malay canoe with an outrigger and a lateen sail.

prob″a·bil'i·ty (prob″ə-bil′ə-tè) n. **1,** likelihood. **2,** that which appears true or likely. **3,** (pl.) relative chances of occurrence; expectancy.

prob'a·ble (prob′ə-bəl) adj. to be expected; likely. **—prob'a·bly,** adv.

pro'bate (prō′bāt) n. (Law) official proof of a will. —adj. **1,** related to the proof of wills. **2,** having jurisdiction over wills, as a probate court. —v.t. submit for probate.

pro·ba'tion (prō-bā′shən) n. **1,** a method or period of test or trial. **2,** conditional release of a prisoner. **—pro·ba'tion·a·ry,** adj. **—pro·ba'tion·er,** n. one who is being tested.

pro'ba·tive (prō′bə-tiv) adj. **1,** serving to test or prove. **2,** pert. to proof. Also, **pro'ba·to″ry** (-tôr″e).

probe (prōb) n. **1,** a surgical instrument for exploring cavities, etc. **2,** a searching investigation. —v.t. & i. search (into); explore.

pro'bi·ty (prō′bə-tè) n. integrity.

prob'lem (prob′ləm) n. **1,** a difficult or perplexing matter; a troublesome person. **2,** a proposition to be worked out. **—prob″lem·at'ic, prob″lem·at'i·cal,** adj. questionable; doubtful.

pro·bos'cis (prō-bos′is) n. a long flexible nose or snout.

pro·caine' (prō-kān′) n. a local anesthetic.

pro·ce'dure (prə-sē′jər) n. **1,** a course or mode of action; a step taken. **2,** customary process. **—pro·ce'dur·al,** adj.

pro·ceed' (prə-sēd′) v.i. **1,** go forward; continue or renew progress. **2,** issue; come forth. **3,** begin and carry on legal action.

pro·ceed'ing n. **1,** a measure or step taken; a legal action. **2,** (pl.) business done; a record of it.

pro'ceeds (prō′sēdz) n.pl. money taken in.

proc'ess (pros′es) n. **1,** course; progress; lapse (of time). **2,** a series of changes leading to some result. **3,** a series of operations, as in manufacturing. **4,** (Anatomy) an outgrowth; protuberance. **5,** (Law) a summons. —v.t. subject to a special treatment.

pro·ces'sion (prə-sesh′ən) n. an array, formal march, or orderly series; those constituting it.

pro·ces'sion·al (-əl) adj. pert. to a procession. —n. **1,** a hymn to which clergy and choir enter. **2,** a procession.

pro·claim' (prō-klām') v.t. declare publicly; announce officially.

proc''la·ma'tion (prok''lə-mā'shən) n. act or result of proclaiming; announcement.

pro·cliv'i·ty (prō-kliv'ə-tē) n. inclination; tendency; predisposition.

pro·con'sul n. in ancient Rome, the governor of a province. —**pro·con'su·lar,** adj. —**pro·con'sul·ate, pro·con'sul·ship,** n.

pro·cras'ti·nate'' (prō-kras'tə-nāt'') v.i. delay action. —**pro·cras''ti·na'tion,** n. —**pro·cras'ti·na''tor,** n.

pro'cre·ate'' (prō'krē-āt'') v.t. engender. —**pro''cre·a'tion,** n.

proc·tol'o·gy (prok-tol'ə-jē) n. (Med.) the study and treatment of rectal and anal diseases.

proc'tor (prok'tər) n. **1,** a supervising official, esp. in a college. **2,** a representative in a church court. —**proc·to'ri·al** (-tôr'ē-əl) adj.

proc'u·ra''tor (prok'yū-rā''tər) n. a manager, spec. a colonial financial officer for ancient Rome.

pro·cure' (prō-kyūr') v.t. **1,** contrive and effect. **2,** obtain. —**pro·cure'ment,** n.

pro·cur'er (prō-kyūr'ər) n. a pimp. —**pro·cur'ess,** n.fem.

prod n. a goad. —v.t. [**prod'ded, -ding**] goad; poke.

prod'i·gal (prod'i-gəl) adj. **1,** lavish; wasteful. **2,** bountiful. —n. a spendthrift. —**prod''i·gal'i·ty,** n.

pro·di'gious (prə-dij'əs) adj. vast; huge; immense. —**pro·di'gious·ness,** n.

prod'i·gy (prod'ə-jē) n. **1,** something remarkable; a marvel. **2,** a portent.

pro·duce' (prə-dūs') v.t. **1,** bring out; exhibit. **2,** bear, yield. **3,** bring about; effect. **4,** make; manufacture. —v.i. yield. —n. (prod'ūs) yield; products, esp. agricultural.

prod'uct (prod'ukt) n. **1,** that which is produced; an effect; result. **2,** the number resulting from multiplication.

pro·duc'tion (prə-duk'shən) n. **1,** act of bringing forward. **2,** a product of physical or mental labor; esp., a theatrical presentation.

pro·duc'tive (prə-duk'tiv) adj. **1,** creative; fertile. **2,** profitable. —**pro·duc'tive·ness,** n.

pro'em (prō'em) n. an introduction; preface. —**pro·e'mi·al** (-ē'mē-əl) adj.

pro·fane' (prə-fān') adj. **1,** not sacred; irreverent; blasphemous. **2,** vulgar. —v.t. **1,** desecrate. **2,** pollute; debase. —**prof''a·na'tion** (prof''ə-nā'shən) n.

pro·fan'i·ty (prə-fan'ə-tē) n. **1,** blasphemy; swearing. **2,** irreverence.

pro·fess' (prə-fes') v.t. **1,** declare openly. **2,** affirm faith in. **3,** make a pretense of. —**pro·fessed',** adj. avowed.

pro·fes'sion (prə-fesh'ən) n. **1,** an avowal. **2,** a vocation, esp. in a branch of science or learning; the body of persons engaged in such a vocation.

pro·fes'sion·al adj. pert. to or engaged in a profession, or in a sport for pay. —n. one working for pay, not an amateur. —**pro·fes'sion·al·ism,** n.

pro·fes'sor (prə-fes'ər) n. a teacher of high rank. Also, slang, **prof.** —**pro''fes·sor'i·al** (prō''fə-sôr'ē-əl) adj.

prof'fer (prof'ər) v.t. tender. —n. an offer.

pro·fi'cient (prə-fish'ənt) adj. skilled. —n. an expert. —**pro·fi'cien·cy,** n.

pro'file (prō'fīl) n. **1,** a side view of a face. **2,** a contour. **3,** a colorful biographical sketch. —v.t. draw or make a profile of.

prof'it n. **1,** advantage; benefit. **2,** monetary gain; excess of returns over costs; benefit. —v.t. benefit. —v.i. **1,** improve; make progress. **2,** gain; become richer. —**prof'it·a·ble,** adj. yielding a profit.

prof''it·eer' (prof''i-tir') n. one who profits unduly from the sale of necessities. —v.i. profit unduly.

prof'li·gate (prof'li-gət) adj. dissolute; recklessly extravagant. —n. a spendthrift. —**prof'li·ga·cy,** n.

pro·found' (prə-fownd') adj. **1,** deep; thorough. **2,** intense; deeply felt. —**pro·found'ness,** n.

pro·fun'di·ty (prə-fun'də-tē) n. **1,** profoundness; intellectual deepness. **2,** that which is profound.

pro·fuse' (prə-fūs') adj. liberal to excess; copious; abundant. —**pro·fu'sion** (-zhən) n.

pro·gen'i·tor (prō-jen'ə-tər) n. an ancestor in the direct line.

prog'e·ny (proj'ə-nē) n. offspring; descendants.

pro·ges'ter·one'' (prō-jes'tə-rōn'') n. a sex hormone.

prog·no'sis (prog-nō'sis) n. a forecast. adj. —**prog·nos'ti·cal·ly,** adv.

prog·nos'tic (prog-nos'tik) adj. **1,** pert. to, or serving as a ground for, prognosis. **2,** foretelling. —n. **1,** an omen. **2,** a prediction. **3,** a prognostic symptom.

prog·nos'ti·cate'' (prog-nos'tə-kāt'') v.t. foretell; predict. —**prog·nos''ti·ca'tion,** n.

pro'gram'' (prō'gram'') n. **1,** a printed list of events, performers, etc., in any public entertainment. **2,** a plan of procedure. **3,** a sequence of coded instructions for a digital computer. —*v.t.* schedule. Also, **pro′-gramme**. —**pro′gram·mer**, *n.*

prog′ress (prog′res) *n.* **1**, a moving forward. **2**, advance; development. —*v.i.* (prə-gres′) **1**, proceed; advance. **2**, grow; develop.

pro·gres′sion (prə-gresh′ən) *n.* **1**, a moving forward. **2**, a sequence, as of events. **3**, a series in which there is a constant relation between each item and the one preceding it.

pro·gres′sive (prə-gres′iv) *adj.* **1**, moving forward. **2**, advocating new ideas, methods, etc. **3**, (*Gram.*) indicating action going on at the time, as *is going; was going.* —*n.* one who is not conservative. —**pro·gres′sive·ness**, *n.*

pro·hib′it (prō-hib′it) *v.t.* **1**, forbid. **2**, prevent; hinder. —**pro·hib′i·to·ry**, *adj.*

pro″hi·bi′tion (prō″ə-bish′ən) *n.* act or effect of forbidding; esp. (*U.S.*) the period 1920–33 when the 18th Amendment was in effect. —**pro″hi·bi′tion·ist**, *n.* one favoring prohibition of alcoholic liquors.

pro·hib′i·tive (prə-hib′ə-tiv) *adj.* tending to preclude or discourage, as a high price. —**pro·hib′i·tive·ness**, *n.*

proj′ect (proj′ekt) *n.* **1**, a plan; scheme. **2**, a piece of research; a problem undertaken in school. **3**, a public works development, esp. in housing. —*v.t.* (prə-jekt′) **1**, cast forward; impose. **2**, devise. **3**, cause (light, shadow) to fall on a surface, as a screen. —*v.i.* jut out; protrude.

pro·jec′tile (prə-jek′til) *n.* a missile, as a bullet. —*adj.* impelling, or impelled, forward.

pro·jec′tion (prə-jek′shən) *n.* **1**, act or effect of projecting. **2**, a part that juts out. **3**, the act or result of projecting a figure on another surface, esp. an image on a screen or the surface of the earth on a plane surface. —**pro·jec′tion·ist**, *n.*

pro·jec′tor (prə-jek′tər) *n.* an optical instrument that projects an image, as a motion picture.

pro·lac′tin (prō-lak′tin) *n.* a pituitary hormone that stimulates the secretion of milk.

pro′lapse (prō′laps) *n.* a falling or slipping out of normal position, as of the uterus.

pro′late (prō′lāt) *adj.* extended; elongated, as a spheroid.

pro″le·tar′i·at (prō″lə-tär′é-ət) *n.* the laboring class. —**pro″le·tar′i·an**, *adj. & n.*

pro·lif′er·ate″ (prō-lif′ə-rāt″) *v.i.* **1**, grow by multiplication of elementary parts, as in budding. **2**, spread or multiply rapidly. —**pro·lif″er·a′tion**, *n.*

pro·lif′ic (prō-lif′ik) *adj.* **1**, producing young, fruit, etc., abundantly. **2**, produc-ing much work, etc. —**pro·lif′i·cal·ly**, *adv.*

pro·lix′ (prō-liks′) *adj.* long and wordy; tedious. —**pro·lix′i·ty**, *n.*

pro′logue (prō′lâg) *n.* the introduction to a poem, play, etc.

pro·long′ (prə-lâng′) *v.t.* extend in time or length. —**pro″lon·ga′tion** (prōlôg-gä′shən) *n.*

prom″e·nade′ (prom″ə-nād′) *n.* **1**, a stroll for pleasure; a place for strolling. **2**, [also (*Colloq.*) **prom**] a dance; ball. —*v.i. & t.* take a stroll.

pro·me′thi·um (prə-mē′thé-əm) *n.* a rare-earth metallic element, no. 61, symbol Pm.

prom′i·nent (prom′ə-nənt) *adj.* **1**, standing out; jutting. **2**, conspicuous; distinguished. —**prom′i·nence**, *n.*

pro·mis′cu·ous (prə-mis′kü-əs) *adj.* **1**, of all sorts and kinds; indiscriminate. **2**, not discriminating in choice of companions, esp. in sexual relations. —**prom″is·cu′i·ty** (prom″-is-kü′ə-tè) *n.*

prom′ise (prom′is) *n.* **1**, one's pledge to another that one will or will not do something. **2**, ground for hope. **3**, indication of future excellence. —*v.t.* **1**, engage to do or give; give one's word to. **2**, afford hope or expectation (of). —**prom′is·ing**, *adj.* encouraging; apparently due to succeed.

prom′is·so·ry (-sôr-ė) *adj.* stating an obligation to pay, as, *a promissory note.*

prom′on·to″ry (prom′ən-tôr″ė) *n.* high land jutting into the sea; a headland.

pro·mote′ (prə-mōt′) *v.t.* **1**, encourage the growth or improvement of. **2**, raise to a higher rank, class, or position. —**pro·mot′-er**, *n.* one who helps to start an enterprise.

pro·mo′tion (prə-mō′shən) *n.* **1**, act or effect of promoting. **2**, advancement in rank. **3**, an enterprise being promoted.

prompt *adj.* **1**, quick to act. **2**, given without delay. **3**, on time. —*v.t.* **1**, move or incite to action. **2**, remind (an actor, speaker) of his lines. —**promp′ti·tude** (-ti-tood) *n.* —**prompt′ness**, *n.*

prom′ul·gate″ (prom′əl-gāt″) *v.t.* make known publicly; proclaim. —**prom″ul·ga′-tion**, *n.*

prone (prōn) *adj.* **1**, lying face downward. **2**, having a natural tendency; inclined. —**prone′ness**, *n.*

prong *n.* a sharp point, as a tine.

prong′horn″ *n.* a No. Amer. ruminant resembling an antelope.

pro′noun (prō′nown) *n.* a word (as *he, it*) used to represent a noun previously stated or understood. —**pro·nom′in·al**, (-nom′-i-nəl) *adj.*

pro·nounce′ (prə-nowns′) *v.t.* **1**, declare;

utter. **2,** utter the recognized sound of (a word, etc.). —*v.i.* **1,** give as one's opinion. **2,** articulate words. —**pro·nounced′,** *adj.* clearly so; decided. —**pro·nounce′ment,** *n.* a formal announcement.

pron′to (pron′tō) *adv.* (*Colloq.*) at once; immediately.

pro·nun″ci·a′tion (prə-nun″sē-ā′shən) *n.* the uttering of words, esp. with correct sounds and accents.

proof *n.* **1,** evidence that establishes a fact. **2,** a test; trial. **3,** an impression from composed type, taken for correction. —*adj.* **1,** (often as a *suf.*) able to withstand. **2,** of liquors, times ½ of 1% absolute alcohol, as, 90 proof is 45% alcohol. —**proof′ing,** *n.* a treatment to make something water-proof, fireproof, etc.; the chemical used.

proof′read″ *v.t. & i.* [*pret. & p.p.* **-read** (-red)] read and correct.

prop *v.t.* [**propped, prop′ping**] support or keep from falling, as by placing something under or against. —*n.* **1,** a support. **2,** an airplane propeller. **3,** a property (def. 4).

prop″a·gan′da (prop″ə-gan′də) *n.* ideas disseminated to support a doctrine. —**prop″·a·gan′dist,** *n.* —**prop″a·gan′dize″** (-dīz″) *v.t. & i.*

prop′a·gate (prop′ə-gāt″) *v.t.* **1,** cause to multiply by natural processes. **2,** spread; disseminate. —*v.i.* have offspring. —**prop″·a·ga′tion,** *n.*

pro′pane (prō′pān) *n.* (*Chem.*) a hydro-carbon, found in petroleum.

pro·pel′ (prə-pel′) *v.t.* [**pro·pelled′, -pel′-ling**] drive forward by force. —**pro·pel′lant** (-ənt) *n.* a propelling agent, as a fuel or an explosive.

pro·pel′ler (prə-pel′ər) *n.* a device with revolving blades for driving forward a ship or airplane.

pro·pen′si·ty (prə-pen′sə-tē) *n.* a natural tendency; bent.

prop′er (prop′ər) *adj.* **1,** particularly suit-ed; natural. **2,** fit; appropriate. **3,** taken in a strict sense. **4,** accurate. **5,** decent; respect-able. **6,** of a noun, naming one particular person, place, etc. —**prop′er·ness,** *n.*

prop′er·ty (prop′ər-tē) *n.* **1,** an essential attribute or quality. **2,** ownership. **3,** a thing owned, esp. real estate; a possession. **4,** (usu. *pl.*) items in a stage setting. —**prop′-er·tied,** *adj.* owning real estate.

proph′e·cy (prof′ə-sē) *n.* a prediction of the future.

proph′e·sy″ (prof′ə-sī″) *v.t. & i.* predict; foretell.

proph′et (prof′it) *n.* **1,** one who predicts. **2,** a spokesman, esp. one inspired by God. —**proph′et·ess,** *n.fem.*

pro·phet′ic (prə-fet′ik) *adj.* **1,** pert. to prophecy or a prophet. **2,** presaging. —**pro·phet′i·cal·ly,** *adv.*

pro″phy·lax′is (prō″fə-lak′sis) *n.* (*Med.*) preventive treatment. —**pro″phy·lac′tic,** *n. & adj.*

pro·pin′qui·ty (prō-ping′kwi-tē) *n.* near-ness, in time, place, or blood.

pro·pi′ti·ate″ (prō-pish′ē-āt″) *v.t.* appease; conciliate. —**pro·pi″ti·a′tion,** *n.* —**pro·pi′-ti·a·to·ry** (-ē-ə-tôr-ē) *adj.*

pro·pi′tious (prə-pish′əs) *adj.* **1,** kindly disposed. **2,** favorable. —**pro·pi′tious·ness,** *n.*

prop′jet engine a turbo-propeller engine.

pro·po′nent (prə-pō′nənt) *n.* one who proposes or supports something.

pro·por′tion (prə-pôr′shən) *n.* **1,** the re-lation of one thing or part to another in respect to size, degree, or quantity. **2,** sym-metrical arrangement; harmony. **3,** just or proper share. **4,** (*pl.*) dimensions. —**pro·por′tion·al,** *adj.* —**pro·por′tion·ate** (-ət) *adj.*

pro·pose′ (prə-pōz′) *v.t.* **1,** offer for con-sideration, acceptance, admission, or adop-tion. **2,** put forward as a plan; suggest. —*v.i.* **1,** intend. **2,** make an offer of mar-riage. —**pro·pos′al,** *n.*

prop″o·si′tion (prop″ə-zish′ən) *n.* **1,** a subject for study, discussion, etc.; a prob-lem. **2,** (*Colloq.*) a project, undertaking, situation, etc. **3,** a proposal. —*v.t.* (*Slang*) make a proposal to, esp. of sexual rela-tions.

pro·pound′ (prə-pownd′) *v.t.* offer for consideration, as a question; set forth (a theory, etc.).

pro·pri·e·tar″y (prə-prī′ə-ter″ē) *adj.* **1,** pert. to an owner; holding property. **2,** privately owned; patented.

pro·pri′e·tor *n.* an owner. —**pro·pri′e·tress,** *n.fem.* —**pro·pri′e·tor·ship″,** *n.*

pro·pri′e·ty (prə-prī′ə-tē) *n.* **1,** fitness; rightness. **2,** correct behavior; decorum. **3,** (*pl.*) the standards of conduct approved by society.

pro·pul′sion (prə-pul′shən) *n.* **1,** a pro-pelling forward. **2,** driving force.

pro ra′ta (prō″rā′tə) (*Lat.*) in proportion.

pro·rate′ (prō′-rāt′) *v.t.* divide proportion-ally. —**pro·ra′tion,** *n.*

pro·rogue′ (prō-rōg′) *v.t.* temporarily dis-continue meetings of, esp. the British Par-liament. —**pro″ro·ga′tion,** *n.*

pro·sa′ic (prō-zā′ik) *adj.* unromantic; commonplace. —**pro·sa′i·cal·ly,** *adv.*

pro·sce′ni·um (prō-sē′nē-əm) *n.* **1,** a stage. **2,** the front of the stage, before the curtain.

pro·scribe' (prō-skrīb') *v.t.* **1,** prohibit. **2,** banish. —**pro·scrip'tion** (-skrip'shən) *n.* —**pro·scrip'tive** (-tiv) *adj.*

prose (prōz) *n.* ordinary language; not poetry. —**pros'y,** *adj.* dull.

pros'e·cute" (pros'ə-kūt") *v.t.* **1,** institute legal proceedings against. **2,** pursue (an object). —*v.i.* **1,** sue. **2,** act as prosecutor. —**prosecuting attorney,** the state's attorney.

pros"e·cu'tion (-kū'shən) *n.* **1,** act or result of prosecuting. **2,** the side that prosecutes. **3,** the prosecutor and his staff.

pros'e·cu"tor (pros'ə-kū"tər) *n.* one who prosecutes, esp. the public prosecutor or state's attorney.

pros'e·lyte" (pros'ə-līt") *n.* a convert from one creed, sect, or party to another. —**pros'e·ly·tize"** (-lə-tīz") *v.t. & i.* attempt to convert.

pro'sit (prō'sit) *interj.* (*Ger.*) (as a toast) may it do good!

pros'o·dy (pros'ə-dē) *n.* the science of metrical versification.

pros'pect (pros'pekt) *n.* **1,** a view; scene. **2,** what one hopes for; expectation. **3,** a possible buyer, client, etc. —*v.t. & i.* explore (a district) for ores, oil, etc. —**pro·spec'tive,** *adj.* expected. —**pros'pec·tor,** *n.* one who seeks ores.

pros·pec'tus (prə-spek'təs) *n.* a descriptive pamphlet; catalog.

pros'per (pros'pər) *v.i.* succeed; thrive. —**pros'per·ous,** *adj.* prospering.

pros·per'i·ty (pros-per'ə-tē) *n.* **1,** success. **2,** a period of economic well-being.

pros'per·ous (-pər-əs) *adj.* **1,** thriving; successful. **2,** favorable.

pros'tate (pros'tāt) *n. & adj.* a gland in males which surrounds the base of the urethra and discharges into it. —**pros·tat'ic** (prō-stat'ik), *adj.*

pros'the·sis (pros'thə-sis) *n.* the supplying of an artificial part of the body; such a part.

pros'ti·tute" (pros'tə-tūt") *v.t.* devote (one's honor, talents, person) to base purposes. —*n.* a harlot. —**pros"ti·tu'tion,** *n.*

pros'trate (pros'trāt) *adj.* **1,** lying flat; laid low. **2,** bowing low. —*v.t.* **1,** throw (oneself) down; lay flat. **2,** overthrow. **3,** cause to succumb. —**pros·tra'tion,** *n.*

pro"tac·tin'i·um (prō"tak-tin'ē-əm) *n.* a short-lived radioactive chemical element formed from uranium 235, No. 91, symbol Pa. Also, **pro"to·ac·tin'i·um** (prō"tō-).

pro·tag'o·nist (prō-tag'ə-nist) *n.* the leading figure, as in a play.

pro'te·an (prō'tē-ən) *adj.* readily assuming many shapes.

pro·tect' (prə-tekt') *v.t.* shield from harm, damage, etc. —**pro·tec'tor,** *n.*

pro·tec'tion *n.* **1,** act or effect of protecting; that which keeps safe. **2,** support of domestic prices by a tariff. **3,** immunity from arrest, purchased by bribery. —**pro·tec'tion·ist,** *n. & adj.* —**pro·tec'tion·ism,** *n.*

pro·tec'tive *adj.* **1,** serving to protect or supply protection. **2,** wishing to protect. —**pro·tec'tive·ness,** *n.*

pro·tec'tor·ate (-ət) *n.* a state controlled and protected by a stronger state.

pro'té·gé" (prō'tə-zhā") *n.* a person protected or aided by another. —**pro'té·gée",** *n. fem.*

pro'te·in (prō'tē-in) *n.* an organic substance, an essential element of diet.

pro'test (prō'test) *v.i. & t.* **1,** declare solemnly. **2,** remonstrate; formally object to. **3,** declare to be dishonored by nonpayment, as a check, etc. —*n.* a formal declaration of disapproval. —**prot"es·ta'tion** (prot"is-tā'shən) *n.*

Prot'es·tant (prot'is-tənt) *adj.* pert. to a Christian church not Roman or Orthodox Catholic. —*n.* a member of such a church. —**Prot'es·tant·ism,** *n.*

pro"tha·la'mi·um (prō"thə-lā'mē-əm) *n.* a pre-wedding ode.

pro·to- (prō-tō) *pref.* first in time; principal; chief.

pro'to·col" (prō'tə-kol") *n.* **1,** a draft of a treaty or agreement. **2,** the formal procedure in official or diplomatic society.

pro'ton (prō'ton) *n.* a particle of the atom, carrying a positive charge of electricity.

pro'to·plasm" (prō'tə-plaz-əm") *n.* the substance of which all animal and plant cells are composed. —**pro"to·plas'mic,** *adj.*

pro'to·type" (prō'tə-tīp") *n.* the original form; pattern; model.

Pro"to·zo'a (prō"tə-zō'ə) *n.pl.* all animals that consist of a single cell. —**pro"to·zo'an,** *adj. & n.*

pro·tract' (prō-trakt') *v.t.* **1,** prolong. **2,** draw to scale; chart. —**pro·trac'tion,** *n.*

pro·trac'tor (-ər) *n.* **1,** a muscle that extends a part of the body. **2,** a device for measuring or drawing angles.

pro·trude' (prō-trood') *v.i. & t.* stick out; project. —**pro·tru'sion** (-troo'zhən) *n.*

pro·tu'ber·ant (prō-tū'bər-ənt) *adj.* bulging out; prominent. —**pro·tu'ber·ance,** *n.*

proud (prowd) *adj.* **1,** haughty; arrogant. **2,** self-respectful. **3,** being gratified or elated. **4,** imposing; splendid. **5,** spirited. —**proud'ness,** *n.* —**proud flesh,** excessive granulation of a healing wound or sore.

---

prove (proov) *v.t.* **1,** test the qualities of. **2,** make certain, by adducing evidence. **3,** probate. **4,** make a proof of (type). —*v.i.* turn out (to be). —**prov'en,** *adj.* proved. —**proving ground,** a place or occasion for testing.

prov'e·nance (prov'ə-nəns) *n.* source; derivation.

prov'en·der (prov'ən-dər) *n.* dry food for animals; fodder.

prov'erb (prov'ĕrb) *n.* **1,** a well-known truth expressed as a maxim. **2,** a byword. —**pro·ver'bi·al,** (prə-vĕr'bē-əl) *adj.*

pro·vide' (prə-vīd') *v.t.* **1,** procure beforehand. **2,** (with *with*) furnish —*v.i.* **1,** furnish supplies; take precautions. **2,** supply what is needed. **3,** stipulate. —**pro·vid'ed, pro·vid'ing,** *conj.* on the condition that.

prov'i·dence (prov'i-dəns) *n.* **2,** thrift; economy. **2,** (*Cap.*) God; divine care.

prov'i·dent (prov'i-dənt) *adj.* thrifty; foresighted.

prov''i·den'tial (prov''i-den'shəl) *adj.* **1,** of or by divine guidance. **2,** opportune.

prov'ince (prov'ins) *n.* **1,** an administrative division of a country. **2,** (*pl.*) rural regions. **3,** a proper sphere of action. **4,** a division or department of knowledge.

pro·vin'cial (prə-vin'shəl) *adj.* **1,** of a province. **2,** rustic. **3,** narrow; not cosmopolitan. —**pro·vin'cial·ism,** *n.*

pro·vi'sion (prə-vizh'ən) *n.* **1,** preparation. **2,** (*pl.*) stores; supplies, as of food. **3,** a proviso; condition, as in a contract. —*v.t.* supply with a store of food.

pro·vi'sion·al *adj.* **1,** conditional. **2,** temporary.

pro·vi'so (prə-vī'zō) *n.* [*pl.* **-sos** (-zōz)] a condition, esp. in a contract. —**pro·vi'so·ry** (-zə-rē) *adj.*

prov''o·ca'tion (prov''ə-kā'shən) *n.* **1,** act or effect of provoking. **2,** a cause of anger or resentment. **3,** stimulus; incitement.

pro·voc'a·tive (prə-vok'ə-tiv) *adj.* serving to provoke, arouse, or stimulate. —**pro·voc'a·tive·ness,** *n.*

pro·voke' (prə-vōk') *v.t.* **1,** incense; irritate. **2,** arouse; goad. **3,** incite; stir up.

pro·vo·lo'ne (prō-və-lō'nē) *n.* a mild Ital. cheese.

prov'ost (prov'əst) *n.* a supervisor or head. —**provost marshal,** a chief of military police.

prow *n.* the foremost surface of a ship; bow.

prow'ess (prow'is) *n.* **1,** valor. **2,** great skill or ability.

prowl *v.i. & t.* roam about stealthily. —*n.* act of prowling. —**prowl car,** a radio-equipped police automobile.

prox''i·mate (prok'si-mət) *adj.* next; immediate.

prox·im'i·ty (prok-sim'ə-tē) *n.* nearness. —**proximity fuse,** a device to explode a bomb when it approaches its object.

prox'y (prok'sē) *n.* **1,** authority to act for another. **2,** the person so authorized.

prude (prood) *n.* an affectedly modest person. —**prud'er·y,** *n.* —**prud'ish,** *adj.* —**prud'ish·ness,** *n.*

pru'dence (proo'dəns) *n.* discretion; foresight; careful judgment. —**pru·den'tial** (-den'shəl) *adj.*

pru'dent (proo'dənt) *adj.* **1,** judicious; wise. **2,** discreet; circumspect. —**pru·den'tial** (-den'shəl) *adj.*

prune (proon) *n.* a dried plum. —*v.t. & i.* trim off something superfluous, esp. branches.

pru'ri·ent (prûr'ē-ənt) *adj.* lewd in thought. —**pru'ri·ence,** *n.*

Prus'sian (prush'ən) *adj.* pert. to Prussia or its people. —**Prussian blue,** a dark blue dye or pigment.

pry (prī) *n.* a lever. —*v.t.* **1,** raise or move by a lever. **2,** extract or move with difficulty. —*v.i.* peer curiously or impertinently.

psalm (säm) *n.* a sacred song or poem. —**psalm'ist,** *n.* —**psal'mo·dy** (sä'mə-dē; sal'-) *n.*

Psal'ter (sâl'tər) *n.* the Book of Psalms.

psal'ter·y (sâl'tə-rē) *n.* an ancient musical instrument like the zither.

pseu'do (soo'dō) *adj.* feigned; sham.

pseu·do- *pref.* false; sham.

pseu'do·nym'' (soo'də-nim'') *n.* a false name; pen name. —**pseu·don'y·mous** (soo-don'ə-məs) *adj.*

pshaw (shà) *interj.* of disdain.

psi (sī) *n.* the twenty-third letter of the Greek alphabet (Ψ, ψ).

psit''ta·co'sis (sit''ə-kō'sis) *n.* a contagious disease of birds, transferable to man: *parrot fever.*

pso·ri'a·sis (sô-rī'ə-sis) *n.* a chronic skin disease characterized by scaly, reddish patches.

psych (sīk) *v.i.* (*Slang*) **1,** (with *out*) figure out (the motives or behavior of); outwit. **2,** talk oneself out of or into; lose one's nerve. **3,** (with *up*) prepare mentally and emotionally.

psy'che (sī'kē) *n.* the human soul.

psy''che·del'ic (sī''kə-del'ik) *adj.* pert. to or causing a state of extreme calm, heightened senses, esthetic perception, and frequently hallucination and distortion of perception.

psy·chi'a·try (sī-kī'ə-trē) *n.* (*Med.*) the science dealing with mental diseases. —**psy''chi·at'ric** (sī''kē-at'rik) *adj.* —**psy·chi'a·trist,** *n.*

psy'chic (sī'kik) *adj.* **1,** pert. to the mental or spiritual life. **2,** pert. to mysterious mental forces. **3,** sensitive to such forces. —*n.* a person esp. susceptible to psychic forces. —**psy'chi·cal·ly**, *adv.*.

psy'cho (sī'kō) *n.* (*Slang*) a deranged person.

psycho- (sī-kō) *pref.* of the mind; by mental processes.

psy"cho·a·nal'y·sis *n.* a method of relieving mental disorders by a study of the subconscious emotional life of the patient. —**psy"cho·an·a'lyze**, *v.t.* —**psy"cho·an'a·lyst**, *n.*

psy'cho·dra"ma *n.* the use of improvisational theater in treating mental patients; such theater.

psy"cho·ki·ne'sis (-kə-nē'səs) *n.* the displacement of an object by strength of will.

psy·chol'o·gy (sī-kol'ə-jē) *n.* **1,** the science of the mind and mental activities. **2,** (*Colloq.*) attitude. **3,** (*Colloq.*) the use of stratagems. —**psy"cho·log'i·cal,** *adj.* —**psy'chol'o·gist,** *n.*

psy"cho·path'ic (-ik) *adj.* pert. to any mental disorder, its study or treatment. —**psy"cho·path'i·cal·ly,** *adv.*

psy"cho·pa·thol'o·gy *n.* the science dealing with mental illness and abnormality.

psy·chop'a·thy (sī-kop'ə-thē) *n.* mental disease.

psy'cho·path" (sī'kō-path") *n.* one mentally afflicted.

psy·cho'sis (sī-kō'sis) *n.* [*pl.* **-ses** (sēz)] a mental disease. —**psy·chot'ic** (-kot'ik) *adj.*

psy"cho·so·mat'ic (sī"kō-sō-mat'ik) *adj.* pert. to the relation between mental and physical disorders, as a physical disease induced by emotional factors.

psy"cho·ther'a·py *n.* treatment of mental disease, esp. by psychoanalysis, psychodrama, etc. —**psy"cho·ther'a·pist,** *n.*

ptar'mi·gan (tär'mə-gən) *n.* a kind of grouse.

PT boat a small, lightly armored motor torpedo boat.

pter"o·dac'tyl (ter"ə-dak'til) *n.* an extinct large flying reptile.

ptis'an (tiz'ən) *n.* **1,** a mild herbal drink; barley water. **2,** tisane.

pto'maine (tō'mān) *n.* a chemical compound, often poisonous, found in decaying organic matter. —**ptomaine poisoning,** an acute intestinal disorder caused by toxic bacilli; formerly attributed to ptomaines.

pub *n.* (*Brit.*) public house; tavern.

pu'ber·ty (pū'bər·tē) *n.* the age at which a person first can procreate.

pu'bes (pū'bēz) *n.* the front bone of the

pelvis, or its region, where hair grows at puberty; the hair itself. —**pu'bic,** *adj.*

pu·bes'cent (pū-bes'ənt) *adj.* arrived, or arriving, at puberty. —**pu·bes'cence,** *n.*

pub'lic (pub'lik) *adj.* **1,** pert. to the people at large. **2,** open to, or shared by, the people. **3,** known to all; not secret. **4,** engaged in service to the people. —*n.* the entire community or a specified group. —**public address system,** the necessary apparatus to provide amplified sound for public assemblies. —**public domain, 1,** public land. **2,** works whose copyrights have expired. —**public defender,** a lawyer available for people without the means to hire an attorney. —**public enemy,** a criminal at large. —**public house,** (*Brit.*) a bar; pub. —**public relations,** organized publicity. —**public school, 1,** a school paid for by public funds. **2,** (*Brit.*) a private boarding school. —**public servant,** an elected or appointed employee of the government. —**pub"lic-spir'it·ed,** seeking the best interests of the community. —**public television,** public service and educational television not accepting commercial advertising.

pub'li·can (pub'lə-kən) *n.* **1,** (*Brit.*) an innkeeper. **2,** in ancient Rome, a tax collector.

pub"li·ca'tion (pub"li-kā'shən) *n.* **1,** the act or business of publishing. **2,** a book, periodical, etc.

pub'li·cist (pub'li-sist) *n.* **1,** a writer on current affairs, esp. international. **2,** one who is retained to manage publicity for another.

pub·lic'i·ty (pub-lis'ə-tē) *n.* **1,** a bringing to public attention. **2,** common knowledge; notoriety

pub'li·cize" (pub'li-sīz") *v.t.* make known by publicity.

pub'lish *v.t.* **1,** make generally known; proclaim. **2,** print and offer for sale, as a book, etc.

puce (pūs) *adj.* of a purple-brown color.

puck (puk) *n.* **1,** the sliding disk used in hockey. **2,** (*cap.*) a mischievous sprite.

puck'er (puk'ər) *v.i. & t.* draw up into small bulges or wrinkles. —*n.* **1,** a furrow. **2,** a state of agitation.

puck'ish (puk'ish) *adj.* mischievous. —**puck'ish·ness,** *n.*

pud'ding (pûd'ing) *n.* a soft, bulky dessert.

pud'dle (pud'əl) *n.* **1,** a small pool of muddy water. **2,** a watertight covering of clay mixed with water. —*v.t.* convert (pig iron) into wrought iron. —**pud'dling,** *n.*

pu·den'dum (poo-den'dəm) *n.* [*pl.* **-da** (-də)] **1,** (usu. *pl.*) the external genital parts of the female; vulva. **2,** (*pl.*) all the female genital parts.

pudg′y (puj′ē) *adj.* short and fat.

pueb′lo (pweb′lō) *n.* [*pl.* **-los** (lōz)] a Lat. Amer. or Indian village of adobe houses.

pu′er·ile (pū′ər-il) *adj.* childish; trivial. —**pu″er·il′i·ty,** *n.*

pu·er′per·al (pū-ēr′pər-əl) *adj.* pert. to childbirth.

puff (puf) *n.* **1,** a short blast, as of wind, smoke, etc. **2,** a light, fluffy pad. **3,** a light, porous pastry. **4,** (*Colloq.*) undue praise; a plug. —*v.i.* **1,** emit a puff. **2,** breathe hard. —*v.t.* **1,** expel with puffs; smoke with puffs. **2,** (usually with *up* or *out*) distend; inflate. **3,** praise. —**puff′y,** *adj.* —**puff adder, 1,** a large, extremely venomous Afr. snake. **2,** a small, harmless snake of No. Amer.

puff′ball″ *n.* a ball-shaped mushroom.

puff′er·y (puf′ər-ē) *n.* extravagant praise, as in advertising.

puf′fin (puf′in) *n.* a bird of the auk family.

pug *n.* **1,** a small dog with a squat, wrinkled face. **2,** a short, tip-tilted nose: *pugnose.* **3,** (*Slang*) pugilist.

pu′gil·ist (pū′jə-list) *n.* a professional boxer. —**pu′gil·ism,** *n.* —**pu″gi·lis′tic,** *adj.*

pug·na′cious (pug-nā′shəs) *adj.* given to fighting; quarrelsome. —**pug·nac′i·ty** (-nas′-ə-tē) *n.*

puke (pūk) *v.t. & i.* (*Vulgar*) vomit.

puk′ka (puk′ə) *adj.* **1,** genuine. **2,** first-rate.

pul′chri·tude″ (pul′kri-tood″) *n.* beauty. —**pul″chri·tu′di·nous,** *adj.*

pule (pūl) *v.i.* whine; whimper.

pu′li (poo′lē) *n.* a Hungarian breed of farm dog.

pull (pûl) *v.i.* **1,** draw with force toward one; tug. **2,** extract, as a tooth. **3,** pluck; gather. **4,** rip; rend. **5,** hit (a ball) so as to cause it to go toward the left (for a right-handed batter). —*v.i.* **1,** draw, drag, tug, etc. **2,** move; be under away. —*n.* **1,** the effort exerted in hauling, drawing, etc. **2,** a device for pulling. **3,** a hard climb. **4,** (*Slang*) influence. —**pull one's leg,** perpetrate a hoax; trick; fool. —**pull through,** help or come through a danger, illness, etc., successfully.

pul′let (pûl′it) *n.* a young hen.

pul′ley (pûl′ē) *n.* a wheel, or series of wheels, used with a rope or belt to transmit power.

Pull′man (pûl′mən) *n.* (*T.N.*) an extra-fare railroad car for sleeping or lounging.

pull′o″ver *n.* a sweater pulled on over the head.

pull-′out″ *n.* **1,** the maneuver of bringing an airplane to level flight from a dive. **2,** a retreat; evacuation.

pull-′up″ *n.* **1,** the maneuver of putting an airplane into a sharp climb from level flight. **2,** chin-up.

pul′mo·nar″y (pûl′mə-ner″ē) *adj.* pert. to the lungs.

pul′mo″tor (pûl′mo″tər) *n.* (*T.N.*) an apparatus for pumping air into the lungs.

pulp *n.* **1,** the fleshy part of a fruit. **2,** a moist mixture of wood fibers, etc., from which paper is made. **3,** a cheap paper; a magazine printed on it. —*v.t.* reduce to a pulp. —**pulp′y,** *adj.*

pul′pit (pûl′pit) *n.* **1,** the stand from which a sermon is preached. **2,** preachers collectively.

pulp′wood″ *n.* soft wood mashed to a pulp for making paper.

pul′que (pûl′kē) *n.* a Mexican fermented drink made from agave juice.

pul′sar (pul′sär) *n.* a rapidly pulsating radio source from space of very short but gradually lengthening period.

pul′sate (pul′sāt) *v.i.* beat; throb. —**pul·sa′tion,** *n.*

pulse (puls) *n.* the throbbing of arteries as blood is pumped along them by the heart. —*v.i.* pulsate.

pul′ver·ize″ (pul′və-rīz″) *v.t.* grind or crush into a fine powder.

pu′ma (pū′mə) *n.* the cougar.

pum′ice (pum′is) *n.* a light spongy volcanic rock used in polishing, etc.

pum′mel (pum′əl) *v.t.* beat with the fists.

pump *n.* **1,** a machine for moving, or compressing, liquids or gases. **2,** a shoe without straps or lacings. —*v.t.* **1,** move (a fluid) by means of a pump. **2,** draw information from. **3,** (often with *up*) inflate.

pum′per·nick″el (pum′pər-nik″əl) *n.* a coarse, dark brown rye bread.

pump′kin *n.* a vine or its large, deep-yellow, gourdlike fruit.

pun *n.* a humorous play on words of similar sound. —**pun′ster,** *n.*

punch *n.* **1,** a blow, as with the fist. **2,** a tool for stamping holes. **3,** a mixed beverage. **4,** energy; force. —*v.t.* **1,** strike, as with the fist. **2,** poke; prod; hence, herd, as cattle. **3,** perforate or impress with a punch. —**punch′drunk″,** *adj.* having confused or dazed actions, due to head injuries. —**punch line,** the final line of a joke, story, etc., that makes the principal point.

punch′card″ *n.* a card having holes or notches punched in particular positions with assigned meaning for use in automatic data-processing machines.

pun′cheon (pun′chən) n. **1,** a large cask. **2,** an upright timber. **3,** a punching tool.

punch′y (-ē) adj. (Colloq.) confused; dazed; punch-drunk.

punc·til′i·o (punk-til′ē-ō) n. correct formal behavior.

punc·til′i·ous (punk-til′ē-əs) adj. scrupulously careful. —**punc·til′i·ous·ness,** n.

punc′tu·al (punk′choo-əl) adj. seldom late; prompt. —**punc″tu·al′i·ty,** n.

punc′tu·ate″ (punk′choo-āt″) v.t. separate into sentences, clauses, and the like, by means of certain marks, as period, comma, dash, etc. —**punc″tu·a′tion,** n.

punc′ture (punk′chər) v.t. prick; make a small hole in. —n. act or effect of puncturing.

pun′dit n. a learned man.

pung n. a low horse-drawn sleigh.

pun′gent (pun′jənt) adj. **1,** stinging to the taste or smell. **2,** caustic; biting. —**pun′gen·cy,** n.

pun′ish v.t. inflict a penalty on (a person) or for (an offense). —**pun′ish·a·ble,** adj.

pun′ish·ment (-mənt) n. act or effect of punishing; penalty.

pu′ni·tive (pū′nə-tiv) adj. pert. to, or inflicting, punishment. Also, **pu′ni·to·ry,** adj.

punk n. **1,** dry, crumbly wood, or a fungus, used as a tinder. **2,** (Slang) a worthless youth. **3,** (Slang) a style of clothing and makeup associated with punk rock. —adj. **1,** (Slang) of low quality. —**punk rock,** a variety of rock music characterized by violence and obscenity.

punt n. **1,** a flat-bottomed boat. **2,** a kick of a football dropped from the hands, before it touches the ground. —v.t. & i. **1,** propel a punt. **2,** kick (a football).

pu′ny (pū′nē) adj. feeble; petty. —**pu′-ni·ness,** n.

pup n. **1,** [also, **pup′py**] a young dog. **2,** the young of various mammals. —**pup tent,** a small tent.

pu′pa (pū′pə) n. [pl. -**pae** (pē)] the stage in an insect's life between the larval and adult stages.

pu′pil (pū′pəl) n. **1,** a person receiving instruction. **2,** the dark center of the eye.

pup′pet (pup′it) n. a doll moved by wires; hence, a person or state controlled by another. —**pup″pet·eer′** (-ir′) n. —**pup′pet·ry** (-rē) n.

pup′py (pup′ē) n. **1,** a pup. **2,** a conceited, impertinent young man. —**puppy love,** immature love.

pur′blind (pēr′blīnd″) adj. partly blind; hence, obtuse; dull. —**pur′blind″ness,** n.

pur′chase (pēr′chəs) v.t. buy. —n. **1,** the act of buying; something bought. **2,** a hold or leverage for moving heavy bodies.

pur′dah (pēr′də) n. **1,** a curtain. **2,** seclusion of women, in India.

pure (pyûr) adj. **1,** free from pollution. **2,** chaste. **3,** genuine; sincere. **4,** abstract, as sciences. **5,** sheer; simple. —**pure′ness,** n.

pure′bred″ adj. & n. of a breed that has maintained certain desirable characteristics through generations of descent.

pu·rée′ (pyû-rā′) n. a thick soup or sauce of sieved vegetables, fruit, etc. —v.t. rub or pass through a sieve to make a smooth sauce; make into a similar sauce by means of a blender, etc.

pur′ga·tive (pēr′gə-tiv) n. that which purges. —adj. purging.

pur′ga·to″ry (pēr′gə-tôr″ē) n. (Rom. Cath.) a place where penitent souls are purified.

purge (pērj) v.t. **1,** cleanse from impurities, bodily or spiritual. **2,** flush (the bowels) by a physic. **3,** remove disloyal members from (a state or party). —n. **1,** the act of purging. **2,** a physic; purgative. —**pur·ga′tion** (pēr-gā′shən) n.

pu′ri·fy (pyûr′i-fī″) v.t. make pure. —**pu″ri·fi·ca′tion,** n.

Pu·rim′ (poo-rēm′) n.sing. a Jewish holiday, the Feast of Lots.

pur′ist (pyûr′ist) n. & adj. (a person) insistent on exactness. —**pur′ism,** n.

pu′ri·tan (pyûr′ə-tən) n. a religious zealot who frowns on frivolity. —**pu″ri·tan′i·cal,** adj.

pu′ri·ty (pyûr′i-tē) n. pureness.

purl (pērl) n. a knitting stitch. **2,** a ripple; eddy. —v.i. make purls.

pur′lieus (pēr′looz) n.pl. outskirts, environs.

pur·loin′ (pər-loin′) v.t. steal.

pur′ple (pēr′pəl) n. **1,** a bluish-red color. **2,** an emperor's robe of this color; regal power. —adj. **1,** of a purple color. **2,** hence, regal. —**pur′plish,** adj. —**Purple Heart,** a medal awarded to one wounded in action.

pur·port′ (pər-pôrt′) v.t. profess; seem to mean. —n. (pēr′pôrt) meaning; import.

pur′pose (pēr′pəs) v.t. intend; mean. —n. **1,** intention; aim. **2,** intended effect; use. —**pur′pos·ive,** adj. —**on purpose,** intentionally.

pur′pose·ful adj. **1,** determined; resolved. **2,** serving a purpose. —**pur′pose·ful·ness,** n.

pur′pose·ly adj. deliberately; intentionally.

purr (pēr) v.t. make a low vibrating sound, as a contented cat. —n. this sound.

purse (pērs) n. **1,** any small receptacle for carrying money; hence, means; finances.

2, a sum of money collected as a gift or offered as a prize. —*v.t.* pucker (the lips). —**purse strings,** power or control over money or spending.

purs′er (pėr′sər) *n.* an officer on a ship or airplane in charge of accounts and passenger welfare.

purs′lane (pėrs′lān) *n.* a low, spreading plant used as a potherb and in salads.

pur·su′ant (pər-soo′ənt) *adj.* **1,** following. **2,** (with *to*) according. —**pur·su′ance,** *n.*

pur·sue′ (pər-soo′) *v.t.* **1,** follow with intent to catch. **2,** proceed along; continue. **3,** seek after. **4,** be engaged in.

pur·suit′ (pər-soot′) *n.* **1,** act of following. **2,** carrying out. **3,** an occupation.

pur′sy (pėr′sė) *adj.* fat and short-winded.

pu′ru·lent (pyûr′ə-lənt) *adj.* full of, or discharging, pus. —**pur′u·lence,** *n.*

pur·vey′ (pər-vā′) *v.t. & i.* provide (food supplies). —**pur·vey′or,** *n.*

pur′view (pėr′vū) *n.* **1,** scope; extent of anything. **2,** range of physical or mental vision.

pus *n.* the yellowish-white matter in an inflamed sore. —**pus′sy** (pus′ė) *adj.*

push (pûsh) *v.t.* **1,** thrust forcibly against, in order to move. **2,** advance or extend by effort. —*v.i.* **1,** exert impelling pressure. **2,** force one's way. —*n.* **1,** a shove. **2,** a crowd of people. **3,** (*Colloq.*) energy; enterprise. —**push′er,** *n.* (*Slang*) a dealer in illegal drugs.

push-′but″ton *adj.* automatic; done by, or as though by, merely pushing an electrical signal.

push′cart″ *n.* a cart pushed by hand, used by a vendor, etc.

push′o″ver *n.* (*Slang*) a weak-willed person; an easy task.

push′pin″ *n.* a thumbtack.

push′up″ *n.* a physical exercise of raising the body with the arms.

push′y *adj.* aggressive.

pu″sil·lan′i·mous (pū″sə-lan′ə-məs) *adj.* mean-spirited; cowardly. —**pu″sil·la·nim′i·ty** (-lə-nim′ə-tė) *n.*

puss (pûs) *n.* **1,** [also, **pus′sy, pus′sy·cat″**] a cat. **2,** (*Slang*) the face or mouth.

puss′y·foot″ *v.t.* move warily or fearfully; hedge.

pussy willow a small willow tree.

pus′tule (pus′chûl) *n.* a small, pus-filled pimple. —**pus′tu·lar,** *adj.*

put (pût) *v.t.* [**put, put′ting**] **1,** set, lay, or cause to be in any place, position, or condition. **2,** assign; attribute. **3,** propound; propose for attention. **4,** (with *across* or *over*) accomplish; effect the acceptance of. **5,**

(with *by*) save, as money. **6,** (with *up*) give lodging to. **7,** (with *up with*) tolerate. —*v.i.* **1,** (with *about*) turn. **2,** (with *on*) pretend. **3,** (with *out*) set forth. —**put down** (*Slang*) **1,** suppress; smash. **2,** snub. **3,** attribute. **4,** inscribe; write down. —**put forward,** propose. —**put in, 1,** interpose; insert. **2,** spend, as time. —**put off, 1,** postpone. **2,** get rid of (a person) by evasion. **3,** take off. —**put on,** (*Slang*) kid; mock. —**put out, 1,** vex; offend. **2,** inconvenience. **3,** extinguish; blind. **4,** expel. **5,** expend. —**put** (something) **over on,** deceive. —**put upon,** impose on.

pu′ta·tive (pū′tə-tiv) *adj.* supposed; reputed.

put′down″ *n.* (*Slang*) insult; slight; rejection.

put-′on″ *n.* (*Colloq.*) a deception; hoax.

pu′tre·fy″ (pū′trə-fī″) *v.i. & t.* decay or cause to decay. —**pu″tre·fac′tion,** *n.*

pu·tres′cence (pū-tres′əns) *n.* process of becoming rotten. —**pu·tres′cent,** *adj.*

pu′trid (pū′trid) *adj.* rotten; foul.

putsch (pûch) *n.* (*Ger.*) a minor rebellion or uprising; a coup.

putt (put) *n.* (*Golf*) a stroke made to send a ball along the ground. —*v.t. & i.* make (the ball) so roll. —**putt′er,** *n.* a golf club for this purpose.

put′tee (put′ė) *n.* a legging.

put′ter (put′ər) *v.i.* busy oneself in an ineffective manner.

put′ty (put′ė) *n.* a soft, doughy cement for filling cracks, etc.

put-′up″ *adj.* fraudulently prearranged.

puz′zle (puz′əl) *n.* a perplexing problem; a device or toy to test one's ingenuity. —*v.t.* perplex. —*v.i.* ponder. —**puz′zle·ment,** *n.*

Pyg′my (pig′mė) *n.* one of a dwarf race of central Africa; hence (*l.c.*) a dwarf.

py·jam′as (pə-jäm′əs) *n.pl.* pajamas.

py′lon (pī′lon) *n.* **1,** a gateway formed of one or two truncated pyramids. **2,** a high tower.

py·lo′rus (pī-lôr′əs) *n.* the opening from the stomach to the intestines. —**py·lor′ic,** *adj.*

py″or·rhe′a (pī″ə-rē′ə) *n.* inflammation of the gums, with discharge of pus.

pyr′a·mid (pir′ə-mid) *n.* (*Geom.*) a solid whose base is a polygon and whose sides are all triangles meeting in a common point; anything so shaped. —*v.i. & t.* reinvest (profits or winnings) for greater profit. —**py·ram′i·dal** (pi-ram′ə-dəl) *adj.*

pyre (pīr) *n.* a heap of wood for burning a corpse.

py′rex (pī′reks) *n.* (*T.N.*) a heat-resistant glassware used for cooking utensils.

py·rex′i·a (pī-rek′sē-ə) *n.* (*Med.*) fever. —**py·ret′ic,** *adj.*

pyr′i·dine″ (pir′ə-dēn″) *n.* a colorless liquid, of pungent odor, used as a solvent, germicide, and in medicine.

py′rite (pī′rīt) *n.* fool's gold. —**py·rit′ic** (-rit′ik) *adj.*

py′ro- (pī-rə) *pref.* heat; fire.

py″ro·ma′ni·a *n.* a mania for starting fires. —**py″ro·ma′ni·ac,** *n.*

py″ro·tech′nics *n.* a display of fireworks.

py·rox′y·lin (pī-rok′sə-lin) *n.* gun-cotton; nitrocellulose, esp. in solution.

Pyr′rhic victory (pir′ik) a victory gained at too great cost.

py′thon (pī′thon) *n.* a large snake that crushes its prey.

py′tho·ness (pī′thə-nis) *n.* a woman with the gift of prophecy; a witch.

pyx (piks) *n.* **1,** a small box or vase in which the consecrated wafer of the Eucharist is kept. **2,** a chest in which specimen coins are deposited.

Q

Q, q (kū) *n.* seventeenth letter of the English alphabet.

Qi·a′na (kē-ä′nə) *n.* (*T.N.*) a silklike nylon fabric.

qua (kwā; kwä) *adv.* as being; in the manner or capacity of.

quack (kwak) *n.* **1,** the cry of a duck; a similar harsh; flat sound. **2,** a false pretender to medical skill. —*v.i.* make a noise as a duck. —*adj.* fraudulent. —**quack′er·y,** *n.* deceptive practice.

quad (kwod) *n.* **1,** the square-shaped court of a college or like group of buildings. **2,** blank metal used to space type. **3,** (*Colloq.*) a quadruplet.

quadr- *pref.* four; fourth.

Quad″ra·ges′i·ma (kwod″rə-jes′ə-mə) *n.* the first Sunday in Lent.

quad′ran″gle (kwod′rang″gəl) *n.* **1,** a plane figure with four sides and four angles. **2,** quad. —**quad·ran′gu·lar** (kwə-drang′gyə-lər) *adj.*

quad′rant (kwod′rənt) *n.* **1,** the fourth part. **2,** a quarter of a circle. **3,** an instrument for measuring altitudes.

quad′ra·phon″ic (kwod′rə-fon″ik) *adj.* recorded or reproduced in four separate channels.

quad·rat′ic (kwod-rat′ik) *adj.* **1,** belonging to a square. **2,** (*Math.*) concerning the square as the highest power of an unknown quantity. —**quad·rat′ics,** *n. sing.* (*Math.*) the study of quadratic equations.

quad·ren′ni·al (kwod-ren′ē-əl) *adj.* **1,** every four years. **2,** for four years' duration. —*n.* a fourth anniversary.

quad″ri·lat′er·al (kwod″rə-lat′ər-əl) *n.* a plane figure with four straight sides. —*adj.* four-sided.

qua·drille′ (kwə-dril′) *n.* a dance for four or more couples.

quad·riv′i·um (kwod-riv′ē-əm) *n.* geometry, astronomy, arithmetic and music.

quad·roon′ (kwod-roon′) *n.* a person of one-quarter Negro blood.

quad′ru·ped″ (kwod′rŭ-ped″) *n.* a four-footed animal. —*adj.* four-footed.

quad′ru·ple (kwod′rŭ-pəl) *adj.* four times. —*v.t.* (kwod-rŭ′pəl) multiply by four. —**quad′ru·plet,** *n.* one of four offspring born of one birth.

quad·ru′pli·cate (kwod-rŭp′li-kət) *n. & adj.* four identical copies; the fourth such copy. —*v.t.* (-kāt″) make four copies of.

quaff (kwäf) *v.t. & i.* drink deeply.

quag′ga (kwag′ə) *n.* a zebralike animal of So. Afr., now extinct.

quag′mire″ (kwag′mīr″) *n.* **1,** an area of muddy ground; a marsh. **2,** a difficult position or situation. —**quag′gy,** *adj.*

qua′hog (kwä′hog) *n.* a large, edible clam of the Atlantic coast.

quail (kwāl) *v.i.* cower; shrink away; flinch; lose courage. —*n.* **1,** a game bird related to the partridge, esp. the bobwhite. **2,** the partridge.

quaint (kwānt) *adj.* pleasingly odd or unusual. —**quaint′ness,** *n.*

quake (kwāk) *v.i.* tremble; shake; shudder. —*n.* a shaking or tremulous agitation, esp. an earthquake.

Quak′er (kwā′ker) *n.* a member of the Society of Friends, a Christian religious sect. —**Quak′er·ism,** *n.* —**Quak·er·ess,** *n. fem.*

qual″i·fi·ca′tion (kwol″i-fi-kā′shən) *n.* **1,** act or result of qualifying. **2,** a quality that meets some requirement. **3,** modification; restriction.

qual′i·fied″ (kwol′i-fīd″) *adj.* **1,** fit; competent. **2,** limited; restricted.

qual′i·fy″ (kwol′i-fī″) *v.t.* **1,** modify; limit; restrict. **2,** establish the authority of; empower; instruct; fit. **3,** soften; assuage. —*v.t.* fill requirements for a place or occupation.

qual′i·ta″tive (kwol′ə-tā″tiv) *adj.* in quality, not quantity.

qual′i·ty (kwol′ə-tē) *n.* **1,** essential nature. **2,** a trait; characteristic. **3,** high birth or rank. **4,** superiority, relatively considered.

qualm (kwäm) *n.* **1,** a twinge of conscience;

compunction. **2,** a sudden sensation of nausea.

quan'da·ry (kwon'də-rē) *n.* state of bewilderment or perplexity; a dilemma.

quan'ti·ta"tive (kwon'ti-tā"tiv) *adj.* relating to quantity of measurement.

quan'ti·ty (kwon'tə-tē) *n.* **1,** amount; weight; bulk. **2,** a portion, esp. a large amount. **3,** a number. **4,** duration (of a sound).

quan'tum (kwon'təm) *n.* [*pl.* **-ta** (tə)] **1,** amount. **2,** the smallest unit of radiant energy. **—quantum theory,** a hypothesis in physics that the emission of radiant energy is not continuous.

quar'an·tine" (kwor'ən-tēn") *n.* **1,** time during which an incoming ship is held for inspection for contagious disease or plant and animal pests. **2,** the place where such ship is held. **3,** a period of enforced seclusion, usually to prevent contagion. *—v.t.* isolate.

quark (kwärk) *n.* a hypothetical particle.

quar'rel (kwor'əl) *n.* a squabble; disagreement; dispute; petty fight. *—v.i.* find fault; dispute. **—quar'rel·some,** *adj.* disposed to quarrel.

quar'ry (kwor'ē) *n.* **1,** an open excavation from which building materials, as stone, are taken. **2,** prey; any object of eager pursuit.

quart (kwôrt) *n.* a unit of capacity; in liquid measure equal to two pints or one-fourth gallon, in dry measure, one-eighth peck.

quar'ter (kwôr'tər) *n.* **1,** one-fourth of the whole. **2,** a U.S. silver coin; one-fourth dollar or 25 cents. **3,** three consecutive months. **4,** section; region; locality. **5,** one leg of an animal with bordering parts for use as meat. **6,** mercy. **7,** (*pl.*) a specific dwelling place; station; lodgings. *—v.t.* **1,** divide into four equal parts. **2,** furnish with lodgings. **—quarter horse,** a breed of horse noted for its endurance. **—quarter note,** (*Music*) a crotchet (see *note*).

quar'ter·back" *n.* (*Football*) the back who directs the play of his team.

quar'ter·deck" *n.* (*Naut.*) an upper deck used by officers.

quar'ter·ly (-lē) *n. & adj.* (of) a periodical published each three months.

quar'ter·mas"ter *n.* (*Mil.*) a supply officer.

quar'ter·staff" *n.* an old Eng. weapon consisting of a stout pole about 6½ ft. long.

quar·tet' (kwôr-tet') *n.* **1,** a group of four. **2,** (*Music*) a composition in four parts. Also, **quar·tette'.**

quar'to (kwôr'tō) *n.* [*pl.* **-tos**] a book whose pages are about 9½ by 12 inches.

quartz (kwôrts) *n.* a common hard mineral occurring in many varieties, some prized as semiprecious stones.

qua'sar (kwā'zär) *n.* **1,** a quasi-stellar radio source, one of the brightest and most distant bodies in the universe, emitter of very intense radio and visible radiation. **2,** [also, **quasi-stellar object** or **QSO**] a quasar not emitting any radio signals but producing very intense visible radiation.

quash (kwosh) *v.t.* **1,** crush; subdue. **2,** annul.

qua'si (kwā'sī; kwā'sē) *adj.* seeming; as though. *—adv.* seemingly; almost.

qua·si- (kwā'sī) *pref.* almost; purportedly but not wholly genuine.

quas'sia (kwosh'ə) *n.* a medicinal bitter extracted from the bark and wood of an Amer. tree.

qua·ter'na·ry (kwə-tēr'nə-rē) *adj.* consisting of or arranged in fours. *—n.* **1,** the number four. **2,** a group of four.

quat'rain (kwot'rān) *n.* a stanza of four lines, usually rhyming alternately.

qua'ver (kwā'vər) *v.i.* **1,** shake; tremble; vibrate. **2,** sing or speak in a tremulous tone. **3,** (*Music*) trill. **4,** (*Music*) an eighthnote (see *note*). *—n.* a shaking or trembling, esp. of the voice.

quay (kē) *n.* a dock for landing and loading a ship's cargo.

quea'sy (kwē'zē) *adj.* **1,** sick at the stomach. **2,** easily nauseated; squeamish. **—quea'si·ness,** *n.*

queen (kwēn) *n.* **1,** the wife of a king. **2,** a female sovereign. **3,** the most notable woman in a particular sphere. **4,** the perfect female bee, ant, or termite. **5,** a playing card depicting a queen. **6,** the most valuable piece in chess. **7,** (*Offensive*) a homosexual. **—queen mother,** the widow of a king and mother of a present sovereign.

queen-'size" *adj.* a bed size, usu. 60 by 72 inches.

queer (kwir) *adj.* **1,** odd; strange; eccentric. **2,** (*Offensive*) homosexual. *—v.t.* (*Colloq.*) spoil; upset. *—n.* (*Slang*) counterfeit money. **—queer'ness,** *n.*

quell (kwel) *v.t.* **1,** subdue; crush. **2,** allay; quiet.

quench (kwench) *v.t.* **1,** satisfy, as thirst. **2,** extinguish or put out, as a fire. **3,** repress or still, as anger. **4,** cool (hot metal) suddenly.

quer'cine (kwēr'sin) *adj.* of or pert. to the oak tree.

quer'u·lous (kwer'ə-ləs) *adj.* habitually complaining; fretful.

que′ry (kwir′ė) *n.* a question; an inquiry. —*v.t. & i.* question; doubt.

quest (kwest) *n.* a search; pursuit. —*v.i.* go in search.

ques′tion (kwes′chən) *n.* **1**, an interrogation; inquiry. **2**, doubt; dispute; controversy. **3**, a subject under discussion; a motion to be voted upon. —*v.t.* ask; examine. —*v.t.* **1**, inquire of. **2**, doubt; challenge; take exception to. —**ques′tion·a·ble**, *adj.* subject to doubt. —**ques′tion·ing·ly**, *adv.* —**question mark**, the mark of punctuation (?) denoting inquiry or doubt; the interrogation point.

ques″tion·naire′ (-nâr′) *n.* a series of questions to be answered.

quet·zal′ (ket-säl′) *n.* **1**, a Central Amer. bird. **2**, the monetary unit of Guatemala.

queue (kū) *n.* **1**, a waiting line. **2**, hair braided and worn as a pigtail. —*v.i.* (with *up*) get in line.

quib′ble (kwib′əl) *v.i.* equivocate; bring up trifling objections. —*n.* an evasive argument.

quiche (kēsh) *n.* a custard pie, often made with cheese and bacon.

quick (kwik) *adj.* **1**, fast; speedy; rapid. **2**, perceptive; alert. **3**, hasty; easily aroused. **4**, (*Archaic*) living. —*n.* **1**, living beings. **2**, sensitive flesh. **3**, the most sensitive part. —*adv.* quickly. —**quick′ness**, *n.*

quick′en (kwik′ən) *v.t. & i.* make or become faster and more active.

quick-′fro″zen *adj.* (of food) frozen rapidly to zero or below, for preservation.

quick′ie (-ė) *n.* (*Slang*) something produced in haste; a drink consumed in haste.

quick′lime″ *n.* a caustic substance made from limestone.

quick′sand″ *n.* a bog.

quick′sil″ver *n.* metallic mercury.

quick′step″ *n.* a fast marching pace, as of soldiers.

quick-′tem″pered *adj.* irascible.

quick-′wit″ted *adj.* mentally alert; quick to think and act. —**quick-′wit″ted·ness**, *n.*

quid (kwid) *n.* **1**, a cud; a lump for chewing, as gum or tobacco. **2**, (*Brit. slang*) a pound sterling.

quid′di·ty (kwid′ə-tė) *n.* **1**, essence. **2**, a trifling nicety.

quid′nunc″ (kwid′nungk″) *n.* a gossip.

quid pro quo (kwid′prō-kwō′) (*Lat.*) something given in return; an exchange.

qui·es′cent (kwī-es′ənt) *adj.* still; resting; tranquil. —**qui·es′cence**, *n.*

qui′et (kwī′ət) *adj.* **1**, still; smooth; tranquil. **2**, silent; noiseless. **3**, composed; subdued. **4**, modest; not glaring. —*v.t.* calm; pacify; hush; allay. —*v.i.* become calm;

abate. —*n.* **1**, repose; rest; stillness. **2**, peace. **3**, composure; calmness. **4**, silence. —**qui′et·ness**, *n.*

qui′e·tude (kwī′ə-tood) *n.* repose; rest; tranquillity.

qui·e′tus (kwī-ē-təs) *n.* **1**, release, as from debts. **2**, death.

quill (kwil) *n.* **1**, a stiff feather from a bird; its stem. **2**, a pen made from a feather. **3**, a sharp spine, as of a porcupine. **4**, a pick used for playing certain string instruments.

quilt (kwilt) *n.* a warm, padded bed cover. —*v.t. & i.* make a quilt.

quince (kwins) *n.* a fruit tree or its yellow applelike fruit.

qui′nine (kwī′nīn) *n.* a bitter alkaloid obtained from cinchona bark, used medicinally, esp. for malaria.

Quin″qua·ges′i·ma (kwing″kwə-jes′ə-mə) *n.* the Sunday before Lent; Shrove Sunday.

quin·que- (kwin′kwe) *pref.* five.

quin′sy (kwin′zė) *n.* severe inflammation of the throat and tonsils accompanied by swelling and pus.

quint (kwint) *n.* **1**, a set or sequence of five. **2**, (*Music*) a fifth. **3**, (*Colloq.*) a quintuplet.

quin′tal (kwin′təl) *n.* a weight, orig. 100 pounds, now varying in different countries.

quin·tes′sence (kwin-tes′əns) *n.* the concentrated and purest essence of anything; the perfect form. —**quin″tes·sen′tial**, *adj.*

quin·tet′ (kwin-tet′) *n.* a group of five. Also, **quin·tette′**.

quin′tu·ple (kwin′tyû-pəl) *adj.* five times. —*v.t.* multiply by five. —**quin′tu·plet**, *n.* one of five offspring born of one birth.

quin·tup′li·cate (kwin-tup′lə-kət) *n.* five identical copies; the fifth such copy. —*v.t.* (-kāt″) make five copies of.

quip (kwip) *n.* a witty remark. —*v.i.* [**quipped, quip′ping**] make quips. —**quip′-ster**, *n.*

quire (kwīr) *n.* one-twentieth of a ream; 24 (sometimes 25) uniform sheets of paper.

quirk (kwėrk) *n.* **1**, idiosyncrasy; deviation. **2**, a quick turn.

quirt (kwėrt) *n.* a riding whip.

quis′ling (kwiz′ling) *n.* a traitor who helps an enemy occupy his country.

quit (kwit) *v.t. & i.* [**quit′ted, -ting**] **1**, leave; abandon; resign. **2**, satisfy; clear. —*adj.* (with *of*) discharged or released from (a debt, obligation, etc.).

quit′claim″ *n.* (*Law*) **1**, a document by which a claim, right, or title to an estate is relinquished to another. **2**, a transfer without warranty. —*v.t.* give up a claim to; relinquish.

quite (kwīt) *adv.* **1,** wholly; completely. **2,** considerably; very.

quits (kwits) *adj. (Colloq.)* on even terms; released from obligation.

quit'tance (kwit'əns) *n.* **1,** a discharge from obligation; receipt. **2,** recompense.

quit'ter (kwit'ər) *n. (Colloq.)* one who abandons a task through discouragement or fear.

quiv'er (kwiv'ər) *v.i.* quake; shiver; flutter. —*n.* **1,** a tremor; shiver. **2,** a case for holding arrows.

qui vive' (kē-vēv') *(Fr.)* **1,** who goes there? **2,** alertness.

quix·ot'ic (kwiks-ot'ik) *adj.* absurdly or extravagantly romantic or chivalrous; impractical; visionary.

quiz (kwiz) *n.* **1,** a puzzling question or series of questions; bantering. **2,** an examination in school; a question-and-answer program on radio or television. —*v.t.* **[quizzed, quiz'zing] 1,** chaff; make sport of. **2,** question. **3,** peer at.

quiz'zi·cal (kwiz'i-kəl) *adj.* **1,** bantering; teasing. **2,** odd; comical.

quoin (koin) *n.* **1,** an external angle of a building; a stone forming such an angle. **2,** a wedgelike device used in printing for locking up type.

quoits (kwoits) *n. sing.* a game of pitching rings, as of iron or rubber, at a peg. —**quoit,** *n.* such a ring.

quon'dam (kwon'dam) *adj.* former; in time past.

Quon'set hut (kwon'sət) a prefabricated metal shelter.

quo'rum (kwôr'əm) *n.* the number of members who must be present to validate a meeting.

quo'ta (kwō'tə) *n.* the share or proportion assigned to one of a group.

quo·ta'tion (kwō-tā'shən) *n.* **1,** repetition of words previously uttered or written. **2,** a citation of a price. —**quotation mark,** a mark of punctuation: '' or ' *(quote)*, '' or ' *(unquote)*.

quote (kwōt) *v.t. & i.* **1,** repeat, copy or cite words previously uttered. **2,** give the current market price of. **3,** enclose within quotation marks. —*n. (Colloq.)* quotation.

quoth (kwōth) *v. (Archaic)* says.

quo·tid'i·an (kwō-tid'ē-ən) *adj.* daily.

quo'tient (kwō'shənt) *n.* the number produced by dividing a given number by another.

R

R, r (är) the eighteenth letter of the English alphabet.

rab'bet (rab'it) *n.* a slot or groove made in a board to receive the edge of another board; a joint so made. —*v.t. & i.* **1,** cut a rabbet in. **2,** join or be joined by a rabbet.

rab'bi (rab'ī) *n.* master; a Jewish doctor of scriptural law. —**rab'bin·ate** (-ə-nət) *n.* —**rab·bin'i·cal** (rə-bin'i-kəl) *adj.*

rab'bit (rab'it) *n.* **1,** a small rodent related to the hare. **2,** Welsh rabbit. —**rabbit punch,** a blow on the back of the neck.

rab'ble (rab'əl) *n.* crowd; mob; the masses.

rab'ble·rou"ser (-row"zər) *n.* one who stirs up the masses; demagogue.

rab'id *adj.* **1,** furious; raging. **2,** zealous; fanatical. **3,** affected with or pert. to rabies. —**ra·bid'i·ty** (rə-bid'ə-tfi) *n.*

ra'bies (rā'bēz) *n.* an infectious disease: *hydrophobia.*

rac·coon' (ra-koon') *n.* a small carnivorous No. Amer. mammal.

race (rās) *n.* **1,** a contest or effort to reach a goal first; a rush. **2,** a rapid current of water. **3,** an ethical, tribal, or national stock. **4,** any class or group, esp. of persons, considered as a class apart. —*v.i. & t.* engage in a contest of speed; run swiftly; cause to run. —**rac'er,** *n.* a racing car or its driver.

race'track" *n.* a track for racing, esp. for horse racing.

race'way" *n.* **1,** a channel for water. **2,** a racetrack.

ra·chi'tis (rə-kī'tis) *n.* rickets. —**ra·chit'ic** (rə-kit'ik) *adj.*

ra'cial (rā'shəl) *adj.* pert. to a race (of people).

rac'ism (rās'iz-əm) *n.* prejudice against certain peoples. —**rac'ist** *n. & adj.*

rack (rak) *n.* **1,** an open framework or stand for holding articles. **2,** a toothed bar engaging a gear. **3,** an ancient instrument of torture; hence, pain or distress. **4,** a gait of a horse between a trot and a gallop. **5,** the neck of mutton, pork, or veal. —*v.t.* **1,** strain; worry. **2,** place on a rack. **3,** (of a horse) go at a rack. —**rack rent,** excessive rent.

rack'et (rak'it) *n.* **1,** a disorderly, confused noise; din; hurly-burly. **2,** a dishonest enterprise. **3,** [also, **rac'quet**] the bat used in tennis, squash, etc. **4,** *(pl.)* an indoor ball game. —*v.i.* engage in an illegal activity.

rack"et·eer' (-ə-tir') *n.* one engaged in a dishonest enterprise; a gangster.

rac"on·teur' (rak"on-tēr') *n.* a skillful narrator of anecdotes.

rac'quet·ball" *n.* a game combining elements of tennis and squash played on an indoor court.

rac'y (rās'fi) *adj.* **1,** piquant; spicy. **2,**

(*Colloq.*) suggestive; off-color. —**rac'i·ness,** *n.*

ra'dar (rā'där) *n.* a device timing the echo of radio waves to detect objects they strike.

ra'dar·scope" *n.* an oscilloscope used to display radar signals.

ra'di·al (rā'dē-əl) *n.* **1,** pert. to a radius; of or being radii. **2,** pert. to a type of tire construction in which the belts are placed directly across the direction of travel.

ra'di·an (rā'dē-ən) *n.* (*Math.*) in a circle, the angle opposing an arc, equal in length to the radius, approx. 57°.

ra'di·ant (rā'dē-ənt) *adj.* **1,** emitting rays; shining; sparkling. **2,** beaming, as with kindness or joy. —**ra'di·ance,** *n.*

ra'di·ate" (rā'dē-āt") *v.i.* & *t.* **1,** issue and proceed in rays from a point, as heat or light. **2,** spread in all directions from a central source. —**ra"di·a'tion,** *n.* —**radiation sickness** or **syndrome,** sickness caused by exposure to radiation (as from nuclear explosion or from X-rays), characterized by loss of hair, nausea, bleeding, etc.

ra'di·a"tor (rā'dē-ā"tər) *n.* an apparatus, as a grill, that radiates heat waves, as to warm a room, dispel the heat from an automobile engine, etc.

rad'i·cal (rad'i-kəl) *adj.* **1,** (*Math*) pert. to a root. **2,** drastic. **3,** advocating drastic reform of existing institutions. —*n.* **1,** an extreme liberal in politics. **2,** (*Math.*) a root; the sign (√) expressing it. **3,** (*Gram.*) a root. **4,** (*Chem.*) a group of atoms remaining unchanged in many reactions. —**rad'i·cal·ism,** *n.*—**rad'i·cal·ize",** *v.t.*

ra'di·o" (rā'dē-ō") *n.* **1,** wireless telephone and telegraph transmission and reception. **2,** a receiving set for sounds so transmitted. —*v.t.* & *i.* send (a message) by radio. —**radio astronomy,** a branch of astronomy dealing with radio signals received from outer space or with the use of radar for celestial observation. —**radio station,** a place from which radio broadcasts are made. —**radio telescope,** a combination of radio receiver and antenna used for celestial observations.

ra"di·o·ac'tive *adj.* spontaneously radiating energy in atoms or particles of atoms. —**ra"di·o·ac·tiv'i·ty,** *n.*

ra'di·o·car'bon *n.* radioactive carbon, used in dating organic remains.

ra'di·o·gram" *n.* a message sent by radio.

ra'di·o·graph" *n.* an image produced on a sensitized surface by radiation other than light, as x-rays or gamma rays. —**ra"di·og'ra·phy** (-og'rə-fē) *n.*

ra"di·ol'o·gy (rā'dē-ol'ə-jē) *n.* the study or use of x-rays and radioactive substances —**ra"di·ol'o·gist,** *n.*

ra"di·om'e·ter (rā"dē-om'ə-tər) *n.* an instrument for detecting and measuring small amounts of radiant energy.

ra'di·o·phone" *n.* **1,** a device for communication by radio waves rather than by wires. **2,** an apparatus for the production of sound by means of radiant energy. Also, **ra"di·o·te'lephone,** —**ra'di·o·te·leph'o·ny,** *n.*

ra"di·os'co·py (rā"dē-os'kə-pē) *n.* the examination of the interior of opaque objects by x-rays or gamma rays.

ra'di·o·sonde" (-sönd") *n.* (*Meteor.*) a radio transmitter held aloft by a balloon for broadcasting atmospheric temperature, pressure, etc.

ra"di·o·tel'e·graph" *n.* a wireless telegraph. —*v.t.* telegraph by radio. —**ra"di·o·te·leg'ra·phy,** *n.*

ra"di·o·ther'a·py *n.* treatment by x-rays or radioactive rays.

rad'ish *n.* the crisp, pungent root of a garden plant; the plant.

ra'di·um (rā'dē-əm) *n.* a metallic chemical element, no. 88, symbol Ra, found in pitchblende.

ra'di·us (rā'dē-əs) *n.* [*pl.* **-i** (-ī)] **1,** a line drawn from the center of a circle or sphere to the circumference or surface. **2,** the measure of this line; any limited area.

ra'dix (rā'diks) *n.* [*pl.* **rad'i·ces** (rad'ə-sēz)] **1,** the root of a plant. **2,** (*Math*) the base number of a system, as 10 in the decimal system. **3,** a root word.

ra'dome" (rā'dōm") *n.* on an airplane, the exterior dome-shaped housing for the radar antenna.

ra'don (rā'don) *n.* a radioactive gaseous element formed in the disintegration of radium, no. 86, symbol Rn.

raf'fi·a (raf'ē-ə) *n.* a species of palm, used for weaving.

raff'ish (raf'ish) *adj.* rowdy. —**raff'ish·ness,** *n.*

raf'fle (raf'əl) *n.* a lottery to dispose of one prize, usually merchandise. —*v.t.* (often with *off*) dispose of by raffle.

raft (räft) *n.* **1,** a wooden platform to float in water. **2,** (*Colloq.*) an accumulation; a collection.

raft'er (räf'tər) *n.* a sloping beam of a roof.

rag *n.* **1,** a worn or worthless piece of cloth. **2,** (*pl.*) shabby clothes. **3,** (*pl.*) (*Slang*) any clothes, as **glad rags.** **4,** (*Colloq.*) jazz music: **ragtime.** —*adj.* made of or with rags, as paper. —*v.t.* [**ragged, rag'ging**] (*Slang*) badger; tease.

ra'ga (rä'gä) *n.* (*Music*) any of the traditional modal patterns of Hindu music.

rag'a·muf"fin (rag'ə-muf"in) *n.* a ragged person.

rage (rāj) *n.* **1,** violent anger; fury. **2,** extreme violence; intensity. **3,** enthusiasm; vogue; a fad. —*v.i.* **1,** be furious with anger. **2,** storm. **3,** have furious course or effect.

rag'ged (rag'id) *adj.* **1,** tattered; frayed; shaggy; dressed in wornout clothes. **2,** slipshod. —**rag'ged·ness,** *n.*

rag'lan (rag'lən) *n.* a topcoat with the sleeves extending down from the collar without shoulder seams.

ra·gout' (ra-goo') *n.* a highly seasoned stew of meat and vegetables.

rag'tag" *n.* (*Contemptuous*) ragged people; the rabble. Also, **ragtag and bobtail** (bob'tāl").

rag'time" *n.* an early form of jazz music.

rag'weed" (rag'wēd") *n.* a herb whose pollen aggravates some asthmatic symptoms.

raid (rād) *n.* a hostile or predatory incursion; a sudden onset. —*v.t. & i.* attack; rob.

rail (rāl) *n.* **1,** a bar passing from one support to another, as for a barrier. **2,** a metal bar used to form a track for a wheeled vehicle. **3,** transportation by railroad. **4,** a small wading bird. —*v.i.* (with *in* or *off*) enclose with rails. —**rail'ing,** *n.* a barrier made of rails; a fence.

rail'head" *n.* **1,** a railroad supply center. **2,** the farthest point to which rails have been laid.

rail'ler·y (rā'lə-rē) *n.* banter.

rail'road" *n.* [also, **rail'way"**] a common carrier operating trains over permanent tracks of rails; the tracks. —*v.t.* (*Slang*) **1,** force and speed to a conclusion. **2,** devise false evidence against; frame. —**rail'road"ing,** *n.* work pert. to the operation of a railroad.

rail'way" *n.* railroad.

rai'ment (rā'mənt) *n.* clothing.

rain (rān) *n.* **1,** water falling in drops from the clouds. **2,** a shower or outpouring of anything. —*v.i.* produce water falling in drops. —*v.t.* shower down; give abundantly. —**rain check,** a ticket for future use, given to ticketholders of an event stopped by rain or other natural phenomenon; hence, a standing invitation.

rain'bow" *n.* an arc of prismatic colors.

rain'coat" *n.* a light waterproof outer coat.

rain'drop" *n.* a drop of rain.

rain'fall" *n.* rain.

rain'storm" *n.* a heavy rain.

rain'y *adj.* constantly or often raining. —**rain'i·ness,** *n.*

raise (rāz) *v.t.* **1,** move to a higher place; hoist; elevate. **2,** increase the height or amount of; build up. **3,** cause to rise. **4,** grow or breed, as crops, cattle; bring up. **5,** muster; collect; procure, as an army or money. —*n.* (*Colloq.*) an increase in pay.

raised (rāzd) *adj.* **1,** leavened. **2,** in relief, as carving.

rai'sin (rā'zən) *n.* a dried grape.

rai"son d'ê'tre (rā"zōn-de'trə) (*Fr.*) reason for being; justification for existence.

ra'jah (rä'jə) *n.* an E. Indian prince.

rake (rāk) *n.* **1,** a long-handled toothed implement for scraping loose materials together; a similar implement. **2,** an idle, dissolute man; a libertine. **3,** a slope. —*v.t.* **1,** gather or smooth with or as with a rake; (with *up*) glean. **2,** ransack. **3,** scratch. **4,** (*Mil.*) fire upon, lengthwise. **5,** cause to incline.

rake-'off" *n.* (*Slang*) a rebate or commission, usually illegal.

rak'ish (rāk'ish) *adj.* **1,** (*Naut.*) inclined, as a mast. **2,** jaunty. **3,** dissolute. —**rak'-ish·ness,** *n.*

ral"len·tan'do (räl"ən-tän'dō) *adv., adj. & n.* (*Ital.*) slowing gradually.

ral'ly (ral'ē) *v.t.* **1,** draw or call together for a common purpose. **2,** assemble and reconstitute as a disorganized army. **3,** banter; tease. —*v.i.*, **1,** reunite. **2,** recover energy or effectiveness. —*n.* **1,** a renewal of energy in joint action. **2,** in tennis, a sustained exchange. **3,** a quick recovery. **4,** a mass meeting. **5,** a race or test among sport cars.

ram *n.* **1,** a male sheep. **2,** (*cap.*) Aries, a sign of the Zodiac. **3,** an instrument of war for battering; the armored prow of a warship. —*v.t.* [**rammed, ram'ming**] **1,** batter. **2,** force or drive down. **3,** stuff; cram.

ram'ble (ram'bəl) *v.i.* **1,** roam or wander about; rove. **2,** digress. —*n.* a sauntering walk. —**ram'bler,** *n.* **1,** a wanderer. **2,** a climbing rose. —**ram'bling,** *adj.* wandering; roundabout; digressive.

ram'bler *n.* **1,** a wanderer. **2,** a climbing rose.

ram·bunc'tious (ram-bunk'shəs) *adj.* boisterous. —**ram·bunc'tious·ness,** *n.*

ram'e·kin (ram'ə-kin) *n.* an individual baking dish. Also, **ram'e·quin.**

ram'ie (ram'ē) *n.* an Asiatic perennial shrub; its fiber.

ram"i·fi·ca'tion (ram"i-fi-kā'shən) *n.* a branch; subdivision.

ram'i·fy" (ram'ə-fī") *v.i. & t.* form or divide into branches.

ram'jet engine the simplest type of jet engine.

ramp *n.* **1,** a sloping passageway. **2,** a vegetable. —*v.i.* rear or spring up; act violently.

ram′page (ram′pāj) *n.* violent, furious, or excited behavior. —*v.i.* (ram-pāj′) act or move violently. **—ram·pa′geous,** *adj.*

ram′pant (ram′pənt) *adj.* raging and unchecked.

ram′part (ram′pärt) *n.* **1,** a mound, usually with a parapet, surrounding a fortified place. **2,** a bulwark; a protective barrier.

ram′rod″ *n.* **1,** a rod for tamping the charge of a muzzle-loading gun. **2,** someone very strict.

ram′shack″le (ram′shak″əl) *adj.* tumble-down; rickety.

ran *v.* pret. of *run.*

ranch *n.* a large farm for raising livestock. —*v.i.* conduct, or work on, a ranch. **—ranch′-er,** *n.* owner of a ranch.

ran·che′ro (ran-châ′rō) *n.* a rancher.

ran′cho (ran′chō) *n.* [*pl.* **-chos**] **1,** a rude hut. **2,** a ranch.

ran′cid (ran′sid) *adj.* having a rank, tainted smell or taste. **—ran·cid′i·ty,** *n.*

ran′cor (rang′kər) *n.* bitter animosity; spitefulness. Also, **ran′cour. —ran′cor-ous,** *adj.*

rand *n.* the monetary unit of the Union of So. Africa.

ran′dom (ran′dəm) *adj.* haphazard; casual. **—at random,** haphazardly.

ran′dom·ize″ (-īz″) *v.t.* make random. **—ran″dom·i·za′tion,** *n.*

rand′y (ran′dē) *adj.* **1,** vulgar; bawdy. **2,** (*Slang*) lascivious.

ra′nee (rä′nē) *n.* rani.

rang *v.* pret. of *ring.*

range (rānj) *v.t.* **1,** dispose in a row or rows of; set in definite order. **2,** oppose. **3,** rove over or along. —*v.i.* **1,** be in or form a parallel line or direction. **2,** roam; wander. **3,** travel a certain distance or direction. **4,** vary, within specified limits. —*n.* **1,** a series in a lane or row. **2,** scope; extent. **3,** distance from one point to another. **4,** a large tract of land for grazing. **5,** a course for shooting or target practice. **6,** a cooking stove. **7,** a chain of mountains. **—range finder,** an instrument for determining the distance of a target from a gun, etc.

rang′er (rān′jər) *n.* **1,** a trooper patrolling a wide area. **2,** (*cap.*) an Amer. soldier trained for raiding.

rang′y (rān′jē) *adj.* **1,** tall and slender. **2,** spacious; roomy.

ra′ni (rä′nē) *n.* in India, the wife of a rajah, or a reigning princess. Also, **ra′nee.**

rank *n.* **1,** a row, esp. one conceived as horizontal; a line; formation. **2,** a class,

order. **3,** relative position; standing, as social, ordinal, etc. **4,** (*pl.*) (*Mil.*) enlisted men. —*v.t.* **1,** arrange in lines or formations. **2,** assign to a particular class. **3,** take precedence of or over; rate above. —*v.i.* occupy a relative position. —*adj.* **1,** strong in growth, as weeds; rich and fertile. **2,** offensive; unmitigated. **3,** obscene; indecent. **—rank′ing,** *adj.* **—rank and file,** the common people; people indiscriminately.

ran′kle (rang′kəl) *v.i.* fester; be irritating.

ran′sack (ran′sak) *v.t.* **1,** search thoroughly. **2,** plunder.

ran′som (ran′səm) *n.* the price or cost of redeeming a hostage. —*v.t.* redeem by paying.

rant *v.i.* declaim violently and with little sense; rave.

rap *v.i. & t.* [**rapped, rap′ping**] **1,** strike (with) a quick sharp blow. **2,** (with *out*) utter sharply; communicate by raps. **3,** criticize adversely. **4,** (*Colloq.*) converse. —*n.* (*Colloq.*) **1,** a cutting remark. **2,** a bit. **3,** (*Slang*) penalty. **4,** a blow. **—rap session,** (*Colloq.*) a free-wheeling conversation. **—rap sheet,** a police record of arrests and convictions.

ra·pa′cious (rə-pā′shəs) *adj.* greedy; grasping; predatory. **—ra·pa′cious·ness,** *n.*

ra·pac′i·ty (rə-pas′ə-tē) *n.* rapaciousness.

rape (rāp) *n.* **1,** forcible seizing and violation; ravishing. **2,** carrying off by force. **3,** a plant grown for fodder and oil. —*v.t.* **1,** ravish. **2,** carry off violently.

rap′id *adj.* **1,** moving swiftly. **2,** requiring little time. —*n.* (usu. *pl.*) a swift current in a river. **—rap′id·ness,** *n.* **—rapid transit,** subway or trolley lines.

rap′id-fire″ *adj.* **1,** capable of firing shots in rapid succession. **2,** characterized by rapidity, sharpness, etc., as questioning.

ra·pid′i·ty (rə-pid′ə-tē) *n.* rapidness; swiftness; speed.

ra′pi·er (rā′pē-ər) *n.* a long, narrow, pointed two-edged sword.

rap′ine (rap′in) *n.* plundering.

rap·port′ (ra-pôr′) *n.* harmonious relation; accord.

rap″proche″ment′ (rä″prâsh″män′) *n.* (*Fr.*) an establishment of harmonious relations.

rap·scal′lion (rap-skal′yən) *n.* (*Colloq.*) a scamp; a rascal.

rapt *adj.* ecstatically engrossed or bemused. **—rapt′ness,** *n.*

rap·tor′i·al (rap-tôr′ē-əl) *adj.* **1,** predatory. **2,** fitted for seizing and holding prey, as claws of birds.

rap′ture (rap′chər) *n.* ecstatic joy. **—rap′tur·ous,** *adj.*

ra′ra a′vis (rär′ə-ā′vis) (*Lat.*) a rare bird; an unusual thing.

rare (rär) *adj.* **1,** thin, not dense; sparse. **2,** very uncommon; remarkable; excellent; choice. **3,** (of meat) not thoroughly cooked. —**rare′ness,** *n.*

rare′bit (rär′bit) *n.* Welsh rabbit.

rare-earth element or **metal** any of a series of metallic elements, nos. 58-71, whose oxides are found in relatively scarce minerals and are very difficult to separate.

rar′e·fy″ (rär′ə-fī″) *v.t. & i.* make or become thin or less dense. —**rar″e·fac′tion,** *n.*

rare′ly (rär′lē) *adv.* seldom; uncommonly.

rare′ripe″ *adj.* ripening early. —*n.* a rareripe fruit, esp. a variety of peach.

rar′ing *adj.* eager.

rar′i·ty (rär′ə-tē) *n.* **1,** state of being uncommon. **2,** something unusual.

ras′cal (ras′kəl) *n.* **1,** a scoundrel. **2,** a scamp. —**ras·cal′i·ty,** *n.*

rash *adj.* too hasty in judgment, speech, or action; reckless; precipitate. —*n.* an eruption on the skin. —**rash′ness,** *n.*

rash′er (rash′ər) *n.* a slice, or small serving, of bacon or ham.

rasp *v.t.* grate with a coarse, rough instrument. —*v.i.* irritate (one's nerves). —*n.* a coarse file. —**rasp′ing,** *adj.* (of a voice, etc.) harsh.

rasp′ber″ry (räz′ber″ē) *n.* **1,** a sweet, red or black, edible berry from a plant of the rose family. **2,** (*Slang*) an expression of derision.

ras′ter (ras′tər) *n.* in television, the parallel lines produced on the screen by the scanner.

rat *n.* **1,** a rodent similar to the mouse but larger. **2,** (*Slang*) a betrayer or informer; a contemptible person. **3,** a bulging roll of hair. —*v.i.* [**rat′ted, -ting**] **1,** catch or kill rats. **2,** (*Slang*) be a betrayer; inform. —**rat race,** the competitive, pointless daily routine of life.

ratch′et (rach′it) *n.* **1,** a pivoted piece or part that checks backward motion of a toothed bar or wheel. **2,** the wheel or bar itself.

rate (rät) *n.* **1,** amount, quantity, range, or degree, measured according to some standard. **2,** a price; a fixed charge. —*v.t.* **1,** appraise; fix the relative scale, rank, or position of. **2,** scold; censure. **3,** (*Colloq.*) deserve. —*v.i.* (*Colloq.*) have (a certain) standing. —**at any rate,** in any case; at least.

rath′er (rà*th*′ər) *adv.* **1,** sooner; preferably. **2,** more correctly. **3,** on the contrary. **4,** somewhat considerably.

raths′kel′ler (rots′kel″ər) *n.* a barroom in a cellar.

rat′i·fy″ (rat′ə-fī″) *v.t.* **1,** accept and sanction formally. **2,** confirm; establish. —**rat″i·fi·ca′tion,** *n.*

rat′ing (rā′ting) *n.* **1,** relative standing; appraisal. **2,** rank of a noncommissioned sailor or seaman. **3,** a scolding.

ra′tio (rā′shō) *n.* the relation between two quantities; proportion.

ra″ti·oc′i·nate″ (rash″ē-os′ə-nāt″) *v.i.* reason. —**ra″ti·oc″i·na′tion,** *n.*

ra′tion (rā′shən) *n.* **1,** an allowance, esp. of a necessity. **2,** (*pl.*) meals. —*v.t.* apportion.

ra′tion·al (rash′ən-əl) *adj.* **1,** of, pert. to, or attributable to, reason or the power of reasoning; sane. **2,** acting in accordance with reason. **3,** (*Math.*) designating a number that can be represented as the quotient of two integers or polynomials. —**ra″tion·al′i·ty,** *n.*

ra″tion·ale′ (rash″ə-nal′) *n.* the rational basis for something; justification.

ra′tion·al·ism (-iz-əm) *n.* a doctrine that places reason above faith. —**ra′tion·al·ist,** *n.*

ra′tion·al·ize″ (-īz″) *v.t. & i.* explain or interpret according to supposed reason. —**ra″tion·al·i·za′tion,** *n.*

rat′line (rat′lin) *n.* (*Naut.*) a rope hung horizontally, used as a step in climbing. Also, **rat′lin.**

rats′bane″ (rats′bān″) *n.* rat poison, esp. white arsenic.

rat·tan′ (ra-tan′) *n.* **1,** a climbing palm whose stems are used for wickerwork, canes, etc. **2,** a cane.

rat·teen′ (ra-tēn′) *n.* a heavy woolen cloth used for linings.

rat′ter (rat′ər) *n.* a dog or cat that kills rats.

rat′tle (rat′əl) *v.i. & t.* **1,** make or cause to make a rapid succession of clicking sounds. **2,** talk rapidly. **3,** move with a clatter. **4,** (*Colloq.*) confuse. —*n.* **1,** the act or effect of rattling. **2,** a toy that produces a clattering sound. **3,** one of the horny cells at the end of a rattlesnake's tail.

rat′tle·brain″ *n.* a giddy, chattering person.

rat′tle·snake″ *n.* a venomous Amer. snake whose tail rattles when shaken. Also (*colloq.*) **rat′tler** (rat′lər).

rat′tle·trap″ *n.* a shaky, rickety object. —*adj.* shaky.

rat′trap″ *n.* (*Slang*) **1,** a hopeless situation. **2,** a shabby, disreputable place.

rat'ty (rat'ē) *adj.* seedy. **—rat'ti·ness,** *n.*

rau'cous (râ'kəs) *adj.* harsh of voice; hoarse. **—rau'ci·ty** (râ'sə-tē) *n.*

raunch'y (rân'chē) *adj.* (*Slang*) **1,** obscene; indecent. **2,** lustful.

rav'age (rav'ij) *v.t. & i.* lay waste; devastate; pillage. **—n.** devastation.

rave (rāv) *v.i.* **& t.** talk insanely, extravagantly, or overenthusiastically. **—n.** (*Colloq.*) unrestrained praise; the object of it. **—adj.** (*Colloq.*) extremely enthusiastic.

rav'el (rav'əl) *v.t. & i.* **1,** draw apart thread by thread; fray. **2,** disentangle or become disentangled.

ra'ven (rā'vən) *n.* a large, glossy, black crow. **—adj.** deep, lustrous black.

rav'en (rav'ən) *v.t. & i.* **1,** obtain by violence. **2,** swallow greedily. **—rav'en·ing,** *adj.* eager for prey. **—rav'en·ous** (-əs) *adj.* furiously hungry or greedy.

ra·vine' (rə-vēn') *n.* a deep valley.

rav'ing (rā'ving) *adj.* **1,** talking wildly; mad. **2,** (*Colloq.*) superlative. **—n.** (often *pl.*) irrational, incoherent talk.

ra"vi·o'li (ra"vē-ō'lē) *n.pl.* an Ital. dish of chopped meat, cheese, etc., wrapped in dough.

rav'ish *v.t.* **1,** seize and carry off. **2,** enrapture. **3,** rape. **—rav'ish·ing,** *adj.* entrancing. **—rav'ish·ment,** *n.*

raw (râ) *adj.* **1,** uncooked. **2,** in a natural state or condition; not processed by manufacture, etc. **3,** harsh, sharp, or chilly; bleak, as of weather. **4,** without covering, as of skin; naked. **5,** untried; untrained; inexperienced. **6,** crude; rough. **—n.** **1,** a raw article or condition. **2,** a sore place. **—raw material,** a substance of which manufactured goods are made. **—raw'ness,** *n.*

raw'boned' (-bōnd') *adj.* gaunt.

raw'hide' *n.* **1,** untanned leather. **2,** aᵃ leather whip.

ray (rā) *n.* **1,** a line of light; a similar emanation from a central source. **2,** a beam of intellectual light. **3,** a stripe. **4,** one of several lines emanating from a point. **5,** a sea fish, as the skate, etc. **—v.i.** radiate.

ray'on (rā'on) *n.* a silklike cellulose yarn or fabric.

raze (rāz) *v.t.* level to the ground; tear down; demolish.

ra'zor (rā'zər) *n.* a sharp-edged instrument used for shaving. **—adj.** extremely sharp.

ra'zor·back' *n.* **1,** a hog with a back like a sharp ridge. **2,** a whale with a similar back.

razz (raz) *v.t. & i.* (*Colloq.*) tease; heckle.

raz'zle-daz'zle (raz'əl-daz'əl) *n.* (*Slang*) **1,** bewildering or noisy confusion. **2,** ostentatious display; deceptive maneuverings.

re (rā) *n.* (*Music*) the second tone in the diatonic scale.

re (rē) *n.* (*Law*) (preceded by *in*) in the case of.

re- (rē) *pref.* **1,** back; denoting reverse action. **2,** (with hyphen when necessary to avoid ambiguity), again; anew. [In addition to words defined in the text, the following words may be defined by adding *again* to the root word.]

re"ad·just'	re"en·force'
re"ap·pear'	re"en'ter
re"ap·point'	re"es·tab'lish
re"arm'	re·fit'
re"ar·range'	re·heat'
re"as·sem'ble	re·kin'dle
re"as·sert'	re·load'
re·born'	re·mar'ry
re·build'	re·name'
re"com·mence'	re·o'pen
re·con'quer	re·paid'
re·con'sti·tute	re"pub·li·ca'tion
re-"cre·ate'	re·pub'lish
re"dis·cov'er	re·read'
re·ech'o	re·set'
re"e·lect'	re"u·nite'
re"em·bark'	re·vis'it

reach (rēch) *v.t. & i.* **1,** stretch out; extend outward. **2,** attain; arrive at; extend as far as. **3,** obtain access to; establish communication with. **4,** influence. **5,** hand over; deliver. **6,** strive. **—n.** **1,** the act or capacity of stretching out for something. **2,** a continuous stretch or course. **3,** the distance one can reach. **4,** range of capacity or ability.

re·act' *v.i.* **1,** act in a reverse or opposite direction. **2,** act mutually or reciprocally upon each other. **3,** respond. **4,** return to a former condition.

re·act'ance (-əns) *n.* impedance due to capacitance or inductance or both.

re·act'ant (rē-ak'tənt) *n.* an initial factor in a chemical reaction.

re·ac'tion (rē-ak'shən) *n.* **1,** an opposed or return action. **2,** a response. **3,** a tendency to revert, as to former customs or ideology. **4,** mutual or reciprocal action. **5,** a chemical change.

re·ac'tion·ar·y *adj. & n.* (one) favoring a return to old, esp. conservative, ways and methods.

re·act'i·vate *v.t.* make active or functional again.

re·ac'tor (rē-ak'tər) *n.* **1,** a chemical reagent. **2,** a device in which a nuclear chain reaction may be initiated and controlled to produce heat or for production of other fissionable materials. Also, **atomic reactor** or **pile, nuclear reactor.**

read (rēd) *v.t. & i.* [*pret. & p.p.* **read**

red)] **1**, understand (something written or printed) by interpretation of the signs used. **2**, understand by observation or scrutiny. **3**, utter aloud (written words); recite. **4**, peruse (a book, etc.); study. **5**, infer. **6**, solve (a riddle); tell fortunes. **7**, perform music at sight. **8**, interpret in a certain way, as music, etc.

read′a·ble *adj.* **1**, legible. **2**, interesting.

read′er *n.* **1**, a person who reads or likes to read. **2**, in some churches, a minor clerical order. **3**, a book for the teaching of reading. **4**, an interpreter. **5**, an anthology. —**read′er·ship″**, *n.*

read′i·ly (red′ə-lē) *adv.* **1**, willingly. **2**, easily.

read′ing (rē′ding) *n.* **1**, act of reading. **2**, a recital; rendition. **3**, interpretation; inference. **4**, the study of reading. **5**, printed matter. **6**, the indication on a graduated instrument.

read′out″ *n.* **1**, presentation of computer data, usu. on a screen in digital form. **2**, printout.

read′y (red′ē) *adj.* **1**, prepared for immediate use or action. **2**, willing. **3**, about (to). **4**, immediately available; handy. **5**, prompt; facile; quick. —**read′i·ness**, *n.*

read′y·made″ *adj.* **1**, manufactured before being offered for sale, as clothes. **2**, un-original.

re·a′gent *n.* a substance that causes chemical reaction.

re′al (rē′əl) *adj.* **1**, existing, not imaginary; actual. **2**, genuine; true; authentic. **3**, of property, immovable, as lands. —**real estate**, land, together with any buildings on it. —**real number**, a number without an imaginary part. —**real time**, the time a computer is engaged in actual computation.

re′al·ism (rē′ə-liz-əm) *n.* **1**, interest only in the actual or real, not in the ideal or abstract. **2**, fidelity to actual appearance or fact, as in art.

re′al·ist (rē′əl-ist) *n.* one who tries to see or portray things as they are, not idealized. —**re″al·is′tic**, *adj.* —**re″al·is′ti·cal·ly**, *adv.*

re·al′i·ty (rē-al′ə-tē) *n.* **1**, state of actual existence. **2**, fact; truth.

re′al·ize (rē′ə-līz″) *v.t.* **1**, recognize the nature or existence of. **2**, comprehend; understand, or feel distinctly. **3**, achieve. **4**, make a profit of or on. **5**, exchange for cash. —*v.i.* convert property into cash; profit. —**re″al·i·za′tion**, *n.*

re′al·ly (rē′ə-lē) *adv.* **1**, as a fact; truly; actually. **2**, indeed.

realm (relm) *n.* a domain; sphere.

Re·al″po·li·tik″ (rē-al″po-li-tēk′) *n.* (*Ger.*) a policy of national development and expansion.

Re·al′tor″ (rē′əl-tôr″) *n.* (*T.N.*) a member of a certain real-estate brokers' organization.

re′al·ty (rē′əl-tē) *n.* real estate.

ream (rēm) *n.* **1**, a quantity of paper, usually 500 sheets. **2**, (*pl.*) (*Colloq.*) a large quantity. —*v.t.* enlarge and smooth (a hole).

ream′er (rē′mər) *n.* **1**, a tool for enlarging holes. **2**, a device for extracting juice from an orange, etc.

reap (rēp) *v.t.* **1**, cut with a sickle or other implement and gather; harvest. **2**, garner as the fruit of one's labors. —**reap′er**, *n.* a machine for reaping.

rear (rir) *n.* **1**, the back; a position lying backward; the background. **2**, (*Mil.*) the body of an army or fleet that comes last. —*adj.* hindmost. —*v.t.* **1**, set or hold up; elevate. **2**, build; construct; erect. **3**, foster; nurture; train, as children. **4**, raise, as plants or animals. —*v.i.* **1**, rise on the hind legs, as a horse. **2**, (with *up*) express resentment. —**rear admiral**, a naval officer ranking above captain and commodore. —**rear guard**, a detachment to follow and protect a marching army.

rear′most *adj.* last of all.

rear′ward (-wərd) *adj.* at or toward the rear. —**rear′wards**, *adv.*

rea′son (rē′zən) *n.* **1**, a statement given to create, confirm, or justify a belief, conclusion, or action; a promise; ground; excuse. **2**, intellect; the faculty of understanding, inferring, and deducing, esp. as man does. **3**, sanity. **4**, moderation; right. —*v.t.* exercise the mind; reflect; think. —**rea′son·ing**, *n.*

rea′son·a·ble *adj.* **1**, rational. **2**, amenable to sound sense. **3**, not exceeding the bounds of common sense; sensible. **4**, moderate in amount or price.

re″as·sur′ance *n.* **1**, restored confidence. **2**, something that reassures.

re″as·sure′ *v.t.* instill confidence in.

Ré′au·mur scale (rā′ə-myûr) a temperature calibration scale on which the freezing and boiling points of water are 0°R and 80°R, respectively.

re′bate (rē′bāt) *n.* a return of part of a payment. —*v.t.* (rē-bāt′) return (part of a payment received).

re′bec (rē′bek) *n.* (*Music*) a medieval string instrument, played with a bow.

re·bel′ (ri-bel′) *v.i.* **1**, make war against one's government; revolt against any authority or order. **2**, refuse or dislike to do something expected. —*n.* (reb′əl) **1**, one who rebels. **2**, an unconventional person.

re·bel′lion (ri-bel′yən) *n.* **1**, an armed revolt. **2**, a spirit of resistance to authority.

re·bel'lious (ri-bel'yəs) *adj.* rebelling; defiant; resisting control. **—re·bel'lious·ness,** *n.*

re'birth" *n.* **1,** a new or second birth; reincarnation. **2,** a revival; renaissance.

re·bound' *v.i.* spring back; bounce. *—n.* (rē'bownd) **1,** the act of flying back; recoil. **2,** (*Colloq.*) recovery from an unhappy love affair.

re·buff' (ri-buf') *v.t.* & *n.* snub.

re·buke' (ri-būk') *v.t.* chide; reprimand. *—n.* reproof.

re'bus (rē'bəs) *n.* a representation of words or phrases by means of figures or pictures.

re·but' (ri-but') *v.t.* disprove by argument or evidence; refute, esp. in a debate. **—re·but'tal,** *n.*

re·cal'ci·trant (ri-kal'si-trənt) *adj.* refusing to submit; refractory. *—n.* a recalcitrant person. **—re·cal'ci·trance,** *n.*

re·call' (ri-kâl') *v.t.* **1,** remember; recollect. **2,** call back; summon anew. **3,** revoke; countermand. *—n.* **1,** the act of recalling; revocation. **2,** the right to vote an elected official out of office. **3,** a signal (by flag, bugle, etc.).

re·cant' (ri-kant') *v.t.* & *i.* contradict formally one's previous assertion; retract. **—re"can·ta'tion** (rē"kan-tā'shən) *n.*

re·cap' (rē-kap') *v.t.* put a new tread on (a worn tire). *—n.* **1,** (rē'kap) a recapped tire. **2,** (*Colloq.*) recapitulation.

re"ca·pit'u·late" *v.t.* **1,** summarize; review. **2,** repeat (past stages of evolution) in development. **—re"ca·pit'u·la'tion,** *n.*

re·cap'ture *v.t.* seize, remember, or enjoy again. *—n.* **1,** a taking again; recovery. **2,** lawful seizure of property or earnings by a government.

re·cede' (ri-sēd') *v.i.* **1,** withdraw; fall away. **2,** turn back or aside. **3,** incline or slope backward.

re·ceipt' (ri-sēt') *n.* **1,** the act or state of receiving. **2,** something received, esp. (*pl.*) money taken in. **3,** a written acknowledgment of having received something, esp. money. **4,** a recipe. *—v.t.* give a receipt for; acknowledge payment of.

re·ceiv'a·ble *adj.* owing to oneself. *—n.* (usu. *pl.*) an account due from another.

re·ceive' (ri-sēv') *v.t.* **1,** get by transfer as from a primary source, as money, a wound, an impression, etc. **2,** give admission, recognition, or welcome to. **3,** hold; contain. *—v.i.* **1,** come into custody of something by transfer. **2,** greet and entertain visitors. **3,** deal in stolen goods.

re·ceiv'er *n.* **1,** one who or that which receives (taxes, etc.). **2,** a dealer in stolen goods. **3,** one appointed to handle the affairs of a bankrupt. **4,** an instrument for receiving signals, sounds, etc. **5,** a receptacle.

re·ceiv'er·ship" *n.* (*Law*) **1,** the office or function of a receiver (def. 3). **2,** state of being in the hands of a receiver.

re·cen'sion (ri-sen'shən) *n.* a critical revision, as of a book; the revised text.

re'cent (rē'sənt) *adj.* **1,** of or pert. to time not long past. **2,** of relatively modern date; fresh. **—re'cent·ly,** *adv.* not long ago.

re·cep'ta·cle (ri-sep'tə-kəl) *n.* **1,** a container, as a wastebasket. **2,** an electrical outlet.

re·cep'tion (ri-sep'shən) *n.* **1,** the act or manner of receiving; a letting in. **2,** a greeting or welcome. **3,** a formal entertainment of guests. **—re·cep'tion·ist,** *n.* one employed to greet visitors.

re·cep'tive (ri-sep'tiv) *adj.* **1,** willing to receive or accept. **2,** able to hold and contain. **—re·cep'tive·ness, re·cep·tiv'i·ty,** *n.*

re·cep'tor (ri-sep'tər) *n,* a sensory nerve ending; a sense organ.

re'cess (rē'ses) *n.* **1,** an interval of relief; a rest period. **2,** an alcove; a niche; a nook. **3,** (*pl.*) a place of retirement or seclusion. *—v.t.* (rē-ses') **1,** put in, make, or order a recess. **2,** set back. *—v.i.* adjourn for a short time.

re·ces'sion (rē-sesh'ən) *n.* **1,** act of receding. **2,** a recessed place. **3,** a brief decline in business prosperity.

re·ces'sion·al (rē-sesh'ən-əl) *n.* a hymn sung while clergy and choir retire at the end of a church service.

re·ces'sive (rē-ses'iv) *adj.* **1,** tending to recede. **2,** tending to yield.

re·cher·ché' (rə-sher-shā') *adj.* (*Fr.*) **1,** studied or refined; careful. **2,** rare.

re·cid'i·vism (ri-sid'ə-viz-əm) *n.* relapse into crime by a convicted criminal. **—re·cid'i·vist,** *n.* **—re·cid'i·vous,** *adj.*

rec'i·pe (res'ə-pē) *n.* **1,** directions, as for preparing a specific dish. **2,** a medical prescription. **3,** any formula for producing a desired effect.

re·cip'i·ent (ri-sip'ē-ənt) *n.* one who receives or accepts something. *—adj.* receiving; receptive.

re·cip'ro·cal (ri-sip'rə-kəl) *adj.* in mutual relation; concerning, given, or owed by each with regard to the other. *—n.* (*Math.*) **1,** the quotient resulting from the division of unity by a quantity, as the reciprocal of 4 is ¼. **2,** a complement.

re·cip'ro·cate" (ri-sip'rə-kāt") *v.t.* & *i.* **1,** give and return mutually; act in return or response. **2,** (*Mech.*) move backward and forward. **—re·cip″ro·ca′tion,** *n.* **—reciprocating engine,** one in which the pistons move back and forth.

rec″i·proc′i·ty (res″i-pros′ə-tē) *n.* mutual exchange or aid; cooperation.

re·ci′sion (ri-sizh′ən) *n.* a cutting off; resection or annulment.

re·cit′al (ri-sīt′əl) *n.* act of reciting; esp. a musical performance.

rec″i·ta′tion (res″i-tā′shən) *n.* **1,** a reciting or recital. **2,** a piece recited; a declamation.

rec″i·ta·tive′ (res″i-tə-tēv′) *n.* a passage in an opera or oratorio intermediate between speaking and singing.

re·cite′ (ri-sīt′) *v.t.* **1,** deliver orally (something memorized); rehearse. **2,** give an account or statement of; tell. **3,** enumerate. *—v.i.* state or perform a lesson, etc.

reck (rek) *v.t. & i.* heed.

reck′less (rek′ləs) *adj.* daring; imprudent; foolhardy. **—reck′less·ness,** *n.*

reck′on (rek′ən) *v.t.* **1,** count; compute. **2,** hold in estimation; regard. *—v.i.* **1,** figure up. **2,** rely; depend. **3,** (*Colloq.*) think; suppose; guess.

reck′on·ing *n.* **1,** an accounting. **2,** a final settlement.

re·claim′ *v.t.* **1,** recover or assert right to (something lost or surrendered). **2,** redeem; save (something abandoned or neglected). **3,** fit for cultivation or other use. **4,** reform; tame. **—rec″la·ma′tion** (rek″lə-mā′shən) *n.*

re·cline′ (ri-klīn′) *v.i.* lie down.

re·cluse′ (ri-kloos′) *n.* a person who lives in seclusion; a hermit. **—re·clu′sion,** *n.* **—re·clu′sive,** *adj.*

rec″og·ni′tion (rek″əg-nish′ən) *n.* the act of recognizing; acceptance; notice.

re·cog′ni·zance (ri-kog′nə-zəns) *n.* **1,** (*Law*) a surety bond. **2,** recognition.

rec′og·nize″ (rek′əg-nīz″) *v.t.* **1,** identify or acknowledge something or someone as previously known. **2,** acknowledge or accept formally. **3,** appreciate. **—rec′og·niz″a·ble,** *adj.*

re·coil′ (ri-koil′) *v.i.* spring back; react. *—n.* (rē′koil″) the act or extent of recoiling.

rec″ol·lect′ (rek″ə-lekt′) *v.t.* bring back to the mind; remember. **—rec″ol·lec′tion,** *n.* the act of recalling; something remembered.

re·com′bi·nant (ri-kom′bə-nənt) *adj.* pert. to the combination of genetic materials in new ways.

rec″om·mend′ (rek″ə-mend′) *v.t.* **1,** put in a favorable light before another; state to be worthy. **2,** advise. **—rec″om·men·da′tion,** *n.*

rec′om·pense″ (rek′əm-pens″) *v.t.* pay, in return for something. *—n.* remuneration; repayment.

rec″on·cile″ (rek′ən-sīl″) *v.t.* **1,** restore to union and friendship after estrangement. **2,** adjust; settle. **3,** bring to agreement. **4,** make consistent. **—rec″on·cil″i·a′tion** (-sil″ē-ā′shən) *n.*

rec″on·dite″ (rek′ən-dīt″) *adj.* hard to understand; deep in meaning.

re″con·di′tion *v.t.* restore to original condition; repair; renovate.

re·con′nais·sance (ri-kon′ə-səns) *n.* act of reconnoitering.

re″con·noi′ter (rē″kə-noi′tər) *v.t. & i.* make a preliminary inspection of (a region, enemy's position, etc.).

re″con·sid′er *v.t.* think about again, esp. to change a decision. **—re″con·sid·er·a′tion,** *n.*

re″con·struct′ *v.t.* construct again; rebuild.

re″con·struc′tion *n.* **1,** act of rebuilding. **2,** (*cap.*) the return of the Confederate States to the Union after the Civil War.

re·cord′ (ri-kôrd′) *v.t.* **1,** write down, so as to keep as evidence. **2,** register; enroll, as voters or pupils. **3,** transcribe for reproduction by phonograph, etc. *—n.* (rek′ərd) **1,** the act of recording; an account or report. **2,** all the known facts; previous experience. **3,** a disk, etc., to reproduce sound on. **4,** the highest achievement in a competition. *—adj.* exceeding all others; best of its kind to date.

re·cord′er *n.* **1,** an official who keeps records. **2,** a registering instrument. **3,** a type of flute.

re·cord′ing *n.* a phonograph record, recorded tape, etc.

re·count′ (ri-kownt′) *v.t.* **1,** tell; relate; narrate in order or detail. **2,** (rē″kownt′) count again. *—n.* (rē′kownt″) a second enumeration.

re·coup′ (ri-koop′) *v.t. & i.* recover (one's losses).

re′course (rē′kôrs) *n.* a source of or appeal for help.

re·cov′er (ri-kuv′ər) *v.t.* get or obtain (something lost) again; regain; save. *—v.i.* **1,** grow well again after illness; come back to a former, better state. **2,** (*Law*) obtain a judgment, as for damages.

re·cov′er·y (-ə-rē) *n.* act or fact of recovering; what is recovered.

rec′re·ant (rek′rē-ənt) *adj.* **1,** craven; cowardly. **2,** unfaithful to duty. *—n.* a coward or traitor. **—rec′re·an·cy** (-ən-sē) *n.*

rec′re·ate″ (rek′rē-āt″) *v.t.* refresh after toil or exertion; divert. *—v.i.* take recreation.

rec″re·a′tion (rek″rē-ā′shən) *n.* diversion

from toil; play. —**rec″re·a′tion·al**, *adj.*
—**rec″re·a′tive**, *adj.*

re·crim′i·nate′ (ri-krim′ə-nāt″) *v.i.* answer an accusation with another. —**re·crim″i·na′tion**, *n.*

re″cru·desce′ (rē″kroo-des′) *v.i.* **1**, become raw or sore again. **2**, break out afresh. —**re″cru·des′cence**, *n.* —**re″cru·des′cent**, *adj.*

re·cruit′ (ri-kroot′) *v.t. & i.* **1**, enlist (new men), esp. for an army, **2**, gather or recover (strength, provisions, etc.). —*n.* a newly enlisted member, esp. a soldier or sailor. —**re·cruit′ment**, *n.*

rec′tal (rek′təl) *adj.* of or pert. to the rectum.

rec′tan″gle (rek′tang″gəl) *n.* a parallelogram having all right angles. —**rec·tan′gu·lar**, (-gyə-lər) *adj.*

rec·ti- (rek-tə) *pref.* straight.

rec′ti·fy″ (rek′ti-fī″) *v.t.* make right or straight; correct; amend. —**rec″ti·fi·ca′tion**, *n.* —**rec′ti·fi″er**, *n.*

rec″ti·lin′e·ar (rek′ti-lin″ē-ər) *adj.* composed of straight lines.

rec′ti·tude″ (rek′ti-tūd″) *n.* **1**, rightness of principle or practice. **2**, correctness; freedom from error.

rec′to (rek′tō) *n.* [*pl.* **-tos**] the right-hand, odd-numbered page of an open book.

rec′tor (rek′tər) *n.* **1**, a priest or clergyman in charge of a parish. **2**, the head of a school or college. —**rec′tor·ate** (-ət) *n.*

rec′to·ry (rek′tə-rē) *n.* a parsonage.

rec′tum (rek′təm) *n.* the terminal section of the intestine.

re·cum′bent (ri-kum′bənt) *adj.* leaning, reclining. —**re·cum′ben·cy**, *n.*

re·cu′per·ate″ (ri-kū′pə-rāt″) *v.i.* **1**, recover health. **2**, recover from pecuniary loss. —*v.t.* regain. —**re·cu″per·a′tion**, *n.* —**re·cu′per·a·tive**, *adj.*

re·cur′ (ri-kėr′) *v.i.* [**-curred′, -cur′ring**] appear again; return. —**re·cur′rence**, *n.* —**re·cur′rent**, *adj.*

rec′u·sant (rek′yə-zənt) *n. & adj.* (one who is) obstinate in refusal to comply. —**rec′u·san·cy** (-zən-sē) *n.*

re·cy′cle *v.t.* reuse, esp. by reducing to component parts or materials.

red *n.* **1**, a bright color, the color of fresh blood; any dark shade of this color, as crimson, scarlet, etc. **2**, a radical; specif., a communist. —*adj.* [**red′der, -dest**] of this color. —**red′dish**, *adj.* —**red′ness**, *n.* —**Red Cross**, an organization that helps victims of war and disaster. —**red flag**, a signal of danger. —**red hat**, (*Colloq.*) a Rom. Cath. cardinal. —**red herring**, a false, diversionary clue. —**red light**, a signal to

stop. —**red light district**, one where brothels are located. —**red pepper**, **1**, cayenne pepper. **2**, the sweet pepper. —**red shift**, a shift in the spectrum toward longer wavelengths, sometimes caused by the Doppler effect. —**red tape**, excessive and tedious adherence to form and routine. —**red tide**, seawater colored red by presence of large quantities of an organism fatal to certain marine life.

re·dact′ (ri-dakt′) *v.t.* edit. —**re·dac′tion**, *n.*

red-′blood″ed *adj.* virile.

red′breast″ *n.* a robin.

red′cap″ *n.* a porter in a railroad station.

red′coat″ *n.* (*Hist.*) a Brit. soldier.

red′den (red′ən) *v.t. & i.* make or become red; blush.

re·deem′ (ri-dēm′) *v.t.* **1**, buy back; pay off (a loan or debt). **2**, liberate from captivity or obligation by paying ransom. **3**, perform or fulfill a promise. **4**, atone for; compensate for. —**re·deem′a·ble**, *adj.*

re·deem′er *n.* one who ransoms or atones for another; (*cap.*) Jesus Christ.

re·demp′tion (ri-dem′shən) *n.* act or result of redeeming; salvation. —**re·demp′tive**, *adj.*

red′hand″ed *adj.* overtly guilty.

red′head″ *n.* a person with red hair. —**red′head″ed**, *adj.*

red-′hot′ *adj.* **1**, very hot; intense. **2**, very new; affording unusual opportunity.

red′in·gote″ (red′ing-gōt″) *n.* a long, double-breasted overcoat, now worn only by women.

re″di·rect′ *adj.* (*Law*) designating the examination of a witness by the party calling him, after cross-examination. —*v.t.* direct again.

re·dis′trict *v.t.* divide again into districts.

red′let″ter *adj.* memorable; auspicious.

red′lin″ing *n.* the practice of banks of designating certain areas, esp. ghetto areas, as bad risks for mortgage loans.

red′man″ *n.* (*Offensive*) a No. Amer. Indian.

red′o·lent (red′ə-lənt) *adj.* having or diffusing a sweet (or, sometimes, offensive) scent; fragrant. —**red′o·lence**, *n.*

re·dou′ble *v.t. & i.* **1**, double again. **2**, increase greatly. **3**, echo.

re·doubt′ (ri-dowt′) *n.* a small fort.

re·doubt′a·ble (ri-dow′tə-bəl) *adj.* causing dread or respect; formidable.

re·dound′ (ri-downd′) *v.i.* **1**, roll or flow back. **2**, accrue.

re·dress′ (ri-dress′) *v.t.* set right; remedy. —*n.* (rē′dres″) relief; atonement; compensation.

red'skin'' *n.* (*Offensive*) an Amer. Indian. Also, **red-man**.

re·duce' (ri-doos') *v.t.* **1**, bring down; diminish in size, quantity, or value. **2**, weaken; degrade. **3**, bring to any specified state, condition, or form. **4**, subdue; raze. —*v.i.* (*Colloq.*) make oneself less fat, esp. by diet. —**re·duc'tion** (ri-duk'shən) *n.*

re·dun'dant (ri-dun'dənt) *adj.* superfluous; esp., using more words than are needed. —**re·dun'dance, —re·dun'dan·cy**, *n.*

red'wood'' *n.* a sequoia.

reed (rēd) *n.* **1**, any tall, broadleaved grass growing near water, or its hollow or pulp-filled stem. **2**, a musical pipe; reed instrument. **3**, (*Music*) a thin, vibratory tongue used in a mouthpiece. —**reed'y**, *adj.*

reef (rēf) *n.* **1**, a low rocky or sandy ridge near the water line; a shoal; a sand bar. **2**, (*Naut.*) a part of a sail that can be rolled up. —*v.t.* roll up. —**reef knot**, a square not.

reef'er *n.* **1**, a short outer coat. **2**, (*Slang*) a marijuana cigarette.

reek (rēk) *v.i.* **1**, give off an offensive odor. **2**, be full of something offensive. —*n.* an offensive odor.

reel (rēl) *n.* **1**, any of various revolving devices for winding yarn, fishing lines, etc. **2**, a spool of motion-picture film. **3**, a lively dance; a staggering motion; a sensation of dizziness. —*v.t.* **1**, wind upon a reel. **2**, (with *off*) utter fluently and rapidly. **3**, (with *in*) draw in with a reel. —*v.i.* **1**, whirl. **2**, stagger.

re-en'try *n.* a return, as of a spacecraft into the earth's atmosphere.

reeve (rēv) *v.t.* (*Naut.*) pass the end of a rope through a hole, as in a block. —*n.* **1**, a bird, the female of the ruff. **2**, a sheriff, bailiff, or similar officer.

re·fec'tion (ri-fek'shən) *n.* refreshment; a repast.

re·fec'to·ry (ri-fek'tə-rē) *n.* a dining room.

re·fer' (ri-fēr') *v.t.* [**re·ferred', -fer'ring**] **1**, submit (to another person of authority) for consideration and decision. **2**, direct (someone to another person or source). **3**, assign. —*v.i.* **1**, relate. **2**, have recourse; appeal. **3**, allude; direct the attention (to). —**re·fer'ral**, *n.*

ref''er·ee' (ref''ə-rē') *n.* a person deputed to settle a matter in dispute; an umpire. —*v.t. & i.* arbitrate. Also, *colloq.*, **ref**.

ref'er·ence (ref'ə-rəns) *n.* **1**, act of referring; consultation. **2**, a casual mention. **3**, a written recommendation. **4**, a citation. —**reference book**, a book of classified information. —**ref''er·en'dum** (ref''ə-ren'dəm) *n.* a popular vote; plebiscite.

re·fill' (rē-fil') *v.t.* fill again. —*n.* (rē'fil'') a supply to replace one used or worn out.

re·fine' (ri-fīn') *v.t.* **1**, bring or reduce to a pure state. **2**, give culture to; polish. —**re·fined'**, *adj.* cultivated; pure.

re·fine'ment (-mənt) *n.* **1**, act of refining; cultivation. **2**, elegance.

re·fin'er (ri-fīn'ər) *n.* a person or establishment that makes gasoline from petroleum, sugar from cane, etc. —**re·fin'er·y**, *n.* a refiner's factory.

re·flect' (ri-flekt') *v.t.* **1**, throw back, as rays of light or heat after they strike a surface. **2**, present an image of; mirror. **3**, bring about. **4**, ponder. —*v.i.* **1**, throw back rays, etc. **2**, meditate. **3**, (with *on*) bring reproach or blame.

re·flec'tion (ri-flek'shən) *n.* **1**, act or result of reflecting. **2**, an image, as in a mirror. **3**, meditation. **4**, comment. **5**, an unfavorable remark; slur. Also, **re·flex'-ion**.

re·flec'tive (ri-flek'tiv) *adj.* **1**, reflecting. **2**, being, or pert. to, reflection.

re·flec'tor (ri-flek'tər) *n.* **1**, a part for reflecting light. **2**, a reflecting telescope.

re'flex (rē'fleks) *n.* an involuntary action of the nervous system in response to some stimulus. —*adj.* **1**, pert. to such an action. **2**, cast, bent, or turned back. —*v.t.* (ri-fleks') bend or turn back. —**reflex camera**, a camera in which viewing is accomplished by means of a ground glass screen upon which the image focused by the lens is reflected by a mirror.

re·flex'ive (ri-flek'siv) *adj.* (*Gram.*) denoting action upon the subject, as in *he wrongs himself.*

re'flux'' (rē'fluks'') *n.* a flowing back, as of a tide; ebb.

re·for'est (rē-fôr'əst) *v.t.* replant with trees. —**re''for·es·ta'tion**, *n.*

re·form' (ri-fôrm') *v.t.* **1**, make over; change, esp. to a better state; improve. **2**, cause (a person) to abandon evil ways. —*v.i.* abandon evil ways. —*n.* **1**, change or improvement, esp. in social institutions. **2**, betterment of conduct. —**re·form'er**, *n.* one who urges betterment of conditions or morals. —**reform school**, a reformatory.

re-"form' (rē-''fôrm') *v.t. & i.* **1**, form again; reconstruct. **2**, make different in shape or form.

ref''or·ma'tion (ref''ər-mā'shən) *n.* **1**, a change for the better. **2**, (*cap.*) the 16th-century movement that led to the formation of Protestant churches.

re·form'a·to·ry (ri-fôr'mə-tôr-ē) *n.* a place of detention for juvenile criminals.

re·fract' (ri-frakt') *v.t.* bend abruptly; esp., deflect a ray of light. —**re·frac'tive**, *adj.*

re·frac'tion (ri-frak'shən) *n.* an oblique direction given a ray of heat, light, or sound, passing into a different medium or through a medium of varying density.

re·frac'to·ry (ri-frak'tə-rè) *adj.* **1,** unmanageable; unyielding. **2,** resistant.

re·frain' (ri-frān') *v.i.* hold oneself back; abstain; forbear. —*n.* something repeated, esp. a phrase or verse in a poem or song; a chorus.

re·fran'gi·ble (ri-fran'jə-bəl) *adj.* capable of being refracted. —**re·fran'gi·bil'i·ty,** *n.*

re·fresh' (ri-fresh') *v.t.* make fresh again; invigorate; stimulate. —*v.i.* become fresh.

re·fresh'er (-ər) *adj.* serving as a review of a subject already studied. —*n.* something that refreshes.

re·fresh'ment (-mənt) *n.* **1,** act or result of refreshing. **2,** (*pl.*) a light meal served at a party.

re·frig'er·ant (ri-frij'ər-ənt) *n. & adj.* a substance that causes cooling.

re·frig'er·ate (ri-frij'ə-rāt") *v.t.* make cold; freeze (food or liquids). —**re·frig"er·a'tion,** *n.*

re·frig'er·a"tor (ri-frij'ə-rā"tər) *n.* a cabinet for cold storage.

re"fu'el *v.t. & i.* supply or take in fresh fuel.

ref'uge (ref'ūj) *n.* a shelter or protection from danger or distress; an asylum.

ref"u·gee' (ref"ū-jē') *n.* one who flees for safety.

re·ful'gence (rè-ful'jəns) *n.* brilliant light; splendor. —**re·ful'gent,** *adj.*

re·fund' (rè-fund') *v.t.* **1,** pay back. **2,** (rē-") refinance, as by a new bond issue. —*n.* (rē'fund") a repayment.

re·fur'bish *v.t.* clean and polish; renovate.

re·fus'al (ri-fūz'əl) *n.* **1,** act or result of refusing. **2,** first option (to buy, sell, etc.).

re·fuse' (ri-fūz') *v.t. & i.* **1,** decline to do or grant; deny. **2,** decline to accept; reject.

ref'use (ref'ūs) *n.* garbage; rubbish.

ref"u·ta'tion (ref"ū-tā'shən) *n.* act or result of refuting; that which refutes.

re·fute' (ri-fūt') *v.t.* defeat by argument or proof; disprove.

re·gain' (ri-gān') *v.t.* **1,** get again; recover. **2,** get back to; reach again.

re·gal (rē'gəl) *adj.* royal; majestic. —**re·gal'i·ty,** (ri'gal'ə-tè) *n.*

re·gale' (ri-gāl') *v.t. & i.* entertain sumptuously; divert; feast. —**re·gale'ment,** *n.*

re·ga'li·a (re-gā'lè-ə) *n. pl.* **1,** emblems; insignia. **2,** personal finery.

re·gard' (ri-gärd') *v.t.* **1,** look upon; observe; consider. **2,** have a particular atti-

tude toward; esteem. **3,** have relation to; concern. —*n.* **1,** reference; respect. **2,** a particular feeling, esp. of respect. **3,** scrutiny. **4,** concern; interest. —**re·gard'ful,** *adj.* thoughtful; attentive. —**re·gard'ing,** *prep.* in reference to; concerning.

re·gard'less *adj.* indifferent; not caring. —*adv.* notwithstanding.

re·gat'ta (ri-gä'tə) *n.* a boat race, esp. of yachts.

re·gen·cy (rē'jən-sè) *n.* **1,** a board of regents. **2,** state of being a regent. **3,** government by a regent. **4,** a style of furniture and interior decoration.

re·gen'er·ate" (rè-jen'ər-āt") *v.t.* **1,** make over completely; reform thoroughly. **2,** bring into existence again. **3,** (*Electricity*) amplify the input by part of the output. —*v.i.* be formed again or improved. —*adj.* (-ət) reformed. —**re"gen·er·a'tion,** *n.* —**re·gen'er·a·tive,** *adj.*

re·gent (rē'jənt) *n.* **1,** one who governs when the legitimate ruler cannot. **2,** one of a board governing education, a college, etc.

reg'i·cide (rej'ə-sīd") *n.* the killing or killer of a king. —**reg'i·ci'dal,** *adj.*

re·gime' (rā-zhēm') *n.* **1,** the mode, system, style, or rule of management or government. **2,** regimen.

reg'i·men (rej'ə-mən) *n.* a system of regulation or remedy.

reg'i·ment (rej'ə-mənt) *n.* a body of soldiers, usu. two or three battalions commanded by a colonel. —*v.t.* systematize; bring under strict and uniform control. —**reg'i·men'tal,** *adj.* pert. to a regiment. —**reg'i·men'tals,** *n.pl.* military dress. —**reg'i·men·ta'tion,** *n.* act or effect of regimenting.

re·gion (rē'jən) *n.* **1,** a large area of indefinite extent; a country. **2,** a district; section. **3,** a sphere or realm. —**re'gion·al,** *adj.* —**re'gion·al·ism,** *n.*

reg'is·ter (rej'is-tər) *n.* **1,** an official written record; a record book; a recording device. **2,** (*Music*) a part or all of the compass or range of a voice or instrument. **3,** a device for regulating the passage of heat or air. **4,** in printing, exact adjustment of position. **5,** a recording office. —*v.t.* **1,** enter in a register; record. **2,** mark or indicate on a scale. **3,** demonstrate (some kind of emotion). **4,** insure delivery of (a letter). —*v.i.* **1,** cause one's name to be recorded. **2,** place printing type or plates in proper position. **3,** (*Colloq.*) create an impression. —**registered nurse,** a graduate trained nurse licensed by a state authority.

reg'is·trar" (rej'is-trär") *n.* a recording officer.

reg″is·tra′tion (rej″is-trā′shən) *n.* **1**, act of registering or being registered. **2**, the number of persons registered. **3**, in organ and harpsichord playing, the stops used for a particular work or passage.

reg′is·try (rej′is-trē) *n.* act or place of recording.

reg′nal (reg′nəl) *adj.* of or pert. to a reign or reigning.

reg′nant (reg′nənt) *adj.* reigning.

re′gress (rē′gres) *n.* passage back; return. —*v.i.* (ri-gres′) go back; retrogress. —**re·gres′sion** (ri-gresh′ən) *n.* —**re·gres′sive** (ri-gres′iv) *adj.*

re·gret′ (ri-gret′) *v.t.* **1**, look back at with sorrow; lament. **2**, be distressed on account of; rue. —*n.* **1**, grief; a painful sense of loss. **2**, (*pl.*) an oral or written message note declining an invitation. —**re·gret′ful,** *adj.*

re·group′ *v.i. & t.* form again into groups.

reg′u·lar (reg′yə-lər) *adj.* **1**, conforming to a rule, law, type, prescribed mode, customary form, or design; normal; customary. **2**, steady; rhythmical. **3**, (*Mil.*) professional. **4**, (*Colloq.*) thorough; sportsman-like. —**reg′u·lar′i·ty** (-lar′ə-tē) *n.*

reg′u·late″ (reg′yə-lāt″) *v.t.* **1**, direct or govern by rule. **2**, put or keep in good order. **3**, adjust (an instrument, as a clock). —**reg″u·la′tion,** *n.* —**reg′u·la″tor,** *n.*

re·gur′gi·tate″ (rē-gêr′ji-tāt″) *v.t. & i.* **1**, bring back (specif., food from the stomach). **2**, (*Slang*) recite from memory. —**re·gur″·gi·ta′tion,** *n.*

re″ha·bil′i·tate″ (rē″hə-bil′ə-tāt″) *v.t.* restore to good condition or respectable position. —**re″ha·bil″i·ta′tion,** *n.*

re′hash (rē′hash) *n.* something made over but with nothing new in substance. —*v.t.* (rē-hash′) **1**, make into a different form. **2**, go over again, as an argument.

re·hearse′ (ri-hêrs′) *v.t.* **1**, practice (as a play) for a public performance. **2**, repeat. **3**, enumerate. —*v.i.* perform for practice. —**re·hears′al,** *n.*

Reich (rīkh) *n.* Germany; the German state.

reign (rān) *n.* **1**, sovereignty; royal or supreme power. **2**, the time during which a sovereign rules. —*v.i.* rule.

re″im·burse′ (rē″im-bêrs′) *v.t.* pay back; restore; refund. —**re″im·burse′ment,** *n.*

rein (rān) *n.* **1**, a long strap attached to a bridle, by which the rider or driver controls a horse. **2**, (usually *pl.*) any means of restraint or control. —*v.t.* restrain.

re″in·car′nate *v.t.* endow a spirit with a new or different body.

re″in·car·na′tion *n.* **1**, a rebirth in a new

embodiment. **2**, the belief that souls are reborn.

rein′deer″ (rān′dir″) *n.* a deer used as a draft animal in Arctic regions.

re″in·force′ (rē″in-fôrs′) *v.t.* strengthen by supplying additional men, materials, support, etc. Also, **re″en·force′.**

re″in·force′ment (-mənt) *n.* **1**, act or effect of reinforcing. **2**, that which reinforces; (*Mil.*, often *pl.*) new troops, ships, etc.

re″in·state′ (rē″in-stāt′) *v.t.* restore to a former position. —**re″in·state′ment,** *n.*

re·it′er·ate″ *v.t.* repeat; iterate. —**re·it″·er·a′tion,** *n.*

re·ject′ (ri-jekt′) *v.t.* **1**, throw away as useless; discard. **2**, refuse to accept; decline. **3**, refuse to grant; deny. —*n.* (rē′jekt) **1**, an imperfect article; a second. **2**, something rejected. —**re·jec′tion,** *n.*

re·joice′ (ri-jois′) *v.i. & t.* feel joy and gladness; exult; gladden.

re·join′ (ri-join′) *v.t. & i.* **1**, answer. **2**, (rē″join′) unite or join again.

re·join′der (-dər) *n.* a reply.

re·ju′ve·nate″ (ri-joo′və-nāt″) *v.t.* make youthful; renew; refresh. —**re·ju″ve·na′·tion,** *n.*

re·ju″ve·nes′cence (ri-joo″və-nes′əns) *n.* a renewal of the appearance, powers, or feeling of youth. —**re·ju″ve·nes′cent,** *adj.*

re·lapse′ (ri-laps′) *v.i.* slip back into a former state, as illness or evil ways. —*n.* (rē′laps″) a recurrence of illness; a backsliding.

re·late′ (ri-lāt′) *v.t.* **1**, connect with (something else). **2**, tell; narrate. **3**, ally by kinship. —*v.i.* have reference, kinship, or connection with something. —**re·lat′ed,** *adj.* associated; connected; akin.

re·la′tion (ri-lā′shən) *n:* **1**, narration; a narrative. **2**, kinship; a kinsman. **3**, (*pl.*) affairs; dealings. **4**, bearing; close connection. **5**, reference. **6**, proportion; ratio. —**re·la′tion·ship,** *n.*

rel′a·tive (rel′ə-tiv) *adj.* **1**, having bearing on something; close in connection. **2**, belonging to or respecting something else. **3**, comparative, not absolute. **4**, (*Gram.*) referring to an antecedent. —*n.* a person connected by blood or affinity. —**rel′a·tiv·is′tic,** *adj.* —**relative humidity,** the ratio of the water vapor in the atmosphere to the amount required to saturate it.

rel″a·tiv′i·ty (rel″ə-tiv′ə-tē) *n.* **1**, quality or state of being connected with; interdependence. **2**, a theory in physics (the Einstein theory) that motion, time, space, etc., are not absolute; that time is a dimension; etc.

re·lax' (ri-laks') *v.t.* & *i.* make or become less·tense, severe, assiduous, or the like; slacken; ease; unbend. —**re·lax'ant** (-ənt) *n.* & *adj.* —**re"lax·a'tion** (rē"-) *n.*

re·lay (rē'lā) *n.* **1,** a fresh supply of men or animals held in readiness; a shift. **2,** a race among teams of successive runners. —*v.t.* send by a series of messengers or media.

re·lease' (ri-lēs') *v.t.* **1,** set free; unfasten. **2,** free from pain, obligation, penalty, etc. **3,** let be shown or sold, as a motion picture or book. —*n.* **1,** liberation, as from prison. **2,** discharge or freedom from any burden. **3,** a news item, motion picture, etc., made available for publication. **4,** a surrender of a claim.

rel'e·gate" (rel'ə-gāt") *v.t.* send away or out of the way; consign. —**rel"e·ga'tion,** *n.*

re·lent' (ri-lent') *v.i.* become less obdurate; feel compassion; soften; yield. —**re·lent'less,** *adj.* ever harsh or pressing.

rel'e·vant (rel'ə-vənt) *adj.* concerning the case in question; pertinent; applicable. —**rel'e·vance,** *n.*

re·li·a·ble (ri-lī'ə-bəl) *adj.* dependable; trustworthy. —**re·li"a·bil'i·ty,** *n.*

re·li'ance (ri-lī'əns) *n.* confidence; trust. —**re·li'ant,** *adj.*

rel'ic (rel'ik) *n.* **1,** that which remains after decay of the rest. **2,** a memento held in religious veneration. **3,** (*pl.*) remains.

rel'ict (rel'ikt) *n.* a widower or, esp., a widow.

re·lief' (ri-lēf') *n.* **1,** the act of relieving; alleviation; comfort. **2,** that which removes or lessens pain, want, etc. **3,** assistance given to the poor. **4,** release from a post of duty by a substitute; the substitute. **5,** the projection of a figure from a plane surface.

re·lieve' (ri-lēv') *v.t.* **1,** remove or lessen anything that weighs down or pains; allevi-ate. **2,** free from pain, want, anxiety, etc.; comfort. **3,** substitute for. **4,** heighten the effect or interest of, by contrast or variety. **5,** remove (an officer, etc.) from a post of duty.

re·li'gion (ri-lij'ən) *n.* **1,** a system of faith in and worship of a deity. **2,** devoutness; dedication to a holy life. **3,** a doctrine or custom accepted on faith.

re·lig"i·os'i·ty (ri-lij"ē-os'ə-tē) *n.* exces-sive or affected religiousness; religious sentimentality.

re·li'gious (ri-lij'əs) *adj.* **1,** pert. to a religion. **2,** devout. **3,** conscientious; dili-gent. —*n.* a monk or nun.

re·lin'quish (ri-ling'kwish) *v.t.* give up; desist from; quit; surrender. —**re·lin'quish-ment,** *n.*

rel'i·quar"y (rel'ə-kwār"ē) *n.* a reposi-tory for relics.

rel'ish *v.t.* be pleased with; enjoy; esp., eat with pleasure. —*n.* **1,** a pleasing taste; flavor. **2,** appreciation; gusto. **3,** an appe-tizer.

re·live' (rē-liv') *v.t.* live or experience again.

re·lo'cate *v.t.* & *i.* move. —**re"lo·ca'tion,** *n.*

re·luc'tant (ri-luk'tənt) *adj.* acting or doing with positive disinclination; unwilling. —**re·luc'tance,** *n.*

re·ly' (ri-lī') *v.i.* (with *on*) have confidence; trust; depend.

rem *n.* a measure of radiation.

re·main' (ri-mān') *v.i.* **1,** continue in a place; stay. **2,** continue in a specified state without change. **3,** endure; last. **4,** be left after something has been taken away. **5,** be held in reserve. —*n.* (*pl.*) that which is left; a dead body; relics.

re·main'der (-dər) *n.* **1,** anything left after the removal of a part. **2,** a surplus. **3,** (*Math.*) the sum left after subtraction, or left over after division. —*v.t.* sell leftover stock at a loss.

re·mand' (ri-mand') *v.t.* send, call, or order back.

re·mark' (ri-märk') *v.t.* & *i.* **1,** note in the mind; observe. **2,** express by way of comment. —*n.* a casual statement.

re·mark'a·ble *adj.* worthy of notice; ex-traordinary.

re·me'di·al (ri-mē'dē-əl) *adj.* serving to cure or correct.

rem'e·dy (rem'ə-dē) *n.* **1,** any treatment that cures a disease. **2,** anything that cor-rects or counteracts an evil. **3,** (*Law*) re-dress. —*v.t.* **1,** cure; heal. **2,** remove something evil from; counteract; redress. —**re·me'di·a·ble** (rə-mē'dē-ə-bəl) *adj.*

re·mem'ber (ri-mem'bər) *v.t.* **1,** retain in the mind; recall; recollect. **2,** observe, as an anniversary. **3,** acknowledge (some ser-vice) with money; tip. **4,** (with *to*) convey regards from someone (to someone). —*v.i.* utilize the memory.

re·mem'brance (ri-mem'brəns) *n.* **1,** act of remembering; something remembered. **2,** memory. **3,** a souvenir; a greeting card, gift, etc. —**Remembrance Day,** a legal holiday in Canada, Nov. 11.

re·mem'bran·cer (ri-mem'brən-sər) *n.* one who or that which reminds; a reminder.

re·mind' (ri-mīnd') *v.t.* put in mind; re-call to the memory or notice of. —**re·mind'-ful,** *adj.* reminiscent.

rem"i·nisce' (rem"ə-nis') *v.t.* recall the past to mind.

rem'i·nis'cence (rem″ə-nis′əns) *n.* **1,** recollection. **2,** something remembered, esp. nostalgically. —**rem'i·nis'cent,** *adj.*

re·mise' (ri-mīz′) *n.* (*Law*) a surrender or release, as of a claim. —*v.t.* release.

re·miss' (ri-mis′) *adj.* negligent; dilatory. —**re·miss'ness,** *n.*

re·mis'sion (ri-mish′ən) *n.* **1,** a giving up or discharge, as of a debt. **2,** the act of forgiving; pardon. **3,** abatement.

re·mit' (ri-mit′) *v.t.* [**re·mit'ted, -ting**] **1,** pardon; forgive. **2,** refrain from enacting. **3,** make less intense or violent; slacken. **4,** restore; replace. **5,** send in payment for goods received. **6,** (*Law*) transfer (a case) to a lower court. —*v.i.* **1,** abate. **2,** send payment. —**re·mit'tal,** *n.*

re·mit'tance (ri-mit′əns) *n.* money sent. —**remittance man,** an exile living on remittances from home.

re·mit'tent (ri-mit′ənt) *adj.* temporarily abating; esp. of a disease the symptoms of which diminish considerably but never disappear entirely. —*n.* a remittent fever.

rem'nant (rem′nənt) *n.* **1,** a small remainder; a remainder of a bolt of cloth, ribbon, etc. **2,** a last trace; vestige.

re·mod'el *v.t.* make over; reform; recondition.

re·mon'strance (ri-mon′strəns) *n.* an objection; protest.

re·mon'strate (ri-mon′strāt) *v.i.* present strong reasons against something; object; protest. —**re″mon·stra'tion** (ri″mən-strā′-shən) *n.* —**re·mon'stra·tive″,** *adj.*

rem'o·ra (rem′ə-rə) *n.* a parasitical marine fish.

re·morse' (ri-môrs′) *n.* self-accusatory regret. —**re·morse'ful,** *adj.* regretful and conscious of guilt. —**re·morse'less,** *adj.* relentless.

re·mote' (ri-mōt′) *adj.* **1,** far away; distant; not closely connected. **2,** alien; foreign. **3,** slight; inconsiderable. —**remote'ness,** *n.* —**remote control,** a device for controlling something (as a television set) from a distance.

re·mount' *v.t. & i.* mount again, as a horse.

re·mov'a·ble (ri-moov′ə-bəl) *adj.* not fixed. —*n.* (usu. *pl.*) furniture and loose possessions.

re·move' (ri-moov′) *v.t.* **1,** change from one place to another; transfer; move. **2,** displace, as from an office. **3,** destroy. —*v.i.* transfer from one residence, place, etc., to another. —*n.* **1,** change of place. **2,** interval; distance. —**re·mov'al,** *n.*

re·mu'ner·ate″ (ri-mū′nə-rāt″) *v.t.* pay (a person) for any service, loss, or expense;

recompense. —**re·mu″ner·a'tion,** *n.* —**re·mu'ner·a·tive,** *adj.* profitable.

ren'ais·sance' (ren″ə-säns′) *n. & adj.* a new emergence or revival, specific (*cap.*) of art and literature after the Dark Ages.

re'nal (rē′nəl) *adj.* pert. to the kidneys.

re·nas'cence (ri-nas′əns) *n.* a rebirth; renaissance. —**re·nas'cent,** *adj.*

ren·coun'ter (ren-kown′tər) *n.* **1,** a combat or engagement. **2,** a contest; debate. **3,** a casual meeting. Also, **ren·con'tre** (-kän′-tər). —*v.* meet; encounter.

rend *v.t. & i.* [*pret. & p.p.* **rent**] tear apart violently; split.

ren'der (ren′dər) *v.t.* **1,** cause to be or become. **2,** afford for use or benefit; present. **3,** give or pay back; return. **4,** translate. **5,** reproduce; represent, as a part in a play. **6,** reduce; melt; clarify by frying.

ren'dez·vous″ (rän′dā-voo″) *n.* [*pl.* **-vous″** (-vooz″)] **1,** a place of meeting. **2,** an appointment. —*v. t. & i.* assemble.

ren·di'tion (ren-dish′ən) *n.* the act of rendering; a translation; interpretation; performance.

ren'e·gade (ren′ə-gād″) *n.* one who deserts his faith, cause, party, etc.; a turncoat; a traitor.

re·nege' (ri-nig′) *v.i.* **1,** in card-playing, deviate from rule, esp. by revoking. **2,** (*Colloq.*) back down. —*n.* a reneging.

re·new' (ri-nū′) *v.t.* **1,** make fresh or vigorous again. **2,** make again; reaffirm, as a promise. **3,** replenish. **4,** grant again; extend the term of. —**re·new'al,** *n.* act or effect of renewing; extension of a contract.

ren·i- (ren-i; rē-ni) *pref.* kidney.

ren'net (ren′it) *n.* **1,** the fourth stomach of a calf. **2,** a substance derived from this stomach, used to curdle milk; rennin.

ren'nin (ren′in) *n.* a substance that coagulates milk; rennet.

re·nounce' (ri-nowns′) *v.t. & i.* refuse to acknowledge; abandon. —**re·nounce'ment,** *n.*

ren'o·vate″ (ren′ə-vāt″) *v.t.* restore to freshness or new condition. —**ren'o·va'-tion,** *n.* —**ren'o·va'tor,** *n.*

re·nown' (ri-nown′) *n.* a great reputation for achievements; fame. —**re·nowned'** (ri-nownd′) *adj.* famous.

rent *n.* **1,** payment for the use of property. **2,** an opening made by tearing; a separation. —*adj.* torn. —*v.t.* **1,** let; grant the use of, for payment. **2,** hire. —*v.i.* be leased or let out. —*v.* pret. & p.p. of *rend*.

rent'al (ren′təl) *n.* **1,** the rate paid as rent. **2,** income from rented property. —*adj.* pert. to rent.

re·nun″ci·a'tion (ri-nun″sē-ā′shən) *n.* act

of renouncing, esp. as a voluntary sacrifice. **—re·nun'ci·a·to"ry,** *adj.*

re·or'gan·ize" *v.t. & i.* organize again or in a new way, esp. of a business or corporation, **—re·or"gan·i·za'tion,** *n.*

rep *n.* **1,** a corded fabric. **2,** (*Slang*) reputation. **3,** (*Colloq.*) representative.

re·pair' (ri-pâr') *v.i.* go to a specified place. **—v.t. 1,** restore to good condition. **2,** make amends for; make good. **—n. 1,** act of restoring to good condition. **2,** good condition. **—re·pair'man",** *n.* [*pl.* **-men**]

rep'a·ra·ble (rep'ə-rə-bəl) *adj.* capable of being repaired.

rep"a·ra'tion (rep"ə-rā'shən) *n.* the act of making amends; (*pl.*) compensation for damage.

rep"ar·tee' (rep"ər-tē') *n.* a ready, pertinent, and witty reply; an exchange of such replies.

re·past' (ri-pàst') *n.* a meal.

re·pa·tri·ate" (rē-pā'trē-āt") *v.t. & i.* **1,** restore to one's own country. **2,** restore to citizenship. **—re·pa"tri·a'tion,** *n.*

re·pay' (rē-pā') *v.t.* **1,** pay back; refund. **2,** requite; return, as a visit. **—re·pay'ment,** *n.*

re·peal' (rē-pēl') *v.t.* recall or annul (a law); revoke; abrogate. **—n.** act of repealing; esp. (U.S., often *cap.*) the 21st Amendment, repealing the 18th (Prohibition) Amendment.

re·peat' (rē-pēt') *v.t.* **1,** do, make, or perform again. **2,** say again; reiterate. **3,** say over from memory; recite. **—v.i. 1,** say or do as before. **2,** vote more than once for one candidate at one election. **—n.** (*Music*) a sign (:) that a passage is to be repeated. **—re·peat'ed,** *adj.* frequent.

re·peat'er *n.* **1,** one who repeats. **2,** a watch that strikes. **3,** an automatic firearm.

re·pel' (ri-pel') *v.t.* [**re·pelled', -pel"ling**] **1,** drive back; force to return; check the advance of. **2,** resist; oppose; reject. **3,** arouse repulsion in; disgust. **—v.i.** be disgusting. **—re·pel'lence,** *n.* **—re·pel'lent,** *adj.*

re·pent' (ri-pent') *v.i. & t.* regret, grieve for, or do penance for (a sin or crime). **—re·pent'ance,** *n.* **—re·pent'ant,** *adj.*

re"per·cus'sion (rē"pər-kush'ən) *n.* **1,** the reaction to, or result of, an action. **2,** a rebounding; echo. **—re"per·cus'sive,** *adj.*

rep'er·toire" (rep'ər-twär") *n.* a list of the works a performer or company can perform.

rep'er·to·ry (rep'ər-tôr-ē) *n.* **1,** repertoire. **2,** an inventory; a stock. **3,** a storage location. **—adj.** designating a theatrical company performing various plays or operas.

rep"e·ti'tion (rep"ə-tish'ən) *n.* the act or result of repeating. **—re·pet'i·tive** (ri-pet'ə-tiv) *adj.*

rep"e·ti'tious (rep"ə-tish'əs) *adj.* characterized by undue or tiresome repetition. **—rep"e·ti'tious·ness,** *n.*

re·pine' (ri-pīn') *v.i.* complain; mourn.

re·place' (ri-plās') *v.t.* **1,** put back; restore; return. **2,** take the place of. **3,** substitute for.

re·place'ment (-mənt) *n.* **1,** act or effect of replacing. **2,** a substitute.

re·play' (rē-plā') *v.t.* play again. **—n.** (rē'plā") a playing again.

re·plen'ish (ri-plen'ish) *v.i.* fill again. **—re·plen'ish·ment,** *n.*

re·plete' (ri-plēt') *adj.* completely filled; stuffed. **—re·ple'tion,** *n.*

re·plev'in (ri-plev'ən) *n.* (*Law*) the recovery of one's property held by another, subject to later court judgment. **—v.t.** seize by replevin. Also, **re·plev'y** (-ē).

rep'li·ca (rep'li-kə) *n.* an exact copy; a duplicate; esp., an exact copy (of a work of art) made by the original artist.

re·ply' (ri-plī') *v.t. & i.* say in answer; respond. **—n.** an answer.

re·port' (ri-pôrt') *n.* **1,** a statement of facts or figures ascertained by investigation; an account or accounting. **2,** a rumor. **3,** (*pl.*) a record of court judgments and opinions. **4,** the sound of an explosion. **—v.i. 1,** serve as a reporter. **2,** present oneself for duty. **—v.t. 1,** give an account of; relate. **2,** say. **—re·port'ed·ly,** *adv.* **—report card, 1,** a school report giving a student's grades, teachers' comments, etc. **2,** an evaluation of work done, etc. (as of a politician).

re·port'age (rə-pôr'tij) *n.* the act or result of reporting, as of news.

re·port'er *n.* one who reports: a newspaper writer; a court stenographer.

rep"or·tor'i·al (rep"ər-tôr'ē-əl) *adj.* pert. to reporters or their work.

re·pose' (ri-pōz') *n.* **1,** a state of rest; sleep. **2,** tranquility; composure. **—v.i. 1,** lie at rest; be tranquil. **2,** be situated. **3,** rely. **—v.t. 1,** lay; place. **2,** set at rest. **—re·pos'al,** *n.* **—re·pose'ful,** *adj.*

re·pos'i·to·ry (ri-poz'i-tôr-ē) *n.* a place where things are situated or stored.

re"pos·sess' *v.t.* regain possession of, esp. something leased or sold conditionally. **—re"pos·ses'sion,** *n.*

rep"re·hend' (rep"ri-hend') *v.t.* chide sharply; reprove; censure. **—rep"re·hen'sion** (-hen'shən) *n.* **—rep"re·hen'sive,** *adj.* censorious.

rep"re·hen'si·ble (rep"ri-hens'ə-bəl) *adj.* highly blameworthy.

rep″re·sent′ (rep″ri-zent′) *v.t.* **1,** portray; depict; describe. **2,** play the rôle of; impersonate. **3,** denote; symbolize; stand for. **4,** speak and act for; be a substitute for. **5,** set forth; assert. **6,** be composed of; consist in. **7,** be a representative for, as in a legislature.

rep″re·sen·ta′tion (-zen-tā′shən) *n.* **1,** act or result of representing; a portrayal; description. **2,** a statement; a claim; a complaint. **3,** the right to be represented in a governing body. **4,** a delegation.

rep″re·sen′ta·tive (-zen′tə-tiv) *adj.* **1,** serving to represent. **2,** composed of delegates of the people. **3,** typical; characteristic. —*n.* one who or that which represents; an agent, delegate, or substitute; (*cap.*) a U.S. Congressman, member of the House of Representatives.

re·press′ (ri-pres′) *v.t.* **1,** put down; subdue; crush. **2,** keep under due restraint. —**re·pres′sion**(-presh′ən)*n.* —**re·pres′sive** (-pres′iv) *adj.*

re·prieve′ (ri-prēv′) *v.t.* **1,** grant a respite to; spare for a time. **2,** suspend or delay the execution of (a criminal). —*n.* a respite.

rep′ri·mand (rep′rə-mand″) *v.t.* reprove severely; censure, esp. publicly. —*n.* a severe reproof.

re·print′ *v.t.* print again. —*n.* (rē′print″) a reproduction or new edition of something printed.

re·pris′al (ri-prī′zəl) *n.* any act done in retaliation.

re·prise′ (ri-prēz′) *n.* (*Music*) a repetition of a main theme.

re·proach′ (ri-prōch′) *v.t.* charge with a fault; upbraid. —*n.* **1,** a severe expression of censure. **2,** shame; disgrace. **3,** a cause or object of disgrace. —**re·proach′ful,** *adj.* accusing; expressing blame.

rep′ro·bate″ (rep′rə-bāt″) *n.* one who is profligate or unprincipled; wicked. —*adj.* unprincipled; wicked. —*v.t.* **1,** condemn; censure. **2,** reject. —**rep″ro·ba′tion,** *n.*

re″pro·duce′ *v.t.* **1,** make a copy of; duplicate. **2,** procreate. **3,** produce again. —*v.i.* **1,** beget; generate offspring. **2,** be capable of being copied, as by printing.

re″pro·duc′tion *n.* **1,** act, process, or result of reproducing. **2,** a copy, picture, etc. —**re″pro·duc′tive,** *adj.*

re·prog′ra·phy (rē-prog′rə-fē) *n.* the photocopying of graphic material.

re·proof′ (ri-proof′) *n.* an expression of blame; rebuke.

re·prove′ (ri-proov′) *v.t.* censure; chide. —**re·prov′al,** *n.*

rep′tile (rep′til, -tīl) *n.* **1,** a creeping animal, as the snake, lizard, crocodile, etc. **2,** a low, mean person. —**rep·til′i·an,** *adj.*

re·pub′lic (ri-pub′lik) *n.* a nation whose government is wholly elected, having no king.

re·pub′li·can (ri-pub′li-kən)*adj.* **1,** being, pert. to, or favoring a republic. **2,** (*cap.*) designating one of the two chief political parties in the U.S. —*n.* **1,** one who favors republican government. **2,** (*cap.*) a member or adherent of the Republican party. —**re·pub′li·can·ism,** *n.*

re·pu′di·ate″ (ri-pū′dē-āt″) *v.t.* **1,** refuse to acknowledge or to pay. **2,** cast away; reject; renounce. —**re·pu″di·a′tion,** *n.*

re·pug′nance (ri-pug′nəns) *n.* **1,** a feeling of distaste or aversion. **2,** state of being repugnant.

re·pug′nant (ri-pug′nənt) *adj.* **1,** highly distasteful; offensive. **2,** contrary in nature.

re·pulse′ (ri-puls′) *v.t.* **1,** beat or drive back; repel. **2,** refuse; reject. —*n.* **1,** a driving back. **2,** refusal; denial.

re·pul′sion (ri-pul′shən) *n.* **1,** act or effect of repulsing. **2,** repugnance.

re·pul′sive (ri-pul′siv) *adj.* **1,** repelling. **2,** offensive; causing intense aversion. —**re·pul′sive·ness,** *n.*

rep′u·ta·ble (rep′yə-tə-bəl) *adj.* held in esteem; respectable. —**rep″u·ta·bil′i·ty,** *n.*

rep″u·ta′tion (rep″yə-tā′shən) *n.* **1,** the estimation of a person or thing by the community. **2,** fame.

re·pute′ (ri-pūt′) *n.* reputation; esp., good reputation. —*v.t.* hold in thought; regard; deem; estimate. —**re·put′ed,** *adj.* supposed to be. —**re·put′ed·ly,** *adv.* supposedly.

re·quest′ (ri-kwest′) *n.* **1,** an asking for something; a petition; demand. **2,** that which is asked for. —*v.t.* express desire for; ask. —*adj.* at someone's request.

re′qui·em (rek′wē-əm) *n.* a Mass for the dead; music for such a Mass.

re·quire′ (ri-kwīr′) *v.t.* **1,** ask or claim, as by right; demand; exact. **2,** order to do something; call on. **3,** need; want. —**re·quire′ment,** *n.*

req′ui·site (rek′wə-zit) *adj.* required; indispensable. —*n.* something essential or indispensable.

req″ui·si′tion (rek″wi-zish′ən) *n.* **1,** act of demanding. **2,** a written order, as for supplies. —*v.t.* order; seize officially.

re·quite′ (ri-kwīt′) *v.t.* repay (either good or evil); recompense; retaliate. —**re·quit′al,** *n.*

rere′dos (rir′dos) *n.* a screen or background, esp. behind an altar.

re′run′ (rē′run″) *v.t. & n.* replay.

re·scind′ (ri-sind′) *v.t.* abrogate; repeal; take back.

---

tub, cūte, pûll; labəl; oil, owl, go, chip, she, thin, *th*en, sing, ink; *see p. 6*

re·scis′sion (ri-sizh′ən) *n.* act of re-
scinding.

re′script (rē′skript) *n.* an edict.

res′cue (res′kū) *v.t.* deliver from danger
or evil; liberate. —*n.* an act of rescuing.

re·search′ (ri-sėrch′) *n.* study or investigation of facts, esp. scientific, not readily
available. —*v.t.* conduct researches into or
concerning. —**re′search″er**, *n.* one who
does research, esp. in assembling facts for
a writer.

re·sec′tion (ri-sek′shən) *n.* a cutting or
paring off, esp. of a bone.

re·sem′blance (ri-zem′bləns) *n.* similarity, esp. in appearance.

re·sem′ble (ri-zem′bəl) *v.t.* have similarity to; look alike.

re·sent′ (ri-zent′) *v.t.* consider to be an
injury or an affront. —**re·sent′ful**, *adj.* angry
at having been injured. —**re·sent′ment**, *n.*

re·ser′pine (ri-sûr′pin) *n.* a tranquilizer
and sedative.

res″er·va′tion (rez″ər-vā′shən) *n.* **1,** the
act of keeping back or withholding. **2,** anything withheld, as a qualification on a statement or contract. **3,** something reserved for
future use or occupation. **4,** a misgiving. **5,**
a qualification of approval. **6,** a tract of
public land set aside for some special use.

re·serve′ (ri-zėrv′) *v.t.* **1,** retain or set
apart for future or special use. **2,** keep as
one's own. —*n.* **1,** that which is kept for
future or special use, esp. capital retained
for future or contingent liabilities. **2,** a res-
ervation. **3,** self-restraint; a distant manner.
4, fighting men subject to call but not on
active duty. —**re·served′**, *adj.* reticent;
self-restrained.

re·serv′ist (ri-zėrv′ist) *n.* a member of a
military reserve force.

res′er·voir″ (rez′ər-vwär″) *n.* a supply
stored for future use; a place of such storage, esp. of water.

re·side′ (ri-zīd′) *v.i.* **1,** dwell permanently
or for a considerable time. **2,** be inherent
in, as a quality.

res′i·dence (rez′i-dəns) *n.* **1,** act or period of residing. **2,** a dwelling.

res′i·den·cy (rez′i-dən-sē) *n.* **1,** residence.
2, an official residence. **3,** living where
one's official duties lie.

res′i·dent (rez′i-dənt) *n.* one who dwells
(in a certain place). —**res″i·den′tial** (-den′-
shəl) *adj.* pert. to or consisting of dwellings.

re·sid′u·al (rə-zij′oo-əl) *adj.* remaining;
left over. —*n.* **1,** a residual quantity or
substance. **2,** (usu. *pl.*) payment given to a
performer in a recorded advertisement, concert, etc., each time it is replayed.

re·sid′u·ar·y (rə-zij′oo-er-ē) *adj.* **1,** remaining in an estate after deducting specific bequests. **2,** inheriting a residuary estate.

res′i·due″ (rez′i-dū″) *n.* that which is left
over; the remainder; the rest.

re·sid′u·um (ri-zij′oo-əm) *n.* [*pl.* **-a** (-ə)]
1, a residue. **2,** any residual product.

re·sign′ (ri-zīn′) *v.i.* **1,** submit oneself; be
reconciled; endure with patience. **2,** give
up an office, position, or post. —*v.t.* **1,**
relinquish. **2,** submit. —**re·signed′**, *adj.*
reconciled (to some ill).

res″ig·na′tion (rez″ig-nā′shən) *n.* **1,** act
or result of resigning. **2,** uncomplaining
acceptance of misfortune.

re·sil′i·ent (ri-zil′yənt) *adj.* **1,** springing
back; rebounding. **2,** buoyant; not readily
discouraged. —**re·sil′ience, re·sil′ien·cy,**
n.

res′in (rez′in) *n.* **1,** a hardened secretion
of many plants, esp. trees, used in varnish,
medicines, etc. **2,** rosin. —**res′in·ous,** *adj.*

re·sist′ (ri-zist′) *v.t.* **1,** oppose, exert physical or moral force against. **2,** withstand.
—*v.i.* make opposition to. —**re·sist′i·ble,**
adj. —**re·sis′tive,** *adj.*

re·sist′ance (-əns) *n.* **1,** the act or power
of resisting; the degree of an opposing force.
2, the extent to which an electrical conductor impedes a flow of current. —*adj.* utilizing electrical resistance.

re·sist′ant (-ənt) *adj.* resisting.

re·sis′to·jet″ (rē-zis′tō-jet″) *n.* a small
hydrogen- or ammonia-powered jet engine.

re·sist′or (ri₂-zis′tər) *n.* a resistant device
used in an electric circuit for protection or
control.

re·sole′ (rē-sōl′) *v.t.* put a new sole on (a
shoe).

res′o·lute (rez′ə-loot) *adj.* having a fixed
purpose; unwavering.

res″o·lu′tion (rez″ə-loo′shən) *n.* **1,** the
quality of having a fixed purpose; determination; firmness. **2,** something determined
upon; a decision of a legislative body. **3,**
the act of resolving; an analysis; a solution
or answer.

re·solve′ (ri-zolv′) *v.t.* **1,** determine; decide; express as a resolution. **2,** separate
into constituent parts; reduce by mental analysis; solve. —*v.i.* **1,** establish a purpose;
determine in the mind. **2,** become by analysis. —*n.* **1,** a resolution. **2,** firmness or
fixedness of purpose; determination.
—**re·solved′**, *adj.* determined; firm.

res′o·nant (rez′ə-nənt) *adj.* **1,** resounding; capable of decided sympathetic vibrations. **2,** having a rich, vibrant tone. —**res′-
o·nance,** *n.*

res'o·nate" (rez'ə-nāt") *v.i.* have or produce resonance; vibrate sympathetically.

res'o·na"tor (-ər) *n.* **1,** a device for increasing the vibrancy of tone. **2,** an instrument used in the analysis of sound. **3,** the high-frequency circuits of a radio receiving set. **4,** a small auxiliary muffler.

res·or'cin·ol (rez-ôr'si-nol) *n.* a derivative of benzene, used in medicines.

re·sort' (ri-zôrt') *v.i.* **1,** (with *to*) have recourse; apply. **2,** go customarily or frequently. —*n.* **1,** a place frequently visited. **2,** the act of having recourse to; a source of aid.

re·sound' (ri-zownd') *v.i.* **1,** ring with echoing sounds; reverberate; be filled with sound. **2,** give forth a loud sound.

re·sound'ing *adj.* **1,** ringing. **2,** thorough.

re·source' (ri-sôrs') *n.* **1,** any source of aid or support; an expedient to which one may resort. **2,** (*pl.*) available means; funds or supplies; assets. **3,** (*pl.*) the natural or collective wealth of a country. —**re·source'ful,** *adj.* clever in finding and utilizing resources. —**re·source'ful·ness,** *n.*

re·spect' (ri-spekt') *v.t.* **1,** treat with special consideration or high regard; heed. **2,** have reference to; relate to. —*n.* **1,** high esteem; courteous or considerate treatment. **2,** a point; a particular; a feature. **3,** (*pl.*) compliments.

re·spect'a·ble *adj.* **1,** worthy of esteem; highly regarded. **2,** decent. **3,** fairly good or large. —**re·spect"a·bil'i·ty,** *n.*

re·spect'ful *adj.* deferent.

re·spect'ing *prep.* regarding; concerning.

re·spec'tive (-spek'tiv) *adj.* pertaining individually to each. —**re·spec'tive·ly,** *adv.* with each in proper order.

res"pi·ra'tion (res"pə-rā'shən) *n.* breathing. —**re·spir'a·to·ry** (ri-spīr'ə-tôr-ē) *adj.*

res'pi·ra"tor (res'pə-rā"tər) *n.* **1,** a device to produce involuntary breathing. **2,** a mask to exclude noxious gases or substances.

re·spire' (ri-spīr') *v.i. & t.* breathe.

res'pite (res'pit) *n.* **1,** an interval of rest or relief. **2,** a postponement. —*v.t.* relieve temporarily; delay; postpone.

re·splend'ent (ri-splen'dənt) *adj.* shining with brilliant luster; splendid. —**re·splend'ence,** *n.*

re·spond' (ri-spond') *v.i.* **1,** give an answer; make a reply. **2,** show reaction to a force or stimulus.

re·spond'ent (ri-spon'dənt) *adj.* answering; responsive. —*n.* (*Law*) defendant.

re·sponse' (ri-spons') *n.* **1,** an answer or reply. **2,** a reaction. **3,** a verse said or sung by choir or congregation in reply to one

read by the pastor. —**re"spon·sor'i·al** (ri"-spon-sôr'ē-əl) *adj.*

re·spon"si·bil'i·ty (ri-spon"sə-bil'ə-tē) *n.* **1,** the state of being responsible. **2,** a duty; charge.

re·spon'si·ble (ri-spon'sə-bəl) *adj.* **1,** answerable; accountable. **2,** able to satisfy any reasonable claim. **3,** involving important work or trust.

re·spon'sive (ri-spon'siv) *adj.* **1,** readily answering or reacting. **2,** constituting an answer or reaction. **3,** pert. to the use of responses. —**re·spon'sive·ness,** *n.*

rest *n.* **1,** a state of quiet or repose. **2,** freedom from care; peace; quiet. **3,** sleep. **4,** a place of quiet; a shelter. **5,** that on or in which anything leans for support. **6,** (*Music*) a silence or pause between tones; the symbol for this silence. **7,** that which is left; remainder. —*v.i.* **1,** cease action or performance; be without motion; pause. **2,** take repose; be tranquil. **3,** have a foundation; be supported. **4,** remain. **5,** lean; trust; rely. —*v.t.* **1,** place at rest; give repose to. **2,** lay or place, as on a foundation. **3,** leave; allow to stand. —**rest room,** a water closet.

res'tau·rant (res'tə-rənt) *n.* a place where meals are sold; a public eating house.

res"tau·ra·teur' (res"tə-rə-tẽr') *n.* the proprietor or manager of a restaurant.

rest'ful *adj.* promoting comfort or tranquillity. —**rest'ful·ness,** *n.*

res"ti·tu'tion (res"tə-tū'shən) *n.* **1,** the act of returning or restoring to someone what is his. **2,** the act of making amends. **3,** restoration.

res'tive (res'tiv) *adj.* **1,** uneasy; impatient. **2,** refractory.

rest'less (-ləs) *adj.* **1,** unable to rest or sleep; uneasy. **2,** unsettled; continually moving. —**rest'less·ness,** *n.*

res"to·ra'tion (res"tə-rā'shən) *n.* **1,** the act of restoring or being restored. **2,** that which is restored. **3,** (*cap.*) the reestablishment of the British monarchy in 1660.

re·stor'a·tive (ri-stôr'ə-tiv) *adj.* healing; stimulating. —*n.* a food, drink, or medicine that heals or stimulates.

re·store' (ri-stôr') *v.t.* **1,** bring back to a former state; return to a former position. **2,** heal; cure. **3,** renew or reestablish after interruption. **4,** return (something lost or taken) to the owner.

re·strain' (ri-strān') *v.t.* hold back; check; repress; restrict; confine.

re·straint' (ri-strānt') *n.* **1,** the act of holding back; hindrance; confinement. **2,** reserve; self-control. **3,** a limitation.

re·strict' (ri-strikt') *v.t.* attach limitations to; limit; restrain. —**re·stric'tion,** *n.* —**re·stric'tive,** *adj.*

re·sult' (ri-zult') *v.i.* **1,** proceed or arise as a consequence or effect; be the outcome. **2,** (with *in*) terminate. —*n:* **1,** a consequence; effect; outcome. **2,** (*Math.*) a quantity or value obtained by calculation.

re·sult'ant (ri-zul'tənt) *adj.* following as a result or consequence. —*n.* that which follows as a consequence.

re·sume' (ri-zoom') *v.t.* take up again after interruption; begin again. —*v.i.* proceed after interruption.

ré''su·mé' (rez''oo-mā') *n.* a summary, esp. of a person's achievements.

re·sump'tion (ri-zum'shən) *n.* act or effect of resuming.

re·surge' (rĕ-sērj') *v.i.* rise again; revive; reappear. —**re·sur'gent,** *adj.* —**re·sur'gence,** *n.*

res''ur·rect' (rez''ə-rekt') *v.t.* **1,** restore to life; reanimate; renew; reconstruct. **2,** bring back from the dead. **3,** disinter.

res''ur·rec'tion (rez''ə-rek'shən) *n.* **1,** act or result of resurrecting. **2,** (*cap.*) the rebirth of souls on the judgment day. **3,** (*cap.,* with *the*) the rising of Christ from the dead.

re·sus'ci·tate'' (ri-sus'ə-tāt'') *v.t. & i.* revive; bring to life again. —**re·sus''ci·ta'tion,** *n.*

re·ta'ble (ri-tā'bəl) *n.* a shelf above an altar for candles, flowers, etc.

re'tail (rē'tāl) *n.* the sale of commodities in small quantities to the ultimate consumer. —*adj.* pert. to such sales. —*v.t.* **1,** sell to the ultimate consumer. **2,** (ri-tāl') tell in detail. —**re'tail''er,** *n.* the keeper of a store.

re·tain' (ri-tān') *v.t.* **1,** hold or keep in possession, use, or practice. **2,** keep in mind; remember. **3,** engage the services of. —**retaining wall,** a wall to prevent a mass of earth from slipping.

re·tain'er (ri-tān'ər) *n.* **1,** that which holds in, as a retaining wall. **2,** a servant long employed. **3,** a fee paid to secure services, esp. of a lawyer.

re·take' (rē-tāk') *v.t.* **1,** take again; recapture. **2,** photograph again. —*n.* (rē'tāk'') a second photographing, as of a motion picture scene.

re·tal'i·ate'' (ri-tal'ē-āt'') *v.t. & i.* return like for like, esp. evil for evil. —**re·tal''i·a'tion,** *n.* —**re·tal'i·a·to·ry,** *adj.*

re·tard' (ri-tärd') *v.t.* **1,** make slow or slower; obstruct. **2,** defer; postpone. —**re·tar'dant,** *adj.* —**re''tar·da'tion,** *n.* —**re·tar'ded,** *adj.*

re·tard'ate (rē-tär'dāt) *n.* a mentally retarded person.

retch (rech) *v.i.* strain, as in vomiting; try to vomit.

re·ten'tion (ri-ten'shən) *n.* **1,** act or re-

sult of retaining. **2,** memory. —**re·ten'tive,** *adj.* serving or tending to retain.

ret'i·cent (ret'ə-sənt) *adj.* disposed to be silent; reserved. —**ret'i·cence,** *n.*

ret'i·cle (ret'i-kəl) *n.* a glass plate divided into small squares by fine lines, as used in a telescope to locate stars, etc.

re·tic'u·late'' (ri-tik'yə-lāt'') *adj.* being or resembling a network. Also, **re·tic'u·lar** (-lər). —*v.t. & i.* form or form into a network.

ret'i·cule'' (ret'ə-kūl'') *n.* a woman's handbag, orig. of network.

ret'i·na (ret'i-nə) *n.* the innermost coating of the back of the eye, extending in to the optic nerve and receiving the images of vision. —**ret'i·nal,** *adj.*

ret'i·nue'' (ret'ə-nū'') *n.* a body of followers or attendants.

re·tire' (ri-tīr') *v.i.* **1,** draw back; retreat. **2,** go into a private place. **3,** withdraw from business or public life. **4,** go to bed. —*v.t.* **1,** take or lead back; withdraw. **2,** make inactive; relieve of duty. **3,** withdraw from circulation, as bonds. —**re·tire'ment,** *n.*

re·tired' *adj.* **1,** having discontinued work after long service. **2,** sequestered; secluded.

re·tir'ing *adj.* diffident; shy.

re·tort' (ri-tôrt') *v.t.* **1,** return or turn back, as an argument upon the originator; retaliate. **2,** reply sharply. —*v.i.* make a sharp reply. —*n.* **1,** a retaliatory remark. **2,** a glass vessel with a long neck, used in chemistry.

re·touch' (rē-tuch') *v.t.* alter details of (a painting, photograph, film, or engraving) for improvement.

re·trace' (rē-trās') *v.t.* **1,** go back over; trace backward. **2,** trace again, as a drawing.

re·tract' (ri-trakt') *v.t.* **1,** draw back or in, as a cat's claws. **2,** take back; undo; recant. —*v.i.* **1,** shrink back; recede. **2,** undo or unsay what has been previously done or said.

re·trac'tile (ri-trak'til) *adj.* capable of being drawn back in.

re·trac'tion (ri-trak'shən) *n.* a disclaimer of, or apology for, an incorrect statement.

re·trac'tive (-tiv) *adj.* drawing back in.

re·trac'tor *n.* **1,** a muscle that draws back a part of the body. **2,** anything that serves to retract.

re·tread' (rē-tred') *v.t.* **1,** tread again. **2,** recap or cut grooves in (a tire). —*n.* (rē'tred'') a retreaded tire.

re·treat' (ri-trēt') *n.* **1,** the act of withdrawing; a backward movement under enemy pressure. **2,** a state of seclusion;

retirement. **3,** a place of retirement, privacy, or security. **4,** an asylum. **5,** (*Mil.*) the bugle call that signals retirement from action. —*v.i.* go back; run from an enemy.

re·trench' (ri-trench') *v.t. & i.* cut down; curtail, esp. expenses; economize. —**re·trench'ment,** *n.*

ret''ri·bu'tion (ret''rə-bū'shən) *n.* reward or punishment for past good or evil, esp. punishment for evil. —**re·trib'u·tive** (ri-trib'yû-tiv) *adj.*

re·trieve' (ri-trēv') *v.t. & i.* **1,** find again; recover; regain. **2,** search for and bring in killed or wounded game.

re·triev'er (ri-trē'vər) *n.* a dog bred or trained to bring in game.

ret·ro- (ret-rō) *pref.* back; backward; behind.

ret''ro·ac'tive *adj.* applicable to past events, as a law. —**ret''ro·ac·tiv'i·ty,** *n.*

ret''ro·grade'' (ret'rə-grād'') *adj.* **1,** moving or directed backward; retreating. **2,** deteriorating. —*v.i.* go or move backward; lose ground; deteriorate. —**ret''ro·gra·da'tion,** *n.*

ret''ro·gress'' (ret'rə-gres'') *v.i.* revert to a worse condition; decline. —**ret''ro·gres'sion** (-gresh'ən) backward movement; deterioration. —**ret''ro·gres'sive,** *adj.*

ret''ro·rock'et *n.* an auxiliary rocket or jet engine on a spacecraft or satellite used to slow down its speed, as for landing on a celestial body.

ret'ro·spect'' (ret'rə-spekt'') *n.* the act of looking backward; contemplation of the past.

ret''ro·spec'tion (-spek'shən) *n.* the act of looking backward (in time).

ret''ro·spec'tive (-iv) *adj.* **1,** looking back on or occurring in the past. **2,** retroactive. —*n.* an exhibition of the works of an artist, composer, etc., covering a wide period of his career.

re''trous·sé' (ret''roo-sā') *adj.* (of a nose) turned up.

re·turn' (ri-tẽrn') *v.i.* **1,** come or go back to a former place, position, or state. **2,** recur. **3,** make a reply; retort. —*v.t.* **1,** send or give back; restore. **2,** cast back; reflect. **3,** repay; requite. **4,** report. **5,** elect or reelect to office. **6,** yield (a profit). —*n.* **1,** the act or an act of returning; a recurrence; repayment. **2,** (*pl.*) a result, esp. of an election. **3,** a profit or yield. **4,** a reply. **5,** a report on one's earnings, for income tax purposes. —**re·turn'ee'',** *n.*

Reu'ben (roo'bən) *adj.* denoting a toasted sandwich of corned beef, sauerkraut, and Swiss cheese.

re·un'ion (rē-ūn'yən) *n.* **1,** the act of uniting again. **2,** a gathering of friends, relatives, etc.

re·up' *v.i.* (*Slang*) reenlist.

rev (*Slang*) *v.t.* [**revved, rev'ving**] increase the number of revolutions per minute of (a motor). —*n.* a revolution.

re·vamp' (rē-vamp') *v.t.* remodel; renovate.

re·veal' (ri-vēl') *v.t.* make known; disclose; divulge.

rev·eil'le (rev'ə-lē) *n.* (*Mil.*) a bugle call sounded at daybreak.

rev'el (rev'əl) *v.i.* **1,** join in merrymaking; carouse. **2,** take great pleasure (in); delight (in). —*n.* a boisterous merrymaking. —**rev'el·ry,** *n.*

rev''e·la'tion (rev''ə-lā'shən) *n.* **1,** the act of revealing; a disclosure, esp. by supernatural means. **2,** a striking accession of information.

re·venge' (ri-venj') *v.t.* inflict punishment because of; avenge. —*n.* retaliation for wrongs. —**re·venge'ful,** *adj.* seeking vengeance.

rev'e·nue'' (rev'ə-nū'') *n.* **1,** income from real or personal property. **2,** the income of a state from taxation. **3,** the department that collects such taxes, etc. —**revenue sharing,** the return of part of federal tax revenues to the states, state to city, etc.

re·ver'ber·ate'' (ri-vẽr'bə-rāt'') *v.t.* return as sound; reecho. —**re·ver''ber·a'tion,** *n.* a series of echoes. Also, *colloq.,* **re'verb''** (rē'vẽrb'') *n.*

re·vere' (ri-vir') *v.t.* regard with deepest respect and awe; venerate. —*n.* revers.

rev'er·ence (rev'ər-əns) *n.* **1,** act of revering; veneration. **2,** title of certain clergymen. **3,** a bow or curtsy.

rev'er·end (rev'ər-ənd) *adj.* deserving of respect: applied to a clergyman. —*n.* (*Colloq.*) a clergyman.

rev'er·ent (rev'ər-ənt) *adj.* **1,** respectful. **2,** devout. —**rev''er·en'tial** (-en'shəl) *adj.* characterized by awe or respect.

rev'er·ie (rev'ə-rē) *n.* a state of fanciful meditation; a daydream.

re·vers' (rə-vir') *n. sing. & pl.* a part of a garment turned back, as a lapel. Also, **re·vere'.**

re·verse' (ri-vẽrs') *adj.* turned backward; opposite; contrary. —*n.* **1,** a change to an opposite form, state, condition, or direction. **2,** a change of fortune, specif. for the worse. **3,** the opposite; the contrary, esp., the back of a coin or medal. —*v.t.* **1,** turn about, around, upside down, or in an opposite direction. **2,** set aside; annul, as a legal decree. —*v.i.* change to an opposite position, direction, motion, etc. —**re·ver'sal,** *n.* —**re·vers'i·ble,** *adj.*

re·ver'sion (ri-vẽr'shən) *n.* **1,** act or result of reverting. **2,** the right of future possession of a property. —**re·ver′sion·ar·y,** *adj.*

re·vert′ (ri-vẽrt′) *v.i.* go back to a former place, position, or state.

re·vet′ (ri-vet′) *v.t.* put a facing of masonry on an embankment, etc. —**re·vet′ment,** *n.*

re·view′ (ri-vū′) *n.* **1,** a going over anything again; an examination. **2,** a survey of the past. **3,** a critical report, as of a book or play; a periodical devoted to critical articles. **4,** (*Mil.*) a formal inspection; parade. **5,** (*Law*) a judicial reconsideration by a higher court. —*v.t.* **1,** look back upon. **2,** repeat; examine again. **3,** write about critically. **4,** (*Mil.*) make a formal inspection of. —**re·view′er,** *n.* one who reviews; a critic.

re·vile′ (ri-vīl′) *v.t.* abuse in speech or writing. —**re·vile′ment,** *n.*

re·vise′ (ri-vīz′) *v.t.* make changes or corrections in; amend. —*n.* **1,** a review and correction. **2,** a proof sheet taken after corrections have been made.

re·vi′sion (ri-vizh′ən) *n.* act or result of revising.

re·viv′al (ri-vīv′əl) *n.* **1,** act or effect of reviving; restoration. **2,** a meeting to promote religious awakening. **3,** the reproduction of a play, film, etc., formerly presented.

re·vive′ (ri-vīv′) *v.i.* come back to life after apparent death; be renewed or refreshed. —*v.t.* **1,** bring back to life or use. **2,** refresh; recall; reawaken. **3,** produce again (a play, etc., formerly presented).

rev′o·ca·ble (rev′ə-kə-bəl) *adj.* subject to being revoked.

rev″o·ca′tion (rev″ə-kā′shən) *n.* annulment; recall.

re·voke′ (ri-vōk′) *v.t.* annul by taking back; repeal; cancel. —*v.i.* in card playing, fail to follow suit when able and obliged to do so. —*n.* in card playing, act or instance of revoking.

re·volt′ (ri-vōlt′) *n.* an uprising against government or authority; rebellion; insurrection. —*v.i.* break away from established authority; rebel. —*v.t.* repel; shock. —**re·volt′ing,** *adj.* repulsive.

rev″o·lu′tion (rev″ə-loo′shən) *n.* **1,** the act of revolting. **2,** a complete rotation. **3,** the act of traveling completely around a circuit. **4,** a cycle. **5,** a total change of conditions, specif. a radical social or political change; a major revolt.

rev″o·lu′tion·ar·y (-er-ē) *adj.* **1,** pert. to a revolution. **2,** revolving. **3,** drastic; radical. —*n.* a revolutionist.

rev″o·lu′tion·ist *n.* one who participates in a revolution.

rev″o·lu′tion·ize (-īz″) *v.t.* effect an extreme change in.

re·volve′ (ri-volv′) *v.i.* **1,** turn or roll around on an axis; rotate. **2,** move about a center. **3,** pass through periodic changes; recur. —*v.t.* turn or cause to roll around, as on an axis. —**revolving charge account,** a charge account that charges a fixed rate of interest each month on the balance remaining due at the beginning or end of that month or on the average balance due during that month. —**revolving fund,** one maintained by balanced borrowings and repayments.

re·volv′er *n.* a repeating pistol having a revolving cylinder to hold cartridges.

re·vue′ (ri-vū′) *n.* a musical variety show, usually of parodies.

re·vul′sion (ri-vul′shən) *n.* a sudden, violent change of feeling.

re·ward′ (ri-wôrd′) *v.t.* **1,** repay, as for good conduct or merit; recompense. **2,** make a return for. —*n.* **1,** a repayment or prize for merit or accomplishment. **2,** profit. **3,** a sum of money offered for the finding of a criminal or of a lost article. —**re·ward′ing,** *adj.*

re·write′ (rē-rīt′) *v.t.* write again in different words or form. —*n.* (rē′rīt″) something rewritten, esp. a newspaper story from oral report.

rex (reks) *n.* [*pl.* **re′ges** (rē′jēz)] a king.

rhap′so·dize″ (rap′sə-dīz″) *v.t. & i.* speak or write rhapsodically.

rhap′so·dy (rap′sə-dē) *n.* **1,** an expression of extravagant enthusiasm. **2,** a musical composition in irregular form with striking changes of tempo and rhythm. —**rhap·sod′ic** (-sod′ik) *adj.* —**rhap·sod′i·cal·ly,** *adv.*

rhe′a (rē′ə) *n.* the three-toed ostrich.

-rhe·a (rē-ə) *suf.* flow; discharge.

rhe′ni·um (rē′nē-əm) *n.* a rare heavy metallic element, symbol Re, no. 75.

rhe·o- (rē-ō, rē-ə) *pref.* flow; current.

rhe′o·stat″ (rē′ə-stat″) *n.* a resistance coil for regulating or adjusting electric current. Also, **resistance box.**

rhe′sus (rē′səs) *n.* a macaque.

rhet′o·ric (ret′ə-rik) *n.* **1,** the art of using language effectively. **2,** (*Colloq.*) inflammatory language. —**rhet″o·ri′cian** (-rish′ən) *n.*

rhe·tor′i·cal (rə-tôr′i-kəl) *adj.* **1,** pert. to rhetoric. **2,** for effect only; not intended to be taken literally.

rheum (room) *n.* a cold.

rheu·mat′ic (roo-mat′ik) *adj.* pert. to rheumatism. —*n.* one subject to rheumatism. —**rheumatic fever,** a disease, usually of children, affecting the joints and heart. —**rheu·mat′i·cal·ly,** *adv.*

rheu′ma·tism (roo′mə-tiz-əm) *n.* a disease characterized by inflammation of the joints. —**rheu'ma·toid,** *adj.*

Rh factor a property of the blood which when present (Rh positive) may cause agglutination of the red cells.

rhi'nal (rī'nəl) *adj.* pert. to the nose; nasal.

rhine'stone" (rīn'stōn") *n.* **1,** imitation diamond. **2,** rock crystal.

rhi·ni'tis (rī-nī'tis) *n.* an inflammation of the nasal mucous membrane.

rhi·no- (rī-nō) *pref.* nose.

rhi·noc'er·os (rī-nos'ər-əs) *n.* a large pachyderm with one or two upright horns on the snout. Also, **rhi'no** (rī'nō).

rho (rō) *n.* the 17th letter of the Greek alphabet (P, ρ).

rho'di·um (rō'dē-əm) *n.* a metallic chemical element, no. 45, symbol Rh.

rho"do·den'dron (rō"də-den'drən) *n.* any of various hardy shrubs bearing flowers in clusters.

rhom'boid (rom'boid) *n.* a parallelogram with opposite sides equal and no right angle.

rhom'bus (rom'bəs) *n.* an equilateral parallelogram with no right angle.

rhu'barb (roo'bärb) *n.* **1,** a garden plant with tender, pink, acid leafstalks, used for sauce, pies, etc. **2,** the root of an Oriental rhubarb, used in medicines. **3,** (*Slang*) noisy objection to an arbiter's decision.

rhyme (rīm) *n.* **1,** agreement in the terminal sounds of words or verses. **2,** a couplet or short poem containing rhymes. **3,** a word that rhymes with another. —*v.i. & t.* make a rhyme or rhymes. Also, **rime.** —**rhyme'-ster,** *n.* a writer of light or mediocre verse.

rhythm (ri*th*'əm) *n.* **1,** movement characterized by equal or regularly alternating beats. **2,** that quality in music or poetry which is produced by a regular succession of accents; cadence. **3,** recurrence at regular or uniform intervals. —**rhyth'mic, rhyth'mi·cal,** *adj.* —**rhythm and blues,** a style of popular music characterized by strong, driving rhythm. —**rhythm method,** a method of birth control based on abstention from sexual intercourse during ovulation.

ri·al' (rē-äl') *n.* a monetary unit of Iran.

ri·al'to (rē-al'tō) *n.* **1,** a theatrical district, esp. in New York City. **2,** a market place, esp. (*cap.*) in Venice.

ri·a'ta (rē-ä'tə) *n.* a lariat.

rib *n.* **1,** one of the series of curved bones enclosing the chest of man and animals. **2,** something likened to such a bone; a slender elongated member, timber, or ridge. —*v.t.* [**ribbed, rib'bing**] **1,** strengthen or support by ribs. **2,** (*Colloq.*) tease.

rib'ald (rib'əld) *adj.* coarsely humorous. —**rib'ald·ry,** *n.*

rib'bon (rib'ən) *n.* **1,** a narrow strip of fabric, as silk; a similar strip of paper, metal, etc., or of color. **2,** a tape for trimming. **3,** (*pl.*) shreds. **4,** an inked tape for a typewriter. Also, **rib'and** (-ənd). —*v.t.* **1,** adorn with ribbons. **2,** streak; stripe. **3,** shred.

ri"bo·fla'vin (rī"bō-flā'vin) *n.* a vitamin property, esp. vitamin B$_2$.

rice (rīs) *n.* the grain from a plant grown in warm climates. —*v.t.* press into shreds. —**ric'er,** *n.* a utensil for ricing potatoes, etc. —**rice paper,** a thin paper made from rice, straw, or from the pith of a shrub.

rich *adj.* **1,** having much money or great possessions; wealthy. **2,** abundantly supplied; abounding. **3,** productive; fertile. **4,** elegant; luxurious; costly. **5,** full in tone; strong in color; vivid. **6,** containing desirable, nutritious, or fattening ingredients. **7,** (*Colloq.*) preposterous. —**rich'es,** *n.pl.* wealth. —**rich'ness,** *n.*

Rich'ter scale (rikh'tər) a logarithmic scale from 1 to 10, used to indicate the force of an earthquake.

rick (rik) *n.* a heap or pile, as of hay.

rick'ets (rik'its) *n.* a disease characterized by softness of the bones and distortions, usu. caused by malnutrition.

rick·ett'si·a (ri-ket'sē-ə) *n.* the microorganisms which cause typhus and other diseases.

rick'et·y (rik'ə-tē) *adj.* **1,** tottering; shaky. **2,** affected with rickets.

rick'ey (rik'ē) *n.* a cold drink made of lime juice, carbonated water, and gin: *gin rickey.*

rick'rack" (rik'rak") *n.* a narrow zigzag openwork braid used for trimming.

rick'sha (rik'shä) *n.* (*Colloq.*) jinrikisha.

ric"o·chet' (rik"ə-shā') *n.* a rebounding or a skipping of an object passing over a flat surface. —*v.i.* rebound and glance off.

ri·cot'ta (rē-kot'ə) *n.* Ital. cottage cheese.

rid *v.t.* [**rid, rid'ding**] free from anything superfluous or objectionable. —*adj.* clear or relieved (of). —**get rid of, 1,** get free of. **2,** do away with.

rid'dance (rid'əns) *n.* the act of ridding; deliverance. —**good riddance,** a welcome relief.

rid'den (rid'ən) *v.* p.p. of **ride.**

rid'dle (rid'əl) *n.* **1,** a puzzling question; an enigma; a perplexing person or thing. **2,** a coarse sieve. —*v.t.* **1,** fill with holes, by or as by shot. **2,** sift through a coarse sieve.

ride (rīd) *v.i.* [**rode** (rōd), **rid'den** (rid'ən), **rid'ing**] **1,** be carried on an animal's back or in a vehicle, ship, or plane. **2,** (of a ship) float. **3,** move on or about something. **4,** carry passengers. **5,** climb up, as an ill-fitting coat. —*v.t.* **1,** sit on and manage (a horse) in motion. **2,** travel on, through, or over. **3,** treat harshly; tease; harass. —*n.* a journey on which one is borne.

rid′er (rīd′ər) *n.* **1,** one who or that which rides. **2,** a clause added to a document. —**rid′er·ship″,** *n.* the people who ride (as the subway, etc.).

ridge (rij) *n.* **1,** the crest of two sloping surfaces rising to meet at an angle. **2,** a mountain or hill in this form. —*v.t. & i.* form into, provide with, or mark with, ridges.

ridge′pole″ *n.* the horizontal timber at the top of a roof.

rid′i·cule″ (rid′ə-kūl″) *n.* incitement of contemptuous laughter; derision. —*v.t.* make to appear absurd.

ri·dic′u·lous (ri-dik′yə-ləs) *adj.* laughable; absurd; preposterous. —**ri·dic′u·lous·ness,** *n.*

rid′ing (rīd′ing) *n.* (*Brit.*) a district.

rife (rīf) *adj.* prevalent; current.

riff (rif) *n.* a note or phrase serving to punctuate swing music.

rif′fle (rif′əl) *n.* **1,** a ripple, as on water. **2,** a method of shuffling cards. **3,** grooves on the bottom of a sluice for catching particles of mineral. —*v.* [**-fled** (-əld), **-fling**] **1,** form or become a riffle. **2,** flutter, as pages. **3,** shuffle (cards).

riff′raff″ (rif′raf″) *n.* **1,** scraps; rubbish; trash. **2,** the rabble.

ri′fle (rī′fəl) *v.t.* **1,** search, esp. to rob; ransack; plunder. **2,** cut spiral grooves in (the bore of a gun barrel). —*n.* a portable firearm or a cannon having a rifled bore. —**ri′fle·man** (-mən) *n.* —**ri′fling,** *n.* spiral grooves cut in the bore of a gun causing the bullet to spin.

rift *n.* an opening made by splitting; a cleft or crevice; a fissure.

rig *v.t.* [**rigged, rig′ging**] **1,** fit with necessary equipment, as a ship with sails. **2,** (with *out*) dress, oddly or gaudily. **3,** raise or lower (prices) artificially. —*n.* **1,** (*Naut.*) arrangement of masts, sails, etc. **2,** dress; equipment. **3,** a light, horse-drawn vehicle.

rig″a·doon′ (rig″ə-doon′) *n.* a former lively dance for one couple; the music for this dance.

rig′a·ma·role″ (rig′ə-mə-rōl″) *n.* rigmarole.

rig′ger (rig′ər) *n.* a mover of heavy objects.

rig′ging (rig′ing) *n.* (*Naut.*) rig, especially sails, masts, etc.

right (rīt) *adj.* **1,** in conformity with the moral law or standards; just; good. **2,** in conformity with truth, fact, or reason; correct; also orderly. **3,** proper; fitting; convenient. **4,** in good condition. **5,** pert. to the side or direction that is eastward when one faces north. **6,** conservative, in politics. **7,** straight; direct. —*adv.* **1,** directly. **2,** justly. **3,** properly. **4,** correctly; exactly. **5,** very. **6,** toward the right side. —*n.* **1,** conformity to an authoritative standard. **2,** that which conforms to a rule. **3,** a just claim or title. **4,** the right side or direction. **5,** (*cap.*) the Conservative party. —*v.t.* **1** set straight; adjust or correct. **2,** vindicate. —*v.i.* resume a vertical position. —**right angle,** an angle of 90° —**right of way, 1,** the right to proceed before another. **2,** land over which a railroad, etc., may pass. **3,** a right of passage. —**right on!,** (*Slang*) exactly right! —**right triangle,** a triangle with one right angle. —**right wing,** ultraconservative.

right′a·bout″ *n.* the opposite direction. —*adv.* in a half circle.

right′eous (rī′chəs) *adj.* virtuous; devout. —**right′eous·ness,** *n.*

right′ful *adj.* having or based on a just claim. —**right′ful·ness,** *n.*

right-′hand″ *adj.* to the right; for the right hand. —**right-hand man,** a chief assistant. —**right-′hand″ed,** *adj.* more adept with the right hand than with the left.

right′ist *n.* a conservative in politics. —**right′ism,** *n.*

rig′id (rij′id) *adj.* **1,** stiff, not pliant or easily bent; inflexible; unyielding. **2,** strict; exacting. —**ri·gid′i·ty,** *n.*

rig′ma·role″ (rig′mə-rōl″) *n.* long, incoherent discourse; nonsense; unnecessary formalities.

rig′or (rig′ər) *n.* **1,** stiffness; inflexibility. **2,** strictness; austerity; sternness. Also, **rig′our.** —**rig′or·ous,** *adj.* —**ri″gor mor′tis** (rig″ər-môr′tis) the stiffening of the body after death.

rile (rīl) *v.t.* (*Colloq.*) annoy; vex.

rill (ril) *n.* a small brook.

rim *n.* **1,** the border, edge, or margin of anything. **2,** of a wheel, the outer part. —*v.t.* [**rimmed, rim′ming**] surround with a rim or border.

rime (rīm) *n.* **1,** rhyme. **2,** white frost; hoarfrost. —*v.t. & i.* rhyme. —**rim′y,** *adj.*

rind (rīnd) *n.* an outer covering; a thick skin.

ring *v.i.* [**rang, rung, ring′ing**] **1,** resound, as a bell when struck. **2,** give a signal with a bell. **3,** sound loudly and clearly. **4,** have the sensation of a humming or buzzing sound. **5,** reverberate; re-echo. —*v.t.* **1,** cause (a bell, etc.) to sound. **2,** announce;

celebrate. **3**, (with *up*) (*Brit.*) telephone to. **4**, (with *in*) introduce unfairly. **5**, [*pret. & p.p.* **ringed**] encircle; surround with, or as with, a ring. —*n.* **1**, the sound of a bell; a peal or clang; resonance. **2**, a telephone call. **3**, a circular band or hoop; an ornamental band for the finger, etc. **4**, anything circular; arrangement or array in a circle. **5**, a group. **6**, an area for sports, exhibitions, etc.; arena. **7**, prizefighting.

ringed (ringd) *adj.* **1**, encircled. **2**, formed into or like a ring. **3**, wearing a ring or rings. **4**, marked with rings.

ring'er *n.* **1**, in quoits, a cast that encircles the pin. **2**, (*Slang*) a person who greatly resembles another: *dead ringer*. **3**, (*Slang*) a superior athlete, race horse, performer, etc., usu. entered at the last minute, often under an assumed name. **4**, (*Slang*) one who votes fraudulently.

ring'lead"er *n.* a leader in mischief or objectionable acts.

ring'let *n.* a curl of hair.

ring'mas"ter *n.* one in charge of the performances in a circus ring, or, often, of the entire circus.

ring'side" *n.* the seating space next to a boxing ring.

ring'worm" *n.* a contagious skin disease.

rink *n.* a section of ice, or a floor, for skating; the building containing it.

rink'y-dink" (ring'kē-dink") *adj.* (*Slang*) cheap; shabby.

rinse (rins) *v.t.* wash lightly, esp. wash out (soap) with fresh water. —*n.* a light wash, as for removing soap, dyeing hair, etc.

ri'ot (rī'ət) *n.* **1**, a disturbance arising from disorderly conduct; a brawl. **2**, revelry. **3**, confusion; a haphazard mixture. **4**, (*Slang*) a cause of hearty laughter. —*v.i.* act without restraint. —**ri'ot·ous**, *adj.*

rip *v.t. & i.* [**ripped, rip'ping**] **1**, tear or cut open or off; slit; undo a seam. **2**, saw (wood) with the grain. **3**, (*Colloq.*) utter with violence. **4**, (with *off*) (*Slang*) cheat; steal. —*v.i.* **1**, be torn or split open. **2**, (*Colloq.*) rush headlong. —*n.* **1**, a rent or tear made by ripping. **2**, a rapid. **3**, (*Colloq.*) a roué. —**rip'per**, *n.* —**rip cord**, a cord for opening a parachute during descent.

ri·par'i·an (ri-pār'ē-ən) *adj.* pert. to, or situated on, the bank of a river, lake, etc.

ripe (rīp) *adj.* **1**, ready for harvest; mature. **2**, in the best condition for use. **3**, ready for action or effect. —**ripe'ness**, *n.*

rip'en (rī'pən) *v.t. & i.* make or become ripe; mature.

rip'off" *n.* (*Slang*) a deception; swindle.

ri·poste' (ri-pōst') *n.* a return thrust in fencing; a clever retort.

rip'ping (rip'ing) *adj.* splendid.

rip'ple (rip'əl) *n.* **1**, the light ruffling of the surface of the water; a little wave. **2**, a sound of or like that of water running over a stony bottom. —*v.t. & i.* **1**, form ripples (in). **2**, make a sound like rippling water. —*v.t.* agitate; mark with ripples. —**rip'plet**, *n.* a small ripple.

rip'roar"ing *adj.* boisterously exhilarating; hilarious; jolly.

rip'saw" *n.* a saw with coarse teeth, for sawing with the grain.

rip'snort"er (rip'snôr"tər) *n.* (*Slang*) **1**, a violent storm, person, etc. **2**, a person of striking energy or ability.

rip'tide" *n.* a strong undertow.

rise (rīz) *v.i.* [**rose** (rōz), **ris'en** (riz'ən), **ris'ing**] **1**, move from a lower to a higher position; move upward. **2**, stand up. **3**, slope or extend upward; stand in height. **4**, swell, as dough. **5**, emerge; come into sight or existence. **6**, increase in force, value, position, etc. **7**, elevation in rank, wealth, or importance. **8**, take up arms; rebel. **9**, (*Slang*) an irritated reaction or retort. —*n.* **1**, ascent; emergence; appearance. **2**, degree of ascent. **3**, an elevated place. **4**, spring; source; origin. **5**, increase.

ris'er (rī'zər) *n.* **1**, one who rises, esp. from sleep. **2**, the vertical piece which separates two stairs. **3**, (*pl.*) sets of stairs used as a multileveled platform, as for singers.

ris'i·ble (riz'ə-bəl) *adj.* **1**, having the faculty of laughing. **2**, exciting laughter. —**ris"i·bil'i·ty**, *n.*

risk *n.* **1**, exposure to loss or harm; danger; peril. **2**, chance; hazard. **3**, a contingency covered by insurance. —*v.t.* **1**, expose to injury or loss. **2**, take the chance of. —**risk'y**, *adj.*

ri·sot'to (rē-zot'tō) *n.* (*Ital.*) rice cooked with meat stock and flavorings.

ris·qué' (ris-kā') *adj.* somewhat indelicate, as a story; daring.

ris·sole' (rē-sōl') *n.* a small fried roll of chopped meat or fish.

ri"tar·dan'do (rē"tär-dän'dō) *adj., adv. & n.* (*Music*) becoming slower gradually.

rite (rīt) *n.* a ceremonial, religious, or other solemn service; ritual.

rit'u·al (rich'oo-əl) *adj.* pert. to or consisting of ceremonials. —*n.* a prescribed form or manner.

rit'u·al·ism (rich'oo-ə-liz-əm) *n.* **1**, insistence upon or fondness for ritual. **2**, the study of rituals. —**rit'u·al·ist**, *n.* —**rit"u·al·is'tic**, *adj.* —**rit"u·al·is'ti·cal·ly**, *adv.*

ritz'y (rit'sē) *adj.* (*Slang*) luxurious; showy and costly.

ri'val (rī'vəl) *n.* one who is in pursuit of

the same object or thing; an opponent. —*adj.* competing. —*v.t.* **1,** stand in competition with. **2,** emulate. **3,** be equal to. —**ri'val·ry,** *n.*

rive (rīv) *v.t. & i.* [*p.p.* **riv'en** (riv'ən)] rend asunder by force.

riv'er (riv'ər) *n.* **1,** a large stream of water flowing throughout the year. **2,** a copious flow.

riv'et (riv'it) *n.* a malleable metal pin or bolt used to fasten pieces together. —*v.t.* fasten with such a pin; fasten firmly.

Ri·vie'ra (ri-vye'rä) *n.* the Mediterranean coast of France and Italy.

riv'u·let (riv'yə-lət) *n.* a small stream or brook.

roach (rōch) *n.* **1,** a common freshwater fish. **2,** a cockroach.

road (rōd) *n.* **1,** a public way for passage or travel; a highway. **2,** any means or way of approach. **3,** an anchorage. —**on the road,** traveling; on tour. —**road company,** the touring cast of a play, musical, etc.

road'a·bil'i·ty *n.* the ease of handling of a vehicle on a road.

road'bed" *n.* the foundation of a railroad track or highway.

road'house" *n.* a restaurant and dance hall by a road.

road'run"ner *n.* a fast-running crested cuckoo of southwest No. Amer.

road'stead" (-sted") *n.* an anchorage.

road'ster (-stər) *n.* **1,** a small open automobile. **2,** a driving horse.

road'way" *n.* a road.

roam (rōm) *v.i. & t.* travel aimlessly; rove; wander over.

roan (rōn) *adj.* of a horse, having a bay, sorrel, or chestnut color interspersed with gray or white. —*n.* **1,** a roan animal. **2,** a sheepskin leather, used in imitation of morocco, used in bookbinding.

roar (rôr) *v.i.* **1,** bellow; cry aloud. **2,** make a full, deep sound, as of wind, waves, or a crowd. **3,** guffaw. —*v.t.* shout. —*n.* a roaring sound, as of a lion.

roar'ing *adj.* **1,** that roars. **2,** extremely active; outstanding.

roast (rōst) *v.t.* **1,** cook (as meat) before an open fire, or in an oven. **2,** heat to excess. **3,** (*Slang*) ridicule or castigate. —*v.i.* be heated; be cooked by roasting. —*n.* a cut of meat suitable for roasting. —**roast'er,** *n.* a pan or chamber for roasting; a pig, chicken, etc., suitable for roasting.

rob *v.t.* [**robbed, rob'bing**] strip or deprive of something by force. —**rob'ber,** *n.* —**rob'ber·y,** *n.*

robe (rōb) *n.* **1,** a gown or a long, loose outer garment, sometimes symbolizing honor

or authority. **2,** (*pl.*) dress; attire. **3,** a dressed pelt, blanket, etc., used as a wrap. —*v.t.* clothe.

rob'in *n.* a red-breasted, migratory thrush of No. Amer.

ro'bot (rō'bət) *n.* an automaton resembling a man. —**robot bomb, robot plane,** one that guides itself or is controlled by radio.

ro·bust' (rō-bust') *adj.* **1,** strong; vigorous. **2,** rough; boisterous; rude. **3,** requiring vigor. —**ro·bust'ness,** *n.*

roc (rok) *n.* a fabulous large bird.

roc'am·bole" (rōk'əm-bōl") *n.* a European plant of the onion family used in seasoning.

rock (rok) *n.* **1,** a mass of stony material; a fragment or piece of it. **2,** a foundation; strength. **3,** (*pl.*) (*Slang*) money; jewels. **4,** a backward and forward movement. —*v.t. & i.* move backward and forward; sway. —**on the rocks, 1,** in or into a state of disaster or bankruptcy. **2,** poured straight over ice (as whiskey). —**rock and rye,** rye whiskey flavored with sugar crystals (rock candy). —**rock crystal,** a transparent variety of quartz. —**rock garden,** one grown among rocks. —**rocking horse,** a child's riding toy. —**rock salt,** a mineral salt. —**rock wool,** an insulating material.

rock'a·bil'ly (rok'ə-bil"ē) *n.* a combination of country-Western and rock music.

rock"bot'tom *adj.* **1,** lowest possible. **2,** basic; fundamental.

rock'bound" *adj.* **1,** surrounded by rocks. **2,** impenetrable.

rock'er *n.* **1,** a curved piece on which a cradle or chair moves backward and forward. **2,** a chair so mounted: *rocking chair.* **3,** an oscillating part in a machine.

rock'et (rok'it) *n.* a tube propelled into the air by self-contained explosives, used in fireworks, warfare, etc. —*v.i.* rise with great rapidity.

rock'et·ry (-rē) *n.* the science and technology of rockets.

rock'ribbed" (rok'ribd") *adj.* **1,** marked by rocky ridges. **2,** inflexible; unyielding.

rock'y (-ē) *adj.* **1,** of or like stone; rough with, or as with, crushed stone. **2,** shaky. —**rock'i·ness,** *n.*

Rocky Mountain spotted fever an infectious disease transmitted by ticks.

ro·co'co (rə-kō'kō) *n.* an excessively ornate style of ornamentation. —*adj.* in this style.

rod *n.* **1,** a slender, straight stick. **2,** a scepter; fig., authority. **3,** a switch used for chastisement. **4,** a measure of length, 16½ feet. **5,** a fishing pole. **6,** a nerve ending in the retina. **7,** (*Slang*) a pistol.

rode (rōd) v. pret. of *ride*.

ro'dent (rō'dənt) n. a member of an order of gnawing mammals with sharp, strong teeth.

ro·de'o (rō-dā'ō) n. 1, a roundup of cattle. 2, a public performance of horsemanship, lassoing, etc.

rod"o·mon·tade' (rod"ə-mon-tād') n. vainglorious boasting; bravado.

roe (rō) n. 1, a small, agile, very graceful deer of Europe and Asia. 2, the doe of the stag or red deer. 3, the eggs of a fish or of various crustaceans. 4, a mottled appearance in wood, esp. in mahogany.

roe'buck" n. the male of a species of deer, the roe deer.

roent'gen (rent'gən) n. a unit of x-radiation. —**Roent'gen ray,** x-ray.

ro·ga'tion (rō-gā'shən) n. a litany or supplication.

rog'er (roj'ər) interj. (*Slang*) very well; order received.

rogue (rōg) n. 1, a dishonest person; a knave. 2, a mischievous or playful person. —**ro'guish** (-gish) adj. —**rogue's gallery,** a collection of photographs of known criminals.

ro'guer·y (rō'gə-rē) n. 1, knavishness. 2, a Knavish act.

roil v.t. 1, make turbid by stirring up (water, etc.). 2, annoy; vex.

roist'er (rois'tər) v.i. bluster; swagger; bully; be noisy. —**roist'er·er,** n.

rôle (rōl) n. an actor's part.

roll (rōl) v.i. 1, move along a surface by turning over and over. 2, travel on wheels. 3, revolve. 4, sway. 5, move in ripples, as waves. 6, make a deep prolonged sound. 7, be wound or curled in cylindrical form. 8, turn over and over while lying down; wallow. —v.t. 1, cause to roll or rotate; whirl. 2, give expression to a prolonged deep sound. 3, (often with *up*) wrap around an axis. 4, press or level with rollers. 5, trill, esp. the letter R. —n. 1, something wound into a cylinder. 2, a small bread; a biscuit. 3, a list of names. 4, the act of rolling. 5, a deep, prolonged, or sustained sound. 6, a swell or undulation of the surface. 7, a swagger. —**roll call,** a calling of names to which those present must answer. —**rolling mill,** an establishment that makes steel sheets, bars, etc. —**rolling pin,** a wooden cylinder for rolling dough. —**rolling stock,** railroad cars.

roll'back" n. a reduction to a previous, lower level, as of prices.

roll'bar" n. a rigid curved bar covering the passenger area of an automobile to protect occupants if the car should overturn.

roll'er n. 1, a cylinder used as a wheel, bearing, core, pressing surface, etc. 2, a heavy wave. —**roller bearing,** a bearing in which revolving cylinders bear the shaft. —**roller coaster,** a miniature railway used at amusement parks. —**roller derby,** a contest played between two teams on roller skates. —**roller skate,** a shoe or attachment with small wheels.

rol'lick (rol'ik) v.i. frolic; be gay. —**rol'-lick·ing,** adj.

roll'o"ver n. 1, a rolling over. 2, the extension of the term of an obligation.

roll'top" desk a desk with a cover that slides upward.

ro·ly·po"ly (rō'lē-pō"lē) adj. round; pudgy. —n. a kind of dessert.

Ro'man (rō'mən) adj. 1, pert. to Rome. 2, (*l.c.*) denoting any printing type not italic. 3, denoting the numerals (as I = 1, V = 5, X = 10, etc.) used in ancient Rome. —n. a citizen or inhabitant of Rome. —**Roman candle,** a kind of colorful firework. —**Roman nose,** a nose with a prominent bridge.

Roman Catholic a member of the Christian church of which the Pope, or Bishop of Rome, is the pontiff.

ro·mance' (rō-mans') n. 1, a tale or novel of extraordinary, not real or familiar, life. 2, a fiction; a falsehood. 3, a love affair. —adj. (*cap.*) denoting a language almost wholly derived from Latin, as Italian, Spanish, French. —v.i. 1, make up fanciful tales. 2, (*Colloq.*) make love.

Ro"man·esque' (rō"mən-esk') n. the early medieval style of architecture in W. Europe. —adj. pert. to or designating this style.

Ro·ma'ni·an (rō-mā'nē-ən) n. & adj. Rumanian.

ro·man'tic (rō-man'tik) adj. 1, fanciful; fabulous; pert. to romance. 2, given to sentimental or amorous feelings. 3, in art and literature, imaginative and free from classical rule. —n. a romantic person; romanticist. —**ro·man'ti·cal·ly,** adv. —**ro·man'ti·cism,** n.

Rom'a·ny (rōm'ə-nē) n. a gypsy; the gypsy language. —adj. belonging to or relating to the gypsies. —**Romany rye** (rī) a person, not a gypsy, who associates with gypsies.

Ro'me·o (rō'mē-ō) n. (*Colloq.*) a lover.

romp v.i. 1, leap and frisk about in play. 2, win easily. —n. 1, boisterous play. 2, an easy win. —**romp'ers,** n.pl. a small child's overalls.

ron'deau (ron'dō) n. [pl. **-deaux** (-dōz)] a French lyric poem.

ron'do (ron'dō) n. [pl. **-dos**] (*Music*) a work in which the principal theme is often repeated.

rood *n.* **1**, a crucifix. **2**, a varying unit of measurement.

roof *n.* **1**, the external upper covering of a building, car, etc. **2**, any house. **3**, an upper limit. —*v.t.* cover with a roof; shelter. —**roof′er**, *n.* —**roof′ing**, *n.* a material for making a roof. —**roof garden**, a restaurant on top of a building.

roof′tree″ *n.* **1**, the ridgepole of a roof. **2**, a roof. **3**, home.

rook (rŭk) *n.* **1**, a Europ. crow. **2**, a piece used in chess; a castle. —*v.i.* & *t.* cheat. —**rook′er·y**, *n.* a roost for rooks.

rook′ie (rŭk′ē) *n.* (*Slang*) an inexperienced recruit; a beginner, as a policeman in training, etc.

room *n.* **1**, extent of space, great or small. **2**, space or place unoccupied or unobstructed. **3**, freedom; opportunity. **4**, an apartment; chamber. —*v.i.* (*Colloq.*) lodge. —**room′er**, *n.* a lodger. —**room′ful**, *n.* —**rooming house**, a house where rooms are let.

room·ette′ (rû-met′) *n.* a small private compartment in a railroad sleeping car.

room′mate″ *n.* one with whom one shares living quarters.

room′y (rûm′ē) *adj.* spacious. —**room′-i·ness**, *n.*

roor′back (rûr′bak) *n.* a false story defaming a political candidate.

roost *n.* **1**, a pole, a perch, or a place, for fowls to rest at night. **2**, (*Colloq.*) a temporary abiding place. —*v.i.* **1**, perch, as a bird. **2**, (*Colloq.*) lodge.

roost′er (roos′tər) *n.* the male of the domestic chicken; a cock.

root *n.* **1**, the part of a plant that grows downward into the soil. **2**, the foundation of anything. **3**, a source, origin, or cause. **4**, (*Math.*) a quantity that when multiplied by itself a certain number of times will produce a given quantity. **5**, (*Math.*) a quantity that, when substituted for the unknown quantity in an equation, satisfies the equation. **6**, the part of a word that conveys its essential meaning. —*v.t.* **1**, plant firmly; fix. **2**, tear up or out, as by the roots. —*v.i.* **1**, take root; be firmly fixed; be established. **2**, turn up the earth with the snout. **3**, (*Colloq.*) cheer; (with *for*) wish well. —**root′er**, *n.* (*Colloq.*) a supporter; one who applauds. —**root beer**, a beverage flavored with aromatic roots.

root′stock″ *n.* **1**, a plant stem resembling a root. **2**, the primary ground or cause of anything.

rope (rōp) *n.* **1**, a thick, strong cord made of several strands twisted together. **2**, a row or string of things. **3**, a stringy, glutinous formation. **4**, death by hanging. —*v.t.* **1**,

fasten or enclose with a strong cord; catch; lasso. **2**, (*Slang*) (with *in*) fool; trick.

Roque′fort (rōk′fərt) *n.* a strong French cheese, veined with mold.

ror′qual (rôr′kwəl) *n.* a finback whale.

Ror′schach test (rôr′shäk) a personality and intelligence test consisting of 10 inkblot designs to be described by the subject in his own terms.

ro′sa·ry (rō′zə-rē) *n.* **1**, (*Rom. Cath.*) a string of beads used in counting prayers. **2**, a garland or bed of roses. **3**, an anthology.

rose (rōz) *n.* **1**, a thorny shrub bearing flowers in various colors. **2**, a light crimson color. —*adj.* light crimson. —*v.* pret. of *rise.* —**rose diamond**, one with a faceted top and flat bottom. —**rose fever**, a form of hay fever caused by grass pollen, occurring in the spring. —**rose window**, a circular window with elaborate radiating tracery.

ros′e·ate (rō′zē-ət) *adj.* **1**, rose-colored; blushing. **2**, optimistic.

rose′bud″ *n.* the bud of a rose.

rose′bush″ *n.* the bush on which roses grow.

rose′mar″y (rōz′mãr″ē) *n.* a fragrant evergreen shrub.

ro·sette′ (rō-zet′) *n.* a design or ornament in circular, roselike form.

rose′wa″ter *n.* a water scented with oil of roses.

rose′wood″ *n.* a tree, or its reddish, fragrant wood.

Rosh″ Ha·sha′na (rosh″hä-shä′nə) the Jewish New Year.

Ro″si·cru′cian (rō″zi-kroo′shən) *n.* a member of a supposed secret society claiming knowledge of the occult sciences. —*adj.* pert. to this society.

ros′in (roz′in) *n.* the solid substance (*resin*) left after the distillation of the oil of turpentine. —*v.t.* rub with rosin.

ros′ter (ros′tər) *n.* **1**, a list of names. **2**, a schedule; a program.

ros′trum (ros′trəm) *n.* a pulpit or platform for a speaker.

ros′y (rō′zē) *adj.* **1**, rose-colored. **2**, favorable; promising. **3**, blushing; blooming. —**ros′i·ness**, *n.*

rot *v.i.* [**rot′ted, -ting**] **1**, undergo natural decomposition; decay. **2**, become corrupt; deteriorate. —*n.* **1**, the process or result of decaying. **2**, a parasitic disease. **3**, (*Slang*) nonsense; humbug.

ro′ta·ry (rō′tə-rē) *adj.* turning, as a wheel on its axis. —*n.* a traffic circle.

ro′tate (rō′tāt) *v.i.* & *t.* **1**, revolve or move around a center or axis. **2**, alternate serially. —**ro·ta′tion**, *n.*

rote (rōt) *n.* **1**, mechanical routine in

learning; repetition without attention to meaning. **2,** a medieval string musical instrument.

ro·tis'se·rie (rō-tis'ə-rē) *n.* a broiler with a rotating spit for roasting meat.

ro''to·gra·vure' (rō''tə-grə-vyûr') *n.* a process for gravure printing from cylindrical plates.

ro'tor (rō'tər) *n.* a rotating part of a machine.

rot'ten (rot'ən) *adj.* **1,** having rotted; decayed. **2,** (*Colloq.*) very bad. **3,** (*Slang*) contemptible. —**rot'ten·ness,** *n.*

rot'ter (rot'ər) *n.* a scoundrel; cad.

rott'wei''ler (rot'wī''lər) *n.* a German breed of cattle dog.

ro·tund' (rō-tund') *adj.* round or rounded out; bulbous; obese. —**ro·tun'di·ty,** *n.*

ro·tun'da (rō-tun'də) *n.* a round building or room, esp. one with a dome.

rou'ble (roo'bəl) *n.* ruble.

rou·é' (roo-ā') *n.* a dissolute man; a rake.

rouge (roozh) *n.* **1,** a red cosmetic or coloring for the skin. **2,** a red powder or paste used for polishing. —*v.t. & i.* apply rouge (to).

rough (ruf) *adj.* **1,** not smooth to the touch or to the sight; uneven. **2,** left in a natural or incomplete state; crude; approximate. **3,** severe; harsh. **4,** lacking refinement; uncouth. **5,** boisterously violent. —*n.* **1,** (with *the*) crudeness; rawness. **2,** in golf, the untrimmed grass bordering the fairway. —*adv.* in a crude, coarse, or harsh manner. —**rough it,** endure hardships. —**rough'ness,** *n.*

rough'age (ruf'ij) *n.* coarse, bulky food.

rough-'and-read'y *adj.* crude but effective.

rough-'and-tum'ble *adj. & n.* (characterized by) rough action or fighting.

rough'en (-ən) *v.t.* make rough.

rough-''hew' *v.t.* **1,** hew without smoothing, as timber. **2,** give a crude form to.

rough'house'' *n.* boisterous play. —*v.t.* treat violently but in fun.

rough'neck'' *n.* a boor; a rowdy.

rough'rid''er *n.* **1,** one who breaks in wild horses. **2,** (*cap.*) in the Span. Amer. war, a member of a volunteer cavalry regiment organized and commanded by Theodore Roosevelt.

rough'shod'' *adj.* **1,** shod with spiked horseshoes. **2,** ruthless.

rou·lade' (roo-läd') *n.* **1,** meat rolled around a filling and cooked. **2,** (*Music*) a rapid succession of notes in a melody.

rou·lette' (roo-let') *n.* **1,** a game of betting on the number at which a revolving

wheel will stop. **2,** a cutting tool using a rowel.

round (rownd) *adj.* **1,** having the shape, or approximately the shape, of a circle, cylinder, or sphere. **2,** having curved sections, lines, or surfaces; convex. **3,** easy, smooth and brisk in motion. **4,** full; liberal. **5,** approximate. —*n.* **1,** a round object. **2,** series; circuit; course or tour of duty. **3,** a period of action between intermissions. **4,** a rung of a ladder or chair. **5,** a cut of beef. **6,** ammunition for a single shot or volley. —*v.t.* **1,** give rotundity to. **2,** (with *out*) complete or perfect. **3,** encircle; encompass. **4,** make a course along or around. **5,** (with *up*) drive or gather (cattle, etc.) together. —*v.i.* **1,** grow or become rotund. **2,** mature; develop. —*adv.* **1,** on all sides, so as to surround. **2,** with a rotating movement. **3,** in, within, or through a circuit. **4,** in circumference. **5,** from beginning to end. —*prep.* around; about. —**round'ness,** *n.* —**round robin,** an act in which all members of a group participate. —**round table,** a group assembled for discussion. —**round trip,** one to a place and back again.

round'a·bout'' *adj.* circuitous; indirect. —*n.* **1,** a circuitous course, statement, etc. **2,** a merry-go-round. **3,** (*Brit.*) a rotary.

round'el (rown'dəl) *n.* **1,** a rondeau. **2,** something round, esp. a window.

roun'de·lay' (rown'də-lā'') *n.* **1,** any song in which an idea, line, or refrain is continually repeated. **2,** a dance in a circle.

round'er *n.* **1,** one who travels a circuit. **2,** a dissolute person; an idler.

round'house'' *n.* a circular building where locomotives are repaired.

round'ly (-lē) *adv.* vigorously; earnestly; frankly.

round-'the-clock' *adj.* lasting more than 24 hours; continual.

round'up' *n.* **1,** a gathering or driving together. **2,** a summation.

round'worm'' *n.* a parasitic worm, esp. one infesting the human intestine.

rouse (rowz) *v.t.* cause to start up from sleep, inactivity, indifference, etc.; stir up; provoke. —*v.i.* start or rise up; be stirred to action.

roust'a·bout'' (rowst'ə-bowt'') *n.* **1,** a laborer on a wharf or river boat. **2,** a laborer at odd jobs.

rout (rowt) *n.* **1,** a confused retreat after a defeat. **2,** a disorderly crowd; the rabble. —*v.t.* **1,** disperse by defeating; drive away in disorder. **2,** (with *out*) turn out. **3,** cut away. —**rout'er,** *n.* a tool for cutting grooves, recesses, etc.

route (root) *n.* **1,** a way; road. **2,** a course; line of travel. —*v.t.* send by a certain route.

rou·tine' (roo-tēn') *n.* a customary procedure or course of action. —*adj.* entirely customary; not deviating from routine.

roux (roo) *n.* a mixture of flour and melted butter for thickening gravy or soup.

rove (rōv) *v.i. & t.* wander at pleasure; roam; ramble.

rov'er (-ər) *n.* **1,** a pirate or a pirate ship. **2,** a wanderer. **3,** a fickle person.

row (rō) *n.* **1,** a series of persons or things in a straight line. **2,** a ride in a rowboat. —*v.t. & i.* propel (a boat) by means of oars.

row *n.* a noisy disturbance; a quarrel. —*v.i.* quarrel.

row'boat" (rō'bōt") *n.* a small boat propelled by oars.

row'dy (row'dĕ) *n.* a rough, quarrelsome person. —*adj.* rough; disreputable. —**row'dy·ish,** *adj.* —**row'dy·ism,** *n.*

row'el (row'əl) *n.* **1,** the wheel of a horseman's spur. **2,** a similar wheel for cutting, perforating, etc.

row'lock (rō'-) *n.* an oarlock.

roy'al (roi'əl) *adj.* **1,** pert. or related to a king or queen. **2,** majestic. **3,** large or superior of its kind.

roy'al·ist *n.* an adherent of a king or monarchy. —*adj.* pert. to royalists. —**roy'al·ism,** *n.*

roy'al·ty (-tĕ) *n.* **1,** the state or condition of being royal; royal persons collectively. **2,** a fee paid for the use of prerogatives such as a patent, copyright, etc.

rub *v.t.* [**rubbed, rub'bing**] **1,** apply pressure and friction by motion over the surface of. **2,** smooth, polish, clean, etc., by rubbing. **3,** affect as if by friction; annoy; disturb. —*v.i.* move or act with friction; rub something. —*n.* **1,** the act of rubbing. **2,** (*Colloq.*) a disturbing factor. —**rub it in,** emphasize or reiterate something disagreeable. —**rub out,** (*Slang*) murder.

rub-'a-dub" (rub'ə-dub") *n.* the sound of a drum when beaten.

ru·ba'to (roo-bä'tō) *adj. & adv.* performed with a certain freedom of rhythm, to heighten the effect. —*n.* **1,** a rubato style of performance. **2,** a passage so played.

rub'ber (rub'ər) *n.* **1,** one who or that which rubs. **2,** something made of rubber, esp. a pencil eraser. **3,** an elastic, tough, waterproof substance obtained from the sap of various tropical trees. **4,** a series of games, usually three. —*adj.* made of rubber. —**rubber cement,** an adhesive containing rubber and naphtha. —**rubber check,** (*Slang*) a check that is worthless.

rub'ber·ize" (-īz") *v.t.* waterproof (as cloth) with rubber.

rub'ber·neck" *n.* (*Slang*) **1,** an inquisitive person. **2,** a sight-seeing bus. —*v.i.* stretch the neck to look.

rub"ber·stamp' *v.t.* **1,** imprint with inked rubber type. **2,** (*Colloq.*) approve without scrutiny.

rub'ber·y *adj.* tough and elastic. —**rub'ber·i·ness,** *n.*

rub'bish (rub'ish) *n.* waste material; trash; litter.

rub'ble (rub'əl) *n.* **1,** rough broken stones. **2,** trash.

rub'down" *n.* a massage of the body, esp. after exercise.

rube (roob) *n.* (*Slang*) a crude or clownish countryman.

ru·bel'la (roo-bel'ə) *n.* a mild contagious disease: *German measles.*

ru'bi·cund" (roo'bə-kund") *adj.* inclining to redness; ruddy.

ru·bid'i·um (roo-bid'ē-əm) *n.* a metallic element, no. 37, symbol Rb.

ru'ble (roo'bəl) *n.* the monetary unit of Russia. Also, **rou'ble.**

ru'bric (roo'brik) *n.* **1,** a heading or caption in a book or other writing. **2,** a rule for the conduct of religious worship.

ru'by (roo'bĕ) *n.* **1,** a clear, red precious stone, a variety of corundum. **2,** a pure crimson red color.

ruche (roosh) *n.* a frill or strip of dress trimming. Also, **ruch'ing** (roo'shing).

ruck (ruk) *n.* **1,** a fold or crease. **2,** the common run of persons or things.

ruck'sack" *n.* a knapsack.

ruck'us (ruk'əs) *n.* (*Slang*) a noisy disturbance.

ruc'tion (ruk'shən) *n.* a disturbance; a row; rumpus.

rud'der (rud'ər) *n.* a flat piece hinged vertically, used for directing a ship or airplane.

rud'dy (rud'ĕ) *adj.* of a red color, esp. healthily red. —**rud'di·ness,** *n.*

rude (rood) *adj.* **1,** rough; crude; primitive. **2,** ill-bred; discourteous; impolite. **3,** sturdy; rugged. **4,** tempestuous, as weather. —**rude'ness,** *n.*

ru'di·ment (roo'di-mənt) *n.* **1,** an undeveloped state. **2,** (usu. *pl.*) an element or first principle, as of an art or science. —**ru"di·men'ta·ry** (-men'tə-rē) *adj.*

rue (roo) *v.t.* repent of; regret; feel sorrow or suffering on account of. —*n.* a garden plant used in medicine. —**rue'ful,** *adj.* sorrowful.

ruff (ruf) *n.* **1,** a large, projecting, frilled collar of fine material. **2,** a breed of domestic pigeons. **3,** in card playing, an act of

trumping. —*v*. in cards, play a trump.
—**ruffed grouse,** partridge.

ruf′fi·an (ruf′é-ən) *n*. a brutal man; a thug; rowdy. —**ruf′fi·an·ly,** *adj*.

ruf′fle (ruf′əl) *v.t*. **1,** draw up into gathers, folds, or pleats. **2,** disturb the arrangement, orderliness, or composure of; rumple; ripple; agitate. —*n*. **1,** a gathered border or trimming. **2,** a low beat of a drum.

rug *n*. **1,** a thick, heavy floor covering. **2,** a lap robe.

Rug′by (rug′bé) *n*. a Brit. form of football.

rug′ged (rug′id) *adj*. **1,** having a rough surface; shaggy; hilly; uneven. **2,** unpolished; uncultivated. **3,** harsh; austere. **4,** fierce; tempestuous. **5,** (*Colloq*.) robust; strong. —**rug′ged·ness,** *n*.

ru′in (roo′in) *n*. **1,** collapse, moral or physical; downfall; overthrow. **2,** that which promotes decay or destruction. **3,** (often *pl*.) anything, as a building, in a state of destruction, decay, or wreck. —*v.t*. damage essentially and irreparably. —**ru″in·a′-tion,** *n*. —**ru′in·ous,** *adj*.

rule (rool) *n*. **1,** a regulation for standard procedure; a law. **2,** an established method or way of doing anything. **3,** government; supreme authority. **4,** a scaled strip; ruler. **5,** a printed or drawn straight line. —*v.t*. **1,** determine; settle. **2,** govern; control. **3,** mark with lines. —*v.i*. **1,** have power or command. **2,** prevail; decide. —**rule of thumb,** a practical method; a rough guide.

rul′er (roo′lər) *n*. **1,** one who governs. **2,** a scaled strip of wood, metal, etc., with a straight edge, used for measuring and drawing lines.

rul′ing *n*. an authoritative decision. —*adj*. governing; chief; prevalent.

rum *n*. **1,** an alcoholic liquor distilled from sugar cane. **2,** any strong alcoholic drink. **3,** a card game; rummy. —*adj*. (*Slang*) queer; odd; droll. —**rum runner,** *n*. a smuggler of, or vehicle or ship carrying, contraband liquor.

Ru·ma′ni·an (roo-mā′né-ən) *n. & adj*. of or pert. to Rumania, its people, or their language. Also, **Ro·ma′ni·an, Rou·ma′-ni·an.**

rum′ba (rum′bə) *n*. a fast dance, originally Cuban, or the music for it.

rum′ble (rum′bəl) *v.i*. **1,** make a deep, heavy, continous sound. **2,** move with such a sound; roll heavily or noisily. **3,** (*Slang*) fight. —*v.t*. utter, or cause to make, such a sound. —*n*. **1,** a rumbling sound. **2,** an open seat at the back of a roadster or coupé. **3,** (*Slang*) a street fight.

ru′men (roo′min) *n*. **1,** the first stomach of a cow or other ruminant. **2,** the cud.

ru′mi·nant (roo′mi-nənt) *n*. a cud-chewing animal. —*adj*. **1,** cud-chewing. **2,** contemplative.

ru′mi·nate (roo′mə-nāt″) *v.i*. **1,** chew the cud. **2,** meditate; ponder. —*v.t*. **1,** chew again. **2,** turn over in the mind. —**ru″mi·na′tion,** *n*.

rum′mage (rum′ij) *v.t. & i*. hunt through; ransack. —*n*. **1,** a search. **2,** odds and ends. —**rummage sale,** a sale of miscellaneous articles.

rum′my (rum′é) *n*. **1,** a card game. **2,** (*Slang*) an alcoholic. —*adj*. rum.

ru′mor (roo′mər) *n*. **1,** popular report. **2,** an unconfirmed but widely circulated story; a piece of gossip. Also, **ru′mour.**

rump *n*. **1,** the back parts of an animal; the buttocks. **2,** a remnant.

rum′ple (rum′pəl) *v.t. & i*. make uneven; wrinkle; become mussed. —*n*. a wrinkle.

rum′pus (rum′pəs) *n*. (*Colloq*.) a noisy or disorderly commotion; a brawl. —**rumpus room,** a room for games and play.

run *v.i*. [**ran, run, run′ning**] **1,** move swiftly on foot. **2,** make haste; rush; flee; steal away; abscond. **3,** pursue a course; travel. **4,** perform a regular passage from place to place. **5,** flow. **6,** discharge a fluid, as tears; become fluid. **7,** extend from point to point; spread. **8,** operate; work. **9,** be a candidate for office; compete in a race. **10,** go or pass by; elapse, as time. **11,** (with *to*) have a proclivity or general tendency. **12,** have a certain direction, course, tenor, or form. **13,** keep going; continue. **14,** ravel. **15,** average. —*v.t*. **1,** cause (anything) to go or to function; direct; operate. **2,** accomplish; undertake. **3,** travel past or through successfully. **4,** smuggle. **5,** sew several stitches at the same time. —*n*. **1,** the act of moving at a rapid pace. **2,** a passage; journey; trip; distance covered. **3,** a current; a flow. **4,** course; progress; a continued course. **5,** a tendency; general character. **6,** a general and extraordinary demand, as on a bank. **7,** in baseball, the act of making a score. **8,** in certain card games, a sequence. **9,** free access to a place. **10,** a place where animals may range. **11,** a herd or school moving together. **12,** a small stream of water; a brook. **13,** a ravel, as in hose. **14,** a series of successes. **15,** (*Music*) a roulade. —**run′ny,** *adj*. —**run down, 1,** disparage. **2,** enumerate; list. **3,** unwind, as a clock. —**run in,** arrest and confine. —**run-of-the-mill,** *adj*. average.

run′a·bout″ *n*. a light, open automobile or motor boat.

run′a·round″ *n*. **1,** (*Colloq*.) an abscess near a finger- or toenail. **2,** (*Slang*) an evasion. **3,** type set around an illustration.

run′a·way″ *adj*. **1,** escaped; out of control. **2,** eloping. —*n*. **1,** a horse, etc., that has escaped. **2,** an easy victory, as in a race.

run′ci·ble spoon (run′si-bəl) a fork with three broad tines, one edged, curved like a spoon.

run-″down″ *adj*. **1,** in poor health or condition. **2,** of a clock, etc., not wound. —*n*. (*Colloq*.) narrative.

rune (roon) *n*. **1,** a character of an ancient Europ. alphabet. **2,** an obscure saying. —**ru′nic,** *adj*.

rung *n*. a rounded bar forming the crosspiece of a ladder, a brace on a chair, a spoke, etc. —*v*. p.p. of *ring*.

run′nel (run′əl) *n*. a small stream.

run′ner (run′ər) *n*. **1,** one who runs; a messenger; a racer. **2,** the base on which a sled, etc., slides. **3,** a shoot from a plant. **4,** a narrow rug or table scarf.

run″ner-up′ *n*. the contestant finishing in second place.

run′ning (-ing) *n*. **1,** act of one who or that which runs. **2,** competition. —*adj*. **1,** that runs. **2,** cursory; hasty. **3,** continuous; persistent. —**running board,** a ledge at the side of a vehicle. —**running head,** the heading at the top of each page of a book. —**running light,** a light (for visibility, navigation, etc.) on a boat, ship, or aircraft. —**running mate,** a competitor or candidate allied with another.

run-′off″ *n*. **1,** water flowing off the land. **2,** a deciding contest.

runt *n*. **1,** any undersized animal, esp. the smallest of a litter. **2,** a small or contemptible person.

run-′through″ *n*. a rehearsal at which a work is performed complete, with few stops.

run′way″ *n*. a channel; course; a level strip for airplanes landing and taking off.

ru·pee′ (roo-pē′) *n*. a monetary unit of India.

rup′ture (rup′chər) *n*. **1,** the act or result of breaking; a breach of peace. **2,** hernia, esp. abdominal hernia. —*v.t*. **1,** break; burst. **2,** cause to suffer from hernia. —*v.i*. suffer a break.

ru′ral (rûr′əl) *adj*. pert. to the country or to country life. —**rural free delivery,** free delivery of mail in rural districts. Abbrev., **RFD.**

ruse (rooz) *n*. artifice; trickery; a stratagem.

rush *v.i*. **1,** move or drive forward with violent haste. **2,** move or act with undue eagerness; hurry. —*v.t*. **1,** cause to go swiftly or violently. **2,** (*Football*) carry (the ball) forward. **3,** cause to hasten; push. **4,** (*Slang*) entertain, to induce to join a fraternity or sorority. **5,** (*Colloq*.) court. —*n*. **1,** a driving

forward with eagerness and haste. **2,** an eager demand; a run. **3,** (*Colloq*.) urgent pressure. **4,** a scrimmage. **5,** (*pl*.) the first prints of a motion picture film, for inspection. **6,** any of various hollow-stemmed water plants. —**rush hour,** a time of heaviest traffic.

rusk *n*. a sweet, toasted bread or biscuit; zwieback.

rus′set (rus′it) *n*. **1,** a reddish-brown color. **2,** a kind of winter apple with a brownish skin. —*adj*. reddish-brown.

Rus′sian (rush′ən) *adj*. pert. to Russia, its people, or its language. —**Russian roulette,** a type of duel or act of bravado performed with a gun loaded with one bullet.

rust *n*. **1,** the reddish coating that forms on iron exposed to air and moisture. **2,** any corrosive formation. **3,** an orange-red color. —*v.i*. become rusty.

rus′tic (rus′tik) *adj*. **1,** pert. to the country; rural. **2,** unsophisticated; simple. **3,** rude; simply constructed. —*n*. a country person. —**rus′ti·cal·ly,** *adv*. —**rus·tic′i·ty** (-tis′ə-tē) *n*.

rus′ti·cate″ (rus′ti-kāt″) *v.t*. & *i*. send or go to live in the country. —**rus″ti·ca′tion,** *n*.

rus′tle (rus′əl) *v.i*. & *t*. **1,** make a murmuring sound by the rubbing of parts against each other. **2,** (*Colloq*.) stir about. **3,** (*Slang*) steal (cattle). —*n*. the sound of rustling. —**rus′tler,** *n*. a cattle thief.

rust′y (rus′tē) *adj*. **1,** covered with rust. **2,** out of practice. **3,** reddish. **4,** hoarse. —**rust′i·ness,** *n*.

rut *n*. **1,** a narrow track worn or cut in the ground. **2,** an established habit or mode of procedure. **3,** the period of heat in various animals. —*v.t*. [**rut′ted, rut′ting**] trace furrows in. —**rut′ted,** *adj*. furrowed.

ru″ta·ba′ga (roo″tə-bā′gə) *n*. a variety of nutritious turnip.

ru·the′ni·um (roo-thē′né-əm) *n*. a rare metallic element, no. 44, symbol Ru.

ruth′less (rooth′lis) *adj*. having no pity; merciless. —**ruth′less·ness,** *n*.

rye (rī) *n*. **1,** a hardy cereal plant or its seeds. **2,** whiskey made of rye.

S

S, s (es) the nineteenth letter of the English alphabet.

′s (s or z; see p. 8) *suf*. marking the possessive form of nouns. —*contr*. is: as, *he′s* (he is).

Sab′bath (sab′əth) *n*. a day of rest and religious dedication.

sab·bat'i·cal (sə-bat'i-kəl) *adj.* pert. to a rest period or (*cap.*) to the Sabbath. —**sabbatical year**, a year's leave of absence (every seventh year).

sa'ber (sā'bər) *n.* a one-edged, curved sword. —**saber-rattling**, *n.* actions or policies that threaten war. —**saber saw**, a portable electric jigsaw.

Sa'bin vaccine (sā'bin) a live attenuated virus taken orally to combat infantile paralysis.

sa'ble (sā'bəl) *n.* **1,** an animal of the marten family; its fur. **2,** the color black. **3,** (*pl.*) mourning garments. —*adj.* **1,** made of sable fur. **2,** black.

sa·bot' (sa-bō') *n.* a wooden shoe.

sab'o·tage (sab'ə-täzh") *n.* malicious destruction. —*v.t.* wilfully and maliciously destroy or impede.

sab'o·teur' (sab"ə-tēr') *n.* one who commits sabotage.

sa'bra (sä'brə) *n.* a native born Israeli.

sab'u·lous (sab'yə-ləs) *adj.* sandy; gritty. —**sab"u·los'i·ty** (-los'ə-tē) *n.*

sac (sak) *n.* a pouch or cavity in an animal or plant.

sac'cha·rin (sak'ə-rin) *n.* a chemical sweetening compound.

sac'cha·rine (sak'ə-rin) *adj.* **1,** sweet; sugary. **2,** insincerely polite, sympathetic, or flattering; fulsome.

sac"er·do'tal (sas"ər-dō'təl) *adj.* pert. to a priest or to priestly functions.

sa'chem (sā'chəm) *n.* **1,** a No. Amer. Indian chief. **2,** a high official of a political party.

sa·chet' (sa-shā') *n.* a small bag of perfuming herbs, etc.

sack (sak) *n.* **1,** a bag, esp. a large one. **2,** (*Slang*) discharge from employment. **3,** pillage. **4,** a strong white wine. —*v.t.* **1,** put into a sack. **2,** plunder. **3,** (*Colloq.*) discharge.

sack'but (sak'but) *n.* an early form of trombone.

sack'cloth" *n.* a coarse cloth, symbol of mourning.

sac'ral (sak'rəl) *adj.* **1,** sacred. **2,** of the sacrum.

sac'ra·ment (sak'rə-mənt) *n.* a devotional rite or symbol. —**sac"ra·men'tal,** *adj.*

sa'cred (sā'krid) *adj.* dedicated to a deity; holy; inviolable. —**sac'red·ness,** *n.* —**sacred cow,** something beyond question; a taboo.

sac'ri·fice (sak'rə-fīs") *n.* **1,** an offering, as to God or a deity. **2,** a voluntary loss. **3,** in baseball, a hit made to advance a runner, although the batter is put out. —*v.i.* make a sacrifice of. —*v.i.* make a sacrifice hit.

sac'ri·lege (sak'rə-lij) *n.* profanation of something sacred. —**sac"ri·le'gious** (-lij'əs) *adj.*

sac'ris·ty (sak'ris-tē) *n.* the place where sacred vessels and vestments are kept. —**sac'ris·tan** (-tən) *n.* the church official in charge of them.

sac"ro·il'i·ac (sak"rō-il'ē-ak) *n.* & *adj.* (pert. to) the region between the sacrum and the small intestine.

sac'ro·sanct" (sak'rə-sankt") *adj.* exceedingly sacred.

sac'rum (sak'rum) *n.* the posterior wall of the pelvis.

sad *adj.* sorrowful; causing sorrow. —**sad'ness,** *n.* —**sad sack,** (*Slang*) an ineffectual or hopeless person.

sad'den (sad'ən) *v.t.* & *i.* make or become sad.

sad'dle (sad'əl) *n.* **1,** a seat for a rider. **2,** a cut of meat. —*v.t.* **1,** put a saddle on. **2,** burden.

sad'i"ron *n.* a flatiron.

sad'ism (sad'iz-əm) *n.* gratification derived from causing pain. —**sad'ist,** *n.* —**sa·dis'tic** (sə-dis'tik) *adj.* —**sa·dis'ti·cal·ly,** *adv.*

sa"do·mas'och·ism (sa"do-mas'ə-kiz-əm) *n.* combined sadism and masochism.

sa·fa'ri (sə-fär'ē) *n.* an expedition, esp. for hunting.

safe (sāf) *adj.* **1,** free from danger or injury; secure. **2,** unharmed. **3,** trustworthy. —*n.* a repository for valuables. —**safe'ness,** *n.*

safe-"con'duct *n.* the right to go unmolested from one place to another, as during a war; a document granting such a right.

safe'crack"er *n.* a burglar who opens and robs safes.

safe-"de·pos'it box a steel box kept in a bank's vault.

safe'guard" *n.* a means of security or protection. —*v.t.* protect.

safe'keep"ing *n.* care.

safe'ty (-tē) *n.* **1,** safeness. **2,** protection; safekeeping. **3,** a device to prevent injury or accident. **4,** in football, a down behind one's own goal line, scoring 2 points for the opponents. —**safety belt,** a belt fastened across the body for protection, in an airplane, automobile, etc. —**safety glass,** unshatterable glass. —**safety match,** a match requiring a prepared surface for striking. —**safety pin,** a pin with a sheathed point. —**safety razor,** one with a guarded blade. —**safety valve, 1,** an automatic escape valve. **2,** an outlet for the emotions.

saf'flow"er (saf'low"ər) *n.* a plant whose florets are used in some drugs and dyes and whose oil is used for cooking, etc.

saf'fron (saf'rən) n. 1, a crocus. 2, a deep orange color.

sag v.i. [**sagged, sag'ging**] 1, droop; hang unevenly. 2, decline in price. —n. a sinking; a dip.

sa'ga (sä'gə) n. a narrative of heroic exploits.

sa·ga'cious (sə-gā'shəs) adj. wise. —**sa·gac'i·ty** (sə-gas'ə-tē) n.

sag'a·more (sag'ə-môr) n. a No. Amer. Indian chief.

sage (sāj) adj. profoundly wise. —n. 1, a wise man. 2, a herb for seasoning. 3, a bush: sagebrush.

Sag·it·ta'ri·us (saj''i-tär'ē-əs) n. a constellation, the Archer (see zodiac).

sa'go (sä'gō) n. [pl. -gos] a starch obtained from certain palms.

sa·gua'ro (sə-wä'rō) n. [pl. -ros] a giant cactus.

sa'hib (sä'ib) n. (Indian) master.

said (sed) v. pret. & p.p. of say.

sail (sāl) n. 1, a piece of canvas, etc., spread to the wind to propel a ship. 2, a voyage. —v.i. move along in or as in a vessel. —v.t. 1, manage (a vessel). 2, travel over. —**set sail**, begin a voyage.

sail'board'' n. a small flat sailboat.

sail'boat'' n. a boat equipped with sails.

sail'cloth'' n. heavy canvas or duck suitable for making ship's sails.

sail'fish'' n. 1, a large sea-fish with a high dorsal fin. 2, a small sailboat.

sail'or n. 1, a mariner; an enlisted seaman. 2, a flat-brimmed hat, usually of straw.

sain'foin (san'foin) n. a wild grass used as a ground cover and for forage.

saint (sānt) n. 1, a person who has been canonized. 2, a person who has died and is in heaven. 3, a person of great purity. —**saint'hood**, n.

Saint Ber·nard' (bər-närd') one of a breed of large, shaggy working dogs.

saint'ed adj. 1, canonized. 2, sacred. 3, saintly.

Saint El'mo's fire (el'mōz) a glow due to atmospheric electricity.

saint'ly adj. being or befitting a saint. —**saint'li·ness**, n.

saith (seth) v. (Archaic) says.

sake (sāk) n. 1, interest; account. 2, purpose.

sa'ke (sä'kē) n. a Jap. rice liquor.

sa·laam' (sə-läm') n. an obeisance.

sal'a·ble (sāl'ə-bəl) adj. sellable.

sa·la'cious (sə-lā'shəs) adj. impure; obscene. —**sa·la'cious·ness**, n.

sal'ad (sal'əd) n. a dish of uncooked green herbs, fruit, cold vegetables, etc. —**salad days**, a period of youth, inexperience, and usu. poverty.

sal'a·man''der (sal'ə-man''dər) n. 1, a lizardlike amphibian. 2, a mythical animal able to live in fire.

sa·la'mi (sə-lä'mē) n. a spicy Italian sausage.

sal'a·ry (sal'ə-rē) n. compensation for work. —**sal'a·ried**, adj.

sale (sāl) n. 1, an act of selling. 2, a selling at a reduced price. —**sales tax**, a tax on retail sales.

sales'man (sālz'mən) n. [pl. -men] one whose profession or specialty is selling. —**sales'clerk''**, n. —**sales'girl**, **sales'la''dy**, **sales'wom''an**, n.fem. —**sales'man·ship**, n. ability to sell. —**sales'per''son**, n.

sa'li·ent (sā'lē-ənt) adj. conspicuous; projecting. —n. a projecting angle. —**sa'li·ence**, n.

sa'line (sā'līn) adj. pert. to salt.

sa·li'va (sə-lī'və) n. a fluid secreted in the mouth. —**sal'i·va·ry** (sal'ə-ver-ē) adj. —**sal'i·vate''** (sal'ə-vāt'') v.i. secrete saliva.

Salk vaccine (sāk) a vaccine used to combat infantile paralysis.

sal'low (sal'ō) adj. of an unhealthy, yellowish complexion. —**sal'low·ness**, n.

sal'ly (sal'ē) n. 1, a rushing forth; a sortie. 2, a witty remark. —v.i. set out briskly.

sal'ma·gun'di (sal''mə-gun'dē) n. 1, a hash or stew. 2, any mixture.

sal'mi (sal'mē) n. a ragout of the meat of game birds, stewed in wine. Also, **sal'mis.**

salm'on (sam'ən) n. a marine and freshwater food fish.

sal''mon·el'la (sal''mə-nel'ə) n. a rod-shaped pathogenic bacterium.

sa·lon' (sə-lon') n. 1, a drawing room. 2, a fashionable gathering. 3, beauty parlor.

sa·loon' (sə-loon') n. 1, a barroom. 2, a public hall. 3, a sedan.

sal·sa (säl'sə) n. 1, a Latin Amer. dance. 2, a sauce.

sal'si·fy (sal'sə-fē) n. a vegetable, the oyster plant.

salt (sält) n. 1, a mineral, sodium chloride, found in deposits or in sea water, used as a seasoning. 2, (pl.) a medicinal compound. 3, piquancy; spice; wit. 4, (Colloq.) a sailor. —v.t. season or preserve with salt. —**salt'ed**, adj. —**salt'y**, adj. —**salt away**, (Colloq.) store up; save. —**salt lick**, a natural deposit of salt, which animals come to lick. —**salt water**, 1, sea water; the sea. 2, a solution of salt in water.

sal·ta'tion (sal-tā'shən) n. 1, leaping; dancing. 2, an abrupt change or transition.

salt'cel''lar n. a dish or shaker for salt.

sal·tine' (săl-tēn') *n.* (*T.N.*) a crisp, square cracker topped with coarse salt.

salt"pe'ter (sălt"pē'tər) *n.* niter.

salt'wa"ter *adj.* **1,** inhabiting ocean waters. **2,** pert. to or consisting of salt water. —**saltwater taffy,** a flavored sugar candy.

salt'y (sâl'tē) *adj.* **1,** containing or tasting of salt. **2,** piquant; witty; racy. —**salt'i·ness,** *n.*

sa·lu'bri·ous (sə-loo'brē-əs) *adj.* favorable to health. —**sa·lu'bri·ous·ness, sa·lu'bri·ty,** *n.*

sa·lu'ki (sə-loo'kē) *n.* an Asiatic breed of hunting dog.

sal'u·tar·y (sal'yə-ter-ē) *adj.* **1,** healthful. **2,** beneficial.

sal"u·ta'tion (sal"yū-tā'shən) *n.* **1,** act of greeting or saluting. **2,** the formal opening of a letter.

sa·lu'ta·to·ry (sə-loo'tə-tôr-ē) *adj.* pert. to a salutation. —*n.* an address of welcome. —**sa·lu'ta·to'ri·an,** *n.*

sa·lute' (sə-loot') *v.t. & i.* **1,** greet; kiss. **2,** honor formally. —*n.* an act of greeting or tribute.

sal'vage (sal'vij) *n.* the saving of property from danger of loss; the property saved. —*v.t.* save.

sal·va'tion (sal-vā'shən) *n.* **1,** deliverance; that which saves. **2,** redemption. —**Salvation Army,** a religious and charitable body, organized on military lines.

salve (sáv) *n.* **1,** a healing ointment. **2,** anything that soothes. —*v.t.* heal; soothe.

sal'ver (sal'vər) *n.* a tray.

sal'vo (sal'vō) *n.* **1,** a discharge of artillery. **2,** a round of applause.

sa·mar'i·um (sə-mar'ē-əm) *n.* a rare-earth metallic element, no. 62, symbol Sm.

sam'ba (sám'bə) *n.* **1,** a So. Amer. dance. **2,** a card game, three-pack canasta.

sam'bo (sam'bō) *n.* a style of wrestling related to judo.

same (sām) *adj.* **1,** identical; agreeing in kind, degree, or amount. **2,** just mentioned. **3,** unchanged. —*pron.* the same person or thing.

same'ness (-nis) *n.* **1,** identity. **2,** monotony.

sam'i·sen (sam'ə-sen") *n.* a Jap. three-stringed musical instrument.

sa'miz·dat" (sa'mĕz-dat") *n.* a system in the U.S.S.R. for printing and distributing government-banned literature.

sam'o·var" (sam'ə-vär") *n.* a copper urn for making tea.

Sam"o·yed' (sam"ə-yed') *n.* a white-haired Siberian dog.

sam'pan" *n.* a small skifflike boat of China, Indochina, etc.

sam'ple (sam'pəl) *n.* a representative specimen. —*v.t.* test; taste.

sam'pler *n.* **1,** a piece of embroidery. **2,** one who samples.

sam'u·rai" (sam'û-rī") *n. sing. & pl.* a member of the Jap. military class.

san"a·to'ri·um (san"ə-tôr'ē-əm) [*pl.* **-a** (-ə)] *n.* a sanitarium.

sanc'ti·fy" (sank'tə-fī") *v.t.* **1,** make holy; purify. **2,** consecrate. —**sanc"ti·fi·ca'tion,** *n.*

sanc"ti·mo'ny (sank'tə-mō'nē) *n.* hypocritical devoutness. —**sanc"ti·mo'ni·ous,** *adj.*

sanc'tion (sank'shən) *n.* **1,** authorization. **2,** ratification. **3,** a nonmilitary punitive act by one nation against another. —*v.t.* **1,** countenance; approve. **2,** ratify.

sanc'ti·ty (sank'tə-tē) *n.* holiness; sacredness.

sanc'tu·ar"y (sank'chû-er"ē) *n.* **1,** a sacred place. **2,** a place of refuge. **3,** a wildlife preserve.

sanc'tum (sank'təm) *n.* **1,** a sacred place. **2,** a private retreat.

sand *n.* **1,** the fine debris of rocks, in soil-like particles. **2,** (*pl.*) a desert or beach. **3,** (*Colloq.*) grit; pluck. —*v.t.* **1,** sprinkle with sand. **2,** sandpaper. —**sand'er,** *n.* —**sand bar,** a ridge of sand. —**sand dollar,** a sea urchin.

san'dal (san'dəl) *n.* a low shoe.

san'dal·wood" (san'dəl-wûd") *n.* a fragrant Asiatic tree.

san'da·rac (san'də-rak) *n.* a No. Afr. tree; a resin obtained from it, used in varnish, incense, etc.

sand'bag" *n.* a sand-filled bag. —*v.t.* (*Slang*) hit or betray unexpectedly.

sand'blast" *v.t.* clean (stone, etc.) with sand driven by air.

sand'hog" *n.* a worker in tunnel construction.

sand-'lot" *adj.* pert. to amateur sports, esp. baseball, played in a city on undeveloped lots.

sand'man" *n.* [*pl.* **-men"**] a fabled spirit that makes children sleepy.

sand'pa"per *n.* paper coated with an abrasive, esp. sand. —*v.t.* rub sandpaper on, to smooth.

sand'pi"per (sand'pī"pər) *n.* a small wading bird.

sand'stone" *n.* soft, crumbly rock.

sand'wich *n.* **1,** meat, cheese, etc., between two slices of bread. **2,** something similarly compacted. —*v.t.* insert between two other things. —**sandwich man,** (*Colloq.*) a man who carries advertising placards (*sand-*

wich boards) held in front and in back of him by two straps over the shoulders.

sand'y (san'dē) *adj.* **1,** of or like sand. **2,** yellowish, as *sandy hair.* **3,** gritty. —**sand'i·ness,** *n.*

sane (sān) *adj.* **1,** mentally sound. **2,** reasonable. —**sane'ness,** *n.*

San'for·ized" (san'fə-rīzd") *adj.* (*T.N.*) designating a process to prevent shrinking.

sang *v.* pret. of *sing.*

sang-froid' (sän-frwä') *n.* (*Fr.*) calmness; indifference.

san·gri'a (san-grē'ə) *n.* a punch made of wine and fruit juice.

san'gui·nar"y (sang'gwi-ner"ē) *adj.* **1,** bloody. **2,** bloodthirsty.

san'guine (sang'gwin) *adj.* **1,** hopeful; confident; cheerful. **2,** ruddy.

san"i·tar'i·um (san"ə-tār'ē-əm) *n.* an establishment for invalids.

san'i·tar"y (san'ə-ter"ē) *adj.* **1,** pert. to conditions affecting health. **2,** hygienic. —**san'i·tize,** *v.t.* —**sanitary napkin,** an absorbent worn by women during menstruation.

san"i·ta'tion (san"ə-tā'shən) *n.* the process of garbage disposal, sewage, etc.

san'i·ty (san'ə-tē) *n.* saneness.

sank *v.* pret. of *sink.*

sans (sanz) *prep.* (*Archaic*) without.

San'skrit *n.* the ancient literary language of India.

sap *n.* **1,** the fluid that circulates in a plant. **2,** (*Slang*) a fool. **3,** (*Mil.*) a ditch dug to approach an enemy position. —*v.t.* [**sapped, sap'ping**] undermine. —**sap'per,** *n.* a soldier who digs or fights in saps.

sap'id *adj.* tasty; agreeable. —**sa·pid'i·ty** (sə-pid'ə-tē) *n.* —**sap'or** (sā'pər) *n.*

sa'pi·ent (sā'pē-ənt) *adj.* wise. —**sa'pi·ence,** *n.*

sap'ling *n.* a young tree.

sap'phire (saf'īr) *n.* **1,** a precious stone, a transparent blue variety of corundum. **2,** deep blue.

sap'py (sap'ē) *adj.* **1,** full of sap or vitality. **2,** (*Slang*) foolish. —**sap'pi·ness,** *n.*

sap'suck"er *n.* a small spotted woodpecker of the U.S.

sar'a·band" (sar'ə-band") *n.* **1,** a lively Span. castanet dance. **2,** a slow, stately Span. dance.

Sar'a·cen (sar'ə-sən) *n.* (formerly) a Mohammedan.

sa·ran' (sə-ran') *n.* a thermoplastic vinyl used for packaging, etc.

sar'casm (sär'kaz-əm) *n.* bitter irony; taunting comment.

sar·cas'tic (sär-kas'tik) *adj.* being or using sarcasm. —**sar·cas'ti·cal·ly,** *adv.*

sar·co'ma (sär-kō'mə) *n.* a malignant tumor of the connective tissue.

sar·coph'a·gus (sär-kof'ə-gəs) *n.* an ornamental stone coffin.

sard (särd) *n.* a reddish chalcedony.

sar·dine' (sär-dēn') *n.* a small fish allied to the herring, often canned in oil.

sar·don'ic (sär-don'ik) *adj.* sneering; sarcastic. —**sar·don'i·cal·ly,** *adv.*

sar'do·nyx (sär'də-niks) *n.* a semiprecious stone.

sar·gas'so (sär-gas'ō) *n.* a seaweed. Also, **sar·gas'sum** (-əm).

sarge (särj) *n.* (*Colloq.*) sergeant.

sa'ri (sä'rē) *n.* a single long piece of silk or cotton, wrapped around the body and over the head, the principal garment of a Hindu woman.

sa·rong' (sä-râng') *n.* a Malay woman's one-piece garment, wrapped around the lower body like a skirt.

sar"sa·pa·ril'la (sas"pə-ril'ə) *n.* a tropical Amer. plant; a soft drink made from its root.

sar·to'ri·al (sär-tôr'ē-əl) *adj.* **1,** pert. to a tailor or his work. **2,** pert. to men's clothing.

sash *n.* **1,** the framed part of a window. **2,** a band worn around the waist.

sa·shay' (sa-shā') *v.i.* (*Colloq.*) move glidingly.

sas'quatch" (sas'kwach") *n.* a large manlike animal believed to exist in the northwest U.S.

sass (sas) (*Slang*) *n.* saucy or insolent talk; sauce. —*v.t.* speak insolently to (a person). —**sass'y,** *adj.* —**sas'si·ness,** *n.*

sas'sa·by (sas'ə-bē) *n.* a large So. Afr. antelope.

sas'sa·fras" (sas'ə-fras") *n.* a No. Amer. tree; the aromatic bark of the root.

sat *v.* pret. & p.p. of *sit.*

Sa'tan (sā'tən) *n.* the chief evil spirit; the devil. —**sa·tan'ic,** *adj.* —**sa·tan'i·cal·ly,** *adv.*

satch'el (sach'əl) *n.* a small bag, used as luggage.

sate (sāt) *v.t.* satisfy; fill.

sa·teen' (sa-tēn') *n.* a cotton fabric resembling satin.

sat'el·lite" (sat'ə-līt") *n.* **1,** a moon. **2,** an attendant; follower. **3,** a country supposedly independent but actually controlled by another.

sa'ti·ate" (sā'shē-āt") *v.t.* surfeit; oversatisfy; glut. —**sa'ti·a·ble,** *adj.* —**sa"ti·a'tion,** *n.*

sa·ti·e·ty (sə-tī′ə-tē) *n.* state of being satiated; surfeit.

sat·in (sat′ən) *n. & adj.* a lustrous fabric. —**sat′in·y,** *adj.*

sat′in·wood″ *n.* an E. Indian tree or its fine, hard wood.

sat′ire (sat′īr) *n.* the use of irony, ridicule, etc., in writing. —**sa·tir′i·cal** (sə-tir′-ə-kəl) *adj.* —**sat′i·rist,** *n.* —**sat′i·rize″** (sat′ə-rīz″) *v.t.*

sat″is·fac′tion (sat″is-fak′shən) *n.* act, means, or result of satisfying. —**sat″is·fac′-to·ry** (-tə-rē) *adj.*

sat′is·fy″ (sat′is-fī″) *v.t.* **1,** gratify completely; supply the needs of. **2,** pay fully. **3,** convince. **4,** fulfill the conditions of. **5,** atone for.

sa·to′ri (sə-tō′rē) *n.* in Zen Buddhism, a state of enlightenment.

sat′rap (sat′rap) *n.* a subordinate but despotic ruler. —**sat′rap·y** (-rə-pē) *n.*

sat′u·rate″ (sach′ə-rāt″) *v.t.* soak; impregnate fully. —**sat″u·ra′tion,** *n.* —**sat′u·rat″-ed,** *adj.* (*Chem.*) a state of animal or vegetable fats, associated with higher concentrations of cholesterol in the blood.

Sat′ur·day (sat′ər-dē) *n.* the seventh day of the week, observed by some Christians and Judaism as the Sabbath. —**Saturday night special,** a cheap handgun.

sat″ur·na′li·a (sat″ər-nā′lē-ə) *n.pl.* unrestrained revelry.

sat′ur·nine″ (sat′ər-nīn″) *adj.* morose; phlegmatic.

sat′yr (sat′ər) *n.* **1,** a sylvan deity, half human and half goat. **2,** a lascivious man.

sat″y·ri′a·sis (sat″ə-rī′ə-sis) *n.* uncontrollable amorous passion in a man.

sauce (sâs) *n.* **1,** a relish or appetizer. **2,** a compote of fruit. **3,** (*Colloq.*) pertness; insolence. **4,** (*Slang*) liquor. —*v.t.* **1,** season; give zest to. **2,** (*Colloq.*) address impertinently.

sauce′pan″ *n.* a small cooking pan with a handle.

sau′cer (sâ′sər) *n.* a small, round dish.

sau′cy (sâ′sē) *adj.* pert; insolent. —**sau′-ci·ness,** *n.*

sau′er·brat″en (sow′ər-brä″tən) *n.* a pot roast of meat marinated in vinegar.

sau′er·kraut″ (sow′ər-krowt″) *n.* fermented, sour cabbage.

sau′na (sâ′nə) *n.* **1,** a Finnish steam bath using water thrown on heated rocks. **2,** a similar bath using dry heat from heated rocks.

saun′ter (sân′tər) *v.i.* walk in a leisurely way; stroll.

sau′sage (sâ′sij) *n.* minced meat, seasoned, often stuffed into a membranous tube.

sau·té′ (sō-tā′) *v.t.* pan fry.

sau·terne′ (sō-tĕrn′) *n.* a sweet, white French wine.

sav′age (sav′ij) *adj.* **1,** uncivilized; uncultivated. **2,** ferocious; barbarous. —*n.* a savage person. —**sav′age·ry** (-rē) *n.*

sa·van′na (sə-van′ə) *n.* a grassy plain with scattered trees. Also, **sa·van′nah.**

sa·vant′ (sa-vänt′) *n.* a man of learning.

save (sāv) *v.t.* **1,** preserve from danger, injury, or loss; deliver from sin. **2,** conserve; set apart; hoard. **3,** (*Theol.*) deliver from the power or penalty of sin. —*v.i.* **1,** put aside money for the future. **2,** be frugal. **3,** last without spoiling, as food. —*prep. & conj.* except. —*n.* (*Hockey*) the prevention by the goalie of a scoring attempt.

sav′ing *n.* **1,** economy. **2,** a reduction in expenditure. **3,** (*pl.*) money put aside. —*adj.* redeeming. —*prep. & conj.* save.

sav′ior (sāv′yər) *n.* **1,** a rescuer. **2,** (*cap.*) [usu., **Sav′iour**] Jesus Christ.

sa′voir-faire′ (sav′wär-fâr′) *n.* (*Fr.*) knowledge of what to do; poise.

sa′vor (sā′vər) *n.* taste; flavor. —*v.i.* taste; season. Also, **sa′vour.**

sa′vor·y (sā′və-rē) *adj.* tasty; agreeable. —*n.* **1,** an appetizing dish. **2,** either of two herbs used for seasoning.

sa·voy′ (sə-voi′) *n.* [*pl.* **-voys**] a variety of cabbage.

sav′vy (sav′ē) (*Slang*) *v.t. & i.* understand. —*adj.* knowledgeable. —*n.* understanding.

saw (sâ) *n.* **1,** a metal blade with teeth, used for cutting. **2,** a proverb. —*v.t. & i.* **1,** cut with or use a saw. **2,** cut or move as a saw does. **3,** pret. of *see.*

saw′bones″ *n.sing.* (*Slang*) a surgeon.

saw′buck″ *n.* **1,** a sawhorse. **2,** (*Slang*) a ten-dollar bill.

saw′dust″ *n.* tiny fragments of wood.

saw′horse″ *n.* a support for holding wood while it is sawed.

saw′mill″ *n.* a mill where logs are sawed into planks.

saw-′toothed″ *adj.* having teeth resembling those of a saw; serrate.

saw′yer (sâ′yər) *n.* **1,** one who saws wood. **2,** a kind of beetle.

sax (saks) *n.* saxophone.

sax′horn″ *n.* any of a family of brass wind instruments used chiefly in military bands.

sax′i·frage″ (sak′si-frij) *n.* any of a genus of perennial herbs.

Sax′on (sak′sən) *adj.* **1,** pert. to an ancient Teutonic people. **2,** pert. to Saxony. —*n.* a Saxon person.

sax′o·phone″ (sak′sə-fōn″) *n.* a brass wind instrument. Also, *colloq.,* **sax.**

---

say (sā) *v.t.* [*pret. & p.p.* **said** (sed)] **1,** utter, express, or declare in words; tell. **2,** suppose. **3,** decide. —*n.* **1,** what one has to say. **2,** the opportunity to speak or decide. —*adv.* for example.

say'ing *n.* a proverbial expression.

say-'so'' *n.* (*Colloq.*) **1,** a personal assertion. **2,** a decision.

scab (skab) *n.* **1,** an incrustation formed over a healing sore. **2,** a strikebreaker. —*v.i.* act as a scab. —**scab'by,** *adj.*

scab'bard (skab'ərd) *n.* a sheath for a sword, etc.

sca'bi·es'' (skā'bē-ēz'') *n.* an infectious parasitic skin disease.

sca'brous (skā'brəs) *adj.* **1,** scabby or scaly. **2,** full of difficulties. **3,** risqué or salacious.

scads (skadz) *n.pl.* (*Slang*) a large amount.

scaf'fold (skaf'əld) *n.* **1,** a temporary supporting platform. **2,** a platform for a gallows. —**scaf'fold·ing,** *n.* a scaffold for workmen.

scag (skag) *n.* (*Slang*) heroin.

sca'lar (skā'lər) *adj.* one-dimensional; having magnitude without direction. —*n.* a scalar quantity.

scal'a·wag'' (skal'ə-wag'') *n.* (*Colloq.*) a worthless fellow; a scamp.

scald (skâld) *v.t.* **1,** burn with a boiling liquid or steam. **2,** cook slightly. **3,** cleanse with boiling water. —*n.* **1,** a sore caused by scalding. **2,** a disease of fruit.

scale (skāl) *n.* **1,** a thin, horny piece of cuticle, as on a fish. **2,** a flake; a scab. **3,** (*sing.* or *pl.*) a balance for weighing. **4,** (*Music*) a series of tones at fixed intervals. **5,** a series of marks for measurement or computation. **6,** a gradation. **7,** a system of proportion. **8,** a table of prices, wages, etc. —*v.t.* **1,** deprive of scales; clean. **2,** skip, as a stone over water. **3,** weigh. **4,** climb up or over. **5,** project or adjust according to scale.

sca·lene' (skā-lēn') *adj.* (*Geom.*) **1,** denoting a triangle with no two sides equal. **2,** having the axis oblique, as a cone.

scal'lion (skal'yən) *n.* a variety of onion with a small bulb.

scal'lop (skal'əp) *n.* **1,** a bivalve mollusk; its wavy-edged shell. **2,** one of a series of small curves cut in the edge of a garment, etc. —*v.t.* **1,** cut (an edge) in a wavy line. **2,** escallop.

scalp (skalp) *n.* the integument of the upper part of the head. —*v.t.* **1,** remove the scalp of. **2,** (*Colloq.*) buy and sell (tickets) for quick profit. —**scalp'er,** *n.* a ticket broker who charges exorbitant prices.

scal'pel (skal'pəl) *n.* a light, straight surgical knife.

scam (skam) *n.* (*Slang*) a swindle.

scamp (skamp) *n.* a rascal.

scam'per (skam'pər) *v.i.* run quickly.

scam'pi (skam'pē) *n.pl.* shrimp cooked in garlic sauce.

scan (skan) *v.t.* [**scanned, scan'ning**] **1,** examine minutely; scrutinize. **2,** glance over hastily. **3,** read for metrical structure. —*v.i.* conform to a meter.

scan'dal (skan'dəl) *n.* **1,** public disgrace; a cause of disgrace. **2,** gossip. —**scan'dal·ize''** (-īz'') *v.t.* shock.

scan'dal·mon''ger (skan'dəl-mung''gər) *n.* one who gossips.

scan'dal·ous (-əs) *adj.* **1,** disgraceful. **2,** defamatory.

Scan''di·na'vi·an (skan''di-nā'vē-ən) *adj. & n.* pert. to Scandinavia, its people or languages.

scan'di·um (skan'dē-əm) *n.* a white metallic element, sometimes included with the rare-earth elements, no. 21, symbol Sc.

scan'sion (skan'shən) *n.* analysis of metrical verse.

scant (skant) *adj.* scarcely sufficient. —**scant'y,** *adj.* small; scant.

scant'ling (-ling) *n.* **1,** timber of small cross-section relative to length, as a joist; such timbers collectively. **2,** an upright piece in a house frame.

scape'goat'' (skāp'gōt'') *n.* one made to bear the blame for others' misdeeds.

scape'grace'' (skāp'grās'') *n.* a graceless fellow; a scamp.

scap'u·la (skap'yə-lə) *n.* the shoulder blade.

scap'u·lar (-lər) *adj.* pert. to the scapula. —*n.* a sleeveless monastic robe hung from the shoulders.

scar (skär) *n.* a mark remaining after a wound has healed. —*v.t. & i.* [**scarred, scar'ring**] mark with a scar; form a scar in healing.

scar'ab (skar'əb) *n.* **1,** a beetle. **2,** an amulet in the form of a beetle.

scarce (skârs) *adj.* **1,** insufficient; not abundant. **2,** uncommon; rare. —**scarce'ness,** *n.*

scarce'ly *adv.* hardly; barely; probably not.

scar'ci·ty (skâr'sə-tē) *n.* scarceness; shortage; dearth.

scare (skâr) *v.t.* **1,** frighten. **2,** (with *up*) get. —*v.i.* become frightened.

scare'crow'' *n.* **1,** a semblance of a man, set up to frighten crows. **2,** a poorly dressed person. **3,** a thin person.

scare'head'' *n.* a headline in very large type.

scarf (skärf) *n.* **1,** a decorative strip of

material; a muffler; a cravat. **2,** a joint for uniting two timbers.

scar'i·fy'' (skar'ə-fī'') *v.t.* **1,** scratch. **2,** harass. —**scar''i·fi·ca'tion,** *n.*

scar''la·ti'na (skär''lə-tē'nə) *n.* scarlet fever, esp. a mild form of it.

scar'let (skär'lit) *n. & adj.* a brilliant red color. —**scarlet fever,** a contagious febrile disease.

scarp (skärp) *n.* **1,** a steep slope. **2,** an escarpment.

scar'y (skār'ē) *adj.* **1,** causing fright. **2,** timid. —**scar'i·ness,** *n.*

scat (skat) *v.t.* [**scat'ted, -ting**] (*Colloq.*) drive off. —*interj.* Go away!

scathe (skāth) *v.t.* **1,** criticize severely. **2,** injure. —**scath'ing,** *adj.*

sca·tol'o·gy (ska-tol'ə-jē) *n.* **1,** the study of animal excretions. **2,** any writing about what is considered morally or physically filthy. —**scat''o·log'i·cal** (skat''ə-loj'i-kəl) *adj.*

scat'ter (skat'ər) *v.t.* **1,** throw loosely about. **2,** dispose. **3,** put to flight. —*v.i.* disperse. —**scat'ter·brain'',** *n.* a giddy person. —**scatter rug,** a small rug used with others.

scaup (skâp) *n.* any of several common species of duck.

scav'en·ger (skav'in-jər) *n.* **1,** an animal or organism that devours refuse. **2,** a street cleaner. —**scav'enge,** *v.i. & t.*

sce·nar'i·o'' (si-nār'ē-ō'') *n.* the outline of a drama or motion picture; hence, a plan of action.

scene (sēn) *n.* **1,** the place where anything is done or takes place. **2,** a stage setting; a division of a play. **3,** a particular incident. **4,** a view; a picture. **5,** an exhibition of strong feeling. **6,** (*Slang*) situation.

scen'er·y (sē'nə-rē) *n.* **1,** the aggregate of features in a view. **2,** stage settings.

scen'ic (sē'nik) *adj.* pert. to scenery; abounding in fine scenery. —**scen'i·cal·ly,** *adv.* —**scenic railway,** a roller-coaster.

scent (sent) *n.* **1,** an odor. **2,** the course of an animal. **3,** a perfume. **4,** the sense of smell. —*v.t.* **1,** smell. **2,** suspect. **3,** perfume.

scep'ter (sep'tər) *n.* a staff emblematic of royalty. Also, **scep'tre.**

scep'tic (skep'tik) *n.* skeptic.

sched'ule (skej'ûl) *n.* **1,** a statement of contents, details, etc. **2,** agenda. **3,** a time-table. —*v.t.* place on a schedule; plan.

sche'ma (skē'mə) *n.* [*pl.* **-ma·ta** (-mə-tə)] scheme; diagram; plan.

sche·mat'ic (skē-mat'ik) *adj.* pert. to a scheme or diagram. —*n.* a schematic draw-

ing. —**sche·mat'i·cal·ly,** *adv.* —**sche'ma·tize,** *v.t.*

scheme (skēm) *n.* **1,** a regular or formal plan; a system. **2,** a plot; an intrigue. —*v.t. & i.* plan; plot. —**schem'er,** *n.* —**schem'-ing,** *adj.* plotting; crafty.

scher·zan'do (sker-tsän'dō) *adj. & adv.* (*Music*) playful; sportive.

scher'zo (sker'tzō) *n.* (*Music*) a movement of a light or playful nature.

Schick test (shik) a diphtheria immunity test.

schip'per·ke (ship'ər-kē) *n.* a Belgian breed of terrier used as watchdogs.

schism (siz'əm; skiz-) *n.* a division or separation. —**schis·mat'ic,** *adj.*

schist (shist) *n.* a crystalline rock formed in parallel layers.

schizo- (skiz-ō) *pref.* split.

schiz''o·phre'ni·a (skiz''ə-frē'nē-ə) *n.* a mental disorder, splitting of the personality. —**schiz'oid, schiz''o·phren'ic** (-fren'ik) *adj.*

schle·miel' (shlə-mēl') *n.* (*Slang*) an ineffective and somewhat stupid or unpractical person.

schlep (shlep) *v.t.* [**schlepped, schlep'-ping**] (*Slang*) lug awkwardly or with difficulty; transport.

schlock (shlok) *n.* (*Slang*) cheap or tawdry merchandise.

schmaltz (shmalts) *n.* (*Slang*) **1,** flattery. **2,** trite or sentimental writing, music, etc.; corn. —**schmaltz'y,** *adj.*

schmear (shmir) *n.* (*Slang*) the totality of something.

schmo (shmō) *n.* (*Slang*) a stupid person.

schmooze (shmooz) *v.i. & n.* (*Slang*) chat.

schmuck (shmuk) *n.* (*Slang*) a stupid, gullible, or clumsy person.

schnapps (shnäps) *n.* liquor.

schnau'zer (shnow'zər) *n.* a Ger. breed of terrier.

schnit'zel (shnit'zəl) *n.* a veal cutlet.

schnook (shnûk) *n.* (*Slang*) a dupe.

schnor'rer (shnôr'ər) *n.* a parasite.

schnoz'zle (shnoz'əl) *n.* (*Slang*) the nose.

schol'ar (skol'ər) *n.* **1,** a student. **2,** a learned man. —**schol'ar·ly,** *adj.*

schol'ar·ship'' *n.* **1,** learning; erudition. **2,** monetary assistance granted to a scholar.

scho·las'tic (skə-las'tik) *adj.* **1,** pert. to schools, scholars, or education. **2,** pedantic. —*n.* a pedantic person.

scho·las'ti·cism (skə-las'tə-siz-əm) *n.* narrow adherence to traditional doctrines or methods.

school (skool) *n.* **1,** an educational establishment. **2,** a united group or sect. **3,** a specific method, etc. **4,** a large body of fish, whales, etc. —*v.t.* educate; train. **—school board,** a body governing local schools. **—school′book″,** *n.* textbook. **—school′ing,** *n.* education; learning. — **school′marm″** (-märm″)*n.* a woman school-teacher, or any prim woman (formerly thought to be typical of schoolteachers).

schoon′er (skoo′nər) *n.* **1,** a sailing vessel. **2,** a tall glass for beer.

schot′tische (shot′ish) *n.* a Scottish dance, similar to the polka.

schtick (shtik) *n.* (*Slang*) act; bit; routine.

schuss (shûs) *n.* in skiing, a steep, straight run. —*v.i.* make such a run.

schwa (shwä) *n.* the indeterminate vowel sound of most unaccented syllables in English; the symbol (ə) for it.

sci·at′ic (sī-at′ik) *adj.* pert. to or affecting the hip.

sci·at′i·ca (sī-at′i-kə) *n.* pain and tenderness in a sciatic nerve.

sci′ence (sī′əns) *n.* **1,** a branch of knowledge; what is known concerning a subject. **2,** (*Colloq.*) natural science, as physics or chemistry. **3,** special skill. **—natural science, 1,** any of the sciences dealing directly with the physical world, as biology, chemistry, physics, etc. **2,** these sciences collectively. **—science fiction,** fiction based on scientific fact or imagining.

sci″en·tif′ic (sī″ən-tif′ik) *adj.* **1,** pert. to science. **2,** systematic and accurate. **—sci″en·tif′i·cal·ly,** *adv.*

sci′en·tist (sī′ən-tist) *n.* one versed in a science.

scim′i·tar (sim′ə-tər) *n.* a curved, single-edged sword.

scin·til′la (sin-til′ə) *n.* the least particle; a trace.

scin′til·late″ (sin′tə-lāt″) *v.i.* emit sparks; twinkle; shine. **—scin″til·la′tion,** *n.*

sci′on (sī′ən) *n.* **1,** a descendant. **2,** a shoot or twig used for grafting.

scis′sors (siz′ərz) *n.pl.* or *sing.* a cutting instrument consisting of two pivoted blades.

scle·ro′sis (skli-rō′sis) *n.* [*pl.* **-ses** (-sēz)] a hardening of a tissue or part. **—scle·rot′-ic,** *adj.*

scoff (skof) *v.i.* (with *at*) jeer.

scoff′law″ *n.* one who scoffs at or disobeys the law.

scold (skōld) *v.t.* & *i.* chide; find fault. —*n.* a railing woman.

sconce (skons) *n.* **1,** a wall bracket for candles, etc. **2,** a defensive bulwark. **3,** (*Archaic*) the head.

scone (skōn) *n.* a soft cake or biscuit.

scoop (skoop) *n.* **1,** an instrument for hollowing out anything. **2,** a hollow. **3,** the act of scooping. **4,** (*Colloq.*) a journalistic beat. —*v.t.* **1,** (with *out*) remove or hollow with a scoop. **2,** publish news earlier than.

scoot (skoot) *v.i.* go hastily; dart. —*v.t.* eject.

scoot′er *n.* **1,** a child's foot-propelled vehicle. **2,** an iceboat. **3,** a motor scooter.

scope (skōp) *n.* **1,** outlook; intellectual range. **2,** room for free observation or action. **3,** extent; length; sweep.

-scope (skōp) *suf.* a means or instrument for viewing.

sco·pol′a·mine″ (skō-pol′ə-mēn″) *n.* an alkaloid used as a depressant and as an anesthetic in obstetrics.

scor·bu′tic (skôr-bū′tik) *adj.* pert. to or affected with scurvy.

scorch (skôrch) *v.t.* & *i.* **1,** burn superficially; singe. **2,** parch. **3,** criticize caustically. —*n.* a superficial burn. **—scorched earth policy,** total destruction of one's own territory, to impede an invader.

scorch′er *n.* anything that scorches; (*Colloq.*) a very hot day; a caustic statement.

score (skōr) *n.* **1,** the points made in a game or match. **2,** a reckoning; account. **3,** a notch; a scratch. **4,** reason; ground. **5,** twenty; (*pl.*) many. **6,** a copy of a musical composition. —*v.t.* & *t.* **1,** make, record, or write a score. **2,** berate. **3,** orchestrate. **4,** (often with *with*) (*Colloq.*) seduce. **5,** win success or advantage.

sco′ri·a (skôr′é-ə) *n.* [*pl.* **-ae** (-ė)] slag.

scorn (skôrn) *n.* contempt; disdain. —*v.t.* **1,** disdain. **2,** reject.

scorn′ful (-fəl) *adj.* full of or expressing contempt.

Scor′pi·o (skôr′pé-ō) *n.* a constellation, the Scorpion (see *zodiac*).

scor′pi·on (skôr′pė-ən) *n.* a venomous arachnid.

Scot (skot) *n.* a native or inhabitant of Scotland. **—Scots,** *adj.* **—Scots′man,** *n.*

Scotch (skoch) *adj.* Scottish. —*n.* **1,** a whiskey distilled in Scotland. **2,** (*l.c.*) a cut. **3,** (*l.c.*) a block or wedge. —*v.t.* (*l.c.*) **1,** cut; crush. **2,** block (a wheel). **3,** thwart; obstruct; hinder. **—Scotch broth,** a soup made of lamb stock and barley. **—Scotch tape,** (*T. N.*) an adhesive cellulose tape. **—Scotch terrier** [also, **Scot′tie,** **Scot′tie** (skot′é)] a short-legged, small terrier.

scot-′free″ (skot′frē″) *adj.* safe; clear; without charge or tax.

Scotland Yard the police headquarters in London, England.

Scot′tish (skot′ish) *adj.* of or pert. to Scotland.

scoun′drel (skown′drəl) *n.* an unprincipled man; a villain. **—scoun′drel·ly,** *adj.*

scour (skowr) *v.t. & i.* **1,** clean by friction; brighten. **2,** cleanse dirt from. **3,** search through; range.

scourge (skėrj) *n.* **1,** a whip. **2,** an affliction; a cause of affliction. —*v.t.* **1,** whip; **2,** afflict.

scout (skowt) *n.* **1,** a soldier, airplane, etc., sent to reconnoiter. **2,** an observer. **3,** (*cap.*) a Boy Scout or Girl Scout. **4,** (*Colloq.*) fellow. —*v.t. & i.* **1,** reconnoiter. **2,** ridicule.

scout'mas"ter *n.* adult leader of a troop of Scouts. —**scout'mis"tress,** *n.fem.*

scow (skow) *n.* a large, flat-bottomed boat for freight.

scowl (skowl) *v.i.* lower the brows; look gloomy, severe, or angry. —*n.* an angry frown.

scrab'ble (skrab'əl) *v.i.* **1,** scratch. **2,** scrawl. **3,** scramble. —*n.* (*cap.; T. N.*) a parlor game based on crossword puzzles and anagrams.

scrag'gly (skrag'lė) *adj.* irregular; ragged. —**scrag'gy,** *adj.* thin; scrawny.

scram (skram) *v.i.* [**scrammed, scram'ming**] (*Slang*) go away.

scram'ble (skram'bəl) *v.i.* **1,** struggle along as if on all fours. **2,** strive eagerly and rudely. —*v.t.* mix together. —*n.* act of scrambling. —**scrambled eggs, 1,** eggs mixed while frying. **2,** (*Slang*) yellow braid worn by a naval officer.

scram'jet" *n.* a ramjet engine with special thrust at supersonic speeds.

scrap (skrap) *n.* **1,** a detached portion; a fragment. **2,** (*pl.*) fragments of food. **3,** discarded iron or steel. **4,** (*Slang*) a fight or quarrel. —*v.t.* [**scrapped, scrap'ping**] **1,** break up. **2,** discard as useless. —*v.i.* (often with *with*) (*Slang*) fight.

scrap'book" *n.* a blank book for pictures, clippings, etc.

scrape (skrāp) *v.t.* **1,** shave or abrade the surface of. **2,** (with *out* or *off*) remove; erase. **3,** (with *together* or *up*) collect. —*v.i.* **1,** rub lightly. **2,** get by with difficulty. **3,** save. —*n.* **1,** the act or sound of scraping. **2,** an embarrassing predicament. —**scrap'er,** *n.* —**scrap'ing,** *n.*

scrap'ple (skrap'əl) *n.* a highly spiced sausage-like food served at breakfast.

scrap'py (skrap'ė) *adj.* (*Slang*) pugnacious. —**scrap'pi-ness,** *n.*

scratch (skrach) *v.t. & i.* **1,** mark or wound slightly. **2,** rub, as with the fingernails, to relieve itching. **3,** scribble. **4,** dig with the claws. **5,** rub roughly; grate against. **6,** erase. **7,** withdraw from a race. —*n.* **1,** an act or result of scratching. **2,** a position without allowance or penalty. —**scratch'y,**

adj. —**scratch hit,** in baseball, a lightly hit ground ball that makes a hit. —**scratch pad,** a memorandum pad.

scrawl (skrâl) *v.t.* write or draw carelessly. —*n.* a careless script.

scraw'ny (skrâ'nė) *adj.* meager; lean. —**scraw'ni-ness,** *n.*

scream (skrēm) *v.i. & t.* **1,** utter a sharp, piercing outcry. **2,** emit a shrill sound. **3,** (*Colloq.*) laugh immoderately. —*n.* **1,** a screaming sound. **2,** (*Colloq.*) a joker; something funny. —**scream'er,** *n.* a banner headline in a newspaper.

screech (skrēch) *v.i. & t.* scream harshly. —*n.* a shriek. —**screech'y,** *adj.*

screed (skrēd) *n.* **1,** a harangue. **2,** a section of plastering.

screen (skrēn) *n.* **1,** any partition or curtain that conceals or protects. **2,** a protective formation, as of troops. **3,** a pretext. **4,** a sieve. **5,** a surface on which motion pictures are projected; motion pictures collectively. —*v.t. & i.* **1,** conceal; protect. **2,** sift. **3,** film; exhibit.

screen'play" *n.* a play or script followed in making a motion picture.

screw (skroo) *n.* **1,** a nail-like device having an external thread, that turns in a nut or is driven into wood. **2,** a propeller. **3,** coercion. **4,** (*Slang*) a prison guard. —*v.t. & i.* **1,** turn (a screw); attach by a screw. **2,** twist; contort.

screw'ball" *n. & adj.* (*Slang*) an eccentric person.

screw'driv"er *n.* a tool for turning screws. **2,** (*Colloq.*) a cocktail made with vodka and orange juice.

screw'y (-ė) *adj.* **1,** twisted; tortuous; spiral. **2,** (*Slang*) crazy; eccentric; inexplicable. —**screw'i-ness,** *n.*

scrib'ble (skrib'əl) *v.t. & i.* write carelessly. —*n.* a scrawl.

scribe (skrīb) *n.* **1,** a penman; a public writer. **2,** (*Colloq.*) an author. —*v.t.* mark or score with a pointed tool.

scrim (skrim) *n.* coarse cotton or linen fabric.

scrim'mage (skrim'ij) *n.* **1,** a skirmish; a tussle. **2,** (*Football*) the clash of opposing lines; a practice game. —*v.i.* engage in a scrimmage.

scrimp (skrimp) *v.t. & i.* be sparing in or of; pinch. —**scrimp'y,** *adj.* meager.

scrim'shaw" *n.* a carved decoration on ivory, bone, etc. —*v.t. & i.* carve such decorations.

scrip (skrip) *n.* a certificate promising future payment.

script (skript) *n.* **1,** handwriting; printing

type like handwriting. **2,** the manuscript of a play or motion picture.

Scrip′ture (skrip′chər) *n.* **1,** the Bible. **2,** any sacred writing. **—scrip′tur·al,** *adj.*

scrive′ner (skriv′nər) *n.* scribe.

scrod (skrod) *n.* a young codfish.

scrof′u·la (skrof′yə-lə) *n.* a disorder characterized by glandular swelling. **—scrof′-u·lous,** *adj.*

scroll (skrōl) *n.* **1,** a roll of paper or parchment, esp. a writing. **2,** a spiral or coiled ornament. **—scroll′work″,** *n.* spiral decoration. **—scroll saw,** a thin saw for cutting irregular shapes.

Scrooge (skrooj) *n.* a disagreeable, stingy person.

scro′tum (skrō′təm) *n.* the pouch of skin containing the testicles.

scrouge (skrowj) *v.t.* (*Colloq.*) squeeze; crowd.

scrounge (skrownj) *v.t. & i.* obtain by sponging on or pilfering from another person. *—n.* one who does so.

scrub (skrub) *v.t. & i.* **[scrubbed, scrub′bing]** cleanse by rubbing hard. *—n.* **1,** underbrush. **2,** a worn-out or inferior animal. **3,** anything inferior. **4,** (*Sports*) a substitute player. **5,** a form of baseball. *—adj.* makeshift. **—scrub′by,** *adj.*

scruff (skruf) *n.* the nape of the neck. **—scruf′fy,** *adj.* unkempt; shabby.

scrump′tious (skrump′shəs) *adj.* (*Slang*) very fine; first-rate; delicious.

scrunch (skrunch) *v.t. & i.* crunch or crush. *—n.* a crumbling sound.

scru′ple (skroo′pəl) *n.* **1,** a conscientious reluctance. **2,** a small amount. *—v.i.* hesitate.

scru′pu·lous (skroop′yə-ləs) *adj.* **1,** upright; moral. **2,** exact; punctilious. **—scru′-pu·lous·ness,** *n.*

scru′ti·nize″ (skroo′tə-nīz″) *v.t.* observe or investigate closely.

scru′ti·ny (skroo′tə-nē) *n.* close observation; examination.

scu′ba (skoo′bə) *n.* a *Self-Contained Underwater Breathing Apparatus* used for extended periods of underwater swimming. Also, **SCUBA.**

scud (skud) *v.i.* **[scud′ded, -ding] 1,** move quickly. **2,** run before a gale.

scuff (skuf) *v.t.* **1,** spoil the finish by scraping. **2,** scrape with the feet. *—v.i.* shuffle. *—n.* **1,** a blemish; scuffmark. **2,** a type of slipper.

scuf′fle (skuf′əl) *v.i.* **1,** fight or struggle confusedly. **2,** shuffle. *—n.* **1,** a brief, rough fight. **2,** a shuffle.

scull (skul) *n.* **1,** an oar. **2,** a light racing boat for one rower. *—v.t. & i.* propel (a boat) with a scull.

scul′ler·y (skul′ə-rē) *n.* a back kitchen.

scul′lion (skul′yən) *n.* a menial kitchen servant.

sculp′ture (skulp′chər) *n.* **1,** the art of carving or shaping figures. **2,** a piece of such work. *—v.* [also, **sculpt**] carve, chisel, or engrave. **—sculp′tur·al,** *adj.* **—sculp′-tor,** *n.*

scum (skum) *n.* **1,** a film of extraneous matter on a liquid. **2,** refuse. **3,** worthless persons. **—scum′my,** *adj.*

scum′ble (skum′bəl) *v.t.* rub (a painting or drawing) to spread and soften the colors or tones.

scup (skup) *n.* the porgy.

scup′per (skup′ər) *n.* an opening to let water run off the deck of a ship.

scup′per·nong″ (skup′ər-nong″) *n.* a muscadine grape of the U.S.

scurf (skêrf) *n.* flakes of skin that are shed, as dandruff. **—scurf′y,** *adj.*

scur′ril·ous (skēr′ə-ləs) *adj.* indecently or grossly abusive; offensive. **—scur·ril′-i·ty,** *n.*

scur′ry (skēr′ē) *v.i.* hurry along; scamper. *—n.* a scampering rush.

scur′vy (skēr′vē) *n.* a disease characterized by swelling, hemorrhages, etc., caused by improper diet. *—adj.* low; contemptible.

scutch′eon (skuch′ən) *n.* **1,** escutcheon. **2,** a metal plate or shield, as that which covers a keyhole, etc.

scut′tle (skut′əl) *n.* **1,** a container for coal. **2,** a hurried run. **3,** a small opening. *—v.i.* hurry. *—v.t.* sink (a ship) by cutting holes in the bottom.

scut′tle·butt″ *n.* **1,** a cask. **2,** (*Slang*) gossip.

scythe (sīth) *n.* an instrument with a long blade for cutting grass.

sea (sē) *n.* **1,** the salt waters on the earth's surface; the ocean. **2,** a region of the ocean; a large lake. **3,** a swell; a large wave. **4,** an overwhelming quantity. **—at sea,** perplexed. **—sea biscuit, 1,** a large, crisp unleavened cracker. **2,** hardtack. **—sea cucumber,** a small invertebrate sea animal. **—sea dog, 1,** an experienced sailor. **2,** the harbor seal. **—sea elephant,** a large seal. **—sea foam,** meerschaum. **—sea gull,** a marine bird; gull. **—sea horse,** a fish with a head suggesting a horse's. **—sea legs,** ability to walk (as on a ship) without losing balance. **—sea level,** the mean level of the sea. **—sea lion,** a variety of seal. **—sea shell,** the shell of any sea mollusk. **—sea urchin,** a spiny sea animal.

sea′bed″ *n.* bed (def. 3).

---

fat, fāte, fär, fâre, fâll, ȧsk; met, hē, hêr, maybė; pin, pīne; not, nōte, ôr, tool

Sea'bee'' *n.* a member of a U.S. Navy construction battalion.

sea'board'' *n.* coast.

sea'coast'' *n.* seashore.

sea'far''er (-fār''ər) *n.* a traveler by sea. —**sea'far''ing,** *adj.*

sea'food'' *n.* edible marine fish and shell-fish.

sea'go''ing *adj.* used for, or suitable for, ocean travel.

seal (sēl) *n.* **1,** an impressed device used to authenticate a document; a stamp for impressing the device. **2,** a tight closure; a substance used to effect it. **3,** a marine carnivorous mammal; its fur; its skin used for leather. —*v.t.* **1,** authenticate, close, or secure with a seal. **2,** determine irrevocably. **3,** close; confine. **4,** hunt seals. —**seal'ant,** *n.*

Sea'lab'' *n.* a special ship for underwater exploration.

Sea'ly·ham'' (sē'lė-ham'') *n.* a shaggy terrier of Welsh origin.

seam (sēm) *n.* **1,** the line formed by joining two edges, esp. in sewing. **2,** a fissure or gap; a ridge. **3,** a stratum. —*v.t. & i.* sew a seam.

sea'man (-mən) *n.* [*pl.* **-men**] a sailor. —**sea'man·ship,** *n.* skill in the operation of a ship.

seam'stress (-strəs) *n.* a woman who sews.

seam'y (sē'mė) *adj.* sordid.

sé'ance (sā'äns) *n.* a session or meeting of spiritualists.

sea'plane'' *n.* an airplane designed for taking off and landing on water; often with pontoons.

sea'port'' *n.* a city having a harbor on the sea.

sear (sir) *v.t.* **1,** burn or brown the surface of. **2,** make callous. **3,** dry up.

search (sėrch) *v.t.* **1,** go through and examine carefully; explore. **2,** probe. **3,** penetrate. **4,** (with *out*) look for; seek. —*v.i.* seek; investigate. —*n.* process of searching; investigation. —**search warrant,** a legal order authorizing a search.

search'ing *adj.* keen; penetrating.

search'light'' *n.* an electric light that sends a concentrated beam.

sea'scape'' (-skāp'') *n.* a view or picture of the sea.

sea'shore'' *n.* land by the sea; a beach.

sea'sick'' *adj.* nauseated by the rolling of a vessel. —**sea'sick''ness,** *n.*

sea'side'' *n.* seashore.

sea'son (sē'zən) *n.* **1,** a quarter of the year: spring, summer, autumn, or winter. **2,** a particular period as to weather, business activity, fashion, etc. **3,** a suitable time. —*v.t.* **1,** mature; ripen. **2,** render palatable with spices, herbs, etc. **3,** give zest to; qualify; imbue. **4,** inure; accustom. —*v.i.* mature.

sea'son·a·ble *adj.* suitable; opportune; timely.

sea'son·al *adj.* pert. to, or depending upon, the season.

sea'son·ing *n.* spices, etc.

seat (sēt) *n.* **1,** a place or thing to sit on. **2,** that part of a chair, garment, etc., on which one sits. **3,** a site; location. **4,** a right to sit or attend. —*v.t.* **1,** place on a seat; locate; fix. **2,** furnish with seats or room for sitting. —**seat belt,** a protective belt worn in automobiles and aircraft.

sea'way'' *n.* **1,** headway, for a ship. **2,** a channel provided for seagoing ships.

sea'weed'' *n.* a plant growing in the sea.

sea'wor''thy *adj.* in condition for sea travel.

se·ba'ceous (si-bā'shəs) *adj.* being, containing, or secreting fat.

se'cant (sē'kənt) *n.* **1,** (*Geom.*) a line across an arc. **2,** a trigonometric ratio.

se·cede' (si-sēd') *v.i.* withdraw, esp. from a political or religious organization.

se·ces'sion (si-sesh'ən) *n.* act of seceding, as (*cap.*) that of the Confederate States in 1861. —**se·ces'sion·ist,** *n.* one who favors secession.

se·clude' (si-klood') *v.t.* shut away; keep in solitude.

se·clu'sion (si-kloo'zhən) *n.* **1,** act or effect of secluding. **2,** a secluded condition or place; solitude. —**se·clu'sive** (-siv) *adj.*

sec'ond (sek'ənd) *adj.* **1,** next after the first in order, time, value, etc.; the ordinal of two. **2,** subordinate. **3,** another. —*n.* **1,** the one next after the first. **2,** a supporter; an attendant in a prize fight or duel. **3,** an imperfect product. **4,** the sixtieth part of a minute. —*v.t.* support; assist. —**second fiddle,** a minor role. —**second hand,** the pointer on a timepiece that indicates the seconds. —**second nature,** habit. —**second sight,** clairvoyance. —**second thought,** reconsideration. —**second wind,** renewed breath control or energy, after an initial exhaustion.

sec'on·dar·y (sek'ən-der-ė) *adj.* **1,** of a second class or group. **2,** subordinate; derived; not primary. —*n.* in electricity, an induction coil or circuit. —**secondary school,** a high school.

sec''ond·class'' *adj.* **1,** in the next-to-highest class. **2,** inferior.

sec'ond-guess'' *v.t.* **1,** anticipate the actions or decisions of. **2,** criticize or analyze (actions or decisions) with the benefit of hindsight, after the fact.

sec″ond·hand′ *adj.* **1,** not original. **2,** previously used.

sec′ond-rate″ *adj.* inferior.

sec′ond-sto″ry man *adj.* a burglar.

sec′ond-string′ *adj.* of a secondary level of ability, achievement, etc.

se′cre·cy (sē′krə-sē) *n.* **1,** the state of being secret. **2,** secretive manner; strict silence.

se′cret (sē′krit) *adj.* **1,** kept private or concealed. **2,** not apparent; mysterious. —*n.* something not revealed. —**secret service,** a governmental branch that investigates secretly: in the U.S., a bureau of the Treasury Dept.

sec″re·tar′i·at (sek″rə-ter′ē-ət) *n.* an administrative bureau.

sec′re·tar′y (sek′re-ter′ē) *n.* **1,** a recording or corresponding officer. **2,** a stenographer. **3,** a cabinet minister. **4,** a writing desk. —**sec″re·tar′i·al,** *adj.*

sec′re·tar′y-gen′er·al *n.* the head of a secretariat.

se·crete′ (si-krēt′) *v.t.* **1,** hide. **2,** produce by secretion. —**se·cre′to·ry,** *adj.*

se·cre′tion (si-krē′shən) *n.* **1,** the process of preparing substances by glandular activity. **2,** the product secreted. —**se·cre′to·ry,** *adj.*

se·cre′tive (si-krē′tiv) *adj.* maintaining secrecy; reticent.

sect (sekt) *n.* a religious denomination. —**sec·tar′i·an** (sek-tār′ē-ən) *adj. & n.*

sec′ta·ry (sek′tə-rē) *n.* a religious dissenter.

sec′tion (sek′shən) *n.* **1,** a part cut or separated; a distinct portion. **2,** a region. **3,** the act of cutting; a surgical operation. **4,** a tract of U.S. public land, a mile square. **5,** a train scheduled jointly with another.

sec′tion·al *adj.* **1,** composed of several sections. **2,** local. —*n.* a piece of furniture made up of several parts. —**sec′tion·al·ism,** *n.* undue regard for local interests.

sec′tor (sek′tər) *n.* **1,** a plane figure enclosed between the arc of a circle and two radii. **2,** a mathematical scale. **3,** a combat area.

sec′u·lar (sek′yə-lər) *adj.* temporal; worldly; not of the church. —**sec′u·lar·ism,** *n.* —**sec′u·lar·ize″,** *v.t.*

se·cure′ (si-kyûr′) *adj.* **1,** free from danger; safe. **2,** firm; stable. **3,** certain. —*v.t.* **1,** make safe; make certain. **2,** obtain. **3,** fasten.

se·cur′i·ty (si-kyûr′ə-tē) *n.* **1,** safety. **2,** a guaranty or pledge. **3,** a bond or stock certificate. —**security blanket,** anything that makes one feel secure, esp. an object.

se·dan′ (si-dan′) *n.* a two-seated closed automobile. —**sedan chair,** a vehicle for one person, borne by two porters.

se·date′ (si-dāt′) *adj.* quiet; composed; serious. —**se·date′ness,** *n.*

sed′a·tive (sed′ə-tiv) *adj.* tending to soothe or calm. —*n.* a calming medicine.

sed′en·tar″y (sed′ən-ter′ē) *adj.* **1,** characterized by a sitting position. **2,** taking little physical exercise.

Se′der (sā′dər) *n.* the Jewish feast of the Exodus.

sedge (sej) *n.* a grasslike plant.

sed′i·ment (sed′ə-mənt) *n.* the matter that settles to the bottom of a liquid; dregs. —**sed″i·men′ta·ry,** *adj.* —**sed″i·men·ta′tion,** *n.*

se·di′tion (si-dish′ən) *n.* incitement of rebellion. —**se·di′tious,** *adj.*

se·duce′ (si-doos′) *v.t.* lead astray; entice away from duty, rectitude, or chastity. —**se·duc′er,** *n.*

se·duc′tion (si-duk′shən) *n.* act or effect of seducing.

se·duc′tive (-tiv) *adj.* tending to seduce; enticing.

sed′u·lous (sej′ə-ləs) *adj.* diligent; persevering. —**se·du′li·ty** (sə-dū′lə-tē) *n.* —**sed′u·lous·ness,** *n.*

see (sē) *v.t.* [saw (sâ), seen (sēn), see′ing] **1,** perceive by the eye; observe; view. **2,** comprehend. **3,** make sure. **4,** escort; attend. **5,** visit. **6,** in poker, etc., meet or call (a bet). —*v.i.* **1,** have the power of sight. **2,** understand. **3,** consider. —*n.* the seat or jurisdiction of a bishop. —**see′ing,** *conj.* inasmuch as. —**See′ing Eye,** an organization that trains dogs to guide blind persons. —**seeing-eye dog,** a dog trained to guide the blind.

seed (sēd) *n.* [*pl.* **seeds** or **seed**] **1,** the fertilized and natural ovule of a plant. **2,** semen, sperm, etc. **3,** offspring; descendants. **4,** origin. —*v.t.* **1,** plant. **2,** distribute (players) evenly in a tournament. —*v.i.* produce seed. —**go to seed,** decline in vigor, freshness, prosperity, etc. —**seed money,** funds given to support the initiation of a project. —**seed pearl,** a very small pearl.

seed′ling *n.* a young plant.

seed′y (sē′dē) *adj.* **1,** gone to seed; shabby. **2,** (*Colloq.*) not well. —**seed′i·ness,** *n.*

seek (sēk) *v.t.* [*pret. & p.p.* **sought** (sât)] **1,** go in search or quest of. **2,** resort to. **3,** attempt; endeavor.

seem (sēm) *v.i.* **1,** appear; appear to be. **2,** appear to oneself.

seem′ing *adj.* ostensible; apparent. —*n.* an appearance.

seem′ly (-lē) *adj.* becoming; proper; decent. —**seem′li·ness,** *n.*

seen (sēn) *v.* p.p. of *see.*

seep (sēp) *v.i.* ooze gently through pores. —*n.* a pool of water, oil, etc., seeping from the ground. —**seep′age** (-ij) *n.*

seer (sir) a prophet; clairvoyant. —**seer′ess**, *n.fem.*

seer′suck″er (sir′suk″ər) *n.* a crinkled cotton fabric.

see′saw″ (sē′sâ″) *n.* **1,** a board balanced on a support, on which two children move alternately up and down. **2,** any up-and-down movement. —*v.i.* move like a see-saw.

seethe (sē*th*) *v.i.* **1,** boil. **2,** be agitated.

seg′ment (seg′mənt) *n.* a part cut off; a section. —*v.t. & i.* divide into segments. —**seg′men·ta′tion**, *n.*

se′go (sē′gō) *n.* a perennial herb. Also, **sego lily.**

seg′re·gate″ (seg′rə-gāt″) *v.t. & i.* separate or detach from others.

seg′re·ga′tion (-gā′shən) *n.* act or effect of segregating; esp., separation of black and white persons. —**seg′ra·ga′tion·ist,** *n.*

seg′ue (seg′wā) *n.* (*Radio & TV*) a brief musical passage between episodes.

seine (sān) *n.* a large fishing net.

seism (sīz′əm) *n.* an earthquake. —**seis′mal** (-məl), **seis′mic** (-mik), *adj.*

seis′mo·graph″ (sīz′mo-gráf″) *n.* a device that records earthquakes.

seis·mol′o·gy (sīz-mol′ə-jē) *n.* the science of earthquakes. —**seis″mo·log′i·cal,** *adj.*

seize (sēz) *v.t.* **1,** grasp suddenly. **2,** comprehend. **3,** take legal or forcible possession of. **4,** afflict.

sei′zure (sē′zhər) *n.* **1,** the act of seizing. **2,** a sudden attack; a fit.

sel′dom (sel′dəm) *adv.* rarely; infrequently.

se·lect′ (si-lekt′) *v.t.* choose. —*adj.* **1,** choice. **2,** fastidious; exclusive. —**se·lec′tee′,** *n.* one drafted for military service.

se·lec′tion (si-lek′shən) *n.* act of choosing; a thing or things chosen.

se·lec′tive (-tiv) *adj.* **1,** pert. to or determined by selection. **2,** careful in choosing. —**selective service,** conscription of selected persons.

se·lec″tiv′i·ty (-tiv′ə-tē) *n.* (*Radio & TV*) precision in tuning qualities.

se·lect′man (-mən) *n.* [*pl.* **-men**] a member of a town governing board.

sel′e·nite″ (sel′ə-nīt″) *n.* a variety of gypsum.

se·le′ni·um (sə-lē′nē-əm) *n.* a nonmetallic toxic chemical element, no. 34, symbol Se.

sel″e·nol′o·gy (sel″ə-nol′ə-jē) *n.* the study of the moon.

self *n.* [*pl.* **selves** (selvz)] **1,** a person in his relations to his own person. **2,** nature; individuality. **3,** personal interest and benefit. —*pron.* (*Colloq.*) myself, himself, etc. —*adj.* single; uniform; unmixed.

self- *pref.* **1,** expressing reflexive action: on or to oneself or itself. **2,** in or by oneself or itself. [In addition to words defined in the text, the following words formed by prefixing *self-* may be defined by reference to the root word.]

self-″ad·dressed′	self-″in·flict′ed
self-″as·sur′ance	self-″load′ing
self-″com·mand′	self-″love′
self-″com·pla′cent	self-″pit′y
self-″con·tained′	self-″pol·li·na′tion
self-″con·trol′	self-″pres″er·va′tion
self-″de·cep′tion	self-″pro·pelled′
self-″de·ni′al	self-″pro·tec′tion
self-″de·struc′tion	self-″re·li′ance
self-″dis′ci·pline	self-″re·proach′
self-″ed′u·cat″ed	self-″re·straint′
self-″es·teem′	self-″sac′ri·fice″
self-″ex·plan′a·to·ry	self-″ser′vice
self-″gov′erning	self-″styled′
self-″help′	self-″sup·port′
self-″im·posed′	self-″sus·tain′ing
self-″in·duced′	self-″taught′
self-″in·dul′gent	self-″wind′ing

self-″cen′tered *adj.* absorbed in oneself.

self-″con′fi·dence *n.* the state of not feeling the need of assistance. —**self-″con′fi·dent,** *adj.*

self-″con′scious *adj.* ill at ease when with others. —**self-″con′scious·ness,** *n.*

self-″de·feat′ing *adj.* having a result opposed to its purpose.

self-″de·fense′ *n.* protection of oneself when attacked.

self-″des·truct′ *v.i.* be destroyed by means of a self-contained mechanism.

self-″de·ter″mi·na′tion *n.* determination of one's own course; autonomy.

self-″ef·fac′ing *adj.* diffident; very modest. —**self-″ef·face′ment,** *n.*

self-″ev′i·dent *adj.* obvious; requiring no proof.

self-″ex·pres′sion *n.* utilization or pursuit of an outlet for one's personality.

self-″im·por′tant *adj.* pompous. —**self-″im·por′tance,** *n.*

self-″in′ter·est *n.* personal advantage.

self′ish *adj.* devoted only to oneself. —**self′ish·ness,** *n.*

self′less *adj.* entirely unselfish. —**self′less·ness,** *n.*

self-″made′ *adj.* successful wholly by one's own efforts.

self-″pos·sessed′ *adj.* composed.

self-"re·al·i·za'tion *n.* the development of one's potential abilities, personality, etc.

self-"re·li'ance *n.* self-confidence. —**self-"re·li'ant,** *adj.*

self-"re·spect' *n.* becoming pride.

self-"right'eous *adj.* righteous in one's own esteem. —**self-"right'eous·ness,** *n.*

self'same" *adj.* identical.

self-"sat'is·fied" *adj.* complacent. —**self-'sat"is·fac'tion,** *n.*

self-"seek'ing *adj.* selfish.

self-"start'er *n.* an electric motor that cranks an automobile engine.

self-"suf·fi'cient *adj.* **1,** requiring no help, companionship, etc. **2,** unduly self-confident.

self-"willed' *adj.* obstinate.

sell (sel) *v.t.* [*pret. & p.p.* **sold** (sōld)] **1,** transfer to another for money. **2,** keep for sale. **3,** betray. **4,** cause acceptance. —*v.i.* **1,** engage in selling. **2,** be in demand; be sold. **3,** (with *out*) yield. —*n.* (*Slang*) a swindle or hoax. —**sell'er's market,** a market in which goods are relatively scarce and prices are relatively high.

sell'out" *n.* **1,** a complete disposal by selling, as of theater seats. **2,** a betrayal.

sel'tzer (sel'tsər) *n.* an effervescent mineral water, or carbonated water resembling it.

sel'vage (sel'vij) *n.* the finished edge of a fabric. Also, **sel'vedge.**

se·man'tic (si-man'tik) *adj.* pert. to meaning in language. —**se·man'tics,** *n. sing.* the study of meaning.

sem'a·phore" (sem'ə-fôr") *n.* a signaling device or method.

sem'blance (sem'bləns) *n.* **1,** a likeness; an image. **2,** outward appearance.

se'men (sē'mən) *n.* the male reproductive fluid.

se·mes'ter (si-mes'tər) *n.* a major division of the academic year, usu. one half.

sem·i- (sem-ē) *pref.* **1,** half. **2,** partly. **3,** once every half, as *semiannual.*

sem"i·an'nu·al *adj.* once every six months.

sem'i·breve" (-brēv") *n.* (*Music*) a whole note (see *note*).

sem"i·cir"cle *n.* half a circle. —**sem"i·cir'cu·lar,** *adj.*

sem'i·co"lon *n.* a mark of punctuation (;) used to separate major sentence elements more distinctly than the comma.

sem"i·con·duc'tor *n.* a solid (such as silicon or germanium) having more conductivity than an insulator but less than good conductors; used in transistors, etc.

sem"i·fi'nal *adj.* a round or match in a contest, next to the final one. —*n.* [*also,*

sem"i·fi'nals] this round, match, or matches. —**sem"i·fi'nal·ist,** *n.*

sem"i·month'ly *adj.* once every two weeks.

sem'i·nal (sem'ə-nəl) *adj.* **1,** pert. to seed or semen. **2,** being the germ of something that develops.

sem'i·nar" (sem'ə-när") *n.* a small group, or course, for advanced study.

sem'i·nar"y (sem'ə-ner"ē) *n.* a school, esp. one for the ministry or for young women.

sem"i·pre'cious *adj.* of less than the highest (gem) value.

sem"i·pri'vate *adj.* used or shared by two (or three) persons.

sem"i·pro·fes'sion·al *adj. & n.* (of or for) one who is professional part of the time. Also, **sem"i·pro'.**

sem'i·qua"ver (-kwā"vər) *n.* (*Music*) a sixteenth note (see *note*).

Sem'ite (sem'īt) *n.* a member of any Semitic people.

Se·mit'ic (sə-mit'ik) *adj.* relating to the Semites or their languages, such as Hebrew, Aramaic, Assyrian, and Arabic.

sem'i·tone" *n.* (*Music*) the interval between adjacent tones of the chromatic scale, as A to A#.

sem"i·trail'er *n.* a trailer with no wheels in the front, that part being supported by the tractor.

sem"o·li'na (sem"ə-lē'nə) *n.* the hard, coarse part of the wheat, used for pasta.

sen *n.* a Jap. coin, 1/100 yen.

sen'ate (sen'it) *n.* a legislative assembly; (*cap.*) the upper legislative house of the U.S.

sen'a·tor (sen'ə-tər) *n.* a member of a senate, as (*cap.*) of the U.S. Senate. —**sen"a·to'ri·al** (-tôr'ē-əl) *adj.*

send *v.t. & i.* [*pret. & p.p.* **sent**] **1,** cause to go; dispatch. **2,** impel. **3,** (with *out*, etc.) produce or give off. **4,** (*Slang*) stimulate or excite. —**send'er,** *n.* **1,** one who sends. **2,** a transmitter.

send-'off" *n.* **1,** a start. **2,** a farewell demonstration.

send-'up" *n.* (*Slang*) parody.

se·nes'cent (sə-nes'ənt) *adj.* growing old. —**se·nes'cence,** *n.*

sen'es·chal (sen'ə-shəl) *n.* the manager of a nobleman's estate.

se'nile (sē'nīl) *adj.* pert. to or characterizing old age. —**se·nil'i·ty** (sə-nil'ə-tē) *n.*

sen'ior (sēn'yər) *adj.* **1,** older; elder. **2,** older in office or service. **3,** pert. to the last year of a high school or college course. —*n.* **1,** a person who is older or of higher rank. **2,** a member of the senior class.

—senior citizen, an elderly person, esp. one 65 years old or older.

sen·ior′i·ty (sē-nyor′ə-tē) *n.* state of being older in years, service, etc.

sen′na (sen′ə) *n.* a cathartic·drug derived from cassia.

se·ñor′ (sā-nyôr′) *n.* (*Span.*) **1,** mister. **2,** sir. **—se·ño′ra** (-nyō′rə) *n.fem.* a married woman; Mrs. **—se″ño·ri′ta** (sā″nyə-rē′tə) *n.fem.* Miss.

sen′sate (sen′sāt) *adj.* perceived by the senses.

sen·sa′tion (sen-sā′shən) *n.* **1,** a mental impression caused by an affection of a bodily organism; sensitive apprehension. **2,** a state of, or the cause of, excited interest or feeling.

sen·sa′tion·al (-əl) *adj.* intended to thrill. **—sen·sa′tion·al·ism,** *n.*

sense (sens) *n.* **1,** a special faculty of sensation: sight, smell, taste, touch, or hearing. **2,** consciousness; understanding; discriminative perception. **3,** practical intelligence. **4,** meaning. **5,** intention. **6,** consensus. **7,** algebraic sign (+ or —). —*v.t.* perceive by or as by the senses.

sense′less (-ləs) *adj.* **1,** unconscious. **2,** stupid. **3,** nonsensical. **—sense′less·ness,** *n.*

sen″si·bil′i·ty (sen″sə-bil′ə-tē) *n.* **1,** mental receptivity. **2,** capacity for the more refined feelings.

sen′si·ble (sen′sə-bəl) *adj.* **1,** reasonable. **2,** aware; cognizant. **3,** perceptible through the senses. **4,** capable of sensation.

sen′si·tive (sen′sə-tiv) *adj.* **1,** pert. to the senses; capable of receiving sensations. **2,** of keen sensibility; easily hurt. **3,** quickly responsive; readily affected. —*n.* one with heightened sensory perceptions. **—sen′si·tive·ness, sen″si·tiv′i·ty,** *n.*

sen′si·tize″ (-tīz″) *v.t.* treat so as to make sensitive.

sen′sor (sen′sər) *n.* a device that responds to a physical stimulus (as heat or light) by emitting a signal for measurement, operating a control, etc.

sen′so·ry (sen′sə-rē) *adj.* pert. to sensation or the senses.

sen′su·al (sen′shû-əl) *adj.* pert. to the senses; not intellectual; carnal; voluptuous. **—sen′su·al·ism,** *n.* **—sen′su·al·ist,** *n.*

sen″su·al′i·ty (sen″shoo-al′ə-tē) *n.* unrestrained self-gratification.

sen′su·ous (sen′shû-əs) *adj.* affecting, or affected through, the senses.

sent *v.* pret. & p.p.p. of *send.*

sen′tence (sen′təns) *n.* **1,** a number of words constituting a complete statement, inquiry, etc. **2,** the punishment determined for a convicted criminal. **3,** an opinion. —*v.t.* pronounce sentence upon.

sen·ten′tious (sen-ten′shəs) *adj.* given to the use of maxims; didactic.

sen′tient (sen′shənt) *adj.* having the power of feeling or perception. **—sen′tience,** *n.*

sen′ti·ment (sen′tə-mənt) *n.* **1,** higher feeling; emotion. **2,** tender susceptibility. **3,** an opinion; mental attitude. **4,** an expression of feeling.

sen″ti·men′tal (sen″tə-men′təl) *adj.* **1,** of a tender nature. **2,** mawkish. **3,** appealing to the feelings. **—sen″ti·men′tal·ist,** *n.* a sentimental person. **—sen″ti·men·tal′i·ty** (-tal′ə-tē) *n.* state of being sentimental; emotionalism.

sen′ti·nel (sen′tə-nəl) *n.* a soldier stationed as a guard.

sen′try (sen′trē) *n.* a guard; a sentinel.

se′pal (sē′pəl) *n.* a small leaf forming part of a flower.

sep′a·rate″ (sep′ə-rāt″) *v.t.* **1,** disunite; disconnect. **2,** divide, place, or keep apart. —*v.i.* **1,** part. **2,** come apart; open. —*adj.* (-rət) **1,** divided; apart. **2,** distinct; individual. **—sep′a·ra·ble,** *adj.* **—sep′a·rat·ist** (-rə-tist) *adj. & n.*

sep″a·ra′tion *n.* **1,** act or effect of separating. **2,** that which separates; a partition, etc. **3,** a limited divorce.

sep′a·ra″tor *n.* an apparatus for separating cream from milk.

se′pi·a (sē′pē-ə) *n. & adj.* a dark brown color.

sep′pu·ku (sep′oo-koo) *n.* harakiri.

sep′sis *n.* bacterial infection accompanied by formation of pus.

sept *n.* a group believing itself descended from a common ancestor.

sept- *pref.* seven.

Sep·tem′ber (sep-tem′bər) *n.* the ninth month of the year.

sep·tet′ *n.* **1,** a group of seven. **2,** a composition in seven parts. Also, **sep·tette′.**

sep′tic (sep′tik) *adj.* pertaining to decay. **—septic tank,** a tank for sewage disposal.

sep″ti·ce′mi·a (sep″tə-sē′mē-ə) *n.* blood poisoning.

sep″tu·a·ge·nar′i·an (sep″choo-ə-ji-nār′ē-ən) *n. & adj.* (a person) aged 70 or more years.

Sep″tu·a·ges′i·ma (sep″choo-ə-jes′ə-mə) *n.* the third Sunday before Lent.

sep′tum (sep′təm) *n.* [*pl.* **-ta** (-tə)] a dividing wall or membrane.

sep′tu·ple (sep′tə-pəl) *adj.* seven times. —*v.t.* multiply by seven. **—sep′tu·plet,** *n.* one of seven offspring born of one birth.

sep′ul·cher (sep′əl-kər) *n.* a tomb; a burial vault. Also, **sep′ul·chre.**

---

tub, cūte, pûll; labəl; oil, owl, go, chip, she, thin, *th*en, sing, ink; *see p. 6*

se·pul′chral (sə-pul′krəl) *adj.* **1,** pert. to burial. **2,** deep; hollow in tone. **3,** gloomy.

sep′ul·ture (sep′əl-chər) *n.* **1,** burial. **2,** sepulcher. —*v.t.* bury.

se′quel (sē′kwəl) *n.* **1,** a continuation. **2,** a consequence.

se′quence (sē′kwəns) *n.* **1,** a succession. **2,** order of succession. **3,** a series; (*Music*) three or more repetitions of a phrase at different pitch levels. —**se′quent,** *adj. & n.* —**se·quen′tial** (si-kwen′shəl) *adj.*

se·ques′ter (si-kwes′tər) *v.t.* put aside; seclude. —**se″ques·tra′tion** (sē″-) *n.*

se′quin (sē′kwin) *n.* **1,** a spangle. **2,** a former gold coin.

se·quoi′a (si-kwoi′ə) *n.* either of two very large coniferous trees of California.

se·ragl′io (si-ral′yō) *n.* **1,** a harem. **2,** a Turkish palace.

se·ra′pe (se-rä′pē) *n.* a bright-colored shawl or wrap.

ser′aph (ser′əf) *n.* [*pl.* **ser′a·phim** (-ə-fim) or **ser′aphs**] an angel. —**se·raph′ic** (sə-raf′ik) *adj.*

Serb (sėrb) *adj. &* pert. to Serbia, its people, language, etc. Also, **Ser′bi·an** (sėr′bē-ən).

sere (sir) *adj.* withered; dry.

ser″e·nade′ (ser′ə-nād′) *n.* an evening song of love. —*v.t.* entertain with a serenade.

ser″e·na′ta (ser″ə-nä′tə) *n.* (*Music*) **1,** a secular cantata. **2,** an instrumental composition in several movements.

ser″en·dip′i·ty (ser″ən-dip′ə-tē) *n.* an assumed talent for making discoveries by accident.

se·rene′ (sə-rēn′) *adj.* **1,** tranquil; calm. **2,** clear. —**se·rene′ness,** *n.*

se·ren′i·ty (sə-ren′ə-tē) *n.* tranquillity; sereneness.

serf (sėrf) *n.* a peasant attached to a feudal estate. —**serf′dom,** *n.*

serge (sėrj) *n.* a twilled worsted fabric.

ser′geant (sär′jənt) *n.* **1,** a noncommissioned officer, ranking above a corporal. **2,** a police or court officer. —**sergeant-at-arms,** an official appointed to maintain order, as in a court.

se′ri·al (sir′ē-əl) *adj.* **1,** published in installments. **2,** successive. **3,** (*Music*) composed on the basis of predetermined series of pitches, numbers, etc. —*n.* a serial story. —**serial number,** an identifying number for something produced as part of a series, as a manufactured article, etc.

se′ri·al·ize″ (-īz″) *v.t.* **1,** publish in installments. **2,** (*Music*) compose a work with the use of series of numbers, pitches, etc.

se′ries (sir′ēz) *n.* a continued succession of similar things. —**in series,** in sequence.

ser′if *n.* a short cross-line on a letter of type.

se′ri·ous (sir′ē-əs) *adj.* **1,** grave; solemn. **2,** in earnest. **3,** weighty; critical. —**se′ri·ous·ness,** *n.*

ser′mon (sėr′mən) *n.* **1,** a religious discourse. **2,** any admonitory speech. —**ser′-mon·ize″** (-īz″) *v.t.* preach; moralize.

ser′pent (sėr′pənt) *n.* **1,** a snake. **2,** (*cap.*) Satan. **3,** an obsolete wooden bass trumpet.

ser′pen·tine″ (sėr′pən-tēn″) *adj.* **1,** winding about; tortuous. **2,** wily; treacherous. —*n.* a greenish silicate mineral.

ser′rate (ser′it) *adj.* having sharp teeth. —**ser·ra′tion,** *n.*

ser′ried (ser′ēd) *adj.* pressed closely together.

se′rum (sir′əm) *n.* **1,** the clear liquid in the blood. **2,** immunized blood serum. —**se′rous,** *adj.*

ser′vant (sėr′vənt) *n.* one who serves, esp. a domestic employee.

serve (sėrv) *v.t.* **1,** attend or wait upon; work for. **2,** aid. **3,** (with *for*) be a substitute for. **4,** avail. **5,** (*Law*) give a summons, etc.) to. **6,** (*Tennis*) put (the ball) in play. **7,** (of animals) mate with. **8,** supply. —*v.i.* **1,** act as a servant or waiter. **2,** suffice; be convenient. **3,** serve something. —*n.* (*Tennis*) the act or manner of serving. —**ser′ver,** *n.* a waiter. —**serv′ing,** *n.* a portion of something served, as food.

ser′vice (sėr′vis) *n.* **1,** act or result of serving; duty performed or needs supplied. **2,** (often *pl.*) religious worship. **3,** a set of dishes, etc. —**ser′vice·a·ble,** *adj.* useful. —**service man,** a member of an armed force. —**service mark,** trademark. —**service module,** the part of a spacecraft containing fuel cells, the engines, and propellant tanks. —**service station, 1,** a filling station. **2,** a place where a service is offered.

ser″vi·ette′ (sėr″vė-et′) *n.* a napkin.

ser′vile (sėr′vil) *adj.* menial; obsequious. —**ser·vil′i·ty,** *n.*

ser′vi·tor (sėr′vi-tər) *n.* an attendant; a waiter.

ser′vi·tude″ (sėr′vi-tood″) *n.* slavery.

ser″vo·mech′a·nism (sėr″vō-mek′ə-niz-əm) *n.* an automatic control device, triggered by mechanical or electrical impulses that operates a machine or maintains performance of a machine at a desired standard. —**ser′vo** (*Colloq.*).

ser′vo·mo″tor *n.* a motor that supplements a control device (such as a servomechanism).

ses′a·me (ses′ə-mē) *n.* a tropical herbaceous plant; its edible seed.

ses·qui- (ses′kwė) *pref.* one and a half.

---

ses'sile (ses'əl) *adj.* attached by the base; permanently attached.

ses'sion (sesh'ən) *n.* **1**, the sitting of a court, council, etc. **2**, one period in a series.

set *v.t.* [**set, set'ting**] **1**, put in a certain place or position; fix; establish. **2**, adjust. **3**, start; employ; assign. **4**, mount, as a gem. **5**, adapt to music. **6**, (with *down*) write. **7**, arrange (type) for printing. **8**, (with *forth*) express. —*v.i.* **1**, sink; settle. **2**, become fixed. **3**, (with *out* or *forth*) begin. **4**, sit on eggs, as a hen. —*n.* **1**, a related group; a collection. **2**, a number of persons customarily associated. **3**, a hardening. **4**, a tendency. **5**, build; carriage. **6**, a stage setting; scenery. **7**, a scoring unit, as in tennis. **8**, (of a saw, the bending of adjacent teeth in opposite directions. —*adj.* **1**, placed; fixed. **2**, obstinate. **3**, prescribed. —**set back**, hinder; delay. —**set up**, establish. —**set upon**, attack.

set'back″ *n.* **1**, a reverse; a recession. **2**, a setting of part of a building behind a lower part.

set'screw″ *n.* a screw for clamping an adjustable part on another.

set·tee' (se-tē') *n.* a small sofa; a bench with a back.

set'ter (set'ər) *n.* a kind of long-haired hunting dog.

set'ting *n.* **1**, environment; scene; scenery. **2**, a mounting, as for a jewel. **3**, music composed for a text, libretto, etc.

set'tle (set'əl) *v.t.* **1**, fix in position or condition; establish; decide. **2**, adjust, as a dispute. **3**, calm. **4**, colonize. **5**, clear of dregs. **6**, pay (a bill). —*v.i.* **1**, become fixed; come to rest. **2**, establish a permanent residence. **3**, become clear. **4**, sink. **5**, decide; arrange; agree. —*n.* a bench.

set'tle·ment *n.* **1**, act or result of settling; an adjustment; payment. **2**, a small colony. **3**, a welfare establishment.

set'tler (-lər) *n.* a colonizer.

set·'to″ *n.* (*Colloq.*) a fight.

set'up″ *n.* **1**, a system. **2**, (*Slang*) a contest easy to win. **3**, ice, etc., for mixing a drink.

sev'en (sev'ən) *n. & adj.* the cardinal number between six and eight, expressed by 7. —**sev'enth**, *adj. & n.* —**seventh heaven**, bliss.

sev'en·teen' (-tēn') *n. & adj.* seven plus ten; also expressed by 17. —**sev″en·teenth'** (-tēnth') *n. & adj.*

sev'en·ty (-tē) *n. & adj.* ten times seven; also expressed by 70. —**sev'en·ti·eth** (-tē-əth) *n. & adj.*

sev'er (sev'ər) *v.t. & i.* separate; divide into parts; cut apart. —**sev'er·ance,** *n.*

sev'er·al (sev'ər-əl) *adj.* **1**, three or more, but not many. **2**, various. **3**, individual; separate. **4**, distinct. —*n.* a few.

se·vere' (si-vir') *adj.* **1**, serious or earnest; austere. **2**, rigorous; trying. **3**, harsh. **4**, sharp; distressing; extreme. —**se·ver'i·ty** (-ver'ə-tē) *n.*

sew (sō) *v.t. & i.* join or attach by means of a thread, wire, etc.

sew'age (soo'ij) *n.* waste matter.

sew'er (soo'ər) *n.* a conduit for carrying off waste water and refuse. —**sew'er·age,** *n.* a system of sewers.

sex (seks) *n.* **1**, the anatomical and physiological distinction between male and female. **2**, either males or females, considered collectively. —**sex appeal,** the quality of attracting amatory interest. —**sex object,** (*Colloq.*) someone appreciated or exploited for sexual reasons alone. —**sex symbol,** a person considered especially sexually appealing. —**sex'less,** *adj.*

sex- *pref.* six.

sex″a·ge·nar'i·an (seks″ə-jə-nār'ē-ən) *adj. & n.* (a person) aged 60 or more years.

sex'ism (sekz'iz-əm) *n.* bias or discrimination by one sex against the other. —**sex'ist,** *n. & adj.*

sex'pot″ *n.* (*Colloq.*) a sexy woman.

sex'tant (seks'tənt) *n.* **1**, one-sixth of a circle. **2**, an instrument used in navigation.

sex·tet' (seks-tet') *n.* **1**, a group of six, esp. musicians. **2**, a composition for six instruments. Also, **sex·tette'.**

sex'ton (seks'tən) *n.* a minor official of a church.

sex'tu·ple (seks'tə-pəl) *adj.* of six parts; six times as great; sixfold. —*v.* make or become six times as great. —**sex'tu·plet,** *n.* a set of six.

sex'u·al (sek'shoo-əl) *adj.* **1**, pert. to sex. **2**, (*Colloq.*) pert. to carnal love. —**sex″u·al'i·ty** (-al'ə-tē) *n.* —**sexual intercourse,** coitus.

sex'y *adj.* (*Slang*) concerned with or suggesting carnal love. —**sex'i·ness,** *n.*

sfor·zan'do (sfôr-tsän'dō) *adj.* (*Music*) strongly accented. —*n.* a strong accent.

shab'by (shab'ē) *adj.* **1**, seedy; (of clothes) much worn. **2**, mean; contemptible. —**shab'bi·ness,** *n.*

shack (shak) *n.* a rough cabin. —**shack up,** (*Slang*) live with.

shack'le (shak'əl) *n.* **1**, a fetter; hobble. **2**, a coupling device. **3**, the bar of a padlock. —*v.t.* **1**, chain with shackles; hamper.

shad *n.* an Amer. food fish.

shad'dock (shad'ək) *n.* an E. Indian tree; its pear-shaped citrus fruit.

shade (shād) *n.* **1,** darkness caused by interception of rays of light. **2,** a shaded place. **3,** a dark area. **4,** a trace. **5,** a ghost. **6,** a screen against light. **7,** a gradation of color; a hue to which black has been added. —*v.t.* **1,** screen from light. **2,** obscure; darken.

shad'ing (shā'ding) *n.* **1,** a slight difference. **2,** application of shade.

shad'ow (shad'ō) *n.* **1,** the dark image of a body intercepting the light. **2,** shade. **3,** an inseparable companion. **4,** a spy. **5,** a phantom. —*v.t.* **1,** shade; cloud. **2,** trail; stay near. —**shad'ow·y,** *adj.*

shad'ow·box"ing *n.* exercise by boxing with an imaginary opponent. —**shad'ow·box",** *v.i.*

shad'ow·graph" *n.* a picture produced by casting a shadow, as of the hands, on a screen.

shad'y (shā'dē) *adj.* **1,** affording shade. **2,** (*Colloq.*) of doubtful character. —**shad'i·ness,** *n.*

shaft (shàft) *n.* **1,** a long, slender, cylindrical body, as an arrow, spear handle, etc. **2,** a bar transmitting motion. **3,** passage, as in a mine, or for an elevator. **4,** harsh criticism. —*v.t.* criticize harshly.

shag *v.t.* [**shagged, shag'ging**] roughen. —*n.* **1,** a rough surface; a coarse material. **2,** a fabric with a nap.

shag'gy (shag'ē) *adj.* having rough hair or nap; unkempt. —**shag'gi·ness,** *n.*

shah (shä) *n.* king: the former monarch of Iran.

shake (shāk) *v.t.* [**shook** (shŭk), **shak'en, shak'ing**] **1,** cause to vibrate or tremble; agitate. **2,** loosen. **3,** weaken; cause to doubt. **4,** (with *up*) disturb; upset; jar. **5,** (with *down*) (*Slang*) extort money from. —*v.i.* be agitated; tremble; totter. —*n.* **1,** an act of shaking. **2,** (*pl.*) the ague. **3,** (*Colloq.*) an instant. **4,** a shaken drink, often with ice cream. **5,** (*Music*) a trill. —**shake a leg,** (*Slang*) bestir oneself. —**fair shake,** just treatment.

shake'down" *n.* **1,** preparation or conditioning, as of a new ship. **2,** (*Slang*) extortion. **3,** a makeshift bed, as of straw.

shak'er *n.* **1,** a perforated container for dispensing salt, etc. **2,** (*cap.*) a member of a celibate religious sect.

shake'up" *n.* a reorganization.

shak'o (shā'kō) *n.* [*pl.* **-os**] a high, plumed, military hat.

shak'y *adj.* **1,** trembling. **2,** insecure; wavering. —**shak'i·ness,** *n.*

shale (shāl) *n.* a rock that splits readily into thin leaves.

shall (shal) *aux. v.* [*pret.* **should** (shŭd)] **1,** (first person) expressing the future: am or are going to or sure to. **2,** (second and third persons) must.

shal'lop (shal'əp) *n.* a light open boat.

shal·lot' (shə-lot') *n.* an onionlike vegetable.

shal'low (shal'ō) *adj.* **1,** not deep. **2,** superficial. —*n.* a shoal.

sha·lom' (shä-lōm') *interj.* (*Hebrew*) peace.

sham *adj.* counterfeit; pretended. —*n.* an imposture; make-believe; an imitation. —*v.i. & t.* [**shammed, sham'ming**] pretend; feign.

sha'man (shā'mən) *n.* a religious man.

sham'ble (sham'bəl) *v.i.* walk awkwardly. —*n.* **1,** a shambling walk. **2,** (*pl.*) a slaughterhouse. **3,** (*pl.*) a scene of devastation.

shame (shām) *n.* **1,** a remorseful consciousness of guilt. **2,** disgrace or dishonor; a cause of it. —*v.t.* **1,** make ashamed. **2,** disgrace. **3,** influence by reproach. —**shame'-faced",** *adj.* ashamed; showing shame. —**shame'ful,** *adj.* disgraceful. —**shame'-less,** *adj.* overbold; conscienceless.

sham·poo' *v.t.* wash (the hair). —*n.* a washing of the hair; a preparation for it.

sham'rock" (sham'rok") *n.* a three-leaved plant, emblem of Ireland.

sham'us (shām'əs) *n.* (*Slang*) a private detective.

shan'dy (shan'de) *n.* a beverage of lemonade and beer.

shang'hai (shang'hī) *v.t.* abduct and force to serve as a seaman; hence, abduct (a person.)

shan"gri-la' (shang"gri-lä') *n.* a hidden or remote paradise.

shank *n.* **1,** the leg between the knee and the ankle. **2,** the part of a tool, etc., that connects the acting part with the handle. **3,** (*Colloq.*) the latter part, as, *shank of the evening*. —**by shank's-'mare",** on foot.

shan'tung' *n.* a silk fabric.

shan'ty (shan'tē) *n.* a rough or flimsy hut or house.

shape (shāp) *n.* **1,** form; outward contour; appearance. **2,** proper form. **3,** condition. —*v.t.* **1,** give form to; create. **2,** adapt. **3,** express. —*v.i.* **1,** take form. **2,** (with *up*) come out; reach proper form. —**shape'ly,** *adj.* pleasingly formed.

shard (shärd) *n.* a fragment of a brittle substance, as glass.

share (shâr) *n.* **1,** a portion; an allotted part. **2,** a unit of stock in a corporation. **3,** a plow blade. —*v.t.* **1,** divide; apportion. **2,** have jointly. —*v.i.* **1,** partake. **2,** give a portion to others.

share'crop"per *n.* a farmer who divides the crop with his landlord.

share'hold"er *n.* stockholder.

shark (shärk) *n.* **1,** a large and ferocious marine fish. **2,** a predatory person. **3,** (*Slang*) an expert.

shark'skin" *n.* a heavy suiting fabric.

sharp (shärp) *adj.* **1,** having a fine cutting edge or point. **2,** well-defined; distinct. **3,** abrupt; angular. **4,** keenly affecting a sense: pungent, shrill, keenly cold, etc. **5,** acute; keen. **6,** barely honest. **7,** (*Music*) of a note, marked (#), raised a half tone. **8,** (*Music*) above the intended pitch. —*adv.* sharply; quickly; exactly. —*n.* **1,** (*Music*) a tone raised half a step. **2,** a sharper. **3,** (*Colloq.*) an expert. —**sharp'ness,** *n.*

sharp'en (shär'pən) *v.t. & i.* make or become sharp. —**sharp'en·er,** *n.* a tool or machine for sharpening an edge or point.

sharp'er *n.* a swindler.

sharp'ie (shär'pē) *n.* a type of small sailboat.

sharp'shoot"er *n.* **1,** an expert marksman. **2,** a sharper.

shat'ter (shat'ər) *v.i. & t.* **1,** break in pieces. **2,** disorder; impair.

shave (shāv) *v.t.* **1,** slice with a keen instrument. **2,** make bare. **3,** cut down gradually. **4,** come very close to. —*v.i.* remove hair with a razor. —*n.* **1,** an act of shaving. **2,** (*Colloq.*) a narrow escape. —**close shave,** a near miss; a success by a very small margin.

shav'er *n.* **1,** one who shaves. **2,** (*Colloq.*) a youngster.

shave'tail" *n.* (*Slang*) a newly-appointed second lieutenant.

shav'ing *n.* a thin slice, esp. of wood.

shawl (shâl) *n.* a loose covering for the shoulders.

shay (shā) *n.* a light carriage.

she (shē) *pron.* [*poss.* **her** (hēr), **hers**; *obj.* **her**] **1,** the third person, sing., fem., nominative; a female person other than the speaker and the person addressed. **2,** any female.

sheaf (shēf) *n.* [*pl.* **sheaves** (shēvz)] a bundle, as of grain, papers, etc.

shear (shir) *v.t.* **1,** clip or cut. **2,** remove by clipping, as fleece. —**shears,** *n.sing. & pl.* large scissors.

sheath (shēth) *n.* a case or covering; a scabbard.

sheathe (shē*th*) *v.t.* put into a sheath; enclose; cover.

sheath'ing (shē'*thi*ng) *n.* **1,** a covering or outer layer. **2,** the boards first put on the framework of a house.

she·bang' (shə-bang') *n.* (*Slang*) establishment; outfit.

shed *v.t.* [**shed, shed'ding**] **1,** throw off, molt, or cause to flow off. **2,** disperse, as

light. —*v.i.* cast or let fall a covering, etc. —*n.* a rude structure for shelter or storage.

sheen (shēn) *n.* luster.

sheep (shēp) *n.sing. & pl.* **1,** a ruminant mammal, valued for its flesh, skin, fleece, etc. **2,** a timid person. **3,** ignorant imitators. —**sheep'ish,** *adj.* embarrassed, timid.

sheep'dog" *n.* any of several dogs trained to herd and guard sheep.

sheep'fold" *n.* a pen or shelter for sheep.

sheep'shank" *n.* a kind of knot made in a rope to shorten it temporarily.

sheep'skin" *n.* **1,** sheep's fur; a garment made of it. **2,** parchment; (*Colloq.*) a diploma.

sheer (shir) *adj.* **1,** very thin; diaphanous. **2,** unmixed; absolute. **3,** precipitous. —*adv.* **1,** absolutely; quite. **2,** steeply. —*v.i.* (with *off*) swerve.

sheet (shēt) *n.* **1,** a rectangular piece of cloth bedding. **2,** a broad, flat, very thin piece of anything. **3,** a newspaper. **4,** an expanse or surface. **5,** a rope fastened to a sail. —**sheet'ing,** *n.*

sheik (shēk) *n.* **1,** an Arab chief. **2,** (*Slang*) a bold lover.

shek'el (shek'əl) *n.* **1,** a silver coin of the ancient Jews. **2,** (*pl., slang*) money.

shelf *n.* [*pl.* **shelves**] **1,** a horizontal plank for supporting objects. **2,** a ledge. **3,** a reef. —**on the shelf,** discarded or retired.

shell (shel) *n.* **1,** a hard outer case or covering. **2,** something flimsy, hollow, or concave. **3,** a light racing boat. **4,** a projectile; a cartridge. —*v.t.* **1,** remove, or take out of, the shell. **2,** bombard. —**shell game,** a swindling game. —**shell out,** (*Colloq.*) hand over; pay. —**shell shock,** a psychoneurosis caused by battle strain.

shel·lac' (shə-lak') *n.* a purified plastic resin; a varnish made from it. —*v.t.* paint with shellac.

shell'fish" *n.* an aquatic animal having a shell, as an oyster, lobster, etc.

shel'ter (shel'tər) *n.* whatever shields or protects; a refuge; a roofed place. —*v.t. & i.* house; protect.

shelve (shelv) *v.t.* **1,** put on a shelf. **2,** put aside; put off. **3,** furnish with shelves.

she·nan'i·gan (shə-nan'ə-gən) *n.* (*Colloq.*) foolery; a prank.

shep'herd (shep'ərd) *n.* **1,** a sheep-herder. **2,** a pastor; (*cap.*) Jesus Christ. **3,** a breed of dog. —**shep'herd·ess,** *n.fem.*

sher'bet (shēr'bət) *n.* an ice containing milk.

sher'iff (sher'if) *n.* the chief law-enforcement officer of a county.

sher'ry (sher'ē) *n.* a strong wine of southern Spain.

Shet'land (shet'lənd) n. **1,** a small, rough-coated pony. **2,** a soft, loosely-twisted wool.

shew (shō) v. (*Brit.*) show.

shib'bo·leth" (shib'ə-leth") n. a password; a slogan.

shield (shēld) n. **1,** a broad plate of defensive armor. **2,** anything that protects. **3,** an escutcheon. —v.t. protect; screen.

shift v.t. transfer to another place or person; change; exchange. —v.i. **1,** change place, position, direction, etc. **2,** alter. **3,** get along. —n. **1,** a change; a turning. **2,** a group of workmen; the time they work. **3,** an expedient; a resource. **4,** a woman's chemise. —**shift'less,** adj. lazy. —**shift'y,** adj. tricky; evasive.

Shih Tzu (shē'tzoo') n. a Chinese breed of dog.

shill (shil) n. (*Slang*) an accomplice to a peddler, gambler, etc.

shil·le'lagh (shə-lā'lē) n. (*Ireland*) a cudgel.

shil'ling (shil'ing) n. **1,** a former Brit. monetary unit. **2,** the monetary unit of Kenya and other Afr. states.

shil'ly-shal'ly (shil'ē-shal'ē) v.i. act in an irresolute manner.

shim n. a wedge or strip of wood, metal, etc., used to fill in or bring one part level with another. —v.t. adjust with a shim.

shim'mer (shim'ər) v.i. shine with a tremulous light. —**shim'mer·y,** adj.

shim'my (shim'ē) n. **1,** abnormal vibration; jiggling. **2,** a jazz dance. **3,** (*Colloq.*) a chemise. —v.i. dance the shimmy.

shin n. **1,** the front of the leg from knee to ankle. **2,** the tibia. —v.t. & i. [**shinned, shin'ning**] [also, **shin'ny**] climb by hugging with arms and legs.

shin'bone" n. the tibia.

shin'dig" n. (*Slang*) a dance or party.

shin'dy (shin'dē) n. (*Slang*) **1,** shindig. **2,** an uproar or fracas.

shine (shīn) v.t. **1,** cause to gleam. **2,** polish. —v.i. [*pret. & p.p.* **shone** (shōn)] **1,** glow; appear bright; gleam. **2,** excel. —n. **1,** light; luster. **2,** fair weather. —**shin'y,** adj.

shin'er n. **1,** a minnow. **2,** (*Slang*) a black eye. **3,** (*Colloq.*) a liking. **4,** (*Colloq.*) a prank.

shin'gle (shing'gəl) n. **1,** a thin piece of wood, etc., used as roofing. **2,** closely bobbed hair. **3,** a small signboard. **4,** a gravelly beach. —v.t. **1,** roof with shingles. **2,** cut (hair) short.

shin'gles (shing'gəlz) n. an inflammatory skin disease.

shin'ny (shin'ē) n. a game similar to hockey. —v.i. (with *up*) climb; shin.

Shin'to (shin'tō) n. a Jap. religion; ancestor worship.

ship n. **1,** a large vessel, usually seagoing. **2,** an aircraft. —v.t. [**shipped, ship'ping**] **1,** put or take on board a ship or boat. **2,** send or transport. —v.i. embark. —**ship'per,** n. one who ships goods; consignor.

-ship suf. denoting office, occupation, condition, character, etc.

ship'board" n. any deck or interior part of a ship.

ship'build"ing n. construction of ships.

ship'load" n. a full load for a (particular) ship.

ship'mate" n. a fellow sailor.

ship'ment n. **1,** act or result of shipping. **2,** a quantity of goods shipped.

ship'ping n. **1,** the business of transporting goods. **2,** ships collectively.

ship'shape" adj. in good order.

ship'wreck" n. **1,** the sinking or destruction of a ship. **2,** ruin. —v.t. ruin.

ship'wright" n. a shipbuilder.

ship'yard" n. a place where ships are built.

shire (shīr) n. a county.

shirk (shērk) v.t. & i. evade work, responsibility, etc. —**shirk'er,** n.

shirr (shēr) v.t. **1,** draw up (a fabric). **2,** bake (eggs).

shirt (shērt) n. a garment for the upper body. —**shirt'ing,** n. material for shirts.

shirt'waist" n. an outer shirt.

shish'ke·bab" (shish'kə-bob") n. meat cubes and vegetables roasted and served on skewers.

shiv n. (*Slang*) a knife used as a weapon.

shiv'a·ree" (shiv'ə-rē") n. a mock serenade of newlyweds.

shiv'er (shiv'ər) v.i. tremble or quiver with cold or fear. —n. shake. —**shiv'er·y,** adj.

shlep v.t. (*Slang*) schlep.

shoal (shōl) n. **1,** a sandbank in the water. **2,** a group of fish. **3,** a crowd. —adj. shallow. —v.i. **1,** throng together. **2,** become shallow.

shoat (shōt) n. a young weaned pig.

shock (shok) n. **1,** a violent collision. **2,** any sudden, violent impact. **3,** a condition of prostration; a stroke. **4,** the sensory impression caused by an electric current. **5,** a group of sheaves of grain in a field. **6,** a thick mass, as of hair. —v.t. **1,** affect with a shock; surprise; outrage; horrify. **2,** stack (grain). —**shock'er,** n. a sensational novel, film, etc. —**shock absorber,** a device for retarding rebound. —**shock therapy**, treatment of certain diseases by inducing electric or other shock. —**shock troops**, experienced assault troops. —**shock wave, 1,** the blast caused by an explosion. **2,** caused when the speed of an object in a medium exceeds the speed at which the medium can transmit sound (as when an aircraft exceeds the speed of sound).

shock'ing *adj.* causing surprise, consternation, or indignation.

shod *v.* pret. & p.p. of *shoe*.

shod'dy (shod'ē) *n.* **1,** a low quality fabric; anything inferior. **2,** sham. —*adj.* **1,** inferior. **2,** sham; ungenerous. —**shod'di·ness,** *n.*

shoe (shoo) *n.* **1,** a covering for the human foot. **2,** a horseshoe. **3,** an outer covering or housing, as a tire. **4,** part of a brake. **5,** a block in sliding contact with a third rail to transmit current to an electric motor. —*v.t.* [*pret. & p.p.* **shod**] put shoes on.

shoe'bill" *n.* an African wading bird.

shoe'horn" *n.* a device used to slip one's feet into shoes.

shoe'lace" *n.* shoestring.

shoe'mak"er *n.* cobbler.

shoe'string" *n.* **1,** a lace for tying a shoe. **2,** very limited capital, in business.

shoe'tree" *n.* a form for keeping shoes in shape.

sho'gun (shō'gən) *n.* a member of the former ruling aristocracy of Japan.

shone (shōn) *v.* pret. & p.p. of *shine*.

shoo *interj.* begone! —**shoo-'in",** *n.* an easy victory, esp. in an election.

shook (shuk) *v.* p.t. of *shake*.

shoot *v.t.* [*pret. & p.p.* **shot**] **1,** hit, wound, or kill with a missile from a weapon. **2,** discharge (a weapon). **3,** send out or forth. **4,** traverse rapidly. **5,** take a picture of. —*v.i.* **1,** discharge a missile; fire. **2,** hunt. **3,** dart forth or along. **4,** be emitted; sprout. **5,** (with *up*) grow rapidly. **6,** (with *up*) (*Slang*) inject oneself with a drug, esp. heroin. —*n.* **1,** a shooting party. **2,** a sprout. —**shooting gallery,** an establishment where one can shoot at targets. —**shooting iron,** (*Slang*) a firearm. —**shooting star,** a meteor.

shoot'out" *n.* a gunfight.

shop *n.* **1,** a store. **2,** a workroom; a factory; (*Colloq.*) an office. **3,** one's own business. —*v.i. & t.* [**shopped, shop'ping**] visit stores as a customer. —**talk shop,** talk about one's business or profession.

shop'keep"er *n.* a tradesman.

shop'lift"er *n.* one who steals from shop counters. —**shop'lift",** *v.i. & t.*

shoppe (shop) *n.* shop.

shop'per (shop'ər) *n.* **1,** one who shops. **2,** one sent to buy from a competitor, for comparison of goods.

shop'worn" *adj.* deteriorated by display.

shore (shōr) *n.* **1,** land adjacent to water. **2,** a prop. —*v.t.* (with *up*) prop. —**shor'ing,** *n.* props.

shorn (shôrn) *v.* p.p. of *shear*.

short (shôrt) *adj.* **1,** not long; not tall. **2,** brief; concise. **3,** deficient; (with *of*) insufficiently supplied with. **4,** of vowels, not prolonged in utterance. **5,** of stocks, not possessed at time of sale. **6,** crumbling readily, as pastry. **7,** curt. **8,** of odds, almost even. —*adv.* **1,** briefly. **2,** abruptly. **3,** insufficiently. —*n.* **1,** whatever is short. **2,** (*pl.*) short trousers or drawers. —**in short order,** quickly and efficiently. —**short cir-cuit,** a low-resistance electrical connection, usually accidental. —**short cut,** a shorter route or method. —**short shrift,** little delay or mercy. —**short story,** a relatively brief prose narrative. —**short wave,** a radio wave sixty meters or less in length.

short'age (-ij) *n.* deficiency.

short'bread" *n.* a rich cake made short with butter.

short'cake" *n.* a cake or biscuit covered with fruit.

short-"change' *v.t.* (*Colloq.*) give inadequate change to; cheat.

short'com"ing *n.* a failing.

short'en *v.t.* make shorter.

short'en·ing *n.* fat used in baking.

short'fall" *n.* the amount by which the actual number falls short of the expected or desired amount.

short'hand" *n.* a system of taking notes.

short'hand"ed *adj.* having too few workers.

Shorthand Outlines

_____

short'horn" *n.* one of a breed of cattle.

short'lived" (-līvd") *adj.* of brief life or duration.

short'ly (-lē) *adv.* **1,** in a short time; soon. **2,** briefly; concisely. **3,** curtly.

short'sight'ed *adj.* **1,** nearsighted. **2,** lacking foresight; not provident. —**short'-sight'ed·ness,** *n.*

short'stop" *n.* (*Baseball*) an infield position between second and third base.

short-"tem'pered *adj.* easily roused to anger.

short-'term" *adj.* lasting for a relatively short time.

short-'wind"ed (-win"did) *adj.* tending to be out of breath after little exertion. **—short-'wind"ed·ness,** *n.*

shot *n.* **1,** an act of shooting; range. **2,** small pellets. **3,** one who shoots. **4,** a move or stroke in a game. **5,** (*Slang*) a guess. **6,** (*Slang*) a drink; one injection of a drug. **7,** a photograph. **8,** the ball used in the shot put. **—adj.** woven with threads of different colors. **—v.** pret. & p.p. of *shoot.*

shot'gun" *n.* a gun firing charges of small shot. **—shotgun wedding,** (*Jocular*) a wedding forced upon the bridegroom.

shot-'put" *n.* a contest at hurling a heavy metal ball.

should (shŭd) *aux.v.* **1,** pret. or subjunctive of *shall.* **2,** ought to.

shoul'der (shōl'dər) *n.* **1,** a part of the body from the side of the neck to the upper joint of the arm (or foreleg). **2,** a ledge. **3,** the unpaved side of a road. **—v.t. & i. 1,** carry on, or as on, the shoulder. **2,** push with the shoulder.

shoul'der·blade" *n.* a flat bone in the shoulder; scapula.

shout (showt) *v.i. & t.* **1,** cry out. **2,** laugh noisily. **—n.** a loud cry.

shove (shuv) *v.t.* **1,** push along a surface. **2,** jostle. **—v.i. 1,** push. **2,** (with *off*) depart. **—n.** a push.

shov'el (shuv'əl) *n.* **1,** a long-handled implement with a broad scoop. **2,** a machine for excavating. **—v.t. & i.** transfer with a shovel.

show (shō) *v.t.* [*p.p.* **shown** (shōn) or **showed**] **1,** allow to be seen; exhibit; indicate. **2,** instruct; guide. **3,** (with *up*) expose the faults of. **—v.i. 1,** be seen; appear. **2,** finish third in a horse race. **3,** (with *off*) perform ostentatiously. **4,** (with *up*) appear; stand out. **—n. 1,** a theatrical performance. **2,** an exhibition. **3,** ostentatious display. **4,** (*Colloq.*) a chance.

show'boat" *n.* **1,** a river boat used as a traveling theater. **—v.i.** show off; parade.

show'case" *n.* **1,** a glass case for the display of articles, as in a store or museum. **2,** any situation or location that displays talent, beauty, etc.

show'down" *n.* a final disclosure or test.

show'er (show'ər) *n.* **1,** a light rain; a spray. **2,** a large number. **3,** a bestowal of gifts. **4,** a shower bath. **—v.t. 1,** wet copiously. **2,** bestow or scatter abundantly. **—v.i. 1,** rain. **2,** take a shower bath. **—show'er·y,** *adj.* raining intermittently. **—shower bath,** a bath in water poured down from above.

show'ing *n.* **1,** act of displaying. **2,** performance.

show'man (-mən) *n.* [*pl.* **-men**] one who puts on a show. **—show'man·ship,** *n.*

shown (shōn) *v.* pret. & p.p. of *show.*

show-'off" *n.* one given to ostentation.

show'piece" *n.* something on display, esp. a particularly good example of a style, etc.

show'place" *n.* a place that is noted for its beauty, interest, etc.

show'room" *n.* a room for exhibition of goods for sale.

show'y *adj.* **1,** imposing. **2,** gaudy. **—show'i·ness,** *n.*

shrank *v.* pret. of *shrink.*

shrap'nel (shrap'nəl) *n.* a bursting projectile that showers missiles.

shred *v.t.* [**shred'ded, -ding**] tear or cut into small pieces or strips. **—n.** **1,** a small strip. **2,** a particle.

shrew (shroo) *n.* **1,** a scolding woman. **2,** a small mouselike animal. **—shrew'ish,** *adj.*

shrewd (shrood) *adj.* astute; quickwitted. **—shrewd'ness,** *n.*

shriek (shrēk) *n.* a shrill outcry or utterance. **—v.t. & i.** utter such a cry.

shrift *n.* a shriving. **—short shrift,** disposition without delay.

shrike (shrīk) *n.* the butcherbird.

shrill (shril) *adj.* sharp, high, and piercing in sound. **—v.t. & i.** utter (such a sound). **—shrill'ness,** *n.*

shrimp *n.* **1,** an edible, long-tailed crustacean. **2,** a small person.

shrine (shrīn) *n.* a consecrated or hallowed place.

shrink *v.i.* [**shrank, shrunk, shrink'ing**] **1,** contract spontaneously; diminish; shrivel. **2,** draw back; recoil. **—n.** (*Slang*) a psychiatrist or psychoanalyst. **—v.t.** cause to contract; lessen. **—shrink'age,** *n.* **—shrinking violet,** (*Colloq.*) a shy person.

shrive (shrīv) *v.t. & i.* [**shrived** or **shrove, shriv'en**] grant absolution to; impose penance on; confess.

shriv'el (shriv'əl) *v.t. & i.* contract; wrinkle; wither.

shroud (shrowd) *n.* **1,** a burial cloth. **2,** something that envelops or conceals. **3,** (*pl.*) (*Naut.*) strong guy ropes. **—v.t.** cover; obscure.

Shrove Tuesday (shrōv) the day before Lent.

shrub *n.* a woody plant smaller than a tree. **—shrub'ber·y,** *n.*

shrug *v.t. & i.* [**shrugged, shrug'ging**] raise and contract the shoulders, expressing doubt, indifference, etc. **—n.** such a gesture.

shrunk *v.* p.p. of *shrink.*

shrunk′en *adj.* having shrunk.

shtick (shtik) *n.* (*Slang*) schtick.

shuck (shuk) *n.* **1,** a husk or pod, as of corn. **2,** a shell. **3,** (*Slang*) a put-on; deception. —*v.t.* **1,** remove the husk or shell from. **2,** deceive. —**shucks,** *interj.* expressing deprecation, frustration, etc.

shud′der (shud′ər) *n.* a convulsive tremor of the body, as from horror, etc. —*v.i.* tremble violently.

shuf′fle (shuf′əl) *v.t. & i.* **1,** move with scraping feet. **2,** mix. **3,** shift evasively. —*n.* an act of shuffling.

shuf′fle·board″ *n.* a game played by pushing disks toward marked squares on a board or court.

shun *v.t.* [**shunned, shun′ning**] keep away from; avoid; refrain from.

shun′pike″ *n.* a road taken to avoid the tollgates of a toll road.

shunt *v.t.* **1,** turn aside. **2,** shift (as a train). **3,** (with *off*) relegate; foist. —*n.* **1,** a shift or shifting. **2,** a conductor carrying off a small part of the current in a circuit.

shush *v.t. & interj.* silence.

shut *v.t.* [**shut, shut′ting**] **1,** close; bring together. **2,** (with *in* or *up*) confine; prevent access to. **3,** (with *out*) exclude; prevent from scoring. —*v.i.* **1,** become closed; close. **2,** (with *down*) discontinue. **3,** (with *up*) (*Colloq.*) stop talking. —*adj.* closed.

shut′down″ *n.* a temporary closing or discontinuance.

shut′-'eye″ *n.* (*Colloq.*) sleep.

shut-′in″ *adj.* confined to a house, hospital, etc. —*n.* one so confined.

shut-′off″ *n.* a device for shutting off, as a valve.

shut′out″ *n.* **1,** exclusion. **2,** a game in which one team does not score.

shut′ter (-ər) *n.* one who or that which shuts, esp. a hinged panel for a window, a device for a camera lens, a movable slide, etc.

shut′ter·bug″ *n.* (*Colloq.*) an avid amateur photographer.

shut′tle (shut′əl) *n.* **1,** a device for passing thread in a loom or sewing machine. **2,** a train running back and forth for a short distance. —*v.t. & i.* move to and fro.

shut′tle·cock″ *n.* a ball, usu. of cork, with a tail of feathers, used in badminton and *battledore and shuttlecock.*

shy (shī) *adj.* **1,** timid; bashful. **2,** cautious; wary. **3,** scant; short. —*v.i.* start back in fear. —*v.t.* throw. —*n.* a start, as in fear. —**shy′ness,** *n.*

Shy′lock (shī′lok) *n.* (often *l.c.*) a usurious moneylender.

shy′ster (shī′stər) *n.* a professional person, esp. a lawyer, who uses underhand or unethical methods.

si (sē) *n.* (*Music*) the seventh tone of the diatonic scale. Also, **ti** (tē).

si′a·mang (sē′ə-mang) *n.* a large black gibbon of Sumatra.

Si′a·mese′ (sī″ə-mēz′) *adj. & n.* pert. to Siam (Thailand), its people, language, etc.; Thai. —**Siamese twins,** twins born with joined bodies.

sib *n.* a kinsman.

sib′i·lant (sib′ə-lənt) *adj.* having a hissing sound. —**sib′i·lance,** *n.* —**sib′i·late,** *v.t. & i.* pronounce with a hiss. —**sib″i·la′tion,** *n.*

sib′ling *n.* a full brother or sister.

sib′yl (sib′il) *n.* a prophetess.

sic (sik) *adv.* (quoted) exactly as written, even though incorrect.

sick (sik) *adj.* **1,** ill. **2,** nauseated. **3,** depressed. **4,** disgusted. **5,** (with *of*) satiated. —*n.* sick people. —*v.t.* set upon, esp. of a dog. —**sick bay,** a ship's hospital. —**sick′-ness,** *n.*

sick′bed″ *n.* a sick person's bed.

sick′en (-ən) *v.t. & i.* make or become sick. —**sick′en·ing,** *adj.* causing nausea or disgust.

sick′le (sik′əl) *n.* a short-handled scythe with a curved blade. —**sickle cell anemia,** a disease of the blood occurring most frequently in black people.

sick′ly *adj.* **1,** unhealthy in fact or appearance. **2,** mawkish. **3,** feeble. —**sick′li·ness,** *n.*

sick′out″ *n.* an organized work protest in which employees feign illness to stay away from the job.

side (sīd) *n.* **1,** a terminal surface or line. **2,** either half, as of the body, right or left. **3,** an aspect; a point of view. **4,** a position in a lawsuit, game, etc. —*adj.* being on, coming from, or aimed toward, one side. —*v.i.* (with *with*) ally oneself. —**side effect,** a reaction or result produced (as by a drug) in addition to the desired effect. —**side line, 1,** an additional business or line of merchandise. **2,** (*Sports*) a side boundary. —**side show,** an incidental attraction, as at a circus.

side′arm″ *adj.* thrown with the arm held between the shoulder and the hip. —**side arm,** a small weapon carried at the side, as a pistol.

side′board″ *n.* a piece of dining-room furniture.

side′burns″ *n.pl.* short side whiskers.

side′car″ *n.* **1,** a small car attached to a motorcycle. **2,** a cocktail made with brandy and Cointreau.

---

tub, cūte, pûll; labəl; oil, owl, go, chip, she, thin, *th*en, sing, ink; *see p. 6*

side'kick" *n.* (*Colloq.*) buddy.

side'light" *n.* **1,** an incidental aspect of anything. **2,** a narrow window beside a door.

side'long" *adj.* to the side; sidewise. —*adv.* sidewise.

side'man" *n.* an instrumental musician in a jazz or rock band.

side'piece" *n.* a handgun.

si·de're·al (sī-dir'ē-əl) *adj.* pert. to the stars; based on fixed stars.

side'sad"dle *n.* a saddle allowing a person to sit with both legs on the same side of the horse.

side'slip" *n.* of a banked airplane, a sliding sideways and down.

side'split"ting *adj.* uproariously funny.

side'step" *v.t.* & *i.* evade.

side'stroke" *n.* a stroke in swimming.

side'swipe" *v.t.* strike glancingly. —*n.* a glancing collision.

side'track" *v.t.* **1,** move to a siding. **2,** divert.

side'walk" *n.* the paved path for foot traffic beside a street.

side'wall" *n.* the lateral surface of a vehicle tire.

side'ward" *adj.* directed or moving to one side. —*adv.* [also, **side'wards"**] toward the side.

side'ways" *adj.* & *adv.* to the side; from one side. Also, **side'wise".**

side'wind"er (-wīn"dər) *n.* **1,** a small rattlesnake. **2,** (*Slang*) a blow from the side. **3,** a kind of air-to-air missile fired from an aircraft.

sid'ing (sī'ding) *n.* **1,** a track for idle railroad cars. **2,** boards for the sides of a frame house.

si'dle (sī'dəl) *v.i.* move obliquely; edge along. —*n.* this movement.

siege (sēj) *n.* **1,** a prolonged surrounding of a place by an enemy. **2,** a long illness. —**siege guns,** artillery used to bombard a fortress.

si·en'na (sē-en'ə) *n.* a brown pigment or color.

si·er'ra (sē-er'ə) *n.* mountains in a succession of peaks.

si·es'ta (sē-es'tə) *n.* a midday nap.

sieve (siv) *n.* **1,** a straining pan. **2,** a leakage of information. —*v.t.* sift.

sift *v.t.* **1,** separate the large from the small. **2,** scrutinize.

sigh (sī) *v.i.* & *t.* breathe out audibly, expressing disappointment. —*n.* an act or sound of sighing.

sight (sīt) *n.* **1,** the faculty of vision; visual perception. **2,** point of view. **3,** a coming into view. **4,** something seen; something unusual (interesting, distressing) to see. **5,** (*Colloq.*) a surprising number. **6,** an aid to aiming. **7,** aim. —*v.t.* get sight of; aim at. —**sight'ed,** *adj.* able to see. —**sight'less,** *adj.* blind. —**sight'ly,** *adj.* pleasing to the eye. —**at sight, 1,** as soon as seen. **2,** on demand.

sight'read" (-rēd") *v.t.* & *i.* read at sight.

sight'see"ing *n.* brief visiting of places of interest. —**sight'see"** (*Colloq.*) *v.i.* —**sight'se"er,** *n.*

sig'ma (sig'mə) *n.* the eighteenth letter of the Greek alphabet (Σ, σ, ς).

sign (sīn) *n.* **1,** a mark or symbol. **2,** a display board. **3,** a gesture. **4,** a symptom. **5,** a trace. —*v.t.* **1,** affix a signature to; write (one's name). **2,** indicate by sign. **3,** (with *on*) engage to do service. —*v.i.* **1,** write one's signature. **2,** (with *off*) end.

sig'nal (sig'nəl) *n.* **1,** a sign carrying a messsage, often in code. **2,** a radio wave. —*adj.* **1,** serving as a signal. **2,** eminent; conspicuous. —*v.t.* & *i.* make a signal (to). —**sig'nal·ize"** (-īz") *v.t.* indicate distinctly. —**sig'nal·ly,** *adv.* notably.

sig'na·to·ry (sig'nə-tôr-ē) *n.* one who signs. —*adj.* signing.

sig'na·ture (sig'nə-tyûr) *n.* **1,** a person's name in his own handwriting. **2,** any distinguishing sign. **3,** (*Printing*) a batch of pages resulting from a single sheet folded and cut; the sheet; a sign printed on the first page of each batch for identification.

sign'board" *n.* a large mounting for advertising signs.

sig'net (sig'nət) *n.* a small seal.

sig·nif'i·cance (sig-nif'i-kəns) *n.* **1,** the real or implied meaning. **2,** consequence. **3,** expressiveness. —**sig·nif'i·cant,** *adj.*

sig'ni·fy" (sig'niəfī") *v.t.* mean; suggest. —**sig"ni·fi·ca'tion,** *n.*

si·gnor' (sē-nyôr') *n.* (*Ital.*) a gentleman; Mr.; sir. Also, **si·gno're** (-e) [*pl.* **-ri** (-ē)] —**si·gno'ra,** (-ä) **si"gno·ri'na** (-rē'nä) *n. fem.*

sign'post" *n.* a post bearing a sign or signs.

Sikh (sēk) *n.* a member of a certain Hindu religious sect.

si'lage (sī'lij) *n.* fodder stored in a silo.

si'lence (sī'ləns) *n.* **1,** the absence of sound. **2,** abstention from speech or noise. **3,** absence of mention. **4,** secrecy. —*v.t.* restrain from making sound or speech. —**si'lencer,** *n.* a device to silence a firearm.

si'lent (sī'lənt) *adj.* **1,** making no sound. **2,** tacit. —**silent partner,** an inactive partner.

si'lex (sī'leks) *n.* **1,** a heat-resistant glass

of fused quartz. **2**, (*T.N.*) a thin beaker of this glass.

sil·hou·ette' (sil″û-et′) *n.* **1**, an outline drawing. **2**, a two-dimensional outline, as of a ship. —*v.t.* represent in silhouette.

sil'i·ca (sil′ə-kə) *n.* **1**, silicon dioxide. **2**, sandlike particles of hard stone. —**si·li'ceous** (si-lish′əs) *adj.*

sil'i·cate (sil′i-kət) *n.* a salt derived from silica.

sil'i·con (sil′i-kən) *n.* a crystalline chemical element, no. 14, symbol Si.

sil'i·cone" (sil′ə-kōn″) *n.* any of various silicon compounds having high resistance to heat and water.

sil'i·co'sis (sil″i-kō′sis) *n.* a disease caused by inhaling stone dust.

silk *n.* a fine soft fiber, produced by the silkworm; a thread or fabrics made from it. —**silk'en, silk'y,** *adj.*

silk-'screen" *adj.* designating a method of reproducing by means of a stencil of silk cloth. —*v.t. & i.* print by this method.

silk-'stock"ing *adj.* luxurious. —*n.* a rich or aristocratic person.

silk'worm" *n.* a moth larva from whose cocoon silk is spun.

sill (sil) *n.* a horizontal foundation, as of a door.

sil'ly (sil′ē) *adj.* **1**, foolish; witless. **2**, ridiculous. **3**, stunned. —**sil'li·ness,** *n.*

si'lo (sī′lō) *n.* an airtight storehouse for grain, etc.

silt *n.* earthy sediment.

sil'ver (sil′vər) *n. & adj.* **1**, a precious metallic chemical element, no. 47, symbol Ag. **2**, silver coin; money. **3**, silver tableware. **4**, a lustrous, grayish-white color. **5**, the 25th anniversary. —**sil'ver·y,** *adj.* —**silver certificate,** a U.S. piece of paper money formerly redeemable in silver. —**silver fox,** a fox with black, silver-gray tipped fur; the fur. —**silver lining,** a fortunate or hopeful circumstance in an otherwise gloomy situation. —**silver screen, 1**, a projection screen. **2**, (*cap.*) motion pictures.

sil'ver·fish" *n.* **1**, any of various fish. **2**, a wingless insect common as a household pest.

sil'ver·plate" *n.* tableware or other item plated with silver.

sil'ver·smith" *n.* a craftsman who makes articles of silver.

sil'ver·ware" *n.* tableware and dishes of silver.

sim'i·an (sim′ē-ən) *adj.* pert. to an ape or monkey. —*n.* monkey or ape.

sim'i·lar (sim′ə-lər) *adj.* resembling. —**sim"i·lar'i·ty** (-lar′ə-tē) *n.*

sim'i·le" (sim′ə-lē″) *n.* a comparison, as a figure of speech.

si·mil'i·tude" (si-mil′i-tood″) *n.* **1**, resemblance. **2**, a comparison.

sim'mer (sim′ər) *v.i. & t.* continue in a state just below the boiling point. —*n.* this state of heat.

si·mol'e·on (si-mō′lē-ən) *n.* (*Slang*) a dollar.

Si'mon·ize" (sī′mən-īz″) *v.t.* (*T.N.*) clean and polish (an enameled surface, as of an automobile).

si"mon·pure' (sī″mən-pyûr′) *adj.* genuine.

si'mo·ny (sī′mə-nē) *n.* the selling of ecclesiastical offices, indulgences, etc. —**si'mo·nist,** *n.*

si·moom' *n.* a hot wind.

simp *n.* (*Slang*) a fool.

sim·pa'ti·co (sim-pä′tē-kō) *adj.* of similar or compatible temperament; congenial.

sim'per (sim′pər) *v.i. & t.* smile or say in a silly manner.

sim'ple (sim′pəl) *adj.* **1**, elementary; not complicated. **2**, plain; not elaborate. **3**, pure; absolute. **4**, unaffected; unassuming. **5**, insignificant. **6**, humble. **7**, easily deceived; silly. **8**, (*Archaic*) a medicinal herb.

sim'ple-mind"ed *adj.* foolish.

sim'ple·ton (-tən) *n.* a fool.

sim·plic'i·ty (sim-plis′ə-tē) *n.* condition of being simple.

sim'pli·fy" (sim′pli-fī″) *v.t.* make easier or less complex. —**sim"pli·fi·ca'tion,** *n.*

sim·plis'tic (sim-plis′tik) *adj.* tending to oversimplify; naïve.

sim"u·la'crum (sim″yə-lā′krəm) *n.* [*pl.* **-cra** (-krə)] an unreal semblance; a shadowy image.

sim'u·late" (sim′yə-lāt″) *v.t.* **1**, pretend. **2**, imitate; resemble. —**sim"u·la'tion,** *n.*

si'mul·cast" (sī′məl-) *v.t.* **1**, broadcast simultaneously by radio and television. **2**, broadcast at the same moment that it happens. —*n.* such a broadcast.

si"mul·ta'ne·ous (sī″məl-tā′nē-əs) *adj.* existing, occurring, or operating at the same time. —**si"mul·ta·ne'i·ty** (-tə-nā′ə-tē), **si"mul·ta'ne·ous·ness,** *n.*

sin *n.* **1**, a transgression of the law of God. **2**, a serious fault; an error. —*v.i.* [**sinned, sin'ning**] commit a sin. —**sin'ful,** *adj.* —**sin'ner,** *n.*

since (sins) *adv.* **1**, from then till now. **2**, subsequently. **3**, before now; ago. —*prep.* throughout all the time, or at some time, following. —*conj.* **1**, from the time when; during the time after. **2**, because.

sin·cere' (sin-sir′) *adj.* free from falsehood, pretense, or deceit. —**sin·cer′i·ty** (-ser′ə-tē) *n.*

sine (sīn) *n.* a trigonometric ratio.

si′ne·cure″ (sī′nə-kyûr″) *n.* an easy job.

si′ne di′e (sē′ne-dē′e) (*Lat.*) without (setting) a day (to meet again).

si′ne qua non′ (sē′ne-kwä-nōn′) (*Lat.*) an absolute necessity.

sin′ew (sin′ū) *n,* **1,** a tendon. **2,** strength; vigor. **3,** a mainstay.

sin′ew·y (-ė) *adj.* **1,** strong. **2,** vigorous. **3,** stringy.

sing *v.i.* [**sang, sung, sing′ing**] **1,** utter words or sounds musically. **2,** murmur, whistle, etc. —*v.t.* utter musically; chant. —*n.* a gathering of persons for singing.

singe (sinj) *v.t.* burn superficially.

Sing″gha·lese′ (sing″gə-lēz′) *adj.* of Ceylon. —*n.* a native of Ceylon; its language.

sin′gle (sing′gəl) *adj.* **1,** pert. to one person or thing; individual. **2,** alone; detached. **3,** unmarried. —*v.t.* (with *out*) select individually. —*n.* **1,** that which is single. **2,** (*Baseball*) a one-base hit. **3,** (*pl.*) (*Tennis*) a contest between two players. —*v.i.* (*Baseball*) hit a single. —**sin′gle·ness,** *n.* —**single file,** a line of people or things, one behind the other.

sin″gle-breast′ed (-bres′tid) *adj.* (of a coat or vest) overlapping only enough to allow fastening.

sin″gle-hand′ed *adj. & adv.* **1,** unaided. **2,** done with one hand.

single-lens reflex a camera which allows viewing through the same lens which exposes the film.

sin′gle-mind″ed *adj.* undeviating. —**sin′-gle·mind″ed·ness,** *n.*

sin′gle·ton (-tən) *n.* (*Card Games*) a holding of one card in a suit.

sin′gle-tree″ *n.* a pivoted bar on a carriage, etc., to which a horse's harness is attached. Also, **whif′fle·tree″.**

sin′gly (sing′glė) *adv.* **1,** separately; individually. **2,** one at a time.

sing′song″ *adj.* monotonously rhythmical.

sin′gu·lar (sing′gyə-lər) *adj.* **1,** unusual. **2,** eccentric. **3,** (*Gram.*) denoting or relating to one person or thing. —**sin″gu·lar′i·ty** (-lar′ə-tē) *n.*

sin′is·ter (sin′is-tər) *adj.* **1,** malicious; harmful; ominous. **2,** bad; corrupt. **3,** on the left side.

sink *v.i.* [**sank, sunk, sink′ing**] **1,** fall or decline; settle. **2,** become submerged. **3,** incline downward. **4,** decrease. —*v.t.* **1,** force downward. **2,** place by excavation. **3,** diminish. **4,** suppress; overwhelm. —*n.* **1,** a basin, esp. in a kitchen; a drain. **2,** a low area. —**sink′a·ble,** *adj.* —**sinking fund,** a fund held in reserve to pay off the principal of a debt.

sink′er *n.* **1,** a weight on a fishing line. **2,** (*Slang*) a doughnut.

Sinn Fein (shin fān) a revolutionary Irish society.

Si·no- (sī-nō-) *pref.* Chinese.

sin′u·ous (sin′ū-əs) *adj.* **1,** full of curves; winding. **2,** devious. —**sin″u·os′i·ty, sin′u·ous·ness,** *n.*

si′nus (sī′nəs) *n.* a cavity or recess, esp. in the skull. —**si″nus·i′tis** (-ī′təs) *n.* inflammation of the sinuses.

Sioux (soo) *adj. & n.sing. & pl.* (pert. to) a tribe of No. Amer. Indians.

sip *v.t. & i.* [**sipped, sip′ping**] drink little by little. —*n.* a small quantity sipped.

si′phon (sī′fən) *n.* **1,** a bent tube used to draw a liquid over an elevation. **2,** a bottle for aerated water. —*v.t.* draw off with a siphon.

sip′per (sip′ər) *n.* a tube for sipping.

sir (sėr) *n.* **1,** a respectful term of address to a man. **2,** (*cap.*) the title of a knight or baronet.

sire (sīr) *n.* **1,** a father; a male parent. **2,** a term of address to a sovereign. —*v.t.* beget.

si′ren (sī′rən) *n.* **1,** a mythical alluring sea nymph. **2,** an alluring and dangerous woman. **3,** a device for producing a whistle; its sound.

sir′loin (sėr′loin) *n.* a cut of beef.

si·roc′co (sə-rok′ō) *n.* a hot southeast wind from N. Afr.

sir′up *n.* syrup.

si′sal (sī′səl) *n.* a hemplike fiber taken from the agave.

sis′sy (sis′ė) *n.* (*Colloq.*) **1,** an effeminate boy. **2,** a timid or cowardly boy or girl.

sis′ter (sis′tər) *n.* **1,** [also, *colloq.*, **sis**] a female relative having the same parents as another. **2,** a fellow person, female. **3,** one of a sisterhood; a nun.

sis′ter·hood″ *n.* **1,** state of being a sister or sisters. **2,** an association of women.

sis′ter-in-law″ *n.* [*pl.* **sis′ters-**] **1,** the sister of one's spouse. **2,** the wife of one's brother.

sis′ter·ly *adj.* befitting a sister. —**sis′ter·li·ness,** *n.*

sit *v.i.* [**sat, sit′ting**] **1,** take a posture with back erect, body bent at the hips; be seated. **2,** perch. **3,** remain. **4,** be located; be in office; convene. —**sit′ter,** *n.* a part-time nurse for children. —**sit′ting,** *n.* the act or period of sitting; session. —**sit-down strike,** occupation of an employer's premises by strikers. —**sitting duck,** an easy target. —**sitting room,** a parlor.

si·tar' (sē-tär') *n.* an Indian plucked-string instrument with a long neck and sympathetic strings.

sit'com'' (sit'kom'') *n.* a situation comedy.

site (sīt) *n.* location.

sit-'in'' *n.* a nonviolent demonstration, usu. involving the obstruction of a public place by sitting there and refusing to move unless carried away.

sit'u·ate'' (sich'oo-āt'') *v.t.* place in a particular place. —*adj.* located.

sit''u·a'tion (sich''oo-ā'shən) *n.* **1,** location. **2,** condition. **3,** a job. —**situation comedy,** a dramatic comedy, esp. on television, in which characters in a certain situation find themselves in different comic, often grotesque, circumstances.

sit'up'' *n.* an exercise.

si'tus (sī'təs) *n.* location; situation.

sitz bath (sits; zits) a tub bath taken with water covering only the legs and hips.

six (siks) *n. & adj.* the cardinal number between five and seven, expressed by 6. —**sixth,** *n. & adj.* —**sixth sense,** intuition.

six'pence (-pəns) *n.* a Brit. coin worth six pennies. —**six'pen''ny,** *adj.*

six-'shoot''er *n.* (*Colloq.*) a revolver, esp. of .45 caliber.

six·teen' (-tēn') *n. & adj.* ten plus six, also expressed by 16. —**six·teenth'** (-tēnth') *adj. & n.*

six'ty (-tē) *n. & adj.* ten times six, also expressed by 60. —**six'ti·eth** (-tē-əth) *adj. & n.*

size (sīz) *n.* **1,** bulk; volume; extent. **2,** a standard measure for clothes, etc. **3,** a gluey substance for bonding or glazing, as starch. —*v.t.* **1,** (with *up*) estimate. **2,** starch, glaze, etc. —**siz'a·ble,** *adj.* fairly large. —**siz'ing,** *n.* material for glazing, etc.

siz'zle (siz'əl) [**siz'zled, siz'zling**] *v.i.* **1,** sputter. **2,** (*Colloq.*) be very hot. —*n.* a sputtering sound.

skag *n.* (*Slang*) heroin.

skate (skāt) *n.* **1,** a steel runner for gliding. **2,** a roller skate. **3,** a fish of the ray family. —*v.i.* glide or roll on skates.

skate'board'' *n.* a short board mounted on roller-skate wheels.

ske·dad'dle (ski-dad'əl) *v.i.* (*Slang*) run away.

skeet (skēt) *n.* a form of trapshooting.

skein (skān) *n.* a coiled length of yarn or thread.

skel'e·ton (skel'ə-tən) *n.* **1,** the assemblage of bones of the body. **2,** an inner framework. **3,** an outline. —*adj.* **1,** skeletal. **2,** condensed or synoptic in form. —**skel'e·tal,** *adj.* pert. to or like a skeleton.

—**skeleton key,** a key for opening many different locks.

skep'tic (skep'tik) *n.* one inclined to doubt. Also, **scep'tic.** —**skep'ti·cal,** *adj.* doubting; incredulous.

skep'ti·cism (skep'ti-siz-əm) *n.* inclination to doubt; questioning nature. Also, **scep'ti·cism.**

sketch (skech) *n.* **1,** a rough drawing. **2,** an outline; synopsis. **3,** a short humorous act; skit. —*v.t.* delineate or describe roughly. —**sketch'y,** *adj.* not detailed.

skew (skū) *v.i.* swerve. —*adj.* oblique or distorted.

skew'er (skū'ər) *n.* a long pin; a spit used in roasting meat. —*v.t.* fasten or pierce with or as with a skewer.

ski (skē) *n.* a long wooden runner for gliding on snow. —*v.i.* [**skied, ski'ing**] travel on skis. —**ski'er,** *n.*

ski'bob'' *n.* a small, steerable vehicle on skis.

skid *n.* **1,** a timber or metal band forming a track. **2,** a supporting runner. **3,** a friction brake. **4,** a framework. **5,** an act of skidding. —*v.t. & i.* [**skid'ded, -ding**] **1,** slide without rotating. **2,** swerve. —**skid row** or **road,** a street or section where vagrants and alcoholics live.

skid·doo' (ski-doo') *interj.* (*Slang*) go away!

skiff (skif) *n.* a small boat.

skif'fle (skif'əl) *n.* music played on unusual instruments.

ski·jor'ing (skē-jôr'ing) *n.* a sport in which a skier is pulled by a horse.

skill (skil) *n.* technical ability or knowledge; expertness. —**skill'ful, skil'ful, skilled,** *adj.*

skil'let (skil'it) *n.* **1,** a frying pan. **2,** a long-handled saucepan.

skim *v.t. & i.* [**skimmed, skim'ming**] **1,** lift or scrape off the top of (a liquid). **2,** read superficially. **3,** glide lightly (over). —**skim milk,** milk without its natural cream.

skimp *v.t. & i.* provide meagerly; scrimp. —**skimp'y,** *adj.* meager.

skin *n.* **1,** the outer covering of a body. **2,** a pelt. **3,** a rind or peel. —*v.t.* [**skinned, skin'ning**] **1,** remove the skin from; peel. **2,** (*Slang*) swindle. —*v.i.* (*Slang*) abscond. —**skin flick,** (*Slang*) a pornographic movie. —**skin game,** (*Colloq.*) a fraud; swindle.

skin-'deep'' *adj. & adv.* superficial; slight.

skin'div''er *n.* a diver who penetrates deep water carrying a supply of oxygen but not wearing a diver's suit. —**skin'div''ing,** *n.*

skin'flint'' *n.* a stingy, grasping person; tightwad.

skink *n.* a small, smooth-scaled lizard.

skin'ner *n.* **1**, one who skins. **2**, a driver of teams of mules.

skin'ny (skin'ē) *adj.* lean; underweight; thin. —**skin'ni·ness,** *n.*

skin'ny-dip' *v.i.* swim in the nude.

skin'tight' *adj.* fitting closely to or like the skin.

skip *v.i.* [**skipped, skip'ping**] **1**, jump lightly. **2**, bounce; ricochet. **3**, pass over something. **4**, (*Colloq.*) flee. —*v.t.* **1**, jump over. **2**, cause to ricochet. **3**, (*Colloq.*) evade. —*n.* act of skipping.

skip'per (skip'ər) *n.* captain of a ship; chief; master. —*v.t.* act as skipper of.

skirl (skẽrl) *n.* the sound of the bagpipe. —*v.t.* sound loudly and shrilly.

skir'mish (skẽr'mish) *n.* a minor battle. —*v.i.* engage in a skirmish.

skirt (skẽrt) *n.* **1**, a garment, or part of it, hanging down from the waist. **2**, an apron. **3**, (*Slang*) a woman. —*v.t.* lie or pass along the border of.

skit *n.* a short, comic play.

skit'ter (skit'ər) *v.i. & t.* glide lightly or swiftly; skim along the surface.

skit'tish (skit'ish) *adj.* **1**, apt to shy. **2**, restless. **3**, coy.

skit'tles (skit'əlz) *n.pl.* ninepins.

skive (skīv) *v.t.* slice (leather) thinly.

skiv'er (skī'vər) *n.* **1**, a thin slice of leather. **2**, a knife for skiving.

skiv'vy (skiv'ē) *n.* **1**, a man's undershirt. **2**, (*pl.*) a man's undershirt and briefs.

skoal (skōl) *interj.* of salutation in toasting.

skul·dug'ger·y (skul-dug'ə-rē) *n.* dishonest trickery.

skulk *v.i.* **1**, sneak away. **2**, slink. **3**, malinger.

skull (skul) *n.* the bony framework of the head. —**skull and crossbones,** a human skull above two crossed bones, used to label poisons (formerly, an emblem on pirates' flags).

skull'cap' *n.* a brimless, close-fitting cap.

skunk *n.* **1**, a small fur-bearing animal of the weasel family that ejects a fetid fluid. **2**, (*Colloq.*) a contemptible person. —*v.t.* (*Slang*) keep scoreless. —**skunk cabbage,** a foul-smelling plant.

sky (skī) *n.* the surrounding space as seen from the earth. —**sky pilot,** (*Slang*) a clergyman.

sky'cap' *n.* a porter at an airport.

sky'div'ing *n.* the sport of jumping from an airplane and performing various gymnastic maneuvers before opening the parachute. —**sky'dive',** *v.i.*

Skye terrier a small, short-legged, usually white terrier.

sky-'high' *adj. & adv.* very high.

sky'jack' (-jak") *v.t.* to hijack an airplane, esp. when in the air.

Sky'lab' *n.* an orbiting space station.

sky'lark' *n.* a lark that sings as it flies.

sky'light' *n.* a window in a ceiling.

sky'line' *n.* **1**, tall buildings seen outlined against the sky. **2**, the visible horizon.

sky'rock"et *n.* a small rocket used in fireworks. —*v.i.* achieve wealth, fame, etc., rapidly.

sky'scrap"er *n.* a tall building.

sky'ward (-wərd) *adj.* toward the sky. —*adv.* [also, **sky'wards**] at or toward the sky.

sky'writ"ing *n.* writing trailed in smoke from an airplane.

slab *n.* a flat, thick piece.

slack (slak) *adj.* **1**, loose, not taut. **2**, slow; sluggish. **3**, negligent. —*n.* **1**, a slack condition or part. **2**, a decrease in activity. **3**, (*pl.*) loose trousers. —**slack'en,** *v.t. & i.* make or become more slack. —**slack'er,** *n.* a shirker, esp. of military service.

slag *n.* **1**, the waste matter from smelting. **2**, lava. —**slag'gy,** *adj.*

slain (slān) *v.* p.p. of *slay.*

slake (slāk) *v.t.* **1**, appease, as thirst, wrath, etc. **2**, abate. **3**, treat (lime) with water.

sla'lom (slä'ləm) *n.* a skiing race.

slam *v.t. & i.* [**slammed, slam'ming**] **1**, shut or strike with violence or noise. **2**, (*Slang*) criticize adversely. —*n.* **1**, a bang. **2**, (*Slang*) criticism. **3**, in card playing, the winning of all the tricks.

slam-'bang' *adv.* (*Colloq.*) suddenly, noisily, or violently.

slan'der (slan'dər) *n.* **1**, aspersion. **2**, (*Law*) defamation by oral utterance. —*v.t.* defame. —**slan'der·ous,** *adj.*

slang *n.* **1**, language of coarse, familiar, or jocular character, regarded as below the level of written or colloquial speech. **2**, jargon; cant.

slant (slànt) *v.i. & t.* **1**, lie obliquely. **2**, have a bias; incline. —*n.* **1**, an oblique direction or position. **2**, bias. **3**, point of view.

slap *v.t.* [**slapped, slap'ping**] **1**, strike with the open hand or with something flat. **2**, strike with. **3**, rebuke. —*n.* act of slapping; a slapping blow. —**slap'dash",** *adv. & adj.* hastily and carelessly.

slap-'hap'py *adj.* (*Slang*) **1**, dazed or mentally impaired from blows on the head. **2**, silly; foolish.

slap'jack" *n.* a children's card game.

slap'stick" *n.* **1**, a device used to make a slapping sound. **2**, rough comedy. —*adj.* like or characteristic of slapstick.

slash *v.t.* **1**, hack violently. **2**, make slits

in. —*v.i.* make a wide cutting stroke. —*n.* **1,** a slashing stroke; a wound. **2,** an ornamental slit. **3,** debris of felled trees. **4,** (usu. *pl.*) a swampy tract.

slat *n.* a strip of wood, etc.; a lath.

slate (slāt) *n.* **1,** a fine-grained rock, easily split. **2,** a plate of this rock, as for writing upon. **3,** a written record. **4,** a dull bluish-gray color. **5,** a list of candidates. —*v.t.* **1,** cover with slate. **2,** destine.

slath′er (slath′ər) *v.t.* **1,** spread thickly with or on. **2,** apply liberally; lavish.

slat′tern (slat′ərn) *n.* a slovenly woman. —**slat′tern·ly,** *adj.*

slaugh′ter (slâ′tər) *n.* **1,** the killing of domestic animals for food. **2,** massacre; carnage. —*v.t.* kill; massacre. —**slaugh′ter-house″,** *n.*

Slav (släv) *n. & adj.* a member of one of the peoples dominant in eastern Europe.

slave (slāv) *n.* **1,** a person who is the property of another. **2,** an addict. **3,** a drudge. —*v.i.* drudge. —**slav′ish,** *adj.* —**slave driver,** a hard taskmaster. —**slave trade,** the buying and selling of human beings as slaves.

slave′hold″ing *n.* the ownership of slaves. —*adj.* owning slaves. —**slave′hol″der,** *n.* one who owns slaves.

slav′er (slā′vər) *n.* **1,** a trader in slaves. **2,** a ship carrying slaves.

slav′er (slā′ər) *v.i.* **1,** let saliva dribble from the mouth. **2,** show inordinate desire. —*n.* **1,** saliva. **2,** drivel.

slav′er·y (slā′və-rē) *n.* **1,** the condition of a slave; bondage. **2,** the practice of enslaving humans. **3,** drudgery.

slav′ey (slā′vē) *n.* (*Colloq.*) a maid of all work.

Slav′ic (släv′ik) *adj.* pert. to the Slavs, as Russians, Poles, etc., and their languages.

slaw (slâ) *n.* chopped cabbage served as a salad; coleslaw.

slay (slā) *v.t.* [**slew, slain, slay′ing**] **1,** kill by violence. **2,** (*Slang*) affect powerfully.

slea′zy (slē′zē; slā′-) *adj.* flimsy, unsubstantial. —**slea′zi·ness,** *n.*

sled *n.* a vehicle mounted on runners for moving on snow or ice. —**sled′ding,** *n.* (*Colloq.*) going.

sledge (slej) *n.* **1,** a large sled. **2,** a large, heavy hammer: *sledgehammer.*

sleek (slēk) *adj.* **1,** smooth and glossy. **2,** well groomed. **3,** suave. —*v.t.* preen. —**sleek′ness,** *n.*

sleep (slēp) *n.* **1,** the natural state of bodily rest, marked by suspension of consciousness. **2,** inactivity; repose. —*v.i.* [*pret. & p.p.* **slept**] **1,** get to sleep. **2,** lie in death. **3,** (with *away, off,* etc.) pass, as time, a

condition, etc. —*v.t.* furnish sleeping accommodations for. —**sleeping bag,** a lined bag in which to sleep on the ground. —**sleeping car,** a railroad car having berths, and sometimes compartments, for sleeping. —**sleeping pill,** a barbiturate. —**sleeping sickness,** a disease that causes extreme lethargy.

sleep′er *n.* **1,** one who sleeps. **2,** a railroad car with berths. **3,** a railroad tie. **4,** (*Colloq.*) an unexpected success.

sleep′less *adj.* **1,** without sleep. **2,** never resting; vigilant.

sleep′walk″ *v.i.* somnambulate.

sleep′y (-ē) *adj.* **1,** anxious to sleep; drowsy. **2,** tranquil; quiet. —**sleep′i·ness,** *n.*

sleet (slēt) *n.* partly frozen rain.

sleeve (slēv) *n.* **1,** the part of a garment that covers the arm. **2,** a tubular covering or jacket.

sleigh (slā) *n.* a horse-drawn sled.

sleight (slīt) *n.* an artful feat, esp. of conjuring: *sleight-of-hand.*

slen′der (slen′dər) *adj.* **1,** small in width or diameter. **2,** scanty. **3,** weak. —**slen′der-ness,** *n.*

slen′der·ize″ (-īz″) *v.i. & t.* (*Colloq.*) make, or become, or make to seem, more slender.

slept *v.,* p.t. & p.p. of *sleep.*

sleuth (slooth) *n.* **1,** (*Colloq.*) a detective. **2,** a bloodhound.

slew (sloo) *v.* pret. of *slay.* —*v.i.* veer; twist. —*n.* [also, **slue**] **1,** a twist. **2,** (*Colloq.*) a great number.

slice (slīs) *n.* **1,** a thin, broad piece. **2,** an act of cutting. **3,** a slicer. **4,** (*Golf*) an oblique stroke, veering to the right. —*v.t. & i.* cut into slices. —**slic′er,** *n.*

slick (slik) *adj.* **1,** sleek. **2,** ingenious; sly. —*n.* **1,** a smooth patch. **2,** a magazine printed on coated paper. —*v.t.* (often with *up*) make smooth, sleek, or elegant.

slick′er *n.* **1,** an oilskin coat. **2,** (*Colloq.*) a sly fellow; a swindler.

slide (slīd) *v.i.* [*pret. & p.p.* **slid**] **1,** slip over a smooth surface. **2,** go smoothly. **3,** deteriorate. —*v.t.* cause to glide. —*n.* **1,** an act of sliding; a place for sliding. **2,** an avalanche. **3,** a sliding part. **4,** a picture on glass, for projection on a screen. —**slide fastener,** a zipper. —**slide rule,** a device for calculating, by the relative position of two graduated rulers. —**sliding scale,** a basis for varying prices, wages, etc., according to conditions.

slight (slīt) *adj.* **1,** small. **2,** of little importance. **3,** slender; frail. —*v.t.* **1,** disdain; ignore. **2,** do negligently. —*n.* discourteous neglect.

slim *adj.* [slim′mer, -mest] **1**, slender; thin. **2**, meager. —**slim′ness**, *n.*

slime (slīm) *n.* an offensive viscous liquid. —**slim′y**, *adj.*

sling *n.* **1**, a device for hurling a missile by hand: *slingshot*. **2**, a loop for suspending a load. —*v.t.* [*pret. & p.p.* **slung**] **1**, fling. **2**, suspend, etc., by a sling.

sling′shot″ *n.* a forked stick with an elastic band for shooting small missiles.

slink *v.i.* [*pret. & p.p.* **slunk**] go in a furtive manner.

slip *v.i.* [**slipped, slip′ping**] **1**, lose hold; slide back. **2**, (often with *up*) err. **3**, slide; decline; deteriorate. **4**, move quietly. —*v.t.* **1**, put or move quietly. **2**, cast off. **3**, of animals, bring forth (young). —*n.* **1**, an act of slipping. **2**, a woman's undergarment. **3**, a pillowcase. **4**, the space between two wharves. **5**, a strip, as of paper. **6**, a slender person. —**slip cover**, a removable cloth cover for a piece of furniture. —**slip stream**, the air forced back by an aircraft propeller.

slip′knot″ *n.* **1**, a knot used to form a noose of variable size. **2**, a knot easily untied.

slip-′on″ *adj.* designed to be slipped on easily. —*n.* a slip-on garment.

slip′o′ver *n.* a sweater, etc., to be pulled over the head.

slip′page (-ij) *n.* act, result, or extent of slipping.

slip′per (-ər) *n.* a low shoe.

slip′per·y *adj.* **1**, offering little friction, as though greasy. **2**, sly; insecure. —**slip′per·i·ness**, *n.*

slip′shod′ *adj.* negligent; careless; slovenly.

slip-′up″ *n.* a careless error.

slit *v.t.* [**slit′ted** or **slit, slit′ting**] **1**, make a long narrow cut in. **2**, cut into strips. —*n.* a long, narrow, straight cut or aperture.

slith′er (slith′ər) *v.i.* slide; go unsteadily; slip. —**slith′er·y**, *adj.*

sliv′er (sliv′ər) *n.* a fragment broken off; a splinter.

slob *n.* (*Slang*) a slovenly or uncultivated person.

slob′ber (slob′ər) *v.i. & t., & n.* slaver; drool. —**slob′ber·y**, *adj.*

sloe (slō) *n.* an small, black plum. —**sloe′-eyed′**, *adj.* dark-eyed. —**sloe gin**, an alcoholic beverage flavored with sloes.

slog *v.i.* [**slogged, slog′ging**] plod.

slo′gan (slō′gən) *n.* a distinctive phrase or cry, used as a rallying cry, motto, catchphrase in advertising, etc.

sloop *n.* a one-masted sailboat.

slop *n.* **1**, a puddle. **2**, an unappetizing mess. **3**, (*pl.*) waste liquid; sewage. —*v.t. & i.* [**slopped, slop′ping**] **1**, spill, splash. **2**, (*Colloq.*) be effusive.

slope (slōp) *n.* a slanting surface; slant. —*v.i.* be slanting or oblique. —*v.t.* cause to slant.

slop′py (-ē) *adj.* **1**, untidy. **2**, splashing. —**slop′pi·ness**, *n.* —**sloppy Joe**, **1**, a dish of ground meat and a sauce, served on a bun. **2**, a baggy sweater worn by girls.

slosh *n.* **1**, slush. **2**, nonsense. —*v.t. & i.* muddle; mix; splash.

slot *n.* a long narrow aperture or recess. —**slot′ted**, *adj.* —**slot car**, a small, electric toy car raced on a special track. —**slot machine**, a device for vending, etc., activated by dropping a coin in a slot.

sloth (slôth) *n.* **1**, laziness; indolence. **2**, a small arboreal mammal of So. America. —**sloth′ful**, *adj.*

slouch (slowch) *v.i.* bend downward; droop. —*n.* **1**, a drooping posture. **2**, an inept person.

slough (slow) *n.* **1**, a mudhole; bog. **2**, condition of helplessness or degradation. **3**, (sloo) a swamp.

slough (sluf) *n.* a molted part, as the skin of a snake. —*v.t.* **1**, molt; cast off; shed. **2**, discard. Also, **sluff.**

slov′en (sluv′ən) *n.* one who is habitually untidy. —**slov′en·ly**, *adj.*

slow (slō) *adj.* **1**, taking a relatively long time. **2**, dull-witted. **3**, tardy; sluggish. **4**, slack. **5**, tedious. —*v.t. & i.* make or become slow. —*adv.* (*Colloq.*) slowly. —**slow′ness**, *n.*

slow′down″ *n.* a slowing down, esp. of the rate of production, as by workers to enforce demands upon the management.

slow-′mo′tion *adj.* denoting a technique that depicts motion at less than its actual speed.

slow′poke″ *n.* (*Slang*) one who thinks or acts slowly.

slow-′wit″ted *adj.* dull in mind.

sludge (sluj) *n.* slush; ooze.

slue (sloo) *n. & v.* slew.

sluff (sluf) *v.t. & n.* in bridge, discard a card (so as to avoid losing a trick).

slug *n.* **1**, a billet or ingot; a lead weight or bullet; a counterfeit coin; a bar of metal. **2**, a snail-like terrestrial mollusk. **3**, a heavy blow. **4**, a drink of liquor or other beverage. —*v.t.* [**slugged, slug′ging**] strike heavily. —**slug′ger**, *n.*

slug′gard (slug′ərd) *n.* one habitually lazy or slow.

slug′gish (slug′ish) *adj.* lazy; torpid.

sluice (sloos) *n.* a channel for carrying off

surplus water; the stream of water. —*v.t.* drench.

slum *n.* (often *pl.*) a squalid residential section. —*v.i.* [**slummed, slum′ming**] visit the slums, esp. as a sightseer.

slum′ber (slum′bər) *v.i. & t.,* & *n.* sleep. —**slum′ber·ous,** *adj.*

slum′lord″ *n.* the landlord of a slum.

slump *v.i.* sink heavily. —*n.* a sudden sinking or decline.

slump″fla′tion *n.* (*Colloq.*) an economic period of combined inflation and recession.

slung *v.* pret. & p.p. of *sling.*

slunk *v.* pret. & p.p. of *slink.*

slur (slêr) [**slurred, slur′ring**] *v.t.* **1,** run together (as separate words or notes). **2,** (usually *over*) treat slightingly; ignore. **3,** disparage. —*n.* **1,** a slurred utterance; (*Music*) a curved line indicating a slur. **2,** a disparaging remark. **3,** a blot or stain. —**slur′ry,** *adj.*

slurp (slêrp) *v.t. & i.* sip or eat noisily.

slush *n.* **1,** watery snow. **2,** a watery mixture of mud, etc. **3,** drivel. **4,** bribery. —*v.t.* splash; flush. —**slush fund,** a fund, usu. secret, of money used for bribery.

slut *n.* **1,** a slovenly woman. **2,** a female dog. —**slut′tish,** *adj.*

sly (slī) *adj.* [**sly′er, sly′est**] **1,** meanly artful; cunning; shrewd. **2,** stealthy; insidious. **3,** roguish. —**sly′ness,** *n.*

sly′boots″ *n.* (*Colloq.*) a sly person.

smack (smak) *v.t.* **1,** separate (the lips) with a sharp sound. **2,** slap. **3,** kiss noisily. —*v.i.* **1,** make a sharp sound; slap. **2,** (with *of*) suggest. —*n.* **1,** a smacking noise. **2,** a resounding blow. **3,** a trace; suggestion. **4,** a small fishing vessel. —*adv.* squarely and abruptly. —**smack′er,** *n.* (*Slang*) a dollar.

small (smâl) *adj.* **1,** little; of limited scope; restricted. **2,** humble. **3,** mean; petty. —*n.* a thin or narrow part. —**small arms,** hand guns. —**small fry,** youngsters. —**small hours,** late hours. —**small potatoes,** (*Colloq.*) of little consequence. —**small talk,** chatter.

small-′mind″ed *adj.* narrow in outlook, sympathy, etc.

small′pox″ *n.* an acute contagious disease often leaving pockmarks on its survivors.

small-′time″ *adj.* (*Slang*) of minor importance.

smart (smärt) *v.i.* **1,** sting. **2,** feel physical or mental distress. —*v.t.* cause to smart. —*n.* **1,** a sting. **2,** mental distress. —*adj.* **1,** keen; acute; severe. **2,** brisk. **3,** clever; shrewd. **4,** vivacious; witty. **5,** fashionably groomed. —**smart′en,** *v.t.* make neat, spruce, etc. —**smart′ness,** *n.* —**smart**

a′leck (a′lək) a cocky person. —**smart bomb,** a bomb with its own internal guidance system. —**smart money,** (*Colloq.*) money bet or invested by one supposed to have superior judgment. —**smart set,** (*Colloq.*) those who are up-to-date, esp. in clothing styles, etc.; fashionable society.

smash *v.t.* **1,** break to pieces. **2,** defeat utterly. **3,** strike against something. —*v.i.* **1,** break to pieces; be ruined, bankrupt, etc. **2,** dash against something. —*n.* **1,** a violent blow. **2,** destruction. **3,** a sweet drink. —**smash-′up″,** *n.* a collision.

smat′ter·ing (smat′ər-ing) *n.* a slight or superficial knowledge or assortment.

smear (smir) *v.t.* **1,** overspread with grease, dirt, paint, etc.; daub. **2,** soil; sully. —*n.* a smudge.

smear′case″ *n.* cottage cheese.

smell (smel) *v.t.* **1,** perceive through the nose. **2,** inhale the odor of. **3,** detect or discover as though by smell. —*v.i.* inhale or give out an odor, esp. an offensive odor. —*n.* **1,** the sense of smell. **2,** odor; scent; aroma. **3,** the act of smelling. **4,** a trace. —**smell′y,** *adj.* having a strong or offensive odor. —**smelling salts,** a pungent restorative.

smelt *v.t.* melt (ore). —*n.* a small food fish.

smelt′er (smel′tər) *n.* a place where ore is melted, to yield metal.

smid′gen (smid′jən) *n.* a very small amount.

smi′lax (smī′laks) *n.* any of various woody vines.

smile (smīl) *n.* **1,** a widening of the mouth, with parted lips, indicating pleasure, amusement, or favor. **2,** a favoring aspect. —*v.i. & t.* **1,** assume, or express by, a smile. **2,** favor.

smirch (smêrch) *v.t.* soil; discolor; sully. —*n.* a stain; smear.

smirk (smêrk) *n.* an affected or knowing smile. —*v.i.* so smile.

smite (smīt) *v.t.* [**smote** (smōt), **smit′ten** (smit′ən)] **1,** strike with a hard blow; afflict. **2,** affect; captivate.

smith *n.* a worker in metal; a blacksmith. —**smith′y,** *n.* his workshop.

smith′er·eens″ (smith′ə-rēnz″) *n.pl.* (*Colloq.*) fragments.

smith′son·ite″ (smith′sən-īt″) *n.* zinc carbonate, an ore of zinc.

smock (smok) *n.* a thin, loose outer robe. —*v.t.* apply smocking to.

smock′ing (-ing) *n.* embroidery stitches that gather material into folds.

smog *n.* (*Colloq.*) smoke and fog.

smoke (smōk) *n.* **1,** the visible vapor given

off by a burning substance. **2,** something unsubstantial. **3,** a cigar or cigarette. —*v.i.* **1,** emit smoke. **2,** draw and emit the fumes of burning tobacco. —*v.t.* **1,** puff the smoke of (tobacco, opium, etc.). **2,** treat with smoke. **3,** (with *out*) drive into view. —**smokeless powder,** white gunpowder, which burns with little smoke. —**smoke screen,** an obscuring cloud of, or as of, smoke. —**smoking jacket,** a jacket worn for indoor lounging.

smoke′house″ *n.* a shed for smoking meat.

smok′er *n.* **1,** one who smokes. **2,** a car in which smoking is permitted. **3,** a social meeting for men.

smoke′stack″ *n.* an upright pipe carrying off smoke.

smok′y (smō′kė) *adj.* **1,** smoking; visibly vaporous. **2,** dark; cloudy; grayish-blue. —**smok′i·ness,** *n.*

smol′der (smōl′dər) *v.i.* **1,** burn and smoke without flame. **2,** exist in a suppressed state.

smooch *v.i.* (*Slang*) make love; pet.

smooth (smooth) *adj.* **1,** having an even surface; not obstructed. **2,** without sudden jolts or breaks; uniform. **3,** not lumpy. **4,** bland. **5,** harmonious. **6,** tranquil. **7,** mild. **8,** flowing, as speech. —*v.t.* **1,** make smoother. **2,** calm; allay; mollify; palliate. —**smooth′ness,** *n.*

smor′gas·bord″ (smôr′gəs-bôrd″) *n.* Swedish hors d'oeuvres.

smote (smōt) *v.* p.t. of *smite*.

smoth′er (smuth′ər) *v.t.* **1,** suffocate; cover so as to deprive of air. **2,** stifle; repress or suppress. —*v.i.* be smothered. —**smoth′er·y,** *adj.*

smoul′der (smōl′dər) *v.i.* smolder.

smudge (smuj) *n.* **1,** a dirty mark; a blot or smear. **2,** a smoky fire. —*v.t. & i.* stain; blacken. —**smudg′y,** *adj.*

smug *adj.* [**smug′ger, -gest**] self-satisfied. —**smug′ness,** *n.*

smug′gle (smug′əl) *v.t. & i.* transport (goods) secretly, esp. to avoid payment of duties. —**smug′gler,** *n.*

smut *n.* **1,** sooty matter. **2,** obscenity. —**smut′ty,** *adj.*

smutch (smuch) *v. & n.* smudge.

snack (snak) *n.* a small portion, esp. of food.

sna″fu′ (sna″foo′) *adj.* (*Slang*) in disorder (Situation Normal—All Fouled Up).

snag *n.* an obstruction; an obstacle. —*v.t.* [**snagged, snag′ging**] **1,** impede; entangle. **2,** trap, as with a snag. —**snag-′toothed″, snag′gle-toothed″,** *adj.* with teeth projecting awry.

snail (snāl) *n.* **1,** a mollusk with a spiral shell. **2,** a slow mover.

snail′paced″ *adj.* sluggish.

snake (snāk) *n.* **1,** any of an order of reptiles with elongated, tubular, limbless bodies: serpent. **2,** a treacherous person. —*v.t.* drag by jerks; haul at the end of a chain or rope.

snak′y *adj.* **1,** pert. to snakes. **2,** flexible; sinuous. **3,** treacherous.

snap *v.i.* [**snapped, snap′ping**] **1,** make a sudden sharp sound; click. **2,** break suddenly. **3,** move suddenly. **4,** (with *at*) bite suddenly. **5,** speak sharply. —*v.t.* **1,** make a clicking sound. **2,** break. **3,** retort. **4,** (with *up*) grab. **5,** take an instantaneous photograph of. —*n.* **1,** a sharp sound; a click. **2,** a quick motion. **3,** something that snaps. **4,** a thin, brittle cake. **5,** briskness; vigor. **6,** a brief spell. **7,** (*Slang*) an easy task. —*adj.* **1,** offhand. **2,** easy. **3,** operated by a device that snaps.

snap′drag″on (snap′drag″ən) *n.* a flowering plant.

snap′per (-ər) *n.* **1,** a large marine fish. **2,** a snapping turtle.

snap′pish (-ish) *adj.* apt to bite or snap. —**snap′pish·ness,** *n.*

snap′py (-ė) *adj.* **1,** snapping; crackling. **2,** brisk; cold and stimulating, as weather. **3,** (*Colloq.*) smart, as dress; lively and clever, as repartee; quick. **4,** snappish. —**snap′pi·ness,** *n.*

snap′shot″ *n.* a photograph.

snare (snâr) *n.* **1,** a trap. **2,** a cord, as one stretched across a head of a drum (*snare drum*). —*v.t.* catch, entangle.

snarl (snärl) *v.t. & i.* **1,** utter an angry cry, as a dog; speak angrily. **2,** entangle; become entangled. —*n.* **1,** act of snarling; a surly tone. **2,** a tangled mass.

snatch (snach) *v.t.* seize abruptly or violently. —*v.i.* grab hastily. —*n.* **1,** the act of snatching; (*Slang*) a kidnaping. **2,** a fragment or bit.

sneak (snēk) *v.i.* go or act in a stealthy, furtive manner; slink; skulk. —*v.t.* **1,** do furtively. **2,** (*Colloq.*) steal. —*n.* **1,** one who sneaks. **2,** (*pl.*) (*Slang*) [also, **sneak′ers**] soft-soled low shoes. —**sneak′y,** *adj.* —**sneak thief,** a thief who does not break his way in.

sneer (snir) *v.i.* express scorn, as by a grimace. —*v.t.* utter with a sneer. —*n.* a contemptuous expression or utterance.

sneeze (snēz) *n.* a sudden, involuntary, spasmodic expulsion of air through the nose and mouth. —*v.i.* make a sneeze. —**sneeze at,** (*Colloq.*) treat with scorn.

snick′er (snik′ər) *v.i. & t.* laugh in a suppressed manner. —*n.* giggle.

snick′er·snee″ *n.* (usu. *jocular*) a cutting weapon.

snide (snīd) *adj.* mean; invidious.

sniff (snif) *v.i.* & *t.* **1,** draw in air audibly. **2,** (with *at*) show scorn or disdain (of). —*n.* a sniffling. —**snif'fy,** *adj.*

snif'fle (-əl) *v.i.* sniff repeatedly.

snif'ter (snif'tər) *n.* **1,** a pear-shaped brandy glass. **2,** (*Slang*) a small drink.

snip *v.t.* & *i.* cut off with one light stroke. —*n.* **1,** the act or result of snipping. **2,** (*Colloq.*) an insignificant person. **3,** (*pl.*) shears.

snipe (snīp) *n.* a long-billed wading bird. —*v.i.* **1,** hunt snipe. **2,** shoot, esp. from a concealed position. —**snip'er,** *n.* a sharpshooter.

snip'pet (snip'ət) *n.* **1,** a small piece snipped off. **2,** (*Colloq.*) a small or insignificant person.

snip'py (-ē) *adj.* snappish; curt. —**snip'-pi-ness,** *n.*

snitch (snich) (*Slang*) *v.t.* steal. —*v.i.* turn informer.

sniv'el (sniv'əl) *v.i.* **1,** weep and sniffle. **2,** pretend contrition; whine.

snob *n.* one who unduly esteems social position. —**snob'bish,** *adj.* —**snob'bish-ness, snob'ber-y,** *n.*

snood *n.* a band or fillet to confine the hair.

snook'er (snûk'ər) *n.* a form of pocket billiards.

snoop (*Colloq.*) *v.i.* prowl and spy. —*n.* one who snoops. —**snoop'y,** *adj.*

snoot *n.* (*Colloq.*) the nose or face. —**snoot'y,** *adj.* (*Slang*) snobbish. —**snoot'i-ness,** *n.*

snooze (snooz) *n.* & *v.i.* (*Colloq.*) sleep; doze; nap.

snore (snôr) *v.i.* breathe with a hoarse noise during sleep. —*n.* a snoring sound.

snor'kel (snôr'kəl) *n.* a device to supply air to the engine of a submarine or to an underwater swimmer.

snort (snôrt) *v.i.* **1,** force air audibly through the nose. **2,** scoff. —*n.* a snorting sound or act. —*v.t.* (*Slang*) inhale cocaine.

snot *n.* (*Vulgar*) mucus from the nose.

snot'ty *adj.* (*Colloq.*) snobbish; impudent. —**snot'ti-ness,** *n.*

snout (snowt) *n.* the forepart of an animal's head, esp. the nose.

snow (snō) *n.* **1,** water vapor frozen into crystals, falling to earth in flakes; a fall of snow; fallen snow. **2,** something very white. **3,** (*Slang*) cocaine or heroin. —*v.i.* & *t.* send down or fall as snow. —*v.t.* (*Slang*) flatter. —**snow job,** (*Slang*) flattery to attain a desired favor. —**snow under,** bury.

snow'ball" *n.* snow, pressed into a ball. —*v.i.* (*Colloq.*) increase rapidly.

snow'bank" *n.* a heap of snow.

snow'belt" *n.* a region of unusually heavy snowfall.

snow'bird" *n.* (*Slang*) a drug addict.

snow-'blind" *adj.* having the eyesight impaired by the glare of snow.

snow'bound" *adj.* confined by impassable snow.

snow'clad" *adj.* topped with snow, as a mountain.

snow'drift" *n.* drifted snow.

snow'drop" *n.* a white flower blooming in the spring.

snow'fall" *n.* a fall of snow.

snow'flake" *n.* **1,** a snow crystal. **2,** a bulbous plant with white flowers.

snow'man" *n.* **1,** a crude statue of a human figure, made of snow. **2,** a humanoid beast, by some supposed to exist in Tibet, also called *abominable snowman* or *yeti* (yet'ē).

snow'mo-bile" *n.* a small motor vehicle on skis, driven by a belt, for traveling on snow.

snow'plow" *n.* a blade for pushing aside snow.

snow'shoe" *n.* a network in a frame, worn for walking on snow.

snow'storm" *n.* a heavy snowfall; blizzard.

snow'y *adj.* **1,** pert. to snow. **2,** clear white; spotless; immaculate. —**snow'i-ness,** *n.*

snub *v.t.* [**snubbed, snub'bing**] **1,** check or stop suddenly. **2,** slight; ignore. —*adj.* (of the nose) turned up at the tip. —**snub'by,** *adj.*

snuff (snuf) *v.t.* & *i.* sniff. —*v.t.* extinguish, as a candle. —*n.* **1,** sniff. **2,** powdered tobacco.

snuff'box" *n.* a pocket container for snuff.

snuf'fle (snuf'əl) *v.i.* & *t.,* & *n.* sniff or sniffle.

snug *adj.* [**snug'ger, -gest**] **1,** comfortable; cozy. **2,** fitting closely. **3,** compact; neat. —**snug'ness,** *n.*

snug'gle (snug'əl) *v.i.* & *t.* cuddle; nestle.

so (sō) *adv.* **1,** in the degree, amount, manner, etc., expressed or implied. **2,** very; extremely. **3,** such being the case. **4,** consequently. —*interj.* expressing mild surprise.

soak (sōk) *v.i.* be permeated by a liquid; become thoroughly wet; permeate. —*v.t.* **1,** drench; saturate. **2,** absorb. **3,** (*Slang*) charge exorbitantly. —*n.* (*Slang*) an immoderate drinker.

so-'and-so" *pron.* **1,** someone whose name is now known or specified. **2,** (*Slang*) a contemptible person.

soap (sōp) *n.* **1,** a substance used for cleansing. **2,** (*Slang*) flattery: *soft soap.* **3,** (*Slang*) money used for building. —*v.t.* cover or treat with soap. —**no soap,** (*Slang*) definitely not. —**soap opera,** a sentimental radio or television drama.

soap′box″ *n.* the podium of an unauthorized orator.

soap′er (-ər) *n.* (*Slang*) soap opera.

soap′stone″ *n.* a soft stone, a variety of talc.

soap′suds″ *n.* suds.

soap′y (-ė) *adj.* **1,** containing soap. **2,** flattering. —**soap′i·ness,** *n.*

soar (sôr) *v.i.* **1,** fly upward; glide in air. **2,** rise higher, or to great height.

sob *v.i.* & *t.* [**sobbed, sob′bing**] weep convulsively. —*n.* a convulsive catching of the breath in weeping. —**sob sister,** (*Slang*) a writer of sentimental human-interest stories. —**sob story,** a story told to arouse pity or generosity.

so′ber (-bər) *adj.* **1,** not intoxicated. **2,** sedate; serious; solemn. **3,** subdued, as in color. —*v.t.* & *i.* make or become sober. —**so′ber·ly,** *adv.* seriously. —**so′ber·ness,** *n.*

so·bri′e·ty (sō-brī′ə-tė) *n.* soberness, not drunkenness.

so′bri·quet″ (sō′bri-kā″) *n.* a nickname. Also, **sou′bri·quet.**

so-″called″ *adj.* thus (perhaps unjustifiably) designated.

soc′cer (sok′ər) *n.* a form of football.

so′cia·ble (sō′shə-bəl) *adj.* gregarious; friendly; amiable. —*n.* a social gathering. —**so″cia·bil′i·ty,** *n.*

so′cial (sō′shəl) *adj.* **1,** pert. to communal activities; gregarious; friendly. **2,** pert. to or tending to advance human society. **3,** fashionable. **4,** of disease, venereal. —*n.* a social gathering. —**social climber,** one who seeks social advancement. —**Social Register,** (*T.N.*) a book listing members of fashionable society. —**social security,** a general insurance and old-age-pension plan. —**social science,** a science dealing with society and its institutions. —**social work,** a profession dealing with the problems of the underprivileged persons of society.

so′cial·ism (-iz-əm) *n.* ownership of exploitable capital and means of production by the government, not by individuals or by private enterprise. —**so′cial·ist,** *n.* —**so″cial·ist′ic** (-is′tik) *adj.*

so′cial·ite″ (sō′shə-līt″) *n.* a member of fashionable society.

so″ci·al′i·ty (sō″shė-al′ə-tė) *n.* the state, tendency, or practice of being social.

so′cial·ize″ (-īz″) *v.t.* make social or socialistic. —**socialized medicine,** medical

care provided by the state. —**so″cial·i·za′-tion,** *n.*

so·ci′e·ty (sō-sī′ə-tė) *n.* **1,** human beings collectively. **2,** the fashionable world. **3,** a community. **4,** an association. **5,** companionship. —**so·ci′e·tal,** *adj.*

so·ci·o- (sō-shė-ō) *pref.* society; social; sociological.

so″ci·ol′o·gy (sō″shė-ol′ə-jė) *n.* the science of human society. —**so″ci·o·log′i·cal** (-ə-loj′i-kəl) *adj.* —**so″ci·ol′o·gist,** *n.*

so″ci·o·path′ic (-path′ik) *adj.* antisocial.

sock (sok) *n.* **1,** a short stocking. **2,** (*Slang*) a hard blow. —*v.t.* (*Slang*) hit hard. —**socked in,** (*Slang*) closed because of bad weather.

sock″dol′a·ger (sok″dol′ə-jər) *n.* (*Slang*) something that brings decisive defeat.

sock′et (sok′it) *n.* a hollow into which something is fitted.

sock′eye″ *n.* a species of red salmon.

sod *n.* **1,** the upper layer of grassy land. **2,** a piece of turf. —*v.t.* cover with sods.

so′da (sō′də) *n.* **1,** sodium or one of its oxides. **2,** water charged with carbon dioxide; any drink prepared with it: *soda water.* —**soda fountain,** a counter at which ice cream and drinks are served. —**soda jerk,** (*Slang*) a clerk at a soda fountain. —**soda pop,** a carbonated soft drink.

so·dal′i·ty (sō-dal′ə-tė) *n.* an association.

sod′den (sod′ən) *adj.* soaked; bloated.

so′di·um (sō′dė-əm) *n.* a metallic chemical element, no. 11, symbol Na. —**sodium chloride,** salt. —**sodium silicate,** waterglass.

sod′om·y (sod′əm-ė) *n.* unnatural sexual intercourse.

so′fa (sō′fə) *n.* a long, upholstered seat with a back and arms.

so′far″ *n.* a system for locating very distant underwater objects.

soft (sâft) *adj.* **1,** yielding readily to pressure; not hard or stiff. **2,** agreeable to the touch; mild, bland, delicate, melodious, etc. **3,** kind, lenient, etc. **4,** not robust. **5,** easy. **6,** (of water) relatively free of mineral salts. **7,** not sharp, as outlines. —*adv.* in a soft manner. —*interj.* (*Archaic*) be quiet! not so fast! —**soft′ness,** *n.* —**soft coal,** bituminous coal. —**soft drink,** a sweet beverage containing no alcohol. —**soft soap,** (*Colloq.*) flattery.

soft′ball″ *n.* baseball played with a larger, softer ball; the ball used.

soft-′bound″ *adj.* paperback.

soft-′core″ *adj.* less explicit than hardcore.

sof′ten (sâf′ən) *v.t.* & *i.* make or become softer. —**sof′ten·er,** *n.*

soft′heart″ed *adj.* very sympathetic.

soft-'ped"al *v.t.* suppress.

soft-'shoe" *adj.* of a type of exhibition dancing without metal taps on the shoes.

soft-'spo"ken *adj.* beguiling; persuasive.

soft'ware" *n.* written or printed information or data for use with computers.

soft'y (sâf'tè) *n.* (*Colloq.*) **1,** a weak-willed or softhearted person. **2,** a person of scant endurance.

sog'gy (sog'é) *adj.* sodden. —**sog'gi·ness,** *n.*

soi·gné' (swä-nyä') *adj.* well-groomed; neat in personal appearance.

soil *n.* **1,** the portion of the earth's surface in which plants grow. **2,** land. **3,** filth. —*v.t.* stain; defile; make dirty or foul. —*v.i.* become soiled.

soi·rée' (swä-rā') *n.* a social gathering in the evening.

so'journ (sō'jērn) *v.i.* dwell temporarily. —*n.* a temporary stay.

sol *n.* (sōl) **1,** (*Music*) the fifth tone of the diatonic scale. **2,** the monetary unit of Peru. **3,** (sol) (*cap.*) the sun.

sol'ace (sol'is) *n.* comfort in sorrow. —*v.t.* comfort.

so'lar (sō'lər) *adj.* pert. to the sun. —**solar energy,** the energy which can be produced from the sun's rays or the effects of the sun's rays or gravity. —**solar plex'us** (plek'səs) the system of nerves behind the stomach. —**solar sail,** a flat sail attached to a spacecraft to receive propulsive force from the sun's radiation. —**solar system,** a sun and the planets revolving around it. —**solar wind,** charged particles emitted from the sun's surface.

so·lar'i·um (sō-lâr'é-əm) *n.* [*pl.* **-a** (-ə)] a glass-enclosed room; sunroom.

sold (sōld) *v.* pret. & p.p. of *sell.*

sol'der (sod'ər) *n.* a fusible metal. —*v.t.* join with solder. —**soldering iron,** a tool for melting solder.

sol'dier (sōl'jər) *n.* a man engaged in military service; one of an army. —*v.i.* **1,** serve as a soldier. **2,** (*Colloq.*) malinger. —**sol'dier·ly,** *adj.* —**sol'dier·y,** *n.* soldiers collectively. —**soldier of fortune,** a mercenary or adventurer.

sole (sōl) *n.* **1,** the under surface of the foot, or of a shoe. **2,** any of several flatfishes. —*adj.* unique; only; alone.

sol'e·cism (sol'ə-siz-əm) *n.* a formal error, as in grammar.

sol'emn (sol'əm) *adj.* **1,** sober in manner or aspect. **2,** gravely impressive. —**so·lem'ni·fy,** *v.t.* —**so·lem'ni·ty** (sə-lem'nə-tè) *n.*

sol'em·nize" (-nīz") *v.t.* **1,** perform (a ceremony); celebrate with ceremonies. **2,**

render solemn. —**sol"em·ni·za'tion,** *n.*

so'le·noid" (sol'ə-noid") *n.* a tubular wire coil for producing a magnetic field.

so·lic'it (sə-lis'it) *v.t.* **1,** seek to obtain; request. **2,** address entreaties to; petition. —*v.i.* seek to obtain something. —**so·lic'i·ta'tion,** *n.*

so·lic'i·tor (sə-lis'ə-tər) *n.* **1,** one who solicits. **2,** (*Brit.*) a lawyer who prepares cases for barristers. —**solicitor general, 1,** a high officer of the U.S. Dept. of Justice, ranking next below the Attorney General. **2,** the chief law officer in some U.S. states.

so·lic'i·tous (sə-lis'ə-təs) *adj.* anxious.

so·lic'i·tude" (sə-lis'ə-tood") *n.* anxiety or concern for the welfare of others.

sol'id *adj.* **1,** existing in three-dimensional space. **2,** compact; undivided; dense. **3,** firm; hard; strong. **4,** united; unanimous. **5,** reliable; financially sound. —*n.* **1,** a three-dimensional body. **2,** a solid substance. —**so·lid'i·ty,** *n.* —**solid-state,** *adj.* using only semiconductors, such as transistors and diodes.

sol"i·dar'i·ty (sol"i-dar'ə-tè) *n.* union; community of interests.

so·lid'i·fy" (sə-lid'ə-fī") *v.t. & i.* make or become solid. —**so·lid"i·fi·ca'tion,** *n.*

sol'i·dus (sol'ə-dəs) *n.* **1,** a gold coin of ancient Rome. **2,** the slant line (/).

so·lil'o·quy (sə-lil'ə-kwè) *n.* the act of talking to oneself. —**so·lil'o·quize"** (-kwīz") *v.i. & t.*

sol'ip·sism" (sol'ip-siz"əm) *n.* the doctrine that since all knowledge is subjective, the self is the only entity directly known.

sol'i·taire" (sol'ə-tār') *n.* **1,** a puzzle or game played by one person alone. **2,** a precious stone, esp. a diamond, set alone.

sol'i·tar"y (sol'ə-ter'è) *adj.* **1,** alone. **2,** single; sole. **3,** characterized by solitude; not social.

sol'i·tude" (sol'ə-tood") *n.* the state of being alone or remote.

so'lo (sō'lō) *n.* [*pl.* **-los**] **1,** a performance by one person alone. **2,** a composition performed by one performer. —*adj.* alone; performed alone. —**so'lo·ist,** *n.*

sol'o·mon (sol'ə-mən) *n.* a wise man.

so'lon (sō'lon) *n.* a lawmaker.

so long (*Colloq.*) goodbye.

sol'stice (sol'stis) *n.* either of the two times when the sun is at its greatest distance from the celestial equator, about June 21 and Dec. 21.

sol'u·ble (sol'yə-bəl) *adj.* **1,** capable of being dissolved. **2,** capable of being solved. —**sol"u·bil'i·ty,** *n.*

sol'ute (sol'oot) *n.* a dissolved substance. —*adj.* dissolved.

so·lu'tion (sə-loo'shən) *n.* **1,** an explanation or answer. **2,** a fluid containing something dissolved.

solve (solv) *v.t.* find the answer to (a problem, puzzle, etc.); clear up.

sol'ven·cy (sol'vən-sē) *n.* ability to pay all just debts.

sol'vent (sol'vənt) *adj.* **1,** able to pay all just debts. **2,** having the power of dissolving. —*n.* a fluid that dissolves a specified substance.

so'ma (sō'mə) *n.* [*pl.* **-ma·ta** (-mə-tə)] the whole body of an organism, excluding its germ cells. —**so·mat'ic** (-mat'ik) *adj.*

som'ber (som'bər) *adj.* **1,** dark in color; dull. **2,** gloomy; dismal. Also, **som'bre.** —**som'ber·ness,** *n.*

som·bre'ro (som-brâr'ō) *n.* [*pl.* **-ros**] a broad-brimmed Mexican hat.

some (sum) *adj.* **1,** of an unspecified but considerable number or quantity. **2,** certain (one or ones) not specified. **3,** (*Slang*) considerable; notable. —*pron.* an unspecified number or portion. —*adv.* (*Slang*) somewhat or considerably.

-some (səm) *suf.* **1,** showing a tendency (to), as *meddlesome.* **2,** a group, as *threesome.*

some'bod"y *pron.* a person unspecified. —*n.* a person of consequence.

some'day" *adv.* on some indefinite day.

some'how" *adv.* in an unspecified way.

some'one" *pron.* somebody.

some'place" *adv. & n.* somewhere.

som'er·sault" (sum'ər-sâlt") *n.* an acrobatic turning over of the body.

some'thing" *n.* an unspecified thing.

some'time" *adv.* at some indefinite time. —*adj.* **1,** former. **2,** occasional.

some'times" *adv.* occasionally.

some'way" *adv.* in some way or manner not specified or known. Also, **some'ways".**

some'what" *adv.* to some extent. —*n.* some part.

some'where" *adv.* in, at, or to some unspecified place. —*n.* an unspecified place.

som·nam'bu·lism" (som-nam'byə-liz"əm) *n.* sleepwalking. —**som·nam'bu·late"** (-lāt") *v.i. & t.* walk, etc., in one's sleep. —**som·nam'bu·list,** *n.*

som'no·lent (som'nə-lənt) *adj.* **1,** sleepy. **2,** causing sleep. —**som'no·lence,** *n.*

son (sun) *n.* **1,** a male in relation to his parents. **2,** (*cap.*) Jesus Christ.

so'nar (sō'när) *n.* a device to time the echo of sound waves in water, used in detecting submarines or obstructions and measuring depths.

so·na'ta (sə-nä'tə) *n.* a musical composition in contrasted movements. —**so"na·ti'na** (sä"nə-tē'nə) *n.* a simplified sonata.

song (sâng) *n.* **1,** a short poem set to music. **2,** poetry. **3,** the act or sound of singing. —**song'ster,** *n.* singer. —**song'-stress,** *n.fem.*

song'bird" *n.* a bird or woman that sings.

song'fest" *n.* a gathering for communal singing.

song'ster (-stər) *n.* a singer, poet, or songbird. —**song'stress,** *n. fem.*

son'ic (son'ik) *adj.* **1,** of or pert. to sound. **2,** of the speed of sound. —**sonic boom,** a sound like the blast of an explosion produced by a shock wave when it reaches the ground.

son-'in-law" *n.* [*pl.* **sons-'-**] the husband of one's daughter.

son'net (son'it) *n.* a fourteen-line poem. —**son"ne·teer',** *n.*

son'ny (sun'ē) *n.* a term of address to a boy.

so·no'rous (sə-nôr'əs) *adj.* richly resonant in sound; deep; full. —**so·nor'i·ty** (sə-nôr'-ə-tē) *n.*

soon *adv.* **1,** in a short time; before long. **2,** promptly; quickly.

soot (sût) *n.* a black substance, chiefly carbon, produced by faulty combustion. —**soot'y,** *adj.*

sooth *n.* (*Archaic*) truth. —**sooth'say"er,** *n.* a fortune-teller.

soothe (sooth) *v.t.* **1,** calm; mollify. **2,** allay (pain, etc.).

sop *n.* **1,** something dipped in a liquid, as bread. **2,** something that pacifies; a bribe. —*v.t. & i.* [**sopped, sop'ping**] **1,** dip; soak. **2,** (with *up*) absorb. —**sop'ping,** *adj.* drenched.

soph'ism (sof'iz-əm) *n.* an adroit but fallacious argument. —**soph'ist,** *n.* —**so·phis'tic** (sə-fis'tik) *adj.* —**so·phis'ti·cal·ly,** *adv.*

so·phis'ti·cate" (sə-fis'ti-kāt") *v.t.* make less natural, more worldly. —*n.* a sophisticated person. —**so·phis"ti·ca'tion,** *n.*

so·phis'ti·cat"ed *adj.* **1,** experienced and worldly-wise; artificial. **2,** complex; advanced.

soph'ist·ry *n.* use of sophisms.

soph'o·more" (sof'ə-môr") *n.* a second-year student. —**soph"o·mor'ic,** *adj.* immature; superficial.

so'por (sō'pər) *n.* an unnaturally deep sleep; lethargy; stupor.

so"po·rif'ic (sop"ə-rif'ik) *adj.* **1,** causing sleep. **2,** sleepy. —*n.* something that causes sleep.

sop'py (-ē) *adj.* **1,** soaked. **2,** rainy. **3,** (*Slang*) mawkish. —**sop'pi·ness,** *n.*

---

so·pran′o (sə-prän′ō) n. [pl. -os] the highest singing voice in women; the singer; the voice part.

sor′cer·y (sôr′sə-rē) n. witchcraft; magic. —**sor′cer·er,** n. —**sor′cer·ess,** n.fem.

sor′did (sôr′did) adj. 1, mercenary. 2, ignoble; base. 3, squalid. —**sor′did·ness,** n.

sore (sôr) adj. 1, sensitive; painful. 2, suffering pain. 3, (Colloq.) offended; angry. —n. an inflamed or infected spot. —**sore′head″,** n. (Slang) a disgruntled person. —**sore′ness,** n.

sor′ghum (sôr′gəm) n. a cereal grass; a syrup made from it.

so·ror′i·ty (sə-rôr′ə-tē) n. a women's society, esp. in college.

sor′rel (sor′əl) n. 1, any of various plants. 2, a light reddish-brown color; a horse of this color.

sor′row (sor′ō) n. 1, distress of mind; sadness; grief. 2, a cause of grief. —v.i. grieve. —**sor′row·ful,** adj.

sor′ry (sor′ē) adj. 1, feeling sorrow, regret, or pity. 2, deplorable. 3, worthless; mean; poor.

sort (sôrt) n. 1, a class, kind, variety, species, etc. 2, manner; character. 3, way; fashion. —v.t. 1, classify. 2, separate from others that differ.

sor′tie (sôr′tē) n. 1, a sally of troops. 2, a combat mission of aircraft.

S O S (es′ō″es′) a call for help.

so-′so″ adj. & adv. fair; mediocre; indifferently.

sot n. a habitual drunkard. —**sot′tish,** adj.

sot′to vo′ce (sot′tō-vō′che) (Ital.) under the breath; softly.

sou (soo) n. a Fr. coin of low value.

sou·brette′ (soo-bret′) n. an actress who plays a pert young woman.

souf·flé′ (soo-flā′) n. a fluffy baked dish.

sought (sât) v. pret. & p.p. of seek.

soul (sōl) n. 1, the spiritual part of man. 2, emotional feeling. 3, nobility; courage. 4, the essential part of anything; a leader. 5, the personification of a quality. 6, a human being. 7, (Slang) a unique quality attributed to U.S. Blacks, resulting from a combination of racial pride, tradition, and social customs. —adj. (Slang) pert. to the usages, customs, and traditions of U.S. Blacks: applied to food, music, etc. —**soul′ful,** adj. expressing deep feeling. —**soul brother** or **sister,** (Slang) a Black; occasionally applied to a person who is not a Black who is known to be sympathetic to the Black cause.

sound (sownd) n. 1, the sensation produced in the organs of hearing by certain vibrations in the air. 2, these vibrations; any auditory effect. 3, the general effect or tone. 4, a narrow passage of water; an inlet. —v.i. 1, make a sound. 2, make a particular sound or impression. 3, measure depth at sea. 4, seek information. —v.t. 1, cause to make a sound. 2, utter. 3, measure the depth of water. 4, investigate. —adj. 1, in good condition; healthy. 2, reliable; substantial. 3, honorable. —**sound′ness,** n. —**sounding board, 1,** a thin plate of wood adding resonance. 2, a sound-reflecting canopy, as over a pulpit. 3, an agency, device, etc., that serves to spread information, etc. —**sound off, 1,** call out one's name. 2, (Slang) utter complaint, reproof, etc. —**sound track,** that part of a movie film carrying the sound record.

sound′ly (-lē) adv. 1, in a sound state or manner. 2, completely; thoroughly.

sound′proof″ adj. insulating against or resisting the passage of sound.

soup (soop) n. 1, a cooked liquid food. 2, (Slang) any potent liquid, as nitroglycerin. —**soup up** (Slang) make more powerful; speed up (an automobile engine).

soup′y (soo′pē) adj. like soup; (of fog) thick. —**soup′i·ness,** n.

sour (sowr) adj. 1, having an acid or tart taste. 2, fermented. 3, unpleasant. 4, morose in disposition. 5, excessively acid, as soil. —v.t. & i. make or become sour; spoil. —**sour′ness,** n. —**sour grapes,** a pretense of not wanting something unobtainable.

source (sôrs) n. a place from which something comes; origin.

sour′dough″ n. 1, fermented dough, used in breadmaking. 2, a seasoned prospector.

sour′puss″ (sowr′pus″) n. (Slang) a person with a peevish disposition.

sou′sa·phone″ (soo′sə-fōn″) n. a form of tuba.

souse (sows) v.t. & i. 1, drench; soak. 2, pickle. 3, (Slang) intoxicate. —n. (Slang) a drunkard; a drinking spree.

south (sowth) n. 1, the point of the compass opposite north. 2, (often cap.) [also, **south′land″**] a region in this direction, esp. the former Confederate States. —adj. & adv. toward, in, or from the south.

south″east′ n., adj., & adv. midway between south and east. —**south″east′er·ly,** adj. & adv. —**south″east′ern,** adj.

south″east′er n. a wind or storm from the southeast.

south′er·ly (suth′ər-lē) adj. & adv. toward or from the south.

south′ern (suth′ərn) adj. in or pert. to the south. —**south′ern·er,** n. —**southern lights,** aurora australis.

south'paw" n. & adj. (Slang) a left-handed person.

south"west' n., adj., & adv. midway between south and west. **—south"west'er·ly,** adj. **—south"west'ern,** adj.

south"west'er n. **1,** a storm from the southwest. **2,** a waterproof hat.

sou"ve·nir' (soo"və-nir') n. **1,** a memento or keepsake. **2,** a memory.

sov'er·eign (sov'rin) n. **1,** one having supreme power; a monarch. **2,** a Brit. gold coin worth one pound. **—adj. 1,** having supreme power. **2,** supreme; greatest. **—sov'er·eign·ty,** n.

so'vi·et" (sō'vē-et") n. **1,** in Russia, a council, esp. a town meeting. **2,** (cap.) (often pl.) the U.S.S.R. **—adj.** pert. to a soviet or (cap.) the U.S.S.R.

sow (sō) v.t. & i. **1,** scatter or plant (seed). **2,** scatter seed over (land). **3,** disseminate.

sow (sow) n. a female hog.

soy (soi) n. a plant or its edible seed (soybean). Also, **soy'a** (-ə).

sox (soks) n.pl. socks.

spa (spä) n. **1,** a mineral spring. **2,** a health resort.

space (spās) n. **1,** the unlimited expanse in all directions in which material objects exist. **2,** a particular portion of this expanse. **3,** enough room. **4,** a blank area. **—v.t.** place a certain distance apart. **—space heater,** a small heater used to heat a relatively small space. **—space shuttle,** a spacecraft designed to enter space and return to earth to be used again. **—space station,** a structure with living spaces, laboratories, etc., placed in permanent orbit in space. **—space suit,** a protective garment worn in space that provides pressurized air for breathing and other life-supporting necessities.

space'craft" (spās'kraft") n. a vehicle built for travel in space.

spaced-'out" adj. (Slang) confused or dazed by or as if by use of drugs.

space'ship" n. an aircraft that can travel beyond the atmosphere of the earth.

space-'time" n. the four-dimensional continuum in which all things exist.

space'walk" n. activity outside a spacecraft in space.

spa'cious (spā'shəs) adj. roomy; broad. **—spa'cious·ness,** n.

spade (spād) n. **1,** a long-handled tool for digging. **2,** the symbol (♠); a playing card so marked. **—v.t.** dig with a spade.

spa'dix (spā'diks) n. a spikelike flower head.

spa·ghet'ti (spə-get'ē) n. a cordlike, solid food paste of Ital. origin. **—spaghetti western,** a western movie made in Italy.

span n. **1,** the full extent or stretch of anything; a space of time. **2,** the distance between two supports of a bridge; a bridge. **3,** the distance between thumb and little finger when extended: about 9 inches. **4,** a pair (of horses). **—v.t.** [**spanned, span'ning**] **1,** measure. **2,** extend or reach over.

span'gle (spang'gəl) n. a small glittering piece. **—v.t.** decorate with spangles.

span'iel (span'yəl) n. any of various hunting or pet dogs.

Span'ish adj. of or pert. to Spain, its people, or their language. **—n. 1,** the language of Spain. **2,** the Spanish people. **—Spanish fly,** a diuretic and aphrodisiac medicine.

spank v.t. strike on the buttocks with the open hand; punish. **—n.** a slap. **—spank'ing,** adj. **1,** exceptional. **2,** brisk.

span'ner (span'ər) n. (Brit.) a wrench.

spar (spär) n. **1,** a pole on a mast; a mast. **2,** a part of the frame of an airplane. **3,** any of various lustrous minerals. **4,** (cap.) a member of the women's reserve of the U.S. Coast Guard. **—v.i.** [**sparred, spar'ring**] **1,** box cautiously or for practice. **2,** wrangle; dispute. **3,** fight with spurs, as cocks do.

spare (spār) v.t. & i. **1,** show mercy to. **2,** refrain from injuring, using, saying, etc. **3,** dispense with. **—adj. 1,** in excess; in reserve. **2,** meager. **3,** lean. **4,** frugal. **—n.** an extra or reserve thing, as a tire.

spare'rib" n. an upper pork rib.

spar'ing (spâr'ing) adj. economical; scanty; restricted.

spark (spärk) n. **1,** a fiery particle. **2,** an electrical discharge or arc. **3,** (Colloq.) a suitor. **—v.i. & t. 1,** produce or issue as sparks. **2,** (Colloq.) court; woo. **—spark plug, 1,** the sparking device in an engine. **2,** (Slang) one who encourages or inspires others.

spar'kle (spär'kəl) v.i. **1,** emit little sparks. **2,** glitter. **3,** effervesce. **4,** be vivacious. **—n.** scintillation.

spar'kler (spär'klər) n. something that sparkles: a gem; a kind of firework.

spar'row (spar'ō) n. any of various small birds.

sparse (spärs) adj. **1,** thinly distributed. **2,** thin; scanty. **—sparse'ness, spar'si·ty,** n.

Spar'tan (spär'tən) adj. strictly disciplined and courageous. **—n.** a person of enduring courage.

spasm (spaz'əm) n. **1,** a sudden, involuntary contraction of the muscles. **2,** a brief burst of activity or feeling.

spas·mod'ic (spaz-mod'ik) adj. **1,** pert.

to or like a spasm. **2,** violent but intermittent. **—spas·mod'i·cal·ly,** *adv.*

spas'tic (spas'tik) *adj.* characterized by spasms. **—***n.* one afflicted with a spastic disease. **—spas'ti·cal·ly,** *adv.*

spat *n.* **1,** a petty dispute. **2,** a light blow. **3,** a splash, as of rain. **4,** (*pl.*) short cloth gaiters. **5,** a young oyster. **—***v.i.* & *t.* **[spat'ted, -ting]** quarrel; strike lightly.

spate (spāt) *n.* a freshet; storm.

spa'tial (spā'shəl) *adj.* pert. to, being, or existing in space.

spat'ter (spat'ər) *v.t.* & *i.* **1,** scatter or sprinkle in small drops. **2,** a splash. **—***n.* a sprinkling.

spat'u·la (spach'ə-lə) *n.* a flat-bladed implement for mixing or spreading. **—spat'-u·late** (-lət) *adj.* shaped like a spatula.

spav'in *n.* a diseased condition of the hock of a horse. **—spav'ined,** *adj.*

spawn (spân) *n.* **1,** the eggs of fishes, etc. **2,** offspring. **—***v.t.* & *i.* (esp. of fishes) produce offspring.

spay (spā) *v.t.* remove the ovaries of (a female animal).

speak (spēk) *v.i.* & *t.* **[spoke, spo'ken, speak'ing] 1,** utter words; express. **2,** talk; converse. **3,** deliver a public address.

speak'eas"y *n.* (*Slang*) an illegal barroom.

speak'er (-ər) *n.* **1,** one who speaks. **2,** an orator. **3,** a presiding officer, as (*cap.*) of the U.S. House of Representatives. **4,** loudspeaker. **—speak'er·ship",** *n.*

speak'er·phone" *n.* a combination microphone and loudspeaker for telephone communication.

speak'ing *adj.* **1,** talking. **2,** lifelike.

spear (spir) *n.* **1,** a long-handled, sharp-headed weapon; any similar instrument. **2,** a blade of grass; a shoot. **—***v.t.* **1,** pierce with a spear. **2,** capture.

spear'head" *n.* **1,** the sharp point of a spear. **2,** a leader or leading force.

spear'mint" *n.* the common mint used for flavoring.

spe'cial (spesh'əl) *adj.* **1,** of a particular kind; being a particular one. **2,** peculiar to a particular person, thing, or purpose. **3,** unusual; exceptional. **—***n.* **1,** a special person or thing. **2,** a radio or TV program not appearing regularly.

spe'cial·ist *n.* one who specializes, esp. in a medical field.

spe"ci·al'i·ty (spesh"ē-al'ə-tē) *n.* **1,** a special characteristic; a distinctive feature or quality. **2,** (*pl.*) details; particulars.

spe'cial·ize" (-īz") *v.i.* pursue a particular course of study or work. **—spe"cial·i·za'-tion,** *n.*

spe'cial·ty (-tē) *n.* **1,** a particular or pre-ferred item, subject, skill, etc. **2,** a novelty.

spe'cie (spē'shē) *n.* a coin.

spe'cies (spē'shēz) *n.sing.* & *pl.* **1,** a category of biological classification, lower than a genus. **2,** any class of persons or things.

spe·cif'ic (spə-sif'ik) *adj.* **1,** explicit; definite. **2,** of a particular kind. **—***n.* **1,** something specific. **2,** a medicinal remedy. **—spe·cif'i·cal·ly,** *adv.* **—specific gravity,** the density of a substance relative to that of water.

spec"i·fi·ca'tion (spes"ə-fi-kā'shən) *n.* **1,** a statement of particulars, as of dimensions, materials, etc. **2,** act or result of specifying.

spec'i·fy" (spes'ə-fī") *v.t.* **1,** name expressly. **2,** state as a condition.

spec'i·men (spes'ə-mən) *n.* an individual or part used as a typical example of the whole.

spe'cious (spē'shəs) *adj.* apparently, but not actually, sound; deceptive. **—spe"ci·os'i·ty** (-os'i-tē) *n.*

speck (spek) *n.* a tiny particle; a spot. **—***v.t.* spot.

speck'le (spek'əl) *v.t.* mark with small spots.

spec'ta·cle (spek'tə-kəl) *n.* **1,** a striking sight or view. **2,** a large public display. **3,** (*pl.*) [also, *colloq.,* **specs**] eyeglasses.

spec·tac'u·lar (spek-tak'yə-lər) *adj.* impressive; thrilling.

spec'ta·tor (spek'tā-tər) *n.* an onlooker; a witness.

spec'ter (spek'tər) *n.* **1,** a ghost. **2,** a source of terror. Also, **spec'tre. —spec'-tral,** (-trəl) *adj.*

spec'tro·gram" *n.* a graph of a spectrum.

spec'tro·graph" *n.* **1,** a spectroscope designed to graph spectra. **2,** a spectrogram.

spec·trol'o·gy (spek-trol'ə-jē) *n.* the study of spectra, esp. to determine the constituent elements of bodies. **—spec·trol'o·gist,** *n.*

spec·trom'e·ter (spek-trom'ə-tər) *n.* any of various optical instruments, for measuring wave length, index of refraction, etc.

spec'tro·scope" (spek'trə-skōp") *n.* an instrument for producing the spectrum of any light. **—spec"tro·scop'ic** (-skop'ik) *adj.* **—spec"tro·scop'i·cal·ly,** *adv.*

spec'trum (spek'trəm) *n.* the band of colors formed by dispersed light.

spec'u·late" (spek'yə-lāt") *v.i.* **1,** meditate or ponder; reflect. **2,** theorize; conjecture. **3,** make a risky investment. **—spec"u·la'tion,** *n.* **—spec'u·la"tive,** *adj.* **—spec'-u·la"tor,** *n.*

speech (spēch) *n.* **1,** the power of speaking. **2,** a particular utterance; an address. **3,** a language. **4,** a manner of speaking.

—**speech′less**, *adj.* deprived of speech by emotion, as surprise.

speech′i·fy″ (-ə-fī″) *v.i.* (*Derogatory*) make speeches.

speed (spēd) *n.* **1,** rapidity of motion or performance. **2,** rate of progress or motion. **3,** (*Slang*) any amphetamine, esp. methedrine. —*v.t.* [*pret. & p.p.* **speed′ed** or **sped**] **1,** expedite. **2,** (with *up*) increase the speed of. —*v.i.* **1,** move, etc., with rapidity. **2,** (with *up*) increase speed. —**speed′er**, *n.* one who drives at an illegally high speed.

speed′boat″ *n.* a motorboat built and powered for speed.

speed·om′e·ter (spē-dom′i-tər) *n.* a device that indicates the rate of speed of an automobile, etc.

speed′ster (-stər) *n.* **1,** a speeder. **2,** a low two-seated automobile.

speed′way″ *n.* a road designed for fast automobile travel or for races.

speed′y *adj.* **1,** rapid. **2,** prompt; not delayed. —**speed′i·ness**, *n.*

spe·le·ol′o·gy (spē″lē-ol′ə-jē) *n.* the scientific study of caves. —**spe·le′an** (spə-lē′ən) *adj.* pert. to caves.

spell (spel) *v.t.* **1,** form or express by or in letters. **2,** (of letters) form or constitute (a word). **3,** replace temporarily; relieve. **4,** (with *out*) make plain. **5,** —*v.i.* form words with the proper letters. —*n.* **1,** a charm; an enchantment. **2,** a turn of work. **3,** a short period. **4,** (*Colloq.*) an ailment. —**spell′er**, *n.* **1,** one who spells. **2,** an elementary spelling textbook.

spell′bind″ *v.t.* entrance; fascinate. —**spell′bound″**, *adj.*

spell′down″ *n.* a spelling bee in which a contestant is eliminated after a certain number of mistakes.

spell′ing *n.* **1,** orthography. **2,** the letters forming a word. —**spelling bee**, a contest in spelling words.

spe·lunk′er (spē-lung′kər) *n.* one who explores caves.

spend *v.t.* [*pret. & p.p.* **spent**] **1,** pay or give out (money, etc.). **2,** consume; use up. **3,** employ or while away (time). —*v.i.* pay out money, etc.

spend′thrift″ *n. & adj.* an extravagant person; a prodigal.

spent *adj.* exhausted. —*v.* pret. & p.p. of *spend.*

sperm (spėrm) *n.* the male reproductive cell: *spermatozoön.* —**sperm oil,** oil from the head of the *sperm whale.*

sper″ma·ce′ti (spėr′mə-sē′tē) *n.* a waxy residue of sperm oil, used in making ointments, cosmetics, etc.

spew (spū) *v.t. & i.,* & *n.* vomit.

sphere (sfir) *n.* **1,** a round solid body; a globe. **2,** a field of knowledge, influence, or activity. —**spher′i·cal** (sfer′i-kəl) *adj.*

sphe′roid (sfir′oid) *n.* the solid generated by rotation of an ellipse. —**sphe·roid′al,** *adj.*

sphinc′ter (sfink′tər) *n.* a ringlike muscle.

sphinx (sfinks) *n.* **1,** a mythical creature, usually half human and half lion. **2,** an enigmatic or inscrutable person.

spice (spīs) *n.* **1,** an aromatic or pungent vegetable substance used for seasoning food. **2,** anything that gives zest or piquancy. —*v.t.* add spice to. —**spic′y,** *adj.*

spick-′and-span′ (spik′ən-span′) *adj.* **1,** neat. **2,** new and fresh.

spic′ule (spik′ūl) *n.* a small piece of hard material, as bone or rock, esp. one needle-shaped. —**spic′u·late** (-lāt) *adj.*

spi′der (spī′dər) *n.* **1,** an eight-legged arachnid, esp. one that spins a web. **2,** something resembling a spider, esp. a frying pan. —**spi′der·y,** *adj.*

spiel (spēl) *n.* (*Slang*) a persuasive talk. —**spiel′er,** *n.* a barker.

spiff′y (spif′ē) *adj.* (*Slang*) spruce; smart.

spig′ot (spig′ət) *n.* a faucet.

spike (spīk) *n.* **1,** a large metal nail. **2,** a sharp-pointed projection. **3,** an ear, as of wheat. —*v.t.* **1,** pierce with a spike; furnish with spikes. **2,** make useless; frustrate. **3,** (*Slang*) add alcohol or liquor to (a drink).

spill (spil) *v.t.* **1,** cause or allow to run or fall out. **2,** shed (blood). **3,** let the wind out (of a sail). **4,** divulge. —*v.i.* run or fall out; overflow. —*n.* **1,** a running out. **2,** (*Colloq.*) a fall.

spill′way″ *n.* an outlet for surplus water.

spilt *adj.* spilled.

spin *v.t.* [**spun, spin′ning**] **1,** draw out and twist into threads, as wool, etc. **2,** make with threads; fabricate. **3,** cause to revolve rapidly. **4,** (with *out*) prolong. —*v.i.* **1,** revolve rapidly. **2,** move, ride, etc., rapidly. —*n.* **1,** a spinning motion; a spiral course. **2,** a rapid ride. —**spinning reel,** a type of fishing reel in which the line is wound on a stationary spool by a bail. —**spinning rod,** a rod designed for use with a spinning reel. —**spinning wheel,** a machine once used in the home to make thread or yarn.

spin′ach (spin′ich) *n.* a vegetable having edible green leaves.

spi′nal (spī′nəl) *adj.* of, in, or pert. to the spine. —**spinal column,** the series of vertebrae. —**spinal cord,** the nervous tissue inside the spinal column.

spin′dle (spin′dəl) *n.* a slender pointed

rod or pin, esp. one used in spinning.
—**spin′dling, spin′dly,** *adj.* tall and slender.

spin′drift″ *n.* a windswept spray.

spine (spīn) *n.* **1,** the backbone. **2,** any bony part, as a quill. **3,** a thorn. —**spine′less,** *adj.* feeble; irresolute.

spin′et (spin′it) *n.* a small piano or harpsichord.

spin′na·ker (spin′ə-kər) *n.* a triangular sail.

spin′ner *n.* **1,** one who or that which spins. **2,** an artificial fly used in angling.

spin-′off″ *n.* **1,** the transfer of a branch of a corporation's activities to a smaller corporation controlled by it. **2,** any product derived from a larger, usu. unrelated, enterprise. **3,** a radio or TV program whose characters or situation derive from another program.

spin′ster (spin′stər) *n.* an unmarried woman.

spin′y (spī′nė) *adj.* **1,** having or covered with spines. **2,** spinelike. —**spin′i·ness,** *n.*

spi′ra·cle (spī′rə-kəl) *n.* a small aperture; a vent or air hole.

spi·rae′a (spī-rē′ə) *n.* any of various flower-bearing shrubs.

spi′ral (spī′rəl) *n.* **1,** a curve winding around a fixed point and continually receding from it. **2,** a coil; a helix. —*adj.* coiled. —*v.i. & t.* go or cause to go in a spiral or winding course.

spire (spīr) *n.* **1,** an upright structure tapering to a point, as a steeple. **2,** the top. **3,** the shoot of a plant.

spir′it *n.* **1,** the inspiring principle or dominant influence. **2,** soul. **3,** the nature of a person; disposition; attitude. **4,** (often *pl.*) vivacity; optimism. **5,** (*cap.*) in the Trinity, the Holy Spirit. **6,** the essence or real meaning. **7,** a supernatural being; an angel; a fairy; a ghost. **8,** a chemical distillation; (*pl.*) strong distilled alcoholic liquor. —*v.t.* (with *away*) carry off secretly. —**spir′it·ed,** *adj.* full of courage, vigor, etc. —**spir′it·u·ous,** *adj.* alcoholic. —**spirit level,** a level (def. 2) using an air bubble in a glass tube full of liquid.

spir′it·u·al (spir′i-choo-əl) *adj.* **1,** pert. to the soul or spirit. **2,** relating to sacred things. —*n.* a religious song, esp. of Negro origin. —**spir′it·u·al′i·ty,** *n.*

spir′it·u·al·ism *n.* belief in communication with the spirits of the dead. —**spir′it·u·al·ist,** *n.*

spi′ro·graph″ (spī′rə-graf″) *n.* **1,** an instrument for recording movements in breathing. **2,** (*T.N.*) a device for drawing various geometric figures.

spit *v.i. & t.* [**spat** or **spit, spit′ting**] **1,** eject saliva from the mouth. **2,** spew out. **3,** [*pret. & p.p.* **spit′ted**] impale on a sharp stick, etc. —*n.* **1,** saliva. **2,** the image of a person. **3,** a sharp stick or bar. **4,** a narrow point of land. —**spitting image,** (*Colloq.*) perfect likeness.

spit′ball″ *n.* **1,** a wad of paper chewed and rolled into a ball for use as a missile. **2,** in baseball, a curve pitched by moistening the ball with saliva (now against the rules).

spite (spīt) *n.* ill will; malevolence. —*v.t.* thwart. —**spite′ful,** *adj.* malicious. —**in spite of,** notwithstanding.

spit′fire″ *n.* **1,** a hot-tempered person. **2,** (*cap.*) a Brit. fighter plane.

spit′tle (-əl) *n.* **1,** saliva. **2,** a frothy insect secretion.

spit·toon′ (spi-toon′) *n.* a cuspidor.

spitz (spits) *n.* a kind of Pomeranian dog.

splash *v.t.* **1,** spatter, as with water or mud. **2,** dash or throw about (water, etc.). —*v.i.* spatter water, or in water. —*n.* **1,** the act or sound of splashing. **2,** a quantity splashed. **3,** an ostentatious display. —**splash′y,** *adj.*

splash-′down″ *n.* the return landing of a spacecraft or missile on the water; hence, any landing on water.

splat *n.* the center upright member of the back of a chair.

splat′ter (splat′ər) *v.t. & i.* splash.

splay (splā) *v.i. & t.* spread out. —*adj.* spread out; turned outward; awkward. —**splay′foot″,** *n.*

spleen (splēn) *n.* **1,** an organ in the abdomen in which the blood is modified. **2,** ill humor; melancholy. **3,** anger; malice. —**splen′ic** (-ik), **sple·net′ic** (spli-net′ik) *adj.*

splen′did *adj.* excellent; admirable; grand.

splen·dif′er·ous (splen-dif′ə-rəs) *adj.* (*Colloq.*) extremely gorgeous or sumptuous.

splen′dor (splen′dər) *n.* brilliant luster; magnificence; grandeur. Also, **splen′dour.** —**splen′dor·ous,** *adj.*

splice (splīs) *v.t.* join together, as two ropes. —*n.* a joint of ropes.

spline (splīn) *n.* a thin strip of wood.

splint *n.* **1,** a thin piece of wood, etc., used to immobilize a fractured bone. **2,** a thin strip for weaving a basket, etc.

splin′ter (splin′tər) *n.* a sharp, thin, split-off piece of wood, bone, etc. —*v.t. & i.* break into splinters.

split *v.t. & i.* [**split, split′ting**] **1,** rend or cleave lengthwise. **2,** burst asunder. **3,** divide; disunite. **4,** (*Slang*) leave; depart. —*n.* **1,** a crack or rent. **2,** a division; a schism. **3,** a split willow twig. **4,** (*Colloq.*) a bottle of half the usual size. —*adj.* divided; cleft.

—**split'ting,** *adj.* extreme; severe, as a headache.

split-'lev"el *adj.* having two levels, one higher than, and adjacent to, the other.

splotch (sploch) *n.* a large, ill-defined spot. —*v.t.* blot.

splurge (splėrj) *n.* an extravagant display or expenditure. —*v.i.* spend extravagantly or ostentatiously.

splut'ter (splut'ər) *v.i. & t.* talk or utter incoherently; sputter.

spoil *v.t.* **1,** seriously impair. **2,** overindulge, as a child. **3,** plunder; despoil. —*v.i.* decay; become tainted. —*n.* (*pl.*) plunder. —**spoil'age,** *n.*

spoil'er *n.* a hinged flap on an airplane wing used to regulate lift.

spoil'sport" *n.* one who spoils the pleasure or enjoyment of others.

spoke (spōk) *n.* one of the bars joining the hub and rim of a wheel. —*v.* pret. of *speak.*

spo'ken (spō'kən) *v.* p.p. of *speak.* —*adj.* oral, not written.

spokes'man (spōks'mən) *n.* [*pl.* **-men**] one who speaks for others. —**spokes'-per"son,** *n.* —**spokes'wom"an,** *n.fem.*

spo'li·ate" (spō'lė-āt") *v.t.* despoil; plunder. —**spo"li·a'tion,** *n.*

spon'dee (spon'dė) *n.* a poetic foot comprising two long syllables. —**spon·da'ic** (-dā'ik) *adj.*

sponge (spunj) *n.* **1,** a marine invertebrate; its dried, absorbent framework. **2,** any similar absorbent substance. **3,** (*Colloq.*) a parasitical person. —*v.t. & i.* **1,** wipe with a sponge. **2,** (*Colloq.*) live at the expense of another. —**spon'gy,** *adj.* —**sponge cake,** a light cake made without shortening.

spon'sor (spon'sər) *n.* **1,** one who vouches for another; a godparent. **2,** a buyer of radio or television time. —*v.t.* vouch for; be a patron of. —**spon'sor·ship,** *n.*

spon"ta·ne'i·ty (spon"tə-nė'ə-tė) *n.* natural, impulsive action; spontaneousness.

spon·ta'ne·ous (spon-tā'nė-əs) *adj.* **1,** proceeding from internal impulse. **2,** arising naturally; instinctive. —**spon·ta'ne·ous-ness,** *n.* —**spontaneous combustion,** a burning ignited by the heat of internal chemical action.

spoof *v.t. & i.,* & *n.* (*Slang*) hoax; tease.

spook (spŏŏk) *n.* (*Colloq.*) a ghost. —*v.t. & i.* frighten. —**spook'y,** *adj.* —**spook'i-ness,** *n.*

spool *n.* a small cylinder on which thread, wire, etc., are wound.

spoon *n.* **1,** a utensil consisting of a concave bowl and a handle. **2,** any implement or object resembling this. **3,** a wooden-faced golf club (No. 3 wood). —*v.t. & i.* **1,**

convey in a spoon. **2,** (*Colloq.*) pet; make love. —**spoon'ful** (-fūl) *n.* [*pl.* **-fuls**].

spoon'bill" *n.* any of various wading birds, as the shovelbill.

spoo'ner·ism" (spoo'nər-iz"əm) *n.* a slip of the tongue in which sounds are transposed.

spoon'fed" *adj.* **1,** given food with a spoon, as a child. **2,** pampered.

spoor (spŭr) *n.* the track or trail of a wild animal.

spo·rad'ic (spô-rad'ik) *adj.* appearing at irregular intervals; occasional. —**spo-rad'i·cal·ly,** *adv.*

spore (spôr) *n.* a germ; a seed; a source of being.

spor'ran (spôr'ən) *n.* a large purse worn suspended from the belt by Scottish highlanders.

sport (spôrt) *n.* **1,** an outdoor or athletic pastime. **2,** fun; diversion. **3,** jesting; a subject of diversion. **4,** (*Colloq.*) a sportsmanlike person; a sporting man. —*v.t.* (*Colloq.*) display ostentatiously. —*v.i.* play; frolic.

sport'ing *adj.* **1,** relating to outdoor pastimes. **2,** sportsmanlike. **3,** pert. to gambling. —**sporting house,** house of prostitution.

spor'tive (spôr'tiv) *adj.* frolicsome; jesting. —**spor'tive·ness,** *n.*

sports'cast" *n.* a broadcast of a sporting event. —**sports'cast"er,** *n.*

sports'man (spôrts'mən) *n.* [*pl.* **-men**] **1,** one who engages in field sports. **2,** a fair contestant. —**sports'man·like",** *adj.* —**sports'man·ship",** *n.*

sports'wear" *n.* clothes for engaging in or attending sporting events.

sport'y (spôr'tė) *adj.* **1,** sporting. **2,** flashy. —**sport'i·ness,** *n.*

spot *n.* **1,** a stain; a blemish. **2,** a small mark; a speck. **3,** a place; a site. —*v.t.* [**spot'ted, -ting**] **1,** stain; mark with spots. **2,** note; recognize. **3,** place. **4,** (*Colloq.*) give a handicap of or to. —*v.i.* become spotted. —**on the spot, 1,** handy. **2,** in an embarrassing position.

spot'less *adj.* unsullied; clean.

spot'light" *n.* **1,** a device, often movable, that focuses brilliant light in a small area. **2,** the center of attraction.

spot'ter (-ər) *n.* one who watches and locates.

spot'ty (-ė) *adj.* occurring in spots; irregular. —**spot'ti·ness,** *n.*

spouse (spows) *n.* one's husband or wife.

spout (spowt) *v.t. & i.* **1,** discharge or issue forth, in a stream. **2,** utter or declaim volubly. —*n.* a tube or opening that guides a flow.

sprain (sprān) *n.* a violent straining of muscles and ligaments.

sprang *v.* pret. of *spring*.

sprat *n.* a small European herring.

sprawl (srâl) *v.i. & t.* **1,** be stretched out carelessly; be spread out aimlessly. **2,** scramble. —*n.* a sprawling posture.

spray (sprā) *n.* **1,** finely divided water or other liquid blown by air. **2,** an atomizer. **3,** a branch of a tree or of a flowering plant; a similar ornament or design. —*v.t. & i.* scatter or apply as a spray. —**spray gun,** a pistol-shaped device for spraying paint.

spread (spred) *v.t. & i.* [*pret. & p.p.* **spread**] **1,** stretch out; unfold. **2,** flatten out in a sheet; distribute evenly. **3,** set out; display. **4,** disperse; scatter; disseminate. **5,** extend. **6,** push apart. —*n.* **1,** extension or expansion. **2,** an expanse. **3,** a feast; a spread food, as jam. **4,** a coverlet. —**spread'er,** *n.* **5,** a layout.

spread-'ea"gle *adj.* **1,** sprawling. **2,** (*Colloq.*) boastful or bombastic. —*v.t.* stretch out; send sprawling.

spree (sprē) *n.* a lively frolic.

sprig *n.* a small branch; a shoot.

spright'ly (sprīt'lē) *adj. & adv.* lively; animated. —**spright'li·ness,** *n.*

spring *v.i.* [**sprang, sprung, spring'ing**] **1,** leap. **2,** rise up or issue forth suddenly. **3,** recoil; warp. —*v.t.* **1,** cause to leap or rise. **2,** disclose or produce suddenly. **3,** release the spring of, as a trap; (*Slang*) provide bail for. —*n.* **1,** a leap. **2,** (often *cap.*) the vernal season, in No. Amer. approx. March 21 to June 21. **3,** the beginning or freshest time of anything. **4,** water rising to the surface of the earth. **5,** any source of supply. **6,** an elastic strip of steel or spiral wire. **7,** elasticity; motive power. **8,** a split; a warp. —**spring chicken,** a young, naïve person, esp. a woman. —**spring fever,** a lazy feeling that comes with spring weather.

spring'board" *n.* a diving board.

spring'bok *n.* a So. Afr. gazelle.

spring'er *n.* a spaniel used in hunting.

spring'time" *n.* the spring.

spring'y *adj.* resilient; elastic; agile. —**spring'i·ness,** *n.*

sprin'kle (spring'kəl) *v.t.* **1,** scatter in drops or particles. **2,** bespatter. **3,** distribute; diversify. —*v.i.* rain slightly. —*n.* a light rain; a spray. —**sprin'kler,** *n.* a device for sprinkling water. —**sprin'kling,** *n.* a small scattered amount.

sprint *n.* a short run at full speed. —*v.i.* run at full speed.

sprit *n.* a small spar that crosses a sail diagonally.

sprite (sprīt) *n.* an elf; a fairy.

sprock'et (sprok'it) *n.* a projection on a wheel that engages a chain or a hole.

sprout (sprowt) *v.i. & t.* **1,** begin to grow. **2,** put forth shoots. —*n.* a shoot or bud.

spruce (sproos) *adj.* trim and neat in appearance. —*v.t. & i.* (with *up*) make neat. —*n.* a coniferous evergreen tree; its wood.

sprung *v.* p.p. of *spring*.

spry (sprī) *adj.* nimble; lively. —**spry'ness,** *n.*

spud *n.* **1,** a small-bladed spade or chisel. **2,** (*Colloq.*) a potato.

spume (spūm) *v.t. & i.,* & *n.* foam; froth.

spu·mo'ne (spoo-mō'nè) *n.* Ital. ice cream containing chopped fruit or nuts.

spun *v.* pret. & p.p. of *spin*.

spunk *n.* (*Colloq.*) mettle; pluck. —**spunk'y,** *adj.* bold; courageous.

spur (spêr) *n.* **1,** a pointed instrument worn on the heel, to goad a horse; any similar projection. **2,** an incentive. **3,** a short ridge, a railroad track, etc., branching from a main line. —*v.t.* [**spurred, spur'ring**] goad; incite. —*v.i.* press forward; hasten.

spu'ri·ous (spyûr'ē-əs) *adj.* not genuine or authentic; counterfeit. —**spu'ri·ous·ness,** *n.*

spurn (spêrn) *v.t.* **1,** reject with disdain. **2,** kick.

spurt (spêrt) *n.* **1,** a forcible gush of liquid. **2,** a short, sudden effort. —*v.i. & t.* gush or advance suddenly.

sput'nik *n.* artificial satellite, esp. one launched by the U.S.S.R.

sput'ter (sput'ər) *v.i. & t.* **1,** spit out or emit small particles explosively. **2,** speak or utter explosively and incoherently. —*n.* an act or result of sputtering.

spu'tum (spū'təm) *n.* [*pl.* **-ta** (-tə)] spittle, esp. when mixed with mucus.

spy (spī) *n.* **1,** a secret watcher. **2,** a secret agent in enemy territory. —*v.i.* observe secretly. —*v.t.* **1,** (with *on*) observe secretly. **2,** (with *out*) discover by observation. **3,** catch sight of; see.

spy'glass" *n.* a hand telescope.

squab (skwob) *n.* a young, unfledged pigeon. —**squab'by,** *adj.* short and stout.

squab'ble (skwob'əl) *n.* a petty quarrel. —*v.i.* bicker.

squad (skwod) *n.* a small party or group, esp. of soldiers. —**squad car,** a cruising police car.

squad'ron (skwod'rən) *n.* an operating unit of warships, cavalry, aircraft, etc.

squal'id (skwol'id) *adj.* dirty; filthy; degraded. —**squal'id·ness,** *n.*

squall (skwâl) *n.* **1,** a sudden, violent gust of wind. **2,** (*Colloq.*) a commotion. **3,** a scream or cry. —v.i. cry violently. —**squall'y**, n.

squal'or (skwol'ər; skwä'lər) n. filthy and depressed condition.

squan'der (skwon'dər) v.t. spend wastefully; dissipate.

square (skwâr) n. **1**, a plane figure having four equal sides and four right angles. **2**, an open area in a city. **3**, a city block. **4**, an instrument for determining right angles. **5**, the result obtained by multiplying a number by itself. —*adj.* **1**, like a square; at right angles. **2**, straight, level, or even. **3**, equitable; honest. **4**, unequivocal. **5**, satisfying, as a meal. —v.t. **1**, make square. **2**, adjust; true. **3**, settle (a debt). —v.i. **1**, agree (with). **2**, (with *off*) prepare to box. —**square dance**, one for four or more couples. —**square deal**, (*Colloq.*) a mutually honest transaction. —**square knot**, a secure but easily untied knot formed of two interlocking half loops. —**square root**, the number of which a given number is the square. —**square shooter**, (*Colloq.*) an honest person.

square-'rigged" *adj.* see *rig*.

squash (skwosh) v.t. **1**, press into pulp; crush. **2**, (*Colloq.*) suppress; silence. —v.i. **1**, be crushed. **2**, make a splashing sound. —n. **1**, the act or sound of squashing. **2**, a game played with rackets in a walled court: *squash rackets*. **3**, a trailing plant of the melon family; its green or yellow fruit, used as a vegetable. —**squash'y**, *adj.* soft and wet; easily crushed.

squat (skwot) v.i. [**squat'ted, -ting**] **1**, sit close to the ground; crouch. **2**, settle on public land. —*adj.* [**squat'ter, -test**] short and thick. —n. a squatting posture. —**squat'ter**, n.

squaw (skwâ) n. a No. Amer. Indian woman, esp. a wife.

squawk (skwâk) v.i. **1**, make a loud, harsh outcry. **2**, (*Colloq.*) complain loudly. —n. act of squawking.

squaw'man" n. [pl. **-men**] a white man living with a squaw.

squeak (skwēk) n. **1**, a short, sharp, shrill sound. **2**, (*Colloq.*) a narrow escape; a close thing. —v.t. & i. make a squeaking sound.

squeal (skwēl) n. **1**, a prolonged shrill cry. **2**, (*Slang*) the act of an informer. —v.t. & i. utter a squeal. —v.i. (often with *on*) (*Slang*) inform (on someone).

squeam'ish (skwē'mish) *adj.* easily nauseated; fastidious; prudish.

squee'gee (skwē'jē) n. a rubber blade for wiping water from panes.

squeeze (skwēz) v.t. **1**, exert pressure upon; compress force; cram. **2**, express; extract. —v.i. press; push. —n. **1**, the act of squeez-

ing. **2**, a handshake; a hug; an embrace. **3**, (*Colloq.*) a predicament.

squelch (skwelch) v.t. suppress. —n. (*Colloq.*) a crushing remark.

squib (skwib) n. **1**, a short, satirical writing. **2**, a firecracker. —v.t. & i. write or assail with a squib.

squid (skwid) n. any of various members of the octopus family.

squig'gle (skwig'əl) n. a wriggly line or scrawl. —v.i. wriggle and squirm.

squint (skwint) v.i. look askance, obliquely, or with narrowed eyes.

squire (skwīr) n. **1**, a landed proprietor. **2**, a lady's escort. **3**, an attendant. **4**, a justice of the peace. —v.t. attend; escort.

squirm (skwêrm) v.i. **1**, wriggle. **2**, writhe mentally. —n. a wriggle.

squir'rel (skwêr'əl) n. a bushy-tailed, arboreal rodent.

squirt (skwêrt) v.t. & i. eject or issue suddenly in a thin stream. —n. **1**, a thin stream of water, etc. **2**, (*Colloq.*) a small, insignificant fellow.

stab v.t. & i. [**stabbed, stab'bing**] **1**, pierce with, or thrust with, a pointed weapon. **2**, betray. —n. act of stabbing; a thrust or wound.

sta'bile (stā'bəl) *adj.* fixed in position; stationary.

sta·bil'i·ty (stə-bil'ə-tē) n. firmness; permanence.

sta'bi·lize" (stā'bə-līz") v.t. make stable; steady. —**sta"bi·li·za'tion**, n.

sta'ble (stā'bəl) n. **1**, a building for horses, cattle, etc. **2**, a collection of racing horses. —*adj.* **1**, firmly fixed; steady. **2**, not changing or wavering. —v.t. lodge in a stable.

stac·ca'to (stə-kä'tō) *adj.* (*Music*) **1**, abrupt. **2**, separated by slight pauses.

stack (stak) n. **1**, an orderly pile or heap. **2**, a chimney or funnel. **3**, (*pl.*) bookshelves. —v.t. **1**, pile in a stack. **2**, prearrange dishonestly.

sta'di·um (stā'dē-əm) n. a structure of tiers of seats enclosing an athletic field.

staff (stâf) n. **1**, a stick or pole; a cane. **2**, a body of workers or assistants. **3**, the lines and spaces on which musical notes are written. —v.t. provide with a staff. —**staff'er**, n. (*Colloq.*) a member of a staff.

stag n. **1**, an adult male deer. **2**, (*Colloq.*) a man not accompanied by a woman. —*adj.* (*Colloq.*) for men only.

stage (stāj) n. **1**, a single time, period, or step of a gradual process. **2**, a raised platform, esp. in a theater. **3**, the theatrical profession; drama. **4**, a station for changing horses. —v.t. exhibit on a stage. —**stage fright**, nervousness caused by public appearance. —**stage whisper,** a whisper intended to be overheard.

stage′coach″ *n.* a horse-drawn public passenger coach.

stage′hand″ *n.* a worker who handles the sets, etc., in a theater.

stage-′struck″ *adj.* obsessed with a desire to act.

stag″fla′tion *n.* (*Colloq.*) combined recession and inflation.

stag′ger (stag′ər) *v.i.* move unsteadily; falter. —*v.t.* **1,** cause to falter; shock. **2,** arrange in a zigzag order. —*n.* **1,** an unsteady movement. **2,** (*pl.*) a cerebral and spinal disease of horses, etc.

stag′ing (stā′jing) *n.* **1,** the act of putting a play, etc., on a stage. **2,** scaffolding.

stag′nant (stag′nənt) *adj.* not moving; stagnating. —**stag′nan·cy,** *n.*

stag′nate (stag′nāt) *v.i.* **1,** cease to run or flow; lose freshness. **2,** be or become inactive. —**stag·na′tion,** *n.*

stag′y (stā′jē) *adj.* theatrical. —**stag′i·ness,** *n.*

staid (stād) *adj.* sober and sedate; not flighty. —**staid′ness,** *n.*

stain (stān) *n.* **1,** a discoloration. **2,** a blot; a taint. **3,** a liquid for coloring wood. —*v.t. & i.* discolor. —**stainless steel,** an alloy of steel with chrome, nickel, etc., to inhibit rusting.

stair (stâr) *n.* **1,** a step, or series of steps, rising to a higher level. **2,** (*pl.*) such steps collectively.

stair′case″ *n.* a flight of stairs. Also, **stair′-way″.**

stair′well″ *n.* a vertical opening containing a staircase.

stake (stāk) *n.* **1,** a pointed stick or post. **2,** money wagered; (*Colloq.*) capital. **3,** that which is risked or to be gained. —*v.t.* **1,** mark, support, etc., with stakes. **2,** hazard or wager.

stake-′out″ *n.* a concealed location for surveillance, usu. used by police.

Stak·han′o·vite″ (stə-kän′ə-vīt″) *adj.* pert. to an incentive system for increasing workers′ productiveness, in the U.S.S.R.

sta·lac′tite (stə-lak′tīt) *n.* a calcium deposit hanging from the roof of a cave.

stal′ag *n.* a German prisoner-of-war camp.

sta·lag′mite (stə-lag′mīt) *n.* a formation similar to a stalactite, but rising from the floor.

stale (stāl) *adj.* **1,** not fresh. **2,** trite. **3,** physically overtrained. —*v.t. & i.* make or become stale. —**stale′ness,** *n.*

stale′mate″ *n.* a deadlocked situation. —*v.t.* deadlock; thwart.

stalk (stâk) *v.i.* **1,** walk with slow, digni-

fied strides. **2,** approach game stealthily. —*v.t.* approach stealthily. —*n.* **1,** an act of stalking. **2,** the principal stem or support, esp. of a plant. —**stalk′y,** *adj.* tall and thin.

stall (stâl) *n.* **1,** a compartment, esp. one for an animal in a stable; a booth; a seat or pew. **2,** a state of arrested operation or motion. **3,** (*Colloq.*) a delaying pretext. —*v.t. & i.* **1,** cause to stick or stop. **2,** (*Colloq.*) evade; delay.

stal′lion (stal′yən) *n.* a male horse kept for breeding.

stal′wart (stâl′wərt) *adj.* strong and brave. —*n.* a stalwart person.

sta′men (stā′mən) *n.* the pollen-bearing organ of a plant.

stam′i·na (stam′ə-nə) *n.* lasting strength; endurance.

stam′mer (stam′ər) *v.i. & t.* speak or utter with involuntary breaks and repetitions. —*n.* a stammering.

stamp *v.t.* **1,** crush or pound; strike the foot down on. **2,** impress; seal. **3,** characterize. **4,** affix a stamp on. —*v.i.* strike the foot down; walk heavily. —*n.* **1,** a downward thrust of the foot. **2,** a device for stamping; a die. **3,** a mark; a seal; a piece of adhesive paper, as postage. —**stamp′-ing ground,** a place one frequents.

stam·pede′ (stam-pēd′) *n.* a concerted, panic-stricken rush. —*v.i. & t.* move in a stampede.

stance (stans) *n.* posture; in golf, the position of the feet.

stanch (stänch) *v.t.* stop the flow of a liquid, esp. blood. —*adj.* **1,** firm. **2,** trustworthy; loyal. **3,** watertight, as a ship. Also, **staunch.** —**stanch′ness,** *n.*

stan′chion (stan′shən) *n.* a post or pillar.

stand *v.i.* [*pret. & p.p.* **stood** (stûd)] **1,** be in or assume an upright position. **2,** be stagnant; stop. **3,** be situated. **4,** continue. **5,** (with *for*) be representative. **6,** move (back, aside, etc.). —*v.t.* **1,** set upright. **2,** (with *for*) tolerate. **3,** endure. **4,** (with *by*) support; abide by. —*n.* **1,** an act of standing. **2,** a determined position. **3,** a structure, platform, or piece of furniture; a grandstand, etc. **4,** a growth, as of grain. —**stand down,** withdraw. —**stand pat,** decline to change.

stan′dard (stan′dərd) *n.* **1,** a basis of comparison; a criterion; measure. **2,** a flag or emblem. **3,** something upright or standing. —*adj.* serving as a basis of comparison.

stan′dard·ize″ (-īz″) *v.t.* make uniform. —**stan″dard·i·za′tion,** *n.*

stand-′by″ *n.* a reliable supporter or resource.

stand'ee *n.* (*Colloq.*) one who stands, as at a theatrical performance.

stand-'in'' *n.* a temporary substitute for a motion-picture actor, etc.

stand'ing *n.* **1**, rank; reputation. **2**, length of experience, etc. —*adj.* **1**, upright. **2**, continuing; permanent.

stand-'off'' *n.* **1**, a state of being evenly matched. **2**, a tie. —**stand-off'ish**, *adj.* aloof.

stand-'out'' *n.* something conspicuous, esp. for excellence.

stand'pipe'' *n.* a large vertical pipe or water tower.

stand'point'' *n.* point of view.

stand'still''·*n.* a halt.

stan'za (stan'zə) *n.* a unit, several lines, of a poem or song.

staph'y·lo·coc''cus (staf'ə-lə-kok''əs) *n.* [*pl.* **-coc''ci** (-kok''sī)] a parasitic bacterium. Also, *colloq.*, **staph.**

sta'ple (stā'pəl) *n.* **1**, a loop of wire, driven as a nail or fastener. **2**, a principal commodity. **3**, a raw material. —*adj.* chief or principal, as commodities; basic. —*v.t.* fasten with staples. —**sta'pler**, *n.* a device for driving staples.

star (stär) *n.* **1**, a body in space, esp. one outside the solar system; a sun. **2**, a figure (★) representing this. **3**, an asterisk (*). **4**, a distinguished or leading performer. —*v.t. & i.* [**starred, star'ring**] **1**, mark with a star. **2**, feature. —*adj.* brilliant; leading. —**star'dom**, *n.* —**star chamber**, a severe and arbitrary court.

star'board (stär'bôrd'') *n.*, *adj. & adv.* (*Naut.*) the right side, as one faces the bow of a vessel.

starch (stärch) *n.* **1**, a carbohydrate occurring in cereals, potatoes, etc.; this substance prepared for stiffening, etc. **2**, formality. —*v.t.* stiffen with starch.

starch'y (stär'chē) *adj.* **1**, full of starch. **2**, (*Colloq.*) formal in manner. —**starch'-i·ness**, *n.*

stare (stär) *v.i. & t.* gaze steadily and fixedly. —*n.* a steady gaze.

star'fish'' *n.* a star-shaped fish.

star'gaz''er *n.* an idle dreamer. —**star'-gaze''**, *v.i.*

stark (stärk) *adj.* **1**, sheer; downright. **2**, rigid. **3**, desolate; naked. —*adv.* entirely; absolutely. —**stark'ness**, *n.*

star'let (stär'lət) *n.* a young motion picture actress.

star'light'' *n.* light from the stars, or a time when stars can be seen.

star'ling (stär'ling) *n.* any of various birds.

star'ry (-ė) *adj.* sparkling with, or as with, stars. —**star'ri·ness**, *n.*

Stars and Stripes the flag of the U.S.A.

star-'span''gled *adj.* dotted with stars. —**the Star-Spangled Banner,** the U.S. flag or the U.S. national anthem.

start (stärt) *v.i.* **1**, begin or enter upon an action, etc.; set out. **2**, make a sudden involuntary move; jerk. —*v.t.* originate; set in motion; establish; begin. —*n.* **1**, a beginning; the outset. **2**, a lead. **3**, a twitch; a jerk.

star'tle (stär'təl) *v.t.* surprise; alarm; shock. —**star'tling,**

star·va'tion (stär-va'shən) *n.* act or process of starving; famishment.

starve (stärv) *v.i.* **1**, die of hunger. **2**, suffer from hunger or want. —*v.t.* cause to starve.

starve'ling *adj.* **1**, starving. **2**, emaciated. **3**, meager, as in supply. —*n.* someone or something that is starved.

stash *v.t.* (*Slang*) put away; hide. —*n.* a place where something is hidden; something hidden.

stat *n.* (*Colloq.*) a photostat.

-stat *suf.* **1**, stationary. **2**, a device for various purposes. **3**, an agent that inhibits growth.

state (stāt) *n.* **1**, mode or form of existence; position; situation; condition; structure. **2**, dignity; ceremony; great style. **3**, the whole people; a nation; a civil community, esp. (often *cap.*) one of the states of the U.S. —*adj.* **1**, pert. to civil government. **2**, pert. to a state of the U.S. **3**, ceremonious. —*v.t.* declare. —**state'hood,** *n.* —**state of the art,** as advanced as permitted by current technology.

stat'ed (stā'tid) *adj.* **1**, settled. **2**, explicit.

state'house'' *n.* a state capitol.

state'ly (-lė) *adj.* majestic; dignified. —**state'li·ness,** *n.*

state'ment (-mənt) *n.* **1**, a spoken or written declaration. **2**, an accounting.

state'room'' *n.* a private room on a train or ship.

state'side'' *adj. & adv.* in or toward the United States.

states'man (-mən) *n.* [*pl.* **men**] a leader in government. —**states'man·ship,** *n.*

stat'ic (stat'ik) *adj.* **1**, fixed; stationary; stagnant. **2**, pert. to a stationary charge of electricity. **3**, (*Radio & TV*) pert. to atmospheric electrical interference. —*n.* (*Radio & TV*) static interference. —**stat'i·cal·ly,** *adv.*

sta'tion (stā'shən) *n.* **1**, an assigned place or position. **2**, a headquarters. **3**, standing. —*v.t.* assign; place. —**station break,** a break in programming during which a radio or

TV station identifies itself, and often commercials are presented. —**station house**, a police station. —**station wagon**, a large automobile designed to carry both passengers and baggage.

sta'tion·ar"y (stā'shə-ner"ē) *adj.* not moving; fixed; not changing.

sta'tion·er (stā'shə-nər) *n.* a dealer in stationery.

sta'tion·er·y (stā'shə-ner"ē) *n.* writing materials, esp. paper.

sta'tion·mas"ter *n.* a person in charge of a railroad station.

sta·tis'tics (stə-tis'tiks) *n.sing.* **1,** the science of collecting and interpreting numerical data. **2,** (constr. as *pl.*) the data. —**sta·tis'ti·cal**, *adj.* —**stat"is·ti'cian** (stat"-is-tish'ən) *n.*

stat'u·ar·y (stach'oo-er-ē) *n.* statues collectively.

stat'ue (stach'oo) *n.* a carved or molded figure, esp. of a person.

stat'u·esque' (stach"oo-esk') *adj.* of dignified bodily form and posture.

stat'u·ette" (stach'oo-et") *n.* a small statue.

stat'ure (stach'ər) *n.* **1,** a person's natural height. **2,** elevation; standing.

sta'tus (stā'təs; stat'əs) *n.* **1,** relative standing. **2,** position; condition.

sta'tus quo (kwō) (*Lat.*) the existing state or condition.

stat'ute (stach'ūt) *n.* an ordinance or law. —**stat'u·to·ry**, *adj.*

staunch (stânch) *adj.* stanch.

stave (stāv) *n.* **1,** a pale or piece of wood, esp. for the side of a barrel. **2,** a stanza. **3,** (*Music*) a staff. —*v.t.* **1,** (with *in*) crush in; break. **2,** (with *off*) avert; keep off.

stay (stā) *v.i.* **1,** remain. **2,** hold out; persevere. **3,** stop; pause; linger. —*v.t.* **1,** halt; restrain. **2,** suspend; delay. **3,** prop up; support. —*n.* **1,** a pause or halt; an indefinite sojourn. **2,** a stoppage or suspension. **3,** a prop. **4,** (*pl.*) a corset. **5,** (*Naut.*) a guy rope or wire.

stead (sted) *n.* place.

stead'fast" *adj.* firm; resolute. —**stead'-fast·ness**, *n.*

stead'y (sted'ē) *adj.* **1,** firmly fixed. **2,** regular; uniform. **3,** resolute. **4,** industrious. —*v.t. & i.* make or become steady. —*n.* (*Colloq.*) a regular sweetheart. —**stead'-i·ness**, *n.*

steak (stāk) *n.* a thick slice of meat, esp. beef.

steal (stēl) *v.t.* [**stole** (stōl) **sto'len**, **steal'-ing**] **1,** take dishonestly and secretly. **2,** obtain surreptitiously or by surprise. —*v.i.*

1, practice theft. **2,** move stealthily. —*n.* (*Colloq.*) a great bargain.

stealth (stelth) *n.* a secret or furtive procedure. —**stealth'y**, *adj.*

steam (stēm) *n.* **1,** water in a gaseous state, esp. when produced by boiling. **2,** (*Colloq.*) energy; enthusiasm. —*v.i.* give out, or move by, steam. —*v.t.* **1,** treat with steam. **2,** (*Colloq.*) (with *up*) arouse enthusiasm in. —**steam engine**, an engine in which steam supplies the power.

steam roller 1, a steam-driven engine for leveling roads. **2,** (*Colloq.*) any agency that ruthlessly overrides and crushes. —**steam'-roll"er**, *v.t.* (*Colloq.*) crush. —**steam shovel**, a steam-powered machine for excavating.

steam'boat" *n.* steamship.

steam'er *n.* **1,** a device for steaming. **2,** a steamship.

steam'fit"ter *n.* a skilled worker who installs pipes, etc., that carry steam at high pressure.

steam'ship" *n.* a ship propelled by a steam engine.

steam'y *adj.* **1,** vaporous; misty. **2,** (*Colloq.*) excited or energetic; sensual. —**steam·i·ness**, *n.*

steed (stēd) *n.* a horse.

steel (stēl) *n.* **1,** iron modified to increase its hardness, toughness, etc. **2,** something made of steel. —*v.t.* instill with courage or resolution. —**steel wool**, long steel shavings compressed into a pad for use as an abrasive.

steel'y (stē'lē) *adj.* hard; unflinching. —**steel·i·ness**, *n.*

steel'yard" *n.* a balance scale.

steen'bok (stēn'bok) *n.* a small So.Afr. antelope.

steep (stēp) *adj.* **1,** almost perpendicular; precipitous. **2,** (*Colloq.*) excessive, as a price. —*v.i. & t.* soak; saturate. —**steep'en**, *v.i. & t.* —**steep'ness**, *n.*

stee'ple (stē'pəl) *n.* a lofty tower, esp. on a church; a spire.

stee'ple·chase" *n.* a horse race over obstacles.

stee'ple·jack" *n.* a person who repairs steeples, etc.

steer (stir) *v.t. & i.* **1,** direct and govern; guide; pilot. **2,** follow (a course). —*n.* a castrated male bovine, raised for beef. —**steering wheel**, a wheel used to guide a ship, automobile, etc.

steer'age (-ij) *n.* third, or lowest, class in a passenger ship.

steers'man (stirz'mən) *n.* [*pl.* **-men**] a pilot.

stein (stīn) *n.* a mug for beer.

stele (stēl) *n.* **1,** an upright slab of stone, usu. bearing an inscription or sculptured design. **2,** the central cylinder in the stem of a plant.

stel'lar (stel'ər) *adj.* starlike; pert. to stars.

stem *n.* **1,** the main body of a plant, the supporting stalk. **2,** a stemlike part, as of a goblet. **3,** ancestry. **4,** (*Gram.*) the unchanged part in a series of inflectional forms. **5,** (*Slang*) a street. —*v.t.* [**stemmed, stem'ming**] stop; check; stanch.

stem'ware *n.* glassware having a stem.

stench *n.* an offensive odor.

sten'cil (sten'səl) *n.* a form cut so that a design or letters can be rubbed through it; such a design or letters.

ste·nog'ra·phy (stə-nog'rə-fē) *n.* the art of writing in shorthand. —**ste·nog'ra·pher,** *n.* —**sten"o·graph'ic** (sten"ə-graf'ik) *adj.* —**sten"o·graph'i·cal·ly,** *adv.*

sten'o·type" (sten'ə-tīp") *n.* (*T.N.*) a keyboard instrument for writing phonetic shorthand.

sten·to'ri·an (sten-tôr'ē-ən) *adj.* loud and powerful in sound.

step *n.* **1,** one completed movement in walking, running, or dancing. **2,** the distance of a step; a short distance. **3,** gait; pace. **4,** a support for the foot. **5,** gradation; degree; interval. **6,** an expedient; a measure. —*v.i.* [**stepped, step'ping**] **1,** walk; go. **2,** dance. **3,** press with the foot. —*v.t.* **1,** (with *off*) measure by steps. **2,** perform, as a dance. **3,** grade; vary. —**step·ping stone,** something to step and pause on briefly.

step- *pref.* indicating relationship through the marriage of a parent, as *stepfather, stepson,* etc.

step-'down" *adj.* (*Electricity*) converting from a higher to a lower voltage. —*n.* a decrease.

step-'ins" *n.pl.* a woman's undergarment.

step'lad"der *n.* a short ladder held erect by a frame.

steppe (step) *n.* an extensive, treeless plain.

step-'up" *adj.* (*Electricity*) converting from a lower to a higher voltage. —*n.* an increase.

-ster (stər) *suf.* occupation.

stere (stir) *n.* a cubic meter.

ster'e·o (ster'ē-ō) *n.* (*Colloq.*) **1,** a stereoscopic photograph. **2,** stereophonic reproduction. **3,** a stereophonic sound system. —*adj.* (*Colloq.*) **1,** stereoscopic. **2,** stereophonic.

ster'e·o- *pref.* solid; three-dimensional.

ster"e·o·phon'ic (ster"ē-ə-fän'ik) *adj.* pert. to or rendering the illusion of true auditory perspective, usu. through the use of two or more microphones for recording and speakers for playback.

ster'e·o·scope" (ster'ē-ə-skōp") *n.* an optical instrument that makes photographs appear three-dimensional. —**ster"e·o·scop'ic** (-skōp'ik) *adj.*

ster'e·o·type" (ster'ē-ə-tīp") *n.* **1,** a type plate cast from a mold. **2,** a convention. —*v.t.* make a stereotype of. —*adj.* hackneyed; unoriginal.

ster'ile (ster'il) *adj.* **1,** free from living germs. **2,** barren; unproductive. —**ste·ril'i·ty,** *n.* —**ster'i·lize"** (-līz") *v.t.*

ster'ling (stēr'ling) *adj.* **1,** (of silver) of standard pureness, 92½%. **2,** (of money) in Brit. money, measured by the pound sterling. **3,** of great excellence.

stern (stērn) *adj.* harsh; austere; severe. —*n.* the hinder part, esp. of a ship. —**stern'ness,** *n.*

ster'num (stēr'nəm) *n.* [*pl.* **-nums; -na** (-nə)] the breastbone.

ster'to·rous (stēr'tə-rəs) *adj.* characterized by noisy breathing.

stet (*Lat.*) *n.* a proofreader's mark: *let it stand.*

steth'o·scope" (steth'ə-skōp") *n.* (*Med.*) an instrument for listening to sounds in the chest.

ste've·dore" (stē'və-dôr") *n.* one who loads or unloads vessels.

stew (stoo) *v.t. & i.* **1,** cook by simmering or slowly boiling. **2,** (*Colloq.*) fret; worry. —*n.* **1,** a dish of stewed meat, etc. **2,** (*Colloq.*) a state of agitation; a predicament. —**stewed,** *adj.* (*Colloq.*) drunk.

stew'ard (stoo'ərd) *n.* **1,** a manager or trustee; a chief servant. **2,** a servant, esp. in a club or ship. —*v.t. & i.* guard; conserve. —**stew'ard·ess,** *n.fem.* —**stew'ard·ship,** *n.*

stick (stik) *n.* **1,** a piece of wood, generally small and slender. **2,** a club; a rod; a cane. **3,** any slender piece. **4,** (*pl.*) (*Colloq.*) rural regions. **5,** a stab. —*v.t.* [*pret. & p.p.* **stuck** (stuk)] **1,** stab; pierce; prod. **2,** thrust (a pin, etc.). **3,** put. **4,** attach; fasten. **5,** (*Colloq.*) nonplus; puzzle. **6,** (*Slang*) impose upon. —*v.i.* **1,** remain; adhere; cling; abide. **2,** extend or protrude. **3,** (with *at*) scruple. **4,** be held fast; stall. —**stick-in-the-mud,** an old-fashioned, ultraconservative person. —**stick shift,** a manual transmission.

stick'er *n.* **1,** a persistent person. **2,** an adhesive label. **3,** (*Colloq.*) a puzzling problem. —**sticker price,** the retail price before any discounts.

stick'ler (stik'lər) *n.* one who is insistently precise. —**stick'le,** *v.i.*

stick-'to-it"ive·ness" *n.* determination; tenacity.

stick-'up" *n.* (*Slang*) a hold-up robbery.
stick'y (-ē) *adj.* **1,** adhesive. **2,** humid. —**stick'i·ness,** *n.*
stiff (stif) *adj.* **1,** rigid; not easily bent. **2,** moving with difficulty. **3,** formal; unbending. **4,** awkward. **5,** strong; hard; severe. **6,** expensive. —*n.* (*Slang*) a corpse. —**stiff'-ness,** *n.*
stiff'en (stif'ən) *v.t. & i.* make or become stiff. —**stiff'en·ing,** *n.*
stiff-'necked" (-nekt") *adj.* **1,** suffering from stiffness of the neck. **2,** (*Colloq.*) obstinate. **3,** (*Colloq.*) haughty.
sti'fle (stī'fəl) *v.t.* **1,** smother; suffocate. **2,** extinguish. **3,** suppress. —*v.i.* suffocate.
stig'ma (stig'mə) *n.* **1,** a brand or mark of infamy; a disgrace. **2,** [*pl.* **stig'ma·ta** (-mə-tə)] wounds corresponding to those of Christ crucified. **3,** (*Bot.*) the part of the pistil that receives the pollen. —**stig·mat'ic** (-mat'ik) *adj.* —**stig·mat'i·cal·ly,** *adv.* —**stig'ma·tize"** (-mə-tīz") *v.t.*
stile (stīl) *n.* a series of steps over a fence or wall.
sti·let'to (sti-let'ō) *n.* [*pl.* **-tos**] a slender, triangular-bladed dagger.
still (stil) *adj.* **1,** motionless; tranquil; silent. **2,** not sparkling, as wine. —*v.t.* silence. —*n.* **1,** silence. **2,** a distilling apparatus. **3,** a single photograph from a motion picture film. —*adv.* **1,** now as previously. **2,** nevertheless. —*conj.* nevertheless. —**still'ness,** *n.* —**still'y,** *adj.* quiet. —**still life,** a painting of inanimate objects.
still'born" *adj.* dead when born.
Still'son wrench (stil'sən) (*T.N.*) a monkey wrench used esp. for round objects.
stilt *n.* **1,** a high post. **2,** (*pl.*) two poles to extend the length of the legs, for walking above ground level. —**stilt'ed,** *adj.* stiffly formal.
Stil'ton cheese a rich waxy English mold cheese.
stim'u·lant (stim'yə-lənt) *n.* that which stimulates.
stim'u·late" (stim'yə-lāt") *v.t.* **1,** excite to action; invigorate. **2,** quicken. —**stim"-u·la'tion,** *n.*
stim'u·lus (stim'yə-ləs) *n.* [*pl.* **-li"** (-lī")] **1,** an excitation of a sense organ; what excites it. **2,** an incentive; any prod to action.
sting *v.t. & i.* [*pret. & p.p.* **stung**] **1,** pain by pricking. **2,** distress. **3,** goad into action. —*n.* **1,** the venomous organ of a bee, etc. **2,** a sharp pain.
sting'er *n.* **1,** that which stings or astounds. **2,** a sting of a bee, etc. **3,** a cocktail of brandy and liqueur.

sting'ray" *n.* a flat fish with a barbed tail. Also, **sting'a·ree** (-ə-rē).
stin'gy (stin'jē) *adj.* **1,** niggardly. **2,** scanty. —**stin'gi·ness,** *n.*
stink *v.i.* [**stank, stunk, stink'ing**] **1,** emit a strong offensive smell. **2,** have a bad reputation. **3,** (*Slang*) be incompetent, mediocre, or very bad. —*n.* **1,** a bad smell. **2,** (*Slang*) a protest. —**stink'er,** *n.* (*Slang*) a mean or dishonorable person.
stint *v.t. & i.* be stingy toward; restrict. —*n.* **1,** limitation. **2,** an allotted task.
sti'pend (stī'pend) *n.* fixed pay.
stip'ple (stip'əl) *v.t.* mark with dots or a grained pattern.
stip'u·late" (stip'yə-lāt") *v.t. & i.* **1,** settle by agreement. **2,** make a condition of; require. —**stip"u·la'tion,** *n.* a condition; requirement.
stir (stėr) *v.t. & i.* [**stirred, stir'ring**] **1,** set in motion; arouse; awake. **2,** circulate; agitate. **3,** move; move briskly. —*n.* **1,** activity; bustle; commotion. **2,** emotion. **3,** (*Slang*) a prison.
stir'ring (stėr'ing) *adj.* **1,** moving; affecting. **2,** rousing; thrilling.
stir'rup (stėr'əp) *n.* a loop to support a rider's foot. —**stirrup cup,** a farewell drink.
stitch (stich) *n.* **1,** in sewing, knitting, etc., one whole movement of the needle; its result. **2,** (*Colloq.*) a bit of clothing. **3,** a sudden muscular pain. **4,** (*pl.*) (*Colloq.*) unrestrained laughter. —*v.t. & i.* **1,** make stitches; sew. **2,** staple.
stoat (stōt) *n.* an ermine.
stock (stok) *n.* **1,** a stem; a race or line of descent; a breed. **2,** a family of languages. **3,** livestock. **4,** a principal supporting part. **5,** a supply of merchandise for sale. **6,** a reserve supply. **7,** the shares of a corporation: *capital stock.* **8,** the broth from boiling meat. **9,** a flowering garden plant. **10,** a wide necktie reaching to the chin. **11,** (*pl.*) a framework for confining petty offenders. **12,** the shoulder support of a gun; butt. —*adj.* **1,** kept on hand; staple; commonplace. **2,** pert. to a repertory theatrical company. —*v.t.* **1,** furnish with stock. **2,** keep on hand. —*v.i.* (with *up*) lay in a supply. —**stock exchange,** an association of stockbrokers. —**stock-in-trade,** *n.* the equipment necessary to ply one's trade; hence, the abilities, tricks, etc., of one's profession. —**stock market,** stock exchange. —**take stock in,** attach importance to.
stock·ade' (stok-ād') *n.* an enclosure of upright posts.
stock'brok"er *n.* a broker in corporate stocks.
stock'hold"er *n.* an owner of corporate stock.

stock′i·net″ an elastic machine-knitted fabric.

stock′ing (stok′ing) *n.* a knitted covering for the foot and lower leg.

stock′pile″ *n.* a reserve supply.

stock-″still′ *adj.* motionless.

stock′y (-ė) *adj.* short and thick. —**stock′-i·ness,** *n.*

stock′yard″ *n.* **1,** an enclosure for livestock. **2,** a slaughterhouse.

stodg′y (stoj′ė) *adj.* heavy and dull. —**stodg′i·ness,** *n.*

sto′gy (stō′gė) *n.* **1,** a long, coarse cigar. **2,** a heavy shoe.

sto′ic (stō′ik) *n.* one indifferent to pain or pleasure. —**sto′i·cal,** *adj.* —**sto′i·cal·ly,** *adv.* —**sto′i·cism** (-siz-əm) *n.*

stoke (stōk) *v.t.* & *i.* supply with fuel; tend. —**stok′er,** *n.*

stole (stōl) *n.* **1,** an ecclesiastical vestment. **2,** a woman's long neckpiece of fur, etc. —*v.* pret. of *steal.*

sto′len (stō′lən) *v.* p.p. of *steal.*

stol′id *adj.* impassive. —**sto·lid′i·ty** (stə-lid′i-tė) *n.*

stom′ach (stum′ək) *n.* **1,** the digestive organ. **2,** the abdomen or belly. **3,** appetite for food. **4,** inclination; liking. —*v.t.* put up with; endure.

stom′ach-ache″ *n.* indigestion.

stom′ach·er (-ər) *n.* a garment covering the stomach.

sto·mach′ic (stō-mak′ik) *adj.* aiding digestions. —*n.* a tonic.

stomp *v.* (*Dial.*) stamp. —*n.* **1,** (*Dial.*) stamp. **2,** a heavy dance.

stone (stōn) *n.* **1,** the substance of rock; a piece of rock; something made of rocks. **2,** a gem. **3,** a hard, rounded object, as a *hailstone.* **4,** a unit of weight, 14 lbs. **5,** a playing piece in various games (as go, bowls, etc.). —*adj.* of stone. —*adv.* (in compounds) completely, as *stone-deaf.* —*v.t.* throw stones at. —**stoned,** *adj.* (*Slang*) intoxicated with alcohol or drugs. —**Stone Age,** the era when stone implements were first used. —**a stone's throw,** a short distance.

stone′wall″ *v.i.* (*Slang*) refuse to give information so as to obstruct an investigation.

stone′ware″ *n.* a coarse pottery.

ston′y (stō′nė) *adj.* **1,** pert. to, or abounding in, stone. **2,** unfeeling; merciless. —**ston′-i·ness,** *n.*

stood (stůd) *v.* pret. & p.p. of *stand.*

stooge (stooj) *n.* (*Colloq.*) the foil for a comedian; a compliant dupe.

stool *n.* **1,** a single seat or rest without arms or back. **2,** an evacuation of the bowels. **3,** a decoy. —**stool pigeon,** (*Slang*) a spy; an informer.

stoop *v.i.* **1,** bend the body forward and downward. **2,** descend; condescend; lower oneself (to). —*n.* **1,** a stooping movement or position. **2,** a small porch and the steps to it.

stop *v.t.* [**stopped, stop′ping**] **1,** close up or block up, as a hole. **2,** check; impede; restrain. **3,** cease from; discontinue. —*v.i.* **1,** halt. **2,** cease; desist. **3,** tarry; make a stay. **4,** (with *by*) (*Colloq.*) drop in. —*n.* **1,** the act or result of stopping. **2,** a place where trains, etc., stop. **3,** an obstacle. **4,** (*Music*) a hole, fret, organ control, etc. —**stop′page** (-ij) *n.*

stop′cock″ *n.* a valve.

stop′gap″ *n.* & *adj.* a temporary expedient.

stop′light″ *n.* **1,** a red light displayed as a signal to traffic to stop. **2,** a warning light at the rear of an automobile.

stop′o′ver *n.* a brief stay, esp. one imposed by carrier schedules.

stop′per (stop′ər) *n.* one who or that which stops, esp. a closure for a bottle.

stop′ple *n.* a stopper in an organ pipe, flute, etc., to regulate pitch. —*v.t.* close or fit with a stopple.

stop′watch″ *n.* a watch whose movement can be stopped, as for timing races; chronograph.

stor′age (stôr′ij) *n.* act or fact of storing; safekeeping.

store (stôr) *n.* **1,** a place where goods are stored or kept for sale. **2,** a supply for future use. —*v.t.* **1,** stock. **2,** put away. —**store′room″, store′house″,** *n.* a repository. —**set store by,** esteem highly.

store′keep″er *n.* **1,** the proprietor of a store or ship. **2,** one in charge of stores, as in a military depot.

sto′ried (stôr′ėd) *adj.* **1,** celebrated in story. **2,** having stories.

stork (stôrk) *n.* a wading bird.

storm (stôrm) *n.* **1,** an atmospheric disturbance, with high wind, rain, or snow, etc. **2,** a vehement outbreak; a tumult. **3,** a violent assault. —*v.i.* **1,** blow, rain, etc. **2,** fume; rage. **3,** move with violence. —*v.t.* attack. —**storm′y,** *adj.* —**storm cellar,** an underground room for refuge from storms. —**storm window,** an insulating window outside a window.

sto′ry (stôr′ė) *n.* **1,** a literary narrative; an account. **2,** the plot of a novel, drama, etc. **3,** (*Colloq.*) a lie. **4,** [also, **sto′rey**] a floor of a building.

sto′ry·tell″er *n.* **1,** one who tells stories. **2,** a liar.

stoup (stoop) *n.* a basin for holy water.

stout (stowt) *adj.* **1,** bulky in figure; corpulent. **2,** bold and brave; firm. —*n.* strong ale, beer, or porter. **—stout'ness,** *n.*

stout'heart'ed *adj.* courageous; resolute.

stove (stōv) *n.* an apparatus for furnishing heat or for cooking. —*v.* pret. of stave (*in*). **—stove'pipe",** *n.* a pipe for carrying off smoke from a stove. **—stovepipe hat** (*Colloq.*) a tall silk hat.

stow (stō) *v.t.* **1,** pack (cargo, etc.); put away. **2,** (*Slang*) desist from. **—stow'age,** *n.*

stow'a·way" *n.* one who hides aboard a ship.

stra·bis'mus (strə-biz'məs) *n.* an ailment of the eye; cross-eyes. **—stra·bis'mal** (-məl) *adj.*

strad'dle (strad'əl) *v.i.* & *t.* **1,** sit or stand astride. **2,** (*Colloq.*) favor both sides. —*n.* a straddling.

Strad'i·var'i·us (strad"ə-vār'ē-əs) *n.* a fine violin made by one of the Stradivari family.

strafe (strāf) *v.t.* fire at (ground troops) from an airplane.

strag'gle (strag'əl) *v.i.* **1,** wander away; stray. **2,** spread irregularly or untidily. **—strag'gly,** *adj.*

straight (strāt) *adj.* **1,** without bend or deviation. **2,** upright; honorable. **3,** regular; unmodified; undiluted. **4,** consecutive. **5,** (*Colloq.*) heterosexual. —*n.* in cards, four cards in sequence. —*adv.* directly; at once. **—straight'ness,** *n.***—straight man,** the foil for a comedian.

straight-'arm" *v.t.* ward off (an opponent) by holding the arm out straight.

straight'a·way" *adj.* & *n.* without a curve, as a race course. —*adv.* (*Colloq.*) straightway.

straight'edge" *n.* a ruler.

straight'en *v.t.* & *i.* make or become straight.

straight"for'ward *adj.* **1,** direct. **2,** honest; open.

straight'way" *adv.* at once.

strain (strān) *v.t.* **1,** stretch to the utmost or beyond the proper limit. **2,** sprain. **3,** press through a filter. —*v.i.* exert oneself. —*n.* **1,** a stretching or deforming force or effect. **2,** great effort. **3,** a passage of music, **4,** streak; trace. **—strained,** *adj.* affected; forced. **—strain'er,** *n.* a filter or sieve.

strait (strāt) *n.* [Also, **straits**] **1,** a narrow connecting passage of water. **2,** a position of difficulty or need. —*adj.* narrow; confined; strict. **—strait jacket,** a restraining coat.

strait'en (strā'tən) *v.t.* impoverish; confine.

strait-'laced" *adj.* strict; puritanical.

strand *v.t.* & *i.* **1,** drive or run aground.

2, leave in a helpless position. —*n.* **1,** a piece of twisted yarn; a filament; a tress of hair; a string, as of pearls. **2,** a beach.

strange (strānj) *adj.* **1,** unfamiliar; new; unusual; surprising. **2,** alien; foreign. **3,** reserved; distant. **—strange'ness,** *n.*

stran'ger (strān'jər) *n.* **1,** a person not known. **2,** a newcomer.

stran'gle (strang'gəl) *v.t.* & *i.* kill by choking.

stran'gu·late" (strang'gyə-lāt") *v.t.* obstruct; compress. **—stran"gu·la'tion,** *n.*

strap *n.* a narrow strip of leather, etc. —*v.t.* [**strapped, strap'ping**] fasten, sharpen, or chastise with a strap. **—strapped,** *adj.* (*Colloq.*) without funds. **—strap'ping,** *adj.* (*Colloq.*) tall and robust.

strap'hang"er *n.* (*Colloq.*) a standing passenger on a bus or streetcar.

stra'ta (strā'tə; strat'ə) *n.* pl. of *stratum*.

strat'a·gem (strat'ə-jəm) *n.* a means of deception; a trick.

stra·te'gic (strə-tē'jik) *adj.* **1,** pert. to strategy. **2,** of vital importance. Also, **stra·te'gi·cal.**

strat'e·gy (strat'ə-jē) *n.* **1,** the skillful employment and coordination of tactics. **2,** artful planning and management. **—strat'e·gist,** *n.*

strat'i·fy" (strat'ə-fī") *v.t.* form in layers. **—strat"i·fi·ca'tion,** *n.*

strat'o·sphere" (strat'ə-sfir") *n.* the region of the earth's atmosphere 6 to 60 miles above sea level.

stra'tum (strā'təm) *n.* [*pl.* **stra'ta, stra'tums**] a layer, as of the earth's crust, of the atmosphere, etc.

straw (strâ) *n.* **1,** a single stalk of grain; such stalks when dried. **2,** a paper tube. **3,** a trifle. —*adj.* **1,** of straw. **2,** ineffective. **3,** pale yellow. **—straw boss,** (*Colloq.*) a subforeman. **—straw vote,** an unofficial test vote.

straw'ber"ry *n.* a low herb, its red fruit, or the color of the fruit.

stray (strā) *v.i.* wander; deviate. —*n.* **1,** a lost domestic animal. **2,** a homeless person. —*adj.* **1,** wandering. **2,** isolated; casual.

streak (strēk) *n.* **1,** a line, stripe, or mark. **2,** a stratum or vein. **3,** a disposition; a trait. **4,** (*Colloq.*) a run of good or bad luck. —*v.t.* mark with streaks. —*v.i.* **1,** move rapidly. **2,** become streaked. **3,** (*Slang*) run naked in public. **—streak'y,** *adj.*

stream (strēm) *n.* **1,** a course of running water. **2,** any continuous flow. —*v.t.* & *i.* flow in a stream.

stream'er *n.* **1,** a pennant. **2,** a headline across five or more newspaper columns.

stream′let *n.* a small stream, as of droplets.

stream′line″ *v.t.* **1,** shape so as to offer little wind resistance, like a drop of water. **2,** modernize by eliminating superfluities.

stream′lin″er *n.* a streamlined train.

street (strēt) *n.* **1,** a passageway for vehicles and pedestrians in a town or city. **2,** the part of such a passageway used by vehicles. **3,** such passageway and its abutting properties. **4,** a stock exchange.

street′car″ *n.* a trolley car.

street′walk″er *n.* a prostitute.

street′wise′ *adj.* (*Colloq.*) having experience with and understanding of conditions in urban areas, esp. those characterized by poverty and a high crime rate.

strength (strength) *n.* **1,** the power of exerting muscular force; power; vigor. **2,** potency; efficacy. **—strength′en,** *v.t. & i.* make or grow stronger.

stren′u·ous (stren′ū-əs) *adj.* energetic; vigorous. **—stren′u·ous·ness,** *n.*

strep″to·coc′cus (strep″tə-kok′əs) *n.* [*pl.* **-coc′ci**″ (-kok′sī″)] a microorganism that forms chains, causing certain diseases. Also, **strep. —strep throat,** sore throat with fever caused by streptococcus infection.

strep″to·my′cin (strep″tə-mī′sin) *n.* an antibiotic effective against certain diseases.

stress (stres) *n.* **1,** importance; emphasis; accent on a word or syllable. **2,** a strain. *—v.t.* **1,** emphasize; accent. **2,** subject to strain.

stretch (strech) *v.t.* **1,** draw out or extend to full length or extent. **2,** extend too far. **3,** (*Colloq.*) exaggerate. *—v.i.* **1,** extend over a distance, period of time, etc. **2,** be elastic. **3,** reach. **4,** (with *out*) recline; be prolonged. **5,** extend one′s limbs. *—n.* **1,** an extent of distance, area, or time. **2,** the act of stretching. **3,** a straightaway. **4,** (*Slang*) a term of imprisonment.

stretch′er (-ər) *n.* **1,** a litter. **2,** a device for stretching.

strew (stroo) *v.t.* [*p.p.* **strewed** or **strewn** (stroon)] **1,** scatter. **2,** overspread by scattering.

stri′a (strī′ə) *n.* [*pl.* **-ae** (ē)] a groove or ridge. **—stri′ate** (-āt) *adj.*

strick′en (strik′ən) *adj.* strongly affected or afflicted; struck; wounded.

strict (strikt) *adj.* **1,** precise. **2,** exacting; severe. **—strict′ness,** *n.*

stric′ture (strik′chər) *n.* **1,** a sharp criticism; censure. **2,** a morbid contraction of a canal in the body.

stride (strīd) *v.i.* [**strode** (strōd), **strid′-den** (strid′ən), **strid′ing**] walk with long steps. *—n.* **1,** a long step or its distance; a striding gait. **2,** (usu. *pl.*) progress.

stri′dent (strī′dənt) *adj.* creaking; harsh; grating. **—stri′den·cy,** *n.*

strife (strīf) *n.* conflict; discord; a quarrel.

strike (strīk) *v.t.* [**struck** (struk), **strik′-ing**] **1,** give a blow to; hit; attack. **2,** inflict (a blow, etc.). **3,** cause to ignite. **4,** stamp out; print. **5,** effect. **6,** come upon suddenly. **7,** appear to. **8,** lower; pull down. **9,** cancel. **10,** assume (a posture, pose, etc.). **11,** form (an acquaintance, etc.). *—v.i.* **1,** inflict a blow. **2,** run aground. **3,** grab at bait. **4,** (*Naut.*) yield. **5,** (with *out*) go; proceed. **6,** (with *upon*) discover. **7,** (with *out*) in baseball, have three strikes; (*Colloq.*) fail. **8,** engage in a strike. *—n.* **1,** a refusal by employees to work. **2,** (*Baseball*) a suitable pitch not hit. **3,** (*Bowling*) a knocking down of all pins with the first bowl. **4,** a discovery; an accession. **—strik′er,** *n.*

strike′break″er *n.* a worker who replaces striking employees.

strike′out″ *n.* in baseball, the act or instance of striking out.

strik′ing *adj.* impressive.

string *n.* **1,** a line, thread, cord, or thong; a tendril. **2,** (*pl.*) stringed musical instruments. **3,** a series; a chain. **4,** (*Colloq.*) a limitation or condition. *—v.t.* [*pret. & p.p.* **strung**] **1,** make a string of. **2,** (with *up*) hang. **3,** (*Slang*) hoax. **—string′y,** *adj.* **—stringed** (stringd) *adj.* having strings. **—string bean, 1,** a leguminous garden vegetable. **2,** (*Slang*) a tall, thin person.

strin′gent (strin′jənt) *adj.* **1,** vigorous; exacting; urgent. **2,** straitened. **—strin′-gen·cy,** *n.*

string′er *n.* **1,** a long horizontal timber. **2,** one of the sloping sides of a stairway. **3,** a part-time newspaper reporter.

strip *v.t.* [**stripped, strip′ping**] **1,** (with *of*) take away; deprive; divest. **2,** deprive of clothing. **3,** tear off (the thread of a screw, the teeth of a gear, etc.). *—v.i.* **1,** remove one′s clothes. **2,** (with *off*) separate. *—n.* **1,** a narrow piece, as of cloth or territory. **2,** a continuous series. **3,** a runway. **—strip′-per,** *n.* **—strip tease,** a dance in which the dancer gradually disrobes.

stripe (strīp) *n.* **1,** a streak or band of a different color or nature. **2,** a kind; character. **3,** (*pl.*) insignia. **4,** a whip stroke given in punishment.

strip′ling *n.* a youth.

strive (strīv) *v.i.* [**strove** (strōv), **striv′en** (striv′ən), **striv′ing**] **1,** make strenuous effort; endeavor. **2,** struggle; fight.

strob′o·scope″ (strob′ə-skōp″) *n.* an instrument for studying rapid revolution or motion. Also, **strobe.**

---

strode (strōd) *v.* pret. of *stride*.

stroke (strōk) *n.* **1,** a sweeping movement. **2,** a mark, as of a pen. **3,** an act of striking; a blow; a sudden affliction. **4,** a coup. **5,** a caress. —*v.t.* rub gently.

stroll (strōl) *v.i.* walk leisurely; saunter. —*v.t.* saunter through. —*n.* a walk for pleasure. —**stroll'er,** *n.* a baby carriage.

strong (strâng) *adj.* **1,** possessing or exerting great physical or moral power. **2,** powerful. **3,** extreme in kind; intense. **4,** rancid. —**strong'ness,** *n.*

strong-'arm'' *adj.* violent. —*v.t.* coerce by violence.

strong'box'' *n.* chest; coffer; safe.

strong'hold'' *n.* a fortress.

stron'ti·um (strän'tē-əm; -chəm) *n.* a metallic element, no. 38, symbol Sr. —**strontium 90,** a heavy radioactive isotope of strontium found in nuclear fallout.

strop *n.* a strap to sharpen razors.

stro'phe (strō'fē) *n.* a stanza or longer section of a poem.

strove (strōv) *v.* pret. of *strive*.

struck *v.* pret. & p.p. of *strike*.

struc'ture (struk'chər) *n.* **1,** that which is built. **2,** form; the mode of construction or organization. —**struc'tur·al,** *adj.*

stru'del (stroo'dəl) *n.* a filled pastry made of very thin dough.

strug'gle (strug'əl) *v.i. & t.* labor or contend urgently or strenuously.

strum *v.i. & t.* [**strummed, strum'ming**] play carelessly on a stringed instrument.

strum'pet (strum'pət) *n.* a harlot.

strung *v.* pret. & p.p. of *string*.

strut *v.i.* [**strut'ted, -ting**] walk pompously. —*n.* **1,** a strutting walk. **2,** a brace or support.

strych'nine (strik'nin) *n.* a colorless, odorless crystalline poison.

stub *n.* **1,** a projection; a short remaining piece. **2,** a space for memoranda, as in a checkbook. —*v.t.* [**stubbed, stub'bing**] strike (the toe).

stub'ble (-əl) *n.* **1,** stubs of grain. **2,** rough growth, as of beard.

stub'born (stub'ərn) *adj.* **1,** obstinately determined or perverse. **2,** tough. —**stub'born·ness,** *n.*

stub'by (-ē) *adj.* thickset; bristly. —**stub'bi·ness,** *n.*

stuc'co (stuk'ō) *n.* daubed plaster or cement on walls.

stuck (stuk) *v.* pret. & p.p. of *stick*. —**stuck-''up',** *adj.* haughty.

stud *n.* **1,** a protuberance, as a knob. **2,** an upright support. **3,** a buttonlike fastener. **4,** an establishment for breeding, as horses or dogs. **5,** a male animal or (*Slang*) person used for breeding. **6,** a form of poker. —*v.i.* [**stud'ded, -ding**] **1,** set with studs. **2,** scatter over at intervals. —**stud farm,** **stud** (def. 4).

stu'dent (stoo'dənt) *n.* one who studies; a pupil; a scholar.

stud'ied (stud'ēd) *adj.* **1,** deliberate. **2,** carefully considered

stu'di·o'' (stoo'dē-ō'') *n.* an artist's workroom; a place for painting, broadcasting, etc.

stu'di·ous (stoo'dē-əs) *adj.* **1,** diligent in study. **2,** thoughtfully attentive. —**stu'di·ous·ness,** *n.*

stud'y (stud'ē) *n.* **1,** the mental effort of understanding. **2,** an exercise. **3,** a branch of learning. **4,** deep meditation. **5,** deliberate contrivance. **6,** a portrait or sketch. **7,** a room for study. —*v.i.* try to learn; ponder; plan. —*v.t.* examine thoughtfully.

stuff (stuf) *n.* **1,** material. **2,** rubbish. —*v.t.* **1,** cram full. **2,** pack tightly. —*v.i.* eat greedily. —**stuffed shirt,** (*Slang*) a pompous person. —**stuff'ing,** *n.* filling.

stuff'y (-ē) *adj.* **1,** poorly ventilated. **2,** dull; prudish. —**stuff'i·ness,** *n.*

stul'ti·fy'' (stul'tə-fī'') *v.t.* make absurd or ineffectual. —**stul'ti·fi·ca'tion,** *n.*

stum'ble (stum'bəl) *v.i.* **1,** strike the foot; trip. **2,** stagger. **3,** blunder. **4,** (with *on* or *across*) discover accidentally. —*n.* a false step; a blunder. —**stumbling block,** an obstacle; a cause of downfall.

stump *n.* **1,** the truncated lower part of a tree. **2,** any remaining part or stub. **3,** (*pl.*) (*Colloq.*) legs. **4,** a political rostrum. —*v.t.* **1,** nonplus. **2,** (*Colloq.*) make political speeches in. —*v.i.* **1,** walk heavily. **2,** make political speeches.

stump'y *adj.* **1,** stocky. **2,** abounding in stumps.

stun *v.t.* [**stunned, stun'ning**] **1,** deprive of consciousness by a blow, etc. **2,** astound; bewilder; stupefy. —**stun'ning,** *adj.* (*Colloq.*) strikingly beautiful.

stung *v.* pret. & p.p. of *sting*.

stunk *v.* p.p. of *stink*.

stunt *v.t.* check or hinder the growth or development of. —*v.i.* (*Colloq.*) perform a stunt. —*n.* an athletic or other feat done to impress an audience.

stu'pe·fy'' (stū'pə-fī'') *v.t.* deprive of sensibility; shock. —**stu'pe·fac'tion** (-fak'shən) *n.*

stu·pen'dous (stū-pen'dəs) *adj.* astounding; prodigious.

stu'pid (stū'pid) *adj.* **1,** lacking ordinary activity of mind. **2,** inane. —**stu·pid'i·ty** (stū-pid'ə-tē) *n.*

stu'por (stoo'pər) *n.* insensibility.

stur′dy (stėr′dė) *adj.* strong; robust; unyielding. —**stur′di·ness**, *n.*

stur′geon (stėr′jən) *n.* any of various large fishes.

stut′ter (stut′ər) *v.t. & i.* utter or speak with breaks and repetitions; stammer. —*n.* a stuttering.

sty (stī) *n.* **1,** a pen for swine. **2,** any filthy place. **3,** an inflammation of the eyelid.

styg′i·an (stij′ė-ən) *adj.* dark; infernal.

style (stīl) *n.* **1,** a characteristic mode of expression or action. **2,** the prevalent fashion. **3,** a stylus; the pointer on a sundial; any pen, pin, or peg. **4,** a trade name. —*v.t.* **1,** design. **2,** name. **3,** shape the hair. —**styl′ish,** *adj.* fashionably elegant. —**styl′ist,** *n.* one whose style is distinctive.

styl′ize *v.t.* conform to a particular style, esp. in an artificial manner; conventionalize. —**sty″li·za′tion,** *n.*

sty′lo·graph″ *n.* a fountain pen having a fine tube instead of a nib.

sty′lus (stī′ləs) *n.* **1,** a pointed instrument, as for writing on wax. **2,** a phonograph needle.

sty′mie (stī′mė) *n.* in golf, obstruction by the opponent's ball; hence, any minor but insurmountable obstacle. —**sty′mied,** *adj.*

styp′tic (stip′tik) *adj.* checking bleeding.

sty′rene (stī′rēn) *n.* a thermoplastic substance.

sty′ro·foam″ (stī′rə-fōm″) *n.* a rigid plastic foam made from polystyrene.

sua′sion (swā′zhən) *n.* a persuasive effort.

suave (swäv) *adj.* urbane; bland. —**suav′i·ty,** *n.*

sub *n.* (*Colloq.*) substitute, submarine, etc.

sub- *pref.* **1,** under. **2,** inferior.

sub·al′tern (sub-âl′tərn) *n.* a junior officer.

sub″a·tom′ic *adj.* pert. to the particles or phenomena inside the atom.

sub″com·mit′tee *n.* a committee acting for a larger committee.

sub″com″pact *n. & adj.* (of) an automobile smaller than a compact.

sub·con′scious (sub-kon′shəs) *adj.* present in the mind but beyond consciousness.

sub·con′ti·nent *n.* a large area of land smaller than a continent.

sub·con′tract *n.* a contract to provide services or materials necessary for another contract. —*v.t. & i.* make a subcontract for.

sub′cul″ture *n.* a unified group or movement within a culture from which it is in some way distinguished.

sub″cu·ta′ne·ous (sub″kū-tā′nė-əs) *adj.* beneath the skin.

sub′deb″ *n.* (*Colloq.*) a teen-age girl, usually under 18, not yet a debutante. Also, **sub″deb·u·tante′.**

sub″di·vide′ *v.t.* divide (esp. real estate) into smaller parts. —**sub′di·vi″sion,** *n.*

sub·due′ (səb-doo′) *v.t.* **1,** overcome by force; conquer. **2,** prevail over. **3,** repress. **4,** soften; allay.

sub′head″ *n.* **1,** the title of a section under a main title; a subordinate heading. **2,** an official ranking next below the head.

sub·in′dex *n.* a symbol written to the right of and slightly below another symbol, as x_0 (read ''x sub-zero'').

sub′ject (sub′jikt) *n.* **1,** a topic; a theme; a person or idea being discussed. **2,** one under the authority of another, esp. a king. **3,** a recipient of treatment. **4,** (*Gram.*) the word representing the person or thing acting. —*adj.* **1,** under the power of another. **2,** (with *to*) exposed or liable to; conditioned upon. —*v.t.* (sub-jekt′) **1,** treat. **2,** expose. —**sub″jec′tion** (-jek′shən) *n.* —**subject matter,** substance (of a book, etc.).

sub·jec′tive (sub-jek′tiv) *adj.* **1,** pert. to the thinking subject. **2,** introspective. —**sub″jec·tiv′i·ty,** *n.*

sub″join′ *v.t.* add below.

sub′ju·gate″ (sub′jə-gāt″) *v.t.* **1,** vanquish. **2,** make subservient. —**sub″ju·ga′tion,** *n.*

sub·junc′tive (səb-junk′tiv) *adj.* (*Gram.*) expressing contingency, doubt, or supposition, not reality.

sub′lease″ *n.* a lease granted by a lessee. —*v.t.* [*also,* **sub′let″**] grant or receive a sublease.

sub′li·mate″ (sub′lə-māt″) *v.t.* **1,** elevate; purify. **2,** turn into, or replace with, more wholesome interests or activities. **3,** vaporize by heat and allow to solidify again. —**sub″li·ma′tion,** *n.*

sub·lime′ (sə-blīm′) *adj.* exalted; lofty. —**sub·lim′i·ty** (-lim′ə-tė) *n.*

sub·lim′i·nal (sub-lim′ə-nəl) *adj.* subconscious.

sub″ma·chine′ gun a portable machine gun.

sub″ma·rine′ *adj.* under water. —*n.* **1,** a boat able to submerge. **2,** (*Colloq.*) a large sandwich; a hero.

sub·merge′ (səb-mėrj′) *v.t. & i.* sink below the surface, as of water. Also, **sub·merse′.** —**sub·mer′gence, sub·mer′sion,** *n.*

sub·mers′i·ble (sub-mėr′sə-bəl) *adj.* capable of being submerged. —*n.* a submarine.

sub″mi·cro·scop′ic *adj.* too small to be seen with an optical microscope.

sub·min′i·a·ture *adj.* smaller than miniature.

sub·mis′sion (-mish′ən) *n.* act or effect of submitting.

sub·mis′sive (-mis′iv) *adj.* yielding; obedient.

sub·mit′ (səb-mit′) *v.t. & i.* [**sub·mit′ted, -ting**] **1,** yield. **2,** refer to another. **3,** propose.

sub·nor′mal *adj.* below average, esp. in intelligence.

sub·or′bi·tal *adj.* following a path too low for an orbit.

sub·or′di·nate (sə-bôr′di-nət) *adj. & n.* secondary; inferior. —**sub·or″di·na′tion,** *n.*

sub·orn′ (sə-bôrn′) *v.t.* bribe to perform an unlawful act. —**sub″or·na′tion** (sub″ər-nā′shən) *n.*

sub·poe′na (səb-pē′nə) *n.* a writ summoning a witness. —*n.* serve a subpoena on. Also, **sub·pe′na.**

sub′ro·gate″ (sub′rə-gāt″) *v.t.* transfer (a claim, etc.). —**sub″ro·ga′tion,** *n.*

sub·scribe′ (səb-skrīb′) *v.t. & i.* **1,** give consent to. **2,** endorse. **3,** engage to receive a magazine, etc., periodically.

sub′script″ *n.* something written low, as a subindex.

sub·scrip′tion (-skrip′shən) *n.* **1,** a signature; assent. **2,** agreement to pay, contribute, etc. **3,** an order for a periodical, season tickets, etc.

sub′se·quent (sub′sə-kwənt) *adj.* following in time; later; succeeding. —**sub′se·quence,** *n.*

sub·serve′ *v.t.* serve to promote (a purpose, plan, etc.); be useful to.

sub·ser′vi·ent (səb-sêr′vē-ənt) *adj.* **1,** subordinate. **2,** servile. —**sub·ser′vi·ence,** *n.*

sub′set″ *n.* (*Math.*) a set, each of whose elements belongs to a given set.

sub·side′ (səb-sīd′) *v.i.* **1,** abate. **2,** sink lower. —**sub·sid′ence,** *n.*

sub·sid′i·ar″y (səb-sid′ē-er″ē) *adj.* lending assistance; supplementary; secondary. —*n.* **1,** a subsidiary thing or person. **2,** a company owned or controlled by a larger company.

sub′si·dize″ (sub′si-dīz″) *v.t.* support financially.

sub′si·dy (sub′sə-dē) *n.* pecuniary aid.

sub·sist′ (səb-sist′) *v.i.* **1,** exist; have the means to live. **2,** continue. —**sub·sist′ence,** *n.*

sub′soil″ *n.* the soil next below the topsoil.

sub″son′ic *adj.* **1,** pert. to speed less than that of sound in air. **2,** moving or capable of moving at subsonic speed.

sub′stance (sub′stəns) *n.* **1,** any particular kind of corporeal matter; material. **2,** subject matter. **3,** wealth.

sub·stan″dard *adj.* of a level of quality, size, etc., below an established standard.

sub·stan′tial (-stan′shəl) *adj.* **1,** real; actual. **2,** genuine.

sub·stan′ti·ate″ (-stan′shē-āt″) *v.t.* establish by evidence. —**sub·stan″ti·a′tion,** *n.*

sub′stan·tive (-stən-tiv) *n.* (*Gram.*) a noun or pronoun; something that exists. —*adj.* **1,** pert. to a noun, etc. **2,** real; existing independently; essential.

sub′sti·tute″ (sub′stə-tūt″) *n.* a person or thing serving in place of another. —*v.t. & i.* supply or serve as a substitute. —**sub″sti·tu′tion,** *n.*

sub·sume′ (-soom′) *v.t.* bring (a class, case, etc.) under a larger class. —**sub·sump′tion** (-sump′shən) *n.*

sub·teen′ *n. & adj.* younger than thirteen.

sub·tend′ *v.t.* **1,** lie under or opposite to. **2,** enclose.

sub′ter·fuge″ (sub′tər-fūj″) *n.* an artifice; an evasion.

sub″ter·ra′ne·an (sub″tə-rā′nē-ən) *adj.* underground; hidden.

sub·ti′tle *n.* **1,** a secondary title. **2,** printed words shown in the course of a motion picture, usu. translating the dialogue into a different language.

sub′tle (sut′əl) *adj.* **1,** delicate; refined. **2,** artful; crafty. **3,** discerning; discriminating; shrewd. Also, **sub′tile.** —**sub′tle·ness, sub′tle·ty,** *n.*

sub·tract′ (səb-trakt′) *v.t. & i.* take away; deduct. —**sub·trac′tion,** *n.*

sub′tra·hend″ (sub′trə-hend″) *n.* a quantity to be subtracted.

sub·trop′i·cal *adj.* near the tropics; almost tropical.

sub′urb (sub′êrb) *n.* a district outside of, but adjoining, a city. —**sub·ur′ban** (sə-bêr′bən) *adj.* —**sub·ur′ban·ite,** *n.*

sub·urb′i·a (sə-bêr′bē-ə) *n.* the suburbs collectively.

sub·ven′tion *n.* a financial grant, esp. from governments.

sub·ver′sive (-vêr′siv) *adj.* tending or intended to overthrow (a government, etc.).

sub·vert′ (səb-vêrt′) *v.t.* overthrow; destroy. —**sub·ver′sion,** *n.*

sub′way″ *n.* **1,** an underground railway. **2,** an underground pedestrian passage.

suc·ceed′ (sək-sēd′) *v.i.* **1,** accomplish what is attempted; terminate, usually well. **2,** follow; come next. —*v.t.* come after; be heir to.

suc·cess' (sək-ses') *n.* **1,** a favorable termination. **2,** a person or thing that prospers. —**suc·cess'ful,** *adj.*

suc·ces'sion (-sesh'ən) *n.* **1,** a following in order; descent. **2,** the act or right of succeeding.

suc·ces'sive (-ses'iv) *adj.* following in order.

suc·ces'sor (-ses'ər) *n.* one who follows or replaces another.

suc·cinct' (sək-sinkt') *adj.* concise; brief. —**suc·cinct'ness,** *n.*

suc'cor (suk'ər) *n.* help. Also, **suc'cour.**

suc'co·tash (suk'ə-tash") *n.* a dish of lima beans and corn.

suc'cu·lent (suk'yə-lənt) *adj.* **1,** juicy. **2,** interesting. —**suc'cu·lence, suc'cu·len·cy,** *n.*

suc·cumb' (sə-kum') *v.i.* **1,** give way under pressure; yield. **2,** die.

such *adj.* **1,** of that kind, character, or extent; like; similar. **2,** the same as previously specified or mentioned. **3,** of that class or character. —*pron.* **1,** such a person or thing; such persons or things. **2,** the same.

such'like" *adj.* of this same kind; similar. —*pron.* persons or things of an indicated kind.

suck (suk) *v.t. & i.* **1,** draw into the mouth by creating a partial vacuum with the lips and tongue. **2,** absorb; inhale.

suck'er *n.* **1,** one who or that which sucks. **2,** any of various fishes. **3,** (*Colloq.*) a lollipop. **4,** (*Colloq.*) a dupe; a gull.

suck'le (suk'əl) *v.i. & t.* nurse at the breast. —**suck'ling,** *n.* a baby at the breast.

su'cre (soo'kre) *n.* the monetary unit of Ecuador.

su'crose (soo'krōs) *n.* cane sugar.

suc'tion (suk'shən) *n.* the process or condition of sucking; sucking force.

sud'den (sud'ən) *adj.* happening or done unexpectedly; abrupt. —**sud'den·ness,** *n.* —**sudden death,** in sports, games, etc., a method of breaking a tie in which the first contestant to score a point wins.

su'dor (soo'dər) *n.* sweat; perspiration.

suds (sudz) *n.pl.* **1,** water foaming with soap. **2,** (*Slang*) beer.

sue (soo) *v.t. & i.* **1,** institute process in law against. **2,** make a petition; woo.

suede (swād) *n.* undressed leather, esp. kid.

su'et (soo'it) *n.* fatty tissue.

suf'fer (suf'ər) *v.i. & t.* **1,** feel or undergo pain; sustain damage or loss. **2,** allow; permit; tolerate.

suf'fer·ance (suf'ər-əns) *n.* **1,** tacit consent. **2,** endurance.

suf·fice' (sə-fīs') *v.i.* be enough or adequate. —*v.t.* satisfy.

suf·fi'cien·cy (sə-fish'ən-sè) *n.* **1,** adequacy. **2,** a sufficient income.

suf·fi'cient (sə-fish'ənt) *adj.* adequate; enough.

suf'fix (suf'iks) *n.* a terminal formative element added to a word or root to make a derivative word. —*v.t.* (sə-fiks') attach at the end.

suf'fo·cate (suf'ə-kāt") *v.t. & i.* **1,** kill by impeding respiration. **2,** stifle; smother. —**suf'fo·ca'tion,** *n.*

suf'fra·gan (suf'rə-gan) *adj. & n.* assistant (bishop).

suf'frage (suf'rij) *n.* the political right or act of voting.

suf'fra·gist (suf'rə-jist) *n.* a person advocating female suffrage. Also, (*Colloq.*) **suf'fra·gette'** (-jet') *n.fem.*

suf·fuse' (sə-fūz') *v.t.* overspread, as with a liquid or tincture. —**suf·fu'sion,** *n.*

sug'ar (shûg'ər) *n.* a sweet crystalline substance. —*v.t.* **1,** sweeten. **2,** make agreeable. —*v.i.* form sugar. —**sug'ar·y,** *adj.* —**sugar beet,** a white beet yielding sugar. —**sugar cane,** a tall grass yielding sugar.

sug'ar-coat" *v.t.* **1,** cover with sugar. **2,** make more palatable.

sug'ar·plum" *n.* a candy.

sug·gest' (səg-jest') *v.t.* **1,** propose for consideration. **2,** intimate. **3,** call to mind by association.

sug·gest'i·ble *adj.* **1,** easily influenced. **2,** that may be suggested.

sug·ges'tion (-jes'chən) *n.* **1,** act or result of suggesting; a proposal; hint. **2,** a small amount; a trace.

sug·ges'tive (-jes'tiv) *adj.* **1,** tending to suggest. **2,** suggesting something improper.

su'i·cide" (soo'ə-sīd") *n.* **1,** intentional self-destruction. **2,** one who takes his own life. —**su"i·ci'dal** (-sī'dəl) *adj.*

suit (soot) *n.* **1,** a set of garments. **2,** a suing in a court of law. **3,** a petition or appeal. **4,** a courtship. **5,** a division of the pack of playing cards: spades, hearts, diamonds, or clubs. —*v.t. & i.* **1,** adapt. **2,** be appropriate. **3,** satisfy.

suit'a·ble *adj.* appropriate; becoming. —**suit"a·bil'i·ty,** *n.*

suit'case" *n.* a rectangular traveling bag.

suite (swēt) *n.* **1,** a series or set. **2,** a retinue.

suit'ing *n.* cloth for making a suit.

suit'or *n.* one who courts a woman.

su'ki·ya'ki (soo'kè-yä'kè) *n.* a Japanese dish of sliced meat and vegetables fried together.

Suk'koth" (sū'koth") *n.* the Jewish feast of thanksgiving.

sul'fa (sul'fə) *n. & adj.* designating certain antibacterial compounds, as **sul"fa·nil'·a·mide"** (-nil'ə-mīd") and its derivatives, **sul"fa·di'a·zine"** (-dī'ə-zēn"), **sul"fa·pyr'i·dine"** (-pir'ə-dēn"), **sul"fa·thi'a·zole"** (-thī'ə-zōl").

sul'fur (sul'fər) *n.* a nonmetallic chemical element, no. 16, symbol S, used in medicine, gunpowder, etc. Also, **sul'phur.** —**sul·fur'ic** (-fyûr'ik) *adj.* —**sul'fur·ous,** *adj.*

sulk *v.i.* be silently resentful. —*n.* a sullen mood.

sulk'y (sul'kė) *adj.* morose. —*n.* a light two-wheeled carriage used in trotting races. —**sulk'i·ness,** *n.*

sul'len (sul'ən) *adj.* morose; gloomy. —**sul'len·ness,** *n.*

sul'ly (sul'ė) *v.t.* stain; defile.

sul'phur (sul'fər) *n.* sulfur.

sul'tan (sul'tən) *n.* the sovereign of a Mohammedan country. —**sul·tan'a** (-tä'nə) *n.fem.* —**sul'tan·ate"** (-tə-nāt") *n.*

sul'try (sul'trė) *adj.* **1,** very hot and moist. **2,** passionate. **3,** (*Slang*) salacious. —**sul'tri·ness,** *n.*

sum *n.* **1,** the aggregate; total. **2,** a quantity of money. —*v.t.* [**summed, sum'ming**] **1,** add together. **2,** (with *up*) condense; recapitulate.

su'mac (soo'mak; shoo'-) *n.* a shrub; its leaves, used in tanning.

sum'ma·ry (sum'ə-rė) *n.* a condensed statement. —*adj.* **1,** brief; concise. **2,** (*Law*) immediately judged. —**sum·mar'i·ly** (sə-mär'ə-lė) *adv.* —**sum'ma·rize"** (-rīz") *v.t.*

sum·ma'tion (sə-mā'shən) *n.* a summing up; total.

sum'mer (sum'ər) *n. & adj.* the warm season; in the No. hemisphere, approx. June 21 to Sept. 21. —**sum'mer·y,** *adj.*

sum'mer·house" *n.* a small shelter in a garden.

sum'mer·time *n.* summer.

sum'mit (sum'it) *n.* the top; the highest point or degree.

sum'mit·ry (-rė) *n.* the political strategy of using conferences between heads of state to deal with international problems.

sum'mon (sum'ən) *v.t.* **1,** call or send for, with authority; call together. **2,** (with *up*) rouse. —**sum'mons,** *n.* an order to appear.

su'mo (soo'mō) *n.* a type of Japanese wrestling.

sump *n.* **1,** a pit in which water collects. **2,** an open drain. **3,** a reservoir. **4,** a cesspool.

sump'tu·ous (sump'choo-əs) *adj.* lavish; luxurious; grand. —**sump'tu·ous·ness,** *n.*

sun *n.* **1,** the central body of a solar system. **2,** the sunshine. **3,** anything splendid or luminous. —*v.t. & i.* [**sunned, sun'ning**] expose to the sun. —**sun bath,** exposure of the body to direct rays of the sun. —**sun lamp,** a lamp casting ultraviolet rays.

sun'bathe" *v.i.* take a sun bath, esp. in the nude.

sun'beam" *n.* a beam of sunlight.

sun'bon"net *n.* a bonnet shading the face.

sun'burn" *n.* a burning of the skin from exposure to the sun. —*v.t. & i.* affect or be affected by sunburn.

sun'dae (sun'dė) *n.* ice cream with syrup, fruit, etc.

Sun'day (sun'dė) *n.* the first day of the week, observed by most Christians as the Sabbath.

sun'der (sun'dər) *v.t. & i.* part; sever.

sun'di'al *n.* a device on which a shadow indicates the time.

sun'down" *n.* dusk; nightfall.

sun'dry (sun'drė) *adj.* several; various. —**sun'dries,** *n.pl.* miscellaneous articles.

sun'fish" *n.* **1,** a large seafish. **2,** a type of small sailboat.

sun'flow"er *n.* a tall plant bearing showy yellow flowers.

sung *v.* p.p. of *sing.*

sun'glass" *n.* **1,** a lens for producing heat by focusing the rays of the sun. **2,** (*pl.*) spectacles of tinted glass.

sunk *v.* p.p. of *sink.*

sunk'en (sunk'ən) *adj.* **1,** submerged. **2,** on a lower level. **3,** concave; hollow.

sun'lamp" *n.* an ultraviolet lamp used for therapeutic purposes or to produce artificial sunburn.

sun'light" *n.* light from the sun. —**sun'lit,** *adj.*

sun'ny (-ė) *adj.* **1,** bright with sunshine. **2,** cheerful. —**sun'ni·ness,** *n.*

sun'rise" *n.* appearance of the sun above the horizon.

sun'roof" *n.* a section in an automobile roof which can be opened to let in the sun.

sun'set" *n.* disappearance of the sun below the horizon.

sun'shade" *n.* a shield from the sun, as a parasol.

sun'shine" *n.* **1,** bright sunlight. **2,** cheer.

sun'spot" *n.* a dark patch appearing on the sun.

sun'stroke" *n.* prostration from the sun's rays or heat.

sun'tan" *n. & v.t. & i.* tan.

sun'up" *n.* sunrise.

sup *v.i.* [**supped, sup'ping**] eat the evening meal.

su'per (soo'pər) *n.* (*Colloq.*) superintendent, supernumerary, etc.

su·per- (soo-pər) *pref.* over, above, or beyond; superior; superlative; transcending.

su"per·an'nu·at"ed (-an'ū-ā"tid) *adj.* too old; past retirement age.

su·perb' (sû-pêrb') *adj.* magnificent; elegant; excellent.

su"per·car'go *n.* a person in charge of a cargo in transit.

su'per·charg"er *n.* a mechanism to force air into an engine.

su"per·cil'i·ous (soo"pər-sil'ē-əs) *adj.* haughtily contemptuous. —**su"per·cil'i·ous·ness,** *n.*

su"per·con"duc·tiv'i·ty *n.* unusually high conductivity, esp. in metals at very low temperatures.

su'per·cool" *v.t. & i.* cool (a liquid) below its freezing point without solidifying it.

su'per·e'go *n.* (*Psychoanal.*) a moral conscience that regulates the ego.

su"per·er'o·gate" (soo"pər-er'ə-gāt") *v.i.* do more than duty requires. —**su"per·e·rog'a·to"ry** (-e-rog'ə-tôr-ē) *adj.*

su"per·fec'ta (soo"pər-fek'tə) *n.* a perfecta requiring the correct choice of the first four finishers of a race in order to win.

su"per·fi'cial (soo"pər-fish'əl) *adj.* **1,** lying on the surface; external. **2,** not deep or thorough. —**su"per·fi"ci·al'i·ty** (-fish"ē-al'-ə-tē) *n.*

su·per'flu·ous (soo-pêr'floo-əs) *adj.* more than is needed. —**su"per·flu'i·ty** (-'ə-tē) *n.*

su"per·for'tress *n.* a large bombing plane, the U.S. B-29.

su"per·heat" *v.t. & i.* heat (a liquid) above its boiling point without vaporizing it.

su"per·het'er·o·dyne" (soo"pər-het'ər-ə-dīn") *adj.* pert. to a radio receiver that changes the frequency of the incoming wave.

su"per·high'way *n.* a multi-lane divided highway.

su"per·hu'man *adj.* surpassing ordinary human power.

su"per·im·pose' *v.t.* lay (something) over something else.

su"per·in·tend' (soo"pər-in-tend') *v.t.* have charge of; manage. —**su"per·in·tend'·ent,** *n.*

su·pe'ri·or (sə-pir'ē-ər) *adj.* **1,** higher in rank or office. **2,** more excellent; greater; higher. **3,** proud. —*n.* **1,** one superior to another. **2,** the head of a convent, etc. —**su·pe"ri·or'i·ty** (-or'ə-tē) *n.*

su·per'la·tive (sə-pêr'lə-tiv) *adj.* **1,** surpassing all others; supreme. **2,** excessive.

3, (*Gram.*) expressing the highest degree by being, or as though, modified by *most.*

su'per·man" *n.* [*pl.* **-men**] a man of extraordinary powers.

su'per·mar"ket *n.* a self-service retail market, usu. one of a chain, that sells food and other convenience items.

su·per'nal (soo-pêr'nəl) *adj.* **1,** lofty. **2,** celestial.

su"per·nat'ur·al *adj.* beyond the normal; not to be explained rationally.

su"per·no'va *n.* an explosion of a star and the resulting release of energy and light.

su"per·nu'mer·ar"y (soo"pər-nü'mə-rer"ē) *n.* an extra person or thing; a theatrical extra.

su'per·pose' *v.t.* superimpose. —**su"per·po·si'tion,** *n.*

su'per·pow"er *n.* **1,** the linking together of several power plants. **2,** a leading country of the world.

su"per·scribe" *v.t.* write on or over. —**su"per·scrip'tion,** *n.*

su'per·script" *n.* (*Math.*) a symbol written to the right of and slightly above another symbol, as x' (read ''x-prime'').

su"per·sede' (soo"pər-sēd') *v.t.* **1,** replace; supplant. **2,** set aside.

su"per·son'ic (soo"pər-son'ik) *adj.* **1,** above the audible limit. **2,** exceeding the speed of sound.

su"per·sti'tion (soo"pər-stish'ən) *n.* an unreasoning belief in an omen, supernatural agency, etc. —**su"per·sti'tious,** *adj.*

su"per·struc'ture *n.* something erected on a foundation.

su"per·vene' (soo"pər-vēn') *v.i.* be added; occur unexpectedly. —**su"per·ven'tion,** *n.*

su'per·vise' (soo"pər-vīz") *v.t.* oversee; have charge of. —**su"per·vi'sion** (-vizh'ən) *n.* —**su'per·vi"sor,** *n.* —**su"per·vi'so·ry,** *adj.*

su·pine' (soo-pīn') *adj.* lying on the back. —**su·pine'ness,** *n.*

sup'per (sup'ər) *n.* a light evening meal. —**supper club,** a restaurant offering entertainment; nightclub.

sup·plant' (sə-plânt') *v.t.* displace and take the place of.

sup'ple (sup'əl) *adj.* pliant; flexible; limber. —**sup'ple·ness,** *n.*

sup'ple·ment (sup'lə-mənt) *n.* an addition to something substantially completed. —*v.t.* (-ment") add to. —**sup"ple·men'tal** (-al), **sup"ple·men'ta·ry** (-ə-rē) *adj.*

sup'pli·ant (sup'lē-ənt) *n.* a petitioner. —*adj.* supplicating. Also, **sup'pli·cant** (-li-kənt).

sup'pli·cate" (sup'li-kāt") *v.i. & t.* entreat; petition. —**sup"pli·ca'tion,** *n.*

sup·ply' (sə-plī') *v.t.* furnish; provide. —*n.* **1,** the act of providing. **2,** a store or stock. **3,** the quantity available. **4,** one who fills a vacant position. —**sup·pli'er,** *n.*

sup·port' (sə-pôrt') *v.t.* **1,** bear; hold up. **2,** uphold; back; speak for; encourage; aid. **3,** provide for; maintain. **4,** act with or accompany (a performer). **5,** put up with; endure. —*n.* **1,** maintenance. **2,** a base; something that supports. —**sup·port'a·ble,** *adj.* endurable; tenable.

sup·pose' (sə-pōz') *v.t.* make a hypothesis; assume. —**sup·pos'ed·ly,** *adv.*

sup"po·si'tion (sup"ə-zish'ən) *n.* act or result of supposing.

sup·pos"i·ti'tious (sə-poz"i-tish'əs) *adj.* **1,** pretended; spurious. **2,** supposed. Also, **sup"po·si'tious** (-zish'əs).

sup·pos'i·tor"y (sə-päz'ə-tôr"ē) *n.* a small capsule of medication, usu. cylindrical or oval, introduced into the rectum, vagina, etc., where it is melted by body temperature.

sup·press' (sə-pres') *v.t.* **1,** restrain; abolish. **2,** repress. **3,** withhold from publication. —**sup·press'ant,** *adj.* & *n.* —**sup·pres'sion** (-presh'ən) *n.*

sup'pu·rate" (sup'yə-rāt") *v.i.* produce pus. —**sup"pu·ra'tion,** *n.*

su·pra- (soo-prə) *pref.* above.

su·prem'a·cy (soo-prem'ə-sė) *n.* state of being supreme; highest power. —**su·prem'a·cist,** *n.* one who believes in the supremacy of (a specified thing).

su·preme' (sə-prēm') *adj.* highest; utmost. —**Supreme Being,** God.

sur·cease' (sėr-sēs') *n.* cessation; end.

sur'charge' (sėr'chärj") *n.* an extra charge.

sur'cin"gle (sėr'sing"gəl) *n.* **1,** a girth for a horse. **2,** a girdle.

sur'coat *n.* an outer coat or garment.

surd (sėrd) *n.* (*Math.*) an irrational number.

sure (shûr) *adj.* **1,** confident; undoubting. **2,** certain. **3,** stable; unfailing; infallible. —*adv.* (*Colloq.*) surely. —**sure'ly,** *adv.* securely; certainly; doubtless. —**sure'ness,** *n.*

sure'fire" *adj.* (*Colloq.*) certain; assured of success.

sure'ty (shûr'ə-tē) *n.* **1,** security against loss or damage; a pledge. **2,** a guarantor; a sponsor.

surf (sėrf) *n.* the swell of the sea that breaks on the shore. —*v.i.* ride waves on a surfboard. —**surf'ing,** *n.*

sur'face (sėr'fis) *n.* **1,** the outside; an outer face. **2,** external appearance. —*adj.* pert. to the surface; superficial.

surf'board" *n.* a board on which one

stands in the sport of riding crests of waves.

sur'feit (sėr'fit) *n.* excess, esp. in eating or drinking; satiety. —*v.t.* satiate.

surge (sėrj) *n.* a large wave or billow; swell. —*v.i.* & *t.* swell.

sur'geon (sėr'jən) *n.* a physician who practices surgery.

sur'ger·y (sėr'jə-rē) *n.* **1,** the treatment of disease, injury, etc., by manual or instrumental operations. **2,** an operating room.

sur'gi·cal (sėr'ji-kəl) *adj.* pert. to surgery.

sur'ly (sėr'lē) *adj.* ill-humored; ill-tempered. —**sur'li·ness,** *n.*

sur·mise' (sėr-mīz') *n.* a conjecture; a guess. —*v.t.* & *i.* guess.

sur·mount' (sėr-mownt') *v.t.* **1,** pass over. **2,** overcome; prevail over. —**sur·mount'a·ble,** *adj.*

sur'name" (sėr'nām") *n.* a family name.

sur·pass' (sėr-pàs') *v.t.* be greater than; exceed; transcend. —**sur·pass'ing,** *adj.* greatly excelling; extraordinary.

sur'plice (sėr'plis) *n.* a white, loose-fitting clerical vestment.

sur'plus (sėr'pləs) *n.* **1,** what is left over. **2,** the excess of assets over liabilities. —*adj.* left over; excess. —**sur'plus·age** (-ij) *n.*

sur·prise' (sər-prīz') *v.t.* **1,** come upon unexpectedly. **2,** strike with astonishment. —*n.* **1,** a surprising act or event. **2,** astonishment.

sur·re'al·ism (sə-rē'ə-liz-əm) *n.* art interpreting the workings of the subconscious mind. —**sur·re'al·ist,** *n.* & *adj.*

sur·ren'der (sə-ren'dər) *v.t.* give up; relinquish. —*v.i.* give oneself up; yield. —*n.* a yielding.

sur"rep·ti'tious (sėr"əp-tish'əs) *adj.* **1,** done by stealth; clandestine. **2,** acting in a stealthy way. —**sur"rep·ti'tious·ness,** *n.*

sur'rey (sėr'ē) *n.* a light, four-wheeled carriage.

sur'ro·gate (sėr'ə-gāt") *n.* **1,** a deputy; a substitute. **2,** a judge having jurisdiction over the probate of wills, estates, etc.

sur·round' (sə-rownd') *v.t.* enclose on all sides; encompass; encircle. —**sur·round'ings,** *n.pl.* environment.

sur'tax" (sėr'taks") *n.* an additional tax, esp. on income.

sur·veil'lance (sėr-vā'ləns) *n.* **1,** a careful watch; supervision. —**sur·veil'lant,** *adj.*

sur·vey' (sėr-vā') *v.t.* **1,** view; scrutinize. **2,** determine the boundaries, extent, position, etc., of a piece of land. —*n.* (sėr'vā) **1,** a general view. **2,** a statistical study. **3,** a surveying. —**sur·vey'or,** *n.*

sur·viv'al (sėr-vī'vəl) *n.* **1,** fact of surviving. **2,** something that has survived.

sur·vive (sẽr-vīv′) *v.i.* continue to live. —*v.t.* outlive; outlast. —**sur·vi′vor,** *n.*

sus·cep′ti·ble (sə-sep′tə-bəl) *adj.* **1,** (with *of* or *to*) capable of being affected. **2,** (with *to*) liable. **3,** impressionable. —**sus·cep″·ti·bil′i·ty,** *n.*

su′shi (soo′shē) *n.* a Japanese dish of raw fish and vegetables served with a cake of rice.

sus′lik *n.* a ground squirrel of Asia and Europe; its fur.

sus·pect′ (sə-spekt′) *v.t.* **1,** imagine to be guilty, without proof. **2,** distrust; doubt; mistrust. **3,** surmise. —*n.* (sus′pekt) a suspected person. —*adj.* (sus′pekt) open to suspicion; doubtful.

sus·pend′ (sə-spend′) *v.t.* **1,** hold from above and keep from falling; cause to hang. **2,** interrupt; delay. **3,** defer; postpone. **4,** debar temporarily. —*v.i.* cease; stay.

sus·pend′er *n.* **1,** (*pl.*) straps to hold up the trousers. **2,** a garter.

sus·pense′ (sə-spens′) *n.* anxious expectancy or indecision.

sus·pen′sion (sə-spen′shən) *n.* **1,** act or result of suspending. **2,** a temporary stoppage; stay. —**suspension bridge,** a bridge held up by cables hung between towers.

sus·pen′so·ry (sə-spen′sə-rē) *adj.* suspending. —*n.* a bandage or appliance that holds something up.

sus·pi′cion (sə-spish′ən) *n.* **1,** the act of suspecting. **2,** a slight trace.

sus·pi′cious (sə-spish′əs) *adj.* exciting or feeling suspicion. —**sus·pi′cious·ness,** *n.*

sus·pire′ (sə-spīr′) *v.i.* sigh; breathe.

sus·tain′ (sə-stān′) *v.t.* **1,** maintain; support; keep alive. **2,** assist. **3,** endure; undergo. **4,** corroborate; affirm **5,** of a tone, prolong. —**sustaining program,** a radio or television program that is not sponsored.

sus′te·nance (sus′tə-nəns) *n.* **1,** act of sustaining. **2,** nourishment; means of living.

sut′ler (sut′lər) *n.* a peddler who follows an army.

su′tra (soo′trə) *n.* a Hindu or Buddhist religious text.

sut·tee′ (sut-ē′) *n.* the self-cremation of a widow in her husband's funeral pyre, formerly practiced by Hindus.

su′ture (soo′chər) *n.* **1,** a sewing together of a wound, etc. **2,** the thread used. —*v.t.* sew (a wound).

su′ze·rain (soo′zə-rən) *n.* a sovereign or state that exercises political control over a dependent state. —**su′ze·rain·ty,** *n.*

svelte (svelt) *adj.* slender.

swab (swob) *n.* **1,** a mop. **2,** a bit of cotton for cleansing or medicating. —*v.t.*

[**swabbed, swab′bing**] mop; wipe with a swab.

swad′dle (swod′əl) *v.t.* wrap (a newborn child).

swag *n.* (*Slang*) loot.

swag′ger (swag′ər) *v.i.* **1,** strut. **2,** bluster. —*n.* a gait suggesting arrogance.

swain (swān) *n.* a male escort; a lover.

swal′low (swol′ō) *v.t.* **1,** take into the stomach through the throat. **2,** accept credulously; take patiently. **3,** suppress; retract. —*v.i.* perform the motions of swallowing. —*n.* **1,** the act of swallowing. **2,** a mouthful. **3,** any of various long-winged, graceful birds. —**swal′low·tail′,** *n.* a cutaway dress coat.

swam *v.* pret. of *swim.*

swa′mi (swä′mē) *n.* **1,** lord; master: used of a Hindu religious teacher or monk. **2,** seer; prophet.

swamp (swomp) *n.* **1,** a marsh; a bog. —*v.t. & i.* **1,** flood; fill (a boat) with water. **2,** overwhelm.

swan (swon) *n.* a large, white swimming bird with a gracefully curved neck. —**swan song,** the last work or performance.

swank *n.* (*Slang*) pretentious smartness. —*adj.* [also, **swank′y**] stylish.

swans′·down′ *n.* **1,** very soft down from a swan. **2,** a fabric of similar softness.

swap (swop) *v.t. & i.* [**swapped, swap′-ping**] barter; exchange.

sward (swôrd) *n.* turf.

swarm (swôrm) *n.* **1,** a colony of honeybees. **2,** a mob. —*v.i.* throng.

swarth′y (swôr′thē) *adj.* dark in complexion. Also, **swart.** —**swarth′i·ness,** *n.*

swash (swosh) *v.t. & i.* splash.

swash′buck′ler (-buk″lər) *n.* a swaggering bully.

swas′ti·ka (swos′ti-kə) *n.* a form of cross adopted as the emblem of the Nazi party. Also **swas′ti·ca.**

swat (swot) *v.t.* [**swat′ted, -ting**] (*Colloq.*) hit sharply. —*n.* a blow.

swatch (swoch) *n.* a sample strip of cloth.

swath (swoth) *n.* **1,** a mowed path. **2,** the sweep of a scythe.

swathe (swāth) *v.t.* bind with a bandage; wrap.

sway (swā) *v.t. & i.* **1,** bend back and forth. **2,** rule. **3,** prejudice; influence. **4,** vacillate. —*n.* rule.

sway-′back″ *n.* abnormal sagging of the back, esp. in horses.

swear (swâr) *v.i. & t.* [**swore** (swôr), **sworn, swear′ing**] **1,** affirm something on oath. **2,** promise on oath; vow. **3,** curse. **4,** (*Colloq.*) (with *off*) give up (a habit, etc.).

sweat (swet) *v.i.* **1,** perspire heavily. **2,**

exude or condense moisture. **3,** (*Colloq.*) drudge; suffer; wait impatiently. —*v.t.* **1,** excrete or exude. **2,** cause to sweat. —*n.* the process or product of sweating. —**sweat′y,** *adj.* perspiring.

sweat′er (swet′ər) *n.* a knitted garment for the upper body.

sweat′shirt″ *n.* a warm pullover shirt, worn by athletes.

sweat′shop″ *n.* a factory where workers are oppressed.

Swed′ish (swē′dish) *adj.* & *n.* of or pert. to Sweden, its people, language, etc.

sweep (swēp) *v.t.* [*pret.* & *p.p.* **swept**] **1,** move by, or as by, a long brushing stroke. **2,** brush over with a broom; clear. **3,** pass over. **4,** drag over; trail. —*v.i.* **1,** clear with a broom. **2,** move steadily. **3,** extend. **4,** move ceremoniously. —*n.* **1,** an act of sweeping. **2,** reach; range; an extent; a curve. **3,** one who sweeps. —**sweep′ing,** *adj.* of wide range; overwhelming.

sweep′stakes″ *n.* a gambling transaction; a lottery.

sweet (swēt) *adj.* **1,** having the taste of sugar or honey. **2,** pleasing. **3,** amiable. **4,** dear; precious. **5,** nonacid; fresh. **6,** fragrant. —*n.* a candy, dessert, etc. —**sweet′ness,** *n.* —**sweet pea,** a climbing plant or its fragrant flower. —**sweet potato,** a climbing plant or its edible yellow root. —**sweet spot,** the area of a tennis, squash, etc., racquet designed to produce optimum rebound. —**sweet tooth,** (*Colloq.*) a liking for candy, etc. —**sweet William,** a plant of the pink family.

sweet′bread″ *n.* the pancreas of an animal, used as meat.

sweet′bri″er *n.* a long-stemmed rose; the eglantine.

sweet′en (-ən) *v.t.* & *i.* **1,** make or become sweet or sweeter. **2,** (*Colloq.*) render more pleasant or palatable. —**sweet′ening,** *n.*

sweet′heart *n.* a person beloved.

sweet′ie (-ē) *n.* (*Colloq.*) sweetheart.

sweet′meat″ *n.* a candy.

sweet-′talk″ *v.t.* cajole; flatter.

swell (swel) *v.i.* & *t.* [*p.p.* **swelled** or **swol′len** (swō′lən)] **1,** grow in bulk; bulge; expand. **2,** rise, as a wave. **3,** show elation. —*n.* **1,** an increase; a bulge. **2,** a wave. **3,** (*Music*) an increase in loudness followed by a decrease; the sign (< >) indicating this. **4,** (*Slang*) a socially prominent person. —*adj.* (*Slang*) **1,** elegant. **2,** excellent.

swell′ing *n.* a swollen part; a protuberance.

swel′ter (swel′tər) *v.i.* & *t.* suffer from heat. —**swel′ter·ing,** *adj.* sultry.

swept *v.* pret. & p.p. of *sweep.*

swerve (swėrv) *v.i.* & *t.* turn aside suddenly. —*n.* a sudden veering.

swift *adj.* **1,** moving with great speed; rapid. **2,** prompt. —*n.* a long-winged bird. —**swift′ness,** *n.*

swig *v.t.* & *i.* [**swigged, swig′ging**] drink by large drafts. —*n.* a drink; a deep draft. (*Colloq.*)

swill (swil) *n.* garbage; hogwash. —*v.t.* & *i.* drink greedily.

swim *v.i.* [**swam, swum, swim′ming**] **1,** propel oneself through the water. **2,** be immersed. **3,** be dizzy. —*v.t.* swim across. —*n.* **1,** act or period of swimming. **2,** a smooth, easy movement. **3,** (*Colloq.*) the trend of fashion, etc. —**swim′mer,** *n.* —**swim′ming·ly,** *adv.* easily; prosperously.

swin′dle (swin′dəl) *v.t.* & *i.* cheat; defraud. —*n.* an act or instance of swindling. —**swin′dler,** *n.*

swine (swīn) *n.sing.* & *pl.* **1,** the domestic hog. **2,** any animal of the hog family. **3,** a contemptible person. —**swin′ish,** *adj.*

swing *v.i.* & *t.* [*pret.* & *p.p.* **swung**] **1,** move to and fro, while suspended; sway. **2,** (*Colloq.*) be hanged. **3,** (*Colloq.*) manage. **4,** (*Slang*) be promiscuous. —*n.* **1,** a seat suspended by ropes. **2,** steady rhythm. **3,** the natural rhythm or movement (of something). **4,** (*Colloq.*) a style of dance music. —**swing shift,** (*Colloq.*) a shift of work from 4 p.m. to midnight.

swing′er *n.* (*Slang*) one who adopts in his life-style the permissive moral and intellectual attitudes of present-day youth: said esp. of members of the older generations.

swipe (swīp) *v.t.* & *i.* **1,** strike with a long, sweeping blow. **2,** (*Colloq.*) steal. —*n.* a sweeping blow.

swirl (swėrl) *v.i.* & *t.* whirl; eddy. —*n.* a twist; a curl. —**swirl′y,** *adj.*

swish *v.i.* & *t.* **1,** whisk; flourish. **2,** rustle. —*n.* a swishing sound or act.

Swiss (swis) *adj.* pert. to Switzerland, its people, etc. —*n.* a Swiss citizen.

switch (swich) *n.* **1,** a flexible twig or rod. **2,** a device for making or breaking an electric current. **3,** a change; a device for changing, as a *railroad switch.* **4,** a tress of hair. —*v.t.* **1,** whip. **2,** shift; divert. —*v.i.* change course.

switch′back″ *n.* **1,** a zigzag road or railroad. **2,** a roller coaster.

switch′blade″ *n.* a pocket knife with an automatic mechanism for opening.

switch′board″ *n.* a device for making telephone connections.

switched-′on″ *adj.* (*Colloq.*) in an elated mood; high (as on drugs).

switch-'hit"ter *n.* a batter who can bat right- or left-handed.

switch'man (-mən) *n.* [*pl.* **-men**] a tender of a railroad switch.

swiv'el (swiv'əl) *n.* a pivoted support. —*v.t. & i.* pivot.

swiz'zle stick (swiz'əl) a stick for stirring drinks.

swol'len (swō'lən) *adj.* swelled.

swoon *v.i. & n.* faint.

swoop *v.i.* sweep down. —*n.* a sudden sweeping down.

sword (sôrd) *n.* **1,** a weapon with a long edged blade. **2,** (*Fig.*) warfare; military power.

sword'bill" *n.* a hummingbird of So. Amer.

sword'fish" *n.* a large fish with a hard, pointed nose.

sword'play" *n.* the art or practice of fighting with swords; fencing.

swords'man (sôrdz'mən) *n.* [*pl.* **-men**] a skilled fencer.

swore (swôr) *v.* pret. of *swear*.

sworn (swôrn) *v.* p.p. of *swear*.

swum *v.* p.p. of *swim*.

swung *v.* pret. & p.p. of *swing*.

syb'a·rite" (sib'ə-rīt") *n.* a self-indulgent, luxury-loving person. —**syb"a·rit'ic** (-rit'ik) *adj.* —**syb"a·rit'i·cal·ly,** *adv.*

syc'a·more" (sik'ə-môr") *n.* **1,** (*U.S.*) the buttonwood or any plane tree. **2,** (*Eng.*) the maple.

syc'o·phant (sīk'ə-fənt) *n.* a servile flatterer. —**syc'o·phan·cy** (-fən-sē) *n.*

syl·lab'i·cate" (si-lab'i-kāt") *v.t.* form or divide into syllables. Also, **syl·lab'i·fy"** (-fī"). —**syl·lab"i·ca'tion, syl·lab"i·fi·ca'tion,** *n.*

syl'la·ble (sil'ə-bəl) *n.* the smallest separately articulated element in human utterance; one of the parts into which a word is divided. —**syl·lab'ic** (si-lab'ik) *adj.* —**syl·lab'i·cal·ly,** *adv.*

syl'la·bus (sil'ə-bəs) *n.* a compendium; an abstract.

syl'lo·gism (sil'ə-jiz-əm) *n.* two premises and a conclusion. —**syl"lo·gis'tic,** *adj.*

sylph (silf) *n.* **1,** an imaginary being. **2,** a slender woman.

syl'van (sil'vən) *adj.* **1,** pert. to the woods. **2,** wooded; woody.

sym"bi·o'sis (sim"bī-ō'sis) *n.* the living together of different species of organisms.

sym'bol (sim'bəl) *n.* **1,** an object standing for or representing something else; an emblem. **2,** a letter, figure, or character. —**sym·bol'ic** (-bol'ik) *adj.* —**sym·bol'i·cal·ly,** *adv.* —**sym'bol·ize"** (-līz") *v.t.*

sym'bol·ism (-iz-əm) *n.* **1,** a set of symbols. **2,** symbolic meaning.

sym'me·try (sim'ə-trē) *n.* **1,** regularity of accordance of form. **2,** excellence of proportion. —**sym·met'ri·cal** (si-met'ri-kəl) *adj.*

sym"pa·thet'ic (sim"pə-thet'ik) *adj.* **1,** feeling sympathy; compassionate. **2,** sharing a feeling. —**sym"pa·thet'i·cal·ly,** *adv.*

sym'pa·thize" (-thīz") *v.i.* feel or express sympathy.

sym'pa·thy (sim'pə-thē) *n.* **1,** fellow-feeling; compassion. **2,** condolence. **3,** agreement; approval; accord.

sym'pho·ny (sim'fə-nē) *n.* **1,** an elaborate musical composition for an orchestra. **2,** any harmony of sounds, words, or colors. —**sym·phon'ic** (-fon'ik) *adj.* —**symphon'i·cal·ly,** *adv.*

sym·po'si·um (sim-pō'zē-əm) *n.* **1,** a meeting for discussion. **2,** a collection of writings on one subject. [

symp'tom (simp'təm) *n.* a sign or indication, esp. of a particular disease. —**symp"to·mat'ic,** *adj.* —**symp"to·mat'i·cal·ly,** *adv.*

syn- (sin) *pref.* with; together.

syn'a·gogue" (sin'ə-gog") *n.* an organization or assembly of the Jews for religious instruction and worship; the building where this is held.

syn'apse (sin'aps) *n.* the place where impulses pass between cells.

sync (sink) *n.* (*Colloq.*) synchronization.

syn'chro·mesh" (sin'krə-mesh") *adj.* designed to produce synchronized, smooth shifting of gears: a *synchromesh transmission*.

syn'chro·nize" (sing'krə-nīz") *v.i.* agree in time; occur at the same time. —*v.t.* cause to agree in time. —**syn"chro·ni·za'tion,** *n.* —**syn'chro·nous** (-nəs) *adj.*

syn'co·pate" (sing'kə-pāt") *v.t.* (*Music*) accent beats normally unaccented. —**syn"co·pa'tion,** *n.*

syn'cope (sin'cōp) *n.* **1,** a contraction. **2,** brief loss of consciousness.

syn'dic (sin'dik) *n.* **1,** a person appointed to transact business for a corporation, estate, etc. **2,** a civil magistrate of various countries.

syn'di·cate (sin'di-kət) *n.* **1,** an association of persons or corporations in a particular enterprise. **2,** an agency that supplies features for simultaneous publication in different newspapers. —*v.t.* (-kāt") **1,** combine. **2,** distribute (newspaper features). —**syn"di·ca'tion,** *n.*

syn'drome (sin'drōm) *n.* a set of symptoms that characterize a certain disease or condition.

syn′er·gism (sĭn′ər-jĭz-əm) *n.* the combined effect of two or more agents (as drugs) that is greater than the effect of either of the agents used alone. —**syn″er·gis′tics,** *n.sing.*

syn′er·gy (sĭn′ər-jē) *n.* combined action or operation, as of muscles, drugs, etc. —**syn·er·get′ic,** *adj.*

syn′od (sĭn′əd) *n.* an ecclesiastical council. —**syn′od·al,** *adj.*

syn′o·nym (sĭn′ə-nĭm) *n.* a word having the same, or nearly the same, meaning as another. —**syn·on′y·mous** (sĭ-nŏn′ə-məs) *adj.*

syn·op′sis (sĭ-nŏp′sĭs) *n.* [*pl.* **-ses** (-sēz)] a summary; outline. —**syn·op′tic,** *adj.* —**syn·op′ti·cal·ly,** *adv.*

syn′tax (sĭn′tăks) *n.* the due arrangement of words and phrases in a sentence. —**syn·tac′ti·cal** (sĭn-tăk′tĭ-kəl) *adj.*

syn′the·sis (sĭn′thə-sĭs) *n.* [*pl.* **-ses″** (-sēz″)] the combination of separate elements into a complex whole; the product. —**syn′the·size″** (-sīz″) *v.t.*

syn′the·si″zer (sĭn′thə-sī″zər) *n.* someone or something that synthesizes; esp., a machine that reconstructs a given sound by recreating and combining its component frequencies.

syn·thet′ic (sĭn-thĕt′ĭk) *adj.* **1,** pert. to or based on synthesis. **2,** artificial. —**syn·thet′i·cal·ly,** *adv.*

syph′i·lis (sĭf′ə-lĭs) *n.* a chronic, infectious venereal disease. —**syph″i·lit′ic,** *adj. & n.*

sy·rin′ga (sə-rĭng′gə) *n.* a flowering shrub, esp. the mock orange.

sy·ringe′ (sə-rĭnj′) *n.* a device used to draw in and eject a liquid.

syr′up (sĭr′əp) *n.* any concentrated solution of sugar, flavored or medicated. Also, **sirup.** —**syr′up·y,** *adj.*

sys′tem (sĭs′təm) *n.* **1,** a number of things adjusted as a connected whole; a scheme, plan, or method. **2,** regular method or order. **3,** a concurrence of bodily parts. **4,** the entire body.

sys″te·mat′ic (-ăt′ĭk) *adj.* following a system; methodical. —**sys″te·mat′i·cal·ly,** *adv.*

sys′tem·a·tize″ (-ə-tīz″) *v.t.* make systematic.

sys·tem′ic (sĭs-tĕm′ĭk) *adj.* pert. to a system, esp. the body. —**sys·tem′i·cal·ly,** *adv.*

sys′to·le (sĭs′tə-lē) *n.* the normal contraction of the heart.

T

T, t (tē) the twentieth letter of the English alphabet. —**to a T,** exactly.

-′t contraction of *it.*

tab *n.* **1,** a flap or strap. **2,** a tag; label. **3,** a bill; accounting.

Ta·bas′co (tə-băs′kō) *n.* (*T.N.*) a seasoning made from pepper.

tab′by (tăb′ē) *n.* **1,** a female cat. **2,** an old maid. **3,** any watered silk fabric. —*adj.* striped or brindled.

tab′er·nac″le (tăb′ər-nak″əl) *n.* **1,** a place or house of worship. **2,** a receptacle for the Eucharist.

tab′la (täb′lä) *n.* a small tuned hand drum of India.

tab′la·ture (tăb′lə-chər) *n.* a system of musical notation using letters, numbers, or symbols other than notes.

ta′ble (tā′bəl) *n.* **1,** an article of furniture having a flat top supported on legs. **2,** a plane surface; a level tract of ground; a plateau. **3,** food served; fare. **4,** persons gathered at a table. **5,** an arrangement of written or printed information for classification in small space. **6,** a list. —*v.t.* **1,** place on a table. **2,** postpone discussion of. —**table tennis,** a game like tennis, usually played indoors on a large table; ping-pong. —**turn the tables,** bring about a reversal of circumstances or relations.

tab′leau (tăb′lō) *n.* [*pl.* **-leaux** (-lō; -lōz)] **1,** a picture. **2,** a striking scene. **3,** an arrangement or array.

ta′ble·cloth″ *n.* a cloth cover for a table.

ta′ble d'hôte′ (tä′blə-dōt′) (*Fr.*) a fixed meal of several courses served at a fixed price.

ta′ble·hop″ *v.i.* (*Colloq.*) go from table to table, visiting friends, as in a restaurant.

ta′ble·land″ *n.* a plateau.

ta′ble·spoon″ *n.* a spoon holding 1/2 fluid ounce. —**ta′ble·spoon″ful** *n.* [*pl.* **-fuls**].

tab′let (tăb′lĭt) *n.* **1,** a small flat slab or piece, esp. one intended to receive an inscription. **2,** a number of sheets of paper bound together. **3,** a flattish cake, as of soap; a pill.

tab′loid *n.* a newspaper printed on sheets about 15″ x 11″ in size. —*adj.* smaller than the usual size.

ta·boo′ *n.* a ban or prohibition. —*adj.* prohibited; ostracized. Also, **ta·bu′.**

ta′bor (tā′bər) *n.* a small drum.

tab″o·ret′ (tăb″ə-ret′) *n.* **1,** a low stand. **2,** a frame for embroidery. **3,** a stool.

tab′u·la ra′sa (täb′yə-lə-rä′sə) (*Lat.*) a blank slate or tablet; hence, the mind before it has received any sensory information.

tab′u·lar (tăb′yə-lər) *adj.* pert. to, or in the form of, a table.

tab′u·late″ (tăb′yə-lāt″) *v.t.* enter in a table

or list; put in the form of a table. —**tab″u·la′tion,** *n.* —**tab′u·la″tor,** *n.*

ta·chom′e·ter (tə-kom′ə-tər) *n.* an instrument for measuring velocity.

tach″y·car′di·a (tak″ē-kär′dē-ə) *n.* relatively rapid heart beat.

tac′it (tas′it) *adj.* **1,** implied or understood, not expressed. **2,** silent. —**tac′it·ness,** *n.*

tac′i·turn″ (tas′ə-tērn″) *adj.* saying little; reserved in speech. —**tac″i·turn′i·ty,** *n.*

tack (tak) *n.* **1,** a small, short nail with a large head. **2,** any temporary fastening; a basting stitch. **3,** a course in sailing, esp. one obliquely toward the wind; a leg of a zigzag course. **4,** a course in general; a line of procedure. **5,** food; fare. —*v.t.* **1,** nail with tacks; attach, esp. temporarily. **2,** steer (a sailing vessel) on a tack. —*v.i.* change course. **3,** baste.

tack′le (tak′əl) *n.* **1,** an apparatus for moving heavy loads. **2,** equipment or gear, as for fishing. **3,** the act of seizing or tackling. **4,** a position on a football team. —*v.t.* **1,** grasp. **2,** undertake to deal with.

tack′y (tak′ē) *adj.* **1,** sticky; adhesive. **2,** (*Colloq.*) dowdy. —**tack′i·ness,** *n.*

ta′co (tä′kō) *n.* a Mexican dish of a tortilla filled with meat, cheese, etc.

tact (takt) *n.* good judgment in dealing with persons; diplomacy. —**tact′ful,** *adj.* —**tact′less,** *adj.*

tac′tic (tak′tik) *n.* a particular expedient. —**tac′ti·cal,** *adj.* —**tac·ti′cian** (-tish′ən) *n.*

tac′tics (tak′tiks) *n.sing.* the art of maneuvering forces in battle.

tac′tile (tak′til) *adj.* pert. to the sense of touch. —**tac·til′i·ty,** *n.*

tac′tu·al (tak′choo-əl) *adj.* **1,** pert. to or arising from the sense of touch. **2,** communicating the feeling of contact.

tad *n.* (*Colloq.*) **1,** a small child. **2,** a small amount.

tad′pole″ (tad′pōl″) *n.* a frog or toad in the larval stage.

tael (tāl) *n.* a Chinese unit of weight; a money based on this weight.

taf′fe·ta (taf′i-tə) *n. & adj.* a lustrous silk or rayon fabric.

taf′fy (taf′ē) *n.* a candy made of molasses and sugar. Also, **tof′fee.**

tag *n.* **1,** a label tied or attached to something. **2,** a tatter. **3,** a binding on the end of a cord, ribbon, etc. **4,** something added, or at the end; a refrain, a moral, etc. **5,** a children's game in which one must pursue and touch another. —*v.t.* [**tagged, tag′ging**] **1,** furnish with a tag. **2,** (*Colloq.*) follow closely. —*v.i.* (with *along*) go as a follower. —**tag day,** a day on which contributions are solicited in exchange for tags.

—**tag sale,** a sale of used and unwanted items.

tai chi (tī′jē′) a Chinese system of exercise, characterized by slow, stylized movement. Also, **t′ai chi ch′uan** (chwän′).

tai′ga (tī′gə) *n.* a subarctic forest, as in Siberia.

tail (tāl) *n.* **1,** the posterior extremity of an animal, esp. a projecting appendage. **2,** any flexible appendage. **3,** the rear, bottom, concluding, or inferior part of anything. **4,** (*pl.*) the reverse of a coin. —*v.t. & i.* follow after. —**tail spin,** a spiral, nearly vertical descent by an airplane. —**tail wind,** a wind blowing in the direction of travel of an airplane.

tail′board″ *n.* the hinged platform at the rear of a truck. Also, **tail′gate″.**

tail′coat″ *n.* a man's coat with a long tail, for formal dress.

tail′gate″ *n.* tailboard. —*v.t.* (*Colloq.*) to follow a vehicle very closely, in another vehicle.

tail′light″ *n.* a warning light at the rear of a vehicle.

tai′lor (tā′lər) *n.* one whose business is to make and mend outer garments. —*v.t.* **1,** shape (a garment) to fit the body. **2,** outfit with clothing. —**tai′lor-made″,** *adj.* made to exact order.

tail′pipe″ *n.* the pipe discharging exhaust gases from the muffler.

taint (tānt) *n.* **1,** a stain or blemish. **2,** contamination. —*v.t.* tinge with something deleterious; corrupt.

take (tāk) *v.t.* [**took** (tûk), **tak′en**] **1,** get by one's own action. **2,** seize; capture. **3,** accept willingly; receive; swallow, absorb, etc. **4,** understand; construe. **5,** be affected by or infected with. **6,** attack and surmount. **7,** (often with *in*) deceive; trick. **8,** carry; carry off; remove. **9,** conduct; escort. **10,** choose; select. **11,** be the subject of; experience. **12,** need; require. **13,** subtract. **14,** (with *up*) enter into or upon. **15,** attract; please. **16,** (with *on*) undertake to do; employ; consume; acquire. **17,** ascertain, as by measurement. **18,** (often with *down*) write down; record. **19,** do; make; perform; execute, etc. **20,** (with *after*) resemble. —*v.i.* **1,** have effect; operate; develop. **2,** be successful; win favor. **3,** apply oneself. **4,** make one's ways; proceed. **5,** admit of being taken. —*n.* **1,** the act of taking; what is taken. **2,** (*Slang*) gross income or net profit. —**take the cake,** (*Colloq.*) win first prize. —**take a powder,** (*Slang*) leave. —**take out, 1,** date. **2,** (*Slang*) kill.

take-′home″ pay net wages received after deduction of taxes, etc.

take-′off″ *n.* **1,** a beginning, as of an

airplane flight. **2,** (*Colloq.*) a burlesque; an imitation.

take'o"ver *n.* the act or an instance of taking over, as of a company.

tak'ing *adj.* captivating.

talc (talk) *n.* a soft mineral, magnesium silicate.

tal'cum (tal'kəm) *n.* pulverized talc used as a powder.

tale (tāl) *n.* **1,** a narrative of events, real or imaginary. **2,** rumor. **—tale-'bear'er,** *n.* informer.

tal'ent (tal'ənt) *n.* **1,** an inborn ability or aptitude. **2,** persons of ability. **3,** performers. **4,** an ancient widely variable unit of weight. **—tal'ent-ed,** *adj.*

ta'les (tā'lēz) *n.* a number of persons summoned to serve on a jury panel. **—tales'man** (tālz'mən) *n.* a person so summoned.

tal'is·man (tal'is-mən) *n.* [*pl.* **-mans**] an inscribed amulet or charm.

talk (tâk) *v.i.* **1,** utter words by the voice; speak. **2,** interchange thoughts; converse. **3,** chatter; prate; gossip. **—v.t. 1,** say; speak. **2,** discuss. **—n. 1,** the act of talking; speech. **2,** a conference or discussion. **3,** report; rumor. **4,** a subject of talk. **5,** manner of talking; language; dialect. **—talking machine,** a phonograph. **—talking** picture [also, *colloq.,* **talkie**], a motion picture with vocal sound. **—talk show,** (*Colloq.*) a radio or TV program consisting of interviews, sometimes with viewers or listeners participating by telephone.

talk'a·tive (-ə-tiv) *adj.* inclined to talk much. **—talk'a·tive·ness,** *n.*

talk'ing-to" *n.* (*Colloq.*) a scolding.

tall (tâl) *adj.* **1,** having relatively great stature; high. **2,** having a specified height. **3,** (*Colloq.*) difficult to believe; extraordinary. **—tall'ness,** *n.*

tall'boy" *n.* highboy.

tal'low (tal'ō) *n.* an oily substance used for making candles, soap, etc.

tal'ly (tal'ē) *n.* **1,** an account kept of items; a reckoning or score. **2,** a tag or label. **3,** agreement. **—v.t. 1,** record; register; score. **2,** count; enumerate. **3,** furnish with a tally; tag. **4,** cause to correspond. **—v.i.** be in correspondence; accord.

tal'ly-ho" (tal'ē-hō") *n.* a coach drawn by four horses. **—interj.** used by hunters on sighting a fox.

Tal'mud *n.* a collection of authoritative dicta on the Jewish religious law and life.

tal'on (tal'ən) *n.* **1,** a claw, esp. of a bird of prey. **2,** playing cards remaining after the deal.

ta'lus (tā'ləs) *n.* **1,** [*pl.* **-li** (-lī)] the ankle-bone. **2,** a slope.

tam *n.* tam o'shanter.

ta·ma'le (tə-mä'lē) *n.* a Mexican dish of corn and minced meat.

tam'a·rack" (tam'ə-rak") *n.* an American larch tree.

tam'a·rind (tam'ə-rind) *n.* a tropical tree or its sweet fruit.

tam"bou·rine' (tam"bə-rēn') *n.* a small single-headed drum with jingling metal disks set in its frame.

tame (tām) *adj.* **1,** changed from the wild state; domesticated. **2,** gentle; tractable; docile. **3,** dull; insipid. **—v.t.** make tame. **—tam'a·ble,** *adj.* **—tame'ness,** *n.*

tam"o'shan'ter (tam"ə-shan'tər) *n.* [also, **tam**] a Scottish flat cap or hat.

tamp *v.t.* press down by repeated strokes; pound lightly. **—tamp'er,** *n.*

tam'per (tam'pər) *v.i.* meddle; touch improperly or harmfully.

tam'pon *n.* **1,** an absorbent plug to stop or absorb hemorrhage. **2,** a type of sanitary napkin.

tan *v.t.* [**tanned, tan'ning**] **1,** convert (a hide) into leather. **2,** make brown by exposure to the sun. **3,** (*Colloq.*) thrash. **—n.** become tanned. **—n. & adj.** a yellowish-brown color, as from exposure to the sun.

tan'a·ger (tan'ə-jər) *n.* a small songbird.

tan'bark" *n.* crushed bark used for tanning.

tan'dem (tan'dəm) *adv.* one behind another.

tang *n.* **1,** a strong or distinctive taste or flavor. **2,** a sharp sound; a twang. **3,** a slender projecting part of an object. **—v.i.** clang; twang. **—tang'y,** *adj.*

tan'ge·lo (tan'jə-lō) *n.* a cross between a tangerine and a grapefruit.

tan'gent (tan'jənt) *n.* **1,** a straight line marking the direction of motion of a point at any instant in generating a plane curve. **2,** a sudden divergence from one course to another. **3,** a trigonometric ratio. **—adj. 1,** touching. **2,** being a tangent. **—tan·gen'tial** (-jen'shəl) *adj.*

tan"ge·rine' (tan"jə-rēn') *n.* **1,** a small, loose-skinned variety of orange. **2,** a reddish-orange color.

tan'gi·ble (tan'jə-bəl) *adj.* **1,** capable of being touched; having corporeal existence. **2,** definite or concrete; capable of being realized. **—tan"gi·bil'i·ty,** *n.*

tan'gle (tang'gəl) *v.t.* **1,** unite confusedly; snarl. **2,** catch, as in a trap; perplex. **—v.i.** be or become tangled. **—n.** a mass of tangled fibers; a confused jumble.

tan′go (tang′gō) *n.* a So. Amer. round dance for couples.

tan′gram (tang′grəm) *n.* a Chinese puzzle.

tank *n.* **1**, a large receptacle for storing fluids. **2**, a pool of water. **3**, an armored self-propelled combat vehicle. —**tank′age** *n.* —**tanked**, *adj.* (*Slang*) drunk. —**tank suit**, a one-piece bathing suit. —**tank top**, a type of T-shirt. —**tank up**, (*Colloq.*) **1**, fill a gas tank. **2**, drink.

tank′ard (tank′ərd) *n.* a large drinking cup with a hinged lid.

tank′er *n.* a ship for transporting oil.

tan′ner (tan′ər) *n.* **1**, one who tans hides. **2**, (*Brit.*) a sixpence. —**tan′ner·y**, *n.* a tanner's place of business.

tan′nin *n.* a substance used in tanning hides: *tannic acid*.

tan′sy (tan′zē) *n.* a flowering weed.

tan′ta·lize″ (tan′tə-līz″) *v.t.* tease by arousing and disappointing expectation.

tan′ta·lum (tan′tə-ləm) *n.* a corrosion-resistant metallic element with high melting point, no. 73, symbol Ta.

tan′ta·mount″ (tan′tə-mownt″) *adj.* equivalent, as in value, force, or effect.

tan′trum (tan′trəm) *n.* (*often used in pl.*) a fit of temper.

Tao′ism (dow′iz-əm) *n.* a Chinese religious system. —**Tao′ist**, *adj. & n.*

tap *v.t.* [**tapped, tap′ping**] **1**, strike lightly; pat. **2**, pierce or unplug (a container) to draw off liquid. **3**, provide outlets for (an electric wire, etc.). **4**, cut an internal screw thread in. **5**, connect into so as to listen, as a telephone line. —*v.i.* strike light blows; rap audibly. —*n.* **1**, a gentle blow; an audible rap. **2**, (*pl.*) a military signal on a bugle or drum: *lights out*. **3**, a piece of leather or metal fastened to the bottom of a shoe. **4**, a plug, faucet, or spigot in a hole. **5**, an outlet. **6**, an instrument for cutting internal screw threads. —**on tap, 1**, ready to be drawn, as liquor from a cask. **2**, ready for use. —**tap dance**, one in which the rhythm is tapped with the feet.

tape (tāp) *n.* a long, narrow band of flexible material. —*v.t.* bind or fasten with tape. —**tape deck**, a tape recorder without an amplifier included. —**tape measure**, a tape marked for measuring distance. —**tape recording**, a recording of sound on magnetized plastic tape, by means of an electronic device called a *tape recorder*.

ta′per (tā′pər) *v.i.* **1**, become gradually slenderer at one end. **2**, become gradually less; diminish. —*v.t.* make in tapered form; cause to diminish. —*v.i.* (with *off*) gradually reduce consumption of something. —*n.* **1**,

gradual diminution of width. **2**, a slender candle.

tap′es·try (tap′is-trē) *n.* a woven fabric reproducing elaborate designs, often pictorial.

tape′worm″ *n.* a parasitic worm that lives in the intestines of humans and animals.

tap″i·o′ca (tap″ē-ō′kə) *n.* a starchy food substance.

ta′pir (tā′pər) *n.* a tropical hoofed mammal resembling swine.

tap′pet (tap′it) *n.* a cam.

tap′room″ *n.* a barroom.

tap′root″ *n.* a main root.

taps *n.sing.* see *tap, n.*, def. 2.

tap′ster *n.* a bartender.

tar (tär) *n.* **1**, any of various dark, viscid products obtained from organic substances, as wood, coal, etc.; pitch. **2**, a sailor. —*v.t.* [**tarred, tar′ring**] smear with, or as with, tar. —**tar′ry** (tär′ē) *adj.*

tar″an·tel′la (tar″ən-tel′ə) *n.* a whirling Ital. dance; its music.

ta·ran′tu·la (tə-ran′chə-lə) *n.* any of various large spiders.

tar′dy (tär′dē) *adj.* **1**, not punctual; late. **2**, moving slowly; sluggish. —**tar′di·ness**, *n.*

tare (tār) *n.* **1**, a weed; vetch. **2**, the weight of a container or vehicle without contents.

tar′get (tär′git) *n.* **1**, a design of concentric circles, aimed at in a shooting contest. **2**, anything aimed or shot at. **3**, a goal or objective.

tar′iff (tar′if) *n.* **1**, the duties levied on imports; customs. **2**, any table or system of charges; a price list.

Tar′mac (tär′mak) *n.* (*T.N.*) a paving substance.

tarn (tärn) *n.* a small mountain lake or pool.

tar′nish (tär′nish) *v.t.* **1**, dull the luster of; discolor. **2**, cast a stain upon; sully. —*v.i.* become tarnished. —*n.* discoloration or impurity.

ta′ro (tä′rō) *n.* a starchy, tuberous plant of tropical regions.

ta′rot (ta′rō) *n.* **1**, any of a set of 22 pictorial playing cards used for fortune-telling. **2**, a card game played with the 22 tarots added to 52 cards of the usual suits.

tar·pau′lin (tär-pâ′lin) *n.* a cloth cover of waterproofed canvas.

tar′pon (tär′pon) *n.* a large game fish of warm Atlantic regions.

tar′ra·gon″ (tar′ə-gon″) *n.* a plant whose leaves are used in seasoning.

tar′ry (tar′ē) *v.i.* **1**, remain in a place; stay; sojourn. **2**, delay or be tardy; linger.

tar′sus (tär′səs) *n.* [*pl.* **-si** (-sī)] a bone structure joining ankle and foot. —**tar′sal,** *adj.*

tart (tärt) *adj.* **1,** acid or sour to the taste. **2,** sharp in character or expression; biting; sarcastic, etc. —*n.* **1,** a small fruit pie. **2,** (*Slang*) a woman of low character. —**tart′-ness,** *n.*

tar′tan (tär′tən) *n.* a woolen or worsted cloth with a pattern of crossing varicolored stripes; a plaid.

Tar′tar (tär′tər) *n.* Tatar.

tar′tar (tär′tər) *n.* **1,** an earthy substance deposited on the teeth by the saliva. **2,** potassium tartrate as used in various drugs. **3,** an adversary hard to overcome. —**tar-tar′ic** (-tär′ik) *adj.*—**cream of tartar,** purified tartar, used in baking. —**tartar sauce,** mayonnaise dressing with chopped pickles, herbs, olives, and capers. —**tartar steak,** chopped beef, eaten raw.

task (tàsk) *n.* **1,** a definite amount of work to be done; a job or stint. **2,** a burdensome piece of work. —*v.t.* put a strain upon. —**task force,** a naval force acting as a unit.

task′mas″ter *n.* one who assigns tasks (esp., hard tasks) to others.

Tas·ma′ni·an devil (taz-mā′nē-ən) a burrowing carnivorous marsupial of Tasmania.

Tass (tas) *n.* the official news agency of the U.S.S.R.

tas′sel (tas′əl) *n.* a pendent fringe of threads.

taste (tāst) *v.t.* & *i.* **1,** try or perceive the flavor of by taking into the mouth. **2,** eat or drink a little of. —*v.i.* have a specified flavor. —*n.* **1,** the sense by which flavor or savor is perceived, operating through organs in the mouth. **2,** flavor or quality as perceived by these organs. **3,** the act of tasting. **4,** a portion tasted; a morsel. **5,** a liking; predilection; relish. **6,** particular preference. **7,** good judgment in aesthetic matters. —**taste′ful,** *adj.* showing good taste. —**tast′y,** *adj.* palatable. —**taste bud,** one of special organs of taste, a group of cells on the tongue.

tat *v.t.* & *i.* [**tat′ted, -ting**] knot thread with a shuttle, to make lace.

ta·ta′mi (tə-tä′mē) *n.* a Japanese floor covering.

Ta′tar (tä′tər) *n.* one of an Asiatic people related to the Turks.

tat′ter (tat′ər) *n.* **1,** a torn piece of cloth hanging from a garment. **2,** (*pl.*) ragged or torn clothing.

tat″ter·de·mal′i·on (tat″ər-də-māl′yən) *n.* a ragged fellow.

tat′ter·sall″ (tat′ər-sâl″) *n.* & *adj.* (of cloth) consisting of dark squares on a light background.

tat′ting (tat′ing) *n.* a kind of knotted lace made of thread.

tat′tle (tat′əl) *v.i.* **1,** gossip; divulge secrets. **2,** talk idly; chatter. —*v.t.* disclose by tattling. —*n.* idle talk; gossip. —**tat′tler, tat′tle·tale″,** *n.* a gossip; an informer.

tat·too′ (ta-too′) *n.* **1,** a picture, etc., inscribed on the skin by the insertion of pigments. **2,** a bugle or drumming signal calling soldiers to their quarters. —*v.t.* mark with tattoos.

tau (tow) *n.* the nineteenth letter of the Greek alphabet (T, τ).

taught (tât) *v.* pret. & p.pl. of *teach.*

taunt (tânt) *v.t.* **1,** reproach scornfully; ridicule. **2,** twit; provoke. —*n.* a gibe; taunting statement.

taupe (tōp) *n.* & *adj.* mole-colored; gray-brown.

tau′rine (tä′rīn) *adj.* pert. to, or resembling, a bull.

Tau′rus (tôr′əs) *n.* a constellation, the Bull (see *zodiac*).

taut (tât) *adj.* **1,** stretched or drawn tight; tense, not slack. **2,** tidy; neat. —**taut′en,** *v.t.* & *i.* make or become taut. —**taut′ness,** *n.*

tau·tog′ (tâ-tog′) *n.* a food fish of the U.S. Atlantic coast.

tau·tol′o·gy (tâ-tol′ə-jē) *n.* needless repetition of the same idea in other words. —**tau″to·log′i·cal** (tâ″tə-loj′ə-kəl) *adj.*

tav′ern (tav′ərn) *n.* **1,** a house in which liquor is sold to be drunk on the premises. **2,** an inn.

taw (tâ) *n.* a game played with marbles; a marble; a line from which the players shoot.

taw′dry (tâ′drē) *adj.* showy but tasteless; gaudy; cheap. —**taw′dri·ness,** *n.*

taw′ny (tâ′nē) *adj.* & *n.* of a yellowish-brown color; tan. —**taw′ni·ness,** *n.*

tax (taks) *n.* **1,** an enforced contribution to the public funds, levied on persons, property, or income by governmental authority. **2,** a burdensome charge, obligation, or task. **3,** (*Colloq.*) any charge. —*v.t.* & *i.* **1,** levy a tax (on). **2,** lay a burden on. **3,** accuse; blame.

tax·a′tion (tak-sā′shən) *n.* act or effect of levying a tax.

tax′i (tak′sē) *n.* [also, **tax′i·cab″**] an automobile for public hire for short trips. —*v.i.* **1,** go by taxicab. **2,** (of an airplane) move on land or water. —**taxi dancer,** a girl who acts as dancing partner for pay.

tax′i·der″my (tak′sə-dēr″mē) *n.* the art of preserving and stuffing the skins of animals. —**tax′i·der″mist,** *n.*

tax′i·me″ter *n.* a device installed in a taxi for computing the fare.

tax·on'o·my (taks-on'ə-mē) *n.* the science of classification. **—tax"o·nom'i·cal** (-ə-nom'ə-kəl) *adj.* **—tax·on'o·mist,** *n.*

tax'pay"er *n.* one who pays taxes, esp. as a landowner.

tea (tē) *n.* **1,** an oriental plant whose dried leaves, infused with hot water, make a beverage; the beverage; a similar beverage made of other plants. **2,** a light evening meal. **3,** an afternoon reception. **—tea ball,** a small, porous bag or container of tea leaves. **—tea rose,** a small, yellowish-pink rose; its color. **—tea wagon,** a small serving table on wheels.

teach (tēch) *v.t.* [*pret.* & *p.p.* **taught** (tât)] **1,** impart knowledge or practical skill to; educate; instruct. **2,** impart knowledge of. —*v.i.* give lessons.

teach'er (-ər) *n.* one who teaches, esp. in a school.

teach-'in" *n.* an extended series of classes, lectures, and seminars on a certain subject.

tea'cup" *n.* a cup in which tea or another hot beverage is served. **—tea'cup·ful,** *n.*

teak (tēk) *n.* a large Indian tree; its hard, durable wood.

tea'ket"tle *n.* a kettle with a spout, in which water is boiled.

teal (tēl) *n.* a wild duck.

team (tēm) *n.* **1,** a group of persons joined together in an action, esp. in a game. **2,** two or more horses, oxen, etc., harnessed together. —*v.t.* & *i.* join together in a team.

team'mate" *n.* a member of the same team.

team'ster (-stər) *n.* a driver of a team or truck.

team'work" *n.* coordination of effort.

tea'pot" *n.* a pot with a spout, in which tea is steeped.

tear (tir) *n.* **1,** [also, **tear'drop"**] a drop of the liquid flowing from the eye. **2,** (*pl.*) sorrow; grief. **3,** a drop of any liquid.

tear (tār) *v.t.* [**tore** (tôr), **torn** (tôrn), **tear'-ing**] **1,** pull apart or into pieces. **2,** make (holes, etc.) by rending forcibly. **3,** lacerate. **4,** (with *off, out, down,* etc.) drag violently; remove; raze; wrench; etc. **5,** affect with grief or pity. —*v.i.* **1,** become torn. **2,** move or act with haste or violence. —*n.* **1,** a rip, rent, or fissure. **2,** turbulent motion; violent haste; an outburst of emotion. **3,** (*Slang*) a spree. **—tear gas** (tir) a gas that temporarily blinds, used as a weapon.

tear'drop" (tir'-) *n.* a tear.

tear'ful (tir'fəl) *adj.* weeping; sorrowful. **—tear'ful·ness,** *n.*

tear'jerk"er (tir'jēr"kər) *n.* an overly sentimental play, movie, etc.

tea'room" *n.* a small restaurant.

tear'y (tir'ē) *adj.* nearly weeping. **—tear'i·ness,** *n.*

tease (tēz) *v.t.* **1,** worry or plague with persistent requests, insinuations, etc.; chaff with good-humored jests. **2,** separate the fibers of (wool, etc.). —*n.* one who teases. **—teas'er,** *n.* (*Colloq.*) an intriguing problem.

tea'sel (tē'zəl) *n.* **1,** a plant with thorny leaves or blooms. **2,** a device for raising the nap of cloth.

tea'spoon" *n.* a small spoon for table use, 1/3 tablespoon in capacity. **—tea'spoon·ful** (-fûl) *n.* [*pl.* **-fuls**].

teat (tēt) *n.* a nipple of the mammary gland.

tech·ne'ti·um (tek-nē'shē-əm) *n.* a radioactive metallic element, no. 43, symbol Tc, produced artificially.

tech'nic (tek'nik) *n.* **1,** technique. **2,** (*pl.*) technical rules, terms, etc. —*adj.* technical.

tech'ni·cal (tek'ni-kəl) *adj.* **1,** pert. to the methods or technique of an art, science, etc. **2,** peculiar to a particular art, etc.; esoteric. **3,** `insistent on exact details or construction.

tech"ni·cal'i·ty (tek"ni-kal'ə-tē) *n.* **1,** technical character. **2,** detail of technique; a technical term or point. **3,** an insignificant point.

tech·ni'cian (tek-nish'ən) *n.* **1,** a skilled worker in a technical field. **2,** one skilled in technique.

tech'ni·col"or (tek'ni-kul"ər) *n.* (*T.N.*) a method of making motion pictures in color.

tech·nique' (tek-nēk') *n.* **1,** method of performance. **2,** technical skill.

tech·noc'ra·cy (tek-nok'rə-sē) *n.* a plan of social reform based on greater control and utilization of industrial power. **—tech'-no·crat",** *n.*

tech·nol'o·gy (tek-nol'ə-jē) *n.* industrial arts collectively; the systematic knowledge of a particular art. **—tech"no·log'i·cal,** *adj.*

tec·ton'ics (tek-ton'iks) *n.* **1,** constructive arts. **2,** structural geology. **—tec·ton'ic,** *adj.*

ted'dy bear (ted'ē-bâr") a child's toy stuffed bear.

te'di·ous (tē'dē-əs) *adj.* long, slow, and tiresome. **—te'di·ous·ness,** *n.*

te'di·um (tē'dē-əm) *n.* boresomeness.

tee (tē) *n.* **1,** the letter *T*; something shaped like it. **2,** the starting place in the play of a hole of golf. **3,** a small heap or peg to elevate a golf ball. **—tee off,** drive a golf ball. **—teed off,** (*Slang*) annoyed. **—tee shirt,** T-shirt.

fat, fāte, fär, fâre, fâll, ásk; met, hē, hêr, maybė; pin, pīne; not, nōte, ôr, tool

teem (tēm) *v.i.* be full, prolific, or abundant.

-teen (tēn) *suf.* plus ten, as in *fourteen.*

teen′age″ *adj.* 13 to 19 years old. **—teen′a″ger**, *n.*

teens (tēnz) *n.pl.* the ages 13 to 19 inclusive.

tee′ny (tē′nē) *adj.* (*Colloq.*) tiny.

tee′ny-bop″per (tē′nē-bäp″ər) *n.* (*Slang*) a young teenage girl who follows the latest fads; used esp. in the 1960s.

tee′pee (tē′pē) *n.* a tent of No. Amer. Indians. Also, **te′pee.**

tee′ter (tē′tər) *v.i. & t.* move back and forth; seesaw; move unsteadily. *—n.* a seesaw; a seesaw motion.

tee′ter-tot″ter *n.* a seesaw.

teeth (tēth) *n.* pl. of *tooth.*

teethe (tēth) *v.i.* grow teeth.

tee·to′tal (tē-tō′təl) *adj.* **1,** pert. to total abstinence from intoxicating liquor. **2,** absolute; entire. **—tee·to′tal·er,** *n.*

tee·to′tum (tē-tō′təm) *n.* a top spun with the fingers.

Tef′lon *n.* (*T.N.*) a substance used as a coating on cooking utensils, razor blades, etc., to prevent sticking or catching.

teg′u·ment (teg′yə-mənt) *n.* a natural covering; integument.

tek′tite (tek′tīt) *n.* glass objects of uncertain (prob. extraterrestrial) origin found in various parts of the world.

tel·au′to·graph″ (tel-â′tə-gráf″) *n.* an apparatus and system for transmitting handwriting electrically.

tel′e- (tel-ə) *pref.* **1,** distant; far off. **2,** television.

tel′e·cast″ (-kást″) *n. & v.* broadcast by television.

tel″e·com·mu′ni·ca′tion (tel″ə-) *n.* the science of communication at a distance (by radio, cable, etc.).

tel″e·gen′ic (tel″ə-jen′ik) *adj.* well suited for television.

tel′e·gram″ *n.* a message sent by telegraph.

tel′e·graph″ (-gráf″) *n.* an apparatus and system for transmitting code messages by electric currents in wires. *—v.t. & i.* send a telegram (to or about). **2,** (*Colloq.*) give advance notice (of). **—te·leg′ra·pher** (tə-leg′rə-fər) *n.* **—te·leg′ra·phy,** *n.*

tel″e·ki·ne′sis (tel″ə-kə-nē′sis) *n.* the movement of objects by methods not explainable by natural laws.

tel′e·mark″ (tel′ə-märk) *n.* a skiing maneuver.

te·lem′e·try (tə-lem′ə-trē) *n.* transmission of radio signals and coded data from a space vehicle or satellite to a station on the earth, or vice versa. **—te·lem′e·ter,** *n.* a device used in telemetry.

te″le·ol′o·gy (tē″lē-ol′ə-jē) *n.* **1,** the study of purpose in nature. **2,** the doctrine that natural phenomena tend to a final purpose. **—te″le·o·log′i·cal,** *adj.*

te·lep′a·thy (tə-lep′ə-thē) *n.* communication between minds by means other than the ordinary and normal. **—tel″e·path′ic** (tel″ə-path′ik) *adj.* **—tel″e·path′i·cal·ly,** *adv.*

tel′e·phone″ (-fōn″) *n.* an apparatus and system for transmitting speech and sounds by electric currents in wires. *—v.t. & i.* speak to or call by telephone. **—tel″e·phon′ic** (-fon′ik) *adj.* **—tel″e·phon′i·cal·ly,** *adv.* **—te·leph′o·ny** (tə-lef′ə-nē) *n.*

tel″e·pho′to *adj.* (of a lens) permitting photography at a distance. **2,** a picture transmitted by electric wire: *telephotograph.* **—tel″e·pho′to·graph′ic,** *adj.* **—tel″e·pho·tog′ra·phy** (-tog′rə-fē) *n.*

tel′e·play″ *n.* a play written for television.

tel′e·port″ (-pôrt″) *v.t.* move (a person or object) without physical contact either by mystical means or by conversion of matter to energy for transmission. **—tel″e·por·ta′tion,** *n.*

tel′e·print″er *n.* a teletypewriter.

tel′e·promp″ter *n.* (*T.N.*) a device used in television for cueing a performer's lines.

tel′e·ran″ *n.* a system of aircraft navigation.

tel′e·scope″ *n.* an optical instrument by means of which distant objects are made to appear nearer and larger. *—v.t. & i.* slide, fit, or come together like a collapsing telescope; shorten.

tel″e·scop′ic (-skop′ik) *adj.* **1,** pert. to a telescope; visible only through a telescope. **2,** farseeing. **—tel″e·scop′i·cal·ly,** *adv.*

tel′e·thon″ *n.* a lengthy, continuous television program, usu. for raising money for charity.

Tel′e·type″ *n.* an apparatus and system for transmitting typewritten messages electrically.

tel′e·vise″ (-vīz″) *v.t.* send (a picture, show, etc.) by television.

tel′e·vi″sion (-vizh″ən) *n.* an apparatus and system for transmitting visual images by wireless electrical or electronic means.

tell (tel) *v.t.* [*pret. & p.p.* **told** (tōld)] **1,** make known; disclose; communicate. **2,** give an account of; narrate; relate. **3,** express in words; say. **4,** explain. **5,** inform. **6,** discern; recognize. **7,** command; bid. **8,** assert positively. **9,** count; enumerate. *—v.i.* **1,** given an account; make a report. **2,** be an indication or evidence of something. **3,** have force or effect; produce a severe effect. **—tell off,** rebuke. **—tell on,** inform against.

tell'er *n.* one who tells or counts; esp., a bank clerk.

tell'ing *adj.* effective; striking.

tell'tale" (tem'plit) *n.* **1,** a tattler. **2,** an indicator or gauge. **—adj.** that reveals or betrays; significant.

tel·lur'i·an (te-lûr'ē-ən) *adj.* of the Earth. **—n.** an inhabitant of the planet Earth.

tel·lu'ri·um (te-lûr'ē-əm) *n.* a chemical element, symbol Te, no. 52.

tel'ly (tel'ē) *n.* (*Brit.*) television.

tem'blor" (tem'blôr") *n.* an earthquake; one tremor of an earthquake.

te·mer'i·ty (tə-mer'ə-tē) *n.* boldness; rashness. **—tem"er·ar'i·ous** (tem"ə-râr'ē-əs) *adj.*

tem'per (tem'pər) *n.* **1,** state of mind or feelings; mood; disposition. **2,** irritability. **3,** calmness of mind; self-restraint. **4,** the state of a metal as to hardness and elasticity. **5,** a modifying substance. **—v.t. 1,** moderate; mitigate. **2,** bring to a desired condition. **3,** modify by admixture. **4,** (*Music*) adjust the pitch of.

tem'per·a (tem'pər-ə) *n.* in painting, distemper.

tem'per·a·ment (tem'pər-ə-mənt) *n.* **1,** the tendencies peculiar to an individual; natural disposition. **2,** tendency to act without self-restraint. **3,** the plan of tuning for a musical instrument.

tem"per·a·men'tal (-men'təl) *adj.* **1,** having a strongly marked temperament; irritable or sensitive. **2,** constitutional; innate.

tem'per·ance (tem'pər-əns) *n.* moderation, esp. in the use of intoxicating liquors.

tem'per·ate (tem'pər-ət) *adj.* moderate. **—tem'per·ate·ness,** *n.* **—Temperate Zone,** either of two portions of the earth's surface lying between the tropics and the polar circles.

tem'per·a·ture" (tem'pər-ə-chûr") *n.* **1,** condition with respect to hotness or coldness. **2,** (*Colloq.*) fever.

tem'pered (tem'pərd) *adj.* **1,** moderated; made less violent. **2,** having a specified disposition, as *good-tempered*. **3,** of metals, modified by heat treatment. **4,** (*Music*) tuned to a certain temperament.

tem'pest (tem'pist) *n.* a violent windstorm; any great commotion or tumult.

tem·pes'tu·ous (tem-pes'choo-əs) *adj.* stormy; tumultuous. **—tem·pes'tu·ous·ness,** *n.*

tem'plate (tem'plāt) *n.* templet.

tem'ple (tem'pəl) *n.* **1,** an edifice dedicated to the service of a deity; a church. **2,** a revered headquarters. **3,** the flattened area at the side of the head above the cheek.

tem'plet (tem'plit) *n.* a pattern or guide used in shaping a piece of work. Also, **tem'plate.**

tem'po (tem'pō) *n.* **1,** rate of movement, as in music. **2,** a favorable movement for action.

tem'po·ral (tem'pə-rəl) *adj.* **1,** pert. to time. **2,** of the present life or this world; worldly; secular.

tem'po·rar"y (tem'pə-rer"ē) *adj.* lasting for a time only.

tem'po·rize" (tem'pə-rīz") *v.i.* **1,** defer action or decision to gain time; delay. **2,** yield temporarily.

tempt *v.t.* **1,** induce or incite; entice; dispose to evil. **2,** be attractive to; allure; invite. **3,** risk provoking; defy. **—tempt'er,** *n.* **—tempt'ress,** *n.fem.*

temp·ta'tion (temp-tā'shən) *n.* act or effect of tempting; an inducement; enticement.

tem·pu'ra (tem-pû'rə) *n.* a Japanese dish of meat, fish, etc., cooked with butter and fried.

ten *n. & adj.* the cardinal number between 9 and 11, expressed by 10.

ten'a·ble (ten'ə-bəl) *adj.* capable of being held or maintained. **—ten·a·bil'i·ty, ten'a·ble·ness,** *n.*

ten'ace" (ten'is) *n.* in card playing, a holding of two cards near but not adjacent in rank.

te·na'cious (tə-nā'shəs) *adj.* **1,** holding fast; retentive. **2,** persistent in an opinion or view; stubborn. **3,** sticky or viscous. **4,** highly cohesive; tough.

te·nac'i·ty (tə-nas'ə-tē) *n.* quality of being tenacious.

ten'ant (ten'ənt) *n.* one who holds property by lease or rent. **—v.t. & i.** inhabit. **—ten'an·cy,** *n.* **—ten'ant·ry,** *n.* tenants collectively.

Ten Commandments a series of rules for moral behavior, given by God to Moses (Ex. 20).

tend *v.i.* **1,** be inclined or disposed. **2,** lead in a particular direction. **3,** attend. **—v.t.** take care of; wait upon; attend.

ten'den·cy (ten'dən-sē) *n.* **1,** disposition to act in a particular way. **2,** a particular inclination; a mode, direction, or outcome.

ten·den'tious (ten-den'shəs) *adj.* serving or written as propaganda. **—ten·den'tious·ness,** *n.*

ten'der (ten'dər) *adj.* **1,** soft in substance, not hard or tough. **2,** delicate in constitution, health, etc.; gentle; sensitive. **3,** affectionate; sentimental; considerate. **4,** immature. **5,** requiring careful handling; critical. **—n. 1,** one who tends; an attendant. **2,** an auxiliary boat or railroad car. **3,**

an offer; the act of tendering. **4,** something offered; money that must be accepted in payment of a debt: *legal tender.* —*v.t.* offer; present for acceptance. —**ten′der·ness,** *n.*

ten′der·foot″ *n.* a soft or inexperienced person; a novice.

ten″der·heart′ed *adj.* kind; sympathetic. —**ten″der·heart′ed·ness,** *n.*

ten′der·ize″ (-īz″) *v.t.* make tender.

ten′der·loin″ *n.* **1,** a cut of tender meat. **2,** the underworld section of a city.

ten′don (ten′dən) *n.* a band of tough, fibrous tissue; a sinew.

ten′dril *n.* a threadlike growth from the stem of a vine.

ten′e·brous (ten′ə-brəs) *adj.* dark; gloomy.

ten′e·ment (ten′ə-mənt) *n.* **1,** a multiple dwelling, esp. of inferior class. **2,** any dwelling occupied by a tenant. **3,** an apartment in a multiple dwelling. **4,** any place of abode.

ten′et (ten′ət) *n.* any opinion, principle, or doctrine held to be true.

ten′nis (ten′is) *n.* a game of propelling a ball, struck by a racket, across a net.

ten′on (ten′ən) *n.* a projecting end for insertion into a mortise. —*v.t.* make or join by a tenon.

ten′or (ten′ər) *n.* **1,** the general course of a thought, saying, discourse, etc.; purport; drift. **2,** a male singing voice of high range.

ten′pen″ny (ten′pē-nē) *adj.* **1,** [also, **ten′pence** (-pəns)] 10 Brit. pennies in value. **2,** of a nail, 3 in. long.

ten′pins″ *n.sing.* a bowling game.

ten′rec (ten′rik) *n.* a mammal of Madagascar.

tense (tens) *adj.* **1,** stretched tight; strained to stiffness; taut. **2,** in a state of mental strain or nervous tension. —*v.t. & i.* make or become tense. —*n.* (*Gram.*) time, of the action of a verb. —**tense′ness,** *n.*

ten′sile (ten′sil) *adj.* **1,** pert. to tension. **2,** ductile.

ten′sion (ten′shən) *n.* **1,** the act of stretching; the state of being strained or tense. **2,** mental strain; excitement. **3,** an opposition of physical or electrical forces; pressure. —**ten′sion·al,** *adj.*

ten′si·ty (ten′sə-tē) *n.* a state of tension.

ten′sor (ten′sər) *n.* **1,** a muscle that tightens or stretches a part. **2,** a set of equations describing the properties of space.

tent *n.* a portable shelter of cloth, skins, etc., supported by one or more poles. —*v.i.* live in a tent.

ten′ta·cle (ten′tə-kəl) *n.* **1,** a slender appendage of an animal; a feeler. **2,** any sensitive filament.

ten′ta·tive (ten′tə-tiv) *adj.* based on or

done as a trial; experimental. —**ten′ta·tive·ness,** *n.*

ten′ter·hook″ (ten′tər-hûk″) *n.* a hook used to hold cloth stretched on a drying frame. —**on tenterhooks,** in a state of suspense; apprehensive.

tenth *adj.* the ordinal of ten, also written 10th. —*n.* one of ten equal parts.

ten′u·ous (ten′ū-əs) *adj.* **1,** thin in consistency; rarefied. **2,** slender or small. **3,** of slight significance. —**ten′u·ous·ness,** *n.*

ten′ure (ten′yər) *n.* **1,** the holding of something, as property, office, etc. **2,** the period of such holding.

te·nu′to (te-noo′tō) *adj.* (*Music*) held; sustained.

te′pee (tē′pē) *n.* teepee.

tep′id *adj.* moderately warm; lukewarm. —**te·pid′i·ty,** *n.*

te·qui′la (te-kē′lə) *n.* an alcholic liquor of Mexico and Central Amer.

ter′bi·um (tēr′bē-əm) *n.* a metallic rare-earth chemical element, symbol Tb, no. 65.

ter·cen′te·nar″y (tēr-sen′tə-nār″ē) *adj.* pert. to or comprising 300 years. —*n.* the 300th anniversary.

ter″gi·ver·sate″ (tēr′ji-vər-sāt″) *v.i.* change one's opinions or principles; be fickle. —**ter″gi·ver·sa′tion,** *n.*

ter″i·ya′ki (ter″i-yä′kē) *n.* a Japanese dish of marinated meat and fish broiled on a skewer.

term (tērm) *n.* **1,** a word or phrase, esp. one particular to some branch of knowledge. **2,** the period of time through which something lasts, as a course of instruction in a school or college. **3,** (*pl.*) conditions offered for acceptance; rates. **4,** (*pl.*) relative position; circumstances. **5,** a mathematical expression treated as a unit. —*v.t.* apply a term to; name; call; designate. —**term insurance,** life insurance effective for a limited number of years.

ter′ma·gant (tēr′mə-gənt) *n.* a quarrelsome or shrewish woman.

ter′mi·na·ble (tēr′mə-nə-bəl) *adj.* that may be terminated.

ter′mi·nal (tēr′mə-nəl) *adj.* **1,** situated at or forming the extremity, boundary, or limit of something. **2,** final. **3,** pert. to a terminus. —*n.* **1,** a terminal part or structure. **2,** a principal railroad, bus, etc., station. **3,** an electrical connection. —**terminal leave,** leave with pay (accumulated unused leave) given to a member of the armed forces before discharge.

ter′mi·nate″ (tēr′mə-nāt″) *v.t.* **1,** bring to an end; finish; conclude. **2,** form the end, boundary, or limit of. —*v.i.* **1,** come to an end; cease. **2,** result. —**ter″mi·na′tion,** *n.*

ter'mi·na"tor (tẽr'mə-nā"tər) *n.* the line between the light and dark portions of the moon's or a planet's disk.

ter"mi·nol'o·gy (tẽr'mə-nol'ə-jē) *n.* the vocabulary of terms peculiar to a science or art.

ter'mi·nus (tẽr'mə-nəs) *n.* [*pl.* **-ni"** (-nī")] an end, extremity, boundary, or limit.

ter'mite (tẽr'mīt) *n.* a social insect that burrows into and undermines wooden structures; white ant.

tern (tẽrn) *n.* an aquatic bird of the gull family.

ter'na·ry (tẽr'nə-rē) *adj.* **1,** based on the number three. **2,** having two parts. **3,** third in order or rank.

terp"si·cho·re'an (tẽrp"si-kə-rē'ən) *adj.* pert. to dancing. —*n.* a dancer.

ter'race (tẽr'əs) *n.* **1,** an elevated tract of flat ground; one of a series of tracts at different levels. **2,** an outdoor promenade; a balcony. **3,** a street cut in a slope. —*v.t.* cut in a series of terraces.

ter'ra cot'ta (tẽr'ə-kot'ə) **1,** a hard earthenware; something made of it. **2,** an orange-brown color.

ter'ra fir'ma (tẽr'ə-fẽr'mə) (*Lat.*) solid ground.

ter·rain' (tə-rān') *n.* a tract of land with regard to its suitability to a particular purpose.

ter"ra·my'cin (tẽr"ə-mī'sin) *n.* an antibiotic drug.

ter'ra·pin (tẽr'ə-pin) *n.* any of several fresh-water and tidewater turtles.

ter·rar'i·um (tə-rār'ē-əm) *n.* **1,** a place where land animals are kept. **2,** a small indoor glass-enclosed garden.

ter·raz'zo (te-rät'tsō) *n.* a flooring of cemented stone or marble chips.

ter·res'tri·al (tə-res'trē-əl) *adj.* **1,** pert. to the earth or dry land. **2,** worldly; mundane. **3,** living on land.

ter'ri·ble (tẽr'ə-bəl) *adj.* **1,** such as to excite terror; dreadful; fearsome. **2,** excessive; severe. **3,** (*Colloq.*) unpleasant; unskillful. —**ter'ri·ble·ness,** *n.* —**ter'ri·bly,** *adv.* (*Colloq.*) very.

ter'ri·er (tẽr'ē-ər) *n.* any of several breeds of small dog.

ter·rif'ic (tə-rif'ik) *adj.* **1,** causing terror. **2,** (*Colloq.*) extraordinary; extreme. —**ter·rif'i·cal·ly,** *adv.* —**ter·rif'ic·ness,** *n.*

ter'ri·fy" (tẽr'i-fī") *v.t.* fill with terror; frighten.

ter'ri·to"ry (tẽr'i-tôr"ē) *n.* **1,** a tract of land; a region or district. **2,** a domain; realm. **3,** (*cap.*) a region belonging to the U.S., not a state. —**ter"ri·to'ri·al,** *adj.*

ter'ror (tẽr'ər) *n.* **1,** intense fear, fright,

or dread; a cause of fear. **2,** the use of violence as a political instrument; (*cap.*) a period of such violence; a terrorist group.

ter'ror·ism (tẽr'ər-iz-əm) *n.* the use of terror and intimidation to gain one's political objectives. —**ter'ror·ist,** *n. & adj.*

ter'ror·ize" (-īz") *v.i. & t.* dominate by intimidation; fill with dread.

ter'ry (tẽr'ē) *n.* [also, *terry cloth*] a fabric with a pile of loops.

terse (tẽrs) *adj.* saying much in few words; brief and pithy; concise. —**terse'ness,** *n.*

ter'ti·ar"y (tẽr'shē-er'ē) *adj.* third in order or rank.

tes'sel·late" (tes'ə-lāt") *v.t.* form into a variegated pattern of small squares.

tes'ser·a (tes'ər-ə) *n.* [*pl.* **-ae** (-ē)] a small square of marble, glass, etc., used in mosaic work.

test *n.* a critical trial or examination; a trial. —*v.t.* subject to a test; try; assay. —**test tube,** a hollow glass cylinder, closed at one end, used in chemical experiments.

tes'ta·ment (tes'tə-mənt) *n.* **1,** a document directing disposition of property after death of the owner; a will. **2,** an agreement; a covenant between God and man. **3,** (*cap.*) either of the two major parts of the Bible; the Mosaic dispensation (*Old Testament*) or Christian dispensation (*New Testament*). —**tes"ta·men'ta·ry,** *adj.*

tes'tate" (tes'tāt") *adj.* having made a valid will.

tes'ta"tor (tes'tā"tər) *n.* one who makes a will. —**tes·ta'trix** (tes-tā'triks) *n.fem.*

test-'drive" *v.t.* drive before buying, to test for roadworthiness.

tes'ter (tes'tər) *n.* a canopy.

tes'ti·cle (tes'tə-kəl) *n.* the male sex gland. Also, **tes'tis** [*pl.* **-tes** (-tēz)].

tes'ti·fy" (tes'ti-fī") *v.i.* give testimony, esp. under oath; attest to facts. —*v.t.* give evidence of.

tes"ti·mo'ni·al (tes"tə-mō'nē-əl) *n.* **1,** a written recommendation or certificate. **2,** an expression of esteem or appreciation. —*adj.* pert. to testimony or a testimonial.

tes'ti·mo"ny (tes'tə-mō"nē) *n.* **1,** a statement made under oath by a witness. **2,** evidence; proof. **3,** open declaration, as of faith.

tes·tos'ter·one" (tes-tos'tə-rōn") *n.* the hormone secreted by the testicles, used medicinally.

tes'ty (tes'tē) *adj.* ill-tempered; irascible; petulant. —**tes'ti·ness,** *n.*

tet'a·nus (tet'ə-nəs) *n.* an infectious, often fatal, bacillic disease, marked by rigid spasm of voluntary muscles, as lockjaw.

tetch′y (tech′ē) *adj.* (*Dial.*) touchy; peevish. —**tetch′i·ness,** *n.*

tête-′à-tête′ (tāt′ə-tāt′) *n.* a private conversation, esp. between two persons. —*adj. & adv.* (in) private.

teth′er (teth′ər) *n.* a rope to restrain a grazing animal; a halter or leash. —*v.t.* restrain with a tether.

tet·ra- (tet-rə) *pref.* four.

tet′ra·chord″ *n.* (*Music*) a diatonic series of four tones.

tet′ra·eth′yl *adj.* pert. to tetraethyl lead: see *ethyl.*

Tet′ra·gram′ma·ton″ (-gram′ə-ton″) *n.* the letters JHVH (or YHWH, etc.), representing the name of God, rendered in English as Jehovah (or Yahweh, etc.).

te·tral′o·gy (te·trăl′ə-jē) *n.* a series of four related dramas, operas, etc.

te′trarch (te′trärk) *n.* one of four joint rulers. —**te′trar·chy** (-kē) *n.*

Teu·ton′ic (tū-ton′ik) *adj.* pert. to the Teutons, or Germanic peoples.

Tex′as lea′guer (tek′səs-lē′gər) in baseball, a batted ball that falls safely between infielders and outfielders.

text (tekst) *n.* **1,** the main body of a book; the actual wording of anything written or printed; the author's words. **2,** the subject of a discourse; a theme or topic. **3,** a passage of Scripture taken as a theme. **4,** the words of a song, oratorio, etc. **5,** a style of printing type (𝔄); Old English.

text′book″ *n.* a book used for instruction.

tex′tile (teks′til) *adj.* pert. to weaving or fabrics. —*n.* cloth.

tex′tu·al (teks′chû-əl) *adj.* being or pert. to a text.

tex′ture (teks′chər) *n.* **1,** the particular arrangement of the constituent parts of any body; structure. **2,** surface characteristics.

-th *suf.* **1,** condition of being, as *warmth.* **2,** denoting ordinal numbers, as *fourth.* **3,** denoting an equal part of a division.

tha·las′sic (thə-las′ik) *adj.* pert. to the sea; marine.

tha·lid′o·mide (thə-lid′ə-mīd) *n.* a sedative drug found to cause birth defects.

thal′li·um (thal′ē-əm) *n.* a metallic chemical element, no. 81, symbol Tl.

than (than) *conj.* a particle used to introduce the second member of a comparison.

than″a·top′sis (than″ə-top′sis) *n.* a view or contemplation of death.

thane (thān) *n.* **1,** a knight or baron. **2,** a Scottish chief.

thank *v.t.* express gratitude to. —*n.* (*pl.*) an expression of gratitude. —**thanks to,** as a result of; due to. —**thank you,** *interj.* expressing gratitude. Also, **thanks.**

thank′ful (-fəl) *adj.* grateful. —**thank′-ful·ness,** *n.*

thank′less (-ləs) *adj.* **1,** unappreciated. **2,** ungrateful. —**thank′less·ness,** *n.*

thanks″giv′ing *n.* **1,** the act or occasion of giving thanks, esp. to God. **2,** (*cap.*) a U.S. holiday, the last Thursday in November.

that (that) *adj. & pron.* [*pl.* **those**] **1,** (*demonstrative*) indicating or emphasizing a person or thing. **2,** (*relative*) as a subject or object in a relative clause, usually when defining or restricting its antecedent. —*adv.* to such an extent or degree. —*conj.* **1,** the following; namely. **2,** for this purpose.

thatch (thach) *n.* **1,** a covering, as for a roof, of straw, rushes, leaves, etc. **2,** the hair covering the head. —*v.t.* cover with a thatch.

thaw (thâ) *v.i.* **1,** of ice, melt. **2,** become so warm as to melt ice. **3,** become less formal or reserved. —*v.t.* cause to thaw. —*n.* the act or process of thawing.

the (thə; emphatic or isolated, thē) *def. art.* used before a noun or pronoun to particularize it, indicate an individual, mark a generic term, emphasize preeminence, etc.

the′a·ter (thē′ə-tər) *n.* **1,** a building or room fitted with a stage or screen and tiers of seats for spectators. **2,** dramatic works or performances collectively. **3,** a field of operations. Also, **the′a·tre.**

the·at′ri·cal (thē-at′ri-kəl) *adj.* **1,** pert. to the theater. **2,** affected; histrionic. —*n.* (*pl.*) dramatic productions.

the·at′rics (thē-at′riks) *n.* **1,** the art of staging dramatic performances. **2,** histrionics.

thee (thē) *pron.* **1,** (*Archaic or poetic*) obj. sing of *thou.* **2,** (*Dial. and among Quakers*) you.

theft *n.* the act or an instance of stealing; larceny.

their (thâr) *pron.* poss. of *they;* in the predicate, **theirs** (-z).

the′ism (thē′iz-əm) *n.* the belief in the existence of a God. —**the′ist,** *n.* —**the·is′tic,** *adj.* —**the·is′ti·cal·ly,** *adv.*

them (them) *pron.* obj. of *they.*

theme (thēm) *n.* **1,** a subject of discourse or discussion; a topic. **2,** a brief essay. **3,** a principal subject in a musical composition. **4,** an identifying melody. —**the·mat′ic** (thē-mat′ik) *adj.* —**theme park,** an amusement park organized around a central idea.

them·selves′ (-selvz′) *pron.* emphatic form of *them;* reflexive form of *they.*

then (then) *adv.* **1,** at that time. **2,** afterward; next in order. **3,** at another time. **4,**

in that case; for this reason; therefore. **5,** on the other hand. —*adj.* being at that time.

thence (*thens*) *adv.* **1,** from that place. **2,** from that time; afterward. **3,** from that source; for that reason. —**thence′forth″,** *adv.* from that time or place onward.

the·o- (thē-ō) *pref.* of God or gods.

the·oc′ra·cy (thē-ok′rə-sē) *n.* government by priests.

the·ol′o·gy (thē-ol′ə-jē) *n.* the systematic study of God and His divinity. —**the″o·log′i·cal** (-ə-loj′ə-kəl) *adj.* —**the″o·lo′gi·an** (-lō′jē-ən) *n.*

the·or′bo (thé-ôr′bō) *n.* a lutelike musical instrument of the 17th century.

the′o·rem (thē′ə-rəm) *n.* **1,** a statement of something to be proved; a theoretical proposition. **2,** a formula or equation expressing a natural law.

the″o·ret′i·cal (thē″ə-ret′i-kəl) *adj.* **1,** in accordance with a theory. **2,** impractical.

the′o·rist (thē′ə-rist) *n.* one who studies or draws conclusions from theory.

the′o·ry (thē′ə-rē) *n.* **1,** a set of propositions describing the operation and causes of natural phenomena. **2,** a proposed but unverified explanation. **3,** the principles of an art, as distinguished from its practice. —**the′o·rize″** (-rīz″) *v.i.*

the·os′o·phy (thē-os′ə-fē) *n.* any philosophical or religious system based on a claim of special insight into the divine nature; specif. Brahmanism or metempsychosis. —**the″o·soph′i·cal** (-sof′i-kəl) *adj.* —**the·os′o·phist,** *n.*

ther″a·peu′tic (ther″ə-pū′tik) *adj.* pert. to the curing of disease; having remedial effect. —**ther″a·peu′ti·cal·ly,** *adv.* —**ther″·a·peu′tics,** *n.* the branch of medicine concerned with this.

ther′a·py (ther′ə-pē) *n.* the treatment of a disease; a remedial process. —**ther′a·pist,** *n.*

there (thâr) *adv.* **1,** in, at, or to that place. **2,** at that point in time, action, etc. **3,** in that respect; in those circumstances. **4,** an introductory word before the verb *be* when the subject is placed after it, as in *there is hope.* —*interj.* see!

there- *pref.* adding a sense of time, place, direction, or agency, as in:

there′a·bout″	there″in·af′ter
there′a·bouts″	there·in′to
there·af′ter	there·of′
there·at′	there·on′
there·by′	there·to′
there·from′	there·un′der
there·in′	there·with′

there′for″ *adv.* for that person or thing.

there′fore″ *adv.* for that reason; as a result; consequently.

ther′e·min (ther′ə-min) *n.* an electronic musical instrument played by moving the hands between two antennas.

there″to·fore′ (*thâr*″tə-fôr′) *adv.* before that time.

there″up·on′ *adv.* then; after that.

there″with·al′ *adv.* in addition to that; following that.

therm- (thêrm) *pref.* heat. Also, **ther·mo-** (thêr-mə; -mō).

ther′mal (thêr′məl) *adj.* pert. to heat or temperature. —**thermal pollution,** the pollution of a body of water by the addition of heated water, as from the cooling system of a nuclear reactor, thereby changing the mean temperature and affecting wildlife.

therm·is′tor (ther-mis′tər) *n.* an electrical resistor sensitive to heat.

ther′mo·cou″ple (thêr′mō-kup″əl) *n.* a device for measuring temperature.

ther″mo·dy·nam′ics *n.* the science concerned with the conversion of heat to energy, the control of temperature, etc. —**ther″mo·dy·nam′ic,** *adj.*

ther·mom′e·ter (thêr-mom′i-tər) *n.* an instrument for measuring temperature. —**ther″mo·met′ric,** *adj.*

ther″mo·nu′cle·ar *adj.* pert. to the extremely high temperatures required to initiate nuclear fusion, as in a hydrogen bomb, or released as a result of nuclear fission, as in the bombardment of uranium.

ther″mo·plas′tic *n. & adj.* a plastic that may be heated and molded more than once.

ther′mos (thêr′məs) *n.* (*T.N.*) a container insulated so as to maintain the temperature of its contents; a vacuum bottle. Also, **Thermos bottle.**

ther″mo·set′ting *adj.* pert. to a plastic that can be molded only once.

ther′mo·sphere″ *n.* the outermost layer of atmosphere, in which temperatures increase with altitude.

ther′mo·stat″ (thêr′mə-stat″) *n.* an instrument for maintaining a desired temperature.

-ther·my (thêr-mé) *suf.* heat.

the·sau′rus (thē-sôr′əs) *n.* [*pl.* **-ri** (rī)] **1,** a collection of words classified by meaning. **2,** any repository; treasury.

these (thēz) *pron. & adj.* pl. of *this.*

the′sis (thē′sis) *n.* [*pl.* **-ses** (sēs)] **1,** a proposition advanced for discussion, proof, etc. **2,** the subject of a composition. **3,** an essay or dissertation, esp. by a candidate for a degree.

Thes′pi·an (thes′pē-ən) *adj.* of the drama. —*n.* an actor.

the′ta (thā′tə) *n.* the eighth letter of the Greek alphabet (Θ, θ).

thew (thū) *n.* muscle; sinew.

they (*th*ā) *pl. pron.* [*poss.* **their** or **theirs**; *obj.* **them**] nominative plural of *he, she,* and *it*.

thi'a·mine (thī'ə-min) *n.* vitamin B₁.

thick (thik) *adj.* **1,** having relatively great extent between opposite sides. **2,** having a specified measure between opposite sides. **3,** compactly arranged; dense. **4,** abundant; abounding with something. **5,** heavy; profound; obscure; intense, etc. **6,** mentally dull. **7,** (*Colloq.*) close in friendship; intimate. **8,** (*Colloq.*) disagreeable; unacceptable. —*n.* the thickest part. —**thick'en,** *v.t. & i.* make or become thick. —**thick'ness,** *n.*

thick'et (thik'it) *n.* a concentration of shrubs, trees, etc.

thick'set" *adj.* **1,** growing or occurring close together. **2,** heavily built; stout.

thick-'skinned" *adj.* not sensitive.

thief (thēf) *n.* [*pl.* **thieves** (thēvz)] **1,** one who steals; one who commits larceny or robbery. **2,** any lawless wrongdoer.

thieve (thēv) *v.i.* be a thief; steal. —**thiev'er·y,** *n.* —**thiev'ing, thiev'ish,** *adj.*

thigh (thī) *n.* the part of the leg between the hip and the knee in man; a corresponding part.

thim'ble (thim'bəl) *n.* **1,** a metal cap worn on the finger to push a needle in sewing. **2,** a sleeve; bushing. —**thim'ble·ful,** *n.* a very small amount.

thim'ble·rig" *v.t.* [-rigged", -rig"ging] swindle.

thin *adj.* [**thin'ner, -nest**] **1,** having relatively little extent between opposite sides; very narrow. **2,** having the constituent parts loose or sparse; not dense. **3,** lacking richness or strength; flimsy; transparent; weak, etc. —*v.t. & i.* make to become thin or thinner. —**thin'ness,** *n.*

thine (*th*īn) *pron.* poss. of *thou.*

thing *n.* **1,** a material object without life. **2,** a matter, affair, fact, circumstance, action, deed, etc. **3,** (*pl.*) personal possessions. **4,** a living being. **5,** (*Colloq.*) what one is most comfortable or most adept at doing. —**the thing,** (*Colloq.*) that which is proper or fashionable.

thing'um·a·bob" (thing'əm-ə-bob") *n.* (*Colloq.*) thing. Also, **thing'um·bob",** **thing'um·a·jig".**

think *v.t.* [*pret. & p.p.* **thought** (thât)] **1,** hold as a belief or opinion; judge; consider. **2,** form a mental concept of; imagine. **3,** hold or bear in mind; recollect. **4,** reflect upon; meditate; ponder. **5,** expect. **6,** (with *up*) invent. —*v.i.* **1,** exercise the mind; cogitate; reflect. **2,** have an opinion or belief. **3,** (with *of*) bring something to mind; remember; make a discovery or invention;

have expectation; show consideration. —**think tank,** (*Colloq.*) a group of experts engaged in research and problem-solving.

thin'ner (-ər) *n.* a solvent.

thin-'skinned" *adj.* very sensitive; touchy.

third (thėrd) *n. & adj.* the member of a series next after the second. —*n.* one of 3 equal parts. —**third class, 1,** a class of mail, comprising printed matter such as advertising circulars, books, etc. **2,** next below second class. —**third degree,** an examination accompanied by torture or intimidation. —**third estate,** the commons. —**third person,** (*Gram.*) one other than the speaker and person spoken to. —**third rail,** a live rail supplying power to an electric locomotive. —**third-rate',** *adj.* inferior. —**third world,** (often *cap.*) the underdeveloped countries of the world, esp. in Asia and Africa.

thirst (thėrst) *n.* **1,** bodily need of drink. **2,** an ardent desire or craving for anything. —*v.i.* feel thirst. —**thirst'y,** *adj.* feeling thirst.

thir·teen' (thėr-tēn') *n. & adj.* three plus ten, also expressed by 13. —**thir·teenth',** *adj. & n.*

thir'ty (thėr'tē) *n. & adj.* three times ten, also expressed by 30. —**thir'ti·eth,** *adj. & n.*

this (*th*is) *pron.* [*pl.* **these** (*th*ēz)] *& adj.* a demonstrative term indicating a person or thing immediately present, nearby, nearer than another, or previously referred to. —*adv.* to the specified extent or degree.

this'tle (this'əl) *n.* any of several thistles having prickly stems and leaves.

this'tle·down" *n.* the silky fibers attached to the dried flower head of the thistle.

thith'er (thith'ər) *adv.* to or toward that place.

tho (thō) *adv.* though.

thole (thōl) *n.* a pin that acts as the fulcrum for an oar.

thong (thâng) *n.* a narrow strip of leather.

tho'rax (thôr'aks) *n.* the part of the body between the neck and abdomen. —**thorac'ic** (thə-ras'ik) *adj.*

tho'ri·um (thôr'ē-əm) *n.* a radioactive chemical element, symbol Th, no. 90.

thorn (thôrn) *n.* **1,** a sharp excrescence on a plant; a spine or prickle. **2,** any of various thorny shrubs. **3,** something that wounds or annoys. —**thorn'y,** *adj.*

thor'ough (thėr'ə) *adj.* **1,** done completely or perfectly; fully executed. **2,** leaving nothing undone; exhaustive in action or operation. **3,** being completely such. —**thor'ough·ness,** *n.*

thor'ough·bred" *adj.* **1,** bred from the

best stock. **2,** superior. —*n.* a thoroughbred person or animal, esp. a racehorse.

thor'ough·fare" *n.* a main road.

thor'ough·go"ing *adj.* complete; consummate.

thorp (thôrp) *n.* a hamlet; village.

those (thōz) *pron.* pl. of *that.*

thou (thow) *pron.* [*poss.* **thy** (thī), **thine** (thīn)] (*Archaic*) sing. pron. of the second person.

though (thō) *conj.* **1,** in spite of the fact that; although. **2,** even if. **3,** nevertheless; yet. **4,** if. —*adv.* however.

thought (thât) *n.* **1,** the act or product of thinking; mental activity; an idea, opinion, etc. **2,** attention; regard or care. —*v.* pret. & p.p. of *think*

thought'ful (-fəl) *adj.* **1,** pensive. **2,** considerate. —**thought'ful·ness,** *n.*

thought'less (-ləs) *adj.* inconsiderate; careless. —**thought'less·ness,** *n.*

thou'sand (thow'zənd) *n.* & *adj.* ten times one hundred, expressed by 1,000. —**thou'sandth,** *adj.* & *n.*

thrall (thrâl) *n.* **1,** one in bondage; a serf or slave. **2,** slavery. —**thral'dom, thrall'-dom,** *n.*

thrash *v.t.* **1,** beat or whip, as for punishment. **2,** defeat thoroughly. **3,** thresh. —*v.i.* toss about violently.

thrash'er (thrash'ər) *n.* a thrushlike songbird.

thread (thred) *n.* **1,** a fine cord made of twisted fibers, used in weaving or sewing. **2,** any fine filament. **3,** something thin and long. **4,** the spiral groove or ridge of a screw. **5,** a theme; sequence. —*v.t.* **1,** pass a thread through the eye of (a needle). **2,** string, as beads. **3,** form a screwthread on or in. **4,** pervade; steer through (something narrow or intricate). —*v.i.* move in a winding course.

thread'bare" *adj.* **1,** shabby; scanty. **2,** trite; hackneyed.

thread'y *adj.* **1,** like thread; filamentous. **2,** very thin, slight, or feeble. —**thread'i·ness,** *n.*

threat (thret) *n.* **1,** a declaration of intention or determination to harm another. **2,** an indication of impending danger or evil.

threat'en (thret'ən) *v.t.* & *i.* utter or be a threat (against).

three (thrē) *n.* & *adj.* the cardinal number between 2 and 4, expressed by 3 (ordinal, *third*).

three-'deck'er *n.* something with three layers, esp. a sandwich made with three slices of bread.

three-"di·men'sion·al *adj.* **1,** having three dimensions, i.e., height, width, and depth. **2,** lifelike; realistic. **3,** having an illusion of depth, often achieved through stereoscopic means. Also, **3-D.**

three'fold" *adj.* times three; in three parts.

three'pence (thrip'əns) *n.* a Brit. coin worth three pennies. —**three'pen"ny** (thrip'-ə-nē) *adj.*

thren'o·dy (thren'ə-dē) *n.* a song of lamentation; a dirge.

thresh *v.t.* **1,** beat (a cereal plant) with a flail, to separate the grain or seeds. **2,** discuss (a matter) exhaustively.

thresh'old (thresh'ōld) *n.* **1,** a doorsill. **2,** a point of beginning.

threw (throo) *v.* pret. of *throw.*

thrice (thrīs) *adj.* three times.

thrift *n.* economical management; the saving of money. —**thrift'y,** *adj.* —**thrift shop,** a store selling used or donated items, usu. to raise money for charity.

thrill (thril) *v.t.* **1,** affect with a sudden wave of emotion or sensation, esp. of pleasure. **2,** cause to vibrate or quiver. —*v.i.* **1,** be thrilled. **2,** produce a thrill. —*n.* **1,** a sudden keen emotion. **2,** a tremor, or tingling; vibration. —**thrill'er,** *n.* an exciting story, play, etc., esp. when of small artistic value.

thrive (thrīv) *v.i.* be fortunate or successful; prosper; flourish.

throat (thrōt) *n.* **1,** the passage from the mouth to the stomach or lungs. **2,** the front of the neck. **3,** any narrowed part or passage.

throat'y (-ē) *adj.* (of sounds) produced or modified in the throat. —**throat'i·ness,** *n.*

throb *v.i.* [**throbbed, throb'bing**] **1,** beat, as the heart, with increased force or rapidity. **2,** pulsate; vibrate. **3,** feel emotion. —*n.* a strong pulsation.

throe (thrō) *n.* **1,** a violent pang; a spasm or paroxysm. **2,** (*pl.*) convulsive pain.

throm·bo'sis (throm-bō'sis) *n.* clotting of the blood in any part of the circulatory system.

throm'bus (throm'bəs) *n.* [*pl.* **-bi** (-bī)] a clot in a blood vessel.

throne (thrōn) *n.* **1,** the ceremonial chair of a sovereign, bishop, etc. **2,** sovereign power.

throng (thrâng) *n.* a large crowd or multitude. —*v.i.* assemble in large numbers. —*v.t.* fill with a crowd.

thros'tle (thros'əl) *n.* a Europ. thrush.

throt'tle (throt'əl) *n.* a valve regulating the admission of fuel to an engine. —*v.t.* **1,** strangle; suffocate. **2,** silence. **3,** check.

through (throo) *prep.* **1,** from one side or end of to the other; completely across or over. **2,** between or among the parts of. **3,**

within the limits of; during the period of. **4,** to the end of. **5,** by agency of. **6,** by reason or in consequence of. —*adv.* **1,** from one side or end to the other. **2,** from beginning to end; all the way. **3,** thoroughly. **4,** to the end or completion. —*adj.* passing or extending to a destination with little or no interruption.

through·out' *pret. & adv.* in every part (of).

through'way" *n.* thruway.

throw (thrō) *v.t.* [**threw** (throo), **thrown** (thrōn), **throw'ing**] **1,** toss or fling through the air with a jerk of the arm; propel in any way; cast; hurl. **2,** put carelessly. **3,** bring to the ground. **4,** shape, as on a lathe. **5,** lose (a contest) intentionally. —*v.i.* make a cast, etc. —*n.* **1,** the act or a result of throwing. **2,** the distance traveled or displacement of a moving part. **3,** a scarf or blanket. —**throw up,** vomit.

throw'a·way" *n.* an advertising circular.

throw'back" *n.* an instance of atavism.

thrown (thrōn) *v.* p.p. of *throw.* —**thrown in,** added without extra charge.

thrum *v.t. & i.* [**thrummed, thrum'ming**] play (a stringed instrument) by plucking; drum or tap idly (on).

thrush *n.* **1,** any of numerous songbirds. **2,** a disease caused by a fungus.

thrust *v.t.* [*pret. & p.p.* **thrust**] **1,** push forcibly; shove. **2,** compel; drive; force. **3,** stab. —*v.i.* make a thrust; lunge. —*n.* **1,** a push, lunge, or stab. **2,** force exerted linearly.

thru'way (throo'wā) *n.* a highspeed divided highway, sometimes having a toll.

thud *n.* a dull, blunt, or hollow sound. —*v.i. & t.* [**thud'ded, -ding**] make a thud.

thug *n.* a professional cutthroat.

thu'li·um (thoo'lē-əm) *n.* a rare-earth metallic element, no. 69, symbol Tm.

thumb (thum) *n.* the shortest and thickest finger of the hand. —*v.i.* **1,** run through with the thumb; handle. **2,** solicit (a ride) by pointing with the thumb. —**all thumbs,** awkward. —**under one's thumb, 1,** readily available. **2,** controlled by.

thumb'nail" *n.* the nail on the thumb. —*adj.* very small or brief.

thumb'screw" *n.* **1,** a screw that may be turned by hand. **2,** an instrument of torture.

thumb'tack" *n.* a tack that may be driven by the thumb.

thump *n.* **1,** a heavy blow. **2,** the dull sound of a blow. —*v.t. & i.* pound.

thump'ing *adj.* (*Colloq.*) heavy; big; excellent.

thun'der (thun'dər) *n.* **1,** the loud atmospheric noise that often follows lightning.

2, any loud noise. **3,** vehement and threatening utterance. —*v.i.* **1,** give forth a resounding noise. **2,** utter denunciation. —*v.t.* utter or move with great noise. —**thun'der·ous,** *adj.*

thun'der·bird" *n.* in Amer. Ind. folklore, the spirit or god of thunder, lightning, and rain.

thun'der·bolt" *n.* **1,** a flash of lightning. **2,** a sudden, violent, or astonishing event.

thun'der·clap" *n.* a crash of thunder.

thun'der·cloud" *n.* an electrically charged cloud producing thunder and lightning.

thun'der·head" *n.* one of the round swelling cumulus clouds which frequently develop into thunderclouds.

thun'der·show"er *n.* a brief rain and electrical storm.

thun'der·storm" *n.* a storm of lightning and thunder and, usually, heavy but brief rain.

thun'der·struck" *adj.* very astonished; thrown into consternation.

thur'i·ble (thûr'ə-bəl) *n.* a censer.

Thurs'day (thērz'dē) *n.* the fifth day of the week.

thus (*th*us) *adv.* **1,** in this way. **2,** in consequence; accordingly. **3,** so.

thwack (thwak) *v.t.* strike with something flat. —*n.* a whack.

thwart (thwôrt) *v.t.* prevent from accomplishing a purpose; frustrate; baffle. —*n.* a transverse part.

thy (*th*ī) *pron.* poss. of *thou.* —**thy·self'**, *pron.* reflexive and emphatic form of *thou.*

thyme (tīm) *n.* a plant of the mint family; a seasoning.

thy'mus (thī'məs) *n.* a ductless gland near the neck.

thy'roid (thī'roid) *n.* a ductless gland near the neck, which regulates metabolism.

ti (tē) *n.* (*Music*) si.

ti·ar'a (tē-âr'ə) *n.* **1,** an ornament worn on the head by women. **2,** a diadem worn by the Pope.

tib'i·a (tib'ē-ə) *n.* [*pl.* **-ae** (-ē)] the shinbone.

tic (tik) *n.* a twitching of the face.

tick (tik) *n.* **1,** a slight, sharp sound, as of a clock. **2,** a small mark; a dot. **3,** a small quantity; an instant of time. **4,** any of various parasitic insects or arachnids. **5,** the cloth case of a mattress, pillow, etc., made of ticking. **6,** (*Colloq.*) score or account; credit. —*v.i.* make a slight, esp. a recurrent, sound. —*v.t.* mark with a tick.

tick'er *n.* **1,** something that ticks; (*Slang*) a watch; the heart. **2,** a telegraph instrument that prints on a tape.

tick'et (tik'it) *n.* **1,** a slip of paper entitling one to admission, service, etc. **2**, a label or tag. **3**, a party's list of candidates. **4**, a license. **5**, (*Colloq.*) proper procedure. **6**, a police summons. —*v.t.* **1**, furnish with a ticket; label. **2**, schedule.

tick'ing *n.* a strong material of linen or cotton, usu. striped.

tick'le (tik'əl) *v.t.* **1**, touch so as to produce a tingling sensation. **2**, amuse; gratify. —*v.i.* produce or feel a tingling sensation. —**tick'ler,** *n.* a reminder.

tick'lish *adj.* **1**, sensitive to tickling. **2**, requiring careful handling; risky. —**tick'-lish·ness,** *n.*

tick″tack·toe′ (tik″tak-tō′) *n.* a game of placing three naughts or crosses in a row. Also, **tit″tat·toe′.**

tick'tock″ (-tok″) *n.* the sound of a clock ticking.

tid'al (tī'dəl) *adj.* pert. to or being a tide. —**tidal wave,** a very large ocean wave.

tid'bit″ *n.* a savory bit, esp. of food.

tid'dly·winks″ (tid'lē-winks″) *n.* a table game of snapping small disks into a cup.

tide (tīd) *n.* **1**, the periodic rise and fall of terrestrial water. **2**, a movement; a flow, current or stream. —*v.t.* bear; carry.

tide'land″ *n.* land which is alternately covered and left dry by the ebb and flow of the tide.

tide'wa″ter *n.* water that rises and falls with the tides.

tid'ings (tī'dingz) *n.pl.* news.

ti'dy (tī'dē) *adj.* **1**, kept in good order; neat. **2**, (*Colloq.*) fairly large; apt. —*v.t.* & *i.* make neat. —**tid'i·ness,** *n.*

tie (tī) *v.t.* [**tied, ty'ing**] **1**, attach or make fast by a knotted cord, etc.; bind; fasten or join in any way. **2**, restrict; constrain. **3**, make the same score, as in a contest. —*v.i.* **1**, make equal scores. **2**, join. —*n.* **1**, anything that binds or unites. **2**, a cravat; neck-tie. **3**, a connecting beam; a transverse timber. **4**, equality of scores. —**tie down, 1**, confine; restrict. **2**, keep occupied. —**tie up, 1**, keep busy. **2**, hinder; prevent. **3**, fasten securely.

tie-'dye″ *v.t.* a method of dying fabric in which certain parts are tied in knots to reduce or eliminate penetration of the dye.

tie-'in″ *n.* **1**, connection; relationship. **2**, a newspaper article mentioning merchandise advertised nearby. **3**, a retailer's advertisement placed near that of the manufacturer.

tier (tir) *n.* a row or rank, esp. one of several at different levels.

tie-'up″ *n.* a stoppage.

tiff (tif) *n.* **1**, a petty quarrel. **2**, a peevish mood. —*v.i.* quarrel.

tif'fa·ny (tif'ə-nē) *n.* a kind of gauze mus-

lin; silk. —**Tiffany glass,** a stained glass used in lamps, windows, and other objects.

ti'ger (tī'gər) *n.* **1**, a large, carnivorous feline of Asia. **2**, a person of great fierceness. —**ti'gress,** *n.fem.* —**tiger lily,** a variety of lily bearing showy yellow flowers with black spots.

ti'ger's-eye″ *n.* an ornamental quartz stone.

tight (tīt) *adj.* **1**, firmly fixed in place. **2**, fitting closely, esp. too closely. **3**, stretched taut; tense. **4**, compact in texture; dense. **5**, hard to obtain. **6**, (*Colloq.*) stingy. **7**, (*Slang*) drunk; tipsy. —*adv.* securely; tensely. —**tight'en,** *v.t.* & *i.* —**tight'ness,** *n.*

tight-'fist″ed *adj.* parsimonious.

tight-'lipped″ *adj.* secretive.

tight'rope″ *n.* a stretched rope on which acrobats walk.

tights *n.pl.* close-fitting trousers worn by acrobats, dancers, etc., and as an undergarment.

tight'wad″ *n.* (*Slang*) a stingy person.

ti'glon (tī'glon) *n.* the offspring of a male tiger and a female lion.

til'de (til'də) *n.* a diacritical mark (˜) as on *ñ* to indicate a nasal sound resembling *nyuh* (nyə).

tile (tīl) *n.* **1**, a thin slab or plate of baked clay, etc., used as building material. **2**, a block used in masonry construction. **3**, a pottery tube or pipe. **4**, tiles collectively. —*v.t.* construct, cover, or drain with tiles.

till (til) *n.* a drawer, tray, or box for keeping money or valuables. —*v.t.* & *i.* cultivate (land); plow. —*prep.* & *conj.* until.

till'age (-ij) *n.* cultivation of land; tilled land.

till'er (-ər) *n.* **1**, a farmer. **2**, a lever that controls a rudder.

tilt *v.i.* & *t.* **1**, lean or incline away from a vertical or normal position; slant. **2**, engage in a joust or combat; make thrusts (at); charge. **3**, forge (steel). —*n.* **1**, a sloping position. **2**, a joust, contest, or dispute; a thrust. **3**, an awning. —**full tilt,** full speed.

tilth *n.* **1**, act or result of tilling. **2**, depth of cultivation. **3**, crop.

tim'bale (tim'bəl) *n.* a small pastry cup filled with cooked food.

tim'ber (tim'bər) *n.* **1**, growing trees. **2**, wood; a wooden member or beam. **3**, personal character; quality. —*v.t.* furnish with timber. —**timber line,** the height or line, on mountains or in polar regions, beyond which trees do not grow.

tim'bre (tim'bər) *n.* the quality or tone color of a sound.

tim'brel (tim'brəl) *n.* a tambourine.

time (tīm) *n.* **1**, the relationship of any event to any other, as being before, simultaneous, or after; continuous duration. **2**, the measurement of duration, as by a clock. **3**, an epoch, era, period, season, etc. **4**, an extent of duration, as an hour, day, etc.; hours worked, or the pay therefor; a prison term. **5**, a point of time; a particular occasion. **6**, (often *pl.*) a historical period; a state of affairs. **7**, leisure; opportunity. **8**, one of several recurrent instances. **9**, (*pl.*) a term denoting multiplication, as in *two times six*. **10**, rhythm; tempo; meter; rate. —*adj.* **1**, pert. to time **2**, equipped with a timing device. **3**, pert. to installment buying. —*v.t.* **1**, determine the moment, duration, or rate of. **2**, choose the time or occasion for. **3**, regulate as to time. —**at times**, occasionally. —**on time**, **1**, punctual. **2**, by installment payments. —**serve time**, be imprisoned. —**time clock**, one that records hours worked. —**time exposure**, exposure of film for more than one-half second; a picture so taken. —**time frame**, period of time. —**time out**, a rest period. —**time signature**, (*Music*) a sign indicating the meter. —**time zone**, an area throughout which standard time is the same.

time-'hon"ored *adj.* respected by reason of age.

time'keep"er *n.* **1**, one who records a worker's hours worked and wages due. **2**, one who watches the time, as in a contest.

time'less (-ləs) *adj.* unending. —**time'less·ness**, *n.*

time'ly *adj.* opportune. —**time'li·ness**, *n.*

time'piece" *n.* a clock, watch, etc.

tim'er (tī'mər) *n.* **1**, one who or that which measures or records time. **2**, a device for supplying the spark in an internal combustion engine.

time'ta"ble *n.* a schedule of the times of planned occurrences, esp. a railroad schedule.

time'worn" *adj.* **1**, worn or impaired by time or use. **2**, out-of-date.

tim'id *adj.* **1**, easily alarmed; fearful; shy. **2**, characterized by fear. —**ti·mid'i·ty**, **tim'id·ness**, *n.*

tim'ing (tī'ming) *n.* synchronization; effective choice of a time.

tim'or·ous (tim'ə-rəs) *adj.* timid. —**tim'or·ous·ness**, *n.*

tim'o·thy (tim'ə-thè) *n.* a grass grown for hay.

tim'pa·ni (tim'pə-nè) *n.* tympani.

tin *n.* **1**, a metallic chemical element, no. 50, symbol Sn. **2**, sheet iron or steel coated with tin: *tin plate*. **3**, a container made of tin plate: *tin can*. —*adj.* **1**, made of tin, as tin plate. **2**, worthless; counterfeit. —*v.t.* [**tinned**, **tin'ning**] **1**, coat with tin. **2**, pre-

serve in tin cans. —**tin foil**, a thin sheet of tin, used to wrap various merchandise.

tin'a·mou (tin'ə-moo) *n.* a So. Amer. bird resembling a partridge.

tinc'ture (tink'chər) *n.* **1**, a solution of a medicinal substance in alcohol. **2**, a tinge. —*v.t.* tinge.

tin'der (tin'dər) *n.* any easily-ignited material. —**tin'der·box**, *n.* (*Colloq.*) something easily inflammable.

tine (tīn) *n.* a slender projection; a prong, as of a fork.

ting *n.* a high-pitched metallic sound. —*v.t. & t.* make this sound.

tinge (tinj) *v.t.* **1**, color slightly; tint. **2**, imbue slightly with something, as flavor. —*n.* **1**, a moderate degree of coloration. **2**, a slight admixture of anything.

tin'gle (ting'gəl) *v.i.* have a prickling or stinging sensation. —*n.* this sensation.

tin'horn" *n.* a professional gambler who bets small amounts; a piker. —*adj.* a gambler or gambling game despised for cheapness.

tink'er (tink'ər) *n.* **1**, a mender of metal household utensils. **2**, a bungler. **3**, a handyman. —*v.i. & t.* work as a tinker; meddle (with). —**tinker's dam**, something worthless.

tin'kle (ting'kəl) *v.i.* give forth a short, light, metallic sound. —*n.* such a sound.

tin'ny (tin'é) *adj.* like tin; flimsy; metallic in sound; sour in taste. —**tin'ni·ness**, *n.*

tin-'pan" alley a street or district largely occupied by publishers and composers of popular music; also, the composers, etc., collectively.

tin'sel (tin'səl) *n.* **1**, a glittering material of metal in sheets or strips. **2**, false show. —*v.t.* decorate.

tint *n.* **1**, a variety of a color; a hue to which white has been added. **2**, a pale color. —*v.t.* color slightly.

tin"tin·nab"u·la'tion (tin"ti-nab"yə-lā'shən) *n.* the sound of bells ringing.

tin'type" *n.* a photograph on a metal plate.

ti'ny (tī'nè) *adj.* very small.

-tion (shən) *suf.* see *-ation*.

tip *n.* **1**, the extremity of something long and slender; an outermost point; the top or apex. **2**, a small piece attached to an extremity. **3**, a light blow; a tap. **4**, the state of being tilted. **5**, a small present of money. **6**, a bit of information or advice. —*v.t.* [**tipped**, **tip'ping**] **1**, form the tip of. **2**, strike lightly or obliquely. **3**, tilt; overturn. **4**, give a tip to. —*v.i.* **1**, tilt; incline; be overturned; topple. **2**, give tips.

tip'off" *n.* a warning or hint.

tip'pet (tip'it) *n.* a covering for the neck

and shoulders, esp. a scarf or muffler wound around the neck.

tip′ple (tip′əl) v.i. & t. drink (intoxicating liquor) habitually. —**tip′pler,** n. a habitual drinker.

tip′staff″ n. a minor police or court officer.

tip′ster (-stər) n. (*Colloq.*). one who furnishes private information.

tip′sy (-sè) adj. slightly intoxicated. —**tip′si·ness,** n.

tip′toe″ n. a movement or posture on the toes. —adj. standing or moving on tiptoe, to reach high or walk quietly. —v.i. move on tiptoe.

tip′top″ n. & adj. the highest point or quality.

ti′rade (tī′rād) n. a long speech or writing of censure or denunciation.

tire (tīr) v.i. become weary or jaded. —v.t. make weary; fatigue. —n. [also, *Brit.*, **tyre**] a rubber or iron hoop around a wheel. —**tired,** adj. weary; impatient; dissatisfied. —**tire′less,** adj. diligent; untiring. —**tire′some,** adj. tedious.

ti·sane′ (ti-zän′) n. an infusion of dried leaves or flowers used medicinally or as a beverage.

tis′sue (tish′oo) n. **1,** the cellular substance of which living bodies are composed. **2,** a woven fabric, esp. one very light and thin. **3,** thin, translucent paper: *tissue paper.*

tit n. **1,** a small bird, esp. the titmouse. **2,** (*Vulgar*) teat. —**tit for tat,** equivalent given in return or as retribution; an eye for an eye.

ti′tan (tī′tən) n. a person or thing of enormous size and strength. —**ti·tan′ic,** adj. —**ti·tan′i·cal·ly,** adv.

ti·ta′ni·um (tī-tā′né-əm) n. a metallic chemical element, no. 22, symbol Ti.

tit′bit″ n. tidbit.

tithe (tīth) n. a tenth part; a tax; a contribution to a church, etc. —v.t. & i. pay a tithe.

ti′tian (tish′ən) n. & adj. a yellow-red color.

tit′il·late″ (tit′ə-lāt″) v.t. excite agreeably; tickle. —**tit′il·la′tion,** n.

tit′i·vate″ (tit′i-vāt″) v.t. (*Colloq.*) dress smartly; spruce up. —**tit′i·va′tion,** n.

ti′tle (tī′təl) n. **1,** a name assigned to distinguish an individual thing. **2,** a descriptive heading or caption. **3,** a word or phrase denoting rank, honors, etc. **4,** the rank of champion. **5,** right to the possession of property. **6,** a division of a statute or law. —v.t. give a name or appellation to. —**title rôle** the rôle from which the name of a play is derived.

ti′tled (tī′təld) adj. bearing a title, esp. of nobility.

tit′mouse″ (tit′mows″) n. [*pl.* **-mice″**] a small bird.

tit′ter (tit′ər) v.i. & n. laugh in a restrained manner; giggle; snicker.

tit′tle (tit′əl) n. a very small mark, dot, thing, etc.; a particle.

tit′tle-tat″tle n. & v.i. chatter; gossip.

tit′u·lar (tit′yə-lər) adj. of, being, or pert. to a title; by virtue of one's title. —**tit″u·lar′i·ty,** n.

tiz′zy (tiz′é) n. dither.

T-′man″ n. (*Colloq.*) a law enforcement agent employed by the U.S. Treasury.

TNT (tē′en-tē′) n. trinitrotoluene, a powerful explosive.

to (too) prep. **1,** indicating motion or purpose toward something. **2,** indicating a destination, result, outcome, limit, or point of space, time, or degree. **3,** indicating relations, as comparison, opposition, agreement, accompaniment, contiguity. **4,** a particle used before the infinitive of a verb. —adv. toward someone or something, usually implied; in an inward direction. —**to and fro,** alternately toward and away from a point.

toad (tōd) n. a terrestrial member of the frog family.

toad′stool″ (tōd′stool″) n. a fungus having an umbrellalike cap on a stalk.

toad′y (tō′dé) n. a servile, fawning person; a sycophant. —v.i. fawn.

toast (tōst) n. **1,** sliced bread browned by heat. **2,** a complimentary sentiment endorsed by drinking; the person complimented. —v.t. **1,** expose to heat. **2,** compliment by a toast. —**toast′er,** n. a device for making toast.

toast′mas″ter n. a master of ceremonies at a dinner.

to·bac′co (tə-bak′ō) n. a plant whose large leaves, containing nicotine, are prepared for smoking and chewing, and snuff. —**to·bac′co·nist** (-ə-nist) n. a dealer in tobacco.

to·bog′gan (tə-bog′ən) n. a boardlike sled with low or no runners. —v.i. **1,** coast on snow. **2,** fall rapidly or abruptly. **3,** move without effort.

to′by (tō′bé) n. **1,** a small jug or mug. **2,** (*Slang*) a long, cheap cigar.

toc·ca′ta (tə-kä′tə) n. (*Music*) a virtuosic keyboard composition.

toc′sin (tok′sin) n. a warning bell or signal.

to·day′ (tə-dā′) n. & adj. **1,** the present day. **2,** the present period.

tod′dle (tod′əl) v.i. walk with short, unsteady steps. —n. a toddling walk.

tod'dy (tod'ē) n. a hot drink of whiskey diluted and sweetened.

to-do' (tə-doo') n. commotion; fuss.

toe (tō) n. **1,** a digit of the foot. **2,** the forepart of a hoof. **3,** the part of a stocking or shoe that covers the toes. **4,** a part resembling a toe; a projection, stud, etc. —v.t. & i. touch, reach, strike, etc., with the toes. —**toe the mark,** behave as instructed. —**toe hold, 1,** a slight or precarious grip, with or as with the toes. **2,** a wrestling grip upon an opponent's foot. —**toe'nail″,** n.

tof'fee (tof'ē) n. taffy. Also, **tof'fy.**

to'fu″ (tä'foo″) n. bean curd.

tog n. (Colloq.) (usually pl.) a garment. —**tog'ge·ry** (tog'ə-rē) n. (Colloq.) clothes; togs. —**togged out,** dressed.

to'ga (tō'gə) n. a loose outer garment, as that of the ancient Romans; a robe.

to·geth'er (tə-geth'ər) adv. **1,** in conjunction; in one gathering, mass, or body. **2,** simultaneously; contemporaneously. **3,** with each other; in common; mutually. **4,** in or into junction or union. **5,** without intermission or interruption.

tog'gle (tog'əl) n. **1,** a transverse pin or bar. **2,** a linkage of levers to produce motion at right angles to a thrust. —**toggle switch,** an electric switch actuated by a toggle lever.

toil v.i. **1,** work hard; labor. **2,** move or travel with difficulty or weariness. —n. **1,** fatiguing labor. **2,** a laborious task. **3,** (pl.) a net for trapping game.

toile (twäl) n. a thin linen fabric.

toi'let (toi'lit) n. **1,** a water closet, bathroom, or dressing room. **2,** the process of dressing, including bathing, make-up, etc.; personal appearance as a result of this. **3,** a dressing table. —**toilet set,** articles as comb, brush, etc. —**toilet water,** a light perfume.

toi'let·ry (-rē) n. an article or preparation used in dressing, as a cosmetic.

toi·lette' (twä-let') n. **1,** toilet (def. 2). **2,** one's style of dress.

toil'worn″ adj. affected by much toil or use.

To·kay' (tō-kā') n. **1,** a rich, heavy Hungarian wine. **2,** a similar California wine. **3,** a sweet variety of grape.

toke (tōk) n. (Slang) a puff on a cigarette, esp. of marijuana. —v.t. puff (on a cigarette).

to'ken (tō'kən) n. **1,** something regarded as representing something else; a sign or symbol; a keepsake or memento. **2,** an indication, expression, or evidence. **3,** a special coin issued as a ticket. —adj. serving

only as an expression of good faith. —**to'ken·ism,** n.

tol·bu'ta·mide″ (tol-byoo'tə-mīd″) n. a drug used in the treatment of diabetes.

told (tōld) v. pret. & p.p. of tell.

tole (tōl) n. lacquered or enameled metalware, usu. decorated.

tol'er·a·ble (tol'ər-ə-bəl) adj. **1,** endurable. **2,** somewhat good; not bad. —**tol'er·a·ble·ness,** n.

tol'er·ance (tol'ər-əns) n. **1,** disposition to be patient and fair; freedom from bigotry. **2,** power of enduring or resisting the action of a drug. **3,** allowed variation from standard dimensions. —**tol'er·ant,** adj.

tol'er·ate (tol'ə-rāt″) v.t. **1,** allow to be, be done, or be practiced; permit. **2,** bear with patience; endure without complaint or ill effect. —**tol″er·a'tion,** n.

toll (tōl) n. **1,** a fee or tax collected for a particular service. **2,** a succession of slow single strokes of a bell; one such stroke. —v.t. **1,** cause (a bell) to toll. **2,** announce, signal, etc., by a bell. —v.i. give forth slow repeated sounds. —**toll call,** a long-distance telephone call.

toll'house″ n. a booth, cabin, etc., at which tolls are paid. Also, **toll'booth″.** —**tollhouse cookies,** chocolate chip cookies.

toll'gate″ n. a point at which tolls are collected.

tol'u·ene″ (tol'yū-ēn″) n. a liquid derivative of coal tar, used as a solvent, detonator, etc. Also, **tol'u·ol** (-ol).

tom n. the male of various animals, as the cat.

tom'a·hawk″ (tom'ə-hâk″) n. an Amer. Ind. stone-headed hatchet.

to·ma'to (tə-mā'tō) n. a plant bearing a pulpy fruit, usu. red.

tomb (toom) n. **1,** an excavation made to receive a dead body; a grave. **2,** a monument to one dead: tombstone. **3,** death.

tom'boy″ n. an athletic, boylike girl.

tomb'stone″ n. a stone marker for a grave.

tom'cat″ n. a male cat.

Tom Col'lins (kol'inz) a tall iced drink of gin, lemon or lime juice, sugar, and carbonated water.

tome (tōm) n. a large book.

tom″fool'er·y n. silly or prankish behavior.

Tom'my (tom'ē) n. a British soldier.

tom'my·gun″ n. (Slang) a machine gun.

tom'my·rot″ (tom'ē-rot″) n. (Slang) nonsense.

to·mor'row (tə-mor'ō) n. & adj. **1,** the day after this day. **2,** the future; a future day.

tom'tit″ n. a small bird.

tom-'tom'' *n.* **1,** a primitive drum. **2,** a drum used in bands.

-to·my (tə-mē) *suf.* cutting, denoting a surgical operation.

ton (tun) *n.* **1,** a unit of weight: 2,000 lbs. avoirdupois (*short ton*) or 2,240 lbs. (*long ton*), or 1,000 kilograms (*metric ton*). **2,** a variable unit of volume or capacity, as 40 cubic feet (*shipping ton*) or 35 cubic feet of salt water (*displacement ton*). **3,** (*Colloq.*) any large amount.

ton'al (tōn'əl) *adj.* pert. to a tone or to tonality.

to·nal'i·ty (tō-nal'ə-tē) *n.* **1,** (*Music*) a system of tones; key. **2,** a color scheme.

tone (tōn) *n.* **1,** any resonant sound. **2,** a sound of definite pitch; a musical note. **3,** a sound with respect to its pitch, volume, and timbre. **4,** accent, inflection, or modulation, esp. of the voice. **5,** a color; a shade or tint. **6,** the state of tension or firmness proper to bodily tissues. **7,** prevailing character; style; temper; spirit; tenor. **8,** elegance; stylishness. —*v.t.* give a proper or desired tone to. —**tone arm,** a phonograph pick-up. —**tone color,** timbre. —**tone deaf,** unable to perceive differences in musical tones by hearing. —**tone down,** reduce, in intensity of sound, color, etc.; subdue. —**tone poem,** a musical composition suggestive of poetic images or sentiments.

tong (tong) *n.* a Chinese political party or private society.

tongs (tângz) *n.pl.* an implement for grasping and lifting something.

tongue (tung) *n.* **1,** a fleshy, freely movable organ in the mouth, the principal organ of taste (in man, also of speech). **2,** an animal's tongue as meat. **3,** speech or talk; a language or dialect. **4,** a tonguelike part, as the clapper of a bell, a strip of leather in a shoe, a small strip of land projecting into water, etc. —*v.t.* **1,** sound with the tongue. **2,** put a tongue on. —**tongue and groove,** a joint formed by a projecting strip on one piece of wood which fits into a groove in another. —**tongue in cheek,** facetiously.

tongue-'lash''ing *n.* a scolding.

tongue-'tied'' *adj.* **1,** having an impediment of the speech. **2,** speechless from shyness or astonishment.

tongue'twist''er *n.* a word or phrase difficult to pronounce because of an unusual combination of sounds.

ton'ic (ton'ik) *n.* **1,** a medicine that improves the bodily tone. **2,** anything that imparts strength or vigor. **3,** the first degree of a musical scale; the keynote. **4,** quinine water. **5,** pop. —*adj.* **1,** invigorating. **2,** pert. to a musical tone or tones. **3,** pert. to muscular tension. —**ton·ic'i·ty** (-is'ə-tē) *n.*

to·night' (tə-nīt') *n. & adj.* the present or coming night. Also, *colloq.,* **to·nite'.**

ton'nage (tun'ij) *n.* **1,** capacity or displacement in tons. **2,** ships collectively.

ton·neau' (tə-nō') *n.* the interior of a closed automobile body.

ton'sil (ton'səl) *n.* either of two masses of lymphoid tissue at the back of the mouth.

ton''sil·lec'to·my (-lek'tə-mē) *n.* removal of the tonsils.

ton''sil·li'tis (-lī'tis) *n.* inflammation of the tonsils.

ton·sor'i·al (ton-sôr'ē-əl) *adj.* pert. to a barber.

ton'sure (ton'shər) *n.* **1,** the cutting or shaving of hair from the head. **2,** a shaved spot on the head of a priest or monk.

ton'y (tōn'ē) *adj.* (*Colloq.*) stylish. —**ton'i·ness,** *n.*

too *adv.* **1,** in addition; also; furthermore. **2,** more than enough; beyond what is normal or proper. **3,** exceedingly; extremely.

took (tûk) *v.* pret. of *take.*

tool *n.* **1,** any implement for working, cutting, shaping, etc. **2,** an unwitting or compliant agent of another. —*v.t. & i.* shape, etc., with a tool; ornament (the cover of a book, etc.).

toot *n.* **1,** the sound of a horn. **2,** (*Slang*) drunken revelry. —*v.t. & i.* blow or make the sound of a horn.

tooth *n.* [*pl.* **teeth** (tēth)] **1,** one of the hard bodies set in a row in the jaw. **2,** any toothlike projection, as on a comb; a cog on a wheel. **3,** something sharp, distressing, or destructive. **4,** taste; relish. —**tooth'y,** *adj.* —**in the teeth of,** in defiance of; straight against. —**tooth and nail,** with all one's strength and means. —**tooth powder,** a powder used for cleaning the teeth.

tooth'ache'' *n.* pain in a tooth.

tooth'brush'' *n.* a small, long-handled brush for cleaning the teeth.

tooth'paste'' *n.* a paste used for cleaning the teeth.

tooth'pick'' *n.* a small pointed piece for cleaning the teeth.

tooth'some (-səm) *adj.* palatable. —**tooth'some·ness,** *n.*

too'tle (too'təl) *v.i.* toot gently or repeatedly. —*n.* a tootling sound.

toot'sy (tût'sē) *n.* a woman's foot, esp. a small foot.

top *n.* **1,** the highest point or part of anything; the summit or apex. **2,** the highest position in rank, etc. **3,** the most perfect example or type; the best. **4,** a lid or cover; a roof. **5,** a toy, made to spin on its point. —*adj.* highest; uppermost; foremost; chief; principal. —*v.t.* [**topped, top'ping**] **1,** be the top of. **2,** furnish with a top. **3,** reach the top of. **4,** rise above; surpass. **5,** get over; vault; cross. **6,** complete; perfect. **7,** remove the top of; prune. **8,** hit (a ball) above the center. —**top hat,** a high silk hat. —**top kick,** (*Colloq.*) a first sergeant; a boss. —**top secret,** the highest classification of secrecy in the U.S. government.

to′paz (tō′paz) *n.* **1,** a gem, silicate of aluminum. **2,** a yellow variety of sapphire or quartz. —*adj.* yellow.

top′coat″ *n.* a light overcoat.

top-′drawer′ *adj.* first-rate.

tope (tōp) *v.i.* drink intoxicating liquor habitually. —**top′er,** *n.*

top′flight″ *adj.* of highest class.

top′gal′lant *n.* (*Naut.*) the mast, sail, or rigging above the topmast and below the royal.

top-′heav″y *adj.* likely to topple; structurally unsound. —**top-′heav″i·ness,** *n.*

top-′hole′ *adj.* (*Brit.*) excellent.

top′ic (top′ik) *n.* a subject or theme of a discourse, etc.

top′i·cal (top′i-kəl) *adj.* **1,** pert. to matters of current interest. **2,** pert. to the topic. **3,** local. —**top″i·cal′i·ty,** *n.*

top′knot″ *n.* a tuft of hair on top of the head; a crest.

top′less (top′ləs) *adj.* wearing nothing above the waist.

top′mast″ *n.* (*Naut.*) a mast on top of a lower mast.

top′most″ *adj.* highest.

top′notch″ *adj.* (*Colloq.*) excellent.

to·pog′ra·phy (tə-pog′rə-fē) *n.* the relief features of a land area; the surface configuration of anything. —**top″o·graph′i·cal,** *adj.*

top′per *n.* **1,** top hat. **2,** a woman's topcoat.

top′ping *n.* a top layer or covering. —*adj.* (*Colloq.*) excellent.

top′ple (top′əl) *v.i.* fall down with the top or head foremost; tumble as from being too heavy at the top.

tops *adj.* (*Slang*) the very best.

top′sail″ (top′səl) *n.* a sail above a lower sail.

top′side″ *n.* the upper part of a ship's side.

top′soil″ *n.* surface soil, essential to agriculture.

top′sy-tur′vy (top′sē-tēr′vē) *adj. & adv.* upside down; in reverse of normal position or order; disorderly. —**top′sy-tur′vi·ness,** *n.*

toque (tōk) *n.* **1,** a woman's hat with little or no brim. **2,** a knitted winter cap.

To′rah (tō′rə) *n.* **1,** the Pentateuch. **2,** the Scriptures of Judaism.

torch (tôrch) *n.* **1,** something burning carried in the hand to give light; (*Brit.*) a flashlight. **2,** a portable instrument producing a jet of flame. **3,** any source of illumination or enlightenment. —**torch song,** a song of unrequited love.

torch′bear″er *n.* a leader; (*Colloq.*) a zealous adherent.

torch′light″ *n.* light given by a torch.

tore (tôr) *v.* pret. of *tear.*

tor′e·a·dor″ (tôr′ē-ə-dôr″) *n.* in bullfighting, an assistant of the matador.

tor·ment′ (tôr-ment′) *v.t.* **1,** afflict with pain or misery; distress, worry, or annoy. **2,** stir up; disturb. —*n.* (tôr′ment) suffering; something that torments. —**tor·men′tor,** *n.*

torn (tôrn) *v.* p.p. of *tear.*

tor·na′do (tôr-nā′dō) *n.* a destructive whirlwind.

tor·pe′do (tôr-pē′dō) *n.* **1,** a self-propelled missile containing an explosive charge, launched in water. **2,** a submarine mine. **3,** a charge of explosive. **4,** (*Slang*) a hired ruffian.

tor′pid (tôr′pid) *adj.* sluggish; slow; inactive. —**tor·pid′i·ty,** *n.*

tor′por (tôr′pər) *n.* **1,** sluggishness in bodily functioning; stupor. **2,** stupidity. **3,** inactivity; lethargy.

torque (tôrk) *n.* a force that tends to cause torsion or rotation.

tor′re·fy (tôr′ə-fī) *v.t.* dry or parch with heat. —**tor″re·fac′tion,** *n.*

tor′rent (tor′ənt) *n.* **1,** an abundant and violent flow of water; a heavy rain. **2,** an overwhelming flow of anything. —**tor·ren′tial** (-shəl) *adj.*

tor′rid (tor′id) *adj.* **1,** hot, dry, and arid in climate. **2,** ardent; passionate. —**Torrid Zone,** the zone centered on the Equator.

tor′sion (tôr′shən) *n.* the act or result of twisting. —**tor′sion·al,** *adj.*

tor′so (tôr′sō) *n.* [*pl.* **-sos**] the trunk of the human body.

tort (tôrt) *n.* (*Law*) a civil wrong calling for compensation in damages.

tor″ti·col′lis (tôr″ti-kol′is) *n.* a twisted neck; wryneck.

tor·til′la (tôr-tē′yə) *n.* a Mexican cake of unleavened corn meal.

tor′toise (tôr′təs) *n.* a turtle of a terrestrial variety. —**tor′toise-shell″,** *adj.* of tortoise shell, or its yellow-and-brown coloring.

tor·to′ni (tôr-tō′nē) *n.* a rich Italian ice cream with fruit and nuts.

tor′tu·ous (tôr′choo-əs) *adj.* full of twists and turns; winding; crooked. —**tor′tu·ous·ness,** *n.*

tor′ture (tôr′chər) *n.* **1,** the act of willfully

inflicting severe pain. **2,** excruciating pain or anguish. **3,** a cause of anguish. —*v.t.* **1,** subject to torture. **2,** distort. —**tor′tur·er,** *n.*

to′ry (tôr′ē) *n. & adj.* one who is conservative in political views, esp. a supporter of an established monarchy or aristocracy.

toss (tâs) *v.t.* **1,** throw or fling, esp. with little effort. **2,** tumble about; agitate. **3,** jerk. —*v.i.* **1,** be pitched or rocked about; sway. **2,** move restlessly. **3,** decide something by the way a tossed coin falls. —*n.* a throw, fling, jerk, or pitch.

toss′pot″ (tâs′pot″) *n.* (*Colloq.*) a heavy drinker; toper; tippler.

toss-′up″ *n.* **1,** the tossing of a coin. **2,** (*Colloq.*) an even chance.

tot *n.* **1,** a small child. **2,** a small quantity. —*v.t.* [**tot′ted, -ting**] (usu. with *up*) add.

to′tal (tō′təl) *adj.* **1,** pert. to the whole; taking all together. **2,** being or comprising the whole. **3,** complete; absolute. —*n.* **1,** the sum; the whole or aggregate. —*v.t. & i.* **1,** ascertain the sum of; add up. **2,** amount to. **3,** (*Slang*) destroy totally. —**total war,** war waged with greatest possible effort.

to·tal″i·tar′i·an (tō-tal″i-târ′ē-ən) *adj.* pert. to a government that suppresses opposition. —*n.* an adherent of such government. —**to·tal″i·tar′i·an·ism,** *n.*

to·tal′i·ty (tō-tal′ə-tē) *n.* an entirety; a whole.

to′tal·i·za″tor (tō′təl-i-zā″tər) *n.* (*T.N.*) a device for registering parimutuel ticket sales. Also, **to′tal·iz″er.**

tote (tōt) *v.t.* (*Colloq.*) carry. —**tote bag,** a large handbag. —**tote board,** (*Colloq.*) an electrical display board for racetrack calculations.

to′tem (tō′təm) *n.* an emblem of a clan or family. —**to′tem·ism,** *n.* —**totem pole,** a post carved or painted with totems, erected by certain American Indians.

tot′ter (tot′ər) *v.i.* **1,** walk unsteadily. **2,** sway or shake as if about to fall. —*n.* an act of tottering.

tou·can′ (too-kän′) *n.* a tropical Amer. bird with an enormous beak and brilliant plumage.

touch (tuch) *v.t.* **1,** perceive by physical contact; feel by tactile sense. **2,** be or come in contact with. **3,** reach; stop at; equal; attain. **4,** put the hand on; handle. **5,** refer or allude to; deal with. **6,** pertain or relate to. **7,** (with *up*) modify; improve. **8,** affect, as with pity. **9,** tinge; imbue. **10,** (*Slang*) borrow or beg money from. —*v.i.* **1,** come or be in contact. **2,** (with *on* or *upon*) allude to something briefly. —*n.* **1,** the sense of feeling. **2,** the act of touching; adjacency. **3,** communication. **4,** a quality perceptible

to the touch. **5,** a small quantity or degree. **6,** a detail of handiwork. **7,** skill or style in execution. —**touch and go,** a precarious state of affairs.

touch′back″ *n.* in football, the grounding of the ball by a player behind his own goal line.

touch′down″ *n.* a scoring play in football.

tou·ché′ (too-shā′) *interj.* acknowledgment of a point scored, in fencing, conversation, etc.

touched (tucht) *adj.* **1,** affected with emotion. **2,** mentally feeble; eccentric.

touch′ing *prep.* in reference to. —*adj.* emotionally affecting.

touch′stone″ *n.* a test or criterion.

touch′tone″ *adj.* (*T.N.*) designating a telephone operated by push-buttons.

touch′y *adj.* **1,** irritable. **2,** risky; delicate. —**touch′i·ness,** *n.*

tough (tuf) *adj.* **1,** not easily broken or cut. **2,** flexible without brittleness; hardy. **3,** stiff in consistency; difficult to chew. **4,** unyielding; hardened; incorrigible. **5,** troublesome; hard to do or bear. **6,** violent; severe. **7,** rowdy; vicious. —*n.* a ruffian or bully. —**tough′en,** *v.t.* make tougher. —**tough′ness,** *n.*

tou·pee′ (too-pā′) *n.* a hairpiece.

tour (tûr) *n.* **1,** a journey to several places in succession. **2,** a period of work or duty. —*v.i. & t.* travel about. —**touring car,** an open automobile for five or more passengers. —**tour′ist,** *n.* a traveler for pleasure. —**tourist class,** service next below first class; second class.

tour de force (toor′də-fôrs′) (*Fr.*) a feat of skill or strength.

tour′ism (tûr′iz-əm) *n.* **1,** travel for pleasure. **2,** the economic activities related to and dependent on tourism.

tour′ma·line (tûr′mə-lēn) *n.* a mineral, a gem when transparent.

tour′na·ment (tûr′nə-mənt) *n.* a meeting for contests.

tour′ney (tûr′nē) *n.* tournament.

tour′ni·quet (tûr′ni-ket) *n.* a tight bandage to stop bleeding.

tou′sle (tow′zəl) *v.t.* rumple.

tout (towt) *v.i.* **1,** sell horse-race betting information. **2,** solicit business, votes, etc. **3,** spy. —*v.t.* **1,** praise highly. **2,** sell a betting tip to. —*n.* one who touts.

to·var′isch (tō-vä′rish) *n.* (*Russ.*) comrade; citizen.

tow (tō) *v.t.* drag by a rope, chain, etc. —*n.* **1,** the act or means of towing. **2,** the fiber of flax, hemp, or jute. —**tow′age,** *n.*

to·ward′ (tôrd, twôrd) *prep.* **1,** in the

direction of. **2,** in furtherance of. **3,** with respect to; concerning. **4,** near. Also, **towards'.**

tow'el (tow'əl) *n.* a cloth or paper for wiping. **—tow'el·ing,** *n.* material used for towels.

tow'er (tow'ər) *n.* a high, slender building or structure. *—v.i.* rise aloft; stand high. **—tow'er·ing,** *adj.*

tow'head"ed *adj.* having flax-colored hair.

tow'hee (tō'hē) *n.* any of several Amer. finches, esp. the chewink.

town *n.* **1,** an inhabited place, larger than a village. **2,** [also, **town'ship**] a division of a county. **3,** a city or borough. **—town hall,** headquarters of a town's government. **—town meeting,** a meeting of the citizens of a town.

town'house" *n.* a house in the city, esp. one of a row of such houses sharing common side walls.

town'ship" *n.* **1,** a unit of territory, varying in size and function in different states and countries, in the U.S. usually 6 miles square. **2,** a town.

towns'man (townz'mən) *n.* [*pl.* **-men**] an inhabitant of a town or of the same town. **—towns'peo"ple, towns'folk",** *n.pl.*

tow'path" *n.* the path on the bank of a canal or river traveled by animal or man towing a boat.

tow'truck" *n.* a truck equipped for towing vehicles.

tox·e'mi·a (tok-sē'mē-ə) *n.* the presence of toxins in the blood. **—tox·e'mic,** *adj.*

tox'ic (tok'sik) *adj.* **1,** poisonous. **2,** pert. to a toxin. **—tox·ic'i·ty** (toks-is'ə-tē) *n.*

tox"i·col'o·gy (tok"si-kol'ə-jē) *n.* the science of poisons. **—tox"i·co·log'i·cal,** *adj.* **—tox"i·col'o·gist,** *n.*

tox'in (tok'sin) *n.* a poisonous product of microorganisms.

toy (toi) *n.* **1,** any article played with by a child; a plaything. **2,** a trinket; a trifle. **3,** a dog of small size. *—adj.* **1,** made as a plaything. **2,** diminutive. *—v.i.* **1,** play. **2,** trifle idly; trifle.

toy'on (toi'ən) *n.* an evergreen shrub with white flowers and red berries.

trace (trās) *n.* **1,** a mark, track, or any evidence of someone or something formerly present or existent. **2,** a very small quantity of something. **3,** a line or sketch. **4,** a strap, rope, or chain for hitching a draft animal. **5,** a bar or lever for transferring motion. *—v.i.* **1,** follow the footprints or track of. **2,** determine the course, development, or history of. **3,** find evidence of; investigate. **4,** copy (a drawing, etc.) by marking the lines on superimposed transparent paper. **5,** make a plan of.

trac'er (trās'ər) *n.* one who or that which traces. *—adj.* that traces. **—skip tracer,** detective who seeks debt-evaders. **—tracer bullet,** one that blazes in flight, to indicate its course.

trac'er·y (trā'sə-rē) *n.* **1,** ornamental openwork built in a window. **2,** any delicate interlacing.

tra'che·a (trā'kē-ə) *n.* [*pl.* **-ae"** (-ē")] the tube that conveys air from the larynx to the lungs; the windpipe. **—tra'che·al,** *adj.*

tra"che·ot'o·my (trā"kē-ot'ə-mē) *n.* the cutting of an opening into the trachea.

trac'ing (trās'ing) *n.* a traced copy.

track (trak) *n.* **1,** marks left in the ground, as footprints, a rut, etc. **2,** a system of rails to support and guide a moving vehicle, esp. a railroad. **3,** a path laid out for a race; running and field sports. **4,** a path or trail. **5,** a course of motion, travel, action, etc. *—v.t.* **1,** pursue; trace. **2,** make a track on; make footprints with (mud, etc.). **3,** traverse; explore. **—keep track of,** keep within sight or knowledge. **—make tracks,** (*Slang*) go away. **—track (and field) meet,** a series of track and field contests. **—track record,** (*Colloq.*) performance record in a certain job, duty, etc.

tract (trakt) *n.* **1,** an expanse of land or water; a region. **2,** a particular system in the body. **3,** a brief printed treatise.

trac'ta·ble (trak'tə-bəl) *adj.* **1,** easily led; docile; compliant. **2,** easily managed, worked, or wrought. **—trac"ta·bil'i·ty,** *n.*

trac'tion (trak'shən) *n.* **1,** the act of dragging or hauling; the state of being drawn. **2,** power of pulling or attracting. **3,** adhesive friction. **—trac'tive,** *adj.*

trac'tate (trak'tāt) *n.* a tract (def. 3).

trac'tor (trak'tər) *n.* a self-propelled vehicle that pulls heavy loads.

trade (trād) *n.* **1,** the business of buying and selling; commerce. **2,** a sale or exchange. **3,** an occupation, esp. skilled mechanical work. **4,** the persons engaged in the same occupation. **5,** customers. *—v.t.* buy, sell, barter, or exchange. *—v.i.* engage in commerce. **—trad'er,** *n.* **—trade name,** a name coined to identify a product; trademark. **—trade union,** an organization of workers in a skilled trade. **—trade wind,** a prevailing wind relied upon by ships. **—trading post,** a station of a trader in a sparsely settled region.

trade-'in" *n.* property given in part payment of a purchase.

trade-'last" *n.* a compliment reported to another on condition of receiving one oneself.

trade'mark" *n.* a patented name or visual mark attached to a product.

trade-'off" *n.* **1,** a stalemate. **2,** an exchange.

trades'man (trādz'mən) *n.* [*pl.* **-men**] a shopkeeper; merchant.

tra·di'tion (trə-dish'ən) *n.* the handing down of customs, practices, etc.; something so handed down. **—tra·di'tion·al,** *adj.* **—tra·di'tion·al·ism,** *n.* **—tra·di'tion·al·ist,** *n.*

tra·duce' (trə-dūs') *v.t.* defame; slander.

traf'fic (traf'ik) *n.* **1,** the coming and going of persons, vehicles, etc. **2,** commercial dealings; the transportation of goods. **—traf'fick·er,** *n.*—*v.i.* [**-ficked, -fick·ing**] carry on traffic; deal. **—traffic circle,** a road intersection designed to avoid cross traffic. **—traffic light,** a stoplight (def. 1).

tra·ge'di·an (trə-jē'dē-ən) *n.* an actor in a tragedy. **—tra·ge'di·enne'** (-en') *n.fem.*

trag'e·dy (traj'ə-dē) *n.* **1,** a lamentable event or state of affairs; a disaster or calamity. **2,** a drama with an unhappy ending.

trag'ic (traj'ik) *adj.* being or suggesting a tragedy; very unhappy. Also, **trag'i·cal.**

trag'i·com'e·dy (traj'i-) *n.* a drama or incident of mixed tragic and comic character. **—trag'i·com'ic,** *adj.*

trail (trāl) *v.t.* **1,** drag loosely, as along the ground; draw along behind. **2,** follow the trail of; track. **3,** (*Colloq.*) follow behind, as in a race. **4,** make a path through; mark out. **—***v.i.* **1,** hang down or be dragged loosely behind something. **2,** proceed idly or lazily; loiter or straggle. **3,** be dispersed. **—***n.* **1,** a rough path. **2,** a track or scent. **3,** something that trails behind. **—trail bike,** a motorcycle designed for use on trails and other rough terrain.

trail'blaz"er *n.* one who goes first, a pioneer or originator.

trail'er (trā'lər) r *n.* **1,** a vehicle drawn by another. **2,** a kind of mobile house drawn by an automobile. **3,** a trailing plant. **4,** brief excerpts from a motion picture to advertise it.

train (trān) *n.* **1,** a railroad locomotive and the cars connected to it. **2,** a procession of persons, vehicles, etc., traveling together. **3,** a body of attendants; a retinue. **4,** something that trails along behind; a trailing skirt. **5,** a series of events, ideas, etc. **—***v.t.* **1,** subject to discipline and instruction; make proficient or fit. **2,** aim or direct, as a gun. **—***v.i.* undergo or impart training.

train·ee' (trā-nē') *n.* one who receives training, esp. military.

train'er *n.* **1,** one who trains others. **2,** in some sports, one who gives rubdowns, applies bandages, etc.

train'man (-mən) *n.* [*pl.* **-men**] a member of a railroad conductor's crew.

traipse (trāps) *v.i.* **1,** walk carelessly or idly. **2,** trail untidily.

trait (trāt) *n.* a distinguishing feature or quality.

trai'tor (trā'tər) *n.* one who betrays; one guilty of treason. **—trai'tor·ous,** *adj.*

tra·jec'to·ry (trə-jek'tə-rē) *n.* the curve described by a projectile in flight.

tram *n.* a wheeled car; (*Brit.*) a streetcar. **—tram'way",** *n.*

tram'mel (tram'əl) *n.* **1,** an impediment. **2,** an instrument for drawing ellipses. **3,** a shackle. **—***v.t.* shackle; hamper.

tramp *v.i.* **1,** walk with a heavy step. **2,** walk steadily or resolutely; trudge. **3,** travel about as a vagabond. **—***v.t.* **1,** traverse on foot. **2,** trample underfoot. **—***n.* **1,** a heavy tread. **2,** the sound of a heavy footstep. **3,** a long walk. **4,** a vagabond who lives by begging or stealing. **5,** a freight ship without fixed ports of call. **6,** (*Slang*) a prostitute.

tram'ple (tram'pəl) *v.t.* **1,** step heavily upon; crush with the feet. **2,** suppress by force.

tram"po·line' (tram"pə-lēn') *n.* a sheet of canvas attached by springs to a frame used for tumbling.

trance (trăns) *n.* **1,** a state of partial unconsciousness. **2,** a daze.

tran'quil (trang'kwil) *adj.* calm; serene; undisturbed. **—tran·quil'li·ty,** *n.* **—tran'·quil·ize"** (-īz") *v.t.* **—tran'quil·iz"er,** *n.* a drug used to reduce tension.

trans- *pref.* across; beyond.

trans·act' *v.t. & i.* carry through (dealings, etc.) to a conclusion; perform; do. **—trans·ac'tion,** *n.* performance; a deal.

trans"at·lan'tic *adj.* **1,** crossing the Atlantic Ocean. **2,** situated across the Atlantic.

trans·ceiv'er (tran-sē'vər) *n.* a combined radio transmitter and receiver.

tran·scend' (tran-send') *v.t.* go or be beyond (a limit, etc.); surpass; excel. **—tran·scend'ence,** *n.* **—tran·scend'ent,** *adj.*

tran"scen·den'tal (tran"sən-den'təl) *adj.* beyond ordinary experience. **—Transcendental Meditation,**™ (*T.N.*) a method of meditation for increasing mental effectiveness and reducing anxiety and tension. Also, **T.M.**™

tran"scen·den'tal·ism (-iz-əm) *n.* a philosophy based on reasoning or intuition, not empiricism.

trans"con·ti·nen'tal *adj.* crossing, or situated across, a continent; (*U.S.*) coast-to-coast.

tran·scribe' (tran-skrīb') *v.t.* **1,** make a

written copy of. **2,** put into writing; write in other characters; transliterate. **3,** make a phonograph recording of. **4,** arrange (a musical composition) for other instruments.

tran'script (tran'skript) *n.* a written copy.

tran·scrip'tion (-skrip'shən) *n.* **1,** act or result of transcribing. **2,** a transcript. **3,** a record for broadcasting.

trans·du'cer (-doo'sər) *n.* a device that converts energy from one form to another.

tran'sept *n.* that part of a cross-shaped church at right angles to the nave.

trans·fer' (trans-fēr') *v.t.* [**trans·ferred', -fer'ring**] **1,** move or convey from one place to another. **2,** make over custody or ownership of. **3,** copy or impress (a design, etc.) from one surface to another. —*n.* (trans'fēr) **1,** the act or means of transferring. **2,** a ticket valid as fare on another car of a transit system. **3,** something to be transferred, as a design. —**trans"fer·ee'**, *n.* —**trans'fer·ence**, *n.* —**trans·fer'or**, *n.*

trans·fig"u·ra'tion (trans-fig"yə-rā'shən) *n.* **1,** transfiguration. **2,** (*cap.*) the change in appearance of Christ on the Mount.

trans·fig'ure *v.t.* **1,** change the outward form or appearance of; transform. **2,** give a glorified appearance to; exalt. —**trans·fig'ure·ment**, *n.*

trans·fix' *v.t.* **1,** pierce through; fasten by pinning down. **2,** make motionless with amazement, etc. —**trans·fix'ion**, *n.*

trans·form' *v.t.* change in form, appearance, or condition.

trans"for·ma'tion *n.* **1,** act or effect of transforming. **2,** a wig.

trans·form'er *n.* an apparatus for changing electric current.

trans·fuse' (trans-fūz') *v.t.* transfer (liquid) by or as by pouring; inject; infuse. —**trans·fu'sion**, *n.* a transfer of blood from one person to another.

trans·gress' (trans-gres') *v.t. & i.* **1,** go beyond (a limit, etc.). **2,** break or violate (a law or rule.). —**trans·gres'sion** (-gresh'ən) *n.* —**trans·gres'sor** (-gres'ər) *n.*

tran'sient (tran'shənt) *adj.* passing with time; not enduring; temporary; momentary. —*n.* one who stays briefly, as a guest. —**tran'sience**, *n.*

tran·sis'tor (tran-sis'tər) *n.* a small electronic device used instead of a tube, to modify the signal.

tran'sit *n.* **1,** passage or conveyance from one place to another. **2,** a surveying instrument for measuring angles.

tran·si'tion (-zish'ən) *n.* a change from one place or state to another. —**tran·si'tion·al**, *adj.*

tran'si·tive (tran'sə-tiv) *adj.* **1,** (of a verb)

taking a direct object. **2,** making, or having power to make, a transition.

tran'si·to"ry (tran'sə-tôr"ē) *adj.* lasting only for a time; fleeting.

trans·late' (trans-lāt') *v.t.* **1,** express the sense of in words of another language. **2,** explain by using other words. **3,** transfer. —**trans·la'tion**, *n.* —**trans·la'tor**, *n.*

trans·lit'er·ate' (trans-lit'ər-āt") *v.t.* spell in another alphabet or language. —**trans'-lit·er·a'tion**, *n.*

trans·lu'cent (trans-loo'sənt) *adj.* transmitting light without being transparent. —**trans·lu'cence**, *n.*

trans"mi·gra'tion *n.* passage, esp. of a soul reborn in another body. —**trans·mi'grate**, *v.i.*

trans·mis'si·ble *adj.* capable of being transmitted. —**trans·mis'si·bil'i·ty**, *n.*

trans·mis'sion (trans-mish'ən) *n.* **1,** the act or result of transmitting. **2,** a system of gears for transmitting power in an automobile.

trans·mit' *v.t.* [**trans·mit'ted, -ting**] **1,** send onward or along; hand over, or down to, a recipient or destination. **2,** communicate; emit. —**trans·mit'tal**, *n.*

trans·mit'ter (-ər) *n.* the sending part of a radio or telephone apparatus.

trans·mog'ri·fy' (-mog'rə-fī") *v.t.* (*Humorous*) transform, as by magic. —**trans·mog"ri·fi·ca'tion**, *n.*

trans·mute' (trans-mūt') *v.t. & i.* change from one nature, form, or substance to another. —**trans"mu·ta'tion**, *n.*

tran'som (tran'səm) *n.* **1,** a beam above a door separating it from a window. **2,** a hinged window or panel above a door. **3,** any crossbeam.

trans·par'ent (trans-par'ənt) *adj.* **1,** permitting distinct vision through a solid substance. **2,** easily understood; manifest. —**trans·par'ence, trans·par'en·cy**, *n.*

tran·spire' (tran-spīr') *v.i.* **1,** emit a vapor; exhale or perspire. **2,** escape through pores. **3,** become known. **4,** happen; occur. —**tran"spi·ra'tion**, *n.*

trans·plant' *v.t.* remove from one place and plant, fix, or establish in another.

trans·pon'der (tran-spon'dər) *n.* a transceiver activated by a predetermined signal.

trans·port' (trans-pôrt') *v.t.* **1,** carry from one place to another; convey. **2,** imbue with strong emotion. **3,** carry into banishment. —*n.* (trans'pôrt) **1,** the act or business of transporting. **2,** a means of transport, esp. a ship for carrying troops. **3,** rapture.

trans"por·ta'tion (trans"pôr-tā'shən) *n.*

1, act or result, or a means, of conveying. **2,** traveling expenses.

trans·pose' (trans-pōz') v.t. **1,** alter the position or order of. **2,** exchange the places of. **3,** [also v.i.] arrange or perform (music) in a different key. —**trans"po·si'tion,** n.

trans·sex'u·al n. & adj. a person who has undergone, or desires to undergo, a change of sex.

trans·ship' v.t. & i. ship by more than one carrier.

tran"sub·stan'ti·ate (tran"səb-stan'shē-āt") v.t. **1,** change from one substance into another. **2,** (*Theol.*) change (the bread and wine of the Eucharist) into the body and blood of Christ. —**tran"sub·stan"ti·a'tion,** n.

trans·ver'sal (trans-vērs'əl) n. a line intersecting two or more other lines.

trans·verse' (trans-vērs') adj. lying across something; extending from side to side.

trans·vest'ism (tranz-vest'iz-əm) n. desire to wear the clothes of the opposite sex. Also, **trans·ves'ti·tism.** —**trans·vest'ite,** n.

trap n. **1,** any contrivance for catching animals; a pitfall or snare; a stratagem. **2,** a U-bend in a pipe. **3,** (*pl.*) baggage; equipment; the percussion instruments of a band. **4,** a door in a floor, ceiling, or roof; trapdoor. **5,** a light two-wheeled carriage. —v.t. [**trapped, trap'ping**] catch in a trap; ensnare in any way. —v.i. trap animals.

trap'door" n. a door in a floor, ceiling, or roof.

tra·peze' (trə-pēz') n. a horizontal bar suspended by two ropes, used for gymnastic exercises.

tra·pe'zi·um (trə-pē'zē-əm) n. a quadrilateral plane figure having no two sides parallel.

trap'e·zoid" (trap'i-zoid") n. a quadrilateral figure with two sides parallel.

trap'per (-ər) n. one who traps animals, esp. fur-bearing animals.

trap'pings (-ingz) n.pl. equipment.

Trap'pist (trap'ist) adj. pert. to a Rom. Cath. order of monks.

trap'rock" n. an igneous rock, as basalt.

trap'shoot"ing n. the sport of shooting at flying targets.

trash n. anything worthless or useless; waste material; rubbish. —v.t. (*Slang*) **1,** vandalize. **2,** run down; disparage. **3,** discard. —**trash'y,** adj.

trau'ma (trâ'mə) n. **1,** a bodily injury. **2,** a mental shock. —**trau·mat'ic,** adj. —**trau·mat'i·cal·ly,** adv.

trav'ail (trav'āl) n. painful labor. —v.i. suffer the pangs of childbirth.

trav'el (trav'əl) v.i. **1,** go from place to

place; make a journey. **2,** move on a fixed track, as a mechanical part. **3,** advance; proceed. **4,** (*Colloq.*) move speedily. —v.t. pass over or through. —n. the act of traveling. —**tra'vel·er,** n.

trav'eled (trav'əld) adj. **1,** having traveled widely. **2,** experienced. **3,** used by travelers, as a road.

trav'e·logue" (trav'ə-lâg") n. a lecture or motion picture describing a journey. Also, **trav'e·log".**

trav'erse (trav'ərs) v.t. **1,** pass across, over, or through. **2,** contradict; obstruct. **3,** turn and aim (a gun). —n. something that lies or moves crosswise; a crosswise barrier. —adj. transverse. —**traverse rod,** a mechanical curtain rod.

trav'er·tine" (trav'ər-tīn") n. a soft, straw-colored form of limestone.

trav'es·ty (trav'is-tē) n. a burlesque of a literary or dramatic composition; any debased likeness. —v.t. imitate grotesquely.

trawl (trål) n. a fishing net or line dragged by a boat. —v.i. fish with a trawl. —**trawl'er,** n. a fishing boat.

tray (trā) n. a flat vessel or shallow box for holding something.

treach'er·ous (trech'ə-rəs) adj. **1,** committing treachery. **2,** deceptive; unreliable. —**treach'er·ous·ness,** n.

treach'er·y (trech'ə-rē) n. violation of allegiance or faith; betrayal of trust; treason or perfidy.

trea'cle (trē'kəl) n. molasses.

tread (tred) v.i. [**trod, trod'den** (-dən), **tread'ing**] set the foot down; step; walk. —v.t. **1,** walk on, in, or along. **2,** trample. **3,** execute by walking or dancing. —n. **1,** a stepping; the sound of a step; a single step. **2,** the undermost surface, as of a shoe, tire, etc., that touches the ground or road. **3,** a bearing surface, as of a rail or stair. —**tread water, 1,** swim so as to remain upright with the head above water. **2,** barely survive without improving one's lot. **3,** not make progress.

trea'dle (tred'əl) n. a lever operated by the foot.

tread'mill" n. **1,** a mill powered by animals walking on a wheel, etc. **2,** any monotonous and wearisome routine.

trea'son (trē'zən) n. violation of the allegiance due a state. —**trea'son·a·ble,** adj. constituting treason. —**trea'son·ous,** adj.

treas'ure (trezh'ər) n. **1,** an accumulation of money or jewels. **2,** anything prized highly. —v.t. **1,** collect and save; retain carefully. **2,** regard as precious; prize. —**treasure trove** (trōv) money or valuables (of an unknown owner) found in the earth.

treas'ur·er (trezh'ər-ər) *n.* the officer in charge of funds.

treas'ur·y (trezh'ə-rē) *n.* **1,** the funds of a government, corporation, etc.; the department administering them. **2,** a place where money or valuables are kept.

treat (trēt) *v.t.* **1,** regard, behave toward, or deal with; discuss. **2,** apply methods of relief or cure to (a patient or disease). **3,** subject to a process. **4,** entertain by paying for food, drink, amusement, etc. —*v.i.* **1,** discuss something. **2,** carry on negotiations. **3,** bear the expense of regalement. —*n.* **1,** entertainment paid for; one's turn to pay. **2,** (*Colloq.*) anything enjoyable.

trea'tise (trē'tis) *n.* a book treating of a particular subject.

treat'ment (-mənt) *n.* **1,** act or manner of dealing with something. **2,** therapy.

trea'ty (trē'tē) *n.* a written agreement between nations.

tre'ble (treb'əl) *adj.* **1,** threefold. **2,** high in pitch; soprano. —*n.* a high-pitched part, tone, etc. —*v.t. & i.* triple. —**treble clef,** a G clef on the second line of a staff.

tree (trē) *n.* **1,** a large perennial plant with a single permanent woody trunk. **2,** any of various devices or parts in the form of a pole, bar, etc. **3,** a genealogical diagram: *family tree.* —*v.t.* drive into a tree.

tre'foil″ (trē'foil″) *n.* a three-leaved plant, esp. the clover.

trek *v.i.* [**trekked, trek'king**] travel; migrate. —*n.* a journey.

trel'lis (trel'is) *n.* a framework of cross-bars; a lattice.

trem'a·tode″ (trem'ə-tōd″) *n.* any of a class of parasitic flatworms.

trem'ble (trem'bəl) *v.i.* **1,** shake or vibrate with continued movement; shiver; quake. **2,** be agitated by fear. **3,** vacillate. —*n.* a shivering or vibratory motion. —**trem'bly,** *adj.*

tre·men'dous (tri-men'dəs) *adj.* **1,** very great in size, amount, degree, etc.; huge; gigantic. **2,** (*Colloq.*) excellent. —**tre·men'dous·ness,** *n.*

trem'o·lo″ (trem'ə-lō″) *n.* [*pl.* **-los″**] rapid reiteration of a musical tone.

trem'or (trem'ər) *n.* a shake, quiver, or vibration; a trembling or vibratory movement.

trem'u·lous (trem'yə-ləs) *adj.* **1,** trembling; unsteady. **2,** fearful; timid; irresolute. **3,** wavy, as a line. —**trem'u·lous·ness,** *n.*

trench *n.* a long, narrow excavation in the ground, esp. as a shelter in warfare; a ditch or furrow. —*v.t. & i.* dig a trench (in); fortify. —**trench coat,** a heavy raincoat. —**trench mouth,** an infectious disease of the mucous membranes of the throat and mouth.

trench'ant (tren'chənt) *adj.* **1,** keenly effective; incisive. **2,** thoroughgoing. —**trench'-an·cy,** *n.*

trench'er *n.* a wooden platter for serving meat.

trench'er·man (tren'chər-mən) *n.* [*pl.* **-men**] a heavy eater.

trend *n.* tendency to go in a particular direction or course; drift, bent, or inclination. —**trend'y,** *adj.* (*Colloq.*).

tre·pan' (trə-pan') *n.* a cylindrical saw; a boring instrument. —*v.t.* [**-panned', -pan'ning**] cut with a trepan.

tre·pang' (trē-pang') *n.* a sea cucumber, often dried, smoked, and used as food. Also, **bêche-de-mer.**

tre·phine' (tri-fīn') *n.* a cylindrical saw used in brain surgery.

trep″i·da'tion (trep″ə-dā'shən) *n.* tremulous agitation, as from alarm.

tres'pass (tres'pəs) *v.i.* **1,** enter without right upon another's land; encroach. **2,** commit a wrong; transgress; sin. —*n.* an offense; sin.

tress (tres) *n.* **1,** a lock or braid of hair. **2,** (*pl.*) the hair of the head.

tres'tle (tres'əl) *n.* **1,** a short horizontal bar supported by legs; a sawhorse. **2,** a bridge supported by framework.

trey (trā) *n.* a playing card, die, domino, etc., with three spots.

tri- (trī) *pref.* three.

tri'ad (trī'ad) *n.* **1,** a group of three closely-related things. **2,** (*Music*) a chord of three tones.

tri·age' (trē-äzh') *n.* the act of sorting, esp. of combat casualties for treatment.

tri'al (trī'əl) *n.* **1,** an action in a judicial court to determine a cause. **2,** a test; an examination. **3,** a try or attempt. **4,** the state of being tried or tested; probation. **5,** a hardship. —*adj.* **1,** pert. to a trial. **2,** done as a test or experiment. —**trial and error,** a method of solving a problem by a series of guesses. —**trial balance,** a statement of the current totals in a ledger. —**trial balloon,** an act or statement to test public reaction.

tri'an″gle (trī'ang″gəl) *n.* **1,** a plane figure formed by three straight lines. **2,** a drawing instrument in this shape. **3,** a steel bar bent into a triangle used as a musical percussion instrument. **4,** two men and a woman, or two women and a man involved in emotional conflict. —**tri·an'gu·lar** (trī-ang'gyû-lər) *adj.*

tri·an″gu·la'tion (trī-ang″gyû-lā'shən) *n.* a measuring by inferring unknown sides or angles of a triangle. —**tri·ang′u·late″** (-lāt″) *v.t.*

tribe (trīb) *n.* **1**, an aggregate of people united by common ancestry, intermarriage, or allegiance. **2**, any class or body of individuals. —**trib′al**, *adj.* —**tribes′man**, *n.*

trib″u·la′tion (trib″yə-lā′shən) *n.* a state, cause, or instance of affliction or suffering.

tri·bu′nal (trī-bū′nəl) *n.* a court of justice.

trib′une (trib′ūn) *n.* **1**, a person who upholds or defends popular rights. **2**, a dais or pulpit.

trib′u·tar″y (trib′yə-ter″ē) *n.* **1**, a river, brook, etc., that flows into another body of water. **2**, one who pays tribute. —*adj.* contributory.

trib′ute (trib′ūt) *n.* **1**, a gift or compliment as a mark of gratitude or respect. **2**, any forced payment.

trice (trīs) *n.* an instant; moment.

tri″cen·ten′ni·al *adj. & n.* tercentenary.

tri′ceps (trī′seps) *n.* a three-headed muscle, esp. the extensor muscle along the back of the upper arm.

trich″i·no′sis (trik″ə-nō′sis) *n.* a disease caused by a parasitic worm.

trick (trik) *n.* **1**, any method of deceiving; a stratagem, ruse, or wile. **2**, a practical joke, prank, or hoax. **3**, a peculiar habit or mannerism. **4**, a batch of playing cards, one played from each hand. **5**, (*Colloq.*) a girl. **6**, a turn of work or duty. —*adj.* fraudulent; crafty; unreliable; unusual. —*v.t. & i.* **1**, dupe; swindle. **2**, (with *out*) dress; array.

trick′er·y (-ə-rē) *n.* deception.

trick′le (trik′əl) *v.i.* flow slowly, irregularly, or by drops. —*v.t.* cause to trickle. —*n.* a trickling flow.

trick′ster (-stər) *n.* a deceiver; a joker.

trick′track″ *n.* a variety of backgammon. Also, **tric′trac″**.

trick′y *adj.* **1**, crafty. **2**, unreliable; ticklish. —**trick′i·ness**, *n.*

tri′col″or (trī′kul″ər) *n.* a flag of three colors.

tri′corne (trī′kôrn) *n.* a three-cornered cocked hat.

tri′cot (trē′kō) *n.* a knitted fabric.

tri′cy·cle (trī′sik-əl) *n.* a three-wheeled vehicle for a child; a velocipede.

tri′dent (trī′dənt) *n. & adj.* a spear or fork having three prongs.

tried (trīd) *v.* pret. & p.p. of *try.*

tri·fec′ta (trī-fek′tə) *n.* a kind of perfecta.

tri′fle (trī′fəl) *n.* something trivial or insignificant. —*v.i.* **1**, deal with something lightly or idly. **2**, waste time; dally. —**tri′fler** (-flər) *n.* —**tri′fling**, *adj.* insignificant.

tri·fo′cal (trī-fō′kəl) *adj.* having three

lenses. —*n.* (*pl.*) eyeglasses having lenses of three different strengths.

trig *adj.* [**trig′ger, -gest**] **1**, neat; spruce. **2**, in good condition. —*n.* a block used to check the motion of a wheel, cask, etc.

trig′ger (trig′ər) *n.* a lever for releasing a spring, esp. on a firearm.

trig″o·nom′e·try (trig″ə-nom′ə-trē) *n.* the branch of mathematics that deals with measurement of and by means of triangles. —**trig″o·no·met′ric** (-nə-met′rik) *adj.*

trill (tril) *n.* **1**, a rapid alternation of two adjacent musical tones. **2**, any quavering, tremulous sound. **3**, a warbling, as of a bird. —*v.i. & t.* sound vibrantly.

tril′lion (tril′yən) *n. & adj.* the cardinal number represented by 1 followed by 12 zeros (U.S. & Fr.) or 18 zeros (Brit. & Ger.).

tril′li·um (tril′ē-əm) *n.* a plant of the lily family.

tril′o·gy (tril′ə-jē) *n.* a group of three related things, as plays.

trim *v.t.* [**trimmed, trim′ming**] **1**, make neat or orderly. **2**, remove by clipping or pruning. **3**, deck with ornaments. **4**, (*Colloq.*) defeat. —*v.i.* come to a desired adjustment or position. —*n.* **1**, position, condition, or order. **2**, dress, equipment, or decoration; ornamental borders or furnishings. —*adj.* [**trim′mer, -mest**] **1**, neat; spruce; smart. **2**, in good order or condition. —**trim′mer**, *n.* —**trim′ming**, *n.* —**trim′ness**, *n.*

tri·mes′ter (trī-mes′tər) *n.* a period of three months.

trin′i·ty (trin′ə-tē) *n.* a group of three, esp. (*cap.*) Father, Son, and Holy Ghost or Spirit.

trin′ket (tring′kit) *n.* a trifling ornament or keepsake.

tri′o (trē′ō) *n.* a group of three.

tri′ode (trī′ōd) *n.* an electron tube containing three elements.

trip *n.* **1**, a journey or voyage. **2**, a catching of the foot against an obstacle; a stumble. **3**, a slip or error. **4**, a light, short step. **5**, a catch or trigger; a sudden release, as by a trigger. **6**, (*Slang*) the hallucinations, heightened perceptions, etc., experienced under the influence of a hallucinogenic drug. —*v.i.* [**tripped, trip′ping**] **1**, stumble. **2**, make a mistake. **3**, run or step lightly; skip. **4**, have a psychedelic experience. —*v.t.* **1**, cause to stumble, fall, or err. **2**, perform with a tripping step. **3**, release suddenly. —**trip′per**, *n.*

tri·par′tite (trī-pär′tīt) *adj.* embracing three parties, as a treaty.

tripe (trīp) *n.* **1**, the stomach of a cow or

ox, prepared as food. **2**, (*Slang*) anything worthless.

trip'ham'mer *n.* a heavy hammer allowed to fall by a tripping device.

tri'ple (trip'əl) *adj.* consisting of three parts; threefold; of three kinds. —*n.* a three-fold object or amount; (*Baseball*) a three-base hit. —*v.t. & i.* multiply by three.

trip'let *n.* one of three offspring born at one birth; one of a group of three; (*pl.*) the three collectively.

tri'plex (trip'leks) *adj.* threefold. —*n.* something triple; an apartment having three stories.

trip'li·cate" (trip'li-kāt") *v.t.* make in three copies. —*adj.* (-kət) made in three copies. —*n.* (-kət) the third copy. —**trip"li·ca'tion,** *n.*

tri'pod (trī'pod) *n.* a stand having three legs. —**trip'o·dal** (trip'ə-dəl) *adj.*

trip'ping *adj.* light and lively.

trip'tych (trip'tik) *n.* three pictures, etc., esp. in hinged frames.

tri'reme (trī'rēm) *n.* a galley with three tiers of oars.

tri·sect' (trī-sekt') *v.t.* divide in three parts. —**tri·sec'tion,** *n.*

trite (trīt) *adj.* stale; hackneyed. —**trite'-ness,** *n.*

tri'tium (trish'yəm) *n.* an isotope of hydrogen.

trit'u·rate" (trich'ə-rāt") *v.t.* grind to powder. —**trit"u·ra'tion,** *n.*

tri'umph (trī'umf) *n.* **1,** the winning of a war or contest; success. **2,** exultation over victory or success. —*v.i.* win; succeed.

tri·um'phal (trī-um'fəl) *adj.* pert. to or commemorating a victory.

tri·um'phant (trī-um'fənt) *adj.* victorious; exulting in victory.

tri·um'vir (trī-um'vər) *n.* a member of a triumvirate.

tri·um'vi·rate (trī-um'və-rit) *n.* three joint rulers; their government.

triv'et (triv'it) *n.* **1,** a three-legged stool or stand. **2,** a short-legged plate to put under a hot platter.

triv'i·a (triv'ē-ə) *n.pl.* trivial matters or things.

triv'i·al (triv'ē-əl) *adj.* of little importance or significance. —**triv"i·al'i·ty,** *n.*

triv'i·um (triv'ē-əm) *n.* grammar, logic, and rhetoric, three of the seven liberal arts.

-trix *suf.* denoting a feminine agent, as *executrix*.

tro'che (trō'kē) *n.* a medicinal tablet or pill.

tro'chee (trō'kē) *n.* (*Prosody*) a metrical foot of two syllables, long then short. —**tro·cha'ic** (-kā'ik) *adj. & n.*

trod *v.* pret. of *tread*.

trod'den (trod'ən) *v.* p.p. of *tread*.

trog'lo·dyte" (trog'lə-dīt") *n.* **1,** a dweller in a cave. **2,** one who lives in seclusion. —**trog"lo·dyt'ic** (-dit'ik) *adj.*

troi'ka (troi'kə) *n.* a team of three horses; the carriage they draw.

Tro'jan horse (trō'jən) an ostensible gift intended as a trap.

troll (trōl) *v.i. & t.* **1,** sing in a full, jovial tone; sing a round. **2,** fish with a moving line. **3,** turn around; roll. —*n.* **1,** a round song. **2,** equipment for trolling. **3,** a fairy dwarf.

trol'ley (trol'ē) *n.* **1,** a pulley or block moving on an overhead wire, to convey loads or feed electric current. **2,** a streetcar.

trol'lop (trol'əp) *n.* **1,** a slovenly woman. **2,** a prostitute.

trom'bone (trom'bōn) *n.* a musical wind instrument having a sliding U-shaped section. —**trom'bon·ist,** *n.*

tromp *v.i.* (*Slang*) **1,** defeat soundly. **2,** trample upon. —*v.i.* walk noisily or heavily.

troop *n.* **1,** an assemblage of people; a herd or flock; a multitude. **2,** a unit of armed forces; (*pl.*) a body of soldiers. —*v.i. & t.* flock together; march or maneuver. —**troop'er,** *n.* a policeman or soldier.

trope (trōp) *n.* a figure of speech; metaphor.

tro'phy (trō'fē) *n.* **1,** something captured in war, hunting, etc. **2,** a prize or medal, etc.

-tro·phy (trə-fē) *suf.* denoting nourishment.

trop'ic (trop'ik) *n.* **1,** either of the two parallels of latitude 23½° distant from the equator, north (tropic of Cancer) or south (tropic of Capricorn). **2,** (*pl.*) the region lying between these two parallels; the Torrid Zone. —**trop'i·cal,** *adj.* pert. to the Torrid Zone.

trop'o·sphere" (trop'ə-sfir") *n.* the layer of atmosphere about 6 to 12 miles above the earth's surface.

-tro·py (trə-pē) *suf.* growth. Also, **-tro·pism.**

trot *v.i.* [**trot'ted, -ting**] go at a pace between a walk and a run. —*v.t.* **1,** cause (a horse) to trot. **2,** (with *out*) produce for inspection. —*n.* **1,** a trotting gait. **2,** (*Colloq.*) an illicit translation used by students; a crib. **3,** a long fishing line with numerous hooks.

troth (trâth) *n.* **1,** a promise to marry. **2,** (*Archaic*) truth.

trot'ter (trot'ər) *n.* **1,** a trotting horse. **2,** pig's foot, as food.

---

tub, cūte, pûll; labəl; oil, owl, go, chip, she, thin, *th*en, sing, ink; *see p.* 6

trou'ba·dour" (troo'bə-dôr") *n.* an itinerant lyric poet or singer, esp. of So. France.

trou'ble (trub'əl) *v.t.* **1,** disturb in the mind; annoy; worry. **2,** put to inconvenience. —*n.* **1,** discomfort; distress; inconvenience. **2,** a cause or source of trouble. —**trou'ble·some,** *adj.* causing trouble. —**trou'blous,** *adj.*

trou'ble·shoot"er *n.* one who locates and eliminates sources of trouble.

trough (trâf) *n.* **1,** a long narrow container for water, food for animals, etc. **2,** a shallow open ditch; a deep groove.

trounce (trowns) *v.t.* defeat decisively; thrash.

troupe (troop) *n.* a traveling theatrical company. —*v.i.* travel as member of a troupe. —**troup'er,** *n.*

trou'sers (trow'zərz) *n.pl.* a garment for men, extending downward from the waist, covering each leg separately. —**trou'ser,** *adj.*

trous·seau' (troo-sō') *n.* a bride's clothes and other outfit.

trout (trowt) *n.* [*pl.* **trout**] a freshwater game fish.

trou·vère' (troo-vär') *n.* a medieval narrative or epic poet of No. France.

trow (trō) *v.i.* (*Archaic*) believe.

trow'el (trow'əl) *n.* a short-handled tool with a flat or concave blade, for digging, spreading, etc.

troy (troi) *adj.* pert. to a system of weights used for gold, silver, etc.

tru'ant (troo'ənt) *n. & adj.* one who is absent without leave, esp. a student. —**tru'an·cy,** *n.*

truce (troos) *n.* **1,** a negotiated suspension of hostilities. **2,** a respite.

truck (truk) *n.* **1,** an automotive vehicle for carrying heavy loads. **2,** a frame on wheels for carrying loads; such a frame supporting a railway car or locomotive. **3,** the top of a mast. **4,** vegetables raised for marketing. **5,** miscellaneous articles. **6,** dealings; barter. —*v.t.* **1,** transport by truck. **2,** barter; peddle. —*v.i.* **1,** use or drive a truck. **2,** deal; bargain. —**truck'age,** *n.* the act or cost of transporting goods. —**truck'er,** *n.* truckman. —**truck farm,** a farm raising garden vegetables for sale.

truck'le (truk'əl) *n.* a small wheel, pulley, or caster. —*v.i.* be tamely submissive or obsequious. —**truckle bed,** a bed that can be pushed under another bed when not in use.

truck'man (-mən) *n.* [*pl.* **-men**] the owner or operator of a motor truck used as a common carrier.

truc'u·lent (truk'yə-lənt) *adj.* overbearing; cruel. —**truc'u·lence,** *n.*

trudge (truj) *v.i.* walk, esp. laboriously or wearily.

true (troo) *adj.* **1,** being in accordance with fact; not false. **2,** correct; accurate. **3,** genuine. **4,** firm in adherence to principles; faithful; loyal; truthful. **5,** sure; reliable. **6,** rightful; legitimate. —*n.* that which is true. —*v.t.* make true; shape or adjust exactly. —*adv.* in a true or truthful manner. —**true'ness,** *n.* —**tru'ly,** *adv.* —**true bill,** an indictment by a grand jury. —**true blue,** loyal.

true'love" *n.* a sweetheart.

truf'fle (truf'əl) *n.* a subterranean edible fungus.

tru'ism (troo'iz-əm) *n.* an obvious truth.

trump *n.* **1,** a playing card or suit given temporary rank higher than all cards of other suits. **2,** (*Colloq.*) a delightful person. —*v.t.* **1,** take with a trump card. **2,** (with *up*) fabricate deceitfully. —*v.i.* play a trump card.

trump'er·y (-ə-rē) *n. & adj.* something showy but of little value.

trum'pet (trum'pit) *n.* **1,** a musical wind instrument of the brass family. **2,** a noise-making toy. **3,** a loud cry, as of an elephant. **4,** a hearing aid: *ear trumpet.* —*v.i. & t.* **1,** make a trumpet's sound. **2,** proclaim. —**trum'pet·er,** *n.*

trun'cate (trung'kāt) *v.t.* reduce in size by cutting off a part. —**trun·ca'tion,** *n.*

trun'cheon (trun'chən) *n.* a baton or staff of office; a policeman's club.

trun'dle (trun'dəl) *n.* a small wheel, roller, or caster. —*v.t. & i.* **1,** move on trundles. **2,** roll along; whirl; rotate. —**trundle bed,** truckle bed.

trunk *n.* **1,** the main stem of a tree. **2,** the human or animal body without the head and limbs. **3,** the proboscis of an elephant. **4,** a large box or chest for carrying clothes in traveling. **5,** the main part or line of something having branches. **6,** (*pl.*) short trousers or breeches. —*adj.* pert. to a main line. —**trunk'ful,** *n.* —**trunk line, 1,** a transportation or supply route for long distance through traffic; main line. **2,** a direct link between two telephone offices or switchboards.

truss (trus) *v.t.* fasten; bind securely; confine closely. —*n.* **1,** a rigid framework, as to support a bridge. **2,** a belt worn for support, as of a hernia. **3,** a bundle or pack.

trust *n.* **1,** reliance on the integrity, veracity, etc. of a person; confidence. **2,** confident expectation. **3,** expectation of future payment; credit. **4,** management of property by one party (trustee) for the benefit of another (beneficiary); property given or held in trust. **5,** a group or company controlling a number of other companies. **6,** any monopolistic organization. —*adj.* pert. to a trust. —*v.t.* rely on; believe; give credit to. —*v.i.* have confidence; be trustful. —**trust company,** a bank that administers trusts.

trus·tee' (trus-tē') *n.* one to whom property is entrusted for management. —**trustee'ship,** *n.*

trust'ful *adj.* confiding. —**trust'ful·ness,** *n.*

trust'wor''thy *adj.* reliable. —**trust'wor''thi·ness,** *n.*

trust'y *adj.* reliable. —*n.* a convict trusted not to escape. —**trust'i·ness,** *n.*

truth (trooth) *n.* **1,** conformity of assertion to fact or reality; the state of being true. **2,** that which is true; a fact; reality. —**truth serum,** a drug used to induce a person to talk freely.

truth'ful *adj.* **1,** speaking the truth, esp. habitually. **2,** correct; true. —**truth'fulness,** *n.*

try (trī) *v.t.* [*pret. & p.p.* **tried** (trīd)] **1,** attempt to do or accomplish; essay; undertake. **2,** test. **3,** examine judicially; subject to trial. **4,** subject to strain, trouble, or affliction. **5,** (with *out*) refine; render. —*v.i.* make an attempt to trial. —*n.* an attempt or effort. —**try'ing,** *adj.* annoying; tiring.

try'out' *n.* a trial to determine fitness.

tryst (trist) *n.* an appointed meeting, esp. between lovers.

tsar (tsär) *n.* czar. —**tsar'e·vitch,** *n.* son of a czar. —**tsa·ri'na** (-rē'nə) *n. fem.*

tset'se (tset'sė) *n.* an Afr. blood-sucking fly that transmits diseases.

T·'shirt'' *n.* a shirt with short sleeves and no collar, used both as an undershirt for men, and as an outer shirt by both sexes.

tsim'mis (tsim'is) *n.* (*Colloq.*) a complicated affair.

T square a T-shaped ruler for drawing parallel lines.

tsu·na'mi (tsoo-nä'mė) *n.* a sea wave caused by a submarine earthquake.

tub *n.* **1,** a tanklike vessel for bathing: *bathtub.* **2,** a shallow cylindrical vessel. **3,** (*Colloq.*) a slow or clumsy boat. **4,** (*Colloq.*) a bath.

tu'ba (too'bə) *n.* a musical wind instrument of the brass family.

tub'by (tub'ė) *adj.* **1,** short and fat. **2,** having a dull sound. —**tub'bi·ness,** *n.*

tube (toob) *n.* **1,** a long, hollow cylinder of metal, glass, etc. **2,** a duct, canal, pipe, etc., for containing or conveying fluid. **3,** a bulb of glass fitted with electrodes. **4,** a tunnel; a subway. **5,** (*Slang*) a television receiver. —**tubing,** *n.* a piece of tube; material for tubes; tubes collectively.

tu'ber (too'bər) *n.* a plant having an enlarged fleshy rootlike part, as the potato. —**tu'ber·ous,** *adj.*

tu'ber·cle (too'bər-kəl) *n.* a small, rounded protuberance or excrescence, as on a bone. —**tubercle bacillus,** the organism causing tuberculosis.

tu·ber'cu·lin (too-bēr'kyə-lin) *n.* a preparation used in treating and testing for tuberculosis.

tu·ber'cu·lo'sis (too-bēr''kyŭ-lō'sis) *n.* **1,** an infectious disease marked by the formation of tubercles. **2,** this disease affecting the lungs; consumption. —**tu·ber'cu·lar, tu·ber'cu·lous,** *adj.*

tube'rose' *n.* a bulbous plant bearing white flowers.

tu'bu·lar (too'byû-lər) *adj.* being or pert. to a tube or tubes.

tuck (tuk) *v.t.* **1,** press into a narrow space; cram. **2,** cover snugly with wrappings. **3,** make tucks in. —*v.i.* draw together; contract. —*n.* a flat fold in cloth. —**tuck shop,** (*Brit.*) a variety store.

tuck'er (-ər) *n.* **1,** one who tucks. **2,** a neckcloth. —**tuckered out,** (*Colloq.*) fatigued.

-tude (tūd) *suf.* quality, state, etc.

Tu'dor (too'dər) *adj.* pert. to an Eng. dynasty or its period, 1485–1603.

Tues'day (tūz'dė) *n.* the third day of the week.

tuft *n.* a small bunch of fibrous material, as hair, feathers, grass, etc., bound at one end. —**tuft'ed,** *adj.*

tug *v.t.* [**tugged, tug'ging**] pull with force or effort; drag; haul; tow. —*v.i.* exert effort in pulling or otherwise. —*n.* **1,** a strong pull; a sudden jerk. **2,** a boat for towing: *tugboat.* **3,** a strenuous contest or struggle. **4,** a strap; trace. —**tug of war,** a pulling contest.

tu·i'tion (too-ish'ən) *n.* **1,** a fee for instruction. **2,** the act or business of teaching. —**tu·i'tion·al,** *adj.*

tu'lip (too'lip) *n.* a bulbous plant bearing cup-shaped flowers.

tulle (tool) *n.* a fine fabric; silk or rayon net.

tum'ble (tum'bəl) *v.i.* **1,** lose footing or support; fall down. **2,** descend rapidly, as prices. **3,** roll about; toss; pitch. **4,** perform gymnastic exercises. **5,** (*Slang*) (often with *to*) become suddenly aware of something. —*v.t.* **1,** cast down; upset. **2,** throw or move about; put in disorder. **3,** rotate in a box of abrasive material, for cleaning. —*n.* **1,** an act of tumbling; a fall or turn. **2,** a state of confusion. **3,** (*Slang*) a sign of recognition.

tum'ble-down" *adj.* dilapidated; ruinous; ready to fall.

tum'bler (tum'blər) *n.* **1,** a drinking glass. **2,** a gymnast; an acrobat. **3,** a lever, pin, etc., that holds the bolt of a lock. **4,** a cog or rotating part.

tum'ble-weed" *n.* a U.S. weed that breaks off at the roots in the fall.

tum'brel (tum'brəl) *n.* a dump cart. Also, **tum'bril.**

tu·mes'cent (tū-mes'ənt) *adj.* swelling; forming into a tumor. **—tu·mes'cence,** *n.*

tu'mid (too'mid) *adj.* **1,** swollen; protuberant. **2,** pompous. **—tu·mid'i·ty,** *n.*

tum'my (tum'ē) *n.* stomach; belly.

tu'mor (too'mər) *n.* an abnormal swelling in the body. Also, **tu'mour.**

tu'mult (too'mult) *n.* **1,** the commotion and uproar of a multitude. **2,** violent disturbance; high excitement. **—tu·mul'tu·ous,** *adj.*

tun *n.* a large cask.

tu'na (too'nə) *n.* a large, oceanic food and game fish.

tun'dra (tun'drə) *n.* a level, treeless plain of arctic regions.

tune (toon) *n.* **1,** a succession of tones having musical coherence; an air or melody. **2,** adjustment to proper pitch or frequency. **3,** harmony; accord. **4,** good condition. *—v.t. & i.* adjust to a proper pitch or frequency; bring or come into harmony. **—tune'ful,** *adj.* melodious. **—tune'less,** *adj.* **—tuning fork,** a pronged instrument that vibrates at an exact pitch.

tun'er *n.* **1,** one who or that which tunes. **2,** a radio receiver without amplifier or speakers.

tune-'up" *n.* (*Colloq.*) an adjustment of an engine to return it to optimal functional efficiency.

tung'sten (tung'stən) *n.* a metallic chemical element, no. 74, symbol W.

tu'nic (too'nik) *n.* a short coat or shirt; a blouse.

tun'nel (tun'əl) *n.* **1,** an underground roadway or passage. **2,** the burrow of an animal. *—v.t. & i.* penetrate by digging. **—tunnel vision,** a lack of peripheral vision.

tun'ny (tun'ē) *n.* a large food fish of the mackerel family.

tu'pe·lo (too'pə-lō) *n.* any of several No. Amer. trees; their wood.

tur'ban (tėr'bən) *n.* **1,** a headdress formed by winding a long scarf around the head. **2,** a brimless hat.

tur'bid (tėr'bid) *adj.* **1,** clouded, opaque, or muddy, as a liquid. **2,** confused, muddled. **—tur·bid'i·ty,** *n.*

tur'bine (tėr'bin) *n.* a motor in which a vaned wheel is made to revolve by a flow of liquid or gas.

tur·bo- (tėr-bō) *pref.* turbine-driven.

tur'bo·fan" *n.* a type of turbojet engine with added thrust.

tur'bo·jet" *n.* a jet-propulsion engine supercharged by a turbine.

tur'bo-pro·pel"ler engine an engine combining the thrust of a turbine-powered propeller with the additional thrust of hot exhaust gases. Also, **tur'bo-prop".**

tur'bot (tėr'bət) *n.* a variety of flatfish.

tur'bu·lent (tėr'byû-lənt) *adj.* disturbed; tumultuous; riotous. **—tur'bu·lence,** *n.*

tu·reen' (tû-rēn') *n.* a deep dish with a cover, for holding soup.

turf (tėrf) *n.* **1,** the matted grass, roots, earth, mold, etc., covering grassland. **2,** a section of this cut out; a sod. **3,** a racetrack for horses; horse-racing. **4,** peat. *—v.t.* cover with turf. **—turf'y,** *adj.*

tur'gid (tėr'jid) *adj.* tumid.

tur'key (tėr'kē) *n.* **1,** a large American fowl. **2,** (*Slang*) a failure, esp. a play; a flop. **—turkey buzzard,** a vulture. **—turkey trot,** a ragtime dance.

Turk'ish (tėr'kish) *adj.* pert. to Turkey, its people, language, etc. **—Turkish bath,** a steam bath. **—Turkish towel,** a thick towel with a long nap.

tur'mer·ic (tėr'mər-ik) *n.* an E. Indian plant, used for making a condiment, a yellow dye, etc.

tur'moil (tėr'moil) *n.* commotion; tumult; agitation.

turn (tėrn) *v.t.* **1,** move to or from a position; shift or twist. **2,** move to a new direction, course, or purpose. **3,** reverse; fold back. **4,** revolve or rotate; shape or perform by rotating. **5,** alter or change in a specified way. **6,** make sour or fermented. **7,** meditate on. **8,** go around; pass beyond. *—v.i.* **1,** rotate or revolve. **2,** assume a new direction, course, position, etc. **3,** change; become different. **4,** (with *on*) be dependent. **5,** become sour; ferment. **6,** be or become curved; bend. *—n.* **1,** movement about a center; a rotation or revolution; a twist. **2,** a change of direction, course, or position. **3,** a bend, curve, angle, fold, etc. **4,** one's occasion to act; a spell of work, duty, etc. **5,** a change in appearance, condition, or character. **6,** trend; tendency; bent. **7,** (*Colloq.*) a nervous shock. **—to a turn,** perfectly. **—turn in,** go to bed. **—turn off,** **1,** extinguish, shut off, etc. **2,** turn away (from); esp., exit (from), as a road. **3,** (*Slang*) lose or cause to lose interest, enthusiasm, etc. **—turn on,** (*Slang*) **1,** use or cause to use a hallucinogenic drug. **2,**

experience or cause to experience without drugs the sense stimulation usu. associated with their use. **3,** make or become elated, excited, etc.

turn′a·bout″ n. **1,** a turning to the opposite direction. **2,** alternation of privileges.

turn′coat″ n. a renegade.

turn′er n. **1,** a woodworker. **2,** a gymnast.

turn′ing n. **1,** act or result of turning. **2,** place of turning; a bend; curve. —**turning point, 1,** a critical point. **2,** a change for the better.

tur′nip (tẽr′nip) n. a plant whose root and leaves are used as vegetables.

turn′key″ n. a jailer.

turn′off″ n. **1,** a branch of a road; an exit, esp. from a main thoroughfare. **2,** (Slang) something that causes one to lose interest, enthusiasm, etc.

turn′out″ n. **1,** those who attend a meeting, etc. **2,** output. **3,** costume; outfit.

turn′o″ver n. **1,** rate or volume of business. **2,** rate of change in personnel employed. **3,** a small semicircular pie.

turn′pike″ n. a toll highway.

turn′stile″ n. a device of revolving arms to bar passage or count those passing through.

turn′ta″ble n. **1,** a revolving platform to change the direction of a locomotive. **2,** the rotating disk of a phonograph.

tur′pen·tine″ (tẽr′pən-tīn″) n. an oily sub‚ stance extracted from several trees, used in making paint.

tur′pi·tude″ (tẽr′pi-tood″) n. wickedness; depravity. —**tur″pi·tud′i·nous,** adj.

tur′quoise″ (tẽr′kwoiz) n. an opaque semiprecious stone; its blue-green color.

tur′ret (tẽr′it) n. **1,** a small tower rising from a larger building. **2,** an attachment on a lathe for holding and applying several tools. **3,** a gun tower on a tank or battleship.

tur′tle (tẽr′təl) n. any of an order of reptiles having two surfaces of strong shell, from between which the head and limbs protrude. —**turn turtle,** capsize; upset.

tur′tle·dove″ (-duv″) n. a variety of dove.

tur′tle·neck″ n. a shirt or sweater with a high, tight-fitting collar.

tush interj. of disapproval.

tusk n. **1,** a long pointed tooth. **2,** a tooth-like part, as a prong. —**tusk′er,** n. a tusked animal.

tus′sle (tus′əl) n. scuffle.

tus′sock (tus′ək) n. a clump or tuft of growing grass.

tut interj. of mild reproach.

tu′te·lage (too′tə-lij) n. guardianship; instruction. —**tu′te·lar·y,** adj.

tu′tor (too′tər) n. a teacher, esp. one engaged for private instruction. —v.t. & i. **1,** instruct, esp. privately. **2,** study under a tutor. —**tu′tor·age,** n. —**tu·tor′i·al** (-tôr′ē-əl) adj.

tut′ti-frut′ti (too′tē-froo′tē) n. a preserve of mixed fruits.

tu′tu (too′too) n. a short ballet skirt of several layers.

tu·whit′, tu·whoo′ (tû-hwit′tû-hwoo′) the cry of the owl.

tux (tuks) n. (Colloq.) tuxedo.

tux·e′do (tuk-sē′dō) n. a man's tailless evening coat; dinner jacket.

TV (tee′vee′) n. (Colloq.) television. —**TV dinner,** (Colloq.) a pre-cooked, packaged dinner which requires only to be heated for use.

twad′dle (twod′əl) v.i. & t. talk in a trivial and tedious manner. —n. idle, senseless talk or writing.

twain (twān) n. (Archaic) two.

twang n. **1,** the sharp sound of a tense string when plucked. **2,** a nasal tone of voice. —v.i. & t. make such a sound.

tweak (twēk) v.t. pinch and pull or twist. —n. a jerk or twist.

tweed (twēd) n. a coarse wool cloth; (pl.) garments of this fabric.

tweet (twēt) n. & v. chirp.

tweet′er (twē′tər) n. a loudspeaker responsive only to the higher frequencies and used for reproducing high-pitched sounds.

tweez′ers (twē′zərz) n.pl. a small two-pronged gripping tool. —**tweeze,** v.t.

Twelfth Night the evening preceding the twelfth day after Christmas.

twelve (twelv) n. the cardinal number, 10 plus 2, expressed by 12. —**twelfth,** adj. & n.

twelve′month″ n. a year.

twen′ty (twen′tē) n. a cardinal number, twice ten, expressed by 20. —**twen′ti·eth,** adj. & n.

twen″ty-one′ n. **1,** twenty plus one. **2,** a card game, blackjack.

twerp (twẽrp) n. (Colloq.) an insignificant, ineffective person.

twice (twīs) adv. **1,** two times. **2,** doubly.

twice-′told″ adj. hackneyed.

twid′dle (twid′əl) v.t. twirl, esp. with the fingers. —v.i. play idly.

twig n. a small shoot of a tree or other plant.

twi′light″ (twī′līt″) n. **1,** light from the sky when the sun is below the horizon. **2,** early evening. —**twilight sleep,** relief from the pain of childbirth, given by scopolamine.

twill (twil) n. a fabric woven so as to show parallel diagonal lines.

twin *n.* **1,** one of two offspring brought forth at a birth. **2,** one of two persons or things closely alike. —*adj.* **1,** being one of twins. **2,** occurring in pairs.

twine (twīn) *n.* **1,** a strong cord or string. **2,** something twisted. —*v.t. & i.* **1,** twist together; interweave. **2,** meander.

twinge (twinj) *n.* a sudden sharp pain.

twi'night" (twī'-) *adj.* beginning during twilight and continuing into the evening. Also, **twi'nite".**

twin'kle (twing'kəl) *v.i.* **1,** shine with quick, irregular gleams. **2,** (of the eyes) sparkle with amusement or kindliness. —*n.* a gleam; gleams of light.

twin'kling *n.* **1,** intermittent shining. **2,** an instant.

twirl (twērl) *v.t.* cause to revolve rapidly; spin; whirl. —*v.i.* **1,** rotate; be whirled about. **2,** wind; coil. —*n.* **1,** a rapid spin; a gyration. **2,** a curl or convolution. —**twirl'er,** *n.* (*Baseball*) a pitcher.

twist *v.t.* **1,** wrap (something flexible) around and around; combine by winding. **2,** wring out of shape; distort; warp. **3,** cause to rotate; turn. **4,** form by bending, curving, etc. **5,** pervert in meaning; misinterpret; misapply. —*v.i.* **1,** be bent or coiled; wind; twine. **2,** rotate or revolve; move in a spiral course. **3,** change direction. **4,** be or become distorted in shape. —*n.* **1,** a bend, curve, knot, etc. **2,** a tangle, kink, crook, etc. **3,** a twisting motion or course. **4,** spin imparted to a ball. **5,** something formed by twisting. **6,** a dance in which one contorts the torso. —**twist'er,** *n.* a tornado.

twit *v.t.* taunt; reproach. —*n.* a gibe or reproach.

twitch (twich) *v.t.* **1,** pull or move with a quick jerk. **2,** pinch; squeeze. —*v.t.* jerk suddenly, as from muscular spasm. —*n.* **1,** a sudden muscular contraction; a twinge. **2,** a slight, sudden movement. **3,** a tug or jerk.

twit'ter (twit'ər) *v.i.* **1,** chirp rapidly or excitedly. **2,** giggle.

two (too) *n.* the cardinal number, one plus one, expressed by 2 (ordinal, *second*).

two-'bit" *adj.* (*Slang*) cheap; worthless. —**two bits,** twenty-five cents.

two-'by-four" *n.* a timber 2 inches thick and 4 inches wide.

two-'edged" *adj.* **1,** having two sharp edges. **2,** doubly effective.

two-'faced" *adj.* deceitful; hypocritical.

two'fer (too'fər) *n.* (*Slang*) two tickets for the price of one.

two-'fist"ed *adj.* strong in a fight.

two'fold" *adj.* times two; double.

two'pence (tup'əns) *n.* (*Brit.*) two pennies. —**two'pen"ny** (tup'nē) *adj.*

two'some" *n.* two persons; a duo.

two-'step" *n.* a dance.

two-'time" *v.t.* (*Colloq.*) deceive; esp., be unfaithful to.

two-'way" *adj.* operating, or permitting operation, in either of two directions.

-ty (tē) *suf.* **1,** of numerals, times ten, as *sixty*. **2,** quality, state, etc.

ty'coon' (tī-koon') *n.* (*Colloq.*) a wealthy and powerful businessman.

tyke (tīk) *n.* **1,** a dog. **2,** a child.

tym'pa·ni (tim'pə-nē) *n.pl.* [*sing.* **-no** (-nō)] orchestral kettledrums. —**tym'pa·nist,** *n.*

tym'pa·num (tim'pə-nəm) *n.* **1,** a stretched membrane; a drum or tambourine. **2,** the eardrum or middle ear. **3,** a vibrating device, as the diaphragm of a telephone. —**tym·pan'ic,** *adj.*

type (tīp) *n.* **1,** a kind or class. **2,** a typical person or thing. **3,** a model or pattern. **4,** a rectangular block bearing a letter or character in relief, used in printing; such printing blocks collectively. —*v.t. & i.* **1,** ascertain the type of. **2,** symbolize. **3,** typewrite.

type'cast" *v.t.* **1,** cast (an actor, etc.) in a role especially appropriate for him. **2,** cast repeatedly in the same type of role.

type'face" *n.* a particular style of printing type.

type'script" *n.* typewritten copy.

type'set"ter *n.* compositor.

type'writ"er (tīp'rī"tər) *n.* a machine for writing letters and characters like those produced by printing type. —**type'write",** *v.t. & i.* —**type'writ"ing,** *n.*

ty'phoid fever (tī'foid) *n.* an infectious bacillic disease marked by inflammation and ulceration of the intestines.

ty·phoon' (tī-foon') *n.* a cyclone of the W. Pacific ocean.

ty'phus (tī'fəs) *n.* an acute infectious disease carried by lice.

typ'i·cal (tip'i-kəl) *adj.* **1,** pert. to a type. **2,** conforming to a type; being a representative specimen.

typ'i·fy" (tip'i-fī") *v.t.* **1,** exemplify. **2,** represent by a type of symbol.

typ'ist (tīp'ist) *n.* one who operates a typewriter.

ty'po (tī'pō) *n.* (*Colloq.*) a typographical error.

ty·pog'ra·phy (tī-pog'rə-fē) *n.* **1,** the art or work of setting type. **2,** the style of printed matter. —**ty·pog'ra·pher,** *n.* —**ty"po·graph'i·cal,** *adj.* —**typographical error,** an error made in the setting of type or in typing [also, *colloq.,* **ty'po** (tī'pō)].

tyr·an·nize" (tir'ə-nīz") *v.i. & t.* dominate tyrannically.

tyr·an"no·saur'us (tir-an"ə-sâ'rəs) *n.* a great carnivorous dinosaur.

tyr·an·ny (tir'ə-nē) *n.* unrestrained exercise of power; unmerciful rule. —**ty·ran'ni·cal** (tī-ran'i-kəl), **tyr·an'nous** (tir'ə-nəs) *adj.*

ty'rant (tī'rənt) *n.* a despot; an absolute ruler.

ty'ro (tī'ro) *n.* a beginner in learning something; a novice.

tzar (tsär) *n.* czar.

tzet'ze (tset'sė) *n.* tsetse.

U

U, u (ū) the 21st letter of the English alphabet.

u·biq'ui·tous (ū-bik'wə-təs) *adj.* existing everywhere; inescapable. —**u·biq'ui·tous·ness,** *n.* —**u·biq'ui·ty,** *n.*

U-'boat" (ū'bōt") *n.* a submarine, esp. German.

ud'der (ud'ər) *n.* the baggy mammary gland of a cow.

u·dom'e·ter (ū-dom'ə-tər) *n.* a rain gauge.

ugh (u; ug; ukh) *interj.* expressing aversion, disgust, or horror.

ug'ly (ug'lė) *adj.* **1,** unpleasing or repulsive in appearance. **2,** disagreeable; inclement; threatening. —**ug'li·ness,** *n.* —**ugly duckling,** an unpromising child who becomes beautiful as an adult.

u'kase (ū'kās) *n.* an edict; decree.

U·krain'i·an (ū-krā'nė-ən) *n. & adj.* of or pert. to the Ukraine, a large region and republic in the Soviet Union, its people, language, etc.

u"ku·le'le (ū"kə-lā'lė) *n.* a Hawaiian stringed musical instrument resembling a small guitar.

ul'cer (ul'sər) *n.* **1,** an infected sore. **2,** a moral blemish. —**ul'cer·ous,** *adj.*

ul'cer·ate" (-āt") *v.t. & i.* (cause to) become ulcerous. —**ul"cer·a'tion,** *n.*

ul'na (ul'nə) *n.* [*pl.* **-nae** (-nė)] the large bone of the forearm. —**ul'nar,** *adj.*

ul'ster (ul'stər) *n.* an overcoat.

ul·te'ri·or (ul-tir'ė-ər) *adj.* **1,** kept concealed. **2,** in the future.

ul'ti·mate (ul'tə-mət) *adj.* **1,** being the last, as of a series; most remote. **2,** eventual; final; decisive. —*n.* the final stage or degree.

ul"ti·ma'tum (ul"tə-mā'təm) *n.* a final statement of conditions.

ul'ti·mo (ul'tə-mō) *adv.* in the month which preceded the present.

ul'tra (ul'trə) *adj.* beyond the ordinary; extreme; superlative; excessive.

ul·tra- *pref.* beyond; excessive; superlative. [In the following compounds, the prefix adds merely the sense of "overmuch" to the adjective.] —**ul"tra·con·serv'a·tive,** *adj.* —**ul"tra·fash'ion·a·ble,** *adj.* —**ul"tra·mod'ern,** *adj.* —**ul"tra·re·li'gious,** *adj.*

ul'tra·fiche" (-fēsh") *n.* a very small size of microfiche.

ultra-high frequency designating frequencies from 300 to 3000 megacycles. Also, **UHF.**

ul"tra·ma·rine' *n.* a deep blue color.

ul"tra·mon'tane (-mon'tān) *adj.* **1,** south of the Alps; in Italy. **2,** recognizing the Pope as head of all Christianity.

ul'tra·son'ic *adj.* supersonic.

ul'tra·sound" *n.* ultrasonic sound.

ul"tra·vi'o·let *adj.* pert. to invisible rays lying beyond violet in the spectrum.

ul'u·late" (ūl'yə-lāt") *v.i.* howl like a wolf; wail. —**ul"u·la'tion,** *n.*

um'ber (um'bər) *n.* a reddish-brown pigment.

um·bil'i·cal (um-bil'i-kəl) *adj.* pert. to the umbilicus. —**umbilical cord,** the tube through which a mother nourishes a fetus.

um·bil'i·cus (um-bil'i-kəs) *n.* [*pl.* **-i·ci** (-sī)] the depression in the middle of the abdomen.

um'bra (um'brə) *n.* [*pl.* **-brae** (-brė)] shadow; a dark spot.

um'brage (um'brij) *n.* **1,** resentment. **2,** foliage. —**um·bra'geous** (-brā'jəs) *adj.*

um·brel'la (um-brel'ə) *n.* **1,** a portable screen from rain or the sun. **2,** aerial protection given by fighter planes to troops or ships below. **3,** a name, organization, etc., which includes a variety of small entities, often unrelated, under its control.

u'mi·ak (oo'mė-ak) *n.* an open boat used by Eskimos.

um'laut (ûm'lowt) *n.* (*Ger.*) modification of a vowel sound, or the diacritical mark (") as in ä, ö, ü, in transliteration indicated by *e* following the vowel.

um'pire (um'pīr) *n.* an arbiter; referee. Also, *colloq.,* **ump.**

ump'teen" (ump'tēn) *adj.* (*Colloq.*) a fairly large, but indefinite, number.

un- *pref.* not; signifying the converse, reversal, or absence of some quality, action, or condition.

un"a·bridged' (un"ə-brijd') *adj.* **1,** not shortened; not restricted. **2,** (of a dictionary) not a condensation or shorter version of a larger dictionary; omitting no applicable material.

un·ad·vised' (un-əd-vīzd') *adj.* ill-advised.

un-"A·mer'i·can *adj.* **1,** not befitting a loyal U.S. citizen. **2,** not consistent with American beliefs, customs, etc.

u·nan'i·mous (ū-nan'ə-məs) *adj.* being of one mind; all agreeing, without exception. —**u"na·nim'i·ty** (ū"nə-nim'ə-tē) *n.*

un·as·sum'ing *adj.* modest; retiring.

un·at·tached' *adj.* **1,** free; loose. **2,** (*Mil.*) not assigned to any unit or duty. **3,** (*Colloq.*) not betrothed, romantically commited, escorted, etc.

un"a·ware' *adj.* not conscious (of something); not knowing or realizing. —**un"a·wares'**, *adv.*

un·bal'anced *adj.* mentally deranged.

un"be·known' (un"bē-nōn') *adj.* (*Colloq.*) unknown. Also, **un"be·knownst'** (-nōnst').

un"be·lief' *n.* lack of belief, esp. in religious dogma. —**un"be·liev'er,** *n.*

un·bend' *v.t.* [**-bent', -bend'ing**] **1,** release from strain or tension. **2,** straighten; untie. —*v.i.* **1,** relax; become less formal, etc. **2,** become unbent. —**un·bend'ing,** *adj.*

un·blessed' *adj.* **1,** denied a blessing. **2,** wretched; unhappy. Also, **un·blest'.**

un·blush'ing *adj.* shameless.

un·bos'om (un-bûz'əm) *v.t. & i.* disclose (thoughts, feelings).

un·bound'ed *adj.* without boundaries or limits; vast.

un·break'a·ble *adj.* **1,** incapable of being broken. **2,** resistant to breaking.

un·bri'dled (un-brī'dəld) *adj.* unrestrained; uncontrolled.

un·called-'for" (un-kâld'fôr") *adj.* **1,** unwarranted; impertinent; improper. **2,** not claimed, as merchandise.

un·can'ny *adj.* eerie; weird; mysterious. —**un·can'ni·ness,** *n.*

un·cap' *v.t.* [**-capped', -cap'ping**] remove the cap or cover from.

un·cer'tain *adj.* **1,** not certain; doubtful. **2,** unsteady or hesitant; not firm. —**un·cer'tain·ty,** *n.*

un·chal'lenged (un-chal'ənjd) *adj.* unquestioned; acknowledged; agreed.

un'ci·al (un'shē-əl) *adj.* designating a style of majuscule writing used from the 4th to 10th century. —*n.* an uncial letter or manuscript.

un'cle (ung'kəl) *n.* **1,** a brother of one's father or mother. **2,** the husband of one's aunt. **3,** any elderly man, regarded familiarly. **4,** (*Slang*) a pawnbroker. —**Uncle Sam,** the U.S., its government or people. —**Uncle Tom,** a black having a submissive attitude toward whites.

un·com'mon *adj.* not common or usual; out of the ordinary; exceptional. —**un·com'mon·ness,** *n.*

un"con·cern' *n.* lack of anxiety; indifference. —**un"con·cerned',** *adj.*

un·con'scion·a·ble *adj.* **1,** not in accord with conscience; unscrupulous. **2,** unduly excessive.

un·con'scious *adj.* **1,** not aware (of something). **2,** having lost consciousness; being in a stupor, faint, etc. **3,** not endowed with

[In the following words, formed of words defined elsewhere in the dictionary, the prefix *un-* forms an antonym of the root word.]

un"a·bashed'	un"ap·pe·tiz"ing	un"be·liev'ing
un"a·bat'ed'	un"ap·pre'ci·a"tive	un·bi'ased
un·a'ble	un"ap·proach'a·ble	un·bid'den
un·ac·cent'ed	un·apt'	un·bind'
un"ac·cept'a·ble	un·arm'	un·bleached'
un"ac·com'pa·nied	un"a·shamed'	un·blink'ing
un"ac·count'a·ble	un·asked'	un·bolt'
un"ac·cus'tomed	un"as·sail'a·ble	un·born'
un"ac·quaint'ed	un"as·sist'ed	un·bound'
un"a·dorned'	un"at·tain'a·ble	un·bowed'
un"a·dul'ter·at"ed	un"at·trac'tive	un·brace'
un"af·fect'ed	un"at·tend'ed	un·braid'
un"a·fraid'	un·au'thor·ized	un·bro'ken
un"aid'ed	un"a·vail'a·ble	un·buck'le
un"al'ien·a·ble	un"a·vail'ing	un·bur'den
un"al·loyed'	un"a·void'a·ble	un·busi'ness·like"
un·al'ter·a·ble	un·bal'ance	un·but'ton
un"am·big'u·ous	un·bar'	un·caused'
un"am·bi'tious	un·bear'a·ble	un·ceas'ing
un"an·nounced'	un·beat'en	un"cer·e·mo'ni·ous
un"an'swer·a·ble	un"be·com'ing	un·chain'
un"an·tic'i·pat"ed	un"be·liev'a·ble	un·change'a·ble

fat, fāte, fär, fâre, fâll, àsk; met, hē, hẽr, maybē; pin, pīne; not, nōte, ôr, tool awareness of one's own existence. **4,** pert. to mental processes not consciously perceived. **—un·con'scious·ness,** *n.*

un·couth' *adj.* **1,** ill-mannered; clumsy. **2,** strange; unusual. **—un·couth'ness,** *n.*

un·cov'er *v.t.* remove a cover from; lay bare; reveal. *—v.i.* take off one's hat.

unc'tion (unk'shən) *n.* **1,** the act of anointing with oil. **2,** anything soothing; a divine or spiritual influence. **—extreme unction,** a sacrament administered to one in imminent danger of death.

unc'tu·ous (unk'choo-əs) *adj.* oily; suave. **—unc'tu·ous·ness,** *n.*

un·cut' *adj.* **1,** (of a stone) not cut or polished. **2,** (of a book) not separated into leaves. **3,** unabridged; complete.

un'de·ceive' *v.t.* free from a mistaken idea or belief.

un'der (un'dər) *prep.* **1,** beneath and covered by; below the surface of. **2,** in a lower place or position. **3,** receiving; bearing; undergoing. **4,** less than. **5,** inferior to. **6,** subject to. **7,** in accordance with. **8,** in. **9,** during the existence of. *—adv.* lower. *—adj.* **1,** beneath. **2,** lower; subordinate.

un·der- *pref.* **1,** below; lower in place or rank. **2,** lesser in degree, esp. less than a proper or usual degree.

[In the following words, the prefix *under-* implies sense 1.]

un"der·arm'	un"der·clothes"
un'der·bel"ly	un"der·cov'er
un'der·bod"ice	un'der·cur"rent
un'der·car"riage	un"der·gar'ment
un"der·class'man	un"der·grad'u·ate

un'der·growth"	un"der·side"
un'der·hung"	un"der·sign'
un'der·laid'	un'der·skirt"
un'der·prop'	un'der·slung"
un'der·sea"	un"der·soil"
un'der·shirt"	un'der·waist"
un'der·shorts"	un'der·wa'ter

[In the following words, the prefix *under-* implies sense 2.]

un"der·act'	un"der·pay'
un"der·armed'	un"der·play'
un"der·bid'	un'der·priv'i·leged
un"der·bred'	un'der·sized"
un'der·charge'	un"der·staffed'
un"der·de·vel'op	un"der·stock'
un"der·do'	un"der·trump'
un"der·ex·pose'	un"der·val'ue
un"der·feed'	un'der·weight"
un"der·nour'ish	

un"der·a·chieve' *v.i.* not produce results (as in school) commensurate with one's assumed potential. **—un"der·a·chiev'er,** *n.*

un"der·age' *adj.* of less than legal or suitable age.

un'der·brush" *n.* shrubs, etc., growing under trees.

un'der·coat" *n.* **1,** a protective coating to the underside of a vehicle. **2,** a preparatory coating, as of paint.

un"der·cut' *v.t.* **1,** cut so as to leave an overhanging edge. **2,** undersell. **3,** strike (a ball) on the underside.

un'der·dog" *n.* one who gets the worst of it, or is at a disadvantage, in a struggle.

un'der·drawers" *n. pl.* drawers.

un·changed'	un"com·par'a·ble	un·curl'
un·chang'ing	un"com·plain'ing	un·dam'aged
un·char'i·ta·ble	un"com·pli·men'ta·ry	un·daunt'ed
un·chart'ed	un"com·pro·mis"ing	un·de·cid'ed
un·chaste'	un·con·di'tion·al	un"de·feat'ed
un·checked'	un"con·di'tioned	un"de·fend'ed
un·Chris'tian	un"con·form'i·ty	un·de·filed'
un·cir'cum·cised	un"con·nect'ed	un"de·fined'
un·civ'il	un·con'quer·a·ble	un"dem·o·crat'ic
un·civ'i·lized"	un"con·sti·tu'tion·al	un"de·mon'stra·tive
un·clad'	un"con·trol'la·ble	un·de·ni'a·ble
un·claimed'	un"con·ven'tion·al	un"de·nom'i·na'tion·al
un·clasp'	un·cooked'	un"de·served'
un·clean'	un·cork'	un'de·sign'ing
un·clench'	un"cor·rupt'ed	un·de·sir'a·ble
un·cloak'	un·count'ed	un"de·vel'oped
un·clog'	un·cou'ple	un·dig'ni·fied"
un·close'	un·cov'er	un"di·min'ished
un·clothe'	un·crit'i·cal	un"dip·lo·mat'ic
un·cloud'ed	un·crossed'	un"di·rect'ed
un·coil'	un·crowned'	un"dis·cov'ered
un·com'fort·a·ble	un·cul'ti·vat"ed	un"dis·mayed'
un"com·mit'ted	un·cul'tured	un"dis·patched'
un"com·mu'ni·ca"tive	un·cured'	un"dis·put'ed

un"der·es'ti·mate" (-es'ti-māt') *v.t.* estimate at too low a value, amount, rate, etc. —*n.* (-mət) too low an estimate. —un"der·es"ti·ma'tion, *n.*

un"der·fed' *adj.* very thin, from malnutrition.

un"der·foot' *adj. & adv.* 1, under the foot; lying on the ground. 2, in the way.

un"der·go' *v.t.* [-went', -gone', -go'ing] be subjected to; experience; sustain.

un'der·ground" *adj.* 1, sunken, buried. 2, done or acting in secrecy. 3, pert. to anything (as movies, publications, etc.) that is experimental, radical, unconventional, etc. —*n.* 1, (*Brit.*) subway. 2, a secret organization opposing government or occupation forces.

un"der·hand" *adj. & adv.* 1, secret and mean; sly; deceitful. 2, with the hand below the shoulder or under the object.

un'der·hand"ed *adj.* underhand.

un"der·lie' *v.t.* [-lay', -ly'ing] 1, be situated under. 2, be the basis or foundation of.

un'der·line' *v.t. & n.* underscore.

un'der·ling (-ling) *n.* one in a subordinate or inferior position (usually in disparagement).

un"der·mine' *v.t.* 1, dig a hole or passage under. 2, weaken or injure by secret or underhand means.

un'der·most" *adj.* lowest.

un"der·neath' (-nēth') *prep. & adv.* beneath; under; below.

un'der·pants" *n.pl.* drawers.

un'der·pass" *n.* a passage or road under a railroad, road, etc.

un"der·pin' *v.t.* [-pinned', -pin'ning] support; stay. —un'der·pin"ning, *n.*

un"der·rate' *v.t.* rate too low; underestimate.

un"der·score" *v.t.* print or draw a line under; emphasize. —*n.* such a line.

un"der·sec're·ta·ry *n.* a deputy to a secretary in a U.S. government department, ranking next under the head.

un"der·sell' *v.t.* [-sold', -sell'ing] 1, sell for a lower price than. 2, understate the virtues of.

un'der·shot' *adj.* 1, driven by water underneath. 2, (of the lower jaw) protruding.

un"der·stand' *v.t. & i.* 1, grasp the meaning (of); comprehend. 2, have full knowledge (of). 3, be told (of); realize; believe. 4, sympathize (with).

un"der·stand'ing *n.* 1, intelligence; mental apprehension and appreciation. 2, good relations. 3, a private or unexpressed agreement. 4, sympathy. —*adj.* intelligent; sympathetic.

un"der·state' *v.t.* state with less than due emphasis; represent in lesser degree than the reality. —un"der·state'ment, *n.*

un'der·steer" *n.* the tendency of an automobile to turn less than normal as the wheel is turned.

un"der·stood' (un"dər-stůd') *adj.* 1, inferred. 2, agreed.

un'der·stud"y *n.* one trained to substitute for an actor or actress. —*v.t.* act as an understudy to.

un"der·take' *v.t.* 1, try to do; attempt. 2,

[In the following words, formed of words defined elsewhere in the dictionary, the prefix *un-* forms an antonym of the root word.]

un"dis·tin'guished
un"dis·turbed'
un"di·vid'ed
un·dou'ble
un·drape'
un·dress'
un·dy'ing
un·earned'
un·eat'a·ble
un·ed'u·cat'ed
un"em·bar'rassed
un"e·mo'tion·al
un"en·dur'a·ble
un"en·force'a·ble
un"en·light'ened
un·en'vied
un·e'qual
un·e'qualed
un"e·quiv'o·cal
un·err'ing
un"es·sen'tial
un·eth'i·cal

un·e'ven
un"e·vent'ful
un"ex·cep'tion·a·ble
un"ex·cep'tion·al
un"ex·pect'ed
un"ex·pired'
un"ex·plained'
un"ex·plored'
un"ex·pressed'
un·ex·pres'sive
un·ex'pur·gat'ed
un·fail'ing
un·fair'
un·faith'ful
un·fal'ter·ing
un"fa·mil'iar
un·fash'ion·a·ble
un·fas'ten
un·fath'om·a·ble
un·fa'vor·a·ble
un·feigned'
un·fenced'

un·fet'ter
un·fet'tered
un·fil'ial
un·fin'ished
un·fit'
un·flinch'ing
un"fore·seen'
un"for·get'ta·ble
un"for·giv'a·ble
un·for·got'ten
un·formed'
un"fre·quen'ted
un·friend'ly
un·fruit'ful
un"ful·filled'
un·gen'er·ous
un·gird'
un·gov'ern·a·ble
un·grace'ful
un·gra'cious
un·grate'ful
un·grudg'ing

---

fat, fāte, fär, fâre, fâll, ȧsk; met, hē, hẽr, maybé; pin, pīne; not, nōte, ôr, tool engage to perform or execute. —**un′der·tak″er,** *n.* a funeral director.

un″der·tak′ing *n.* **1,** a project, esp. a business venture. **2,** the business of preparing the dead for burial and arranging funerals.

un″der-the-coun′ter *adj.* illegal; illicit; unlawful.

un′der·things″ *n.pl.* underclothes.

un′der·tone″ *n.* **1,** a tone of less than normal loudness in speaking. **2,** a tone, hue, etc., lying under another.

un′der·tow″ *n.* a strong current below the surface of water, as the backflow from a beach.

un′der·wear″ *n.* garments worn beneath the outer clothing; underclothes.

un′der·world″ *n.* **1,** the community of criminal or degraded persons. **2,** Hades or hell.

un″der·write′ *v.t.* **1,** subscribe to; endorse; guarantee; indemnify. **2,** insure against loss.

un′der·writ″er *n.* **1,** one in the insurance business. **2,** one who subscribes to bonds, etc., for resale.

un·dis′ci·plined (un-dis′ə-plind) *adj.* unruly; not controllable.

un″dis·guised′ (un″dis-gīzd′) *adj.* lacking disguise or pretense; candid; open.

un·do′ *v.t.* [**-done′ -do′ing**] **1,** annul; reverse (the effect of). **2,** spoil; ruin. **3,** unfasten. —**un·do′ing,** *n.* ruin; destruction.

un·doubt′ed (un-dow′tid) *adj.* not questioned: obviously true. —**un·doubt′ed·ly** *adv.* surely.

un·due′ *adj.* **1,** unwarranted; disproportionate; excessive. **2,** not yet payable.

un′du·lant (un′dyə-lənt) *adj.* waving; wavy. —**undulant fever,** a recurrent disease usually contracted from bacteria in raw milk.

un′du·late″ (un′dyə-lāt″) *v.i. & t.* move or be formed in waves; rise and fall. —*adj.* (-lət) wavy. —**un″du·la′tion,** *n.*

un·du′ly *adv.* **1,** without warrant or right. **2,** excessively.

un·earth′ *v.t.* **1,** discover; bring to light. **2,** dig up; disinter.

un·earth′ly *adj.* **1,** supernatural; weird. **2,** (*Colloq.*) extraordinary.

un·eas′y *adj.* **1,** not comfortable in mind or body; disturbed; restless. **2,** not easy in manner; constrained. —**un·eas′i·ly,** *adv.* —**un·eas′i·ness,** *n.*

un″em·ployed′ (un″əm-ploid′) *adj.* **1,** without a job; out of work. **2,** not in use. —**un″em·ploy′ment,** *n.*

un·end′ing *adj.* without end, or seemingly so.

un″ex·am′pled (un″eg-zam′pəld) *adj.* without precedent.

un·feel′ing *adj.* **1,** hardhearted; unsympathetic. **2,** insensitive; devoid of feeling. —**un·feel′ing·ness,** *n.*

un·flap′pa·ble *adj.* (*Slang*) not easily confused or excited.

un·fledged′ (-flejd′) *adj.* **1,** too young to fly. **2,** undeveloped; immature.

un·fold′ *v.t. & i.* **1,** open or spread out. **2,** reveal or become revealed.

un·for′tu·nate *adj.* **1,** not lucky. **2,** regrettable. —*n.* a pitiable person.

un·found′ed (un-fown′did) *adj.* without

---

un·guard′ed	un″in·hab′it·ed	un·link′
un·hal′lowed	un″in·hib′it·ed	un·list′ed
un·ham′pered	un″in·i′ti·at″ed	un·lit′
un·harmed′	un·in′jured	_un·load′
un·harm′ful	un″in·spired′	un·lock′
un·har′ness	un″in·tel′li·gent	un·love′ly
un·hatched′	un″in·tel′li·gi·ble	un·luck′y
un·health′ful	un″in·ten′tion·al	un·make′
un·heard′	un″in·ter·est·ed	un·man′age·a·ble
un·heed′ed	un″in·ter·est·ing	un·manned′
un·hes′i·tat″ing	un″in·ter·rupt′ed	un·man′ner·ly
un·hitch′	un″in·vit′ed	un·marked′
un·hook′	un·is′sued	un·mar′ried
un·hur′ried	un·just′	un·mask′
un·hurt′	un·kind′	un·matched′
un″i·den′ti·fied	un·knot′	un·meas′ured
un″im·ag′i·na·ble	un·lace′	un·mer′ci·ful
un″im·ag′i·na″tive	un″la·ment′ed	un·mer′it·ed
un″im·paired′	un·lash′	un·mind′ful
un″im·peach′a·ble	un·latch′	un″mis·tak′a·ble
un″im·proved′	un·leash′	un·mit′i·gat·ed
un″in·flect′ed	un·li′censed	un·mixed′
un″in·formed′	un·lim′ber	un″mo·lest′ed
un″in·hab′it·a·ble	un·lim′it·ed	un·moved′

---

foundation; not based on fact; unwarranted.

un·frock' *v.t.* deprive of ecclesiastical rank or status.

un·furl' *v.t.* spread out, as a flag; display.

un·fur'nished (un-fĕr'nisht) *adj.* without furniture. —

un·gain'ly (un-gān'lē) *adj.* clumsy; awkward; uncouth. —*adv.* awkwardly.

un·god'ly *adj.* **1,** wicked; sinful. **2,** (*Colloq.*) outrageous; atrocious. —**un·god'·li·ness,** *n.*

un''gram·mat'i·cal *adj.* not in conformity to rules of grammar.

un'guent (ung'gwənt) *n.* an ointment; salve.

un'gu·late (ung'gyə-lət) *adj.* **1,** having hoofs. **2,** hooflike. —*n.* a hoofed mammal.

un·hand' *v.t.* take the hand from; let go; release.

un·hand'y *adj.* **1,** not easy to manage; inconvenient. **2,** not skillful.

un·hap'py *adj.* **1,** sad. **2,** unfortunate. —**un·hap'pi·ness,** *n.*

un·health'y *adj.* **1,** in poor health. **2,** unwholesome; likely to turn out badly. —**un·health'i·ness,** *n.*

un·heard-'of'' (un-hĕrd'uv'') *adj.* not hitherto known or existent; unprecedented.

un·hinge' *v.t.* **1,** remove the hinges of; take off of hinges. **2,** detach; derange. **3,** unbalance mentally; discompose; craze. —**un·hinged',** *adj.*

un·hol'y *adj.* **1,** sinful; impious. **2,** (*Colloq.*) extreme; unseemly. —**un·ho'li·ness,** *n.*

un·horse' *v.t.* **1,** throw down from a horse. **2,** dislodge.

u·ni- (ū-nə) *pref.* one; having only one; single.

u''ni·cam'er·al (ū'nə-kam'ə-rəl) *adj.* (of a legislature) having only one chamber.

u''ni·cel'lu·lar *adj.* consisting of a single cell.

u'ni·corn'' (ū'nə-kôrn'') *n.* a fabulous animal with a single long horn and usually the body of a horse.

u'ni·cy''cle *n.* a one-wheeled vehicle with footpedals.

u'ni·form'' (ū'nə-fôrm'') *adj.* **1,** unchanging; even; regular. **2,** the same as others. —*n.* a distinctive dress worn by all the members of a military force, a society, etc. —**u''ni·form'i·ty,** *n.*

u'ni·fy'' (ū'nə-fī'') *v.t.* collect, class, or form into a single whole; make uniform. —**u''ni·fi·ca'tion,** *n.*

u''ni·lat'er·al (ū''nə-lat'ər-əl) *adj.* **1,** affecting or done by only one party (of two or more). **2,** having or pert. to only one side.

un''im·por'tant *adj.* not important; insignificant. —**un''im·por'tance,** *n.*

un'ion (ūn'yən) *n.* **1,** the act of joining two or more things into one. **2,** something made by uniting; a league, combination, compound, etc. **3,** marriage. **4,** an organization of workers: a labor or trade union. **5,** a flag symbolizing union; a jack: *union jack.* **6,** a coupling device. —**un'ion·ism,** *n.* —**un'ion·ize''** (-īz'') *v.t. & i.* organize in a labor union. —**union shop,** a shop where labor relations are controlled by

---

[In the following words, formed of words defined elsewhere in the dictionary, the prefix *un-* forms an antonym of the root word.]

un·mov'ing	un·peo'pled	un''pro·tect'ed
un·mus'i·cal	un''per·turbed'	un''pro·voked'
un·muz'zle	un·pin'	un·pub'lished
un·named'	un·planned'	un·pun'ished
un·nat'u·ral	un·pleas'ing	un·qual'i·fied''
un''nec'es·sar''y	un·plowed'	un·quench'a·ble
un·neigh'bor·ly	un·plug'	un·ques'tion·a·ble
un·no'ticed	un·pol'ished	un·ques'tioned
un''ob·served'	un''pol·lut'ed	un·qui'et
un''ob·struct'ed	un''prec'e·dent·ed	un·read'
un''ob·tru'sive	un''pre·dict'a·ble	un·read'a·ble
un·oc'cu·pied''	un''prej'u·diced	un·read'y
un''of·fend'ing	un''pre·med'i·tat''ed	un·real'
un·o'pened	un''pre·pared'	un·rea'son·a·ble
un·or'gan·ized''	un''pre·tend'ing	un·rea'son·ing
un·or'tho·dox	un''pre·ten'tious	un''rec·og·niz'a·ble
un·pack'	un·print'a·ble	un·rec'og·nized''
un·paid'	un''pro·duc'tive	un''re·cord'ed
un·pal'at·a·ble	un''pro·fes'sion·al	un·reel'
un·par'don·a·ble	un·prof'it·a·ble	un''re·fined'
un''par·lia·men'ta·ry	un·prom'is·ing	un''re·flect'ing
un·pen'	un''pro·nounce'a·ble	un''re·gen'er·ate

---

fixed contract between employer and labor union. —**union suit,** a one-piece undergarment.

u·nique' (ū-nēk') *adj.* **1,** being the only one of its kind. **2,** unusual; rare. —**u·nique'-ness,** *n.*

u"ni·sex" *adj.* designed for both sexes alike, as clothing.

u'ni·son (ū'nə-sən) *n.* **1,** coincidence in pitch of two or more tones. **2,** accord in sentiment or action.

u'nit (ū'nit) *n.* **1,** a single thing or person. **2,** a group of things or persons regarded as a single entity. **3,** a component part. **4,** any standard quantity used as a measure. **5,** the quantity and integer 1. —**u'ni·tar"y** (ū'ni-ter"ē) *adj.* —**u'ni·tize",** *v.t.*

U"ni·ta'ri·an (ū"ni-târ'ē-ən) *adj.* & *n.* of a sect that believes God exists in one person, not the Trinity.

u·nite' (ū-nīt') *v.t.* & *i.* **1,** combine so as to form one; make a union (of); connect. **2,** join in feeling or sympathy; agree. —**u·nit'-ed,** *adj.* —**United Nations,** an organization comprising representatives of most of the countries of the world.

u'ni·ty (ū'nə-tē) *n.* **1,** the state of being united or uniform. **2,** the quantity and integer 1. **3,** harmony among elements.

u'ni·valve" (ū'ni-valv") *n.* a mollusk having only one shell.

u"ni·ver'sal (ū"nə-vēr'səl) *adj.* **1,** pert. to the, or a, universe; generally applicable. **2,** comprehensive; wide in scope. **3,** widely adaptable or effective in different directions, as of a mechanical contrivance. —**u"ni·ver'sal·i·ty,** *n.* —**universal joint** or **coupling,** a coupling of two shafts, so designed that one of them can change direction.

U"ni·ver'sal·ist *adj.* & *n.* pert. to a Christian denomination or its doctrine of universal salvation.

u'ni·verse" (ū'nə-vērs") *n.* **1,** the totality of all existing things. **2,** the whole world; all mankind. **3,** an individual's own sphere or ken. —**island universe,** any of the collections of stars in space; a galaxy.

u"ni·ver'si·ty (ū"nə-vēr'sə-tē) *n.* an institution of higher learning, embracing both colleges and postgraduate schools.

un·kempt' *adj.* not combed, as hair; untidy. —**un·kempt'ness,** *n.*

un·known' *adj.* **1,** not known, discovered, determined, or identified. **2,** unfamiliar. —*n.* something unknown; (*Math.*) a symbol for an unknown quantity. —**un·know'a·ble,** *adj.* beyond the range of human knowledge. —**un·know'ing,** *adj.* ignorant; unsophisticated.

un·law'ful *adj.* against the law. —**un·law'ful·ness,** *n.*

un·learn' *v.t.* put out of the mind or memory; forget.

un·leash' *v.t.* release from, or as from, a leash; let loose.

un·leav'ened (un-lev'ənd) *adj.* (of bread) not raised with yeast, etc.

un·less' (un-les') *conj.* if it be not that; if not; except in case that.—*prep.* except.

un"re·lat'ed	un"sat·is·fac'to·ry	un·shod'
un"re·lent'ing	un·sat'is·fied	un·sight'ly
un"re·li'a·ble	un·sat'u·rat·ed	un·skilled'
un"re·lieved'	un·sa'vo·ry	un·skill'ful
un"re·li'gious	un·schooled'	un·sling'
un"re·mem'bered	un"sci·en·tif'ic	un·snap'
un"re·mit'ting	un·screw'	un·snarl'
un"re·quit'ed	un·seal'	un·so'ber
un"re·served'	un·sea'son·a·ble	un·so'cia·ble
un"re·sist'ing	un·sea'soned	un·sold'
un"re·strained'	un·seat'	un·sol'dier·ly
un"re·strict'ed	un"se·cured'	un"so·phis'ti·cat"ed
un·rig'	un·see'ing	un·sought'
un·right'eous	un·seem'ly	un·spar'ing
un·ripe'	un·seen'	un·spoiled'
un·ri'valed	un·set'	un·spo'ken
un·robe'	un·set'tle	un·sports'man·like"
un·roll'	un·set'tled	un·spot'ted
un·ruf'fled	un·shack'le	un·sta'ble
un·sad'dle	un·shad'ed	un·stained'
un·safe'	un·shaped'	un·states'man·like"
un·said'	un·shape'ly	un·strained'
un·sal'a·ble	un·shav'en	un·strap'
un·san'i·tar·y	un·sheathe'	un·string'

un·let'tered (un-let'ərd) *adj.* lacking book knowledge; uneducated.

un·like' *adj.* not like; different; dissimilar. —*prep.* differently from. —**un·like'ness,** *n.*

un·like'ly *adj. & adv.* **1,** not probable. **2,** having little prospect of success; unpromising. —**un·like'li·ness,** *n.*

un·looked-'for" (un-lûkt'fôr") *adj.* unexpected.

un·loose' (un-loos') *v.t.* loosen; untie; release.

un·luck'y *adj.* **1,** having bad luck. **2,** regrettable. —**un·luck'i·ness,** *n.*

un·make' *v.t.* **1,** take apart; reduce to original components. **2,** ruin; destroy; depose.

un·man' *v.t.* **1,** deprive of manly spirit; dishearten. **2,** emasculate. **3,** deprive of men, as a ship. —**un·man'ly,** *adj.* weak; womanish.

un·mean'ing (un-mē'ning) *adj.* **1,** without meaning or significance. **2,** expressionless, as a face.

un·men'tion·a·ble *adj.* not fit to be mentioned. —*n.* (usu. *pl.*) any undergarment.

un·mor'al *adj.* **1,** having no moral aspect. **2,** neither moral nor immoral.

un·nerve' *v.t.* cause to lose courage or resolution.

un·num'bered (un-num'bərd) *adj.* **1,** innumerable; very many. **2,** not numbered.

un"of·fi'cial *adj.* **1,** lacking official sanction. **2,** tentative.

un·pack' *v.t. & i.* remove a packing or something that has been packed (from).

un·par'al·leled" (un-par'ə-leld") *adj.* having no parallel or equal; unmatched.

un"per'son *n.* a person treated as, or as if, nonexistent.

un·pleas'ant *adj.* **1,** displeasing. **2,** disagreeable in manner, disposition, etc. —**un·pleas'ant·ness,** *n.*

un"plumbed' *adj.* unfathomed; unexplored.

un·pop'u·lar *adj.* disliked by a majority of persons. —**un·pop"u·lar'i·ty,** *n.*

un·prac'ticed (un-prak'tist) *adj.* **1,** not done usually or at all. **2,** not trained; unskillful.

un·prec'e·dent"ed (un-pres'ə-den"tid) *adj.* having no precedent; unexampled.

un·prin'ci·pled (un-prin'sə-pəld) *adj.* lacking moral principles; unscrupulous; wicked.

un·quote' *v.t.* close a quotation. —*n.* a mark (as '') so signifying.

un·rav'el *v.t.* **1,** separate the threads or fibers of; disentangle. **2,** free from perplexity; solve.

un·re'al (un-rē'əl) *adj.* **1,** not real. **2,** unpractical; visionary. **3,** (*Slang*) unbelievable.

un·re"con·struct'ed *adj.* not ready for social change.

un·rest' *n.* lack of rest or quiet; a state of agitation.

un·rid'dle *v.t.* solve, as a riddle; interpret; fathom.

[In the following words, formed of words defined elsewhere in the dictionary, the prefix *un-* forms an antonym of the root word.]

un"sub·dued'
un"sub·stan'tial
un"suc·cess'ful
un·suit'a·ble
un·suit'ed
un·sul'lied
un"sup·port'ed
un"sur·passed'
un"sus·pect'ed
un"sus·pect'ing
un"sus·pi'cious
un"sus·tained'
un·sweet'ened
un·swept'
un·swerv'ing
un"sym·pa·thet'ic
un·tack'
un·taint'ed
un·tak'en
un·tamed'
un·tan'gle
un·tar'nished
un·tast'ed

un·taught'
un·ten'a·ble
un·ten'ant·ed
un·teth'er
un·thank'ful
un·thread'
un·throne'
un·ti'dy
un·touched'
un·trained'
un·tram'meled
un·tried'
un·trimmed'
un·trou'bled
un·true'
un·tu'tored
un·twist'
un·used'
un·ut'ter·a·ble
un·var'y·ing
un·veil'
un·ver'i·fied'
un·vexed'

un·vis'it·ed
un·voiced'
un·want'ed
un·warped'
un·war'y
un·wa'ver·ing
un·wea'ried
un·weave'
un·wed'
un·wel'come
un·well'
un·wept'
un·wil'ling
un·wind'
un·wise'
un·wom'an·ly
un·work'a·ble
un·world'ly
un·wor'thy
un·wound'ed
un·wrap'
un·yoke'
un·youth'ful
un·zip'

---

un·rip' v.t. [-ripped', -rip'ping] rip; tear apart.

un·rul'y (un-roo'lē) adj. not submissive; balky; ungovernable. —**un·ru'li·ness,** n.

un·say' v.t. retract or recant (something said).

un·scathed' (un-skāthd') adj. not injured; unharmed.

un·scram'ble v.t. make orderly; disentangle.

un·scru'pu·lous adj. not honest, ethical, etc. —**un·scru'pu·lous·ness,** n.

un·self'ish adj. not putting one's own interests first. —**un·self'ish·ness,** n.

un·sex' (un-seks') v.t. deprive (a person) of the qualities of his or her sex.

un·shake'a·ble (un-shāk'ə-bəl) adj. determined; not open to persuasion.

un·shak'en adj. having lost no faith, resolution, force, etc.

un·smil'ing (un-smī'ling) adj. serious in demeanor; dour.

un·sound' adj. **1,** not sound; diseased, decayed, or defective. **2,** not well-founded; invalid. **3,** financially insecure; unreliable.

un·speak'a·ble (un-spē'kə-bəl) adj. inexpressible; very bad.

un·stead'y adj. **1,** not steady; shaky. **2,** not reliable or resolute. —**un·stead'i·ness,** n.

un·stop' v.t. open; release.

un·strung' adj. **1,** removed from a string; with strings relaxed. **2,** nervously upset; distraught.

un·stud'ied (un-stud'ēd) adj. not affected in manner; artless; natural.

un·sung' adj. not duly honored.

un·sure' adj. **1,** not sure. **2,** not confident; hesitant.

un·think'a·ble (un-think'ə-bəl) adj. **1,** unworthy of consideration. **2,** inconceivable. —**un·think'ing,** adj. showing lack of thought; heedless.

un·tie' v.t. undo (a knot); release the fastenings of; set free.

un·til' conj. & prep. up to the time that; when or before.

un·time'ly adj. **1,** premature. **2,** inopportune; inconvenient. —**un·time'li·ness,** n.

un·tir'ing (un-tīr'ing) adj. unceasing in effort; not yielding to fatigue. —**un·tir'ing·ness,** n.

un'to prep. (Archaic) to; until.

un·told' adj. **1,** not told or revealed. **2,** not counted; too vast to be measured.

un·touch'a·ble (un-tuch'ə-bəl) adj. **1,** loathsome to the touch. **2,** that cannot be reached. **3,** impalpable; intangible. —n. a member of the lowest caste in India, whose touch is thought to pollute.

un·to·ward' (un-tôrd') adj. unfavorable; troublesome.

un·truth' n. a falsehood; lie. —**un·truth'·ful,** adj.

un·u'su·al adj. strange; uncommon. —**un·u'su·al·ness,** n.

un·var'nished (un-vär'nisht) adj. **1,** not varnished. **2,** not embellished or disguised; stark.

un·war'rant·a·ble (-ə-bəl) adj. lacking justification; without authority; unjust. Also, **un·war'rant·ed.**

un·washed' (un-wosht') adj. not washed; (of persons) unclean and vulgar.

un·whole'some adj. not healthful; unhealthy. —**un·whole'some·ness,** n.

un·wield'y (un-wēl'dē) adj. too large or bulky to be easily handled. —**un·wield'·i·ness,** n.

un·wit'ting (un-wit'ing) adj. not knowing or realizing; unaware.

un·wont'ed adj. not usual or customary.

un·writ'ten adj. not written. —**unwritten law,** a custom that is observed as though it were formal law; esp., that crimes in defense of honor should not be punished.

up adv. **1,** in, toward, or to a more elevated position; to an erect position; higher. **2,** at or to a source or point of importance. **3,** to an equally advanced point or extent. **4,** well prepared or equipped. **5,** into activity. **6,** in process of happening. **7,** ended. **8,** together or close. —prep. **1,** to a higher position on or in; near the top of. **2,** toward the source, center, interior, etc., of. —adj. going or tending to higher position. —n. an upward movement; improvement. —v.t. [**upped,** **up'ping**] (Colloq.) make larger; bid or bet higher than. —**up-and-coming,** adj. promising. —**up to snuff,** sharp; alert.

up'beat" n. (Music) a beat preceding a downbeat. —adj. (Colloq.) lively; brisk.

up·braid' v.t. blame; rebuke.

up'bring"ing n. childhood training; rearing.

up'chuck" v.i. (Slang) vomit.

up'com"ing adj. coming soon.

up'coun"try n. a region away from the seacoast or lowlands. —adj. & adv. in or toward such a region.

up'date" n. a revision incorporating latest news, documents, etc. —v.t. so revise.

up'draft" n. a rising air current.

up·end' v.t. set on end; turn the top upward. —v.i. stand on end.

up'front" adj. in view; in cash.

up'grade" n. **1,** an upward slope; rising grade. **2,** improvement. —adj. & adv. upward. —*v.t.* **1,** put in a higher grade or classification than previously. **2,** improve.

up·heav'al (up-hēv'əl) *n.* **1,** a bursting upward, as in an earthquake. **2,** a violent disturbance, as a revolution.

up'hill" *adj. & adv.* on or toward the top of a hill.

up·hold" *v.t.* [-**held'**, -**hold'ing**] support; advocate; confirm.

up·hol'ster (up-hōl'stər) *v.t.* provide (the framework of furniture) with cushions, covering, etc. —**up·hol'ster·er,** *n.* —**up·hol'ster·y,** *n.*

up'keep" *n.* maintenance.

up'land (-lənd) *n. & adj.* **1,** upcountry. **2,** high land.

up·lift' *v.t.* elevate. —*n.* (up'lift) **1,** raising; elevation. **2,** moral advancement; inspiration.

up'most *adj.* uppermost.

up·on' (ə-pon') *prep.* **1,** up and on. **2,** on.

up'per (up'ər) *adj.* **1,** higher in place or position. **2,** superior in rank, station, etc. —*n.* **1,** an upper part or section; the part of a shoe above the sole. **2,** (*Slang*) a stimulant drug. —**on one's uppers,** poverty-stricken. —**upper house,** the senior or smaller of two legislative bodies, as the U.S. Senate. —**the upper hand,** mastery.

up"per·case' *adj. & n.* capital (of a letter).

up"per·class' *adj.* pert. to or characteristic of a high-ranking social or scholastic class. —**up"per·class'man,** *n.*

up'per·cut" *n.* an upward blow.

up"per·most' *adj. & adv.* highest in place, position, rank, power, etc.

up'pish (up'ish) *adj.* insolent; haughty. Also, **up'pi·ty** (up'ə-tē). —**up'pish·ness,** *n.*

up·raise' *v.t.* raise; lift up.

up'right" *adj.* **1,** vertical or erect. **2,** honest; righteous. —*n.* something standing erect or vertical, as a supporting post. —*adv.* vertically. —**up'right"ness,** *n.* —**upright piano,** one in which the strings and sounding board are placed vertically.

up·ris'ing (up"rīz'ing) *n.* rebellion; insurrection.

up'roar" *n.* violent disturbance and noise; bustle and clamor.

up·roar'i·ous (up-rôr'ē-əs) *adj.* **1,** clamorous. **2,** hilarious. —**up·roar'i·ous·ness,** *n.*

up·root' *v.t.* tear out by the roots; remove forcibly.

up·set' *v.t.* **1,** knock down from an erect or normal posture; overturn; throw into confusion. **2,** overthrow; spoil. **3,** perturb. —*n.* (up'set) **1,** a fall; an overturning. **2,** an

unexpected result. —*adj.* overturned; disordered; disturbed.

up'shift" *n.* **1,** an improvement. **2,** a shift from a lower gear to a higher gear. —*v.i.* so shift.

up'shot" *n.* result.

up'side-"down' *adj. & adv.* **1,** having on top the side that should be on the bottom. **2,** in total disorder.

up'si·lon" (ūp'sə-lon") *n.* the twentieth letter of the Greek alphabet (γ, υ).

up'stage" *adj. & adv.* (*Theater*) at or to the back of the stage; (*Colloq.*) haughty. —*v.t.* **1,** cause (an actor, singer, etc.) to face away from the audience. **2,** draw attention from (a person, subject, etc.)

up'stairs" *adj., adv. & n.* (in, to, etc.) the second or a higher story.

up·stand'ing *adj.* highly respectable; upright.

up'start" *n.* a presumptuous person.

up'state" *adj. & n.* (*Colloq.*) (of or from) the interior or northern part of a state.

up'stream" *adj. & adv.* to or toward the source of a river, etc.; against the current.

up'surge" *n.* an increasing wave or movement, as of emotion.

up'swing" *n.* a marked improvement.

up'take" *n.* **1,** a ventilating pipe or shaft. **2,** comprehension; awareness.

up-"tight" *adj.* (*Slang*) **1,** tense; nervous. **2,** conventional in attitude.

up-'to-date" *adj.* **1,** in accordance with, or conforming to, the latest ideas or fashions; modern. **2,** extending to the present time.

up'town" *adj., adv. & n.* (in or to) a section away from the main business district.

up'turn" *n.* **1,** a turning over or up. **2,** a change for the better.

up'ward (up'wərd) *adv.* **1,** toward a higher position, degree, etc. **2,** toward the source, interior, etc. **3,** in the upper part. **4,** more. —*adj.* moving or directed upward. —**upward mobility,** the possibility or ability to improve one's financial, social, or professional position.

up'wards (-wərdz) *adv.* in an upward direction. —**upwards of,** somewhat more than.

u·ra'ni·um (yû-rā'nē-əm) *n.* a radioactive chemical element, no. 92, symbol U.

urb (ērb) *n.* an urban area.

ur'ban (ēr'bən) *adj.* pert. to, comprising, living in, or characteristic of a city. —**ur'ban·ite,** *n.* —**urban renewal,** reconstruction or rehabilitation of blighted urban areas. —**urban sprawl,** the tendency of the city to expand.

---

ur·bane' (ẽr-bān') *adj.* affable; suave. **—ur·ban'i·ty** (-ban'ə-tē) *n.*

ur"ban·ol'o·gy *n.* the study of urban problems.

ur'chin (ẽr'chin) *n.* a mischievous boy; any small boy.

-ure (-yər) *suf.* forming abstract nouns of action, agency, state, or result.

u·re'a (yū-rē'ə) *n.* a substance found in urine, used in plastics.

u·re'mi·a (yū-rē'mē-ə) *n.* a morbid bodily condition due to retention of waste products. **—u·re'mic,** *adj.*

u·re'ter (yū-rē'tər) *n.* the tube carrying urine from kidney to bladder.

u·re'thra (yū-rē'thrə) *n.* the tube through which urine is discharged from the bladder.

urge (ẽrj) *v.t.* **1,** push onward; drive vigorously. **2,** exhort. **3,** advocate earnestly. *—n.* an impelling force; an impulse.

ur'gen·cy (ẽr'jən-sē) *n.* **1,** insistence. **2,** imperative necessity.

ur'gent (ẽr'jənt) *adj.* **1,** imperative; needed at once. **2,** insistent.

-ur·gy (ẽr-jē) *suf.* technology.

u'ric (yůr'ik) *adj.* of or pert. to urine or urea.

u'rin·al (yůr'i-nəl) *n.* a receptacle to receive urine.

u"ri·nal'y·sis (yůr"i-nal'ə-sis) *n.* an analysis of a specimen of urine, made for medical purposes.

u'ri·na·ry (-ner-ē) *adj.* pert. to the organs that excrete urine.

u'ri·nate" (-nāt") *v.t.* discharge urine. **—u"ri·na'tion,** *n.*

u'rine (yůr'in) *n.* a fluid secretion of the kidneys, excreting waste products.

urn (ẽrn) *n.* **1,** a vase with a base. **2,** a vessel for making tea, coffee, etc.

u·rol'o·gy (yůr-ol'ə-jē) *n.* the study and treatment of organs that excrete urine. **—u"ro·log'i·cal,** *adj.* **—u·rol'o·gist,** *n.*

ur'sine (ẽr'sīn) *adj.* pert. to a bear; bearlike.

ur"ti·car'i·a (ẽr"ti-kär'ē-ə) *n.* an eruptive skin disease; hives. **—ur"ti·car'i·al,** *adj.*

us *pron.* obj. pl. of *I.*

us'age (ū'sij) *n.* **1,** customary practice or way of acting or doing; an established way of using words or phrases. **2,** the use or enjoyment of something.

us'ance (ū'zəns) *n.* **1,** the time allowed by custom for payment of foreign bills of exchange. **2,** income derived from ownership of wealth.

use (ūz) *v.t.* **1,** employ for a purpose; put to service. **2,** consume or expend. **3,** treat. *—n.* (ūs) **1,** the act of using, employing, or putting to service; the state of being used. **2,** utility; service. **3,** an instance or

way of using something. **—us'a·ble** (ū'-zə-bəl) *adj.* **—us'er** (ū'zər) *n.* **—used to** (ūs'tū) accustomed to (with a noun); in past time did.

use'ful (ūs'fəl) *adj.* having a practical function, purpose, or effect; worthwhile. **—use'ful·ness,** *n.*

use'less (ūs'ləs) *adj.* without function or effect; not useful. **—use'less·ness,** *n.*

ush'er (ush'ər) *n.* **1,** one who escorts persons to seats in a church, theater, etc. **2,** one in charge of a door. *—v.t.* **1,** escort. **2,** (with *in*) introduce; contribute to the beginning of. **—ush'er·ette",** *n.fem.*

u'su·al (ū'zhū-əl) *adj.* **1,** ordinary; normal. **2,** customary; habitual. **—u'su·al·ly,** *adv.* on most occasions.

u'su·fruct" (ū'zū-frukt") *n.* the right to use; the yield from use.

u·surp' (ū-sẽrp') *v.t.* seize and hold (office, power, etc.) by force and without right. **—u"sur·pa'tion,** *n.*

u'su·ry (ū'zhə-rē) *n.* exorbitant interest paid or charged. **—u'su·rer,** *n.* **—u·sur'i·ous** (ū-zhůr'ē-əs) *adj.*

ut (ût) *n.* (*Music*) do.

u·ten'sil (ū-ten'səl) *n.* an implement, instrument, or vessel, esp. one used in preparing food.

u'ter·us (ū'tər-əs) *n.* [*pl.* **-i** (-ī)] the organ in which the fetus rests and grows; the womb. **—u"ter·ine** (-in) *adj.*

u'tile (ū'təl) *adj.* useful.

u·til"i·tar'i·an (ū-til"ə-tār'ē-ən) *adj.* useful rather than ornamental.

u·til'i·ty (ū-til'ə-tē) *n.* **1,** the state of being useful; something useful. **2,** a public service, as an agency supplying electricity, water, etc. **—utility man,** one who does any odd jobs.

u'ti·lize" (ū'tə-līz") *v.t.* make use of; put to service. **—u"ti·li·za'tion,** *n.*

ut'most" (ut'mōst") *adj.* **1,** of the greatest degree, quantity, etc. **2,** at the farthest or outermost point. *—n.* the limit. Also, **ut'-ter·most.**

U·to'pi·an (ū-tō'pē-ən) *adj.* relating to an imaginary ideal state (Utopia) or condition; hence, idealistic but not practical.

ut'ter (ut'ər) *v.t.* **1,** give audible expression to; say. **2,** issue; emit. *—adj.* complete; absolute; unconditional.

ut'ter·ance *n.* **1,** act of uttering; issuance; something said. **2,** manner of speaking.

ut'ter·most" *adj. & n.* utmost.

u'vu·la (ū'vyə-lə) *n.* the fleshy conical body hanging down from the soft palate in the back of the mouth. **—u'vu·lar** (-lər) *adj.*

ux·o'ri·ous (uk-sôr'é-əs) *adj.* excessively fond of one's wife. **—ux·o'ri·ous·ness,** *n.*

V

V, v (vē) **1,** the 22nd letter of the English alphabet. **2,** (*cap.*) five, 5, the Rom. numeral.

va'can·cy (vā'kən-sè) *n.* **1,** state of being vacant; a vacant space. **2,** an available job, space, etc.

va'cant (vā'kənt) *adj.* **1,** having no contents; empty; devoid of something. **2,** having no occupant; untenanted. **3,** idle; disengaged. **4,** vacuous; stupid.

va'cate" (vā'kāt") *v.t.* **1,** make vacant; quit; empty. **2,** make void; annul.

va·ca'tion (vā-kā'shən) *n.* **1,** a period of release from work; holiday. **2,** act of vacating. **—va·ca'tion·ist,** *n.*

vac'ci·nate" (vak'sə-nāt") *v.t.* innoculate with a vaccine, esp. to immunize against smallpox. **—vac"ci·na'tion,** *n.*

vac·cine' (vak-sēn') *n.* a weakened virus introduced into a healthy body to induce immunity against the disease.

vac·cin'i·a (vak-sin'é-ə) *n.* cowpox.

vac'il·late" (vas'ə-lāt") *v.i.* **1,** waver in opinion, sentiment, determination, etc.; be irresolute. **2,** sway; stagger. **—vac"il·la'-tion,** *n.*

vac'u·ole" (vak'ū-ōl") *n.* **1,** a cavity in the protoplasm of a cell. **2,** a tiny cell or cavity in the tissue of organisms.

vac'u·ous (vak'ū-əs) *adj.* **1,** showing no intelligence; blank. **2,** empty; unfilled. **—va·cu'i·ty** (-kū'ə-tè) *n.*

vac'u·um (vak'ū-əm) *n.* **1,** space void of matter. **2,** a space largely exhausted of air or gas. **—v.t. & i.** (*Colloq.*) clean with a vacuum cleaner. **—vacuum bottle,** thermos. **—vacuum cleaner,** a device that sucks in dust, etc., for housecleaning. **—vacuum-packed,** *adj.* packed in a container from which the air is removed. **—vacuum tube,** a sealed tube of glass or metal, used in electronic devices, as radio.

va'de me'cum (vä'dē-mā'kəm) (*Lat.*) a guide, esp., a guidebook.

vag'a·bond" (vag'ə-bond") *adj.* having no settled habitation; wandering; nomadic. **—n.** a wanderer; esp. a worthless vagrant; a tramp.

va·gar'y (və-gār'é) *n.* a capricious or extravagant thought or action.

va·gi'na (və-jī'nə) *n.* the passage from vulva to uterus in a female animal. **—vag'i·nal** (vaj'i-nəl) *adj.*

va'grant (vā'grənt) *adj.* **1,** vagabond. **2,**

uncertain; erratic (as ideas). **—n. 1,** a vagabond. **2,** one without visible or reputable means of support. **—va'gran·cy,** *n.*

vague (vāg) *adj.* **1,** not definite, precise, or clear. **2,** mentally confused. **3,** indistinct to sight or other sense. **—vague'ness,** *n.*

vain (vān) *adj.* **1,** ineffective; futile. **2,** of no real value; trivial. **3,** excessively proud of oneself; conceited. **—vain'ness,** *n.*

vain·glo'ri·ous *adj.* inordinately proud, boasting, or pretentious. **—vain·glo'ri·ous·ness,** *n.* **—vain"glo'ry,** *n.*

val'ance (val'əns) *n.* a short drape or curtain used as an ornamental border.

vale (vāl) *n.* (*Poetic*) valley. **—interj.** (vā'le) farewell.

val"e·dic'tion (val'ə-dik'shən) *n.* a farewell; a bidding farewell.

val"e·dic'to·ry (val''ə-dik'tə-rè) *adj.* bidding farewell; farewell. **—n.** an oration of farewell, esp. by a member of a graduating class. **—val"e·dic·to'ri·an,** *n.* one who delivers a valedictory, usu. the top academic student in the graduating class.

va'lence (vā'ləns) *n.* (*Chem.*) the relative combining capacity of an atom compared with the hydrogen atom. Also, **va'len·cy.**

Va·len'ci·ennes' (və-len"sè-enz') *n.* a kind of fine lace.

-va·lent (vā-lənt) *suf.* having a valency of, as *univalent.*

val'en·tine" (val'ən-tīn") *n.* **1,** a sentimental missive sent on St. Valentine's day, Feb. 14. **2,** a sweetheart chosen on this day.

va·le'ri·an (və-lir'é-ən) *n.* **1,** a perennial herb. **2,** a drug made from it, used to quiet the nerves.

val'et (val'ət, va-lā') *n.* **1,** a personal servant. **2,** one whose business is pressing and cleaning clothes. **—valet parking,** a parking system in which an employee parks the car for the client.

val"e·tu"di·nar'i·an (val''ə-tū"də-nār'é-ən) *n. & adj.* (one) in poor health; invalid.

Val·hal'la (val-hal'ə) *n.* in Norse mythology, the final resting place for the souls of heros slain in battle.

val'iant (val'yənt) *adj.* **1,** brave; courageous. **2,** showing valor. **—val'ian·cy,** *n.*

val'id (val'id) *adj.* **1,** well supported by fact; sound; just. **2,** legally effective or binding. **—va·lid'i·ty** (və-lid'ə-tè) *n.*

val'i·date" (val'i-dāt") *v.t.* make valid. **—val"i·da'tion,** *n.*

va·lise' (və-lēs') *n.* a small leather traveling bag.

Val'i·um (val'è-əm) *n.* (*T.N.*) a tranquilizing drug.

val'ley (val'è) *n.* **1,** a relatively low tract

of land between hills. **2**, the lowlands along the course of a river. **3**, any hollow, depression, or dip.

val′or (val′ər) *n.* strength of mind in braving danger. Also, **val′our.** —**val′or·ous,** *adj.*

val′or·ize″ (val′ə-rīz″) *v.t.* fix and maintain an arbitrary price of (a commodity) by governmental action. —**val″or·i·za′tion,** *n.*

val′u·a·ble (val′ū-ə-bəl) *adj.* of great value or price. —*n.* (usually *pl.*) an expensive personal possession, as a jewel. —**val′u·a·ble·ness,** *n.*

val″u·a′tion (val″ū-ā′shən) *n.* **1**, act of appraising or estimating value. **2**, estimated worth.

val′ue (val′ū) *n.* **1**, that for which something is regarded as useful or desirable; utility, merit, or worth. **2**, price. **3**, import. **4**, degree; number; amount; duration, etc. —*v.t.* **1**, regard as desirable or useful. **2**, estimate the value of. —**val′ued,** *adj.* highly regarded. —**val′ue·less,** *adj.* worthless. —**value-added tax,** a tax based on the cost added to the value of a product at each stage of production.

valve (valv) *n.* **1**, any device used to control the flow of a fluid through a pipe, vent, etc. **2**, a hinged lid or flap, as of the shell of a clam, etc. **3**, an electron tube. —**val′vu·lar** (val′vyə-lər) *adj.*

va·moose′ (va-moos′) *v.i.* depart rapidly; run away.

vamp *n.* **1**, the front part of the upper of a shoe or boot. **2**, a patch added to something old. **3**, an improvised musical accompaniment. **4**, (*Slang*) a flirtatious woman. —*v.t.* **1**, repair; patch; renovate. **2**, (*Slang*) use feminine wiles on.

vam′pire (vam′pīr) *n.* **1**, a supposed blood-sucking monster. **2**, any of various blood-sucking or similar bats. **3**, an extortionist, esp. a flirtatious or predatory woman.

van *n.* **1**, a large covered wagon or truck. **2**, (*Brit.*) a light delivery truck; a baggage or freight car. **3**, vanguard.

va·na′di·um (və-nā′dē-əm) *n.* a rare element, no. 23, symbol V, used to harden steel.

Van Al′len radiation belt (van-al′ən) a belt of ionizing radiation surrounding the earth and extending from approx. 500 miles to approx. 30,000 miles into space.

van′dal *n.* one who willfully destroys things of beauty. —**van′dal·ism,** *n.* wanton destruction. —**van′dal·ize″,** *v.t.*

van·dyke′ (-dīke′) *n.* (often *cap.*) a short pointed beard.

vane (vān) *n.* **1**, a device that turns with the wind and shows its direction: *weather-vane*. **2**, blade, plate, fin, etc., moved by a fluid stream.

van′guard″ (van′gärd″) *n.* the foremost units, as of an advancing army; the leaders, as of a social movement.

va·nil′la (və-nil′ə) *n.* a tropical orchid; a flavoring extract made from its bean.

va·nil′lin (və-nil′ən) *n.* an artificial compound giving a vanilla flavor.

van′ish *v.i.* **1**, fade from sight; disappear. **2**, pass away; cease to exist. **3**, (*Math.*) become zero. —**vanishing point,** the point toward which receding parallel lines seem to converge.

van′i·ty (van′ə-tē) *n.* **1**, excessive pride; excessive attention to one's appearance. **2**, futility; worthlessness. **3**, a thing or trait regarded as vain. **4**, a small cosmetic case carried by a woman. **5**, a woman's dressing table.

van′quish (vang′kwish) *v.t.* defeat in battle or contest.

van′tage (van′tij) *n.* a position affording superior power or opportunity.

vap′id *adj.* lacking animation or flavor. —**va·pid′i·ty** (və-pid′ə-tē), **vap′id·ness,** *n.*

va′por (vā′pər) *n.* **1**, a gas made visible by particles of liquid or dust, as steam, fog, smoke. **2**, any matter in gaseous state. **3**, something unsubstantial or transitory. **4**, (*Archaic*) hypochondria. —*v.t. & i.* change to vapor. Also, **va′pour.** —**vapor trail,** contrail.

va′por·ize″ (-īz″) *v.t. & i.* make or become vapor. —**va″por·i·za′tion,** *n.*

va′por·ous (-əs) *adj.* **1**, pert. to or of vapor. **2**, unsubstantial; vague. —**va′por·ous·ness,** *n.*

va·que′ro (va-kā′rō) *n.* (*Span.*) a herdsman or cowboy.

var·ac′tor (var-ak′tər) *n.* a type of semiconductor capacitor.

var′i·a·ble (vār′ē-ə-bəl) *adj.* **1**, tending to change; not constant. **2**, capable of being varied. —*n.* that which varies. —**var″i·a·bil′i·ty,** *n.*

var′i·ance (vār′ē-əns) *n.* act or effect of varying; difference. —**at variance,** in disagreement.

var′i·ant (vār′ē-ənt) *adj.* tending to change; different; diverse. —*n.* an altered form of something.

var″i·a′tion (vār″ē-ā′shən) *n.* **1**, the act or process of varying; change; modification. **2**, a point or aspect of difference. **3**, the amount of change; variance. **4**, a different form. **5**, (*Music*) a theme repeated with changes or elaborations.

var″i·cel′la (var″i-sel′lə) *n.* chicken pox.

var'i·col″ored (vãr'ĕ-kul″ərd) *adj.* variegated; motley.

var'i·cose″ (vãr'i-kōs″) *adj.* dilated; abnormally swollen, esp. of veins. —**var'i·cos'i·ty** (-kos'ə-tĕ) *n.*

var'ied (vãr'ĕd) *adj.* **1,** assorted; differing. **2,** altered.

var'i·e·gat'ed (vãr'ĕ-ə-gāt″ed) *adj.* marked with different colors. —**var'i·e·gate″,** *v.t.* —**var″i·e·ga'tion,** *n.*

va·ri'e·ty (və-rī'ə-tĕ) *n.* **1,** a mixture of different things. **2,** difference or discrepancy. **3,** a variant; a subdivision. **4,** vaudeville. —**variety store,** a store offering a wide variety of merchandise.

var'i·fo″cal lens (var'ə-fō″kəl) zoom lens.

var'i·form (var'ə-fôrm″) *adj.* varied in form; having different shapes.

va·ri'o·la (və-rī'ə-lə) *n.* smallpox. —**va·ri'o·lous,** *adj.*

var″i·om'e·ter (vãr″ĕ-om'ə-tər) *n.* an instrument for regulating or measuring electrical variations.

var″i·o'rum (vãr″ĕ-ôr'əm) *adj.* presenting several versions (of a text).

var'i·ous (vãr'ĕ-əs) *adj.* **1,** differing; having diverse features; not uniform. **2,** some; several; many. —**var'i·ous·ness,** *n.*

var'let (vär'lit) *n.* (*Archaic*) a rascal. —**var'let·ry,** *n.* (*Archaic*) the rabble.

var'mint (vär'mənt) *n.* (*Dial.*) **1,** an insect; bug; any undesirable creature. **2,** a low or rascally person.

var'nish (vär'nish) *n.* **1,** a resinous coating material that produces a glossy surface. **2,** superficial social polish. —*v.t.* finish with, or as with, varnish.

var'si·ty (vär'sə·tĕ) *n.* the principal team of a school or college in a given sport.

var'y (vãr'ĕ) *v.t.* **1,** make different; alter. **2,** make of different kinds; diversify. **3,** (*Music*) embellish with variations. —*v.i.* **1,** be different or diverse. **2,** undergo change. **3,** be variable.

vas'cu·lar (vas'kyə-lər) *adj.* pert. to bodily ducts that convey fluid, as blood and lymph. —**vas″cu·lar'i·ty** (-lar'ə-tĕ) *n.*

vase (vās) *n.* a hollow vessel, as for holding cut flowers, etc.

va·sec'to·my (va-sek'tə-mĕ) *n.* a surgical method of sterilization of a male.

vas'e·line″ (vas'ə-lēn″) *n.* (*T.N.*) a greasy petroleum product used as an ointment and lubricant.

vas″o·mo'tor (vas″ō-mō'tər) *adj.* regulating the blood vessels.

vas'sal (vas'əl) *n.* **1,** a feudal tenant. **2,** a subject, follower, or retainer. —**vas'sal·age,** *n.*

vast (vàst) *adj.* very great in extent, quantity, etc. —**vast'ness,** *n.*

vat *n.* a large container for liquids.

vat'ic (vat'ik) *adj.* prophetic.

Vat'i·can (vat'i-kən) *n.* the palace of the Pope, at Rome.

vaude'ville (vod'vil) *n.* a theatrical show comprising separate acts of different kinds. —**vaude·vil'lian** (-yən) *n. & adj.*

vault (vâlt) *n.* **1,** a chamber with an arched or concave roof, esp. one underground; any underground room. **2,** a chamber used as a safe. **3,** a jump; the act of vaulting. —*v.i. & t.* jump or leap, esp. with aid of the hands resting on something.

vaunt (vânt) *v.t.* speak of boastfully.

V-'Day″ day of victory (in World War II): in Europe (*V-E Day*), May 8, 1945, and over Japan (*V-J Day*), Sept. 2, 1945.

veal (vēl) *n.* the meat of a calf.

vec'tor (vek'tər) *n. & adj.* a line graphically representing both magnitude and direction; a quantity which may be represented by such a line.

Ve'da (vā'də) *n.* one of the Hindu scriptures. —**Ve'dic,** *adj.*

Ve·dan'ta (vā-dän'tə) *n.* a Hindu philosophy, a derivation of the Vedas.

ve·dette' (və-det') *n.* (*Naval*) a small scouting boat.

veep (vēp) *n.* (*Slang*) vice-president.

veer (vir) *v.i.* change direction, as wind. —*n.* a change of direction.

veer'y (vir'ĕ) *n.* a thrush of eastern U.S. noted for its song.

veg'e·ta·ble (vej'tə-bəl) *n.* **1,** any herbaceous plant used wholly or in part for food. **2,** any plant. —*adj.* **1,** being an edible plant. **2,** belonging to the plant kingdom. —**veg'e·tal** (vej'ə-təl) *adj.* —**vegetable marrow,** a kind of oblong squash.

veg″e·tar'i·an (vej″ə-tãr'ĕ-ən) *n. & adj.* one who eats no meat.

veg'e·tate″ (vej'ə-tāt″) *v.i.* **1,** grow or live like a plant. **2,** be mentally inactive. —**veg'e·ta·tive,** *adj.*

veg″e·ta'tion (vej″ə-tā'shən) *n.* **1,** plants collectively. **2,** the act of vegetating.

ve'he·ment (vē'ə-mənt) *adj.* showing strength or impetuosity in feeling; eager, fervent, or passionate. —**ve'he·mence,** *n.*

ve'hi·cle (vē'ə-kəl) *n.* **1,** any carriage or conveyance on wheels or runners. **2,** any medium for producing effects. **3,** (*Painting*) a liquid, as linseed oil, with which a pigment is mixed. —**ve·hic'u·lar** (vĕ-hik'yŭ-lər) *adj.*

veil (vāl) *n.* **1,** a piece of light fabric worn over the face or head. **2,** anything that screens or conceals. —*v.t.* **1,** cover with a veil. **2**, hide; disguise. —**take the veil,** become a nun.

vein (vān) *n.* **1**, one of the tubes that convey blood to the heart. **2**, a riblike part supporting a membrane, as a leaf. **3**, a stratum or deposit; a lode. **4**, a fissure or cavity; a small natural watercourse. **5**, a streak or stripe. —*v.t.* furnish or mark with veins. —**vein′y**, *adj.*

Vel′cro (vel′krō) *n.* (*T.N.*) a plastic fastener consisting of interlocking hooks.

veldt (velt) *n.* the open, scrubby country of So. Afr. Also, **veld.**

vel′lum (vel′əm) *n.* **1**, parchment made from calfskin. **2**, a paper of similar texture.

ve·loc′i·pede″ (və-los′ə-pēd″) *n.* a light vehicle with three wheels propelled by foot power; a tricycle.

ve·loc′i·ty (və-los′ə-tē) *n.* quickness or rate of motion; speed.

ve·lours′ (və-loor′) *n.* (*Fr.*) velvet.

ve·lure′ (və-lūr′) *n.* a velvet.

vel′vet (vel′vit) *n.* **1**, a fabric with a thick, soft pile. **2**, something of similar texture. **3**, (*Slang*) net profit. —**vel′vet·y**, *adj.*

vel″ve·teen′ (vel″və-tēn′) *n.* a cotton fabric woven like velvet.

ve′nal (vē′nəl) *adj.* open to bribery; corrupt. —**ve·nal′i·ty** (vē-nal′ə-tē) *n.*

vend *v.t. & i.* sell; purvey. —**vend·ee′**, *n.* buyer. —**vend′i·ble**, *adj.* —**vending machine**, a coin-slot machine for selling merchandise.

ven·det′ta (ven-det′ə) *n.* a feud.

ven′dor (ven′dər) *n.* **1**, a seller; a peddler. **2**, a vending machine. Also, **vend′er.**

ven·due′ (ven-dū′) *n.* a public auction.

ve·neer′ (və-nir′) *n.* **1**, a thin layer of fine wood or other material applied as an outercoating. **2**, one of the layers in plywood. **3**, outward show to give a fair appearance; superficial ornamentation. —*v.t.* **1**, cover with veneer. **2**, make into plywood.

ven′er·a·ble (ven′ər-ə-bəl) *adj.* **1**, worthy of veneration. **2**, old and dignified; ancient. —**ven″er·a·bil′i·ty, ven′er·a·ble·ness,** *n.*

ven′er·ate″ (ven′ə-rāt″) *v.t.* regard with reverence. —**ven″er·a′tion,** *n.*

ve·ne′re·al (və-nir′ē-əl) *adj.* pert. to diseases arising from copulation.

ven′er·y (ven′ə-rē) *n.* hunting; the chase.

Ve·ne′tian (və-nē′shən) *adj. & n.* of or pert. to Venice. —**Venetian blind,** a screen for a window, having adjustable horizontal slats.

venge′ance (ven′jəns) *n.* retributive punishment; revenge.

venge′ful (venj′fəl) *adj.* seeking revenge. —**venge′ful·ness,** *n.*

ve′ni·al (vē′nē-əl) *adj.* pardonable; excusable. —**ve″ni·al′i·ty,** *n.*

ve·ni′re (və-nī′rē) *n.* (*Law*) a writ requiring a sheriff to summon qualified citizens to act as jurors.

ve·ni′re·man (vi-nī′rē-mən) *n.* [*pl.* **-men**] one summoned to be a juror.

ven′i·son (ven′ə-zən) *n.* the flesh of a deer or like animal.

ven′om (ven′əm) *n.* **1**, poison secreted by snakes, spiders, etc. **2**, spite; malice; virulence. —**ven′om·ous,** *adj.*

ve′nous (vē′nəs) *adj.* of or pert. to the veins.

vent *n.* **1**, a small aperture or passage; an outlet. **2**, an emission or discharge. **3**, utterance. —*v.t.* **1**, let out; discharge. **2**, utter.

ven′ti·late″ (ven′tə-lāt″) *v.t.* let fresh air into; expose to the action of air. —**ven″ti·la′tion,** *n.* —**ven′ti·la″tor,** *n.* a device, as an opening, shaft, fan, etc., for ventilating.

ven′tral (ven′trəl) *adj.* pert. to the abdominal side of the body.

ven′tri·cle (ven′tri-kəl) *n.* a small cavity or hollow organ of the body; esp., a chamber of the heart. —**ven·tric′u·lar** (-yû-lər) *adj.*

ven·tril′o·quism (ven-tril′ə-kwiz-əm) *n.* the art of uttering sounds so that they seem to come from a source other than the speaker. —**ven·tril′o·quist,** *n.*

ven′ture (ven′chər) *n.* a hazardous enterprise. —*v.t.* **1**, expose to risk; stake. **2**, expose oneself to the risk of; utter daringly. —*v.i.* risk. —**ven′tur·ous,** *adj.* venturesome. —**at a venture,** at random.

ven′ture·some (-səm) *adj.* **1**, daring. **2**, hazardous; dangerous. —**ven′ture·some·ness,** *n.*

ven·ue (ven′ū) *n.* the scene of a crime or the jurisdiction of a court.

ve·ra′cious (və-rā′shəs) *adj.* **1**, disposed to tell the truth. **2**, true. —**ve·ra′cious·ness,** *n.*

ve·rac′i·ty (və-ras′ə-tē) *n.* truthfulness; accuracy.

ve·ran′da (və-ran′də) *n.* an open porch or gallery, usually roofed.

verb (vẽrb) *n.* a word that expresses action or existence; a part of speech that predicates and combines with a subject to form a sentence.

verb′al (vẽr′bəl) *adj.* **1**, expressed in words. **2**, oral, not written. **3**, pert. to a verb.

ver′bal·ism *n.* **1**, something expressed orally. **2**, wordiness. **3**, a wordy expression. —**ver′bal·ist,** *n.*

ver'bal·ize" (-īz") *v.i.* be verbose. —*v.t.* express in words. —**ver"bal·i·za'tion,** *n.*

ver·ba'tim (vər-bā'təm) *adj.* in exactly the same words.

ver·be'na (vər-bē'nə) *n.* a plant with showy flowers.

ver'bi·age (vēr'bē-ij) *n.* wordiness; verbosity.

ver·bose' (vər-bōs') *adj.* using more words than are necessary; wordy. —**ver·bos'i·ty** (-bos'ə-tē) *n.*

ver'dant (vēr'dənt) *adj.* **1,** green with vegetation. **2,** inexperienced. —**ver'dan·cy,** *n.*

ver'dict (vēr'dikt) *n.* **1,** the finding of a jury. **2,** any judgment or decision.

ver'di·gris" (vēr'də-grēs") *n.* a greenish patina that forms on copper, etc.

ver'dure (vēr'jər) *n.* **1,** green vegetation. **2,** greenness, esp. of growing plants. **3,** fresh or healthy condition.

verge (vērj) *n.* **1,** brink; edge; rim. **2,** a point or limit beyond which something begins. **3,** a staff of authority. —*v.i.* be at a border; approach.

ver'ger (vēr'jər) *n.* a minor church officer, as an usher or sexton.

ver'i·fy" (ver'ə-fī") *v.t.* ascertain or prove to be true. —**ver"i·fi·ca'tion,** *n.*

ver'i·ly (ver'ə-lē) *adv.* (*Archaic*) truly; really.

ver"i·si·mil'i·tude" (ver"i-si-mil'ə-tūd") *n.* an appearance of truth.

ver'ism (ver'iz-əm) *n.* the attempt to depict reality in art and literature.

ver'i·ta·ble (ver'i-tə-bəl) *adj.* true; genuine. —**ver"i·ta·bil'i·ty,** *n.*

ver'i·ty (ver'ə-tē) *n.* **1,** the quality of being true or real. **2,** a truth; a reality.

ver'juice" (vēr'joos") *n.* **1,** the juice of a sour fruit. **2,** tartness.

ver·mi– (vēr-mə) *pref.* wormlike.

ver"mi·cel'li (vēr"mə-sel'ē) *n.* a thin spaghetti.

ver·mic'u·late (vēr-mik'yû-lət) *adj.* **1,** marked with wavy lines. **2,** infested with worms.

ver·mi·form" (vēr'mə-fôrm") *adj.* long and slender, resembling a worm.

ver·mil'ion (vər-mil'yən) *n. & adj.* a bright yellow-red color.

ver'min (vēr'min) *n.pl.* or *sing.* **1,** small noxious animals collectively, esp. insects that infest the body, houses, etc. **2,** an obnoxious person or persons. —**ver'min·ous,** *adj.*

ver·mouth' (vər-mooth') *n.* a spiced wine. Also, **ver·muth'.**

ver·nac'u·lar (vər-nak'yə-lər) *adj. & n.*

pert. to the native or common language of a place or group.

ver'nal (vēr'nəl) *adj.* **1,** pert. to spring. **2,** pert. to early age; youthful.

ver'ni·er (vēr'nē-ər) *n.* an auxiliary device to measure fractional parts of subdivisions of a graduated scale.

ve·ron'i·ca (və-ron'i-kə) *n.* **1,** any of various plants or shrubs. **2,** a napkin or piece of cloth impressed with the face of Christ.

ver'sa·tile (vēr'sə-til) *adj.* **1,** having ability in many different fields. **2,** pivoted so as to swing or turn freely. —**ver"sa·til'i·ty,** *n.*

verse (vērs) *n.* **1,** metrical composition; poetry. **2,** a line of poetry or prose. **3,** a poem. **4,** a stanza.

versed (vērsd) *adj.* experienced; practiced; skilled.

ver'si·cle (vēr'sə-kəl) *n.* one of a succession of short verses said or sung alternately.

ver·si·fy" (vēr'sə-fī") *v.t. & i.* write in poetry. —**ver"si·fi·ca'tion,** *n.*

ver'sion (vēr'shən) *n.* **1,** a particular form or variant of something; a particular translation. **2,** a narration from a particular point of view.

ver'so (vēr'sō) *n.* **1,** a left-hand page of a book. **2,** the reverse side.

verst (vērst) *n.* a Russian measure of distance, equaling 3500 ft.

ver'sus (vēr'səs) *prep.* against, as opposing parties in a lawsuit or contest.

ver'te·bra (vēr'tə-brə) *n.* [*pl.* **-brae** (-brē) or **-bras**] any of the bone segments forming the spinal column. —**ver'te·bral,** *adj.*

ver'te·brate" (vēr'tə-brāt") *adj.* having a spine or backbone. —*n.* a vertebrate animal.

ver'tex (vēr'teks) *n.* [*pl.* **-es** or **ver'ti·ces"** (-tə-sēz")] the highest point; a point where two lines intersect.

ver'ti·cal (vēr'tə-kəl) *adj.* being perpendicular to the horizon; upright. —*n.* **1,** something vertical, as a line, supporting post, etc. **2,** an upright position. —**ver'ti·cal·ness,** *n.*

ver·tig'i·nous (vēr-tij'ə-nəs) *adj.* **1,** turning around; whirling; **2,** unstable.

ver'ti·go" (vēr'tə-gō") *n.* a disordered condition marked by dizziness.

ver'vain (ver'vān) *n.* a weedy plant with small flowers.

verve (vērv) *n.* enthusiasm; dash.

ver'y (ver'ē) *adv.* to a high degree; greatly; extremely. —*adj.* **1,** [*superl.* **ver'i·est**] true; actual; genuine. **2,** exact; innermost.

very high frequency designating radio

frequencies from 30 to 300 megacycles. Also, **VHF.**

ve·si′ca (və-sē′kə) *n.* [*pl.* **-cae** (-sè)] a bladder or sac. —**ves′i·cal** (ves′ə-kəl) *adj.*

ves′i·cle (ves′ə-kəl) *n.* a bladderlike structure, cavity, sac, or cyst.

ve·sic′u·lar (ve-sik′yû-lər) *adj.* pert. to or like a vesicle. —**ve·sic′u·late** (-lət) *adj.* having vesicles.

ves′per (ves′pər) *n.* **1,** evening; the evening star. **2,** (*pl.*) a religious service held in late afternoon; evensong.

ves′per·tine (ves′pər-tīn″) *adj.* pert. to, or happening in, the evening.

ves′sel (ves′əl) *n.* **1,** a ship or other craft for traveling on water. **2,** a hollow container. **3,** a tube or duct.

vest *n.* a short sleeveless garment worn by men under the coat; any similar garment. —*v.t.* **1,** clothe; cover or adorn with fabric. **2,** endow with something, as authority. **3,** put (rights, property, etc.) in possession of someone.

ves′tal (ves′təl) *adj.* virginal; chaste. —*n.* **1,** a virgin. **2,** a nun.

vest′ed (ves′tid) *adj.* **1,** owned securely. **2,** clothed; robed.

vest·ee′ (ves-tē′) *n.* a vestlike front piece in a woman's dress.

ves′ti·bule″ (ves′tə-būl″) *n.* a hall or antechamber between an outer door and inner room.

ves′tige (ves′tij) *n.* a remainder or evidence of something no longer present; a trace. —**ves·tig′i·al** (-tij′əl) *adj.*

vest′ment (-mənt) *n.* a garment, esp. an official or ceremonial dress.

vest-′pock″et *adj.* small enough to fit in a vest pocket; miniature.

ves′try (ves′trè) *n.* **1,** a room in a church where vestments are kept. **2,** a chapel. **3,** a church committee. —**ves′try·man,** *n.*

ves′ture (ves′chər) *n.* **1,** garments. **2,** any covering. —*v.t.* clothe.

vet *n.* **1,** veteran (of a war). **2,** veterinarian. —*v.t.* **1,** (*Colloq.*) work as a veterinarian. **2,** examine thoroughly.

vetch (vech) *n.* any of several leguminous plants used for forage.

vet′er·an (vet′ər-ən) *n.* **1,** one who has had long experience. **2,** a former soldier or other serviceman. —*adj.* having long experience. —**Veteran's Day,** a Federal legal holiday, Nov. 11.

vet′er·in·ar″y (vet′ər-ə-ner″è) *adj.* pert. to medical and surgical care of domestic animals. —*n.* [also, **vet″er·i·nar′i·an**] one who practices veterinary medicine.

ve′to (vē′tō) *n.* **1,** rejection by one branch of government of measures proposed by another. **2,** the right to reject. **3,** any ban or prohibition. —*v.t.* reject; prohibit; refuse to endorse.

vex (veks) *v.t.* **1,** make angry or displeased. **2,** annoy; worry; harass.

vex·a′tion (veks-ā′shən) *n.* annoyance; irritation. —**vex·a′tious,** *adj.*

vi′a (vī′ə) *prep.* by way of; by a route through.

vi′a·ble (vī′ə-bəl) *adj.* **1,** capable of living, esp., able to live outside the womb. **2,** (*Colloq.*) workable; practical. —**vi″a·bil′i·ty,** *n.*

vi′a·duct″ (vī′ə-dukt″) *n.* a bridge for carrying a road, railroad, waterway, etc., over a depression.

vi′al (vī′əl) *n.* a small bottle or flask.

vi′and (vī′ənd) *n.* an article of food.

vi·at′i·cum (vī-at′ə-kəm) *n.* **1,** communion given to a dying person. **2,** an allowance for traveling expenses.

vibes (vībz) *n.pl.* (*Slang*) **1,** vibrations; intuitive feelings. **2,** vibraharp.

vi′bra·harp″ (vī′brə-) *n.* a musical percussion instrument similar to a marimba but having metal chimes and an electric mechanism for producing vibrato. Also, **vi′-bra·phone″.**

vi′brant (vī′brənt) *adj.* **1,** vibrating; resonant. **2,** full of vigorous enthusiasm. —**vi′bran·cy,** *n.*

vi′brate (vī′brāt) *v.i.* **1,** swing to and fro, as a pendulum; oscillate. **2,** move rapidly to and fro, as a plucked string; quiver; resound; thrill. —**vi·bra′tion,** *n.* —**vi′-bra·tor,** *n.* —**vi′bra·to·ry** (-brə-tôr-è) *adj.*

vi·bra′to (vi-brä′tō) *n.* a tremulous effect or tremolo produced in singing and on various instruments.

vi·bur′num (vi-bēr′nəm) *n.* any of various shrubs or small trees, usu. bearing white flowers.

vic′ar (vik′ər) *n.* **1,** an assistant clergyman. **2,** one in charge of a dependent parish or chapel. **3,** a deputy. —**Vicar of Christ,** the Pope.

vic′ar·age (-ij) *n.* the residence or office of a vicar.

vi·car′i·ous (vī-kâr′è-əs) *adj.* substituting for, or feeling in place of, another. —**vi·car′i·ous·ness,** *n.*

vice (vīs) *n.* **1,** any immoral or evil practice. **2,** prostitution. **3,** a defect; a bad habit. **4,** vise. —*prep.* instead of; in place of.

vice- (vīs) *pref.* denoting a deputy or subordinate.

vice″ge′rent (-jir′ənt) *n.* a deputy.

vi·cen′ni·al (vī-sen′è-əl) *n. & adj.* **1,** 20 years. **2,** the 20th anniversary.

vice-″pres′i·dent *n.* an officer of a government, corporation, etc., ranking next below the president. —**vice-″pres′i·den·cy,** *n.*

vice′roy (-roi) *n.* a deputy king. —**vice″re′gal,** *adj.* —**vice′roy·ship,** *n.*

vi′ce ver′sa (vī′sə-vėr′sə) conversely; denoting reciprocal relationship or reversal of order.

vi′chy (vish′ē) *n.* **1,** a carbonated, naturally effervescent water; soda. **2,** (*cap.*) an alkaline, still water from Vichy, France (*eau de Vichy*).

vi′chys·soise″ (vish′ē-swäz″) *n.* a soup made with potatoes, leeks, and heavy cream, and served chilled.

vi·cin′i·ty (vi-sin′ə-tē) *n.* the region surrounding or near a place; the neighborhood.

vi′cious (vish′əs) *adj.* **1,** addicted to vice; wicked; depraved. **2,** evil; pernicious. **3,** faulty; defective. **4,** malicious; spiteful. —**vi′cious·ness,** *n.* —**vicious circle,** a series of successively consequent effects in which the last affects the first.

vi·cis′si·tude″ (vi-sis′i-tūd″) *n.* **1,** change of condition; succession of one set of circumstances by another. **2,** (*pl.*) good or bad fortune.

vic′tim (vik′tim) *n.* **1,** one who suffers from a harmful agency. **2,** one who is cheated or duped. —**vic′tim·ize″** (-mīz″) *v.t.*

vic′tor (vik′tər) *n.* one who wins.

Vic·to′ri·a (vik-tôr′e-ə) *n.* a kind of horse-drawn carriage. —**Victoria Day,** a legal holiday in Canada, the Monday before May 25.

Vic·to′ri·an (vik-tôr′ē-ən) *adj.* **1,** pert. to the time of Queen Victoria of England, 1837–1901. **2,** prudish; smug.

vic′to·ry (vik′tə-rē) *n.* **1,** the winning of a contest or battle. **2,** any successful performance. —**vic·to′ri·ous** (-tôr′ē-əs) *adj.*

vic·tro′la (vik-trō′lə) *n.* (*T.N.*) an early phonograph.

vict′ual (vit′əl) *n.* (*pl.*) food or provisions, esp. for human beings. —*v.t. & i.* supply with or obtain provisions. —**vict′ual·er,** *n.* a supplier of food; a restaurateur.

vi·cu′ña (vī-kū′nyə) *n.* **1,** a wild ruminant of the Andes, related to the llama. **2,** a fabric made from the wool of this animal.

vid′e·o (vid′ē-ō) *adj.* pert. to television. —*n.* television.

vid′e·o·disc″ *n.* (*T.N.*) a disc on which video images and sound are recorded, to be played back later.

vid″e·o·g′ra·phy (vid″ē-og′rə-fē) *n.* picture-taking with a television camera recording on videotape. —**vid″e·og′ra·pher,** *n.* —**vid″e·o·graph′ic,** *adj.*

vid′e·o·phone″ *n.* a Picturephone.

vid′e·o·tape″ *n.* a tape for recording video images for playback; the process by which this is done. —*v.t. & i.* record on videotape.

vid′kid″ *n.* (*Slang*) a child who watches television excessively.

vie (vī) *v.i.* [**vied, vy′ing**] strive for superiority; compete.

Vi″en·nese′ (vē″ə-nēz′) *adj. & n.* of or pert. to Vienna.

Viet″cong′ (vyet″kong′) *n.* [*pl.* **Viet″cong′**] a member of the former National Liberation Front of So. Vietnam; the Front itself.

view (vū) *n.* **1,** examination by eye; inspection; survey. **2,** range of vision. **3,** what is seen; scene, prospect, etc. **4,** mental contemplation; visualization. **5,** a particular aspect or mental attitude; an opinion, judgment, theory, etc. **6,** purpose; aim. —*v.t.* **1,** look at. **2,** consider; regard in a particular way. —**in view of,** in consideration of.

view′er *n.* **1,** one who or that which views. **2,** a device used for viewing, as of photographic slides, etc.

view′find′er *n.* a finder.

view′point″ *n.* **1,** a place from which something may be seen. **2,** attitude of mind: *point of view.*

vi·ges′i·mal (vi-jes′i-məl) *adj.* twentieth; by twenties.

vig′il (vij′əl) *n.* **1,** a keeping awake; a watch kept at night. **2,** watchful attention at any time.

vig′i·lant (vij′ə-lənt) *adj.* alert to detect danger. —**vig′i·lance,** *n.*

vig″i·lan′te (vij″ə-lan′tē) *n.* one of a group of self-appointed citizens acting to maintain order.

vi·gnette′ (vin-yet′) *n.* **1,** a photograph shaded at the edges so as to have no clear border. **2,** a descriptive literary sketch. **3,** a decorative illustration in a book. —*v.t.* **1,** outline; describe. **2,** make a (photographic) vignette of.

vig′or (vig′ər) *n.* **1,** active strength of body; good physical condition. **2,** mental energy. **3,** strength or force in general; powerful action; potency. Also, **vig′our.** —**vig′or·ous,** *adj.*

vi′king (vī′king) *n.* a Scandinavian mariner of the Middle Ages.

vile (vīl) *adj.* **1,** morally base; depraved; villainous. **2,** repulsive; obnoxious; disgusting. **3,** low in station; mean. **4,** of small value; paltry. —**vile′ness,** *n.*

vil′i·fy″ (vil′ə-fī″) *v.t.* defame. —**vil″i·fi·ca′tion,** *n.*

vil′i·pend″ *v.t.* **1,** treat contemptuously. **2,** vilify.

vil'la (vil'ə) *n.* a rural or suburban mansion; a large country residence.

vil'lage (vil'ij) *n.* a small assemblage of houses, less than a town. —**vil'lag·er,** *n.*

vil'lain (vil'ən) *n.* 1, the chief antagonist of the hero in a play or novel. 2, a wicked person; rascal; scoundrel. —**vil'lain·ess,** *n.fem.* —**vil'lain·ous,** *adj.* —**vil'lain·y,** *n.*

vil"la·nelle' (vil"ə-nel') *n.* a French verse form.

vil'lein (vil'ən) *n.* under the feudal system, a member of the class who were serfs with respect to their lords, but freemen with respect to others. —**vil'lein·age,** *n.*

vim *n.* energy; impetuosity.

vin"ai·grette' (vin"ə-gret') *n.* a small ornamental bottle or box for holding smelling salts, etc. —**vinaigrette sauce,** a sauce of vinegar, oil, etc.

vin'ci·ble (vin'sə-bəl) *adj.* conquerable. —**vin"ci·bil'i·ty,** *n.*

vin'cu·lum (ving'kyə-ləm) *n.* [*pl.* **-la** (-lə)] 1, a bond of union; a tie. 2, (*Math.*) a line drawn over two or more algebraic quantities to show that they are to be treated as one term.

vin'di·cate" (vin'də-kāt") *v.t.* 1, clear, as from an accusation or imputation. 2, maintain as true or correct. 3, regain possession of (property) by legal procedure. —**vin"·di·ca'tion,** *n.*

vin·dic'tive (vin-dik'tiv) *adj.* disposed to seek revenge; bitter. —**vin·dic'tive·ness,** *n.*

vine (vīn) *n.* 1, any plant with a long slender stem that trails on the ground or climbs upright objects. 2, the grape plant. 3, wine.

vin'e·gar (vin'ə-gər) *n.* 1, a sour liquid obtained by fermentation of fruit juices. 2, sourness of speech, temper, etc. —**vin"e·gar·y,** *adj.*

vine'yard" (vin'yərd) *n.* a plantation for grapes, esp., for wine-making.

vin'i·cul'ture (vin'ə-) *n.* the cultivation of grapes for wine.

vi'nous (vī'nəs) *adj.* pert. to wine or vines.

vin'tage (vin'tij) *n.* 1, the wine from a particular crop of grapes; the crop or output of anything. 2, the gathering of grapes; the harvest season. 3, wine-making. —*adj.* exceptionally fine.

vint'ner (vint'nər) *n.* a dealer in wines.

vi'nyl (vī'nil) *n.* pert. to certain compounds used in plastics (**vinyl resins,** as styrene, vinylite, koroseal, etc.).

vi'ol (vī'əl) *n.* a stringed musical instrument similar in shape to a violin but with more than four strings. —**vi'ol·ist,** *n.*

vi·o'la (vē-ō'lə) *n.* the alto instrument of the violin family. —**vi·o'list,** *n.*

vi'o·late" (vī'ə-lāt") *v.t.* 1, break or infringe, as a contract. 2, break in upon; do violence to. 3, treat with irreverence; desecrate; profane. 4, ravish (a woman). —**vi'o·la·ble,** *adj.* —**vi"o·la'tion,** *n.* —**vi'o·la·tor,** *n.*

vi'o·lent (vī'ə-lənt) *adj.* 1, acting with, or characterized by, strong physical force. 2, vehement; passionate; furious. —**vi'o·lence,** *n.*

vi'o·let (vī'ə-lit) *n.* 1, any of numerous herbs bearing small short-stemmed flowers; the flower. 2, a blue or reddish-blue color; the spectrum color of highest frequency visible to the eye.

vi"o·lin' (vī"ə-lin') *n.* a stringed musical instrument played with a bow; the treble member of the modern family of such instruments. —**vi"o·lin'ist,** *n.*

vi"o·lon·cel'lo (vē"ə-lon-chel'ō) *n.* the tenor instrument of the violin family. Also, **cel'lo.** —**vi"o·lon·cel'list,** *n.*

vi"o·lo'ne (vē"ə-lō'nā) *n.* a contrabass viol.

vi·os'ter·ol" (vī-os'tər-ol") *n.* a prepared oil that supplies vitamin D.

VIP (vē'ī'pē') *n.* (*Slang*) very important personage.

vi'per (vī'pər) *n.* 1, a venomous snake. 2, a malignant or treacherous person. —**vi'per·ous,** **vi'per·ish,** *adj.*

vi·ra'go (vi-rä'gō) *n.* an ill-tempered or violent woman.

vi'ral (vī'rəl) *adj.* pert. to, or resulting from, a virus.

vir'e·lay (vir'ə-lā) *n.* an old French poetic form.

vir'e·o (vir'ē-ō) *n.* [*pl.* **-e·os**] any of several small Amer. songbirds.

vir'gin (vėr'jin) *n.* 1, a person, esp. a woman, who has not had sexual intercourse. 2, (*cap.*) Mary, mother of Jesus. —*adj.* 1, being a virgin; pure. 2, fresh; new; unused. —**vir·gin'i·ty,** *n.* —**virgin birth,** the doctrine that Jesus was miraculously born of a virgin mother.

vir'gin·al (-əl) *adj.* pure; fresh. —*n.* a small harpsichord.

Virginia creeper a No. Amer. vine; woodbine.

Virginia reel a type of square dance.

vir·gin'i·um (vər-jin'ē-əm) *n.* francium.

Vir'go (vėr'gō) *n.* a constellation, the Virgin (see *zodiac*).

vir"i·des'cent (vir"ə-des'ənt) *adj.* greenish. —**vir"i·des'cence,** *n.*

vir'ile (vir'əl) *adj.* 1, of or like a man; masculine; manly. 2, capable of procreating. 3, forceful. —**vi·ril'i·ty** (və-ril'ə-tē) *n.*

vir·tu' (vər-too') *n.* the quality of being artistic, rare, etc.; objects having this quality.

vir'tu·al (vēr'choo-əl) *adj.* **1,** existing in power or effect, but not actually. **2,** equivalent to, though somewhat different or deficient. —**vir"tu·al'i·ty,** *n.*

vir'tue (vēr'choo) *n.* **1,** conformity to moral law; uprightness; rectitude. **2,** a commendable quality. **3,** chastity. **4,** inherent power; effect. —**by virtue of,** by authority of; because of.

vir"tu·os'i·ty (vēr"choo-os'ə-tē) *n.* great individual skill.

vir"tu·o'so (vēr"choo-ō'sō) *n.* [*pl.* **-sos, si** (-sē)] **1,** one who has great skill in a fine art, as music. **2,** a connoisseur.

vir'tu·ous (vēr'choo-əs) *adj.* moral; upright; chaste. —**vir'tu·ous·ness,** *n.*

vir'u·lent (vir'yə-lənt) *adj.* **1,** like a poison; deadly; malignant. **2,** bitterly hostile; acrimonious. —**vir'u·lence,** *n.*

vi'rus (vī'rəs) *n.* **1,** an agent of infection, esp. one smaller than common bacteria. **2,** a pernicious influence.

vi'sa (vē'zə) *n.* an endorsement making a passport valid for entry into a particular country. Also, **vi·sé'** (-zā').

vis'age (viz'ij) *n.* **1,** the face, esp. of a human being. **2,** countenance; appearance; aspect.

vis"-à-vis' (vē"zä-vē') *prep.* (*Fr.*) face to face.

vis'cer·a (vis'ər-ə) *n.pl.* [*sing.* **vis'cus** (-kəs)] **1,** the soft interior parts of the body. **2,** the bowels. —**vis'cer·al,** *adj.*

vis'cid (vis'id) *adj.* having a glutinous consistency; sticky. —**vis·cid'i·ty, vis'cid·ness,** *n.*

vis'cose (vis'kōs) *n. & adj.* a solution of cellulose used in making rayon.

vis·cos'i·ty (vis-kos'ə-tē) *n.* thickness or consistency of a liquid; resistance to flow.

vis'count (vī'kownt) *n.* a nobleman ranking next below a count (or earl). —**vis'count"ess,** *n.fem.*

vis'cous (vis'kəs) *adj.* **1,** viscid. **2,** having high viscosity.

vise (vīs) *n.* an apparatus for gripping and holding an object while work is performed on it. Also, **vice.**

vis'i·ble (viz'ə-bəl) *adj.* **1,** capable of being seen. **2,** open to view; conspicuous. **3,** perceptible to the mind. —**vis"i·bil'i·ty,** *n.*

vi'sion (vizh'ən) *n.* **1,** the sense of sight; ability to see. **2,** the ability to visualize; foresight. **3,** a pleasing or vivid scene. **4,** a supernatural or prophetic presentiment, as in a dream or trance. **5,** a fanciful or unpractical view.

vi'sion·ar·y (-er-ē) *adj.* **1,** unpractical. **2,**

given to idealistic theorizing. —*n.* a dreamer; theorizer.

vis'it (viz'it) *v.t.* **1,** go to see (a person, place, etc.); call upon. **2,** stay with, as a guest. **3,** afflict, as with suffering; assail. —*v.i.* make calls. —*n.* a friendly or official call; a stay as a guest. —**vis'i·tor,** *n.*

vis'it·ant (viz'i-tənt) *n.* one visiting for a short period.

vis"i·ta'tion (viz"i-tā'shən) *n.* **1,** an official visit. **2,** a boon or affliction regarded as an act of God. **3,** (*cap.*) the visit of the Virgin Mary to her cousin Elizabeth (Luke 1:39).

vi'sor (vī'zər) *n.* a part projecting above the eyes, as on a cap, to shade or protect them. Also, **vi'zor.**

vis'ta (vis'tə) *n.* a view or prospect, esp. one of great depth.

vis'u·al (vizh'ū-əl) *adj.* **1,** pert. to vision; used in seeing; optical. **2,** visible to the eye or mind. —**visual arts,** the arts whose objects are appreciated by viewing, as painting, sculpture, photography, etc.

vis'u·al·ize" (vizh'ū-ə-līz") *v.t.* **1,** form a mental image of. **2,** make perceptible. —*v.i.* form mental images. —**vis"u·al·i·za'tion,** *n.*

vi'tal (vī'təl) *adj.* **1,** pert. to life; alive. **2,** essential to existence or well-being. **3,** critically important. **4,** invigorating. **5,** fatal. —**vi'tal·ness,** *n.* —**vital signs,** bodily symptoms indicative of basic bodily functions, as heartbeat, pulse rate, etc. —**vital statistics,** birth and death records. —**vi'tals,** *n.pl.* vital organs of the body.

vi·tal'i·ty (vī-tal'ə-tē) *n.* **1,** the power to live; the principle of life. **2,** vigor; energy.

vi'tal·ize" (vī'təl-īz") *v.t.* give life, vigor, or vitality to. —**vi"tal·i·za'tion,** *n.*

vi'ta·min (vī'tə-min) *n.* a food constituent essential to the proper functioning of the body. Also, **vi'ta·mine.**

vi'ti·ate" (vish'ē-āt") *v.t.* make faulty or imperfect; contaminate; spoil; invalidate. —**vi"ti·a'tion,** *n.*

vit'i·cul'ture (vit'ə-) *n.* the cultivation of grapes. —**vit"i·cul'tur·al,** *adj.*

vit're·ous (vit'rē-əs) *adj.* **1,** pert. to or consisting of glass. **2,** resembling glass, as in hardness, finish, etc. —**vit're·ous·ness,** *n.* —**vitreous humor,** the jellylike fluid in the eye.

vit'ri·fy" (vit'ri-fī") *v.t. & i.* change to a glassy state by heat. —**vit"ri·fi·ca'tion, vit"ri·fac'tion,** *n.*

vit'ri·ol (vit'rē-əl) *n.* **1,** sulfuric acid. **2,** any metallic sulfate of glassy appearance. **3,** something extremely caustic, as criticism. —**vit"ri·ol'ic,** *adj.* —**vit"ri·ol'i·cal·ly,** *adv.*

vi·tu'per·ate" (vī-tū"pə-rāt") *v.t.* address

or find fault with abusively. —**vi·tu″per·a′tion,** *n.* —**vi·tu′per·a·tive** (-ə-tiv), **vi·tu′per·ous** (-əs) *adj.*

vi′va (vē′və) *interj.* long live (the person or thing named). —*n.* a shout of "viva."

vi·va′cious (vī-vā′shəs) *adj.* animated; lively; sprightly. —**vi·va′cious·ness,** *n.*

vi·vac′i·ty (vi-vas′ə-tē) *n.* high spirits; vivaciousness.

vi·var′i·um (vi-vâr′ē-əm) *n.* a place where animals are kept in a natural setting.

vi′va vo′ce (vī′və-vō′che) (*Lat.*) orally.

viv′id *adj.* **1,** lifelike; animated; bright. **2,** clearly perceptible. **3,** vigorous or lively in action. —**viv′id·ness,** *n.*

viv′i·fy″ (viv′ə-fī″) *v.t.* enliven; give life to.

vi·vip′a·rous (vī-vip′ə-rəs) *adj.* bearing young alive, not in eggs. —**vi·vip′a·rous·ness,** *n.*

viv′i·sect″ (viv′ə-sekt″) *v.t.* dissect the living body of (an animal), for experimental purposes. —**viv″i·sec′tion,** *n.*

vix′en (vik′sən) *n.fem.* **1,** a female fox. **2,** an ill-tempered woman. —**vix′en·ish,** *adj.*

vi·zier′ (vi-zir′) *n.* a chief minister of a Mohammedan sovereign.

vi′zor (vī′zər) *n.* visor.

vizs′la (vish′lə) *n.* a Hungarian breed of hunting dog.

vo′ca·ble (vō′kə-bəl) *n.* any word, regarded as a group of letters or sounds, without reference to meaning. —*adj.* that may be spoken.

vo·cab′u·lar″y (vō-kab′yū-ler′ē) *n.* **1,** the words of a language collectively. **2,** the stock of words used by a particular person, group, etc. **3,** a written list of words, as a dictionary.

vo′cal (vō′kəl) *adj.* **1,** pert. to the voice, speech, or singing. **2,** pert. to expression in speech; able or insistent in speaking. —*n.* **1,** a vocal sound, esp. a vowel. **2,** (*Colloq.*) the singing part of a musical performance. —**vo′cal·ist,** *n.* a singer. —**vo′cal·ize″** (-īz″) *v.t. & i.* utter; sing. —**vocal cords,** membranes in the larynx that vibrate to produce sound.

vo·ca′tion (vō-kā′shən) *n.* **1,** a particular profession, business, or occupation; calling. **2,** a summons or feeling of being called to a particular activity, esp. religious. —**vo·ca′tion·al,** *adj.* pert. to an occupation; giving training for a trade.

voc′a·tive (vok′ə-tiv) *adj. & n.* calling by name; (*Gram.*) designating the case of one directly addressed.

vo·cif′er·ate″ (vō-sif′ə-rāt″) *v.i. & t.* cry out noisily; shout. —**vo·cif″er·a′tion,** *n.*

vo·cif′er·ous (vō-sif′ə-rəs) *adj.* exclaiming; clamorous; noisy. —**vo·cif′er·ous·ness,** *n.*

vod′ka (vod′kə) *n.* a Russian alcoholic liquor distilled from cereals or potatoes.

vogue (vōg) *n.* prevalent fashion; popularity.

voice (vois) *n.* **1,** sound uttered by the mouth of a living creature, esp. human. **2,** the vocal sounds characteristic of a particular person. **3,** expression by, or as though by, speaking, singing, etc. **4,** the right to speak, vote, etc. **5,** a person or agency by which something is revealed. **6,** a singer; his rôle or part. **7,** (*Gram.*) a relative verb inflection, active (as, *I do it*) or passive (as, *it is done by me*). —*v.t.* give utterance to. —**voiced,** *adj.* —**voice′less,** *n.* —**voice box,** larynx.

-voiced *suf.* having a specified kind of voice, as *soft-voiced.*

voice-′o″ver *n.* (*Colloq.*) in motion pictures and television, a voice of a narrator, etc., not actually appearing on camera.

voice′print″ *n.* the distinctive pattern of wavy lines made by an individual's voice on a sound spectrograph: used for identification.

void *adj.* **1,** not legally binding; invalid; null. **2,** having no contents; vacant. **3,** ineffectual. —*v.t.* **1,** nullify. **2,** empty; evacuate. —*n.* a vacuum; empty place. —**void′·ness,** *n.*

voile (voil) *n.* a thinly-woven dress fabric.

vol′a·tile (vol′ə-til) *adj.* **1,** changing to vapor readily or rapidly. **2,** fickle; frivolous. **3,** transient; unstable. —**vol″a·til′i·ty,** *n.*

vol·can′ic (vol-kan′ik) *adj.* **1,** pert. to a volcano. **2,** violently eruptive. —**vol·can′i·cal·ly,** *adv.* —**vol′can·ism** (vol′kən-iz-əm) *n.*

vol·ca′no (vol-kā′nō) *n.* a vent in the earth's surface, commonly at the top of a mountain, from which molten rock and heated gases issue or have issued.

vole (vōl) *n.* a small rodent of the rat family.

vo·li′tion (vō-lish′ən) *n.* the act or power of willing; voluntary action. —**vo·li′tion·al,** *adj.*

vol′i·tive (vol′ə-tiv) *adj.* expressing a wish.

vol′ley (vol′ē) *n.* **1,** a flight or discharge of a number of missiles at one time. **2,** the sound of concerted explosions. **3,** (in games) the striking of a ball before it touches the ground. —*v.t. & i.* send or fly in a volley.

vol′ley·ball″ *n.* a game played by volleying a large ball back and forth over a high net.

vol′plane (vol′plān) *v.i.* glide in an airplane without motor power. —*n.* a glide without motor power.

volt (vōlt) *n.* **1,** a unit of electrical force. **2,** a sideward step.

volt'age (vōl'tij) *n.* the force of an electric current, expressed in volts.

vol·ta'ic (vol-tā'ik) *adj.* pert. to electric current. —**voltaic cell,** a device for generating electricity.

volte-"face' (vōlt"fäs') *n.* (*Fr.*) a reversal.

volt'me"ter *n.* a device for measuring voltage.

vol'u·ble (vol'yə-bəl) *adj.* speaking fluently; glib. —**vol"u·bil'i·ty,** *n.*

vol'ume (vol'ūm) *n.* **1,** a book, esp. one of a set. **2,** amount or capacity measured in three dimensions; cubic magnitude. **3,** mass or quantity, esp. a large amount. **4,** loudness or softness; roundness of tone.

vol"u·met'ric (vol"yə-met'rik) *adj.* pert. to measurement or analysis by volume.

vo·lu'mi·nous (və-loo'mi-nəs) *adj.* **1,** having many volumes; copious; prolix. **2,** large in bulk. —**vo·lu'mi·nous·ness,** *n.*

vol'un·tar"y (vol'ən-ter'ē) *adj.* **1,** done of one's own accord or free choice. **2,** controlled by the will. **3,** having the power of making free choice. —*n.* a piece of music interpolated in a church service. —**vol'un·tar"i·ness,** *n.*

vol"un·teer' (vol"ən-tir') *n. & adj.* one who enters into any service of his own free will. —*v.i.* offer or undertake to do something. —*v.t.* offer or state voluntarily.

vo·lup'tu·ar·y (və-lup'choo-er-ē) *n.* a sensualist.

vo·lup'tu·ous (və-lup'choo-əs) *adj.* seeking, affording, or suggestive of pleasure. —**vo·lup'tu·ous·ness,** *n.*

vo·lute' (və-loot') *n. & adj.* a spiral or whorled formation.

vom'it *v.i.* **1,** eject the contents of the stomach through the mouth; throw up. **2,** be emitted; come out with force or violence. —*v.t.* throw up; emit. —*n.* the act of vomiting; what is thrown up.

vom'i·to·ry (vom'i-tôr-ē) *n.* **1,** an emetic. **2,** a doorway for entrance and exit.

voo'doo *n. & adj.* **1,** a form of witchcraft or conjuration. **2,** a fetish of voodoo worship. —**voo'doo·ism,** *n.*

vo·ra'cious (vō-rā'shəs) *adj.* greedily devouring; ravenous. —**vo·ra'cious·ness, vo·rac'i·ty** (vō-ras'ə-tē) *n.*

vor'tex (vôr'teks) *n.* **1,** a whirling motion or mass; a whirlpool or eddy. **2,** destructive force that draws one in. —**vor'ti·cal** (-tə-kəl) *adj.*

vo'ta·ry (vō'tə-rē) *n. & adj.* **1,** one bound by a vow, as a monk or nun. **2,** a devotee.

vote (vōt) *n.* **1,** a formal expression of choice. **2,** the right to choose or elect; franchise; suffrage. **3,** votes collectively; a decision made by voting. **4,** a ballot. —*v.i.* indicate a choice. —*v.t.* (often with *in*) enact, establish, grant, declare, etc., by voting. —**vot'er,** *n.*

vo'tive (vō'tiv) *adj.* **1,** in accordance with a vow. **2,** optional, not prescribed. —**vo'tive·ness,** *n.*

vouch (vowch) *v.t.* assert; attest. —*v.i.* (with *for*) attest or warrant to be true, reliable, etc.

vouch'er (-ər) *n.* a receipt or authorization for an expenditure.

vouch"safe' *v.t.* bestow or grant condescendingly.

vow *n.* a solemn promise or pledge. —*v.t.* promise solemnly; swear. —**take vows,** enter a religious order.

vow'el (vow'əl) *n. & adj.* **1,** a speech sound uttered without friction and with more or less open mouth. **2,** a letter standing for such a sound: in English, *a, e, i, o, u,* sometimes *y.*

voy'age (voi'ij) *n.* a journey to a distant place, esp. by water. —*v.i. & t.* travel (to). —**voy'ag·er,** *n.*

vo·ya·geur' (vwä-yä-zhēr') *n.* [*pl.* **-geurs'** (-zhēr')] **1,** in Canada, one of those employed by fur companies to maintain communication and transportation with distant stations. **2,** traveler.

voy·eur' (vwä-yēr') *n.* a person who enjoys observing sexual acts or organs.

vul'can·ite" (vul'kən-īt") *n.* hard rubber, used for making combs, etc.

vul'can·ize" (vul'kə-nīz") *v.t.* **1,** treat (rubber) with sulfur and heat. **2,** patch (as a tire) with rubber fused by heat. —**vul"can·i·za'tion,** *n.*

vul'gar (vul'gər) *adj.* **1,** ignorant or deficient of good taste; coarse; unrefined. **2,** plebeian. **3,** ordinary; common. —**vul'gar·ness,** *n.*

vul·gar'i·an (vul-gâr'ē-ən) *n.* a vulgar person.

vul'gar·ism (vul'gə-riz-əm) *n.* a word or expression not in good usage.

vul·gar'i·ty (vul-gâr'ə-tē) *n.* **1,** the state of being vulgar. **2,** something vulgar.

Vul'gate (vul'gāt) *n.* a Latin version of the Bible, the authorized version of the Rom. Cath. Church. —*adj.* (*l.c.*) common; in popular use.

vul'ner·a·ble (vul'nər-ə-bəl) *adj.* **1,** susceptible of being wounded, assaulted, or conquered. **2,** open to reproof. **3,** not resistant to evil influence. **—vul″ner·a·bil′i·ty,** *n.*

vul′pine (vul′pīn) *adj.* pert. to a fox; foxlike.

vul′ture (vul′chər) *n.* **1,** a large carrion-eating bird. **2,** a rapacious or ruthless person. **—vul′tur·ine** (-rīn), **vul′tur·ous,** *adj.*

vul′va (vul′və) *n.* the external parts of the female genital organs.

W

W, w (dub′əl-yû) the 23rd letter of the English alphabet.

wab′ble (wob′əl) *v.i.* wobble.

Wac (wak) *n.* a member of the U.S. Women's Army Corps.

wack′y (wak′ē) *adj.* (*Slang*) **1,** slightly demented. **2,** odd. **—wack,** *n.* an eccentric person. **—wack′i·ness,** *n.*

wad (wod) *n.* **1,** a small mass of soft material; a packing or filling. **2,** (*Slang*) a roll of money. *—v.t.* **[wad′ded, -ding]** form into or pack with a wad.

wad′ding (wod′ing) *n.* material for stuffing; wads collectively.

wad′dle (wod′əl) *v.i.* rock from side to side in walking. *—n.* a rocking gait. **—wad′dler** (-dlər) *n.*

wad′dy (wäd′ē) *n.* **1,** a native war club. **2,** a walking stick.

wade (wād) *v.i.* **1,** walk through a substance that impedes, as water, sand, etc. **2,** make progress against obstacles. **3,** (with *in*) begin vigorously. *—v.t.* pass or cross by wading.

wad′er (wād′ər) *n.* **1,** one who wades. **2,** a long-legged bird. **3,** (*pl.*) high boots.

wa′di (wä′dē) *n.* in No. Afr., a river channel, usually dry.

Waf *n.* a member of Women in the Air Force.

wa′fer (wā′fər) *n.* **1,** a thin, usu. sweetened, delicate cake. **2,** any similar disk. **—wa′fer·y,** *adj.*

waf′fle (wof′əl) *n.* a flat battercake baked in a mold. *—v.i.* (*Colloq.*) speak or write in a weighty style, but communicate little. **—waffle iron,** a griddle with a hinged cover, both having indented surfaces.

waft (wäft) *v.t.* bear or convey through, or as through, a buoyant medium, as water or air. *—n.* something wafted; a gust.

wag *v.i. & t.* **[wagged, wag′ging]** move or cause to move from side to side. *—n.* **1,** a shake; an oscillation. **2,** one who jokes; a wit. **—wag the tongue,** (*Colloq.*) talk.

wage (wāj) *v.t.* engage in; carry on, as a

war. *—n.* rate of payment for work; (*pl.*) recompense; pay.

wa′ger (wā′jər) *n.* a bet. *—v.t. & i.* bet.

wag′ger·y (wag′ə-rē) *n.* **1,** jocularity; waggishness. **2,** a joke.

wag′gish (wag′ish) *adj.* jocular. **—wag′-gish·ness,** *n.*

wag′gle (wag′əl) *v.t. & i.* wag.

wag′on (wag′ən) *n.* **1,** a wheeled vehicle, esp. a four-wheeled freight vehicle. **2,** a railroad freight car. Also, (*Brit.*) **wag′gon. —wag′on·er,** *n.* **—on the wagon,** abstaining from liquor.

wag″on·ette′ (wag″ə-net′) *n.* a four-wheeled pleasure vehicle with two lengthwise seats facing each other, and a cross seat in front.

wag′tail″ *n.* any of several small birds with a wagging tail.

wa·hoo′ (wä-hoo′) *n.* **1,** any of several trees or shrubs. **2,** a food fish.

waif (wāf) *n.* **1,** a homeless person, esp. a child. **2,** a stray animal or thing.

wail (wāl) *v.i. & t.* express sorrow by a mournful sound; lament. *—n.* a plaintive cry or sound. **—wail′ful,** *adj.*

wain′scot (wān′skət) *n.* a wooden lining, usually paneled, of the walls of a room. **—wain′scot″ing,** *n.*

wain′wright″ (wān′rīt″) *n.* a wagon maker.

waist (wāst) *n.* **1,** the part of the human body between the ribs and the hips. **2,** a middle part. **3,** an undergarment. **4,** a bodice; a blouse.

waist′coat″ (wāst′kōt; (*Brit.*) wes′kət) *n.* a man's vest.

waist′line″ *n.* the body between ribs and hips.

wait (wāt) *v.i.* **1,** remain, expecting something. **2,** (with *on*) attend as a servant. **3,** (*Archaic*) call (upon); visit. *—n.* a stay; a delay.

wait′er (-ər) *n.* **1,** a server at the table. **2,** a tray. **—wait′ress,** *n.fem.*

waive (wāv) *v.t.* relinquish; forgo; defer for the present.

waiv′er (wāv′ər) *n.* (*Law*) the intentional relinquishment of a right or claim.

wake (wāk) *v.i.* [*pret.* **waked** or **woke** (wōk)] **1,** stop sleeping; be unable to sleep. **2,** become active. *—v.t.* **1,** rouse from sleep. **2,** arouse; reanimate. *—n.* **1,** an all-night watch over a corpse; a vigil. **2,** the track left by a boat in the water.

wake′ful (-fəl) *adj.* unable to sleep. **—wake′ful·ness,** *n.*

wak′en (wāk′ən) *v.t.* wake.

wake-′rob″in *n.* **1,** (*U.S.*) any of several trilliums. **2,** (*Brit.*) a plant of the arum family.

Wal'dorf salad (wâl'dôrf) a salad of diced apples, walnuts, and vegetables mixed with mayonnaise.

wale (wāl) n. 1, a streak or stripe produced by a blow; a welt. 2, a ridge or plank along the edge of a ship. 3, a ridge in cloth.

walk (wâk) v.i. 1, move by steps with a moderate gait; go or travel on foot. 2, wander about. 3, behave in any particular manner. 4, in baseball, achieve first base on balls. —v.t. 1, move over on foot at a moderate gait. 2, lead or drive at a moderate speed; carry. 3, take for a stroll. —n. 1, a stroll; a distance covered by walking. 2, way of living. 3, range or sphere of action. 4, gait; carriage. 5, a path. 6, a slow pace or gait. 7, in baseball, a base on balls. —**walking papers**, (Slang) notice of dismissal. —**walking stick**, a cane.

walk'a·way" n. an easy victory. Also, **walk'o"ver.**

walk'ie-talk'ie (-ē) n. (Slang) a portable radio receiving and transmitting set.

walk-'in" adj. & n. 1, large enough to walk into, as a closet. 2, having a direct entrance from the street.

walk-'on" n. a minor, nonspeaking role in a theatrical production.

walk'out" n. (Colloq.) a labor strike.

walk'o"ver n. (Colloq.) an easy victory.

walk'up" n. (Colloq.) an apartment not served by an elevator.

walk'way" n. a pedestrian passage.

wall (wâl) n. 1, a structure of stone, brick, or other materials, serving to enclose, divide, support, or defend. 2, a solid fence. 3, any enclosing part or shell. —v.t. enclose or seal with, or as with, a wall; fortify.

wal'la·by (wol'ə-bē) n. any of the smaller kangaroos of Australia.

wal"la·roo' (wol"ə-roo') n. any of several large kangaroos.

wall'board" n. fibers, minerals, etc. pressed into thick sheets.

wal'let (wol'it) n. 1, a pocketbook, esp. one in which bank notes, papers, etc., lie flat. 2, a bag or kit.

wall'eye" n. 1, an eye in which the iris is light-colored. 2, strabismus. 3, a large staring eye. 4, any of various fishes with large staring eyes. —**wall'eyed"**, adj.

wall'flow"er n. 1, a Europ. perennial plant. 2, (Colloq.) a person unable to attract a partner at a dance, esp. a woman.

wal'lop (wol'əp) v.t. 1, beat soundly. 2, defeat conclusively. —n. a heavy blow.

wal'low (wol'ō) v.i. 1, roll the body in sand, mire, etc. 2, dwell with satisfaction in. —n. 1, the act of wallowing. 2, a place where animals, as hogs, wallow.

wall'pa"per n. paper for covering the walls of a room. —v.t. cover with wallpaper.

Wall Street 1, a street in New York City, the financial center of the U.S. 2, the financial interests of the U.S. collectively.

wal'nut (wâl'nut) n. 1, any of various trees bearing edible, hard-shelled nuts; the wood or nut of such a tree. 2, a shade of brown.

wal'rus (wol'rəs) n. a large, carnivorous Arctic sea mammal related to the seal. —**walrus mustache**, a mustache with the ends hanging down.

waltz (wâlts) n. 1, a dance for couples, in 3/4 time; music for such a dance. 2, (Slang) easy or effortless progress. —v.i. & i. dance (a waltz).

wam'pum (wom'pəm) n. 1, small shell beads used for money by No. Amer. Indians. 2, (Slang) money.

wan (won) adj. [wan'ner, -nest] of a sickly hue; pale; colorless. —**wan'ness,** n.

wand (wond) n. a slender stick; a rod, esp. one used by a conjurer.

wan'der (won'dər) v.i. 1, roam; ramble; stroll. 2, go astray; err. 3, be delirious. —v.t. travel aimlessly about. —**wan'der·er,** n. —**Wandering Jew,** 1, a legendary character who insulted Christ and was condemned to wander on the earth until Christ's return. 2, (l.c.) any of several trailing plants.

wan'der·lust" n. restless desire to roam.

wane (wān) v.i. decrease, as in size; decline. —n. decreasing.

wan'gle (wang'gəl) v.i. & t. (Colloq.) contrive; accomplish or obtain by shrewdness.

Wan'kel engine (wäng'kəl) an internal-combustion engine in which pistons are replaced by a single rotor.

want (wont) v.t. 1, feel a desire for. 2, be without; lack. 3, require; need. —v.i. be lacking or deficient; be in need. —n. 1, lack or scarcity of what is needed or desired; poverty. 2, a desire. —**want'ing,** adj. lacking; needed. —**want ad,** (Colloq.) a short advertisement for something desired.

wan'ton (won'tən) adj. 1, unrestrained; wild; reckless. 2, heartless; malicious. 3, dissolute. —n. an unrestrained or dissolute person. —v.i. revel. —v.t. squander. —**wan'ton·ness,** n.

wap'i·ti (wop'ə-tē) n. the No. Amer. stag or elk.

war (wôr) n. 1, armed conflict among nations; such conflict between parties in the same state (civil war). 2, any strife or conflict. **3,** the profession of arms. —*v.i.* **[warred, war′ring]** carry on a war. —**at war,** engaged in warfare; warring. —**war game,** a military training exercise. —**war dance, war paint, war whoop,** respectively, a dance, a facial paint worn, or a cry, used by primitive peoples to arouse warlike emotions or frighten an enemy. —**war horse, 1,** a horse trained for battle; hence, an experienced campaigner of any sort. **2,** (*Colloq.*) a work of art which has become hackneyed through constant repetition.

war′ble (wôr′bəl) *v.i. & t.* **1,** carol or sing. **2,** sound vibratingly; quaver. —*n.* a song, esp. of a bird. —**war′bler,** *n.* any of various songbirds.

ward (wôrd) *v.t.* (with *off*) fend off; turn aside; repel. —*n.* **1,** the act of keeping guard. **2,** one under guardianship, esp. a minor. **3,** a political division of a city. **4,** one of the sections of a hospital. **5,** a curved ridge of metal inside a lock; a notch on a key that fits it. —**ward heeler,** (*Colloq.*) a minor political worker.

-ward (wərd) *suf.* forming adjectives and adverbs, in the direction of. Also, **-wards** (wərdz) *suf.* forming adverbs.

ward′en (wôr′dən) *n.* **1,** a guard or guardian. **2,** the chief officer of a prison. **3,** the title of various chief officers. **4,** a kind of pear.

ward′er (wôr′dər) *n.* a keeper; a guard.

ward′robe″ (wôrd′rōb″) *n.* **1,** a cabinet for clothes. **2,** one's supply of clothing.

ward′room″ (wôrd′room″) *n.* the quarters of officers, except the captain, on a war vessel.

ward′ship″ *n.* custody.

ware (wâr) *n.* **1,** (usually *pl.*) articles of merchandise. **2,** a term used in compounds, denoting articles, as *chinaware.*

ware′house″ *n.* a place for storage.

war′fare″ *n.* the waging of war.

war′head″ *n.* a compartment containing an explosive charge, at the forward part of a torpedo or other missile.

war′like″ *adj.* disposed to make war.

war′lock″ *n.* (*Archaic*) one in league with the devil; a sorcerer or wizard.

war′lord″ *n.* a military commander exercising civil authority.

warm (wôrm) *adj.* **1,** having a moderate degree of heat; communicating or causing heat. **2,** having the sensation of heat. **3,** hearty; earnest; affectionate; intimate. **4,** new; fresh. **5,** close, in a guessing game. —*v.t. & i.* make or become warm. —**warm′ness,** *n.* —**warm up, 1,** practice before a contest, performance, etc. **2,** reheat.

warm′blood″ed *adj.* **1,** denoting animals,

esp. mammals, with warm blood. **2,** ardent; impulsive. —**warm′blood″ed·ness,** *n.*

warm′heart″ed *adj.* kindly; generous; sympathetic. —**warm′heart″ed·ness,** *n.*

war′mong″er (-mong″gər) *n.* one who incites to warfare.

warmth (wôrmth) *n.* warmness; ardor.

warn (wôrn) *v.t.* **1,** put on guard; caution. **2,** advise; notify.

warn′ing *n.* **1,** a caution; admonition. **2,** (*Brit.*) notice of dismissal or resignation from a job. —*adj.* that warns.

warp (wôrp) *v.t.* **1,** turn or twist out of shape; distort; pervert. **2,** pull (a ship) with a rope. **3,** twist (the wings of an airplane) to maintain balance. —*v.i.* **1,** be twisted out of proper shape. **2,** swerve. —*n.* **1,** a twist; distortion. **2,** the lengthwise threads on a loom. —**warp′age,** *n.*

war′path″ *n.* among Amer. Indians, a warring campaign. —**on the warpath,** bellicose; wrathful.

war′plane″ *n.* a plane designed for fighting.

war′rant (wor′ənt) *n.* **1,** that which attests or proves; a guarantee. **2,** sanction; justification. **3,** (*Law*) a writ authorizing an arrest, search, or seizure. —*v.t.* **1,** guarantee; indemnify. **2,** authorize; justify. **3,** affirm. —**war′ran·tor,** *n.* —**warrant officer,** an Army or Navy officer below commissioned but above noncommissioned rank.

war′ran·ty (wor′ən-tē) *n.* a guarantee; assurance.

war′ren (wor′ən) *n.* **1,** a shelter or pen for rabbits or game. **2,** any crowded section.

war′rior (wôr′yər) *n.* a fighting man.

war′ship″ *n.* a ship designed for fighting.

wart (wôrt) *n.* a small, hard growth on the skin. —**wart′y,** *adj.*

wart′hog″ *n.* a large, ugly, African wild swine.

war′y (wâr′ė) *adj.* cautious of danger; alert. —**war′i·ness,** *n.*

was (wuz) *v.* pret. of *be.* —**was′n′t** (wuz′ənt) contraction of *was not.*

wash (wosh) *v.t.* **1,** cleanse in or with a liquid, esp. water. **2,** flow over or against; wet. **3,** (with *away*) remove; absolve. **4,** sweep. **5,** process by immersing in a liquid. —*v.i.* **1,** cleanse oneself, etc., in or with water. **2,** stand cleansing by water without injury. **3,** flow. **4,** (*Colloq.*) hold up under scrutiny, as a theory. —*n.* **1,** a cleansing by water; articles to be cleansed. **2,** the flow, sweep, or sound of a body of water. **3,** the wake of a vessel. **4,** waste articles or liquid; alluvia. **5,** a liquid for washing. **6,** a body of water. —**wash′a·ble**, *adj.* that can safely be washed in water. —**washed out, 1,** faded. **2,** fatigued. **3,** expelled after failure. —**washed up,** (*Colloq.*) spent; finished. —**wash out,** (*Slang*) fail.

wash′board″ *n.* a corrugated board for scrubbing clothes.

wash′bowl″ *n.* a basin.

wash′cloth″ *n.* a cloth for use in washing oneself. Also, **wash′rag″**.

wash′er (-ər) *n.* **1,** one who or that which washes; a washing machine. **2,** a small metal gasket.

wash′er·wom″an *n.* [*pl.* **-wom″en**] a laundress.

wash′ing *n.* clothes to be washed. —**washing machine**, a machine for washing clothes. —**washing soda**, sodium bicarbonate.

wash′out″ *n.* **1,** a place where soil or a foundation has been eroded. **2,** (*Slang*) a failure.

wash′rag″ *n.* washcloth.

wash′room″ *n.* a lavatory and toilet.

wash′stand″ *n.* a cabinet or fixture for holding a washbowl.

wash′tub″ *n.* a tub for washing clothes.

wash′wom″an *n.* [*pl.* **-wom″en**] a laundress.

wash′y (wosh′ē) *adj.* **1,** watery; moist. **2,** weak; diluted. **3,** insubstantial; feeble. —**wash′i·ness**, *n.*

wasp (wosp) *n.* an insect allied to the bee.

wasp′ish *adj.* **1,** peevish. **2,** slenderwaisted. —**wasp′ish·ness**, *n.*

was′sail (wos′əl) *n.* **1,** a toast. **2,** a drink of spiced ale. **3,** a drinking party. —*v.i.* carouse.

Was′ser·mann test (wäs′ər-mən) a test for syphilis.

waste (wāst) *adj.* **1,** desolate; uninhabited; untilled; unproductive. **2,** rejected as unfit for use; unused. —*v.t.* **1,** devastate; ruin. **2,** consume or wear away the strength and substance of. **3,** squander; throw away. **4,** (*Slang*) kill. —*v.i.* decay or diminish in strength, substance, or value; wear or pine away. —*n.* **1,** a desolate place or region. **2,** gradual loss or decay. **3,** broken, spoiled, useless, or superfluous material; refuse. **4,** useless expenditure. **5,** a drain pipe. —**wast′age**, *n.*

waste′bas″ket *n.* a receptacle for unwanted papers.

waste′ful (-fəl) *adj.* needlessly spending or spent. —**waste′ful·ness**, *n.*

waste′land″ *n.* **1,** a barren uncultivated region. **2,** a place without artistic, intellectual, etc., resources.

wast′rel (wās′trəl) *n.* a spendthrift; a profligate.

watch (woch) *v.i.* **1,** be attentive, circumspect, or closely observant. **2,** keep vigil. **3,** keep guard. **4,** wait. —*v.t.* **1,** look at attentively. **2,** take care of; tend; guard. —*n.* **1,** a keeping awake for the purpose of attending, guarding, or preserving; vigil. **2,** close, constant observation; supervision. **3,** a force on duty, esp. for guarding; a sentinel. **4,** a period of duty; on a ship, four hours. **5,** a timepiece carried in the pocket or worn on the wrist.

watch′band″ *n.* a strap or bracelet of leather, metal, etc., used to hold a wristwatch.

watch′dog″ *n.* **1,** a dog trained to bark a warning. **2,** a guardian.

watch′ful (-fəl) *adj.* alert. —**watch′ful·ness**, *n.*

watch′man (-mən) *n.* [*pl.* **-men**] a guard.

watch′night″ *n.* a prayer service held on New Year's Eve.

watch′tow″er *n.* a tower in which to post a lookout.

watch′word″ *n.* **1,** a secret password. **2,** a slogan; a rallying cry.

wa′ter (wot′ər, wä′-) *n.* **1,** the transparent, odorless, tasteless fluid, H_2O, that falls in rain. **2,** a body of water; (*pl.*) a flood. **3,** any liquid secretion of an animal body. **4,** transparency denoting the fine properties of a precious stone. —*v.t.* **1,** moisten; irrigate. **2,** supply with water. **3,** dilute; assign unjustified value to (a stock). **4,** produce a gleaming, wavy pattern upon (a fabric). —*v.i.* **1,** give off or fill up with liquid. **2,** get or take in water. —**of the first water**, of the finest quality. —**water ballet**, choreographed movements performed in the water. —**water biscuit**, a kind of cracker. —**water buffalo**, a carabao. —**water chestnut**, a plant or its edible nutlike fruit. —**water closet, 1,** a device, with a seat, for disposing of excrement. **2,** a toilet room. —**water cooler**, a device for cooling and dispensing drinking water. —**water gap**, a cleft in a mountain ridge through which a stream flows. —**water ice**, a frozen dessert like ice cream, made without milk. —**watering hole, 1,** a place where animals drink. **2,** (*Colloq.*) a place, as a bar, where one can get something to drink. —**watering place**, a spa. —**watering pot**, a can with a perforated spout, for spraying on flowers. —**water lily**, a plant with floating leaves and showy flowers, that grows in water. —**water moccasin, 1,** a venomous snake of the so. U.S. **2,** any of several harmless snakes. —**water nymph**, a naiad. —**water pipe**, a hookah. —**water polo**, a ball game played by swimmers. —**water power**, power derived from a flow or fall of water.

—**water rat,** an aquatic rodent, as the musk-rat. —**water repellent,** treated to repel water, as cloth, but not entirely waterproof. —**water resistant,** resistant to penetration by water, but not entirely waterproof. —**water table,** the level below which the soil is saturated with water. —**water tower, 1,** a tower used as a reservoir for water. **2,** a fire-fighting apparatus. —**water wheel,** a wheel turned by water power. —**water wings,** inflated bags used to support a person in water.

wa'ter·bed" *n.* a watertight sac filled with heated water, used as a bed.

wa'ter·col"or, *n.* **1,** a paint soluble in water. **2,** a picture painted with such paint.

wa'ter·course" *n.* a stream or river, or its bed.

wa'ter·craft" *n.* **1,** any boat or ship. **2,** skill in sailing or in aquatic sports.

wa'ter·cress" *n.* a salad herb.

wa'ter·fall" *n.* a cascade; a cataract.

wa'ter·front" *n.* docks, etc., at the water's edge.

wa'ter·glass" *n.* a substance that forms a protective coating.

wa'ter·line" *n.* the line at which a floating body is out of the water.

wa'ter·logged" (-lâgd") *adj.* saturated so as to sink in water.

Wa'ter·loo *n.* a final defeat.

wa'ter·mark" *n.* a design impressed in paper during its manufacture.

wa'ter·mel"on *n.* a large edible melon.

wa'ter·proof" *adj.* impervious or resistant to water.

wa'ter·shed" *n.* **1,** a ridge off which water flows or drains. **2,** the area drained by a river.

wa'ter·side" *n.* a shore or bank.

wa'ter·ski" *v.i.* ski on water while being pulled by a motorboat.

wa'ter·spout" *n.* a gyrating column of rising moisture, caused by a whirlwind at sea.

wa'ter·tight" *adj.* **1,** impenetrable by water. **2,** that cannot be evaded or controverted.

wa'ter·way" *n.* a course navigable by water.

wa'ter·works" *n.* a system for supplying water to a city.

wa'ter·y (-è) *adj.* **1,** pert. to or consisting of water; wet; dripping. **2,** thin, as a liquid. —**wa'ter·i·ness,** *n.*

watt (wot) *n.* a unit of electrical activity or power. —**watt'age,** *n.*

wat'tle (wot'əl) *n.* **1,** a framework of poles. **2,** a rod; a twig. **3,** a fleshy lobe hanging from the throat of a bird or the mouth of a fish. —*v.t.* interweave.

wave (wāv) *v.i.* **1,** move up and down or to and fro; undulate; flutter. **2,** have a curved form or direction. **3,** give a signal by waving the hands. —*v.t.* **1,** move to and fro; brandish. **2,** shape in undulations or curves. —*n.* **1,** a ridge in the surface of a liquid. **2,** (*pl.*) the sea. **3,** an influx of anything. **4,** a gesture or signal made by moving the hand. **5,** a curl in the hair. **6,** (*cap.*) a woman serving in the U.S. Navy. —**wave band,** a range of frequencies assigned to a particular form of broadcasting, as television, AM radio, etc. —**wave length,** the distance between two particles in the same phase of a wave: now applied chiefly to the band assigned to a radio or television transmitting station.

wave'let *n.* a ripple.

wa'ver (wā'vər) *v.i.* **1,** sway; falter. **2,** be irresolute; vacillate. —*n.* a wavering motion.

wav'y (wāv'è) *adj.* **1,** abounding in waves. **2,** curly. —**wav'i·ness,** *n.*

wax (waks) *v.i.* increase in size; grow, specif. of the moon. —*v.t.* put wax on. —*n.* a thick, sticky substance secreted by bees; any similar oily substance. —**wax bean,** a yellow string bean. —**wax paper,** paper coated with paraffin. —**wax'works",** *n.* an exhibit of forms modeled in wax.

wax'en (wak'sən) *adj.* **1,** yellowish, as wax. **2,** of the consistency of wax.

wax'wing" *n.* a passerine bird.

wax'work" *n.* **1,** a figure, or figures, modeled in wax. **2,** (*pl.*) an exhibit of such figures.

wax'y (-è) *adj.* like wax. —**wax'i·ness,** *n.*

way (wā) *n.* **1,** a course leading from one place to another; a road, passage, route, etc. **2,** room for passage. **3,** a journey. **4,** distance. **5,** direction. **6,** a respect; a particular. **7,** condition or state. **8,** a plan; mode; method. **9,** progress; headway. **10,** (*pl.*) the timbers on which a ship is built and launched. —**give way, 1,** make way. **2,** break down. —**out of the way,** unusual; extraordinary. —**under way,** in motion. —**way station,** a minor railroad station, or similar station for other mode of travel.

way'bill" *n.* a descriptive list of goods sent by a common carrier.

way'far"er *n.* a traveler, esp. on foot.

way'lay" *v.t.* ambush.

way-'out" *adj.* (*Slang*) **1,** unusual; strange. **2,** excellent.

-ways (wāz) *suf.* indicating manner, direction, or position.

way'side" *n.* the side of a road; a secluded place.

---

way'ward" (-wərd) *adj.* **1,** rebellious; perverse. **2,** irregular; accidental. **—way'-ward·ness,** *n.*

we (wē) *pron. pl.* of *I* (*poss.* **our, ours;** *obj.* **us**) the first person, nominative, pl.; used as sing. by monarchs and editors (the editorial *we*).

weak (wēk) *adj.* **1,** lacking physical strength or endurance. **2,** lacking moral or mental strength or firmness. **3,** inadequate or unsatisfactory; faulty. **4,** (*Com.*) tending downward in price. **—weak'ly,** *adj. & adv.*

weak'en (-ən) *v.t. & i.* make or become weaker.

weak'fish" *n.* an edible sea fish.

weak-'kneed" *adj.* irresolute; easily controlled.

weak'ling *n.* a weak person.

weak'ness *n.* **1,** state of being weak. **2,** a weak point; fault or defect. **3,** (*Colloq.*) a fondness; an uncontrollable desire.

wealth (welth) *n.* **1,** valuable and large material possessions; riches. **2,** profusion; abundance. **3,** all property. **—wealth'i-ness,** *n.* **—wealth'y,** *adj.*

wean (wēn) *v.t.* **1,** accustom (a child or young animal) to food other than mother's milk. **2,** alienate.

weap'on (wep'ən) *n.* any instrument used in fighting. **—weap'on·ry,** *n.*

wear (wâr) *v.t.* [**wore** (wôr), **worn** (wôrn), **wear'ing**] **1,** carry or bear on the body, as clothing. **2,** consume or deteriorate by friction or frequent use. **3,** make weary. **4,** bear; show. —*v.i.* **1,** last or hold out. **2,** waste; diminish. —*n.* **1,** use; deterioration. **2,** garments. **—wear'a·ble,** *adj.* **—wear'-ing,** *adj.* tiring. **—wear and tear,** loss by waste, deterioration, etc., sustained in ordinary use.

wea'ry (wir'ē) *adj.* **1,** exhausted either physically or mentally; tired. **2,** discontented. **3,** causing fatigue. —*v.t. & i.* tire. **—wea'ri·ness,** *n.* **—wea'ri·some,** *adj.* tiresome.

wea'sel (wē'zəl) *n.* a small carnivorous mammal. **—weasel words,** evasive language.

weath'er (weth'ər) *n.* **1,** the state of the atmosphere in regard to heat, cold, wetness, dryness, humidity, storm, etc. **2,** bad or stormy weather. —*v.t.* **1,** bear up against and survive. **2,** condition by exposure. **3,** (*Naut.*) sail to windward of. —*adj.* (*Naut.*) windward. **—under the weather,** (*Colloq.*) **1,** ill. **2,** drunk. **—weather strip,** a strip to seal a crack around a window, etc. **—weather vane,** a device that turns with the wind, to show its direction.

weath'er·beat"en *adj.* marked or hardened by exposure.

weath'er·board" *n.* clapboard.

weath'er·bound" *adj.* delayed by bad weather.

weath'er·cock" *n.* a figure of a bird, on top of a weather vane.

weath'er·glass" *n.* an instrument for indicating the state of the atmosphere, as a barometer.

weath'er·ing *n.* the action of the elements on rock, wood, etc.

weath'er·man" *n.* [*pl.* **-men**] **1,** a man whose job is to forecast the weather. **2,** (*cap.*) a member of a radical political organization.

weath'er·proof" *adj.* resistant to rain, wind, etc.

weave (wēv) *v.t.* [**wove** (wōv), **wo'ven, weav'ing**] **1,** form by interlacing flexible parts, as threads; produce (a fabric) on a loom. **2,** contrive or construct. —*v.i.* **1,** become interlaced. **2,** wind in and out. —*n.* a pattern produced by weaving.

web *n.* **1,** that which is woven. **2,** a trap, plot, or scheme. **3,** the membrane of skin connecting the toes of a bird or animal, as a duck. **—webbed,** *adj.* **—web'bing,** *n.* **—web'foot"ed,** *adj.*

wed *v.t. & i.* [**wed'ded** or **wed, wed'ding**] take for husband or wife; marry; unite closely.

wed'ding (wed'ing) *n.* an occasion or anniversary of marriage.

wedge (wej) *n.* **1,** a triangular-shaped solid, used to separate, split, or raise objects. **2,** an act that serves to introduce or divide. —*v.t.* **1,** use a wedge on. **2,** compress closely. —*v.i.* force one's way.

wedg'ie (wej'ē) *n.* a woman's shoe giving elevation as with a high heel but with the sole almost flat.

wed'lock" *n.* matrimony.

Wednes'day (wenz'dē) *n.* the fourth day of the week.

wee (wē) *adj.* [**we'er, we'est**] tiny.

weed (wēd) *n.* **1,** a useless or characteristically unwanted plant. **2,** (*Colloq.*) tobacco. **3,** (*pl.*) a widow's mourning attire. **4,** (*Slang*) marijuana. —*v.t.* free from obnoxious plants. —*v.i.* root up weeds. **—weed out,** remove weeds or other undesirable elements (from).

weed'y (-ē) *adj.* **1,** like a weed; lanky. **2,** being or like widow's weeds. **3,** abounding in weeds. **—weed'i·ness,** *n.*

week (wēk) *n.* **1,** a period of seven consecutive days. **2,** the working days of the week. **—week'day",** *n.* any day but Sunday. **—week'ly,** *adj. & adv.* occurring once each week.

week'end" *n.* the period from the end of

the working week through Sunday. —*adj.* of or on a weekend. —*v.i.* spend the weekend. —**week′end″er,** *n.*

ween′ie (wē′nē) *n.* (*Colloq.*) a frankfurter.

weep (wēp) *v.i.* [*pret. & p.p.* **wept**] **1,** shed tears; lament. **2,** drip; give out moisture. **3,** droop. —*v.t.* shed, as tears. —**weep′-ing,** *adj.* drooping, as the branches of a tree: as, *weeping willow.* —**weep′y,** *adj.*

wee′vil (wē′vəl) *n.* any of various beetles.

weft *n.* the woof.

weigh (wā) *v.t.* **1,** determine the heaviness of. **2,** consider; ponder. **3,** (*Naut.*) raise or lift up. **4,** (with *down*) burden; oppress. —*v.i.* have weight or influence.

weight (wāt) *n.* **1,** the downward force of a body; heaviness. **2,** mass. **3,** something used on account of its heaviness. **4,** a system of units for expressing the heaviness of bodies. **5,** pressure; care; burden. **6,** importance; influence. —*v.t.* **1,** add to the heaviness of. **2,** adjust the proportions of.

weight′less *adj.* having no weight, esp. as a result of a lack of gravitational pull, as in space. —**weight′less·ness,** *n.*

weight′y (-ē) *adj.* **1,** momentous; influential. **2,** burdensome. —**weight′i·ness,** *n.*

wei′ma·ran″er (vī′mə-rän″ər) *n.* German breed of sporting dog.

weir (wir) *n.* **1,** a dam. **2,** a fence set in a stream for catching fish.

weird (wird) *adj.* unearthly; uncanny. —**weird′ness,** *n.* —**Weird Sisters,** the Fates.

weird′o (-ō) *n.* (*Slang*) an eccentric person.

welch *v.i.* welsh.

wel′come (wel′kəm) *adj.* gladly received or permitted. —*n.* a kindly, warm greeting; hospitable reception. —*v.t.* receive gladly.

weld *v.t.* unite (pieces of metal); join. —*n.* a solid union; a welt where union was made.

wel′fare″ (wel′fâr″) *n.* **1,** prosperous or healthy condition. **2,** charity. —**welfare state, 1,** a social system under which the state assumes primary responsibility for the physical, mental, and social well-being of its citizens. **2,** a nation, state, etc., in which the system of the welfare state is adopted.

wel′kin *n.* (*Archaic*) the sky; the firmament.

well (wel) *n.* **1,** an excavation in the ground as a source of water, oil, gas, etc.; a spring. **2,** any source of origin or supply; a fount. **3,** a dangerous depression; a whirlpool. —*v.i.* issue; pour forth. —*adv.* [**bet′ter, best**] **1,** in a good, right, or worthy manner; abundantly. **2,** favorably. **3,** conveniently. —*adj.* in good health. —**as well (as),** also.

well-″ap·point′ed *adj.* furnished with all requisites.

well-″bal′anced *adj.* **1,** properly adjusted or proportioned. **2,** sensible.

well-″be′ing *n.* good health; welfare.

well″born′ *adj.* of gentle or noble birth.

well″bred′ *adj.* having good manners.

well-″de·fined′ *adj.* leaving no room for doubt; clear.

well-″dis·posed′ *adj.* favorable.

well-′done″ *adj.* cooked thoroughly.

well-′fed′ *adj.* prosperous-looking.

well-′fixed″ *adj.* (*Colloq.*) well-to-do.

well-″found′ed *adj.* based on good reasons or grounds.

well′head″ *n.* a source.

well-″heeled′ *adj.* (*Slang*) wealthy.

well-″in·formed′ *adj.* abreast of current events.

well-′known″ *adj.* **1,** famous. **2,** fully known. **3,** generally acknowledged.

well-′man″nered *adj.* polite; courteous.

well-″mean′ing *adj.* having good intentions. —**well-″meant′,** *adj.*

well-′nigh″ *adv.* very nearly.

well-″off′ *adj.* wealthy or fortunate.

well-″read′ (-red′) *adj.* having read many books; educated.

well-″round′ed *adj.* complete.

well′spring″ *n.* a constant source.

well-′to-do′ *adj.* prosperous; wealthy.

welsh *v.i.* fail to pay a gambling loss. Also, **welch.**

Welsh *adj. & n.* of or pert. to Wales, its people, language, etc. —**Welsh′man,** *n.* —**Welsh corgi** (kôr′gē) a Welsh breed of short-legged dog. —**Welsh rabbit** [or, **rare′bit**], melted cheese served on toast.

welt *n.* **1,** a strip of material, esp. leather, standing out. **2,** a wale.

wel′ter (wel′tər) *v.i.* **1,** wallow (in something). **2,** roll or toss; be tossed. —*n.* **1,** rolling or wallowing motion. **2,** turmoil; ferment.

wel′ter·weight″ (wel′tər-wāt″) *n.* a boxer weighing 136 to 147 pounds.

wen *n.* a small, benign tumor.

wench *n.* **1,** a girl or young woman. **2,** a strumpet. —*v.i.* consort with strumpets.

wend *v.i.* proceed; go. —*v.t.* direct (one's way or course).

went *v.* pret. of *go.*

wept *v.* pret. & p.p. of *weep.*

were (wêr) *v.* pret. & subjunctive of *be.*

were′wolf″ (wêr′wûlf″) *n.* [*pl.* **-wolves**] in folklore, a human being turned into a wolf.

---

tŭb, cūte, pûll; labəl; oil, owl, go, chip, she, thin, *t*hen, sing, ink; *see p.* 6

Wes'ley·an (wez'lē-ən) *n.* a Methodist.

west *n.* **1,** the direction lying on the left hand when one faces the north; the point where the sun sets at the equinox. **2,** any place to the west; (*cap.*) Europe and the Americas. —*adj. & adv.* toward the sunset. —**west'er·ly,** *adj.* toward the west. —**west'·ward,** *adv.* —**West Point,** the site of the U.S. Military Academy.

west'ern (wes'tərn) *adj.* pert. to the west. —*n.* (*Colloq.*) a story or motion picture depicting cowboy life in the western U.S. —**west'ern·er,** *n.* —**west'ern·most",** *adj.*

wes'tern·ize" *v.t. & i.* adopt the social, economic, etc., customs of Europe or, esp., America.

wet *adj.* [**wet'ter, -test**] **1,** covered with or permeated by a moist or fluid substance. **2,** rainy. **3,** (*Colloq.*) opposed to Prohibition. —*n.* **1,** moisture, specif. rain. **2,** (*Colloq.*) a person, state, etc., opposed to Prohibition. —*v.t. & i.* [**wet'ted, -ting**] drench with water or other fluid; urinate. —**wet'ness,** *n.* —**wet blanket,** (*Slang*) a depressing person. —**wet nurse,** a woman employed to suckle the infant of another. —**wet suit,** a close-fitting heat-retaining suit worn in cold water.

wet'back" *n.* a person who enters the U.S. illegally, usually from Mexico, to take a temporary job.

weth'er (we*th*'ər) *n.* a castrated ram.

whack (hwak) *v.t. & i.* strike a smart, resounding blow. —*n.* **1,** a heavy blow. **2,** (*Colloq.*) an attempt. —**whack'ing,** *adj.* (*Slang*) enormous.

whale (hwāl) *n.* **1,** any of an order of marine mammals; the largest known animals. **2,** (*Colloq.*) anything huge. —*v.i.* pursue the business of whale fishing. —*v.t.* (*Colloq.*) thrash; castigate. —**whal'er,** *n.* a whaling ship.

whale'back" *n.* a type of freight steamer.

whale'boat" *n.* a large rowboat originally used by whale fishermen.

whale'bone" *n.* baleen; a flexible strip of it, used to stiffen a corset.

whal'ing 1, the work or business of whale fishing. **2,** a thrashing. —*adj.* (*Colloq.*) whopping.

wham (hwam) *n.* a powerful blow; its sound. —*v.t. & i.* [**whammed, wham'ming**] smash (into) with great force and noise.

wham'my (hwam'ē) *n.* (*Slang*) a hex; a magic spell.

whang (hwang) (*Colloq.*) *n.* a resounding blow; a bang. —*v.t.* strike with a blow or bang.

whang'ee (hwang'ē) *n.* **1,** a Chinese species of bamboo. **2,** walking stick made of the stalk of the plant.

wharf (wôrf) *n.* [*pl.* **wharves** (wôrvz)] a mooring platform for ships; a dock; a pier. —**wharf'age,** *n.*

wharf'in·ger (hwôr'fin-jər) *n.* one who owns or has charge of a wharf.

what (hwot) *pron. sing. & pl.* **1,** which thing or things. **2,** that which. —*adj.* **1,** (*interrogative*) which. **2,** any; whatever. **3,** (*exclamatory*) how extraordinary!; how large! **4,** in part; partly. —*conj.* but that.

what"ev'er *pron.* **1,** anything which; all that. **2,** no matter what. —*adj.* **1,** any or all that. **2,** of any kind.

what'not" *n.* **1,** a stand to display small ornaments. **2,** anything indiscriminately.

what'so·ev"er *adj. & pron.* of whatever nature or kind.

wheal (hwēl) *n.* **1,** a pimple or small itching swelling on the skin. **2,** a wale.

wheat (hwēt) *n.* any of various cereal plants whose grain is ground into flour and makes bread. —**wheat'en,** *adj.* of wheat. —**wheat germ,** the embryo of the wheat kernel, used as a source of vitamins.

whee'dle (hwē'dəl) *v.t. & i.* cajole; gain by flattery; coax.

wheel (hwēl) *n.* **1,** a circular frame or disk capable of turning on an axis. **2,** a bicycle. **3,** a firework that revolves while burning. **4,** the office of pilot or driver. **5,** a turning maneuver; a circular course. **6,** (*pl.*) machinery. **7,** (*Slang*) an important person. **8,** an instrument of torture. **9,** (*pl.*) (*Slang*) an automobile or other vehicle. —*v.t.* cause to turn; cause to move on or as on wheels. —*v.i.* **1,** turn; rotate. **2,** move on wheels or on a bicycle. —**fifth wheel,** something superfluous or useless. —**wheel horse, 1,** the horse at the pivot of a team. **2,** an essential worker. —**wheel housing,** the space reserved from an automobile seat or body to give play to the wheels.

wheel'bar"row *n.* a vehicle for pushing light loads.

wheel'base" *n.* the distance between centers of axles on a vehicle.

wheel'chair" *n.* a conveyance for an invalid.

wheeled *adj.* having (such, or so many) wheels.

wheel'er-deal'er *n.* (*Slang*) a clever operator.

wheel'wright" *n.* a maker of wheels.

wheeze (hwēz) *v.i.* breathe with difficulty and audibly. —*n.* **1,** the sound of such a breath. **2,** a joke. —**wheez'y,** *adj.*

whelk (hwelk) *n.* **1,** an edible, spiral-shelled mollusk. **2,** a wheal.

whelm (hwelm) *v.t.* **1,** engulf; submerge.

2, overcome; overwhelm. —*v.i.* roll so as to engulf.

whelp (hwelp) *n.* the young of certain animals, as the dog. —*v.i. & t.* bring forth young.

when (hwen) *adv.* **1,** at what or which time. —*conj.* **1,** as soon as. **2,** at which time. —*n.* a time specified.

whence (hwens) *adv.* from that or which place.

when″ev′er *adv. & conj.* at whatever time.

where (hwâr) *adv.* **1,** at or in what place. **2,** to which place? whither? —*conj.* **1,** at, in, or to the place in which. **2,** whereas. **3,** when. —*n.* place; situation.

where′a·bouts″ *n.* location.

where·as′ *conj.* this being the case.

where·at′ *adv.* at which. —*conj.* whereupon.

where′by″ *adv.* for which reason; how.

where′fore″ *adv. & conj.* **1,** why? **2,** consequently. —*n.* a reason.

where·from′ *conj.* from which; whence.

where·in′ *adv.* in which.

where·of′ *conj.* of what, which, or whom.

where·to′ *adv.* to what place, point, or end. —*conj.* to which or whom.

where′up·on′ *adv.* at which juncture.

wher·ev′er *conj.* in, at, or to whatever place. Also, **where″so·ev′er.**

where·with′ *adv.* with which.

where′with·al″ *n.* the means; money.

wher′ry (hwer′ē) *n.* a light boat.

whet (hwet) *v.t.* [**whet′ted, -ting**] **1,** sharpen. **2,** excite.

wheth′er (hwe*th*′ər) *conj.* **1,** introducing the first of two or more alternatives, the second being introduced by *or.* **2,** introducing a single alternative, the other being implied.

whet′stone″ *n.* a stone for sharpening knives, etc.

whey (hwā) *n.* the watery part of milk. —**whey′ey** (hwā′ē) *adj.*

which (hwich) *pron.* **1,** (*interrogative*) what one? (of several). **2,** (*relative*) the one that. **3,** (*relative*) that (with additional information). —*adj.* indicating one of a number of known or specified things.

which·ev′er *pron. & adj.* any one. Also, **which″so·ev′er.**

whid′ah bird (hwi′də) an Afr. weaver bird.

whiff (hwif) *n.* a puff; a slight current or gust of air, smoke, etc. —*v.i. & t.* blow; puff.

whif′fet (hwif′ət) *n.* **1,** (*Colloq.*) an insignificant person. **2,** a snappish little dog.

whif′fle (hwif′əl) *v.i.* **1,** blow in gusts;

veer, as the wind. **2,** be fickle or unsteady. —*v.t.* disperse; scatter.

whif″fle·tree″ (hwif′əl-trē″) *n.* whippletree.

Whig (hwig) *n.* (*Hist.*) a member of: **1,** an English political party, later known as Liberals. **2,** a 19th-century U.S. political party.

while (hwīl) *n.* a space of time, esp. a short time. —*conj.* [also, **whilst**] **1,** during or in the time that; as long as. **2,** though; whereas. —*v.t.* cause (time) to pass.

whi′lom (hwī′ləm) *adj.* former. —*adv.* (*Archaic*) formerly; at times.

whim (hwim) *n.* a fancy; a capricious desire.

whim′per (hwim′pər) *v.i. & t.* cry with a low, whining voice; utter plaintively. —*n.* a low, peevish cry.

whim′si·cal (hwim′zi-kəl) *adj.* quaintly humorous; odd. —**whim″si·cal′i·ty, whim′-si·cal·ness,** *n.*

whim′sy (hwim′zē) *n.* a fanciful notion.

whine (hwīn) *v.i. & t.* **1,** utter a plaintive, prolonged nasal sound. **2,** complain in a feeble way. —*n.* a whining utterance or tone.

whin′ny (hwin′ē) *n.* the cry of a horse; a low or gentle neigh. —*v.i.* utter this sound.

whip (hwip) *v.t.* [**whipped, whip′ping**] **1,** punish with a scourge, rod, etc.; flog; beat. **2,** move or pull with a sudden quick motion; jerk; snatch. **3,** overlay or wrap with cord. **4,** bring or keep together. **5,** sew with an over-and-over stitch. **6,** beat into a froth. —*v.i.* **1,** move suddenly and nimbly; thrash around. **2,** in fishing, cast. —*n.* **1,** an instrument for lashing; a scourge. **2,** a driver. **3,** a swishing or whipping motion. **4,** a conveyance for hoisting. **5,** a preparation of beaten eggs, cream, etc. **6,** a party disciplinarian in a legislature. —**whip hand,** control. —**whipping boy,** a scapegoat.

whip′cord″ *n.* a ribbed fabric.

whip′lash″ *n.* **1,** the flexible striking end of a whip. **2,** a twisting of the spine, as from an accident.

whip′per·snap″per (hwip′ər-snap″ər) *n.* an insignificant, but presumptuous, person, esp. male.

whip′pet (hwip′it) *n.* **1,** a kind of dog, a cross between a greyhound and a terrier. **2,** something slight and speedy; a small, fast tank.

whip′ple·tree″ (hwip′əl-trē″) *n.* a crossbar at the front of a horse-drawn vehicle to which the harness is attached.

whip′poor·will″ (hwip′ər-wil″) *n.* an Amer. nocturnal bird; its cry.

whip′saw″ *n.* a narrow saw in a frame. —*v.t.* (*Slang*) defeat doubly.

whir (hwêr) *v.i.* [**whirred, whir′ring**] fly,

dart, revolve, or move quickly with a buzzing sound. —*n.* a buzzing sound.

whirl (hwērl) *v.t.* **1,** cause to revolve rapidly; rotate. **2,** carry swiftly away. —*v.i.* **1,** revolve swiftly. **2,** reel. —*n.* **1,** a spinning movement or sensation. **2,** a round of parties, events, etc.

whirl′i·gig (hwērl′ə-gig) *n.* something that revolves.

whirl′pool″ *n.* a circular eddy in a body of water.

whirl′wind″ *n.* **1,** a destructive wind moving in a vortical path. **2,** a rushing force.

whir′ly·bird″ (hwer′lē-) *n.* (*Colloq.*) a helicopter.

whish (hwish) *v.i.* move with, or make, a swishing or whistling sound. —*n.* such a sound.

whisk (hwisk) *v.t.* **1,** sweep or brush with a light, rapid motion. **2,** move quickly. **3,** (with *away, off,* etc.) carry suddenly and rapidly. —*v.i.* move nimbly and swiftly. —*n.* **1,** a small brush: *whiskbroom.* **2,** a rapid, light, sweeping motion.

whisk′er (hwisk′ər) *n.* a hair on the face, esp. (*pl.*) those on a man's face. —**whisk′-ered,** *adj.*

whis′key (hwis′kē) *n.* a strong alcoholic liquor, made chiefly from grain. Also, **whis′ky.**

whis′per (hwis′pər) *v.i.* **1,** speak softly with the breath, without vibration of the vocal cords. **2,** gossip; plot. **3,** make a low rustling sound. —*v.t.* say under the breath; say secretly. —*n.* **1,** a whispering voice or utterance. **2,** a hint or insinuation. **3,** a low, rustling sound.

whist (hwist) *n.* a game of cards, the forerunner of bridge. —*interj.* hush!

whis′tle (hwis′əl) *v.i.* **1,** make a shrill or musical sound by forcing the breath through pursed lips or air through a pipe. **2,** move with a whizzing sound. **3,** (*Colloq.*) desire in vain. —*v.t.* **1,** sound by whistling. **2,** signal to, by whistling. —*n.* **1,** a whistling sound; a device for producing it. **2,** (*Colloq.*) the throat. —**whis′tler,** *n.* —**whistle stop,** a short stop, as for a political speech.

whit (hwit) *n.* a little; a jot.

white (hwīt) *adj.* **1,** of the color of pure snow. **2,** of a light color; gray. **3,** fair-skinned. **4,** pale. **5,** pure. **6,** blank; unprinted. **7,** (*Colloq.*) sportsmanlike; honorable. —*n.* a white color; something of this color, as: the albumen of an egg; a member of the Caucasian race; a part of the eyeball. —*v.t.* make white. —**white′ness,** *n.* —**whit′ish,** *adj.* —**white ant,** a termite. —**white elephant,** an embarrassing possession. —**white feather,** a symbol of cowardice. —**white flag,** a symbol of surrender or peaceful intent. —**white gold,** a white alloy of gold, used for jewelry. —**white heat,** intense heat, excitement, etc. —**white lead,** lead carbonate, used in paints; a paint containing it. —**white lie,** a harmless falsehood. —**white noise,** a mixture of sound waves spreading over a wide frequency range. —**white paper,** a government report; hence, any authoritative report. —**white plague,** tuberculosis. —**white sale,** a sale of household articles, esp. linens. —**white slave,** a woman forced into prostitution. —**white whale,** the beluga.

white′cap″ *n.* a wave with a foaming crest.

white-′col″lar *adj.* pert. to clerical or professional workers.

white′fish″ *n.* any of various white or silvery food fish.

White′hall″ *n.* **1,** a former palace in London. **2,** a street in London bordered by government offices, hence the British government.

white-″hot″ *adj.* intensely hot.

White House 1, the residence of the president of the U.S. in Washington, D.C. **2,** the presidential office, authority, etc.

white-′liv″ered *adj.* cowardly.

whit′en (hwīt′ən) *v.t. & i.* make or become whiter.

white′wall″ *n.* a tire having a band of white around the visible outer side.

white′wash″ *v.t.* **1,** paint with whitewash. **2,** cover up the faults or defects of. **3,** (*Colloq.*) defeat, when the loser fails to score. —*n.* **1,** a white paint, usu. of quicklime and water. **2,** the covering up of wrongdoing or defects. **3,** (*Colloq.*) a victory over a scoreless opponent.

whith′er (hwi*th*′ər) *adv.* wherever; to which place.

whit′ing (hwīt′ing) *n.* **1,** any of various edible fish. **2,** a powdered chalk.

Whit′sun·tide″ (hwit′sən-tīd″) *n.* the 8th week after Easter, beginning with *Whitsunday.* —**Whit′sun,** *adj.*

whit′tle (hwit′əl) *v.t. & i.* cut or form with a knife; pare. —**whit′tler** (-lər) *n.*

whiz *v.i.* [**whizzed, whiz′zing**] **1,** make a humming or hissing sound. **2,** move rapidly; rush. —*n.* **1,** a sound made by rapid motion through the air. **2,** (*Slang*) someone very capable. —**whiz′zer,** *n.*

who (hoo) *pron. sing. & pl.* [*poss.* **whose** (hooz), *obj.* **whom** (hoom)] **1,** what or which person or persons? **2,** that person; those persons.

whoa (hwō) *interj.* stop!

who·dun′it (hoo-dun′it) *n.* (*Slang*) a detective story or drama.

who·ev′er *pron.* no matter who. Also, **who″so·ev′er.**

whole (hōl) *adj.* **1,** not broken or injured; intact; unimpaired. **2,** entire; complete. **3,** having full blood relationship. —*n.* **1,** the complete thing; the total. **2,** an organic unity. —**whole′ness,** *n.* —**whol′ly,** *adv.* —**out of whole cloth,** fabricated. —**whole hog,** (*Slang*) all the way. —**whole note,** a semibreve (see *note*). —**whole number,** an integer.

whole′heart″ed *adj.* sincere; enthusiastic. —**whole′heart″ed·ness,** *n.*

whole′sale″ (hōl′sāl″) *n.* sale of goods in quantity to retailers. —*adj.* **1,** pert. to trade with dealers. **2,** in great quantities; extensive; indiscriminate. —*v.t.* sell by wholesale. —**whole′sal″er,** *n.*

whole′some (hōl′səm) *adj.* **1,** contributing to health of body, mind, or character. **2,** healthy or sound-looking. —**whole′some·ness,** *n.*

whole′wheat″ *adj.* made of the complete wheat kernel.

whom (hoom) *pron.* objective of *who*.

whoop (hwoop) *v.i.* **1,** shout; halloo; hoot. **2,** gasp after coughing, as in the disease *whooping cough*. —*n.* **1,** a loud call or shout. **2,** a gasp.

whoo′pee (hwoo′pē) *n.* (*Slang*) hilarity.

whoops (hwoops) *interj.* expressing enthusiasm, or surprise at an error.

whoosh (hwoosh) *v.i.* move rapidly with a rushing sound. —*n.* a rushing sound.

whop′per (hwop′ər) *n.* (*Colloq.*) anything unusually large, esp. a lie. —**whop′ping,** *adj.* (*Colloq.*) very large.

whore (hôr) *n.* an unchaste woman; a prostitute. —*v.i.* **1,** act as a whore. **2,** consort with whores. —**whore′dom** (-dəm) *n.* —**whor′ish,** *adj.*

whorl (hwêrl) *n.* a spiral or coil-shaped part or pattern.

whose (hooz) *pron.* poss. of *who* or *which*.

why (hwī) *adv.* **1,** used interrogatively, for what cause, reason, or purpose? **2,** on account of which. —*n.* the reason or cause. —*interj.* used as an expletive.

wick (wik) *n.* a strip or cord that draws up the fuel that burns in a lamp or candle.

wick′ed (wik′id) *adj.* **1,** evil; sinful. **2,** harmful; pernicious. **3,** difficult; disagreeable. **4,** (*Colloq.*) mischievous. —**wick′ed·ness,** *n.*

wick′er (wik′ər) *n. & adj.* a small pliant twig. —**wick′er·work″,** *n.* anything made of wicker.

wick′et (wik′it) *n.* **1,** a small gate or window. **2,** in croquet, an arch. **3,** in cricket, one of the goals.

wick′i·up″ (wik′ē-up″) *n.* the rude hut of certain Amer. Indians.

wide (wīd) *adj.* **1,** having considerable extension from side to side; broad. **2,** having a specified width. **3,** vast; spacious. **4,** embracing many subjects. **5,** spread apart; open. **6,** deviating or far from a point. —*adv.* **1,** a long way; afar. **2,** extensively; far apart. **3,** astray. —**wide′ness,** *n.*

wide-′an′gle *adj.* of a lens, having greater than a 50° angle of coverage.

wide-′a·wake″ *adj.* fully awake.

wide-′eyed″ (-īd″) *adj. & adv.* having the eyes widely open, as with astonishment.

wid′en (wīd′ən) *v.t. & i.* make or become wider.

wide-′o′pen *adj.* (*Colloq.*) **1,** of a town, lax in enforcement of laws. **2,** of liquor sales, gambling, etc., unrestrained.

wide′spread″ *adj.* covering a great area, or known to many persons.

widg′eon (wij′ən) *n.* a duck, the baldpate. Also, **wi′geon.**

wid′ow (wid′ō) *n.* **1,** a woman who has not remarried since the death of her husband. **2,** in some card games, additional cards dealt to the table. —*v.t.* bereave of a spouse. —**wid′ow·er,** *n.masc.* —**wid′ow·hood″,** *n.*

width *n.* linear extent from side to side.

wield (wēld) *v.t.* **1,** use or exert (power, etc.). **2,** handle; brandish.

wie′ner (wē′nər) *n.* a kind of small sausage. Also, **wie′ner·wurst″** (-wûrst″).

wife (wīf) *n.* [*pl.* **wives** (wīvz)] a woman wedded to a man; a man's spouse. —**wife′hood,** *n.* —**wife′ly,** *adj.* befitting a wife.

wig *n.* an artificial covering of hair for the head. —**wigged,** *adj.*

wig′gle (wig′əl) *v.t. & i., & n.* wobble; wriggle. —**wig′gly,** *adj.*

wight (wīt) *n.* (*Archaic*) a person.

wig′wag″ *v.i. & t.* [**wig′wagged″, -wag″-ging**] **1,** move or cause to move to and fro. **2,** signal by waving flags. —*n.* a system of signaling with two flags.

wig′wam (wig′wom) *n.* the tent or hut of a No. Amer. Indian; teepee.

wild (wīld) *adj.* **1,** living or growing in a natural state; not domesticated; not cultivated. **2,** stormy; violent. **3,** savage; ferocious. **4,** extravagant; fantastic. **5,** reckless; rash. **6,** wide of the mark. **7,** disorderly; boisterous. **8,** (*Colloq.*) ardent; enthusiastic. —*n.* (often *pl.*) an uninhabited or uncultivated region. —**wild′ness,** *n.* —**wild fowl,** ducks, geese, etc. —**wild oats,** youthful indiscretions.

wild′cat″ (wīld′kat″) *n.* **1,** any of various small, untamed cats, as the lynx. **2,** a quick-tempered person. —*adj.* **1,** speculative; unsound. **2,** of a strike, unsanctioned. —*v.t.* **[-cat″ted, -ting]** drill wells experimentally for oil or gas.

wil′de·beest″ (wil′də-bēst″) *n.* a gnu.

wil′der·ness (wil′dər-nəs) *n.* an uninhabited tract of land; a desert.

wild-′eyed″ *adj.* staring wildly; wildly excited or angry.

wild′fire″ *n.* a spreading, uncontrollable fire.

wild-goose′ chase the pursuit of something unattainable; a futile chase or search.

wild′life″ *n.* wild, undomesticated animals living in their natural habitat.

wild′wood″ *n.* a wild or unfrequented wood; a forest.

wile (wil) *n.* a sly trick; a stratagem. —*v.t.* **1,** lure; entice. **2,** (with *away*) pass (time) pleasantly. —**wil′y,** *adj.*

will (wil) *n.* **1,** the faculty of conscious and deliberate action; volition. **2,** desire; choice; pleasure. **3,** purpose; determination. **4,** a legal document to dispose of property after the owner's death. —*aux. v.* [*pret.* **would**] **1,** expressing the future: am, is, are, etc., about to, sure to, determined to, etc. **2,** expressing desire; wish, want. **3,** is able to; can. —*v.t.* [*pret. & p.p.* **willed**] **1,** determine; decide. **2,** bequeath. **3,** influence.

will′ful (-fəl) *adj.* **1,** deliberate; intentional. **2,** obstinate; headstrong. Also, **wil′ful.** —**will′ful·ness,** *n.*

wil′lies (wil′ēs) *n.pl.* (*Colloq.*) nervousness; the jitters.

will′ing *adj.* **1,** favorably disposed; amenable. **2,** voluntary. **3,** eager to serve or comply. —**will′ing·ness,** *n.*

wil′li·waw″ *n.* a cold wind blowing from the coastal mountains toward the sea; any gust or squall.

will-′o′-the-wisp′ (wil′ə-*th*ə-wisp′) *n.* **1,** a light (from burning gas) that flits over marshes. **2,** an elusive or misleading hope.

wil′low (wil′ō) *n.* **1,** any of a genus of trees or shrubs with slender flexible twigs, valuable for wickerwork; its wood. **2,** in baseball and cricket, the bat. —**wil′low·y,** *adj.* supple.

will′pow″er *n.* strength of will; self-discipline.

wil′ly-nil′ly (wil′ē-nil′ē) *adv.* regardless of one's wishes.

wilt *v.i. & t.* **1,** become or make limp or drooping. **2,** weaken.

Wil′ton (wil′tən) *n.* a heavy carpet, orig. made at Wilton, Eng.

wim′ble (wim′bəl) *n.* a tool for boring.

wimp *n.* an ineffectual person.

wim′ple (wim′pəl) *n.* a woman's head covering, as worn by nuns.

win *v.t.* [**won,** (wun), **win′ning**] **1,** acquire by effort; gain. **2,** be victorious in. **3,** gain the favor of. **4,** prevail on; induce. **5,** reach; attain. —*v.i.* gain one's end; be successful or victorious. —*n.* (*Colloq.*) a victory. —**win′ner,** *n.*

wince (wins) *v.i.* shrink, as in pain or from a blow; start back. —*n.* a flinch.

winch *n.* hoisting machine.

wind *n.* **1,** a natural current of air. **2,** air artificially put in motion. **3,** breath; the power of respiration. **4,** idle talk; bombast. **5,** scent. **6,** flatulence. **7,** (*pl.*) wind instruments. —*v.t.* put out of breath. —**wind′ed,** *adj.* out of breath. —**wind instrument,** any musical instrument sounded by air. —**wind sleeve,** a windsock. —**wind tunnel,** a tunnellike structure for testing wind resistance.

wind (wīnd) *v.i.* [**wound** (wownd), **wind′ing**] **1,** go in a devious course; twist. **2,** entwine itself round something. **3,** (*Colloq.*) (with *up*) come to a conclusion; end. —*v.t.* **1,** turn; coil; twist. **2,** entwine; enfold. **3,** insinuate; worm. **4,** (*Colloq.*) (with *up*) bring to a conclusion. —*n.* [also, **wind′ing**] a turn; a bend. —**winding sheet,** a cloth in which a corpse is wrapped for burial.

wind′bag″ (wind′-) *n.* (*Slang*) a chatterer; a braggart.

wind′blown″ (wind′-) *adj.* made disorderly by the wind, as hair.

wind′break″ (wind′-) *n.* something to break the force of the wind, as a fence or a growth of trees.

wind′break″er (wind′-) *n.* an outer jacket.

wind′bro″ken (wind′-) *adj.* of a horse, having the heaves.

wind′burn″ (wind′-) *n.* skin burn caused by the wind.

wind′chill″ (wind′-) *n.* the cooling effect of wind, expressed as a combination of wind speed and temperature.

wind′cane″ (wind′-) *n.* a windsock.

wind′fall″ (wind′-) *n.* an unexpected and fortunate acquisition.

wind′flow″er (wind′-) *n.* the anemone.

wind′jam″mer (wind′jam″ər) *n.* a sailing ship.

wind′lass (wind′ləs) *n.* a machine for hoisting.

wind′mill″ (wind′-) *n.* a mill driven by blades turned by the wind.

win′dow (win′dō) *n.* **1,** an opening in the wall of a building to let in light and air. **2,** any similar opening. —**window box,** a box of soil in which to grow plants, placed below a window. —**window dressing,** a display in a store's window; any display designed to impress. —**window envelope,** an envelope with a transparent panel.

win′dow·pane″ n. a glass pane in a window.

win′dow·shop″ v.i. [**-shopped″ -shop″-ping**] look at display windows without intending to buy.

wind′pipe″ (wind′-) n. the trachea.

wind′row″ (wind′rō″) n. a ridge of hay, etc., arranged for drying.

wind′shield″ (wind′-) n. a glass shield before a driver of an automobile.

wind′sock″ (wind′-) n. a device used to show the direction of the wind. Also, **wind sleeve, wind′cone″,** n.

wind′storm″ (wind′-) n. a violent wind with little or no rain.

wind′surf″ing (wind′-) n. a type of sailing on a surfboard equipped with a sail.

wind′up″ (wīnd′-) n. (Colloq.) **1,** a conclusion. **2,** a baseball pitcher's preparatory movements.

wind′ward (wind′wərd) adv. & adj. toward the wind.

wind′y (win′dē) adj. **1,** marked by much blowing of wind. **2,** voluble; wordy. —**wind′i·ness,** n.

wine (wīn) n. the fermented juice of fruit or plants, specif. of the grape. —v.t. regale with alcoholic liquors. —v.i. drink wine. —adj. a dark red color. —**wine′bib″ber,** n. a heavy drinker. —**win′er·y,** n. a place where wine is made.

wine′sap″ n. a red apple.

wine′skin″ n. a goatskin container for wine.

wing n. **1,** a limb, usually occurring in pairs, by which certain animals fly; any similar appendage. **2,** flight. **3,** one of the chief supporting planes of an airplane. **4,** a part of a building projecting from the main part. **5,** one of the sides of a stage of a theater. **6,** anything projecting to the side. **7,** (pl.) an emblem worn by a military flier. **8,** protection. —v.t. **1,** equip with wings. **2,** traverse in flight. **3,** accomplish by means of flight. **4,** shoot; wound; disable. —v.i. **1,** fly; soar. **2,** (with it) (Colloq.) improvise; do without forethought. —**wing chair,** an upholstered chair with winglike projections of the back. —**wing collar,** a high, stiff man's collar with pointed winglike corners.

wing′ding″ adj. (Slang) a wild, lavish party.

winged (wingd) adj. **1,** having wings. **2,** swift; rapid. **3,** lofty; elevated; sublime.

wing′spread″ n. the distance, tip to tip, of outstretched wings. Also, **wing′span″.**

wink v.i. **1,** close and open the eye quickly, as a signal. **2,** (with at) condone. —n. an act of winking. —**forty winks,** a short nap. —**wink at,** overlook; condone.

win′kle (wing′kəl) n. **1,** a large sea snail with a spiral shell. **2,** a periwinkle.

win′ning (win′ing) adj. **1,** that wins. **2,** attractive. —n.pl. gains.

win′now (win′ō) v.t. **1,** drive off chaff from (grain) by a current of air. **2,** sift; weed out; test. —v.i. **1,** winnow grain. **2,** flutter.

wi′no (wī′nō) n. (Slang) a person habitually drunk on wine.

win′some (-səm) adj. charming. —**win′-some·ness,** n.

win′ter (win′tər) n. & adj. **1,** (often cap.) the cold season; in the No. hemisphere, approximately Dec. 22 to March 21. **2,** a period of dreariness or adversity. **3,** old age. —v.i. spend or pass the winter. —v.t. keep or shelter during the winter. —**win′-ter·ize″** (-īz″) v.t. prepare for winter. —**winter wheat,** wheat planted in the fall.

win′ter·green″ (win′tər-grēn″) n. an evergreen plant bearing aromatic leaves and berries.

win′ter·kill″ v.t. kill (a plant) by exposure to winter cold. —v.i. die from exposure to the cold.

win′ter·time″ n. winter.

win′try (win′trē) adj. of or like winter; cold; forbidding. —**win′tri·ness,** n.

wipe (wīp) v.t. **1,** clean or dry by gently rubbing, as with a soft cloth. **2,** remove, as dirt. **3,** cleanse. —n. **1,** an act of wiping. **2,** (Slang) a handkerchief. —**wipe out, 1,** destroy. **2,** (Colloq.) murder. **3,** in skiing, etc., lose balance and fall.

wire (wīr) n. **1,** a pliable thread or slender rod of metal; a piece of this material. **2,** a telegram. —v.t. **1,** provide with wire. **2,** snare. **3,** send a telegram; telegraph to. —v.i. telegraph. —**wire recording,** recording of sound on magnetized wire.

wire′hair″ n. a type of fox terrier: wirehaired terrier.

wire′less (-ləs) n. a telegraph or telephone not requiring connection by wires; radio.

wire′pho″to n. [pl. -tos] a method or apparatus for transmitting photographs by wire; a photograph so transmitted.

wire′pull″ing n. the use of influence to gain unfair advantage.

wire′tap″per (wīr′tap″ər) n. one who gets information, messages, etc., by electronically listening to someone's telephone conversations. —**wire′tap″,** n. & v.t. & i.

wir′ing n. a system of connected wires.

wir′y (wīr′ē) adj. lean but muscular. —**wir′i·ness,** n.

wis'dom (wiz'dəm) *n.* **1,** the power or faculty of forming a sound judgment in any matter; sagacity; experience. **2,** erudition. —**wisdom tooth,** the third molar, in the back of the jaw.

wise (wīz) *adj.* **1,** having the power of discerning and judging rightly. **2,** having knowledge; learned. **3,** experienced; cunning. **4,** judicious. **5,** (*Slang*) too smart; aware. **6,** (*Colloq.*) impudent; rude. —*n.* **1,** wise persons collectively. **2,** manner; way; mode.

-wise *suf.* forming adverbs: in the manner of, as *likewise;* in the direction of, as *sidewise.*; (*Colloq.*) with respect to, as *performance-wise.*

wise'a"cre *n.* one who affects wit or cleverness.

wise'crack" *n.* & *v.i.* (*Slang*) quip. —**wise'crack"er,** *n.*

wish *v.t.* **1,** long for; desire; crave. **2,** (*Colloq.*) (with *on*) shunt off. —*v.i.* form or express a desire. —*n.* **1,** eager desire or longing. **2,** a request. **3,** the thing desired.

wish'bone" *n.* the forked bone in front of the breast of a fowl.

wish'ful (-fəl) *adj.* based on desire; desirous. —**wish'ful-ness,** *n.*

wish'y-wash'y (wish'ē-wosh'ē) *adj.* (*Colloq.*) **1,** feeble. **2,** vacillating.

wisp *n.* **1,** a tuft of hay or straw, hair, etc. **2,** a fragment. —**wisp'y,** *adj.*

wist *v.* (*Archaic*) knew.

wis·ta'ri·a (wis-tār'ē-ə) *n.* a climbing shrub bearing clusters of purplish or white flowers. Also, **wis·te'ri·a** (-tir'ē-ə).

wist'ful (wist'fəl) *adj.* longing, but with little hope. —**wist'ful·ness,** *n.*

wit *n.* **1,** cleverness; intelligence; sense; (often *pl.*) power to reason. **2,** clever, amusing sayings and writings; one apt at making them. —**to wit,** namely.

witch (wich) *n.* **1,** a woman with magic powers derived from evil spirits; a sorceress. **2,** a hag; a crone. **3,** (*Colloq.*) a fascinating woman. —*v.t.* **1,** work witchcraft on. **2,** effect by witchcraft. **3,** charm; fascinate. —**witch'er·y,** *n.* —**witch'ing,** *adj.* bewitching; fascinating. —**witch doctor,** a medicine man. —**witch hazel,** a shrub bearing yellow flowers; a soothing lotion prepared from its bark. —**witch hunt,** a search for and prosecution of political dissidents on the pretext of the public good.

witch'craft" *n.* magic.

with *prep.* **1,** accompanying; beside; carrying. **2,** possessing; holding. **3,** opposed to; against; compared to. **4,** using. **5,** having in association or connection, or as a reason. **6,** away from. —**with it,** (*Slang*) hip; up-to-date; aware.

with·al' (with-âl') *adv.* & *prep.* considering everything; besides.

with·draw' (with-drâ') *v.t.* take back; recall; retract. —*v.i.* retire; retreat. —**withdraw'al,** *n.*

withe (with) *n.* a tough, flexible twig, esp. of willow.

with'er (with'ər) *v.i.* & *t.* **1,** shrivel up; dry out; decay. **2,** languish. **3,** abash.

with'ers (with'ərz) *n.pl.* the highest part of the back of a horse.

with·hold' (with-hōld') *v.t.* [-**held'**, -**hold'ing**] **1,** restrain. **2,** refuse to grant or release. —**withholding tax,** a deduction from wages for payment of tax.

with·in' (with-in') *adv.* **1,** pert. to the inside; indoors; internally; inwardly. —*prep.* in; inside of; not exceeding.

with·out' (with-owt') *adv.* on or as to the outside; outdoors; externally. —*prep.* **1,** outside of; beyond. **2,** lacking; independent of.

with·stand' *v.t.* [*pret.* & *p.p.* **with·stood'**] resist successfully; oppose.

wit'less (-ləs) *adj.* stupid; foolish. —**wit'less·ness,** *n.*

wit'ness (wit'nəs) *v.t.* **1,** see or know by personal presence. **2,** attest to (a document) by one's signature. **3,** testify. —*n.* **1,** one who sees personally. **2,** one who gives evidence or witnesses a document. **3,** testimony.

wit'ti·cism (wit'i-siz-əm) *n.* a witty remark.

wit'ting·ly (wit'ing-lē) *adv.* knowingly.

wit'ty (wit'ē) *adj.* characterized by or apt at making original and clever remarks. —**wit'ti·ness,** *n.*

wive (wīv) *v.t.* & *i.* marry.

wives (wīvz) *n.* pl. of *wife.*

wiz'ard (wiz'ərd) *n.* **1,** one supposed to have magic powers; a sorcerer. **2,** an unusually skilled person. —*adj.* **1,** enchanting. **2,** (*Brit. slang*) superb. —**wiz'ard·ry,** *n.* **1,** sorcery. **2,** admirable skill.

wiz'ened (wiz'ənd) *adj.* dried up; shriveled.

woad (wōd) *n.* a European plant formerly cultivated for the blue dye obtained from its leaves; the dye.

wob'ble (wob'əl) *v.i.* **1,** move from side to side; rock. **2,** tremble. —*n.* a rocking motion. —**wob'bly,** (-lē) *adj.*

woe (wō) *n.* **1,** intense unhappiness; grief; sorrow. **2,** an affliction.

woe'be·gone" *adj.* sorrowful.

woe'ful (-fəl) *adj.* **1,** sorrowful. **2,** causing or expressing woe. —**woe'ful·ness,** *n.*

wok (wäk) *n.* a Chinese bowl-shaped cooking utensil.

---

woke (wōk) v. pret. of *wake*.

wold (wōld) n. in England, a tract of treeless, rolling country; a down or moor.

wolf (wûlf) n. [pl. **wolves** (wûlvz)] **1**, a wild, carnivorous animal of the dog family. **2**, a cruel, cunning, greedy person. **3**, (*Slang*) a man who makes advances to many women. —v.t. devour ravenously. —**wolf′ish**, adj. —**cry wolf**, raise a false alarm. —**wolf pack**, a group of submarines hunting together for enemy shipping.

wolf′hound″ n. a large hound used to hunt wolves.

wolf′ram (wûl′frəm) n. a mineral, a source of tungsten. Also, **wolf′ram·ite″** (-īt″).

wolfs′bane″ n. aconite or monkshood.

wol″ver·ine″ (wûl″və-rēn′) n. **1**, a small, ferocious, carnivorous animal, related to the marten. **2**, (*cap.*) (*Colloq.*) an inhabitant of Michigan.

wom′an (wûm′ən) n. [pl. **wom′en** (wim′ən)] **1**, an adult human female; a wife; a female attendant. **2**, the female sex. **3**, feminine nature. —**wom′an·hood″**, n. the state of being a woman; womanly qualities. —**wom′an·ish**, adj. unbecomingly feminine. —**wom′an·kind″**, n. —**wom′an·like″**, adj. —**wom′an·ly**, adj. befitting a woman.

wom′an·ize″ v.t. make more feminine. —v.i. (*Slang*) chase after women.

womb (woom) n. the uterus.

wom′bat n. an Australian marsupial resembling a small bear.

wom′en (wim′ən) n. pl. of *woman*. —**wom′en·folk″**, n.

won (wun) v. pret. & p.p. of *win*.

won′der (wun′dər) n. **1**, a strange thing; a cause of surprise or admiration; a marvel; a prodigy. **2**, astonishment. —v.i. **1**, entertain doubt or curiosity; speculate. **2**, marvel. —**won′der·ment**, n. —**won′drous**, adj.

won′der·ful (-fəl) adj. **1**, extraordinary; marvelous. **2**, delightful. —**won′der·ful·ness**, n.

won′der·land″ n. a wonderful place.

wont adj. accustomed; in the habit. —n. custom; habit; practice. —**wont′ed**, adj.

woo v.t. & i. seek the favor or love of; court. —**woo′er**, n.

wood (wûd) n. **1**, the hard, fibrous substance of the body of a tree. **2**, (often *pl.*) a forest. **3**, timber. —**wood alcohol**, methyl alcohol. —**wood pulp**, wood fibers, prepared for use in manufacturing paper.

wood′bine″ (wûd′bīn″) n. **1**, honeysuckle. **2**, the Virginia creeper.

wood′block″ n. **1**, a woodcut. **2**, a musical percussion instrument.

wood′chuck″ (wûd′chuk″) n. a burrowing hibernating marmot; the ground hog.

wood′cock″ n. a game bird. —**Scotch woodcock**, a dish of scrambled eggs on toast or crackers spread with anchovy paste.

wood′craft″ n. the art of living on nature.

wood′cut″ n. a printing block of wood; a print made from one.

wood′ed adj. thick with trees.

wood′en (-ən) adj. **1**, made of wood. **2**, inflexible; unimaginative. **3**, not sensitive; expressionless. —**wood′en·head″ed**, adj. stupid; obstinate.

wood′land (-lənd) n. a forest.

wood′man (-mən) n. [pl. **-men**] **1**, a woodcutter; lumberman. **2**, one who dwells in the woods. **3**, a forester.

wood′note″ n. a wild or natural song, as of a forest bird.

wood′peck″er n. a bird that bores into trees with its bill.

wood′ruff″ (-ruf″) n. a small sweet-scented European herb.

wood′shed″ n. a shed for storing cut firewood. —v.i. (*Colloq.*) do extra study.

woods′man (wûdz′mən) n. [pl. **-men**] a forester.

woods′y adj. belonging to, associated with, or suggestive of the woods.

wood′wind″ n. a musical wind instrument, as the flute, clarinet, etc.

wood′work″ n. interior trim and fixtures made of wood.

wood′y (-ē) adj. **1**, wooded. **2**, of or resembling wood. —**wood′i·ness**, n.

woof n. **1**, the crosswise threads in weaving. **2**, a suppressed bark or growl of a dog. —v.i. make such a sound.

woof′er (wûf′ər) n. a loudspeaker responsive only to the lower frequencies and used for reproducing low-pitched sounds.

wool (wûl) n. **1**, the fleece of the sheep; any fabric or yarn made of it. **2**, kinky hair.

wool′en (-ən) adj. & n. made of wool. Also, **wool′len**.

wool′gath″er·ing n. desultory thought causing inattention.

wool′ly (-ē) adj. **1**, of or like wool. **2**, (*Colloq.*) confused; blurred. **3**, (*Colloq.*) exciting. —**wool′lies**, n.pl. woolen clothes. —**wool′li·ness**, n. —**woolly bear**, a hairy caterpillar.

wool′sack″ n. the wool-stuffed seat of the Lord Chancellor, in the Eng. House of Lords.

wooz′y (woo′zē) adj. (*Slang*) **1**, confused; befuddled. **2**, shaky. —**wooz′i·ness**, n.

Worces′ter·shire sauce (wus′tər-shər) a piquant sauce of soy, vinegar, and many other ingredients.

word (wērd) n. **1**, a sound or combination

of sounds, or its graphic representation, expressing an idea; a term. **2,** (*pl.*) speech; written words; a song lyric; a quarrel. **3,** information; a report; a command; a signal or password; a motto. **4,** a promise. **5,** (*cap.*) Holy Scripture. —*v.t.* express in words; phrase. —**word'age,** *n.* —**word'-ing,** *n.* phrasing. —**word'less,** *adj.* silent; tacit. —**the last word,** the ultimate authority; (*Slang*) the latest thing. —**word for word,** verbatim; literally. —**word process-ing,** electronic processing of written material, as letters, contracts, etc.

word'book" *n.* **1,** a dictionary; vocabulary. **2,** an opera libretto.

word'y (-ē) *adj.* verbose. —**word'i·ness,** *n.*

wore (wôr) *v.* pret. of *wear.*

work (wêrk) *v.i.* **1,** put forth effort; labor; toil; strive. **2,** act; operate, esp. effectively. **3,** ferment; seethe. **4,** make way slowly. **5,** be employed; perform labor. —*v.t.* **1,** prepare or fashion by labor; operate; employ. **2,** sew; embroider. **3,** do; accomplish. **4,** (often with *on,* etc.) affect; influence; persuade; provoke. **5,** exact labor or service from. **6,** solve. —*n.* **1,** effort or exertion; toil; labor. **2,** employment; a job; an undertaking; a project. **3,** a product of effort; deed; performance. **4,** (*pl.*) a factory. **5,** (*pl.*) a mechanism, as of a watch. **6,** (*pl.*) the entire output of an artist, writer, etc. **7,** (*pl.*) engineering structures, esp. public ones. **8,** (*pl., colloq.*) everything; the whole thing. —**work out, 1,** develop; study. **2,** solve. **3,** exhaust, as a mine. **4,** exercise.

-work *suf.* product of (what is specified).

work'a·ble (-ə-bəl) *adj.* **1,** feasible; practicable. **2,** tractable. —**work"a·bil'i·ty,** *n.*

work"a·hol'ic (-ə-hol'ik) *n.* (*Slang*) one who works excessively, as though addicted to work.

work'a·day" *adj.* commonplace; matter-of-fact.

work'bench" *n.* a table on which to do work.

work'book" *n.* an instructive manual or drill book.

work'day" *n.* hours worked in a day. Also, **working day.**

work'er (-ər) *n.* one who works; esp., a laborer.

work'horse" *n.* **1,** a horse used for labor. **2,** (*Colloq.*) a hard-working person.

work'house" *n.* a poorhouse or small prison.

work'ing *adj.* **1,** that works. **2,** effective; in operation. —*n.* **1,** operation; fermentation. **2,** (*pl.*) the parts of a mine. —**work'-ing·man",** *n.* a laborer.

work'man (-mən) *n.* [*pl.* **-men**] a skilled worker. —**work'man·like",** *adj.* competently executed. —**work'man·ship",** *n.*

work'out" *n.* **1,** a performance for practice or exercise. **2,** (*Colloq.*) a trying experience.

work'shop" *n.* a building or room in which work is done.

world (wērld) *n.* **1,** the whole creation; the universe; the earth. **2,** the human race; mankind. **3,** a class or society of persons; a sphere; realm. **4,** material concerns. **5,** public or social life. **6,** a particular part of the earth. **7,** a great number or quantity.

world'beat"er *n.* one who is unusually good at what he does.

world'ling *n.* one devoted to the pleasures and interests of this life.

world'ly (-lē) *adj.* **1,** mundane; material; not spiritual. **2,** sophisticated. —**world'li-ness,** *n.* —**world'ly-wise",** *adj.* experienced; knowing; shrewd.

world'wide" *adj.* throughout the earth.

worm (wērm) *n.* **1,** any small, creeping tube-shaped animal. **2,** a contemptible person; an unfortunate person. **3,** something that silently harasses. **4,** any device resembling a worm, as a spiral part. **5,** (*pl.*) any disease caused by parasitic worms. —*v.i.* work or act slowly, stealthily, or secretly. —*v.t.* free from worms. —**worm'y,** *adj.* —**worm gear,** a wheel driven by a screw.

worm-'eat"en *adj.* **1,** eaten or bored into by worms. **2,** old; worn-out; worthless.

worm'wood" (wērm'wûd') *n.* **1,** a bitter herb used in tonics and in absinthe. **2,** bitterness.

worn (wôrn) *v.* pret. & p.p. of *wear.* —*adj.* weary. —**worn'ness,** *n.*

worn-"out' *adj.* **1,** unfit for use. **2,** exhausted.

wor'ry (wēr'ē) *v.t.* **1,** cause to feel anxious; harass; bother. **2,** grasp with the teeth and shake. —*v.i.* **1,** be anxious; fret. **2,** (*Colloq.*) manage somehow. —*n.* anxiety; trouble. —**wor'ri·er,** *n.* —**wor'ri·ment** (-mənt) *n.* (*Colloq.*) worry. —**wor'ri·some** (-səm) *adj.* causing worry.

wor'ry·wart" (-wôrt) *n.* (*Colloq.*) someone who worries excessively.

worse (wērs) *adj.* & *adv.* comp. of *bad, ill, badly.* —**wors'en,** *v.t.* & *i.*

wor'ship (wēr'ship) *n.* **1,** reverence and homage, esp. to God. **2,** religious services. **3,** a title of honor. —*v.t.* **1,** pay divine honors to; adore (God). **2,** love or admire inordinately. —*v.i.* perform or attend religious services. —**wor'ship·er,** *n.* —**wor'-ship·ful,** *adj.*

worst (wērst) *adj.* & *adv.* superl. of *bad,*

ill, badly. —*v.t.* defeat. —*n.* that which is worst.

wor´sted (wûs´tid) *n.* **1,** a tight-twisted woolen yarn; fabric made of it. **2,** a woolen yarn for knitting.

wort (wêrt) *n.* **1,** a plant, herb, or vegetable: used in old plant names, as *colewort*. **2,** the infusion of malt which, after fermentation, becomes beer.

worth (wêrth) *adj.* **1,** meriting; deserving. **2,** having a specified value. **3,** equivalent in value to. **4,** possessing. —*n.* **1,** value, esp. in money. **2,** excellence; merit.

worth´less (-ləs) *adj.* useless; worth nothing; undeserving. —**worth´less·ness,** *n.*

worth´while´´ *adj.* serving a useful purpose. —**worth´´while´ness,** *n.*

wor´thy (wēr´thė) *adj.* deserving respect. —**wor´thi·ness,** *n.*

would (wûd) *v.* pret. of *will.*

would-´be´´ *adj.* hoping or pretending to be.

wound (woond) *n.* **1,** an injury to flesh or tissue, esp. one caused by violence. **2,** any injury; something that hurts. —*v.t. & i.* **1,** hurt by violence. **2,** hurt the feelings (of).

wound (wownd) *v.* pret. & p.p. of *wind.*

wove (wōv) *v.* pret. of *weave.*

wo´ven (wō´vən) *v.* p.p. of *weave.*

wow *interj.* expressing admiration or wonder. —*v.t.* (*Slang*) captivate. —*n.* **1,** a distortion of fidelity in sound reproduction. **2,** (*Slang*) a wonderful person, thing, or performance.

wrack (rak) *n.* wreck.

wraith (rāth) *n.* an apparition; a specter; a ghost. —**wraith´y,** *adj.*

wran´gle (rang´gəl) *v.i.* argue noisily; dispute. —*v.t.* round up (livestock). —*n.* a noisy quarrel. —**wran´gler,** *n.*

wrap (rap) *v.t.* [**wrapped, wrap´ping**] **1,** cover with (paper, etc.); envelop; make into a bundle. **2,** roll or fold (paper, etc.) around. —*n.* a cloak or shawl; (*Colloq.*) an overcoat. —**wrapped up in,** engrossed.

wrap´a·round´´ *adj.* designating a garment that wraps around the body before being fastened.

wrap´per (-ər) *n.* **1,** any covering. **2,** a dressing gown.

wrap´ping (rap´ing) *n.* that which wraps; material for wrapping.

wrap´up´´ *n.* summary; précis. —**wrap up, 1,** conclude; work out the details of. **2,** summarize.

wrasse (ras) *n.* any of various marine fishes.

wrath (rǎth) *n.* **1,** fierce anger; rage. **2,** vengeance. —**wrath´ful,** *adj.*

wreak (rēk) *v.t.* inflict.

wreath (rēth) *n.* something twisted or formed into a circular band; a garland.

wreathe (rēth) *v.t.* form by twisting; intertwine; encircle.

wreck (rek) *n.* **1,** destruction, disruption, or ruin. **2,** one who or that which is in a state of ruin; remains; a shipwrecked vessel. —*v.t.* cause the ruin or demolition of. —**wreck´age,** *n.*

wreck´er (-ər) *n.* **1,** one who wrecks. **2,** a car for removing or towing wrecked cars.

wren (ren) *n.* any of a family of small, migratory songbirds.

wrench (rench) *n.* **1,** a violent, sudden twist or jerk; a sprain. **2,** a grasping tool. —*v.t.* **1,** give a sudden twist to; distort. **2,** sprain. **3,** wrest forcibly.

wrest (rest) *v.t.* remove or seize by, or as if by, violent twisting; wring; wrench.

wres´tle (res´əl) *v.i.* **1,** struggle, as two persons each trying to throw the other to the mat in a contest. **2,** contend; grapple; strive. —*v.t.* contest with in wrestling. —*n.* a wrestling match. —**wres´tler,** *n.* —**wres´tling,** *n.*

wretch (rech) *n.* **1,** one who is very unhappy or unfortunate. **2,** a contemptible person.

wretch´ed *adj.* **1,** miserable. **2,** mean; lowly. —**wretch´ed·ness,** *n.*

wrig´gle (rig´əl) *v.i.* **1,** move along sinuously; writhe; squirm. **2,** make way by opportunism and shrewdness. —*n.* a squirming motion. —**wrig´gler,** *n.* —**wrig´gly,** *adj.*

wright (rīt) *n.* a workman.

wring (ring) *v.t.* [**wrung** (rung), **wring´ing**] **1,** twist or flex forcibly. **2,** distress. **3,** squeeze out; extort. —*v.i.* writhe. —*n.* a twist. —**wring´er,** *n.* a device for pressing water from washed clothes. —**wring´ing wet,** drenched.

wrin´kle (ring´kəl) *n.* **1,** a slight ridge or furrow in a surface; a crease in the skin, esp. one caused by old age. **2,** (*Colloq.*) a good or new idea. —*v.t. & i.* crease; pucker.

wrist (rist) *n.* **1,** the joint between the hand and the forearm. **2,** a connecting stud or pin: *wrist pin.* —**wrist watch,** a watch strapped to the wrist.

wrist´let *n.* a band around the wrist.

writ (rit) *n.* **1,** (*Law*) a written order or document. **2,** Scripture.

write (rīt) *v.t.* [**wrote** (rōt), **writ´ten** (rit´ən) **writ´ing**] **1,** form (letters or characters) on a surface by hand. **2,** set down for reading, as with a pen or typewriter; cause to be written, as by dictation. **3,** cover with writing. **4,** (with *off*) treat as a loss; forget about. —*v.i.* **1,** write words or characters.

2, work as an author. **3,** conduct a correspondence. —**writer's cramp,** a muscular spasm in the hand caused by holding a writing implement for a long period of time.

write-'in″ *adj.* pert. to votes, written or sent in, or to a candidate voted for or elected by such votes.

write-'off″ *n.* an amount, person, etc., considered lost and hence canceled.

write-'up″ *n.* a written account, esp. a laudatory description.

writhe (rīth) *v.i.* twist one's body, as from pain.

writ'ing (rīt'ing) *n.* **1,** written matter; a literary work. **2,** handwriting.

writ'ten (rit'ən) *v.* p.p. of *write.*

wrong (râng) *adj.* **1,** deviating from right, truth, or morals. **2,** not correct in fact; mistaken. **3,** unsuitable; improper. —*adv.* not rightly; incorrectly; amiss. —*n.* evil; harm; injury. —*v.t.* **1,** do harm to; treat unfairly. **2,** unjustly blame or disapprove of.

wrong'do″**er** (-doo″ər) *n.* a sinner. —**wrong'do**″**ing,** *n.*

wrong'ful (-fəl) *adj.* injurious; unlawful. —**wrong'ful·ness,** *n.*

wrong'head″**ed** *adj.* obstinately opinionated; misguided and stubborn. —**wrong'head**″**ed·ness,** *n.*

wrote (rōt) *v.* pret. of *write.*

wroth (roth) *adj.* very angry.

wrought (rât) *v.* & *adj.* worked; formed, fashioned, or hammered. —**wrought iron,** iron purified of carbon. —**wrought-'up**′, *adj.* disturbed; excited.

wrung (rung) *v.* pret. & p.p. of *wring.*

wry (rī) *adj.* **1,** twisted to one side; askew; distorted. **2,** ironic. —**wry'ness,** *n.*

wry'neck″ *n.* **1,** spasmodic contraction of the neck muscles; torticollis. **2,** a bird resembling a woodpecker.

wy'an·dotte″ (wī'ən-dot″) *n.* a breed of domestic fowl.

X

X, x (eks) **1,** the 24th letter of the English alphabet. **2,** the legal signature of an illiterate person. **3,** (*cap.*) ten, 10, the Rom. numeral.

xan·tho- (zan-thə) *pref.* yellow.

xan'thous (zan'thəs) *adj.* yellow; yellow-skinned.

X'-chro″**mo·some** *n.* a female sex chromosome.

xe'bec (zē'bek) *n.* a small Mediterranean three-masted vessel. Also, **ze'bec.**

xe'ni·a (zē'nē-ə) *n.* (*Bot.*) the effect of pollen on a seed or fruit, other than on the embryo.

xen·o- (zen-ō; -ə) *pref.* alien.

xe'non (zē'non) *n.* an inert gaseous chemical element, no. 54, symbol Xe.

xen″**o·pho'bi·a** (zen″ə-fō'bē-ə) *n.* fear or hatred of foreigners.

xe·ro- (zē-rə) *pref.* dry.

xe·rog'ra·phy (zi-räg'rə-fē) *n.* copying by use of light action on an electrically charged photo-conductive insulating surface that transfers a special printing powder only from those areas that remain electrically charged, thereby reproducing the image to be copied.

xe'ro·phyte (zē'rə-fīt) *n.* a plant that grows in arid regions, as the cactus. —**xe**″**ro·phyt'ic** (-fit'ik) *adj.* —**xe**″**ro·phyt'i·cal·ly,** *adv.*

Xe'rox (zi'-räks) *n.* (*T.N.*) **1,** a machine that copies by xerography. **2,** a copy made by xerography. —*v.t.* (*l.c.*) to copy by xerography.

xi (zī or sī) *n.* the 14th letter of the Greek alphabet (Ξ, ξ).

X'mas *abbr.* Christmas.

x-'ray″ (eks'rā″) *n.* **1,** (*pl.*) electromagnetic radiations of extremely short wave length and high penetrating power, commonly used to photograph the interior of solids and for the treatment of skin or cancerous diseases. **2,** a photograph made by x-rays. —*v.t.* examine, photograph, or treat by x-rays. —**x-'ra·di·a'tion,** *n.*

xy'lem (zī'lem) *n.* the woody tissue of plants.

xy·lo- (zī-lə) *pref.* wood; wooden.

xy·log'ra·phy (zī-log'rə-fē) *n.* wood engraving. —**xy'lo·graph**″, *n.* —**xy**″**lo·graph'ic,** *adj.* —**xy**″**lo·graph'i·cal·ly,** *adv.*

xy'loid (zī'loid) *adj.* resembling wood.

xy'lo·phone″ (zī'lə-fōn″) *n.* a musical instrument comprising a series of wooden bars processed to sound musical tones when struck with wooden hammers. —**xy'lo·phon**″**ist,** *n.*

Y

Y, y (wī) the 25th letter of the English alphabet.

-y (ē; i) *suf.* forming adjectives; **1,** of the nature of, as *misty.* **2,** being, as *guilty.*

yacht (yot) *n.* a pleasure ship used solely for its owner's personal purposes. —*v.i.* travel in a yacht. —**yacht'ing,** *n.* —**yachts'-man** (-mən) *n.,* **yachts'wom**″**an,** *n. fem.* the owner of a yacht.

ya'hoo (yä'hoo) *n*. a coarse, uncouth person.

Yah'weh (yä'we) *n*. variant transliteration of Jehovah.

yak *n*. a long-haired Asiatic ox.

yam *n*. **1**, a tuberous root cultivated as food. **2**, the sweet potato.

yam'mer (yam'ər) (*Colloq.*) *v.i.* **1**, whimper; whine. **2**, shout; yell. **3**, talk persistently. **4**, lament. —*n*. an act of yammering.

yang *n*. the masculine force in Chinese philosophy, opposed to yin.

yank *v.t. & i.* pull suddenly; jerk. —*n*. **1**, a jerk. **2**, (*cap.*) (*Slang*) Yankee.

Yan'kee (yang'kè) *n*. **1**, a citizen of the U.S. **2**, a native of the N. E. states. **3**, in the southern U.S., any native of the northern states. —*adj*. pert. to Yankees.

yap *v.i.* [**yapped, yap'ping**] **1**, yelp. **2**, talk foolishly, or in a barking manner. —*n*. a yelp.

ya·pok' *n*. a small, aquatic opossum of Central and So. Amer.

yard (yärd) *n*. **1**, the ground adjoining a building. **2**, an enclosure or area in which any work is carried on. **3**, a unit of linear measure, equal to 3 ft. **4**, a rod or spar, esp. a crosswise piece on a mast. —**yard goods,** goods sold by length, as fabrics, etc.

yard'age (-ij) *n*. distance or area in yards.

yard'arm" *n*. (*Naut.*) an end of a yard.

yard'mas"ter *n*. one who superintends a railway yard.

yard'stick" (yärd'stik") *n*. **1**, a calibrated stick one yard long. **2**, any standard of measurement.

yar'mul·ke (yar'məl-kə) *n*. a skullcap worn by Jewish males.

yarn (yärn) *n*. **1**, fibers of cotton, wool, etc., twisted together. **2**, a tale, esp., a fabricated one. —*v.i.* tell or exchange stories.

yar'row (yar'ō) *n*. a plant related to the aster; milfoil.

yaw (yä) *v.i.* turn to one side, heading off course. —*n*. a deviation.

yawl (yäl) *n*. a small two-masted sailing vessel.

yawn (yân) *v.i.* **1**, open the mouth involuntarily in reaction from fatigue or sleepiness. **2**, open wide; extend far. —*n*. a yawning.

yawp (yâp) (*Colloq.*) *v.i.* **1**, yelp. **2**, make a loud, uncouth sound, as an audible yawn. **3**, talk noisily. —*n*. **1**, a yelp. **2**, a loud sound or cry. **3**, noisy talk.

yaws (yâz) *n.pl.* a skin disease.

Y'-chro"mo·some *n*. a male sex chromosome.

y·clept' (i-klept') *v*. (*Archaic*) named.

ye (yē) *pron. pl.* (*Obs.*) you.

yea (yā) *adv*. **1**, yes. **2**, truly; indeed. —*n*. an affirmative vote.

year (yir) *n*. **1**, the period of one revolution of the earth about the sun, about 365 days. **2**, the period from Jan. 1 to the next Dec. 31 inclusive (calendar year); any period of 365 or 366 consecutive calendar days. **3**, the period of an annually-recurring activity, as a school year. **4**, (*pl.*) age; old age; time. —**year'ly,** *adj. & adv*.

year'book" *n*. an annual publication, usually dealing with events of the past year.

year'ling (yir'ling) *n*. an animal one year old, or in its second year.

yearn (yērn) *v.i.* desire strongly; long for something. —**yearn'ing,** *n*.

yeast (yēst) *n*. **1**, a yellowish substance, an aggregate of minute fungi, used to leaven bread and ferment liquors. **2**, any froth or spume. —*v.i.* ferment.

yeast'y (-ē) *adj*. frothy; light. —**yeast'i-ness,** *n*.

yegg (yeg) *n*. (*Slang*) a robber, esp. one who cracks safes.

yell (yel) *v.i.* cry out; shout. —*v.t.* utter in a loud, piercing tone. —*n*. **1**, a shout or scream. **2**, a cry or slogan uttered in concert by a crowd.

yel'low (yel'ō) *n*. the color of lemons, the yolk of an egg, etc.; a hue between orange and green in the spectrum. —*adj*. **1**, of this color. **2**, yellow-skinned; belonging to the Mongolian race. **3**, (*Colloq.*) cowardly; contemptible. **4**, offensively sensational (of newspapers). —**yellow-dog contract,** (*Slang*) a contract in which workers agree not to join a union. —**yellow fever,** an infectious febrile disease, also called *yellow jack.* —**yellow jacket,** a variety of wasp. —**yellow pages,** a telephone directory of businesses and services. —**yellow peril,** (*Offensive*) Oriental peoples, when viewed as dangerous because so numerous.

yel'low·bel'ly *n*. (*Slang*) a coward.

yelp *v.i.* give a quick, shrill cry, like a dog. —*n*. a sharp cry; a bark.

yen *n*. **1**, the monetary unit of Japan. **2**, (*Colloq.*) yearning.

yen'ta (yen'tə) *n*. (*Slang*) a nosy, gossiping woman.

yeo'man (yō'mən) *n*. [*pl.* **-men**] **1**, a petty officer of the U.S. Navy whose duties are clerical. **2**, (*Brit.*) an independent farmer; (*Archaic*) an attendant or servant. —**yeo'man·ry,** *n*. yeomen collectively. —**yeoman service,** vigorous and effective work.

yes *adv*. a word expressing affirmation, agreement, consent. —**yes'man",** *n*. one who always agrees with a superior.

ye·shi'va (ye-shē'və) *n.* an Orthodox Jewish school.

yes'ter- (yes'tər) *adj.* past. **—yes"ter·eve'**, **yes"ter·night'**, **yes"ter·year'**, *n.*

yes'ter·day (yes'tər-dā) *n.* **1,** the day preceding the present day. **2,** time of the immediate past. *—adv.* on yesterday.

yet *adv.* **1,** at or up to the present or some future time; hitherto; already. **2,** as formerly; still; in continuation. **3,** in addition; besides; moreover. *—conj.* nevertheless; notwithstanding.

ye'ti (ye'tē) *n.* the abominable snowman.

yew (ū) *n.* an evergreen coniferous tree; its wood.

Yid'dish (yid'ish) *n.* a language of the Jews, incorporating Hebrew, German, and other words.

yield (yēld) *v.t. & i.* **1,** produce in payment. **2,** bring forth by natural process; bear (as fruit); produce. **3,** surrender; relinquish. *—v.i.* give way; assent; comply. *—n.* what is produced. **—yield'ing**, *adj.* compliant; tractable.

yin *n.* the female force in Chinese philosophy, opposed to yang.

yip *v.i.* [**yipped, yip'ping**] (*Colloq.*) bark sharply; yelp. *—n.* a yelp.

yip'pie (yip'ē) *n.* a radical hippie activist.

yo'del (yō'dəl) *v.i. & t.* sing with alternation between ordinary voice and falsetto.

yo'ga (yō'gə) *n.* a Hindu ascetic philosophy.

yo'gi (yō'gē) *n.* one who practices or teaches yoga.

yo'gurt (yō'gûrt) *n.* a curdled milk food.

yoicks (yoiks) *interj.* a cry of fox hunters.

yoke (yōk) *n.* **1,** a contrivance for fastening together the necks of two draft animals, as oxen. **2,** anything resembling a yoke in form or use, as the collar-piece of a garment. **3,** something that binds or holds parts together. **4,** servitude; slavery. *—v.t.* put a yoke on; couple; link.

yo'kel (yō'kəl) *n.* a rustic or countryman; an awkward person.

yolk (yōk) *n.* **1,** the yellow substance of an egg. **2,** the vital or essential part of anything.

Yom Kip'pur (yom kip'ər) a fast day, the Day of Atonement, in Judaism.

yon *adj.* (*Poetic*) yonder.

yon'der (yon'dər) *adv. & adj.* in that (distant or more distant) place.

yore (yôr) *adv.* (*Archaic*) long ago.

York'shire pudding (yôrk'shər) a batter pudding baked in roast-meat drippings.

you (ū) *pron. sing. & pl.* [*poss.* **your** (yûr), **yours**] the personal pronoun of the second person; in nominative it always takes a plural verb.

young (yung) *adj.* **1,** being in an early stage of life or growth; not yet mature. **2,** recent; not fully developed. **3,** having the appearance and vigor of youth. **4,** inexperienced. *—n.* offspring. **—young'ish**, *adj.* **—young'ness**, *n.* **—young blood, 1,** youthful vigor, ideas, etc. **2,** a relatively young person or persons.

young'ling *n.* **1,** any young person or thing. **2,** a beginner. *—adj.* youthful; young.

young'ster (-stər) *n.* a young person.

your (yûr) *pron.* poss. of *you*. **—yours**, poss. of *you*, used predicatively. **—your-self'**, emphatic and reflexive form of *you*.

youth (ūth) *n.* **1,** the period of life from puberty to maturity; adolescence. **2,** the earliest stage. **3,** the condition of being young. **4,** the qualities of early age, as vigor. **5,** a young person, esp. male; young persons collectively. **—youth'ful**, *adj.* **—youth'ful·ness**, *n.*

yowl *v.i.* utter a long wailing cry; howl. *—n.* such a cry.

yo'yo (yō'yō) *n.* **1,** a dish-shaped toy designed to be spun out and reeled in by a string. **2,** (*Slang*) an eccentric or crazy person.

yt·ter'bi·um (i-tēr'bē-əm) *n.* a metallic chemical element, no. 70, symbol Yb.

yt'tri·um (it'rē-əm) *n.* a metallic chemical element, no. 39, symbol Yt.

yu·an' (ū-än') *n. sing. & pl.* the monetary unit of China, formerly worth about .50 dollar.

yuc'ca (yuk'ə) *n.* a plant of the lily family.

Yu'go·slav" (ū'gō-släv") *adj. & n.* of or pert. to Yugoslavia, its people, language, etc.

yule (ūl) *n.* Christmas or the Christmas season. Also, **yule'tide"**.

yum'my (yum'ē) *adj.* (*Colloq.*) delicious.

Z

Z, z (zē) the 26th letter of the English alphabet.

za'ny (zā'nē) *n.* **1,** a clownish person; an amusing fool, a simpleton.

zap *v.t.* (*Slang*) kill or wipe out with a sudden burst, as of electricity, firepower, etc.

zeal (zēl) *n.* fervent ardor; eagerness; enthusiasm; diligence.

zeal'ot (zel'ət) *n.* one who is fanatically earnest.

zeal'ous (zel'əs) *adj.* diligent; earnest. **—zeal'ous·ness**, *n.*

ze′bec (zē′bek) *n.* xebec.

ze′bra (zē′brə) *n.* an Afr. mammal related to the horse, marked with alternate light and dark stripes.

ze′bu (zē′bū) *n.* a bovine animal having a hump over the shoulders, domesticated in the Orient.

zed *n.* (*Brit.*) the letter z.

Zeit′geist (tsīt′gīst″) *n.* (*Ger.*) the spirit of the time; the moral and intellectual thought or feeling characteristic of an age or period.

Zen *n.* a school of Buddhism which stresses meditation.

ze·na′na (ze-nä′nə) *n.* in India, the living quarters of the women; the harem.

ze′nith (zē′nith) *n.* **1,** the point in the sky directly above an observer or place on the earth. **2,** the highest point of anything; culmination.

zeph′yr (zef′ər) *n.* a mild, gentle breeze.

Zep′pe·lin (zep′ə-lin) *n.* a type of dirigible balloon with a cigar-shaped bag.

ze′ro (zir′ō) [*pl.* **-ros**] *n.* **1,** the symbol 0, meaning the absence of quantity; the cipher. **2,** the first or lowest point on a scale of measurement, as a thermometer. **3,** naught; nothing. **—zero hour,** a time set for the commencement of action. **—zero-base budgeting,** a process in which the entire budget is reviewed every year. **—zero population growth,** the principle that births and deaths in a given year should be equal.

ze′ro-ze′ro *adj.* of an atmospheric condition characterized by zero ceiling and zero visibility.

zest *n.* **1,** keen relish; hearty enjoyment; gusto. **2,** piquant or appealing flavor; an enjoyable quality. **—zest′ful,** *adj.* **—zest′y,** *adj.*

ze′ta (zā′tə) *n.* the sixth letter of the Greek alphabet (Z, ζ).

zig′zag″ *n.* a sharp angle or series of such angles; a line or course that turns abruptly from side to side. **—adj.** having sharp turnings or angles. **—v.i. & t.** [**-zagged″,** **-zag″ging**] advance or form in zigzags.

zilch *n.* (*Slang*) zero.

zil′lion (zil′yən) *adj.* an indefinite, very large number.

zinc (zink) *n.* a metallic chemical element, no. 30, symbol Zn. **—zinc ointment,** a salve containing zinc oxide. **—zinc oxide,** an oxide of zinc, an antiseptic.

zing *n.* **1,** a high-pitched humming sound. **2,** (*Colloq.*) vitality; energy. **—interj.** an exclamation of enthusiasm. **—v.i.** make a high-pitched humming sound.

zin′ni·a (zin′ē-ə) *n.* a plant having showy yellow or red flowers.

Zi′on (zī′ən) *n.* **1,** a hill in Jerusalem, designated as holy. **2,** heaven.

Zi′on·ism (zī′ə-niz-əm) *n.* advocacy of the establishment and support of a Jewish nation (now Israel) in Palestine. **—Zi′onist,** *n.*

zip *n.* **1,** the sound of a bullet in flight. **2,** energy; vim. **3,** (*Colloq.*) zero. **—v.i.** [**zipped,** **zip′ping**] sound or move with a zip. **—v.t.** fasten with a zipper.

ZIP code 1, [also, **ZIP code number**] a special 5-digit number assigned by the U.S. Postal Service to each of the many postal districts throughout the U.S. to speed the distribution of mail. **2,** the entire system of ZIP code numbers.

zip′per (zip′ər) *n.* a fastening device that causes two strips of metal or plastic studs to interlock.

zip′py (-ē) *adj.* pert; lively. **—zip′pi·ness,** *n.*

zir′con (zėr′kon) *n.* a common silicate mineral used as a gem.

zir·co′ni·um (zėr-kō′nē-əm) *n.* a metallic element, no. 40, symbol Zr.

zith′er (zith′ər) *n.* a musical instrument comprising a number of strings stretched over a flat sounding board, played with the fingers or a plectrum.

zlo′ty (zlâ′tē) *n.* [*pl.* **-tys**] the monetary unit of Poland, formerly worth about .20 dollar.

zo·di′ac″ (zō′dē-ak″) *n.* the imaginary belt in the sky in which lie the apparent paths of the sun, moon, and principal planets. There are twelve signs of the zodiac:

Aquarius (*Water Bearer*)	**Virgo** (*Virgin*)
	Libra (*Balance*)
Pisces (*Fish*)	**Scorpio** (*Scorpion*)
Aries (*Ram*)	
Taurus (*Bull*)	**Sagittarius** (*Archer*)
Gemini (*Twins*)	
Cancer (*Crab*)	**Capricorn** (*Goat*)
Leo (*Lion*)	

zo·di′a·cal (zō-dī′ə-kəl) *adj.* pert. to the zodiac.

zo′ic (zō′ik) *adj.* pert. to animal life.

zom′bi (zom′bē) *n.* **1,** a snake deity worshiped by certain tribes of Afr. and the W.I. **2,** a dead body brought to life. Also, **zom′bie.**

zone (zōn) *n.* **1,** a part of the surface of a sphere lying between two parallel planes. **2,** any of the five arbitrary divisions of the surface of the earth: North Frigid, North Temperate, Torrid, South Temperate, South Frigid. **3,** region; district; any distinct, defined, or delimited area. **—v.t. 1,** encircle like a belt. **2,** divide into or mark with zones. **—zon′al,** *adj.*

zonked (zänkt) *adj.* (*Slang*) under or as if under the influence of a hallucinogenic drug. **—zonk,** *v.t.*

zoo *n.* an enclosure where live animals are kept for public exhibition.

zo·o- (zō-ə) *pref.* pert. to living animals.

zo″o·log′i·cal (zō″ə-loj′i-kəl) *adj.* pert. to zoology. **—zoological garden,** a zoo.

zo·ol′o·gy (zō-ol′ə-jē) *n.* the general science of animal life. **—zo·ol′o·gist,** *n.*

zoom *v.i. & t.* fly (an aircraft) on a sudden upward course. **—zoom lens** [also, **var′i·fo″cal lens**], a motion-picture or television camera lens permitting change in the image size without loss of focus.

zo′o·phyte″ (zō′ə-fīt″) *n.* an animal that looks like a plant, as a coral. **—zo″o·phyt′ic** (-fit′ik) *adj.*

zoot suit (*Slang*) an extreme costume popular during the 1940's among young male jitterbugs.

zor′il (zôr′il) *n.* a South African animal resembling the skunk.

Zo″ro·as′tri·an (zō″rə-as′trē-ən) *adj.* pert. to Zoroaster, Persian prophet of 1000 B.C., his religion or philosophy.

Zou·ave′ (zoo-äv′) *n.* formerly, a brightly-dressed French infantryman.

zounds (zowndz) *interj.* of surprise.

zo′ys·ia (zō′is-ē-ə) *n.* a type of grass.

zuc·chet′to (zû-ket′tō) *n.* [*pl.* **-tos**] a small round skullcap worn by Rom. Cath. clergymen.

zuc·chi′ni (zû-kē′nē) *n.* [*pl.* **-nis**] a variety of summer squash, used as a vegetable.

Zu′lu (zoo′loo) *adj. & n.* of or pert. to a So. African people, their language, etc.

zwie′back″ (tswē′bäk″) *n.* a kind of toasted bread prepared in small pieces.

Zwing′li·an (zwing′lē-ən) *adj.* pert. to Ulrich Zwingli, 1484–1531, Swiss Protestant reformer.

zyme (zīm) *n.* the specific principle regarded as the cause of a zymotic disease.

zy·mo- (zī-mō) *pref.* pert. to leaven.

zy·mo′sis (zī-mō′sis) *n.* **1,** an infectious or contagious disease. **2,** fermentation as a supposed cause of disease. **—zy·mot′ic** (-mot′ik) *adj.*

zy′mur·gy (zī′mər-jē) *n.* (*Chem.*) the science and study of fermentation, as in brewing.

ABBREVIATIONS
Including all abbreviations used in this
Dictionary.

A.A., Alcoholics Anonymous.

AAA, American Automobile Association.

A. & M., Agricultural and Mechanical.

A.A.U., Amateur Athletic Union.

A.B., Bachelor of Arts.

ABA, American Bar Association; American Basketball Association.

abbr., abbreviation.

ABC, American Broadcasting Company; Argentina, Brazil, and Chile.

A.C., alternating current; before Christ.

A/C, account.

acct., account; accountant.

A.D., Anno Domini; active duty.

A.D.A., Americans for Democratic Action.

adj., adjective; (*cap.*) Adjutant.

Adm., Admiral.

adv., adverb.

advt., advertisement.

a.e., aet., aetat., aetatis, (*Lat.*) aged.

AEC, Atomic Energy Commission.

AEF, American Expeditionary Force.

aero., aeronautical; aeronautics.

A.F. & A.M., Ancient Free and Accepted Masons.

AFB, Air Force Base.

AFC, automatic frequency control.

A.F.L., A.F. of L., American Federation of Labor.

Afr., Africa, African.

A.F.T., American Federation of Teachers.

AID, Agency for International Development.

AK, Ak., Alaska.

A.k.a., also known as; alias.

AL, Al., Ala., Alabama.

Alas., Alaska.

A.L.P., American Labor Party.

Alta., Alberta.

AM, amplitude modulation. **A.M.,** Master of Arts. **A.M., a.m.,** ante meridiem.

A.M.A., American Medical Association.

Amer., America; American.

AMG, Allied Military Government.

amp., ampere; amperage.

AMVETS, American Veterans of World War II.

anat., anatomical; anatomy.

anon., anonymous.

AP, Associated Press.

APB, all points bulletin.

APO, Army Post Office.

Apr., April.

apt(s)., apartment(s).

AR, Ar., Arkansas.

A.R.C., American (National) Red Cross.

Arch., Archbishop; (*l.c.*) architect.

archit., architect; architecture.

arith., arithmetic; arithmetical.

Ariz., Arizona.

Ark., Arkansas.

art., article.

AS, American Samoa.

A-S., A.S., Anglo-Saxon.

A.S.C., American Society of Cinematographers.

ASCAP, American Society of Composers, Authors, and Publishers.

ASEAN, Association of Southeast Asian Nations.

assn., association.

assoc., associate; association.

asst., assistant.

Assyr., Assyrian.

astron., astronomy.

Atl., Atlantic.

att., atty., attorney.

Aug., August.

Aus., Austl., Australia.

Aust., Austria; Austrian.

aux., auxiliary.

A.V., Authorized Version (of the Bible); audiovisual.

av., average.

avdp., avoirdupois.

Ave., Av., Avenue.

AWOL, absent without official leave.

AZ, Az., Arizona.

B.A., Bachelor of Arts; Buenos Aires.

Bart., Bt., Baronet.

B.B.A., Bachelor of Business Administration.

B.B.C., British Broadcasting Corporation.

Bbl., barrel; barrels.

B.C., British Columbia; before Christ.

bd., board.

BEF, British Expeditionary Force or Forces.

Belg., Belgian; Belgium.

Benj., Benjamin.

b.f., boldface (type).

B.F.A., Bachelor of Fine Arts.

Bib., Bible: Biblical.

b.i.d., twice a day (in prescription).

biol., biology.

B/L, bill of lading.

bldg., blg., building.

Blvd., Boulevard.

BLT, bacon, lettuce, and tomato (sandwich).

BMI, Broadcast Music, Inc.

bn., battalion.

bot., botany.

B.P.O.E., Benevolent and Protective Order of Elks.

Braz., Brazil; Brazilian.

Brig., Brigadier.
Brit., British.
bro., bros., brother(s).
B.S., B.Sc., Bachelor of Science.
B/S, bill of sale.
B.S.A., Boy Scouts of America.
bsh., bushel; bushels.
B.T.U., British thermal unit(s).
Bulg., Bulgaria; Bulgarian.
B.V., B.V.M., Blessed Virgin (Mary).
BX, base exchange.
B.W.I., British West Indies.

C., Celsius; centigrade.
C.A., Central America; Coast Artillery; chartered accountant.
CA, Ca., California.
ca., circ., circa (about).
CAA, Civil Aeronautics Authority.
CAB, Civil Aeronautics Board.
Cal., Calif. California.
Can., Canada; Canadian.
cap., capital(ized).
Capt., Captain.
car., carat.
CARE, Cooperative for American Relief Everywhere.
CATV, Community Antenna Television.
CB, citizens band.
C.B., Companion of the Bath.
CBC, Canadian Broadcasting Corporation.
C.B.I., China, Burma, India.
CBS, Columbia Broadcasting System.
c.c., carbon copy; cubic centimeters.
CCC, Civilian Conservation Corps; Commodity Credit Corporation.
CCTV, closed-circuit television.
cd., cord.
Cdr., commander.
C.E., Civil Engineer.
cent., centigrade; centimeter; century.
CENTO, Central Treaty Organization.
cert., certificate, certify.
CETA, Comprehensive Employment and Training Act.
cf., compare; (Baseball) center fielder.
C.G., Coast Guard.
Ch., China; Chinese; church; (*l.c.*) chapter.
Chas., Charles.
Ch.E., Chemical Engineer.
chem., chemistry; chemical; chemist.
chm., chairman.
Chr., Christian.
Chron., Chronicles.
CIA, Central Intelligence Agency.
CID, Criminal Investigation Department.
Cie., (*Fr.*) company.
C. in C., Commander in Chief.
C.I.O., Congress of Industrial Organizations.
cit., cited; citation.
ck., check.
cl., centiliter(s).
CLU, Civil Liberties Union.
cm., centimeter(s).
Cmdr., commander.

CO, conscientious objector; Colorado.
C.O., Commanding Officer.
Co., company; county; Colorado.
c/o, care of.
C.O.D., cash on delivery; collect on delivery.
Col., Colonel; Columbia; Colorado.
colloq., colloquial.
Colo., Colorado.
Com., Commander; Commodore; commerce.
comp., comparative.
Comr., Commissioner.
Cong., Congregational; Congress; Congressional.
conj. conjunction.
Conn., Connecticut.
cont., continued.
contr., contract; contralto.
Cor., Corinthians.
CORE, Congress of Racial Equality.
Corp., Corporal; Corporation.
C.P.A., Certified Public Accountant.
CPI, consumer price index.
Cpl., Corporal.
C.P.O., Chief Petty Officer.
C. R., Costa Rica.
cr., credit; creditor.
C.S.A., Confederate States of America.
C.S.T., Central Standard Time.
CT, Ct., Connecticut.
ct., cent(s); carat.
cu., cubic.
cwt., hundredweight.
CYO, Catholic Youth Organization
CZ, C. Z., Canal Zone (Panama).
Czech., Czechoslovakia.

D.A., District Attorney.
D.A.R., Daughters of the American Revolution.
DAV, Disabled American Veterans.
dB, decibel.
D.C., District of Columbia, direct current.
D.C.M., Distinguished Conduct Medal.
D.D., Doctor of Divinity.
D.D.S., Doctor of Dental Surgery.
DDT, dichloro-diphenyl-trichloroethane (an insecticide).
DE, De., Delaware.
Dec., December.
Del., Delaware.
Dem., Democratic; Democrat.
Den., Denmark
dept., department.
Deut., Deuteronomy.
DEW, distant early warning.
DFC, Distinguished Flying Cross.
DFM, Distinguished Flying Medal.
dial., dialect(ical).
dir., director.
dl, deciliter; deciliters.
D.Litt., Doctor of Letters.
dm, decimeter; decimeters.
DMZ, demilitarized zone.

DNA, deoxyribonucleic acid.
do., ditto.
DOA, dead on arrival.
doz., dozen; dozens.
DP, displaced person.
dpt., department.
Dr., Doctor; (*l.c.*) debit; debtor; dram.
D.Sc., Doctor of Science.
DSC, Distinguished Service Cross.
DSO, Distinguished Service Order.
DST, Daylight Saving Time.
d.t., delirium tremens.
D.V.M., Doctor of Veterinary Medicine.
dwt., pennyweight.
dz., dozen; dozens.

E., east.
ECA, Economic Cooperation Administration.
Eccl., Ecclesiastes.
econ., economics.
Ecua., Ecuador.
ed., editor(ial).
EDT, Eastern daylight time.
Edw., Edward.
E.E., Electrical Engineer.
EEC, European Economic Community.
EEG, electroencephalogram.
EFTA, European Free Trade Association.
Eg., Egypt; Egyptian.
e.g., for example.
EKG, electrocardiogram.
Eliz., Elizabeth; Elizabethan.
ENE, east-northeast.
Eng., England; English.
engr., engineer.
Ens., Ensign.
EPA, Environmental Protection Agency.
ERA, earned-run average; Equal Rights Amendment.
ESE, east-southeast.
ESP, extrasensory perception.
esp., especially.
Esq., Esqr., Esquire.
EST, Eastern Standard Time.
Est., Estonia; established.
Esth., Esther.
et al., and others.
etc., et cetera.
Eth., Ethiopia.
ETO, European Theater of Operations.
et seq., and the following.
Eu., Europ., European.
EVA, extravehicular activity.
Ex., Exodus.
Ez., Ezr., Ezra.
Ezek., Ezekiel.

F., Fahrenheit; Fellow.
F. & A. M., Free and Accepted Masons.
FAO, Food and Agriculture Organization.
FBI, Federal Bureau of Investigation.
FCA, Farm Credit Administration.
FCC, Federal Communications Commission.

FDA, Food and Drug Administration.
FDIC, Federal Deposit Insurance Corporation.
Feb., February.
Fed., Federal.
fem., feminine.
F.E.T., Federal Excise Tax.
ff., following pages.
F.F.V., First Families of Virginia.
FHA, Federal Housing Administration.
F.I.C.A., Federal Insurance Contributions Act.
fig., figuratively.
Fin., Finland; Finnish.
FL, Fl., Fla., Florida.
Flem., Flemish.
FM, frequency modulation.
fn., footnote.
f.o.b., free on board.
F.O.E., Fraternal Order of Eagles *or* Elks.
FPC, Federal Power Commission.
FPO, Fleet Post Office.
Fr., Father; French.
Fri., Friday.
ft., feet; foot; fort.
FTC, Federal Trade Commission.
fwd., forward.

G, general audiences (a motion picture rating).
GA, Ga., Georgia.
Gal., Galatians.
gal., gallon; gallons.
GAO, General Accounting Office.
G. B., Great Britain.
gent., gentleman.
Geo., George.
geom., geometrical; geometry.
Ger., German; Germany.
GHQ, General Headquarters.
GI, General (or Government) Issue; a private soldier.
Gk., Greek.
gm., gram; grams.
GMT, Greenwich mean time.
GNP, gross national product.
G.O.P., Grand Old Party (Republican party).
Gov., governor.
Govt., government.
G.P., general practitioner.
G.P.O., Government Printing Office.
GPU, (formerly) Soviet Secret Police.
gr., grain, gross.
gram., grammar.
Gr. Br., Gr. Brit., Great Britain.
G.S.A., Girl Scouts of America.
GU, Guam.

Hag., Haggai.
hdqrs., headquarters.
hdw., hardware.
Heb., Hebrew(s).
HI, H.I., Hawaiian Islands.
hist., historical.
H. J., here lies.

H. M., His (Her) Majesty.
H.M.S., His (Her) Majesty's Ship.
Hon., Honorable.
hp, horsepower.
HQ, headquarters.
H.R., House of Representatives.
hr., hour; hours.
H.R.H., His (Her) Royal Highness.
ht., height.
Hz, hertz.

I., Island(s); Isle(s).
IA, Ia., Iowa.
ibid., in the same place.
IC, integrated circuit.
ICBM, Intercontinentl Ballistic Missile.
ICC, Interstate Commerce Commission.
I.D., identification.
ID, Ida., Idaho.
i.e., that is.
IHS, Jesus.
IL, Il., Ill., Illinois.
ILGWU. International Ladies' Garment Workers' Union.
I.L.O. International Labor Organization.
IMF, International Monetary Fund.
in., inch: inches.
IN, In., Ind., Indiana.
inc., inclosure; (*cap.*) incorporated.
incl., inclusive.
inf., infinitive.
I.N.R.I., Jesus of Nazareth, King of the Jews.
INS, International News Service.
inst., the present month.
interj., interjection.
intl., international.
I.O.O.F., Independent Order of Odd Fellows.
I.O.U., I owe you.
I.Q., intelligence quotient.
Ire., Ireland.
IRA, Irish Republican Army; individual retirement account.
IRO, International Refugee Organization.
IRBM, Intermediate Range Ballistic Missile.
IRS, Internal Revenue Service.
Is., is., island; islands; (*cap.*) Isaiah.
ISBN, International Standard Book Number.
Ital., Italian; (*l.c.*) italic (type).
ITO, International Trade Organization.
IUD, intrauterine device.
IWW, Industrial Workers of the World.

Jan., January.
Jap., Japan; Japanese.
Jas., James.
jct., junction.
JDL, Jewish Defense League.
j.g., junior grade.
Jno., John.
Jos., Joseph; Josiah.
Josh., Joshua.
J.P., Justice of the Peace.
jr., junior.

Judg., Judges.
JV, junior varsity.

K, king (Chess); thousand.
Kan., Kans., Kas., Kansas.
K.C., King's Counsel; Knights of Columbus.
kc., kilocycle(s).
K.G., Knight (of the Order) of the Garter.
kg., keg(s); kilogram(s).
kilo., kilogram(s); kilometer(s).
K.K.K., Ku Klux Klan.
km., kilometer; kilometers.
K.O., knockout.
K. of P., Knights of Pythias.
KP, kitchen police.
K.T., Knight Templar.
Kt., knight.
kw., kilowatt(s).
KY, Ky., Kentucky.

L, large.
LA, La., Louisiana.
Lab., Labrador.
Lam., Lamentations.
Lat., Latin.
lb., pound(s).
LC, landing craft; **LS,** landing ship; **LCI,** landing craft, infantry; **LCP,** landing craft, personnel; **LST,** landing ship, tank; etc.
l. c., lower case (type).
LCD, liquid crystal diode.
LED, light-emitting diode.
LM, LEM, lunar (excursion) module.
L. I., Long Island.
Lieut., Lt., Lieutenant.
Litt.D., Doctor of Letters.
LL.B., Bachelor of Laws.
LL.D., Doctor of Laws.
LNG, liquefied natural gas.
L.O.O.M., Loyal Order of Moose.
LP, long play.
LSD, lysergic acid diethylamide (a hallucinogenic drug).
Ltd., Limited.

M, medium.
M., Monsieur; meridies, midday.
m., meter(s); noon.
MA, Ma., Mass., Massachusetts.
M.A., Master of Arts.
Macc., Maccabees.
Maj., Major.
Man., Manitoba.
Mar., March.
masc., masculine.
MASH, mobile army surgical hospital.
math., mathematics.
M.B.A., Master of Business Administration.
M.C., Master of Ceremonies; Member of Congress.
M.D., Doctor of Medicine.
MD, Md., Maryland.
mdse., merchandise.

ME, Me., Maine.
M.E., Methodist Episcopal; Mechanical Engineer.
mech., mechanics.
med., medicine.
Medit., Mediterranean.
memo., memorandum.
Messrs:, Messieurs.
meteorol., meteorology.
Mex., Mexican.
mfg., manufacturing.
mfr., manufacturer.
Mgr., Manager; Monsignor.
MI, Mi., Mich., Michigan.
MIA, missing in action.
Mic., Micah.
mil., military.
min., mineral; mineralogy.
Minn., Minnesota.
MIRV, multiple independent re-entry vehicle.
misc., miscellaneous.
Miss., Mississippi.
Mlle., Mademoiselle.
MM., Messieurs.
mm., millimeter(s).
Mme., Madame.
MN, Mn., Minnesota.
MO, Mo., Missouri.
M.O., money order.
mo., month(s).
Mon., Monday.
Mont., Montana.
M.P., military police; Member of Parliament.
m.p.h., miles per hour.
Mr., Mister.
Mrs., Mistress.
MS, Ms., Mississippi.
Ms., a title for an unmarried woman, or for one whose marital status is unknown.
ms, manuscript.
MSG, monosodium glutamate.
Msgr., Monsignor.
M/Sgt., Master Sergeant.
M.S.T., Mountain Standard Time.
MT, Montana.
Mt., mountain; Montana.
MVD, the Soviet Ministry of Internal Affairs.
MVP, most valuable player.
myth., mythology.

n., noun.
N., north.
N.A.A.C.P., National Association for the Advancement of Colored People.
NAB, National Association of Broadcasters.
N.A.M., National Association of Manufacturers.
NASA, National Aeronautics and Space Administration.
natl., national.
NATO, North Atlantic Treaty Organization.

naut., nautical.
NB, Nb., Nebraska.
N. B., New Brunswick; note well.
NBA, National Basketball Association.
NBC, National Broadcasting Company.
NC, N.C., North Carolina.
N.C.A.A., National Collegiate Athletic Association.
NCO, non-commissioned officer.
ND, N.D., North Dakota.
NE, northeast.
N. E., New England.
Nebr., Neb., Nebraska.
Neh., Nehemiah.
NET, National Educational Television.
Neth., Netherlands.
Nev., Nevada.
NFL, National Football League.
N. F., Newf., Newfoundland.
NG, no good.
NH, N.H., New Hampshire.
NHL, National Hockey League.
NJ, N.J., New Jersey.
NKVD, the Soviet Secret Police.
NLRB, National Labor Relations Board.
NM, N.M., New Mexico.
NNE, north-northeast.
NNW, north-northwest.
No., north; northern; number.
nom., nominative.
Nor., Norwegian; Norway.
Nov., November.
NOW, negotiable order of withdrawal.
N.P., no protest.
NRA, National Recovery Administration; National Rifle Association.
N. S., New Style; Nova Scotia.
NSA, National Student Association; National Security Agency.
NSF, National Science Foundation.
N. T., New Testament.
NTA, sodiumnitrilotriacetate, used in some detergents as a substitute for phosphates.
Num., Numbers.
NV, Nevada.
NW, northwest.
NY, N.Y., New York.
N.Y.C., New York City.
N.Z., New Zealand.

O., Ohio.
OAS, Organization of American States.
OAU, Organization of African Unity.
ob., he (she) died.
Obad., Obadiah.
O.B.E., Officer (of the Order) of the British Empire.
obj., objective; object.
OCS, Officer Candidate School.
Oct., October.
O.D., Officer of the Day; overdraft; olive drab (uniforms).
O.E.D., Oxford English Dictionary.
OEO, Office of Economic Opportunity.

O. E. S., Order of the Eastern Star.
OH, Oh., Ohio.
OK, Ok., Okla., Oklahoma.
Ont., Ontario.
OPA, Office of Price Administration.
OR, Or., Ore., Oreg., Oregon.
orch., orchestra.
orig., original(ly).
O.S., Old Style; ordinary seaman.
OSS, Office of Strategic Services.
O. T., Old Testament.
OTB, off-track betting.
OTC, one-stop inclusive tour charter.
OTS, Officers' Training School.
OWI, Office of War Information.
Ox., Oxford.
oz., ounce(s).

PA, Pa., Pennsylvania.
PA, public address.
P.A., Purchasing Agent; Press Agent.
Pac., Pacif., Pacific.
p. adj., participial adjective.
Pan., Panama.
par., paragraph; parallel.
Para., Paraguay.
paren., parentheses.
part., participle.
pathol., pathology.
pat. pend., patent pending.
payt., payment.
PBS, Public Broadcasting Service.
PBX, private branch (telephone) exchange.
pc., piece.
p. c., per cent; post card.
PCB, polychlorinated biphenyl (a poisonous industrial chemical).
PCP, phencyclidine (a hallucinogenic drug).
pct., percent.
P.D., Police Department.
pd., paid.
P.D.Q., (slang) pretty damn quick.
P.D.T., Pacific daylight time.
P.E.N., (International Association of) Poets, Playwrights, Editors, Essayists and Novelists.
Penn., Penns., Pennsylvania.
Pers., Persia; Persian.
pert., pertaining.
Peruv., Peruvian.
Pfc., Private, First Class.
PG, parental guidance recommended (a motion picture rating).
PGA, Professional Golfers' Association.
phar., pharm., pharmaceutical; pharmacopoeia; pharmacy.
Ph.B., Bachelor of Philosophy.
Ph.D., Doctor of Philosophy.
Phil., Philemon; Philip; Philippians; Philippine.
Phila., Philadelphia.
photog., photography.
P. I., Philippine Islands.
pkg., package(s).
pkwy., parkway.

pl., plural.
PLO, Palestine Liberation Organization.
plupf., pluperfect.
P.M., p.m., post meridiem; post-mortem; (*cap.*) Prime Minister; Postmaster.
P.O., post office.
POE, port of entry.
Pol., Poland; Polish.
Port., Portugal; Portuguese.
pos., possessive.
POW, prisoner of war.
p.p., parcel post; past participle; postpaid.
P.P.S., post postscriptum.
P.Q., Province of Quebec.
PR, P. R., Puerto Rico; public relations.
pr., pair.
pref., prefix.
prep., preposition; preparatory.
pret., preterit.
Prof., professor.
pron., pronoun.
Prot., Protestant.
pro tem., for the time being.
Prov., Proverbs; (*l.c.*) province.
prox., (*Lat.*) proximo; next (month).
P.S., postscript.
Ps., Psalm(s).
P.S.T., Pacific Standard Time.
psychonanal., psychoanalysis.
pt., point.
P.T.A., Parent-Teacher Association.
PT boat, patrol torpedo boat.
p.t.o., please turn over (the page).
Pvt., Private.
PVC, polyvinyl chloride.
PWA, Public Works Administration.
PX, Post Exchange.

Q., Quebec.
Q.E.D., which was to be demonstrated.
QMC, Quartermaster Corps.
qt., quart.
qty., quantity.
Que., Quebec.
q.v., which see.

R, restricted (a motion picture rating).
RAF, Royal Air Force.
R & B, rhythm and blues.
R & D, research and development.
R. C., Red Cross; Reserve Corps; Roman Catholic.
RCAF, Royal Canadian Air Force.
RCMP, Royal Canadian Mounted Police.
R.D., Rural Delivery.
REM, rapid eye movement.
Rep., Republican; Representative.
Rev., Revelation; Reverend.
R.F.D., Rural Free Delivery.
RI, R.I., Rhode Island.
R.I.P., rest in peace.
rm., ream (paper); room.
R.N., Registered Nurse.
RNA, ribonucleic acid.
Robt., Robert.

Rom., Roman; Romans.
Rom. Cath., Roman Catholic.
ROTC, Reserve Officers' Training Corps.
r.p.m., revolutions per minute.
R.R., railroad; Right Reverend.
RRSP, Registered Retirement Savings Plan.
R.S.V., Revised Standard Version (of the Bible).
R.S.V.P., please reply.
rt., right.
Rum., Rumania; Rumanian.
Rus., Russ., Russia; Russian.
RV, recreational vehicle.
Rx, (*Med.*) prescription.
Ry., Railway.

S., small.
S., south.
S.A., South Africa; South America; corporation; (*Slang*) sex appeal.
SAC., Strategic Air Command.
SALT, strategic arms limitation treaty.
Salv., Salvador; Salvator.
SAM, surface-to-air missile.
Sam., Saml., Samuel.
S.A.R., Sons of the American Revolution.
Sask., Saskatchewan.
Sat., Saturday; Saturn.
sc., science.
SC, S.C., South Carolina.
Scot., Scottish; Scotland.
SD, S.D., South Dakota.
SDA, Students for Democratic Action; Seventh-Day Adventist.
SDS, Students for a Democratic Society.
SE, southeast.
SEATO, Southeast Asia Treaty Organization.
SEC, Securities and Exchange Commission.
Sept., September.
SF, sf, science fiction.
sgd., signed.
Sgt., Sergeant.
SHAEF, Supreme Headquarters Allied Expeditionary Forces.
Shak., Shakespeare.
S. I., Staten Island.
Sib., Siberia; Siberian.
Sic., Sicily; Sicilian.
Sig., sig., signor.
sing., singular.
S. J., Society of Jesus.
Slav., Slavic; Slavonian.
SLR, single-lens reflex (camera).
So., south; southern.
sop., soprano.
SOS, a radio distress signal.
SP, shore patrol.
Span., Sp., Spain; Spaniard; Spanish.
SPAR, Women's Coast Guard Reserves.
S.P.C.A., Society for Prevention of Cruelty to Animals.
S.P.C.C., Society for Prevention of Cruelty to Children.
sq., square.

sqq., and the following ones.
Sr., Senior; Señor; Sister.
Sra., Señora.
SRO, standing room only.
SS., Saints.
S.S., steamship.
SSE, south-southeast.
S/Sgt., Staff Sergeant.
S.S.R., Soviet Socialist Republic.
SSS, Selective Service System.
SST, supersonic transport.
SSW, south-southwest.
St., Saint (*fem.* **Ste.**); Strait; Street.
STOL, short takeoff and landing (aircraft).
suf., suff., suffix.
Sun., Sund., Sunday.
superl., superlative.
supt., superintendent.
S.W., southwest.
Swed., Sweden; Swedish.
Swtz., Swit., Switz., Switzerland.
Syr., Syria.

TB, t.b., tuberculosis.
tbsp., tablespoon.
TD, touchdown.
Tenn., Tennessee.
Tex., Texas.
THC, tetra-hydrocannabinol (the principal chemical in marijuana).
Th.D., Doctor of Theology.
Theo., Theodore; Theodosia.
Thos., Thomas.
Thurs., Thursday.
Tim., Timothy.
TKO, technical knockout.
TLC, tender loving care.
TN, Tn., Tennessee.
T.N., trade name.
tp., twp., township.
Tr., Troop.
treas., treasurer; treasury.
tsp., teaspoon.
TT, Trust Territories.
Tues., Tuesday.
TV, television.
TVA, Tennessee Valley Authority.
TX, Tx., Texas.

U.A.W., United Auto, Aircraft, or Agricultural Implements Workers.
u.c., upper case (type).
U.D.C., United Daughters of the Confederacy.
UFO, unidentified flying object.
UHF, ultrahigh frequency.
U. K., United Kingdom.
Ukr., Ukraine.
UL, Underwriters Laboratories.
ult., last month.
U.M.W., United Mine Workers.
U.N., United Nations.
UNESCO, United Nations Educational, Scientific and Cultural Organization.
UNICEF, United Nations Children's Fund.

UNRRA, United Nations Relief and Reha-
bilitation Administration..
UP, United Press.
UPS, United Parcel Service.
Uru., Uruguay.
U. S., United States (of America).
U. S. A., Union of South Africa; United
States Army; United States of America.
USAF, United States Air Force.
USCG, United States Coast Guard.
USES, United States Employment Service.
USIA, United States Information Agency.
U.S.M.A. United States Military Academy.
USMC, United States Marine Corps.
USN, United States Navy.
U.S.N.A., United States Naval Academy.
USNR, United States Naval Reserve.
USO, United Service Organizations.
U.S.P., United States Pharmacopoeia.
U.S.S., United States Ship, or Steamer.
U.S.S.R., Union of Soviet Socialist Re-
publics.
usu., usually.
UT, Ut., Utah.

v., verb.
VA, Veterans' Administration.
VA, Va., Virginia.
VAT, value-added tax.
V.C., Victoria Cross; Vietcong.
V.D., venereal disease.
Venez., Venezuela.
vet., veteran; veterinarian.
V.F.W., Veterans of Foreign Wars.
VHF, very high frequency.
VI, V. I., Virgin Islands.
v.i., verb intransitive.
V.I.P., very important personage.
VISTA, Volunteers in Service to America.
vis., namely.
V.M.D., Doctor of Veterinary Medicine.
VOA, Voice of America.
vol., volume.
V.P., Vice-President.
V.S., Veterinary Surgeon.
vs., versus.
VT, Vt., Vermont.
v.t., verb transitive.
VTOL, vertical takeoff and landing (air-
craft).

W., west.
w/, with.
WA, Wa., Washington.
WAAC, Women's Auxiliary Army Corps.

WAAF, Women's Auxiliary Air Force.
WAC, Women's Army Corps.
WAF, Women in the Air Force.
Wash., Washington.
WASP, Women's Air Force Service Pilots;
(usu. offensive) White Anglo-Saxon Pro-
testant.
WATS, wide area telephone service.
WAVES, Women for Volunteer Emergency
Service (U. S. Navy).
W.C., WC, water closet.
W. C. T. U., Women's Christian Temper-
ance Union.
Wed., Wednesday.
WHO, World Health Organization.
W. I., West Indies.
WI, Wi., Wis., Wisc., Wisconsin.
wk., week; work.
Wm., William.
WNW, west-northwest.
W.O., Warrant Officer.
w/o, without.
WPA, Works Progress Administration.
WPB, War Production Board.
w.p.m., words per minute.
WRENS, Women's Royal Naval Service.
WSW, west-southwest.
WV, Wv., W.Va., West Virginia.
WW, World War.
WY, Wy., Wyo., Wyoming.

X, restricted to adults only (a motion pic-
ture rating).
XL, extra large.
Xmas, Christmas.

Y., Young Men's Christian Association.
yd., yard(s).
Y.M.C.A., Young Men's Christian Asso-
ciation.
Y.M.H.A., Young Men's Hebrew Asso-
ciation.
yr., year(s).
Y.T., Yukon Territory.
Yuc., Yucatan.
Y.W.C.A., Young Women's Christian
Association.
Y.W.H.A., Young Women's Hebrew Asso-
ciation.

Zech., Zechariah.
Zeph., Zephaniah.
ZIP, Zone Improvement Plan.
ZPG, zero population growth.

GAZETTEER

An otherwise unidentified entry in the Gazetteer denotes an independent or self-governing country. A dependency is indicated by the name of the mother country, in parentheses. The following special abbreviations are used: *Fr. C.*, French Community; *Br. C. of N.*, (British) Commonwealth of Nations; and *Trust.*, Trusteeship. Population figures for the U.S.S.R. are based on 1981 estimates; for the United States, the 1980 census has been used, and for Canada, the 1981 census. United States Government and United Nations reports or estimates have been followed for most other countries, and for the majority of countries the estimates are as of July 1979. For some cities, population figures are also given for the urbanized area (urb.), which includes the city proper and its suburban fringe.

Abidjan (ä″bi-jän′) City (cap. of Ivory Coast) pop. 700,000.

Abu Dhabi (ä′boo *thä*′bē) City (cap. United Arab Emirates) pop. 72,000.

Abyssinia, see *Ethiopia*.

Accra (ə-krä′) City (cap. of Ghana) pop. 615,800.

Addis Ababa (ad′is ab′ə-bə) City (cap. of Ethiopia) pop. 950,000.

Adelaide (ad′ə-lād) City (Australia) pop. 742,300.

Aden (a′dən) City (cap. of Yemen) pop. 150,000.

Admiralty Is. part of Papua New Guinea, 820 sq. mi. pop. 25,000.

Adriatic Sea (a″drē-at′ik) between Italy & Yugoslavia 50,000 sq. mi.

Aegean Sea (ē-jē′ən) between Greece & Turkey, 40,000 sq. mi.

Afghanistan (af-gan′is-tan″) 250,000 sq. mi., pop. 14,702,000, cap. Kabul.

Africa (af′ri-kə) Continent, 11,530,000 sq. mi., pop. 458,231,000.

Ahmedabad (ä′məd-ä-bäd) City (India) pop. 1,720,000.

Akron (ak′rən) City (Ohio) pop. 237,177.

Alabama (al″-ə-ba′mə) State (U.S.) 50,767 sq. mi., pop. 3,893,888, cap. Montgomery.

Alaska (ə-las′kə) State (U.S.) 570,833 sq. mi., pop. 401,851, cap. Juneau.

Albania (al-bān′yə) 11,096 sq. mi., pop. 2,626,000, cap. Tiranë (Tirana).

Albany (âl′bə-ne) City (cap. of N.Y.) pop. 101,727.

Alberta (al-bêr′tə) Prov. (Canada) 248,800 sq. mi., pop. 2,237,724, cap. Edmonton (ed′mən-tən) (pop. 532,246).

Albuquerque (al″boo-kêr′kē) City (N.M.) pop. 331,767.

Aleutian Is. (ə-loo′shən) (U.S.) 6,800 sq. mi., pop. 7,768.

Alexandria (al″ig-zạn′drē-ə) City (Egypt) pop. 2,200,000.

Algeria (al-jir′ē-ə) 851,284 sq. mi., pop. 18,249,000, cap. Algiers.

Algiers (*Fr.* Alger) (al-jirz′, al-zhe′) City (cap. of Algeria) pop. 903,530.

Amazon River (am′ə-zon) (Brazil) 4,000 miles.

Amman (äm′män) City (cap. of Jordan) pop. 655,000.

Amsterdam (am′stər-dam″) City (cap. of Netherlands) pop. 852,479.

Andaman Is. (an′də-man) (India) 2,508 sq. mi., pop. 128,000, cap. Port Blair (blär).

Andaman Sea (an′də-man) part of Bay of Bengal, 218,100 sq. mi.

Andorra (an-dôr′ə) 191 sq. mi., pop. 29,000, cap. Andorra la Velia (Andorra la Vieja) (lä vä′yä, lä vē-ä′hä), pop. 3,000.

Angola (ang-gō′lə) 481,351 sq. mi., pop. 6,606,000, cap. Luanda.

Ankara (ang′kə-rə) City (cap. of Turkey) pop. 1,701,000.

Annapolis (ə-nap′ə-lis) City (cap. of Md.) pop. 31,740.

Antananarivo (än-tä-nä-nä-rē′vō) City (cap. of Madagascar) pop. 366,500.

Antarctica (ant-ärk′ti-kə) Continent, 5,000,000 sq. mi.

Antigua (an-tē′gwə) I. (Br.) 108 sq. mi., pop. 74,000, cap. St. Johns.

Antilles, Greater Lesser (an-til′lēz) two groups of Caribbean islands.

Antilles, Netherlands (an-til′lēz) (Neth. 390 sq. mi., pop. 241,000, cap. Willemstad.

Antwerp (ant′wərp) City (Belgium) pop. 234,099.

Apia (ä-pē′ä) City (cap. of W. Samoa) pop. 25,480.

Arabia (ə-rā′bē-ə) Peninsula, SW Asia; includes Saudi Arabia, Yemen, Oman, Kuwait, Qatar, and Bahrain.

Arab Republic of Egypt (ē′jipt) 386,659 sq. mi., pop. 40,958,000, cap. Cairo.

Aral, Lake (ar′əl) (U.S.S.R.) 26,233 sq. mi.

Arctic Ocean (ärk′tik) 5,450,000 sq. mi.

Argentina (är-jən-tē′nə) 1,078,266 sq. mi., pop. 26,829,000, cap. Buenos Aires.

Arizona (ar-i-zō′nə) State (U.S.) 113,508 sq. mi., pop. 2,718,215, cap. Phoenix.

Arkansas (är′kən-sâ) State (U.S.) 52,078 sq. mi., pop. 2,286,435, cap. Little Rock.

tub, cūte, pûll; labəl; oil, owl, go, chip, she, thin, *th*en, sing, ink; *see p. 6*

Armenian S.S.R. (är-mē'nē-ən) (U.S.S.R.) 11,544 sq. mi., pop. 3,119,000, cap. Yerevan.

Ascension I. (ə-sen'shən) (Br.) 34 sq. mi., pop. 1,486, cap. Georgetown.

Asia (ā'zhə) Continent, 17,000,000 sq. mi., pop. (without U.S.S.R.) 2,582,861,000.

Asunción (ä-soon-syän') City (cap. of Paraguay) pop. 441,000.

Athens (ath'ənz) City (cap. of Greece) pop. 867,023, urb. 2,101,103.

Atlanta (at-lan'tə) City (cap. of Ga.) pop. 425,022, urb. 1,613,357.

Atlantic Ocean (at-lan'tik) 41,000,000 sq. mi., inc. Arctic Ocean.

Augusta (ə-gus'tə) City (cap. of Me.) pop. 21,819.

Austin (âs'tin) City (cap. of Tex.) pop. 345,496.

Australia (âs-trāl'yə) **1, Commonwealth of** (Br. C. of N.) 2,974,581 sq. mi., pop. 14,400,000, cap. Canberra. **2,** Continent, 2,948,366 sq. mi.

Austria (âs'trē-ə) 82,369 sq. mi., pop. 7,498,000, cap. Vienna.

Azerbaijan S.S.R. (ä"zər-bī-jän') (U.S.S.R.) 33,011 sq. mi., pop. 6,202,000, cap. Baku.

Azores Is. (ə-zōrz') (Port.) 890 sq. mi., pop. 336,100, cap. Ponta Delgada (pon'tə del-gä'də).

Azov, Sea of (ā'zof) No. of the Black Sea, 14,000 sq. mi.

Baffin Bay (baf'in) between Greenland & Baffin Island, approx. 180,000 sq. mi.

Baghdad (bag'dad) City (cap. of Iraq) pop. 2,200,000.

Bahama (bə-hä'mə; -hä'-) (Br. C. of N.) 4,375 sq. mi., pop. 233,000, cap. Nassau.

Bahrain Is. (bä'rān) 213 sq. mi., pop. 365,000 cap. Manama.

Baikal, Lake (bī-kal') (U.S.S.R.) 11,780 sq. mi.

Baku (bä-koo') City (cap. of Azerbaijan S.S.R.) pop. 1,046,000.

Balearic Is. (bal"ē-a'rik) (Sp.) 1,936 sq. mi., pop. 558,287, cap. Palma (päl'mä).

Balkan States (bâl'kən) Albania, Bulgaria, Greece, Rumania, Turkey & Yugoslavia.

Baltic Sea (bâl'tik) between Germany & Scandinavia, 163,000 sq. mi.

Baltimore (bâl'ti-môr') City (Md.) pop. 786,775, urb. 1,755,477.

Bamako (bä-mä-kä') City (cap. of Mali) pop. 300,000.

Bandar Seri Begawan (bän-där' se'rē be-gä'wän) City (cap. of Brunei) pop. 180,000.

Bangkok (bang'kok) City (cap. of Thailand) pop. 2,750,000.

Bangladesh [formerly **East Pakistan**] (bang'glə-desh") 54,501 sq. mi., pop. 88,092, cap. Dacca.

Bangui (bäng'gē) City (cap. of C. African Republic) pop. 235,000.

Banjul əban-jool') City, [formerly **Bathurst**] (cap. of Gambia) pop. 39,000.

Barbados (bär-bā'dōz) (Br. C. of N.) 166 sq. mi., pop. 273,000, cap. Bridgetown.

Barcelona (bär-sə-lō'nə) City (Spain) pop. 1,794,881.

Barents Sea (bar'ənts) No. of Scandinavia & U.S.S.R., 529,096 sq. mi.

Basse-Terre (bäs-tär') **1,** City (cap. of St. Kitts) pop. 15,726. **2,** City (cap. of Guadeloupe) pop. 14,000.

Basutoland (bə-soo'tō-land) see *Lesotho.*

Bathurst (bath'ērst) see **Banjul.**

Baton Rouge (bat'ən roozh) City (cap. of La.) pop. 219,419.

Bechuanaland (bech"û-ä'nə-land) see *Botswana.*

Beijing: see *Peking.*

Beirut [*Fr.* **Beyrouth**] (bā-root') City (cap. of Lebanon) pop. 900,000.

Belfast (bel'fast) City (cap. of No. Ireland) pop. 390,700.

Belgium (bel'jəm) 11,775 sq. mi., pop. 9,874,000, cap. Brussels.

Belgrade [*Serb.* **Beograd**] (bel'-grād, be' ə-gräd) City (cap. of Yugoslavia) pop. 820,000.

Belize (be-lēz') (Br.) 8,766 sq. mi., pop. 156,000, cap. Belmopan, (pop. 5,500).

Belo Horizonte (be"lō-rē-zon'te) City (Brazil) pop. 1,335,000.

Bengal, Bay of (ben-gäl') between India and Indo-China, approx. 650,000 sq. mi.

Benghazi (ben-gä'zē) City (cap. of Libya) pop. 137,295.

Benin (benēn') [formerly **Dahomey**] 42,471 sq. mi., pop. 3,379,000, cap. Porto-Novo.

Bering Sea (bir'ing) between Alaska & Siberia, 878,000 sq. mi.

Berlin (bēr-lin') City, pop. 3,221,000; East Berlin (cap. of East Germany) 1,086,000; West Berlin (West Germany) 2,135,000.

Bermuda (bər-mūd'ə) I. (Br.) 21 sq. mi., pop. 61,000 cap. Hamilton.

Bern (bērn) City (cap. of Switzerland) pop. 166,800.

Bhutan (boo"tän') 18,000 sq. mi., pop. 1,297,000 cap. Thimphu.

Birmingham 1, (bēr'ming-əm) City (England) pop. 1,074,900. **2,** (bēr'ming-ham") City (Ala.) pop. 284,413.

Biscay, Bay of (bis'kā) bay off coasts of France & Spain, 160,000 sq. mi.

Bismarck (biz'märk) City (cap. of N.D.) pop. 44,485.

Bismarck Archipelago (biz'märk) part of Papua New Guinea; includes New Britain, New Ireland, New Hanover, and the Admiralty Is.

---

fat, fāte, fär, fâre, fâll, ásk; met, hē, hêr, maybē; pin, pīne; not, nōte, ôr, tool

Bissau (bi-sow') City (cap. of Port. Guinea) pop. 71,000.

Black Sea, between Europe & Asia, 170,000 sq. mi.

Bogotá (bō″go-tä') City (cap. of Columbia) pop. 3,100,000.

Boise (bol'zē) City (cap. of Ida.) pop. 102,451.

Bolivia (bə-liv'é-ə) 412,777 sq. mi., pop. 5,216,000, cap. La Paz, also Sucre.

Bombay (bom-bā') City (India) pop. 5,534,358.

Bonn (bân) City (cap. of West Germany) pop. 138,090.

Bordeaux (bôr-dō') City (France) pop. 266,662.

Borneo (bôr'né-ō) I. (Indonesia & Malaysia) 289,000 sq. mi., pop. 6,800,000.

Boston (bäs'tən) City (cap. of Mass.) pop. 562,994, urb. 2,678,762.

Bothnia, Gulf of (both'né-ə) between Sweden & Finland, 43,000 sq. mi.

Botswana (bot-swä'nə) [formerly **Bechuanaland**] (Br. C. of N.) 238,605 sq. mi., pop. 770,000, cap. Gaborone.

Brazil (brə-zil') 3,286,170 sq. mi., pop. 124,428,000, cap. Brasilia (brə-zil'é-ə) (pop. 379,699).

Brazzaville (brä″zä-vēl') City (cap. of People's Republic of Congo) pop. 279,000.

Bridgetown (brij'town) city (cap. of Barbados) pop. 68,000.

Brisbane (briz'bän) City (Australia) pop. 720,000.

British Columbia (kə-lum'bé-ə) Prov. (Canada) 359,279 sq. mi., pop. 2,744,467, cap. Victoria (pop. 64,379).

Brunei (brû-nī') Br. Protect. (Borneo) 2,226 sq. mi., pop. 199,000, cap. Bandar Seri Begawan.

Brussels [*Fr.* **Bruxelles**] (brus'əlz, brook-sel') City (cap. of Belgium) pop. 1,500,000.

Bucharest [*Rom.* **Bucuresti**] (boo'-kə-rest″, boo″koo-resht') City (cap. of Rumania) pop. 1,431,993.

Budapest (boo'du-pest″) City (cap. of Hungary) pop. 2,000,000.

Buenos Aires (bwä'nes ī'res) City (cap. of Argentina) pop. 2,983,000, urb. 9,910,000.

Buffalo (buf″ə-lō) City (N.Y.) pop. 357,870, urb. 1,002,285.

Bujumbura (boo″jam-bûr'ə) City (cap. of Burundi), pop. 71,000.

Bulgaria (bul-ger'é-ə) 42,796 sq. mi., pop. 8,892,000 cap. Sofia.

Burma (bēr'mə) 261,610 sq. mi., pop. 33,517,000, cap. Rangoon.

Burundi (bû-rûn'dē) 10,744, sq. mi., pop. 4,314,000, cap. Bujumbura.

Byelorussian S.S.R. (bye″lə-rush'ən) (U.S.S.R.) 80,100 sq. mi., pop. 9,675,000 cap. Minsk (pop. 1,333,000).

Cairo (kī'rō) City (cap. of Arab Rep. of Egypt) pop, 5,715,000.

Calcutta (kal-kut'ə) City (India) pop. 3,148,746, urb. 7,031,382.

Calgary (kal'gə-ré) City (Canada) pop. 592,743.

California (kal-i-fôr'né-ə) State (U.S.) 156,299 sq. mi., pop. 23,667,902, cap. Sacramento.

Cambodia (kam-bō'dé-ə) see *Kampuchea*.

Cameroon (käm-roon') 161,787 sq. mi., pop. 8,168,000, cap. Yaoundé.

Canada (kan'ə-də) (Br. C. of N.) 3,621,616 sq. mi., pop. 24,343,181, cap. Ottawa.

Canal Zone (U.S.) 362 sq. mi., pop. 44,650, cap. Balboa Heights (bal-bō'ə)

Canary Is. (kə-ner'é) (Sp.) 2,894 sq. mi., pop. 944,448, cap. Las Palmas, Santa Cruz (läs päl'mäs, san'tə krooz).

Canberra (kan'ber-ə) City (cap. of Australia, pop. 204,500.

Canton [*Chinese* **Kwangchou**] (kan-ton', gwäng-jō') City (China) pop. 1,840,000.

Cape Town City (cap. of Union of South Africa) pop. 691,000.

Cape Verde Is. (käp vērd) 1,557 sq. mi., pop. 328,000, cap. Praia.

Caracas (kə-rä'kəs) City (cap. of Venezuela) pop. 956,000.

Caribbean Sea (kar″ə-bé'ən) between So. American & West Indies, 750,000 sq. mi.

Caroline Is. (kar'ə-lin) U.S. Trust., 525 sq. mi., pop. 66,900, cap. Truk (trûk).

Carson City (kär'sən) City (cap. of Nev.) pop. 32,022.

Casablanca (kas″ə-blang'kə) City (Morocco) pop. 1,495,000.

Caspian Sea (kas'pé-ən) between Europe & Asia, 169,383 sq. mi.

Castries (kä'strēz) City (cap. of St. Lucia) pop. 41,000.

Cayenne (kī-en') City (cap. of Fr. Guinea) pop. 21,050.

Cayman Is. (kī-män') (Br.) 104 sq. mi., pop. 12,000, cap. Georgetown.

Celebes (sel'ə-bēz) (Indonesia) 72,986 sq. mi., pop. 8,925,000, cap. Makasaar (mə-kas'ər) (pop. 384,159).

Central African Republic (af'ri-kən) (Fr. C.) 238,000 sq. mi., pop. 2,418,000, cap. Bangui.

Central America (ə-mer'i-kə) district comprising Guatemala, Honduras, El Salvador, Nicaragua, Costa Rica, and Panama.

Ceylon (sé-lon') see *Sri Lanka*.

Chad (chäd) (Fr. C.) 455,598 sq. mi., pop. 4,523,000, cap. Ndjamena.

Changsha (chäng'shä) City (cap. of Hunan China) pop. 703,000.

Channel Is. (chan'əl) (Br.) 75 sq. mi., pop. 117,000.

Charleston (chärls'tən) **1,** City (cap. of

---

tub, cūte, pûll; labəl; oil, owl, go, chip, she, thin, *th*en, sing, ink; *see p. 6

W. Va.) pop. 63,968; **2,** City (S.C.) pop. 69,510.

Charlotte (shär′lət) City (N.C.)ʳ pop. 314,447.

Chengtu (chung-doo′) City (China) pop. 1,107,000.

Cheyenne (shī-en′) City (cap. of Wyo.) pop. 47,283.

Chicago (shi-kä′go) City (Ill.) pop. 3,005,072, urb. 6,779,799.

Chile (chil′é) 286,396 sq. mi., pop. 10,850,000, cap. Santiago.

China (chī′nə) **1,** [People's Republic of China] 3,768,727 sq. mi., pop. 1,017,-477,000, cap. Peking (Beijing). **2,** [The Republic of China] see *Taiwan.*

Chosen (chō′sen′) see *Korea.*

Christmas (kris′məs) **1, I.** (Australia) 64 sq. mi., pop. 3,524. **2, Is.** (Kiribati) 184 sq. mi.

Chongking [*Chinese* **Pahsien**] (chung′king′, bä-shyen′) City (China) pop. 2,121,000.

Cincinnati (sin-si-na′té) City (Ohio) pop. 385,457, urb. 1,123,412.

Ciudad Trujillo (thyoo′*thäth* troo-hē′yō) former name of capital of Dominican Republic.

Cleveland (klēv′lənd) City (Ohio) pop. 573,822, urb. 1,752,424.

Cocos Is. (ko′kəs) (Australia) 5 sq. mi., pop. 1,000.

Cologne [*Ger.* **Köln**] (kə-lōn, köln) City (West Germany) pop. 853,864.

Colombia (kə-lum′bē-ə) 439,828 sq. mi., pop. 26,115,000, cap. Bogota.

Colombo (kə-lum′bō) City (cap. of Sri Lanka) pop. 551,200.

Colorado (kol-ə-rad′ō) State (U.S.) 103,595 sq. mi., pop. 2,889,964, cap. Denver.

Columbia (kə-lum′bē-ə) City (cap. of S.C.) pop. 101,208.

Columbus (kə-lum′bəs) City (cap. of Ohio) pop. 564,871.

Comoros Is. (ko-mō′rō) 863 sq. mi., pop. 323,000, cap. Moroni.

Conakry (kon′ə-krē″) City (cap. of Guinea) pop. 525,000.

Concord (kon′kôrd) City (cap. of N.H.) pop. 30,400.

Congo (kon′gō) region in C. Africa, now: Democratic Republic of Congo [formerly Belgian Congo] 902,274 sq. mi., pop. 17,100,000, cap. Kinshasa; and People's Republic of Congo [formerly Moyen Congo] (Fr. C.) 175,676 sq. mi., pop. 1,504,000, cap. Brazzaville.

Connecticut (kə-net′i-kət) State (U.S.) 4,872 sq. mi., pop. 3,107,576, cap. Hartford.

Constantinople, see *Istanbul.*

Cook Is. (kůk) (New Zeal.) 90 sq. mi., pop. 20,000, cap. Rarotonga.

Copenhagen (kō″pən-hä′gən) City (cap. of Denmark) pop. 1,100,000.

Coral Sea, part of Pacific Ocean NE of Australia.

Corsica (kôr′si-kə) I. (Fr.) 3,367 sq. mi., pop. 269,831, cap. Ajaccio (ä-yät′chō).

Costa Rica (kos′tə-rē′kə) 19,239 sq. mi., pop. 2,168,000, cap. San José.

Contonou (kō-tō-noo′) City (de facto cap. of Benin) pop. 175,000.

Crete (krēt) I. (Greece) 3,232 sq. mi., pop. 483,075, cap. Canea (kə-nē′ə).

Cuba (kū′bə) 42,857 sq. mi., pop. 9,824,000, cap. Havana.

Curaçao (kûr′ə-sow) see *Antilles, Netherlands.*

Cyprus (si′prəs) (Br. C. of N.) 3,572 sq. mi., pop. 614,000, cap. Nicosia.

Czechoslovakia (chek′ō-slō-väk″-yə) 49,356 sq. mi., pop. 15,240,000, cap. Prague.

Dacca (dak′a) City (cap. of Bangladesh) pop. 1,679,572.

Dahomey (da-ho′mé) see *Benin.*

Dakar (dä-kär′) City (cap. of Senegal) pop. 581,000.

Dallas (dal′əs) City (Tex.) pop. 904,078, urb. 2,451,390.

Damascus [*Arabic* **Esh Shâm**] (də-mas′kəs, ash-sham′) City (cap. of Syria) pop. 789,840.

Danzig [*Pol.* **Gdansk**] (dan′tsig, gə-däny′-sk) City (Poland) pop. 364,000.

Dar es Salaam (där′es-sə-läm′) City (cap. of Tanzania) pop. 527,000.

Davis Strait (dä′vis) between Greenland & Baffin Island.

Dayton (dā′tən) City (Ohio) pop. 203,371.

Dead Sea, between Palestine & Jordan, 340 sq. mi.

Delaware (del′ə-wär) State (U.S.) 1,932 sq. mi., pop. 594,338, cap. Dover.

Denmark (den′märk) 16,556 sq. mi., pop. 5,118,000, cap. Copenhagen.

Denver (den′vər) City (cap. of Colo.) pop. 492,365, urb. 1,352,070.

Des Moines (di-moin′) City (cap. of Iowa) pop. 191,003.

Detroit (dé-troit′) City (Mich.) pop. 1,203,339, urb. 3,809,327.

Dili (dil′é) City (cap. of Port. Timor) pop. 52,158.

District of Columbia (kə-lum′-bē-ə) (U.S.) 63 sq. mi., pop. 638,333.

Djakarta (jə-kär′tə) City (cap. of Indonesia) pop. 4,564,000.

Djibouti (ji-boo′té) [formerly **French Territory of the Afars and Issas**] 9,000 sq. mi., pop. 314,000, cap. Djibouti, pop. 100,000.

Dodecanese Is. (dō-dek′ə-nēz) (Greece) 1,030 sq. mi., pop. 123,021.

---

fat, fāte, fär, fâre, fâll, ásk; met, hē, hêr, maybè; pin, pīne; not, nōte, ôr, tool

Doha (dō'hə) City (cap. of Qatar) pop. 65,000.

Dominica (dō-min'i-kə) (Br. C. of N.) 290 sq. mi., pop. 78,000, cap. Roseau.

Dominican Republic (də-min'ə-kən) 19,129 sq. mi., pop. 5,539,000, cap. Santo Domingo.

Douglas (dug'ləs) City (cap. of Isle of Man) pop. 20,400.

Dover (dō'vər) City (cap. of Del.) pop. 23,512.

Dresden (drez'dən) City (East Germany) pop. 499,848.

Dublin [*Gaelic* **Baile Atha Cliath**] (dub'lin, blâ-klē'ə) cap. of Republic of Ireland, pop. 568,772.

Durban (dēr'bən) City (So. Africa) pop. 560,010.

Ecuador (ek'wə-dôr) 115,000 sq. mi., pop. 7,781,000 cap. Quito.

Edinburgh (ed'ən-bēr'ə) City (cap. of Scotland) pop. 470,404.

Egypt (ē'jipt) see *Arab Republic of Egypt.*

Eire (er'ə) former name for the *Republic of Ireland.*

Ellesmere I. (elz'mèr) (Canada) 82,119 sq. mi., pop. 150.

El Paso (el pas'o) City (Tex.) pop. 425,259.

El Salvador (el säl-və-dôr') 13,176 sq. mi., pop. 4,646,000, cap. San Salvador.

England and Wales (ing'glənd, wälz) 58,340 sq. mi., pop. 48,827,000, cap. London.

Erie, Lake (ir'ė) (Great Lakes) 9,940, sq. mi.

Eritrea (er-i-trē'ə) (Ethiopia) 15,754 sq. mi., pop. 1,589,400, cap. Asmara (äs-mä'rä).

Erivan, see *Yerevan.*

Estonia or Estonian S.S.R. (es-tō'nyə) (U.S.S.R.) 17,838 sq. mi., pop. 1,485,000, cap. Tallinn (täl'-lin) (pop. 442,000).

Ethiopia (ē'thë-ō'pé-ə) 350,000 sq. mi., pop. 31,743,000, cap. Addis Ababa.

Europe (ū'rəp) Continent, 1,920,000 sq. mi., pop. 640,000,000. (without U.S.S.R.).

Faroe Is. (fer'ō) (Den.) 540 sq. mi., pop. 43,000, cap. Torshavn.

Falkland Is. (fâk'lənd) (Br.) incl. S. Georgia, 5,618 sq. mi., pop. 2,721, cap. Stanley.

Fiji (fē'jè) Is. (Br. C. of N.) 7,055 sq. mi., pop. 621,000, cap. Suva.

Finland (fin'lənd) 130,500 sq. mi., pop. 4,771,000, cap. Helsinki.

Florida (flor'i-də) State (U.S.) 54,153 sq. mi., pop. 9,746,324, cap. Tallahassee.

Formosa, see *Taiwan.*

Fort-de-France (fôr'dė-fräns') City (cap. of Martinique) pop. 40,380.

Fort Lauderdale (lâ'dər-dāl") City (Florida) pop. 153,279, urb. 1,008,526.

Fort Worth (wêrth) City (Tex.) pop. 385,164.

France (frans) 212,736 sq. mi., pop. 53,451,000, cap. Paris.

Frankfort (frank'fərt) City (cap. of Ky.) pop. 25,973.

Franz Josef Land (fränts' yō'zef-länt") Arctic archipelago (U.S.S.R.) 8,000 sq. mi.

Freetown (frē'town) City (cap. of Sierra Leone) pop. 310,000.

French Indo-China (in'dō-chī'nə) former Fr. terr., now: Kampuchea, Laos, Vietnam.

French Sudan (soo-dan') see *Mali.*

Friendly Is., see *Tonga.*

Funafuti (foo-nä-foo'ti) City (cap. of Tuvalu) pop. 2,000.

Fundy, Bay of (fun'dė) between Nova Scotia & New Brunswick, 6,300 sq. mi.

Gabon (gâ-bân') (Fr. C.) 103,088 sq. mi., pop. 580,000, cap. Libreville.

Gaborone (gä-bə-rō'nē) City (cap. of Botswana) pop. 34,000.

Galapagos Is. (gä-lä'pä-gâs) (Ecuador) 3,042 sq. mi., pop. 2,391, cap. San Cristobal (san krəs-tō'bəl).

Galilee, Sea of (gal'ə-lē") (Israel) 64 sq. mi.

Gambia (gam'bé-ə) (Br. C. of N.) 3,999 sq. mi., pop. 584,000, cap. Banjul.

Gangtok City (cap. of Sikkim) pop. not known.

Gdansk, see *Danzig.*

Geneva (jə-nē'və) City (Switzerland) pop. 331,600.

Genoa [*Ital.* **Genova**] (jen'ō-ə, je-nō'və) City (Italy) pop. 843,632.

Georgetown (jôrj'town) **1,** City (cap. of Cayman) pop. 2,573. **2,** City (cap. of Guyana) pop. 97,160.

Georgia (jôr'jə) State (U.S.) 58,056 sq. mi., pop. 5,463,105, cap. Atlanta.

Georgian S.S.R. (jôr'jyən) (U.S.S.R.) 28,687 sq. mi., pop. 5,071,000, cap. Tiflis (Tbilisi) (tif'-lis, tbi'lė-se) (pop. 1,095,000).

Germany (jēr'mə-nė) former German Empire, now: German Democratic Republic (East Germany), 41,479 sq. mi., pop. 16,793,000, cap. East Berlin; and Federal Republic of Germany (West Germany), 95,737 sq. mi., pop. 61,181,000, cap. Bonn.

Ghana (gä'nə) (Br. C. of N.) 88,802 sq. mi., pop. 11,741,000, cap. Accra.

Gibraltar (ji-brâl'tər) (Br.) 2 sq. mi., pop. 27,000.

Gibraltar, Strait of, between Spain & Africa.

Gilbert Is. (gil'bərt) (Br.) 349 sq. mi., pop. 54,000, cap. Tarawa.

Glasgow (glas'kō) City (Scotland) pop. 927,948.

Goa (gō'ə) (India) 1,313 sq. mi., pop.

tub, cūte, půll; labəl; oil, owl, go, chip, she, thin, *th*en, sing, ink; *see p. 6*

626,978, cap. Pangim (bän-zhen').

Godháb (gât'hâp) City (cap. of Greenland) pop. 9,000.

Gold Coast, former name of *Ghana.*

Gorky (gôr'kė) City (U.S.S.R.) pop. 1,367,000.

Great Bear Lake (Canada) 12,275 sq. mi.

Great Britain, see *United Kingdom.*

Great Lakes, chain of 5 lakes between U.S. & Canada: Erie, Huron, Michigan, Ontario, Superior.

Great Salt Lake (Utah) 2,560 sq. mi.

Great Slave Lake (Canada) 10,980 sq. mi.

Greece (grēs) 51,182 sq. mi., pop. 9,390,-000 cap. Athens.

Greenland (grēn'lənd) (Den.) 839,999 sq. mi., pop. 47,000, cap. Godháb.

Grenada (grə-nä'də) (Br.) 133 sq. mi., pop. 105,000, cap. St. George's.

Guadalajara (gwä"*th*ä-lä-hä'rä) City (Mexico) pop. 1,352,109.

Guadeloupe (gwä"də-loop') (Fr.) 688 sq. mi., pop. 323,000, cap. Basse-Terre.

Guam (gwäm) U.S. Terr., 206 sq. mi., pop. 105,821, cap. Agaña (ä-gä'nyə).

Guatemala (gwät'ə-mä-lə) 45,452 sq. mi., pop. 6,817,000, cap. Guatemala City (pop. 701,000).

Guiana (gė-ä'nə) see *Guyana.*

Guiana, Dutch (gė-ä'nə) see *Surinam.*

Guiana, French (gė-ä'nə) (Fr.) 35,135 sq. mi., pop. 61,000, cap. Cayenne (kī-en').

Guinea (gin'ė) 96,525 sq. mi., pop. 5,276,-000, cap. Conakry.

Guinea-Bissau (gin'ė bi-sow') [formerly *Portuguese Guinea*] 13,948 sq. mi., pop. 634,000, cap. Bissau.

Guinea, Equatorial (gin'ė) 10,830 sq. mi., pop. 341,000, cap. Malabo.

Guyana (gė-ä'nə) (Br. C. of N.) 89,480 sq. mi., pop. 824,000, cap. Georgetown.

Hague, The [*Dutch* 's Gravenhage] (häg, skrä"vən-hä'kə) City (Netherlands) pop. 570,765.

Haiti (hä'tė) 10,714 sq. mi., pop. 5,666,-000, cap. Port-au-Prince.

Hamburg (ham'bėrg) City (West Germany) pop. 1,826,411.

Hamilton (ham'il-tən) **1,** City (cap. of Bermuda) pop. 3,000. **2,** City (Canada) pop. 306,434.

Hanoi (ha-noi') City (cap. of Vietnam) pop. 1,375,000.

Harbin (här'bin) City (Manchuria) pop. 2,800,000.

Harrisburg (har'is-bėrg) City (cap. of Pa.) pop. 53,264.

Hartford (härt'fərd) City (cap. of Conn.) pop. 136,392.

Havana [*Span.* **La Habana**] (hə-van'ə, lä ä-vä'nə) City (cap. of Cuba) pop. 1,600,000.

Hawaii (hä-wī'ė) State (U.S.) 6,425 sq. mi., pop. 964,691, cap. Honolulu.

Helena (hel'ə-nə) City (cap. of Mont.) pop. 23,938.

Helsinki (hel'sing-kė) City (Cap. of Finland) pop. 532,051.

Hiroshima (hi"rŏ-shē' mə, *Jap.* hē-râsh'mä) City (Japan) pop. 542,000.

Hispaniola (his-pan"ė-ō'lə) I.; includes Haiti and Dominican Republic.

Holland, see *Netherlands.*

Honduras (hon-door'əs) 43,277 sq. mi., pop. 3,639,000, cap. Tegucigalpa.

Hong Kong (hong'kong') (Br.) 391 sq. mi., pop. 4,693,000, cap. none.

Honiara (hŏ'nē-är"ə) City (cap. of Solomon Is.) pop. 14,000.

Honolulu (hŏ"n∂-loo'loo) City (cap. of Hawaii) pop. 365,048.

Honshu (hon'shoo) I. (Jap.) 88,000 sq. mi., pop. 81,560,000, cap. Tokyo.

Houston (hūs'tən) City (Tex.) pop. 1,595,138 urb. 2,412,664.

Huang or **Yellow River** (hwäng) (China) 3,000 miles.

Hudson Bay, bay of No. Canada, 281,900 sq. mi.

Hungary (hung'gə-rė) 35,875 sq. mi., pop. 10,735,000, cap. Budapest.

Huron, Lake (hyū'rən) (Great Lakes) 23,010 sq. mi.

Hyderabad (hi'dēr-ə-bád") City (India) pop. 1,612,000.

Iceland (īs'lənd) 39,709 sq. mi., pop. 225,000, cap. Reykjavik.

Idaho (i'də-hō) State (U.S.) 82,413 sq. mi., pop. 943,935, cap. Boise.

Ifni (ēf'nė) (Morocco) 579 sq. mi., pop. 52,000.

Illinois (il-ə-noi') State (U.S.) 55,645 sq. mi., pop. 11,426,518, cap. Springfield.

India (in'dė-ə) (Br. C. of N.) 1,059,342 sq. mi., pop. 669,785,000, cap. New Delhi.

Indiana (in"dė-an'ə) State (U.S.) 35,932 sq. mi., pop. 5,490,224, cap. Indianapolis (in"dė-ən-ap'ə-lis) (pop. 700,807, urb. 1,166,575).

Indian Ocean, between Africa & Australia, 28,350,000 sq. mi.

Indo-China (in'dō chī'nə) Peninsula comprising Burma, Thailand, Kampuchea, Laos, Vietnam, and Malaya.

Indonesia (in"dō-nē'zhə) 575,892 sq. mi., pop. 148,085,000, cap. Djakarta.

Iowa (i'ə-wə) State (U.S.) 55,965 sq. mi., pop. 2,913,808, cap. Des Moines.

Iran [formerly **Persia**] (ī-ran', pēr'zhə) 628,000 sq. mi., pop. 37,582,000, cap. Tehran.

Iraq [formerly **Mesopotamia**] (i-rak', mes"ō-pō-tā'mé-ə) 116,600 sq. mi., pop. 12,-

907,000, cap. Baghdad.

Ireland, Northern (ir'lənd) (U.K.) 5,238 sq. mi., pop. 1,513,000, cap. Belfast.

Ireland, Republic of (ir'lənd) 26,601 sq. mi., pop. 3,267,000, cap. Dublin.

Irish Sea, between Ireland & Great Britain, 75,000 sq. mi.

Islamabad (is-läm'ə-bäd") City (cap. of Pakistan), pop. 85,000.

Isle of Man (Br.) 221 sq. mi., pop. 50,000, cap. Douglas.

Israel (iz-rē-əl) 7,992 sq. mi., pop. 3,663,-000, cap. Jerusalem.

Istanbul [formerly **Constantinople**] (is"tan-bool', kon"stan-ti-nō'pəl) City (Turkey) pop. 2,248,000.

Italy (it'ə-lē) 116,000 sq. mi., pop. 56,-924,000, cap. Rome.

Ivory Coast 124,503 sq. mi., pop. 7,465,-000, cap. Abidjan.

Jackson (jak'sən) City (cap. of Miss.) pop. 202,895.

Jacksonville (jak'sən-vil) City (Fla.) pop. 540,920.

Jakarta (jə-kär'tə) see *Djakarta*.

Jamaica (jə-mā'kə) I. (Br. C. of N.) 4,450 sq. mi., pop. 2,233,000, cap. Kingston.

Japan (jə-pan') 144,550 sq. mi., pop. 116,051,000, cap. Tokyo.

Japan, Sea of (jə-pan') between Japan and Korea, 391,100 sq. mi.

Java and Madura (jä'və, mä-doo'rä) (Indonesia) 51,032 sq. mi., pop. 78,000,000.

Jefferson City (jef'ər-sən) City (cap. of Mo.) pop. 33,619.

Jersey City (jër'zē) City (N.J.) pop. 223,532.

Jerusalem (jə-roo'sə-lem) City (cap. of Israel) pop. 350,000.

Johannesburg (jō-han'is-bərg") City (Union of So. Africa) pop. 740,000.

Jordan [formerly **Transjordan**] (jōr'dən) 37,300 sq. mi., pop. 3,055,000, cap. Amman.

Juneau (joo'nō) City (cap. of Alaska) pop. 19,528.

Kabul (kä'bůl) City (cap. of Afghanistan) pop. 289,703.

Kampala (käm-pä'lä) City (cap. of Uganda) pop. 325,000.

Kampuchea (käm-pū-chē'ə) [formerly **Cambodia**] 161,787 sq. mi., pop. 7,957,-000, cap. Phnom Penh.

Kanpur (kän' půr) City (India) pop. 1,163,-524.

Kansas (kan'zəs) State (U.S.) 81,781 sq. mi., pop. 2,363,679, cap. Topeka.

Kansas City (kan'zəs) **1,** City (Mo.) pop. 448,159, urb. 1,097,793. **2,** City (Kan.) pop. 161,087.

Karachi (ke-rä'chē) City (former cap. of Pakistan) pop. 3,469,000.

Katmandu (kät-män-doo') City (cap. of Nepal) pop. 145,000.

Kazakh S.S.R. (kä-zäk') (U.S.S.R.) 1,064,092 sq. mi., pop. 15,053,000, cap. Alma-Ata (pop. 975,000).

Keeling Is. (kē'ling) see *Cocos Is.*

Kentucky (kən-tuk'ē) State (U.S.) 39,669 sq. mi., pop. 3,660,777, cap. Frankfort.

Kenya (kēn'yə) (Br. C. of N.) 224,960 sq. mi., pop. 15,364,000, cap. Nairobi.

Kharkov (kär'kof) City (Russia) pop. 1,485,000.

Khartoum (kär-toom') City (cap. of Sudan) pop. 334,000.

Kiev (kē'yef) City (Russia) pop. 2,248,000.

Kigali (kē-gä'lē) City (cap. of Rwanda) pop. 89,800.

Kingston (kings'tən) City (cap. of Jamaica) pop. 550,000.

Kingstown City (cap. of St. Vincent) pop. 22,500.

Kinshasa [formerly **Leopoldville**] (kin-shä'sä) City (cap. of Zaire) pop. 901,520..

Kirghiz S.S.R. (kir-gēz') (U.S.S.R.) 77,838 sq. mi., pop. 3,653,000, cap. Frunze (froon'zə) (pop. 552,000).

Kiribati (ki-ri-bäss') 264 sq. mi., pop. 60,000, cap. Tarawa.

Kitakyushu (kē"tä-kyoo'shoo) City (Japan) pop. 1,050,000.

Kiubyshev (kyoo'bi-shef") City (U.S.S.R) pop. 1,238,000.

Kobe (kō'be) City (Japan) pop. 1,253,000.

Korea (kō-rē'ə) **1,** Democratic People's Republic of Korea (North Korea) 47,862 sq. mi., pop. 18,717,000, cap. Pyongyang. **2,** Republic of Korea (South Korea) 37,424 sq. mi., pop. 39,544,000, cap. Seoul.

Kuala Lumpur (kwä'lä lûm'půr) City (cap. of Malaysia) pop. 475,000.

Kuching (koo'ching) City (cap. of Sarawak, E. Malaysia) pop. 63,491.

Kuril Is. or **Chishima** (koo-rēl', chē-shē'mä) (U.S.S.R.) 6,020 sq.,mi., pop. 15,000.

Kuwait (ků-wät') 5,991 sq. mi., pop. 1,278,000, cap. Kuwait pop. 99,609.

Kwangchou, see *Canton.*

Kyoto (kyō'tō) City (Japan) pop. 1,410,000.

Labrador (lab'rə-dôr") (Newfoundland) 112,000 sq. mi., pop. 21,300, cap. Battle Harbour.

Lagos (lä'gâs) City (cap. of Nigeria) pop. 1,061,000.

Lahore (lə'hôr) City (Pakistan) pop. 1,823,-000.

Lansing (lan'sing) City (cap. of Mich.) pop. 130,414.

Laos (lä'ōs) 89,343 sq. mi., pop. 3,630,000, cap. Vientiane.

La Paz (lä-päz') City (cap. of Bolivia) pop. 652,000.

Latvia or **Latvian S.S.R.** (lat'vē-ə)

(U.S.S.R.) 24,954 sq. mi., pop. 2,539,000,
cap. Riga (rē'gä) (pop. 850,000).

Lebanon (leb'ə-nən) 3,475 sq. mi., pop.
2,943,000, cap. Beirut.

Leeds (lēdz) City (England) pop. 506,100.

Leeward Is. (lē'wərd) (Br.) 423 sq. mi.,
pop. 32,000, cap. St. John's.

Leipzig (līp'sig) City (East Germany) pop.
590,291.

Leningrad (len'in-grad") City (Russia) pop.
4,676,000.

Leopoldville (lē'ə-pōld-vil) see *Kinshasa.*

Lesotho [formerly **Basutoland**] (lə-sō'tō)
(Br. C. of N.) 11,716 sq. mi., pop.
1,306,000, cap. Maseru.

Liberia (lī-bir'ē-ə) 43,000 sq. mi., pop.
1,789,000, cap. Monrovia.

Libreville (le'brə-vēl") City (cap. of Gabon)
pop. 57,000.

Libya (lib'ē-ə) 679,358 sq. mi., pop.
2,873,000, cap. Tripoli.

Liechtenstein (lik'tən-stīn) 65 sq. mi., pop.
25,000, cap. Vaduz.

Lilongwe (li-lâng'wä) City (cap. of Malawi)
pop. 105,000.

Lima (lē'mə) City (cap. of Peru) pop.
2,855,000.

Lincoln (link'ən) City (cap. of Neb.) pop.
171,932.

Lisbon [*Port.* **Lisboa**] (liz'bən, lēzh-bō'ə)
City (cap. of Portugal) pop. 828,000.

Lithuania or **Lithuanian S.S.R.** (lith"ū-
ā'nyə) (U.S.S.R.) 24,151 sq. mi., pop.
3,445,000, cap. Vilnyus (Vilna) vil'nē-ūs,
vil'nə) (pop. 503,000).

Little Rock (lit'əl-rok") City (cap. of Ark.)
pop. 158,461.

Liverpool (liv'ər-pool) City (England) pop.
688,000.

Lomé (lō-mā') City (cap. of Togo) pop.
220,000.

London (lun'dən) City (cap. of England)
pop. 7,763,800.

Long Beach (lâng'bēch') City (Calif.) pop.
361,334.

Los Angeles (los an'jə-ləs) City (Calif.)
pop. 2,966,850, urb. 9,479,436.

Louisiana (lū-ēz"ē-an'ə) State (U.S.) 44,521
sq. mi., pop. 4,205,900, cap. Baton Rouge.

Louisville (loo'i-vil) City (Ky.) pop. 298,451,
urb. 761,002.

Loyalty Is. (lâ'yəl-tē) (Fr.) 800 sq. mi.,
pop. 11,500, cap. Lifou (lē-foo').

Luanda (lū-än'də) City (cap. of Angola)
pop. 400,000.

Lusaka (loo-sä'kə) City (cap. of Zambia)
pop. 599,000.

Lüshun [formerly **Port Arthur**] (lyoo'shûn)
City (People's Republic of China) pop.
126,000.

Luxembourg (luk'səm-bērg) 999 sq. mi.,

pop. 337,000, cap. Luxembourg (pop.
77,458).

Lyon (lē-ôn') City (France) pop. 527,800.

Macao (mə-kow') (Port.) 6 sq. mi., pop.
272,000, cap. none.

Madagascar [formerly **Malagasy Republic**] (mad-ə-gas'kər, mä-lä-ga'sė) 241,094
sq. mi., pop. 8,358,000, cap. Antananarivo.

Madeira Is. (mə-dir'ə) (Port.) 308 sq. mi.,
pop. 268,600, cap. Funchal (fûn-shäl').

Madison (mad'i-sən) City (cap. of Wis.)
pop. 170,616.

Madras (ma-dräs') City (India) pop. 2,047,-
735.

Madrid (mə-drid') City (cap. of Spain)
pop. 3,140,000.

Madura (mä-doo'rə) I. (Indonesia) 1,725
sq. mi., pop. 2,400,000, cap. Pamekasan
(pä"mä-kə-sän').

Magellan, Straits of (mə-jel'ən) at so. tip
of So. America.

Maine (mān) State (U.S.) 30,995 sq. mi.,
pop. 1,124,660, cap. Augusta.

Malabo [formerly **Santa Isabel**] (mal'ə-bō,
sän'tä ē-sä-bel') City (cap. of Equatorial
Guinea) pop. 35,000.

Malacca, Straits of (mə-lak'ə) between
Sumatra & Malaya.

Malawi [formerly **Nyasaland**] (mä-lä'wē)
(Br. C. of N.) 48,443 sq. mi., pop.
5,861,000, cap. Lilongwe.

Malaysia [formerly **Federation of Malaya**]
(mə-lā'zhə) (Br. C. of N.) 128,430 sq.
mi., pop. 13,280,000, cap. Kuala Lumpur.

Maldive Is. (mal'dīv) 115 sq. mi., pop.
144,000, cap. Male (mä-lā') (pop. 16,000).

Mali Republic [formerly **French Sudan**]
(mä'lē) 584,942 sq. mi., pop. 6,350,000,
cap. Bamako.

Malta (mâl'tə) (Br. C. of N.) 122 sq. mi.,
pop. 343,000, cap. Valletta.

Managua (mä-nä'gwä) City (cap. of Nicaragua) pop. 480,000.

Manama (mä-nä'mə) City (cap. of Bahrain)
pop. 99,369.

Manchester (man'ches-tər) City (England)
pop. 602,800.

Manchuria (man-chûr'ē-ə) (People's Republic of China) 412,801 sq. mi., pop.
53,000,000, cap. Shenyang.

Manila (mə-nil'ə) City (cap. of Philippines)
pop. 1,499,000.

Manitoba (man-i-tō'bə) Prov. (Canada)
219,723 sq. mi., pop. 1,026,241, cap.
Winnipeg.

Maputo (mə-pū'tō) City (cap. of Mozambique) pop. 375,000.

Marianas Is. (mar"ē-an'əs) U.S. Trust.,
247 sq. mi., pop. 16,600, cap. Saipan
(sī-pan').

Marquesas Is. (mär-kā'səs) (Fr.) 480 sq.
mi., pop. 4,838, cap. Atuana (ä"tū-ä'nä).

---

fat, fāte, fär, fāre, fâll, ȧsk; met, hē, hėr, maybė; pin, pīne; not, nōte, ôr, tool

Marseille (mär-sā') City (France) pop. 889,029.

Marshall Is. (mär'shəl) U.S. Trust., 74 sq. mi., pop. 22,888, cap. Kwajalein (kwä'jä-län).

Martinique (mär-ti-nēk') (Fr.) 425 sq. mi., pop. 315,000, cap. Fort-de-France.

Maryland (mer'i-lənd) State (U.S.) 9,837 sq. mi., pop. 4,216,975, cap. Annapolis.

Maseru (maz'ə-roo") City (cap. of Lesotho) pop. 27,000.

Masqat, see *Muscat*.

Massachusetts (mas-ə-choo'səts) State (U.S.) 7,824 sq. mi., pop. 5,737,037, cap. Boston.

Mata Utu (ma'ta o'too) City (cap. of Wallis and Futuna Is.) pop. 3,000.

Mauritania (mâ-rə-tā'nē-ə) 328,185 sq. mi., pop. 1,558,000, cap. Nouakchott.

Mauritius (mâ-rish'əs) **I.** (Br. C. of N.) 720 sq. mi., pop. 933,000, cap. Port Louis.

Mbabane (m-bä-bä'nə) City (cap. of Swaziland) pop. 16,000.

Medellin (mā"thä-yēn') City (Colombia) pop. 1,039,800.

Mediterranean Sea (med"i-tə-rā'nē-ən) between Europe & Africa, 1,145,000 sq. mi.

Melbourne (mel'bərn) City (Australia) pop. 76,200.

Memphis (mem'fis) City (Tenn.) pop. 646,305.

Mesopotamia, see *Iraq*.

Mexico (mek'si-kō) 760,373 sq. mi., pop. 66,114,000, cap. Mexico City (pop. 8,600,000, urb. 14,000,000).

Mexico Gulf of, off so. U.S. and east Mexico, 700,000 sq. mi.

Miami (mī-am'ē) City (Fla.) pop. 346,865, urb. 1,608,159.

Michigan (mish'i-gən) State (U.S.) 56,954 sq. mi., pop. 9,262,078, cap. Lansing.

Michigan, Lake (Great Lakes) 22,400 sq. mi.

Micronesia (mī"krə-nē'zhə) see *Pacific Islands*.

Midway I. (U.S.) 2 sq. mi., pop. 2,000.

Milan [*Ital.* **Milano**] (mi-lan', mē-lä'nō) City (Italy) pop. 1,724,000.

Milwaukee (mil-wâ'kē) City (Wis.) pop. 636,212, urb. 1,207,008.

Minneapolis (min-ē-ap'ə-lis) City (Minn.) pop. 370,951, urb. 1,787,564.

Minnesota (min-i-sō'tə) State (U.S.) 79,548 sq. mi., pop. 4,075,970, cap. St. Paul.

Mississippi (mis"i-sip'ē) State (U.S.) 47,233 sq. mi., pop. 2,520,638, cap. Jackson.

Mississippi-Missouri River (U.S.) 3,710 miles.

Missouri (mə-zûr'ē) State (U.S.) 68,945 sq. mi., pop. 4,916,686, cap. Jefferson City.

Mobile (mō'bēl) City (Ala.) pop. 200,452.

Mogadishu (mog"ə-dish'oo) City (cap. of Somalia) pop. 235,000.

Moldavian S.S.R. (mol-dä'vē-ən) (U.S.S.R). 13,012 sq. mi., pop. 3,995,000, cap. Kishinev (pop. 539,000).

Monaco (mon'ə-kō) 370 acres, pop. 25,000, cap. Monaco, pop. same.

Mongolia (mon-gō'lē-ə) 625,946 sq. mi., pop. 1,639,000, cap. Ulan Bator.

Monrovia (mən-rō'vē-ə) City (cap. of Liberia) pop. 194,000.

Montana (mon-tan'ə) State (U.S.) 145,392 sq. mi., pop. 786,690, cap. Helena.

Monterrey (mon"tə-rā') City (Mexico) pop. 1,011,887.

Montevideo (mon"ti-vi-dā'ō) City (cap. of Uruguay) pop. 1,154,465.

Montgomery (mont-gum'ə-rē) City (cap. of Ala.) pop. 177,857.

Montpelier (mont-pēl'yər) City (cap. of Vt.) pop. 8,241.

Montreal (mon"trē-âl') City (Que.) pop. 980,354, urb. 2,828,349.

Montserrat Is. (mont-sə-rat') (Br.) 32 sq. mi., pop. 15,000, cap. Plymouth (plim'əth).

Morocco (mə-rok'ō) 171,031 sq. mi., pop. 19,751,000, cap. Rabat.

Moroni (mô-rō'nē) City (cap. of Comoros Is.) pop. 17,800.

Moscow [*Russ.* **Moskva**] (mos'kō, mus-kvä') City (cap. of U.S.S.R.) pop. 8,203,000.

Mozambique (mō"zəm-bēk') (Port.) 297,-731 sq. mi., pop. 10,108,000, cap. Maputo.

Mukden, see *Shenyang*.

Munich [*Ger.* **München**] (mü'nik, myûn'-chən) City (W. Germany) pop. 1,260,553.

Muscat (mus'kat) City (cap. of Oman) pop. 11,000.

Nagoya (nə-goi'ə) City (Japan) pop. 1,996,-000.

Naha (nä-hä) City (cap. of Ryukyu) pop. 284,000.

Nairobi (nī-rō'bē) City (cap. of Kenya) pop. 619,000.

Namibia (nä-mē'bē-ə) (in dispute) 318,261 sq. mi., pop. 992,000, cap. Windhoek.

Nanjing (nan'jing') City (China) pop. 1,419,000.

Naples [*Ital.* **Napoli**] (nā'pəlz, nä'pō-lē) City (Italy) pop. 1,267,073.

Nashville (nash'vil) City (cap. of Tenn.) pop. (Nashville-Davidson City) 455,651.

Nassau (nas'â) City (cap. of Bahamas) pop. 100,000.

Nauru [formerly **Pleasant Island**] (nä-oo'roo) 8.22 sq. mi., pop. 7,000, cap. none.

Ndjamena (en-jä'mä-nä) City (cap. of Chad) pop. 180,000.

Nebraska (nə-bras'kə) State (U.S.) 76,644

sq. mi., pop. 1,569,825, cap. Lincoln.

Nepal (ni-pâl′) 54,000 sq. mi., pop. 14,-028,000, cap. Katmandu.

Netherlands or **Holland** (neth′ər-ləndz, hol′ənd) 12,883 sq. mi., pop. 14,015,000, cap. Amsterdam (seat of government, The Hague).

Nevada (ni-vä′də) State (U.S.) 109,893 sq. mi., pop. 800,493, cap. Carson City.

Newark (noo′ərk) City (N.J.) pop. 329,248.

New Britain Is. (brit′ən) part of Papua New Guinea) 14,600 sq. mi., pop. 154,-000.

New Brunswick (brunz′wik) Prov. (Canada) 27,895 sq. mi., pop. 696,403, cap. Fredericton (fred′rik-tən) (pop. 43,723).

New Caledonia (kal″ə-dō′né-ə) (Fr.) 7,201 sq. mi., pop. 141,000, cap. Nouméa.

New Delhi (del′é) City (cap. of India) pop. 3,750,000.

Newfoundland (noo′fənd-lənd) Prov. (Canada) 152,734 sq. mi., pop. 567,681, cap. St. John's (pop. 83,370).

New Guinea (gin′é): see *Indonesia* and *Papua New Guinea.*

New Guinea, Netherlands (gin′é) see *Indonesia.*

New Hampshire (hamp′shər) State (U.S.) 8,993 sq. mi., pop. 920,610, cap. Concord.

New Hebrides Is. (heb′ri-dēz) see *Vanuatu.*

New Ireland (īr′lənd) I. (part of Papua New Guinea) 3,800 sq. mi., pop. 50,129.

New Jersey (jėr′zé) State (U.S.) 7,468 sq. mi., pop. 7,364,823, cap. Trenton.

New Mexico (mek′si-kō) State (U.S.) 121,335 sq. mi., pop. 1,302,894, cap. Santa Fe.

New Orleans (ôr′lé-ənz) City (La.) pop. 557,515, urb. 1,078,299.

New York (yôrk) **1,** State (U.S.) 47,377 sq. mi., pop. 17,558,072, cap. Albany. **2,** City (N.Y.) pop. 7,071,369, urb. 15,590,274.

New Zealand (zē′-lənd) (Br. C. of N.) 103,934 sq. mi., pop. 3,119,000, cap. Wellington.

Niamey (né-ə-mā′) City (cap. of Niger) pop. 135,000.

Nicaragua (nik″ə-rä′gwə) 57,143 sq. mi., pop. 2,485,000 cap. Managua.

Nicobar Is. (nik-ō-bär′) see *Andaman Is.*

Nicosia (nik″ō-sē′ə) City (cap. of Cyprus) pop. 112,000.

Niger (nī′jər) 501,930 sq. mi., pop. 5,133,-000, cap. Niamey.

Nigeria (nī-jir′é-ə) (Br. C. of N.) 372,674 sq. mi., pop. 74,604,000, cap. Lagos.

Nile River (nīl) (Arab Republic of Egypt) 4,145 miles.

Norfolk (nôr′fək) **1,** City (Va.) pop. 266,979. **2,** I. (Austl.) 13 sq. mi., pop. 1,000.

North America (ə-mer′i-kə) Continent,

8,500,000 sq. mi., pop. 347,000,000.

North Carolina (kar-ə-lī′nə) State (U.S.) 48,843 sq. mi., pop. 5,881,766, cap. Raleigh.

North Dakota (də-kō′tə) State (U.S.) 69,300 sq. mi., pop. 652,717, cap. Bismarck.

Northern Rhodesia (rō-dē′zhə) see *Zambia.*

North Sea, off NW Europe, 222,000 sq. mi.

Northwest Territories (Canada) 1,258,217 sq. mi., pop. 45,741, cap. Yellowknife.

Norway (nôr′wā) 124,560 sq. mi., pop. 4,077,000, cap. Oslo.

Nouakchott (nwäk′-shôt) City (cap. of Mauritania) pop. 130,000.

Nouméa (noo-mä′ə) City (cap. of New Caledonia) pop. 41,853.

Nova Scotia (nō-və skō′shə) Prov. (Canada) 20,743 sq. mi., pop. 847,442, cap. Halifax (hal′i-faks) (pop. 114,594).

Novosibirsk (nō-vō-si-birsk′) City (U.S.S.R.) pop. 1,343,000.

Nukualofa (noo-koo″ə-lō′fə) City (cap. of Tonga) pop. 24,000.

Nyasa Lake (nī-as′ə) (Africa) 11,430 sq. mi.

Nyasaland (nī-as′ə-land) see *Malawi.*

Oakland (ōk′lənd) City (Calif.) pop. 339,337.

Ob-Irtysh River (ôb′-ir-tish′) (U.S.S.R.) 3,460 miles.

Ohio (ō-hī′ō) State (U.S.) 41,004 sq. mi., pop. 10,797,630, cap. Columbus.

Okhotsk, Sea of (ō-kotsk′) (U.S.S.R.) 537,500 sq. mi.

Oklahoma (ōk-lə-hō′mə) State (U.S.) 68,655 sq. mi., pop. 3,025,290, cap. Oklahoma City (pop. 403,213).

Olympia (ō-lim′pyə) City (cap. of Wash.) pop. 27,447.

Omaha (ō′mə-hâ) City (Nebr.) pop. 314,255.

Oman (ō′man) 82,000 sq. mi., pop. 565,-000, cap. Muscat.

Ontario (on-tār′é-o) Prov. (Canada) 363,282 sq. mi., pop. 8,625,107, cap. Toronto.

Ontario, Lake (Great Lakes) 7,540 sq. mi.

Oregon (or′ə-gon) State (U.S.) 96,184 sq. mi., pop. 2,633,105, cap. Salem.

Orkney Is. (ôrk′né) (Scotland) 376 sq. mi., pop. 17,300, cap. Kirkwall (kērk′wâl).

Osaka (ō-sä′kə) City (Japan) pop. 3,078,000.

Oslo (oz′lō) City (cap. of Norway) pop. 487,916.

Ottawa (ot′ə-wə) City (cap. of Canada) pop. 295,163.

Ouagadougou (wä″gä-doo′goo) City (cap. of Upper Volta) pop. 165,000.

Pacific Is. (pə-sif′ik) U.S. Trust., consisting of the Caroline, Marshall, and Marianas Is., 687 sq. mi., pop. 136,810, cap. Saipan.

Pacific Ocean, 70,000,000 sq. mi.

Pakistan [formerly **West Pakistan**] (pak'is-tan) (Br. C. of N.) 310,236 sq. mi., pop. 80,171,000, cap. Islamabad.

Palau Is. (pä-low') U.S. Trust. (part of Caroline Is.) 175 sq. mi., pop. 10,280, cap. Korror (kâ-rôr').

Palestine (pal'əs-tīn") see *Israel*.

Panama (excluding Canal Zone) (pan'ə-mä) 28,576 sq. mi., pop. 1,862,000, cap. Panama (pop. 460,000).

Panama Canal, between Pacific Ocean & Gulf of Mexico, 50 mi.

Papeete (pä-pē-ā'te) City (cap. of Fr. Polynesia) pop. 22,278.

Papua New Guinea (pap'yoo-ə) (Br. C. of N.) 90,540 sq. mi., pop. 3,064,000, cap. Port Moresby.

Paraguay (par'ə-gwā) 150,518 sq. mi., pop. 3,160,000, cap. Asunción.

Paramaribo (par"ə-mar'i-bō) City (cap. of Surinam) pop. 110,867.

Paris (par'is) City (cap. of France) pop. 2,590,771, urb. 8,612,531.

Peking [formerly **Peiping**] (pe-king', bā'ping) City (cap. of People's Republic of China) pop. 15,000,000.

Pennsylvania (pen"sil-vā'ni-ə) State (U.S.) 44,888 sq. mi., pop. 11,863,895, cap. Harrisburg.

Pernambuco, see *Recife*.

Persia, see *Iran*.

Persian Gulf, between Iran & Arabia, 88,800 sq. mi.

Peru (pə-roo') 513,000 sq. mi., pop. 17,287,000, cap. Lima.

Philadelphia (fil-ə-del'fē-ə) City (Pa.) pop. 1,688,210, urb. 4,112,933.

Philippines, Republic of the (fil'e-pēnz") 115,600 sq. mi., pop. 46,893,000, cap. Manila.

Phnom Penh (nom-pen') City (cap. of Kampuchea) pop. 455,000.

Phoenix (fē'niks) City (cap. of Ariz.) pop. 789,704, urb. 1,409,279.

Phoenix Is. (fē'niks) (Kiribati) 16 sq. mi., pop. 850.

Pierre (pir) City (cap. of S.D.) pop. 11,973.

Pitcairn I. (pit'kärn) (Br.) 2 sq. mi., pop. 97.

Pittsburgh (pits'bėrg) City (Pa.) pop. 423,938, urb. 1,810,038.

Poland (pō'lənd) 119,734 sq. mi., pop. 35,391,000, cap. Warsaw.

Polynesia, French (pol"i-nē'zhə) Fr. Terr., 1,544 sq. mi., pop. 144,000 cap. Papeete.

Port Arthur and Dairen see *Lüshun, Talien*.

Port-au-Prince (por"tō-prins') City (cap. of Haiti) pop. 470,000.

Portland (pôrt'lənd) City (Ore.) pop. 366,383, urb. 1,026,144.

Port-Louis (pôr"lwē') City (cap. of Mauritius) pop. 134,900.

Port Moresby (môrz'bė) City (cap. of Papua) pop. 91,000.

Port-of-Spain, City (cap. of Trinidad) pop. 93,954.

Porto-Novo (pôr"tō-nō'vō) City (cap. of Benin) pop. 102,000.

Portugal (pôr'chə-gəl) 35,413 sq. mi., pop. 9,866,000, cap. Lisbon.

Prague [*Czech* **Praha**] (präg, prä'hä) City (cap of Czechoslovakia) pop.1,031,870.

Praia (prī'ə) City (cap. of Cape Verde Is.) pop. 25,000.

Pretoria (pri-tôr'ė-ə) City (cap. of Republic of South Africa) pop. 535,000.

Prince Edward I., Prov. (Canada) 2,184 sq. mi., pop. 122,506, cap. Charlottetown.

Providence (prov'i-dəns) City (cap. of R.I.) pop. 156,804, urb. 796,250.

Puerto Rico (pwer"tō-rē'kō) (U.S.) 3,423 sq. mi., pop. 3,186,076, cap. San Juan.

Pusan (pū-sän) City (So. Korea) pop. 1,425,703.

Pyong Yang (pyûng'yäng') City (cap. of No. Korea) pop. 1,350,000.

Qatar (kä'tär) 4,000 sq. mi., pop. 167,000, cap. Doha.

Québec (kwi-bek'; *Fr.* kā-) Prov. (Canada) 523,860 sq. mi., pop. 6,438,403, cap. Québec (pop. 166,474).

Queen Elizabeth Is. (i-liz'ə-bəth) (Canada) 134,920 sq. mi., pop. 310.

Quito (kē'tō) City (cap. of Ecuador) pop. 555,000,

Rabat (rə-bät') City (cap. of Morocco) pop. 485,000.

Raleigh (râ'lė) City (cap. of N.C.) pop. 150,255.

Rangoon (rang-goon') City (cap. of Burma) pop. 1,821,000.

Rarotonga (rä-rō-tông'gä) City (cap. of Cook Is.) pop. 11,000.

Recife or **Pernambuco** (re-sē'fə, pėr'nəmboo'kō) City (Brazil) pop. 1,100,464.

Red Sea, between Asia & Africa, 178,000 sq. mi.

Réunion (rä-û-nyōn') I. (Fr.) 970 sq. mi., pop. 503,000, cap. St. Denis.

Reykjavik (rä'kyə-vēk") City (cap. of Iceland) pop. 91,000.

Rhode Island (rōd-ī'lənd) State (U.S.) 1,055 sq. mi., pop. 947,154, cap. Providence.

Rhodesia, see *Zimbabwe Rhodesia*.

Richmond (rich'mənd) City (cap. of Va.) pop. 219,214.

Rio de Janeiro (rē"ō-dā-jə-nā'rō) City (Brazil) pop. 5,394,900.

Rio de Oro (rē"ō-dā-ō'rō) see *Spanish Sahara*.

---

tŭb, cūte, pŭll; labəl; oil, owl, go, chip, she, thin, *th*en, sing, ink; *see p. 6*

Rio Muni or **Continental Spanish Guinea** (rē'ō moo'nē) see *Equatorial Guinea*.

Riyadh (ri-yäd') City (cap. of Saudi Arabia) pop. 665,000.

Rochester (ro'ches-tər) City (N.Y.) pop. 241,741, urb. 606,070.

Romania see *Rumania*.

Rome [*Ital.* **Roma**] (rōm, rō'mä) City (cap. of Italy) pop. 2,656,104.

Roseau (rō-zū') City (cap. of Dominica) pop. 25,000.

Rotterdam (rot'ər-dam") City (Netherlands) pop. 704,858.

Ruanda-Urundi (roo-än'dä-û-rûn'dē) see *Rwanda* and *Burundi*.

Rumania (roo-mān'yə) 91,671 sq. mi., pop. 22,057,000 cap. Bucharest.

Russia (rush'ə) see *Union of Soviet Socialist Republics*.

Russian S.F.S.R. (rush'ən) (U.S.S.R.) 6,593,391 sq. mi., pop. 139,165,000, cap. Moscow.

Rwanda (rwän'dä) 10,170 sq. mi., pop. 4,573,000, cap. Kigali.

Ryukyu Is. (ryoo'kyoo) (Japan) 1,850 sq. mi., pop. 1,245,000, cap. Naha (nä'hä).

Sabah (sä'bə) State (Malaysia) pop. 633,-000, cap. Kota Kinabalu.

Sacramento (sak-rə-men'to) City (cap. of Calif.) pop. 275,741.

St. Croix (sänt kroi) (Virgin Is., U.S.) 80 sq. mi., pop. 49,013, cap. Christiansted (kris'tyän-sted).

St. Denis (san də-nē') City (cap. of Réunion) pop. 65,614.

St. Georges (sänt jôr'jəs) City (cap. of Grenada) pop. 26,000.

St. Helena (sänt he-lē'nə) I. (Br.) 47 sq. mi., pop. 5,060, cap. Jamestown.

St. John (sänt jon) (Virgin Is., U.S.) 20 sq. mi., pop. 2,360.

St. Johns, City (cap. of Antigua) pop. 24,000.

St. Kitts-Nevis-Anguilla (kits; ne'vis; ang-gwil'ə) (Br.) 155 sq. mi., pop. 56,000, cap. Basse-Terre.

St. Louis (sänt lū'əs) City (Mo.) pop. 453,085, urb. 1,848,590.

St. Lucia (sänt loo'shē-ə) I. (Br.) 233 sq. mi., pop. 113,000, cap. Castries (käs'trēs).

St. Paul (sänt pâl) City (cap. of Minn.) pop. 270,230.

St. Petersburg (sant pē'tərz-bərg) City (Florida) pop. 238,647.

St. Thomas (sänt tom'əs) (Virgin Is., U.S.) 32 sq. mi., pop. 44,218, cap. Charlotte Amalie (am'ə-lē).

St. Vincent (sänt vin'sənt) (Br.) 150 sq. mi., pop. 113,000, cap. Kingstown.

Sakhalin (sä-kä-lēn') I. (U.S.S.R.) 29,000 sq. mi., pop. 669,000, cap. Yuzhno-Sakhalinsk (yoo"zhnə-suk"həl-yēnsk').

Salem (sä'ləm) City (cap. of Ore.) pop. 89,233.

Salisbury (sôlz'bēr-ė) City (cap. of Zimbabwe Rhodesia) pop. 180,000.

Salt Lake City (sält läk) City (cap. of Utah) pop. 163,033.

Samoa, American (sä-mō'ə) Is. (U.S.) 76 sq. mi., pop. 32,395, cap. Pago Pago (päng'gō päng'gō).

Samoa, Western (sä-mō'ə) Is. (Br. C. of N.) 1,133 sq. mi., pop. 155,000, cap. Apia.

San'a (sä-nä') City (cap. of Yemen) pop. 60,000.

San Antonio (san an-tō'nē-ō) City (Tex.) pop. 785,880.

San Diego (san dė-ä'gō) City (Calif.) 875,538, urb. 1,704,352.

San Francisco (san fran-sis'kō) City (Calif.) pop. 678,974, urb. 3,190,698.

San Jose (sän"hō-zā') **1**, City (cap. of Costa Rica) pop. 728,000. **2**, City (Calif.) pop. 629,442, urb. 1,243,952.

San Juan (sän hwän) City (cap. of Puerto Rico) pop. 432,973, urb. 1,083,664.

San Marino (san mə-rē'nō) 38 sq. mi., pop. 19,000, cap. San Marino (pop. 4,450).

San Salvador (sän säl-vä-dôr') City (cap. of El Salvador) pop. 368,000.

Sante Fe (sän"tə-fā') City (cap. of N.M.) pop. 48,953.

Santiago (sän"tē-ä'gō) City (cap. of Chile) pop. 3,185,000.

Santo Domingo (sän"tō dō-ming'-gō) City (cap. of Dominican Republic) pop. 950,-000.

São Paulo (sow pow'lō) City (Brazil) pop. 8,407,500.

São Tome and Principe (sowṅ tō-mā'; prēn'sė-pe) 372 sq. mi., pop. 82,000, cap. São Tome (pop. 8,800).

Sarawak (sərä'wäk) (Malaysia) 50,000 sq. mi., pop. 977,000, cap. Kuching.

Sardinia (sär-din'yə) I. (Ital.) 9,301 sq. mi., pop. 1,468,737, cap. Cagliari (kä'lyä-rė).

Saskatchewan (sas-kach'ə-wän) Prov. (Canada) 251,700 sq. mi., pop. 968,313, cap. Regina (rė-jī'nə) (pop. 162,613).

Saudi Arabia, Kingdom of (sä-oo'dė) 350,000 sq. mi., pop. 8,103,000, cap. Riyadh.

Scotland (skot'lənd) (U.K.) 30,405 sq. mi., pop. 5,195,000, cap. Edinburgh.

Seattle (sė-at'əl) City (Wash.) pop. 493,846, urb. 1,391,535).

Senegal (sen-əgâl') (Fr. C.) 77,401 sq. mi., pop. 5,519,000., cap. Dakar.

Seoul [*Jap.* **Keijo**] (sōl, su'ool, kä'jō") City (cap. of South Korea) pop. 5,500,000.

Seychelles (sa-shel') Is. (Br. C. of N.) 156 sq. mi., pop. 65,000, cap. Victoria.

fat, fāte, fär, fâre, fâll, ásk; met, hē, hėr, maybė; pin, pīne; not, nōte, ôr, tool

Shanghai (shang'hi) City (China) pop. 6,900,000.

Shenyang [formerly **Mukden**] (Shung-yäng', muk'den) City (cap. of Manchuria) pop. 2,411,000.

Shetland Is. (shet'lǝnd) (Scotland) 550 sq. mi., pop. 17,812, cap. Lerwick (lër'wik).

Siam, see *Thailand*.

Sian (shē'än) City (China) pop. 1,310,000.

Sicily (sis'ǝ-lē) I. (Ital.) 9,926 sq. mi., pop. 4,721,000, cap. Palermo (pǝ-ler'mō).

Sierra Leone (sē-er'ǝ lē-ō'nē) (Br. C. of N.) 27,295 sq. mi., pop. 3,351,000, cap. Freetown.

Sikkim (sik'im) (India) 2,818 sq. mi., pop. 215,000, cap. Gangtok.

Singapore (sing-ǝ-pōr') (Br. C. of N.) 220 sq. mi., pop. 2,361,000, cap. Singapore (pop. 1,987,000).

Society Is. (sō-sī'ǝ-tē) (Fr.) (part of French Polynesia) 650 sq. mi., pop. 68,245, cap. Papeete.

Socotra (sō-kō'trǝ) I. (Dem. Rep. of Yemen) 1,400 sq. mi., pop. 12,000, cap. Tamridah.

Sofia (sō'fē-ǝ) City (cap. of Bulgaria) pop. 960,000.

Solomon Is. (sol'ǝ-mǝn) 11,497 sq. mi., pop. 219,000, cap. Honiara.

Somalia (sō-mä'lē-ǝ) 262,000 sq. mi., pop. 3,469,000, cap. Mogadishu.

Somaliland, French (sō-mä'li-land) see *Djibouti*.

South Africa, Republic of 472,494 sq. mi., pop. 28,094,000, cap. Cape Town, also, Pretoria.

South America (ǝ-mer'i-kǝ) Continent, 6,814,000 sq. mi., pop. 235,444,000.

South Carolina (kar-ǝ-lī'nǝ) State (U.S.) 30,203 sq. mi., pop. 3,121,820, cap. Columbia.

South China Sea, between China, Vietnam & the Philippines, 1,148,500 sq. mi..

South Dakota (dǝ-kō'tǝ) State (U.S.) 75,952 sq. mi., pop. 690,768, cap. Pierre.

South-West Africa, see *Namibia*.

Spain (spān) 195,258 sq. mi., pop. 37,-551,000, cap. Madrid.

Spanish Sahara (sǝ-hēr'ǝ; -här'ǝ) 102,700 sq. mi., pop. 75,000.

Spitsbergen [*Nor.* **Svalbard**] (spits'bǝrg-ǝn, sväl'bär) Is. (Norway) 15,075 sq. mi., pop 3,431.

Springfield (spring'fēld) **1,** City (cap. of Ill.) pop. 99,637. **2,** City (Mass.) pop. 152,319. **3,** City (Mo.) pop. 133,116.

Sri Lanka [formerly **Ceylon**] (srē läng'kǝ) (Br. C. of N.) 25,332 sq. mi., pop. 14,502,000, cap. Colombo.

Stanley (stan'lē) City (Cap. of Falkland Is.) pop. 1,000.

Stockholm (stok'hōm″) City (cap. of Swe-

den) pop. 756,697, urb. 1,380,426.

Sucre (soo'krä) City (cap. of Bolivia) pop. 63,000.

Sudan (soo-dan') 967,500 sq. mi., pop. 20,941,000, cap. Khartoum.

Sudanese Republic, see *Mali Republic*.

Suez Canal (soo'ez) between Mediterranean & Red Seas, 107 mi.

Sulu Sea (soo'loo) between Philippine Is. & Borneo.

Sumatra (sû-mä'trǝ) I. (Indonesia) 164,148 sq. mi., pop. 20,800,000, cap. Padang (pä'däng').

Superior Lake (Great Lakes) 31,810 sq. mi.

Surabaja (sûr″ǝ-bä'yǝ) City (Indonesia) pop. 1,283,000.

Surinam [formerly **Dutch Guiana**] (soo-ri-näm') 63,037 sq. mi., pop. 398,000, cap. Paramaribo.

Suva (soo'vä) City (cap. of Fiji) pop. 84,000.

Sverdlovsk (svûrd-lôvsk') City (U.S.S.R.) pop. 1,239,000.

Swan Is. (swän) U.S.) 1 sq. mi., pop. 28.

Swaziland (swä'zi-land) (Br. C. of N.) 6,704 sq. mi., pop. 535,000, cap. Mbabane.

Sweden (swē'dǝn) 173,394 sq. mi., pop. 8,300,000, cap. Stockholm.

Switzerland (swit'zǝr-lǝnd) 15,944 sq. mi.,; pop. 6,230,000, cap. Bern.

Sydney (sid'nē) City (Australia) pop. 155,-480.

Syracuse (sir'ǝ-kyoos) City (N.Y.) pop. 170,105.

Syria (sir'ē-ǝ) 71,227 sq. mi., pop. 8,395,-000, cap. Damascus.

Tadzhik S.S.R. (tä-jik') (U.S.S.R.) 54,019 sq. mi., pop. 4,007,000, cap. Dushanbe (pop. 510,000).

Tahiti (tä-hē'tē) see *French Polynesia*.

Taipei (tī-pā') City (cap. of Taiwan) pop. 1,850,000.

Taiwan or Formosa (tī-wän', fôr-mō'sǝ) [The Republic of China] 13,885 sq. mi., pop. 17,440,000, cap. Taipei.

Taiyuan (tī-yü-än') City (China) pop. 1,020,000.

Talien or Dalien [formerly **Dairen**] (dä'lē-en') City (People's Republic of China) pop. 595,000.

Tallahassee (tal-ǝ-has'ē) City (cap. of Fla.) pop. 81,548.

Tampa (tam'pǝ) City (Fla.) pop. 271,523.

Tanganyika (tan-gǝn-yē'kǝ) see *Tanzania*.

Tanganyika, Lake (Africa) 12,700 sq. mi.

Tangier (tan-jir') City (Morocco) pop. 160,000.

Tanzania (tan″zǝ-nē'ǝ; tan-zä'nē-ǝ) (Br. C. of N.) 362,820 sq. mi., pop. 17,358,000, cap. Dar es Salaam.

---

tub, cūte, pûll; labǝl; oil, owl, go, chip, she, thin, *th*en, sing, ink; *see p.* 6

Tarawa (tar'ə-wä") City (cap. of Gilbert Is.) pop. 15,000.

Tashkent (tash-kent') City (cap. of Uzbek S.S.R.) pop. 1,858,000.

Tasmania (taz-mā'nē-ə) I. (Austl.) 26,215 sq. mi., pop. 389,500, cap. Hobart (hō'bərt).

Tegucigalpa (te-goo"sē-gäl'pä) City (cap. of Honduras) pop. 314,000.

Tehran (te-rän') City (cap. of Iran) pop. 4,496,159.

Tel Aviv-Jaffa (tel a-vēv', jaf'ə) City (Israel) pop. 384,700, seat of government of Israel.

Tennessee (ten-ə-sē') State (U.S.) 41,155 sq. mi., pop. 4,591,120, cap. Nashville.

Texas (tek'səs) State (U.S.) 262,017 sq. mi., pop. 14,229,191, cap. Austin.

Thailand [formerly **Siam**] (tī'land, sī-am') 200,148 sq. mi., pop. 46,350,000, cap. Bangkok.

Thimphu (tim'poo) City (cap. of Bhutan) pop. 9,000.

Tibet (ti-bet') (People's Republic of China) 469,413 sq. mi., pop. 1,300,000, cap, Lhasa (lä'sə).

Tientsin (tin'sin) City (China) pop. 3,220,-000.

Timbuktu (tim-buk'too) City (Mali) pop. 12,000.

Timor (tē'môr) I. (Indonesia & Port.) 13,071 sq. mi., pop. 850,000.

Timor, Portuguese (tē'môr) e. part of Timor (Port.) 7,330 sq. mi., pop. 465,000, cap. Dili.

Tiranë (tè-rä'nə) City (cap. of Albania) pop. 169,300.

Tobago, see *Trinidad and Tobago.*

Togo (tō'gō) 20,733 sq. mi., pop. 2,528,-000, cap. Lomé.

Togoland (tō'gō-land) former Br. Trust., now part of Ghana.

Tokelau Is. (tō"kə-low') (New Zeal.) 4 sq. mi., pop. 2,000.

Tokyo (tō'kē-ō) City (cap. of Japan) pop. 9,012,000, Greater Tokyo, 11,350,000.

Toledo (tə-lē'dō) City (Ohio) pop. 354,635.

Tonga (Friendly) Is. (tong'gə) (Br. C. of N.) 269 sq. mi., pop. 92,000, cap. Nukualofa.

Topeka (tə-pē'kə) City (cap. of Kan.) pop. 115,266.

Toronto (tə-ron'to) City (Ont.) pop. 599,217, urb. 2,998,947.

Torshavn (tôrs-hown') City (cap. of Faroe Is.) pop. 15,000.

Transjordan, see *Jordan.*

Trenton (tren'tən) City (cap. of N.J.) pop. 92,124.

Trieste (trē-est') (Italy, Yugoslavia) 287 sq. mi., pop. 280,017.

Trinidad and Tobago (trin'ə-dad, tə-bä'gō)

Is. (Br. C. of N.) 1,980 sq. mi., pop. 1,136,000, cap. Port of Spain.

Tripoli (trip'ə-lē) City (cap. of Libya) pop. 247,365.

Tristan da Cunha (tris'tan dä koon'yə) I. (Br.) 40 sq. mi., pop. 262.

Tsingtao (ching'dow') City (China) pop. 1,121,000.

Tucson (too'son) City (Ariz.) pop. 330,537.

Tulsa (tul'sə) City (Okla.) pop. 360,919.

Tunis (too'nis) City (cap. of Tunisia) pop. 550,400.

Tunisia (too-nizh'ə) 48,300 sq. mi., pop. 6,412,000, cap. Tunis.

Turin [*Ital:* **Torino**] (tûr'in, tō-rē'nō) City (Italy) pop. 1,177,900.

Turkey (tēr'kē) 296,185 sq. mi., pop. 44,236,000, cap. Ankara.

Turkmen S.S.R. (tûrk'men) (U.S.S.R.) 188,417 sq. mi., pop. 9,897,000, cap. Ashkhabad (pop. 325,000)).

Turks and Caicos Is. (Jamaica) (tērks, kī'kōs) (Br.) 166 sq. mi., pop. 6,148, cap. Grand Turk.

Tuvalu [formerly **Ellice Is.**] (too"-və-loo') (Br. C. of N.) 10 sq. mi., pop. 7,400, cap. Funafuti.

Uganda (yoo-gan'də) (Br. C. of N.) 80,292 sq. mi., pop. 13,225,000, cap. Kampala.

Ukrainian S.S.R. (yû-krän'yən) (U.S.S.R.) 226,687 sq. mi., pop. 50,135,000 cap. Kiev.

Ulan Bator (oo'län bä'tôr) City (cap. of Mongolia) pop. 220,000.

Union of South Africa, see *South Africa, Republic of.*

Union of Soviet Socialist Republics 8,649,798 sq. mi., pop. 267,7000,000, cap. Moscow.

United Arab Emirates [formerly **Trucial States**] 31,992 sq. mi., pop. 862,000, cap. Abu Dhabi.

United Kingdom (of Great Britain and Northern Ireland) 94,279 sq. mi., pop. 55,534,000, cap. London.

United States of America 3,554,613 sq. mi., pop. 226,504,825 (50 states), cap. Washington.

Upper Volta (vôl'tə) (Fr. C.) 105,538 sq. mi., pop. 6,656,000, cap. Ouagadougou.

Uruguay (yûr'ə-gwā) 72,172 sq. mi., pop. 2,910,000, cap. Montevideo.

Utah (yoo'tä", -tä") State (U.S.) 82,073 sq. mi., pop. 1,461,307, cap. Salt Lake City.

Uzbek S.S.R. (ûz'bek) (U.S.S.R.) 158,069 sq. mi., pop. 16,158,000, cap Tashkent.

Vaduz (vä'dûts) City (cap. of Liechtenstein) pop. 4,500.

Valencia (və-len"shė-ə) City (Spain) pop. 653,700.

Valletta (və-let'ə) City (cap. of Malta) pop. 17,600.

---

fat, fāte, fär, fåre, fåll, ȧsk; met, hē, hêr, maybė; pin, pīne; not, nōte, ôr, tool

Vancouver (van-koo′vər) City (B.C.) pop. 414,281, urb. 1,268,183.

Vanuatu (vä-noo-ä′too) (formerly New Hebrides) 57,000 sq. mi., pop. 112,600, cap. Vila (vēlä).

Vatican City (vat′i-kən) 109 acres, pop. 1,025.

Venezuela (ven-i-zwā′lə) 325,143 sq. mi., pop. 14,534,000, cap. Caracas.

Venice [Ital. Venezia] (ven′is, vä-nā′tsyə) City (Italy) pop. 367,327.

Vermont (vər-mont′) State (U.S.) 9,273 sq. mi., pop. 511,456, cap. Montpelier.

Versailles (ver-sī′) City (France) pop. 94,900.

Victoria (vik-tôr′é-ə) City (cap. of Seychelles) pop. 16,000.

Victoria I. (vik-tôr′é-ə) (Canada) 81,930 sq. mi., pop. 61,800.

Victoria, Lake (vik-tôr′é-ə) (Africa) 26,000 sq. mi.

Vienna [Ger. Wien] (vē-en′ə, vēn) City (cap. of Austria) pop. 1,642,072.

Vientiane (ven-tyen′) City (cap. of Laos) pop. 173,000.

Viet-Nam or Vietnam (vēt′näm; vyet-näm′) 127,267 sq. mi., pop. 52,558,000. cap. Hanoi.

Vila (vē′la) City (cap. of New Hebrides) pop. 15,000.

Virgin Is. (vēr′jin) 1, (U.S.) 132 sq. mi., pop. 95,591, cap. Charlotte Amalie. 2, (Br.) 58 sq. mi., pop. 9,000, cap. Road Town.

Virginia (vər-jin′yə) State (U.S.) 39,703 sq. mi., pop. 5,346,818. cap. Richmond.

Vladivostok (vlad″i-və-stok′) City (Asian U.S.S.R.) pop. 565,000.

Wake (wāk) I. (U.S.) 3 sq. mi., pop. 300.

Wales (wālz) (U.K.) 7,466 sq. mi., pop. 2,724,000, cap. Cardiff (kär′-dif).

Wallis and Futuna Is. (wol′is; foo-too′nə) Fr. Terr., 106 sq. mi., pop. 9,000, cap. Mata-Utu.

Warsaw [Pol. Warszawa] (wôr-sâ, vär-shä′və) City (cap. of Poland) pop. 1,463,-000.

Washington (wosh′ing-tən) 1, City (cap. of U.S.) pop. 638,333, urb. 2,763,105 2, State (U.S.) 66,511 sq. mi., pop. 4,132,156, cap. Olympia.

Wellington (wel′ing-tən) City (cap. of New Zealand) pop. 351,000.

West Indies (in′dèz) Archipelago, 100,000 sq. mi., pop. 9,000,000.

West Virginia (vər-jin′yə) State (U.S.)

24,119 sq. mi., pop. 1,949,644, cap. Charleston.

White Russian S.S.R., see Byelorussian S.S.R.

Whtie Sea, off no. U.S.S.R. (Eur.), 36,680 sq. mi.

Wichita (wich′i-tâ) City (Kan.) pop. 279,-272.

Willemstad (vil′əm-stät) City (cap. of Netherlands Antilles) pop. 47,000.

Wilmington (wil′ming-tən) City (Delaware) pop. 70,195.

Windhoek (vint′hûk) City (cap. of Namibia) pop. 36,051.

Windward Is. (wind′wərd) (Br.) 821 sq. mi., pop. 367,416, cap. St. George's.

Winnipeg (win′ə-peg) City (Manitoba) pop. 564,473.

Winnipeg, Lake (Canada) 9,398 sq. mi.

Wisconsin (wis-kon′sin) State (U.S.) 54,426 sq. mi., pop. 4,705,767, cap. Madison.

Wuhan (woo′hän′) City (China) pop. 2,146,000.

Wyoming (wī-ō′ming) State (U.S.) 96,989 sq. mi., pop. 469,557, cap. Cheyenne.

Yangtze River (yang′tsē″) (China) 3,400 miles.

Yaoundé (yä-oon-dā) City (cap. of Cameroon) pop. 272,000.

Yellow Sea, between Korea & China.

Yemen (yem′ən) 1, (Democratic Republic of Yemen) 110,971 sq. mi., pop. 1,781,000 cap. Aden. 2, (Arab Republic of Yemen) 74,981 sq. mi., pop. 5,125,000, cap. Sana.

Yerevan [Russ. Erivan] (ye-rə-vän′, er″yə-vän′yə) City (cap. of Armenian S.S.R.) pop. 1,055,000.

Yokohama (yōk″ə-hä′mə) City (Japan) pop. 2,047,000.

Yugoslavia (yoo-gō-slä′vé-ə) 99,079 sq. mi., pop. 22,174,00, cap. Belgrade.

Yukon Territory (yoo′kon) (Canada) 205,-346 sq. mi., pop. 23,153, cap. Whitehorse.

Zaire [formerly Democratic Republic of the Congo; Belgian Congo] (zī′ēr) 904,764 sq. mi., pop. 27,869,000, cap. Kinshasa.

Zambia (zam′bé-ə) (Br. C. of N.) 290,586 sq. mi., pop. 5,647,000. cap. Lusaka.

Zanzibar (zan-zi-bär′) see Tanzania.

Zetland (zet′lənd) see Shetland Is.

Zimbabwe Rhodesia [formerly Southern Rhodesia] (zim-bäb′wä rō-dēzhə) 150,-333 sq. mi., pop. 7,560,000, cap. Salisbury.

Zurich (zûr′ik) City (Switzerland) pop. 432,400.

tub, cūte, pûll; labəl; oil, owl, go, chip, she, thin, then, sing, ink; see p. 6

FOREIGN WORDS AND PHRASES

Many foreign words and phrases used frequently in English speech and writing are listed in the main vocabulary. Below are found many others used less frequently.

An effort has been made to adapt the pronunciations of foreign words to the sounds that English-speaking persons are accustomed to use. The following sounds, however, have no near equivalents in English:

ü—the French *u*, German ü: *ē* with the lips rounded as though to say *oo*.
ö—the French *eu*, German ö: *ā* with the lips rounded as though to say *ō*.
ṅ—as in French *bon*: a nasal sound given to the preceding vowel; it is not completed by the touch of the tongue, as is the English *n*.
kh—as in German *ach*: an *h* (breathing) sound with the tongue in position for *k*.

ab in·i′ti·o (ab i-nish′ē-ō) (*Lat.*) from the beginning.

ad in″fi·ni′tum (ad in″fə-nī′təm) (*Lat.*) to infinity: without end.

ad va·lo′rem (ad və-lôr′em) (*Lat.*) according to value.

af·faire′ d'a·mour′ (ä-fär′ dä-moor′) (*Fr.*) a love affair. **—af·faire′ d'hon·neur′** (dä-nör′) a duel. **—af·faire′ de coeur′** (də kör′) a love affair.

a·gent′ pro·vo·ca·teur′ (ä-zhäṅ′ prä-vä-kä-tör′) (*Fr.*) a professional agitator.

Ag′nus De′i (ag′nəs dē′ī; än′yoos de′ē) (*Lat.*) Lamb of God.

al den′te (al den′te) (*Ital.*) undercooked.

al fres′co (al fres′kō) (*Ital.*) in the open air.

a·mi′cus cu′ri·a (a-mī′kəs kū′rē-ē) (*Lat.*) a friend of the court.

a·mour-″pro′pre (ä-moor″prä′pr) n. (*Fr.*) self-esteem.

an′nu·it coep′tis (an′ū-it sep′tis) (*Lat.*) He (God) approves our undertakings: motto on the reverse of the great seal of the U.S.

An′schluss (än′shlŭs) n. (*Ger.*) an alliance; union.

an′te bel′lum (an′tē bel′əm) (*Lat.*) before the war.

a·près moi le dé·luge′ (ä-pre mwä′ lə dä-lüzh′) (*Fr.*) after me, the deluge.

a·ri″ve·der′ci (ä-rē″vä-dār′chē) *interj.* (*Ital.*) until we meet again.

ars lon′ga vi′ta bre′vis (ärz läng′gə vī′tə brē′vis) (*Lat.*) art is long, life is short.

au con·traire′ (ō käṅ-trär′) (*Fr.*) on the contrary.

au cou·rant′ (ō koo-räṅ′) (*Fr.*) up-to-date.

au fait (ō fe′) (*Fr.*) well-informed; sophisticated.

auf Wie′der·seh″en (owf vē′dər-zā″ən)(*Ger.*) till we meet again; goodbye.

au na·tu·rel′ (ō nä-tū-rel′) (*Fr.*) in the natural state; nude.

au re·voir′ (ō rə-vwär′) (*Fr.*) till we meet again; goodbye.

Au′to·bahn″ (ä′tō-bän″) (*Ger.*), **au′to·route″** (ō′tō-root″) (*Fr.*), **au′to·stra″da** (ow′tō-strä″dä) (*Ital.*) superhighway.

a′ve at′que va′le (ä′vē at′kwē vä′lē) (*Lat.*) hail and farewell.

à vo″tre san·té (ä vätr″ sän-tä′) (*Fr.*) to your health.

beau geste (bō′ jest′) (*Fr.*) a beautiful gesture; a futile gesture.

beau monde (bō′ mōnd′) (*Fr.*) fashionable society.

belles-let′tres (bel-let′r) n. pl. & sing. (*Fr.*) fine literature.

bien″ve·nue′ (byaṅ″və-nü′) (*Fr.*) welcome.

bon mot (bôṅ′ mō′) (*Fr.*) a witty saying.

bon ton (bôṅ′tôṅ′) (*Fr.*) good manners or breeding.

bon vi·vant′ (bôṅ vē-väṅ′) (*Fr.*) an epicure; a good companion.

bon vo·yage′ (bôṅ vwä-yäzh′) (*Fr.*) happy trip; farewell.

ca″ba·lle′ro (kab″əl-yär′ō) n. (*Span.*) cavalier.

can′tus fir′mus (kan′təs fēr′məs) (*Lat.*) a chant or musical theme.

car′pe di′em (kär′pē dī′əm) (*Lat.*) make use of the day.

carte blanche (kärt′blänsh′) (*Fr.*) unlimited authority.

ca′ve ca′nem (kā′vē kā′nəm) (*Lat.*) beware the dog.

cha·cun à son goût′ (shä-kuṅ′nä sôṅ goo′) (*Fr.*) each to his own taste.

cher·chez′ la femme′ (sher-shä′lä fäm′) (*Fr.*) look for the woman.

che se·ra′ se·ra′ (kā se-rä′ se-rä′) (*Ital.*) what will be, will be.

co″gno·scen′te (ko″nyo-shen′te) n. (*Ital.*) a connoisseur.

com·bien′ (käṅ-byeṅ′) *adv.* (*Fr.*) how much?

com·ment″al·lez-vous′? (kə-mäṅ″tä-lä-voo′) (*Fr.*) how are you?

com·ment′ vous″ por·tez-vous′? (kə-mäṅ′-voo″pôr-tä-voo′) (*Fr.*) how are you?

comme il faut′ (ku-mēl-fō′) (*Fr.*) as is required; as it should be.

cor′don bleu′ (kôr′dôṅ blö′) (*Fr.*) blue ribbon; one entitled to wear one.

cor′pus de·lic′ti (kôr′pəs di-lik′tī) (*Lat.*) the facts connected with a crime.

danse ma·ca′bre (däns mä-kä′br) (*Fr.*) dance of death.

De′i gra′ti·a (dē′ī grä′shē·ə; de″ē grä′tsē·ə) (*Lat.*) by the grace of God.

de gus′ti·bus non est dis″pu·tan″dum (dē gus′ti-bəs non est dis″pū-tan′dəm) (*Lat.*) there is no disputing about tastes.

dé″jà vu′ (dā″ zhä vü′) (*Fr.*) already seen;

the illusion of having previously experienced something now actually experienced for the first time.

de ju're (dē jūr'e) (*Lat.*) by right or lawful title.

de mor'tu·is nil ni'si bo'num (dē môr'tū-is nil nī'sī bō'nəm) (*Lat.*) of the dead speak nothing but good.

de no'vo (dē nō'vō) (*Lat.*) from the beginning.

De'o gra'ti·as (dē'ō grä'shē-əs; de'ō grä'tsē-əs) (*Lat.*) thanks be to God.

De'o vo·len'te (dē'ō vō-len'tē; de'ō) (*Lat.*) God being willing.

de pro·fun'dis (dē prō-fun'dis) (*Lat.*) out of the depths.

de rè'gle (də re'gl) (*Fr.*) according to rule.

de ri·gueur' (də-rē-gör') (*Fr.*) obligatory.

de trop' (də trō') (*Fr.*) too much.

Di'es ir'ae (dē"ās ir'ī) (*Lat.*) day of wrath; Judgment Day.

Dieu et mon droit (dyö' ā môn drwä') (*Fr.*) God and my right: motto on British royal arms.

di'tat De'us (dī'tat dē'əs) (*Lat.*) God enriches: motto of Arizona.

dol'ce far nien'te (dōl'che fär nyen'te) (*Ital.*) sweet to do nothing; (*fig.*) sweet idleness.

dra'ma·tis per·so'nae (dram'ə-tis pər-sō'nē) (*Lat.*) the characters in a play.

eau"de vie' (ō"də vē') (*Fr.*) brandy.

ec'ce ho'mo (ek'sē hō'mō) (*Lat.*) behold the man.

em·bar·ras' de ri·chesses' (än-bä-rä' də rē-shes') (*Fr.*) an embarrassment of wealth.

en fa·mille' (än"fä-mē'ə) (*Fr.*) at home; informally.

en·fant ter·ri'ble (än-fän te-rēbl') (*Fr.*) an unruly child.

en·fin' (än-fan') (*Fr.*) finally.

en garde' (än gärd') (*Fr.*) on guard; watch out!

en masse' (än-mäs') (*Fr.*) all together; collectively.

en pass·ant' (än"pä-sän') (*Fr.*) in passing; by the way.

en rap·port' (än rä-pôr') (*Fr.*) in harmony.

en·tre nous' (än-trə-noo') (*Fr.*) between us.

e plu'ri·bus u'num (ē plūr'i-bəs ū'nəm) (*Lat.*) one out of many: motto of the U.S.

ex ca·the'dra (eks kə-thē'drə) (*Lat.*) from the chair (of office); with authority.

ex·em'pli gra'ti·a (eg-zem'plī grä'shē-ə) (*Lat.*) for example.

ex'e·unt (ek'sē-ənt) (*Lat.*) they go out.

ex par'te (eks pär'tē) (*Lat.*) from one side only; from a partisan point of view.

ex post fac'to (eks pōst fak'tō) (*Lat.*) after the deed (is done).

fait ac·com·pli' (fe"tä-kän-plē') (*Fr.*) an accomplished fact.

femme fa·tale' (fäm fä-täl') (*Fr.*) a dangerous woman; a seductress.

fin de siè'cle (fan də sye'kl) (*Fr.*) end of the century.

fla·gran'te de·lic'to (flə-gran'tē dē-lik'tō)

(*Lat.*) during the commission of the crime.

Ge·sund'heit (gə-zŭnt'hīt) (*Ger.*) good health.

grand prix (grän' prē') (*Fr.*) first prize.

haut monde (ō' mônd') (*Fr.*) high society.

heil (hīl) *interj.* (*Ger.*) hail!

hic ja'cet (hik jä'set) (*Lat.*) here lies.

ho·ni soit' qui mal y pense' (ō"nē swä' kē mäl ē pāns') (*Fr.*) shamed be he who thinks evil of it.

hors de com·bat' (ôr"də-kän-bä') (*Fr.*) out of the fight; disabled.

i·bi'dem (i-bī'dəm; ib'ə-dem) (*Lat.*) in the same place.

i·dée fixe (ē-dā' fēks') (*Fr.*) a fixed idea; obsession.

i'dem (ī'dem) (*Lat.*) the same.

id est (*Lat.*) that is.

in ab·sen'tia (in ab-sen'shə) (*Lat.*) in absence.

in ex·tre'mis (in eks-trē'mis) (*Lat.*) at the very end; near death.

in'fra dig"ni·ta'tem (in'frə dig"ni-tä'təm) (*Lat.*) beneath one's dignity.

in lo'co pa·ren'tis (in lō'kō pə-ren'tis) (*Lat.*) in the place of a parent.

in re (in rä) (*Lat.*) re; concerning.

in sta'tu quo (in stä'tū kwō') (*Lat.*) in the same condition.

in'ter nos' (in'tər nōs') (*Lat.*) between us.

in to'to (in tō'tō) (*Lat.*) in full; wholly.

ip'se dix'it (ip'sē dik'sit) (*Lat.*) he himself has said it.

ip'so fac'to (ip'sō fak'tō) (*Lat.*) by virtue of the same fact.

je ne sais quoi (zhə nə sā kwä') (*Fr.*) I don't know what.

jeu·nesse' do·rée' (zhö-nes' dâ-rä') (*Fr.*) gilded youth.

joie" de vivre' (zhwä' də vēvr') (*Fr.*) joy of life; enthusiasm.

Ka·pell'meis"ter (kä-pel'mīs"tər) *n.* (*Ger.*) a musical conductor of a choir or orchestra.

Kul·tur' (kŭl-tūr') (*Ger.*) culture, esp. that of the Germans.

lap'sus lin'guae (lap'səs ling'gwē) (*Lat.*) a slip of the tongue.

la'res et pe·na'tes (lär'ēz et pē-nä'tēz) (*Lat.*) household gods.

Le'bens·raum" (lā'bənz-rowm") *n.* (*Ger.*) living space; room for expansion.

le roi est mort (lə rwä' ā môr') (*Fr.*) the king is dead.

l'é·tat', c'est moi (lā-tä' sā mwä') (*Fr.*) I am the state.

let'tre de ca·chet' (let'r də kä-she') (*Fr.*) a sealed letter (ordering arrest).

lo'co ci·ta'to (lō'kō sī-tä'tō) (*Lat.*) in the place cited.

lo'cum te'nens (lō'kəm tē'nenz) (*Lat.*) a substitute.

lo'cus si·gil'li (lō'kəs si-jil'ī) (*Lat.*) the place of the seal.

mal de mer (mäl'də mär') (*Fr.*) seasickness.

man sagt (män zäkt) (*Ger.*) they say.

ma're nos'trum (mä'rē nos'trəm) (*Lat.*) our sea.

ma·ter (mā′tər) (*Lat.*) mother.

me·a cul′pa (me′a-kŭl′pa) (*Lat.*) I am to blame.

mens sa′na in cor′por·e sa′no (menz sä′nə in kôr′pôr-ĕ sä′nō) (*Lat.*) a sound mind in a sound body.

mi·ra′bi·le dic′tu (mi-rab′ə-lĕ dik′too) (*Lat.*) marvelous to relate.

mo′dus op″e·ran′di (mō′dəs op″ə-ran′dī) (*Lat.*) method of working.

mo′dus vi·ven′di (mō′dəs vi-ven′dī) (*Lat.*) way of living or getting along.

mo″ri·tu′ri te sa″lu·ta′mus (môr″ĕ-tyûr′ĕ te sal″ū-tä′məs) (*Lat.*) we about to die salute thee.

ne″ plus ul′tra (nē″plus ul′trə) (*Lat.*) no more beyond; the ultimate.

n'est-ce pas? (nes-pä′) (*Fr.*) is it not?

nicht wahr? (nikht vär″) (*Ger.*) not true?

nil des″pe·ran′dum (nil des″pə-ran′dem) (*Lat.*) despair of nothing.

ni′si (nīsī) (*Lat.*) unless.

no′lens vo′lens (nō′lənz vō′lənz) (*Lat.*) willy-nilly.

nol′le pros′e·qui (nol′e pros′ĕ-kwī) (*Lat.*) to be unwilling to prosecute.

no′lo con·ten′de·re (nō′lō kon-ten′də-re) (*Lat.*) I am unwilling to contest.

non com′pos men′tis (non kom′pos men′tis) (*Lat.*) not of sound mind.

no′ta be′ne (nō′tə be′ne) (*Lat.*) note well.

ob′i·it (ob′ĕ-it) (*Lat.*) he (she) died.

on dit′ (ôn dē′) (*Fr.*) they say.

par′ti·ceps cri′mi·nis (pär′ti-seps krim′in-is) (*Lat.*) an accomplice.

pa′ter (pä′tər) (*Lat.*) father.

pa″ter nos′ter (pä″tər nâ′stər) (*Lat.*) our father; the Lord's prayer.

pec·ca′vi (pe-kä′vĕ) (*Lat.*) I have sinned.

per an′num (pər an′əm) (*Lat.*) by the year.

per se (pər sē′; sā′) (*Lat.*) by itself.

pièce de ré″sis′tance (pyes də räz″ĕs″täns′) (*Fr.*) the main dish, event, etc.

porte″-co·chère′ (pôrt″kō-shär′) *n.* (*Fr.*) a covered carriage entrance.

pour·boire′ (pûr′bwär′) (*Fr.*) a tip to a servant.

pre·si′di·o (prä-sē′dyō) (*Span.*) a fort.

pri′ma fa′cie (prī′mə fä′shē) (*Lat.*) at first sight.

prix fixe (prē″fēks′) (*Fr.*) (at a) fixed price; table d'hôte.

pro bo″no pub′li·ca (prō bō″nō poo′blĕ-kō) (*Lat.*) for the public good.

pro for′ma (prō fôr′mə) (*Lat.*) as a matter of form.

pro tem′po·re (prō tem′pə-rĕ) (*Lat.*) for the time being.

¿quién sa′be? (kyen sä′bĕ) (*Span.*) who knows?

qui va là? (kē″vä-lä′) (*Fr.*) who goes there?

quod e′rat de″mon·stran′dum (kwod er′at dem″ən-stran′dəm) (*Lat.*) which was to be proved.

quod vi′de (kwod vī′dē) (*Lat.*) which see.

re·duc′ti·o ad ab·sur′dum (ri-duk′shē-ō ad ab-sēr′dəm) (*Lat.*) reduction to absurdity.

re″qui·es′cat in pa′ce (rek″wĕ-es′kat in pä′che) (*Lat.*) may he (she) rest in peace.

res ges′tae (räs ges′tĕ) (*Lat.*) things done; exploits.

ro·man à clef (râ-män′nä-klä′) (*Fr.*) a novel in which real persons are concealed under fictitious names.

sanc′tum sanc·to′rum (sank′təm sank-tôr′əm) (*Lat.*) Holy of Holies.

sauve qui peut (sōv′ kĕ pö′) (*Fr.*) save (himself) who can; a disorderly retreat.

se hab′la Es″pa·ñol′ (sā ä′blä es″pä-nyōl′) (*Span.*) Spanish is spoken here.

sem′per fi·de′lis (sem′pər fi-de′lis) (*Lat.*) ever faithful.

sem′per pa·ra′tus (sem′per pə-rä′təs) (*Lat.*) ever ready.

sha·lom′ (shä-lōm′) *n.* (*Hebrew*) peace. **—shalom a·lei′chem** (a-lä′kəm) be with you.

sic (sik) *adv.* (*Lat.*) so; thus.

sic tran′sit glo′ri·a mun′di (sik tran′sit glôr′ē-ə mun′dĕ) (*Lat.*) so passes away the glory of the world.

s'il vous plaît (sēl voo plä′) (*Fr.*) if you please; please.

Sturm und Drang (shtoorm′ ûnt dräng′) (*Ger.*) storm and stress; an early development of German romanticism.

sub ju′di·ce (sub joo′di-sē) (*Lat.*) before the court; under consideration.

sub ro′sa (sub rō′zə) (*Lat.*) secretly.

su′i gen′e·ris (soo′ĕ jen′ər-is) (*Lat.*) of its own kind; unique.

ta·bleau′ vi·vant′ (ta-blō′ vē-vän′) (*Fr.*) living tableau; a representation of a scene by posed costumed persons.

thé dan·sant′ (tā dän-sän′) (*Fr.*) a tea dance.

tout à fait (too′ tä fe′) (*Fr.*) entirely.

tout de suite (toot′swēt′) (*Fr.*) at once; immediately.

vae vic′tis (vē vik′tis) (*Lat.*) woe to the vanquished.

ve′ni, vi′di, vi′ci (vä′nĕ vē′dĕ vē′sĕ) (*Lat.*) I came, I saw, I conquered.

ver′bum sa″pi·en′ti (vēr′bəm sä″pē-en′tĕ) (*Lat.*) a word to the wise.

vi′de (vī′dĕ) (*Lat.*) see.

vi·de·li·cat (vi-del′i-set) (*Lat.*) to wit; namely.

vive (vēv) (*Fr.*) long live: **vive le roi** (lə rwä) long live the king.

vox pop′u·li vox De′i (voks pop′ū-lī voks dē′ī) (*Lat.*) the voice of the people (is) the voice of God.

Welt′schmerz″ (velt′shmerts″) *n.* (*Ger.*) dejection at the state of the world; pessimism.

wie geht's? (vē gāts′) (*Ger.*) how goes it?; how are you?

Zoll′ver·ein″ (tsâl′fer-īn″) *n.* (*Ger.*) customs union.

FORMS OF ADDRESS

The following are the forms of address most commonly used in correspondence.

When two different salutations are given, the first is the more formal of the two; if the forms are separated by *or*, however, they are interchangeable. A salutation of "Sir:", "Madam:", Dear Sir:", or "Dear Madam:" is acceptable in practically any situation.

If the husband or wife of a person of rank or title is to be included in the address, he or she is listed second. If the husband has the title, the form is

> (*title*) and Mrs. (*full name*)
> e.g., The Honorable and Mrs. John Doe.

If the wife has the title, the form is

> (*title*) (*wife's full name*) and Mr. (*surname*)
> e.g., The Honorable Jane Doe and Mr. Doe.

The salutation in these cases would be "Dear Mr. & Mrs. Doe:". If the person of rank has a specific title of office (as President, Attorney General, etc.) the salutation is

> Dear Mr. (Madam) (*title*) and Mrs. (Mr.) (*surname*)
> e.g. Dear Mr. President and Mrs. Doe.

In general, a complimentary close of "Sincerely yours," or "Very truly yours," is proper, with the latter being slightly the more formal of the two.

If the addressee is the holder of one or more academic degrees, these follow the name, preceded by a comma:

> (*title*) (*full name*), (*degrees*)
> e.g., Professor John Doe, Ph.D., Ll.D.

If the addressee holds a doctorate, he or she may be addressed as "Dr.", instead of Mr. (Mrs., Ms., Miss).

Full addresses are given only when appropriate; otherwise, a proper local address is to be supplied.

ALDERMAN

Address
Alderman (*full name*)
Salutation
Dear Sir (Madam):
Dear Mr. (Mrs., Ms., Miss) (*surname*):

AMBASSADOR

AMERICAN
Address
The Honorable (*full name*)
American Ambassador to (*country*)
American Embassy
Salutation
Dear Mr. (Madam) Ambassador:

FOREIGN
Address
His (Her) Excellency the Ambassador of (*country*)
Embassy of (*country*)
Salutation
Your Excellency:
Sir (Madam):

ARCHBISHOP

ANGLICAN (Great Britain)
Address
His Grace the Lord Archbishop of (*city*)
Salutation
My Lord Archbishop:
Your Grace:

ANGLICAN (Canada)
Address
The Most Reverend (*full name*)

Archbishop of (name)
Salutation
Most Reverend Sir:
Dear Archbishop:

ARMY OFFICERS

Be careful to use the exact rank. A qualifying adjective is not used in the salutation (e.g., Lieutenant Colonel Smith becomes "Dear Colonel Smith:"). Warrant officers are addressed as "Mister".

Address
(*rank*) (*full name*)
(*military unit*), U.S.A.
Salutation
Sir:
Dear (*rank*) (*surname*):

ASSEMBLYMAN
(see REPRESENTATIVE, U.S., LOCAL)

ASSOCIATE JUSTICE OF THE SUPREME COURT

FEDERAL
Address
The Honorable (*full name*)
Associate Justice of the Supreme Court
Washington, D.C. 20543
Salutation
Dear Mr. (Madam) Justice:
Dear Justice (*surname*):

STATE
Address
The Honorable (*full name*)

Associate Justice of the Supreme Court
(*capital city, state, ZIP*)
Salutation
　Dear Sir (Madam):
　Dear Mr. (Madam) Justice:
ATTORNEY GENERAL
FEDERAL
Address
　The Honorable (*full name*)
　Attorney General
　Washington, D.C. 20530
Salutation
　Dear Sir: (Madam): *or*
　Dear Mr. (Madam) Attorney General:
STATE
Address
　The Honorable (*full name*)
　Attorney General of (*state*)
　(*capital city, state, ZIP*)
Salutation
　Dir Sir (Madam): *or*
　Dear Mr. (Madam) Attorney General:
BARON (BARONESS)
Address
　The Right Honourable Lord (Baroness)
　(*surname*)
Salutation
　My Lord: (Madam:)
BARONET
Address
　Sir (*full name*), Bart.
Salutation
　Sir:

BISHOP
ANGLICAN (Great Britain)
Address
　The Right Reverend the Lord Bishop of
　(*place*)
Salutation
　My Lord Bishop:
*ANGLICAN (Canadian) / PROTESTANT
EPISCOPAL*
Address
　The Right Reverend (*full name*)
　Bishop of (*place*)
Salutation
　Right Reverend Sir:
　Dear Bishop (*surname*):
METHODIST
Address
　Bishop (*full name*)
Salutation
　Dear Bishop (*surname*):
ROMAN CATHOLIC
Address
　The Most Reverend (*full name*)
　Bishop of (*place*)
Salutation
　Your Excellency:
BROTHER OF A RELIGIOUS ORDER
Address
　The Reverend Brother (*full or given name*)

Salutation
　Dear Brother (*given name*):
CABINET OFFICER OR MINISTER
AMERICAN
Address
　, The Honorable (*full name*)
　Secretary of (*name of Dept.*)
　Washington, D.C. (*ZIP of Dept.*)
Salutation
　Dear Sir (Madam): *or*
　Dear Mr. (Madam) Secretary:
CANADIAN
Address
　The Honourable (*full name*)
　Minister of (*function*)
　House of Commons
　Parliament Buildings
　Ottawa, Ontario KIA 0A2
Salutation
　Dear Sir (Madam):
　Dear Mr. (Mrs., Ms., Miss) (*surname*):
CARDINAL
Address
　His Eminence (given name), Cardinal
　(*surname*)
　Archbishop of (*place*)
Salutation
　Your Eminence:
CHIEF JUSTICE
AMERICAN (Federal)
Address
　The Chief Justice of the United States
　The Supreme Court of the United States
　Washington, D.C. 20543
Salutation
　Dear Mr. (Madam) Chief Justice:
AMERICAN (State)
Address
　The Chief Justice
　Supreme Court of the State (Common-
　wealth) of (*name*)
　(*capital city, state, ZIP*)
Salutation
　Dear Mr. (Madam) Chief Justice:
CANADIAN
Address
　The Right Honourable (*full name*)
　Chief Justice of Canada
　Supreme Court Building
　Ottawa, Ontario K1A 0J1
CLERGYMAN
Address
　The Reverend (*full name*)
Salutation
　Reverend Sir (Madam):
　Dear Mr. (Mrs., MS., Miss) (*surname*):
CONSUL
Address
　Mr. (Mrs., Ms., Miss) (*full name*)
　American Consul at (*place*)
Salutation
　Dear Sir (Madam):
　Dear Mr. (Mrs., Ms., Miss) (*surname*):

DEACON

Address
  The Reverend Deacon (*surname*)
Salutation
  Reverend Sir (Madam):

DEAN (Ecclesiastic)

Address
  The Very Reverend (*full name*)
  Dean of (*church or place*)
Salutation
  Very Reverend Sir:
  Dear Dean (*surname*):

DELEGATE
(see REPRESENTATIVE, U.S., LOCAL)

DUKE (DUCHESS)

Address
  His (Her) Grace, the Duke (Duchess) of
  (*place*)
Salutation
  Your Grace:

WHEN OF ROYAL BLOOD
Address
  His (Her) Royal Highness the Duke
  (Duchess) of (*place*)
Salutation
  May it please your Royal Highness:

EARL (COUNTESS)

Address
  The Right Honourable the Earl (Coun-
  tess) of (*place*)
Salutation
  Sir (Madam):

GOVERNOR GENERAL (Canada)

Address
  His (Her) Excellency (*full name*)
  Government House
  Ottawa, Ontario K1A 0A1
Salutation
  Sir (Madam):
  Dear Governor General:

GOVERNOR
(LIEUTENANT GOVERNOR)

Address
  The Honorable (*full name*)
  Governor (Lieutenant Governor) of (*state*)
  (*capital city, state, ZIP*)
Salutation
  Governor: Dear Governor (*surname*):
  Lieutenant Governor: Dear Mr. (Mrs.,
  Ms., Miss) (*surname*):

JUDGE (JUSTICE)

Address
  The Honorable (*full name*)
  Judge (Justice) of the (*name of court;
  district, if any*)
Salutation
  Dear Judge (*surname*):

KING (QUEEN)

Address
  His (Her) Majesty, (*full name*), King
  (Queen) of (*place*)

Salutation
  May it please your Majesty:
  Sir (Madam):

LADY

A Lady is a peeress under the rank of
Duchess; a wife of a Baronet, knight, or
Lord of session; or a daughter of a Duke,
Marquis, or Earl.

Address
  Lady (*full name*)
Salutation
  Madam: *or*
  Your Ladyship:

MARINE OFFICER

Same form as Army officers, except that
U.S.M.C. follows name of military unit.

MARQUIS (MARCHIONESS)

Address
  The Most Honourable the Marquis
  (Marchioness) of (*place*)
Salutation
  My Lord (*place*): (Madam:)

MAYOR

AMERICAN
Address
  The Honorable (*full name*)
  Mayor of (*city*)
  City Hall
  (*city, state, ZIP*)
Salutation
  Dear Sir (Madam): *or*
  Dear Mr. (Madam) Mayor:

CANADIAN
Address
  His (Her) Worship Mayor (*full name*)
  City Hall
  (*city, province, code*)
Salutation
  Dear Sir (Madam):

MINISTER (Diplomatic)

Address
  His (Her) Excellency (*surname*) *or*
  The Honorable (*surname*)
  Minister of (*country*)
Salutation
  Your Excellency:
  Dear Mr. (Madam) Minister:

MONSIGNOR

Address
  The Right Reverend Monsignor (*surname*)
Salutation
  Right Reverend Monsignor:

WHEN A PAPAL CHAMBERLAIN
Address
  The Very Reverend Monsignor (*surname*)
Salutation
  Very Reverend Monsignor:

NAVAL OFFICER

Same form as Army officers, except: Officers under the rank of Commander are addressed as "Mister"; a naval officer regard-

less of rank who is in command of a ship is addressed as "Captain" for the period of his command; U.S.N. follows military unit.

POPE

Address
His Holiness, the Pope *or*
His Holiness, Pope (*official name*)
Salutation
Your Holiness: *or*
Most Holy Father:

PRESIDENT OF THE UNITED STATES

Address
The President
The White House
Washington, D.C. 20500
Salutation
Sir (Madam): *or*
Dear Mr. (Madam) President:

RABBI

Address
Rabbi (*full name*)
Salutation
Dear Rabbi (*surname*):

REPRESENTATIVE

U.S., FEDERAL
Address
The Honorable (*full name*)
The House of Representatives
Washington, D.C. 20515
Salutation
Sir (Madam):
Dear Congressman (Congresswoman) (*surname*):

U.S., LOCAL
Address
The Honorable (*full name*)
(*place*) House of Representatives (*or* Assembly *or* House of Delegates)
(*city, state, ZIP*)
Salutation
Dear Mr. (Mrs., Ms., Miss) (*surname*):

CANADIAN, FEDERAL
Address
Mr. (Mrs., Ms., Miss) (*full name*), M.P.
House of Commons
Parliament Buildings
Ottawa, Ontario K1A 0A6
Salutation
Dear Sir (Madam):

Dear Mr. (Mrs., Ms., Miss) (*surname*):

CANADIAN, PROVINCIAL
Address
Mr. (Mrs., Ms., Miss) (*full name*), M.L.A.
(*Ontario*: M.P.P.; *Quebec*: M.N.A.)
Member of Legislative Assembly
(*city, province, code*)
Salutation
Dear Sir (Madam):
Dear Mr. (Mrs., Ms., Miss) (*surname*):

SENATOR

U.S., FEDERAL
Address
The Honorable (*full name*)
United States Senate
Washington, D.C. 20510
Salutation
Sir (Madam):
Dear Senator (*surname*):

U.S., STATE
Address
The Honorable (*full name*)
(*place*) Senate
(*capital, city, state, ZIP*)
Salutation
Dear Mr. (Mrs., Ms., Miss) (*surname*):

CANADIAN
Address
The Honourable (*full name*)
The Senate
Parliament Buildings
Ottawa, Ontario K1A 0A4
Salutation
Dear Sir (Madam):
Dear Senator (*surname*):

SISTER OF A RELIGIOUS ORDER

Address
The Reverend Sister (*full or given name*)
Salutation
Dear Sister (*given name*):

VICE PRESIDENT OF THE UNITED STATES

Address
The Honorable (*full name*)
Vice President of the United States
Washington, D.C. 20501
Salutation
Sir (Madam):
Dear Mr. (Madam) Vice President:

TABLES OF WEIGHTS AND MEASURES
U.S. SYSTEM

Linear Measure

		1 inch (in)	= 2.54 centimeters (cm)
12 inches	=	1 foot (ft)	0.3048 meter (m)
3 feet		1 yard (yd)	0.9144 meter
5½ yards		1 rod (rd)	5.029 meters
40 rods		1 furlong (fur)	201.168 meters
8 furlongs		1 (statute) mile (mi)	1609.344 meters
3 (statute) miles		1 (land) league	4.828 kilometers
6 feet		1 fathom	1.828 meters
1000 fathoms or 1.1508 statute miles		1 nautical mile (knot)	1.852 kilometers

Area or Square Measure

		1 square inch (sq in)	= 6.452 square centimeters
144 square inches	=	1 square foot (sq ft)	929.030 square centimeters
9 square feet		1 square yard (sq yd)	0.836 square meter
30¼ square yards		1 square rod (sq rd)	25.293 square meters
160 square rods		1 acre	0.405 hectare
640 acres		1 square mile (sq mi)	258.999 hectares
1 square mile		1 section (of land)	
36 square miles		1 township	

Volume or Cubic Measure

		1 cubic inch (cu in)	= 16.387 cubic centimeters
1,728 cubic inches	=	1 cubic foot (cu ft)	0.028 cubic meter
27 cubic feet		1 cubic yard (cu yd)	0.765 cubic meter
16 cubic feet		1 cord foot	
8 cord feet		1 cord	3.625 cubic meters

Capacity Measures
Dry Measure

1 pint (pt)	=	(33.60 cubic inches)	= 0.551 liter
2 pints		1 quart (qt)	1.101 liters
8 quarts		1 peck (pk)	8.810 liters
4 pecks		1 bushel (bu)	35.238 liters

Liquid Measure

1 minim	=	(0.004 cubic inch)	= 0.062 milliliter
60 minims		1 fluid dram (fl dr)	3.697 milliliters
8 fluid drams		1 fluid ounce (fl oz)	0.030 liter
4 fluid ounces		1 gill	0.118 liter

8 fluid ounces	1 cup	0.236 liter
2 cups	1 pint (pt)	0.473 liter
2 pints	1 quart (qt)	0.946 liter
4 quarts	1 gallon	3.785 liters

| 1 teaspoon (tsp) | 1⅓ fluid drams |
| 1 tablespoon (tsb) | 3 teaspoons |

Angular and Circular Measure

60 seconds (″)	=	1 minute (′)
60 minutes		1 degree (°)
90 degrees		1 right angle, or 1 quadrant of a circle
4 quadrants or 360 degrees	=	1 circle

Weights
Avoirdupois Weight

	1 grain (gr)	= 0.065 gram
27.34 grains =	1 dram (dr)	1.772 grams
16 drams	1 ounce (oz)	28.350 grams
16 ounces	1 pound (lb)	453.592 grams
100 pounds	1 hundredweight (cwt)	45.359 kilograms.
2000 pounds	1 ton (tn)	907.18 kilograms
14 pounds (Great Britain)	1 stone	6.35 kilograms

Troy Weight

	1 grain	= 0.065 gram
3.086 grains =	1 carat (c)	200. miligrams
24 grains	1 pennyweight (dwt)	1.555 grams
20 pennyweights	1 ounce (oz)	31.104 grams
12 ounces	1 pound (lb)	373.242 grams

Apothecaries' Weight

	1 grain	= 0.065 gram
20 grains =	1 scruple	1.296 grams
3 scruples	1 dram	3.888 grams
8 drams or 480 grains	1 ounce	31.104 grams
12 ounces or 5,760 grains	1 pound	373.24 grams

METRIC SYSTEM

Linear Measure

		1 millimeter (mm)	=	0.039 inch
10 millimeters	=	1 centimeter (cm)		0.394 inch
10 centimeters		1 decimeter (dm)		3.937 inches
10 decimeters		1 meter (m)		39.37 inches
10 meters		1 decameter (dam)		32.8 feet
10 decameters		1 hectometer (hm)		328. feet
10 hectometers		1 kilometer (km)		0.621 mile

Square Measure

		1 square millimeter (sq mm)	= 0.002 square inch
100 square millimeters	=	1 square centimeter (cm²)	0.155 square inch
100 square centimeters		1 square decimeter (dm²)	15.499 square inches
100 square decimeters		1 square meter (m²)	1549. square inches
1 square meter		1 centare	10.76 square feet
100 centares		1 are (a)	119.6 square yards
100 ares		1 hectare (ha)	2.471 acres
100 hectares		1 square kilometer (km²)	0.386 square mile

Volume Measure

		1 cubic centimeter (cm³)	= .061 cubic inch
1000 cubic centimeters	=	1 cubic decimeter (dm³)	61.02 cubic inches
1000 cubic decimeters		1 cubic meter (cm³)	35.314 cubic feet

Capacity Measure

		1 milliliter (ml)	=	.027 fluid drams
10 milliliters	=	1 centiliter (cl)		.338 fluid ounce
10 centiliters		1 deciliter (dl)		3.38 fluid ounces
10 deciliters		1 liter (l)		1.057 liquid quarts or 0.908 dry quart
10 liters		1 decaliter (dal)		2.64 gallons or 0.284 bushel
10 decaliters		1 hectoliter (hl)		264.18 gallons or 2.838 bushels
10 hectoliters		1 kiloliter (kl)		264.18 gallons or 28.38 bushels

Weights

		1 milligram (mg)	=	0.015 grain
10 milligrams	=	1 centigram (cg)		0.154 grain
10 centigrams		1 decigram (dg)		1.543 grains
10 decigrams		1 gram (g)		15.432 grains

10 grams	1 decagram (dag)	0.353 ounce
10 decagrams	1 hectogram (hg)	3.527 ounces
10 hectograms	1 kilogram (kg)	2.205 pounds
100 kilograms	1 quintal	220.46 pounds
10 quintals	1 metric ton (t)	2204.6 pounds

CONVERSION FACTORS

These conversion factors are provided as an aid in quickly converting selected units of weight and measure from the U.S. System to the Metric System and back. To make the opposite conversion from that given below, simply divide by the number given instead of multiplying.

To Change	To	Multiply By
inches	centimeters	2.54
feet	meters	.305
miles	kilometers	1.609
kilometers	miles	.621
square inches	square centimeters	6.452
square yards	square meters	.836
square meters	square yards	1.196
ounces (fluid)	cubic centimeters	29.57
quarts	liters	.946
cubic inches	cubic centimeters	16.387
cubic yards	cubic meters	.765
grains	milligrams	64.799
ounces (dry)	grams	28.35
pounds	grams	454
pounds	kilograms	.454
degrees Centigrade	degrees Fahrenheit	$\frac{9}{5}$ and add 32
degrees Fahrenheit	degrees Centigrade	subtract 32, then multiply by $\frac{5}{9}$

Other conversion factors of use include:

Multiply	By	To Obtain
Diameter circle	3.1416	Circumference of circle
Diameter circle	.8862	Side of equal square
Diameter circle squared	.7854	Area of circle
Diameter sphere squared	3.1416	Area of sphere
Diameter sphere cubed	.5236	Volume of sphere
U.S. gallons	.8327	Imperial gallons (British)
U.S. gallons	.1337	Cubic feet
U.S. gallons	8.330	Pounds of water at 20° C.
Cubic feet	62.427	Pounds of water at 4° C.
Feet of water at 4° C.	.4335	Pounds per square inch
Inch of mercury at 0° C.	.4912	Pounds per square inch
Knots	1.1516	Miles per hour

SIGNS AND SYMBOLS

Accents and Punctuation:

´	acute
&	ampersand
{ }	braces
[ ]	brackets
˘	breve
¸	cedilla
^	circumflex
¨	dieresis
"	ditto
. . .	ellipsis
& c or etc	et cetera
!	exclamation mark
`	grave
¯	macron
¶	paragraph mark
( )	parentheses
§	section mark
~	tilde
/	virgule

Business and Finance:

a/c	account
@	at or each
B/L	bill of lading
B/S	bill of sale
¢	cent
$	dollar
L/C	letter of credit
#	number (before a figure); pound (weight) (after a figure)
%	per cent
£	pound (currency—sterling)
lb	pound (weight)

Electrical:

⇄	alternating current
▽	antenna
⊣⊢	battery
⊣⊢	capacitor
▶⊢	diode
→	direct current; or direction of flow
⊟	fuse
⏚	ground
⬤	inductor
⊸	lamp
▷⊂	microphone
Ω	ohm
−	polarity, negative
+	polarity, positive
▶⊢	rectifier
⟋\/\/\⟍	resistor
↗	switch
⬤	transformer
⊕	transistor—position of arrow indicates type

Mathematical:

∥	parallel
× or ·	multiplied by
÷ or /	divided by
:	ratio; is to
∴	therefore
∵	because
>	greater than
≧	greater than or equal to
≷	greater than or less than
<	less than
≦	less than or equal to
≐	approaches
=	equal to
≠ or ≠	not equal to
≡	identical with
≢ or ≢	not identical with
~	equivalent to
~	difference
√	radical
	root
π	pi
ε	epsilon
±	plus or minus
#	number
%	per cent
→	approaches limit of
Σ	sum; sigma
sin	sine of angle
cos	cosine of angle
tan	tangent of angle
log	logarithm

!	factorial	⅄	Leo; Lion
∞	infinity	ⅧP	Virgo; Virgin
		♎	Libra; Balance
	Medical:	♏	Scorpio; Scorpion
		♐	Sagittarius; Archer
*	birth	♑	Capricornus; Goat
†	death	♒	Aquarius; Water Bearer
♀	female	♓	Pisces; Fish
○	female, in charts		
♂ or ♂	male		*Weather:*
□	male, in charts		
Rh −	Rhesus factor, negative	T	thunder
Rh +	Rhesus factor, positive	℞	thunderstorm
		↓	precipitate
	Planets and Zodiac:	⑪	rain
		▲	hail
☿	Mercury	⊗	sleet
♀	Venus	∨	frost
⊕	Earth	*	snow
♂	Mars	≡	fog
♃	Jupiter	∞	haze
♄	Saturn	◑	cloudy
♅	Uranus	◎	calm
♆	Neptune	○	clear
♇	Pluto	⌒	tropical storm
☌	conjunction	▬▬▬	cold front
☍	opposition	▬▬▬	warm front
☉	Sun	◥◥◣	stationary front
●	Moon		
●	New Moon		*Miscellaneous:*
☽	Moon: first quarter		
☾	Moon: last quarter	©	copyright
○	full Moon	®	registered trademark
♈	Aries; Ram	℞	prescription; recipe
♉	Taurus; Bull	†	dagger ⎫ used
♊	Gemini; Twins	‡	double dagger ⎭
♋	Cancer; Crab		in text for reference